PRESENTED

TO:

BY:

ON:

NIV
INVESTIGATOR'S
HOLY BIBLE
NEW INTERNATIONAL VERSION

NIV
INVESTIGATOR'S
HOLY BIBLE
NEW INTERNATIONAL VERSION

ZONDERVAN®

Library of Congress Catalog Card Number 2016951042

17 18 19 20 21 22 /DSC/ 20 19 18 17 16 15 14 13 12 11 10 9 8 7 6 5 4 3 2 1

A portion of the purchase price of your NIV® Bible is provided to Biblica so together we support the mission of *Transforming lives through God's Word.*

Biblica provides God's Word to people through translation, publishing and Bible engagement in Africa, Asia Pacific, Europe, Latin America, Middle East, and North America. Through its worldwide reach, Biblica engages people with God's Word so that their lives are transformed through a relationship with Jesus Christ.

TABLE OF CONTENTS

INTRODUCTION

Welcome! We're Mateo and Isabella, and this is our super-sniffer dog, Clooney. We love to solve mysteries and do detective work. We love to look for clues with our detective tools. And we love to read books that give us clues to how things happened and the way things work. Some of our favorite books are ones where kids help solve problems. But our favorite book of all is the Bible. The Bible is a very special book that is a gift from God. And even though it's a great gift, it's sometimes hard for kids like us to understand.

We are often confused by things we read in the Bible. Sometimes that's because the Bible can use very big words. Sometimes it's because there are a ton of names in there. And, boy, are some of them long! Sometimes we don't understand because the Bible talks about places that are far away from our home. These are lands where people speak different languages, the weather is different, and the food everyone eats is different.

So, we decided to put our detective skills to use. We both sat down with pastors, parents, and teachers to find as many clues as we could about the Bible. They helped us find books written by Bible experts. These experts have studied the Bible for many years. Some of them speak ancient languages and can read ancient writings.

Then we sat down and helped the grown-ups write these notes for you. With a few comments from us too!

To use this Bible, you can read from front to back and read our notes along the way. Or, you can read your favorite passages and pick and choose which notes to read. There's an index in the back to help you with that. Or, if you are studying a certain passage in church or school, you may want to read that first. Younger kids might want to read with a grown-up or a big kid. We did try hard to put this in kid language. But the Bible still has some pretty special Bible words that may be a bit tricky.

So here's what you'll find in the *NIV Investigator's Bible*:

The Evidence

These introduce each book of the Bible. They answer what kind of book it is, who wrote it, what happens, and what we think is the "best part."

Breakthrough!

This feature answers questions you might have about what you read. For example, if the Bible verse uses special words you don't know. Or, if you can't understand why God or a character acted in the way that they did. We try to help you understand life in Bible times, and how that time period might have affected people's actions.

The Witnesses

Have you ever looked up the meaning of your name? It's kind of fun, right? Well, as you'll find out, names in ancient times often meant even more than they do today. This feature explains the meaning and history behind the names of Bible characters.

The Scene

This feature tells you about where events took place. They might be regions of the world, ancient countries, mountains, lakes, rivers, oceans or cities. We hope you'll be able to better imagine each Bible story when you know where it took place.

Check the Facts

These are short quizzes. We didn't want to make this too tough for you. So, each quiz is just one question. We hope they help you remember what you have read.

Case Closed!

This feature is kind of like a summary. We tell you how we felt after we read each book. Or we tell you how we think we can all use what we read to be better Christians. And sometimes these help get you ready for the next book of the Bible.

PREFACE

The goal of the New International Version (NIV) is to enable English-speaking people from around the world to read and hear God's eternal Word in their own language. Our work as translators is motivated by our conviction that the Bible is God's Word in written form. We believe that the Bible contains the divine answer to the deepest needs of humanity, sheds unique light on our path in a dark world and sets forth the way to our eternal well-being. Out of these deep convictions, we have sought to recreate as far as possible the experience of the original audience—blending transparency to the original text with accessibility for the millions of English speakers around the world. We have prioritized accuracy, clarity and literary quality with the goal of creating a translation suitable for public and private reading, evangelism, teaching, preaching, memorizing and liturgical use. We have also sought to preserve a measure of continuity with the long tradition of translating the Scriptures into English.

The complete NIV Bible was first published in 1978. It was a completely new translation made by over a hundred scholars working directly from the best available Hebrew, Aramaic and Greek texts. The translators came from the United States, Great Britain, Canada, Australia and New Zealand, giving the translation an international scope. They were from many denominations and churches—including Anglican, Assemblies of God, Baptist, Brethren, Christian Reformed, Church of Christ, Evangelical Covenant, Evangelical Free, Lutheran, Mennonite, Methodist, Nazarene, Presbyterian, Wesleyan and others. This breadth of denominational and theological perspective helped to safeguard the translation from sectarian bias. For these reasons, and by the grace of God, the NIV has gained a wide readership in all parts of the English-speaking world.

The work of translating the Bible is never finished. As good as they are, English translations must be regularly updated so that they will continue to communicate accurately the meaning of God's Word. Updates are needed in order to reflect the latest developments in our understanding of the biblical world and its languages and to keep pace with changes in English usage. Recognizing, then, that the NIV would retain its ability to communicate God's Word accurately only if it were regularly updated, the original translators established the Committee on Bible Translation (CBT). The Committee is a self-perpetuating group of biblical scholars charged with keeping abreast of advances in biblical scholarship and changes in English and issuing periodic updates to the NIV. The CBT is an independent, self-governing body and has sole responsibility for the NIV text. The Committee mirrors the original group of translators in its diverse international and denominational makeup and in its unifying commitment to the Bible as God's inspired Word.

In obedience to its mandate, the Committee has issued periodic updates to the NIV. An initial revision was released in 1984. A more thorough revision process was completed in 2005, resulting in the separately published TNIV. The updated NIV you now have in your hands builds on both the original NIV and the TNIV and represents the latest effort of the Committee to articulate God's unchanging Word in the way the original authors might have said it had they been speaking in English to the global English-speaking audience today.

Translation Philosophy

The Committee's translating work has been governed by three widely accepted principles about the way people use words and about the way we understand them.

First, the meaning of words is determined by the way that users of the language actually use them at any given time. For the biblical languages, therefore, the Committee utilizes the best and most recent scholarship on the way Hebrew, Aramaic and Greek words were being used in biblical times. At the same time, the Committee carefully studies the state of modern English. Good translation is like good communication: one must know the target audience so that the appropriate choices can be made about which English words to use to represent the original words of Scripture. From its inception, the NIV has had as its target the general English-speaking population all over the world, the "International" in its title reflecting this concern. The aim of the Committee is to put the Scriptures into natural English that will communicate effectively with the broadest possible audience of English speakers.

Modern technology has enhanced the Committee's ability to choose the right English words to convey the meaning of the original text. The field of computational linguistics harnesses the power of computers to provide broadly applicable and current data about the state of the language. Translators can now access huge databases of modern English to better understand the current meaning and usage of key words. The Committee utilized this resource in preparing the 2011 edition of the NIV. An area of especially rapid and significant change in English is the way certain nouns and pronouns are used to refer to human beings. The Committee therefore requested experts in computational linguistics at Collins Dictionaries to pose some key questions about this usage to its database of English—the largest in the world, with over 4.4 billion words, gathered from several English-speaking countries and including both spoken and written English. (The Collins Study, called "The Development and Use of Gender Language in Contemporary English," can be accessed at *http://www.thenivbible.com/about-the-niv/about-the-2011-edition/*.) The study revealed that the most popular words to describe the human race in modern U.S. English were "humanity," "man" and "mankind." The Committee then used this data in the updated NIV, choosing from among these three words (and occasionally others also) depending on the context.

A related issue creates a larger problem for modern translations: the move away from using the third-person masculine singular pronouns—"he/him/his"—to refer to men and women equally. This usage does persist in some forms of English, and this revision therefore occasionally uses these pronouns in a generic sense. But the tendency, recognized in day-to-day usage and confirmed by the Collins study, is away from the generic use of "he," "him" and "his." In recognition of this shift in language and in an effort to translate into the natural English that people are actually using, this revision of the NIV generally uses other constructions when the biblical text is plainly addressed to men and women equally. The reader will encounter especially frequently a "they," "their" or "them" to express a generic singular idea. Thus, for instance, Mark 8:36 reads: "What good is it for someone to gain the whole world, yet forfeit their soul?" This generic use of the "distributive" or "singular" "they/them/their" has been used for many centuries by respected writers of English and has now become established as standard English, spoken and written, all over the world.

A second linguistic principle that feeds into the Committee's translation work is that meaning is found not in individual words, as vital as they are, but in larger clusters: phrases, clauses, sentences, discourses. Translation is not, as many people think, a matter of word substitution: English word *x* in place of Hebrew word *y*. Translators must first determine the meaning of the words of the biblical languages in the context of the passage and then select English words that accurately communicate that meaning to modern listeners and readers. This means that accurate translation will not always reflect the exact structure of the original language. To be sure, there is debate over the degree to which translators should try to preserve the "form" of the original text in English. From the beginning, the NIV has taken a mediating position on this issue. The manual produced when the translation that became the NIV was first being planned states: "If the Greek or Hebrew syntax has a good parallel in modern English, it should be used. But if there is no good parallel, the English syntax appropriate to the meaning of the original is to be chosen." It is fine, in other words, to carry over the form of the biblical languages into English—but not at the expense of natural expression. The principle that meaning resides in larger clusters of words means that the Committee has not insisted on a "word-for-word" approach to translation. We certainly believe that every word of Scripture is inspired by God and therefore to be carefully studied to determine what God is saying to us. It is for this reason that the Committee labors over every single word of the original texts, working hard to determine how each of those words contributes to what the text is saying. Ultimately, however, it is how these individual words function in combination with other words that determines meaning.

A third linguistic principle guiding the Committee in its translation work is the recognition that words have a spectrum of meaning. It is popular to define a word by using another word, or "gloss," to substitute for it. This substitute word is then sometimes called the "literal" meaning of a word. In fact, however, words have a range of possible meanings. Those meanings will vary depending on the context, and words in one language will usually not occupy the same semantic range as words in another language. The Committee therefore studies each original word of Scripture in its context to identify its meaning in a particular verse and then chooses an appropriate English word (or phrase) to represent it. It is impossible, then, to translate any given Hebrew, Aramaic or Greek word with the same English word all the time. The Committee does try to translate related occurrences of a word in the original languages with the same English word in order to preserve the connection for the English reader. But the Committee generally privileges clear natural meaning over a concern with consistency in rendering particular words.

Textual Basis

For the Old Testament the standard Hebrew text, the Masoretic Text as published in the latest edition of *Biblia Hebraica*, has been used throughout. The Masoretic Text tradition contains marginal notations that offer variant readings. These have sometimes been followed instead of the text itself. Because such instances involve variants within the Masoretic tradition, they have not been indicated in the textual notes. In a few cases, words in the basic consonantal text have been divided differently than in the Masoretic Text. Such cases are usually indicated in the textual footnotes. The Dead Sea Scrolls contain biblical texts that represent an earlier stage of the transmission of the Hebrew text. They have been consulted, as have been the Samaritan Pentateuch and the ancient scribal traditions concerning deliberate textual changes. The translators also consulted the more important early versions. Readings from these versions, the Dead Sea Scrolls and the scribal traditions were occasionally followed where the Masoretic Text seemed doubtful and where accepted principles of textual criticism showed that one or more of these textual witnesses appeared to provide the correct reading. In rare cases, the translators have emended the Hebrew text where it appears to have become corrupted at an even earlier stage of its transmission. These departures from the Masoretic Text are also indicated in the textual footnotes. Sometimes the vowel indicators (which are later additions to the basic consonantal text) found in the Masoretic Text did not, in the judgment of the translators, represent the correct vowels for the original text. Accordingly, some words have been read with a different set of vowels. These instances are usually not indicated in the footnotes.

The Greek text used in translating the New Testament has been an eclectic one, based on the latest editions of the Nestle-Aland/United Bible Societies' Greek New Testament. The translators have made their choices among the variant readings in accordance with widely accepted principles of New Testament textual criticism. Footnotes call attention to places where uncertainty remains.

The New Testament authors, writing in Greek, often quote the Old Testament from its ancient Greek version, the Septuagint. This is one reason why some of the Old Testament quotations in the NIV New Testament are not identical to the corresponding passages in the NIV Old Testament. Such quotations in the New Testament are indicated with the footnote "(see Septuagint)."

Footnotes and Formatting

Footnotes in this version are of several kinds, most of which need no explanation. Those giving alternative translations begin with "Or" and generally introduce the alternative with the last word preceding it in the text, except when it is a single-word alternative. When poetry is quoted in a footnote a slash mark indicates a line division.

It should be noted that references to diseases, minerals, flora and fauna, architectural details, clothing, jewelry, musical instruments and other articles cannot always be identified with precision. Also, linear measurements and measures of capacity can only be approximated (see the Table of Weights and Measures). Although Selah, used mainly in the Psalms, is probably a musical term, its meaning is uncertain. Since it may interrupt reading and distract the reader, this word has not been kept in the English text, but every occurrence has been signaled by a footnote.

As an aid to the reader, sectional headings have been inserted. They are not to be regarded as part of the biblical text and are not intended for oral reading. It is the Committee's hope that these headings may prove more helpful to the reader than the traditional chapter divisions, which were introduced long after the Bible was written.

Sometimes the chapter and/or verse numbering in English translations of the Old Testament differs from that found in published Hebrew texts. This is particularly the case in the Psalms, where the traditional titles are included in the Hebrew verse numbering. Such differences are indicated in the footnotes at the bottom of the page. In the New Testament, verse numbers that marked off portions of the traditional English text not supported by the best Greek manuscripts now appear in brackets, with a footnote indicating the text that has been omitted (see, for example, Matthew 17:[21]).

Mark 16:9–20 and John 7:53—8:11, although long accorded virtually equal status with the rest of the Gospels in which they stand, have a questionable standing in the textual history of the New Testament, as noted in the bracketed annotations with which they are set off. A different typeface has been chosen for these passages to indicate their uncertain status.

Basic formatting of the text, such as lining the poetry, paragraphing (both prose and poetry), setting up of (administrative-like) lists, indenting letters and lengthy prayers within narratives and the insertion of sectional headings, has been the work of the Committee. However, the choice between single-column and double-column formats has been left to the publishers. Also the issuing of "red-letter" editions is a publisher's choice—one that the Committee does not endorse.

The Committee has again been reminded that every human effort is flawed—including this revision of the NIV. We trust, however, that many will find in it an improved representation of the Word of God, through which they hear his call to faith in our Lord Jesus Christ and to service in his kingdom. We offer this version of the Bible to him in whose name and for whose glory it has been made.

The Committee on Bible Translation

OLD TESTAMENT

GENESIS

THE EVIDENCE:

WHO WROTE IT?
To be honest, nobody really knows who wrote Genesis. Most likely, it was written by several authors. Many Bible experts think Moses wrote this book.

HOW LONG AGO?
We don't know much about this either. People who study the Bible say the material was gathered and written about 700 years before Christ, and that the final writing was finished 400 years before Christ. (I suppose you know that the years before Christ have to be subtracted up until the year he was born, don't you?)

WHAT'S IT ABOUT?
Genesis is the first book of the Bible, and it is part of a group of five books that are called the Pentateuch. This word means "five books" in Greek.

Genesis is a word that also comes from the Greek language, and it means "origin" or "beginning." That's exactly what this book is about. Its main ideas have to do with the beginnings of the world and the universe, of the animals, the plants and the human beings, of sin and evil, of life and death, of peoples and cultures, of different languages and of the rainbow. It also tells us the story of a family, Abraham's family. His son was Isaac, his grandson was Jacob and his great-grandson was Joseph. This family was the beginning of a new people called Israel, the people of God. And this book tells the story of the beginning of the relationship of God with his people.

The most wonderful thing about this book is that it tells us God acts in the history of men and women. He doesn't act as a mean or mischievous God who finds fun in watching humans suffer. He acts as a loving father who is always near his children, caring for them and teaching them how to really be happy.

THE BEST PART
The best part is in the first two chapters, when God creates everything and each part finishes with, "And God saw that it was good." How wonderful that God was happy after he created such an amazing world!

The Beginning

1 In the beginning God created the heavens and the earth. ²Now the earth was formless and empty, darkness was over the surface of the deep, and the Spirit of God was hovering over the waters.

³And God said, "Let there be light," and there was light. ⁴God saw that the light was good, and he separated the light from the darkness. ⁵God called the light "day," and the darkness he called "night." And there was evening, and there was morning—the first day.

⁶And God said, "Let there be a vault between the waters to separate water

BREAK THROUGH!

What existed before God began to create the heavens and the earth?

(GENESIS 1:1)

This book tells us that before creation, nothing alive was here. Only God existed. He was the one who made it possible for everything we can see and enjoy now to exist: light, land, sky, animals, plants and even the men and women who live here.

BREAK THROUGH!

What kind of book is Genesis?

(GENESIS 1:1)

Although it does talk about the creation of the world, Genesis is not a science book. And although it does give us a lot of historical information, it isn't a history book either. Genesis is actually a very old book that was written to explain the beginning of the universe, of humankind, of sin, of the struggles between brothers and of the people God chose to spread his blessing to the rest of humankind.

from water." ⁷So God made the vault and separated the water under the vault from the water above it. And it was so. ⁸God called the vault "sky." And there was evening, and there was morning—the second day.

⁹And God said, "Let the water under the sky be gathered to one place, and let dry ground appear." And it was so. ¹⁰God called the dry ground "land," and the gathered waters he called "seas." And God saw that it was good.

¹¹Then God said, "Let the land produce vegetation: seed-bearing plants and trees on the land that bear fruit with seed in it, according to their various kinds." And it was so. ¹²The land produced vegetation: plants bearing seed according to their kinds and

trees bearing fruit with seed in it according to their kinds. And God saw that it was good. ¹³And there was evening, and there was morning—the third day.

¹⁴And God said, "Let there be lights in the vault of the sky to separate the day from the night, and let them serve as signs to mark sacred times, and days and years, ¹⁵and let them be lights in the vault of the sky to give light on the earth." And it was so. ¹⁶God made two great lights—the greater light to govern the day and the lesser light to govern the night. He also made the stars. ¹⁷God set them in the vault of the sky to give light on the earth, ¹⁸to govern the day and the night, and to separate light from darkness. And God saw that it was good. ¹⁹And there was evening, and there was morning—the fourth day.

²⁰And God said, "Let the water teem

BREAKTHROUGH!

The Spirit of God

(GENESIS 1:2)

In the language this book was written in, Hebrew, the word *spirit* can also mean "wind" or "breath." So the Spirit of God is like strength. It's the "breath" of God that makes living beings come to life.

with living creatures, and let birds fly above the earth across the vault of the sky." ²¹So God created the great creatures of the sea and every living thing with which the water teems and that moves about in it, according to their kinds, and every winged bird according to its kind. And God saw that it was good. ²²God blessed them and said, "Be fruitful and increase in number and fill the water in the seas, and let the birds increase on the earth." ²³And there was evening, and there was morning—the fifth day.

²⁴And God said, "Let the land produce living creatures according to their kinds: the livestock, the creatures that move along the ground, and the wild animals, each according to its kind." And it was so. ²⁵God made the wild animals according to their kinds, the livestock according to their kinds, and all the creatures that move along the ground according to their kinds. And God saw that it was good.

²⁶Then God said, "Let us make mankind in our image, in our likeness, so that they may rule over the fish in the sea and the birds in the sky, over the livestock and all the wild animals,ᵃ and over all the creatures that move along the ground."

²⁷So God created mankind in his own image,
in the image of God he created them;
male and female he created them.

²⁸God blessed them and said to them, "Be fruitful and increase in number; fill the earth and subdue it. Rule over the fish in the sea and the birds in the sky and over every living creature that moves on the ground." ²⁹Then God said, "I give you every seed-bearing plant on the face of the whole earth and every tree that has fruit with seed in it. They will be yours for food. ³⁰And to all the

---

ᵃ 26 Probable reading of the original Hebrew text (see Syriac); Masoretic Text *the earth* beasts of the earth and all the birds in the sky and all the creatures that move along the ground—everything that has the breath of life in it—I give every green plant for food." And it was so. ³¹God saw all that he had made, and it was very good. And there was evening, and there was morning—the sixth day.

2 Thus the heavens and the earth were completed in all their vast array.

²By the seventh day God had finished the work he had been doing; so on the seventh day he rested from all his work. ³Then God blessed the seventh day and made it holy, because on it he rested from all the work of creating that he had done.

Adam and Eve

⁴This is the account of the heavens and the earth when they were created, when the Lord God made the earth and the heavens.

⁵Now no shrub had yet appeared on the earthª and no plant had yet sprung up, for the Lord God had not sent rain on the earth and there was no one to work the ground, ⁶but streamsᵇ came up from the earth and watered the whole surface of the ground. ⁷Then the Lord God formed a manᶜ from the dust of the ground and breathed into his nostrils the breath of life, and the man became a living being.

⁸Now the Lord God had planted a garden in the east, in Eden; and there he put the man he had formed. ⁹The Lord God made all kinds of trees grow out of the ground—trees that were pleasing to the eye and good for food. In the middle of the garden were the tree of life and the tree of the knowledge of good and evil.

¹⁰A river watering the garden flowed from Eden; from there it was separated into four headwaters. ¹¹The name of the first is the Pishon; it winds through the entire land of Havilah, where there is gold. ¹²(The gold of that land is good; aromatic resinᵈ and onyx are also there.)

¹³The name of the second river is the Gihon; it winds through the entire land of Cush.ᵉ ¹⁴The name of the third river is the Tigris; it runs along the east side of Ashur. And the fourth river is the Euphrates.

¹⁵The Lord God took the man and put him in the Garden of Eden to work it and take care of it. ¹⁶And the Lord God commanded the man, "You are free to eat from any tree in the garden; ¹⁷but you must not eat from the tree of the knowledge of good and evil, for when you eat from it you will certainly die."

¹⁸The Lord God said, "It is not good for the man to be alone. I will make a helper suitable for him."

¹⁹Now the Lord God had formed out of the ground all the wild animals and all the birds in the sky. He brought them to the man to see what he would name them; and whatever the man called each living creature, that was its name. ²⁰So the man gave names to all the livestock, the birds in the sky and all the wild animals.

But for Adamᶠ no suitable helper was found. ²¹So the Lord God caused the man to fall into a deep sleep; and while he was sleeping, he took one of the man's ribsᵍ and then closed up the place with flesh. ²²Then the Lord God made a woman from the ribʰ he had taken out of the man, and he brought her to the man.

²³The man said,

"This is now bone of my bones
    and flesh of my flesh;
she shall be called 'woman,'
    for she was taken out of man."

²⁴That is why a man leaves his father and mother and is united to his wife, and they become one flesh.

²⁵Adam and his wife were both naked, and they felt no shame.

The Fall

3 Now the serpent was more crafty than any of the wild animals the Lord God had made. He said to the woman, "Did

---

ª 5 Or *land*; also in verse 6   ᵇ 6 Or *mist*   ᶜ 7 The Hebrew for *man (adam)* sounds like and may be related to the Hebrew for *ground (adamah)*; it is also the name *Adam* (see verse 20).   ᵈ 12 Or *good; pearls*   ᵉ 13 Possibly southeast Mesopotamia   ᶠ 20 Or *the man*   ᵍ 21 Or *took part of the man's side*   ʰ 22 Or *part*

THE
WITNESSES

✓ **ADAM** (GENESIS 2:20)
This is the name of the first man who lived on the earth. In some verses, like Genesis 1:26, Adam really means "human being" (man and woman). But there are other things you should know about this name. There's a play on the Hebrew words *Adam*, which means "man," and *Adama*, which means "earth." This is because God created him from the soil of the earth. This play on words shows us the relationship between human beings and the earth.

God really say, 'You must not eat from any tree in the garden'?"

²The woman said to the serpent, "We may eat fruit from the trees in the garden, ³but God did say, 'You must not eat fruit from the tree that is in the middle of the garden, and you must not touch it, or you will die.' "

⁴"You will not certainly die," the serpent said to the woman. ⁵"For God knows that when you eat from it your eyes will be opened, and you will be like God, knowing good and evil."

⁶When the woman saw that the fruit of the tree was good for food and pleasing to the eye, and also desirable for gaining wisdom, she took some and ate it. She also gave some to her husband, who was with her, and he ate it. ⁷Then the eyes of both of them were opened, and they realized they were naked; so they sewed fig leaves together and made coverings for themselves.

⁸Then the man and his wife heard the sound of the LORD God as he was walking in the garden in the cool of the day, and they hid from the LORD God among the trees of the garden. ⁹But the LORD God called to the man, "Where are you?"

¹⁰He answered, "I heard you in the garden, and I was afraid because I was naked; so I hid."

¹¹And he said, "Who told you that you were naked? Have you eaten from the tree that I commanded you not to eat from?"

¹²The man said, "The woman you put here with me—she gave me some fruit from the tree, and I ate it."

¹³Then the LORD God said to the woman, "What is this you have done?"

The woman said, "The serpent deceived me, and I ate."

¹⁴So the LORD God said to the serpent, "Because you have done this,

"Cursed are you above all livestock
    and all wild animals!
You will crawl on your belly
    and you will eat dust
    all the days of your life.
¹⁵ And I will put enmity
    between you and the woman,
    and between your offspring[a] and
        hers;
he will crush[b] your head,
    and you will strike his heel."

¹⁶To the woman he said,

"I will make your pains in childbearing
        very severe;

---

[a] 15 Or seed   [b] 15 Or strike

BREAKTHROUGH!

Offspring
(GENESIS 3:15)

These are the people who belong to the same family, starting with the oldest and going on down to the youngest. For example, I'm an offspring of my mother and she's an offspring of her mother, who is my grandmother, and so on. When I have a son or daughter, that child will be my offspring.

with painful labor you will give birth
    to children.
Your desire will be for your husband,
    and he will rule over you."

¹⁷To Adam he said, "Because you listened to your wife and ate fruit from the tree about which I commanded you, 'You must not eat from it,'

"Cursed is the ground because of you;
    through painful toil you will eat food
      from it
    all the days of your life.
¹⁸It will produce thorns and thistles for
    you,
    and you will eat the plants of the
      field.
¹⁹By the sweat of your brow
    you will eat your food
until you return to the ground,
    since from it you were taken;

for dust you are
    and to dust you will return."

²⁰Adam[a] named his wife Eve,[b] because she would become the mother of all the living.

²¹The Lᴏʀᴅ God made garments of skin for Adam and his wife and clothed them. ²²And the Lᴏʀᴅ God said, "The man has now become like one of us, knowing good and evil. He must not be allowed to reach out his hand and take also from the tree of life and eat, and live forever." ²³So the Lᴏʀᴅ God banished him from the Garden of Eden to work the ground from which he had been taken. ²⁴After he drove the man out, he placed on the east side[c] of the Garden of Eden cherubim and a flaming sword flashing back and forth to guard the way to the tree of life.

Cain and Abel

4 Adam[a] made love to his wife Eve, and she became pregnant and gave birth

---

[a] *20,1 Or The man*   [b] *20 Eve probably means* living.
[c] *24 Or placed in front*

BREAKTHROUGH!

Cherubim
(GENESIS 3:24)

These are heavenly beings with wings who serve God, but they're not God. That's why we don't worship them.

to Cain.[a] She said, "With the help of the LORD I have brought forth[b] a man." [2]Later she gave birth to his brother Abel.

Now Abel kept flocks, and Cain worked

THE
WITNESSES

✓ **EVE** (GENESIS 3:20)
This is the name of the first woman. In Hebrew, the name Eve and the word that means "life" or "living" sound alike. God called her Eve because she would be able to create new life through her children.

✓ **CAIN** (GENESIS 4:1)
Cain was the name of Adam and Eve's first son. The name Cain sounds very much like the Hebrew action word that means "acquire." Cain is best known as the first murderer in history, because he killed his own brother, Abel, just because he was jealous of him. How terrible!

✓ **ABEL** (GENESIS 4:2)
Abel was Adam and Eve's second son. The Hebrew word *hebel* means anything that doesn't last long. Abel was killed by his brother, Cain.

the soil. [3]In the course of time Cain brought some of the fruits of the soil as an offering to the LORD. [4]And Abel also brought an offering—fat portions from some of the firstborn of his flock. The LORD looked with favor on Abel and his offering, [5]but on Cain and his offering he did not look with favor. So Cain was very angry, and his face was downcast.

[6]Then the LORD said to Cain, "Why are you angry? Why is your face downcast? [7]If you do what is right, will you not be accepted? But if you do not do what is right, sin is crouching at your door; it desires to have you, but you must rule over it."

[8]Now Cain said to his brother Abel, "Let's go out to the field."[c] While they were in the field, Cain attacked his brother Abel and killed him.

[9]Then the LORD said to Cain, "Where is your brother Abel?"

"I don't know," he replied. "Am I my brother's keeper?"

[10]The LORD said, "What have you done? Listen! Your brother's blood cries out to me from the ground. [11]Now you are under a curse and driven from the ground, which opened its mouth to receive your brother's blood from your hand. [12]When you work the ground, it will no longer yield its crops for you. You will be a restless wanderer on the earth."

[13]Cain said to the LORD, "My punishment is more than I can bear. [14]Today you are driving me from the land, and I will be hidden from your presence; I will be a restless wanderer on the earth, and whoever finds me will kill me."

[15]But the LORD said to him, "Not so[d]; anyone who kills Cain will suffer vengeance seven times over." Then the LORD put a mark on Cain so that no one who found him would kill him. [16]So Cain went out from the LORD's presence and lived in the land of Nod,[e] east of Eden.

[17]Cain made love to his wife, and she became pregnant and gave birth to Enoch. Cain was then building a city, and

---

[a] 1 *Cain* sounds like the Hebrew for *brought forth* or *acquired.*   [b] 1 Or *have acquired*   [c] 8 Samaritan Pentateuch, Septuagint, Vulgate and Syriac; Masoretic Text does not have *"Let's go out to the field."*
[d] 15 Septuagint, Vulgate and Syriac; Hebrew *Very well*
[e] 16 *Nod* means *wandering* (see verses 12 and 14).

he named it after his son Enoch. ¹⁸To Enoch was born Irad, and Irad was the father of Mehujael, and Mehujael was the father of Methushael, and Methushael was the father of Lamech.

¹⁹Lamech married two women, one named Adah and the other Zillah. ²⁰Adah gave birth to Jabal; he was the father of those who live in tents and raise livestock. ²¹His brother's name was Jubal; he was the father of all who play stringed instruments and pipes. ²²Zillah also had a son, Tubal-Cain, who forged all kinds of tools out of[a] bronze and iron. Tubal-Cain's sister was Naamah.

²³Lamech said to his wives,

"Adah and Zillah, listen to me;
    wives of Lamech, hear my words.
I have killed a man for wounding me,
    a young man for injuring me.
²⁴If Cain is avenged seven times,
    then Lamech seventy-seven times."

²⁵Adam made love to his wife again, and she gave birth to a son and named him Seth,[b] saying, "God has granted me another child in place of Abel, since Cain killed him." ²⁶Seth also had a son, and he named him Enosh.

At that time people began to call on[c] the name of the LORD.

From Adam to Noah

5 This is the written account of Adam's family line.

When God created mankind, he made them in the likeness of God. ²He created them male and female and blessed them. And he named them "Mankind"[d] when they were created.

³When Adam had lived 130 years, he had a son in his own likeness, in his own image; and he named him Seth. ⁴After Seth was born, Adam lived 800 years and had other sons and daughters. ⁵Altogether, Adam lived a total of 930 years, and then he died.

⁶When Seth had lived 105 years, he became the father[e] of Enosh. ⁷After he became the father of Enosh, Seth lived 807 years and had other sons and daughters. ⁸Altogether, Seth lived a total of 912 years, and then he died.

⁹When Enosh had lived 90 years, he became the father of Kenan. ¹⁰After he became the father of Kenan, Enosh lived 815 years and had other sons and daughters. ¹¹Altogether, Enosh lived a total of 905 years, and then he died.

¹²When Kenan had lived 70 years, he became the father of Mahalalel. ¹³After he became the father of Mahalalel, Kenan lived 840 years and had other sons and daughters. ¹⁴Altogether, Kenan lived a total of 910 years, and then he died.

¹⁵When Mahalalel had lived 65 years, he became the father of Jared. ¹⁶After he became the father of Jared, Mahalalel lived 830 years and had other sons and daughters. ¹⁷Altogether, Mahalalel lived a total of 895 years, and then he died.

¹⁸When Jared had lived 162 years, he became the father of Enoch. ¹⁹After he became the father of Enoch, Jared lived 800 years and had other sons and daughters. ²⁰Altogether, Jared lived a total of 962 years, and then he died.

²¹When Enoch had lived 65 years, he became the father of Methuselah. ²²After he became the father of Methuselah, Enoch walked faithfully with God 300 years and had other sons and daughters. ²³Altogether, Enoch lived a total of 365 years. ²⁴Enoch walked faithfully with God; then he was no more, because God took him away.

²⁵When Methuselah had lived 187 years, he became the father of Lamech. ²⁶After he became the father of Lamech, Methuselah lived 782 years and had other sons and daughters. ²⁷Altogether, Methuselah lived a total of 969 years, and then he died.

²⁸When Lamech had lived 182 years, he had a son. ²⁹He named him Noah[f] and said, "He will comfort us in the labor and painful toil of our hands caused by the ground the LORD has cursed." ³⁰After Noah was born, Lamech lived 595 years and

---

[a] 22 Or *who instructed all who work in*   [b] 25 *Seth* probably means *granted.*   [c] 26 Or *to proclaim*   [d] 2 Hebrew *adam*   [e] 6 *Father* may mean *ancestor*; also in verses 7-26.   [f] 29 *Noah* sounds like the Hebrew for *comfort.*

had other sons and daughters. ³¹Altogether, Lamech lived a total of 777 years, and then he died.

³²After Noah was 500 years old, he became the father of Shem, Ham and Japheth.

Wickedness in the World

6 When human beings began to increase in number on the earth and daughters were born to them, ²the sons of God saw that the daughters of humans were beautiful, and they married any of them they chose. ³Then the LORD said, "My Spirit will not contend with*ᵃ* humans forever, for they are mortal*ᵇ*; their days will be a hundred and twenty years."

⁴The Nephilim were on the earth in those days—and also afterward—when the sons of God went to the daughters of humans and had children by them. They were the heroes of old, men of renown.

⁵The LORD saw how great the wickedness of the human race had become on the earth, and that every inclination of the

---

ᵃ 3 Or *My spirit will not remain in*   *ᵇ* 3 Or *corrupt*

THE WITNESSES

✓ **SETH** (GENESIS 4:25)
Seth was Adam and Eve's third son. His name means "substitute," because he took Abel's place as the father of a family who did God's will, unlike Cain, who turned his back on God and didn't give him a place in his life.

✓ **NOAH** (GENESIS 5:29)
The name Noah sounds a little like the Hebrew word that means "comfort" or "rest." God chose him to bring comfort and rest to humanity. First of all, he warned them that God's judgment was coming in the form of a flooding rain. Second, he built a huge floating house that saved the lives of his family and a lot of animals.

BREAKTHROUGH!

Who were these "sons of God"?
(GENESIS 6:2)
It isn't easy to understand who they were. Experts have several ideas. Some say they were divine beings who lived in heaven. Others say they were people who had important jobs. And others think they were a famous group of heroes who existed in the times Genesis 6:4 talks about.

thoughts of the human heart was only evil all the time. ⁶The LORD regretted that he had made human beings on the earth, and his heart was deeply troubled. ⁷So the LORD said, "I will wipe from the face of the earth the human race I have created—and with them the animals, the birds and the creatures that move along the ground—for I regret that I have made them." ⁸But Noah found favor in the eyes of the LORD.

Noah and the Flood

⁹This is the account of Noah and his family.

Noah was a righteous man, blameless among the people of his time, and he

BREAKTHROUGH!

Was God sorry he had created human beings?

(GENESIS 6:5-7)

Sinfulness in people makes God sad, because it hurts him that people have turned away and don't pay attention to him. From what the Bible says here, we can understand that God really was sorry. We also need to understand that many times the Bible says God does "human" things and acts as if he were a person. That's just so we can make sense of it. It doesn't mean that he really thinks or acts exactly the way we would.

walked faithfully with God. ¹⁰Noah had three sons: Shem, Ham and Japheth.

¹¹Now the earth was corrupt in God's sight and was full of violence. ¹²God saw how corrupt the earth had become, for all the people on earth had corrupted their ways. ¹³So God said to Noah, "I am going to put an end to all people, for the earth is filled with violence because of them. I am surely going to destroy both them and the earth. ¹⁴So make yourself an ark of cypress*a* wood; make rooms in it and coat it with pitch inside and out. ¹⁵This is how you are to build it: The ark is to be three hundred cubits long, fifty cubits wide and thirty cubits high.*b* ¹⁶Make a roof for it, leaving below the roof an opening one cubit*c* high all around.*d* Put a door in the side of the ark and make lower, middle and upper decks. ¹⁷I am going to bring floodwaters on the earth to destroy all life under the heavens, every creature that has the breath of life in it. Everything on earth will perish. ¹⁸But I will establish my covenant with you, and you will enter the ark—you and your sons and your wife and your sons' wives with you. ¹⁹You are to bring into the ark two of all living creatures, male and female, to keep them alive with you. ²⁰Two of every kind of bird, of every kind of animal and of every kind of creature that moves along the ground will come to you to be kept alive. ²¹You are to take every kind of food that is to be eaten and store it away as food for you and for them."

²²Noah did everything just as God commanded him.

7 The LORD then said to Noah, "Go into the ark, you and your whole family, because I have found you righteous in this generation. ²Take with you seven pairs of every kind of clean animal, a male and its mate, and one pair of every kind of unclean animal, a male and its mate, ³and also seven pairs of every kind of bird, male and female, to keep their various kinds alive throughout the earth. ⁴Seven days from now I will send rain on the

---

a 14 The meaning of the Hebrew for this word is uncertain.   *b* 15 That is, about 450 feet long, 75 feet wide and 45 feet high or about 135 meters long, 23 meters wide and 14 meters high   *c* 16 That is, about 18 inches or about 45 centimeters   *d* 16 The meaning of the Hebrew for this clause is uncertain.

earth for forty days and forty nights, and I will wipe from the face of the earth every living creature I have made."

⁵And Noah did all that the LORD commanded him.

⁶Noah was six hundred years old when the floodwaters came on the earth. ⁷And Noah and his sons and his wife and his sons' wives entered the ark to escape the waters of the flood. ⁸Pairs of clean and unclean animals, of birds and of all creatures that move along the ground, ⁹male and female, came to Noah and entered the ark, as God had commanded Noah. ¹⁰And after the seven days the floodwaters came on the earth.

¹¹In the six hundredth year of Noah's life, on the seventeenth day of the second month—on that day all the springs of the great deep burst forth, and the floodgates of the heavens were opened. ¹²And rain fell on the earth forty days and forty nights.

¹³On that very day Noah and his sons, Shem, Ham and Japheth, together with his wife and the wives of his three sons, entered the ark. ¹⁴They had with them every wild animal according to its kind, all livestock according to their kinds, every creature that moves along the ground according to its kind and every bird according to its kind, everything with wings. ¹⁵Pairs of all creatures that have the breath of life in them came to Noah and entered the ark. ¹⁶The animals going in were male and female of every living thing, as God had commanded Noah. Then the LORD shut him in.

¹⁷For forty days the flood kept coming on the earth, and as the waters increased they lifted the ark high above the earth. ¹⁸The waters rose and increased greatly on the earth, and the ark floated on the surface of the water. ¹⁹They rose greatly on the earth, and all the high mountains under the entire heavens were covered. ²⁰The waters rose and covered the mountains to a depth of more than fifteen cubits.[a,b] ²¹Every living thing that moved on land perished—birds, livestock, wild animals, all the creatures that swarm over the earth, and all mankind. ²²Everything on dry land that had the breath of life in

its nostrils died. ²³Every living thing on the face of the earth was wiped out; people and animals and the creatures that move along the ground and the birds were wiped from the earth. Only Noah was left, and those with him in the ark.

²⁴The waters flooded the earth for a hundred and fifty days.

8 But God remembered Noah and all the wild animals and the livestock that were with him in the ark, and he sent a wind over the earth, and the waters receded. ²Now the springs of the deep and the floodgates of the heavens had been closed, and the rain had stopped falling from the sky. ³The water receded steadily from the earth. At the end of the hundred and fifty days the water had gone down, ⁴and on the seventeenth day of the

---

[a] 20 That is, about 23 feet or about 6.8 meters
[b] 20 Or rose more than fifteen cubits, and the mountains were covered

ARARAT

(GENESIS 8:4)

Ararat is the highest mountain in Turkey. It's more than 16,945 feet (5,195 m) high. It is an inactive volcano, and its peak is always covered with snow.

seventh month the ark came to rest on the mountains of Ararat. ⁵The waters continued to recede until the tenth month, and on the first day of the tenth month the tops of the mountains became visible.

⁶After forty days Noah opened a window he had made in the ark ⁷and sent out a raven, and it kept flying back and forth until the water had dried up from the earth. ⁸Then he sent out a dove to see if the water had receded from the surface of the ground. ⁹But the dove could find nowhere to perch because there was water over all the surface of the earth; so it returned to Noah in the ark. He reached out his hand and took the dove and brought it back to himself in the ark. ¹⁰He waited seven more days and again sent out the dove from the ark. ¹¹When the dove returned to him in the evening, there in its beak was a freshly plucked olive leaf!

BREAK THROUGH!

Tenth month
(GENESIS 8:5)
It is Tebeth, the tenth month of the Jewish lunar calendar. It would be from the middle of December to the middle of January in our solar calendar.

BREAK THROUGH!

Seventh month
(GENESIS 8:4)
In other languages, the months of the year have different names. And the Jews organized months differently than our calendar. The seventh month belongs to the old Jewish calendar. Its real name in Hebrew is *Ethanim*. In our solar calendar, this is from the middle of September to the middle of October. It rains a lot in this month.

Then Noah knew that the water had receded from the earth. ¹²He waited seven more days and sent the dove out again, but this time it did not return to him.

¹³By the first day of the first month of Noah's six hundred and first year, the water had dried up from the earth. Noah then removed the covering from the ark and saw that the surface of the ground was dry. ¹⁴By the twenty-seventh day of the second month the earth was completely dry.

¹⁵Then God said to Noah, ¹⁶"Come out of the ark, you and your wife and your sons and their wives. ¹⁷Bring out every kind of living creature that is with you—the birds, the animals, and all the creatures that move along the ground—so they can multiply on the earth and be fruitful and increase in number on it."

¹⁸So Noah came out, together with his sons and his wife and his sons' wives. ¹⁹All the animals and all the creatures that move along the ground and all the birds—everything that moves on land—came out of the ark, one kind after another.

20Then Noah built an altar to the Lord and, taking some of all the clean animals and clean birds, he sacrificed burnt offerings on it. 21The Lord smelled the pleasing aroma and said in his heart: "Never again will I curse the ground because of humans, even though[a] every inclination of the human heart is evil from childhood. And never again will I destroy all living creatures, as I have done.

22 "As long as the earth endures,
  seedtime and harvest,
  cold and heat,
  summer and winter,
  day and night
  will never cease."

God's Covenant With Noah

9 Then God blessed Noah and his sons, saying to them, "Be fruitful and increase in number and fill the earth. 2The fear and dread of you will fall on all the

Altar
(GENESIS 8:20)

An altar was a high place, a pile of dirt where they offered the sacrifices. The offering was made by sacrificing (that means killing) an animal and then burning it completely on the altar, because nothing could be left to be used for any other thing.

beasts of the earth, and on all the birds in the sky, on every creature that moves along the ground, and on all the fish in the sea; they are given into your hands. 3Everything that lives and moves about will be food for you. Just as I gave you the green plants, I now give you everything.

4"But you must not eat meat that has its lifeblood still in it. 5And for your lifeblood I will surely demand an accounting. I will demand an accounting from every animal. And from each human being, too, I will demand an accounting for the life of another human being.

6 "Whoever sheds human blood,
  by humans shall their blood be
    shed;
for in the image of God
  has God made mankind.

7As for you, be fruitful and increase in number; multiply on the earth and increase upon it."

8Then God said to Noah and to his sons with him: 9"I now establish my covenant with you and with your descendants after you 10and with every living creature that was with you—the birds, the livestock and all the wild animals, all those that came out of the ark with you—every living creature on earth. 11I establish my covenant with you: Never again will all life be destroyed by the waters of a flood; never again will there be a flood to destroy the earth."

12And God said, "This is the sign of the covenant I am making between me and you and every living creature with you, a covenant for all generations to come: 13I have set my rainbow in the clouds, and it will be the sign of the covenant between me and the earth. 14Whenever I bring clouds over the earth and the rainbow appears in the clouds, 15I will remember my covenant between me and you and all living creatures of every kind. Never again will the waters become a flood to destroy all life. 16Whenever the rainbow appears in the clouds, I will see it and remember the everlasting covenant between God and all living creatures of every kind on the earth."

17So God said to Noah, "This is the

---

a 21 Or humans, for

sign of the covenant I have established between me and all life on the earth."

The Sons of Noah

¹⁸The sons of Noah who came out of the ark were Shem, Ham and Japheth. (Ham was the father of Canaan.) ¹⁹These were the three sons of Noah, and from them came the people who were scattered over the whole earth.

THE
WITNESSES

✓ **SHEM, HAM AND JAPHETH**
(GENESIS 9:18)
These were the names of Noah's three sons. The word "Semite" comes from Shem. Semites are a group of people who have related languages called Semitic languages. The people of Israel are one of these groups. Ham is the father of the Canaanites, the people of the promised land. Japheth is the father of the people who are not Semite. They live on the coasts of the Mediterranean Sea and Asia Minor.

²⁰Noah, a man of the soil, proceeded*a* to plant a vineyard. ²¹When he drank some of its wine, he became drunk and lay uncovered inside his tent. ²²Ham, the father of Canaan, saw his father naked and told his two brothers outside. ²³But Shem and Japheth took a garment and laid it across their shoulders; then they walked in backward and covered their father's naked body. Their faces were turned the other way so that they would not see their father naked.

²⁴When Noah awoke from his wine and found out what his youngest son had done to him, ²⁵he said,

"Cursed be Canaan!
The lowest of slaves
will he be to his brothers."

²⁶He also said,

"Praise be to the LORD, the God of
Shem!
May Canaan be the slave of Shem.
²⁷May God extend Japheth's*b* territory;
may Japheth live in the tents of
Shem,
and may Canaan be the slave of
Japheth."

²⁸After the flood Noah lived 350 years. ²⁹Noah lived a total of 950 years, and then he died.

The Table of Nations

10 This is the account of Shem, Ham and Japheth, Noah's sons, who themselves had sons after the flood.

The Japhethites

²The sons*c* of Japheth:
Gomer, Magog, Madai, Javan, Tubal, Meshek and Tiras.
³The sons of Gomer:
Ashkenaz, Riphath and Togarmah.
⁴The sons of Javan:
Elishah, Tarshish, the Kittites and the Rodanites.*d* ⁵(From these the

---

a 20 Or *soil, was the first*   *b* 27 *Japheth* sounds like the Hebrew for *extend.*   *c* 2 *Sons* may mean *descendants* or *successors* or *nations;* also in verses 3, 4, 6, 7, 20-23, 29 and 31.   *d* 4 Some manuscripts of the Masoretic Text and Samaritan Pentateuch (see also Septuagint and 1 Chron. 1:7); most manuscripts of the Masoretic Text *Dodanites* maritime peoples spread out into their territories by their clans within their nations, each with its own language.)

The Hamites

6 The sons of Ham:

Cush, Egypt, Put and Canaan.

7 The sons of Cush:

Seba, Havilah, Sabtah, Raamah and Sabteka.

The sons of Raamah:

Sheba and Dedan.

8 Cush was the father*a* of Nimrod, who became a mighty warrior on the earth. 9 He was a mighty hunter before the LORD; that is why it is said, "Like Nimrod, a mighty hunter before the LORD." 10 The first centers of his kingdom were Babylon, Uruk, Akkad and Kalneh, in*b* Shinar.*c* 11 From that land he went to Assyria, where he built Nineveh, Rehoboth Ir,*d* Calah 12 and

THE SCENE

BABYLON

(GENESIS 10:10)

Babylon is the southern region of Mesopotamia. An important ancient empire also had this name. This is where the history of writing started 5,000 years ago.

BREAKTHROUGH!

Philistines

(GENESIS 10:14)

The Philistines were a group of people who weren't from Canaan. They arrived by sea along what is now the coast of Israel and Palestine. In the Bible, they're described as fearsome warriors, almost like pirates! For centuries, they were enemies of the Israelites. The Bible stories of Samson, Samuel, Saul and David tell about the fights between the Philistines and the Israelites. That famous giant that David killed with his slingshot, Goliath, was a Philistine.

Resen, which is between Nineveh and Calah—which is the great city.

13 Egypt was the father of

the Ludites, Anamites, Lehabites, Naphtuhites, 14 Pathrusites, Kasluhites (from whom the Philistines came) and Caphtorites.

15 Canaan was the father of

Sidon his firstborn,*e* and of the Hittites, 16 Jebusites, Amorites, Girgashites, 17 Hivites, Arkites, Sinites, 18 Arvadites, Zemarites and Hamathites.

a 8 Father *may mean* ancestor *or* predecessor *or* founder; also in verses 13, 15, 24 and 26.   *b 10* Or Uruk and Akkad—all of them in   *c 10* That is, Babylonia   *d 11* Or Nineveh with its city squares   *e 15* Or of the Sidonians, the foremost

Later the Canaanite clans scattered [19]and the borders of Canaan reached from Sidon toward Gerar as far as Gaza, and then toward Sodom, Gomorrah, Admah and Zeboyim, as far as Lasha.

[20]These are the sons of Ham by their clans and languages, in their territories and nations.

The Semites

[21]Sons were also born to Shem, whose older brother was[a] Japheth; Shem was the ancestor of all the sons of Eber.

[22]The sons of Shem:

Elam, Ashur, Arphaxad, Lud and Aram.

[23]The sons of Aram:

Uz, Hul, Gether and Meshek.[b]

[24]Arphaxad was the father of[c] Shelah, and Shelah the father of Eber.

[25]Two sons were born to Eber:

One was named Peleg,[d] because in his time the earth was divided; his brother was named Joktan.

[26]Joktan was the father of

Almodad, Sheleph, Hazarmaveth, Jerah, [27]Hadoram, Uzal, Diklah, [28]Obal, Abimael, Sheba, [29]Ophir, Havilah and Jobab. All these were sons of Joktan.

[30]The region where they lived stretched from Mesha toward Sephar, in the eastern hill country.

[31]These are the sons of Shem by their clans and languages, in their territories and nations.

[32]These are the clans of Noah's sons, according to their lines of descent, within their nations. From these the nations spread out over the earth after the flood.

The Tower of Babel

11 Now the whole world had one language and a common speech. [2]As people moved eastward,[e] they found a plain in Shinar[f] and settled there.

[3]They said to each other, "Come, let's make bricks and bake them thoroughly." They used brick instead of stone, and tar for mortar. [4]Then they said, "Come, let us build ourselves a city, with a tower that reaches to the heavens, so that we may make a name for ourselves; otherwise we will be scattered over the face of the whole earth."

[5]But the LORD came down to see the city and the tower the people were building. [6]The LORD said, "If as one people speaking the same language they have begun to do this, then nothing they plan to do will be impossible for them. [7]Come, let us go down and confuse their language so they will not understand each other."

---

[a] 21 Or Shem, the older brother of and 1 Chron. 1:17; Hebrew Mash.   [b] 23 See Septuagint   [c] 24 Hebrew; Septuagint father of Cainan, and Cainan was the father of   [d] 25 Peleg means division.   [e] 2 Or from the east; or in the east   [f] 2 That is, Babylonia

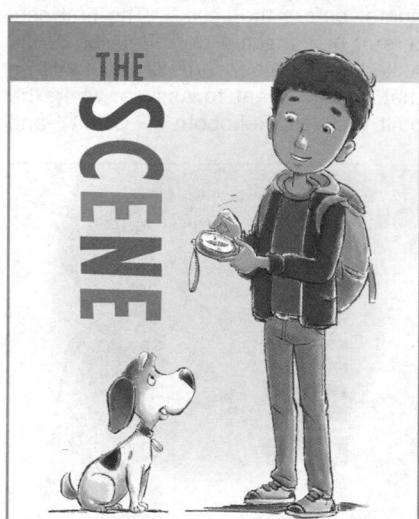

THE SCENE

BABEL

(GENESIS 11:9)

Babel is located on a plain in the land of Shinar, where the people wanted to build a tower so high, it would reach heaven. That was the famous Tower of Babel. The story is probably talking about building a *ziggurat*. These were temples in ancient Mesopotamia that had the shape of a tower or a sloping pyramid with steps at different levels.

⁸So the LORD scattered them from there over all the earth, and they stopped building the city. ⁹That is why it was called Babel *ᵃ* —because there the LORD confused the language of the whole world. From there the LORD scattered them over the face of the whole earth.

THE WITNESSES

✓ ABRAM (GENESIS 11:26)
He was the first of the patriarchs (fathers) of the people of Israel after the flood. During his life, he had two names. For the early Hebrews, the name of a person wasn't used just to know who that person was. It also said something about what that person was like. So a change of name meant a change of lifestyle. When he got to the land of Canaan, he was called Abram, which meant "my father is important." But then God made an agreement with him and made him the father of a nation and the owner of the land of Canaan. God changed his name and called him Abraham, which means "father of many."

From Shem to Abram

¹⁰This is the account of Shem's family line.

Two years after the flood, when Shem was 100 years old, he became the father *ᵇ* of Arphaxad. ¹¹And after he became the father of Arphaxad, Shem lived 500 years and had other sons and daughters.

¹²When Arphaxad had lived 35 years, he became the father of Shelah. ¹³And after he became the father of Shelah, Arphaxad lived 403 years and had other sons and daughters. *ᶜ*

¹⁴When Shelah had lived 30 years, he became the father of Eber. ¹⁵And after he became the father of Eber, Shelah lived 403 years and had other sons and daughters.

¹⁶When Eber had lived 34 years, he became the father of Peleg. ¹⁷And after he became the father of Peleg, Eber lived 430 years and had other sons and daughters.

¹⁸When Peleg had lived 30 years, he became the father of Reu. ¹⁹And after he became the father of Reu, Peleg lived 209 years and had other sons and daughters.

²⁰When Reu had lived 32 years, he became the father of Serug. ²¹And after he became the father of Serug, Reu lived 207 years and had other sons and daughters.

²²When Serug had lived 30 years, he became the father of Nahor. ²³And after he became the father of Nahor, Serug lived 200 years and had other sons and daughters.

²⁴When Nahor had lived 29 years, he became the father of Terah. ²⁵And after he became the father of Terah, Nahor lived 119 years and had other sons and daughters.

²⁶After Terah had lived 70 years, he became the father of Abram, Nahor and Haran.

ᵃ 9 That is, Babylon; *Babel* sounds like the Hebrew for confused.   *ᵇ 10 Father* may mean *ancestor;* also in verses 11-25.   *ᶜ 12,13* Hebrew; Septuagint (see also Luke 3:35, 36 and note at Gen. 10:24) *35 years, he became the father of Cainan.* ¹³*And after he became the father of Cainan, Arphaxad lived 430 years and had other sons and daughters, and then he died. When Cainan had lived 130 years, he became the father of Shelah. And after he became the father of Shelah, Cainan lived 330 years and had other sons and daughters*

Abram's Family

²⁷This is the account of Terah's family line.

Terah became the father of Abram, Nahor and Haran. And Haran became the father of Lot. ²⁸While his father Terah was still alive, Haran died in Ur of the Chaldeans, in the land of his birth. ²⁹Abram and Nahor both married. The name of Abram's wife was Sarai, and the name of Nahor's wife was Milkah; she was the daughter of Haran, the father of both Milkah and Iskah. ³⁰Now Sarai was childless because she was not able to conceive.

³¹Terah took his son Abram, his grandson Lot son of Haran, and his daughter-in-law Sarai, the wife of his son Abram, and together they set out from Ur of the Chaldeans to go to Canaan. But when they came to Harran, they settled there.

³²Terah lived 205 years, and he died in Harran.

The Call of Abram

12 The Lᴏʀᴅ had said to Abram, "Go from your country, your people and your father's household to the land I will show you.

² "I will make you into a great nation,
　　and I will bless you;
　I will make your name great,
　　and you will be a blessing.ᵃ
³ I will bless those who bless you,
　　and whoever curses you I will curse;
　and all peoples on earth
　　will be blessed through you."ᵇ

⁴So Abram went, as the Lᴏʀᴅ had told him; and Lot went with him. Abram was seventy-five years old when he set out from Harran. ⁵He took his wife Sarai, his nephew Lot, all the possessions they had accumulated and the people they had acquired in Harran, and they set out for the land of Canaan, and they arrived there.

⁶Abram traveled through the land as far as the site of the great tree of Moreh at Shechem. At that time the Canaanites were in the land. ⁷The Lᴏʀᴅ appeared to Abram and said, "To your offspringᶜ I will give this land." So he built an altar there to the Lᴏʀᴅ, who had appeared to him.

THE
WITNESSES

✓ SARAI (ɢᴇɴᴇsɪs 11:29)
The same thing that happened to Abraham also happened to Sarai. God changed her name too. (Look up Genesis 17:15.) Her name changed from "Sarai" (*princess*) to "Sarah" (*my princess*) when God gave her the blessing of becoming the mother of a great nation.

✓ LOT (ɢᴇɴᴇsɪs 12:4)
This name means "covered." He was Haran's son and Abraham's nephew. Because his father had died, he traveled to Haran with his grandfather, and then he continued on with Abraham and his family to Canaan. Abraham and Lot both had a lot of cattle. They decided to live in different places so their animals would have enough food to eat.

⁸From there he went on toward the hills east of Bethel and pitched his tent, with Bethel on the west and Ai on the east.

ᵃ 2 Or *be seen as blessed*   ᵇ 3 Or *earth / will use your name in blessings* (see 48:20)   ᶜ 7 Or *seed*

THE SCENE

CANAANITES

(GENESIS 12:6)

They lived in the land God promised Abraham and his offspring—the land he gave them to make their home. The promise was completely fulfilled when the Israelites reached Canaan after they had been freed from slavery in Egypt.

There he built an altar to the LORD and called on the name of the LORD.

⁹Then Abram set out and continued toward the Negev.

Abram in Egypt

¹⁰Now there was a famine in the land, and Abram went down to Egypt to live there for a while because the famine was severe. ¹¹As he was about to enter Egypt, he said to his wife Sarai, "I know what a beautiful woman you are. ¹²When the Egyptians see you, they will say, 'This is his wife.' Then they will kill me but will let you live. ¹³Say you are my sister, so that I will be treated well for your sake and my life will be spared because of you."

¹⁴When Abram came to Egypt, the Egyptians saw that Sarai was a very beautiful woman. ¹⁵And when Pharaoh's officials saw her, they praised her to Pharaoh, and she was taken into his palace. ¹⁶He treated Abram well for her sake, and Abram acquired sheep and cattle, male and female donkeys, male and female servants, and camels.

¹⁷But the LORD inflicted serious diseases on Pharaoh and his household because of Abram's wife Sarai. ¹⁸So Pharaoh summoned Abram. "What have you done to me?" he said. "Why didn't you tell me she was your wife? ¹⁹Why did you say, 'She is my sister,' so that I took her to be

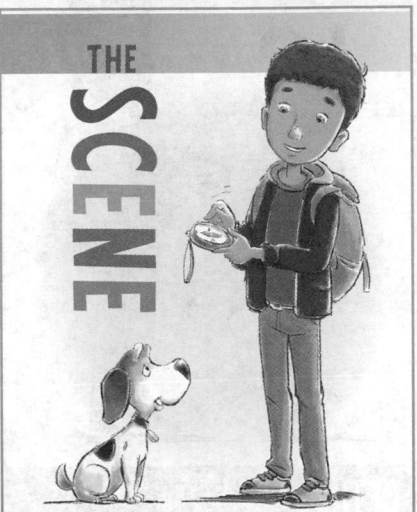

THE SCENE

EGYPT

(GENESIS 12:10)

Egypt is the name of the region in the northeastern part of Africa. Its borders have changed from time to time, but generally speaking, it was bordered by the Mediterranean Sea on the north. The huge waterfalls formed by the Nile River as it goes down toward the sea marked the southern boundary. The Red Sea was on the east, and the country belonging to the Libyans was on the west.

my wife? Now then, here is your wife. Take her and go!" ²⁰Then Pharaoh gave orders about Abram to his men, and they sent him on his way, with his wife and everything he had.

Abram and Lot Separate

13 So Abram went up from Egypt to the Negev, with his wife and everything he had, and Lot went with him. ²Abram had become very wealthy in livestock and in silver and gold.

THE SCENE

BETHEL

(GENESIS 13:3)

This is the name of a Canaanite city in the ancient region of Samaria, which was in the central section of the land of Canaan. The people decided to settle there because there was a lot of water, like many other areas in this region. The Canaanites who lived there had a sanctuary dedicated to the god "El." The Hebrew name of the city means "House of God" and comes from the vision Jacob had there. If you want to know more about that story, you can read Genesis 28:10–22.

³From the Negev he went from place to place until he came to Bethel, to the place between Bethel and Ai where his tent had been earlier ⁴and where he had first built an altar. There Abram called on the name of the LORD.

⁵Now Lot, who was moving about with Abram, also had flocks and herds and tents. ⁶But the land could not support them while they stayed together, for their possessions were so great that they were not able to stay together. ⁷And quarreling arose between Abram's herders and Lot's. The Canaanites and Perizzites were also living in the land at that time.

⁸So Abram said to Lot, "Let's not have any quarreling between you and me, or between your herders and mine, for we

BREAKTHROUGH!

Canaanites

(GENESIS 13:7)

I've been told that the Canaanites lived in the region of Canaan. That was the land where Abraham, Isaac, Jacob and later on the Israelites who were freed in Egypt all went to live. The Canaanites lived in a large region of the ancient Near East located between the Mediterranean Sea and the Jordan River. It's a very fertile area. This is where Israel, Palestine, part of Jordan and some parts of Syria and Lebanon are today.

BREAK THROUGH!

Perizzites

(GENESIS 13:7)

These people belonged to one of the groups that lived in Canaan before the Israelites arrived. The Israelites tried many times to make them leave but they couldn't ever get completely rid of them, because the Perizzites would hide in the mountains and defend themselves very bravely against their attacks.

are close relatives. ⁹Is not the whole land before you? Let's part company. If you go to the left, I'll go to the right; if you go to the right, I'll go to the left."

¹⁰Lot looked around and saw that the whole plain of the Jordan toward Zoar was well watered, like the garden of the LORD, like the land of Egypt. (This was before the LORD destroyed Sodom and Gomorrah.) ¹¹So Lot chose for himself the whole plain of the Jordan and set out toward the east. The two men parted company: ¹²Abram lived in the land of Canaan, while Lot lived among the cities of the plain and pitched his tents near Sodom. ¹³Now the people of Sodom were wicked and were sinning greatly against the LORD.

¹⁴The LORD said to Abram after Lot had parted from him, "Look around from where you are, to the north and south, to the east and west. ¹⁵All the land that you see I will give to you and your offspring*ᵃ* forever. ¹⁶I will make your offspring like the dust of the earth, so that if anyone could count the dust, then your offspring could be counted. ¹⁷Go, walk through the length and breadth of the land, for I am giving it to you."

¹⁸So Abram went to live near the great trees of Mamre at Hebron, where he pitched his tents. There he built an altar to the LORD.

Abram Rescues Lot

14 At the time when Amraphel was king of Shinar,*ᵇ* Arioch king of El-lasar, Kedorlaomer king of Elam and Tidal king of Goyim, ²these kings went to war against Bera king of Sodom, Birsha king of Gomorrah, Shinab king of Admah, Shemeber king of Zeboyim, and the king of Bela (that is, Zoar). ³All these latter kings joined forces in the Valley of Siddim (that is, the Dead Sea Valley). ⁴For twelve years they had been subject to Kedorlaomer, but in the thirteenth year they rebelled.

⁵In the fourteenth year, Kedorlaomer and the kings allied with him went out and defeated the Rephaites in Ashteroth Karnaim, the Zuzites in Ham, the Emites in Shaveh Kiriathaim ⁶and the Horites in the hill country of Seir, as far as El Paran near the desert. ⁷Then they turned back and went to En Mishpat (that is, Kadesh), and they conquered the whole territory of the Amalekites, as well as the Amorites who were living in Hazezon Tamar.

⁸Then the king of Sodom, the king of Gomorrah, the king of Admah, the king of Zeboyim and the king of Bela (that is, Zoar) marched out and drew up their battle lines in the Valley of Siddim ⁹against Kedorlaomer king of Elam, Tidal king of Goyim, Amraphel king of Shinar and Arioch king of Ellasar—four kings against five. ¹⁰Now the Valley of Siddim was full of tar pits, and when the kings of Sodom and Gomorrah fled, some of the men fell into them and the rest fled to the hills. ¹¹The four kings seized all the goods of

---

ᵃ 15 Or *seed*; also in verse 16   *ᵇ* 1 That is, Babylonia; also in verse 9

Sodom and Gomorrah and all their food; then they went away. ¹²They also carried off Abram's nephew Lot and his possessions, since he was living in Sodom.

¹³A man who had escaped came and reported this to Abram the Hebrew. Now Abram was living near the great trees of Mamre the Amorite, a brother*ᵃ* of Eshkol and Aner, all of whom were allied with Abram. ¹⁴When Abram heard that his relative had been taken captive, he called out the 318 trained men born in his household and went in pursuit as far as Dan. ¹⁵During the night Abram divided his men

to attack them and he routed them, pursuing them as far as Hobah, north of Damascus. ¹⁶He recovered all the goods and brought back his relative Lot and his possessions, together with the women and the other people.

¹⁷After Abram returned from defeating Kedorlaomer and the kings allied with him, the king of Sodom came out to meet him in the Valley of Shaveh (that is, the King's Valley).

¹⁸Then Melchizedek king of Salem brought out bread and wine. He was priest of God Most High, ¹⁹and he blessed Abram, saying,

"Blessed be Abram by God Most
    High,
    Creator of heaven and earth.
²⁰And praise be to God Most High,
    who delivered your enemies into
        your hand."

Then Abram gave him a tenth of everything.

²¹The king of Sodom said to Abram, "Give me the people and keep the goods for yourself."

²²But Abram said to the king of Sodom, "With raised hand I have sworn an oath to the Lord, God Most High, Creator of heaven and earth, ²³that I will accept nothing belonging to you, not even a thread or the strap of a sandal, so that you will never be able to say, 'I made Abram rich.' ²⁴I will accept nothing but what my men have eaten and the share that belongs to the men who went with me—to Aner, Eshkol and Mamre. Let them have their share."

The Lord's Covenant With Abram

15 After this, the word of the Lord came to Abram in a vision:

"Do not be afraid, Abram.
    I am your shield,*ᵇ*
    your very great reward.*ᶜ*"

²But Abram said, "Sovereign Lord, what can you give me since I remain childless and the one who will inherit*ᵈ* my estate is Eliezer of Damascus?" ³And Abram said,

THE
WITNESSES

✓ **MELCHIZEDEK** (GENESIS 14:18)
Melchizedek is a really mysterious person. His name means "Zedek is my king." Zedek was one of the gods worshiped in Salem. It also could mean "king of justice." He was both priest and king, like many kings and rulers in the ancient Near East.

ᵃ 13 Or a relative; or an ally   *ᵇ* 1 Or sovereign   *ᶜ* 1 Or shield; / your reward will be very great   *ᵈ* 2 The meaning of the Hebrew for this phrase is uncertain.

"You have given me no children; so a servant in my household will be my heir."

⁴Then the word of the LORD came to him: "This man will not be your heir, but a son who is your own flesh and blood will be your heir." ⁵He took him outside and said, "Look up at the sky and count the stars—if indeed you can count them." Then he said to him, "So shall your offspringᵃ be."

⁶Abram believed the LORD, and he credited it to him as righteousness.

⁷He also said to him, "I am the LORD, who brought you out of Ur of the Chaldeans to give you this land to take possession of it."

⁸But Abram said, "Sovereign LORD, how can I know that I will gain possession of it?"

⁹So the LORD said to him, "Bring me a heifer, a goat and a ram, each three years old, along with a dove and a young pigeon."

¹⁰Abram brought all these to him, cut them in two and arranged the halves opposite each other; the birds, however, he did not cut in half. ¹¹Then birds of prey came down on the carcasses, but Abram drove them away.

¹²As the sun was setting, Abram fell into a deep sleep, and a thick and dreadful darkness came over him. ¹³Then the LORD said to him, "Know for certain that for four hundred years your descendants will be strangers in a country not their own and that they will be enslaved and mistreated there. ¹⁴But I will punish the nation they serve as slaves, and afterward they will come out with great possessions. ¹⁵You, however, will go to your ancestors in peace and be buried at a good old age. ¹⁶In the fourth generation your descendants will come back here, for the sin of the Amorites has not yet reached its full measure."

¹⁷When the sun had set and darkness had fallen, a smoking firepot with a blazing torch appeared and passed between the pieces. ¹⁸On that day the LORD made a covenant with Abram and said, "To your descendants I give this land, from the Wadiᵇ of Egypt to the great river, the Euphrates— ¹⁹the land of the Kenites, Ken-

THE SCENE

EUPHRATES RIVER

(GENESIS 15:18)

This is a very important river in Western Asia. Its waters flow through Armenia, Syria and Iraq, joining the Tigris River to empty into the Persian Gulf. It flows through plains and mountains for more than 1,678 miles (2,700 km). This makes the land around it very fertile. I'm sure you'll remember that in the first part of this book (in 2:10–14), it mentions that this was one of the four rivers that flowed out of the river that watered the Garden of Eden.

izzites, Kadmonites, ²⁰Hittites, Perizzites, Rephaites, ²¹Amorites, Canaanites, Girgashites and Jebusites."

Hagar and Ishmael

16 Now Sarai, Abram's wife, had borne him no children. But she had an Egyptian slave named Hagar; ²so she said to Abram, "The LORD has kept me from having children. Go, sleep with my slave; perhaps I can build a family through her."

ᵃ 5 Or seed   ᵇ 18 Or river

Abram agreed to what Sarai said. ³So after Abram had been living in Canaan ten years, Sarai his wife took her Egyptian slave Hagar and gave her to her husband to be his wife. ⁴He slept with Hagar, and she conceived.

When she knew she was pregnant, she began to despise her mistress. ⁵Then Sarai said to Abram, "You are responsible for the wrong I am suffering. I put my slave in your arms, and now that she knows she is pregnant, she despises me. May the LORD judge between you and me."

⁶"Your slave is in your hands," Abram said. "Do with her whatever you think best." Then Sarai mistreated Hagar; so she fled from her.

⁷The angel of the LORD found Hagar near a spring in the desert; it was the spring that is beside the road to Shur. ⁸And he said, "Hagar, slave of Sarai, where have you come from, and where are you going?"

"I'm running away from my mistress Sarai," she answered.

⁹Then the angel of the LORD told her, "Go back to your mistress and submit to her." ¹⁰The angel added, "I will increase your descendants so much that they will be too numerous to count."

¹¹The angel of the LORD also said to her:

"You are now pregnant
    and you will give birth to a son.
You shall name him Ishmael,ᵃ
    for the LORD has heard of your
        misery.
¹² He will be a wild donkey of a man;
    his hand will be against everyone
    and everyone's hand against him,
and he will live in hostility
    towardᵇ all his brothers."

¹³She gave this name to the LORD who spoke to her: "You are the God who sees me," for she said, "I have now seenᶜ the One who sees me." ¹⁴That is why the well was called Beer Lahai Roiᵈ; it is still there, between Kadesh and Bered.

¹⁵So Hagar bore Abram a son, and Abram gave the name Ishmael to the son she had borne. ¹⁶Abram was eighty-six years old when Hagar bore him Ishmael.

The Covenant of Circumcision

17 When Abram was ninety-nine years old, the LORD appeared to him and said, "I am God Almightyᵉ; walk before me faithfully and be blameless. ²Then I will make my covenant between me and you and will greatly increase your numbers."

³Abram fell facedown, and God said to him, ⁴"As for me, this is my covenant with you: You will be the father of many nations. ⁵No longer will you be called Abramᶠ; your name will be Abraham,ᵍ for I have made you a father of many nations. ⁶I will make you very fruitful; I will make nations of you, and kings will come from you. ⁷I will establish my covenant as an everlasting covenant between me and you and your descendants after you for the generations to come, to be your God and the God of your descendants after you. ⁸The whole land of Canaan, where you now reside as a foreigner, I will give as an everlasting possession to you and your descendants after you; and I will be their God."

⁹Then God said to Abraham, "As for you, you must keep my covenant, you and your descendants after you for the generations to come. ¹⁰This is my covenant with you and your descendants after you, the covenant you are to keep: Every male among you shall be circumcised. ¹¹You are to undergo circumcision, and it will be the sign of the covenant between me and you. ¹²For the generations to come every male among you who is eight days old must be circumcised, including those born in your household or bought with money from a foreigner—those who are not your offspring. ¹³Whether born in your household or bought with your money, they must be circumcised. My covenant in your flesh is to be an everlasting covenant. ¹⁴Any uncircumcised male, who has not been circumcised in the flesh, will be cut off from his people; he has broken my covenant."

¹⁵God also said to Abraham, "As for Sarai your wife, you are no longer to call

---

ᵃ 11 *Ishmael* means *God hears.*   ᵇ 12 Or *live to the east / of*   ᶜ 13 Or *seen the back of*   ᵈ 14 *Beer Lahai Roi* means *well of the Living One who sees me.*   ᵉ 1 Hebrew *El-Shaddai*   ᶠ 5 *Abram* means *exalted father.*   ᵍ 5 *Abraham* probably means *father of many.*

her Sarai; her name will be Sarah. ¹⁶I will bless her and will surely give you a son by her. I will bless her so that she will be the mother of nations; kings of peoples will come from her."

¹⁷Abraham fell facedown; he laughed and said to himself, "Will a son be born to a man a hundred years old? Will Sarah bear a child at the age of ninety?" ¹⁸And Abraham said to God, "If only Ishmael might live under your blessing!"

¹⁹Then God said, "Yes, but your wife Sarah will bear you a son, and you will call him Isaac.ᵃ I will establish my covenant with him as an everlasting covenant for his descendants after him. ²⁰And as for Ishmael, I have heard you: I will surely bless him; I will make him fruitful and will greatly increase his numbers. He will be the father of twelve rulers, and I will make him into a great nation. ²¹But my covenant I will establish with Isaac, whom Sarah will bear to you by this time next year."

ᵃ *19 Isaac means he laughs.*

THE
WITNESSES

✓ HAGAR (GENESIS 16:1–3)
Hagar was the name of the Egyptian slave that gave Abraham his son Ishmael. The Arabs believe that Abraham's real wife was Hagar and not Sarah. That's why they believe they're the direct offspring of Abraham.

✓ ISHMAEL (GENESIS 16:11)
Ishmael means "God hears" or "God has heard." Ishmael's offspring are the Arab tribes that lived like nomads in the desert. They moved around from one place to another.

✓ ISAAC (GENESIS 17:21)
He's the Israelites' second great head of family. His name sounds a lot like a Hebrew action word that means "laugh," because that's what his mother, Sarah, did when she found out she was going to have a baby boy. Why wouldn't she laugh, since she was 90 years old and her husband, Abraham, was 100?

BREAKTHROUGH!

Circumcised
(GENESIS 17:10)
Circumcision is a practice where the skin that covers the end of the penis is cut off. This custom is a reminder of the covenant God made with Abraham.

²²When he had finished speaking with Abraham, God went up from him.

²³On that very day Abraham took his son Ishmael and all those born in his household or bought with his money, every male in his household, and circumcised them, as God told him. ²⁴Abraham was ninety-nine years old when he was circumcised, ²⁵and his son Ishmael was thirteen; ²⁶Abraham and his son Ishmael were both circumcised on that very day. ²⁷And every male in Abraham's household, including those born in his household or bought from a foreigner, was circumcised with him.

The Three Visitors

18 The LORD appeared to Abraham near the great trees of Mamre while he was sitting at the entrance to his tent in the heat of the day. ²Abraham looked up and saw three men standing nearby. When he saw them, he hurried from the entrance of his tent to meet them and bowed low to the ground.

³He said, "If I have found favor in your eyes, my lord,ᵃ do not pass your servant by. ⁴Let a little water be brought, and then you may all wash your feet and rest under this tree. ⁵Let me get you something to eat, so you can be refreshed and then go on your way—now that you have come to your servant."

"Very well," they answered, "do as you say."

⁶So Abraham hurried into the tent to Sarah. "Quick," he said, "get three seahsᵇ of the finest flour and knead it and bake some bread."

⁷Then he ran to the herd and selected a choice, tender calf and gave it to a servant, who hurried to prepare it. ⁸He then brought some curds and milk and the calf that had been prepared, and set these before them. While they ate, he stood near them under a tree.

⁹"Where is your wife Sarah?" they asked him.

"There, in the tent," he said.

¹⁰Then one of them said, "I will surely return to you about this time next year, and Sarah your wife will have a son."

Now Sarah was listening at the entrance to the tent, which was behind him. ¹¹Abraham and Sarah were already very old, and Sarah was past the age of childbearing. ¹²So Sarah laughed to herself as she thought, "After I am worn out and my lord is old, will I now have this pleasure?"

¹³Then the LORD said to Abraham, "Why did Sarah laugh and say, 'Will I really have a child, now that I am old?' ¹⁴Is anything too hard for the LORD? I will return to you at the appointed time next year, and Sarah will have a son."

¹⁵Sarah was afraid, so she lied and said, "I did not laugh."

But he said, "Yes, you did laugh."

Abraham Pleads for Sodom

¹⁶When the men got up to leave, they looked down toward Sodom, and Abraham walked along with them to see them on their way. ¹⁷Then the LORD said, "Shall I hide from Abraham what I am about to do? ¹⁸Abraham will surely become a great and powerful nation, and all nations on earth will be blessed through him.ᶜ ¹⁹For I have chosen him, so that he will direct his children and his household after him to keep the way of the LORD by doing what is right and just, so that the LORD will bring about for Abraham what he has promised him."

²⁰Then the LORD said, "The outcry against Sodom and Gomorrah is so great and their sin so grievous ²¹that I will go down and see if what they have done is as bad as the outcry that has reached me. If not, I will know."

²²The men turned away and went toward Sodom, but Abraham remained standing before the LORD.ᵈ ²³Then Abraham approached him and said: "Will you sweep away the righteous with the wicked? ²⁴What if there are fifty righteous people in the city? Will you really sweep it away and not spareᵉ the place for the sake of the fifty righteous people in it? ²⁵Far be it from you to do such a thing— to kill the righteous with the wicked, treating the righteous and the wicked alike. Far

---

ᵃ 3 Or *eyes, Lord*   ᵇ 6 That is, probably about 36 pounds or about 16 kilograms   ᶜ 18 Or *will use his name in blessings* (see 48:20)   ᵈ 22 Masoretic Text; an ancient Hebrew scribal tradition *but the LORD remained standing before Abraham*   ᵉ 24 Or *forgive*; also in verse 26 be it from you! Will not the Judge of all the earth do right?"

²⁶The LORD said, "If I find fifty righteous people in the city of Sodom, I will spare the whole place for their sake."

²⁷Then Abraham spoke up again: "Now that I have been so bold as to speak to the Lord, though I am nothing but dust and ashes, ²⁸what if the number of the righteous is five less than fifty? Will you destroy the whole city for lack of five people?"

"If I find forty-five there," he said, "I will not destroy it."

²⁹Once again he spoke to him, "What if only forty are found there?"

He said, "For the sake of forty, I will not do it."

³⁰Then he said, "May the Lord not be angry, but let me speak. What if only thirty can be found there?"

He answered, "I will not do it if I find thirty there."

³¹Abraham said, "Now that I have been so bold as to speak to the Lord, what if only twenty can be found there?"

He said, "For the sake of twenty, I will not destroy it."

³²Then he said, "May the Lord not be angry, but let me speak just once more. What if only ten can be found there?"

He answered, "For the sake of ten, I will not destroy it."

³³When the LORD had finished speaking with Abraham, he left, and Abraham returned home.

Sodom and Gomorrah Destroyed

19 The two angels arrived at Sodom in the evening, and Lot was sitting in the gateway of the city. When he saw them, he got up to meet them and bowed down with his face to the ground. ²"My lords," he said, "please turn aside to your servant's house. You can wash your feet and spend the night and then go on your way early in the morning."

"No," they answered, "we will spend the night in the square."

³But he insisted so strongly that they did go with him and entered his house. He prepared a meal for them, baking bread without yeast, and they ate. ⁴Before

BREAK THROUGH!

Angels

(GENESIS 19:1)

The Hebrew word translated here as "angels" also means "messengers."

they had gone to bed, all the men from every part of the city of Sodom—both young and old—surrounded the house. ⁵They called to Lot, "Where are the men who came to you tonight? Bring them out to us so that we can have sex with them."

⁶Lot went outside to meet them and shut the door behind him ⁷and said, "No, my friends. Don't do this wicked thing. ⁸Look, I have two daughters who have never slept with a man. Let me bring them out to you, and you can do what you like with them. But don't do anything to these men, for they have come under the protection of my roof."

⁹"Get out of our way," they replied. "This fellow came here as a foreigner, and now he wants to play the judge! We'll treat you worse than them." They kept bringing pressure on Lot and moved forward to break down the door.

¹⁰But the men inside reached out and pulled Lot back into the house and shut the door. ¹¹Then they struck the men who were at the door of the house, young and old, with blindness so that they could not find the door.

¹²The two men said to Lot, "Do you have anyone else here — sons-in-law, sons or daughters, or anyone else in the city who belongs to you? Get them out of here, ¹³because we are going to destroy this place. The outcry to the LORD against its people is so great that he has sent us to destroy it."

¹⁴So Lot went out and spoke to his sons-in-law, who were pledged to marry[a] his daughters. He said, "Hurry and get out of this place, because the LORD is about to destroy the city!" But his sons-in-law thought he was joking.

¹⁵With the coming of dawn, the angels urged Lot, saying, "Hurry! Take your wife and your two daughters who are here, or you will be swept away when the city is punished."

¹⁶When he hesitated, the men grasped his hand and the hands of his wife and of his two daughters and led them safely out of the city, for the LORD was merciful to them. ¹⁷As soon as they had brought them out, one of them said, "Flee for your lives! Don't look back, and don't stop anywhere in the plain! Flee to the mountains or you will be swept away!"

¹⁸But Lot said to them, "No, my lords,[b] please! ¹⁹Your[c] servant has found favor in your[c] eyes, and you[c] have shown great kindness to me in sparing my life. But I can't flee to the mountains; this disaster will overtake me, and I'll die. ²⁰Look, here is a town near enough to run to, and it is small. Let me flee to it—it is very small, isn't it? Then my life will be spared."

²¹He said to him, "Very well, I will grant this request too; I will not overthrow the town you speak of. ²²But flee there quickly, because I cannot do anything until you reach it." (That is why the town was called Zoar.[d])

²³By the time Lot reached Zoar, the sun had risen over the land. ²⁴Then the LORD rained down burning sulfur on Sodom and Gomorrah—from the LORD out of the heavens. ²⁵Thus he overthrew those cities and the entire plain, destroying all those living in the cities—and also the vegetation in the land. ²⁶But Lot's wife looked back, and she became a pillar of salt.

²⁷Early the next morning Abraham got

THE SCENE

SODOM AND GOMORRAH

(GENESIS 19:1–29)

These are the two most important cities on the plain near the Dead Sea. They became famous because God destroyed them with "burning sulfur" due to the sin of its people who lived there.

up and returned to the place where he had stood before the LORD. ²⁸He looked down toward Sodom and Gomorrah, toward all the land of the plain, and he saw dense smoke rising from the land, like smoke from a furnace.

²⁹So when God destroyed the cities of the plain, he remembered Abraham, and he brought Lot out of the catastrophe that overthrew the cities where Lot had lived.

Lot and His Daughters

³⁰Lot and his two daughters left Zoar and settled in the mountains, for he was afraid to stay in Zoar. He and his two daughters lived in a cave. ³¹One day the older daughter said to the younger, "Our father is old, and there is no man around

---

a 14 Or were married to   b 18 Or No, Lord; or No, my lord   c 19 The Hebrew is singular.   d 22 Zoar means small.

here to give us children—as is the custom all over the earth. ³²Let's get our father to drink wine and then sleep with him and preserve our family line through our father."

³³That night they got their father to drink wine, and the older daughter went in and slept with him. He was not aware of it when she lay down or when she got up.

³⁴The next day the older daughter said to the younger, "Last night I slept with my father. Let's get him to drink wine again tonight, and you go in and sleep with him so we can preserve our family line through our father." ³⁵So they got their father to drink wine that night also, and the younger daughter went in and slept with him. Again he was not aware of it when she lay down or when she got up.

³⁶So both of Lot's daughters became pregnant by their father. ³⁷The older daughter had a son, and she named him Moab[a]; he is the father of the Moabites of today. ³⁸The younger daughter also had a son, and she named him Ben-Ammi[b]; he is the father of the Ammonites[c] of today.

BREAKTHROUGH!

Lot and his daughters
(GENESIS 19:30-38)
Since the Moabites and the Ammonites were Lot's offspring, they were related to the Israelites, but they were never their friends.

Abraham and Abimelek

20 Now Abraham moved on from there into the region of the Negev and lived between Kadesh and Shur. For a while he stayed in Gerar, ²and there Abraham said of his wife Sarah, "She is my sister." Then Abimelek king of Gerar sent for Sarah and took her.

³But God came to Abimelek in a dream one night and said to him, "You are as good as dead because of the woman you have taken; she is a married woman."

⁴Now Abimelek had not gone near her, so he said, "Lord, will you destroy an innocent nation? ⁵Did he not say to me, 'She is my sister,' and didn't she also say, 'He is my brother'? I have done this with a clear conscience and clean hands."

⁶Then God said to him in the dream, "Yes, I know you did this with a clear conscience, and so I have kept you from sinning against me. That is why I did not let you touch her. ⁷Now return the man's wife, for he is a prophet, and he will pray for you and you will live. But if you do not return her, you may be sure that you and all who belong to you will die."

⁸Early the next morning Abimelek summoned all his officials, and when he told them all that had happened, they were very much afraid. ⁹Then Abimelek called Abraham in and said, "What have you done to us? How have I wronged you that you have brought such great guilt upon me and my kingdom? You have done things to me that should never be done." ¹⁰And Abimelek asked Abraham, "What was your reason for doing this?"

¹¹Abraham replied, "I said to myself, 'There is surely no fear of God in this place, and they will kill me because of my wife.' ¹²Besides, she really is my sister, the daughter of my father though not of my mother; and she became my wife. ¹³And when God had me wander from my father's household, I said to her, 'This is how you can show your love to me: Everywhere we go, say of me, "He is my brother." ' "

---

a 37 Moab sounds like the Hebrew for from father.
b 38 Ben-Ammi means son of my father's people.
c 38 Hebrew Bene-Ammon

¹⁴Then Abimelek brought sheep and cattle and male and female slaves and gave them to Abraham, and he returned Sarah his wife to him. ¹⁵And Abimelek said, "My land is before you; live wherever you like."

¹⁶To Sarah he said, "I am giving your brother a thousand shekels*a* of silver. This is to cover the offense against you before all who are with you; you are completely vindicated."

¹⁷Then Abraham prayed to God, and God healed Abimelek, his wife and his female slaves so they could have children again, ¹⁸for the LORD had kept all the women in Abimelek's household from conceiving because of Abraham's wife Sarah.

The Birth of Isaac

21 Now the LORD was gracious to Sarah as he had said, and the LORD did for Sarah what he had promised. ²Sarah became pregnant and bore a son to Abraham in his old age, at the very time God had promised him. ³Abraham gave the name Isaac*b* to the son Sarah bore him. ⁴When his son Isaac was eight days old, Abraham circumcised him, as God commanded him. ⁵Abraham was a hundred years old when his son Isaac was born to him.

⁶Sarah said, "God has brought me laughter, and everyone who hears about this will laugh with me." ⁷And she added, "Who would have said to Abraham that Sarah would nurse children? Yet I have borne him a son in his old age."

Hagar and Ishmael Sent Away

⁸The child grew and was weaned, and on the day Isaac was weaned Abraham held a great feast. ⁹But Sarah saw that the son whom Hagar the Egyptian had borne to Abraham was mocking, ¹⁰and she said to Abraham, "Get rid of that slave woman and her son, for that woman's son will never share in the inheritance with my son Isaac."

¹¹The matter distressed Abraham greatly because it concerned his son. ¹²But God said to him, "Do not be so distressed

about the boy and your slave woman. Listen to whatever Sarah tells you, because it is through Isaac that your offspring*c* will be reckoned. ¹³I will make the son of the slave into a nation also, because he is your offspring."

¹⁴Early the next morning Abraham took some food and a skin of water and gave them to Hagar. He set them on her shoulders and then sent her off with the boy. She went on her way and wandered in the Desert of Beersheba.

¹⁵When the water in the skin was gone, she put the boy under one of the bushes. ¹⁶Then she went off and sat down about a bowshot away, for she thought, "I cannot watch the boy die." And as she sat there, she*d* began to sob.

¹⁷God heard the boy crying, and the angel of God called to Hagar from heaven and said to her, "What is the matter, Hagar? Do not be afraid; God has heard the boy crying as he lies there. ¹⁸Lift the boy up and take him by the hand, for I will make him into a great nation."

¹⁹Then God opened her eyes and she saw a well of water. So she went and filled the skin with water and gave the boy a drink.

²⁰God was with the boy as he grew up. He lived in the desert and became an archer. ²¹While he was living in the Desert of Paran, his mother got a wife for him from Egypt.

The Treaty at Beersheba

²²At that time Abimelek and Phicol the commander of his forces said to Abraham, "God is with you in everything you do. ²³Now swear to me here before God that you will not deal falsely with me or my children or my descendants. Show to me and the country where you now reside as a foreigner the same kindness I have shown to you."

²⁴Abraham said, "I swear it."

²⁵Then Abraham complained to Abimelek about a well of water that Abimelek's servants had seized. ²⁶But Abimelek said, "I don't know who has done this. You did

---

a 16 That is, about 25 pounds or about 12 kilograms
b 3 Isaac means he laughs.　　*c* 12 Or seed
d 16 Hebrew; Septuagint the child

THE SCENE

PARAN

(GENESIS 21:21)

This is the largest desert in the southern part of Canaan. It's northeast of the Sinai Peninsula.

not tell me, and I heard about it only today."

²⁷So Abraham brought sheep and cattle and gave them to Abimelek, and the two men made a treaty. ²⁸Abraham set apart seven ewe lambs from the flock, ²⁹and Abimelek asked Abraham, "What is the meaning of these seven ewe lambs you have set apart by themselves?"

³⁰He replied, "Accept these seven lambs from my hand as a witness that I dug this well."

³¹So that place was called Beersheba,ᵃ because the two men swore an oath there.

³²After the treaty had been made at Beersheba, Abimelek and Phicol the commander of his forces returned to the land of the Philistines. ³³Abraham planted a tamarisk tree in Beersheba, and there he called on the name of the LORD, the Eternal God. ³⁴And Abraham stayed in the land of the Philistines for a long time.

Abraham Tested

22 Some time later God tested Abraham. He said to him, "Abraham!"

"Here I am," he replied.

²Then God said, "Take your son, your only son, whom you love—Isaac—and go to the region of Moriah. Sacrifice him there as a burnt offering on a mountain I will show you."

³Early the next morning Abraham got up and loaded his donkey. He took with him two of his servants and his son Isaac. When he had cut enough wood for the burnt offering, he set out for the place God had told him about. ⁴On the third day Abraham looked up and saw the place in the distance. ⁵He said to his servants, "Stay here with the donkey while I and the boy go over there. We will worship and then we will come back to you."

⁶Abraham took the wood for the burnt offering and placed it on his son Isaac, and he himself carried the fire and the knife. As the two of them went on together, ⁷Isaac spoke up and said to his father Abraham, "Father?"

"Yes, my son?" Abraham replied.

"The fire and wood are here," Isaac said, "but where is the lamb for the burnt offering?"

⁸Abraham answered, "God himself will provide the lamb for the burnt offering, my son." And the two of them went on together.

⁹When they reached the place God had told him about, Abraham built an altar there and arranged the wood on it. He bound his son Isaac and laid him on the altar, on top of the wood. ¹⁰Then he reached out his hand and took the knife to slay his son. ¹¹But the angel of the LORD called out to him from heaven, "Abraham! Abraham!"

"Here I am," he replied.

¹²"Do not lay a hand on the boy," he said. "Do not do anything to him. Now I know that you fear God, because you have not withheld from me your son, your only son."

¹³Abraham looked up and there in a

ᵃ 31 *Beersheba* can mean *well of seven* and *well of the oath*.

thicket he saw a ram[a] caught by its horns. He went over and took the ram and sacrificed it as a burnt offering instead of his son. [14]So Abraham called that place The LORD Will Provide. And to this day it is said, "On the mountain of the LORD it will be provided."

[15]The angel of the LORD called to Abraham from heaven a second time [16]and said, "I swear by myself, declares the LORD, that because you have done this and have not withheld your son, your only son, [17]I will surely bless you and make

BREAK THROUGH!

How could God ask Abraham to kill his son?

(GENESIS 22:1-19)

This is a very dramatic story, and it's very hard to understand. God gives Abraham a very hard test. Abraham finally got the son that God had promised him, and he was very happy about that. But then God asks him to give that son back and to sacrifice him. So Abraham takes Isaac and prepares to offer the sacrifice. When everything is ready, Abraham doesn't hesitate and — with a great sadness, for sure — offers his son to God. Then an angel steps in and doesn't let him harm the boy. God blesses him and he says that because Abraham was obedient, all his offspring will also be blessed.

your descendants as numerous as the stars in the sky and as the sand on the seashore. Your descendants will take possession of the cities of their enemies, [18]and through your offspring[b] all nations on earth will be blessed,[c] because you have obeyed me."

[19]Then Abraham returned to his servants, and they set off together for Beersheba. And Abraham stayed in Beersheba.

Nahor's Sons

[20]Some time later Abraham was told, "Milkah is also a mother; she has borne sons to your brother Nahor: [21]Uz the firstborn, Buz his brother, Kemuel (the father of Aram), [22]Kesed, Hazo, Pildash, Jidlaph and Bethuel." [23]Bethuel became the father of Rebekah. Milkah bore these eight sons to Abraham's brother Nahor. [24]His concubine, whose name was Reumah, also had sons: Tebah, Gaham, Tahash and Maakah.

The Death of Sarah

23 Sarah lived to be a hundred and twenty-seven years old. [2]She died at Kiriath Arba (that is, Hebron) in the land of Canaan, and Abraham went to mourn for Sarah and to weep over her.

[3]Then Abraham rose from beside his dead wife and spoke to the Hittites.[d] He said, [4]"I am a foreigner and stranger among you. Sell me some property for a burial site here so I can bury my dead."

[5]The Hittites replied to Abraham, [6]"Sir, listen to us. You are a mighty prince among us. Bury your dead in the choicest of our tombs. None of us will refuse you his tomb for burying your dead."

[7]Then Abraham rose and bowed down before the people of the land, the Hittites. [8]He said to them, "If you are willing to let me bury my dead, then listen to me and intercede with Ephron son of Zohar on my behalf [9]so he will sell me the cave of Machpelah, which belongs to him and is at the end of his field. Ask him to sell

---

[a] 13 Many manuscripts of the Masoretic Text, Samaritan Pentateuch, Septuagint and Syriac; most manuscripts of the Masoretic Text *a ram behind him*   [b] 18 Or *seed*
[c] 18 Or *and all nations on earth will use the name of your offspring in blessings* (see 48:20)   [d] 3 Or *the descendants of Heth*; also in verses 5, 7, 10, 16, 18 and 20

Hittites
(GENESIS 23:3)

The Hittites were Heth's offspring. He was Canaan's second son.

it to me for the full price as a burial site among you."

[10]Ephron the Hittite was sitting among his people and he replied to Abraham in the hearing of all the Hittites who had come to the gate of his city. [11]"No, my lord," he said. "Listen to me; I give[a] you the field, and I give[a] you the cave that is in it. I give[a] it to you in the presence of my people. Bury your dead."

[12]Again Abraham bowed down before the people of the land [13]and he said to Ephron in their hearing, "Listen to me, if you will. I will pay the price of the field. Accept it from me so I can bury my dead there."

[14]Ephron answered Abraham, [15]"Listen to me, my lord; the land is worth four hundred shekels[b] of silver, but what is that between you and me? Bury your dead."

[16]Abraham agreed to Ephron's terms and weighed out for him the price he had named in the hearing of the Hittites: four hundred shekels of silver, according to the weight current among the merchants.

[17]So Ephron's field in Machpelah near Mamre—both the field and the cave in it, and all the trees within the borders of the field—was deeded [18]to Abraham as his property in the presence of all the Hittites who had come to the gate of the city. [19]Afterward Abraham buried his wife Sarah in the cave in the field of Machpelah near Mamre (which is at Hebron) in the land of Canaan. [20]So the field and the cave in it were deeded to Abraham by the Hittites as a burial site.

Isaac and Rebekah

24 Abraham was now very old, and the LORD had blessed him in every way. [2]He said to the senior servant in his

[a] 11 Or sell   [b] 15 That is, about 10 pounds or about 4.6 kilograms

THE
WITNESSES

✓ **REBEKAH** (GENESIS 24:1)
We're not really sure what this name means. It might be either "tie" or "ensnaring." She was Isaac's wife. They didn't have any children for 20 years, and then God gave them twins: Jacob and Esau.

household, the one in charge of all that he had, "Put your hand under my thigh. ³I want you to swear by the LORD, the God of heaven and the God of earth, that you will not get a wife for my son from the daughters of the Canaanites, among whom I am living, ⁴but will go to my country and my own relatives and get a wife for my son Isaac."

⁵The servant asked him, "What if the woman is unwilling to come back with me to this land? Shall I then take your son back to the country you came from?"

⁶"Make sure that you do not take my son back there," Abraham said. ⁷"The LORD, the God of heaven, who brought me out of my father's household and my native land and who spoke to me and promised me on oath, saying, 'To your offspring[a] I will give this land' — he will send his angel before you so that you can get a wife for my son from there. ⁸If the woman is unwilling to come back with you, then you will be released from this oath of mine. Only do not take my son back there." ⁹So the servant put his hand under the thigh of his master Abraham and swore an oath to him concerning this matter.

¹⁰Then the servant left, taking with him ten of his master's camels loaded with all kinds of good things from his master. He set out for Aram Naharaim[b] and made his way to the town of Nahor. ¹¹He had the camels kneel down near the well outside the town; it was toward evening, the time the women go out to draw water.

¹²Then he prayed, "LORD, God of my master Abraham, make me successful today, and show kindness to my master Abraham. ¹³See, I am standing beside this spring, and the daughters of the townspeople are coming out to draw water. ¹⁴May it be that when I say to a young woman, 'Please let down your jar that I may have a drink,' and she says, 'Drink, and I'll water your camels too' — let her be the one you have chosen for your servant Isaac. By this I will know that you have shown kindness to my master."

¹⁵Before he had finished praying, Rebekah came out with her jar on her shoulder. She was the daughter of Bethuel son of Milkah, who was the wife of Abraham's brother Nahor. ¹⁶The woman was very beautiful, a virgin; no man had ever slept with her. She went down to the spring, filled her jar and came up again.

¹⁷The servant hurried to meet her and said, "Please give me a little water from your jar."

¹⁸"Drink, my lord," she said, and quickly lowered the jar to her hands and gave him a drink.

¹⁹After she had given him a drink, she said, "I'll draw water for your camels too, until they have had enough to drink." ²⁰So she quickly emptied her jar into the trough, ran back to the well to draw more water, and drew enough for all his camels. ²¹Without saying a word, the man watched her closely to learn whether or not the LORD had made his journey successful.

²²When the camels had finished drinking, the man took out a gold nose ring weighing a beka[c] and two gold bracelets weighing ten shekels.[d] ²³Then he asked, "Whose daughter are you? Please tell me, is there room in your father's house for us to spend the night?"

²⁴She answered him, "I am the daughter of Bethuel, the son that Milkah bore to Nahor." ²⁵And she added, "We have plenty of straw and fodder, as well as room for you to spend the night."

²⁶Then the man bowed down and worshiped the LORD, ²⁷saying, "Praise be to the LORD, the God of my master Abraham, who has not abandoned his kindness and faithfulness to my master. As for me, the LORD has led me on the journey to the house of my master's relatives."

²⁸The young woman ran and told her mother's household about these things. ²⁹Now Rebekah had a brother named Laban, and he hurried out to the man at the spring. ³⁰As soon as he had seen the nose ring, and the bracelets on his sister's arms, and had heard Rebekah tell what the man said to her, he went out to the man and found him standing by the camels near the spring. ³¹"Come, you who are blessed by the LORD," he said.

---

a 7 Or *seed*   *b 10* That is, Northwest Mesopotamia
c 22 That is, about 1/5 ounce or about 5.7 grams
d 22 That is, about 4 ounces or about 115 grams

THE
WITNESSES

✓ **LABAN** (GENESIS 24:29–30)
Laban was Rebekah's brother. His name refers to the color white. He was the one who let Rebekah marry Isaac. Years later, he let Jacob (who was Rebekah and Isaac's son) marry his two daughters, Rachel and Leah.

"Why are you standing out here? I have prepared the house and a place for the camels."

³²So the man went to the house, and the camels were unloaded. Straw and fodder were brought for the camels, and water for him and his men to wash their feet. ³³Then food was set before him, but he said, "I will not eat until I have told you what I have to say."

"Then tell us," Laban said.

³⁴So he said, "I am Abraham's servant. ³⁵The LORD has blessed my master abundantly, and he has become wealthy. He has given him sheep and cattle, silver and gold, male and female servants, and camels and donkeys. ³⁶My master's wife Sarah has borne him a son in her old age, and he has given him everything he owns. ³⁷And my master made me swear an oath, and said, 'You must not get a wife for my son from the daughters of the Canaanites, in whose land I live, ³⁸but go to my father's family and to my own clan, and get a wife for my son.'

³⁹"Then I asked my master, 'What if the woman will not come back with me?'

⁴⁰"He replied, 'The LORD, before whom I have walked faithfully, will send his angel with you and make your journey a success, so that you can get a wife for my son from my own clan and from my father's family. ⁴¹You will be released from my oath if, when you go to my clan, they refuse to give her to you—then you will be released from my oath.'

⁴²"When I came to the spring today, I said, 'LORD, God of my master Abraham, if you will, please grant success to the journey on which I have come. ⁴³See, I am standing beside this spring. If a young woman comes out to draw water and I say to her, "Please let me drink a little water from your jar," ⁴⁴and if she says to me, "Drink, and I'll draw water for your camels too," let her be the one the LORD has chosen for my master's son.'

⁴⁵"Before I finished praying in my heart, Rebekah came out, with her jar on her shoulder. She went down to the spring and drew water, and I said to her, 'Please give me a drink.'

⁴⁶"She quickly lowered her jar from her shoulder and said, 'Drink, and I'll water your camels too.' So I drank, and she watered the camels also.

⁴⁷"I asked her, 'Whose daughter are you?'

"She said, 'The daughter of Bethuel son of Nahor, whom Milkah bore to him.'

"Then I put the ring in her nose and the bracelets on her arms, ⁴⁸and I bowed down and worshiped the LORD. I praised the LORD, the God of my master Abraham, who had led me on the right road to get the granddaughter of my master's brother for his son. ⁴⁹Now if you will show kindness and faithfulness to my master, tell me; and if not, tell me, so I may know which way to turn."

⁵⁰Laban and Bethuel answered, "This is from the LORD; we can say nothing to you one way or the other. ⁵¹Here is Rebekah; take her and go, and let her become the wife of your master's son, as the LORD has directed."

⁵²When Abraham's servant heard what they said, he bowed down to the ground before the LORD. ⁵³Then the servant brought out gold and silver jewelry and articles of clothing and gave them to Rebekah; he also gave costly gifts to her brother and to her mother. ⁵⁴Then he and the men who were with him ate and drank and spent the night there.

When they got up the next morning, he said, "Send me on my way to my master."

⁵⁵But her brother and her mother replied, "Let the young woman remain with us ten days or so; then you*a* may go."

⁵⁶But he said to them, "Do not detain me, now that the LORD has granted success to my journey. Send me on my way so I may go to my master."

⁵⁷Then they said, "Let's call the young woman and ask her about it." ⁵⁸So they called Rebekah and asked her, "Will you go with this man?"

"I will go," she said.

⁵⁹So they sent their sister Rebekah on her way, along with her nurse and Abraham's servant and his men. ⁶⁰And they blessed Rebekah and said to her,

"Our sister, may you increase
    to thousands upon thousands;
may your offspring possess
    the cities of their enemies."

⁶¹Then Rebekah and her attendants got ready and mounted the camels and went back with the man. So the servant took Rebekah and left.

⁶²Now Isaac had come from Beer Lahai Roi, for he was living in the Negev. ⁶³He went out to the field one evening to meditate,*b* and as he looked up, he saw camels approaching. ⁶⁴Rebekah also looked up and saw Isaac. She got down from her camel ⁶⁵and asked the servant, "Who is that man in the field coming to meet us?"

"He is my master," the servant answered. So she took her veil and covered herself.

⁶⁶Then the servant told Isaac all he had done. ⁶⁷Isaac brought her into the tent of his mother Sarah, and he married Rebekah. So she became his wife, and he loved her; and Isaac was comforted after his mother's death.

The Death of Abraham

25 Abraham had taken another wife, whose name was Keturah. ²She bore him Zimran, Jokshan, Medan, Midian, Ishbak and Shuah. ³Jokshan was the father of Sheba and Dedan; the descendants of Dedan were the Ashurites, the Letushites and the Leummites. ⁴The sons of Midian were Ephah, Epher, Hanok, Abida and Eldaah. All these were descendants of Keturah.

⁵Abraham left everything he owned to Isaac. ⁶But while he was still living, he gave gifts to the sons of his concubines and sent them away from his son Isaac to the land of the east.

⁷Abraham lived a hundred and seventy-five years. ⁸Then Abraham breathed his last and died at a good old age, an old man and full of years; and he was gathered to his people. ⁹His sons Isaac and Ishmael buried him in the cave of Machpelah near Mamre, in the field of Ephron son of Zohar the Hittite, ¹⁰the field Abraham had bought from the Hittites.*c* There Abraham was buried with his wife Sarah. ¹¹After Abraham's death, God blessed his son Isaac, who then lived near Beer Lahai Roi.

Ishmael's Sons

¹²This is the account of the family line of Abraham's son Ishmael, whom Sarah's slave, Hagar the Egyptian, bore to Abraham.

¹³These are the names of the sons of Ishmael, listed in the order of their birth: Nebaioth the firstborn of Ishmael, Kedar, Adbeel, Mibsam, ¹⁴Mishma, Dumah, Massa, ¹⁵Hadad, Tema, Jetur, Naphish and Kedemah. ¹⁶These were the sons

---

a 55 Or *she*   *b 63* The meaning of the Hebrew for this word is uncertain.   *c 10* Or *the descendants of Heth*

THE
WITNESSES

✓ **ESAU** (GENESIS 25:25)
The name Esau sounds a little like the Hebrew word that means "hairy." He was Isaac and Rebekah's oldest son. He was also called Edom, which means "red," because he traded his rights as the oldest son for a red stew his brother, Jacob, had cooked. He was famous for being rough and not very smart. His brother, Jacob, took advantage of this and tricked him.

✓ **JACOB** (GENESIS 25:26)
The Hebrew word for "heel" sounds a lot like the name Jacob. He and Esau were Isaac and Rebekah's twin sons. He spent most of his life fighting with his brother. But the night before they made up, something very strange happened. He wrestled with a mysterious person who changed his name. (Afterward, he realized it was God himself!) After that he was called Israel, which means "he who wrestles with God." This name became the name of God's chosen people.

of Ishmael, and these are the names of the twelve tribal rulers according to their settlements and camps. ¹⁷Ishmael lived a hundred and thirty-seven years. He breathed his last and died, and he was gathered to his people. ¹⁸His descendants settled in the area from Havilah to Shur, near the eastern border of Egypt, as you go toward Ashur. And they lived in hostility toward*ᵃ* all the tribes related to them.

Jacob and Esau

¹⁹This is the account of the family line of Abraham's son Isaac.

Abraham became the father of Isaac, ²⁰and Isaac was forty years old when he married Rebekah daughter of Bethuel the Aramean from Paddan Aram*ᵇ* and sister of Laban the Aramean.
²¹Isaac prayed to the LORD on behalf of his wife, because she was childless. The LORD answered his prayer, and his wife Rebekah became pregnant. ²²The babies jostled each other within her, and she said, "Why is this happening to me?" So she went to inquire of the LORD.
²³The LORD said to her,

"Two nations are in your womb,
　and two peoples from within you will
　　be separated;
one people will be stronger than the
　　other,
　and the older will serve the
　　younger."

²⁴When the time came for her to give birth, there were twin boys in her womb. ²⁵The first to come out was red, and his whole body was like a hairy garment; so they named him Esau.*ᶜ* ²⁶After this, his brother came out, with his hand grasping Esau's heel; so he was named Jacob.*ᵈ* Isaac was sixty years old when Rebekah gave birth to them.
²⁷The boys grew up, and Esau became a skillful hunter, a man of the open country, while Jacob was content to stay at home among the tents. ²⁸Isaac, who had

---

ᵃ 18 Or *lived to the east of*　　*ᵇ 20* That is, Northwest Mesopotamia　　*ᶜ 25 Esau* may mean *hairy*.
ᵈ 26 Jacob means *he grasps the heel*, a Hebrew idiom for *he deceives*.

a taste for wild game, loved Esau, but Rebekah loved Jacob. ²⁹Once when Jacob was cooking some stew, Esau came in from the open country, famished. ³⁰He said to Jacob, "Quick, let me have some of that red stew! I'm famished!" (That is why he was also called Edom.^a)

³¹Jacob replied, "First sell me your birthright."

³²"Look, I am about to die," Esau said. "What good is the birthright to me?"

³³But Jacob said, "Swear to me first." So he swore an oath to him, selling his birthright to Jacob.

³⁴Then Jacob gave Esau some bread and some lentil stew. He ate and drank, and then got up and left.

So Esau despised his birthright.

Isaac and Abimelek

26 Now there was a famine in the land—besides the previous famine in Abraham's time—and Isaac went to Abimelek king of the Philistines in Gerar. ²The LORD appeared to Isaac and said, "Do not go down to Egypt; live in the land where I tell you to live. ³Stay in this land for a while, and I will be with you and will bless you. For to you and your descendants I will give all these lands and will confirm the oath I swore to your father Abraham. ⁴I will make your descendants as numerous as the stars in the sky and will give them all these lands, and through your offspring^b all nations on earth will be blessed,^c ⁵because Abraham obeyed me and did everything I required of him, keeping my commands, my decrees and my instructions." ⁶So Isaac stayed in Gerar.

⁷When the men of that place asked him about his wife, he said, "She is my sister," because he was afraid to say, "She is my wife." He thought, "The men of this place might kill me on account of Rebekah, because she is beautiful."

⁸When Isaac had been there a long time, Abimelek king of the Philistines looked down from a window and saw Isaac caressing his wife Rebekah. ⁹So Abimelek summoned Isaac and said, "She is really your wife! Why did you say, 'She is my sister'?"

Isaac answered him, "Because I thought I might lose my life on account of her."

¹⁰Then Abimelek said, "What is this you have done to us? One of the men might well have slept with your wife, and you would have brought guilt upon us."

¹¹So Abimelek gave orders to all the people: "Anyone who harms this man or his wife shall surely be put to death."

¹²Isaac planted crops in that land and the same year reaped a hundredfold, because the LORD blessed him. ¹³The man became rich, and his wealth continued to grow until he became very wealthy. ¹⁴He had so many flocks and herds and servants that the Philistines envied him. ¹⁵So all the wells that his father's servants had dug in the time of his father Abraham, the Philistines stopped up, filling them with earth.

¹⁶Then Abimelek said to Isaac, "Move away from us; you have become too powerful for us."

¹⁷So Isaac moved away from there and encamped in the Valley of Gerar, where he settled. ¹⁸Isaac reopened the wells that had been dug in the time of his father Abraham, which the Philistines had stopped up after Abraham died, and he gave them the same names his father had given them.

¹⁹Isaac's servants dug in the valley and discovered a well of fresh water there. ²⁰But the herders of Gerar quarreled with those of Isaac and said, "The water is ours!" So he named the well Esek,^d because they disputed with him. ²¹Then they dug another well, but they quarreled over that one also; so he named it Sitnah.^e ²²He moved on from there and dug another well, and no one quarreled over it. He named it Rehoboth,^f saying, "Now the LORD has given us room and we will flourish in the land."

²³From there he went up to Beersheba. ²⁴That night the LORD appeared to him and said, "I am the God of your father Abraham. Do not be afraid, for I am with you;

---

^a 30 Edom means red.   ^b 4 Or seed   ^c 4 Or and all nations on earth will use the name of your offspring in blessings (see 48:20)   ^d 20 Esek means dispute.   ^e 21 Sitnah means opposition.   ^f 22 Rehoboth means room.

I will bless you and will increase the number of your descendants for the sake of my servant Abraham."

25Isaac built an altar there and called on the name of the LORD. There he pitched his tent, and there his servants dug a well.

26Meanwhile, Abimelek had come to him from Gerar, with Ahuzzath his personal adviser and Phicol the commander of his forces. 27Isaac asked them, "Why have you come to me, since you were hostile to me and sent me away?"

28They answered, "We saw clearly that the LORD was with you; so we said, 'There ought to be a sworn agreement between us'—between us and you. Let us make a treaty with you 29that you will do us no harm, just as we did not harm you but always treated you well and sent you away peacefully. And now you are blessed by the LORD."

30Isaac then made a feast for them, and they ate and drank. 31Early the next morning the men swore an oath to each other. Then Isaac sent them on their way, and they went away peacefully.

32That day Isaac's servants came and told him about the well they had dug. They said, "We've found water!" 33He called it Shibah,a and to this day the name of the town has been Beersheba.b

Jacob Takes Esau's Blessing

34When Esau was forty years old, he married Judith daughter of Beeri the Hittite, and also Basemath daughter of Elon the Hittite. 35They were a source of grief to Isaac and Rebekah.

27 When Isaac was old and his eyes were so weak that he could no longer see, he called for Esau his older son and said to him, "My son."

"Here I am," he answered.

2Isaac said, "I am now an old man and don't know the day of my death. 3Now then, get your equipment—your quiver and bow—and go out to the open country to hunt some wild game for me. 4Prepare me the kind of tasty food I like and bring it to me to eat, so that I may give you my blessing before I die."

5Now Rebekah was listening as Isaac spoke to his son Esau. When Esau left for the open country to hunt game and bring it back, 6Rebekah said to her son Jacob, "Look, I overheard your father say to your brother Esau, 7'Bring me some game and prepare me some tasty food to eat, so that I may give you my blessing in the presence of the LORD before I die.' 8Now, my son, listen carefully and do what I tell you: 9Go out to the flock and bring me two choice young goats, so I can prepare some tasty food for your father, just the way he likes it. 10Then take it to your father to eat, so that he may give you his blessing before he dies."

11Jacob said to Rebekah his mother, "But my brother Esau is a hairy man while I have smooth skin. 12What if my father touches me? I would appear to be tricking him and would bring down a curse on myself rather than a blessing."

13His mother said to him, "My son, let the curse fall on me. Just do what I say; go and get them for me."

14So he went and got them and brought them to his mother, and she prepared some tasty food, just the way his father liked it. 15Then Rebekah took the best clothes of Esau her older son, which she had in the house, and put them on her younger son Jacob. 16She also covered his hands and the smooth part of his neck with the goatskins. 17Then she handed to her son Jacob the tasty food and the bread she had made.

18He went to his father and said, "My father."

"Yes, my son," he answered. "Who is it?"

19Jacob said to his father, "I am Esau your firstborn. I have done as you told me. Please sit up and eat some of my game, so that you may give me your blessing."

20Isaac asked his son, "How did you find it so quickly, my son?"

"The LORD your God gave me success," he replied.

21Then Isaac said to Jacob, "Come near so I can touch you, my son, to know

---

a 33 Shibah can mean oath or seven.   b 33 Beersheba can mean well of the oath and well of seven.

whether you really are my son Esau or not."

²²Jacob went close to his father Isaac, who touched him and said, "The voice is the voice of Jacob, but the hands are the hands of Esau." ²³He did not recognize him, for his hands were hairy like those of his brother Esau; so he proceeded to bless him. ²⁴"Are you really my son Esau?" he asked.

"I am," he replied.

²⁵Then he said, "My son, bring me some of your game to eat, so that I may give you my blessing."

Jacob brought it to him and he ate; and he brought some wine and he drank. ²⁶Then his father Isaac said to him, "Come here, my son, and kiss me."

²⁷So he went to him and kissed him. When Isaac caught the smell of his clothes, he blessed him and said,

"Ah, the smell of my son
    is like the smell of a field
    that the LORD has blessed.
²⁸ May God give you heaven's dew
    and earth's richness—
    an abundance of grain and new
    wine.
²⁹ May nations serve you
    and peoples bow down to you.
Be lord over your brothers,
    and may the sons of your mother
    bow down to you.
May those who curse you be
    cursed
    and those who bless you be
    blessed."

³⁰After Isaac finished blessing him, and Jacob had scarcely left his father's presence, his brother Esau came in from hunting. ³¹He too prepared some tasty food and brought it to his father. Then he said to him, "My father, please sit up and eat some of my game, so that you may give me your blessing."

³²His father Isaac asked him, "Who are you?"

"I am your son," he answered, "your firstborn, Esau."

³³Isaac trembled violently and said, "Who was it, then, that hunted game and brought it to me? I ate it just before you came and I blessed him—and indeed he will be blessed!"

³⁴When Esau heard his father's words, he burst out with a loud and bitter cry and said to his father, "Bless me—me too, my father!"

³⁵But he said, "Your brother came deceitfully and took your blessing."

³⁶Esau said, "Isn't he rightly named Jacob[a]? This is the second time he has taken advantage of me: He took my birthright, and now he's taken my blessing!" Then he asked, "Haven't you reserved any blessing for me?"

³⁷Isaac answered Esau, "I have made him lord over you and have made all his relatives his servants, and I have sustained him with grain and new wine. So what can I possibly do for you, my son?"

³⁸Esau said to his father, "Do you have only one blessing, my father? Bless me too, my father!" Then Esau wept aloud.

³⁹His father Isaac answered him,

"Your dwelling will be
    away from the earth's richness,
    away from the dew of heaven
    above.
⁴⁰ You will live by the sword
    and you will serve your brother.
But when you grow restless,
    you will throw his yoke
    from off your neck."

⁴¹Esau held a grudge against Jacob because of the blessing his father had given him. He said to himself, "The days of mourning for my father are near; then I will kill my brother Jacob."

⁴²When Rebekah was told what her older son Esau had said, she sent for her younger son Jacob and said to him, "Your brother Esau is planning to avenge himself by killing you. ⁴³Now then, my son, do what I say: Flee at once to my brother Laban in Harran. ⁴⁴Stay with him for a while until your brother's fury subsides. ⁴⁵When your brother is no longer angry with you and forgets what you did to him, I'll send word for you to come back from there. Why should I lose both of you in one day?"

---

*a 36 Jacob means he grasps the heel, a Hebrew idiom for
he takes advantage of or he deceives.*

⁴⁶Then Rebekah said to Isaac, "I'm disgusted with living because of these Hittite women. If Jacob takes a wife from among the women of this land, from Hittite women like these, my life will not be worth living."

28 So Isaac called for Jacob and blessed him. Then he commanded him: "Do not marry a Canaanite woman. ²Go at once to Paddan Aram,ᵃ to the house of your mother's father Bethuel. Take a wife for yourself there, from among the daughters of Laban, your mother's brother. ³May God Almightyᵇ bless you and make you fruitful and increase your numbers until you become a community of peoples. ⁴May he give you and your descendants the blessing given to Abraham, so that you may take possession of the land where you now reside as a foreigner, the land God gave to Abraham." ⁵Then Isaac sent Jacob on his way, and he went to Paddan Aram, to Laban son of Bethuel the Aramean, the brother of Rebekah, who was the mother of Jacob and Esau.

⁶Now Esau learned that Isaac had blessed Jacob and had sent him to Paddan Aram to take a wife from there, and that when he blessed him he commanded him, "Do not marry a Canaanite woman," ⁷and that Jacob had obeyed his father and mother and had gone to Paddan Aram. ⁸Esau then realized how displeasing the Canaanite women were to his father Isaac; ⁹so he went to Ishmael and married Mahalath, the sister of Nebaioth and daughter of Ishmael son of Abraham, in addition to the wives he already had.

Jacob's Dream at Bethel

¹⁰Jacob left Beersheba and set out for Harran. ¹¹When he reached a certain place, he stopped for the night because the sun had set. Taking one of the stones there, he put it under his head and lay down to sleep. ¹²He had a dream in which he saw a stairway resting on the earth, with its top reaching to heaven, and the angels of God were ascending and descending on it. ¹³There above itᶜ stood the Lord, and he said: "I am the Lord, the God of your father Abraham and the God of Isaac. I will give you and your descendants the land on which you are lying. ¹⁴Your descendants will be like the dust of the earth, and you will spread out to the west and to the east, to the north and to the south. All peoples on earth will be blessed through you and your offspring.ᵈ ¹⁵I am with you and will watch over you wherever you go, and I will bring you back to this land. I will not leave you until I have done what I have promised you."

¹⁶When Jacob awoke from his sleep, he thought, "Surely the Lord is in this place, and I was not aware of it." ¹⁷He was afraid and said, "How awesome is this place! This is none other than the house of God; this is the gate of heaven."

¹⁸Early the next morning Jacob took the stone he had placed under his head and set it up as a pillar and poured oil on top of it. ¹⁹He called that place Bethel,ᵉ though the city used to be called Luz.

²⁰Then Jacob made a vow, saying, "If God will be with me and will watch over me on this journey I am taking and will give me food to eat and clothes to wear ²¹so that I return safely to my father's household, then the Lordᶠ will be my God ²²andᵍ this stone that I have set up as a pillar will be God's house, and of all that you give me I will give you a tenth."

Jacob Arrives in Paddan Aram

29 Then Jacob continued on his journey and came to the land of the eastern peoples. ²There he saw a well in the open country, with three flocks of sheep lying near it because the flocks were watered from that well. The stone over the mouth of the well was large. ³When all the flocks were gathered there, the shepherds would roll the stone away from the well's mouth and water the sheep. Then they would return the stone to its place over the mouth of the well.

⁴Jacob asked the shepherds, "My brothers, where are you from?"

"We're from Harran," they replied.

ᵃ 2 That is, Northwest Mesopotamia; also in verses 5, 6 and 7   ᵇ 3 Hebrew *El-Shaddai*   ᶜ 13 Or *There beside him*   ᵈ 14 Or *will use your name and the name of your offspring in blessings* (see 48:20)   ᵉ 19 *Bethel* means *house of God.*   ᶠ 20,21 Or *Since God . . . father's household, the Lord*   ᵍ 21,22 Or *household, and the Lord will be my God,* ²²*then*

THE SCENE

HARAN

(GENESIS 29:4)

Haran was an important money-making city in ancient Mesopotamia. Now it belongs to Turkey. It was cleverly located along the market roads leading to Damascus. Abraham lived there at one time with his father, Terah, after they left Ur of the Chaldeans. Isaac's wife, Rebecca, was born there. Jacob found refuge there when he was running for his life. He ended up marrying two women from Haran—Leah and Rachel. The city has been discovered, and archeologists are finding very interesting things there.

⁵He said to them, "Do you know Laban, Nahor's grandson?"

"Yes, we know him," they answered.

⁶Then Jacob asked them, "Is he well?"

"Yes, he is," they said, "and here comes his daughter Rachel with the sheep."

⁷"Look," he said, "the sun is still high; it is not time for the flocks to be gathered. Water the sheep and take them back to pasture."

⁸"We can't," they replied, "until all the flocks are gathered and the stone has been rolled away from the mouth of the well. Then we will water the sheep."

⁹While he was still talking with them, Rachel came with her father's sheep, for she was a shepherd. ¹⁰When Jacob saw Rachel daughter of his uncle Laban, and Laban's sheep, he went over and rolled the stone away from the mouth of the well and watered his uncle's sheep. ¹¹Then Jacob kissed Rachel and began to weep aloud. ¹²He had told Rachel that he was a relative of her father and a son of Rebekah. So she ran and told her father.

¹³As soon as Laban heard the news about Jacob, his sister's son, he hurried to meet him. He embraced him and kissed him and brought him to his home, and there Jacob told him all these things. ¹⁴Then Laban said to him, "You are my own flesh and blood."

Jacob Marries Leah and Rachel

After Jacob had stayed with him for a whole month, ¹⁵Laban said to him, "Just because you are a relative of mine, should you work for me for nothing? Tell me what your wages should be."

¹⁶Now Laban had two daughters; the name of the older was Leah, and the name of the younger was Rachel. ¹⁷Leah had weak[a] eyes, but Rachel had a lovely figure and was beautiful. ¹⁸Jacob was in love with Rachel and said, "I'll work for you seven years in return for your younger daughter Rachel."

¹⁹Laban said, "It's better that I give her to you than to some other man. Stay here with me." ²⁰So Jacob served seven years to get Rachel, but they seemed like only a few days to him because of his love for her.

²¹Then Jacob said to Laban, "Give me my wife. My time is completed, and I want to make love to her."

²²So Laban brought together all the people of the place and gave a feast. ²³But when evening came, he took his daughter Leah and brought her to Jacob, and Jacob made love to her. ²⁴And Laban

---

a 17 Or delicate

gave his servant Zilpah to his daughter as her attendant.

25When morning came, there was Leah! So Jacob said to Laban, "What is this you have done to me? I served you for Rachel, didn't I? Why have you deceived me?"

26Laban replied, "It is not our custom here to give the younger daughter in marriage before the older one. 27Finish this daughter's bridal week; then we will give you the younger one also, in return for another seven years of work."

28And Jacob did so. He finished the week with Leah, and then Laban gave him his daughter Rachel to be his wife. 29Laban gave his servant Bilhah to his daughter Rachel as her attendant. 30Jacob made love to Rachel also, and his love for Rachel was greater than his love for Leah. And he worked for Laban another seven years.

Jacob's Children

31When the LORD saw that Leah was not loved, he enabled her to conceive, but Rachel remained childless. 32Leah became pregnant and gave birth to a son. She named him Reuben,*a* for she said, "It is because the LORD has seen my misery. Surely my husband will love me now."

33She conceived again, and when she gave birth to a son she said, "Because the LORD heard that I am not loved, he gave me this one too." So she named him Simeon.*b*

34Again she conceived, and when she gave birth to a son she said, "Now at last my husband will become attached to me, because I have borne him three sons." So he was named Levi.*c*

35She conceived again, and when she gave birth to a son she said, "This time I will praise the LORD." So she named him Judah.*d* Then she stopped having children.

30 When Rachel saw that she was not bearing Jacob any children, she became jealous of her sister. So she said to Jacob, "Give me children, or I'll die!"

2Jacob became angry with her and said, "Am I in the place of God, who has kept you from having children?"

THE
WITNESSES

✓ **RACHEL** (GENESIS 29:10)
The name Rachel has to do with the Hebrew word that means "lamb." She and her sister both married the same man, Jacob. They could do that in those days. Rachel couldn't have babies, but her sister, Leah, had several. Then God performed a miracle so Rachel could have children, and she had Joseph and Benjamin.

✓ **LEAH** (GENESIS 29:16)
Of all the possible meanings, "worthy cow" seems the most likely. She was Laban's daughter and Jacob's first wife. Although Jacob had wanted to marry Rachel (Leah's sister), Laban (their father) made Jacob marry Leah first. They had six sons: Reuben, Simeon, Levi, Judah, Issachar and Zebulun.

---

a 32 Reuben sounds like the Hebrew for *he has seen my misery;* the name means *see, a son.*   *b 33 Simeon* probably means *one who hears.*   *c 34 Levi* sounds like and may be derived from the Hebrew for *attached.*   *d 35 Judah* sounds like and may be derived from the Hebrew for *praise.*

³Then she said, "Here is Bilhah, my servant. Sleep with her so that she can bear children for me and I too can build a family through her."

⁴So she gave him her servant Bilhah as a wife. Jacob slept with her, ⁵and she became pregnant and bore him a son. ⁶Then Rachel said, "God has vindicated me; he has listened to my plea and given me a son." Because of this she named him Dan.ᵃ

⁷Rachel's servant Bilhah conceived again and bore Jacob a second son. ⁸Then Rachel said, "I have had a great struggle with my sister, and I have won." So she named him Naphtali.ᵇ

⁹When Leah saw that she had stopped having children, she took her servant Zilpah and gave her to Jacob as a wife. ¹⁰Leah's servant Zilpah bore Jacob a son. ¹¹Then Leah said, "What good fortune!"ᶜ So she named him Gad.ᵈ

¹²Leah's servant Zilpah bore Jacob a second son. ¹³Then Leah said, "How happy I am! The women will call me happy." So she named him Asher.ᵉ

¹⁴During wheat harvest, Reuben went out into the fields and found some mandrake plants, which he brought to his mother Leah. Rachel said to Leah, "Please give me some of your son's mandrakes."

¹⁵But she said to her, "Wasn't it enough that you took away my husband? Will you take my son's mandrakes too?"

"Very well," Rachel said, "he can sleep with you tonight in return for your son's mandrakes."

¹⁶So when Jacob came in from the fields that evening, Leah went out to meet him. "You must sleep with me," she said. "I have hired you with my son's mandrakes." So he slept with her that night.

¹⁷God listened to Leah, and she became pregnant and bore Jacob a fifth son. ¹⁸Then Leah said, "God has rewarded me for giving my servant to my husband." So she named him Issachar.ᶠ

¹⁹Leah conceived again and bore Jacob a sixth son. ²⁰Then Leah said, "God has presented me with a precious gift. This time my husband will treat me with honor, because I have borne him six sons." So she named him Zebulun.ᵍ

THE
WITNESSES

✓ BILHAH (GENESIS 30:3)
Her name means "bashful." She was the slave that Laban gave Rachel when she married Jacob. Since Rachel couldn't have children, she gave her slave to Jacob so she could have children with him. Bilhah had two sons, Dan and Naphtali.

✓ ZILPAH (GENESIS 30:9)
She was the slave Leah's father had given her. When Leah couldn't have any more children, she gave her slave to Jacob so he could have more sons with her. They had Gad and Asher.

²¹Some time later she gave birth to a daughter and named her Dinah.

²²Then God remembered Rachel; he listened to her and enabled her to conceive. ²³She became pregnant and gave birth to

---

ᵃ 6 *Dan* here means *he has vindicated.*   ᵇ 8 *Naphtali* means *my struggle.*   ᶜ 11 Or *"A troop is coming!"*
ᵈ 11 *Gad* can mean *good fortune* or *a troop.*   ᵉ 13 *Asher* means *happy.*   ᶠ 18 *Issachar* sounds like the Hebrew for *reward.*   ᵍ 20 *Zebulun* probably means *honor.*

a son and said, "God has taken away my disgrace." ²⁴She named him Joseph,ᵃ and said, "May the LORD add to me another son."

Jacob's Flocks Increase

²⁵After Rachel gave birth to Joseph, Jacob said to Laban, "Send me on my way so I can go back to my own homeland. ²⁶Give me my wives and children, for whom I have served you, and I will be on my way. You know how much work I've done for you."

²⁷But Laban said to him, "If I have found favor in your eyes, please stay. I have learned by divination that the LORD has blessed me because of you." ²⁸He added, "Name your wages, and I will pay them."

²⁹Jacob said to him, "You know how I

BREAK THROUGH!

Mandrakes

(GENESIS 30:14)

This plant has large green leaves all year round. Its fruit is like small, sweet-smelling apples. Its roots have odd, humanlike shapes, so people thought that if women ate mandrakes, they'd have babies. The truth is that this plant makes a person sleepy, and it's also used as a medicine to help you go to the bathroom.

have worked for you and how your livestock has fared under my care. ³⁰The little you had before I came has increased greatly, and the LORD has blessed you wherever I have been. But now, when may I do something for my own household?"

³¹"What shall I give you?" he asked.

"Don't give me anything," Jacob replied. "But if you will do this one thing for me, I will go on tending your flocks and watching over them: ³²Let me go through all your flocks today and remove from them every speckled or spotted sheep, every dark-colored lamb and every spotted or speckled goat. They will be my wages. ³³And my honesty will testify for me in the future, whenever you check on the wages you have paid me. Any goat in my possession that is not speckled or spotted, or any lamb that is not dark-colored, will be considered stolen."

³⁴"Agreed," said Laban. "Let it be as you have said." ³⁵That same day he removed all the male goats that were streaked or spotted, and all the speckled or spotted female goats (all that had white on them) and all the dark-colored lambs, and he placed them in the care of his sons. ³⁶Then he put a three-day journey between himself and Jacob, while Jacob continued to tend the rest of Laban's flocks.

³⁷Jacob, however, took fresh-cut branches from poplar, almond and plane trees and made white stripes on them by peeling the bark and exposing the white inner wood of the branches. ³⁸Then he placed the peeled branches in all the watering troughs, so that they would be directly in front of the flocks when they came to drink. When the flocks were in heat and came to drink, ³⁹they mated in front of the branches. And they bore young that were streaked or speckled or spotted. ⁴⁰Jacob set apart the young of the flock by themselves, but made the rest face the streaked and dark-colored animals that belonged to Laban. Thus he made separate flocks for himself and did not put them with Laban's animals. ⁴¹Whenever the stronger females were in heat, Jacob

---

ᵃ 24 *Joseph* means *may he add.*

would place the branches in the troughs in front of the animals so they would mate near the branches, ⁴²but if the animals were weak, he would not place them there. So the weak animals went to Laban and the strong ones to Jacob. ⁴³In this way the man grew exceedingly prosperous and came to own large flocks, and female and male servants, and camels and donkeys.

Jacob Flees From Laban

31 Jacob heard that Laban's sons were saying, "Jacob has taken everything our father owned and has gained all this wealth from what belonged to our father." ²And Jacob noticed that Laban's attitude toward him was not what it had been.

³Then the LORD said to Jacob, "Go back to the land of your fathers and to your relatives, and I will be with you."

⁴So Jacob sent word to Rachel and Leah to come out to the fields where his flocks were. ⁵He said to them, "I see that your father's attitude toward me is not what it was before, but the God of my father has been with me. ⁶You know that I've worked for your father with all my strength, ⁷yet your father has cheated me by changing my wages ten times. However, God has not allowed him to harm me. ⁸If he said, 'The speckled ones will be your wages,' then all the flocks gave birth to speckled young; and if he said, 'The streaked ones will be your wages,' then all the flocks bore streaked young. ⁹So God has taken away your father's livestock and has given them to me.

¹⁰"In breeding season I once had a dream in which I looked up and saw that the male goats mating with the flock were streaked, speckled or spotted. ¹¹The angel of God said to me in the dream, 'Jacob.' I answered, 'Here I am.' ¹²And he said, 'Look up and see that all the male goats mating with the flock are streaked, speckled or spotted, for I have seen all that Laban has been doing to you. ¹³I am the God of Bethel, where you anointed a pillar and where you made a vow to me. Now leave this land at once and go back to your native land.' "

¹⁴Then Rachel and Leah replied, "Do we still have any share in the inheritance of our father's estate? ¹⁵Does he not regard us as foreigners? Not only has he sold us, but he has used up what was paid for us. ¹⁶Surely all the wealth that God took away from our father belongs to us and our children. So do whatever God has told you."

¹⁷Then Jacob put his children and his wives on camels, ¹⁸and he drove all his livestock ahead of him, along with all the goods he had accumulated in Paddan Aram,ᵃ to go to his father Isaac in the land of Canaan.

¹⁹When Laban had gone to shear his sheep, Rachel stole her father's household gods. ²⁰Moreover, Jacob deceived Laban the Aramean by not telling him he was running away. ²¹So he fled with all

---

ᵃ *18* That is, Northwest Mesopotamia

BREAKTHROUGH!

Household gods
(GENESIS 31:19)

These were statues of gods that people believed protected family members and their possessions. When a member of the family had one of these gods, it meant that he was the one who would be left the family's possessions. This explains why Rachel stole them, and why Laban wanted to get them back.

he had, crossed the Euphrates River, and headed for the hill country of Gilead.

Laban Pursues Jacob

²²On the third day Laban was told that Jacob had fled. ²³Taking his relatives with him, he pursued Jacob for seven days and caught up with him in the hill country of Gilead. ²⁴Then God came to Laban the Aramean in a dream at night and said to him, "Be careful not to say anything to Jacob, either good or bad."

²⁵Jacob had pitched his tent in the hill country of Gilead when Laban overtook him, and Laban and his relatives camped there too. ²⁶Then Laban said to Jacob, "What have you done? You've deceived me, and you've carried off my daughters like captives in war. ²⁷Why did you run off secretly and deceive me? Why didn't you tell me, so I could send you away with joy and singing to the music of timbrels and harps? ²⁸You didn't even let me kiss my grandchildren and my daughters goodbye. You have done a foolish thing. ²⁹I have the power to harm you; but last night the God of your father said to me, 'Be careful not to say anything to Jacob, either good or bad.' ³⁰Now you have gone off because you longed to return to your father's household. But why did you steal my gods?"

³¹Jacob answered Laban, "I was afraid, because I thought you would take your daughters away from me by force. ³²But if you find anyone who has your gods, that person shall not live. In the presence of our relatives, see for yourself whether there is anything of yours here with me; and if so, take it." Now Jacob did not know that Rachel had stolen the gods.

³³So Laban went into Jacob's tent and into Leah's tent and into the tent of the two female servants, but he found nothing. After he came out of Leah's tent, he entered Rachel's tent. ³⁴Now Rachel had taken the household gods and put them inside her camel's saddle and was sitting on them. Laban searched through everything in the tent but found nothing.

³⁵Rachel said to her father, "Don't be angry, my lord, that I cannot stand up in your presence; I'm having my period." So he searched but could not find the household gods.

³⁶Jacob was angry and took Laban to task. "What is my crime?" he asked Laban. "How have I wronged you that you hunt me down? ³⁷Now that you have searched through all my goods, what have you found that belongs to your household? Put it here in front of your relatives and mine, and let them judge between the two of us.

³⁸"I have been with you for twenty years now. Your sheep and goats have not miscarried, nor have I eaten rams from your flocks. ³⁹I did not bring you animals torn by wild beasts; I bore the loss myself. And you demanded payment from me for whatever was stolen by day or night. ⁴⁰This was my situation: The heat consumed me in the daytime and the cold at night, and sleep fled from my eyes. ⁴¹It was like this for the twenty years I was in your household. I worked for you fourteen years for your two daughters and six years for your flocks, and you changed my wages ten times. ⁴²If the God of my father, the God of Abraham and the Fear of Isaac, had not been with me, you would surely have sent me away empty-handed. But God has seen my hardship and the toil of my hands, and last night he rebuked you."

⁴³Laban answered Jacob, "The women are my daughters, the children are my children, and the flocks are my flocks. All you see is mine. Yet what can I do today about these daughters of mine, or about the children they have borne? ⁴⁴Come now, let's make a covenant, you and I, and let it serve as a witness between us."

⁴⁵So Jacob took a stone and set it up as a pillar. ⁴⁶He said to his relatives, "Gather some stones." So they took stones and piled them in a heap, and they ate there by the heap. ⁴⁷Laban called it Jegar Sahadutha, and Jacob called it Galeed.ᵃ

⁴⁸Laban said, "This heap is a witness between you and me today." That is why it was called Galeed. ⁴⁹It was also called Mizpah,ᵇ because he said, "May the Lord

---

ᵃ 47 The Aramaic *Jegar Sahadutha* and the Hebrew *Galeed* both mean *witness heap.*   ᵇ 49 *Mizpah* means *watchtower.*

keep watch between you and me when we are away from each other. [50]If you mistreat my daughters or if you take any wives besides my daughters, even though no one is with us, remember that God is a witness between you and me."

[51]Laban also said to Jacob, "Here is this heap, and here is this pillar I have set up between you and me. [52]This heap is a witness, and this pillar is a witness, that I will not go past this heap to your side to harm you and that you will not go past this heap and pillar to my side to harm me. [53]May the God of Abraham and the God of Nahor, the God of their father, judge between us."

So Jacob took an oath in the name of the Fear of his father Isaac. [54]He offered a sacrifice there in the hill country and invited his relatives to a meal. After they had eaten, they spent the night there.

[55]Early the next morning Laban kissed his grandchildren and his daughters and blessed them. Then he left and returned home.[a]

Jacob Prepares to Meet Esau

32[b] Jacob also went on his way, and the angels of God met him. [2]When Jacob saw them, he said, "This is the camp of God!" So he named that place Mahanaim.[c]

[3]Jacob sent messengers ahead of him to his brother Esau in the land of Seir, the country of Edom. [4]He instructed them: "This is what you are to say to my lord Esau: 'Your servant Jacob says, I have been staying with Laban and have remained there till now. [5]I have cattle and donkeys, sheep and goats, male and female servants. Now I am sending this message to my lord, that I may find favor in your eyes.'"

[6]When the messengers returned to Jacob, they said, "We went to your brother Esau, and now he is coming to meet you, and four hundred men are with him."

[7]In great fear and distress Jacob divided the people who were with him into two groups,[d] and the flocks and herds and camels as well. [8]He thought, "If Esau comes and attacks one group,[e] the group[e] that is left may escape."

THE SCENE

EDOM

(GENESIS 32:3)

Edom is a mountain land rich in copper. It is south of Judea and the Red Sea. Its inhabitants are related to the Israelites because they are offspring of Esau. Esau was renamed Edom (meaning "red" in the Hebrew language) when he decided to give up his rights as the oldest son for a red-colored stew. In spite of the fact that they were related, the Israelites and the Edomites were almost always enemies. During the time of the Romans, this region was called Idumea. King Herod was Idumean.

[9]Then Jacob prayed, "O God of my father Abraham, God of my father Isaac, LORD, you who said to me, 'Go back to your country and your relatives, and I will make you prosper,' [10]I am unworthy of all the kindness and faithfulness you have shown your servant. I had only my

---

[a] 55 In Hebrew texts this verse (31:55) is numbered 32:1.
[b] In Hebrew texts 32:1-32 is numbered 32:2-33.
[c] 2 Mahanaim means two camps.   [d] 7 Or camps
[e] 8 Or camp

staff when I crossed this Jordan, but now I have become two camps. ¹¹Save me, I pray, from the hand of my brother Esau, for I am afraid he will come and attack me, and also the mothers with their children. ¹²But you have said, 'I will surely make you prosper and will make your descendants like the sand of the sea, which cannot be counted.' "

¹³He spent the night there, and from what he had with him he selected a gift for his brother Esau: ¹⁴two hundred female goats and twenty male goats, two hundred ewes and twenty rams, ¹⁵thirty female camels with their young, forty cows and ten bulls, and twenty female donkeys and ten male donkeys. ¹⁶He put them in the care of his servants, each herd by itself, and said to his servants, "Go ahead of me, and keep some space between the herds."

¹⁷He instructed the one in the lead: "When my brother Esau meets you and asks, 'Who do you belong to, and where are you going, and who owns all these animals in front of you?' ¹⁸then you are to say, 'They belong to your servant Jacob. They are a gift sent to my lord Esau, and he is coming behind us.' "

¹⁹He also instructed the second, the third and all the others who followed the herds: "You are to say the same thing to Esau when you meet him. ²⁰And be sure to say, 'Your servant Jacob is coming behind us.' " For he thought, "I will pacify him with these gifts I am sending on ahead; later, when I see him, perhaps he will receive me." ²¹So Jacob's gifts went on ahead of him, but he himself spent the night in the camp.

Jacob Wrestles With God

²²That night Jacob got up and took his two wives, his two female servants and his eleven sons and crossed the ford of the Jabbok. ²³After he had sent them across the stream, he sent over all his possessions. ²⁴So Jacob was left alone, and a man wrestled with him till daybreak. ²⁵When the man saw that he could not overpower him, he touched the socket of Jacob's hip so that his hip was wrenched as he wrestled with the man.

²⁶Then the man said, "Let me go, for it is daybreak."

But Jacob replied, "I will not let you go unless you bless me."

²⁷The man asked him, "What is your name?"

"Jacob," he answered.

²⁸Then the man said, "Your name will no longer be Jacob, but Israel,ᵃ because you have struggled with God and with humans and have overcome."

²⁹Jacob said, "Please tell me your name."

But he replied, "Why do you ask my name?" Then he blessed him there.

³⁰So Jacob called the place Peniel,ᵇ saying, "It is because I saw God face to face, and yet my life was spared."

³¹The sun rose above him as he passed Peniel,ᶜ and he was limping because of his hip. ³²Therefore to this day the Israelites do not eat the tendon attached to the socket of the hip, because the socket of Jacob's hip was touched near the tendon.

Jacob Meets Esau

33 Jacob looked up and there was Esau, coming with his four hundred men; so he divided the children among Leah, Rachel and the two female servants. ²He put the female servants and their children in front, Leah and her children next, and Rachel and Joseph in the rear. ³He himself went on ahead and bowed down to the ground seven times as he approached his brother.

⁴But Esau ran to meet Jacob and embraced him; he threw his arms around his neck and kissed him. And they wept. ⁵Then Esau looked up and saw the women and children. "Who are these with you?" he asked.

Jacob answered, "They are the children God has graciously given your servant."

⁶Then the female servants and their children approached and bowed down. ⁷Next, Leah and her children came and bowed down. Last of all came Joseph and Rachel, and they too bowed down.

⁸Esau asked, "What's the meaning of all these flocks and herds I met?"

ᵃ 28 *Israel* probably means *he struggles with God.*
ᵇ 30 *Peniel* means *face of God.*   ᶜ 31 Hebrew *Penuel,* a variant of *Peniel*

"To find favor in your eyes, my lord," he said.

⁹But Esau said, "I already have plenty, my brother. Keep what you have for yourself."

¹⁰"No, please!" said Jacob. "If I have found favor in your eyes, accept this gift from me. For to see your face is like seeing the face of God, now that you have received me favorably. ¹¹Please accept the present that was brought to you, for God has been gracious to me and I have all I need." And because Jacob insisted, Esau accepted it.

¹²Then Esau said, "Let us be on our way; I'll accompany you."

¹³But Jacob said to him, "My lord knows that the children are tender and that I must care for the ewes and cows that are nursing their young. If they are driven hard just one day, all the animals will die. ¹⁴So let my lord go on ahead of his servant, while I move along slowly at the pace of the flocks and herds before me and the pace of the children, until I come to my lord in Seir."

¹⁵Esau said, "Then let me leave some of my men with you."

"But why do that?" Jacob asked. "Just let me find favor in the eyes of my lord."

¹⁶So that day Esau started on his way back to Seir. ¹⁷Jacob, however, went to Sukkoth, where he built a place for himself and made shelters for his livestock. That is why the place is called Sukkoth.ᵃ

¹⁸After Jacob came from Paddan Aram,ᵇ he arrived safely at the city of Shechem in Canaan and camped within sight of the city. ¹⁹For a hundred pieces of silver,ᶜ he bought from the sons of Hamor, the father of Shechem, the plot of ground where he pitched his tent. ²⁰There he set up an altar and called it El Elohe Israel.ᵈ

Dinah and the Shechemites

34 Now Dinah, the daughter Leah had borne to Jacob, went out to visit the women of the land. ²When Shechem son of Hamor the Hivite, the ruler of that area, saw her, he took her and raped her. ³His heart was drawn to Dinah daughter of Jacob; he loved the young woman and spoke tenderly to her. ⁴And Shechem said

THE
WITNESSES

✓ **DINAH** (GENESIS 34:1)
She was Jacob and Leah's only daughter.

to his father Hamor, "Get me this girl as my wife."

⁵When Jacob heard that his daughter Dinah had been defiled, his sons were in the fields with his livestock; so he did nothing about it until they came home.

⁶Then Shechem's father Hamor went out to talk with Jacob. ⁷Meanwhile, Jacob's sons had come in from the fields as soon as they heard what had happened. They were shocked and furious, because Shechem had done an outrageous thing inᵉ Israel by sleeping with Jacob's daughter—a thing that should not be done.

⁸But Hamor said to them, "My son She-

ᵃ 17 *Sukkoth* means *shelters*.   ᵇ 18 That is, Northwest Mesopotamia   ᶜ 19 Hebrew *hundred kesitahs*; a kesitah was a unit of money of unknown weight and value.
ᵈ 20 *El Elohe Israel* can mean *El is the God of Israel* or *mighty is the God of Israel*.   ᵉ 7 Or *against*

chem has his heart set on your daughter. Please give her to him as his wife. ⁹Intermarry with us; give us your daughters and take our daughters for yourselves. ¹⁰You can settle among us; the land is open to you. Live in it, trade*ᵃ* in it, and acquire property in it."

¹¹Then Shechem said to Dinah's father and brothers, "Let me find favor in your eyes, and I will give you whatever you ask. ¹²Make the price for the bride and the gift I am to bring as great as you like, and I'll pay whatever you ask me. Only give me the young woman as my wife."

¹³Because their sister Dinah had been defiled, Jacob's sons replied deceitfully as they spoke to Shechem and his father Hamor. ¹⁴They said to them, "We can't do such a thing; we can't give our sister to a man who is not circumcised. That would be a disgrace to us. ¹⁵We will enter into an agreement with you on one condition only: that you become like us by circumcising all your males. ¹⁶Then we will give you our daughters and take your daughters for ourselves. We'll settle among you and become one people with you. ¹⁷But if you will not agree to be circumcised, we'll take our sister and go."

¹⁸Their proposal seemed good to Hamor and his son Shechem. ¹⁹The young man, who was the most honored of all his father's family, lost no time in doing what they said, because he was delighted with Jacob's daughter. ²⁰So Hamor and his son Shechem went to the gate of their city to speak to the men of their city. ²¹"These men are friendly toward us," they said. "Let them live in our land and trade in it; the land has plenty of room for them. We can marry their daughters and they can marry ours. ²²But the men will agree to live with us as one people only on the condition that our males be circumcised, as they themselves are. ²³Won't their livestock, their property and all their other animals become ours? So let us agree to their terms, and they will settle among us."

²⁴All the men who went out of the city gate agreed with Hamor and his son Shechem, and every male in the city was circumcised.

²⁵Three days later, while all of them were still in pain, two of Jacob's sons, Simeon and Levi, Dinah's brothers, took their swords and attacked the unsuspecting city, killing every male. ²⁶They put Hamor and his son Shechem to the sword and took Dinah from Shechem's house and left. ²⁷The sons of Jacob came upon the dead bodies and looted the city where*ᵇ* their sister had been defiled. ²⁸They seized their flocks and herds and donkeys and everything else of theirs in the city and out in the fields. ²⁹They carried off all their wealth and all their women and children, taking as plunder everything in the houses.

³⁰Then Jacob said to Simeon and Levi, "You have brought trouble on me by making me obnoxious to the Canaanites and Perizzites, the people living in this land. We are few in number, and if they join forces against me and attack me, I and my household will be destroyed."

³¹But they replied, "Should he have treated our sister like a prostitute?"

Jacob Returns to Bethel

35 Then God said to Jacob, "Go up to Bethel and settle there, and build an altar there to God, who appeared to you when you were fleeing from your brother Esau."

²So Jacob said to his household and to all who were with him, "Get rid of the foreign gods you have with you, and purify yourselves and change your clothes. ³Then come, let us go up to Bethel, where I will build an altar to God, who answered me in the day of my distress and who has been with me wherever I have gone." ⁴So they gave Jacob all the foreign gods they had and the rings in their ears, and Jacob buried them under the oak at Shechem. ⁵Then they set out, and the terror of God fell on the towns all around them so that no one pursued them.

⁶Jacob and all the people with him came to Luz (that is, Bethel) in the land of Canaan. ⁷There he built an altar, and he called the place El Bethel,*ᶜ* because

ᵃ 10 Or move about freely; also in verse 21   ᵇ 27 Or because   ᶜ 7 El Bethel means God of Bethel.

it was there that God revealed himself to him when he was fleeing from his brother.

[8]Now Deborah, Rebekah's nurse, died and was buried under the oak outside Bethel. So it was named Allon Bakuth.[a]

[9]After Jacob returned from Paddan Aram,[b] God appeared to him again and blessed him. [10]God said to him, "Your name is Jacob,[c] but you will no longer be called Jacob; your name will be Israel.[d]" So he named him Israel.

[11]And God said to him, "I am God Almighty[e]; be fruitful and increase in number. A nation and a community of nations will come from you, and kings will be among your descendants. [12]The land I gave to Abraham and Isaac I also give to you, and I will give this land to your descendants after you." [13]Then God went

THE SCENE

EPHRATH/BETHLEHEM

(GENESIS 35:16–19)

This small city in Judah is 5 miles (8 km) southeast of Jerusalem. It's one of the most famous places in Bible history. Bethlehem is where King David lived and where Samuel anointed him as king. However, it's most famous for Jesus, who was born there.

THE WITNESSES

✓ BENJAMIN (GENESIS 35:18)

He was Jacob and Rachel's second and last son. He was the youngest of all Jacob's sons. Unfortunately, Rachel died when he was born. Benjamin means "son of my right hand." This might mean that he was the favorite son. Did you

up from him at the place where he had talked with him.

[14]Jacob set up a stone pillar at the place where God had talked with him, and he poured out a drink offering on it; he also poured oil on it. [15]Jacob called the place where God had talked with him Bethel.[f]

The Deaths of Rachel and Isaac

[16]Then they moved on from Bethel. While they were still some distance from

---

[a] 8 *Allon Bakuth* means *oak of weeping.*   [b] 9 That is, Northwest Mesopotamia; also in verse 26   [c] 10 *Jacob* means *he grasps the heel,* a Hebrew idiom for *he deceives.*   [d] 10 *Israel* probably means *he struggles with God.*   [e] 11 Hebrew *El-Shaddai*   [f] 15 *Bethel* means *house of God.*

know that King Saul and the apostle Paul were two famous members of the tribe of Benjamin? The youngest son is sometimes called the "Benjamin of the family."

✓ **REUBEN** (GENESIS 35:23)
He was Jacob and Leah's first son. His name sounds like the Hebrew word that means "look, a son" or "he saw my sadness." Although he was the first of Jacob's twelve sons, he didn't get the blessing of the oldest son. His brother Judah got that.

✓ **SIMEON** (GENESIS 35:23)
He was Jacob and Leah's second son. His name sounds like the Hebrew action word that means "heard."

✓ **LEVI** (GENESIS 35:23)
He was Jacob and Leah's third son. His name sounds like the Hebrew action word that means "unite." Moses and his brother were two important members of the tribe of Levi. This tribe was very important, because God had said that all priests had to belong to this family.

✓ **JUDAH** (GENESIS 35:23)
He was Jacob and Leah's fourth son. His name sounds like the Hebrew action word that means "praise." Just before Jacob died, he gave Judah the blessing reserved for the oldest son, which meant more wealth for his family. Both King David and Jesus were Judah's offspring.

✓ **ISSACHAR** (GENESIS 35:23)
He was Jacob and Leah's fifth son. His name sounds like the Hebrew word that means "the person who earns a salary."

✓ **ZEBULUN** (GENESIS 35:23)
He was Jacob and Leah's sixth and last son. His name is related to the Hebrew action word that means "to stay." It's also like the Hebrew word that means "residence" or "dwelling place." Zebulun and his brother Issachar must have been close friends, because their names are always mentioned together in the Bible.

✓ **JOSEPH** (GENESIS 35:24)
Joseph was the eleventh of the twelve sons Jacob had. His father loved him very much, because he was the first son he had with Rachel, the wife he loved. Joseph's name sounds like the Hebrew action word that means "to add." Joseph was a special person even when he was a child, because he could understand dreams. This gift made his life tricky several times. But it also saved his life and the lives of his family members.

✓ **DAN** (GENESIS 35:25)
His name is related to the Hebrew word translated as "judge." His mother was Bilhah, one of Rachel's slaves. Dan was the father of one of the twelve tribes of Israel. Dan's tribe is famous for being fighters. Samson was one of his most famous offspring.

✓ **NAPHTALI** (GENESIS 35:25)
He was the second son Jacob had with Bilhah, Rachel's servant. His name sounds like the Hebrew word that means "my fight."

Ephrath, Rachel began to give birth and had great difficulty. ¹⁷And as she was having great difficulty in childbirth, the midwife said to her, "Don't despair, for you have another son." ¹⁸As she breathed her last—for she was dying—she named her son Ben-Oni.^a But his father named him Benjamin.^b ¹⁹So Rachel died and was buried on the way to Ephrath (that is, Bethlehem). ²⁰Over her tomb Jacob set up a pillar, and to this day that pillar marks Rachel's tomb.

²¹Israel moved on again and pitched his tent beyond Migdal Eder. ²²While Israel was living in that region, Reuben went in and slept with his father's concubine Bilhah, and Israel heard of it.

Jacob had twelve sons:
²³The sons of Leah:
Reuben the firstborn of Jacob,
Simeon, Levi, Judah, Issachar and Zebulun.
²⁴The sons of Rachel:
Joseph and Benjamin.
²⁵The sons of Rachel's servant Bilhah:
Dan and Naphtali.

^a 18 Ben-Oni means son of my trouble.   ^b 18 Benjamin means son of my right hand.

26 The sons of Leah's servant Zilpah:
Gad and Asher.

These were the sons of Jacob, who were born to him in Paddan Aram.

27 Jacob came home to his father Isaac in Mamre, near Kiriath Arba (that is, Hebron), where Abraham and Isaac had stayed. 28 Isaac lived a hundred and eighty years. 29 Then he breathed his last and died and was gathered to his people, old and full of years. And his sons Esau and Jacob buried him.

Esau's Descendants

36 This is the account of the family line of Esau (that is, Edom).

2 Esau took his wives from the women of Canaan: Adah daughter of Elon the Hittite, and Oholibamah daughter of Anah and granddaughter of Zibeon the Hivite— 3 also Basemath daughter of Ishmael and sister of Nebaioth.

4 Adah bore Eliphaz to Esau, Basemath bore Reuel, 5 and Oholibamah bore Jeush, Jalam and Korah. These were the sons of Esau, who were born to him in Canaan.

6 Esau took his wives and sons and daughters and all the members of his household, as well as his livestock and all his other animals and all the goods he had acquired in Canaan, and moved to a land some distance from his brother Jacob. 7 Their possessions were too great for them to remain together; the land where they were staying could not support them both because of their livestock. 8 So Esau (that is, Edom) settled in the hill country of Seir.

9 This is the account of the family line of Esau the father of the Edomites in the hill country of Seir.

10 These are the names of Esau's sons:
Eliphaz, the son of Esau's wife Adah, and Reuel, the son of Esau's wife Basemath.
11 The sons of Eliphaz:
Teman, Omar, Zepho, Gatam and Kenaz.

THE
WITNESSES

✓ **GAD** (GENESIS 35:26)
Gad was another of Jacob's sons. His mother was Zilpah, and she was one of Leah's servants. His name means "fortune." It was the name of a false god.

✓ **ASHER** (GENESIS 35:26)
Asher was the other son of Jacob and Zilpah. In Hebrew, his name sounds like the action word that means "being happy."

12 Esau's son Eliphaz also had a concubine named Timna, who bore him Amalek. These were grandsons of Esau's wife Adah.
13 The sons of Reuel:
Nahath, Zerah, Shammah and Mizzah. These were grandsons of Esau's wife Basemath.
14 The sons of Esau's wife Oholibamah daughter of Anah and granddaughter of Zibeon, whom she bore to Esau:
Jeush, Jalam and Korah.

15These were the chiefs among Esau's descendants:

The sons of Eliphaz the firstborn of Esau:

Chiefs Teman, Omar, Zepho, Kenaz, 16Korah,ª Gatam and Amalek. These were the chiefs descended from Eliphaz in Edom; they were grandsons of Adah.

17The sons of Esau's son Reuel:

Chiefs Nahath, Zerah, Shammah and Mizzah. These were the chiefs descended from Reuel in Edom; they were grandsons of Esau's wife Basemath.

18The sons of Esau's wife Oholibamah:

Chiefs Jeush, Jalam and Korah. These were the chiefs descended from Esau's wife Oholibamah daughter of Anah.

19These were the sons of Esau (that is, Edom), and these were their chiefs.

20These were the sons of Seir the Horite, who were living in the region:

Lotan, Shobal, Zibeon, Anah, 21Dishon, Ezer and Dishan. These sons of Seir in Edom were Horite chiefs.

22The sons of Lotan:

Hori and Homam.ᵇ Timna was Lotan's sister.

23The sons of Shobal:

Alvan, Manahath, Ebal, Shepho and Onam.

24The sons of Zibeon:

Aiah and Anah. This is the Anah who discovered the hot springsᶜ in the desert while he was grazing the donkeys of his father Zibeon.

25The children of Anah:

Dishon and Oholibamah daughter of Anah.

26The sons of Dishonᵈ:

Hemdan, Eshban, Ithran and Keran.

27The sons of Ezer:

Bilhan, Zaavan and Akan.

28The sons of Dishan:

Uz and Aran.

29These were the Horite chiefs:

Lotan, Shobal, Zibeon, Anah, 30Dishon, Ezer and Dishan. These were the Horite chiefs, according to their divisions, in the land of Seir.

The Rulers of Edom

31These were the kings who reigned in Edom before any Israelite king reigned:

32Bela son of Beor became king of Edom. His city was named Dinhabah.

33When Bela died, Jobab son of Zerah from Bozrah succeeded him as king.

34When Jobab died, Husham from the land of the Temanites succeeded him as king.

35When Husham died, Hadad son of Bedad, who defeated Midian in the country of Moab, succeeded him as king. His city was named Avith.

36When Hadad died, Samlah from Masrekah succeeded him as king.

37When Samlah died, Shaul from Rehoboth on the river succeeded him as king.

38When Shaul died, Baal-Hanan son of Akbor succeeded him as king.

39When Baal-Hanan son of Akbor died, Hadadᵉ succeeded him as king. His city was named Pau, and his wife's name was Mehetabel daughter of Matred, the daughter of Me-Zahab.

40These were the chiefs descended from Esau, by name, according to their clans and regions:

Timna, Alvah, Jetheth, 41Oholibamah, Elah, Pinon, 42Kenaz, Teman, Mibzar, 43Magdiel and Iram. These were the chiefs of Edom, according to their settlements in the land they occupied.

This is the family line of Esau, the father of the Edomites.

ª 16 Masoretic Text; Samaritan Pentateuch (also verse 11 and 1 Chron. 1:36) does not have Korah.   ᵇ 22 Hebrew Hemam, a variant of Homam (see 1 Chron. 1:39)
ᶜ 24 Vulgate; Syriac discovered water; the meaning of the Hebrew for this word is uncertain.   ᵈ 26 Hebrew Dishan, a variant of Dishon   ᵉ 39 Many manuscripts of the Masoretic Text, Samaritan Pentateuch and Syriac (see also 1 Chron. 1:50); most manuscripts of the Masoretic Text Hadar

Joseph's Dreams

37 Jacob lived in the land where his father had stayed, the land of Canaan.

²This is the account of Jacob's family line.

Joseph, a young man of seventeen, was tending the flocks with his brothers, the sons of Bilhah and the sons of Zilpah, his father's wives, and he brought their father a bad report about them. ³Now Israel loved Joseph more than any of his other sons, because he had been born to him in his old age; and he made an ornate*ᵃ* robe for him. ⁴When his brothers saw that their father loved him more than any of them, they hated him and could not speak a kind word to him.

⁵Joseph had a dream, and when he told it to his brothers, they hated him all the more. ⁶He said to them, "Listen to this dream I had: ⁷We were binding sheaves of grain out in the field when suddenly my sheaf rose and stood upright, while your sheaves gathered around mine and bowed down to it."

⁸His brothers said to him, "Do you intend to reign over us? Will you actually rule us?" And they hated him all the more because of his dream and what he had said.

⁹Then he had another dream, and he told it to his brothers. "Listen," he said, "I had another dream, and this time the sun and moon and eleven stars were bowing down to me."

¹⁰When he told his father as well as his brothers, his father rebuked him and said, "What is this dream you had? Will your mother and I and your brothers actually come and bow down to the ground before you?" ¹¹His brothers were jealous of him, but his father kept the matter in mind.

Joseph Sold by His Brothers

¹²Now his brothers had gone to graze their father's flocks near Shechem, ¹³and Israel said to Joseph, "As you know, your brothers are grazing the flocks near Shechem. Come, I am going to send you to them."

THE
WITNESSES

✓ **POTIPHAR** (GENESIS 37:36)
Potiphar (in ancient Egyptian, "He whom the gods help") was the name of Pharaoh's official. He was the captain of the guard who bought Joseph as a slave from some Midianite traders.

✓ **TAMAR** (GENESIS 38:6)
This name means "date palm." She was Judah's daughter-in-law. She was his son Er's first wife. Then she was his son Onan's wife also. She became a widow both times she was married, so then she had twins with Judah himself. Their names were Perez and Zerah.

"Very well," he replied.

¹⁴So he said to him, "Go and see if all is well with your brothers and with the flocks, and bring word back to me." Then he sent him off from the Valley of Hebron.

When Joseph arrived at Shechem, ¹⁵a

ᵃ 3 The meaning of the Hebrew for this word is uncertain; also in verses 23 and 32.

man found him wandering around in the fields and asked him, "What are you looking for?"

¹⁶He replied, "I'm looking for my brothers. Can you tell me where they are grazing their flocks?"

¹⁷"They have moved on from here," the man answered. "I heard them say, 'Let's go to Dothan.'"

So Joseph went after his brothers and found them near Dothan. ¹⁸But they saw him in the distance, and before he reached them, they plotted to kill him.

¹⁹"Here comes that dreamer!" they said to each other. ²⁰"Come now, let's kill him and throw him into one of these cisterns and say that a ferocious animal devoured him. Then we'll see what comes of his dreams."

²¹When Reuben heard this, he tried to rescue him from their hands. "Let's not take his life," he said. ²²"Don't shed any blood. Throw him into this cistern here in the wilderness, but don't lay a hand on him." Reuben said this to rescue him from them and take him back to his father.

²³So when Joseph came to his brothers, they stripped him of his robe—the ornate robe he was wearing— ²⁴and they took him and threw him into the cistern. The cistern was empty; there was no water in it.

²⁵As they sat down to eat their meal, they looked up and saw a caravan of Ishmaelites coming from Gilead. Their camels were loaded with spices, balm and myrrh, and they were on their way to take them down to Egypt.

²⁶Judah said to his brothers, "What will we gain if we kill our brother and cover up his blood? ²⁷Come, let's sell him to the Ishmaelites and not lay our hands on him; after all, he is our brother, our own flesh and blood." His brothers agreed.

²⁸So when the Midianite merchants came by, his brothers pulled Joseph up out of the cistern and sold him for twenty shekels*a* of silver to the Ishmaelites, who took him to Egypt.

²⁹When Reuben returned to the cistern and saw that Joseph was not there, he tore his clothes. ³⁰He went back to his brothers and said, "The boy isn't there! Where can I turn now?"

³¹Then they got Joseph's robe, slaughtered a goat and dipped the robe in the blood. ³²They took the ornate robe back to their father and said, "We found this. Examine it to see whether it is your son's robe."

³³He recognized it and said, "It is my son's robe! Some ferocious animal has devoured him. Joseph has surely been torn to pieces."

³⁴Then Jacob tore his clothes, put on sackcloth and mourned for his son many days. ³⁵All his sons and daughters came to comfort him, but he refused to be comforted. "No," he said, "I will continue to mourn until I join my son in the grave." So his father wept for him.

³⁶Meanwhile, the Midianites*b* sold Joseph in Egypt to Potiphar, one of Pharaoh's officials, the captain of the guard.

Judah and Tamar

38 At that time, Judah left his brothers and went down to stay with a man of Adullam named Hirah. ²There Judah met the daughter of a Canaanite man named Shua. He married her and made love to her; ³she became pregnant and gave birth to a son, who was named Er. ⁴She conceived again and gave birth to a son and named him Onan. ⁵She gave birth to still another son and named him Shelah. It was at Kezib that she gave birth to him.

⁶Judah got a wife for Er, his firstborn, and her name was Tamar. ⁷But Er, Judah's firstborn, was wicked in the LORD's sight; so the LORD put him to death. ⁸Then Judah said to Onan, "Sleep with your brother's wife and fulfill your duty to her as a brother-in-law to raise up offspring for your brother." ⁹But Onan knew that the child would not be his; so whenever he slept with his brother's wife, he spilled his semen on the ground

---

a 28 That is, about 8 ounces or about 230 grams
b 36 Samaritan Pentateuch, Septuagint, Vulgate and Syriac (see also verse 28); Masoretic Text *Medanites*

BREAKTHROUGH!

Fulfill your duty

(GENESIS 38:8)

This refers to an old Jewish law called *Levirate*. It said that when a man died but didn't have any children, his brother or brother-in-law had to marry his widow so she could have children. Then their first child was considered the son of the husband who died, and he received the land and property of that man.

to keep from providing offspring for his brother. ¹⁰What he did was wicked in the LORD's sight; so the LORD put him to death also.

¹¹Judah then said to his daughter-in-law Tamar, "Live as a widow in your father's household until my son Shelah grows up." For he thought, "He may die too, just like his brothers." So Tamar went to live in her father's household.

¹²After a long time Judah's wife, the daughter of Shua, died. When Judah had recovered from his grief, he went up to Timnah, to the men who were shearing his sheep, and his friend Hirah the Adullamite went with him.

¹³When Tamar was told, "Your father-in-law is on his way to Timnah to shear his sheep," ¹⁴she took off her widow's clothes, covered herself with a veil to dis-

guise herself, and then sat down at the entrance to Enaim, which is on the road to Timnah. For she saw that, though Shelah had now grown up, she had not been given to him as his wife.

¹⁵When Judah saw her, he thought she was a prostitute, for she had covered her face. ¹⁶Not realizing that she was his daughter-in-law, he went over to her by the roadside and said, "Come now, let me sleep with you."

"And what will you give me to sleep with you?" she asked.

¹⁷"I'll send you a young goat from my flock," he said.

"Will you give me something as a pledge until you send it?" she asked.

¹⁸He said, "What pledge should I give you?"

"Your seal and its cord, and the staff in your hand," she answered. So he gave them to her and slept with her, and she became pregnant by him. ¹⁹After she left, she took off her veil and put on her widow's clothes again.

²⁰Meanwhile Judah sent the young goat by his friend the Adullamite in order to get his pledge back from the woman, but he did not find her. ²¹He asked the men who lived there, "Where is the shrine prostitute who was beside the road at Enaim?"

"There hasn't been any shrine prostitute here," they said.

²²So he went back to Judah and said, "I didn't find her. Besides, the men who lived there said, 'There hasn't been any shrine prostitute here.' "

²³Then Judah said, "Let her keep what she has, or we will become a laughing-stock. After all, I did send her this young goat, but you didn't find her."

²⁴About three months later Judah was told, "Your daughter-in-law Tamar is guilty of prostitution, and as a result she is now pregnant."

Judah said, "Bring her out and have her burned to death!"

²⁵As she was being brought out, she sent a message to her father-in-law. "I am pregnant by the man who owns these," she said. And she added, "See if you recognize whose seal and cord and staff these are."

²⁶Judah recognized them and said, "She is more righteous than I, since I wouldn't give her to my son Shelah." And he did not sleep with her again.

²⁷When the time came for her to give birth, there were twin boys in her womb. ²⁸As she was giving birth, one of them put out his hand; so the midwife took a scarlet thread and tied it on his wrist and said, "This one came out first." ²⁹But when he drew back his hand, his brother came out, and she said, "So this is how you have broken out!" And he was named Perez.ᵃ ³⁰Then his brother, who had the scarlet thread on his wrist, came out. And he was named Zerah.ᵇ

Joseph and Potiphar's Wife

39 Now Joseph had been taken down to Egypt. Potiphar, an Egyptian who was one of Pharaoh's officials, the captain of the guard, bought him from the Ishmaelites who had taken him there.

²The Lord was with Joseph so that he prospered, and he lived in the house of his Egyptian master. ³When his master saw that the Lord was with him and that the Lord gave him success in everything he did, ⁴Joseph found favor in his eyes and became his attendant. Potiphar put him in charge of his household, and he entrusted to his care everything he owned. ⁵From the time he put him in charge of his household and of all that he owned, the Lord blessed the household of the Egyptian because of Joseph. The blessing of the Lord was on everything Potiphar had, both in the house and in the field. ⁶So Potiphar left everything he had in Joseph's care; with Joseph in charge, he did not concern himself with anything except the food he ate.

Now Joseph was well-built and handsome, ⁷and after a while his master's wife took notice of Joseph and said, "Come to bed with me!"

⁸But he refused. "With me in charge," he told her, "my master does not concern himself with anything in the house; everything he owns he has entrusted to my care. ⁹No one is greater in this house than I am. My master has withheld nothing from me except you, because you

are his wife. How then could I do such a wicked thing and sin against God?" ¹⁰And though she spoke to Joseph day after day, he refused to go to bed with her or even be with her.

¹¹One day he went into the house to attend to his duties, and none of the household servants was inside. ¹²She caught him by his cloak and said, "Come to bed with me!" But he left his cloak in her hand and ran out of the house.

¹³When she saw that he had left his cloak in her hand and had run out of the house, ¹⁴she called her household servants. "Look," she said to them, "this Hebrew has been brought to us to make sport of us! He came in here to sleep with me, but I screamed. ¹⁵When he heard me scream for help, he left his cloak beside me and ran out of the house."

¹⁶She kept his cloak beside her until his master came home. ¹⁷Then she told him this story: "That Hebrew slave you brought us came to me to make sport of me. ¹⁸But as soon as I screamed for help, he left his cloak beside me and ran out of the house."

¹⁹When his master heard the story his wife told him, saying, "This is how your slave treated me," he burned with anger. ²⁰Joseph's master took him and put him in prison, the place where the king's prisoners were confined.

But while Joseph was there in the prison, ²¹the Lord was with him; he showed him kindness and granted him favor in the eyes of the prison warden. ²²So the warden put Joseph in charge of all those held in the prison, and he was made responsible for all that was done there. ²³The warden paid no attention to anything under Joseph's care, because the Lord was with Joseph and gave him success in whatever he did.

The Cupbearer and the Baker

40 Some time later, the cupbearer and the baker of the king of Egypt offended their master, the king of Egypt. ²Pharaoh was angry with his two officials, the chief cupbearer and the chief baker,

---

ᵃ 29 *Perez* means *breaking out.*   ᵇ 30 *Zerah* can mean *scarlet* or *brightness.*

³and put them in custody in the house of the captain of the guard, in the same prison where Joseph was confined. ⁴The captain of the guard assigned them to Joseph, and he attended them.

After they had been in custody for some time, ⁵each of the two men—the cupbearer and the baker of the king of Egypt, who were being held in prison—had a dream the same night, and each dream had a meaning of its own.

⁶When Joseph came to them the next morning, he saw that they were dejected. ⁷So he asked Pharaoh's officials who were in custody with him in his master's house, "Why do you look so sad today?"

⁸"We both had dreams," they answered, "but there is no one to interpret them."

Then Joseph said to them, "Do not interpretations belong to God? Tell me your dreams."

⁹So the chief cupbearer told Joseph his dream. He said to him, "In my dream I saw a vine in front of me, ¹⁰and on the vine were three branches. As soon as it budded, it blossomed, and its clusters ripened into grapes. ¹¹Pharaoh's cup was in my hand, and I took the grapes, squeezed them into Pharaoh's cup and put the cup in his hand."

¹²"This is what it means," Joseph said to him. "The three branches are three days. ¹³Within three days Pharaoh will lift up your head and restore you to your position, and you will put Pharaoh's cup in his hand, just as you used to do when you were his cupbearer. ¹⁴But when all goes well with you, remember me and show me kindness; mention me to Pharaoh and get me out of this prison. ¹⁵I was forcibly carried off from the land of the Hebrews, and even here I have done nothing to deserve being put in a dungeon."

¹⁶When the chief baker saw that Joseph had given a favorable interpretation, he said to Joseph, "I too had a dream: On my head were three baskets of bread.ᵃ ¹⁷In the top basket were all kinds of baked goods for Pharaoh, but the birds were eating them out of the basket on my head."

¹⁸"This is what it means," Joseph said. "The three baskets are three days. ¹⁹With-in three days Pharaoh will lift off your head and impale your body on a pole. And the birds will eat away your flesh."

²⁰Now the third day was Pharaoh's birthday, and he gave a feast for all his officials. He lifted up the heads of the chief cupbearer and the chief baker in the presence of his officials: ²¹He restored the chief cupbearer to his position, so that he once again put the cup into Pharaoh's hand— ²²but he impaled the chief baker, just as Joseph had said to them in his interpretation.

²³The chief cupbearer, however, did not remember Joseph; he forgot him.

Pharaoh's Dreams

41 When two full years had passed, Pharaoh had a dream: He was standing by the Nile, ²when out of the river there came up seven cows, sleek and fat, and they grazed among the reeds. ³After them, seven other cows, ugly and gaunt, came up out of the Nile and stood beside those on the riverbank. ⁴And the cows that were ugly and gaunt ate up the seven sleek, fat cows. Then Pharaoh woke up.

⁵He fell asleep again and had a second dream: Seven heads of grain, healthy and good, were growing on a single stalk. ⁶After them, seven other heads of grain sprouted—thin and scorched by the east wind. ⁷The thin heads of grain swallowed up the seven healthy, full heads. Then Pharaoh woke up; it had been a dream.

⁸In the morning his mind was troubled, so he sent for all the magicians and wise men of Egypt. Pharaoh told them his dreams, but no one could interpret them for him.

⁹Then the chief cupbearer said to Pharaoh, "Today I am reminded of my shortcomings. ¹⁰Pharaoh was once angry with his servants, and he imprisoned me and the chief baker in the house of the captain of the guard. ¹¹Each of us had a dream the same night, and each dream had a meaning of its own. ¹²Now a young Hebrew was there with us, a servant of the captain of the guard. We told him our

---

ᵃ 16 Or three wicker baskets

THE SCENE

THE NILE RIVER

(GENESIS 41:1)

This is one of the longest rivers in the world. It starts in Burundi, in the heart of Africa. It flows nearly 4,350 miles (7,000 km) until it reaches Egypt to join the Mediterranean Sea. It's practically desert all the way. It is possible to fish and sail in this river. Once a year, the Nile overflows and covers the land with black silt, which is a very soft, fertile soil that can be planted in. Swamps form, and papyrus grows there. Special technology can turn this plant into writing paper.

I have heard it said of you that when you hear a dream you can interpret it."

16 "I cannot do it," Joseph replied to Pharaoh, "but God will give Pharaoh the answer he desires."

17 Then Pharaoh said to Joseph, "In my dream I was standing on the bank of the Nile, 18 when out of the river there came up seven cows, fat and sleek, and they grazed among the reeds. 19 After them, seven other cows came up—scrawny and very ugly and lean. I had never seen such ugly cows in all the land of Egypt. 20 The lean, ugly cows ate up the seven fat cows that came up first. 21 But even after they ate them, no one could tell that they had done so; they looked just as ugly as before. Then I woke up.

22 "In my dream I saw seven heads of grain, full and good, growing on a single stalk. 23 After them, seven other heads sprouted—withered and thin and scorched by the east wind. 24 The thin

CHECK THE FACTS

Who did the pharaoh of Egypt put in charge of the entire country?

A) Abraham

B) Moses

C) Joseph

CORRECT ANSWER: C

dreams, and he interpreted them for us, giving each man the interpretation of his dream. 13 And things turned out exactly as he interpreted them to us: I was restored to my position, and the other man was impaled."

14 So Pharaoh sent for Joseph, and he was quickly brought from the dungeon. When he had shaved and changed his clothes, he came before Pharaoh.

15 Pharaoh said to Joseph, "I had a dream, and no one can interpret it. But

heads of grain swallowed up the seven good heads. I told this to the magicians, but none of them could explain it to me." 25Then Joseph said to Pharaoh, "The dreams of Pharaoh are one and the same. God has revealed to Pharaoh what he is about to do. 26The seven good cows are seven years, and the seven good heads of grain are seven years; it is one and the same dream. 27The seven lean, ugly cows that came up afterward are seven years, and so are the seven worthless heads of grain scorched by the east wind: They are seven years of famine.

28"It is just as I said to Pharaoh: God has shown Pharaoh what he is about to do. 29Seven years of great abundance are coming throughout the land of Egypt, 30but seven years of famine will follow them. Then all the abundance in Egypt will be forgotten, and the famine will ravage the land. 31The abundance in the land will not be remembered, because the famine that follows it will be so severe. 32The reason the dream was given to Pharaoh in two forms is that the matter has been firmly decided by God, and God will do it soon.

33"And now let Pharaoh look for a discerning and wise man and put him in charge of the land of Egypt. 34Let Pharaoh appoint commissioners over the land to take a fifth of the harvest of Egypt during the seven years of abundance. 35They should collect all the food of these good years that are coming and store up the grain under the authority of Pharaoh, to be kept in the cities for food. 36This food should be held in reserve for the country, to be used during the seven years of famine that will come upon Egypt, so that the country may not be ruined by the famine."

37The plan seemed good to Pharaoh and to all his officials. 38So Pharaoh asked them, "Can we find anyone like this man, one in whom is the spirit of God*a*?"

39Then Pharaoh said to Joseph, "Since God has made all this known to you, there is no one so discerning and wise as you. 40You shall be in charge of my palace, and all my people are to submit to your orders. Only with respect to the throne will I be greater than you."

Joseph in Charge of Egypt

41So Pharaoh said to Joseph, "I hereby put you in charge of the whole land of Egypt." 42Then Pharaoh took his signet ring from his finger and put it on Joseph's finger. He dressed him in robes of fine linen and put a gold chain around his neck. 43He had him ride in a chariot as his second-in-command,*b* and people shouted before him, "Make way*c*!" Thus he put him in charge of the whole land of Egypt.

44Then Pharaoh said to Joseph, "I am Pharaoh, but without your word no one will lift hand or foot in all Egypt." 45Pharaoh gave Joseph the name Zaphenath-Paneah and gave him Asenath daughter of Potiphera, priest of On,*d* to be his wife. And Joseph went throughout the land of Egypt.

46Joseph was thirty years old when he entered the service of Pharaoh king of Egypt. And Joseph went out from Pharaoh's presence and traveled throughout Egypt. 47During the seven years of abundance the land produced plentifully. 48Joseph collected all the food produced in those seven years of abundance in Egypt and stored it in the cities. In each city he put the food grown in the fields surrounding it. 49Joseph stored up huge quantities of grain, like the sand of the sea; it was so much that he stopped keeping records because it was beyond measure.

50Before the years of famine came, two sons were born to Joseph by Asenath daughter of Potiphera, priest of On. 51Joseph named his firstborn Manasseh*e* and said, "It is because God has made me forget all my trouble and all my father's household." 52The second son he named Ephraim*f* and said, "It is because God has made me fruitful in the land of my suffering."

53The seven years of abundance in Egypt came to an end, 54and the seven years of famine began, just as Joseph had said. There was famine in all the other lands, but in the whole land of Egypt

---

a 38 Or *of the gods*   *b 43* Or *in the chariot of his second-in-command; or in his second chariot*   *c 43* Or *Bow down*   *d 45* That is, Heliopolis; also in verse 50   *e 51 Manasseh* sounds like and may be derived from the Hebrew for *forget.*   *f 52 Ephraim* sounds like the Hebrew for *twice fruitful.*

THE
WITNESSES

✓ **MANASSEH** (GENESIS 41:51)

Manasseh was the name of the son Joseph had with his Egyptian wife, Asenath. In Hebrew, his name sounds like the verb that means "forget." This might be because Joseph wanted to forget all his past sufferings. His grandfather, Jacob, adopted him and his brother Ephraim as his own sons, so they also became leaders of two of the twelve tribes of Israel.

✓ **EPHRAIM** (GENESIS 41:52)

He was Joseph and Asenath's son, so he was Manasseh's brother. His name sounds like the Hebrew action word that means "be fruitful." Joseph gave him that name because God had allowed him to have children and riches in the land where he had arrived as a slave. His grandfather, Jacob, adopted him as a son so Ephraim could also become one of the leaders of the twelve tribes of Israel.

there was food. ⁵⁵When all Egypt began to feel the famine, the people cried to Pharaoh for food. Then Pharaoh told all the Egyptians, "Go to Joseph and do what he tells you."

⁵⁶When the famine had spread over the whole country, Joseph opened all the storehouses and sold grain to the Egyptians, for the famine was severe throughout Egypt. ⁵⁷And all the world came to Egypt to buy grain from Joseph, because the famine was severe everywhere.

Joseph's Brothers Go to Egypt

42 When Jacob learned that there was grain in Egypt, he said to his sons, "Why do you just keep looking at each other?" ²He continued, "I have heard that there is grain in Egypt. Go down there and buy some for us, so that we may live and not die."

³Then ten of Joseph's brothers went down to buy grain from Egypt. ⁴But Jacob did not send Benjamin, Joseph's brother, with the others, because he was afraid that harm might come to him. ⁵So Israel's sons were among those who went to buy grain, for there was famine in the land of Canaan also.

⁶Now Joseph was the governor of the land, the person who sold grain to all its people. So when Joseph's brothers arrived, they bowed down to him with their faces to the ground. ⁷As soon as Joseph saw his brothers, he recognized them, but he pretended to be a stranger and spoke harshly to them. "Where do you come from?" he asked.

"From the land of Canaan," they replied, "to buy food."

⁸Although Joseph recognized his brothers, they did not recognize him. ⁹Then he remembered his dreams about them and said to them, "You are spies! You have come to see where our land is unprotected."

¹⁰"No, my lord," they answered. "Your servants have come to buy food. ¹¹We are all the sons of one man. Your servants are honest men, not spies."

¹²"No!" he said to them. "You have come to see where our land is unprotected."

¹³But they replied, "Your servants were twelve brothers, the sons of one man, who lives in the land of Canaan. The youngest is now with our father, and one is no more."

¹⁴Joseph said to them, "It is just as I told you: You are spies! ¹⁵And this is how you will be tested: As surely as Pharaoh lives, you will not leave this place unless your youngest brother comes here. ¹⁶Send one of your number to get your brother; the rest of you will be kept in prison, so that your words may be tested to see if you are telling the truth. If you are not, then as surely as Pharaoh lives, you are spies!" ¹⁷And he put them all in custody for three days.

¹⁸On the third day, Joseph said to them, "Do this and you will live, for I fear God: ¹⁹If you are honest men, let one of your brothers stay here in prison, while the rest of you go and take grain back for your starving households. ²⁰But you must bring your youngest brother to me, so that your words may be verified and that you may not die." This they proceeded to do.

²¹They said to one another, "Surely we are being punished because of our brother. We saw how distressed he was when he pleaded with us for his life, but we would not listen; that's why this distress has come on us."

²²Reuben replied, "Didn't I tell you not to sin against the boy? But you wouldn't listen! Now we must give an accounting for his blood." ²³They did not realize that Joseph could understand them, since he was using an interpreter.

²⁴He turned away from them and began to weep, but then came back and spoke to them again. He had Simeon taken from them and bound before their eyes.

²⁵Joseph gave orders to fill their bags with grain, to put each man's silver back in his sack, and to give them provisions for their journey. After this was done for them, ²⁶they loaded their grain on their donkeys and left.

²⁷At the place where they stopped for the night one of them opened his sack to get feed for his donkey, and he saw his silver in the mouth of his sack. ²⁸"My silver has been returned," he said to his brothers. "Here it is in my sack."

Their hearts sank and they turned to each other trembling and said, "What is this that God has done to us?"

²⁹When they came to their father Jacob in the land of Canaan, they told him all that had happened to them. They said, ³⁰"The man who is lord over the land spoke harshly to us and treated us as though we were spying on the land. ³¹But we said to him, 'We are honest men; we are not spies. ³²We were twelve brothers, sons of one father. One is no more, and the youngest is now with our father in Canaan.'

³³"Then the man who is lord over the land said to us, 'This is how I will know whether you are honest men: Leave one of your brothers here with me, and take food for your starving households and go. ³⁴But bring your youngest brother to me so I will know that you are not spies but honest men. Then I will give your brother back to you, and you can trade[a] in the land.' "

³⁵As they were emptying their sacks, there in each man's sack was his pouch of silver! When they and their father saw the money pouches, they were frightened. ³⁶Their father Jacob said to them, "You have deprived me of my children. Joseph is no more and Simeon is no more, and now you want to take Benjamin. Everything is against me!"

³⁷Then Reuben said to his father, "You may put both of my sons to death if I do not bring him back to you. Entrust him to my care, and I will bring him back."

³⁸But Jacob said, "My son will not go down there with you; his brother is dead and he is the only one left. If harm comes to him on the journey you are taking, you will bring my gray head down to the grave in sorrow."

The Second Journey to Egypt

43 Now the famine was still severe in the land. ²So when they had eaten all the grain they had brought from Egypt, their father said to them, "Go back and buy us a little more food."

---

a 34 Or *move about freely*

³But Judah said to him, "The man warned us solemnly, 'You will not see my face again unless your brother is with you.' ⁴If you will send our brother along with us, we will go down and buy food for you. ⁵But if you will not send him, we will not go down, because the man said to us, 'You will not see my face again unless your brother is with you.' "

⁶Israel asked, "Why did you bring this trouble on me by telling the man you had another brother?"

⁷They replied, "The man questioned us closely about ourselves and our family. 'Is your father still living?' he asked us. 'Do you have another brother?' We simply answered his questions. How were we to know he would say, 'Bring your brother down here'?"

⁸Then Judah said to Israel his father, "Send the boy along with me and we will go at once, so that we and you and our children may live and not die. ⁹I myself will guarantee his safety; you can hold me personally responsible for him. If I do not bring him back to you and set him here before you, I will bear the blame before you all my life. ¹⁰As it is, if we had not delayed, we could have gone and returned twice."

¹¹Then their father Israel said to them, "If it must be, then do this: Put some of the best products of the land in your bags and take them down to the man as a gift—a little balm and a little honey, some spices and myrrh, some pistachio nuts and almonds. ¹²Take double the amount of silver with you, for you must return the silver that was put back into the mouths of your sacks. Perhaps it was a mistake. ¹³Take your brother also and go back to the man at once. ¹⁴And may God Almighty[a] grant you mercy before the man so that he will let your other brother and Benjamin come back with you. As for me, if I am bereaved, I am bereaved."

¹⁵So the men took the gifts and double the amount of silver, and Benjamin also. They hurried down to Egypt and presented themselves to Joseph. ¹⁶When Joseph saw Benjamin with them, he said to the steward of his house, "Take these men to my house, slaughter an animal and pre-

BREAKTHROUGH!

Myrrh
(GENESIS 43:11)

This plant was used to make perfume. It was also a medicine, and was used to preserve dead bodies. Myrrh was one of the gifts the wise men gave Jesus when he was a baby.

pare a meal; they are to eat with me at noon."

¹⁷The man did as Joseph told him and took the men to Joseph's house. ¹⁸Now the men were frightened when they were taken to his house. They thought, "We were brought here because of the silver that was put back into our sacks the first time. He wants to attack us and overpower us and seize us as slaves and take our donkeys."

¹⁹So they went up to Joseph's steward and spoke to him at the entrance to the house. ²⁰"We beg your pardon, our lord," they said, "we came down here the first time to buy food. ²¹But at the place where we stopped for the night we opened our sacks and each of us found his silver—the exact weight—in the mouth of his sack. So we have brought it back with us. ²²We have also brought additional silver with us to buy food. We don't know who put our silver in our sacks."

---

[a] 14 Hebrew *El-Shaddai*

²³"It's all right," he said. "Don't be afraid. Your God, the God of your father, has given you treasure in your sacks; I received your silver." Then he brought Simeon out to them.

²⁴The steward took the men into Joseph's house, gave them water to wash their feet and provided fodder for their donkeys. ²⁵They prepared their gifts for Joseph's arrival at noon, because they had heard that they were to eat there.

²⁶When Joseph came home, they presented to him the gifts they had brought into the house, and they bowed down before him to the ground. ²⁷He asked them how they were, and then he said, "How is your aged father you told me about? Is he still living?"

²⁸They replied, "Your servant our father is still alive and well." And they bowed down, prostrating themselves before him.

²⁹As he looked about and saw his brother Benjamin, his own mother's son, he asked, "Is this your youngest brother, the one you told me about?" And he said, "God be gracious to you, my son." ³⁰Deeply moved at the sight of his brother, Joseph hurried out and looked for a place to weep. He went into his private room and wept there.

³¹After he had washed his face, he came out and, controlling himself, said, "Serve the food."

³²They served him by himself, the brothers by themselves, and the Egyptians who ate with him by themselves, because Egyptians could not eat with Hebrews, for that is detestable to Egyptians. ³³The men had been seated before him in the order of their ages, from the firstborn to the youngest; and they looked at each other in astonishment. ³⁴When portions were served to them from Joseph's table, Benjamin's portion was five times as much as anyone else's. So they feasted and drank freely with him.

A Silver Cup in a Sack

44 Now Joseph gave these instructions to the steward of his house: "Fill the men's sacks with as much food as they can carry, and put each man's silver in the mouth of his sack. ²Then put my cup, the silver one, in the mouth of the youngest one's sack, along with the silver for his grain." And he did as Joseph said.

³As morning dawned, the men were sent on their way with their donkeys. ⁴They had not gone far from the city when Joseph said to his steward, "Go after those men at once, and when you catch up with them, say to them, 'Why have you repaid good with evil? ⁵Isn't this the cup my master drinks from and also uses for divination? This is a wicked thing you have done.' "

⁶When he caught up with them, he repeated these words to them. ⁷But they said to him, "Why does my lord say such things? Far be it from your servants to do anything like that! ⁸We even brought back to you from the land of Canaan the silver we found inside the mouths of our sacks. So why would we steal silver or gold from your master's house? ⁹If any of your servants is found to have it, he will die; and the rest of us will become my lord's slaves."

¹⁰"Very well, then," he said, "let it be as you say. Whoever is found to have it will become my slave; the rest of you will be free from blame."

¹¹Each of them quickly lowered his sack to the ground and opened it. ¹²Then the steward proceeded to search, beginning with the oldest and ending with the youngest. And the cup was found in Benjamin's sack. ¹³At this, they tore their clothes. Then they all loaded their donkeys and returned to the city.

¹⁴Joseph was still in the house when Judah and his brothers came in, and they threw themselves to the ground before him. ¹⁵Joseph said to them, "What is this you have done? Don't you know that a man like me can find things out by divination?"

¹⁶"What can we say to my lord?" Judah replied. "What can we say? How can we prove our innocence? God has uncovered your servants' guilt. We are now my lord's slaves—we ourselves and the one who was found to have the cup."

¹⁷But Joseph said, "Far be it from me to do such a thing! Only the man who was found to have the cup will become

my slave. The rest of you, go back to your father in peace."

[18]Then Judah went up to him and said: "Pardon your servant, my lord, let me speak a word to my lord. Do not be angry with your servant, though you are equal to Pharaoh himself. [19]My lord asked his servants, 'Do you have a father or a brother?' [20]And we answered, 'We have an aged father, and there is a young son born to him in his old age. His brother is dead, and he is the only one of his mother's sons left, and his father loves him.'

[21]"Then you said to your servants, 'Bring him down to me so I can see him for myself.' [22]And we said to my lord, 'The boy cannot leave his father; if he leaves him, his father will die.' [23]But you told your servants, 'Unless your youngest brother comes down with you, you will not see my face again.' [24]When we went back to your servant my father, we told him what my lord had said.

[25]"Then our father said, 'Go back and buy a little more food.' [26]But we said, 'We cannot go down. Only if our youngest brother is with us will we go. We cannot see the man's face unless our youngest brother is with us.'

[27]"Your servant my father said to us, 'You know that my wife bore me two sons. [28]One of them went away from me, and I said, "He has surely been torn to pieces." And I have not seen him since. [29]If you take this one from me too and harm comes to him, you will bring my gray head down to the grave in misery.'

[30]"So now, if the boy is not with us when I go back to your servant my father, and if my father, whose life is closely bound up with the boy's life, [31]sees that the boy isn't there, he will die. Your servants will bring the gray head of our father down to the grave in sorrow. [32]Your servant guaranteed the boy's safety to my father. I said, 'If I do not bring him back to you, I will bear the blame before you, my father, all my life!'

[33]"Now then, please let your servant remain here as my lord's slave in place of the boy, and let the boy return with his brothers. [34]How can I go back to my father if the boy is not with me? No! Do not let me see the misery that would come on my father."

Joseph Makes Himself Known

45 Then Joseph could no longer control himself before all his attendants, and he cried out, "Have everyone leave my presence!" So there was no one with Joseph when he made himself known to his brothers. [2]And he wept so loudly that the Egyptians heard him, and Pharaoh's household heard about it.

[3]Joseph said to his brothers, "I am Joseph! Is my father still living?" But his brothers were not able to answer him, because they were terrified at his presence.

[4]Then Joseph said to his brothers, "Come close to me." When they had done so, he said, "I am your brother Joseph, the one you sold into Egypt! [5]And now, do not be distressed and do not be angry with yourselves for selling me here, because it was to save lives that God sent me ahead of you. [6]For two years now there has been famine in the land, and for the next five years there will be no plowing and reaping. [7]But God sent me ahead of you to preserve for you a remnant on earth and to save your lives by a great deliverance.[a]

[8]"So then, it was not you who sent me here, but God. He made me father to Pharaoh, lord of his entire household and ruler of all Egypt. [9]Now hurry back to my father and say to him, 'This is what your son Joseph says: God has made me lord of all Egypt. Come down to me; don't delay. [10]You shall live in the region of Goshen and be near me—you, your children and grandchildren, your flocks and herds, and all you have. [11]I will provide for you there, because five years of famine are still to come. Otherwise you and your household and all who belong to you will become destitute.'

[12]"You can see for yourselves, and so can my brother Benjamin, that it is really I who am speaking to you. [13]Tell my father about all the honor accorded me in Egypt and about everything you have seen. And bring my father down here quickly."

---

[a] 7 Or *save you as a great band of survivors*

THE SCENE

GOSHEN

(GENESIS 45:10)

This land is located on the eastern delta of the Nile River. It was good pastureland and an ideal region for cattle and farming, so the Israelites settled there during the time of Joseph. They lived there in peace for 400 years until a pharaoh who didn't know anything about Joseph's past made them slaves and made them work really hard building new cities.

[14]Then he threw his arms around his brother Benjamin and wept, and Benjamin embraced him, weeping. [15]And he kissed all his brothers and wept over them. Afterward his brothers talked with him.

[16]When the news reached Pharaoh's palace that Joseph's brothers had come, Pharaoh and all his officials were pleased. [17]Pharaoh said to Joseph, "Tell your brothers, 'Do this: Load your animals and return to the land of Canaan, [18]and bring your father and your families back to me. I will give you the best of the land of Egypt and you can enjoy the fat of the land.'

[19]"You are also directed to tell them, 'Do this: Take some carts from Egypt for your children and your wives, and get your father and come. [20]Never mind about your belongings, because the best of all Egypt will be yours.'"

[21]So the sons of Israel did this. Joseph gave them carts, as Pharaoh had commanded, and he also gave them provisions for their journey. [22]To each of them he gave new clothing, but to Benjamin he gave three hundred shekels[a] of silver and five sets of clothes. [23]And this is what he sent to his father: ten donkeys loaded with the best things of Egypt, and ten female donkeys loaded with grain and bread and other provisions for his journey. [24]Then he sent his brothers away, and as they were leaving he said to them, "Don't quarrel on the way!"

[25]So they went up out of Egypt and came to their father Jacob in the land of Canaan. [26]They told him, "Joseph is still alive! In fact, he is ruler of all Egypt." Jacob was stunned; he did not believe them. [27]But when they told him everything Joseph had said to them, and when he saw the carts Joseph had sent to carry him back, the spirit of their father Jacob revived. [28]And Israel said, "I'm convinced! My son Joseph is still alive. I will go and see him before I die."

Jacob Goes to Egypt

46 So Israel set out with all that was his, and when he reached Beersheba, he offered sacrifices to the God of his father Isaac.

[2]And God spoke to Israel in a vision at night and said, "Jacob! Jacob!"

"Here I am," he replied.

[3]"I am God, the God of your father," he said. "Do not be afraid to go down to Egypt, for I will make you into a great nation there. [4]I will go down to Egypt with you, and I will surely bring you back again. And Joseph's own hand will close your eyes."

[5]Then Jacob left Beersheba, and Israel's sons took their father Jacob and their children and their wives in the carts

---

[a] 22 That is, about 7 1/2 pounds or about 3.5 kilograms

that Pharaoh had sent to transport him. ⁶So Jacob and all his offspring went to Egypt, taking with them their livestock and the possessions they had acquired in Canaan. ⁷Jacob brought with him to Egypt his sons and grandsons and his daughters and granddaughters—all his offspring.

⁸These are the names of the sons of Israel (Jacob and his descendants) who went to Egypt:

Reuben the firstborn of Jacob. ⁹The sons of Reuben:

Hanok, Pallu, Hezron and Karmi. ¹⁰The sons of Simeon:

Jemuel, Jamin, Ohad, Jakin, Zohar and Shaul the son of a Canaanite woman.

BREAKTHROUGH!

Sacrifices

(GENESIS 46:1)

This was offering God something a person had. It could be food, a drink, incense or the life of an animal. The Israelites did this to thank God for giving them everything they needed, to ask for God's blessing or to ask God to forgive the sin of the person offering the sacrifice. When the high priest presented the sacrifice, it was to ask for the forgiveness of the sins of all the people.

¹¹The sons of Levi:

Gershon, Kohath and Merari. ¹²The sons of Judah:

Er, Onan, Shelah, Perez and Zerah (but Er and Onan had died in the land of Canaan).

The sons of Perez:

Hezron and Hamul. ¹³The sons of Issachar:

Tola, Puah,ᵃ Jashubᵇ and Shimron. ¹⁴The sons of Zebulun:

Sered, Elon and Jahleel.

¹⁵These were the sons Leah bore to Jacob in Paddan Aram,ᶜ besides his daughter Dinah. These sons and daughters of his were thirty-three in all.

¹⁶The sons of Gad:

Zephon,ᵈ Haggi, Shuni, Ezbon, Eri, Arodi and Areli. ¹⁷The sons of Asher:

Imnah, Ishvah, Ishvi and Beriah.

Their sister was Serah.

The sons of Beriah:

Heber and Malkiel. ¹⁸These were the children born to Jacob by Zilpah, whom Laban had given to his daughter Leah—sixteen in all.

¹⁹The sons of Jacob's wife Rachel:

Joseph and Benjamin. ²⁰In Egypt, Manasseh and Ephraim were born to Joseph by Asenath daughter of Potiphera, priest of On.ᵉ ²¹The sons of Benjamin:

Bela, Beker, Ashbel, Gera, Naaman, Ehi, Rosh, Muppim, Huppim and Ard. ²²These were the sons of Rachel who were born to Jacob—fourteen in all.

²³The son of Dan:

Hushim. ²⁴The sons of Naphtali:

Jahziel, Guni, Jezer and Shillem. ²⁵These were the sons born to Jacob by Bilhah, whom Laban had given to his daughter Rachel—seven in all.

---

a 13 Samaritan Pentateuch and Syriac (see also 1 Chron. 7:1); Masoretic Text *Puvah*   *b 13* Samaritan Pentateuch and some Septuagint manuscripts (see also Num. 26:24 and 1 Chron. 7:1); Masoretic Text *Iob*   *c 15* That is, Northwest Mesopotamia   *d 16* Samaritan Pentateuch and Septuagint (see also Num. 26:15); Masoretic Text *Ziphion*   *e 20* That is, Heliopolis

26All those who went to Egypt with Jacob—those who were his direct descendants, not counting his sons' wives—numbered sixty-six persons. 27With the two sons[a] who had been born to Joseph in Egypt, the members of Jacob's family, which went to Egypt, were seventy[b] in all.

28Now Jacob sent Judah ahead of him to Joseph to get directions to Goshen. When they arrived in the region of Goshen, 29Joseph had his chariot made ready and went to Goshen to meet his father Israel. As soon as Joseph appeared before him, he threw his arms around his father[c] and wept for a long time.

30Israel said to Joseph, "Now I am ready to die, since I have seen for myself that you are still alive."

31Then Joseph said to his brothers and to his father's household, "I will go up and speak to Pharaoh and will say to him, 'My brothers and my father's household, who were living in the land of Canaan, have come to me. 32The men are shepherds; they tend livestock, and they have brought along their flocks and herds and everything they own.' 33When Pharaoh calls you in and asks, 'What is your occupation?' 34you should answer, 'Your servants have tended livestock from our boyhood on, just as our fathers did.' Then you will be allowed to settle in the region of Goshen, for all shepherds are detestable to the Egyptians."

47 Joseph went and told Pharaoh, "My father and brothers, with their flocks and herds and everything they own, have come from the land of Canaan and are now in Goshen." 2He chose five of his brothers and presented them before Pharaoh.

3Pharaoh asked the brothers, "What is your occupation?"

"Your servants are shepherds," they replied to Pharaoh, "just as our fathers were." 4They also said to him, "We have come to live here for a while, because the famine is severe in Canaan and your servants' flocks have no pasture. So now, please let your servants settle in Goshen."

5Pharaoh said to Joseph, "Your father and your brothers have come to you, 6and the land of Egypt is before you; settle your father and your brothers in the best part of the land. Let them live in Goshen. And if you know of any among them with special ability, put them in charge of my own livestock."

7Then Joseph brought his father Jacob in and presented him before Pharaoh. After Jacob blessed[d] Pharaoh, 8Pharaoh asked him, "How old are you?"

9And Jacob said to Pharaoh, "The years of my pilgrimage are a hundred and thirty. My years have been few and difficult, and they do not equal the years of the pilgrimage of my fathers." 10Then Jacob blessed[e] Pharaoh and went out from his presence.

11So Joseph settled his father and his brothers in Egypt and gave them property in the best part of the land, the district of Rameses, as Pharaoh directed. 12Joseph also provided his father and his brothers and all his father's household with food, according to the number of their children.

Joseph and the Famine

13There was no food, however, in the whole region because the famine was severe; both Egypt and Canaan wasted away because of the famine. 14Joseph collected all the money that was to be found in Egypt and Canaan in payment for the grain they were buying, and he brought it to Pharaoh's palace. 15When the money of the people of Egypt and Canaan was gone, all Egypt came to Joseph and said, "Give us food. Why should we die before your eyes? Our money is all gone."

16"Then bring your livestock," said Joseph. "I will sell you food in exchange for your livestock, since your money is gone." 17So they brought their livestock to Joseph, and he gave them food in exchange for their horses, their sheep and goats, their cattle and donkeys. And he brought them through that year with food in exchange for all their livestock.

18When that year was over, they came to him the following year and said, "We cannot hide from our lord the fact that

---

a 27 Hebrew; Septuagint the nine children   b 27 Hebrew (see also Exodus 1:5 and note); Septuagint (see also Acts 7:14) seventy-five   c 29 Hebrew around him   d 7 Or greeted   e 10 Or said farewell to since our money is gone and our livestock belongs to you, there is nothing left for our lord except our bodies and our land. ¹⁹Why should we perish before your eyes—we and our land as well? Buy us and our land in exchange for food, and we with our land will be in bondage to Pharaoh. Give us seed so that we may live and not die, and that the land may not become desolate."

²⁰So Joseph bought all the land in Egypt for Pharaoh. The Egyptians, one and all, sold their fields, because the famine was too severe for them. The land became Pharaoh's, ²¹and Joseph reduced the people to servitude,ᵃ from one end of Egypt to the other. ²²However, he did not buy the land of the priests, because they received a regular allotment from Pharaoh and had food enough from the allotment Pharaoh gave them. That is why they did not sell their land.

²³Joseph said to the people, "Now that I have bought you and your land today for Pharaoh, here is seed for you so you can plant the ground. ²⁴But when the crop comes in, give a fifth of it to Pharaoh. The other four-fifths you may keep as seed for the fields and as food for yourselves and your households and your children."

²⁵"You have saved our lives," they said. "May we find favor in the eyes of our lord; we will be in bondage to Pharaoh."

²⁶So Joseph established it as a law concerning land in Egypt—still in force today—that a fifth of the produce belongs to Pharaoh. It was only the land of the priests that did not become Pharaoh's.

²⁷Now the Israelites settled in Egypt in the region of Goshen. They acquired property there and were fruitful and increased greatly in number.

²⁸Jacob lived in Egypt seventeen years, and the years of his life were a hundred and forty-seven. ²⁹When the time drew near for Israel to die, he called for his son Joseph and said to him, "If I have found favor in your eyes, put your hand under my thigh and promise that you will show me kindness and faithfulness. Do not bury me in Egypt, ³⁰but when I rest with my fathers, carry me out of Egypt and bury me where they are buried."

"I will do as you say," he said.

³¹"Swear to me," he said. Then Joseph swore to him, and Israel worshiped as he leaned on the top of his staff.ᵇ

Manasseh and Ephraim

48 Some time later Joseph was told, "Your father is ill." So he took his two sons Manasseh and Ephraim along with him. ²When Jacob was told, "Your son Joseph has come to you," Israel rallied his strength and sat up on the bed.

³Jacob said to Joseph, "God Almightyᶜ appeared to me at Luz in the land of Canaan, and there he blessed me ⁴and said to me, 'I am going to make you fruitful and increase your numbers. I will make you a community of peoples, and I will give this land as an everlasting possession to your descendants after you.'

⁵"Now then, your two sons born to you in Egypt before I came to you here will be reckoned as mine; Ephraim and Manasseh will be mine, just as Reuben and Simeon are mine. ⁶Any children born to you after them will be yours; in the territory they inherit they will be reckoned under the names of their brothers. ⁷As I was returning from Paddan,ᵈ to my sorrow Rachel died in the land of Canaan while we were still on the way, a little distance from Ephrath. So I buried her there beside the road to Ephrath" (that is, Bethlehem).

⁸When Israel saw the sons of Joseph, he asked, "Who are these?"

⁹"They are the sons God has given me here," Joseph said to his father.

Then Israel said, "Bring them to me so I may bless them."

¹⁰Now Israel's eyes were failing because of old age, and he could hardly see. So Joseph brought his sons close to him, and his father kissed them and embraced them.

¹¹Israel said to Joseph, "I never expected to see your face again, and now God has allowed me to see your children too."

¹²Then Joseph removed them from Israel's knees and bowed down with his face

---

ᵃ **21** Samaritan Pentateuch and Septuagint (see also Vulgate); Masoretic Text *and he moved the people into the cities*   ᵇ **31** Or *Israel bowed down at the head of his bed*   ᶜ **3** Hebrew *El-Shaddai*   ᵈ **7** That is, Northwest Mesopotamia to the ground. ¹³And Joseph took both of them, Ephraim on his right toward Israel's left hand and Manasseh on his left toward Israel's right hand, and brought them close to him. ¹⁴But Israel reached out his right hand and put it on Ephraim's head, though he was the younger, and crossing his arms, he put his left hand on Manasseh's head, even though Manasseh was the firstborn.

¹⁵Then he blessed Joseph and said,

"May the God before whom my fathers
　　Abraham and Isaac walked
　　faithfully,
the God who has been my shepherd
　all my life to this day,
¹⁶the Angel who has delivered me from
　　all harm
　—may he bless these boys.
May they be called by my name
　and the names of my fathers
　　Abraham and Isaac,
and may they increase greatly
　on the earth."

¹⁷When Joseph saw his father placing his right hand on Ephraim's head he was displeased; so he took hold of his father's hand to move it from Ephraim's head to Manasseh's head. ¹⁸Joseph said to him, "No, my father, this one is the firstborn; put your right hand on his head."

¹⁹But his father refused and said, "I know, my son, I know. He too will become a people, and he too will become great. Nevertheless, his younger brother will be greater than he, and his descendants will become a group of nations." ²⁰He blessed them that day and said,

"In your[a] name will Israel pronounce
　this blessing:
'May God make you like Ephraim
　and Manasseh.' "

So he put Ephraim ahead of Manasseh. ²¹Then Israel said to Joseph, "I am about to die, but God will be with you[b] and take you[b] back to the land of your[b] fathers. ²²And to you I give one more ridge of land[c] than to your brothers, the ridge I took from the Amorites with my sword and my bow."

Jacob Blesses His Sons

49 Then Jacob called for his sons and said: "Gather around so I can tell you what will happen to you in days to come.

² "Assemble and listen, sons of Jacob;
　listen to your father Israel.

³ "Reuben, you are my firstborn,
　my might, the first sign of my
　　strength,
　excelling in honor, excelling in
　　power.
⁴Turbulent as the waters, you will no
　　longer excel,
　for you went up onto your father's
　　bed,
　onto my couch and defiled it.

⁵ "Simeon and Levi are brothers—
　their swords[d] are weapons of
　　violence.
⁶Let me not enter their council,
　let me not join their assembly,
　for they have killed men in their anger
　and hamstrung oxen as they
　　pleased.
⁷Cursed be their anger, so fierce,
　and their fury, so cruel!
I will scatter them in Jacob
　and disperse them in Israel.

⁸ "Judah,[e] your brothers will praise you;
　your hand will be on the neck of
　　your enemies;
　your father's sons will bow down to
　　you.
⁹You are a lion's cub, Judah;
　you return from the prey, my son.
Like a lion he crouches and lies down,
　like a lioness—who dares to rouse
　　him?
¹⁰The scepter will not depart from
　　Judah,
　nor the ruler's staff from between
　　his feet,[f]

---

a 20 The Hebrew is singular.　　*b 21* The Hebrew is plural.
c 22 The Hebrew for *ridge of land* is identical with the place name Shechem.　　*d 5* The meaning of the Hebrew for this word is uncertain.　　*e 8 Judah* sounds like and may be derived from the Hebrew for *praise.*　　*f 10* Or *from his descendants*

until he to whom it belongs*a* shall
     come
     and the obedience of the nations
          shall be his.
11 He will tether his donkey to a vine,
     his colt to the choicest branch;
     he will wash his garments in wine,
          his robes in the blood of grapes.
12 His eyes will be darker than wine,
     his teeth whiter than milk.*b*

13 "Zebulun will live by the seashore
     and become a haven for ships;
     his border will extend toward Sidon.

14 "Issachar is a rawboned*c* donkey
     lying down among the sheep pens.*d*
15 When he sees how good is his resting
          place
     and how pleasant is his land,
     he will bend his shoulder to the
          burden
     and submit to forced labor.

16 "Dan*e* will provide justice for his
          people
     as one of the tribes of Israel.
17 Dan will be a snake by the roadside,
     a viper along the path,
     that bites the horse's heels
     so that its rider tumbles backward.

18 "I look for your deliverance, LORD.

19 "Gad*f* will be attacked by a band of
          raiders,
     but he will attack them at their
          heels.

20 "Asher's food will be rich;
     he will provide delicacies fit for a
          king.

21 "Naphtali is a doe set free
     that bears beautiful fawns.*g*

22 "Joseph is a fruitful vine,
     a fruitful vine near a spring,
     whose branches climb over a wall.*h*
23 With bitterness archers attacked him;
     they shot at him with hostility.
24 But his bow remained steady,
     his strong arms stayed*i* limber,
     because of the hand of the Mighty
          One of Jacob,
     because of the Shepherd, the Rock
          of Israel,

25 because of your father's God, who
          helps you,
     because of the Almighty,*j* who
          blesses you
     with blessings of the skies above,
     blessings of the deep springs
          below,
     blessings of the breast and womb.
26 Your father's blessings are greater
     than the blessings of the ancient
          mountains,
     than*k* the bounty of the age-old hills.
     Let all these rest on the head of
          Joseph,
     on the brow of the prince among*l*
          his brothers.

27 "Benjamin is a ravenous wolf;
     in the morning he devours the prey,
     in the evening he divides the
          plunder."

28 All these are the twelve tribes of Israel, and this is what their father said to
them when he blessed them, giving each
the blessing appropriate to him.

The Death of Jacob

29 Then he gave them these instructions: "I am about to be gathered to my
people. Bury me with my fathers in the
cave in the field of Ephron the Hittite,
30 the cave in the field of Machpelah, near
Mamre in Canaan, which Abraham bought
along with the field as a burial place from
Ephron the Hittite. 31 There Abraham and
his wife Sarah were buried, there Isaac
and his wife Rebekah were buried, and
there I buried Leah. 32 The field and the
cave in it were bought from the Hittites.*m*"
33 When Jacob had finished giving instructions to his sons, he drew his feet up
into the bed, breathed his last and was
gathered to his people.

---

a 10 Or *to whom tribute belongs; the meaning of the
Hebrew for this phrase is uncertain.*   *b* 12 Or *will be
dull from wine, / his teeth white from milk*   *c* 14 Or
strong   *d* 14 Or *the campfires; or the saddlebags*
e 16 *Dan* here means *he provides justice.*   *f* 19 *Gad*
sounds like the Hebrew for *attack* and also for *band of
raiders.*   *g* 21 Or *free; / he utters beautiful words*
h 22 Or *Joseph is a wild colt, / a wild colt near a spring, /
a wild donkey on a terraced hill*   *i* 23,24 Or *archers will
attack . . . will shoot . . . will remain . . . will stay*
j 25 Hebrew *Shaddai*   *k* 26 Or *of my progenitors, / as
great as*   *l* 26 Or *of the one separated from*   *m* 32 Or
the descendants of Heth

50 Joseph threw himself on his father and wept over him and kissed him. ²Then Joseph directed the physicians in his service to embalm his father Israel. So the physicians embalmed him, ³taking a full forty days, for that was the time required for embalming. And the Egyptians mourned for him seventy days.

⁴When the days of mourning had passed, Joseph said to Pharaoh's court, "If I have found favor in your eyes, speak to Pharaoh for me. Tell him, ⁵'My father made me swear an oath and said, "I am about to die; bury me in the tomb I dug for myself in the land of Canaan." Now let me go up and bury my father; then I will return.'"

⁶Pharaoh said, "Go up and bury your father, as he made you swear to do."

⁷So Joseph went up to bury his father. All Pharaoh's officials accompanied him—the dignitaries of his court and all the dignitaries of Egypt— ⁸besides all the members of Joseph's household and his brothers and those belonging to his father's household. Only their children and their flocks and herds were left in Goshen. ⁹Chariots and horsemen*ª* also went up with him. It was a very large company.

¹⁰When they reached the threshing floor of Atad, near the Jordan, they lamented loudly and bitterly; and there Joseph observed a seven-day period of mourning for his father. ¹¹When the Canaanites who lived there saw the mourning at the threshing floor of Atad, they said, "The Egyptians are holding a solemn ceremony of mourning." That is why that place near the Jordan is called Abel Mizraim.*ᵇ*

¹²So Jacob's sons did as he had commanded them: ¹³They carried him to the land of Canaan and buried him in the cave in the field of Machpelah, near Mam-

---

ª 9 Or *charioteers*   *ᵇ* 11 *Abel Mizraim* means *mourning of the Egyptians.*

CASE CLOSED!

God made a good creation. He put humans in the midst of nature so we can care for it and enjoy it without hurting it or destroying it. But we human beings let down God's trust and separated ourselves from him. So sin took over our world, and bad things like suffering and death came in. In spite of all this, God is still very close to us.

It's true that we alone can't solve the problem of sin. Only God can do that. But Genesis teaches us that not everything was lost. There was still hope, because God didn't stay quiet when humans disobeyed. He looked for a way to help them.

If you want to know how he did this, then you'll have to keep on reading the other books of the Bible!

re, which Abraham had bought along with the field as a burial place from Ephron the Hittite. [14]After burying his father, Joseph returned to Egypt, together with his brothers and all the others who had gone with him to bury his father.

Joseph Reassures His Brothers

[15]When Joseph's brothers saw that their father was dead, they said, "What if Joseph holds a grudge against us and pays us back for all the wrongs we did to him?" [16]So they sent word to Joseph, saying, "Your father left these instructions before he died: [17]'This is what you are to say to Joseph: I ask you to forgive your brothers the sins and the wrongs they committed in treating you so badly.' Now please forgive the sins of the servants of the God of your father." When their message came to him, Joseph wept.

[18]His brothers then came and threw themselves down before him. "We are your slaves," they said.

[19]But Joseph said to them, "Don't be afraid. Am I in the place of God? [20]You intended to harm me, but God intended it for good to accomplish what is now being done, the saving of many lives. [21]So then, don't be afraid. I will provide for you and your children." And he reassured them and spoke kindly to them.

The Death of Joseph

[22]Joseph stayed in Egypt, along with all his father's family. He lived a hundred and ten years [23]and saw the third generation of Ephraim's children. Also the children of Makir son of Manasseh were placed at birth on Joseph's knees.[a]

[24]Then Joseph said to his brothers, "I am about to die. But God will surely come to your aid and take you up out of this land to the land he promised on oath to Abraham, Isaac and Jacob." [25]And Joseph made the Israelites swear an oath and said, "God will surely come to your aid, and then you must carry my bones up from this place."

[26]So Joseph died at the age of a hundred and ten. And after they embalmed him, he was placed in a coffin in Egypt.

---

[a] 23 That is, were counted as his

EXODUS

THE EVIDENCE:

WHO WROTE IT?
It was probably written by several different authors. Even if Moses was really the person who received God's message, it is still most likely that it was written by several authors. Some people call it the Second Book of Moses.

HOW LONG AGO?
We don't know this for sure either. We have to understand that a long time ago, everything was learned by hearing it, and people just talked to each other to pass on information. That was called "oral tradition." It is thought that this book was written about 700 years before Christ and that it was edited, or left the way we know it now, more or less 400 years before Christ.

WHAT'S IT ABOUT?
The Greek name of this book means "departure." Exodus tells us how God freed the Israelite people from slavery in the country of Egypt. He did this through Moses so the people could serve God and show God's love to other people.

After he had freed them, God gave the Israelites laws and commandments. This was so they would know what was good and what was bad. If they did not obey these laws, God would punish them.

This book shows us that God is always present in the midst of his people. He defends them, cares for them and gives them what they need. But God holds people responsible for their actions.

THE BEST PART
We think the nicest part is in 34:6-7, where it says, "The LORD, the LORD, the compassionate and gracious God, slow to anger, abounding in love and faithfulness, maintaining love to thousands, and forgiving wickedness, rebellion and sin."

The Israelites Oppressed

1 These are the names of the sons of Israel who went to Egypt with Jacob, each with his family: ²Reuben, Simeon, Levi and Judah; ³Issachar, Zebulun and Benjamin; ⁴Dan and Naphtali; Gad and Asher. ⁵The descendants of Jacob numbered seventy[a] in all; Joseph was already in Egypt.

⁶Now Joseph and all his brothers and all that generation died, ⁷but the Israelites were exceedingly fruitful; they multiplied greatly, increased in numbers and became so numerous that the land was filled with them.

---

[a] 5 Masoretic Text (see also Gen. 46:27); Dead Sea Scrolls and Septuagint (see also Acts 7:14 and note at Gen. 46:27) *seventy-five*

⁸Then a new king, to whom Joseph meant nothing, came to power in Egypt. ⁹"Look," he said to his people, "the Israelites have become far too numerous for us. ¹⁰Come, we must deal shrewdly with them or they will become even more numerous and, if war breaks out, will join our enemies, fight against us and leave the country."

¹¹So they put slave masters over them to oppress them with forced labor, and they built Pithom and Rameses as store cities for Pharaoh. ¹²But the more they were oppressed, the more they multiplied and spread; so the Egyptians came to dread the Israelites ¹³and worked them ruthlessly. ¹⁴They made their lives bitter with harsh labor in brick and mortar and with all kinds of work in the fields; in all their harsh labor the Egyptians worked them ruthlessly.

¹⁵The king of Egypt said to the Hebrew midwives, whose names were Shiphrah and Puah, ¹⁶"When you are helping the Hebrew women during childbirth on the

BREAKTHROUGH!

Why were the Israelites slaves?

(EXODUS 1:1-14)

When Jacob's son Joseph was governor of all of Egypt, he sent people to look for his father so his brothers and their families could all go to live comfortably in Egypt, because there wasn't much food in their country. But time passed and Joseph and all his close relatives died, and even the pharaoh of Egypt, who had been so good to Joseph, died too. Then one of the rulers who took over later (I think his name was Ramses II) realized that there were a lot of Israelites living there, and he was afraid they could become enemies. So he made them work really hard as slaves. In other words, he made them work for him and for his kingdom. This king thought that if the Israelites worked hard all day, they wouldn't have enough strength to stand up to him or be able to have a lot of children. In old times, it was very common for a strong nation to make slaves of a weaker nation. What an injustice!

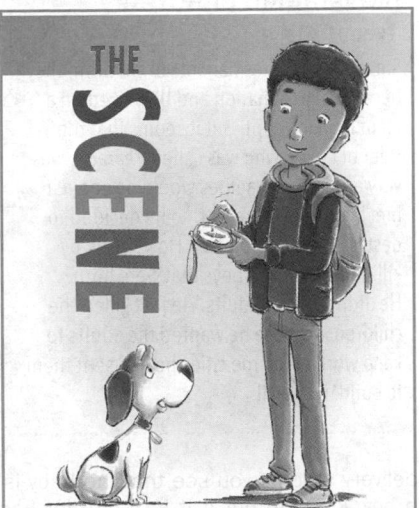

THE SCENE

PITHOM AND RAMESES

(EXODUS 1:11)

Cities built by the Israelites under the orders of the Egyptian pharaoh (or king) Rameses II. We don't know exactly where they were located, but most likely they were on the Nile River delta.

BREAKTHROUGH!

The king's order to kill the Israelite children

(EXODUS 1:15-22)

Since the Israelites had lots of children, they became a great nation and they lived on a lot of land in Egypt. But it seems that the ruler of Egypt, who was called *Pharaoh*, was very afraid the Israelites would be against him and try to make war, so he decided to destroy them completely. How? Well, by killing all the baby boys that were born. He didn't kill the adults. He just killed the children, because he wanted the adults to keep working on the cities he had sent them to build. How evil!

delivery stool, if you see that the baby is a boy, kill him; but if it is a girl, let her live." ¹⁷The midwives, however, feared God and did not do what the king of Egypt had told them to do; they let the boys live. ¹⁸Then the king of Egypt summoned the midwives and asked them, "Why have you done this? Why have you let the boys live?"

¹⁹The midwives answered Pharaoh, "Hebrew women are not like Egyptian women; they are vigorous and give birth before the midwives arrive."

²⁰So God was kind to the midwives and the people increased and became even more numerous. ²¹And because the midwives feared God, he gave them families of their own.

²²Then Pharaoh gave this order to all his people: "Every Hebrew boy that is born you must throw into the Nile, but let every girl live."

The Birth of Moses

2 Now a man of the tribe of Levi married a Levite woman, ²and she became pregnant and gave birth to a son. When she saw that he was a fine child, she hid him for three months. ³But when she could hide him no longer, she got a papyrus basket[a] for him and coated it with tar and pitch. Then she placed the child in it and put it among the reeds along the bank of the Nile. ⁴His sister stood at a distance to see what would happen to him.

⁵Then Pharaoh's daughter went down to the Nile to bathe, and her attendants were walking along the riverbank. She saw the basket among the reeds and sent her female slave to get it. ⁶She opened it and saw the baby. He was crying, and she felt sorry for him. "This is one of the Hebrew babies," she said.

⁷Then his sister asked Pharaoh's daughter, "Shall I go and get one of the Hebrew women to nurse the baby for you?"

⁸"Yes, go," she answered. So the girl went and got the baby's mother. ⁹Pharaoh's daughter said to her, "Take this baby and nurse him for me, and I will pay you." So the woman took the baby and nursed him. ¹⁰When the child grew older, she took him to Pharaoh's daughter and he became her son. She named him Moses,[b] saying, "I drew him out of the water."

Moses Flees to Midian

¹¹One day, after Moses had grown up, he went out to where his own people were and watched them at their hard labor. He saw an Egyptian beating a Hebrew, one of his own people. ¹²Looking this way

---

[a] 3 The Hebrew can also mean *ark*, as in Gen. 6:14.
[b] 10 *Moses* sounds like the Hebrew for *draw out*.

Moses was afraid and thought, "What I did must have become known."

¹⁵When Pharaoh heard of this, he tried to kill Moses, but Moses fled from Pharaoh and went to live in Midian, where he sat down by a well. ¹⁶Now a priest of Midian had seven daughters, and they came to draw water and fill the troughs to water their father's flock. ¹⁷Some shepherds came along and drove them away, but Moses got up and came to their rescue and watered their flock.

¹⁸When the girls returned to Reuel their father, he asked them, "Why have you returned so early today?"

¹⁹They answered, "An Egyptian rescued us from the shepherds. He even drew water for us and watered the flock."

²⁰"And where is he?" Reuel asked his daughters. "Why did you leave him? Invite him to have something to eat."

THE
WITNESSES

✓ MOSES (EXODUS 2:10)

This Egyptian name means "a son born." But the Egyptian princess who found Moses in the river probably tried to say the name in Hebrew, which sounded more like "taken from the water." We notice that this baby was important from the time of his birth. God amazingly saved him from death when the king of Egypt ordered that all the Israelite baby boys be killed. Moses became the rescuer of the Israelites when they were slaves in Egypt.

and that and seeing no one, he killed the Egyptian and hid him in the sand. ¹³The next day he went out and saw two Hebrews fighting. He asked the one in the wrong, "Why are you hitting your fellow Hebrew?"

¹⁴The man said, "Who made you ruler and judge over us? Are you thinking of killing me as you killed the Egyptian?" Then

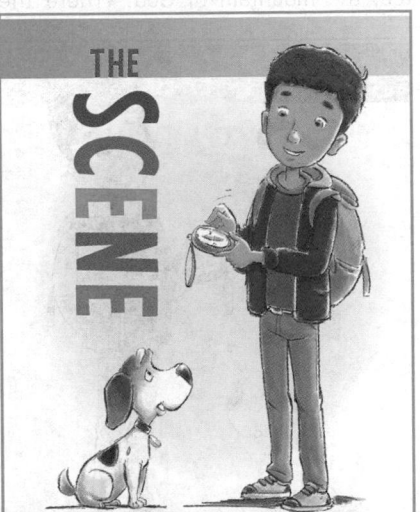

THE
SCENE

MIDIAN

(EXODUS 2:15)

This name means "strife." It was pastureland east of Horeb, in the Sinai Peninsula. It covers a large amount of desert that stretches from the eastern border of Egypt to Arabia and Transjordan.

²¹Moses agreed to stay with the man, who gave his daughter Zipporah to Moses in marriage. ²²Zipporah gave birth to a son, and Moses named him Gershom,ᵃ saying, "I have become a foreigner in a foreign land."

²³During that long period, the king of Egypt died. The Israelites groaned in their slavery and cried out, and their cry for help because of their slavery went up to God. ²⁴God heard their groaning and he remembered his covenant with Abraham, with Isaac and with Jacob. ²⁵So God looked on the Israelites and was concerned about them.

Moses and the Burning Bush

3 Now Moses was tending the flock of Jethro his father-in-law, the priest of Midian, and he led the flock to the far side of the wilderness and came to Horeb, the mountain of God. ²There the

THE SCENE

MOUNT HOREB

(EXODUS 3:1)

This is the mountain where Moses received the Ten Commandments. Nobody knows exactly where it was. It's also called "Sinai."

BREAK THROUGH!

Take off your sandals
(EXODUS 3:5)

That was a sign of respect. God wanted Moses to understand that the place was sacred, or holy, because he was there.

angel of the LORD appeared to him in flames of fire from within a bush. Moses saw that though the bush was on fire it did not burn up. ³So Moses thought, "I will go over and see this strange sight — why the bush does not burn up."

⁴When the LORD saw that he had gone over to look, God called to him from within the bush, "Moses! Moses!"

And Moses said, "Here I am."

⁵"Do not come any closer," God said. "Take off your sandals, for the place where you are standing is holy ground." ⁶Then he said, "I am the God of your father,ᵇ the God of Abraham, the God of Isaac and the God of Jacob." At this, Moses hid his face, because he was afraid to look at God.

⁷The LORD said, "I have indeed seen the misery of my people in Egypt. I have heard them crying out because of their slave drivers, and I am concerned about their suffering. ⁸So I have come down to res-

---

ᵃ 22 *Gershom* sounds like the Hebrew for *a foreigner there.*
ᵇ 6 Masoretic Text; Samaritan Pentateuch (see Acts 7:32) *fathers*

cue them from the hand of the Egyptians and to bring them up out of that land into a good and spacious land, a land flowing with milk and honey—the home of the Canaanites, Hittites, Amorites, Perizzites, Hivites and Jebusites. 9And now the cry of the Israelites has reached me, and I have seen the way the Egyptians are oppressing them. 10So now, go. I am sending you to Pharaoh to bring my people the Israelites out of Egypt."

11But Moses said to God, "Who am I that I should go to Pharaoh and bring the Israelites out of Egypt?"

12And God said, "I will be with you. And this will be the sign to you that it is I who have sent you: When you have brought the people out of Egypt, you^a will worship God on this mountain."

13Moses said to God, "Suppose I go to the Israelites and say to them, 'The God

a 12 The Hebrew is plural.

THE
WITNESSES

✓ ZIPPORAH (EXODUS 2:21)
Her name means "little bird" as well as "brilliance." She was Jethro's daughter and Moses' wife. They had two sons, Gershom and Eliezer. It seems that Zipporah stayed with her father until Moses was able to get all the people out of Egypt.

✓ GERSHOM (EXODUS 2:22)
This name means "foreigner," because Moses was considered a foreigner in Midian. That's why he gave this name to his first son who was born in Midian.

✓ JETHRO (EXODUS 3:1)
This name means "superiority." He was a priest of Midian who worshiped the God of Israel (read Exodus 18:10 – 12). He also was Moses' father-in-law. He had seven daughters. The daughter Moses married was Zipporah.

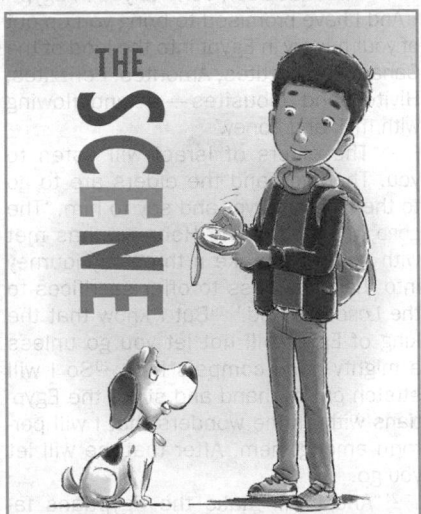

THE SCENE

CANAAN

(EXODUS 3:7 – 9)
It is between the Mediterranean Sea and the Jordan River. It extends from the Nile River to the Euphrates River. The land was very rich and fertile. It was settled by a different people that didn't know God. Later, it was called the "promised land."

of your fathers has sent me to you,' and they ask me, 'What is his name?' Then what shall I tell them?"

¹⁴God said to Moses, "I AM WHO I AM.ᵃ This is what you are to say to the Israelites: 'I AM has sent me to you.' "

¹⁵God also said to Moses, "Say to the Israelites, 'The LORD,ᵇ the God of your fathers—the God of Abraham, the God of Isaac and the God of Jacob—has sent me to you.'

"This is my name forever,
    the name you shall call me
    from generation to generation.

¹⁶"Go, assemble the elders of Israel and say to them, 'The LORD, the God of your fathers—the God of Abraham, Isaac and Jacob—appeared to me and said: I have watched over you and have seen what has been done to you in Egypt. ¹⁷And I have promised to bring you up out of your misery in Egypt into the land of the Canaanites, Hittites, Amorites, Perizzites, Hivites and Jebusites—a land flowing with milk and honey.'

¹⁸"The elders of Israel will listen to you. Then you and the elders are to go to the king of Egypt and say to him, 'The LORD, the God of the Hebrews, has met with us. Let us take a three-day journey into the wilderness to offer sacrifices to the LORD our God.' ¹⁹But I know that the king of Egypt will not let you go unless a mighty hand compels him. ²⁰So I will stretch out my hand and strike the Egyptians with all the wonders that I will perform among them. After that, he will let you go.

²¹"And I will make the Egyptians favorably disposed toward this people, so that when you leave you will not go empty-handed. ²²Every woman is to ask her neighbor and any woman living in her house for articles of silver and gold and for clothing, which you will put on your sons and daughters. And so you will plunder the Egyptians."

Signs for Moses

4 Moses answered, "What if they do not believe me or listen to me and say, 'The LORD did not appear to you'?"

²Then the LORD said to him, "What is that in your hand?"

"A staff," he replied.

³The LORD said, "Throw it on the ground." Moses threw it on the ground and it became a snake, and he ran from it. ⁴Then the LORD said to him, "Reach out your hand and take it by the tail." So Moses reached out and took hold of the snake and it turned back into a staff in his hand. ⁵"This," said the LORD, "is so that they may believe that the LORD, the God of their fathers—the God of Abraham, the God of Isaac and the God of Jacob—has appeared to you."

⁶Then the LORD said, "Put your hand inside your cloak." So Moses put his hand into his cloak, and when he took it out, the skin was leprousᶜ—it had become as white as snow.

⁷"Now put it back into your cloak," he said. So Moses put his hand back into his cloak, and when he took it out, it was restored, like the rest of his flesh.

⁸Then the LORD said, "If they do not believe you or pay attention to the first sign, they may believe the second. ⁹But if they do not believe these two signs or listen to you, take some water from the Nile and pour it on the dry ground. The water you take from the river will become blood on the ground."

¹⁰Moses said to the LORD, "Pardon your servant, Lord. I have never been eloquent, neither in the past nor since you have spoken to your servant. I am slow of speech and tongue."

¹¹The LORD said to him, "Who gave human beings their mouths? Who makes them deaf or mute? Who gives them sight or makes them blind? Is it not I, the LORD? ¹²Now go; I will help you speak and will teach you what to say."

¹³But Moses said, "Pardon your servant, Lord. Please send someone else."

¹⁴Then the LORD's anger burned against Moses and he said, "What about your brother, Aaron the Levite? I know he can speak well. He is already on his way to

---

ᵃ 14 Or *I WILL BE WHAT I WILL BE*   ᵇ 15 The Hebrew for LORD sounds like and may be related to the Hebrew for *I AM* in verse 14.   ᶜ 6 The Hebrew word for *leprous* was used for various diseases affecting the skin.

THE
WITNESSES

✓ AARON (EXODUS 4:14)

He was Moses' brother and a priest in the tribe of Levi. He was the first high priest in Israel. He had four sons. Since he was a good speaker, he helped his brother, Moses, with everything God asked them to do in order to free the Israelites in Egypt. God allowed him to go up into the sacred mountain, and there he ate and drank and worshiped God. But he made the big mistake of making a golden calf and telling the Israelites that it was their God. What a pity!

meet you, and he will be glad to see you. 15You shall speak to him and put words in his mouth; I will help both of you speak and will teach you what to do. 16He will speak to the people for you, and it will be as if he were your mouth and as if you were God to him. 17But take this staff in your hand so you can perform the signs with it."

Moses Returns to Egypt

18Then Moses went back to Jethro his father-in-law and said to him, "Let me return to my own people in Egypt to see if any of them are still alive."

Jethro said, "Go, and I wish you well." 19Now the LORD had said to Moses in Midian, "Go back to Egypt, for all those who wanted to kill you are dead." 20So Moses took his wife and sons, put them on a donkey and started back to Egypt. And he took the staff of God in his hand.

21The LORD said to Moses, "When you return to Egypt, see that you perform before Pharaoh all the wonders I have given you the power to do. But I will harden his heart so that he will not let the people go. 22Then say to Pharaoh, 'This is what the LORD says: Israel is my firstborn son, 23and I told you, "Let my son go, so he may worship me." But you refused to let him go; so I will kill your firstborn son.' "

24At a lodging place on the way, the LORD met Moses[a] and was about to kill him. 25But Zipporah took a flint knife, cut off her son's foreskin and touched Moses' feet with it.[b] "Surely you are a bridegroom of blood to me," she said. 26So the LORD let him alone. (At that time she said "bridegroom of blood," referring to circumcision.)

27The LORD said to Aaron, "Go into the wilderness to meet Moses." So he met Moses at the mountain of God and kissed him. 28Then Moses told Aaron everything the LORD had sent him to say, and also about all the signs he had commanded him to perform.

29Moses and Aaron brought together all the elders of the Israelites, 30and Aaron told them everything the LORD had said to Moses. He also performed the signs before the people, 31and they believed. And when they heard that the LORD was concerned about them and had seen their misery, they bowed down and worshiped.

Bricks Without Straw

5 Afterward Moses and Aaron went to Pharaoh and said, "This is what the LORD, the God of Israel, says: 'Let my

---

a 24 Hebrew *him*   *b* 25 The meaning of the Hebrew for this clause is uncertain.

people go, so that they may hold a festival to me in the wilderness.' "

²Pharaoh said, "Who is the Lord, that I should obey him and let Israel go? I do not know the Lord and I will not let Israel go." ³Then they said, "The God of the Hebrews has met with us. Now let us take a three-day journey into the wilderness to offer sacrifices to the Lord our God, or he may strike us with plagues or with the sword."

⁴But the king of Egypt said, "Moses and Aaron, why are you taking the people away from their labor? Get back to your work!" ⁵Then Pharaoh said, "Look, the people of the land are now numerous, and you are stopping them from working."

⁶That same day Pharaoh gave this order to the slave drivers and overseers in charge of the people: ⁷"You are no longer to supply the people with straw for making bricks; let them go and gather their own straw. ⁸But require them to make the same number of bricks as before; don't reduce the quota. They are lazy; that is why they are crying out, 'Let us go and sacrifice to our God.' ⁹Make the work harder for the people so that they keep working and pay no attention to lies."

¹⁰Then the slave drivers and the overseers went out and said to the people, "This is what Pharaoh says: 'I will not give you any more straw. ¹¹Go and get your own straw wherever you can find it, but your work will not be reduced at all.' " ¹²So the people scattered all over Egypt to gather stubble to use for straw. ¹³The slave drivers kept pressing them, saying, "Complete the work required of you for each day, just as when you had straw." ¹⁴And Pharaoh's slave drivers beat the Israelite overseers they had appointed, demanding, "Why haven't you met your quota of bricks yesterday or today, as before?"

¹⁵Then the Israelite overseers went and appealed to Pharaoh: "Why have you treated your servants this way? ¹⁶Your servants are given no straw, yet we are told, 'Make bricks!' Your servants are being beaten, but the fault is with your own people."

¹⁷Pharaoh said, "Lazy, that's what you are — lazy! That is why you keep saying, 'Let us go and sacrifice to the Lord.' ¹⁸Now get to work. You will not be given any straw, yet you must produce your full quota of bricks."

¹⁹The Israelite overseers realized they were in trouble when they were told, "You are not to reduce the number of bricks required of you for each day." ²⁰When they left Pharaoh, they found Moses and Aaron waiting to meet them, ²¹and they said, "May the Lord look on you and judge you! You have made us obnoxious to Pharaoh and his officials and have put a sword in their hand to kill us."

God Promises Deliverance

²²Moses returned to the Lord and said, "Why, Lord, why have you brought trouble on this people? Is this why you sent me? ²³Ever since I went to Pharaoh to speak in your name, he has brought trouble on this people, and you have not rescued your people at all."

6 Then the Lord said to Moses, "Now you will see what I will do to Pharaoh: Because of my mighty hand he will let them go; because of my mighty hand he will drive them out of his country."

²God also said to Moses, "I am the Lord. ³I appeared to Abraham, to Isaac and to Jacob as God Almighty,ᵃ but by my name the Lordᵇ I did not make myself fully known to them. ⁴I also established my covenant with them to give them the land of Canaan, where they resided as foreigners. ⁵Moreover, I have heard the groaning of the Israelites, whom the Egyptians are enslaving, and I have remembered my covenant.

⁶"Therefore, say to the Israelites: 'I am the Lord, and I will bring you out from under the yoke of the Egyptians. I will free you from being slaves to them, and I will redeem you with an outstretched arm and with mighty acts of judgment. ⁷I will take you as my own people, and I will be your God. Then you will know that I am the Lord your God, who brought you out from under the yoke of the Egyptians. ⁸And I will bring you to the land I swore with uplifted hand to give to Abraham, to Isaac

---

ᵃ 3 Hebrew *El-Shaddai*   ᵇ 3 See note at 3:15.

and to Jacob. I will give it to you as a possession. I am the LORD.' "

⁹Moses reported this to the Israelites, but they did not listen to him because of their discouragement and harsh labor.

¹⁰Then the LORD said to Moses, ¹¹"Go, tell Pharaoh king of Egypt to let the Israelites go out of his country."

¹²But Moses said to the LORD, "If the Israelites will not listen to me, why would Pharaoh listen to me, since I speak with faltering lips*ᵃ*?"

Family Record of Moses and Aaron

¹³Now the LORD spoke to Moses and Aaron about the Israelites and Pharaoh king of Egypt, and he commanded them to bring the Israelites out of Egypt.

¹⁴These were the heads of their families*ᵇ*:

The sons of Reuben the firstborn son of Israel were Hanok and Pallu, Hezron and Karmi. These were the clans of Reuben.

¹⁵The sons of Simeon were Jemuel, Jamin, Ohad, Jakin, Zohar and Shaul the son of a Canaanite woman. These were the clans of Simeon.

¹⁶These were the names of the sons of Levi according to their records: Gershon, Kohath and Merari. Levi lived 137 years.

¹⁷The sons of Gershon, by clans, were Libni and Shimei.

¹⁸The sons of Kohath were Amram, Izhar, Hebron and Uzziel. Kohath lived 133 years.

¹⁹The sons of Merari were Mahli and Mushi.

These were the clans of Levi according to their records.

²⁰Amram married his father's sister Jochebed, who bore him Aaron and Moses. Amram lived 137 years.

²¹The sons of Izhar were Korah, Nepheg and Zikri.

²²The sons of Uzziel were Mishael, Elzaphan and Sithri.

²³Aaron married Elisheba, daughter of Amminadab and sister of Nahshon, and she bore him Nadab and Abihu, Eleazar and Ithamar.

²⁴The sons of Korah were Assir, Elkanah and Abiasaph. These were the Korahite clans.

²⁵Eleazar son of Aaron married one of the daughters of Putiel, and she bore him Phinehas.

These were the heads of the Levite families, clan by clan.

²⁶It was this Aaron and Moses to whom the LORD said, "Bring the Israelites out of Egypt by their divisions." ²⁷They were the ones who spoke to Pharaoh king of Egypt about bringing the Israelites out of Egypt— this same Moses and Aaron.

Aaron to Speak for Moses

²⁸Now when the LORD spoke to Moses in Egypt, ²⁹he said to him, "I am the LORD. Tell Pharaoh king of Egypt everything I tell you."

³⁰But Moses said to the LORD, "Since I speak with faltering lips, why would Pharaoh listen to me?"

7 Then the LORD said to Moses, "See, I have made you like God to Pharaoh, and your brother Aaron will be your prophet. ²You are to say everything I command you, and your brother Aaron is to tell Pharaoh to let the Israelites go out of his country. ³But I will harden Pharaoh's heart, and though I multiply my signs and wonders in Egypt, ⁴he will not listen to you. Then I will lay my hand on Egypt and with mighty acts of judgment I will bring out my divisions, my people the Israelites. ⁵And the Egyptians will know that I am the LORD when I stretch out my hand against Egypt and bring the Israelites out of it."

⁶Moses and Aaron did just as the LORD commanded them. ⁷Moses was eighty years old and Aaron eighty-three when they spoke to Pharaoh.

Aaron's Staff Becomes a Snake

⁸The LORD said to Moses and Aaron, ⁹"When Pharaoh says to you, 'Perform a miracle,' then say to Aaron, 'Take your

---

ᵃ 12 Hebrew *I am uncircumcised of lips*; also in verse 30
ᵇ 14 The Hebrew for *families* here and in verse 25 refers to units larger than clans.

BREAKTHROUGH!

Did God make the ruler of Egypt hard-hearted?

(EXODUS 7:3-5)

God let the ruler be hard-hearted. He let him be stubborn. And he gave him the chance to let all the evil he had inside come to the surface. In other parts of Exodus, it says clearly that it was Pharaoh himself who hardened his heart (8:15,32). In other words, God didn't make him do this. The king himself did what he wanted to do and went his own stubborn way, but God already knew what he was going to do.

staff and throw it down before Pharaoh,' and it will become a snake."

¹⁰So Moses and Aaron went to Pharaoh and did just as the Lord commanded. Aaron threw his staff down in front of Pharaoh and his officials, and it became a snake. ¹¹Pharaoh then summoned wise men and sorcerers, and the Egyptian magicians also did the same things by their secret arts: ¹²Each one threw down his staff and it became a snake. But Aaron's staff swallowed up their staffs. ¹³Yet Pharaoh's heart became hard and he would not listen to them, just as the Lord had said.

The Plague of Blood

¹⁴Then the Lord said to Moses, "Pharaoh's heart is unyielding; he refuses to let the people go. ¹⁵Go to Pharaoh in the morning as he goes out to the river. Confront him on the bank of the Nile, and take in your hand the staff that was changed into a snake. ¹⁶Then say to him, 'The Lord, the God of the Hebrews, has sent me to say to you: Let my people go, so that they may worship me in the wilderness. But until now you have not listened. ¹⁷This is what the Lord says: By this you will know that I am the Lord: With the staff that is in my hand I will strike the water of the Nile, and it will be changed into blood. ¹⁸The fish in the Nile will die, and the river will stink; the Egyptians will not be able to drink its water.' "

¹⁹The Lord said to Moses, "Tell Aaron, 'Take your staff and stretch out your hand over the waters of Egypt—over the streams and canals, over the ponds and all the reservoirs—and they will turn to blood.' Blood will be everywhere in Egypt, even in vessels[a] of wood and stone."

²⁰Moses and Aaron did just as the Lord had commanded. He raised his staff in the presence of Pharaoh and his officials and struck the water of the Nile, and all the water was changed into blood. ²¹The fish in the Nile died, and the river smelled so bad that the Egyptians could not drink its water. Blood was everywhere in Egypt.

²²But the Egyptian magicians did the same things by their secret arts, and Pharaoh's heart became hard; he would not listen to Moses and Aaron, just as the Lord had said. ²³Instead, he turned and went into his palace, and did not take even this to heart. ²⁴And all the Egyptians dug along the Nile to get drinking water, because they could not drink the water of the river.

The Plague of Frogs

²⁵Seven days passed after the Lord **8**[b] struck the Nile.¹Then the Lord said to Moses, "Go to Pharaoh and say to him, 'This is what the Lord says: Let my people go, so that they may worship me. ²If you refuse to let them go, I will send a plague of frogs on your whole country.

---

a 19 Or even on their idols   b In Hebrew texts 8:1-4 is numbered 7:26-29, and 8:5-32 is numbered 8:1-28.

³The Nile will teem with frogs. They will come up into your palace and your bedroom and onto your bed, into the houses of your officials and on your people, and into your ovens and kneading troughs. ⁴The frogs will come up on you and your people and all your officials.' "

⁵Then the LORD said to Moses, "Tell Aaron, 'Stretch out your hand with your staff over the streams and canals and ponds, and make frogs come up on the land of Egypt.' "

⁶So Aaron stretched out his hand over the waters of Egypt, and the frogs came up and covered the land. ⁷But the magicians did the same things by their secret arts; they also made frogs come up on the land of Egypt.

⁸Pharaoh summoned Moses and Aaron and said, "Pray to the LORD to take the frogs away from me and my people, and I will let your people go to offer sacrifices to the LORD."

⁹Moses said to Pharaoh, "I leave to you the honor of setting the time for me to pray for you and your officials and your people that you and your houses may be rid of the frogs, except for those that remain in the Nile."

¹⁰"Tomorrow," Pharaoh said.

Moses replied, "It will be as you say, so that you may know there is no one like the LORD our God. ¹¹The frogs will leave you and your houses, your officials and your people; they will remain only in the Nile."

¹²After Moses and Aaron left Pharaoh, Moses cried out to the LORD about the frogs he had brought on Pharaoh. ¹³And the LORD did what Moses asked. The frogs died in the houses, in the courtyards and in the fields. ¹⁴They were piled into heaps, and the land reeked of them. ¹⁵But when Pharaoh saw that there was relief, he hardened his heart and would not listen to Moses and Aaron, just as the LORD had said.

The Plague of Gnats

¹⁶Then the LORD said to Moses, "Tell Aaron, 'Stretch out your staff and strike the dust of the ground,' and throughout the land of Egypt the dust will become gnats." ¹⁷They did this, and when Aaron stretched out his hand with the staff and struck the dust of the ground, gnats came on people and animals. All the dust throughout the land of Egypt became gnats. ¹⁸But when the magicians tried to produce gnats by their secret arts, they could not.

Since the gnats were on people and animals everywhere, ¹⁹the magicians said to Pharaoh, "This is the finger of God." But Pharaoh's heart was hard and he would not listen, just as the LORD had said.

The Plague of Flies

²⁰Then the LORD said to Moses, "Get up early in the morning and confront Pharaoh as he goes to the river and say to him, 'This is what the LORD says: Let my people go, so that they may worship me. ²¹If you do not let my people go, I will send swarms of flies on you and your officials, on your people and into your houses. The houses of the Egyptians will be full of flies; even the ground will be covered with them.

²²" 'But on that day I will deal differently with the land of Goshen, where my people live; no swarms of flies will be there, so that you will know that I, the LORD, am in this land. ²³I will make a distinction*a* between my people and your people. This sign will occur tomorrow.' "

²⁴And the LORD did this. Dense swarms of flies poured into Pharaoh's palace and into the houses of his officials; throughout Egypt the land was ruined by the flies.

²⁵Then Pharaoh summoned Moses and Aaron and said, "Go, sacrifice to your God here in the land."

²⁶But Moses said, "That would not be right. The sacrifices we offer the LORD our God would be detestable to the Egyptians. And if we offer sacrifices that are detestable in their eyes, will they not stone us? ²⁷We must take a three-day journey into the wilderness to offer sacrifices to the LORD our God, as he commands us."

²⁸Pharaoh said, "I will let you go to offer sacrifices to the LORD your God in the wilderness, but you must not go very far. Now pray for me."

---

a 23 Septuagint and Vulgate; Hebrew *will put a deliverance*

²⁹Moses answered, "As soon as I leave you, I will pray to the LORD, and tomorrow the flies will leave Pharaoh and his officials and his people. Only let Pharaoh be sure that he does not act deceitfully again by not letting the people go to offer sacrifices to the LORD." ³⁰Then Moses left Pharaoh and prayed to the LORD, ³¹and the LORD did what Moses asked. The flies left Pharaoh and his officials and his people; not a fly remained. ³²But this time also Pharaoh hardened his heart and would not let the people go.

The Plague on Livestock

9 Then the LORD said to Moses, "Go to Pharaoh and say to him, 'This is what the LORD, the God of the Hebrews, says: "Let my people go, so that they may worship me." ²If you refuse to let them go and continue to hold them back, ³the hand of the LORD will bring a terrible plague on your livestock in the field—on your horses, donkeys and camels and on your cattle, sheep and goats. ⁴But the LORD will make a distinction between the livestock of Israel and that of Egypt, so that no animal belonging to the Israelites will die.' "

⁵The LORD set a time and said, "Tomorrow the LORD will do this in the land." ⁶And the next day the LORD did it: All the livestock of the Egyptians died, but not one animal belonging to the Israelites died. ⁷Pharaoh investigated and found that not even one of the animals of the Israelites had died. Yet his heart was unyielding and he would not let the people go.

The Plague of Boils

⁸Then the LORD said to Moses and Aaron, "Take handfuls of soot from a furnace and have Moses toss it into the air in the presence of Pharaoh. ⁹It will become fine dust over the whole land of Egypt, and festering boils will break out on people and animals throughout the land."

¹⁰So they took soot from a furnace and stood before Pharaoh. Moses tossed it into the air, and festering boils broke out on people and animals. ¹¹The magicians could not stand before Moses because of the boils that were on them and on all the Egyptians. ¹²But the LORD hardened Pharaoh's heart and he would not listen to Moses and Aaron, just as the LORD had said to Moses.

The Plague of Hail

¹³Then the LORD said to Moses, "Get up early in the morning, confront Pharaoh and say to him, 'This is what the LORD, the God of the Hebrews, says: Let my people go, so that they may worship me, ¹⁴or this time I will send the full force of my plagues against you and against your officials and your people, so you may know that there is no one like me in all the earth. ¹⁵For by now I could have stretched out my hand and struck you and your people with a plague that would have wiped you off the earth. ¹⁶But I have raised you up[a] for this very purpose, that I might show you my power and that my name might be proclaimed in all the earth. ¹⁷You still set yourself against my people and will not let them go. ¹⁸Therefore, at this time tomorrow I will send the worst hailstorm that has ever fallen on Egypt, from the day it was founded till now. ¹⁹Give an order now to bring your livestock and everything you have in the field to a place of shelter, because the hail will fall on every person and animal that has not been brought in and is still out in the field, and they will die.' "

²⁰Those officials of Pharaoh who feared the word of the LORD hurried to bring their slaves and their livestock inside. ²¹But those who ignored the word of the LORD left their slaves and livestock in the field. ²²Then the LORD said to Moses, "Stretch out your hand toward the sky so that hail will fall all over Egypt—on people and animals and on everything growing in the fields of Egypt." ²³When Moses stretched out his staff toward the sky, the LORD sent thunder and hail, and lightning flashed down to the ground. So the LORD rained hail on the land of Egypt; ²⁴hail fell and lightning flashed back and forth. It was the worst storm in all the land of Egypt since it had become a nation. ²⁵Throughout Egypt hail struck everything in the

---

a 16 Or have spared you

fields—both people and animals; it beat down everything growing in the fields and stripped every tree. 26The only place it did not hail was the land of Goshen, where the Israelites were.

27Then Pharaoh summoned Moses and Aaron. "This time I have sinned," he said to them. "The LORD is in the right, and I and my people are in the wrong. 28Pray to the LORD, for we have had enough thunder and hail. I will let you go; you don't have to stay any longer."

29Moses replied, "When I have gone out of the city, I will spread out my hands in prayer to the LORD. The thunder will stop and there will be no more hail, so you may know that the earth is the LORD's. 30But I know that you and your officials still do not fear the LORD God."

31(The flax and barley were destroyed, since the barley had headed and the flax was in bloom. 32The wheat and spelt, however, were not destroyed, because they ripen later.)

33Then Moses left Pharaoh and went out of the city. He spread out his hands toward the LORD; the thunder and hail stopped, and the rain no longer poured down on the land. 34When Pharaoh saw that the rain and hail and thunder had stopped, he sinned again: He and his officials hardened their hearts. 35So Pharaoh's heart was hard and he would not let the Israelites go, just as the LORD had said through Moses.

The Plague of Locusts

10 Then the LORD said to Moses, "Go to Pharaoh, for I have hardened his heart and the hearts of his officials so that I may perform these signs of mine among them 2that you may tell your children and grandchildren how I dealt harshly with the Egyptians and how I performed my signs among them, and that you may know that I am the LORD."

3So Moses and Aaron went to Pharaoh and said to him, "This is what the LORD, the God of the Hebrews, says: 'How long will you refuse to humble yourself before me? Let my people go, so that they may worship me. 4If you refuse to let them go, I will bring locusts into your country to-morrow. 5They will cover the face of the ground so that it cannot be seen. They will devour what little you have left after the hail, including every tree that is growing in your fields. 6They will fill your houses and those of all your officials and all the Egyptians—something neither your parents nor your ancestors have ever seen from the day they settled in this land till now.' " Then Moses turned and left Pharaoh.

7Pharaoh's officials said to him, "How long will this man be a snare to us? Let the people go, so that they may worship the LORD their God. Do you not yet realize that Egypt is ruined?"

8Then Moses and Aaron were brought back to Pharaoh. "Go, worship the LORD your God," he said. "But tell me who will be going."

9Moses answered, "We will go with our young and our old, with our sons and our daughters, and with our flocks and herds, because we are to celebrate a festival to the LORD."

10Pharaoh said, "The LORD be with you—if I let you go, along with your women and children! Clearly you are bent on evil.ᵃ 11No! Have only the men go and worship the LORD, since that's what you have been asking for." Then Moses and Aaron were driven out of Pharaoh's presence.

12And the LORD said to Moses, "Stretch out your hand over Egypt so that locusts swarm over the land and devour everything growing in the fields, everything left by the hail."

13So Moses stretched out his staff over Egypt, and the LORD made an east wind blow across the land all that day and all that night. By morning the wind had brought the locusts; 14they invaded all Egypt and settled down in every area of the country in great numbers. Never before had there been such a plague of locusts, nor will there ever be again. 15They covered all the ground until it was black. They devoured all that was left after the hail—everything growing in the fields and the fruit on the trees. Nothing green remained on tree or plant in all the land of Egypt.

ᵃ 10 Or Be careful, trouble is in store for you!

16Pharaoh quickly summoned Moses and Aaron and said, "I have sinned against the LORD your God and against you. 17Now forgive my sin once more and pray to the LORD your God to take this deadly plague away from me." 18Moses then left Pharaoh and prayed to the LORD. 19And the LORD changed the wind to a very strong west wind, which caught up the locusts and carried them into the Red Sea.a Not a locust was left anywhere in Egypt. 20But the LORD hardened Pharaoh's heart, and he would not let the Israelites go.

The Plague of Darkness

21Then the LORD said to Moses, "Stretch out your hand toward the sky so that darkness spreads over Egypt—darkness that can be felt." 22So Moses stretched out his hand toward the sky, and total darkness covered all Egypt for three days. 23No one could see anyone else or move about for three days. Yet all the Israelites had light in the places where they lived.

24Then Pharaoh summoned Moses and said, "Go, worship the LORD. Even your women and children may go with you; only leave your flocks and herds behind."

25But Moses said, "You must allow us to have sacrifices and burnt offerings to present to the LORD our God. 26Our livestock too must go with us; not a hoof is to be left behind. We have to use some of them in worshiping the LORD our God, and until we get there we will not know what we are to use to worship the LORD."

27But the LORD hardened Pharaoh's heart, and he was not willing to let them go. 28Pharaoh said to Moses, "Get out of my sight! Make sure you do not appear before me again! The day you see my face you will die."

29"Just as you say," Moses replied. "I will never appear before you again."

The Plague on the Firstborn

11 Now the LORD had said to Moses, "I will bring one more plague on Pharaoh and on Egypt. After that, he will let you go from here, and when he does, he will drive you out completely. 2Tell the

people that men and women alike are to ask their neighbors for articles of silver and gold." 3(The LORD made the Egyptians favorably disposed toward the people, and Moses himself was highly regarded in Egypt by Pharaoh's officials and by the people.)

4So Moses said, "This is what the LORD says: 'About midnight I will go throughout Egypt. 5Every firstborn son in Egypt will die, from the firstborn son of Pharaoh, who sits on the throne, to the firstborn son of the female slave, who is at her hand mill, and all the firstborn of the cattle as well. 6There will be loud wailing throughout Egypt—worse than there has ever been or ever will be again. 7But among the Israelites not a dog will bark at any person or animal.' Then you will know that the LORD makes a distinction between Egypt and Israel. 8All these officials of yours will come to me, bowing down before me and saying, 'Go, you and all the people who follow you!' After that I will leave." Then Moses, hot with anger, left Pharaoh.

9The LORD had said to Moses, "Pharaoh will refuse to listen to you—so that my wonders may be multiplied in Egypt." 10Moses and Aaron performed all these wonders before Pharaoh, but the LORD hardened Pharaoh's heart, and he would not let the Israelites go out of his country.

The Passover and the Festival of Unleavened Bread

12 The LORD said to Moses and Aaron in Egypt, 2"This month is to be for you the first month, the first month of your year. 3Tell the whole community of Israel that on the tenth day of this month each man is to take a lambb for his family, one for each household. 4If any household is too small for a whole lamb, they must share one with their nearest neighbor, having taken into account the number of people there are. You are to determine the amount of lamb needed in accordance with what each person will eat. 5The animals you choose must be year-

---

a 19 Or the Sea of Reeds   b 3 The Hebrew word can mean lamb or kid; also in verse 4.

BREAKTHROUGH!

The Passover

(EXODUS 12:1-30)

Here are the instructions for killing the lamb and preparing the family meal that was celebrated in the homes. That little animal had to be roasted and then eaten. Every house had to be marked clearly with the animal's blood in order to avoid God's punishment. God asked that this meal be celebrated every year so they would remember when they had left Egypt, where they had been slaves.

old males without defect, and you may take them from the sheep or the goats. 6Take care of them until the fourteenth day of the month, when all the members of the community of Israel must slaughter them at twilight. 7Then they are to take some of the blood and put it on the sides and tops of the doorframes of the houses where they eat the lambs. 8That same night they are to eat the meat roasted over the fire, along with bitter herbs, and bread made without yeast. 9Do not eat the meat raw or boiled in water, but roast it over a fire—with the head, legs and internal organs. 10Do not leave any of it till morning; if some is left till morning, you must burn it. 11This is how you are to eat it: with your cloak tucked into your

belt, your sandals on your feet and your staff in your hand. Eat it in haste; it is the LORD's Passover.

12"On that same night I will pass through Egypt and strike down every first-born of both people and animals, and I will bring judgment on all the gods of Egypt. I am the LORD. 13The blood will be a sign for you on the houses where you are, and when I see the blood, I will pass over you. No destructive plague will touch you when I strike Egypt.

14"This is a day you are to commemorate; for the generations to come you shall celebrate it as a festival to the LORD—a lasting ordinance. 15For seven days you are to eat bread made without yeast. On the first day remove the yeast from your houses, for whoever eats anything with yeast in it from the first day through the seventh must be cut off from Israel. 16On the first day hold a sacred assembly, and another one on the seventh day. Do no work at all on these days, except to prepare food for everyone to eat; that is all you may do.

17"Celebrate the Festival of Unleavened Bread, because it was on this very day that I brought your divisions out of Egypt. Celebrate this day as a lasting ordinance for the generations to come. 18In the first month you are to eat bread made without yeast, from the evening of the fourteenth day until the evening of the twenty-first day. 19For seven days no yeast is to be found in your houses. And anyone, whether foreigner or native-born, who eats anything with yeast in it must be cut off from the community of Israel. 20Eat nothing made with yeast. Wherever you live, you must eat unleavened bread."

21Then Moses summoned all the elders of Israel and said to them, "Go at once and select the animals for your families and slaughter the Passover lamb. 22Take a bunch of hyssop, dip it into the blood in the basin and put some of the blood on the top and on both sides of the doorframe. None of you shall go out of the door of your house until morning. 23When the LORD goes through the land to strike down the Egyptians, he will see the blood on the top and sides of the doorframe

BREAK THROUGH!

Hyssop
(EXODUS 12:22)
This plant has a little bunch of flowers at the tip of each branch.

and will pass over that doorway, and he will not permit the destroyer to enter your houses and strike you down.

24 "Obey these instructions as a lasting ordinance for you and your descendants. 25 When you enter the land that the LORD will give you as he promised, observe this ceremony. 26 And when your children ask you, 'What does this ceremony mean to you?' 27 then tell them, 'It is the Passover sacrifice to the LORD, who passed over the houses of the Israelites in Egypt and spared our homes when he struck down the Egyptians.'" Then the people bowed down and worshiped. 28 The Israelites did just what the LORD commanded Moses and Aaron.

29 At midnight the LORD struck down all the firstborn in Egypt, from the firstborn of Pharaoh, who sat on the throne, to the firstborn of the prisoner, who was in the dungeon, and the firstborn of all the livestock as well. 30 Pharaoh and all his officials and all the Egyptians got up during the night, and there was loud wailing in Egypt, for there was not a house without someone dead.

The Exodus

31 During the night Pharaoh summoned Moses and Aaron and said, "Up! Leave my people, you and the Israelites! Go, worship the LORD as you have requested. 32 Take your flocks and herds, as you have said, and go. And also bless me."

33 The Egyptians urged the people to hurry and leave the country. "For otherwise," they said, "we will all die!" 34 So the people took their dough before the yeast was added, and carried it on their shoulders in kneading troughs wrapped in clothing. 35 The Israelites did as Moses instructed and asked the Egyptians for articles of silver and gold and for clothing. 36 The LORD had made the Egyptians favorably disposed toward the people, and they gave them what they asked for; so they plundered the Egyptians.

37 The Israelites journeyed from Rameses to Sukkoth. There were about six

CHECK THE FACTS

What is Passover really?

A) An oriental dish made with lamb

B) A celebration to remember when the Israelites left Egypt

C) A party where we eat chocolate Easter eggs and bunnies

CORRECT ANSWER: B

hundred thousand men on foot, besides women and children. ³⁸Many other people went up with them, and also large droves of livestock, both flocks and herds. ³⁹With the dough the Israelites had brought from Egypt, they baked loaves of unleavened bread. The dough was without yeast because they had been driven out of Egypt and did not have time to prepare food for themselves.

⁴⁰Now the length of time the Israelite people lived in Egypt* was 430 years. ⁴¹At the end of the 430 years, to the very day, all the Lord's divisions left Egypt. ⁴²Because the Lord kept vigil that night to bring them out of Egypt, on this night all the Israelites are to keep vigil to honor the Lord for the generations to come.

Passover Restrictions

⁴³The Lord said to Moses and Aaron, "These are the regulations for the Passover meal:

"No foreigner may eat it. ⁴⁴Any slave you have bought may eat it after you have circumcised him, ⁴⁵but a temporary resident or a hired worker may not eat it.

⁴⁶"It must be eaten inside the house; take none of the meat outside the house. Do not break any of the bones. ⁴⁷The whole community of Israel must celebrate it.

⁴⁸"A foreigner residing among you who wants to celebrate the Lord's Passover must have all the males in his household circumcised; then he may take part like one born in the land. No uncircumcised male may eat it. ⁴⁹The same law applies both to the native-born and to the foreigner residing among you."

⁵⁰All the Israelites did just what the Lord had commanded Moses and Aaron. ⁵¹And on that very day the Lord brought the Israelites out of Egypt by their divisions.

Consecration of the Firstborn

13 The Lord said to Moses, ²"Consecrate to me every firstborn male. The first offspring of every womb among the Israelites belongs to me, whether human or animal."

³Then Moses said to the people, "Commemorate this day, the day you came out of Egypt, out of the land of slavery, because the Lord brought you out of it with a mighty hand. Eat nothing containing yeast. ⁴Today, in the month of Aviv, you are leaving. ⁵When the Lord brings you into the land of the Canaanites, Hittites, Amorites, Hivites and Jebusites—the land he swore to your ancestors to give you, a land flowing with milk and honey—you are to observe this ceremony in this month: ⁶For seven days eat bread made without yeast and on the seventh day hold a festival to the Lord. ⁷Eat unleavened bread during those seven days; nothing with yeast in it is to be seen among you, nor shall any

^a 40 Masoretic Text; Samaritan Pentateuch and Septuagint Egypt and Canaan

Festival of Unleavened Bread
(EXODUS 13:1-16)
This celebration lasted seven days. The Israelites had to eat unleavened bread, a flatbread made without yeast, like tortillas. They couldn't even have yeast in their homes. Later on, this celebration became part of the Passover, because both celebrations were a time to remember that God had taken them out of Egypt.

yeast be seen anywhere within your borders. [8]On that day tell your son, 'I do this because of what the LORD did for me when I came out of Egypt.' [9]This observance will be for you like a sign on your hand and a reminder on your forehead that this law of the LORD is to be on your lips. For the LORD brought you out of Egypt with his mighty hand. [10]You must keep this ordinance at the appointed time year after year.

[11]"After the LORD brings you into the land of the Canaanites and gives it to you, as he promised on oath to you and your ancestors, [12]you are to give over to the LORD the first offspring of every womb. All the firstborn males of your livestock belong to the LORD. [13]Redeem with a lamb every firstborn donkey, but if you do not redeem it, break its neck. Redeem every firstborn among your sons.

[14]"In days to come, when your son asks you, 'What does this mean?' say to him, 'With a mighty hand the LORD brought us out of Egypt, out of the land of slavery. [15]When Pharaoh stubbornly refused to let us go, the LORD killed the firstborn of both people and animals in Egypt. This is why I sacrifice to the LORD the first male offspring of every womb and redeem each of my firstborn sons.' [16]And it will be like a sign on your hand and a symbol on your forehead that the LORD brought us out of Egypt with his mighty hand.'"

Crossing the Sea

[17]When Pharaoh let the people go, God did not lead them on the road through the Philistine country, though that was shorter. For God said, "If they face war, they might change their minds and return to Egypt." [18]So God led the people around by the desert road toward the Red Sea.[a] The Israelites went up out of Egypt ready for battle.

[19]Moses took the bones of Joseph with him because Joseph had made the Israelites swear an oath. He had said, "God will surely come to your aid, and then you must carry my bones up with you from this place."[b]

[20]After leaving Sukkoth they camped at Etham on the edge of the desert. [21]By day the LORD went ahead of them in a pillar of

THE SCENE

RED SEA OR SEA OF REEDS?

(EXODUS 13:18)

This is more like a lake than a sea. The water is fresh, and reeds grow there (of course!). It's near the Nile River delta. For many years, it was thought that it was the Red Sea, but now people who study the Bible have decided that's not so.

cloud to guide them on their way and by night in a pillar of fire to give them light, so that they could travel by day or night. [22]Neither the pillar of cloud by day nor the pillar of fire by night left its place in front of the people.

14 Then the LORD said to Moses, [2]"Tell the Israelites to turn back and encamp near Pi Hahiroth, between Migdol and the sea. They are to encamp by the sea, directly opposite Baal Zephon. [3]Pharaoh will think, 'The Israelites are wandering around the land in confusion, hemmed in by the desert.' [4]And I will harden Pharaoh's heart, and he will pursue them. But I will gain glory for myself through Pharaoh and all his army, and the Egyptians

---

[a] 18 Or the Sea of Reeds   [b] 19 See Gen. 50:25.

will know that I am the Lord." So the Israelites did this.

5When the king of Egypt was told that the people had fled, Pharaoh and his officials changed their minds about them and said, "What have we done? We have let the Israelites go and have lost their services!" 6So he had his chariot made ready and took his army with him. 7He took six hundred of the best chariots, along with all the other chariots of Egypt, with officers over all of them. 8The Lord hardened the heart of Pharaoh king of Egypt, so that he pursued the Israelites, who were marching out boldly. 9The Egyptians—all Pharaoh's horses and chariots, horsemen[a] and troops—pursued the Israelites and overtook them as they camped by the sea near Pi Hahiroth, opposite Baal Zephon.

BREAKTHROUGH!

Is it true that they crossed the sea on dry land?

(EXODUS 14)

This happened because God got involved and showed his great power. God made the wind blow very hard during the night, so the sea divided and the people could cross on dry land. Then God made the sea go back to normal again when the Egyptians appeared, so all the Egyptians were killed. After that, the Israelites were free. Finally!

10As Pharaoh approached, the Israelites looked up, and there were the Egyptians, marching after them. They were terrified and cried out to the Lord. 11They said to Moses, "Was it because there were no graves in Egypt that you brought us to the desert to die? What have you done to us by bringing us out of Egypt? 12Didn't we say to you in Egypt, 'Leave us alone; let us serve the Egyptians'? It would have been better for us to serve the Egyptians than to die in the desert!"

13Moses answered the people, "Do not be afraid. Stand firm and you will see the deliverance the Lord will bring you today. The Egyptians you see today you will never see again. 14The Lord will fight for you; you need only to be still."

15Then the Lord said to Moses, "Why are you crying out to me? Tell the Israelites to move on. 16Raise your staff and stretch out your hand over the sea to divide the water so that the Israelites can go through the sea on dry ground. 17I will harden the hearts of the Egyptians so that they will go in after them. And I will gain glory through Pharaoh and all his army, through his chariots and his horsemen. 18The Egyptians will know that I am the Lord when I gain glory through Pharaoh, his chariots and his horsemen."

19Then the angel of God, who had been traveling in front of Israel's army, withdrew and went behind them. The pillar of cloud also moved from in front and stood behind them, 20coming between the armies of Egypt and Israel. Throughout the night the cloud brought darkness to the one side and light to the other side; so neither went near the other all night long.

21Then Moses stretched out his hand over the sea, and all that night the Lord drove the sea back with a strong east wind and turned it into dry land. The waters were divided, 22and the Israelites went through the sea on dry ground, with a wall of water on their right and on their left.

23The Egyptians pursued them, and all Pharaoh's horses and chariots and horsemen followed them into the sea.

---

a 9 Or charioteers; also in verses 17, 18, 23, 26 and 28

²⁴During the last watch of the night the LORD looked down from the pillar of fire and cloud at the Egyptian army and threw it into confusion. ²⁵He jammed*a* the wheels of their chariots so that they had difficulty driving. And the Egyptians said, "Let's get away from the Israelites! The LORD is fighting for them against Egypt."

²⁶Then the LORD said to Moses, "Stretch out your hand over the sea so that the waters may flow back over the Egyptians and their chariots and horsemen." ²⁷Moses stretched out his hand over the sea, and at daybreak the sea went back to its place. The Egyptians were fleeing toward*b* it, and the LORD swept them into the sea. ²⁸The water flowed back and covered the chariots and horsemen—the entire army of Pharaoh that had followed the Israelites into the sea. Not one of them survived.

²⁹But the Israelites went through the sea on dry ground, with a wall of water on their right and on their left. ³⁰That day the LORD saved Israel from the hands of the Egyptians, and Israel saw the Egyptians lying dead on the shore. ³¹And when the Israelites saw the mighty hand of the LORD displayed against the Egyptians, the people feared the LORD and put their trust in him and in Moses his servant.

The Song of Moses and Miriam

15 Then Moses and the Israelites sang this song to the LORD:

"I will sing to the LORD,
  for he is highly exalted.
Both horse and driver
  he has hurled into the sea.
² "The LORD is my strength and my
    defense*c*;
  he has become my salvation.
He is my God, and I will praise him,
  my father's God, and I will exalt
    him.
³ The LORD is a warrior;
  the LORD is his name.
⁴ Pharaoh's chariots and his army
  he has hurled into the sea.
The best of Pharaoh's officers
  are drowned in the Red Sea.*d*

⁵ The deep waters have covered them;
  they sank to the depths like a
    stone.
⁶ Your right hand, LORD,
  was majestic in power.
Your right hand, LORD,
  shattered the enemy.
⁷ "In the greatness of your majesty
  you threw down those who opposed
    you.
You unleashed your burning anger;
  it consumed them like stubble.
⁸ By the blast of your nostrils
  the waters piled up.
The surging waters stood up like a
    wall;
  the deep waters congealed in the
    heart of the sea.
⁹ The enemy boasted,
  'I will pursue, I will overtake
    them.
I will divide the spoils;
  I will gorge myself on them.
I will draw my sword
  and my hand will destroy them.'
¹⁰ But you blew with your breath,
  and the sea covered them.
They sank like lead
  in the mighty waters.
¹¹ Who among the gods
  is like you, LORD?
Who is like you—
  majestic in holiness,
awesome in glory,
  working wonders?

¹² "You stretch out your right hand,
  and the earth swallows your
    enemies.
¹³ In your unfailing love you will lead
  the people you have redeemed.
In your strength you will guide them
  to your holy dwelling.
¹⁴ The nations will hear and tremble;
  anguish will grip the people of
    Philistia.
¹⁵ The chiefs of Edom will be terrified,
  the leaders of Moab will be seized
    with trembling,
the people*e* of Canaan will melt away;

---

a 25 See Samaritan Pentateuch, Septuagint and Syriac; Masoretic Text *removed*   *b* 27 Or *from*   *c* 2 Or *song*   *d* 4 Or *the Sea of Reeds*; also in verse 22   *e* 15 Or *rulers*

16 terror and dread will fall on them.
   By the power of your arm
      they will be as still as a stone—
   until your people pass by, LORD,
      until the people you bought[a] pass by.
17 You will bring them in and plant them
      on the mountain of your
         inheritance—
   the place, LORD, you made for your
      dwelling,
   the sanctuary, Lord, your hands
      established.

18 "The LORD reigns
      for ever and ever."

19 When Pharaoh's horses, chariots and horsemen[b] went into the sea, the LORD brought the waters of the sea back over them, but the Israelites walked through the sea on dry ground. 20 Then Miriam the prophet, Aaron's sister, took a timbrel in her hand, and all the women followed her, with timbrels and dancing. 21 Miriam sang to them:

"Sing to the LORD,
   for he is highly exalted.
Both horse and driver
   he has hurled into the sea."

The Waters of Marah and Elim

22 Then Moses led Israel from the Red Sea and they went into the Desert of Shur. For three days they traveled in the desert without finding water. 23 When they came to Marah, they could not drink its water because it was bitter. (That is why the place is called Marah.[c]) 24 So the people grumbled against Moses, saying, "What are we to drink?"

25 Then Moses cried out to the LORD, and the LORD showed him a piece of wood. He threw it into the water, and the water became fit to drink.

There the LORD issued a ruling and instruction for them and put them to the test. 26 He said, "If you listen carefully to the LORD your God and do what is right in his eyes, if you pay attention to his commands and keep all his decrees, I will not bring on you any of the diseases I brought on the Egyptians, for I am the LORD, who heals you."

27 Then they came to Elim, where there were twelve springs and seventy palm trees, and they camped there near the water.

---

[a] 16 Or created   [b] 19 Or charioteers   [c] 23 Marah means bitter.

THE
WITNESSES

✓ MIRIAM THE PROPHET
(EXODUS 15:20)

She was Moses' sister and the daughter of Amram and Jochebed. Miriam was the woman who took care of baby Moses when he was left in a basket in the water. She told the king's daughter that she could find a Hebrew mother to tend him. After crossing the Red Sea so incredibly, Miriam became a prophet, and she led the Israelite women in a song of praise to God. Unfortunately, God punished her with leprosy after she spoke badly about Moses, but she recovered later. (Read about it in Numbers 12:1–15.)

Manna and Quail

16 The whole Israelite community set out from Elim and came to the Desert of Sin, which is between Elim and Sinai, on the fifteenth day of the second month after they had come out of Egypt. ²In the desert the whole community grumbled against Moses and Aaron. ³The Israelites said to them, "If only we had died by the LORD's hand in Egypt! There we sat around pots of meat and ate all the food we wanted, but you have brought us out into this desert to starve this entire assembly to death."

⁴Then the LORD said to Moses, "I will rain down bread from heaven for you. The people are to go out each day and gather enough for that day. In this way I will test them and see whether they will follow my instructions. ⁵On the sixth day they are to prepare what they bring in, and that is to be twice as much as they gather on the other days."

⁶So Moses and Aaron said to all the Israelites, "In the evening you will know that it was the LORD who brought you out of Egypt, ⁷and in the morning you will see the glory of the LORD, because he has heard your grumbling against him. Who are we, that you should grumble against us?" ⁸Moses also said, "You will know that it was the LORD when he gives you meat to eat in the evening and all the bread you want in the morning, because he has heard your grumbling against him. Who are we? You are not grumbling against us, but against the LORD."

⁹Then Moses told Aaron, "Say to the entire Israelite community, 'Come before the LORD, for he has heard your grumbling.'"

¹⁰While Aaron was speaking to the whole Israelite community, they looked toward the desert, and there was the glory of the LORD appearing in the cloud.

¹¹The LORD said to Moses, ¹²"I have heard the grumbling of the Israelites. Tell them, 'At twilight you will eat meat, and in the morning you will be filled with bread. Then you will know that I am the LORD your God.'"

¹³That evening quail came and covered the camp, and in the morning there was a layer of dew around the camp. ¹⁴When the dew was gone, thin flakes like frost on the ground appeared on the desert floor. ¹⁵When the Israelites saw it, they said to each other, "What is it?" For they did not know what it was.

Moses said to them, "It is the bread the LORD has given you to eat. ¹⁶This is what the LORD has commanded: 'Everyone is to gather as much as they need. Take an omer*a* for each person you have in your tent.'"

¹⁷The Israelites did as they were told; some gathered much, some little. ¹⁸And when they measured it by the omer, the one who gathered much did not have too much, and the one who gathered little did not have too little. Everyone had gathered just as much as they needed.

¹⁹Then Moses said to them, "No one is to keep any of it until morning."

²⁰However, some of them paid no attention to Moses; they kept part of it until morning, but it was full of maggots and began to smell. So Moses was angry with them.

²¹Each morning everyone gathered as much as they needed, and when the sun grew hot, it melted away. ²²On the sixth day, they gathered twice as much—two omers*b* for each person—and the leaders of the community came and reported this to Moses. ²³He said to them, "This is what the LORD commanded: 'Tomorrow is to be a day of sabbath rest, a holy sabbath to the LORD. So bake what you want to bake and boil what you want to boil. Save whatever is left and keep it until morning.'"

²⁴So they saved it until morning, as Moses commanded, and it did not stink or get maggots in it. ²⁵"Eat it today," Moses said, "because today is a sabbath to the LORD. You will not find any of it on the ground today. ²⁶Six days you are to gather it, but on the seventh day, the Sabbath, there will not be any."

²⁷Nevertheless, some of the people went out on the seventh day to gather it,

---

a 16 That is, possibly about 3 pounds or about 1.4 kilograms; also in verses 18, 32, 33 and 36   *b* 22 That is, possibly about 6 pounds or about 2.8 kilograms but they found none. 28Then the LORD said to Moses, "How long will you[a] refuse to keep my commands and my instructions? 29Bear in mind that the LORD has given you the Sabbath; that is why on the sixth day he gives you bread for two days. Everyone is to stay where they are on the seventh day; no one is to go out." 30So the people rested on the seventh day.

31The people of Israel called the bread manna.[b] It was white like coriander seed and tasted like wafers made with honey. 32Moses said, "This is what the LORD has commanded: 'Take an omer of manna and keep it for the generations to come, so they can see the bread I gave you to eat in the wilderness when I brought you out of Egypt.' "

33So Moses said to Aaron, "Take a jar and put an omer of manna in it. Then place it before the LORD to be kept for the generations to come."

34As the LORD commanded Moses, Aaron put the manna with the tablets of

BREAK THROUGH!

Manna
(EXODUS 16:31)
God provided this special food for the Israelites during the time they were walking out in the desert after leaving Egypt. It was white, like little white coriander seeds, and it was sweet like honey.

the covenant law, so that it might be preserved. 35The Israelites ate manna forty years, until they came to a land that was settled; they ate manna until they reached the border of Canaan.

36(An omer is one-tenth of an ephah.)

Water From the Rock

17 The whole Israelite community set out from the Desert of Sin, traveling from place to place as the LORD commanded. They camped at Rephidim, but there was no water for the people to drink. 2So they quarreled with Moses and said, "Give us water to drink."

Moses replied, "Why do you quarrel with me? Why do you put the LORD to the test?"

3But the people were thirsty for water there, and they grumbled against Moses. They said, "Why did you bring us up out of Egypt to make us and our children and livestock die of thirst?"

4Then Moses cried out to the LORD, "What am I to do with these people? They are almost ready to stone me."

5The LORD answered Moses, "Go out in front of the people. Take with you some of the elders of Israel and take in your hand the staff with which you struck the Nile, and go. 6I will stand there before you by the rock at Horeb. Strike the rock, and water will come out of it for the people to drink." So Moses did this in the sight of the elders of Israel. 7And he called the place Massah[c] and Meribah[d] because the Israelites quarreled and because they tested the LORD saying, "Is the LORD among us or not?"

The Amalekites Defeated

8The Amalekites came and attacked the Israelites at Rephidim. 9Moses said to Joshua, "Choose some of our men and go out to fight the Amalekites. Tomorrow I will stand on top of the hill with the staff of God in my hands."

10So Joshua fought the Amalekites as Moses had ordered, and Moses, Aaron

---

[a] 28 The Hebrew is plural.   [b] 31 *Manna* sounds like the Hebrew for *What is it?* (see verse 15).   [c] 7 *Massah* means *testing*.   [d] 7 *Meribah* means *quarreling*.

and Hur went to the top of the hill. ¹¹As long as Moses held up his hands, the Israelites were winning, but whenever he lowered his hands, the Amalekites were winning. ¹²When Moses' hands grew tired, they took a stone and put it under him and he sat on it. Aaron and Hur held his hands up—one on one side, one on the other—so that his hands remained steady till sunset. ¹³So Joshua overcame the Amalekite army with the sword.

¹⁴Then the LORD said to Moses, "Write this on a scroll as something to be remembered and make sure that Joshua hears it, because I will completely blot out the name of Amalek from under heaven."

¹⁵Moses built an altar and called it The LORD is my Banner. ¹⁶He said, "Because hands were lifted up against[a] the throne of the LORD,[b] the LORD will be at war against the Amalekites from generation to generation."

Jethro Visits Moses

18 Now Jethro, the priest of Midian and father-in-law of Moses, heard of everything God had done for Moses and for his people Israel, and how the LORD had brought Israel out of Egypt.

²After Moses had sent away his wife Zipporah, his father-in-law Jethro received her ³and her two sons. One son was named Gershom,[c] for Moses said, "I have become a foreigner in a foreign land"; ⁴and the other was named Eliezer,[d] for he said, "My father's God was my helper; he saved me from the sword of Pharaoh."

⁵Jethro, Moses' father-in-law, together with Moses' sons and wife, came to him in the wilderness, where he was camped near the mountain of God. ⁶Jethro had sent word to him, "I, your father-in-law Jethro, am coming to you with your wife and her two sons."

⁷So Moses went out to meet his father-in-law and bowed down and kissed him. They greeted each other and then went into the tent. ⁸Moses told his father-in-law about everything the LORD had done to Pharaoh and the Egyptians for Israel's sake and about all the hardships they had met along the way and how the LORD had saved them.

THE WITNESSES

✓ JOSHUA (EXODUS 17:9)
His name was originally Hoshea, and he was the son of Nun from the tribe of Ephraim. Moses changed his name and called him Joshua. He was Moses' assistant and later his replacement. Joshua means "God saves." It is the Hebrew name for Jesus.

✓ ELIEZER (EXODUS 18:4)
This name means "God is my help." Moses remembered that the God of his father had helped him and had also freed him from the king of Egypt. He was Moses' second son.

⁹Jethro was delighted to hear about all the good things the LORD had done for Israel in rescuing them from the hand of the Egyptians. ¹⁰He said, "Praise be to the LORD, who rescued you from the hand

---

a 16 Or *to*   *b 16* The meaning of the Hebrew for this clause is uncertain.   *c 3* *Gershom* sounds like the Hebrew for *a foreigner there.*   *d 4* *Eliezer* means *my God is helper.*

of the Egyptians and of Pharaoh, and who rescued the people from the hand of the Egyptians. ¹¹Now I know that the LORD is greater than all other gods, for he did this to those who had treated Israel arrogantly." ¹²Then Jethro, Moses' father-in-law, brought a burnt offering and other sacrifices to God, and Aaron came with all the elders of Israel to eat a meal with Moses' father-in-law in the presence of God.

¹³The next day Moses took his seat to serve as judge for the people, and they stood around him from morning till evening. ¹⁴When his father-in-law saw all that Moses was doing for the people, he said, "What is this you are doing for the people? Why do you alone sit as judge, while all these people stand around you from morning till evening?"

¹⁵Moses answered him, "Because the people come to me to seek God's will. ¹⁶Whenever they have a dispute, it is brought to me, and I decide between the parties and inform them of God's decrees and instructions."

¹⁷Moses' father-in-law replied, "What you are doing is not good. ¹⁸You and these people who come to you will only wear yourselves out. The work is too heavy for you; you cannot handle it alone. ¹⁹Listen now to me and I will give you some advice, and may God be with you. You must be the people's representative before God and bring their disputes to him. ²⁰Teach them his decrees and instructions, and show them the way they are to live and how they are to behave. ²¹But select capable men from all the people—men who fear God, trustworthy men who hate dishonest gain—and appoint them as officials over thousands, hundreds, fifties and tens. ²²Have them serve as judges for the people at all times, but have them bring every difficult case to you; the simple cases they can decide themselves. That will make your load lighter, because they will share it with you. ²³If you do this and God so commands, you will be able to stand the strain, and all these people will go home satisfied."

²⁴Moses listened to his father-in-law and did everything he said. ²⁵He chose capable men from all Israel and made them leaders of the people, officials over thousands, hundreds, fifties and tens. ²⁶They served as judges for the people at all times. The difficult cases they brought to Moses, but the simple ones they decided themselves.

²⁷Then Moses sent his father-in-law on his way, and Jethro returned to his own country.

At Mount Sinai

19 On the first day of the third month after the Israelites left Egypt—on that very day—they came to the Desert of Sinai. ²After they set out from Rephidim, they entered the Desert of Sinai, and

THE SCENE

DESERT OF SINAI

(EXODUS 19:1–2)

This is the desert region that we call the Sinai Peninsula now. It was the place where Moses saw the burning bush (Exodus 3:2). And it was where water burst out of the rock (Exodus 17:5–6). There's a mountain there that many times is called the "Mount" or "Mountain of God." We don't know the exact location of that mountain.

Israel camped there in the desert in front of the mountain.

³Then Moses went up to God, and the LORD called to him from the mountain and said, "This is what you are to say to the descendants of Jacob and what you are to tell the people of Israel: ⁴'You yourselves have seen what I did to Egypt, and how I carried you on eagles' wings and brought you to myself. ⁵Now if you obey me fully and keep my covenant, then out of all nations you will be my treasured possession. Although the whole earth is mine, ⁶you*ᵃ* will be for me a kingdom of priests and a holy nation.' These are the words you are to speak to the Israelites."

⁷So Moses went back and summoned the elders of the people and set before them all the words the LORD had commanded him to speak. ⁸The people all responded together, "We will do everything the LORD has said." So Moses brought their answer back to the LORD.

⁹The LORD said to Moses, "I am going to come to you in a dense cloud, so that the people will hear me speaking with you and will always put their trust in you." Then Moses told the LORD what the people had said.

¹⁰And the LORD said to Moses, "Go to the people and consecrate them today and tomorrow. Have them wash their clothes ¹¹and be ready by the third day, because on that day the LORD will come down on Mount Sinai in the sight of all the people. ¹²Put limits for the people around the mountain and tell them, 'Be careful that you do not approach the mountain or touch the foot of it. Whoever touches the mountain is to be put to death. ¹³They are to be stoned or shot with arrows; not a hand is to be laid on them. No person or animal shall be permitted to live.' Only when the ram's horn sounds a long blast may they approach the mountain."

¹⁴After Moses had gone down the mountain to the people, he consecrated them, and they washed their clothes. ¹⁵Then he said to the people, "Prepare yourselves for the third day. Abstain from sexual relations."

¹⁶On the morning of the third day there was thunder and lightning, with a thick cloud over the mountain, and a very loud trumpet blast. Everyone in the camp trembled. ¹⁷Then Moses led the people out of the camp to meet with God, and they stood at the foot of the mountain. ¹⁸Mount Sinai was covered with smoke, because the LORD descended on it in fire. The smoke billowed up from it like smoke from a furnace, and the whole mountain*ᵇ* trembled violently. ¹⁹As the sound of the trumpet grew louder and louder, Moses spoke and the voice of God answered him.*ᶜ*

²⁰The LORD descended to the top of Mount Sinai and called Moses to the top of the mountain. So Moses went up ²¹and the LORD said to him, "Go down and warn the people so they do not force their way through to see the LORD and many of them perish. ²²Even the priests, who approach the LORD, must consecrate themselves, or the LORD will break out against them."

²³Moses said to the LORD, "The people cannot come up Mount Sinai, because you yourself warned us, 'Put limits around the mountain and set it apart as holy.' "

²⁴The LORD replied, "Go down and bring Aaron up with you. But the priests and the people must not force their way through to come up to the LORD, or he will break out against them."

²⁵So Moses went down to the people and told them.

The Ten Commandments

20 And God spoke all these words:

²"I am the LORD your God, who brought you out of Egypt, out of the land of slavery.

³"You shall have no other gods before*ᵈ* me.

⁴"You shall not make for yourself an image in the form of anything in heaven above or on the earth beneath or in the waters below. ⁵You shall not bow down to them or worship them; for I, the LORD your God, am a jealous God,

---

ᵃ 5,6 Or possession, for the whole earth is mine. ⁶You
ᵇ 18 Most Hebrew manuscripts; a few Hebrew manuscripts and Septuagint and all the people   ᶜ 19 Or and God answered him with thunder   ᵈ 3 Or besides

BREAK THROUGH!

The Ten Commandments explained

(EXODUS 20:1-21)

These are ten important orders that God himself gave to Moses so he could explain them to the people of Israel. But they can be for us today too. God asks us to:

1. Not have other gods except him.
2. Not have idols or images. That means we shouldn't make sculptures, statues or drawings of God to worship them as if they were god.
3. Not use God's name without respect.
4. Understand that Saturday is a day dedicated to God. Or it can be Sunday. It really means that we have to set aside one day to worship God and rest.
5. Obey our parents.
6. Not kill anyone. God considers life as something very precious.
7. Not be unfaithful in marriage. That's a great rule for parents!
8. Not steal. Obviously!
9. Not talk badly about other people or tell lies.
10. Not want to have what other people have. We should be happy with what we have.

punishing the children for the sin of the parents to the third and fourth generation of those who hate me, ⁶but showing love to a thousand generations of those who love me and keep my commandments.

⁷"You shall not misuse the name of the LORD your God, for the LORD will not hold anyone guiltless who misuses his name.

⁸"Remember the Sabbath day by keeping it holy. ⁹Six days you shall labor and do all your work, ¹⁰but the seventh day is a sabbath to the LORD your God. On it you shall not do any work, neither you, nor your son or daughter, nor your male or female servant, nor your animals, nor any foreigner residing in your towns. ¹¹For in six days the LORD made the heavens and the earth, the sea, and all that is in them, but he rested on the seventh day. Therefore the LORD blessed the Sabbath day and made it holy.

¹²"Honor your father and your mother, so that you may live long in the land the LORD your God is giving you.

¹³"You shall not murder.

¹⁴"You shall not commit adultery.

¹⁵"You shall not steal.

¹⁶"You shall not give false testimony against your neighbor.

¹⁷"You shall not covet your neighbor's house. You shall not covet your neighbor's wife, or his male or female servant, his ox or donkey, or anything that belongs to your neighbor."

¹⁸When the people saw the thunder and lightning and heard the trumpet and saw the mountain in smoke, they trembled with fear. They stayed at a distance ¹⁹and said to Moses, "Speak to us yourself and we will listen. But do not have God speak to us or we will die."

²⁰Moses said to the people, "Do not be afraid. God has come to test you, so that

the fear of God will be with you to keep you from sinning."

²¹The people remained at a distance, while Moses approached the thick darkness where God was.

Idols and Altars

²²Then the Lᴏʀᴅ said to Moses, "Tell the Israelites this: 'You have seen for yourselves that I have spoken to you from heaven: ²³Do not make any gods to be alongside me; do not make for yourselves gods of silver or gods of gold.

²⁴" 'Make an altar of earth for me and sacrifice on it your burnt offerings and fellowship offerings, your sheep and goats and your cattle. Wherever I cause my name to be honored, I will come to you and bless you. ²⁵If you make an altar of stones for me, do not build it with dressed stones, for you will defile it if you use a tool on it. ²⁶And do not go up to my altar on steps, or your private parts may be exposed.'

21 "These are the laws you are to set before them:

Hebrew Servants

²"If you buy a Hebrew servant, he is to serve you for six years. But in the seventh year, he shall go free, without paying anything. ³If he comes alone, he is to go free alone; but if he has a wife when he comes, she is to go with him. ⁴If his master gives him a wife and she bears him sons or daughters, the woman and her children shall belong to her master, and only the man shall go free.

⁵"But if the servant declares, 'I love my master and my wife and children and do not want to go free,' ⁶then his master must take him before the judges.ᵃ He shall take him to the door or the doorpost and pierce his ear with an awl. Then he will be his servant for life.

⁷"If a man sells his daughter as a servant, she is not to go free as male servants do. ⁸If she does not please the master who has selected her for himself,ᵇ

he must let her be redeemed. He has no right to sell her to foreigners, because he has broken faith with her. ⁹If he selects her for his son, he must grant her the rights of a daughter. ¹⁰If he marries another woman, he must not deprive the first one of her food, clothing and marital rights. ¹¹If he does not provide her with these three things, she is to go free, without any payment of money.

Personal Injuries

¹²"Anyone who strikes a person with a fatal blow is to be put to death. ¹³However, if it is not done intentionally, but God lets it happen, they are to flee to a place I will designate. ¹⁴But if anyone schemes and kills someone deliberately, that person is to be taken from my altar and put to death.

¹⁵"Anyone who attacksᶜ their father or mother is to be put to death.

¹⁶"Anyone who kidnaps someone is to be put to death, whether the victim has been sold or is still in the kidnapper's possession.

¹⁷"Anyone who curses their father or mother is to be put to death.

¹⁸"If people quarrel and one person hits another with a stone or with their fistᵈ and the victim does not die but is confined to bed, ¹⁹the one who struck the blow will not be held liable if the other can get up and walk around outside with a staff; however, the guilty party must pay the injured person for any loss of time and see that the victim is completely healed.

²⁰"Anyone who beats their male or female slave with a rod must be punished if the slave dies as a direct result, ²¹but they are not to be punished if the slave recovers after a day or two, since the slave is their property.

²²"If people are fighting and hit a pregnant woman and she gives birth prematurelyᵉ but there is no serious injury, the offender must be fined whatever the woman's husband demands and the court allows. ²³But if there is serious injury, you are to take life for life, ²⁴eye for eye, tooth

---

ᵃ 6 Or *before God*   ᵇ 8 Or *master so that he does not choose her*   ᶜ 15 Or *kills*   ᵈ 18 Or *with a tool*   ᵉ 22 Or *she has a miscarriage* for tooth, hand for hand, foot for foot, [25]burn for burn, wound for wound, bruise for bruise.

[26]"An owner who hits a male or female slave in the eye and destroys it must let the slave go free to compensate for the eye. [27]And an owner who knocks out the tooth of a male or female slave must let the slave go free to compensate for the tooth.

[28]"If a bull gores a man or woman to death, the bull is to be stoned to death, and its meat must not be eaten. But the owner of the bull will not be held responsible. [29]If, however, the bull has had the habit of goring and the owner has been warned but has not kept it penned up and it kills a man or woman, the bull is to be stoned and its owner also is to be put to death. [30]However, if payment is demanded, the owner may redeem his life by the payment of whatever is demanded. [31]This law also applies if the bull gores a son or daughter. [32]If the bull gores a male or female slave, the owner must pay thirty shekels[a] of silver to the master of the slave, and the bull is to be stoned to death.

[33]"If anyone uncovers a pit or digs one and fails to cover it and an ox or a donkey falls into it, [34]the one who opened the pit must pay the owner for the loss and take the dead animal in exchange.

[35]"If anyone's bull injures someone else's bull and it dies, the two parties are to sell the live one and divide both the money and the dead animal equally. [36]However, if it was known that the bull had the habit of goring, yet the owner did not keep it penned up, the owner must pay, animal for animal, and take the dead animal in exchange.

Protection of Property

22[b] "Whoever steals an ox or a sheep and slaughters it or sells it must pay back five head of cattle for the ox and four sheep for the sheep.

[2]"If a thief is caught breaking in at night and is struck a fatal blow, the defender is not guilty of bloodshed; [3]but if it happens after sunrise, the defender is guilty of bloodshed.

"Anyone who steals must certainly make restitution, but if they have nothing, they must be sold to pay for their theft. [4]If the stolen animal is found alive in their possession—whether ox or donkey or sheep—they must pay back double.

[5]"If anyone grazes their livestock in a field or vineyard and lets them stray and they graze in someone else's field, the offender must make restitution from the best of their own field or vineyard.

[6]"If a fire breaks out and spreads into thornbushes so that it burns shocks of grain or standing grain or the whole field, the one who started the fire must make restitution.

[7]"If anyone gives a neighbor silver or goods for safekeeping and they are stolen from the neighbor's house, the thief, if caught, must pay back double. [8]But if the thief is not found, the owner of the house must appear before the judges, and they must[c] determine whether the owner of the house has laid hands on the other person's property. [9]In all cases of illegal possession of an ox, a donkey, a sheep, a garment, or any other lost property about which somebody says, 'This is mine,' both parties are to bring their cases before the judges.[d] The one whom the judges declare[e] guilty must pay back double to the other.

[10]"If anyone gives a donkey, an ox, a sheep or any other animal to their neighbor for safekeeping and it dies or is injured or is taken away while no one is looking, [11]the issue between them will be settled by the taking of an oath before the Lord that the neighbor did not lay hands on the other person's property. The owner is to accept this, and no restitution is required. [12]But if the animal was stolen from the neighbor, restitution must be made to the owner. [13]If it was torn to pieces by a wild animal, the neighbor shall bring in the remains as evidence and shall not be required to pay for the torn animal.

[14]"If anyone borrows an animal from their neighbor and it is injured or dies

---

[a] 32 That is, about 12 ounces or about 345 grams
[b] In Hebrew texts 22:1 is numbered 21:37, and 22:2-31 is numbered 22:1-30.   [c] 8 Or before God, and he will
[d] 9 Or before God   [e] 9 Or whom God declares

while the owner is not present, they must make restitution. ¹⁵But if the owner is with the animal, the borrower will not have to pay. If the animal was hired, the money paid for the hire covers the loss.

Social Responsibility

¹⁶"If a man seduces a virgin who is not pledged to be married and sleeps with her, he must pay the bride-price, and she shall be his wife. ¹⁷If her father absolutely refuses to give her to him, he must still pay the bride-price for virgins.

¹⁸"Do not allow a sorceress to live.

¹⁹"Anyone who has sexual relations with an animal is to be put to death.

²⁰"Whoever sacrifices to any god other than the LORD must be destroyed.ᵃ

²¹"Do not mistreat or oppress a foreigner, for you were foreigners in Egypt.

²²"Do not take advantage of the widow or the fatherless. ²³If you do and they cry out to me, I will certainly hear their cry. ²⁴My anger will be aroused, and I will kill you with the sword; your wives will become widows and your children fatherless.

²⁵"If you lend money to one of my people among you who is needy, do not treat it like a business deal; charge no interest. ²⁶If you take your neighbor's cloak as a pledge, return it by sunset, ²⁷because that cloak is the only covering your neighbor has. What else can they sleep in? When they cry out to me, I will hear, for I am compassionate.

²⁸"Do not blaspheme Godᵇ or curse the ruler of your people.

²⁹"Do not hold back offerings from your granaries or your vats.ᶜ

"You must give me the firstborn of your sons. ³⁰Do the same with your cattle and your sheep. Let them stay with their mothers for seven days, but give them to me on the eighth day.

³¹"You are to be my holy people. So do not eat the meat of an animal torn by wild beasts; throw it to the dogs.

Laws of Justice and Mercy

23 "Do not spread false reports. Do not help a guilty person by being a malicious witness.

²"Do not follow the crowd in doing wrong. When you give testimony in a lawsuit, do not pervert justice by siding with the crowd, ³and do not show favoritism to a poor person in a lawsuit.

⁴"If you come across your enemy's ox or donkey wandering off, be sure to return it. ⁵If you see the donkey of someone who hates you fallen down under its load, do not leave it there; be sure you help them with it.

⁶"Do not deny justice to your poor people in their lawsuits. ⁷Have nothing to do with a false charge and do not put an innocent or honest person to death, for I will not acquit the guilty.

⁸"Do not accept a bribe, for a bribe blinds those who see and twists the words of the innocent.

⁹"Do not oppress a foreigner; you yourselves know how it feels to be foreigners, because you were foreigners in Egypt.

Sabbath Laws

¹⁰"For six years you are to sow your fields and harvest the crops, ¹¹but during the seventh year let the land lie unplowed and unused. Then the poor among your people may get food from it, and the wild animals may eat what is left. Do the same with your vineyard and your olive grove.

¹²"Six days do your work, but on the seventh day do not work, so that your ox and your donkey may rest, and so that the slave born in your household and the foreigner living among you may be refreshed.

¹³"Be careful to do everything I have said to you. Do not invoke the names of other gods; do not let them be heard on your lips.

The Three Annual Festivals

¹⁴"Three times a year you are to celebrate a festival to me.

¹⁵"Celebrate the Festival of Unleavened Bread; for seven days eat bread made without yeast, as I commanded you. Do this at the appointed time in the month

---

ᵃ 20 The Hebrew term refers to the irrevocable giving over of things or persons to the LORD, often by totally destroying them.   ᵇ 28 Or Do not revile the judges   ᶜ 29 The meaning of the Hebrew for this phrase is uncertain.

of Aviv, for in that month you came out of Egypt.

"No one is to appear before me empty-handed.

¹⁶"Celebrate the Festival of Harvest with the firstfruits of the crops you sow in your field.

"Celebrate the Festival of Ingathering at the end of the year, when you gather in your crops from the field.

¹⁷"Three times a year all the men are to appear before the Sovereign LORD.

¹⁸"Do not offer the blood of a sacrifice to me along with anything containing yeast.

"The fat of my festival offerings must not be kept until morning.

¹⁹"Bring the best of the firstfruits of your soil to the house of the LORD your God.

"Do not cook a young goat in its mother's milk.

God's Angel to Prepare the Way

²⁰"See, I am sending an angel ahead of you to guard you along the way and to

BREAK THROUGH!

Aviv
(EXODUS 23:15)

The Israelites counted the months differently than we do. Aviv was the first month of the Jewish lunar calendar. In our solar calendar, that would be more or less from the middle of March to the middle of April.

bring you to the place I have prepared. ²¹Pay attention to him and listen to what he says. Do not rebel against him; he will not forgive your rebellion, since my Name is in him. ²²If you listen carefully to all he says and do all that I say, I will be an enemy to your enemies and will oppose those who oppose you. ²³My angel will go ahead of you and bring you into the land of the Amorites, Hittites, Perizzites, Canaanites, Hivites and Jebusites, and I will wipe them out. ²⁴Do not bow down before their gods or worship them or follow their practices. You must demolish them and break their sacred stones to pieces. ²⁵Worship the LORD your God, and his blessing will be on your food and water. I will take away sickness from among you, ²⁶and none will miscarry or be barren in your land. I will give you a full life span.

²⁷"I will send my terror ahead of you and throw into confusion every nation you encounter. I will make all your enemies turn their backs and run. ²⁸I will send the hornet ahead of you to drive the Hivites, Canaanites and Hittites out of your way. ²⁹But I will not drive them out in a single year, because the land would become desolate and the wild animals too numerous for you. ³⁰Little by little I will drive them out before you, until you have increased enough to take possession of the land.

³¹"I will establish your borders from the Red Sea*a* to the Mediterranean Sea,*b* and from the desert to the Euphrates River. I will give into your hands the people who live in the land, and you will drive them out before you. ³²Do not make a covenant with them or with their gods. ³³Do not let them live in your land or they will cause you to sin against me, because the worship of their gods will certainly be a snare to you."

The Covenant Confirmed

24 Then the LORD said to Moses, "Come up to the LORD, you and Aaron, Nadab and Abihu, and seventy of the elders of Israel. You are to worship

---

a 31 Or *the Sea of Reeds*   *b* 31 Hebrew *to the Sea of the Philistines*

THE
WITNESSES

✓ **NADAB AND ABIHU** (EXODUS 24:1)
Nadab means "generous" and *Abihu* means "he's my father." They were two of Aaron's four sons. Nadab was the oldest. They were consecrated as priests after they went up into the mountain of God. But then God struck them dead because they hadn't offered incense the way they were supposed to. What a pity!

sent young Israelite men, and they offered burnt offerings and sacrificed young bulls as fellowship offerings to the LORD. ⁶Moses took half of the blood and put it in bowls, and the other half he splashed against the altar. ⁷Then he took the Book of the Covenant and read it to the people. They responded, "We will do everything the LORD has said; we will obey."

⁸Moses then took the blood, sprinkled it on the people and said, "This is the blood of the covenant that the LORD has made with you in accordance with all these words."

⁹Moses and Aaron, Nadab and Abihu, and the seventy elders of Israel went up ¹⁰and saw the God of Israel. Under his feet was something like a pavement made of lapis lazuli, as bright blue as the sky. ¹¹But God did not raise his hand against these leaders of the Israelites; they saw God, and they ate and drank.

¹²The LORD said to Moses, "Come up to me on the mountain and stay here, and I will give you the tablets of stone with the law and commandments I have written for their instruction."

¹³Then Moses set out with Joshua his aide, and Moses went up on the mountain of God. ¹⁴He said to the elders, "Wait here for us until we come back to you. Aaron and Hur are with you, and anyone involved in a dispute can go to them."

¹⁵When Moses went up on the mountain, the cloud covered it, ¹⁶and the glory of the LORD settled on Mount Sinai. For six days the cloud covered the mountain, and on the seventh day the LORD called to Moses from within the cloud. ¹⁷To the Israelites the glory of the LORD looked like a consuming fire on top of the mountain. ¹⁸Then Moses entered the cloud as he went on up the mountain. And he stayed on the mountain forty days and forty nights.

Offerings for the Tabernacle

25 The LORD said to Moses, ²"Tell the Israelites to bring me an offering. You are to receive the offering for me from everyone whose heart prompts them to give. ³These are the offerings you are to receive from them: gold, silver and bronze; ⁴blue, purple and scarlet yarn

at a distance, ²but Moses alone is to approach the LORD; the others must not come near. And the people may not come up with him."

³When Moses went and told the people all the LORD's words and laws, they responded with one voice, "Everything the LORD has said we will do." ⁴Moses then wrote down everything the LORD had said.

He got up early the next morning and built an altar at the foot of the mountain and set up twelve stone pillars representing the twelve tribes of Israel. ⁵Then he rings of this ark; they are not to be removed. [16]Then put in the ark the tablets of the covenant law, which I will give you.

[17]"Make an atonement cover of pure gold—two and a half cubits long and a cubit and a half wide. [18]And make two cherubim out of hammered gold at the ends of the cover. [19]Make one cherub on one end and the second cherub on the other; make the cherubim of one piece with the cover, at the two ends. [20]The cherubim are to have their wings spread upward, overshadowing the cover with them. The cherubim are to face each other, looking toward the cover. [21]Place the

---

[a] 5 Possibly the hides of large aquatic mammals
[b] 10 That is, a chest　　[c] 10 That is, about 3 3/4 feet long and 2 1/4 feet wide and high or about 1.1 meters long and 68 centimeters wide and high; similarly in verse 17

BREAKTHROUGH!

Anointing oil

(EXODUS 25:6)

In order to make a person or something special, to be used only for God, they poured oil over them. This meant that the Spirit of God was on that person or that object.

and fine linen; goat hair; [5]ram skins dyed red and another type of durable leather[a]; acacia wood; [6]olive oil for the light; spices for the anointing oil and for the fragrant incense; [7]and onyx stones and other gems to be mounted on the ephod and breastpiece.

[8]"Then have them make a sanctuary for me, and I will dwell among them. [9]Make this tabernacle and all its furnishings exactly like the pattern I will show you.

The Ark

[10]"Have them make an ark[b] of acacia wood—two and a half cubits long, a cubit and a half wide, and a cubit and a half high.[c] [11]Overlay it with pure gold, both inside and out, and make a gold molding around it. [12]Cast four gold rings for it and fasten them to its four feet, with two rings on one side and two rings on the other. [13]Then make poles of acacia wood and overlay them with gold. [14]Insert the poles into the rings on the sides of the ark to carry it. [15]The poles are to remain in the

BREAKTHROUGH!

Did Moses travel through the desert with the Ten Commandments?

(EXODUS 25:10-22)

Yes! Well, Moses really put them in the ark of the covenant (a wooden box covered in gold) that was in the Most Holy Place (a kind of tent where God was present). When the Israelites moved from place to place, the priests carried the box and everything that was in it. (Read Exodus 40:20-21.)

BREAKTHROUGH!

Cherubim
(EXODUS 25:18)
They are heavenly beings with wings that serve God and carry out his orders. In this case, they were cherub statues.

cover on top of the ark and put in the ark the tablets of the covenant law that I will give you. ²²There, above the cover between the two cherubim that are over the ark of the covenant law, I will meet with you and give you all my commands for the Israelites.

The Table

²³"Make a table of acacia wood—two cubits long, a cubit wide and a cubit and a half high.ᵃ ²⁴Overlay it with pure gold and make a gold molding around it. ²⁵Also make around it a rim a handbreadthᵇ wide and put a gold molding on the rim. ²⁶Make four gold rings for the table and fasten them to the four corners, where the four legs are. ²⁷The rings are to be close to the rim to hold the poles used in carrying the table. ²⁸Make the poles of acacia wood, overlay them with gold and carry the table with them. ²⁹And make its plates and dishes of pure gold, as well as its pitchers and bowls for the pouring out of offerings. ³⁰Put the bread of the Presence on this table to be before me at all times.

The Lampstand

³¹"Make a lampstand of pure gold. Hammer out its base and shaft, and make its flowerlike cups, buds and blossoms of one piece with them. ³²Six branches are to extend from the sides of the lampstand—three on one side and three on the other. ³³Three cups shaped like almond flowers with buds and blossoms are to be on one branch, three on the next branch, and the same for all six branches extending from the lampstand. ³⁴And on the lampstand there are to be four cups shaped like almond flowers with buds and blossoms. ³⁵One bud shall be under the first pair of branches extending from the lampstand, a second bud under the second pair, and a third bud under the third pair—six branches in all. ³⁶The buds and branches shall all be of one piece with the lampstand, hammered out of pure gold.

³⁷"Then make its seven lamps and set them up on it so that they light the space in front of it. ³⁸Its wick trimmers and trays are to be of pure gold. ³⁹A talentᶜ of pure gold is to be used for the lampstand and all these accessories. ⁴⁰See that you make them according to the pattern shown you on the mountain.

The Tabernacle

26 "Make the tabernacle with ten curtains of finely twisted linen and blue, purple and scarlet yarn, with cherubim woven into them by a skilled worker. ²All the curtains are to be the same size—twenty-eight cubits long and four cubits wide.ᵈ ³Join five of the curtains together, and do the same with the other five. ⁴Make loops of blue material along the edge of the end curtain in one set, and do the same with the end curtain in the other set. ⁵Make fifty loops on one curtain and fifty loops on the end curtain of the other set, with the loops opposite each other. ⁶Then make fifty gold clasps

---

ᵃ 23 That is, about 3 feet long, 1 1/2 feet wide and 2 1/4 feet high or about 90 centimeters long, 45 centimeters wide and 68 centimeters high
ᵇ 25 That is, about 3 inches or about 7.5 centimeters
ᶜ 39 That is, about 75 pounds or about 34 kilograms
ᵈ 2 That is, about 42 feet long and 6 feet wide or about 13 meters long and 1.8 meters wide

and use them to fasten the curtains together so that the tabernacle is a unit.

7 "Make curtains of goat hair for the tent over the tabernacle — eleven altogether. 8All eleven curtains are to be the same size — thirty cubits long and four cubits wide.[a] 9Join five of the curtains together into one set and the other six into another set. Fold the sixth curtain double at the front of the tent. 10Make fifty loops along the edge of the end curtain in one set and also along the edge of the end curtain in the other set. 11Then make fifty bronze clasps and put them in the loops to fasten the tent together as a unit. 12As for the additional length of the tent curtains, the half curtain that is left over is to hang down at the rear of the tabernacle. 13The tent curtains will be a cubit[b] longer on both sides; what is left will hang over the sides of the tabernacle so as to cover it. 14Make for the tent a covering of ram skins dyed red, and over that a covering of the other durable leather.[c]

15 "Make upright frames of acacia wood for the tabernacle. 16Each frame is to be ten cubits long and a cubit and a half wide,[d] 17with two projections set parallel to each other. Make all the frames of the tabernacle in this way. 18Make twenty frames for the south side of the tabernacle 19and make forty silver bases to go under them — two bases for each frame, one under each projection. 20For the other side, the north side of the tabernacle, make twenty frames 21and forty silver bases — two under each frame. 22Make six frames for the far end, that is, the west end of the tabernacle, 23and make two frames for the corners at the far end. 24At these two corners they must be double from the bottom all the way to the top and fitted into a single ring; both shall be like that. 25So there will be eight frames and sixteen silver bases — two under each frame.

26 "Also make crossbars of acacia wood: five for the frames on one side of the tabernacle, 27five for those on the other side, and five for the frames on the west, at the far end of the tabernacle. 28The center crossbar is to extend from end to end at the middle of the frames.

29Overlay the frames with gold and make gold rings to hold the crossbars. Also overlay the crossbars with gold.

30 "Set up the tabernacle according to the plan shown you on the mountain.

31 "Make a curtain of blue, purple and scarlet yarn and finely twisted linen, with cherubim woven into it by a skilled worker. 32Hang it with gold hooks on four posts of acacia wood overlaid with gold and standing on four silver bases. 33Hang the curtain from the clasps and place the ark of the covenant law behind the curtain. The curtain will separate the Holy Place from the Most Holy Place. 34Put the atonement cover on the ark of the covenant law in the Most Holy Place. 35Place the table outside the curtain on the north side of the tabernacle and put the lampstand opposite it on the south side.

36 "For the entrance to the tent make a curtain of blue, purple and scarlet yarn and finely twisted linen — the work of an embroiderer. 37Make gold hooks for this curtain and five posts of acacia wood overlaid with gold. And cast five bronze bases for them.

The Altar of Burnt Offering

27 "Build an altar of acacia wood, three cubits[e] high; it is to be square, five cubits long and five cubits wide.[f] 2Make a horn at each of the four corners, so that the horns and the altar are of one piece, and overlay the altar with bronze. 3Make all its utensils of bronze — its pots to remove the ashes, and its shovels, sprinkling bowls, meat forks and firepans. 4Make a grating for it, a bronze network, and make a bronze ring at each of the four corners of the network. 5Put it under the ledge of the altar so that it is halfway up the altar. 6Make poles of acacia wood for the altar and overlay them with bronze. 7The poles

---

a 8 That is, about 45 feet long and 6 feet wide or about 13.5 meters long and 1.8 meters wide   *b 13* That is, about 18 inches or about 45 centimeters   *c 14* Possibly the hides of large aquatic mammals (see 25:5)
d 16 That is, about 15 feet long and 2 1/4 feet wide or about 4.5 meters long and 68 centimeters wide
e 1 That is, about 4 1/2 feet or about 1.4 meters
f 1 That is, about 7 1/2 feet or about 2.3 meters long and wide

are to be inserted into the rings so they will be on two sides of the altar when it is carried. ⁸Make the altar hollow, out of boards. It is to be made just as you were shown on the mountain.

The Courtyard

⁹"Make a courtyard for the tabernacle. The south side shall be a hundred cubits^a long and is to have curtains of finely twisted linen, ¹⁰with twenty posts and twenty bronze bases and with silver hooks and bands on the posts. ¹¹The north side shall also be a hundred cubits long and is to have curtains, with twenty posts and twenty bronze bases and with silver hooks and bands on the posts.

¹²"The west end of the courtyard shall be fifty cubits^b wide and have curtains, with ten posts and ten bases. ¹³On the east end, toward the sunrise, the courtyard shall also be fifty cubits wide. ¹⁴Curtains fifteen cubits^c long are to be on one side of the entrance, with three posts and three bases, ¹⁵and curtains fifteen cubits long are to be on the other side, with three posts and three bases.

¹⁶"For the entrance to the courtyard, provide a curtain twenty cubits^d long, of blue, purple and scarlet yarn and finely twisted linen — the work of an embroiderer — with four posts and four bases. ¹⁷All the posts around the courtyard are to have silver bands and hooks, and bronze bases. ¹⁸The courtyard shall be a hundred cubits long and fifty cubits wide,^e with curtains of finely twisted linen five cubits^f high, and with bronze bases. ¹⁹All the other articles used in the service of the tabernacle, whatever their function, including all the tent pegs for it and those for the courtyard, are to be of bronze.

Oil for the Lampstand

²⁰"Command the Israelites to bring you clear oil of pressed olives for the light so that the lamps may be kept burning. ²¹In the tent of meeting, outside the curtain that shields the ark of the covenant law, Aaron and his sons are to keep the lamps burning before the Lord from evening till morning. This is to be a lasting ordinance

among the Israelites for the generations to come.

The Priestly Garments

28 "Have Aaron your brother brought to you from among the Israelites, along with his sons Nadab and Abihu, Eleazar and Ithamar, so they may serve me as priests. ²Make sacred garments for your brother Aaron to give him dignity and honor. ³Tell all the skilled workers to whom I have given wisdom in such matters that they are to make garments for Aaron, for his consecration, so he may serve me as priest. ⁴These are the garments they are to make: a breastpiece, an ephod, a robe, a woven tunic, a turban and a sash. They are to make these sacred garments for your brother Aaron and his sons, so they may serve me as priests. ⁵Have them use gold, and blue, purple and scarlet yarn, and fine linen.

The Ephod

⁶"Make the ephod of gold, and of blue, purple and scarlet yarn, and of finely twisted linen — the work of skilled hands. ⁷It is to have two shoulder pieces attached to two of its corners, so it can be fastened. ⁸Its skillfully woven waistband is to be like it — of one piece with the ephod and made with gold, and with blue, purple and scarlet yarn, and with finely twisted linen.

⁹"Take two onyx stones and engrave on them the names of the sons of Israel ¹⁰in the order of their birth — six names on one stone and the remaining six on the other. ¹¹Engrave the names of the sons of Israel on the two stones the way a gem cutter engraves a seal. Then mount the stones in gold filigree settings ¹²and fasten them on the shoulder pieces of the ephod as memorial stones for the sons of Israel. Aaron is to bear the names on his shoulders as a memorial before the Lord.

---

^a 9 That is, about 150 feet or about 45 meters; also in verse 11   ^b 12 That is, about 75 feet or about 23 meters; also in verse 13   ^c 14 That is, about 23 feet or about 6.8 meters; also in verse 15   ^d 16 That is, about 30 feet or about 9 meters   ^e 18 That is, about 150 feet long and 75 feet wide or about 45 meters long and 23 meters wide   ^f 18 That is, about 7 1/2 feet or about 2.3 meters

13Make gold filigree settings 14and two braided chains of pure gold, like a rope, and attach the chains to the settings.

The Breastpiece

15"Fashion a breastpiece for making decisions — the work of skilled hands. Make it like the ephod: of gold, and of blue, purple and scarlet yarn, and of finely twisted linen. 16It is to be square — a span*a* long and a span wide — and folded double. 17Then mount four rows of precious stones on it. The first row shall be carnelian, chrysolite and beryl; 18the second row shall be turquoise, lapis lazuli and emerald; 19the third row shall be jacinth, agate and amethyst; 20the fourth row shall be topaz, onyx and jasper.*b* Mount them in gold filigree settings. 21There are to be twelve stones, one for each of the names of the sons of Israel, each engraved like a seal with the name of one of the twelve tribes.

22"For the breastpiece make braided chains of pure gold, like a rope. 23Make two gold rings for it and fasten them to two corners of the breastpiece. 24Fasten the two gold chains to the rings at the corners of the breastpiece, 25and the other ends of the chains to the two settings, attaching them to the shoulder pieces of the ephod at the front. 26Make two gold rings and attach them to the other two corners of the breastpiece on the inside edge next to the ephod. 27Make two more gold rings and attach them to the bottom of the shoulder pieces on the front of the ephod, close to the seam just above the waistband of the ephod. 28The rings of the breastpiece are to be tied to the rings of the ephod with blue cord, connecting it to the waistband, so that the breastpiece will not swing out from the ephod.

29"Whenever Aaron enters the Holy Place, he will bear the names of the sons of Israel over his heart on the breastpiece of decision as a continuing memorial before the Lord. 30Also put the Urim and the Thummim in the breastpiece, so they may be over Aaron's heart whenever he enters the presence of the Lord. Thus Aaron will always bear the means of

BREAKTHROUGH!

Urim and Thummim
(EXODUS 28:30)
They were two stones that God used to make his will known. When it was hard to decide something, the Israelites tossed the stones like we throw dice. Then they considered the result to be God's will in the matter.

making decisions for the Israelites over his heart before the Lord.

Other Priestly Garments

31"Make the robe of the ephod entirely of blue cloth, 32with an opening for the head in its center. There shall be a woven edge like a collar*c* around this opening, so that it will not tear. 33Make pomegranates of blue, purple and scarlet yarn around the hem of the robe, with gold bells between them. 34The gold bells and the pomegranates are to alternate around the hem of the robe. 35Aaron must wear it when he ministers. The sound of the bells will be heard when he enters the Holy Place before the Lord and when he comes out, so that he will not die.

36"Make a plate of pure gold and engrave on it as on a seal: HOLY TO THE LORD.

---

a 16 That is, about 9 inches or about 23 centimeters   *b* 20 The precise identification of some of these precious stones is uncertain.   *c* 32 The meaning of the Hebrew for this word is uncertain.

37 Fasten a blue cord to it to attach it to the turban; it is to be on the front of the turban. 38 It will be on Aaron's forehead, and he will bear the guilt involved in the sacred gifts the Israelites consecrate, whatever their gifts may be. It will be on Aaron's forehead continually so that they will be acceptable to the LORD. 39 "Weave the tunic of fine linen and make the turban of fine linen. The sash is to be the work of an embroiderer. 40 Make tunics, sashes and caps for Aaron's sons to give them dignity and honor. 41 After you put these clothes on your brother Aaron and his sons, anoint and ordain them. Consecrate them so they may serve me as priests.

42 "Make linen undergarments as a covering for the body, reaching from the waist to the thigh. 43 Aaron and his sons must wear them whenever they enter the tent of meeting or approach the altar to minister in the Holy Place, so that they will not incur guilt and die.

"This is to be a lasting ordinance for Aaron and his descendants.

Consecration of the Priests

29 "This is what you are to do to consecrate them, so they may serve me as priests: Take a young bull and two rams without defect. 2 And from the finest wheat flour make round loaves without yeast, thick loaves without yeast and with olive oil mixed in, and thin loaves without yeast and brushed with olive oil. 3 Put them in a basket and present them along with the bull and the two rams. 4 Then bring Aaron and his sons to the entrance to the tent of meeting and wash them with water. 5 Take the garments and dress Aaron with the tunic, the robe of the ephod, the ephod itself and the breastpiece. Fasten the ephod on him by its skillfully woven waistband. 6 Put the turban on his head and attach the sacred emblem to the turban. 7 Take the anointing oil and anoint him by pouring it on his head. 8 Bring his sons and dress them in tunics 9 and fasten caps on them. Then tie sashes on Aaron and his sons.ᵃ The priesthood is theirs by a lasting ordinance.

"Then you shall ordain Aaron and his sons.

10 "Bring the bull to the front of the tent of meeting, and Aaron and his sons shall lay their hands on its head. 11 Slaughter it in the LORD's presence at the entrance to the tent of meeting. 12 Take some of the bull's blood and put it on the horns of the altar with your finger, and pour out the rest of it at the base of the altar. 13 Then take all the fat on the internal organs, the long lobe of the liver, and both kidneys with the fat on them, and burn them on the altar. 14 But burn the bull's flesh and its hide and its intestines outside the camp. It is a sin offering.ᵇ

15 "Take one of the rams, and Aaron and his sons shall lay their hands on its head. 16 Slaughter it and take the blood and splash it against the sides of the altar. 17 Cut the ram into pieces and wash the internal organs and the legs, putting them with the head and the other pieces. 18 Then burn the entire ram on the altar. It is a burnt offering to the LORD, a pleasing aroma, a food offering presented to the LORD.

19 "Take the other ram, and Aaron and his sons shall lay their hands on its head. 20 Slaughter it, take some of its blood and put it on the lobes of the right ears of Aaron and his sons, on the thumbs of their right hands, and on the big toes of their right feet. Then splash blood against the sides of the altar. 21 And take some blood from the altar and some of the anointing oil and sprinkle it on Aaron and his garments and on his sons and their garments. Then he and his sons and their garments will be consecrated.

22 "Take from this ram the fat, the fat tail, the fat on the internal organs, the long lobe of the liver, both kidneys with the fat on them, and the right thigh. (This is the ram for the ordination.) 23 From the basket of bread made without yeast, which is before the LORD, take one round loaf, one thick loaf with olive oil mixed in, and one thin loaf. 24 Put all these in the hands of Aaron and his sons and have them wave them before the LORD as a

---

ᵃ 9 Hebrew; Septuagint on them   ᵇ 14 Or purification offering; also in verse 36 wave offering. ²⁵Then take them from their hands and burn them on the altar along with the burnt offering for a pleasing aroma to the LORD, a food offering presented to the LORD. ²⁶After you take the breast of the ram for Aaron's ordination, wave it before the LORD as a wave offering, and it will be your share.

²⁷"Consecrate those parts of the ordination ram that belong to Aaron and his sons: the breast that was waved and the thigh that was presented. ²⁸This is always to be the perpetual share from the Israelites for Aaron and his sons. It is the contribution the Israelites are to make to the LORD from their fellowship offerings.

²⁹"Aaron's sacred garments will belong to his descendants so that they can be anointed and ordained in them. ³⁰The son who succeeds him as priest and comes to the tent of meeting to minister in the Holy Place is to wear them seven days.

³¹"Take the ram for the ordination and cook the meat in a sacred place. ³²At the entrance to the tent of meeting, Aaron and his sons are to eat the meat of the ram and the bread that is in the basket. ³³They are to eat these offerings by which atonement was made for their ordination and consecration. But no one else may eat them, because they are sacred. ³⁴And if any of the meat of the ordination ram or any bread is left over till morning, burn it up. It must not be eaten, because it is sacred.

³⁵"Do for Aaron and his sons everything I have commanded you, taking seven days to ordain them. ³⁶Sacrifice a bull each day as a sin offering to make atonement. Purify the altar by making atonement for it, and anoint it to consecrate it. ³⁷For seven days make atonement for the altar and consecrate it. Then the altar will be most holy, and whatever touches it will be holy.

³⁸"This is what you are to offer on the altar regularly each day: two lambs a year old. ³⁹Offer one in the morning and the other at twilight. ⁴⁰With the first lamb offer a tenth of an ephah*ᵃ* of the finest flour mixed with a quarter of a hin*ᵇ* of oil from pressed olives, and a quarter of a hin of wine as a drink offering. ⁴¹Sacrifice the other lamb at twilight with the same grain offering and its drink offering as in the morning—a pleasing aroma, a food offering presented to the LORD.

⁴²"For the generations to come this burnt offering is to be made regularly at the entrance to the tent of meeting, before the LORD. There I will meet you and speak to you; ⁴³there also I will meet with the Israelites, and the place will be consecrated by my glory.

⁴⁴"So I will consecrate the tent of meeting and the altar and will consecrate Aaron and his sons to serve me as priests. ⁴⁵Then I will dwell among the Israelites and be their God. ⁴⁶They will know that I am the LORD their God, who brought them out of Egypt so that I might dwell among them. I am the LORD their God.

The Altar of Incense

30 "Make an altar of acacia wood for burning incense. ²It is to be square, a cubit long and a cubit wide, and two cubits high*ᶜ*—its horns of one piece with it. ³Overlay the top and all the sides and the horns with pure gold, and make a gold molding around it. ⁴Make two gold rings for the altar below the molding—two on each of the opposite sides—to hold the poles used to carry it. ⁵Make the poles of acacia wood and overlay them with gold. ⁶Put the altar in front of the curtain that shields the ark of the covenant law—before the atonement cover that is over the tablets of the covenant law—where I will meet with you.

⁷"Aaron must burn fragrant incense on the altar every morning when he tends the lamps. ⁸He must burn incense again when he lights the lamps at twilight so incense will burn regularly before the LORD for the generations to come. ⁹Do not offer on this altar any other incense or any burnt offering or grain offering, and do not pour a drink offering on it. ¹⁰Once a year Aaron shall make atonement on its horns. This annual atonement must be made with the blood of the atoning sin offering*ᵈ*

ᵃ 40 That is, probably about 3 1/2 pounds or about 1.6 kilograms   *ᵇ 40* That is, probably about 1 quart or about 1 liter   *ᶜ 2* That is, about 1 1/2 feet long and wide and 3 feet high or about 45 centimeters long and wide and 90 centimeters high   *ᵈ 10* Or *purification offering*

BREAKTHROUGH!

Sacrifices and offerings
(EXODUS 29-30)

These are special things offered to God to show adoration or thankfulness for everything he gives us. A sacrifice was when an animal was killed and presented to God, but offerings could be grains, wine, oil, incense and salt.

for the generations to come. It is most holy to the LORD."

Atonement Money

¹¹Then the LORD said to Moses, ¹²"When you take a census of the Israelites to count them, each one must pay the LORD a ransom for his life at the time he is counted. Then no plague will come on them when you number them. ¹³Each one who crosses over to those already counted is to give a half shekel,ᵃ according to the sanctuary shekel, which weighs twenty gerahs. This half shekel is an offering to the LORD. ¹⁴All who cross over, those twenty years old or more, are to give an offering to the LORD. ¹⁵The rich are not to give more than a half shekel and the poor are not to give less when you make the offering to the LORD to atone for your lives. ¹⁶Receive the atonement money from the Israelites and use

it for the service of the tent of meeting. It will be a memorial for the Israelites before the LORD, making atonement for your lives."

Basin for Washing

¹⁷Then the LORD said to Moses, ¹⁸"Make a bronze basin, with its bronze stand, for washing. Place it between the tent of meeting and the altar, and put water in it. ¹⁹Aaron and his sons are to wash their hands and feet with water from it. ²⁰Whenever they enter the tent of meeting, they shall wash with water so that they will not die. Also, when they approach the altar to minister by presenting a food offering to the LORD, ²¹they shall wash their hands and feet so that they will not die. This is to be a lasting ordinance for Aaron and his descendants for the generations to come."

Anointing Oil

²²Then the LORD said to Moses, ²³"Take the following fine spices: 500 shekelsᵇ of liquid myrrh, half as much (that is, 250 shekels) of fragrant cinnamon, 250 shekelsᶜ of fragrant calamus, ²⁴500 shekels of cassia—all according to the sanctuary shekel—and a hinᵈ of olive oil. ²⁵Make these into a sacred anointing oil, a fragrant blend, the work of a perfumer. It will be the sacred anointing oil. ²⁶Then use it to anoint the tent of meeting, the ark of the covenant law, ²⁷the table and all its articles, the lampstand and its accessories, the altar of incense, ²⁸the altar of burnt offering and all its utensils, and the basin with its stand. ²⁹You shall consecrate them so they will be most holy, and whatever touches them will be holy.

³⁰"Anoint Aaron and his sons and consecrate them so they may serve me as priests. ³¹Say to the Israelites, 'This is to be my sacred anointing oil for the generations to come. ³²Do not pour it on anyone else's body and do not make any other

---

ᵃ 13 That is, about 1/5 ounce or about 5.8 grams; also in verse 15   ᵇ 23 That is, about 12 1/2 pounds or about 5.8 kilograms; also in verse 24   ᶜ 23 That is, about 6 1/4 pounds or about 2.9 kilograms   ᵈ 24 That is, probably about 1 gallon or about 3.8 liters oil using the same formula. It is sacred, and you are to consider it sacred. [33]Whoever makes perfume like it and puts it on anyone other than a priest must be cut off from their people.' "

Incense

[34]Then the LORD said to Moses, "Take fragrant spices—gum resin, onycha and galbanum—and pure frankincense, all in equal amounts, [35]and make a fragrant blend of incense, the work of a perfumer. It is to be salted and pure and sacred. [36]Grind some of it to powder and place it in front of the ark of the covenant law in the tent of meeting, where I will meet with you. It shall be most holy to you. [37]Do not make any incense with this formula; consider it holy to the LORD. [38]Whoever makes incense like it to enjoy its fragrance must be cut off from their people."

Bezalel and Oholiab

31 Then the LORD said to Moses, [2]"See, I have chosen Bezalel son of Uri, the son of Hur, of the tribe of Judah, [3]and I have filled him with the Spirit of God, with wisdom, with understanding, with knowledge and with all kinds of skills— [4]to make artistic designs for work in gold, silver and bronze, [5]to cut and set stones, to work in wood, and to engage in all kinds of crafts. [6]Moreover, I have appointed Oholiab son of Ahisamak, of the tribe of Dan, to help him. Also I have given ability to all the skilled workers to make everything I have commanded you: [7]the tent of meeting, the ark of the covenant law with the atonement cover on it, and all the other furnishings of the tent— [8]the table and its articles, the pure gold lampstand and all its accessories, the altar of incense, [9]the altar of burnt offering and all its utensils, the basin with its stand— [10]and also the woven garments, both the sacred garments for Aaron the priest and the garments for his sons when they serve as priests, [11]and the anointing oil and fragrant incense for the Holy Place. They are to make them just as I commanded you."

The Sabbath

[12]Then the LORD said to Moses, [13]"Say to the Israelites, 'You must observe my Sabbaths. This will be a sign between me and you for the generations to come, so you may know that I am the LORD, who makes you holy.

[14]" 'Observe the Sabbath, because it is holy to you. Anyone who desecrates it is to be put to death; those who do any work on that day must be cut off from their people. [15]For six days work is to be done, but the seventh day is a day of sabbath rest, holy to the LORD. Whoever does any work on the Sabbath day is to be put to death. [16]The Israelites are to observe the Sabbath, celebrating it for the generations to come as a lasting covenant. [17]It will be a sign between me and the Israelites forever, for in six days the LORD made the heavens and the earth, and on the seventh day he rested and was refreshed.' "

[18]When the LORD finished speaking to Moses on Mount Sinai, he gave him the two tablets of the covenant law, the tablets of stone inscribed by the finger of God.

The Golden Calf

32 When the people saw that Moses was so long in coming down from the mountain, they gathered around Aaron and said, "Come, make us gods[a] who will go before us. As for this fellow Moses who brought us up out of Egypt, we don't know what has happened to him."

[2]Aaron answered them, "Take off the gold earrings that your wives, your sons and your daughters are wearing, and bring them to me." [3]So all the people took off their earrings and brought them to Aaron. [4]He took what they handed him and made it into an idol cast in the shape of a calf, fashioning it with a tool. Then they said, "These are your gods,[b] Israel, who brought you up out of Egypt."

[5]When Aaron saw this, he built an altar in front of the calf and announced, "Tomorrow there will be a festival to the LORD." [6]So the next day the people rose early and sacrificed burnt offerings and

---

a 1 Or a god; also in verses 23 and 31   *b 4 Or This is your god; also in verse 8* presented fellowship offerings. Afterward they sat down to eat and drink and got up to indulge in revelry.

⁷Then the LORD said to Moses, "Go down, because your people, whom you brought up out of Egypt, have become corrupt. ⁸They have been quick to turn away from what I commanded them and have made themselves an idol cast in the shape of a calf. They have bowed down to it and sacrificed to it and have said, 'These are your gods, Israel, who brought you up out of Egypt.'

⁹"I have seen these people," the LORD said to Moses, "and they are a stiff-necked people. ¹⁰Now leave me alone so that my anger may burn against them and that I may destroy them. Then I will make you into a great nation."

¹¹But Moses sought the favor of the LORD his God. "LORD," he said, "why should your anger burn against your people, whom you brought out of Egypt with great power and a mighty hand? ¹²Why should the Egyptians say, 'It was with evil intent that he brought them out, to kill them in the mountains and to wipe them off the face of the earth'? Turn from your fierce anger; relent and do not bring disaster on your people. ¹³Remember your servants Abraham, Isaac and Israel, to whom you swore by your own self: 'I will make your descendants as numerous as the stars in the sky and I will give your descendants all this land I promised them, and it will be their inheritance forever.'" ¹⁴Then the LORD relented and did not bring on his people the disaster he had threatened.

¹⁵Moses turned and went down the mountain with the two tablets of the covenant law in his hands. They were inscribed on both sides, front and back. ¹⁶The tablets were the work of God; the writing was the writing of God, engraved on the tablets.

¹⁷When Joshua heard the noise of the people shouting, he said to Moses, "There is the sound of war in the camp."

¹⁸Moses replied:

"It is not the sound of victory,
    it is not the sound of defeat;
    it is the sound of singing that I hear."

¹⁹When Moses approached the camp and saw the calf and the dancing, his anger burned and he threw the tablets out of his hands, breaking them to pieces at the foot of the mountain. ²⁰And he took the calf the people had made and burned it in the fire; then he ground it to powder, scattered it on the water and made the Israelites drink it.

²¹He said to Aaron, "What did these people do to you, that you led them into such great sin?"

²²"Do not be angry, my lord," Aaron answered. "You know how prone these people are to evil. ²³They said to me, 'Make us gods who will go before us. As for this fellow Moses who brought us up out of Egypt, we don't know what has happened to him.' ²⁴So I told them, 'Whoever has any gold jewelry, take it off.' Then they gave me the gold, and I threw it into the fire, and out came this calf!"

²⁵Moses saw that the people were running wild and that Aaron had let them get out of control and so become a laughingstock to their enemies. ²⁶So he stood at the entrance to the camp and said, "Whoever is for the LORD, come to me." And all the Levites rallied to him.

²⁷Then he said to them, "This is what the LORD, the God of Israel, says: 'Each man strap a sword to his side. Go back and forth through the camp from one end to the other, each killing his brother and friend and neighbor.'" ²⁸The Levites did as Moses commanded, and that day about three thousand of the people died. ²⁹Then Moses said, "You have been set apart to the LORD today, for you were against your own sons and brothers, and he has blessed you this day."

³⁰The next day Moses said to the people, "You have committed a great sin. But now I will go up to the LORD; perhaps I can make atonement for your sin."

³¹So Moses went back to the LORD and said, "Oh, what a great sin these people have committed! They have made themselves gods of gold. ³²But now, please forgive their sin—but if not, then blot me out of the book you have written."

³³The LORD replied to Moses, "Whoever has sinned against me I will blot out of

my book. [34]Now go, lead the people to the place I spoke of, and my angel will go before you. However, when the time comes for me to punish, I will punish them for their sin."

[35]And the Lord struck the people with a plague because of what they did with the calf Aaron had made.

33 Then the Lord said to Moses, "Leave this place, you and the people you brought up out of Egypt, and go up to the land I promised on oath to Abraham, Isaac and Jacob, saying, 'I will give it to your descendants.' [2]I will send an angel before you and drive out the Canaanites, Amorites, Hittites, Perizzites, Hivites and Jebusites. [3]Go up to the land flowing with milk and honey. But I will not go with you, because you are a stiff-necked people and I might destroy you on the way."

[4]When the people heard these distressing words, they began to mourn and no one put on any ornaments. [5]For the Lord had said to Moses, "Tell the Israelites, 'You are a stiff-necked people. If I were to go with you even for a moment, I might destroy you. Now take off your ornaments and I will decide what to do with you.' " [6]So the Israelites stripped off their ornaments at Mount Horeb.

The Tent of Meeting

[7]Now Moses used to take a tent and pitch it outside the camp some distance away, calling it the "tent of meeting." Anyone inquiring of the Lord would go to the tent of meeting outside the camp. [8]And whenever Moses went out to the tent, all the people rose and stood at the entrances to their tents, watching Moses until he entered the tent. [9]As Moses went into the tent, the pillar of cloud would come down and stay at the entrance, while the Lord spoke with Moses. [10]Whenever the people saw the pillar of cloud standing at the entrance to the tent, they all stood and worshiped, each at the entrance to their tent. [11]The Lord would speak to Moses face to face, as one speaks to a friend. Then Moses would return to the camp, but his young aide Joshua son of Nun did not leave the tent.

Moses and the Glory of the Lord

[12]Moses said to the Lord, "You have been telling me, 'Lead these people,' but you have not let me know whom you will send with me. You have said, 'I know you by name and you have found favor with me.' [13]If you are pleased with me, teach me your ways so I may know you and continue to find favor with you. Remember that this nation is your people."

[14]The Lord replied, "My Presence will go with you, and I will give you rest."

[15]Then Moses said to him, "If your Presence does not go with us, do not send us up from here. [16]How will anyone know that you are pleased with me and with your people unless you go with us? What else will distinguish me and your people from all the other people on the face of the earth?"

[17]And the Lord said to Moses, "I will do the very thing you have asked, because I am pleased with you and I know you by name."

[18]Then Moses said, "Now show me your glory."

[19]And the Lord said, "I will cause all my goodness to pass in front of you, and I will proclaim my name, the Lord, in your presence. I will have mercy on whom I will have mercy, and I will have compassion on whom I will have compassion. [20]But," he said, "you cannot see my face, for no one may see me and live."

[21]Then the Lord said, "There is a place near me where you may stand on a rock. [22]When my glory passes by, I will put you in a cleft in the rock and cover you with my hand until I have passed by. [23]Then I will remove my hand and you will see my back; but my face must not be seen."

The New Stone Tablets

34 The Lord said to Moses, "Chisel out two stone tablets like the first ones, and I will write on them the words that were on the first tablets, which you broke. [2]Be ready in the morning, and then come up on Mount Sinai. Present yourself to me there on top of the mountain. [3]No one is to come with you or be seen anywhere on the mountain; not even the flocks and herds may graze in front of the mountain."

⁴So Moses chiseled out two stone tablets like the first ones and went up Mount Sinai early in the morning, as the LORD had commanded him; and he carried the two stone tablets in his hands. ⁵Then the LORD came down in the cloud and stood there with him and proclaimed his name, the LORD. ⁶And he passed in front of Moses, proclaiming, "The LORD, the LORD, the compassionate and gracious God, slow to anger, abounding in love and faithfulness, ⁷maintaining love to thousands, and forgiving wickedness, rebellion and sin. Yet he does not leave the guilty unpunished; he punishes the children and their children for the sin of the parents to the third and fourth generation."

⁸Moses bowed to the ground at once and worshiped. ⁹"Lord," he said, "if I have found favor in your eyes, then let the Lord go with us. Although this is a stiff-necked people, forgive our wickedness and our sin, and take us as your inheritance."

¹⁰Then the LORD said: "I am making a covenant with you. Before all your people I will do wonders never before done in any nation in all the world. The people you live among will see how awesome is the work that I, the LORD, will do for you. ¹¹Obey what I command you today. I will drive out before you the Amorites, Canaanites, Hittites, Perizzites, Hivites and Jebusites. ¹²Be careful not to make a treaty with those who live in the land where you are going, or they will be a snare among you. ¹³Break down their altars, smash their sacred stones and cut down their Asherah poles.ᵃ ¹⁴Do not worship any other god, for the LORD, whose name is Jealous, is a jealous God.

¹⁵"Be careful not to make a treaty with those who live in the land; for when they prostitute themselves to their gods and sacrifice to them, they will invite you and you will eat their sacrifices. ¹⁶And when you choose some of their daughters as wives for your sons and those daughters prostitute themselves to their gods, they will lead your sons to do the same.

¹⁷"Do not make any idols.

¹⁸"Celebrate the Festival of Unleavened Bread. For seven days eat bread made without yeast, as I commanded you. Do this at the appointed time in the month of Aviv, for in that month you came out of Egypt.

¹⁹"The first offspring of every womb belongs to me, including all the firstborn males of your livestock, whether from herd or flock. ²⁰Redeem the firstborn donkey with a lamb, but if you do not redeem it, break its neck. Redeem all your firstborn sons.

"No one is to appear before me empty-handed.

²¹"Six days you shall labor, but on the seventh day you shall rest; even during the plowing season and harvest you must rest.

²²"Celebrate the Festival of Weeks with the firstfruits of the wheat harvest, and the Festival of Ingathering at the turn of the year.ᵇ ²³Three times a year all your men are to appear before the Sovereign LORD, the God of Israel. ²⁴I will drive out nations before you and enlarge your territory, and no one will covet your land when you go up three times each year to appear before the LORD your God.

²⁵"Do not offer the blood of a sacrifice to me along with anything containing yeast, and do not let any of the sacrifice from the Passover Festival remain until morning.

²⁶"Bring the best of the firstfruits of your soil to the house of the LORD your God.

"Do not cook a young goat in its mother's milk."

²⁷Then the LORD said to Moses, "Write down these words, for in accordance with these words I have made a covenant with you and with Israel." ²⁸Moses was there with the LORD forty days and forty nights without eating bread or drinking water. And he wrote on the tablets the words of the covenant—the Ten Commandments.

The Radiant Face of Moses

²⁹When Moses came down from Mount Sinai with the two tablets of the covenant

---

ᵃ 13 That is, wooden symbols of the goddess Asherah
ᵇ 22 That is, in the autumn

law in his hands, he was not aware that his face was radiant because he had spoken with the Lord. 30When Aaron and all the Israelites saw Moses, his face was radiant, and they were afraid to come near him. 31But Moses called to them; so Aaron and all the leaders of the community came back to him, and he spoke to them. 32Afterward all the Israelites came near him, and he gave them all the commands the Lord had given him on Mount Sinai.

33When Moses finished speaking to them, he put a veil over his face. 34But whenever he entered the Lord's presence to speak with him, he removed the veil until he came out. And when he came out and told the Israelites what he had been

BREAKTHROUGH!

Festival of Ingathering
(EXODUS 34:22)

This is a one-week celebration in the fall, from the 15th to the 21st of the month of Ethanim, which was the seventh month in the Hebrew calendar. That means it was from the middle of September to the middle of October in our solar calendar. The Israelites celebrated this feast to remember the time when they were slaves in Egypt, as well as their freedom and the years they spent wandering in the desert. An ingathering was a very simple hut made with some rather weak poles and a few branches that served as the walls and roof. The people had to live in these huts during the seven days of the celebration. That was how they showed other nations that they were a people who depended entirely on God and not on the things they had.

BREAKTHROUGH!

Festival of Weeks
(EXODUS 34:22)

This celebration was in the spring, on the 6th day of the month of Sivan. That was the third month in the Hebrew calendar, so it was from the middle of May to the middle of June in our solar calendar. In the Greek language, this celebration was called *Pentecost* because *pentecostós* means fiftieth. It was celebrated fifty days after the barley harvest had begun, and that was just at the end of the wheat harvest. It was a celebration to give thanks to God for the blessing of a good harvest.

commanded, 35they saw that his face was radiant. Then Moses would put the veil back over his face until he went in to speak with the Lord.

Sabbath Regulations

35 Moses assembled the whole Israelite community and said to them, "These are the things the Lord has commanded you to do: 2For six days, work is to be done, but the seventh day shall be your holy day, a day of sabbath rest to the Lord. Whoever does any work on it is to be put to death. ³Do not light a fire in any of your dwellings on the Sabbath day."

Materials for the Tabernacle

⁴Moses said to the whole Israelite community, "This is what the Lord has commanded: ⁵From what you have, take an offering for the Lord. Everyone who is willing is to bring to the Lord an offering of gold, silver and bronze; ⁶blue, purple and scarlet yarn and fine linen; goat hair; ⁷ram skins dyed red and another type of durable leather*a*; acacia wood; ⁸olive oil for the light; spices for the anointing oil and for the fragrant incense; ⁹and onyx stones and other gems to be mounted on the ephod and breastpiece.

¹⁰"All who are skilled among you are to come and make everything the Lord has commanded: ¹¹the tabernacle with its tent and its covering, clasps, frames, crossbars, posts and bases; ¹²the ark with its poles and the atonement cover and the curtain that shields it; ¹³the table with its poles and all its articles and the bread of the Presence; ¹⁴the lampstand that is for light with its accessories, lamps and oil for the light; ¹⁵the altar of incense with its poles, the anointing oil and the fragrant incense; the curtain for the doorway at the entrance to the tabernacle; ¹⁶the altar of burnt offering with its bronze grating, its poles and all its utensils; the bronze basin with its stand; ¹⁷the curtains of the courtyard with its posts and bases, and the curtain for the entrance to the courtyard; ¹⁸the tent pegs for the tabernacle and for the courtyard, and their ropes; ¹⁹the woven garments worn for ministering in the sanctuary—both the sacred garments for Aaron the priest and the garments for his sons when they serve as priests."

²⁰Then the whole Israelite community withdrew from Moses' presence, ²¹and everyone who was willing and whose heart moved them came and brought an offering to the Lord for the work on the tent of meeting, for all its service, and for the sacred garments. ²²All who were willing,

men and women alike, came and brought gold jewelry of all kinds: brooches, earrings, rings and ornaments. They all presented their gold as a wave offering to the Lord. ²³Everyone who had blue, purple or scarlet yarn or fine linen, or goat hair, ram skins dyed red or the other durable leather brought them. ²⁴Those presenting an offering of silver or bronze brought it as an offering to the Lord, and everyone who had acacia wood for any part of the work brought it. ²⁵Every skilled woman spun with her hands and brought what she had spun—blue, purple or scarlet yarn or fine linen. ²⁶And all the women who were willing and had the skill spun the goat hair. ²⁷The leaders brought onyx stones and other gems to be mounted on the ephod and breastpiece. ²⁸They also brought spices and olive oil for the light and for the anointing oil and for the fragrant incense. ²⁹All the Israelite men and women who were willing brought to the Lord freewill offerings for all the work the Lord through Moses had commanded them to do.

Bezalel and Oholiab

³⁰Then Moses said to the Israelites, "See, the Lord has chosen Bezalel son of Uri, the son of Hur, of the tribe of Judah, ³¹and he has filled him with the Spirit of God, with wisdom, with understanding, with knowledge and with all kinds of skills— ³²to make artistic designs for work in gold, silver and bronze, ³³to cut and set stones, to work in wood and to engage in all kinds of artistic crafts. ³⁴And he has given both him and Oholiab son of Ahisamak, of the tribe of Dan, the ability to teach others. ³⁵He has filled them with skill to do all kinds of work as engravers, designers, embroiderers in blue, purple and scarlet yarn and fine linen, and weavers—all of them skilled workers and **36** designers. ¹So Bezalel, Oholiab and every skilled person to whom the Lord has given skill and ability to know how to carry out all the work of constructing the sanctuary are to do the work just as the Lord has commanded."

---

a 7 Possibly the hides of large aquatic mammals; also in verse 23

[2]Then Moses summoned Bezalel and Oholiab and every skilled person to whom the LORD had given ability and who was willing to come and do the work. [3]They received from Moses all the offerings the Israelites had brought to carry out the work of constructing the sanctuary. And the people continued to bring freewill offerings morning after morning. [4]So all the skilled workers who were doing all the work on the sanctuary left what they were doing [5]and said to Moses, "The people are bringing more than enough for doing the work the LORD commanded to be done."

[6]Then Moses gave an order and they sent this word throughout the camp: "No man or woman is to make anything else as an offering for the sanctuary." And so the people were restrained from bringing more, [7]because what they already had was more than enough to do all the work.

The Tabernacle

[8]All those who were skilled among the workers made the tabernacle with ten curtains of finely twisted linen and blue, purple and scarlet yarn, with cherubim woven into them by expert hands. [9]All the curtains were the same size—twenty-eight cubits long and four cubits wide.[a] [10]They joined five of the curtains together and did the same with the other five. [11]Then they made loops of blue material along the edge of the end curtain in one set, and the same was done with the end curtain in the other set. [12]They also made fifty loops on one curtain and fifty loops on the end curtain of the other set, with the loops opposite each other. [13]Then they made fifty gold clasps and used them to fasten the two sets of curtains together so that the tabernacle was a unit.

[14]They made curtains of goat hair for the tent over the tabernacle—eleven altogether. [15]All eleven curtains were the same size—thirty cubits long and four cubits wide.[b] [16]They joined five of the curtains into one set and the other six into another set. [17]Then they made fifty loops along the edge of the end curtain in one set and also along the edge of the end curtain in the other set. [18]They made fifty bronze clasps to fasten the tent together

as a unit. [19]Then they made for the tent a covering of ram skins dyed red, and over that a covering of the other durable leather.[c]

[20]They made upright frames of acacia wood for the tabernacle. [21]Each frame was ten cubits long and a cubit and a half wide,[d] [22]with two projections set parallel to each other. They made all the frames of the tabernacle in this way. [23]They made twenty frames for the south side of the tabernacle [24]and made forty silver bases to go under them—two bases for each frame, one under each projection. [25]For the other side, the north side of the tabernacle, they made twenty frames [26]and forty silver bases—two under each frame. [27]They made six frames for the far end, that is, the west end of the tabernacle, [28]and two frames were made for the corners of the tabernacle at the far end. [29]At these two corners the frames were double from the bottom all the way to the top and fitted into a single ring; both were made alike. [30]So there were eight frames and sixteen silver bases—two under each frame.

[31]They also made crossbars of acacia wood: five for the frames on one side of the tabernacle, [32]five for those on the other side, and five for the frames on the west, at the far end of the tabernacle. [33]They made the center crossbar so that it extended from end to end at the middle of the frames. [34]They overlaid the frames with gold and made gold rings to hold the crossbars. They also overlaid the crossbars with gold.

[35]They made the curtain of blue, purple and scarlet yarn and finely twisted linen, with cherubim woven into it by a skilled worker. [36]They made four posts of acacia wood for it and overlaid them with gold. They made gold hooks for them and cast their four silver bases. [37]For the entrance to the tent they made a curtain of blue, purple and scarlet yarn and finely twisted

---

a 9 That is, about 42 feet long and 6 feet wide or about 13 meters long and 1.8 meters wide   *b 15* That is, about 45 feet long and 6 feet wide or about 14 meters long and 1.8 meters wide   *c 19* Possibly the hides of large aquatic mammals (see 35:7)   *d 21* That is, about 15 feet long and 2 1/4 feet wide or about 4.5 meters long and 68 centimeters wide linen—the work of an embroiderer; ³⁸and they made five posts with hooks for them. They overlaid the tops of the posts and their bands with gold and made their five bases of bronze.

The Ark

37 Bezalel made the ark of acacia wood—two and a half cubits long, a cubit and a half wide, and a cubit and a half high.ª ²He overlaid it with pure gold, both inside and out, and made a gold molding around it. ³He cast four gold rings for it and fastened them to its four feet, with two rings on one side and two rings on the other. ⁴Then he made poles of acacia wood and overlaid them with gold. ⁵And he inserted the poles into the rings on the sides of the ark to carry it.

⁶He made the atonement cover of pure gold—two and a half cubits long and a cubit and a half wide. ⁷Then he made two cherubim out of hammered gold at the ends of the cover. ⁸He made one cherub on one end and the second cherub on the other; at the two ends he made them of one piece with the cover. ⁹The cherubim had their wings spread upward, overshadowing the cover with them. The cherubim faced each other, looking toward the cover.

The Table

¹⁰Theyᵇ made the table of acacia wood—two cubits long, a cubit wide and a cubit and a half high.ᶜ ¹¹Then they overlaid it with pure gold and made a gold molding around it. ¹²They also made around it a rim a handbreadthᵈ wide and put a gold molding on the rim. ¹³They cast four gold rings for the table and fastened them to the four corners, where the four legs were. ¹⁴The rings were put close to the rim to hold the poles used in carrying the table. ¹⁵The poles for carrying the table were made of acacia wood and were overlaid with gold. ¹⁶And they made from pure gold the articles for the table—its plates and dishes and bowls and its pitchers for the pouring out of drink offerings.

The Lampstand

¹⁷They made the lampstand of pure gold. They hammered out its base and shaft, and made its flowerlike cups, buds and blossoms of one piece with them. ¹⁸Six branches extended from the sides of the lampstand—three on one side and three on the other. ¹⁹Three cups shaped like almond flowers with buds and blossoms were on one branch, three on the next branch and the same for all six branches extending from the lampstand. ²⁰And on the lampstand were four cups shaped like almond flowers with buds and blossoms. ²¹One bud was under the first pair of branches extending from the lampstand, a second bud under the second pair, and a third bud under the third pair—six branches in all. ²²The buds and the branches were all of one piece with the lampstand, hammered out of pure gold.

²³They made its seven lamps, as well as its wick trimmers and trays, of pure gold. ²⁴They made the lampstand and all its accessories from one talentᵉ of pure gold.

The Altar of Incense

²⁵They made the altar of incense out of acacia wood. It was square, a cubit long and a cubit wide and two cubits highᶠ—its horns of one piece with it. ²⁶They overlaid the top and all the sides and the horns with pure gold, and made a gold molding around it. ²⁷They made two gold rings below the molding—two on each of the opposite sides—to hold the poles used to carry it. ²⁸They made the poles of acacia wood and overlaid them with gold.

²⁹They also made the sacred anointing oil and the pure, fragrant incense—the work of a perfumer.

ª 1 That is, about 3 3/4 feet long and 2 1/4 feet wide and high or about 1.1 meters long and 68 centimeters wide and high; similarly in verse 6   ᵇ 10 Or He; also in verses 11-29   ᶜ 10 That is, about 3 feet long, 1 1/2 feet wide and 2 1/4 feet high or about 90 centimeters long, 45 centimeters wide and 68 centimeters high   ᵈ 12 That is, about 3 inches or about 7.5 centimeters   ᵉ 24 That is, about 75 pounds or about 34 kilograms   ᶠ 25 That is, about 1 1/2 feet long and wide and 3 feet high or about 45 centimeters long and wide and 90 centimeters high

The Altar of Burnt Offering

38 They[a] built the altar of burnt offering of acacia wood, three cubits[b] high; it was square, five cubits long and five cubits wide.[c] ²They made a horn at each of the four corners, so that the horns and the altar were of one piece, and they overlaid the altar with bronze. ³They made all its utensils of bronze — its pots, shovels, sprinkling bowls, meat forks and firepans. ⁴They made a grating for the altar, a bronze network, to be under its ledge, halfway up the altar. ⁵They cast bronze rings to hold the poles for the four corners of the bronze grating. ⁶They made the poles of acacia wood and overlaid them with bronze. ⁷They inserted the poles into the rings so they would be on the sides of the altar for carrying it. They made it hollow, out of boards.

The Basin for Washing

⁸They made the bronze basin and its bronze stand from the mirrors of the women who served at the entrance to the tent of meeting.

The Courtyard

⁹Next they made the courtyard. The south side was a hundred cubits[d] long and had curtains of finely twisted linen, ¹⁰with twenty posts and twenty bronze bases, and with silver hooks and bands on the posts. ¹¹The north side was also a hundred cubits long and had twenty posts and twenty bronze bases, with silver hooks and bands on the posts.

¹²The west end was fifty cubits[e] wide and had curtains, with ten posts and ten bases, with silver hooks and bands on the posts. ¹³The east end, toward the sunrise, was also fifty cubits wide. ¹⁴Curtains fifteen cubits[f] long were on one side of the entrance, with three posts and three bases, ¹⁵and curtains fifteen cubits long were on the other side of the entrance to the courtyard, with three posts and three bases. ¹⁶All the curtains around the courtyard were of finely twisted linen. ¹⁷The bases for the posts were bronze. The hooks and bands on the posts were silver, and their tops were overlaid with silver; so all the posts of the courtyard had silver bands.

¹⁸The curtain for the entrance to the courtyard was made of blue, purple and scarlet yarn and finely twisted linen — the work of an embroiderer. It was twenty cubits[g] long and, like the curtains of the courtyard, five cubits[h] high, ¹⁹with four posts and four bronze bases. Their hooks and bands were silver, and their tops were overlaid with silver. ²⁰All the tent pegs of the tabernacle and of the surrounding courtyard were bronze.

The Materials Used

²¹These are the amounts of the materials used for the tabernacle, the tabernacle of the covenant law, which were recorded at Moses' command by the Levites under the direction of Ithamar son of Aaron, the priest. ²²(Bezalel son of Uri, the son of Hur, of the tribe of Judah, made everything the LORD commanded Moses; ²³with him was Oholiab son of Ahisamak, of the tribe of Dan — an engraver and designer, and an embroiderer in blue, purple and scarlet yarn and fine linen.) ²⁴The total amount of the gold from the wave offering used for all the work on the sanctuary was 29 talents and 730 shekels,[i] according to the sanctuary shekel.

²⁵The silver obtained from those of the community who were counted in the census was 100 talents[j] and 1,775 shekels,[k] according to the sanctuary shekel — ²⁶one beka per person, that is, half a shekel,[l] according to the sanctuary shekel, from everyone who had crossed over to those counted, twenty years old or more, a total of 603,550 men. ²⁷The 100 talents of silver were used to cast the

---

a 1 Or *He*; also in verses 2-9   *b 1* That is, about 4 1/2 feet or about 1.4 meters   *c 1* That is, about 7 1/2 feet or about 2.3 meters long and wide   *d 9* That is, about 150 feet or about 45 meters   *e 12* That is, about 75 feet or about 23 meters   *f 14* That is, about 22 feet or about 6.8 meters   *g 18* That is, about 30 feet or about 9 meters   *h 18* That is, about 7 1/2 feet or about 2.3 meters   *i 24* The weight of the gold was a little over a ton or about 1 metric ton.   *j 25* That is, about 3 3/4 tons or about 3.4 metric tons; also in verse 27   *k 25* That is, about 44 pounds or about 20 kilograms; also in verse 28   *l 26* That is, about 1/5 ounce or about 5.7 grams

THE
WITNESSES

✓ **ITHAMAR** (EXODUS 38:21)
We don't know what this name really means. Probably it's "island of palm trees" or it might be "where Tamar is." He was Aaron's fourth son, and he was a priest like his father.

bases for the sanctuary and for the curtain—100 bases from the 100 talents, one talent for each base. ²⁸They used the 1,775 shekels to make the hooks for the posts, to overlay the tops of the posts, and to make their bands.

²⁹The bronze from the wave offering was 70 talents and 2,400 shekels.ᵃ ³⁰They used it to make the bases for the entrance to the tent of meeting, the bronze altar with its bronze grating and all its utensils, ³¹the bases for the surrounding courtyard and those for its entrance and all the tent pegs for the tabernacle and those for the surrounding courtyard.

The Priestly Garments

39 From the blue, purple and scarlet yarn they made woven garments for ministering in the sanctuary. They also made sacred garments for Aaron, as the LORD commanded Moses.

The Ephod

²Theyᵇ made the ephod of gold, and of blue, purple and scarlet yarn, and of finely twisted linen. ³They hammered out thin sheets of gold and cut strands to be worked into the blue, purple and scarlet yarn and fine linen—the work of skilled hands. ⁴They made shoulder pieces for the ephod, which were attached to two of its corners, so it could be fastened. ⁵Its skillfully woven waistband was like it—of one piece with the ephod and made with gold, and with blue, purple and scarlet yarn, and with finely twisted linen, as the LORD commanded Moses.

⁶They mounted the onyx stones in gold filigree settings and engraved them like a seal with the names of the sons of Israel. ⁷Then they fastened them on the shoulder pieces of the ephod as memorial stones for the sons of Israel, as the LORD commanded Moses.

The Breastpiece

⁸They fashioned the breastpiece—the work of a skilled craftsman. They made it like the ephod: of gold, and of blue, purple and scarlet yarn, and of finely twisted linen. ⁹It was square—a spanᶜ long and a span wide—and folded double. ¹⁰Then they mounted four rows of precious stones on it. The first row was carnelian, chrysolite and beryl; ¹¹the second row was turquoise, lapis lazuli and emerald; ¹²the third row was jacinth, agate and amethyst; ¹³the fourth row was topaz, onyx and jasper.ᵈ They were mounted in gold filigree settings. ¹⁴There were twelve stones, one for each of the names of the sons of Israel, each engraved like a seal with the name of one of the twelve tribes.

ᵃ 29 The weight of the bronze was about 2 1/2 tons or about 2.4 metric tons.   ᵇ 2 Or He; also in verses 7, 8 and 22   ᶜ 9 That is, about 9 inches or about 23 centimeters   ᵈ 13 The precise identification of some of these precious stones is uncertain.

¹⁵For the breastpiece they made braided chains of pure gold, like a rope. ¹⁶They made two gold filigree settings and two gold rings, and fastened the rings to two of the corners of the breastpiece. ¹⁷They fastened the two gold chains to the rings at the corners of the breastpiece, ¹⁸and the other ends of the chains to the two settings, attaching them to the shoulder pieces of the ephod at the front. ¹⁹They made two gold rings and attached them to the other two corners of the breastpiece on the inside edge next to the ephod. ²⁰Then they made two more gold rings and attached them to the bottom of the shoulder pieces on the front of the ephod, close to the seam just above the waistband of the ephod. ²¹They tied the rings of the breastpiece to the rings of the ephod with blue cord, connecting it to the waistband so that the breastpiece would not swing out from the ephod—as the Lord commanded Moses.

Other Priestly Garments

²²They made the robe of the ephod entirely of blue cloth—the work of a weaver— ²³with an opening in the center of the robe like the opening of a collar,ᵃ and a band around this opening, so that it would not tear. ²⁴They made pomegranates of blue, purple and scarlet yarn and finely twisted linen around the hem of the robe. ²⁵And they made bells of pure gold and attached them around the hem between the pomegranates. ²⁶The bells and pomegranates alternated around the hem of the robe to be worn for ministering, as the Lord commanded Moses.

²⁷For Aaron and his sons, they made tunics of fine linen—the work of a weaver— ²⁸and the turban of fine linen, the linen caps and the undergarments of finely twisted linen. ²⁹The sash was made of finely twisted linen and blue, purple and scarlet yarn—the work of an embroiderer—as the Lord commanded Moses.

³⁰They made the plate, the sacred emblem, out of pure gold and engraved on it, like an inscription on a seal: HOLY TO THE LORD. ³¹Then they fastened a blue cord to it to attach it to the turban, as the Lord commanded Moses.

Moses Inspects the Tabernacle

³²So all the work on the tabernacle, the tent of meeting, was completed. The Israelites did everything just as the Lord commanded Moses. ³³Then they brought the tabernacle to Moses: the tent and all its furnishings, its clasps, frames, crossbars, posts and bases; ³⁴the covering of ram skins dyed red and the covering of another durable leatherᵇ and the shielding curtain; ³⁵the ark of the covenant law with its poles and the atonement cover; ³⁶the table with all its articles and the bread of the Presence; ³⁷the pure gold lampstand with its row of lamps and all its accessories, and the olive oil for the light; ³⁸the gold altar, the anointing oil, the fragrant incense, and the curtain for the entrance to the tent; ³⁹the bronze altar with its bronze grating, its poles and all its utensils; the basin with its stand; ⁴⁰the curtains of the courtyard with its posts and bases, and the curtain for the entrance to the courtyard; the ropes and tent pegs for the courtyard; all the furnishings for the tabernacle, the tent of meeting; ⁴¹and the woven garments worn for ministering in the sanctuary, both the sacred garments for Aaron the priest and the garments for his sons when serving as priests.

⁴²The Israelites had done all the work just as the Lord had commanded Moses. ⁴³Moses inspected the work and saw that they had done it just as the Lord had commanded. So Moses blessed them.

Setting Up the Tabernacle

40 Then the Lord said to Moses: ²"Set up the tabernacle, the tent of meeting, on the first day of the first month. ³Place the ark of the covenant law in it and shield the ark with the curtain. ⁴Bring in the table and set out what belongs on it. Then bring in the lampstand and set up its lamps. ⁵Place the gold altar of incense in front of the ark of the covenant law and put the curtain at the entrance to the tabernacle.

ᵃ 23 The meaning of the Hebrew for this word is uncertain.
ᵇ 34 Possibly the hides of large aquatic mammals

⁶"Place the altar of burnt offering in front of the entrance to the tabernacle, the tent of meeting; ⁷place the basin between the tent of meeting and the altar and put water in it. ⁸Set up the courtyard around it and put the curtain at the entrance to the courtyard.

⁹"Take the anointing oil and anoint the tabernacle and everything in it; consecrate it and all its furnishings, and it will be holy. ¹⁰Then anoint the altar of burnt offering and all its utensils; consecrate the altar, and it will be most holy. ¹¹Anoint the basin and its stand and consecrate them.

¹²"Bring Aaron and his sons to the entrance to the tent of meeting and wash them with water. ¹³Then dress Aaron in the sacred garments, anoint him and consecrate him so he may serve me as priest. ¹⁴Bring his sons and dress them in tunics. ¹⁵Anoint them just as you anointed their father, so they may serve me as priests. Their anointing will be to a priesthood that will continue throughout their generations." ¹⁶Moses did everything just as the LORD commanded him.

¹⁷So the tabernacle was set up on the first day of the first month in the second year. ¹⁸When Moses set up the tabernacle, he put the bases in place, erected the frames, inserted the crossbars and set up the posts. ¹⁹Then he spread the tent over the tabernacle and put the covering over the tent, as the LORD commanded him.

²⁰He took the tablets of the covenant law and placed them in the ark, attached the poles to the ark and put the atonement cover over it. ²¹Then he brought the ark into the tabernacle and hung the shielding curtain and shielded the ark of the covenant law, as the LORD commanded him.

²²Moses placed the table in the tent of meeting on the north side of the tabernacle outside the curtain ²³and set out the bread on it before the LORD, as the LORD commanded him.

²⁴He placed the lampstand in the tent of meeting opposite the table on the south side of the tabernacle ²⁵and set up the lamps before the LORD, as the LORD commanded him.

²⁶Moses placed the gold altar in the tent of meeting in front of the curtain ²⁷and burned fragrant incense on it, as the LORD commanded him.

²⁸Then he put up the curtain at the entrance to the tabernacle. ²⁹He set the

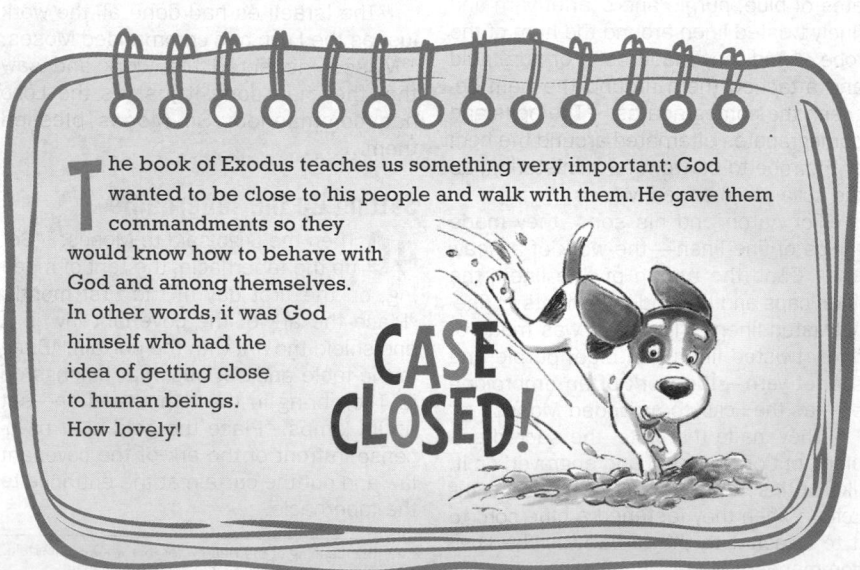

The book of Exodus teaches us something very important: God wanted to be close to his people and walk with them. He gave them commandments so they would know how to behave with God and among themselves. In other words, it was God himself who had the idea of getting close to human beings. How lovely!

CASE CLOSED!

altar of burnt offering near the entrance to the tabernacle, the tent of meeting, and offered on it burnt offerings and grain offerings, as the LORD commanded him.

30He placed the basin between the tent of meeting and the altar and put water in it for washing, 31and Moses and Aaron and his sons used it to wash their hands and feet. 32They washed whenever they entered the tent of meeting or approached the altar, as the LORD commanded Moses.

33Then Moses set up the courtyard around the tabernacle and altar and put up the curtain at the entrance to the courtyard. And so Moses finished the work.

The Glory of the LORD

34Then the cloud covered the tent of meeting, and the glory of the LORD filled the tabernacle. 35Moses could not enter the tent of meeting because the cloud had settled on it, and the glory of the LORD filled the tabernacle.

36In all the travels of the Israelites, whenever the cloud lifted from above the tabernacle, they would set out; 37but if the cloud did not lift, they did not set out— until the day it lifted. 38So the cloud of the LORD was over the tabernacle by day, and fire was in the cloud by night, in the sight of all the Israelites during all their travels.

LEVITICUS

THE EVIDENCE:

WHO WROTE IT?
It seems this book was written by Moses, but we're not super sure. People who study the Bible say the book of Leviticus was based on "priestly tradition." They call it that because it contains most of the laws and ordinances the priests had to make the people obey, according to God's orders.

HOW LONG AGO?
It was probably written 500 to 400 years before Christ. The final edition — in other words, the book the way we have it now — was finished more or less 400 years before Christ.

WHAT'S IT ABOUT?
The real name of this book in Hebrew comes from the first word in the book, "called," because God called Moses and gave him a message for the Israelites. In Leviticus, we can read about the different kinds of offerings God asked for, the things the priests had to do, and the rules and laws that show how God wants people to live. God appears as a God who is with his people and wants to be in contact with them, but he's a holy God, which means there are a lot of instructions so they could be holy and stay near him.

THE BEST PART
We really like chapter 25, because God says the people did not have to work on the land for a whole year! They could work for six years, and then they did not have to work on the seventh year. In that way, the people, the land, the animals, and everything could rest. And God kept giving them food so nobody had to work. How great! That shows us how important it is to rest and spend time enjoying life. We just need to trust God, who will give us what we need.

The Burnt Offering

1 The Lord called to Moses and spoke to him from the tent of meeting. He said, 2 "Speak to the Israelites and say to them: 'When anyone among you brings an offering to the Lord, bring as your offering an animal from either the herd or the flock.

3 " 'If the offering is a burnt offering from the herd, you are to offer a male without defect. You must present it at the entrance to the tent of meeting so that it will be acceptable to the Lord. 4 You are to lay your hand on the head of the burnt offering, and it will be accepted on your behalf to make atonement for you. 5 You are to slaughter the young bull before the

10 " 'If the offering is a burnt offering from the flock, from either the sheep or the goats, you are to offer a male without defect. 11You are to slaughter it at the north side of the altar before the LORD, and Aaron's sons the priests shall splash its blood against the sides of the altar. 12You are to cut it into pieces, and the priest shall arrange them, including the head and the fat, on the wood that is burning on the altar. 13You are to wash the internal organs and the legs with water,

BREAK THROUGH!

Why did they have to kill animals for the offerings they gave God?

(LEVITICUS 1)

A sacrifice was about giving the life of an animal to God like a gift. It wasn't to get God's kindness. They were thanking God for what he was giving them. Or they were asking him to forgive them for something bad they had done. When they killed the animal God asked for, the animal's blood was spilled. It was like the animal was taking the place of the person who had done something that God didn't like. So God took the animal's life instead of the person's life. It was a trade.

LORD, and then Aaron's sons the priests shall bring the blood and splash it against the sides of the altar at the entrance to the tent of meeting. 6You are to skin the burnt offering and cut it into pieces. 7The sons of Aaron the priest are to put fire on the altar and arrange wood on the fire. 8Then Aaron's sons the priests shall arrange the pieces, including the head and the fat, on the wood that is burning on the altar. 9You are to wash the internal organs and the legs with water, and the priest is to burn all of it on the altar. It is a burnt offering, a food offering, an aroma pleasing to the LORD.

THE
WITNESSES

✓ MOSES (LEVITICUS 1:1)

You remember Moses, don't you? If you don't, then read Exodus 2.

✓ AARON (LEVITICUS 1:5)

We saw him in Exodus! Aaron was Moses' brother and a priest of the tribe of Levi. He was the first high priest of Israel, and he helped his brother free the Israelite people from slavery in Egypt.

and the priest is to bring all of them and burn them on the altar. It is a burnt offering, a food offering, an aroma pleasing to the LORD.

¹⁴ " 'If the offering to the LORD is a burnt offering of birds, you are to offer a dove or a young pigeon. ¹⁵The priest shall bring it to the altar, wring off the head and burn it on the altar; its blood shall be drained out on the side of the altar. ¹⁶He is to remove the crop and the feathers[a] and throw them down east of the altar where the ashes are. ¹⁷He shall tear it open by the wings, not dividing it completely, and then the priest shall burn it on the wood that is burning on the altar. It is a burnt offering, a food offering, an aroma pleasing to the LORD.

The Grain Offering

2 " 'When anyone brings a grain offering to the LORD, their offering is to be of the finest flour. They are to pour olive oil on it, put incense on it ²and take it to Aaron's sons the priests. The priest shall take a handful of the flour and oil, together with all the incense, and burn this as a memorial[b] portion on the altar, a food offering, an aroma pleasing to the LORD. ³The rest of the grain offering belongs to Aaron and his sons; it is a most holy part of the food offerings presented to the LORD.

⁴ " 'If you bring a grain offering baked in an oven, it is to consist of the finest flour: either thick loaves made without yeast and with olive oil mixed in or thin loaves made without yeast and brushed with olive oil. ⁵If your grain offering is prepared on a griddle, it is to be made of the finest flour mixed with oil, and without yeast. ⁶Crumble it and pour oil on it; it is a grain offering. ⁷If your grain offering is cooked in a pan, it is to be made of the finest flour and some olive oil. ⁸Bring the grain offering made of these things to the LORD; present it to the priest, who shall take it to the altar. ⁹He shall take out the memorial portion from the grain offering and burn it on the altar as a food offering, an aroma pleasing to the LORD. ¹⁰The rest of the grain offering belongs to Aaron and his sons; it is a most holy part of the food offerings presented to the LORD.

¹¹ " 'Every grain offering you bring to the LORD must be made without yeast, for you are not to burn any yeast or honey in a food offering presented to the LORD. ¹²You may bring them to the LORD as an offering of the firstfruits, but they are not to be offered on the altar as a pleasing aroma. ¹³Season all your grain offerings with salt. Do not leave the salt of the covenant of your God out of your grain offerings; add salt to all your offerings.

¹⁴ " 'If you bring a grain offering of firstfruits to the LORD, offer crushed heads of new grain roasted in the fire. ¹⁵Put oil and incense on it; it is a grain offering. ¹⁶The priest shall burn the memorial portion of the crushed grain and the oil, together with all the incense, as a food offering presented to the LORD.

The Fellowship Offering

3 " 'If your offering is a fellowship offering, and you offer an animal from the herd, whether male or female, you are to present before the LORD an animal without defect. ²You are to lay your hand on the head of your offering and slaughter it at the entrance to the tent of meeting. Then Aaron's sons the priests shall splash the blood against the sides of the altar. ³From the fellowship offering you are to bring a food offering to the LORD: the internal organs and all the fat that is connected to them, ⁴both kidneys with the fat on them near the loins, and the long lobe of the liver, which you will remove with the kidneys. ⁵Then Aaron's sons are to burn it on the altar on top of the burnt offering that is lying on the burning wood; it is a food offering, an aroma pleasing to the LORD.

⁶ " 'If you offer an animal from the flock as a fellowship offering to the LORD, you are to offer a male or female without defect. ⁷If you offer a lamb, you are to present it before the LORD, ⁸lay your hand on its head and slaughter it in front of the tent of meeting. Then Aaron's sons shall splash its blood against the sides of the altar. ⁹From the fellowship offering you are to bring a food offering to the LORD: its fat,

---

a 16 Or *crop with its contents*; the meaning of the Hebrew for this word is uncertain.   *b 2* Or *representative*; also in verses 9 and 16 the entire fat tail cut off close to the backbone, the internal organs and all the fat that is connected to them, ¹⁰both kidneys with the fat on them near the loins, and the long lobe of the liver, which you will remove with the kidneys. ¹¹The priest shall burn them on the altar as a food offering presented to the Lord.

¹²" 'If your offering is a goat, you are to present it before the Lord, ¹³lay your hand on its head and slaughter it in front of the tent of meeting. Then Aaron's sons shall splash its blood against the sides of the altar. ¹⁴From what you offer you are to present this food offering to the Lord: the internal organs and all the fat that is connected to them, ¹⁵both kidneys with the fat on them near the loins, and the long lobe of the liver, which you will remove with the kidneys. ¹⁶The priest shall burn them on the altar as a food offering, a pleasing aroma. All the fat is the Lord's.

¹⁷" 'This is a lasting ordinance for the generations to come, wherever you live: You must not eat any fat or any blood.' "

The Sin Offering

4 The Lord said to Moses, ²"Say to the Israelites: 'When anyone sins unintentionally and does what is forbidden in any of the Lord's commands—

³" 'If the anointed priest sins, bringing guilt on the people, he must bring to the Lord a young bull without defect as a sin offering[a] for the sin he has committed. ⁴He is to present the bull at the entrance to the tent of meeting before the Lord. He is to lay his hand on its head and slaughter it there before the Lord. ⁵Then the anointed priest shall take some of the bull's blood and carry it into the tent of meeting. ⁶He is to dip his finger into the blood and sprinkle some of it seven times before the Lord, in front of the curtain of the sanctuary. ⁷The priest shall then put some of the blood on the horns of the altar of fragrant incense that is before the Lord in the tent of meeting. The rest of the bull's blood he shall pour out at the base of the altar of burnt offering at the entrance to the tent of meeting. ⁸He shall remove all the fat from the bull of the sin

BREAKTHROUGH!

What is sin really?

(LEVITICUS 4)

Sin is disobeying God's commandments and teachings. It's not doing what God asks us to do. It's also doing something against what God has ordered.

offering—all the fat that is connected to the internal organs, ⁹both kidneys with the fat on them near the loins, and the long lobe of the liver, which he will remove with the kidneys— ¹⁰just as the fat is removed from the ox[b] sacrificed as a fellowship offering. Then the priest shall burn them on the altar of burnt offering. ¹¹But the hide of the bull and all its flesh, as well as the head and legs, the internal organs and the intestines— ¹²that is, all the rest of the bull—he must take outside the camp to a place ceremonially clean, where the ashes are thrown, and burn it there in a wood fire on the ash heap.

¹³" 'If the whole Israelite community sins unintentionally and does what is forbidden in any of the Lord's commands, even though the community is unaware of the matter, when they realize their guilt ¹⁴and the sin they committed becomes known, the assembly must bring a young

---

[a] 3 Or *purification offering*; here and throughout this chapter   [b] 10 The Hebrew word can refer to either male or female.

bull as a sin offering and present it before the tent of meeting. [15]The elders of the community are to lay their hands on the bull's head before the Lord, and the bull shall be slaughtered before the Lord. [16]Then the anointed priest is to take some of the bull's blood into the tent of meeting. [17]He shall dip his finger into the blood and sprinkle it before the Lord seven times in front of the curtain. [18]He is to put some of the blood on the horns of the altar that is before the Lord in the tent of meeting. The rest of the blood he shall pour out at the base of the altar of burnt offering at the entrance to the tent of meeting. [19]He shall remove all the fat from it and burn it on the altar, [20]and do with this bull just as he did with the bull for the sin offering. In this way the priest will make atonement for the community, and they will be forgiven. [21]Then he shall take the bull outside the camp and burn it as he burned the first bull. This is the sin offering for the community.

[22]" 'When a leader sins unintentionally and does what is forbidden in any of the commands of the Lord his God, when he realizes his guilt [23]and the sin he has committed becomes known, he must bring as his offering a male goat without defect. [24]He is to lay his hand on the goat's head and slaughter it at the place where the burnt offering is slaughtered before the Lord. It is a sin offering. [25]Then the priest shall take some of the blood of the sin offering with his finger and put it on the horns of the altar of burnt offering and pour out the rest of the blood at the base of the altar. [26]He shall burn all the fat on the altar as he burned the fat of the fellowship offering. In this way the priest will make atonement for the leader's sin, and he will be forgiven.

[27]" 'If any member of the community sins unintentionally and does what is forbidden in any of the Lord's commands, when they realize their guilt [28]and the sin they have committed becomes known, they must bring as their offering for the sin they committed a female goat without defect. [29]They are to lay their hand on the head of the sin offering and slaughter it at the place of the burnt offering. [30]Then the priest is to take some of the blood with his finger and put it on the horns of the altar of burnt offering and pour out the rest of the blood at the base of the altar. [31]They shall remove all the fat, just as the fat is removed from the fellowship offering, and the priest shall burn it on the altar as an aroma pleasing to the Lord. In this way the priest will make atonement for them, and they will be forgiven.

[32]" 'If someone brings a lamb as their sin offering, they are to bring a female without defect. [33]They are to lay their hand on its head and slaughter it for a sin offering at the place where the burnt offering is slaughtered. [34]Then the priest shall take some of the blood of the sin offering with his finger and put it on the horns of the altar of burnt offering and pour out the rest of the blood at the base of the altar. [35]They shall remove all the fat, just as the fat is removed from the lamb of the fellowship offering, and the priest shall burn it on the altar on top of the food offerings presented to the Lord. In this way the priest will make atonement for them for the sin they have committed, and they will be forgiven.

5 " 'If anyone sins because they do not speak up when they hear a public charge to testify regarding something they have seen or learned about, they will be held responsible.

[2]" 'If anyone becomes aware that they are guilty—if they unwittingly touch anything ceremonially unclean (whether the carcass of an unclean animal, wild or domestic, or of any unclean creature that moves along the ground) and they are unaware that they have become unclean, but then they come to realize their guilt; [3]or if they touch human uncleanness (anything that would make them unclean) even though they are unaware of it, but then they learn of it and realize their guilt; [4]or if anyone thoughtlessly takes an oath to do anything, whether good or evil (in any matter one might carelessly swear about) even though they are unaware of it, but then they learn of it and realize their guilt— [5]when anyone becomes aware

that they are guilty in any of these matters, they must confess in what way they have sinned. [6]As a penalty for the sin they have committed, they must bring to the LORD a female lamb or goat from the flock as a sin offering[a]; and the priest shall make atonement for them for their sin.

[7]" 'Anyone who cannot afford a lamb is to bring two doves or two young pigeons to the LORD as a penalty for their sin— one for a sin offering and the other for a burnt offering. [8]They are to bring them to the priest, who shall first offer the one for the sin offering. He is to wring its head from its neck, not dividing it completely, [9]and is to splash some of the blood of the sin offering against the side of the altar; the rest of the blood must be drained out at the base of the altar. It is a sin offering. [10]The priest shall then offer the other as a burnt offering in the prescribed way and make atonement for them for the sin they have committed, and they will be forgiven.

[11]" 'If, however, they cannot afford two doves or two young pigeons, they are to bring as an offering for their sin a tenth of an ephah[b] of the finest flour for a sin offering. They must not put olive oil or incense on it, because it is a sin offering. [12]They are to bring it to the priest, who shall take a handful of it as a memorial[c] portion and burn it on the altar on top of the food offerings presented to the LORD. It is a sin offering. [13]In this way the priest will make atonement for them for any of these sins they have committed, and they will be forgiven. The rest of the offering will belong to the priest, as in the case of the grain offering.' "

The Guilt Offering

[14]The LORD said to Moses: [15]"When anyone is unfaithful to the LORD by sinning unintentionally in regard to any of the LORD's holy things, they are to bring to the LORD as a penalty a ram from the flock, one without defect and of the proper value in silver, according to the sanctuary shekel.[d] It is a guilt offering. [16]They must make restitution for what they have failed to do in regard to the holy things, pay an additional penalty of a fifth of its value and give it all to the priest. The priest will

make atonement for them with the ram as a guilt offering, and they will be forgiven.

[17]"If anyone sins and does what is forbidden in any of the LORD's commands, even though they do not know it, they are guilty and will be held responsible. [18]They are to bring to the priest as a guilt offering a ram from the flock, one without defect and of the proper value. In this way the priest will make atonement for them for the wrong they have committed unintentionally, and they will be forgiven. [19]It is a guilt offering; they have been guilty of[e] wrongdoing against the LORD."

6[f] The LORD said to Moses: [2]"If anyone sins and is unfaithful to the LORD by deceiving a neighbor about something entrusted to them or left in their care or about something stolen, or if they cheat their neighbor, [3]or if they find lost property and lie about it, or if they swear falsely about any such sin that people may commit— [4]when they sin in any of these ways and realize their guilt, they must return what they have stolen or taken by extortion, or what was entrusted to them, or the lost property they found, [5]or whatever it was they swore falsely about. They must make restitution in full, add a fifth of the value to it and give it all to the owner on the day they present their guilt offering. [6]And as a penalty they must bring to the priest, that is, to the LORD, their guilt offering, a ram from the flock, one without defect and of the proper value. [7]In this way the priest will make atonement for them before the LORD, and they will be forgiven for any of the things they did that made them guilty."

The Burnt Offering

[8]The LORD said to Moses: [9]"Give Aaron and his sons this command: 'These are the regulations for the burnt offering: The burnt offering is to remain on the altar hearth throughout the night, till morning, and the fire must be kept burning on the

---

a 6 Or purification offering; here and throughout this chapter   *b 11 That is, probably about 3 1/2 pounds or about 1.6 kilograms   *c 12 Or representative*
*d 15 That is, about 2/5 ounce or about 12 grams
e 19 Or offering; atonement has been made for their*
f In Hebrew texts 6:1-7 is numbered 5:20-26, and 6:8-30 is numbered 6:1-23.

altar. ¹⁰The priest shall then put on his linen clothes, with linen undergarments next to his body, and shall remove the ashes of the burnt offering that the fire has consumed on the altar and place them beside the altar. ¹¹Then he is to take off these clothes and put on others, and carry the ashes outside the camp to a place that is ceremonially clean. ¹²The fire on the altar must be kept burning; it must not go out. Every morning the priest is to add firewood and arrange the burnt offering on the fire and burn the fat of the fellowship offerings on it. ¹³The fire must be kept burning on the altar continuously; it must not go out.

The Grain Offering

¹⁴" 'These are the regulations for the grain offering: Aaron's sons are to bring it before the LORD, in front of the altar.

Priest

(LEVITICUS 6:10)

That was the person who was in charge of giving the sacrifices and offerings to God. Levi's offspring (he was one of Jacob's twelve sons) were the only ones who could be priests and serve God. Some of them were very important, and the most important one of all of them was called the "high priest."

¹⁵The priest is to take a handful of the finest flour and some olive oil, together with all the incense on the grain offering, and burn the memorial*ᵃ* portion on the altar as an aroma pleasing to the LORD. ¹⁶Aaron and his sons shall eat the rest of it, but it is to be eaten without yeast in the sanctuary area; they are to eat it in the courtyard of the tent of meeting. ¹⁷It must not be baked with yeast; I have given it as their share of the food offerings presented to me. Like the sin offering*ᵇ* and the guilt offering, it is most holy. ¹⁸Any male descendant of Aaron may eat it. For all generations to come it is his perpetual share of the food offerings presented to the LORD. Whatever touches them will become holy.*ᶜ'* "

¹⁹The LORD also said to Moses, ²⁰"This is the offering Aaron and his sons are to bring to the LORD on the day he*ᵈ* is anointed: a tenth of an ephah*ᵉ* of the finest flour as a regular grain offering, half of it in the morning and half in the evening. ²¹It must be prepared with oil on a griddle; bring it well-mixed and present the grain offering broken*ᶠ* in pieces as an aroma pleasing to the LORD. ²²The son who is to succeed him as anointed priest shall prepare it. It is the LORD's perpetual share and is to be burned completely. ²³Every grain offering of a priest shall be burned completely; it must not be eaten."

The Sin Offering

²⁴The LORD said to Moses, ²⁵"Say to Aaron and his sons: 'These are the regulations for the sin offering: The sin offering is to be slaughtered before the LORD in the place the burnt offering is slaughtered; it is most holy. ²⁶The priest who offers it shall eat it; it is to be eaten in the sanctuary area, in the courtyard of the tent of meeting. ²⁷Whatever touches any of the flesh will become holy, and if any of the blood is spattered on a garment, you must wash it in the sanctuary area. ²⁸The clay pot the meat is cooked in must

---

ᵃ 15 Or *representative*   *ᵇ* 17 Or *purification offering*; also in verses 25 and 30   *ᶜ* 18 Or *Whoever touches them must be holy*; similarly in verse 27   *ᵈ* 20 Or *each*   *ᵉ* 20 That is, probably about 3 1/2 pounds or about 1.6 kilograms   *ᶠ* 21 The meaning of the Hebrew for this word is uncertain.

be broken; but if it is cooked in a bronze pot, the pot is to be scoured and rinsed with water. ²⁹Any male in a priest's family may eat it; it is most holy. ³⁰But any sin offering whose blood is brought into the tent of meeting to make atonement in the Holy Place must not be eaten; it must be burned up.

The Guilt Offering

7 " 'These are the regulations for the guilt offering, which is most holy: ²The guilt offering is to be slaughtered in the place where the burnt offering is slaughtered, and its blood is to be splashed against the sides of the altar. ³All its fat shall be offered: the fat tail and the fat that covers the internal organs, ⁴both kidneys with the fat on them near the loins, and the long lobe of the liver, which is to be removed with the kidneys. ⁵The priest shall burn them on the altar as a food offering presented to the LORD. It is a guilt offering. ⁶Any male in a priest's family may eat it, but it must be eaten in the sanctuary area; it is most holy.

⁷ " 'The same law applies to both the sin offering[a] and the guilt offering: They belong to the priest who makes atonement with them. ⁸The priest who offers a burnt offering for anyone may keep its hide for himself. ⁹Every grain offering baked in an oven or cooked in a pan or on a griddle belongs to the priest who offers it, ¹⁰and every grain offering, whether mixed with olive oil or dry, belongs equally to all the sons of Aaron.

The Fellowship Offering

¹¹ " 'These are the regulations for the fellowship offering anyone may present to the LORD:

¹² " 'If they offer it as an expression of thankfulness, then along with this thank offering they are to offer thick loaves made without yeast and with olive oil mixed in, thin loaves made without yeast and brushed with oil, and thick loaves of the finest flour well-kneaded and with oil mixed in. ¹³Along with their fellowship offering of thanksgiving they are to present an offering with thick loaves of bread

made with yeast. ¹⁴They are to bring one of each kind as an offering, a contribution to the LORD; it belongs to the priest who splashes the blood of the fellowship offering against the altar. ¹⁵The meat of their fellowship offering of thanksgiving must be eaten on the day it is offered; they must leave none of it till morning.

¹⁶ " 'If, however, their offering is the result of a vow or is a freewill offering, the sacrifice shall be eaten on the day they offer it, but anything left over may be eaten on the next day. ¹⁷Any meat of the sacrifice left over till the third day must be burned up. ¹⁸If any meat of the fellowship offering is eaten on the third day, the one who offered it will not be accepted. It will not be reckoned to their credit, for it has become impure; the person who eats any of it will be held responsible.

¹⁹ " 'Meat that touches anything ceremonially unclean must not be eaten; it must be burned up. As for other meat, anyone ceremonially clean may eat it. ²⁰But if anyone who is unclean eats any meat of the fellowship offering belonging to the LORD, they must be cut off from their people. ²¹Anyone who touches something unclean — whether human uncleanness or an unclean animal or any unclean creature that moves along the ground[b] — and then eats any of the meat of the fellowship offering belonging to the LORD must be cut off from their people.' "

Eating Fat and Blood Forbidden

²²The LORD said to Moses, ²³"Say to the Israelites: 'Do not eat any of the fat of cattle, sheep or goats. ²⁴The fat of an animal found dead or torn by wild animals may be used for any other purpose, but you must not eat it. ²⁵Anyone who eats the fat of an animal from which a food offering may be[c] presented to the LORD must be cut off from their people. ²⁶And wherever you live, you must not eat the blood of any bird or animal. ²⁷Anyone who eats blood must be cut off from their people.' "

---

^a 7 Or *purification offering*; also in verse 37   ^b 21 A few Hebrew manuscripts, Samaritan Pentateuch, Syriac and Targum (see 5:2); most Hebrew manuscripts *any unclean, detestable thing*   ^c 25 Or *offering is*

The Priests' Share

²⁸The LORD said to Moses, ²⁹"Say to the Israelites: 'Anyone who brings a fellowship offering to the LORD is to bring part of it as their sacrifice to the LORD. ³⁰With their own hands they are to present the food offering to the LORD; they are to bring the fat, together with the breast, and wave the breast before the LORD as a wave offering. ³¹The priest shall burn the fat on the altar, but the breast belongs to Aaron and his sons. ³²You are to give the right thigh of your fellowship offerings to the priest as a contribution. ³³The son of Aaron who offers the blood and the fat of the fellowship offering shall have the right thigh as his share. ³⁴From the fellowship offerings of the Israelites, I have taken the breast that is waved and the thigh that is presented and have given them to Aaron the priest and his sons as their perpetual share from the Israelites.' "

³⁵This is the portion of the food offerings presented to the LORD that were allotted to Aaron and his sons on the day they were presented to serve the LORD as priests. ³⁶On the day they were anointed, the LORD commanded that the Israelites give this to them as their perpetual share for the generations to come.

³⁷These, then, are the regulations for the burnt offering, the grain offering, the sin offering, the guilt offering, the ordination offering and the fellowship offering, ³⁸which the LORD gave Moses at Mount Sinai in the Desert of Sinai on the day he commanded the Israelites to bring their offerings to the LORD.

The Ordination of Aaron and His Sons

8 The LORD said to Moses, ²"Bring Aaron and his sons, their garments, the anointing oil, the bull for the sin offering,ᵃ the two rams and the basket containing bread made without yeast, ³and gather the entire assembly at the entrance to the tent of meeting." ⁴Moses did as the LORD commanded him, and the assembly gathered at the entrance to the tent of meeting.

BREAKTHROUGH!

Anoint

(LEVITICUS 8)

This is when a person or an object is completely faithful to the service of God. Here we see that first they washed Aaron and his sons really well, and then they dressed them in special clothes. Finally, they poured oil on their heads to anoint them.

⁵Moses said to the assembly, "This is what the LORD has commanded to be done." ⁶Then Moses brought Aaron and his sons forward and washed them with water. ⁷He put the tunic on Aaron, tied the sash around him, clothed him with the robe and put the ephod on him. He also fastened the ephod with a decorative waistband, which he tied around him. ⁸He placed the breastpiece on him and put the Urim and Thummim in the breastpiece. ⁹Then he placed the turban on Aaron's head and set the gold plate, the sacred emblem, on the front of it, as the LORD commanded Moses.

¹⁰Then Moses took the anointing oil and anointed the tabernacle and everything in it, and so consecrated them. ¹¹He sprinkled some of the oil on the altar seven times, anointing the altar and all its utensils and the basin with its stand,

---

ᵃ 2 Or *purification offering*; also in verse 14

to consecrate them. ¹²He poured some of the anointing oil on Aaron's head and anointed him to consecrate him. ¹³Then he brought Aaron's sons forward, put tunics on them, tied sashes around them and fastened caps on them, as the LORD commanded Moses.

¹⁴He then presented the bull for the sin offering, and Aaron and his sons laid their hands on its head. ¹⁵Moses slaughtered the bull and took some of the blood, and with his finger he put it on all the horns of the altar to purify the altar. He poured out the rest of the blood at the base of the altar. So he consecrated it to make atonement for it. ¹⁶Moses also took all the fat around the internal organs, the long lobe of the liver, and both kidneys and their fat, and burned it on the altar. ¹⁷But the bull with its hide and its flesh and its intestines he burned up outside the camp, as the LORD commanded Moses.

¹⁸He then presented the ram for the burnt offering, and Aaron and his sons laid their hands on its head. ¹⁹Then Moses slaughtered the ram and splashed the blood against the sides of the altar. ²⁰He cut the ram into pieces and burned the head, the pieces and the fat. ²¹He washed the internal organs and the legs with water and burned the whole ram on the altar. It was a burnt offering, a pleasing aroma, a food offering presented to the LORD, as the LORD commanded Moses.

²²He then presented the other ram, the ram for the ordination, and Aaron and his sons laid their hands on its head. ²³Moses slaughtered the ram and took some of its blood and put it on the lobe of Aaron's right ear, on the thumb of his right hand and on the big toe of his right foot. ²⁴Moses also brought Aaron's sons forward and put some of the blood on the lobes of their right ears, on the thumbs of their right hands and on the big toes of their right feet. Then he splashed blood against the sides of the altar. ²⁵After that, he took the fat, the fat tail, all the fat around the internal organs, the long lobe of the liver, both kidneys and their fat and the right thigh. ²⁶And from the basket of bread made without yeast, which was before the LORD, he took one thick loaf, one

thick loaf with olive oil mixed in, and one thin loaf, and he put these on the fat portions and on the right thigh. ²⁷He put all these in the hands of Aaron and his sons, and they waved them before the LORD as a wave offering. ²⁸Then Moses took them from their hands and burned them on the altar on top of the burnt offering as an ordination offering, a pleasing aroma, a food offering presented to the LORD. ²⁹Moses also took the breast, which was his share of the ordination ram, and waved it before the LORD as a wave offering, as the LORD commanded Moses.

³⁰Then Moses took some of the anointing oil and some of the blood from the altar and sprinkled them on Aaron and his garments and on his sons and their garments. So he consecrated Aaron and his garments and his sons and their garments.

³¹Moses then said to Aaron and his sons, "Cook the meat at the entrance to the tent of meeting and eat it there with the bread from the basket of ordination

BREAKTHROUGH!

Consecration

(LEVITICUS 8:30)

This means to be free from anything that makes a person or thing "unclean." No person or thing that hadn't been made holy could come near God or be in contact with him.

offerings, as I was commanded: 'Aaron and his sons are to eat it.' ³²Then burn up the rest of the meat and the bread. ³³Do not leave the entrance to the tent of meeting for seven days, until the days of your ordination are completed, for your ordination will last seven days. ³⁴What has been done today was commanded by the LORD to make atonement for you. ³⁵You must stay at the entrance to the tent of meeting day and night for seven days and do what the LORD requires, so you will not die; for that is what I have been commanded."

³⁶So Aaron and his sons did everything the LORD commanded through Moses.

The Priests Begin Their Ministry

9 On the eighth day Moses summoned Aaron and his sons and the elders of Israel. ²He said to Aaron, "Take a bull calf for your sin offering[a] and a ram for your burnt offering, both without defect, and present them before the LORD. ³Then say to the Israelites: 'Take a male goat for a sin offering, a calf and a lamb—both a year old and without defect—for a burnt offering, ⁴and an ox[b] and a ram for a fellowship offering to sacrifice before the LORD, together with a grain offering mixed with olive oil. For today the LORD will appear to you.'"

⁵They took the things Moses commanded to the front of the tent of meeting, and the entire assembly came near and stood before the LORD. ⁶Then Moses said, "This is what the LORD has commanded you to do, so that the glory of the LORD may appear to you."

⁷Moses said to Aaron, "Come to the altar and sacrifice your sin offering and your burnt offering and make atonement for yourself and the people; sacrifice the offering that is for the people and make atonement for them, as the LORD has commanded."

⁸So Aaron came to the altar and slaughtered the calf as a sin offering for himself. ⁹His sons brought the blood to him, and he dipped his finger into the blood and put it on the horns of the altar; the rest of the blood he poured out at the base of the altar. ¹⁰On the altar he burned the fat, the kidneys and the long lobe of the liver from the sin offering, as the LORD commanded Moses; ¹¹the flesh and the hide he burned up outside the camp.

¹²Then he slaughtered the burnt offering. His sons handed him the blood, and he splashed it against the sides of the altar. ¹³They handed him the burnt offering piece by piece, including the head, and he burned them on the altar. ¹⁴He washed the internal organs and the legs and burned them on top of the burnt offering on the altar.

¹⁵Aaron then brought the offering that was for the people. He took the goat for the people's sin offering and slaughtered it and offered it for a sin offering as he did with the first one.

¹⁶He brought the burnt offering and offered it in the prescribed way. ¹⁷He also brought the grain offering, took a handful of it and burned it on the altar in addition to the morning's burnt offering.

¹⁸He slaughtered the ox and the ram as the fellowship offering for the people. His sons handed him the blood, and he splashed it against the sides of the altar. ¹⁹But the fat portions of the ox and the ram—the fat tail, the layer of fat, the kidneys and the long lobe of the liver— ²⁰these they laid on the breasts, and then Aaron burned the fat on the altar. ²¹Aaron waved the breasts and the right thigh before the LORD as a wave offering, as Moses commanded.

²²Then Aaron lifted his hands toward the people and blessed them. And having sacrificed the sin offering, the burnt offering and the fellowship offering, he stepped down.

²³Moses and Aaron then went into the tent of meeting. When they came out, they blessed the people; and the glory of the LORD appeared to all the people. ²⁴Fire came out from the presence of the LORD and consumed the burnt offering and the fat portions on the altar. And when all the people saw it, they shouted for joy and fell facedown.

---

a 2 Or *purification offering*; here and throughout this chapter   *b* 4 The Hebrew word can refer to either male or female; also in verses 18 and 19.

The Death of Nadab and Abihu

10 Aaron's sons Nadab and Abihu took their censers, put fire in them and added incense; and they offered unauthorized fire before the Lord, contrary to his command. [2]So fire came out from the presence of the Lord and consumed them, and they died before the Lord. [3]Moses then said to Aaron, "This is what the Lord spoke of when he said:

" 'Among those who approach me
   I will be proved holy;
in the sight of all the people
   I will be honored.' "

Aaron remained silent.

[4]Moses summoned Mishael and Elzaphan, sons of Aaron's uncle Uzziel, and said to them, "Come here; carry your cousins outside the camp, away from the front of the sanctuary." [5]So they came and carried them, still in their tunics, outside the camp, as Moses ordered.

[6]Then Moses said to Aaron and his sons Eleazar and Ithamar, "Do not let your hair become unkempt[a] and do not tear your clothes, or you will die and the Lord will be angry with the whole community. But your relatives, all the Israelites, may mourn for those the Lord has destroyed by fire. [7]Do not leave the entrance to the tent of meeting or you will die, because the Lord's anointing oil is on you." So they did as Moses said.

[8]Then the Lord said to Aaron, [9]"You and your sons are not to drink wine or other fermented drink whenever you go into the tent of meeting, or you will die. This is a lasting ordinance for the generations to come, [10]so that you can distinguish between the holy and the common, between the unclean and the clean, [11]and so you can teach the Israelites all the decrees the Lord has given them through Moses."

[12]Moses said to Aaron and his remaining sons, Eleazar and Ithamar, "Take the grain offering left over from the food offerings prepared without yeast and presented to the Lord and eat it beside the altar, for it is most holy. [13]Eat it in a sanctuary area, because it is your share and your sons' share of the food offerings presented to the Lord; for so I have been commanded. [14]But you and your sons and your daughters may eat the breast that was waved and the thigh that was presented. Eat them in a ceremonially clean place; they have been given to you and your children as your share of the Israelites' fellowship offerings. [15]The thigh that was presented and the breast that was waved must be brought with the fat portions of the food offerings, to be waved before the Lord as a wave offering. This will be the perpetual share for you and your children, as the Lord has commanded."

[16]When Moses inquired about the goat of the sin offering[b] and found that it had been burned up, he was angry with Eleazar and Ithamar, Aaron's remaining sons, and asked, [17]"Why didn't you eat the sin offering in the sanctuary area? It is most holy; it was given to you to take away the guilt of the community by making atonement for them before the Lord. [18]Since its blood was not taken into the Holy Place, you should have eaten the goat in the sanctuary area, as I commanded."

[19]Aaron replied to Moses, "Today they sacrificed their sin offering and their burnt offering before the Lord, but such things as this have happened to me. Would the Lord have been pleased if I had eaten the sin offering today?" [20]When Moses heard this, he was satisfied.

Clean and Unclean Food

11 The Lord said to Moses and Aaron, [2]"Say to the Israelites: 'Of all the animals that live on land, these are the ones you may eat: [3]You may eat any animal that has a divided hoof and that chews the cud.

[4]" 'There are some that only chew the cud or only have a divided hoof, but you must not eat them. The camel, though it chews the cud, does not have a divided hoof; it is ceremonially unclean for you. [5]The hyrax, though it chews the cud, does not have a divided hoof; it is unclean for you. [6]The rabbit, though it chews the cud,

---

[a] 6 Or *Do not uncover your heads*   [b] 16 Or *purification offering*; also in verses 17 and 19

BREAKTHROUGH!

Clean and unclean animals
(LEVITICUS 11)

God gave laws about which animals were clean (pure) or unclean. Here, "clean" doesn't mean that they weren't dirty. It's talking about a "ritual of cleanliness." In other words, the laws said which animals could be used for sacrifices and which ones people could eat.

Some people think that this also had to do with other people who lived nearby the Israelites. They sometimes worshiped different animals as if they were gods, or they used the animals as offerings to false gods, so God considered those types of creatures unclean.

does not have a divided hoof; it is unclean for you. ⁷And the pig, though it has a divided hoof, does not chew the cud; it is unclean for you. ⁸You must not eat their meat or touch their carcasses; they are unclean for you.

⁹" 'Of all the creatures living in the water of the seas and the streams you may eat any that have fins and scales. ¹⁰But all creatures in the seas or streams that do not have fins and scales — whether among all the swarming things or among all the other living creatures in the water — you are to regard as unclean. ¹¹And since you are to regard them as unclean,

you must not eat their meat; you must regard their carcasses as unclean. ¹²Anything living in the water that does not have fins and scales is to be regarded as unclean by you.

¹³" 'These are the birds you are to regard as unclean and not eat because they are unclean: the eagle,ᵃ the vulture, the black vulture, ¹⁴the red kite, any kind of black kite, ¹⁵any kind of raven, ¹⁶the horned owl, the screech owl, the gull, any kind of hawk, ¹⁷the little owl, the cormorant, the great owl, ¹⁸the white owl, the desert owl, the osprey, ¹⁹the stork, any kind of heron, the hoopoe and the bat.

²⁰" 'All flying insects that walk on all fours are to be regarded as unclean by you. ²¹There are, however, some flying insects that walk on all fours that you may eat: those that have jointed legs for hopping on the ground. ²²Of these you may eat any kind of locust, katydid, cricket or grasshopper. ²³But all other flying insects that have four legs you are to regard as unclean.

²⁴" 'You will make yourselves unclean by these; whoever touches their carcasses will be unclean till evening. ²⁵Whoever picks up one of their carcasses must wash their clothes, and they will be unclean till evening.

²⁶" 'Every animal that does not have a divided hoof or that does not chew the cud is unclean for you; whoever touches the carcass of any of them will be unclean. ²⁷Of all the animals that walk on all fours, those that walk on their paws are unclean for you; whoever touches their carcasses will be unclean till evening. ²⁸Anyone who picks up their carcasses must wash their clothes, and they will be unclean till evening. These animals are unclean for you.

²⁹" 'Of the animals that move along the ground, these are unclean for you: the weasel, the rat, any kind of great lizard, ³⁰the gecko, the monitor lizard, the wall lizard, the skink and the chameleon. ³¹Of all those that move along the ground, these are unclean for you. Whoever touches them when they are dead will be un-

---

ᵃ 13 The precise identification of some of the birds, insects and animals in this chapter is uncertain.

clean till evening. ³²When one of them dies and falls on something, that article, whatever its use, will be unclean, whether it is made of wood, cloth, hide or sackcloth. Put it in water; it will be unclean till evening, and then it will be clean. ³³If one of them falls into a clay pot, everything in it will be unclean, and you must break the pot. ³⁴Any food you are allowed to eat that has come into contact with water from any such pot is unclean, and any liquid that is drunk from such a pot is unclean. ³⁵Anything that one of their carcasses falls on becomes unclean; an oven or cooking pot must be broken up. They are unclean, and you are to regard them as unclean. ³⁶A spring, however, or a cistern for collecting water remains clean, but anyone who touches one of these carcasses is unclean. ³⁷If a carcass falls on any seeds that are to be planted, they remain clean. ³⁸But if water has been put on the seed and a carcass falls on it, it is unclean for you.

³⁹ "'If an animal that you are allowed to eat dies, anyone who touches its carcass will be unclean till evening. ⁴⁰Anyone who eats some of its carcass must wash their clothes, and they will be unclean till evening. Anyone who picks up the carcass must wash their clothes, and they will be unclean till evening.

⁴¹ "'Every creature that moves along the ground is to be regarded as unclean; it is not to be eaten. ⁴²You are not to eat any creature that moves along the ground, whether it moves on its belly or walks on all fours or on many feet; it is unclean. ⁴³Do not defile yourselves by any of these creatures. Do not make yourselves unclean by means of them or be made unclean by them. ⁴⁴I am the LORD your God; consecrate yourselves and be holy, because I am holy. Do not make yourselves unclean by any creature that moves along the ground. ⁴⁵I am the LORD, who brought you up out of Egypt to be your God; therefore be holy, because I am holy.

⁴⁶ "'These are the regulations concerning animals, birds, every living thing that moves about in the water and every creature that moves along the ground. ⁴⁷You

must distinguish between the unclean and the clean, between living creatures that may be eaten and those that may not be eaten.'"

Purification After Childbirth

12 The LORD said to Moses, ²"Say to the Israelites: 'A woman who becomes pregnant and gives birth to a son will be ceremonially unclean for seven days, just as she is unclean during her monthly period. ³On the eighth day the boy is to be circumcised. ⁴Then the woman must wait thirty-three days to be purified from her bleeding. She must not touch anything sacred or go to the sanctuary until the days of her purification are over. ⁵If she gives birth to a daughter, for two weeks the woman will be unclean, as during her period. Then she must wait sixty-six days to be purified from her bleeding.

⁶ "'When the days of her purification for a son or daughter are over, she is to bring to the priest at the entrance to the tent of meeting a year-old lamb for a burnt offering and a young pigeon or a dove for a sin offering.ᵃ ⁷He shall offer them before the LORD to make atonement for her, and then she will be ceremonially clean from her flow of blood.

" 'These are the regulations for the woman who gives birth to a boy or a girl. ⁸But if she cannot afford a lamb, she is to bring two doves or two young pigeons, one for a burnt offering and the other for a sin offering. In this way the priest will make atonement for her, and she will be clean.'"

Regulations About Defiling Skin Diseases

13 The LORD said to Moses and Aaron, ²"When anyone has a swelling or a rash or a shiny spot on their skin that may be a defiling skin disease,ᵇ they must be brought to Aaron the priest or to one of his sonsᶜ who is a priest. ³The priest is to examine the sore on the skin, and if the hair in the sore has turned white and

---

ᵃ 6 Or *purification offering*; also in verse 8   ᵇ 2 The Hebrew word for *defiling skin disease*, traditionally translated "leprosy," was used for various diseases affecting the skin; here and throughout verses 3-46.
ᶜ 2 Or *descendants*

the sore appears to be more than skin deep, it is a defiling skin disease. When the priest examines that person, he shall pronounce them ceremonially unclean. [4]If the shiny spot on the skin is white but does not appear to be more than skin deep and the hair in it has not turned white, the priest is to isolate the affected person for seven days. [5]On the seventh day the priest is to examine them, and if he sees that the sore is unchanged and has not spread in the skin, he is to isolate them for another seven days. [6]On the seventh day the priest is to examine them again, and if the sore has faded and has not spread in the skin, the priest shall pronounce them clean; it is only a rash. They must wash their clothes, and they will be clean. [7]But if the rash does spread in their skin after they have shown themselves to the priest to be pronounced clean, they must appear before the priest again. [8]The priest is to examine that person, and if the rash has spread in the skin, he shall pronounce them unclean; it is a defiling skin disease.

[9]"When anyone has a defiling skin disease, they must be brought to the priest. [10]The priest is to examine them, and if there is a white swelling in the skin that has turned the hair white and if there is raw flesh in the swelling, [11]it is a chronic skin disease and the priest shall pronounce them unclean. He is not to isolate them, because they are already unclean.

[12]"If the disease breaks out all over their skin and, so far as the priest can see, it covers all the skin of the affected person from head to foot, [13]the priest is to examine them, and if the disease has covered their whole body, he shall pronounce them clean. Since it has all turned white, they are clean. [14]But whenever raw flesh appears on them, they will be unclean. [15]When the priest sees the raw flesh, he shall pronounce them unclean. The raw flesh is unclean; they have a defiling disease. [16]If the raw flesh changes and turns white, they must go to the priest. [17]The priest is to examine them, and if the sores have turned white, the priest shall pronounce the affected person clean; then they will be clean.

[18]"When someone has a boil on their skin and it heals, [19]and in the place where the boil was, a white swelling or reddish-white spot appears, they must present themselves to the priest. [20]The priest is to examine it, and if it appears to be more than skin deep and the hair in it has turned white, the priest shall pronounce that person unclean. It is a defiling skin disease that has broken out where the boil was. [21]But if, when the priest examines it, there is no white hair in it and it is not more than skin deep and has faded, then the priest is to isolate them for seven days. [22]If it is spreading in the skin, the priest shall pronounce them unclean; it is a defiling disease. [23]But if the spot is unchanged and has not spread, it is only a scar from the boil, and the priest shall pronounce them clean.

[24]"When someone has a burn on their skin and a reddish-white or white spot appears in the raw flesh of the burn, [25]the priest is to examine the spot, and if the hair in it has turned white, and it appears to be more than skin deep, it is a defiling disease that has broken out in the burn. The priest shall pronounce them unclean; it is a defiling skin disease. [26]But if the priest examines it and there is no white hair in the spot and if it is not more than skin deep and has faded, then the priest is to isolate them for seven days. [27]On the seventh day the priest is to examine that person, and if it is spreading in the skin, the priest shall pronounce them unclean; it is a defiling skin disease. [28]If, however, the spot is unchanged and has not spread in the skin but has faded, it is a swelling from the burn, and the priest shall pronounce them clean; it is only a scar from the burn.

[29]"If a man or woman has a sore on their head or chin, [30]the priest is to examine the sore, and if it appears to be more than skin deep and the hair in it is yellow and thin, the priest shall pronounce them unclean; it is a defiling skin disease on the head or chin. [31]But if, when the priest examines the sore, it does not seem to be more than skin deep and there is no black hair in it, then the priest is to isolate the affected person for seven days.

Skin diseases

(LEVITICUS 13:1 - 46)

In Bible times, all skin diseases — like sores, infections and spots — were called leprosy. But this leprosy was not the terrible disease we know about today that is also called leprosy. So people who had skin problems had to live in groups of people who had the same problem, and they lived in lonely places far away. Visiting them was forbidden, because people thought disease was a punishment from God. And they thought these diseases could spread to them.

³²On the seventh day the priest is to examine the sore, and if it has not spread and there is no yellow hair in it and it does not appear to be more than skin deep, ³³then the man or woman must shave themselves, except for the affected area, and the priest is to keep them isolated another seven days. ³⁴On the seventh day the priest is to examine the sore, and if it has not spread in the skin and appears to be no more than skin deep, the priest shall pronounce them clean. They must wash their clothes, and they will be clean. ³⁵But if the sore does spread in the skin after they are pronounced clean, ³⁶the priest is to examine them, and if he finds that the sore has spread in the skin, he does not need to look for yellow hair; they are unclean. ³⁷If, however, the sore is unchanged so far as the priest can see, and if black hair has grown in it, the affected person is healed. They are clean, and the priest shall pronounce them clean.

³⁸"When a man or woman has white spots on the skin, ³⁹the priest is to examine them, and if the spots are dull white, it is a harmless rash that has broken out on the skin; they are clean.

⁴⁰"A man who has lost his hair and is bald is clean. ⁴¹If he has lost his hair from the front of his scalp and has a bald forehead, he is clean. ⁴²But if he has a reddish-white sore on his bald head or forehead, it is a defiling disease breaking out on his head or forehead. ⁴³The priest is to examine him, and if the swollen sore on his head or forehead is reddish-white like a defiling skin disease, ⁴⁴the man is diseased and is unclean. The priest shall pronounce him unclean because of the sore on his head.

⁴⁵"Anyone with such a defiling disease must wear torn clothes, let their hair be unkempt,[a] cover the lower part of their face and cry out, 'Unclean! Unclean!' ⁴⁶As long as they have the disease they remain unclean. They must live alone; they must live outside the camp.

Regulations About Defiling Molds

⁴⁷"As for any fabric that is spoiled with a defiling mold — any woolen or linen clothing, ⁴⁸any woven or knitted material of linen or wool, any leather or anything made of leather — ⁴⁹if the affected area in the fabric, the leather, the woven or knitted material, or any leather article, is greenish or reddish, it is a defiling mold and must be shown to the priest. ⁵⁰The priest is to examine the affected area and isolate the article for seven days. ⁵¹On the seventh day he is to examine it, and if the mold has spread in the fabric, the woven or knitted material, or the leather, whatever its use, it is a persistent defiling mold; the article is unclean. ⁵²He must burn the fabric, the woven or knitted material of wool or linen, or any leather

---

ᵃ 45 Or clothes, uncover their head

article that has been spoiled; because the defiling mold is persistent, the article must be burned.

53 "But if, when the priest examines it, the mold has not spread in the fabric, the woven or knitted material, or the leather article, 54he shall order that the spoiled article be washed. Then he is to isolate it for another seven days. 55After the article has been washed, the priest is to examine it again, and if the mold has not changed its appearance, even though it has not spread, it is unclean. Burn it, no matter which side of the fabric has been spoiled. 56If, when the priest examines it, the mold has faded after the article has been washed, he is to tear the spoiled part out of the fabric, the leather, or the woven or knitted material. 57But if it reappears in the fabric, in the woven or knitted material, or in the leather article, it is a spreading mold; whatever has the mold must be burned. 58Any fabric, woven or knitted material, or any leather article that has been washed and is rid of the mold, must be washed again. Then it will be clean."

59These are the regulations concerning defiling molds in woolen or linen clothing, woven or knitted material, or any leather article, for pronouncing them clean or unclean.

Cleansing From Defiling Skin Diseases

14 The Lord said to Moses, 2"These are the regulations for any diseased person at the time of their ceremonial cleansing, when they are brought to the priest: 3The priest is to go outside the camp and examine them. If they have been healed of their defiling skin disease,[a] 4the priest shall order that two live clean birds and some cedar wood, scarlet yarn and hyssop be brought for the person to be cleansed. 5Then the priest shall order that one of the birds be killed over fresh water in a clay pot. 6He is then to take the live bird and dip it, together with the cedar wood, the scarlet yarn and the hyssop, into the blood of the bird that was killed over the fresh water. 7Seven times

he shall sprinkle the one to be cleansed of the defiling disease, and then pronounce them clean. After that, he is to release the live bird in the open fields.

8"The person to be cleansed must wash their clothes, shave off all their hair and bathe with water; then they will be ceremonially clean. After this they may come into the camp, but they must stay outside their tent for seven days. 9On the seventh day they must shave off all their hair; they must shave their head, their beard, their eyebrows and the rest of their hair. They must wash their clothes and bathe themselves with water, and they will be clean.

10"On the eighth day they must bring two male lambs and one ewe lamb a year old, each without defect, along with three-tenths of an ephah[b] of the finest flour mixed with olive oil for a grain offering, and one log[c] of oil. 11The priest who pronounces them clean shall present both the one to be cleansed and their offerings before the Lord at the entrance to the tent of meeting.

12"Then the priest is to take one of the male lambs and offer it as a guilt offering, along with the log of oil; he shall wave them before the Lord as a wave offering. 13He is to slaughter the lamb in the sanctuary area where the sin offering[d] and the burnt offering are slaughtered. Like the sin offering, the guilt offering belongs to the priest; it is most holy. 14The priest is to take some of the blood of the guilt offering and put it on the lobe of the right ear of the one to be cleansed, on the thumb of their right hand and on the big toe of their right foot. 15The priest shall then take some of the log of oil, pour it in the palm of his own left hand, 16dip his right forefinger into the oil in his palm, and with his finger sprinkle some of it before the Lord seven times. 17The priest is to put some of the oil remaining in his palm on the lobe of the right ear of the one to be cleansed, on the thumb of their

---

a 3 The Hebrew word for *defiling skin disease*, traditionally translated "leprosy," was used for various diseases affecting the skin; also in verses 7, 32, 54 and 57.
b 10 That is, probably about 11 pounds or about 5 kilograms   *c 10* That is, about 1/3 quart or about 0.3 liter; also in verses 12, 15, 21 and 24   *d 13* Or *purification offering*; also in verses 19, 22 and 31

right hand and on the big toe of their right foot, on top of the blood of the guilt offering. [18]The rest of the oil in his palm the priest shall put on the head of the one to be cleansed and make atonement for them before the LORD.

[19]"Then the priest is to sacrifice the sin offering and make atonement for the one to be cleansed from their uncleanness. After that, the priest shall slaughter the burnt offering [20]and offer it on the altar, together with the grain offering, and make atonement for them, and they will be clean.

[21]"If, however, they are poor and cannot afford these, they must take one male lamb as a guilt offering to be waved to make atonement for them, together with a tenth of an ephah[a] of the finest flour mixed with olive oil for a grain offering, a log of oil, [22]and two doves or two young pigeons, such as they can afford, one for a sin offering and the other for a burnt offering.

[23]"On the eighth day they must bring them for their cleansing to the priest at the entrance to the tent of meeting, before the LORD. [24]The priest is to take the lamb for the guilt offering, together with the log of oil, and wave them before the LORD as a wave offering. [25]He shall slaughter the lamb for the guilt offering and take some of its blood and put it on the lobe of the right ear of the one to be cleansed, on the thumb of their right hand and on the big toe of their right foot. [26]The priest is to pour some of the oil into the palm of his own left hand, [27]and with his right forefinger sprinkle some of the oil from his palm seven times before the LORD. [28]Some of the oil in his palm he is to put on the same places he put the blood of the guilt offering—on the lobe of the right ear of the one to be cleansed, on the thumb of their right hand and on the big toe of their right foot. [29]The rest of the oil in his palm the priest shall put on the head of the one to be cleansed, to make atonement for them before the LORD. [30]Then he shall sacrifice the doves or the young pigeons, such as the person can afford, [31]one as a sin offering and the other as a burnt offering, together with the grain offering. In

this way the priest will make atonement before the LORD on behalf of the one to be cleansed."

[32]These are the regulations for anyone who has a defiling skin disease and who cannot afford the regular offerings for their cleansing.

Cleansing From Defiling Molds

[33]The LORD said to Moses and Aaron, [34]"When you enter the land of Canaan, which I am giving you as your possession, and I put a spreading mold in a house in that land, [35]the owner of the house must go and tell the priest, 'I have seen something that looks like a defiling mold in my house.' [36]The priest is to order the house to be emptied before he goes in to examine the mold, so that nothing in the house will be pronounced unclean. After this the priest is to go in and inspect the house. [37]He is to examine the mold on the walls, and if it has greenish or reddish depressions that appear to be deeper than the surface of the wall, [38]the priest shall go out the doorway of the house and close it up for seven days. [39]On the seventh day the priest shall return to inspect the house. If the mold has spread on the walls, [40]he is to order that the contaminated stones be torn out and thrown into an unclean place outside the town. [41]He must have all the inside walls of the house scraped and the material that is scraped off dumped into an unclean place outside the town. [42]Then they are to take other stones to replace these and take new clay and plaster the house.

[43]"If the defiling mold reappears in the house after the stones have been torn out and the house scraped and plastered, [44]the priest is to go and examine it and, if the mold has spread in the house, it is a persistent defiling mold; the house is unclean. [45]It must be torn down—its stones, timbers and all the plaster—and taken out of the town to an unclean place.

[46]"Anyone who goes into the house while it is closed up will be unclean till evening. [47]Anyone who sleeps or eats in the house must wash their clothes.

---

[a] 21 That is, probably about 3 1/2 pounds or about 1.6 kilograms

⁴⁸"But if the priest comes to examine it and the mold has not spread after the house has been plastered, he shall pronounce the house clean, because the defiling mold is gone. ⁴⁹To purify the house he is to take two birds and some cedar wood, scarlet yarn and hyssop. ⁵⁰He shall kill one of the birds over fresh water in a clay pot. ⁵¹Then he is to take the cedar wood, the hyssop, the scarlet yarn and the live bird, dip them into the blood of the dead bird and the fresh water, and sprinkle the house seven times. ⁵²He shall purify the house with the bird's blood, the fresh water, the live bird, the cedar wood, the hyssop and the scarlet yarn. ⁵³Then he is to release the live bird in the open fields outside the town. In this way he will make atonement for the house, and it will be clean."

⁵⁴These are the regulations for any defiling skin disease, for a sore, ⁵⁵for defiling molds in fabric or in a house, ⁵⁶and for a swelling, a rash or a shiny spot, ⁵⁷to determine when something is clean or unclean.

These are the regulations for defiling skin diseases and defiling molds.

Discharges Causing Uncleanness

15 The LORD said to Moses and Aaron, ²"Speak to the Israelites and say to them: 'When any man has an unusual bodily discharge, such a discharge is unclean. ³Whether it continues flowing from his body or is blocked, it will make him unclean. This is how his discharge will bring about uncleanness:

⁴"'Any bed the man with a discharge lies on will be unclean, and anything he sits on will be unclean. ⁵Anyone who touches his bed must wash their clothes and bathe with water, and they will be unclean till evening. ⁶Whoever sits on anything that the man with a discharge sat on must wash their clothes and bathe with water, and they will be unclean till evening. ⁷"'Whoever touches the man who has a discharge must wash their clothes and bathe with water, and they will be unclean till evening.

⁸"'If the man with the discharge spits on anyone who is clean, they must wash their clothes and bathe with water, and they will be unclean till evening. ⁹"'Everything the man sits on when riding will be unclean, ¹⁰and whoever touches any of the things that were under him will be unclean till evening; whoever picks up those things must wash their clothes and bathe with water, and they will be unclean till evening. ¹¹"'Anyone the man with a discharge touches without rinsing his hands with water must wash their clothes and bathe with water, and they will be unclean till evening.

¹²"'A clay pot that the man touches must be broken, and any wooden article is to be rinsed with water.

¹³"'When a man is cleansed from his discharge, he is to count off seven days for his ceremonial cleansing; he must wash his clothes and bathe himself with fresh water, and he will be clean. ¹⁴On the eighth day he must take two doves or two young pigeons and come before the LORD to the entrance to the tent of meeting and give them to the priest. ¹⁵The priest is to sacrifice them, the one for a sin offering[a] and the other for a burnt offering. In this way he will make atonement before the LORD for the man because of his discharge.

¹⁶"'When a man has an emission of semen, he must bathe his whole body with water, and he will be unclean till evening. ¹⁷Any clothing or leather that has semen on it must be washed with water, and it will be unclean till evening. ¹⁸When a man has sexual relations with a woman and there is an emission of semen, both of them must bathe with water, and they will be unclean till evening.

¹⁹"'When a woman has her regular flow of blood, the impurity of her monthly period will last seven days, and anyone who touches her will be unclean till evening.

²⁰"'Anything she lies on during her period will be unclean, and anything she sits on will be unclean. ²¹Anyone who touches her bed will be unclean; they must wash their clothes and bathe with water, and

_____

a 15 Or *purification offering*; also in verse 30

they will be unclean till evening. ²²Anyone who touches anything she sits on will be unclean; they must wash their clothes and bathe with water, and they will be unclean till evening. ²³Whether it is the bed or anything she was sitting on, when anyone touches it, they will be unclean till evening.

²⁴ "If a man has sexual relations with her and her monthly flow touches him, he will be unclean for seven days; any bed he lies on will be unclean.

²⁵ "When a woman has a discharge of blood for many days at a time other than her monthly period or has a discharge that continues beyond her period, she will be unclean as long as she has the discharge, just as in the days of her period. ²⁶Any bed she lies on while her discharge continues will be unclean, as is her bed during her monthly period, and anything she sits on will be unclean, as during her period. ²⁷Anyone who touches them will be unclean; they must wash their clothes and bathe with water, and they will be unclean till evening.

²⁸ "When she is cleansed from her discharge, she must count off seven days, and after that she will be ceremonially clean. ²⁹On the eighth day she must take two doves or two young pigeons and bring them to the priest at the entrance to the tent of meeting. ³⁰The priest is to sacrifice one for a sin offering and the other for a burnt offering. In this way he will make atonement for her before the LORD for the uncleanness of her discharge.

³¹ "'You must keep the Israelites separate from things that make them unclean, so they will not die in their uncleanness for defiling my dwelling place,ᵃ which is among them.'"

³²These are the regulations for a man with a discharge, for anyone made unclean by an emission of semen, ³³for a woman in her monthly period, for a man or a woman with a discharge, and for a man who has sexual relations with a woman who is ceremonially unclean.

The Day of Atonement

16 The LORD spoke to Moses after the death of the two sons of Aaron who died when they approached the LORD.

²The LORD said to Moses: "Tell your brother Aaron that he is not to come whenever he chooses into the Most Holy Place behind the curtain in front of the atonement cover on the ark, or else he will die. For I will appear in the cloud over the atonement cover.

³ "This is how Aaron is to enter the Most Holy Place: He must first bring a young bull for a sin offeringᵇ and a ram for a burnt offering. ⁴He is to put on the sacred linen tunic, with linen undergarments next to his body; he is to tie the linen sash around him and put on the linen turban. These are sacred garments; so he must

---

ᵃ 31 Or *my tabernacle*   ᵇ 3 Or *purification offering*; here and throughout this chapter

BREAK THROUGH!

The Most Holy Place

(LEVITICUS 16:2)

The Holy Place and the Most Holy Place were the most "sacred" parts of the sanctuary. The incense altar, the pure gold lampstand and the gold table with 12 loaves of bread were kept in the Holy Place. The ark of the covenant with the cherubim was in the Most Holy Place, indicating the presence of God. Only the high priest could go in there, and he went just once a year. That's all different now, because Jesus made it so any one of us, as a child of God, can go to the Father whenever we want.

bathe himself with water before he puts them on. ⁵From the Israelite community he is to take two male goats for a sin offering and a ram for a burnt offering.

⁶"Aaron is to offer the bull for his own sin offering to make atonement for himself and his household. ⁷Then he is to take the two goats and present them before the Lᴏʀᴅ at the entrance to the tent of meeting. ⁸He is to cast lots for the two goats—one lot for the Lᴏʀᴅ and the other for the scapegoat.ᵃ ⁹Aaron shall bring the goat whose lot falls to the Lᴏʀᴅ and sacrifice it for a sin offering. ¹⁰But the goat chosen by lot as the scapegoat shall be presented alive before the Lᴏʀᴅ to be used for making atonement by sending it into the wilderness as a scapegoat.

¹¹"Aaron shall bring the bull for his own sin offering to make atonement for himself and his household, and he is to slaughter the bull for his own sin offering. ¹²He is to take a censer full of burning coals from the altar before the Lᴏʀᴅ and two handfuls of finely ground fragrant incense and take them behind the curtain. ¹³He is to put the incense on the fire before the Lᴏʀᴅ, and the smoke of the incense will conceal the atonement cover above the tablets of the covenant law, so that he will not die. ¹⁴He is to take some of the bull's blood and with his finger sprinkle it on the front of the atonement cover; then he shall sprinkle some of it with his finger seven times before the atonement cover.

¹⁵"He shall then slaughter the goat for the sin offering for the people and take its blood behind the curtain and do with it as he did with the bull's blood: He shall sprinkle it on the atonement cover and in front of it. ¹⁶In this way he will make atonement for the Most Holy Place because of the uncleanness and rebellion of the Israelites, whatever their sins have been. He is to do the same for the tent of meeting, which is among them in the midst of their uncleanness. ¹⁷No one is to be in the tent of meeting from the time Aaron goes in to make atonement in the Most Holy Place until he comes out, having made atonement for himself, his household and the whole community of Israel.

¹⁸"Then he shall come out to the altar that is before the Lᴏʀᴅ and make atonement for it. He shall take some of the bull's blood and some of the goat's blood and put it on all the horns of the altar. ¹⁹He shall sprinkle some of the blood on it with his finger seven times to cleanse it and to consecrate it from the uncleanness of the Israelites.

²⁰"When Aaron has finished making atonement for the Most Holy Place, the tent of meeting and the altar, he shall bring forward the live goat. ²¹He is to lay both hands on the head of the live goat and confess over it all the wickedness and rebellion of the Israelites—all their sins—and put them on the goat's head. He shall send the goat away into the wilderness in the care of someone appointed for the task. ²²The goat will carry on itself all their sins to a remote place; and the man shall release it in the wilderness.

²³"Then Aaron is to go into the tent of meeting and take off the linen garments he put on before he entered the Most Holy Place, and he is to leave them there. ²⁴He shall bathe himself with water in the sanctuary area and put on his regular garments. Then he shall come out and sacrifice the burnt offering for himself and the burnt offering for the people, to make atonement for himself and for the people. ²⁵He shall also burn the fat of the sin offering on the altar.

²⁶"The man who releases the goat as a scapegoat must wash his clothes and bathe himself with water; afterward he may come into the camp. ²⁷The bull and the goat for the sin offerings, whose blood was brought into the Most Holy Place to make atonement, must be taken outside the camp; their hides, flesh and intestines are to be burned up. ²⁸The man who burns them must wash his clothes and bathe himself with water; afterward he may come into the camp.

²⁹"This is to be a lasting ordinance for you: On the tenth day of the seventh month you must deny yourselvesᵇ and not do any work—whether native-born or a foreigner

---

ᵃ 8 The meaning of the Hebrew for this word is uncertain; also in verses 10 and 26.　ᵇ 29 Or *must fast*; also in verse 31

Tenth month
(LEVITICUS 16:29)
This is Tebeth, the tenth month in the Jewish lunar calendar. In our solar calendar, it would be more or less from the middle of December to the middle of January.

residing among you— ³⁰because on this day atonement will be made for you, to cleanse you. Then, before the Lᴏʀᴅ, you will be clean from all your sins. ³¹It is a day of sabbath rest, and you must deny yourselves; it is a lasting ordinance. ³²The priest who is anointed and ordained to succeed his father as high priest is to make atonement. He is to put on the sacred linen garments ³³and make atonement for the Most Holy Place, for the tent of meeting and the altar, and for the priests and all the members of the community.

³⁴"This is to be a lasting ordinance for you: Atonement is to be made once a year for all the sins of the Israelites."

And it was done, as the Lᴏʀᴅ commanded Moses.

Eating Blood Forbidden

17 The Lᴏʀᴅ said to Moses, ²"Speak to Aaron and his sons and to all the Israelites and say to them: 'This is what the Lᴏʀᴅ has commanded: ³Any Israelite who sacrifices an ox,ᵃ a lamb or a goat in the camp or outside of it ⁴instead of bringing it to the entrance to the tent of meeting to present it as an offering to the Lᴏʀᴅ in front of the tabernacle of the Lᴏʀᴅ— that person shall be considered guilty of bloodshed; they have shed blood and must be cut off from their people. ⁵This is so the Israelites will bring to the Lᴏʀᴅ the sacrifices they are now making in the open fields. They must bring them to the priest, that is, to the Lᴏʀᴅ, at the entrance to the tent of meeting and sacrifice them as fellowship offerings. ⁶The priest is to splash the blood against the altar of the Lᴏʀᴅ at the entrance to the tent of meeting and burn the fat as an aroma pleasing to the Lᴏʀᴅ. ⁷They must no longer offer any of their sacrifices to the goat idolsᵇ to whom they prostitute themselves. This is to be a lasting ordinance for them and for the generations to come.'

⁸"Say to them: 'Any Israelite or any foreigner residing among them who offers a burnt offering or sacrifice ⁹and does not bring it to the entrance to the tent of meeting to sacrifice it to the Lᴏʀᴅ must be cut off from the people of Israel.

¹⁰"'I will set my face against any Israelite or any foreigner residing among them who eats blood, and I will cut them off from the people. ¹¹For the life of a creature is in the blood, and I have given it to you to make atonement for yourselves on the altar; it is the blood that makes atonement for one's life.ᶜ ¹²Therefore I say to the Israelites, "None of you may eat blood, nor may any foreigner residing among you eat blood."

¹³"'Any Israelite or any foreigner residing among you who hunts any animal or bird that may be eaten must drain out the blood and cover it with earth, ¹⁴because the life of every creature is its blood. That is why I have said to the Israelites, "You must not eat the blood of any creature, because the life of every creature is its blood; anyone who eats it must be cut off."

¹⁵"'Anyone, whether native-born or foreigner, who eats anything found dead or torn by wild animals must wash their

---

ᵃ 3 The Hebrew word can refer to either male or female.
ᵇ 7 Or *the demons*   ᶜ 11 Or *atonement by the life in the blood*

clothes and bathe with water, and they will be ceremonially unclean till evening; then they will be clean. ¹⁶But if they do not wash their clothes and bathe themselves, they will be held responsible.' "

Unlawful Sexual Relations

18 The LORD said to Moses, ²"Speak to the Israelites and say to them: 'I am the LORD your God. ³You must not do as they do in Egypt, where you used to live, and you must not do as they do in the land of Canaan, where I am bringing you. Do not follow their practices. ⁴You must obey my laws and be careful to follow my decrees. I am the LORD your God. ⁵Keep my decrees and laws, for the person who obeys them will live by them. I am the LORD.

⁶" 'No one is to approach any close relative to have sexual relations. I am the LORD.

⁷" 'Do not dishonor your father by having sexual relations with your mother. She is your mother; do not have relations with her.

⁸" 'Do not have sexual relations with your father's wife; that would dishonor your father.

⁹" 'Do not have sexual relations with your sister, either your father's daughter or your mother's daughter, whether she was born in the same home or elsewhere.

¹⁰" 'Do not have sexual relations with your son's daughter or your daughter's daughter; that would dishonor you.

¹¹" 'Do not have sexual relations with the daughter of your father's wife, born to your father; she is your sister.

¹²" 'Do not have sexual relations with your father's sister; she is your father's close relative.

¹³" 'Do not have sexual relations with your mother's sister, because she is your mother's close relative.

¹⁴" 'Do not dishonor your father's brother by approaching his wife to have sexual relations; she is your aunt.

¹⁵" 'Do not have sexual relations with your daughter-in-law. She is your son's wife; do not have relations with her.

¹⁶" 'Do not have sexual relations with your brother's wife; that would dishonor your brother.

¹⁷" 'Do not have sexual relations with both a woman and her daughter. Do not have sexual relations with either her son's daughter or her daughter's daughter; they are her close relatives. That is wickedness.

¹⁸" 'Do not take your wife's sister as a rival wife and have sexual relations with her while your wife is living.

¹⁹" 'Do not approach a woman to have sexual relations during the uncleanness of her monthly period.

²⁰" 'Do not have sexual relations with your neighbor's wife and defile yourself with her.

²¹" 'Do not give any of your children to be sacrificed to Molek, for you must not profane the name of your God. I am the LORD.

²²" 'Do not have sexual relations with a man as one does with a woman; that is detestable.

²³" 'Do not have sexual relations with an animal and defile yourself with it. A woman must not present herself to an animal to have sexual relations with it; that is a perversion.

²⁴" 'Do not defile yourselves in any of these ways, because this is how the nations that I am going to drive out before you became defiled. ²⁵Even the land was defiled; so I punished it for its sin, and the land vomited out its inhabitants. ²⁶But you must keep my decrees and my laws. The native-born and the foreigners residing among you must not do any of these detestable things, ²⁷for all these things were done by the people who lived in the land before you, and the land became defiled. ²⁸And if you defile the land, it will vomit you out as it vomited out the nations that were before you.

²⁹" 'Everyone who does any of these detestable things—such persons must be cut off from their people. ³⁰Keep my requirements and do not follow any of the detestable customs that were practiced before you came and do not defile yourselves with them. I am the LORD your God.' "

Various Laws

19 The LORD said to Moses, ²"Speak to the entire assembly of Israel and say to them: 'Be holy because I, the LORD your God, am holy.

³ " 'Each of you must respect your mother and father, and you must observe my Sabbaths. I am the LORD your God.

⁴ " 'Do not turn to idols or make metal gods for yourselves. I am the LORD your God.

⁵ " 'When you sacrifice a fellowship offering to the LORD, sacrifice it in such a way that it will be accepted on your behalf. ⁶It shall be eaten on the day you sacrifice it or on the next day; anything left over until the third day must be burned up. ⁷If any of it is eaten on the third day, it is impure and will not be accepted. ⁸Whoever eats it will be held responsible because they have desecrated what is holy to the LORD; they must be cut off from their people.

⁹ " 'When you reap the harvest of your land, do not reap to the very edges of your field or gather the gleanings of your harvest. ¹⁰Do not go over your vineyard a second time or pick up the grapes that have fallen. Leave them for the poor and the foreigner. I am the LORD your God.

¹¹ " 'Do not steal.

" 'Do not lie.

" 'Do not deceive one another.

¹² " 'Do not swear falsely by my name and so profane the name of your God. I am the LORD.

¹³ " 'Do not defraud or rob your neighbor.

" 'Do not hold back the wages of a hired worker overnight.

¹⁴ " 'Do not curse the deaf or put a stumbling block in front of the blind, but fear your God. I am the LORD.

¹⁵ " 'Do not pervert justice; do not show partiality to the poor or favoritism to the great, but judge your neighbor fairly.

¹⁶ " 'Do not go about spreading slander among your people.

" 'Do not do anything that endangers your neighbor's life. I am the LORD.

¹⁷ " 'Do not hate a fellow Israelite in your heart. Rebuke your neighbor frankly so you will not share in their guilt.

¹⁸ " 'Do not seek revenge or bear a grudge against anyone among your people, but love your neighbor as yourself. I am the LORD.

¹⁹ " 'Keep my decrees.

" 'Do not mate different kinds of animals.

" 'Do not plant your field with two kinds of seed.

" 'Do not wear clothing woven of two kinds of material.

²⁰ " 'If a man sleeps with a female slave who is promised to another man but who has not been ransomed or given her freedom, there must be due punishment.ᵃ Yet they are not to be put to death, because she had not been freed. ²¹The man, however, must bring a ram to the entrance to the tent of meeting for a guilt offering to the LORD. ²²With the ram of the guilt offering the priest is to make atonement for him before the LORD for the sin he has committed, and his sin will be forgiven.

ᵃ 20 Or be an inquiry

BREAKTHROUGH!

Why couldn't they wear clothes that were woven of two kinds of materials?
(LEVITICUS 19:17-19)

How strange! We really don't know why God said this. Maybe it was because that was what magicians did in other nations. Remember that in this book, God always said that Israel was different from other nations. Also, Genesis 1 says that God separated elements in nature and put them in order.

23 " 'When you enter the land and plant any kind of fruit tree, regard its fruit as forbidden.[a] For three years you are to consider it forbidden[a]; it must not be eaten. 24In the fourth year all its fruit will be holy, an offering of praise to the LORD. 25But in the fifth year you may eat its fruit. In this way your harvest will be increased. I am the LORD your God.

26 " 'Do not eat any meat with the blood still in it.

" 'Do not practice divination or seek omens.

27 " 'Do not cut the hair at the sides of your head or clip off the edges of your beard.

28 " 'Do not cut your bodies for the dead or put tattoo marks on yourselves. I am the LORD.

29 " 'Do not degrade your daughter by making her a prostitute, or the land will turn to prostitution and be filled with wickedness.

30 " 'Observe my Sabbaths and have reverence for my sanctuary. I am the LORD.

31 " 'Do not turn to mediums or seek out spiritists, for you will be defiled by them. I am the LORD your God.

32 " 'Stand up in the presence of the aged, show respect for the elderly and revere your God. I am the LORD.

33 " 'When a foreigner resides among you in your land, do not mistreat them. 34The foreigner residing among you must be treated as your native-born. Love them as yourself, for you were foreigners in Egypt. I am the LORD your God.

35 " 'Do not use dishonest standards when measuring length, weight or quantity. 36Use honest scales and honest weights, an honest ephah[b] and an honest hin.[c] I am the LORD your God, who brought you out of Egypt.

37 " 'Keep all my decrees and all my laws and follow them. I am the LORD.' "

Punishments for Sin

20 The LORD said to Moses, 2"Say to the Israelites: 'Any Israelite or any foreigner residing in Israel who sacrifices any of his children to Molek is to be put to death. The members of the community are to stone him. 3I myself will set my face against him and will cut him off from his people; for by sacrificing his children to Molek, he has defiled my sanctuary and profaned my holy name. 4If the members of the community close their eyes when that man sacrifices one of his children to Molek and if they fail to put him to death, 5I myself will set my face against him and his family and will cut them off from their people together with all who follow him in prostituting themselves to Molek.

6 " 'I will set my face against anyone who turns to mediums and spiritists to prostitute themselves by following them, and I will cut them off from their people.

7 " 'Consecrate yourselves and be holy, because I am the LORD your God. 8Keep my decrees and follow them. I am the LORD, who makes you holy.

9 " 'Anyone who curses their father or mother is to be put to death. Because they have cursed their father or mother, their blood will be on their own head.

10 " 'If a man commits adultery with another man's wife—with the wife of his neighbor—both the adulterer and the adulteress are to be put to death.

11 " 'If a man has sexual relations with his father's wife, he has dishonored his father. Both the man and the woman are to be put to death; their blood will be on their own heads.

12 " 'If a man has sexual relations with his daughter-in-law, both of them are to be put to death. What they have done is a perversion; their blood will be on their own heads.

13 " 'If a man has sexual relations with a man as one does with a woman, both of them have done what is detestable. They are to be put to death; their blood will be on their own heads.

14 " 'If a man marries both a woman and her mother, it is wicked. Both he and they must be burned in the fire, so that no wickedness will be among you.

15 " 'If a man has sexual relations with an animal, he is to be put to death, and you must kill the animal.

---

[a] 23 Hebrew *uncircumcised*   [b] 36 An ephah was a dry measure having the capacity of about 3/5 of a bushel or about 22 liters.   [c] 36 A hin was a liquid measure having the capacity of about 1 gallon or about 3.8 liters.

16 " 'If a woman approaches an animal to have sexual relations with it, kill both the woman and the animal. They are to be put to death; their blood will be on their own heads.

17 " 'If a man marries his sister, the daughter of either his father or his mother, and they have sexual relations, it is a disgrace. They are to be publicly removed from their people. He has dishonored his sister and will be held responsible.

18 " 'If a man has sexual relations with a woman during her monthly period, he has exposed the source of her flow, and she has also uncovered it. Both of them are to be cut off from their people.

19 " 'Do not have sexual relations with the sister of either your mother or your father, for that would dishonor a close relative; both of you would be held responsible.

20 " 'If a man has sexual relations with his aunt, he has dishonored his uncle. They will be held responsible; they will die childless.

21 " 'If a man marries his brother's wife, it is an act of impurity; he has dishonored his brother. They will be childless.

22 " 'Keep all my decrees and laws and follow them, so that the land where I am bringing you to live may not vomit you out. 23 You must not live according to the customs of the nations I am going to drive out before you. Because they did all these things, I abhorred them. 24 But I said to you, "You will possess their land; I will give it to you as an inheritance, a land flowing with milk and honey." I am the LORD your God, who has set you apart from the nations.

25 " 'You must therefore make a distinction between clean and unclean animals and between unclean and clean birds. Do not defile yourselves by any animal or bird or anything that moves along the ground— those that I have set apart as unclean for you. 26 You are to be holy to me because I, the LORD, am holy, and I have set you apart from the nations to be my own.

27 " 'A man or woman who is a medium or spiritist among you must be put to death. You are to stone them; their blood will be on their own heads.' "

Rules for Priests

21 The LORD said to Moses, "Speak to the priests, the sons of Aaron, and say to them: 'A priest must not make himself ceremonially unclean for any of his people who die, 2 except for a close relative, such as his mother or father, his son or daughter, his brother, 3 or an unmarried sister who is dependent on him since she has no husband—for her he may make himself unclean. 4 He must not make himself unclean for people related to him by marriage,[a] and so defile himself.

5 " 'Priests must not shave their heads or shave off the edges of their beards or cut their bodies. 6 They must be holy to their God and must not profane the name of their God. Because they present the food offerings to the LORD, the food of their God, they are to be holy.

7 " 'They must not marry women defiled by prostitution or divorced from their husbands, because priests are holy to their God. 8 Regard them as holy, because they offer up the food of your God. Consider them holy, because I the LORD am holy—I who make you holy.

9 " 'If a priest's daughter defiles herself by becoming a prostitute, she disgraces her father; she must be burned in the fire.

10 " 'The high priest, the one among his brothers who has had the anointing oil poured on his head and who has been ordained to wear the priestly garments, must not let his hair become unkempt[b] or tear his clothes. 11 He must not enter a place where there is a dead body. He must not make himself unclean, even for his father or mother, 12 nor leave the sanctuary of his God or desecrate it, because he has been dedicated by the anointing oil of his God. I am the LORD.

13 " 'The woman he marries must be a virgin. 14 He must not marry a widow, a divorced woman, or a woman defiled by prostitution, but only a virgin from his own people, 15 so that he will not defile his offspring among his people. I am the LORD, who makes him holy.' "

---

a 4 Or unclean as a leader among his people   b 10 Or not uncover his head

16The LORD said to Moses, 17"Say to Aaron: 'For the generations to come none of your descendants who has a defect may come near to offer the food of his God. 18No man who has any defect may come near: no man who is blind or lame, disfigured or deformed; 19no man with a crippled foot or hand, 20or who is a hunchback or a dwarf, or who has any eye defect, or who has festering or running sores or damaged testicles. 21No descendant of Aaron the priest who has any defect is to come near to present

BREAKTHROUGH!

Why couldn't a priest who had some physical flaw go near the altar of God?

(LEVITICUS 21:17‑23)

This is another strange thing, but it was common in the entire region at that time. The priests had to be completely healthy. And the animals they sacrificed also had to be healthy. Because God is holy, only a person who was physically and honestly "perfect" could come near the altar of the sanctuary to carry out his work. It was the same for the people who waited on the king. They had to be healthy too, and they couldn't have any misshapenness or injury. Thank goodness that has all changed now!

the food offerings to the LORD. He has a defect; he must not come near to offer the food of his God. 22He may eat the most holy food of his God, as well as the holy food; 23yet because of his defect, he must not go near the curtain or approach the altar, and so desecrate my sanctuary. I am the LORD, who makes them holy.' "

24So Moses told this to Aaron and his sons and to all the Israelites.

22 The LORD said to Moses, 2"Tell Aaron and his sons to treat with respect the sacred offerings the Israelites consecrate to me, so they will not profane my holy name. I am the LORD.

3"Say to them: 'For the generations to come, if any of your descendants is ceremonially unclean and yet comes near the sacred offerings that the Israelites consecrate to the LORD, that person must be cut off from my presence. I am the LORD.

4" 'If a descendant of Aaron has a defiling skin disease[a] or a bodily discharge, he may not eat the sacred offerings until he is cleansed. He will also be unclean if he touches something defiled by a corpse or by anyone who has an emission of semen, 5or if he touches any crawling thing that makes him unclean, or any person who makes him unclean, whatever the uncleanness may be. 6The one who touches any such thing will be unclean till evening. He must not eat any of the sacred offerings unless he has bathed himself with water. 7When the sun goes down, he will be clean, and after that he may eat the sacred offerings, for they are his food. 8He must not eat anything found dead or torn by wild animals, and so become unclean through it. I am the LORD.

9" 'The priests are to perform my service in such a way that they do not become guilty and die for treating it with contempt. I am the LORD, who makes them holy.

10" 'No one outside a priest's family may eat the sacred offering, nor may the guest of a priest or his hired worker

---

[a] 4 The Hebrew word for *defiling skin disease*, traditionally translated "leprosy," was used for various diseases affecting the skin.

eat it. ¹¹But if a priest buys a slave with money, or if slaves are born in his household, they may eat his food. ¹²If a priest's daughter marries anyone other than a priest, she may not eat any of the sacred contributions. ¹³But if a priest's daughter becomes a widow or is divorced, yet has no children, and she returns to live in her father's household as in her youth, she may eat her father's food. No unauthorized person, however, may eat it.

¹⁴ " 'Anyone who eats a sacred offering by mistake must make restitution to the priest for the offering and add a fifth of the value to it. ¹⁵The priests must not desecrate the sacred offerings the Israelites present to the LORD ¹⁶by allowing them to eat the sacred offerings and so bring upon them guilt requiring payment. I am the LORD, who makes them holy.' "

Unacceptable Sacrifices

¹⁷The LORD said to Moses, ¹⁸"Speak to Aaron and his sons and to all the Israelites and say to them: 'If any of you— whether an Israelite or a foreigner residing in Israel—presents a gift for a burnt offering to the LORD, either to fulfill a vow or as a freewill offering, ¹⁹you must present a male without defect from the cattle, sheep or goats in order that it may be accepted on your behalf. ²⁰Do not bring anything with a defect, because it will not be accepted on your behalf. ²¹When anyone brings from the herd or flock a fellowship offering to the LORD to fulfill a special vow or as a freewill offering, it must be without defect or blemish to be acceptable. ²²Do not offer to the LORD the blind, the injured or the maimed, or anything with warts or festering or running sores. Do not place any of these on the altar as a food offering presented to the LORD. ²³You may, however, present as a freewill offering an ox*ᵃ* or a sheep that is deformed or stunted, but it will not be accepted in fulfillment of a vow. ²⁴You must not offer to the LORD an animal whose testicles are bruised, crushed, torn or cut. You must not do this in your own land, ²⁵and you must not accept such animals from the hand of a foreigner and offer them as the food of your God. They

will not be accepted on your behalf, because they are deformed and have defects.' "

²⁶The LORD said to Moses, ²⁷"When a calf, a lamb or a goat is born, it is to remain with its mother for seven days. From the eighth day on, it will be acceptable as a food offering presented to the LORD. ²⁸Do not slaughter a cow or a sheep and its young on the same day.

²⁹"When you sacrifice a thank offering to the LORD, sacrifice it in such a way that it will be accepted on your behalf. ³⁰It must be eaten that same day; leave none of it till morning. I am the LORD.

³¹"Keep my commands and follow them. I am the LORD. ³²Do not profane my holy name, for I must be acknowledged as holy by the Israelites. I am the LORD, who made you holy ³³and who brought you out of Egypt to be your God. I am the LORD."

The Appointed Festivals

23 The LORD said to Moses, ²"Speak to the Israelites and say to them: 'These are my appointed festivals, the appointed festivals of the LORD, which you are to proclaim as sacred assemblies.

The Sabbath

³ " 'There are six days when you may work, but the seventh day is a day of sabbath rest, a day of sacred assembly. You are not to do any work; wherever you live, it is a sabbath to the LORD.

The Passover and the Festival of Unleavened Bread

⁴ " 'These are the LORD's appointed festivals, the sacred assemblies you are to proclaim at their appointed times: ⁵The LORD's Passover begins at twilight on the fourteenth day of the first month. ⁶On the fifteenth day of that month the LORD's Festival of Unleavened Bread begins; for seven days you must eat bread made without yeast. ⁷On the first day hold a sacred assembly and do no regular work. ⁸For seven days present a food offering to the LORD. And on the seventh day hold a sacred assembly and do no regular work.' "

ᵃ 23 The Hebrew word can refer to either male or female.

BREAKTHROUGH!

The first month

(LEVITICUS 23:5)

That was the month of Nisan, or Aviv — the first of the Jewish lunar calendar. In our solar calendar, it would be from the middle of March to the middle of April.

Offering the Firstfruits

⁹The LORD said to Moses, ¹⁰"Speak to the Israelites and say to them: 'When you enter the land I am going to give you and you reap its harvest, bring to the priest a sheaf of the first grain you harvest. ¹¹He is to wave the sheaf before the LORD so it will be accepted on your behalf; the priest is to wave it on the day after the Sabbath. ¹²On the day you wave the sheaf, you must sacrifice as a burnt offering to the LORD a lamb a year old without defect, ¹³together with its grain offering of two-tenths of an ephah*ᵃ* of the finest flour mixed with olive oil — a food offering presented to the LORD, a pleasing aroma — and its drink offering of a quarter of a hin*ᵇ* of wine. ¹⁴You must not eat any bread, or roasted or new grain, until the very day you bring this offering to your God. This is to be a lasting ordinance for the generations to come, wherever you live.

The Festival of Weeks

¹⁵" 'From the day after the Sabbath, the day you brought the sheaf of the wave of- fering, count off seven full weeks. ¹⁶Count off fifty days up to the day after the seventh Sabbath, and then present an offering of new grain to the LORD. ¹⁷From wherever you live, bring two loaves made of two-tenths of an ephah of the finest flour, baked with yeast, as a wave offering of firstfruits to the LORD. ¹⁸Present with this bread seven male lambs, each a year old and without defect, one young bull and two rams. They will be a burnt offering to the LORD, together with their grain offerings and drink offerings — a food offering, an aroma pleasing to the LORD. ¹⁹Then sacrifice one male goat for a sin offering*ᶜ* and two lambs, each a year old, for a fellowship offering. ²⁰The priest is to wave the two lambs before the LORD as a wave offering, together with the bread of the firstfruits. They are a sacred offering to the LORD for the priest. ²¹On that same day you are to proclaim a sacred assembly and do no regular work. This is to be a lasting ordinance for the generations to come, wherever you live.

²²" 'When you reap the harvest of your land, do not reap to the very edges of your field or gather the gleanings of your harvest. Leave them for the poor and for the foreigner residing among you. I am the LORD your God.' "

The Festival of Trumpets

²³The LORD said to Moses, ²⁴"Say to the Israelites: 'On the first day of the seventh month you are to have a day of sabbath rest, a sacred assembly commemorated with trumpet blasts. ²⁵Do no regular work, but present a food offering to the LORD.' "

The Day of Atonement

²⁶The LORD said to Moses, ²⁷"The tenth day of this seventh month is the Day of Atonement. Hold a sacred assembly and deny yourselves,*ᵈ* and present a food offering to the LORD. ²⁸Do not do any work on that day, because it is the Day of Atonement, when atonement is made for you before the LORD your God. ²⁹Those

---

ᵃ 13 That is, probably about 7 pounds or about 3.2 kilograms; also in verse 17   *ᵇ 13* That is, about 1 quart or about 1 liter   *ᶜ 19* Or *purification offering*   *ᵈ 27* Or *and fast*; similarly in verses 29 and 32 who do not deny themselves on that day must be cut off from their people. ³⁰I will destroy from among their people anyone who does any work on that day. ³¹You shall do no work at all. This is to be a lasting ordinance for the generations to come, wherever you live. ³²It is a day of sabbath rest for you, and you must deny yourselves. From the evening of the ninth day of the month until the following evening you are to observe your sabbath."

The Festival of Tabernacles

³³The Lᴏʀᴅ said to Moses, ³⁴"Say to the Israelites: 'On the fifteenth day of the seventh month the Lᴏʀᴅ's Festival of Tabernacles begins, and it lasts for seven days. ³⁵The first day is a sacred assembly; do no regular work. ³⁶For seven days present food offerings to the Lᴏʀᴅ, and on the eighth day hold a sacred assembly and present a food offering to the Lᴏʀᴅ. It is the closing special assembly; do no regular work.

³⁷("'These are the Lᴏʀᴅ's appointed

BREAKTHROUGH!

The seventh month

(LEVITICUS 23:24-25,33-43)

That was Ethanim, the seventh month of the Jewish lunar calendar. In our solar calendar, it would be from the middle of September to the middle of October.

festivals, which you are to proclaim as sacred assemblies for bringing food offerings to the Lᴏʀᴅ—the burnt offerings and grain offerings, sacrifices and drink offerings required for each day. ³⁸These offerings are in addition to those for the Lᴏʀᴅ's Sabbaths andᵃ in addition to your gifts and whatever you have vowed and all the freewill offerings you give to the Lᴏʀᴅ.)

³⁹"'So beginning with the fifteenth day of the seventh month, after you have gathered the crops of the land, celebrate the festival to the Lᴏʀᴅ for seven days; the first day is a day of sabbath rest, and the eighth day also is a day of sabbath rest. ⁴⁰On the first day you are to take branches from luxuriant trees—from palms, willows and other leafy trees—and rejoice before the Lᴏʀᴅ your God for seven days. ⁴¹Celebrate this as a festival to the Lᴏʀᴅ for seven days each year. This is to be a lasting ordinance for the generations to come; celebrate it in the seventh month. ⁴²Live in temporary shelters for seven days: All native-born Israelites are to live in such shelters ⁴³so your descendants will know that I had the Israelites live in temporary shelters when I brought them out of Egypt. I am the Lᴏʀᴅ your God.'"

⁴⁴So Moses announced to the Israelites the appointed festivals of the Lᴏʀᴅ.

Olive Oil and Bread Set Before the Lᴏʀᴅ

24 The Lᴏʀᴅ said to Moses, ²"Command the Israelites to bring you clear oil of pressed olives for the light so that the lamps may be kept burning continually. ³Outside the curtain that shields the ark of the covenant law in the tent of meeting, Aaron is to tend the lamps before the Lᴏʀᴅ from evening till morning, continually. This is to be a lasting ordinance for the generations to come. ⁴The lamps on the pure gold lampstand before the Lᴏʀᴅ must be tended continually.

⁵"Take the finest flour and bake twelve loaves of bread, using two-tenths of an ephahᵇ for each loaf. ⁶Arrange them in

---

ᵃ 38 Or These festivals are in addition to the Lᴏʀᴅ's Sabbaths, and these offerings are   ᵇ 5 That is, probably about 7 pounds or about 3.2 kilograms two stacks, six in each stack, on the table of pure gold before the LORD. [7]By each stack put some pure incense as a memorial[a] portion to represent the bread and to be a food offering presented to the LORD. [8]This bread is to be set out before the LORD regularly, Sabbath after Sabbath, on behalf of the Israelites, as a lasting covenant. [9]It belongs to Aaron and his sons, who are to eat it in the sanctuary area, because it is a most holy part of their perpetual share of the food offerings presented to the LORD."

A Blasphemer Put to Death

[10]Now the son of an Israelite mother and an Egyptian father went out among the Israelites, and a fight broke out in the camp between him and an Israelite. [11]The son of the Israelite woman blasphemed the Name with a curse; so they brought him to Moses. (His mother's name was Shelomith, the daughter of Dibri the Danite.) [12]They put him in custody until the will of the LORD should be made clear to them.

[13]Then the LORD said to Moses: [14]"Take the blasphemer outside the camp. All those who heard him are to lay their hands on his head, and the entire assembly is to stone him. [15]Say to the Israelites: 'Anyone who curses their God will be held responsible; [16]anyone who blasphemes the name of the LORD is to be put to death. The entire assembly must stone them. Whether foreigner or native-born, when they blaspheme the Name they are to be put to death.

[17]"'Anyone who takes the life of a human being is to be put to death. [18]Anyone who takes the life of someone's animal must make restitution—life for life. [19]Anyone who injures their neighbor is to be injured in the same manner: [20]fracture for fracture, eye for eye, tooth for tooth. The one who has inflicted the injury must suffer the same injury. [21]Whoever kills an animal must make restitution, but whoever kills a human being is to be put to death. [22]You are to have the same law for the foreigner and the native-born. I am the LORD your God.' "

[23]Then Moses spoke to the Israelites, and they took the blasphemer outside the camp and stoned him. The Israelites did as the LORD commanded Moses.

The Sabbath Year

25 The LORD said to Moses at Mount Sinai, [2]"Speak to the Israelites and say to them: 'When you enter the land I am going to give you, the land itself must observe a sabbath to the LORD. [3]For six years sow your fields, and for six years prune your vineyards and gather their crops. [4]But in the seventh year the land is to have a year of sabbath rest, a sabbath to the LORD. Do not sow your fields or prune your vineyards. [5]Do not reap what grows of itself or harvest the grapes of your untended vines. The land is to have a year of rest. [6]Whatever the land yields during the sabbath year will be food for you—for yourself, your male and female servants, and the hired worker and temporary resident who live among you, [7]as well as for your livestock and the wild animals in your land. Whatever the land produces may be eaten.

The Year of Jubilee

[8]" 'Count off seven sabbath years—seven times seven years—so that the seven sabbath years amount to a period of forty-nine years. [9]Then have the trumpet sounded everywhere on the tenth day of the seventh month; on the Day of Atonement sound the trumpet throughout your land. [10]Consecrate the fiftieth year and proclaim liberty throughout the land to all its inhabitants. It shall be a jubilee for you; each of you is to return to your family property and to your own clan. [11]The fiftieth year shall be a jubilee for you; do not sow and do not reap what grows of itself or harvest the untended vines. [12]For it is a jubilee and is to be holy for you; eat only what is taken directly from the fields.

[13]" 'In this Year of Jubilee everyone is to return to their own property.

[14]" 'If you sell land to any of your own people or buy land from them, do not take advantage of each other. [15]You are to buy from your own people on the basis of the

---

[a] 7 Or *representative*

BREAKTHROUGH!

Temporary residents

(LEVITICUS 25:6)

These were foreigners who had problems in the places where they were born and had to go live in another country. We call them refugees now. These refugees were usually from countries where there was war and people were starving. Many of them decided to accept the religion and laws of the country that had received them.

number of years since the Jubilee. And they are to sell to you on the basis of the number of years left for harvesting crops. ¹⁶When the years are many, you are to increase the price, and when the years are few, you are to decrease the price, because what is really being sold to you is the number of crops. ¹⁷Do not take advantage of each other, but fear your God. I am the LORD your God.

¹⁸ "'Follow my decrees and be careful to obey my laws, and you will live safely in the land. ¹⁹Then the land will yield its fruit, and you will eat your fill and live there in safety. ²⁰You may ask, "What will we eat in the seventh year if we do not plant or harvest our crops?" ²¹I will send you such a blessing in the sixth year that the land will yield enough for three years. ²²While you plant during the eighth year, you will eat from the old crop and will continue to eat from it until the harvest of the ninth year comes in.

²³ "'The land must not be sold permanently, because the land is mine and you reside in my land as foreigners and strangers. ²⁴Throughout the land that you hold as a possession, you must provide for the redemption of the land.

²⁵ "'If one of your fellow Israelites becomes poor and sells some of their property, their nearest relative is to come and redeem what they have sold. ²⁶If, however, there is no one to redeem it for them but later on they prosper and acquire sufficient means to redeem it themselves, ²⁷they are to determine the value for the years since they sold it and refund the balance to the one to whom they sold it; they can then go back to their own property. ²⁸But if they do not acquire the means to repay, what was

CHECK THE FACTS

What happened during the "Year of Jubilee"?

A) The slaves were freed, they got their land back and nobody had to work.

B) A goat was set free, and it took the sins into the desert.

C) All the Israelites celebrated their birthdays.

CORRECT ANSWER: A

sold will remain in the possession of the buyer until the Year of Jubilee. It will be returned in the Jubilee, and they can then go back to their property.

29 " 'Anyone who sells a house in a walled city retains the right of redemption a full year after its sale. During that time the seller may redeem it. 30If it is not redeemed before a full year has passed, the house in the walled city shall belong permanently to the buyer and the buyer's descendants. It is not to be returned in the Jubilee. 31But houses in villages without walls around them are to be considered as belonging to the open country. They can be redeemed, and they are to be returned in the Jubilee.

32 " 'The Levites always have the right to redeem their houses in the Levitical towns, which they possess. 33So the property of the Levites is redeemable—that is, a house sold in any town they hold—and is to be returned in the Jubilee, because the houses in the towns of the Levites are their property among the Israelites. 34But the pastureland belonging to their towns must not be sold; it is their permanent possession.

35 " 'If any of your fellow Israelites become poor and are unable to support themselves among you, help them as you would a foreigner and stranger, so they can continue to live among you. 36Do not take interest or any profit from them, but fear your God, so that they may continue to live among you. 37You must not lend them money at interest or sell them food at a profit. 38I am the LORD your God, who brought you out of Egypt to give you the land of Canaan and to be your God.

39 " 'If any of your fellow Israelites become poor and sell themselves to you, do not make them work as slaves. 40They are to be treated as hired workers or temporary residents among you; they are to work for you until the Year of Jubilee. 41Then they and their children are to be released, and they will go back to their own clans and to the property of their ancestors. 42Because the Israelites are my servants, whom I brought out of Egypt, they must not be sold as slaves. 43Do not rule over them ruthlessly, but fear your God.

44 " 'Your male and female slaves are to come from the nations around you; from them you may buy slaves. 45You may also buy some of the temporary residents living among you and members of their clans born in your country, and they will become your property. 46You can bequeath them to your children as inherited property and can make them slaves for life, but you must not rule over your fellow Israelites ruthlessly.

47 " 'If a foreigner residing among you becomes rich and any of your fellow Israelites become poor and sell themselves to the foreigner or to a member of the foreigner's clan, 48they retain the right of redemption after they have sold themselves. One of their relatives may redeem them: 49An uncle or a cousin or any blood relative in their clan may redeem them. Or if they prosper, they may redeem themselves. 50They and their buyer are to count the time from the year they sold themselves up to the Year of Jubilee. The price for their release is to be based on the rate paid to a hired worker for that number of years. 51If many years remain, they must pay for their redemption a larger share of the price paid for them. 52If only a few years remain until the Year of Jubilee, they are to compute that and pay for their redemption accordingly. 53They are to be treated as workers hired from year to year; you must see to it that those to whom they owe service do not rule over them ruthlessly.

54 " 'Even if someone is not redeemed in any of these ways, they and their children are to be released in the Year of Jubilee, 55for the Israelites belong to me as servants. They are my servants, whom I brought out of Egypt. I am the LORD your God.

Reward for Obedience

26 " 'Do not make idols or set up an image or a sacred stone for yourselves, and do not place a carved stone in your land to bow down before it. I am the LORD your God.

2 " 'Observe my Sabbaths and have reverence for my sanctuary. I am the LORD.

3 " 'If you follow my decrees and are

careful to obey my commands, ⁴I will send you rain in its season, and the ground will yield its crops and the trees their fruit. ⁵Your threshing will continue until grape harvest and the grape harvest will continue until planting, and you will eat all the food you want and live in safety in your land.

⁶" 'I will grant peace in the land, and you will lie down and no one will make you afraid. I will remove wild beasts from the land, and the sword will not pass through your country. ⁷You will pursue your enemies, and they will fall by the sword before you. ⁸Five of you will chase a hundred, and a hundred of you will chase ten thousand, and your enemies will fall by the sword before you.

⁹" 'I will look on you with favor and make you fruitful and increase your numbers, and I will keep my covenant with you. ¹⁰You will still be eating last year's harvest when you will have to move it out to make room for the new. ¹¹I will put my dwelling place^a among you, and I will not abhor you. ¹²I will walk among you and be your God, and you will be my people. ¹³I am the Lord your God, who brought you out of Egypt so that you would no longer be slaves to the Egyptians; I broke the bars of your yoke and enabled you to walk with heads held high.

Punishment for Disobedience

¹⁴" 'But if you will not listen to me and carry out all these commands, ¹⁵and if you reject my decrees and abhor my laws and fail to carry out all my commands and so violate my covenant, ¹⁶then I will do this to you: I will bring on you sudden terror, wasting diseases and fever that will destroy your sight and sap your strength. You will plant seed in vain, because your enemies will eat it. ¹⁷I will set my face against you so that you will be defeated by your enemies; those who hate you will rule over you, and you will flee even when no one is pursuing you.

¹⁸" 'If after all this you will not listen to me, I will punish you for your sins seven times over. ¹⁹I will break down your stubborn pride and make the sky above you like iron and the ground beneath you like

bronze. ²⁰Your strength will be spent in vain, because your soil will not yield its crops, nor will the trees of your land yield their fruit.

²¹" 'If you remain hostile toward me and refuse to listen to me, I will multiply your afflictions seven times over, as your sins deserve. ²²I will send wild animals against you, and they will rob you of your children, destroy your cattle and make you so few in number that your roads will be deserted.

²³" 'If in spite of these things you do not accept my correction but continue to be hostile toward me, ²⁴I myself will be hostile toward you and will afflict you for your sins seven times over. ²⁵And I will bring the sword on you to avenge the breaking of the covenant. When you withdraw into your cities, I will send a plague among you, and you will be given into enemy hands. ²⁶When I cut off your supply of bread, ten women will be able to bake your bread in one oven, and they will dole out the bread by weight. You will eat, but you will not be satisfied.

²⁷" 'If in spite of this you still do not listen to me but continue to be hostile toward me, ²⁸then in my anger I will be hostile toward you, and I myself will punish you for your sins seven times over. ²⁹You will eat the flesh of your sons and the flesh of your daughters. ³⁰I will destroy your high places, cut down your incense altars and pile your dead bodies^b on the lifeless forms of your idols, and I will abhor you. ³¹I will turn your cities into ruins and lay waste your sanctuaries, and I will take no delight in the pleasing aroma of your offerings. ³²I myself will lay waste the land, so that your enemies who live there will be appalled. ³³I will scatter you among the nations and will draw out my sword and pursue you. Your land will be laid waste, and your cities will lie in ruins. ³⁴Then the land will enjoy its sabbath years all the time that it lies desolate and you are in the country of your enemies; then the land will rest and enjoy its sabbaths. ³⁵All the time that it lies desolate, the land will have the rest it did not have during the sabbaths you lived in it.

---

^a 11 Or my tabernacle   ^b 30 Or your funeral offerings

36 " 'As for those of you who are left, I will make their hearts so fearful in the lands of their enemies that the sound of a windblown leaf will put them to flight. They will run as though fleeing from the sword, and they will fall, even though no one is pursuing them. 37They will stumble over one another as though fleeing from the sword, even though no one is pursuing them. So you will not be able to stand before your enemies. 38You will perish among the nations; the land of your enemies will devour you. 39Those of you who are left will waste away in the lands of their enemies because of their sins; also because of their ancestors' sins they will waste away.

40 " 'But if they will confess their sins and the sins of their ancestors—their unfaithfulness and their hostility toward me, 41which made me hostile toward them so that I sent them into the land of their enemies—then when their uncircumcised hearts are humbled and they pay for their sin, 42I will remember my covenant with Jacob and my covenant with Isaac and my covenant with Abraham, and I will remember the land. 43For the land will be deserted by them and will enjoy its sabbaths while it lies desolate without them. They will pay for their sins because they rejected my laws and abhorred my decrees. 44Yet in spite of this, when they are in the land of their enemies, I will not reject them or abhor them so as to destroy them completely, breaking my covenant with them. I am the LORD their God. 45But for their sake I will remember the covenant with their ancestors whom I brought out of Egypt in the sight of the nations to be their God. I am the LORD.' "

46These are the decrees, the laws and the regulations that the LORD established at Mount Sinai between himself and the Israelites through Moses.

Redeeming What Is the LORD's

27 The LORD said to Moses, 2 "Speak to the Israelites and say to them: 'If anyone makes a special vow to dedicate a person to the LORD by giving the equivalent value, 3set the value of a male between the ages of twenty and sixty at fifty shekels[a] of silver, according to the sanctuary shekel[b]; 4for a female, set her value at thirty shekels[c]; 5for a person between the ages of five and twenty, set the value of a male at twenty shekels[d] and of a female at ten shekels[e]; 6for a person between one month and five years, set the value of a male at five shekels[f] of silver and that of a female at three shekels[g] of silver; 7for a person sixty years old or more, set the value of a male at fifteen shekels[h] and of a female at ten shekels. 8If anyone making the vow is too poor to pay the specified amount, the person being dedicated is to be presented to the priest, who will set the value according to what the one making the vow can afford.

9 " 'If what they vowed is an animal that is acceptable as an offering to the LORD, such an animal given to the LORD becomes holy. 10They must not exchange it or substitute a good one for a bad one, or a bad one for a good one; if they should substitute one animal for another, both it and the substitute become holy. 11If what they vowed is a ceremonially unclean animal—one that is not acceptable as an offering to the LORD—the animal must be presented to the priest, 12who will judge its quality as good or bad. Whatever value the priest then sets, that is what it will be. 13If the owner wishes to redeem the animal, a fifth must be added to its value.

14 " 'If anyone dedicates their house as something holy to the LORD, the priest will judge its quality as good or bad. Whatever value the priest then sets, so it will remain. 15If the one who dedicates their house wishes to redeem it, they must add a fifth to its value, and the house will again become theirs.

16 " 'If anyone dedicates to the LORD part of their family land, its value is to be set according to the amount of seed required

---

a 3 That is, about 1 1/4 pounds or about 575 grams; also in verse 16   b 3 That is, about 2/5 ounce or about 12 grams; also in verse 25   c 4 That is, about 12 ounces or about 345 grams   d 5 That is, about 8 ounces or about 230 grams   e 5 That is, about 4 ounces or about 115 grams; also in verse 7   f 6 That is, about 2 ounces or about 58 grams   g 6 That is, about 1 1/4 ounces or about 35 grams   h 7 That is, about 6 ounces or about 175 grams for it—fifty shekels of silver to a homer[a] of barley seed. [17]If they dedicate a field during the Year of Jubilee, the value that has been set remains. [18]But if they dedicate a field after the Jubilee, the priest will determine the value according to the number of years that remain until the next Year of Jubilee, and its set value will be reduced. [19]If the one who dedicates the field wishes to redeem it, they must add a fifth to its value, and the field will again become theirs. [20]If, however, they do not redeem the field, or if they have sold it to someone else, it can never be redeemed. [21]When the field is released in the Jubilee, it will become holy, like a field devoted to the Lord; it will become priestly property.

[22]" 'If anyone dedicates to the Lord a field they have bought, which is not part of their family land, [23]the priest will determine its value up to the Year of Jubilee, and the owner must pay its value on that day as something holy to the Lord. [24]In the Year of Jubilee the field will revert to the person from whom it was bought, the one whose land it was. [25]Every value is to be set according to the sanctuary shekel, twenty gerahs to the shekel.

[26]" 'No one, however, may dedicate the firstborn of an animal, since the firstborn already belongs to the Lord; whether an ox[b] or a sheep, it is the Lord's. [27]If it is one of the unclean animals, it may be bought back at its set value, adding a fifth of the value to it. If it is not redeemed, it is to be sold at its set value.

[28]" 'But nothing that a person owns and devotes[c] to the Lord—whether a human being or an animal or family land—may

---

[a] *16* That is, probably about 300 pounds or about 135 kilograms   [b] *26* The Hebrew word can refer to either male or female.   [c] *28* The Hebrew term refers to the irrevocable giving over of things or persons to the Lord.

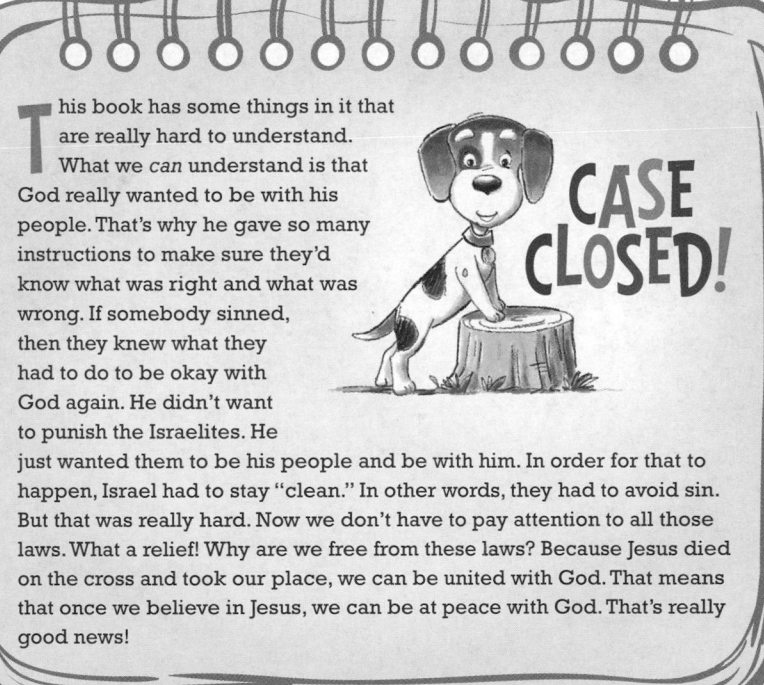

This book has some things in it that are really hard to understand. What we *can* understand is that God really wanted to be with his people. That's why he gave so many instructions to make sure they'd know what was right and what was wrong. If somebody sinned, then they knew what they had to do to be okay with God again. He didn't want to punish the Israelites. He just wanted them to be his people and be with him. In order for that to happen, Israel had to stay "clean." In other words, they had to avoid sin. But that was really hard. Now we don't have to pay attention to all those laws. What a relief! Why are we free from these laws? Because Jesus died on the cross and took our place, we can be united with God. That means that once we believe in Jesus, we can be at peace with God. That's really good news!

CASE CLOSED!

be sold or redeemed; everything so devoted is most holy to the LORD.

29 " 'No person devoted to destruction[a] may be ransomed; they are to be put to death.

30 " 'A tithe of everything from the land, whether grain from the soil or fruit from the trees, belongs to the LORD; it is holy to the LORD. 31Whoever would redeem any of their tithe must add a fifth of the value to it. 32Every tithe of the herd and flock — every tenth animal that passes under the

shepherd's rod — will be holy to the LORD. 33No one may pick out the good from the bad or make any substitution. If anyone does make a substitution, both the animal and its substitute become holy and cannot be redeemed.' "

34These are the commands the LORD gave Moses at Mount Sinai for the Israelites.

---

[a] 29 The Hebrew term refers to the irrevocable giving over of things or persons to the LORD, often by totally destroying them.

NUMBERS

THE EVIDENCE:

WHO WROTE IT?
It is said that this book was also written by many authors, although some people think it was written by Moses.

HOW LONG AGO?
It was probably written 700 years before Christ, and it was edited, or left the way we know it now, more or less 400 years before Christ.

WHAT'S IT ABOUT?
Numbers is the translation of the title it had in Greek. It is called Numbers because in the beginning and at the end of the book, there is a list of the people of Israel. Its title in Hebrew is "In the Desert." Chapter 1 talks about the number of people who left Egypt, and chapter 26 gives a list of who was prepared to enter the promised land. The Israelites wandered around the desert for 40 years, so the people registered in the first list died and didn't get to enter the land that God had promised them. This was because they behaved badly and disobeyed God a bunch of times. They just complained and complained, and they were punished for their disobedience. But there were two people who didn't complain — Joshua and Caleb. They trusted and obeyed, and they entered the promised land with the children and grandchildren of those who had come out of Egypt. And it was this same Joshua that God called to lead the people when Moses died.

THE BEST PART
We thought the funniest part was when Balaam's donkey talked to him and asked why he was beating her. Poor thing! She could see God's angel and Balaam could not! So she taught her master that even a prophet should obey and be faithful to the true God (chapter 22).

The Census

1 The LORD spoke to Moses in the tent of meeting in the Desert of Sinai on the first day of the second month of the second year after the Israelites came out of Egypt. He said: ²"Take a census of the whole Israelite community by their clans and families, listing every man by name, one by one. ³You and Aaron are to count according to their divisions all the men in Israel who are twenty years old or more and able to serve in the army. ⁴One man from each tribe, each of them the head of his family, is to help you. ⁵These are the names of the men who are to assist you:

from Reuben, Elizur son of Shedeur;
⁶from Simeon, Shelumiel son of Zurishaddai;

⁷from Judah, Nahshon son of Amminadab;

⁸from Issachar, Nethanel son of Zuar;

⁹from Zebulun, Eliab son of Helon;

¹⁰from the sons of Joseph:

from Ephraim, Elishama son of Ammihud;

from Manasseh, Gamaliel son of Pedahzur;

¹¹from Benjamin, Abidan son of Gideoni;

¹²from Dan, Ahiezer son of Ammishaddai;

¹³from Asher, Pagiel son of Okran;

¹⁴from Gad, Eliasaph son of Deuel;

¹⁵from Naphtali, Ahira son of Enan."

¹⁶These were the men appointed from the community, the leaders of their ancestral tribes. They were the heads of the clans of Israel.

¹⁷Moses and Aaron took these men whose names had been specified, ¹⁸and they called the whole community together on the first day of the second month. The people registered their ancestry by their clans and families, and the men twenty years old or more were listed by name, one by one, ¹⁹as the LORD commanded Moses. And so he counted them in the Desert of Sinai:

²⁰From the descendants of Reuben the firstborn son of Israel:

All the men twenty years old or more who were able to serve in the army were listed by name, one by one, according to the records of their clans and families. ²¹The number from the tribe of Reuben was 46,500.

²²From the descendants of Simeon:

All the men twenty years old or more who were able to serve in the army were counted and listed by name, one by one, according to the records of their clans and families. ²³The number from the tribe of Simeon was 59,300.

²⁴From the descendants of Gad:

All the men twenty years old or more who were able to serve in the army were listed by name, according to the records of their clans and families. ²⁵The number from the tribe of Gad was 45,650.

²⁶From the descendants of Judah:

All the men twenty years old or more who were able to serve in the army were listed by name, according to the records of their clans and families. ²⁷The number from the tribe of Judah was 74,600.

²⁸From the descendants of Issachar:

All the men twenty years old or more who were able to serve in the army were listed by name, according to the records of their clans and families. ²⁹The number from the tribe of Issachar was 54,400.

³⁰From the descendants of Zebulun:

All the men twenty years old or more who were able to serve in the army were listed by name, according to the records of their clans and families. ³¹The number from the tribe of Zebulun was 57,400.

³²From the sons of Joseph:

From the descendants of Ephraim:

All the men twenty years old or more who were able to serve in the army were listed by name, according to the records of their clans and families. ³³The number from the tribe of Ephraim was 40,500.

³⁴From the descendants of Manasseh:

All the men twenty years old or more who were able to serve in the army were listed by name, according to the records of their clans and families. ³⁵The number from the tribe of Manasseh was 32,200.

³⁶From the descendants of Benjamin:

All the men twenty years old or more who were able to serve in the army were listed by name, according to the records of their clans and families. ³⁷The number from the tribe of Benjamin was 35,400.

³⁸From the descendants of Dan:

All the men twenty years old or more who were able to serve in the army were listed by name, according to the records of their clans and families. ³⁹The number from the tribe of Dan was 62,700.

⁴⁰From the descendants of Asher:
All the men twenty years old or more who were able to serve in the army were listed by name, according to the records of their clans and families. ⁴¹The number from the tribe of Asher was 41,500.

⁴²From the descendants of Naphtali:
All the men twenty years old or more who were able to serve in the army were listed by name, according to the records of their clans and families. ⁴³The number from the tribe of Naphtali was 53,400.

⁴⁴These were the men counted by Moses and Aaron and the twelve leaders of Israel, each one representing his family. ⁴⁵All the Israelites twenty years old or more who were able to serve in Israel's army were counted according to their families. ⁴⁶The total number was 603,550.

⁴⁷The ancestral tribe of the Levites, however, was not counted along with the others. ⁴⁸The LORD had said to Moses: ⁴⁹"You must not count the tribe of Levi or include them in the census of the other Israelites. ⁵⁰Instead, appoint the Levites to be in charge of the tabernacle of the covenant law — over all its furnishings and everything belonging to it. They are to carry the tabernacle and all its furnishings; they are to take care of it and encamp around it. ⁵¹Whenever the tabernacle is to move, the Levites are to take it down, and whenever the tabernacle is to be set up, the Levites shall do it. Anyone else who approaches it is to be put to death. ⁵²The Israelites are to set up their tents by divisions, each of them in their own camp under their standard. ⁵³The Levites, however, are to set up their tents around the tabernacle of the covenant law so that my wrath will not fall on the Israelite community. The Levites are to be responsible for the care of the tabernacle of the covenant law."

⁵⁴The Israelites did all this just as the LORD commanded Moses.

The Arrangement of the Tribal Camps

2 The LORD said to Moses and Aaron: ²"The Israelites are to camp around the tent of meeting some distance from it, each of them under their standard and holding the banners of their family."

³On the east, toward the sunrise, the divisions of the camp of Judah are to encamp under their standard. The leader of the people of Judah is Nahshon son of Amminadab. ⁴His division numbers 74,600.

⁵The tribe of Issachar will camp next to them. The leader of the people of Issachar is Nethanel son of Zuar. ⁶His division numbers 54,400.

⁷The tribe of Zebulun will be next. The leader of the people of Zebulun is Eliab son of Helon. ⁸His division numbers 57,400.

⁹All the men assigned to the camp of Judah, according to their divisions, number 186,400. They will set out first.

¹⁰On the south will be the divisions of the camp of Reuben under their standard. The leader of the people of Reuben is Elizur son of Shedeur. ¹¹His division numbers 46,500.

¹²The tribe of Simeon will camp next to them. The leader of the people of Simeon is Shelumiel son of Zurishaddai. ¹³His division numbers 59,300.

¹⁴The tribe of Gad will be next. The leader of the people of Gad is Eliasaph son of Deuel.ᵃ ¹⁵His division numbers 45,650.

¹⁶All the men assigned to the camp of Reuben, according to their divisions, number 151,450. They will set out second.

¹⁷Then the tent of meeting and the camp of the Levites will set out in

---

ᵃ 14 Many manuscripts of the Masoretic Text, Samaritan Pentateuch and Vulgate (see also 1:14); most manuscripts of the Masoretic Text *Reuel* the middle of the camps. They will set out in the same order as they encamp, each in their own place under their standard.

¹⁸On the west will be the divisions of the camp of Ephraim under their standard. The leader of the people of Ephraim is Elishama son of Ammihud. ¹⁹His division numbers 40,500. ²⁰The tribe of Manasseh will be next to them. The leader of the people of Manasseh is Gamaliel son of Pedahzur. ²¹His division numbers 32,200. ²²The tribe of Benjamin will be next. The leader of the people of Benjamin is Abidan son of Gideoni. ²³His division numbers 35,400.

²⁴All the men assigned to the camp of Ephraim, according to their divisions, number 108,100. They will set out third.

²⁵On the north will be the divisions of the camp of Dan under their standard. The leader of the people of Dan is Ahiezer son of Ammishaddai. ²⁶His division numbers 62,700. ²⁷The tribe of Asher will camp next to them. The leader of the people of Asher is Pagiel son of Okran. ²⁸His division numbers 41,500. ²⁹The tribe of Naphtali will be next. The leader of the people of Naphtali is Ahira son of Enan. ³⁰His division numbers 53,400.

³¹All the men assigned to the camp of Dan number 157,600. They will set out last, under their standards.

³²These are the Israelites, counted according to their families. All the men in the camps, by their divisions, number 603,550. ³³The Levites, however, were not counted along with the other Israelites, as the LORD commanded Moses.

³⁴So the Israelites did everything the LORD commanded Moses; that is the way they encamped under their standards, and that is the way they set out, each of them with their clan and family.

The Levites

3 This is the account of the family of Aaron and Moses at the time the LORD spoke to Moses at Mount Sinai.

²The names of the sons of Aaron were Nadab the firstborn and Abihu, Eleazar and Ithamar. ³Those were the names of Aaron's sons, the anointed priests, who were ordained to serve as priests. ⁴Nadab and Abihu, however, died before the LORD when they made an offering with unauthorized fire before him in the Desert of Sinai. They had no sons, so Eleazar and Ithamar served as priests during the lifetime of their father Aaron.

⁵The LORD said to Moses, ⁶"Bring the tribe of Levi and present them to Aaron the priest to assist him. ⁷They are to perform duties for him and for the whole community at the tent of meeting by doing the work of the tabernacle. ⁸They are to take care of all the furnishings of the tent of meeting, fulfilling the obligations of the Israelites by doing the work of the tabernacle. ⁹Give the Levites to Aaron and his sons; they are the Israelites who are to be given wholly to him.^a ¹⁰Appoint Aaron and his sons to serve as priests; anyone else who approaches the sanctuary is to be put to death."

¹¹The LORD also said to Moses, ¹²"I have taken the Levites from among the Israelites in place of the first male offspring of every Israelite woman. The Levites are mine, ¹³for all the firstborn are mine. When I struck down all the firstborn in Egypt, I set apart for myself every firstborn in Israel, whether human or animal. They are to be mine. I am the LORD."

¹⁴The LORD said to Moses in the Desert of Sinai, ¹⁵"Count the Levites by their families and clans. Count every male a month old or more." ¹⁶So Moses counted them, as he was commanded by the word of the LORD.

¹⁷These were the names of the sons of Levi:

Gershon, Kohath and Merari.

---

^a 9 Most manuscripts of the Masoretic Text; some manuscripts of the Masoretic Text, Samaritan Pentateuch and Septuagint (see also 8:16) *to me*

¹⁸These were the names of the Gershonite clans:
    Libni and Shimei.
¹⁹The Kohathite clans:
    Amram, Izhar, Hebron and Uzziel.
²⁰The Merarite clans:
    Mahli and Mushi.
These were the Levite clans, according to their families.

²¹To Gershon belonged the clans of the Libnites and Shimeites; these were the Gershonite clans. ²²The number of all the males a month old or more who were counted was 7,500. ²³The Gershonite clans were to camp on the west, behind the tabernacle. ²⁴The leader of the families of the Gershonites was Eliasaph son of Lael. ²⁵At the tent of meeting the Gershonites were responsible for the care of the tabernacle and tent, its coverings, the curtain at the entrance to the tent of meeting, ²⁶the curtains of the courtyard, the curtain at the entrance to the courtyard surrounding the tabernacle and altar, and the ropes—and everything related to their use.

²⁷To Kohath belonged the clans of the Amramites, Izharites, Hebronites and Uzzielites; these were the Kohathite clans. ²⁸The number of all the males a month old or more was 8,600.^a The Kohathites were responsible for the care of the sanctuary. ²⁹The Kohathite clans were to camp on the south side of the tabernacle. ³⁰The leader of the families of the Kohathite clans was Elizaphan son of Uzziel. ³¹They were responsible for the care of the ark, the table, the lampstand, the altars, the articles of the sanctuary used in ministering, the curtain, and everything related to their use. ³²The chief leader of the Levites was Eleazar son of Aaron, the priest. He was appointed over those who were responsible for the care of the sanctuary.

³³To Merari belonged the clans of the Mahlites and the Mushites; these were the Merarite clans. ³⁴The number of all the males a month old or more who were counted was 6,200. ³⁵The leader of the families of the Merarite clans was Zuriel

son of Abihail; they were to camp on the north side of the tabernacle. ³⁶The Merarites were appointed to take care of the frames of the tabernacle, its crossbars, posts, bases, all its equipment, and everything related to their use, ³⁷as well as the posts of the surrounding courtyard with their bases, tent pegs and ropes.

³⁸Moses and Aaron and his sons were to camp to the east of the tabernacle, toward the sunrise, in front of the tent of meeting. They were responsible for the care of the sanctuary on behalf of the Israelites. Anyone else who approached the sanctuary was to be put to death.

³⁹The total number of Levites counted at the Lord's command by Moses and Aaron according to their clans, including every male a month old or more, was 22,000.

⁴⁰The Lord said to Moses, "Count all the firstborn Israelite males who are a month old or more and make a list of their names. ⁴¹Take the Levites for me in place of all the firstborn of the Israelites, and the livestock of the Levites in place of all the firstborn of the livestock of the Israelites. I am the Lord."
⁴²So Moses counted all the firstborn of the Israelites, as the Lord commanded him. ⁴³The total number of firstborn males a month old or more, listed by name, was 22,273.

⁴⁴The Lord also said to Moses, ⁴⁵"Take the Levites in place of all the firstborn of Israel, and the livestock of the Levites in place of their livestock. The Levites are to be mine. I am the Lord. ⁴⁶To redeem the 273 firstborn Israelites who exceed the number of the Levites, ⁴⁷collect five shekels^b for each one, according to the sanctuary shekel, which weighs twenty gerahs. ⁴⁸Give the money for the redemption of the additional Israelites to Aaron and his sons."

⁴⁹So Moses collected the redemption money from those who exceeded the

---

^a 28 Hebrew; some Septuagint manuscripts *8,300*
^b 47 That is, about 2 ounces or about 58 grams

number redeemed by the Levites. [50]From the firstborn of the Israelites he collected silver weighing 1,365 shekels,[a] according to the sanctuary shekel. [51]Moses gave the redemption money to Aaron and his sons, as he was commanded by the word of the LORD.

The Kohathites

4 The LORD said to Moses and Aaron: [2]"Take a census of the Kohathite branch of the Levites by their clans and families. [3]Count all the men from thirty to fifty years of age who come to serve in the work at the tent of meeting.

[4]"This is the work of the Kohathites at the tent of meeting: the care of the most holy things. [5]When the camp is to move, Aaron and his sons are to go in and take down the shielding curtain and put it over the ark of the covenant law. [6]Then they are to cover the curtain with a durable leather,[b] spread a cloth of solid blue over that and put the poles in place.

[7]"Over the table of the Presence they are to spread a blue cloth and put on it the plates, dishes and bowls, and the jars for drink offerings; the bread that is continually there is to remain on it. [8]They are to spread a scarlet cloth over them, cover that with the durable leather and put the poles in place.

[9]"They are to take a blue cloth and cover the lampstand that is for light, together with its lamps, its wick trimmers and trays, and all its jars for the olive oil used to supply it. [10]Then they are to wrap it and all its accessories in a covering of the durable leather and put it on a carrying frame.

[11]"Over the gold altar they are to spread a blue cloth and cover that with the durable leather and put the poles in place. [12]"They are to take all the articles used for ministering in the sanctuary, wrap them in a blue cloth, cover that with the durable leather and put them on a carrying frame.

[13]"They are to remove the ashes from the bronze altar and spread a purple cloth over it. [14]Then they are to place on it all the utensils used for ministering at the altar, including the firepans, meat forks,

shovels and sprinkling bowls. Over it they are to spread a covering of the durable leather and put the poles in place.

[15]"After Aaron and his sons have finished covering the holy furnishings and all the holy articles, and when the camp is ready to move, only then are the Kohathites to come and do the carrying. But they must not touch the holy things or they will die. The Kohathites are to carry those things that are in the tent of meeting.

[16]"Eleazar son of Aaron, the priest, is to have charge of the oil for the light, the fragrant incense, the regular grain offering and the anointing oil. He is to be in charge of the entire tabernacle and everything in it, including its holy furnishings and articles."

[17]The LORD said to Moses and Aaron, [18]"See that the Kohathite tribal clans are not destroyed from among the Levites. [19]So that they may live and not die when they come near the most holy things, do this for them: Aaron and his sons are to go into the sanctuary and assign to each man his work and what he is to carry. [20]But the Kohathites must not go in to look at the holy things, even for a moment, or they will die."

The Gershonites

[21]The LORD said to Moses, [22]"Take a census also of the Gershonites by their families and clans. [23]Count all the men from thirty to fifty years of age who come to serve in the work at the tent of meeting.

[24]"This is the service of the Gershonite clans in their carrying and their other work: [25]They are to carry the curtains of the tabernacle, that is, the tent of meeting, its covering and its outer covering of durable leather, the curtains for the entrance to the tent of meeting, [26]the curtains of the courtyard surrounding the tabernacle and altar, the curtain for the entrance to the courtyard, the ropes and all the equipment used in the service of the tent. The Gershonites are to do all that needs to be done with these things.

---

[a] 50 That is, about 35 pounds or about 16 kilograms
[b] 6 Possibly the hides of large aquatic mammals; also in verses 8, 10, 11, 12, 14 and 25

²⁷All their service, whether carrying or doing other work, is to be done under the direction of Aaron and his sons. You shall assign to them as their responsibility all they are to carry. ²⁸This is the service of the Gershonite clans at the tent of meeting. Their duties are to be under the direction of Ithamar son of Aaron, the priest.

The Merarites

²⁹"Count the Merarites by their clans and families. ³⁰Count all the men from thirty to fifty years of age who come to serve in the work at the tent of meeting. ³¹As part of all their service at the tent, they are to carry the frames of the tabernacle, its crossbars, posts and bases, ³²as well as the posts of the surrounding courtyard with their bases, tent pegs, ropes, all their equipment and everything related to their use. Assign to each man the specific things he is to carry. ³³This is the service of the Merarite clans as they work at the tent of meeting under the direction of Ithamar son of Aaron, the priest."

The Numbering of the Levite Clans

³⁴Moses, Aaron and the leaders of the community counted the Kohathites by their clans and families. ³⁵All the men from thirty to fifty years of age who came to serve in the work at the tent of meeting, ³⁶counted by clans, were 2,750. ³⁷This was the total of all those in the Kohathite clans who served at the tent of meeting. Moses and Aaron counted them according to the LORD's command through Moses.

³⁸The Gershonites were counted by their clans and families. ³⁹All the men from thirty to fifty years of age who came to serve in the work at the tent of meeting, ⁴⁰counted by their clans and families, were 2,630. ⁴¹This was the total of those in the Gershonite clans who served at the tent of meeting. Moses and Aaron counted them according to the LORD's command.

⁴²The Merarites were counted by their clans and families. ⁴³All the men from thirty to fifty years of age who came to serve in the work at the tent of meeting, ⁴⁴counted by their clans, were 3,200. ⁴⁵This was the total of those in the Merarite clans. Moses and Aaron counted them according to the LORD's command through Moses.

⁴⁶So Moses, Aaron and the leaders of Israel counted all the Levites by their clans and families. ⁴⁷All the men from thirty to fifty years of age who came to do the work of serving and carrying the tent of meeting ⁴⁸numbered 8,580. ⁴⁹At the LORD's command through Moses, each was assigned his work and told what to carry.

Thus they were counted, as the LORD commanded Moses.

The Purity of the Camp

5 The LORD said to Moses, ²"Command the Israelites to send away from the camp anyone who has a defiling skin disease[a] or a discharge of any kind, or who is ceremonially unclean because of a dead body. ³Send away male and female alike; send them outside the camp so they will not defile their camp, where I dwell among them." ⁴The Israelites did so; they sent them outside the camp. They did just as the LORD had instructed Moses.

Restitution for Wrongs

⁵The LORD said to Moses, ⁶"Say to the Israelites: 'Any man or woman who wrongs another in any way[b] and so is unfaithful to the LORD is guilty ⁷and must confess the sin they have committed. They must make full restitution for the wrong they have done, add a fifth of the value to it and give it all to the person they have wronged. ⁸But if that person has no close relative to whom restitution can be made for the wrong, the restitution belongs to the LORD and must be given to the priest, along with the ram with which atonement is made for the wrongdoer. ⁹All the sacred contributions the Israelites bring to a priest will belong to him. ¹⁰Sacred things belong to their owners, but what they give to the priest will belong to the priest.' "

---

[a] 2 The Hebrew word for *defiling skin disease*, traditionally translated "leprosy," was used for various diseases affecting the skin.   [b] 6 Or *woman who commits any wrong common to mankind*

The Test for an Unfaithful Wife

[11]Then the LORD said to Moses, [12]"Speak to the Israelites and say to them: 'If a man's wife goes astray and is unfaithful to him [13]so that another man has sexual relations with her, and this is hidden from her husband and her impurity is undetected (since there is no witness against her and she has not been caught in the act), [14]and if feelings of jealousy come over her husband and he suspects his wife and she is impure — or if he is jealous and suspects her even though she is not impure — [15]then he is to take his wife to the priest. He must also take an offering of a tenth of an ephah[a] of barley flour on her behalf. He must not pour olive oil on it or put incense on it, because it is a grain offering for jealousy, a reminder-offering to draw attention to wrongdoing.

[16]" 'The priest shall bring her and have her stand before the LORD. [17]Then he shall take some holy water in a clay jar and put some dust from the tabernacle floor into the water. [18]After the priest has had the woman stand before the LORD, he shall loosen her hair and place in her hands the reminder-offering, the grain offering for jealousy, while he himself holds the bitter water that brings a curse. [19]Then the priest shall put the woman under oath and say to her, "If no other man has had sexual relations with you and you have not gone astray and become impure while married to your husband, may this bitter water that brings a curse not harm you. [20]But if you have gone astray while married to your husband and you have made yourself impure by having sexual relations with a man other than your husband" — [21]here the priest is to put the woman under this curse — "may the LORD cause you to become a curse[b] among your people when he makes your womb miscarry and your abdomen swell. [22]May this water that brings a curse enter your body so that your abdomen swells or your womb miscarries."

" 'Then the woman is to say, "Amen. So be it."

[23]" 'The priest is to write these curses on a scroll and then wash them off into the bitter water. [24]He shall make the woman drink the bitter water that brings a curse, and this water that brings a curse and causes bitter suffering will enter her. [25]The priest is to take from her hands the grain offering for jealousy, wave it before the LORD and bring it to the altar. [26]The priest is then to take a handful of the grain offering as a memorial[c] offering and burn it on the altar; after that, he is to have the woman drink the water. [27]If she has made herself impure and been unfaithful to her husband, this will be the result: When she is made to drink the water that brings a curse and causes bitter suffering, it will enter her, her abdomen will swell and her womb will miscarry, and she will become a curse. [28]If, however, the woman has not made herself impure, but is clean, she will be cleared of guilt and will be able to have children.

[29]" 'This, then, is the law of jealousy when a woman goes astray and makes herself impure while married to her husband, [30]or when feelings of jealousy come over a man because he suspects his wife. The priest is to have her stand before the LORD and is to apply this entire law to her. [31]The husband will be innocent of any wrongdoing, but the woman will bear the consequences of her sin.' "

The Nazirite

6 The LORD said to Moses, [2]"Speak to the Israelites and say to them: 'If a man or woman wants to make a special vow, a vow of dedication to the LORD as a Nazirite, [3]they must abstain from wine and other fermented drink and must not drink vinegar made from wine or other fermented drink. They must not drink grape juice or eat grapes or raisins. [4]As long as they remain under their Nazirite vow, they must not eat anything that comes from the grapevine, not even the seeds or skins.

[5]" 'During the entire period of their Nazirite vow, no razor may be used on their

---

[a] 15 That is, probably about 3 1/2 pounds or about 1.6 kilograms   [b] 21 That is, may he cause your name to be used in cursing (see Jer. 29:22); or, may others see that you are cursed; similarly in verse 27.
[c] 26 Or representative

BREAK THROUGH!

Nazirite
(NUMBERS 6:2)
A person devoted to the service of God.
This promise could be for a short time or a
lifetime. (Read Judges 13:4–5.)

head. They must be holy until the period of their dedication to the LORD is over; they must let their hair grow long.

6 " 'Throughout the period of their dedication to the LORD, the Nazirite must not go near a dead body. 7Even if their own father or mother or brother or sister dies, they must not make themselves ceremonially unclean on account of them, because the symbol of their dedication to God is on their head. 8Throughout the period of their dedication, they are consecrated to the LORD.

9 " 'If someone dies suddenly in the Nazirite's presence, thus defiling the hair that symbolizes their dedication, they must shave their head on the seventh day—the day of their cleansing. 10Then on the eighth day they must bring two doves or two young pigeons to the priest at the entrance to the tent of meeting. 11The priest is to offer one as a sin offering[a] and the other as a burnt offering to make atonement for the Nazirite because they sinned by being in the presence of the dead body. That same day they are to consecrate their head again. 12They must rededicate themselves to the LORD for the same period of dedication and must bring a year-old male lamb as a guilt offering. The previous days do not count, because they became defiled during their period of dedication.

13 " 'Now this is the law of the Nazirite when the period of their dedication is over. They are to be brought to the entrance to the tent of meeting. 14There they are to present their offerings to the LORD: a year-old male lamb without defect for a burnt offering, a year-old ewe lamb without defect for a sin offering, a ram without defect for a fellowship offering, 15together with their grain offerings and drink offerings, and a basket of bread made with the finest flour and without yeast—thick loaves with olive oil mixed in, and thin loaves brushed with olive oil.

16 " 'The priest is to present all these before the LORD and make the sin offering and the burnt offering. 17He is to present the basket of unleavened bread and is to sacrifice the ram as a fellowship offering to the LORD, together with its grain offering and drink offering.

18 " 'Then at the entrance to the tent of meeting, the Nazirite must shave off the hair that symbolizes their dedication. They are to take the hair and put it in the fire that is under the sacrifice of the fellowship offering.

19 " 'After the Nazirite has shaved off the hair that symbolizes their dedication, the priest is to place in their hands a boiled shoulder of the ram, and one thick loaf and one thin loaf from the basket, both made without yeast. 20The priest shall then wave these before the LORD as a wave offering; they are holy and belong to the priest, together with the breast that was waved and the thigh that was presented. After that, the Nazirite may drink wine.

21 " 'This is the law of the Nazirite who vows offerings to the LORD in accordance with their dedication, in addition to whatever else they can afford. They must fulfill the vows they have made, according to the law of the Nazirite.' "

---

a 11 Or *purification offering*; also in verses 14 and 16

The Priestly Blessing

²²The LORD said to Moses, ²³"Tell Aaron and his sons, 'This is how you are to bless the Israelites. Say to them:

²⁴ " ' "The LORD bless you
and keep you;
²⁵the LORD make his face shine on you
and be gracious to you;
²⁶the LORD turn his face toward you
and give you peace." '

²⁷"So they will put my name on the Israelites, and I will bless them."

Offerings at the Dedication of the Tabernacle

7 When Moses finished setting up the tabernacle, he anointed and consecrated it and all its furnishings. He also anointed and consecrated the altar and all its utensils. ²Then the leaders of Israel, the heads of families who were the tribal leaders in charge of those who were counted, made offerings. ³They brought as their gifts before the LORD six covered carts and twelve oxen—an ox from each leader and a cart from every two. These they presented before the tabernacle.

⁴The LORD said to Moses, ⁵"Accept these from them, that they may be used in the work at the tent of meeting. Give them to the Levites as each man's work requires."

⁶So Moses took the carts and oxen and gave them to the Levites. ⁷He gave two carts and four oxen to the Gershonites, as their work required, ⁸and he gave four carts and eight oxen to the Merarites, as their work required. They were all under the direction of Ithamar son of Aaron, the priest. ⁹But Moses did not give any to the Kohathites, because they were to carry on their shoulders the holy things, for which they were responsible.

¹⁰When the altar was anointed, the leaders brought their offerings for its dedication and presented them before the altar. ¹¹For the LORD had said to Moses, "Each day one leader is to bring his offering for the dedication of the altar."

¹²The one who brought his offering on the first day was Nahshon son of Amminadab of the tribe of Judah.

¹³His offering was one silver plate weighing a hundred and thirty shekels[a] and one silver sprinkling bowl weighing seventy shekels,[b] both according to the sanctuary shekel, each filled with the finest flour mixed with olive oil as a grain offering; ¹⁴one gold dish weighing ten shekels,[c] filled with incense; ¹⁵one young bull, one ram and one male lamb a year old for a burnt offering; ¹⁶one male goat for a sin offering[d]; ¹⁷and two oxen, five rams, five male goats and five male lambs a year old to be sacrificed as a fellowship offering. This was the offering of Nahshon son of Amminadab.

¹⁸On the second day Nethanel son of Zuar, the leader of Issachar, brought his offering.

¹⁹The offering he brought was one silver plate weighing a hundred and thirty shekels and one silver sprinkling bowl weighing seventy shekels, both according to the sanctuary shekel, each filled with the finest flour mixed with olive oil as a grain offering; ²⁰one gold dish weighing ten shekels, filled with incense; ²¹one young bull, one ram and one male lamb a year old for a burnt offering; ²²one male goat for a sin offering; ²³and two oxen, five rams, five male goats and five male lambs a year old to be sacrificed as a fellowship offering. This was the offering of Nethanel son of Zuar.

²⁴On the third day, Eliab son of Helon, the leader of the people of Zebulun, brought his offering.

²⁵His offering was one silver plate weighing a hundred and thirty shekels and one silver sprinkling bowl weighing seventy shekels, both according to the sanctuary shekel, each filled with the finest flour mixed with olive oil as a grain offering; ²⁶one gold dish weighing ten shekels, filled

---

a 13 That is, about 3 1/4 pounds or about 1.5 kilograms; also elsewhere in this chapter   *b 13* That is, about 1 3/4 pounds or about 800 grams; also elsewhere in this chapter   *c 14* That is, about 4 ounces or about 115 grams; also elsewhere in this chapter   *d 16* Or *purification offering*; also elsewhere in this chapter with incense; [27]one young bull, one ram and one male lamb a year old for a burnt offering; [28]one male goat for a sin offering; [29]and two oxen, five rams, five male goats and five male lambs a year old to be sacrificed as a fellowship offering. This was the offering of Eliab son of Helon.

[30]On the fourth day Elizur son of Shedeur, the leader of the people of Reuben, brought his offering.

[31]His offering was one silver plate weighing a hundred and thirty shekels and one silver sprinkling bowl weighing seventy shekels, both according to the sanctuary shekel, each filled with the finest flour mixed with olive oil as a grain offering; [32]one gold dish weighing ten shekels, filled with incense; [33]one young bull, one ram and one male lamb a year old for a burnt offering; [34]one male goat for a sin offering; [35]and two oxen, five rams, five male goats and five male lambs a year old to be sacrificed as a fellowship offering. This was the offering of Elizur son of Shedeur.

[36]On the fifth day Shelumiel son of Zurishaddai, the leader of the people of Simeon, brought his offering.

[37]His offering was one silver plate weighing a hundred and thirty shekels and one silver sprinkling bowl weighing seventy shekels, both according to the sanctuary shekel, each filled with the finest flour mixed with olive oil as a grain offering; [38]one gold dish weighing ten shekels, filled with incense; [39]one young bull, one ram and one male lamb a year old for a burnt offering; [40]one male goat for a sin offering; [41]and two oxen, five rams, five male goats and five male lambs a year old to be sacrificed as a fellowship offering. This was the offering of Shelumiel son of Zurishaddai.

[42]On the sixth day Eliasaph son of Deuel, the leader of the people of Gad, brought his offering.

[43]His offering was one silver plate weighing a hundred and thirty shek-

els and one silver sprinkling bowl weighing seventy shekels, both according to the sanctuary shekel, each filled with the finest flour mixed with olive oil as a grain offering; [44]one gold dish weighing ten shekels, filled with incense; [45]one young bull, one ram and one male lamb a year old for a burnt offering; [46]one male goat for a sin offering; [47]and two oxen, five rams, five male goats and five male lambs a year old to be sacrificed as a fellowship offering. This was the offering of Eliasaph son of Deuel.

[48]On the seventh day Elishama son of Ammihud, the leader of the people of Ephraim, brought his offering.

[49]His offering was one silver plate weighing a hundred and thirty shekels and one silver sprinkling bowl weighing seventy shekels, both according to the sanctuary shekel, each filled with the finest flour mixed with olive oil as a grain offering; [50]one gold dish weighing ten shekels, filled with incense; [51]one young bull, one ram and one male lamb a year old for a burnt offering; [52]one male goat for a sin offering; [53]and two oxen, five rams, five male goats and five male lambs a year old to be sacrificed as a fellowship offering. This was the offering of Elishama son of Ammihud.

[54]On the eighth day Gamaliel son of Pedahzur, the leader of the people of Manasseh, brought his offering.

[55]His offering was one silver plate weighing a hundred and thirty shekels and one silver sprinkling bowl weighing seventy shekels, both according to the sanctuary shekel, each filled with the finest flour mixed with olive oil as a grain offering; [56]one gold dish weighing ten shekels, filled with incense; [57]one young bull, one ram and one male lamb a year old for a burnt offering; [58]one male goat for a sin offering; [59]and two oxen, five rams, five male goats and five male lambs a year old to be sacrificed as a fellowship offering. This was the offering of Gamaliel son of Pedahzur.

⁶⁰On the ninth day Abidan son of Gideoni, the leader of the people of Benjamin, brought his offering.

⁶¹His offering was one silver plate weighing a hundred and thirty shekels and one silver sprinkling bowl weighing seventy shekels, both according to the sanctuary shekel, each filled with the finest flour mixed with olive oil as a grain offering; ⁶²one gold dish weighing ten shekels, filled with incense; ⁶³one young bull, one ram and one male lamb a year old for a burnt offering; ⁶⁴one male goat for a sin offering; ⁶⁵and two oxen, five rams, five male goats and five male lambs a year old to be sacrificed as a fellowship offering. This was the offering of Abidan son of Gideoni.

⁶⁶On the tenth day Ahiezer son of Ammishaddai, the leader of the people of Dan, brought his offering.

⁶⁷His offering was one silver plate weighing a hundred and thirty shekels and one silver sprinkling bowl weighing seventy shekels, both according to the sanctuary shekel, each filled with the finest flour mixed with olive oil as a grain offering; ⁶⁸one gold dish weighing ten shekels, filled with incense; ⁶⁹one young bull, one ram and one male lamb a year old for a burnt offering; ⁷⁰one male goat for a sin offering; ⁷¹and two oxen, five rams, five male goats and five male lambs a year old to be sacrificed as a fellowship offering. This was the offering of Ahiezer son of Ammishaddai.

⁷²On the eleventh day Pagiel son of Okran, the leader of the people of Asher, brought his offering.

⁷³His offering was one silver plate weighing a hundred and thirty shekels and one silver sprinkling bowl weighing seventy shekels, both according to the sanctuary shekel, each filled with the finest flour mixed with olive oil as a grain offering; ⁷⁴one gold dish weighing ten shekels, filled with incense; ⁷⁵one young bull, one ram and one male lamb a year old for a burnt offering; ⁷⁶one male goat for a sin offering; ⁷⁷and two oxen, five rams, five male goats and five male lambs a year old to be sacrificed as a fellowship offering. This was the offering of Pagiel son of Okran.

⁷⁸On the twelfth day Ahira son of Enan, the leader of the people of Naphtali, brought his offering.

⁷⁹His offering was one silver plate weighing a hundred and thirty shekels and one silver sprinkling bowl weighing seventy shekels, both according to the sanctuary shekel, each filled with the finest flour mixed with olive oil as a grain offering; ⁸⁰one gold dish weighing ten shekels, filled with incense; ⁸¹one young bull, one ram and one male lamb a year old for a burnt offering; ⁸²one male goat for a sin offering; ⁸³and two oxen, five rams, five male goats and five male lambs a year old to be sacrificed as a fellowship offering. This was the offering of Ahira son of Enan.

⁸⁴These were the offerings of the Israelite leaders for the dedication of the altar when it was anointed: twelve silver plates, twelve silver sprinkling bowls and twelve gold dishes. ⁸⁵Each silver plate weighed a hundred and thirty shekels, and each sprinkling bowl seventy shekels. Altogether, the silver dishes weighed two thousand four hundred shekels,ᵃ according to the sanctuary shekel. ⁸⁶The twelve gold dishes filled with incense weighed ten shekels each, according to the sanctuary shekel. Altogether, the gold dishes weighed a hundred and twenty shekels.ᵇ ⁸⁷The total number of animals for the burnt offering came to twelve young bulls, twelve rams and twelve male lambs a year old, together with their grain offering. Twelve male goats were used for the sin offering. ⁸⁸The total number of animals for the sacrifice of the fellowship offering came to twenty-four oxen, sixty rams, sixty male goats and sixty male lambs a year old. These were the offerings for the dedication of the altar after it was anointed.

---

a 85 That is, about 60 pounds or about 28 kilograms
b 86 That is, about 3 pounds or about 1.4 kilograms

[89]When Moses entered the tent of meeting to speak with the LORD, he heard the voice speaking to him from between the two cherubim above the atonement cover on the ark of the covenant law. In this way the LORD spoke to him.

Setting Up the Lamps

8 The LORD said to Moses, [2]"Speak to Aaron and say to him, 'When you set up the lamps, see that all seven light up the area in front of the lampstand.'"

[3]Aaron did so; he set up the lamps so that they faced forward on the lampstand, just as the LORD commanded Moses. [4]This is how the lampstand was made: It was made of hammered gold—from its base to its blossoms. The lampstand was made exactly like the pattern the LORD had shown Moses.

The Setting Apart of the Levites

[5]The LORD said to Moses: [6]"Take the Levites from among all the Israelites and make them ceremonially clean. [7]To purify them, do this: Sprinkle the water of cleansing on them; then have them shave their whole bodies and wash their clothes. And so they will purify themselves. [8]Have them take a young bull with its grain offering of the finest flour mixed with olive oil; then you are to take a second young bull for a sin offering.[a] [9]Bring the Levites to the front of the tent of meeting and assemble the whole Israelite community. [10]You are to bring the Levites before the LORD, and the Israelites are to lay their hands on them. [11]Aaron is to present the Levites before the LORD as a wave offering from the Israelites, so that they may be ready to do the work of the LORD.

[12]"Then the Levites are to lay their hands on the heads of the bulls, using one for a sin offering to the LORD and the other for a burnt offering, to make atonement for the Levites. [13]Have the Levites stand in front of Aaron and his sons and then present them as a wave offering to the LORD. [14]In this way you are to set the Levites apart from the other Israelites, and the Levites will be mine.

[15]"After you have purified the Levites and presented them as a wave offering, they are to come to do their work at the tent of meeting. [16]They are the Israelites who are to be given wholly to me. I have taken them as my own in place of the firstborn, the first male offspring from every Israelite woman. [17]Every firstborn male in Israel, whether human or animal, is mine. When I struck down all the firstborn in Egypt, I set them apart for myself. [18]And I have taken the Levites in place of all the firstborn sons in Israel. [19]From among all the Israelites, I have given the Levites as gifts to Aaron and his sons to do the work at the tent of meeting on behalf of the Israelites and to make atonement for them so that no plague will strike the Israelites when they go near the sanctuary."

[20]Moses, Aaron and the whole Israelite community did with the Levites just as the LORD commanded Moses. [21]The Levites purified themselves and washed their clothes. Then Aaron presented them as a wave offering before the LORD and made atonement for them to purify them. [22]After that, the Levites came to do their work at the tent of meeting under the supervision of Aaron and his sons. They did with the Levites just as the LORD commanded Moses.

[23]The LORD said to Moses, [24]"This applies to the Levites: Men twenty-five years old or more shall come to take part in the work at the tent of meeting, [25]but at the age of fifty, they must retire from their regular service and work no longer. [26]They may assist their brothers in performing their duties at the tent of meeting, but they themselves must not do the work. This, then, is how you are to assign the responsibilities of the Levites."

The Passover

9 The LORD spoke to Moses in the Desert of Sinai in the first month of the second year after they came out of Egypt. He said, [2]"Have the Israelites celebrate the Passover at the appointed

---

[a] 8 Or *purification offering*; also in verse 12

time. ³Celebrate it at the appointed time, at twilight on the fourteenth day of this month, in accordance with all its rules and regulations."

⁴So Moses told the Israelites to celebrate the Passover, ⁵and they did so in the Desert of Sinai at twilight on the fourteenth day of the first month. The Israelites did everything just as the LORD commanded Moses.

⁶But some of them could not celebrate the Passover on that day because they were ceremonially unclean on account of a dead body. So they came to Moses and Aaron that same day ⁷and said to Moses, "We have become unclean because of a dead body, but why should we be kept from presenting the LORD's offering with the other Israelites at the appointed time?"

⁸Moses answered them, "Wait until I find out what the LORD commands concerning you."

⁹Then the LORD said to Moses, ¹⁰"Tell the Israelites: 'When any of you or your

BREAK THROUGH!

Passover

(NUMBERS 9:1-14)

This is a family meal where the Israelites eat lamb and remember that God took them out of Egypt. You can learn more about the Passover in Exodus 12.

BREAK THROUGH!

First month

(NUMBERS 9:5)

This was Aviv, the first month of the Jewish lunar calendar. In our solar calendar, it would be from the middle of March to the middle of April.

descendants are unclean because of a dead body or are away on a journey, they are still to celebrate the LORD's Passover, ¹¹but they are to do it on the fourteenth day of the second month at twilight. They are to eat the lamb, together with unleavened bread and bitter herbs. ¹²They must not leave any of it till morning or break any of its bones. When they celebrate the Passover, they must follow all the regulations. ¹³But if anyone who is ceremonially clean and not on a journey fails to celebrate the Passover, they must be cut off from their people for not presenting the LORD's offering at the appointed time. They will bear the consequences of their sin.

¹⁴" 'A foreigner residing among you is also to celebrate the LORD's Passover in accordance with its rules and regulations. You must have the same regulations for both the foreigner and the native-born.' "

The Cloud Above the Tabernacle

¹⁵On the day the tabernacle, the tent of the covenant law, was set up, the cloud

covered it. From evening till morning the cloud above the tabernacle looked like fire. ¹⁶That is how it continued to be; the cloud covered it, and at night it looked like fire. ¹⁷Whenever the cloud lifted from above the tent, the Israelites set out; wherever the cloud settled, the Israelites encamped. ¹⁸At the LORD's command the Israelites set out, and at his command they encamped. As long as the cloud stayed over the tabernacle, they remained in camp. ¹⁹When the cloud remained over the tabernacle a long time, the Israelites obeyed the LORD's order and did not set out. ²⁰Sometimes the cloud was over the tabernacle only a few days; at the LORD's command they would encamp, and then at his command they would set out. ²¹Sometimes the cloud stayed only from evening till morning, and when it lifted in the morning, they set out. Whether by day or by night, whenever the cloud lifted, they set out. ²²Whether the cloud stayed over the tabernacle for two days or a month or a year, the Israelites would remain in camp and not set out; but when it lifted, they would set out. ²³At the LORD's command they encamped, and at the LORD's command they set out. They obeyed the LORD's order, in accordance with his command through Moses.

The Silver Trumpets

10 The LORD said to Moses: ²"Make two trumpets of hammered silver, and use them for calling the community together and for having the camps set out. ³When both are sounded, the whole community is to assemble before you at the entrance to the tent of meeting. ⁴If only one is sounded, the leaders—the heads of the clans of Israel—are to assemble before you. ⁵When a trumpet blast is sounded, the tribes camping on the east are to set out. ⁶At the sounding of a second blast, the camps on the south are to set out. The blast will be the signal for setting out. ⁷To gather the assembly, blow the trumpets, but not with the signal for setting out.

⁸"The sons of Aaron, the priests, are to blow the trumpets. This is to be a lasting ordinance for you and the generations to

BREAKTHROUGH!

Second month

(NUMBERS 9:11)
The second month of the Jewish lunar calendar is called Ziv. It would be from the middle of April to the middle of May in our solar calendar.

come. ⁹When you go into battle in your own land against an enemy who is oppressing you, sound a blast on the trumpets. Then you will be remembered by the LORD your God and rescued from your enemies. ¹⁰Also at your times of rejoicing—your appointed festivals and New Moon feasts—you are to sound the trumpets over your burnt offerings and fellowship offerings, and they will be a memorial for you before your God. I am the LORD your God."

The Israelites Leave Sinai

¹¹On the twentieth day of the second month of the second year, the cloud lifted from above the tabernacle of the covenant law. ¹²Then the Israelites set out from the Desert of Sinai and traveled from place to place until the cloud came to rest in the Desert of Paran. ¹³They set out, this first time, at the LORD's command through Moses.

¹⁴The divisions of the camp of Judah went first, under their standard. Nahshon

son of Amminadab was in command. 15Nethanel son of Zuar was over the division of the tribe of Issachar, 16and Eliab son of Helon was over the division of the tribe of Zebulun. 17Then the tabernacle was taken down, and the Gershonites and Merarites, who carried it, set out.

18The divisions of the camp of Reuben went next, under their standard. Elizur son of Shedeur was in command. 19Shelumiel son of Zurishaddai was over the division of the tribe of Simeon, 20and Eliasaph son of Deuel was over the division of the tribe of Gad. 21Then the Kohathites set out, carrying the holy things. The tabernacle was to be set up before they arrived.

22The divisions of the camp of Ephraim went next, under their standard. Elishama son of Ammihud was in command. 23Gamaliel son of Pedahzur was over the division of the tribe of Manasseh, 24and Abidan son of Gideoni was over the division of the tribe of Benjamin.

25Finally, as the rear guard for all the units, the divisions of the camp of Dan set out under their standard. Ahiezer son of Ammishaddai was in command. 26Pagiel son of Okran was over the division of the tribe of Asher, 27and Ahira son of Enan was over the division of the tribe of Naphtali. 28This was the order of march for the Israelite divisions as they set out.

29Now Moses said to Hobab son of Reuel the Midianite, Moses' father-in-law, "We are setting out for the place about which the Lord said, 'I will give it to you.' Come with us and we will treat you well, for the Lord has promised good things to Israel."

30He answered, "No, I will not go; I am going back to my own land and my own people."

31But Moses said, "Please do not leave us. You know where we should camp in the wilderness, and you can be our eyes. 32If you come with us, we will share with you whatever good things the Lord gives us."

33So they set out from the mountain of the Lord and traveled for three days. The ark of the covenant of the Lord went before them during those three days to find them a place to rest. 34The cloud of the Lord was over them by day when they set out from the camp.

35Whenever the ark set out, Moses said,

"Rise up, Lord!
  May your enemies be scattered;
  may your foes flee before you."

36Whenever it came to rest, he said,

"Return, Lord,
  to the countless thousands of
    Israel."

BREAKTHROUGH!

Ark of the covenant

(NUMBERS 10:33-36)

This was a wooden box covered in gold that God told Moses to make. They kept the stone tablets of the Ten Commandments and some manna in it. Manna was the white food that looked like breadcrumbs that God gave them to eat in the desert. Later, they put Aaron's staff in it too. (Read Numbers 17.) The ark was kept in the most special place of the sanctuary, and it stood for the presence of God in the midst of his people. The Israelites believed that if the ark went with them in their battles, they were super sure to win. But they had to learn that the presence of the ark wasn't magic, and that what was most important was to obey God and his commandments.

Fire From the Lord

11 Now the people complained about their hardships in the hearing of the Lord, and when he heard them his anger was aroused. Then fire from the Lord burned among them and consumed some of the outskirts of the camp. ²When the people cried out to Moses, he prayed to the Lord and the fire died down. ³So that place was called Taberah,ª because fire from the Lord had burned among them.

Quail From the Lord

⁴The rabble with them began to crave other food, and again the Israelites started wailing and said, "If only we had meat to eat! ⁵We remember the fish we ate in Egypt at no cost—also the cucumbers, melons, leeks, onions and garlic. ⁶But now we have lost our appetite; we never see anything but this manna!"

⁷The manna was like coriander seed and looked like resin. ⁸The people went around gathering it, and then ground it in a hand mill or crushed it in a mortar. They cooked it in a pot or made it into loaves. And it tasted like something made with olive oil. ⁹When the dew settled on the camp at night, the manna also came down.

¹⁰Moses heard the people of every family wailing at the entrance to their tents. The Lord became exceedingly angry, and Moses was troubled. ¹¹He asked the Lord, "Why have you brought this trouble on your servant? What have I done to displease you that you put the burden of all these people on me? ¹²Did I conceive all these people? Did I give them birth? Why do you tell me to carry them in my arms, as a nurse carries an infant, to the land you promised on oath to their ancestors? ¹³Where can I get meat for all these people? They keep wailing to me, 'Give us meat to eat!' ¹⁴I cannot carry all these people by myself; the burden is too heavy for me. ¹⁵If this is how you are going to treat me, please go ahead and kill me—if I have found favor in your eyes—and do not let me face my own ruin."

¹⁶The Lord said to Moses: "Bring me seventy of Israel's elders who are known to you as leaders and officials among the people. Have them come to the tent of meeting, that they may stand there with you. ¹⁷I will come down and speak with you there, and I will take some of the power of the Spirit that is on you and put it on them. They will share the burden of the people with you so that you will not have to carry it alone.

¹⁸"Tell the people: 'Consecrate yourselves in preparation for tomorrow, when you will eat meat. The Lord heard you when you wailed, "If only we had meat to eat! We were better off in Egypt!" Now the Lord will give you meat, and you will eat it. ¹⁹You will not eat it for just one day, or two days, or five, ten or twenty days, ²⁰but for a whole month—until it comes out of your nostrils and you loathe it—because you have rejected the Lord, who is among you, and have wailed before him, saying, "Why did we ever leave Egypt?"'"

²¹But Moses said, "Here I am among six hundred thousand men on foot, and you say, 'I will give them meat to eat for a whole month!' ²²Would they have enough if flocks and herds were slaughtered for them? Would they have enough if all the fish in the sea were caught for them?"

²³The Lord answered Moses, "Is the Lord's arm too short? Now you will see whether or not what I say will come true for you."

²⁴So Moses went out and told the people what the Lord had said. He brought together seventy of their elders and had them stand around the tent. ²⁵Then the Lord came down in the cloud and spoke with him, and he took some of the power of the Spirit that was on him and put it on the seventy elders. When the Spirit rested on them, they prophesied—but did not do so again.

²⁶However, two men, whose names were Eldad and Medad, had remained in the camp. They were listed among the elders, but did not go out to the tent. Yet the Spirit also rested on them, and they prophesied in the camp. ²⁷A young man ran and told Moses, "Eldad and Medad are prophesying in the camp."

ª 3 *Taberah* means *burning.*

²⁸Joshua son of Nun, who had been Moses' aide since youth, spoke up and said, "Moses, my lord, stop them!"

²⁹But Moses replied, "Are you jealous for my sake? I wish that all the LORD's people were prophets and that the LORD would put his Spirit on them!" ³⁰Then Moses and the elders of Israel returned to the camp.

³¹Now a wind went out from the LORD and drove quail in from the sea. It scattered them up to two cubits*ᵃ* deep all around the camp, as far as a day's walk in any direction. ³²All that day and night and all the next day the people went out and gathered quail. No one gathered less than ten homers.*ᵇ* Then they spread them out all around the camp. ³³But while the meat was still between their teeth and before it could be consumed, the anger

of the LORD burned against the people, and he struck them with a severe plague. ³⁴Therefore the place was named Kibroth Hattaavah,*ᶜ* because there they buried the people who had craved other food.

³⁵From Kibroth Hattaavah the people traveled to Hazeroth and stayed there.

Miriam and Aaron Oppose Moses

12 Miriam and Aaron began to talk against Moses because of his Cushite wife, for he had married a Cushite. ²"Has the LORD spoken only through Moses?" they asked. "Hasn't he also spoken through us?" And the LORD heard this.

³(Now Moses was a very humble man, more humble than anyone else on the face of the earth.)

⁴At once the LORD said to Moses, Aaron and Miriam, "Come out to the tent of meeting, all three of you." So the three of them went out. ⁵Then the LORD came down in a pillar of cloud; he stood at the entrance to the tent and summoned Aaron and Miriam. When the two of them stepped forward, ⁶he said, "Listen to my words:

> "When there is a prophet among you,
> I, the LORD, reveal myself to them in
>   visions,
> I speak to them in dreams.
> ⁷But this is not true of my servant
>   Moses;
> he is faithful in all my house.
> ⁸With him I speak face to face,
>   clearly and not in riddles;
> he sees the form of the LORD.
> Why then were you not afraid
>   to speak against my servant
>   Moses?"

⁹The anger of the LORD burned against them, and he left them.

¹⁰When the cloud lifted from above the tent, Miriam's skin was leprous*ᵈ*— it became as white as snow. Aaron turned toward her and saw that she had a defiling skin disease, ¹¹and he said to Moses, "Please, my lord, I ask you not to hold against us the sin we have

THE WITNESSES

✓ **JOSHUA (NUMBERS 11:28)**
Read Exodus 17:9.

ᵃ *31* That is, about 3 feet or about 90 centimeters
ᵇ *32* That is, possibly about 1 3/4 tons or about
1.6 metric tons   *ᶜ* *34* *Kibroth Hattaavah* means *graves of craving.*   *ᵈ* *10* The Hebrew for *leprous* was used for various diseases affecting the skin.

so foolishly committed. ¹²Do not let her be like a stillborn infant coming from its mother's womb with its flesh half eaten away."

¹³So Moses cried out to the LORD, "Please, God, heal her!"

¹⁴The LORD replied to Moses, "If her father had spit in her face, would she not have been in disgrace for seven days? Confine her outside the camp for seven days; after that she can be brought back." ¹⁵So Miriam was confined outside the camp for seven days, and the people did not move on till she was brought back.

¹⁶After that, the people left Hazeroth and encamped in the Desert of Paran.

Exploring Canaan

13 The LORD said to Moses, ²"Send some men to explore the land of Canaan, which I am giving to the Israelites. From each ancestral tribe send one of its leaders."

³So at the LORD's command Moses

CANAAN

(NUMBERS 13:1)

The biblical name for Palestine west of the Jordan River. This is the land God promised to give Abraham and his offspring so they could live there.

DESERT OF PARAN

(NUMBERS 12:16)

This desert is north of the Sinai Desert.

sent them out from the Desert of Paran. All of them were leaders of the Israelites. ⁴These are their names:

from the tribe of Reuben, Shammua son of Zakkur;
⁵from the tribe of Simeon, Shaphat son of Hori;
⁶from the tribe of Judah, Caleb son of Jephunneh;
⁷from the tribe of Issachar, Igal son of Joseph;
⁸from the tribe of Ephraim, Hoshea son of Nun;
⁹from the tribe of Benjamin, Palti son of Raphu;
¹⁰from the tribe of Zebulun, Gaddiel son of Sodi;
¹¹from the tribe of Manasseh (a tribe of Joseph), Gaddi son of Susi;
¹²from the tribe of Dan, Ammiel son of Gemalli;

13from the tribe of Asher, Sethur son of Michael;
14from the tribe of Naphtali, Nahbi son of Vophsi;
15from the tribe of Gad, Geuel son of Maki.

16These are the names of the men Moses sent to explore the land. (Moses gave Hoshea son of Nun the name Joshua.)

17When Moses sent them to explore

THE WITNESSES

✓ **CALEB** (NUMBERS 13:6,30)
This name means "dog." His father's name was Jephunneh, and he was from the tribe of Judah. Caleb was one of the twelve spies that Moses sent to check out the land of Canaan. He went with Joshua, and these two men were the only ones who came back with a good report. God rewarded them for that. God let them live during the 40 years the Israelites wandered the desert. Then he gave Caleb the land of Hebron.

Canaan, he said, "Go up through the Negev and on into the hill country. 18See what the land is like and whether the people who live there are strong or weak, few or many. 19What kind of land do they live in? Is it good or bad? What kind of towns do they live in? Are they unwalled or fortified? 20How is the soil? Is it fertile or poor? Are there trees in it or not? Do your best to bring back some of the fruit of the land." (It was the season for the first ripe grapes.)

21So they went up and explored the land from the Desert of Zin as far as Rehob, toward Lebo Hamath. 22They went up through the Negev and came to Hebron, where Ahiman, Sheshai and Talmai, the descendants of Anak, lived. (Hebron had been built seven years before Zoan in Egypt.) 23When they reached the Valley of Eshkol,ᵃ they cut off a branch bearing a single cluster of grapes. Two of them carried it on a pole between them, along with some pomegranates and figs. 24That place was called the Valley of Eshkol because of the cluster of grapes the Israelites cut off there. 25At the end of forty days they returned from exploring the land.

Report on the Exploration

26They came back to Moses and Aaron and the whole Israelite community at Kadesh in the Desert of Paran. There they reported to them and to the whole assembly and showed them the fruit of the land. 27They gave Moses this account: "We went into the land to which you sent us, and it does flow with milk and honey! Here is its fruit. 28But the people who live there are powerful, and the cities are fortified and very large. We even saw descendants of Anak there. 29The Amalekites live in the Negev; the Hittites, Jebusites and Amorites live in the hill country; and the Canaanites live near the sea and along the Jordan."

30Then Caleb silenced the people before Moses and said, "We should go up and take possession of the land, for we can certainly do it."

31But the men who had gone up with

ᵃ 23 *Eshkol* means *cluster*; also in verse 24.

BREAKTHROUGH!

Amalekites, Hittites, Jebusites, Amorites and Canaanites

(NUMBERS 13:29)

These were people who lived in Canaan, a fertile region in the ancient Near East between the Mediterranean Sea and the Jordan River. It's where Israel, Palestine, part of Jordan and some areas of Syria and Lebanon are now.

him said, "We can't attack those people; they are stronger than we are." ³²And they spread among the Israelites a bad report about the land they had explored. They said, "The land we explored devours those living in it. All the people we saw there are of great size. ³³We saw the Nephilim there (the descendants of Anak come from the Nephilim). We seemed like grasshoppers in our own eyes, and we looked the same to them."

The People Rebel

14 That night all the members of the community raised their voices and wept aloud. ²All the Israelites grumbled against Moses and Aaron, and the whole assembly said to them, "If only we had died in Egypt! Or in this wilderness! ³Why is the Lord bringing us to this land only to let us fall by the sword? Our wives and children will be taken as plunder. Wouldn't it be better for us to go back to Egypt?" ⁴And they said to each other, "We should choose a leader and go back to Egypt."

⁵Then Moses and Aaron fell facedown in front of the whole Israelite assembly gathered there. ⁶Joshua son of Nun and Caleb son of Jephunneh, who were among those who had explored the land, tore their clothes ⁷and said to the entire Israelite assembly, "The land we passed through and explored is exceedingly good. ⁸If the Lord is pleased with us, he will lead us into that land, a land flowing with milk and honey, and will give it to us. ⁹Only do not rebel against the Lord. And do not be afraid of the people of the land, because we will devour them. Their protection is gone, but the Lord is with us. Do not be afraid of them."

¹⁰But the whole assembly talked about stoning them. Then the glory of the Lord

CHECK THE FACTS

Who were the only two spies that brought back good reports from the land of Canaan?

A) Moses and Aaron

B) Joshua and Caleb

C) Balak and Balaam

appeared at the tent of meeting to all the Israelites. ¹¹The LORD said to Moses, "How long will these people treat me with contempt? How long will they refuse to believe in me, in spite of all the signs I have performed among them? ¹²I will strike them down with a plague and destroy them, but I will make you into a nation greater and stronger than they."

¹³Moses said to the LORD, "Then the Egyptians will hear about it! By your power you brought these people up from among them. ¹⁴And they will tell the inhabitants of this land about it. They have already heard that you, LORD, are with these people and that you, LORD, have been seen face to face, that your cloud stays over them, and that you go before them in a pillar of cloud by day and a pillar of fire by night. ¹⁵If you put all these people to death, leaving none alive, the nations who have heard this report about you will say, ¹⁶'The LORD was not able to bring these people into the land he promised them on oath, so he slaughtered them in the wilderness.'

¹⁷"Now may the Lord's strength be displayed, just as you have declared: ¹⁸'The LORD is slow to anger, abounding in love and forgiving sin and rebellion. Yet he does not leave the guilty unpunished; he punishes the children for the sin of the parents to the third and fourth generation.' ¹⁹In accordance with your great love, forgive the sin of these people, just as you have pardoned them from the time they left Egypt until now."

²⁰The LORD replied, "I have forgiven them, as you asked. ²¹Nevertheless, as surely as I live and as surely as the glory of the LORD fills the whole earth, ²²not one of those who saw my glory and the signs I performed in Egypt and in the wilderness but who disobeyed me and tested me ten times— ²³not one of them will ever see the land I promised on oath to their ancestors. No one who has treated me with contempt will ever see it. ²⁴But because my servant Caleb has a different spirit and follows me wholeheartedly, I will bring him into the land he went to, and his descendants will inherit it. ²⁵Since the Amalekites and the Canaanites are living

in the valleys, turn back tomorrow and set out toward the desert along the route to the Red Sea.ᵃ"

²⁶The LORD said to Moses and Aaron: ²⁷"How long will this wicked community grumble against me? I have heard the complaints of these grumbling Israelites. ²⁸So tell them, 'As surely as I live, declares the LORD, I will do to you the very thing I heard you say: ²⁹In this wilderness your bodies will fall—every one of you twenty years old or more who was counted in the census and who has grumbled against me. ³⁰Not one of you will enter the land I swore with uplifted hand to make your home, except Caleb son of Jephunneh and Joshua son of Nun. ³¹As for your children that you said would be taken as plunder, I will bring them in to enjoy the land you have rejected. ³²But as for you, your bodies will fall in this wilderness. ³³Your children will be shepherds here for forty years, suffering for your unfaithfulness, until the last of your bodies lies in the wilderness. ³⁴For forty years—one year for each of the forty days you explored the land—you will suffer for your sins and know what it is like to have me against you.' ³⁵I, the LORD, have spoken, and I will surely do these things to this whole wicked community, which has banded together against me. They will meet their end in this wilderness; here they will die."

³⁶So the men Moses had sent to explore the land, who returned and made the whole community grumble against him by spreading a bad report about it— ³⁷these men who were responsible for spreading the bad report about the land were struck down and died of a plague before the LORD. ³⁸Of the men who went to explore the land, only Joshua son of Nun and Caleb son of Jephunneh survived.

³⁹When Moses reported this to all the Israelites, they mourned bitterly. ⁴⁰Early the next morning they set out for the highest point in the hill country, saying, "Now we are ready to go up to the land the LORD promised. Surely we have sinned!"

⁴¹But Moses said, "Why are you disobeying the LORD's command? This will not succeed! ⁴²Do not go up, because the

---

ᵃ 25 Or the Sea of Reeds

LORD is not with you. You will be defeated by your enemies, [43]for the Amalekites and the Canaanites will face you there. Because you have turned away from the LORD, he will not be with you and you will fall by the sword."

[44]Nevertheless, in their presumption they went up toward the highest point in the hill country, though neither Moses nor the ark of the LORD's covenant moved from the camp. [45]Then the Amalekites and the Canaanites who lived in that hill country came down and attacked them and beat them down all the way to Hormah.

Supplementary Offerings

15 The LORD said to Moses, [2]"Speak to the Israelites and say to them: 'After you enter the land I am giving you as a home [3]and you present to the LORD food offerings from the herd or the flock, as an aroma pleasing to the LORD—whether burnt offerings or sacrifices, for special vows or freewill offerings or festival offerings— [4]then the person who brings an offering shall present to the LORD a grain offering of a tenth of an ephah[a] of the finest flour mixed with a quarter of a hin[b] of olive oil. [5]With each lamb for the burnt offering or the sacrifice, prepare a quarter of a hin of wine as a drink offering.

[6]" 'With a ram prepare a grain offering of two-tenths of an ephah[c] of the finest flour mixed with a third of a hin[d] of olive oil, [7]and a third of a hin of wine as a drink offering. Offer it as an aroma pleasing to the LORD.

[8]" 'When you prepare a young bull as a burnt offering or sacrifice, for a special vow or a fellowship offering to the LORD, [9]bring with the bull a grain offering of three-tenths of an ephah[e] of the finest flour mixed with half a hin[f] of olive oil, [10]and also bring half a hin of wine as a drink offering. This will be a food offering, an aroma pleasing to the LORD. [11]Each bull or ram, each lamb or young goat, is to be prepared in this manner. [12]Do this for each one, for as many as you prepare.

[13]" 'Everyone who is native-born must do these things in this way when they present a food offering as an aroma pleasing to the LORD. [14]For the generations to come, whenever a foreigner or anyone else living among you presents a food offering as an aroma pleasing to the LORD, they must do exactly as you do. [15]The community is to have the same rules for you and for the foreigner residing among you; this is a lasting ordinance for the generations to come. You and the foreigner shall be the same before the LORD: [16]The same laws and regulations will apply both to you and to the foreigner residing among you.' "

[17]The LORD said to Moses, [18]"Speak to the Israelites and say to them: 'When you enter the land to which I am taking you [19]and you eat the food of the land, present a portion as an offering to the LORD. [20]Present a loaf from the first of your ground meal and present it as an offering from the threshing floor. [21]Throughout the generations to come you are to give this offering to the LORD from the first of your ground meal.

Offerings for Unintentional Sins

[22]" 'Now if you as a community unintentionally fail to keep any of these commands the LORD gave Moses— [23]any of the LORD's commands to you through him, from the day the LORD gave them and continuing through the generations to come— [24]and if this is done unintentionally without the community being aware of it, then the whole community is to offer a young bull for a burnt offering as an aroma pleasing to the LORD, along with its prescribed grain offering and drink offering, and a male goat for a sin offering.[g] [25]The priest is to make atonement for the whole Israelite community, and they will be forgiven, for it was not intentional and they have presented to the LORD for their wrong a food offering and a sin offering. [26]The whole Israelite community and the foreigners residing among them will be forgiven, because all the people were involved in the unintentional wrong.

---

[a] 4 That is, probably about 3 1/2 pounds or about 1.6 kilograms   [b] 4 That is, about 1 quart or about 1 liter; also in verse 5   [c] 6 That is, probably about 7 pounds or about 3.2 kilograms   [d] 6 That is, about 1 1/3 quarts or about 1.3 liters; also in verse 7   [e] 9 That is, probably about 11 pounds or about 5 kilograms   [f] 9 That is, about 2 quarts or about 1.9 liters; also in verse 10   [g] 24 Or *purification offering*; also in verses 25 and 27

27 " 'But if just one person sins unintentionally, that person must bring a year-old female goat for a sin offering. 28The priest is to make atonement before the LORD for the one who erred by sinning unintentionally, and when atonement has been made, that person will be forgiven. 29One and the same law applies to everyone who sins unintentionally, whether a native-born Israelite or a foreigner residing among you.

30 " 'But anyone who sins defiantly, whether native-born or foreigner, blasphemes the LORD and must be cut off from the people of Israel. 31Because they have despised the LORD's word and broken his commands, they must surely be cut off; their guilt remains on them.' "

The Sabbath-Breaker Put to Death

32While the Israelites were in the wilderness, a man was found gathering wood on the Sabbath day. 33Those who found him gathering wood brought him to Moses and Aaron and the whole assembly, 34and they kept him in custody, because it was not clear what should be done to him. 35Then the LORD said to Moses, "The man must die. The whole assembly must stone him outside the camp." 36So the assembly took him outside the camp and stoned him to death, as the LORD commanded Moses.

Tassels on Garments

37The LORD said to Moses, 38"Speak to the Israelites and say to them: 'Throughout the generations to come you are to make tassels on the corners of your garments, with a blue cord on each tassel. 39You will have these tassels to look at and so you will remember all the commands of the LORD, that you may obey them and not prostitute yourselves by chasing after the lusts of your own hearts and eyes. 40Then you will remember to obey all my commands and will be consecrated to your God. 41I am the LORD your God, who brought you out of Egypt to be your God. I am the LORD your God.' "

Korah, Dathan and Abiram

16 Korah son of Izhar, the son of Kohath, the son of Levi, and certain

BREAKTHROUGH!

Why was the punishment for disobedience so harsh?

(NUMBERS 15:32-36)

Because God didn't want them to get used to disobeying him. In this case, God had said that Saturday was the day to rest, and that they didn't have to work. They should just rest and worship him. When this man disobeyed, that meant he didn't think God was his master or his superior, so he didn't pay him any attention. If his disobedience went unpunished, then everybody could just do anything they pleased.

Reubenites—Dathan and Abiram, sons of Eliab, and On son of Peleth—became insolent[a] 2and rose up against Moses. With them were 250 Israelite men, well-known community leaders who had been appointed members of the council. 3They came as a group to oppose Moses and Aaron and said to them, "You have gone too far! The whole community is holy, every one of them, and the LORD is with them. Why then do you set yourselves above the LORD's assembly?"

4When Moses heard this, he fell facedown. 5Then he said to Korah and all his followers: "In the morning the LORD will show who belongs to him and who is holy,

a 1 Or Peleth — took men

and he will have that person come near him. The man he chooses he will cause to come near him. ⁶You, Korah, and all your followers are to do this: Take censers ⁷and tomorrow put burning coals and incense in them before the LORD. The man the LORD chooses will be the one who is holy. You Levites have gone too far!"

⁸Moses also said to Korah, "Now listen, you Levites! ⁹Isn't it enough for you that the God of Israel has separated you from the rest of the Israelite community and brought you near himself to do the work at the LORD's tabernacle and to stand before the community and minister to them? ¹⁰He has brought you and all your fellow Levites near himself, but now you are trying to get the priesthood too. ¹¹It is against the LORD that you and all your followers have banded together. Who is Aaron that you should grumble against him?"

¹²Then Moses summoned Dathan and Abiram, the sons of Eliab. But they said, "We will not come! ¹³Isn't it enough that you have brought us up out of a land flowing with milk and honey to kill us in the wilderness? And now you also want to lord it over us! ¹⁴Moreover, you haven't brought us into a land flowing with milk and honey or given us an inheritance of fields and vineyards. Do you want to treat these men like slaves*? No, we will not come!"

¹⁵Then Moses became very angry and said to the LORD, "Do not accept their offering. I have not taken so much as a donkey from them, nor have I wronged any of them."

¹⁶Moses said to Korah, "You and all your followers are to appear before the LORD tomorrow—you and they and Aaron. ¹⁷Each man is to take his censer and put incense in it—250 censers in all—and present it before the LORD. You and Aaron are to present your censers also." ¹⁸So each of them took his censer, put burning coals and incense in it, and stood with Moses and Aaron at the entrance to the tent of meeting. ¹⁹When Korah had gathered all his followers in opposition to them at the entrance to the tent of meeting, the glory of the LORD appeared to the entire assembly. ²⁰The LORD said to Moses and Aaron, ²¹"Separate yourselves from this assembly so I can put an end to them at once."

²²But Moses and Aaron fell facedown and cried out, "O God, the God who gives breath to all living things, will you be angry with the entire assembly when only one man sins?"

ᵃ 14 Or to deceive these men; Hebrew *Will you gouge out the eyes of these men*

THE
WITNESSES

✓ KORAH (NUMBERS 16:1–40)
This name means "bald." He was the leader of the people who rebelled against Moses and Aaron in the Paran Desert.

✓ DATHAN AND ABIRAM
(NUMBERS 16:1–40)
Dathan means "fountain" or "law." *Abiram* means "my father is exalted." They were brothers who led the Israelites when they rebelled against Moses and Aaron.

23Then the LORD said to Moses, 24"Say to the assembly, 'Move away from the tents of Korah, Dathan and Abiram.' "

25Moses got up and went to Dathan and Abiram, and the elders of Israel followed him. 26He warned the assembly, "Move back from the tents of these wicked men! Do not touch anything belonging to them, or you will be swept away because of all their sins." 27So they moved away from the tents of Korah, Dathan and Abiram. Dathan and Abiram had come out and were standing with their wives, children and little ones at the entrances to their tents.

28Then Moses said, "This is how you will know that the LORD has sent me to do all these things and that it was not my idea: 29If these men die a natural death and suffer the fate of all mankind, then the LORD has not sent me. 30But if the LORD brings about something totally new, and the earth opens its mouth and swallows them, with everything that belongs to them, and they go down alive into the realm of the dead, then you will know that these men have treated the LORD with contempt."

31As soon as he finished saying all this, the ground under them split apart 32and the earth opened its mouth and swallowed them and their households, and all those associated with Korah, together with their possessions. 33They went down alive into the realm of the dead, with everything they owned; the earth closed over them, and they perished and were gone from the community. 34At their cries, all the Israelites around them fled, shouting, "The earth is going to swallow us too!"

35And fire came out from the LORD and consumed the 250 men who were offering the incense.

36The LORD said to Moses, 37"Tell Eleazar son of Aaron, the priest, to remove the censers from the charred remains and scatter the coals some distance away, for the censers are holy— 38the censers of the men who sinned at the cost of their lives. Hammer the censers into sheets to overlay the altar, for they were presented before the LORD and have become holy. Let them be a sign to the Israelites."

39So Eleazar the priest collected the bronze censers brought by those who had been burned to death, and he had them hammered out to overlay the altar, 40as the LORD directed him through Moses. This was to remind the Israelites that no one except a descendant of Aaron should come to burn incense before the LORD, or he would become like Korah and his followers.

41The next day the whole Israelite community grumbled against Moses and Aaron. "You have killed the LORD's people," they said.

42But when the assembly gathered in opposition to Moses and Aaron and turned toward the tent of meeting, suddenly the cloud covered it and the glory of the LORD appeared. 43Then Moses and Aaron went to the front of the tent of meeting, 44and the LORD said to Moses, 45"Get away from this assembly so I can put an end to them at once." And they fell facedown.

46Then Moses said to Aaron, "Take your censer and put incense in it, along with burning coals from the altar, and hurry to the assembly to make atonement for them. Wrath has come out from the LORD; the plague has started." 47So Aaron did as Moses said, and ran into the midst of the assembly. The plague had already started among the people, but Aaron offered the incense and made atonement for them. 48He stood between the living and the dead, and the plague stopped. 49But 14,700 people died from the plague, in addition to those who had died because of Korah. 50Then Aaron returned to Moses at the entrance to the tent of meeting, for the plague had stopped.[a]

The Budding of Aaron's Staff

17[b] The LORD said to Moses, 2"Speak to the Israelites and get twelve staffs from them, one from the leader of each of their ancestral tribes. Write the name of each man on his staff. 3On the staff of Levi write Aaron's name, for there

---

[a] 50 In Hebrew texts 16:36-50 is numbered 17:1-15.
[b] In Hebrew texts 17:1-13 is numbered 17:16-28.

must be one staff for the head of each ancestral tribe. ⁴Place them in the tent of meeting in front of the ark of the covenant law, where I meet with you. ⁵The staff belonging to the man I choose will sprout, and I will rid myself of this constant grumbling against you by the Israelites."

⁶So Moses spoke to the Israelites, and their leaders gave him twelve staffs, one for the leader of each of their ancestral tribes, and Aaron's staff was among them. ⁷Moses placed the staffs before the LORD in the tent of the covenant law.

⁸The next day Moses entered the tent and saw that Aaron's staff, which represented the tribe of Levi, had not only sprouted but had budded, blossomed and produced almonds. ⁹Then Moses brought out all the staffs from the LORD's presence to all the Israelites. They looked at them, and each of the leaders took his own staff.

¹⁰The LORD said to Moses, "Put back Aaron's staff in front of the ark of the covenant law, to be kept as a sign to the rebellious. This will put an end to their grumbling against me, so that they will not die." ¹¹Moses did just as the LORD commanded him.

¹²The Israelites said to Moses, "We will die! We are lost, we are all lost! ¹³Anyone who even comes near the tabernacle of the LORD will die. Are we all going to die?"

Duties of Priests and Levites

18 The LORD said to Aaron, "You, your sons and your family are to bear the responsibility for offenses connected with the sanctuary, and you and your sons alone are to bear the responsibility for offenses connected with the priesthood. ²Bring your fellow Levites from your ancestral tribe to join you and assist you when you and your sons minister before the tent of the covenant law. ³They are to be responsible to you and are to perform all the duties of the tent, but they must not go near the furnishings of the sanctuary or the altar. Otherwise both they and you will die. ⁴They are to join you and be responsible for the care of the tent of meeting—all the work at the tent—and no one else may come near where you are.

⁵"You are to be responsible for the care of the sanctuary and the altar, so that my wrath will not fall on the Israelites again. ⁶I myself have selected your fellow Levites from among the Israelites as a gift to you, dedicated to the LORD to do the work at the tent of meeting. ⁷But only you and your sons may serve as priests in connection with everything at the altar and inside the curtain. I am giving you the service of the priesthood as a gift. Anyone else who comes near the sanctuary is to be put to death."

Offerings for Priests and Levites

⁸Then the LORD said to Aaron, "I myself have put you in charge of the offerings presented to me; all the holy offerings the Israelites give me I give to you and your sons as your portion, your perpetual share. ⁹You are to have the part of the most holy offerings that is kept from the fire. From all the gifts they bring me as most holy offerings, whether grain or sin*a* or guilt offerings, that part belongs to you and your sons. ¹⁰Eat it as something most holy; every male shall eat it. You must regard it as holy.

¹¹"This also is yours: whatever is set aside from the gifts of all the wave offerings of the Israelites. I give this to you and your sons and daughters as your perpetual share. Everyone in your household who is ceremonially clean may eat it.

¹²"I give you all the finest olive oil and all the finest new wine and grain they give the LORD as the firstfruits of their harvest. ¹³All the land's firstfruits that they bring to the LORD will be yours. Everyone in your household who is ceremonially clean may eat it.

¹⁴"Everything in Israel that is devoted*b* to the LORD is yours. ¹⁵The first offspring of every womb, both human and animal, that is offered to the LORD is yours. But you must redeem every firstborn son and every firstborn male of unclean animals. ¹⁶When they are a month old, you must redeem

---

a 9 Or *purification*   *b* 14 The Hebrew term refers to the irrevocable giving over of things or persons to the LORD.

them at the redemption price set at five shekels[a] of silver, according to the sanctuary shekel, which weighs twenty gerahs.

[17] "But you must not redeem the firstborn of a cow, a sheep or a goat; they are holy. Splash their blood against the altar and burn their fat as a food offering, an aroma pleasing to the LORD. [18]Their meat is to be yours, just as the breast of the wave offering and the right thigh are yours. [19]Whatever is set aside from the holy offerings the Israelites present to the LORD I give to you and your sons and daughters as your perpetual share. It is an everlasting covenant of salt before the LORD for both you and your offspring."

[20]The LORD said to Aaron, "You will have no inheritance in their land, nor will you have any share among them; I am your share and your inheritance among the Israelites.

[21] "I give to the Levites all the tithes in Israel as their inheritance in return for the work they do while serving at the tent of meeting. [22]From now on the Israelites must not go near the tent of meeting, or they will bear the consequences of their sin and will die. [23]It is the Levites who are to do the work at the tent of meeting and bear the responsibility for any offenses they commit against it. This is a lasting ordinance for the generations to come. They will receive no inheritance among the Israelites. [24]Instead, I give to the Levites as their inheritance the tithes that the Israelites present as an offering to the LORD. That is why I said concerning them: 'They will have no inheritance among the Israelites.' "

[25]The LORD said to Moses, [26] "Speak to the Levites and say to them: 'When you receive from the Israelites the tithe I give you as your inheritance, you must present a tenth of that tithe as the LORD's offering. [27]Your offering will be reckoned to you as grain from the threshing floor or juice from the winepress. [28]In this way you also will present an offering to the LORD from all the tithes you receive from the Israelites. From these tithes you must give the LORD's portion to Aaron the priest. [29]You must present as the LORD's portion the best and holiest part of everything given to you.'

[30] "Say to the Levites: 'When you present the best part, it will be reckoned to you as the product of the threshing floor or the winepress. [31]You and your households may eat the rest of it anywhere, for it is your wages for your work at the tent of meeting. [32]By presenting the best part of it you will not be guilty in this matter; then you will not defile the holy offerings of the Israelites, and you will not die.' "

The Water of Cleansing

19 The LORD said to Moses and Aaron: [2] "This is a requirement of the law that the LORD has commanded: Tell the Israelites to bring you a red heifer without defect or blemish and that has never been under a yoke. [3]Give it to Eleazar the priest; it is to be taken outside the camp and slaughtered in his presence. [4]Then Eleazar the priest is to take some of its blood on his finger and sprinkle it seven times toward the front of the tent of meeting. [5]While he watches, the heifer is to be

---

[a] 16 That is, about 2 ounces or about 58 grams

BREAKTHROUGH!

Tent of meeting
(NUMBERS 19:4)
This is another way to say "sanctuary." It was a portable tent, where God met with the Israelites.

burned—its hide, flesh, blood and intestines. ⁶The priest is to take some cedar wood, hyssop and scarlet wool and throw them onto the burning heifer. ⁷After that, the priest must wash his clothes and bathe himself with water. He may then come into the camp, but he will be ceremonially unclean till evening. ⁸The man who burns it must also wash his clothes and bathe with water, and he too will be unclean till evening.

⁹"A man who is clean shall gather up the ashes of the heifer and put them in a ceremonially clean place outside the camp. They are to be kept by the Israelite community for use in the water of cleansing; it is for purification from sin. ¹⁰The man who gathers up the ashes of the heifer must also wash his clothes, and he too will be unclean till evening. This will be a lasting ordinance both for the Israelites and for the foreigners residing among them.

¹¹"Whoever touches a human corpse will be unclean for seven days. ¹²They must purify themselves with the water on the third day and on the seventh day; then they will be clean. But if they do not purify themselves on the third and seventh days, they will not be clean. ¹³If they fail to purify themselves after touching a human corpse, they defile the Lord's tabernacle. They must be cut off from Israel. Because the water of cleansing has not been sprinkled on them, they are unclean; their uncleanness remains on them.

¹⁴"This is the law that applies when a person dies in a tent: Anyone who enters the tent and anyone who is in it will be unclean for seven days, ¹⁵and every open container without a lid fastened on it will be unclean.

¹⁶"Anyone out in the open who touches someone who has been killed with a sword or someone who has died a natural death, or anyone who touches a human bone or a grave, will be unclean for seven days.

¹⁷"For the unclean person, put some ashes from the burned purification offering into a jar and pour fresh water over them. ¹⁸Then a man who is ceremonially clean is to take some hyssop, dip it in the water and sprinkle the tent and all the furnishings and the people who were there. He must also sprinkle anyone who has touched a human bone or a grave or anyone who has been killed or anyone who has died a natural death. ¹⁹The man who is clean is to sprinkle those who are unclean on the third and seventh days, and on the seventh day he is to purify them. Those who are being cleansed must wash their clothes and bathe with water, and that evening they will be clean. ²⁰But if those who are unclean do not purify themselves, they must be cut off from the community, because they have defiled the sanctuary of the Lord. The water of cleansing has not been sprinkled on them, and they are unclean. ²¹This is a lasting ordinance for them.

"The man who sprinkles the water of cleansing must also wash his clothes, and anyone who touches the water of cleansing will be unclean till evening. ²²Anything that an unclean person touches becomes unclean, and anyone who touches it becomes unclean till evening."

Water From the Rock

20 In the first month the whole Israelite community arrived at the Desert of Zin, and they stayed at Kadesh. There Miriam died and was buried.

²Now there was no water for the community, and the people gathered in opposition to Moses and Aaron. ³They quarreled with Moses and said, "If only we had died when our brothers fell dead before the Lord! ⁴Why did you bring the Lord's community into this wilderness, that we and our livestock should die here? ⁵Why did you bring us up out of Egypt to this terrible place? It has no grain or figs, grapevines or pomegranates. And there is no water to drink!"

⁶Moses and Aaron went from the assembly to the entrance to the tent of meeting and fell facedown, and the glory of the Lord appeared to them. ⁷The Lord said to Moses, ⁸"Take the staff, and you and your brother Aaron gather the assembly together. Speak to that rock before their eyes and it will pour out its water. You will bring water out of the rock for the

community so they and their livestock can drink."

⁹So Moses took the staff from the Lord's presence, just as he commanded him. ¹⁰He and Aaron gathered the assembly together in front of the rock and Moses said to them, "Listen, you rebels, must we bring you water out of this rock?" ¹¹Then Moses raised his arm and struck the rock twice with his staff. Water gushed out, and the community and their livestock drank.

¹²But the Lord said to Moses and Aaron, "Because you did not trust in me enough to honor me as holy in the sight of the Israelites, you will not bring this community into the land I give them."

¹³These were the waters of Meribah,ᵃ where the Israelites quarreled with the Lord and where he was proved holy among them.

Edom Denies Israel Passage

¹⁴Moses sent messengers from Kadesh to the king of Edom, saying:

"This is what your brother Israel says: You know about all the hardships that have come on us. ¹⁵Our ancestors went down into Egypt, and we lived there many years. The Egyptians mistreated us and our ancestors, ¹⁶but when we cried out to the Lord, he heard our cry and sent an angel and brought us out of Egypt.

"Now we are here at Kadesh, a town on the edge of your territory. ¹⁷Please let us pass through your country. We will not go through any field or vineyard, or drink water from any well. We will travel along the King's Highway and not turn to the right or to the left until we have passed through your territory."

¹⁸But Edom answered:

"You may not pass through here; if you try, we will march out and attack you with the sword."

¹⁹The Israelites replied:

"We will go along the main road, and if we or our livestock drink any of your water, we will pay for it. We only want to pass through on foot—nothing else."

²⁰Again they answered:

"You may not pass through."

Then Edom came out against them with a large and powerful army. ²¹Since Edom refused to let them go through their territory, Israel turned away from them.

The Death of Aaron

²²The whole Israelite community set out from Kadesh and came to Mount Hor. ²³At Mount Hor, near the border of Edom, the Lord said to Moses and Aaron, ²⁴"Aaron will be gathered to his people. He will not enter the land I give the Israelites, because both of you rebelled against my command at the waters of Meribah. ²⁵Get Aaron and his son Eleazar and take them up Mount Hor. ²⁶Remove Aaron's garments and put them on his son Eleazar, for Aaron will be gathered to his people; he will die there."

²⁷Moses did as the Lord commanded: They went up Mount Hor in the sight of the whole community. ²⁸Moses removed Aaron's garments and put them on his son Eleazar. And Aaron died there on top of the mountain. Then Moses and Eleazar came down from the mountain, ²⁹and when the whole community learned that Aaron had died, all the Israelites mourned for him thirty days.

Arad Destroyed

21 When the Canaanite king of Arad, who lived in the Negev, heard that Israel was coming along the road to Atharim, he attacked the Israelites and captured some of them. ²Then Israel made this vow to the Lord: "If you will deliver these people into our hands, we will totally destroyᵇ their cities." ³The Lord listened to Israel's plea and gave the Canaanites over to them. They completely destroyed them and their towns; so the place was named Hormah.ᶜ

ᵃ 13 Meribah means quarreling.   ᵇ 2 The Hebrew term refers to the irrevocable giving over of things or persons to the Lord, often by totally destroying them; also in verse 3. ᶜ 3 Hormah means destruction.

The Bronze Snake

[4]They traveled from Mount Hor along the route to the Red Sea,[a] to go around Edom. But the people grew impatient on the way; [5]they spoke against God and against Moses, and said, "Why have you brought us up out of Egypt to die in the wilderness? There is no bread! There is no water! And we detest this miserable food!"

[6]Then the LORD sent venomous snakes among them; they bit the people and many Israelites died. [7]The people came to Moses and said, "We sinned when we spoke against the LORD and against you. Pray that the LORD will take the snakes away from us." So Moses prayed for the people.

[8]The LORD said to Moses, "Make a snake and put it up on a pole; anyone who is bitten can look at it and live." [9]So Moses made a bronze snake and put it up on a pole. Then when anyone was bitten by a snake and looked at the bronze snake, they lived.

The Journey to Moab

[10]The Israelites moved on and camped at Oboth. [11]Then they set out from Oboth and camped in Iye Abarim, in the wilderness that faces Moab toward the sunrise. [12]From there they moved on and camped in the Zered Valley. [13]They set out from there and camped alongside the Arnon, which is in the wilderness extending into Amorite territory. The Arnon is the border of Moab, between Moab and the Amorites. [14]That is why the Book of the Wars of the LORD says:

> ". . . Zahab[b] in Suphah and the
> ravines,
> the Arnon [15]and[c] the slopes of the
> ravines
> that lead to the settlement of Ar
> and lie along the border of
> Moab."

[16]From there they continued on to Beer, the well where the LORD said to Moses, "Gather the people together and I will give them water."

[17]Then Israel sang this song:

BREAKTHROUGH!

The Book of the Wars of the LORD

(NUMBERS 21:14)

This must have been a collection of songs about war, but this book no longer exists. It probably listed the wars Israel had with neighboring nations.

> "Spring up, O well!
> Sing about it,
> [18]about the well that the princes dug,
> that the nobles of the people sank—
> the nobles with scepters and staffs."

Then they went from the wilderness to Mattanah, [19]from Mattanah to Nahaliel, from Nahaliel to Bamoth, [20]and from Bamoth to the valley in Moab where the top of Pisgah overlooks the wasteland.

Defeat of Sihon and Og

[21]Israel sent messengers to say to Sihon king of the Amorites:

[22]"Let us pass through your country. We will not turn aside into any field or vineyard, or drink water from any well. We will travel along the King's Highway until we have passed through your territory."

---

[a] 4 Or the Sea of Reeds   [b] 14 Septuagint; Hebrew Waheb   [c] 14,15 Or "I have been given from Suphah and the ravines / of the Arnon [15]to

²³But Sihon would not let Israel pass through his territory. He mustered his entire army and marched out into the wilderness against Israel. When he reached Jahaz, he fought with Israel. ²⁴Israel, however, put him to the sword and took over his land from the Arnon to the Jabbok, but only as far as the Ammonites, because their border was fortified. ²⁵Israel captured all the cities of the Amorites and occupied them, including Heshbon and all its surrounding settlements. ²⁶Heshbon was the city of Sihon king of the Amorites, who had fought against the former king of Moab and had taken from him all his land as far as the Arnon.

²⁷That is why the poets say:

"Come to Heshbon and let it be rebuilt;
    let Sihon's city be restored.

²⁸ "Fire went out from Heshbon,
    a blaze from the city of Sihon.
It consumed Ar of Moab,
    the citizens of Arnon's heights.
²⁹Woe to you, Moab!
    You are destroyed, people of
        Chemosh!
He has given up his sons as fugitives
    and his daughters as captives
    to Sihon king of the Amorites.

³⁰ "But we have overthrown them;
    Heshbon's dominion has been
        destroyed all the way to Dibon.
We have demolished them as far as
        Nophah,
    which extends to Medeba."

³¹So Israel settled in the land of the Amorites.

³²After Moses had sent spies to Jazer, the Israelites captured its surrounding settlements and drove out the Amorites who were there. ³³Then they turned and went up along the road toward Bashan, and Og king of Bashan and his whole army marched out to meet them in battle at Edrei. ³⁴The Lᴏʀᴅ said to Moses, "Do not be afraid of him, for I have delivered him into your hands, along with his whole army and his land. Do to him what you did to Sihon king of the Amorites, who reigned in Heshbon." ³⁵So they struck him down, together

THE
WITNESSES

✓ OG (NUMBERS 21:33)
He was an Amorite and he was the king of Bashan. The Israelites beat him before they crossed the Jordan River. It seems he was the last of the giants (see Deuteronomy 3:11).

✓ BALAK AND BALAAM (NUMBERS 22:1)
Balak was the Moabite king. He wanted to put a curse on the Israelites so he wouldn't have to go to war against them. But God blessed the Israelites and Balak couldn't hurt them. Balaam was the prophet Balak looked for in order to get him to put the curse on the Israelites. Balaam wasn't an Israelite and he worshiped other gods. In the old times in the East, people thought that when one of these prophets put a curse or a blessing on someone, it would happen. However, thanks to Balaam's donkey, Balaam realized that it was God who was talking to him and telling him not to curse Israel.

with his sons and his whole army, leaving them no survivors. And they took possession of his land.

Balak Summons Balaam

22 Then the Israelites traveled to the plains of Moab and camped along the Jordan across from Jericho.

²Now Balak son of Zippor saw all that Israel had done to the Amorites, ³and Moab was terrified because there were so many people. Indeed, Moab was filled with dread because of the Israelites.

⁴The Moabites said to the elders of Midian, "This horde is going to lick up everything around us, as an ox licks up the grass of the field."

So Balak son of Zippor, who was king of Moab at that time, ⁵sent messengers to summon Balaam son of Beor, who was at Pethor, near the Euphrates River, in his native land. Balak said:

> "A people has come out of Egypt; they cover the face of the land and have settled next to me. ⁶Now come and put a curse on these people, because they are too powerful for me. Perhaps then I will be able to defeat them and drive them out of the land. For I know that whoever you bless is blessed, and whoever you curse is cursed."

⁷The elders of Moab and Midian left, taking with them the fee for divination. When they came to Balaam, they told him what Balak had said.

⁸"Spend the night here," Balaam said to them, "and I will report back to you with the answer the Lord gives me." So the Moabite officials stayed with him.

⁹God came to Balaam and asked, "Who are these men with you?"

¹⁰Balaam said to God, "Balak son of Zippor, king of Moab, sent me this message: ¹¹'A people that has come out of Egypt covers the face of the land. Now come and put a curse on them for me. Perhaps then I will be able to fight them and drive them away.' "

¹²But God said to Balaam, "Do not go with them. You must not put a curse on those people, because they are blessed."

THE SCENE

MOAB

(NUMBERS 22:1)

This was a strip of land east of the Dead Sea. It was good for growing crops.

¹³The next morning Balaam got up and said to Balak's officials, "Go back to your own country, for the Lord has refused to let me go with you."

¹⁴So the Moabite officials returned to Balak and said, "Balaam refused to come with us."

¹⁵Then Balak sent other officials, more numerous and more distinguished than the first. ¹⁶They came to Balaam and said:

> "This is what Balak son of Zippor says: Do not let anything keep you from coming to me, ¹⁷because I will reward you handsomely and do whatever you say. Come and put a curse on these people for me."

¹⁸But Balaam answered them, "Even if Balak gave me all the silver and gold in his palace, I could not do anything great or small to go beyond the command of the Lord my God. ¹⁹Now spend the night here so that I can find out what else the Lord will tell me."

20That night God came to Balaam and said, "Since these men have come to summon you, go with them, but do only what I tell you."

Balaam's Donkey

21Balaam got up in the morning, saddled his donkey and went with the Moabite officials. 22But God was very angry when he went, and the angel of the LORD stood in the road to oppose him. Balaam was riding on his donkey, and his two servants were with him. 23When the donkey saw the angel of the LORD standing in the road with a drawn sword in his hand, it turned off the road into a field. Balaam beat it to get it back on the road.

24Then the angel of the LORD stood in a narrow path through the vineyards, with walls on both sides. 25When the donkey saw the angel of the LORD, it pressed close to the wall, crushing Balaam's foot against it. So he beat the donkey again.

26Then the angel of the LORD moved on ahead and stood in a narrow place where there was no room to turn, either to the right or to the left. 27When the donkey saw the angel of the LORD, it lay down under Balaam, and he was angry and beat it with his staff. 28Then the LORD opened the donkey's mouth, and it said to Balaam, "What have I done to you to make you beat me these three times?"

29Balaam answered the donkey, "You have made a fool of me! If only I had a sword in my hand, I would kill you right now."

30The donkey said to Balaam, "Am I not your own donkey, which you have always ridden, to this day? Have I been in the habit of doing this to you?"

"No," he said.

31Then the LORD opened Balaam's eyes, and he saw the angel of the LORD standing in the road with his sword drawn. So he bowed low and fell facedown.

32The angel of the LORD asked him, "Why have you beaten your donkey these three times? I have come here to oppose you because your path is a reckless one before me.[a] 33The donkey saw me and turned away from me these three times.

If it had not turned away, I would certainly have killed you by now, but I would have spared it."

34Balaam said to the angel of the LORD, "I have sinned. I did not realize you were standing in the road to oppose me. Now if you are displeased, I will go back."

35The angel of the LORD said to Balaam, "Go with the men, but speak only what I tell you." So Balaam went with Balak's officials.

36When Balak heard that Balaam was coming, he went out to meet him at the Moabite town on the Arnon border, at the edge of his territory. 37Balak said to Balaam, "Did I not send you an urgent summons? Why didn't you come to me? Am I really not able to reward you?"

38"Well, I have come to you now," Balaam replied. "But I can't say whatever I please. I must speak only what God puts in my mouth."

39Then Balaam went with Balak to Kiriath Huzoth. 40Balak sacrificed cattle and sheep, and gave some to Balaam and the officials who were with him. 41The next morning Balak took Balaam up to Bamoth Baal, and from there he could see the outskirts of the Israelite camp.

Balaam's First Message

23 Balaam said, "Build me seven altars here, and prepare seven bulls and seven rams for me." 2Balak did as Balaam said, and the two of them offered a bull and a ram on each altar.

3Then Balaam said to Balak, "Stay here beside your offering while I go aside. Perhaps the LORD will come to meet with me. Whatever he reveals to me I will tell you." Then he went off to a barren height.

4God met with him, and Balaam said, "I have prepared seven altars, and on each altar I have offered a bull and a ram."

5The LORD put a word in Balaam's mouth and said, "Go back to Balak and give him this word."

6So he went back to him and found him standing beside his offering, with all the Moabite officials. 7Then Balaam spoke his message:

---

a 32 The meaning of the Hebrew for this clause is uncertain.

"Balak brought me from Aram,
   the king of Moab from the eastern
      mountains.
'Come,' he said, 'curse Jacob for me;
   come, denounce Israel.'
⁸How can I curse
   those whom God has not cursed?
How can I denounce
   those whom the Lᴏʀᴅ has not
      denounced?
⁹From the rocky peaks I see them,
   from the heights I view them.
I see a people who live apart
   and do not consider themselves
      one of the nations.
¹⁰Who can count the dust of Jacob
   or number even a fourth of Israel?
Let me die the death of the righteous,
   and may my final end be like
      theirs!"

¹¹Balak said to Balaam, "What have you done to me? I brought you to curse my enemies, but you have done nothing but bless them!"

¹²He answered, "Must I not speak what the Lᴏʀᴅ puts in my mouth?"

Balaam's Second Message

¹³Then Balak said to him, "Come with me to another place where you can see them; you will not see them all but only the outskirts of their camp. And from there, curse them for me." ¹⁴So he took him to the field of Zophim on the top of Pisgah, and there he built seven altars and offered a bull and a ram on each altar.

¹⁵Balaam said to Balak, "Stay here beside your offering while I meet with him over there."

¹⁶The Lᴏʀᴅ met with Balaam and put a word in his mouth and said, "Go back to Balak and give him this word."

¹⁷So he went to him and found him standing beside his offering, with the Moabite officials. Balak asked him, "What did the Lᴏʀᴅ say?"

¹⁸Then he spoke his message:

"Arise, Balak, and listen;
   hear me, son of Zippor.
¹⁹God is not human, that he should lie,
   not a human being, that he should
      change his mind.

THE SCENE

MOUNT PISGAH

(NUMBERS 23:14)

This probably means "the divided." It's a mountain across from Jericho. God let Moses see the promised land from this mountain.

Does he speak and then not act?
   Does he promise and not fulfill?
²⁰I have received a command to
      bless;
   he has blessed, and I cannot
      change it.

²¹"No misfortune is seen in Jacob,
   no misery observedᵃ in Israel.
The Lᴏʀᴅ their God is with them;
   the shout of the King is among
      them.
²²God brought them out of Egypt;
   they have the strength of a wild ox.
²³There is no divination againstᵇ Jacob,
   no evil omens againstᵇ Israel.
It will now be said of Jacob
   and of Israel, 'See what God has
      done!'
²⁴The people rise like a lioness;
   they rouse themselves like a lion

ᵃ 21 Or He has not looked on Jacob's offenses / or on the wrongs found   ᵇ 23 Or in

that does not rest till it devours its
　　prey
and drinks the blood of its victims."

²⁵Then Balak said to Balaam, "Neither
curse them at all nor bless them at all!"
²⁶Balaam answered, "Did I not tell you I
must do whatever the LORD says?"

Balaam's Third Message

²⁷Then Balak said to Balaam, "Come,
let me take you to another place. Perhaps
it will please God to let you curse them
for me from there." ²⁸And Balak took Balaam to the top of Peor, overlooking the
wasteland.

²⁹Balaam said, "Build me seven altars
here, and prepare seven bulls and sev-
en rams for me." ³⁰Balak did as Balaam
had said, and offered a bull and a ram on
each altar.

24 Now when Balaam saw that it
pleased the LORD to bless Israel,
he did not resort to divination as at other
times, but turned his face toward the wilderness. ²When Balaam looked out and
saw Israel encamped tribe by tribe, the
Spirit of God came on him ³and he spoke
his message:

"The prophecy of Balaam son of Beor,
　　the prophecy of one whose eye
　　　sees clearly,
⁴the prophecy of one who hears the
　　words of God,
who sees a vision from the
　　Almighty,ᵃ
who falls prostrate, and whose eyes
　　are opened:

⁵ "How beautiful are your tents, Jacob,
　　your dwelling places, Israel!

⁶ "Like valleys they spread out,
　　like gardens beside a river,
like aloes planted by the LORD,
　　like cedars beside the waters.
⁷Water will flow from their buckets;
　　their seed will have abundant water.

"Their king will be greater than Agag;
　　their kingdom will be exalted.

⁸ "God brought them out of Egypt;
　　they have the strength of a wild ox.

They devour hostile nations
　　and break their bones in pieces;
　　with their arrows they pierce them.
⁹ Like a lion they crouch and lie down,
　　like a lioness—who dares to rouse
　　　them?

"May those who bless you be blessed
　　and those who curse you be
　　　cursed!"

¹⁰Then Balak's anger burned against
Balaam. He struck his hands together
and said to him, "I summoned you to
curse my enemies, but you have blessed
them these three times. ¹¹Now leave at
once and go home! I said I would reward
you handsomely, but the LORD has kept
you from being rewarded."

¹²Balaam answered Balak, "Did I not
tell the messengers you sent me, ¹³'Even
if Balak gave me all the silver and gold in
his palace, I could not do anything of my
own accord, good or bad, to go beyond
the command of the LORD—and I must
say only what the LORD says'? ¹⁴Now I am
going back to my people, but come, let
me warn you of what this people will do
to your people in days to come."

Balaam's Fourth Message

¹⁵Then he spoke his message:

"The prophecy of Balaam son of Beor,
　　the prophecy of one whose eye
　　　sees clearly,
¹⁶the prophecy of one who hears the
　　words of God,
who has knowledge from the Most
　　High,
who sees a vision from the Almighty,
who falls prostrate, and whose eyes
　　are opened:

¹⁷ "I see him, but not now;
　　I behold him, but not near.
A star will come out of Jacob;
　　a scepter will rise out of Israel.
He will crush the foreheads of Moab,
　　the skullsᵇ ofᶜ all the people of
　　　Sheth.ᵈ

ᵃ 4 Hebrew *Shaddai*; also in verse 16　　ᵇ 17 Samaritan
Pentateuch (see also Jer. 48:45); the meaning of the word
in the Masoretic Text is uncertain.　　ᶜ 17 Or possibly
Moab, / batter　　ᵈ 17 Or *all the noisy boasters*

18 Edom will be conquered;
　Seir, his enemy, will be conquered,
　but Israel will grow strong.
19 A ruler will come out of Jacob
　and destroy the survivors of the
　　city."

Balaam's Fifth Message

20 Then Balaam saw Amalek and spoke his message:

"Amalek was first among the nations,
　but their end will be utter
　　destruction."

Balaam's Sixth Message

21 Then he saw the Kenites and spoke his message:

"Your dwelling place is secure,
　your nest is set in a rock;
22 yet you Kenites will be destroyed
　when Ashur takes you captive."

Balaam's Seventh Message

23 Then he spoke his message:

"Alas! Who can live when God does
　this?[a]
24　Ships will come from the shores of
　　Cyprus;
　they will subdue Ashur and Eber,
　but they too will come to ruin."

25 Then Balaam got up and returned home, and Balak went his own way.

Moab Seduces Israel

25 While Israel was staying in Shittim, the men began to indulge in sexual immorality with Moabite women, 2 who invited them to the sacrifices to their gods. The people ate the sacrificial meal and bowed down before these gods. 3 So Israel yoked themselves to the Baal of Peor. And the LORD's anger burned against them.

4 The LORD said to Moses, "Take all the leaders of these people, kill them and expose them in broad daylight before the LORD, so that the LORD's fierce anger may turn away from Israel."

5 So Moses said to Israel's judges, "Each of you must put to death those of

THE
WITNESSES

✓ **BAAL OF PEOR** (NUMBERS 25:3)
This was a god the Moabites worshiped. The Israelites worshiped him too. What a pity! It all happened because the men married Moabite women, and those women had that god. But the true God was angry and ordered that everyone who had worshiped Baal be killed.

your people who have yoked themselves to the Baal of Peor."

6 Then an Israelite man brought into the camp a Midianite woman right before the eyes of Moses and the whole assembly of Israel while they were weeping at the entrance to the tent of meeting. 7 When Phinehas son of Eleazar, the son of Aaron, the priest, saw this, he left the assembly, took a spear in his hand 8 and followed the Israelite into the tent. He drove the

---

[a] 23 Masoretic Text; with a different word division of the Hebrew *The people from the islands will gather from the north.*

spear into both of them, right through the Israelite man and into the woman's stomach. Then the plague against the Israelites was stopped; [9]but those who died in the plague numbered 24,000.

[10]The LORD said to Moses, [11]"Phinehas son of Eleazar, the son of Aaron, the priest, has turned my anger away from the Israelites. Since he was as zealous for my honor among them as I am, I did not put an end to them in my zeal. [12]Therefore tell him I am making my covenant of peace with him. [13]He and his descendants will have a covenant of a lasting priesthood, because he was zealous for the honor of his God and made atonement for the Israelites."

[14]The name of the Israelite who was killed with the Midianite woman was Zimri son of Salu, the leader of a Simeonite family. [15]And the name of the Midianite woman who was put to death was Kozbi daughter of Zur, a tribal chief of a Midianite family.

[16]The LORD said to Moses, [17]"Treat the Midianites as enemies and kill them. [18]They treated you as enemies when they deceived you in the Peor incident involving their sister Kozbi, the daughter of a Midianite leader, the woman who was killed when the plague came as a result of that incident."

The Second Census

26 After the plague the LORD said to Moses and Eleazar son of Aaron, the priest, [2]"Take a census of the whole Israelite community by families—all those twenty years old or more who are able to serve in the army of Israel." [3]So on the plains of Moab by the Jordan across from Jericho, Moses and Eleazar the priest spoke with them and said, [4]"Take a census of the men twenty years old or more, as the LORD commanded Moses."

These were the Israelites who came out of Egypt:

[5]The descendants of Reuben, the firstborn son of Israel, were:

through Hanok, the Hanokite clan;
through Pallu, the Palluite clan;

[6]through Hezron, the Hezronite clan;
through Karmi, the Karmite clan.

[7]These were the clans of Reuben; those numbered were 43,730.

[8]The son of Pallu was Eliab, [9]and the sons of Eliab were Nemuel, Dathan and Abiram. The same Dathan and Abiram were the community officials who rebelled against Moses and Aaron and were among Korah's followers when they rebelled against the LORD. [10]The earth opened its mouth and swallowed them along with Korah, whose followers died when the fire devoured the 250 men. And they served as a warning sign. [11]The line of Korah, however, did not die out.

[12]The descendants of Simeon by their clans were:

through Nemuel, the Nemuelite clan;
through Jamin, the Jaminite clan;
through Jakin, the Jakinite clan;
[13]through Zerah, the Zerahite clan;
through Shaul, the Shaulite clan.

[14]These were the clans of Simeon; those numbered were 22,200.

[15]The descendants of Gad by their clans were:

through Zephon, the Zephonite clan;
through Haggi, the Haggite clan;
through Shuni, the Shunite clan;
[16]through Ozni, the Oznite clan;
through Eri, the Erite clan;
[17]through Arodi,[a] the Arodite clan;
through Areli, the Arelite clan.

[18]These were the clans of Gad; those numbered were 40,500.

[19]Er and Onan were sons of Judah, but they died in Canaan. [20]The descendants of Judah by their clans were:

through Shelah, the Shelanite clan;
through Perez, the Perezite clan;
through Zerah, the Zerahite clan.

[21]The descendants of Perez were:

through Hezron, the Hezronite clan;
through Hamul, the Hamulite clan.

[22]These were the clans of Judah; those numbered were 76,500.

---

[a] 17 Samaritan Pentateuch and Syriac (see also Gen. 46:16); Masoretic Text Arod

²³The descendants of Issachar by their clans were:

through Tola, the Tolaite clan;
through Puah, the Puite[a] clan;
²⁴through Jashub, the Jashubite clan;
through Shimron, the Shimronite clan.

²⁵These were the clans of Issachar; those numbered were 64,300.

²⁶The descendants of Zebulun by their clans were:

through Sered, the Seredite clan;
through Elon, the Elonite clan;
through Jahleel, the Jahleelite clan.

²⁷These were the clans of Zebulun; those numbered were 60,500.

²⁸The descendants of Joseph by their clans through Manasseh and Ephraim were:

²⁹The descendants of Manasseh:

through Makir, the Makirite clan (Makir was the father of Gilead);
through Gilead, the Gileadite clan.

³⁰These were the descendants of Gilead:

through Iezer, the Iezerite clan;
through Helek, the Helekite clan;
³¹through Asriel, the Asrielite clan;
through Shechem, the Shechemite clan;
³²through Shemida, the Shemidaite clan;
through Hepher, the Hepherite clan.

³³(Zelophehad son of Hepher had no sons; he had only daughters, whose names were Mahlah, Noah, Hoglah, Milkah and Tirzah.)

³⁴These were the clans of Manasseh; those numbered were 52,700.

³⁵These were the descendants of Ephraim by their clans:

through Shuthelah, the Shuthelahite clan;
through Beker, the Bekerite clan;
through Tahan, the Tahanite clan.

³⁶These were the descendants of Shuthelah:

through Eran, the Eranite clan.

³⁷These were the clans of Ephraim; those numbered were 32,500.

These were the descendants of Joseph by their clans.

³⁸The descendants of Benjamin by their clans were:

through Bela, the Belaite clan;
through Ashbel, the Ashbelite clan;
through Ahiram, the Ahiramite clan;
³⁹through Shupham,[b] the Shuphamite clan;
through Hupham, the Huphamite clan.

⁴⁰The descendants of Bela through Ard and Naaman were:

through Ard,[c] the Ardite clan;
through Naaman, the Naamite clan.

⁴¹These were the clans of Benjamin; those numbered were 45,600.

⁴²These were the descendants of Dan by their clans:

through Shuham, the Shuhamite clan.

These were the clans of Dan: ⁴³All of them were Shuhamite clans; and those numbered were 64,400.

⁴⁴The descendants of Asher by their clans were:

through Imnah, the Imnite clan;
through Ishvi, the Ishvite clan;
through Beriah, the Beriite clan;
⁴⁵and through the descendants of Beriah:

through Heber, the Heberite clan;
through Malkiel, the Malkielite clan.

⁴⁶(Asher had a daughter named Serah.)

⁴⁷These were the clans of Asher; those numbered were 53,400.

⁴⁸The descendants of Naphtali by their clans were:

through Jahzeel, the Jahzeelite clan;
through Guni, the Gunite clan;
⁴⁹through Jezer, the Jezerite clan;
through Shillem, the Shillemite clan.

⁵⁰These were the clans of Naphtali; those numbered were 45,400.

[a] 23 Samaritan Pentateuch, Septuagint, Vulgate and Syriac (see also 1 Chron. 7:1); Masoretic Text *through Puvah, the Punite*   [b] 39 A few manuscripts of the Masoretic Text, Samaritan Pentateuch, Vulgate and Syriac (see also Septuagint); most manuscripts of the Masoretic Text *Shephupham*   [c] 40 Samaritan Pentateuch and Vulgate (see also Septuagint); Masoretic Text does not have *through Ard*.

⁵¹The total number of the men of Israel was 601,730.

⁵²The LORD said to Moses, ⁵³"The land is to be allotted to them as an inheritance based on the number of names. ⁵⁴To a larger group give a larger inheritance, and to a smaller group a smaller one; each is to receive its inheritance according to the number of those listed. ⁵⁵Be sure that the land is distributed by lot. What each group inherits will be according to the names for its ancestral tribe. ⁵⁶Each inheritance is to be distributed by lot among the larger and smaller groups."

⁵⁷These were the Levites who were counted by their clans:

through Gershon, the Gershonite clan;
through Kohath, the Kohathite clan;
through Merari, the Merarite clan.
⁵⁸These also were Levite clans:
the Libnite clan,
the Hebronite clan,
the Mahlite clan,
the Mushite clan,
the Korahite clan.

(Kohath was the forefather of Amram; ⁵⁹the name of Amram's wife was Jochebed, a descendant of Levi, who was born to the Levites*a* in Egypt. To Amram she bore Aaron, Moses and their sister Miriam. ⁶⁰Aaron was the father of Nadab and Abihu, Eleazar and Ithamar. ⁶¹But Nadab and Abihu died when they made an offering before the LORD with unauthorized fire.)

⁶²All the male Levites a month old or more numbered 23,000. They were not counted along with the other Israelites because they received no inheritance among them.

⁶³These are the ones counted by Moses and Eleazar the priest when they counted the Israelites on the plains of Moab by the Jordan across from Jericho. ⁶⁴Not one of them was among those counted by Moses and Aaron the priest when they counted the Israelites in the Desert of Sinai. ⁶⁵For the LORD had told those Israelites they would surely die in the wilderness, and not one of them was left except Caleb son of Jephunneh and Joshua son of Nun.

Zelophehad's Daughters

27 The daughters of Zelophehad son of Hepher, the son of Gilead, the son of Makir, the son of Manasseh, belonged to the clans of Manasseh son of Joseph. The names of the daughters were Mahlah, Noah, Hoglah, Milkah and Tirzah. They came forward ²and stood before Moses, Eleazar the priest, the leaders and the whole assembly at the entrance to the tent of meeting and said, ³"Our father died in the wilderness. He was not among Korah's followers, who banded together against the LORD, but he died for his own sin and left no sons. ⁴Why should our father's name disappear from his clan because he had no son? Give us property among our father's relatives."

⁵So Moses brought their case before the LORD, ⁶and the LORD said to him, ⁷"What Zelophehad's daughters are saying is right. You must certainly give them property as an inheritance among their father's relatives and give their father's inheritance to them.

⁸"Say to the Israelites, 'If a man dies and leaves no son, give his inheritance to his daughter. ⁹If he has no daughter, give his inheritance to his brothers. ¹⁰If he has no brothers, give his inheritance to his father's brothers. ¹¹If his father had no brothers, give his inheritance to the nearest relative in his clan, that he may possess it. This is to have the force of law for the Israelites, as the LORD commanded Moses.' "

Joshua to Succeed Moses

¹²Then the LORD said to Moses, "Go up this mountain in the Abarim Range and see the land I have given the Israelites. ¹³After you have seen it, you too will be gathered to your people, as your brother Aaron was, ¹⁴for when the community rebelled at the waters in the Desert of Zin, both of you disobeyed my command to honor me as holy before their eyes." (These were the waters of Meribah Kadesh, in the Desert of Zin.) ¹⁵Moses said to the LORD, ¹⁶"May the

---

a 59 Or Jochebed, a daughter of Levi, who was born to Levi

Lord, the God who gives breath to all living things, appoint someone over this community [17]to go out and come in before them, one who will lead them out and bring them in, so the Lord's people will not be like sheep without a shepherd." [18]So the Lord said to Moses, "Take Joshua son of Nun, a man in whom is the spirit of leadership,[a] and lay your hand on him. [19]Have him stand before Eleazar the priest and the entire assembly and commission him in their presence. [20]Give him some of your authority so the whole Israelite community will obey him. [21]He is to stand before Eleazar the priest, who will obtain decisions for him by inquiring of the Urim before the Lord. At his command he and the entire community of the Israelites will go out, and at his command they will come in." [22]Moses did as the Lord commanded him. He took Joshua and had him stand before Eleazar the priest and the whole assembly. [23]Then he laid his hands on him and commissioned him, as the Lord instructed through Moses.

Daily Offerings

28 The Lord said to Moses, [2]"Give this command to the Israelites and say to them: 'Make sure that you present to me at the appointed time my food offerings, as an aroma pleasing to me.' [3]Say to them: 'This is the food offering you are to present to the Lord: two lambs a year old without defect, as a regular burnt offering each day. [4]Offer one lamb in the morning and the other at twilight, [5]together with a grain offering of a tenth of an ephah[b] of the finest flour mixed with a quarter of a hin[c] of oil from pressed olives. [6]This is the regular burnt offering instituted at Mount Sinai as a pleasing aroma, a food offering presented to the Lord. [7]The accompanying drink offering is to be a quarter of a hin of fermented drink with each lamb. Pour out the drink offering to the Lord at the sanctuary. [8]Offer the second lamb at twilight, along with the same kind of grain offering and drink offering that you offer in the morning. This is a food offering, an aroma pleasing to the Lord.

Sabbath Offerings

[9]" 'On the Sabbath day, make an offering of two lambs a year old without defect, together with its drink offering and a grain offering of two-tenths of an ephah[d] of the finest flour mixed with olive oil. [10]This is the burnt offering for every Sabbath, in addition to the regular burnt offering and its drink offering.

Monthly Offerings

[11]" 'On the first of every month, present to the Lord a burnt offering of two young bulls, one ram and seven male lambs a year old, all without defect. [12]With each bull there is to be a grain offering of three-tenths of an ephah[e] of the finest flour mixed with oil; with the ram, a grain offering of two-tenths of an ephah of the finest flour mixed with oil; [13]and with each lamb, a grain offering of a tenth of an ephah of the finest flour mixed with oil. This is for a burnt offering, a pleasing aroma, a food offering presented to the Lord. [14]With each bull there is to be a drink offering of half a hin[f] of wine; with the ram, a third of a hin[g]; and with each lamb, a quarter of a hin. This is the monthly burnt offering to be made at each new moon during the year. [15]Besides the regular burnt offering with its drink offering, one male goat is to be presented to the Lord as a sin offering.[h]

The Passover

[16]" 'On the fourteenth day of the first month the Lord's Passover is to be held. [17]On the fifteenth day of this month there is to be a festival; for seven days eat bread made without yeast. [18]On the first day hold a sacred assembly and do no regular work. [19]Present to the Lord a food offering consisting of a burnt offering of two young bulls, one ram and seven male lambs a year old, all without

a 18 Or *the Spirit*   *b 5* That is, probably about 3 1/2 pounds or about 1.6 kilograms; also in verses 13, 21 and 29   *c 5* That is, about 1 quart or about 1 liter; also in verses 7 and 14   *d 9* That is, probably about 7 pounds or about 3.2 kilograms; also in verses 12, 20 and 28   *e 12* That is, probably about 11 pounds or about 5 kilograms; also in verses 20 and 28   *f 14* That is, about 2 quarts or about 1.9 liters   *g 14* That is, about 1 1/3 quarts or about 1.3 liters   *h 15* Or *purification offering*; also in verse 22 defect. ²⁰With each bull offer a grain offering of three-tenths of an ephah of the finest flour mixed with oil; with the ram, two-tenths; ²¹and with each of the seven lambs, one-tenth. ²²Include one male goat as a sin offering to make atonement for you. ²³Offer these in addition to the regular morning burnt offering. ²⁴In this way present the food offering every day for seven days as an aroma pleasing to the LORD; it is to be offered in addition to the regular burnt offering and its drink offering. ²⁵On the seventh day hold a sacred assembly and do no regular work.

The Festival of Weeks

²⁶ " 'On the day of firstfruits, when you present to the LORD an offering of new grain during the Festival of Weeks, hold a sacred assembly and do no regular work. ²⁷Present a burnt offering of two young bulls, one ram and seven male lambs a year old as an aroma pleasing to the LORD. ²⁸With each bull there is to be a grain offering of three-tenths of an ephah of the finest flour mixed with oil; with the ram, two-tenths; ²⁹and with each of the seven lambs, one-tenth. ³⁰Include one male goat to make atonement for you. ³¹Offer these together with their drink offerings, in addition to the regular burnt offering and its grain offering. Be sure the animals are without defect.

The Festival of Trumpets

29 " 'On the first day of the seventh month hold a sacred assembly and do no regular work. It is a day for you to sound the trumpets. ²As an aroma pleasing to the LORD, offer a burnt offering of one young bull, one ram and seven male lambs a year old, all without defect. ³With the bull offer a grain offering of three-tenths of an ephah*ᵃ* of the finest flour mixed with olive oil; with the ram, two-tenths*ᵇ*; ⁴and with each of the seven lambs, one-tenth.*ᶜ* ⁵Include one male goat as a sin offering*ᵈ* to make atonement for you. ⁶These are in addition to the monthly and daily burnt offerings with their grain offerings and drink offerings as specified. They are food offerings presented to the LORD, a pleasing aroma.

BREAKTHROUGH!

Seventh month

(NUMBERS 29:1)

Ethanim was the seventh month in the Jewish lunar calendar. In our solar calendar, it would be from the middle of September to the middle of October.

The Day of Atonement

⁷ " 'On the tenth day of this seventh month hold a sacred assembly. You must deny yourselves*ᵉ* and do no work. ⁸Present as an aroma pleasing to the LORD a burnt offering of one young bull, one ram and seven male lambs a year old, all without defect. ⁹With the bull offer a grain offering of three-tenths of an ephah of the finest flour mixed with oil; with the ram, two-tenths; ¹⁰and with each of the seven lambs, one-tenth. ¹¹Include one male goat as a sin offering, in addition to the sin offering for atonement and the regular burnt offering with its grain offering, and their drink offerings.

The Festival of Tabernacles

¹² " 'On the fifteenth day of the seventh month, hold a sacred assembly and do

---

ᵃ 3 That is, probably about 11 pounds or about 5 kilograms; also in verses 9 and 14   *ᵇ 3* That is, probably about 7 pounds or about 3.2 kilograms; also in verses 9 and 14   *ᶜ 4* That is, probably about 3 1/2 pounds or about 1.6 kilograms; also in verses 10 and 15   *ᵈ 5* Or *purification offering*; also elsewhere in this chapter   *ᵉ 7* Or *must fast* no regular work. Celebrate a festival to the Lord for seven days. ¹³Present as an aroma pleasing to the Lord a food offering consisting of a burnt offering of thirteen young bulls, two rams and fourteen male lambs a year old, all without defect. ¹⁴With each of the thirteen bulls offer a grain offering of three-tenths of an ephah of the finest flour mixed with oil; with each of the two rams, two-tenths; ¹⁵and with each of the fourteen lambs, one-tenth. ¹⁶Include one male goat as a sin offering, in addition to the regular burnt offering with its grain offering and drink offering.

¹⁷ " 'On the second day offer twelve young bulls, two rams and fourteen male lambs a year old, all without defect. ¹⁸With the bulls, rams and lambs, offer their grain offerings and drink offerings according to the number specified. ¹⁹Include one male goat as a sin offering, in addition to the regular burnt offering with its grain offering, and their drink offerings.

²⁰ " 'On the third day offer eleven bulls, two rams and fourteen male lambs a year old, all without defect. ²¹With the bulls, rams and lambs, offer their grain offerings and drink offerings according to the number specified. ²²Include one male goat as a sin offering, in addition to the regular burnt offering with its grain offering and drink offering.

²³ " 'On the fourth day offer ten bulls, two rams and fourteen male lambs a year old, all without defect. ²⁴With the bulls, rams and lambs, offer their grain offerings and drink offerings according to the number specified. ²⁵Include one male goat as a sin offering, in addition to the regular burnt offering with its grain offering and drink offering.

²⁶ " 'On the fifth day offer nine bulls, two rams and fourteen male lambs a year old, all without defect. ²⁷With the bulls, rams and lambs, offer their grain offerings and drink offerings according to the number specified. ²⁸Include one male goat as a sin offering, in addition to the regular burnt offering with its grain offering and drink offering.

²⁹ " 'On the sixth day offer eight bulls, two rams and fourteen male lambs a

year old, all without defect. ³⁰With the bulls, rams and lambs, offer their grain offerings and drink offerings according to the number specified. ³¹Include one male goat as a sin offering, in addition to the regular burnt offering with its grain offering and drink offering.

³² " 'On the seventh day offer seven bulls, two rams and fourteen male lambs a year old, all without defect. ³³With the bulls, rams and lambs, offer their grain offerings and drink offerings according to the number specified. ³⁴Include one male goat as a sin offering, in addition to the regular burnt offering with its grain offering and drink offering.

³⁵ " 'On the eighth day hold a closing special assembly and do no regular work. ³⁶Present as an aroma pleasing to the Lord a food offering consisting of a burnt offering of one bull, one ram and seven male lambs a year old, all without defect. ³⁷With the bull, the ram and the lambs, offer their grain offerings and drink offerings according to the number specified. ³⁸Include one male goat as a sin offering, in addition to the regular burnt offering with its grain offering and drink offering.

³⁹ " 'In addition to what you vow and your freewill offerings, offer these to the Lord at your appointed festivals: your burnt offerings, grain offerings, drink offerings and fellowship offerings.' "

⁴⁰Moses told the Israelites all that the Lord commanded him.ᵃ

Vows

30 ᵇ Moses said to the heads of the tribes of Israel: "This is what the Lord commands: ²When a man makes a vow to the Lord or takes an oath to obligate himself by a pledge, he must not break his word but must do everything he said.

³"When a young woman still living in her father's household makes a vow to the Lord or obligates herself by a pledge ⁴and her father hears about her vow or pledge but says nothing to her, then all her vows and every pledge by which she obligated herself will stand. ⁵But if her

---

ᵃ 40 In Hebrew texts this verse (29:40) is numbered 30:1.
ᵇ In Hebrew texts 30:1-16 is numbered 30:2-17.

father forbids her when he hears about it, none of her vows or the pledges by which she obligated herself will stand; the LORD will release her because her father has forbidden her.

6 "If she marries after she makes a vow or after her lips utter a rash promise by which she obligates herself 7and her husband hears about it but says nothing to her, then her vows or the pledges by which she obligated herself will stand. 8But if her husband forbids her when he hears about it, he nullifies the vow that obligates her or the rash promise by which she obligates herself, and the LORD will release her.

9 "Any vow or obligation taken by a widow or divorced woman will be binding on her.

10 "If a woman living with her husband makes a vow or obligates herself by a pledge under oath 11and her husband hears about it but says nothing to her and does not forbid her, then all her vows or the pledges by which she obligated herself will stand. 12But if her husband nullifies them when he hears about them, then none of the vows or pledges that came from her lips will stand. Her husband has nullified them, and the LORD will release her. 13Her husband may confirm or nullify any vow she makes or any sworn pledge to deny herself.ª 14But if her husband says nothing to her about it from day to day, then he confirms all her vows or the pledges binding on her. He confirms them by saying nothing to her when he hears about them. 15If, however, he nullifies them some time after he hears about them, then he must bear the consequences of her wrongdoing."

16These are the regulations the LORD gave Moses concerning relationships between a man and his wife, and between a father and his young daughter still living at home.

Vengeance on the Midianites

31 The LORD said to Moses, 2 "Take vengeance on the Midianites for the Israelites. After that, you will be gathered to your people."

3So Moses said to the people, "Arm some of your men to go to war against the Midianites so that they may carry out the LORD's vengeance on them. 4Send into battle a thousand men from each of the tribes of Israel." 5So twelve thousand men armed for battle, a thousand from each tribe, were supplied from the clans of Israel. 6Moses sent them into battle, a thousand from each tribe, along with Phinehas son of Eleazar, the priest, who took with him articles from the sanctuary and the trumpets for signaling.

7They fought against Midian, as the LORD commanded Moses, and killed every man. 8Among their victims were Evi, Rekem, Zur, Hur and Reba—the five kings of Midian. They also killed Balaam son of Beor with the sword. 9The Israelites captured the Midianite women and children and took all the Midianite herds, flocks and goods as plunder. 10They burned all the towns where the Midianites had settled, as well as all their camps. 11They took all the plunder and spoils, including the people and animals, 12and brought the captives, spoils and plunder to Moses and Eleazar the priest and the Israelite assembly at their camp on the plains of Moab, by the Jordan across from Jericho.

13Moses, Eleazar the priest and all the leaders of the community went to meet them outside the camp. 14Moses was angry with the officers of the army—the commanders of thousands and commanders of hundreds—who returned from the battle.

15 "Have you allowed all the women to live?" he asked them. 16 "They were the ones who followed Balaam's advice and enticed the Israelites to be unfaithful to the LORD in the Peor incident, so that a plague struck the LORD's people. 17Now kill all the boys. And kill every woman who has slept with a man, 18but save for yourselves every girl who has never slept with a man.

19 "Anyone who has killed someone or touched someone who was killed must stay outside the camp seven days. On the third and seventh days you must purify yourselves and your captives. 20Purify every garment as well as everything made of leather, goat hair or wood."

ª 13 Or to fast

21Then Eleazar the priest said to the soldiers who had gone into battle, "This is what is required by the law that the Lord gave Moses: 22Gold, silver, bronze, iron, tin, lead 23and anything else that can withstand fire must be put through the fire, and then it will be clean. But it must also be purified with the water of cleansing. And whatever cannot withstand fire must be put through that water. 24On the seventh day wash your clothes and you will be clean. Then you may come into the camp."

Dividing the Spoils

25The Lord said to Moses, 26"You and Eleazar the priest and the family heads of the community are to count all the people and animals that were captured. 27Divide the spoils equally between the soldiers who took part in the battle and the rest of the community. 28From the soldiers who fought in the battle, set apart as tribute for the Lord one out of every five hundred, whether people, cattle, donkeys or sheep. 29Take this tribute from their half share and give it to Eleazar the priest as the Lord's part. 30From the Israelites' half, select one out of every fifty, whether people, cattle, donkeys, sheep or other animals. Give them to the Levites, who are responsible for the care of the Lord's tabernacle." 31So Moses and Eleazar the priest did as the Lord commanded Moses.

32The plunder remaining from the spoils that the soldiers took was 675,000 sheep, 3372,000 cattle, 3461,000 donkeys 35and 32,000 women who had never slept with a man.

36The half share of those who fought in the battle was:

337,500 sheep, 37of which the tribute for the Lord was 675;
3836,000 cattle, of which the tribute for the Lord was 72;
3930,500 donkeys, of which the tribute for the Lord was 61;
4016,000 people, of whom the tribute for the Lord was 32.

41Moses gave the tribute to Eleazar the priest as the Lord's part, as the Lord commanded Moses.

42The half belonging to the Israelites, which Moses set apart from that of the fighting men— 43the community's half— was 337,500 sheep, 4436,000 cattle, 4530,500 donkeys 46and 16,000 people. 47From the Israelites' half, Moses selected one out of every fifty people and animals, as the Lord commanded him, and gave them to the Levites, who were responsible for the care of the Lord's tabernacle.

48Then the officers who were over the units of the army—the commanders of thousands and commanders of hundreds—went to Moses 49and said to him, "Your servants have counted the soldiers under our command, and not one is missing. 50So we have brought as an offering to the Lord the gold articles each of us acquired—armlets, bracelets, signet rings, earrings and necklaces—to make atonement for ourselves before the Lord."

51Moses and Eleazar the priest accepted from them the gold—all the crafted articles. 52All the gold from the commanders of thousands and commanders of hundreds that Moses and Eleazar presented as a gift to the Lord weighed 16,750 shekels.a 53Each soldier had taken plunder for himself. 54Moses and Eleazar the priest accepted the gold from the commanders of thousands and commanders of hundreds and brought it into the tent of meeting as a memorial for the Israelites before the Lord.

The Transjordan Tribes

32 The Reubenites and Gadites, who had very large herds and flocks, saw that the lands of Jazer and Gilead were suitable for livestock. 2So they came to Moses and Eleazar the priest and to the leaders of the community, and said, 3"Ataroth, Dibon, Jazer, Nimrah, Heshbon, Elealeh, Sebam, Nebo and Beon— 4the land the Lord subdued before the people of Israel—are suitable for livestock, and your servants have livestock. 5If we have found favor in your eyes," they said, "let this land be given to your servants as our possession. Do not make us cross the Jordan."

a 52 That is, about 420 pounds or about 190 kilograms

THE SCENE

JAZER AND GILEAD

(NUMBERS 32:1)

Not much is known about where these two places were. They probably were east of the Jordan River, somewhere inside the land of the tribe of Gad. Jazer was an Amorite city-state that Israel conquered while they were moving toward the promised land. The tribe of Gad rebuilt Jazer and stayed there. The Jabbok River divides Gilead.

⁶Moses said to the Gadites and Reubenites, "Should your fellow Israelites go to war while you sit here? ⁷Why do you discourage the Israelites from crossing over into the land the LORD has given them? ⁸This is what your fathers did when I sent them from Kadesh Barnea to look over the land. ⁹After they went up to the Valley of Eshkol and viewed the land, they discouraged the Israelites from entering the land the LORD had given them. ¹⁰The LORD's anger was aroused that day and he swore this oath: ¹¹'Because they have not followed me wholeheartedly, not one of those who were twenty years old or more when they came up out of Egypt will see the land I promised on oath to Abraham, Isaac and Jacob— ¹²not one except Caleb son of Jephunneh the Kenizzite and Joshua son of Nun, for they followed the LORD wholeheartedly.' ¹³The LORD's anger burned against Israel and he made them wander in the wilderness forty years, until the whole generation of those who had done evil in his sight was gone.

¹⁴"And here you are, a brood of sinners, standing in the place of your fathers and making the LORD even more angry with Israel. ¹⁵If you turn away from following him, he will again leave all this people in the wilderness, and you will be the cause of their destruction."

¹⁶Then they came up to him and said, "We would like to build pens here for our livestock and cities for our women and children. ¹⁷But we will arm ourselves for battle*ᵃ* and go ahead of the Israelites until we have brought them to their place. Meanwhile our women and children will live in fortified cities, for protection from the inhabitants of the land. ¹⁸We will not return to our homes until each of the Israelites has received their inheritance. ¹⁹We will not receive any inheritance with them on the other side of the Jordan, because our inheritance has come to us on the east side of the Jordan."

²⁰Then Moses said to them, "If you will do this—if you will arm yourselves before the LORD for battle ²¹and if all of you who are armed cross over the Jordan before the LORD until he has driven his enemies out before him— ²²then when the land is subdued before the LORD, you may return and be free from your obligation to the LORD and to Israel. And this land will be your possession before the LORD.

²³"But if you fail to do this, you will be sinning against the LORD; and you may be sure that your sin will find you out. ²⁴Build cities for your women and children, and pens for your flocks, but do what you have promised."

²⁵The Gadites and Reubenites said to Moses, "We your servants will do as our lord commands. ²⁶Our children and wives, our flocks and herds will remain here in

---

ᵃ 17 Septuagint; Hebrew will be quick to arm ourselves

the cities of Gilead. ²⁷But your servants, every man who is armed for battle, will cross over to fight before the Lord, just as our lord says."

²⁸Then Moses gave orders about them to Eleazar the priest and Joshua son of Nun and to the family heads of the Israelite tribes. ²⁹He said to them, "If the Gadites and Reubenites, every man armed for battle, cross over the Jordan with you before the Lord, then when the land is subdued before you, you must give them the land of Gilead as their possession. ³⁰But if they do not cross over with you armed, they must accept their possession with you in Canaan."

³¹The Gadites and Reubenites answered, "Your servants will do what the Lord has said. ³²We will cross over before the Lord into Canaan armed, but the property we inherit will be on this side of the Jordan."

³³Then Moses gave to the Gadites, the Reubenites and the half-tribe of Manasseh son of Joseph the kingdom of Sihon king of the Amorites and the kingdom of Og king of Bashan—the whole land with its cities and the territory around them.

³⁴The Gadites built up Dibon, Ataroth, Aroer, ³⁵Atroth Shophan, Jazer, Jogbehah, ³⁶Beth Nimrah and Beth Haran as fortified cities, and built pens for their flocks. ³⁷And the Reubenites rebuilt Heshbon, Elealeh and Kiriathaim, ³⁸as well as Nebo and Baal Meon (these names were changed) and Sibmah. They gave names to the cities they rebuilt.

³⁹The descendants of Makir son of Manasseh went to Gilead, captured it and drove out the Amorites who were there. ⁴⁰So Moses gave Gilead to the Makirites, the descendants of Manasseh, and they settled there. ⁴¹Jair, a descendant of Manasseh, captured their settlements and called them Havvoth Jair.[a] ⁴²And Nobah captured Kenath and its surrounding settlements and called it Nobah after himself.

Stages in Israel's Journey

33 Here are the stages in the journey of the Israelites when they came out of Egypt by divisions under the leadership of Moses and Aaron. ²At the Lord's command Moses recorded the stages in their journey. This is their journey by stages:

³The Israelites set out from Rameses on the fifteenth day of the first month, the day after the Passover. They marched out defiantly in full view of all the Egyptians, ⁴who were burying all their firstborn, whom the Lord had struck down among them; for the Lord had brought judgment on their gods.

⁵The Israelites left Rameses and camped at Sukkoth.

⁶They left Sukkoth and camped at Etham, on the edge of the desert.

⁷They left Etham, turned back to Pi Hahiroth, to the east of Baal Zephon, and camped near Migdol.

⁸They left Pi Hahiroth[b] and passed through the sea into the desert, and when they had traveled for three days in the Desert of Etham, they camped at Marah.

⁹They left Marah and went to Elim, where there were twelve springs and seventy palm trees, and they camped there.

¹⁰They left Elim and camped by the Red Sea.[c]

¹¹They left the Red Sea and camped in the Desert of Sin.

¹²They left the Desert of Sin and camped at Dophkah.

¹³They left Dophkah and camped at Alush.

¹⁴They left Alush and camped at Rephidim, where there was no water for the people to drink.

¹⁵They left Rephidim and camped in the Desert of Sinai.

¹⁶They left the Desert of Sinai and camped at Kibroth Hattaavah.

¹⁷They left Kibroth Hattaavah and camped at Hazeroth.

¹⁸They left Hazeroth and camped at Rithmah.

---

[a] 41 Or them the settlements of Jair   [b] 8 Many manuscripts of the Masoretic Text, Samaritan Pentateuch and Vulgate; most manuscripts of the Masoretic Text left from before Hahiroth   [c] 10 Or the Sea of Reeds; also in verse 11

¹⁹They left Rithmah and camped at Rimmon Perez.
²⁰They left Rimmon Perez and camped at Libnah.
²¹They left Libnah and camped at Rissah.
²²They left Rissah and camped at Kehelathah.
²³They left Kehelathah and camped at Mount Shepher.
²⁴They left Mount Shepher and camped at Haradah.
²⁵They left Haradah and camped at Makheloth.
²⁶They left Makheloth and camped at Tahath.
²⁷They left Tahath and camped at Terah.
²⁸They left Terah and camped at Mithkah.
²⁹They left Mithkah and camped at Hashmonah.
³⁰They left Hashmonah and camped at Moseroth.
³¹They left Moseroth and camped at Bene Jaakan.
³²They left Bene Jaakan and camped at Hor Haggidgad.
³³They left Hor Haggidgad and camped at Jotbathah.
³⁴They left Jotbathah and camped at Abronah.
³⁵They left Abronah and camped at Ezion Geber.
³⁶They left Ezion Geber and camped at Kadesh, in the Desert of Zin.
³⁷They left Kadesh and camped at Mount Hor, on the border of Edom.
³⁸At the LORD's command Aaron the priest went up Mount Hor, where he died on the first day of the fifth month of the fortieth year after the Israelites came out of Egypt. ³⁹Aaron was a hundred and twenty-three years old when he died on Mount Hor.
⁴⁰The Canaanite king of Arad, who lived in the Negev of Canaan, heard that the Israelites were coming.
⁴¹They left Mount Hor and camped at Zalmonah.
⁴²They left Zalmonah and camped at Punon.
⁴³They left Punon and camped at Oboth.

BREAKTHROUGH!

Fifth month

(NUMBERS 33:38)

Ab was the fifth month in the Jewish lunar calendar, which would be like the middle of July to the middle of August for us.

⁴⁴They left Oboth and camped at Iye Abarim, on the border of Moab.
⁴⁵They left Iye Abarim and camped at Dibon Gad.
⁴⁶They left Dibon Gad and camped at Almon Diblathaim.
⁴⁷They left Almon Diblathaim and camped in the mountains of Abarim, near Nebo.
⁴⁸They left the mountains of Abarim and camped on the plains of Moab by the Jordan across from Jericho. ⁴⁹There on the plains of Moab they camped along the Jordan from Beth Jeshimoth to Abel Shittim.

⁵⁰On the plains of Moab by the Jordan across from Jericho the LORD said to Moses, ⁵¹"Speak to the Israelites and say to them: 'When you cross the Jordan into Canaan, ⁵²drive out all the inhabitants of the land before you. Destroy all their carved images and their cast idols, and demolish all their high places. ⁵³Take possession of the land and settle in it, for I have given you the land to possess.

⁵⁴Distribute the land by lot, according to your clans. To a larger group give a larger inheritance, and to a smaller group a smaller one. Whatever falls to them by lot will be theirs. Distribute it according to your ancestral tribes.

⁵⁵ "But if you do not drive out the inhabitants of the land, those you allow to remain will become barbs in your eyes and thorns in your sides. They will give you trouble in the land where you will live. ⁵⁶And then I will do to you what I plan to do to them.' "

Boundaries of Canaan

34 The LORD said to Moses, ²"Command the Israelites and say to them: 'When you enter Canaan, the land that will be allotted to you as an inheritance is to have these boundaries:

³" 'Your southern side will include some of the Desert of Zin along the border of Edom. Your southern boundary will start in the east from the southern end of the Dead Sea, ⁴cross south of Scorpion Pass, continue on to Zin and go south of Kadesh Barnea. Then it will go to Hazar Addar and over to Azmon, ⁵where it will turn, join the Wadi of Egypt and end at the Mediterranean Sea.

⁶" 'Your western boundary will be the coast of the Mediterranean Sea. This will be your boundary on the west.

⁷" 'For your northern boundary, run a line from the Mediterranean Sea to Mount Hor ⁸and from Mount Hor to Lebo Hamath. Then the boundary will go to Zedad, ⁹continue to Ziphron and end at Hazar Enan. This will be your boundary on the north.

¹⁰" 'For your eastern boundary, run a line from Hazar Enan to Shepham. ¹¹The boundary will go down from Shepham to Riblah on the east side of Ain and continue along the slopes east of the Sea of Galilee.ᵃ ¹²Then the boundary will go down along the Jordan and end at the Dead Sea.

" 'This will be your land, with its boundaries on every side.' "

¹³Moses commanded the Israelites: "Assign this land by lot as an inheritance.

The LORD has ordered that it be given to the nine and a half tribes, ¹⁴because the families of the tribe of Reuben, the tribe of Gad and the half-tribe of Manasseh have received their inheritance. ¹⁵These two and a half tribes have received their inheritance east of the Jordan across from Jericho, toward the sunrise."

¹⁶The LORD said to Moses, ¹⁷"These are the names of the men who are to assign the land for you as an inheritance: Eleazar the priest and Joshua son of Nun. ¹⁸And appoint one leader from each tribe to help assign the land. ¹⁹These are their names:

Caleb son of Jephunneh,
   from the tribe of Judah;
²⁰Shemuel son of Ammihud,
   from the tribe of Simeon;
²¹Elidad son of Kislon,
   from the tribe of Benjamin;
²²Bukki son of Jogli,
   the leader from the tribe of Dan;
²³Hanniel son of Ephod,
   the leader from the tribe of Manasseh son of Joseph;
²⁴Kemuel son of Shiphtan,
   the leader from the tribe of Ephraim son of Joseph;
²⁵Elizaphan son of Parnak,
   the leader from the tribe of Zebulun;
²⁶Paltiel son of Azzan,
   the leader from the tribe of Issachar;
²⁷Ahihud son of Shelomi,
   the leader from the tribe of Asher;
²⁸Pedahel son of Ammihud,
   the leader from the tribe of Naphtali."

²⁹These are the men the LORD commanded to assign the inheritance to the Israelites in the land of Canaan.

Towns for the Levites

35 On the plains of Moab by the Jordan across from Jericho, the LORD said to Moses, ²"Command the Israelites to give the Levites towns to live in from the inheritance the Israelites will possess. And give them pasturelands around the

ᵃ 11 Hebrew Kinnereth

towns. ³Then they will have towns to live in and pasturelands for the cattle they own and all their other animals.

⁴"The pasturelands around the towns that you give the Levites will extend a thousand cubits[a] from the town wall. ⁵Outside the town, measure two thousand cubits[b] on the east side, two thousand on the south side, two thousand on the west and two thousand on the north, with the town in the center. They will have this area as pastureland for the towns.

Cities of Refuge

⁶"Six of the towns you give the Levites will be cities of refuge, to which a person who has killed someone may flee. In addition, give them forty-two other towns. ⁷In all you must give the Levites forty-eight towns, together with their pasturelands. ⁸The towns you give the Levites from the land the Israelites possess are to be given in proportion to the inheritance of each tribe: Take many towns from a tribe that has many, but few from one that has few."

⁹Then the LORD said to Moses: ¹⁰"Speak to the Israelites and say to them: 'When you cross the Jordan into Canaan, ¹¹select some towns to be your cities of refuge, to which a person who has killed someone accidentally may flee. ¹²They will be places of refuge from the avenger, so that anyone accused of murder may not die before they stand trial before the assembly. ¹³These six towns you give will be your cities of refuge. ¹⁴Give three on this side of the Jordan and three in Canaan as cities of refuge. ¹⁵These six towns will be a place of refuge for Israelites and for foreigners residing among them, so that anyone who has killed another accidentally can flee there.

¹⁶"'If anyone strikes someone a fatal blow with an iron object, that person is a murderer; the murderer is to be put to death. ¹⁷Or if anyone is holding a stone and strikes someone a fatal blow with it, that person is a murderer; the murderer is to be put to death. ¹⁸Or if anyone is holding a wooden object and strikes someone a fatal blow with it, that person is a murderer; the murderer is to be put

to death. ¹⁹The avenger of blood shall put the murderer to death; when the avenger comes upon the murderer, the avenger shall put the murderer to death. ²⁰If anyone with malice aforethought shoves another or throws something at them intentionally so that they die ²¹or if out of enmity one person hits another with their fist so that the other dies, that person is to be put to death; that person is a murderer. The avenger of blood shall put the murderer to death when they meet.

²²"'But if without enmity someone suddenly pushes another or throws something at them unintentionally ²³or, without seeing them, drops on them a stone heavy enough to kill them, and they die, then since that other person was not an

---

[a] 4 That is, about 1,500 feet or about 450 meters
[b] 5 That is, about 3,000 feet or about 900 meters

BREAKTHROUGH!

The Year of Jubilee
(NUMBERS 36:4)

It was celebrated once every 50 years in remembrance of the slaves who were freed and the people who got their land back after they had lost it. It was a year when nobody planted or took care of the land, and the land just produced the food they needed without them having to work. This story is in Leviticus 25:8 – 19.

enemy and no harm was intended, ²⁴the assembly must judge between the accused and the avenger of blood according to these regulations. ²⁵The assembly must protect the one accused of murder from the avenger of blood and send the accused back to the city of refuge to which they fled. The accused must stay there until the death of the high priest, who was anointed with the holy oil.

²⁶" 'But if the accused ever goes outside the limits of the city of refuge to which they fled ²⁷and the avenger of blood finds them outside the city, the avenger of blood may kill the accused without being guilty of murder. ²⁸The accused must stay in the city of refuge until the death of the high priest; only after the death of the high priest may they return to their own property.

²⁹" 'This is to have the force of law for you throughout the generations to come, wherever you live.

³⁰" 'Anyone who kills a person is to be put to death as a murderer only on the testimony of witnesses. But no one is to be put to death on the testimony of only one witness.

³¹" 'Do not accept a ransom for the life of a murderer, who deserves to die. They are to be put to death.

³²" 'Do not accept a ransom for anyone who has fled to a city of refuge and so allow them to go back and live on their own land before the death of the high priest.

³³" 'Do not pollute the land where you are. Bloodshed pollutes the land, and atonement cannot be made for the land on which blood has been shed, except by the blood of the one who shed it. ³⁴Do not defile the land where you live and where I dwell, for I, the LORD, dwell among the Israelites.' "

Inheritance of Zelophehad's Daughters

36 The family heads of the clan of Gilead son of Makir, the son of Manasseh, who were from the clans of the descendants of Joseph, came and spoke before Moses and the leaders, the heads of the Israelite families. ²They said,

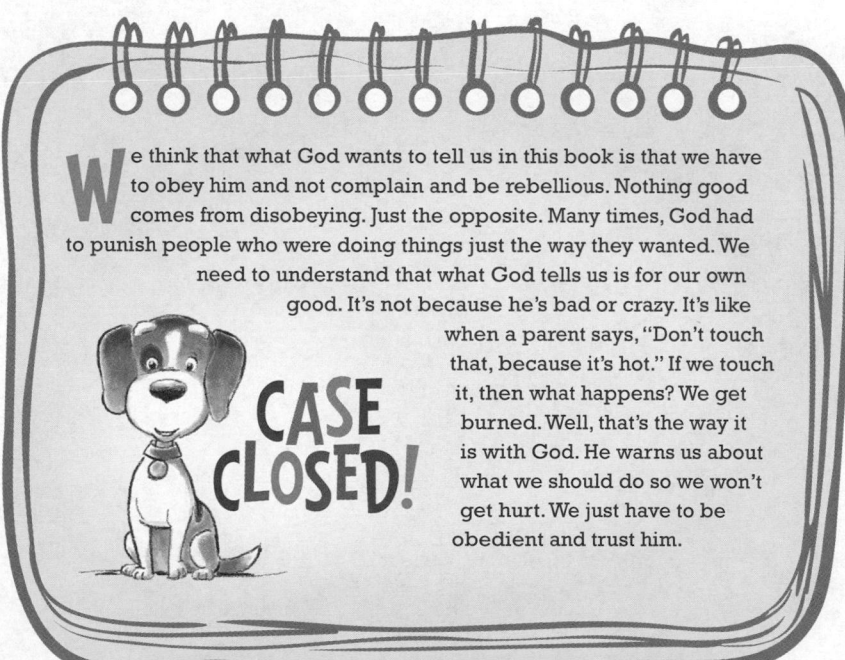

We think that what God wants to tell us in this book is that we have to obey him and not complain and be rebellious. Nothing good comes from disobeying. Just the opposite. Many times, God had to punish people who were doing things just the way they wanted. We need to understand that what God tells us is for our own good. It's not because he's bad or crazy. It's like when a parent says, "Don't touch that, because it's hot." If we touch it, then what happens? We get burned. Well, that's the way it is with God. He warns us about what we should do so we won't get hurt. We just have to be obedient and trust him.

CASE CLOSED!

"When the Lord commanded my lord to give the land as an inheritance to the Israelites by lot, he ordered you to give the inheritance of our brother Zelophehad to his daughters. ³Now suppose they marry men from other Israelite tribes; then their inheritance will be taken from our ancestral inheritance and added to that of the tribe they marry into. And so part of the inheritance allotted to us will be taken away. ⁴When the Year of Jubilee for the Israelites comes, their inheritance will be added to that of the tribe into which they marry, and their property will be taken from the tribal inheritance of our ancestors."

⁵Then at the Lord's command Moses gave this order to the Israelites: "What the tribe of the descendants of Joseph is saying is right. ⁶This is what the Lord commands for Zelophehad's daughters: They may marry anyone they please as long as they marry within their father's tribal clan. ⁷No inheritance in Israel is to pass from one tribe to another, for every Israelite shall keep the tribal inheritance of their ancestors. ⁸Every daughter who inherits land in any Israelite tribe must marry someone in her father's tribal clan, so that every Israelite will possess the inheritance of their ancestors. ⁹No inheritance may pass from one tribe to another, for each Israelite tribe is to keep the land it inherits."

¹⁰So Zelophehad's daughters did as the Lord commanded Moses. ¹¹Zelophehad's daughters—Mahlah, Tirzah, Hoglah, Milkah and Noah—married their cousins on their father's side. ¹²They married within the clans of the descendants of Manasseh son of Joseph, and their inheritance remained in their father's tribe and clan.

¹³These are the commands and regulations the Lord gave through Moses to the Israelites on the plains of Moab by the Jordan across from Jericho.

DEUTERONOMY

THE EVIDENCE:

WHO WROTE IT?
Like the other books of the Pentateuch (remember that little word that comes from Greek and means "five books"), Deuteronomy was also probably written by several authors, although some experts say that Moses wrote it.

HOW LONG AGO?
Some people think it was written about 700 years before Christ and that it was edited, or left the way we know it now, about 400 years before Christ.

WHAT'S IT ABOUT?
The word *Deuteronomy* comes from the Greek language and means "second law or instruction." That's because it is a repetition of teachings and commandments that had already been written before. In Hebrew, the name of this book would be something like "these are the words," because those are precisely the first words of the book. In some Bibles like this one, that is the exact way this book starts.

God thought it was important to repeat to the Israelites everything he had taught them and ordered them to do when he took them out of Egypt 40 years before. The people who were listening were the children of the people who had complained so much about God and had disobeyed his teachings. The complainers' punishment was to wander around in the desert for a long time, and they all died without being able to enter the promised land. What a pity!

Moses reminds them about the important teachings that were given to their parents. He tells them that these teachings need to be taught and obeyed by them and their children and their grandchildren so they can live peacefully in the promised land.

THE BEST PART
This book has many nice parts, because it says that if we love God, we'll follow his teachings and he'll bless us. But what we like best is "Love the LORD your God with all your heart and with all your soul and with all your strength" (6:5), because that means loving God with everything you've got!

The Command to Leave Horeb

1 These are the words Moses spoke to all Israel in the wilderness east of the Jordan—that is, in the Arabah—opposite Suph, between Paran and Tophel, Laban, Hazeroth and Dizahab. ²(It takes eleven days to go from Horeb to Kadesh Barnea by the Mount Seir road.)

³In the fortieth year, on the first day of the eleventh month, Moses proclaimed to the Israelites all that the LORD had commanded him concerning them. ⁴This was after he had defeated Sihon king of the Amorites, who reigned in Heshbon, and at Edrei had defeated Og king of Bashan, who reigned in Ashtaroth.

⁵East of the Jordan in the territory of Moab, Moses began to expound this law, saying:

⁶The LORD our God said to us at Horeb, "You have stayed long enough at this mountain. ⁷Break camp and advance into the hill country of the Amorites; go to all the neighboring peoples in the Arabah, in the mountains, in the western foothills, in the Negev and along the coast, to the land of the Canaanites and to Lebanon, as far as the great river, the Euphrates. ⁸See, I have given you this land. Go in and take possession of the land the LORD swore he would give to your fathers—to Abraham, Isaac and Jacob—and to their descendants after them."

The Appointment of Leaders

⁹At that time I said to you, "You are too heavy a burden for me to carry alone. ¹⁰The LORD your God has increased your numbers so that today you are as numerous as the stars in the sky. ¹¹May the LORD, the God of your ancestors, increase you a thousand times and bless you as he has promised! ¹²But how can I bear your problems and your burdens and your disputes all by myself? ¹³Choose some wise, understanding and respected men from each of your tribes, and I will set them over you."

¹⁴You answered me, "What you propose to do is good."

¹⁵So I took the leading men of your tribes, wise and respected men, and appointed them to have authority over you—as commanders of thousands, of hundreds, of fifties and of tens and as tribal officials. ¹⁶And I charged your judges at that time, "Hear the disputes between your people and judge fairly, whether the case is between two Israelites or between an Israelite and a foreigner residing among you. ¹⁷Do not show partiality in judging; hear both small and great alike. Do not be afraid of anyone, for judgment belongs to God. Bring me any case too hard for you, and I will hear it." ¹⁸And at that time I told you everything you were to do.

Spies Sent Out

¹⁹Then, as the LORD our God commanded us, we set out from Horeb and went toward the hill country of the Amorites through all that vast and dreadful wilderness that you have seen, and so we reached Kadesh Barnea. ²⁰Then I said to you, "You have reached the hill country of the Amorites, which the LORD our God is giving us. ²¹See, the LORD your God has

BREAKTHROUGH!

The eleventh month

(DEUTERONOMY 1:3)

This was Shebat in the Jewish lunar calendar. In our solar calendar, it's more or less from the middle of January to the middle of February.

HOREB

(DEUTERONOMY 1:6)

This is the mountain where Moses received the Ten Commandments. Nobody knows exactly where it is. It's also called Mount Sinai.

tents and said, "The LORD hates us; so he brought us out of Egypt to deliver us into the hands of the Amorites to destroy us. ²⁸Where can we go? Our brothers have made our hearts melt in fear. They say, 'The people are stronger and taller than we are; the cities are large, with walls up to the sky. We even saw the Anakites there.' "

²⁹Then I said to you, "Do not be terrified; do not be afraid of them. ³⁰The LORD your God, who is going before you, will fight for you, as he did for you in Egypt, before your very eyes, ³¹and in the wilderness. There you saw how the LORD your God carried you, as a father carries his son, all the way you went until you reached this place."

³²In spite of this, you did not trust in the LORD your God, ³³who went ahead of you on your journey, in fire by night and in a cloud by day, to search out places for you to camp and to show you the way you should go.

given you the land. Go up and take possession of it as the LORD, the God of your ancestors, told you. Do not be afraid; do not be discouraged."

²²Then all of you came to me and said, "Let us send men ahead to spy out the land for us and bring back a report about the route we are to take and the towns we will come to."

²³The idea seemed good to me; so I selected twelve of you, one man from each tribe. ²⁴They left and went up into the hill country, and came to the Valley of Eshkol and explored it. ²⁵Taking with them some of the fruit of the land, they brought it down to us and reported, "It is a good land that the LORD our God is giving us."

Rebellion Against the LORD

²⁶But you were unwilling to go up; you rebelled against the command of the LORD your God. ²⁷You grumbled in your

ARABAH

(DEUTERONOMY 1:7)

This word means "dry region." It was a hot desert and didn't get much rain.

³⁴When the LORD heard what you said, he was angry and solemnly swore: ³⁵"No one from this evil generation shall see the good land I swore to give your ancestors, ³⁶except Caleb son of Jephunneh. He will see it, and I will give him and his descendants the land he set his feet on, because he followed the LORD wholeheartedly."

³⁷Because of you the LORD became angry with me also and said, "You shall not enter it, either. ³⁸But your assistant, Joshua son of Nun, will enter it. Encourage him, because he will lead Israel to inherit it. ³⁹And the little ones that you said would be taken captive, your children who do not yet know good from bad—they will enter the land. I will give it to them and they will take possession of it.

✓ **JOSHUA** (DEUTERONOMY 1:38)
Read Exodus 17:9.

⁴⁰But as for you, turn around and set out toward the desert along the route to the Red Sea.ᵃ"

⁴¹Then you replied, "We have sinned against the LORD. We will go up and fight, as the LORD our God commanded us." So every one of you put on his weapons, thinking it easy to go up into the hill country.

⁴²But the LORD said to me, "Tell them, 'Do not go up and fight, because I will not be with you. You will be defeated by your enemies.'"

⁴³So I told you, but you would not listen. You rebelled against the LORD's command and in your arrogance you marched up into the hill country. ⁴⁴The Amorites who lived in those hills came out against you; they chased you like a swarm of bees and beat you down from Seir all the way to Hormah. ⁴⁵You came back and wept before the LORD, but he paid no attention to your weeping and turned a deaf ear to you. ⁴⁶And so you stayed in Kadesh many days—all the time you spent there.

Wanderings in the Wilderness

2 Then we turned back and set out toward the wilderness along the route to the Red Sea,ᵃ as the LORD had directed me. For a long time we made our way around the hill country of Seir.

²Then the LORD said to me, ³"You have made your way around this hill country long enough; now turn north. ⁴Give the people these orders: 'You are about to pass through the territory of your relatives the descendants of Esau, who live in Seir. They will be afraid of you, but be very careful. ⁵Do not provoke them to war, for I will not give you any of their land, not even enough to put your foot on. I have given Esau the hill country of Seir as his own. ⁶You are to pay them in silver for the food you eat and the water you drink.'"

⁷The LORD your God has blessed you in all the work of your hands. He has watched over your journey through this vast wilderness. These forty years the LORD your God has been with you, and you have not lacked anything.

ᵃ 40,1 Or the Sea of Reeds

8So we went on past our relatives the descendants of Esau, who live in Seir. We turned from the Arabah road, which comes up from Elath and Ezion Geber, and traveled along the desert road of Moab.

9Then the LORD said to me, "Do not harass the Moabites or provoke them to war, for I will not give you any part of their land. I have given Ar to the descendants of Lot as a possession."

10(The Emites used to live there—a people strong and numerous, and as tall as the Anakites. 11Like the Anakites, they too were considered Rephaites, but the Moabites called them Emites. 12Horites used to live in Seir, but the descendants of Esau drove them out. They destroyed the Horites from before them and settled in their place, just as Israel did in the land the LORD gave them as their possession.)

13And the LORD said, "Now get up and cross the Zered Valley." So we crossed the valley.

14Thirty-eight years passed from the time we left Kadesh Barnea until we crossed the Zered Valley. By then, that entire generation of fighting men had perished from the camp, as the LORD had sworn to them. 15The LORD's hand was against them until he had completely eliminated them from the camp.

16Now when the last of these fighting men among the people had died, 17the LORD said to me, 18"Today you are to pass by the region of Moab at Ar. 19When you come to the Ammonites, do not harass them or provoke them to war, for I will not give you possession of any land belonging to the Ammonites. I have given it as a possession to the descendants of Lot."

20(That too was considered a land of the Rephaites, who used to live there; but the Ammonites called them Zamzummites. 21They were a people strong and numerous, and as tall as the Anakites. The LORD destroyed them from before the Ammonites, who drove them out and settled in their place. 22The LORD had done the same for the descendants of Esau, who lived in Seir, when he destroyed the Horites from before them. They drove them out and have lived in their place to

this day. 23And as for the Avvites who lived in villages as far as Gaza, the Caphtorites coming out from Caphtor[a] destroyed them and settled in their place.)

Defeat of Sihon King of Heshbon

24"Set out now and cross the Arnon Gorge. See, I have given into your hand Sihon the Amorite, king of Heshbon, and his country. Begin to take possession of it and engage him in battle. 25This very day I will begin to put the terror and fear of you on all the nations under heaven. They will hear reports of you and will tremble and be in anguish because of you."

26From the Desert of Kedemoth I sent messengers to Sihon king of Heshbon offering peace and saying, 27"Let us pass through your country. We will stay on the main road; we will not turn aside to the right or to the left. 28Sell us food to eat and water to drink for their price in silver. Only let us pass through on foot— 29as the descendants of Esau, who live in Seir, and the Moabites, who live in Ar, did for us—until we cross the Jordan into the land the LORD our God is giving us." 30But Sihon king of Heshbon refused to let us pass through. For the LORD your God had made his spirit stubborn and his heart obstinate in order to give him into your hands, as he has now done.

31The LORD said to me, "See, I have begun to deliver Sihon and his country over to you. Now begin to conquer and possess his land."

32When Sihon and all his army came out to meet us in battle at Jahaz, 33the LORD our God delivered him over to us and we struck him down, together with his sons and his whole army. 34At that time we took all his towns and completely destroyed[b] them—men, women and children. We left no survivors. 35But the livestock and the plunder from the towns we had captured we carried off for ourselves. 36From Aroer on the rim of the Arnon Gorge, and from the town in the gorge, even as far as Gilead, not one town was too strong for us. The LORD our God gave us all of them.

---

a 23 That is, Crete   b 34 The Hebrew term refers to the irrevocable giving over of things or persons to the LORD, often by totally destroying them.

[37]But in accordance with the command of the LORD our God, you did not encroach on any of the land of the Ammonites, neither the land along the course of the Jabbok nor that around the towns in the hills.

Defeat of Og King of Bashan

3 Next we turned and went up along the road toward Bashan, and Og king of Bashan with his whole army marched out to meet us in battle at Edrei. [2]The LORD said to me, "Do not be afraid of him, for I have delivered him into your hands, along with his whole army and his land. Do to him what you did to Sihon king of the Amorites, who reigned in Heshbon."

[3]So the LORD our God also gave into our hands Og king of Bashan and all his army. We struck them down, leaving no survivors. [4]At that time we took all his cities. There was not one of the sixty cities that we did not take from them—the whole region of Argob, Og's kingdom in Bashan. [5]All these cities were fortified with high walls and with gates and bars, and there were also a great many unwalled villages. [6]We completely destroyed[a] them, as we had done with Sihon king of Heshbon, destroying[a] every city—men, women and children. [7]But all the livestock and the plunder from their cities we carried off for ourselves.

[8]So at that time we took from these two kings of the Amorites the territory east of the Jordan, from the Arnon Gorge as far as Mount Hermon. [9](Hermon is called Sirion by the Sidonians; the Amorites call it Senir.) [10]We took all the towns on the plateau, and all Gilead, and all Bashan as far as Salekah and Edrei, towns of Og's kingdom in Bashan. [11](Og king of Bashan was the last of the Rephaites. His bed was decorated with iron and was more than nine cubits long and four cubits wide.[b] It is still in Rabbah of the Ammonites.)

Division of the Land

[12]Of the land that we took over at that time, I gave the Reubenites and the Gadites the territory north of Aroer by the Arnon Gorge, including half the hill country of Gilead, together with its towns. [13]The rest of Gilead and also all of Bashan, the kingdom of Og, I gave to the half-tribe of Manasseh. (The whole region of Argob in Bashan used to be known as a land of the Rephaites. [14]Jair, a descendant of Manasseh, took the whole region of Argob as far as the border of the Geshurites and the Maakathites; it was named after him, so that to this day Bashan is called Havvoth Jair.[c]) [15]And I gave Gilead to Makir. [16]But to the Reubenites and the Gadites I gave the territory extending from Gilead down to the Arnon Gorge (the middle of the gorge being the border) and out to the Jabbok River, which is the border of the Ammonites. [17]Its western border was the Jordan in the Arabah, from Kinnereth to the Sea of the Arabah (that is, the Dead Sea), below the slopes of Pisgah.

[18]I commanded you at that time: "The LORD your God has given you this land to take possession of it. But all your able-bodied men, armed for battle, must cross over ahead of the other Israelites. [19]However, your wives, your children and your livestock (I know you have much livestock) may stay in the towns I have given you, [20]until the LORD gives rest to your fellow Israelites as he has to you, and they too have taken over the land that the LORD your God is giving them across the Jordan. After that, each of you may go back to the possession I have given you."

Moses Forbidden to Cross the Jordan

[21]At that time I commanded Joshua: "You have seen with your own eyes all that the LORD your God has done to these two kings. The LORD will do the same to all the kingdoms over there where you are going. [22]Do not be afraid of them; the LORD your God himself will fight for you."

[23]At that time I pleaded with the LORD: [24]"Sovereign LORD, you have begun to show to your servant your greatness and your strong hand. For what god is there in heaven or on earth who can do the

---

[a] 6 The Hebrew term refers to the irrevocable giving over of things or persons to the LORD, often by totally destroying them.   [b] 11 That is, about 14 feet long and 6 feet wide or about 4 meters long and 1.8 meters wide   [c] 14 Or called the settlements of Jair

deeds and mighty works you do? ²⁵Let me go over and see the good land beyond the Jordan—that fine hill country and Lebanon."

²⁶But because of you the LORD was angry with me and would not listen to me. "That is enough," the LORD said. "Do not speak to me anymore about this matter. ²⁷Go up to the top of Pisgah and look west and north and south and east. Look at the land with your own eyes, since you are not going to cross this Jordan. ²⁸But commission Joshua, and encourage and strengthen him, for he will lead this people across and will cause them to inherit the land that you will see." ²⁹So we stayed in the valley near Beth Peor.

Obedience Commanded

4 Now, Israel, hear the decrees and laws I am about to teach you. Follow them so that you may live and may go in and take possession of the land the LORD, the God of your ancestors, is giving you. ²Do not add to what I command you and do not subtract from it, but keep the commands of the LORD your God that I give you.

³You saw with your own eyes what the LORD did at Baal Peor. The LORD your God destroyed from among you everyone who followed the Baal of Peor, ⁴but all of you who held fast to the LORD your God are still alive today.

⁵See, I have taught you decrees and laws as the LORD my God commanded me, so that you may follow them in the land you are entering to take possession of it. ⁶Observe them carefully, for this will show your wisdom and understanding to the nations, who will hear about all these decrees and say, "Surely this great nation is a wise and understanding people." ⁷What other nation is so great as to have their gods near them the way the LORD our God is near us whenever we pray to him? ⁸And what other nation is so great as to have such righteous decrees and laws as this body of laws I am setting before you today?

⁹Only be careful, and watch yourselves closely so that you do not forget the things your eyes have seen or let them fade from your heart as long as you live. Teach them to your children and to their children after them. ¹⁰Remember the day you stood before the LORD your God at Horeb, when he said to me, "Assemble the people before me to hear my words so that they may learn to revere me as long as they live in the land and may teach them to their children." ¹¹You came near and stood at the foot of the mountain while it blazed with fire to the very heavens, with black clouds and deep darkness. ¹²Then the LORD spoke to you out of the fire. You heard the sound of words but saw no form; there was only a voice. ¹³He declared to you his covenant, the Ten Commandments, which he commanded you to follow and then wrote them on two stone tablets. ¹⁴And the LORD directed me at that time to teach you the decrees and laws you are to follow in the land that you are crossing the Jordan to possess.

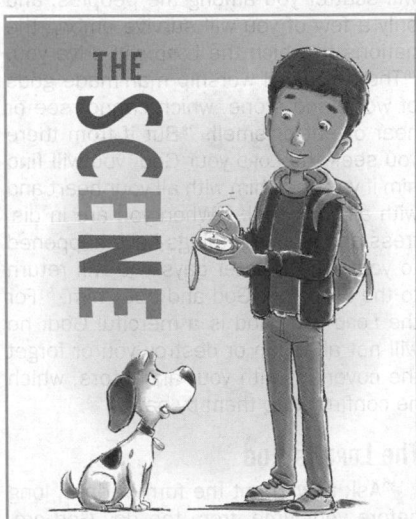

THE SCENE

LEBANON

(DEUTERONOMY 3:25)

This name means "white." It was the north border of Palestine. This land was famous for its fruits and vegetables and beautiful forests.

Idolatry Forbidden

[15]You saw no form of any kind the day the LORD spoke to you at Horeb out of the fire. Therefore watch yourselves very carefully, [16]so that you do not become corrupt and make for yourselves an idol, an image of any shape, whether formed like a man or a woman, [17]or like any animal on earth or any bird that flies in the air, [18]or like any creature that moves along the ground or any fish in the waters below. [19]And when you look up to the sky and see the sun, the moon and the stars—all the heavenly array—do not be enticed into bowing down to them and worshiping things the LORD your God has apportioned to all the nations under heaven. [20]But as for you, the LORD took you and brought you out of the iron-smelting furnace, out of Egypt, to be the people of his inheritance, as you now are.

[21]The LORD was angry with me because of you, and he solemnly swore that I would not cross the Jordan and enter

BREAKTHROUGH!

Idols

(DEUTERONOMY 4:16)

This is about little statues or figures made of wood, stone or metal, like the ones the people of other nations made to represent their gods.

the good land the LORD your God is giving you as your inheritance. [22]I will die in this land; I will not cross the Jordan; but you are about to cross over and take possession of that good land. [23]Be careful not to forget the covenant of the LORD your God that he made with you; do not make for yourselves an idol in the form of anything the LORD your God has forbidden. [24]For the LORD your God is a consuming fire, a jealous God.

[25]After you have had children and grandchildren and have lived in the land a long time—if you then become corrupt and make any kind of idol, doing evil in the eyes of the LORD your God and arousing his anger, [26]I call the heavens and the earth as witnesses against you this day that you will quickly perish from the land that you are crossing the Jordan to possess. You will not live there long but will certainly be destroyed. [27]The LORD will scatter you among the peoples, and only a few of you will survive among the nations to which the LORD will drive you. [28]There you will worship man-made gods of wood and stone, which cannot see or hear or eat or smell. [29]But if from there you seek the LORD your God, you will find him if you seek him with all your heart and with all your soul. [30]When you are in distress and all these things have happened to you, then in later days you will return to the LORD your God and obey him. [31]For the LORD your God is a merciful God; he will not abandon or destroy you or forget the covenant with your ancestors, which he confirmed to them by oath.

The LORD Is God

[32]Ask now about the former days, long before your time, from the day God created human beings on the earth; ask from one end of the heavens to the other. Has anything so great as this ever happened, or has anything like it ever been heard of? [33]Has any other people heard the voice of God[a] speaking out of fire, as you have, and lived? [34]Has any god ever tried to take for himself one nation out of another nation, by testings, by signs and

_____

[a] 33 Or of a god

after you and that you may live long in the land the Lord your God gives you for all time.

Cities of Refuge

⁴¹Then Moses set aside three cities east of the Jordan, ⁴²to which anyone who had killed a person could flee if they had unintentionally killed a neighbor without malice aforethought. They could flee into one of these cities and save their life. ⁴³The cities were these: Bezer in the wilderness plateau, for the Reubenites; Ramoth in Gilead, for the Gadites; and Golan in Bashan, for the Manassites.

Introduction to the Law

⁴⁴This is the law Moses set before the Israelites. ⁴⁵These are the stipulations, decrees and laws Moses gave them when they came out of Egypt ⁴⁶and were in the valley near Beth Peor east of the Jordan, in the land of Sihon king of the Amorites, who reigned in Heshbon and was defeated by Moses and the Israelites as they came out of Egypt. ⁴⁷They took possession of his land and the land of Og king of Bashan, the two Amorite kings east of the Jordan. ⁴⁸This land extended from Aroer on the rim of the Arnon Gorge to Mount Sirionᵃ (that is, Hermon), ⁴⁹and included all the Arabah east of the Jordan, as far as the Dead Sea,ᵇ below the slopes of Pisgah.

The Ten Commandments

5 Moses summoned all Israel and said: Hear, Israel, the decrees and laws I declare in your hearing today. Learn them and be sure to follow them. ²The Lord our God made a covenant with us at Horeb. ³It was not with our ancestorsᶜ that the Lord made this covenant, but with us, with all of us who are alive here today. ⁴The Lord spoke to you face to face out of the fire on the mountain. ⁵(At that time I stood between the Lord and you to declare to you the word of the Lord, because you were afraid of the fire and did not go up the mountain.) And he said:

BREAKTHROUGH!

Signs and wonders

(DEUTERONOMY 4:34)

These are acts of God that are supernatural for us. It's when God makes the impossible happen. Only God can do this, because he is super powerful!

wonders, by war, by a mighty hand and an outstretched arm, or by great and awesome deeds, like all the things the Lord your God did for you in Egypt before your very eyes?

³⁵You were shown these things so that you might know that the Lord is God; besides him there is no other. ³⁶From heaven he made you hear his voice to discipline you. On earth he showed you his great fire, and you heard his words from out of the fire. ³⁷Because he loved your ancestors and chose their descendants after them, he brought you out of Egypt by his Presence and his great strength, ³⁸to drive out before you nations greater and stronger than you and to bring you into their land to give it to you for your inheritance, as it is today.

³⁹Acknowledge and take to heart this day that the Lord is God in heaven above and on the earth below. There is no other. ⁴⁰Keep his decrees and commands, which I am giving you today, so that it may go well with you and your children

---

ᵃ 48 Syriac (see also 3:9); Hebrew *Siyon*　　ᵇ 49 Hebrew *the Sea of the Arabah*　　ᶜ 3 Or *not only with our parents*

[6] "I am the LORD your God, who brought you out of Egypt, out of the land of slavery.

[7] "You shall have no other gods before[a] me.

[8] "You shall not make for yourself an image in the form of anything in heaven above or on the earth beneath or in the waters below. [9]You shall not bow down to them or worship them; for I, the LORD your God, am a jealous God, punishing the children for the sin of the parents to the third and fourth generation of those who hate me, [10]but showing love to a thousand generations of those who love me and keep my commandments.

[11] "You shall not misuse the name of the LORD your God, for the LORD will not hold anyone guiltless who misuses his name.

[12] "Observe the Sabbath day by keeping it holy, as the LORD your God has commanded you. [13]Six days you shall labor and do all your work, [14]but the seventh day is a sabbath to the LORD your God. On it you shall not do any work, neither you, nor your son or daughter, nor your male or female servant, nor your ox, your donkey or any of your animals, nor any foreigner residing in your towns, so that your male and female servants may rest, as you do. [15]Remember that you were slaves in Egypt and that the LORD your God brought you out of there with a mighty hand and an outstretched arm. Therefore the LORD your God has commanded you to observe the Sabbath day.

[16] "Honor your father and your mother, as the LORD your God has commanded you, so that you may live long and that it may go well with you in the land the LORD your God is giving you.

[17] "You shall not murder.

[18] "You shall not commit adultery.

[19] "You shall not steal.

[20] "You shall not give false testimony against your neighbor.

[21] "You shall not covet your neighbor's wife. You shall not set your desire on your neighbor's house or land, his male or female servant, his ox or donkey, or anything that belongs to your neighbor."

[22]These are the commandments the LORD proclaimed in a loud voice to your whole assembly there on the mountain from out of the fire, the cloud and the deep darkness; and he added nothing more. Then he wrote them on two stone tablets and gave them to me.

[23]When you heard the voice out of the darkness, while the mountain was ablaze with fire, all the leaders of your tribes and your elders came to me. [24]And you said, "The LORD our God has shown us his glory and his majesty, and we have heard his voice from the fire. Today we have seen that a person can live even if God speaks with them. [25]But now, why should we die? This great fire will consume us, and we will die if we hear the voice of the LORD our God any longer. [26]For what mortal has ever heard the voice of the living God speaking out of fire, as we have, and survived? [27]Go near and listen to all that the LORD our God says. Then tell us whatever the LORD our God tells you. We will listen and obey."

[28]The LORD heard you when you spoke to me, and the LORD said to me, "I have heard what this people said to you. Everything they said was good. [29]Oh, that their hearts would be inclined to fear me and keep all my commands always, so that it might go well with them and their children forever!

[30] "Go, tell them to return to their tents. [31]But you stay here with me so that I may give you all the commands, decrees and laws you are to teach them to follow in the land I am giving them to possess."

[32]So be careful to do what the LORD your God has commanded you; do not turn aside to the right or to the left. [33]Walk in obedience to all that the LORD your God

---

[a] 7 Or *besides*

has commanded you, so that you may live and prosper and prolong your days in the land that you will possess.

Love the LORD Your God

6 These are the commands, decrees and laws the LORD your God directed me to teach you to observe in the land that you are crossing the Jordan to possess, ²so that you, your children and their children after them may fear the LORD your God as long as you live by keeping all his decrees and commands that I give you, and so that you may enjoy long life. ³Hear, Israel, and be careful to obey so that it may go well with you and that you may increase greatly in a land flowing with milk and honey, just as the LORD, the God of your ancestors, promised you.

⁴Hear, O Israel: The LORD our God, the LORD is one.ᵃ ⁵Love the LORD your God with all your heart and with all your soul and with all your strength. ⁶These commandments that I give you today are to be on your hearts. ⁷Impress them on your children. Talk about them when you sit at home and when you walk along the road, when you lie down and when you get up. ⁸Tie them as symbols on your hands and bind them on your foreheads. ⁹Write them on the doorframes of your houses and on your gates.

¹⁰When the LORD your God brings you into the land he swore to your fathers, to Abraham, Isaac and Jacob, to give you—a land with large, flourishing cities you did not build, ¹¹houses filled with all kinds of good things you did not provide, wells you did not dig, and vineyards and olive groves you did not plant—then when you eat and are satisfied, ¹²be careful that you do not forget the LORD, who brought you out of Egypt, out of the land of slavery.

¹³Fear the LORD your God, serve him only and take your oaths in his name. ¹⁴Do not follow other gods, the gods of the peoples around you; ¹⁵for the LORD your God, who is among you, is a jealous God and his anger will burn against you, and he will destroy you from the face of the land. ¹⁶Do not put the LORD your God to the test as you did at Massah. ¹⁷Be sure to keep

MASSAH

(DEUTERONOMY 6:16)

This name means "doubt." It was the name Moses gave the place where the Israelites complained about being thirsty, so God gave them water from a rock. He called it this name because they had doubted the power of God to care for them. Read the story in Exodus 17:1–7.

the commands of the LORD your God and the stipulations and decrees he has given you. ¹⁸Do what is right and good in the LORD's sight, so that it may go well with you and you may go in and take over the good land the LORD promised on oath to your ancestors, ¹⁹thrusting out all your enemies before you, as the LORD said.

²⁰In the future, when your son asks you, "What is the meaning of the stipulations, decrees and laws the LORD our God has commanded you?" ²¹tell him: "We were slaves of Pharaoh in Egypt, but the LORD brought us out of Egypt with a mighty hand. ²²Before our eyes the LORD sent signs and wonders—great and terrible—on Egypt

---

ᵃ 4 Or *The LORD our God is one LORD*; or *The LORD is our God, the LORD is one*; or *The LORD is our God, the LORD alone* and Pharaoh and his whole household. ²³But he brought us out from there to bring us in and give us the land he promised on oath to our ancestors. ²⁴The LORD commanded us to obey all these decrees and to fear the LORD our God, so that we might always prosper and be kept alive, as is the case today. ²⁵And if we are careful to obey all this law before the LORD our God, as he has commanded us, that will be our righteousness."

Driving Out the Nations

7 When the LORD your God brings you into the land you are entering to possess and drives out before you many nations—the Hittites, Girgashites, Amorites, Canaanites, Perizzites, Hivites and Jebusites, seven nations larger and stronger than you— ²and when the LORD your God has delivered them over to you and you have defeated them, then you must destroy them totally.ᵃ Make no treaty with them, and show them no mercy. ³Do not intermarry with them. Do not give your daughters to their sons or take their daughters for your sons, ⁴for they will turn your children away from following me to serve other gods, and the LORD's anger will burn against you and will quickly destroy you. ⁵This is what you are to do to them: Break down their altars, smash their sacred stones, cut down their Asherah polesᵇ and burn their idols in the fire. ⁶For you are a people holy to the LORD your God. The LORD your God has chosen you out of all the peoples on the face of the earth to be his people, his treasured possession.

⁷The LORD did not set his affection on you and choose you because you were more numerous than other peoples, for you were the fewest of all peoples. ⁸But it was because the LORD loved you and kept the oath he swore to your ancestors that he brought you out with a mighty hand and redeemed you from the land of slavery, from the power of Pharaoh king of Egypt. ⁹Know therefore that the LORD your God is God; he is the faithful God, keeping his covenant of love to a thousand generations of those who love him and keep his commandments. ¹⁰But

those who hate him he will repay to
  their face by destruction;
he will not be slow to repay to their
  face those who hate him.

¹¹Therefore, take care to follow the commands, decrees and laws I give you today.

¹²If you pay attention to these laws and are careful to follow them, then the LORD your God will keep his covenant of love with you, as he swore to your

---

ᵃ 2 The Hebrew term refers to the irrevocable giving over of things or persons to the LORD, often by totally destroying them; also in verse 26.   ᵇ 5 That is, wooden symbols of the goddess Asherah; here and elsewhere in Deuteronomy

BREAK THROUGH!

Who were the Hittites, Girgashites, Amorites, Canaanites, Perizzites, Hivites and Jebusites?

(DEUTERONOMY 7:1)

These were all the foreign people who were living in the land God has promised the Israelites. They worshiped other gods, especially the goddess Ashtoreth. In spite of the fact that these nations were powerful, God told the Israelites that he would help them conquer these people, and that they'd be able to destroy everything those people had. And he warned them to be careful and not worship other gods!

ancestors. ¹³He will love you and bless you and increase your numbers. He will bless the fruit of your womb, the crops of your land—your grain, new wine and olive oil—the calves of your herds and the lambs of your flocks in the land he swore to your ancestors to give you. ¹⁴You will be blessed more than any other people; none of your men or women will be childless, nor will any of your livestock be without young. ¹⁵The LORD will keep you free from every disease. He will not inflict on you the horrible diseases you knew in Egypt, but he will inflict them on all who hate you. ¹⁶You must destroy all the peoples the LORD your God gives over to you. Do not look on them with pity and do not serve their gods, for that will be a snare to you.

¹⁷You may say to yourselves, "These nations are stronger than we are. How can we drive them out?" ¹⁸But do not be afraid of them; remember well what the LORD your God did to Pharaoh and to all Egypt. ¹⁹You saw with your own eyes the great trials, the signs and wonders, the mighty hand and outstretched arm, with which the LORD your God brought you out. The LORD your God will do the same to all the peoples you now fear. ²⁰Moreover, the LORD your God will send the hornet among them until even the survivors who hide from you have perished. ²¹Do not be terrified by them, for the LORD your God, who is among you, is a great and awesome God. ²²The LORD your God will drive out those nations before you, little by little. You will not be allowed to eliminate them all at once, or the wild animals will multiply around you. ²³But the LORD your God will deliver them over to you, throwing them into great confusion until they are destroyed. ²⁴He will give their kings into your hand, and you will wipe out their names from under heaven. No one will be able to stand up against you; you will destroy them. ²⁵The images of their gods you are to burn in the fire. Do not covet the silver and gold on them, and do not take it for yourselves, or you will be ensnared by it, for it is detestable to the LORD your God. ²⁶Do not bring a detestable thing into your house or you, like it,

will be set apart for destruction. Regard it as vile and utterly detest it, for it is set apart for destruction.

Do Not Forget the LORD

8 Be careful to follow every command I am giving you today, so that you may live and increase and may enter and possess the land the LORD promised on oath to your ancestors. ²Remember how the LORD your God led you all the way in the wilderness these forty years, to humble and test you in order to know what was in your heart, whether or not you would keep his commands. ³He humbled you, causing you to hunger and then feeding you with manna, which neither you nor your ancestors had known, to teach you that man does not live on bread alone but on every word that comes from the mouth of the LORD. ⁴Your clothes did not wear out and your feet did not swell during these forty years. ⁵Know then in your heart that as a man disciplines his son, so the LORD your God disciplines you.

⁶Observe the commands of the LORD your God, walking in obedience to him and revering him. ⁷For the LORD your God is bringing you into a good land—a land with brooks, streams, and deep springs gushing out into the valleys and hills; ⁸a land with wheat and barley, vines and fig trees, pomegranates, olive oil and honey; ⁹a land where bread will not be scarce and you will lack nothing; a land where the rocks are iron and you can dig copper out of the hills.

¹⁰When you have eaten and are satisfied, praise the LORD your God for the good land he has given you. ¹¹Be careful that you do not forget the LORD your God, failing to observe his commands, his laws and his decrees that I am giving you this day. ¹²Otherwise, when you eat and are satisfied, when you build fine houses and settle down, ¹³and when your herds and flocks grow large and your silver and gold increase and all you have is multiplied, ¹⁴then your heart will become proud and you will forget the LORD your God, who brought you out of Egypt, out of the land of slavery. ¹⁵He led you through the vast and dreadful wilderness, that thirsty and

waterless land, with its venomous snakes and scorpions. He brought you water out of hard rock. ¹⁶He gave you manna to eat in the wilderness, something your ancestors had never known, to humble and test you so that in the end it might go well with you. ¹⁷You may say to yourself, "My power and the strength of my hands have produced this wealth for me." ¹⁸But remember the Lord your God, for it is he who gives you the ability to produce wealth, and so confirms his covenant, which he swore to your ancestors, as it is today.

¹⁹If you ever forget the Lord your God and follow other gods and worship and bow down to them, I testify against you today that you will surely be destroyed. ²⁰Like the nations the Lord destroyed before you, so you will be destroyed for not obeying the Lord your God.

Not Because of Israel's Righteousness

9 Hear, Israel: You are now about to cross the Jordan to go in and dispossess nations greater and stronger than you, with large cities that have walls up to the sky. ²The people are strong and tall—Anakites! You know about them and have heard it said: "Who can stand up against the Anakites?" ³But be assured today that the Lord your God is the one who goes across ahead of you like a devouring fire. He will destroy them; he will subdue them before you. And you will drive them out and annihilate them quickly, as the Lord has promised you.

⁴After the Lord your God has driven them out before you, do not say to yourself, "The Lord has brought me here to take possession of this land because of my righteousness." No, it is on account of the wickedness of these nations that the Lord is going to drive them out before you. ⁵It is not because of your righteousness or your integrity that you are going in to take possession of their land; but on account of the wickedness of these nations, the Lord your God will drive them out before you, to accomplish what he swore to your fathers, to Abraham, Isaac and Jacob. ⁶Understand, then, that it is not because of your righteousness that

the Lord your God is giving you this good land to possess, for you are a stiff-necked people.

The Golden Calf

⁷Remember this and never forget how you aroused the anger of the Lord your God in the wilderness. From the day you left Egypt until you arrived here, you have been rebellious against the Lord. ⁸At Horeb you aroused the Lord's wrath so that he was angry enough to destroy you. ⁹When I went up on the mountain to receive the tablets of stone, the tablets of the covenant that the Lord had made with you, I stayed on the mountain forty days and forty nights; I ate no bread and drank no water. ¹⁰The Lord gave me two stone tablets inscribed by the finger of God. On them were all the commandments the Lord proclaimed to you on the mountain out of the fire, on the day of the assembly.

¹¹At the end of the forty days and forty nights, the Lord gave me the two stone tablets, the tablets of the covenant. ¹²Then the Lord told me, "Go down from here at once, because your people whom you brought out of Egypt have become corrupt. They have turned away quickly from what I commanded them and have made an idol for themselves."

¹³And the Lord said to me, "I have seen this people, and they are a stiff-necked people indeed! ¹⁴Let me alone, so that I may destroy them and blot out their name from under heaven. And I will make you into a nation stronger and more numerous than they."

¹⁵So I turned and went down from the mountain while it was ablaze with fire. And the two tablets of the covenant were in my hands. ¹⁶When I looked, I saw that you had sinned against the Lord your God; you had made for yourselves an idol cast in the shape of a calf. You had turned aside quickly from the way that the Lord had commanded you. ¹⁷So I took the two tablets and threw them out of my hands, breaking them to pieces before your eyes.

¹⁸Then once again I fell prostrate before the Lord for forty days and forty nights; I ate no bread and drank no water, because of all the sin you had committed,

doing what was evil in the Lord's sight and so arousing his anger. ¹⁹I feared the anger and wrath of the Lord, for he was angry enough with you to destroy you. But again the Lord listened to me. ²⁰And the Lord was angry enough with Aaron to destroy him, but at that time I prayed for Aaron too. ²¹Also I took that sinful thing of yours, the calf you had made, and burned it in the fire. Then I crushed it and ground it to powder as fine as dust and threw the dust into a stream that flowed down the mountain.

²²You also made the Lord angry at Taberah, at Massah and at Kibroth Hattaavah.

²³And when the Lord sent you out from Kadesh Barnea, he said, "Go up and take possession of the land I have given you." But you rebelled against the command of the Lord your God. You did not trust him or obey him. ²⁴You have been rebellious against the Lord ever since I have known you.

²⁵I lay prostrate before the Lord those forty days and forty nights because the Lord had said he would destroy you. ²⁶I prayed to the Lord and said, "Sovereign Lord, do not destroy your people, your own inheritance that you redeemed by your great power and brought out of Egypt with a mighty hand. ²⁷Remember your servants Abraham, Isaac and Jacob. Overlook the stubbornness of this people, their wickedness and their sin. ²⁸Otherwise, the country from which you brought us will say, 'Because the Lord was not able to take them into the land he had promised them, and because he hated them, he brought them out to put them to death in the wilderness.' ²⁹But they are your people, your inheritance that you brought out by your great power and your outstretched arm."

Tablets Like the First Ones

10 At that time the Lord said to me, "Chisel out two stone tablets like the first ones and come up to me on the mountain. Also make a wooden ark.ᵃ ²I will write on the tablets the words that were on the first tablets, which you broke. Then you are to put them in the ark."

³So I made the ark out of acacia wood and chiseled out two stone tablets like the first ones, and I went up on the mountain with the two tablets in my hands. ⁴The Lord wrote on these tablets what he had written before, the Ten Commandments he had proclaimed to you on the mountain, out of the fire, on the day of the assembly. And the Lord gave them to me. ⁵Then I came back down the mountain and put the tablets in the ark I had made, as the Lord commanded me, and they are there now.

⁶(The Israelites traveled from the wells of Bene Jaakan to Moserah. There Aaron died and was buried, and Eleazar his son succeeded him as priest. ⁷From there they traveled to Gudgodah and on to Jotbathah, a land with streams of water. ⁸At that time the Lord set apart the tribe of Levi to carry the ark of the covenant of the Lord, to stand before the Lord to minister and to pronounce blessings in his name, as they still do today. ⁹That is why the Levites have no share or inheritance among their fellow Israelites; the Lord is their inheritance, as the Lord your God told them.)

¹⁰Now I had stayed on the mountain forty days and forty nights, as I did the first time, and the Lord listened to me at this time also. It was not his will to destroy you. ¹¹"Go," the Lord said to me, "and lead the people on their way, so that they may enter and possess the land I swore to their ancestors to give them."

Fear the Lord

¹²And now, Israel, what does the Lord your God ask of you but to fear the Lord your God, to walk in obedience to him, to love him, to serve the Lord your God with all your heart and with all your soul, ¹³and to observe the Lord's commands and decrees that I am giving you today for your own good?

¹⁴To the Lord your God belong the heavens, even the highest heavens, the earth and everything in it. ¹⁵Yet the Lord set his affection on your ancestors and loved

---

ᵃ 1 That is, a chest

them, and he chose you, their descendants, above all the nations—as it is today. ¹⁶Circumcise your hearts, therefore, and do not be stiff-necked any longer. ¹⁷For the LORD your God is God of gods and Lord of lords, the great God, mighty and awesome, who shows no partiality and accepts no bribes. ¹⁸He defends the cause of the fatherless and the widow, and loves the foreigner residing among you, giving them food and clothing. ¹⁹And you are to love those who are foreigners, for you yourselves were foreigners in Egypt. ²⁰Fear the LORD your God and serve him. Hold fast to him and take your oaths in his name. ²¹He is the one you praise; he is your God, who performed for you those great and awesome wonders you saw with your own eyes. ²²Your ancestors who went down into Egypt were seventy in all, and now the LORD your God has made you as numerous as the stars in the sky.

Love and Obey the LORD

11 Love the LORD your God and keep his requirements, his decrees, his laws and his commands always. ²Remember today that your children were not the ones who saw and experienced the discipline of the LORD your God: his majesty, his mighty hand, his outstretched arm; ³the signs he performed and the things he did in the heart of Egypt, both to Pharaoh king of Egypt and to his whole country; ⁴what he did to the Egyptian army, to its horses and chariots, how he overwhelmed them with the waters of the Red Sea[a] as they were pursuing you, and how the LORD brought lasting ruin on them. ⁵It was not your children who saw what he did for you in the wilderness until you arrived at this place, ⁶and what he did to Dathan and Abiram, sons of Eliab the Reubenite, when the earth opened its mouth right in the middle of all Israel and swallowed them up with their households, their tents and every living thing that belonged to them. ⁷But it was your own eyes that saw all these great things the LORD has done.

⁸Observe therefore all the commands I am giving you today, so that you may have the strength to go in and take over the land that you are crossing the Jordan to possess, ⁹and so that you may live long in the land the LORD swore to your ancestors to give to them and their descendants, a land flowing with milk and honey. ¹⁰The land you are entering to take over is not like the land of Egypt, from which you have come, where you planted your seed and irrigated it by foot as in a vegetable garden. ¹¹But the land you are crossing the Jordan to take possession of is a land of mountains and valleys that drinks rain from heaven. ¹²It is a land the LORD your God cares for; the eyes of the LORD your God are continually on it from the beginning of the year to its end.

¹³So if you faithfully obey the commands I am giving you today—to love the LORD your God and to serve him with all your heart and with all your soul— ¹⁴then I will send rain on your land in its season, both autumn and spring rains, so that you may gather in your grain, new wine and olive oil. ¹⁵I will provide grass in the fields for your cattle, and you will eat and be satisfied.

¹⁶Be careful, or you will be enticed to turn away and worship other gods and bow down to them. ¹⁷Then the LORD's anger will burn against you, and he will shut up the heavens so that it will not rain and the ground will yield no produce, and you will soon perish from the good land the LORD is giving you. ¹⁸Fix these words of mine in your hearts and minds; tie them as symbols on your hands and bind them on your foreheads. ¹⁹Teach them to your children, talking about them when you sit at home and when you walk along the road, when you lie down and when you get up. ²⁰Write them on the doorframes of your houses and on your gates, ²¹so that your days and the days of your children may be many in the land the LORD swore to give your ancestors, as many as the days that the heavens are above the earth.

²²If you carefully observe all these commands I am giving you to follow—to love the LORD your God, to walk in obedience

---

a 4 Or *the Sea of Reeds*

to him and to hold fast to him— ²³then the LORD will drive out all these nations before you, and you will dispossess nations larger and stronger than you. ²⁴Every place where you set your foot will be yours: Your territory will extend from the desert to Lebanon, and from the Euphrates River to the Mediterranean Sea. ²⁵No one will be able to stand against you. The LORD your God, as he promised you, will put the terror and fear of you on the whole land, wherever you go.

²⁶See, I am setting before you today a blessing and a curse— ²⁷the blessing if you obey the commands of the LORD your God that I am giving you today; ²⁸the curse if you disobey the commands of the LORD your God and turn from the way that I command you today by following other gods, which you have not known. ²⁹When the LORD your God has brought you into the land you are entering to possess, you are to proclaim on Mount Gerizim the blessings, and on Mount Ebal the curses. ³⁰As you know, these mountains are across the Jordan, westward, toward the setting sun, near the great trees of Moreh, in the territory of those Canaanites living in the Arabah in the vicinity of Gilgal. ³¹You are about to cross the Jordan to enter and take possession of the land the LORD your God is giving you. When you have taken it over and are living there, ³²be sure that you obey all the decrees and laws I am setting before you today.

The One Place of Worship

12 These are the decrees and laws you must be careful to follow in the land that the LORD, the God of your ancestors, has given you to possess—as long as you live in the land. ²Destroy completely all the places on the high mountains, on the hills and under every spreading tree, where the nations you are dispossessing worship their gods. ³Break down their altars, smash their sacred stones and burn their Asherah poles in the fire; cut down the idols of their gods and wipe out their names from those places.

⁴You must not worship the LORD your God in their way. ⁵But you are to seek the place the LORD your God will choose from among all your tribes to put his Name there for his dwelling. To that place you must go; ⁶there bring your burnt offerings and sacrifices, your tithes and special gifts, what you have vowed to give and your freewill offerings, and the firstborn of your herds and flocks. ⁷There, in the presence of the LORD your God, you and your families shall eat and shall rejoice in everything you have put your hand to, because the LORD your God has blessed you.

⁸You are not to do as we do here today, everyone doing as they see fit, ⁹since you have not yet reached the resting place and the inheritance the LORD your God is giving you. ¹⁰But you will cross the Jordan and settle in the land the LORD your God is giving you as an inheritance, and he will give you rest from all your enemies around you so that you will live in safety. ¹¹Then to the place the LORD your God will choose as a dwelling for his Name—there you are to bring everything I command you: your burnt offerings and sacrifices, your tithes and special gifts, and all the choice possessions you have vowed to the LORD. ¹²And there rejoice before the LORD your God—you, your sons and daughters, your male and female servants, and the Levites from your towns who have no allotment or inheritance of their own. ¹³Be careful not to sacrifice your burnt offerings anywhere you please. ¹⁴Offer them only at the place the LORD will choose in one of your tribes, and there observe everything I command you.

¹⁵Nevertheless, you may slaughter your animals in any of your towns and eat as much of the meat as you want, as if it were gazelle or deer, according to the blessing the LORD your God gives you. Both the ceremonially unclean and the clean may eat it. ¹⁶But you must not eat the blood; pour it out on the ground like water. ¹⁷You must not eat in your own towns the tithe of your grain and new wine and olive oil, or the firstborn of your herds and flocks, or whatever you have vowed to give, or your freewill offerings or special gifts. ¹⁸Instead, you are to eat them in the presence of the LORD your God at the place the LORD your God will

BREAKTHROUGH!

Why couldn't they eat meat with blood?

(DEUTERONOMY 12:16)

Life is in the blood (see Genesis 9:4 and Leviticus 17:11–12), and life is a gift from God. Therefore, blood is "sacred" and was used only in the sacrifices for the forgiveness of sins and in other kinds of offerings. Also, the foreign nations ate and drank the blood from the sacrifices they made to their gods, so God didn't want his people to do what they did.

choose—you, your sons and daughters, your male and female servants, and the Levites from your towns—and you are to rejoice before the LORD your God in everything you put your hand to. ¹⁹Be careful not to neglect the Levites as long as you live in your land.

²⁰When the LORD your God has enlarged your territory as he promised you, and you crave meat and say, "I would like some meat," then you may eat as much of it as you want. ²¹If the place where the LORD your God chooses to put his Name is too far away from you, you may slaughter animals from the herds and flocks the LORD has given you, as I have commanded you, and in your own towns you may eat as much of them as you want. ²²Eat them as

you would gazelle or deer. Both the ceremonially unclean and the clean may eat. ²³But be sure you do not eat the blood, because the blood is the life, and you must not eat the life with the meat. ²⁴You must not eat the blood; pour it out on the ground like water. ²⁵Do not eat it, so that it may go well with you and your children after you, because you will be doing what is right in the eyes of the LORD.

²⁶But take your consecrated things and whatever you have vowed to give, and go to the place the LORD will choose. ²⁷Present your burnt offerings on the altar of the LORD your God, both the meat and the blood. The blood of your sacrifices must be poured beside the altar of the LORD your God, but you may eat the meat. ²⁸Be careful to obey all these regulations I am giving you, so that it may always go well with you and your children after you, because you will be doing what is good and right in the eyes of the LORD your God.

²⁹The LORD your God will cut off before you the nations you are about to invade and dispossess. But when you have driven them out and settled in their land, ³⁰and after they have been destroyed before you, be careful not to be ensnared by inquiring about their gods, saying, "How do these nations serve their gods? We will do the same." ³¹You must not worship the LORD your God in their way, because in worshiping their gods, they do all kinds of detestable things the LORD hates. They even burn their sons and daughters in the fire as sacrifices to their gods.

³²See that you do all I command you; do not add to it or take away from it.ᵃ

Worshiping Other Gods

13ᵇ If a prophet, or one who foretells by dreams, appears among you and announces to you a sign or wonder, ²and if the sign or wonder spoken of takes place, and the prophet says, "Let us follow other gods" (gods you have not known) "and let us worship them," ³you must not listen to the words of that prophet or dreamer. The LORD your God is testing you to

ᵃ 32 In Hebrew texts this verse (12:32) is numbered 13:1.
ᵇ In Hebrew texts 13:1-18 is numbered 13:2-19.

find out whether you love him with all your heart and with all your soul. ⁴It is the LORD your God you must follow, and him you must revere. Keep his commands and obey him; serve him and hold fast to him. ⁵That prophet or dreamer must be put to death for inciting rebellion against the LORD your God, who brought you out of Egypt and redeemed you from the land of slavery. That prophet or dreamer tried to turn you from the way the LORD your God commanded you to follow. You must purge the evil from among you.

⁶If your very own brother, or your son or daughter, or the wife you love, or your closest friend secretly entices you, saying, "Let us go and worship other gods" (gods that neither you nor your ancestors have known, ⁷gods of the peoples around you, whether near or far, from one end of the land to the other), ⁸do not yield to them or listen to them. Show them no pity. Do not spare them or shield them. ⁹You must certainly put them to death. Your hand must be the first in putting them to death, and then the hands of all the people. ¹⁰Stone them to death, because they tried to turn you away from the LORD your God, who brought you out of Egypt, out of the land of slavery. ¹¹Then all Israel will hear and be afraid, and no one among you will do such an evil thing again.

¹²If you hear it said about one of the towns the LORD your God is giving you to live in ¹³that troublemakers have arisen among you and have led the people of their town astray, saying, "Let us go and worship other gods" (gods you have not known), ¹⁴then you must inquire, probe and investigate it thoroughly. And if it is true and it has been proved that this detestable thing has been done among you, ¹⁵you must certainly put to the sword all who live in that town. You must destroy it completely,ᵃ both its people and its livestock. ¹⁶You are to gather all the plunder of the town into the middle of the public square and completely burn the town and all its plunder as a whole burnt offering to the LORD your God. That town is to remain a ruin forever, never to be rebuilt, ¹⁷and none of the condemned thingsᵃ are

to be found in your hands. Then the LORD will turn from his fierce anger, will show you mercy, and will have compassion on you. He will increase your numbers, as he promised on oath to your ancestors — ¹⁸because you obey the LORD your God by keeping all his commands that I am giving you today and doing what is right in his eyes.

Clean and Unclean Food

14 You are the children of the LORD your God. Do not cut yourselves or shave the front of your heads for the dead, ²for you are a people holy to the LORD your God. Out of all the peoples on the face of the earth, the LORD has chosen you to be his treasured possession.

³Do not eat any detestable thing. ⁴These are the animals you may eat: the ox, the sheep, the goat, ⁵the deer, the gazelle, the roe deer, the wild goat, the ibex, the antelope and the mountain sheep.ᵇ ⁶You may eat any animal that has a divided hoof and that chews the cud. ⁷However, of those that chew the cud or that have a divided hoof you may not eat the camel, the rabbit or the hyrax. Although they chew the cud, they do not have a divided hoof; they are ceremonially unclean for you. ⁸The pig is also unclean; although it has a divided hoof, it does not chew the cud. You are not to eat their meat or touch their carcasses.

⁹Of all the creatures living in the water, you may eat any that has fins and scales. ¹⁰But anything that does not have fins and scales you may not eat; for you it is unclean.

¹¹You may eat any clean bird. ¹²But these you may not eat: the eagle, the vulture, the black vulture, ¹³the red kite, the black kite, any kind of falcon, ¹⁴any kind of raven, ¹⁵the horned owl, the screech owl, the gull, any kind of hawk, ¹⁶the little owl, the great owl, the white owl, ¹⁷the desert owl, the osprey, the cormorant, ¹⁸the stork, any kind of heron, the hoopoe and the bat.

ᵃ 15,17 The Hebrew term refers to the irrevocable giving over of things or persons to the LORD, often by totally destroying them.   ᵇ 5 The precise identification of some of the birds and animals in this chapter is uncertain.

¹⁹All flying insects are unclean to you; do not eat them. ²⁰But any winged creature that is clean you may eat.

²¹Do not eat anything you find already dead. You may give it to the foreigner residing in any of your towns, and they may eat it, or you may sell it to any other foreigner. But you are a people holy to the LORD your God.

Do not cook a young goat in its mother's milk.

Tithes

²²Be sure to set aside a tenth of all that your fields produce each year. ²³Eat the tithe of your grain, new wine and olive oil, and the firstborn of your herds and flocks in the presence of the LORD your God at

BREAKTHROUGH!

Why couldn't they cook a young goat in its mother's milk?

(DEUTERONOMY 14:21)

That's really weird! It might be because the mother's milk was supposed to make the little goat grow and develop, but if it was used for the opposite purpose, which was to use the milk to cook the animal after it had died, well, that was just too cruel! God wanted his people to be good and compassionate. But it was also possible that God prohibited this because the Canaanites performed this as a kind of magic practice, and they didn't believe in the true God.

BREAKTHROUGH!

Why couldn't they eat certain animals?

(DEUTERONOMY 14:3-21)

There were two main reasons. One was because some animals were used in the religious practices of the foreign nations. God didn't want the Israelites to be affected by this and try to be like them. The second reason was because those animals ate garbage and spoiled food. They lived in dirty surroundings, so they might spread diseases and make the Israelites sick.

the place he will choose as a dwelling for his Name, so that you may learn to revere the LORD your God always. ²⁴But if that place is too distant and you have been blessed by the LORD your God and cannot carry your tithe (because the place where the LORD will choose to put his Name is so far away), ²⁵then exchange your tithe for silver, and take the silver with you and go to the place the LORD your God will choose. ²⁶Use the silver to buy whatever you like: cattle, sheep, wine or other fermented drink, or anything you wish. Then you and your household shall eat there in the presence of the LORD your God and rejoice. [27]And do not neglect the Levites living in your towns, for they have no allotment or inheritance of their own.

[28]At the end of every three years, bring all the tithes of that year's produce and store it in your towns, [29]so that the Levites (who have no allotment or inheritance of their own) and the foreigners, the fatherless and the widows who live in your towns may come and eat and be satisfied, and so that the LORD your God may bless you in all the work of your hands.

The Year for Canceling Debts

15 At the end of every seven years you must cancel debts. [2]This is how it is to be done: Every creditor shall cancel any loan they have made to a fellow Israelite. They shall not require payment from anyone among their own people, because the LORD's time for canceling debts has been proclaimed. [3]You may require payment from a foreigner, but you must cancel any debt your fellow Israelite owes you. [4]However, there need be no poor people among you, for in the land the LORD your God is giving you to possess as your inheritance, he will richly bless you, [5]if only you fully obey the LORD your God and are careful to follow all these commands I am giving you today. [6]For the LORD your God will bless you as he has promised, and you will lend to many nations but will borrow from none. You will rule over many nations but none will rule over you.

[7]If anyone is poor among your fellow Israelites in any of the towns of the land the LORD your God is giving you, do not be hardhearted or tightfisted toward them. [8]Rather, be openhanded and freely lend them whatever they need. [9]Be careful not to harbor this wicked thought: "The seventh year, the year for canceling debts, is near," so that you do not show ill will toward the needy among your fellow Israelites and give them nothing. They may then appeal to the LORD against you, and you will be found guilty of sin. [10]Give generously to them and do so without a grudging heart; then because of this the LORD your God will bless you in all your work and in everything you put your hand to. [11]There will always be poor people in the land. Therefore I command you to be openhanded toward your fellow Israelites who are poor and needy in your land.

Freeing Servants

[12]If any of your people—Hebrew men or women—sell themselves to you and serve you six years, in the seventh year you must let them go free. [13]And when you release them, do not send them away empty-handed. [14]Supply them liberally from your flock, your threshing floor and your winepress. Give to them as the LORD your God has blessed you. [15]Remember that you were slaves in Egypt and the LORD your God redeemed you. That is why I give you this command today.

[16]But if your servant says to you, "I do not want to leave you," because he loves you and your family and is well off with you, [17]then take an awl and push it through his earlobe into the door, and he will become your servant for life. Do the same for your female servant.

[18]Do not consider it a hardship to set your servant free, because their service to you these six years has been worth twice as much as that of a hired hand. And the LORD your God will bless you in everything you do.

The Firstborn Animals

[19]Set apart for the LORD your God every firstborn male of your herds and flocks. Do not put the firstborn of your cows to work, and do not shear the firstborn of your sheep. [20]Each year you and your family are to eat them in the presence of the LORD your God at the place he will choose. [21]If an animal has a defect, is lame or blind, or has any serious flaw, you must not sacrifice it to the LORD your God. [22]You are to eat it in your own towns. Both the ceremonially unclean and the clean may eat it, as if it were gazelle or deer. [23]But you must not eat the blood; pour it out on the ground like water.

The Passover

16 Observe the month of Aviv and celebrate the Passover of the LORD your God, because in the month of Aviv he brought you out of Egypt by night. [2]Sacrifice

Aviv

(DEUTERONOMY 16:1)
The first month of the Jewish lunar calendar.
It would be more or less from the middle
of March to the middle of April in our solar
calendar.

as the Passover to the LORD your God
an animal from your flock or herd at the
place the LORD will choose as a dwelling
for his Name. ³Do not eat it with bread
made with yeast, but for seven days eat
unleavened bread, the bread of affliction,
because you left Egypt in haste—so that
all the days of your life you may remember the time of your departure from Egypt.
⁴Let no yeast be found in your possession in all your land for seven days. Do
not let any of the meat you sacrifice on
the evening of the first day remain until
morning.

⁵You must not sacrifice the Passover
in any town the LORD your God gives you
⁶except in the place he will choose as a
dwelling for his Name. There you must
sacrifice the Passover in the evening,
when the sun goes down, on the anni-
versary^a of your departure from Egypt.
⁷Roast it and eat it at the place the LORD
your God will choose. Then in the morning return to your tents. ⁸For six days eat
unleavened bread and on the seventh

day hold an assembly to the LORD your
God and do no work.

The Festival of Weeks

⁹Count off seven weeks from the time
you begin to put the sickle to the standing grain. ¹⁰Then celebrate the Festival of
Weeks to the LORD your God by giving a
freewill offering in proportion to the blessings the LORD your God has given you.
¹¹And rejoice before the LORD your God at
the place he will choose as a dwelling for
his Name—you, your sons and daughters, your male and female servants, the
Levites in your towns, and the foreigners, the fatherless and the widows living
among you. ¹²Remember that you were
slaves in Egypt, and follow carefully these
decrees.

The Festival of Tabernacles

¹³Celebrate the Festival of Tabernacles
for seven days after you have gathered
the produce of your threshing floor and
your winepress. ¹⁴Be joyful at your festival—you, your sons and daughters, your
male and female servants, and the Levites, the foreigners, the fatherless and
the widows who live in your towns. ¹⁵For
seven days celebrate the festival to the
LORD your God at the place the LORD will
choose. For the LORD your God will bless
you in all your harvest and in all the work
of your hands, and your joy will be complete.

¹⁶Three times a year all your men must
appear before the LORD your God at the
place he will choose: at the Festival of
Unleavened Bread, the Festival of Weeks
and the Festival of Tabernacles. No one
should appear before the LORD empty-
handed: ¹⁷Each of you must bring a gift in
proportion to the way the LORD your God
has blessed you.

Judges

¹⁸Appoint judges and officials for each
of your tribes in every town the LORD your
God is giving you, and they shall judge
the people fairly. ¹⁹Do not pervert justice
or show partiality. Do not accept a bribe,

---

^a 6 Or down, at the time of day

for a bribe blinds the eyes of the wise and twists the words of the innocent. [20]Follow justice and justice alone, so that you may live and possess the land the LORD your God is giving you.

Worshiping Other Gods

[21]Do not set up any wooden Asherah pole beside the altar you build to the LORD your God, [22]and do not erect a sacred stone, for these the LORD your God hates.

17 Do not sacrifice to the LORD your God an ox or a sheep that has any defect or flaw in it, for that would be detestable to him.

[2]If a man or woman living among you in one of the towns the LORD gives you is found doing evil in the eyes of the LORD your God in violation of his covenant, [3]and contrary to my command has worshiped other gods, bowing down to them or to the sun or the moon or the stars in the sky, [4]and this has been brought to your attention, then you must investigate it thoroughly. If it is true and it has been proved that this detestable thing has been done in Israel, [5]take the man or woman who has done this evil deed to your city gate and stone that person to death. [6]On the testimony of two or three witnesses a person is to be put to death, but no one is to be put to death on the testimony of only one witness. [7]The hands of the witnesses must be the first in putting that person to death, and then the hands of all the people. You must purge the evil from among you.

Law Courts

[8]If cases come before your courts that are too difficult for you to judge—whether bloodshed, lawsuits or assaults—take them to the place the LORD your God will choose. [9]Go to the Levitical priests and to the judge who is in office at that time. Inquire of them and they will give you the verdict. [10]You must act according to the decisions they give you at the place the LORD will choose. Be careful to do everything they instruct you to do. [11]Act according to whatever they teach you and the decisions they give you. Do not turn aside from what they tell you, to the right

BREAKTHROUGH!

Why did God order death by stoning as a punishment for sin?

(DEUTERONOMY 17:7)

Maybe it was so all the people could participate. In that way, everyone could judge the wrongdoer and enforce justice. Everyone would evaluate what had happened, and everyone would be part of that death.

or to the left. [12]Anyone who shows contempt for the judge or for the priest who stands ministering there to the LORD your God is to be put to death. You must purge the evil from Israel. [13]All the people will hear and be afraid, and will not be contemptuous again.

The King

[14]When you enter the land the LORD your God is giving you and have taken possession of it and settled in it, and you say, "Let us set a king over us like all the nations around us," [15]be sure to appoint over you a king the LORD your God chooses. He must be from among your fellow Israelites. Do not place a foreigner over you, one who is not an Israelite. [16]The king, moreover, must not acquire great numbers of horses for himself or make the people return to Egypt to get more of

them, for the Lord has told you, "You are not to go back that way again." [17]He must not take many wives, or his heart will be led astray. He must not accumulate large amounts of silver and gold.

[18]When he takes the throne of his kingdom, he is to write for himself on a scroll a copy of this law, taken from that of the Levitical priests. [19]It is to be with him, and he is to read it all the days of his life so that he may learn to revere the Lord his God and follow carefully all the words of this law and these decrees [20]and not consider himself better than his fellow Israelites and turn from the law to the right or to the left. Then he and his descendants will reign a long time over his kingdom in Israel.

Offerings for Priests and Levites

18 The Levitical priests—indeed, the whole tribe of Levi—are to have no allotment or inheritance with Israel. They shall live on the food offerings presented to the Lord, for that is their inheritance. [2]They shall have no inheritance among their fellow Israelites; the Lord is their inheritance, as he promised them.

[3]This is the share due the priests from the people who sacrifice a bull or a sheep: the shoulder, the internal organs and the meat from the head. [4]You are to give them the firstfruits of your grain, new wine and olive oil, and the first wool from the shearing of your sheep, [5]for the Lord your God has chosen them and their descendants out of all your tribes to stand and minister in the Lord's name always.

[6]If a Levite moves from one of your towns anywhere in Israel where he is living, and comes in all earnestness to the place the Lord will choose, [7]he may minister in the name of the Lord his God like all his fellow Levites who serve there in the presence of the Lord. [8]He is to share equally in their benefits, even though he has received money from the sale of family possessions.

Occult Practices

[9]When you enter the land the Lord your God is giving you, do not learn to imitate the detestable ways of the nations there.

[10]Let no one be found among you who sacrifices their son or daughter in the fire, who practices divination or sorcery, interprets omens, engages in witchcraft, [11]or casts spells, or who is a medium or spiritist or who consults the dead. [12]Anyone who does these things is detestable to the Lord; because of these same detestable practices the Lord your God will drive out those nations before you. [13]You must be blameless before the Lord your God.

The Prophet

[14]The nations you will dispossess listen to those who practice sorcery or divination. But as for you, the Lord your God has not permitted you to do so. [15]The Lord your God will raise up for you a prophet like me from among you, from your fellow Israelites. You must listen to him. [16]For this is what you asked of the Lord your God at Horeb on the day of the assembly when you said, "Let us not hear the voice of the Lord our God nor see this great fire anymore, or we will die."

[17]The Lord said to me: "What they say is good. [18]I will raise up for them a prophet like you from among their fellow Israelites, and I will put my words in his mouth. He will tell them everything I command him. [19]I myself will call to account anyone who does not listen to my words that the prophet speaks in my name. [20]But a prophet who presumes to speak in my name anything I have not commanded, or a prophet who speaks in the name of other gods, is to be put to death."

[21]You may say to yourselves, "How can we know when a message has not been spoken by the Lord?" [22]If what a prophet proclaims in the name of the Lord does not take place or come true, that is a message the Lord has not spoken. That prophet has spoken presumptuously, so do not be alarmed.

Cities of Refuge

19 When the Lord your God has destroyed the nations whose land he is giving you, and when you have driven them out and settled in their towns and houses, [2]then set aside for yourselves three cities in the land the Lord your God is giving you to possess. ³Determine the distances involved and divide into three parts the land the Lᴏʀᴅ your God is giving you as an inheritance, so that a person who kills someone may flee for refuge to one of these cities.

⁴This is the rule concerning anyone who kills a person and flees there for safety—anyone who kills a neighbor unintentionally, without malice aforethought. ⁵For instance, a man may go into the forest with his neighbor to cut wood, and as he swings his ax to fell a tree, the head may fly off and hit his neighbor and kill him. That man may flee to one of these cities and save his life. ⁶Otherwise, the avenger of blood might pursue him in a rage, overtake him if the distance is too great, and kill him even though he is not deserving of death, since he did it to his neighbor without malice aforethought. ⁷This is why I command you to set aside for yourselves three cities.

⁸If the Lᴏʀᴅ your God enlarges your territory, as he promised on oath to your ancestors, and gives you the whole land he promised them, ⁹because you carefully follow all these laws I command you today—to love the Lᴏʀᴅ your God and to walk always in obedience to him—then you are to set aside three more cities. ¹⁰Do this so that innocent blood will not be shed in your land, which the Lᴏʀᴅ your God is giving you as your inheritance, and so that you will not be guilty of bloodshed.

¹¹But if out of hate someone lies in wait, assaults and kills a neighbor, and then flees to one of these cities, ¹²the killer shall be sent for by the town elders, be brought back from the city, and be handed over to the avenger of blood to die. ¹³Show no pity. You must purge from Israel the guilt of shedding innocent blood, so that it may go well with you.

¹⁴Do not move your neighbor's boundary stone set up by your predecessors in the inheritance you receive in the land the Lᴏʀᴅ your God is giving you to possess.

Witnesses

¹⁵One witness is not enough to convict anyone accused of any crime or offense they may have committed. A matter must be established by the testimony of two or three witnesses.

¹⁶If a malicious witness takes the stand to accuse someone of a crime, ¹⁷the two people involved in the dispute must stand in the presence of the Lᴏʀᴅ before the priests and the judges who are in office at the time. ¹⁸The judges must make a thorough investigation, and if the witness proves to be a liar, giving false testimony against a fellow Israelite, ¹⁹then do to the false witness as that witness intended to do to the other party. You must purge the evil from among you. ²⁰The rest of the people will hear of this and be afraid, and never again will such an evil thing be done among you. ²¹Show no pity: life for life, eye for eye, tooth for tooth, hand for hand, foot for foot.

Going to War

20 When you go to war against your enemies and see horses and chariots and an army greater than yours, do not be afraid of them, because the Lᴏʀᴅ your God, who brought you up out of Egypt, will be with you. ²When you are about to go into battle, the priest shall come forward and address the army. ³He shall say: "Hear, Israel: Today you are going into battle against your enemies. Do not be fainthearted or afraid; do not panic or be terrified by them. ⁴For the Lᴏʀᴅ your God is the one who goes with you to fight for you against your enemies to give you victory."

⁵The officers shall say to the army: "Has anyone built a new house and not yet begun to live in it? Let him go home, or he may die in battle and someone else may begin to live in it. ⁶Has anyone planted a vineyard and not begun to enjoy it? Let him go home, or he may die in battle and someone else enjoy it. ⁷Has anyone become pledged to a woman and not married her? Let him go home, or he may die in battle and someone else marry her." ⁸Then the officers shall add, "Is anyone afraid or fainthearted? Let him go home so that his fellow soldiers will not become disheartened too." ⁹When the officers have finished speaking to the army, they shall appoint commanders over it.

BREAK THROUGH!

Why does God say not to forgive any fault? Aren't we supposed to forgive?

(DEUTERONOMY 19:19-21)

God wanted his people to be holy and just and not allow any kind of sin. That way they could all live peacefully and happily. These rules have to do with the "eye for an eye" law (something like "making the punishment fit the crime"). These laws were set up like a punishment or like fair pay in order to avoid an uneven punishment of the crime committed. For example, if somebody broke another person's tooth in a fight, the punishment shouldn't be more than making the attacker lose his own tooth.

Thank God that now these laws have been improved or annulled by the fair and loving laws that Jesus taught us when he was here on earth. (You can read them in Matthew 5:21-26,38-48 and Luke 6:27-36.)

BREAK THROUGH!

Is it God who makes bad things happen?

(DEUTERONOMY 20)

All those people had become very bad. They worshiped other gods and did sinful things. They were so bad that God couldn't stand them anymore, so he decided to get rid of them and give their land to the Israelites. But then notice this: God ordered the Israelites to kill the men in the cities, but only the king and his court, the most important military officers and the priests who lived in the cities. The common people, who were most of the people, lived in unprotected small villages.

---

¹⁰When you march up to attack a city, make its people an offer of peace. ¹¹If they accept and open their gates, all the people in it shall be subject to forced labor and shall work for you. ¹²If they refuse to make peace and they engage you in battle, lay siege to that city. ¹³When the LORD your God delivers it into your hand, put to the sword all the men in it. ¹⁴As for the women, the children, the livestock and everything else in the city, you may take these as plunder for yourselves. And you may use the plunder the LORD your God gives you from your enemies. ¹⁵This is how you are to treat all the cities that are at a distance from you and do not belong to the nations nearby.

¹⁶However, in the cities of the nations the LORD your God is giving you as an inheritance, do not leave alive anything that breathes. ¹⁷Completely destroy*ᵃ* them—

ᵃ 17 The Hebrew term refers to the irrevocable giving over of things or persons to the LORD, often by totally destroying them.

the Hittites, Amorites, Canaanites, Perizzites, Hivites and Jebusites—as the Lord your God has commanded you. [18]Otherwise, they will teach you to follow all the detestable things they do in worshiping their gods, and you will sin against the Lord your God.

[19]When you lay siege to a city for a long time, fighting against it to capture it, do not destroy its trees by putting an ax to them, because you can eat their fruit. Do not cut them down. Are the trees people, that you should besiege them?[a] [20]However, you may cut down trees that you know are not fruit trees and use them to build siege works until the city at war with you falls.

Atonement for an Unsolved Murder

21 If someone is found slain, lying in a field in the land the Lord your God is giving you to possess, and it is not known who the killer was, [2]your elders and judges shall go out and measure the distance from the body to the neighboring towns. [3]Then the elders of the town nearest the body shall take a heifer that has never been worked and has never worn a yoke [4]and lead it down to a valley that has not been plowed or planted and where there is a flowing stream. There in the valley they are to break the heifer's neck. [5]The Levitical priests shall step forward, for the Lord your God has chosen them to minister and to pronounce blessings in the name of the Lord and to decide all cases of dispute and assault. [6]Then all the elders of the town nearest the body shall wash their hands over the heifer whose neck was broken in the valley, [7]and they shall declare: "Our hands did not shed this blood, nor did our eyes see it done. [8]Accept this atonement for your people Israel, whom you have redeemed, Lord, and do not hold your people guilty of the blood of an innocent person." Then the bloodshed will be atoned for, [9]and you will have purged from yourselves the guilt of shedding innocent blood, since you have done what is right in the eyes of the Lord.

Marrying a Captive Woman

[10]When you go to war against your enemies and the Lord your God delivers them into your hands and you take captives, [11]if you notice among the captives a beautiful woman and are attracted to her, you may take her as your wife. [12]Bring her into your home and have her shave her head, trim her nails [13]and put aside the clothes she was wearing when captured. After she has lived in your house and mourned her father and mother for a full month, then you may go to her and be her husband and she shall be your wife. [14]If you are not pleased with her, let her go wherever she wishes. You must not sell her or treat her as a slave, since you have dishonored her.

The Right of the Firstborn

[15]If a man has two wives, and he loves one but not the other, and both bear him sons but the firstborn is the son of the wife he does not love, [16]when he wills his property to his sons, he must not give the rights of the firstborn to the son of the wife he loves in preference to his actual firstborn, the son of the wife he does not love. [17]He must acknowledge the son of his unloved wife as the firstborn by giving him a double share of all he has. That son is the first sign of his father's strength. The right of the firstborn belongs to him.

A Rebellious Son

[18]If someone has a stubborn and rebellious son who does not obey his father and mother and will not listen to them when they discipline him, [19]his father and mother shall take hold of him and bring him to the elders at the gate of his town. [20]They shall say to the elders, "This son of ours is stubborn and rebellious. He will not obey us. He is a glutton and a drunkard." [21]Then all the men of his town are to stone him to death. You must purge the evil from among you. All Israel will hear of it and be afraid.

Various Laws

[22]If someone guilty of a capital offense is put to death and their body is exposed on a pole, [23]you must not leave the body

---

[a] 19 Or down to use in the siege, for the fruit trees are for the benefit of people.

hanging on the pole overnight. Be sure to bury it that same day, because anyone who is hung on a pole is under God's curse. You must not desecrate the land the LORD your God is giving you as an inheritance.

22 If you see your fellow Israelite's ox or sheep straying, do not ignore it but be sure to take it back to its owner. ²If they do not live near you or if you do not know who owns it, take it home with you and keep it until they come looking for it. Then give it back. ³Do the same if you find their donkey or cloak or anything else they have lost. Do not ignore it.

⁴If you see your fellow Israelite's donkey or ox fallen on the road, do not ignore it. Help the owner get it to its feet.

⁵A woman must not wear men's clothing, nor a man wear women's clothing, for the LORD your God detests anyone who does this.

⁶If you come across a bird's nest beside the road, either in a tree or on the ground, and the mother is sitting on the young or on the eggs, do not take the mother with the young. ⁷You may take the young, but be sure to let the mother go, so that it may go well with you and you may have a long life.

⁸When you build a new house, make a parapet around your roof so that you may not bring the guilt of bloodshed on your house if someone falls from the roof.

⁹Do not plant two kinds of seed in your vineyard; if you do, not only the crops you plant but also the fruit of the vineyard will be defiled.ᵃ

¹⁰Do not plow with an ox and a donkey yoked together.

¹¹Do not wear clothes of wool and linen woven together.

¹²Make tassels on the four corners of the cloak you wear.

Marriage Violations

¹³If a man takes a wife and, after sleeping with her, dislikes her ¹⁴and slanders her and gives her a bad name, saying, "I married this woman, but when I approached her, I did not find proof of her virginity," ¹⁵then the young woman's father and mother shall bring to the town elders at the gate proof that she was a virgin. ¹⁶Her father will say to the elders, "I gave my daughter in marriage to this man, but he dislikes her. ¹⁷Now he has slandered her and said, 'I did not find your daughter to be a virgin.' But here is the proof of my daughter's virginity." Then her parents shall display the cloth before the elders of the town, ¹⁸and the elders shall take the man and punish him. ¹⁹They shall fine him a hundred shekelsᵇ of silver and give them to the young woman's father, because this man has given an Israelite virgin a bad name. She shall continue to be his wife; he must not divorce her as long as he lives.

²⁰If, however, the charge is true and no proof of the young woman's virginity can be found, ²¹she shall be brought to the door of her father's house and there the men of her town shall stone her to death. She has done an outrageous thing in Israel by being promiscuous while still in her father's house. You must purge the evil from among you.

²²If a man is found sleeping with another man's wife, both the man who slept with her and the woman must die. You must purge the evil from Israel.

²³If a man happens to meet in a town a virgin pledged to be married and he sleeps with her, ²⁴you shall take both of them to the gate of that town and stone them to death—the young woman because she was in a town and did not scream for help, and the man because he violated another man's wife. You must purge the evil from among you.

²⁵But if out in the country a man happens to meet a young woman pledged to be married and rapes her, only the man who has done this shall die. ²⁶Do nothing to the woman; she has committed no sin deserving death. This case is like that of someone who attacks and murders a neighbor, ²⁷for the man found the young woman out in the country, and though the betrothed woman screamed, there was no one to rescue her.

²⁸If a man happens to meet a virgin who is not pledged to be married and rapes

---

ᵃ 9 Or be forfeited to the sanctuary   ᵇ 19 That is, about 2 1/2 pounds or about 1.2 kilograms her and they are discovered, ²⁹he shall pay her father fifty shekels*ª* of silver. He must marry the young woman, for he has violated her. He can never divorce her as long as he lives.

³⁰A man is not to marry his father's wife; he must not dishonor his father's bed.*ᵇ*

Exclusion From the Assembly

23*ᶜ* No one who has been emasculated by crushing or cutting may enter the assembly of the LORD.

²No one born of a forbidden marriage*ᵈ* nor any of their descendants may enter the assembly of the LORD, not even in the tenth generation.

³No Ammonite or Moabite or any of their descendants may enter the assembly of the LORD, not even in the tenth generation. ⁴For they did not come to meet you with bread and water on your way when you came out of Egypt, and they hired Balaam son of Beor from Pethor in Aram Naharaim*ᵉ* to pronounce a curse on you. ⁵However, the LORD your God would not listen to Balaam but turned the curse into a blessing for you, because the LORD your God loves you. ⁶Do not seek a treaty of friendship with them as long as you live.

⁷Do not despise an Edomite, for the Edomites are related to you. Do not despise an Egyptian, because you resided as foreigners in their country. ⁸The third generation of children born to them may enter the assembly of the LORD.

Uncleanness in the Camp

⁹When you are encamped against your enemies, keep away from everything impure. ¹⁰If one of your men is unclean because of a nocturnal emission, he is to go outside the camp and stay there. ¹¹But as evening approaches he is to wash himself, and at sunset he may return to the camp.

¹²Designate a place outside the camp where you can go to relieve yourself. ¹³As part of your equipment have something to dig with, and when you relieve yourself, dig a hole and cover up your excrement. ¹⁴For the LORD your God moves about in your camp to protect you and to deliver your enemies to you. Your camp must be holy, so that he will not see among you anything indecent and turn away from you.

Miscellaneous Laws

¹⁵If a slave has taken refuge with you, do not hand them over to their master. ¹⁶Let them live among you wherever they like and in whatever town they choose. Do not oppress them.

¹⁷No Israelite man or woman is to become a shrine prostitute. ¹⁸You must not bring the earnings of a female prostitute or of a male prostitute*ᶠ* into the house of the LORD your God to pay any vow, because the LORD your God detests them both.

¹⁹Do not charge a fellow Israelite interest, whether on money or food or anything else that may earn interest. ²⁰You may charge a foreigner interest, but not a fellow Israelite, so that the LORD your God may bless you in everything you put your hand to in the land you are entering to possess.

²¹If you make a vow to the LORD your God, do not be slow to pay it, for the LORD your God will certainly demand it of you and you will be guilty of sin. ²²But if you refrain from making a vow, you will not be guilty. ²³Whatever your lips utter you must be sure to do, because you made your vow freely to the LORD your God with your own mouth.

²⁴If you enter your neighbor's vineyard, you may eat all the grapes you want, but do not put any in your basket. ²⁵If you enter your neighbor's grainfield, you may pick kernels with your hands, but you must not put a sickle to their standing grain.

24 If a man marries a woman who becomes displeasing to him because he finds something indecent about her, and he writes her a certificate of divorce, gives it to her and sends her from his house, ²and if after she leaves his house

---

ª 29 That is, about 1 1/4 pounds or about 575 grams
ᵇ 30 In Hebrew texts this verse (22:30) is numbered 23:1.
ᶜ In Hebrew texts 23:1-25 is numbered 23:2-26.
ᵈ 2 Or one of illegitimate birth   *ᵉ* 4 That is, Northwest Mesopotamia   *ᶠ* 18 Hebrew of a dog

she becomes the wife of another man, [3]and her second husband dislikes her and writes her a certificate of divorce, gives it to her and sends her from his house, or if he dies, [4]then her first husband, who divorced her, is not allowed to marry her again after she has been defiled. That would be detestable in the eyes of the LORD. Do not bring sin upon the land the LORD your God is giving you as an inheritance.

[5]If a man has recently married, he must not be sent to war or have any other duty laid on him. For one year he is to be free to stay at home and bring happiness to the wife he has married.

[6]Do not take a pair of millstones—not even the upper one—as security for a debt, because that would be taking a person's livelihood as security.

[7]If someone is caught kidnapping a fellow Israelite and treating or selling them as a slave, the kidnapper must die. You must purge the evil from among you.

[8]In cases of defiling skin diseases,[a] be very careful to do exactly as the Levitical priests instruct you. You must follow carefully what I have commanded them. [9]Remember what the LORD your God did to Miriam along the way after you came out of Egypt.

[10]When you make a loan of any kind to your neighbor, do not go into their house to get what is offered to you as a pledge. [11]Stay outside and let the neighbor to whom you are making the loan bring the pledge out to you. [12]If the neighbor is poor, do not go to sleep with their pledge in your possession. [13]Return their cloak by sunset so that your neighbor may sleep in it. Then they will thank you, and it will be regarded as a righteous act in the sight of the LORD your God.

[14]Do not take advantage of a hired worker who is poor and needy, whether that worker is a fellow Israelite or a foreigner residing in one of your towns. [15]Pay them their wages each day before sunset, because they are poor and are counting on it. Otherwise they may cry to the LORD against you, and you will be guilty of sin.

[16]Parents are not to be put to death for their children, nor children put to death for their parents; each will die for their own sin.

[17]Do not deprive the foreigner or the fatherless of justice, or take the cloak of the widow as a pledge. [18]Remember that you were slaves in Egypt and the LORD your God redeemed you from there. That is why I command you to do this.

[19]When you are harvesting in your field and you overlook a sheaf, do not go back to get it. Leave it for the foreigner, the fatherless and the widow, so that the LORD your God may bless you in all the work of your hands. [20]When you beat the olives from your trees, do not go over the branches a second time. Leave what remains for the foreigner, the fatherless and the widow. [21]When you harvest the grapes in your vineyard, do not go over the vines again. Leave what remains for the foreigner, the fatherless and the widow. [22]Remember that you were slaves in Egypt. That is why I command you to do this.

25 When people have a dispute, they are to take it to court and the judges will decide the case, acquitting the innocent and condemning the guilty. [2]If the guilty person deserves to be beaten, the judge shall make them lie down and have them flogged in his presence with the number of lashes the crime deserves, [3]but the judge must not impose more than forty lashes. If the guilty party is flogged more than that, your fellow Israelite will be degraded in your eyes.

[4]Do not muzzle an ox while it is treading out the grain.

[5]If brothers are living together and one of them dies without a son, his widow must not marry outside the family. Her husband's brother shall take her and marry her and fulfill the duty of a brother-in-law to her. [6]The first son she bears shall carry on the name of the dead brother so that his name will not be blotted out from Israel.

[7]However, if a man does not want to marry his brother's wife, she shall go to the elders at the town gate and say, "My

---

[a] 8 The Hebrew word for *defiling skin diseases*, traditionally translated "leprosy," was used for various diseases affecting the skin.

husband's brother refuses to carry on his brother's name in Israel. He will not fulfill the duty of a brother-in-law to me." ⁸Then the elders of his town shall summon him and talk to him. If he persists in saying, "I do not want to marry her," ⁹his brother's widow shall go up to him in the presence of the elders, take off one of his sandals, spit in his face and say, "This is what is done to the man who will not build up his brother's family line." ¹⁰That man's line shall be known in Israel as The Family of the Unsandaled.

¹¹If two men are fighting and the wife of one of them comes to rescue her husband from his assailant, and she reaches out and seizes him by his private parts, ¹²you shall cut off her hand. Show her no pity.

¹³Do not have two differing weights in your bag—one heavy, one light. ¹⁴Do not have two differing measures in your house—one large, one small. ¹⁵You must have accurate and honest weights and measures, so that you may live long in the land the Lᴏʀᴅ your God is giving you. ¹⁶For the Lᴏʀᴅ your God detests anyone who does these things, anyone who deals dishonestly.

¹⁷Remember what the Amalekites did to you along the way when you came out of Egypt. ¹⁸When you were weary and worn out, they met you on your journey and attacked all who were lagging behind; they had no fear of God. ¹⁹When the Lᴏʀᴅ your God gives you rest from all the enemies around you in the land he is giving you to possess as an inheritance, you shall blot out the name of Amalek from under heaven. Do not forget!

Firstfruits and Tithes

26 When you have entered the land the Lᴏʀᴅ your God is giving you as an inheritance and have taken possession of it and settled in it, ²take some of the firstfruits of all that you produce from the soil of the land the Lᴏʀᴅ your God is giving you and put them in a basket. Then go to the place the Lᴏʀᴅ your God will choose as a dwelling for his Name ³and say to the priest in office at the time, "I declare today to the Lᴏʀᴅ your God that I have come to the land the Lᴏʀᴅ swore to our ancestors to give us." ⁴The priest shall take the basket from your hands and set it down in front of the altar of the Lᴏʀᴅ your God. ⁵Then you shall declare before the Lᴏʀᴅ your God: "My father was a wandering Aramean, and he went down into Egypt with a few people and lived there and became a great nation, powerful and numerous. ⁶But the Egyptians mistreated us and made us suffer, subjecting us to harsh labor. ⁷Then we cried out to the Lᴏʀᴅ, the God of our ancestors, and the Lᴏʀᴅ heard our voice and saw our misery, toil and oppression. ⁸So the Lᴏʀᴅ brought us out of Egypt with a mighty hand and an outstretched arm, with great terror and with signs and wonders. ⁹He brought us to this place and gave us this land, a land flowing with milk and honey; ¹⁰and now I bring the firstfruits of the soil that you, Lᴏʀᴅ, have given me." Place the basket before the Lᴏʀᴅ your God and bow down before him. ¹¹Then you and the Levites and the foreigners residing among you shall rejoice in all the good things the Lᴏʀᴅ your God has given to you and your household.

¹²When you have finished setting aside a tenth of all your produce in the third year, the year of the tithe, you shall give it to the Levite, the foreigner, the fatherless and the widow, so that they may eat in your towns and be satisfied. ¹³Then say to the Lᴏʀᴅ your God: "I have removed from my house the sacred portion and have given it to the Levite, the foreigner, the fatherless and the widow, according to all you commanded. I have not turned aside from your commands nor have I forgotten any of them. ¹⁴I have not eaten any of the sacred portion while I was in mourning, nor have I removed any of it while I was unclean, nor have I offered any of it to the dead. I have obeyed the Lᴏʀᴅ my God; I have done everything you commanded me. ¹⁵Look down from heaven, your holy dwelling place, and bless your people Israel and the land you have given us as you promised on oath to our ancestors, a land flowing with milk and honey."

Follow the Lord's Commands

16The Lord your God commands you this day to follow these decrees and laws; carefully observe them with all your heart and with all your soul. 17You have declared this day that the Lord is your God and that you will walk in obedience to him, that you will keep his decrees, commands and laws—that you will listen to him. 18And the Lord has declared this day that you are his people, his treasured possession as he promised, and that you are to keep all his commands. 19He has declared that he will set you in praise, fame and honor high above all the nations he has made and that you will be a people holy to the Lord your God, as he promised.

The Altar on Mount Ebal

27 Moses and the elders of Israel commanded the people: "Keep all these commands that I give you today. 2When you have crossed the Jordan into the land the Lord your God is giving you, set up some large stones and coat them with plaster. 3Write on them all the words of this law when you have crossed over to enter the land the Lord your God is giving you, a land flowing with milk and honey, just as the Lord, the God of your ancestors, promised you. 4And when you have crossed the Jordan, set up these stones on Mount Ebal, as I command you today, and coat them with plaster. 5Build there an altar to the Lord your God, an altar of stones. Do not use any iron tool on them. 6Build the altar of the Lord your God with fieldstones and offer burnt offerings on it to the Lord your God. 7Sacrifice fellowship offerings there, eating them and rejoicing in the presence of the Lord your God. 8And you shall write very clearly all the words of this law on these stones you have set up."

Curses From Mount Ebal

9Then Moses and the Levitical priests said to all Israel, "Be silent, Israel, and listen! You have now become the people of the Lord your God. 10Obey the Lord your God and follow his commands and decrees that I give you today."

11On the same day Moses commanded the people:

12When you have crossed the Jordan, these tribes shall stand on Mount Gerizim to bless the people: Simeon, Levi, Judah, Issachar, Joseph and Benjamin. 13And these tribes shall stand on Mount Ebal to pronounce curses: Reuben, Gad, Asher, Zebulun, Dan and Naphtali.

14The Levites shall recite to all the people of Israel in a loud voice:

15"Cursed is anyone who makes an idol—a thing detestable to the Lord, the work of skilled hands—and sets it up in secret."

Then all the people shall say, "Amen!"

16"Cursed is anyone who dishonors their father or mother."

Then all the people shall say, "Amen!"

17"Cursed is anyone who moves their neighbor's boundary stone."

Then all the people shall say, "Amen!"

18"Cursed is anyone who leads the blind astray on the road."

Then all the people shall say, "Amen!"

19"Cursed is anyone who withholds justice from the foreigner, the fatherless or the widow."

Then all the people shall say, "Amen!"

20"Cursed is anyone who sleeps with his father's wife, for he dishonors his father's bed."

Then all the people shall say, "Amen!"

21"Cursed is anyone who has sexual relations with any animal."

Then all the people shall say, "Amen!"

22"Cursed is anyone who sleeps with his sister, the daughter of his father or the daughter of his mother."

Then all the people shall say, "Amen!"

23"Cursed is anyone who sleeps with his mother-in-law."

Then all the people shall say, "Amen!"

24 "Cursed is anyone who kills their neighbor secretly."

Then all the people shall say, "Amen!"

25 "Cursed is anyone who accepts a bribe to kill an innocent person."

Then all the people shall say, "Amen!"

26 "Cursed is anyone who does not uphold the words of this law by carrying them out."

Then all the people shall say, "Amen!"

Blessings for Obedience

28 If you fully obey the LORD your God and carefully follow all his commands I give you today, the LORD your God will set you high above all the nations on earth. 2All these blessings will come on you and accompany you if you obey the LORD your God:

3You will be blessed in the city and blessed in the country.

4The fruit of your womb will be blessed, and the crops of your land and the young of your livestock—the calves of your herds and the lambs of your flocks.

5Your basket and your kneading trough will be blessed.

6You will be blessed when you come in and blessed when you go out.

7The LORD will grant that the enemies who rise up against you will be defeated before you. They will come at you from one direction but flee from you in seven.

8The LORD will send a blessing on your barns and on everything you put your hand to. The LORD your God will bless you in the land he is giving you.

9The LORD will establish you as his holy people, as he promised you on oath, if you keep the commands of the LORD your God and walk in obedience to him. 10Then all the peoples on earth will see that you are called by the name of the LORD, and they will fear you. 11The LORD will grant you abundant prosperity—in the fruit of your womb, the young of your livestock and the crops of your ground—in the land he swore to your ancestors to give you.

12The LORD will open the heavens, the storehouse of his bounty, to send rain on your land in season and to bless all the work of your hands. You will lend to many nations but will borrow from none. 13The LORD will make you the head, not the tail. If you pay attention to the commands of the LORD your God that I give you this day and carefully follow them, you will always be at the top, never at the bottom. 14Do not turn aside from any of the commands I give you today, to the right or to the left, following other gods and serving them.

Curses for Disobedience

15However, if you do not obey the LORD your God and do not carefully follow all his commands and decrees I am giving you today, all these curses will come on you and overtake you:

16You will be cursed in the city and cursed in the country.

17Your basket and your kneading trough will be cursed.

18The fruit of your womb will be cursed, and the crops of your land, and the calves of your herds and the lambs of your flocks.

19You will be cursed when you come in and cursed when you go out.

20The LORD will send on you curses, confusion and rebuke in everything you put your hand to, until you are destroyed and come to sudden ruin because of the evil you have done in forsaking him.[a] 21The LORD will plague you with diseases until he has destroyed you from the land you are entering to possess. 22The LORD will strike you with wasting disease, with fever and inflammation, with scorching heat and drought, with blight and mildew, which will plague you until you perish. 23The sky over your head will be bronze, the ground beneath you iron. 24The LORD will turn the rain of your country into dust and powder; it will come down from the skies until you are destroyed.

25The LORD will cause you to be defeated before your enemies. You will come at them from one direction but flee from

a 20 Hebrew me

them in seven, and you will become a thing of horror to all the kingdoms on earth. ²⁶Your carcasses will be food for all the birds and the wild animals, and there will be no one to frighten them away. ²⁷The Lord will afflict you with the boils of Egypt and with tumors, festering sores and the itch, from which you cannot be cured. ²⁸The Lord will afflict you with madness, blindness and confusion of mind. ²⁹At midday you will grope about like a blind person in the dark. You will be unsuccessful in everything you do; day after day you will be oppressed and robbed, with no one to rescue you.

³⁰You will be pledged to be married to a woman, but another will take her and rape her. You will build a house, but you will not live in it. You will plant a vineyard, but you will not even begin to enjoy its fruit. ³¹Your ox will be slaughtered before your eyes, but you will eat none of it. Your donkey will be forcibly taken from you and will not be returned. Your sheep will be given to your enemies, and no one will rescue them. ³²Your sons and daughters will be given to another nation, and you will wear out your eyes watching for them day after day, powerless to lift a hand. ³³A people that you do not know will eat what your land and labor produce, and you will have nothing but cruel oppression all your days. ³⁴The sights you see will drive you mad. ³⁵The Lord will afflict your knees and legs with painful boils that cannot be cured, spreading from the soles of your feet to the top of your head.

³⁶The Lord will drive you and the king you set over you to a nation unknown to you or your ancestors. There you will worship other gods, gods of wood and stone. ³⁷You will become a thing of horror, a byword and an object of ridicule among all the peoples where the Lord will drive you.

³⁸You will sow much seed in the field but you will harvest little, because locusts will devour it. ³⁹You will plant vineyards and cultivate them but you will not drink the wine or gather the grapes, because worms will eat them. ⁴⁰You will have olive trees throughout your country but you will not use the oil, because the olives will drop off. ⁴¹You will have sons and daughters but you will not keep them, because they will go into captivity. ⁴²Swarms of locusts will take over all your trees and the crops of your land.

⁴³The foreigners who reside among you will rise above you higher and higher, but you will sink lower and lower. ⁴⁴They will lend to you, but you will not lend to them. They will be the head, but you will be the tail.

⁴⁵All these curses will come on you. They will pursue you and overtake you until you are destroyed, because you did not obey the Lord your God and observe the commands and decrees he gave you. ⁴⁶They will be a sign and a wonder to you and your descendants forever. ⁴⁷Because you did not serve the Lord your God joyfully and gladly in the time of prosperity, ⁴⁸therefore in hunger and thirst, in nakedness and dire poverty, you will serve the enemies the Lord sends against you. He will put an iron yoke on your neck until he has destroyed you.

⁴⁹The Lord will bring a nation against you from far away, from the ends of the earth, like an eagle swooping down, a nation whose language you will not understand, ⁵⁰a fierce-looking nation without respect for the old or pity for the young. ⁵¹They will devour the young of your livestock and the crops of your land until you are destroyed. They will leave you no grain, new wine or olive oil, nor any calves of your herds or lambs of your flocks until you are ruined. ⁵²They will lay siege to all the cities throughout your land until the high fortified walls in which you trust fall down. They will besiege all the cities throughout the land the Lord your God is giving you.

⁵³Because of the suffering your enemy will inflict on you during the siege, you will eat the fruit of the womb, the flesh of the sons and daughters the Lord your God has given you. ⁵⁴Even the most gentle and sensitive man among you will have no compassion on his own brother or the wife he loves or his surviving children, ⁵⁵and he will not give to one of them

any of the flesh of his children that he is eating. It will be all he has left because of the suffering your enemy will inflict on you during the siege of all your cities. ⁵⁶The most gentle and sensitive woman among you—so sensitive and gentle that she would not venture to touch the ground with the sole of her foot—will begrudge the husband she loves and her own son or daughter ⁵⁷the afterbirth from her womb and the children she bears. For in her dire need she intends to eat them secretly because of the suffering your enemy will inflict on you during the siege of your cities.

⁵⁸If you do not carefully follow all the words of this law, which are written in this book, and do not revere this glorious and awesome name—the Lᴏʀᴅ your God— ⁵⁹the Lᴏʀᴅ will send fearful plagues on you and your descendants, harsh and prolonged disasters, and severe and lingering illnesses. ⁶⁰He will bring on you all the diseases of Egypt that you dreaded, and they will cling to you. ⁶¹The Lᴏʀᴅ will also bring on you every kind of sickness and disaster not recorded in this Book of the Law, until you are destroyed. ⁶²You who were as numerous as the stars in the sky will be left but few in number, because you did not obey the Lᴏʀᴅ your God. ⁶³Just as it pleased the Lᴏʀᴅ to make you prosper and increase in number, so it will please him to ruin and destroy you. You will be uprooted from the land you are entering to possess.

⁶⁴Then the Lᴏʀᴅ will scatter you among all nations, from one end of the earth to the other. There you will worship other gods—gods of wood and stone, which neither you nor your ancestors have known. ⁶⁵Among those nations you will find no repose, no resting place for the sole of your foot. There the Lᴏʀᴅ will give you an anxious mind, eyes weary with longing, and a despairing heart. ⁶⁶You will live in constant suspense, filled with dread both night and day, never sure of your life. ⁶⁷In the morning you will say, "If only it were evening!" and in the evening, "If only it were morning!"—because of the terror that will fill your hearts and the sights that your eyes will see. ⁶⁸The Lᴏʀᴅ

will send you back in ships to Egypt on a journey I said you should never make again. There you will offer yourselves for sale to your enemies as male and female slaves, but no one will buy you.

Renewal of the Covenant

29 ᵃ These are the terms of the covenant the Lᴏʀᴅ commanded Moses to make with the Israelites in Moab, in addition to the covenant he had made with them at Horeb.

²Moses summoned all the Israelites and said to them:

Your eyes have seen all that the Lᴏʀᴅ did in Egypt to Pharaoh, to all his officials and to all his land. ³With your own eyes you saw those great trials, those signs and great wonders. ⁴But to this day the Lᴏʀᴅ has not given you a mind that understands or eyes that see or ears that hear. ⁵Yet the Lᴏʀᴅ says, "During the forty years that I led you through the wilderness, your clothes did not wear out, nor did the sandals on your feet. ⁶You ate no bread and drank no wine or other fermented drink. I did this so that you might know that I am the Lᴏʀᴅ your God."

⁷When you reached this place, Sihon king of Heshbon and Og king of Bashan came out to fight against us, but we defeated them. ⁸We took their land and gave it as an inheritance to the Reubenites, the Gadites and the half-tribe of Manasseh.

⁹Carefully follow the terms of this covenant, so that you may prosper in everything you do. ¹⁰All of you are standing today in the presence of the Lᴏʀᴅ your God—your leaders and chief men, your elders and officials, and all the other men of Israel, ¹¹together with your children and your wives, and the foreigners living in your camps who chop your wood and carry your water. ¹²You are standing here in order to enter into a covenant with the Lᴏʀᴅ your God, a covenant the Lᴏʀᴅ is making with you this day and sealing with an oath, ¹³to confirm you this day as his people, that he may be your God

ᵃ In Hebrew texts 29:1 is numbered 28:69, and 29:2-29 is numbered 29:1-28.

as he promised you and as he swore to your fathers, Abraham, Isaac and Jacob. ¹⁴I am making this covenant, with its oath, not only with you ¹⁵who are standing here with us today in the presence of the Lord our God but also with those who are not here today.

¹⁶You yourselves know how we lived in Egypt and how we passed through the countries on the way here. ¹⁷You saw among them their detestable images and idols of wood and stone, of silver and gold. ¹⁸Make sure there is no man or woman, clan or tribe among you today whose heart turns away from the Lord our God to go and worship the gods of those nations; make sure there is no root among you that produces such bitter poison.

¹⁹When such a person hears the words of this oath and they invoke a blessing on themselves, thinking, "I will be safe, even though I persist in going my own way," they will bring disaster on the watered land as well as the dry. ²⁰The Lord will never be willing to forgive them; his wrath and zeal will burn against them. All the curses written in this book will fall on them, and the Lord will blot out their names from under heaven. ²¹The Lord will single them out from all the tribes of Israel for disaster, according to all the curses of the covenant written in this Book of the Law.

²²Your children who follow you in later generations and foreigners who come from distant lands will see the calamities that have fallen on the land and the diseases with which the Lord has afflicted it. ²³The whole land will be a burning waste of salt and sulfur—nothing planted, nothing sprouting, no vegetation growing on it. It will be like the destruction of Sodom and Gomorrah, Admah and Zeboyim, which the Lord overthrew in fierce anger. ²⁴All the nations will ask: "Why has the Lord done this to this land? Why this fierce, burning anger?"

²⁵And the answer will be: "It is because this people abandoned the covenant of the Lord, the God of their ancestors, the covenant he made with them when he brought them out of Egypt. ²⁶They went

THE SCENE

SODOM, GOMORRAH, ADMAH AND ZEBOYIM

(DEUTERONOMY 29:23)

These were nations that God destroyed because they were very bad and did very unjust and ugly things.

off and worshiped other gods and bowed down to them, gods they did not know, gods he had not given them. ²⁷Therefore the Lord's anger burned against this land, so that he brought on it all the curses written in this book. ²⁸In furious anger and in great wrath the Lord uprooted them from their land and thrust them into another land, as it is now."

²⁹The secret things belong to the Lord our God, but the things revealed belong to us and to our children forever, that we may follow all the words of this law.

Prosperity After Turning to the Lord

30 When all these blessings and curses I have set before you come on you and you take them to heart wherever the Lord your God disperses you among the nations, ²and when you and your children return to the Lord your God and obey him with all your heart and with all your soul according to everything I command you today, [3]then the Lord your God will restore your fortunes[a] and have compassion on you and gather you again from all the nations where he scattered you. [4]Even if you have been banished to the most distant land under the heavens, from there the Lord your God will gather you and bring you back. [5]He will bring you to the land that belonged to your ancestors, and you will take possession of it. He will make you more prosperous and numerous than your ancestors. [6]The Lord your God will circumcise your hearts and the hearts of your descendants, so that you may love him with all your heart and with all your soul, and live. [7]The Lord your God will put all these curses on your enemies who hate and persecute you. [8]You will again obey the Lord and follow all his commands I am giving you today. [9]Then the Lord your God will make you most prosperous in all the work of your hands and in the fruit of your womb, the young of your livestock and the crops of your land. The Lord will again delight in you and make you prosperous, just as he delighted in your ancestors, [10]if you obey the Lord your God and keep his commands and decrees that are written in this Book of the Law and turn to the Lord your God with all your heart and with all your soul.

The Offer of Life or Death

[11]Now what I am commanding you today is not too difficult for you or beyond your reach. [12]It is not up in heaven, so that you have to ask, "Who will ascend into heaven to get it and proclaim it to us so we may obey it?" [13]Nor is it beyond the sea, so that you have to ask, "Who will cross the sea to get it and proclaim it to us so we may obey it?" [14]No, the word is very near you; it is in your mouth and in your heart so you may obey it.

[15]See, I set before you today life and prosperity, death and destruction. [16]For I command you today to love the Lord your God, to walk in obedience to him, and to keep his commands, decrees and laws;

then you will live and increase, and the Lord your God will bless you in the land you are entering to possess.

[17]But if your heart turns away and you are not obedient, and if you are drawn away to bow down to other gods and worship them, [18]I declare to you this day that you will certainly be destroyed. You will not live long in the land you are crossing the Jordan to enter and possess.

[19]This day I call the heavens and the earth as witnesses against you that I have set before you life and death, blessings and curses. Now choose life, so that you and your children may live [20]and that you may love the Lord your God, listen to his voice, and hold fast to him. For the Lord is your life, and he will give you many years in the land he swore to give to your fathers, Abraham, Isaac and Jacob.

Joshua to Succeed Moses

31 Then Moses went out and spoke these words to all Israel: [2]"I am now a hundred and twenty years old and I am no longer able to lead you. The Lord has said to me, 'You shall not cross the Jordan.' [3]The Lord your God himself will cross over ahead of you. He will destroy these nations before you, and you will take possession of their land. Joshua also will cross over ahead of you, as the Lord said. [4]And the Lord will do to them what he did to Sihon and Og, the kings of the Amorites, whom he destroyed along with their land. [5]The Lord will deliver them to you, and you must do to them all that I have commanded you. [6]Be strong and courageous. Do not be afraid or terrified because of them, for the Lord your God goes with you; he will never leave you nor forsake you."

[7]Then Moses summoned Joshua and said to him in the presence of all Israel, "Be strong and courageous, for you must go with this people into the land that the Lord swore to their ancestors to give them, and you must divide it among them as their inheritance. [8]The Lord himself goes before you and will be with you;

---

[a] 3 Or *will bring you back from captivity*

CHECK THE FACTS

Who was Moses' successor?

A) Jesus

B) Aaron

C) Joshua

CORRECT ANSWER: C

he will never leave you nor forsake you. Do not be afraid; do not be discouraged."

Public Reading of the Law

⁹So Moses wrote down this law and gave it to the Levitical priests, who carried the ark of the covenant of the Lord, and to all the elders of Israel. ¹⁰Then Moses commanded them: "At the end of every seven years, in the year for canceling debts, during the Festival of Tabernacles, ¹¹when all Israel comes to appear before the Lord your God at the place he will choose, you shall read this law before them in their hearing. ¹²Assemble the people—men, women and children, and the foreigners residing in your towns—so they can listen and learn to fear the Lord your God and follow carefully all the words of this law. ¹³Their children, who do not know this law, must hear it and learn to fear the Lord your God as long as you live in the land you are crossing the Jordan to possess."

Israel's Rebellion Predicted

¹⁴The Lord said to Moses, "Now the day of your death is near. Call Joshua and present yourselves at the tent of meeting, where I will commission him." So Moses and Joshua came and presented themselves at the tent of meeting.

¹⁵Then the Lord appeared at the tent in a pillar of cloud, and the cloud stood over the entrance to the tent. ¹⁶And the Lord said to Moses: "You are going to rest with your ancestors, and these people will soon prostitute themselves to the foreign gods of the land they are entering. They will forsake me and break the covenant I made with them. ¹⁷And in that day I will become angry with them and forsake them; I will hide my face from them, and they will be destroyed. Many disasters and calamities will come on them, and in that day they will ask, 'Have not these disasters come on us because our God is not with us?' ¹⁸And I will certainly hide my face in that day because of all their wickedness in turning to other gods.

¹⁹"Now write down this song and teach it to the Israelites and have them sing it, so that it may be a witness for me against them. ²⁰When I have brought them into the land flowing with milk and honey, the land I promised on oath to their ancestors, and when they eat their fill and thrive, they will turn to other gods and worship them, rejecting me and breaking my covenant. ²¹And when many disasters and calamities come on them, this song will testify against them, because it will not be forgotten by their descendants. I know what they are disposed to do, even before I bring them into the land I promised them on oath." ²²So Moses wrote down this song that day and taught it to the Israelites.

²³The Lord gave this command to Joshua son of Nun: "Be strong and courageous, for you will bring the Israelites into the land I promised them on oath, and I myself will be with you."

²⁴After Moses finished writing in a book the words of this law from beginning to end, ²⁵he gave this command to the Levites who carried the ark of the covenant

of the LORD: ²⁶"Take this Book of the Law and place it beside the ark of the covenant of the LORD your God. There it will remain as a witness against you. ²⁷For I know how rebellious and stiff-necked you are. If you have been rebellious against the LORD while I am still alive and with you, how much more will you rebel after I die! ²⁸Assemble before me all the elders of your tribes and all your officials, so that I can speak these words in their hearing and call the heavens and the earth to testify against them. ²⁹For I know that after my death you are sure to become utterly corrupt and to turn from the way I have commanded you. In days to come, disaster will fall on you because you will do evil in the sight of the LORD and arouse his anger by what your hands have made."

The Song of Moses

³⁰And Moses recited the words of this song from beginning to end in the hearing of the whole assembly of Israel:

32 Listen, you heavens, and I will
    speak;
  hear, you earth, the words of my
    mouth.
²Let my teaching fall like rain
  and my words descend like dew,
like showers on new grass,
  like abundant rain on tender plants.

³I will proclaim the name of the LORD.
  Oh, praise the greatness of our
    God!
⁴He is the Rock, his works are perfect,
  and all his ways are just.
A faithful God who does no wrong,
  upright and just is he.

⁵They are corrupt and not his children;
  to their shame they are a warped
    and crooked generation.
⁶Is this the way you repay the LORD,
  you foolish and unwise people?
Is he not your Father, your Creator,ᵃ
  who made you and formed you?

⁷Remember the days of old;
  consider the generations long past.
Ask your father and he will tell you,
  your elders, and they will explain to
    you.

⁸When the Most High gave the nations
  their inheritance,
  when he divided all mankind,
he set up boundaries for the peoples
  according to the number of the
    sons of Israel.ᵇ
⁹For the LORD's portion is his people,
  Jacob his allotted inheritance.

¹⁰In a desert land he found him,
  in a barren and howling waste.
He shielded him and cared for him;
  he guarded him as the apple of his
    eye,
¹¹like an eagle that stirs up its nest
  and hovers over its young,
that spreads its wings to catch
    them
  and carries them aloft.
¹²The LORD alone led him;
  no foreign god was with him.

¹³He made him ride on the heights of
    the land
  and fed him with the fruit of the
    fields.
He nourished him with honey from the
    rock,
  and with oil from the flinty crag,
¹⁴with curds and milk from herd and
    flock
  and with fattened lambs and goats,
with choice rams of Bashan
  and the finest kernels of wheat.
You drank the foaming blood of the
    grape.

¹⁵Jeshurunᶜ grew fat and kicked;
  filled with food, they became heavy
    and sleek.
They abandoned the God who made
    them
  and rejected the Rock their Savior.
¹⁶They made him jealous with their
    foreign gods
  and angered him with their
    detestable idols.
¹⁷They sacrificed to false gods, which
    are not God—
  gods they had not known,
gods that recently appeared,
  gods your ancestors did not fear.

ᵃ 6 Or *Father, who bought you*   ᵇ 8 Masoretic Text;
Dead Sea Scrolls (see also Septuagint) *sons of God*
ᶜ 15 *Jeshurun* means *the upright one*, that is, Israel.

¹⁸ You deserted the Rock, who fathered
you;
you forgot the God who gave you
birth.

¹⁹ The LORD saw this and rejected them
because he was angered by his
sons and daughters.

²⁰ "I will hide my face from them," he
said,
"and see what their end will be;
for they are a perverse generation,
children who are unfaithful.

²¹ They made me jealous by what is no
god
and angered me with their
worthless idols.
I will make them envious by those who
are not a people;
I will make them angry by a nation
that has no understanding.

²² For a fire will be kindled by my wrath,
one that burns down to the realm of
the dead below.
It will devour the earth and its
harvests
and set afire the foundations of the
mountains.

²³ "I will heap calamities on them
and spend my arrows against them.

²⁴ I will send wasting famine against
them,
consuming pestilence and deadly
plague;
I will send against them the fangs of
wild beasts,
the venom of vipers that glide in the
dust.

²⁵ In the street the sword will make them
childless;
in their homes terror will reign.
The young men and young women will
perish,
the infants and those with gray hair.

²⁶ I said I would scatter them
and erase their name from human
memory,

²⁷ but I dreaded the taunt of the enemy,
lest the adversary misunderstand
and say, 'Our hand has triumphed;
the LORD has not done all this.' "

²⁸ They are a nation without sense,
there is no discernment in them.

²⁹ If only they were wise and would
understand this
and discern what their end will be!

³⁰ How could one man chase a
thousand,
or two put ten thousand to flight,
unless their Rock had sold them,
unless the LORD had given them up?

³¹ For their rock is not like our Rock,
as even our enemies concede.

³² Their vine comes from the vine of
Sodom
and from the fields of Gomorrah.
Their grapes are filled with poison,
and their clusters with bitterness.

³³ Their wine is the venom of serpents,
the deadly poison of cobras.

³⁴ "Have I not kept this in reserve
and sealed it in my vaults?

³⁵ It is mine to avenge; I will repay.
In due time their foot will slip;
their day of disaster is near
and their doom rushes upon them."

³⁶ The LORD will vindicate his people
and relent concerning his servants
when he sees their strength is gone
and no one is left, slave or free.ᵃ

³⁷ He will say: "Now where are their
gods,
the rock they took refuge in,

³⁸ the gods who ate the fat of their
sacrifices
and drank the wine of their drink
offerings?
Let them rise up to help you!
Let them give you shelter!

³⁹ "See now that I myself am he!
There is no god besides me.
I put to death and I bring to life,
I have wounded and I will heal,
and no one can deliver out of my
hand.

⁴⁰ I lift my hand to heaven and solemnly
swear:
As surely as I live forever,

⁴¹ when I sharpen my flashing sword
and my hand grasps it in judgment,
I will take vengeance on my
adversaries
and repay those who hate me.

ᵃ 36 Or *and they are without a ruler or leader*

⁴²I will make my arrows drunk with blood,
  while my sword devours flesh:
the blood of the slain and the
    captives,
  the heads of the enemy leaders."

⁴³Rejoice, you nations, with his people,ᵃ·ᵇ
  for he will avenge the blood of his
    servants;
he will take vengeance on his enemies
  and make atonement for his land
    and people.

⁴⁴Moses came with Joshuaᶜ son of Nun and spoke all the words of this song in the hearing of the people. ⁴⁵When Moses finished reciting all these words to all Israel, ⁴⁶he said to them, "Take to heart all the words I have solemnly declared to you this day, so that you may command your children to obey carefully all the words of this law. ⁴⁷They are not just idle words for you—they are your life. By them you will live long in the land you are crossing the Jordan to possess."

Moses to Die on Mount Nebo

⁴⁸On that same day the Lᴏʀᴅ told Moses, ⁴⁹"Go up into the Abarim Range to Mount Nebo in Moab, across from Jericho, and view Canaan, the land I am giving the Israelites as their own possession. ⁵⁰There on the mountain that you have climbed you will die and be gathered to your people, just as your brother Aaron died on Mount Hor and was gathered to his people. ⁵¹This is because both of you broke faith with me in the presence of the Israelites at the waters of Meribah Kadesh in the Desert of Zin and because you did not uphold my holiness among the Israelites. ⁵²Therefore, you will see the land only from a distance; you will not enter the land I am giving to the people of Israel."

Moses Blesses the Tribes

33 This is the blessing that Moses the man of God pronounced on the Israelites before his death. ²He said:

"The Lᴏʀᴅ came from Sinai
  and dawned over them from Seir;
he shone forth from Mount Paran.

He came withᵈ myriads of holy ones
  from the south, from his mountain
    slopes.ᵉ
³Surely it is you who love the people;
  all the holy ones are in your hand.
At your feet they all bow down,
  and from you receive instruction,
⁴the law that Moses gave us,
  the possession of the assembly of
    Jacob.
⁵He was king over Jeshurunᶠ
  when the leaders of the people
    assembled,
  along with the tribes of Israel.

⁶"Let Reuben live and not die,
  norᵍ his people be few."

⁷And this he said about Judah:

"Hear, Lᴏʀᴅ, the cry of Judah;
  bring him to his people.
With his own hands he defends his
    cause.
  Oh, be his help against his foes!"

⁸About Levi he said:

"Your Thummim and Urim belong
  to your faithful servant.
You tested him at Massah;
  you contended with him at the
    waters of Meribah.
⁹He said of his father and mother,
  'I have no regard for them.'
He did not recognize his brothers
  or acknowledge his own children,
but he watched over your word
  and guarded your covenant.
¹⁰He teaches your precepts to Jacob
  and your law to Israel.
He offers incense before you
  and whole burnt offerings on your
    altar.
¹¹Bless all his skills, Lᴏʀᴅ,
  and be pleased with the work of his
    hands.
Strike down those who rise against
    him,
  his foes till they rise no more."

ᵃ 43 Or *Make his people rejoice, you nations*
ᵇ 43 Masoretic Text; Dead Sea Scrolls (see also Septuagint) *people, / and let all the angels worship him, /*
ᶜ 44 Hebrew *Hoshea,* a variant of *Joshua*   ᵈ 2 Or *from*
ᵉ 2 The meaning of the Hebrew for this phrase is uncertain.   ᶠ 5 *Jeshurun* means *the upright one,* that is, Israel; also in verse 26.   ᵍ 6 Or *but let*

¹²About Benjamin he said:

"Let the beloved of the Lᴏʀᴅ rest
    secure in him,
  for he shields him all day long,
  and the one the Lᴏʀᴅ loves rests
    between his shoulders."

¹³About Joseph he said:

"May the Lᴏʀᴅ bless his land
  with the precious dew from heaven
    above
  and with the deep waters that lie
    below;
¹⁴with the best the sun brings forth
  and the finest the moon can yield;
¹⁵with the choicest gifts of the ancient
    mountains
  and the fruitfulness of the
    everlasting hills;
¹⁶with the best gifts of the earth and its
    fullness
  and the favor of him who dwelt in
    the burning bush.
Let all these rest on the head of
    Joseph,
  on the brow of the prince among*ᵃ*
    his brothers.
¹⁷In majesty he is like a firstborn bull;
  his horns are the horns of a wild ox.
With them he will gore the nations,
  even those at the ends of the earth.
Such are the ten thousands of
    Ephraim;
  such are the thousands of
    Manasseh."

¹⁸About Zebulun he said:

"Rejoice, Zebulun, in your going out,
  and you, Issachar, in your tents.
¹⁹They will summon peoples to the
    mountain
  and there offer the sacrifices of the
    righteous;
they will feast on the abundance of
    the seas,
  on the treasures hidden in the sand."

²⁰About Gad he said:

"Blessed is he who enlarges Gad's
    domain!
  Gad lives there like a lion,
    tearing at arm or head.

²¹He chose the best land for himself;
  the leader's portion was kept for
    him.
When the heads of the people
    assembled,
  he carried out the Lᴏʀᴅ's righteous
    will,
  and his judgments concerning
    Israel."

²²About Dan he said:

"Dan is a lion's cub,
  springing out of Bashan."

²³About Naphtali he said:

"Naphtali is abounding with the favor
    of the Lᴏʀᴅ
  and is full of his blessing;
  he will inherit southward to the
    lake."

²⁴About Asher he said:

"Most blessed of sons is Asher;
  let him be favored by his
    brothers,
  and let him bathe his feet in oil.
²⁵The bolts of your gates will be iron
    and bronze,
  and your strength will equal your
    days.

²⁶"There is no one like the God of
    Jeshurun,
  who rides across the heavens to
    help you
  and on the clouds in his majesty.
²⁷The eternal God is your refuge,
  and underneath are the everlasting
    arms.
He will drive out your enemies before
    you,
  saying, 'Destroy them!'
²⁸So Israel will live in safety;
  Jacob will dwellᵇ secure
in a land of grain and new wine,
  where the heavens drop dew.
²⁹Blessed are you, Israel!
  Who is like you,
  a people saved by the Lᴏʀᴅ?
He is your shield and helper
  and your glorious sword.

ᵃ 16 Or *of the one separated from*   *ᵇ 28* Septuagint;
Hebrew *Jacob's spring is*

Your enemies will cower before you,
　and you will tread on their heights."

The Death of Moses

34 Then Moses climbed Mount Nebo from the plains of Moab to the top of Pisgah, across from Jericho. There the LORD showed him the whole land—from Gilead to Dan, ²all of Naphtali, the territory of Ephraim and Manasseh, all the land of Judah as far as the Mediterranean Sea, ³the Negev and the whole region from the Valley of Jericho, the City of Palms, as far as Zoar. ⁴Then the LORD said to him, "This is the land I promised on oath to Abraham, Isaac and Jacob when I said, 'I will give it to your descendants.' I have let you see it with your eyes, but you will not cross over into it."

⁵And Moses the servant of the LORD died there in Moab, as the LORD had said. ⁶He buried him[a] in Moab, in the valley opposite Beth Peor, but to this day no one knows where his grave is. ⁷Moses was a hundred and twenty years old when he died, yet his eyes were not weak nor his strength gone. ⁸The Israelites grieved for Moses in the plains of Moab thirty days, until the time of weeping and mourning was over.

⁹Now Joshua son of Nun was filled with the spirit[b] of wisdom because Moses had laid his hands on him. So the Israelites listened to him and did what the LORD had commanded Moses.

¹⁰Since then, no prophet has risen in Israel like Moses, whom the LORD knew face to face, ¹¹who did all those signs and wonders the LORD sent him to do in Egypt—to Pharaoh and to all his officials and to his whole land. ¹²For no one has ever shown the mighty power or performed the awesome deeds that Moses did in the sight of all Israel.

---

[a] 6 Or He was buried　　[b] 9 Or Spirit

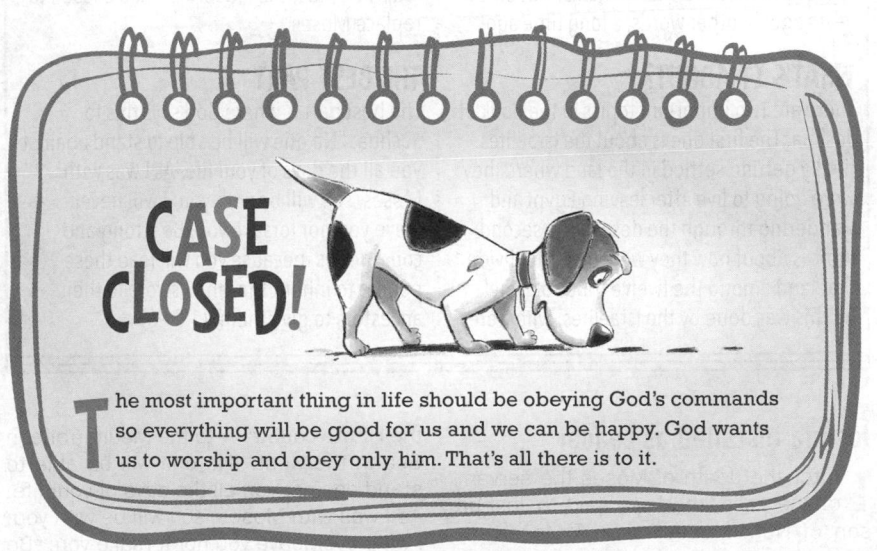

CASE CLOSED!

The most important thing in life should be obeying God's commands so everything will be good for us and we can be happy. God wants us to worship and obey only him. That's all there is to it.

JOSHUA

THE EVIDENCE:

WHO WROTE IT?

We do not know the name of the person who wrote this. It seems it may have been written by several people who were prophets. This book is part of a collection of books that include Joshua, Judges, the two books of Samuel, the two books of Kings and the two books of Chronicles.

HOW LONG AGO?

The book of Joshua was written about 2,600 years ago. In other words, a long time ago!

WHAT'S IT ABOUT?

There are two important topics in the book of Joshua. The first one is about the Israelites finally getting settled in the land where they were going to live after leaving Egypt and wandering through the desert. The second topic is about how they were going to divide that land among the twelve tribes of Israel. All this was done by the Israelites, who were led by Joshua, the leader God had chosen to replace Moses.

THE BEST PART

The best part is where God says this to Joshua: "No one will be able to stand against you all the days of your life. As I was with Moses, so I will be with you; I will never leave you nor forsake you. Be strong and courageous, because you will lead these people to inherit the land I swore to their ancestors to give them" (1:5 – 6).

Joshua Installed as Leader

1 After the death of Moses the servant of the LORD, the LORD said to Joshua son of Nun, Moses' aide: ²"Moses my servant is dead. Now then, you and all these people, get ready to cross the Jordan River into the land I am about to give to them—to the Israelites. ³I will give you every place where you set your foot, as I promised Moses. ⁴Your territory will extend from the desert to Lebanon, and from the great river, the Euphrates—all the Hittite country—to the Mediterranean Sea in the west. ⁵No one will be able to stand against you all the days of your life. As I was with Moses, so I will be with you; I will never leave you nor forsake you. ⁶Be strong and courageous, because you will lead these people to inherit the land I swore to their ancestors to give them.

⁷"Be strong and very courageous. Be careful to obey all the law my servant Moses gave you; do not turn from it to the right or to the left, that you may be successful wherever you go. ⁸Keep this Book

THE
WITNESSES

✓ **JOSHUA SON OF NUN (JOSHUA 1:1)**
Joshua means "God saves," and it's the Hebrew
name for Jesus. He was Moses' successor and is
the main character of the whole story told in this
book that has his name. He was from the tribe of
Ephraim.

of the Law always on your lips; meditate
on it day and night, so that you may be
careful to do everything written in it. Then
you will be prosperous and successful.
⁹Have I not commanded you? Be strong
and courageous. Do not be afraid; do not
be discouraged, for the LORD your God will
be with you wherever you go."

¹⁰So Joshua ordered the officers of the
people: ¹¹"Go through the camp and tell
the people, 'Get your provisions ready.
Three days from now you will cross the
Jordan here to go in and take possession
of the land the LORD your God is giving you
for your own.'"

¹²But to the Reubenites, the Gadites
and the half-tribe of Manasseh, Joshua
said, ¹³"Remember the command that
Moses the servant of the LORD gave you
after he said, 'The LORD your God will give
you rest by giving you this land.' ¹⁴Your
wives, your children and your livestock
may stay in the land that Moses gave you
east of the Jordan, but all your fighting
men, ready for battle, must cross over
ahead of your fellow Israelites. You are
to help them ¹⁵until the LORD gives them
rest, as he has done for you, and until
they too have taken possession of the
land the LORD your God is giving them. After that, you may go back and occupy your
own land, which Moses the servant of the
LORD gave you east of the Jordan toward
the sunrise."

¹⁶Then they answered Joshua, "Whatever you have commanded us we will do,
and wherever you send us we will go.
¹⁷Just as we fully obeyed Moses, so we
will obey you. Only may the LORD your God

BREAK THROUGH!

Book of the Law

(JOSHUA 1:8)

These are the first five books of the Bible:
Genesis, Exodus, Leviticus, Numbers
and Deuteronomy. Now we call them the
Pentateuch, because that word means "five
books."

be with you as he was with Moses. ¹⁸Whoever rebels against your word and does not obey it, whatever you may command them, will be put to death. Only be strong and courageous!"

Rahab and the Spies

2 Then Joshua son of Nun secretly sent two spies from Shittim. "Go, look over the land," he said, "especially Jericho." So they went and entered the house of a prostitute named Rahab and stayed there.

²The king of Jericho was told, "Look, some of the Israelites have come here tonight to spy out the land." ³So the king of Jericho sent this message to Rahab: "Bring out the men who came to you and entered your house, because they have come to spy out the whole land."

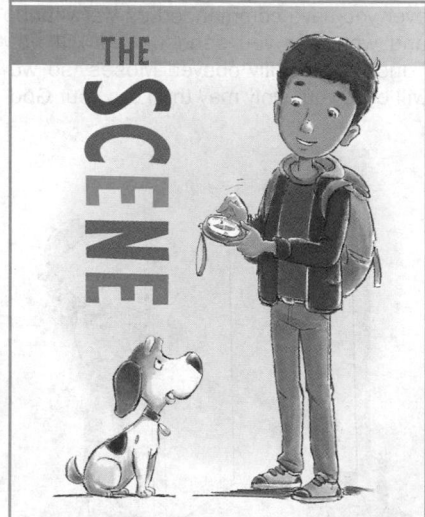

THE SCENE

JERICHO

(JOSHUA 2:1)

Jericho is also called the "City of Palms." It's a very old city. It may be the oldest city in the world. It's about 6 miles (10 km) north of the Dead Sea, and it's 274 yards (250 m) below sea level. Jericho was an important place in Bible history, in the Old Testament as well as in the New Testament.

THE WITNESSES

✓ RAHAB (JOSHUA 2:1)

She was a Canaanite woman who was possibly forced to be a prostitute in order to feed her family and give them a place to live. But God saw her faith, so Rahab became the first person who wasn't an Israelite to belong to the people of God. In the New Testament, Rahab appears as a model of a person who trusts God (Hebrews 11:31; James 2:25). She is one of David's and Jesus' great-grandmothers (Matthew 1:5).

⁴But the woman had taken the two men and hidden them. She said, "Yes, the men came to me, but I did not know where they had come from. ⁵At dusk, when it was time to close the city gate, they left. I don't know which way they went. Go after them quickly. You may catch up with them." ⁶(But she had taken them up to the roof and hidden them under the stalks of flax she had laid out on the roof.) ⁷So the men set out in pursuit

THE SCENE

SHITTIM

(JOSHUA 2:1)

This city is in Moab near Mount Nebo, close to Jericho on the other side of the Jordan River. In Shittim, God gave Joshua the order to become Moses' replacement (Numbers 27:18–23).

of the spies on the road that leads to the fords of the Jordan, and as soon as the pursuers had gone out, the gate was shut.

⁸Before the spies lay down for the night, she went up on the roof ⁹and said to them, "I know that the LORD has given you this land and that a great fear of you has fallen on us, so that all who live in this country are melting in fear because of you. ¹⁰We have heard how the LORD dried up the water of the Red Seaᵃ for you when you came out of Egypt, and what you did to Sihon and Og, the two kings of the Amorites east of the Jordan, whom you completely destroyed.ᵇ ¹¹When we heard of it, our hearts melted in fear and everyone's courage failed because of you, for the LORD your God is God in heaven above and on the earth below.

¹²"Now then, please swear to me by the LORD that you will show kindness to my family, because I have shown kindness to you. Give me a sure sign ¹³that you will spare the lives of my father and mother, my brothers and sisters, and all who belong to them—and that you will save us from death."

¹⁴"Our lives for your lives!" the men assured her. "If you don't tell what we are doing, we will treat you kindly and faithfully when the LORD gives us the land."

¹⁵So she let them down by a rope through the window, for the house she lived in was part of the city wall. ¹⁶She said to them, "Go to the hills so the pursuers will not find you. Hide yourselves there three days until they return, and then go on your way."

ᵃ 10 Or the Sea of Reeds   ᵇ 10 The Hebrew term refers to the irrevocable giving over of things or persons to the LORD, often by totally destroying them.

BREAKTHROUGH!

Close the city gate

(JOSHUA 2:5)

At the time the Israelites reached the promised land (Palestine), several cities, like Jericho, were surrounded and protected by enormous walls about 11 yards (10 m) high and 4–7 yards (4–6 m) thick. Usually, there was only one huge entrance with wooden doors, which they closed at night.

BREAKTHROUGH!

Stalks of flax
(JOSHUA 2:6)

Flax is a plant that has small, narrow leaves and grows to about three feet (1 m) in height. Its fruit looks like a capsule full of small seeds, which produce an oil that can be used as food or also to make paint. Stalks are just the long stems that were laid out to dry.

RED SEA OR SEA OF REEDS?

(JOSHUA 2:10)

There are Bibles that call this "Red Sea" and others that call it "Sea of Reeds." But the truth is that they are two different seas! Experts who study the Bible say that according to the route the Israelites took when they left Egypt, this is Sea of Reeds or Reed Lake, because that's what the Hebrew words *yam suf* mean.

¹⁷Now the men had said to her, "This oath you made us swear will not be binding on us ¹⁸unless, when we enter the land, you have tied this scarlet cord in the window through which you let us down, and unless you have brought your father and mother, your brothers and all your family into your house. ¹⁹If any of them go outside your house into the street, their blood will be on their own heads; we will not be responsible. As for those who are in the house with you, their blood will be on our head if a hand is laid on them. ²⁰But if you tell what we are doing, we will be released from the oath you made us swear."

²¹"Agreed," she replied. "Let it be as you say."

So she sent them away, and they departed. And she tied the scarlet cord in the window.

²²When they left, they went into the hills and stayed there three days, until the pursuers had searched all along the road and returned without finding them. ²³Then the two men started back. They went down out of the hills, forded the river and came to Joshua son of Nun and told him everything that had happened to them. ²⁴They said to Joshua, "The LORD has surely given the whole land into our hands; all the people are melting in fear because of us."

Crossing the Jordan

3 Early in the morning Joshua and all the Israelites set out from Shittim and went to the Jordan, where they camped before crossing over. ²After three days the officers went throughout the camp, ³giving orders to the people: "When you see the ark of the covenant of the LORD your God, and the Levitical priests carrying it, you are to move out from your positions and follow it. ⁴Then you will know which way to go, since you have never been this way before. But keep a distance of about two thousand cubitsᵃ between you and the ark; do not go near it."

⁵Joshua told the people, "Consecrate yourselves, for tomorrow the LORD will do amazing things among you."

⁶Joshua said to the priests, "Take up the ark of the covenant and pass on ahead of the people." So they took it up and went ahead of them.

⁷And the LORD said to Joshua, "Today I will begin to exalt you in the eyes of all Israel, so they may know that I am with you as I was with Moses. ⁸Tell the priests who carry the ark of the covenant: 'When you reach the edge of the Jordan's waters, go and stand in the river.' "

BREAKTHROUGH!

Consecrate

(JOSHUA 3:5)

This was what they had to do to get ready to present themselves before God. It was a very special preparation for war or for a special religious activity, which consisted of bathing very well, washing the clothes and having them very clean. (See Exodus 19:10 – 15.)

⁹Joshua said to the Israelites, "Come here and listen to the words of the LORD your God. ¹⁰This is how you will know that the living God is among you and that he will certainly drive out before you the Canaanites, Hittites, Hivites, Perizzites, Girgashites, Amorites and Jebusites. ¹¹See, the ark of the covenant of the Lord of all the earth will go into the Jordan ahead of you. ¹²Now then, choose twelve men from the tribes of Israel, one from each tribe. ¹³And as soon as the priests who carry the ark of the LORD—the Lord of all the earth—set foot in the Jordan, its waters flowing downstream will be cut off and stand up in a heap."

¹⁴So when the people broke camp to cross the Jordan, the priests carrying the ark of the covenant went ahead of them. ¹⁵Now the Jordan is at flood stage all during harvest. Yet as soon as the priests who carried the ark reached the Jordan and their feet touched the water's edge, ¹⁶the water from upstream stopped flowing. It piled up in a heap a great distance away, at a town called Adam in the vicinity of Zarethan, while the water flowing down to the Sea of the Arabah (that is, the Dead Sea) was completely cut off. So the people crossed over opposite Jericho. ¹⁷The priests who carried the ark of the covenant of the LORD stopped in the middle of the Jordan and stood on dry ground, while all Israel passed by until the whole nation had completed the crossing on dry ground.

4 When the whole nation had finished crossing the Jordan, the LORD said to Joshua, ²"Choose twelve men from among the people, one from each tribe, ³and tell them to take up twelve stones from the middle of the Jordan, from right where the priests are standing, and carry them over with you and put them down at the place where you stay tonight."

⁴So Joshua called together the twelve men he had appointed from the Israelites, one from each tribe, ⁵and said to them, "Go over before the ark of the LORD your God into the middle of the Jordan. Each of you is to take up a stone on his

ᵃ 4 That is, about 3,000 feet or about 900 meters

THE SCENE

DEAD SEA

(JOSHUA 3:16)

The Dead Sea isn't really a sea at all! It's a big salt water lake 438 yards (400 m) below sea level. It's the lowest body of water on the planet! The Jordan River and some other smaller rivers all end here. It's 50 miles (80 km) long and almost 10 miles (16 km) wide at one point. The water in this lake has so much salt and other minerals that fish can't live here! That's why it is called the "Dead" Sea. The water is so salty that people can float on top and don't need to swim.

shoulder, according to the number of the tribes of the Israelites, ⁶to serve as a sign among you. In the future, when your children ask you, 'What do these stones mean?' ⁷tell them that the flow of the Jordan was cut off before the ark of the covenant of the LORD. When it crossed the Jordan, the waters of the Jordan were cut off. These stones are to be a memorial to the people of Israel forever."

⁸So the Israelites did as Joshua commanded them. They took twelve stones from the middle of the Jordan, according to the number of the tribes of the Israelites, as the LORD had told Joshua; and they carried them over with them to their camp, where they put them down. ⁹Joshua set up the twelve stones that had beenᵃ in the middle of the Jordan at the spot where the priests who carried the ark of the covenant had stood. And they are there to this day.

¹⁰Now the priests who carried the ark remained standing in the middle of the Jordan until everything the LORD had commanded Joshua was done by the people, just as Moses had directed Joshua. The people hurried over, ¹¹and as soon as all of them had crossed, the ark of the LORD and the priests came to the other side while the people watched. ¹²The men of Reuben, Gad and the half-tribe of Manasseh crossed over, ready for battle, in front of the Israelites, as Moses had directed them. ¹³About forty thousand armed for battle crossed over before the LORD to the plains of Jericho for war.

¹⁴That day the LORD exalted Joshua in the sight of all Israel; and they stood in awe of him all the days of his life, just as they had stood in awe of Moses.

¹⁵Then the LORD said to Joshua, ¹⁶"Command the priests carrying the ark of the covenant law to come up out of the Jordan."

¹⁷So Joshua commanded the priests, "Come up out of the Jordan."

¹⁸And the priests came up out of the river carrying the ark of the covenant of the LORD. No sooner had they set their feet on the dry ground than the waters of the Jordan returned to their place and ran at flood stage as before.

¹⁹On the tenth day of the first month the people went up from the Jordan and camped at Gilgal on the eastern border of Jericho. ²⁰And Joshua set up at Gilgal the twelve stones they had taken out of the Jordan. ²¹He said to the Israelites, "In the future when your descendants ask their parents, 'What do these stones mean?' ²²tell them, 'Israel crossed the Jordan on

ᵃ 9 Or Joshua also set up twelve stones

THE SCENE

GILGAL

(JOSHUA 4:19)

This city is located between the Jordan River and Jericho. It was the first place the Israelites camped when they crossed the river to enter the Holy Land. From that moment on, Gilgal became Joshua's center of operations. Later, in the time of the judges and when they started having kings, it became an important center for rulers, priests and soldiers.

dry ground.' ²³For the LORD your God dried up the Jordan before you until you had crossed over. The LORD your God did to the Jordan what he had done to the Red Sea^a when he dried it up before us until we had crossed over. ²⁴He did this so that all the peoples of the earth might know that the hand of the LORD is powerful and so that you might always fear the LORD your God."

5 Now when all the Amorite kings west of the Jordan and all the Canaanite kings along the coast heard how the LORD had dried up the Jordan before the Israelites until they^b had crossed over, their hearts melted in fear and they no longer had the courage to face the Israelites.

Circumcision and Passover at Gilgal

²At that time the LORD said to Joshua, "Make flint knives and circumcise the Israelites again." ³So Joshua made flint knives and circumcised the Israelites at Gibeath Haaraloth.^c

⁴Now this is why he did so: All those who came out of Egypt—all the men of military age—died in the wilderness on the way after leaving Egypt. ⁵All the people that came out had been circumcised, but all the people born in the wilderness during the journey from Egypt had not. ⁶The Israelites had moved about in the wilderness forty years until all the men who were of military age when they left Egypt had died, since they had not obeyed the LORD. For the LORD had sworn to them that they would not see the land he had solemnly promised their ancestors to give us, a land flowing with milk and honey. ⁷So he raised up their sons in their place, and these were the ones Joshua circumcised. They were still uncircumcised because they had not been circumcised on the way. ⁸And after the whole nation had been circumcised, they remained where they were in camp until they were healed.

⁹Then the LORD said to Joshua, "Today I have rolled away the reproach of Egypt from you." So the place has been called Gilgal^d to this day.

¹⁰On the evening of the fourteenth day of the month, while camped at Gilgal on the plains of Jericho, the Israelites celebrated the Passover. ¹¹The day after the Passover, that very day, they ate some of the produce of the land: unleavened bread and roasted grain. ¹²The manna stopped the day after^e they ate this food from the land; there was no longer any manna for the Israelites, but that year they ate the produce of Canaan.

The Fall of Jericho

¹³Now when Joshua was near Jericho, he looked up and saw a man standing in front of him with a drawn sword in his

---

^a 23 Or the Sea of Reeds   ^b 1 Another textual tradition we   ^c 3 Gibeath Haaraloth means the hill of foreskins.
^d 9 Gilgal sounds like the Hebrew for roll.   ^e 12 Or the day

BREAKTHROUGH!

Unleavened bread
(JOSHUA 5:11)

Unleavened bread doesn't have any ingredient that make the dough rise. It looks like a thick tortilla. They ate this bread during the Passover celebration to remember that when they left Egypt in a hurry, they didn't have time to wait for the bread dough to ferment and "puff up."

hand. Joshua went up to him and asked, "Are you for us or for our enemies?"

¹⁴"Neither," he replied, "but as commander of the army of the LORD I have now come." Then Joshua fell facedown to the ground in reverence, and asked him, "What message does my Lord*a* have for his servant?"

¹⁵The commander of the LORD's army replied, "Take off your sandals, for the place where you are standing is holy." And Joshua did so.

6 Now the gates of Jericho were securely barred because of the Israelites. No one went out and no one came in.

²Then the LORD said to Joshua, "See, I have delivered Jericho into your hands, along with its king and its fighting men. ³March around the city once with all the armed men. Do this for six days. ⁴Have seven priests carry trumpets of rams'

horns in front of the ark. On the seventh day, march around the city seven times, with the priests blowing the trumpets. ⁵When you hear them sound a long blast on the trumpets, have the whole army give a loud shout; then the wall of the city will collapse and the army will go up, everyone straight in."

⁶So Joshua son of Nun called the priests and said to them, "Take up the ark of the covenant of the LORD and have seven priests carry trumpets in front of it." ⁷And he ordered the army, "Advance!

---

a 14 Or lord

THE SCENE

CANAAN

(JOSHUA 5:12)

This is another name for the promised land. It's called Canaan because of the different nations who lived in Palestine many years before the Israelites arrived. They were the Hittites, Amorites, Canaanites, Perizzites, Girgashites, Hivites and Jebusites. They were people who lived in the mountains, in the valley and along the eastern shore of the Mediterranean Sea as far as Mount Lebanon.

March around the city, with an armed guard going ahead of the ark of the LORD."

8When Joshua had spoken to the people, the seven priests carrying the seven trumpets before the LORD went forward, blowing their trumpets, and the ark of the LORD's covenant followed them. 9The armed guard marched ahead of the priests who blew the trumpets, and the rear guard followed the ark. All this time the trumpets were sounding. 10But Joshua had commanded the army, "Do not give a war cry, do not raise your voices, do not say a word until the day I tell you to shout. Then shout!" 11So he had the ark of the LORD carried around the city, circling it once. Then the army returned to camp and spent the night there.

12Joshua got up early the next morning and the priests took up the ark of the LORD. 13The seven priests carrying the seven trumpets went forward, marching before the ark of the LORD and blowing the trumpets. The armed men went ahead of them and the rear guard followed the ark of the LORD, while the trumpets kept sounding. 14So on the second day they marched around the city once and returned to the camp. They did this for six days.

15On the seventh day, they got up at daybreak and marched around the city seven times in the same manner, except that on that day they circled the city seven times. 16The seventh time around, when the priests sounded the trumpet blast, Joshua commanded the army, "Shout! For the LORD has given you the city! 17The city and all that is in it are to be devoted*a* to the LORD. Only Rahab the prostitute and all who are with her in her house shall be spared, because she hid the spies we sent. 18But keep away from the devoted things, so that you will not bring about your own destruction by taking any of them. Otherwise you will make the camp of Israel liable to destruction and bring trouble on it. 19All the silver and gold and the articles of bronze and iron are sacred to the LORD and must go into his treasury."

20When the trumpets sounded, the army shouted, and at the sound of the trumpet, when the men gave a loud shout, the wall collapsed; so everyone charged straight in, and they took the city. 21They devoted the city to the LORD and destroyed with the sword every living thing in it—men and women, young and old, cattle, sheep and donkeys.

22Joshua said to the two men who had spied out the land, "Go into the prostitute's house and bring her out and all who belong to her, in accordance with your oath to her." 23So the young men who had done the spying went in and brought out Rahab, her father and mother, her brothers and sisters and all who belonged to her. They brought out her entire family and put them in a place outside the camp of Israel.

24Then they burned the whole city and everything in it, but they put the silver and gold and the articles of bronze and iron into the treasury of the LORD's house. 25But Joshua spared Rahab the prostitute, with her family and all who belonged to her, because she hid the men Joshua had sent as spies to Jericho—and she lives among the Israelites to this day.

26At that time Joshua pronounced this solemn oath: "Cursed before the LORD is the one who undertakes to rebuild this city, Jericho:

"At the cost of his firstborn son
    he will lay its foundations;
at the cost of his youngest
    he will set up its gates."

27So the LORD was with Joshua, and his fame spread throughout the land.

Achan's Sin

7 But the Israelites were unfaithful in regard to the devoted things*b*; Achan son of Karmi, the son of Zimri,*c* the son of Zerah, of the tribe of Judah, took some of them. So the LORD's anger burned against Israel.

2Now Joshua sent men from Jericho to Ai, which is near Beth Aven to the east

---

a 17 The Hebrew term refers to the irrevocable giving over of things or persons to the LORD, often by totally destroying them; also in verses 18 and 21.   *b* 1 The Hebrew term refers to the irrevocable giving over of things or persons to the LORD, often by totally destroying them; also in verses 11, 12, 13 and 15.   *c* 1 See Septuagint and 1 Chron. 2:6; Hebrew *Zabdi*; also in verses 17 and 18.

BREAKTHROUGH!

"They ... destroyed with the sword every living thing"

(JOSHUA 6:21)

How hard is this matter of violence in the Old Testament?! People who study the Bible a lot say that this story was told many years after it happened, to explain that it was God who helped the Israelites in a special way to get settled in the new land where they were going to live.

Only a few people lived inside the cities that had walls like Jericho. Just the richest and most powerful in the nation lived in the cities. They were the kings, the military officers and the religious leaders. Most of the common people lived in small villages or towns that didn't have walls to protect them. So the destruction of Jericho that God ordered was damage to the powerful people but not the common people.

Another important thing to know is that archeological studies haven't been able to find terrible killings of entire groups of people in these walled cities during the times of Joshua and the judges. The words used here in Joshua 6:21 seem to be larger-than-life and made by a person who, despite being weak, had managed to overcome an enemy.

CHECK THE FACTS

How did the walls of the city of Jericho fall?

A) The giant Anak blew them down with one big breath.

B) God gave the Israelites a special plan that they followed to the letter.

C) All the people threw giant rocks against the wall for seven days, until the walls fell down.

B :ЯƎWSИA TƆƎЯЯOƆ

of Bethel, and told them, "Go up and spy out the region." So the men went up and spied out Ai.

³When they returned to Joshua, they said, "Not all the army will have to go up against Ai. Send two or three thousand men to take it and do not weary the whole army, for only a few people live there." ⁴So about three thousand went up; but they were routed by the men of Ai, ⁵who killed about thirty-six of them. They chased the Israelites from the city gate as far as the stone quarries and struck them down on the slopes. At this the hearts of the people melted in fear and became like water.

⁶Then Joshua tore his clothes and fell facedown to the ground before the ark of the LORD, remaining there till evening.

The elders of Israel did the same, and sprinkled dust on their heads. ⁷And Joshua said, "Alas, Sovereign LORD, why did you ever bring this people across the Jordan to deliver us into the hands of the Amorites to destroy us? If only we had been content to stay on the other side of the Jordan! ⁸Pardon your servant, Lord. What can I say, now that Israel has been routed by its enemies? ⁹The Canaanites and the other people of the country will hear about this and they will surround us and wipe out our name from the earth. What then will you do for your own great name?"

¹⁰The LORD said to Joshua, "Stand up! What are you doing down on your face? ¹¹Israel has sinned; they have violated my covenant, which I commanded them to keep. They have taken some of the devoted things; they have stolen, they have lied, they have put them with their own possessions. ¹²That is why the Israelites cannot stand against their enemies; they turn their backs and run because they have been made liable to destruction. I will not be with you anymore unless you destroy whatever among you is devoted to destruction.

¹³"Go, consecrate the people. Tell them, 'Consecrate yourselves in preparation for tomorrow; for this is what the LORD, the God of Israel, says: There are devoted things among you, Israel. You cannot stand against your enemies until you remove them.

¹⁴"'In the morning, present yourselves tribe by tribe. The tribe the LORD chooses shall come forward clan by clan; the clan the LORD chooses shall come forward family by family; and the family the LORD chooses shall come forward man by man. ¹⁵Whoever is caught with the devoted things shall be destroyed by fire, along with all that belongs to him. He has violated the covenant of the LORD and has done an outrageous thing in Israel!'"

¹⁶Early the next morning Joshua had Israel come forward by tribes, and Judah was chosen. ¹⁷The clans of Judah came forward, and the Zerahites were chosen. He had the clan of the Zerahites come forward by families, and Zimri was

chosen. ¹⁸Joshua had his family come forward man by man, and Achan son of Karmi, the son of Zimri, the son of Zerah, of the tribe of Judah, was chosen.

¹⁹Then Joshua said to Achan, "My son, give glory to the LORD, the God of Israel, and honor him. Tell me what you have done; do not hide it from me."

²⁰Achan replied, "It is true! I have sinned against the LORD, the God of Israel. This is what I have done: ²¹When I saw in the plunder a beautiful robe from Babylonia,ᵃ two hundred shekelsᵇ of silver and a bar of gold weighing fifty shekels,ᶜ I coveted them and took them. They are hidden in the ground inside my tent, with the silver underneath."

²²So Joshua sent messengers, and they ran to the tent, and there it was,

---

ᵃ 21 Hebrew *Shinar* about 2.3 kilograms or about 575 grams
ᵇ 21 That is, about 5 pounds or
ᶜ 21 That is, about 1 1/4 pounds

BREAK THROUGH!

Tear your clothes and sprinkle dust or ashes on your head

(JOSHUA 7:6)

In Bible times, this was a way to show a lot of pain and sadness because a family member or dear friend had died. It was also done when a battle was lost in a war.

hidden in his tent, with the silver underneath. ²³They took the things from the tent, brought them to Joshua and all the Israelites and spread them out before the Lord.

²⁴Then Joshua, together with all Israel, took Achan son of Zerah, the silver, the robe, the gold bar, his sons and daughters, his cattle, donkeys and sheep, his tent and all that he had, to the Valley of Achor. ²⁵Joshua said, "Why have you brought this trouble on us? The Lord will bring trouble on you today."

Then all Israel stoned him, and after they had stoned the rest, they burned them. ²⁶Over Achan they heaped up a large pile of rocks, which remains to this day. Then the Lord turned from his fierce anger. Therefore that place has been called the Valley of Achor*ᵃ* ever since.

Ai Destroyed

8 Then the Lord said to Joshua, "Do not be afraid; do not be discouraged. Take the whole army with you, and go up and attack Ai. For I have delivered into your hands the king of Ai, his people, his city and his land. ²You shall do to Ai and its king as you did to Jericho and its king, except that you may carry off their plunder and livestock for yourselves. Set an ambush behind the city."

³So Joshua and the whole army moved out to attack Ai. He chose thirty thousand of his best fighting men and sent them out at night ⁴with these orders: "Listen carefully. You are to set an ambush behind the city. Don't go very far from it. All of you be on the alert. ⁵I and all those with me will advance on the city, and when the men come out against us, as they did before, we will flee from them. ⁶They will pursue us until we have lured them away from the city, for they will say, 'They are running away from us as they did before.' So when we flee from them, ⁷you are to rise up from ambush and take the city. The Lord your God will give it into your hand. ⁸When you have taken the city, set it on fire. Do what the Lord has commanded. See to it; you have my orders."

⁹Then Joshua sent them off, and they went to the place of ambush and lay in wait between Bethel and Ai, to the west of Ai—but Joshua spent that night with the people.

¹⁰Early the next morning Joshua mustered his army, and he and the leaders of Israel marched before them to Ai. ¹¹The entire force that was with him marched up and approached the city and arrived in front of it. They set up camp north of Ai, with the valley between them and the city. ¹²Joshua had taken about five thousand men and set them in ambush between Bethel and Ai, to the west of the city. ¹³So the soldiers took up their positions—with the main camp to the north of the city and the ambush to the west of it. That night Joshua went into the valley.

¹⁴When the king of Ai saw this, he and all the men of the city hurried out early in the morning to meet Israel in battle at a certain place overlooking the Arabah. But he did not know that an ambush had been set against him behind the city. ¹⁵Joshua and all Israel let themselves be driven back before them, and they fled toward the wilderness. ¹⁶All the men of Ai were called to pursue them, and they pursued Joshua and were lured away from the city. ¹⁷Not a man remained in Ai or Bethel who did not go after Israel. They left the city open and went in pursuit of Israel.

¹⁸Then the Lord said to Joshua, "Hold out toward Ai the javelin that is in your hand, for into your hand I will deliver the city." So Joshua held out toward the city the javelin that was in his hand. ¹⁹As soon as he did this, the men in the ambush rose quickly from their position and rushed forward. They entered the city and captured it and quickly set it on fire.

²⁰The men of Ai looked back and saw the smoke of the city rising up into the sky, but they had no chance to escape in any direction; the Israelites who had been fleeing toward the wilderness had turned back against their pursuers. ²¹For when Joshua and all Israel saw that the ambush had taken the city and that smoke was going up from it, they turned around and attacked the men of Ai. ²²Those in the ambush also came out of the city

---

ᵃ 26 Achor means trouble.

against them, so that they were caught in the middle, with Israelites on both sides. Israel cut them down, leaving them neither survivors nor fugitives. ²³But they took the king of Ai alive and brought him to Joshua.

²⁴When Israel had finished killing all the men of Ai in the fields and in the wilderness where they had chased them, and when every one of them had been put to the sword, all the Israelites returned to Ai and killed those who were in it. ²⁵Twelve thousand men and women fell that day— all the people of Ai. ²⁶For Joshua did not draw back the hand that held out his javelin until he had destroyed*a* all who lived in Ai. ²⁷But Israel did carry off for themselves the livestock and plunder of this city, as the LORD had instructed Joshua.

²⁸So Joshua burned Ai*b* and made it a permanent heap of ruins, a desolate

THE SCENE

MOUNT EBAL

(JOSHUA 8:30)

It is north of the city of Shechem, and it is 1,094 yards (1,000 m) above sea level. According to Deuteronomy 11:29, it's the mountain of "curses," because the people didn't respect their pact with God.

place to this day. ²⁹He impaled the body of the king of Ai on a pole and left it there until evening. At sunset, Joshua ordered them to take the body from the pole and throw it down at the entrance of the city gate. And they raised a large pile of rocks over it, which remains to this day.

The Covenant Renewed at Mount Ebal

³⁰Then Joshua built on Mount Ebal an altar to the LORD, the God of Israel, ³¹as Moses the servant of the LORD had commanded the Israelites. He built it according to what is written in the Book of the Law of Moses—an altar of uncut stones, on which no iron tool had been used. On it they offered to the LORD burnt offerings

BREAK THROUGH!

Why did they hang the body of the king of Ai on a pole?

(JOSHUA 8:29)

They did this to shame the enemy nation. They also did it to scare the people who were planning to go to battle with the people who had beaten them. The same thing happened with the five kings (10:26).

---

a 26 The Hebrew term refers to the irrevocable giving over of things or persons to the LORD, often by totally destroying them.   *b 28 Ai* means *the ruin*.

and sacrificed fellowship offerings. ³²There, in the presence of the Israelites, Joshua wrote on stones a copy of the law of Moses. ³³All the Israelites, with their elders, officials and judges, were standing on both sides of the ark of the covenant of the LORD, facing the Levitical priests who carried it. Both the foreigners living among them and the native-born were there. Half of the people stood in front of Mount Gerizim and half of them in front of Mount Ebal, as Moses the servant of the LORD had formerly commanded when he gave instructions to bless the people of Israel.

³⁴Afterward, Joshua read all the words of the law—the blessings and the curses—just as it is written in the Book of

BREAKTHROUGH!

Blessings and curses
(JOSHUA 8:34)

Blessings and curses were an important part of all the agreements they made in that time. The people who made the deal promised to do everything the agreement paper said. If a person didn't keep the bargain, then he deserved the curses. But if he carried out all the responsibilities, then he was given a life full of blessings.

THE SCENE

MOUNT GERIZIM
(JOSHUA 8:33)

This mountain is southeast of the city of Shechem. It is 984 yards (900 m) above sea level. According to Deuteronomy 11:29, it's the mountain of the "blessings" the people received when they obeyed their pact with God. A long time later, the Samaritans built their main temple here on this mountain (read John 4:20).

the Law. ³⁵There was not a word of all that Moses had commanded that Joshua did not read to the whole assembly of Israel, including the women and children, and the foreigners who lived among them.

The Gibeonite Deception

9 Now when all the kings west of the Jordan heard about these things—the kings in the hill country, in the western foothills, and along the entire coast of the Mediterranean Sea as far as Lebanon (the kings of the Hittites, Amorites, Canaanites, Perizzites, Hivites and Jebusites)— ²they came together to wage war against Joshua and Israel.

³However, when the people of Gibeon heard what Joshua had done to Jericho and Ai, ⁴they resorted to a ruse: They went as a delegation whose donkeys

were loaded[a] with worn-out sacks and old wineskins, cracked and mended. [5]They put worn and patched sandals on their feet and wore old clothes. All the bread of their food supply was dry and moldy. [6]Then they went to Joshua in the camp at Gilgal and said to him and the Israelites, "We have come from a distant country; make a treaty with us."

[7]The Israelites said to the Hivites, "But perhaps you live near us, so how can we make a treaty with you?"

[8]"We are your servants," they said to Joshua.

But Joshua asked, "Who are you and where do you come from?"

[9]They answered: "Your servants have come from a very distant country because of the fame of the LORD your God. For we have heard reports of him: all that he did in Egypt, [10]and all that he did to the two kings of the Amorites east of the Jordan— Sihon king of Heshbon, and Og king of Bashan, who reigned in Ashtaroth. [11]And our

BREAKTHROUGH!

People of Gibeon

(JOSHUA 9:3)

These people lived in a city called Gibeon. It was 11 km southeast of the city of Ai. Unlike the other nations in the region, the Gibeonites didn't have a king. Experts think their government was like a board of elders.

elders and all those living in our country said to us, 'Take provisions for your journey; go and meet them and say to them, "We are your servants; make a treaty with us." ' [12]This bread of ours was warm when we packed it at home on the day we left to come to you. But now see how dry and moldy it is. [13]And these wineskins that we filled were new, but see how cracked they are. And our clothes and sandals are worn out by the very long journey."

[14]The Israelites sampled their provisions but did not inquire of the LORD. [15]Then Joshua made a treaty of peace with them to let them live, and the leaders of the assembly ratified it by oath.

[16]Three days after they made the treaty with the Gibeonites, the Israelites heard that they were neighbors, living near them. [17]So the Israelites set out and on the third day came to their cities: Gibeon, Kephirah, Beeroth and Kiriath Jearim. [18]But the Israelites did not attack them, because the leaders of the assembly had sworn an oath to them by the LORD, the God of Israel.

The whole assembly grumbled against the leaders, [19]but all the leaders answered, "We have given them our oath by the LORD, the God of Israel, and we cannot touch them now. [20]This is what we will do to them: We will let them live, so that God's wrath will not fall on us for breaking the oath we swore to them." [21]They continued, "Let them live, but let them be woodcutters and water carriers in the service of the whole assembly." So the leaders' promise to them was kept.

[22]Then Joshua summoned the Gibeonites and said, "Why did you deceive us by saying, 'We live a long way from you,' while actually you live near us? [23]You are now under a curse: You will never be released from service as woodcutters and water carriers for the house of my God."

[24]They answered Joshua, "Your servants were clearly told how the LORD your God had commanded his servant Moses to give you the whole land and to wipe out all its inhabitants from before you. So we feared for our lives because of you,

---

[a] 4 Most Hebrew manuscripts; some Hebrew manuscripts, Vulgate and Syriac (see also Septuagint) *They prepared provisions and loaded their donkeys*

and that is why we did this. 25We are now in your hands. Do to us whatever seems good and right to you."

26So Joshua saved them from the Israelites, and they did not kill them. 27That day he made the Gibeonites woodcutters and water carriers for the assembly, to provide for the needs of the altar of the LORD at the place the LORD would choose. And that is what they are to this day.

The Sun Stands Still

10 Now Adoni-Zedek king of Jerusalem heard that Joshua had taken Ai and totally destroyed[a] it, doing to Ai and its king as he had done to Jericho and its king, and that the people of Gibeon had made a treaty of peace with Israel and had become their allies. 2He and his people were very much alarmed at this, because Gibeon was an important city, like one of the

THE
WITNESSES

✓ **ADONI-ZEDEK** (JOSHUA 10:1)
This name means "my LORD is justice." It might also refer to the name of a god called Zedek that was worshiped in the ancient city of Jerusalem. Adoni-Zedek was the king of Jerusalem during Joshua's life, when the city belonged to the Jebusites.

royal cities; it was larger than Ai, and all its men were good fighters. 3So Adoni-Zedek king of Jerusalem appealed to Hoham king of Hebron, Piram king of Jarmuth, Japhia king of Lachish and Debir king of Eglon. 4"Come up and help me attack Gibeon," he said, "because it has made peace with Joshua and the Israelites."

5Then the five kings of the Amorites— the kings of Jerusalem, Hebron, Jarmuth,

THE SCENE

JERUSALEM, HEBRON, JARMUTH, LACHISH AND EGLON

(JOSHUA 10:1–6)

In Joshua's time, all these cities belonged to different Amorite nations.

---

a 1 The Hebrew term refers to the irrevocable giving over of things or persons to the LORD, often by totally destroying them; also in verses 28, 35, 37, 39 and 40.

THE SCENE

GIBEON

(JOSHUA 10:5)

This place didn't have any protection walls. It was located 5 miles (8 km) northeast of Jerusalem. In the time of the judges and before the temple was built in Jerusalem, Gibeon was an important religious center. God's sanctuary was there. (Read about this in 1 Chronicles 16:39.)

Lachish and Eglon—joined forces. They moved up with all their troops and took up positions against Gibeon and attacked it.

⁶The Gibeonites then sent word to Joshua in the camp at Gilgal: "Do not abandon your servants. Come up to us quickly and save us! Help us, because all the Amorite kings from the hill country have joined forces against us."

⁷So Joshua marched up from Gilgal with his entire army, including all the best fighting men. ⁸The LORD said to Joshua, "Do not be afraid of them; I have given them into your hand. Not one of them will be able to withstand you."

⁹After an all-night march from Gilgal, Joshua took them by surprise. ¹⁰The LORD threw them into confusion before Israel, so Joshua and the Israelites defeated them completely at Gibeon. Israel pursued them along the road going up to Beth Horon and cut them down all the way to Azekah and Makkedah. ¹¹As they fled before Israel on the road down from Beth Horon to Azekah, the LORD hurled large hailstones down on them, and more of them died from the hail than were killed by the swords of the Israelites.

¹²On the day the LORD gave the Amorites over to Israel, Joshua said to the LORD in the presence of Israel:

"Sun, stand still over Gibeon,
    and you, moon, over the Valley of
        Aijalon."
¹³So the sun stood still,
    and the moon stopped,
        till the nation avenged itself onᵃ its
            enemies,

as it is written in the Book of Jashar.

ᵃ 13 Or *nation triumphed over*

BREAK THROUGH!

Did the sun stand still?

(JOSHUA 10:12-13)

This idea is part of a poem, so it's like a symbol. It was a way to explain how the people of Israel managed to defeat their enemies in a spectacular way with God's supernatural help.

The sun stopped in the middle of the sky and delayed going down about a full day. ¹⁴There has never been a day like it before or since, a day when the LORD listened to a human being. Surely the LORD was fighting for Israel!

¹⁵Then Joshua returned with all Israel to the camp at Gilgal.

Five Amorite Kings Killed

¹⁶Now the five kings had fled and hidden in the cave at Makkedah. ¹⁷When Joshua was told that the five kings had been found hiding in the cave at Makkedah, ¹⁸he said, "Roll large rocks up to the mouth of the cave, and post some men there to guard it. ¹⁹But don't stop; pursue your enemies! Attack them from the rear and don't let them reach their cities, for the LORD your God has given them into your hand."

²⁰So Joshua and the Israelites defeated them completely, but a few survivors managed to reach their fortified cities. ²¹The whole army then returned safely to Joshua in the camp at Makkedah, and no one uttered a word against the Israelites.

²²Joshua said, "Open the mouth of the cave and bring those five kings out to me." ²³So they brought the five kings out of the cave—the kings of Jerusalem, Hebron, Jarmuth, Lachish and Eglon. ²⁴When they had brought these kings to Joshua, he summoned all the men of Israel and said to the army commanders who had come with him, "Come here and put your feet on the necks of these kings." So they came forward and placed their feet on their necks.

²⁵Joshua said to them, "Do not be afraid; do not be discouraged. Be strong and courageous. This is what the LORD will do to all the enemies you are going to fight." ²⁶Then Joshua put the kings to death and exposed their bodies on five poles, and they were left hanging on the poles until evening.

²⁷At sunset Joshua gave the order and they took them down from the poles and threw them into the cave where they had been hiding. At the mouth of the cave they placed large rocks, which are there to this day.

Southern Cities Conquered

²⁸That day Joshua took Makkedah. He put the city and its king to the sword and totally destroyed everyone in it. He left no survivors. And he did to the king of Makkedah as he had done to the king of Jericho.

²⁹Then Joshua and all Israel with him moved on from Makkedah to Libnah and attacked it. ³⁰The LORD also gave that city and its king into Israel's hand. The city and everyone in it Joshua put to the sword. He left no survivors there. And he did to its king as he had done to the king of Jericho.

³¹Then Joshua and all Israel with him moved on from Libnah to Lachish; he took up positions against it and attacked it. ³²The LORD gave Lachish into Israel's hands, and Joshua took it on the second day. The city and everyone in it he put to the sword, just as he had done to Libnah. ³³Meanwhile, Horam king of Gezer had come up to help Lachish, but Joshua defeated him and his army—until no survivors were left.

³⁴Then Joshua and all Israel with him moved on from Lachish to Eglon; they took up positions against it and attacked it. ³⁵They captured it that same day and put it to the sword and totally destroyed everyone in it, just as they had done to Lachish.

³⁶Then Joshua and all Israel with him went up from Eglon to Hebron and attacked it. ³⁷They took the city and put it to the sword, together with its king, its villages and everyone in it. They left no survivors. Just as at Eglon, they totally destroyed it and everyone in it.

³⁸Then Joshua and all Israel with him turned around and attacked Debir. ³⁹They took the city, its king and its villages, and put them to the sword. Everyone in it they totally destroyed. They left no survivors. They did to Debir and its king as they had done to Libnah and its king and to Hebron.

⁴⁰So Joshua subdued the whole region, including the hill country, the Negev, the western foothills and the mountain slopes, together with all their kings. He left no survivors. He totally destroyed all who breathed, just as the LORD, the God of Israel, had commanded. ⁴¹Joshua

subdued them from Kadesh Barnea to Gaza and from the whole region of Goshen to Gibeon. [42]All these kings and their lands Joshua conquered in one campaign, because the LORD, the God of Israel, fought for Israel.

[43]Then Joshua returned with all Israel to the camp at Gilgal.

Northern Kings Defeated

11 When Jabin king of Hazor heard of this, he sent word to Jobab king of Madon, to the kings of Shimron and Akshaph, [2]and to the northern kings who were in the mountains, in the Arabah south of Kinnereth, in the western foothills and in Naphoth Dor on the west; [3]to the Canaanites in the east and west; to the Amorites, Hittites, Perizzites and Jebusites in the hill country; and to the Hivites below Hermon in the region of Mizpah. [4]They came out with all their troops and a large number of horses and chariots—a huge army, as numerous as the sand on the seashore. [5]All these kings joined forces and made camp together at the Waters of Merom to fight against Israel.

[6]The LORD said to Joshua, "Do not be afraid of them, because by this time tomorrow I will hand all of them, slain, over to Israel. You are to hamstring their horses and burn their chariots."

[7]So Joshua and his whole army came against them suddenly at the Waters of Merom and attacked them, [8]and the LORD gave them into the hand of Israel. They defeated them and pursued them all the way to Greater Sidon, to Misrephoth Maim, and to the Valley of Mizpah on the east, until no survivors were left. [9]Joshua did to them as the LORD had directed: He hamstrung their horses and burned their chariots.

[10]At that time Joshua turned back and captured Hazor and put its king to the sword. (Hazor had been the head of all these kingdoms.) [11]Everyone in it they put to the sword. They totally destroyed[a] them, not sparing anyone that breathed, and he burned Hazor itself.

[12]Joshua took all these royal cities and their kings and put them to the sword. He totally destroyed them, as Moses the servant of the LORD had commanded. [13]Yet Israel did not burn any of the cities built on their mounds—except Hazor, which Joshua burned. [14]The Israelites carried off for themselves all the plunder and livestock of these cities, but all the people they put to the sword until they completely destroyed them, not sparing anyone that breathed. [15]As the LORD commanded his servant Moses, so Moses commanded Joshua, and Joshua did it; he left nothing undone of all that the LORD commanded Moses.

[16]So Joshua took this entire land: the hill country, all the Negev, the whole region of Goshen, the western foothills, the Arabah and the mountains of Israel with their foothills, [17]from Mount Halak, which rises toward Seir, to Baal Gad in the Valley of Lebanon below Mount Hermon. He captured all their kings and put them to death. [18]Joshua waged war against all these kings for a long time. [19]Except for the Hivites living in Gibeon, not one city made a treaty of peace with the Israelites, who took them all in battle. [20]For it was the LORD himself who hardened their hearts to wage war against Israel, so that he might destroy them totally, exterminating them without mercy, as the LORD had commanded Moses.

[21]At that time Joshua went and destroyed the Anakites from the hill country: from Hebron, Debir and Anab, from all the hill country of Judah, and from all the hill country of Israel. Joshua totally destroyed them and their towns. [22]No Anakites were left in Israelite territory; only in Gaza, Gath and Ashdod did any survive.

[23]So Joshua took the entire land, just as the LORD had directed Moses, and he gave it as an inheritance to Israel according to their tribal divisions. Then the land had rest from war.

List of Defeated Kings

12 These are the kings of the land whom the Israelites had defeated and whose territory they took over east of the Jordan, from the Arnon Gorge to

---

[a] 11 The Hebrew term refers to the irrevocable giving over of things or persons to the LORD, often by totally destroying them; also in verses 12, 20 and 21.

Mount Hermon, including all the eastern side of the Arabah:

²Sihon king of the Amorites, who reigned in Heshbon.

He ruled from Aroer on the rim of the Arnon Gorge—from the middle of the gorge—to the Jabbok River, which is the border of the Ammonites. This included half of Gilead. ³He also ruled over the eastern Arabah from the Sea of Galilee[a] to the Sea of the Arabah (that is, the Dead Sea), to Beth Jeshimoth, and then southward below the slopes of Pisgah.

⁴And the territory of Og king of Bashan, one of the last of the Rephaites, who reigned in Ashtaroth and Edrei.

⁵He ruled over Mount Hermon, Salekah, all of Bashan to the border of the people of Geshur and Maakah, and half of Gilead to the border of Sihon king of Heshbon.

⁶Moses, the servant of the LORD, and the Israelites conquered them. And Moses the servant of the LORD gave their land to the Reubenites, the Gadites and the half-tribe of Manasseh to be their possession.

⁷Here is a list of the kings of the land that Joshua and the Israelites conquered on the west side of the Jordan, from Baal Gad in the Valley of Lebanon to Mount Halak, which rises toward Seir. Joshua gave their lands as an inheritance to the tribes of Israel according to their tribal divisions. ⁸The lands included the hill country, the western foothills, the Arabah, the mountain slopes, the wilderness and the Negev. These were the lands of the Hittites, Amorites, Canaanites, Perizzites, Hivites and Jebusites. These were the kings:

⁹the king of Jericho	one
the king of Ai (near Bethel)	one
¹⁰the king of Jerusalem	one
the king of Hebron	one
¹¹the king of Jarmuth	one
the king of Lachish	one
¹²the king of Eglon	one
the king of Gezer	one
¹³the king of Debir	one
the king of Geder	one
¹⁴the king of Hormah	one
the king of Arad	one
¹⁵the king of Libnah	one
the king of Adullam	one
¹⁶the king of Makkedah	one
the king of Bethel	one
¹⁷the king of Tappuah	one
the king of Hepher	one
¹⁸the king of Aphek	one
the king of Lasharon	one
¹⁹the king of Madon	one
the king of Hazor	one
²⁰the king of Shimron Meron	one
the king of Akshaph	one
²¹the king of Taanach	one
the king of Megiddo	one
²²the king of Kedesh	one
the king of Jokneam in Carmel	one
²³the king of Dor (in Naphoth Dor)	one
the king of Goyim in Gilgal	one
²⁴the king of Tirzah	one
thirty-one kings in all.	

Land Still to Be Taken

13 When Joshua had grown old, the LORD said to him, "You are now very old, and there are still very large areas of land to be taken over.

²"This is the land that remains: all the regions of the Philistines and Geshurites, ³from the Shihor River on the east of Egypt to the territory of Ekron on the north, all of it counted as Canaanite though held by the five Philistine rulers in Gaza, Ashdod, Ashkelon, Gath and Ekron; the territory of the Avvites ⁴on the south; all the land of the Canaanites, from Arah of the Sidonians as far as Aphek and the border of the Amorites; ⁵the area of Byblos; and all Lebanon to the east, from Baal Gad below Mount Hermon to Lebo Hamath.

⁶"As for all the inhabitants of the mountain regions from Lebanon to Misrephoth Maim, that is, all the Sidonians, I myself

---

a 3 Hebrew *Kinnereth*

will drive them out before the Israelites. Be sure to allocate this land to Israel for an inheritance, as I have instructed you, [7]and divide it as an inheritance among the nine tribes and half of the tribe of Manasseh."

Division of the Land East of the Jordan

[8]The other half of Manasseh,[a] the Reubenites and the Gadites had received the inheritance that Moses had given them east of the Jordan, as he, the servant of the LORD, had assigned it to them.

[9]It extended from Aroer on the rim of the Arnon Gorge, and from the town in the middle of the gorge, and included the whole plateau of Medeba as far as Dibon, [10]and all the towns of Sihon king of the Amorites, who ruled in Heshbon, out to the border of the Ammonites. [11]It also included Gilead, the territory of the people of Geshur and Maakah, all of Mount Hermon and all Bashan as far as Salekah— [12]that is, the whole kingdom of Og in Bashan, who had reigned in Ashtaroth and Edrei. (He was the last of the Rephaites.) Moses had defeated them and taken over their land. [13]But the Israelites did not drive out the people of Geshur and Maakah, so they continue to live among the Israelites to this day.

[14]But to the tribe of Levi he gave no inheritance, since the food offerings presented to the LORD, the God of Israel, are their inheritance, as he promised them.

[15]This is what Moses had given to the tribe of Reuben, according to its clans:

[16]The territory from Aroer on the rim of the Arnon Gorge, and from the town in the middle of the gorge, and the whole plateau past Medeba [17]to Heshbon and all its towns on the plateau, including Dibon, Bamoth Baal, Beth Baal Meon, [18]Jahaz, Kedemoth, Mephaath, [19]Kiriathaim, Sibmah, Zereth Shahar on the hill in the valley, [20]Beth Peor, the slopes of Pisgah, and Beth Jeshimoth—

[21]all the towns on the plateau and the entire realm of Sihon king of the Amorites, who ruled at Heshbon. Moses had defeated him and the Midianite chiefs, Evi, Rekem, Zur, Hur and Reba—princes allied with Sihon—who lived in that country. [22]In addition to those slain in battle, the Israelites had put to the sword Balaam son of Beor, who practiced divination. [23]The boundary of the Reubenites was the bank of the Jordan. These towns and their villages were the inheritance of the Reubenites, according to their clans.

[24]This is what Moses had given to the tribe of Gad, according to its clans:

[25]The territory of Jazer, all the towns of Gilead and half the Ammonite country as far as Aroer, near Rabbah; [26]and from Heshbon to Ramath Mizpah and Betonim, and from Mahanaim to the territory of Debir; [27]and in the valley, Beth Haram, Beth Nimrah, Sukkoth and Zaphon with the rest of the realm of Sihon king of Heshbon (the east side of the Jordan, the territory up to the end of the Sea of Galilee[b]). [28]These towns and their villages were the inheritance of the Gadites, according to their clans.

[29]This is what Moses had given to the half-tribe of Manasseh, that is, to half the family of the descendants of Manasseh, according to its clans:

[30]The territory extending from Mahanaim and including all of Bashan, the entire realm of Og king of Bashan— all the settlements of Jair in Bashan, sixty towns, [31]half of Gilead, and Ashtaroth and Edrei (the royal cities of Og in Bashan). This was for the descendants of Makir son of Manasseh—for half of the sons of Makir, according to their clans.

[32]This is the inheritance Moses had given when he was in the plains of Moab

a 8 Hebrew With it (that is, with the other half of Manasseh)   b 27 Hebrew Kinnereth across the Jordan east of Jericho. [33]But to the tribe of Levi, Moses had given no inheritance; the LORD, the God of Israel, is their inheritance, as he promised them.

Division of the Land West of the Jordan

14 Now these are the areas the Israelites received as an inheritance in the land of Canaan, which Eleazar the priest, Joshua son of Nun and the heads of the tribal clans of Israel allotted to them. [2]Their inheritances were assigned by lot to the nine and a half tribes, as the LORD had commanded through Moses. [3]Moses had granted the two and a half tribes their inheritance east of the Jordan but had not granted the Levites an inheritance among the rest, [4]for Joseph's descendants had become two tribes—Manasseh and Ephraim. The Levites received no share of the land but only towns to live in, with pasturelands for their flocks and herds. [5]So the Israelites divided the land, just as the LORD had commanded Moses.

Allotment for Caleb

[6]Now the people of Judah approached Joshua at Gilgal, and Caleb son of Jephunneh the Kenizzite said to him, "You know what the LORD said to Moses the man of God at Kadesh Barnea about you and me. [7]I was forty years old when Moses the servant of the LORD sent me from Kadesh Barnea to explore the land. And I brought him back a report according to my convictions, [8]but my fellow Israelites who went up with me made the hearts of the people melt in fear. I, however, followed the LORD my God wholeheartedly. [9]So on that day Moses swore to me, 'The land on which your feet have walked will be your inheritance and that of your children forever, because you have followed the LORD my God wholeheartedly.'[a]

[10]"Now then, just as the LORD promised, he has kept me alive for forty-five years since the time he said this to Moses, while Israel moved about in the wilderness. So here I am today, eighty-five years old! [11]I am still as strong today as the day Moses sent me out; I'm just as vigorous to go out to battle now as I was then. [12]Now give me this hill country that the LORD promised me that day. You yourself heard then that the Anakites were there and their cities were large and fortified, but, the LORD helping me, I will drive them out just as he said."

[13]Then Joshua blessed Caleb son of Jephunneh and gave him Hebron as his inheritance. [14]So Hebron has belonged to Caleb son of Jephunneh the Kenizzite ever since, because he followed the LORD, the God of Israel, wholeheartedly. [15](Hebron used to be called Kiriath Arba after Arba, who was the greatest man among the Anakites.)

Then the land had rest from war.

Allotment for Judah

15 The allotment for the tribe of Judah, according to its clans, extended down to the territory of Edom, to the Desert of Zin in the extreme south.

[2]Their southern boundary started from the bay at the southern end of the Dead Sea, [3]crossed south of Scorpion Pass, continued on to Zin and went over to the south of Kadesh Barnea. Then it ran past Hezron up to Addar and curved around to Karka. [4]It then passed along to Azmon and joined the Wadi of Egypt, ending at the Mediterranean Sea. This is their[b] southern boundary.

[5]The eastern boundary is the Dead Sea as far as the mouth of the Jordan.

The northern boundary started from the bay of the sea at the mouth of the Jordan, [6]went up to Beth Hoglah and continued north of Beth Arabah to the Stone of Bohan son of Reuben. [7]The boundary then went up to Debir from the Valley of Achor and turned north to Gilgal, which faces the Pass of Adummim south of the gorge. It continued along to the waters of En Shemesh and came out at En Rogel. [8]Then it ran up the Valley of Ben Hinnom along the southern

---

[a] 9 Deut. 1:36   [b] 4 Septuagint; Hebrew *your*

THE
WITNESSES

✓ ARBA (JOSHUA 15:13)
Here, it says Arba was an ancestor of Anak. Anak was one of those giants called "Anakites." In Joshua 14:15, it says that Arba was the most important giant. His name means "four."

✓ AKSAH (JOSHUA 15:16)
She was Caleb's daughter and Othniel's wife. Othniel was the first judge mentioned in the book of Judges (1:13; 3:9 – 11). Aksah's name seems to mean something like "charming," but we can't be sure about that. In the book of Judges, she appears as a very brave woman.

✓ OTHNIEL SON OF KENAZ
(JOSHUA 15:17)
He was Aksah's husband, and he was the first judge. Although he was a foreigner, he became an example for the Israelite people. All the other judges who belonged to the Israelite people were compared to Othniel, the foreigner.

slope of the Jebusite city (that is, Jerusalem). From there it climbed to the top of the hill west of the Hinnom Valley at the northern end of the Valley of Rephaim. ⁹From the hilltop the boundary headed toward the spring of the waters of Nephtoah, came out at the towns of Mount Ephron and went down toward Baalah (that is, Kiriath Jearim). ¹⁰Then it curved westward from Baalah to Mount Seir, ran along the northern slope of Mount Jearim (that is, Kesalon), continued down to Beth Shemesh and crossed to Timnah. ¹¹It went to the northern slope of Ekron, turned toward Shikkeron, passed along to Mount Baalah and reached Jabneel. The boundary ended at the sea.

¹²The western boundary is the coastline of the Mediterranean Sea.

These are the boundaries around the people of Judah by their clans.

¹³In accordance with the Lᴏʀᴅ's command to him, Joshua gave to Caleb son of Jephunneh a portion in Judah — Kiriath Arba, that is, Hebron. (Arba was the forefather of Anak.) ¹⁴From Hebron Caleb drove out the three Anakites — Sheshai, Ahiman and Talmai, the sons of Anak. ¹⁵From there he marched against the people living in Debir (formerly called Kiriath Sepher). ¹⁶And Caleb said, "I will give my daughter Aksah in marriage to the man who attacks and captures Kiriath Sepher." ¹⁷Othniel son of Kenaz, Caleb's brother, took it; so Caleb gave his daughter Aksah to him in marriage.

¹⁸One day when she came to Othniel, she urged him*a* to ask her father for a field. When she got off her donkey, Caleb asked her, "What can I do for you?"

¹⁹She replied, "Do me a special favor. Since you have given me land in the Negev, give me also springs of water." So Caleb gave her the upper and lower springs.

²⁰This is the inheritance of the tribe of Judah, according to its clans:

---

a 18 Hebrew and some Septuagint manuscripts; other Septuagint manuscripts (see also note at Judges 1:14) *Othniel, he urged her*

BREAKTHROUGH!

Anakites, Perizzites and Rephaites

(JOSHUA 15:13-14; 17:15)

They were different groups of giants and other people who lived in the land of Palestine. The Israelites were trying to get settled in the promised land, and they were really afraid of these people. However, the Word of God teaches us that God didn't give the promised land to the powerful giants. Instead, he gave it to the weak people he had rescued from slavery in Egypt.

²¹The southernmost towns of the tribe of Judah in the Negev toward the boundary of Edom were:

Kabzeel, Eder, Jagur, ²²Kinah, Dimonah, Adadah, ²³Kedesh, Hazor, Ithnan, ²⁴Ziph, Telem, Bealoth, ²⁵Hazor Hadattah, Kerioth Hezron (that is, Hazor), ²⁶Amam, Shema, Moladah, ²⁷Hazar Gaddah, Heshmon, Beth Pelet, ²⁸Hazar Shual, Beersheba, Biziothiah, ²⁹Baalah, Iyim, Ezem, ³⁰Eltolad, Kesil, Hormah, ³¹Ziklag, Madmannah, Sansannah, ³²Lebaoth, Shilhim, Ain and Rimmon—a total of twenty-nine towns and their villages.

³³In the western foothills:

Eshtaol, Zorah, Ashnah, ³⁴Zanoah, En Gannim, Tappuah, Enam,

³⁵Jarmuth, Adullam, Sokoh, Azekah, ³⁶Shaaraim, Adithaim and Gederah (or Gederothaim)*ᵃ*—fourteen towns and their villages.

³⁷Zenan, Hadashah, Migdal Gad, ³⁸Dilean, Mizpah, Joktheel, ³⁹Lachish, Bozkath, Eglon, ⁴⁰Kabbon, Lahmas, Kitlish, ⁴¹Gederoth, Beth Dagon, Naamah and Makkedah—sixteen towns and their villages.

⁴²Libnah, Ether, Ashan, ⁴³Iphtah, Ashnah, Nezib, ⁴⁴Keilah, Akzib and Mareshah—nine towns and their villages.

⁴⁵Ekron, with its surrounding settlements and villages; ⁴⁶west of Ekron, all that were in the vicinity of Ashdod, together with their villages; ⁴⁷Ashdod, its surrounding settlements and villages; and Gaza, its settlements and villages, as far as the Wadi of Egypt and the coastline of the Mediterranean Sea.

⁴⁸In the hill country:

Shamir, Jattir, Sokoh, ⁴⁹Dannah, Kiriath Sannah (that is, Debir), ⁵⁰Anab, Eshtemoh, Anim, ⁵¹Goshen, Holon and Giloh—eleven towns and their villages.

⁵²Arab, Dumah, Eshan, ⁵³Janim, Beth Tappuah, Aphekah, ⁵⁴Humtah, Kiriath Arba (that is, Hebron) and Zior—nine towns and their villages.

⁵⁵Maon, Carmel, Ziph, Juttah, ⁵⁶Jezreel, Jokdeam, Zanoah, ⁵⁷Kain, Gibeah and Timnah—ten towns and their villages.

⁵⁸Halhul, Beth Zur, Gedor, ⁵⁹Maarath, Beth Anoth and Eltekon—six towns and their villages.*ᵇ*

⁶⁰Kiriath Baal (that is, Kiriath Jearim) and Rabbah—two towns and their villages.

⁶¹In the wilderness:

Beth Arabah, Middin, Sekakah, ⁶²Nibshan, the City of Salt and En Gedi—six towns and their villages.

⁶³Judah could not dislodge the Jebusites, who were living in Jerusalem; to

---

ᵃ 36 Or *Gederah and Gederothaim*   *ᵇ 59* The Septuagint adds another district of eleven towns, including Tekoa and Ephrathah (Bethlehem).

this day the Jebusites live there with the people of Judah.

Allotment for Ephraim and Manasseh

16 The allotment for Joseph began at the Jordan, east of the springs of Jericho, and went up from there through the desert into the hill country of Bethel. ²It went on from Bethel (that is, Luz),ᵃ crossed over to the territory of the Arkites in Ataroth, ³descended westward to the territory of the Japhletites as far as the region of Lower Beth Horon and on to Gezer, ending at the Mediterranean Sea.

⁴So Manasseh and Ephraim, the descendants of Joseph, received their inheritance.

⁵This was the territory of Ephraim, according to its clans:

The boundary of their inheritance went from Ataroth Addar in the east to Upper Beth Horon ⁶and continued to the Mediterranean Sea. From Mikmethath on the north it curved eastward to Taanath Shiloh, passing by it to Janoah on the east. ⁷Then it went down from Janoah to Ataroth and Naarah, touched Jericho and came out at the Jordan. ⁸From Tappuah the border went west to the Kanah Ravine and ended at the Mediterranean Sea. This was the inheritance of the tribe of the Ephraimites, according to its clans. ⁹It also included all the towns and their villages that were set aside for the Ephraimites within the inheritance of the Manassites.

¹⁰They did not dislodge the Canaanites living in Gezer; to this day the Canaanites live among the people of Ephraim but are required to do forced labor.

17 This was the allotment for the tribe of Manasseh as Joseph's firstborn, that is, for Makir, Manasseh's firstborn. Makir was the ancestor of the Gileadites, who had received Gilead and Bashan because the Makirites were great soldiers. ²So this allotment was for the rest of the people of Manasseh—the clans of Abie-

zer, Helek, Asriel, Shechem, Hepher and Shemida. These are the other male descendants of Manasseh son of Joseph by their clans.

³Now Zelophehad son of Hepher, the son of Gilead, the son of Makir, the son of Manasseh, had no sons but only daughters, whose names were Mahlah, Noah, Hoglah, Milkah and Tirzah. ⁴They went to Eleazar the priest, Joshua son of Nun, and the leaders and said, "The Lᴏʀᴅ commanded Moses to give us an inheritance among our relatives." So Joshua gave them an inheritance along with the brothers of their father, according to the Lᴏʀᴅ's command. ⁵Manasseh's share consisted of ten tracts of land besides Gilead and Bashan east of the Jordan, ⁶because the daughters of the tribe of Manasseh received an inheritance among the sons. The land of Gilead belonged to the rest of the descendants of Manasseh.

⁷The territory of Manasseh extended from Asher to Mikmethath east of Shechem. The boundary ran southward from there to include the people living at En Tappuah. ⁸(Manasseh had the land of Tappuah, but Tappuah itself, on the boundary of Manasseh, belonged to the Ephraimites.) ⁹Then the boundary continued south to the Kanah Ravine. There were towns belonging to Ephraim lying among the towns of Manasseh, but the boundary of Manasseh was the northern side of the ravine and ended at the Mediterranean Sea. ¹⁰On the south the land belonged to Ephraim, on the north to Manasseh. The territory of Manasseh reached the Mediterranean Sea and bordered Asher on the north and Issachar on the east. ¹¹Within Issachar and Asher, Manasseh also had Beth Shan, Ibleam and the people of Dor, Endor, Taanach and Megiddo, together with their surrounding settlements (the third in the list is Naphothᵇ).

¹²Yet the Manassites were not able to occupy these towns, for the Canaanites were determined to live in that region.

ᵃ 2 Septuagint; Hebrew *Bethel to Luz*   ᵇ 11 That is, Naphoth Dor

13However, when the Israelites grew stronger, they subjected the Canaanites to forced labor but did not drive them out completely.

14The people of Joseph said to Joshua, "Why have you given us only one allotment and one portion for an inheritance? We are a numerous people, and the Lord has blessed us abundantly."

15"If you are so numerous," Joshua answered, "and if the hill country of Ephraim is too small for you, go up into the forest and clear land for yourselves there in the land of the Perizzites and Rephaites."

16The people of Joseph replied, "The hill country is not enough for us, and all the Canaanites who live in the plain have chariots fitted with iron, both those in Beth Shan and its settlements and those in the Valley of Jezreel."

17But Joshua said to the tribes of Joseph—to Ephraim and Manasseh—"You are numerous and very powerful. You will have not only one allotment 18but the forested hill country as well. Clear it, and its farthest limits will be yours; though the Canaanites have chariots fitted with iron and though they are strong, you can drive them out."

Division of the Rest of the Land

18 The whole assembly of the Israelites gathered at Shiloh and set up the tent of meeting there. The country was brought under their control, 2but there were still seven Israelite tribes who had not yet received their inheritance.

3So Joshua said to the Israelites: "How long will you wait before you begin to take possession of the land that the Lord, the God of your ancestors, has given you? 4Appoint three men from each tribe. I will send them out to make a survey of the land and to write a description of it, according to the inheritance of each. Then they will return to me. 5You are to divide the land into seven parts. Judah is to remain in its territory on the south and the tribes of Joseph in their territory on the north. 6After you have written descriptions of the seven parts of the land, bring them here to me and I will cast lots for you in the presence of the Lord our God. 7The

THE SCENE

SHILOH

(JOSHUA 18:1)

This was an important religious center for Israel. It's about 10 miles (16 km) north of Bethel in an area that was given to the tribe of Ephraim. God's sanctuary was set up here. This is the place where they cast lots to decide which tribes of Israel would get the different parts of land. The sanctuary was kept in Shiloh until the Philistines captured the ark of the covenant during the time of Eli, who was a priest of Israel. (Read 1 Samuel 4.)

Levites, however, do not get a portion among you, because the priestly service of the Lord is their inheritance. And Gad, Reuben and the half-tribe of Manasseh have already received their inheritance on the east side of the Jordan. Moses the servant of the Lord gave it to them."

8As the men started on their way to map out the land, Joshua instructed them, "Go and make a survey of the land and write a description of it. Then return to me, and I will cast lots for you here at Shiloh in the presence of the Lord." 9So the men left and went through the land. They wrote its description on a scroll, town by town, in seven parts, and returned to Joshua in the camp at Shiloh. ¹⁰Joshua then cast lots for them in Shiloh in the presence of the Lᴏʀᴅ, and there he distributed the land to the Israelites according to their tribal divisions.

Allotment for Benjamin

¹¹The first lot came up for the tribe of Benjamin according to its clans. Their allotted territory lay between the tribes of Judah and Joseph:

¹²On the north side their boundary began at the Jordan, passed the northern slope of Jericho and headed west into the hill country, coming out at the wilderness of Beth Aven. ¹³From there it crossed to the south slope of Luz (that is, Bethel) and went down to Ataroth Addar on the hill south of Lower Beth Horon.

¹⁴From the hill facing Beth Horon on the south the boundary turned south along the western side and came out at Kiriath Baal (that is, Kiriath Jearim), a town of the people of Judah. This was the western side.

¹⁵The southern side began at the outskirts of Kiriath Jearim on the west, and the boundary came out at the spring of the waters of Nephtoah. ¹⁶The boundary went down to the foot of the hill facing the Valley of Ben Hinnom, north of the Valley of Rephaim. It continued down the Hinnom Valley along the southern slope of the Jebusite city and so to En Rogel. ¹⁷It then curved north, went to En Shemesh, continued to Geliloth, which faces the Pass of Adummim, and ran down to the Stone of Bohan son of Reuben. ¹⁸It continued to the northern slope of Beth Arabahᵃ and on down into the Arabah. ¹⁹It then went to the northern slope of Beth Hoglah and came out at the northern bay of the Dead Sea, at the mouth of the Jordan in the south. This was the southern boundary.

²⁰The Jordan formed the boundary on the eastern side.

These were the boundaries that marked out the inheritance of the clans of Benjamin on all sides.

²¹The tribe of Benjamin, according to its clans, had the following towns:

Jericho, Beth Hoglah, Emek Keziz, ²²Beth Arabah, Zemaraim, Bethel, ²³Avvim, Parah, Ophrah, ²⁴Kephar Ammoni, Ophni and Geba—twelve towns and their villages.

²⁵Gibeon, Ramah, Beeroth, ²⁶Mizpah, Kephirah, Mozah, ²⁷Rekem, Irpeel, Taralah, ²⁸Zelah, Haeleph, the Jebusite city (that is, Jerusalem), Gibeah and Kiriath—fourteen towns and their villages.

This was the inheritance of Benjamin for its clans.

Allotment for Simeon

19 The second lot came out for the tribe of Simeon according to its clans. Their inheritance lay within the territory of Judah. ²It included:

Beersheba (or Sheba),ᵇ Moladah, ³Hazar Shual, Balah, Ezem, ⁴Eltolad, Bethul, Hormah, ⁵Ziklag, Beth Markaboth, Hazar Susah, ⁶Beth Lebaoth and Sharuhen—thirteen towns and their villages;

⁷Ain, Rimmon, Ether and Ashan—four towns and their villages— ⁸and all the villages around these towns as far as Baalath Beer (Ramah in the Negev).

This was the inheritance of the tribe of the Simeonites, according to its clans. ⁹The inheritance of the Simeonites was taken from the share of Judah, because Judah's portion was more than they needed. So the Simeonites received their inheritance within the territory of Judah.

Allotment for Zebulun

¹⁰The third lot came up for Zebulun according to its clans:

The boundary of their inheritance went as far as Sarid. ¹¹Going west it ran to Maralah, touched Dabbesheth, and extended to the ravine

---

ᵃ 18 Septuagint; Hebrew *slope facing the Arabah*   ᵇ 2 Or *Beersheba, Sheba*; 1 Chron. 4:28 does not have *Sheba*.

near Jokneam. ¹²It turned east from Sarid toward the sunrise to the territory of Kisloth Tabor and went on to Daberath and up to Japhia. ¹³Then it continued eastward to Gath Hepher and Eth Kazin; it came out at Rimmon and turned toward Neah. ¹⁴There the boundary went around on the north to Hannathon and ended at the Valley of Iphtah El. ¹⁵Included were Kattath, Nahalal, Shimron, Idalah and Bethlehem. There were twelve towns and their villages.
¹⁶These towns and their villages were the inheritance of Zebulun, according to its clans.

Allotment for Issachar

¹⁷The fourth lot came out for Issachar according to its clans. ¹⁸Their territory included:

Jezreel, Kesulloth, Shunem, ¹⁹Hapharaim, Shion, Anaharath, ²⁰Rabbith, Kishion, Ebez, ²¹Remeth, En Gannim, En Haddah and Beth Pazzez. ²²The boundary touched Tabor, Shahazumah and Beth Shemesh, and ended at the Jordan. There were sixteen towns and their villages.

²³These towns and their villages were the inheritance of the tribe of Issachar, according to its clans.

Allotment for Asher

²⁴The fifth lot came out for the tribe of Asher according to its clans. ²⁵Their territory included:

Helkath, Hali, Beten, Akshaph, ²⁶Allammelek, Amad and Mishal. On the west the boundary touched Carmel and Shihor Libnath. ²⁷It then turned east toward Beth Dagon, touched Zebulun and the Valley of Iphtah El, and went north to Beth Emek and Neiel, passing Kabul on the left. ²⁸It went to Abdon,ᵃ Rehob, Hammon and Kanah, as far as Greater Sidon. ²⁹The boundary then turned back toward Ramah and went to the fortified city of Tyre, turned toward Hosah and came out at the Mediterranean Sea in the region of Akzib, ³⁰Ummah, Aphek and Rehob.

There were twenty-two towns and their villages.
³¹These towns and their villages were the inheritance of the tribe of Asher, according to its clans.

Allotment for Naphtali

³²The sixth lot came out for Naphtali according to its clans:

³³Their boundary went from Heleph and the large tree in Zaanannim, passing Adami Nekeb and Jabneel to Lakkum and ending at the Jordan. ³⁴The boundary ran west through Aznoth Tabor and came out at Hukkok. It touched Zebulun on the south, Asher on the west and the Jordanᵇ on the east. ³⁵The fortified towns were Ziddim, Zer, Hammath, Rakkath, Kinnereth, ³⁶Adamah, Ramah, Hazor, ³⁷Kedesh, Edrei, En Hazor, ³⁸Iron, Migdal El, Horem, Beth Anath and Beth Shemesh. There were nineteen towns and their villages.

³⁹These towns and their villages were the inheritance of the tribe of Naphtali, according to its clans.

Allotment for Dan

⁴⁰The seventh lot came out for the tribe of Dan according to its clans. ⁴¹The territory of their inheritance included:

Zorah, Eshtaol, Ir Shemesh, ⁴²Shaalabbin, Aijalon, Ithlah, ⁴³Elon, Timnah, Ekron, ⁴⁴Eltekeh, Gibbethon, Baalath, ⁴⁵Jehud, Bene Berak, Gath Rimmon, ⁴⁶Me Jarkon and Rakkon, with the area facing Joppa.

⁴⁷(When the territory of the Danites was lost to them, they went up and attacked Leshem, took it, put it to the sword and occupied it. They settled in Leshem and named it Dan after their ancestor.) ⁴⁸These towns and their villages were the inheritance of the tribe of Dan, according to its clans.

Allotment for Joshua

⁴⁹When they had finished dividing the land into its allotted portions, the Israel-

---

ᵃ 28 Some Hebrew manuscripts (see also 21:30); most Hebrew manuscripts Ebron　　ᵇ 34 Septuagint; Hebrew west, and Judah, the Jordan, ites gave Joshua son of Nun an inheritance among them, ⁵⁰as the LORD had commanded. They gave him the town he asked for—Timnath Serahᵃ in the hill country of Ephraim. And he built up the town and settled there.

⁵¹These are the territories that Eleazar the priest, Joshua son of Nun and the heads of the tribal clans of Israel assigned by lot at Shiloh in the presence of the LORD at the entrance to the tent of meeting. And so they finished dividing the land.

Cities of Refuge

20 Then the LORD said to Joshua: ²"Tell the Israelites to designate the cities of refuge, as I instructed you through Moses, ³so that anyone who kills a person accidentally and unintentionally may flee there and find protection from

BREAK THROUGH!

Cities of refuge
(JOSHUA 20)

These places protected people who had accidentally killed another person. They found protection here from the relatives of the person who had been killed, because that person's family wanted revenge. There were cities like this in most ancient cultures.

the avenger of blood. ⁴When they flee to one of these cities, they are to stand in the entrance of the city gate and state their case before the elders of that city. Then the elders are to admit the fugitive into their city and provide a place to live among them. ⁵If the avenger of blood comes in pursuit, the elders must not surrender the fugitive, because the fugitive killed their neighbor unintentionally and without malice aforethought. ⁶They are to stay in that city until they have stood trial before the assembly and until the death of the high priest who is serving at that time. Then they may go back to their own home in the town from which they fled."

⁷So they set apart Kedesh in Galilee in the hill country of Naphtali, Shechem in the hill country of Ephraim, and Kiriath Arba (that is, Hebron) in the hill country of Judah. ⁸East of the Jordan (on the other

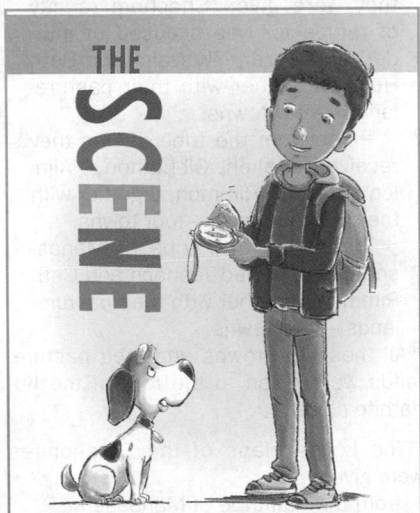

THE SCENE

TIMNATH SERAH

(JOSHUA 19:50)

It's in the territory of the tribe of Ephraim about 11 miles (18 km) southwest of Shiloh. It belonged to Joshua and his family, and that's where that great leader of Israel was buried. (Read Joshua 24:30.)

ᵃ 50 Also known as *Timnath Heres* (see Judges 2:9)

side from Jericho) they designated Bezer in the wilderness on the plateau in the tribe of Reuben, Ramoth in Gilead in the tribe of Gad, and Golan in Bashan in the tribe of Manasseh. ⁹Any of the Israelites or any foreigner residing among them who killed someone accidentally could flee to these designated cities and not be killed by the avenger of blood prior to standing trial before the assembly.

Towns for the Levites

21 Now the family heads of the Levites approached Eleazar the priest, Joshua son of Nun, and the heads of the other tribal families of Israel ²at Shiloh in Canaan and said to them, "The Lord commanded through Moses that you give us towns to live in, with pasturelands for our livestock." ³So, as the Lord had commanded, the Israelites gave the Levites the following towns and pasturelands out of their own inheritance:

⁴The first lot came out for the Kohathites, according to their clans. The Levites who were descendants of Aaron the priest were allotted thirteen towns from the tribes of Judah, Simeon and Benjamin. ⁵The rest of Kohath's descendants were allotted ten towns from the clans of the tribes of Ephraim, Dan and half of Manasseh.

⁶The descendants of Gershon were allotted thirteen towns from the clans of the tribes of Issachar, Asher, Naphtali and the half-tribe of Manasseh in Bashan.

⁷The descendants of Merari, according to their clans, received twelve towns from the tribes of Reuben, Gad and Zebulun.

⁸So the Israelites allotted to the Levites these towns and their pasturelands, as the Lord had commanded through Moses.

⁹From the tribes of Judah and Simeon they allotted the following towns by name ¹⁰(these towns were assigned to the descendants of Aaron who were from the Kohathite clans of the Levites, because the first lot fell to them):

¹¹They gave them Kiriath Arba (that is, Hebron), with its surrounding pastureland, in the hill country of Judah. (Arba was the forefather of Anak.)

¹²But the fields and villages around the city they had given to Caleb son of Jephunneh as his possession.

¹³So to the descendants of Aaron the priest they gave Hebron (a city of refuge for one accused of murder), Libnah, ¹⁴Jattir, Eshtemoa, ¹⁵Holon, Debir, ¹⁶Ain, Juttah and Beth Shemesh, together with their pasturelands—nine towns from these two tribes.

¹⁷And from the tribe of Benjamin they gave them Gibeon, Geba, ¹⁸Anathoth and Almon, together with their pasturelands—four towns.

¹⁹The total number of towns for the priests, the descendants of Aaron, came to thirteen, together with their pasturelands.

²⁰The rest of the Kohathite clans of the Levites were allotted towns from the tribe of Ephraim:

²¹In the hill country of Ephraim they were given Shechem (a city of refuge for one accused of murder) and Gezer, ²²Kibzaim and Beth Horon, together with their pasturelands—four towns.

²³Also from the tribe of Dan they received Eltekeh, Gibbethon, ²⁴Aijalon and Gath Rimmon, together with their pasturelands—four towns.

²⁵From half the tribe of Manasseh they received Taanach and Gath Rimmon, together with their pasturelands—two towns.

²⁶All these ten towns and their pasturelands were given to the rest of the Kohathite clans.

²⁷The Levite clans of the Gershonites were given:

from the half-tribe of Manasseh,
Golan in Bashan (a city of refuge for one accused of murder) and Be Eshterah, together with their pasturelands—two towns;

²⁸from the tribe of Issachar,
Kishion, Daberath, ²⁹Jarmuth and En Gannim, together with their pasturelands—four towns;

³⁰from the tribe of Asher,
Mishal, Abdon, ³¹Helkath and Rehob, together with their pasturelands—four towns;

³²from the tribe of Naphtali,
Kedesh in Galilee (a city of refuge for one accused of murder), Hammoth Dor and Kartan, together with their pasturelands—three towns.
³³The total number of towns of the Gershonite clans came to thirteen, together with their pasturelands.

³⁴The Merarite clans (the rest of the Levites) were given:
from the tribe of Zebulun,
Jokneam, Kartah, ³⁵Dimnah and Nahalal, together with their pasturelands—four towns;
³⁶from the tribe of Reuben,
Bezer, Jahaz, ³⁷Kedemoth and Mephaath, together with their pasturelands—four towns;
³⁸from the tribe of Gad,
Ramoth in Gilead (a city of refuge for one accused of murder), Mahanaim, ³⁹Heshbon and Jazer, together with their pasturelands—four towns in all.
⁴⁰The total number of towns allotted to the Merarite clans, who were the rest of the Levites, came to twelve.
⁴¹The towns of the Levites in the territory held by the Israelites were forty-eight in all, together with their pasturelands.
⁴²Each of these towns had pasturelands surrounding it; this was true for all these towns.

⁴³So the Lord gave Israel all the land he had sworn to give their ancestors, and they took possession of it and settled there. ⁴⁴The Lord gave them rest on every side, just as he had sworn to their ancestors. Not one of their enemies withstood them; the Lord gave all their enemies into their hands. ⁴⁵Not one of all the Lord's good promises to Israel failed; every one was fulfilled.

Eastern Tribes Return Home

22 Then Joshua summoned the Reubenites, the Gadites and the half-tribe of Manasseh ²and said to them, "You have done all that Moses the servant of the Lord commanded, and you have obeyed me in everything I commanded. ³For a long time now—to this very

day—you have not deserted your fellow Israelites but have carried out the mission the Lord your God gave you. ⁴Now that the Lord your God has given them rest as he promised, return to your homes in the land that Moses the servant of the Lord gave you on the other side of the Jordan. ⁵But be very careful to keep the commandment and the law that Moses the servant of the Lord gave you: to love the Lord your God, to walk in obedience to him, to keep his commands, to hold fast to him and to serve him with all your heart and with all your soul."

⁶Then Joshua blessed them and sent them away, and they went to their homes. ⁷(To the half-tribe of Manasseh Moses had given land in Bashan, and to the other half of the tribe Joshua gave land on the west side of the Jordan along with their fellow Israelites.) When Joshua sent them home, he blessed them, ⁸saying, "Return to your homes with your great wealth—with large herds of livestock, with silver, gold, bronze and iron, and a great quantity of clothing—and divide the plunder from your enemies with your fellow Israelites."

⁹So the Reubenites, the Gadites and the half-tribe of Manasseh left the Israelites at Shiloh in Canaan to return to Gilead, their own land, which they had acquired in accordance with the command of the Lord through Moses.

¹⁰When they came to Geliloth near the Jordan in the land of Canaan, the Reubenites, the Gadites and the half-tribe of Manasseh built an imposing altar there by the Jordan. ¹¹And when the Israelites heard that they had built the altar on the border of Canaan at Geliloth near the Jordan on the Israelite side, ¹²the whole assembly of Israel gathered at Shiloh to go to war against them.

¹³So the Israelites sent Phinehas son of Eleazar, the priest, to the land of Gilead—to Reuben, Gad and the half-tribe of Manasseh. ¹⁴With him they sent ten of the chief men, one from each of the tribes of Israel, each the head of a family division among the Israelite clans. ¹⁵When they went to Gilead—to Reuben, Gad and the half-tribe of Manasseh—

they said to them: ¹⁶"The whole assembly of the LORD says: 'How could you break faith with the God of Israel like this? How could you turn away from the LORD and build yourselves an altar in rebellion against him now? ¹⁷Was not the sin of Peor enough for us? Up to this very day we have not cleansed ourselves from that sin, even though a plague fell on the community of the LORD! ¹⁸And are you now turning away from the LORD?

" 'If you rebel against the LORD today, tomorrow he will be angry with the whole community of Israel. ¹⁹If the land you possess is defiled, come over to the LORD's land, where the LORD's tabernacle stands, and share the land with us. But do not rebel against the LORD or against us by building an altar for yourselves, other than the altar of the LORD our God. ²⁰When Achan son of Zerah was unfaithful in regard to the devoted things,ᵃ did not wrath come on the whole community of Israel? He was not the only one who died for his sin.' "

²¹Then Reuben, Gad and the half-tribe of Manasseh replied to the heads of the clans of Israel: ²²"The Mighty One, God, the LORD! The Mighty One, God, the LORD! He knows! And let Israel know! If this has been in rebellion or disobedience to the LORD, do not spare us this day. ²³If we have built our own altar to turn away from the LORD and to offer burnt offerings and grain offerings, or to sacrifice fellowship offerings on it, may the LORD himself call us to account.

²⁴"No! We did it for fear that some day your descendants might say to ours, 'What do you have to do with the LORD, the God of Israel? ²⁵The LORD has made the Jordan a boundary between us and you—you Reubenites and Gadites! You have no share in the LORD.' So your descendants might cause ours to stop fearing the LORD.

²⁶"That is why we said, 'Let us get ready and build an altar—but not for burnt offerings or sacrifices.' ²⁷On the contrary, it is to be a witness between us and you and the generations that follow, that we will worship the LORD at his sanctuary with our burnt offerings, sacrifices and fellowship offerings. Then in the future your descendants will not be able to say to ours, 'You have no share in the LORD.'

²⁸"And we said, 'If they ever say this to us, or to our descendants, we will answer: Look at the replica of the LORD's altar, which our ancestors built, not for burnt offerings and sacrifices, but as a witness between us and you.'

²⁹"Far be it from us to rebel against the LORD and turn away from him today by building an altar for burnt offerings, grain offerings and sacrifices, other than the altar of the LORD our God that stands before his tabernacle."

³⁰When Phinehas the priest and the leaders of the community—the heads of the clans of the Israelites—heard what Reuben, Gad and Manasseh had to say, they were pleased. ³¹And Phinehas son of Eleazar, the priest, said to Reuben, Gad and Manasseh, "Today we know that the LORD is with us, because you have not been unfaithful to the LORD in this matter. Now you have rescued the Israelites from the LORD's hand."

³²Then Phinehas son of Eleazar, the priest, and the leaders returned to Canaan from their meeting with the Reubenites and Gadites in Gilead and reported to the Israelites. ³³They were glad to hear the report and praised God. And they talked no more about going to war against them to devastate the country where the Reubenites and the Gadites lived.

³⁴And the Reubenites and the Gadites gave the altar this name: A Witness Between Us—that the LORD is God.

Joshua's Farewell to the Leaders

23 After a long time had passed and the LORD had given Israel rest from all their enemies around them, Joshua, by then a very old man, ²summoned all Israel—their elders, leaders, judges and officials—and said to them: "I am very old. ³You yourselves have seen everything the LORD your God has done to all these nations for your sake; it was the LORD your God who fought for you. ⁴Remember how I have allotted as an inheritance for

---

ᵃ *20* The Hebrew term refers to the irrevocable giving over of things or persons to the LORD, often by totally destroying them.

BREAK THROUGH!

Why were other nations enemies?

(JOSHUA 23:1)

The people who lived in the promised land were considered "enemies" for two reasons. The first was that if those people continued living there, the people of Israel couldn't live peacefully on the best land of the country. The second reason was that their customs and religious practices were different from what God had ordered the Israelites to do in Moses' Law. If the Israelites disobeyed God and followed the wrong practices of those nations, then God wouldn't help them beat those enemies.

your tribes all the land of the nations that remain—the nations I conquered—between the Jordan and the Mediterranean Sea in the west. ⁵The LORD your God himself will push them out for your sake. He will drive them out before you, and you will take possession of their land, as the LORD your God promised you.

⁶"Be very strong; be careful to obey all that is written in the Book of the Law of Moses, without turning aside to the right or to the left. ⁷Do not associate with these nations that remain among you; do not invoke the names of their gods or swear by them. You must not serve them or bow down to them. ⁸But you are to hold fast to the LORD your God, as you have until now.

⁹"The LORD has driven out before you great and powerful nations; to this day no one has been able to withstand you. ¹⁰One of you routs a thousand, because the LORD your God fights for you, just as he promised. ¹¹So be very careful to love the LORD your God.

¹²"But if you turn away and ally yourselves with the survivors of these nations that remain among you and if you intermarry with them and associate with them, ¹³then you may be sure that the LORD your God will no longer drive out these nations before you. Instead, they will become snares and traps for you, whips on your backs and thorns in your eyes, until you perish from this good land, which the LORD your God has given you.

¹⁴"Now I am about to go the way of all the earth. You know with all your heart and soul that not one of all the good promises the LORD your God gave you has failed. Every promise has been fulfilled; not one has failed. ¹⁵But just as all the good things the LORD your God has promised you have come to you, so he will bring on you all the evil things he has threatened, until the LORD your God has destroyed you from this good land he has given you. ¹⁶If you violate the covenant of the LORD your God, which he commanded you, and go and serve other gods and bow down to them, the LORD's anger will burn against you, and you will quickly perish from the good land he has given you."

The Covenant Renewed at Shechem

24 Then Joshua assembled all the tribes of Israel at Shechem. He summoned the elders, leaders, judges and officials of Israel, and they presented themselves before God.

²Joshua said to all the people, "This is what the LORD, the God of Israel, says: 'Long ago your ancestors, including Terah the father of Abraham and Nahor, lived beyond the Euphrates River and worshiped other gods. ³But I took your father Abraham from the land beyond the Euphrates and led him throughout Canaan and gave

THE SCENE

SHECHEM

(JOSHUA 24:1)

It was 40 miles (65 km) north of Jerusalem in the territory of Manasseh, although there were times when it belonged to the tribe of Ephraim too. It was a city of refuge controlled by Levite priests. This place is important in the history of the Old Testament. Shechem was on an important road. There were many sources of water, so there was pastureland and it was good for farming. In Shechem, Joshua challenged all the people to be faithful only to God. As a result, the entire nation and its leader renewed their deal with God.

him many descendants. I gave him Isaac, ⁴and to Isaac I gave Jacob and Esau. I assigned the hill country of Seir to Esau, but Jacob and his family went down to Egypt.

⁵" 'Then I sent Moses and Aaron, and I afflicted the Egyptians by what I did there, and I brought you out. ⁶When I brought your people out of Egypt, you came to the sea, and the Egyptians pursued them with chariots and horsemen[a] as far as the Red Sea.[b] ⁷But they cried to the Lord for help, and he put darkness between you and the Egyptians; he brought the sea over them and covered them. You saw with your own eyes what I did to the Egyptians. Then you lived in the wilderness for a long time.

⁸" 'I brought you to the land of the Amorites who lived east of the Jordan. They fought against you, but I gave them into your hands. I destroyed them from before you, and you took possession of their land. ⁹When Balak son of Zippor, the king of Moab, prepared to fight against Israel, he sent for Balaam son of Beor to put a curse on you. ¹⁰But I would not listen to Balaam, so he blessed you again and again, and I delivered you out of his hand.

¹¹" 'Then you crossed the Jordan and came to Jericho. The citizens of Jericho fought against you, as did also the Amorites, Perizzites, Canaanites, Hittites, Girgashites, Hivites and Jebusites, but I gave them into your hands. ¹²I sent the hornet ahead of you, which drove them out before you—also the two Amorite kings. You did not do it with your own sword and bow. ¹³So I gave you a land on which you did not toil and cities you did not build; and you live in them and eat from vineyards and olive groves that you did not plant.'

¹⁴"Now fear the Lord and serve him with all faithfulness. Throw away the gods your ancestors worshiped beyond the Euphrates River and in Egypt, and serve the Lord. ¹⁵But if serving the Lord seems undesirable to you, then choose for yourselves this day whom you will serve, whether the gods your ancestors served beyond the Euphrates, or the gods of the Amorites, in whose land you are living. But as for me and my household, we will serve the Lord."

¹⁶Then the people answered, "Far be it from us to forsake the Lord to serve other gods! ¹⁷It was the Lord our God himself who brought us and our parents up out of Egypt, from that land of slavery, and performed those great signs before our eyes. He protected us on our entire journey and among all the nations through which we traveled. ¹⁸And the Lord drove out before us all the nations, including the Amorites,

---

a 6 Or charioteers   *b 6 Or the Sea of Reeds*

who lived in the land. We too will serve the LORD, because he is our God."

¹⁹Joshua said to the people, "You are not able to serve the LORD. He is a holy God; he is a jealous God. He will not forgive your rebellion and your sins. ²⁰If you forsake the LORD and serve foreign gods, he will turn and bring disaster on you and make an end of you, after he has been good to you."

²¹But the people said to Joshua, "No! We will serve the LORD."

²²Then Joshua said, "You are witnesses against yourselves that you have chosen to serve the LORD."

"Yes, we are witnesses," they replied.

²³"Now then," said Joshua, "throw away the foreign gods that are among you and yield your hearts to the LORD, the God of Israel."

²⁴And the people said to Joshua, "We will serve the LORD our God and obey him."

²⁵On that day Joshua made a covenant for the people, and there at Shechem he reaffirmed for them decrees and laws. ²⁶And Joshua recorded these things in the Book of the Law of God. Then he took a large stone and set it up there under the oak near the holy place of the LORD.

²⁷"See!" he said to all the people. "This stone will be a witness against us. It has heard all the words the LORD has said to us. It will be a witness against you if you are untrue to your God."

²⁸Then Joshua dismissed the people, each to their own inheritance.

Buried in the Promised Land

²⁹After these things, Joshua son of Nun, the servant of the LORD, died at the age of a hundred and ten. ³⁰And they buried him in the land of his inheritance, at Timnath Serah*a* in the hill country of Ephraim, north of Mount Gaash.

³¹Israel served the LORD throughout the lifetime of Joshua and of the elders who outlived him and who had experienced everything the LORD had done for Israel.

³²And Joseph's bones, which the Israelites had brought up from Egypt, were buried at Shechem in the tract of land that Jacob bought for a hundred pieces of silver*b* from the sons of Hamor, the father of Shechem. This became the inheritance of Joseph's descendants.

³³And Eleazar son of Aaron died and was buried at Gibeah, which had been allotted to his son Phinehas in the hill country of Ephraim.

---

a 30 Also known as *Timnath Heres* (see Judges 2:9)
b 32 Hebrew *hundred kesitahs*; a kesitah was a unit of money of unknown weight and value.

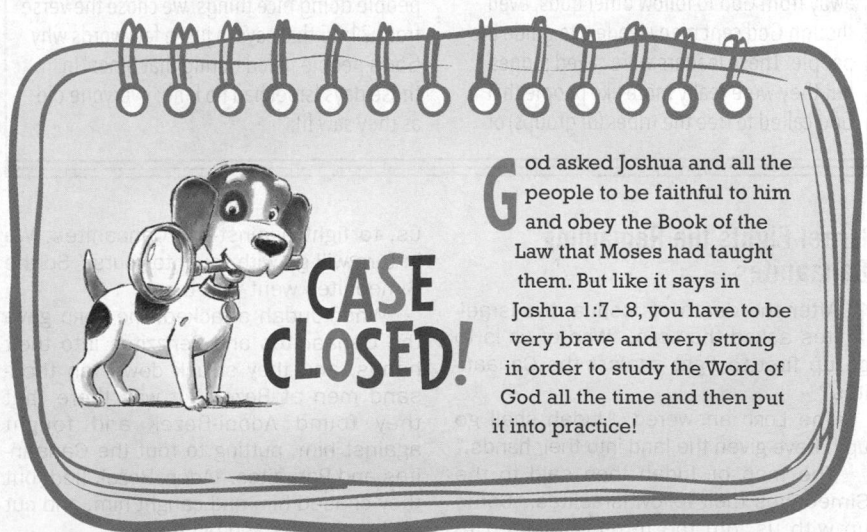

CASE CLOSED!

God asked Joshua and all the people to be faithful to him and obey the Book of the Law that Moses had taught them. But like it says in Joshua 1:7–8, you have to be very brave and very strong in order to study the Word of God all the time and then put it into practice!

JUDGES

THE EVIDENCE:

WHO WROTE IT?

We do not know the name of the person who wrote this book. It seems that it was written by a group of people—a group of prophets. This book is part of a collection of books that also include Joshua, the two books of Samuel, the two books of Kings and the two books of Chronicles.

HOW LONG AGO?

The book of Judges was written about 2,600 years ago, so that's a long time ago!

WHAT'S IT ABOUT?

This book is pretty much the opposite of the book of Joshua. In Joshua, he and the people lived according to the Word of God. In the book of the Judges, it's all about disobedience, evil, violence and running away from God to follow other gods, even though God sent many leaders to guide the people. These leaders were called judges, but they were really more like people that God called to free the tribes (or groups) of people from the hands of their enemies. There were twelve: six major judges (Othniel, Ehud, Deborah, Gideon, Jephthah and Samson) and six minor judges (Shamgar, Tola, Jair, Ibzan, Elon and Abdon).

THE BEST PART

Since the book of Judges doesn't have many people doing nice things, we chose the verse from 21:25 that says in just a few words why God's people failed during that time: "In those days Israel had no king; everyone did as they saw fit."

Israel Fights the Remaining Canaanites

1 After the death of Joshua, the Israelites asked the LORD, "Who of us is to go up first to fight against the Canaanites?"

²The LORD answered, "Judah shall go up; I have given the land into their hands."

³The men of Judah then said to the Simeonites their fellow Israelites, "Come up with us into the territory allotted to us, to fight against the Canaanites. We in turn will go with you into yours." So the Simeonites went with them.

⁴When Judah attacked, the LORD gave the Canaanites and Perizzites into their hands, and they struck down ten thousand men at Bezek. ⁵It was there that they found Adoni-Bezek and fought against him, putting to rout the Canaanites and Perizzites. ⁶Adoni-Bezek fled, but they chased him and caught him, and cut off his thumbs and big toes.

¹³Othniel son of Kenaz, Caleb's younger brother, took it; so Caleb gave his daughter Aksah to him in marriage.

¹⁴One day when she came to Othniel, she urged him*ᵃ* to ask her father for a field. When she got off her donkey, Caleb asked her, "What can I do for you?"

¹⁵She replied, "Do me a special favor. Since you have given me land in the Negev, give me also springs of water." So Caleb gave her the upper and lower springs.

ᵃ 14 Hebrew; Septuagint and Vulgate *Othniel, he urged her*

BREAK THROUGH!

What does cutting off the thumbs and big toes mean?

(JUDGES 1:6–7)

It means shaming and disabling a person. That person was usually a king, a priest or an important military officer. In this case, Adoni-Bezek, as king, couldn't use weapons anymore. Since parts of his body had been cut off, he couldn't be the high priest of the nation, because a priest had to be "perfect."

⁷Then Adoni-Bezek said, "Seventy kings with their thumbs and big toes cut off have picked up scraps under my table. Now God has paid me back for what I did to them." They brought him to Jerusalem, and he died there.

⁸The men of Judah attacked Jerusalem also and took it. They put the city to the sword and set it on fire.

⁹After that, Judah went down to fight against the Canaanites living in the hill country, the Negev and the western foothills. ¹⁰They advanced against the Canaanites living in Hebron (formerly called Kiriath Arba) and defeated Sheshai, Ahiman and Talmai. ¹¹From there they advanced against the people living in Debir (formerly called Kiriath Sepher).

¹²And Caleb said, "I will give my daughter Aksah in marriage to the man who attacks and captures Kiriath Sepher."

BREAK THROUGH!

Did they kill all the people in that city and then set fire to it?

(JUDGES 1:8)

Did you know that archaeologists have found that the walled cities like Jerusalem were usually very small? For example, Jerusalem was only a little bigger than two soccer fields. Only the richest and most powerful people of the nation lived there. They were the kings, the military officials and the religious leaders. So most of the people lived outside those cities in small villages or in towns that didn't have any kind of protection. God ordered the people in the cities, not the common people, to be killed—they were the ones in power, and they were usually evil.

chariots fitted with iron. ²⁰As Moses had promised, Hebron was given to Caleb, who drove from it the three sons of Anak. ²¹The Benjamites, however, did not drive out the Jebusites, who were living in Jerusalem; to this day the Jebusites live there with the Benjamites.

²²Now the tribes of Joseph attacked Bethel, and the Lᴏʀᴅ was with them. ²³When they sent men to spy out Bethel (formerly called Luz), ²⁴the spies saw a man coming out of the city and they said to him, "Show us how to get into the city and we will see that you are treated well."

ᵃ 16 That is, Jericho   *ᵇ 17* The Hebrew term refers to the irrevocable giving over of things or persons to the Lᴏʀᴅ, often by totally destroying them.   *ᶜ 17 Hormah* means *destruction.*   *ᵈ 18* Hebrew; Septuagint *Judah did not take*

THE
WITNESSES

✓ **SHESHAI, AHIMAN AND TALMAI**
(JUDGES 1:10)
They were groups of families that were descendants of the giant Anak (see Numbers 13:22).

---

¹⁶The descendants of Moses' father-in-law, the Kenite, went up from the City of Palmsᵃ with the people of Judah to live among the inhabitants of the Desert of Judah in the Negev near Arad.

¹⁷Then the men of Judah went with the Simeonites their fellow Israelites and attacked the Canaanites living in Zephath, and they totally destroyedᵇ the city. Therefore it was called Hormah.ᶜ ¹⁸Judah also tookᵈ Gaza, Ashkelon and Ekron—each city with its territory.

¹⁹The Lᴏʀᴅ was with the men of Judah. They took possession of the hill country, but they were unable to drive the people from the plains, because they had

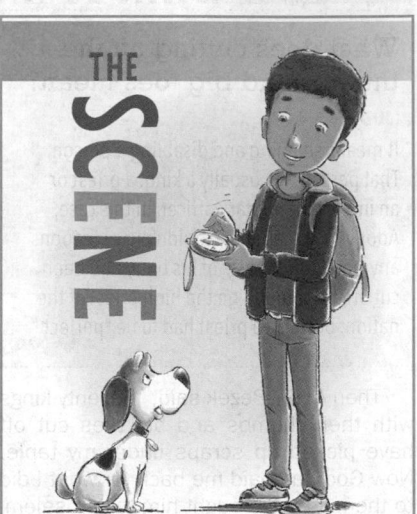

THE
SCENE

GAZA, ASHKELON AND EKRON

(JUDGES 1:18)

These places are on the coastal plain (along the Mediterranean Sea). Gaza is in the south, Ashkelon is in the middle and Ekron is in the north. The five Philistine cities are located along an important commercial route that joins Egypt with Syria and Mesopotamia.

²⁵So he showed them, and they put the city to the sword but spared the man and his whole family. ²⁶He then went to the land of the Hittites, where he built a city and called it Luz, which is its name to this day.

²⁷But Manasseh did not drive out the people of Beth Shan or Taanach or Dor or Ibleam or Megiddo and their surrounding settlements, for the Canaanites were determined to live in that land. ²⁸When Israel became strong, they pressed the Canaanites into forced labor but never drove them out completely. ²⁹Nor did Ephraim drive out the Canaanites living in Gezer, but the Canaanites continued to live there among them. ³⁰Neither did Zebulun drive out the Canaanites living in Kitron or Nahalol, so these Canaanites lived among them, but Zebulun did subject them to forced labor. ³¹Nor did Asher drive out those living in Akko or Sidon or Ahlab or Akzib or Helbah or Aphek or Rehob. ³²The Asherites lived among the Canaanite inhabitants of the land because they did not drive them out. ³³Neither did Naphtali drive out those living in Beth Shemesh or Beth Anath; but the Naphtalites too lived among the Canaanite inhabitants of the land, and those living in Beth Shemesh and Beth Anath became forced laborers for them. ³⁴The Amorites confined the Danites to the hill country, not allowing them to come down into the plain. ³⁵And the Amorites were determined also to hold out in Mount Heres, Aijalon and Shaalbim, but when the power of the tribes of Joseph increased, they too were pressed into forced labor. ³⁶The boundary of the Amorites was from Scorpion Pass to Sela and beyond.

The Angel of the Lᴏʀᴅ at Bokim

2 The angel of the Lᴏʀᴅ went up from Gilgal to Bokim and said, "I brought you up out of Egypt and led you into the land I swore to give to your ancestors. I said, 'I will never break my covenant with you, ²and you shall not make a covenant with the people of this land, but you shall break down their altars.' Yet you have disobeyed me. Why have you done this? ³And I have also said, 'I will not drive them out before you; they will become traps for you, and their gods will become snares to you.'"

⁴When the angel of the Lᴏʀᴅ had spoken these things to all the Israelites, the people wept aloud, ⁵and they called that place Bokim.ᵃ There they offered sacrifices to the Lᴏʀᴅ.

Disobedience and Defeat

⁶After Joshua had dismissed the Israelites, they went to take possession of the land, each to their own inheritance. ⁷The

THE SCENE

BETH SHAN, TAANACH, DOR, IBLEAM AND MEGIDDO

(JUDGES 1:27)

These places are in the territory that belongs to the tribe of Manasseh. That means they're in the northern part, south of the Sea of Galilee. Beth Shan controlled an important road near the Jordan River. Taanach, Ibleam and Megiddo controlled the Esdrelon Valley in the southern part of Mount Carmel.

ᵃ 5 *Bokim* means *weepers.*

people served the LORD throughout the lifetime of Joshua and of the elders who outlived him and who had seen all the great things the LORD had done for Israel.

8 Joshua son of Nun, the servant of the LORD, died at the age of a hundred and ten. 9 And they buried him in the land of his inheritance, at Timnath Heres[a] in the hill country of Ephraim, north of Mount Gaash.

10 After that whole generation had been gathered to their ancestors, another generation grew up who knew neither the LORD nor what he had done for Israel. 11 Then the Israelites did evil in the eyes of the LORD and served the Baals. 12 They forsook the LORD, the God of their ancestors, who had brought them out of Egypt. They followed and worshiped various gods of the peoples around them. They aroused the LORD's anger 13 because they forsook him and served Baal and the Ashtoreths. 14 In his anger against Israel the LORD gave them into the hands of raiders who plundered them. He sold them into the hands of their enemies all around, whom they were no longer able to resist. 15 Whenever Israel went out to fight, the hand of the LORD was against them to defeat them, just as he had sworn to them. They were in great distress.

16 Then the LORD raised up judges,[b] who saved them out of the hands of these raiders. 17 Yet they would not listen to their judges but prostituted themselves to other gods and worshiped them. They quickly turned from the ways of their ancestors, who had been obedient to the LORD's commands. 18 Whenever the LORD raised up a judge for them, he was with the judge and saved them out of the hands of their enemies as long as the judge lived; for the LORD relented because of their groaning under those who oppressed and afflicted them. 19 But when the judge died, the people returned to ways even more corrupt than those of their ancestors, following other gods and serving and worshiping them. They refused to give up their evil practices and stubborn ways.

20 Therefore the LORD was very angry with Israel and said, "Because this nation has violated the covenant I ordained

BREAKTHROUGH!

Who were Baal and Ashtoreth?

(JUDGES 2:13)

They were gods the Canaanites had. Their most important god was called *'El* or *'Ilu*. That's the same word for God in Hebrew! *Baal* means "lord" or "master." His symbol was a bull, and he was considered to be the god of life, of storms and of war. That's why the Israelites were so tempted to follow and serve him instead of being faithful to the God of Israel. Ashtoreth was the goddess of fertility (that means being able to have many babies, or in the case of the land, produce a lot of fruit). In several regions of the ancient Near East, especially the city of Ashtoreth in Sidon, they believed she was Baal's wife.

for their ancestors and has not listened to me, 21 I will no longer drive out before them any of the nations Joshua left when he died. 22 I will use them to test Israel and see whether they will keep the way of the LORD and walk in it as their ancestors did." 23 The LORD had allowed those nations to remain; he did not drive them out at once by giving them into the hands of Joshua.

---

a 9 Also known as *Timnath Serah* (see Joshua 19:50 and 24:30)   *b* 16 Or *leaders*; similarly in verses 17-19

3 These are the nations the Lord left to test all those Israelites who had not experienced any of the wars in Canaan ²(he did this only to teach warfare to the descendants of the Israelites who had not had previous battle experience): ³the five rulers of the Philistines, all the Canaanites, the Sidonians, and the Hivites living in the Lebanon mountains from Mount Baal Hermon to Lebo Hamath. ⁴They were left to test the Israelites to see whether they would obey the Lord's commands, which he had given their ancestors through Moses.

⁵The Israelites lived among the Canaanites, Hittites, Amorites, Perizzites, Hivites and Jebusites. ⁶They took their daughters in marriage and gave their own daughters to their sons, and served their gods.

Othniel

⁷The Israelites did evil in the eyes of the Lord; they forgot the Lord their God and served the Baals and the Asherahs. ⁸The anger of the Lord burned against Israel so that he sold them into the hands of Cushan-Rishathaim king of Aram Naharaim,ᵃ to whom the Israelites were subject for eight years. ⁹But when they cried out to the Lord, he raised up for them a deliverer, Othniel son of Kenaz, Caleb's younger

ᵃ 8 That is, Northwest Mesopotamia

BREAKTHROUGH!

Why couldn't the Israelites marry people from other nations?

(JUDGES 3:6)

It was to prevent the foreign women from making their husbands and children separate themselves from the true God in order to follow their false gods. Their marriages with foreigners always happened with Israelite men marrying women from other countries, because it was the men who went away to war or came into contact with people from other nations. The Israelite women usually stayed at home and very rarely came into contact with men outside the family, much less men from other nations.

THE WITNESSES

✓ **CUSHAN-RISHATHAIM, KING OF ARAM NAHARAIM** (JUDGES 3:8)
This name means "Cushan of the two sins."

brother, who saved them. ¹⁰The Spirit of the LORD came on him, so that he became Israel's judge[a] and went to war. The LORD gave Cushan-Rishathaim king of Aram into the hands of Othniel, who overpowered him. ¹¹So the land had peace for forty years, until Othniel son of Kenaz died.

Ehud

¹²Again the Israelites did evil in the eyes of the LORD, and because they did this evil the LORD gave Eglon king of Moab power over Israel. ¹³Getting the Ammonites and Amalekites to join him, Eglon came and attacked Israel, and they took possession of the City of Palms.[b] ¹⁴The Israelites were subject to Eglon king of Moab for eighteen years.

¹⁵Again the Israelites cried out to the LORD, and he gave them a deliverer— Ehud, a left-handed man, the son of Gera the Benjamite. The Israelites sent him with tribute to Eglon king of Moab. ¹⁶Now Ehud had made a double-edged sword about a cubit[c] long, which he strapped to his right thigh under his clothing. ¹⁷He presented the tribute to Eglon king of Moab, who was a very fat man. ¹⁸After Ehud had presented the tribute, he sent on their way those who had carried it. ¹⁹But on reaching the stone images near Gilgal he himself went back to Eglon and said, "Your Majesty, I have a secret message for you."

The king said to his attendants, "Leave us!" And they all left.

²⁰Ehud then approached him while he was sitting alone in the upper room of his palace[d] and said, "I have a message from God for you." As the king rose from his seat, ²¹Ehud reached with his left hand, drew the sword from his right thigh and plunged it into the king's belly. ²²Even the handle sank in after the blade, and his bowels discharged. Ehud did not pull the sword out, and the fat closed in over it. ²³Then Ehud went out to the porch[e]; he shut the doors of the upper room behind him and locked them.

²⁴After he had gone, the servants came and found the doors of the upper room locked. They said, "He must be relieving himself in the inner room of the palace."

²⁵They waited to the point of embarrassment, but when he did not open the doors of the room, they took a key and unlocked them. There they saw their lord fallen to the floor, dead.

²⁶While they waited, Ehud got away. He passed by the stone images and escaped to Seirah. ²⁷When he arrived there, he blew a trumpet in the hill country of Ephraim, and the Israelites went down with him from the hills, with him leading them.

---

[a] 10 Or *leader*   [b] 13 That is, Jericho   [c] 16 That is, about 18 inches or about 45 centimeters   [d] 20 The meaning of the Hebrew for this word is uncertain; also in verse 24.   [e] 23 The meaning of the Hebrew for this word is uncertain.

Ammonites and Amalekites

(JUDGES 3:13)

The Ammonites were a nomad tribe. That means they moved from one place to another and didn't settle down in just one place. They lived in the south of Canaan and the north part of the Arabian Peninsula. When the Israelite people were wandering around the desert, these people were the first enemies they came upon (see Exodus 17:8–16). That tribe came from Lot, Abraham's nephew (Genesis 19:36–38). The Amalekites were another nomad tribe that lived south of Palestine, near the country of Edom and the Negev Desert in the south.

28"Follow me," he ordered, "for the LORD has given Moab, your enemy, into your hands." So they followed him down and took possession of the fords of the Jordan that led to Moab; they allowed no one to cross over. 29At that time they struck down about ten thousand Moabites, all vigorous and strong; not one escaped. 30That day Moab was made

BREAK THROUGH!

Moabites

(JUDGES 3:29)

They were always enemies of Israel (see Numbers 21:29; 22–24; Deuteronomy 23:3–4; 1 Samuel 14:47). They made the Israelites worship their gods (read about it in Numbers 25:1–4). Like the Ammonites, they were the offspring of Lot, Abraham's nephew. They lived north of the Dead Sea in the area where the people of Israel lived until they entered the promised land.

THE WITNESSES

✓ EGLON, KING OF MOAB (JUDGES 3:12)
This king was very bad, and he was the enemy of God's people. Do you know what his name meant? It was "fat bull ready to be slaughtered." A pretty good name for him!

✓ EHUD (JUDGES 3:15–16)
This name can be translated as "Where is the glory?" or "Majesty of God." It's interesting that Ehud was from the tribe of Benjamin, which in Hebrew means "son of the right hand," but that was the hand he had "tied up" or "disabled."

subject to Israel, and the land had peace for eighty years.

Shamgar

31After Ehud came Shamgar son of Anath, who struck down six hundred Philistines with an oxgoad. He too saved Israel.

Deborah

4 Again the Israelites did evil in the eyes of the LORD, now that Ehud was dead. 2So the LORD sold them into the hands of Jabin king of Canaan, who reigned in Hazor. Sisera, the commander of his army, was based in Harosheth Haggoyim. 3Because he had nine hundred chariots fitted with iron and had cruelly oppressed

✓ DEBORAH (JUDGES 4:1)
Her name means "bee." This judge and prophet was key in helping the Israelites defeat the Canaanite army and its commander, Sisera. Just like a little bee, she didn't stop "stinging" Barak until he decided to lead the Israelite army.

✓ SISERA (JUDGES 4:2)
This was the name of the commander of the Hazor armies. His ancestors possibly were Philistines, the ones called "sea peoples." Sisera was a very powerful and brave military officer. But he not only was defeated by a small Israelite army, he was also killed by Jael, a very brave, smart woman.

✓ BARAK (JUDGES 4:8)
His name means "lightning," but he wasn't very brave, and he needed to be pushed to make his "lightning" strike and defeat Sisera's army.

✓ HEBER (JUDGES 4:11)
He was Jael's husband, and he belonged to the Kenites (see Judges 1:16). He was the leader of a group that separated from the Kenites. His group was friendly with King Jabin.

✓ JAEL (JUDGES 4:17)
Her name means "mountain goat." The story explains how this "mountain goat" became the first to "give milk" (like a goat would) to Sisera, and then she finished off the enemy with her "horn" that was really a tent peg.

THE WITNESSES

the Israelites for twenty years, they cried to the LORD for help.

⁴Now Deborah, a prophet, the wife of Lappidoth, was leading[a] Israel at that time. ⁵She held court under the Palm of Deborah between Ramah and Bethel in the hill country of Ephraim, and the Israelites went up to her to have their disputes decided. ⁶She sent for Barak son of Abinoam from Kedesh in Naphtali and said to him, "The LORD, the God of Israel, commands you: 'Go, take with you ten thousand men of Naphtali and Zebulun and lead them up to Mount Tabor. ⁷I will lead Sisera, the commander of Jabin's army, with his chariots and his troops to the Kishon River and give him into your hands.'"

⁸Barak said to her, "If you go with me,

I will go; but if you don't go with me, I won't go."

⁹"Certainly I will go with you," said Deborah. "But because of the course you are taking, the honor will not be yours, for the LORD will deliver Sisera into the hands of a woman." So Deborah went with Barak to Kedesh. ¹⁰There Barak summoned Zebulun and Naphtali, and ten thousand men went up under his command. Deborah also went up with him.

¹¹Now Heber the Kenite had left the other Kenites, the descendants of Hobab, Moses' brother-in-law,[b] and pitched his tent by the great tree in Zaanannim near Kedesh.

¹²When they told Sisera that Barak son

---

[a] 4 Traditionally judging   [b] 11 Or father-in-law

THE SCENE

MOUNT TABOR

(JUDGES 4:6)

It's in the northern part of the country between Mount Carmel and the Sea of Galilee, bordering on the limits of the tribes of Naphtali and Issachar.

of Abinoam had gone up to Mount Tabor, [13] Sisera summoned from Harosheth Haggoyim to the Kishon River all his men and his nine hundred chariots fitted with iron.

[14] Then Deborah said to Barak, "Go! This is the day the LORD has given Sisera into your hands. Has not the LORD gone ahead of you?" So Barak went down Mount Tabor, with ten thousand men following him. [15] At Barak's advance, the LORD routed Sisera and all his chariots and army by the sword, and Sisera got down from his chariot and fled on foot.

[16] Barak pursued the chariots and army as far as Harosheth Haggoyim, and all Sisera's troops fell by the sword; not a man was left. [17] Sisera, meanwhile, fled on foot to the tent of Jael, the wife of Heber the Kenite, because there was an alliance between Jabin king of Hazor and the family of Heber the Kenite.

[18] Jael went out to meet Sisera and said to him, "Come, my lord, come right in. Don't be afraid." So he entered her tent, and she covered him with a blanket.

[19] "I'm thirsty," he said. "Please give me some water." She opened a skin of milk, gave him a drink, and covered him up.

[20] "Stand in the doorway of the tent," he told her. "If someone comes by and asks you, 'Is anyone in there?' say 'No.'"

[21] But Jael, Heber's wife, picked up a tent peg and a hammer and went quietly to him while he lay fast asleep, exhausted. She drove the peg through his temple into the ground, and he died.

[22] Just then Barak came by in pursuit of Sisera, and Jael went out to meet him. "Come," she said, "I will show you the man you're looking for." So he went in with her, and there lay Sisera with the tent peg through his temple—dead.

[23] On that day God subdued Jabin king of Canaan before the Israelites. [24] And the hand of the Israelites pressed harder and harder against Jabin king of Canaan until they destroyed him.

The Song of Deborah

5 On that day Deborah and Barak son of Abinoam sang this song:

[2] "When the princes in Israel take the
        lead,
   when the people willingly offer
        themselves—
   praise the LORD!

[3] "Hear this, you kings! Listen, you
        rulers!
   I, even I, will sing to[a] the LORD;
   I will praise the LORD, the God of
        Israel, in song.

[4] "When you, LORD, went out from
        Seir,
   when you marched from the land of
        Edom,
   the earth shook, the heavens
        poured,
   the clouds poured down water.
[5] The mountains quaked before the
        LORD, the One of Sinai,
   before the LORD, the God of Israel.

---

[a] 3 Or of

6 "In the days of Shamgar son of Anath,
    in the days of Jael, the highways
        were abandoned;
    travelers took to winding paths.
7 Villagers in Israel would not fight;
    they held back until I, Deborah,
        arose,
    until I arose, a mother in Israel.
8 God chose new leaders
    when war came to the city gates,
    but not a shield or spear was seen
        among forty thousand in Israel.
9 My heart is with Israel's princes,
    with the willing volunteers among
        the people.
    Praise the LORD!

10 "You who ride on white donkeys,
    sitting on your saddle blankets,
    and you who walk along the road,
    consider 11 the voice of the singers*a* at
        the watering places.
    They recite the victories of the
        LORD,
    the victories of his villagers in
        Israel.

    "Then the people of the LORD
        went down to the city gates.
12 'Wake up, wake up, Deborah!
    Wake up, wake up, break out in
        song!
    Arise, Barak!
    Take captive your captives, son of
        Abinoam.'
13 "The remnant of the nobles came
        down;
    the people of the LORD came down
        to me against the mighty.
14 Some came from Ephraim, whose
        roots were in Amalek;
    Benjamin was with the people who
        followed you.
    From Makir captains came down,
    from Zebulun those who bear a
        commander's*a* staff.
15 The princes of Issachar were with
        Deborah;
    yes, Issachar was with Barak,
    sent under his command into the
        valley.
    In the districts of Reuben
        there was much searching of heart.

16 Why did you stay among the sheep
        pens*b*
    to hear the whistling for the flocks?
    In the districts of Reuben
        there was much searching of heart.
17 Gilead stayed beyond the Jordan.
    And Dan, why did he linger by the
        ships?
    Asher remained on the coast
        and stayed in his coves.
18 The people of Zebulun risked their
        very lives;
    so did Naphtali on the terraced
        fields.

19 "Kings came, they fought,
    the kings of Canaan fought.
    At Taanach, by the waters of Megiddo,
    they took no plunder of silver.
20 From the heavens the stars fought,
    from their courses they fought
        against Sisera.
21 The river Kishon swept them away,
    the age-old river, the river Kishon.
    March on, my soul; be strong!
22 Then thundered the horses' hooves—
    galloping, galloping go his mighty
        steeds.
23 'Curse Meroz,' said the angel of the
        LORD.
    'Curse its people bitterly,
    because they did not come to help
        the LORD,
    to help the LORD against the
        mighty.'

24 "Most blessed of women be Jael,
    the wife of Heber the Kenite,
    most blessed of tent-dwelling
        women.
25 He asked for water, and she gave him
        milk;
    in a bowl fit for nobles she brought
        him curdled milk.
26 Her hand reached for the tent peg,
    her right hand for the workman's
        hammer.
    She struck Sisera, she crushed his
        head,
    she shattered and pierced his
        temple.

---

a 11,14 The meaning of the Hebrew for this word is
uncertain.   *b* 16 Or *the campfires*; or *the saddlebags*

27 At her feet he sank,
　　he fell; there he lay.
　At her feet he sank, he fell;
　　where he sank, there he fell—
　　　dead.

28 "Through the window peered Sisera's
　　　mother;
　　behind the lattice she cried out,
　'Why is his chariot so long in coming?
　　Why is the clatter of his chariots
　　　delayed?'
29 The wisest of her ladies answer her;
　　indeed, she keeps saying to herself,
30 'Are they not finding and dividing the
　　　spoils:
　　a woman or two for each man,
　colorful garments as plunder for
　　　Sisera,
　　colorful garments embroidered,
　highly embroidered garments for my
　　　neck—
　　all this as plunder?'

31 "So may all your enemies perish, Lord!
　　But may all who love you be like the
　　　sun
　　when it rises in its strength."

Then the land had peace forty years.

Gideon

6 The Israelites did evil in the eyes of
the Lord, and for seven years he gave
them into the hands of the Midianites.
²Because the power of Midian was so op-
pressive, the Israelites prepared shelters
for themselves in mountain clefts, caves
and strongholds. ³Whenever the Israelites
planted their crops, the Midianites, Amalekites and other eastern peoples invaded the country. ⁴They camped on the land
and ruined the crops all the way to Gaza
and did not spare a living thing for Israel, neither sheep nor cattle nor donkeys.
⁵They came up with their livestock and
their tents like swarms of locusts. It was
impossible to count them or their camels;
they invaded the land to ravage it. ⁶Midian
so impoverished the Israelites that they
cried out to the Lord for help.

⁷When the Israelites cried out to the
Lord because of Midian, ⁸he sent them a
prophet, who said, "This is what the Lord,

BREAK THROUGH!

Midianites

(JUDGES 6:1)

They lived in the desert in northeastern
Arabia. They were related to the Israelites,
because Midian was one of the sons Abraham
had with his wife Keturah. (Read about it in
Genesis 25:1–5.)

the God of Israel, says: I brought you up
out of Egypt, out of the land of slavery. ⁹I
rescued you from the hand of the Egyptians. And I delivered you from the hand
of all your oppressors; I drove them out
before you and gave you their land. ¹⁰I
said to you, 'I am the Lord your God; do
not worship the gods of the Amorites, in
whose land you live.' But you have not listened to me."

¹¹The angel of the Lord came and sat
down under the oak in Ophrah that belonged to Joash the Abiezrite, where his
son Gideon was threshing wheat in a
winepress to keep it from the Midianites.
¹²When the angel of the Lord appeared
to Gideon, he said, "The Lord is with you,
mighty warrior."

¹³"Pardon me, my lord," Gideon replied,
"but if the Lord is with us, why has all
this happened to us? Where are all his
wonders that our ancestors told us about
when they said, 'Did not the Lord bring us
up out of Egypt?' But now the Lord has

abandoned us and given us into the hand of Midian."

¹⁴The Lᴏʀᴅ turned to him and said, "Go in the strength you have and save Israel out of Midian's hand. Am I not sending you?"

¹⁵"Pardon me, my lord," Gideon replied, "but how can I save Israel? My clan is the weakest in Manasseh, and I am the least in my family."

¹⁶The Lᴏʀᴅ answered, "I will be with you, and you will strike down all the Midianites, leaving none alive."

THE
WITNESSES

✓ **GIDEON/JERUB-BAAL (JUDGES 6:11,32)**
He was the fifth judge in the book of Judges. Gideon means "he who pulls out or destroys." That was a good name for him, because his task was to stop the worshiping of the god Baal and get rid of the image of that god. But this rescuer had another name too. It was Jerub-Baal, and that meant "Baal is great" or "Baal is master."

¹⁷Gideon replied, "If now I have found favor in your eyes, give me a sign that it is really you talking to me. ¹⁸Please do not go away until I come back and bring my offering and set it before you."

And the Lᴏʀᴅ said, "I will wait until you return."

¹⁹Gideon went inside, prepared a young goat, and from an ephah[a] of flour he made bread without yeast. Putting the meat in a basket and its broth in a pot, he brought them out and offered them to him under the oak.

²⁰The angel of God said to him, "Take the meat and the unleavened bread, place them on this rock, and pour out the broth." And Gideon did so. ²¹Then the angel of the Lᴏʀᴅ touched the meat and the unleavened bread with the tip of the staff that was in his hand. Fire flared from the rock, consuming the meat and the bread. And the angel of the Lᴏʀᴅ disappeared. ²²When Gideon realized that it was the angel of the Lᴏʀᴅ, he exclaimed, "Alas, Sovereign Lᴏʀᴅ! I have seen the angel of the Lᴏʀᴅ face to face!"

²³But the Lᴏʀᴅ said to him, "Peace! Do not be afraid. You are not going to die."

²⁴So Gideon built an altar to the Lᴏʀᴅ there and called it The Lᴏʀᴅ Is Peace. To this day it stands in Ophrah of the Abiezrites.

²⁵That same night the Lᴏʀᴅ said to him, "Take the second bull from your father's herd, the one seven years old.[b] Tear down your father's altar to Baal and cut down the Asherah pole[c] beside it. ²⁶Then build a proper kind of[d] altar to the Lᴏʀᴅ your God on the top of this height. Using the wood of the Asherah pole that you cut down, offer the second[e] bull as a burnt offering."

²⁷So Gideon took ten of his servants and did as the Lᴏʀᴅ told him. But because he was afraid of his family and the townspeople, he did it at night rather than in the daytime.

²⁸In the morning when the people of the town got up, there was Baal's altar,

---

[a] 19 That is, probably about 36 pounds or about 16 kilograms   [b] 25 Or *Take a full-grown, mature bull from your father's herd*   [c] 25 That is, a wooden symbol of the goddess Asherah; also in verses 26, 28 and 30   [d] 26 Or *build with layers of stone an*   [e] 26 Or *full-grown*; also in verse 28

BREAKTHROUGH!

Goddess Asherah

(JUDGES 6:25)

This Canaanite goddess was the wife of the supreme god 'El (also called 'Ilu), and she was the mother of all the gods. In the Old Testament, the word *Asherah* also means "sacred tree" and the "sacred poles" that they placed next to the sanctuaries.

demolished, with the Asherah pole beside it cut down and the second bull sacrificed on the newly built altar!

²⁹They asked each other, "Who did this?"

When they carefully investigated, they were told, "Gideon son of Joash did it."

³⁰The people of the town demanded of Joash, "Bring out your son. He must die, because he has broken down Baal's altar and cut down the Asherah pole beside it."

³¹But Joash replied to the hostile crowd around him, "Are you going to plead Baal's cause? Are you trying to save him? Whoever fights for him shall be put to death by morning! If Baal really is a god, he can defend himself when someone breaks down his altar." ³²So because Gideon broke down Baal's altar, they gave him the name Jerub-Baal*ᵃ* that day, saying, "Let Baal contend with him."

³³Now all the Midianites, Amalekites and other eastern peoples joined forces

and crossed over the Jordan and camped in the Valley of Jezreel. ³⁴Then the Spirit of the LORD came on Gideon, and he blew a trumpet, summoning the Abiezrites to follow him. ³⁵He sent messengers throughout Manasseh, calling them to arms, and also into Asher, Zebulun and Naphtali, so that they too went up to meet them.

³⁶Gideon said to God, "If you will save Israel by my hand as you have promised— ³⁷look, I will place a wool fleece on the threshing floor. If there is dew only on the fleece and all the ground is dry, then I will know that you will save Israel by my hand, as you said." ³⁸And that is what happened. Gideon rose early the next day; he squeezed the fleece and wrung out the dew—a bowlful of water.

³⁹Then Gideon said to God, "Do not be angry with me. Let me make just one more request. Allow me one more test with the fleece, but this time make the

---

ᵃ 32 Jerub-Baal probably means *let Baal contend.*

THE SCENE

VALLEY OF JEZREEL

(JUDGES 6:33)

It is south of Mount Tabor and the hill of Moreh, and it stretches south to the border of the tribe of Issachar.

BREAKTHROUGH!

Abiezrites

(JUDGES 6:34)

These were the descendants of Abiezer. Gideon belonged to the tribe of Manasseh and the family of Abiezer. When Gideon called the men to battle, they came right away because they were people from his own clan.

fleece dry and let the ground be covered with dew." ⁴⁰That night God did so. Only the fleece was dry; all the ground was covered with dew.

Gideon Defeats the Midianites

7 Early in the morning, Jerub-Baal (that is, Gideon) and all his men camped at the spring of Harod. The camp of Midian was north of them in the valley near the hill of Moreh. ²The LORD said to Gideon, "You have too many men. I cannot deliver Midian into their hands, or Israel would boast against me, 'My own strength has saved me.' ³Now announce to the army, 'Anyone who trembles with fear may turn back and leave Mount Gilead.' " So twenty-two thousand men left, while ten thousand remained.

⁴But the LORD said to Gideon, "There are still too many men. Take them down to the water, and I will thin them out for you there. If I say, 'This one shall go with you,' he shall go; but if I say, 'This one shall not go with you,' he shall not go."

⁵So Gideon took the men down to the water. There the LORD told him, "Separate those who lap the water with their tongues as a dog laps from those who kneel down to drink." ⁶Three hundred of them drank from cupped hands, lapping like dogs. All the rest got down on their knees to drink.

⁷The LORD said to Gideon, "With the three hundred men that lapped I will save you and give the Midianites into your hands. Let all the others go home." ⁸So Gideon sent the rest of the Israelites home but kept the three hundred, who took over the provisions and trumpets of the others.

Now the camp of Midian lay below him in the valley. ⁹During that night the LORD said to Gideon, "Get up, go down against the camp, because I am going to give it into your hands. ¹⁰If you are afraid to attack, go down to the camp with your servant Purah ¹¹and listen to what they are saying. Afterward, you will be encouraged to attack the camp." So he and Purah his servant went down to the outposts of the camp. ¹²The Midianites, the Amalekites and all the other eastern peoples had settled in the valley, thick as locusts. Their camels could no more be counted than the sand on the seashore.

¹³Gideon arrived just as a man was telling a friend his dream. "I had a dream," he was saying. "A round loaf of barley bread came tumbling into the Midianite camp. It struck the tent with such force that the tent overturned and collapsed."

¹⁴His friend responded, "This can be nothing other than the sword of Gideon son of Joash, the Israelite. God has given the Midianites and the whole camp into his hands."

¹⁵When Gideon heard the dream and its interpretation, he bowed down and worshiped. He returned to the camp of Israel and called out, "Get up! The LORD has given the Midianite camp into your hands." ¹⁶Dividing the three hundred men into three companies, he placed trumpets and empty jars in the hands of all of them, with torches inside.

¹⁷"Watch me," he told them. "Follow my lead. When I get to the edge of the camp, do exactly as I do. ¹⁸When I and all who are with me blow our trumpets, then from all around the camp blow yours and shout, 'For the Lᴏʀᴅ and for Gideon.'"

¹⁹Gideon and the hundred men with him reached the edge of the camp at the beginning of the middle watch, just after they had changed the guard. They blew their trumpets and broke the jars that were in their hands. ²⁰The three companies blew the trumpets and smashed the jars. Grasping the torches in their left hands and holding in their right hands the trumpets they were to blow, they shout-

ed, "A sword for the Lᴏʀᴅ and for Gideon!" ²¹While each man held his position around the camp, all the Midianites ran, crying out as they fled.

²²When the three hundred trumpets sounded, the Lᴏʀᴅ caused the men throughout the camp to turn on each other with their swords. The army fled to Beth Shittah toward Zererah as far as the border of Abel Meholah near Tabbath. ²³Israelites from Naphtali, Asher and all Manasseh were called out, and they pursued the Midianites. ²⁴Gideon sent messengers throughout the hill country of Ephraim, saying, "Come down against the Midianites and seize the waters of the Jordan ahead of them as far as Beth Barah."

So all the men of Ephraim were called out and they seized the waters of the Jordan as far as Beth Barah. ²⁵They also captured two of the Midianite leaders, Oreb and Zeeb. They killed Oreb at the rock of Oreb, and Zeeb at the winepress of Zeeb. They pursued the Midianites and brought the heads of Oreb and Zeeb to Gideon, who was by the Jordan.

Zebah and Zalmunna

8 Now the Ephraimites asked Gideon, "Why have you treated us like this? Why didn't you call us when you went to fight Midian?" And they challenged him vigorously.

²But he answered them, "What have I accomplished compared to you? Aren't the gleanings of Ephraim's grapes better than the full grape harvest of Abiezer? ³God gave Oreb and Zeeb, the Midianite leaders, into your hands. What was I able to do compared to you?" At this, their resentment against him subsided.

⁴Gideon and his three hundred men, exhausted yet keeping up the pursuit, came to the Jordan and crossed it. ⁵He said to the men of Sukkoth, "Give my troops some bread; they are worn out, and I am still pursuing Zebah and Zalmunna, the kings of Midian."

⁶But the officials of Sukkoth said, "Do you already have the hands of Zebah and Zalmunna in your possession? Why should we give bread to your troops?"

THE
WITNESSES

✓ **PURAH** (JUDGES 7:10)
He was Gideon's military assistant. That means he was in charge of Gideon's shield and weapons. His name means "be the best" or "be fruitful."

THE SCENE

SUKKOTH

(JUDGES 8:5)

It is 4.5 miles (7 km) east of Jordan, exactly where the Jabbok River flows into the Jordan River.

⁷Then Gideon replied, "Just for that, when the LORD has given Zebah and Zalmunna into my hand, I will tear your flesh with desert thorns and briers."

⁸From there he went up to Peniel*ᵃ* and made the same request of them, but they answered as the men of Sukkoth had. ⁹So he said to the men of Peniel, "When I return in triumph, I will tear down this tower."

¹⁰Now Zebah and Zalmunna were in Karkor with a force of about fifteen thousand men, all that were left of the armies of the eastern peoples; a hundred and twenty thousand swordsmen had fallen. ¹¹Gideon went up by the route of the nomads east of Nobah and Jogbehah and attacked the unsuspecting army. ¹²Zebah and Zalmunna, the two kings of Midian, fled, but he pursued them and captured them, routing their entire army.

¹³Gideon son of Joash then returned from the battle by the Pass of Heres. ¹⁴He caught a young man of Sukkoth and questioned him, and the young man wrote down for him the names of the seventy-seven officials of Sukkoth, the elders of the town. ¹⁵Then Gideon came and said to the men of Sukkoth, "Here are Zebah and Zalmunna, about whom you taunted me by saying, 'Do you already have the hands of Zebah and Zalmunna in your possession? Why should we give bread to your exhausted men?'" ¹⁶He took the elders of the town and taught the men of Sukkoth a lesson by punishing them with desert thorns and briers. ¹⁷He also pulled down the tower of Peniel and killed the men of the town.

¹⁸Then he asked Zebah and Zalmunna, "What kind of men did you kill at Tabor?"

"Men like you," they answered, "each one with the bearing of a prince."

¹⁹Gideon replied, "Those were my brothers, the sons of my own mother. As surely as the LORD lives, if you had spared their

---

ᵃ 8 Hebrew *Penuel*, a variant of *Peniel*; also in verses 9 and 17

THE SCENE

PENIEL

(JUDGES 8:8)

It is in the vicinity of Sukkoth, about 4 miles (6 km) east of Sukkoth, along the Jabbok River.

lives, I would not kill you." [20]Turning to Jether, his oldest son, he said, "Kill them!" But Jether did not draw his sword, because he was only a boy and was afraid.

[21]Zebah and Zalmunna said, "Come, do it yourself. 'As is the man, so is his strength.' " So Gideon stepped forward and killed them, and took the ornaments off their camels' necks.

Gideon's Ephod

[22]The Israelites said to Gideon, "Rule over us—you, your son and your grandson—because you have saved us from the hand of Midian."

[23]But Gideon told them, "I will not rule over you, nor will my son rule over you. The Lord will rule over you." [24]And he said, "I do have one request, that each of you give me an earring from your share of the plunder." (It was the custom of the Ishmaelites to wear gold earrings.)

[25]They answered, "We'll be glad to give them." So they spread out a garment, and each of them threw a ring from his plunder onto it. [26]The weight of the gold rings he asked for came to seventeen hundred shekels,[a] not counting the ornaments, the pendants and the purple garments worn by the kings of Midian or the chains that were on their camels' necks. [27]Gideon made the gold into an ephod, which he placed in Ophrah, his town. All Israel prostituted themselves by worshiping it there, and it became a snare to Gideon and his family.

Gideon's Death

[28]Thus Midian was subdued before the Israelites and did not raise its head again. During Gideon's lifetime, the land had peace forty years.

[29]Jerub-Baal son of Joash went back home to live. [30]He had seventy sons of his own, for he had many wives. [31]His concubine, who lived in Shechem, also bore him a son, whom he named Abimelek. [32]Gideon son of Joash died at a good old age and was buried in the tomb of his father Joash in Ophrah of the Abiezrites.

[33]No sooner had Gideon died than the Israelites again prostituted themselves

THE
WITNESSES

✓ **ABIMELEK (JUDGES 8:31)**
The name of this person means "my father is king." It shows that Gideon really wanted to become king. Abimelek killed all 70 of his stepbrothers except one. What a jerk!

✓ **BAAL-BERITH (JUDGES 8:33)**
This means "Baal of the alliance" or "Lord of the alliance." God's people and their leaders had abandoned the true God and they were serving and worshiping this false god.

to the Baals. They set up Baal-Berith as their god [34]and did not remember the Lord their God, who had rescued them from the hands of all their enemies on every side. [35]They also failed to show any loyalty to the family of Jerub-Baal (that is, Gideon) in spite of all the good things he had done for them.

---

[a] 26 That is, about 43 pounds or about 20 kilograms

Abimelek

9 Abimelek son of Jerub-Baal went to his mother's brothers in Shechem and said to them and to all his mother's clan, [2] "Ask all the citizens of Shechem, 'Which is better for you: to have all seventy of Jerub-Baal's sons rule over you, or just one man?' Remember, I am your flesh and blood."

[3] When the brothers repeated all this to the citizens of Shechem, they were inclined to follow Abimelek, for they said, "He is related to us." [4] They gave him seventy shekels[a] of silver from the temple of Baal-Berith, and Abimelek used it to hire reckless scoundrels, who became his followers. [5] He went to his father's home in Ophrah and on one stone murdered his seventy brothers, the sons of Jerub-Baal. But Jotham, the youngest son of Jerub-Baal, escaped by hiding. [6] Then all the citizens of Shechem and Beth Millo gathered beside the great tree at the pillar in Shechem to crown Abimelek king.

[7] When Jotham was told about this, he climbed up on the top of Mount Gerizim and shouted to them, "Listen to me, citizens of Shechem, so that God may listen to you. [8] One day the trees went out to anoint a king for themselves. They said to the olive tree, 'Be our king.'

[9] "But the olive tree answered, 'Should I give up my oil, by which both gods and humans are honored, to hold sway over the trees?'

[10] "Next, the trees said to the fig tree, 'Come and be our king.'

[11] "But the fig tree replied, 'Should I give up my fruit, so good and sweet, to hold sway over the trees?'

[12] "Then the trees said to the vine, 'Come and be our king.'

[13] "But the vine answered, 'Should I give up my wine, which cheers both gods and humans, to hold sway over the trees?'

[14] "Finally all the trees said to the thornbush, 'Come and be our king.'

[15] "The thornbush said to the trees, 'If you really want to anoint me king over you, come and take refuge in my shade; but if not, then let fire come out of the thornbush and consume the cedars of Lebanon!'

[16] "Have you acted honorably and in good faith by making Abimelek king? Have you been fair to Jerub-Baal and his family? Have you treated him as he deserves? [17] Remember that my father fought for you and risked his life to rescue you from the hand of Midian. [18] But today you have revolted against my father's family. You have murdered his seventy sons on a single stone and have made Abimelek, the son of his female slave, king over the citizens of Shechem because he is related to you. [19] So have you acted honorably and in good faith toward Jerub-Baal and his family today? If you have, may Abimelek be your joy, and may you be his, too! [20] But if you have not, let fire come out from Abimelek and consume you, the citizens of Shechem and Beth Millo, and let fire come out from you, the citizens of Shechem and Beth Millo, and consume Abimelek!"

[21] Then Jotham fled, escaping to Beer, and he lived there because he was afraid of his brother Abimelek.

[22] After Abimelek had governed Israel three years, [23] God stirred up animosity between Abimelek and the citizens of Shechem so that they acted treacherously against Abimelek. [24] God did this in order that the crime against Jerub-Baal's seventy sons, the shedding of their blood, might be avenged on their brother Abimelek and on the citizens of Shechem, who had helped him murder his brothers. [25] In opposition to him these citizens of Shechem set men on the hilltops to ambush and rob everyone who passed by, and this was reported to Abimelek.

[26] Now Gaal son of Ebed moved with his clan into Shechem, and its citizens put their confidence in him. [27] After they had gone out into the fields and gathered the grapes and trodden them, they held a festival in the temple of their god. While they were eating and drinking, they cursed Abimelek. [28] Then Gaal son of Ebed said, "Who is Abimelek, and why should we Shechemites be subject to him? Isn't he Jerub-Baal's son, and isn't Zebul his deputy? Serve the family of Hamor,

---

[a] 4 That is, about 1 3/4 pounds or about 800 grams

Shechem's father! Why should we serve Abimelek? ²⁹If only this people were under my command! Then I would get rid of him. I would say to Abimelek, 'Call out your whole army!' "ᵃ

³⁰When Zebul the governor of the city heard what Gaal son of Ebed said, he was very angry. ³¹Under cover he sent messengers to Abimelek, saying, "Gaal son of Ebed and his clan have come to Shechem and are stirring up the city against you. ³²Now then, during the night you and your men should come and lie in wait in the fields. ³³In the morning at sunrise, advance against the city. When Gaal and his men come out against you, seize the opportunity to attack them."

³⁴So Abimelek and all his troops set out by night and took up concealed positions near Shechem in four companies. ³⁵Now Gaal son of Ebed had gone out and was standing at the entrance of the city gate just as Abimelek and his troops came out from their hiding place.

³⁶When Gaal saw them, he said to Zebul, "Look, people are coming down from the tops of the mountains!"

Zebul replied, "You mistake the shadows of the mountains for men."

³⁷But Gaal spoke up again: "Look, people are coming down from the central hill,ᵇ and a company is coming from the direction of the diviners' tree."

³⁸Then Zebul said to him, "Where is your big talk now, you who said, 'Who is Abimelek that we should be subject to him?' Aren't these the men you ridiculed? Go out and fight them!"

³⁹So Gaal led outᶜ the citizens of Shechem and fought Abimelek. ⁴⁰Abimelek chased him all the way to the entrance of the gate, and many were killed as they fled. ⁴¹Then Abimelek stayed in Arumah, and Zebul drove Gaal and his clan out of Shechem.

⁴²The next day the people of Shechem went out to the fields, and this was reported to Abimelek. ⁴³So he took his men, divided them into three companies and set an ambush in the fields. When he saw the people coming out of the city, he rose to attack them. ⁴⁴Abimelek and the companies with him rushed forward to a posi-

tion at the entrance of the city gate. Then two companies attacked those in the fields and struck them down. ⁴⁵All that day Abimelek pressed his attack against

ᵃ 29 Septuagint; Hebrew *him." Then he said to Abimelek, "Call out your whole army!"*   ᵇ 37 The Hebrew for this phrase means *the navel of the earth.*   ᶜ 39 Or *Gaal went out in the sight of*

THE
WITNESSES

✓ **JOTHAM** (JUDGES 9:5)
He was the only one who survived the massacre committed by Abimelek. His name means "the LORD is perfect."

✓ **GAAL** (JUDGES 9:26)
In Hebrew, this name sounds like the word "despicable" or "repugnant." And that's exactly what he was: powerless and dreadful.

✓ **ZEBUL** (JUDGES 9:28)
This name means "supreme" or "elevated." He was the governor and military leader of Shechem under Abimelek, who he helped defeat Gaal.

the city until he had captured it and killed its people. Then he destroyed the city and scattered salt over it.

⁴⁶On hearing this, the citizens in the tower of Shechem went into the stronghold of the temple of El-Berith. ⁴⁷When Abimelek heard that they had assembled there, ⁴⁸he and all his men went up Mount Zalmon. He took an ax and cut off some branches, which he lifted to his shoulders. He ordered the men with him, "Quick! Do what you have seen me do!" ⁴⁹So all the men cut branches and followed Abimelek. They piled them against the stronghold and set it on fire with the people still inside. So all the people in the tower of Shechem, about a thousand men and women, also died.

⁵⁰Next Abimelek went to Thebez and besieged it and captured it. ⁵¹Inside the city, however, was a strong tower, to which all the men and women—all the people of the city—had fled. They had locked themselves in and climbed up on the tower roof. ⁵²Abimelek went to the tower and attacked it. But as he approached the entrance to the tower to set it on fire, ⁵³a woman dropped an upper millstone on his head and cracked his skull.

⁵⁴Hurriedly he called to his armor-bearer, "Draw your sword and kill me, so that they can't say, 'A woman killed him.' " So his servant ran him through, and he died. ⁵⁵When the Israelites saw that Abimelek was dead, they went home.

⁵⁶Thus God repaid the wickedness that Abimelek had done to his father by murdering his seventy brothers. ⁵⁷God also made the people of Shechem pay for all their wickedness. The curse of Jotham son of Jerub-Baal came on them.

Tola

10 After the time of Abimelek, a man of Issachar named Tola son of Puah, the son of Dodo, rose to save Israel. He lived in Shamir, in the hill country of Ephraim. ²He led[a] Israel twenty-three years; then he died, and was buried in Shamir.

Jair

³He was followed by Jair of Gilead, who led Israel twenty-two years. ⁴He had thirty sons, who rode thirty donkeys. They controlled thirty towns in Gilead, which to this day are called Havvoth Jair.[b] ⁵When Jair died, he was buried in Kamon.

Jephthah

⁶Again the Israelites did evil in the eyes of the LORD. They served the Baals and the Ashtoreths, and the gods of Aram, the gods of Sidon, the gods of Moab, the gods of the Ammonites and the gods of the Philistines. And because the Israelites forsook the LORD and no longer served him, ⁷he became angry with them. He sold them into the hands of the Philistines and the Ammonites, ⁸who that year shattered and crushed them. For eighteen years they oppressed all the Israelites on the east side of the Jordan in Gilead, the land of the Amorites. ⁹The Ammonites also crossed the Jordan to fight against Judah, Benjamin and Ephraim; Israel was in great distress. ¹⁰Then the Israelites cried out to the LORD, "We have sinned against you, forsaking our God and serving the Baals."

¹¹The LORD replied, "When the Egyptians, the Amorites, the Ammonites, the Philistines, ¹²the Sidonians, the Amalekites and the Maonites[c] oppressed you and you cried to me for help, did I not save you from their hands? ¹³But you have forsaken me and served other gods, so I will no longer save you. ¹⁴Go and cry out to the gods you have chosen. Let them save you when you are in trouble!"

¹⁵But the Israelites said to the LORD, "We have sinned. Do with us whatever you think best, but please rescue us now." ¹⁶Then they got rid of the foreign gods among them and served the LORD. And he could bear Israel's misery no longer.

¹⁷When the Ammonites were called to arms and camped in Gilead, the Israelites

---

assembled and camped at Mizpah. ¹⁸The leaders of the people of Gilead said to each other, "Whoever will take the lead in attacking the Ammonites will be head over all who live in Gilead."

11 Jephthah the Gileadite was a mighty warrior. His father was Gilead; his mother was a prostitute. ²Gilead's wife also bore him sons, and when they were grown up, they drove Jephthah away. "You are not going to get any inheritance in our family," they said, "because you are the son of another woman." ³So Jephthah fled from his brothers and settled in the land of Tob, where a gang of scoundrels gathered around him and followed him.

⁴Some time later, when the Ammonites were fighting against Israel, ⁵the elders of Gilead went to get Jephthah from the land of Tob. ⁶"Come," they said, "be our commander, so we can fight the Ammonites."

⁷Jephthah said to them, "Didn't you hate me and drive me from my father's house? Why do you come to me now, when you're in trouble?"

⁸The elders of Gilead said to him, "Nevertheless, we are turning to you now; come with us to fight the Ammonites, and you will be head over all of us who live in Gilead."

⁹Jephthah answered, "Suppose you take me back to fight the Ammonites and the Lord gives them to me—will I really be your head?"

¹⁰The elders of Gilead replied, "The Lord is our witness; we will certainly do as you say." ¹¹So Jephthah went with the elders of Gilead, and the people made him head and commander over them. And he repeated all his words before the Lord in Mizpah.

¹²Then Jephthah sent messengers to the Ammonite king with the question: "What do you have against me that you have attacked my country?"

¹³The king of the Ammonites answered Jephthah's messengers, "When Israel came up out of Egypt, they took away my land from the Arnon to the Jabbok, all the way to the Jordan. Now give it back peaceably."

¹⁴Jephthah sent back messengers to the Ammonite king, ¹⁵saying:

"This is what Jephthah says: Israel did not take the land of Moab or the land of the Ammonites. ¹⁶But when

THE
WITNESSES

✓ TOLA (JUDGES 10:1)
This name means "worm" or "scarlet worm." He was the second minor judge. They are called "minor" judges because their stories are very short.

✓ JAIR (JUDGES 10:3)
This name means "let God make you shine." This judge's rule was very peaceful. That may be because the Israelites had so much. They had a lot of animals, and there were many villages.

✓ JEPHTHAH (JUDGES 11:1)
He was the fifth major judge. His name means "God frees the captive." During his time, the Israelite nation went downhill.

they came up out of Egypt, Israel went through the wilderness to the Red Sea[a] and on to Kadesh. [17]Then Israel sent messengers to the king of Edom, saying, 'Give us permission to go through your country,' but the king of Edom would not listen. They sent also to the king of Moab, and he refused. So Israel stayed at Kadesh.

[18]"Next they traveled through the wilderness, skirted the lands of Edom and Moab, passed along the eastern side of the country of Moab, and camped on the other side of the Arnon. They did not enter the territory of Moab, for the Arnon was its border.

[19]"Then Israel sent messengers to Sihon king of the Amorites, who ruled in Heshbon, and said to him, 'Let us pass through your country to our own place.' [20]Sihon, however, did not trust Israel[b] to pass through his territory. He mustered all his troops and encamped at Jahaz and fought with Israel.

[21]"Then the LORD, the God of Israel, gave Sihon and his whole army into Israel's hands, and they defeated them. Israel took over all the land of the Amorites who lived in that country, [22]capturing all of it from the Arnon to the Jabbok and from the desert to the Jordan.

[23]"Now since the LORD, the God of Israel, has driven the Amorites out before his people Israel, what right have you to take it over? [24]Will you not take what your god Chemosh gives you? Likewise, whatever the LORD our God has given us, we will possess. [25]Are you any better than Balak son of Zippor, king of Moab? Did he ever quarrel with Israel or fight with them? [26]For three hundred years Israel occupied Heshbon, Aroer, the surrounding settlements and all the towns along the Arnon. Why didn't you retake them during that time? [27]I have not wronged you, but you are doing me wrong by waging war against me. Let the LORD, the

Judge, decide the dispute this day between the Israelites and the Ammonites."

[28]The king of Ammon, however, paid no attention to the message Jephthah sent him.

[29]Then the Spirit of the LORD came on Jephthah. He crossed Gilead and Manasseh, passed through Mizpah of Gilead, and from there he advanced against the Ammonites. [30]And Jephthah made a vow to the LORD: "If you give the Ammonites into my hands, [31]whatever comes out of the door of my house to meet me when I return in triumph from the Ammonites will be the LORD's, and I will sacrifice it as a burnt offering."

[32]Then Jephthah went over to fight the Ammonites, and the LORD gave them into his hands. [33]He devastated twenty towns from Aroer to the vicinity of Minnith, as far as Abel Keramim. Thus Israel subdued Ammon.

[34]When Jephthah returned to his home in Mizpah, who should come out to meet him but his daughter, dancing to the sound of timbrels! She was an only child. Except for her he had neither son nor daughter. [35]When he saw her, he tore his clothes and cried, "Oh no, my daughter! You have brought me down and I am devastated. I have made a vow to the LORD that I cannot break."

[36]"My father," she replied, "you have given your word to the LORD. Do to me just as you promised, now that the LORD has avenged you of your enemies, the Ammonites. [37]But grant me this one request," she said. "Give me two months to roam the hills and weep with my friends, because I will never marry."

[38]"You may go," he said. And he let her go for two months. She and her friends went into the hills and wept because she would never marry. [39]After the two months, she returned to her father, and he did to her as he had vowed. And she was a virgin.

From this comes the Israelite tradition [40]that each year the young women of Israel

---

[a] 16 Or the Sea of Reeds   [b] 20 Or however, would not make an agreement for Israel

go out for four days to commemorate the daughter of Jephthah the Gileadite.

Jephthah and Ephraim

12 The Ephraimite forces were called out, and they crossed over to Zaphon. They said to Jephthah, "Why did you go to fight the Ammonites without calling us to go with you? We're going to burn down your house over your head."

²Jephthah answered, "I and my people were engaged in a great struggle with the Ammonites, and although I called, you didn't save me out of their hands. ³When I saw that you wouldn't help, I took my life in my hands and crossed over to fight the Ammonites, and the Lord gave me the victory over them. Now why have you come up today to fight me?"

⁴Jephthah then called together the men of Gilead and fought against Ephraim. The Gileadites struck them down because the Ephraimites had said, "You Gileadites are renegades from Ephraim and Manasseh." ⁵The Gileadites captured the fords of the Jordan leading to Ephraim, and whenever a survivor of Ephraim said, "Let me cross over," the men of Gilead asked him, "Are you an Ephraimite?" If he replied, "No," ⁶they said, "All right, say 'Shibboleth.' " If he said, "Sibboleth," because he could not pronounce the word correctly, they seized him and killed him at the fords of the Jordan. Forty-two thousand Ephraimites were killed at that time.

⁷Jephthah led*ᵃ* Israel six years. Then Jephthah the Gileadite died and was buried in a town in Gilead.

Ibzan, Elon and Abdon

⁸After him, Ibzan of Bethlehem led Israel. ⁹He had thirty sons and thirty daughters. He gave his daughters away in marriage to those outside his clan, and for his sons he brought in thirty young women as wives from outside his clan. Ibzan led Israel seven years. ¹⁰Then Ibzan died and was buried in Bethlehem.

¹¹After him, Elon the Zebulunite led Israel ten years. ¹²Then Elon died and was buried in Aijalon in the land of Zebulun.

¹³After him, Abdon son of Hillel, from Pirathon, led Israel. ¹⁴He had forty sons and thirty grandsons, who rode on seventy donkeys. He led Israel eight years. ¹⁵Then Abdon son of Hillel died and was buried at Pirathon in Ephraim, in the hill country of the Amalekites.

The Birth of Samson

13 Again the Israelites did evil in the eyes of the Lord, so the Lord delivered them into the hands of the Philistines for forty years.

ᵃ 7 Traditionally *judged*; also in verses 8–14

THE
WITNESSES

✓ **IBZAN, ELON AND ABDON**
(JUDGES 12:8–15)
They were the last three minor judges. During the time they were leaders, there was peace and wealth. *Ibzan* means "rapid," *Elon* means "oak" and *Abdon* can mean "service" or "serving."

er fermented drink and that you do not eat anything unclean. ⁵You will become pregnant and have a son whose head is never to be touched by a razor because the boy is to be a Nazirite, dedicated to God from the womb. He will take the lead in delivering Israel from the hands of the Philistines."

⁶Then the woman went to her husband and told him, "A man of God came to me. He looked like an angel of God, very awesome. I didn't ask him where he came from, and he didn't tell me his name. ⁷But he said to me, 'You will become pregnant

BREAK THROUGH!

Why did people have so many kids in olden times?

(JUDGES 12:8–15)

Having many children was a way to make sure that a family or clan would continue on, and that their land would stay in the same family. Having many boys meant more people who could work and protect them. Having many girls made sure the parents could collect belongings like cattle. (When the women married, their future husbands had to pay with animals or other things in order to take a girl from her father's home. This was because the father would be losing someone who could work for his family.) And when the sons married women from other countries or nations, that also meant they would get more land and make important friends. We also know that at that time it was legal to have many wives, so that resulted in people having a lot of children.

THE WITNESSES

✓ **SAMSON** (JUDGES 13:1)
This name means "little sun." Some Bible experts say that Samson's long hair stands for the rays of the sun. Samson lost his hair because of Delilah. Her name is related to the word for "night." So, the idea of the story is that Samson — the "little sun" — fell into the trap of the "night."

²A certain man of Zorah, named Manoah, from the clan of the Danites, had a wife who was childless, unable to give birth. ³The angel of the Lᴏʀᴅ appeared to her and said, "You are barren and childless, but you are going to become pregnant and give birth to a son. ⁴Now see to it that you drink no wine or oth-

and have a son. Now then, drink no wine or other fermented drink and do not eat anything unclean, because the boy will be a Nazirite of God from the womb until the day of his death.' "

⁸Then Manoah prayed to the LORD: "Pardon your servant, Lord. I beg you to let the man of God you sent to us come again to teach us how to bring up the boy who is to be born."

⁹God heard Manoah, and the angel of God came again to the woman while she was out in the field; but her husband Manoah was not with her. ¹⁰The woman hurried to tell her husband, "He's here! The man who appeared to me the other day!"

¹¹Manoah got up and followed his wife. When he came to the man, he said, "Are you the man who talked to my wife?"

"I am," he said.

¹²So Manoah asked him, "When your words are fulfilled, what is to be the rule that governs the boy's life and work?"

CHECK THE FACTS

Where did Samson get his strength?

A) His long hair

B) His muscular body

C) His obedience to God

CORRECT ANSWER: A

BREAKTHROUGH!

Nazirite

(JUDGES 13:4-5)

This was a man who was made holy, often even before he was born, for special service to God. He couldn't cut his hair or drink alcohol or eat certain kinds of food or do other things that might dirty him. (Read Numbers 6:1-21.)

¹³The angel of the LORD answered, "Your wife must do all that I have told her. ¹⁴She must not eat anything that comes from the grapevine, nor drink any wine or other fermented drink nor eat anything unclean. She must do everything I have commanded her."

¹⁵Manoah said to the angel of the LORD, "We would like you to stay until we prepare a young goat for you."

¹⁶The angel of the LORD replied, "Even though you detain me, I will not eat any of your food. But if you prepare a burnt offering, offer it to the LORD." (Manoah did not realize that it was the angel of the LORD.)

¹⁷Then Manoah inquired of the angel of the LORD, "What is your name, so that we may honor you when your word comes true?"

¹⁸He replied, "Why do you ask my name? It is beyond understanding.ᵃ"

ᵃ 18 Or is wonderful

¹⁹Then Manoah took a young goat, together with the grain offering, and sacrificed it on a rock to the Lᴏʀᴅ. And the Lᴏʀᴅ did an amazing thing while Manoah and his wife watched: ²⁰As the flame blazed up from the altar toward heaven, the angel of the Lᴏʀᴅ ascended in the flame. Seeing this, Manoah and his wife fell with their faces to the ground. ²¹When the angel of the Lᴏʀᴅ did not show himself again to Manoah and his wife, Manoah realized that it was the angel of the Lᴏʀᴅ.

²²"We are doomed to die!" he said to his wife. "We have seen God!"

²³But his wife answered, "If the Lᴏʀᴅ had meant to kill us, he would not have accepted a burnt offering and grain offering from our hands, nor shown us all these things or now told us this."

²⁴The woman gave birth to a boy and named him Samson. He grew and the Lᴏʀᴅ blessed him, ²⁵and the Spirit of the Lᴏʀᴅ began to stir him while he was in Mahaneh Dan, between Zorah and Eshtaol.

Samson's Marriage

14 Samson went down to Timnah and saw there a young Philistine woman. ²When he returned, he said to his father and mother, "I have seen a Philistine woman in Timnah; now get her for me as my wife."

³His father and mother replied, "Isn't there an acceptable woman among your relatives or among all our people? Must you go to the uncircumcised Philistines to get a wife?"

But Samson said to his father, "Get her for me. She's the right one for me." ⁴(His parents did not know that this was from the Lᴏʀᴅ, who was seeking an occasion to confront the Philistines; for at that time they were ruling over Israel.)

⁵Samson went down to Timnah together with his father and mother. As they approached the vineyards of Timnah, suddenly a young lion came roaring toward him. ⁶The Spirit of the Lᴏʀᴅ came powerfully upon him so that he tore the lion apart with his bare hands as he might have torn a young goat. But he told neither his father nor his mother what he

THE SCENE

TIMNAH
(JUDGES 14:1)

I t is east of the cities of Zorah and Eshtaol, in the land of the tribe of Dan, next to Philistine territory and the Valley of Sorek.

had done. ⁷Then he went down and talked with the woman, and he liked her.

⁸Some time later, when he went back to marry her, he turned aside to look at the lion's carcass, and in it he saw a swarm of bees and some honey. ⁹He scooped out the honey with his hands and ate as he went along. When he rejoined his parents, he gave them some, and they too ate it. But he did not tell them that he had taken the honey from the lion's carcass.

¹⁰Now his father went down to see the woman. And there Samson held a feast, as was customary for young men. ¹¹When the people saw him, they chose thirty men to be his companions.

¹²"Let me tell you a riddle," Samson said to them. "If you can give me the answer within the seven days of the feast, I will give you thirty linen garments and thirty sets of clothes. ¹³If you can't tell me the answer, you must give me thirty linen garments and thirty sets of clothes."

"Tell us your riddle," they said. "Let's hear it."

¹⁴He replied,

> "Out of the eater, something to eat;
>   out of the strong, something
>   sweet."

For three days they could not give the answer.

¹⁵On the fourth*ᵃ* day, they said to Samson's wife, "Coax your husband into explaining the riddle for us, or we will burn you and your father's household to death. Did you invite us here to steal our property?"

¹⁶Then Samson's wife threw herself on him, sobbing, "You hate me! You don't really love me. You've given my people a riddle, but you haven't told me the answer."

BREAK THROUGH!

Philistines

(JUDGES 14:1)

This group was called the "Sea Peoples." They came from the islands and coastal area of the Aegean Sea. A little after the year 1200 before Christ, they tried to enter Egypt. When they couldn't, they finally ended up on the Palestine coast. They had weapons made of iron and they had an organized army, so that's why they had an advantage over the Israelites (13:19–22).

"I haven't even explained it to my father or mother," he replied, "so why should I explain it to you?" ¹⁷She cried the whole seven days of the feast. So on the seventh day he finally told her, because she continued to press him. She in turn explained the riddle to her people.

¹⁸Before sunset on the seventh day the men of the town said to him,

> "What is sweeter than honey?
>   What is stronger than a lion?"

Samson said to them,

> "If you had not plowed with my heifer,
>   you would not have solved my riddle."

¹⁹Then the Spirit of the Lᴏʀᴅ came powerfully upon him. He went down to Ashkelon, struck down thirty of their men, stripped them of everything and gave their clothes to those who had explained the riddle. Burning with anger, he returned to his father's home. ²⁰And Samson's wife was given to one of his companions who had attended him at the feast.

Samson's Vengeance on the Philistines

15 Later on, at the time of wheat harvest, Samson took a young goat and went to visit his wife. He said, "I'm going to my wife's room." But her father would not let him go in.

²"I was so sure you hated her," he said, "that I gave her to your companion. Isn't her younger sister more attractive? Take her instead."

³Samson said to them, "This time I have a right to get even with the Philistines; I will really harm them." ⁴So he went out and caught three hundred foxes and tied them tail to tail in pairs. He then fastened a torch to every pair of tails, ⁵lit the torches and let the foxes loose in the standing grain of the Philistines. He burned up the shocks and standing grain, together with the vineyards and olive groves.

⁶When the Philistines asked, "Who did this?" they were told, "Samson,

---

ᵃ 15 Some Septuagint manuscripts and Syriac; Hebrew *seventh*

BREAK THROUGH!

Why did they make Samson's wife marry one of the guests who had been invited to the feast?

(JUDGES 14:20)

When Samson left home after he got married, he didn't go to live with his new wife. Since he was very violent against the Philistine people, the girl's father thought that Samson didn't mean to live with her and really be his daughter's husband.

the Timnite's son-in-law, because his wife was given to his companion."

⁷So the Philistines went up and burned her and her father to death. ⁷Samson said to them, "Since you've acted like this, I swear that I won't stop until I get my revenge on you." ⁸He attacked them viciously and slaughtered many of them. Then he went down and stayed in a cave in the rock of Etam.

⁹The Philistines went up and camped in Judah, spreading out near Lehi. ¹⁰The people of Judah asked, "Why have you come to fight us?"

"We have come to take Samson prisoner," they answered, "to do to him as he did to us."

¹¹Then three thousand men from Judah went down to the cave in the rock of Etam

and said to Samson, "Don't you realize that the Philistines are rulers over us? What have you done to us?"

He answered, "I merely did to them what they did to me."

¹²They said to him, "We've come to tie you up and hand you over to the Philistines."

Samson said, "Swear to me that you won't kill me yourselves."

¹³"Agreed," they answered. "We will only tie you up and hand you over to them. We will not kill you." So they bound him with two new ropes and led him up from the rock. ¹⁴As he approached Lehi, the Philistines came toward him shouting. The Spirit of the LORD came powerfully upon him. The ropes on his arms became like charred flax, and the bindings dropped from his hands. ¹⁵Finding a fresh jawbone of a donkey, he grabbed it and struck down a thousand men.

¹⁶Then Samson said,

"With a donkey's jawbone
  I have made donkeys of them.ᵃ
With a donkey's jawbone
  I have killed a thousand men."

¹⁷When he finished speaking, he threw away the jawbone; and the place was called Ramath Lehi.ᵇ

¹⁸Because he was very thirsty, he cried out to the LORD, "You have given your servant this great victory. Must I now die of thirst and fall into the hands of the uncircumcised?" ¹⁹Then God opened up the hollow place in Lehi, and water came out of it. When Samson drank, his strength returned and he revived. So the spring was called En Hakkore,ᶜ and it is still there in Lehi.

²⁰Samson ledᵈ Israel for twenty years in the days of the Philistines.

Samson and Delilah

16 One day Samson went to Gaza, where he saw a prostitute. He went in to spend the night with her. ²The peo-

---

ᵃ 16 Or *made a heap or two*; the Hebrew for *donkey* sounds like the Hebrew for *heap*.   ᵇ 17 *Ramath Lehi* means *jawbone hill*.   ᶜ 19 *En Hakkore* means *caller's spring*.   ᵈ 20 Traditionally *judged* ple of Gaza were told, "Samson is here!" So they surrounded the place and lay in wait for him all night at the city gate. They made no move during the night, saying, "At dawn we'll kill him."

3But Samson lay there only until the middle of the night. Then he got up and took hold of the doors of the city gate, together with the two posts, and tore them loose, bar and all. He lifted them to his shoulders and carried them to the top of the hill that faces Hebron.

4Some time later, he fell in love with a woman in the Valley of Sorek whose name was Delilah. 5The rulers of the Philistines went to her and said, "See if you can lure him into showing you the secret of his great strength and how we can overpower him so we may tie him up and subdue him. Each one of us will give you eleven hundred shekels*a* of silver."

6So Delilah said to Samson, "Tell me the secret of your great strength and how you can be tied up and subdued."

7Samson answered her, "If anyone ties me with seven fresh bowstrings that have not been dried, I'll become as weak as any other man."

8Then the rulers of the Philistines brought her seven fresh bowstrings that had not been dried, and she tied him with them. 9With men hidden in the room, she called to him, "Samson, the Philistines are upon you!" But he snapped the bowstrings as easily as a piece of string snaps when it comes close to a flame. So the secret of his strength was not discovered.

10Then Delilah said to Samson, "You have made a fool of me; you lied to me. Come now, tell me how you can be tied."

11He said, "If anyone ties me securely with new ropes that have never been used, I'll become as weak as any other man."

12So Delilah took new ropes and tied him with them. Then, with men hidden in the room, she called to him, "Samson, the Philistines are upon you!" But he snapped the ropes off his arms as if they were threads.

13Delilah then said to Samson, "All this time you have been making a fool of me

and lying to me. Tell me how you can be tied."

He replied, "If you weave the seven braids of my head into the fabric on the loom and tighten it with the pin, I'll become as weak as any other man." So while he was sleeping, Delilah took the seven braids of his head, wove them into the fabric 14and*b* tightened it with the pin.

Again she called to him, "Samson, the Philistines are upon you!" He awoke from his sleep and pulled up the pin and the loom, with the fabric.

a 5 That is, about 28 pounds or about 13 kilograms
b 13,14 Some Septuagint manuscripts; Hebrew *replied, "I can if you weave the seven braids of my head into the fabric on the loom."* 14So she

THE
WITNESSES

✓ **DELILAH** (JUDGES 16:4)
This name refers to "night." Of all the women that appear in the story of Samson, this "night" was the one whose cleverness and patience outsmarted the "little sun."

¹⁵Then she said to him, "How can you say, 'I love you,' when you won't confide in me? This is the third time you have made a fool of me and haven't told me the secret of your great strength." ¹⁶With such nagging she prodded him day after day until he was sick to death of it.

¹⁷So he told her everything. "No razor has ever been used on my head," he said, "because I have been a Nazirite dedicated to God from my mother's womb. If my head were shaved, my strength would leave me, and I would become as weak as any other man."

¹⁸When Delilah saw that he had told her everything, she sent word to the rulers of the Philistines, "Come back once more; he has told me everything." So the rulers of the Philistines returned with the silver in their hands. ¹⁹After putting him to sleep on her lap, she called for someone to shave off the seven braids of his hair, and so began to subdue him.ᵃ And his strength left him.

²⁰Then she called, "Samson, the Philistines are upon you!"

He awoke from his sleep and thought, "I'll go out as before and shake myself free." But he did not know that the LORD had left him.

²¹Then the Philistines seized him, gouged out his eyes and took him down to Gaza. Binding him with bronze shackles, they set him to grinding grain in the prison. ²²But the hair on his head began to grow again after it had been shaved.

The Death of Samson

²³Now the rulers of the Philistines assembled to offer a great sacrifice to Dagon their god and to celebrate, saying, "Our god has delivered Samson, our enemy, into our hands."

²⁴When the people saw him, they praised their god, saying,

"Our god has delivered our enemy
        into our hands,
    the one who laid waste our land
        and multiplied our slain."

²⁵While they were in high spirits, they shouted, "Bring out Samson to entertain

THE
WITNESSES

✓ **THE GOD DAGON (JUDGES 16:23)**
This was the most important Philistine god of Canaanite origin. He was considered the god of grain—that meant the god of harvests.

us." So they called Samson out of the prison, and he performed for them.

When they stood him among the pillars, ²⁶Samson said to the servant who held his hand, "Put me where I can feel the pillars that support the temple, so that I may lean against them." ²⁷Now the temple was crowded with men and women; all the rulers of the Philistines were there, and on the roof were about three thousand men and women watching Samson perform. ²⁸Then Samson prayed to the LORD, "Sovereign LORD, remember me. Please, God, strengthen me just once more, and let me with one blow get

---

ᵃ 19 Hebrew; some Septuagint manuscripts *and he began to weaken* revenge on the Philistines for my two eyes." ²⁹Then Samson reached toward the two central pillars on which the temple stood. Bracing himself against them, his right hand on the one and his left hand on the other, ³⁰Samson said, "Let me die with the Philistines!" Then he pushed with all his might, and down came the temple on the rulers and all the people in it. Thus he killed many more when he died than while he lived.

³¹Then his brothers and his father's whole family went down to get him. They brought him back and buried him between Zorah and Eshtaol in the tomb of Manoah his father. He had led*ᵃ* Israel twenty years.

Micah's Idols

17 Now a man named Micah from the hill country of Ephraim ²said to his mother, "The eleven hundred shekels*ᵇ* of silver that were taken from you and about which I heard you utter a curse—I have that silver with me; I took it."

Then his mother said, "The LORD bless you, my son!"

³When he returned the eleven hundred shekels of silver to his mother, she said, "I solemnly consecrate my silver to the LORD for my son to make an image overlaid with silver. I will give it back to you."

⁴So after he returned the silver to his mother, she took two hundred shekels*ᶜ* of silver and gave them to a silversmith, who used them to make the idol. And it was put in Micah's house.

⁵Now this man Micah had a shrine, and he made an ephod and some household gods and installed one of his sons as his priest. ⁶In those days Israel had no king; everyone did as they saw fit.

⁷A young Levite from Bethlehem in Judah, who had been living within the clan of Judah, ⁸left that town in search of some other place to stay. On his way*ᵈ* he came to Micah's house in the hill country of Ephraim.

⁹Micah asked him, "Where are you from?"

"I'm a Levite from Bethlehem in Judah," he said, "and I'm looking for a place to stay."

¹⁰Then Micah said to him, "Live with me and be my father and priest, and I'll give you ten shekels*ᵉ* of silver a year, your clothes and your food." ¹¹So the Levite agreed to live with him, and the young man became like one of his sons to him. ¹²Then Micah installed the Levite, and the young man became his priest and lived in his house. ¹³And Micah said, "Now I know that the LORD will be good to me, since this Levite has become my priest."

The Danites Settle in Laish

18 In those days Israel had no king.

And in those days the tribe of the Danites was seeking a place of their own where they might settle, because they had not yet come into an inheritance among the tribes of Israel. ²So the Danites sent five of their leading men from Zorah and

---

ᵃ 31 Traditionally *judged*   *ᵇ 2* That is, about 28 pounds or about 13 kilograms   *ᶜ 4* That is, about 5 pounds or about 2.3 kilograms   *ᵈ 8* Or *To carry on his profession*   *ᵉ 10* That is, about 4 ounces or about 115 grams

ZORAH AND ESHTAOL

(JUDGES 18:2)

Both places are in the territory of the tribe of Dan, near the northern border with Judah.

Eshtaol to spy out the land and explore it. These men represented all the Danites. They told them, "Go, explore the land."

So they entered the hill country of Ephraim and came to the house of Micah, where they spent the night. ³When they were near Micah's house, they recognized the voice of the young Levite; so they turned in there and asked him, "Who brought you here? What are you doing in this place? Why are you here?"

⁴He told them what Micah had done for him, and said, "He has hired me and I am his priest."

⁵Then they said to him, "Please inquire of God to learn whether our journey will be successful."

⁶The priest answered them, "Go in peace. Your journey has the LORD's approval."

⁷So the five men left and came to Laish, where they saw that the people were living in safety, like the Sidonians, at peace and secure. And since their land lacked nothing, they were prosperous.ᵃ Also, they lived a long way from the Sidonians and had no relationship with anyone else.ᵇ

⁸When they returned to Zorah and Eshtaol, their fellow Danites asked them, "How did you find things?"

⁹They answered, "Come on, let's attack them! We have seen the land, and it is very good. Aren't you going to do something? Don't hesitate to go there and take it over. ¹⁰When you get there, you will find an unsuspecting people and a spacious land that God has put into your hands, a land that lacks nothing whatever."

¹¹Then six hundred men of the Danites, armed for battle, set out from Zorah and Eshtaol. ¹²On their way they set up camp near Kiriath Jearim in Judah. This is why the place west of Kiriath Jearim is called Mahaneh Danᶜ to this day. ¹³From there they went on to the hill country of Ephraim and came to Micah's house.

¹⁴Then the five men who had spied out the land of Laish said to their fellow Danites, "Do you know that one of these houses has an ephod, some household gods and an image overlaid with silver? Now you know what to do." ¹⁵So they

THE SCENE

LAISH

(JUDGES 18:7)

It is about 25 miles (40 km) north of the Sea of Galilee, where the Jordan River starts.

turned in there and went to the house of the young Levite at Micah's place and greeted him. ¹⁶The six hundred Danites, armed for battle, stood at the entrance of the gate. ¹⁷The five men who had spied out the land went inside and took the idol, the ephod and the household gods while the priest and the six hundred armed men stood at the entrance of the gate.

¹⁸When the five men went into Micah's house and took the idol, the ephod and the household gods, the priest said to them, "What are you doing?"

¹⁹They answered him, "Be quiet! Don't say a word. Come with us, and be our father and priest. Isn't it better that you serve a tribe and clan in Israel as priest rather than just one man's household?" ²⁰The priest was very pleased. He took the ephod, the household gods and the idol and went along with the people.

ᵃ 7 The meaning of the Hebrew for this clause is uncertain.   ᵇ 7 Hebrew; some Septuagint manuscripts *with the Arameans*   ᶜ 12 *Mahaneh Dan* means *Dan's camp.*

²¹Putting their little children, their livestock and their possessions in front of them, they turned away and left.

²²When they had gone some distance from Micah's house, the men who lived near Micah were called together and overtook the Danites. ²³As they shouted after them, the Danites turned and said to Micah, "What's the matter with you that you called out your men to fight?" ²⁴He replied, "You took the gods I made, and my priest, and went away. What else do I have? How can you ask, 'What's the matter with you?' " ²⁵The Danites answered, "Don't argue with us, or some of the men may get angry and attack you, and you and your family will lose your lives." ²⁶So the Danites went their way, and Micah, seeing that they were too strong for him, turned around and went back home.

²⁷Then they took what Micah had made, and his priest, and went on to Laish, against a people at peace and secure. They attacked them with the sword and burned down their city. ²⁸There was no one to rescue them because they lived a long way from Sidon and had no relationship with anyone else. The city was in a valley near Beth Rehob.

The Danites rebuilt the city and settled there. ²⁹They named it Dan after their ancestor Dan, who was born to Israel—though the city used to be called Laish. ³⁰There the Danites set up for themselves the idol, and Jonathan son of Gershom, the son of Moses,ᵃ and his sons were priests for the tribe of Dan until the time of the captivity of the land. ³¹They continued to use the idol Micah had made, all the time the house of God was in Shiloh.

A Levite and His Concubine

19 In those days Israel had no king.
Now a Levite who lived in a remote area in the hill country of Ephraim took a concubine from Bethlehem in Judah. ²But she was unfaithful to him. She left him and went back to her parents' home in Bethlehem, Judah. After she had been there four months, ³her husband went to her to persuade her to return. He had with him his servant and two donkeys.

She took him into her parents' home, and when her father saw him, he gladly welcomed him. ⁴His father-in-law, the woman's father, prevailed on him to stay; so he remained with him three days, eating and drinking, and sleeping there.

⁵On the fourth day they got up early and he prepared to leave, but the woman's father said to his son-in-law, "Refresh yourself with something to eat; then you can go." ⁶So the two of them sat down to eat and drink together. Afterward the woman's father said, "Please stay tonight and enjoy yourself." ⁷And when the man got up to go, his father-in-law persuaded him, so he stayed there that night. ⁸On the morning of the fifth day, when he rose to go, the woman's father said, "Refresh yourself. Wait till afternoon!" So the two of them ate together.

⁹Then when the man, with his concubine and his servant, got up to leave, his father-in-law, the woman's father, said, "Now look, it's almost evening. Spend the night here; the day is nearly over. Stay and enjoy yourself. Early tomorrow morning you can get up and be on your way home." ¹⁰But, unwilling to stay another night, the man left and went toward Jebus (that is, Jerusalem), with his two saddled donkeys and his concubine.

¹¹When they were near Jebus and the day was almost gone, the servant said to his master, "Come, let's stop at this city of the Jebusites and spend the night." ¹²His master replied, "No. We won't go into any city whose people are not Israelites. We will go on to Gibeah." ¹³He added, "Come, let's try to reach Gibeah or Ramah and spend the night in one of those places." ¹⁴So they went on, and the sun set as they neared Gibeah in Benjamin. ¹⁵There they stopped to spend the night. They went and sat in the city square, but no one took them in for the night.

¹⁶That evening an old man from the hill country of Ephraim, who was living in Gibeah (the inhabitants of the place were Benjamites), came in from his work in

---

ᵃ 30 Many Hebrew manuscripts, some Septuagint manuscripts and Vulgate; many other Hebrew manuscripts and some other Septuagint manuscripts *Manasseh*

THE SCENE

GIBEAH

(JUDGES 19:12)

I t is in the territory of the tribe of Benjamin north of Jerusalem.

the fields. ¹⁷When he looked and saw the traveler in the city square, the old man asked, "Where are you going? Where did you come from?"

¹⁸He answered, "We are on our way from Bethlehem in Judah to a remote area in the hill country of Ephraim where I live. I have been to Bethlehem in Judah and now I am going to the house of the LORD.ᵃ No one has taken me in for the night. ¹⁹We have both straw and fodder for our donkeys and bread and wine for ourselves your servants—me, the woman and the young man with us. We don't need anything."

²⁰"You are welcome at my house," the old man said. "Let me supply whatever you need. Only don't spend the night in the square." ²¹So he took him into his house and fed his donkeys. After they had washed their feet, they had something to eat and drink.

²²While they were enjoying themselves, some of the wicked men of the city sur-

rounded the house. Pounding on the door, they shouted to the old man who owned the house, "Bring out the man who came to your house so we can have sex with him."

²³The owner of the house went outside and said to them, "No, my friends, don't be so vile. Since this man is my guest, don't do this outrageous thing. ²⁴Look, here is my virgin daughter, and his concubine. I will bring them out to you now, and you can use them and do to them whatever you wish. But as for this man, don't do such an outrageous thing."

²⁵But the men would not listen to him. So the man took his concubine and sent her outside to them, and they raped her and abused her throughout the night, and at dawn they let her go. ²⁶At daybreak the woman went back to the house where her master was staying, fell down at the door and lay there until daylight.

²⁷When her master got up in the morning and opened the door of the house and stepped out to continue on his way, there lay his concubine, fallen in the doorway of the house, with her hands on the threshold. ²⁸He said to her, "Get up; let's go." But there was no answer. Then the man put her on his donkey and set out for home.

²⁹When he reached home, he took a knife and cut up his concubine, limb by limb, into twelve parts and sent them into all the areas of Israel. ³⁰Everyone who saw it was saying to one another, "Such a thing has never been seen or done, not since the day the Israelites came up out of Egypt. Just imagine! We must do something! So speak up!"

The Israelites Punish the Benjamites

20 Then all Israel from Dan to Beersheba and from the land of Gilead came together as one and assembled before the LORD in Mizpah. ²The leaders of all the people of the tribes of Israel took their places in the assembly of God's people, four hundred thousand men armed with swords. ³(The Benjamites heard that

ᵃ 18 Hebrew, Vulgate, Syriac and Targum; Septuagint *going home* the Israelites had gone up to Mizpah.) Then the Israelites said, "Tell us how this awful thing happened."

⁴So the Levite, the husband of the murdered woman, said, "I and my concubine came to Gibeah in Benjamin to spend the night. ⁵During the night the men of Gibeah came after me and surrounded the house, intending to kill me. They raped my concubine, and she died. ⁶I took my concubine, cut her into pieces and sent one piece to each region of Israel's inheritance, because they committed this lewd and outrageous act in Israel. ⁷Now, all you Israelites, speak up and tell me what you have decided to do."

⁸All the men rose up together as one, saying, "None of us will go home. No, not one of us will return to his house. ⁹But now this is what we'll do to Gibeah: We'll go up against it in the order decided by casting lots. ¹⁰We'll take ten men out of every hundred from all the tribes of Israel, and a hundred from a thousand, and a thousand from ten thousand, to get provisions for the army. Then, when the army arrives at Gibeahᵃ in Benjamin, it can give them what they deserve for this outrageous act done in Israel." ¹¹So all the Israelites got together and united as one against the city.

¹²The tribes of Israel sent messengers throughout the tribe of Benjamin, saying, "What about this awful crime that was committed among you? ¹³Now turn those wicked men of Gibeah over to us so that we may put them to death and purge the evil from Israel."

But the Benjamites would not listen to their fellow Israelites. ¹⁴From their towns they came together at Gibeah to fight against the Israelites. ¹⁵At once the Benjamites mobilized twenty-six thousand swordsmen from their towns, in addition to seven hundred able young men from those living in Gibeah. ¹⁶Among all these soldiers there were seven hundred select troops who were left-handed, each of whom could sling a stone at a hair and not miss.

¹⁷Israel, apart from Benjamin, mustered four hundred thousand swordsmen, all of them fit for battle.

¹⁸The Israelites went up to Bethelᵇ and inquired of God. They said, "Who of us is to go up first to fight against the Benjamites?"

The Lᴏʀᴅ replied, "Judah shall go first."

¹⁹The next morning the Israelites got up and pitched camp near Gibeah. ²⁰The Israelites went out to fight the Benjamites and took up battle positions against them at Gibeah. ²¹The Benjamites came out of Gibeah and cut down twenty-two thousand Israelites on the battlefield that day. ²²But the Israelites encouraged one another and again took up their positions where they had stationed themselves the first day. ²³The Israelites went up and wept before the Lᴏʀᴅ until evening, and they inquired of the Lᴏʀᴅ. They said, "Shall we go up again to fight against the Benjamites, our fellow Israelites?"

The Lᴏʀᴅ answered, "Go up against them."

²⁴Then the Israelites drew near to Benjamin the second day. ²⁵This time, when the Benjamites came out from Gibeah to oppose them, they cut down another eighteen thousand Israelites, all of them armed with swords.

²⁶Then all the Israelites, the whole army, went up to Bethel, and there they sat weeping before the Lᴏʀᴅ. They fasted that day until evening and presented burnt offerings and fellowship offerings to the Lᴏʀᴅ. ²⁷And the Israelites inquired of the Lᴏʀᴅ. (In those days the ark of the covenant of God was there, ²⁸with Phinehas son of Eleazar, the son of Aaron, ministering before it.) They asked, "Shall we go up again to fight against the Benjamites, our fellow Israelites, or not?"

The Lᴏʀᴅ responded, "Go, for tomorrow I will give them into your hands."

²⁹Then Israel set an ambush around Gibeah. ³⁰They went up against the Benjamites on the third day and took up positions against Gibeah as they had done before. ³¹The Benjamites came out to meet them and were drawn away from the city. They began to inflict casualties

ᵃ 10 One Hebrew manuscript; most Hebrew manuscripts *Geba,* a variant of *Gibeah*   ᵇ 18 Or *to the house of God;* also in verse 26 on the Israelites as before, so that about thirty men fell in the open field and on the roads—the one leading to Bethel and the other to Gibeah. ³²While the Benjamites were saying, "We are defeating them as before," the Israelites were saying, "Let's retreat and draw them away from the city to the roads."

³³All the men of Israel moved from their places and took up positions at Baal Tamar, and the Israelite ambush charged out of its place on the west*ᵃ* of Gibeah.*ᵇ* ³⁴Then ten thousand of Israel's able young men made a frontal attack on Gibeah. The fighting was so heavy that the Benjamites did not realize how near disaster was. ³⁵The Lᴏʀᴅ defeated Benjamin before Israel, and on that day the Israelites struck down 25,100 Benjamites, all armed with swords. ³⁶Then the Benjamites saw that they were beaten.

Now the men of Israel had given way before Benjamin, because they relied on the ambush they had set near Gibeah. ³⁷Those who had been in ambush made a sudden dash into Gibeah, spread out and put the whole city to the sword. ³⁸The Israelites had arranged with the ambush that they should send up a great cloud of smoke from the city, ³⁹and then the Israelites would counterattack.

The Benjamites had begun to inflict casualties on the Israelites (about thirty), and they said, "We are defeating them as in the first battle." ⁴⁰But when the column of smoke began to rise from the city, the Benjamites turned and saw the whole city going up in smoke. ⁴¹Then the Israelites counterattacked, and the Benjamites were terrified, because they realized that disaster had come on them. ⁴²So they fled before the Israelites in the direction of the wilderness, but they could not escape the battle. And the Israelites who came out of the towns cut them down there. ⁴³They surrounded the Benjamites, chased them and easily*ᶜ* overran them in the vicinity of Gibeah on the east. ⁴⁴Eighteen thousand Benjamites fell, all of them valiant fighters. ⁴⁵As they turned and fled toward the wilderness to the rock of Rimmon, the Israelites cut down

five thousand men along the roads. They kept pressing after the Benjamites as far as Gidom and struck down two thousand more.

⁴⁶On that day twenty-five thousand Benjamite swordsmen fell, all of them valiant fighters. ⁴⁷But six hundred of them turned and fled into the wilderness to the rock of Rimmon, where they stayed four months. ⁴⁸The men of Israel went back to Benjamin and put all the towns to the sword, including the animals and everything else they found. All the towns they came across they set on fire.

Wives for the Benjamites

21 The men of Israel had taken an oath at Mizpah: "Not one of us will give his daughter in marriage to a Benjamite."

²The people went to Bethel,*ᵈ* where they sat before God until evening, raising their voices and weeping bitterly. ³"Lᴏʀᴅ, God of Israel," they cried, "why has this happened to Israel? Why should one tribe be missing from Israel today?"

⁴Early the next day the people built an altar and presented burnt offerings and fellowship offerings.

⁵Then the Israelites asked, "Who from all the tribes of Israel has failed to assemble before the Lᴏʀᴅ?" For they had taken a solemn oath that anyone who failed to assemble before the Lᴏʀᴅ at Mizpah was to be put to death.

⁶Now the Israelites grieved for the tribe of Benjamin, their fellow Israelites. "Today one tribe is cut off from Israel," they said. ⁷"How can we provide wives for those who are left, since we have taken an oath by the Lᴏʀᴅ not to give them any of our daughters in marriage?" ⁸Then they asked, "Which one of the tribes of Israel failed to assemble before the Lᴏʀᴅ at Mizpah?" They discovered that no one from Jabesh Gilead had come to the camp for the assembly. ⁹For when they counted the people, they found that none of the people of Jabesh Gilead were there.

ᵃ 33 Some Septuagint manuscripts and Vulgate; the meaning of the Hebrew for this word is uncertain.
ᵇ 33 Hebrew *Geba*, a variant of *Gibeah*   *ᶜ 43* The meaning of the Hebrew for this word is uncertain.
ᵈ 2 Or *to the house of God*

¹⁰So the assembly sent twelve thousand fighting men with instructions to go to Jabesh Gilead and put to the sword those living there, including the women and children. ¹¹"This is what you are to do," they said. "Kill every male and every woman who is not a virgin." ¹²They found among the people living in Jabesh Gilead four hundred young women who had never slept with a man, and they took them to the camp at Shiloh in Canaan.

¹³Then the whole assembly sent an offer of peace to the Benjamites at the rock of Rimmon. ¹⁴So the Benjamites returned at that time and were given the women of Jabesh Gilead who had been spared. But there were not enough for all of them.

¹⁵The people grieved for Benjamin, because the LORD had made a gap in the tribes of Israel. ¹⁶And the elders of the assembly said, "With the women of Benjamin destroyed, how shall we provide wives for the men who are left? ¹⁷The Benjamite survivors must have heirs," they said, "so that a tribe of Israel will not be wiped out. ¹⁸We can't give them our daughters as wives, since we Israelites have taken this oath: 'Cursed be anyone who gives a wife to a Benjamite.' ¹⁹But look, there is the annual festival of the LORD in Shiloh, which lies north of Bethel, east of the road that goes from Bethel to Shechem, and south of Lebonah."

²⁰So they instructed the Benjamites, saying, "Go and hide in the vineyards ²¹and watch. When the young women of Shiloh come out to join in the dancing, rush from the vineyards and each of you seize one of them to be your wife. Then return to the land of Benjamin. ²²When their fathers or brothers complain to us, we will say to them, 'Do us the favor of helping them, because we did not get wives for them during the war. You will

While Joshua and the leaders of the country were alive, the Israelites obeyed God's teachings. But when the leaders died, all the people of Israel turned away from God because they didn't believe that the Lord was the true God. It seems they hadn't been told about everything that God had done for them in the past. That's really sad! And that's exactly why God sent the judges to them, so they could guide the people and teach them to trust God. When the Israelites disobeyed God, their enemies beat them in battle. But when they asked forgiveness and prayed to God, then God helped them. The book of Judges teaches us that God watches over us and that he cares about what happens to us. We just have to love him and obey him.

CASE CLOSED!

not be guilty of breaking your oath because you did not give your daughters to them.' "

²³So that is what the Benjamites did. While the young women were dancing, each man caught one and carried her off to be his wife. Then they returned to their inheritance and rebuilt the towns and settled in them.

²⁴At that time the Israelites left that place and went home to their tribes and clans, each to his own inheritance.

²⁵In those days Israel had no king; everyone did as they saw fit.

RUTH

THE EVIDENCE:

WHO WROTE IT?

There's no signature or date in this book, so we don't know who wrote it. But we do know that in the Hebrew Bible, the book of Ruth is in the section called *Ketuvim*, which means "writings." It was customary to read it during the Feast of Pentecost.

HOW LONG AGO?

It was written many, many years ago. The experts don't agree. Some say it was written before the Babylonian exile (that means the book was written before the Israelite people were taken prisoners to live in Babylon). Others think it was written later, more or less during the time of Ezra and Nehemiah.

WHAT'S IT ABOUT?

Ruth is a really short book that tells the story of a family from a town in Judah called Bethlehem, who one day decided to move and live in Moab. The father and his sons died there, so the mother and the sons' wives were left alone. They didn't have any money or anyone to help them. When they saw that life was getting really hard in Moab,

Naomi (she was the mother) and Ruth (she was one of the daughters-in-law) decided to return to Bethlehem and start their lives over there. God was with them, and he blessed them.

THE BEST PART

It's very nice when Ruth finds one of her husband's relatives, and he tells her that he had heard about how she had helped her mother-in-law. He says, "May the LORD repay you for what you have done. May you be richly rewarded by the LORD, the God of Israel, under whose wings you have come to take refuge" (2:12).

Naomi Loses Her Husband and Sons

1 In the days when the judges ruled,[a] there was a famine in the land. So a man from Bethlehem in Judah, together with his wife and two sons, went to live for a while in the country of Moab. [2]The man's name was Elimelek, his wife's name was Naomi, and the names of his two sons were Mahlon and Kilion. They were Ephrathites from Bethlehem, Judah. And they went to Moab and lived there.

[3]Now Elimelek, Naomi's husband, died, and she was left with her two sons. [4]They married Moabite women, one named Orpah and the other Ruth. After they had lived there about ten years, [5]both Mahlon

---

[a] 1 Traditionally *judged*

THE SCENE

BETHLEHEM

(RUTH 1:1)

In Hebrew, it means "house of bread." How strange! Elimelek's family left their "house of bread" because they didn't have anything to eat! Bethlehem was a small village more or less 5 miles (8 km) from Jerusalem. Before it was called Bethlehem, it was called Ephrathah. Many years later, Jesus was born there.

and Kilion also died, and Naomi was left without her two sons and her husband.

Naomi and Ruth Return to Bethlehem

⁶When Naomi heard in Moab that the LORD had come to the aid of his people by providing food for them, she and her daughters-in-law prepared to return home from there. ⁷With her two daughters-in-law she left the place where she had been living and set out on the road that would take them back to the land of Judah.

⁸Then Naomi said to her two daughters-in-law, "Go back, each of you, to your mother's home. May the LORD show you kindness, as you have shown kindness to your dead husbands and to me. ⁹May the LORD grant that each of you will find rest in the home of another husband."

Then she kissed them goodbye and they wept aloud ¹⁰and said to her, "We will go back with you to your people."

¹¹But Naomi said, "Return home, my daughters. Why would you come with me? Am I going to have any more sons, who could become your husbands? ¹²Return home, my daughters; I am too old to have another husband. Even if I thought there was still hope for me—even if I had a husband tonight and then gave birth to sons— ¹³would you wait until they grew up? Would you remain unmarried for them? No, my daughters. It is more bitter for me than for you, because the LORD's hand has turned against me!"

¹⁴At this they wept aloud again. Then Orpah kissed her mother-in-law goodbye, but Ruth clung to her.

THE SCENE

MOAB

(RUTH 1:2)

This means "seed" in Hebrew. It was a village east of the Dead Sea in a mountainous region. People here were often at war with the people of Israel.

THE WITNESSES

✓ **ELIMELEK** (RUTH 1:2)
He was a man from Judah. His name means "God is King." He was married to Naomi.

✓ **NAOMI** (RUTH 1:2)
Naomi means "sweet." She was Elimelek's wife.

✓ **MAHLON AND KILION** (RUTH 1:2)
Mahlon and Kilion means "sick or weak people." Those are the names of Elimelek and Naomi's sons. Mahlon was Ruth's husband. Kilion was Orpah's husband.

✓ **ORPAH** (RUTH 1:4)
Orpah is a woman's name. It's like saying "turning your back." She was one of Naomi's daughters-in-law.

✓ **RUTH** (RUTH 1:4)
This name means "friend" or "companion." She was a Moabite, so that means she was born in Moab. She was one of Naomi's daughters-in-law. Ruth traveled to Israel with her mother-in-law. She became King David's great-grandmother.

---

¹⁵"Look," said Naomi, "your sister-in-law is going back to her people and her gods. Go back with her."

¹⁶But Ruth replied, "Don't urge me to leave you or to turn back from you. Where you go I will go, and where you stay I will stay. Your people will be my people and your God my God. ¹⁷Where you die I will die, and there I will be buried. May the LORD deal with me, be it ever so severely, if even death separates you and me." ¹⁸When Naomi realized that Ruth was determined to go with her, she stopped urging her.

¹⁹So the two women went on until they came to Bethlehem. When they arrived in Bethlehem, the whole town was stirred because of them, and the women exclaimed, "Can this be Naomi?"

²⁰"Don't call me Naomi,ᵃ" she told them. "Call me Mara,ᵇ because the Almightyᶜ has made my life very bitter. ²¹I

went away full, but the LORD has brought me back empty. Why call me Naomi? The LORD has afflictedᵈ me; the Almighty has brought misfortune upon me."

²²So Naomi returned from Moab accompanied by Ruth the Moabite, her daughter-in-law, arriving in Bethlehem as the barley harvest was beginning.

Ruth Meets Boaz in the Grain Field

2 Now Naomi had a relative on her husband's side, a man of standing from the clan of Elimelek, whose name was Boaz.

²And Ruth the Moabite said to Naomi, "Let me go to the fields and pick up the leftover grain behind anyone in whose eyes I find favor."

Naomi said to her, "Go ahead, my daughter." ³So she went out, entered a

---

ᵃ 20 Naomi means pleasant.   ᵇ 20 Mara means bitter.
ᶜ 20 Hebrew Shaddai; also in verse 21   ᵈ 21 Or has testified against

BREAKTHROUGH!

Why didn't Ruth want to leave her mother-in-law alone?
(RUTH 1:16-17)

Because Ruth was good and she loved Naomi as if she were her own mother. Besides, Naomi was old, and she didn't have anyone else who could help her in her old age. Ruth wanted to go with her, because Naomi couldn't work or find food. If Naomi had been left alone, she would surely have become poor and homeless.

field and began to glean behind the harvesters. As it turned out, she was working in a field belonging to Boaz, who was from the clan of Elimelek.

⁴Just then Boaz arrived from Bethlehem and greeted the harvesters, "The LORD be with you!"

"The LORD bless you!" they answered.

⁵Boaz asked the overseer of his harvesters, "Who does that young woman belong to?"

⁶The overseer replied, "She is the Moabite who came back from Moab with Naomi. ⁷She said, 'Please let me glean and gather among the sheaves behind the harvesters.' She came into the field and has remained here from morning till now, except for a short rest in the shelter."

⁸So Boaz said to Ruth, "My daughter, listen to me. Don't go and glean in another field and don't go away from here. Stay here with the women who work for me. ⁹Watch the field where the men are harvesting, and follow along after the women. I have told the men not to lay a hand on you. And whenever you are thirsty, go and get a drink from the water jars the men have filled."

¹⁰At this, she bowed down with her face to the ground. She asked him, "Why have I found such favor in your eyes that you notice me—a foreigner?"

THE WITNESSES

✓ **BOAZ** (RUTH 2:3)

The name Boaz means "strong" or "fortress." It's just the opposite of the meaning of the name of Ruth's husband who died, whose name meant "weak." Boaz was Elimelek's relative, who married Ruth and rescued her from poverty. Boaz and Ruth had a son they called Obed.

[11]Boaz replied, "I've been told all about what you have done for your mother-in-law since the death of your husband—how you left your father and mother and your homeland and came to live with a people you did not know before. [12]May the LORD repay you for what you have done. May you be richly rewarded by the LORD, the God of Israel, under whose wings you have come to take refuge."

[13]"May I continue to find favor in your eyes, my lord," she said. "You have put me at ease by speaking kindly to your servant—though I do not have the standing of one of your servants."

[14]At mealtime Boaz said to her, "Come over here. Have some bread and dip it in the wine vinegar."

When she sat down with the harvesters, he offered her some roasted grain. She ate all she wanted and had some left over. [15]As she got up to glean, Boaz gave orders to his men, "Let her gather among the sheaves and don't reprimand her. [16]Even pull out some stalks for her from the bundles and leave them for her to pick up, and don't rebuke her."

[17]So Ruth gleaned in the field until evening. Then she threshed the barley she had gathered, and it amounted to about an ephah.[a] [18]She carried it back to town, and her mother-in-law saw how much she had gathered. Ruth also brought out and gave her what she had left over after she had eaten enough.

[19]Her mother-in-law asked her, "Where did you glean today? Where did you work? Blessed be the man who took notice of you!"

Then Ruth told her mother-in-law about the one at whose place she had been working. "The name of the man I worked with today is Boaz," she said.

[20]"The LORD bless him!" Naomi said to her daughter-in-law. "He has not stopped showing his kindness to the living and the dead." She added, "That man is our close relative; he is one of our guardian-redeemers.[b]"

[21]Then Ruth the Moabite said, "He even said to me, 'Stay with my workers until they finish harvesting all my grain.' "

[22]Naomi said to Ruth her daughter-in-law, "It will be good for you, my daughter, to go with the women who work for him, because in someone else's field you might be harmed."

[23]So Ruth stayed close to the women of Boaz to glean until the barley and wheat harvests were finished. And she lived with her mother-in-law.

Ruth and Boaz at the Threshing Floor

3 One day Ruth's mother-in-law Naomi said to her, "My daughter, I must find a home[c] for you, where you will be well provided for. [2]Now Boaz, with whose women you have worked, is a relative of ours. Tonight he will be winnowing barley on the threshing floor. [3]Wash, put on perfume, and get dressed in your best clothes. Then go down to the threshing floor, but don't let him know you are there until he has finished eating and drinking. [4]When he lies down, note the place where he is lying. Then go and uncover his feet and lie down. He will tell you what to do."

[5]"I will do whatever you say," Ruth answered. [6]So she went down to the threshing floor and did everything her mother-in-law told her to do.

[7]When Boaz had finished eating and drinking and was in good spirits, he went over to lie down at the far end of the grain pile. Ruth approached quietly, uncovered his feet and lay down. [8]In the middle of the night something startled the man; he turned—and there was a woman lying at his feet!

[9]"Who are you?" he asked.

"I am your servant Ruth," she said. "Spread the corner of your garment over me, since you are a guardian-redeemer[d] of our family."

[10]"The LORD bless you, my daughter," he replied. "This kindness is greater than that which you showed earlier: You have

---

[a] 17 That is, probably about 30 pounds or about 13 kilograms   [b] 20 The Hebrew word for *guardian-redeemer* is a legal term for one who has the obligation to redeem a relative in serious difficulty (see Lev. 25:25-55).   [c] 1 Hebrew *find rest* (see 1:9)   [d] 9 The Hebrew word for *guardian-redeemer* is a legal term for one who has the obligation to redeem a relative in serious difficulty (see Lev. 25:25-55); also in verses 12 and 13.

not run after the younger men, whether rich or poor. ¹¹And now, my daughter, don't be afraid. I will do for you all you ask. All the people of my town know that you are a woman of noble character. ¹²Although it is true that I am a guardian-redeemer of our family, there is another who is more closely related than I. ¹³Stay here for the night, and in the morning if he wants to do his duty as your guardian-redeemer, good; let him redeem you. But if he is not willing, as surely as the LORD lives I will do it. Lie here until morning."

¹⁴So she lay at his feet until morning, but got up before anyone could be recognized; and he said, "No one must

Did her mother-in-law have to find a husband for Ruth?
(RUTH 3:1)

Yes. A long time ago, in Bible times, girls and boys had to marry the person their parents chose for them. So when Ruth was living with Naomi, it was like Naomi was her mother. Besides, Ruth was a widow, so she was supposed to marry the closest relative her husband had. That was the law called Levirate.

Why did the family member need to protect Ruth and her mother-in-law?
(RUTH 3)

In Bible times, women were like little girls. That means they weren't treated like adults. That's why they were told they couldn't make their own decisions. Imagine! There was always someone over them like a father, a husband or a son. The unusual part about the story in this book is that although the laws of Israel at that time said that a man had to be the protector, Ruth took on that role to take care of Naomi.

know that a woman came to the threshing floor."

¹⁵He also said, "Bring me the shawl you are wearing and hold it out." When she did so, he poured into it six measures of barley and placed the bundle on her. Then he*a* went back to town.

¹⁶When Ruth came to her mother-in-law, Naomi asked, "How did it go, my daughter?"

Then she told her everything Boaz had done for her ¹⁷and added, "He gave me these six measures of barley, saying, 'Don't go back to your mother-in-law empty-handed.' "

¹⁸Then Naomi said, "Wait, my daughter, until you find out what happens. For the

---
a 15 Most Hebrew manuscripts; many Hebrew manuscripts, Vulgate and Syriac *she*

man will not rest until the matter is settled today."

Boaz Marries Ruth

4 Meanwhile Boaz went up to the town gate and sat down there just as the guardian-redeemer[a] he had mentioned came along. Boaz said, "Come over here, my friend, and sit down." So he went over and sat down.

²Boaz took ten of the elders of the town and said, "Sit here," and they did so. ³Then he said to the guardian-redeemer, "Naomi, who has come back from Moab, is selling the piece of land that belonged to our relative Elimelek. ⁴I thought I should bring the matter to your attention and suggest that you buy it in the presence of these seated here and in the presence of the elders of my people. If you will redeem it, do so. But if you[b] will not, tell me, so I will know. For no one has the right to do it except you, and I am next in line."

"I will redeem it," he said.

BREAK THROUGH!

Taking off a sandal
(RUTH 4:7 - 8)
This very old custom is mentioned in Deuteronomy 25:9 - 10. It was like signing a contract.

THE WITNESSES

✓ **OBED** (RUTH 4:17)
He was the son of Boaz and Ruth. Obed became King David's grandfather. His name means "server."

⁵Then Boaz said, "On the day you buy the land from Naomi, you also acquire Ruth the Moabite, the[c] dead man's widow, in order to maintain the name of the dead with his property."

⁶At this, the guardian-redeemer said, "Then I cannot redeem it because I might endanger my own estate. You redeem it yourself. I cannot do it."

⁷(Now in earlier times in Israel, for the redemption and transfer of property to become final, one party took off his sandal

---

^a 1 The Hebrew word for *guardian-redeemer* is a legal term for one who has the obligation to redeem a relative in serious difficulty (see Lev. 25:25-55); also in verses 3, 6, 8 and 14.   ^b 4 Many Hebrew manuscripts, Septuagint, Vulgate and Syriac; most Hebrew manuscripts *he*
^c 5 Vulgate and Syriac; Hebrew (see also Septuagint) *Naomi and from Ruth the Moabite, you acquire the*

and gave it to the other. This was the method of legalizing transactions in Israel.)

⁸So the guardian-redeemer said to Boaz, "Buy it yourself." And he removed his sandal.

⁹Then Boaz announced to the elders and all the people, "Today you are witnesses that I have bought from Naomi all the property of Elimelek, Kilion and Mahlon. ¹⁰I have also acquired Ruth the Moabite, Mahlon's widow, as my wife, in order to maintain the name of the dead with his property, so that his name will not disappear from among his family or from his hometown. Today you are witnesses!"

¹¹Then the elders and all the people at the gate said, "We are witnesses. May the LORD make the woman who is coming into your home like Rachel and Leah, who together built up the family of Israel. May you have standing in Ephrathah and be famous in Bethlehem. ¹²Through the offspring the LORD gives you by this young woman, may your family be like that of Perez, whom Tamar bore to Judah."

Naomi Gains a Son

¹³So Boaz took Ruth and she became his wife. When he made love to her, the LORD enabled her to conceive, and she gave birth to a son. ¹⁴The women said to Naomi: "Praise be to the LORD, who this day has not left you without a guardian-redeemer. May he become famous throughout Israel! ¹⁵He will renew your life and sustain you in your old age. For your daughter-in-law, who loves you and who is better to you than seven sons, has given him birth."

¹⁶Then Naomi took the child in her arms and cared for him. ¹⁷The women living there said, "Naomi has a son!" And they named him Obed. He was the father of Jesse, the father of David.

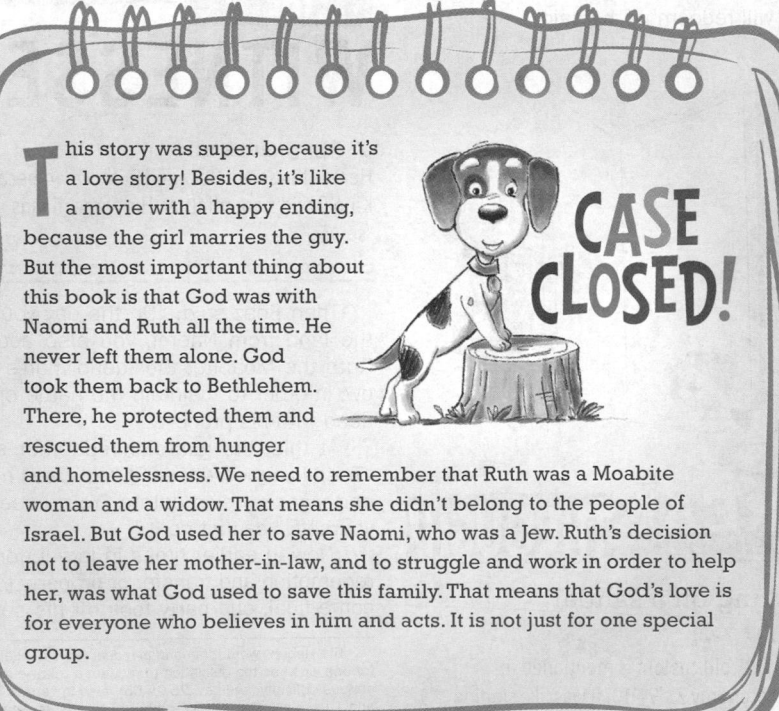

This story was super, because it's a love story! Besides, it's like a movie with a happy ending, because the girl marries the guy. But the most important thing about this book is that God was with Naomi and Ruth all the time. He never left them alone. God took them back to Bethlehem. There, he protected them and rescued them from hunger and homelessness. We need to remember that Ruth was a Moabite woman and a widow. That means she didn't belong to the people of Israel. But God used her to save Naomi, who was a Jew. Ruth's decision not to leave her mother-in-law, and to struggle and work in order to help her, was what God used to save this family. That means that God's love is for everyone who believes in him and acts. It is not just for one special group.

CASE CLOSED!

The Genealogy of David

18 This, then, is the family line of Perez:

Perez was the father of Hezron,
19 Hezron the father of Ram,
   Ram the father of Amminadab,
20 Amminadab the father of Nahshon,
   Nahshon the father of Salmon,[a]

21 Salmon the father of Boaz,
   Boaz the father of Obed,
22 Obed the father of Jesse,
   and Jesse the father of David.

---

[a] 20 A few Hebrew manuscripts, some Septuagint manuscripts and Vulgate (see also verse 21 and Septuagint of 1 Chron. 2:11); most Hebrew manuscripts *Salma*

1 SAMUEL

THE EVIDENCE:

WHO WROTE IT?

This book is called "Samuel" because he is the first important person who appears in it. But we know Samuel didn't write the whole book, since it talks about things that happened after he died. Maybe Samuel wrote part of it and Nathan and Gad wrote other parts. The truth is that we don't really know who the author was. Experts who study the Bible think that several people wrote it.

HOW LONG AGO?

People who know a lot about the Bible can't agree about when this book was written. Almost all of them think it was while Samuel was alive or a short time later, more or less between 1,000 and 930 years before Christ. Some think it might have been during the time of the exile in Babylon, when the Israelites were taken prisoners. That was around 500 years before Jesus (B.C.).

WHAT'S IT ABOUT?

In the Hebrew Bible, this book is in a part called Prophets. The books that now are called First and Second Samuel used to be just one book. Samuel, Saul and David are the three most important people in this book. It's like a history book of Israel told through the lives of these three people. It's also about how God always took control of everything that happened. For example, in First Samuel, we read how Samuel was born, how his parents took him to live in the temple and how the monarchy started (*monarchy* means a government with a king). This book also tells about how Saul became the first king of Israel. It explains that he was disobedient, and that's why God was angry and chose a different king, whose name was David.

THE BEST PART

We picked 3:19: "The Lord was with Samuel as he grew up ..." because that means that God takes care of us kids.

The Birth of Samuel

1 There was a certain man from Ramathaim, a Zuphite[a] from the hill country of Ephraim, whose name was Elkanah son of Jeroham, the son of Elihu, the son of Tohu, the son of Zuph, an Ephraimite. [2]He had two wives; one was called Hannah and the other Peninnah. Peninnah had children, but Hannah had none.

[3]Year after year this man went up from his town to worship and sacrifice to the LORD Almighty at Shiloh, where Hophni and Phinehas, the two sons of Eli, were priests of the LORD. [4]Whenever the day came for Elkanah to sacrifice, he would give portions of the meat to his wife Peninnah and to all her sons and daughters. [5]But to Hannah he gave a double portion because he loved her, and the LORD had closed her womb. [6]Because the LORD had closed Hannah's womb, her

THE
WITNESSES

✓ **ELKANAH** (1 SAMUEL 1:1)
In Hebrew, this name means "God obtained." He was a Levite who lived in the mountainous region of Ephraim, northeast of Jerusalem. He was Samuel's father.

rival kept provoking her in order to irritate her. [7]This went on year after year. Whenever Hannah went up to the house of the LORD, her rival provoked her till she wept and would not eat. [8]Her husband Elkanah would say to her, "Hannah, why are you weeping? Why don't you eat? Why are you downhearted? Don't I mean more to you than ten sons?"

[9]Once when they had finished eating and drinking in Shiloh, Hannah stood up. Now Eli the priest was sitting on his chair by the doorpost of the LORD's house. [10]In her deep anguish Hannah prayed to the

THE
SCENE

RAMATHAIM

(1 SAMUEL 1:1)

In Hebrew, *Rama* means "high." The experts really don't know where this city was, but they think it was an important city belonging to the tribe of Benjamin. It was west of the territory of Ephraim, between Lydda and Ekron.

---

[a] 1 See Septuagint and 1 Chron. 6:26-27,33-35; *or from* Ramathaim Zuphim.

THE SCENE

SHILOH

(1 SAMUEL 1:3)

It was a city in the territory of Ephraim, 31 miles (50 km) northwest of Ramathaim and 9 miles (15 km) north of Bethel. It was very important because God's sanctuary was there. Later, with David, the sanctuary was moved to Jerusalem.

LORD, weeping bitterly. ¹¹And she made a vow, saying, "LORD Almighty, if you will only look on your servant's misery and remember me, and not forget your servant but give her a son, then I will give him to the LORD for all the days of his life, and no razor will ever be used on his head."

¹²As she kept on praying to the LORD, Eli observed her mouth. ¹³Hannah was praying in her heart, and her lips were moving but her voice was not heard. Eli thought she was drunk ¹⁴and said to her, "How long are you going to stay drunk? Put away your wine."

¹⁵"Not so, my lord," Hannah replied, "I am a woman who is deeply troubled. I have not been drinking wine or beer; I was pouring out my soul to the LORD. ¹⁶Do not take your servant for a wicked woman;

I have been praying here out of my great anguish and grief."

¹⁷Eli answered, "Go in peace, and may the God of Israel grant you what you have asked of him."

¹⁸She said, "May your servant find favor in your eyes." Then she went her way and ate something, and her face was no longer downcast.

BREAK THROUGH!

Why did not cutting one's hair prove that a person was dedicated to God?

(1 SAMUEL 1:11)

This was a very old custom with the Israelite people. You can find it in the book of Numbers, chapter 6. That custom was called the Nazirite Law. Nazirite means "separated" or "dedicated." It was more or less like this: When a man or a woman promised to dedicate his or her life to God during their lifetime or for a short period of time, they didn't cut their hair. This was a way of showing that they had made this promise. They also used special clothes and didn't drink alcoholic beverages. Here, Hannah, who was Samuel's mother, promises that her son will always be a Nazirite. There are other Nazirites in the Bible. Samson and John the Baptist are two examples.

THE WITNESSES

✓ **PENINNAH** (1 SAMUEL 1:2)
This name means "pearl." She was one of Elkanah's wives, but she was very bad. She was always making fun of Hannah, because she had babies and Hannah didn't.

✓ **HANNAH** (1 SAMUEL 1:2)
Hannah means "grace" or "gracious." She was one of Elkanah's wives. She couldn't have babies, but she prayed with a lot of faith in God, and God gave her several sons. The first one was Samuel, who became a very important judge and prophet of God for Israel.

✓ **ELI** (1 SAMUEL 1:3)
He was the priest at Shiloh. When Hannah left the boy Samuel in the temple, she left him under Eli's care. He was Hophni and Phinehas' father, but he didn't teach them very well, and they were disobedient to God.

✓ **SAMUEL** (1 SAMUEL 1:20)
This name means "ear of God." Right! Because God heard his mother's prayer! He was an important Israelite judge and prophet. He went to live in the sanctuary when he was just a little boy. He learned to hear and obey the voice of God.

¹⁹Early the next morning they arose and worshiped before the LORD and then went back to their home at Ramah. Elkanah made love to his wife Hannah, and the LORD remembered her. ²⁰So in the course of time Hannah became pregnant and gave birth to a son. She named him Samuel,ᵃ saying, "Because I asked the LORD for him."

Hannah Dedicates Samuel

²¹When her husband Elkanah went up with all his family to offer the annual sacrifice to the LORD and to fulfill his vow, ²²Hannah did not go. She said to her husband, "After the boy is weaned, I will take him and present him before the LORD, and he will live there always."ᵇ
²³"Do what seems best to you," her husband Elkanah told her. "Stay here until you have weaned him; only may the LORD make good hisᶜ word." So the woman stayed at home and nursed her son until she had weaned him.

²⁴After he was weaned, she took the boy with her, young as he was, along with a three-year-old bull,ᵈ an ephahᵉ of flour and a skin of wine, and brought him to the house of the LORD at Shiloh. ²⁵When the bull had been sacrificed, they brought the boy to Eli, ²⁶and she said to him, "Pardon me, my lord. As surely as you live, I am the woman who stood here beside you praying to the LORD. ²⁷I prayed for this child, and the LORD has granted me what I asked of him. ²⁸So now I give him to the LORD. For his whole life he will be given over to the LORD." And he worshiped the LORD there.

ᵃ *20 Samuel* sounds like the Hebrew for *heard by God.*
ᵇ *22* Masoretic Text; Dead Sea Scrolls *always. I have dedicated him as a Nazirite—all the days of his life.*
ᶜ *23* Masoretic Text; Dead Sea Scrolls, Septuagint and Syriac *your*   ᵈ *24* Dead Sea Scrolls, Septuagint and Syriac; Masoretic Text *with three bulls*   ᵉ *24* That is, probably about 36 pounds or about 16 kilograms

but those who were hungry are
    hungry no more.
She who was barren has borne seven
    children,
    but she who has had many sons
        pines away.

6 "The LORD brings death and makes
    alive;
    he brings down to the grave and
        raises up.
7 The LORD sends poverty and wealth;
    he humbles and he exalts.
8 He raises the poor from the dust
    and lifts the needy from the ash
        heap;
he seats them with princes
    and has them inherit a throne of
        honor.

"For the foundations of the earth are
        the LORD's;
    on them he has set the world.

a 1 *Horn* here symbolizes strength; also in verse 10.

BREAK THROUGH!

What does "worship" God mean exactly?

(1 SAMUEL 1:19)

The word in Hebrew is *shachah*, which means "to kneel." Worshiping is really a sign of humility before God. In other words, we are showing that before God we're small and he's powerful. It's accepting in our heart that God is the King of our life.

Hannah's Prayer

2 Then Hannah prayed and said:

"My heart rejoices in the LORD;
    in the LORD my horn*a* is lifted high.
My mouth boasts over my enemies,
    for I delight in your deliverance.

2 "There is no one holy like the LORD;
    there is no one besides you;
    there is no Rock like our God.

3 "Do not keep talking so proudly
    or let your mouth speak such
        arrogance,
for the LORD is a God who knows,
    and by him deeds are weighed.

4 "The bows of the warriors are broken,
    but those who stumbled are armed
        with strength.
5 Those who were full hire themselves
        out for food,

BREAK THROUGH!

How old was Samuel when his parents gave him to Priest Eli?

(1 SAMUEL 1:23-28)

Bible experts think he was three years old, because that's the age when his mother would have stopped breastfeeding him.

[9] He will guard the feet of his faithful
    servants,
    but the wicked will be silenced in
    the place of darkness.

"It is not by strength that one prevails;
[10] those who oppose the LORD will be
    broken.
    The Most High will thunder from
    heaven;
    the LORD will judge the ends of the
    earth.

"He will give strength to his king
    and exalt the horn of his anointed."

[11] Then Elkanah went home to Ramah,
but the boy ministered before the LORD under Eli the priest.

Eli's Wicked Sons

[12] Eli's sons were scoundrels; they had no regard for the LORD. [13] Now it was the practice of the priests that, whenever any of the people offered a sacrifice, the priest's servant would come with a three-pronged fork in his hand while the meat was being boiled [14] and would plunge the fork into the pan or kettle or caldron or pot. Whatever the fork brought up the priest would take for himself. This is how they treated all the Israelites who came to Shiloh. [15] But even before the fat was burned, the priest's servant would come and say to the person who was sacrificing, "Give the priest some meat to roast; he won't accept boiled meat from you, but only raw."

[16] If the person said to him, "Let the fat be burned first, and then take whatever you want," the servant would answer, "No, hand it over now; if you don't, I'll take it by force."

[17] This sin of the young men was very great in the LORD's sight, for they[a] were treating the LORD's offering with contempt.

[18] But Samuel was ministering before the LORD—a boy wearing a linen ephod. [19] Each year his mother made him a little robe and took it to him when she went up with her husband to offer the annual sacrifice. [20] Eli would bless Elkanah and his wife, saying, "May the LORD give you

children by this woman to take the place of the one she prayed for and gave to[b] the LORD." Then they would go home. [21] And the LORD was gracious to Hannah; she gave birth to three sons and two daughters. Meanwhile, the boy Samuel grew up in the presence of the LORD.

[22] Now Eli, who was very old, heard about everything his sons were doing to all Israel and how they slept with the women who served at the entrance to the tent of meeting. [23] So he said to them, "Why do you do such things? I hear from all the people about these wicked deeds of yours. [24] No, my sons; the report I hear spreading among the LORD's people is not good. [25] If one person sins against another, God[c] may mediate for the offender; but if anyone sins against the LORD, who will intercede for them?" His sons, however, did not listen to their father's rebuke, for it was the LORD's will to put them to death.

[26] And the boy Samuel continued to grow in stature and in favor with the LORD and with people.

Prophecy Against the House of Eli

[27] Now a man of God came to Eli and said to him, "This is what the LORD says: 'Did I not clearly reveal myself to your ancestor's family when they were in Egypt under Pharaoh? [28] I chose your ancestor out of all the tribes of Israel to be my priest, to go up to my altar, to burn incense, and to wear an ephod in my presence. I also gave your ancestor's family all the food offerings presented by the Israelites. [29] Why do you[d] scorn my sacrifice and offering that I prescribed for my dwelling? Why do you honor your sons more than me by fattening yourselves on the choice parts of every offering made by my people Israel?'

[30] "Therefore the LORD, the God of Israel, declares: 'I promised that members of your family would minister before me forever.' But now the LORD declares: 'Far be it from me! Those who honor me I will honor,

---

a 17 Dead Sea Scrolls and Septuagint; Masoretic Text
people   *b* 20 Dead Sea Scrolls; Masoretic Text *and
asked from*   *c* 25 Or *the judges*   *d* 29 The Hebrew is
plural.

but those who despise me will be disdained. [31]The time is coming when I will cut short your strength and the strength of your priestly house, so that no one in it will reach old age, [32]and you will see distress in my dwelling. Although good will be done to Israel, no one in your family line will ever reach old age. [33]Every one of you that I do not cut off from serving at my altar I will spare only to destroy your sight and sap your strength, and all your descendants will die in the prime of life. [34]" 'And what happens to your two sons, Hophni and Phinehas, will be a sign to you—they will both die on the same day. [35]I will raise up for myself a faithful priest, who will do according to what is in my heart and mind. I will firmly establish his priestly house, and they will minister before my anointed one always. [36]Then everyone left in your family line will come and bow down before him for a piece of silver and a loaf of bread and plead, "Appoint me to some priestly office so I can have food to eat." ' "

The Lord Calls Samuel

3 The boy Samuel ministered before the Lord under Eli. In those days the word of the Lord was rare; there were not many visions.

[2]One night Eli, whose eyes were becoming so weak that he could barely see, was lying down in his usual place. [3]The lamp of God had not yet gone out, and Samuel was lying down in the house of the Lord, where the ark of God was. [4]Then the Lord called Samuel.

Samuel answered, "Here I am." [5]And he ran to Eli and said, "Here I am; you called me."

But Eli said, "I did not call; go back and lie down." So he went and lay down.

[6]Again the Lord called, "Samuel!" And Samuel got up and went to Eli and said, "Here I am; you called me."

"My son," Eli said, "I did not call; go back and lie down."

[7]Now Samuel did not yet know the Lord: The word of the Lord had not yet been revealed to him.

[8]A third time the Lord called, "Samuel!" And Samuel got up and went to Eli and said, "Here I am; you called me."

Then Eli realized that the Lord was calling the boy. [9]So Eli told Samuel, "Go and lie down, and if he calls you, say, 'Speak, Lord, for your servant is listening.' " So Samuel went and lay down in his place.

[10]The Lord came and stood there, calling as at the other times, "Samuel! Samuel!"

Then Samuel said, "Speak, for your servant is listening."

[11]And the Lord said to Samuel: "See, I am about to do something in Israel that will make the ears of everyone who hears about it tingle. [12]At that time I will carry out against Eli everything I spoke against his family—from beginning to end. [13]For I told him that I would judge his family forever because of the sin he knew about; his sons blasphemed God,[a] and he failed to restrain them. [14]Therefore I swore to the house of Eli, 'The guilt of Eli's house will never be atoned for by sacrifice or offering.' "

[15]Samuel lay down until morning and then opened the doors of the house of the Lord. He was afraid to tell Eli the vision, [16]but Eli called him and said, "Samuel, my son."

Samuel answered, "Here I am."

[17]"What was it he said to you?" Eli asked. "Do not hide it from me. May God deal with you, be it ever so severely, if you hide from me anything he told you." [18]So Samuel told him everything, hiding nothing from him. Then Eli said, "He is the Lord; let him do what is good in his eyes."

[19]The Lord was with Samuel as he grew up, and he let none of Samuel's words fall to the ground. [20]And all Israel from Dan to Beersheba recognized that Samuel was attested as a prophet of the Lord. [21]The Lord continued to appear at Shiloh, and there he revealed himself to Samuel through his word.

4 And Samuel's word came to all Israel.

The Philistines Capture the Ark

Now the Israelites went out to fight against the Philistines. The Israelites

---

[a] 13 An ancient Hebrew scribal tradition (see also Septuagint); Masoretic Text *sons made themselves contemptible*

camped at Ebenezer, and the Philistines at Aphek. [2]The Philistines deployed their forces to meet Israel, and as the battle spread, Israel was defeated by the Philistines, who killed about four thousand of them on the battlefield. [3]When the soldiers returned to camp, the elders of Israel asked, "Why did the LORD bring defeat on us today before the Philistines? Let us bring the ark of the LORD's covenant from Shiloh, so that he may go with us and save us from the hand of our enemies."

[4]So the people sent men to Shiloh, and they brought back the ark of the covenant of the LORD Almighty, who is enthroned between the cherubim. And Eli's two sons, Hophni and Phinehas, were there with the ark of the covenant of God.

[5]When the ark of the LORD's covenant came into the camp, all Israel raised such a great shout that the ground shook. [6]Hearing the uproar, the Philistines asked, "What's all this shouting in the Hebrew camp?"

When they learned that the ark of the LORD had come into the camp, [7]the Philistines were afraid. "A god has[a] come into the camp," they said. "Oh no! Nothing like this has happened before. [8]We're doomed! Who will deliver us from the hand of these mighty gods? They are the gods who struck the Egyptians with all kinds of plagues in the wilderness. [9]Be strong, Philistines! Be men, or you will be subject to the Hebrews, as they have been to you. Be men, and fight!"

[10]So the Philistines fought, and the Israelites were defeated and every man fled to his tent. The slaughter was very great; Israel lost thirty thousand foot soldiers. [11]The ark of God was captured, and Eli's two sons, Hophni and Phinehas, died.

Death of Eli

[12]That same day a Benjamite ran from the battle line and went to Shiloh with his clothes torn and dust on his head. [13]When he arrived, there was Eli sitting on his chair by the side of the road, watching, because his heart feared for the ark of God. When the man entered the town and told what had happened, the whole town sent up a cry.

[14]Eli heard the outcry and asked, "What is the meaning of this uproar?"

The man hurried over to Eli, [15]who was ninety-eight years old and whose eyes had failed so that he could not see. [16]He told Eli, "I have just come from the battle line; I fled from it this very day."

Eli asked, "What happened, my son?"

[17]The man who brought the news replied, "Israel fled before the Philistines, and the army has suffered heavy losses. Also your two sons, Hophni and Phinehas, are dead, and the ark of God has been captured."

[18]When he mentioned the ark of God, Eli fell backward off his chair by the side of the gate. His neck was broken and he died, for he was an old man, and he was heavy. He had led[b] Israel forty years.

[19]His daughter-in-law, the wife of Phinehas, was pregnant and near the time of delivery. When she heard the news that the ark of God had been captured and that her father-in-law and her husband were dead, she went into labor and gave birth, but was overcome by her labor pains. [20]As she was dying, the women attending her said, "Don't despair; you have given birth to a son." But she did not respond or pay any attention.

[21]She named the boy Ichabod,[c] saying, "The Glory has departed from Israel!" — because of the capture of the ark of God and the deaths of her father-in-law and her husband. [22]She said, "The Glory has departed from Israel, for the ark of God has been captured."

The Ark in Ashdod and Ekron

5 After the Philistines had captured the ark of God, they took it from Ebenezer to Ashdod. [2]Then they carried the ark into Dagon's temple and set it beside Dagon. [3]When the people of Ashdod rose early the next day, there was Dagon, fallen on his face on the ground before the ark of the LORD! They took Dagon and put him back in his place. [4]But the following morning when they rose, there was Dagon, fallen on his face on the ground before the ark of the LORD! His head and

---

[a] 7 Or "Gods have (see Septuagint)   [b] 18 Traditionally judged   [c] 21 Ichabod means no glory.

hands had been broken off and were lying on the threshold; only his body remained. ⁵That is why to this day neither the priests of Dagon nor any others who enter Dagon's temple at Ashdod step on the threshold.

⁶The LORD's hand was heavy on the people of Ashdod and its vicinity; he brought devastation on them and afflicted them with tumors.ᵃ ⁷When the people of Ashdod saw what was happening, they said, "The ark of the god of Israel must not stay here with us, because his hand is heavy on us and on Dagon our god." ⁸So they called together all the rulers of the Philistines and asked them, "What shall we do with the ark of the god of Israel?"

They answered, "Have the ark of the god of Israel moved to Gath." So they moved the ark of the God of Israel.

THE SCENE

ASHDOD

(1 SAMUEL 5:1)

This was one of the five main cities of the Philistines. It was 20 miles (32 km) northwest of Gaza and about 3 miles (5 km) from the shore of the Mediterranean Sea. When the land of Canaan was divided, the tribe of Judah got Ashdod.

BREAKTHROUGH!

The god Dagon
(1 SAMUEL 5:2)

He was one of the Philistines' most important gods. However, he was really just a statue. He wasn't alive, and he couldn't see or hear anything. In the city of Gaza, there was a temple dedicated to this god, but Samson destroyed it. We can read that story in Judges 16.

⁹But after they had moved it, the LORD's hand was against that city, throwing it into a great panic. He afflicted the people of the city, both young and old, with an outbreak of tumors.ᵇ ¹⁰So they sent the ark of God to Ekron.

As the ark of God was entering Ekron, the people of Ekron cried out, "They have brought the ark of the god of Israel around to us to kill us and our people." ¹¹So they called together all the rulers of the Philistines and said, "Send the ark of the god of Israel away; let it go back to its own place, or itᶜ will kill us and our people." For death had filled the city with panic; God's hand was very heavy on it. ¹²Those who did not die were afflicted with tumors, and the outcry of the city went up to heaven.

ᵃ 6 Hebrew; Septuagint and Vulgate *tumors. And rats appeared in their land, and there was death and destruction throughout the city*   ᵇ 9 Or *with tumors in the groin* (see Septuagint)   ᶜ 11 Or *he*

THE SCENE

GATH

(1 SAMUEL 5:8)

This was another one of the five important cities of the Philistines. Goliath was from Gath.

The Ark Returned to Israel

6 When the ark of the LORD had been in Philistine territory seven months, ²the Philistines called for the priests and the diviners and said, "What shall we do with the ark of the LORD? Tell us how we should send it back to its place."

³They answered, "If you return the ark of the god of Israel, do not send it back to him without a gift; by all means send a guilt offering to him. Then you will be healed, and you will know why his hand has not been lifted from you."

⁴The Philistines asked, "What guilt offering should we send to him?"

They replied, "Five gold tumors and five gold rats, according to the number of the Philistine rulers, because the same plague has struck both you and your rulers. ⁵Make models of the tumors and of the rats that are destroying the country, and give glory to Israel's god. Perhaps he will lift his hand from you and your gods and your land. ⁶Why do you harden your hearts as the Egyptians and Pharaoh did? When Israel's god dealt harshly with them, did they not send the Israelites out so they could go on their way?

⁷"Now then, get a new cart ready, with two cows that have calved and have never been yoked. Hitch the cows to the cart, but take their calves away and pen them up. ⁸Take the ark of the LORD and put it on the cart, and in a chest beside it put the gold objects you are sending back to him as a guilt offering. Send it on its way, ⁹but keep watching it. If it goes up to its own territory, toward Beth Shemesh, then the LORD has brought this great disaster on us. But if it does not, then we will know that it was not his hand that struck us but that it happened to us by chance."

¹⁰So they did this. They took two such cows and hitched them to the cart and penned up their calves. ¹¹They placed the ark of the LORD on the cart and along

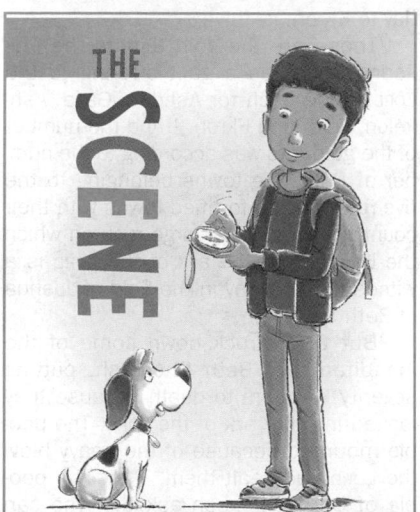

THE SCENE

EKRON

(1 SAMUEL 5:10)

This was also one of the five important cities of the Philistines. It was far north on the border, between Judah and Dan.

with it the chest containing the gold rats and the models of the tumors. ¹²Then the cows went straight up toward Beth Shemesh, keeping on the road and lowing all the way; they did not turn to the right or to the left. The rulers of the Philistines followed them as far as the border of Beth Shemesh.

¹³Now the people of Beth Shemesh were harvesting their wheat in the valley, and when they looked up and saw the ark, they rejoiced at the sight. ¹⁴The cart came to the field of Joshua of Beth Shemesh, and there it stopped beside a large rock. The people chopped up the wood of the cart and sacrificed the cows as a burnt offering to the LORD. ¹⁵The Levites took down the ark of the LORD, together with the chest containing the gold objects, and placed them on the large rock. On that day the people of Beth Shemesh offered burnt offerings and made sacrifices to the LORD. ¹⁶The five rulers of the Philistines saw all this and then returned that same day to Ekron.

¹⁷These are the gold tumors the Philistines sent as a guilt offering to the LORD—one each for Ashdod, Gaza, Ashkelon, Gath and Ekron. ¹⁸And the number of the gold rats was according to the number of Philistine towns belonging to the five rulers—the fortified towns with their country villages. The large rock on which the Levites set the ark of the LORD is a witness to this day in the field of Joshua of Beth Shemesh.

¹⁹But God struck down some of the inhabitants of Beth Shemesh, putting seventy[a] of them to death because they looked into the ark of the LORD. The people mourned because of the heavy blow the LORD had dealt them. ²⁰And the people of Beth Shemesh asked, "Who can stand in the presence of the LORD, this holy God? To whom will the ark go up from here?"

²¹Then they sent messengers to the people of Kiriath Jearim, saying, "The Philistines have returned the ark of the LORD. Come down and take it up to your town."

7 ¹So the men of Kiriath Jearim came and took up the ark of the LORD. They brought it to Abinadab's house on the hill

and consecrated Eleazar his son to guard the ark of the LORD. ²The ark remained at Kiriath Jearim a long time—twenty years in all.

Samuel Subdues the Philistines at Mizpah

Then all the people of Israel turned back to the LORD. ³So Samuel said to all the Israelites, "If you are returning to the LORD with all your hearts, then rid yourselves of the foreign gods and the Ashtoreths and commit yourselves to the LORD and serve him only, and he will deliver you out of the hand of the Philistines." ⁴So the Israelites put away their Baals and Ashtoreths, and served the LORD only.

⁵Then Samuel said, "Assemble all Israel at Mizpah, and I will intercede with the

---

a 19 A few Hebrew manuscripts; most Hebrew manuscripts and Septuagint 50,070

BREAK THROUGH!

Images of Baal and Ashtoreth

(1 SAMUEL 7:3–4)

Baal means "lord." He was the Canaanite god of fertility (that means being able to have many babies). Ashtoreth was a Canaanite goddess, and was represented by a pole or a rod. The Canaanites usually worshiped these two gods together.

THE SCENE

MIZPAH

(1 SAMUEL 7:5)

It belonged to the territory of Benjamin and was near Ramathaim. Samuel anointed Saul and declared him king in Mizpah.

LORD for you." ⁶When they had assembled at Mizpah, they drew water and poured it out before the LORD. On that day they fasted and there they confessed, "We have sinned against the LORD." Now Samuel was serving as leader*a* of Israel at Mizpah.

⁷When the Philistines heard that Israel had assembled at Mizpah, the rulers of the Philistines came up to attack them. When the Israelites heard of it, they were afraid because of the Philistines. ⁸They said to Samuel, "Do not stop crying out to the LORD our God for us, that he may rescue us from the hand of the Philistines." ⁹Then Samuel took a suckling lamb and sacrificed it as a whole burnt offering to the LORD. He cried out to the LORD on Israel's behalf, and the LORD answered him.

¹⁰While Samuel was sacrificing the burnt offering, the Philistines drew near to engage Israel in battle. But that day the LORD thundered with loud thunder against the Philistines and threw them into such a panic that they were routed before the Israelites. ¹¹The men of Israel rushed out of Mizpah and pursued the Philistines, slaughtering them along the way to a point below Beth Kar.

¹²Then Samuel took a stone and set it up between Mizpah and Shen. He named it Ebenezer,*b* saying, "Thus far the LORD has helped us."

¹³So the Philistines were subdued and they stopped invading Israel's territory. Throughout Samuel's lifetime, the hand of the LORD was against the Philistines.

---

a 6 Traditionally *judge*; also in verse 15   *b* 12 *Ebenezer* means *stone of help.*

BREAKTHROUGH!

Fasting

(1 SAMUEL 7:6)

This is when someone doesn't eat for a time in order to spend time praying and preparing to receive a message from God, It is sometimes also done before a person leaves to carry out a special mission for God. Chapter 58 of Isaiah says that "the kind of fasting [God] has chosen" has a very important social job: carrying out justice, feeding poor people, giving shelter to people who don't have a home, giving clothes to people who need them and so on.

¹⁴The towns from Ekron to Gath that the Philistines had captured from Israel were restored to Israel, and Israel delivered the neighboring territory from the hands of the Philistines. And there was peace between Israel and the Amorites.

¹⁵Samuel continued as Israel's leader all the days of his life. ¹⁶From year to year he went on a circuit from Bethel to Gilgal to Mizpah, judging Israel in all those places. ¹⁷But he always went back to Ramah, where his home was, and there he also held court for Israel. And he built an altar there to the Lᴏʀᴅ.

Israel Asks for a King

8 When Samuel grew old, he appointed his sons as Israel's leaders.ᵃ ²The name of his firstborn was Joel and the

name of his second was Abijah, and they served at Beersheba. ³But his sons did not follow his ways. They turned aside after dishonest gain and accepted bribes and perverted justice.

⁴So all the elders of Israel gathered together and came to Samuel at Ramah. ⁵They said to him, "You are old, and your sons do not follow your ways; now appoint a king to leadᵇ us, such as all the other nations have."

⁶But when they said, "Give us a king to lead us," this displeased Samuel; so he prayed to the Lᴏʀᴅ. ⁷And the Lᴏʀᴅ told him: "Listen to all that the people are saying to you; it is not you they have rejected, but they have rejected me as their king. ⁸As they have done from the day I brought them up out of Egypt until this day, forsaking me and serving other gods, so they are doing to you. ⁹Now listen to them; but warn them solemnly and let them know what the king who will reign over them will claim as his rights."

¹⁰Samuel told all the words of the Lᴏʀᴅ to the people who were asking him for a king. ¹¹He said, "This is what the king who will reign over you will claim as his rights: He will take your sons and make them serve with his chariots and horses, and they will run in front of his chariots. ¹²Some he will assign to be commanders of thousands and commanders of fifties, and others to plow his ground and reap his harvest, and still others to make weapons of war and equipment for his chariots. ¹³He will take your daughters to be perfumers and cooks and bakers. ¹⁴He will take the best of your fields and vineyards and olive groves and give them to his attendants. ¹⁵He will take a tenth of your grain and of your vintage and give it to his officials and attendants. ¹⁶Your male and female servants and the best of your cattleᶜ and donkeys he will take for his own use. ¹⁷He will take a tenth of your flocks, and you yourselves will become his slaves. ¹⁸When that day comes, you will cry out for relief from the king you have chosen, but the Lᴏʀᴅ will not answer you in that day."

THE SCENE

BETHEL

(1 SAMUEL 7:16)

In Hebrew, this means "house of God." It was a city of the tribe of Benjamin 19 miles (30 km) north of Jerusalem and south of Shiloh. During the time of the judges, the ark of the covenant was in Bethel. Later, it was taken to Shiloh.

ᵃ 1 Traditionally *judges*   ᵇ 5 Traditionally *judge*; also in verses 6 and 20   ᶜ 16 Septuagint; Hebrew *young men*

¹⁹But the people refused to listen to Samuel. "No!" they said. "We want a king over us. ²⁰Then we will be like all the other nations, with a king to lead us and to go out before us and fight our battles."

²¹When Samuel heard all that the people said, he repeated it before the LORD. ²²The LORD answered, "Listen to them and give them a king."

Then Samuel said to the Israelites, "Everyone go back to your own town."

Samuel Anoints Saul

9 There was a Benjamite, a man of standing, whose name was Kish son of Abiel, the son of Zeror, the son of Bekorath, the son of Aphiah of Benjamin. ²Kish had a son named Saul, as handsome a young man as could be found anywhere in Israel, and he was a head taller than anyone else.

³Now the donkeys belonging to Saul's father Kish were lost, and Kish said to his son Saul, "Take one of the servants with you and go and look for the donkeys." ⁴So he passed through the hill country of Ephraim and through the area around Shalisha, but they did not find them. They went on into the district of Shaalim, but the donkeys were not there. Then he passed through the territory of Benjamin, but they did not find them.

⁵When they reached the district of Zuph, Saul said to the servant who was with him, "Come, let's go back, or my father will stop thinking about the donkeys and start worrying about us."

⁶But the servant replied, "Look, in this town there is a man of God; he is highly respected, and everything he says comes true. Let's go there now. Perhaps he will tell us what way to take."

⁷Saul said to his servant, "If we go, what can we give the man? The food in our sacks is gone. We have no gift to take to the man of God. What do we have?"

⁸The servant answered him again. "Look," he said, "I have a quarter of a shekelᵃ of silver. I will give it to the man of God so that he will tell us what way to take." ⁹(Formerly in Israel, if someone went to inquire of God, they would say, "Come, let us go to the seer," because

THE
WITNESSES

✓ **SAUL** (1 SAMUEL 9:2)
Saul means "wanted." He was the first king of Israel. He was very poor, but he was very brave. Saul triumphed in the war against the Amalekites, but he never conquered the Philistines. Over time, Saul began to disobey God. For that reason, God was upset with him.

the prophet of today used to be called a seer.)

¹⁰"Good," Saul said to his servant. "Come, let's go." So they set out for the town where the man of God was.

¹¹As they were going up the hill to the town, they met some young women coming out to draw water, and they asked them, "Is the seer here?"

¹²"He is," they answered. "He's ahead of you. Hurry now; he has just come to our town today, for the people have a sacrifice

ᵃ 8 That is, about 1/10 ounce or about 3 grams

at the high place. [13]As soon as you enter the town, you will find him before he goes up to the high place to eat. The people will not begin eating until he comes, because he must bless the sacrifice; afterward, those who are invited will eat. Go up now; you should find him about this time."

[14]They went up to the town, and as they were entering it, there was Samuel, coming toward them on his way up to the high place.

[15]Now the day before Saul came, the LORD had revealed this to Samuel: [16]"About this time tomorrow I will send you a man from the land of Benjamin. Anoint him ruler over my people Israel; he will deliver them from the hand of the Philistines. I have looked on my people, for their cry has reached me."

[17]When Samuel caught sight of Saul, the LORD said to him, "This is the man I spoke to you about; he will govern my people."

[18]Saul approached Samuel in the gateway and asked, "Would you please tell me where the seer's house is?"

[19]"I am the seer," Samuel replied. "Go up ahead of me to the high place, for today you are to eat with me, and in the morning I will send you on your way and will tell you all that is in your heart. [20]As for the donkeys you lost three days ago, do not worry about them; they have been found. And to whom is all the desire of Israel turned, if not to you and your whole family line?"

[21]Saul answered, "But am I not a Benjamite, from the smallest tribe of Israel, and is not my clan the least of all the clans of the tribe of Benjamin? Why do you say such a thing to me?"

[22]Then Samuel brought Saul and his servant into the hall and seated them at the head of those who were invited — about thirty in number. [23]Samuel said to the cook, "Bring the piece of meat I gave you, the one I told you to lay aside."

[24]So the cook took up the thigh with what was on it and set it in front of Saul. Samuel said, "Here is what has been kept for you. Eat, because it was set aside for you for this occasion from the time I said, 'I have invited guests.'" And Saul dined with Samuel that day.

[25]After they came down from the high place to the town, Samuel talked with Saul on the roof of his house. [26]They rose about daybreak, and Samuel called to Saul on the roof, "Get ready, and I will send you on your way." When Saul got ready, he and Samuel went outside together. [27]As they were going down to the edge of the town, Samuel said to Saul, "Tell the servant to go on ahead of us" — and the servant did so — "but you stay here for a while, so that I may give you a message from God."

10 Then Samuel took a flask of olive oil and poured it on Saul's head and kissed him, saying, "Has not the LORD anointed you ruler over his inheritance?[a] [2]When you leave me today, you will meet two men near Rachel's tomb, at Zelzah on the border of Benjamin. They will say to you, 'The donkeys you set out to look for have been found. And now your father has stopped thinking about them and is worried about you. He is asking, "What shall I do about my son?"'

[3]"Then you will go on from there until you reach the great tree of Tabor. Three men going up to worship God at Bethel will meet you there. One will be carrying three young goats, another three loaves of bread, and another a skin of wine. [4]They will greet you and offer you two loaves of bread, which you will accept from them.

[5]"After that you will go to Gibeah of God, where there is a Philistine outpost. As you approach the town, you will meet a procession of prophets coming down from the high place with lyres, timbrels, pipes and harps being played before them, and they will be prophesying. [6]The Spirit of the LORD will come powerfully upon you, and you will prophesy with them; and you will be changed into a different person. [7]Once these signs are fulfilled, do whatever your hand finds to do, for God is with you.

---

[a] 1 Hebrew; Septuagint and Vulgate *over his people Israel?
You will reign over the LORD's people and save them from the
power of their enemies round about. And this will be a sign
to you that the LORD has anointed you ruler over his
inheritance:*

[8]"Go down ahead of me to Gilgal. I will surely come down to you to sacrifice burnt offerings and fellowship offerings, but you must wait seven days until I come to you and tell you what you are to do."

Saul Made King

[9]As Saul turned to leave Samuel, God changed Saul's heart, and all these signs were fulfilled that day. [10]When he and his servant arrived at Gibeah, a procession of prophets met him; the Spirit of God came powerfully upon him, and he joined in their prophesying. [11]When all those who had formerly known him saw him prophesying with the prophets, they asked each other, "What is this that has happened to the son of Kish? Is Saul also among the prophets?"

[12]A man who lived there answered, "And who is their father?" So it became a saying: "Is Saul also among the prophets?" [13]After Saul stopped prophesying, he went to the high place.

[14]Now Saul's uncle asked him and his servant, "Where have you been?"

"Looking for the donkeys," he said. "But when we saw they were not to be found, we went to Samuel." [15]Saul's uncle said, "Tell me what Samuel said to you."

[16]Saul replied, "He assured us that the donkeys had been found." But he did not tell his uncle what Samuel had said about the kingship.

[17]Samuel summoned the people of Israel to the Lord at Mizpah [18]and said to them, "This is what the Lord, the God of Israel, says: 'I brought Israel up out of Egypt, and I delivered you from the power of Egypt and all the kingdoms that oppressed you.' [19]But you have now rejected your God, who saves you out of all your disasters and calamities. And you have said, 'No, appoint a king over us.' So now present yourselves before the Lord by your tribes and clans."

[20]When Samuel had all Israel come forward by tribes, the tribe of Benjamin was taken by lot. [21]Then he brought forward the tribe of Benjamin, clan by clan, and Matri's clan was taken. Finally Saul son of Kish was taken. But when they looked for him, he was not to be found. [22]So they inquired further of the Lord, "Has the man come here yet?"

And the Lord said, "Yes, he has hidden himself among the supplies."

[23]They ran and brought him out, and as he stood among the people he was a head taller than any of the others. [24]Samuel said to all the people, "Do you see the man the Lord has chosen? There is no one like him among all the people."

Then the people shouted, "Long live the king!"

[25]Samuel explained to the people the rights and duties of kingship. He wrote them down on a scroll and deposited it before the Lord. Then Samuel dismissed the people to go to their own homes.

[26]Saul also went to his home in Gibeah, accompanied by valiant men whose hearts God had touched. [27]But some scoundrels said, "How can this fellow save us?" They despised him and brought him no gifts. But Saul kept silent.

Saul Rescues the City of Jabesh

11 Nahash[a] the Ammonite went up and besieged Jabesh Gilead. And all the men of Jabesh said to him, "Make a treaty with us, and we will be subject to you."

[2]But Nahash the Ammonite replied, "I will make a treaty with you only on the condition that I gouge out the right eye of every one of you and so bring disgrace on all Israel."

[3]The elders of Jabesh said to him, "Give us seven days so we can send messengers throughout Israel; if no one comes to rescue us, we will surrender to you."

[4]When the messengers came to Gibeah of Saul and reported these terms to the people, they all wept aloud. [5]Just then Saul was returning from the fields, behind his oxen, and he asked, "What is wrong with everyone? Why are they weeping?"

---

a 1 Masoretic Text; Dead Sea Scrolls gifts. Now Nahash king of the Ammonites oppressed the Gadites and Reubenites severely. He gouged out all their right eyes and struck terror and dread in Israel. Not a man remained among the Israelites beyond the Jordan whose right eye was not gouged out by Nahash king of the Ammonites, except that seven thousand men fled from the Ammonites and entered Jabesh Gilead. About a month later, [1]Nahash

BREAKTHROUGH!

Ammonites

(1 SAMUEL 11:1)

This was a nation that was formed by the family line of Ben-Ammi, who was Lot's son (Lot was Abraham's nephew). The Ammonites were constantly at war with Israel. The Ammonites worshiped the gods Milcom and Molek. Their king was Nahash, which means "serpent."

Then they repeated to him what the men of Jabesh had said.

⁶When Saul heard their words, the Spirit of God came powerfully upon him, and he burned with anger. ⁷He took a pair of oxen, cut them into pieces, and sent the pieces by messengers throughout Israel, proclaiming, "This is what will be done to the oxen of anyone who does not follow Saul and Samuel." Then the terror of the LORD fell on the people, and they came out together as one. ⁸When Saul mustered them at Bezek, the men of Israel numbered three hundred thousand and those of Judah thirty thousand.

⁹They told the messengers who had come, "Say to the men of Jabesh Gilead, 'By the time the sun is hot tomorrow, you will be rescued.'" When the messengers went and reported this to the men of Jabesh, they were elated. ¹⁰They said to the Ammonites, "Tomorrow we will surrender to you, and you can do to us whatever you like."

¹¹The next day Saul separated his men into three divisions; during the last watch of the night they broke into the camp of the Ammonites and slaughtered them until the heat of the day. Those who survived were scattered, so that no two of them were left together.

Saul Confirmed as King

¹²The people then said to Samuel, "Who was it that asked, 'Shall Saul reign over us?' Turn these men over to us so that we may put them to death."

¹³But Saul said, "No one will be put to death today, for this day the LORD has rescued Israel."

¹⁴Then Samuel said to the people, "Come, let us go to Gilgal and there renew the kingship." ¹⁵So all the people went to Gilgal and made Saul king in the presence of the LORD. There they sacrificed fellowship offerings before the LORD, and Saul and all the Israelites held a great celebration.

Samuel's Farewell Speech

12 Samuel said to all Israel, "I have listened to everything you said to me and have set a king over you. ²Now you have a king as your leader. As for me, I am old and gray, and my sons are here with you. I have been your leader from my youth until this day. ³Here I stand. Testify against me in the presence of the LORD and his anointed. Whose ox have I taken? Whose donkey have I taken? Whom have I cheated? Whom have I oppressed? From whose hand have I accepted a bribe to make me shut my eyes? If I have done any of these things, I will make it right."

⁴"You have not cheated or oppressed us," they replied. "You have not taken anything from anyone's hand."

⁵Samuel said to them, "The LORD is witness against you, and also his anointed is witness this day, that you have not found anything in my hand."

"He is witness," they said.

⁶Then Samuel said to the people, "It is the Lᴏʀᴅ who appointed Moses and Aaron and brought your ancestors up out of Egypt. ⁷Now then, stand here, because I am going to confront you with evidence before the Lᴏʀᴅ as to all the righteous acts performed by the Lᴏʀᴅ for you and your ancestors.

⁸"After Jacob entered Egypt, they cried to the Lᴏʀᴅ for help, and the Lᴏʀᴅ sent Moses and Aaron, who brought your ancestors out of Egypt and settled them in this place.

⁹"But they forgot the Lᴏʀᴅ their God; so he sold them into the hand of Sisera, the commander of the army of Hazor, and into the hands of the Philistines and the king of Moab, who fought against them. ¹⁰They cried out to the Lᴏʀᴅ and said, 'We have sinned; we have forsaken the Lᴏʀᴅ and served the Baals and the Ashtoreths. But now deliver us from the hands of our enemies, and we will serve you.' ¹¹Then the Lᴏʀᴅ sent Jerub-Baal,ᵃ Barak,ᵇ Jephthah and Samuel,ᶜ and he delivered you from the hands of your enemies all around you, so that you lived in safety.

¹²"But when you saw that Nahash king of the Ammonites was moving against you, you said to me, 'No, we want a king to rule over us'—even though the Lᴏʀᴅ your God was your king. ¹³Now here is the king you have chosen, the one you asked for; see, the Lᴏʀᴅ has set a king over you. ¹⁴If you fear the Lᴏʀᴅ and serve and obey him and do not rebel against his commands, and if both you and the king who reigns over you follow the Lᴏʀᴅ your God—good! ¹⁵But if you do not obey the Lᴏʀᴅ, and if you rebel against his commands, his hand will be against you, as it was against your ancestors.

¹⁶"Now then, stand still and see this great thing the Lᴏʀᴅ is about to do before your eyes! ¹⁷Is it not wheat harvest now? I will call on the Lᴏʀᴅ to send thunder and rain. And you will realize what an evil thing you did in the eyes of the Lᴏʀᴅ when you asked for a king."

¹⁸Then Samuel called on the Lᴏʀᴅ, and that same day the Lᴏʀᴅ sent thunder and rain. So all the people stood in awe of the Lᴏʀᴅ and of Samuel.

¹⁹The people all said to Samuel, "Pray to the Lᴏʀᴅ your God for your servants so that we will not die, for we have added to all our other sins the evil of asking for a king."

²⁰"Do not be afraid," Samuel replied. "You have done all this evil; yet do not turn away from the Lᴏʀᴅ, but serve the Lᴏʀᴅ with all your heart. ²¹Do not turn away after useless idols. They can do you no good, nor can they rescue you, because they are useless. ²²For the sake of his great name the Lᴏʀᴅ will not reject his people, because the Lᴏʀᴅ was pleased to make you his own. ²³As for me, far be it from me that I should sin against the Lᴏʀᴅ by failing to pray for you. And I will teach you the way that is good and right. ²⁴But be sure to fear the Lᴏʀᴅ and serve him faithfully with all your heart; consider what great things he has done for you. ²⁵Yet if you persist in doing evil, both you and your king will perish."

Samuel Rebukes Saul

13 Saul was thirtyᵈ years old when he became king, and he reigned over Israel forty-ᵉ two years.

²Saul chose three thousand men from Israel; two thousand were with him at Mikmash and in the hill country of Bethel, and a thousand were with Jonathan at Gibeah in Benjamin. The rest of the men he sent back to their homes.

³Jonathan attacked the Philistine outpost at Geba, and the Philistines heard about it. Then Saul had the trumpet blown throughout the land and said, "Let the Hebrews hear!" ⁴So all Israel heard the news: "Saul has attacked the Philistine outpost, and now Israel has become obnoxious to the Philistines." And the people were summoned to join Saul at Gilgal.

⁵The Philistines assembled to fight Israel, with three thousandᶠ chariots, six

---

ᵃ 11 Also called *Gideon*   ᵇ 11 Some Septuagint manuscripts and Syriac; Hebrew *Bedan*   ᶜ 11 Hebrew; some Septuagint manuscripts and Syriac *Samson*   ᵈ 1 A few late manuscripts of the Septuagint; Hebrew does not have *thirty*.   ᵉ 1 Probable reading of the original Hebrew text (see Acts 13:21); Masoretic Text does not have *forty-*.   ᶠ 5 Some Septuagint manuscripts and Syriac; Hebrew *thirty thousand*

THE
WITNESSES

✓ **JONATHAN** (1 SAMUEL 13:2)
He was Saul's first son. He was very good and loving, but he was also a brave warrior. Jonathan and David were inseparable friends.

thousand charioteers, and soldiers as numerous as the sand on the seashore. They went up and camped at Mikmash, east of Beth Aven. ⁶When the Israelites saw that their situation was critical and that their army was hard pressed, they hid in caves and thickets, among the rocks, and in pits and cisterns. ⁷Some Hebrews even crossed the Jordan to the land of Gad and Gilead.

Saul remained at Gilgal, and all the troops with him were quaking with fear. ⁸He waited seven days, the time set by Samuel; but Samuel did not come to Gilgal, and Saul's men began to scatter. ⁹So he said, "Bring me the burnt offering and the fellowship offerings." And Saul of-

fered up the burnt offering. ¹⁰Just as he finished making the offering, Samuel arrived, and Saul went out to greet him.

¹¹"What have you done?" asked Samuel.

Saul replied, "When I saw that the men were scattering, and that you did not come at the set time, and that the Philistines were assembling at Mikmash, ¹²I thought, 'Now the Philistines will come down against me at Gilgal, and I have not sought the LORD's favor.' So I felt compelled to offer the burnt offering."

¹³"You have done a foolish thing," Samuel said. "You have not kept the command the LORD your God gave you; if you had, he would have established your kingdom over Israel for all time. ¹⁴But now your kingdom will not endure; the LORD has sought out a man after his own heart and appointed him ruler of his people, because you have not kept the LORD's command."

¹⁵Then Samuel left Gilgal[a] and went up to Gibeah in Benjamin, and Saul counted the men who were with him. They numbered about six hundred.

Israel Without Weapons

¹⁶Saul and his son Jonathan and the men with them were staying in Gibeah[b] in Benjamin, while the Philistines camped at Mikmash. ¹⁷Raiding parties went out from the Philistine camp in three detachments. One turned toward Ophrah in the vicinity of Shual, ¹⁸another toward Beth Horon, and the third toward the borderland overlooking the Valley of Zeboyim facing the wilderness.

¹⁹Not a blacksmith could be found in the whole land of Israel, because the Philistines had said, "Otherwise the Hebrews will make swords or spears!" ²⁰So all Israel went down to the Philistines to have their plow points, mattocks, axes and sickles[c] sharpened. ²¹The price was two-thirds of a shekel[d] for sharpening

---

[a] 15 Hebrew; Septuagint *Gilgal and went his way; the rest of the people went after Saul to meet the army, and they went out of Gilgal*   [b] 16 Two Hebrew manuscripts; most Hebrew manuscripts *Geba,* a variant of *Gibeah*
[c] 20 Septuagint; Hebrew *plow points*   [d] 21 That is, about 1/4 ounce or about 8 grams

plow points and mattocks, and a third of a shekel[a] for sharpening forks and axes and for repointing goads.

²²So on the day of the battle not a soldier with Saul and Jonathan had a sword or spear in his hand; only Saul and his son Jonathan had them.

Jonathan Attacks the Philistines

14 ²³Now a detachment of Philistines had gone out to the pass at Mikmash. ¹One day Jonathan son of Saul said to his young armor-bearer, "Come, let's go over to the Philistine outpost on the other side." But he did not tell his father.

²Saul was staying on the outskirts of Gibeah under a pomegranate tree in Migron. With him were about six hundred men, ³among whom was Ahijah, who was wearing an ephod. He was a son of Ichabod's brother Ahitub son of Phinehas, the son of Eli, the LORD's priest in Shiloh. No one was aware that Jonathan had left.

⁴On each side of the pass that Jonathan intended to cross to reach the Philistine outpost was a cliff; one was called Bozez and the other Seneh. ⁵One cliff stood to the north toward Mikmash, the other to the south toward Geba.

⁶Jonathan said to his young armor-bearer, "Come, let's go over to the outpost of those uncircumcised men. Perhaps the LORD will act in our behalf. Nothing can hinder the LORD from saving, whether by many or by few."

⁷"Do all that you have in mind," his armor-bearer said. "Go ahead; I am with you heart and soul."

⁸Jonathan said, "Come on, then; we will cross over toward them and let them see us. ⁹If they say to us, 'Wait there until we come to you,' we will stay where we are and not go up to them. ¹⁰But if they say, 'Come up to us,' we will climb up, because that will be our sign that the LORD has given them into our hands."

¹¹So both of them showed themselves to the Philistine outpost. "Look!" said the Philistines. "The Hebrews are crawling out of the holes they were hiding in." ¹²The men of the outpost shouted to Jon-

BREAK THROUGH!

Why did God always get the Israelites into wars?

(1 SAMUEL 14)

Sometimes the Israelites obeyed God and sometimes they disobeyed him. The wars they had with other nations often happened when they disobeyed God. Then, when they felt threatened, they had to pray and ask God to help them. But sometimes God let them have wars so they could take over their enemies' lands.

athan and his armor-bearer, "Come up to us and we'll teach you a lesson."

So Jonathan said to his armor-bearer, "Climb up after me; the LORD has given them into the hand of Israel."

¹³Jonathan climbed up, using his hands and feet, with his armor-bearer right behind him. The Philistines fell before Jonathan, and his armor-bearer followed and killed behind him. ¹⁴In that first attack Jonathan and his armor-bearer killed some twenty men in an area of about half an acre.

Israel Routs the Philistines

¹⁵Then panic struck the whole army—those in the camp and field, and those in the outposts and raiding parties—and

---

ᵃ 21 That is, about 1/8 ounce or about 4 grams

the ground shook. It was a panic sent by God.[a]

[16] Saul's lookouts at Gibeah in Benjamin saw the army melting away in all directions. [17] Then Saul said to the men who were with him, "Muster the forces and see who has left us." When they did, it was Jonathan and his armor-bearer who were not there. [18] Saul said to Ahijah, "Bring the ark of God." (At that time it was with the Israelites.)[b] [19] While Saul was talking to the priest, the tumult in the Philistine camp increased more and more. So Saul said to the priest, "Withdraw your hand."

[20] Then Saul and all his men assembled and went to the battle. They found the Philistines in total confusion, striking each other with their swords. [21] Those Hebrews who had previously been with the Philistines and had gone up with them to their camp went over to the Israelites who were with Saul and Jonathan. [22] When all the Israelites who had hidden in the hill country of Ephraim heard that the Philistines were on the run, they joined the battle in hot pursuit. [23] So on that day the LORD saved Israel, and the battle moved on beyond Beth Aven.

Jonathan Eats Honey

[24] Now the Israelites were in distress that day, because Saul had bound the people under an oath, saying, "Cursed be anyone who eats food before evening comes, before I have avenged myself on my enemies!" So none of the troops tasted food.

[25] The entire army entered the woods, and there was honey on the ground. [26] When they went into the woods, they saw the honey oozing out; yet no one put his hand to his mouth, because they feared the oath. [27] But Jonathan had not heard that his father had bound the people with the oath, so he reached out the end of the staff that was in his hand and dipped it into the honeycomb. He raised his hand to his mouth, and his eyes brightened.[c] [28] Then one of the soldiers told him, "Your father bound the army under a strict oath, saying, 'Cursed be anyone who eats food today!' That is why the men are faint."

[29] Jonathan said, "My father has made trouble for the country. See how my eyes brightened when I tasted a little of this honey. [30] How much better it would have been if the men had eaten today some of the plunder they took from their enemies. Would not the slaughter of the Philistines have been even greater?"

[31] That day, after the Israelites had struck down the Philistines from Mikmash to Aijalon, they were exhausted. [32] They pounced on the plunder and, taking sheep, cattle and calves, they butchered them on the ground and ate them, together with the blood. [33] Then someone said to Saul, "Look, the men are sinning against the LORD by eating meat that has blood in it."

"You have broken faith," he said. "Roll a large stone over here at once." [34] Then he said, "Go out among the men and tell them, 'Each of you bring me your cattle and sheep, and slaughter them here and eat them. Do not sin against the LORD by eating meat with blood still in it.' "

So everyone brought his ox that night and slaughtered it there. [35] Then Saul built an altar to the LORD; it was the first time he had done this.

[36] Saul said, "Let us go down and pursue the Philistines by night and plunder them till dawn, and let us not leave one of them alive."

"Do whatever seems best to you," they replied.

But the priest said, "Let us inquire of God here."

[37] So Saul asked God, "Shall I go down and pursue the Philistines? Will you give them into Israel's hand?" But God did not answer him that day.

[38] Saul therefore said, "Come here, all you who are leaders of the army, and let us find out what sin has been committed today. [39] As surely as the LORD who rescues Israel lives, even if the guilt lies with my son Jonathan, he must die." But not one of them said a word.

[40] Saul then said to all the Israelites, "You stand over there; I and Jonathan my son will stand over here."

---

[a] 15 Or a terrible panic   [b] 18 Hebrew; Septuagint "Bring the ephod." (At that time he wore the ephod before the Israelites.)   [c] 27 Or his strength was renewed; similarly in verse 29

"Do what seems best to you," they replied.

⁴¹Then Saul prayed to the LORD, the God of Israel, "Why have you not answered your servant today? If the fault is in me or my son Jonathan, respond with Urim, but if the men of Israel are at fault,ᵃ respond with Thummim." Jonathan and Saul were taken by lot, and the men were cleared. ⁴²Saul said, "Cast the lot between me and Jonathan my son." And Jonathan was taken.

⁴³Then Saul said to Jonathan, "Tell me what you have done."

So Jonathan told him, "I tasted a little honey with the end of my staff. And now I must die!"

⁴⁴Saul said, "May God deal with me, be it ever so severely, if you do not die, Jonathan."

⁴⁵But the men said to Saul, "Should Jonathan die—he who has brought about this great deliverance in Israel? Never! As surely as the LORD lives, not a hair of his head will fall to the ground, for he did this today with God's help." So the men rescued Jonathan, and he was not put to death.

⁴⁶Then Saul stopped pursuing the Philistines, and they withdrew to their own land.

⁴⁷After Saul had assumed rule over Israel, he fought against their enemies on every side: Moab, the Ammonites, Edom, the kingsᵇ of Zobah, and the Philistines. Wherever he turned, he inflicted punishment on them.ᶜ ⁴⁸He fought valiantly and defeated the Amalekites, delivering Israel from the hands of those who had plundered them.

Saul's Family

⁴⁹Saul's sons were Jonathan, Ishvi and Malki-Shua. The name of his older daughter was Merab, and that of the younger was Michal. ⁵⁰His wife's name was Ahinoam daughter of Ahimaaz. The name of the commander of Saul's army was Abner son of Ner, and Ner was Saul's uncle. ⁵¹Saul's father Kish and Abner's father Ner were sons of Abiel.

⁵²All the days of Saul there was bitter war with the Philistines, and whenever Saul saw a mighty or brave man, he took him into his service.

The LORD Rejects Saul as King

15 Samuel said to Saul, "I am the one the LORD sent to anoint you king over his people Israel; so listen now to the message from the LORD. ²This is what the LORD Almighty says: 'I will punish the Amalekites for what they did to Israel when they waylaid them as they came up from Egypt. ³Now go, attack the Amalekites and totally destroyᵈ all that belongs to them. Do not spare them; put to death men and women, children and infants, cattle and sheep, camels and donkeys.' "

⁴So Saul summoned the men and mustered them at Telaim—two hundred thousand foot soldiers and ten thousand from

ᵃ 41 Septuagint; Hebrew does not have "Why . . . at fault.
ᵇ 47 Masoretic Text; Dead Sea Scrolls and Septuagint king
ᶜ 47 Hebrew; Septuagint he was victorious   ᵈ 3 The Hebrew term refers to the irrevocable giving over of things or persons to the LORD, often by totally destroying them; also in verses 8, 9, 15, 18, 20 and 21.

BREAKTHROUGH!

Amalekites

(1 SAMUEL 15:2)

These people were nomads from Negev in ancient times. (A nomad is a person who doesn't settle down in just one place and moves around from one place to another.) They were warriors and almost always allies of the Canaanites and Moabites in their wars against Israel. Not fair!

BREAK THROUGH!

Why did they have to kill even the children?

(1 SAMUEL 15:2 - 3)

How terrible! They killed everybody! Everybody! God had told the Israelites to destroy everything so nothing would be left that had been contaminated by the statues the people living there believed were gods. In Hebrew, that was called *jerem*, which meant "curse." The real enemies of the Israelites were other nations, but the statues of their gods were also considered enemies. God wanted to be their only God, so nothing of the others that were thought to be gods or what they worshiped could be left.

Judah. ⁵Saul went to the city of Amalek and set an ambush in the ravine. ⁶Then he said to the Kenites, "Go away, leave the Amalekites so that I do not destroy you along with them; for you showed kindness to all the Israelites when they came up out of Egypt." So the Kenites moved away from the Amalekites.

⁷Then Saul attacked the Amalekites all the way from Havilah to Shur, near the eastern border of Egypt. ⁸He took Agag king of the Amalekites alive, and all his people he totally destroyed with the sword. ⁹But Saul and the army spared Agag and the best of the sheep and cat-

tle, the fat calves^a and lambs — everything that was good. These they were unwilling to destroy completely, but everything that was despised and weak they totally destroyed.

¹⁰Then the word of the LORD came to Samuel: ¹¹"I regret that I have made Saul king, because he has turned away from me and has not carried out my instructions." Samuel was angry, and he cried out to the LORD all that night.

¹²Early in the morning Samuel got up and went to meet Saul, but he was told, "Saul has gone to Carmel. There he has set up a monument in his own honor and has turned and gone on down to Gilgal."

¹³When Samuel reached him, Saul said, "The LORD bless you! I have carried out the LORD's instructions."

¹⁴But Samuel said, "What then is this bleating of sheep in my ears? What is this lowing of cattle that I hear?"

¹⁵Saul answered, "The soldiers brought them from the Amalekites; they spared

---

^a 9 Or *the grown bulls*; the meaning of the Hebrew for this phrase is uncertain.

BREAK THROUGH!

Kenites

(1 SAMUEL 15:6)

They were descendants of Moses' father-in-law. They were friends of Israel, and they joined the tribe of Judah.

the best of the sheep and cattle to sacrifice to the Lord your God, but we totally destroyed the rest."

[16] "Enough!" Samuel said to Saul. "Let me tell you what the Lord said to me last night."

"Tell me," Saul replied.

[17] Samuel said, "Although you were once small in your own eyes, did you not become the head of the tribes of Israel? The Lord anointed you king over Israel. [18] And he sent you on a mission, saying, 'Go and completely destroy those wicked people, the Amalekites; wage war against them until you have wiped them out.' [19] Why did you not obey the Lord? Why did you pounce on the plunder and do evil in the eyes of the Lord?"

[20] "But I did obey the Lord," Saul said. "I went on the mission the Lord assigned me. I completely destroyed the Amalekites and brought back Agag their king. [21] The soldiers took sheep and cattle from the plunder, the best of what was devoted to God, in order to sacrifice them to the Lord your God at Gilgal."

[22] But Samuel replied:

"Does the Lord delight in burnt
        offerings and sacrifices
    as much as in obeying the Lord?
To obey is better than sacrifice,
    and to heed is better than the fat of
        rams.
[23] For rebellion is like the sin of divination,
    and arrogance like the evil of
        idolatry.
Because you have rejected the word
        of the Lord,
    he has rejected you as king."

[24] Then Saul said to Samuel, "I have sinned. I violated the Lord's command and your instructions. I was afraid of the men and so I gave in to them. [25] Now I beg you, forgive my sin and come back with me, so that I may worship the Lord."

[26] But Samuel said to him, "I will not go back with you. You have rejected the word of the Lord, and the Lord has rejected you as king over Israel!"

[27] As Samuel turned to leave, Saul caught hold of the hem of his robe, and it tore. [28] Samuel said to him, "The Lord

has torn the kingdom of Israel from you today and has given it to one of your neighbors—to one better than you. [29] He who is the Glory of Israel does not lie or change his mind; for he is not a human being, that he should change his mind."

[30] Saul replied, "I have sinned. But please honor me before the elders of my people and before Israel; come back with me, so that I may worship the Lord your God." [31] So Samuel went back with Saul, and Saul worshiped the Lord.

[32] Then Samuel said, "Bring me Agag king of the Amalekites."

Agag came to him in chains.[a] And he thought, "Surely the bitterness of death is past."

[33] But Samuel said,

"As your sword has made women
        childless,
    so will your mother be childless
        among women."

And Samuel put Agag to death before the Lord at Gilgal.

[34] Then Samuel left for Ramah, but Saul went up to his home in Gibeah of Saul. [35] Until the day Samuel died, he did not go to see Saul again, though Samuel mourned for him. And the Lord regretted that he had made Saul king over Israel.

Samuel Anoints David

16 The Lord said to Samuel, "How long will you mourn for Saul, since I have rejected him as king over Israel? Fill your horn with oil and be on your way; I am sending you to Jesse of Bethlehem. I have chosen one of his sons to be king."

[2] But Samuel said, "How can I go? If Saul hears about it, he will kill me."

The Lord said, "Take a heifer with you and say, 'I have come to sacrifice to the Lord.' [3] Invite Jesse to the sacrifice, and I will show you what to do. You are to anoint for me the one I indicate."

[4] Samuel did what the Lord said. When he arrived at Bethlehem, the elders of the town trembled when they met him. They asked, "Do you come in peace?"

---

[a] 32 The meaning of the Hebrew for this phrase is uncertain.

said to him, "The LORD has not chosen these." ¹¹So he asked Jesse, "Are these all the sons you have?"

"There is still the youngest," Jesse answered. "He is tending the sheep."

Samuel said, "Send for him; we will not sit down until he arrives."

¹²So he sent for him and had him brought in. He was glowing with health and had a fine appearance and handsome features.

Then the LORD said, "Rise and anoint him; this is the one."

¹³So Samuel took the horn of oil and anointed him in the presence of his brothers, and from that day on the Spirit of the LORD came powerfully upon David. Samuel then went to Ramah.

BREAK THROUGH!

Why did Samuel kill Agag?
(1 SAMUEL 15:33)

He applied the "eye for an eye" rule to Agag. That means that when someone does something bad to a person, as punishment the same kind of thing is done to them. Since Agag had left so many mothers without their children, Samuel killed him the way that Agag had killed others.

⁵Samuel replied, "Yes, in peace; I have come to sacrifice to the LORD. Consecrate yourselves and come to the sacrifice with me." Then he consecrated Jesse and his sons and invited them to the sacrifice.

⁶When they arrived, Samuel saw Eliab and thought, "Surely the LORD's anointed stands here before the LORD."

⁷But the LORD said to Samuel, "Do not consider his appearance or his height, for I have rejected him. The LORD does not look at the things people look at. People look at the outward appearance, but the LORD looks at the heart."

⁸Then Jesse called Abinadab and had him pass in front of Samuel. But Samuel said, "The LORD has not chosen this one either." ⁹Jesse then had Shammah pass by, but Samuel said, "Nor has the LORD chosen this one." ¹⁰Jesse had seven of his sons pass before Samuel, but Samuel

THE SCENE

BETHLEHEM

(1 SAMUEL 16:4)

This means "house of bread." It was a city in the territory of Judah. It was 5 miles (8 km) southwest of Jerusalem, near the road that connects that city with Hebron. At first, it was called Ephrath. David lived in this city, but Bethlehem is most famous because Jesus was born there.

David in Saul's Service

¹⁴Now the Spirit of the Lᴏʀᴅ had departed from Saul, and an evilᵃ spirit from the Lᴏʀᴅ tormented him.

¹⁵Saul's attendants said to him, "See, an evil spirit from God is tormenting you. ¹⁶Let our lord command his servants here to search for someone who can play the lyre. He will play when the evil spirit from God comes on you, and you will feel better."

¹⁷So Saul said to his attendants, "Find someone who plays well and bring him to me."

¹⁸One of the servants answered, "I have seen a son of Jesse of Bethlehem who knows how to play the lyre. He is a brave man and a warrior. He speaks well and is a fine-looking man. And the Lᴏʀᴅ is with him."

¹⁹Then Saul sent messengers to Jesse and said, "Send me your son David, who is with the sheep." ²⁰So Jesse took a donkey loaded with bread, a skin of wine and a young goat and sent them with his son David to Saul.

²¹David came to Saul and entered his service. Saul liked him very much, and David became one of his armor-bearers. ²²Then Saul sent word to Jesse, saying, "Allow David to remain in my service, for I am pleased with him."

²³Whenever the spirit from God came on Saul, David would take up his lyre and play. Then relief would come to Saul; he would feel better, and the evil spirit would leave him.

THE WITNESSES

✓ **JESSE** (1 SAMUEL 16:1)
His name means "It's over there." He was King David's father. He lived in Bethlehem. He had sheep, and David took care of them.

✓ **DAVID** (1 SAMUEL 16:13)
This name probably means "beloved" or "loved." He was the second king of Israel, and he ruled after Saul. Before he became king, he was a sheepherder for his father. He was very strong and brave. He wasn't afraid of the giant Goliath, so he defeated him. He was also a good musician and a poet. Many of the songs in the book called Psalms were written by David.

David and Goliath

17 Now the Philistines gathered their forces for war and assembled at Sokoh in Judah. They pitched camp at Ephes Dammim, between Sokoh and Azekah. ²Saul and the Israelites assembled and camped in the Valley of Elah and drew up their battle line to meet the Philistines. ³The Philistines occupied one hill and the Israelites another, with the valley between them.

⁴A champion named Goliath, who was from Gath, came out of the Philistine camp. His height was six cubits and a span.ᵇ ⁵He had a bronze helmet on his head and wore a coat of scale armor of bronze weighing five thousand shekelsᶜ; ⁶on his legs he wore bronze greaves, and a bronze javelin was slung on his back.

ᵃ 14 Or *and a harmful*; similarly in verses 15, 16 and 23
ᵇ 4 That is, about 9 feet 9 inches or about 3 meters
ᶜ 5 That is, about 125 pounds or about 58 kilograms

CHECK THE FACTS

What nation did the giant Goliath belong to?

A) The Ammonites

B) The Philistines

C) The North Americans

CORRECT ANSWER: B

---

the war: The firstborn was Eliab; the second, Abinadab; and the third, Shammah. [14]David was the youngest. The three oldest followed Saul, [15]but David went back and forth from Saul to tend his father's sheep at Bethlehem.

[16]For forty days the Philistine came forward every morning and evening and took his stand.

[17]Now Jesse said to his son David, "Take this ephah[b] of roasted grain and these ten loaves of bread for your brothers and hurry to their camp. [18]Take along

---

[a] 7 That is, about 15 pounds or about 6.9 kilograms
[b] 17 That is, probably about 36 pounds or about 16 kilograms

---

[7]His spear shaft was like a weaver's rod, and its iron point weighed six hundred shekels.[a] His shield bearer went ahead of him.

[8]Goliath stood and shouted to the ranks of Israel, "Why do you come out and line up for battle? Am I not a Philistine, and are you not the servants of Saul? Choose a man and have him come down to me. [9]If he is able to fight and kill me, we will become your subjects; but if I overcome him and kill him, you will become our subjects and serve us." [10]Then the Philistine said, "This day I defy the armies of Israel! Give me a man and let us fight each other." [11]On hearing the Philistine's words, Saul and all the Israelites were dismayed and terrified.

[12]Now David was the son of an Ephrathite named Jesse, who was from Bethlehem in Judah. Jesse had eight sons, and in Saul's time he was very old. [13]Jesse's three oldest sons had followed Saul to

THE WITNESSES

✓ **GOLIATH** (1 SAMUEL 17:4–7)
Some people think that this name means "exile" (to send out of the country). He was a Philistine warrior. Since he was super tall, everybody was afraid of him — everybody except David.

these ten cheeses to the commander of their unit. See how your brothers are and bring back some assurance[a] from them. 19They are with Saul and all the men of Israel in the Valley of Elah, fighting against the Philistines."

20Early in the morning David left the flock in the care of a shepherd, loaded up and set out, as Jesse had directed. He reached the camp as the army was going out to its battle positions, shouting the war cry. 21Israel and the Philistines were drawing up their lines facing each other. 22David left his things with the keeper of supplies, ran to the battle lines and asked his brothers how they were. 23As he was talking with them, Goliath, the Philistine champion from Gath, stepped out from his lines and shouted his usual defiance, and David heard it. 24Whenever the Israelites saw the man, they all fled from him in great fear.

25Now the Israelites had been saying, "Do you see how this man keeps coming out? He comes out to defy Israel. The king will give great wealth to the man who kills him. He will also give him his daughter in marriage and will exempt his family from taxes in Israel."

26David asked the men standing near him, "What will be done for the man who kills this Philistine and removes this disgrace from Israel? Who is this uncircumcised Philistine that he should defy the armies of the living God?"

27They repeated to him what they had been saying and told him, "This is what will be done for the man who kills him."

28When Eliab, David's oldest brother, heard him speaking with the men, he burned with anger at him and asked, "Why have you come down here? And with whom did you leave those few sheep in the wilderness? I know how conceited you are and how wicked your heart is; you came down only to watch the battle."

29"Now what have I done?" said David. "Can't I even speak?" 30He then turned away to someone else and brought up the same matter, and the men answered him as before. 31What David said was overheard and reported to Saul, and Saul sent for him.

32David said to Saul, "Let no one lose heart on account of this Philistine; your servant will go and fight him."

33Saul replied, "You are not able to go out against this Philistine and fight him; you are only a young man, and he has been a warrior from his youth."

34But David said to Saul, "Your servant has been keeping his father's sheep. When a lion or a bear came and carried off a sheep from the flock, 35I went after it, struck it and rescued the sheep from its mouth. When it turned on me, I seized it by its hair, struck it and killed it. 36Your servant has killed both the lion and the bear; this uncircumcised Philistine will be like one of them, because he has defied the armies of the living God. 37The Lord who rescued me from the paw of the lion and the paw of the bear will rescue me from the hand of this Philistine."

Saul said to David, "Go, and the Lord be with you."

38Then Saul dressed David in his own tunic. He put a coat of armor on him and a bronze helmet on his head. 39David fastened on his sword over the tunic and tried walking around, because he was not used to them.

"I cannot go in these," he said to Saul, "because I am not used to them." So he took them off. 40Then he took his staff in his hand, chose five smooth stones from the stream, put them in the pouch of his shepherd's bag and, with his sling in his hand, approached the Philistine.

41Meanwhile, the Philistine, with his shield bearer in front of him, kept coming closer to David. 42He looked David over and saw that he was little more than a boy, glowing with health and handsome, and he despised him. 43He said to David, "Am I a dog, that you come at me with sticks?" And the Philistine cursed David by his gods. 44"Come here," he said, "and I'll give your flesh to the birds and the wild animals!"

45David said to the Philistine, "You come against me with sword and spear and javelin, but I come against you in the name of the Lord Almighty, the God of the armies of Israel, whom you have defied. ⁴⁶This day the LORD will deliver you into my hands, and I'll strike you down and cut off your head. This very day I will give the carcasses of the Philistine army to the birds and the wild animals, and the whole world will know that there is a God in Israel. ⁴⁷All those gathered here will know that it is not by sword or spear that the LORD saves; for the battle is the LORD's, and he will give all of you into our hands."

⁴⁸As the Philistine moved closer to attack him, David ran quickly toward the battle line to meet him. ⁴⁹Reaching into his bag and taking out a stone, he slung it and struck the Philistine on the forehead. The stone sank into his forehead, and he fell facedown on the ground.

⁵⁰So David triumphed over the Philistine with a sling and a stone; without a sword in his hand he struck down the Philistine and killed him.

⁵¹David ran and stood over him. He took hold of the Philistine's sword and drew it from the sheath. After he killed him, he cut off his head with the sword.

When the Philistines saw that their hero was dead, they turned and ran. ⁵²Then the men of Israel and Judah surged forward with a shout and pursued the Philistines to the entrance of Gath[a] and to the gates of Ekron. Their dead were strewn along the Shaaraim road to Gath and Ekron. ⁵³When the Israelites returned from chasing the Philistines, they plundered their camp.

⁵⁴David took the Philistine's head and brought it to Jerusalem; he put the Philistine's weapons in his own tent.

⁵⁵As Saul watched David going out to meet the Philistine, he said to Abner, commander of the army, "Abner, whose son is that young man?"

Abner replied, "As surely as you live, Your Majesty, I don't know."

⁵⁶The king said, "Find out whose son this young man is."

⁵⁷As soon as David returned from killing the Philistine, Abner took him and brought him before Saul, with David still holding the Philistine's head.

⁵⁸"Whose son are you, young man?" Saul asked him.

David said, "I am the son of your servant Jesse of Bethlehem."

Saul's Growing Fear of David

18 After David had finished talking with Saul, Jonathan became one in spirit with David, and he loved him as himself. ²From that day Saul kept David with him and did not let him return home to his family. ³And Jonathan made a covenant with David because he loved him as himself. ⁴Jonathan took off the robe he was wearing and gave it to David, along with his tunic, and even his sword, his bow and his belt.

⁵Whatever mission Saul sent him on, David was so successful that Saul gave him a high rank in the army. This pleased all the troops, and Saul's officers as well.

⁶When the men were returning home after David had killed the Philistine, the women came out from all the towns of Israel to meet King Saul with singing and dancing, with joyful songs and with timbrels and lyres. ⁷As they danced, they sang:

"Saul has slain his thousands,
    and David his tens of thousands."

⁸Saul was very angry; this refrain displeased him greatly. "They have credited David with tens of thousands," he thought, "but me with only thousands. What more can he get but the kingdom?" ⁹And from that time on Saul kept a close eye on David.

¹⁰The next day an evil[b] spirit from God came forcefully on Saul. He was prophesying in his house, while David was playing the lyre, as he usually did. Saul had a spear in his hand ¹¹and he hurled it, saying to himself, "I'll pin David to the wall." But David eluded him twice.

¹²Saul was afraid of David, because the LORD was with David but had departed from Saul. ¹³So he sent David away from him and gave him command over a thousand men, and David led the troops in their campaigns. ¹⁴In everything he did he had great success, because the LORD was

---

[a] 52 Some Septuagint manuscripts; Hebrew *of a valley*
[b] 10 Or *a harmful*

with him. ¹⁵When Saul saw how successful he was, he was afraid of him. ¹⁶But all Israel and Judah loved David, because he led them in their campaigns.

¹⁷Saul said to David, "Here is my older daughter Merab. I will give her to you in marriage; only serve me bravely and fight the battles of the LORD." For Saul said to himself, "I will not raise a hand against him. Let the Philistines do that!"

¹⁸But David said to Saul, "Who am I, and what is my family or my clan in Israel, that I should become the king's son-in-law?" ¹⁹So*a* when the time came for Merab, Saul's daughter, to be given to David, she was given in marriage to Adriel of Meholah.

²⁰Now Saul's daughter Michal was in love with David, and when they told Saul about it, he was pleased. ²¹"I will give her to him," he thought, "so that she may be a snare to him and so that the hand of the Philistines may be against him." So Saul said to David, "Now you have a second opportunity to become my son-in-law."

²²Then Saul ordered his attendants: "Speak to David privately and say, 'Look, the king likes you, and his attendants all love you; now become his son-in-law.' "

²³They repeated these words to David. But David said, "Do you think it is a small matter to become the king's son-in-law? I'm only a poor man and little known."

²⁴When Saul's servants told him what David had said, ²⁵Saul replied, "Say to David, 'The king wants no other price for the bride than a hundred Philistine foreskins, to take revenge on his enemies.' " Saul's plan was to have David fall by the hands of the Philistines.

²⁶When the attendants told David these things, he was pleased to become the king's son-in-law. So before the allotted time elapsed, ²⁷David took his men with him and went out and killed two hundred Philistines and brought back their foreskins. They counted out the full number to the king so that David might become the king's son-in-law. Then Saul gave him his daughter Michal in marriage.

²⁸When Saul realized that the LORD was with David and that his daughter Michal loved David, ²⁹Saul became still more afraid of him, and he remained his enemy the rest of his days.

³⁰The Philistine commanders continued to go out to battle, and as often as they did, David met with more success than the rest of Saul's officers, and his name became well known.

Saul Tries to Kill David

19 Saul told his son Jonathan and all the attendants to kill David. But Jonathan had taken a great liking to David ²and warned him, "My father Saul is looking for a chance to kill you. Be on your guard tomorrow morning; go into hiding and stay there. ³I will go out and stand with my father in the field where you are. I'll speak to him about you and will tell you what I find out."

⁴Jonathan spoke well of David to Saul his father and said to him, "Let not the king do wrong to his servant David; he has not wronged you, and what he has done has benefited you greatly. ⁵He took his life in his hands when he killed the Philistine. The LORD won a great victory for all Israel, and you saw it and were glad. Why then would you do wrong to an innocent man like David by killing him for no reason?"

⁶Saul listened to Jonathan and took this oath: "As surely as the LORD lives, David will not be put to death."

⁷So Jonathan called David and told him the whole conversation. He brought him to Saul, and David was with Saul as before.

⁸Once more war broke out, and David went out and fought the Philistines. He struck them with such force that they fled before him.

⁹But an evil*b* spirit from the LORD came on Saul as he was sitting in his house with his spear in his hand. While David was playing the lyre, ¹⁰Saul tried to pin him to the wall with his spear, but David eluded him as Saul drove the spear into the wall. That night David made good his escape.

¹¹Saul sent men to David's house to watch it and to kill him in the morning. But Michal, David's wife, warned him, "If

a 19 Or However,   *b 9 Or But a harmful*

you don't run for your life tonight, tomorrow you'll be killed." ¹²So Michal let David down through a window, and he fled and escaped. ¹³Then Michal took an idol and laid it on the bed, covering it with a garment and putting some goats' hair at the head.

¹⁴When Saul sent the men to capture David, Michal said, "He is ill."

¹⁵Then Saul sent the men back to see David and told them, "Bring him up to me in his bed so that I may kill him." ¹⁶But when the men entered, there was the idol in the bed, and at the head was some goats' hair.

¹⁷Saul said to Michal, "Why did you deceive me like this and send my enemy away so that he escaped?"

Michal told him, "He said to me, 'Let me get away. Why should I kill you?'"

¹⁸When David had fled and made his escape, he went to Samuel at Ramah and told him all that Saul had done to him. Then he and Samuel went to Naioth and stayed there. ¹⁹Word came to Saul: "David is in Naioth at Ramah"; ²⁰so he sent men to capture him. But when they saw a group of prophets prophesying, with Samuel standing there as their leader, the Spirit of God came on Saul's men, and they also prophesied. ²¹Saul was told about it, and he sent more men, and they prophesied too. Saul sent men a third time, and they also prophesied. ²²Finally, he himself left for Ramah and went to the great cistern at Seku. And he asked, "Where are Samuel and David?"

"Over in Naioth at Ramah," they said.

²³So Saul went to Naioth at Ramah. But the Spirit of God came even on him, and he walked along prophesying until he came to Naioth. ²⁴He stripped off his garments, and he too prophesied in Samuel's presence. He lay naked all that day and all that night. This is why people say, "Is Saul also among the prophets?"

David and Jonathan

20 Then David fled from Naioth at Ramah and went to Jonathan and asked, "What have I done? What is my crime? How have I wronged your father, that he is trying to kill me?"

²"Never!" Jonathan replied. "You are not going to die! Look, my father doesn't do anything, great or small, without letting me know. Why would he hide this from me? It isn't so!"

³But David took an oath and said, "Your father knows very well that I have found favor in your eyes, and he has said to himself, 'Jonathan must not know this or he will be grieved.' Yet as surely as the LORD lives and as you live, there is only a step between me and death."

⁴Jonathan said to David, "Whatever you want me to do, I'll do for you."

⁵So David said, "Look, tomorrow is the New Moon feast, and I am supposed to dine with the king; but let me go and hide in the field until the evening of the day after tomorrow. ⁶If your father misses me at all, tell him, 'David earnestly asked my permission to hurry to Bethlehem, his hometown, because an annual sacrifice is being made there for his whole clan.' ⁷If he says, 'Very well,' then your servant is safe. But if he loses his temper, you can

BREAKTHROUGH!

New Moon feast
(1 SAMUEL 20:5)

During this feast that was celebrated the first day of every month, they offered special sacrifices to God. They also prepared a special sacred meal.

be sure that he is determined to harm me. ⁸As for you, show kindness to your servant, for you have brought him into a covenant with you before the LORD. If I am guilty, then kill me yourself! Why hand me over to your father?"

⁹"Never!" Jonathan said. "If I had the least inkling that my father was determined to harm you, wouldn't I tell you?"

¹⁰David asked, "Who will tell me if your father answers you harshly?"

¹¹"Come," Jonathan said, "let's go out into the field." So they went there together.

¹²Then Jonathan said to David, "I swear by the LORD, the God of Israel, that I will surely sound out my father by this time the day after tomorrow! If he is favorably disposed toward you, will I not send you word and let you know? ¹³But if my father intends to harm you, may the LORD deal with Jonathan, be it ever so severely, if I do not let you know and send you away in peace. May the LORD be with you as he has been with my father. ¹⁴But show me unfailing kindness like the LORD's kindness as long as I live, so that I may not be killed, ¹⁵and do not ever cut off your kindness from my family—not even when the LORD has cut off every one of David's enemies from the face of the earth."

¹⁶So Jonathan made a covenant with the house of David, saying, "May the LORD call David's enemies to account." ¹⁷And Jonathan had David reaffirm his oath out of love for him, because he loved him as he loved himself.

¹⁸Then Jonathan said to David, "Tomorrow is the New Moon feast. You will be missed, because your seat will be empty. ¹⁹The day after tomorrow, toward evening, go to the place where you hid when this trouble began, and wait by the stone Ezel. ²⁰I will shoot three arrows to the side of it, as though I were shooting at a target. ²¹Then I will send a boy and say, 'Go, find the arrows.' If I say to him, 'Look, the arrows are on this side of you; bring them here,' then come, because, as surely as the LORD lives, you are safe; there is no danger. ²²But if I say to the boy, 'Look, the arrows are beyond you,' then you must go, because the LORD has sent you away.

²³And about the matter you and I discussed—remember, the LORD is witness between you and me forever."

²⁴So David hid in the field, and when the New Moon feast came, the king sat down to eat. ²⁵He sat in his customary place by the wall, opposite Jonathan,[a] and Abner sat next to Saul, but David's place was empty. ²⁶Saul said nothing that day, for he thought, "Something must have happened to David to make him ceremonially unclean—surely he is unclean." ²⁷But the next day, the second day of the month, David's place was empty again. Then Saul said to his son Jonathan, "Why hasn't the son of Jesse come to the meal, either yesterday or today?"

²⁸Jonathan answered, "David earnestly asked me for permission to go to Bethlehem. ²⁹He said, 'Let me go, because our family is observing a sacrifice in the town and my brother has ordered me to be there. If I have found favor in your eyes, let me get away to see my brothers.' That is why he has not come to the king's table."

³⁰Saul's anger flared up at Jonathan and he said to him, "You son of a perverse and rebellious woman! Don't I know that you have sided with the son of Jesse to your own shame and to the shame of the mother who bore you? ³¹As long as the son of Jesse lives on this earth, neither you nor your kingdom will be established. Now send someone to bring him to me, for he must die!"

³²"Why should he be put to death? What has he done?" Jonathan asked his father. ³³But Saul hurled his spear at him to kill him. Then Jonathan knew that his father intended to kill David.

³⁴Jonathan got up from the table in fierce anger; on that second day of the feast he did not eat, because he was grieved at his father's shameful treatment of David.

³⁵In the morning Jonathan went out to the field for his meeting with David. He had a small boy with him, ³⁶and he said to the boy, "Run and find the arrows I shoot." As the boy ran, he shot an arrow beyond him. ³⁷When the boy came to the place where Jonathan's arrow had fallen, Jonathan called out after him, "Isn't the

---

a 25 Septuagint; Hebrew *wall. Jonathan arose*

arrow beyond you?" ³⁸Then he shouted, "Hurry! Go quickly! Don't stop!" The boy picked up the arrow and returned to his master. ³⁹(The boy knew nothing about all this; only Jonathan and David knew.) ⁴⁰Then Jonathan gave his weapons to the boy and said, "Go, carry them back to town."

⁴¹After the boy had gone, David got up from the south side of the stone and bowed down before Jonathan three times, with his face to the ground. Then they kissed each other and wept together — but David wept the most.

⁴²Jonathan said to David, "Go in peace, for we have sworn friendship with each other in the name of the LORD, saying, 'The LORD is witness between you and me, and between your descendants and my descendants forever.' " Then David left, and Jonathan went back to the town.ᵃ

David at Nob

21 ᵇ David went to Nob, to Ahimelek the priest. Ahimelek trembled when he met him, and asked, "Why are you alone? Why is no one with you?"

²David answered Ahimelek the priest, "The king sent me on a mission and said to me, 'No one is to know anything about the mission I am sending you on.' As for my men, I have told them to meet me at a certain place. ³Now then, what do you have on hand? Give me five loaves of bread, or whatever you can find."

⁴But the priest answered David, "I don't have any ordinary bread on hand; however, there is some consecrated bread here — provided the men have kept themselves from women."

⁵David replied, "Indeed women have been kept from us, as usual wheneverᶜ I set out. The men's bodies are holy even on missions that are not holy. How much more so today!" ⁶So the priest gave him the consecrated bread, since there was no bread there except the bread of the Presence that had been removed from before the LORD and replaced by hot bread on the day it was taken away.

⁷Now one of Saul's servants was there that day, detained before the LORD; he was Doeg the Edomite, Saul's chief shepherd.

⁸David asked Ahimelek, "Don't you have a spear or a sword here? I haven't brought my sword or any other weapon, because the king's mission was urgent."

⁹The priest replied, "The sword of Goliath the Philistine, whom you killed in the Valley of Elah, is here; it is wrapped in a cloth behind the ephod. If you want it, take it; there is no sword here but that one."

David said, "There is none like it; give it to me."

ᵃ 42 In Hebrew texts this sentence (20:42b) is numbered 21:1.   ᵇ In Hebrew texts 21:1-15 is numbered 21:2-16.   ᶜ 5 Or *from us in the past few days since*

THE WITNESSES

✓ **PRIEST AHIMELEK** (1 SAMUEL 21:1)
His name means "brother of the king." He was the priest of Nob who gave David the bread that was used as an offering to God, and he also gave him Goliath's sword — all when David was running from Saul. That's why Saul sent men to kill Ahimelek and the 85 priests of Nob.

David at Gath

[10] That day David fled from Saul and went to Achish king of Gath. [11] But the servants of Achish said to him, "Isn't this David, the king of the land? Isn't he the one they sing about in their dances:

" 'Saul has slain his thousands,
   and David his tens of thousands'?"

[12] David took these words to heart and was very much afraid of Achish king of Gath. [13] So he pretended to be insane in their presence; and while he was in their hands he acted like a madman, making marks on the doors of the gate and letting saliva run down his beard.

[14] Achish said to his servants, "Look at the man! He is insane! Why bring him to me? [15] Am I so short of madmen that you have to bring this fellow here to carry on like this in front of me? Must this man come into my house?"

David at Adullam and Mizpah

22 David left Gath and escaped to the cave of Adullam. When his brothers and his father's household heard about it, they went down to him there. [2] All those who were in distress or in debt or discontented gathered around him, and he became their commander. About four hundred men were with him.

[3] From there David went to Mizpah in Moab and said to the king of Moab, "Would you let my father and mother come and stay with you until I learn what God will do for me?" [4] So he left them with the king of Moab, and they stayed with him as long as David was in the stronghold.

[5] But the prophet Gad said to David, "Do not stay in the stronghold. Go into the land of Judah." So David left and went to the forest of Hereth.

Saul Kills the Priests of Nob

[6] Now Saul heard that David and his men had been discovered. And Saul was seated, spear in hand, under the tamarisk tree on the hill at Gibeah, with all his officials standing at his side. [7] He said to them, "Listen, men of Benjamin! Will the son of Jesse give all of you fields and vineyards? Will he make all of you commanders of thousands and commanders of hundreds? [8] Is that why you have all conspired against me? No one tells me when my son makes a covenant with the son of Jesse. None of you is concerned about me or tells me that my son has incited my servant to lie in wait for me, as he does today."

[9] But Doeg the Edomite, who was standing with Saul's officials, said, "I saw the son of Jesse come to Ahimelek son of Ahitub at Nob. [10] Ahimelek inquired of the LORD for him; he also gave him provisions and the sword of Goliath the Philistine."

[11] Then the king sent for the priest Ahimelek son of Ahitub and all the men of his family, who were the priests at Nob, and they all came to the king. [12] Saul said, "Listen now, son of Ahitub."

"Yes, my lord," he answered.

[13] Saul said to him, "Why have you conspired against me, you and the son of Jesse, giving him bread and a sword and inquiring of God for him, so that he has rebelled against me and lies in wait for me, as he does today?"

[14] Ahimelek answered the king, "Who of all your servants is as loyal as David, the king's son-in-law, captain of your bodyguard and highly respected in your household? [15] Was that day the first time I inquired of God for him? Of course not! Let not the king accuse your servant or any of his father's family, for your servant knows nothing at all about this whole affair."

[16] But the king said, "You will surely die, Ahimelek, you and your whole family."

[17] Then the king ordered the guards at his side: "Turn and kill the priests of the LORD, because they too have sided with David. They knew he was fleeing, yet they did not tell me."

But the king's officials were unwilling to raise a hand to strike the priests of the LORD.

[18] The king then ordered Doeg, "You turn and strike down the priests." So Doeg the Edomite turned and struck them down. That day he killed eighty-five men who wore the linen ephod. [19] He also put to the sword Nob, the town of the priests, with its men and women, its children and infants, and its cattle, donkeys and sheep.

²⁰But one son of Ahimelek son of Ahitub, named Abiathar, escaped and fled to join David. ²¹He told David that Saul had killed the priests of the LORD. ²²Then David said to Abiathar, "That day, when Doeg the Edomite was there, I knew he would be sure to tell Saul. I am responsible for the death of your whole family. ²³Stay with me; don't be afraid. The man who wants to kill you is trying to kill me too. You will be safe with me."

David Saves Keilah

23 When David was told, "Look, the Philistines are fighting against Keilah and are looting the threshing floors," ²he inquired of the LORD, saying, "Shall I go and attack these Philistines?"

The LORD answered him, "Go, attack the Philistines and save Keilah."

³But David's men said to him, "Here in Judah we are afraid. How much more, then, if we go to Keilah against the Philistine forces!"

⁴Once again David inquired of the LORD, and the LORD answered him, "Go down to Keilah, for I am going to give the Philistines into your hand." ⁵So David and his men went to Keilah, fought the Philistines and carried off their livestock. He inflicted heavy losses on the Philistines and saved the people of Keilah. ⁶(Now Abiathar son of Ahimelek had brought the ephod down with him when he fled to David at Keilah.)

Saul Pursues David

⁷Saul was told that David had gone to Keilah, and he said, "God has delivered him into my hands, for David has imprisoned himself by entering a town with gates and bars." ⁸And Saul called up all his forces for battle, to go down to Keilah to besiege David and his men.

⁹When David learned that Saul was plotting against him, he said to Abiathar the priest, "Bring the ephod." ¹⁰David said, "LORD, God of Israel, your servant has heard definitely that Saul plans to come to Keilah and destroy the town on account of me. ¹¹Will the citizens of Keilah surrender me to him? Will Saul come down, as your servant has heard? LORD, God of Israel, tell your servant."

And the LORD said, "He will."

¹²Again David asked, "Will the citizens of Keilah surrender me and my men to Saul?"

And the LORD said, "They will."

¹³So David and his men, about six hundred in number, left Keilah and kept moving from place to place. When Saul was told that David had escaped from Keilah, he did not go there.

¹⁴David stayed in the wilderness strongholds and in the hills of the Desert of Ziph. Day after day Saul searched for him, but God did not give David into his hands.

¹⁵While David was at Horesh in the Desert of Ziph, he learned that[a] Saul had come out to take his life. ¹⁶And Saul's son Jonathan went to David at Horesh and helped him find strength in God. ¹⁷"Don't be afraid," he said. "My father Saul will not lay a hand on you. You will be king over Israel, and I will be second to you. Even my father Saul knows this." ¹⁸The two of them made a covenant before the LORD. Then Jonathan went home, but David remained at Horesh.

¹⁹The Ziphites went up to Saul at Gibeah and said, "Is not David hiding among us in the strongholds at Horesh, on the hill of Hakilah, south of Jeshimon? ²⁰Now, Your Majesty, come down whenever it pleases you to do so, and we will be responsible for giving him into your hands."

²¹Saul replied, "The LORD bless you for your concern for me. ²²Go and get more information. Find out where David usually goes and who has seen him there. They tell me he is very crafty. ²³Find out about all the hiding places he uses and come back to me with definite information. Then I will go with you; if he is in the area, I will track him down among all the clans of Judah."

²⁴So they set out and went to Ziph ahead of Saul. Now David and his men were in the Desert of Maon, in the Arabah south of Jeshimon. ²⁵Saul and his men began the search, and when David was told about it, he went down to the rock and stayed in the Desert of Maon. When

---

^a 15 Or he was afraid because

Saul heard this, he went into the Desert of Maon in pursuit of David.

²⁶Saul was going along one side of the mountain, and David and his men were on the other side, hurrying to get away from Saul. As Saul and his forces were closing in on David and his men to capture them, ²⁷a messenger came to Saul, saying, "Come quickly! The Philistines are raiding the land." ²⁸Then Saul broke off his pursuit of David and went to meet the Philistines. That is why they call this place Sela Hammahlekoth.ᵃ ²⁹And David went up from there and lived in the strongholds of En Gedi.ᵇ

David Spares Saul's Life

24 ᶜ After Saul returned from pursuing the Philistines, he was told, "David is in the Desert of En Gedi." ²So Saul took three thousand able young men from all Israel and set out to look for David and his men near the Crags of the Wild Goats.

³He came to the sheep pens along the way; a cave was there, and Saul went in to relieve himself. David and his men were far back in the cave. ⁴The men said, "This is the day the LORD spoke of when he saidᵈ to you, 'I will give your enemy into your hands for you to deal with as you wish.'" Then David crept up unnoticed and cut off a corner of Saul's robe.

⁵Afterward, David was conscience-stricken for having cut off a corner of his robe. ⁶He said to his men, "The LORD forbid that I should do such a thing to my master, the LORD's anointed, or lay my hand on him; for he is the anointed of the LORD." ⁷With these words David sharply rebuked his men and did not allow them to attack Saul. And Saul left the cave and went his way.

⁸Then David went out of the cave and called out to Saul, "My lord the king!" When Saul looked behind him, David bowed down and prostrated himself with his face to the ground. ⁹He said to Saul, "Why do you listen when men say, 'David is bent on harming you'? ¹⁰This day you have seen with your own eyes how the LORD delivered you into my hands in the cave. Some urged me to kill you, but I spared you; I said, 'I will not lay my hand on my lord, because he is the LORD's anointed.' ¹¹See, my father, look at this piece of your robe in my hand! I cut off the corner of your robe but did not kill you. See that there is nothing in my hand to indicate that I am guilty of wrongdoing or rebellion. I have not wronged you, but you are hunting me down to take my life. ¹²May the LORD judge between you and me. And may the LORD avenge the wrongs you have done to me, but my hand will not touch you. ¹³As the old saying goes, 'From evildoers come evil deeds,' so my hand will not touch you.

¹⁴"Against whom has the king of Israel come out? Who are you pursuing? A dead dog? A flea? ¹⁵May the LORD be our judge and decide between us. May he consider my cause and uphold it; may he vindicate me by delivering me from your hand."

¹⁶When David finished saying this, Saul asked, "Is that your voice, David my son?" And he wept aloud. ¹⁷"You are more righteous than I," he said. "You have treated me well, but I have treated you badly. ¹⁸You have just now told me about the good you did to me; the LORD delivered me into your hands, but you did not kill me. ¹⁹When a man finds his enemy, does he let him get away unharmed? May the LORD reward you well for the way you treated me today. ²⁰I know that you will surely be king and that the kingdom of Israel will be established in your hands. ²¹Now swear to me by the LORD that you will not kill off my descendants or wipe out my name from my father's family."

²²So David gave his oath to Saul. Then Saul returned home, but David and his men went up to the stronghold.

David, Nabal and Abigail

25 Now Samuel died, and all Israel assembled and mourned for him; and they buried him at his home in Ramah. Then David moved down into the Desert of Paran.ᵉ

ᵃ 28 Sela Hammahlekoth means rock of parting.
ᵇ 29 In Hebrew texts this verse (23:29) is numbered 24:1.   ᶜ In Hebrew texts 24:1-22 is numbered 24:2-23.
ᵈ 4 Or "Today the LORD is saying   ᵉ 1 Hebrew and some Septuagint manuscripts; other Septuagint manuscripts Maon

²A certain man in Maon, who had property there at Carmel, was very wealthy. He had a thousand goats and three thousand sheep, which he was shearing in Carmel. ³His name was Nabal and his wife's name was Abigail. She was an intelligent and beautiful woman, but her husband was surly and mean in his dealings—he was a Calebite.

⁴While David was in the wilderness, he heard that Nabal was shearing sheep. ⁵So he sent ten young men and said to them, "Go up to Nabal at Carmel and greet him in my name. ⁶Say to him: 'Long life to you! Good health to you and your household! And good health to all that is yours!

⁷" 'Now I hear that it is sheep-shearing time. When your shepherds were with us, we did not mistreat them, and the whole time they were at Carmel nothing of theirs was missing. ⁸Ask your own servants and they will tell you. Therefore be favorable toward my men, since we come at a festive time. Please give your servants and your son David whatever you can find for them.' "

⁹When David's men arrived, they gave Nabal this message in David's name. Then they waited.

¹⁰Nabal answered David's servants, "Who is this David? Who is this son of Jesse? Many servants are breaking away from their masters these days. ¹¹Why should I take my bread and water, and the meat I have slaughtered for my shearers, and give it to men coming from who knows where?"

¹²David's men turned around and went back. When they arrived, they reported every word. ¹³David said to his men, "Each of you strap on your sword!" So they did, and David strapped his on as well. About four hundred men went up with David, while two hundred stayed with the supplies.

¹⁴One of the servants told Abigail, Nabal's wife, "David sent messengers from the wilderness to give our master his greetings, but he hurled insults at them. ¹⁵Yet these men were very good to us. They did not mistreat us, and the whole time we were out in the fields near them

THE
WITNESSES

✓ **ABIGAIL** (1 SAMUEL 25:3)
Abigail means "my father is joy." She was a beautiful woman and also sensible. She was married to a man named Nabal. Later, she married David.

nothing was missing. ¹⁶Night and day they were a wall around us the whole time we were herding our sheep near them. ¹⁷Now think it over and see what you can do, because disaster is hanging over our master and his whole household. He is such a wicked man that no one can talk to him."

¹⁸Abigail acted quickly. She took two hundred loaves of bread, two skins of wine, five dressed sheep, five seahsᵃ of roasted grain, a hundred cakes of raisins and two hundred cakes of pressed figs,

---

ᵃ 18 That is, probably about 60 pounds or about 27 kilograms and loaded them on donkeys. [19]Then she told her servants, "Go on ahead; I'll follow you." But she did not tell her husband Nabal.

[20]As she came riding her donkey into a mountain ravine, there were David and his men descending toward her, and she met them. [21]David had just said, "It's been useless—all my watching over this fellow's property in the wilderness so that nothing of his was missing. He has paid me back evil for good. [22]May God deal with David,[a] be it ever so severely, if by morning I leave alive one male of all who belong to him!"

[23]When Abigail saw David, she quickly got off her donkey and bowed down before David with her face to the ground. [24]She fell at his feet and said: "Pardon your servant, my lord, and let me speak to you; hear what your servant has to say. [25]Please pay no attention, my lord, to that wicked man Nabal. He is just like his name—his name means Fool, and folly goes with him. And as for me, your servant, I did not see the men my lord sent. [26]And now, my lord, as surely as the LORD your God lives and as you live, since the LORD has kept you from bloodshed and from avenging yourself with your own hands, may your enemies and all who are intent on harming my lord be like Nabal. [27]And let this gift, which your servant has brought to my lord, be given to the men who follow you.

[28]"Please forgive your servant's presumption. The LORD your God will certainly make a lasting dynasty for my lord, because you fight the LORD's battles, and no wrongdoing will be found in you as long as you live. [29]Even though someone is pursuing you to take your life, the life of my lord will be bound securely in the bundle of the living by the LORD your God, but the lives of your enemies he will hurl away as from the pocket of a sling. [30]When the LORD has fulfilled for my lord every good thing he promised concerning him and has appointed him ruler over Israel, [31]my lord will not have on his conscience the staggering burden of needless bloodshed or of having avenged himself. And when the LORD your God has

brought my lord success, remember your servant."

[32]David said to Abigail, "Praise be to the LORD, the God of Israel, who has sent you today to meet me. [33]May you be blessed for your good judgment and for keeping me from bloodshed this day and from avenging myself with my own hands. [34]Otherwise, as surely as the LORD, the God of Israel, lives, who has kept me from harming you, if you had not come quickly to meet me, not one male belonging to Nabal would have been left alive by daybreak."

[35]Then David accepted from her hand what she had brought him and said, "Go home in peace. I have heard your words and granted your request."

[36]When Abigail went to Nabal, he was in the house holding a banquet like that of a king. He was in high spirits and very drunk. So she told him nothing at all until daybreak. [37]Then in the morning, when Nabal was sober, his wife told him all these things, and his heart failed him and he became like a stone. [38]About ten days later, the LORD struck Nabal and he died.

[39]When David heard that Nabal was dead, he said, "Praise be to the LORD, who has upheld my cause against Nabal for treating me with contempt. He has kept his servant from doing wrong and has brought Nabal's wrongdoing down on his own head."

Then David sent word to Abigail, asking her to become his wife. [40]His servants went to Carmel and said to Abigail, "David has sent us to you to take you to become his wife."

[41]She bowed down with her face to the ground and said, "I am your servant and am ready to serve you and wash the feet of my lord's servants." [42]Abigail quickly got on a donkey and, attended by her five female servants, went with David's messengers and became his wife. [43]David had also married Ahinoam of Jezreel, and they both were his wives. [44]But Saul had given his daughter Michal, David's wife, to Paltiel[b] son of Laish, who was from Gallim.

---

[a] 22 Some Septuagint manuscripts; Hebrew *with David's enemies*   [b] 44 Hebrew *Palti*, a variant of *Paltiel*

David Again Spares Saul's Life

26 The Ziphites went to Saul at Gibeah and said, "Is not David hiding on the hill of Hakilah, which faces Jeshimon?"

²So Saul went down to the Desert of Ziph, with his three thousand select Israelite troops, to search there for David. ³Saul made his camp beside the road on the hill of Hakilah facing Jeshimon, but David stayed in the wilderness. When he saw that Saul had followed him there, ⁴he sent out scouts and learned that Saul had definitely arrived.

⁵Then David set out and went to the place where Saul had camped. He saw where Saul and Abner son of Ner, the commander of the army, had lain down. Saul was lying inside the camp, with the army encamped around him.

⁶David then asked Ahimelek the Hittite and Abishai son of Zeruiah, Joab's brother, "Who will go down into the camp with me to Saul?"

"I'll go with you," said Abishai.

⁷So David and Abishai went to the army by night, and there was Saul, lying asleep inside the camp with his spear stuck in the ground near his head. Abner and the soldiers were lying around him.

⁸Abishai said to David, "Today God has delivered your enemy into your hands. Now let me pin him to the ground with one thrust of the spear; I won't strike him twice."

⁹But David said to Abishai, "Don't destroy him! Who can lay a hand on the LORD's anointed and be guiltless? ¹⁰As surely as the LORD lives," he said, "the LORD himself will strike him, or his time will come and he will die, or he will go into battle and perish. ¹¹But the LORD forbid that I should lay a hand on the LORD's anointed. Now get the spear and water jug that are near his head, and let's go."

¹²So David took the spear and water jug near Saul's head, and they left. No one saw or knew about it, nor did anyone wake up. They were all sleeping, because the LORD had put them into a deep sleep.

¹³Then David crossed over to the other side and stood on top of the hill some distance away; there was a wide space between them. ¹⁴He called out to the army and to Abner son of Ner, "Aren't you going to answer me, Abner?"

Abner replied, "Who are you who calls to the king?"

¹⁵David said, "You're a man, aren't you? And who is like you in Israel? Why didn't you guard your lord the king? Someone came to destroy your lord the king. ¹⁶What you have done is not good. As surely as the LORD lives, you and your men must die, because you did not guard your master, the LORD's anointed. Look around you. Where are the king's spear and water jug that were near his head?"

¹⁷Saul recognized David's voice and said, "Is that your voice, David my son?"

David replied, "Yes it is, my lord the king." ¹⁸And he added, "Why is my lord pursuing his servant? What have I done, and what wrong am I guilty of? ¹⁹Now let my lord the king listen to his servant's words. If the LORD has incited you against me, then may he accept an offering. If, however, people have done it, may they be cursed before the LORD! They have driven me today from my share in the LORD's inheritance and have said, 'Go, serve other gods.' ²⁰Now do not let my blood fall to the ground far from the presence of the LORD. The king of Israel has come out to look for a flea—as one hunts a partridge in the mountains."

²¹Then Saul said, "I have sinned. Come back, David my son. Because you considered my life precious today, I will not try to harm you again. Surely I have acted like a fool and have been terribly wrong."

²²"Here is the king's spear," David answered. "Let one of your young men come over and get it. ²³The LORD rewards everyone for their righteousness and faithfulness. The LORD delivered you into my hands today, but I would not lay a hand on the LORD's anointed. ²⁴As surely as I valued your life today, so may the LORD value my life and deliver me from all trouble."

²⁵Then Saul said to David, "May you be blessed, David my son; you will do great things and surely triumph."

So David went on his way, and Saul returned home.

David Among the Philistines

27 But David thought to himself, "One of these days I will be destroyed by the hand of Saul. The best thing I can do is to escape to the land of the Philistines. Then Saul will give up searching for me anywhere in Israel, and I will slip out of his hand." ²So David and the six hundred men with him left and went over to Achish son of Maok king of Gath. ³David and his men settled in Gath with Achish. Each man had his family with him, and David had his two wives: Ahinoam of Jezreel and Abigail of Carmel, the widow of Nabal. ⁴When Saul was told that David had fled to Gath, he no longer searched for him.

⁵Then David said to Achish, "If I have found favor in your eyes, let a place be assigned to me in one of the country towns, that I may live there. Why should your servant live in the royal city with you?"

⁶So on that day Achish gave him Ziklag, and it has belonged to the kings of Judah ever since. ⁷David lived in Philistine territory a year and four months.

⁸Now David and his men went up and raided the Geshurites, the Girzites and the Amalekites. (From ancient times these peoples had lived in the land extending to Shur and Egypt.) ⁹Whenever David attacked an area, he did not leave a man or woman alive, but took sheep and cattle, donkeys and camels, and clothes. Then he returned to Achish. ¹⁰When Achish asked, "Where did you go raiding today?" David would say, "Against the Negev of Judah" or "Against the Negev of Jerahmeel" or "Against the Negev of the Kenites." ¹¹He did not leave a man or woman alive to be brought to Gath, for he thought, "They might inform on us and say, 'This is what David did.' " And such was his practice as long as he lived in Philistine territory. ¹²Achish trusted David and said to himself, "He has become so obnoxious to his people, the Israelites, that he will be my servant for life."

28 In those days the Philistines gathered their forces to fight against Israel. Achish said to David, "You must understand that you and your men will accompany me in the army."

²David said, "Then you will see for yourself what your servant can do."

Achish replied, "Very well, I will make you my bodyguard for life."

Saul and the Medium at Endor

³Now Samuel was dead, and all Israel had mourned for him and buried him in his own town of Ramah. Saul had expelled the mediums and spiritists from the land.

⁴The Philistines assembled and came and set up camp at Shunem, while Saul gathered all Israel and set up camp at Gilboa. ⁵When Saul saw the Philistine army, he was afraid; terror filled his heart. ⁶He inquired of the LORD, but the LORD did not answer him by dreams or Urim or prophets. ⁷Saul then said to his attendants, "Find me a woman who is a medium, so I may go and inquire of her."

"There is one in Endor," they said.

⁸So Saul disguised himself, putting on other clothes, and at night he and two men went to the woman. "Consult a spirit

BREAKTHROUGH!

Medium

(1 SAMUEL 28:3-7)

These are people who talk to the spirits of dead people. How awful! God prohibits this.

for me," he said, "and bring up for me the one I name."

9But the woman said to him, "Surely you know what Saul has done. He has cut off the mediums and spiritists from the land. Why have you set a trap for my life to bring about my death?"

10Saul swore to her by the LORD, "As surely as the LORD lives, you will not be punished for this."

11Then the woman asked, "Whom shall I bring up for you?"

"Bring up Samuel," he said.

12When the woman saw Samuel, she cried out at the top of her voice and said to Saul, "Why have you deceived me? You are Saul!"

13The king said to her, "Don't be afraid. What do you see?"

The woman said, "I see a ghostly figure*a* coming up out of the earth."

14"What does he look like?" he asked.

"An old man wearing a robe is coming up," she said.

Then Saul knew it was Samuel, and he bowed down and prostrated himself with his face to the ground.

15Samuel said to Saul, "Why have you disturbed me by bringing me up?"

"I am in great distress," Saul said. "The Philistines are fighting against me, and God has departed from me. He no longer answers me, either by prophets or by dreams. So I have called on you to tell me what to do."

16Samuel said, "Why do you consult me, now that the LORD has departed from you and become your enemy? 17The LORD has done what he predicted through me. The LORD has torn the kingdom out of your hands and given it to one of your neighbors—to David. 18Because you did not obey the LORD or carry out his fierce wrath against the Amalekites, the LORD has done this to you today. 19The LORD will deliver both Israel and you into the hands of the Philistines, and tomorrow you and your sons will be with me. The LORD will also give the army of Israel into the hands of the Philistines."

20Immediately Saul fell full length on the ground, filled with fear because of Samuel's words. His strength was gone,

BREAK THROUGH!

Is it possible to talk to dead people?

(1 SAMUEL 28:8-20)

Experts who study the Bible don't agree about what happened here. Some think that it was a bad spirit appearing as Samuel. Others think that God unexpectedly got involved and let Samuel appear in order to tell Saul what was really going to happen. That's why the medium was scared.

for he had eaten nothing all that day and all that night.

21When the woman came to Saul and saw that he was greatly shaken, she said, "Look, your servant has obeyed you. I took my life in my hands and did what you told me to do. 22Now please listen to your servant and let me give you some food so you may eat and have the strength to go on your way."

23He refused and said, "I will not eat."

But his men joined the woman in urging him, and he listened to them. He got up from the ground and sat on the couch.

24The woman had a fattened calf at the house, which she butchered at once. She took some flour, kneaded it and baked bread without yeast. 25Then she set it before Saul and his men, and

a 13 Or see spirits; or see gods

they ate. That same night they got up and left.

Achish Sends David Back to Ziklag

29 The Philistines gathered all their forces at Aphek, and Israel camped by the spring in Jezreel. ²As the Philistine rulers marched with their units of hundreds and thousands, David and his men were marching at the rear with Achish. ³The commanders of the Philistines asked, "What about these Hebrews?"

Achish replied, "Is this not David, who was an officer of Saul king of Israel? He has already been with me for over a year, and from the day he left Saul until now, I have found no fault in him."

⁴But the Philistine commanders were angry with Achish and said, "Send the man back, that he may return to the place you assigned him. He must not go with us into battle, or he will turn against us during the fighting. How better could he regain his master's favor than by taking the heads of our own men? ⁵Isn't this the David they sang about in their dances:

" 'Saul has slain his thousands,
    and David his tens of thousands'?"

⁶So Achish called David and said to him, "As surely as the LORD lives, you have been reliable, and I would be pleased to have you serve with me in the army. From the day you came to me until today, I have found no fault in you, but the rulers don't approve of you. ⁷Now turn back and go in peace; do nothing to displease the Philistine rulers."

⁸"But what have I done?" asked David. "What have you found against your servant from the day I came to you until now? Why can't I go and fight against the enemies of my lord the king?"

⁹Achish answered, "I know that you have been as pleasing in my eyes as an angel of God; nevertheless, the Philistine commanders have said, 'He must not go up with us into battle.' ¹⁰Now get up early, along with your master's servants who have come with you, and leave in the morning as soon as it is light."

¹¹So David and his men got up early in the morning to go back to the land of the Philistines, and the Philistines went up to Jezreel.

David Destroys the Amalekites

30 David and his men reached Ziklag on the third day. Now the Amalekites had raided the Negev and Ziklag. They had attacked Ziklag and burned it, ²and had taken captive the women and everyone else in it, both young and old. They killed none of them, but carried them off as they went on their way.

³When David and his men reached Ziklag, they found it destroyed by fire and their wives and sons and daughters taken captive. ⁴So David and his men wept aloud until they had no strength left to weep. ⁵David's two wives had been captured—Ahinoam of Jezreel and Abigail, the widow of Nabal of Carmel. ⁶David was greatly distressed because the men were talking of stoning him; each one was bitter in spirit because of his sons and daughters. But David found strength in the LORD his God.

⁷Then David said to Abiathar the priest, the son of Ahimelek, "Bring me the ephod." Abiathar brought it to him, ⁸and David inquired of the LORD, "Shall I pursue this raiding party? Will I overtake them?"

"Pursue them," he answered. "You will certainly overtake them and succeed in the rescue."

⁹David and the six hundred men with him came to the Besor Valley, where some stayed behind. ¹⁰Two hundred of them were too exhausted to cross the valley, but David and the other four hundred continued the pursuit.

¹¹They found an Egyptian in a field and brought him to David. They gave him water to drink and food to eat— ¹²part of a cake of pressed figs and two cakes of raisins. He ate and was revived, for he had not eaten any food or drunk any water for three days and three nights.

¹³David asked him, "Who do you belong to? Where do you come from?"

He said, "I am an Egyptian, the slave of an Amalekite. My master abandoned me when I became ill three days ago. ¹⁴We raided the Negev of the Kerethites, some territory belonging to Judah and the Negev of Caleb. And we burned Ziklag."

¹⁵David asked him, "Can you lead me down to this raiding party?"

He answered, "Swear to me before God that you will not kill me or hand me over to my master, and I will take you down to them."

¹⁶He led David down, and there they were, scattered over the countryside, eating, drinking and reveling because of the great amount of plunder they had taken from the land of the Philistines and from Judah. ¹⁷David fought them from dusk until the evening of the next day, and none of them got away, except four hundred young men who rode off on camels and fled. ¹⁸David recovered everything the Amalekites had taken, including his two wives. ¹⁹Nothing was missing: young or old, boy or girl, plunder or anything else they had taken. David brought everything back.

²⁰He took all the flocks and herds, and his men drove them ahead of the other livestock, saying, "This is David's plunder."

²¹Then David came to the two hundred men who had been too exhausted to follow him and who were left behind at the Besor Valley. They came out to meet David and the men with him. As David and his men approached, he asked them how they were. ²²But all the evil men and troublemakers among David's followers said, "Because they did not go out with us, we will not share with them the plunder we recovered. However, each man may take his wife and children and go."

²³David replied, "No, my brothers, you must not do that with what the LORD has given us. He has protected us and delivered into our hands the raiding party that came against us. ²⁴Who will listen to what you say? The share of the man who stayed with the supplies is to be the

What a nice book! We really liked it. Isabella's favorite is the story of Hannah and all the faith she had when she prayed and God gave her a baby. But she did feel a bit sad when Hannah took Samuel to the temple and left him there. Poor little thing! He must have really missed his mother after that. But God watched over him so he wouldn't miss her too much. And because he grew up in the temple, Samuel learned to hear the voice of God and obey him.

Mateo liked the stories of David and Jonathan and their friendship. He also enjoyed the stories of the battles. The one he liked the best was David's battle with Goliath.

The most important lesson in this book is that we should always have faith in God and be obedient to him. God sees and hears everything. He watches over his children just like he did with Hannah and Samuel and David.

CASE CLOSED!

same as that of him who went down to the battle. All will share alike." ²⁵David made this a statute and ordinance for Israel from that day to this.

²⁶When David reached Ziklag, he sent some of the plunder to the elders of Judah, who were his friends, saying, "Here is a gift for you from the plunder of the LORD's enemies."

²⁷David sent it to those who were in Bethel, Ramoth Negev and Jattir; ²⁸to those in Aroer, Siphmoth, Eshtemoa ²⁹and Rakal; to those in the towns of the Jerahmeelites and the Kenites; ³⁰to those in Hormah, Bor Ashan, Athak ³¹and Hebron; and to those in all the other places where he and his men had roamed.

Saul Takes His Life

31 Now the Philistines fought against Israel; the Israelites fled before them, and many fell dead on Mount Gilboa. ²The Philistines were in hot pursuit of Saul and his sons, and they killed his sons Jonathan, Abinadab and Malki-Shua. ³The fighting grew fierce around Saul, and when the archers overtook him, they wounded him critically.

⁴Saul said to his armor-bearer, "Draw your sword and run me through, or these uncircumcised fellows will come and run me through and abuse me."

But his armor-bearer was terrified and would not do it; so Saul took his own sword and fell on it. ⁵When the armor-bearer saw that Saul was dead, he too fell on his sword and died with him. ⁶So Saul and his three sons and his armor-bearer and all his men died together that same day.

⁷When the Israelites along the valley and those across the Jordan saw that the Israelite army had fled and that Saul and his sons had died, they abandoned their towns and fled. And the Philistines came and occupied them.

⁸The next day, when the Philistines came to strip the dead, they found Saul and his three sons fallen on Mount Gilboa. ⁹They cut off his head and stripped off his armor, and they sent messengers throughout the land of the Philistines to proclaim the news in the temple of their idols and among their people. ¹⁰They put his armor in the temple of the Ashtoreths and fastened his body to the wall of Beth Shan.

¹¹When the people of Jabesh Gilead heard what the Philistines had done to Saul, ¹²all their valiant men marched through the night to Beth Shan. They took down the bodies of Saul and his sons from the wall of Beth Shan and went to Jabesh, where they burned them. ¹³Then they took their bones and buried them under a tamarisk tree at Jabesh, and they fasted seven days.

2 SAMUEL

THE EVIDENCE:

WHO WROTE IT?
Samuel didn't write anything in this book, because he had already died when the events took place! Gad and Nathan probably had something to do with it, just like in the first book of Samuel.

HOW LONG AGO?
We don't know very well when this book was written, but it was during the same time as the other one (1 Samuel), because they were just one book at first.

WHAT'S IT ABOUT?
This book tells the story of how David became the king of Israel after Saul died. That wasn't easy, because there were other people who also wanted to be king, so they went to war against each other. The book also has other stories, like the one about David and Bathsheba and the one about Tamar.

THE BEST PART
We chose this verse:

"In my distress I called to the LORD;
    I called out to my God.
From his temple he heard my voice;
    my cry came to his ears" (22:7).

We like this because it means that God hears us when we pray. We already knew that was true!

David Hears of Saul's Death

1 After the death of Saul, David returned from striking down the Amalekites and stayed in Ziklag two days. ²On the third day a man arrived from Saul's camp with his clothes torn and dust on his head. When he came to David, he fell to the ground to pay him honor.

³"Where have you come from?" David asked him.

He answered, "I have escaped from the Israelite camp."

⁴"What happened?" David asked. "Tell me."

"The men fled from the battle," he replied. "Many of them fell and died. And Saul and his son Jonathan are dead."

⁵Then David said to the young man who brought him the report, "How do you know that Saul and his son Jonathan are dead?"

⁶"I happened to be on Mount Gilboa," the young man said, "and there was Saul, leaning on his spear, with the chariots and their drivers in hot pursuit. ⁷When he turned around and saw me, he called out to me, and I said, 'What can I do?'

8 "He asked me, 'Who are you?'

" 'An Amalekite,' I answered.

9 "Then he said to me, 'Stand here by me and kill me! I'm in the throes of death, but I'm still alive.'

10 "So I stood beside him and killed him, because I knew that after he had fallen he could not survive. And I took the crown that was on his head and the band on his arm and have brought them here to my lord."

11 Then David and all the men with him took hold of their clothes and tore them. 12 They mourned and wept and fasted till evening for Saul and his son Jonathan, and for the army of the LORD and for the nation of Israel, because they had fallen by the sword.

13 David said to the young man who brought him the report, "Where are you from?"

"I am the son of a foreigner, an Amalekite," he answered.

14 David asked him, "Why weren't you afraid to lift your hand to destroy the LORD's anointed?"

15 Then David called one of his men and said, "Go, strike him down!" So he struck him down, and he died. 16 For David had said to him, "Your blood be on your own head. Your own mouth testified against you when you said, 'I killed the LORD's anointed.' "

David's Lament for Saul and Jonathan

17 David took up this lament concerning Saul and his son Jonathan, 18 and he ordered that the people of Judah be taught this lament of the bow (it is written in the Book of Jashar):

19 "A gazelle^a lies slain on your heights,
    Israel.
    How the mighty have fallen!

20 "Tell it not in Gath,
    proclaim it not in the streets of
      Ashkelon,
    lest the daughters of the Philistines
      be glad,
    lest the daughters of the
      uncircumcised rejoice.

21 "Mountains of Gilboa,
    may you have neither dew nor rain,
    may no showers fall on your
      terraced fields.^b
For there the shield of the mighty was
    despised,
    the shield of Saul—no longer
      rubbed with oil.

22 "From the blood of the slain,
    from the flesh of the mighty,
    the bow of Jonathan did not turn
      back,
    the sword of Saul did not return
      unsatisfied.

23 Saul and Jonathan—
    in life they were loved and admired,
    and in death they were not parted.
They were swifter than eagles,
    they were stronger than lions.

24 "Daughters of Israel,
    weep for Saul,
who clothed you in scarlet and finery,
    who adorned your garments with
      ornaments of gold.

25 "How the mighty have fallen in battle!
    Jonathan lies slain on your heights.
26 I grieve for you, Jonathan my brother;
    you were very dear to me.
Your love for me was wonderful,
    more wonderful than that of women.

27 "How the mighty have fallen!
    The weapons of war have perished!"

David Anointed King Over Judah

2 In the course of time, David inquired of the LORD. "Shall I go up to one of the towns of Judah?" he asked.

The LORD said, "Go up."

David asked, "Where shall I go?"

"To Hebron," the LORD answered.

2 So David went up there with his two wives, Ahinoam of Jezreel and Abigail, the widow of Nabal of Carmel. 3 David also took the men who were with him, each with his family, and they settled in Hebron and its towns. 4 Then the men of Judah came to Hebron, and there they anointed David king over the tribe of Judah.

---

^a 19 *Gazelle* here symbolizes a human dignitary.
^b 21 Or / *nor fields that yield grain for offerings*

When David was told that it was the men from Jabesh Gilead who had buried Saul, ⁵he sent messengers to them to say to them, "The LORD bless you for showing this kindness to Saul your master by burying him. ⁶May the LORD now show you kindness and faithfulness, and I too will show you the same favor because you have done this. ⁷Now then, be strong and brave, for Saul your master is dead, and the people of Judah have anointed me king over them."

War Between the Houses of David and Saul

⁸Meanwhile, Abner son of Ner, the commander of Saul's army, had taken Ish-Bosheth son of Saul and brought him over to Mahanaim. ⁹He made him king over Gilead, Ashuri and Jezreel, and also over Ephraim, Benjamin and all Israel.

¹⁰Ish-Bosheth son of Saul was forty years old when he became king over Israel, and he reigned two years. The tribe of Judah, however, remained loyal to David. ¹¹The length of time David was king in Hebron over Judah was seven years and six months.

¹²Abner son of Ner, together with the men of Ish-Bosheth son of Saul, left Mahanaim and went to Gibeon. ¹³Joab son of Zeruiah and David's men went out and met them at the pool of Gibeon. One group sat down on one side of the pool and one group on the other side. ¹⁴Then Abner said to Joab, "Let's have some of the young men get up and fight hand to hand in front of us."

"All right, let them do it," Joab said.

¹⁵So they stood up and were counted off—twelve men for Benjamin and Ish-Bosheth son of Saul, and twelve for David. ¹⁶Then each man grabbed his opponent by the head and thrust his dagger into his opponent's side, and they fell down together. So that place in Gibeon was called Helkath Hazzurim.ᵃ

¹⁷The battle that day was very fierce, and Abner and the Israelites were defeated by David's men.

¹⁸The three sons of Zeruiah were there: Joab, Abishai and Asahel. Now Asahel was as fleet-footed as a wild gazelle. ¹⁹He

THE SCENE

GIBEON

(2 SAMUEL 2:12)

This name means "hill." This city was very famous, because it had a big pond of water. It was 5 miles (8 km) from Jerusalem.

chased Abner, turning neither to the right nor to the left as he pursued him. ²⁰Abner looked behind him and asked, "Is that you, Asahel?"

"It is," he answered.

²¹Then Abner said to him, "Turn aside to the right or to the left; take on one of the young men and strip him of his weapons." But Asahel would not stop chasing him.

²²Again Abner warned Asahel, "Stop chasing me! Why should I strike you down? How could I look your brother Joab in the face?"

²³But Asahel refused to give up the pursuit; so Abner thrust the butt of his spear into Asahel's stomach, and the spear came out through his back. He fell there and died on the spot. And every man stopped when he came to the place where Asahel had fallen and died.

ᵃ 16 *Helkath Hazzurim* means *field of daggers* or *field of hostilities.*

²⁴But Joab and Abishai pursued Abner, and as the sun was setting, they came to the hill of Ammah, near Giah on the way to the wasteland of Gibeon. ²⁵Then the men of Benjamin rallied behind Abner. They formed themselves into a group and took their stand on top of a hill.

²⁶Abner called out to Joab, "Must the sword devour forever? Don't you real-

THE
WITNESSES

✓ ISH-BOSHETH (2 SAMUEL 2:8–10)
This name means "man of shame," but he was called Ish-Baal before he had this name. He was Saul's son, so when his father died, Abner proclaimed him king of Israel. Ish-Bosheth was king for two years.

✓ JOAB (2 SAMUEL 2:13)
He was David's nephew. His name means "God is father." When Saul died, Joab was the leader of David's army. He was very brave, and he led David's army in many victories.

ize that this will end in bitterness? How long before you order your men to stop pursuing their fellow Isra-elites?"

²⁷Joab answered, "As sure-ly as God lives, if you had not spoken, the men would have con-tinued pursuing them until morning."

²⁸So Joab blew the trumpet, and all the troops came to a halt; they no longer pur-sued Israel, nor did they fight anymore.

²⁹All that night Abner and his men marched through the Arabah. They crossed the Jordan, continued through the morning hours*a* and came to Maha-naim.

³⁰Then Joab stopped pursuing Abner and assembled the whole army. Besides Asahel, nineteen of David's men were found missing. ³¹But David's men had killed three hundred and sixty Benjamites who were with Abner. ³²They took Asa-hel and buried him in his father's tomb at Bethlehem. Then Joab and his men marched all night and arrived at Hebron by daybreak.

3 The war between the house of Saul and the house of David lasted a long time. David grew stronger and stronger, while the house of Saul grew weaker and weaker.

²Sons were born to David in Hebron:

His firstborn was Amnon the son of Ahinoam of Jezreel;

³his second, Kileab the son of Abi-gail the widow of Nabal of Carmel; the third, Absalom the son of Maa-kah daughter of Talmai king of Ge-shur;

⁴the fourth, Adonijah the son of Haggith; the fifth, Shephatiah the son of Abital;

⁵and the sixth, Ithream the son of David's wife Eglah.

These were born to David in He-bron.

Abner Goes Over to David
⁶During the war between the house of Saul and the house of David, Abner had

---

a 29 See Septuagint; the meaning of the Hebrew for this phrase is uncertain.

BREAKTHROUGH!

Why did David have so many wives?

(2 SAMUEL 3:2-5; 5:13; 15:16)

At that time, a king had to have many wives (called a "harem") and many sons. It was the way to show that he was very rich. Also, that's how David stayed related to the most important families in the kingdom and made sure that other foreign kings didn't attack them. There were two kinds of wives in a harem. There were the principal wives, who were given a great celebration when they got married. Then there were the concubines, who were also wives but they didn't get any ceremony when they went to live in the palace and their children were also less important.

Abner, be it ever so severely, if I do not do for David what the LORD promised him on oath ¹⁰and transfer the kingdom from the house of Saul and establish David's throne over Israel and Judah from Dan to Beersheba." ¹¹Ish-Bosheth did not dare to say another word to Abner, because he was afraid of him.

¹²Then Abner sent messengers on his behalf to say to David, "Whose land is it? Make an agreement with me, and I will help you bring all Israel over to you."

¹³"Good," said David. "I will make an agreement with you. But I demand one thing of you: Do not come into my presence unless you bring Michal daughter of Saul when you come to see me." ¹⁴Then

been strengthening his own position in the house of Saul. ⁷Now Saul had had a concubine named Rizpah daughter of Aiah. And Ish-Bosheth said to Abner, "Why did you sleep with my father's concubine?"

⁸Abner was very angry because of what Ish-Bosheth said. So he answered, "Am I a dog's head—on Judah's side? This very day I am loyal to the house of your father Saul and to his family and friends. I haven't handed you over to David. Yet now you accuse me of an offense involving this woman! ⁹May God deal with

THE WITNESSES

✓ **RIZPAH** (2 SAMUEL 3:7)
This name means "hot stone" as well as "burning charcoal." She was one of King Saul's concubines (not as important as a wife).

David sent messengers to Ish-Bosheth son of Saul, demanding, "Give me my wife Michal, whom I betrothed to myself for the price of a hundred Philistine foreskins." ¹⁵So Ish-Bosheth gave orders and had her taken away from her husband Paltiel son of Laish. ¹⁶Her husband, however, went with her, weeping behind her all the way to Bahurim. Then Abner said to him, "Go back home!" So he went back.

¹⁷Abner conferred with the elders of Israel and said, "For some time you have wanted to make David your king. ¹⁸Now do it! For the LORD promised David, 'By my servant David I will rescue my people Israel from the hand of the Philistines and from the hand of all their enemies.' "

¹⁹Abner also spoke to the Benjamites in person. Then he went to Hebron to tell David everything that Israel and the whole tribe of Benjamin wanted to do. ²⁰When Abner, who had twenty men with him, came to David at Hebron, David prepared a feast for him and his men. ²¹Then Abner said to David, "Let me go at once and assemble all Israel for my lord the king, so that they may make a covenant with you, and that you may rule over all that your heart desires." So David sent Abner away, and he went in peace.

Joab Murders Abner

²²Just then David's men and Joab returned from a raid and brought with them a great deal of plunder. But Abner was no longer with David in Hebron, because David had sent him away, and he had gone in peace. ²³When Joab and all the soldiers with him arrived, he was told that Abner son of Ner had come to the king and that the king had sent him away and that he had gone in peace.

²⁴So Joab went to the king and said, "What have you done? Look, Abner came to you. Why did you let him go? Now he is gone! ²⁵You know Abner son of Ner; he came to deceive you and observe your movements and find out everything you are doing."

²⁶Joab then left David and sent messengers after Abner, and they brought him back from the cistern at Sirah. But David did not know it. ²⁷Now when Abner returned to Hebron, Joab took him aside into an inner chamber, as if to speak with him privately. And there, to avenge the blood of his brother Asahel, Joab stabbed him in the stomach, and he died.

²⁸Later, when David heard about this, he said, "I and my kingdom are forever innocent before the LORD concerning the blood of Abner son of Ner. ²⁹May his blood fall on the head of Joab and on his whole family! May Joab's family never be without someone who has a running sore or leprosyᵃ or who leans on a crutch or who falls by the sword or who lacks food."

³⁰(Joab and his brother Abishai murdered Abner because he had killed their brother Asahel in the battle at Gibeon.)

³¹Then David said to Joab and all the people with him, "Tear your clothes and put on sackcloth and walk in mourning in front of Abner." King David himself walked behind the bier. ³²They buried Abner in Hebron, and the king wept aloud at Abner's tomb. All the people wept also.

³³The king sang this lament for Abner:

"Should Abner have died as the
        lawless die?
34   Your hands were not bound,
        your feet were not fettered.
    You fell as one falls before the
        wicked."

And all the people wept over him again. ³⁵Then they all came and urged David to eat something while it was still day; but David took an oath, saying, "May God deal with me, be it ever so severely, if I taste bread or anything else before the sun sets!"

³⁶All the people took note and were pleased; indeed, everything the king did pleased them. ³⁷So on that day all the people there and all Israel knew that the king had no part in the murder of Abner son of Ner.

³⁸Then the king said to his men, "Do you not realize that a commander and a great man has fallen in Israel this day? ³⁹And today, though I am the anointed king, I am weak, and these sons of

---

ᵃ 29 The Hebrew for *leprosy* was used for various diseases affecting the skin.

BREAKTHROUGH!

Why did the people love David so much?

(2 SAMUEL 3:36)

David didn't fight with anybody in order to become king. It was God himself who chose David when he was just a sheepherder. David always respected Saul, who was the king God had chosen before David, even though Saul wanted to kill David and chased him for a long time. David always tried to obey God, and that's why God promised him that in Israel, there would be a king in his family. David had other virtues too. He was a great warrior as well as a poet and a musician.

Zeruiah are too strong for me. May the LORD repay the evildoer according to his evil deeds!"

Ish-Bosheth Murdered

4 When Ish-Bosheth son of Saul heard that Abner had died in Hebron, he lost courage, and all Israel became alarmed. ²Now Saul's son had two men who were leaders of raiding bands. One was named Baanah and the other Rekab; they were sons of Rimmon the Beerothite from the tribe of Benjamin—Beeroth is considered part of Benjamin, ³because the people of Beeroth fled to Gittaim and have resided there as foreigners to this day.

⁴(Jonathan son of Saul had a son who was lame in both feet. He was five years old when the news about Saul and Jonathan came from Jezreel. His nurse picked him up and fled, but as she hurried to leave, he fell and became disabled. His name was Mephibosheth.)

⁵Now Rekab and Baanah, the sons of Rimmon the Beerothite, set out for the house of Ish-Bosheth, and they arrived there in the heat of the day while he was taking his noonday rest. ⁶They went into the inner part of the house as if to get some wheat, and they stabbed him in the stomach. Then Rekab and his brother Baanah slipped away.

⁷They had gone into the house while he was lying on the bed in his bedroom. After they stabbed and killed him, they cut off his head. Taking it with them, they traveled all night by way of the Arabah. ⁸They brought the head of Ish-Bosheth to David at Hebron and said to the king, "Here

CHECK THE FACTS

Who was the second king of Israel?

A) David

B) Samuel

C) Mephibosheth

CORRECT ANSWER: A

is the head of Ish-Bosheth son of Saul, your enemy, who tried to kill you. This day the LORD has avenged my lord the king against Saul and his offspring."

9David answered Rekab and his brother Baanah, the sons of Rimmon the Beerothite, "As surely as the LORD lives, who has delivered me out of every trouble, 10when someone told me, 'Saul is dead,' and thought he was bringing good news,

THE
WITNESSES

✓ **BAANAH AND REKAB** (2 SAMUEL 4:2)
They were brothers, and Ish-Bosheth killed them. *Baanah* means "affliction" and *Rekab* means "rider."

✓ **MEPHIBOSHETH** (2 SAMUEL 4:4)
This name means "make shame disappear." There are two men who have this name. One was Saul and Rizpah's son. But the one mentioned here was Jonathan's son. He couldn't walk because of an accident he had when he was a boy.

I seized him and put him to death in Ziklag. That was the reward I gave him for his news! 11How much more—when wicked men have killed an innocent man in his own house and on his own bed—should I not now demand his blood from your hand and rid the earth of you!"

12So David gave an order to his men, and they killed them. They cut off their hands and feet and hung the bodies by the pool in Hebron. But they took the head of Ish-Bosheth and buried it in Abner's tomb at Hebron.

David Becomes King Over Israel

5 All the tribes of Israel came to David at Hebron and said, "We are your own flesh and blood. 2In the past, while Saul was king over us, you were the one who led Israel on their military campaigns. And the LORD said to you, 'You will shepherd my people Israel, and you will become their ruler.'"

3When all the elders of Israel had come to King David at Hebron, the king made a covenant with them at Hebron before the LORD, and they anointed David king over Israel.

4David was thirty years old when he became king, and he reigned forty years. 5In Hebron he reigned over Judah seven years and six months, and in Jerusalem he reigned over all Israel and Judah thirty-three years.

David Conquers Jerusalem

6The king and his men marched to Jerusalem to attack the Jebusites, who lived there. The Jebusites said to David, "You will not get in here; even the blind and the lame can ward you off." They thought, "David cannot get in here." 7Nevertheless, David captured the fortress of Zion—which is the City of David.

8On that day David had said, "Anyone who conquers the Jebusites will have to use the water shaft to reach those 'lame and blind' who are David's enemies.[a]" That is why they say, "The 'blind and lame' will not enter the palace."

9David then took up residence in the fortress and called it the City of David.

---

[a] 8 Or *are hated by David*

BREAKTHROUGH!

Did David hate blind or disabled people?

(2 SAMUEL 5:8)

This part is really hard to understand, because it seems that the original writing – the first time it was written down – was in Hebrew, and it's a little damaged and hard to read. Many people think that maybe this was David's revenge against the Jebusites, who were very proud and didn't like David or his army. Some people who study the Bible a lot think it really refers to the idols – the statues of their gods. Maybe, because those statues couldn't see or walk.

He built up the area around it, from the terraces[a] inward. [10]And he became more and more powerful, because the LORD God Almighty was with him.

[11]Now Hiram king of Tyre sent envoys to David, along with cedar logs and carpenters and stonemasons, and they built a palace for David. [12]Then David knew that the LORD had established him as king over Israel and had exalted his kingdom for the sake of his people Israel.

[13]After he left Hebron, David took more concubines and wives in Jerusalem, and more sons and daughters were born to him. [14]These are the names of the children born to him there: Shammua, Sho-

bab, Nathan, Solomon, [15]Ibhar, Elishua, Nepheg, Japhia, [16]Elishama, Eliada and Eliphelet.

David Defeats the Philistines

[17]When the Philistines heard that David had been anointed king over Israel, they went up in full force to search for him, but David heard about it and went down to the stronghold. [18]Now the Philistines had come and spread out in the Valley of Rephaim; [19]so David inquired of the LORD, "Shall I go and attack the Philistines? Will you deliver them into my hands?"

The LORD answered him, "Go, for I will surely deliver the Philistines into your hands."

[20]So David went to Baal Perazim, and there he defeated them. He said, "As waters break out, the LORD has broken out against my enemies before me." So that place was called Baal Perazim.[b] [21]The Philistines abandoned their idols there, and David and his men carried them off.

[22]Once more the Philistines came up and spread out in the Valley of Rephaim; [23]so David inquired of the LORD, and he answered, "Do not go straight up, but circle around behind them and attack them in front of the poplar trees. [24]As soon as you hear the sound of marching in the tops of the poplar trees, move quickly, because that will mean the LORD has gone out in front of you to strike the Philistine army." [25]So David did as the LORD commanded him, and he struck down the Philistines all the way from Gibeon[c] to Gezer.

The Ark Brought to Jerusalem

6 David again brought together all the able young men of Israel—thirty thousand. [2]He and all his men went to Baalah[d] in Judah to bring up from there the ark of God, which is called by the Name,[e] the name of the LORD Almighty, who is enthroned between the cherubim on the ark. [3]They set the ark of God on a new cart and brought it from the house of Abinadab,

---

[a] 9 Or the Millo　[b] 20 Baal Perazim means the lord who breaks out.　[c] 25 Septuagint (see also 1 Chron. 14:16); Hebrew Geba　[d] 2 That is, Kiriath Jearim (see 1 Chron. 13:6)　[e] 2 Hebrew; Septuagint and Vulgate do not have the Name.

THE SCENE

VALLEY OF REPHAIM

(2 SAMUEL 5:22)

It was a place on the border of the tribes of Judah and Benjamin, quite close to Jerusalem. David fought the Philistines there.

which was on the hill. Uzzah and Ahio, sons of Abinadab, were guiding the new cart ⁴with the ark of God on it,ᵃ and Ahio was walking in front of it. ⁵David and all Israel were celebrating with all their might before the Lord, with castanets,ᵇ harps, lyres, timbrels, sistrums and cymbals.

⁶When they came to the threshing floor of Nakon, Uzzah reached out and took hold of the ark of God, because the oxen stumbled. ⁷The Lord's anger burned against Uzzah because of his irreverent act; therefore God struck him down, and he died there beside the ark of God.

⁸Then David was angry because the Lord's wrath had broken out against Uzzah, and to this day that place is called Perez Uzzah.ᶜ

⁹David was afraid of the Lord that day and said, "How can the ark of the Lord ever come to me?" ¹⁰He was not willing to take the ark of the Lord to be with him in the City of David. Instead, he took it to

the house of Obed-Edom the Gittite. ¹¹The ark of the Lord remained in the house of Obed-Edom the Gittite for three months, and the Lord blessed him and his entire household.

¹²Now King David was told, "The Lord has blessed the household of Obed-Edom and everything he has, because of the ark of God." So David went to bring up the ark of God from the house of Obed-Edom to the City of David with rejoicing. ¹³When

---

ᵃ 3,4 Dead Sea Scrolls and some Septuagint manuscripts; Masoretic Text *cart* ⁴*and they brought it with the ark of God from the house of Abinadab, which was on the hill*
ᵇ 5 Masoretic Text; Dead Sea Scrolls and Septuagint (see also 1 Chron. 13:8) *songs*   ᶜ 8 *Perez Uzzah* means *outbreak against Uzzah.*

THE WITNESSES

✓ **ABINADAB** (2 SAMUEL 6:3–4)
This means "father of generosity" or "giver." This man lived in Kiriath Jearim. For a long time, he took care of the ark of the covenant, which had been left in his house.

those who were carrying the ark of the LORD had taken six steps, he sacrificed a bull and a fattened calf. ¹⁴Wearing a linen ephod, David was dancing before the LORD with all his might, ¹⁵while he and all Israel were bringing up the ark of the LORD with shouts and the sound of trumpets.

¹⁶As the ark of the LORD was entering the City of David, Michal daughter of Saul watched from a window. And when she saw King David leaping and dancing before the LORD, she despised him in her heart.

¹⁷They brought the ark of the LORD and set it in its place inside the tent that David had pitched for it, and David sacrificed burnt offerings and fellowship offerings before the LORD. ¹⁸After he had finished sacrificing the burnt offerings and fellowship offerings, he blessed the people in the name of the LORD Almighty. ¹⁹Then he gave a loaf of bread, a cake of dates and a cake of raisins to each person in the whole crowd of Israelites, both men and women. And all the people went to their homes.

²⁰When David returned home to bless his household, Michal daughter of Saul came out to meet him and said, "How the king of Israel has distinguished himself today, going around half-naked in full view of the slave girls of his servants as any vulgar fellow would!"

²¹David said to Michal, "It was before the LORD, who chose me rather than your father or anyone from his house when he appointed me ruler over the LORD's people Israel—I will celebrate before the LORD. ²²I will become even more undignified than this, and I will be humiliated in my own eyes. But by these slave girls you spoke of, I will be held in honor."

²³And Michal daughter of Saul had no children to the day of her death.

God's Promise to David

7 After the king was settled in his palace and the LORD had given him rest from all his enemies around him, ²he said to Nathan the prophet, "Here I am, living in a house of cedar, while the ark of God remains in a tent."

³Nathan replied to the king, "Whatever you have in mind, go ahead and do it, for the LORD is with you."

⁴But that night the word of the LORD came to Nathan, saying:

⁵"Go and tell my servant David, 'This is what the LORD says: Are you the one to build me a house to dwell in? ⁶I have not dwelt in a house from the day I brought the Israelites up out of Egypt to this day. I have been moving from place to place with a tent as my dwelling. ⁷Wherever I have moved with all the Israelites, did I ever say to any of their rulers whom I commanded to shepherd my people

THE
WITNESSES

✓ NATHAN THE PROPHET
(2 SAMUEL 7:1–2)

His name means "given" or "paid." He was a prophet of God who traveled with David a lot. David paid attention to him and obeyed him, because he knew that Nathan always spoke for God.

Israel, "Why have you not built me a house of cedar?" '

[8] "Now then, tell my servant David, 'This is what the LORD Almighty says: I took you from the pasture, from tending the flock, and appointed you ruler over my people Israel. [9] I have been with you wherever you have gone, and I have cut off all your enemies from before you. Now I will make your name great, like the names of the greatest men on earth. [10] And I will provide a place for my people Israel and will plant them so that they can have a home of their own and no longer be disturbed. Wicked people will not oppress them anymore, as they did at the beginning [11] and have done ever since the time I appointed leaders[a] over my people Israel. I will also give you rest from all your enemies.

" 'The LORD declares to you that the LORD himself will establish a house for you: [12] When your days are over and you rest with your ancestors, I will raise up your offspring to succeed you, your own flesh and blood, and I will establish his kingdom. [13] He is the one who will build a house for my Name, and I will establish the throne of his kingdom forever. [14] I will be his father, and he will be my son. When he does wrong, I will punish him with a rod wielded by men, with floggings inflicted by human hands. [15] But my love will never be taken away from him, as I took it away from Saul, whom I removed from before you. [16] Your house and your kingdom will endure forever before me[b]; your throne will be established forever.' "

[17] Nathan reported to David all the words of this entire revelation.

David's Prayer

[18] Then King David went in and sat before the LORD, and he said:

"Who am I, Sovereign LORD, and what is my family, that you have brought me this far? [19] And as if this were not enough in your sight, Sovereign LORD, you have also spoken about the future of the house of your servant—and this decree, Sovereign LORD, is for a mere human![c]

[20] "What more can David say to you? For you know your servant, Sovereign LORD. [21] For the sake of your word and according to your will, you have done this great thing and made it known to your servant.

[22] "How great you are, Sovereign LORD! There is no one like you, and there is no God but you, as we have heard with our own ears. [23] And who is like your people Israel—the one nation on earth that God went out to redeem as a people for himself, and to make a name for himself, and to perform great and awesome wonders by driving out nations and their gods from before your people, whom you redeemed from Egypt?[d] [24] You have established your people Israel as your very own forever, and you, LORD, have become their God.

[25] "And now, LORD God, keep forever the promise you have made concerning your servant and his house. Do as you promised, [26] so that your name will be great forever. Then people will say, 'The LORD Almighty is God over Israel!' And the house of your servant David will be established in your sight.

[27] "LORD Almighty, God of Israel, you have revealed this to your servant, saying, 'I will build a house for you.' So your servant has found courage to pray this prayer to you. [28] Sovereign LORD, you are God! Your covenant is trustworthy, and you have promised these good things to your servant. [29] Now be pleased to bless the house of your servant, that it may continue forever in your sight; for you, Sovereign LORD, have spoken, and with your blessing the house of your servant will be blessed forever."

---

[a] 11 Traditionally *judges*   [b] 16 Some Hebrew manuscripts and Septuagint; most Hebrew manuscripts *you*   [c] 19 Or *for the human race*   [d] 23 See Septuagint and 1 Chron. 17:21; Hebrew *wonders for your land and before your people, whom you redeemed from Egypt, from the nations and their gods.*

David's Victories

8 In the course of time, David defeated the Philistines and subdued them, and he took Metheg Ammah from the control of the Philistines.

² David also defeated the Moabites. He made them lie down on the ground and measured them off with a length of cord. Every two lengths of them were put to death, and the third length was allowed to live. So the Moabites became subject to David and brought him tribute.

³ Moreover, David defeated Hadadezer son of Rehob, king of Zobah, when he went to restore his monument at^a the Euphrates River. ⁴ David captured a thousand of his chariots, seven thousand charioteers^b and twenty thousand foot soldiers. He hamstrung all but a hundred of the chariot horses.

⁵ When the Arameans of Damascus came to help Hadadezer king of Zobah, David struck down twenty-two thousand of them. ⁶ He put garrisons in the Aramean kingdom of Damascus, and the Arameans became subject to him and brought tribute. The Lᴏʀᴅ gave David victory wherever he went.

⁷ David took the gold shields that belonged to the officers of Hadadezer and brought them to Jerusalem. ⁸ From Tebah^c and Berothai, towns that belonged to Hadadezer, King David took a great quantity of bronze.

⁹ When Tou^d king of Hamath heard that David had defeated the entire army of Hadadezer, ¹⁰ he sent his son Joram^e to King David to greet him and congratulate him on his victory in battle over Hadadezer, who had been at war with Tou. Joram brought with him articles of silver, of gold and of bronze.

¹¹ King David dedicated these articles to the Lᴏʀᴅ, as he had done with the silver and gold from all the nations he had subdued: ¹² Edom^f and Moab, the Ammonites and the Philistines, and Amalek. He also dedicated the plunder taken from Hadadezer son of Rehob, king of Zobah.

¹³ And David became famous after he returned from striking down eighteen thousand Edomites^g in the Valley of Salt.

BREAKTHROUGH!

Arameans

(2 SAMUEL 8:6‑8)

These were desert people who later went to live farther north, and they stayed in Mesopotamia and had very good land there. Later on, they went south to the territory between the Euphrates River and the Mediterranean Sea.

¹⁴ He put garrisons throughout Edom, and all the Edomites became subject to David. The Lᴏʀᴅ gave David victory wherever he went.

David's Officials

¹⁵ David reigned over all Israel, doing what was just and right for all his people. ¹⁶ Joab son of Zeruiah was over the army; Jehoshaphat son of Ahilud was recorder; ¹⁷ Zadok son of Ahitub and Ahimelek son of Abiathar were priests; Seraiah was secretary; ¹⁸ Benaiah son of Jehoiada was over the Kerethites and Pelethites; and David's sons were priests.^h

---

^a 3 Or *his control along*   ^b 4 Septuagint (see also Dead Sea Scrolls and 1 Chron. 18:4); Masoretic Text *captured seventeen hundred of his charioteers*   ^c 8 See some Septuagint manuscripts (see also 1 Chron. 18:8); Hebrew *Betah.*   ^d 9 Hebrew *Toi,* a variant of *Tou;* also in verse 10   ^e 10 A variant of *Hadoram*   ^f 12 Some Hebrew manuscripts, Septuagint and Syriac (see also 1 Chron. 18:11); most Hebrew manuscripts *Aram*   ^g 13 A few Hebrew manuscripts, Septuagint and Syriac (see also 1 Chron. 18:12); most Hebrew manuscripts *Aram* (that is, Arameans)   ^h 18 Or *were chief officials* (see Septuagint and Targum; see also 1 Chron. 18:17)

David and Mephibosheth

9 David asked, "Is there anyone still left of the house of Saul to whom I can show kindness for Jonathan's sake?"

[2] Now there was a servant of Saul's household named Ziba. They summoned him to appear before David, and the king said to him, "Are you Ziba?"

"At your service," he replied.

[3] The king asked, "Is there no one still alive from the house of Saul to whom I can show God's kindness?"

Ziba answered the king, "There is still a son of Jonathan; he is lame in both feet."

[4] "Where is he?" the king asked.

Ziba answered, "He is at the house of Makir son of Ammiel in Lo Debar."

[5] So King David had him brought from Lo Debar, from the house of Makir son of Ammiel.

[6] When Mephibosheth son of Jonathan, the son of Saul, came to David, he bowed down to pay him honor.

David said, "Mephibosheth!"

"At your service," he replied.

[7] "Don't be afraid," David said to him, "for I will surely show you kindness for the sake of your father Jonathan. I will restore to you all the land that belonged to your grandfather Saul, and you will always eat at my table."

[8] Mephibosheth bowed down and said, "What is your servant, that you should notice a dead dog like me?"

[9] Then the king summoned Ziba, Saul's steward, and said to him, "I have given your master's grandson everything that belonged to Saul and his family. [10] You and your sons and your servants are to farm the land for him and bring in the crops, so that your master's grandson may be provided for. And Mephibosheth, grandson of your master, will always eat at my table." (Now Ziba had fifteen sons and twenty servants.)

[11] Then Ziba said to the king, "Your servant will do whatever my lord the king commands his servant to do." So Mephibosheth ate at David's[a] table like one of the king's sons.

[12] Mephibosheth had a young son named Mika, and all the members of Zi-

THE WITNESSES

✓ **ZIBA** (2 SAMUEL 9:2)

He was one of King Saul's slaves. Later, David put him to work for Mephibosheth, Jonathan's son. Ziba did some good things, but he also did some bad things, like lie about Mephibosheth. In the end, his lie was discovered and justice was done!

ba's household were servants of Mephibosheth. [13] And Mephibosheth lived in Jerusalem, because he always ate at the king's table; he was lame in both feet.

David Defeats the Ammonites

10 In the course of time, the king of the Ammonites died, and his son Hanun succeeded him as king. [2] David thought, "I will show kindness to Hanun son of Nahash, just as his father showed kindness to me." So David sent a delegation to

---

[a] 11 Septuagint; Hebrew *my*

express his sympathy to Hanun concerning his father.

When David's men came to the land of the Ammonites, ³the Ammonite commanders said to Hanun their lord, "Do you think David is honoring your father by sending envoys to you to express sympathy? Hasn't David sent them to you only to explore the city and spy it out and overthrow it?" ⁴So Hanun seized David's envoys, shaved off half of each man's beard, cut off their garments at the buttocks, and sent them away.

⁵When David was told about this, he sent messengers to meet the men, for they were greatly humiliated. The king said, "Stay at Jericho till your beards have grown, and then come back."

⁶When the Ammonites realized that they had become obnoxious to David,

BREAKTHROUGH!

Why did Hanun shave off half of the messengers' beards?

(2 SAMUEL 10:4)

For a man at that time, his beard showed that he was a real man. That's why they only shaved during times when they were suffering a lot, like when somebody had died. Shaving the beards of those messengers was a big embarrassment.

they hired twenty thousand Aramean foot soldiers from Beth Rehob and Zobah, as well as the king of Maakah with a thousand men, and also twelve thousand men from Tob.

⁷On hearing this, David sent Joab out with the entire army of fighting men. ⁸The Ammonites came out and drew up in battle formation at the entrance of their city gate, while the Arameans of Zobah and Rehob and the men of Tob and Maakah were by themselves in the open country.

⁹Joab saw that there were battle lines in front of him and behind him; so he selected some of the best troops in Israel and deployed them against the Arameans. ¹⁰He put the rest of the men under the command of Abishai his brother and deployed them against the Ammonites. ¹¹Joab said, "If the Arameans are too strong for me, then you are to come to my rescue; but if the Ammonites are too strong for you, then I will come to rescue you. ¹²Be strong, and let us fight bravely for our people and the cities of our God. The Lᴏʀᴅ will do what is good in his sight."

¹³Then Joab and the troops with him advanced to fight the Arameans, and they fled before him. ¹⁴When the Ammonites realized that the Arameans were fleeing, they fled before Abishai and went inside the city. So Joab returned from fighting the Ammonites and came to Jerusalem.

¹⁵After the Arameans saw that they had been routed by Israel, they regrouped. ¹⁶Hadadezer had Arameans brought from beyond the Euphrates River; they went to Helam, with Shobak the commander of Hadadezer's army leading them.

¹⁷When David was told of this, he gathered all Israel, crossed the Jordan and went to Helam. The Arameans formed their battle lines to meet David and fought against him. ¹⁸But they fled before Israel, and David killed seven hundred of their charioteers and forty thousand of their foot soldiers.ᵃ He also struck down Shobak the commander of their army, and he died there. ¹⁹When all the kings who were vassals of Hadadezer saw that they had been routed by Israel,

---

ᵃ 18 Some Septuagint manuscripts (see also 1 Chron. 19:18); Hebrew horsemen they made peace with the Israelites and became subject to them.

So the Arameans were afraid to help the Ammonites anymore.

David and Bathsheba

11 In the spring, at the time when kings go off to war, David sent Joab out with the king's men and the whole Israelite army. They destroyed the Ammonites and besieged Rabbah. But David remained in Jerusalem.

²One evening David got up from his bed and walked around on the roof of the palace. From the roof he saw a woman bathing. The woman was very beautiful, ³and David sent someone to find out about her. The man said, "She is Bathsheba, the daughter of Eliam and the wife of Uriah the Hittite." ⁴Then David sent messengers to get her. She came to him, and he slept with her. (Now she was purifying herself from her monthly uncleanness.) Then she went back home. ⁵The woman conceived and sent word to David, saying, "I am pregnant."

⁶So David sent this word to Joab: "Send me Uriah the Hittite." And Joab sent him to David. ⁷When Uriah came to him, David asked him how Joab was, how the soldiers were and how the war was going. ⁸Then David said to Uriah, "Go down to your house and wash your feet." So Uriah left the palace, and a gift was sent after him. ⁹But Uriah slept at the entrance to the palace with all his master's servants and did not go down to his house.

¹⁰David was told, "Uriah did not go home." So he asked Uriah, "Haven't you just come from a military campaign? Why didn't you go home?"

¹¹Uriah said to David, "The ark and Israel and Judah are staying in tents,ᵃ and my commander Joab and my lord's men are camped in the open country. How could I go to my house to eat and drink and make love to my wife? As surely as you live, I will not do such a thing!"

¹²Then David said to him, "Stay here one more day, and tomorrow I will send you back." So Uriah remained in Jerusalem that day and the next. ¹³At David's

invitation, he ate and drank with him, and David made him drunk. But in the evening Uriah went out to sleep on his mat among his master's servants; he did not go home.

¹⁴In the morning David wrote a letter to Joab and sent it with Uriah. ¹⁵In it he wrote, "Put Uriah out in front where the fighting is fiercest. Then withdraw from him so he will be struck down and die."

¹⁶So while Joab had the city under siege, he put Uriah at a place where he knew

---

ᵃ 11 Or *staying at Sukkoth*

THE WITNESSES

✓ **BATHSHEBA** (2 SAMUEL 11:3)
This name means "daughter of oath." She was David's wife and Solomon's mother. Solomon was the third king of Israel. She was married to Uriah, but David ordered him to the front line of war so he would be killed. That way Bathsheba could belong to him. What he did was wrong!

the strongest defenders were. [17]When the men of the city came out and fought against Joab, some of the men in David's army fell; moreover, Uriah the Hittite died. [18]Joab sent David a full account of the battle. [19]He instructed the messenger: "When you have finished giving the king this account of the battle, [20]the king's anger may flare up, and he may ask you, 'Why did you get so close to the city to fight? Didn't you know they would shoot arrows from the wall? [21]Who killed Abimelek son of Jerub-Besheth[a]? Didn't a woman drop an upper millstone on him from the wall, so that he died in Thebez? Why did you get so close to the wall?' If he asks you this, then say to him, 'Moreover, your servant Uriah the Hittite is dead.'"

[22]The messenger set out, and when he arrived he told David everything Joab had sent him to say. [23]The messenger said to David, "The men overpowered us and came out against us in the open, but we drove them back to the entrance of the city gate. [24]Then the archers shot arrows at your servants from the wall, and some of the king's men died. Moreover, your servant Uriah the Hittite is dead."

[25]David told the messenger, "Say this to Joab: 'Don't let this upset you; the sword devours one as well as another. Press the attack against the city and destroy it.' Say this to encourage Joab."

[26]When Uriah's wife heard that her husband was dead, she mourned for him. [27]After the time of mourning was over, David had her brought to his house, and she became his wife and bore him a son. But the thing David had done displeased the LORD.

Nathan Rebukes David

12 The LORD sent Nathan to David. When he came to him, he said, "There were two men in a certain town, one rich and the other poor. [2]The rich man had a very large number of sheep and cattle, [3]but the poor man had nothing except one little ewe lamb he had bought. He raised it, and it grew up with him and his children. It shared his food, drank from his cup and even slept in his arms. It was like a daughter to him.

[4]"Now a traveler came to the rich man, but the rich man refrained from taking one of his own sheep or cattle to prepare a meal for the traveler who had come to him. Instead, he took the ewe lamb that belonged to the poor man and prepared it for the one who had come to him."

[5]David burned with anger against the man and said to Nathan, "As surely as the LORD lives, the man who did this must die! [6]He must pay for that lamb four times over, because he did such a thing and had no pity."

[7]Then Nathan said to David, "You are the man! This is what the LORD, the God of Israel, says: 'I anointed you king over Israel, and I delivered you from the hand of Saul. [8]I gave your master's house to you, and your master's wives into your arms. I gave you all Israel and Judah. And if all this had been too little, I would have given you even more. [9]Why did you despise the word of the LORD by doing what is evil in his eyes? You struck down Uriah the Hittite with the sword and took his wife to be your own. You killed him with the sword of the Ammonites. [10]Now, therefore, the sword will never depart from your house, because you despised me and took the wife of Uriah the Hittite to be your own.'

[11]"This is what the LORD says: 'Out of your own household I am going to bring calamity on you. Before your very eyes I will take your wives and give them to one who is close to you, and he will sleep with your wives in broad daylight. [12]You did it in secret, but I will do this thing in broad daylight before all Israel.'"

[13]Then David said to Nathan, "I have sinned against the LORD."

Nathan replied, "The LORD has taken away your sin. You are not going to die. [14]But because by doing this you have shown utter contempt for[b] the LORD, the son born to you will die."

[15]After Nathan had gone home, the LORD struck the child that Uriah's wife had borne to David, and he became ill. [16]David pleaded with God for the child. He fasted

---

[a] 21 Also known as *Jerub-Baal* (that is, Gideon)   [b] 14 An ancient Hebrew scribal tradition; Masoretic Text *for the enemies of*

and spent the nights lying in sackcloth[a] on the ground. [17]The elders of his household stood beside him to get him up from the ground, but he refused, and he would not eat any food with them.

[18]On the seventh day the child died. David's attendants were afraid to tell him that the child was dead, for they thought, "While the child was still living, he wouldn't listen to us when we spoke to him. How can we now tell him the child is dead? He may do something desperate."

[19]David noticed that his attendants were whispering among themselves, and he realized the child was dead. "Is the child dead?" he asked.

"Yes," they replied, "he is dead."

[20]Then David got up from the ground. After he had washed, put on lotions and changed his clothes, he went into the house of the LORD and worshiped. Then he went to his own house, and at his request they served him food, and he ate.

[21]His attendants asked him, "Why are you acting this way? While the child was alive, you fasted and wept, but now that the child is dead, you get up and eat!"

[22]He answered, "While the child was still alive, I fasted and wept. I thought, 'Who knows? The LORD may be gracious to me and let the child live.' [23]But now that he is dead, why should I go on fasting? Can I bring him back again? I will go to him, but he will not return to me."

[24]Then David comforted his wife Bathsheba, and he went to her and made love to her. She gave birth to a son, and they named him Solomon. The LORD loved him; [25]and because the LORD loved him, he sent word through Nathan the prophet to name him Jedidiah.[b]

[26]Meanwhile Joab fought against Rabbah of the Ammonites and captured the royal citadel. [27]Joab then sent messengers to David, saying, "I have fought against Rabbah and taken its water supply. [28]Now muster the rest of the troops and besiege the city and capture it. Otherwise I will take the city, and it will be named after me."

[29]So David mustered the entire army and went to Rabbah, and attacked and captured it. [30]David took the crown from

THE
WITNESSES

✓ SOLOMON (2 SAMUEL 12:24)

This name means "peaceful." He was David and Bathsheba's son. He became king after David. The Bible says he was the wisest man in the world, and that people came from all over to hear him speak.

their king's[c] head, and it was placed on his own head. It weighed a talent[d] of gold, and it was set with precious stones. David took a great quantity of plunder from the city [31]and brought out the people who were there, consigning them to labor with saws and with iron picks and axes, and he made them work at brickmaking.[e] David did this to all the Ammonite towns. Then he and his entire army returned to Jerusalem.

[a] 16 Dead Sea Scrolls and Septuagint; Masoretic Text does not have *in sackcloth*.   [b] 25 *Jedidiah* means *loved by the* LORD.   [c] 30 Or *from Milkom's* (that is, Molek's)
[d] 30 That is, about 75 pounds or about 34 kilograms
[e] 31 The meaning of the Hebrew for this clause is uncertain.

Amnon and Tamar

13 In the course of time, Amnon son of David fell in love with Tamar, the beautiful sister of Absalom son of David.

2 Amnon became so obsessed with his sister Tamar that he made himself ill. She was a virgin, and it seemed impossible for him to do anything to her.

3 Now Amnon had an adviser named Jonadab son of Shimeah, David's brother. Jonadab was a very shrewd man. 4 He asked Amnon, "Why do you, the king's son, look so haggard morning after morning? Won't you tell me?"

Amnon said to him, "I'm in love with Tamar, my brother Absalom's sister."

5 "Go to bed and pretend to be ill," Jonadab said. "When your father comes to see you, say to him, 'I would like my sister Tamar to come and give me something to eat. Let her prepare the food in my sight so I may watch her and then eat it from her hand.' "

6 So Amnon lay down and pretended to be ill. When the king came to see him, Amnon said to him, "I would like my sister Tamar to come and make some special bread in my sight, so I may eat from her hand."

7 David sent word to Tamar at the palace: "Go to the house of your brother Amnon and prepare some food for him." 8 So Tamar went to the house of her brother Amnon, who was lying down. She took some dough, kneaded it, made the bread in his sight and baked it. 9 Then she took the pan and served him the bread, but he refused to eat.

"Send everyone out of here," Amnon said. So everyone left him. 10 Then Amnon said to Tamar, "Bring the food here into my bedroom so I may eat from your hand." And Tamar took the bread she had prepared and brought it to her brother Amnon in his bedroom. 11 But when she took it to him to eat, he grabbed her and said, "Come to bed with me, my sister."

12 "No, my brother!" she said to him. "Don't force me! Such a thing should not be done in Israel! Don't do this wicked thing. 13 What about me? Where could I

THE
WITNESSES

✓ ABSALOM (2 SAMUEL 13:1)

This name means "father of peace." He was David's son, and his mother was Maakah. He defended his sister, Tamar, when her brother Amnon attacked her. Later, Absalom wanted to be king instead of David, his father.

✓ TAMAR (2 SAMUEL 13:1)

This means "palm tree." She was David and Maakah's daughter. She was beautiful and her stepbrother Amnon fell in love with her. It's not a pretty story—it's really very terrible, and chapter 13 of this book talks about it.

✓ AMNON (2 SAMUEL 13:1)

This name means "faithful." He was David and Ahinoam's son. He was very cruel to his sister, Tamar.

get rid of my disgrace? And what about you? You would be like one of the wicked fools in Israel. Please speak to the king; he will not keep me from being married to you." ¹⁴But he refused to listen to her, and since he was stronger than she, he raped her.

¹⁵Then Amnon hated her with intense hatred. In fact, he hated her more than he had loved her. Amnon said to her, "Get up and get out!"

¹⁶"No!" she said to him. "Sending me away would be a greater wrong than what you have already done to me."

But he refused to listen to her. ¹⁷He called his personal servant and said, "Get this woman out of my sight and bolt the door after her." ¹⁸So his servant put her out and bolted the door after her. She was wearing an ornate*ᵃ* robe, for this was the kind of garment the virgin daughters of the king wore. ¹⁹Tamar put ashes on her head and tore the ornate robe she was wearing. She put her hands on her head and went away, weeping aloud as she went.

²⁰Her brother Absalom said to her, "Has that Amnon, your brother, been with you? Be quiet for now, my sister; he is your brother. Don't take this thing to heart." And Tamar lived in her brother Absalom's house, a desolate woman.

²¹When King David heard all this, he was furious. ²²And Absalom never said a word to Amnon, either good or bad; he hated Amnon because he had disgraced his sister Tamar.

Absalom Kills Amnon

²³Two years later, when Absalom's sheepshearers were at Baal Hazor near the border of Ephraim, he invited all the king's sons to come there. ²⁴Absalom went to the king and said, "Your servant has had shearers come. Will the king and his attendants please join me?"

²⁵"No, my son," the king replied. "All of us should not go; we would only be a burden to you." Although Absalom urged him, he still refused to go but gave him his blessing.

²⁶Then Absalom said, "If not, please let my brother Amnon come with us."

The king asked him, "Why should he go with you?" ²⁷But Absalom urged him, so he sent with him Amnon and the rest of the king's sons.

²⁸Absalom ordered his men, "Listen! When Amnon is in high spirits from drinking wine and I say to you, 'Strike Amnon down,' then kill him. Don't be afraid. Haven't I given you this order? Be strong and brave." ²⁹So Absalom's men did to Amnon what Absalom had ordered. Then all the king's sons got up, mounted their mules and fled.

³⁰While they were on their way, the report came to David: "Absalom has struck down all the king's sons; not one of them is left." ³¹The king stood up, tore his clothes and lay down on the ground; and all his attendants stood by with their clothes torn.

³²But Jonadab son of Shimeah, David's brother, said, "My lord should not think that they killed all the princes; only Amnon is dead. This has been Absalom's express intention ever since the day Amnon raped his sister Tamar. ³³My lord the king should not be concerned about the report that all the king's sons are dead. Only Amnon is dead."

³⁴Meanwhile, Absalom had fled.

Now the man standing watch looked up and saw many people on the road west of him, coming down the side of the hill. The watchman went and told the king, "I see men in the direction of Horonaim, on the side of the hill."*ᵇ*

³⁵Jonadab said to the king, "See, the king's sons have come; it has happened just as your servant said."

³⁶As he finished speaking, the king's sons came in, wailing loudly. The king, too, and all his attendants wept very bitterly.

³⁷Absalom fled and went to Talmai son of Ammihud, the king of Geshur. But King David mourned many days for his son.

³⁸After Absalom fled and went to Geshur, he stayed there three years. ³⁹And King David longed to go to Absalom, for he was consoled concerning Amnon's death.

ᵃ *18* The meaning of the Hebrew for this word is uncertain; also in verse 19.　　*ᵇ* *34* Septuagint; Hebrew does not have this sentence.

THE SCENE

GESHUR

(2 SAMUEL 13:37)

This city was on the east side of the Jordan River. The people of Israel were never able to conquer it completely. Geshur had its own kings, but they paid taxes to Israel. Absalom found refuge in this city after his brother Amnon died. His mother, Maakah, was Talmai's daughter, and he was the king of Geshur.

Absalom Returns to Jerusalem

14 Joab son of Zeruiah knew that the king's heart longed for Absalom. ² So Joab sent someone to Tekoa and had a wise woman brought from there. He said to her, "Pretend you are in mourning. Dress in mourning clothes, and don't use any cosmetic lotions. Act like a woman who has spent many days grieving for the dead. ³ Then go to the king and speak these words to him." And Joab put the words in her mouth.

⁴ When the woman from Tekoa went*ᵃ* to the king, she fell with her face to the ground to pay him honor, and she said, "Help me, Your Majesty!"

⁵ The king asked her, "What is troubling you?"

She said, "I am a widow; my husband is dead. ⁶ I your servant had two sons. They got into a fight with each other in the field, and no one was there to separate them. One struck the other and killed him. ⁷ Now the whole clan has risen up against your servant; they say, 'Hand over the one who struck his brother down, so that we may put him to death for the life of his brother whom he killed; then we will get rid of the heir as well.' They would put out the only burning coal I have left, leaving my husband neither name nor descendant on the face of the earth."

⁸ The king said to the woman, "Go home, and I will issue an order in your behalf."

⁹ But the woman from Tekoa said to him, "Let my lord the king pardon me and my family, and let the king and his throne be without guilt."

¹⁰ The king replied, "If anyone says anything to you, bring them to me, and they will not bother you again."

¹¹ She said, "Then let the king invoke the LORD his God to prevent the avenger of blood from adding to the destruction, so that my son will not be destroyed."

"As surely as the LORD lives," he said, "not one hair of your son's head will fall to the ground."

¹² Then the woman said, "Let your servant speak a word to my lord the king."

"Speak," he replied.

¹³ The woman said, "Why then have you devised a thing like this against the people of God? When the king says this, does he not convict himself, for the king has not brought back his banished son? ¹⁴ Like water spilled on the ground, which cannot be recovered, so we must die. But that is not what God desires; rather, he devises ways so that a banished person does not remain banished from him.

¹⁵ "And now I have come to say this to my lord the king because the people have made me afraid. Your servant thought, 'I will speak to the king; perhaps he will

---

ᵃ 4 Many Hebrew manuscripts, Septuagint, Vulgate and Syriac; most Hebrew manuscripts *spoke* grant his servant's request. [16]Perhaps the king will agree to deliver his servant from the hand of the man who is trying to cut off both me and my son from God's inheritance.'

[17]"And now your servant says, 'May the word of my lord the king secure my inheritance, for my lord the king is like an angel of God in discerning good and evil. May the LORD your God be with you.' "

[18]Then the king said to the woman, "Don't keep from me the answer to what I am going to ask you."

"Let my lord the king speak," the woman said.

[19]The king asked, "Isn't the hand of Joab with you in all this?"

The woman answered, "As surely as you live, my lord the king, no one can turn to the right or to the left from anything my lord the king says. Yes, it was your servant Joab who instructed me to do this and who put all these words into the mouth of your servant. [20]Your servant Joab did this to change the present situation. My lord has wisdom like that of an angel of God—he knows everything that happens in the land."

[21]The king said to Joab, "Very well, I will do it. Go, bring back the young man Absalom."

[22]Joab fell with his face to the ground to pay him honor, and he blessed the king. Joab said, "Today your servant knows that he has found favor in your eyes, my lord the king, because the king has granted his servant's request."

[23]Then Joab went to Geshur and brought Absalom back to Jerusalem. [24]But the king said, "He must go to his own house; he must not see my face." So Absalom went to his own house and did not see the face of the king.

[25]In all Israel there was not a man so highly praised for his handsome appearance as Absalom. From the top of his head to the sole of his foot there was no blemish in him. [26]Whenever he cut the hair of his head—he used to cut his hair once a year because it became too heavy for him—he would weigh it, and its weight was two hundred shekels[a] by the royal standard.

[27]Three sons and a daughter were born to Absalom. His daughter's name was Tamar, and she became a beautiful woman.

[28]Absalom lived two years in Jerusalem without seeing the king's face. [29]Then Absalom sent for Joab in order to send him to the king, but Joab refused to come to him. So he sent a second time, but he refused to come. [30]Then he said to his servants, "Look, Joab's field is next to mine, and he has barley there. Go and set it on fire." So Absalom's servants set the field on fire.

[31]Then Joab did go to Absalom's house, and he said to him, "Why have your servants set my field on fire?"

[32]Absalom said to Joab, "Look, I sent word to you and said, 'Come here so I can send you to the king to ask, "Why have I come from Geshur? It would be better for me if I were still there!" ' Now then, I want to see the king's face, and if I am guilty of anything, let him put me to death."

[33]So Joab went to the king and told him this. Then the king summoned Absalom, and he came in and bowed down with his face to the ground before the king. And the king kissed Absalom.

Absalom's Conspiracy

15 In the course of time, Absalom provided himself with a chariot and horses and with fifty men to run ahead of him. [2]He would get up early and stand by the side of the road leading to the city gate. Whenever anyone came with a complaint to be placed before the king for a decision, Absalom would call out to him, "What town are you from?" He would answer, "Your servant is from one of the tribes of Israel." [3]Then Absalom would say to him, "Look, your claims are valid and proper, but there is no representative of the king to hear you." [4]And Absalom would add, "If only I were appointed judge in the land! Then everyone who has a complaint or case could come to me and I would see that they receive justice."

[5]Also, whenever anyone approached

---

[a] 26 That is, about 5 pounds or about 2.3 kilograms

him to bow down before him, Absalom would reach out his hand, take hold of him and kiss him. ⁶Absalom behaved in this way toward all the Israelites who came to the king asking for justice, and so he stole the hearts of the people of Israel.

⁷At the end of four*ᵃ* years, Absalom said to the king, "Let me go to Hebron and fulfill a vow I made to the LORD. ⁸While your servant was living at Geshur in Aram, I made this vow: 'If the LORD takes me back to Jerusalem, I will worship the LORD in Hebron.*ᵇ*' "

⁹The king said to him, "Go in peace." So he went to Hebron.

¹⁰Then Absalom sent secret messengers throughout the tribes of Israel to say, "As soon as you hear the sound of the trumpets, then say, 'Absalom is king in Hebron.' " ¹¹Two hundred men from Jerusalem had accompanied Absalom. They had been invited as guests and went quite innocently, knowing nothing about the matter. ¹²While Absalom was offering sacrifices, he also sent for Ahithophel the Gilonite, David's counselor, to come from Giloh, his hometown. And so the conspiracy gained strength, and Absalom's following kept on increasing.

David Flees

¹³A messenger came and told David, "The hearts of the people of Israel are with Absalom."

¹⁴Then David said to all his officials who were with him in Jerusalem, "Come! We must flee, or none of us will escape from Absalom. We must leave immediately, or he will move quickly to overtake us and bring ruin on us and put the city to the sword."

¹⁵The king's officials answered him, "Your servants are ready to do whatever our lord the king chooses."

¹⁶The king set out, with his entire household following him; but he left ten concubines to take care of the palace. ¹⁷So the king set out, with all the people following him, and they halted at the edge of the city. ¹⁸All his men marched past him, along with all the Kerethites and Pelethites; and all the six hundred

Gittites who had accompanied him from Gath marched before the king.

¹⁹The king said to Ittai the Gittite, "Why should you come along with us? Go back and stay with King Absalom. You are a foreigner, an exile from your homeland. ²⁰You came only yesterday. And today shall I make you wander about with us, when I do not know where I am going? Go back, and take your people with you. May the LORD show you kindness and faithfulness."*ᶜ*

²¹But Ittai replied to the king, "As surely as the LORD lives, and as my lord the king lives, wherever my lord the king may be, whether it means life or death, there will your servant be."

²²David said to Ittai, "Go ahead, march on." So Ittai the Gittite marched on with all his men and the families that were with him.

²³The whole countryside wept aloud as all the people passed by. The king also crossed the Kidron Valley, and all the people moved on toward the wilderness.

²⁴Zadok was there, too, and all the Levites who were with him were carrying the ark of the covenant of God. They set down the ark of God, and Abiathar offered sacrifices until all the people had finished leaving the city.

²⁵Then the king said to Zadok, "Take the ark of God back into the city. If I find favor in the LORD's eyes, he will bring me back and let me see it and his dwelling place again. ²⁶But if he says, 'I am not pleased with you,' then I am ready; let him do to me whatever seems good to him."

²⁷The king also said to Zadok the priest, "Do you understand? Go back to the city with my blessing. Take your son Ahimaaz with you, and also Abiathar's son Jonathan. You and Abiathar return with your two sons. ²⁸I will wait at the fords in the wilderness until word comes from you to inform me." ²⁹So Zadok and Abiathar took the ark of God back to Jerusalem and stayed there.

ᵃ 7 Some Septuagint manuscripts, Syriac and Josephus; Hebrew *forty*   *ᵇ 8* Some Septuagint manuscripts; Hebrew does not have *in Hebron.*   *ᶜ 20* Septuagint; Hebrew *May kindness and faithfulness be with you*

³⁰But David continued up the Mount of Olives, weeping as he went; his head was covered and he was barefoot. All the people with him covered their heads too and were weeping as they went up. ³¹Now David had been told, "Ahithophel is among the conspirators with Absalom." So David prayed, "LORD, turn Ahithophel's counsel into foolishness."

³²When David arrived at the summit, where people used to worship God, Hushai the Arkite was there to meet him, his robe torn and dust on his head. ³³David said to him, "If you go with me, you will be a burden to me. ³⁴But if you return to the city and say to Absalom, 'Your Majesty, I will be your servant; I was your father's servant in the past, but now I will be your servant,' then you can help me

THE
WITNESSES

✓ ZADOK (2 SAMUEL 15:24)

It means "fair." He was a priest of God. He was very obedient to King David and accompanied him during very difficult times. He was also in charge of anointing Solomon as king after David.

by frustrating Ahithophel's advice. ³⁵Won't the priests Zadok and Abiathar be there with you? Tell them anything you hear in the king's palace. ³⁶Their two sons, Ahimaaz son of Zadok and Jonathan son of Abiathar, are there with them. Send them to me with anything you hear."

³⁷So Hushai, David's confidant, arrived at Jerusalem as Absalom was entering the city.

David and Ziba

16 When David had gone a short distance beyond the summit, there was Ziba, the steward of Mephibosheth, waiting to meet him. He had a string of

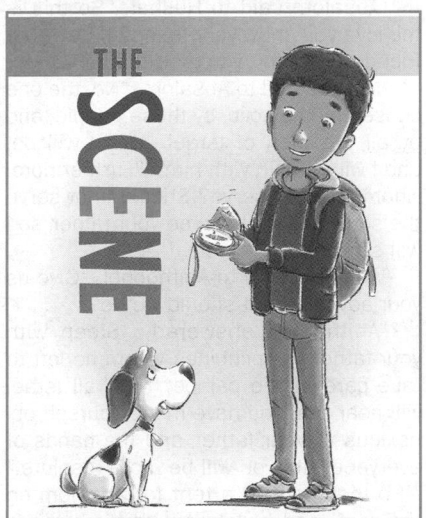

THE
SCENE

KIDRON VALLEY

(2 SAMUEL 15:23)

This stream separates Jerusalem from the Mount of Olives. It's between Stephen's Gate and the Garden of Gethsemane. It is 33 yards (30 meters) deep and 131 yards (120 meters) wide. David probably crossed it when he escaped from his son Absalom.

donkeys saddled and loaded with two hundred loaves of bread, a hundred cakes of raisins, a hundred cakes of figs and a skin of wine. ²The king asked Ziba, "Why have you brought these?"

Ziba answered, "The donkeys are for the king's household to ride on, the bread and fruit are for the men to eat, and the wine is to refresh those who become exhausted in the wilderness." ³The king then asked, "Where is your master's grandson?"

Ziba said to him, "He is staying in Jerusalem, because he thinks, 'Today the Israelites will restore to me my grandfather's kingdom.'"

⁴Then the king said to Ziba, "All that belonged to Mephibosheth is now yours."

"I humbly bow," Ziba said. "May I find favor in your eyes, my lord the king."

Shimei Curses David

⁵As King David approached Bahurim, a man from the same clan as Saul's family came out from there. His name was Shimei son of Gera, and he cursed as he came out. ⁶He pelted David and all the king's officials with stones, though all the troops and the special guard were on David's right and left. ⁷As he cursed, Shimei said, "Get out, get out, you murderer, you scoundrel! ⁸The LORD has repaid you for all the blood you shed in the household of Saul, in whose place you have reigned. The LORD has given the kingdom into the hands of your son Absalom. You have come to ruin because you are a murderer!"

⁹Then Abishai son of Zeruiah said to the king, "Why should this dead dog curse my lord the king? Let me go over and cut off his head."

¹⁰But the king said, "What does this have to do with you, you sons of Zeruiah? If he is cursing because the LORD said to him, 'Curse David,' who can ask, 'Why do you do this?'"

¹¹David then said to Abishai and all his officials, "My son, my own flesh and blood, is trying to kill me. How much more, then, this Benjamite! Leave him alone; let him curse, for the LORD has told him to. ¹²It may be that the LORD will look upon my misery and restore to me his covenant blessing instead of his curse today."

¹³So David and his men continued along the road while Shimei was going along the hillside opposite him, cursing as he went and throwing stones at him and showering him with dirt. ¹⁴The king and all the people with him arrived at their destination exhausted. And there he refreshed himself.

The Advice of Ahithophel and Hushai

¹⁵Meanwhile, Absalom and all the men of Israel came to Jerusalem, and Ahithophel was with him. ¹⁶Then Hushai the Arkite, David's confidant, went to Absalom and said to him, "Long live the king! Long live the king!"

¹⁷Absalom said to Hushai, "So this is the love you show your friend? If he's your friend, why didn't you go with him?"

¹⁸Hushai said to Absalom, "No, the one chosen by the LORD, by these people, and by all the men of Israel—his I will be, and I will remain with him. ¹⁹Furthermore, whom should I serve? Should I not serve the son? Just as I served your father, so I will serve you."

²⁰Absalom said to Ahithophel, "Give us your advice. What should we do?"

²¹Ahithophel answered, "Sleep with your father's concubines whom he left to take care of the palace. Then all Israel will hear that you have made yourself obnoxious to your father, and the hands of everyone with you will be more resolute." ²²So they pitched a tent for Absalom on the roof, and he slept with his father's concubines in the sight of all Israel.

²³Now in those days the advice Ahithophel gave was like that of one who inquires of God. That was how both David and Absalom regarded all of Ahithophel's advice.

17 Ahithophel said to Absalom, "I would*ᵃ* choose twelve thousand men and set out tonight in pursuit of David. ²I would attack him while he is weary and weak. I would strike him with terror, and then all the people with him will flee.

ᵃ 1 Or Let me

I would strike down only the king [3]and bring all the people back to you. The death of the man you seek will mean the return of all; all the people will be unharmed." [4]This plan seemed good to Absalom and to all the elders of Israel.

[5]But Absalom said, "Summon also Hushai the Arkite, so we can hear what he has to say as well." [6]When Hushai came to him, Absalom said, "Ahithophel has given this advice. Should we do what he says? If not, give us your opinion."

[7]Hushai replied to Absalom, "The advice Ahithophel has given is not good this time. [8]You know your father and his men; they are fighters, and as fierce as a wild bear robbed of her cubs. Besides, your father is an experienced fighter; he will not spend the night with the troops. [9]Even now, he is hidden in a cave or some other place. If he should attack your troops first,[a] whoever hears about it will say, 'There has been a slaughter among the troops who follow Absalom.' [10]Then even the bravest soldier, whose heart is like the heart of a lion, will melt with fear, for all Israel knows that your father is a fighter and that those with him are brave.

[11]"So I advise you: Let all Israel, from Dan to Beersheba—as numerous as the sand on the seashore—be gathered to you, with you yourself leading them into battle. [12]Then we will attack him wherever he may be found, and we will fall on him as dew settles on the ground. Neither he nor any of his men will be left alive. [13]If he withdraws into a city, then all Israel will bring ropes to that city, and we will drag it down to the valley until not so much as a pebble is left."

[14]Absalom and all the men of Israel said, "The advice of Hushai the Arkite is better than that of Ahithophel." For the LORD had determined to frustrate the good advice of Ahithophel in order to bring disaster on Absalom.

[15]Hushai told Zadok and Abiathar, the priests, "Ahithophel has advised Absalom and the elders of Israel to do such and such, but I have advised them to do so and so. [16]Now send a message at once and tell David, 'Do not spend the night at the fords in the wilderness; cross over without fail, or the king and all the people with him will be swallowed up.' "

[17]Jonathan and Ahimaaz were staying at En Rogel. A female servant was to go and inform them, and they were to go and tell King David, for they could not risk being seen entering the city. [18]But a young man saw them and told Absalom. So the two of them left at once and went to the house of a man in Bahurim. He had a well in his courtyard, and they climbed down into it. [19]His wife took a covering and spread it out over the opening of the well and scattered grain over it. No one knew anything about it.

[20]When Absalom's men came to the woman at the house, they asked, "Where are Ahimaaz and Jonathan?"

The woman answered them, "They crossed over the brook."[b] The men searched but found no one, so they returned to Jerusalem.

[21]After they had gone, the two climbed out of the well and went to inform King David. They said to him, "Set out and cross the river at once; Ahithophel has advised such and such against you." [22]So David and all the people with him set out and crossed the Jordan. By daybreak, no one was left who had not crossed the Jordan.

[23]When Ahithophel saw that his advice had not been followed, he saddled his donkey and set out for his house in his hometown. He put his house in order and then hanged himself. So he died and was buried in his father's tomb.

Absalom's Death

[24]David went to Mahanaim, and Absalom crossed the Jordan with all the men of Israel. [25]Absalom had appointed Amasa over the army in place of Joab. Amasa was the son of Jether,[c] an Ishmaelite[d] who had married Abigail,[e] the daughter of Nahash and sister of Zeruiah the mother of Joab. [26]The Israelites and Absalom camped in the land of Gilead.

[a] 9 Or When some of the men fall at the first attack
[b] 20 Or "They passed by the sheep pen toward the water."
[c] 25 Hebrew Ithra, a variant of Jether   [d] 25 Some Septuagint manuscripts (see also 1 Chron. 2:17); Hebrew and other Septuagint manuscripts Israelite   [e] 25 Hebrew Abigal, a variant of Abigail

27When David came to Mahanaim, Shobi son of Nahash from Rabbah of the Ammonites, and Makir son of Ammiel from Lo Debar, and Barzillai the Gileadite from Rogelim 28brought bedding and bowls and articles of pottery. They also brought wheat and barley, flour and roasted grain, beans and lentils,*a* 29honey and curds, sheep, and cheese from cows' milk for David and his people to eat. For they said, "The people have become exhausted and hungry and thirsty in the wilderness."

18 David mustered the men who were with him and appointed over them commanders of thousands and commanders of hundreds. 2David sent out his troops, a third under the command of Joab, a third under Joab's brother Abishai son of Zeruiah, and a third under Ittai the Gittite. The king told the troops, "I myself will surely march out with you."

3But the men said, "You must not go out; if we are forced to flee, they won't care about us. Even if half of us die, they won't care; but you are worth ten thousand of us.*b* It would be better now for you to give us support from the city."

4The king answered, "I will do whatever seems best to you."

So the king stood beside the gate while all his men marched out in units of hundreds and of thousands. 5The king commanded Joab, Abishai and Ittai, "Be gentle with the young man Absalom for my sake." And all the troops heard the king giving orders concerning Absalom to each of the commanders.

6David's army marched out of the city to fight Israel, and the battle took place in the forest of Ephraim. 7There Israel's troops were routed by David's men, and the casualties that day were great—twenty thousand men. 8The battle spread out over the whole countryside, and the forest swallowed up more men that day than the sword.

9Now Absalom happened to meet David's men. He was riding his mule, and as the mule went under the thick branches of a large oak, Absalom's hair got caught in the tree. He was left hanging in midair, while the mule he was riding kept on going.

10When one of the men saw what had happened, he told Joab, "I just saw Absalom hanging in an oak tree."

11Joab said to the man who had told him this, "What! You saw him? Why didn't you strike him to the ground right there? Then I would have had to give you ten shekels*c* of silver and a warrior's belt."

12But the man replied, "Even if a thousand shekels*d* were weighed out into my hands, I would not lay a hand on the king's son. In our hearing the king commanded you and Abishai and Ittai, 'Protect the young man Absalom for my sake.*e*' 13And if I had put my life in jeopardy*f*—and nothing is hidden from the king—you would have kept your distance from me."

14Joab said, "I'm not going to wait like this for you." So he took three javelins in his hand and plunged them into Absalom's heart while Absalom was still alive in the oak tree. 15And ten of Joab's armor-bearers surrounded Absalom, struck him and killed him.

16Then Joab sounded the trumpet, and the troops stopped pursuing Israel, for Joab halted them. 17They took Absalom, threw him into a big pit in the forest and piled up a large heap of rocks over him. Meanwhile, all the Israelites fled to their homes.

18During his lifetime Absalom had taken a pillar and erected it in the King's Valley as a monument to himself, for he thought, "I have no son to carry on the memory of my name." He named the pillar after himself, and it is called Absalom's Monument to this day.

David Mourns

19Now Ahimaaz son of Zadok said, "Let me run and take the news to the king that the LORD has vindicated him by delivering him from the hand of his enemies."

---

a 28 Most Septuagint manuscripts and Syriac; Hebrew *lentils, and roasted grain*   *b* 3 Two Hebrew manuscripts, some Septuagint manuscripts and Vulgate; most Hebrew manuscripts *care; for now there are ten thousand like us*   *c* 11 That is, about 4 ounces or about 115 grams   *d* 12 That is, about 25 pounds or about 12 kilograms   *e* 12 A few Hebrew manuscripts, Septuagint, Vulgate and Syriac; most Hebrew manuscripts may be translated *Absalom, whoever you may be.*   *f* 13 Or *Otherwise, if I had acted treacherously toward him*

20"You are not the one to take the news today," Joab told him. "You may take the news another time, but you must not do so today, because the king's son is dead."

21Then Joab said to a Cushite, "Go, tell the king what you have seen." The Cushite bowed down before Joab and ran off.

22Ahimaaz son of Zadok again said to Joab, "Come what may, please let me run behind the Cushite."

But Joab replied, "My son, why do you want to go? You don't have any news that will bring you a reward."

23He said, "Come what may, I want to run."

So Joab said, "Run!" Then Ahimaaz ran by way of the plain*a* and outran the Cushite.

24While David was sitting between the inner and outer gates, the watchman went up to the roof of the gateway by the wall. As he looked out, he saw a man running alone. 25The watchman called out to the king and reported it.

The king said, "If he is alone, he must have good news." And the runner came closer and closer.

26Then the watchman saw another runner, and he called down to the gatekeeper, "Look, another man running alone!"

The king said, "He must be bringing good news, too."

27The watchman said, "It seems to me that the first one runs like Ahimaaz son of Zadok."

"He's a good man," the king said. "He comes with good news."

28Then Ahimaaz called out to the king, "All is well!" He bowed down before the king with his face to the ground and said, "Praise be to the LORD your God! He has delivered up those who lifted their hands against my lord the king."

29The king asked, "Is the young man Absalom safe?"

Ahimaaz answered, "I saw great confusion just as Joab was about to send the king's servant and me, your servant, but I don't know what it was."

30The king said, "Stand aside and wait here." So he stepped aside and stood there.

31Then the Cushite arrived and said, "My lord the king, hear the good news! The LORD has vindicated you today by delivering you from the hand of all who rose up against you."

32The king asked the Cushite, "Is the young man Absalom safe?"

The Cushite replied, "May the enemies of my lord the king and all who rise up to harm you be like that young man."

33The king was shaken. He went up to the room over the gateway and wept. As he went, he said: "O my son Absalom! My son, my son Absalom! If only I had died instead of you—O Absalom, my son, my son!"*b*

19*c* Joab was told, "The king is weeping and mourning for Absalom." 2And for the whole army the victory that day was turned into mourning, because on that day the troops heard it said, "The king is grieving for his son." 3The men stole into the city that day as men steal in who are ashamed when they flee from battle. 4The king covered his face and cried aloud, "O my son Absalom! O Absalom, my son, my son!"

5Then Joab went into the house to the king and said, "Today you have humiliated all your men, who have just saved your life and the lives of your sons and daughters and the lives of your wives and concubines. 6You love those who hate you and hate those who love you. You have made it clear today that the commanders and their men mean nothing to you. I see that you would be pleased if Absalom were alive today and all of us were dead. 7Now go out and encourage your men. I swear by the LORD that if you don't go out, not a man will be left with you by nightfall. This will be worse for you than all the calamities that have come on you from your youth till now."

8So the king got up and took his seat in the gateway. When the men were told, "The king is sitting in the gateway," they all came before him.

Meanwhile, the Israelites had fled to their homes.

---

a 23 That is, the plain of the Jordan   *b* 33 In Hebrew texts this verse (18:33) is numbered 19:1.   *c* In Hebrew texts 19:1-43 is numbered 19:2-44.

David Returns to Jerusalem

⁹Throughout the tribes of Israel, all the people were arguing among themselves, saying, "The king delivered us from the hand of our enemies; he is the one who rescued us from the hand of the Philistines. But now he has fled the country to escape from Absalom; ¹⁰and Absalom, whom we anointed to rule over us, has died in battle. So why do you say nothing about bringing the king back?"

¹¹King David sent this message to Zadok and Abiathar, the priests: "Ask the elders of Judah, 'Why should you be the last to bring the king back to his palace, since what is being said throughout Israel has reached the king at his quarters? ¹²You are my relatives, my own flesh and blood. So why should you be the last to bring back the king?' ¹³And say to Amasa, 'Are you not my own flesh and blood? May God deal with me, be it ever so severely, if you are not the commander of my army for life in place of Joab.' "

¹⁴He won over the hearts of the men of Judah so that they were all of one mind. They sent word to the king, "Return, you and all your men." ¹⁵Then the king returned and went as far as the Jordan.

Now the men of Judah had come to Gilgal to go out and meet the king and bring him across the Jordan. ¹⁶Shimei son of Gera, the Benjamite from Bahurim, hurried down with the men of Judah to meet King David. ¹⁷With him were a thousand Benjamites, along with Ziba, the steward of Saul's household, and his fifteen sons and twenty servants. They rushed to the Jordan, where the king was. ¹⁸They crossed at the ford to take the king's household over and to do whatever he wished.

When Shimei son of Gera crossed the Jordan, he fell prostrate before the king ¹⁹and said to him, "May my lord not hold me guilty. Do not remember how your servant did wrong on the day my lord the king left Jerusalem. May the king put it out of his mind. ²⁰For I your servant know that I have sinned, but today I have come here as the first from the tribes of Joseph to come down and meet my lord the king."

²¹Then Abishai son of Zeruiah said, "Shouldn't Shimei be put to death for this? He cursed the Lord's anointed." ²²David replied, "What does this have to do with you, you sons of Zeruiah? What right do you have to interfere? Should anyone be put to death in Israel today? Don't I know that today I am king over Israel?" ²³So the king said to Shimei, "You shall not die." And the king promised him on oath.

²⁴Mephibosheth, Saul's grandson, also went down to meet the king. He had not taken care of his feet or trimmed his mustache or washed his clothes from the day the king left until the day he returned safely. ²⁵When he came from Jerusalem to meet the king, the king asked him, "Why didn't you go with me, Mephibosheth?"

²⁶He said, "My lord the king, since I your servant am lame, I said, 'I will have my donkey saddled and will ride on it, so I can go with the king.' But Ziba my servant betrayed me. ²⁷And he has slandered your servant to my lord the king. My lord the king is like an angel of God; so do whatever you wish. ²⁸All my grandfather's descendants deserved nothing but death from my lord the king, but you gave your servant a place among those who eat at your table. So what right do I have to make any more appeals to the king?"

²⁹The king said to him, "Why say more? I order you and Ziba to divide the land." ³⁰Mephibosheth said to the king, "Let him take everything, now that my lord the king has returned home safely."

³¹Barzillai the Gileadite also came down from Rogelim to cross the Jordan with the king and to send him on his way from there. ³²Now Barzillai was very old, eighty years of age. He had provided for the king during his stay in Mahanaim, for he was a very wealthy man. ³³The king said to Barzillai, "Cross over with me and stay with me in Jerusalem, and I will provide for you."

³⁴But Barzillai answered the king, "How many more years will I live, that I should go up to Jerusalem with the king? ³⁵I am now eighty years old. Can I tell the difference between what is enjoyable and

what is not? Can your servant taste what he eats and drinks? Can I still hear the voices of male and female singers? Why should your servant be an added burden to my lord the king? ³⁶Your servant will cross over the Jordan with the king for a short distance, but why should the king reward me in this way? ³⁷Let your servant return, that I may die in my own town near the tomb of my father and mother. But here is your servant Kimham. Let him cross over with my lord the king. Do for him whatever you wish."

³⁸The king said, "Kimham shall cross over with me, and I will do for him whatever you wish. And anything you desire from me I will do for you."

³⁹So all the people crossed the Jordan, and then the king crossed over. The king kissed Barzillai and bid him farewell, and Barzillai returned to his home.

⁴⁰When the king crossed over to Gilgal, Kimham crossed with him. All the troops of Judah and half the troops of Israel had taken the king over.

⁴¹Soon all the men of Israel were coming to the king and saying to him, "Why did our brothers, the men of Judah, steal the king away and bring him and his household across the Jordan, together with all his men?"

⁴²All the men of Judah answered the men of Israel, "We did this because the king is closely related to us. Why are you angry about it? Have we eaten any of the king's provisions? Have we taken anything for ourselves?"

⁴³Then the men of Israel answered the men of Judah, "We have ten shares in the king; so we have a greater claim on David than you have. Why then do you treat us with contempt? Weren't we the first to speak of bringing back our king?"

But the men of Judah pressed their claims even more forcefully than the men of Israel.

Sheba Rebels Against David

20 Now a troublemaker named Sheba son of Bikri, a Benjamite, happened to be there. He sounded the trumpet and shouted,

"We have no share in David,
no part in Jesse's son!
Every man to his tent, Israel!"

²So all the men of Israel deserted David to follow Sheba son of Bikri. But the men of Judah stayed by their king all the way from the Jordan to Jerusalem.

³When David returned to his palace in Jerusalem, he took the ten concubines he had left to take care of the palace and put them in a house under guard. He provided for them but had no sexual relations with them. They were kept in confinement till the day of their death, living as widows.

⁴Then the king said to Amasa, "Summon the men of Judah to come to me

THE
WITNESSES

✓ **SHEBA SON OF BIKRI** (2 SAMUEL 20:1)
Sheba means "seven." He was from the tribe of Benjamin. He was the leader of a rebellion against David.

within three days, and be here yourself."
⁵But when Amasa went to summon Judah, he took longer than the time the king had set for him.

⁶David said to Abishai, "Now Sheba son of Bikri will do us more harm than Absalom did. Take your master's men and pursue him, or he will find fortified cities and escape from us."*ᵃ ⁷So Joab's men and the Kerethites and Pelethites and all the mighty warriors went out under the command of Abishai. They marched out from Jerusalem to pursue Sheba son of Bikri.

⁸While they were at the great rock in Gibeon, Amasa came to meet them. Joab was wearing his military tunic, and strapped over it at his waist was a belt with a dagger in its sheath. As he stepped forward, it dropped out of its sheath.

⁹Joab said to Amasa, "How are you, my brother?" Then Joab took Amasa by the beard with his right hand to kiss him. ¹⁰Amasa was not on his guard against the dagger in Joab's hand, and Joab plunged it into his belly, and his intestines spilled out on the ground. Without being stabbed again, Amasa died. Then Joab and his brother Abishai pursued Sheba son of Bikri.

¹¹One of Joab's men stood beside Amasa and said, "Whoever favors Joab, and whoever is for David, let him follow Joab!" ¹²Amasa lay wallowing in his blood in the middle of the road, and the man saw that all the troops came to a halt there. When he realized that everyone who came up to Amasa stopped, he dragged him from the road into a field and threw a garment over him. ¹³After Amasa had been removed from the road, everyone went on with Joab to pursue Sheba son of Bikri.

¹⁴Sheba passed through all the tribes of Israel to Abel Beth Maakah and through the entire region of the Bikrites,ᵇ who gathered together and followed him. ¹⁵All the troops with Joab came and besieged Sheba in Abel Beth Maakah. They built a siege ramp up to the city, and it stood against the outer fortifications. While they were battering the wall to bring it down, ¹⁶a wise woman called

from the city, "Listen! Listen! Tell Joab to come here so I can speak to him." ¹⁷He went toward her, and she asked, "Are you Joab?"

"I am," he answered.

She said, "Listen to what your servant has to say."

"I'm listening," he said.

¹⁸She continued, "Long ago they used to say, 'Get your answer at Abel,' and that settled it. ¹⁹We are the peaceful and faithful in Israel. You are trying to destroy a city that is a mother in Israel. Why do you want to swallow up the Lᴏʀᴅ's inheritance?"

²⁰"Far be it from me!" Joab replied, "Far be it from me to swallow up or destroy! ²¹That is not the case. A man named Sheba son of Bikri, from the hill country of Ephraim, has lifted up his hand against the king, against David. Hand over this one man, and I'll withdraw from the city."

The woman said to Joab, "His head will be thrown to you from the wall."

²²Then the woman went to all the people with her wise advice, and they cut off the head of Sheba son of Bikri and threw it to Joab. So he sounded the trumpet, and his men dispersed from the city, each returning to his home. And Joab went back to the king in Jerusalem.

David's Officials

²³Joab was over Israel's entire army; Benaiah son of Jehoiada was over the Kerethites and Pelethites; ²⁴Adoniramᶜ was in charge of forced labor; Jehoshaphat son of Ahilud was recorder; ²⁵Sheva was secretary; Zadok and Abiathar were priests; ²⁶and Ira the Jairiteᵈ was David's priest.

The Gibeonites Avenged

21 During the reign of David, there was a famine for three successive years; so David sought the face of the Lᴏʀᴅ. The Lᴏʀᴅ said, "It is on account of

---

ᵃ 6 Or and do us serious injury   ᵇ 14 See Septuagint and Vulgate; Hebrew Berites.   ᶜ 24 Some Septuagint manuscripts (see also 1 Kings 4:6 and 5:14); Hebrew Adoram   ᵈ 26 Hebrew; some Septuagint manuscripts and Syriac (see also 23:38) Ithrite

Saul and his blood-stained house; it is because he put the Gibeonites to death." ²The king summoned the Gibeonites and spoke to them. (Now the Gibeonites were not a part of Israel but were survivors of the Amorites; the Israelites had sworn to spare them, but Saul in his zeal for Israel and Judah had tried to annihilate them.) ³David asked the Gibeonites, "What shall I do for you? How shall I make atonement so that you will bless the LORD's inheritance?"

⁴The Gibeonites answered him, "We have no right to demand silver or gold from Saul or his family, nor do we have the right to put anyone in Israel to death."

"What do you want me to do for you?" David asked.

⁵They answered the king, "As for the man who destroyed us and plotted against us so that we have been decimated and have no place anywhere in Israel, ⁶let seven of his male descendants be given to us to be killed and their bodies exposed before the LORD at Gibeah of Saul—the LORD's chosen one."

So the king said, "I will give them to you."

⁷The king spared Mephibosheth son of Jonathan, the son of Saul, because of the oath before the LORD between David and Jonathan son of Saul. ⁸But the king took Armoni and Mephibosheth, the two sons of Aiah's daughter Rizpah, whom she had borne to Saul, together with the five sons of Saul's daughter Merab,ᵃ whom she had borne to Adriel son of Barzillai the Meholathite. ⁹He handed them over to the Gibeonites, who killed them and exposed their bodies on a hill before the LORD. All seven of them fell together; they were put to death during the first days of the harvest, just as the barley harvest was beginning.

¹⁰Rizpah daughter of Aiah took sackcloth and spread it out for herself on a rock. From the beginning of the harvest till the rain poured down from the heavens on the bodies, she did not let the birds touch them by day or the wild animals by night. ¹¹When David was told what Aiah's daughter Rizpah, Saul's concubine, had done, ¹²he went and took

the bones of Saul and his son Jonathan from the citizens of Jabesh Gilead. (They had stolen their bodies from the public square at Beth Shan, where the Philistines had hung them after they struck Saul down on Gilboa.) ¹³David brought the bones of Saul and his son Jonathan from there, and the bones of those who had been killed and exposed were gathered up.

¹⁴They buried the bones of Saul and his son Jonathan in the tomb of Saul's father Kish, at Zela in Benjamin, and did everything the king commanded. After that, God answered prayer in behalf of the land.

Wars Against the Philistines

¹⁵Once again there was a battle between the Philistines and Israel. David went down with his men to fight against the Philistines, and he became exhausted. ¹⁶And Ishbi-Benob, one of the descendants of Rapha, whose bronze spearhead weighed three hundred shekelsᵇ and who was armed with a new sword, said he would kill David. ¹⁷But Abishai son of Zeruiah came to David's rescue; he struck the Philistine down and killed him. Then David's men swore to him, saying, "Never again will you go out with us to battle, so that the lamp of Israel will not be extinguished."

¹⁸In the course of time, there was another battle with the Philistines, at Gob. At that time Sibbekai the Hushathite killed Saph, one of the descendants of Rapha.

¹⁹In another battle with the Philistines at Gob, Elhanan son of Jairᶜ the Bethlehemite killed the brother ofᵈ Goliath the Gittite, who had a spear with a shaft like a weaver's rod.

²⁰In still another battle, which took place at Gath, there was a huge man with six fingers on each hand and six toes on each foot—twenty-four in all. He also was descended from Rapha. ²¹When he

---

ᵃ 8 Two Hebrew manuscripts, some Septuagint manuscripts and Syriac (see also 1 Samuel 18:19); most Hebrew and Septuagint manuscripts Michal   ᵇ 16 That is, about 7 1/2 pounds or about 3.5 kilograms   ᶜ 19 See 1 Chron. 20:5; Hebrew Jaare-Oregim.   ᵈ 19 See 1 Chron. 20:5; Hebrew does not have the brother of.

taunted Israel, Jonathan son of Shimeah, David's brother, killed him.

²²These four were descendants of Rapha in Gath, and they fell at the hands of David and his men.

David's Song of Praise

22 David sang to the Lᴏʀᴅ the words of this song when the Lᴏʀᴅ delivered him from the hand of all his enemies and from the hand of Saul. ²He said:

"The Lᴏʀᴅ is my rock, my fortress and
   my deliverer;
³ my God is my rock, in whom I take
   refuge,
  my shield*ᵃ* and the horn*ᵇ* of my
   salvation.
He is my stronghold, my refuge and
   my savior—
from violent people you save me.

⁴"I called to the Lᴏʀᴅ, who is worthy of
   praise,
  and have been saved from my
   enemies.
     ⁵The waves of death swirled
       about me;
      the torrents of destruction
       overwhelmed me.
     ⁶The cords of the grave
       coiled around me;
     the snares of death
       confronted me.
⁷"In my distress I called to the Lᴏʀᴅ;
  I called out to my God.
From his temple he heard my voice;
  my cry came to his ears.
⁸The earth trembled and quaked,
  the foundations of the heavens*ᶜ*
   shook;
  they trembled because he was
   angry.
⁹Smoke rose from his nostrils;
  consuming fire came from his
   mouth,
  burning coals blazed out of it.
¹⁰He parted the heavens and came
   down;
  dark clouds were under his feet.
¹¹He mounted the cherubim and
   flew;
  he soared*ᵈ* on the wings of the
   wind.

¹²He made darkness his canopy around
   him—
  the dark*ᵉ* rain clouds of the sky.
¹³Out of the brightness of his
   presence
  bolts of lightning blazed forth.
¹⁴The Lᴏʀᴅ thundered from
   heaven;
  the voice of the Most High
   resounded.
¹⁵He shot his arrows and scattered the
   enemy,
  with great bolts of lightning he
   routed them.
¹⁶The valleys of the sea were exposed
  and the foundations of the earth
   laid bare
at the rebuke of the Lᴏʀᴅ,
  at the blast of breath from his
   nostrils.

¹⁷"He reached down from on high and
   took hold of me;
  he drew me out of deep waters.
¹⁸He rescued me from my powerful
   enemy,
  from my foes, who were too strong
   for me.
¹⁹They confronted me in the day of my
   disaster,
  but the Lᴏʀᴅ was my support.
²⁰He brought me out into a spacious
   place;
  he rescued me because he
   delighted in me.

²¹"The Lᴏʀᴅ has dealt with me according
   to my righteousness;
  according to the cleanness of my
   hands he has rewarded me.
²²For I have kept the ways of the
   Lᴏʀᴅ;
  I am not guilty of turning from my
   God.
²³All his laws are before me;
  I have not turned away from his
   decrees.
²⁴I have been blameless before
   him
  and have kept myself from sin.

ᵃ 3 Or *sovereign*   *ᵇ 3 Horn* here symbolizes strength.
ᶜ 8 Hebrew; Vulgate and Syriac (see also Psalm 18:7)
mountains   *ᵈ 11* Many Hebrew manuscripts (see also
Psalm 18:10); most Hebrew manuscripts *appeared*
ᵉ 12 Septuagint (see also Psalm 18:11); Hebrew *massed*

25 The LORD has rewarded me according
  to my righteousness,
  according to my cleanness*a* in his
  sight.
26 "To the faithful you show yourself
  faithful,
  to the blameless you show yourself
  blameless,
27 to the pure you show yourself pure,
  but to the devious you show
  yourself shrewd.
28 You save the humble,
  but your eyes are on the haughty to
  bring them low.
29 You, LORD, are my lamp;
  the LORD turns my darkness into
  light.
30 With your help I can advance against
  a troop*b*;
  with my God I can scale a wall.

31 "As for God, his way is perfect:
  The LORD's word is flawless;
  he shields all who take refuge in
  him.
32 For who is God besides the LORD?
  And who is the Rock except our
  God?
33 It is God who arms me with
  strength*c*
  and keeps my way secure.
34 He makes my feet like the feet of a
  deer;
  he causes me to stand on the
  heights.
35 He trains my hands for battle;
  my arms can bend a bow of
  bronze.
36 You make your saving help my
  shield;
  your help has made*d* me great.
37 You provide a broad path for my
  feet,
  so that my ankles do not give
  way.

38 "I pursued my enemies and crushed
  them;
  I did not turn back till they were
  destroyed.
39 I crushed them completely, and they
  could not rise;
  they fell beneath my feet.

40 You armed me with strength for
  battle;
  you humbled my adversaries before
  me.
41 You made my enemies turn their
  backs in flight,
  and I destroyed my foes.
42 They cried for help, but there was no
  one to save them—
  to the LORD, but he did not answer.
43 I beat them as fine as the dust of the
  earth;
  I pounded and trampled them like
  mud in the streets.

44 "You have delivered me from the
  attacks of the peoples;
  you have preserved me as the head
  of nations.
  People I did not know now serve me,
45   foreigners cower before me;
  as soon as they hear of me, they
  obey me.
46 They all lose heart;
  they come trembling*e* from their
  strongholds.

47 "The LORD lives! Praise be to my
  Rock!
  Exalted be my God, the Rock, my
  Savior!
48 He is the God who avenges me,
  who puts the nations under me,
49   who sets me free from my
  enemies.
  You exalted me above my foes;
  from a violent man you
  rescued me.
50 Therefore I will praise you, LORD,
  among the nations;
  I will sing the praises of your
  name.

51 "He gives his king great victories;
  he shows unfailing kindness to his
  anointed,
  to David and his descendants
  forever."

---

a 25 Hebrew; Septuagint and Vulgate (see also Psalm
18:24) *to the cleanness of my hands*   *b* 30 Or *can run
through a barricade*   *c* 33 Dead Sea Scrolls, some
Septuagint manuscripts, Vulgate and Syriac (see also
Psalm 18:32); Masoretic Text *who is my strong refuge*
d 36 Dead Sea Scrolls; Masoretic Text *shield; / you stoop
down to make*   *e* 46 Some Septuagint manuscripts and
Vulgate (see also Psalm 18:45); Masoretic Text *they arm
themselves*

David's Last Words

23 These are the last words of David:

"The inspired utterance of David son
　of Jesse,
　the utterance of the man exalted by
　　the Most High,
　the man anointed by the God of Jacob,
　the hero of Israel's songs:

² "The Spirit of the LORD spoke through
　me;
　his word was on my tongue.
³ The God of Israel spoke,
　the Rock of Israel said to me:
'When one rules over people in
　righteousness,
　when he rules in the fear of God,
⁴ he is like the light of morning at
　sunrise
on a cloudless morning,
like the brightness after rain
　that brings grass from the earth.'

⁵ "If my house were not right with God,
　surely he would not have made
　　with me an everlasting
　　covenant,
　arranged and secured in every part;
surely he would not bring to fruition
　my salvation
　and grant me my every desire.
⁶ But evil men are all to be cast aside
　like thorns,
　which are not gathered with the
　hand.
⁷ Whoever touches thorns
　uses a tool of iron or the shaft of a
　spear;
　they are burned up where they lie."

David's Mighty Warriors

⁸These are the names of David's mighty
warriors:

Josheb-Basshebeth,ᵃ a Tahkemonite,ᵇ
was chief of the Three; he raised his
spear against eight hundred men, whom
he killedᶜ in one encounter.

⁹Next to him was Eleazar son of Dodai
the Ahohite. As one of the three mighty
warriors, he was with David when they
taunted the Philistines gathered at Pas
Dammimᵈ for battle. Then the Israelites

retreated, ¹⁰but Eleazar stood his ground
and struck down the Philistines till his
hand grew tired and froze to the sword.
The LORD brought about a great victory
that day. The troops returned to Eleazar,
but only to strip the dead.

¹¹Next to him was Shammah son of
Agee the Hararite. When the Philistines
banded together at a place where there
was a field full of lentils, Israel's troops
fled from them. ¹²But Shammah took his
stand in the middle of the field. He defended it and struck the Philistines down,
and the LORD brought about a great victory.

¹³During harvest time, three of the
thirty chief warriors came down to David
at the cave of Adullam, while a band of
Philistines was encamped in the Valley
of Rephaim. ¹⁴At that time David was in
the stronghold, and the Philistine garrison
was at Bethlehem. ¹⁵David longed for water and said, "Oh, that someone would
get me a drink of water from the well near
the gate of Bethlehem!" ¹⁶So the three
mighty warriors broke through the Philistine lines, drew water from the well near
the gate of Bethlehem and carried it back
to David. But he refused to drink it; instead, he poured it out before the LORD.
¹⁷"Far be it from me, LORD, to do this!"
he said. "Is it not the blood of men who
went at the risk of their lives?" And David
would not drink it.

Such were the exploits of the three
mighty warriors.

¹⁸Abishai the brother of Joab son of
Zeruiah was chief of the Three.ᵉ He raised
his spear against three hundred men,
whom he killed, and so he became as famous as the Three. ¹⁹Was he not held in
greater honor than the Three? He became
their commander, even though he was not
included among them.

²⁰Benaiah son of Jehoiada, a valiant
fighter from Kabzeel, performed great ex-

ᵃ 8 Hebrew; some Septuagint manuscripts suggest *Ish-
Bosheth*, that is, *Esh-Baal* (see also 1 Chron. 11:11
Jashobeam).   ᵇ 8 Probably a variant of *Hakmonite* (see
1 Chron. 11:11)   ᶜ 8 Some Septuagint manuscripts (see
also 1 Chron. 11:11); Hebrew and other Septuagint
manuscripts *Three; it was Adino the Eznite who killed eight
hundred men*   ᵈ 9 See 1 Chron. 11:13; Hebrew *gathered
there*.   ᵉ 18 Most Hebrew manuscripts (see also
1 Chron. 11:20); two Hebrew manuscripts and Syriac *Thirty*

ploits. He struck down Moab's two mightiest warriors. He also went down into a pit on a snowy day and killed a lion. ²¹And he struck down a huge Egyptian. Although the Egyptian had a spear in his hand, Benaiah went against him with a club. He snatched the spear from the Egyptian's hand and killed him with his own spear. ²²Such were the exploits of Benaiah son of Jehoiada; he too was as famous as the three mighty warriors. ²³He was held in greater honor than any of the Thirty, but he was not included among the Three. And David put him in charge of his bodyguard.

²⁴Among the Thirty were:
Asahel the brother of Joab,
Elhanan son of Dodo from Bethlehem,
²⁵Shammah the Harodite,
Elika the Harodite,
²⁶Helez the Paltite,
Ira son of Ikkesh from Tekoa,
²⁷Abiezer from Anathoth,
Sibbekaiᵃ the Hushathite,
²⁸Zalmon the Ahohite,
Maharai the Netophathite,
²⁹Heledᵇ son of Baanah the Netophathite,
Ithai son of Ribai from Gibeah in Benjamin,
³⁰Benaiah the Pirathonite,
Hiddaiᶜ from the ravines of Gaash,
³¹Abi-Albon the Arbathite,
Azmaveth the Barhumite,
³²Eliahba the Shaalbonite,
the sons of Jashen,
Jonathan ³³son ofᵈ Shammah the Hararite,
Ahiam son of Shararᵉ the Hararite,
³⁴Eliphelet son of Ahasbai the Maakathite,
Eliam son of Ahithophel the Gilonite,
³⁵Hezro the Carmelite,
Paarai the Arbite,
³⁶Igal son of Nathan from Zobah,
the son of Hagri,ᶠ
³⁷Zelek the Ammonite,
Naharai the Beerothite, the armorbearer of Joab son of Zeruiah,
³⁸Ira the Ithrite,
Gareb the Ithrite

³⁹and Uriah the Hittite.
There were thirty-seven in all.

David Enrolls the Fighting Men

24 Again the anger of the LORD burned against Israel, and he incited David against them, saying, "Go and take a census of Israel and Judah."

²So the king said to Joab and the army commandersᵍ with him, "Go throughout the tribes of Israel from Dan to Beersheba and enroll the fighting men, so that I may know how many there are."

³But Joab replied to the king, "May the LORD your God multiply the troops a hundred times over, and may the eyes of my lord the king see it. But why does my lord the king want to do such a thing?"

⁴The king's word, however, overruled Joab and the army commanders; so they left the presence of the king to enroll the fighting men of Israel.

⁵After crossing the Jordan, they camped near Aroer, south of the town in the gorge, and then went through Gad and on to Jazer. ⁶They went to Gilead and the region of Tahtim Hodshi, and on to Dan Jaan and around toward Sidon. ⁷Then they went toward the fortress of Tyre and all the towns of the Hivites and Canaanites. Finally, they went on to Beersheba in the Negev of Judah.

⁸After they had gone through the entire land, they came back to Jerusalem at the end of nine months and twenty days.

⁹Joab reported the number of the fighting men to the king: In Israel there were eight hundred thousand able-bodied men who could handle a sword, and in Judah five hundred thousand.

¹⁰David was conscience-stricken after he had counted the fighting men, and he

---

ᵃ 27 Some Septuagint manuscripts (see also 21:18; 1 Chron. 11:29); Hebrew *Mebunnai* ᵇ 29 Some Hebrew manuscripts and Vulgate (see also 1 Chron. 11:30); most Hebrew manuscripts *Heleb* ᶜ 30 Hebrew; some Septuagint manuscripts (see also 1 Chron. 11:32) *Hurai* ᵈ 33 Some Septuagint manuscripts (see also 1 Chron. 11:34); Hebrew does not have *son of.* ᵉ 33 Hebrew; some Septuagint manuscripts (see also 1 Chron. 11:35) *Sakar* ᶠ 36 Some Septuagint manuscripts (see also 1 Chron. 11:38); Hebrew *Haggadi* ᵍ 2 Septuagint (see also verse 4) and 1 Chron. 21:2); Hebrew *Joab the army commander*

THE
WITNESSES

✓ **GAD** (2 SAMUEL 24:11)
This name means "fortune." He was a prophet of God during the time of David. It's possible that he wrote part of this book and 1 Samuel too.

said to the LORD, "I have sinned greatly in what I have done. Now, LORD, I beg you, take away the guilt of your servant. I have done a very foolish thing."

¹¹Before David got up the next morning, the word of the LORD had come to Gad the prophet, David's seer: ¹²"Go and tell David, 'This is what the LORD says: I am giving you three options. Choose one of them for me to carry out against you.'"

¹³So Gad went to David and said to him, "Shall there come on you three*ᵃ* years of famine in your land? Or three months of fleeing from your enemies while they pursue you? Or three days of plague in your land? Now then, think it over and de-

cide how I should answer the one who sent me."

¹⁴David said to Gad, "I am in deep distress. Let us fall into the hands of the LORD, for his mercy is great; but do not let me fall into human hands."

¹⁵So the LORD sent a plague on Israel from that morning until the end of the time designated, and seventy thousand of the people from Dan to Beersheba died. ¹⁶When the angel stretched out his hand to destroy Jerusalem, the LORD relented concerning the disaster and said to the angel who was afflicting the people, "Enough! Withdraw your hand." The angel of the LORD was then at the threshing floor of Araunah the Jebusite.

¹⁷When David saw the angel who was striking down the people, he said to the LORD, "I have sinned; I, the shepherd,*ᵇ* have done wrong. These are but sheep. What have they done? Let your hand fall on me and my family."

David Builds an Altar

¹⁸On that day Gad went to David and said to him, "Go up and build an altar to the LORD on the threshing floor of Araunah the Jebusite." ¹⁹So David went up, as the LORD had commanded through Gad. ²⁰When Araunah looked and saw the king and his officials coming toward him, he went out and bowed down before the king with his face to the ground.

²¹Araunah said, "Why has my lord the king come to his servant?"

"To buy your threshing floor," David answered, "so I can build an altar to the LORD, that the plague on the people may be stopped."

²²Araunah said to David, "Let my lord the king take whatever he wishes and offer it up. Here are oxen for the burnt offering, and here are threshing sledges and ox yokes for the wood. ²³Your Majesty, Araunah*ᶜ* gives all this to the king." Araunah also said to him, "May the LORD your God accept you."

ᵃ 13 Septuagint (see also 1 Chron. 21:12); Hebrew *seven*
ᵇ 17 Dead Sea Scrolls and Septuagint; Masoretic Text does not have *the shepherd.*   *ᶜ* 23 Some Hebrew manuscripts and Septuagint; most Hebrew manuscripts *King Araunah*

²⁴But the king replied to Araunah, "No, I insist on paying you for it. I will not sacrifice to the LORD my God burnt offerings that cost me nothing."

So David bought the threshing floor and the oxen and paid fifty shekels[a] of silver for them. ²⁵David built an altar to the LORD there and sacrificed burnt offerings and fellowship offerings. Then the LORD answered his prayer in behalf of the land, and the plague on Israel was stopped.

---

[a] 24 That is, about 1 1/4 pounds or about 575 grams

CASE CLOSED!

We think the most important thing about this book is seeing that David did some very good things, but he also did some bad things and made mistakes. However, God forgave him, because David was always sorry and wanted to be faithful and obedient to God. We should be like that too. When we make mistakes, we should be sorry and look for God.

Another good lesson to be learned is the example of the prophet Nathan. He was very faithful to God, even when he had to scold David for what he had done with Bathsheba and her husband, Uriah. Nathan wasn't afraid to talk to David. That was a really hard task, because David was the king and could get angry and even kill him. But Nathan stayed brave, and he gave David God's message in spite of the fact that the message was very tough. True prophets are very important, because they bring us God's message whether he's angry or happy with us.

1 KINGS

THE EVIDENCE:

WHO WROTE IT?
Although we see two books here called Kings, they are really like one book. Nobody knows who wrote this. Maybe a group of people wrote it or revised it, or they wrote parts at different times. What we can be sure about is that this book, like the books of Joshua, Judges and Samuel, is based on the orders God gave in the book of Deuteronomy. Do you remember that book? It is the fifth book of the Old Testament.

HOW LONG AGO?
It was written about 609 to 562 years before Christ, but it talks about kingdoms of Israel that existed about 961 to 587 years before Christ.

WHAT'S IT ABOUT?
This first book talks about the end of David's reign, the reign of Solomon and the division of the kingdom between the northern kingdom (Israel) and the southern kingdom (Judah). Besides talking about the kings and their kingdoms, it also talks about several prophets, like Elijah, who was the most important prophet.

THE BEST PART
We really like it when Solomon, who was very young, had to start ruling over his people and didn't know what to do, so he asked God for something very special: "I am only a little child and do not know how to carry out my duties. Your servant is here among the people you have chosen, a great people, too numerous to count or number. So give your servant a discerning heart to govern your people and to distinguish between right and wrong. For who is able to govern this great people of yours?" (3:7 – 9).

Adonijah Sets Himself Up as King

1 When King David was very old, he could not keep warm even when they put covers over him. ²So his attendants said to him, "Let us look for a young virgin to serve the king and take care of him. She can lie beside him so that our lord the king may keep warm."

³Then they searched throughout Israel for a beautiful young woman and found Abishag, a Shunammite, and brought her to the king. ⁴The woman was very beautiful; she took care of the king and waited on him, but the king had no sexual relations with her.

⁵Now Adonijah, whose mother was Hag-

gith, put himself forward and said, "I will be king." So he got chariots and horses[a] ready, with fifty men to run ahead of him. [6](His father had never rebuked him by asking, "Why do you behave as you do?" He was also very handsome and was born next after Absalom.)

[7]Adonijah conferred with Joab son of Zeruiah and with Abiathar the priest, and they gave him their support. [8]But Zadok

THE
WITNESSES

✓ **ABISHAG** (1 KINGS 1:3)
This name means "my father is a wanderer." She was the girl who took care of King David when he was very old. She was from Shunem in the Valley of Jezreel.

✓ **ADONIJAH** (1 KINGS 1:5)
This name means "God is LORD." He was David and Haggith's son. He tried to take the kingdom away from Solomon, his half brother, so Solomon had him killed.

the priest, Benaiah son of Jehoiada, Nathan the prophet, Shimei and Rei and David's special guard did not join Adonijah.

[9]Adonijah then sacrificed sheep, cattle and fattened calves at the Stone of Zoheleth near En Rogel. He invited all his brothers, the king's sons, and all the royal officials of Judah, [10]but he did not invite Nathan the prophet or Benaiah or the special guard or his brother Solomon.

[11]Then Nathan asked Bathsheba, Solomon's mother, "Have you not heard that Adonijah, the son of Haggith, has become king, and our lord David knows nothing about it? [12]Now then, let me advise you how you can save your own life and the life of your son Solomon. [13]Go in to King David and say to him, 'My lord the king, did you not swear to me your servant: "Surely Solomon your son shall be king after me, and he will sit on my throne"? Why then has Adonijah become king?' [14]While you are still there talking to the king, I will come in and add my word to what you have said."

[15]So Bathsheba went to see the aged king in his room, where Abishag the Shunammite was attending him. [16]Bathsheba bowed down, prostrating herself before the king.

"What is it you want?" the king asked.

[17]She said to him, "My lord, you yourself swore to me your servant by the LORD your God: 'Solomon your son shall be king after me, and he will sit on my throne.' [18]But now Adonijah has become king, and you, my lord the king, do not know about it. [19]He has sacrificed great numbers of cattle, fattened calves, and sheep, and has invited all the king's sons, Abiathar the priest and Joab the commander of the army, but he has not invited Solomon your servant. [20]My lord the king, the eyes of all Israel are on you, to learn from you who will sit on the throne of my lord the king after him. [21]Otherwise, as soon as my lord the king is laid to rest with his ancestors, I and my son Solomon will be treated as criminals."

[22]While she was still speaking with the king, Nathan the prophet arrived. [23]And the king was told, "Nathan the prophet

---

[a] 5 Or charioteers

is here." So he went before the king and bowed with his face to the ground.

²⁴Nathan said, "Have you, my lord the king, declared that Adonijah shall be king after you, and that he will sit on your throne? ²⁵Today he has gone down and sacrificed great numbers of cattle, fattened calves, and sheep. He has invited all the king's sons, the commanders of the army and Abiathar the priest. Right now they are eating and drinking with him and saying, 'Long live King Adonijah!' ²⁶But me your servant, and Zadok the priest, and Benaiah son of Jehoiada, and your servant Solomon he did not invite. ²⁷Is this something my lord the king has done without letting his servants know who should sit on the throne of my lord the king after him?"

David Makes Solomon King

²⁸Then King David said, "Call in Bathsheba." So she came into the king's presence and stood before him.

²⁹The king then took an oath: "As surely as the LORD lives, who has delivered me out of every trouble, ³⁰I will surely carry out this very day what I swore to you by the LORD, the God of Israel: Solomon your son shall be king after me, and he will sit on my throne in my place."

³¹Then Bathsheba bowed down with her face to the ground, prostrating herself before the king, and said, "May my lord King David live forever!"

³²King David said, "Call in Zadok the priest, Nathan the prophet and Benaiah son of Jehoiada." When they came before the king, ³³he said to them: "Take your lord's servants with you and have Solomon my son mount my own mule and take him down to Gihon. ³⁴There have Zadok the priest and Nathan the prophet anoint him king over Israel. Blow the trumpet and shout, 'Long live King Solomon!' ³⁵Then you are to go up with him, and he is to come and sit on my throne and reign in my place. I have appointed him ruler over Israel and Judah."

³⁶Benaiah son of Jehoiada answered the king, "Amen! May the LORD, the God of my lord the king, so declare it. ³⁷As the LORD was with my lord the king, so may

THE
WITNESSES

✓ **SOLOMON** (1 KINGS 1:30)
This name is related to the Hebrew word *shalom*, which means "peace." Read more about him in 2 Samuel 12:24.

he be with Solomon to make his throne even greater than the throne of my lord King David!"

³⁸So Zadok the priest, Nathan the prophet, Benaiah son of Jehoiada, the Kerethites and the Pelethites went down and had Solomon mount King David's mule, and they escorted him to Gihon. ³⁹Zadok the priest took the horn of oil from the sacred tent and anointed Solomon. Then they sounded the trumpet and all the people shouted, "Long live King Solomon!" ⁴⁰And all the people went up after him, playing pipes and rejoicing greatly, so that the ground shook with the sound.

⁴¹Adonijah and all the guests who were with him heard it as they were finishing

their feast. On hearing the sound of the trumpet, Joab asked, "What's the meaning of all the noise in the city?" [42]Even as he was speaking, Jonathan son of Abiathar the priest arrived. Adonijah said, "Come in. A worthy man like you must be bringing good news."

[43]"Not at all!" Jonathan answered. "Our lord King David has made Solomon king. [44]The king has sent with him Zadok the priest, Nathan the prophet, Benaiah son of Jehoiada, the Kerethites and the Pelethites, and they have put him on the king's mule, [45]and Zadok the priest and Nathan the prophet have anointed him king at Gihon. From there they have gone up cheering, and the city resounds with it. That's the noise you hear. [46]Moreover, Solomon has taken his seat on the royal throne. [47]Also, the royal officials have come to congratulate our lord King David, saying, 'May your God make Solomon's name more famous than yours and his throne greater than yours!' And the king bowed in worship on his bed [48]and said, 'Praise be to the LORD, the God of Israel, who has allowed my eyes to see a successor on my throne today.'"

[49]At this, all Adonijah's guests rose in alarm and dispersed. [50]But Adonijah, in fear of Solomon, went and took hold of the horns of the altar. [51]Then Solomon was told, "Adonijah is afraid of King Solomon and is clinging to the horns of the altar. He says, 'Let King Solomon swear to me today that he will not put his servant to death with the sword.'"

[52]Solomon replied, "If he shows himself to be worthy, not a hair of his head will fall to the ground; but if evil is found in him, he will die." [53]Then King Solomon sent men, and they brought him down from the altar. And Adonijah came and bowed down to King Solomon, and Solomon said, "Go to your home."

David's Charge to Solomon

2 When the time drew near for David to die, he gave a charge to Solomon his son.

[2]"I am about to go the way of all the earth," he said. "So be strong, act like a man, [3]and observe what the LORD your God requires: Walk in obedience to him, and keep his decrees and commands, his laws and regulations, as written in the Law of Moses. Do this so that you may prosper in all you do and wherever you go [4]and that the LORD may keep his promise to me: 'If your descendants watch how they live, and if they walk faithfully before me with all their heart and soul, you will never fail to have a successor on the throne of Israel.'

[5]"Now you yourself know what Joab son of Zeruiah did to me—what he did to the two commanders of Israel's armies, Abner son of Ner and Amasa son of Jether. He killed them, shedding their blood in peacetime as if in battle, and with that blood he stained the belt around his waist and the sandals on his feet. [6]Deal with him according to your wisdom, but do not let his gray head go down to the grave in peace.

[7]"But show kindness to the sons of Barzillai of Gilead and let them be among those who eat at your table. They stood by me when I fled from your brother Absalom.

[8]"And remember, you have with you Shimei son of Gera, the Benjamite from Bahurim, who called down bitter curses on me the day I went to Mahanaim. When he came down to meet me at the Jordan, I swore to him by the LORD: 'I will not put you to death by the sword.' [9]But now, do not consider him innocent. You are a man of wisdom; you will know what to do to him. Bring his gray head down to the grave in blood."

[10]Then David rested with his ancestors and was buried in the City of David. [11]He had reigned forty years over Israel—seven years in Hebron and thirty-three in Jerusalem. [12]So Solomon sat on the throne of his father David, and his rule was firmly established.

Solomon's Throne Established

[13]Now Adonijah, the son of Haggith, went to Bathsheba, Solomon's mother. Bathsheba asked him, "Do you come peacefully?"

He answered, "Yes, peacefully." [14]Then he added, "I have something to say to you."

"You may say it," she replied.

¹⁹When Bathsheba went to King Solomon to speak to him for Adonijah, the king stood up to meet her, bowed down to her and sat down on his throne. He had a throne brought for the king's mother, and she sat down at his right hand. ²⁰"I have one small request to make of you," she said. "Do not refuse me."

The king replied, "Make it, my mother; I will not refuse you."

²¹So she said, "Let Abishag the Shunammite be given in marriage to your brother Adonijah."

²²King Solomon answered his mother, "Why do you request Abishag the Shunammite for Adonijah? You might as well request the kingdom for him—after all, he is my older brother—yes, for him and for Abiathar the priest and Joab son of Zeruiah!"

²³Then King Solomon swore by the LORD: "May God deal with me, be it ever so severely, if Adonijah does not pay with his life for this request! ²⁴And now, as surely as the LORD lives—he who has established me securely on the throne of my father David and has founded a dynasty for me as he promised—Adonijah shall be put to death today!" ²⁵So King Solomon gave orders to Benaiah son of Jehoiada, and he struck down Adonijah and he died.

²⁶To Abiathar the priest the king said, "Go back to your fields in Anathoth. You deserve to die, but I will not put you to death now, because you carried the ark of the Sovereign LORD before my father David and shared all my father's hardships." ²⁷So Solomon removed Abiathar from the priesthood of the LORD, fulfilling the word the LORD had spoken at Shiloh about the house of Eli.

²⁸When the news reached Joab, who had conspired with Adonijah though not with Absalom, he fled to the tent of the LORD and took hold of the horns of the altar. ²⁹King Solomon was told that Joab had fled to the tent of the LORD and was beside the altar. Then Solomon ordered Benaiah son of Jehoiada, "Go, strike him down!"

³⁰So Benaiah entered the tent of the LORD and said to Joab, "The king says, 'Come out!' "

BREAKTHROUGH!

Why did Solomon get so angry about his brother Adonijah's request?

(1 KINGS 2:13–25)

Because Adonijah wanted to take the place of David, his father, after he died. When a king died, his successor would take over everything that was in his house or palace, even the women (the group that was called a "harem"). Adonijah and Solomon were brothers. They were David's sons, but they had different mothers. God had chosen Solomon as the successor to the throne of his father in spite of the fact that the position really belonged to Adonijah, because he was the oldest son.

¹⁵"As you know," he said, "the kingdom was mine. All Israel looked to me as their king. But things changed, and the kingdom has gone to my brother; for it has come to him from the LORD. ¹⁶Now I have one request to make of you. Do not refuse me."

"You may make it," she said.

¹⁷So he continued, "Please ask King Solomon—he will not refuse you—to give me Abishag the Shunammite as my wife."

¹⁸"Very well," Bathsheba replied, "I will speak to the king for you."

But he answered, "No, I will die here."
Benaiah reported to the king, "This is
how Joab answered me."

³¹Then the king commanded Benaiah,
"Do as he says. Strike him down and bury
him, and so clear me and my whole family of the guilt of the innocent blood that
Joab shed. ³²The Lord will repay him for
the blood he shed, because without my
father David knowing it he attacked two
men and killed them with the sword. Both
of them—Abner son of Ner, commander
of Israel's army, and Amasa son of Jether,
commander of Judah's army—were better men and more upright than he. ³³May
the guilt of their blood rest on the head
of Joab and his descendants forever. But
on David and his descendants, his house
and his throne, may there be the Lord's
peace forever."

³⁴So Benaiah son of Jehoiada went
up and struck down Joab and killed him,
and he was buried at his home out in
the country. ³⁵The king put Benaiah son
of Jehoiada over the army in Joab's position and replaced Abiathar with Zadok
the priest.

³⁶Then the king sent for Shimei and
said to him, "Build yourself a house in Jerusalem and live there, but do not go anywhere else. ³⁷The day you leave and cross
the Kidron Valley, you can be sure you will
die; your blood will be on your own head."

³⁸Shimei answered the king, "What
you say is good. Your servant will do as
my lord the king has said." And Shimei
stayed in Jerusalem for a long time.

³⁹But three years later, two of Shimei's
slaves ran off to Achish son of Maakah,
king of Gath, and Shimei was told, "Your
slaves are in Gath." ⁴⁰At this, he saddled
his donkey and went to Achish at Gath
in search of his slaves. So Shimei went
away and brought the slaves back from
Gath.

⁴¹When Solomon was told that Shimei had gone from Jerusalem to Gath and
had returned, ⁴²the king summoned Shimei and said to him, "Did I not make you
swear by the Lord and warn you, 'On the
day you leave to go anywhere else, you
can be sure you will die'? At that time you
said to me, 'What you say is good. I will

obey.' ⁴³Why then did you not keep your
oath to the Lord and obey the command
I gave you?"

⁴⁴The king also said to Shimei, "You
know in your heart all the wrong you did
to my father David. Now the Lord will repay you for your wrongdoing. ⁴⁵But King
Solomon will be blessed, and David's
throne will remain secure before the Lord
forever."

⁴⁶Then the king gave the order to Benaiah son of Jehoiada, and he went out and
struck Shimei down and he died.

The kingdom was now established in
Solomon's hands.

Solomon Asks for Wisdom

3 Solomon made an alliance with Pharaoh king of Egypt and married his
daughter. He brought her to the City of
David until he finished building his palace
and the temple of the Lord, and the wall
around Jerusalem. ²The people, however, were still sacrificing at the high places, because a temple had not yet been
built for the Name of the Lord. ³Solomon
showed his love for the Lord by walking
according to the instructions given him by
his father David, except that he offered
sacrifices and burned incense on the high
places.

⁴The king went to Gibeon to offer sacrifices, for that was the most important
high place, and Solomon offered a thousand burnt offerings on that altar. ⁵At Gibeon the Lord appeared to Solomon during
the night in a dream, and God said, "Ask
for whatever you want me to give you."

⁶Solomon answered, "You have shown
great kindness to your servant, my father
David, because he was faithful to you and
righteous and upright in heart. You have
continued this great kindness to him and
have given him a son to sit on his throne
this very day.

⁷"Now, Lord my God, you have made
your servant king in place of my father
David. But I am only a little child and do
not know how to carry out my duties.
⁸Your servant is here among the people
you have chosen, a great people, too numerous to count or number. ⁹So give your
servant a discerning heart to govern your

people and to distinguish between right and wrong. For who is able to govern this great people of yours?"

¹⁰The Lord was pleased that Solomon had asked for this. ¹¹So God said to him, "Since you have asked for this and not for long life or wealth for yourself, nor have asked for the death of your enemies but for discernment in administering justice, ¹²I will do what you have asked. I will give you a wise and discerning heart, so that there will never have been anyone like you, nor will there ever be. ¹³Moreover, I will give you what you have not asked for—both wealth and honor—so that in your lifetime you will have no equal among kings. ¹⁴And if you walk in obedience to me and keep my decrees and commands as David your father did, I will give you a long life." ¹⁵Then Solomon awoke—and he realized it had been a dream.

He returned to Jerusalem, stood before the ark of the Lord's covenant and sacrificed burnt offerings and fellowship offerings. Then he gave a feast for all his court.

A Wise Ruling

¹⁶Now two prostitutes came to the king and stood before him. ¹⁷One of them said, "Pardon me, my lord. This woman and I live in the same house, and I had a baby while she was there with me. ¹⁸The third day after my child was born, this woman also had a baby. We were alone; there was no one in the house but the two of us.

¹⁹"During the night this woman's son died because she lay on him. ²⁰So she got up in the middle of the night and took my son from my side while I your servant was asleep. She put him by her breast and put her dead son by my breast. ²¹The next morning, I got up to nurse my son—and he was dead! But when I looked at him closely in the morning light, I saw that it wasn't the son I had borne."

²²The other woman said, "No! The living one is my son; the dead one is yours."

But the first one insisted, "No! The dead one is yours; the living one is mine." And so they argued before the king.

²³The king said, "This one says, 'My son is alive and your son is dead,' while

that one says, 'No! Your son is dead and mine is alive.' "

²⁴Then the king said, "Bring me a sword." So they brought a sword for the king. ²⁵He then gave an order: "Cut the living child in two and give half to one and half to the other."

²⁶The woman whose son was alive was deeply moved out of love for her son and said to the king, "Please, my lord, give her the living baby! Don't kill him!"

But the other said, "Neither I nor you shall have him. Cut him in two!"

²⁷Then the king gave his ruling: "Give the living baby to the first woman. Do not kill him; she is his mother."

²⁸When all Israel heard the verdict the king had given, they held the king in awe, because they saw that he had wisdom from God to administer justice.

Solomon's Officials and Governors

4 So King Solomon ruled over all Israel. ²And these were his chief officials:

Azariah son of Zadok—the priest;
³Elihoreph and Ahijah, sons of Shisha—secretaries;
Jehoshaphat son of Ahilud—recorder;
⁴Benaiah son of Jehoiada—commander in chief;
Zadok and Abiathar—priests;
⁵Azariah son of Nathan—in charge of the district governors;
Zabud son of Nathan—a priest and adviser to the king;
⁶Ahishar—palace administrator;
Adoniram son of Abda—in charge of forced labor.

⁷Solomon had twelve district governors over all Israel, who supplied provisions for the king and the royal household. Each one had to provide supplies for one month in the year. ⁸These are their names:

Ben-Hur—in the hill country of Ephraim;
⁹Ben-Deker—in Makaz, Shaalbim, Beth Shemesh and Elon Bethhanan;
¹⁰Ben-Hesed—in Arubboth (Sokoh and all the land of Hepher were his);

¹¹Ben-Abinadab—in Naphoth Dor (he was married to Taphath daughter of Solomon);

¹²Baana son of Ahilud—in Taanach and Megiddo, and in all of Beth Shan next to Zarethan below Jezreel, from Beth Shan to Abel Meholah across to Jokmeam;

¹³Ben-Geber—in Ramoth Gilead (the settlements of Jair son of Manasseh in Gilead were his, as well as the region of Argob in Bashan and its sixty large walled cities with bronze gate bars);

¹⁴Ahinadab son of Iddo—in Mahanaim;

¹⁵Ahimaaz—in Naphtali (he had married Basemath daughter of Solomon);

¹⁶Baana son of Hushai—in Asher and in Aloth;

¹⁷Jehoshaphat son of Paruah—in Issachar;

¹⁸Shimei son of Ela—in Benjamin;

¹⁹Geber son of Uri—in Gilead (the country of Sihon king of the Amorites and the country of Og king of Bashan). He was the only governor over the district.

Solomon's Daily Provisions

²⁰The people of Judah and Israel were as numerous as the sand on the seashore; they ate, they drank and they were happy. ²¹And Solomon ruled over all the kingdoms from the Euphrates River to the land of the Philistines, as far as the border of Egypt. These countries brought tribute and were Solomon's subjects all his life.

²²Solomon's daily provisions were thirty cors*ᵃ* of the finest flour and sixty cors*ᵇ* of meal, ²³ten head of stall-fed cattle, twenty of pasture-fed cattle and a hundred sheep and goats, as well as deer, gazelles, roebucks and choice fowl. ²⁴For he ruled over all the kingdoms west of the Euphrates River, from Tiphsah to Gaza, and had peace on all sides. ²⁵During Solomon's lifetime Judah and Israel, from Dan to Beersheba, lived in safety, everyone under their own vine and under their own fig tree.

²⁶Solomon had four*ᶜ* thousand stalls for chariot horses, and twelve thousand horses.*ᵈ*

²⁷The district governors, each in his month, supplied provisions for King Solomon and all who came to the king's table. They saw to it that nothing was lacking. ²⁸They also brought to the proper place their quotas of barley and straw for the chariot horses and the other horses.

Solomon's Wisdom

²⁹God gave Solomon wisdom and very great insight, and a breadth of understanding as measureless as the sand on the seashore. ³⁰Solomon's wisdom was greater than the wisdom of all the people of the East, and greater than all the wisdom of Egypt. ³¹He was wiser than anyone else, including Ethan the Ezrahite—wiser than Heman, Kalkol and Darda, the sons of Mahol. And his fame spread to all the surrounding nations. ³²He spoke three thousand proverbs and his songs numbered a thousand and five. ³³He spoke about plant life, from the cedar of Lebanon to the hyssop that grows out of walls. He also spoke about animals and birds, reptiles and fish. ³⁴From all nations people came to listen to Solomon's wisdom, sent by all the kings of the world, who had heard of his wisdom.*ᵉ*

Preparations for Building the Temple

5ᶠ When Hiram king of Tyre heard that Solomon had been anointed king to succeed his father David, he sent his envoys to Solomon, because he had always been on friendly terms with David. ²Solomon sent back this message to Hiram:

³"You know that because of the wars waged against my father David from all sides, he could not build a temple for the Name of the Lᴏʀᴅ his God until the Lᴏʀᴅ put his enemies under his feet. ⁴But now the Lᴏʀᴅ

ᵃ 22 That is, probably about 5 1/2 tons or about 5 metric tons   *ᵇ 22* That is, probably about 11 tons or about 10 metric tons   *ᶜ 26* Some Septuagint manuscripts (see also 2 Chron. 9:25); Hebrew *forty*   *ᵈ 26* Or *charioteers*   *ᵉ 34* In Hebrew texts 4:21-34 is numbered 5:1-14.   *ᶠ* In Hebrew texts 5:1-18 is numbered 5:15-32.

my God has given me rest on every side, and there is no adversary or disaster. ⁵I intend, therefore, to build a temple for the Name of the Lᴏʀᴅ my God, as the Lᴏʀᴅ told my father David, when he said, 'Your son whom I will put on the throne in your place will build the temple for my Name.'

⁶"So give orders that cedars of Lebanon be cut for me. My men will work with yours, and I will pay you for your men whatever wages you set. You know that we have no one so skilled in felling timber as the Sidonians."

⁷When Hiram heard Solomon's message, he was greatly pleased and said, "Praise be to the Lᴏʀᴅ today, for he has given David a wise son to rule over this great nation."

⁸So Hiram sent word to Solomon:

"I have received the message you sent me and will do all you want in providing the cedar and juniper logs. ⁹My men will haul them down from Lebanon to the Mediterranean Sea, and I will float them as rafts by sea to the place you specify. There I will separate them and you can take them away. And you are to grant my wish by providing food for my royal household."

¹⁰In this way Hiram kept Solomon supplied with all the cedar and juniper logs he wanted, ¹¹and Solomon gave Hiram twenty thousand cors*ᵃ* of wheat as food for his household, in addition to twenty thousand baths*ᵇ,ᶜ* of pressed olive oil. Solomon continued to do this for Hiram year after year. ¹²The Lᴏʀᴅ gave Solomon wisdom, just as he had promised him. There were peaceful relations between Hiram and Solomon, and the two of them made a treaty.

¹³King Solomon conscripted laborers from all Israel — thirty thousand men. ¹⁴He sent them off to Lebanon in shifts of ten thousand a month, so that they spent one month in Lebanon and two months at home. Adoniram was in charge of the forced labor. ¹⁵Solomon had seventy thousand carriers and eighty thousand stonecutters in the hills, ¹⁶as well as thirty-three hundred*ᵈ* foremen who supervised the

project and directed the workers. ¹⁷At the king's command they removed from the quarry large blocks of high-grade stone to provide a foundation of dressed stone for the temple. ¹⁸The craftsmen of Solomon and Hiram and workers from Byblos cut and prepared the timber and stone for the building of the temple.

ᵃ 11 That is, probably about 3,600 tons or about 3,250 metric tons　　*ᵇ 11* Septuagint (see also 2 Chron. 2:10); Hebrew *twenty cors*　　*ᶜ 11* That is, about 120,000 gallons or about 440,000 liters　　*ᵈ 16* Hebrew; some Septuagint manuscripts (see also 2 Chron. 2:2,18) *thirty-six hundred*

Why was God's temple and everything in it made of gold and so rich?

(1 KINGS 5 - 7)

Because God's presence was in the temple. God lived in the temple. During the time that Solomon was king, people were rich in Israel, and they had good neighbors who could give them anything they needed. Gold is a beautiful metal that's pure and doesn't break when it's being worked on. It symbolizes that before God, there can't be any "bad" or "impure" things. All the walls, the columns and the elements had to be made very carefully, paying attention to all the details God himself ordered. That symbolizes that the best is always for God.

extended the width of the temple, that is twenty cubits,^{c} and projected ten cubits^d from the front of the temple. ^{4}He made narrow windows high up in the temple walls. ^{5}Against the walls of the main hall and inner sanctuary he built a structure around the building, in which there were side rooms. ^{6}The lowest floor was five cubits^e wide, the middle floor six cubits^f and the third floor seven.^{g} He made offset ledges around the outside of the temple so that nothing would be inserted into the temple walls.

^{7}In building the temple, only blocks dressed at the quarry were used, and no hammer, chisel or any other iron tool was heard at the temple site while it was being built.

---

^{a} 1 Hebrew; Septuagint *four hundred and fortieth*
^{b} 2 That is, about 90 feet long, 30 feet wide and 45 feet high or about 27 meters long, 9 meters wide and 14 meters high ^{c} 3 That is, about 30 feet or about 9 meters; also in verses 16 and 20 ^{d} 3 That is, about 15 feet or about 4.5 meters; also in verses 23-26
^{e} 6 That is, about 7 1/2 feet or about 2.3 meters; also in verses 10 and 24 ^{f} 6 That is, about 9 feet or about 2.7 meters ^{g} 6 That is, about 11 feet or about 3.2 meters

THE
WITNESSES

✓ **HIRAM** (1 **KINGS** 5:1)
His name means "brother of the exalted." He was the king of Tyre, and he joined David and Solomon in building the temple. He became king when he was 17 years old. He improved his kingdom and made it grow a lot. He got along really well with David and with Solomon too. Jerusalem, which was an interior city, used the port of Tyre for commerce.

Solomon Builds the Temple

6 In the four hundred and eightieth^a year after the Israelites came out of Egypt, in the fourth year of Solomon's reign over Israel, in the month of Ziv, the second month, he began to build the temple of the LORD.

^{2}The temple that King Solomon built for the LORD was sixty cubits long, twenty wide and thirty high.^{b} ^{3}The portico at the front of the main hall of the temple

BREAK THROUGH!

Ziv

(1 KINGS 6:1)
The second month of the Jewish lunar calendar. In our solar calendar, that would be the middle of April to the middle of May.

[8]The entrance to the lowest[a] floor was on the south side of the temple; a stairway led up to the middle level and from there to the third. [9]So he built the temple and completed it, roofing it with beams and cedar planks. [10]And he built the side rooms all along the temple. The height of each was five cubits, and they were attached to the temple by beams of cedar.

[11]The word of the LORD came to Solomon: [12]"As for this temple you are building, if you follow my decrees, observe my laws and keep all my commands and obey them, I will fulfill through you the promise I gave to David your father. [13]And I will live among the Israelites and will not abandon my people Israel."

[14]So Solomon built the temple and completed it. [15]He lined its interior walls with cedar boards, paneling them from the floor of the temple to the ceiling, and covered the floor of the temple with planks of juniper. [16]He partitioned off twenty cubits at the rear of the temple with cedar boards from floor to ceiling to form within the temple an inner sanctuary, the Most Holy Place. [17]The main hall in front of this room was forty cubits[b] long. [18]The inside of the temple was cedar, carved with gourds and open flowers. Everything was cedar; no stone was to be seen.

[19]He prepared the inner sanctuary within the temple to set the ark of the covenant of the LORD there. [20]The inner sanctuary was twenty cubits long, twenty wide and twenty high. He overlaid the inside with pure gold, and he also overlaid the altar of cedar. [21]Solomon covered the inside of the temple with pure gold, and he extended gold chains across the front of the inner sanctuary, which was overlaid with gold. [22]So he overlaid the whole interior with gold. He also overlaid with gold the altar that belonged to the inner sanctuary.

[23]For the inner sanctuary he made a pair of cherubim out of olive wood, each ten cubits high. [24]One wing of the first cherub was five cubits long, and the other wing five cubits—ten cubits from wing tip to wing tip. [25]The second cherub also measured ten cubits, for the two cherubim were identical in size and shape. [26]The height of each cherub was ten cubits. [27]He placed the cherubim inside the innermost room of the temple, with their wings spread out. The wing of one cherub touched one wall, while the wing of the other cherub touched the other wall, and their wings touched each other in the middle of the room. [28]He overlaid the cherubim with gold.

[29]On the walls all around the temple, in both the inner and outer rooms, he carved cherubim, palm trees and open flowers. [30]He also covered the floors of both the inner and outer rooms of the temple with gold.

[31]For the entrance to the inner sanctuary he made doors out of olive wood that were one fifth of the width of the sanctuary. [32]And on the two olive-wood doors he carved cherubim, palm trees and open flowers, and overlaid the cherubim and palm trees with hammered gold. [33]In the same way, for the entrance to the main hall he made doorframes out of olive wood that were one fourth of the width of the hall. [34]He also made two doors out of juniper wood, each having two leaves that turned in sockets. [35]He carved cherubim, palm trees and open flowers on them and overlaid them with gold hammered evenly over the carvings.

[36]And he built the inner courtyard of three courses of dressed stone and one course of trimmed cedar beams.

[37]The foundation of the temple of the LORD was laid in the fourth year, in the month of Ziv. [38]In the eleventh year in the month of Bul, the eighth month, the temple was finished in all its details according to its specifications. He had spent seven years building it.

Solomon Builds His Palace

7 It took Solomon thirteen years, however, to complete the construction of his palace. [2]He built the Palace of the Forest of Lebanon a hundred cubits long, fifty wide and thirty high,[c] with four rows of cedar columns supporting trimmed cedar beams. [3]It was roofed with cedar above the beams that rested on the columns—

---

[a] 8 Septuagint; Hebrew middle   [b] 17 That is, about 60 feet or about 18 meters   [c] 2 That is, about 150 feet long, 75 feet wide and 45 feet high or about 45 meters long, 23 meters wide and 14 meters high

BREAKTHROUGH!

Bul

(1 KINGS 6:38; 12:32–33)
The eighth month in the Jewish lunar calendar. That would be from the middle of October to the middle of November in our calendar.

forty-five beams, fifteen to a row. [4]Its windows were placed high in sets of three, facing each other. [5]All the doorways had rectangular frames; they were in the front part in sets of three, facing each other.[a]

[6]He made a colonnade fifty cubits long and thirty wide.[b] In front of it was a portico, and in front of that were pillars and an overhanging roof.

[7]He built the throne hall, the Hall of Justice, where he was to judge, and he covered it with cedar from floor to ceiling.[c] [8]And the palace in which he was to live, set farther back, was similar in design. Solomon also made a palace like this hall for Pharaoh's daughter, whom he had married.

[9]All these structures, from the outside to the great courtyard and from foundation to eaves, were made of blocks of high-grade stone cut to size and smoothed on their inner and outer faces. [10]The foundations were laid with large stones of good quality, some measuring ten cubits[d] and some eight.[e] [11]Above were high-grade stones, cut to size, and cedar beams.

[12]The great courtyard was surrounded by a wall of three courses of dressed stone and one course of trimmed cedar beams, as was the inner courtyard of the temple of the LORD with its portico.

The Temple's Furnishings

[13]King Solomon sent to Tyre and brought Huram,[f] [14]whose mother was a widow from the tribe of Naphtali and whose father was from Tyre and a skilled craftsman in bronze. Huram was filled with wisdom, with understanding and with knowledge to do all kinds of bronze work. He came to King Solomon and did all the work assigned to him.

[15]He cast two bronze pillars, each eighteen cubits high and twelve cubits in circumference.[g] [16]He also made two capitals of cast bronze to set on the tops of the pillars; each capital was five cubits[h] high. [17]A network of interwoven chains adorned the capitals on top of the pillars, seven for each capital. [18]He made pomegranates in two rows[i] encircling each network to decorate the capitals on top of the pillars.[j] He did the same for each capital. [19]The capitals on top of the pillars in the portico were in the shape of lilies, four cubits[k] high. [20]On the capitals of both pillars, above the bowl-shaped part next to the network, were the two hundred pomegranates in rows all around. [21]He erected the pillars at the portico of the temple. The pillar to the south he named Jakin[l] and the one to the north Boaz.[m] [22]The capitals on top were in the shape of lilies. And so the work on the pillars was completed.

[23]He made the Sea of cast metal, circular in shape, measuring ten cubits from

---

[a] 5 The meaning of the Hebrew for this verse is uncertain.
[b] 6 That is, about 75 feet long and 45 feet wide or about 23 meters long and 14 meters wide   [c] 7 Vulgate and Syriac; Hebrew *floor*   [d] 10 That is, about 15 feet or about 4.5 meters; also in verse 23   [e] 10 That is, about 12 feet or about 3.6 meters   [f] 13 Hebrew *Hiram*, a variant of *Huram*; also in verses 40 and 45   [g] 15 That is, about 27 feet high and 18 feet in circumference or about 8.1 meters high and 5.4 meters in circumference   [h] 16 That is, about 7 1/2 feet or about 2.3 meters; also in verse 23   [i] 18 Two Hebrew manuscripts and Septuagint; most Hebrew manuscripts *made the pillars, and there were two rows*   [j] 18 Many Hebrew manuscripts and Syriac; most Hebrew manuscripts *pomegranates*   [k] 19 That is, about 6 feet or about 1.8 meters; also in verse 38   [l] 21 *Jakin* probably means *he establishes.*   [m] 21 *Boaz* probably means *in him is strength.*

rim to rim and five cubits high. It took a line of thirty cubits[a] to measure around it. ²⁴Below the rim, gourds encircled it—ten to a cubit. The gourds were cast in two rows in one piece with the Sea.

²⁵The Sea stood on twelve bulls, three facing north, three facing west, three facing south and three facing east. The Sea rested on top of them, and their hindquarters were toward the center. ²⁶It was a handbreadth[b] in thickness, and its rim was like the rim of a cup, like a lily blossom. It held two thousand baths.[c]

²⁷He also made ten movable stands of bronze; each was four cubits long, four wide and three high.[d] ²⁸This is how the stands were made: They had side panels attached to uprights. ²⁹On the panels between the uprights were lions, bulls and cherubim—and on the uprights as well. Above and below the lions and bulls were wreaths of hammered work. ³⁰Each stand had four bronze wheels with bronze axles, and each had a basin resting on four supports, cast with wreaths on each side. ³¹On the inside of the stand there was an opening that had a circular frame one cubit[e] deep. This opening was round, and with its basework it measured a cubit and a half.[f] Around its opening there was engraving. The panels of the stands were square, not round. ³²The four wheels were under the panels, and the axles of the wheels were attached to the stand. The diameter of each wheel was a cubit and a half. ³³The wheels were made like chariot wheels; the axles, rims, spokes and hubs were all of cast metal.

³⁴Each stand had four handles, one on each corner, projecting from the stand. ³⁵At the top of the stand there was a circular band half a cubit[g] deep. The supports and panels were attached to the top of the stand. ³⁶He engraved cherubim, lions and palm trees on the surfaces of the supports and on the panels, in every available space, with wreaths all around. ³⁷This is the way he made the ten stands. They were all cast in the same molds and were identical in size and shape.

³⁸He then made ten bronze basins, each holding forty baths[h] and measuring four cubits across, one basin to go on

each of the ten stands. ³⁹He placed five of the stands on the south side of the temple and five on the north. He placed the Sea on the south side, at the southeast corner of the temple. ⁴⁰He also made the pots[i] and shovels and sprinkling bowls.

So Huram finished all the work he had undertaken for King Solomon in the temple of the LORD:

⁴¹the two pillars;
  the two bowl-shaped capitals on top of the pillars;
  the two sets of network decorating the two bowl-shaped capitals on top of the pillars;
⁴²the four hundred pomegranates for the two sets of network (two rows of pomegranates for each network decorating the bowl-shaped capitals on top of the pillars);
⁴³the ten stands with their ten basins;
⁴⁴the Sea and the twelve bulls under it;
⁴⁵the pots, shovels and sprinkling bowls.

All these objects that Huram made for King Solomon for the temple of the LORD were of burnished bronze. ⁴⁶The king had them cast in clay molds in the plain of the Jordan between Sukkoth and Zarethan. ⁴⁷Solomon left all these things unweighed, because there were so many; the weight of the bronze was not determined.

⁴⁸Solomon also made all the furnishings that were in the LORD's temple:

the golden altar;
the golden table on which was the bread of the Presence;
⁴⁹the lampstands of pure gold (five on the right and five on the left, in front of the inner sanctuary);

ᵃ 23 That is, about 45 feet or about 14 meters
ᵇ 26 That is, about 3 inches or about 7.5 centimeters
ᶜ 26 That is, about 12,000 gallons or about 44,000 liters; the Septuagint does not have this sentence.   ᵈ 27 That is, about 6 feet long and wide and about 4 1/2 feet high or about 1.8 meters long and wide and 1.4 meters high
ᵉ 31 That is, about 18 inches or about 45 centimeters
ᶠ 31 That is, about 2 1/4 feet or about 68 centimeters; also in verse 32   ᵍ 35 That is, about 9 inches or about 23 centimeters   ʰ 38 That is, about 240 gallons or about 880 liters   ⁱ 40 Many Hebrew manuscripts, Septuagint, Syriac and Vulgate (see also verse 45 and 2 Chron. 4:11); many other Hebrew manuscripts basins

the gold floral work and lamps and tongs;

50 the pure gold basins, wick trimmers, sprinkling bowls, dishes and censers;

and the gold sockets for the doors of the innermost room, the Most Holy Place, and also for the doors of the main hall of the temple.

51 When all the work King Solomon had done for the temple of the LORD was finished, he brought in the things his father David had dedicated—the silver and gold and the furnishings—and he placed them in the treasuries of the LORD's temple.

The Ark Brought to the Temple

8 Then King Solomon summoned into his presence at Jerusalem the elders of Israel, all the heads of the tribes and the chiefs of the Israelite families, to bring up the ark of the LORD's covenant from Zion, the City of David. 2 All the Israelites came together to King Solomon at the time of the festival in the month of Ethanim, the seventh month.

3 When all the elders of Israel had arrived, the priests took up the ark, 4 and they brought up the ark of the LORD and the tent of meeting and all the sacred furnishings in it. The priests and Levites carried them up, 5 and King Solomon and the entire assembly of Israel that had gathered about him were before the ark, sacrificing so many sheep and cattle that they could not be recorded or counted.

6 The priests then brought the ark of the LORD's covenant to its place in the inner sanctuary of the temple, the Most Holy Place, and put it beneath the wings of the cherubim. 7 The cherubim spread their wings over the place of the ark and overshadowed the ark and its carrying poles. 8 These poles were so long that their ends could be seen from the Holy Place in front of the inner sanctuary, but not from outside the Holy Place; and they are still there today. 9 There was nothing in the ark except the two stone tablets that Moses had placed in it at Horeb, where the LORD made a covenant with the Israelites after they came out of Egypt.

10 When the priests withdrew from the Holy Place, the cloud filled the temple of the LORD. 11 And the priests could not perform their service because of the cloud, for the glory of the LORD filled his temple.

12 Then Solomon said, "The LORD has said that he would dwell in a dark cloud; 13 I have indeed built a magnificent temple for you, a place for you to dwell forever."

14 While the whole assembly of Israel was standing there, the king turned around and blessed them. 15 Then he said:

"Praise be to the LORD, the God of Israel, who with his own hand has fulfilled what he promised with his own mouth to my father David. For he said, 16 'Since the day I brought my people Israel out of Egypt, I have not chosen a city in any tribe of Israel to have a temple built so that my Name might be there, but I have chosen David to rule my people Israel.'

17 "My father David had it in his heart to build a temple for the Name

BREAKTHROUGH!

Ethanim

(1 KINGS 8:2)

The seventh month in the Jewish lunar calendar, which would be from the middle of September to the middle of October in our solar calendar.

of the Lord, the God of Israel. ¹⁸But the Lord said to my father David, 'You did well to have it in your heart to build a temple for my Name. ¹⁹Nevertheless, you are not the one to build the temple, but your son, your own flesh and blood—he is the one who will build the temple for my Name.'

²⁰"The Lord has kept the promise he made: I have succeeded David my father and now I sit on the throne of Israel, just as the Lord promised, and I have built the temple for the Name of the Lord, the God of Israel. ²¹I have provided a place there for the ark, in which is the covenant of the Lord that he made with our ancestors when he brought them out of Egypt."

Solomon's Prayer of Dedication

²²Then Solomon stood before the altar of the Lord in front of the whole assembly of Israel, spread out his hands toward heaven ²³and said:

"Lord, the God of Israel, there is no God like you in heaven above or on earth below—you who keep your covenant of love with your servants who continue wholeheartedly in your way. ²⁴You have kept your promise to your servant David my father; with your mouth you have promised and with your hand you have fulfilled it— as it is today.

²⁵"Now Lord, the God of Israel, keep for your servant David my father the promises you made to him when you said, 'You shall never fail to have a successor to sit before me on the throne of Israel, if only your descendants are careful in all they do to walk before me faithfully as you have done.' ²⁶And now, God of Israel, let your word that you promised your servant David my father come true.

²⁷"But will God really dwell on earth? The heavens, even the highest heaven, cannot contain you. How much less this temple I have built! ²⁸Yet give attention to your servant's prayer and his plea for mercy, Lord my God. Hear the cry and the prayer that your servant is praying in your presence this day. ²⁹May your eyes be open toward this temple night and day, this place of which you said, 'My Name shall be there,' so that you will hear the prayer your servant prays toward this place. ³⁰Hear the supplication of your servant and of your people Israel when they pray toward this place. Hear from heaven, your dwelling place, and when you hear, forgive.

³¹"When anyone wrongs their neighbor and is required to take an oath and they come and swear the oath before your altar in this temple, ³²then hear from heaven and act. Judge between your servants, condemning the guilty by bringing down on their heads what they have done, and vindicating the innocent by treating them in accordance with their innocence.

³³"When your people Israel have been defeated by an enemy because they have sinned against you, and when they turn back to you and give praise to your name, praying and making supplication to you in this temple, ³⁴then hear from heaven and forgive the sin of your people Israel and bring them back to the land you gave to their ancestors.

³⁵"When the heavens are shut up and there is no rain because your people have sinned against you, and when they pray toward this place and give praise to your name and turn from their sin because you have afflicted them, ³⁶then hear from heaven and forgive the sin of your servants, your people Israel. Teach them the right way to live, and send rain on the land you gave your people for an inheritance.

³⁷"When famine or plague comes to the land, or blight or mildew, locusts or grasshoppers, or when an enemy besieges them in any of their cities, whatever disaster or disease may come, ³⁸and when a prayer or plea is made by anyone among your people Israel—being aware of the afflictions of their own hearts, and spreading out their hands toward

this temple— ³⁹then hear from heaven, your dwelling place. Forgive and act; deal with everyone according to all they do, since you know their hearts (for you alone know every human heart), ⁴⁰so that they will fear you all the time they live in the land you gave our ancestors.

⁴¹"As for the foreigner who does not belong to your people Israel but has come from a distant land because of your name— ⁴²for they will hear of your great name and your mighty hand and your outstretched arm— when they come and pray toward this temple, ⁴³then hear from heaven, your dwelling place. Do whatever the foreigner asks of you, so that all the peoples of the earth may know your name and fear you, as do your own people Israel, and may know that this house I have built bears your Name.

⁴⁴"When your people go to war against their enemies, wherever you send them, and when they pray to the Lᴏʀᴅ toward the city you have chosen and the temple I have built for your Name, ⁴⁵then hear from heaven their prayer and their plea, and uphold their cause.

⁴⁶"When they sin against you—for there is no one who does not sin— and you become angry with them and give them over to their enemies, who take them captive to their own lands, far away or near; ⁴⁷and if they have a change of heart in the land where they are held captive, and repent and plead with you in the land of their captors and say, 'We have sinned, we have done wrong, we have acted wickedly'; ⁴⁸and if they turn back to you with all their heart and soul in the land of their enemies who took them captive, and pray to you toward the land you gave their ancestors, toward the city you have chosen and the temple I have built for your Name; ⁴⁹then from heaven, your dwelling place, hear their prayer and their plea, and uphold their cause. ⁵⁰And forgive your people, who have sinned against you; forgive all the offenses they have committed

against you, and cause their captors to show them mercy; ⁵¹for they are your people and your inheritance, whom you brought out of Egypt, out of that iron-smelting furnace.

⁵²"May your eyes be open to your servant's plea and to the plea of your people Israel, and may you listen to them whenever they cry out to you. ⁵³For you singled them out from all the nations of the world to be your own inheritance, just as you declared through your servant Moses when you, Sovereign Lᴏʀᴅ, brought our ancestors out of Egypt."

⁵⁴When Solomon had finished all these prayers and supplications to the Lᴏʀᴅ, he rose from before the altar of the Lᴏʀᴅ, where he had been kneeling with his hands spread out toward heaven. ⁵⁵He stood and blessed the whole assembly of Israel in a loud voice, saying:

⁵⁶"Praise be to the Lᴏʀᴅ, who has given rest to his people Israel just as he promised. Not one word has failed of all the good promises he gave through his servant Moses. ⁵⁷May the Lᴏʀᴅ our God be with us as he was with our ancestors; may he never leave us nor forsake us. ⁵⁸May he turn our hearts to him, to walk in obedience to him and keep the commands, decrees and laws he gave our ancestors. ⁵⁹And may these words of mine, which I have prayed before the Lᴏʀᴅ, be near to the Lᴏʀᴅ our God day and night, that he may uphold the cause of his servant and the cause of his people Israel according to each day's need, ⁶⁰so that all the peoples of the earth may know that the Lᴏʀᴅ is God and that there is no other. ⁶¹And may your hearts be fully committed to the Lᴏʀᴅ our God, to live by his decrees and obey his commands, as at this time."

The Dedication of the Temple

⁶²Then the king and all Israel with him offered sacrifices before the Lᴏʀᴅ. ⁶³Solomon offered a sacrifice of fellowship offerings to the Lᴏʀᴅ: twenty-two thousand

cattle and a hundred and twenty thousand sheep and goats. So the king and all the Israelites dedicated the temple of the LORD.

⁶⁴On that same day the king consecrated the middle part of the courtyard in front of the temple of the LORD, and there he offered burnt offerings, grain offerings and the fat of the fellowship offerings, because the bronze altar that stood before the LORD was too small to hold the burnt offerings, the grain offerings and the fat of the fellowship offerings.

⁶⁵So Solomon observed the festival at that time, and all Israel with him—a vast assembly, people from Lebo Hamath to the Wadi of Egypt. They celebrated it before the LORD our God for seven days and seven days more, fourteen days in all. ⁶⁶On the following day he sent the people away. They blessed the king and then went home, joyful and glad in heart for all the good things the LORD had done for his servant David and his people Israel.

The LORD Appears to Solomon

9 When Solomon had finished building the temple of the LORD and the royal palace, and had achieved all he had desired to do, ²the LORD appeared to him a second time, as he had appeared to him at Gibeon. ³The LORD said to him:

"I have heard the prayer and plea you have made before me; I have consecrated this temple, which you have built, by putting my Name there forever. My eyes and my heart will always be there.

⁴"As for you, if you walk before me faithfully with integrity of heart and uprightness, as David your father did, and do all I command and observe my decrees and laws, ⁵I will establish your royal throne over Israel forever, as I promised David your father when I said, 'You shall never fail to have a successor on the throne of Israel.'

⁶"But if you[a] or your descendants turn away from me and do not observe the commands and decrees I have given you[a] and go off to serve other gods and worship them, ⁷then

FROM LEBO HAMATH TO THE WADI OF EGYPT

(1 KINGS 8:65)

The boundaries of the territory of Judah extended from as far in the northeast as Hamath, which was the valley between the two Lebanons, to the valley of Egypt in the southwest.

I will cut off Israel from the land I have given them and will reject this temple I have consecrated for my Name. Israel will then become a byword and an object of ridicule among all peoples. ⁸This temple will become a heap of rubble. All[b] who pass by will be appalled and will scoff and say, 'Why has the LORD done such a thing to this land and to this temple?' ⁹People will answer, 'Because they have forsaken the LORD their God, who brought their ancestors out of Egypt, and have embraced other gods, worshiping and serving them—that is why the LORD brought all this disaster on them.' "

---

a 6 The Hebrew is plural.   *b 8* See some Septuagint manuscripts, Old Latin, Syriac, Arabic and Targum; Hebrew *And though this temple is now imposing, all*

Solomon's Other Activities

[10]At the end of twenty years, during which Solomon built these two buildings—the temple of the LORD and the royal palace— [11]King Solomon gave twenty towns in Galilee to Hiram king of Tyre, because Hiram had supplied him with all the cedar and juniper and gold he wanted. [12]But when Hiram went from Tyre to see the towns that Solomon had given him, he was not pleased with them. [13]"What kind of towns are these you have given me, my brother?" he asked. And he called them the Land of Kabul,[a] a name they have to this day. [14]Now Hiram had sent to the king 120 talents[b] of gold.

[15]Here is the account of the forced labor King Solomon conscripted to build the LORD's temple, his own palace, the terraces,[c] the wall of Jerusalem, and Hazor, Megiddo and Gezer. [16](Pharaoh king of Egypt had attacked and captured Gezer. He had set it on fire. He killed its Canaanite inhabitants and then gave it as a wedding gift to his daughter, Solomon's wife. [17]And Solomon rebuilt Gezer.) He built up Lower Beth Horon, [18]Baalath, and Tadmor[d] in the desert, within his land, [19]as well as all his store cities and the towns for his chariots and for his horses[e]—whatever he desired to build in Jerusalem, in Lebanon and throughout all the territory he ruled.

[20]There were still people left from the Amorites, Hittites, Perizzites, Hivites and Jebusites (these peoples were not Israelites). [21]Solomon conscripted the descendants of all these peoples remaining in the land—whom the Israelites could not exterminate[f]—to serve as slave labor, as it is to this day. [22]But Solomon did not make slaves of any of the Israelites; they were his fighting men, his government officials, his officers, his captains, and the commanders of his chariots and charioteers. [23]They were also the chief officials in charge of Solomon's projects—550 officials supervising those who did the work.

[24]After Pharaoh's daughter had come up from the City of David to the palace Solomon had built for her, he constructed the terraces.

[25]Three times a year Solomon sacrificed burnt offerings and fellowship offerings on the altar he had built for the LORD, burning incense before the LORD along with them, and so fulfilled the temple obligations.

[26]King Solomon also built ships at Ezion Geber, which is near Elath in Edom, on the shore of the Red Sea.[g] [27]And Hiram sent his men—sailors who knew the sea—to serve in the fleet with Solomon's men. [28]They sailed to Ophir and brought back 420 talents[h] of gold, which they delivered to King Solomon.

---

[a] 13 *Kabul* sounds like the Hebrew for *good-for-nothing.*
[b] 14 That is, about 4 1/2 tons or about 4 metric tons
[c] 15 Or *the Millo;* also in verse 24   [d] 18 The Hebrew may also be read *Tamar.*   [e] 19 Or *charioteers*
[f] 21 The Hebrew term refers to the irrevocable giving over of things or persons to the LORD, often by totally destroying them.   [g] 26 Or *the Sea of Reeds*   [h] 28 That is, about 16 tons or about 14 metric tons

OPHIR

(1 KINGS 9:28)

Gold wasn't easily found where the Israelites lived. On the other hand, there was a lot in Ophir. We don't know exactly where that was. It was probably in India or in Arabia.

The Queen of Sheba Visits Solomon

10 When the queen of Sheba heard about the fame of Solomon and his relationship to the LORD, she came to test Solomon with hard questions. ²Arriving at Jerusalem with a very great caravan—with camels carrying spices, large quantities of gold, and precious stones—she came to Solomon and talked with him about all that she had on her mind. ³Solomon answered all her questions; nothing was too hard for the king to explain to her. ⁴When the queen of Sheba saw all the wisdom of Solomon and the palace he had built, ⁵the food on his table, the seating of his officials, the attending servants in their robes, his cupbearers, and the burnt offerings he made at*ᵃ* the temple of the LORD, she was overwhelmed.

⁶She said to the king, "The report I heard in my own country about your achievements and your wisdom is true. ⁷But I did not believe these things until I came and saw with my own eyes. Indeed, not even half was told me; in wisdom and wealth you have far exceeded the report I heard. ⁸How happy your people must be! How happy your officials, who continually stand before you and hear your wisdom! ⁹Praise be to the LORD your God, who has delighted in you and placed you on the throne of Israel. Because of the LORD's eternal love for Israel, he has made you king to maintain justice and righteousness."

¹⁰And she gave the king 120 talents*ᵇ* of gold, large quantities of spices, and precious stones. Never again were so many spices brought in as those the queen of Sheba gave to King Solomon.

¹¹(Hiram's ships brought gold from Ophir; and from there they brought great cargoes of almugwood*ᶜ* and precious stones. ¹²The king used the almugwood to make supports*ᵈ* for the temple of the LORD and for the royal palace, and to make harps and lyres for the musicians. So much almugwood has never been imported or seen since that day.)

¹³King Solomon gave the queen of Sheba all she desired and asked for, besides what he had given her out of his royal bounty. Then she left and returned with her retinue to her own country.

Solomon's Splendor

¹⁴The weight of the gold that Solomon received yearly was 666 talents,*ᵉ* ¹⁵not including the revenues from merchants and traders and from all the Arabian kings and the governors of the territories.

¹⁶King Solomon made two hundred large shields of hammered gold; six hundred shekels*ᶠ* of gold went into each shield. ¹⁷He also made three hundred small shields of hammered gold, with three minas*ᵍ* of gold in each shield. The king put them in the Palace of the Forest of Lebanon.

ᵃ 5 Or *the ascent by which he went up to* the temple of the LORD; also in verse 12   *ᵇ 10* That is, about 4 1/2 tons or about 4 metric tons   *ᶜ 11* Probably a variant of *algumwood*; also in verse 12   *ᵈ 12* The meaning of the Hebrew for this word is uncertain.   *ᵉ 14* That is, about 25 tons or about 23 metric tons   *ᶠ 16* That is, about 15 pounds or about 6.9 kilograms; also in verse 29   *ᵍ 17* That is, about 3 3/4 pounds or about 1.7 kilograms; or perhaps reference is to double minas, that is, about 7 1/2 pounds or about 3.5 kilograms.

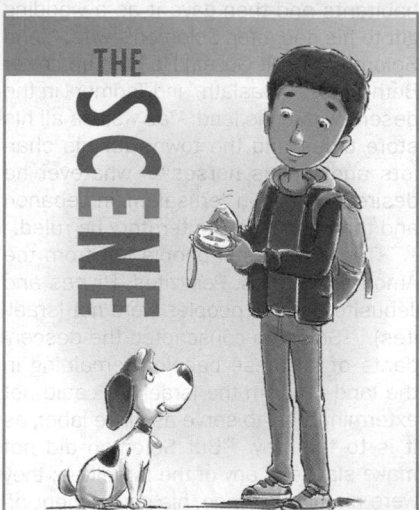

SHEBA

(1 KINGS 10:1)

Today, this place is called Yemen. It is in the southwestern part of Arabia, more than 994 miles (1,600 km) from Jerusalem.

18Then the king made a great throne covered with ivory and overlaid with fine gold. 19The throne had six steps, and its back had a rounded top. On both sides of the seat were armrests, with a lion standing beside each of them. 20Twelve lions stood on the six steps, one at either end of each step. Nothing like it had ever been made for any other kingdom. 21All King Solomon's goblets were gold, and all the household articles in the Palace of the Forest of Lebanon were pure gold. Nothing was made of silver, because silver was considered of little value in Solomon's days. 22The king had a fleet of trading ships*a* at sea along with the ships of Hiram. Once every three years it returned, carrying gold, silver and ivory, and apes and baboons.

23King Solomon was greater in riches and wisdom than all the other kings of the earth. 24The whole world sought audience with Solomon to hear the wisdom God had put in his heart. 25Year after year, everyone who came brought a gift — articles of silver and gold, robes, weapons and spices, and horses and mules.

26Solomon accumulated chariots and horses; he had fourteen hundred chariots and twelve thousand horses,*b* which he kept in the chariot cities and also with him in Jerusalem. 27The king made silver as common in Jerusalem as stones, and cedar as plentiful as sycamore-fig trees in the foothills. 28Solomon's horses were imported from Egypt and from Kue*c* — the royal merchants purchased them from Kue at the current price. 29They imported a chariot from Egypt for six hundred shekels of silver, and a horse for a hundred and fifty.*d* They also exported them to all the kings of the Hittites and of the Arameans.

Solomon's Wives

11 King Solomon, however, loved many foreign women besides Pharaoh's daughter — Moabites, Ammonites, Edomites, Sidonians and Hittites. 2They were from nations about which the LORD had told the Israelites, "You must not intermarry with them, because they will surely turn your hearts after their gods." Nev-

ertheless, Solomon held fast to them in love. 3He had seven hundred wives of royal birth and three hundred concubines, and his wives led him astray. 4As Solomon grew old, his wives turned his heart after other gods, and his heart was not fully devoted to the LORD his God, as the heart of David his father had been. 5He followed Ashtoreth the goddess of the Sidonians, and Molek the detestable god of the Ammonites. 6So Solomon did evil in the eyes of the LORD; he did not follow the LORD completely, as David his father had done.

7On a hill east of Jerusalem, Solomon built a high place for Chemosh the detestable god of Moab, and for Molek the detestable god of the Ammonites. 8He did the same for all his foreign wives, who burned incense and offered sacrifices to their gods.

9The LORD became angry with Solomon because his heart had turned away from the LORD, the God of Israel, who had appeared to him twice. 10Although he had forbidden Solomon to follow other gods, Solomon did not keep the LORD's command. 11So the LORD said to Solomon, "Since this is your attitude and you have not kept my covenant and my decrees, which I commanded you, I will most certainly tear the kingdom away from you and give it to one of your subordinates. 12Nevertheless, for the sake of David your father, I will not do it during your lifetime. I will tear it out of the hand of your son. 13Yet I will not tear the whole kingdom from him, but will give him one tribe for the sake of David my servant and for the sake of Jerusalem, which I have chosen."

Solomon's Adversaries

14Then the LORD raised up against Solomon an adversary, Hadad the Edomite, from the royal line of Edom. 15Earlier when David was fighting with Edom, Joab the commander of the army, who had gone up to bury the dead, had struck down all the men in Edom. 16Joab and all the Israelites stayed there for six months, until they

---

a 22 Hebrew *of ships of Tarshish*   *b* 26 Or *charioteers*
c 28 Probably *Cilicia*   *d* 29 That is, about 3 3/4 pounds or about 1.7 kilograms

had destroyed all the men in Edom. [17]But Hadad, still only a boy, fled to Egypt with some Edomite officials who had served his father. [18]They set out from Midian and went to Paran. Then taking people from Paran with them, they went to Egypt, to Pharaoh king of Egypt, who gave Hadad a house and land and provided him with food.

[19]Pharaoh was so pleased with Hadad that he gave him a sister of his own wife, Queen Tahpenes, in marriage. [20]The sister of Tahpenes bore him a son named Genubath, whom Tahpenes brought up in the royal palace. There Genubath lived with Pharaoh's own children.

[21]While he was in Egypt, Hadad heard that David rested with his ancestors and that Joab the commander of the army was also dead. Then Hadad said to Pharaoh, "Let me go, that I may return to my own country."

[22]"What have you lacked here that you want to go back to your own country?" Pharaoh asked.

"Nothing," Hadad replied, "but do let me go!"

[23]And God raised up against Solomon another adversary, Rezon son of Eliada, who had fled from his master, Hadadezer king of Zobah. [24]When David destroyed Zobah's army, Rezon gathered a band of men around him and became their leader; they went to Damascus, where they settled and took control. [25]Rezon was Israel's adversary as long as Solomon lived, adding to the trouble caused by Hadad. So Rezon ruled in Aram and was hostile toward Israel.

Jeroboam Rebels Against Solomon

[26]Also, Jeroboam son of Nebat rebelled against the king. He was one of Solomon's officials, an Ephraimite from Zeredah, and his mother was a widow named Zeruah.

[27]Here is the account of how he rebelled against the king: Solomon had built the terraces[a] and had filled in the gap in the wall of the city of David his father. [28]Now Jeroboam was a man of standing, and when Solomon saw how well the young man did his work, he put him in charge of the whole labor force of the tribes of Joseph.

[29]About that time Jeroboam was going out of Jerusalem, and Ahijah the prophet of Shiloh met him on the way, wearing a new cloak. The two of them were alone out in the country, [30]and Ahijah took hold of the new cloak he was wearing and tore it into twelve pieces. [31]Then he said to Jeroboam, "Take ten pieces for yourself, for this is what the Lord, the God of Israel, says: 'See, I am going to tear the kingdom out of Solomon's hand and give you ten tribes. [32]But for the sake of my servant David and the city of Jerusalem, which I have chosen out of all the tribes of Israel, he will have one tribe. [33]I will do this because they have[b] forsaken me and worshiped Ashtoreth the goddess of the Sidonians, Chemosh the god of the Moabites, and Molek the god of the Ammonites, and have not walked in obedience to me, nor done what is right in my eyes, nor kept my decrees and laws as David, Solomon's father, did.

[34]" 'But I will not take the whole kingdom out of Solomon's hand; I have made him ruler all the days of his life for the sake of David my servant, whom I chose and who obeyed my commands and decrees. [35]I will take the kingdom from his son's hands and give you ten tribes. [36]I will give one tribe to his son so that David my servant may always have a lamp before me in Jerusalem, the city where I chose to put my Name. [37]However, as for you, I will take you, and you will rule over all that your heart desires; you will be king over Israel. [38]If you do whatever I command you and walk in obedience to me and do what is right in my eyes by obeying my decrees and commands, as David my servant did, I will be with you. I will build you a dynasty as enduring as the one I built for David and will give Israel to you. [39]I will humble David's descendants because of this, but not forever.' "

[40]Solomon tried to kill Jeroboam, but Jeroboam fled to Egypt, to Shishak the king, and stayed there until Solomon's death.

---

a 27 Or the Millo   *b* 33 Hebrew; Septuagint, Vulgate and Syriac *because he has*

THE
WITNESSES

✓ JEROBOAM (1 KINGS 11:26)
His name means "he who fights for the justice of the people." He was the first king of the northern kingdom. Jeroboam wasn't a good king, because he built other temples with golden bulls to represent God. At that time, the image of a bull was considered the symbol of the presence of Baal, the false god.

✓ AHIJAH THE PROPHET (1 KINGS 11:29)
His name means "God is my brother." God told this prophet that he was going to divide the kingdom of Israel into two parts because Solomon, who was the king at that time, had disobeyed God. So God took the kingdom away from him. Well, he really let Solomon's family rule over two tribes (Judah and Benjamin). He made Jeroboam king of the other ten tribes.

✓ REHOBOAM (1 KINGS 11:43)
His name means "God makes the people great." He was one of Solomon's sons. He became king after his father. At the beginning of his reign, the northern tribes rebelled against him because he was very hard on the people. They chose Jeroboam as their king. Rehoboam ruled over only the two southern tribes (Judah and Benjamin). He followed the custom of worshiping other gods. What a dreadful practice!

Solomon's Death

⁴¹As for the other events of Solomon's reign—all he did and the wisdom he displayed—are they not written in the book of the annals of Solomon? ⁴²Solomon reigned in Jerusalem over all Israel forty years. ⁴³Then he rested with his ancestors and was buried in the city of David his father. And Rehoboam his son succeeded him as king.

Israel Rebels Against Rehoboam

12 Rehoboam went to Shechem, for all Israel had gone there to make him king. ²When Jeroboam son of Nebat heard this (he was still in Egypt, where he had fled from King Solomon), he returned from*ᵃ* Egypt. ³So they sent for Jeroboam, and he and the whole assembly of Israel went to Rehoboam and said to him:

⁴"Your father put a heavy yoke on us, but now lighten the harsh labor and the heavy yoke he put on us, and we will serve you."

⁵Rehoboam answered, "Go away for three days and then come back to me." So the people went away.

⁶Then King Rehoboam consulted the elders who had served his father Solomon during his lifetime. "How would you advise me to answer these people?" he asked.

⁷They replied, "If today you will be a servant to these people and serve them and give them a favorable answer, they will always be your servants."

⁸But Rehoboam rejected the advice the elders gave him and consulted the young men who had grown up with him and were serving him. ⁹He asked them, "What is

ᵃ 2 Or he remained in

your advice? How should we answer these people who say to me, 'Lighten the yoke your father put on us'?"

¹⁰The young men who had grown up with him replied, "These people have said to you, 'Your father put a heavy yoke on us, but make our yoke lighter.' Now tell them, 'My little finger is thicker than my father's waist. ¹¹My father laid on you a heavy yoke; I will make it even heavier. My father scourged you with whips; I will scourge you with scorpions.'"

¹²Three days later Jeroboam and all the people returned to Rehoboam, as the king had said, "Come back to me in three days." ¹³The king answered the people harshly. Rejecting the advice given him by the elders, ¹⁴he followed the advice of the young men and said, "My father made your yoke heavy; I will make it even heavier. My father scourged you with whips; I will scourge you with scorpions." ¹⁵So the king did not listen to the people, for this turn of events was from the LORD, to fulfill the word the LORD had spoken to Jeroboam son of Nebat through Ahijah the Shilonite.

¹⁶When all Israel saw that the king refused to listen to them, they answered the king:

"What share do we have in David,
   what part in Jesse's son?
To your tents, Israel!
Look after your own house, David!"

So the Israelites went home. ¹⁷But as for the Israelites who were living in the towns of Judah, Rehoboam still ruled over them.

¹⁸King Rehoboam sent out Adoniram,ᵃ who was in charge of forced labor, but all Israel stoned him to death. King Rehoboam, however, managed to get into his chariot and escape to Jerusalem. ¹⁹So Israel has been in rebellion against the house of David to this day.

²⁰When all the Israelites heard that Jeroboam had returned, they sent and called him to the assembly and made him king over all Israel. Only the tribe of Judah remained loyal to the house of David.

²¹When Rehoboam arrived in Jerusalem, he mustered all Judah and the tribe of Benjamin—a hundred and eighty thousand able young men—to go to war against Israel and to regain the kingdom for Rehoboam son of Solomon.

²²But this word of God came to Shemaiah the man of God: ²³"Say to Rehoboam son of Solomon king of Judah, to all Judah and Benjamin, and to the rest of the people, ²⁴'This is what the LORD says: Do not go up to fight against your brothers, the Israelites. Go home, every one of you, for this is my doing.'" So they obeyed the word of the LORD and went home again, as the LORD had ordered.

Golden Calves at Bethel and Dan

²⁵Then Jeroboam fortified Shechem in the hill country of Ephraim and lived there. From there he went out and built up Peniel.ᵇ

²⁶Jeroboam thought to himself, "The kingdom will now likely revert to the house of David. ²⁷If these people go up to offer sacrifices at the temple of the LORD in Jerusalem, they will again give their allegiance to their lord, Rehoboam king of Judah. They will kill me and return to King Rehoboam."

²⁸After seeking advice, the king made two golden calves. He said to the people, "It is too much for you to go up to Jerusalem. Here are your gods, Israel, who brought you up out of Egypt." ²⁹One he set up in Bethel, and the other in Dan. ³⁰And this thing became a sin; the people came to worship the one at Bethel and went as far as Dan to worship the other.ᶜ

³¹Jeroboam built shrines on high places and appointed priests from all sorts of people, even though they were not Levites. ³²He instituted a festival on the fifteenth day of the eighth month, like the festival held in Judah, and offered sacrifices on the altar. This he did in Bethel, sacrificing to the calves he had made. And at Bethel he also installed priests at the high places he had made. ³³On the fifteenth day of the eighth month, a month of his own choosing, he offered sacrifices on the altar he had built at Bethel. So

---

ᵃ 18 Some Septuagint manuscripts and Syriac (see also 4:6 and 5:14); Hebrew *Adoram*   ᵇ 25 Hebrew *Penuel,* a variant of *Peniel*   ᶜ 30 Probable reading of the original Hebrew text; Masoretic Text *people went to the one as far as Dan* he instituted the festival for the Israelites and went up to the altar to make offerings.

The Man of God From Judah

13 By the word of the LORD a man of God came from Judah to Bethel, as Jeroboam was standing by the altar to make an offering. ²By the word of the LORD he cried out against the altar: "Altar, altar! This is what the LORD says: 'A son named Josiah will be born to the house of David. On you he will sacrifice the priests of the high places who make offerings here, and human bones will be burned on you.'" ³That same day the man of God gave a sign: "This is the sign the LORD has declared: The altar will be split apart and the ashes on it will be poured out."

⁴When King Jeroboam heard what the man of God cried out against the altar at Bethel, he stretched out his hand from the altar and said, "Seize him!" But the hand he stretched out toward the man shriveled up, so that he could not pull it back. ⁵Also, the altar was split apart and its ashes poured out according to the sign given by the man of God by the word of the LORD.

⁶Then the king said to the man of God, "Intercede with the LORD your God and pray for me that my hand may be restored." So the man of God interceded with the LORD, and the king's hand was restored and became as it was before.

⁷The king said to the man of God, "Come home with me for a meal, and I will give you a gift."

⁸But the man of God answered the king, "Even if you were to give me half your possessions, I would not go with you, nor would I eat bread or drink water here. ⁹For I was commanded by the word of the LORD: 'You must not eat bread or drink water or return by the way you came.'" ¹⁰So he took another road and did not return by the way he had come to Bethel.

¹¹Now there was a certain old prophet living in Bethel, whose sons came and told him all that the man of God had done there that day. They also told their father what he had said to the king. ¹²Their father asked them, "Which way did he go?"

And his sons showed him which road the man of God from Judah had taken. ¹³So he said to his sons, "Saddle the donkey for me." And when they had saddled the donkey for him, he mounted it ¹⁴and rode after the man of God. He found him sitting under an oak tree and asked, "Are you the man of God who came from Judah?"

"I am," he replied.

¹⁵So the prophet said to him, "Come home with me and eat."

¹⁶The man of God said, "I cannot turn back and go with you, nor can I eat bread or drink water with you in this place. ¹⁷I have been told by the word of the LORD: 'You must not eat bread or drink water there or return by the way you came.'"

¹⁸The old prophet answered, "I too am a prophet, as you are. And an angel said to me by the word of the LORD: 'Bring him back with you to your house so that he may eat bread and drink water.'" (But he was lying to him.) ¹⁹So the man of God returned with him and ate and drank in his house.

²⁰While they were sitting at the table, the word of the LORD came to the old prophet who had brought him back. ²¹He cried out to the man of God who had come from Judah, "This is what the LORD says: 'You have defied the word of the LORD and have not kept the command the LORD your God gave you. ²²You came back and ate bread and drank water in the place where he told you not to eat or drink. Therefore your body will not be buried in the tomb of your ancestors.'"

²³When the man of God had finished eating and drinking, the prophet who had brought him back saddled his donkey for him. ²⁴As he went on his way, a lion met him on the road and killed him, and his body was left lying on the road, with both the donkey and the lion standing beside it. ²⁵Some people who passed by saw the body lying there, with the lion standing beside the body, and they went and reported it in the city where the old prophet lived.

²⁶When the prophet who had brought him back from his journey heard of it, he said, "It is the man of God who defied the

word of the LORD. The LORD has given him over to the lion, which has mauled him and killed him, as the word of the LORD had warned him."

²⁷The prophet said to his sons, "Saddle the donkey for me," and they did so. ²⁸Then he went out and found the body lying on the road, with the donkey and the lion standing beside it. The lion had neither eaten the body nor mauled the donkey. ²⁹So the prophet picked up the body of the man of God, laid it on the donkey, and brought it back to his own city to mourn for him and bury him. ³⁰Then he laid the body in his own tomb, and they mourned over him and said, "Alas, my brother!"

³¹After burying him, he said to his sons, "When I die, bury me in the grave where the man of God is buried; lay my bones beside his bones. ³²For the message he declared by the word of the LORD against the altar in Bethel and against all the shrines on the high places in the towns of Samaria will certainly come true."

³³Even after this, Jeroboam did not change his evil ways, but once more appointed priests for the high places from all sorts of people. Anyone who wanted to become a priest he consecrated for the high places. ³⁴This was the sin of the house of Jeroboam that led to its downfall and to its destruction from the face of the earth.

Ahijah's Prophecy Against Jeroboam

14 At that time Abijah son of Jeroboam became ill, ²and Jeroboam said to his wife, "Go, disguise yourself, so you won't be recognized as the wife of Jeroboam. Then go to Shiloh. Ahijah the prophet is there—the one who told me I would be king over this people. ³Take ten loaves of bread with you, some cakes and a jar of honey, and go to him. He will tell you what will happen to the boy." ⁴So Jeroboam's wife did what he said and went to Ahijah's house in Shiloh.

Now Ahijah could not see; his sight was gone because of his age. ⁵But the LORD had told Ahijah, "Jeroboam's wife is coming to ask you about her son, for he is ill,

and you are to give her such and such an answer. When she arrives, she will pretend to be someone else."

⁶So when Ahijah heard the sound of her footsteps at the door, he said, "Come in, wife of Jeroboam. Why this pretense? I have been sent to you with bad news. ⁷Go, tell Jeroboam that this is what the LORD, the God of Israel, says: 'I raised you up from among the people and appointed you ruler over my people Israel. ⁸I tore the kingdom away from the house of David and gave it to you, but you have not been like my servant David, who kept my commands and followed me with all his heart, doing only what was right in my eyes. ⁹You have done more evil than all who lived before you. You have made for yourself other gods, idols made of metal; you have aroused my anger and turned your back on me.

¹⁰"'Because of this, I am going to bring disaster on the house of Jeroboam. I will cut off from Jeroboam every last male in Israel—slave or free.ᵃ I will burn up the house of Jeroboam as one burns dung, until it is all gone. ¹¹Dogs will eat those belonging to Jeroboam who die in the city, and the birds will feed on those who die in the country. The LORD has spoken!'

¹²"As for you, go back home. When you set foot in your city, the boy will die. ¹³All Israel will mourn for him and bury him. He is the only one belonging to Jeroboam who will be buried, because he is the only one in the house of Jeroboam in whom the LORD, the God of Israel, has found anything good.

¹⁴"The LORD will raise up for himself a king over Israel who will cut off the family of Jeroboam. Even now this is beginning to happen.ᵇ ¹⁵And the LORD will strike Israel, so that it will be like a reed swaying in the water. He will uproot Israel from this good land that he gave to their ancestors and scatter them beyond the Euphrates River, because they aroused the LORD's anger by making Asherah poles.ᶜ ¹⁶And he will give Israel up because of the sins

---

ᵃ 10 Or Israel—every ruler or leader   ᵇ 14 The meaning of the Hebrew for this sentence is uncertain.   ᶜ 15 That is, wooden symbols of the goddess Asherah; here and elsewhere in 1 Kings

Jeroboam has committed and has caused Israel to commit."

¹⁷Then Jeroboam's wife got up and left and went to Tirzah. As soon as she stepped over the threshold of the house, the boy died. ¹⁸They buried him, and all Israel mourned for him, as the LORD had said through his servant the prophet Ahijah.

¹⁹The other events of Jeroboam's reign, his wars and how he ruled, are written in the book of the annals of the kings of Israel. ²⁰He reigned for twenty-two years and then rested with his ancestors. And Nadab his son succeeded him as king.

Rehoboam King of Judah

²¹Rehoboam son of Solomon was king in Judah. He was forty-one years old when he became king, and he reigned seventeen years in Jerusalem, the city the LORD had chosen out of all the tribes of Israel in which to put his Name. His mother's name was Naamah; she was an Ammonite.

²²Judah did evil in the eyes of the LORD. By the sins they committed they stirred up his jealous anger more than those who were before them had done. ²³They also set up for themselves high places, sacred stones and Asherah poles on every high hill and under every spreading tree. ²⁴There were even male shrine prostitutes in the land; the people engaged in all the detestable practices of the nations the LORD had driven out before the Israelites.

²⁵In the fifth year of King Rehoboam, Shishak king of Egypt attacked Jerusalem. ²⁶He carried off the treasures of the temple of the LORD and the treasures of the royal palace. He took everything, including all the gold shields Solomon had made. ²⁷So King Rehoboam made bronze shields to replace them and assigned these to the commanders of the guard on duty at the entrance to the royal palace. ²⁸Whenever the king went to the LORD's temple, the guards bore the shields, and afterward they returned them to the guardroom.

²⁹As for the other events of Rehoboam's reign, and all he did, are they not written in the book of the annals of the kings of Judah? ³⁰There was continual warfare between Rehoboam and Jeroboam. ³¹And Rehoboam rested with his ancestors and was buried with them in the City of David. His mother's name was Naamah; she was an Ammonite. And Abijah[a] his son succeeded him as king.

Abijah King of Judah

15 In the eighteenth year of the reign of Jeroboam son of Nebat, Abijah[b] became king of Judah, ²and he reigned in Jerusalem three years. His mother's name was Maakah daughter of Abishalom.[c]

³He committed all the sins his father had done before him; his heart was not fully devoted to the LORD his God, as the heart of David his forefather had been. ⁴Nevertheless, for David's sake the LORD his God gave him a lamp in Jerusalem by raising up a son to succeed him and by making Jerusalem strong. ⁵For David had done what was right in the eyes of the LORD and had not failed to keep any of the LORD's commands all the days of his life—except in the case of Uriah the Hittite.

⁶There was war between Abijah[d] and Jeroboam throughout Abijah's lifetime. ⁷As for the other events of Abijah's reign, and all he did, are they not written in the book of the annals of the kings of Judah? There was war between Abijah and Jeroboam. ⁸And Abijah rested with his ancestors and was buried in the City of David. And Asa his son succeeded him as king.

Asa King of Judah

⁹In the twentieth year of Jeroboam king of Israel, Asa became king of Judah, ¹⁰and he reigned in Jerusalem forty-one years. His grandmother's name was Maakah daughter of Abishalom.

¹¹Asa did what was right in the eyes of the LORD, as his father David had done. ¹²He expelled the male shrine prostitutes

---

a 31 Some Hebrew manuscripts and Septuagint (see also 2 Chron. 12:16); most Hebrew manuscripts *Abijam*
b 1 Some Hebrew manuscripts and Septuagint (see also 2 Chron. 12:16); most Hebrew manuscripts *Abijam*; also in verses 7 and 8   *c 2* A variant of *Absalom*; also in verse 10   *d 6* Some Hebrew manuscripts and Syriac *Abijam* (that is, Abijah); most Hebrew manuscripts *Rehoboam*

from the land and got rid of all the idols his ancestors had made. ¹³He even deposed his grandmother Maakah from her position as queen mother, because she had made a repulsive image for the worship of Asherah. Asa cut it down and burned it in the Kidron Valley. ¹⁴Although he did not remove the high places, Asa's heart was fully committed to the Lᴏʀᴅ all his life. ¹⁵He brought into the temple of the Lᴏʀᴅ the silver and gold and the articles that he and his father had dedicated.

¹⁶There was war between Asa and Baasha king of Israel throughout their reigns. ¹⁷Baasha king of Israel went up against Judah and fortified Ramah to prevent anyone from leaving or entering the territory of Asa king of Judah.

¹⁸Asa then took all the silver and gold that was left in the treasuries of the Lᴏʀᴅ's temple and of his own palace. He entrusted it to his officials and sent them to Ben-Hadad son of Tabrimmon, the son of Hezion, the king of Aram, who was ruling in Damascus. ¹⁹"Let there be a treaty between me and you," he said, "as there was between my father and your father. See, I am sending you a gift of silver and gold. Now break your treaty with Baasha king of Israel so he will withdraw from me."

²⁰Ben-Hadad agreed with King Asa and sent the commanders of his forces against the towns of Israel. He conquered Ijon, Dan, Abel Beth Maakah and all Kinnereth in addition to Naphtali. ²¹When Baasha heard this, he stopped building Ramah and withdrew to Tirzah. ²²Then King Asa issued an order to all Judah—no one was exempt—and they carried away from Ramah the stones and timber Baasha had been using there. With them King Asa built up Geba in Benjamin, and also Mizpah.

²³As for all the other events of Asa's reign, all his achievements, all he did and the cities he built, are they not written in the book of the annals of the kings of Judah? In his old age, however, his feet became diseased. ²⁴Then Asa rested with his ancestors and was buried with them in the city of his father David. And Jehoshaphat his son succeeded him as king.

THE
WITNESSES

✓ **ASA** (1 KINGS 15:8–24)
His name means "doctor" or "healer." He was a good king, and he led the people back to worshiping the true God of Israel.

Nadab King of Israel

²⁵Nadab son of Jeroboam became king of Israel in the second year of Asa king of Judah, and he reigned over Israel two years. ²⁶He did evil in the eyes of the Lᴏʀᴅ, following the ways of his father and committing the same sin his father had caused Israel to commit.

²⁷Baasha son of Ahijah from the tribe of Issachar plotted against him, and he struck him down at Gibbethon, a Philistine town, while Nadab and all Israel were besieging it. ²⁸Baasha killed Nadab in the third year of Asa king of Judah and succeeded him as king.

²⁹As soon as he began to reign, he killed Jeroboam's whole family. He did

not leave Jeroboam anyone that breathed, but destroyed them all, according to the word of the Lord given through his servant Ahijah the Shilonite. ³⁰This happened because of the sins Jeroboam had committed and had caused Israel to commit, and because he aroused the anger of the Lord, the God of Israel.

³¹As for the other events of Nadab's reign, and all he did, are they not written in the book of the annals of the kings of Israel? ³²There was war between Asa and Baasha king of Israel throughout their reigns.

Baasha King of Israel

³³In the third year of Asa king of Judah, Baasha son of Ahijah became king of all Israel in Tirzah, and he reigned twenty-four years. ³⁴He did evil in the eyes of the Lord, following the ways of Jeroboam and committing the same sin Jeroboam had caused Israel to commit.

16 Then the word of the Lord came to Jehu son of Hanani concerning Baasha: ²"I lifted you up from the dust and appointed you ruler over my people Israel, but you followed the ways of Jeroboam and caused my people Israel to sin and to arouse my anger by their sins. ³So I am about to wipe out Baasha and his house, and I will make your house like that of Jeroboam son of Nebat. ⁴Dogs will eat those belonging to Baasha who die in the city, and birds will feed on those who die in the country."

⁵As for the other events of Baasha's reign, what he did and his achievements, are they not written in the book of the annals of the kings of Israel? ⁶Baasha rested with his ancestors and was buried in Tirzah. And Elah his son succeeded him as king.

⁷Moreover, the word of the Lord came through the prophet Jehu son of Hanani to Baasha and his house, because of all the evil he had done in the eyes of the Lord, arousing his anger by the things he did, becoming like the house of Jeroboam—and also because he destroyed it.

Elah King of Israel

⁸In the twenty-sixth year of Asa king of Judah, Elah son of Baasha became king of Israel, and he reigned in Tirzah two years.

⁹Zimri, one of his officials, who had command of half his chariots, plotted against him. Elah was in Tirzah at the time, getting drunk in the home of Arza, the palace administrator at Tirzah. ¹⁰Zimri came in, struck him down and killed him in the twenty-seventh year of Asa king of Judah. Then he succeeded him as king.

¹¹As soon as he began to reign and was seated on the throne, he killed off Baasha's whole family. He did not spare a single male, whether relative or friend. ¹²So Zimri destroyed the whole family of Baasha, in accordance with the word of the Lord spoken against Baasha through the prophet Jehu— ¹³because of all the sins Baasha and his son Elah had committed and had caused Israel to commit, so that they aroused the anger of the Lord, the God of Israel, by their worthless idols.

¹⁴As for the other events of Elah's reign, and all he did, are they not written in the book of the annals of the kings of Israel?

Zimri King of Israel

¹⁵In the twenty-seventh year of Asa king of Judah, Zimri reigned in Tirzah seven days. The army was encamped near Gibbethon, a Philistine town. ¹⁶When the Israelites in the camp heard that Zimri had plotted against the king and murdered him, they proclaimed Omri, the commander of the army, king over Israel that very day there in the camp. ¹⁷Then Omri and all the Israelites with him withdrew from Gibbethon and laid siege to Tirzah. ¹⁸When Zimri saw that the city was taken, he went into the citadel of the royal palace and set the palace on fire around him. So he died, ¹⁹because of the sins he had committed, doing evil in the eyes of the Lord and following the ways of Jeroboam and committing the same sin Jeroboam had caused Israel to commit.

²⁰As for the other events of Zimri's reign, and the rebellion he carried out, are they not written in the book of the annals of the kings of Israel?

CHECK THE FACTS

What happened when Elijah challenged the prophets of Baal at Mount Carmel?

A) The prophets of Baal repented and went away with Elijah.

B) The true God sent fire from heaven and burned up the bull, the wood and even the stones and the soil.

C) It rained all day, and they had to cancel the competition.

CORRECT ANSWER: B

Omri King of Israel

21 Then the people of Israel were split into two factions; half supported Tibni son of Ginath for king, and the other half supported Omri. 22 But Omri's followers proved stronger than those of Tibni son of Ginath. So Tibni died and Omri became king.

23 In the thirty-first year of Asa king of Judah, Omri became king of Israel, and he reigned twelve years, six of them in Tirzah. 24 He bought the hill of Samaria from Shemer for two talents*a* of silver and built a city on the hill, calling it Samaria, after Shemer, the name of the former owner of the hill.

25 But Omri did evil in the eyes of the LORD and sinned more than all those be-

fore him. 26 He followed completely the ways of Jeroboam son of Nebat, committing the same sin Jeroboam had caused Israel to commit, so that they aroused the anger of the LORD, the God of Israel, by their worthless idols.

27 As for the other events of Omri's reign, what he did and the things he achieved, are they not written in the book of the annals of the kings of Israel? 28 Omri rested with his ancestors and was buried in Samaria. And Ahab his son succeeded him as king.

Ahab Becomes King of Israel

29 In the thirty-eighth year of Asa king of Judah, Ahab son of Omri became king of Israel, and he reigned in Samaria over Israel twenty-two years. 30 Ahab son of Omri did more evil in the eyes of the LORD than any of those before him. 31 He not only considered it trivial to commit the sins of Jeroboam son of Nebat, but he also married Jezebel daughter of Ethbaal king of the Sidonians, and began to serve Baal and worship him. 32 He set up an altar for Baal in the temple of Baal that he built in Samaria. 33 Ahab also made an Asherah pole and did more to arouse the anger of the LORD, the God of Israel, than did all the kings of Israel before him.

34 In Ahab's time, Hiel of Bethel rebuilt Jericho. He laid its foundations at the cost of his firstborn son Abiram, and he set up its gates at the cost of his youngest son Segub, in accordance with the word of the LORD spoken by Joshua son of Nun.

Elijah Announces a Great Drought

17 Now Elijah the Tishbite, from Tishbe*b* in Gilead, said to Ahab, "As the LORD, the God of Israel, lives, whom I serve, there will be neither dew nor rain in the next few years except at my word."

Elijah Fed by Ravens

2 Then the word of the LORD came to Elijah: 3 "Leave here, turn eastward and hide in the Kerith Ravine, east of the Jordan.

---

a 24 That is, about 150 pounds or about 68 kilograms
b 1 Or *Tishbite, of the settlers*

⁴You will drink from the brook, and I have directed the ravens to supply you with food there."

⁵So he did what the Lord had told him. He went to the Kerith Ravine, east of the Jordan, and stayed there. ⁶The ravens brought him bread and meat in the morning and bread and meat in the evening, and he drank from the brook.

Elijah and the Widow at Zarephath

⁷Some time later the brook dried up because there had been no rain in the land.

THE
WITNESSES

✓ ELIJAH (1 KINGS 17:1)

His name means "my Lord is God." He was a prophet. That means he was someone who spoke for God to the people and to the kings. He was a true messenger of God who fought against the prophets of Baal, and he conquered them. He also performed several miracles, because God was with him.

⁸Then the word of the Lord came to him: ⁹"Go at once to Zarephath in the region of Sidon and stay there. I have directed a widow there to supply you with food." ¹⁰So he went to Zarephath. When he came to the town gate, a widow was there gathering sticks. He called to her and asked, "Would you bring me a little water in a jar so I may have a drink?" ¹¹As she was going to get it, he called, "And bring me, please, a piece of bread."

¹²"As surely as the Lord your God lives," she replied, "I don't have any bread—only a handful of flour in a jar and a little olive oil in a jug. I am gathering a few sticks to take home and make a meal for myself and my son, that we may eat it—and die."

¹³Elijah said to her, "Don't be afraid. Go home and do as you have said. But first make a small loaf of bread for me from what you have and bring it to me, and then make something for yourself and your son. ¹⁴For this is what the Lord, the God of Israel, says: 'The jar of flour will not be used up and the jug of oil will not run dry until the day the Lord sends rain on the land.'"

¹⁵She went away and did as Elijah had told her. So there was food every day for Elijah and for the woman and her family. ¹⁶For the jar of flour was not used up and the jug of oil did not run dry, in keeping with the word of the Lord spoken by Elijah.

¹⁷Some time later the son of the woman who owned the house became ill. He grew worse and worse, and finally stopped breathing. ¹⁸She said to Elijah, "What do you have against me, man of God? Did you come to remind me of my sin and kill my son?"

¹⁹"Give me your son," Elijah replied. He took him from her arms, carried him to the upper room where he was staying, and laid him on his bed. ²⁰Then he cried out to the Lord, "Lord my God, have you brought tragedy even on this widow I am staying with, by causing her son to die?" ²¹Then he stretched himself out on the boy three times and cried out to the Lord, "Lord my God, let this boy's life return to him!"

²²The Lord heard Elijah's cry, and the boy's life returned to him, and he lived. ²³Elijah picked up the child and carried him down from the room into the house. He gave him to his mother and said, "Look, your son is alive!"

²⁴Then the woman said to Elijah, "Now I know that you are a man of God and that the word of the Lord from your mouth is the truth."

Elijah and Obadiah

18 After a long time, in the third year, the word of the Lord came to Elijah: "Go and present yourself to Ahab, and I will send rain on the land." ²So Elijah went to present himself to Ahab.

Now the famine was severe in Samaria, ³and Ahab had summoned Obadiah, his palace administrator. (Obadiah was a devout believer in the Lord. ⁴While Jezebel

SAMARIA

(1 KINGS 18:2)

This means "a watch mountain" (like a watch tower), because it is a mountainous region. It was the fourth capital of the northern kingdom. Now, it is the north part of West Bank (Cisjordan).

was killing off the Lord's prophets, Obadiah had taken a hundred prophets and hidden them in two caves, fifty in each, and had supplied them with food and water.) ⁵Ahab had said to Obadiah, "Go through the land to all the springs and valleys. Maybe we can find some grass to keep the horses and mules alive so we will not have to kill any of our animals." ⁶So they divided the land they were to cover, Ahab going in one direction and Obadiah in another.

⁷As Obadiah was walking along, Elijah met him. Obadiah recognized him, bowed down to the ground, and said, "Is it really you, my lord Elijah?"

⁸"Yes," he replied. "Go tell your master, 'Elijah is here.'"

⁹"What have I done wrong," asked Obadiah, "that you are handing your servant over to Ahab to be put to death? ¹⁰As surely as the Lord your God lives, there is not a nation or kingdom where my master has not sent someone to look for you. And whenever a nation or kingdom claimed you were not there, he made them swear they could not find you. ¹¹But now you tell me to go to my master and say, 'Elijah is here.' ¹²I don't know where the Spirit of the Lord may carry you when I leave you. If I go and tell Ahab and he doesn't find you, he will kill me. Yet I your servant have worshiped the Lord since my youth. ¹³Haven't you heard, my lord, what I did while Jezebel was killing the prophets of the Lord? I hid a hundred of the Lord's prophets in two caves, fifty in each, and supplied them with food and water. ¹⁴And now you tell me to go to my master and say, 'Elijah is here.' He will kill me!"

¹⁵Elijah said, "As the Lord Almighty lives, whom I serve, I will surely present myself to Ahab today."

Elijah on Mount Carmel

¹⁶So Obadiah went to meet Ahab and told him, and Ahab went to meet Elijah. ¹⁷When he saw Elijah, he said to him, "Is that you, you troubler of Israel?"

¹⁸"I have not made trouble for Israel," Elijah replied. "But you and your father's family have. You have abandoned the

THE
WITNESSES

✓ **JEZEBEL** (1 **KINGS** 18:4)
Her name means "Baal is my prince." She was the king of Sidon's daughter and also the wife of King Ahab of Israel. She tried to destroy all of God's prophets and replace them with the prophets of her false gods, Baal and Asherah. She also bothered the prophet Elijah a lot. She did many bad, ugly things, and she finally had a horrible death. She was thrown out of a window, some horses trampled her and then some dogs ate her body. How horrible!

LORD's commands and have followed the Baals. ¹⁹Now summon the people from all over Israel to meet me on Mount Carmel. And bring the four hundred and fifty prophets of Baal and the four hundred prophets of Asherah, who eat at Jezebel's table."

²⁰So Ahab sent word throughout all Israel and assembled the prophets on Mount Carmel. ²¹Elijah went before the people and said, "How long will you waver between two opinions? If the LORD is God, follow him; but if Baal is God, follow him." But the people said nothing.

²²Then Elijah said to them, "I am the only one of the LORD's prophets left, but Baal has four hundred and fifty prophets. ²³Get two bulls for us. Let Baal's prophets choose one for themselves, and let them cut it into pieces and put it on the wood but not set fire to it. I will prepare the other bull and put it on the wood but not set fire to it. ²⁴Then you call on the name of your god, and I will call on the name of the LORD. The god who answers by fire—he is God."

Then all the people said, "What you say is good."

²⁵Elijah said to the prophets of Baal, "Choose one of the bulls and prepare it first, since there are so many of you. Call on the name of your god, but do not light the fire." ²⁶So they took the bull given them and prepared it.

Then they called on the name of Baal from morning till noon. "Baal, answer us!" they shouted. But there was no response; no one answered. And they danced around the altar they had made.

²⁷At noon Elijah began to taunt them. "Shout louder!" he said. "Surely he is a god! Perhaps he is deep in thought, or busy, or traveling. Maybe he is sleeping and must be awakened." ²⁸So they shouted louder and slashed themselves with swords and spears, as was their custom, until their blood flowed. ²⁹Midday passed, and they continued their frantic prophesying until the time for the evening sacrifice. But there was no response, no one answered, no one paid attention.

³⁰Then Elijah said to all the people, "Come here to me." They came to him, and he repaired the altar of the LORD, which had been torn down. ³¹Elijah took twelve stones, one for each of the tribes descended from Jacob, to whom the word of the LORD had come, saying, "Your name shall be Israel." ³²With the stones he built an altar in the name of the LORD, and he dug a trench around it large enough to hold two seahs*a* of seed. ³³He arranged

---

a 32 That is, probably about 24 pounds or about 11 kilograms the wood, cut the bull into pieces and laid it on the wood. Then he said to them, "Fill four large jars with water and pour it on the offering and on the wood."

³⁴"Do it again," he said, and they did it again.

"Do it a third time," he ordered, and they did it the third time. ³⁵The water ran down around the altar and even filled the trench.

³⁶At the time of sacrifice, the prophet Elijah stepped forward and prayed: "Lord, the God of Abraham, Isaac and Israel, let it be known today that you are God in Israel and that I am your servant and have done all these things at your command. ³⁷Answer me, Lord, answer me, so these people will know that you, Lord, are God, and that you are turning their hearts back again."

³⁸Then the fire of the Lord fell and burned up the sacrifice, the wood, the stones and the soil, and also licked up the water in the trench.

³⁹When all the people saw this, they fell prostrate and cried, "The Lord—he is God! The Lord—he is God!"

⁴⁰Then Elijah commanded them, "Seize the prophets of Baal. Don't let anyone get away!" They seized them, and Elijah had them brought down to the Kishon Valley and slaughtered there.

⁴¹And Elijah said to Ahab, "Go, eat and drink, for there is the sound of a heavy rain." ⁴²So Ahab went off to eat and drink, but Elijah climbed to the top of Carmel, bent down to the ground and put his face between his knees.

⁴³"Go and look toward the sea," he told his servant. And he went up and looked.

"There is nothing there," he said.

Seven times Elijah said, "Go back."

⁴⁴The seventh time the servant reported, "A cloud as small as a man's hand is rising from the sea."

So Elijah said, "Go and tell Ahab, 'Hitch up your chariot and go down before the rain stops you.'"

⁴⁵Meanwhile, the sky grew black with clouds, the wind rose, a heavy rain started falling and Ahab rode off to Jezreel. ⁴⁶The power of the Lord came on Elijah and, tucking his cloak into his belt, he ran ahead of Ahab all the way to Jezreel.

Elijah Flees to Horeb

19 Now Ahab told Jezebel everything Elijah had done and how he had killed all the prophets with the sword. ²So Jezebel sent a messenger to Elijah to say, "May the gods deal with me, be it ever so severely, if by this time tomorrow I do not make your life like that of one of them."

³Elijah was afraid^a and ran for his life. When he came to Beersheba in Judah, he left his servant there, ⁴while he himself went a day's journey into the wilderness. He came to a broom bush, sat down under it and prayed that he might die. "I have had enough, Lord," he said. "Take my life; I am no better than my ancestors." ⁵Then he lay down under the bush and fell asleep.

All at once an angel touched him and said, "Get up and eat." ⁶He looked around, and there by his head was some bread baked over hot coals, and a jar of water. He ate and drank and then lay down again.

⁷The angel of the Lord came back a second time and touched him and said, "Get up and eat, for the journey is too much for you." ⁸So he got up and ate and drank. Strengthened by that food, he traveled forty days and forty nights until he reached Horeb, the mountain of God. ⁹There he went into a cave and spent the night.

The Lord Appears to Elijah

And the word of the Lord came to him: "What are you doing here, Elijah?"

¹⁰He replied, "I have been very zealous for the Lord God Almighty. The Israelites have rejected your covenant, torn down your altars, and put your prophets to death with the sword. I am the only one left, and now they are trying to kill me too."

¹¹The Lord said, "Go out and stand on the mountain in the presence of the Lord, for the Lord is about to pass by."

Then a great and powerful wind tore the mountains apart and shattered the rocks before the Lord, but the Lord was not in the wind. After the wind there was an

---

^a 3 Or Elijah saw

earthquake, but the LORD was not in the earthquake. ¹²After the earthquake came a fire, but the LORD was not in the fire. And after the fire came a gentle whisper. ¹³When Elijah heard it, he pulled his cloak over his face and went out and stood at the mouth of the cave.

Then a voice said to him, "What are you doing here, Elijah?"

¹⁴He replied, "I have been very zealous for the LORD God Almighty. The Israelites have rejected your covenant, torn down your altars, and put your prophets

THE WITNESSES

✓ **ELISHA** (1 KINGS 19:19)

His name means "my God is salvation." He was a man who worked as a farmer until the prophet Elijah called him. So Elisha became Elijah's assistant. When Elijah went to heaven, Elisha took over his place as a prophet. God gave him special powers, and Elisha performed many miracles.

to death with the sword. I am the only one left, and now they are trying to kill me too."

¹⁵The LORD said to him, "Go back the way you came, and go to the Desert of Damascus. When you get there, anoint Hazael king over Aram. ¹⁶Also, anoint Jehu son of Nimshi king over Israel, and anoint Elisha son of Shaphat from Abel Meholah to succeed you as prophet. ¹⁷Jehu will put to death any who escape the sword of Hazael, and Elisha will put to death any who escape the sword of Jehu. ¹⁸Yet I reserve seven thousand in Israel—all whose knees have not bowed down to Baal and whose mouths have not kissed him."

The Call of Elisha

¹⁹So Elijah went from there and found Elisha son of Shaphat. He was plowing with twelve yoke of oxen, and he himself was driving the twelfth pair. Elijah went up to him and threw his cloak around him. ²⁰Elisha then left his oxen and ran after Elijah. "Let me kiss my father and mother goodbye," he said, "and then I will come with you."

"Go back," Elijah replied. "What have I done to you?"

²¹So Elisha left him and went back. He took his yoke of oxen and slaughtered them. He burned the plowing equipment to cook the meat and gave it to the people, and they ate. Then he set out to follow Elijah and became his servant.

Ben-Hadad Attacks Samaria

20 Now Ben-Hadad king of Aram mustered his entire army. Accompanied by thirty-two kings with their horses and chariots, he went up and besieged Samaria and attacked it. ²He sent messengers into the city to Ahab king of Israel, saying, "This is what Ben-Hadad says: ³'Your silver and gold are mine, and the best of your wives and children are mine.' "

⁴The king of Israel answered, "Just as you say, my lord the king. I and all I have are yours."

⁵The messengers came again and said, "This is what Ben-Hadad says: 'I sent to demand your silver and gold, your wives

and your children. ⁶But about this time tomorrow I am going to send my officials to search your palace and the houses of your officials. They will seize everything you value and carry it away.' "

⁷The king of Israel summoned all the elders of the land and said to them, "See how this man is looking for trouble! When he sent for my wives and my children, my silver and my gold, I did not refuse him."

⁸The elders and the people all answered, "Don't listen to him or agree to his demands."

⁹So he replied to Ben-Hadad's messengers, "Tell my lord the king, 'Your servant will do all you demanded the first time, but this demand I cannot meet.' " They left and took the answer back to Ben-Hadad.

¹⁰Then Ben-Hadad sent another message to Ahab: "May the gods deal with me, be it ever so severely, if enough dust remains in Samaria to give each of my men a handful."

¹¹The king of Israel answered, "Tell him: 'One who puts on his armor should not boast like one who takes it off.' "

¹²Ben-Hadad heard this message while he and the kings were drinking in their tents,^a and he ordered his men: "Prepare to attack." So they prepared to attack the city.

Ahab Defeats Ben-Hadad

¹³Meanwhile a prophet came to Ahab king of Israel and announced, "This is what the LORD says: 'Do you see this vast army? I will give it into your hand today, and then you will know that I am the LORD.' "

¹⁴"But who will do this?" asked Ahab.

The prophet replied, "This is what the LORD says: 'The junior officers under the provincial commanders will do it.' "

"And who will start the battle?" he asked.

The prophet answered, "You will."

¹⁵So Ahab summoned the 232 junior officers under the provincial commanders. Then he assembled the rest of the Israelites, 7,000 in all. ¹⁶They set out at noon while Ben-Hadad and the 32 kings allied with him were in their tents getting drunk. ¹⁷The junior officers under the provincial commanders went out first.

Now Ben-Hadad had dispatched scouts, who reported, "Men are advancing from Samaria."

¹⁸He said, "If they have come out for peace, take them alive; if they have come out for war, take them alive."

¹⁹The junior officers under the provincial commanders marched out of the city with the army behind them ²⁰and each one struck down his opponent. At that, the Arameans fled, with the Israelites in pursuit. But Ben-Hadad king of Aram escaped on horseback with some of his horsemen. ²¹The king of Israel advanced and overpowered the horses and chariots and inflicted heavy losses on the Arameans.

²²Afterward, the prophet came to the king of Israel and said, "Strengthen your position and see what must be done, because next spring the king of Aram will attack you again."

²³Meanwhile, the officials of the king of Aram advised him, "Their gods are gods of the hills. That is why they were too strong for us. But if we fight them on the plains, surely we will be stronger than they. ²⁴Do this: Remove all the kings from their commands and replace them with other officers. ²⁵You must also raise an army like the one you lost—horse for horse and chariot for chariot—so we can fight Israel on the plains. Then surely we will be stronger than they." He agreed with them and acted accordingly.

²⁶The next spring Ben-Hadad mustered the Arameans and went up to Aphek to fight against Israel. ²⁷When the Israelites were also mustered and given provisions, they marched out to meet them. The Israelites camped opposite them like two small flocks of goats, while the Arameans covered the countryside.

²⁸The man of God came up and told the king of Israel, "This is what the LORD says: 'Because the Arameans think the LORD is a god of the hills and not a god of the valleys, I will deliver this vast army into your hands, and you will know that I am the LORD.' "

---

^a 12 Or in Sukkoth; also in verse 16

²⁹For seven days they camped opposite each other, and on the seventh day the battle was joined. The Israelites inflicted a hundred thousand casualties on the Aramean foot soldiers in one day. ³⁰The rest of them escaped to the city of Aphek, where the wall collapsed on twenty-seven thousand of them. And Ben-Hadad fled to the city and hid in an inner room.

³¹His officials said to him, "Look, we have heard that the kings of Israel are merciful. Let us go to the king of Israel with sackcloth around our waists and ropes around our heads. Perhaps he will spare your life."

³²Wearing sackcloth around their waists and ropes around their heads, they went to the king of Israel and said, "Your servant Ben-Hadad says: 'Please let me live.' "

The king answered, "Is he still alive? He is my brother."

³³The men took this as a good sign and were quick to pick up his word. "Yes, your brother Ben-Hadad!" they said.

"Go and get him," the king said. When Ben-Hadad came out, Ahab had him come up into his chariot.

³⁴"I will return the cities my father took from your father," Ben-Hadad offered. "You may set up your own market areas in Damascus, as my father did in Samaria."

Ahab said, "On the basis of a treaty I will set you free." So he made a treaty with him, and let him go.

A Prophet Condemns Ahab

³⁵By the word of the LORD one of the company of the prophets said to his companion, "Strike me with your weapon," but he refused.

³⁶So the prophet said, "Because you have not obeyed the LORD, as soon as you leave me a lion will kill you." And after the man went away, a lion found him and killed him.

³⁷The prophet found another man and said, "Strike me, please." So the man struck him and wounded him. ³⁸Then the prophet went and stood by the road waiting for the king. He disguised himself with his headband down over his eyes. ³⁹As the king passed by, the prophet called out to him, "Your servant went into the thick of the battle, and someone came to me with a captive and said, 'Guard this man. If he is missing, it will be your life for his life, or you must pay a talent[a] of silver.' ⁴⁰While your servant was busy here and there, the man disappeared."

"That is your sentence," the king of Israel said. "You have pronounced it yourself."

⁴¹Then the prophet quickly removed the headband from his eyes, and the king of Israel recognized him as one of the prophets. ⁴²He said to the king, "This is what the LORD says: 'You have set free a man I had determined should die.[b] Therefore it is your life for his life, your people for his people.' " ⁴³Sullen and angry, the king of Israel went to his palace in Samaria.

Naboth's Vineyard

21 Some time later there was an incident involving a vineyard belonging to Naboth the Jezreelite. The vineyard was in Jezreel, close to the palace of Ahab king of Samaria. ²Ahab said to Naboth, "Let me have your vineyard to use for a vegetable garden, since it is close to my palace. In exchange I will give you a better vineyard or, if you prefer, I will pay you whatever it is worth."

³But Naboth replied, "The LORD forbid that I should give you the inheritance of my ancestors."

⁴So Ahab went home, sullen and angry because Naboth the Jezreelite had said, "I will not give you the inheritance of my ancestors." He lay on his bed sulking and refused to eat.

⁵His wife Jezebel came in and asked him, "Why are you so sullen? Why won't you eat?"

⁶He answered her, "Because I said to Naboth the Jezreelite, 'Sell me your vineyard; or if you prefer, I will give you another vineyard in its place.' But he said, 'I will not give you my vineyard.' "

⁷Jezebel his wife said, "Is this how you act as king over Israel? Get up and eat!

---

a 39 That is, about 75 pounds or about 34 kilograms
b 42 The Hebrew term refers to the irrevocable giving over of things or persons to the LORD, often by totally destroying them.

Cheer up. I'll get you the vineyard of Naboth the Jezreelite."

⁸So she wrote letters in Ahab's name, placed his seal on them, and sent them to the elders and nobles who lived in Naboth's city with him. ⁹In those letters she wrote:

"Proclaim a day of fasting and seat Naboth in a prominent place among the people. ¹⁰But seat two scoundrels opposite him and have them bring charges that he has cursed both God and the king. Then take him out and stone him to death."

¹¹So the elders and nobles who lived in Naboth's city did as Jezebel directed in the letters she had written to them. ¹²They proclaimed a fast and seated Naboth in a prominent place among the people. ¹³Then two scoundrels came and sat opposite him and brought charges against Naboth before the people, saying, "Naboth has cursed both God and the king." So they took him outside the city and stoned him to death. ¹⁴Then they sent word to Jezebel: "Naboth has been stoned to death."

¹⁵As soon as Jezebel heard that Naboth had been stoned to death, she said to Ahab, "Get up and take possession of the vineyard of Naboth the Jezreelite that he refused to sell you. He is no longer alive, but dead." ¹⁶When Ahab heard that Naboth was dead, he got up and went down to take possession of Naboth's vineyard.

¹⁷Then the word of the LORD came to Elijah the Tishbite: ¹⁸"Go down to meet Ahab king of Israel, who rules in Samaria. He is now in Naboth's vineyard, where he has gone to take possession of it. ¹⁹Say to him, 'This is what the LORD says: Have you not murdered a man and seized his property?' Then say to him, 'This is what the LORD says: In the place where dogs licked up Naboth's blood, dogs will lick up your blood—yes, yours!'"

²⁰Ahab said to Elijah, "So you have found me, my enemy!"

"I have found you," he answered, "because you have sold yourself to do evil in the eyes of the LORD. ²¹He says, 'I am going to bring disaster on you. I will wipe out your descendants and cut off from Ahab every last male in Israel—slave or free.[a] ²²I will make your house like that of Jeroboam son of Nebat and that of Baasha son of Ahijah, because you have aroused my anger and have caused Israel to sin.'

²³"And also concerning Jezebel the LORD says: 'Dogs will devour Jezebel by the wall of[b] Jezreel.'

²⁴"Dogs will eat those belonging to Ahab who die in the city, and the birds will feed on those who die in the country."

²⁵(There was never anyone like Ahab, who sold himself to do evil in the eyes of the LORD, urged on by Jezebel his wife. ²⁶He behaved in the vilest manner by going after idols, like the Amorites the LORD drove out before Israel.)

²⁷When Ahab heard these words, he tore his clothes, put on sackcloth and fasted. He lay in sackcloth and went around meekly.

²⁸Then the word of the LORD came to Elijah the Tishbite: ²⁹"Have you noticed how Ahab has humbled himself before me? Because he has humbled himself, I will not bring this disaster in his day, but I will bring it on his house in the days of his son."

Micaiah Prophesies Against Ahab

22 For three years there was no war between Aram and Israel. ²But in the third year Jehoshaphat king of Judah went down to see the king of Israel. ³The king of Israel had said to his officials, "Don't you know that Ramoth Gilead belongs to us and yet we are doing nothing to retake it from the king of Aram?"

⁴So he asked Jehoshaphat, "Will you go with me to fight against Ramoth Gilead?"

Jehoshaphat replied to the king of Israel, "I am as you are, my people as your people, my horses as your horses." ⁵But Jehoshaphat also said to the king of Israel, "First seek the counsel of the LORD."

⁶So the king of Israel brought together the prophets—about four hundred

---

ᵃ 21 Or Israel—every ruler or leader   ᵇ 23 Most Hebrew manuscripts; a few Hebrew manuscripts, Vulgate and Syriac (see also 2 Kings 9:26) the plot of ground at

THE SCENE

RAMOTH GILEAD

(1 KINGS 22:3)

This was a city of refuge, where a person who had accidentally killed somebody could be protected. The name means "highlands of Gilead." It is located east of the Jordan River.

men—and asked them, "Shall I go to war against Ramoth Gilead, or shall I refrain?"

"Go," they answered, "for the Lord will give it into the king's hand."

⁷But Jehoshaphat asked, "Is there no longer a prophet of the Lord here whom we can inquire of?"

⁸The king of Israel answered Jehoshaphat, "There is still one prophet through whom we can inquire of the Lord, but I hate him because he never prophesies anything good about me, but always bad. He is Micaiah son of Imlah."

"The king should not say such a thing," Jehoshaphat replied.

⁹So the king of Israel called one of his officials and said, "Bring Micaiah son of Imlah at once."

¹⁰Dressed in their royal robes, the king of Israel and Jehoshaphat king of Judah were sitting on their thrones at the threshing floor by the entrance of the gate of Samaria, with all the prophets prophesying before them. ¹¹Now Zedekiah son of Kenaanah had made iron horns and he declared, "This is what the Lord says: 'With these you will gore the Arameans until they are destroyed.' "

¹²All the other prophets were prophesying the same thing. "Attack Ramoth Gilead and be victorious," they said, "for the Lord will give it into the king's hand."

¹³The messenger who had gone to summon Micaiah said to him, "Look, the other prophets without exception are predicting success for the king. Let your word agree with theirs, and speak favorably."

¹⁴But Micaiah said, "As surely as the Lord lives, I can tell him only what the Lord tells me."

¹⁵When he arrived, the king asked him, "Micaiah, shall we go to war against Ramoth Gilead, or not?"

"Attack and be victorious," he answered, "for the Lord will give it into the king's hand."

¹⁶The king said to him, "How many times must I make you swear to tell me nothing but the truth in the name of the Lord?"

¹⁷Then Micaiah answered, "I saw all Israel scattered on the hills like sheep without a shepherd, and the Lord said, 'These people have no master. Let each one go home in peace.' "

¹⁸The king of Israel said to Jehoshaphat, "Didn't I tell you that he never prophesies anything good about me, but only bad?"

¹⁹Micaiah continued, "Therefore hear the word of the Lord: I saw the Lord sitting on his throne with all the multitudes of heaven standing around him on his right and on his left. ²⁰And the Lord said, 'Who will entice Ahab into attacking Ramoth Gilead and going to his death there?'

"One suggested this, and another that. ²¹Finally, a spirit came forward, stood before the Lord and said, 'I will entice him.'

²²" 'By what means?' the Lord asked.

" 'I will go out and be a deceiving spirit in the mouths of all his prophets,' he said.

" 'You will succeed in enticing him,' said the Lᴏʀᴅ. 'Go and do it.'

²³"So now the Lᴏʀᴅ has put a deceiving spirit in the mouths of all these prophets of yours. The Lᴏʀᴅ has decreed disaster for you."

²⁴Then Zedekiah son of Kenaanah went up and slapped Micaiah in the face. "Which way did the spirit from*ᵃ the Lᴏʀᴅ go when he went from me to speak to you?" he asked.

²⁵Micaiah replied, "You will find out on the day you go to hide in an inner room."

²⁶The king of Israel then ordered, "Take Micaiah and send him back to Amon the ruler of the city and to Joash the king's son ²⁷and say, 'This is what the king says: Put this fellow in prison and give him nothing but bread and water until I return safely.' "

²⁸Micaiah declared, "If you ever return safely, the Lᴏʀᴅ has not spoken through me." Then he added, "Mark my words, all you people!"

Ahab Killed at Ramoth Gilead

²⁹So the king of Israel and Jehoshaphat king of Judah went up to Ramoth Gilead. ³⁰The king of Israel said to Jehoshaphat, "I will enter the battle in disguise, but you wear your royal robes." So the king of Israel disguised himself and went into battle.

³¹Now the king of Aram had ordered his thirty-two chariot commanders, "Do not fight with anyone, small or great, except the king of Israel." ³²When the chariot commanders saw Jehoshaphat, they thought, "Surely this is the king of Israel." So they turned to attack him, but when Jehoshaphat cried out, ³³the chariot commanders saw that he was not the king of Israel and stopped pursuing him.

³⁴But someone drew his bow at random and hit the king of Israel between the sections of his armor. The king told his chariot driver, "Wheel around and get me out of the fighting. I've been wounded." ³⁵All day long the battle raged, and the king was propped up in his chariot facing the Arameans. The blood from his wound ran onto the floor of the chariot, and that evening he died. ³⁶As the sun was setting, a cry spread through the army: "Every man to his town. Every man to his land!"

³⁷So the king died and was brought to Samaria, and they buried him there. ³⁸They washed the chariot at a pool in Samaria (where the prostitutes bathed),ᵇ and the dogs licked up his blood, as the word of the Lᴏʀᴅ had declared.

³⁹As for the other events of Ahab's reign, including all he did, the palace he built and adorned with ivory, and the cities he fortified, are they not written in the book of the annals of the kings of Israel? ⁴⁰Ahab rested with his ancestors. And Ahaziah his son succeeded him as king.

Jehoshaphat King of Judah

⁴¹Jehoshaphat son of Asa became king of Judah in the fourth year of Ahab king of Israel. ⁴²Jehoshaphat was thirty-five years old when he became king, and he reigned in Jerusalem twenty-five years. His mother's name was Azubah daughter of Shilhi. ⁴³In everything he followed the ways of his father Asa and did not stray from them; he did what was right in the eyes of the Lᴏʀᴅ. The high places, however, were not removed, and the people continued to offer sacrifices and burn incense there.ᶜ ⁴⁴Jehoshaphat was also at peace with the king of Israel.

⁴⁵As for the other events of Jehoshaphat's reign, the things he achieved and his military exploits, are they not written in the book of the annals of the kings of Judah? ⁴⁶He rid the land of the rest of the male shrine prostitutes who remained there even after the reign of his father Asa. ⁴⁷There was then no king in Edom; a provincial governor ruled.

⁴⁸Now Jehoshaphat built a fleet of trading shipsᵈ to go to Ophir for gold, but they never set sail—they were wrecked at Ezion Geber. ⁴⁹At that time Ahaziah son of Ahab said to Jehoshaphat, "Let my men sail with yours," but Jehoshaphat refused.

⁵⁰Then Jehoshaphat rested with his ancestors and was buried with them in the

---

ᵃ 24 Or Spirit of   ᵇ 38 Or Samaria and cleaned the weapons   ᶜ 43 In Hebrew texts this sentence (22:43b) is numbered 22:44, and 22:44-53 is numbered 22:45-54.   ᵈ 48 Hebrew of ships of Tarshish city of David his father. And Jehoram his son succeeded him as king.

Ahaziah King of Israel

⁵¹Ahaziah son of Ahab became king of Israel in Samaria in the seventeenth year of Jehoshaphat king of Judah, and he reigned over Israel two years. ⁵²He did evil in the eyes of the LORD, because he followed the ways of his father and mother and of Jeroboam son of Nebat, who caused Israel to sin. ⁵³He served and worshiped Baal and aroused the anger of the LORD, the God of Israel, just as his father had done.

CASE CLOSED!

After reading this first book of Kings, we were left thinking that this story is very sad. Almost none of the kings of Israel and Judah did things right. They were bad kings, although a few of them started off right. But then, like Solomon, they disobeyed God in the end. The most important thing God had asked them to do was not worship other gods and not treat poor or weak people badly. That wasn't a lot to ask, don't you think? Especially because they were kings who had so much power, and they could do so many good things! We should try not to make those same mistakes now.

2 KINGS

THE EVIDENCE:

WHO WROTE IT?
Since this was just one book along with the book of 1 Kings, we don't know who wrote this part either. Read the explanation in this section for 1 Kings.

HOW LONG AGO?
About 609 to 562 years before Christ.

WHAT'S IT ABOUT?
This book keeps on telling about what happened in 1 Kings. The two books are part of the same big story, but that story ends here. It talks especially about the destruction of the two kingdoms: the northern kingdom in chapter 17 and the southern kingdom in chapter 25.

This book tells us about everything the kings and the people of God did wrong. But it also talks about some of the good people, like the prophets Elijah and Elisha, who were faithful to God and did the right things. At any rate, the people kept on making mistakes. That was disastrous for Israel. In the end, Jerusalem was destroyed.

THE BEST PART
Isabella really likes the story about Naaman, because it was a girl who made everything happen! If that girl hadn't told Naaman's wife that a prophet could heal him, Naaman would never have been cured and the story wouldn't have had a happy ending! It made us realize that we kids can also be part of God's plans. How great! When Naaman got better, he accepted God and said, "Now I know that there is no God in all the world except in Israel. So please accept a gift from your servant" (5:15).

The Lord's Judgment on Ahaziah

1 After Ahab's death, Moab rebelled against Israel. ²Now Ahaziah had fallen through the lattice of his upper room in Samaria and injured himself. So he sent messengers, saying to them, "Go and consult Baal-Zebub, the god of Ekron, to see if I will recover from this injury."

³But the angel of the Lord said to Elijah the Tishbite, "Go up and meet the messengers of the king of Samaria and ask them, 'Is it because there is no God in Israel that you are going off to consult Baal-Zebub, the god of Ekron?' ⁴Therefore this is what the Lord says: 'You will not leave the bed you are lying on. You will certainly die!'" So Elijah went.

⁵When the messengers returned to the king, he asked them, "Why have you come back?"

⁶"A man came to meet us," they replied. "And he said to us, 'Go back to the king

who sent you and tell him, "This is what the LORD says: Is it because there is no God in Israel that you are sending messengers to consult Baal-Zebub, the god of Ekron? Therefore you will not leave the bed you are lying on. You will certainly die!'"'"

⁷The king asked them, "What kind of man was it who came to meet you and told you this?"

⁸They replied, "He had a garment of hair*a* and had a leather belt around his waist."

The king said, "That was Elijah the Tishbite."

⁹Then he sent to Elijah a captain with his company of fifty men. The captain went up to Elijah, who was sitting on the top of a hill, and said to him, "Man of God, the king says, 'Come down!'"

¹⁰Elijah answered the captain, "If I am a man of God, may fire come down from heaven and consume you and your fifty men!" Then fire fell from heaven and consumed the captain and his men.

¹¹At this the king sent to Elijah another captain with his fifty men. The captain said to him, "Man of God, this is what the king says, 'Come down at once!'"

¹²"If I am a man of God," Elijah replied, "may fire come down from heaven and consume you and your fifty men!" Then the fire of God fell from heaven and consumed him and his fifty men.

¹³So the king sent a third captain with his fifty men. This third captain went up and fell on his knees before Elijah. "Man of God," he begged, "please have respect for my life and the lives of these fifty men, your servants! ¹⁴See, fire has fallen from heaven and consumed the first two captains and all their men. But now have respect for my life!"

¹⁵The angel of the LORD said to Elijah, "Go down with him; do not be afraid of him." So Elijah got up and went down with him to the king.

¹⁶He told the king, "This is what the LORD says: Is it because there is no God in Israel for you to consult that you have sent messengers to consult Baal-Zebub, the god of Ekron? Because you have done this, you will never leave the bed you are lying on. You will certainly die!" ¹⁷So he

died, according to the word of the LORD that Elijah had spoken.

Because Ahaziah had no son, Joram*b* succeeded him as king in the second year of Jehoram son of Jehoshaphat king of Judah. ¹⁸As for all the other events of Ahaziah's reign, and what he did, are they not written in the book of the annals of the kings of Israel?

Elijah Taken Up to Heaven

2 When the LORD was about to take Elijah up to heaven in a whirlwind, Elijah and Elisha were on their way from Gilgal.

---

a 8 Or *He was a hairy man*   *b* 17 Hebrew *Jehoram,* a variant of *Joram*

THE
WITNESSES

✓ **AHAZIAH** (2 KINGS 1:1–18)
This name means "God has taken." He was Ahab's son and successor as king of Israel. He wasn't a good king, because he disobeyed God. So his rule was very short. He died tragically.

²Elijah said to Elisha, "Stay here; the LORD has sent me to Bethel."

But Elisha said, "As surely as the LORD lives and as you live, I will not leave you." So they went down to Bethel.

³The company of the prophets at Bethel came out to Elisha and asked, "Do you know that the LORD is going to take your master from you today?"

"Yes, I know," Elisha replied, "so be quiet."

⁴Then Elijah said to him, "Stay here, Elisha; the LORD has sent me to Jericho."

And he replied, "As surely as the LORD lives and as you live, I will not leave you." So they went to Jericho.

⁵The company of the prophets at Jericho went up to Elisha and asked him, "Do you know that the LORD is going to take your master from you today?"

"Yes, I know," he replied, "so be quiet."

⁶Then Elijah said to him, "Stay here; the LORD has sent me to the Jordan."

And he replied, "As surely as the LORD lives and as you live, I will not leave you." So the two of them walked on.

⁷Fifty men from the company of the prophets went and stood at a distance, facing the place where Elijah and Elisha had stopped at the Jordan. ⁸Elijah took his cloak, rolled it up and struck the water with it. The water divided to the right and to the left, and the two of them crossed over on dry ground.

⁹When they had crossed, Elijah said to Elisha, "Tell me, what can I do for you before I am taken from you?"

"Let me inherit a double portion of your spirit," Elisha replied.

¹⁰"You have asked a difficult thing," Elijah said, "yet if you see me when I am taken from you, it will be yours—otherwise, it will not."

¹¹As they were walking along and talking together, suddenly a chariot of fire and horses of fire appeared and separated the two of them, and Elijah went up to heaven in a whirlwind. ¹²Elisha saw this and cried out, "My father! My father! The chariots and horsemen of Israel!" And Elisha saw him no more. Then he took hold of his garment and tore it in two.

BREAKTHROUGH!

Did Elijah's cloak have magical powers?

(2 KINGS 2:8,14)

It wasn't that the cloak had magical powers—it was that its owner counted on God's favor, and he could perform miracles and give signs. God was with Elijah and then he was with Elisha. It was God who made the supernatural signs this book talks about.

¹³Elisha then picked up Elijah's cloak that had fallen from him and went back and stood on the bank of the Jordan. ¹⁴He took the cloak that had fallen from Elijah and struck the water with it. "Where now is the LORD, the God of Elijah?" he asked. When he struck the water, it divided to the right and to the left, and he crossed over.

¹⁵The company of the prophets from Jericho, who were watching, said, "The spirit of Elijah is resting on Elisha." And they went to meet him and bowed to the ground before him. ¹⁶"Look," they said, "we your servants have fifty able men. Let them go and look for your master. Perhaps the Spirit of the LORD has picked him up and set him down on some mountain or in some valley."

"No," Elisha replied, "do not send them."

¹⁷But they persisted until he was too embarrassed to refuse. So he said,

"Send them." And they sent fifty men, who searched for three days but did not find him. ¹⁸When they returned to Elisha, who was staying in Jericho, he said to them, "Didn't I tell you not to go?"

Healing of the Water

¹⁹The people of the city said to Elisha, "Look, our lord, this town is well situated, as you can see, but the water is bad and the land is unproductive." ²⁰"Bring me a new bowl," he said, "and put salt in it." So they brought it to him.

²¹Then he went out to the spring and threw the salt into it, saying, "This is what the LORD says: 'I have healed this water. Never again will it cause death or make the land unproductive.'" ²²And the water has remained pure to this day, according to the word Elisha had spoken.

Elisha Is Jeered

²³From there Elisha went up to Bethel. As he was walking along the road, some boys came out of the town and jeered at him. "Get out of here, baldy!" they said. "Get out of here, baldy!" ²⁴He turned around, looked at them and called down a curse on them in the name of the LORD. Then two bears came out of the woods and mauled forty-two of the boys. ²⁵And he went on to Mount Carmel and from there returned to Samaria.

Moab Revolts

3 Joram[a] son of Ahab became king of Israel in Samaria in the eighteenth year of Jehoshaphat king of Judah, and he reigned twelve years. ²He did evil in the eyes of the LORD, but not as his father and mother had done. He got rid of the sacred stone of Baal that his father had made. ³Nevertheless he clung to the sins of Jeroboam son of Nebat, which he had caused Israel to commit; he did not turn away from them.

⁴Now Mesha king of Moab raised sheep, and he had to pay the king of Israel a tribute of a hundred thousand lambs and the wool of a hundred thousand rams. ⁵But after Ahab died, the king of Moab rebelled against the king of Israel. ⁶So at that time King Joram set out from Samaria and mobilized all Israel. ⁷He also sent this message to Jehoshaphat king of Judah: "The king of Moab has rebelled against me. Will you go with me to fight against Moab?"

"I will go with you," he replied. "I am as you are, my people as your people, my horses as your horses." ⁸"By what route shall we attack?" he asked.

"Through the Desert of Edom," he answered.

⁹So the king of Israel set out with the king of Judah and the king of Edom. After a roundabout march of seven days, the army had no more water for themselves or for the animals with them.

¹⁰"What!" exclaimed the king of Israel. "Has the LORD called us three kings together only to deliver us into the hands of Moab?"

¹¹But Jehoshaphat asked, "Is there no prophet of the LORD here, through whom we may inquire of the LORD?"

An officer of the king of Israel answered, "Elisha son of Shaphat is here. He used to pour water on the hands of Elijah.[b]"

¹²Jehoshaphat said, "The word of the LORD is with him." So the king of Israel and Jehoshaphat and the king of Edom went down to him.

¹³Elisha said to the king of Israel, "Why do you want to involve me? Go to the prophets of your father and the prophets of your mother."

"No," the king of Israel answered, "because it was the LORD who called us three kings together to deliver us into the hands of Moab."

¹⁴Elisha said, "As surely as the LORD Almighty lives, whom I serve, if I did not have respect for the presence of Jehoshaphat king of Judah, I would not pay any attention to you. ¹⁵But now bring me a harpist."

While the harpist was playing, the hand of the LORD came on Elisha ¹⁶and he said, "This is what the LORD says: I will fill this valley with pools of water. ¹⁷For this is what the LORD says: You will see neither

---

[a] 1 Hebrew *Jehoram*, a variant of *Joram*; also in verse 6
[b] 11 That is, he was Elijah's personal servant.

wind nor rain, yet this valley will be filled with water, and you, your cattle and your other animals will drink. ¹⁸This is an easy thing in the eyes of the LORD; he will also deliver Moab into your hands. ¹⁹You will overthrow every fortified city and every major town. You will cut down every good tree, stop up all the springs, and ruin every good field with stones."

²⁰The next morning, about the time for offering the sacrifice, there it was—water flowing from the direction of Edom! And the land was filled with water.

²¹Now all the Moabites had heard that the kings had come to fight against them; so every man, young and old, who could bear arms was called up and stationed on the border. ²²When they got up early in the morning, the sun was shining on the water. To the Moabites across the way, the water looked red—like blood. ²³"That's blood!" they said. "Those kings must have fought and slaughtered each other. Now to the plunder, Moab!"

²⁴But when the Moabites came to the camp of Israel, the Israelites rose up and fought them until they fled. And the Israelites invaded the land and slaughtered the Moabites. ²⁵They destroyed the towns, and each man threw a stone on every good field until it was covered. They stopped up all the springs and cut down every good tree. Only Kir Hareseth was left with its stones in place, but men armed with slings surrounded it and attacked it.

²⁶When the king of Moab saw that the battle had gone against him, he took with him seven hundred swordsmen to break through to the king of Edom, but they failed. ²⁷Then he took his firstborn son, who was to succeed him as king, and offered him as a sacrifice on the city wall. The fury against Israel was great; they withdrew and returned to their own land.

The Widow's Olive Oil

4 The wife of a man from the company of the prophets cried out to Elisha, "Your servant my husband is dead, and you know that he revered the LORD. But now his creditor is coming to take my two boys as his slaves."

²Elisha replied to her, "How can I help you? Tell me, what do you have in your house?"

"Your servant has nothing there at all," she said, "except a small jar of olive oil."

³Elisha said, "Go around and ask all your neighbors for empty jars. Don't ask for just a few. ⁴Then go inside and shut the door behind you and your sons. Pour oil into all the jars, and as each is filled, put it to one side."

⁵She left him and shut the door behind her and her sons. They brought the jars to her and she kept pouring. ⁶When all the jars were full, she said to her son, "Bring me another one."

But he replied, "There is not a jar left." Then the oil stopped flowing.

⁷She went and told the man of God, and he said, "Go, sell the oil and pay your debts. You and your sons can live on what is left."

The Shunammite's Son Restored to Life

⁸One day Elisha went to Shunem. And a well-to-do woman was there, who urged him to stay for a meal. So whenever he came by, he stopped there to eat. ⁹She said to her husband, "I know that this man who often comes our way is a holy man of God. ¹⁰Let's make a small room on the roof and put in it a bed and a table, a chair and a lamp for him. Then he can stay there whenever he comes to us."

¹¹One day when Elisha came, he went up to his room and lay down there. ¹²He said to his servant Gehazi, "Call the Shunammite." So he called her, and she stood before him. ¹³Elisha said to him, "Tell her, 'You have gone to all this trouble for us. Now what can be done for you? Can we speak on your behalf to the king or the commander of the army?'"

She replied, "I have a home among my own people."

¹⁴"What can be done for her?" Elisha asked.

Gehazi said, "She has no son, and her husband is old."

¹⁵Then Elisha said, "Call her." So he called her, and she stood in the doorway.

THE SCENE

SHUNEM

(2 KINGS 4:8)

It was a little village 25 miles (40 km) north of Samaria, the capital of Israel. It was more or less the same distance from Mount Carmel.

¹⁶"About this time next year," Elisha said, "you will hold a son in your arms."

"No, my lord!" she objected. "Please, man of God, don't mislead your servant!"

¹⁷But the woman became pregnant, and the next year about that same time she gave birth to a son, just as Elisha had told her.

¹⁸The child grew, and one day he went out to his father, who was with the reapers. ¹⁹He said to his father, "My head! My head!"

His father told a servant, "Carry him to his mother." ²⁰After the servant had lifted him up and carried him to his mother, the boy sat on her lap until noon, and then he died. ²¹She went up and laid him on the bed of the man of God, then shut the door and went out.

²²She called her husband and said, "Please send me one of the servants and a donkey so I can go to the man of God quickly and return."

²³"Why go to him today?" he asked. "It's not the New Moon or the Sabbath."

"That's all right," she said.

²⁴She saddled the donkey and said to her servant, "Lead on; don't slow down for me unless I tell you." ²⁵So she set out and came to the man of God at Mount Carmel.

When he saw her in the distance, the man of God said to his servant Gehazi, "Look! There's the Shunammite! ²⁶Run to meet her and ask her, 'Are you all right? Is your husband all right? Is your child all right?'"

"Everything is all right," she said.

THE WITNESSES

✓ **GEHAZI** (2 KINGS 4:12–15)

It means "surprised." He was the prophet Elisha's servant. Sometimes he did good things, like when he helped a widow recover her land. He also did bad things, and God punished him with a skin disease.

THE SCENE

MOUNT CARMEL

(2 KINGS 4:25)

This mountain was very beautiful and fertile. Its peak was 574 yards (525 meters) high. This was the place where the prophet Elijah faced and beat the prophets of Baal. (Read about it in 1 Kings 18:20–40.)

27 When she reached the man of God at the mountain, she took hold of his feet. Gehazi came over to push her away, but the man of God said, "Leave her alone! She is in bitter distress, but the Lord has hidden it from me and has not told me why."

28 "Did I ask you for a son, my lord?" she said. "Didn't I tell you, 'Don't raise my hopes'?"

29 Elisha said to Gehazi, "Tuck your cloak into your belt, take my staff in your hand and run. Don't greet anyone you meet, and if anyone greets you, do not answer. Lay my staff on the boy's face."

30 But the child's mother said, "As surely as the Lord lives and as you live, I will not leave you." So he got up and followed her.

31 Gehazi went on ahead and laid the staff on the boy's face, but there was no sound or response. So Gehazi went back to meet Elisha and told him, "The boy has not awakened."

32 When Elisha reached the house, there was the boy lying dead on his couch. 33 He went in, shut the door on the two of them and prayed to the Lord. 34 Then he got on the bed and lay on the boy, mouth to mouth, eyes to eyes, hands to hands. As he stretched himself out on him, the boy's body grew warm. 35 Elisha turned away and walked back and forth in the room and then got on the bed and stretched out on him once more. The boy sneezed seven times and opened his eyes.

36 Elisha summoned Gehazi and said, "Call the Shunammite." And he did. When she came, he said, "Take your son." 37 She came in, fell at his feet and bowed to the ground. Then she took her son and went out.

Death in the Pot

38 Elisha returned to Gilgal and there was a famine in that region. While the company of the prophets was meeting with him, he said to his servant, "Put on the large pot and cook some stew for these prophets."

39 One of them went out into the fields to gather herbs and found a wild vine and picked as many of its gourds as his garment could hold. When he returned, he cut them up into the pot of stew, though no one knew what they were. 40 The stew was poured out for the men, but as they began to eat it, they cried out, "Man of God, there is death in the pot!" And they could not eat it.

41 Elisha said, "Get some flour." He put it into the pot and said, "Serve it to the people to eat." And there was nothing harmful in the pot.

Feeding of a Hundred

42 A man came from Baal Shalishah, bringing the man of God twenty loaves of barley bread baked from the first ripe grain, along with some heads of new grain. "Give it to the people to eat," Elisha said.

43 "How can I set this before a hundred men?" his servant asked.

But Elisha answered, "Give it to the people to eat. For this is what the LORD says: 'They will eat and have some left over.' " ⁴⁴Then he set it before them, and they ate and had some left over, according to the word of the LORD.

Naaman Healed of Leprosy

5 Now Naaman was commander of the army of the king of Aram. He was a great man in the sight of his master and highly regarded, because through him the LORD had given victory to Aram. He was a valiant soldier, but he had leprosy.ᵃ

²Now bands of raiders from Aram had gone out and had taken captive a young girl from Israel, and she served Naaman's wife. ³She said to her mistress, "If only

BREAKTHROUGH!

Leprosy

(2 KINGS 5:1)

In Bible times, all skin diseases like sores, infections and spots were called leprosy. But this leprosy was not the same as the terrible disease we know about today that's called leprosy. People who had skin problems had to live in groups of people who had the same problem, and they lived in lonely places far away. They couldn't come into contact with healthy people, because people thought these diseases could spread.

THE WITNESSES

✓ **NAAMAN** (**2 KINGS 5:1**)
This name means "fair" or "nice." He was the Syrian general (Israel and Syria were friends during his time) who was cured of leprosy, and he started worshiping the God of Israel.

my master would see the prophet who is in Samaria! He would cure him of his leprosy."

⁴Naaman went to his master and told him what the girl from Israel had said. ⁵"By all means, go," the king of Aram replied. "I will send a letter to the king of Israel." So Naaman left, taking with him ten talentsᵇ of silver, six thousand shekelsᶜ of gold and ten sets of clothing. ⁶The letter that he took to the king of Israel read: "With this letter I am sending my servant

---

ᵃ 1 The Hebrew for *leprosy* was used for various diseases affecting the skin; also in verses 3, 6, 7, 11 and 27.
ᵇ 5 That is, about 750 pounds or about 340 kilograms
ᶜ 5 That is, about 150 pounds or about 69 kilograms

Naaman to you so that you may cure him of his leprosy."

⁷As soon as the king of Israel read the letter, he tore his robes and said, "Am I God? Can I kill and bring back to life? Why does this fellow send someone to me to be cured of his leprosy? See how he is trying to pick a quarrel with me!"

⁸When Elisha the man of God heard that the king of Israel had torn his robes, he sent him this message: "Why have you torn your robes? Have the man come to me and he will know that there is a prophet in Israel." ⁹So Naaman went with his horses and chariots and stopped at the door of Elisha's house. ¹⁰Elisha sent a messenger to say to him, "Go, wash yourself seven times in the Jordan, and your flesh will be restored and you will be cleansed."

¹¹But Naaman went away angry and said, "I thought that he would surely come out to me and stand and call on the name of the LORD his God, wave his hand over the spot and cure me of my leprosy. ¹²Are not Abana and Pharpar, the rivers of Damascus, better than all the waters of Israel? Couldn't I wash in them and be cleansed?" So he turned and went off in a rage.

¹³Naaman's servants went to him and said, "My father, if the prophet had told you to do some great thing, would you not have done it? How much more, then, when he tells you, 'Wash and be cleansed'!" ¹⁴So he went down and dipped himself in the Jordan seven times, as the man of God had told him, and his flesh was restored and became clean like that of a young boy.

¹⁵Then Naaman and all his attendants went back to the man of God. He stood before him and said, "Now I know that there is no God in all the world except in Israel. So please accept a gift from your servant."

¹⁶The prophet answered, "As surely as the LORD lives, whom I serve, I will not accept a thing." And even though Naaman urged him, he refused.

¹⁷"If you will not," said Naaman, "please let me, your servant, be given as much earth as a pair of mules can carry, for your servant will never again make burnt offerings and sacrifices to any other god but the LORD. ¹⁸But may the LORD forgive your servant for this one thing: When my master enters the temple of Rimmon to bow down and he is leaning on my arm and I have to bow there also — when I bow down in the temple of Rimmon, may the LORD forgive your servant for this."

¹⁹"Go in peace," Elisha said.

After Naaman had traveled some distance, ²⁰Gehazi, the servant of Elisha the man of God, said to himself, "My master was too easy on Naaman, this Aramean, by not accepting from him what he brought. As surely as the LORD lives, I will run after him and get something from him."

BREAK THROUGH!

Why did Naaman want to take earth from Samaria?

(2 KINGS 5:17)

As it was customary at that time, Naaman probably thought that the God of Israel could only be worshiped on land that belonged to Israel. That's why he wanted to take soil in order to build an altar in his own country on top of soil brought from Israel. He asked Elisha for permission to take the soil so nobody could say he had stolen it.

²¹So Gehazi hurried after Naaman. When Naaman saw him running toward him, he got down from the chariot to meet him. "Is everything all right?" he asked. ²²"Everything is all right," Gehazi answered. "My master sent me to say, 'Two young men from the company of the prophets have just come to me from the hill country of Ephraim. Please give them a talentᵃ of silver and two sets of clothing.'"

²³"By all means, take two talents," said Naaman. He urged Gehazi to accept them, and then tied up the two talents of silver in two bags, with two sets of clothing. He gave them to two of his servants, and they carried them ahead of Gehazi. ²⁴When Gehazi came to the hill, he took the things from the servants and put them away in the house. He sent the men away and they left.

²⁵When he went in and stood before his master, Elisha asked him, "Where have you been, Gehazi?"

"Your servant didn't go anywhere," Gehazi answered.

²⁶But Elisha said to him, "Was not my spirit with you when the man got down from his chariot to meet you? Is this the time to take money or to accept clothes—or olive groves and vineyards, or flocks and herds, or male and female slaves? ²⁷Naaman's leprosy will cling to you and to your descendants forever." Then Gehazi went from Elisha's presence and his skin was leprous—it had become as white as snow.

An Axhead Floats

6 The company of the prophets said to Elisha, "Look, the place where we meet with you is too small for us. ²Let us go to the Jordan, where each of us can get a pole; and let us build a place there for us to meet."

And he said, "Go."

³Then one of them said, "Won't you please come with your servants?"

"I will," Elisha replied. ⁴And he went with them.

They went to the Jordan and began to cut down trees. ⁵As one of them was cutting down a tree, the iron axhead fell into the water. "Oh no, my lord!" he cried out. "It was borrowed!"

⁶The man of God asked, "Where did it fall?" When he showed him the place, Elisha cut a stick and threw it there, and made the iron float. ⁷"Lift it out," he said. Then the man reached out his hand and took it.

Elisha Traps Blinded Arameans

⁸Now the king of Aram was at war with Israel. After conferring with his officers, he said, "I will set up my camp in such and such a place."

⁹The man of God sent word to the king of Israel: "Beware of passing that place, because the Arameans are going down there." ¹⁰So the king of Israel checked on the place indicated by the man of God. Time and again Elisha warned the king, so that he was on his guard in such places.

¹¹This enraged the king of Aram. He summoned his officers and demanded of them, "Tell me! Which of us is on the side of the king of Israel?"

¹²"None of us, my lord the king," said one of his officers, "but Elisha, the prophet who is in Israel, tells the king of Israel the very words you speak in your bedroom."

¹³"Go, find out where he is," the king ordered, "so I can send men and capture him." The report came back: "He is in Dothan." ¹⁴Then he sent horses and chariots and a strong force there. They went by night and surrounded the city.

¹⁵When the servant of the man of God got up and went out early the next morning, an army with horses and chariots had surrounded the city. "Oh no, my lord! What shall we do?" the servant asked.

¹⁶"Don't be afraid," the prophet answered. "Those who are with us are more than those who are with them."

¹⁷And Elisha prayed, "Open his eyes, LORD, so that he may see." Then the LORD opened the servant's eyes, and he looked and saw the hills full of horses and chariots of fire all around Elisha.

¹⁸As the enemy came down toward him, Elisha prayed to the LORD, "Strike this

---

ᵃ 22 That is, about 75 pounds or about 34 kilograms

army with blindness." So he struck them with blindness, as Elisha had asked.

¹⁹Elisha told them, "This is not the road and this is not the city. Follow me, and I will lead you to the man you are looking for." And he led them to Samaria.

²⁰After they entered the city, Elisha said, "LORD, open the eyes of these men so they can see." Then the LORD opened their eyes and they looked, and there they were, inside Samaria.

²¹When the king of Israel saw them, he asked Elisha, "Shall I kill them, my father? Shall I kill them?"

²²"Do not kill them," he answered. "Would you kill those you have captured with your own sword or bow? Set food and water before them so that they may eat and drink and then go back to their master." ²³So he prepared a great feast for them, and after they had finished eating and drinking, he sent them away, and they returned to their master. So the bands from Aram stopped raiding Israel's territory.

Famine in Besieged Samaria

²⁴Some time later, Ben-Hadad king of Aram mobilized his entire army and marched up and laid siege to Samaria. ²⁵There was a great famine in the city; the siege lasted so long that a donkey's head sold for eighty shekels*a* of silver, and a quarter of a cab*b* of seed pods*c* for five shekels.*d*

²⁶As the king of Israel was passing by on the wall, a woman cried to him, "Help me, my lord the king!"

²⁷The king replied, "If the LORD does not help you, where can I get help for you? From the threshing floor? From the winepress?" ²⁸Then he asked her, "What's the matter?"

She answered, "This woman said to me, 'Give up your son so we may eat him today, and tomorrow we'll eat my son.' ²⁹So we cooked my son and ate him. The next day I said to her, 'Give up your son so we may eat him,' but she had hidden him."

³⁰When the king heard the woman's words, he tore his robes. As he went along the wall, the people looked, and

they saw that, under his robes, he had sackcloth on his body. ³¹He said, "May God deal with me, be it ever so severely, if the head of Elisha son of Shaphat remains on his shoulders today!"

³²Now Elisha was sitting in his house, and the elders were sitting with him. The king sent a messenger ahead, but before he arrived, Elisha said to the elders, "Don't you see how this murderer is sending someone to cut off my head? Look, when the messenger comes, shut the door and hold it shut against him. Is not the sound of his master's footsteps behind him?" ³³While he was still talking to them, the messenger came down to him.

The king said, "This disaster is from the LORD. Why should I wait for the LORD any longer?"

7 Elisha replied, "Hear the word of the LORD. This is what the LORD says: About this time tomorrow, a seah*e* of the finest flour will sell for a shekel*f* and two seahs*g* of barley for a shekel at the gate of Samaria."

²The officer on whose arm the king was leaning said to the man of God, "Look, even if the LORD should open the floodgates of the heavens, could this happen?"

"You will see it with your own eyes," answered Elisha, "but you will not eat any of it!"

The Siege Lifted

³Now there were four men with leprosy*h* at the entrance of the city gate. They said to each other, "Why stay here until we die? ⁴If we say, 'We'll go into the city'—the famine is there, and we will die. And if we stay here, we will die. So let's go over to the camp of the Arameans and surrender. If they spare us, we live; if they kill us, then we die."

---

a 25 That is, about 2 pounds or about 920 grams
b 25 That is, probably about 1/4 pound or about 100 grams   *c* 25 Or of doves' dung   *d* 25 That is, about 2 ounces or about 58 grams   *e* 1 That is, probably about 12 pounds or about 5.5 kilograms of flour; also in verses 16 and 18   *f* 1 That is, about 2/5 ounce or about 12 grams; also in verses 16 and 18   *g* 1 That is, probably about 20 pounds or about 9 kilograms of barley; also in verses 16 and 18   *h* 3 The Hebrew for leprosy was used for various diseases affecting the skin; also in verse 8.

⁵At dusk they got up and went to the camp of the Arameans. When they reached the edge of the camp, no one was there, ⁶for the Lord had caused the Arameans to hear the sound of chariots and horses and a great army, so that they said to one another, "Look, the king of Israel has hired the Hittite and Egyptian kings to attack us!" ⁷So they got up and fled in the dusk and abandoned their tents and their horses and donkeys. They left the camp as it was and ran for their lives.

⁸The men who had leprosy reached the edge of the camp, entered one of the tents and ate and drank. Then they took silver, gold and clothes, and went off and hid them. They returned and entered another tent and took some things from it and hid them also.

⁹Then they said to each other, "What we're doing is not right. This is a day of good news and we are keeping it to ourselves. If we wait until daylight, punishment will overtake us. Let's go at once and report this to the royal palace."

¹⁰So they went and called out to the city gatekeepers and told them, "We went into the Aramean camp and no one was there—not a sound of anyone—only tethered horses and donkeys, and the tents left just as they were." ¹¹The gatekeepers shouted the news, and it was reported within the palace.

¹²The king got up in the night and said to his officers, "I will tell you what the Arameans have done to us. They know we are starving; so they have left the camp to hide in the countryside, thinking, 'They will surely come out, and then we will take them alive and get into the city.'"

¹³One of his officers answered, "Have some men take five of the horses that are left in the city. Their plight will be like that of all the Israelites left here—yes, they will only be like all these Israelites who are doomed. So let us send them to find out what happened."

¹⁴So they selected two chariots with their horses, and the king sent them after the Aramean army. He commanded the drivers, "Go and find out what has happened." ¹⁵They followed them as far as the Jordan, and they found the whole road strewn with the clothing and equipment the Arameans had thrown away in their headlong flight. So the messengers returned and reported to the king. ¹⁶Then the people went out and plundered the camp of the Arameans. So a seah of the finest flour sold for a shekel, and two seahs of barley sold for a shekel, as the Lord had said.

¹⁷Now the king had put the officer on whose arm he leaned in charge of the gate, and the people trampled him in the gateway, and he died, just as the man of God had foretold when the king came down to his house. ¹⁸It happened as the man of God had said to the king: "About this time tomorrow, a seah of the finest flour will sell for a shekel and two seahs of barley for a shekel at the gate of Samaria."

¹⁹The officer had said to the man of God, "Look, even if the Lord should open the floodgates of the heavens, could this happen?" The man of God had replied, "You will see it with your own eyes, but you will not eat any of it!" ²⁰And that is exactly what happened to him, for the people trampled him in the gateway, and he died.

The Shunammite's Land Restored

8 Now Elisha had said to the woman whose son he had restored to life, "Go away with your family and stay for a while wherever you can, because the Lord has decreed a famine in the land that will last seven years." ²The woman proceeded to do as the man of God said. She and her family went away and stayed in the land of the Philistines seven years.

³At the end of the seven years she came back from the land of the Philistines and went to appeal to the king for her house and land. ⁴The king was talking to Gehazi, the servant of the man of God, and had said, "Tell me about all the great things Elisha has done." ⁵Just as Gehazi was telling the king how Elisha had restored the dead to life, the woman whose son Elisha had brought back to life came to appeal to the king for her house and land.

Gehazi said, "This is the woman, my lord the king, and this is her son whom Elisha restored to life." ⁶The king asked the woman about it, and she told him.

Then he assigned an official to her case and said to him, "Give back everything that belonged to her, including all the income from her land from the day she left the country until now."

Hazael Murders Ben-Hadad

⁷Elisha went to Damascus, and Ben-Hadad king of Aram was ill. When the king was told, "The man of God has come all the way up here," ⁸he said to Hazael, "Take a gift with you and go to meet the man of God. Consult the LORD through him; ask him, 'Will I recover from this illness?' "

⁹Hazael went to meet Elisha, taking with him as a gift forty camel-loads of all the finest wares of Damascus. He went in and stood before him, and said, "Your son Ben-Hadad king of Aram has sent me to ask, 'Will I recover from this illness?' "

¹⁰Elisha answered, "Go and say to him, 'You will certainly recover.' Nevertheless,ᵃ the LORD has revealed to me that he will in fact die." ¹¹He stared at him with a fixed gaze until Hazael was embarrassed. Then the man of God began to weep.

¹²"Why is my lord weeping?" asked Hazael.

"Because I know the harm you will do to the Israelites," he answered. "You will set fire to their fortified places, kill their young men with the sword, dash their little children to the ground, and rip open their pregnant women."

¹³Hazael said, "How could your servant, a mere dog, accomplish such a feat?"

"The LORD has shown me that you will become king of Aram," answered Elisha.

¹⁴Then Hazael left Elisha and returned to his master. When Ben-Hadad asked, "What did Elisha say to you?" Hazael replied, "He told me that you would certainly recover." ¹⁵But the next day he took a thick cloth, soaked it in water and spread it over the king's face, so that he died. Then Hazael succeeded him as king.

Jehoram King of Judah

¹⁶In the fifth year of Joram son of Ahab king of Israel, when Jehoshaphat was king of Judah, Jehoram son of Jehoshaphat began his reign as king of Judah. ¹⁷He was thirty-two years old when he became king, and he reigned in Jerusalem eight years. ¹⁸He followed the ways of the kings of Israel, as the house of Ahab had done, for he married a daughter of Ahab. He did evil in the eyes of the LORD. ¹⁹Nevertheless, for the sake of his servant David, the LORD was not willing to destroy Judah. He had promised to maintain a lamp for David and his descendants forever.

²⁰In the time of Jehoram, Edom rebelled against Judah and set up its own king. ²¹So Jehoramᵇ went to Zair with all his chariots. The Edomites surrounded him and his chariot commanders, but he rose up and broke through by night; his army, however, fled back home. ²²To this day Edom has been in rebellion against Judah. Libnah revolted at the same time.

²³As for the other events of Jehoram's reign, and all he did, are they not written in the book of the annals of the kings of Judah? ²⁴Jehoram rested with his ancestors and was buried with them in the City of David. And Ahaziah his son succeeded him as king.

Ahaziah King of Judah

²⁵In the twelfth year of Joram son of Ahab king of Israel, Ahaziah son of Jehoram king of Judah began to reign. ²⁶Ahaziah was twenty-two years old when he became king, and he reigned in Jerusalem one year. His mother's name was Athaliah, a granddaughter of Omri king of Israel. ²⁷He followed the ways of the house of Ahab and did evil in the eyes of the LORD, as the house of Ahab had done, for he was related by marriage to Ahab's family.

²⁸Ahaziah went with Joram son of Ahab to war against Hazael king of Aram at Ramoth Gilead. The Arameans wounded Joram; ²⁹so King Joram returned to Jezreel

ᵃ 10 The Hebrew may also be read Go and say, 'You will certainly not recover,' for.   ᵇ 21 Hebrew Joram, a variant of Jehoram; also in verses 23 and 24 to recover from the wounds the Arameans had inflicted on him at Ramoth[a] in his battle with Hazael king of Aram.

Then Ahaziah son of Jehoram king of Judah went down to Jezreel to see Jo-

THE WITNESSES

✓ BEN-HADAD (2 KINGS 8:7)
Many people in the Bible have this name, but this Ben-Hadad was the king of Syria. He was the king mentioned in the two previous chapters. It's possible that he heard that Elisha had healed Naaman, and that's why he wanted the prophet to help him.

✓ HAZAEL (2 KINGS 8:8-15)
He worked for King Ben-Hadad. Then he killed the king and took his place until the year 841 before Christ. He fought against Judah and Israel. He was about to conquer Jerusalem, but he didn't because the Israelites told him to just take anything of value he wanted. He was a very bad king.

ram son of Ahab, because he had been wounded.

Jehu Anointed King of Israel

9 The prophet Elisha summoned a man from the company of the prophets and said to him, "Tuck your cloak into your belt, take this flask of olive oil with you and go to Ramoth Gilead. ²When you get there, look for Jehu son of Jehoshaphat, the son of Nimshi. Go to him, get him away from his companions and take him into an inner room. ³Then take the flask and pour the oil on his head and declare, 'This is what the LORD says: I anoint you king over Israel.' Then open the door and run; don't delay!"

⁴So the young prophet went to Ramoth Gilead. ⁵When he arrived, he found the army officers sitting together. "I have a message for you, commander," he said.

"For which of us?" asked Jehu.

"For you, commander," he replied.

⁶Jehu got up and went into the house. Then the prophet poured the oil on Jehu's head and declared, "This is what the LORD, the God of Israel, says: 'I anoint you king over the LORD's people Israel. ⁷You are to destroy the house of Ahab your master, and I will avenge the blood of my servants the prophets and the blood of all the LORD's servants shed by Jezebel. ⁸The whole house of Ahab will perish. I will cut off from Ahab every last male in Israel—slave or free.[b] ⁹I will make the house of Ahab like the house of Jeroboam son of Nebat and like the house of Baasha son of Ahijah. ¹⁰As for Jezebel, dogs will devour her on the plot of ground at Jezreel, and no one will bury her.' " Then he opened the door and ran.

¹¹When Jehu went out to his fellow officers, one of them asked him, "Is everything all right? Why did this maniac come to you?"

"You know the man and the sort of things he says," Jehu replied.

¹²"That's not true!" they said. "Tell us."

Jehu said, "Here is what he told me: 'This is what the LORD says: I anoint you king over Israel.' "

---

^a 29 Hebrew *Ramah*, a variant of *Ramoth*   ^b 8 Or *Israel — every ruler or leader*

¹³They quickly took their cloaks and spread them under him on the bare steps. Then they blew the trumpet and shouted, "Jehu is king!"

Jehu Kills Joram and Ahaziah

¹⁴So Jehu son of Jehoshaphat, the son of Nimshi, conspired against Joram. (Now Joram and all Israel had been defending Ramoth Gilead against Hazael king of Aram, ¹⁵but King Joram*ᵃ* had returned to Jezreel to recover from the wounds the Arameans had inflicted on him in the battle with Hazael king of Aram.) Jehu said, "If you desire to make me king, don't let anyone slip out of the city to go and tell the news in Jezreel."

¹⁶Then he got into his chariot and rode to Jezreel, because Joram was resting there and Ahaziah king of Judah had gone down to see him.

¹⁷When the lookout standing on the tower in Jezreel saw Jehu's troops approaching, he called out, "I see some troops coming."

"Get a horseman," Joram ordered. "Send him to meet them and ask, 'Do you come in peace?'"

¹⁸The horseman rode off to meet Jehu and said, "This is what the king says: 'Do you come in peace?'"

"What do you have to do with peace?" Jehu replied. "Fall in behind me."

The lookout reported, "The messenger has reached them, but he isn't coming back."

¹⁹So the king sent out a second horseman. When he came to them he said, "This is what the king says: 'Do you come in peace?'"

Jehu replied, "What do you have to do with peace? Fall in behind me."

²⁰The lookout reported, "He has reached them, but he isn't coming back either. The driving is like that of Jehu son of Nimshi—he drives like a maniac."

²¹"Hitch up my chariot," Joram ordered. And when it was hitched up, Joram king of Israel and Ahaziah king of Judah rode out, each in his own chariot, to meet Jehu. They met him at the plot of ground that had belonged to Naboth the Jezreelite.

²²When Joram saw Jehu he asked, "Have you come in peace, Jehu?"

"How can there be peace," Jehu replied, "as long as all the idolatry and witchcraft of your mother Jezebel abound?"

²³Joram turned about and fled, calling out to Ahaziah, "Treachery, Ahaziah!"

²⁴Then Jehu drew his bow and shot Joram between the shoulders. The arrow pierced his heart and he slumped down in his chariot. ²⁵Jehu said to Bidkar, his chariot officer, "Pick him up and throw him on the field that belonged to Naboth the Jezreelite. Remember how you and I were riding together in chariots behind Ahab his father when the Lᴏʀᴅ spoke this prophecy against him: ²⁶'Yesterday I saw the blood of Naboth and the blood of his sons, declares the Lᴏʀᴅ, and I will surely make you pay for it on this plot of ground, declares the Lᴏʀᴅ.'ᵇ Now then, pick him up and throw him on that plot, in accordance with the word of the Lᴏʀᴅ."

²⁷When Ahaziah king of Judah saw what had happened, he fled up the road to Beth Haggan.ᶜ Jehu chased him, shouting, "Kill him too!" They wounded him in his chariot on the way up to Gur near Ibleam, but he escaped to Megiddo and died there. ²⁸His servants took him by chariot to Jerusalem and buried him with his ancestors in his tomb in the City of David. ²⁹(In the eleventh year of Joram son of Ahab, Ahaziah had become king of Judah.)

Jezebel Killed

³⁰Then Jehu went to Jezreel. When Jezebel heard about it, she put on eye makeup, arranged her hair and looked out of a window. ³¹As Jehu entered the gate, she asked, "Have you come in peace, you Zimri, you murderer of your master?"ᵈ

³²He looked up at the window and called out, "Who is on my side? Who?" Two or three eunuchs looked down at him. ³³"Throw her down!" Jehu said. So they threw her down, and some of her blood spattered the wall and the horses as they trampled her underfoot.

ᵃ 15 Hebrew Jehoram, a variant of Joram; also in verses 17 and 21-24   ᵇ 26 See 1 Kings 21:19.   ᶜ 27 Or fled by way of the garden house   ᵈ 31 Or "Was there peace for Zimri, who murdered his master?"

34 Jehu went in and ate and drank. "Take care of that cursed woman," he said, "and bury her, for she was a king's daughter." 35 But when they went out to bury her, they found nothing except her skull, her feet and her hands. 36 They went back and told Jehu, who said, "This is the word of the LORD that he spoke through his servant Elijah the Tishbite: On the plot of ground at Jezreel dogs will devour Jezebel's flesh.[a] 37 Jezebel's body will be like dung on the ground in the plot at Jezreel, so that no one will be able to say, 'This is Jezebel.' "

Ahab's Family Killed

10 Now there were in Samaria seventy sons of the house of Ahab. So Jehu wrote letters and sent them to Samaria: to the officials of Jezreel,[b] to the elders and to the guardians of Ahab's children. He said, 2 "You have your master's sons with you and you have chariots and horses, a fortified city and weapons. Now as soon as this letter reaches you, 3 choose the best and most worthy of your master's sons and set him on his father's throne. Then fight for your master's house."

4 But they were terrified and said, "If two kings could not resist him, how can we?"

5 So the palace administrator, the city governor, the elders and the guardians sent this message to Jehu: "We are your servants and we will do anything you say. We will not appoint anyone as king; you do whatever you think best."

6 Then Jehu wrote them a second letter, saying, "If you are on my side and will obey me, take the heads of your master's sons and come to me in Jezreel by this time tomorrow."

Now the royal princes, seventy of them, were with the leading men of the city, who were rearing them. 7 When the letter arrived, these men took the princes and slaughtered all seventy of them. They put their heads in baskets and sent them to Jehu in Jezreel. 8 When the messenger arrived, he told Jehu, "They have brought the heads of the princes."

Then Jehu ordered, "Put them in two piles at the entrance of the city gate until morning."

9 The next morning Jehu went out. He stood before all the people and said, "You are innocent. It was I who conspired against my master and killed him, but who killed all these? 10 Know, then, that not a word the LORD has spoken against the house of Ahab will fail. The LORD has done what he announced through his servant Elijah." 11 So Jehu killed everyone in Jezreel who remained of the house of Ahab, as well as all his chief men, his close friends and his priests, leaving him no survivor.

12 Jehu then set out and went toward Samaria. At Beth Eked of the Shepherds, 13 he met some relatives of Ahaziah king of Judah and asked, "Who are you?"

They said, "We are relatives of Ahaziah, and we have come down to greet the families of the king and of the queen mother."

14 "Take them alive!" he ordered. So they took them alive and slaughtered them by the well of Beth Eked — forty-two of them. He left no survivor.

15 After he left there, he came upon Jehonadab son of Rekab, who was on his way to meet him. Jehu greeted him and said, "Are you in accord with me, as I am with you?"

"I am," Jehonadab answered.

"If so," said Jehu, "give me your hand." So he did, and Jehu helped him up into the chariot. 16 Jehu said, "Come with me and see my zeal for the LORD." Then he had him ride along in his chariot.

17 When Jehu came to Samaria, he killed all who were left there of Ahab's family; he destroyed them, according to the word of the LORD spoken to Elijah.

Servants of Baal Killed

18 Then Jehu brought all the people together and said to them, "Ahab served Baal a little; Jehu will serve him much. 19 Now summon all the prophets of Baal, all his servants and all his priests. See that no one is missing, because I am going to hold a great sacrifice for Baal. Anyone who fails to come will no longer live." But Jehu was acting deceptively in order to destroy the servants of Baal.

---

a 36 See 1 Kings 21:23.   *b 1* Hebrew; some Septuagint manuscripts and Vulgate *of the city*

²⁰Jehu said, "Call an assembly in honor of Baal." So they proclaimed it. ²¹Then he sent word throughout Israel, and all the servants of Baal came; not one stayed away. They crowded into the temple of Baal until it was full from one end to the other. ²²And Jehu said to the keeper of the wardrobe, "Bring robes for all the servants of Baal." So he brought out robes for them.

²³Then Jehu and Jehonadab son of Rekab went into the temple of Baal. Jehu said to the servants of Baal, "Look around and see that no one who serves the LORD is here with you—only servants of Baal." ²⁴So they went in to make sacrifices and burnt offerings. Now Jehu had posted eighty men outside with this warning: "If one of you lets any of the men I am placing in your hands escape, it will be your life for his life."

²⁵As soon as Jehu had finished making the burnt offering, he ordered the guards and officers: "Go in and kill them; let no one escape." So they cut them down with the sword. The guards and officers threw the bodies out and then entered the inner shrine of the temple of Baal. ²⁶They brought the sacred stone out of the temple of Baal and burned it. ²⁷They demolished the sacred stone of Baal and tore down the temple of Baal, and people have used it for a latrine to this day.

²⁸So Jehu destroyed Baal worship in Israel. ²⁹However, he did not turn away from the sins of Jeroboam son of Nebat, which he had caused Israel to commit—the worship of the golden calves at Bethel and Dan.

³⁰The LORD said to Jehu, "Because you have done well in accomplishing what is right in my eyes and have done to the house of Ahab all I had in mind to do, your descendants will sit on the throne of Israel to the fourth generation." ³¹Yet Jehu was not careful to keep the law of the LORD, the God of Israel, with all his heart. He did not turn away from the sins of Jeroboam, which he had caused Israel to commit.

³²In those days the LORD began to reduce the size of Israel. Hazael overpowered the Israelites throughout their territory ³³east of the Jordan in all the land of Gilead (the region of Gad, Reuben and Manasseh), from Aroer by the Arnon Gorge through Gilead to Bashan.

³⁴As for the other events of Jehu's reign, all he did, and all his achievements, are they not written in the book of the annals of the kings of Israel? ³⁵Jehu rested with his ancestors and was buried in Samaria. And Jehoahaz his son succeeded him as king. ³⁶The time that Jehu reigned over Israel in Samaria was twenty-eight years.

Athaliah and Joash

11 When Athaliah the mother of Ahaziah saw that her son was dead, she proceeded to destroy the whole royal family. ²But Jehosheba, the daughter of King Jehoram[a] and sister of Ahaziah, took Joash son of Ahaziah and stole him away from among the royal princes, who were about to be murdered. She put him and his nurse in a bedroom to hide him from Athaliah; so he was not killed. ³He remained hidden with his nurse at the temple of the LORD for six years while Athaliah ruled the land.

⁴In the seventh year Jehoiada sent for the commanders of units of a hundred, the Carites and the guards and had them brought to him at the temple of the LORD. He made a covenant with them and put them under oath at the temple of the LORD. Then he showed them the king's son. ⁵He commanded them, saying, "This is what you are to do: You who are in the three companies that are going on duty on the Sabbath—a third of you guarding the royal palace, ⁶a third at the Sur Gate, and a third at the gate behind the guard, who take turns guarding the temple— ⁷and you who are in the other two companies that normally go off Sabbath duty are all to guard the temple for the king. ⁸Station yourselves around the king, each of you with weapon in hand. Anyone who approaches your ranks[b] is to be put to death. Stay close to the king wherever he goes."

⁹The commanders of units of a hundred did just as Jehoiada the priest ordered.

---

[a] 2 Hebrew *Joram*, a variant of *Jehoram*   [b] 8 Or *approaches the precincts*

THE
WITNESSES

✓ **JOASH** (2 KINGS 11–12)
His name means "God gives." He was Ahaziah's son, and he became the king of Judah when he was eight years old, about 835 years before Christ. He was the only member of his family who survived when Queen Athaliah killed everybody, because his aunt Jehosheba hid him. He repaired the temple that was about a hundred years old then. He was a good king for some time, but he changed in the end.

✓ **ATHALIAH** (2 KINGS 11:1)
This name means "God is fair." She was Jehoram's wife and Ahaziah's mother. Jehoram was the king of Judah, and so was Ahaziah. Athaliah was very bad and worshiped the false god Baal. When her son died, she governed Judah for six years. The people finally chose another king and they killed her.

✓ **PRIEST JEHOIADA** (2 KINGS 11:4)
This name means "God knows." He was Jehosheba's husband, and Jehosheba was King Jehoram's daughter. Jehoiada was a priest, maybe a high priest. He acted as Joash's tutor, because Joash became king when he was only eight years old. He was a good influence on this boy, and he encouraged him to restore the temple. When Jehoiada died, Joash turned away from God.

Each one took his men—those who were going on duty on the Sabbath and those who were going off duty—and came to Jehoiada the priest. ¹⁰Then he gave the commanders the spears and shields that had belonged to King David and that were in the temple of the LORD. ¹¹The guards, each with weapon in hand, stationed themselves around the king—near the altar and the temple, from the south side to the north side of the temple.

¹²Jehoiada brought out the king's son and put the crown on him; he presented him with a copy of the covenant and proclaimed him king. They anointed him, and the people clapped their hands and shouted, "Long live the king!"

¹³When Athaliah heard the noise made by the guards and the people, she went to the people at the temple of the LORD. ¹⁴She looked and there was the king, standing by the pillar, as the custom was. The officers and the trumpeters were beside the king, and all the people of the land were rejoicing and blowing trumpets. Then Athaliah tore her robes and called out, "Treason! Treason!"

¹⁵Jehoiada the priest ordered the commanders of units of a hundred, who were in charge of the troops: "Bring her out between the ranks[a] and put to the sword anyone who follows her." For the priest had said, "She must not be put to death in the temple of the LORD." ¹⁶So they seized her as she reached the place where the horses enter the palace grounds, and there she was put to death.

¹⁷Jehoiada then made a covenant between the LORD and the king and people that they would be the LORD's people. He

---

ᵃ 15 Or out from the precincts

also made a covenant between the king and the people. ¹⁸All the people of the land went to the temple of Baal and tore it down. They smashed the altars and idols to pieces and killed Mattan the priest of Baal in front of the altars.

Then Jehoiada the priest posted guards at the temple of the LORD. ¹⁹He took with him the commanders of hundreds, the Carites, the guards and all the people of the land, and together they brought the king down from the temple of the LORD and went into the palace, entering by way of the gate of the guards. The king then took his place on the royal throne. ²⁰All the people of the land rejoiced, and the city was calm, because Athaliah had been slain with the sword at the palace.

²¹Joash[a] was seven years old when he began to reign.[b]

Joash Repairs the Temple

12[c] In the seventh year of Jehu, Joash[d] became king, and he reigned in Jerusalem forty years. His mother's name was Zibiah; she was from Beersheba. ²Joash did what was right in the eyes of the LORD all the years Jehoiada the priest instructed him. ³The high places, however, were not removed; the people continued to offer sacrifices and burn incense there.

⁴Joash said to the priests, "Collect all the money that is brought as sacred offerings to the temple of the LORD—the money collected in the census, the money received from personal vows and the money brought voluntarily to the temple. ⁵Let every priest receive the money from one of the treasurers, then use it to repair whatever damage is found in the temple."

⁶But by the twenty-third year of King Joash the priests still had not repaired the temple. ⁷Therefore King Joash summoned Jehoiada the priest and the other priests and asked them, "Why aren't you repairing the damage done to the temple? Take no more money from your treasurers, but hand it over for repairing the temple." ⁸The priests agreed that they would not collect any more money from the people and that they would not repair the temple themselves.

⁹Jehoiada the priest took a chest and bored a hole in its lid. He placed it beside the altar, on the right side as one enters the temple of the LORD. The priests who guarded the entrance put into the chest all the money that was brought to the temple of the LORD. ¹⁰Whenever they saw that there was a large amount of money in the chest, the royal secretary and the high priest came, counted the money that had been brought into the temple of the LORD and put it into bags. ¹¹When the amount had been determined, they gave the money to the men appointed to supervise the work on the temple. With it they paid those who worked on the temple of the LORD— the carpenters and builders, ¹²the masons and stonecutters. They purchased timber and blocks of dressed stone for the repair of the temple of the LORD, and met all the other expenses of restoring the temple.

¹³The money brought into the temple was not spent for making silver basins, wick trimmers, sprinkling bowls, trumpets or any other articles of gold or silver for the temple of the LORD; ¹⁴it was paid to the workers, who used it to repair the temple. ¹⁵They did not require an accounting from those to whom they gave the money to pay the workers, because they acted with complete honesty. ¹⁶The money from the guilt offerings and sin offerings[e] was not brought into the temple of the LORD; it belonged to the priests.

¹⁷About this time Hazael king of Aram went up and attacked Gath and captured it. Then he turned to attack Jerusalem. ¹⁸But Joash king of Judah took all the sacred objects dedicated by his predecessors—Jehoshaphat, Jehoram and Ahaziah, the kings of Judah—and the gifts he himself had dedicated and all the gold found in the treasuries of the temple of the LORD and of the royal palace, and he sent them to Hazael king of Aram, who then withdrew from Jerusalem.

¹⁹As for the other events of the reign of Joash, and all he did, are they not written in the book of the annals of the kings of

---

a 21 Hebrew *Jehoash*, a variant of *Joash*   *b* 21 In Hebrew texts this verse (11:21) is numbered 12:1.   *c* In Hebrew texts 12:1-21 is numbered 12:2-22.   *d* 1 Hebrew *Jehoash*, a variant of *Joash*; also in verses 2, 4, 6, 7 and 18   *e* 16 Or *purification offerings*

Judah? ²⁰His officials conspired against him and assassinated him at Beth Millo, on the road down to Silla. ²¹The officials who murdered him were Jozabad son of Shimeath and Jehozabad son of Shomer. He died and was buried with his ancestors in the City of David. And Amaziah his son succeeded him as king.

Jehoahaz King of Israel

13 In the twenty-third year of Joash son of Ahaziah king of Judah, Jehoahaz son of Jehu became king of Israel in Samaria, and he reigned seventeen years. ²He did evil in the eyes of the LORD by following the sins of Jeroboam son of Nebat, which he had caused Israel to commit, and he did not turn away from them. ³So the LORD's anger burned against Israel, and for a long time he kept them under the power of Hazael king of Aram and Ben-Hadad his son.

⁴Then Jehoahaz sought the LORD's favor, and the LORD listened to him, for he saw how severely the king of Aram was oppressing Israel. ⁵The LORD provided a deliverer for Israel, and they escaped from the power of Aram. So the Israelites lived in their own homes as they had before. ⁶But they did not turn away from the sins of the house of Jeroboam, which he had caused Israel to commit; they continued in them. Also, the Asherah pole*ᵃ* remained standing in Samaria.

⁷Nothing had been left of the army of Jehoahaz except fifty horsemen, ten chariots and ten thousand foot soldiers, for the king of Aram had destroyed the rest and made them like the dust at threshing time. ⁸As for the other events of the reign of Jehoahaz, all he did and his achievements, are they not written in the book of the annals of the kings of Israel? ⁹Jehoahaz rested with his ancestors and was buried in Samaria. And Jehoash*ᵇ* his son succeeded him as king.

Jehoash King of Israel

¹⁰In the thirty-seventh year of Joash king of Judah, Jehoash son of Jehoahaz became king of Israel in Samaria, and he

reigned sixteen years. ¹¹He did evil in the eyes of the LORD and did not turn away from any of the sins of Jeroboam son of Nebat, which he had caused Israel to commit; he continued in them.

¹²As for the other events of the reign of Jehoash, all he did and his achievements, including his war against Amaziah king of Judah, are they not written in the book of the annals of the kings of Israel? ¹³Jehoash rested with his ancestors, and Jeroboam succeeded him on the throne. Jehoash was buried in Samaria with the kings of Israel.

¹⁴Now Elisha had been suffering from the illness from which he died. Jehoash king of Israel went down to see him and wept over him. "My father! My father!" he cried. "The chariots and horsemen of Israel!"

¹⁵Elisha said, "Get a bow and some arrows," and he did so. ¹⁶"Take the bow in your hands," he said to the king of Israel. When he had taken it, Elisha put his hands on the king's hands.

¹⁷"Open the east window," he said, and he opened it. "Shoot!" Elisha said, and he shot. "The LORD's arrow of victory, the arrow of victory over Aram!" Elisha declared. "You will completely destroy the Arameans at Aphek."

¹⁸Then he said, "Take the arrows," and the king took them. Elisha told him, "Strike the ground." He struck it three times and stopped. ¹⁹The man of God was angry with him and said, "You should have struck the ground five or six times; then you would have defeated Aram and completely destroyed it. But now you will defeat it only three times."

²⁰Elisha died and was buried.

Now Moabite raiders used to enter the country every spring. ²¹Once while some Israelites were burying a man, suddenly they saw a band of raiders; so they threw the man's body into Elisha's tomb. When the body touched Elisha's bones, the man came to life and stood up on his feet. ²²Hazael king of Aram oppressed Israel throughout the reign of Jehoahaz. ²³But

---

ᵃ 6 That is, a wooden symbol of the goddess Asherah; here and elsewhere in 2 Kings   ᵇ 9 Hebrew *Joash*, a variant of *Jehoash*; also in verses 12-14 and 25 the Lᴏʀᴅ was gracious to them and had compassion and showed concern for them because of his covenant with Abraham, Isaac and Jacob. To this day he has been unwilling to destroy them or banish them from his presence. ²⁴Hazael king of Aram died, and Ben-Hadad his son succeeded him as king. ²⁵Then Jehoash son of Jehoahaz recaptured from Ben-Hadad son of Hazael the towns he had taken in battle from his father Jehoahaz. Three times Jehoash defeated him, and so he recovered the Israelite towns.

Amaziah King of Judah

14 In the second year of Jehoash*ᵃ* son of Jehoahaz king of Israel, Amaziah son of Joash king of Judah began to reign. ²He was twenty-five years old when he became king, and he reigned in Jerusalem twenty-nine years. His mother's name was Jehoaddan; she was from Jerusalem. ³He did what was right in the eyes of the Lᴏʀᴅ, but not as his father David had done. In everything he followed the example of his father Joash. ⁴The high places, however, were not removed; the people continued to offer sacrifices and burn incense there.

⁵After the kingdom was firmly in his grasp, he executed the officials who had murdered his father the king. ⁶Yet he did not put the children of the assassins to death, in accordance with what is written in the Book of the Law of Moses where the Lᴏʀᴅ commanded: "Parents are not to be put to death for their children, nor children put to death for their parents; each will die for their own sin."*ᵇ*

⁷He was the one who defeated ten thousand Edomites in the Valley of Salt and captured Sela in battle, calling it Joktheel, the name it has to this day.

⁸Then Amaziah sent messengers to Jehoash son of Jehoahaz, the son of Jehu, king of Israel, with the challenge: "Come, let us face each other in battle."

⁹But Jehoash king of Israel replied to Amaziah king of Judah: "A thistle in Lebanon sent a message to a cedar in Lebanon, 'Give your daughter to my son in marriage.' Then a wild beast in Lebanon came along and trampled the thistle underfoot. ¹⁰You have indeed defeated Edom and now you are arrogant. Glory in your victory, but stay at home! Why ask for trouble and cause your own downfall and that of Judah also?"

¹¹Amaziah, however, would not listen, so Jehoash king of Israel attacked. He and Amaziah king of Judah faced each other at Beth Shemesh in Judah. ¹²Judah was routed by Israel, and every man fled to his home. ¹³Jehoash king of Israel captured Amaziah king of Judah, the son of Joash, the son of Ahaziah, at Beth Shemesh. Then Jehoash went to Jerusalem and broke down the wall of Jerusalem from the Ephraim Gate to the Corner Gate—a section about four hundred cubits long.*ᶜ* ¹⁴He took all the gold and silver and all the articles found in the temple of the Lᴏʀᴅ and in the treasuries of the royal palace. He also took hostages and returned to Samaria.

¹⁵As for the other events of the reign of Jehoash, what he did and his achievements, including his war against Amaziah king of Judah, are they not written in the book of the annals of the kings of Israel? ¹⁶Jehoash rested with his ancestors and was buried in Samaria with the kings of Israel. And Jeroboam his son succeeded him as king.

¹⁷Amaziah son of Joash king of Judah lived for fifteen years after the death of Jehoash son of Jehoahaz king of Israel. ¹⁸As for the other events of Amaziah's reign, are they not written in the book of the annals of the kings of Judah?

¹⁹They conspired against him in Jerusalem, and he fled to Lachish, but they sent men after him to Lachish and killed him there. ²⁰He was brought back by horse and was buried in Jerusalem with his ancestors, in the City of David.

²¹Then all the people of Judah took Azariah,*ᵈ* who was sixteen years old, and made him king in place of his father Amaziah. ²²He was the one who rebuilt Elath and restored it to Judah after Amaziah rested with his ancestors.

ᵃ 1 Hebrew *Joash,* a variant of *Jehoash;* also in verses 13, 23 and 27   *ᵇ 6* Deut. 24:16   *ᶜ 13* That is, about 600 feet or about 180 meters   *ᵈ 21* Also called *Uzziah*

Jeroboam II King of Israel

[23]In the fifteenth year of Amaziah son of Joash king of Judah, Jeroboam son of Jehoash king of Israel became king in Samaria, and he reigned forty-one years. [24]He did evil in the eyes of the LORD and did not turn away from any of the sins of Jeroboam son of Nebat, which he had caused Israel to commit. [25]He was the one who restored the boundaries of Israel from Lebo Hamath to the Dead Sea,[a] in accordance with the word of the LORD, the God of Israel, spoken through his servant Jonah son of Amittai, the prophet from Gath Hepher.

[26]The LORD had seen how bitterly everyone in Israel, whether slave or free, was suffering;[b] there was no one to help them. [27]And since the LORD had not said he would blot out the name of Israel from under heaven, he saved them by the hand of Jeroboam son of Jehoash.

[28]As for the other events of Jeroboam's reign, all he did, and his military achievements, including how he recovered for Israel both Damascus and Hamath, which had belonged to Judah, are they not written in the book of the annals of the kings of Israel? [29]Jeroboam rested with his ancestors, the kings of Israel. And Zechariah his son succeeded him as king.

Azariah King of Judah

15 In the twenty-seventh year of Jeroboam king of Israel, Azariah[c] son of Amaziah king of Judah began to reign. [2]He was sixteen years old when he became king, and he reigned in Jerusalem fifty-two years. His mother's name was Jekoliah; she was from Jerusalem. [3]He did what was right in the eyes of the LORD, just as his father Amaziah had done. [4]The high places, however, were not removed; the people continued to offer sacrifices and burn incense there.

[5]The LORD afflicted the king with leprosy[d] until the day he died, and he lived in a separate house.[e] Jotham the king's son had charge of the palace and governed the people of the land.

[6]As for the other events of Azariah's reign, and all he did, are they not written

in the book of the annals of the kings of Judah? [7]Azariah rested with his ancestors and was buried near them in the City of David. And Jotham his son succeeded him as king.

Zechariah King of Israel

[8]In the thirty-eighth year of Azariah king of Judah, Zechariah son of Jeroboam became king of Israel in Samaria, and he reigned six months. [9]He did evil in the eyes of the LORD, as his predecessors had done. He did not turn away from the sins of Jeroboam son of Nebat, which he had caused Israel to commit.

[10]Shallum son of Jabesh conspired against Zechariah. He attacked him in front of the people,[f] assassinated him and succeeded him as king. [11]The other events of Zechariah's reign are written in the book of the annals of the kings of Israel. [12]So the word of the LORD spoken to Jehu was fulfilled: "Your descendants will sit on the throne of Israel to the fourth generation."[g]

Shallum King of Israel

[13]Shallum son of Jabesh became king in the thirty-ninth year of Uzziah king of Judah, and he reigned in Samaria one month. [14]Then Menahem son of Gadi went from Tirzah up to Samaria. He attacked Shallum son of Jabesh in Samaria, assassinated him and succeeded him as king.

[15]The other events of Shallum's reign, and the conspiracy he led, are written in the book of the annals of the kings of Israel.

[16]At that time Menahem, starting out from Tirzah, attacked Tiphsah and everyone in the city and its vicinity, because they refused to open their gates. He sacked Tiphsah and ripped open all the pregnant women.

---

[a] 25 Hebrew *the Sea of the Arabah*   [b] 26 Or *Israel was suffering. They were without a ruler or leader, and*   [c] 1 Also called *Uzziah*; also in verses 6, 7, 8, 17, 23 and 27   [d] 5 The Hebrew for *leprosy* was used for various diseases affecting the skin.   [e] 5 Or *in a house where he was relieved of responsibilities*   [f] 10 Hebrew; some Septuagint manuscripts *in Ibleam*   [g] 12 2 Kings 10:30

Menahem King of Israel

¹⁷In the thirty-ninth year of Azariah king of Judah, Menahem son of Gadi became king of Israel, and he reigned in Samaria ten years. ¹⁸He did evil in the eyes of the LORD. During his entire reign he did not turn away from the sins of Jeroboam son of Nebat, which he had caused Israel to commit.

¹⁹Then Pul*ᵃ* king of Assyria invaded the land, and Menahem gave him a thousand talentsᵇ of silver to gain his support and strengthen his own hold on the kingdom. ²⁰Menahem exacted this money from Israel. Every wealthy person had to contribute fifty shekelsᶜ of silver to be given to the king of Assyria. So the king of Assyria withdrew and stayed in the land no longer.

²¹As for the other events of Menahem's reign, and all he did, are they not written in the book of the annals of the kings of Israel? ²²Menahem rested with his ancestors. And Pekahiah his son succeeded him as king.

Pekahiah King of Israel

²³In the fiftieth year of Azariah king of Judah, Pekahiah son of Menahem became king of Israel in Samaria, and he reigned two years. ²⁴Pekahiah did evil in the eyes of the LORD. He did not turn away from the sins of Jeroboam son of Nebat, which he had caused Israel to commit. ²⁵One of his chief officers, Pekah son of Remaliah, conspired against him. Taking fifty men of Gilead with him, he assassinated Pekahiah, along with Argob and Arieh, in the citadel of the royal palace at Samaria. So Pekah killed Pekahiah and succeeded him as king.

²⁶The other events of Pekahiah's reign, and all he did, are written in the book of the annals of the kings of Israel.

Pekah King of Israel

²⁷In the fifty-second year of Azariah king of Judah, Pekah son of Remaliah became king of Israel in Samaria, and he reigned twenty years. ²⁸He did evil in the eyes of the LORD. He did not turn away from the sins of Jeroboam son of Nebat, which he had caused Israel to commit.

²⁹In the time of Pekah king of Israel, Tiglath-Pileser king of Assyria came and took Ijon, Abel Beth Maakah, Janoah, Kedesh and Hazor. He took Gilead and Galilee, including all the land of Naphtali, and deported the people to Assyria. ³⁰Then Hoshea son of Elah conspired against Pekah son of Remaliah. He attacked and assassinated him, and then succeeded him as king in the twentieth year of Jotham son of Uzziah.

THE **WITNESSES**

✓ **PUL** (2 KINGS 15:19)
Also called Tiglath-Pileser. There were three kings with this name. This one is Tiglath-Pileser III (the Third). He was king of Assyria, which was a very large territory at that time, 745 to 727 years before Christ.

ᵃ 19 Also called *Tiglath-Pileser*   ᵇ 19 That is, about 38 tons or about 34 metric tons   ᶜ 20 That is, about 1 1/4 pounds or about 575 grams

31As for the other events of Pekah's reign, and all he did, are they not written in the book of the annals of the kings of Israel?

Jotham King of Judah

32In the second year of Pekah son of Remaliah king of Israel, Jotham son of Uzziah king of Judah began to reign. 33He was twenty-five years old when he became king, and he reigned in Jerusalem sixteen years. His mother's name was Jerusha daughter of Zadok. 34He did what was right in the eyes of the LORD, just as his father Uzziah had done. 35The high places, however, were not removed; the people continued to offer sacrifices and burn incense there. Jotham rebuilt the Upper Gate of the temple of the LORD.

36As for the other events of Jotham's reign, and what he did, are they not written in the book of the annals of the kings of Judah? 37(In those days the LORD began to send Rezin king of Aram and Pekah son of Remaliah against Judah.) 38Jotham rested with his ancestors and was buried with them in the City of David, the city of his father. And Ahaz his son succeeded him as king.

Ahaz King of Judah

16 In the seventeenth year of Pekah son of Remaliah, Ahaz son of Jotham king of Judah began to reign. 2Ahaz was twenty years old when he became king, and he reigned in Jerusalem sixteen years. Unlike David his father, he did not do what was right in the eyes of the LORD his God. 3He followed the ways of the kings of Israel and even sacrificed his son in the fire, engaging in the detestable practices of the nations the LORD had driven out before the Israelites. 4He offered sacrifices and burned incense at the high places, on the hilltops and under every spreading tree.

5Then Rezin king of Aram and Pekah son of Remaliah king of Israel marched up to fight against Jerusalem and besieged Ahaz, but they could not overpower him. 6At that time, Rezin king of Aram recovered Elath for Aram by driving out the people of Judah. Edomites then moved into Elath and have lived there to this day.

7Ahaz sent messengers to say to Tiglath-Pileser king of Assyria, "I am your servant and vassal. Come up and save me out of the hand of the king of Aram and of the king of Israel, who are attacking me." 8And Ahaz took the silver and gold found in the temple of the LORD and in the treasuries of the royal palace and sent it as a gift to the king of Assyria. 9The king of Assyria complied by attacking Damascus and capturing it. He deported its inhabitants to Kir and put Rezin to death.

10Then King Ahaz went to Damascus to meet Tiglath-Pileser king of Assyria. He saw an altar in Damascus and sent to Uriah the priest a sketch of the altar, with detailed plans for its construction. 11So Uriah the priest built an altar in accordance with all the plans that King Ahaz had sent from Damascus and finished it before King Ahaz returned. 12When the king came back from Damascus and saw the altar, he approached it and presented offerings[a] on it. 13He offered up his burnt offering and grain offering, poured out his drink offering, and splashed the blood of his fellowship offerings against the altar. 14As for the bronze altar that stood before the LORD, he brought it from the front of the temple — from between the new altar and the temple of the LORD — and put it on the north side of the new altar.

15King Ahaz then gave these orders to Uriah the priest: "On the large new altar, offer the morning burnt offering and the evening grain offering, the king's burnt offering and his grain offering, and the burnt offering of all the people of the land, and their grain offering and their drink offering. Splash against this altar the blood of all the burnt offerings and sacrifices. But I will use the bronze altar for seeking guidance." 16And Uriah the priest did just as King Ahaz had ordered.

17King Ahaz cut off the side panels and removed the basins from the movable stands. He removed the Sea from the bronze bulls that supported it and set it

_____

a 12 Or and went up

on a stone base. [18]He took away the Sabbath canopy[a] that had been built at the temple and removed the royal entryway outside the temple of the LORD, in deference to the king of Assyria.

[19]As for the other events of the reign of Ahaz, and what he did, are they not written in the book of the annals of the kings of Judah? [20]Ahaz rested with his ancestors and was buried with them in the City of David. And Hezekiah his son succeeded him as king.

Hoshea Last King of Israel

17 In the twelfth year of Ahaz king of Judah, Hoshea son of Elah became king of Israel in Samaria, and he reigned nine years. [2]He did evil in the eyes of the LORD, but not like the kings of Israel who preceded him.

[3]Shalmaneser king of Assyria came up to attack Hoshea, who had been Shalmaneser's vassal and had paid him tribute. [4]But the king of Assyria discovered that Hoshea was a traitor, for he had sent envoys to So[b] king of Egypt, and he no longer paid tribute to the king of Assyria, as he had done year by year. Therefore Shalmaneser seized him and put him in prison. [5]The king of Assyria invaded the entire land, marched against Samaria and laid siege to it for three years. [6]In the ninth year of Hoshea, the king of Assyria captured Samaria and deported the Israelites to Assyria. He settled them in Halah, in Gozan on the Habor River and in the towns of the Medes.

Israel Exiled Because of Sin

[7]All this took place because the Israelites had sinned against the LORD their God, who had brought them up out of Egypt from under the power of Pharaoh king of Egypt. They worshiped other gods [8]and followed the practices of the nations the LORD had driven out before them, as well as the practices that the kings of Israel had introduced. [9]The Israelites secretly did things against the LORD their God that were not right. From watchtower to fortified city they built themselves high places in all their towns. [10]They set up sacred stones and

Asherah poles on every high hill and under every spreading tree. [11]At every high place they burned incense, as the nations whom the LORD had driven out before them had done. They did wicked things that aroused the LORD's anger. [12]They worshiped idols, though the LORD had said, "You shall not do this."[c] [13]The LORD warned Israel and Judah through all his prophets and seers: "Turn from your evil ways. Observe my commands and decrees, in accordance with the entire Law that I commanded your ancestors to obey and that I delivered to you through my servants the prophets."

[14]But they would not listen and were as stiff-necked as their ancestors, who did not trust in the LORD their God. [15]They rejected his decrees and the covenant he had made with their ancestors and the statutes he had warned them to keep. They followed worthless idols and themselves became worthless. They imitated the nations around them although the LORD had ordered them, "Do not do as they do."

[16]They forsook all the commands of the LORD their God and made for themselves two idols cast in the shape of calves, and an Asherah pole. They bowed down to all the starry hosts, and they worshiped Baal. [17]They sacrificed their sons and daughters in the fire. They practiced divination and sought omens and sold themselves to do evil in the eyes of the LORD, arousing his anger.

[18]So the LORD was very angry with Israel and removed them from his presence. Only the tribe of Judah was left, [19]and even Judah did not keep the commands of the LORD their God. They followed the practices Israel had introduced. [20]Therefore the LORD rejected all the people of Israel; he afflicted them and gave them into the hands of plunderers, until he thrust them from his presence.

[21]When he tore Israel away from the house of David, they made Jeroboam son of Nebat their king. Jeroboam enticed Israel away from following the LORD and

---

[a] 18 Or the dais of his throne (see Septuagint)
[b] 4 So is probably an abbreviation for Osorkon.
[c] 12 Exodus 20:4,5

caused them to commit a great sin. ²²The Israelites persisted in all the sins of Jeroboam and did not turn away from them ²³until the LORD removed them from his presence, as he had warned through all his servants the prophets. So the people of Israel were taken from their homeland into exile in Assyria, and they are still there.

Samaria Resettled

²⁴The king of Assyria brought people from Babylon, Kuthah, Avva, Hamath and Sepharvaim and settled them in the towns of Samaria to replace the Israelites. They took over Samaria and lived in its towns. ²⁵When they first lived there, they did not worship the LORD; so he sent lions among them and they killed some of the people. ²⁶It was reported to the king of Assyria: "The people you deported and resettled in the towns of Samaria do not know what the god of that country requires. He has sent lions among them, which are killing them off, because the people do not know what he requires." ²⁷Then the king of Assyria gave this order: "Have one of the priests you took captive from Samaria go back to live there and teach the people what the god of the land requires." ²⁸So one of the priests who had been exiled from Samaria came to live in Bethel and taught them how to worship the LORD.

²⁹Nevertheless, each national group made its own gods in the several towns where they settled, and set them up in the shrines the people of Samaria had made at the high places. ³⁰The people from Babylon made Sukkoth Benoth, those from Kuthah made Nergal, and those from Hamath made Ashima; ³¹the Avvites made Nibhaz and Tartak, and the Sepharvites burned their children in the fire as sacrifices to Adrammelek and Anammelek, the gods of Sepharvaim. ³²They worshiped the LORD, but they also appointed all sorts of their own people to officiate for them as priests in the shrines at the high places. ³³They worshiped the LORD, but they also served their own gods in accordance with the customs of the nations from which they had been brought.

³⁴To this day they persist in their former practices. They neither worship the LORD nor adhere to the decrees and regulations, the laws and commands that the LORD gave the descendants of Jacob, whom he named Israel. ³⁵When the LORD made a covenant with the Israelites, he commanded them: "Do not worship any other gods or bow down to them, serve them or sacrifice to them. ³⁶But the LORD, who brought you up out of Egypt with mighty power and outstretched arm, is the one you must worship. To him you shall bow down and to him offer sacrifices.

THE
WITNESSES

✓ **SHALMANESER** (2 KINGS 17:3)
His full name was Shalmaneser V (the Fifth), and he ruled Assyria between the years 727 and 722 before Christ. He was the son of Tiglath-Pileser III (the Third). He conquered the Israelites and made them pay taxes.

37You must always be careful to keep the decrees and regulations, the laws and commands he wrote for you. Do not worship other gods. 38Do not forget the covenant I have made with you, and do not worship other gods. 39Rather, worship the LORD your God; it is he who will deliver you from the hand of all your enemies."

40They would not listen, however, but persisted in their former practices. 41Even while these people were worshiping the LORD, they were serving their idols. To this day their children and grandchildren continue to do as their ancestors did.

Hezekiah King of Judah

18 In the third year of Hoshea son of Elah king of Israel, Hezekiah son of Ahaz king of Judah began to reign. 2He was twenty-five years old when he became king, and he reigned in Jerusalem twenty-nine years. His mother's name was Abijah*a* daughter of Zechariah. 3He did what was right in the eyes of the LORD, just as his father David had done. 4He removed the high places, smashed the sacred stones and cut down the Asherah poles. He broke into pieces the bronze snake Moses had made, for up to that time the Israelites had been burning incense to it. (It was called Nehushtan.*b*)

5Hezekiah trusted in the LORD, the God of Israel. There was no one like him among all the kings of Judah, either before him or after him. 6He held fast to the LORD and did not stop following him; he kept the commands the LORD had given Moses. 7And the LORD was with him; he was successful in whatever he undertook. He rebelled against the king of Assyria and did not serve him. 8From watchtower to fortified city, he defeated the Philistines, as far as Gaza and its territory.

9In King Hezekiah's fourth year, which was the seventh year of Hoshea son of Elah king of Israel, Shalmaneser king of Assyria marched against Samaria and laid siege to it. 10At the end of three years the Assyrians took it. So Samaria was captured in Hezekiah's sixth year, which was the ninth year of Hoshea king of Is-

rael. 11The king of Assyria deported Israel to Assyria and settled them in Halah, in Gozan on the Habor River and in towns of the Medes. 12This happened because they had not obeyed the LORD their God, but had violated his covenant—all that Moses the servant of the LORD commanded. They neither listened to the commands nor carried them out.

13In the fourteenth year of King Hezekiah's reign, Sennacherib king of Assyria attacked all the fortified cities of Judah and captured them. 14So Hezekiah king of Judah sent this message to the king of Assyria at Lachish: "I have done wrong. Withdraw from me, and I will pay whatever you demand of me." The king of Assyria exacted from Hezekiah king of Judah three hundred talents*c* of silver and thirty talents*d* of gold. 15So Hezekiah gave him all the silver that was found in the temple of the LORD and in the treasuries of the royal palace.

16At this time Hezekiah king of Judah stripped off the gold with which he had covered the doors and doorposts of the temple of the LORD, and gave it to the king of Assyria.

Sennacherib Threatens Jerusalem

17The king of Assyria sent his supreme commander, his chief officer and his field commander with a large army, from Lachish to King Hezekiah at Jerusalem. They came up to Jerusalem and stopped at the aqueduct of the Upper Pool, on the road to the Washerman's Field. 18They called for the king; and Eliakim son of Hilkiah the palace administrator, Shebna the secretary, and Joah son of Asaph the recorder went out to them.

19The field commander said to them, "Tell Hezekiah:

"'This is what the great king, the king of Assyria, says: On what are you basing this confidence of yours? 20You say you have the counsel and the might for war—but you speak only empty words. On whom are you

---

a 2 Hebrew *Abi,* a variant of *Abijah*   *b 4* Nehushtan sounds like the Hebrew for both *bronze* and *snake.*
c 14 That is, about 11 tons or about 10 metric tons
d 14 That is, about 1 ton or about 1 metric ton

depending, that you rebel against me? ²¹Look, I know you are depending on Egypt, that splintered reed of a staff, which pierces the hand of anyone who leans on it! Such is Pharaoh king of Egypt to all who depend on him. ²²But if you say to me, "We are depending on the LORD our God"—isn't he the one whose high places and altars Hezekiah removed, saying to Judah and Jerusalem, "You must worship before this altar in Jerusalem"?

²³"'Come now, make a bargain with my master, the king of Assyria: I will give you two thousand horses—if you can put riders on them! ²⁴How can you repulse one officer of the least of my master's officials, even though you are depending on Egypt for chariots and horsemen*a*? ²⁵Furthermore, have I come to attack and destroy this place without word from the LORD? The LORD himself told me to march against this country and destroy it.'"

²⁶Then Eliakim son of Hilkiah, and Shebna and Joah said to the field commander, "Please speak to your servants in Aramaic, since we understand it. Don't speak to us in Hebrew in the hearing of the people on the wall."

²⁷But the commander replied, "Was it only to your master and you that my master sent me to say these things, and not to the people sitting on the wall—who, like you, will have to eat their own excrement and drink their own urine?"

²⁸Then the commander stood and called out in Hebrew, "Hear the word of the great king, the king of Assyria! ²⁹This is what the king says: Do not let Hezekiah deceive you. He cannot deliver you from my hand. ³⁰Do not let Hezekiah persuade you to trust in the LORD when he says, 'The LORD will surely deliver us; this city will not be given into the hand of the king of Assyria.'

³¹"Do not listen to Hezekiah. This is what the king of Assyria says: Make peace with me and come out to me. Then each of you will eat fruit from your own vine and fig tree and drink water from your own cistern, ³²until I come and take you to

THE WITNESSES

✓ HEZEKIAH (2 KINGS 18:1)
This name means "God is my strength." He was king of Judah. He did good things for God, like destroy all the altars of other gods. He reopened the temple in Jerusalem. He also built a tunnel through rock in order to get water for the city.

✓ SENNACHERIB (2 KINGS 18:13)
He was king of Assyria between 705 and 681 years before Christ. His name means "the moon-god has replaced my brother."

a land like your own—a land of grain and new wine, a land of bread and vineyards, a land of olive trees and honey. Choose life and not death!

"Do not listen to Hezekiah, for he is misleading you when he says, 'The LORD will deliver us.' ³³Has the god of any nation ever delivered his land from the hand of the king of Assyria? ³⁴Where are the

a 24 Or charioteers

gods of Hamath and Arpad? Where are the gods of Sepharvaim, Hena and Iv-vah? Have they rescued Samaria from my hand? ³⁵Who of all the gods of these countries has been able to save his land from me? How then can the LORD deliver Jerusalem from my hand?"

³⁶But the people remained silent and said nothing in reply, because the king had commanded, "Do not answer him."

³⁷Then Eliakim son of Hilkiah the palace administrator, Shebna the secretary, and Joah son of Asaph the recorder went to Hezekiah, with their clothes torn, and told him what the field commander had said.

Jerusalem's Deliverance Foretold

19 When King Hezekiah heard this, he tore his clothes and put on sackcloth and went into the temple of the LORD. ²He sent Eliakim the palace administrator, Shebna the secretary and the leading priests, all wearing sackcloth, to the prophet Isaiah son of Amoz. ³They told him, "This is what Hezekiah says: This day is a day of distress and rebuke and disgrace, as when children come to the moment of birth and there is no strength to deliver them. ⁴It may be that the LORD your God will hear all the words of the field commander, whom his master, the king of Assyria, has sent to ridicule the living God, and that he will rebuke him for the words the LORD your God has heard. Therefore pray for the remnant that still survives."

⁵When King Hezekiah's officials came to Isaiah, ⁶Isaiah said to them, "Tell your master, 'This is what the LORD says: Do not be afraid of what you have heard — those words with which the underlings of the king of Assyria have blasphemed me. ⁷Listen! When he hears a certain report, I will make him want to return to his own country, and there I will have him cut down with the sword.' "

⁸When the field commander heard that the king of Assyria had left Lachish, he withdrew and found the king fighting against Libnah.

⁹Now Sennacherib received a report that Tirhakah, the king of Cush,ᵃ was marching out to fight against him. So he again sent messengers to Hezekiah with this word: ¹⁰"Say to Hezekiah king of Judah: Do not let the god you depend on deceive you when he says, 'Jerusalem will not be given into the hands of the king of Assyria.' ¹¹Surely you have heard what the kings of Assyria have done to all the countries, destroying them completely. And will you be delivered? ¹²Did the gods of the nations that were destroyed by my predecessors deliver them—the gods of Gozan, Harran, Rezeph and the people of Eden who were in Tel Assar? ¹³Where is the king of Hamath or the king of Arpad? Where are the kings of Lair, Sepharvaim, Hena and Ivvah?"

Hezekiah's Prayer

¹⁴Hezekiah received the letter from the messengers and read it. Then he went up to the temple of the LORD and spread it out before the LORD. ¹⁵And Hezekiah prayed to the LORD: "LORD, the God of Israel, enthroned between the cherubim, you alone are God over all the kingdoms of the earth. You have made heaven and earth. ¹⁶Give ear, LORD, and hear; open your eyes, LORD, and see; listen to the words Sennacherib has sent to ridicule the living God.

¹⁷"It is true, LORD, that the Assyrian kings have laid waste these nations and their lands. ¹⁸They have thrown their gods into the fire and destroyed them, for they were not gods but only wood and stone, fashioned by human hands. ¹⁹Now, LORD our God, deliver us from his hand, so that all the kingdoms of the earth may know that you alone, LORD, are God."

Isaiah Prophesies Sennacherib's Fall

²⁰Then Isaiah son of Amoz sent a message to Hezekiah: "This is what the LORD, the God of Israel, says: I have heard your prayer concerning Sennacherib king of Assyria. ²¹This is the word that the LORD has spoken against him:

" 'Virgin Daughter Zion
    despises you and mocks you.

ᵃ 9 That is, the upper Nile region

Daughter Jerusalem
tosses her head as you flee.
22 Who is it you have ridiculed and
blasphemed?
Against whom have you raised your
voice
and lifted your eyes in pride?
Against the Holy One of Israel!
23 By your messengers
you have ridiculed the Lord.
And you have said,
"With my many chariots
I have ascended the heights of the
mountains,
the utmost heights of Lebanon.

THE
WITNESSES

✓ **ISAIAH** (2 KINGS 19:2)
Isaiah means "the LORD is salvation." He was the
prophet that God used to give a special message
to Israel. In the Bible, there's an entire book that
has his name. It tells about all the adventures
this prophet had.

I have cut down its tallest cedars,
the choicest of its junipers.
I have reached its remotest parts,
the finest of its forests.
24 I have dug wells in foreign lands
and drunk the water there.
With the soles of my feet
I have dried up all the streams of
Egypt."

25 " 'Have you not heard?
Long ago I ordained it.
In days of old I planned it;
now I have brought it to pass,
that you have turned fortified cities
into piles of stone.
26 Their people, drained of power,
are dismayed and put to shame.
They are like plants in the field,
like tender green shoots,
like grass sprouting on the roof,
scorched before it grows up.

27 " 'But I know where you are
and when you come and go
and how you rage against me.
28 Because you rage against me
and because your insolence has
reached my ears,
I will put my hook in your nose
and my bit in your mouth,
and I will make you return
by the way you came.'

29 "This will be the sign for you, Hezekiah:

"This year you will eat what grows by
itself,
and the second year what springs
from that.
But in the third year sow and reap,
plant vineyards and eat their fruit.
30 Once more a remnant of the kingdom
of Judah
will take root below and bear fruit
above.
31 For out of Jerusalem will come a
remnant,
and out of Mount Zion a band of
survivors.

"The zeal of the LORD Almighty will accomplish this.

32 "Therefore this is what the LORD says
concerning the king of Assyria:

" 'He will not enter this city
or shoot an arrow here.
He will not come before it with
shield
or build a siege ramp against it.
³³ By the way that he came he will
return;
he will not enter this city,
declares the LORD.
³⁴ I will defend this city and save it,
for my sake and for the sake of
David my servant.' "

³⁵ That night the angel of the LORD went out and put to death a hundred and eighty-five thousand in the Assyrian camp. When the people got up the next morning—there were all the dead bodies! ³⁶ So Sennacherib king of Assyria broke

CHECK THE FACTS

When King Hezekiah got seriously ill and was about to die, what happened?

A) He prayed to God and cried because he was very sad.

B) God heard his prayer, saw his tears and healed him.

C) Both answers are correct.

CORRECT ANSWER: C

camp and withdrew. He returned to Nineveh and stayed there.

³⁷ One day, while he was worshiping in the temple of his god Nisrok, his sons Adrammelek and Sharezer killed him with the sword, and they escaped to the land of Ararat. And Esarhaddon his son succeeded him as king.

Hezekiah's Illness

20 In those days Hezekiah became ill and was at the point of death. The prophet Isaiah son of Amoz went to him and said, "This is what the LORD says: Put your house in order, because you are going to die; you will not recover."

² Hezekiah turned his face to the wall and prayed to the LORD, ³ "Remember, LORD, how I have walked before you faithfully and with wholehearted devotion and have done what is good in your eyes." And Hezekiah wept bitterly.

⁴ Before Isaiah had left the middle court, the word of the LORD came to him: ⁵ "Go back and tell Hezekiah, the ruler of my people, 'This is what the LORD, the God of your father David, says: I have heard your prayer and seen your tears; I will heal you. On the third day from now you will go up to the temple of the LORD. ⁶ I will add fifteen years to your life. And I will deliver you and this city from the hand of the king of Assyria. I will defend this city for my sake and for the sake of my servant David.' "

⁷ Then Isaiah said, "Prepare a poultice of figs." They did so and applied it to the boil, and he recovered.

⁸ Hezekiah had asked Isaiah, "What will be the sign that the LORD will heal me and that I will go up to the temple of the LORD on the third day from now?"

⁹ Isaiah answered, "This is the LORD's sign to you that the LORD will do what he has promised: Shall the shadow go forward ten steps, or shall it go back ten steps?"

¹⁰ "It is a simple matter for the shadow to go forward ten steps," said Hezekiah. "Rather, have it go back ten steps."

¹¹ Then the prophet Isaiah called on the LORD, and the LORD made the shadow go back the ten steps it had gone down on the stairway of Ahaz.

Envoys From Babylon

[12]At that time Marduk-Baladan son of Baladan king of Babylon sent Hezekiah letters and a gift, because he had heard of Hezekiah's illness. [13]Hezekiah received the envoys and showed them all that was in his storehouses—the silver, the gold, the spices and the fine olive oil—his armory and everything found among his treasures. There was nothing in his palace or in all his kingdom that Hezekiah did not show them.

[14]Then Isaiah the prophet went to King Hezekiah and asked, "What did those men say, and where did they come from?"

"From a distant land," Hezekiah replied. "They came from Babylon."

[15]The prophet asked, "What did they see in your palace?"

"They saw everything in my palace," Hezekiah said. "There is nothing among my treasures that I did not show them."

[16]Then Isaiah said to Hezekiah, "Hear the word of the Lord: [17]The time will surely come when everything in your palace, and all that your predecessors have stored up until this day, will be carried off to Babylon. Nothing will be left, says the Lord. [18]And some of your descendants, your own flesh and blood who will be born to you, will be taken away, and they will become eunuchs in the palace of the king of Babylon."

[19]"The word of the Lord you have spoken is good," Hezekiah replied. For he thought, "Will there not be peace and security in my lifetime?"

[20]As for the other events of Hezekiah's reign, all his achievements and how he made the pool and the tunnel by which he brought water into the city, are they not written in the book of the annals of the kings of Judah? [21]Hezekiah rested with his ancestors. And Manasseh his son succeeded him as king.

Manasseh King of Judah

21 Manasseh was twelve years old when he became king, and he reigned in Jerusalem fifty-five years. His mother's name was Hephzibah. [2]He did evil in the eyes of the Lord, following the detestable practices of the nations the Lord had driven out before the Israelites. [3]He rebuilt the high places his father Hezekiah had destroyed; he also erected altars to Baal and made an Asherah pole, as Ahab king of Israel had done. He bowed down to all the starry hosts and worshiped them. [4]He built altars in the temple of the Lord, of which the Lord had said, "In Jerusalem I will put my Name." [5]In the two courts of the temple of the Lord, he built altars to all the starry hosts. [6]He sacrificed his own son in the fire, practiced divination, sought omens, and consulted mediums and spiritists. He did much evil in the eyes of the Lord, arousing his anger.

[7]He took the carved Asherah pole he had made and put it in the temple, of which the Lord had said to David and to his son Solomon, "In this temple and in Jerusalem, which I have chosen out of all the tribes of Israel, I will put my Name forever. [8]I will not again make the feet of the Israelites wander from the land I gave their ancestors, if only they will be careful to do everything I commanded them and will keep the whole Law that my servant Moses gave them." [9]But the people did not listen. Manasseh led them astray, so that they did more evil than the nations the Lord had destroyed before the Israelites.

[10]The Lord said through his servants the prophets: [11]"Manasseh king of Judah has committed these detestable sins. He has done more evil than the Amorites who preceded him and has led Judah into sin with his idols. [12]Therefore this is what the Lord, the God of Israel, says: I am going to bring such disaster on Jerusalem and Judah that the ears of everyone who hears of it will tingle. [13]I will stretch out over Jerusalem the measuring line used against Samaria and the plumb line used against the house of Ahab. I will wipe out Jerusalem as one wipes a dish, wiping it and turning it upside down. [14]I will forsake the remnant of my inheritance and give them into the hands of enemies. They will be looted and plundered by all their enemies; [15]they have done evil in my eyes and have aroused my anger from the day their ancestors came out of Egypt until this day."

[16]Moreover, Manasseh also shed so

much innocent blood that he filled Jerusalem from end to end—besides the sin that he had caused Judah to commit, so that they did evil in the eyes of the LORD. ¹⁷As for the other events of Manasseh's reign, and all he did, including the sin he committed, are they not written in the book of the annals of the kings of Judah? ¹⁸Manasseh rested with his ancestors and was buried in his palace garden, the garden of Uzza. And Amon his son succeeded him as king.

Amon King of Judah

¹⁹Amon was twenty-two years old when he became king, and he reigned in Jerusalem two years. His mother's name was Meshullemeth daughter of Haruz; she was from Jotbah. ²⁰He did evil in the eyes of the LORD, as his father Manasseh had done. ²¹He followed completely the ways of his father, worshiping the idols his father had worshiped, and bowing down to them. ²²He forsook the LORD, the God of his ancestors, and did not walk in obedience to him.

²³Amon's officials conspired against him and assassinated the king in his palace. ²⁴Then the people of the land killed all who had plotted against King Amon, and they made Josiah his son king in his place.

²⁵As for the other events of Amon's reign, and what he did, are they not written in the book of the annals of the kings of Judah? ²⁶He was buried in his tomb in the garden of Uzza. And Josiah his son succeeded him as king.

The Book of the Law Found

22 Josiah was eight years old when he became king, and he reigned in Jerusalem thirty-one years. His mother's name was Jedidah daughter of Adaiah; she was from Bozkath. ²He did what was right in the eyes of the LORD and followed completely the ways of his father David, not turning aside to the right or to the left.

³In the eighteenth year of his reign, King Josiah sent the secretary, Shaphan son of Azaliah, the son of Meshullam, to the temple of the LORD. He said: ⁴"Go up to Hilkiah the high priest and have him get ready the money that has been

THE
WITNESSES

✓ **JOSIAH** (2 KINGS 22:1)
His name means "God heals." He was a good king, and he governed for 31 years. Once, when he found the Book of the Law of God, he had it read. When he understood what it said, he was very sad, and he repented of everything bad he had done.

brought into the temple of the LORD, which the doorkeepers have collected from the people. ⁵Have them entrust it to the men appointed to supervise the work on the temple. And have these men pay the workers who repair the temple of the LORD— ⁶the carpenters, the builders and the masons. Also have them purchase timber and dressed stone to repair the temple. ⁷But they need not account for the money entrusted to them, because they are honest in their dealings."

⁸Hilkiah the high priest said to Shaphan the secretary, "I have found the Book of

the Law in the temple of the LORD." He gave it to Shaphan, who read it. ⁹Then Shaphan the secretary went to the king and reported to him: "Your officials have paid out the money that was in the temple of the LORD and have entrusted it to the workers and supervisors at the temple." ¹⁰Then Shaphan the secretary informed the king, "Hilkiah the priest has given me a book." And Shaphan read from it in the presence of the king.

¹¹When the king heard the words of the Book of the Law, he tore his robes. ¹²He gave these orders to Hilkiah the priest, Ahikam son of Shaphan, Akbor son of Micaiah, Shaphan the secretary and Asaiah the king's attendant: ¹³"Go and inquire of the LORD for me and for the people and for all Judah about what is written in this book that has been found. Great is the LORD's anger that burns against us because those who have gone before us have not obeyed the words of this book; they have not acted in accordance with all that is written there concerning us."

¹⁴Hilkiah the priest, Ahikam, Akbor, Shaphan and Asaiah went to speak to the prophet Huldah, who was the wife of Shallum son of Tikvah, the son of Harhas, keeper of the wardrobe. She lived in Jerusalem, in the New Quarter.

¹⁵She said to them, "This is what the LORD, the God of Israel, says: Tell the man who sent you to me, ¹⁶'This is what the LORD says: I am going to bring disaster on this place and its people, according to everything written in the book the king of Judah has read. ¹⁷Because they have forsaken me and burned incense to other gods and aroused my anger by all the idols their hands have made,ᵃ my anger will burn against this place and will not be quenched.' ¹⁸Tell the king of Judah, who sent you to inquire of the LORD, 'This is what the LORD, the God of Israel, says concerning the words you heard: ¹⁹Because your heart was responsive and you humbled yourself before the LORD when you heard what I have spoken against this place and its people—that they would become a curseᵇ and be laid waste—and because you tore your robes and wept in my presence, I also have heard you, declares

the LORD. ²⁰Therefore I will gather you to your ancestors, and you will be buried in peace. Your eyes will not see all the disaster I am going to bring on this place.'"

So they took her answer back to the king.

Josiah Renews the Covenant

23 Then the king called together all the elders of Judah and Jerusalem. ²He went up to the temple of the LORD with the people of Judah, the inhabitants of Jerusalem, the priests and the prophets—all the people from the least to the greatest. He read in their hearing all the words of the Book of the Covenant, which had been found in the temple of the LORD. ³The king stood by the pillar and renewed the covenant in the presence of the LORD—to follow the LORD and keep his commands, statutes and decrees with all his heart and all his soul, thus confirming the words of the covenant written in this book. Then all the people pledged themselves to the covenant.

⁴The king ordered Hilkiah the high priest, the priests next in rank and the doorkeepers to remove from the temple of the LORD all the articles made for Baal and Asherah and all the starry hosts. He burned them outside Jerusalem in the fields of the Kidron Valley and took the ashes to Bethel. ⁵He did away with the idolatrous priests appointed by the kings of Judah to burn incense on the high places of the towns of Judah and on those around Jerusalem—those who burned incense to Baal, to the sun and moon, to the constellations and to all the starry hosts. ⁶He took the Asherah pole from the temple of the LORD to the Kidron Valley outside Jerusalem and burned it there. He ground it to powder and scattered the dust over the graves of the common people. ⁷He also tore down the quarters of the male shrine prostitutes that were in the temple of the LORD, the quarters where women did weaving for Asherah.

⁸Josiah brought all the priests from the towns of Judah and desecrated the high

---

ᵃ *17 Or by everything they have done*   ᵇ *19 That is, their names would be used in cursing (see Jer. 29:22); or, others would see that they are cursed.*

places, from Geba to Beersheba, where the priests had burned incense. He broke down the gateway at the entrance of the Gate of Joshua, the city governor, which was on the left of the city gate. ⁹Although the priests of the high places did not serve at the altar of the LORD in Jerusalem, they ate unleavened bread with their fellow priests.

¹⁰He desecrated Topheth, which was in the Valley of Ben Hinnom, so no one could use it to sacrifice their son or daughter in the fire to Molek. ¹¹He removed from the entrance to the temple of the LORD the horses that the kings of Judah had dedicated to the sun. They were in the court[a] near the room of an official named Nathan-Melek. Josiah then burned the chariots dedicated to the sun.

¹²He pulled down the altars the kings of Judah had erected on the roof near the upper room of Ahaz, and the altars Manasseh had built in the two courts of the temple of the LORD. He removed them from there, smashed them to pieces and threw the rubble into the Kidron Valley. ¹³The king also desecrated the high places that were east of Jerusalem on the south of the Hill of Corruption—the ones Solomon king of Israel had built for Ashtoreth the vile goddess of the Sidonians, for Chemosh the vile god of Moab, and for Molek the detestable god of the people of Ammon. ¹⁴Josiah smashed the sacred stones and cut down the Asherah poles and covered the sites with human bones.

¹⁵Even the altar at Bethel, the high place made by Jeroboam son of Nebat, who had caused Israel to sin—even that altar and high place he demolished. He burned the high place and ground it to powder, and burned the Asherah pole also. ¹⁶Then Josiah looked around, and when he saw the tombs that were there on the hillside, he had the bones removed from them and burned on the altar to defile it, in accordance with the word of the LORD proclaimed by the man of God who foretold these things.

¹⁷The king asked, "What is that tombstone I see?"

The people of the city said, "It marks the tomb of the man of God who came from Judah and pronounced against the altar of Bethel the very things you have done to it."

¹⁸"Leave it alone," he said. "Don't let anyone disturb his bones." So they spared his bones and those of the prophet who had come from Samaria.

¹⁹Just as he had done at Bethel, Josiah removed all the shrines at the high places that the kings of Israel had built in the towns of Samaria and that had aroused the LORD's anger. ²⁰Josiah slaughtered all the priests of those high places on the altars and burned human bones on them. Then he went back to Jerusalem.

²¹The king gave this order to all the people: "Celebrate the Passover to the LORD your God, as it is written in this Book of the Covenant." ²²Neither in the days of the judges who led Israel nor in the days of the kings of Israel and the kings of Judah had any such Passover been observed. ²³But in the eighteenth year of King Josiah, this Passover was celebrated to the LORD in Jerusalem.

²⁴Furthermore, Josiah got rid of the mediums and spiritists, the household gods, the idols and all the other detestable things seen in Judah and Jerusalem. This he did to fulfill the requirements of the law written in the book that Hilkiah the priest had discovered in the temple of the LORD. ²⁵Neither before nor after Josiah was there a king like him who turned to the LORD as he did—with all his heart and with all his soul and with all his strength, in accordance with all the Law of Moses.

²⁶Nevertheless, the LORD did not turn away from the heat of his fierce anger, which burned against Judah because of all that Manasseh had done to arouse his anger. ²⁷So the LORD said, "I will remove Judah also from my presence as I removed Israel, and I will reject Jerusalem, the city I chose, and this temple, about which I said, 'My Name shall be there.'[b]

²⁸As for the other events of Josiah's reign, and all he did, are they not written in the book of the annals of the kings of Judah?

²⁹While Josiah was king, Pharaoh Necho king of Egypt went up to the Euphra-

---

[a] 11 The meaning of the Hebrew for this word is uncertain.
[b] 27 1 Kings 8:29

tes River to help the king of Assyria. King Josiah marched out to meet him in battle, but Necho faced him and killed him at Megiddo. ³⁰Josiah's servants brought his body in a chariot from Megiddo to Jerusalem and buried him in his own tomb. And the people of the land took Jehoahaz son of Josiah and anointed him and made him king in place of his father.

Jehoahaz King of Judah

³¹Jehoahaz was twenty-three years old when he became king, and he reigned in Jerusalem three months. His mother's name was Hamutal daughter of Jeremiah; she was from Libnah. ³²He did evil in the eyes of the LORD, just as his predecessors had done. ³³Pharaoh Necho put him in chains at Riblah in the land of Hamath so that he might not reign in Jerusalem, and he imposed on Judah a levy of a hundred talents*ᵃ* of silver and a talent*ᵇ* of gold. ³⁴Pharaoh Necho made Eliakim son of Josiah king in place of his father Josiah and changed Eliakim's name to Jehoiakim. But he took Jehoahaz and carried him off to Egypt, and there he died. ³⁵Jehoiakim paid Pharaoh Necho the silver and gold he demanded. In order to do so, he taxed the land and exacted the silver and gold from the people of the land according to their assessments.

Jehoiakim King of Judah

³⁶Jehoiakim was twenty-five years old when he became king, and he reigned in Jerusalem eleven years. His mother's name was Zebidah daughter of Pedaiah; she was from Rumah. ³⁷And he did evil in the eyes of the LORD, just as his predecessors had done.

24 During Jehoiakim's reign, Nebuchadnezzar king of Babylon invaded the land, and Jehoiakim became his vassal for three years. But then he turned against Nebuchadnezzar and rebelled. ²The LORD sent Babylonian,*ᶜ* Aramean, Moabite and Ammonite raiders against him to destroy Judah, in accordance with the word of the LORD proclaimed by his servants the prophets. ³Surely these things happened to Judah according to the

LORD's command, in order to remove them from his presence because of the sins of Manasseh and all he had done, ⁴including the shedding of innocent blood. For he had filled Jerusalem with innocent blood, and the LORD was not willing to forgive.

⁵As for the other events of Jehoiakim's reign, and all he did, are they not written in the book of the annals of the kings of Judah? ⁶Jehoiakim rested with his ancestors. And Jehoiachin his son succeeded him as king.

⁷The king of Egypt did not march out from his own country again, because the king of Babylon had taken all his territory, from the Wadi of Egypt to the Euphrates River.

ᵃ 33 That is, about 3 3/4 tons or about 3.4 metric tons
ᵇ 33 That is, about 75 pounds or about 34 kilograms
ᶜ 2 Or *Chaldean*

THE
WITNESSES

✓ **NEBUCHADNEZZAR (2 KINGS 24:1)**
Read this explanation in Jeremiah 21:2.

Jehoiachin King of Judah

8 Jehoiachin was eighteen years old when he became king, and he reigned in Jerusalem three months. His mother's name was Nehushta daughter of Elnathan; she was from Jerusalem. 9He did evil in the eyes of the LORD, just as his father had done.

10At that time the officers of Nebuchadnezzar king of Babylon advanced on Jerusalem and laid siege to it, 11and Nebuchadnezzar himself came up to the city while his officers were besieging it. 12Jehoiachin king of Judah, his mother, his attendants, his nobles and his officials all surrendered to him.

In the eighth year of the reign of the king of Babylon, he took Jehoiachin prisoner. 13As the LORD had declared, Nebuchadnezzar removed the treasures from the temple of the LORD and from the royal palace, and cut up the gold articles that Solomon king of Israel had made for the temple of the LORD. 14He carried all Jerusalem into exile: all the officers and fighting men, and all the skilled workers and artisans—a total of ten thousand. Only the poorest people of the land were left.

15Nebuchadnezzar took Jehoiachin captive to Babylon. He also took from Jerusalem to Babylon the king's mother, his wives, his officials and the prominent people of the land. 16The king of Babylon also deported to Babylon the entire force of seven thousand fighting men, strong and fit for war, and a thousand skilled workers and artisans. 17He made Mattaniah, Jehoiachin's uncle, king in his place and changed his name to Zedekiah.

Zedekiah King of Judah

18Zedekiah was twenty-one years old when he became king, and he reigned in Jerusalem eleven years. His mother's name was Hamutal daughter of Jeremiah; she was from Libnah. 19He did evil in the eyes of the LORD, just as Jehoiakim had done. 20It was because of the LORD's anger that all this happened to Jerusalem and Judah, and in the end he thrust them from his presence.

The Fall of Jerusalem

Now Zedekiah rebelled against the king of Babylon.

25 So in the ninth year of Zedekiah's reign, on the tenth day of the tenth month, Nebuchadnezzar king of Babylon marched against Jerusalem with his whole army. He encamped outside the city and built siege works all around it. 2The city was kept under siege until the eleventh year of King Zedekiah.

3By the ninth day of the fourtha month the famine in the city had become so severe that there was no food for the people to eat. 4Then the city wall was broken through, and the whole army fled at night through the gate between the two walls near the king's garden, though the Babyloniansb were surrounding the city. They fled toward the Arabah,c 5but the Babylonian d army pursued the king and overtook

---

a 3 Probable reading of the original Hebrew text (see Jer. 52:6); Masoretic Text does not have *fourth*.   b 4 Or *Chaldeans*; also in verses 13, 25 and 26   c 4 Or *the Jordan Valley*   d 5 Or *Chaldean*; also in verses 10 and 24

The tenth month
(2 KINGS 25:1)

That was Tebeth, the tenth month of the Jewish lunar calendar. In our solar calendar, that would be more or less from the middle of December to the middle of January.

him in the plains of Jericho. All his soldiers were separated from him and scattered, ⁶and he was captured.

He was taken to the king of Babylon at Riblah, where sentence was pronounced on him. ⁷They killed the sons of Zedekiah before his eyes. Then they put out his eyes, bound him with bronze shackles and took him to Babylon.

⁸On the seventh day of the fifth month, in the nineteenth year of Nebuchadnezzar king of Babylon, Nebuzaradan commander of the imperial guard, an official of the king of Babylon, came to Jerusalem. ⁹He set fire to the temple of the Lᴏʀᴅ, the royal palace and all the houses of Jerusalem. Every important building he burned down. ¹⁰The whole Babylonian army under the commander of the imperial guard broke down the walls around Jerusalem. ¹¹Nebuzaradan the commander of the guard carried into exile the people who remained in the city, along with the rest of the populace and those who had deserted to the king of Babylon. ¹²But the commander left

BREAK THROUGH!

The fifth month
(2 KINGS 25:8)

That is called Ab in the Jewish lunar calendar. In our solar calendar, that's the period from the middle of July to the middle of August.

behind some of the poorest people of the land to work the vineyards and fields.

¹³The Babylonians broke up the bronze pillars, the movable stands and the bronze Sea that were at the temple of the Lᴏʀᴅ and they carried the bronze to Babylon. ¹⁴They also took away the pots, shovels, wick trimmers, dishes and all the bronze articles used in the temple service. ¹⁵The commander of the imperial guard took away the censers and sprinkling bowls— all that were made of pure gold or silver.

¹⁶The bronze from the two pillars, the Sea and the movable stands, which Solomon had made for the temple of the Lᴏʀᴅ, was more than could be weighed. ¹⁷Each pillar was eighteen cubits*a* high. The bronze capital on top of one pillar was three cubits*b* high and was decorated with a network and pomegranates of bronze all around. The other pillar, with its network, was similar.

¹⁸The commander of the guard took as prisoners Seraiah the chief priest,

BREAK THROUGH!

The fourth month
(2 KINGS 25:3)

That was Tammuz, the fourth month of the Jewish lunar calendar. In our solar calendar, that would be from the middle of June to the middle of July.

---

a 17 That is, about 27 feet or about 8.1 meters
b 17 That is, about 4 1/2 feet or about 1.4 meters

Zephaniah the priest next in rank and the three doorkeepers. [19]Of those still in the city, he took the officer in charge of the fighting men, and five royal advisers. He also took the secretary who was chief officer in charge of conscripting the people of the land and sixty of the conscripts who were found in the city. [20]Nebuzaradan the commander took them all and brought them to the king of Babylon at Riblah. [21]There at Riblah, in the land of Hamath, the king had them executed.

So Judah went into captivity, away from her land.

[22]Nebuchadnezzar king of Babylon appointed Gedaliah son of Ahikam, the son of Shaphan, to be over the people he had left behind in Judah. [23]When all the army officers and their men heard that the king of Babylon had appointed Gedaliah as governor, they came to Gedaliah at Mizpah—Ishmael son of Nethaniah, Johanan son of Kareah, Seraiah son of Tanhumeth the Netophathite, Jaazaniah the son of the Maakathite, and their men. [24]Gedaliah took an oath to reassure them and their men. "Do not be afraid of the Babylonian officials," he said. "Settle down in the land and serve the king of Babylon, and it will go well with you."

[25]In the seventh month, however, Ishmael son of Nethaniah, the son of Elishama, who was of royal blood, came with ten men and assassinated Gedaliah and also the men of Judah and the Babylonians who were with him at Mizpah. [26]At this, all the people from the least to the greatest, together with the army officers, fled to Egypt for fear of the Babylonians.

Jehoiachin Released

[27]In the thirty-seventh year of the exile of Jehoiachin king of Judah, in the year

THE WITNESSES

✓ **AWEL-MARDUK** (2 KINGS 25:27)
He was Nebuchadnezzar's son. His name is Babylonian and means "worshiper of the god Marduk."

BREAKTHROUGH!

The twelfth month
(2 KINGS 25:27)
This is called Adar in the lunar Jewish calendar. It's from the middle of February to the middle of March in our solar calendar.

Awel-Marduk became king of Babylon, he released Jehoiachin king of Judah from prison. He did this on the twenty-seventh day of the twelfth month. 28He spoke kindly to him and gave him a seat of honor higher than those of the other kings who were with him in Babylon. 29So Jehoiachin put aside his prison clothes and for the rest of his life ate regularly at the king's table. 30Day by day the king gave Jehoiachin a regular allowance as long as he lived.

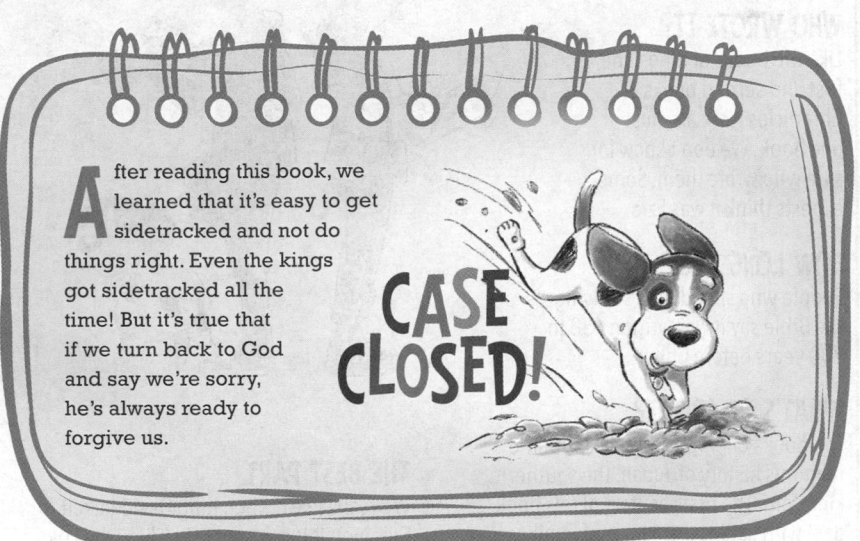

After reading this book, we learned that it's easy to get sidetracked and not do things right. Even the kings got sidetracked all the time! But it's true that if we turn back to God and say we're sorry, he's always ready to forgive us.

CASE CLOSED!

1 CHRONICLES

THE EVIDENCE:

WHO WROTE IT?
Like the books of Kings, the first and second books of Chronicles were also just one book. We don't know for sure who wrote them. Some experts think it was Ezra.

HOW LONG AGO?
People who spend time studying the Bible say it was written 458 to 200 years before Christ.

WHAT'S IT ABOUT?
The books of Chronicles talk about the religious history of Judah, the southern kingdom. The first chapters of this book deal with lists of the names of families and their descendants. Then it talks about David and about Solomon, who built the temple. It also tells how they worshiped and what the priests and their assistants, the Levites, had to do. And there's a lot of talk about feasts, prayers, music and songs. It seems the Hebrews celebrated a lot of feasts as they worshiped God!

THE BEST PART
We really like it when King David talked to Solomon, his son, and said, "May the LORD give you discretion and understanding when he puts you in command over Israel, so that you may keep the law of the LORD your God. Then you will have success if you are careful to observe the decrees and laws that the LORD gave Moses for Israel. Be strong and courageous. Do not be afraid or discouraged" (22:12 – 13).

Historical Records From Adam to Abraham

To Noah's Sons

1 Adam, Seth, Enosh, ²Kenan, Mahalalel, Jared, ³Enoch, Methuselah, Lamech, Noah.

⁴ The sons of Noah:ᵃ
   Shem, Ham and Japheth.

The Japhethites

⁵ The sonsᵇ of Japheth:
   Gomer, Magog, Madai, Javan, Tubal, Meshek and Tiras.

⁶ The sons of Gomer:
   Ashkenaz, Riphathᶜ and Togarmah.
⁷ The sons of Javan:
   Elishah, Tarshish, the Kittites and the Rodanites.

The Hamites

⁸ The sons of Ham:
   Cush, Egypt, Put and Canaan.

ᵃ 4 Septuagint; Hebrew does not have this line.
ᵇ 5 Sons may mean descendants or successors or nations; also in verses 6-9, 17 and 23.   ᶜ 6 Many Hebrew manuscripts and Vulgate (see also Septuagint and Gen. 10:3); most Hebrew manuscripts Diphath

BREAKTHROUGH!

Why does it talk about all these people?

(1 CHRONICLES 1-9)

In this first book of Chronicles, there are names of many families and their children, from Adam up to the time the Hebrews were taken to Babylon (in the year 576 before Christ). With all of this, God wanted to show that he controls history. He was showing how Israel, Judah and David's family are central in God's plan of salvation. This was later fulfilled with the arrival of Jesus, the Messiah. And here, God also reveals why Judah had to be punished by Babylon and how they should behave in order to please God once they return to their own land.

⁹ The sons of Cush:
Seba, Havilah, Sabta, Raamah and Sabteka.
The sons of Raamah:
Sheba and Dedan.
¹⁰ Cush was the father^a of
Nimrod, who became a mighty warrior on earth.
¹¹ Egypt was the father of
the Ludites, Anamites, Lehabites, Naphtuhites, ¹² Pathrusites, Kasluhites (from whom the Philistines came) and Caphtorites.

¹³ Canaan was the father of
Sidon his firstborn,^b and of the Hittites, ¹⁴ Jebusites, Amorites, Girgashites, ¹⁵ Hivites, Arkites, Sinites, ¹⁶ Arvadites, Zemarites and Hamathites.

The Semites

¹⁷ The sons of Shem:
Elam, Ashur, Arphaxad, Lud and Aram.
The sons of Aram:^c
Uz, Hul, Gether and Meshek.
¹⁸ Arphaxad was the father of Shelah, and Shelah the father of Eber.
¹⁹ Two sons were born to Eber:
One was named Peleg,^d because in his time the earth was divided; his brother was named Joktan.
²⁰ Joktan was the father of
Almodad, Sheleph, Hazarmaveth, Jerah, ²¹ Hadoram, Uzal, Diklah, ²² Obal,^e Abimael, Sheba, ²³ Ophir, Havilah and Jobab. All these were sons of Joktan.

²⁴ Shem, Arphaxad,^f Shelah,
²⁵ Eber, Peleg, Reu,
²⁶ Serug, Nahor, Terah
²⁷ and Abram (that is, Abraham).

The Family of Abraham

²⁸ The sons of Abraham:
Isaac and Ishmael.

Descendants of Hagar

²⁹ These were their descendants:
Nebaioth the firstborn of Ishmael, Kedar, Adbeel, Mibsam, ³⁰ Mishma, Dumah, Massa, Hadad, Tema, ³¹ Jetur, Naphish and Kedemah. These were the sons of Ishmael.

Descendants of Keturah

³² The sons born to Keturah, Abraham's concubine:

---

^a 10 Father may mean ancestor or predecessor or founder; also in verses 11, 13, 18 and 20.   ^b 13 Or of the Sidonians, the foremost   ^c 17 One Hebrew manuscript and some Septuagint manuscripts (see also Gen. 10:23); most Hebrew manuscripts do not have this line.   ^d 19 Peleg means division.   ^e 22 Some Hebrew manuscripts and Syriac (see also Gen. 10:28); most Hebrew manuscripts Ebal   ^f 24 Hebrew; some Septuagint manuscripts Arphaxad, Cainan (see also note at Gen. 11:10)

Zimran, Jokshan, Medan, Midian, Ishbak and Shuah.
The sons of Jokshan:
Sheba and Dedan.
³³ The sons of Midian:
Ephah, Epher, Hanok, Abida and Eldaah.
All these were descendants of Keturah.

Descendants of Sarah

³⁴ Abraham was the father of Isaac.
The sons of Isaac:
Esau and Israel.

Esau's Sons

³⁵ The sons of Esau:
Eliphaz, Reuel, Jeush, Jalam and Korah.
³⁶ The sons of Eliphaz:
Teman, Omar, Zepho,^a Gatam and Kenaz;
by Timna: Amalek.^b
³⁷ The sons of Reuel:
Nahath, Zerah, Shammah and Mizzah.

The People of Seir in Edom

³⁸ The sons of Seir:
Lotan, Shobal, Zibeon, Anah, Dishon, Ezer and Dishan.
³⁹ The sons of Lotan:
Hori and Homam. Timna was Lotan's sister.
⁴⁰ The sons of Shobal:
Alvan,^c Manahath, Ebal, Shepho and Onam.
The sons of Zibeon:
Aiah and Anah.
⁴¹ The son of Anah:
Dishon.
The sons of Dishon:
Hemdan,^d Eshban, Ithran and Keran.
⁴² The sons of Ezer:
Bilhan, Zaavan and Akan.^e
The sons of Dishan^f:
Uz and Aran.

The Rulers of Edom

⁴³ These were the kings who reigned in Edom before any Israelite king reigned:

Bela son of Beor, whose city was named Dinhabah.
⁴⁴ When Bela died, Jobab son of Zerah from Bozrah succeeded him as king.
⁴⁵ When Jobab died, Husham from the land of the Temanites succeeded him as king.
⁴⁶ When Husham died, Hadad son of Bedad, who defeated Midian in the country of Moab, succeeded him as king. His city was named Avith.
⁴⁷ When Hadad died, Samlah from Masrekah succeeded him as king.
⁴⁸ When Samlah died, Shaul from Rehoboth on the river^g succeeded him as king.
⁴⁹ When Shaul died, Baal-Hanan son of Akbor succeeded him as king.
⁵⁰ When Baal-Hanan died, Hadad succeeded him as king. His city was named Pau,^h and his wife's name was Mehetabel daughter of Matred, the daughter of Me-Zahab.
⁵¹ Hadad also died.

The chiefs of Edom were:
Timna, Alvah, Jetheth, ⁵² Oholibamah, Elah, Pinon, ⁵³ Kenaz, Teman, Mibzar, ⁵⁴ Magdiel and Iram. These were the chiefs of Edom.

Israel's Sons

2 These were the sons of Israel:
Reuben, Simeon, Levi, Judah, Issachar, Zebulun, ² Dan, Joseph, Benjamin, Naphtali, Gad and Asher.

Judah

To Hezron's Sons

³ The sons of Judah:
Er, Onan and Shelah. These three

---

^a 36 Many Hebrew manuscripts, some Septuagint manuscripts and Syriac (see also Gen. 36:11); most Hebrew manuscripts *Zephi*   ^b 36 Some Septuagint manuscripts (see also Gen. 36:12); Hebrew *Gatam, Kenaz, Timna and Amalek*   ^c 40 Many Hebrew manuscripts and some Septuagint manuscripts (see also Gen. 36:23); most Hebrew manuscripts *Alian*   ^d 41 Many Hebrew manuscripts and some Septuagint manuscripts (see also Gen. 36:26); most Hebrew manuscripts *Hamran*   ^e 42 Many Hebrew and Septuagint manuscripts (see also Gen. 36:27); most Hebrew manuscripts *Zaavan, Jaakan*   ^f 42 See Gen. 36:28; Hebrew *Dishon,* a variant of *Dishan*   ^g 48 Possibly the Euphrates   ^h 50 Many Hebrew manuscripts, some Septuagint manuscripts, Vulgate and Syriac (see also Gen. 36:39); most Hebrew manuscripts *Pai*

were born to him by a Canaanite woman, the daughter of Shua. Er, Judah's firstborn, was wicked in the LORD's sight; so the LORD put him to death. ⁴Judah's daughter-in-law Tamar bore Perez and Zerah to Judah. He had five sons in all.

⁵The sons of Perez:
Hezron and Hamul.

⁶The sons of Zerah:
Zimri, Ethan, Heman, Kalkol and Darda*ᵃ*—five in all.

⁷The son of Karmi:
Achar,*ᵇ* who brought trouble on Israel by violating the ban on taking devoted things.*ᶜ*

⁸The son of Ethan:
Azariah.

⁹The sons born to Hezron were:
Jerahmeel, Ram and Caleb.*ᵈ*

From Ram Son of Hezron

¹⁰Ram was the father of Amminadab, and Amminadab the father of Nahshon, the leader of the people of Judah. ¹¹Nahshon was the father of Salmon,*ᵉ* Salmon the father of Boaz, ¹²Boaz the father of Obed and Obed the father of Jesse.

¹³Jesse was the father of
Eliab his firstborn; the second son was Abinadab, the third Shimea, ¹⁴the fourth Nethanel, the fifth Raddai, ¹⁵the sixth Ozem and the seventh David. ¹⁶Their sisters were Zeruiah and Abigail. Zeruiah's three sons were Abishai, Joab and Asahel. ¹⁷Abigail was the mother of Amasa, whose father was Jether the Ishmaelite.

Caleb Son of Hezron

¹⁸Caleb son of Hezron had children by his wife Azubah (and by Jerioth). These were her sons: Jesher, Shobab and Ardon. ¹⁹When Azubah died, Caleb married Ephrath, who bore him Hur. ²⁰Hur was the father of Uri, and Uri the father of Bezalel.

²¹Later, Hezron, when he was sixty years old, married the daughter of Makir the father of Gilead. He made love to her, and she bore him Segub. ²²Segub was the father of Jair, who controlled twenty-three towns in Gilead. ²³(But Geshur and Aram captured Havvoth Jair,*ᶠ* as well as Kenath with its surrounding settlements—sixty towns.) All these were descendants of Makir the father of Gilead.

²⁴After Hezron died in Caleb Ephrathah, Abijah the wife of Hezron bore him Ashhur the father*ᵍ* of Tekoa.

Jerahmeel Son of Hezron

²⁵The sons of Jerahmeel the firstborn of Hezron:
Ram his firstborn, Bunah, Oren, Ozem and*ʰ* Ahijah. ²⁶Jerahmeel had another wife, whose name was Atarah; she was the mother of Onam.

²⁷The sons of Ram the firstborn of Jerahmeel:
Maaz, Jamin and Eker.

²⁸The sons of Onam:
Shammai and Jada.
The sons of Shammai:
Nadab and Abishur.

²⁹Abishur's wife was named Abihail, who bore him Ahban and Molid.

³⁰The sons of Nadab:
Seled and Appaim. Seled died without children.

³¹The son of Appaim:
Ishi, who was the father of Sheshan.
Sheshan was the father of Ahlai.

³²The sons of Jada, Shammai's brother:
Jether and Jonathan. Jether died without children.

³³The sons of Jonathan:
Peleth and Zaza.

ᵃ 6 Many Hebrew manuscripts, some Septuagint manuscripts and Syriac (see also 1 Kings 4:31); most Hebrew manuscripts *Dara*   *ᵇ 7 Achar* means *trouble; Achar* is called *Achan* in Joshua.   *ᶜ 7* The Hebrew term refers to the irrevocable giving over of things or persons to the LORD, often by totally destroying them.   *ᵈ 9* Hebrew *Kelubai,* a variant of *Caleb*   *ᵉ 11* Septuagint (see also Ruth 4:21); Hebrew *Salma*   *ᶠ 23* Or *captured the settlements of Jair*   *ᵍ 24 Father* may mean *civic leader* or *military leader;* also in verses 42, 45, 49-52 and possibly elsewhere.   *ʰ 25* Or *Oren and Ozem, by*

These were the descendants of Jerahmeel.
34 Sheshan had no sons—only daughters.
He had an Egyptian servant named Jarha. 35 Sheshan gave his daughter in marriage to his servant Jarha, and she bore him Attai.
36 Attai was the father of Nathan,
Nathan the father of Zabad,
37 Zabad the father of Ephlal,
Ephlal the father of Obed,
38 Obed the father of Jehu,
Jehu the father of Azariah,
39 Azariah the father of Helez,
Helez the father of Eleasah,
40 Eleasah the father of Sismai,
Sismai the father of Shallum,
41 Shallum the father of Jekamiah,
and Jekamiah the father of Elishama.

The Clans of Caleb

42 The sons of Caleb the brother of Jerahmeel:
Mesha his firstborn, who was the father of Ziph, and his son Mareshah,[a] who was the father of Hebron.
43 The sons of Hebron:
Korah, Tappuah, Rekem and Shema. 44 Shema was the father of Raham, and Raham the father of Jorkeam. Rekem was the father of Shammai. 45 The son of Shammai was Maon, and Maon was the father of Beth Zur.
46 Caleb's concubine Ephah was the mother of Haran, Moza and Gazez. Haran was the father of Gazez.
47 The sons of Jahdai:
Regem, Jotham, Geshan, Pelet, Ephah and Shaaph.
48 Caleb's concubine Maakah was the mother of Sheber and Tirhanah.
49 She also gave birth to Shaaph the father of Madmannah and to Sheva the father of Makbenah and Gibea. Caleb's daughter was Aksah. 50 These were the descendants of Caleb.

The sons of Hur the firstborn of Ephrathah:

Shobal the father of Kiriath Jearim,
51 Salma the father of Bethlehem, and Hareph the father of Beth Gader.
52 The descendants of Shobal the father of Kiriath Jearim were:
Haroeh, half the Manahathites, 53 and the clans of Kiriath Jearim: the Ithrites, Puthites, Shumathites and Mishraites. From these descended the Zorathites and Eshtaolites.
54 The descendants of Salma:
Bethlehem, the Netophathites, Atroth Beth Joab, half the Manahathites, the Zorites, 55 and the clans of scribes[b] who lived at Jabez: the Tirathites, Shimeathites and Sucathites. These are the Kenites who came from Hammath, the father of the Rekabites.[c]

The Sons of David

3 These were the sons of David born to him in Hebron:
The firstborn was Amnon the son of Ahinoam of Jezreel;
the second, Daniel the son of Abigail of Carmel;
2 the third, Absalom the son of Maakah daughter of Talmai king of Geshur;
the fourth, Adonijah the son of Haggith;
3 the fifth, Shephatiah the son of Abital;
and the sixth, Ithream, by his wife Eglah.
4 These six were born to David in Hebron, where he reigned seven years and six months.
David reigned in Jerusalem thirty-three years, 5 and these were the children born to him there:
Shammua,[d] Shobab, Nathan and Solomon. These four were by Bathsheba[e] daughter of Ammiel.

---

a 42 The meaning of the Hebrew for this phrase is uncertain.   b 55 Or of the Sopherites   c 55 Or father of Beth Rekab   d 5 Hebrew Shimea, a variant of Shammua   e 5 One Hebrew manuscript and Vulgate (see also Septuagint and 2 Samuel 11:3); most Hebrew manuscripts Bathshua

⁶There were also Ibhar, Elishua,ᵃ Eliphelet, ⁷Nogah, Nepheg, Japhia, ⁸Elishama, Eliada and Eliphelet— nine in all. ⁹All these were the sons of David, besides his sons by his concubines. And Tamar was their sister.

The Kings of Judah

¹⁰Solomon's son was Rehoboam,
Abijah his son,
Asa his son,
Jehoshaphat his son,
¹¹Jehoramᵇ his son,
Ahaziah his son,
Joash his son,
¹²Amaziah his son,
Azariah his son,
Jotham his son,
¹³Ahaz his son,
Hezekiah his son,
Manasseh his son,
¹⁴Amon his son,
Josiah his son.
¹⁵The sons of Josiah:
Johanan the firstborn,
Jehoiakim the second son,
Zedekiah the third,
Shallum the fourth.
¹⁶The successors of Jehoiakim:
Jehoiachinᶜ his son,
and Zedekiah.

The Royal Line After the Exile

¹⁷The descendants of Jehoiachin the captive:
Shealtiel his son, ¹⁸Malkiram, Pedaiah, Shenazzar, Jekamiah, Hoshama and Nedabiah.
¹⁹The sons of Pedaiah:
Zerubbabel and Shimei.
The sons of Zerubbabel:
Meshullam and Hananiah.
Shelomith was their sister.
²⁰There were also five others:
Hashubah, Ohel, Berekiah, Hasadiah and Jushab-Hesed.
²¹The descendants of Hananiah:
Pelatiah and Jeshaiah, and the sons of Rephaiah, of Arnan, of Obadiah and of Shekaniah.
²²The descendants of Shekaniah:
Shemaiah and his sons:

Hattush, Igal, Bariah, Neariah and Shaphat—six in all.
²³The sons of Neariah:
Elioenai, Hizkiah and Azrikam— three in all.
²⁴The sons of Elioenai:
Hodaviah, Eliashib, Pelaiah, Akkub, Johanan, Delaiah and Anani—seven in all.

Other Clans of Judah

4 The descendants of Judah:
Perez, Hezron, Karmi, Hur and Shobal.
²Reaiah son of Shobal was the father of Jahath, and Jahath the father of Ahumai and Lahad. These were the clans of the Zorathites.
³These were the sonsᵈ of Etam:
Jezreel, Ishma and Idbash. Their sister was named Hazzelelponi.
⁴Penuel was the father of Gedor, and Ezer the father of Hushah.
These were the descendants of Hur, the firstborn of Ephrathah and fatherᵉ of Bethlehem.
⁵Ashhur the father of Tekoa had two wives, Helah and Naarah.
⁶Naarah bore him Ahuzzam, Hepher, Temeni and Haahashtari. These were the descendants of Naarah.
⁷The sons of Helah:
Zereth, Zohar, Ethnan, ⁸and Koz, who was the father of Anub and Hazzobebah and of the clans of Aharhel son of Harum.

⁹Jabez was more honorable than his brothers. His mother had named him Jabez,ᶠ saying, "I gave birth to him in pain." ¹⁰Jabez cried out to the God of Israel, "Oh, that you would bless me and enlarge my territory! Let your hand be with me, and keep me from harm so that I will be free from pain." And God granted his request.

¹¹Kelub, Shuhah's brother, was the father of Mehir, who was the father

ᵃ 6 Two Hebrew manuscripts (see also 2 Samuel 5:15 and 1 Chron. 14:5); most Hebrew manuscripts Elishama ᵇ 11 Hebrew Joram, a variant of Jehoram ᶜ 16 Hebrew Jeconiah, a variant of Jehoiachin; also in verse 17 ᵈ 3 Some Septuagint manuscripts (see also Vulgate); Hebrew father ᵉ 4 Father may mean civic leader or military leader; also in verses 12, 14, 17, 18 and possibly elsewhere. ᶠ 9 Jabez sounds like the Hebrew for pain.

THE
WITNESSES

✓ **JABEZ** (1 CHRONICLES 4:9)
The name Jabez is similar to the Hebrew word that means "pain."

of Eshton. ¹²Eshton was the father of Beth Rapha, Paseah and Tehinnah the father of Ir Nahash.ᵃ These were the men of Rekah.

¹³The sons of Kenaz:
Othniel and Seraiah.
The sons of Othniel:
Hathath and Meonothai.ᵇ ¹⁴Meonothai was the father of Ophrah.
Seraiah was the father of Joab,
the father of Ge Harashim.ᶜ It was called this because its people were skilled workers.
¹⁵The sons of Caleb son of Jephunneh:
Iru, Elah and Naam.
The son of Elah:
Kenaz.

¹⁶The sons of Jehallelel:
Ziph, Ziphah, Tiria and Asarel.
¹⁷The sons of Ezrah:
Jether, Mered, Epher and Jalon. One of Mered's wives gave birth to Miriam, Shammai and Ishbah the father of Eshtemoa. ¹⁸(His wife from the tribe of Judah gave birth to Jered the father of Gedor, Heber the father of Soko, and Jekuthiel the father of Zanoah.) These were the children of Pharaoh's daughter Bithiah, whom Mered had married.
¹⁹The sons of Hodiah's wife, the sister of Naham:
the father of Keilah the Garmite, and Eshtemoa the Maakathite.
²⁰The sons of Shimon:
Amnon, Rinnah, Ben-Hanan and Tilon.
The descendants of Ishi:
Zoheth and Ben-Zoheth.
²¹The sons of Shelah son of Judah:
Er the father of Lekah, Laadah the father of Mareshah and the clans of the linen workers at Beth Ashbea, ²²Jokim, the men of Kozeba, and Joash and Saraph, who ruled in Moab and Jashubi Lehem. (These records are from ancient times.) ²³They were the potters who lived at Netaim and Gederah; they stayed there and worked for the king.

Simeon

²⁴The descendants of Simeon:
Nemuel, Jamin, Jarib, Zerah and Shaul;
²⁵Shallum was Shaul's son, Mibsam his son and Mishma his son.
²⁶The descendants of Mishma:
Hammuel his son, Zakkur his son and Shimei his son.
²⁷Shimei had sixteen sons and six daughters, but his brothers did not have many children; so their entire clan did not become as numerous as the people of Judah. ²⁸They lived in Beersheba, Moladah,

---

ᵃ 12 Or of the city of Nahash   ᵇ 13 Some Septuagint manuscripts and Vulgate; Hebrew does not have and Meonothai.   ᶜ 14 Ge Harashim means valley of skilled workers.

Hazar Shual, [29]Bilhah, Ezem, Tolad, [30]Bethuel, Hormah, Ziklag, [31]Beth Markaboth, Hazar Susim, Beth Biri and Shaaraim. These were their towns until the reign of David. [32]Their surrounding villages were Etam, Ain, Rimmon, Token and Ashan— five towns— [33]and all the villages around these towns as far as Baalath.[a] These were their settlements. And they kept a genealogical record.

[34]Meshobab, Jamlech, Joshah son of Amaziah, [35]Joel, Jehu son of Joshibiah, the son of Seraiah, the son of Asiel, [36]also Elioenai, Jaakobah, Jeshohaiah, Asaiah, Adiel, Jesimiel, Benaiah, [37]and Ziza son of Shiphi, the son of Allon, the son of Jedaiah, the son of Shimri, the son of Shemaiah.

[38]The men listed above by name were leaders of their clans. Their families increased greatly, [39]and they went to the outskirts of Gedor to the east of the valley in search of pasture for their flocks. [40]They found rich, good pasture, and the land was spacious, peaceful and quiet. Some Hamites had lived there formerly. [41]The men whose names were listed came in the days of Hezekiah king of Judah. They attacked the Hamites in their dwellings and also the Meunites who were there and completely destroyed[b] them, as is evident to this day. Then they settled in their place, because there was pasture for their flocks. [42]And five hundred of these Simeonites, led by Pelatiah, Neariah, Rephaiah and Uzziel, the sons of Ishi, invaded the hill country of Seir. [43]They killed the remaining Amalekites who had escaped, and they have lived there to this day.

Reuben

5 The sons of Reuben the firstborn of Israel (he was the firstborn, but when he defiled his father's marriage bed, his rights as firstborn were given to the sons of Joseph son of Israel; so he could not be listed in the genealogical record in accordance with his birthright, [2]and though Judah was the strongest of his brothers and a ruler came from him, the rights of the firstborn belonged to Joseph)— [3]the sons of Reuben the firstborn of Israel:

Hanok, Pallu, Hezron and Karmi.
[4]The descendants of Joel:
Shemaiah his son, Gog his son,
Shimei his son, [5]Micah his son,
Reaiah his son, Baal his son,
[6]and Beerah his son, whom Tiglath-Pileser[c] king of Assyria took into exile. Beerah was a leader of the Reubenites.
[7]Their relatives by clans, listed according to their genealogical records:
Jeiel the chief, Zechariah, [8]and Bela son of Azaz, the son of Shema, the son of Joel. They settled in the area from Aroer to Nebo and Baal Meon. [9]To the east they occupied the land up to the edge of the desert that extends to the Euphrates River, because their livestock had increased in Gilead.
[10]During Saul's reign they waged war against the Hagrites, who were defeated at their hands; they occupied the dwellings of the Hagrites throughout the entire region east of Gilead.

Gad

[11]The Gadites lived next to them in Bashan, as far as Salekah:
[12]Joel was the chief, Shapham the second, then Janai and Shaphat, in Bashan.
[13]Their relatives, by families, were:
Michael, Meshullam, Sheba, Jorai, Jakan, Zia and Eber—seven in all.
[14]These were the sons of Abihail son of Huri, the son of Jaroah, the son of Gilead, the son of Michael, the son of Jeshishai, the son of Jahdo, the son of Buz.
[15]Ahi son of Abdiel, the son of Guni, was head of their family.
[16]The Gadites lived in Gilead, in Bashan and its outlying villages, and on all the pasturelands of Sharon as far as they extended.

---

a 33 Some Septuagint manuscripts (see also Joshua 19:8); Hebrew *Baal*   *b 41* The Hebrew term refers to the irrevocable giving over of things or persons to the Lord, often by totally destroying them.   *c 6* Hebrew *Tilgath-Pilneser*, a variant of *Tiglath-Pileser*; also in verse 26

¹⁷All these were entered in the genealogical records during the reigns of Jotham king of Judah and Jeroboam king of Israel.

¹⁸The Reubenites, the Gadites and the half-tribe of Manasseh had 44,760 men ready for military service—able-bodied men who could handle shield and sword, who could use a bow, and who were trained for battle. ¹⁹They waged war against the Hagrites, Jetur, Naphish and Nodab. ²⁰They were helped in fighting them, and God delivered the Hagrites and all their allies into their hands, because they cried out to him during the battle. He answered their prayers, because they trusted in him. ²¹They seized the livestock of the Hagrites—fifty thousand camels, two hundred fifty thousand sheep and two thousand donkeys. They also took one hundred thousand people captive, ²²and many others fell slain, because the battle was God's. And they occupied the land until the exile.

The Half-Tribe of Manasseh

²³The people of the half-tribe of Manasseh were numerous; they settled in the land from Bashan to Baal Hermon, that is, to Senir (Mount Hermon). ²⁴These were the heads of their families: Epher, Ishi, Eliel, Azriel, Jeremiah, Hodaviah and Jahdiel. They were brave warriors, famous men, and heads of their families. ²⁵But they were unfaithful to the God of their ancestors and prostituted themselves to the gods of the peoples of the land, whom God had destroyed before them. ²⁶So the God of Israel stirred up the spirit of Pul king of Assyria (that is, Tiglath-Pileser king of Assyria), who took the Reubenites, the Gadites and the half-tribe of Manasseh into exile. He took them to Halah, Habor, Hara and the river of Gozan, where they are to this day.

Levi

6ᵃ The sons of Levi:
Gershon, Kohath and Merari.
²The sons of Kohath:
Amram, Izhar, Hebron and Uzziel.
³The children of Amram:
Aaron, Moses and Miriam.

The sons of Aaron:
Nadab, Abihu, Eleazar and Ithamar.
⁴Eleazar was the father of Phinehas,
Phinehas the father of Abishua,
⁵Abishua the father of Bukki,
Bukki the father of Uzzi,
⁶Uzzi the father of Zerahiah,
Zerahiah the father of Meraioth,
⁷Meraioth the father of Amariah,
Amariah the father of Ahitub,
⁸Ahitub the father of Zadok,
Zadok the father of Ahimaaz,
⁹Ahimaaz the father of Azariah,
Azariah the father of Johanan,
¹⁰Johanan the father of Azariah (it was he who served as priest in the temple Solomon built in Jerusalem),
¹¹Azariah the father of Amariah,
Amariah the father of Ahitub,
¹²Ahitub the father of Zadok,
Zadok the father of Shallum,
¹³Shallum the father of Hilkiah,
Hilkiah the father of Azariah,
¹⁴Azariah the father of Seraiah,
and Seraiah the father of Jozadak.ᵇ
¹⁵Jozadak was deported when the Lᴏʀᴅ sent Judah and Jerusalem into exile by the hand of Nebuchadnezzar.

¹⁶The sons of Levi:
Gershon,ᶜ Kohath and Merari.
¹⁷These are the names of the sons of Gershon:
Libni and Shimei.
¹⁸The sons of Kohath:
Amram, Izhar, Hebron and Uzziel.
¹⁹The sons of Merari:
Mahli and Mushi.
These are the clans of the Levites listed according to their fathers:
²⁰Of Gershon:
Libni his son, Jahath his son,
Zimmah his son, ²¹Joah his son,
Iddo his son, Zerah his son
and Jeatherai his son.

ᵃ In Hebrew texts 6:1-15 is numbered 5:27-41, and 6:16-81 is numbered 6:1-66.   ᵇ 14 Hebrew Jehozadak, a variant of Jozadak; also in verse 15   ᶜ 16 Hebrew Gershom, a variant of Gershon; also in verses 17, 20, 43, 62 and 71

²² The descendants of Kohath:
Amminadab his son, Korah his son,
Assir his son, ²³ Elkanah his son,
Ebiasaph his son, Assir his son,
²⁴ Tahath his son, Uriel his son,
Uzziah his son and Shaul his son.
²⁵ The descendants of Elkanah:
Amasai, Ahimoth,
²⁶ Elkanah his son,^a Zophai his son,
Nahath his son, ²⁷ Eliab his son,
Jeroham his son, Elkanah his son
and Samuel his son.^b
²⁸ The sons of Samuel:
Joel^c the firstborn
and Abijah the second son.
²⁹ The descendants of Merari:
Mahli, Libni his son,
Shimei his son, Uzzah his son,
³⁰ Shimea his son, Haggiah his son
and Asaiah his son.

The Temple Musicians

³¹ These are the men David put in charge of the music in the house of the LORD after the ark came to rest there. ³² They ministered with music before the tabernacle, the tent of meeting, until Solomon built the temple of the LORD in Jerusalem. They performed their duties according to the regulations laid down for them. ³³ Here are the men who served, together with their sons:

From the Kohathites:
Heman, the musician,
the son of Joel, the son of Samuel,
³⁴ the son of Elkanah, the son of Jeroham,
the son of Eliel, the son of Toah,
³⁵ the son of Zuph, the son of Elkanah,
the son of Mahath, the son of Amasai,
³⁶ the son of Elkanah, the son of Joel,
the son of Azariah, the son of Zephaniah,
³⁷ the son of Tahath, the son of Assir,
the son of Ebiasaph, the son of Korah,
³⁸ the son of Izhar, the son of Kohath,
the son of Levi, the son of Israel;

³⁹ and Heman's associate Asaph, who served at his right hand:
Asaph son of Berekiah, the son of Shimea,
⁴⁰ the son of Michael, the son of Baaseiah,^d
the son of Malkijah, ⁴¹ the son of Ethni,
the son of Zerah, the son of Adaiah,
⁴² the son of Ethan, the son of Zimmah,
the son of Shimei, ⁴³ the son of Jahath,
the son of Gershon, the son of Levi;
⁴⁴ and from their associates, the Merarites, at his left hand:
Ethan son of Kishi, the son of Abdi,
the son of Malluk, ⁴⁵ the son of Hashabiah,
the son of Amaziah, the son of Hilkiah,
⁴⁶ the son of Amzi, the son of Bani,
the son of Shemer, ⁴⁷ the son of Mahli,
the son of Mushi, the son of Merari,
the son of Levi.

⁴⁸ Their fellow Levites were assigned to all the other duties of the tabernacle, the house of God. ⁴⁹ But Aaron and his descendants were the ones who presented offerings on the altar of burnt offering and on the altar of incense in connection with all that was done in the Most Holy Place, making atonement for Israel, in accordance with all that Moses the servant of God had commanded.

⁵⁰ These were the descendants of Aaron:
Eleazar his son, Phinehas his son,
Abishua his son, ⁵¹ Bukki his son,
Uzzi his son, Zerahiah his son,

---

^a 26 Some Hebrew manuscripts, Septuagint and Syriac; most Hebrew manuscripts *Ahimoth* ²⁶*and Elkanah. The sons of Elkanah:*   ^b 27 Some Septuagint manuscripts (see also 1 Samuel 1:19,20 and 1 Chron. 6:33,34); Hebrew does not have *and Samuel his son.*   ^c 28 Some Septuagint manuscripts and Syriac (see also 1 Samuel 8:2 and 1 Chron. 6:33); Hebrew does not have *Joel.*
^d 40 Most Hebrew manuscripts; some Hebrew manuscripts, one Septuagint manuscript and Syriac *Maaseiah*

⁵²Meraioth his son, Amariah his son, Ahitub his son, ⁵³Zadok his son and Ahimaaz his son.

⁵⁴These were the locations of their settlements allotted as their territory (they were assigned to the descendants of Aaron who were from the Kohathite clan, because the first lot was for them): ⁵⁵They were given Hebron in Judah with its surrounding pasturelands. ⁵⁶But the fields and villages around the city were given to Caleb son of Jephunneh.

⁵⁷So the descendants of Aaron were given Hebron (a city of refuge), and Libnah,ᵃ Jattir, Eshtemoa, ⁵⁸Hilen, Debir, ⁵⁹Ashan, Juttahᵇ and Beth Shemesh, together with their pasturelands. ⁶⁰And from the tribe of Benjamin they were given Gibeon,ᶜ Geba, Alemeth and Anathoth, together with their pasturelands.

The total number of towns distributed among the Kohathite clans came to thirteen.

⁶¹The rest of Kohath's descendants were allotted ten towns from the clans of half the tribe of Manasseh.

⁶²The descendants of Gershon, clan by clan, were allotted thirteen towns from the tribes of Issachar, Asher and Naphtali, and from the part of the tribe of Manasseh that is in Bashan.

⁶³The descendants of Merari, clan by clan, were allotted twelve towns from the tribes of Reuben, Gad and Zebulun.

⁶⁴So the Israelites gave the Levites these towns and their pasturelands. ⁶⁵From the tribes of Judah, Simeon and Benjamin they allotted the previously named towns.

⁶⁶Some of the Kohathite clans were given as their territory towns from the tribe of Ephraim.

⁶⁷In the hill country of Ephraim they were given Shechem (a city of refuge), and Gezer,ᵈ ⁶⁸Jokmeam, Beth Horon, ⁶⁹Aijalon and Gath Rimmon, together with their pasturelands.

⁷⁰And from half the tribe of Manasseh the Israelites gave Aner and Bileam, together with their pasturelands, to the rest of the Kohathite clans.

⁷¹The Gershonites received the following:
From the clan of the half-tribe of Manasseh
they received Golan in Bashan and also Ashtaroth, together with their pasturelands;
⁷²from the tribe of Issachar
they received Kedesh, Daberath, ⁷³Ramoth and Anem, together with their pasturelands;
⁷⁴from the tribe of Asher
they received Mashal, Abdon, ⁷⁵Hukok and Rehob, together with their pasturelands;
⁷⁶and from the tribe of Naphtali
they received Kedesh in Galilee, Hammon and Kiriathaim, together with their pasturelands.

⁷⁷The Merarites (the rest of the Levites) received the following:
From the tribe of Zebulun
they received Jokneam, Kartah,ᵉ Rimmono and Tabor, together with their pasturelands;
⁷⁸from the tribe of Reuben across the Jordan east of Jericho
they received Bezer in the wilderness, Jahzah, ⁷⁹Kedemoth and Mephaath, together with their pasturelands;
⁸⁰and from the tribe of Gad
they received Ramoth in Gilead, Mahanaim, ⁸¹Heshbon and Jazer, together with their pasturelands.

Issachar

7 The sons of Issachar:
Tola, Puah, Jashub and Shimron — four in all.
²The sons of Tola:
Uzzi, Rephaiah, Jeriel, Jahmai, Ibsam and Samuel — heads of their families. During the reign of David, the descendants of Tola listed as fighting men in their genealogy numbered 22,600.

ᵃ 57 See Joshua 21:13; Hebrew *given the cities of refuge: Hebron, Libnah.*   ᵇ 59 Syriac (see also Septuagint and Joshua 21:16); Hebrew does not have *Juttah.*   ᶜ 60 See Joshua 21:17; Hebrew does not have *Gibeon.*   ᵈ 67 See Joshua 21:21; Hebrew *given the cities of refuge: Shechem, Gezer.*   ᵉ 77 See Septuagint and Joshua 21:34; Hebrew does not have *Jokneam, Kartah.*

³The son of Uzzi:
Izrahiah.
The sons of Izrahiah:
Michael, Obadiah, Joel and Ishiah. All five of them were chiefs. ⁴According to their family genealogy, they had 36,000 men ready for battle, for they had many wives and children.

⁵The relatives who were fighting men belonging to all the clans of Issachar, as listed in their genealogy, were 87,000 in all.

Benjamin

⁶Three sons of Benjamin:
Bela, Beker and Jediael.
⁷The sons of Bela:
Ezbon, Uzzi, Uzziel, Jerimoth and Iri, heads of families—five in all. Their genealogical record listed 22,034 fighting men.
⁸The sons of Beker:
Zemirah, Joash, Eliezer, Elioenai, Omri, Jeremoth, Abijah, Anathoth and Alemeth. All these were the sons of Beker. ⁹Their genealogical record listed the heads of families and 20,200 fighting men.
¹⁰The son of Jediael:
Bilhan.
The sons of Bilhan:
Jeush, Benjamin, Ehud, Kenaanah, Zethan, Tarshish and Ahishahar. ¹¹All these sons of Jediael were heads of families. There were 17,200 fighting men ready to go out to war.
¹²The Shuppites and Huppites were the descendants of Ir, and the Hushites[a] the descendants of Aher.

Naphtali

¹³The sons of Naphtali:
Jahziel, Guni, Jezer and Shillem[b]—the descendants of Bilhah.

Manasseh

¹⁴The descendants of Manasseh:
Asriel was his descendant through his Aramean concubine. She gave birth to Makir the father of Gilead.

¹⁵Makir took a wife from among the Huppites and Shuppites. His sister's name was Maakah. Another descendant was named Zelophehad, who had only daughters.

¹⁶Makir's wife Maakah gave birth to a son and named him Peresh. His brother was named Sheresh, and his sons were Ulam and Rakem.
¹⁷The son of Ulam:
Bedan.
These were the sons of Gilead son of Makir, the son of Manasseh. ¹⁸His sister Hammoleketh gave birth to Ishhod, Abiezer and Mahlah.
¹⁹The sons of Shemida were:
Ahian, Shechem, Likhi and Aniam.

Ephraim

²⁰The descendants of Ephraim:
Shuthelah, Bered his son,
Tahath his son, Eleadah his son,
Tahath his son, ²¹Zabad his son
and Shuthelah his son.
Ezer and Elead were killed by the native-born men of Gath, when they went down to seize their livestock. ²²Their father Ephraim mourned for them many days, and his relatives came to comfort him. ²³Then he made love to his wife again, and she became pregnant and gave birth to a son. He named him Beriah,[c] because there had been misfortune in his family. ²⁴His daughter was Sheerah, who built Lower and Upper Beth Horon as well as Uzzen Sheerah.
²⁵Rephah was his son, Resheph his son,[d]
Telah his son, Tahan his son,
²⁶Ladan his son, Ammihud his son,
Elishama his son, ²⁷Nun his son
and Joshua his son.
²⁸Their lands and settlements included Bethel and its surrounding villages,

---

[a] 12 Or Ir. The sons of Dan: Hushim, (see Gen. 46:23); Hebrew does not have The sons of Dan.   [b] 13 Some Hebrew and Septuagint manuscripts (see also Gen. 46:24 and Num. 26:49); most Hebrew manuscripts Shallum   [c] 23 Beriah sounds like the Hebrew for misfortune.   [d] 25 Some Septuagint manuscripts; Hebrew does not have his son.

BREAKTHROUGH!

A woman built villages?

(1 CHRONICLES 7:24)

That's right! It was very unusual for a woman to do that kind of work, but here we see a brave woman who did just that. Her name was Sheerah. She's the only woman in the entire Old Testament who built villages.

Naaran to the east, Gezer and its villages to the west, and Shechem and its villages all the way to Ayyah and its villages. ²⁹Along the borders of Manasseh were Beth Shan, Taanach, Megiddo and Dor, together with their villages. The descendants of Joseph son of Israel lived in these towns.

Asher

³⁰The sons of Asher:
Imnah, Ishvah, Ishvi and Beriah. Their sister was Serah.
³¹The sons of Beriah:
Heber and Malkiel, who was the father of Birzaith.
³²Heber was the father of Japhlet, Shomer and Hotham and of their sister Shua.
³³The sons of Japhlet:
Pasak, Bimhal and Ashvath. These were Japhlet's sons.
³⁴The sons of Shomer:
Ahi, Rohgah,ᵃ Hubbah and Aram.

³⁵The sons of his brother Helem:
Zophah, Imna, Shelesh and Amal.
³⁶The sons of Zophah:
Suah, Harnepher, Shual, Beri, Imrah, ³⁷Bezer, Hod, Shamma, Shilshah, Ithranᵇ and Beera.
³⁸The sons of Jether:
Jephunneh, Pispah and Ara.
³⁹The sons of Ulla:
Arah, Hanniel and Rizia.

⁴⁰All these were descendants of Asher—heads of families, choice men, brave warriors and outstanding leaders. The number of men ready for battle, as listed in their genealogy, was 26,000.

The Genealogy of Saul the Benjamite

8 Benjamin was the father of Bela his firstborn,
Ashbel the second son, Aharah the third,
²Nohah the fourth and Rapha the fifth.
³The sons of Bela were:
Addar, Gera, Abihud,ᶜ ⁴Abishua, Naaman, Ahoah, ⁵Gera, Shephuphan and Huram.
⁶These were the descendants of Ehud, who were heads of families of those living in Geba and were deported to Manahath:
⁷Naaman, Ahijah, and Gera, who deported them and who was the father of Uzza and Ahihud.
⁸Sons were born to Shaharaim in Moab after he had divorced his wives Hushim and Baara. ⁹By his wife Hodesh he had Jobab, Zibia, Mesha, Malkam, ¹⁰Jeuz, Sakia and Mirmah. These were his sons, heads of families. ¹¹By Hushim he had Abitub and Elpaal.
¹²The sons of Elpaal:
Eber, Misham, Shemed (who built Ono and Lod with its surrounding villages), ¹³and Beriah and Shema, who were heads of families of those living in Aijalon and who drove out the inhabitants of Gath.

ᵃ 34 Or *of his brother Shomer: Rohgah*   ᵇ 37 Possibly a variant of *Jether*   ᶜ 3 Or *Gera the father of Ehud*

¹⁴Ahio, Shashak, Jeremoth, ¹⁵Zebadiah, Arad, Eder, ¹⁶Michael, Ishpah and Joha were the sons of Beriah. ¹⁷Zebadiah, Meshullam, Hizki, Heber, ¹⁸Ishmerai, Izliah and Jobab were the sons of Elpaal.

¹⁹Jakim, Zikri, Zabdi, ²⁰Elienai, Zillethai, Eliel, ²¹Adaiah, Beraiah and Shimrath were the sons of Shimei.

²²Ishpan, Eber, Eliel, ²³Abdon, Zikri, Hanan, ²⁴Hananiah, Elam, Anthothijah, ²⁵Iphdeiah and Penuel were the sons of Shashak.

²⁶Shamsherai, Shehariah, Athaliah, ²⁷Jaareshiah, Elijah and Zikri were the sons of Jeroham.

²⁸All these were heads of families, chiefs as listed in their genealogy, and they lived in Jerusalem.

²⁹Jeiel*ᵃ* the father*ᵇ* of Gibeon lived in Gibeon.

His wife's name was Maakah, ³⁰and his firstborn son was Abdon, followed by Zur, Kish, Baal, Ner,*ᶜ* Nadab, ³¹Gedor, Ahio, Zeker ³²and Mikloth, who was the father of Shimeah. They too lived near their relatives in Jerusalem.

³³Ner was the father of Kish, Kish the father of Saul, and Saul the father of Jonathan, Malki-Shua, Abinadab and Esh-Baal.*ᵈ*

³⁴The son of Jonathan:
Merib-Baal,*ᵉ* who was the father of Micah.

³⁵The sons of Micah:
Pithon, Melek, Tarea and Ahaz.

³⁶Ahaz was the father of Jehoaddah, Jehoaddah was the father of Alemeth, Azmaveth and Zimri, and Zimri was the father of Moza. ³⁷Moza was the father of Binea; Raphah was his son, Eleasah his son and Azel his son.

³⁸Azel had six sons, and these were their names:
Azrikam, Bokeru, Ishmael, Sheariah, Obadiah and Hanan. All these were the sons of Azel.

³⁹The sons of his brother Eshek:
Ulam his firstborn, Jeush the second son and Eliphelet the third.

⁴⁰The sons of Ulam were brave warriors who could handle the bow. They had many sons and grandsons—150 in all.
All these were the descendants of Benjamin.

9

All Israel was listed in the genealogies recorded in the book of the kings of Israel and Judah. They were taken captive to Babylon because of their unfaithfulness.

The People in Jerusalem

²Now the first to resettle on their own property in their own towns were some Israelites, priests, Levites and temple servants.

³Those from Judah, from Benjamin, and from Ephraim and Manasseh who lived in Jerusalem were:

⁴Uthai son of Ammihud, the son of Omri, the son of Imri, the son of Bani, a descendant of Perez son of Judah.

⁵Of the Shelanites*ᶠ*:
Asaiah the firstborn and his sons.

⁶Of the Zerahites:
Jeuel.
The people from Judah numbered 690.

⁷Of the Benjamites:
Sallu son of Meshullam, the son of Hodaviah, the son of Hassenuah;

⁸Ibneiah son of Jeroham; Elah son of Uzzi, the son of Mikri; and Meshullam son of Shephatiah, the son of Reuel, the son of Ibnijah.

⁹The people from Benjamin, as listed in their genealogy, numbered 956. All these men were heads of their families.

¹⁰Of the priests:
Jedaiah; Jehoiarib; Jakin;

¹¹Azariah son of Hilkiah, the son of Meshullam, the son of Zadok, the son of Meraioth, the son of Ahitub,

---

ᵃ 29 Some Septuagint manuscripts (see also 9:35); Hebrew does not have Jeiel.   ᵇ 29 Father may mean civic leader or military leader.   ᶜ 30 Some Septuagint manuscripts (see also 9:36); Hebrew does not have Ner.   ᵈ 33 Also known as Ish-Bosheth   ᵉ 34 Also known as Mephibosheth   ᶠ 5 See Num. 26:20; Hebrew Shilonites.

the official in charge of the house of God;

¹²Adaiah son of Jeroham, the son of Pashhur, the son of Malkijah; and Maasai son of Adiel, the son of Jahzerah, the son of Meshullam, the son of Meshillemith, the son of Immer.

¹³The priests, who were heads of families, numbered 1,760. They were able men, responsible for ministering in the house of God.

¹⁴Of the Levites:

Shemaiah son of Hasshub, the son of Azrikam, the son of Hashabiah, a Merarite; ¹⁵Bakbakkar, Heresh, Galal and Mattaniah son of Mika, the son of Zikri, the son of Asaph; ¹⁶Obadiah son of Shemaiah, the son of Galal, the son of Jeduthun; and Berekiah son of Asa, the son of Elkanah, who lived in the villages of the Netophathites.

¹⁷The gatekeepers:

Shallum, Akkub, Talmon, Ahiman and their fellow Levites, Shallum their chief ¹⁸being stationed at the King's Gate on the east, up to the present time. These were the gatekeepers belonging to the camp of the Levites. ¹⁹Shallum son of Kore, the son of Ebiasaph, the son of Korah, and his fellow gatekeepers from his family (the Korahites) were responsible for guarding the thresholds of the tent just as their ancestors had been responsible for guarding the entrance to the dwelling of the LORD. ²⁰In earlier times Phinehas son of Eleazar was the official in charge of the gatekeepers, and the LORD was with him. ²¹Zechariah son of Meshelemiah was the gatekeeper at the entrance to the tent of meeting.

²²Altogether, those chosen to be gatekeepers at the thresholds numbered 212. They were registered by genealogy in their villages. The gatekeepers had been assigned to their positions of trust by David and Samuel the seer. ²³They and their descendants were in charge of guarding the gates of the house of the LORD—the house called the tent of meeting. ²⁴The gatekeepers were on the four sides: east, west, north and south. ²⁵Their fellow Levites in their villages had to come from time to time and share their duties for seven-day periods. ²⁶But the four principal gatekeepers, who were Levites, were entrusted with the responsibility for the rooms and treasuries in the house of God. ²⁷They would spend the night stationed around the house of God, because they had to guard it; and they had charge of the key for opening it each morning.

²⁸Some of them were in charge of the articles used in the temple service; they counted them when they were brought in and when they were taken out. ²⁹Others were assigned to take care of the furnishings and all the other articles of the sanctuary, as well as the special flour and wine, and the olive oil, incense and spices. ³⁰But some of the priests took care of mixing the spices. ³¹A Levite named Mattithiah, the firstborn son of Shallum the Korahite, was entrusted with the responsibility for baking the offering bread. ³²Some of the Kohathites, their fellow Levites, were in charge of preparing for every Sabbath the bread set out on the table.

³³Those who were musicians, heads of Levite families, stayed in the rooms of the temple and were exempt from other duties because they were responsible for the work day and night.

³⁴All these were heads of Levite families, chiefs as listed in their genealogy, and they lived in Jerusalem.

The Genealogy of Saul

³⁵Jeiel the father[a] of Gibeon lived in Gibeon.

His wife's name was Maakah, ³⁶and his firstborn son was Abdon, followed by Zur, Kish, Baal, Ner, Nadab, ³⁷Gedor, Ahio, Zechariah and Mikloth. ³⁸Mikloth was the father of Shimeam. They too lived near their relatives in Jerusalem.

---

[a] 35 *Father* may mean *civic leader* or *military leader.*

³⁹ Ner was the father of Kish, Kish the father of Saul, and Saul the father of Jonathan, Malki-Shua, Abinadab and Esh-Baal.ᵃ

⁴⁰ The son of Jonathan:
Merib-Baal,ᵇ who was the father of Micah.

⁴¹ The sons of Micah:
Pithon, Melek, Tahrea and Ahaz.ᶜ

⁴² Ahaz was the father of Jadah, Jadahᵈ was the father of Alemeth, Azmaveth and Zimri, and Zimri was the father of Moza. ⁴³ Moza was the father of Binea; Rephaiah was his son, Eleasah his son and Azel his son.

⁴⁴ Azel had six sons, and these were their names:
Azrikam, Bokeru, Ishmael, Sheariah, Obadiah and Hanan. These were the sons of Azel.

Saul Takes His Life

10 Now the Philistines fought against Israel; the Israelites fled before them, and many fell dead on Mount Gilboa. ²The Philistines were in hot pursuit of Saul and his sons, and they killed his sons Jonathan, Abinadab and Malki-Shua. ³The fighting grew fierce around Saul, and when the archers overtook him, they wounded him.

⁴Saul said to his armor-bearer, "Draw your sword and run me through, or these uncircumcised fellows will come and abuse me."

But his armor-bearer was terrified and would not do it; so Saul took his own sword and fell on it. ⁵When the armor-bearer saw that Saul was dead, he too fell on his sword and died. ⁶So Saul and his three sons died, and all his house died together.

⁷When all the Israelites in the valley saw that the army had fled and that Saul and his sons had died, they abandoned their towns and fled. And the Philistines came and occupied them.

⁸The next day, when the Philistines came to strip the dead, they found Saul and his sons fallen on Mount Gilboa. ⁹They stripped him and took his head and his armor, and sent messengers through-out the land of the Philistines to proclaim the news among their idols and their people. ¹⁰They put his armor in the temple of their gods and hung up his head in the temple of Dagon.

¹¹When all the inhabitants of Jabesh Gilead heard what the Philistines had done to Saul, ¹²all their valiant men went and took the bodies of Saul and his sons and brought them to Jabesh. Then they buried their bones under the great tree in Jabesh, and they fasted seven days.

¹³Saul died because he was unfaithful to the Lord; he did not keep the word of the Lord and even consulted a medium for guidance, ¹⁴and did not inquire of the Lord. So the Lord put him to death and turned the kingdom over to David son of Jesse.

David Becomes King Over Israel

11 All Israel came together to David at Hebron and said, "We are your own flesh and blood. ²In the past, even while Saul was king, you were the one who led Israel on their military campaigns. And the Lord your God said to you, 'You will shepherd my people Israel, and you will become their ruler.' "

³When all the elders of Israel had come to King David at Hebron, he made a covenant with them at Hebron before the Lord, and they anointed David king over Israel, as the Lord had promised through Samuel.

David Conquers Jerusalem

⁴David and all the Israelites marched to Jerusalem (that is, Jebus). The Jebusites who lived there ⁵said to David, "You will not get in here." Nevertheless, David captured the fortress of Zion—which is the City of David.

⁶David had said, "Whoever leads the attack on the Jebusites will become commander-in-chief." Joab son of Zeruiah

---

ᵃ *39* Also known as *Ish-Bosheth*   ᵇ *40* Also known as *Mephibosheth*   ᶜ *41* Vulgate and Syriac (see also Septuagint and 8:35); Hebrew does not have *and Ahaz*.   ᵈ *42* Some Hebrew manuscripts and Septuagint (see also 8:36); most Hebrew manuscripts *Jarah, Jarah* went up first, and so he received the command.

⁷David then took up residence in the fortress, and so it was called the City of David. ⁸He built up the city around it, from the terraces*a* to the surrounding wall, while Joab restored the rest of the city. ⁹And David became more and more powerful, because the LORD Almighty was with him.

David's Mighty Warriors

¹⁰These were the chiefs of David's mighty warriors—they, together with all Israel, gave his kingship strong support to extend it over the whole land, as the LORD had promised— ¹¹this is the list of David's mighty warriors:

Jashobeam,*b* a Hakmonite, was chief of the officers*c*; he raised his spear against three hundred men, whom he killed in one encounter.

¹²Next to him was Eleazar son of Dodai the Ahohite, one of the three mighty warriors. ¹³He was with David at Pas Dammim when the Philistines gathered there for battle. At a place where there was a field full of barley, the troops fled from the Philistines. ¹⁴But they took their stand in the middle of the field. They defended it and struck the Philistines down, and the LORD brought about a great victory.

¹⁵Three of the thirty chiefs came down to David to the rock at the cave of Adullam, while a band of Philistines was encamped in the Valley of Rephaim. ¹⁶At that time David was in the stronghold, and the Philistine garrison was at Bethlehem. ¹⁷David longed for water and said, "Oh, that someone would get me a drink of water from the well near the gate of Bethlehem!" ¹⁸So the Three broke through the Philistine lines, drew water from the well near the gate of Bethlehem and carried it back to David. But he refused to drink it; instead, he poured it out to the LORD. ¹⁹"God forbid that I should do this!" he said. "Should I drink the blood of these men who went at the risk of their lives?" Because they risked their lives to bring it back, David would not drink it.

Such were the exploits of the three mighty warriors.

²⁰Abishai the brother of Joab was chief of the Three. He raised his spear against three hundred men, whom he killed, and so he became as famous as the Three. ²¹He was doubly honored above the Three and became their commander, even though he was not included among them.

²²Benaiah son of Jehoiada, a valiant fighter from Kabzeel, performed great exploits. He struck down Moab's two mightiest warriors. He also went down into a pit on a snowy day and killed a lion. ²³And he struck down an Egyptian who was five cubits*d* tall. Although the Egyptian had a spear like a weaver's rod in his hand, Benaiah went against him with a club. He snatched the spear from the Egyptian's hand and killed him with his own spear. ²⁴Such were the exploits of Benaiah son of Jehoiada; he too was as famous as the three mighty warriors. ²⁵He was held in greater honor than any of the Thirty, but he was not included among the Three. And David put him in charge of his bodyguard.

²⁶The mighty warriors were:
Asahel the brother of Joab,
Elhanan son of Dodo from Bethlehem,
²⁷Shammoth the Harorite,
Helez the Pelonite,
²⁸Ira son of Ikkesh from Tekoa,
Abiezer from Anathoth,
²⁹Sibbekai the Hushathite,
Ilai the Ahohite,
³⁰Maharai the Netophathite,
Heled son of Baanah the Netophathite,
³¹Ithai son of Ribai from Gibeah in Benjamin,
Benaiah the Pirathonite,
³²Hurai from the ravines of Gaash,
Abiel the Arbathite,
³³Azmaveth the Baharumite,
Eliahba the Shaalbonite,
³⁴the sons of Hashem the Gizonite,
Jonathan son of Shagee the Hararite,
³⁵Ahiam son of Sakar the Hararite,
Eliphal son of Ur,

---

a 8 Or the Millo   *b* 11 Possibly a variant of Jashob-Baal   *c* 11 Or Thirty; some Septuagint manuscripts Three (see also 2 Samuel 23:8)   *d* 23 That is, about 7 feet 6 inches or about 2.3 meters

36 Hepher the Mekerathite,
Ahijah the Pelonite,
37 Hezro the Carmelite,
Naarai son of Ezbai,
38 Joel the brother of Nathan,
Mibhar son of Hagri,
39 Zelek the Ammonite,
Naharai the Berothite, the armor-bearer of Joab son of Zeruiah,
40 Ira the Ithrite,
Gareb the Ithrite,
41 Uriah the Hittite,
Zabad son of Ahlai,
42 Adina son of Shiza the Reubenite, who was chief of the Reubenites, and the thirty with him,
43 Hanan son of Maakah,
Joshaphat the Mithnite,
44 Uzzia the Ashterathite,
Shama and Jeiel the sons of Hotham the Aroerite,
45 Jediael son of Shimri,
his brother Joha the Tizite,
46 Eliel the Mahavite,
Jeribai and Joshaviah the sons of Elnaam,
Ithmah the Moabite,
47 Eliel, Obed and Jaasiel the Mezobaite.

Warriors Join David

12 These were the men who came to David at Ziklag, while he was banished from the presence of Saul son of Kish (they were among the warriors who helped him in battle; 2they were armed with bows and were able to shoot arrows or to sling stones right-handed or left-handed; they were relatives of Saul from the tribe of Benjamin):

3 Ahiezer their chief and Joash the sons of Shemaah the Gibeathite; Jeziel and Pelet the sons of Azmaveth; Berakah, Jehu the Anathothite, 4and Ishmaiah the Gibeonite, a mighty warrior among the Thirty, who was a leader of the Thirty; Jeremiah, Jahaziel, Johanan, Jozabad the Gederathite,*a* 5Eluzai, Jerimoth, Bealiah, Shemariah and Shephatiah the Haruphite; 6Elkanah, Ishiah, Azarel, Joezer and Jashobeam the Korahites;

7 and Joelah and Zebadiah the sons of Jeroham from Gedor.

8 Some Gadites defected to David at his stronghold in the wilderness. They were brave warriors, ready for battle and able to handle the shield and spear. Their faces were the faces of lions, and they were as swift as gazelles in the mountains.
9 Ezer was the chief,
Obadiah the second in command, Eliab the third,
10 Mishmannah the fourth, Jeremiah the fifth,
11 Attai the sixth, Eliel the seventh,
12 Johanan the eighth, Elzabad the ninth,
13 Jeremiah the tenth and Makbannai the eleventh.
14 These Gadites were army commanders; the least was a match for a hundred, and the greatest for a thousand. 15It was they who crossed the Jordan in the first month when it was overflowing all its banks, and they put to flight everyone living in the valleys, to the east and to the west.
16 Other Benjamites and some men from Judah also came to David in his stronghold. 17David went out to meet them and said to them, "If you have come to me in peace to help me, I am ready for you to join me. But if you have come to betray me to my enemies when my hands are free from violence, may the God of our ancestors see it and judge you."
18 Then the Spirit came on Amasai, chief of the Thirty, and he said:

"We are yours, David!
We are with you, son of Jesse!
Success, success to you,
and success to those who help you,
for your God will help you."

So David received them and made them leaders of his raiding bands.

19 Some of the tribe of Manasseh defected to David when he went with the Philistines to fight against Saul. (He and his men did not help the Philistines because, after consultation, their rulers sent him away. They said, "It will cost us our heads

a 4 In Hebrew texts the second half of this verse (Jeremiah . . . Gederathite) is numbered 12:5, and 12:5-40 is numbered 12:6-41.

if he deserts to his master Saul.") [20]When David went to Ziklag, these were the men of Manasseh who defected to him: Adnah, Jozabad, Jediael, Michael, Jozabad, Elihu and Zillethai, leaders of units of a thousand in Manasseh. [21]They helped David against raiding bands, for all of them were brave warriors, and they were commanders in his army. [22]Day after day men came to help David, until he had a great army, like the army of God.[a]

Others Join David at Hebron

[23]These are the numbers of the men armed for battle who came to David at Hebron to turn Saul's kingdom over to him, as the LORD had said:

[24]from Judah, carrying shield and spear—6,800 armed for battle;

[25]from Simeon, warriors ready for battle—7,100;

[26]from Levi—4,600, [27]including Jehoiada, leader of the family of Aaron, with 3,700 men, [28]and Zadok, a brave young warrior, with 22 officers from his family;

[29]from Benjamin, Saul's tribe—3,000, most of whom had remained loyal to Saul's house until then;

[30]from Ephraim, brave warriors, famous in their own clans—20,800;

[31]from half the tribe of Manasseh, designated by name to come and make David king—18,000;

[32]from Issachar, men who understood the times and knew what Israel should do—200 chiefs, with all their relatives under their command;

[33]from Zebulun, experienced soldiers prepared for battle with every type of weapon, to help David with undivided loyalty—50,000;

[34]from Naphtali—1,000 officers, together with 37,000 men carrying shields and spears;

[35]from Dan, ready for battle—28,600;

[36]from Asher, experienced soldiers prepared for battle—40,000;

[37]and from east of the Jordan, from Reuben, Gad and the half-tribe of Manasseh, armed with every type of weapon—120,000.

[38]All these were fighting men who volunteered to serve in the ranks. They came to Hebron fully determined to make David king over all Israel. All the rest of the Israelites were also of one mind to make David king. [39]The men spent three days there with David, eating and drinking, for their families had supplied provisions for them. [40]Also, their neighbors from as far away as Issachar, Zebulun and Naphtali came bringing food on donkeys, camels, mules and oxen. There were plentiful supplies of flour, fig cakes, raisin cakes, wine, olive oil, cattle and sheep, for there was joy in Israel.

Bringing Back the Ark

13 David conferred with each of his officers, the commanders of thousands and commanders of hundreds. [2]He then said to the whole assembly of Israel, "If it seems good to you and if it is the will of the LORD our God, let us send word far and wide to the rest of our people throughout the territories of Israel, and also to the priests and Levites who are with them in their towns and pasturelands, to come and join us. [3]Let us bring the ark of our God back to us, for we did not inquire of[b] it[c] during the reign of Saul." [4]The whole assembly agreed to do this, because it seemed right to all the people.

[5]So David assembled all Israel, from the Shihor River in Egypt to Lebo Hamath, to bring the ark of God from Kiriath Jearim. [6]David and all Israel went to Baalah of Judah (Kiriath Jearim) to bring up from there the ark of God the LORD, who is enthroned between the cherubim—the ark that is called by the Name.

[7]They moved the ark of God from Abinadab's house on a new cart, with Uzzah and Ahio guiding it. [8]David and all the Israelites were celebrating with all their might before God, with songs and with harps, lyres, timbrels, cymbals and trumpets.

[9]When they came to the threshing floor of Kidon, Uzzah reached out his hand to steady the ark, because the oxen stumbled. [10]The LORD's anger burned against Uzzah, and he struck him down because

---

[a] 22 Or a great and mighty army   [b] 3 Or we neglected   [c] 3 Or him

he had put his hand on the ark. So he died there before God.

¹¹Then David was angry because the LORD's wrath had broken out against Uzzah, and to this day that place is called Perez Uzzah.ᵃ

¹²David was afraid of God that day and asked, "How can I ever bring the ark of God to me?" ¹³He did not take the ark to be with him in the City of David. Instead, he took it to the house of Obed-Edom the Gittite. ¹⁴The ark of God remained with the family of Obed-Edom in his house for three months, and the LORD blessed his household and everything he had.

David's House and Family

14 Now Hiram king of Tyre sent messengers to David, along with cedar logs, stonemasons and carpenters to build a palace for him. ²And David knew that the LORD had established him as king over Israel and that his kingdom had been highly exalted for the sake of his people Israel.

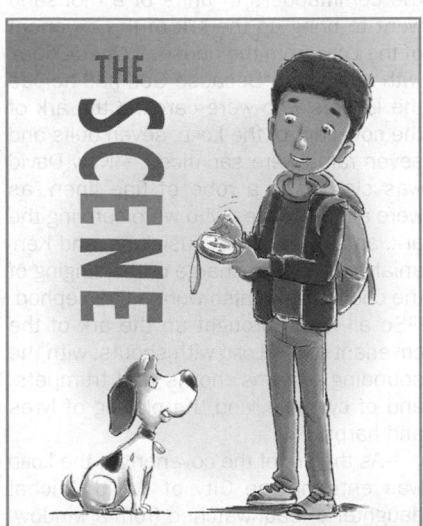

THE SCENE

PEREZ UZZAH

(1 CHRONICLES 13:11)

I n Hebrew, this means "breach of Uzzah," and *Uzzah* alone means "strong."

³In Jerusalem David took more wives and became the father of more sons and daughters. ⁴These are the names of the children born to him there: Shammua, Shobab, Nathan, Solomon, ⁵Ibhar, Elishua, Elpelet, ⁶Nogah, Nepheg, Japhia, ⁷Elishama, Beeliadaᵇ and Eliphelet.

David Defeats the Philistines

⁸When the Philistines heard that David had been anointed king over all Israel, they went up in full force to search for him, but David heard about it and went out to meet them. ⁹Now the Philistines had come and raided the Valley of Rephaim; ¹⁰so David inquired of God: "Shall I go and attack the Philistines? Will you deliver them into my hands?"

The LORD answered him, "Go, I will deliver them into your hands."

¹¹So David and his men went up to Baal Perazim, and there he defeated them. He said, "As waters break out, God has broken out against my enemies by my hand." So that place was called Baal Perazim.ᶜ ¹²The Philistines had abandoned their gods there, and David gave orders to burn them in the fire.

¹³Once more the Philistines raided the valley; ¹⁴so David inquired of God again, and God answered him, "Do not go directly after them, but circle around them and attack them in front of the poplar trees. ¹⁵As soon as you hear the sound of marching in the tops of the poplar trees, move out to battle, because that will mean God has gone out in front of you to strike the Philistine army." ¹⁶So David did as God commanded him, and they struck down the Philistine army, all the way from Gibeon to Gezer.

¹⁷So David's fame spread throughout every land, and the LORD made all the nations fear him.

The Ark Brought to Jerusalem

15 After David had constructed buildings for himself in the City of David, he prepared a place for the ark of God and pitched a tent for it. ²Then David said,

ᵃ 11 *Perez Uzzah* means *outbreak against Uzzah.*
ᵇ 7 A variant of *Eliada*   ᶜ 11 *Baal Perazim* means *the lord who breaks out.*

"No one but the Levites may carry the ark of God, because the Lord chose them to carry the ark of the Lord and to minister before him forever." ³David assembled all Israel in Jerusalem to bring up the ark of the Lord to the place he had prepared for it. ⁴He called together the descendants of Aaron and the Levites:

⁵From the descendants of Kohath,
Uriel the leader and 120 relatives;
⁶from the descendants of Merari,
Asaiah the leader and 220 relatives;
⁷from the descendants of Gershon,ᵃ
Joel the leader and 130 relatives;
⁸from the descendants of Elizaphan,
Shemaiah the leader and 200 relatives;
⁹from the descendants of Hebron,
Eliel the leader and 80 relatives;
¹⁰from the descendants of Uzziel,
Amminadab the leader and 112 relatives.

¹¹Then David summoned Zadok and Abiathar the priests, and Uriel, Asaiah, Joel, Shemaiah, Eliel and Amminadab the Levites. ¹²He said to them, "You are the heads of the Levitical families; you and your fellow Levites are to consecrate yourselves and bring up the ark of the Lord, the God of Israel, to the place I have prepared for it. ¹³It was because you, the Levites, did not bring it up the first time that the Lord our God broke out in anger against us. We did not inquire of him about how to do it in the prescribed way." ¹⁴So the priests and Levites consecrated themselves in order to bring up the ark of the Lord, the God of Israel. ¹⁵And the Levites carried the ark of God with the poles on their shoulders, as Moses had commanded in accordance with the word of the Lord.

¹⁶David told the leaders of the Levites to appoint their fellow Levites as musicians to make a joyful sound with musical instruments: lyres, harps and cymbals.

¹⁷So the Levites appointed Heman son of Joel; from his relatives, Asaph son of Berekiah; and from their relatives the Merarites, Ethan son of Kushaiah; ¹⁸and with them their relatives next in rank: Zecha-riah,ᵇ Jaaziel, Shemiramoth, Jehiel, Unni, Eliab, Benaiah, Maaseiah, Mattithiah, Eliphelehu, Mikneiah, Obed-Edom and Je-iel,ᶜ the gatekeepers.

¹⁹The musicians Heman, Asaph and Ethan were to sound the bronze cymbals; ²⁰Zechariah, Jaaziel,ᵈ Shemiramoth, Jehiel, Unni, Eliab, Maaseiah and Benaiah were to play the lyres according to ala-moth,ᵉ ²¹and Mattithiah, Eliphelehu, Mikneiah, Obed-Edom, Jeiel and Azaziah were to play the harps, directing according to sheminith.ᵉ ²²Kenaniah the head Levite was in charge of the singing; that was his responsibility because he was skillful at it.

²³Berekiah and Elkanah were to be doorkeepers for the ark. ²⁴Shebaniah, Joshaphat, Nethanel, Amasai, Zechariah, Benaiah and Eliezer the priests were to blow trumpets before the ark of God. Obed-Edom and Jehiah were also to be doorkeepers for the ark.

²⁵So David and the elders of Israel and the commanders of units of a thousand went to bring up the ark of the covenant of the Lord from the house of Obed-Edom, with rejoicing. ²⁶Because God had helped the Levites who were carrying the ark of the covenant of the Lord, seven bulls and seven rams were sacrificed. ²⁷Now David was clothed in a robe of fine linen, as were all the Levites who were carrying the ark, and as were the musicians, and Kenaniah, who was in charge of the singing of the choirs. David also wore a linen ephod. ²⁸So all Israel brought up the ark of the covenant of the Lord with shouts, with the sounding of rams' horns and trumpets, and of cymbals, and the playing of lyres and harps.

²⁹As the ark of the covenant of the Lord was entering the City of David, Michal daughter of Saul watched from a window. And when she saw King David dancing and celebrating, she despised him in her heart.

ᵃ 7 Hebrew *Gershom*, a variant of *Gershon*   ᵇ 18 Three Hebrew manuscripts and most Septuagint manuscripts (see also verse 20 and 16:5); most Hebrew manuscripts *Zechariah son and* or *Zechariah, Ben and*   ᶜ 18 Hebrew; Septuagint (see also verse 21) *Jeiel and Azaziah*   ᵈ 20 See verse 18; Hebrew *Aziel*, a variant of *Jaaziel*.   ᵉ 20,21 Probably a musical term

Ministering Before the Ark

16 They brought the ark of God and set it inside the tent that David had pitched for it, and they presented burnt offerings and fellowship offerings before God. ²After David had finished sacrificing the burnt offerings and fellowship offerings, he blessed the people in the name of the LORD. ³Then he gave a loaf of bread, a cake of dates and a cake of raisins to each Israelite man and woman.

⁴He appointed some of the Levites to minister before the ark of the LORD, to extol,ª thank, and praise the LORD, the God of Israel: ⁵Asaph was the chief, and next to him in rank were Zechariah, then Jaaziel,ᵇ Shemiramoth, Jehiel, Mattithiah, Eliab, Benaiah, Obed-Edom and Jeiel. They were to play the lyres and harps, Asaph was to sound the cymbals, ⁶and Benaiah and Jahaziel the priests were to blow the trumpets regularly before the ark of the covenant of God.

⁷That day David first appointed Asaph and his associates to give praise to the LORD in this manner:

⁸Give praise to the LORD, proclaim his name;
    make known among the nations what he has done.
⁹Sing to him, sing praise to him;
    tell of all his wonderful acts.
¹⁰Glory in his holy name;
    let the hearts of those who seek the LORD rejoice.
¹¹Look to the LORD and his strength;
    seek his face always.
¹²Remember the wonders he has done, his miracles, and the judgments he pronounced,
¹³you his servants, the descendants of Israel,
    his chosen ones, the children of Jacob.
¹⁴He is the LORD our God;
    his judgments are in all the earth.
¹⁵He remembersᶜ his covenant forever,
    the promise he made, for a thousand generations,
¹⁶the covenant he made with Abraham, the oath he swore to Isaac.

THE
WITNESSES

✓ **ASAPH** (1 CHRONICLES 16:5–6)
His name means "he collected." He was a Levite musician who David sent to serve in the tabernacle. David gave Asaph psalms for the sanctuary singers. Asaph and his singers ministered every day in the sanctuary.

¹⁷He confirmed it to Jacob as a decree,
    to Israel as an everlasting covenant:
¹⁸"To you I will give the land of Canaan as the portion you will inherit."

¹⁹When they were but few in number, few indeed, and strangers in it,
²⁰theyᵈ wandered from nation to nation, from one kingdom to another.

ª 4 Or petition; or invoke   ᵇ 5 See 15:18,20; Hebrew Jeiel, possibly another name for Jaaziel.   ᶜ 15 Some Septuagint manuscripts (see also Psalm 105:8); Hebrew Remember   ᵈ 18-20 One Hebrew manuscript, Septuagint and Vulgate (see also Psalm 105:12); most Hebrew manuscripts inherit, / ¹⁹though you are but few in number, / few indeed, and strangers in it." / ²⁰They

²¹ He allowed no one to oppress them;
    for their sake he rebuked kings:
²² "Do not touch my anointed ones;
    do my prophets no harm."

²³ Sing to the Lᴏʀᴅ, all the earth;
    proclaim his salvation day after day.
²⁴ Declare his glory among the nations,
    his marvelous deeds among all
    peoples.

²⁵ For great is the Lᴏʀᴅ and most worthy
    of praise;
    he is to be feared above all gods.
²⁶ For all the gods of the nations are
    idols,
    but the Lᴏʀᴅ made the heavens.
²⁷ Splendor and majesty are before him;
    strength and joy are in his dwelling
    place.

²⁸ Ascribe to the Lᴏʀᴅ, all you families of
    nations,
    ascribe to the Lᴏʀᴅ glory and
    strength.
²⁹ Ascribe to the Lᴏʀᴅ the glory due his
    name;
    bring an offering and come before
    him.
    Worship the Lᴏʀᴅ in the splendor of
    his*ᵃ* holiness.
³⁰   Tremble before him, all the earth!
    The world is firmly established; it
    cannot be moved.

³¹ Let the heavens rejoice, let the earth
    be glad;
    let them say among the nations,
    "The Lᴏʀᴅ reigns!"
³² Let the sea resound, and all that is
    in it;
    let the fields be jubilant, and
    everything in them!
³³ Let the trees of the forest sing,
    let them sing for joy before the
    Lᴏʀᴅ,
    for he comes to judge the earth.

³⁴ Give thanks to the Lᴏʀᴅ, for he is good;
    his love endures forever.
³⁵ Cry out, "Save us, God our Savior;
    gather us and deliver us from the
    nations,
    that we may give thanks to your holy
    name,
    and glory in your praise."

³⁶ Praise be to the Lᴏʀᴅ, the God of
    Israel,
    from everlasting to everlasting.

Then all the people said "Amen" and "Praise the Lᴏʀᴅ."

³⁷ David left Asaph and his associates before the ark of the covenant of the Lᴏʀᴅ to minister there regularly, according to each day's requirements. ³⁸ He also left Obed-Edom and his sixty-eight associates to minister with them. Obed-Edom son of Jeduthun, and also Hosah, were gatekeepers.

³⁹ David left Zadok the priest and his fellow priests before the tabernacle of the Lᴏʀᴅ at the high place in Gibeon ⁴⁰ to present burnt offerings to the Lᴏʀᴅ on the altar of burnt offering regularly, morning and evening, in accordance with everything written in the Law of the Lᴏʀᴅ, which he had given Israel. ⁴¹ With them were Heman and Jeduthun and the rest of those chosen and designated by name to give thanks to the Lᴏʀᴅ, "for his love endures forever." ⁴² Heman and Jeduthun were responsible for the sounding of the trumpets and cymbals and for the playing of the other instruments for sacred song. The sons of Jeduthun were stationed at the gate.

⁴³ Then all the people left, each for their own home, and David returned home to bless his family.

God's Promise to David

17 After David was settled in his palace, he said to Nathan the prophet, "Here I am, living in a house of cedar, while the ark of the covenant of the Lᴏʀᴅ is under a tent."

² Nathan replied to David, "Whatever you have in mind, do it, for God is with you."

³ But that night the word of God came to Nathan, saying:

⁴ "Go and tell my servant David, 'This is what the Lᴏʀᴅ says: You are not the one to build me a house to dwell in. ⁵ I have not dwelt in a house from the day I brought Israel up out of Egypt to this day. I have moved

---

ᵃ 29 Or Lᴏʀᴅ with the splendor of

from one tent site to another, from one dwelling place to another. ⁶Wherever I have moved with all the Israelites, did I ever say to any of their leaders^a whom I commanded to shepherd my people, "Why have you not built me a house of cedar?"'

⁷"Now then, tell my servant David, 'This is what the LORD Almighty says: I took you from the pasture, from tending the flock, and appointed you ruler over my people Israel. ⁸I have been with you wherever you have gone, and I have cut off all your enemies from before you. Now I will make your name like the names of the greatest men on earth. ⁹And I will provide a place for my people Israel and will plant them so that they can have a home of their own and no longer be disturbed. Wicked people will not oppress them anymore, as they did at the beginning ¹⁰and have done ever since the time I appointed leaders over my people Israel. I will also subdue all your enemies.

" 'I declare to you that the LORD will build a house for you: ¹¹When your days are over and you go to be with your ancestors, I will raise up your offspring to succeed you, one of your own sons, and I will establish his kingdom. ¹²He is the one who will build a house for me, and I will establish his throne forever. ¹³I will be his father, and he will be my son. I will never take my love away from him, as I took it away from your predecessor. ¹⁴I will set him over my house and my kingdom forever; his throne will be established forever.' "

¹⁵Nathan reported to David all the words of this entire revelation.

David's Prayer

¹⁶Then King David went in and sat before the LORD, and he said:

"Who am I, LORD God, and what is my family, that you have brought me this far? ¹⁷And as if this were not enough in your sight, my God, you have spoken about the future of the house of your servant. You, LORD God, have looked on me as though I were the most exalted of men.

¹⁸"What more can David say to you for honoring your servant? For you know your servant, ¹⁹LORD. For the sake of your servant and according to your will, you have done this great thing and made known all these great promises.

²⁰"There is no one like you, LORD, and there is no God but you, as we have heard with our own ears. ²¹And who is like your people Israel—the one nation on earth whose God went out to redeem a people for himself, and to make a name for yourself, and to perform great and awesome wonders by driving out nations from before your people, whom you redeemed from Egypt? ²²You made your people Israel your very own forever, and you, LORD, have become their God.

²³"And now, LORD, let the promise you have made concerning your servant and his house be established forever. Do as you promised, ²⁴so that it will be established and that your name will be great forever. Then people will say, 'The LORD Almighty, the God over Israel, is Israel's God!' And the house of your servant David will be established before you.

²⁵"You, my God, have revealed to your servant that you will build a house for him. So your servant has found courage to pray to you. ²⁶You, LORD, are God! You have promised these good things to your servant. ²⁷Now you have been pleased to bless the house of your servant, that it may continue forever in your sight; for you, LORD, have blessed it, and it will be blessed forever."

David's Victories

18 In the course of time, David defeated the Philistines and subdued them, and he took Gath and its surrounding villages from the control of the Philistines.

---

^a 6 Traditionally *judges*; also in verse 10

²David also defeated the Moabites, and they became subject to him and brought him tribute.

³Moreover, David defeated Hadadezer king of Zobah, in the vicinity of Hamath, when he went to set up his monument at*a* the Euphrates River. ⁴David captured a thousand of his chariots, seven thousand charioteers and twenty thousand foot soldiers. He hamstrung all but a hundred of the chariot horses.

⁵When the Arameans of Damascus came to help Hadadezer king of Zobah, David struck down twenty-two thousand of them. ⁶He put garrisons in the Aramean kingdom of Damascus, and the Arameans became subject to him and brought him tribute. The LORD gave David victory wherever he went.

⁷David took the gold shields carried by the officers of Hadadezer and brought them to Jerusalem. ⁸From Tebah*b* and Kun, towns that belonged to Hadadezer, David took a great quantity of bronze, which Solomon used to make the bronze Sea, the pillars and various bronze articles.

⁹When Tou king of Hamath heard that David had defeated the entire army of Hadadezer king of Zobah, ¹⁰he sent his son Hadoram to King David to greet him and congratulate him on his victory in battle over Hadadezer, who had been at war with Tou. Hadoram brought all kinds of articles of gold, of silver and of bronze.

¹¹King David dedicated these articles to the LORD, as he had done with the silver and gold he had taken from all these nations: Edom and Moab, the Ammonites and the Philistines, and Amalek.

¹²Abishai son of Zeruiah struck down eighteen thousand Edomites in the Valley of Salt. ¹³He put garrisons in Edom, and all the Edomites became subject to David. The LORD gave David victory wherever he went.

David's Officials

¹⁴David reigned over all Israel, doing what was just and right for all his people. ¹⁵Joab son of Zeruiah was over the army; Jehoshaphat son of Ahilud was recorder; ¹⁶Zadok son of Ahitub and Ahimelek*c* son of Abiathar were priests; Shavsha was sec-

retary; ¹⁷Benaiah son of Jehoiada was over the Kerethites and Pelethites; and David's sons were chief officials at the king's side.

David Defeats the Ammonites

19 In the course of time, Nahash king of the Ammonites died, and his son succeeded him as king. ²David thought, "I will show kindness to Hanun son of Nahash, because his father showed kindness to me." So David sent a delegation to express his sympathy to Hanun concerning his father.

When David's envoys came to Hanun in the land of the Ammonites to express sympathy to him, ³the Ammonite commanders said to Hanun, "Do you think David is honoring your father by sending envoys to you to express sympathy? Haven't his envoys come to you only to explore and spy out the country and overthrow it?" ⁴So Hanun seized David's envoys, shaved them, cut off their garments at the buttocks, and sent them away.

⁵When someone came and told David about the men, he sent messengers to meet them, for they were greatly humiliated. The king said, "Stay at Jericho till your beards have grown, and then come back."

⁶When the Ammonites realized that they had become obnoxious to David, Hanun and the Ammonites sent a thousand talents*d* of silver to hire chariots and charioteers from Aram Naharaim,*e* Aram Maakah and Zobah. ⁷They hired thirty-two thousand chariots and charioteers, as well as the king of Maakah with his troops, who came and camped near Medeba, while the Ammonites were mustered from their towns and moved out for battle.

⁸On hearing this, David sent Joab out with the entire army of fighting men. ⁹The Ammonites came out and drew up in battle formation at the entrance to their city, while the kings who had come were by themselves in the open country.

¹⁰Joab saw that there were battle lines in front of him and behind him; so he

---

a 3 Or *to restore his control over*   *b 8* Hebrew *Tibhath,* a variant of *Tebah*   *c 16* Some Hebrew manuscripts, Vulgate and Syriac (see also 2 Samuel 8:17); most Hebrew manuscripts *Abimelek*   *d 6* That is, about 38 tons or about 34 metric tons   *e 6* That is, Northwest Mesopotamia selected some of the best troops in Israel and deployed them against the Arameans. ¹¹He put the rest of the men under the command of Abishai his brother, and they were deployed against the Ammonites. ¹²Joab said, "If the Arameans are too strong for me, then you are to rescue me; but if the Ammonites are too strong for you, then I will rescue you. ¹³Be strong, and let us fight bravely for our people and the cities of our God. The LORD will do what is good in his sight."

¹⁴Then Joab and the troops with him advanced to fight the Arameans, and they fled before him. ¹⁵When the Ammonites realized that the Arameans were fleeing, they too fled before his brother Abishai and went inside the city. So Joab went back to Jerusalem.

¹⁶After the Arameans saw that they had been routed by Israel, they sent messengers and had Arameans brought from beyond the Euphrates River, with Shophak the commander of Hadadezer's army leading them.

¹⁷When David was told of this, he gathered all Israel and crossed the Jordan; he advanced against them and formed his battle lines opposite them. David formed his lines to meet the Arameans in battle, and they fought against him. ¹⁸But they fled before Israel, and David killed seven thousand of their charioteers and forty thousand of their foot soldiers. He also killed Shophak the commander of their army.

¹⁹When the vassals of Hadadezer saw that they had been routed by Israel, they made peace with David and became subject to him.

So the Arameans were not willing to help the Ammonites anymore.

The Capture of Rabbah

20 In the spring, at the time when kings go off to war, Joab led out the armed forces. He laid waste the land of the Ammonites and went to Rabbah and besieged it, but David remained in Jerusalem. Joab attacked Rabbah and left it in ruins. ²David took the crown from the head of their king*ᵃ*—its weight was found to be a talent*ᵇ* of gold, and it was set with

precious stones—and it was placed on David's head. He took a great quantity of plunder from the city ³and brought out the people who were there, consigning them to labor with saws and with iron picks and axes. David did this to all the Ammonite towns. Then David and his entire army returned to Jerusalem.

War With the Philistines

⁴In the course of time, war broke out with the Philistines, at Gezer. At that time Sibbekai the Hushathite killed Sippai, one of the descendants of the Rephaites, and the Philistines were subjugated.

⁵In another battle with the Philistines, Elhanan son of Jair killed Lahmi the brother

---

ᵃ 2 Or *of Milkom,* that is, Molek   *ᵇ* 2 That is, about 75 pounds or about 34 kilograms

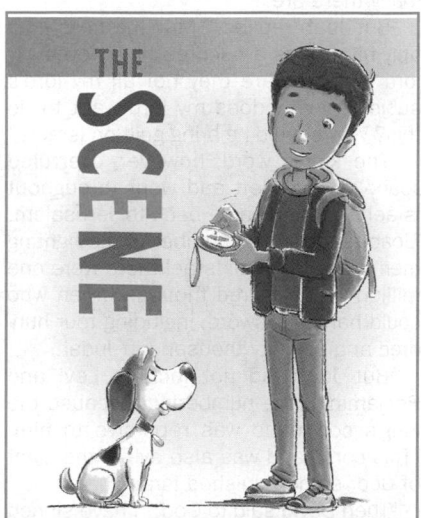

THE SCENE

RABBAH

(1 CHRONICLES 20:1)

It means "greatness." This place is east of the Jordan River. David captured it, and it regained its freedom after Israel had been divided into two kingdoms. It was destroyed in the Babylonian attack from 590 to 559 before Christ.

of Goliath the Gittite, who had a spear with a shaft like a weaver's rod. ⁶In still another battle, which took place at Gath, there was a huge man with six fingers on each hand and six toes on each foot—twenty-four in all. He also was descended from Rapha. ⁷When he taunted Israel, Jonathan son of Shimea, David's brother, killed him.

⁸These were descendants of Rapha in Gath, and they fell at the hands of David and his men.

David Counts the Fighting Men

21 Satan rose up against Israel and incited David to take a census of Israel. ²So David said to Joab and the commanders of the troops, "Go and count the Israelites from Beersheba to Dan. Then report back to me so that I may know how many there are."

³But Joab replied, "May the LORD multiply his troops a hundred times over. My lord the king, are they not all my lord's subjects? Why does my lord want to do this? Why should he bring guilt on Israel?"

⁴The king's word, however, overruled Joab; so Joab left and went throughout Israel and then came back to Jerusalem. ⁵Joab reported the number of the fighting men to David: In all Israel there were one million one hundred thousand men who could handle a sword, including four hundred and seventy thousand in Judah.

⁶But Joab did not include Levi and Benjamin in the numbering, because the king's command was repulsive to him. ⁷This command was also evil in the sight of God; so he punished Israel.

⁸Then David said to God, "I have sinned greatly by doing this. Now, I beg you, take away the guilt of your servant. I have done a very foolish thing."

⁹The LORD said to Gad, David's seer, ¹⁰"Go and tell David, 'This is what the LORD says: I am giving you three options. Choose one of them for me to carry out against you.'"

¹¹So Gad went to David and said to him, "This is what the LORD says: 'Take your choice: ¹²three years of famine, three months of being swept away*ᵃ* before your enemies, with their swords overtaking

THE WITNESSES

✓ **GAD** (1 CHRONICLES 21:9)
This name means "good fortune." He was a prophet who advised David, and he spoke for God.

you, or three days of the sword of the LORD—days of plague in the land, with the angel of the LORD ravaging every part of Israel.' Now then, decide how I should answer the one who sent me."

¹³David said to Gad, "I am in deep distress. Let me fall into the hands of the LORD, for his mercy is very great; but do not let me fall into human hands."

¹⁴So the LORD sent a plague on Israel, and seventy thousand men of Israel fell dead. ¹⁵And God sent an angel to destroy Jerusalem. But as the angel was doing so, the LORD saw it and relented concerning the disaster and said to the angel who was destroying the people, "Enough!

ᵃ 12 Hebrew; Septuagint and Vulgate (see also 2 Samuel 24:13) *of fleeing*

Withdraw your hand." The angel of the LORD was then standing at the threshing floor of Araunah[a] the Jebusite.

[16]David looked up and saw the angel of the LORD standing between heaven and earth, with a drawn sword in his hand extended over Jerusalem. Then David and the elders, clothed in sackcloth, fell facedown.

[17]David said to God, "Was it not I who ordered the fighting men to be counted? I, the shepherd,[b] have sinned and done wrong. These are but sheep. What have they done? LORD my God, let your hand fall on me and my family, but do not let this plague remain on your people."

David Builds an Altar

[18]Then the angel of the LORD ordered Gad to tell David to go up and build an altar to the LORD on the threshing floor of Araunah the Jebusite. [19]So David went up in obedience to the word that Gad had spoken in the name of the LORD.

[20]While Araunah was threshing wheat, he turned and saw the angel; his four sons who were with him hid themselves. [21]Then David approached, and when Araunah looked and saw him, he left the threshing floor and bowed down before David with his face to the ground.

[22]David said to him, "Let me have the site of your threshing floor so I can build an altar to the LORD, that the plague on the people may be stopped. Sell it to me at the full price."

[23]Araunah said to David, "Take it! Let my lord the king do whatever pleases him. Look, I will give the oxen for the burnt offerings, the threshing sledges for the wood, and the wheat for the grain offering. I will give all this."

[24]But King David replied to Araunah, "No, I insist on paying the full price. I will not take for the LORD what is yours, or sacrifice a burnt offering that costs me nothing."

[25]So David paid Araunah six hundred shekels[c] of gold for the site. [26]David built an altar to the LORD there and sacrificed burnt offerings and fellowship offerings. He called on the LORD, and the LORD answered him with fire from heaven on the altar of burnt offering.

[27]Then the LORD spoke to the angel, and he put his sword back into its sheath. [28]At that time, when David saw that the LORD had answered him on the threshing floor of Araunah the Jebusite, he offered sacrifices there. [29]The tabernacle of the LORD, which Moses had made in the wilderness, and the altar of burnt offering were at that time on the high place at Gibeon. [30]But David could not go before it to inquire of God, because he was afraid of the sword of the angel of the LORD.

22 Then David said, "The house of the LORD God is to be here, and also the altar of burnt offering for Israel."

Preparations for the Temple

[2]So David gave orders to assemble the foreigners residing in Israel, and from

---

[a] 15 Hebrew *Ornan*, a variant of *Araunah*; also in verses 18-28   [b] 17 Probable reading of the original Hebrew text (see 2 Samuel 24:17 and note); Masoretic Text does not have *the shepherd*.   [c] 25 That is, about 15 pounds or about 6.9 kilograms

GIBEON

(1 CHRONICLES 21:29)

It means "hill site." It's a business city about 5 miles (8 km) northwest of Jerusalem. Solomon worshiped there before building the temple.

among them he appointed stonecutters to prepare dressed stone for building the house of God. ³He provided a large amount of iron to make nails for the doors of the gateways and for the fittings, and more bronze than could be weighed. ⁴He also provided more cedar logs than could be counted, for the Sidonians and Tyrians had brought large numbers of them to David.

⁵David said, "My son Solomon is young and inexperienced, and the house to be built for the LORD should be of great magnificence and fame and splendor in the sight of all the nations. Therefore I will make preparations for it." So David made extensive preparations before his death.

⁶Then he called for his son Solomon and charged him to build a house for the LORD, the God of Israel. ⁷David said to Solomon: "My son, I had it in my heart to build a house for the Name of the LORD my God. ⁸But this word of the LORD came to me: 'You have shed much blood and have fought many wars. You are not to build a house for my Name, because you have shed much blood on the earth in my sight. ⁹But you will have a son who will be a man of peace and rest, and I will give him rest from all his enemies on every side. His name will be Solomon,ᵃ and I will grant Israel peace and quiet during his reign. ¹⁰He is the one who will build a house for my Name. He will be my son, and I will be his father. And I will establish the throne of his kingdom over Israel forever.'

¹¹"Now, my son, the LORD be with you, and may you have success and build the house of the LORD your God, as he said you would. ¹²May the LORD give you discretion and understanding when he puts you in command over Israel, so that you may keep the law of the LORD your God. ¹³Then you will have success if you are careful to observe the decrees and laws that the LORD gave Moses for Israel. Be strong and courageous. Do not be afraid or discouraged.

¹⁴"I have taken great pains to provide for the temple of the LORD a hundred thousand talentsᵇ of gold, a million talentsᶜ of silver, quantities of bronze and iron too great to be weighed, and wood and stone. And you may add to them. ¹⁵You have

many workers: stonecutters, masons and carpenters, as well as those skilled in every kind of work ¹⁶in gold and silver, bronze and iron—craftsmen beyond number. Now begin the work, and the LORD be with you."

¹⁷Then David ordered all the leaders of Israel to help his son Solomon. ¹⁸He said to them, "Is not the LORD your God with you? And has he not granted you rest on every side? For he has given the inhabitants of the land into my hands, and the land is subject to the LORD and to his people. ¹⁹Now devote your heart and soul to seeking the LORD your God. Begin to build the sanctuary of the LORD God, so that you may bring the ark of the covenant of the LORD and the sacred articles belonging to God into the temple that will be built for the Name of the LORD."

The Levites

23 When David was old and full of years, he made his son Solomon king over Israel.

²He also gathered together all the leaders of Israel, as well as the priests and Levites. ³The Levites thirty years old or more were counted, and the total number of men was thirty-eight thousand. ⁴David said, "Of these, twenty-four thousand are to be in charge of the work of the temple of the LORD and six thousand are to be officials and judges. ⁵Four thousand are to be gatekeepers and four thousand are to praise the LORD with the musical instruments I have provided for that purpose."

⁶David separated the Levites into divisions corresponding to the sons of Levi: Gershon, Kohath and Merari.

Gershonites

⁷Belonging to the Gershonites:
    Ladan and Shimei.
⁸The sons of Ladan:
    Jehiel the first, Zetham and Joel—
    three in all.
⁹The sons of Shimei:
    Shelomoth, Haziel and Haran—
    three in all.

ᵃ 9 *Solomon* sounds like and may be derived from the Hebrew for *peace*.   ᵇ 14 That is, about 3,750 tons or about 3,400 metric tons   ᶜ 14 That is, about 37,500 tons or about 34,000 metric tons

These were the heads of the families of Ladan.

¹⁰And the sons of Shimei:

Jahath, Ziza,ᵃ Jeush and Beriah. These were the sons of Shimei— four in all.

¹¹Jahath was the first and Ziza the second, but Jeush and Beriah did not have many sons; so they were counted as one family with one assignment.

Kohathites

¹²The sons of Kohath:

Amram, Izhar, Hebron and Uzziel— four in all.

¹³The sons of Amram:

Aaron and Moses.

Aaron was set apart, he and his descendants forever, to consecrate the most holy things, to offer sacrifices before the LORD, to minister before him and to pronounce blessings in his name forever. ¹⁴The sons of Moses the man of God were counted as part of the tribe of Levi.

¹⁵The sons of Moses:

Gershom and Eliezer.

¹⁶The descendants of Gershom:

Shubael was the first.

¹⁷The descendants of Eliezer:

Rehabiah was the first.

Eliezer had no other sons, but the sons of Rehabiah were very numerous.

¹⁸The sons of Izhar:

Shelomith was the first.

¹⁹The sons of Hebron:

Jeriah the first, Amariah the second, Jahaziel the third and Jekameam the fourth.

²⁰The sons of Uzziel:

Micah the first and Ishiah the second.

Merarites

²¹The sons of Merari:

Mahli and Mushi.

The sons of Mahli:

Eleazar and Kish.

²²Eleazar died without having sons: he had only daughters. Their cousins, the sons of Kish, married them.

²³The sons of Mushi:

Mahli, Eder and Jerimoth—three in all.

²⁴These were the descendants of Levi by their families—the heads of families as they were registered under their names and counted individually, that is, the workers twenty years old or more who served in the temple of the LORD. ²⁵For David had said, "Since the LORD, the God of Israel, has granted rest to his people and has come to dwell in Jerusalem forever, ²⁶the Levites no longer need to carry the tabernacle or any of the articles used in its service." ²⁷According to the last instructions of David, the Levites were counted from those twenty years old or more.

²⁸The duty of the Levites was to help Aaron's descendants in the service of the temple of the LORD: to be in charge of the courtyards, the side rooms, the purification of all sacred things and the performance of other duties at the house of God. ²⁹They were in charge of the bread set out on the table, the special flour for the grain offerings, the thin loaves made without yeast, the baking and the mixing, and all measurements of quantity and size. ³⁰They were also to stand every morning to thank and praise the LORD. They were to do the same in the evening ³¹and whenever burnt offerings were presented to the LORD on the Sabbaths, at the New Moon feasts and at the appointed festivals. They were to serve before the LORD regularly in the proper number and in the way prescribed for them.

³²And so the Levites carried out their responsibilities for the tent of meeting, for the Holy Place and, under their relatives the descendants of Aaron, for the service of the temple of the LORD.

The Divisions of Priests

24 These were the divisions of the descendants of Aaron:

The sons of Aaron were Nadab, Abihu, Eleazar and Ithamar. ²But Nadab and Abihu died before their father did, and they had no sons; so Eleazar and Ithamar

---

ᵃ 10 One Hebrew manuscript, Septuagint and Vulgate (see also verse 11); most Hebrew manuscripts *Zina* served as the priests. ³With the help of Zadok a descendant of Eleazar and Ahimelek a descendant of Ithamar, David separated them into divisions for their appointed order of ministering. ⁴A larger number of leaders were found among Eleazar's descendants than among Ithamar's, and they were divided accordingly: sixteen heads of families from Eleazar's descendants and eight heads of families from Ithamar's descendants. ⁵They divided them impartially by casting lots, for there were officials of the sanctuary and officials of God among the descendants of both Eleazar and Ithamar.

⁶The scribe Shemaiah son of Nethanel, a Levite, recorded their names in the presence of the king and of the officials: Zadok the priest, Ahimelek son of Abiathar and the heads of families of the priests and of the Levites—one family being taken from Eleazar and then one from Ithamar.

⁷The first lot fell to Jehoiarib,
the second to Jedaiah,
⁸the third to Harim,
the fourth to Seorim,
⁹the fifth to Malkijah,
the sixth to Mijamin,
¹⁰the seventh to Hakkoz,
the eighth to Abijah,
¹¹the ninth to Jeshua,
the tenth to Shekaniah,
¹²the eleventh to Eliashib,
the twelfth to Jakim,
¹³the thirteenth to Huppah,
the fourteenth to Jeshebeab,
¹⁴the fifteenth to Bilgah,
the sixteenth to Immer,
¹⁵the seventeenth to Hezir,
the eighteenth to Happizzez,
¹⁶the nineteenth to Pethahiah,
the twentieth to Jehezkel,
¹⁷the twenty-first to Jakin,
the twenty-second to Gamul,
¹⁸the twenty-third to Delaiah
and the twenty-fourth to Maaziah.

¹⁹This was their appointed order of ministering when they entered the temple of the LORD, according to the regulations prescribed for them by their ancestor Aaron, as the LORD, the God of Israel, had commanded him.

The Rest of the Levites

²⁰As for the rest of the descendants of Levi:
from the sons of Amram: Shubael;
from the sons of Shubael: Jehdeiah.
²¹As for Rehabiah, from his sons:
Ishiah was the first.
²²From the Izharites: Shelomoth;
from the sons of Shelomoth: Jahath.
²³The sons of Hebron: Jeriah the first,ᵃ Amariah the second, Jahaziel the third and Jekameam the fourth.
²⁴The son of Uzziel: Micah;
from the sons of Micah: Shamir.
²⁵The brother of Micah: Ishiah;
from the sons of Ishiah: Zechariah.
²⁶The sons of Merari: Mahli and Mushi.
The son of Jaaziah: Beno.
²⁷The sons of Merari:
from Jaaziah: Beno, Shoham, Zakkur and Ibri.
²⁸From Mahli: Eleazar, who had no sons.
²⁹From Kish: the son of Kish: Jerahmeel.
³⁰And the sons of Mushi: Mahli, Eder and Jerimoth.

These were the Levites, according to their families. ³¹They also cast lots, just as their relatives the descendants of Aaron did, in the presence of King David and of Zadok, Ahimelek, and the heads of families of the priests and of the Levites. The families of the oldest brother were treated the same as those of the youngest.

The Musicians

25 David, together with the commanders of the army, set apart some of the sons of Asaph, Heman and Jeduthun for the ministry of prophesying, accompanied by harps, lyres and cymbals. Here is the list of the men who performed this service:

ᵃ 23 Two Hebrew manuscripts and some Septuagint manuscripts (see also 23:19); most Hebrew manuscripts *The sons of Jeriah:*

²From the sons of Asaph:
Zakkur, Joseph, Nethaniah and Asarelah. The sons of Asaph were under the supervision of Asaph, who prophesied under the king's supervision. ³As for Jeduthun, from his sons:
Gedaliah, Zeri, Jeshaiah, Shimei,ᵃ Hashabiah and Mattithiah, six in all, under the supervision of their father Jeduthun, who prophesied, using the harp in thanking and praising the Lord. ⁴As for Heman, from his sons:
Bukkiah, Mattaniah, Uzziel, Shubael and Jerimoth; Hananiah, Hanani, Eliathah, Giddalti and Romamti-Ezer; Joshbekashah, Mallothi, Hothir and Mahazioth. ⁵(All these were sons of Heman the king's seer. They were given him through the promises of God to exalt him. God gave Heman fourteen sons and three daughters.)

⁶All these men were under the supervision of their father for the music of the temple of the Lord, with cymbals, lyres and harps, for the ministry at the house of God.
Asaph, Jeduthun and Heman were under the supervision of the king. ⁷Along with their relatives—all of them trained and skilled in music for the Lord—they numbered 288. ⁸Young and old alike, teacher as well as student, cast lots for their duties.

⁹The first lot, which was for Asaph,
fell to Joseph,
his sons and relativesᵇ 12ᶜ
the second to Gedaliah,
him and his relatives
and sons 12
¹⁰the third to Zakkur,
his sons and relatives 12
¹¹the fourth to Izri,ᵈ
his sons and relatives 12
¹²the fifth to Nethaniah,
his sons and relatives 12
¹³the sixth to Bukkiah,
his sons and relatives 12
¹⁴the seventh to Jesarelah,ᵉ
his sons and relatives 12
¹⁵the eighth to Jeshaiah,
his sons and relatives 12
¹⁶the ninth to Mattaniah,
his sons and relatives 12
¹⁷the tenth to Shimei,
his sons and relatives 12
¹⁸the eleventh to Azarel,ᶠ
his sons and relatives 12
¹⁹the twelfth to Hashabiah,
his sons and relatives 12
²⁰the thirteenth to Shubael,
his sons and relatives 12
²¹the fourteenth to Mattithiah,
his sons and relatives 12
²²the fifteenth to Jerimoth,
his sons and relatives 12
²³the sixteenth to Hananiah,
his sons and relatives 12
²⁴the seventeenth to
Joshbekashah,
his sons and relatives 12
²⁵the eighteenth to Hanani,
his sons and relatives 12
²⁶the nineteenth to Mallothi,
his sons and relatives 12
²⁷the twentieth to Eliathah,
his sons and relatives 12
²⁸the twenty-first to Hothir,
his sons and relatives 12
²⁹the twenty-second to Giddalti,
his sons and relatives 12
³⁰the twenty-third to Mahazioth,
his sons and relatives 12
³¹the twenty-fourth to Romamti-Ezer,
his sons and relatives 12.

The Gatekeepers

26 The divisions of the gatekeepers:

From the Korahites: Meshelemiah son of Kore, one of the sons of Asaph.
²Meshelemiah had sons:
Zechariah the firstborn,
Jediael the second,
Zebadiah the third,
Jathniel the fourth,
³Elam the fifth,

ᵃ 3 One Hebrew manuscript and some Septuagint manuscripts (see also verse 17); most Hebrew manuscripts do not have *Shimei*.   ᵇ 9 See Septuagint; Hebrew does not have *his sons and relatives*.   ᶜ 9 See the total in verse 7; Hebrew does not have *twelve*.   ᵈ 11 A variant of *Zeri*   ᵉ 14 A variant of *Asarelah*   ᶠ 18 A variant of *Uzziel*

Jehohanan the sixth
and Eliehoenai the seventh.
⁴Obed-Edom also had sons:
Shemaiah the firstborn,
Jehozabad the second,
Joah the third,
Sakar the fourth,
Nethanel the fifth,
⁵Ammiel the sixth,
Issachar the seventh
and Peullethai the eighth.
(For God had blessed Obed-Edom.)

⁶Obed-Edom's son Shemaiah also had sons, who were leaders in their father's family because they were very capable men. ⁷The sons of Shemaiah: Othni, Rephael, Obed and Elzabad; his relatives Elihu and Semakiah were also able men. ⁸All these were descendants of Obed-Edom; they and their sons and their relatives were capable men with the strength to do the work—descendants of Obed-Edom, 62 in all. ⁹Meshelemiah had sons and relatives, who were able men—18 in all.

¹⁰Hosah the Merarite had sons: Shimri the first (although he was not the firstborn, his father had appointed him the first), ¹¹Hilkiah the second, Tabaliah the third and Zechariah the fourth. The sons and relatives of Hosah were 13 in all.

¹²These divisions of the gatekeepers, through their leaders, had duties for ministering in the temple of the Lord, just as their relatives had. ¹³Lots were cast for each gate, according to their families, young and old alike.

¹⁴The lot for the East Gate fell to Shelemiah.ᵃ Then lots were cast for his son Zechariah, a wise counselor, and the lot for the North Gate fell to him. ¹⁵The lot for the South Gate fell to Obed-Edom, and the lot for the storehouse fell to his sons. ¹⁶The lots for the West Gate and the Shalleketh Gate on the upper road fell to Shuppim and Hosah.

Guard was alongside of guard: ¹⁷There were six Levites a day on the east, four a day on the north, four a day on the south and two at a time at the storehouse. ¹⁸As for the courtᵇ to the west, there were four at the road and two at the courtᵇ itself.

¹⁹These were the divisions of the gatekeepers who were descendants of Korah and Merari.

The Treasurers and Other Officials

²⁰Their fellow Levites wereᶜ in charge of the treasuries of the house of God and the treasuries for the dedicated things.

²¹The descendants of Ladan, who were Gershonites through Ladan and who were heads of families belonging to Ladan the Gershonite, were Jehieli, ²²the sons of Jehieli, Zetham and his brother Joel. They were in charge of the treasuries of the temple of the Lord.

²³From the Amramites, the Izharites, the Hebronites and the Uzzielites:

²⁴Shubael, a descendant of Gershom son of Moses, was the official in charge of the treasuries. ²⁵His relatives through Eliezer: Rehabiah his son, Jeshaiah his son, Joram his son, Zikri his son and Shelomith his son. ²⁶Shelomith and his relatives were in charge of all the treasuries for the things dedicated by King David, by the heads of families who were the commanders of thousands and commanders of hundreds, and by the other army commanders. ²⁷Some of the plunder taken in battle they dedicated for the repair of the temple of the Lord. ²⁸And everything dedicated by Samuel the seer and by Saul son of Kish, Abner son of Ner and Joab son of Zeruiah, and all the other dedicated things were in the care of Shelomith and his relatives.

²⁹From the Izharites: Kenaniah and his sons were assigned duties away from the temple, as officials and judges over Israel.

ᵃ 14 A variant of Meshelemiah   ᵇ 18 The meaning of the Hebrew for this word is uncertain.   ᶜ 20 Septuagint; Hebrew As for the Levites, Ahijah was

30 From the Hebronites: Hashabiah and his relatives—seventeen hundred able men—were responsible in Israel west of the Jordan for all the work of the LORD and for the king's service. 31 As for the Hebronites, Jeriah was their chief according to the genealogical records of their families. In the fortieth year of David's reign a search was made in the records, and capable men among the Hebronites were found at Jazer in Gilead. 32 Jeriah had twenty-seven hundred relatives, who were able men and heads of families, and King David put them in charge of the Reubenites, the Gadites and the half-tribe of Manasseh for every matter pertaining to God and for the affairs of the king.

Army Divisions

27 This is the list of the Israelites— heads of families, commanders of thousands and commanders of hundreds, and their officers, who served the king in all that concerned the army divisions that were on duty month by month throughout the year. Each division consisted of 24,000 men.

2 In charge of the first division, for the first month, was Jashobeam son of Zabdiel. There were 24,000 men in his division. 3 He was a descendant of Perez and chief of all the army officers for the first month. 4 In charge of the division for the second month was Dodai the Ahohite; Mikloth was the leader of his division. There were 24,000 men in his division. 5 The third army commander, for the third month, was Benaiah son of Jehoiada the priest. He was chief and there were 24,000 men in his division. 6 This was the Benaiah who was a mighty warrior among the Thirty and was over the Thirty. His son Ammizabad was in charge of his division. 7 The fourth, for the fourth month, was Asahel the brother of Joab; his son Zebadiah was his successor. There were 24,000 men in his division.

8 The fifth, for the fifth month, was the commander Shamhuth the Izrahite. There were 24,000 men in his division. 9 The sixth, for the sixth month, was Ira the son of Ikkesh the Tekoite. There were 24,000 men in his division. 10 The seventh, for the seventh month, was Helez the Pelonite, an Ephraimite. There were 24,000 men in his division. 11 The eighth, for the eighth month, was Sibbekai the Hushathite, a Zerahite. There were 24,000 men in his division. 12 The ninth, for the ninth month, was Abiezer the Anathothite, a Benjamite. There were 24,000 men in his division. 13 The tenth, for the tenth month, was Maharai the Netophathite, a Zerahite. There were 24,000 men in his division. 14 The eleventh, for the eleventh month, was Benaiah the Pirathonite, an Ephraimite. There were 24,000 men in his division. 15 The twelfth, for the twelfth month, was Heldai the Netophathite, from the family of Othniel. There were 24,000 men in his division.

Leaders of the Tribes

16 The leaders of the tribes of Israel:

over the Reubenites: Eliezer son of Zikri;

over the Simeonites: Shephatiah son of Maakah;

17 over Levi: Hashabiah son of Kemuel;

over Aaron: Zadok;

18 over Judah: Elihu, a brother of David;

over Issachar: Omri son of Michael;

19 over Zebulun: Ishmaiah son of Obadiah;

over Naphtali: Jerimoth son of Azriel;

20 over the Ephraimites: Hoshea son of Azaziah;

over half the tribe of Manasseh: Joel son of Pedaiah;

21 over the half-tribe of Manasseh in Gilead: Iddo son of Zechariah;

over Benjamin: Jaasiel son of Abner;

22 over Dan: Azarel son of Jeroham. These were the leaders of the tribes of Israel.

23 David did not take the number of the men twenty years old or less, because the LORD had promised to make Israel as numerous as the stars in the sky. 24 Joab son of Zeruiah began to count the men but did not finish. God's wrath came on Israel on account of this numbering, and the number was not entered in the book[a] of the annals of King David.

The King's Overseers

25 Azmaveth son of Adiel was in charge of the royal storehouses.

Jonathan son of Uzziah was in charge of the storehouses in the outlying districts, in the towns, the villages and the watchtowers.

26 Ezri son of Kelub was in charge of the workers who farmed the land.

27 Shimei the Ramathite was in charge of the vineyards.

Zabdi the Shiphmite was in charge of the produce of the vineyards for the wine vats.

28 Baal-Hanan the Gederite was in charge of the olive and sycamore-fig trees in the western foothills.

Joash was in charge of the supplies of olive oil.

29 Shitrai the Sharonite was in charge of the herds grazing in Sharon.

Shaphat son of Adlai was in charge of the herds in the valleys.

30 Obil the Ishmaelite was in charge of the camels.

Jehdeiah the Meronothite was in charge of the donkeys.

31 Jaziz the Hagrite was in charge of the flocks.

All these were the officials in charge of King David's property.

32 Jonathan, David's uncle, was a counselor, a man of insight and a scribe. Jehiel son of Hakmoni took care of the king's sons.

33 Ahithophel was the king's counselor. Hushai the Arkite was the king's confidant. 34 Ahithophel was succeeded by Jehoiada son of Benaiah and by Abiathar.

Joab was the commander of the royal army.

David's Plans for the Temple

28 David summoned all the officials of Israel to assemble at Jerusalem: the officers over the tribes, the commanders of the divisions in the service of the king, the commanders of thousands and commanders of hundreds, and the officials in charge of all the property and livestock belonging to the king and his sons, together with the palace officials, the warriors and all the brave fighting men.

2 King David rose to his feet and said: "Listen to me, my fellow Israelites, my people. I had it in my heart to build a house as a place of rest for the ark of the covenant of the LORD, for the footstool of our God, and I made plans to build it. 3 But God said to me, 'You are not to build a house for my Name, because you are a warrior and have shed blood.'

4 "Yet the LORD, the God of Israel, chose me from my whole family to be king over Israel forever. He chose Judah as leader, and from the tribe of Judah he chose my family, and from my father's sons he was pleased to make me king over all Israel. 5 Of all my sons—and the LORD has given me many—he has chosen my son Solomon to sit on the throne of the kingdom of the LORD over Israel. 6 He said to me: 'Solomon your son is the one who will build my house and my courts, for I have chosen him to be my son, and I will be his father. 7 I will establish his kingdom forever if he is unswerving in carrying out my commands and laws, as is being done at this time.'

8 "So now I charge you in the sight of all Israel and of the assembly of the LORD, and in the hearing of our God: Be careful to follow all the commands of the LORD your God, that you may possess this good land and pass it on as an inheritance to your descendants forever.

9 "And you, my son Solomon, acknowledge the God of your father, and serve him with wholehearted devotion and with a willing mind, for the LORD searches

---

[a] 24 Septuagint; Hebrew number

every heart and understands every desire and every thought. If you seek him, he will be found by you; but if you forsake him, he will reject you forever. [10]Consider now, for the LORD has chosen you to build a house as the sanctuary. Be strong and do the work."

[11]Then David gave his son Solomon the plans for the portico of the temple, its buildings, its storerooms, its upper parts, its inner rooms and the place of atonement. [12]He gave him the plans of all that the Spirit had put in his mind for the courts of the temple of the LORD and all the surrounding rooms, for the treasuries of the temple of God and for the treasuries for the dedicated things. [13]He gave him instructions for the divisions of the priests and Levites, and for all the work of serving in the temple of the LORD, as well as for all the articles to be used in its service. [14]He designated the weight of gold for all the gold articles to be used in various kinds of service, and the weight of silver for all the silver articles to be used in various kinds of service: [15]the weight of gold for the gold lampstands and their lamps, with the weight for each lampstand and its lamps; and the weight of silver for each silver lampstand and its lamps, according to the use of each lampstand; [16]the weight of gold for each table for consecrated bread; the weight of silver for the silver tables; [17]the weight of pure gold for the forks, sprinkling bowls and pitchers; the weight of gold for each gold dish; the weight of silver for each silver dish; [18]and the weight of the refined gold for the altar of incense. He also gave him the plan for the chariot, that is, the cherubim of gold that spread their wings and overshadow the ark of the covenant of the LORD.

[19]"All this," David said, "I have in writing as a result of the LORD's hand on me, and he enabled me to understand all the details of the plan."

[20]David also said to Solomon his son, "Be strong and courageous, and do the work. Do not be afraid or discouraged, for the LORD God, my God, is with you. He will not fail you or forsake you until all the work for the service of the temple of the LORD is finished. [21]The divisions of the priests and Levites are ready for all the work on the temple of God, and every willing person skilled in any craft will help you in all the work. The officials and all the people will obey your every command."

Gifts for Building the Temple

29 Then King David said to the whole assembly: "My son Solomon, the one whom God has chosen, is young and inexperienced. The task is great, because this palatial structure is not for man but for the LORD God. [2]With all my resources I have provided for the temple of my God—gold for the gold work, silver for the silver, bronze for the bronze, iron for the iron and wood for the wood, as well as onyx for the settings, turquoise,[a] stones of various colors, and all kinds of fine stone and marble—all of these in large quantities. [3]Besides, in my devotion to the temple of my God I now give my personal treasures of gold and silver for the temple of my God, over and above everything I have provided for this holy temple: [4]three thousand talents[b] of gold (gold of Ophir) and seven thousand talents[c] of refined silver, for the overlaying of the walls of the buildings, [5]for the gold work and the silver work, and for all the work to be done by the craftsmen. Now, who is willing to consecrate themselves to the LORD today?"

[6]Then the leaders of families, the officers of the tribes of Israel, the commanders of thousands and commanders of hundreds, and the officials in charge of the king's work gave willingly. [7]They gave toward the work on the temple of God five thousand talents[d] and ten thousand darics[e] of gold, ten thousand talents[f] of silver, eighteen thousand talents[g] of bronze and a hundred thousand talents[h] of iron. [8]Anyone who had precious stones gave them to the treasury of the temple of the

---

[a] 2 The meaning of the Hebrew for this word is uncertain.
[b] 4 That is, about 110 tons or about 100 metric tons
[c] 4 That is, about 260 tons or about 235 metric tons
[d] 7 That is, about 190 tons or about 170 metric tons
[e] 7 That is, about 185 pounds or about 84 kilograms
[f] 7 That is, about 380 tons or about 340 metric tons
[g] 7 That is, about 675 tons or about 610 metric tons
[h] 7 That is, about 3,800 tons or about 3,400 metric tons

LORD in the custody of Jehiel the Gershonite. ⁹The people rejoiced at the willing response of their leaders, for they had given freely and wholeheartedly to the LORD. David the king also rejoiced greatly.

David's Prayer

¹⁰David praised the LORD in the presence of the whole assembly, saying,

"Praise be to you, LORD,
the God of our father Israel,
from everlasting to everlasting.
¹¹Yours, LORD, is the greatness and the power
and the glory and the majesty and the splendor,
for everything in heaven and earth is yours.
Yours, LORD, is the kingdom;
you are exalted as head over all.
¹²Wealth and honor come from you;
you are the ruler of all things.
In your hands are strength and power
to exalt and give strength to all.
¹³Now, our God, we give you thanks,
and praise your glorious name.

¹⁴"But who am I, and who are my people, that we should be able to give as generously as this? Everything comes from you, and we have given you only what comes from your hand. ¹⁵We are foreigners and strangers in your sight, as were all our ancestors. Our days on earth are like a shadow, without hope. ¹⁶LORD our God, all this abundance that we have provided for building you a temple for your Holy Name comes from your hand, and all of it belongs to you. ¹⁷I know, my God, that you test the heart and are pleased with integrity. All these things I have given willingly and with honest intent. And now I have seen with joy how willingly your people who are here have given to you. ¹⁸LORD, the God of our fathers Abraham, Isaac and Israel, keep these desires and thoughts in the hearts of your people forever, and keep their hearts loyal to you. ¹⁹And give my son Solomon the wholehearted devotion to keep your commands, statutes and decrees and to do everything to build the palatial structure for which I have provided."

²⁰Then David said to the whole assembly, "Praise the LORD your God." So they all praised the LORD, the God of their fathers; they bowed down, prostrating themselves before the LORD and the king.

Solomon Acknowledged as King

²¹The next day they made sacrifices to the LORD and presented burnt offerings to him: a thousand bulls, a thousand rams and a thousand male lambs, together with their drink offerings, and other sacrifices in abundance for all Israel. ²²They ate and drank with great joy in the presence of the LORD that day.

Then they acknowledged Solomon son of David as king a second time, anointing him before the LORD to be ruler and Zadok to be priest. ²³So Solomon sat on the throne of the LORD as king in place of his father David. He prospered and all Israel obeyed him. ²⁴All the officers and

CHECK THE FACTS

Which man was David's son, who became king after him?

A) Solomon

B) Rehoboam

C) Jesus

CORRECT ANSWER: A

warriors, as well as all of King David's sons, pledged their submission to King Solomon.

25The LORD highly exalted Solomon in the sight of all Israel and bestowed on him royal splendor such as no king over Israel ever had before.

The Death of David

26David son of Jesse was king over all Israel. 27He ruled over Israel forty years— seven in Hebron and thirty-three in Jeru-salem. 28He died at a good old age, having enjoyed long life, wealth and honor. His son Solomon succeeded him as king.

29As for the events of King David's reign, from beginning to end, they are written in the records of Samuel the seer, the records of Nathan the prophet and the records of Gad the seer, 30together with the details of his reign and power, and the circumstances that surrounded him and Israel and the kingdoms of all the other lands.

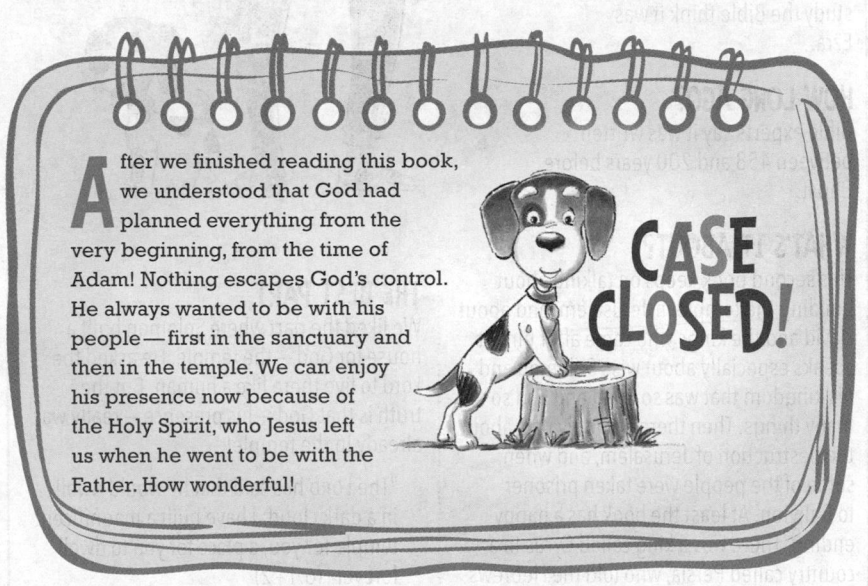

After we finished reading this book, we understood that God had planned everything from the very beginning, from the time of Adam! Nothing escapes God's control. He always wanted to be with his people—first in the sanctuary and then in the temple. We can enjoy his presence now because of the Holy Spirit, who Jesus left us when he went to be with the Father. How wonderful!

CASE CLOSED!

2 CHRONICLES

THE EVIDENCE:

WHO WROTE IT?
Remember that 1 and 2 Chronicles were just one book before. We don't know who wrote it. People who study the Bible think it was Ezra.

HOW LONG AGO?
Bible experts say it was written between 458 and 200 years before Christ.

WHAT'S IT ABOUT?
This second book keeps on talking about building the temple in Jerusalem, and about David and the kings who came after him. It speaks especially about wise Solomon and his kingdom that was so great and had so many things. Then there's an ugly part about the destruction of Jerusalem, and when some of the people were taken prisoner to Babylon. At least the book has a happy ending. There was a king called Cyrus in a country called Persia, who told the Hebrews they could return to their land and worship God.

THE BEST PART
We liked the part where Solomon built a house for God — the temple. He asked the Lord to live there like a human. But the truth is that God — his presence — really was already in the temple!

"The LORD has said that he would dwell in a dark cloud; I have built a magnificent temple for you, a place for you to dwell forever" (6:1 - 2).

Solomon Asks for Wisdom

1 Solomon son of David established himself firmly over his kingdom, for the LORD his God was with him and made him exceedingly great.

²Then Solomon spoke to all Israel — to the commanders of thousands and commanders of hundreds, to the judges and to all the leaders in Israel, the heads of families — ³and Solomon and the whole assembly went to the high place at Gibeon, for God's tent of meeting was there, which Moses the LORD's servant had made in the wilderness. ⁴Now David had brought up the ark of God from Kiriath Jearim to the place he had prepared for it, because he had pitched a tent for it in Jerusalem. ⁵But the bronze altar that Bezalel son of Uri, the son of Hur, had made was in Gibeon in front of the tabernacle of the LORD; so Solomon and the assembly inquired of him there. ⁶Solomon went up to the bronze altar before the LORD in the tent of meeting and offered a thousand burnt offerings on it.

⁷That night God appeared to Solomon and said to him, "Ask for whatever you want me to give you."

⁸Solomon answered God, "You have shown great kindness to David my father and have made me king in his place. ⁹Now, Lord God, let your promise to my father David be confirmed, for you have made me king over a people who are as numerous as the dust of the earth. ¹⁰Give me wisdom and knowledge, that I may lead this people, for who is able to govern this great people of yours?"

¹¹God said to Solomon, "Since this is your heart's desire and you have not asked for wealth, possessions or honor, nor for the death of your enemies, and since you have not asked for a long life but for wisdom and knowledge to govern my people over whom I have made you king, ¹²therefore wisdom and knowledge will be given you. And I will also give you wealth, possessions and honor, such as no king who was before you ever had and none after you will have."

¹³Then Solomon went to Jerusalem from the high place at Gibeon, from before the tent of meeting. And he reigned over Israel.

¹⁴Solomon accumulated chariots and horses; he had fourteen hundred chariots and twelve thousand horses,ᵃ which he kept in the chariot cities and also with him in Jerusalem. ¹⁵The king made silver and gold as common in Jerusalem as stones, and cedar as plentiful as sycamore-fig trees in the foothills. ¹⁶Solomon's horses were imported from Egypt and from Kueᵇ—the royal merchants purchased them from Kue at the current price. ¹⁷They imported a chariot from Egypt for six hundred shekelsᶜ of silver, and a horse for a hundred and fifty.ᵈ They also exported them to all the kings of the Hittites and of the Arameans.

Preparations for Building the Temple

2ᵉ Solomon gave orders to build a temple for the Name of the Lord and a royal palace for himself. ²He conscripted 70,000 men as carriers and 80,000 as stonecutters in the hills and 3,600 as foremen over them.

³Solomon sent this message to Hiramᶠ king of Tyre:

"Send me cedar logs as you did for my father David when you sent him cedar to build a palace to live in. ⁴Now I am about to build a temple for the Name of the Lord my God and to dedicate it to him for burning fragrant incense before him, for setting out the consecrated bread regularly, and for making burnt offerings every morning and evening and on the Sabbaths, at the New Moons and at the appointed festivals of the Lord our God. This is a lasting ordinance for Israel.

⁵"The temple I am going to build will be great, because our God is greater than all other gods. ⁶But who is able to build a temple for him, since the heavens, even the highest heavens, cannot contain him? Who then am I to build a temple for him, except as a place to burn sacrifices before him?

⁷"Send me, therefore, a man skilled to work in gold and silver, bronze and iron, and in purple, crimson and blue yarn, and experienced in the art of engraving, to work in Judah and Jerusalem with my skilled workers, whom my father David provided.

⁸"Send me also cedar, juniper and algumᵍ logs from Lebanon, for I know that your servants are skilled in cutting timber there. My servants will work with yours ⁹to provide me with plenty of lumber, because the temple I build must be large and magnificent. ¹⁰I will give your servants, the woodsmen who cut the timber, twenty thousand corsʰ of ground wheat, twenty thousand corsⁱ of barley, twenty thousand bathsʲ of wine and twenty thousand baths of olive oil."

ᵃ 14 Or charioteers　ᵇ 16 Probably Cilicia　ᶜ 17 That is, about 15 pounds or about 6.9 kilograms　ᵈ 17 That is, about 3 3/4 pounds or about 1.7 kilograms　ᵉ In Hebrew texts 2:1 is numbered 1:18, and 2:2-18 is numbered 2:1-17.　ᶠ 3 Hebrew Huram, a variant of Hiram; also in verses 11 and 12　ᵍ 8 Probably a variant of almug　ʰ 10 That is, probably about 3,600 tons or about 3,200 metric tons of wheat　ⁱ 10 That is, probably about 3,000 tons or about 2,700 metric tons of barley　ʲ 10 That is, about 120,000 gallons or about 440,000 liters

¹¹Hiram king of Tyre replied by letter to Solomon:

"Because the Lᴏʀᴅ loves his people, he has made you their king."

¹²And Hiram added:

"Praise be to the Lᴏʀᴅ, the God of Israel, who made heaven and earth! He has given King David a wise son, endowed with intelligence and discernment, who will build a temple for the Lᴏʀᴅ and a palace for himself.

¹³"I am sending you Huram-Abi, a man of great skill, ¹⁴whose mother was from Dan and whose father was from Tyre. He is trained to work in gold and silver, bronze and iron, stone and wood, and with purple and blue and crimson yarn and fine linen. He is experienced in all kinds of engraving and can execute any design given to him. He will work with your skilled workers and with those of my lord, David your father.

¹⁵"Now let my lord send his servants the wheat and barley and the olive oil and wine he promised, ¹⁶and we will cut all the logs from Lebanon that you need and will float them as rafts by sea down to Joppa. You can then take them up to Jerusalem."

¹⁷Solomon took a census of all the foreigners residing in Israel, after the census his father David had taken; and they were found to be 153,600. ¹⁸He assigned 70,000 of them to be carriers and 80,000 to be stonecutters in the hills, with 3,600 foremen over them to keep the people working.

Solomon Builds the Temple

3 Then Solomon began to build the temple of the Lᴏʀᴅ in Jerusalem on Mount Moriah, where the Lᴏʀᴅ had appeared to his father David. It was on the threshing floor of Araunah*ᵃ* the Jebusite, the place provided by David. ²He began building on the second day of the second month in the fourth year of his reign.

³The foundation Solomon laid for building the temple of God was sixty cubits long and twenty cubits wide*ᵇ* (using the

BREAKTHROUGH!

The second month

(2 CHRONICLES 3:2)

That was Ziv, the second month of the Jewish lunar calendar. In our solar calendar, that would more or less be from the middle of April to the middle of May.

cubit of the old standard). ⁴The portico at the front of the temple was twenty cubits*ᶜ* long across the width of the building and twenty*ᵈ* cubits high.

He overlaid the inside with pure gold. ⁵He paneled the main hall with juniper and covered it with fine gold and decorated it with palm tree and chain designs. ⁶He adorned the temple with precious stones. And the gold he used was gold of Parvaim. ⁷He overlaid the ceiling beams, doorframes, walls and doors of the temple with gold, and he carved cherubim on the walls.

⁸He built the Most Holy Place, its length corresponding to the width of the temple—twenty cubits long and twenty cubits wide. He overlaid the inside with six hundred talents*ᵉ* of fine gold. ⁹The gold nails

---

ᵃ 1 Hebrew *Ornan,* a variant of *Araunah*   *ᵇ* 3 That is, about 90 feet long and 30 feet wide or about 27 meters long and 9 meters wide   *ᶜ* 4 That is, about 30 feet or about 9 meters; also in verses 8, 11 and 13   *ᵈ* 4 Some Septuagint and Syriac manuscripts; Hebrew *and a hundred and twenty*   *ᵉ* 8 That is, about 23 tons or about 21 metric tons weighed fifty shekels.*a* He also overlaid the upper parts with gold.

¹⁰For the Most Holy Place he made a pair of sculptured cherubim and overlaid them with gold. ¹¹The total wingspan of the cherubim was twenty cubits. One wing of the first cherub was five cubits*b* long and touched the temple wall, while its other wing, also five cubits long, touched the wing of the other cherub. ¹²Similarly one wing of the second cherub was five cubits long and touched the other temple wall, and its other wing, also five cubits long, touched the wing of the first cherub. ¹³The wings of these cherubim extended twenty cubits. They stood on their feet, facing the main hall.*c*

¹⁴He made the curtain of blue, purple and crimson yarn and fine linen, with cherubim worked into it.

¹⁵For the front of the temple he made two pillars, which together were thirty-five cubits*d* long, each with a capital five cubits high. ¹⁶He made interwoven chains*e* and put them on top of the pillars. He also made a hundred pomegranates and attached them to the chains. ¹⁷He erected the pillars in the front of the temple, one to the south and one to the north. The one to the south he named Jakin*f* and the one to the north Boaz.*g*

The Temple's Furnishings

4 He made a bronze altar twenty cubits long, twenty cubits wide and ten cubits high.*h* ²He made the Sea of cast metal, circular in shape, measuring ten cubits from rim to rim and five cubits*i* high. It took a line of thirty cubits*j* to measure around it. ³Below the rim, figures of bulls encircled it—ten to a cubit.*k* The bulls were cast in two rows in one piece with the Sea.

⁴The Sea stood on twelve bulls, three facing north, three facing west, three facing south and three facing east. The Sea rested on top of them, and their hindquarters were toward the center. ⁵It was a handbreadth*l* in thickness, and its rim was like the rim of a cup, like a lily blossom. It held three thousand baths.*m*

⁶He then made ten basins for washing and placed five on the south side and five on the north. In them the things to be used for the burnt offerings were rinsed, but the Sea was to be used by the priests for washing.

⁷He made ten gold lampstands according to the specifications for them and placed them in the temple, five on the south side and five on the north.

⁸He made ten tables and placed them in the temple, five on the south side and five on the north. He also made a hundred gold sprinkling bowls.

⁹He made the courtyard of the priests, and the large court and the doors for the court, and overlaid the doors with bronze. ¹⁰He placed the Sea on the south side, at the southeast corner.

¹¹And Huram also made the pots and shovels and sprinkling bowls.

So Huram finished the work he had undertaken for King Solomon in the temple of God:

¹²the two pillars;

the two bowl-shaped capitals on top of the pillars;

the two sets of network decorating the two bowl-shaped capitals on top of the pillars;

¹³the four hundred pomegranates for the two sets of network (two rows of pomegranates for each network, decorating the bowl-shaped capitals on top of the pillars);

¹⁴the stands with their basins;

¹⁵the Sea and the twelve bulls under it;

¹⁶the pots, shovels, meat forks and all related articles.

All the objects that Huram-Abi made for King Solomon for the temple of the Lord were of polished bronze. ¹⁷The king had them cast in clay molds in the plain of the

---

a 9 That is, about 1 1/4 pounds or about 575 grams
b 11 That is, about 7 1/2 feet or about 2.3 meters; also in verse 15　*c* 13 Or *facing inward*　*d* 15 That is, about 53 feet or about 16 meters　*e* 16 Or possibly *made chains in the inner sanctuary*; the meaning of the Hebrew for this phrase is uncertain.　*f* 17 *Jakin* probably means *he establishes.*　*g* 17 *Boaz* probably means *in him is strength.*　*h* 1 That is, about 30 feet long and wide and 15 feet high or about 9 meters long and wide and 4.5 meters high　*i* 2 That is, about 7 1/2 feet or about 2.3 meters　*j* 2 That is, about 45 feet or about 14 meters　*k* 3 That is, about 18 inches or about 45 centimeters　*l* 5 That is, about 3 inches or about 7.5 centimeters　*m* 5 That is, about 18,000 gallons or about 66,000 liters

Jordan between Sukkoth and Zarethan.[a] [18]All these things that Solomon made amounted to so much that the weight of the bronze could not be calculated.

[19]Solomon also made all the furnishings that were in God's temple:

the golden altar;
the tables on which was the bread of the Presence;
[20]the lampstands of pure gold with their lamps, to burn in front of the inner sanctuary as prescribed;
[21]the gold floral work and lamps and tongs (they were solid gold);
[22]the pure gold wick trimmers, sprinkling bowls, dishes and censers; and the gold doors of the temple: the inner doors to the Most Holy Place and the doors of the main hall.

5 When all the work Solomon had done for the temple of the LORD was finished, he brought in the things his father David had dedicated—the silver and gold and all the furnishings—and he placed them in the treasuries of God's temple.

The Ark Brought to the Temple

[2]Then Solomon summoned to Jerusalem the elders of Israel, all the heads of the tribes and the chiefs of the Israelite families, to bring up the ark of the LORD's covenant from Zion, the City of David. [3]And all the Israelites came together to the king at the time of the festival in the seventh month.

[4]When all the elders of Israel had arrived, the Levites took up the ark, [5]and they brought up the ark and the tent of meeting and all the sacred furnishings in it. The Levitical priests carried them up; [6]and King Solomon and the entire assembly of Israel that had gathered about him were before the ark, sacrificing so many sheep and cattle that they could not be recorded or counted.

[7]The priests then brought the ark of the LORD's covenant to its place in the inner sanctuary of the temple, the Most Holy Place, and put it beneath the wings of the cherubim. [8]The cherubim spread their wings over the place of the ark and covered the ark and its carrying poles. [9]These poles were so long that their ends, extending from the ark, could be seen in front of the inner sanctuary, but not from outside the Holy Place; and they are still there today. [10]There was nothing in the ark except the two tablets that Moses had placed in it at Horeb, where the LORD made a covenant with the Israelites after they came out of Egypt.

[11]The priests then withdrew from the Holy Place. All the priests who were there had consecrated themselves, regardless of their divisions. [12]All the Levites who were musicians—Asaph, Heman, Jeduthun and their sons and relatives—stood on the east side of the altar, dressed in fine linen and playing cymbals, harps and lyres. They were accompanied by 120 priests sounding trumpets. [13]The trumpeters and musicians joined in unison to give praise and thanks to the LORD. Accompanied by trumpets, cymbals and other instruments, the singers raised their voices in praise to the LORD and sang:

"He is good;
his love endures forever."

Then the temple of the LORD was filled with the cloud, [14]and the priests could not perform their service because of the cloud, for the glory of the LORD filled the temple of God.

6 Then Solomon said, "The LORD has said that he would dwell in a dark cloud; [2]I have built a magnificent temple for you, a place for you to dwell forever."

[3]While the whole assembly of Israel was standing there, the king turned around and blessed them. [4]Then he said:

"Praise be to the LORD, the God of Israel, who with his hands has fulfilled what he promised with his mouth to my father David. For he said, [5]'Since the day I brought my people out of Egypt, I have not chosen a city in any tribe of Israel to have a temple built so that my Name might be there, nor have I chosen anyone to be ruler over my people Israel. [6]But now I have chosen

---

[a] 17 Hebrew *Zeredatha*, a variant of *Zarethan*

Jerusalem for my Name to be there, and I have chosen David to rule my people Israel.'

⁷"My father David had it in his heart to build a temple for the Name of the Lord, the God of Israel. ⁸But the Lord said to my father David, 'You did well to have it in your heart to build a temple for my Name. ⁹Nevertheless, you are not the one to build the temple, but your son, your own flesh and blood—he is the one who will build the temple for my Name.'

¹⁰"The Lord has kept the promise he made. I have succeeded David my father and now I sit on the throne of Israel, just as the Lord promised, and I have built the temple for the Name of the Lord, the God of Israel. ¹¹There I have placed the ark, in which is the covenant of the Lord that he made with the people of Israel."

Solomon's Prayer of Dedication

¹²Then Solomon stood before the altar of the Lord in front of the whole assembly of Israel and spread out his hands. ¹³Now he had made a bronze platform, five cubits long, five cubits wide and three cubits high,ᵃ and had placed it in the center of the outer court. He stood on the platform and then knelt down before the whole assembly of Israel and spread out his hands toward heaven. ¹⁴He said:

"Lord, the God of Israel, there is no God like you in heaven or on earth—you who keep your covenant of love with your servants who continue wholeheartedly in your way. ¹⁵You have kept your promise to your servant David my father; with your mouth you have promised and with your hand you have fulfilled it—as it is today.

¹⁶"Now, Lord, the God of Israel, keep for your servant David my father the promises you made to him when you said, 'You shall never fail to have a successor to sit before me on the throne of Israel, if only your descendants are careful in all they do to walk before me according to my law, as you have done.' ¹⁷And now, Lord, the God of Israel, let your word that you promised your servant David come true.

¹⁸"But will God really dwell on earth with humans? The heavens, even the highest heavens, cannot contain you. How much less this temple I have built! ¹⁹Yet, Lord my God, give attention to your servant's prayer and his plea for mercy. Hear the cry and the prayer that your servant is praying in your presence. ²⁰May your eyes be open toward this temple day and night, this place of which you said you would put your Name there. May you hear the prayer your servant prays toward this place. ²¹Hear the supplications of your servant and of your people Israel when they pray toward this place. Hear from heaven, your dwelling place; and when you hear, forgive.

²²"When anyone wrongs their neighbor and is required to take an oath and they come and swear the oath before your altar in this temple, ²³then hear from heaven and act. Judge between your servants, condemning the guilty and bringing down on their heads what they have done, and vindicating the innocent by treating them in accordance with their innocence.

²⁴"When your people Israel have been defeated by an enemy because they have sinned against you and when they turn back and give praise to your name, praying and making supplication before you in this temple, ²⁵then hear from heaven and forgive the sin of your people Israel and bring them back to the land you gave to them and their ancestors.

²⁶"When the heavens are shut up and there is no rain because your people have sinned against you, and when they pray toward this place and give praise to your name

---

ᵃ *13* That is, about 7 1/2 feet long and wide and 4 1/2 feet high or about 2.3 meters long and wide and 1.4 meters high and turn from their sin because you have afflicted them, [27]then hear from heaven and forgive the sin of your servants, your people Israel. Teach them the right way to live, and send rain on the land you gave your people for an inheritance.

[28]"When famine or plague comes to the land, or blight or mildew, locusts or grasshoppers, or when enemies besiege them in any of their cities, whatever disaster or disease may come, [29]and when a prayer or plea is made by anyone among your people Israel—being aware of their afflictions and pains, and spreading out their hands toward this temple— [30]then hear from heaven, your dwelling place. Forgive, and deal with everyone according to all they do, since you know their hearts (for you alone know the human heart), [31]so that they will fear you and walk in obedience to you all the time they live in the land you gave our ancestors.

[32]"As for the foreigner who does not belong to your people Israel but has come from a distant land because of your great name and your mighty hand and your outstretched arm—when they come and pray toward this temple, [33]then hear from heaven, your dwelling place. Do whatever the foreigner asks of you, so that all the peoples of the earth may know your name and fear you, as do your own people Israel, and may know that this house I have built bears your Name.

[34]"When your people go to war against their enemies, wherever you send them, and when they pray to you toward this city you have chosen and the temple I have built for your Name, [35]then hear from heaven their prayer and their plea, and uphold their cause.

[36]"When they sin against you— for there is no one who does not sin—and you become angry with them and give them over to the enemy, who takes them captive to a land far away or near; [37]and if they

have a change of heart in the land where they are held captive, and repent and plead with you in the land of their captivity and say, 'We have sinned, we have done wrong and acted wickedly'; [38]and if they turn back to you with all their heart and soul in the land of their captivity where they were taken, and pray toward the land you gave their ancestors, toward the city you have chosen and toward the temple I have built for your Name; [39]then from heaven, your dwelling place, hear their prayer and their pleas, and uphold their cause. And forgive your people, who have sinned against you.

[40]"Now, my God, may your eyes be open and your ears attentive to the prayers offered in this place.

[41]"Now arise, Lord God, and come
    to your resting place,
    you and the ark of your might.
May your priests, Lord God, be
    clothed with salvation,
    may your faithful people rejoice
    in your goodness.
[42]Lord God, do not reject your
    anointed one.
Remember the great love
    promised to David your
    servant."

The Dedication of the Temple

7 When Solomon finished praying, fire came down from heaven and consumed the burnt offering and the sacrifices, and the glory of the Lord filled the temple. [2]The priests could not enter the temple of the Lord because the glory of the Lord filled it. [3]When all the Israelites saw the fire coming down and the glory of the Lord above the temple, they knelt on the pavement with their faces to the ground, and they worshiped and gave thanks to the Lord, saying,

"He is good;
    his love endures forever."

[4]Then the king and all the people offered sacrifices before the Lord. [5]And King Solomon offered a sacrifice of twenty-two thousand head of cattle and a hundred

and twenty thousand sheep and goats. So the king and all the people dedicated the temple of God. ⁶The priests took their positions, as did the Levites with the Lᴏʀᴅ's musical instruments, which King David had made for praising the Lᴏʀᴅ and which were used when he gave thanks, saying, "His love endures forever." Opposite the Levites, the priests blew their trumpets, and all the Israelites were standing.

⁷Solomon consecrated the middle part of the courtyard in front of the temple of the Lᴏʀᴅ, and there he offered burnt offerings and the fat of the fellowship offerings, because the bronze altar he had made could not hold the burnt offerings, the grain offerings and the fat portions.

⁸So Solomon observed the festival at that time for seven days, and all Israel with him—a vast assembly, people from Lebo Hamath to the Wadi of Egypt. ⁹On the eighth day they held an assembly, for they had celebrated the dedication of the altar for seven days and the festival for seven days more. ¹⁰On the twenty-third day of the seventh month he sent the people to their homes, joyful and glad in heart for the good things the Lᴏʀᴅ had done for David and Solomon and for his people Israel.

The Lᴏʀᴅ Appears to Solomon

¹¹When Solomon had finished the temple of the Lᴏʀᴅ and the royal palace, and had succeeded in carrying out all he had in mind to do in the temple of the Lᴏʀᴅ and in his own palace, ¹²the Lᴏʀᴅ appeared to him at night and said:

"I have heard your prayer and have chosen this place for myself as a temple for sacrifices.

¹³"When I shut up the heavens so that there is no rain, or command locusts to devour the land or send a plague among my people, ¹⁴if my people, who are called by my name, will humble themselves and pray and seek my face and turn from their wicked ways, then I will hear from heaven, and I will forgive their sin and will heal their land. ¹⁵Now my eyes will be open and my ears at-

BREAKTHROUGH!

The seventh month
(2 CHRONICLES 7:10)
Called Ethanim, this is the seventh month in the Jewish lunar calendar. In our solar calendar, it would be more or less from the middle of September to the middle of October.

tentive to the prayers offered in this place. ¹⁶I have chosen and consecrated this temple so that my Name may be there forever. My eyes and my heart will always be there.

¹⁷"As for you, if you walk before me faithfully as David your father did, and do all I command, and observe my decrees and laws, ¹⁸I will establish your royal throne, as I covenanted with David your father when I said, 'You shall never fail to have a successor to rule over Israel.'

¹⁹"But if you[a] turn away and forsake the decrees and commands I have given you[a] and go off to serve other gods and worship them, ²⁰then I will uproot Israel from my land, which I have given them, and will reject this temple I have consecrated for my Name. I will make it a byword and an object of ridicule among all

---

a 19 The Hebrew is plural.

peoples. [21]This temple will become a heap of rubble. All[a] who pass by will be appalled and say, 'Why has the LORD done such a thing to this land and to this temple?' [22]People will answer, 'Because they have forsaken the LORD, the God of their ancestors, who brought them out of Egypt, and have embraced other gods, worshiping and serving them—that is why he brought all this disaster on them.' "

Solomon's Other Activities

8 At the end of twenty years, during which Solomon built the temple of the LORD and his own palace, [2]Solomon rebuilt the villages that Hiram[b] had given him, and settled Israelites in them. [3]Solomon then went to Hamath Zobah and captured it. [4]He also built up Tadmor in the desert and all the store cities he had built in Hamath. [5]He rebuilt Upper Beth Horon and Lower Beth Horon as fortified cities, with walls and with gates and bars, [6]as well as Baalath and all his store cities, and all the cities for his chariots and for his horses[c]—whatever he desired to build in Jerusalem, in Lebanon and throughout all the territory he ruled.

[7]There were still people left from the Hittites, Amorites, Perizzites, Hivites and Jebusites (these people were not Israelites). [8]Solomon conscripted the descendants of all these people remaining in the land—whom the Israelites had not destroyed—to serve as slave labor, as it is to this day. [9]But Solomon did not make slaves of the Israelites for his work; they were his fighting men, commanders of his captains, and commanders of his chariots and charioteers. [10]They were also King Solomon's chief officials—two hundred and fifty officials supervising the men.

[11]Solomon brought Pharaoh's daughter up from the City of David to the palace he had built for her, for he said, "My wife must not live in the palace of David king of Israel, because the places the ark of the LORD has entered are holy."

[12]On the altar of the LORD that he had built in front of the portico, Solomon sacrificed burnt offerings to the LORD, [13]according to the daily requirement for offerings commanded by Moses for the Sabbaths, the New Moons and the three annual festivals—the Festival of Unleavened Bread, the Festival of Weeks and the Festival of Tabernacles. [14]In keeping with the ordinance of his father David, he appointed the divisions of the priests for their duties, and the Levites to lead the praise and to assist the priests according to each day's requirement. He also appointed the gatekeepers by divisions for the various gates, because this was what David the man of God had ordered. [15]They did not deviate from the king's commands to the priests or to the Levites in any matter, including that of the treasuries.

[16]All Solomon's work was carried out, from the day the foundation of the temple of the LORD was laid until its completion. So the temple of the LORD was finished.

[17]Then Solomon went to Ezion Geber and Elath on the coast of Edom. [18]And Hiram sent him ships commanded by his own men, sailors who knew the sea. These, with Solomon's men, sailed to Ophir and brought back four hundred and fifty talents[d] of gold, which they delivered to King Solomon.

The Queen of Sheba Visits Solomon

9 When the queen of Sheba heard of Solomon's fame, she came to Jerusalem to test him with hard questions. Arriving with a very great caravan—with camels carrying spices, large quantities of gold, and precious stones—she came to Solomon and talked with him about all she had on her mind. [2]Solomon answered all her questions; nothing was too hard for him to explain to her. [3]When the queen of Sheba saw the wisdom of Solomon, as well as the palace he had built, [4]the food on his table, the seating of his officials, the attending servants in their robes, the cupbearers in their robes and the burnt offerings he made at[e] the temple of the LORD, she was overwhelmed.

---

[a] 21 See some Septuagint manuscripts, Old Latin, Syriac, Arabic and Targum; Hebrew *And though this temple is now so imposing, all*   [b] 2 Hebrew *Huram*, a variant of *Hiram*; also in verse 18   [c] 6 Or *charioteers*   [d] 18 That is, about 17 tons or about 15 metric tons   [e] 4 Or *and the ascent by which he went up to*

CHECK THE FACTS

**Why did the queen of Sheba
visit King Solomon?**

A) To meet him, because she had heard
he was very handsome

B) To ask him some hard questions and find
out if he was as smart as people said

C) To see the wonderful palace and eat the
fantastic food they served

CORRECT ANSWER: B

⁵She said to the king, "The report I heard in my own country about your achievements and your wisdom is true. ⁶But I did not believe what they said until I came and saw with my own eyes. Indeed, not even half the greatness of your wisdom was told me; you have far exceeded the report I heard. ⁷How happy your people must be! How happy your officials, who continually stand before you and hear your wisdom! ⁸Praise be to the LORD your God, who has delighted in you and placed you on his throne as king to rule for the LORD your God. Because of the love of your God for Israel and his desire to uphold them forever, he has made you king over them, to maintain justice and righteousness."

⁹Then she gave the king 120 talents[a] of gold, large quantities of spices, and precious stones. There had never been such spices as those the queen of Sheba gave to King Solomon.

¹⁰(The servants of Hiram and the servants of Solomon brought gold from Ophir; they also brought algumwood[b] and precious stones. ¹¹The king used the algumwood to make steps for the temple of the LORD and for the royal palace, and to make harps and lyres for the musicians. Nothing like them had ever been seen in Judah.)

¹²King Solomon gave the queen of Sheba all she desired and asked for; he gave her more than she had brought to him. Then she left and returned with her retinue to her own country.

Solomon's Splendor

¹³The weight of the gold that Solomon received yearly was 666 talents,[c] ¹⁴not including the revenues brought in by merchants and traders. Also all the kings of Arabia and the governors of the territories brought gold and silver to Solomon.

¹⁵King Solomon made two hundred large shields of hammered gold; six hundred shekels[d] of hammered gold went into each shield. ¹⁶He also made three hundred small shields of hammered gold, with three hundred shekels[e] of gold in each shield. The king put them in the Palace of the Forest of Lebanon.

¹⁷Then the king made a great throne covered with ivory and overlaid with pure gold. ¹⁸The throne had six steps, and a footstool of gold was attached to it. On both sides of the seat were armrests, with a lion standing beside each of them. ¹⁹Twelve lions stood on the six steps, one at either end of each step. Nothing like it had ever been made for any other kingdom. ²⁰All King Solomon's goblets were gold, and all the household articles in the Palace of the Forest of Lebanon were pure gold. Nothing was made of silver, because silver was considered of little value in Solomon's day. ²¹The king had a fleet

[a] 9 That is, about 4 1/2 tons or about 4 metric tons
[b] 10 Probably a variant of *almugwood*   [c] 13 That is, about 25 tons or about 23 metric tons   [d] 15 That is, about 15 pounds or about 6.9 kilograms   [e] 16 That is, about 7 1/2 pounds or about 3.5 kilograms

of trading ships[a] manned by Hiram's[b] servants. Once every three years it returned, carrying gold, silver and ivory, and apes and baboons.

²²King Solomon was greater in riches and wisdom than all the other kings of the earth. ²³All the kings of the earth sought audience with Solomon to hear the wisdom God had put in his heart. ²⁴Year after year, everyone who came brought a gift—articles of silver and gold, and robes, weapons and spices, and horses and mules.

²⁵Solomon had four thousand stalls for horses and chariots, and twelve thousand horses,[c] which he kept in the chariot cities and also with him in Jerusalem. ²⁶He ruled over all the kings from the Euphrates River to the land of the Philistines, as far as the border of Egypt. ²⁷The king made silver as common in Jerusalem as stones, and cedar as plentiful as sycamore-fig trees in the foothills. ²⁸Solomon's horses were imported from Egypt and from all other countries.

Solomon's Death

²⁹As for the other events of Solomon's reign, from beginning to end, are they not written in the records of Nathan the prophet, in the prophecy of Ahijah the Shilonite and in the visions of Iddo the seer concerning Jeroboam son of Nebat? ³⁰Solomon reigned in Jerusalem over all Israel forty years. ³¹Then he rested with his ancestors and was buried in the city of David his father. And Rehoboam his son succeeded him as king.

Israel Rebels Against Rehoboam

10 Rehoboam went to Shechem, for all Israel had gone there to make him king. ²When Jeroboam son of Nebat heard this (he was in Egypt, where he had fled from King Solomon), he returned from Egypt. ³So they sent for Jeroboam, and he and all Israel went to Rehoboam and said to him: ⁴"Your father put a heavy yoke on us, but now lighten the harsh labor and the heavy yoke he put on us, and we will serve you."

⁵Rehoboam answered, "Come back to me in three days." So the people went away.

BREAKTHROUGH!

Where are the books it talks about in 9:29 and 12:15?

(2 CHRONICLES 9:29)

The truth is that we don't have a copy of those books anymore. We think they were records that disciples of Nathan, Ahijah, Iddo and Shemaiah took from the prophecies and stories about things that had happened to their teachers, but no one knows what happened to those papers.

⁶Then King Rehoboam consulted the elders who had served his father Solomon during his lifetime. "How would you advise me to answer these people?" he asked.

⁷They replied, "If you will be kind to these people and please them and give them a favorable answer, they will always be your servants."

⁸But Rehoboam rejected the advice the elders gave him and consulted the young men who had grown up with him and were serving him. ⁹He asked them, "What is your advice? How should we answer these people who say to me, 'Lighten the yoke your father put on us'?"

¹⁰The young men who had grown up with him replied, "The people have said

---

[a] 21 Hebrew *of ships that could go to Tarshish*
[b] 21 Hebrew *Huram,* a variant of *Hiram*   [c] 25 Or *charioteers*

to you, 'Your father put a heavy yoke on us, but make our yoke lighter.' Now tell them, 'My little finger is thicker than my father's waist. ¹¹My father laid on you a heavy yoke; I will make it even heavier. My father scourged you with whips; I will scourge you with scorpions.' "

¹²Three days later Jeroboam and all the people returned to Rehoboam, as the king had said, "Come back to me in three days." ¹³The king answered them harshly. Rejecting the advice of the elders, ¹⁴he followed the advice of the young men and said, "My father made your yoke heavy; I will make it even heavier. My father scourged you with whips; I will scourge you with scorpions." ¹⁵So the king did not listen to the people, for this turn of events was from God, to fulfill the word the Lᴏʀᴅ had spoken to Jeroboam son of Nebat through Ahijah the Shilonite.

¹⁶When all Israel saw that the king refused to listen to them, they answered the king:

"What share do we have in David,
    what part in Jesse's son?
To your tents, Israel!
Look after your own house, David!"

So all the Israelites went home. ¹⁷But as for the Israelites who were living in the towns of Judah, Rehoboam still ruled over them.

¹⁸King Rehoboam sent out Adoniram,[a] who was in charge of forced labor, but the Israelites stoned him to death. King Rehoboam, however, managed to get into his chariot and escape to Jerusalem. ¹⁹So Israel has been in rebellion against the house of David to this day.

11 When Rehoboam arrived in Jerusalem, he mustered Judah and Benjamin—a hundred and eighty thousand able young men—to go to war against Israel and to regain the kingdom for Rehoboam.

²But this word of the Lᴏʀᴅ came to Shemaiah the man of God: ³"Say to Rehoboam son of Solomon king of Judah and to all Israel in Judah and Benjamin, ⁴'This is what the Lᴏʀᴅ says: Do not go up to fight against your fellow Israelites. Go home, every one of you, for this is my doing.'"

So they obeyed the words of the Lᴏʀᴅ and turned back from marching against Jeroboam.

Rehoboam Fortifies Judah

⁵Rehoboam lived in Jerusalem and built up towns for defense in Judah: ⁶Bethlehem, Etam, Tekoa, ⁷Beth Zur, Soko, Adullam, ⁸Gath, Mareshah, Ziph, ⁹Adoraim, Lachish, Azekah, ¹⁰Zorah, Aijalon and Hebron. These were fortified cities in Judah and Benjamin. ¹¹He strengthened their defenses and put commanders in them, with supplies of food, olive oil and wine. ¹²He put shields and spears in all the cities, and made them very strong. So Judah and Benjamin were his.

¹³The priests and Levites from all their districts throughout Israel sided with him. ¹⁴The Levites even abandoned their pasturelands and property and came to Judah and Jerusalem, because Jeroboam and his sons had rejected them as priests of the Lᴏʀᴅ ¹⁵when he appointed his own priests for the high places and for the goat and calf idols he had made. ¹⁶Those from every tribe of Israel who set their hearts on seeking the Lᴏʀᴅ, the God of Israel, followed the Levites to Jerusalem to offer sacrifices to the Lᴏʀᴅ, the God of their ancestors. ¹⁷They strengthened the kingdom of Judah and supported Rehoboam son of Solomon three years, following the ways of David and Solomon during this time.

Rehoboam's Family

¹⁸Rehoboam married Mahalath, who was the daughter of David's son Jerimoth and of Abihail, the daughter of Jesse's son Eliab. ¹⁹She bore him sons: Jeush, Shemariah and Zaham. ²⁰Then he married Maakah daughter of Absalom, who bore him Abijah, Attai, Ziza and Shelomith. ²¹Rehoboam loved Maakah daughter of Absalom more than any of his other wives and concubines. In all, he had eighteen wives and sixty concubines, twenty-eight sons and sixty daughters.

²²Rehoboam appointed Abijah son of Maakah as crown prince among his brothers, in order to make him king. ²³He

---

a 18 Hebrew *Hadoram*, a variant of *Adoniram*

acted wisely, dispersing some of his sons throughout the districts of Judah and Benjamin, and to all the fortified cities. He gave them abundant provisions and took many wives for them.

Shishak Attacks Jerusalem

12 After Rehoboam's position as king was established and he had become strong, he and all Israel[a] with him abandoned the law of the LORD. ²Because they had been unfaithful to the LORD, Shishak king of Egypt attacked Jerusalem in the fifth year of King Rehoboam. ³With twelve hundred chariots and sixty thousand horsemen and the innumerable troops of Libyans, Sukkites and Cushites[b] that came with him from Egypt, ⁴he captured the fortified cities of Judah and came as far as Jerusalem.

⁵Then the prophet Shemaiah came to Rehoboam and to the leaders of Judah who had assembled in Jerusalem for fear of Shishak, and he said to them, "This is what the LORD says, 'You have abandoned me; therefore, I now abandon you to Shishak.'"

⁶The leaders of Israel and the king humbled themselves and said, "The LORD is just."

⁷When the LORD saw that they humbled themselves, this word of the LORD came to Shemaiah: "Since they have humbled themselves, I will not destroy them but will soon give them deliverance. My wrath will not be poured out on Jerusalem through Shishak. ⁸They will, however, become subject to him, so that they may learn the difference between serving me and serving the kings of other lands."

⁹When Shishak king of Egypt attacked Jerusalem, he carried off the treasures of the temple of the LORD and the treasures of the royal palace. He took everything, including the gold shields Solomon had made. ¹⁰So King Rehoboam made bronze shields to replace them and assigned these to the commanders of the guard on duty at the entrance to the royal palace. ¹¹Whenever the king went to the LORD's temple, the guards went with him, bearing the shields, and afterward they returned them to the guardroom.

¹²Because Rehoboam humbled himself, the LORD's anger turned from him, and he was not totally destroyed. Indeed, there was some good in Judah.

¹³King Rehoboam established himself firmly in Jerusalem and continued as king. He was forty-one years old when he became king, and he reigned seventeen years in Jerusalem, the city the LORD had chosen out of all the tribes of Israel in which to put his Name. His mother's name was Naamah; she was an Ammonite. ¹⁴He did evil because he had not set his heart on seeking the LORD.

---

[a] 1 That is, Judah, as frequently in 2 Chronicles
[b] 3 That is, people from the upper Nile region

THE
WITNESSES

✓ **SHEMAIAH** (2 CHRONICLES 12:5)
This means "God heard." He was a prophet who spoke for God during the time of King Rehoboam.

¹⁵As for the events of Rehoboam's reign, from beginning to end, are they not written in the records of Shemaiah the prophet and of Iddo the seer that deal with genealogies? There was continual warfare between Rehoboam and Jeroboam. ¹⁶Rehoboam rested with his ancestors and was buried in the City of David. And Abijah his son succeeded him as king.

Abijah King of Judah

13 In the eighteenth year of the reign of Jeroboam, Abijah became king of Judah, ²and he reigned in Jerusalem three years. His mother's name was Maakah,ᵃ a daughterᵇ of Uriel of Gibeah.

There was war between Abijah and Jeroboam. ³Abijah went into battle with an army of four hundred thousand able fighting men, and Jeroboam drew up a battle line against him with eight hundred thousand able troops.

⁴Abijah stood on Mount Zemaraim, in the hill country of Ephraim, and said, "Jeroboam and all Israel, listen to me! ⁵Don't you know that the LORD, the God of Israel, has given the kingship of Israel to David and his descendants forever by a covenant of salt? ⁶Yet Jeroboam son of Nebat, an official of Solomon son of David, rebelled against his master. ⁷Some worthless scoundrels gathered around him and opposed Rehoboam son of Solomon when he was young and indecisive and not strong enough to resist them.

⁸"And now you plan to resist the kingdom of the LORD, which is in the hands of David's descendants. You are indeed a vast army and have with you the golden calves that Jeroboam made to be your gods. ⁹But didn't you drive out the priests of the LORD, the sons of Aaron, and the Levites, and make priests of your own as the peoples of other lands do? Whoever comes to consecrate himself with a young bull and seven rams may become a priest of what are not gods.

¹⁰"As for us, the LORD is our God, and we have not forsaken him. The priests who serve the LORD are sons of Aaron, and the Levites assist them. ¹¹Every morning and evening they present burnt offerings and fragrant incense to the LORD. They set out the bread on the ceremonially clean table and light the lamps on the gold lampstand every evening. We are observing the requirements of the LORD our God. But you have forsaken him. ¹²God is with us; he is our leader. His priests with their trumpets will sound the battle cry against you. People of Israel, do not fight against the LORD, the God of your ancestors, for you will not succeed."

¹³Now Jeroboam had sent troops around to the rear, so that while he was in front of Judah the ambush was behind them. ¹⁴Judah turned and saw that they were being attacked at both front and rear. Then they cried out to the LORD. The priests blew their trumpets ¹⁵and the men of Judah raised the battle cry. At the sound of their battle cry, God routed Jeroboam and all Israel before Abijah and Judah. ¹⁶The Israelites fled before Judah, and God delivered them into their hands. ¹⁷Abijah and his troops inflicted heavy losses on them, so that there were five hundred thousand casualties among Israel's able men. ¹⁸The Israelites were subdued on that occasion, and the people of Judah were victorious because they relied on the LORD, the God of their ancestors.

¹⁹Abijah pursued Jeroboam and took from him the towns of Bethel, Jeshanah and Ephron, with their surrounding villages. ²⁰Jeroboam did not regain power during the time of Abijah. And the LORD struck him down and he died.

²¹But Abijah grew in strength. He married fourteen wives and had twenty-two sons and sixteen daughters.

²²The other events of Abijah's reign, what he did and what he said, are written in the annotations of the prophet Iddo.

14 ᶜ And Abijah rested with his ancestors and was buried in the City of David. Asa his son succeeded him as king, and in his days the country was at peace for ten years.

ᵃ 2 Most Septuagint manuscripts and Syriac (see also 11:20 and 1 Kings 15:2); Hebrew *Micaiah*   ᵇ 2 Or *granddaughter*   ᶜ In Hebrew texts 14:1 is numbered 13:23, and 14:2-15 is numbered 14:1-14.

Asa King of Judah

[2]Asa did what was good and right in the eyes of the Lord his God. [3]He removed the foreign altars and the high places, smashed the sacred stones and cut down the Asherah poles.[a] [4]He commanded Judah to seek the Lord, the God of their ancestors, and to obey his laws and commands. [5]He removed the high places and incense altars in every town in Judah, and the kingdom was at peace under him. [6]He built up the fortified cities of Judah, since the land was at peace. No one was at war with him during those years, for the Lord gave him rest.

[7]"Let us build up these towns," he said to Judah, "and put walls around them, with towers, gates and bars. The land is still ours, because we have sought the Lord our God; we sought him and he has given us rest on every side." So they built and prospered.

[8]Asa had an army of three hundred thousand men from Judah, equipped with large shields and with spears, and two hundred and eighty thousand from Benjamin, armed with small shields and with bows. All these were brave fighting men.

[9]Zerah the Cushite marched out against them with an army of thousands upon thousands and three hundred chariots, and came as far as Mareshah. [10]Asa went out to meet him, and they took up battle positions in the Valley of Zephathah near Mareshah.

[11]Then Asa called to the Lord his God and said, "Lord, there is no one like you to help the powerless against the mighty. Help us, Lord our God, for we rely on you, and in your name we have come against this vast army. Lord, you are our God; do not let mere mortals prevail against you."

[12]The Lord struck down the Cushites before Asa and Judah. The Cushites fled, [13]and Asa and his army pursued them as far as Gerar. Such a great number of Cushites fell that they could not recover; they were crushed before the Lord and his forces. The men of Judah carried off a large amount of plunder. [14]They destroyed all the villages around Gerar, for the terror of the Lord had fallen on them. They

THE
WITNESSES

✓ **ZERAH** (2 CHRONICLES 14:9)
He was an Ethiopian general who led a big army. Perhaps he served one of the pharaohs.

looted all these villages, since there was much plunder there. [15]They also attacked the camps of the herders and carried off droves of sheep and goats and camels. Then they returned to Jerusalem.

Asa's Reform

15 The Spirit of God came on Azariah son of Oded. [2]He went out to meet Asa and said to him, "Listen to me, Asa and all Judah and Benjamin. The Lord is with you when you are with him. If you seek him, he will be found by you, but if you forsake him, he will forsake you. [3]For a long time Israel was without the true God, without a priest to teach and without

---

[a] 3 That is, wooden symbols of the goddess Asherah; here and elsewhere in 2 Chronicles

the law. ⁴But in their distress they turned to the Lᴏʀᴅ, the God of Israel, and sought him, and he was found by them. ⁵In those days it was not safe to travel about, for all the inhabitants of the lands were in great turmoil. ⁶One nation was being crushed by another and one city by another, because God was troubling them with every kind of distress. ⁷But as for you, be strong and do not give up, for your work will be rewarded."

⁸When Asa heard these words and the prophecy of Azariah son of*ᵃ* Oded the prophet, he took courage. He removed the detestable idols from the whole land of Judah and Benjamin and from the towns he had captured in the hills of Ephraim. He repaired the altar of the Lᴏʀᴅ that was in front of the portico of the Lᴏʀᴅ's temple.

⁹Then he assembled all Judah and Benjamin and the people from Ephraim, Manasseh and Simeon who had settled among them, for large numbers had come over to him from Israel when they saw that the Lᴏʀᴅ his God was with him. ¹⁰They assembled at Jerusalem in the third month of the fifteenth year of Asa's reign. ¹¹At that time they sacrificed to the Lᴏʀᴅ seven hundred head of cattle and seven thousand sheep and goats from the plunder they had brought back. ¹²They entered into a covenant to seek the Lᴏʀᴅ, the God of their ancestors, with all their heart and soul. ¹³All who would not seek the Lᴏʀᴅ, the God of Israel, were to be put to death, whether small or great, man or woman. ¹⁴They took an oath to the Lᴏʀᴅ with loud acclamation, with shouting and with trumpets and horns. ¹⁵All Judah rejoiced about the oath because they had sworn it wholeheartedly. They sought God eagerly, and he was found by them. So the Lᴏʀᴅ gave them rest on every side.

¹⁶King Asa also deposed his grandmother Maakah from her position as queen mother, because she had made a repulsive image for the worship of Asherah. Asa cut it down, broke it up and burned it in the Kidron Valley. ¹⁷Although he did not remove the high places from Israel, Asa's heart was fully committed to the Lᴏʀᴅ all his life. ¹⁸He brought into the

BREAK THROUGH!

The third month
(2 CHRONICLES 15:10)
It was called Sivan in the Jewish lunar calendar. That would be from the middle of May to the middle of June in our solar calendar.

temple of God the silver and gold and the articles that he and his father had dedicated.

¹⁹There was no more war until the thirty-fifth year of Asa's reign.

Asa's Last Years

16 In the thirty-sixth year of Asa's reign Baasha king of Israel went up against Judah and fortified Ramah to prevent anyone from leaving or entering the territory of Asa king of Judah.

²Asa then took the silver and gold out of the treasuries of the Lᴏʀᴅ's temple and of his own palace and sent it to Ben-Hadad king of Aram, who was ruling in Damascus. ³"Let there be a treaty between me and you," he said, "as there was between my father and your father. See, I am sending you silver and gold. Now break your treaty with Baasha king of Israel so he will withdraw from me."

ᵃ 8 Vulgate and Syriac (see also Septuagint and verse 1); Hebrew does not have *Azariah son of*.

⁴Ben-Hadad agreed with King Asa and sent the commanders of his forces against the towns of Israel. They conquered Ijon, Dan, Abel Maim*a* and all the store cities of Naphtali. ⁵When Baasha heard this, he stopped building Ramah and abandoned his work. ⁶Then King Asa brought all the men of Judah, and they carried away from Ramah the stones and timber Baasha had been using. With them he built up Geba and Mizpah.

⁷At that time Hanani the seer came to Asa king of Judah and said to him: "Because you relied on the king of Aram and not on the LORD your God, the army of the king of Aram has escaped from your hand. ⁸Were not the Cushites*b* and Libyans a mighty army with great numbers of chariots and horsemen*c*? Yet when you relied on the LORD, he delivered them into your hand. ⁹For the eyes of the LORD range throughout the earth to strengthen those whose hearts are fully committed to him. You have done a foolish thing, and from now on you will be at war."

BREAKTHROUGH!

Judah

(2 CHRONICLES 16:1)

At that time, the land of Israel was divided into two kingdoms. One was Israel in the north and the other was Judah in the south.

THE WITNESSES

✓ **HANANI** (2 CHRONICLES 16:7)
Hanani means "my grace." He was a prophet who spoke in the name of God during the times of King Asa of Judah.

¹⁰Asa was angry with the seer because of this; he was so enraged that he put him in prison. At the same time Asa brutally oppressed some of the people. ¹¹The events of Asa's reign, from beginning to end, are written in the book of the kings of Judah and Israel. ¹²In the thirty-ninth year of his reign Asa was afflicted with a disease in his feet. Though his disease was severe, even in his illness he did not seek help from the LORD, but only from the physicians. ¹³Then in the forty-first year of his reign Asa died and rested with his ancestors. ¹⁴They buried him in the tomb that he had cut out for

a 4 Also known as *Abel Beth Maakah*   *b 8* That is, people from the upper Nile region   *c 8* Or *charioteers* himself in the City of David. They laid him on a bier covered with spices and various blended perfumes, and they made a huge fire in his honor.

Jehoshaphat King of Judah

17 Jehoshaphat his son succeeded him as king and strengthened himself against Israel. [2] He stationed troops in all the fortified cities of Judah and put garrisons in Judah and in the towns of Ephraim that his father Asa had captured.

[3] The LORD was with Jehoshaphat because he followed the ways of his father David before him. He did not consult the Baals [4] but sought the God of his father and followed his commands rather than the practices of Israel. [5] The LORD established the kingdom under his control; and all Judah brought gifts to Jehoshaphat, so that he had great wealth and honor. [6] His heart was devoted to the ways of the LORD; furthermore, he removed the high places and the Asherah poles from Judah.

[7] In the third year of his reign he sent his officials Ben-Hail, Obadiah, Zechariah, Nethanel and Micaiah to teach in the towns of Judah. [8] With them were certain Levites—Shemaiah, Nethaniah, Zebadiah, Asahel, Shemiramoth, Jehonathan, Adonijah, Tobijah and Tob-Adonijah—and the priests Elishama and Jehoram. [9] They taught throughout Judah, taking with them the Book of the Law of the LORD; they went around to all the towns of Judah and taught the people.

[10] The fear of the LORD fell on all the kingdoms of the lands surrounding Judah, so that they did not go to war against Jehoshaphat. [11] Some Philistines brought Jehoshaphat gifts and silver as tribute, and the Arabs brought him flocks: seven thousand seven hundred rams and seven thousand seven hundred goats.

[12] Jehoshaphat became more and more powerful; he built forts and store cities in Judah [13] and had large supplies in the towns of Judah. He also kept experienced fighting men in Jerusalem. [14] Their enrollment by families was as follows:

From Judah, commanders of units of 1,000:
Adnah the commander, with 300,000 fighting men;
[15] next, Jehohanan the commander, with 280,000;
[16] next, Amasiah son of Zikri, who volunteered himself for the service of the LORD, with 200,000.
[17] From Benjamin:
Eliada, a valiant soldier, with 200,000 men armed with bows and shields;
[18] next, Jehozabad, with 180,000 men armed for battle.

[19] These were the men who served the king, besides those he stationed in the fortified cities throughout Judah.

Micaiah Prophesies Against Ahab

18 Now Jehoshaphat had great wealth and honor, and he allied himself with Ahab by marriage. [2] Some years later he went down to see Ahab in Samaria. Ahab slaughtered many sheep and cattle for him and the people with him and urged him to attack Ramoth Gilead. [3] Ahab king of Israel asked Jehoshaphat king of Judah, "Will you go with me against Ramoth Gilead?"

Jehoshaphat replied, "I am as you are, and my people as your people; we will join you in the war." [4] But Jehoshaphat also said to the king of Israel, "First seek the counsel of the LORD."

[5] So the king of Israel brought together the prophets—four hundred men—and asked them, "Shall we go to war against Ramoth Gilead, or shall I not?"

"Go," they answered, "for God will give it into the king's hand."

[6] But Jehoshaphat asked, "Is there no longer a prophet of the LORD here whom we can inquire of?"

[7] The king of Israel answered Jehoshaphat, "There is still one prophet through whom we can inquire of the LORD, but I hate him because he never prophesies anything good about me, but always bad. He is Micaiah son of Imlah."

"The king should not say such a thing," Jehoshaphat replied.

THE SCENE

RAMOTH GILEAD

(2 CHRONICLES 18:2)

This means "the highlands of Gilead." It was a city of refuge (those cities that protected a person who had accidentally killed someone) east of the Jordan River and south of the Yarmuk River. It was an Israelite city back in the times of Moses. When Chronicles was written, it belonged to Syria.

⁸So the king of Israel called one of his officials and said, "Bring Micaiah son of Imlah at once."

⁹Dressed in their royal robes, the king of Israel and Jehoshaphat king of Judah were sitting on their thrones at the threshing floor by the entrance of the gate of Samaria, with all the prophets prophesying before them. ¹⁰Now Zedekiah son of Kenaanah had made iron horns, and he declared, "This is what the LORD says: 'With these you will gore the Arameans until they are destroyed.'"

¹¹All the other prophets were prophesying the same thing. "Attack Ramoth Gilead and be victorious," they said, "for the LORD will give it into the king's hand."

¹²The messenger who had gone to summon Micaiah said to him, "Look, the other prophets without exception are predicting success for the king. Let your word agree with theirs, and speak favorably."

¹³But Micaiah said, "As surely as the LORD lives, I can tell him only what my God says."

¹⁴When he arrived, the king asked him, "Micaiah, shall we go to war against Ramoth Gilead, or shall I not?"

"Attack and be victorious," he answered, "for they will be given into your hand."

¹⁵The king said to him, "How many times must I make you swear to tell me nothing but the truth in the name of the LORD?"

THE WITNESSES

✓ **MICAIAH** (2 CHRONICLES 18:7)

This name means "Who is like God?" He was a prophet of God, and he was the only prophet who told King Ahab the truth.

16Then Micaiah answered, "I saw all Israel scattered on the hills like sheep without a shepherd, and the LORD said, 'These people have no master. Let each one go home in peace.' "

17The king of Israel said to Jehoshaphat, "Didn't I tell you that he never prophesies anything good about me, but only bad?"

18Micaiah continued, "Therefore hear the word of the LORD: I saw the LORD sitting on his throne with all the multitudes of heaven standing on his right and on his left. 19And the LORD said, 'Who will entice Ahab king of Israel into attacking Ramoth Gilead and going to his death there?'

"One suggested this, and another that. 20Finally, a spirit came forward, stood before the LORD and said, 'I will entice him.'

" 'By what means?' the LORD asked.

21" 'I will go and be a deceiving spirit in the mouths of all his prophets,' he said.

" 'You will succeed in enticing him,' said the LORD. 'Go and do it.'

22"So now the LORD has put a deceiving spirit in the mouths of these prophets of yours. The LORD has decreed disaster for you."

23Then Zedekiah son of Kenaanah went up and slapped Micaiah in the face. "Which way did the spirit from*a* the LORD go when he went from me to speak to you?" he asked.

24Micaiah replied, "You will find out on the day you go to hide in an inner room."

25The king of Israel then ordered, "Take Micaiah and send him back to Amon the ruler of the city and to Joash the king's son, 26and say, 'This is what the king says: Put this fellow in prison and give him nothing but bread and water until I return safely.' "

27Micaiah declared, "If you ever return safely, the LORD has not spoken through me." Then he added, "Mark my words, all you people!"

Ahab Killed at Ramoth Gilead

28So the king of Israel and Jehoshaphat king of Judah went up to Ramoth Gilead. 29The king of Israel said to Jehoshaphat, "I will enter the battle in disguise, but you wear your royal robes." So the king of Israel disguised himself and went into battle.

30Now the king of Aram had ordered his chariot commanders, "Do not fight with anyone, small or great, except the king of Israel." 31When the chariot commanders saw Jehoshaphat, they thought, "This is the king of Israel." So they turned to attack him, but Jehoshaphat cried out, and the LORD helped him. God drew them away from him, 32for when the chariot commanders saw that he was not the king of Israel, they stopped pursuing him.

33But someone drew his bow at random and hit the king of Israel between the breastplate and the scale armor. The king told the chariot driver, "Wheel around and get me out of the fighting. I've been wounded." 34All day long the battle raged, and the king of Israel propped himself up in his chariot facing the Arameans until evening. Then at sunset he died.

19 When Jehoshaphat king of Judah returned safely to his palace in Jerusalem, 2Jehu the seer, the son of Hanani, went out to meet him and said to the king, "Should you help the wicked and love*b* those who hate the LORD? Because of this, the wrath of the LORD is on you. 3There is, however, some good in you, for you have rid the land of the Asherah poles and have set your heart on seeking God."

Jehoshaphat Appoints Judges

4Jehoshaphat lived in Jerusalem, and he went out again among the people from Beersheba to the hill country of Ephraim and turned them back to the LORD, the God of their ancestors. 5He appointed judges in the land, in each of the fortified cities of Judah. 6He told them, "Consider carefully what you do, because you are not judging for mere mortals but for the LORD, who is with you whenever you give a verdict. 7Now let the fear of the LORD be on you. Judge carefully, for with the LORD our God there is no injustice or partiality or bribery."

8In Jerusalem also, Jehoshaphat appointed some of the Levites, priests and heads of Israelite families to administer

---

a 23 Or *Spirit of*   *b* 2 Or *and make alliances with* the law of the Lord and to settle disputes. And they lived in Jerusalem. ⁹He gave them these orders: "You must serve faithfully and wholeheartedly in the fear of the Lord. ¹⁰In every case that comes before you from your people who live in the cities—whether bloodshed or other concerns of the law, commands, decrees or regulations—you are to warn them not to sin against the Lord; otherwise his wrath will come on you and your people. Do this, and you will not sin.

¹¹"Amariah the chief priest will be over you in any matter concerning the Lord, and Zebadiah son of Ishmael, the leader of the tribe of Judah, will be over you in

THE WITNESSES

✓ **AMARIAH (2 CHRONICLES 19:11)**
This name means "God has spoken." He was a high priest and the most important judge. He made decisions about religious matters during the reign of Jehoshaphat.

any matter concerning the king, and the Levites will serve as officials before you. Act with courage, and may the Lord be with those who do well."

Jehoshaphat Defeats Moab and Ammon

20 After this, the Moabites and Ammonites with some of the Meunites^a came to wage war against Jehoshaphat.

²Some people came and told Jehoshaphat, "A vast army is coming against you from Edom,^b from the other side of the Dead Sea. It is already in Hazezon Tamar" (that is, En Gedi). ³Alarmed, Jehoshaphat resolved to inquire of the Lord, and he proclaimed a fast for all Judah. ⁴The people of Judah came together to seek help from the Lord; indeed, they came from every town in Judah to seek him.

⁵Then Jehoshaphat stood up in the assembly of Judah and Jerusalem at the temple of the Lord in the front of the new courtyard ⁶and said:

"Lord, the God of our ancestors, are you not the God who is in heaven? You rule over all the kingdoms of the nations. Power and might are in your hand, and no one can withstand you. ⁷Our God, did you not drive out the inhabitants of this land before your people Israel and give it forever to the descendants of Abraham your friend? ⁸They have lived in it and have built in it a sanctuary for your Name, saying, ⁹'If calamity comes upon us, whether the sword of judgment, or plague or famine, we will stand in your presence before this temple that bears your Name and will cry out to you in our distress, and you will hear us and save us.'

¹⁰"But now here are men from Ammon, Moab and Mount Seir, whose territory you would not allow Israel to invade when they came from Egypt; so they turned away from them and did not destroy them. ¹¹See how they

---

^a 1 Some Septuagint manuscripts; Hebrew *Ammonites*
^b 2 One Hebrew manuscript; most Hebrew manuscripts, Septuagint and Vulgate *Aram*

are repaying us by coming to drive us out of the possession you gave us as an inheritance. [12]Our God, will you not judge them? For we have no power to face this vast army that is attacking us. We do not know what to do, but our eyes are on you."

[13]All the men of Judah, with their wives and children and little ones, stood there before the Lord.

[14]Then the Spirit of the Lord came on Jahaziel son of Zechariah, the son of Benaiah, the son of Jeiel, the son of Mattaniah, a Levite and descendant of Asaph, as he stood in the assembly.

[15]He said: "Listen, King Jehoshaphat and all who live in Judah and Jerusalem! This is what the Lord says to you: 'Do not be afraid or discouraged because of this vast army. For the battle is not yours, but God's. [16]Tomorrow march down against them. They will be climbing up by the Pass of Ziz, and you will find them at the end of the gorge in the Desert of Jeruel. [17]You will not have to fight this battle. Take up your positions; stand firm and see the deliverance the Lord will give you, Judah and Jerusalem. Do not be afraid; do not be discouraged. Go out to face them tomorrow, and the Lord will be with you.' "

[18]Jehoshaphat bowed down with his face to the ground, and all the people of Judah and Jerusalem fell down in worship before the Lord. [19]Then some Levites from the Kohathites and Korahites stood up and praised the Lord, the God of Israel, with a very loud voice.

[20]Early in the morning they left for the Desert of Tekoa. As they set out, Jehoshaphat stood and said, "Listen to me, Judah and people of Jerusalem! Have faith in the Lord your God and you will be upheld; have faith in his prophets and you will be successful." [21]After consulting the people, Jehoshaphat appointed men to sing to the Lord and to praise him for the splendor of his[a] holiness as they went out at the head of the army, saying:

"Give thanks to the Lord,
for his love endures forever."

[22]As they began to sing and praise, the Lord set ambushes against the men of Ammon and Moab and Mount Seir who were invading Judah, and they were defeated. [23]The Ammonites and Moabites rose up against the men from Mount Seir to destroy and annihilate them. After they finished slaughtering the men from Seir, they helped to destroy one another.

[24]When the men of Judah came to the place that overlooks the desert and looked toward the vast army, they saw only dead bodies lying on the ground; no one had escaped. [25]So Jehoshaphat and his men went to carry off their plunder, and they found among them a great amount of equipment and clothing[b] and also articles of value—more than they could take away. There was so much plunder that it took three days to collect it. [26]On the fourth day they assembled in the Valley of Berakah, where they praised the Lord. This is why it is called the Valley of Berakah[c] to this day.

[27]Then, led by Jehoshaphat, all the men of Judah and Jerusalem returned joyfully to Jerusalem, for the Lord had given them cause to rejoice over their enemies. [28]They entered Jerusalem and went to the temple of the Lord with harps and lyres and trumpets.

[29]The fear of God came on all the surrounding kingdoms when they heard how the Lord had fought against the enemies of Israel. [30]And the kingdom of Jehoshaphat was at peace, for his God had given him rest on every side.

The End of Jehoshaphat's Reign

[31]So Jehoshaphat reigned over Judah. He was thirty-five years old when he became king of Judah, and he reigned in Jerusalem twenty-five years. His mother's name was Azubah daughter of Shilhi. [32]He followed the ways of his father Asa and did not stray from them; he did what was right in the eyes of the Lord. [33]The high places, however, were not removed, and the people still had not set their hearts on the God of their ancestors.

[34]The other events of Jehoshaphat's reign, from beginning to end, are written

---

a 21 Or *him with the splendor of*   *b 25* Some Hebrew manuscripts and Vulgate; most Hebrew manuscripts *corpses*   *c 26* Berakah *means* praise.

in the annals of Jehu son of Hanani, which are recorded in the book of the kings of Israel. 35Later, Jehoshaphat king of Judah made an alliance with Ahaziah king of Israel, whose ways were wicked. 36He agreed with him to construct a fleet of trading ships.ª After these were built at Ezion Geber, 37Eliezer son of Dodavahu of Mareshah prophesied against Jehoshaphat, saying, "Because you have made an alliance with Ahaziah, the LORD will destroy what you have made." The ships were wrecked and were not able to set sail to trade.ᵇ

21 Then Jehoshaphat rested with his ancestors and was buried with them in the City of David. And Jehoram his son succeeded him as king. 2Jehoram's brothers, the sons of Jehoshaphat, were Azariah, Jehiel, Zechariah, Azariahu, Michael and Shephatiah. All these were sons of Jehoshaphat king of Israel.ᶜ 3Their father had given them many gifts of silver and gold and articles of value, as well as fortified cities in Judah, but he had given the kingdom to Jehoram because he was his firstborn son.

Jehoram King of Judah

4When Jehoram established himself firmly over his father's kingdom, he put all his brothers to the sword along with some of the officials of Israel. 5Jehoram was thirty-two years old when he became king, and he reigned in Jerusalem eight years. 6He followed the ways of the kings of Israel, as the house of Ahab had done, for he married a daughter of Ahab. He did evil in the eyes of the LORD. 7Nevertheless, because of the covenant the LORD had made with David, the LORD was not willing to destroy the house of David. He had promised to maintain a lamp for him and his descendants forever.

8In the time of Jehoram, Edom rebelled against Judah and set up its own king. 9So Jehoram went there with his officers and all his chariots. The Edomites surrounded him and his chariot commanders, but he rose up and broke through by night. 10To this day Edom has been in rebellion against Judah.

Libnah revolted at the same time, because Jehoram had forsaken the LORD, the God of his ancestors. 11He had also built high places on the hills of Judah and had caused the people of Jerusalem to prostitute themselves and had led Judah astray.

12Jehoram received a letter from Elijah the prophet, which said:

"This is what the LORD, the God of your father David, says: 'You have not followed the ways of your father Jehoshaphat or of Asa king of Judah. 13But you have followed the ways of the kings of Israel, and you have led Judah and the people of Jerusalem to prostitute themselves, just as the house of Ahab did. You have also murdered your own brothers, members of your own family, men who were better than you. 14So now the LORD is about to strike your people, your sons, your wives and everything that is yours, with a heavy blow. 15You yourself will be very ill with a lingering disease of the bowels, until the disease causes your bowels to come out.' "

16The LORD aroused against Jehoram the hostility of the Philistines and of the Arabs who lived near the Cushites. 17They attacked Judah, invaded it and carried off all the goods found in the king's palace, together with his sons and wives. Not a son was left to him except Ahaziah,ᵈ the youngest.

18After all this, the LORD afflicted Jehoram with an incurable disease of the bowels. 19In the course of time, at the end of the second year, his bowels came out because of the disease, and he died in great pain. His people made no funeral fire in his honor, as they had for his predecessors.

20Jehoram was thirty-two years old when he became king, and he reigned in Jerusalem eight years. He passed away, to no one's regret, and was buried in the City of David, but not in the tombs of the kings.

ª 36 Hebrew of ships that could go to Tarshish
ᵇ 37 Hebrew sail for Tarshish　ᶜ 2 That is, Judah, as frequently in 2 Chronicles　ᵈ 17 Hebrew Jehoahaz, a variant of Ahaziah

Ahaziah King of Judah

22 The people of Jerusalem made Ahaziah, Jehoram's youngest son, king in his place, since the raiders, who came with the Arabs into the camp, had killed all the older sons. So Ahaziah son of Jehoram king of Judah began to reign.

²Ahaziah was twenty-two^a years old when he became king, and he reigned in Jerusalem one year. His mother's name was Athaliah, a granddaughter of Omri.

³He too followed the ways of the house of Ahab, for his mother encouraged him to act wickedly. ⁴He did evil in the eyes of the LORD, as the house of Ahab had done, for after his father's death they became his advisers, to his undoing. ⁵He also followed their counsel when he went with Joram^b son of Ahab king of Israel to wage war against Hazael king of Aram at Ramoth Gilead. The Arameans wounded Joram; ⁶so he returned to Jezreel to recover from the wounds they had inflicted on him at Ramoth^c in his battle with Hazael king of Aram.

Then Ahaziah^d son of Jehoram king of Judah went down to Jezreel to see Joram son of Ahab because he had been wounded.

⁷Through Ahaziah's visit to Joram, God brought about Ahaziah's downfall. When Ahaziah arrived, he went out with Joram to meet Jehu son of Nimshi, whom the LORD had anointed to destroy the house of Ahab. ⁸While Jehu was executing judgment on the house of Ahab, he found the officials of Judah and the sons of Ahaziah's relatives, who had been attending Ahaziah, and he killed them. ⁹He then went in search of Ahaziah, and his men captured him while he was hiding in Samaria. He was brought to Jehu and put to death. They buried him, for they said, "He was a son of Jehoshaphat, who sought the LORD with all his heart." So there was no one in the house of Ahaziah powerful enough to retain the kingdom.

Athaliah and Joash

¹⁰When Athaliah the mother of Ahaziah saw that her son was dead, she proceeded to destroy the whole royal family of the house of Judah. ¹¹But Jehosheba,^e the daughter of King Jehoram, took Joash son of Ahaziah and stole him away from among the royal princes who were about to be murdered and put him and his nurse in a bedroom. Because Jehosheba,^e the daughter of King Jehoram and wife of the priest Jehoiada, was Ahaziah's sister, she hid the child from Athaliah so she could not kill him. ¹²He remained hidden with them at the temple of God for six years while Athaliah ruled the land.

23 In the seventh year Jehoiada showed his strength. He made a covenant with the commanders of units of a hundred: Azariah son of Jeroham, Ishmael son of Jehohanan, Azariah son of Obed, Maaseiah son of Adaiah, and Elishaphat son of Zikri. ²They went throughout Judah and gathered the Levites and the heads of Israelite families from all the towns. When they came to Jerusalem, ³the whole assembly made a covenant with the king at the temple of God.

Jehoiada said to them, "The king's son shall reign, as the LORD promised concerning the descendants of David. ⁴Now this is what you are to do: A third of you priests and Levites who are going on duty on the Sabbath are to keep watch at the doors, ⁵a third of you at the royal palace and a third at the Foundation Gate, and all the others are to be in the courtyards of the temple of the LORD. ⁶No one is to enter the temple of the LORD except the priests and Levites on duty; they may enter because they are consecrated, but all the others are to observe the LORD's command not to enter.^f ⁷The Levites are to station themselves around the king, each with weapon in hand. Anyone who enters the temple is to be put to death. Stay close to the king wherever he goes."

⁸The Levites and all the men of Judah did just as Jehoiada the priest ordered. Each one took his men—those who were going on duty on the Sabbath and those

---

^a 2 Some Septuagint manuscripts and Syriac (see also 2 Kings 8:26); Hebrew *forty-two*   ^b 5 Hebrew *Jehoram,* a variant of *Joram*; also in verses 6 and 7   ^c 6 Hebrew *Ramah,* a variant of *Ramoth*   ^d 6 Some Hebrew manuscripts, Septuagint, Vulgate and Syriac (see also 2 Kings 8:29); most Hebrew manuscripts *Azariah*   ^e 11 Hebrew *Jehoshabeath,* a variant of *Jehosheba*   ^f 6 Or *are to stand guard where the LORD has assigned them*

who were going off duty — for Jehoiada the priest had not released any of the divisions. ⁹Then he gave the commanders of units of a hundred the spears and the large and small shields that had belonged to King David and that were in the temple of God. ¹⁰He stationed all the men, each with his weapon in his hand, around the king — near the altar and the temple, from the south side to the north side of the temple.

¹¹Jehoiada and his sons brought out the king's son and put the crown on him; they presented him with a copy of the covenant and proclaimed him king. They anointed him and shouted, "Long live the king!"

¹²When Athaliah heard the noise of the people running and cheering the king, she went to them at the temple of the LORD. ¹³She looked, and there was the king, standing by his pillar at the entrance. The officers and the trumpeters were beside the king, and all the people of the land were rejoicing and blowing trumpets, and musicians with their instruments were leading the praises. Then Athaliah tore her robes and shouted, "Treason! Treason!"

¹⁴Jehoiada the priest sent out the commanders of units of a hundred, who were in charge of the troops, and said to them: "Bring her out between the ranks[a] and put to the sword anyone who follows her." For the priest had said, "Do not put her to death at the temple of the LORD." ¹⁵So they seized her as she reached the entrance of the Horse Gate on the palace grounds, and there they put her to death.

¹⁶Jehoiada then made a covenant that he, the people and the king[b] would be the LORD's people. ¹⁷All the people went to the temple of Baal and tore it down. They smashed the altars and idols and killed Mattan the priest of Baal in front of the altars.

¹⁸Then Jehoiada placed the oversight of the temple of the LORD in the hands of the Levitical priests, to whom David had made assignments in the temple, to present the burnt offerings of the LORD as written in the Law of Moses, with rejoicing and singing, as David had ordered. ¹⁹He also stationed gatekeepers at the gates of the LORD's temple so that no one who was in any way unclean might enter.

²⁰He took with him the commanders of hundreds, the nobles, the rulers of the people and all the people of the land and brought the king down from the temple of the LORD. They went into the palace through the Upper Gate and seated the king on the royal throne. ²¹All the people of the land rejoiced, and the city was calm, because Athaliah had been slain with the sword.

Joash Repairs the Temple

24 Joash was seven years old when he became king, and he reigned in Jerusalem forty years. His mother's name was Zibiah; she was from Beersheba. ²Joash did what was right in the eyes of the LORD all the years of Jehoiada the priest. ³Jehoiada chose two wives for him, and he had sons and daughters.

⁴Some time later Joash decided to restore the temple of the LORD. ⁵He called together the priests and Levites and said to them, "Go to the towns of Judah and collect the money due annually from all Israel, to repair the temple of your God. Do it now." But the Levites did not act at once.

⁶Therefore the king summoned Jehoiada the chief priest and said to him, "Why haven't you required the Levites to bring in from Judah and Jerusalem the tax imposed by Moses the servant of the LORD and by the assembly of Israel for the tent of the covenant law?"

⁷Now the sons of that wicked woman Athaliah had broken into the temple of God and had used even its sacred objects for the Baals.

⁸At the king's command, a chest was made and placed outside, at the gate of the temple of the LORD. ⁹A proclamation was then issued in Judah and Jerusalem that they should bring to the LORD the tax that Moses the servant of God had required of Israel in the wilderness. ¹⁰All

---

a 14 Or *out from the precincts*   *b 16* Or *covenant between the LORD and the people and the king that they* (see 2 Kings 11:17) the officials and all the people brought their contributions gladly, dropping them into the chest until it was full. [11]Whenever the chest was brought in by the Levites to the king's officials and they saw that there was a large amount of money, the royal secretary and the officer of the chief priest would come and empty the chest and carry it back to its place. They did this regularly and collected a great amount of money. [12]The king and Jehoiada gave it to those who carried out the work required for the temple of the LORD. They hired masons and carpenters to restore the LORD's temple, and also workers in iron and bronze to repair the temple.

[13]The men in charge of the work were diligent, and the repairs progressed under them. They rebuilt the temple of God according to its original design and reinforced it. [14]When they had finished, they brought the rest of the money to the king and Jehoiada, and with it were made articles for the LORD's temple: articles for the service and for the burnt offerings, and also dishes and other objects of gold and silver. As long as Jehoiada lived, burnt offerings were presented continually in the temple of the LORD.

[15]Now Jehoiada was old and full of years, and he died at the age of a hundred and thirty. [16]He was buried with the kings in the City of David, because of the good he had done in Israel for God and his temple.

The Wickedness of Joash

[17]After the death of Jehoiada, the officials of Judah came and paid homage to the king, and he listened to them. [18]They abandoned the temple of the LORD, the God of their ancestors, and worshiped Asherah poles and idols. Because of their guilt, God's anger came on Judah and Jerusalem. [19]Although the LORD sent prophets to the people to bring them back to him, and though they testified against them, they would not listen.

[20]Then the Spirit of God came on Zechariah son of Jehoiada the priest. He stood before the people and said, "This is what God says: 'Why do you disobey the LORD's commands? You will not prosper. Because you have forsaken the LORD, he has forsaken you.' "

[21]But they plotted against him, and by order of the king they stoned him to death in the courtyard of the LORD's temple. [22]King Joash did not remember the kindness Zechariah's father Jehoiada had shown him but killed his son, who said as he lay dying, "May the LORD see this and call you to account."

[23]At the turn of the year,[a] the army of Aram marched against Joash; it invaded Judah and Jerusalem and killed all the leaders of the people. They sent all the plunder to their king in Damascus. [24]Although the Aramean army had come with only a few men, the LORD delivered into their hands a much larger army. Because Judah had forsaken the LORD, the God of their ancestors, judgment was executed on Joash. [25]When the Arameans withdrew, they left Joash severely wounded. His officials conspired against him for murdering the son of Jehoiada the priest, and they killed him in his bed. So he died and was buried in the City of David, but not in the tombs of the kings.

[26]Those who conspired against him were Zabad,[b] son of Shimeath an Ammonite woman, and Jehozabad, son of Shimrith[c] a Moabite woman. [27]The account of his sons, the many prophecies about him, and the record of the restoration of the temple of God are written in the annotations on the book of the kings. And Amaziah his son succeeded him as king.

Amaziah King of Judah

25 Amaziah was twenty-five years old when he became king, and he reigned in Jerusalem twenty-nine years. His mother's name was Jehoaddan; she was from Jerusalem. [2]He did what was right in the eyes of the LORD, but not wholeheartedly. [3]After the kingdom was firmly in his control, he executed the officials who had murdered his father the king. [4]Yet he did not put their children to death, but acted in accordance with what is written in the Law, in the Book of Moses, where the LORD commanded:

---

[a] 23 Probably in the spring   [b] 26 A variant of *Jozabad*
[c] 26 A variant of *Shomer*

"Parents shall not be put to death for their children, nor children be put to death for their parents; each will die for their own sin."[a]

5Amaziah called the people of Judah together and assigned them according to their families to commanders of thousands and commanders of hundreds for all Judah and Benjamin. He then mustered those twenty years old or more and found that there were three hundred thousand men fit for military service, able to handle the spear and shield. 6He also hired a hundred thousand fighting men from Israel for a hundred talents[b] of silver.

7But a man of God came to him and said, "Your Majesty, these troops from Israel must not march with you, for the LORD is not with Israel—not with any of the people of Ephraim. 8Even if you go and fight courageously in battle, God will overthrow you before the enemy, for God has the power to help or to overthrow."

9Amaziah asked the man of God, "But what about the hundred talents I paid for these Israelite troops?"

The man of God replied, "The LORD can give you much more than that."

10So Amaziah dismissed the troops who had come to him from Ephraim and sent them home. They were furious with Judah and left for home in a great rage.

11Amaziah then marshaled his strength and led his army to the Valley of Salt, where he killed ten thousand men of Seir. 12The army of Judah also captured ten thousand men alive, took them to the top of a cliff and threw them down so that all were dashed to pieces.

13Meanwhile the troops that Amaziah had sent back and had not allowed to take part in the war raided towns belonging to Judah from Samaria to Beth Horon. They killed three thousand people and carried off great quantities of plunder.

14When Amaziah returned from slaughtering the Edomites, he brought back the gods of the people of Seir. He set them up as his own gods, bowed down to them and burned sacrifices to them. 15The anger of the LORD burned against Amaziah, and he sent a prophet to him, who said,

"Why do you consult this people's gods, which could not save their own people from your hand?"

16While he was still speaking, the king said to him, "Have we appointed you an adviser to the king? Stop! Why be struck down?"

So the prophet stopped but said, "I know that God has determined to destroy you, because you have done this and have not listened to my counsel."

17After Amaziah king of Judah consulted his advisers, he sent this challenge to Jehoash[c] son of Jehoahaz, the son of Jehu, king of Israel: "Come, let us face each other in battle."

18But Jehoash king of Israel replied to Amaziah king of Judah: "A thistle in Lebanon sent a message to a cedar in Lebanon, 'Give your daughter to my son in marriage.' Then a wild beast in Lebanon came along and trampled the thistle underfoot. 19You say to yourself that you have defeated Edom, and now you are arrogant and proud. But stay at home! Why ask for trouble and cause your own downfall and that of Judah also?"

20Amaziah, however, would not listen, for God so worked that he might deliver them into the hands of Jehoash, because they sought the gods of Edom. 21So Jehoash king of Israel attacked. He and Amaziah king of Judah faced each other at Beth Shemesh in Judah. 22Judah was routed by Israel, and every man fled to his home. 23Jehoash king of Israel captured Amaziah king of Judah, the son of Joash, the son of Ahaziah,[d] at Beth Shemesh. Then Jehoash brought him to Jerusalem and broke down the wall of Jerusalem from the Ephraim Gate to the Corner Gate—a section about four hundred cubits[e] long. 24He took all the gold and silver and all the articles found in the temple of God that had been in the care of Obed-Edom, together with the palace treasures and the hostages, and returned to Samaria.

25Amaziah son of Joash king of Judah lived for fifteen years after the death of

---

[a] 4 Deut. 24:16   [b] 6 That is, about 3 3/4 tons or about 3.4 metric tons; also in verse 9   [c] 17 Hebrew Joash, a variant of Jehoash; also in verses 18, 21, 23 and 25   [d] 23 Hebrew Jehoahaz, a variant of Ahaziah   [e] 23 That is, about 600 feet or about 180 meters

Jehoash son of Jehoahaz king of Israel. ²⁶As for the other events of Amaziah's reign, from beginning to end, are they not written in the book of the kings of Judah and Israel? ²⁷From the time that Amaziah turned away from following the LORD, they conspired against him in Jerusalem and he fled to Lachish, but they sent men after him to Lachish and killed him there. ²⁸He was brought back by horse and was buried with his ancestors in the City of Judah.ᵃ

Uzziah King of Judah

26 Then all the people of Judah took Uzziah,ᵇ who was sixteen years old, and made him king in place of his father Amaziah. ²He was the one who rebuilt Elath and restored it to Judah after Amaziah rested with his ancestors.

³Uzziah was sixteen years old when he became king, and he reigned in Jerusalem fifty-two years. His mother's name was Jekoliah; she was from Jerusalem. ⁴He did what was right in the eyes of the LORD, just as his father Amaziah had done. ⁵He sought God during the days of Zechariah, who instructed him in the fearᶜ of God. As long as he sought the LORD, God gave him success.

⁶He went to war against the Philistines and broke down the walls of Gath, Jabneh and Ashdod. He then rebuilt towns near Ashdod and elsewhere among the Philistines. ⁷God helped him against the Philistines and against the Arabs who lived in Gur Baal and against the Meunites. ⁸The Ammonites brought tribute to Uzziah, and his fame spread as far as the border of Egypt, because he had become very powerful.

⁹Uzziah built towers in Jerusalem at the Corner Gate, at the Valley Gate and at the angle of the wall, and he fortified them. ¹⁰He also built towers in the wilderness and dug many cisterns, because he had much livestock in the foothills and in the plain. He had people working his fields and vineyards in the hills and in the fertile lands, for he loved the soil.

¹¹Uzziah had a well-trained army, ready to go out by divisions according to their numbers as mustered by Jeiel the sec-

retary and Maaseiah the officer under the direction of Hananiah, one of the royal officials. ¹²The total number of family leaders over the fighting men was 2,600. ¹³Under their command was an army of 307,500 men trained for war, a powerful force to support the king against his enemies. ¹⁴Uzziah provided shields, spears, helmets, coats of armor, bows and slingstones for the entire army. ¹⁵In Jerusalem he made devices invented for use on the towers and on the corner defenses so that soldiers could shoot arrows and hurl large stones from the walls. His fame spread far and wide, for he was greatly helped until he became powerful.

¹⁶But after Uzziah became powerful, his pride led to his downfall. He was unfaithful to the LORD his God, and entered the temple of the LORD to burn incense on the altar of incense. ¹⁷Azariah the priest with eighty other courageous priests of the

---

ᵃ 28 Most Hebrew manuscripts; some Hebrew manuscripts, Septuagint, Vulgate and Syriac (see also 2 Kings 14:20) *David*　　ᵇ 1 Also called *Azariah*　　ᶜ 5 Many Hebrew manuscripts, Septuagint and Syriac; other Hebrew manuscripts *vision*

BREAKTHROUGH!

The towers

(2 CHRONICLES 26:10)

These were watchtowers, and they often stored grain there. The people who were planting could rest or spend the night there.

LORD followed him in. [18]They confronted King Uzziah and said, "It is not right for you, Uzziah, to burn incense to the LORD. That is for the priests, the descendants of Aaron, who have been consecrated to burn incense. Leave the sanctuary, for you have been unfaithful; and you will not be honored by the LORD God." [19]Uzziah, who had a censer in his hand ready to burn incense, became angry. While he was raging at the priests in their presence before the incense altar in the LORD's temple, leprosy[a] broke out on his forehead. [20]When Azariah the chief priest and all the other priests looked at him, they saw that he had leprosy on his forehead, so they hurried him out. Indeed, he himself was eager to leave, because the LORD had afflicted him. [21]King Uzziah had leprosy until the day he died. He lived in a separate house[b]— leprous, and banned from the temple of the LORD. Jotham his son had charge of the palace and governed the people of the land. [22]The other events of Uzziah's reign, from beginning to end, are recorded by the prophet Isaiah son of Amoz. [23]Uzziah rested with his ancestors and was buried near them in a cemetery that belonged to the kings, for people said, "He had leprosy." And Jotham his son succeeded him as king.

Jotham King of Judah

27 Jotham was twenty-five years old when he became king, and he reigned in Jerusalem sixteen years. His mother's name was Jerusha daughter of Zadok. [2]He did what was right in the eyes of the LORD, just as his father Uzziah had done, but unlike him he did not enter the temple of the LORD. The people, however, continued their corrupt practices. [3]Jotham rebuilt the Upper Gate of the temple of the LORD and did extensive work on the wall at the hill of Ophel. [4]He built towns in the hill country of Judah and forts and towers in the wooded areas.

[5]Jotham waged war against the king of the Ammonites and conquered them. That year the Ammonites paid him a hundred talents[c] of silver, ten thousand cors[d] of wheat and ten thousand cors[e] of barley. The Ammonites brought him the same amount also in the second and third years.

[6]Jotham grew powerful because he walked steadfastly before the LORD his God.

[7]The other events in Jotham's reign, including all his wars and the other things he did, are written in the book of the kings of Israel and Judah. [8]He was twenty-five years old when he became king, and he reigned in Jerusalem sixteen years. [9]Jotham rested with his ancestors and was buried in the City of David. And Ahaz his son succeeded him as king.

Ahaz King of Judah

28 Ahaz was twenty years old when he became king, and he reigned in Jerusalem sixteen years. Unlike David his father, he did not do what was right in the eyes of the LORD. [2]He followed the ways of the kings of Israel and also made idols for worshiping the Baals. [3]He burned sacrifices in the Valley of Ben Hinnom and sacrificed his children in the fire, engaging in the detestable practices of the nations the LORD had driven out before the Israelites. [4]He offered sacrifices and burned incense at the high places, on the hilltops and under every spreading tree.

[5]Therefore the LORD his God delivered him into the hands of the king of Aram. The Arameans defeated him and took many of his people as prisoners and brought them to Damascus.

He was also given into the hands of the king of Israel, who inflicted heavy casualties on him. [6]In one day Pekah son of Remaliah killed a hundred and twenty thousand soldiers in Judah—because Judah had forsaken the LORD, the God of their ancestors. [7]Zikri, an Ephraimite warrior, killed Maaseiah the king's son, Azrikam the officer in charge of the palace, and Elkanah, second to the king.

---

[a] 19 The Hebrew for *leprosy* was used for various diseases affecting the skin; also in verses 20, 21 and 23.
[b] 21 Or *in a house where he was relieved of responsibilities*
[c] 5 That is, about 3 3/4 tons or about 3.4 metric tons
[d] 5 That is, probably about 1,800 tons or about 1,600 metric tons of wheat   [e] 5 That is, probably about 1,500 tons or about 1,350 metric tons of barley

VALLEY OF BEN HINNOM

(2 CHRONICLES 28:3)

I t was south of Jerusalem. The story about this place is really quite nasty, because they sacrificed children to the gods Baal and Molek there. How horrible!

[8]The men of Israel took captive from their fellow Israelites who were from Judah two hundred thousand wives, sons and daughters. They also took a great deal of plunder, which they carried back to Samaria. [9]But a prophet of the Lord named Oded was there, and he went out to meet the army when it returned to Samaria. He said to them, "Because the Lord, the God of your ancestors, was angry with Judah, he gave them into your hand. But you have slaughtered them in a rage that reaches to heaven. [10]And now you intend to make the men and women of Judah and Jerusalem your slaves. But aren't you also guilty of sins against the Lord your God? [11]Now listen to me! Send back your fellow Israelites you have taken as prisoners, for the Lord's fierce anger rests on you."

[12]Then some of the leaders in Ephraim—Azariah son of Jehohanan, Bereki-ah son of Meshillemoth, Jehizkiah son of Shallum, and Amasa son of Hadlai—confronted those who were arriving from the war. [13]"You must not bring those prisoners here," they said, "or we will be guilty before the Lord. Do you intend to add to our sin and guilt? For our guilt is already great, and his fierce anger rests on Israel."

[14]So the soldiers gave up the prisoners and plunder in the presence of the officials and all the assembly. [15]The men designated by name took the prisoners, and from the plunder they clothed all who were naked. They provided them with clothes and sandals, food and drink, and healing balm. All those who were weak they put on donkeys. So they took them back to their fellow Israelites at Jericho, the City of Palms, and returned to Samaria.

[16]At that time King Ahaz sent to the kings[a] of Assyria for help. [17]The Edomites had again come and attacked Judah and carried away prisoners, [18]while the Philistines had raided towns in the foothills and in the Negev of Judah. They captured and occupied Beth Shemesh, Aijalon and Gederoth, as well as Soko, Timnah and Gimzo, with their surrounding villages. [19]The Lord had humbled Judah because of Ahaz king of Israel,[b] for he had promoted wickedness in Judah and had been most unfaithful to the Lord. [20]Tiglath-Pileser[c] king of Assyria came to him, but he gave him trouble instead of help. [21]Ahaz took some of the things from the temple of the Lord and from the royal palace and from the officials and presented them to the king of Assyria, but that did not help him.

[22]In his time of trouble King Ahaz became even more unfaithful to the Lord. [23]He offered sacrifices to the gods of Damascus, who had defeated him; for he thought, "Since the gods of the kings of Aram have helped them, I will sacrifice to them so they will help me." But they were his downfall and the downfall of all Israel. [24]Ahaz gathered together the furnishings from the temple of God and cut them in pieces. He shut the doors of the Lord's

a 16 Most Hebrew manuscripts; one Hebrew manuscript, Septuagint and Vulgate (see also 2 Kings 16:7) king
b 19 That is, Judah, as frequently in 2 Chronicles
c 20 Hebrew Tilgath-Pilneser, a variant of Tiglath-Pileser

temple and set up altars at every street corner in Jerusalem. ²⁵In every town in Judah he built high places to burn sacrifices to other gods and aroused the anger of the LORD, the God of his ancestors.

²⁶The other events of his reign and all his ways, from beginning to end, are written in the book of the kings of Judah and Israel. ²⁷Ahaz rested with his ancestors and was buried in the city of Jerusalem, but he was not placed in the tombs of the kings of Israel. And Hezekiah his son succeeded him as king.

Hezekiah Purifies the Temple

29 Hezekiah was twenty-five years old when he became king, and he reigned in Jerusalem twenty-nine years. His mother's name was Abijah daughter of Zechariah. ²He did what was right in the eyes of the LORD, just as his father David had done.

³In the first month of the first year of his reign, he opened the doors of the temple of the LORD and repaired them.

BREAKTHROUGH!

The first month

(2 CHRONICLES 29:3)

Called Aviv in the Jewish lunar calendar. This means it was the period from the middle of March to the middle of April in our solar calendar.

⁴He brought in the priests and the Levites, assembled them in the square on the east side ⁵and said: "Listen to me, Levites! Consecrate yourselves now and consecrate the temple of the LORD, the God of your ancestors. Remove all defilement from the sanctuary. ⁶Our parents were unfaithful; they did evil in the eyes of the LORD our God and forsook him. They turned their faces away from the LORD's dwelling place and turned their backs on him. ⁷They also shut the doors of the portico and put out the lamps. They did not burn incense or present any burnt offerings at the sanctuary to the God of Israel. ⁸Therefore, the anger of the LORD has fallen on Judah and Jerusalem; he has made them an object of dread and horror and scorn, as you can see with your own eyes. ⁹This is why our fathers have fallen by the sword and why our sons and daughters and our wives are in captivity. ¹⁰Now I intend to make a covenant with the LORD, the God of Israel, so that his fierce anger will turn away from us. ¹¹My sons, do not be negligent now, for the LORD has chosen you to stand before him and serve him, to minister before him and to burn incense."

¹²Then these Levites set to work:

from the Kohathites,
  Mahath son of Amasai and Joel son of Azariah;
from the Merarites,
  Kish son of Abdi and Azariah son of Jehallelel;
from the Gershonites,
  Joah son of Zimmah and Eden son of Joah;
¹³from the descendants of Elizaphan,
  Shimri and Jeiel;
from the descendants of Asaph,
  Zechariah and Mattaniah;
¹⁴from the descendants of Heman,
  Jehiel and Shimei;
from the descendants of Jeduthun,
  Shemaiah and Uzziel.

¹⁵When they had assembled their fellow Levites and consecrated themselves, they went in to purify the temple of the LORD, as the king had ordered, following the word of the LORD. ¹⁶The priests went into the sanctuary of the LORD to purify

it. They brought out to the courtyard of the Lord's temple everything unclean that they found in the temple of the Lord. The Levites took it and carried it out to the Kidron Valley. [17]They began the consecration on the first day of the first month, and by the eighth day of the month they reached the portico of the Lord. For eight more days they consecrated the temple of the Lord itself, finishing on the sixteenth day of the first month.

[18]Then they went in to King Hezekiah and reported: "We have purified the entire temple of the Lord, the altar of burnt offering with all its utensils, and the table for setting out the consecrated bread, with all its articles. [19]We have prepared and consecrated all the articles that King Ahaz removed in his unfaithfulness while he was king. They are now in front of the Lord's altar."

[20]Early the next morning King Hezekiah gathered the city officials together and went up to the temple of the Lord. [21]They brought seven bulls, seven rams, seven male lambs and seven male goats as a sin offering[a] for the kingdom, for the sanctuary and for Judah. The king commanded the priests, the descendants of Aaron, to offer these on the altar of the Lord. [22]So they slaughtered the bulls, and the priests took the blood and splashed it against the altar; next they slaughtered the rams and splashed their blood against the altar; then they slaughtered the lambs and splashed their blood against the altar. [23]The goats for the sin offering were brought before the king and the assembly, and they laid their hands on them. [24]The priests then slaughtered the goats and presented their blood on the altar for a sin offering to atone for all Israel, because the king had ordered the burnt offering and the sin offering for all Israel.

[25]He stationed the Levites in the temple of the Lord with cymbals, harps and lyres in the way prescribed by David and Gad the king's seer and Nathan the prophet; this was commanded by the Lord through his prophets. [26]So the Levites stood ready with David's instruments, and the priests with their trumpets.

[27]Hezekiah gave the order to sacrifice the burnt offering on the altar. As the offering began, singing to the Lord began also, accompanied by trumpets and the instruments of David king of Israel. [28]The whole assembly bowed in worship, while the musicians played and the trumpets sounded. All this continued until the sacrifice of the burnt offering was completed.

[29]When the offerings were finished, the king and everyone present with him knelt down and worshiped. [30]King Hezekiah and his officials ordered the Levites to praise the Lord with the words of David and of Asaph the seer. So they sang praises with gladness and bowed down and worshiped.

[31]Then Hezekiah said, "You have now dedicated yourselves to the Lord. Come and bring sacrifices and thank offerings to the temple of the Lord." So the assembly brought sacrifices and thank offerings, and all whose hearts were willing brought burnt offerings.

[32]The number of burnt offerings the assembly brought was seventy bulls, a hundred rams and two hundred male lambs—all of them for burnt offerings to the Lord. [33]The animals consecrated as sacrifices amounted to six hundred bulls and three thousand sheep and goats. [34]The priests, however, were too few to skin all the burnt offerings; so their relatives the Levites helped them until the task was finished and until other priests had been consecrated, for the Levites had been more conscientious in consecrating themselves than the priests had been. [35]There were burnt offerings in abundance, together with the fat of the fellowship offerings and the drink offerings that accompanied the burnt offerings.

So the service of the temple of the Lord was reestablished. [36]Hezekiah and all the people rejoiced at what God had brought about for his people, because it was done so quickly.

Hezekiah Celebrates the Passover

30 Hezekiah sent word to all Israel and Judah and also wrote letters to Ephraim and Manasseh, inviting them to

---

[a] 21 Or purification offering; also in verses 23 and 24

come to the temple of the LORD in Jerusalem and celebrate the Passover to the LORD, the God of Israel. ²The king and his officials and the whole assembly in Jerusalem decided to celebrate the Passover in the second month. ³They had not been able to celebrate it at the regular time because not enough priests had consecrated themselves and the people had not assembled in Jerusalem. ⁴The plan seemed right both to the king and to the whole assembly. ⁵They decided to send a proclamation throughout Israel, from Beersheba to Dan, calling the people to come to Jerusalem and celebrate the Passover to the LORD, the God of Israel. It had not been celebrated in large numbers according to what was written.

⁶At the king's command, couriers went throughout Israel and Judah with letters from the king and from his officials, which read:

"People of Israel, return to the LORD, the God of Abraham, Isaac and Israel, that he may return to you who are left, who have escaped from the hand of the kings of Assyria. ⁷Do not be like your parents and your fellow Israelites, who were unfaithful to the LORD, the God of their ancestors, so that he made them an object of horror, as you see. ⁸Do not be stiff-necked, as your ancestors were; submit to the LORD. Come to his sanctuary, which he has consecrated forever. Serve the LORD your God, so that his fierce anger will turn away from you. ⁹If you return to the LORD, then your fellow Israelites and your children will be shown compassion by their captors and will return to this land, for the LORD your God is gracious and compassionate. He will not turn his face from you if you return to him."

¹⁰The couriers went from town to town in Ephraim and Manasseh, as far as Zebulun, but people scorned and ridiculed them. ¹¹Nevertheless, some from Asher, Manasseh and Zebulun humbled themselves and went to Jerusalem. ¹²Also in Judah the hand of God was on the people to give them unity of mind to carry out what the king and his officials had ordered, following the word of the LORD.

¹³A very large crowd of people assembled in Jerusalem to celebrate the Festival of Unleavened Bread in the second month. ¹⁴They removed the altars in Jerusalem and cleared away the incense altars and threw them into the Kidron Valley.

¹⁵They slaughtered the Passover lamb on the fourteenth day of the second month. The priests and the Levites were ashamed and consecrated themselves and brought burnt offerings to the temple of the LORD. ¹⁶Then they took up their regular positions as prescribed in the Law of Moses the man of God. The priests splashed against the altar the blood handed to them by the Levites. ¹⁷Since many in the crowd had not consecrated themselves, the Levites had to kill the Passover lambs for all those who were not ceremonially clean and could not consecrate their lambs^a to the LORD.

---

^a 17 Or consecrate themselves

BREAKTHROUGH!

Festival of Unleavened Bread

(2 CHRONICLES 30:13)

Read more in Exodus 13:1–16 and Leviticus 23:6–8.

[18]Although most of the many people who came from Ephraim, Manasseh, Issachar and Zebulun had not purified themselves, yet they ate the Passover, contrary to what was written. But Hezekiah prayed for them, saying, "May the LORD, who is good, pardon everyone [19]who sets their heart on seeking God—the LORD, the God of their ancestors—even if they are not clean according to the rules of the sanctuary." [20]And the LORD heard Hezekiah and healed the people.

[21]The Israelites who were present in Jerusalem celebrated the Festival of Unleavened Bread for seven days with great rejoicing, while the Levites and priests praised the LORD every day with resounding instruments dedicated to the LORD.[a]

[22]Hezekiah spoke encouragingly to all the Levites, who showed good understanding of the service of the LORD. For the seven days they ate their assigned portion and offered fellowship offerings and praised[b] the LORD, the God of their ancestors.

[23]The whole assembly then agreed to celebrate the festival seven more days; so for another seven days they celebrated joyfully. [24]Hezekiah king of Judah provided a thousand bulls and seven thousand sheep and goats for the assembly, and the officials provided them with a thousand bulls and ten thousand sheep and goats. A great number of priests consecrated themselves. [25]The entire assembly of Judah rejoiced, along with the priests and Levites and all who had assembled from Israel, including the foreigners who had come from Israel and also those who resided in Judah. [26]There was great joy in Jerusalem, for since the days of Solomon son of David king of Israel there had been nothing like this in Jerusalem. [27]The priests and the Levites stood to bless the people, and God heard them, for their prayer reached heaven, his holy dwelling place.

31 When all this had ended, the Israelites who were there went out to the towns of Judah, smashed the sacred stones and cut down the Asherah poles. They destroyed the high places and the altars throughout Judah and Benjamin and in Ephraim and Manasseh. After they had destroyed all of them, the Israelites returned to their own towns and to their own property.

Contributions for Worship

[2]Hezekiah assigned the priests and Levites to divisions—each of them according to their duties as priests or Levites—to offer burnt offerings and fellowship offerings, to minister, to give thanks and to sing praises at the gates of the LORD's dwelling. [3]The king contributed from his own possessions for the morning and evening burnt offerings and for the burnt offerings on the Sabbaths, at the New Moons and at the appointed festivals as written in the Law of the LORD. [4]He ordered the people living in Jerusalem to give the portion due the priests and Levites so they could devote themselves to the Law of the LORD. [5]As soon as the order went out, the Israelites generously gave the firstfruits of their grain, new wine, olive oil and honey and all that the fields produced. They brought a great amount, a tithe of everything. [6]The people of Israel and Judah who lived in the towns of Judah also brought a tithe of their herds and flocks and a tithe of the holy things dedicated to the LORD their God, and they piled them in heaps. [7]They began doing this in the third month and finished in the seventh month. [8]When Hezekiah and his officials came and saw the heaps, they praised the LORD and blessed his people Israel.

[9]Hezekiah asked the priests and Levites about the heaps; [10]and Azariah the chief priest, from the family of Zadok, answered, "Since the people began to bring their contributions to the temple of the LORD, we have had enough to eat and plenty to spare, because the LORD has blessed his people, and this great amount is left over."

[11]Hezekiah gave orders to prepare storerooms in the temple of the LORD, and this was done. [12]Then they faithfully

---

[a] 21 Or *priests sang to the LORD every day, accompanied by the LORD's instruments of praise*   [b] 22 Or *and confessed their sins to*

brought in the contributions, tithes and dedicated gifts. Konaniah, a Levite, was the overseer in charge of these things, and his brother Shimei was next in rank. [13] Jehiel, Azaziah, Nahath, Asahel, Jerimoth, Jozabad, Eliel, Ismakiah, Mahath and Benaiah were assistants of Konaniah and Shimei his brother. All these served by appointment of King Hezekiah and Azariah the official in charge of the temple of God.

[14] Kore son of Imnah the Levite, keeper of the East Gate, was in charge of the freewill offerings given to God, distributing the contributions made to the Lord and also the consecrated gifts. [15] Eden, Miniamin, Jeshua, Shemaiah, Amariah and Shekaniah assisted him faithfully in the towns of the priests, distributing to their fellow priests according to their divisions, old and young alike.

[16] In addition, they distributed to the males three years old or more whose names were in the genealogical records — all who would enter the temple of the Lord to perform the daily duties of their various tasks, according to their responsibilities and their divisions. [17] And they distributed to the priests enrolled by their families in the genealogical records and likewise to the Levites twenty years old or more, according to their responsibilities and their divisions. [18] They included all the little ones, the wives, and the sons and daughters of the whole community listed in these genealogical records. For they were faithful in consecrating themselves.

[19] As for the priests, the descendants of Aaron, who lived on the farmlands around their towns or in any other towns, men were designated by name to distribute portions to every male among them and to all who were recorded in the genealogies of the Levites.

[20] This is what Hezekiah did throughout Judah, doing what was good and right and faithful before the Lord his God. [21] In everything that he undertook in the service of God's temple and in obedience to the law and the commands, he sought his God and worked wholeheartedly. And so he prospered.

Sennacherib Threatens Jerusalem

32 After all that Hezekiah had so faithfully done, Sennacherib king of Assyria came and invaded Judah. He laid siege to the fortified cities, thinking to conquer them for himself. [2] When Hezekiah saw that Sennacherib had come and that he intended to wage war against Jerusalem, [3] he consulted with his officials and military staff about blocking off the water from the springs outside the city, and they helped him. [4] They gathered a large group of people who blocked all the springs and the stream that flowed through the land. "Why should the kings[a] of Assyria come and find plenty of water?" they said. [5] Then he worked hard repairing all the broken sections of the wall and building towers on it. He built another wall outside that one and reinforced the terraces[b] of the City of David. He also made large numbers of weapons and shields.

[6] He appointed military officers over the people and assembled them before him in the square at the city gate and encouraged them with these words: [7] "Be strong and courageous. Do not be afraid or discouraged because of the king of Assyria and the vast army with him, for there is a greater power with us than with him. [8] With him is only the arm of flesh, but with us is the Lord our God to help us and to fight our battles." And the people gained confidence from what Hezekiah the king of Judah said.

[9] Later, when Sennacherib king of Assyria and all his forces were laying siege to Lachish, he sent his officers to Jerusalem with this message for Hezekiah king of Judah and for all the people of Judah who were there:

[10] "This is what Sennacherib king of Assyria says: On what are you basing your confidence, that you remain in Jerusalem under siege? [11] When Hezekiah says, 'The Lord our God will save us from the hand of the king of Assyria,' he is misleading you, to let you die of hunger and thirst. [12] Did not Hezekiah himself remove this

---

a 4 Hebrew; Septuagint and Syriac *king*   *b 5* Or *the Millo* god's high places and altars, saying to Judah and Jerusalem, 'You must worship before one altar and burn sacrifices on it'?

¹³"Do you not know what I and my predecessors have done to all the peoples of the other lands? Were the gods of those nations ever able to deliver their land from my hand? ¹⁴Who of all the gods of these nations that my predecessors destroyed has been able to save his people from me? How then can your god deliver you from my hand? ¹⁵Now do not let Hezekiah deceive you and mislead you like this. Do not believe him, for no god of any nation or kingdom has been able to deliver his people from my hand or the hand of my predecessors. How much less will your god deliver you from my hand!"

¹⁶Sennacherib's officers spoke further against the LORD God and against his servant Hezekiah. ¹⁷The king also wrote letters ridiculing the LORD, the God of Israel, and saying this against him: "Just as the gods of the peoples of the other lands did not rescue their people from my hand, so the god of Hezekiah will not rescue his people from my hand." ¹⁸Then they called out in Hebrew to the people of Jerusalem who were on the wall, to terrify them and make them afraid in order to capture the city. ¹⁹They spoke about the God of Jerusalem as they did about the gods of the other peoples of the world—the work of human hands.

²⁰King Hezekiah and the prophet Isaiah son of Amoz cried out in prayer to heaven about this. ²¹And the LORD sent an angel, who annihilated all the fighting men and the commanders and officers in the camp of the Assyrian king. So he withdrew to his own land in disgrace. And when he went into the temple of his god, some of his sons, his own flesh and blood, cut him down with the sword.

²²So the LORD saved Hezekiah and the people of Jerusalem from the hand of Sennacherib king of Assyria and from the hand of all others. He took care of them*a* on every side. ²³Many brought offerings to Jerusalem for the LORD and valuable gifts for Hezekiah king of Judah. From then on he was highly regarded by all the nations.

Hezekiah's Pride, Success and Death

²⁴In those days Hezekiah became ill and was at the point of death. He prayed to the LORD, who answered him and gave him a miraculous sign. ²⁵But Hezekiah's heart was proud and he did not respond to the kindness shown him; therefore the LORD's wrath was on him and on Judah and Jerusalem. ²⁶Then Hezekiah repented of the pride of his heart, as did the people of Jerusalem; therefore the LORD's wrath did not come on them during the days of Hezekiah.

²⁷Hezekiah had very great wealth and honor, and he made treasuries for his silver and gold and for his precious stones, spices, shields and all kinds of valuables. ²⁸He also made buildings to store the harvest of grain, new wine and olive oil; and he made stalls for various kinds of cattle, and pens for the flocks. ²⁹He built villages and acquired great numbers of flocks and herds, for God had given him very great riches.

³⁰It was Hezekiah who blocked the upper outlet of the Gihon spring and channeled the water down to the west side of the City of David. He succeeded in everything he undertook. ³¹But when envoys were sent by the rulers of Babylon to ask him about the miraculous sign that had occurred in the land, God left him to test him and to know everything that was in his heart.

³²The other events of Hezekiah's reign and his acts of devotion are written in the vision of the prophet Isaiah son of Amoz in the book of the kings of Judah and Israel. ³³Hezekiah rested with his ancestors and was buried on the hill where the tombs of David's descendants are. All Judah and the people of Jerusalem honored him when he died. And Manasseh his son succeeded him as king.

---

a 22 Hebrew; Septuagint and Vulgate *He gave them rest*

Manasseh King of Judah

33 Manasseh was twelve years old when he became king, and he reigned in Jerusalem fifty-five years. ²He did evil in the eyes of the Lᴏʀᴅ, following the detestable practices of the nations the Lᴏʀᴅ had driven out before the Israelites. ³He rebuilt the high places his father Hezekiah had demolished; he also erected altars to the Baals and made Asherah poles. He bowed down to all the starry hosts and worshiped them. ⁴He built altars in the temple of the Lᴏʀᴅ, of which the Lᴏʀᴅ had said, "My Name will remain in Jerusalem forever." ⁵In both courts of the temple of the Lᴏʀᴅ, he built altars to all the starry hosts. ⁶He sacrificed his children in the fire in the Valley of Ben Hinnom, practiced divination and witchcraft, sought omens, and consulted mediums and spiritists. He did much evil in the eyes of the Lᴏʀᴅ, arousing his anger.

⁷He took the image he had made and put it in God's temple, of which God had said to David and to his son Solomon, "In this temple and in Jerusalem, which I have chosen out of all the tribes of Israel, I will put my Name forever. ⁸I will not again make the feet of the Israelites leave the land I assigned to your ancestors, if only they will be careful to do everything I commanded them concerning all the laws, decrees and regulations given through Moses." ⁹But Manasseh led Judah and the people of Jerusalem astray, so that they did more evil than the nations the Lᴏʀᴅ had destroyed before the Israelites.

¹⁰The Lᴏʀᴅ spoke to Manasseh and his people, but they paid no attention. ¹¹So the Lᴏʀᴅ brought against them the army commanders of the king of Assyria, who took Manasseh prisoner, put a hook in his nose, bound him with bronze shackles and took him to Babylon. ¹²In his distress he sought the favor of the Lᴏʀᴅ his God and humbled himself greatly before the God of his ancestors. ¹³And when he prayed to him, the Lᴏʀᴅ was moved by his entreaty and listened to his plea; so he brought him back to Jerusalem and to his kingdom. Then Manasseh knew that the Lᴏʀᴅ is God.

¹⁴Afterward he rebuilt the outer wall of the City of David, west of the Gihon spring in the valley, as far as the entrance of the Fish Gate and encircling the hill of Ophel; he also made it much higher. He stationed military commanders in all the fortified cities in Judah. ¹⁵He got rid of the foreign gods and removed the image from the temple of the Lᴏʀᴅ, as well as all the altars he had built on the temple hill and in Jerusalem; and he threw them out of the city. ¹⁶Then he restored the altar of the Lᴏʀᴅ and sacrificed fellowship offerings and thank offerings on it, and told Judah to serve the Lᴏʀᴅ, the God of Israel. ¹⁷The people, however, continued to sacrifice at the high places, but only to the Lᴏʀᴅ their God.

¹⁸The other events of Manasseh's reign, including his prayer to his God and the words the seers spoke to him in the name of the Lᴏʀᴅ, the God of Israel, are written in the annals of the kings of Israel.ᵃ ¹⁹His prayer and how God was moved by his entreaty, as well as all his sins and unfaithfulness, and the sites where he built high places and set up Asherah poles and idols before he humbled himself—all these are written in the records of the seers.ᵇ ²⁰Manasseh rested with his ancestors and was buried in his palace. And Amon his son succeeded him as king.

Amon King of Judah

²¹Amon was twenty-two years old when he became king, and he reigned in Jerusalem two years. ²²He did evil in the eyes of the Lᴏʀᴅ, as his father Manasseh had done. Amon worshiped and offered sacrifices to all the idols Manasseh had made. ²³But unlike his father Manasseh, he did not humble himself before the Lᴏʀᴅ; Amon increased his guilt.

²⁴Amon's officials conspired against him and assassinated him in his palace. ²⁵Then the people of the land killed all who had plotted against King Amon, and they made Josiah his son king in his place.

ᵃ 18 That is, Judah, as frequently in 2 Chronicles
ᵇ 19 One Hebrew manuscript and Septuagint; most Hebrew manuscripts of Hozai

Josiah's Reforms

34 Josiah was eight years old when he became king, and he reigned in Jerusalem thirty-one years. [2]He did what was right in the eyes of the Lord and followed the ways of his father David, not turning aside to the right or to the left.

[3]In the eighth year of his reign, while he was still young, he began to seek the God of his father David. In his twelfth year he began to purge Judah and Jerusalem of high places, Asherah poles and idols. [4]Under his direction the altars of the Baals were torn down; he cut to pieces the incense altars that were above them, and smashed the Asherah poles and the idols. These he broke to pieces and scattered over the graves of those who had sacrificed to them. [5]He burned the bones of the priests on their altars, and so he purged Judah and Jerusalem. [6]In the towns of Manasseh, Ephraim and Simeon, as far as Naphtali, and in the ruins around them, [7]he tore down the altars and the Asherah poles and crushed the idols to powder and cut to pieces all the incense altars throughout Israel. Then he went back to Jerusalem.

[8]In the eighteenth year of Josiah's reign, to purify the land and the temple, he sent Shaphan son of Azaliah and Maaseiah the ruler of the city, with Joah son of Joahaz, the recorder, to repair the temple of the Lord his God.

[9]They went to Hilkiah the high priest and gave him the money that had been brought into the temple of God, which the Levites who were the gatekeepers had collected from the people of Manasseh, Ephraim and the entire remnant of Israel and from all the people of Judah and Benjamin and the inhabitants of Jerusalem. [10]Then they entrusted it to the men appointed to supervise the work on the Lord's temple. These men paid the workers who repaired and restored the temple. [11]They also gave money to the carpenters and builders to purchase dressed stone, and timber for joists and beams for the buildings that the kings of Judah had allowed to fall into ruin.

[12]The workers labored faithfully. Over them to direct them were Jahath and Obadiah, Levites descended from Merari, and Zechariah and Meshullam, descended from Kohath. The Levites—all who were skilled in playing musical instruments— [13]had charge of the laborers and supervised all the workers from job to job. Some of the Levites were secretaries, scribes and gatekeepers.

The Book of the Law Found

[14]While they were bringing out the money that had been taken into the temple of the Lord, Hilkiah the priest found the Book of the Law of the Lord that had been given through Moses. [15]Hilkiah said to Shaphan the secretary, "I have found the Book of the Law in the temple of the Lord." He gave it to Shaphan.

[16]Then Shaphan took the book to the king and reported to him: "Your officials are doing everything that has been committed to them. [17]They have paid out the money that was in the temple of the Lord and have entrusted it to the supervisors and workers." [18]Then Shaphan the secretary informed the king, "Hilkiah the priest has given me a book." And Shaphan read from it in the presence of the king.

[19]When the king heard the words of the Law, he tore his robes. [20]He gave these orders to Hilkiah, Ahikam son of Shaphan, Abdon son of Micah,[a] Shaphan the secretary and Asaiah the king's attendant: [21]"Go and inquire of the Lord for me and for the remnant in Israel and Judah about what is written in this book that has been found. Great is the Lord's anger that is poured out on us because those who have gone before us have not kept the word of the Lord; they have not acted in accordance with all that is written in this book."

[22]Hilkiah and those the king had sent with him[b] went to speak to the prophet Huldah, who was the wife of Shallum son of Tokhath,[c] the son of Hasrah,[d] keeper of the wardrobe. She lived in Jerusalem, in the New Quarter.

---

[a] 20 Also called *Akbor son of Micaiah*   [b] 22 One Hebrew manuscript, Vulgate and Syriac; most Hebrew manuscripts do not have *had sent with him.*   [c] 22 Also called *Tikvah*   [d] 22 Also called *Harhas*

²³She said to them, "This is what the Lᴏʀᴅ, the God of Israel, says: Tell the man who sent you to me, ²⁴'This is what the Lᴏʀᴅ says: I am going to bring disaster on this place and its people—all the curses written in the book that has been read in the presence of the king of Judah. ²⁵Because they have forsaken me and burned incense to other gods and aroused my anger by all that their hands have made,ᵃ my anger will be poured out on this place and will not be quenched.' ²⁶Tell the king of Judah, who sent you to inquire of the Lᴏʀᴅ, 'This is what the Lᴏʀᴅ, the God of Israel, says concerning the words you heard: ²⁷Because your heart was responsive and you humbled yourself before God when you heard what he spoke against this place and its people, and because you humbled yourself before me and tore your robes and wept in my presence, I have heard you, declares the Lᴏʀᴅ. ²⁸Now I will gather you to your ancestors, and you will be buried in peace. Your eyes will not see all the disaster I am going to bring on this place and on those who live here.' "

So they took her answer back to the king.

²⁹Then the king called together all the elders of Judah and Jerusalem. ³⁰He went up to the temple of the Lᴏʀᴅ with the people of Judah, the inhabitants of Jerusalem, the priests and the Levites—all the people from the least to the greatest. He read in their hearing all the words of the Book of the Covenant, which had been found in the temple of the Lᴏʀᴅ. ³¹The king stood by his pillar and renewed the covenant in the presence of the Lᴏʀᴅ—to follow the Lᴏʀᴅ and keep his commands, statutes and decrees with all his heart and all his soul, and to obey the words of the covenant written in this book.

³²Then he had everyone in Jerusalem and Benjamin pledge themselves to it; the people of Jerusalem did this in accordance with the covenant of God, the God of their ancestors.

³³Josiah removed all the detestable idols from all the territory belonging to the Israelites, and he had all who were present in Israel serve the Lᴏʀᴅ their God. As long as he lived, they did not fail to follow the Lᴏʀᴅ, the God of their ancestors.

Josiah Celebrates the Passover

35 Josiah celebrated the Passover to the Lᴏʀᴅ in Jerusalem, and the Passover lamb was slaughtered on the fourteenth day of the first month. ²He appointed the priests to their duties and encouraged them in the service of the Lᴏʀᴅ's temple. ³He said to the Levites, who instructed all Israel and who had been consecrated to the Lᴏʀᴅ: "Put the sacred ark in the temple that Solomon son of David king of Israel built. It is not to be carried about on your shoulders. Now serve the Lᴏʀᴅ your God and his people Israel. ⁴Prepare yourselves by families in your divisions, according to the instructions written by David king of Israel and by his son Solomon.

⁵"Stand in the holy place with a group of Levites for each subdivision of the families of your fellow Israelites, the lay people. ⁶Slaughter the Passover lambs, consecrate yourselves and prepare the lambs for your fellow Israelites, doing what the Lᴏʀᴅ commanded through Moses."

⁷Josiah provided for all the lay people who were there a total of thirty thousand lambs and goats for the Passover offerings, and also three thousand cattle—all from the king's own possessions.

⁸His officials also contributed voluntarily to the people and the priests and Levites. Hilkiah, Zechariah and Jehiel, the officials in charge of God's temple, gave the priests twenty-six hundred Passover offerings and three hundred cattle. ⁹Also Konaniah along with Shemaiah and Nethanel, his brothers, and Hashabiah, Jeiel and Jozabad, the leaders of the Levites, provided five thousand Passover offerings and five hundred head of cattle for the Levites.

¹⁰The service was arranged and the priests stood in their places with the Levites in their divisions as the king had ordered. ¹¹The Passover lambs were slaughtered, and the priests splashed

---

ᵃ 25 Or by everything they have done

against the altar the blood handed to them, while the Levites skinned the animals. 12They set aside the burnt offerings to give them to the subdivisions of the families of the people to offer to the Lord, as it is written in the Book of Moses. They did the same with the cattle. 13They roasted the Passover animals over the fire as prescribed, and boiled the holy offerings in pots, caldrons and pans and served them quickly to all the people. 14After this, they made preparations for themselves and for the priests, because the priests, the descendants of Aaron, were sacrificing the burnt offerings and the fat portions until nightfall. So the Levites made preparations for themselves and for the Aaronic priests.

15The musicians, the descendants of Asaph, were in the places prescribed by David, Asaph, Heman and Jeduthun the king's seer. The gatekeepers at each gate did not need to leave their posts, because their fellow Levites made the preparations for them.

16So at that time the entire service of the Lord was carried out for the celebration of the Passover and the offering of burnt offerings on the altar of the Lord, as King Josiah had ordered. 17The Israelites who were present celebrated the Passover at that time and observed the Festival of Unleavened Bread for seven days. 18The Passover had not been observed like this in Israel since the days of the prophet Samuel; and none of the kings of Israel had ever celebrated such a Passover as did Josiah, with the priests, the Levites and all Judah and Israel who were there with the people of Jerusalem. 19This Passover was celebrated in the eighteenth year of Josiah's reign.

The Death of Josiah

20After all this, when Josiah had set the temple in order, Necho king of Egypt went up to fight at Carchemish on the Euphrates, and Josiah marched out to meet him in battle. 21But Necho sent messengers to him, saying, "What quarrel is there, king of Judah, between you and me? It is not you I am attacking at this time, but the house with which I am at war. God has

told me to hurry; so stop opposing God, who is with me, or he will destroy you."

22Josiah, however, would not turn away from him, but disguised himself to engage him in battle. He would not listen to what Necho had said at God's command but went to fight him on the plain of Megiddo.

23Archers shot King Josiah, and he told his officers, "Take me away; I am badly wounded." 24So they took him out of his chariot, put him in his other chariot and brought him to Jerusalem, where he

THE
WITNESSES

✓ **NECHO** (2 **CHRONICLES** 35:20)
This would be Necho II (Second), an Egyptian king who governed Egypt between the years 609 and 595 before Christ. He wasn't against Josiah, the king of Judah, but he wanted to unite the Assyrians to fight against Babylon. That's why he needed to pass through the territory of Judah, but King Josiah though he was coming to attack him. What a mess!

died. He was buried in the tombs of his ancestors, and all Judah and Jerusalem mourned for him.

25 Jeremiah composed laments for Josiah, and to this day all the male and female singers commemorate Josiah in the laments. These became a tradition in Israel and are written in the Laments.

26 The other events of Josiah's reign and his acts of devotion in accordance with what is written in the Law of the LORD— 27 all the events, from beginning to end, are written in the book of the kings of **36** Israel and Judah. 1 And the people of the land took Jehoahaz son of Josiah and made him king in Jerusalem in place of his father.

Jehoahaz King of Judah

2 Jehoahaz[a] was twenty-three years old when he became king, and he reigned in Jerusalem three months. 3 The king of Egypt dethroned him in Jerusalem and imposed on Judah a levy of a hundred talents[b] of silver and a talent[c] of gold. 4 The king of Egypt made Eliakim, a brother of Jehoahaz, king over Judah and Jerusalem and changed Eliakim's name to Jehoiakim. But Necho took Eliakim's brother Jehoahaz and carried him off to Egypt.

Jehoiakim King of Judah

5 Jehoiakim was twenty-five years old when he became king, and he reigned in Jerusalem eleven years. He did evil in the eyes of the LORD his God. 6 Nebuchadnezzar king of Babylon attacked him and bound him with bronze shackles to take him to Babylon. 7 Nebuchadnezzar also took to Babylon articles from the temple of the LORD and put them in his temple[d] there.

8 The other events of Jehoiakim's reign, the detestable things he did and all that was found against him, are written in the book of the kings of Israel and Judah. And Jehoiachin his son succeeded him as king.

Jehoiachin King of Judah

9 Jehoiachin was eighteen[e] years old when he became king, and he reigned in

Jerusalem three months and ten days. He did evil in the eyes of the LORD. 10 In the spring, King Nebuchadnezzar sent for him and brought him to Babylon, together with articles of value from the temple of the LORD, and he made Jehoiachin's uncle,[f] Zedekiah, king over Judah and Jerusalem.

Zedekiah King of Judah

11 Zedekiah was twenty-one years old when he became king, and he reigned in Jerusalem eleven years. 12 He did evil in the eyes of the LORD his God and did not humble himself before Jeremiah the prophet, who spoke the word of the LORD. 13 He also rebelled against King Nebuchadnezzar, who had made him take an oath in God's name. He became stiff-necked and hardened his heart and would not turn to the LORD, the God of Israel. 14 Furthermore, all the leaders of the priests and the people became more and more unfaithful, following all the detestable practices of the nations and defiling the temple of the LORD, which he had consecrated in Jerusalem.

The Fall of Jerusalem

15 The LORD, the God of their ancestors, sent word to them through his messengers again and again, because he had pity on his people and on his dwelling place. 16 But they mocked God's messengers, despised his words and scoffed at his prophets until the wrath of the LORD was aroused against his people and there was no remedy. 17 He brought up against them the king of the Babylonians,[g] who killed their young men with the sword in the sanctuary, and did not spare young men or young women, the elderly or the infirm. God gave them all into the hands of Nebuchadnezzar. 18 He carried to Babylon all the articles from the temple of God, both large and small, and

---

[a] 2 Hebrew *Joahaz*, a variant of *Jehoahaz*; also in verse 4   [b] 3 That is, about 3 3/4 tons or about 3.4 metric tons   [c] 3 That is, about 75 pounds or about 34 kilograms   [d] 7 Or *palace*   [e] 9 One Hebrew manuscript, some Septuagint manuscripts and Syriac (see also 2 Kings 24:8); most Hebrew manuscripts *eight*   [f] 10 Hebrew *brother*, that is, relative (see 2 Kings 24:17)   [g] 17 Or *Chaldeans*

the treasures of the Lord's temple and the treasures of the king and his officials. ¹⁹They set fire to God's temple and broke down the wall of Jerusalem; they burned all the palaces and destroyed everything of value there.

²⁰He carried into exile to Babylon the remnant, who escaped from the sword, and they became servants to him and his successors until the kingdom of Persia came to power. ²¹The land enjoyed its sabbath rests; all the time of its desolation it rested, until the seventy years were completed in fulfillment of the word of the Lord spoken by Jeremiah.

²²In the first year of Cyrus king of Persia, in order to fulfill the word of the Lord spoken by Jeremiah, the Lord moved the heart of Cyrus king of Persia to make a proclamation throughout his realm and also to put it in writing:

²³"This is what Cyrus king of Persia says:

" 'The Lord, the God of heaven, has given me all the kingdoms of the earth and he has appointed me to build a temple for him at Jerusalem in Judah. Any of his people among you may go up, and may the Lord their God be with them.' "

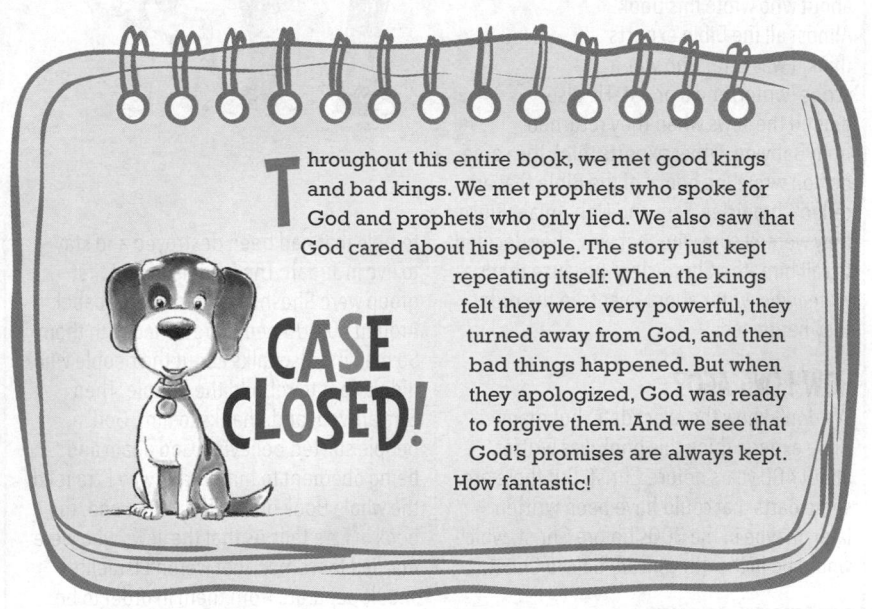

CASE CLOSED!

Throughout this entire book, we met good kings and bad kings. We met prophets who spoke for God and prophets who only lied. We also saw that God cared about his people. The story just kept repeating itself: When the kings felt they were very powerful, they turned away from God, and then bad things happened. But when they apologized, God was ready to forgive them. And we see that God's promises are always kept. How fantastic!

EZRA

THE EVIDENCE:

WHO WROTE IT?

There are several opinions about who wrote this book. Almost all the Bible experts think it was Ezra, who was a scribe (writer) and a priest. He also guided the Jews when they returned from Babylon. Other experts think the same person wrote the books of the Bible that are called Chronicles, Ezra and Nehemiah. Since they weren't sure who that was, they decided to call him "the Chronicler," because that's a writer who writes about events in the order they happened.

HOW LONG AGO?

We don't know the exact date, but many Bible experts think this book was written about 400 years before Christ. But there are some parts that could have been written later, maybe in the 300s before Christ, which would be in the 4th century before Christ.

WHAT'S IT ABOUT?

The book starts by telling about when the first Jews who had been sent away to Babylon returned to Jerusalem. (See what we are saying about this in 4:1.) It says that King Cyrus let them return, rebuild the temple that had been destroyed and stay to live in Judah. The leaders of that first group were Sheshbazzar and Zerubbabel. Around 50,000 people returned with them. So many! It also talks about the people who didn't want to rebuild the temple. Then Ezra arrived, and, thanks to him, God's people started believing God again and being obedient to him. That's why Ezra read the whole Book of the Law. At the end, the book of Ezra tells us that the Jews who were married to women that weren't Israelites should separate from them in order to be obedient to God. That must have been quite sad.

THE BEST PART

This part from 3:11 – 13 is really nice: "He is good; his love toward Israel endures forever."

Cyrus Helps the Exiles to Return

1 In the first year of Cyrus king of Persia, in order to fulfill the word of the LORD spoken by Jeremiah, the LORD moved the heart of Cyrus king of Persia to make a proclamation throughout his realm and also to put it in writing:

2 "This is what Cyrus king of Persia says:

" 'The LORD, the God of heaven, has given me all the kingdoms of the earth and he has appointed me to build a temple for him at Jerusalem in Judah. 3 Any of his people among you may go up to Jerusalem in Judah and build the temple of the LORD, the God of Israel, the God who is in Jerusalem, and may their God be with them. 4 And in any locality where survivors may now be living, the people are to provide them with silver and gold, with goods and livestock, and with freewill offerings for the temple of God in Jerusalem.' "

5 Then the family heads of Judah and Benjamin, and the priests and Levites— everyone whose heart God had moved— prepared to go up and build the house of the LORD in Jerusalem. 6 All their neighbors assisted them with articles of silver and gold, with goods and livestock, and with valuable gifts, in addition to all the freewill offerings. 7 Moreover, King Cyrus brought out the articles belonging to the temple of the LORD, which Nebuchadnezzar had carried away from Jerusalem and had placed in the temple of his god.[a] 8 Cyrus king of Persia had them brought by Mithredath the treasurer, who counted them out to Sheshbazzar the prince of Judah.

9 This was the inventory:

gold dishes	30
silver dishes	1,000
silver pans[b]	29
10 gold bowls	30
matching silver bowls	410
other articles	1,000

11 In all, there were 5,400 articles of gold and of silver. Sheshbazzar brought all these along with the exiles when they came up from Babylon to Jerusalem.

The List of the Exiles Who Returned

2 Now these are the people of the province who came up from the captivity of the exiles, whom Nebuchadnezzar king of Babylon had taken captive to Babylon (they returned to Jerusalem and Judah,

---

[a] 7 Or gods   [b] 9 The meaning of the Hebrew for this word is uncertain.

THE WITNESSES

✓ **CYRUS** (EZRA 1:1)
Cyrus was a very important king who started the Persian empire. He was able to conquer the Babylonian army in the year 539 before Christ. Cyrus was very good to the Hebrews. He let them return to Jerusalem and rebuild the temple.

✓ **JEREMIAH** (EZRA 1:1)
Jeremiah was an important prophet of God. He and the prophets Haggai and Zechariah (see 5:1) announced everything God told them. Jeremiah means "appointed by God."

each to their own town, ²in company with Zerubbabel, Joshua, Nehemiah, Seraiah, Reelaiah, Mordecai, Bilshan, Mispar, Bigvai, Rehum and Baanah):

The list of the men of the people of Israel:

³the descendants of Parosh 2,172
⁴of Shephatiah   372
⁵of Arah   775
⁶of Pahath-Moab (through
    the line of Jeshua
    and Joab)   2,812

THE

WITNESSES

✓ **ZERUBBABEL** (EZRA 2:1–2)
This name means "seed of Babylon," probably because he was born there. He was very important for God's people, because he led the first group of Hebrews who returned to Jerusalem. Zerubbabel was dead set on rebuilding God's temple. He also had them start celebrating Passover again.

⁷of Elam   1,254
⁸of Zattu   945
⁹of Zakkai   760
¹⁰of Bani   642
¹¹of Bebai   623
¹²of Azgad   1,222
¹³of Adonikam   666
¹⁴of Bigvai   2,056
¹⁵of Adin   454
¹⁶of Ater (through Hezekiah)   98
¹⁷of Bezai   323
¹⁸of Jorah   112
¹⁹of Hashum   223
²⁰of Gibbar   95

²¹the men of Bethlehem   123
²²of Netophah   56
²³of Anathoth   128
²⁴of Azmaveth   42
²⁵of Kiriath Jearim,ᵃ
    Kephirah and Beeroth   743
²⁶of Ramah and Geba   621
²⁷of Mikmash   122
²⁸of Bethel and Ai   223
²⁹of Nebo   52
³⁰of Magbish   156
³¹of the other Elam   1,254
³²of Harim   320
³³of Lod, Hadid and Ono   725
³⁴of Jericho   345
³⁵of Senaah   3,630

³⁶The priests:

the descendants of Jedaiah
    (through the family
    of Jeshua)   973
³⁷of Immer   1,052
³⁸of Pashhur   1,247
³⁹of Harim   1,017

⁴⁰The Levites:

the descendants of Jeshua
    and Kadmiel (of the line of
    Hodaviah)   74

⁴¹The musicians:

the descendants of Asaph   128

⁴²The gatekeepers of the temple:

the descendants of
    Shallum, Ater, Talmon,
    Akkub, Hatita and Shobai   139

ᵃ 25 See Septuagint (see also Neh. 7:29); Hebrew *Kiriath Arim.*

⁴³The temple servants:

the descendants of
Ziha, Hasupha, Tabbaoth,
⁴⁴Keros, Siaha, Padon,
⁴⁵Lebanah, Hagabah, Akkub,
⁴⁶Hagab, Shalmai, Hanan,
⁴⁷Giddel, Gahar, Reaiah,
⁴⁸Rezin, Nekoda, Gazzam,
⁴⁹Uzza, Paseah, Besai,
⁵⁰Asnah, Meunim, Nephusim,
⁵¹Bakbuk, Hakupha, Harhur,
⁵²Bazluth, Mehida, Harsha,
⁵³Barkos, Sisera, Temah,
⁵⁴Neziah and Hatipha

⁵⁵The descendants of the servants of Solomon:

the descendants of
Sotai, Hassophereth, Peruda,
⁵⁶Jaala, Darkon, Giddel,
⁵⁷Shephatiah, Hattil,
Pokereth-Hazzebaim and Ami

⁵⁸The temple servants and
the descendants of the
servants of Solomon   392

⁵⁹The following came up from the towns of Tel Melah, Tel Harsha, Kerub, Addon and Immer, but they could not show that their families were descended from Israel:

⁶⁰The descendants of
Delaiah, Tobiah and
Nekoda   652

⁶¹And from among the priests:

The descendants of
Hobaiah, Hakkoz and Barzillai
(a man who had married
a daughter of Barzillai the
Gileadite and was called by
that name).

⁶²These searched for their family records, but they could not find them and so were excluded from the priesthood as unclean. ⁶³The governor ordered them not to eat any of the most sacred food until there was a priest ministering with the Urim and Thummim.

⁶⁴The whole company numbered 42,360, ⁶⁵besides their 7,337 male

and female slaves; and they also had 200 male and female singers. ⁶⁶They had 736 horses, 245 mules, ⁶⁷435 camels and 6,720 donkeys.

⁶⁸When they arrived at the house of the LORD in Jerusalem, some of the heads of the families gave freewill offerings toward the rebuilding of the house of God on its site. ⁶⁹According to their ability they gave to the treasury for this work 61,000 darics*a* of gold, 5,000 minas*b* of silver and 100 priestly garments.

⁷⁰The priests, the Levites, the musicians, the gatekeepers and the temple servants settled in their own towns, along with some of the other people, and the rest of the Israelites settled in their towns.

Rebuilding the Altar

3 When the seventh month came and the Israelites had settled in their towns, the people assembled together as

---

a 69 That is, about 1,100 pounds or about 500 kilograms
b 69 That is, about 3 tons or about 2.8 metric tons

The seventh month
(EZRA 3:1)
The real name in the Jewish calendar was Ethanim. It's from the middle of September to the middle of October in our solar calendar. In Bible lands, that's during the fall.

one in Jerusalem. ²Then Joshua son of Jozadak and his fellow priests and Zerubbabel son of Shealtiel and his associates began to build the altar of the God of Israel to sacrifice burnt offerings on it, in accordance with what is written in the Law of Moses the man of God. ³Despite their fear of the peoples around them, they built the altar on its foundation and sacrificed burnt offerings on it to the LORD, both the morning and evening sacrifices. ⁴Then in accordance with what is written, they celebrated the Festival of Tabernacles with the required number of burnt offerings prescribed for each day. ⁵After that, they presented the regular burnt offerings, the New Moon sacrifices and the sacrifices for all the appointed sacred festivals of the LORD, as well as those brought as freewill offerings to the LORD. ⁶On the first day of the seventh month they began to offer burnt offerings to the LORD, though the foundation of the LORD's temple had not yet been laid.

Rebuilding the Temple

⁷Then they gave money to the masons and carpenters, and gave food and drink and olive oil to the people of Sidon and Tyre, so that they would bring cedar logs by sea from Lebanon to Joppa, as authorized by Cyrus king of Persia.

⁸In the second month of the second year after their arrival at the house of God in Jerusalem, Zerubbabel son of Shealtiel, Joshua son of Jozadak and the rest of the people (the priests and the Levites and all who had returned from the captivity to Jerusalem) began the work. They appointed Levites twenty years old and older to supervise the building of the house of the LORD. ⁹Joshua and his sons and brothers and Kadmiel and his sons (descendants of Hodaviah*a*) and the sons of Henadad and their sons and brothers — all Levites — joined together in supervising those working on the house of God.

¹⁰When the builders laid the foundation of the temple of the LORD, the priests in their vestments and with trumpets, and the Levites (the sons of Asaph) with cymbals, took their places to praise the LORD, as prescribed by David king of Israel.

THE SCENE

SIDON AND TYRE

(EZRA 3:7)

They were big Phoenician cities. A long time ago, Tyre was built on a rocky island 44 miles (40 km) south of Sidon. In Old Testament times, the island was connected to the mainland by a cobblestone road that over time got widened. Now Tyre is part of a peninsula. Sidon was known for business, boating, fishing and the purple dye they got from shellfish and used to dye the fabric. It was super expensive!

¹¹With praise and thanksgiving they sang to the LORD:

"He is good;
　　his love toward Israel endures
　　　　forever."

And all the people gave a great shout of praise to the LORD, because the foundation of the house of the LORD was laid. ¹²But many of the older priests and Levites and family heads, who had seen the former temple, wept aloud when they saw

---

a 9 Hebrew *Yehudah,* a variant of *Hodaviah*

THE SCENE

JOPPA

(EZRA 3:7)

This is a Hebrew word that means "beautiful." It is the only natural port on the Mediterranean Sea. It is 61 miles (56 km) northwest of Jerusalem. For a long time, Joppa was Palestine's only port, so it was super important. The Philistines took over this city, but David took it back. Solomon helped develop it to make it the main port that brought in goods for Jerusalem. For example, the wood they used to rebuild the temple came through this port.

help you build because, like you, we seek your God and have been sacrificing to him since the time of Esarhaddon king of Assyria, who brought us here."

³But Zerubbabel, Joshua and the rest of the heads of the families of Israel answered, "You have no part with us in building a temple to our God. We alone will build it for the LORD, the God of Israel, as King Cyrus, the king of Persia, commanded us."

⁴Then the peoples around them set out to discourage the people of Judah and make them afraid to go on building.ᵃ ⁵They bribed officials to work against them and frustrate their plans during the entire reign of Cyrus king of Persia and down to the reign of Darius king of Persia.

ᵃ 4 Or *and troubled them as they built*

BREAKTHROUGH!

Exile

(EZRA 4:1)

This word means "being forced to move," so it's when a person is taken away and has to live in another country. In this book, it's talking about a time when the king of Babylon, Nebuchadnezzar, took the Israelites to live in Babylon. They were exiled a long time, until King Cyrus arrived. He governed Persia and conquered Babylon, and he let the Israelites return to their own country. Thank goodness!

the foundation of this temple being laid, while many others shouted for joy. ¹³No one could distinguish the sound of the shouts of joy from the sound of weeping, because the people made so much noise. And the sound was heard far away.

Opposition to the Rebuilding

4 When the enemies of Judah and Benjamin heard that the exiles were building a temple for the LORD, the God of Israel, ²they came to Zerubbabel and to the heads of the families and said, "Let us

Later Opposition Under Xerxes and Artaxerxes

⁶At the beginning of the reign of Xerxes,ᵃ they lodged an accusation against the people of Judah and Jerusalem.

⁷And in the days of Artaxerxes king of Persia, Bishlam, Mithredath, Tabeel and the rest of his associates wrote a letter to Artaxerxes. The letter was written in Aramaic script and in the Aramaic language.ᵇ,ᶜ

⁸Rehum the commanding officer and Shimshai the secretary wrote a letter against Jerusalem to Artaxerxes the king as follows:

⁹Rehum the commanding officer and Shimshai the secretary, together with the rest of their associates— the judges, officials and adminis-

BREAK THROUGH!

Why did the Israelites' enemies want to help them? That doesn't make sense!

(EZRA 4:1-2)

It was a trap. It was just the opposite! The enemies were Samaritans, and they wanted to have rights over the temple and be in Jerusalem. God's people realized that it was a trap. Besides, they couldn't accept that help because the enemies worshiped other gods.

BREAK THROUGH!

How long did it take to rebuild the temple?

(EZRA 4:5-7)

It seems that the work took a long time, because it stopped between the years 538 and 522 before Christ, so nothing happened for 16 years! It was finished in the years 516 and 515 before Christ.

trators over the people from Persia, Uruk and Babylon, the Elamites of Susa, ¹⁰and the other people whom the great and honorable Ashurbanipal deported and settled in the city of Samaria and elsewhere in Trans-Euphrates.

¹¹(This is a copy of the letter they sent him.)

To King Artaxerxes,

From your servants in Trans-Euphrates:

¹²The king should know that the people who came up to us from you have gone to Jerusalem and are rebuilding that rebellious and wicked city. They are restoring the walls and repairing the foundations.

ᵃ 6 Hebrew *Ahasuerus*   ᵇ 7 Or *written in Aramaic and translated*   ᶜ 7 The text of 4:8–6:18 is in Aramaic.

THE
WITNESSES

✓ **KING ARTAXERXES** (EZRA 4:7)
In the Old Testament, there are three Persian kings who have this name. We think this one ruled in the years 464 and 424 before Christ. It seems that the throne belonged to another man, but Artaxerxes stole it from him. And he was the one who made the Hebrews stop rebuilding the temple.

---

[13] Furthermore, the king should know that if this city is built and its walls are restored, no more taxes, tribute or duty will be paid, and eventually the royal revenues will suffer.[a] [14] Now since we are under obligation to the palace and it is not proper for us to see the king dishonored, we are sending this message to inform the king, [15] so that a search may be made in the archives of your predecessors. In these records you will find that this city is a rebellious city, troublesome to kings and provinces, a place with a long history of sedition. That is why this city was destroyed. [16] We inform the king that if this city is built and its walls are restored, you will be left with nothing in Trans-Euphrates.

[17] The king sent this reply:

To Rehum the commanding officer, Shimshai the secretary and the rest of their associates living in Samaria and elsewhere in Trans-Euphrates:

Greetings.

[18] The letter you sent us has been read and translated in my presence. [19] I issued an order and a search was made, and it was found that this city has a long history of revolt against kings and has been a place of rebellion and sedition. [20] Jerusalem has had powerful kings ruling over the whole of Trans-Euphrates, and taxes, tribute and duty were paid to them. [21] Now issue an order to these men to stop work, so that this city will not be rebuilt until I so order. [22] Be careful not to neglect this matter. Why let this threat grow, to the detriment of the royal interests?

[23] As soon as the copy of the letter of King Artaxerxes was read to Rehum and Shimshai the secretary and their associates, they went immediately to the Jews in Jerusalem and compelled them by force to stop.

[24] Thus the work on the house of God in Jerusalem came to a standstill until the second year of the reign of Darius king of Persia.

Tattenai's Letter to Darius

5 Now Haggai the prophet and Zechariah the prophet, a descendant of Iddo, prophesied to the Jews in Judah and Jerusalem in the name of the God of Israel, who was over them. [2] Then Zerubbabel son of Shealtiel and Joshua son of

---

[a] 13 The meaning of the Aramaic for this clause is uncertain.

Jozadak set to work to rebuild the house of God in Jerusalem. And the prophets of God were with them, supporting them.

[3]At that time Tattenai, governor of Trans-Euphrates, and Shethar-Bozenai and their associates went to them and asked, "Who authorized you to rebuild this temple and to finish it?" [4]They[a] also asked, "What are the names of those who are constructing this building?" [5]But the eye of their God was watching over the elders of the Jews, and they were not stopped until a report could go to Darius and his written reply be received.

[6]This is a copy of the letter that Tattenai, governor of Trans-Euphrates, and Shethar-Bozenai and their associates, the officials of Trans-Euphrates, sent to King Darius. [7]The report they sent him read as follows:

To King Darius:

Cordial greetings.

[8]The king should know that we went to the district of Judah, to the temple of the great God. The people are building it with large stones and placing the timbers in the walls. The work is being carried on with diligence and is making rapid progress under their direction.

[9]We questioned the elders and asked them, "Who authorized you to rebuild this temple and to finish it?" [10]We also asked them their names, so that we could write down the names of their leaders for your information.

[11]This is the answer they gave us:

"We are the servants of the God of heaven and earth, and we are rebuilding the temple that was built many years ago, one that a great king of Israel built and finished. [12]But because our ancestors angered the God of heaven, he gave them into the hands of Nebuchadnezzar the Chaldean, king of Babylon, who destroyed this temple and deported the people to Babylon.

[13]"However, in the first year of Cyrus king of Babylon, King Cyrus issued a decree to rebuild this house of God. [14]He even removed from the temple[b] of Babylon the gold and silver articles of the house of God, which Nebuchadnezzar had taken from the temple in Jerusalem and brought to the temple[b] in Babylon. Then King Cyrus gave them to a man named Sheshbazzar, whom he had appointed governor, [15]and he told him, 'Take these articles and go and deposit them in the temple in Jerusalem. And rebuild the house of God on its site.'

[16]"So this Sheshbazzar came and laid the foundations of the house of God in Jerusalem. From that day to the present it has been under construction but is not yet finished."

[17]Now if it pleases the king, let a search be made in the royal archives of Babylon to see if King Cyrus did in fact issue a decree to rebuild this house of God in Jerusalem. Then let the king send us his decision in this matter.

The Decree of Darius

6 King Darius then issued an order, and they searched in the archives stored in the treasury at Babylon. [2]A scroll was found in the citadel of Ecbatana in the province of Media, and this was written on it:

Memorandum:

[3]In the first year of King Cyrus, the king issued a decree concerning the temple of God in Jerusalem:

Let the temple be rebuilt as a place to present sacrifices, and let its foundations be laid. It is to be sixty cubits[c] high and sixty cubits wide, [4]with three courses of large stones and one of timbers. The costs are to be paid by the royal treasury. [5]Also, the gold and silver articles of the house of God, which Nebuchadnezzar took from the temple in Jerusalem and brought to Babylon, are to

---

[a] 4 See Septuagint; Aramaic We.　　[b] 14 Or palace
[c] 3 That is, about 90 feet or about 27 meters

be returned to their places in the temple in Jerusalem; they are to be deposited in the house of God.

⁶Now then, Tattenai, governor of Trans-Euphrates, and Shethar-Bozenai and you other officials of that province, stay away from there. ⁷Do not interfere with the work on this temple of God. Let the governor of the Jews and the Jewish elders rebuild this house of God on its site.

⁸Moreover, I hereby decree what you are to do for these elders of the Jews in the construction of this house of God:

Their expenses are to be fully paid out of the royal treasury, from the revenues of Trans-Euphrates, so that the work will not stop. ⁹Whatever is needed—young bulls, rams, male lambs for burnt offerings to the God of heaven, and wheat, salt, wine and olive oil, as requested by the priests in Jerusalem—must be given them daily without fail, ¹⁰so that they may offer sacrifices pleasing to the God of heaven and pray for the well-being of the king and his sons.

¹¹Furthermore, I decree that if anyone defies this edict, a beam is to be pulled from their house and they are to be impaled on it. And for this crime their house is to be made a pile of rubble. ¹²May God, who has caused his Name to dwell there, overthrow any king or people who lifts a hand to change this decree or to destroy this temple in Jerusalem.

I Darius have decreed it. Let it be carried out with diligence.

Completion and Dedication of the Temple

¹³Then, because of the decree King Darius had sent, Tattenai, governor of Trans-Euphrates, and Shethar-Bozenai and their associates carried it out with diligence. ¹⁴So the elders of the Jews continued to build and prosper under the preaching of Haggai the prophet and Zechariah, a descendant of Iddo. They finished building the temple according to the command of the God of Israel and the decrees of Cyrus, Darius and Artaxerxes, kings of Persia. ¹⁵The temple was completed on the third day of the month Adar, in the sixth year of the reign of King Darius.

¹⁶Then the people of Israel—the priests, the Levites and the rest of the exiles—celebrated the dedication of the house of God with joy. ¹⁷For the dedication of this house of God they offered a hundred bulls, two hundred rams, four hundred male lambs and, as a sin offering*ᵃ* for all Israel, twelve male goats, one for each of the tribes of Israel. ¹⁸And they installed the priests in their divisions and the Levites in their groups for the service of God at Jerusalem, according to what is written in the Book of Moses.

The Passover

¹⁹On the fourteenth day of the first month, the exiles celebrated the Passover.

―――――――――――――――――
ᵃ 17 Or purification offering

Adar
(EZRA 6:15)
This is the twelfth month in the Jewish lunar calendar. It's from the middle of February to the middle of March in our solar calendar. In the Middle East, where this is taking place, this would be spring.

BREAK THROUGH!

The first month
(EZRA 6:19)
This was Aviv in the lunar year for the Jews. It's from the middle of March to the middle of April in our solar calendar.

²⁰The priests and Levites had purified themselves and were all ceremonially clean. The Levites slaughtered the Passover lamb for all the exiles, for their relatives the priests and for themselves. ²¹So the Israelites who had returned from the exile ate it, together with all who had separated themselves from the unclean practices of their Gentile neighbors in order to seek the LORD, the God of Israel. ²²For seven days they celebrated with joy the Festival of Unleavened Bread, because the LORD had filled them with joy by changing the attitude of the king of Assyria so that he assisted them in the work on the house of God, the God of Israel.

Ezra Comes to Jerusalem

7 After these things, during the reign of Artaxerxes king of Persia, Ezra son of Seraiah, the son of Azariah, the son of Hilkiah, ²the son of Shallum, the son of Zadok, the son of Ahitub, ³the son of Amariah, the son of Azariah, the son of Meraioth, ⁴the son of Zerahiah, the son of Uzzi, the son of Bukki, ⁵the son of Abishua, the son of Phinehas, the son of Eleazar, the son of Aaron the chief priest— ⁶this Ezra came up from Babylon. He was a teacher well versed in the Law of Moses, which the LORD, the God of Israel, had given. The king had granted him everything he asked, for the hand of the LORD his God was on him. ⁷Some of the Israelites, including priests, Levites, musicians, gatekeepers and temple servants, also came up to Jerusalem in the seventh year of King Artaxerxes.

⁸Ezra arrived in Jerusalem in the fifth month of the seventh year of the king. ⁹He had begun his journey from Babylon on the first day of the first month, and he

THE WITNESSES

✓ **EZRA** **(EZRA 7:1)**
He was an Israelite scribe and priest. He was very important for God's people when they returned from their exile in Babylon. His name in Hebrew means "help."

arrived in Jerusalem on the first day of the fifth month, for the gracious hand of his God was on him. [10]For Ezra had devoted himself to the study and observance of the Law of the LORD, and to teaching its decrees and laws in Israel.

King Artaxerxes' Letter to Ezra

[11]This is a copy of the letter King Artaxerxes had given to Ezra the priest, a teacher of the Law, a man learned in matters concerning the commands and decrees of the LORD for Israel:

[12]Artaxerxes, king of kings,

To Ezra the priest, teacher of the Law of the God of heaven:

Greetings.

[13]Now I decree that any of the Israelites in my kingdom, including priests and Levites, who volunteer to go to Jerusalem with you, may go. [14]You are sent by the king and his seven advisers to inquire about Judah and Jerusalem with regard to the Law of your God, which is in your hand. [15]Moreover, you are to take with you the silver and gold that the king and his advisers have freely given to the God of Israel, whose dwelling is in Jerusalem, [16]together with all the silver and gold you may obtain from the province of Babylon, as well as the freewill offerings of the people and priests for the temple of their God in Jerusalem. [17]With this money be sure to buy bulls, rams and male lambs, together with their grain offerings and drink offerings, and sacrifice them on the altar of the temple of your God in Jerusalem.

[18]You and your fellow Israelites may then do whatever seems best with the rest of the silver and gold, in accordance with the will of your God. [19]Deliver to the God of Jerusalem all the articles entrusted to you for worship in the temple of your God. [20]And anything else needed for the temple of your God that you are responsible to supply, you may provide from the royal treasury.

[21]Now I, King Artaxerxes, decree that all the treasurers of Trans-Euphrates are to provide with diligence whatever Ezra the priest, the teacher of the Law of the God of heaven, may ask of you— [22]up to a hundred talents[a] of silver, a hundred cors[b] of wheat, a hundred baths[c] of wine, a hundred baths[c] of olive oil, and salt without limit. [23]Whatever the God of heaven has prescribed, let it be done with diligence for the temple of the God of heaven. Why should his wrath fall on the realm of the king and of his sons? [24]You are also to know that you have no authority to impose taxes, tribute or duty on any of the priests, Levites, musicians, gatekeepers, temple servants or other workers at this house of God.

[25]And you, Ezra, in accordance with the wisdom of your God, which you possess, appoint magistrates and judges to administer justice to all the people of Trans-Euphrates— all who know the laws of your God. And you are to teach any who do not know them. [26]Whoever does not obey the law of your God and the law of the king must surely be punished by death, banishment, confiscation of property, or imprisonment.[d]

[27]Praise be to the LORD, the God of our ancestors, who has put it into the king's heart to bring honor to the house of the LORD in Jerusalem in this way [28]and who has extended his good favor to me before the king and his advisers and all the king's powerful officials. Because the hand of the LORD my God was on me, I took courage and gathered leaders from Israel to go up with me.

List of the Family Heads Returning With Ezra

8 These are the family heads and those registered with them who came up with me from Babylon during the reign of King Artaxerxes:

---

[a] 22 That is, about 3 3/4 tons or about 3.4 metric tons   [b] 22 That is, probably about 18 tons or about 16 metric tons   [c] 22 That is, about 600 gallons or about 2,200 liters   [d] 26 The text of 7:12-26 is in Aramaic.

2 of the descendants of Phinehas, Gershom;
of the descendants of Ithamar, Daniel;
of the descendants of David, Hattush 3 of the descendants of Shekaniah;
of the descendants of Parosh, Zechariah, and with him were registered 150 men;
4 of the descendants of Pahath-Moab, Eliehoenai son of Zerahiah, and with him 200 men;
5 of the descendants of Zattu,ᵃ Shekaniah son of Jahaziel, and with him 300 men;
6 of the descendants of Adin, Ebed son of Jonathan, and with him 50 men;
7 of the descendants of Elam, Jeshaiah son of Athaliah, and with him 70 men;
8 of the descendants of Shephatiah, Zebadiah son of Michael, and with him 80 men;
9 of the descendants of Joab, Obadiah son of Jehiel, and with him 218 men;
10 of the descendants of Bani,ᵇ Shelomith son of Josiphiah, and with him 160 men;
11 of the descendants of Bebai, Zechariah son of Bebai, and with him 28 men;
12 of the descendants of Azgad, Johanan son of Hakkatan, and with him 110 men;
13 of the descendants of Adonikam, the last ones, whose names were Eliphelet, Jeuel and Shemaiah, and with them 60 men;
14 of the descendants of Bigvai, Uthai and Zakkur, and with them 70 men.

The Return to Jerusalem

15 I assembled them at the canal that flows toward Ahava, and we camped there three days. When I checked among the people and the priests, I found no Levites there. 16 So I summoned Eliezer, Ariel, Shemaiah, Elnathan, Jarib, Elnathan, Nathan, Zechariah and Meshullam, who were leaders, and Joiarib and Elnathan, who were men of learning, 17 and I ordered them to go to Iddo, the leader in Kasiphia. I told them what to say to Iddo and his fellow Levites, the temple servants in Kasiphia, so that they might bring attendants to us for the house of our God. 18 Because the gracious hand of our God was on us, they brought us Sherebiah, a capable man, from the descendants of Mahli son of Levi, the son of Israel, and Sherebiah's sons and brothers, 18 in all; 19 and Hashabiah, together with Jeshaiah from the descendants of Merari, and his brothers and nephews, 20 in all. 20 They also brought 220 of the temple servants—a body that David and the officials had established to assist the Levites. All were registered by name.

21 There, by the Ahava Canal, I proclaimed a fast, so that we might humble ourselves before our God and ask him for a safe journey for us and our children, with all our possessions. 22 I was ashamed to ask the king for soldiers and horsemen to protect us from enemies on the road, because we had told the king, "The gracious hand of our God is on everyone who looks to him, but his great anger is against all who forsake him." 23 So we fasted and petitioned our God about this, and he answered our prayer.

24 Then I set apart twelve of the leading priests, namely, Sherebiah, Hashabiah and ten of their brothers, 25 and I weighed out to them the offering of silver and gold and the articles that the king, his advisers, his officials and all Israel present there had donated for the house of our God. 26 I weighed out to them 650 talentsᶜ of silver, silver articles weighing 100 talents,ᵈ 100 talentsᵈ of gold, 27 20 bowls of gold valued at 1,000 darics,ᵉ and two fine articles of polished bronze, as precious as gold.

28 I said to them, "You as well as these articles are consecrated to the LORD.

ᵃ 5 Some Septuagint manuscripts (also 1 Esdras 8:32); Hebrew does not have Zattu.   ᵇ 10 Some Septuagint manuscripts (also 1 Esdras 8:36); Hebrew does not have Bani.   ᶜ 26 That is, about 24 tons or about 22 metric tons   ᵈ 26 That is, about 3 3/4 tons or about 3.4 metric tons   ᵉ 27 That is, about 19 pounds or about 8.4 kilograms

The silver and gold are a freewill offering to the LORD, the God of your ancestors. ²⁹Guard them carefully until you weigh them out in the chambers of the house of the LORD in Jerusalem before the leading priests and the Levites and the family heads of Israel." ³⁰Then the priests and Levites received the silver and gold and sacred articles that had been weighed out to be taken to the house of our God in Jerusalem.

³¹On the twelfth day of the first month we set out from the Ahava Canal to go to Jerusalem. The hand of our God was on us, and he protected us from enemies and bandits along the way. ³²So we arrived in Jerusalem, where we rested three days.

³³On the fourth day, in the house of our God, we weighed out the silver and gold and the sacred articles into the hands of Meremoth son of Uriah, the priest. Eleazar son of Phinehas was with him, and so were the Levites Jozabad son of Jeshua and Noadiah son of Binnui. ³⁴Everything was accounted for by number and weight, and the entire weight was recorded at that time.

³⁵Then the exiles who had returned from captivity sacrificed burnt offerings to the God of Israel: twelve bulls for all Israel, ninety-six rams, seventy-seven male lambs and, as a sin offering,ᵃ twelve male goats. All this was a burnt offering to the LORD. ³⁶They also delivered the king's orders to the royal satraps and to the governors of Trans-Euphrates, who then gave assistance to the people and to the house of God.

Ezra's Prayer About Intermarriage

9 After these things had been done, the leaders came to me and said, "The people of Israel, including the priests and the Levites, have not kept themselves separate from the neighboring peoples with their detestable practices, like those of the Canaanites, Hittites, Perizzites, Jebusites, Ammonites, Moabites, Egyptians and Amorites. ²They have taken some of their daughters as wives for themselves and their sons, and have mingled the holy race with the peoples around them. And

the leaders and officials have led the way in this unfaithfulness."

³When I heard this, I tore my tunic and cloak, pulled hair from my head and beard and sat down appalled. ⁴Then everyone who trembled at the words of the God of Israel gathered around me because of this unfaithfulness of the exiles. And I sat there appalled until the evening sacrifice.

⁵Then, at the evening sacrifice, I rose from my self-abasement, with my tunic and cloak torn, and fell on my knees with my hands spread out to the LORD my God ⁶and prayed:

"I am too ashamed and disgraced, my God, to lift up my face to you, because our sins are higher than our heads and our guilt has reached to the heavens. ⁷From the days of our ancestors until now, our guilt has been great. Because of our sins, we and our kings and our priests have been subjected to the sword and captivity, to pillage and humiliation at the hand of foreign kings, as it is today.

⁸"But now, for a brief moment, the LORD our God has been gracious in leaving us a remnant and giving us a firm placeᵇ in his sanctuary, and so our God gives light to our eyes and a little relief in our bondage. ⁹Though we are slaves, our God has not forsaken us in our bondage. He has shown us kindness in the sight of the kings of Persia: He has granted us new life to rebuild the house of our God and repair its ruins, and he has given us a wall of protection in Judah and Jerusalem.

¹⁰"But now, our God, what can we say after this? For we have forsaken the commands ¹¹you gave through your servants the prophets when you said: 'The land you are entering to possess is a land polluted by the corruption of its peoples. By their detestable practices they have filled it with their impurity from one end to the other. ¹²Therefore, do not give your daughters in marriage to their sons or take their daughters

---

ᵃ 35 Or *purification offering*   ᵇ 8 Or *a foothold*

CHECK THE FACTS

Which Persian emperor sent a letter to Ezra, along with money to make sacrifices to God?

A) Nebuchadnezzar

B) Zerubbabel

C) Artaxerxes

CORRECT ANSWER: C

for your sons. Do not seek a treaty of friendship with them at any time, that you may be strong and eat the good things of the land and leave it to your children as an everlasting inheritance.'

13 "What has happened to us is a result of our evil deeds and our great guilt, and yet, our God, you have punished us less than our sins deserved and have given us a remnant like this. 14 Shall we then break your commands again and intermarry with the peoples who commit such detestable practices? Would you not be angry enough with us to destroy us, leaving us no remnant or survivor? 15 Lord, the God of Israel, you are righteous! We are left this day as a remnant. Here we are before you in our guilt, though because of it not one of us can stand in your presence."

The People's Confession of Sin

10 While Ezra was praying and confessing, weeping and throwing himself down before the house of God, a large crowd of Israelites—men, women and children—gathered around him. They too wept bitterly. 2 Then Shekaniah son of Jehiel, one of the descendants of Elam, said to Ezra, "We have been unfaithful to our God by marrying foreign women from the peoples around us. But in spite of this, there is still hope for Israel. 3 Now let us make a covenant before our God to send away all these women and their children, in accordance with the counsel of my lord and of those who fear the commands of our God. Let it be done according to

BREAKTHROUGH!

Why did God want the Israelite men to leave their women and children?

(EZRA 10)

For God's people, returning to Jerusalem was like starting anew at God's side. They needed to be very faithful and obedient. The problem was that the women from other lands continued believing in and worshiping their gods. They often wanted the Israelites to worship those gods too. That was very, very bad. That's why God told the men to leave them.

the Law. ⁴Rise up; this matter is in your hands. We will support you, so take courage and do it."

⁵So Ezra rose up and put the leading priests and Levites and all Israel under oath to do what had been suggested. And they took the oath. ⁶Then Ezra withdrew from before the house of God and went to the room of Jehohanan son of Eliashib. While he was there, he ate no food and drank no water, because he continued to mourn over the unfaithfulness of the exiles.

⁷A proclamation was then issued throughout Judah and Jerusalem for all the exiles to assemble in Jerusalem. ⁸Anyone who failed to appear within three days would forfeit all his property, in accordance with the decision of the officials and elders, and would himself be expelled from the assembly of the exiles.

⁹Within the three days, all the men of Judah and Benjamin had gathered in Jerusalem. And on the twentieth day of the ninth month, all the people were sit-

BREAK THROUGH!

The tenth month
(EZRA 10:15-16)

Its real name is Tebet in the Jewish lunar calendar. In our solar calendar, it's from the middle of December to the middle of January. That's during the winter.

ting in the square before the house of God, greatly distressed by the occasion and because of the rain. ¹⁰Then Ezra the priest stood up and said to them, "You have been unfaithful; you have married foreign women, adding to Israel's guilt. ¹¹Now honorᵃ the LORD, the God of your ancestors, and do his will. Separate yourselves from the peoples around you and from your foreign wives."

¹²The whole assembly responded with a loud voice: "You are right! We must do as you say. ¹³But there are many people here and it is the rainy season; so we cannot stand outside. Besides, this matter cannot be taken care of in a day or two, because we have sinned greatly in this thing. ¹⁴Let our officials act for the whole assembly. Then let everyone in our towns who has married a foreign woman come at a set time, along with the elders and judges of each town, until the fierce anger of our God in this matter is turned away

BREAK THROUGH!

The ninth month
(EZRA 10:9)

Called Kislev in the Jewish lunar calendar. In our solar calendar, that would be from the middle of November to the middle of December. It's during the winter.

ᵃ 11 Or *Now make confession to*

from us." ¹⁵Only Jonathan son of Asahel and Jahzeiah son of Tikvah, supported by Meshullam and Shabbethai the Levite, opposed this.

¹⁶So the exiles did as was proposed. Ezra the priest selected men who were family heads, one from each family division, and all of them designated by name. On the first day of the tenth month they sat down to investigate the cases, ¹⁷and by the first day of the first month they finished dealing with all the men who had married foreign women.

Those Guilty of Intermarriage

¹⁸Among the descendants of the priests, the following had married foreign women:

From the descendants of Joshua son of Jozadak, and his brothers: Maaseiah, Eliezer, Jarib and Gedaliah. ¹⁹(They all gave their hands in pledge to put away their wives, and for their guilt they each presented a ram from the flock as a guilt offering.)

²⁰From the descendants of Immer:

Hanani and Zebadiah.

²¹From the descendants of Harim:

Maaseiah, Elijah, Shemaiah, Jehiel and Uzziah.

²²From the descendants of Pashhur:

Elioenai, Maaseiah, Ishmael, Nethanel, Jozabad and Elasah.

²³Among the Levites:

Jozabad, Shimei, Kelaiah (that is, Kelita), Pethahiah, Judah and Eliezer.

²⁴From the musicians:

Eliashib.

From the gatekeepers:

Shallum, Telem and Uri.

CASE CLOSED!

A s we were reading this book, we learned a whole lot about the history of Israel. Because they disobeyed, they were taken to live in Babylon. They were there for many, many years. Their own land was left unattended, and the temple—that was God's house—got totally destroyed. How terribly sad! Afterward, they were able to return, but they had to work really hard to rebuild the temple.

Although the enemies of Judah didn't want them to rebuild the temple, the children of God managed to work together and do it. In this book, we learned that each person has a special role and we're all important. When they worked in the temple, each one did what he or she knew best so they could complete a really big job by working together.

25 And among the other Israelites:

From the descendants of Parosh:
Ramiah, Izziah, Malkijah, Mijamin, Eleazar, Malkijah and Benaiah.
26 From the descendants of Elam:
Mattaniah, Zechariah, Jehiel, Abdi, Jeremoth and Elijah.
27 From the descendants of Zattu:
Elioenai, Eliashib, Mattaniah, Jeremoth, Zabad and Aziza.
28 From the descendants of Bebai:
Jehohanan, Hananiah, Zabbai and Athlai.
29 From the descendants of Bani:
Meshullam, Malluk, Adaiah, Jashub, Sheal and Jeremoth.
30 From the descendants of Pahath-Moab:
Adna, Kelal, Benaiah, Maaseiah, Mattaniah, Bezalel, Binnui and Manasseh.
31 From the descendants of Harim:
Eliezer, Ishijah, Malkijah, Shemaiah, Shimeon, 32 Benjamin, Malluk and Shemariah.

33 From the descendants of Hashum:
Mattenai, Mattattah, Zabad, Eliphelet, Jeremai, Manasseh and Shimei.
34 From the descendants of Bani:
Maadai, Amram, Uel, 35 Benaiah, Bedeiah, Keluhi, 36 Vaniah, Meremoth, Eliashib, 37 Mattaniah, Mattenai and Jaasu.
38 From the descendants of Binnui:[a]
Shimei, 39 Shelemiah, Nathan, Adaiah, 40 Maknadebai, Shashai, Sharai, 41 Azarel, Shelemiah, Shemariah, 42 Shallum, Amariah and Joseph.
43 From the descendants of Nebo:
Jeiel, Mattithiah, Zabad, Zebina, Jaddai, Joel and Benaiah.

44 All these had married foreign women, and some of them had children by these wives.[b]

---

a 37,38 See Septuagint (also 1 Esdras 9:34); Hebrew Jaasu 38and Bani and Binnui,   b 44 Or and they sent them away with their children

NEHEMIAH

THE EVIDENCE:

WHO WROTE IT?

Nehemiah is the name of the main character of this story, but he wasn't the one who wrote it. Since the person who wrote it didn't sign his name, it's called *anonymous*, which means "without a name." But many Bible experts think "the Chronicler" wrote it, just like Ezra, the book that comes just before this one. Also, almost everyone thinks that the books of Ezra and Nehemiah were just one book that later got divided into two.

HOW LONG AGO?

It seems that the writer started writing about 430 years before Christ, when Artaxerxes I (the First) was governing. But some parts of the book, like chapter 12, were written a long time before that, maybe in the year 300 before Christ.

WHAT'S IT ABOUT?

The things this book talks about happened around the year 445 before Christ. It had been about 90 years since the Jews had gone to Babylon and then returned to their own land to rebuild the temple in Jerusalem. However, the walls of the city were still in ruins. This book is part of the book just before it, Ezra, and it tells the twelve-year history of Nehemiah insisting that the people had to rebuild the walls of the city. Also, Nehemiah was angry because the people were disobedient, the priests were dishonest and the men were married to women from other nations that believed in false gods. So Nehemiah prays to God and asks forgiveness for their sins. He also reads the Book of the Law so all the people will understand and obey it. Because if they don't, God won't be able to forgive them.

THE BEST PART

We chose these verses, because we want to worship God: "Blessed be your glorious name, and may it be exalted above all blessing and praise. You alone are the LORD" (9:5 – 6).

Nehemiah's Prayer

1 The words of Nehemiah son of Hakaliah:

In the month of Kislev in the twentieth year, while I was in the citadel of Susa, ²Hanani, one of my brothers, came from Judah with some other men, and I questioned them about the Jewish remnant that had survived the exile, and also about Jerusalem.

³They said to me, "Those who survived the exile and are back in the province are in great trouble and disgrace. The wall of Jerusalem is broken down, and its gates have been burned with fire."

⁴When I heard these things, I sat down and wept. For some days I mourned and fasted and prayed before the God of heaven. ⁵Then I said:

"LORD, the God of heaven, the great and awesome God, who keeps his covenant of love with those who love him and keep his commandments,

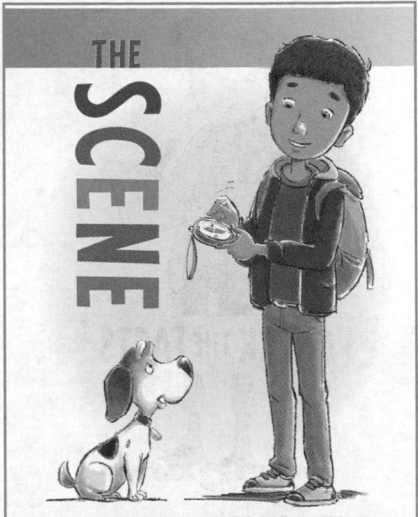

THE SCENE

SUSA

(NEHEMIAH 1:1)

Over the years, Susa belonged to different empires. During the time of Nehemiah, it was one of the main cities of the Persian empire. That's where the Persian kings had their winter palace.

⁶let your ear be attentive and your eyes open to hear the prayer your servant is praying before you day and night for your servants, the people of Israel. I confess the sins we Israelites, including myself and my father's family, have committed against you. ⁷We have acted very wickedly toward you. We have not obeyed the commands, decrees and laws you gave your servant Moses.

⁸"Remember the instruction you gave your servant Moses, saying, 'If you are unfaithful, I will scatter you among the nations, ⁹but if you return to me and obey my commands, then even if your exiled people are at the farthest horizon, I will gather them from there and bring them to the place I have chosen as a dwelling for my Name.'

BREAKTHROUGH!

Kislev

(NEHEMIAH 1:1)

It's the ninth month of the Jewish calendar, which is based on the moon. In our calendar, which is solar, that's from the middle of November to the middle of December.

10 "They are your servants and your people, whom you redeemed by your great strength and your mighty hand. 11Lord, let your ear be attentive to the prayer of this your servant and to the prayer of your servants who delight in revering your name. Give your servant success today by granting him favor in the presence of this man."

I was cupbearer to the king.

Artaxerxes Sends Nehemiah to Jerusalem

2 In the month of Nisan in the twenti-eth year of King Artaxerxes, when wine was brought for him, I took the wine and gave it to the king. I had not been sad in his presence before, 2so the king asked me, "Why does your face look so sad when you are not ill? This can be nothing but sadness of heart."

I was very much afraid, 3but I said to the king, "May the king live forever! Why should my face not look sad when the city where my ancestors are buried lies in ruins, and its gates have been destroyed by fire?"

4The king said to me, "What is it you want?"

Then I prayed to the God of heaven, 5and I answered the king, "If it pleases the king and if your servant has found favor in his sight, let him send me to the city in Judah where my ancestors are buried so that I can rebuild it."

6Then the king, with the queen sitting beside him, asked me, "How long will your journey take, and when will you get back?" It pleased the king to send me; so I set a time.

7I also said to him, "If it pleases the king, may I have letters to the governors of Trans-Euphrates, so that they will provide me safe-conduct until I arrive in Judah?

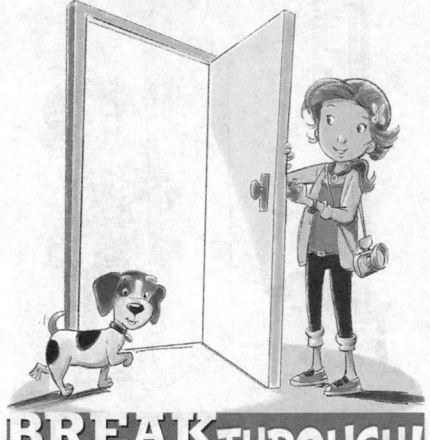

BREAKTHROUGH!

Nisan

(NEHEMIAH 2:1)

It's the first month of the Jewish lunar calendar post-exile. In our solar calendar, that's from the middle of March to the middle of April.

⁸And may I have a letter to Asaph, keeper of the royal park, so he will give me timber to make beams for the gates of the citadel by the temple and for the city wall and for the residence I will occupy?" And because the gracious hand of my God was on me, the king granted my requests. ⁹So I went to the governors of Trans-Euphrates and gave them the king's letters. The king had also sent army officers and cavalry with me.

¹⁰When Sanballat the Horonite and Tobiah the Ammonite official heard about this, they were very much disturbed that someone had come to promote the welfare of the Israelites.

Nehemiah Inspects Jerusalem's Walls

¹¹I went to Jerusalem, and after staying there three days ¹²I set out during the night with a few others. I had not told anyone what my God had put in my heart to do for Jerusalem. There were no mounts with me except the one I was riding on. ¹³By night I went out through the Valley Gate toward the Jackal*ᵃ* Well and the Dung Gate, examining the walls of Jerusalem, which had been broken down, and its gates, which had been destroyed by fire. ¹⁴Then I moved on toward the Fountain Gate and the King's Pool, but there was not enough room for my mount to get through; ¹⁵so I went up the valley by night, examining the wall. Finally, I turned back and reentered through the Valley Gate. ¹⁶The officials did not know where I had gone or what I was doing, because as yet I had said nothing to the Jews or the priests or nobles or officials or any others who would be doing the work.

ᵃ 13 Or Serpent or Fig

THE
WITNESSES

✓ NEHEMIAH (NEHEMIAH 1:1)
He was King Artaxerxes' cupbearer. That means he was in charge of serving the king's wine. He had to taste it first to make sure it wasn't poisoned. A cupbearer was a person of confidence and even he advised the king. Nehemiah was also governor of Jerusalem, and he organized the people when they rebuilt the walls and gates of the city. In Hebrew, *Nehemiah* means "the LORD comforts."

✓ HANANI (NEHEMIAH 1:2)
He was Nehemiah's brother. His name is short for Hananiah, which means "God has had grace." Nehemiah put him in charge of watching over the gates of Jerusalem.

✓ ARTAXERXES (NEHEMIAH 2:1)
This man appeared in Ezra 4:7. He's the same man here—the king of Persia.

✓ SANBALLAT AND TOBIAH (NEHEMIAH 2:10)
Sanballat was a leader in Samaria, which at that time was a Persian province under King Artaxerxes' control. It seems that Tobiah was a minister or a public servant. They were both enemies of the people of Israel, and they were against rebuilding Jerusalem.

¹⁷Then I said to them, "You see the trouble we are in: Jerusalem lies in ruins, and its gates have been burned with fire. Come, let us rebuild the wall of Jerusalem, and we will no longer be in disgrace." ¹⁸I also told them about the gracious hand of my God on me and what the king had said to me.

They replied, "Let us start rebuilding." So they began this good work.

¹⁹But when Sanballat the Horonite, Tobiah the Ammonite official and Geshem the Arab heard about it, they mocked and ridiculed us. "What is this you are doing?"

JERUSALEM

(NEHEMIAH 2:12)

During David's reign, this city became the most important city in the promised land. However, Jerusalem had existed for many, many years before that. It had different names at different times: Salem, Jebus and finally Jerusalem. David made it the capital of the kingdom. His son Solomon built the temple to worship God there. Jerusalem finally fell under the power of Nebuchadnezzar, who destroyed and set fire to it in the year 576 before Christ.

JUDAH

(NEHEMIAH 2:5)

Judah had the largest population of the twelve tribes. It was one of the first to occupy its land in the south of the land God had promised them. It ruled over the city of Jerusalem even though the city belonged to the tribe of Benjamin. The territory of Judah was one of the largest of all the tribes. It extended 37 miles (60 km) from east to west and 50 miles (80 km) from north to south. During the time of Nehemiah, it was a province in the Persian empire.

they asked. "Are you rebelling against the king?"

²⁰I answered them by saying, "The God of heaven will give us success. We his servants will start rebuilding, but as for you, you have no share in Jerusalem or any claim or historic right to it."

Builders of the Wall

3 Eliashib the high priest and his fellow priests went to work and rebuilt the Sheep Gate. They dedicated it and set its and put its doors with their bolts and bars in place. 7Next to them, repairs were made by men from Gibeon and Mizpah—Melatiah of Gibeon and Jadon of Meronoth—places under the authority of the governor of Trans-Euphrates. 8Uzziel son of Harhaiah, one of the goldsmiths, repaired the next section; and Hananiah, one of the perfume-makers, made repairs next to that. They restored Jerusalem as far as the Broad Wall. 9Rephaiah son of Hur, ruler of a half-district of Jerusalem, repaired the next section. 10Adjoining this, Jedaiah son of Harumaph made repairs opposite his house, and Hattush son of

---

a 5 Or *their Lord* or *the governor*   *b* 6 Or *Old*

BREAKTHROUGH!

Why were the walls in ruins and the gates burned?
(NEHEMIAH 2:17)

When Nebuchadnezzar took the people of Judah away as prisoners, he destroyed the entire city of Jerusalem and set fire to it. How evil! Although the Jews had been back in their land for quite a while, they still hadn't gotten busy and rebuilt the walls or the gates.

doors in place, building as far as the Tower of the Hundred, which they dedicated, and as far as the Tower of Hananel. 2The men of Jericho built the adjoining section, and Zakkur son of Imri built next to them.

3The Fish Gate was rebuilt by the sons of Hassenaah. They laid its beams and put its doors and bolts and bars in place. 4Meremoth son of Uriah, the son of Hakkoz, repaired the next section. Next to him Meshullam son of Berekiah, the son of Meshezabel, made repairs, and next to him Zadok son of Baana also made repairs. 5The next section was repaired by the men of Tekoa, but their nobles would not put their shoulders to the work under their supervisors.*a*

6The Jeshanah*b* Gate was repaired by Joiada son of Paseah and Meshullam son of Besodeiah. They laid its beams

BREAKTHROUGH!

Why were there so many helpers, but each one only repaired one small part?
(NEHEMIAH 3)

It was really a shame that the walls were in ruins! Since Nehemiah was a good leader, he called all the heads of families so they would help with the rebuilding. They organized 41 groups for the work, because then everybody had something to do. It was a very big job and it was very important, because the wall would separate God's people from their enemies.

Beth Hakkerem. He rebuilt it and put its doors with their bolts and bars in place.

¹⁵The Fountain Gate was repaired by Shallun son of Kol-Hozeh, ruler of the district of Mizpah. He rebuilt it, roofing it over and putting its doors and bolts and bars in place. He also repaired the wall of the Pool of Siloam,ᵇ by the King's Garden, as far as the steps going down from the City of David. ¹⁶Beyond him, Nehemiah son of Azbuk, ruler of a half-district of Beth Zur, made repairs up to a point opposite the tombsᶜ of David, as far as the artificial pool and the House of the Heroes.

ᵃ *13* That is, about 1,500 feet or about 450 meters
ᵇ *15* Hebrew *Shelah,* a variant of *Shiloah,* that is, Siloam
ᶜ *16* Hebrew; Septuagint, some Vulgate manuscripts and Syriac *tomb*

THE
WITNESSES

✓ **ELIASHIB (NEHEMIAH 3:1)**
He was the high priest who helped Nehemiah rebuild the walls. Later on, he joined Tobiah and set a trap for Nehemiah. No way! That's an injustice!

═══════════════════════════

Hashabneiah made repairs next to him. ¹¹Malkijah son of Harim and Hasshub son of Pahath-Moab repaired another section and the Tower of the Ovens. ¹²Shallum son of Hallohesh, ruler of a half-district of Jerusalem, repaired the next section with the help of his daughters.

¹³The Valley Gate was repaired by Hanun and the residents of Zanoah. They rebuilt it and put its doors with their bolts and bars in place. They also repaired a thousand cubitsᵃ of the wall as far as the Dung Gate.

¹⁴The Dung Gate was repaired by Malkijah son of Rekab, ruler of the district of

THE
SCENE

JERICHO

(NEHEMIAH 3:2)

This was a very old city. Some archaeologists think it might be the oldest city in the world. It was built on very fertile land 19 miles (30 km) northeast of Jerusalem and 4 miles (7 km) west of the Jordan River. During its long history, it was destroyed and rebuilt a number of times.

17 Next to him, the repairs were made by the Levites under Rehum son of Bani. Beside him, Hashabiah, ruler of half the district of Keilah, carried out repairs for his district. 18 Next to him, the repairs were made by their fellow Levites under Binnui[a] son of Henadad, ruler of the other half-district of Keilah. 19 Next to him, Ezer son of Jeshua, ruler of Mizpah, repaired another section, from a point facing the ascent to the armory as far as the angle of the wall. 20 Next to him, Baruch son of Zabbai zealously repaired another section, from the angle to the entrance of the house of Eliashib the high priest. 21 Next to him, Meremoth son of Uriah, the son of Hakkoz, repaired another section, from the entrance of Eliashib's house to the end of it.

THE SCENE

TEKOA

(NEHEMIAH 3:5)

It was a village in Judah 17 miles (16 km) south of Jerusalem. One of God's prophets, who was called Amos, was born in this village. During Nehemiah's time, the leaders there didn't help rebuild the walls of Jerusalem, but some of the poorest people in Tekoa did.

22 The repairs next to him were made by the priests from the surrounding region. 23 Beyond them, Benjamin and Hasshub made repairs in front of their house; and next to them, Azariah son of Maaseiah, the son of Ananiah, made repairs beside his house. 24 Next to him, Binnui son of Henadad repaired another section, from Azariah's house to the angle and the corner, 25 and Palal son of Uzai worked opposite the angle and the tower projecting from the upper palace near the court of the guard. Next to him, Pedaiah son of Parosh 26 and the temple servants living on the hill of Ophel made repairs up to a point opposite the Water Gate toward the east and the projecting tower. 27 Next to them, the men of Tekoa repaired another section, from the great projecting tower to the wall of Ophel.

28 Above the Horse Gate, the priests made repairs, each in front of his own house. 29 Next to them, Zadok son of Immer made repairs opposite his house. Next to him, Shemaiah son of Shekaniah, the guard at the East Gate, made repairs. 30 Next to him, Hananiah son of Shelemiah, and Hanun, the sixth son of Zalaph, repaired another section. Next to them, Meshullam son of Berekiah made repairs opposite his living quarters. 31 Next to him, Malkijah, one of the goldsmiths, made repairs as far as the house of the temple servants and the merchants, opposite the Inspection Gate, and as far as the room above the corner; 32 and between the room above the corner and the Sheep Gate the goldsmiths and merchants made repairs.

Opposition to the Rebuilding

4 [b] When Sanballat heard that we were rebuilding the wall, he became angry and was greatly incensed. He ridiculed the Jews, 2 and in the presence of his associates and the army of Samaria, he

---

a 18 Two Hebrew manuscripts and Syriac (see also Septuagint and verse 24); most Hebrew manuscripts *Bavvai*   *b* In Hebrew texts 4:1-6 is numbered 3:33-38, and 4:7-23 is numbered 4:1-17.

said, "What are those feeble Jews doing? Will they restore their wall? Will they offer sacrifices? Will they finish in a day? Can they bring the stones back to life from those heaps of rubble—burned as they are?"

³Tobiah the Ammonite, who was at his side, said, "What they are building—even a fox climbing up on it would break down their wall of stones!"

⁴Hear us, our God, for we are despised. Turn their insults back on their own heads. Give them over as plunder in a land of captivity. ⁵Do not cover up their guilt or blot out their sins from your sight, for they have thrown insults in the face of*a* the builders.

⁶So we rebuilt the wall till all of it reached half its height, for the people worked with all their heart.

⁷But when Sanballat, Tobiah, the Arabs, the Ammonites and the people of Ashdod heard that the repairs to Jerusalem's walls had gone ahead and that the gaps were being closed, they were very angry. ⁸They all plotted together to come and fight against Jerusalem and stir up trouble against it. ⁹But we prayed to our God and posted a guard day and night to meet this threat.

¹⁰Meanwhile, the people in Judah said, "The strength of the laborers is giving out, and there is so much rubble that we cannot rebuild the wall."

¹¹Also our enemies said, "Before they know it or see us, we will be right there among them and will kill them and put an end to the work."

¹²Then the Jews who lived near them came and told us ten times over, "Wherever you turn, they will attack us."

¹³Therefore I stationed some of the people behind the lowest points of the wall at the exposed places, posting them by families, with their swords, spears and bows. ¹⁴After I looked things over, I stood up and said to the nobles, the officials and the rest of the people, "Don't be afraid of them. Remember the Lord, who is great and awesome, and fight for your families, your sons and your daughters, your wives and your homes."

¹⁵When our enemies heard that we were aware of their plot and that God had frustrated it, we all returned to the wall, each to our own work.

¹⁶From that day on, half of my men did the work, while the other half were equipped with spears, shields, bows and armor. The officers posted themselves behind all the people of Judah ¹⁷who were building the wall. Those who carried materials did their work with one hand and held a weapon in the other, ¹⁸and each of the builders wore his sword at his side as he worked. But the man who sounded the trumpet stayed with me.

¹⁹Then I said to the nobles, the officials and the rest of the people, "The work is extensive and spread out, and we are widely separated from each other along the wall. ²⁰Wherever you hear the sound of the trumpet, join us there. Our God will fight for us!"

²¹So we continued the work with half the men holding spears, from the first light of dawn till the stars came out. ²²At that time I also said to the people, "Have every man and his helper stay inside Jerusalem at night, so they can serve us as guards by night and as workers by day." ²³Neither I nor my brothers nor my men nor the guards with me took off our clothes; each had his weapon, even when he went for water.*b*

Nehemiah Helps the Poor

5 Now the men and their wives raised a great outcry against their fellow Jews. ²Some were saying, "We and our sons and daughters are numerous; in order for us to eat and stay alive, we must get grain."

³Others were saying, "We are mortgaging our fields, our vineyards and our homes to get grain during the famine."

⁴Still others were saying, "We have had to borrow money to pay the king's tax on our fields and vineyards. ⁵Although we are of the same flesh and blood as our fellow Jews and though our children are as good as theirs, yet we have to subject our sons and daughters to slavery. Some of our

---

a 5 Or *have aroused your anger before*   *b 23* The meaning of the Hebrew for this clause is uncertain.

daughters have already been enslaved, but we are powerless, because our fields and our vineyards belong to others."

⁶When I heard their outcry and these charges, I was very angry. ⁷I pondered them in my mind and then accused the nobles and officials. I told them, "You are charging your own people interest!" So I called together a large meeting to deal with them ⁸and said: "As far as possible, we have bought back our fellow Jews who were sold to the Gentiles. Now you are selling your own people, only for them to be sold back to us!" They kept quiet, because they could find nothing to say.

⁹So I continued, "What you are doing is not right. Shouldn't you walk in the fear of our God to avoid the reproach of our Gentile enemies? ¹⁰I and my brothers and my men are also lending the people money and grain. But let us stop charging interest! ¹¹Give back to them immediately their fields, vineyards, olive groves and houses, and also the interest you are charging them—one percent of the money, grain, new wine and olive oil."

¹²"We will give it back," they said. "And we will not demand anything more from them. We will do as you say."

Then I summoned the priests and made the nobles and officials take an oath to do what they had promised. ¹³I also shook out the folds of my robe and said, "In this way may God shake out of their house and possessions anyone who does not keep this promise. So may such a person be shaken out and emptied!"

At this the whole assembly said, "Amen," and praised the LORD. And the people did as they had promised.

¹⁴Moreover, from the twentieth year of King Artaxerxes, when I was appointed to be their governor in the land of Judah, until his thirty-second year—twelve years—neither I nor my brothers ate the food allotted to the governor. ¹⁵But the earlier governors—those preceding me—placed a heavy burden on the people and took forty shekels[a] of silver from them in addition to food and wine. Their assistants also lorded it over the people. But out of reverence for God I did not act

like that. ¹⁶Instead, I devoted myself to the work on this wall. All my men were assembled there for the work; we[b] did not acquire any land.

¹⁷Furthermore, a hundred and fifty Jews and officials ate at my table, as well as those who came to us from the surrounding nations. ¹⁸Each day one ox, six choice sheep and some poultry were prepared for me, and every ten days an abundant supply of wine of all kinds. In spite of all this, I never demanded the food allotted to the governor, because the demands were heavy on these people.

¹⁹Remember me with favor, my God, for all I have done for these people.

Further Opposition to the Rebuilding

6 When word came to Sanballat, Tobiah, Geshem the Arab and the rest of our enemies that I had rebuilt the wall and not a gap was left in it—though up to that time I had not set the doors in the gates— ²Sanballat and Geshem sent me this message: "Come, let us meet together in one of the villages[c] on the plain of Ono."

But they were scheming to harm me; ³so I sent messengers to them with this reply: "I am carrying on a great project and cannot go down. Why should the work stop while I leave it and go down to you?" ⁴Four times they sent me the same message, and each time I gave them the same answer.

⁵Then, the fifth time, Sanballat sent his aide to me with the same message, and in his hand was an unsealed letter ⁶in which was written:

> "It is reported among the nations—and Geshem[d] says it is true—that you and the Jews are plotting to revolt, and therefore you are building the wall. Moreover, according to these reports you are about to become their king ⁷and have even

---

[a] 15 That is, about 1 pound or about 460 grams
[b] 16 Most Hebrew manuscripts; some Hebrew manuscripts, Septuagint, Vulgate and Syriac *I* [c] 2 Or *in Kephirim* [d] 6 Hebrew *Gashmu*, a variant of *Geshem*

appointed prophets to make this proclamation about you in Jerusalem: 'There is a king in Judah!' Now this report will get back to the king; so come, let us meet together."

⁸I sent him this reply: "Nothing like what you are saying is happening; you are just making it up out of your head."

⁹They were all trying to frighten us, thinking, "Their hands will get too weak for the work, and it will not be completed." But I prayed, "Now strengthen my hands."

¹⁰One day I went to the house of Shemaiah son of Delaiah, the son of Mehetabel, who was shut in at his home. He said, "Let us meet in the house of God, inside the temple, and let us close the temple doors, because men are coming to kill you—by night they are coming to kill you."

¹¹But I said, "Should a man like me run away? Or should someone like me go into the temple to save his life? I will not go!" ¹²I realized that God had not sent him, but that he had prophesied against me because Tobiah and Sanballat had hired him. ¹³He had been hired to intimidate me so that I would commit a sin by doing this, and then they would give me a bad name to discredit me.

¹⁴Remember Tobiah and Sanballat, my God, because of what they have done; remember also the prophet Noadiah and how she and the rest of the prophets have been trying to intimidate me. ¹⁵So the wall was completed on the twenty-fifth of Elul, in fifty-two days.

Opposition to the Completed Wall

¹⁶When all our enemies heard about this, all the surrounding nations were afraid and lost their self-confidence, because they realized that this work had been done with the help of our God.

¹⁷Also, in those days the nobles of Judah were sending many letters to Tobiah, and replies from Tobiah kept coming to them. ¹⁸For many in Judah were under oath to him, since he was son-in-law to Shekaniah son of Arah, and his son Jehohanan had married the daughter of Me-

BREAK THROUGH!

Elul

(NEHEMIAH 6:15)

It's the sixth month of the Jewish lunar calendar. In our calendar, which is based on the sun, that's from the middle of August to the middle of September.

shullam son of Berekiah. ¹⁹Moreover, they kept reporting to me his good deeds and then telling him what I said. And Tobiah sent letters to intimidate me.

7 After the wall had been rebuilt and I had set the doors in place, the gatekeepers, the musicians and the Levites were appointed. ²I put in charge of Jerusalem my brother Hanani, along with Hananiah the commander of the citadel, because he was a man of integrity and feared God more than most people do. ³I said to them, "The gates of Jerusalem are not to be opened until the sun is hot. While the gatekeepers are still on duty, have them shut the doors and bar them. Also appoint residents of Jerusalem as guards, some at their posts and some near their own houses."

The List of the Exiles Who Returned

⁴Now the city was large and spacious, but there were few people in it, and the houses had not yet been rebuilt. ⁵So my

God put it into my heart to assemble the nobles, the officials and the common people for registration by families. I found the genealogical record of those who had been the first to return. This is what I found written there:

⁶These are the people of the province who came up from the captivity of the exiles whom Nebuchadnezzar king of Babylon had taken captive (they returned to Jerusalem and Judah, each to his own town, ⁷in company with Zerubbabel, Joshua, Nehemiah, Azariah, Raamiah, Nahamani, Mordecai, Bilshan, Mispereth, Bigvai, Nehum and Baanah):

The list of the men of Israel:

⁸the descendants of		
Parosh	2,172	
⁹of Shephatiah	372	
¹⁰of Arah	652	
¹¹of Pahath-Moab (through		
the line of Jeshua		
and Joab)	2,818	
¹²of Elam	1,254	
¹³of Zattu	845	
¹⁴of Zakkai	760	
¹⁵of Binnui	648	
¹⁶of Bebai	628	
¹⁷of Azgad	2,322	
¹⁸of Adonikam	667	
¹⁹of Bigvai	2,067	
²⁰of Adin	655	
²¹of Ater (through Hezekiah)	98	
²²of Hashum	328	
²³of Bezai	324	
²⁴of Hariph	112	
²⁵of Gibeon	95	

²⁶the men of Bethlehem		
and Netophah	188	
²⁷of Anathoth	128	
²⁸of Beth Azmaveth	42	
²⁹of Kiriath Jearim,		
Kephirah and Beeroth	743	
³⁰of Ramah and Geba	621	
³¹of Mikmash	122	
³²of Bethel and Ai	123	
³³of the other Nebo	52	
³⁴of the other Elam	1,254	
³⁵of Harim	320	
³⁶of Jericho	345	

³⁷of Lod, Hadid and Ono	721
³⁸of Senaah	3,930

³⁹The priests:

the descendants of Jedaiah	
(through the family	
of Jeshua)	973
⁴⁰of Immer	1,052
⁴¹of Pashhur	1,247
⁴²of Harim	1,017

⁴³The Levites:

the descendants of Jeshua	
(through Kadmiel through	
the line of Hodaviah)	74

⁴⁴The musicians:

the descendants of Asaph	148

⁴⁵The gatekeepers:

the descendants of	
Shallum, Ater, Talmon,	
Akkub, Hatita and Shobai	138

⁴⁶The temple servants:

the descendants of
    Ziha, Hasupha, Tabbaoth,
⁴⁷Keros, Sia, Padon,
⁴⁸Lebana, Hagaba, Shalmai,
⁴⁹Hanan, Giddel, Gahar,
⁵⁰Reaiah, Rezin, Nekoda,
⁵¹Gazzam, Uzza, Paseah,
⁵²Besai, Meunim, Nephusim,
⁵³Bakbuk, Hakupha, Harhur,
⁵⁴Bazluth, Mehida, Harsha,
⁵⁵Barkos, Sisera, Temah,
⁵⁶Neziah and Hatipha

⁵⁷The descendants of the servants of Solomon:

the descendants of
    Sotai, Sophereth, Perida,
⁵⁸Jaala, Darkon, Giddel,
⁵⁹Shephatiah, Hattil,
    Pokereth-Hazzebaim and
    Amon

⁶⁰The temple servants and	
the descendants of the	
servants of Solomon	392

⁶¹The following came up from the towns of Tel Melah, Tel Harsha, Kerub, Addon and Immer, but they could

not show that their families were descended from Israel:

⁶²the descendants of
Delaiah, Tobiah and
Nekoda   642

⁶³And from among the priests:

the descendants of
Hobaiah, Hakkoz and Barzillai
(a man who had married
a daughter of Barzillai the
Gileadite and was called by
that name).

⁶⁴These searched for their family records, but they could not find them and so were excluded from the priesthood as unclean. ⁶⁵The governor, therefore, ordered them not to eat any of the most sacred food until there should be a priest ministering with the Urim and Thummim.

⁶⁶The whole company numbered 42,360, ⁶⁷besides their 7,337 male and female slaves; and they also had 245 male and female singers. ⁶⁸There were 736 horses, 245

BREAKTHROUGH!

Seventh month

(NEHEMIAH 7:73)

It was called Ethanim in the Jewish lunar calendar. That is more or less from the middle of September to the middle of October in our solar calendar.

mules,ᵃ ⁶⁹435 camels and 6,720 donkeys.

⁷⁰Some of the heads of the families contributed to the work. The governor gave to the treasury 1,000 daricsᵇ of gold, 50 bowls and 530 garments for priests. ⁷¹Some of the heads of the families gave to the treasury for the work 20,000 daricsᶜ of gold and 2,200 minasᵈ of silver. ⁷²The total given by the rest of the people was 20,000 darics of gold, 2,000 minasᵉ of silver and 67 garments for priests.

⁷³The priests, the Levites, the gatekeepers, the musicians and the temple servants, along with certain of the people and the rest of the Israelites, settled in their own towns.

BREAKTHROUGH!

Urim and Thummim

(NEHEMIAH 7:65)

Those were the two stones they used to cast lots and know what God's will was.

ᵃ 68 Some Hebrew manuscripts (see also Ezra 2:66); most Hebrew manuscripts do not have this verse.
ᵇ 70 That is, about 19 pounds or about 8.4 kilograms
ᶜ 71 That is, about 375 pounds or about 170 kilograms; also in verse 72   ᵈ 71 That is, about 1 1/3 tons or about 1.2 metric tons   ᵉ 72 That is, about 1 1/4 tons or about 1.1 metric tons

Ezra Reads the Law

When the seventh month came and the Israelites had settled in their towns, **8** ¹all the people came together as one in the square before the Water Gate. They told Ezra the teacher of the Law to bring out the Book of the Law of Moses, which the LORD had commanded for Israel.

²So on the first day of the seventh month Ezra the priest brought the Law before the assembly, which was made up of men and women and all who were able to understand. ³He read it aloud from daybreak till noon as he faced the square before the Water Gate in the presence of the men, women and others who could understand. And all the people listened attentively to the Book of the Law.

⁴Ezra the teacher of the Law stood on a high wooden platform built for the occasion. Beside him on his right stood Mattithiah, Shema, Anaiah, Uriah, Hilkiah and Maaseiah; and on his left were Pedaiah, Mishael, Malkijah, Hashum, Hashbaddanah, Zechariah and Meshullam.

⁵Ezra opened the book. All the people could see him because he was standing above them; and as he opened it, the people all stood up. ⁶Ezra praised the LORD, the great God; and all the people lifted their hands and responded, "Amen! Amen!" Then they bowed down and worshiped the LORD with their faces to the ground.

⁷The Levites—Jeshua, Bani, Sherebiah, Jamin, Akkub, Shabbethai, Hodiah, Maaseiah, Kelita, Azariah, Jozabad, Hanan and Pelaiah—instructed the people in the Law while the people were standing there. ⁸They read from the Book of the Law of God, making it clear[a] and giving the meaning so that the people understood what was being read.

⁹Then Nehemiah the governor, Ezra the priest and teacher of the Law, and the Levites who were instructing the people said to them all, "This day is holy to the LORD your God. Do not mourn or weep." For all the people had been weeping as they listened to the words of the Law.

¹⁰Nehemiah said, "Go and enjoy choice food and sweet drinks, and send some

BREAK THROUGH!

Why did they give the meaning of the Book of the Law? Wasn't it already written in Hebrew?

(NEHEMIAH 8:7-8)

The Book of the Law was in Hebrew, but many Jews after the exile didn't speak that language. They spoke Aramaic. That's why they needed it made clear.

to those who have nothing prepared. This day is holy to our Lord. Do not grieve, for the joy of the LORD is your strength."

¹¹The Levites calmed all the people, saying, "Be still, for this is a holy day. Do not grieve."

¹²Then all the people went away to eat and drink, to send portions of food and to celebrate with great joy, because they now understood the words that had been made known to them.

¹³On the second day of the month, the heads of all the families, along with the priests and the Levites, gathered around Ezra the teacher to give attention to the words of the Law. ¹⁴They found written in the Law, which the LORD had commanded through Moses, that the Israelites were to live in temporary shelters during

---

a 8 Or God, translating it

the festival of the seventh month ¹⁵and that they should proclaim this word and spread it throughout their towns and in Jerusalem: "Go out into the hill country and bring back branches from olive and wild olive trees, and from myrtles, palms and shade trees, to make temporary shelters" — as it is written.ᵃ

¹⁶So the people went out and brought back branches and built themselves temporary shelters on their own roofs, in their courtyards, in the courts of the house of God and in the square by the Water Gate and the one by the Gate of Ephraim. ¹⁷The whole company that had returned from exile built temporary shelters and lived in them. From the days of Joshua son of Nun until that day, the Israelites had not celebrated it like this. And their joy was very great.

¹⁸Day after day, from the first day to the last, Ezra read from the Book of the Law of God. They celebrated the festival for seven days, and on the eighth day, in accordance with the regulation, there was an assembly.

The Israelites Confess Their Sins

9 On the twenty-fourth day of the same month, the Israelites gathered together, fasting and wearing sackcloth and putting dust on their heads. ²Those of Israelite descent had separated themselves from all foreigners. They stood in their places and confessed their sins and the sins of their ancestors. ³They stood where they were and read from the Book of the Law of the LORD their God for a quarter of the day, and spent another quarter in confession and in worshiping the LORD their God. ⁴Standing on the stairs of the Levites were Jeshua, Bani, Kadmiel, Shebaniah, Bunni, Sherebiah, Bani and Kenani. They cried out with loud voices to the LORD their God. ⁵And the Levites — Jeshua, Kadmiel, Bani, Hashabneiah, Sherebiah, Hodiah, Shebaniah and Pethahiah — said: "Stand up and praise the LORD your God, who is from everlasting to everlasting.ᵇ"

"Blessed be your glorious name, and may it be exalted above all blessing and praise. ⁶You alone are the LORD. You made the heavens, even the highest heavens, and all their starry host, the earth and all that is on it, the seas and all that is in them. You give life to everything, and the multitudes of heaven worship you.

⁷"You are the LORD God, who chose Abram and brought him out of Ur of the Chaldeans and named him Abraham. ⁸You found his heart faithful to you, and you made a covenant with him to give to his descendants the land of the Canaanites, Hittites, Amorites, Perizzites, Jebusites and Girgashites. You have kept your promise because you are righteous.

⁹"You saw the suffering of our ancestors in Egypt; you heard their cry at the Red Sea.ᶜ ¹⁰You sent signs and wonders against Pharaoh, against all his officials and all the people of his land, for you knew how arrogantly the Egyptians treated them. You made a name for yourself, which remains to this day. ¹¹You divided the sea before them, so that they passed through it on dry ground, but you hurled their pursuers into the depths, like a stone into mighty waters. ¹²By day you led them with a pillar of cloud, and by night with a pillar of fire to give them light on the way they were to take.

¹³"You came down on Mount Sinai; you spoke to them from heaven. You gave them regulations and laws that are just and right, and decrees and commands that are good. ¹⁴You made known to them your holy Sabbath and gave them commands, decrees and laws through your servant Moses. ¹⁵In their hunger you gave them bread from heaven and in their thirst you brought them water from the rock; you told them to go in and take possession of the land you had sworn with uplifted hand to give them.

¹⁶"But they, our ancestors, became arrogant and stiff-necked, and

---

ᵃ 15 See Lev. 23:37-40.   ᵇ 5 Or God for ever and ever
ᶜ 9 Or the Sea of Reeds

they did not obey your commands. [17]They refused to listen and failed to remember the miracles you performed among them. They became stiff-necked and in their rebellion appointed a leader in order to return to their slavery. But you are a forgiving God, gracious and compassionate, slow to anger and abounding in love. Therefore you did not desert them, [18]even when they cast for themselves an image of a calf and said, 'This is your god, who brought you up out of Egypt,' or when they committed awful blasphemies.

[19]"Because of your great compassion you did not abandon them in the wilderness. By day the pillar of cloud did not fail to guide them on their path, nor the pillar of fire by night to shine on the way they were to take. [20]You gave your good Spirit to instruct them. You did not withhold your manna from their mouths, and you gave them water for their thirst. [21]For forty years you sustained them in the wilderness; they lacked nothing, their clothes did not wear out nor did their feet become swollen.

[22]"You gave them kingdoms and nations, allotting to them even the remotest frontiers. They took over the country of Sihon[a] king of Heshbon and the country of Og king of Bashan. [23]You made their children as numerous as the stars in the sky, and you brought them into the land that you told their parents to enter and possess. [24]Their children went in and took possession of the land. You subdued before them the Canaanites, who lived in the land; you gave the Canaanites into their hands, along with their kings and the peoples of the land, to deal with them as they pleased. [25]They captured fortified cities and fertile land; they took possession of houses filled with all kinds of good things, wells already dug, vineyards, olive groves and fruit trees in abundance. They ate to the full and were well-nourished; they reveled in your great goodness.

[26]"But they were disobedient and rebelled against you; they turned their backs on your law. They killed your prophets, who had warned them in order to turn them back to you; they committed awful blasphemies. [27]So you delivered them into the hands of their enemies, who oppressed them. But when they were oppressed they cried out to you. From heaven you heard them, and in your great compassion you gave them deliverers, who rescued them from the hand of their enemies.

[28]"But as soon as they were at rest, they again did what was evil in your sight. Then you abandoned them to the hand of their enemies so that they ruled over them. And when they cried out to you again, you heard from heaven, and in your compassion you delivered them time after time.

[29]"You warned them in order to turn them back to your law, but they became arrogant and disobeyed your commands. They sinned against your ordinances, of which you said, 'The person who obeys them will live by them.' Stubbornly they turned their backs on you, became stiff-necked and refused to listen. [30]For many years you were patient with them. By your Spirit you warned them through your prophets. Yet they paid no attention, so you gave them into the hands of the neighboring peoples. [31]But in your great mercy you did not put an end to them or abandon them, for you are a gracious and merciful God.

[32]"Now therefore, our God, the great God, mighty and awesome, who keeps his covenant of love, do not let all this hardship seem trifling in your eyes—the hardship that has come on us, on our kings and leaders, on our priests and prophets, on our ancestors and all your people, from the days of the kings of Assyria until today. [33]In all that has happened to us, you have remained righteous; you

---

[a] 22 One Hebrew manuscript and Septuagint; most Hebrew manuscripts *Sihon, that is, the country of the*

have acted faithfully, while we acted wickedly. [34] Our kings, our leaders, our priests and our ancestors did not follow your law; they did not pay attention to your commands or the statutes you warned them to keep. [35] Even while they were in their kingdom, enjoying your great goodness to them in the spacious and fertile land you gave them, they did not serve you or turn from their evil ways.

[36] "But see, we are slaves today, slaves in the land you gave our ancestors so they could eat its fruit and the other good things it produces. [37] Because of our sins, its abundant harvest goes to the kings you have placed over us. They rule over our bodies and our cattle as they please. We are in great distress.

The Agreement of the People

[38] "In view of all this, we are making a binding agreement, putting it in writing, and our leaders, our Levites and our priests are affixing their seals to it."[a]

10[b] Those who sealed it were:

Nehemiah the governor, the son of Hakaliah.

Zedekiah, [2] Seraiah, Azariah, Jeremiah,
[3] Pashhur, Amariah, Malkijah,
[4] Hattush, Shebaniah, Malluk,
[5] Harim, Meremoth, Obadiah,
[6] Daniel, Ginnethon, Baruch,
[7] Meshullam, Abijah, Mijamin,
[8] Maaziah, Bilgai and Shemaiah.

These were the priests.

[9] The Levites:

Jeshua son of Azaniah, Binnui of the sons of Henadad, Kadmiel,
[10] and their associates: Shebaniah, Hodiah, Kelita, Pelaiah, Hanan,
[11] Mika, Rehob, Hashabiah,
[12] Zakkur, Sherebiah, Shebaniah,
[13] Hodiah, Bani and Beninu.

[14] The leaders of the people:

Parosh, Pahath-Moab, Elam, Zattu, Bani,

[15] Bunni, Azgad, Bebai,
[16] Adonijah, Bigvai, Adin,
[17] Ater, Hezekiah, Azzur,
[18] Hodiah, Hashum, Bezai,
[19] Hariph, Anathoth, Nebai,
[20] Magpiash, Meshullam, Hezir,
[21] Meshezabel, Zadok, Jaddua,
[22] Pelatiah, Hanan, Anaiah,
[23] Hoshea, Hananiah, Hasshub,
[24] Hallohesh, Pilha, Shobek,
[25] Rehum, Hashabnah, Maaseiah,
[26] Ahiah, Hanan, Anan,
[27] Malluk, Harim and Baanah.

[28] "The rest of the people—priests, Levites, gatekeepers, musicians, temple servants and all who separated themselves from the neighboring peoples for the sake of the Law of God, together with their wives and all their sons and daughters who are able to understand— [29] all these now join their fellow Israelites the nobles, and bind themselves with a curse and an oath to follow the Law of God given through Moses the servant of God and to obey carefully all the commands, regulations and decrees of the LORD our Lord.

[30] "We promise not to give our daughters in marriage to the peoples around us or take their daughters for our sons.

[31] "When the neighboring peoples bring merchandise or grain to sell on the Sabbath, we will not buy from them on the Sabbath or on any holy day. Every seventh year we will forgo working the land and will cancel all debts.

[32] "We assume the responsibility for carrying out the commands to give a third of a shekel[c] each year for the service of the house of our God: [33] for the bread set out on the table; for the regular grain offerings and burnt offerings; for the offerings on the Sabbaths, at the New Moon feasts and at the appointed festivals; for the holy offerings; for sin

---

a 38 In Hebrew texts this verse (9:38) is numbered 10:1.
b In Hebrew texts 10:1-39 is numbered 10:2-40.
c 32 That is, about 1/8 ounce or about 4 grams

offerings[a] to make atonement for Israel; and for all the duties of the house of our God.

³⁴ "We — the priests, the Levites and the people — have cast lots to determine when each of our families is to bring to the house of our God at set times each year a contribution of wood to burn on the altar of the LORD our God, as it is written in the Law.

³⁵ "We also assume responsibility for bringing to the house of the LORD each year the firstfruits of our crops and of every fruit tree.

³⁶ "As it is also written in the Law, we will bring the firstborn of our sons and of our cattle, of our herds and of our flocks to the house of our God, to the priests ministering there.

³⁷ "Moreover, we will bring to the storerooms of the house of our God, to the priests, the first of our ground meal, of our grain offerings, of the fruit of all our trees and of our new wine and olive oil. And we will bring a tithe of our crops to the Levites, for it is the Levites who collect the tithes in all the towns where we work. ³⁸ A priest descended from Aaron is to accompany the Levites when they receive the tithes, and the Levites are to bring a tenth of the tithes up to the house of our God, to the storerooms of the treasury. ³⁹ The people of Israel, including the Levites, are to bring their contributions of grain, new wine and olive oil to the storerooms, where the articles for the sanctuary and for the ministering priests, the gatekeepers and the musicians are also kept.

"We will not neglect the house of our God."

The New Residents of Jerusalem

11 Now the leaders of the people settled in Jerusalem. The rest of the people cast lots to bring one out of every ten of them to live in Jerusalem, the holy city, while the remaining nine were to stay in their own towns. ² The people commended all who volunteered to live in Jerusalem.

³ These are the provincial leaders who settled in Jerusalem (now some Israelites, priests, Levites, temple servants and descendants of Solomon's servants lived in the towns of Judah, each on their own property in the various towns, ⁴ while other people from both Judah and Benjamin lived in Jerusalem):

From the descendants of Judah:

Athaiah son of Uzziah, the son of Zechariah, the son of Amariah, the son of Shephatiah, the son of Mahalalel, a descendant of Perez; ⁵ and Maaseiah son of Baruch, the son of Kol-Hozeh, the son of Hazaiah, the son of Adaiah, the son of Joiarib, the son of Zechariah, a descendant of Shelah. ⁶ The descendants of Perez who lived in Jerusalem totaled 468 men of standing.

⁷ From the descendants of Benjamin:

Sallu son of Meshullam, the son of Joed, the son of Pedaiah, the son of Kolaiah, the son of Maaseiah, the son of Ithiel, the son of Jeshaiah, ⁸ and his followers, Gabbai and Sallai — 928 men. ⁹ Joel son of Zikri was their chief officer, and Judah son of Hassenuah was over the New Quarter of the city.

¹⁰ From the priests:

Jedaiah; the son of Joiarib; Jakin; ¹¹ Seraiah son of Hilkiah, the son of Meshullam, the son of Zadok, the son of Meraioth, the son of Ahitub, the official in charge of the house of God, ¹² and their associates, who carried on work for the temple — 822 men; Adaiah son of Jeroham, the son of Pelaliah, the son of Amzi, the son of Zechariah, the son of Pashhur, the son of Malkijah, ¹³ and his associates, who were heads of families — 242 men; Amashsai son of Azarel, the son of Ahzai, the son of Meshillemoth, the son of Immer, ¹⁴ and his[b] associates, who were men of standing — 128. Their chief officer was Zabdiel son of Haggedolim.

ᵃ 33 Or purification offerings   ᵇ 14 Most Septuagint manuscripts; Hebrew their

¹⁵From the Levites:

Shemaiah son of Hasshub, the son of Azrikam, the son of Hashabiah, the son of Bunni; ¹⁶Shabbethai and Jozabad, two of the heads of the Levites, who had charge of the outside work of the house of God; ¹⁷Mattaniah son of Mika, the son of Zabdi, the son of Asaph, the director who led in thanksgiving and prayer; Bakbukiah, second among his associates; and Abda son of Shammua, the son of Galal, the son of Jeduthun. ¹⁸The Levites in the holy city totaled 284.

¹⁹The gatekeepers:

Akkub, Talmon and their associates, who kept watch at the gates—172 men.

²⁰The rest of the Israelites, with the priests and Levites, were in all the towns of Judah, each on their ancestral property. ²¹The temple servants lived on the hill of Ophel, and Ziha and Gishpa were in charge of them.

²²The chief officer of the Levites in Jerusalem was Uzzi son of Bani, the son of Hashabiah, the son of Mattaniah, the son of Mika. Uzzi was one of Asaph's descendants, who were the musicians responsible for the service of the house of God. ²³The musicians were under the king's orders, which regulated their daily activity.

²⁴Pethahiah son of Meshezabel, one of the descendants of Zerah son of Judah, was the king's agent in all affairs relating to the people.

²⁵As for the villages with their fields, some of the people of Judah lived in Kiriath Arba and its surrounding settlements, in Dibon and its settlements, in Jekabzeel and its villages, ²⁶in Jeshua, in Moladah, in Beth Pelet, ²⁷in Hazar Shual, in Beersheba and its settlements, ²⁸in Ziklag, in Mekonah and its settlements, ²⁹in En Rimmon, in Zorah, in Jarmuth, ³⁰Zanoah, Adullam and their villages, in Lachish and its fields, and in Azekah and its settlements. So they were living all the way from Beersheba to the Valley of Hinnom.

³¹The descendants of the Benjamites from Geba lived in Mikmash, Aija, Bethel and its settlements, ³²in Anathoth, Nob and Ananiah, ³³in Hazor, Ramah and Gittaim, ³⁴in Hadid, Zeboim and Neballat, ³⁵in Lod and Ono, and in Ge Harashim.

³⁶Some of the divisions of the Levites of Judah settled in Benjamin.

Priests and Levites

12 These were the priests and Levites who returned with Zerubbabel son of Shealtiel and with Joshua:

Seraiah, Jeremiah, Ezra,
²Amariah, Malluk, Hattush,
³Shekaniah, Rehum, Meremoth,
⁴Iddo, Ginnethon,ᵃ Abijah,
⁵Mijamin,ᵇ Moadiah, Bilgah,
⁶Shemaiah, Joiarib, Jedaiah,
⁷Sallu, Amok, Hilkiah and Jedaiah.

These were the leaders of the priests and their associates in the days of Joshua. ⁸The Levites were Jeshua, Binnui, Kadmiel, Sherebiah, Judah, and also Mattaniah, who, together with his associates, was in charge of the songs of thanksgiving. ⁹Bakbukiah and Unni, their associates, stood opposite them in the services.

¹⁰Joshua was the father of Joiakim, Joiakim the father of Eliashib, Eliashib the father of Joiada, ¹¹Joiada the father of Jonathan, and Jonathan the father of Jaddua.

¹²In the days of Joiakim, these were the heads of the priestly families:

of Seraiah's family, Meraiah;
of Jeremiah's, Hananiah;
¹³of Ezra's, Meshullam;
of Amariah's, Jehohanan;
¹⁴of Malluk's, Jonathan;
of Shekaniah's,ᶜ Joseph;
¹⁵of Harim's, Adna;
of Meremoth's,ᵈ Helkai;
¹⁶of Iddo's, Zechariah;
of Ginnethon's, Meshullam;
¹⁷of Abijah's, Zikri;
of Miniamin's and of Moadiah's, Piltai;
¹⁸of Bilgah's, Shammua;
of Shemaiah's, Jehonathan;

ᵃ 4 Many Hebrew manuscripts and Vulgate (see also verse 16); most Hebrew manuscripts *Ginnethoi*
ᵇ 5 A variant of *Miniamin*   ᶜ 14 Very many Hebrew manuscripts, some Septuagint manuscripts and Syriac (see also verse 3); most Hebrew manuscripts *Shebaniah's*
ᵈ 15 Some Septuagint manuscripts (see also verse 3); Hebrew *Meraioth's*

¹⁹ of Joiarib's, Mattenai;
of Jedaiah's, Uzzi;
²⁰ of Sallu's, Kallai;
of Amok's, Eber;
²¹ of Hilkiah's, Hashabiah;
of Jedaiah's, Nethanel.

²² The family heads of the Levites in the days of Eliashib, Joiada, Johanan and Jaddua, as well as those of the priests, were recorded in the reign of Darius the Persian. ²³ The family heads among the descendants of Levi up to the time of Johanan son of Eliashib were recorded in the book of the annals. ²⁴ And the leaders of the Levites were Hashabiah, Sherebiah, Jeshua son of Kadmiel, and their associates, who stood opposite them to give praise and thanksgiving, one section responding to the other, as prescribed by David the man of God.

²⁵ Mattaniah, Bakbukiah, Obadiah, Meshullam, Talmon and Akkub were gatekeepers who guarded the storerooms at the gates. ²⁶ They served in the days of Joiakim son of Joshua, the son of Jozadak, and in the days of Nehemiah the governor and of Ezra the priest, the teacher of the Law.

Dedication of the Wall of Jerusalem

²⁷ At the dedication of the wall of Jerusalem, the Levites were sought out from where they lived and were brought to Jerusalem to celebrate joyfully the dedication with songs of thanksgiving and with the music of cymbals, harps and lyres. ²⁸ The musicians also were brought together from the region around Jerusalem—from the villages of the Netophathites, ²⁹ from Beth Gilgal, and from the area of Geba and Azmaveth, for the musicians had built villages for themselves around Jerusalem. ³⁰ When the priests and Levites had purified themselves ceremonially, they purified the people, the gates and the wall.

³¹ I had the leaders of Judah go up on top of^a the wall. I also assigned two large choirs to give thanks. One was to proceed on top of^b the wall to the right, toward the Dung Gate. ³² Hoshaiah and half the leaders of Judah followed them, ³³ along with Azariah, Ezra, Meshullam, ³⁴ Judah, Benjamin, Shemaiah, Jeremiah, ³⁵ as well

as some priests with trumpets, and also Zechariah son of Jonathan, the son of Shemaiah, the son of Mattaniah, the son of Micaiah, the son of Zakkur, the son of Asaph, ³⁶ and his associates—Shemaiah, Azarel, Milalai, Gilalai, Maai, Nethanel, Judah and Hanani—with musical instruments prescribed by David the man of God. Ezra the teacher of the Law led the procession. ³⁷ At the Fountain Gate they continued directly up the steps of the City of David on the ascent to the wall and passed above the site of David's palace to the Water Gate on the east.

³⁸ The second choir proceeded in the opposite direction. I followed them on top of^c the wall, together with half the people—past the Tower of the Ovens to the Broad Wall, ³⁹ over the Gate of Ephraim, the Jeshanah^d Gate, the Fish Gate, the Tower of Hananel and the Tower of the Hundred, as far as the Sheep Gate. At the Gate of the Guard they stopped.

⁴⁰ The two choirs that gave thanks then took their places in the house of God; so did I, together with half the officials, ⁴¹ as well as the priests—Eliakim, Maaseiah, Miniamin, Micaiah, Elioenai, Zechariah and Hananiah with their trumpets—⁴² and also Maaseiah, Shemaiah, Eleazar, Uzzi, Jehohanan, Malkijah, Elam and Ezer. The choirs sang under the direction of Jezrahiah. ⁴³ And on that day they offered great sacrifices, rejoicing because God had given them great joy. The women and children also rejoiced. The sound of rejoicing in Jerusalem could be heard far away.

⁴⁴ At that time men were appointed to be in charge of the storerooms for the contributions, firstfruits and tithes. From the fields around the towns they were to bring into the storerooms the portions required by the Law for the priests and the Levites, for Judah was pleased with the ministering priests and Levites. ⁴⁵ They performed the service of their God and the service of purification, as did also the musicians and gatekeepers, according to the commands of David and his son

---

^{a} 31 Or go alongside ^{b} 31 Or proceed alongside
^{c} 38 Or them alongside ^{d} 39 Or Old

Solomon. [46]For long ago, in the days of David and Asaph, there had been directors for the musicians and for the songs of praise and thanksgiving to God. [47]So in the days of Zerubbabel and of Nehemiah, all Israel contributed the daily portions for the musicians and the gatekeepers. They also set aside the portion for the other Levites, and the Levites set aside the portion for the descendants of Aaron.

Nehemiah's Final Reforms

13 On that day the Book of Moses was read aloud in the hearing of the people and there it was found written that no Ammonite or Moabite should ever be admitted into the assembly of God, [2]because they had not met the Israelites with food and water but had hired Balaam to call a curse down on them. (Our God, however, turned the curse into a blessing.) [3]When the people heard this law, they excluded from Israel all who were of foreign descent.

[4]Before this, Eliashib the priest had been put in charge of the storerooms of the house of our God. He was closely associated with Tobiah, [5]and he had provided him with a large room formerly used to store the grain offerings and incense and temple articles, and also the tithes of grain, new wine and olive oil prescribed for the Levites, musicians and gatekeepers, as well as the contributions for the priests.

[6]But while all this was going on, I was not in Jerusalem, for in the thirty-second year of Artaxerxes king of Babylon I had returned to the king. Some time later I asked his permission [7]and came back to Jerusalem. Here I learned about the evil thing Eliashib had done in providing Tobiah a room in the courts of the house of God. [8]I was greatly displeased and threw all Tobiah's household goods out of the room. [9]I gave orders to purify the rooms, and then I put back into them the equipment of the house of God, with the grain offerings and the incense.

[10]I also learned that the portions assigned to the Levites had not been given to them, and that all the Levites and musicians responsible for the service had gone back to their own fields. [11]So I re-buked the officials and asked them, "Why is the house of God neglected?" Then I called them together and stationed them at their posts.

[12]All Judah brought the tithes of grain, new wine and olive oil into the storerooms. [13]I put Shelemiah the priest, Zadok the scribe, and a Levite named Pedaiah in charge of the storerooms and made Hanan son of Zakkur, the son of Mattaniah, their assistant, because they were considered trustworthy. They were made responsible for distributing the supplies to their fellow Levites.

[14]Remember me for this, my God, and do not blot out what I have so faithfully done for the house of my God and its services.

[15]In those days I saw people in Judah treading winepresses on the Sabbath and bringing in grain and loading it on donkeys, together with wine, grapes, figs and all other kinds of loads. And they were bringing all this into Jerusalem on the Sabbath. Therefore I warned them against selling food on that day. [16]People from Tyre who lived in Jerusalem were bringing in fish and all kinds of merchandise and selling them in Jerusalem on the Sabbath to the people of Judah. [17]I rebuked the nobles of Judah and said to them, "What is this wicked thing you are doing—desecrating the Sabbath day? [18]Didn't your ancestors do the same things, so that our God brought all this calamity on us and on this city? Now you are stirring up more wrath against Israel by desecrating the Sabbath."

[19]When evening shadows fell on the gates of Jerusalem before the Sabbath, I ordered the doors to be shut and not opened until the Sabbath was over. I stationed some of my own men at the gates so that no load could be brought in on the Sabbath day. [20]Once or twice the merchants and sellers of all kinds of goods spent the night outside Jerusalem. [21]But I warned them and said, "Why do you spend the night by the wall? If you do this again, I will arrest you." From that time on they no longer came on the Sabbath. [22]Then I commanded the Levites to purify

themselves and go and guard the gates in order to keep the Sabbath day holy.

Remember me for this also, my God, and show mercy to me according to your great love.

23Moreover, in those days I saw men of Judah who had married women from Ashdod, Ammon and Moab. 24Half of their children spoke the language of Ashdod or the language of one of the other peoples, and did not know how to speak the language of Judah. 25I rebuked them and called curses down on them. I beat some of the men and pulled out their hair. I made them take an oath in God's name and said: "You are not to give your daughters in marriage to their sons, nor are you to take their daughters in marriage for your sons or for yourselves. 26Was it not because of marriages like these that Solomon king of Israel sinned? Among the many nations there

was no king like him. He was loved by his God, and God made him king over all Israel, but even he was led into sin by foreign women. 27Must we hear now that you too are doing all this terrible wickedness and are being unfaithful to our God by marrying foreign women?"

28One of the sons of Joiada son of Eliashib the high priest was son-in-law to Sanballat the Horonite. And I drove him away from me.

29Remember them, my God, because they defiled the priestly office and the covenant of the priesthood and of the Levites.

30So I purified the priests and the Levites of everything foreign, and assigned them duties, each to his own task. 31I also made provision for contributions of wood at designated times, and for the firstfruits.

Remember me with favor, my God.

CASE CLOSED!

When we read this book, we learned a lot about the history of God's people. We found out how they rebuilt the city of Jerusalem. We saw how they worked together to carry out God's will. And we learned how they prayed when their enemies tricked them or wanted to attack them. We also learned that God wants an obedient people. When there's no obedience, God doesn't bless us.

Finally, we understood what the character traits of a good leader for God are: knowing and obeying what God orders, never getting tired of working, praying to God, not turning your back on God's call and scolding people who are disobedient. We can be good leaders like Nehemiah too!

ESTHER

THE EVIDENCE:

WHO WROTE IT?

It seems no one knows exactly who wrote this book, but we say it had to be *someone*. Well-versed people say maybe it was Esther's cousin, whose name was Mordecai, or maybe a man named Ezra, who also appears in the Bible but in another book.

HOW LONG AGO?

No one's sure about this either! It all happened so many years ago — about 470 years before Jesus — and it was written down later. But at any rate, it was a long time ago. Just imagine!

WHAT'S IT ABOUT?

This book is pretty old, but the things it talks about are similar to what happens nowadays. For example, it's like when people order you around and think they have more power than God. That's wrong.

Another thing that's nice is the part about the Purim Festival. Isabella's dad told us that it's a party to celebrate the liberation of the Jews during the time of the Persians, the people who ruled that country at that time. There are several things in this book that are important for us. First of all, there's Esther. She's beautiful and brave. She wasn't afraid, and she helped her people. Then there's Esther's cousin Mordecai. He's the one who discovers the plans the bad people have against the Jews. And then there's the meanest of all — that's Haman. He had a little less power than the king, and he wanted to get rid of Mordecai and all the Jews.

THE BEST PART

The part we like best is where it says, "For if you remain silent at this time, relief and deliverance for the Jews will arise from another place, but you and your father's family will perish. And who knows but that you have come to your royal position for such a time as this?" (4:14).

Queen Vashti Deposed

1 This is what happened during the time of Xerxes,[a] the Xerxes who ruled over 127 provinces stretching from India to Cush[b]: ²At that time King Xerxes reigned from his royal throne in the citadel of Susa, ³and in the third year of his reign he gave a banquet for all his nobles and officials. The military leaders of Persia and Media, the princes, and the nobles of the provinces were present.

⁴For a full 180 days he displayed the vast wealth of his kingdom and the splendor and glory of his majesty. ⁵When these

---

a 1 Hebrew *Ahasuerus*; here and throughout Esther
b 1 That is, the upper Nile region

days were over, the king gave a banquet, lasting seven days, in the enclosed garden of the king's palace, for all the people from the least to the greatest who were in the citadel of Susa. ⁶The garden had hangings of white and blue linen, fastened with cords of white linen and purple material to silver rings on marble pillars. There were couches of gold and silver on a mosaic pavement of porphyry, marble, mother-of-pearl and other costly stones. ⁷Wine was served in goblets of gold, each one different from the other, and the royal wine was abundant, in keeping with the

SUSA

(ESTHER 1:2)

This was the capital of Persia, so it was the most important city and where the king and members of the court lived. Babylonia was in the land that is now called Iraq.

THE
WITNESSES

✓ XERXES (ESTHER 1:1)
Xerxes was a great warrior. He was crowned king of Persia in the year 485 before Christ. He challenged many powerful countries and won many victories. However, when he fought the Greeks, they tricked him and he lost this famous battle called the Battle of Salamis.

king's liberality. ⁸By the king's command each guest was allowed to drink with no restrictions, for the king instructed all the wine stewards to serve each man what he wished.

⁹Queen Vashti also gave a banquet for the women in the royal palace of King Xerxes.

¹⁰On the seventh day, when King Xerxes was in high spirits from wine, he commanded the seven eunuchs who served him—Mehuman, Biztha, Harbona, Bigtha, Abagtha, Zethar and Karkas— ¹¹to bring before him Queen Vashti, wearing her royal crown, in order to display her beauty to the people and nobles, for she was lovely to look at. ¹²But when the attendants delivered the king's command, Queen Vashti refused to come. Then the king became furious and burned with anger.

¹³Since it was customary for the king to consult experts in matters of law and

THE SCENE

PERSIA

(ESTHER 1:3)

This country doesn't exist now, because many years have passed and it has disappeared! It was in the place now called Iran. Persia was a little country at first. Then it grew to be very big, and was the richest country in the world.

justice, he spoke with the wise men who understood the times ¹⁴and were closest to the king—Karshena, Shethar, Admatha, Tarshish, Meres, Marsena and Memukan, the seven nobles of Persia and Media who had special access to the king and were highest in the kingdom.

¹⁵"According to law, what must be done to Queen Vashti?" he asked. "She has not obeyed the command of King Xerxes that the eunuchs have taken to her."

¹⁶Then Memukan replied in the presence of the king and the nobles, "Queen Vashti has done wrong, not only against the king but also against all the nobles and the peoples of all the provinces of King Xerxes. ¹⁷For the queen's conduct will become known to all the women, and so they will despise their husbands and say, 'King Xerxes commanded Queen

Vashti to be brought before him, but she would not come.' ¹⁸This very day the Persian and Median women of the nobility who have heard about the queen's conduct will respond to all the king's nobles in the same way. There will be no end of disrespect and discord.

¹⁹"Therefore, if it pleases the king, let him issue a royal decree and let it be written in the laws of Persia and Media, which cannot be repealed, that Vashti is never again to enter the presence of King Xerxes. Also let the king give her royal position to someone else who is better than she. ²⁰Then when the king's edict is proclaimed throughout all his vast realm, all the women will respect their husbands, from the least to the greatest."

²¹The king and his nobles were pleased with this advice, so the king did as Memukan proposed. ²²He sent dispatches to all parts of the kingdom, to each province in its own script and to each people in their own language, proclaiming that every man should be ruler over his own household, using his native tongue.

Esther Made Queen

2 Later when King Xerxes' fury had subsided, he remembered Vashti and what she had done and what he had decreed about her. ²Then the king's personal attendants proposed, "Let a search be made for beautiful young virgins for the king. ³Let the king appoint commissioners in every province of his realm to bring all these beautiful young women into the harem at the citadel of Susa. Let them be placed under the care of Hegai, the king's eunuch, who is in charge of the women; and let beauty treatments be given to them. ⁴Then let the young woman who pleases the king be queen instead of Vashti." This advice appealed to the king, and he followed it.

⁵Now there was in the citadel of Susa a Jew of the tribe of Benjamin, named Mordecai son of Jair, the son of Shimei, the son of Kish, ⁶who had been carried into exile from Jerusalem by Nebuchadnezzar king of Babylon, among those taken captive with Jehoiachin*ᵃ* king of Judah.

ᵃ 6 Hebrew Jeconiah, a variant of Jehoiachin

⁷Mordecai had a cousin named Hadassah, whom he had brought up because she had neither father nor mother. This young woman, who was also known as Esther, had a lovely figure and was beautiful. Mordecai had taken her as his own daughter when her father and mother died.

⁸When the king's order and edict had been proclaimed, many young women were brought to the citadel of Susa and put under the care of Hegai. Esther also was taken to the king's palace and entrusted to Hegai, who had charge of the harem. ⁹She pleased him and won his favor. Immediately he provided her with her beauty treatments and special food. He assigned to her seven female attendants selected from the king's palace and moved her and her attendants into the best place in the harem.

¹⁰Esther had not revealed her nationality and family background, because Mordecai had forbidden her to do so. ¹¹Every day he walked back and forth near the courtyard of the harem to find out how Esther was and what was happening to her.

¹²Before a young woman's turn came to go in to King Xerxes, she had to complete twelve months of beauty treatments prescribed for the women, six months with oil of myrrh and six with perfumes and

THE
WITNESSES

✓ MORDECAI (ESTHER 2:5)
This was a common man's name. We aren't sure what this name means, but it is similar to the name of a Babylonian god, Marduk. This Mordecai was the son of Jair, of the tribe of Benjamin.

✓ ESTHER (ESTHER 2:7)
This name has been changed. The name Esther comes from the Persian name *Ishtar*, which means "star." Esther's real name in Hebrew was *Hadasshah*, which means "myrrh." Myrrh is a small tree.

BREAKTHROUGH!

Myrrh
(ESTHER 2:12)
This is a plant. In the old days, they used it to make mummies — in other words, to preserve dead bodies. They also used it to make their clothes smell good, and they put it in body oil.

BREAKTHROUGH!

Tebeth

(ESTHER 2:16)

This is the name of the tenth month in Hebrew. It starts in the middle of December and ends in the middle of January. These are winter months.

cosmetics. ¹³And this is how she would go to the king: Anything she wanted was given her to take with her from the harem to the king's palace. ¹⁴In the evening she would go there and in the morning return to another part of the harem to the care of Shaashgaz, the king's eunuch who was in charge of the concubines. She would not return to the king unless he was pleased with her and summoned her by name.

¹⁵When the turn came for Esther (the young woman Mordecai had adopted, the daughter of his uncle Abihail) to go to the king, she asked for nothing other than what Hegai, the king's eunuch who was in charge of the harem, suggested. And Esther won the favor of everyone who saw her. ¹⁶She was taken to King Xerxes in the royal residence in the tenth month, the month of Tebeth, in the seventh year of his reign.

¹⁷Now the king was attracted to Esther more than to any of the other women, and she won his favor and approval more than any of the other virgins. So he set a royal crown on her head and made her queen instead of Vashti. ¹⁸And the king gave a great banquet, Esther's banquet, for all his nobles and officials. He proclaimed a holiday throughout the provinces and distributed gifts with royal liberality.

Mordecai Uncovers a Conspiracy

¹⁹When the virgins were assembled a second time, Mordecai was sitting at the king's gate. ²⁰But Esther had kept secret her family background and nationality just as Mordecai had told her to do, for she continued to follow Mordecai's instructions as she had done when he was bringing her up.

²¹During the time Mordecai was sitting at the king's gate, Bigthana[a] and Teresh, two of the king's officers who guarded the doorway, became angry and conspired to assassinate King Xerxes. ²²But Mordecai found out about the plot and told Queen Esther, who in turn reported it to the king, giving credit to Mordecai. ²³And when the report was investigated and found to be true, the two officials were impaled on poles. All this was recorded in the book of the annals in the presence of the king.

Haman's Plot to Destroy the Jews

3 After these events, King Xerxes honored Haman son of Hammedatha, the Agagite, elevating him and giving him a seat of honor higher than that of all the other nobles. ²All the royal officials at the king's gate knelt down and paid honor to Haman, for the king had commanded this concerning him. But Mordecai would not kneel down or pay him honor.

³Then the royal officials at the king's gate asked Mordecai, "Why do you disobey the king's command?" ⁴Day after day they spoke to him but he refused to comply. Therefore they told Haman about it to see whether Mordecai's behavior would be tolerated, for he had told them he was a Jew.

⁵When Haman saw that Mordecai would not kneel down or pay him honor, he was enraged. ⁶Yet having learned who Mordecai's people were, he scorned the

---

a 21 Hebrew *Bigthan,* a variant of *Bigthana*

idea of killing only Mordecai. Instead Haman looked for a way to destroy all Mordecai's people, the Jews, throughout the whole kingdom of Xerxes.

⁷In the twelfth year of King Xerxes, in the first month, the month of Nisan, the *pur* (that is, the lot) was cast in the presence of Haman to select a day and month. And the lot fell on*ᵃ* the twelfth month, the month of Adar.

⁸Then Haman said to King Xerxes, "There is a certain people dispersed among the peoples in all the provinces of your kingdom who keep themselves separate. Their customs are different from those of all other people, and they do not obey the king's laws; it is not in the king's best interest to tolerate them. ⁹If it pleases the king, let a decree be issued to destroy them, and I will give ten thousand talents*ᵇ* of silver to the king's administrators for the royal treasury."

¹⁰So the king took his signet ring from his finger and gave it to Haman son of Hammedatha, the Agagite, the enemy of the Jews. ¹¹"Keep the money," the king

BREAK THROUGH!

Signet ring
(ESTHER 3:10)

A very long time ago, important people like kings would wear a ring that had a design nobody else had. So when the king wanted people to know that a paper was really from him, he would put a little dab of colored wax on it and then he would place the design of the ring on the soft wax. When the wax dried, it was marked. Done! It was like a signature back then.

said to Haman, "and do with the people as you please."

¹²Then on the thirteenth day of the first month the royal secretaries were summoned. They wrote out in the script of each province and in the language of each people all Haman's orders to the king's satraps, the governors of the various provinces and the nobles of the various peoples. These were written in the name of King Xerxes himself and sealed with his own ring. ¹³Dispatches were sent by couriers to all the king's provinces with the order to destroy, kill and annihilate all the Jews—young and old, women and children—on a single day, the thirteenth day of the twelfth month, the month of

BREAK THROUGH!

Nisan
(ESTHER 3:7)

It's the first month of the Jewish lunar calendar. In our solar calendar, that's from the middle of March to the middle of April.

ᵃ 7 Septuagint; Hebrew does not have *And the lot fell on.*
ᵇ 9 That is, about 375 tons or about 340 metric tons

BREAKTHROUGH!

Edict
(ESTHER 3:14)

This is like when a teacher or the principal of a school tells us to do something. The difference is that this is written, and we have to do it no matter what. It's like the laws of a country—if you don't obey, you get sent to jail.

Adar, and to plunder their goods. ¹⁴A copy of the text of the edict was to be issued as law in every province and made known to the people of every nationality so they would be ready for that day.

¹⁵The couriers went out, spurred on by the king's command, and the edict was issued in the citadel of Susa. The king and Haman sat down to drink, but the city of Susa was bewildered.

Mordecai Persuades Esther to Help

4 When Mordecai learned of all that had been done, he tore his clothes, put on sackcloth and ashes, and went out into the city, wailing loudly and bitterly. ²But he went only as far as the king's gate, because no one clothed in sackcloth was allowed to enter it. ³In every province to which the edict and order of the king came, there was great mourning among the Jews, with fasting, weeping and wailing. Many lay in sackcloth and ashes.

⁴When Esther's eunuchs and female attendants came and told her about Mordecai, she was in great distress. She sent clothes for him to put on instead of his sackcloth, but he would not accept them. ⁵Then Esther summoned Hathak, one of the king's eunuchs assigned to attend her, and ordered him to find out what was troubling Mordecai and why.

⁶So Hathak went out to Mordecai in the open square of the city in front of the king's gate. ⁷Mordecai told him everything that had happened to him, including the exact amount of money Haman had promised to pay into the royal treasury for the destruction of the Jews. ⁸He also gave him a copy of the text of the edict for their annihilation, which had been published in Susa, to show to Esther and explain it to her, and he told him to instruct her to go into the king's presence to beg for mercy and plead with him for her people.

BREAKTHROUGH!

Sackcloth
(ESTHER 4:1)

This was a course fabric so rough, it scratched and hurt. It was worn in Bible times to ask God's forgiveness for some sin or as a way of stating regret in a difficult situation.

BREAKTHROUGH!

Ashes on the head

(ESTHER 4:1)

How strange! Sprinkling dirt or ashes on the head was a way people in the Bible used to show they were sad. It seems they took a little bit of dirt or something like that and rubbed it on their heads or through their beards. Then people would notice this and know they were sad.

⁹Hathak went back and reported to Esther what Mordecai had said. ¹⁰Then she instructed him to say to Mordecai, ¹¹"All the king's officials and the people of the royal provinces know that for any man or woman who approaches the king in the inner court without being summoned the king has but one law: that they be put to death unless the king extends the gold scepter to them and spares their lives. But thirty days have passed since I was called to go to the king."

¹²When Esther's words were reported to Mordecai, ¹³he sent back this answer: "Do not think that because you are in the king's house you alone of all the Jews will escape. ¹⁴For if you remain silent at this time, relief and deliverance for the Jews will arise from another place, but you and your father's family will perish. And who knows but that you have come to your royal position for such a time as this?"

¹⁵Then Esther sent this reply to Mordecai: ¹⁶"Go, gather together all the Jews who are in Susa, and fast for me. Do not eat or drink for three days, night or day. I and my attendants will fast as you do. When this is done, I will go to the king, even though it is against the law. And if I perish, I perish."

¹⁷So Mordecai went away and carried out all of Esther's instructions.

Esther's Request to the King

5 On the third day Esther put on her royal robes and stood in the inner court of the palace, in front of the king's hall. The king was sitting on his royal throne in the hall, facing the entrance. ²When he saw Queen Esther standing in the court, he was pleased with her and held out to her the gold scepter that was in his hand. So Esther approached and touched the tip of the scepter.

BREAKTHROUGH!

Fasting

(ESTHER 4:16)

In the Bible, fasting means not eating in order to ask God from the bottom of your heart for something you need or want. And just fasting isn't enough. We also have to pray so that God will hear us. In Bible times, people prayed and fasted a lot.

Scepter

(ESTHER 5:2)

This is like a cane, but it's made of gold and colored precious stones that are very expensive. Only the king can use it.

³Then the king asked, "What is it, Queen Esther? What is your request? Even up to half the kingdom, it will be given you."

⁴"If it pleases the king," replied Esther, "let the king, together with Haman, come today to a banquet I have prepared for him."

⁵"Bring Haman at once," the king said, "so that we may do what Esther asks."

So the king and Haman went to the banquet Esther had prepared. ⁶As they were drinking wine, the king again asked Esther, "Now what is your petition? It will be given you. And what is your request? Even up to half the kingdom, it will be granted."

⁷Esther replied, "My petition and my request is this: ⁸If the king regards me with favor and if it pleases the king to grant my petition and fulfill my request, let the king and Haman come tomorrow to the banquet I will prepare for them. Then I will answer the king's question."

Haman's Rage Against Mordecai

⁹Haman went out that day happy and in high spirits. But when he saw Mordecai

at the king's gate and observed that he neither rose nor showed fear in his presence, he was filled with rage against Mordecai. ¹⁰Nevertheless, Haman restrained himself and went home.

Calling together his friends and Zeresh, his wife, ¹¹Haman boasted to them about his vast wealth, his many sons, and all the ways the king had honored him and how he had elevated him above the other nobles and officials. ¹²"And that's not all," Haman added. "I'm the only person Queen Esther invited to accompany the king to the banquet she gave. And she has invited me along with the king tomorrow. ¹³But all this gives me no satisfaction as long as I see that Jew Mordecai sitting at the king's gate."

¹⁴His wife Zeresh and all his friends said to him, "Have a pole set up, reaching to a height of fifty cubits,ᵃ and ask the king in the morning to have Mordecai impaled on it. Then go with the king to the banquet and enjoy yourself." This suggestion delighted Haman, and he had the pole set up.

Mordecai Honored

6 That night the king could not sleep; so he ordered the book of the chronicles, the record of his reign, to be brought in and read to him. ²It was found recorded there that Mordecai had exposed Bigthana and Teresh, two of the king's officers who guarded the doorway, who had conspired to assassinate King Xerxes.

³"What honor and recognition has Mordecai received for this?" the king asked.

"Nothing has been done for him," his attendants answered.

⁴The king said, "Who is in the court?" Now Haman had just entered the outer court of the palace to speak to the king about impaling Mordecai on the pole he had set up for him.

⁵His attendants answered, "Haman is standing in the court."

"Bring him in," the king ordered.

⁶When Haman entered, the king asked him, "What should be done for the man the king delights to honor?"

ᵃ 14 That is, about 75 feet or about 23 meters

Now Haman thought to himself, "Who is there that the king would rather honor than me?" [7]So he answered the king, "For the man the king delights to honor, [8]have them bring a royal robe the king has worn and a horse the king has ridden, one with a royal crest placed on its head. [9]Then let the robe and horse be entrusted to one of the king's most noble princes. Let them robe the man the king delights to honor, and lead him on the horse through the city streets, proclaiming before him, 'This is what is done for the man the king delights to honor!' "

[10]"Go at once," the king commanded Haman. "Get the robe and the horse and do just as you have suggested for Mordecai the Jew, who sits at the king's gate. Do not neglect anything you have recommended."

[11]So Haman got the robe and the horse. He robed Mordecai, and led him on horseback through the city streets, proclaiming before him, "This is what is done for the man the king delights to honor!"

[12]Afterward Mordecai returned to the king's gate. But Haman rushed home, with his head covered in grief, [13]and told Zeresh his wife and all his friends everything that had happened to him.

His advisers and his wife Zeresh said to him, "Since Mordecai, before whom your downfall has started, is of Jewish origin, you cannot stand against him—you will surely come to ruin!" [14]While they were still talking with him, the king's eunuchs arrived and hurried Haman away to the banquet Esther had prepared.

Haman Impaled

7 So the king and Haman went to Queen Esther's banquet, [2]and as they were drinking wine on the second day, the king again asked, "Queen Esther, what is your petition? It will be given you. What is your request? Even up to half the kingdom, it will be granted."

[3]Then Queen Esther answered, "If I have found favor with you, Your Majesty, and if it pleases you, grant me my life— this is my petition. And spare my people— this is my request. [4]For I and my people have been sold to be destroyed, killed and annihilated. If we had merely been sold as male and female slaves, I would have kept quiet, because no such distress would justify disturbing the king.[a]"

[5]King Xerxes asked Queen Esther, "Who is he? Where is he—the man who has dared to do such a thing?"

[6]Esther said, "An adversary and enemy! This vile Haman!"

Then Haman was terrified before the king and queen. [7]The king got up in a rage, left his wine and went out into the palace garden. But Haman, realizing that the king had already decided his fate, stayed behind to beg Queen Esther for his life.

[8]Just as the king returned from the palace garden to the banquet hall, Haman was falling on the couch where Esther was reclining.

The king exclaimed, "Will he even molest the queen while she is with me in the house?"

As soon as the word left the king's mouth, they covered Haman's face. [9]Then Harbona, one of the eunuchs attending the king, said, "A pole reaching to a height of fifty cubits[b] stands by Haman's house. He had it set up for Mordecai, who spoke up to help the king."

The king said, "Impale him on it!" [10]So they impaled Haman on the pole he had set up for Mordecai. Then the king's fury subsided.

The King's Edict in Behalf of the Jews

8 That same day King Xerxes gave Queen Esther the estate of Haman, the enemy of the Jews. And Mordecai came into the presence of the king, for Esther had told how he was related to her. [2]The king took off his signet ring, which he had reclaimed from Haman, and presented it to Mordecai. And Esther appointed him over Haman's estate.

[3]Esther again pleaded with the king, falling at his feet and weeping. She begged him to put an end to the evil plan of Haman the Agagite, which he had devised against the Jews. [4]Then the king

---

[a] 4 Or quiet, but the compensation our adversary offers cannot be compared with the loss the king would suffer
[b] 9 That is, about 75 feet or about 23 meters

extended the gold scepter to Esther and she arose and stood before him.

⁵"If it pleases the king," she said, "and if he regards me with favor and thinks it the right thing to do, and if he is pleased with me, let an order be written overruling the dispatches that Haman son of Hammedatha, the Agagite, devised and wrote to destroy the Jews in all the king's provinces. ⁶For how can I bear to see disaster fall on my people? How can I bear to see the destruction of my family?"

⁷King Xerxes replied to Queen Esther and to Mordecai the Jew, "Because Haman attacked the Jews, I have given his estate to Esther, and they have impaled him on the pole he set up. ⁸Now write another decree in the king's name in behalf of the Jews as seems best to you, and seal it with the king's signet ring—for no document written in the king's name and sealed with his ring can be revoked."

⁹At once the royal secretaries were summoned—on the twenty-third day of the third month, the month of Sivan. They wrote out all Mordecai's orders to the

BREAKTHROUGH!

Sivan

(ESTHER 8:9)

This is the third month in the Jewish calendar. It's something like May or June for us. In the Middle East, this month is in the spring.

THE SCENE

CUSH

(ESTHER 8:9)

Also called Ethiopia. This country still exists today, but in Esther's time it was larger than it is now. It's in Africa. Since it rains a lot there, the land is fertile and many different crops are grown there.

Jews, and to the satraps, governors and nobles of the 127 provinces stretching from India to Cush.ᵃ These orders were written in the script of each province and the language of each people and also to the Jews in their own script and language. ¹⁰Mordecai wrote in the name of King Xerxes, sealed the dispatches with the king's signet ring, and sent them by mounted couriers, who rode fast horses especially bred for the king.

¹¹The king's edict granted the Jews in every city the right to assemble and protect themselves; to destroy, kill and annihilate the armed men of any nationality or province who might attack them and their women and children,ᵇ and to plunder the property of their enemies. ¹²The

ᵃ 9 That is, the upper Nile region   ᵇ 11 Or province, together with their women and children, who might attack them;

day appointed for the Jews to do this in all the provinces of King Xerxes was the thirteenth day of the twelfth month, the month of Adar. ¹³A copy of the text of the edict was to be issued as law in every province and made known to the people of every nationality so that the Jews would be ready on that day to avenge themselves on their enemies.

¹⁴The couriers, riding the royal horses, went out, spurred on by the king's command, and the edict was issued in the citadel of Susa.

The Triumph of the Jews

¹⁵When Mordecai left the king's presence, he was wearing royal garments of blue and white, a large crown of gold and a purple robe of fine linen. And the city of Susa held a joyous celebration. ¹⁶For the Jews it was a time of happiness and joy, gladness and honor. ¹⁷In every province and in every city to which the edict of the king came, there was joy and gladness among the Jews, with feasting and celebrating. And many people of other nationalities became Jews because fear of the Jews had seized them.

9 On the thirteenth day of the twelfth month, the month of Adar, the edict commanded by the king was to be carried out. On this day the enemies of the Jews had hoped to overpower them, but now the tables were turned and the Jews got the upper hand over those who hated them. ²The Jews assembled in their cities in all the provinces of King Xerxes to attack those determined to destroy them. No one could stand against them, because the people of all the other nationalities were afraid of them. ³And all the nobles of the provinces, the satraps, the governors and the king's administrators helped the Jews, because fear of Mordecai had seized them. ⁴Mordecai was prominent in the palace; his reputation spread throughout the provinces, and he became more and more powerful.

⁵The Jews struck down all their enemies with the sword, killing and destroying them, and they did what they pleased to those who hated them. ⁶In the citadel of Susa, the Jews killed and destroyed five

BREAKTHROUGH!

Adar
(ESTHER 9:1)

This is the name of a month that has 29 days. It's pretty much like February or March, but it's the last month of the year in the Jewish calendar. In Bible lands, it's in the winter and it's very cold.

hundred men. ⁷They also killed Parshandatha, Dalphon, Aspatha, ⁸Poratha, Adalia, Aridatha, ⁹Parmashta, Arisai, Aridai and Vaizatha, ¹⁰the ten sons of Haman son of Hammedatha, the enemy of the Jews. But they did not lay their hands on the plunder.

¹¹The number of those killed in the citadel of Susa was reported to the king that same day. ¹²The king said to Queen Esther, "The Jews have killed and destroyed five hundred men and the ten sons of Haman in the citadel of Susa. What have they done in the rest of the king's provinces? Now what is your petition? It will be given you. What is your request? It will also be granted."

¹³"If it pleases the king," Esther answered, "give the Jews in Susa permission to carry out this day's edict tomorrow also, and let Haman's ten sons be impaled on poles."

¹⁴So the king commanded that this be done. An edict was issued in Susa, and they impaled the ten sons of Haman.

¹⁵The Jews in Susa came together on the fourteenth day of the month of Adar, and they put to death in Susa three hundred men, but they did not lay their hands on the plunder.

¹⁶Meanwhile, the remainder of the Jews who were in the king's provinces also assembled to protect themselves and get relief from their enemies. They killed seventy-five thousand of them but did not lay their hands on the plunder. ¹⁷This happened on the thirteenth day of the month of Adar, and on the fourteenth they rested and made it a day of feasting and joy.

¹⁸The Jews in Susa, however, had assembled on the thirteenth and fourteenth, and then on the fifteenth they rested and made it a day of feasting and joy.

¹⁹That is why rural Jews—those living in villages—observe the fourteenth of the month of Adar as a day of joy and feasting, a day for giving presents to each other.

CHECK THE FACTS

What is celebrated during the Purim Festival?

A) The beginning of spring

B) The freeing of the exiled Jews from their enemies

C) That the king lowered the taxes

CORRECT ANSWER: B

BREAKTHROUGH!

Purim

(ESTHER 9:20-32)

Purim is a celebration that lasts two days during the winter every year, because it's exactly the 14th and 15th of Adar, when it's cold. It's really to celebrate that Esther helped her friends and that God saved the Jews from Haman's plans to kill all of them. This festival was so important that they couldn't forget to celebrate it, and they gave gifts to each other too. How nice!

Purim Established

²⁰Mordecai recorded these events, and he sent letters to all the Jews throughout the provinces of King Xerxes, near and far, ²¹to have them celebrate annually the fourteenth and fifteenth days of the month of Adar ²²as the time when the Jews got relief from their enemies, and as the month when their sorrow was turned into joy and their mourning into a day of celebration. He wrote them to observe the days as days of feasting and joy and giving presents of food to one another and gifts to the poor.

²³So the Jews agreed to continue the celebration they had begun, doing what Mordecai had written to them. ²⁴For Haman son of Hammedatha, the Agagite, the enemy of all the Jews, had plotted

against the Jews to destroy them and had cast the *pur* (that is, the lot) for their ruin and destruction. ²⁵But when the plot came to the king's attention,ᵃ he issued written orders that the evil scheme Haman had devised against the Jews should come back onto his own head, and that he and his sons should be impaled on poles. ²⁶(Therefore these days were called Purim, from the word *pur*.) Because of everything written in this letter and because of what they had seen and what had happened to them, ²⁷the Jews took it on themselves to establish the custom that they and their descendants and all who join them should without fail observe these two days every year, in the way prescribed and at the time appointed. ²⁸These days should be remembered and observed in every generation by every family, and in every province and in every city. And these days of Purim should never fail to be celebrated by the Jews—nor should the memory of these days die out among their descendants.

²⁹So Queen Esther, daughter of Abihail, along with Mordecai the Jew, wrote with full authority to confirm this second letter concerning Purim. ³⁰And Mordecai sent letters to all the Jews in the 127 provinces of Xerxes' kingdom—words of goodwill and assurance— ³¹to establish these days of Purim at their designated times, as Mordecai the Jew and Queen Esther had decreed for them, and as they had established for themselves and their descendants in regard to their times of fasting and lamentation. ³²Esther's decree confirmed these regulations about Purim, and it was written down in the records.

The Greatness of Mordecai

10 King Xerxes imposed tribute throughout the empire, to its distant shores. ²And all his acts of power and might, together with a full account of the greatness of Mordecai, whom the king had promoted, are they not written in the book of the annals of the kings of Media and Persia? ³Mordecai the Jew was second in rank to King Xerxes, preeminent among the Jews, and held in high esteem by his many fellow Jews, because he worked for the good of his people and spoke up for the welfare of all the Jews.

ᵃ 25 Or *when Esther came before the king*

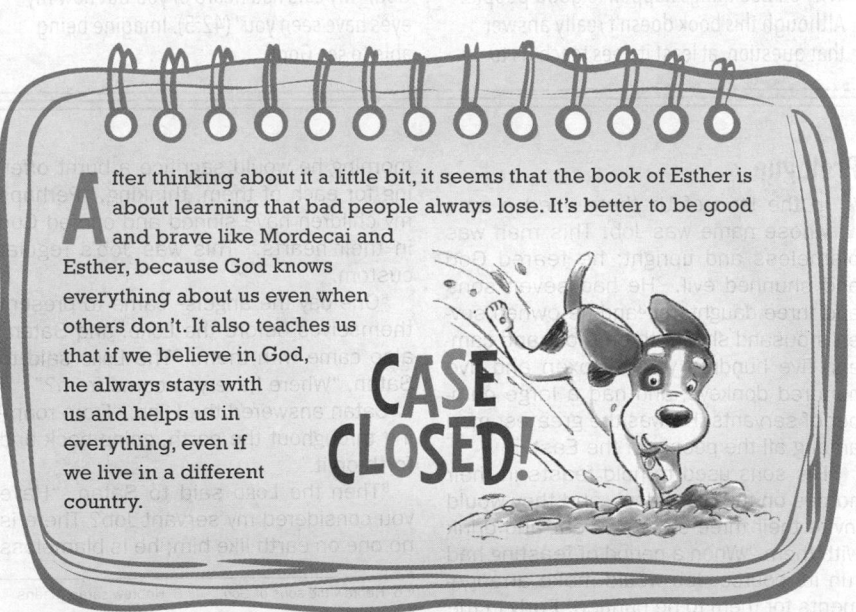

After thinking about it a little bit, it seems that the book of Esther is about learning that bad people always lose. It's better to be good and brave like Mordecai and Esther, because God knows everything about us even when others don't. It also teaches us that if we believe in God, he always stays with us and helps us in everything, even if we live in a different country.

CASE CLOSED!

JOB

THE EVIDENCE:

WHO WROTE IT?
This book has the name of one of its characters — the main one — but it was probably written, and maybe even rewritten, by other people at different times.

HOW LONG AGO?
There's no exact date, but it certainly was written a long time ago. Although it talks about things that happened before Moses' time, many Bible experts say it was written in the 500s before Christ.

WHAT'S IT ABOUT?
It's about something hard to understand: Why do bad things happen to good people? Although this book doesn't really answer that question, at least it does teach us to always trust God, and that God will reward our trust in him.

THE BEST PART
The most exciting part is when Job says to God, "My ears had heard of you but now my eyes have seen you" (42:5). Imagine being able to see God!

Prologue

1 In the land of Uz there lived a man whose name was Job. This man was blameless and upright; he feared God and shunned evil. ²He had seven sons and three daughters, ³and he owned seven thousand sheep, three thousand camels, five hundred yoke of oxen and five hundred donkeys, and had a large number of servants. He was the greatest man among all the people of the East.

⁴His sons used to hold feasts in their homes on their birthdays, and they would invite their three sisters to eat and drink with them. ⁵When a period of feasting had run its course, Job would make arrangements for them to be purified. Early in the morning he would sacrifice a burnt offering for each of them, thinking, "Perhaps my children have sinned and cursed God in their hearts." This was Job's regular custom.

⁶One day the angels[a] came to present themselves before the LORD, and Satan[b] also came with them. ⁷The LORD said to Satan, "Where have you come from?"

Satan answered the LORD, "From roaming throughout the earth, going back and forth on it."

⁸Then the LORD said to Satan, "Have you considered my servant Job? There is no one on earth like him; he is blameless

---

a 6 Hebrew *the sons of God*   *b* 6 Hebrew *satan* means *adversary.*

¹³One day when Job's sons and daughters were feasting and drinking wine at the oldest brother's house, ¹⁴a messenger came to Job and said, "The oxen were plowing and the donkeys were grazing nearby, ¹⁵and the Sabeans attacked and made off with them. They put the servants to the sword, and I am the only one who has escaped to tell you!"

¹⁶While he was still speaking, another messenger came and said, "The fire of God fell from the heavens and burned up the sheep and the servants, and I am the only one who has escaped to tell you!"

¹⁷While he was still speaking, another messenger came and said, "The Chaldeans formed three raiding parties and swept down on your camels and made off

THE
WITNESSES

✓ JOB (JOB 1:1)

Job is the good guy of this book. The meaning of his name isn't clear. Some people say it means "enemy" or "persecuted." Others say it's "he who supports problems."

and upright, a man who fears God and shuns evil."

⁹"Does Job fear God for nothing?" Satan replied. ¹⁰"Have you not put a hedge around him and his household and everything he has? You have blessed the work of his hands, so that his flocks and herds are spread throughout the land. ¹¹But now stretch out your hand and strike everything he has, and he will surely curse you to your face."

¹²The LORD said to Satan, "Very well, then, everything he has is in your power, but on the man himself do not lay a finger."

Then Satan went out from the presence of the LORD.

BREAKTHROUGH!

The angels and Satan
(JOB 1:6)

The words translated as *angels* and *Satan* were related to the Hebrew word for Satan, the word we get "Satan" from. But this really isn't talking about the devil the way we understand him. The Hebrews thought that God was in heaven, surrounded by angels. One of them was an angel that was always contradicting God. When this angel saw that God thought Job was very good, the angel decided to show that God was wrong.

with them. They put the servants to the sword, and I am the only one who has escaped to tell you!"

¹⁸While he was still speaking, yet another messenger came and said, "Your sons and daughters were feasting and drinking wine at the oldest brother's house, ¹⁹when suddenly a mighty wind swept in from the desert and struck the four corners of the house. It collapsed on them and they are dead, and I am the only one who has escaped to tell you!"

²⁰At this, Job got up and tore his robe and shaved his head. Then he fell to the ground in worship ²¹and said:

> "Naked I came from my mother's
> 　　womb,
> 　and naked I will depart.ᵃ
> The LORD gave and the LORD has taken
> 　　away;
> 　may the name of the LORD be
> 　　praised."

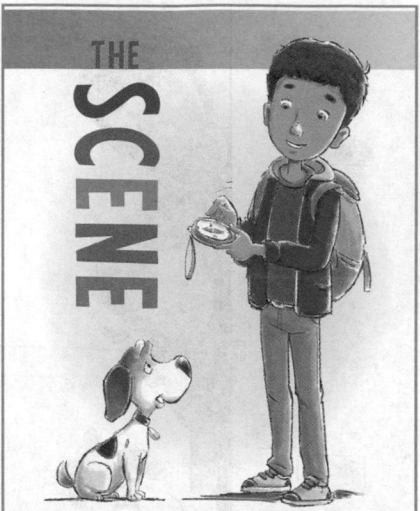

THE SCENE

CHALDEA

(JOB 1:17)

A region in ancient Mesopotamia where the Neo-Babylonian empire began. The people who lived there, the Chaldeans, were famous magicians and fortune tellers.

²²In all this, Job did not sin by charging God with wrongdoing.

2 On another day the angelsᵇ came to present themselves before the LORD, and Satan also came with them to present himself before him. ²And the LORD said to Satan, "Where have you come from?"

Satan answered the LORD, "From roaming throughout the earth, going back and forth on it."

³Then the LORD said to Satan, "Have you considered my servant Job? There is no one on earth like him; he is blameless and upright, a man who fears God and shuns evil. And he still maintains his integrity, though you incited me against him to ruin him without any reason."

⁴"Skin for skin!" Satan replied. "A man will give all he has for his own life. ⁵But

BREAKTHROUGH!

Why did God let the accuser (Satan) do what he wanted?

(JOB 1:12; 2:6)

We might say that God is very "democratic," and he respects everybody's opinion. He also wanted to show this angel that he was wrong about Job.

ᵃ 21 Or *will return there*　　ᵇ 1 Hebrew *the sons of God*

by agreement to go and sympathize with him and comfort him. 12When they saw him from a distance, they could hardly recognize him; they began to weep aloud, and they tore their robes and sprinkled dust on their heads. 13Then they sat on the ground with him for seven days and seven nights. No one said a word to him, because they saw how great his suffering was.

a 10 The Hebrew word rendered *foolish* denotes moral deficiency.

BREAKTHROUGH!

Why did God let this angel (Satan) kill Job's children?

(JOB 1:19)

To prove Job's goodness and patience.

now stretch out your hand and strike his flesh and bones, and he will surely curse you to your face."

6The LORD said to Satan, "Very well, then, he is in your hands; but you must spare his life."

7So Satan went out from the presence of the LORD and afflicted Job with painful sores from the soles of his feet to the crown of his head. 8Then Job took a piece of broken pottery and scraped himself with it as he sat among the ashes.

9His wife said to him, "Are you still maintaining your integrity? Curse God and die!"

10He replied, "You are talking like a foolish*a* woman. Shall we accept good from God, and not trouble?"

In all this, Job did not sin in what he said.

11When Job's three friends, Eliphaz the Temanite, Bildad the Shuhite and Zophar the Naamathite, heard about all the troubles that had come upon him, they set out from their homes and met together

THE WITNESSES

✓ **ELIPHAZ (JOB 2:11)**
One of Job's three friends. His name means "my god is gold."

✓ **BILDAD (JOB 2:11)**
Job's friend. His name means "son of Hadad."

✓ **ZOPHAR (JOB 2:11)**
Job's friend. His name means "little bird."

Job Speaks

3 After this, Job opened his mouth and cursed the day of his birth. ²He said:

³ "May the day of my birth perish,
   and the night that said, 'A boy is
      conceived!'
⁴ That day—may it turn to darkness;
   may God above not care about it;
   may no light shine on it.
⁵ May gloom and utter darkness claim it
      once more;
   may a cloud settle over it;
   may blackness overwhelm it.
⁶ That night—may thick darkness
      seize it;
   may it not be included among the
      days of the year
   nor be entered in any of the
      months.
⁷ May that night be barren;
   may no shout of joy be heard in it.
⁸ May those who curse days*ᵃ* curse that
      day,
   those who are ready to rouse
      Leviathan.
⁹ May its morning stars become dark;
   may it wait for daylight in vain
   and not see the first rays of dawn,
¹⁰ for it did not shut the doors of the
      womb on me
   to hide trouble from my eyes.

¹¹ "Why did I not perish at birth,
   and die as I came from the
      womb?
¹² Why were there knees to receive me
   and breasts that I might be
      nursed?
¹³ For now I would be lying down in
      peace;
   I would be asleep and at rest
¹⁴ with kings and rulers of the earth,
   who built for themselves places
      now lying in ruins,
¹⁵ with princes who had gold,
   who filled their houses with
      silver.
¹⁶ Or why was I not hidden away in the
      ground like a stillborn child,
   like an infant who never saw the
      light of day?
¹⁷ There the wicked cease from turmoil,
   and there the weary are at rest.

¹⁸ Captives also enjoy their ease;
   they no longer hear the slave
      driver's shout.
¹⁹ The small and the great are there,
   and the slaves are freed from their
      owners.

²⁰ "Why is light given to those in misery,
   and life to the bitter of soul,
²¹ to those who long for death that does
      not come,
   who search for it more than for
      hidden treasure,
²² who are filled with gladness
   and rejoice when they reach the
      grave?
²³ Why is life given to a man
   whose way is hidden,
   whom God has hedged in?
²⁴ For sighing has become my daily food;
   my groans pour out like water.
²⁵ What I feared has come upon me;
   what I dreaded has happened to me.
²⁶ I have no peace, no quietness;
   I have no rest, but only turmoil."

ᵃ 8 Or *curse the sea*

BREAKTHROUGH!

Leviathan
(JOB 3:8)

The Hebrews believed that there was a giant serpent in the ocean that stirred up the waves. They called that monster Leviathan.

Eliphaz

4 Then Eliphaz the Temanite replied:

2 "If someone ventures a word with you,
   will you be impatient?
   But who can keep from speaking?
3 Think how you have instructed many,
   how you have strengthened feeble
      hands.
4 Your words have supported those who
      stumbled;
   you have strengthened faltering
      knees.
5 But now trouble comes to you, and
      you are discouraged;
   it strikes you, and you are
      dismayed.
6 Should not your piety be your
      confidence
   and your blameless ways your
      hope?

7 "Consider now: Who, being innocent,
      has ever perished?
   Where were the upright ever
      destroyed?
8 As I have observed, those who plow
      evil
   and those who sow trouble reap it.
9 At the breath of God they perish;
   at the blast of his anger they are no
      more.
10 The lions may roar and growl,
   yet the teeth of the great lions are
      broken.
11 The lion perishes for lack of prey,
   and the cubs of the lioness are
      scattered.

12 "A word was secretly brought to me,
   my ears caught a whisper of it.
13 Amid disquieting dreams in the night,
   when deep sleep falls on people,
14 fear and trembling seized me
   and made all my bones shake.
15 A spirit glided past my face,
   and the hair on my body stood on
      end.
16 It stopped,
   but I could not tell what it was.
   A form stood before my eyes,
   and I heard a hushed voice:
17 'Can a mortal be more righteous than
      God?

Can even a strong man be more
      pure than his Maker?
18 If God places no trust in his servants,
   if he charges his angels with error,
19 how much more those who live in
      houses of clay,
   whose foundations are in the dust,
   who are crushed more readily than
      a moth!
20 Between dawn and dusk they are
      broken to pieces;
   unnoticed, they perish forever.
21 Are not the cords of their tent pulled
      up,
   so that they die without wisdom?'

5 "Call if you will, but who will answer
      you?
   To which of the holy ones will you
      turn?
2 Resentment kills a fool,
   and envy slays the simple.
3 I myself have seen a fool taking root,
   but suddenly his house was cursed.
4 His children are far from safety,
   crushed in court without a defender.
5 The hungry consume his harvest,
   taking it even from among thorns,
   and the thirsty pant after his wealth.
6 For hardship does not spring from the
      soil,
   nor does trouble sprout from the
      ground.
7 Yet man is born to trouble
   as surely as sparks fly upward.

8 "But if I were you, I would appeal to
      God;
   I would lay my cause before him.
9 He performs wonders that cannot be
      fathomed,
   miracles that cannot be counted.
10 He provides rain for the earth;
   he sends water on the countryside.
11 The lowly he sets on high,
   and those who mourn are lifted to
      safety.
12 He thwarts the plans of the crafty,
   so that their hands achieve no
      success.
13 He catches the wise in their
      craftiness,
   and the schemes of the wily are
      swept away.

¹⁴ Darkness comes upon them in the daytime;
  at noon they grope as in the night.
¹⁵ He saves the needy from the sword in their mouth;
  he saves them from the clutches of the powerful.
¹⁶ So the poor have hope,
  and injustice shuts its mouth.

¹⁷ "Blessed is the one whom God corrects;
  so do not despise the discipline of the Almighty.^a
¹⁸ For he wounds, but he also binds up;
  he injures, but his hands also heal.
¹⁹ From six calamities he will rescue you;
  in seven no harm will touch you.
²⁰ In famine he will deliver you from death,
  and in battle from the stroke of the sword.
²¹ You will be protected from the lash of the tongue,
  and need not fear when destruction comes.
²² You will laugh at destruction and famine,
  and need not fear the wild animals.
²³ For you will have a covenant with the stones of the field,
  and the wild animals will be at peace with you.
²⁴ You will know that your tent is secure;
  you will take stock of your property and find nothing missing.
²⁵ You will know that your children will be many,
  and your descendants like the grass of the earth.
²⁶ You will come to the grave in full vigor,
  like sheaves gathered in season.

²⁷ "We have examined this, and it is true.
  So hear it and apply it to yourself."

Job

6 Then Job replied:

² "If only my anguish could be weighed
  and all my misery be placed on the scales!
³ It would surely outweigh the sand of the seas—
  no wonder my words have been impetuous.
⁴ The arrows of the Almighty are in me,
  my spirit drinks in their poison;
  God's terrors are marshaled against me.
⁵ Does a wild donkey bray when it has grass,
  or an ox bellow when it has fodder?
⁶ Is tasteless food eaten without salt,
  or is there flavor in the sap of the mallow^b?
⁷ I refuse to touch it;
  such food makes me ill.

⁸ "Oh, that I might have my request,
  that God would grant what I hope for,
⁹ that God would be willing to crush me,
  to let loose his hand and cut off my life!

^a 17 Hebrew *Shaddai*; here and throughout Job   ^b 6 The meaning of the Hebrew for this phrase is uncertain.

BREAKTHROUGH!

Was it God or Satan who hurt Job?

(JOB 6:4)

It was Satan, but God let him do it. And Job didn't know that it was Satan who had hurt him.

TEMA

(JOB 6:18–21)

A region in northern Arabia that's famous because caravans that were crossing the desert had to stop in its oasis.

10 Then I would still have this
    consolation—
    my joy in unrelenting pain—
    that I had not denied the words of
    the Holy One.

11 "What strength do I have, that I should
    still hope?
    What prospects, that I should be
    patient?
12 Do I have the strength of stone?
    Is my flesh bronze?
13 Do I have any power to help myself,
    now that success has been driven
    from me?

14 "Anyone who withholds kindness from
    a friend
    forsakes the fear of the Almighty.
15 But my brothers are as undependable
    as intermittent streams,
    as the streams that overflow
16 when darkened by thawing ice
    and swollen with melting snow,

17 but that stop flowing in the dry
    season,
    and in the heat vanish from their
    channels.
18 Caravans turn aside from their routes;
    they go off into the wasteland and
    perish.
19 The caravans of Tema look for water,
    the traveling merchants of Sheba
    look in hope.
20 They are distressed, because they had
    been confident;
    they arrive there, only to be
    disappointed.
21 Now you too have proved to be of no
    help;
    you see something dreadful and are
    afraid.
22 Have I ever said, 'Give something on
    my behalf,
    pay a ransom for me from your
    wealth,

SHEBA

(JOB 6:19)

Territory in the south part of Arabia, where Sabeans live (1:15). They were known for their gold, spices, incense and gemstones.

23 deliver me from the hand of the
　　enemy,
　　　rescue me from the clutches of the
　　　　ruthless'?

24 "Teach me, and I will be quiet;
　　show me where I have been
　　　wrong.
25 How painful are honest words!
　　But what do your arguments
　　　prove?
26 Do you mean to correct what I say,
　　and treat my desperate words as
　　　wind?
27 You would even cast lots for the
　　fatherless
　　　and barter away your friend.

28 "But now be so kind as to look
　　at me.
　　　Would I lie to your face?
29 Relent, do not be unjust;
　　reconsider, for my integrity is at
　　　stake.*a*
30 Is there any wickedness on my lips?
　　Can my mouth not discern malice?

7 "Do not mortals have hard service on
　　earth?
　　　Are not their days like those of hired
　　　　laborers?
2 Like a slave longing for the evening
　　shadows,
　　　or a hired laborer waiting to be
　　　　paid,
3 so I have been allotted months of
　　futility,
　　　and nights of misery have been
　　　　assigned to me.
4 When I lie down I think, 'How long
　　before I get up?'
　　　The night drags on, and I toss and
　　　　turn until dawn.
5 My body is clothed with worms and
　　scabs,
　　　my skin is broken and festering.

6 "My days are swifter than a weaver's
　　shuttle,
　　　and they come to an end without
　　　　hope.
7 Remember, O God, that my life is but a
　　breath;
　　　my eyes will never see happiness
　　　　again.

8 The eye that now sees me will see me
　　no longer;
　　　you will look for me, but I will be no
　　　　more.
9 As a cloud vanishes and is gone,
　　so one who goes down to the grave
　　　does not return.
10 He will never come to his house
　　again;
　　　his place will know him no more.

11 "Therefore I will not keep silent;
　　I will speak out in the anguish of my
　　　spirit,
　　　I will complain in the bitterness of
　　　　my soul.
12 Am I the sea, or the monster of the
　　deep,
　　　that you put me under guard?
13 When I think my bed will comfort me
　　and my couch will ease my
　　　complaint,
14 even then you frighten me with
　　dreams
　　　and terrify me with visions,
15 so that I prefer strangling and death,
　　rather than this body of mine.
16 I despise my life; I would not live
　　forever.
　　　Let me alone; my days have no
　　　　meaning.

17 "What is mankind that you make so
　　much of them,
　　　that you give them so much
　　　　attention,
18 that you examine them every morning
　　and test them every moment?
19 Will you never look away from me,
　　or let me alone even for an instant?
20 If I have sinned, what have I done to
　　you,
　　　you who see everything we do?
　　Why have you made me your target?
　　Have I become a burden to you?*b*
21 Why do you not pardon my offenses
　　and forgive my sins?
　　For I will soon lie down in the dust;
　　　you will search for me, but I will be
　　　　no more."

---

a 29 Or *my righteousness still stands*　　*b* 20 A few
manuscripts of the Masoretic Text, an ancient Hebrew
scribal tradition and Septuagint; most manuscripts of the
Masoretic Text *I have become a burden to myself.*

Bildad

8 Then Bildad the Shuhite replied:

2 "How long will you say such things?
  Your words are a blustering wind.
3 Does God pervert justice?
  Does the Almighty pervert what is
    right?
4 When your children sinned against
    him,
  he gave them over to the penalty of
    their sin.
5 But if you will seek God earnestly
  and plead with the Almighty,
6 if you are pure and upright,
  even now he will rouse himself on
    your behalf
  and restore you to your prosperous
    state.
7 Your beginnings will seem humble,
  so prosperous will your future be.

8 "Ask the former generation
  and find out what their ancestors
    learned,
9 for we were born only yesterday and
    know nothing,
  and our days on earth are but a
    shadow.
10 Will they not instruct you and tell you?
  Will they not bring forth words from
    their understanding?
11 Can papyrus grow tall where there is
    no marsh?
  Can reeds thrive without water?
12 While still growing and uncut,
  they wither more quickly than grass.
13 Such is the destiny of all who forget
    God;
  so perishes the hope of the
    godless.
14 What they trust in is fragile*a*;
  what they rely on is a spider's web.
15 They lean on the web, but it gives way;
  they cling to it, but it does not hold.
16 They are like a well-watered plant in
    the sunshine,
  spreading its shoots over the
    garden;
17 it entwines its roots around a pile of
    rocks
  and looks for a place among the
    stones.

18 But when it is torn from its spot,
  that place disowns it and says, 'I
    never saw you.'
19 Surely its life withers away,
  and*b* from the soil other plants
    grow.

20 "Surely God does not reject one who
    is blameless
  or strengthen the hands of
    evildoers.
21 He will yet fill your mouth with
    laughter
  and your lips with shouts of joy.
22 Your enemies will be clothed in
    shame,
  and the tents of the wicked will be
    no more."

Job

9 Then Job replied:

2 "Indeed, I know that this is true.
  But how can mere mortals prove
    their innocence before God?
3 Though they wished to dispute with
    him,
  they could not answer him one time
    out of a thousand.
4 His wisdom is profound, his power is
    vast.
  Who has resisted him and come out
    unscathed?
5 He moves mountains without their
    knowing it
  and overturns them in his anger.
6 He shakes the earth from its place
  and makes its pillars tremble.
7 He speaks to the sun and it does not
    shine;
  he seals off the light of the stars.
8 He alone stretches out the heavens
  and treads on the waves of the
    sea.
9 He is the Maker of the Bear*c* and
    Orion,
  the Pleiades and the constellations
    of the south.
10 He performs wonders that cannot be
    fathomed,
  miracles that cannot be counted.

---

a 14 The meaning of the Hebrew for this word is uncertain.
b 19 Or *Surely all the joy it has / is that*   *c* 9 Or *of Leo*

BREAKTHROUGH!

Why does it talk about the Bear, Orion, the Pleiades and the constellations?

(JOB 9:9)

Because that was the group of stars the Hebrews knew about. Job was saying that God was very powerful and that he had created all the stars.

¹¹ When he passes me, I cannot see
    him;
    when he goes by, I cannot perceive
    him.
¹² If he snatches away, who can stop
    him?
    Who can say to him, 'What are you
    doing?'
¹³ God does not restrain his anger;
    even the cohorts of Rahab cowered
    at his feet.
¹⁴ "How then can I dispute with him?
    How can I find words to argue with
    him?
¹⁵ Though I were innocent, I could not
    answer him;
    I could only plead with my Judge for
    mercy.
¹⁶ Even if I summoned him and he
    responded,
    I do not believe he would give me a
    hearing.

¹⁷ He would crush me with a storm
    and multiply my wounds for no
    reason.
¹⁸ He would not let me catch my breath
    but would overwhelm me with
    misery.
¹⁹ If it is a matter of strength, he is
    mighty!
    And if it is a matter of justice, who
    can challenge him*ª*?
²⁰ Even if I were innocent, my mouth
    would condemn me;
    if I were blameless, it would
    pronounce me guilty.

²¹ "Although I am blameless,
    I have no concern for myself;
    I despise my own life.
²² It is all the same; that is why I say,
    'He destroys both the blameless
    and the wicked.'
²³ When a scourge brings sudden
    death,
    he mocks the despair of the
    innocent.
²⁴ When a land falls into the hands of
    the wicked,
    he blindfolds its judges.
    If it is not he, then who is it?

²⁵ "My days are swifter than a runner;
    they fly away without a glimpse of
    joy.
²⁶ They skim past like boats of papyrus,
    like eagles swooping down on their
    prey.
²⁷ If I say, 'I will forget my complaint,
    I will change my expression, and
    smile,'
²⁸ I still dread all my sufferings,
    for I know you will not hold me
    innocent.
²⁹ Since I am already found guilty,
    why should I struggle in vain?
³⁰ Even if I washed myself with soap
    and my hands with cleansing
    powder,
³¹ you would plunge me into a slime pit
    so that even my clothes would
    detest me.

³² "He is not a mere mortal like me that
    I might answer him,

ª 19 See Septuagint; Hebrew *me.*

that we might confront each other in court.

³³ If only there were someone to mediate between us,
  someone to bring us together,
³⁴ someone to remove God's rod from me,
  so that his terror would frighten me no more.
³⁵ Then I would speak up without fear of him,
  but as it now stands with me, I cannot.

10 "I loathe my very life;
  therefore I will give free rein to my complaint
  and speak out in the bitterness of my soul.
² I say to God: Do not declare me guilty,
  but tell me what charges you have against me.
³ Does it please you to oppress me,
  to spurn the work of your hands,
  while you smile on the plans of the wicked?
⁴ Do you have eyes of flesh?
  Do you see as a mortal sees?
⁵ Are your days like those of a mortal
  or your years like those of a strong man,
⁶ that you must search out my faults
  and probe after my sin—
⁷ though you know that I am not guilty
  and that no one can rescue me from your hand?

⁸ "Your hands shaped me and made me.
  Will you now turn and destroy me?
⁹ Remember that you molded me like clay.
  Will you now turn me to dust again?
¹⁰ Did you not pour me out like milk
  and curdle me like cheese,
¹¹ clothe me with skin and flesh
  and knit me together with bones and sinews?
¹² You gave me life and showed me kindness,
  and in your providence watched over my spirit.

¹³ "But this is what you concealed in your heart,
  and I know that this was in your mind:
¹⁴ If I sinned, you would be watching me
  and would not let my offense go unpunished.
¹⁵ If I am guilty—woe to me!
  Even if I am innocent, I cannot lift my head,
  for I am full of shame
  and drowned in*ᵃ* my affliction.
¹⁶ If I hold my head high, you stalk me like a lion
  and again display your awesome power against me.
¹⁷ You bring new witnesses against me
  and increase your anger toward me;
  your forces come against me wave upon wave.

ᵃ 15 Or and aware of

Does God watch us all the time?

(JOB 10:14)

It would be better to say that God pays attention to us. However, Job feels watched, because he doesn't understand why he's having so many problems.

18 "Why then did you bring me out of the
    womb?
  I wish I had died before any eye
    saw me.
19 If only I had never come into being,
    or had been carried straight from
      the womb to the grave!
20 Are not my few days almost over?
    Turn away from me so I can have a
      moment's joy
21 before I go to the place of no return,
    to the land of gloom and utter
      darkness,
22 to the land of deepest night,
    of utter darkness and disorder,
    where even the light is like
      darkness."

Zophar

11 Then Zophar the Naamathite re-
    plied:

2 "Are all these words to go
    unanswered?
  Is this talker to be vindicated?
3 Will your idle talk reduce others to
    silence?
  Will no one rebuke you when you
    mock?
4 You say to God, 'My beliefs are
    flawless
  and I am pure in your sight.'
5 Oh, how I wish that God would speak,
    that he would open his lips against
      you
6 and disclose to you the secrets of
    wisdom,
  for true wisdom has two sides.
  Know this: God has even forgotten
    some of your sin.

7 "Can you fathom the mysteries of
    God?
  Can you probe the limits of the
    Almighty?
8 They are higher than the heavens
    above—what can you do?
  They are deeper than the depths
    below—what can you know?
9 Their measure is longer than the earth
    and wider than the sea.

10 "If he comes along and confines you
    in prison

and convenes a court, who can
    oppose him?
11 Surely he recognizes deceivers;
    and when he sees evil, does he not
      take note?
12 But the witless can no more become
    wise
  than a wild donkey's colt can be
    born human.[a]

13 "Yet if you devote your heart to him
    and stretch out your hands to him,
14 if you put away the sin that is in your
    hand
  and allow no evil to dwell in your
    tent,
15 then, free of fault, you will lift up your
    face;
  you will stand firm and without fear.
16 You will surely forget your trouble,
    recalling it only as waters gone by.
17 Life will be brighter than noonday,
    and darkness will become like
      morning.
18 You will be secure, because there is
    hope;
  you will look about you and take
    your rest in safety.
19 You will lie down, with no one to make
    you afraid,
  and many will court your favor.
20 But the eyes of the wicked will fail,
    and escape will elude them;
  their hope will become a dying gasp."

Job

12 Then Job replied:

2 "Doubtless you are the only people
    who matter,
  and wisdom will die with you!
3 But I have a mind as well as you;
    I am not inferior to you.
  Who does not know all these
    things?

4 "I have become a laughingstock to my
    friends,
  though I called on God and he
    answered—
  a mere laughingstock, though
    righteous and blameless!

---

a 12 Or *wild donkey can be born tame*

⁵ Those who are at ease have contempt
for misfortune
as the fate of those whose feet are
slipping.
⁶ The tents of marauders are
undisturbed,
and those who provoke God are
secure—
those God has in his hand.ᵃ

⁷ "But ask the animals, and they will
teach you,
or the birds in the sky, and they will
tell you;
⁸ or speak to the earth, and it will teach
you,
or let the fish in the sea inform you.
⁹ Which of all these does not know
that the hand of the LORD has done
this?
¹⁰ In his hand is the life of every creature
and the breath of all mankind.
¹¹ Does not the ear test words
as the tongue tastes food?
¹² Is not wisdom found among the
aged?
Does not long life bring
understanding?

¹³ "To God belong wisdom and power;
counsel and understanding are
his.
¹⁴ What he tears down cannot be rebuilt;
those he imprisons cannot be
released.
¹⁵ If he holds back the waters, there is
drought;
if he lets them loose, they
devastate the land.
¹⁶ To him belong strength and insight;
both deceived and deceiver are his.
¹⁷ He leads rulers away stripped
and makes fools of judges.
¹⁸ He takes off the shackles put on by
kings
and ties a loinclothᵇ around their
waist.
¹⁹ He leads priests away stripped
and overthrows officials long
established.
²⁰ He silences the lips of trusted
advisers
and takes away the discernment of
elders.

²¹ He pours contempt on nobles
and disarms the mighty.
²² He reveals the deep things of
darkness
and brings utter darkness into the
light.
²³ He makes nations great, and destroys
them;
he enlarges nations, and disperses
them.
²⁴ He deprives the leaders of the earth
of their reason;
he makes them wander in a
trackless waste.
²⁵ They grope in darkness with no light;
he makes them stagger like
drunkards.

13 "My eyes have seen all this,
my ears have heard and
understood it.
² What you know, I also know;
I am not inferior to you.
³ But I desire to speak to the Almighty
and to argue my case with God.
⁴ You, however, smear me with lies;
you are worthless physicians, all
of you!
⁵ If only you would be altogether
silent!
For you, that would be wisdom.
⁶ Hear now my argument;
listen to the pleas of my lips.
⁷ Will you speak wickedly on God's
behalf?
Will you speak deceitfully for him?
⁸ Will you show him partiality?
Will you argue the case for God?
⁹ Would it turn out well if he examined
you?
Could you deceive him as you might
deceive a mortal?
¹⁰ He would surely call you to account
if you secretly showed partiality.
¹¹ Would not his splendor terrify you?
Would not the dread of him fall on
you?
¹² Your maxims are proverbs of ashes;
your defenses are defenses of clay.

¹³ "Keep silent and let me speak;
then let come to me what may.

ᵃ 6 Or those whose god is in their own hand   ᵇ 18 Or
shackles of kings / and ties a belt

¹⁴ Why do I put myself in jeopardy
    and take my life in my hands?
¹⁵ Though he slay me, yet will I hope in
      him;
    I will surely*ᵃ* defend my ways to his
      face.
¹⁶ Indeed, this will turn out for my
      deliverance,
    for no godless person would dare
      come before him!
¹⁷ Listen carefully to what I say;
    let my words ring in your ears.
¹⁸ Now that I have prepared my case,
    I know I will be vindicated.
¹⁹ Can anyone bring charges against me?
    If so, I will be silent and die.
²⁰ "Only grant me these two things, God,
    and then I will not hide from you:
²¹ Withdraw your hand far from me,
    and stop frightening me with your
      terrors.
²² Then summon me and I will answer,
    or let me speak, and you reply
      to me.
²³ How many wrongs and sins have I
      committed?
    Show me my offense and my sin.
²⁴ Why do you hide your face
    and consider me your enemy?
²⁵ Will you torment a windblown leaf?
    Will you chase after dry chaff?
²⁶ For you write down bitter things
      against me
    and make me reap the sins of my
      youth.
²⁷ You fasten my feet in shackles;
    you keep close watch on all my
      paths
    by putting marks on the soles of my
      feet.
²⁸ "So man wastes away like something
      rotten,
    like a garment eaten by moths.

14 "Mortals, born of woman,
    are of few days and full of trouble.
² They spring up like flowers and wither
      away;
    like fleeting shadows, they do not
      endure.
³ Do you fix your eye on them?
    Will you bring them*ᵇ* before you for
      judgment?

⁴ Who can bring what is pure from the
      impure?
    No one!
⁵ A person's days are determined;
    you have decreed the number of his
      months
    and have set limits he cannot
      exceed.
⁶ So look away from him and let him
      alone,
    till he has put in his time like a
      hired laborer.

⁷ "At least there is hope for a tree:
    If it is cut down, it will sprout again,
    and its new shoots will not fail.
⁸ Its roots may grow old in the ground
    and its stump die in the soil,
⁹ yet at the scent of water it will bud
    and put forth shoots like a plant.
¹⁰ But a man dies and is laid low;
    he breathes his last and is no
      more.
¹¹ As the water of a lake dries up
    or a riverbed becomes parched and
      dry,
¹² so he lies down and does not rise;
    till the heavens are no more, people
      will not awake
    or be roused from their sleep.

¹³ "If only you would hide me in the grave
    and conceal me till your anger has
      passed!
  If only you would set me a time
    and then remember me!
¹⁴ If someone dies, will they live again?
    All the days of my hard service
    I will wait for my renewal*ᶜ* to come.
¹⁵ You will call and I will answer you;
    you will long for the creature your
      hands have made.
¹⁶ Surely then you will count my steps
    but not keep track of my sin.
¹⁷ My offenses will be sealed up in a
      bag;
    you will cover over my sin.

¹⁸ "But as a mountain erodes and
      crumbles
    and as a rock is moved from its
      place,

ᵃ 15 Or *He will surely slay me; I have no hope* — / *yet I will*
ᵇ 3 Septuagint, Vulgate and Syriac; Hebrew *me*   *ᶜ 14* Or
release

19 as water wears away stones
   and torrents wash away the soil,
   so you destroy a person's hope.
20 You overpower them once for all, and
      they are gone;
   you change their countenance and
      send them away.
21 If their children are honored, they do
      not know it;
   if their offspring are brought low,
      they do not see it.
22 They feel but the pain of their own
      bodies
   and mourn only for themselves."

Eliphaz

15 Then Eliphaz the Temanite replied:

2 "Would a wise person answer with
      empty notions
   or fill their belly with the hot east
      wind?
3 Would they argue with useless words,
   with speeches that have no value?
4 But you even undermine piety
   and hinder devotion to God.
5 Your sin prompts your mouth;
   you adopt the tongue of the crafty.
6 Your own mouth condemns you, not
      mine;
   your own lips testify against you.

7 "Are you the first man ever born?
   Were you brought forth before the
      hills?
8 Do you listen in on God's council?
   Do you have a monopoly on
      wisdom?
9 What do you know that we do not
      know?
   What insights do you have that we
      do not have?
10 The gray-haired and the aged are on
      our side,
   men even older than your father.
11 Are God's consolations not enough for
      you,
   words spoken gently to you?
12 Why has your heart carried you away,
   and why do your eyes flash,
13 so that you vent your rage against God
   and pour out such words from your
      mouth?

14 "What are mortals, that they could be
      pure,
   or those born of woman, that they
      could be righteous?
15 If God places no trust in his holy
      ones,
   if even the heavens are not pure in
      his eyes,
16 how much less mortals, who are vile
      and corrupt,
   who drink up evil like water!

17 "Listen to me and I will explain to
      you;
   let me tell you what I have seen,
18 what the wise have declared,
   hiding nothing received from their
      ancestors
19 (to whom alone the land was given
   when no foreigners moved among
      them):
20 All his days the wicked man suffers
      torment,
   the ruthless man through all the
      years stored up for him.
21 Terrifying sounds fill his ears;
   when all seems well, marauders
      attack him.
22 He despairs of escaping the realm of
      darkness;
   he is marked for the sword.
23 He wanders about for food like a
      vulture;
   he knows the day of darkness is at
      hand.
24 Distress and anguish fill him with
      terror;
   troubles overwhelm him, like a king
      poised to attack,
25 because he shakes his fist at God
   and vaunts himself against the
      Almighty,
26 defiantly charging against him
   with a thick, strong shield.

27 "Though his face is covered with fat
   and his waist bulges with flesh,
28 he will inhabit ruined towns
   and houses where no one lives,
   houses crumbling to rubble.
29 He will no longer be rich and his
      wealth will not endure,
   nor will his possessions spread
      over the land.

30 He will not escape the darkness;
　a flame will wither his shoots,
　and the breath of God's mouth will
　　carry him away.
31 Let him not deceive himself by
　　trusting what is worthless,
　for he will get nothing in return.
32 Before his time he will wither,
　and his branches will not flourish.
33 He will be like a vine stripped of its
　　unripe grapes,
　like an olive tree shedding its
　　blossoms.
34 For the company of the godless will be
　　barren,
　and fire will consume the tents of
　　those who love bribes.
35 They conceive trouble and give birth to
　　evil;
　their womb fashions deceit."

Job

16

Then Job replied:

2 "I have heard many things like these;
　you are miserable comforters, all of
　　you!
3 Will your long-winded speeches never
　　end?
　What ails you that you keep on
　　arguing?
4 I also could speak like you,
　if you were in my place;
　I could make fine speeches against
　　you
　and shake my head at you.
5 But my mouth would encourage you;
　comfort from my lips would bring
　　you relief.

6 "Yet if I speak, my pain is not relieved;
　and if I refrain, it does not go
　　away.
7 Surely, God, you have worn me out;
　you have devastated my entire
　　household.
8 You have shriveled me up—and it has
　　become a witness;
　my gauntness rises up and testifies
　　against me.
9 God assails me and tears me in his
　　anger
　and gnashes his teeth at me;

my opponent fastens on me his
　　piercing eyes.
10 People open their mouths to jeer
　　at me;
　they strike my cheek in scorn
　and unite together against me.
11 God has turned me over to the
　　ungodly
　and thrown me into the clutches of
　　the wicked.
12 All was well with me, but he shattered
　　me;
　he seized me by the neck and
　　crushed me.
　He has made me his target;
13 　his archers surround me.
　Without pity, he pierces my kidneys
　and spills my gall on the ground.
14 Again and again he bursts upon me;
　he rushes at me like a warrior.

15 "I have sewed sackcloth over my
　　skin
　and buried my brow in the dust.
16 My face is red with weeping,
　dark shadows ring my eyes;
17 yet my hands have been free of
　　violence
　and my prayer is pure.

18 "Earth, do not cover my blood;
　may my cry never be laid to rest!
19 Even now my witness is in heaven;
　my advocate is on high.
20 My intercessor is my friend[a]
　as my eyes pour out tears to
　　God;
21 on behalf of a man he pleads with
　　God
　as one pleads for a friend.

22 "Only a few years will pass
　before I take the path of no return.

17

1 My spirit is broken,
　my days are cut short,
　the grave awaits me.
2 Surely mockers surround me;
　my eyes must dwell on their
　　hostility.

3 "Give me, O God, the pledge you
　　demand.
　Who else will put up security
　　for me?

---

a 20 Or *My friends treat me with scorn*

4 You have closed their minds to
    understanding;
    therefore you will not let them
    triumph.
5 If anyone denounces their friends for
    reward,
    the eyes of their children will fail.

6 "God has made me a byword to
    everyone,
    a man in whose face people spit.
7 My eyes have grown dim with grief;
    my whole frame is but a shadow.
8 The upright are appalled at this;
    the innocent are aroused against
    the ungodly.
9 Nevertheless, the righteous will hold
    to their ways,
    and those with clean hands will
    grow stronger.

10 "But come on, all of you, try again!
    I will not find a wise man among
    you.
11 My days have passed, my plans are
    shattered.
    Yet the desires of my heart
12 turn night into day;
    in the face of the darkness light is
    near.
13 If the only home I hope for is the grave,
    if I spread out my bed in the realm
    of darkness,
14 if I say to corruption, 'You are my
    father,'
    and to the worm, 'My mother' or
    'My sister,'
15 where then is my hope—
    who can see any hope for me?
16 Will it go down to the gates of death?
    Will we descend together into the
    dust?"

Bildad

18 Then Bildad the Shuhite replied:

2 "When will you end these speeches?
    Be sensible, and then we can talk.
3 Why are we regarded as cattle
    and considered stupid in your sight?
4 You who tear yourself to pieces in your
    anger,
    is the earth to be abandoned for
    your sake?

Or must the rocks be moved from
    their place?

5 "The lamp of a wicked man is snuffed
    out;
    the flame of his fire stops burning.
6 The light in his tent becomes dark;
    the lamp beside him goes out.
7 The vigor of his step is weakened;
    his own schemes throw him
    down.
8 His feet thrust him into a net;
    he wanders into its mesh.
9 A trap seizes him by the heel;
    a snare holds him fast.
10 A noose is hidden for him on the
    ground;
    a trap lies in his path.
11 Terrors startle him on every side
    and dog his every step.
12 Calamity is hungry for him;
    disaster is ready for him when he
    falls.
13 It eats away parts of his skin;
    death's firstborn devours his
    limbs.
14 He is torn from the security of his
    tent
    and marched off to the king of
    terrors.
15 Fire resides[a] in his tent;
    burning sulfur is scattered over his
    dwelling.
16 His roots dry up below
    and his branches wither above.
17 The memory of him perishes from the
    earth;
    he has no name in the land.
18 He is driven from light into the realm
    of darkness
    and is banished from the world.
19 He has no offspring or descendants
    among his people,
    no survivor where once he lived.
20 People of the west are appalled at his
    fate;
    those of the east are seized with
    horror.
21 Surely such is the dwelling of an evil
    man;
    such is the place of one who does
    not know God."

---

a 15 Or *Nothing he had remains*

Job

19 Then Job replied:

2 "How long will you torment me
and crush me with words?
3 Ten times now you have reproached
me;
shamelessly you attack me.
4 If it is true that I have gone astray,
my error remains my concern
alone.
5 If indeed you would exalt yourselves
above me
and use my humiliation against me,
6 then know that God has wronged me
and drawn his net around me.

7 "Though I cry, 'Violence!' I get no
response;
though I call for help, there is no
justice.
8 He has blocked my way so I cannot
pass;
he has shrouded my paths in
darkness.
9 He has stripped me of my honor
and removed the crown from my
head.
10 He tears me down on every side till I
am gone;
he uproots my hope like a tree.
11 His anger burns against me;
he counts me among his enemies.
12 His troops advance in force;
they build a siege ramp against me
and encamp around my tent.

13 "He has alienated my family from me;
my acquaintances are completely
estranged from me.
14 My relatives have gone away;
my closest friends have forgotten
me.
15 My guests and my female servants
count me a foreigner;
they look on me as on a stranger.
16 I summon my servant, but he does not
answer,
though I beg him with my own
mouth.
17 My breath is offensive to my wife;
I am loathsome to my own family.
18 Even the little boys scorn me;
when I appear, they ridicule me.

19 All my intimate friends detest me;
those I love have turned against
me.
20 I am nothing but skin and bones;
I have escaped only by the skin of
my teeth.[a]

21 "Have pity on me, my friends, have
pity,
for the hand of God has struck me.
22 Why do you pursue me as God
does?
Will you never get enough of my
flesh?

23 "Oh, that my words were recorded,
that they were written on a scroll,
24 that they were inscribed with an iron
tool on[b] lead,
or engraved in rock forever!
25 I know that my redeemer[c] lives,
and that in the end he will stand on
the earth.[d]
26 And after my skin has been destroyed,
yet[e] in[f] my flesh I will see God;
27 I myself will see him
with my own eyes—I, and not
another.
How my heart yearns within me!

28 "If you say, 'How we will hound him,
since the root of the trouble lies in
him,[g]'
29 you should fear the sword yourselves;
for wrath will bring punishment by
the sword,
and then you will know that there is
judgment.[h]"

Zophar

20 Then Zophar the Naamathite replied:

2 "My troubled thoughts prompt me to
answer
because I am greatly disturbed.
3 I hear a rebuke that dishonors me,
and my understanding inspires me
to reply.

---

a 20 Or *only by my gums*   *b 24* Or *and*   *c 25* Or *vindicator*   *d 25* Or *on my grave*   *e 26* Or *And after I awake, / though this body has been destroyed, / then*   *f 26* Or *destroyed, / apart from*   *g 28* Many Hebrew manuscripts, Septuagint and Vulgate; most Hebrew manuscripts *me*   *h 29* Or *sword, / that you may come to know the Almighty*

4 "Surely you know how it has been
from of old,
ever since mankind[a] was placed on
the earth,
5 that the mirth of the wicked is brief,
the joy of the godless lasts but a
moment.
6 Though the pride of the godless
person reaches to the heavens
and his head touches the clouds,
7 he will perish forever, like his own
dung;
those who have seen him will say,
'Where is he?'
8 Like a dream he flies away, no more to
be found,
banished like a vision of the night.
9 The eye that saw him will not see him
again;
his place will look on him no more.
10 His children must make amends to
the poor;
his own hands must give back his
wealth.
11 The youthful vigor that fills his bones
will lie with him in the dust.

12 "Though evil is sweet in his mouth
and he hides it under his tongue,
13 though he cannot bear to let it go
and lets it linger in his mouth,
14 yet his food will turn sour in his
stomach;
it will become the venom of
serpents within him.
15 He will spit out the riches he
swallowed;
God will make his stomach vomit
them up.
16 He will suck the poison of serpents;
the fangs of an adder will kill
him.
17 He will not enjoy the streams,
the rivers flowing with honey and
cream.
18 What he toiled for he must give back
uneaten;
he will not enjoy the profit from his
trading.
19 For he has oppressed the poor and
left them destitute;
he has seized houses he did not
build.

20 "Surely he will have no respite from
his craving;
he cannot save himself by his
treasure.
21 Nothing is left for him to devour;
his prosperity will not endure.
22 In the midst of his plenty, distress will
overtake him;
the full force of misery will come
upon him.
23 When he has filled his belly,
God will vent his burning anger
against him
and rain down his blows on him.
24 Though he flees from an iron weapon,
a bronze-tipped arrow pierces him.
25 He pulls it out of his back,
the gleaming point out of his liver.
Terrors will come over him;
26 total darkness lies in wait
for his treasures.
A fire unfanned will
consume him
and devour what is left in his tent.
27 The heavens will expose his guilt;
the earth will rise up against him.
28 A flood will carry off his house,
rushing waters[b] on the day of God's
wrath.
29 Such is the fate God allots the
wicked,
the heritage appointed for them by
God."

Job

21

Then Job replied:

2 "Listen carefully to my words;
let this be the consolation you give
me.
3 Bear with me while I speak,
and after I have spoken, mock on.

4 "Is my complaint directed to a human
being?
Why should I not be impatient?
5 Look at me and be appalled;
clap your hand over your mouth.
6 When I think about this, I am
terrified;
trembling seizes my body.

---

a 4 Or *Adam*   b 28 Or *The possessions in his house will
be carried off, / washed away*

⁷Why do the wicked live on,
    growing old and increasing in
      power?
⁸They see their children established
    around them,
    their offspring before their eyes.
⁹Their homes are safe and free from
    fear;
    the rod of God is not on them.
¹⁰Their bulls never fail to breed;
    their cows calve and do not
      miscarry.
¹¹They send forth their children as a
    flock;
    their little ones dance about.
¹²They sing to the music of timbrel and
    lyre;
    they make merry to the sound of
      the pipe.
¹³They spend their years in prosperity
    and go down to the grave in peace.^a
¹⁴Yet they say to God, 'Leave us alone!
    We have no desire to know your
      ways.
¹⁵Who is the Almighty, that we should
    serve him?
    What would we gain by praying to
      him?'
¹⁶But their prosperity is not in their own
    hands,
    so I stand aloof from the plans of
      the wicked.

¹⁷"Yet how often is the lamp of the
    wicked snuffed out?
    How often does calamity come upon
      them,
    the fate God allots in his anger?
¹⁸How often are they like straw before
    the wind,
    like chaff swept away by a gale?
¹⁹It is said, 'God stores up the
    punishment of the wicked for
      their children.'
    Let him repay the wicked, so that
      they themselves will experience
      it!
²⁰Let their own eyes see their
    destruction;
    let them drink the cup of the wrath
      of the Almighty.
²¹For what do they care about the
    families they leave behind

when their allotted months come to
    an end?
²²"Can anyone teach knowledge to God,
    since he judges even the highest?
²³One person dies in full vigor,
    completely secure and at ease,
²⁴well nourished in body,^b
    bones rich with marrow.
²⁵Another dies in bitterness of soul,
    never having enjoyed anything
      good.
²⁶Side by side they lie in the dust,
    and worms cover them both.

²⁷"I know full well what you are thinking,
    the schemes by which you would
      wrong me.
²⁸You say, 'Where now is the house of
    the great,
    the tents where the wicked lived?'
²⁹Have you never questioned those who
    travel?
    Have you paid no regard to their
      accounts—
³⁰that the wicked are spared from the
    day of calamity,
    that they are delivered from^c the day
      of wrath?
³¹Who denounces their conduct to their
    face?
    Who repays them for what they have
      done?
³²They are carried to the grave,
    and watch is kept over their tombs.
³³The soil in the valley is sweet to them;
    everyone follows after them,
    and a countless throng goes^d
      before them.

³⁴"So how can you console me with your
    nonsense?
    Nothing is left of your answers but
      falsehood!"

Eliphaz

22 Then Eliphaz the Temanite replied:

²"Can a man be of benefit to God?
    Can even a wise person benefit
      him?

---

^a 13 Or in an instant   ^b 24 The meaning of the Hebrew
for this word is uncertain.   ^c 30 Or wicked are reserved
for the day of calamity, / that they are brought forth to
^d 33 Or them, / as a countless throng went

³ What pleasure would it give the
   Almighty if you were righteous?
   What would he gain if your ways
   were blameless?

⁴ "Is it for your piety that he rebukes you
   and brings charges against you?
⁵ Is not your wickedness great?
   Are not your sins endless?
⁶ You demanded security from your
   relatives for no reason;
   you stripped people of their
   clothing, leaving them naked.
⁷ You gave no water to the weary
   and you withheld food from the
   hungry,
⁸ though you were a powerful man,
   owning land—
   an honored man, living on it.
⁹ And you sent widows away empty-
   handed
   and broke the strength of the
   fatherless.
¹⁰ That is why snares are all around you,
   why sudden peril terrifies you,
¹¹ why it is so dark you cannot see,
   and why a flood of water covers you.

¹² "Is not God in the heights of heaven?
   And see how lofty are the highest
   stars!
¹³ Yet you say, 'What does God know?
   Does he judge through such
   darkness?
¹⁴ Thick clouds veil him, so he does not
   see us
   as he goes about in the vaulted
   heavens.'
¹⁵ Will you keep to the old path
   that the wicked have trod?
¹⁶ They were carried off before their time,
   their foundations washed away by a
   flood.
¹⁷ They said to God, 'Leave us alone!
   What can the Almighty do to us?'
¹⁸ Yet it was he who filled their houses
   with good things,
   so I stand aloof from the plans of
   the wicked.
¹⁹ The righteous see their ruin and
   rejoice;
   the innocent mock them, saying,
²⁰ 'Surely our foes are destroyed,
   and fire devours their wealth.'

²¹ "Submit to God and be at peace with
   him;
   in this way prosperity will come to
   you.
²² Accept instruction from his mouth
   and lay up his words in your
   heart.
²³ If you return to the Almighty, you will
   be restored:
   If you remove wickedness far from
   your tent
²⁴ and assign your nuggets to the dust,
   your gold of Ophir to the rocks in
   the ravines,
²⁵ then the Almighty will be your gold,
   the choicest silver for you.
²⁶ Surely then you will find delight in the
   Almighty
   and will lift up your face to God.
²⁷ You will pray to him, and he will hear
   you,
   and you will fulfill your vows.
²⁸ What you decide on will be done,
   and light will shine on your ways.
²⁹ When people are brought low and you
   say, 'Lift them up!'
   then he will save the downcast.
³⁰ He will deliver even one who is not
   innocent,
   who will be delivered through the
   cleanness of your hands."

Job

23 Then Job replied:

² "Even today my complaint is bitter;
   his hand[a] is heavy in spite of[b] my
   groaning.
³ If only I knew where to find him;
   if only I could go to his dwelling!
⁴ I would state my case before him
   and fill my mouth with arguments.
⁵ I would find out what he would answer
   me,
   and consider what he would say to
   me.
⁶ Would he vigorously oppose me?
   No, he would not press charges
   against me.
⁷ There the upright can establish their
   innocence before him,

---

[a] 2 Septuagint and Syriac; Hebrew / the hand on me
[b] 2 Or heavy on me in

and there I would be delivered
forever from my judge.
⁸ "But if I go to the east, he is not
there;
if I go to the west, I do not find him.
⁹ When he is at work in the north, I do
not see him;
when he turns to the south, I catch
no glimpse of him.
¹⁰ But he knows the way that I take;
when he has tested me, I will come
forth as gold.
¹¹ My feet have closely followed his
steps;
I have kept to his way without
turning aside.
¹² I have not departed from the
commands of his lips;
I have treasured the words of his
mouth more than my daily
bread.
¹³ "But he stands alone, and who can
oppose him?
He does whatever he pleases.
¹⁴ He carries out his decree against me,
and many such plans he still has in
store.
¹⁵ That is why I am terrified before him;
when I think of all this, I fear him.
¹⁶ God has made my heart faint;
the Almighty has terrified me.
¹⁷ Yet I am not silenced by the darkness,
by the thick darkness that covers
my face.

24 "Why does the Almighty not set
times for judgment?
Why must those who know him look
in vain for such days?
² There are those who move boundary
stones;
they pasture flocks they have
stolen.
³ They drive away the orphan's donkey
and take the widow's ox in pledge.
⁴ They thrust the needy from the path
and force all the poor of the land
into hiding.
⁵ Like wild donkeys in the desert,
the poor go about their labor of
foraging food;
the wasteland provides food for
their children.

⁶ They gather fodder in the fields
and glean in the vineyards of the
wicked.
⁷ Lacking clothes, they spend the night
naked;
they have nothing to cover
themselves in the cold.
⁸ They are drenched by mountain
rains
and hug the rocks for lack of
shelter.
⁹ The fatherless child is snatched from
the breast;
the infant of the poor is seized for
a debt.
¹⁰ Lacking clothes, they go about
naked;
they carry the sheaves, but still go
hungry.
¹¹ They crush olives among the
terraces[a];
they tread the winepresses, yet
suffer thirst.
¹² The groans of the dying rise from the
city,
and the souls of the wounded cry
out for help.
But God charges no one with
wrongdoing.

¹³ "There are those who rebel against
the light,
who do not know its ways
or stay in its paths.
¹⁴ When daylight is gone, the murderer
rises up,
kills the poor and needy,
and in the night steals forth like a
thief.
¹⁵ The eye of the adulterer watches for
dusk;
he thinks, 'No eye will see me,'
and he keeps his face concealed.
¹⁶ In the dark, thieves break into
houses,
but by day they shut themselves in;
they want nothing to do with the
light.
¹⁷ For all of them, midnight is their
morning;
they make friends with the terrors
of darkness.

---

a 11 The meaning of the Hebrew for this word is uncertain.

18 "Yet they are foam on the surface of
the water;
their portion of the land is cursed,
so that no one goes to the
vineyards.
19 As heat and drought snatch away the
melted snow,
so the grave snatches away those
who have sinned.
20 The womb forgets them,
the worm feasts on them;
the wicked are no longer remembered
but are broken like a tree.
21 They prey on the barren and childless
woman,
and to the widow they show no
kindness.
22 But God drags away the mighty by his
power;
though they become established,
they have no assurance of life.
23 He may let them rest in a feeling of
security,
but his eyes are on their ways.
24 For a little while they are exalted, and
then they are gone;
they are brought low and gathered
up like all others;
they are cut off like heads of grain.
25 "If this is not so, who can prove me
false
and reduce my words to nothing?"

Bildad

25 Then Bildad the Shuhite replied:

2 "Dominion and awe belong to God;
he establishes order in the heights
of heaven.
3 Can his forces be numbered?
On whom does his light not rise?
4 How then can a mortal be righteous
before God?
How can one born of woman be
pure?
5 If even the moon is not bright
and the stars are not pure in his
eyes,
6 how much less a mortal, who is but a
maggot—
a human being, who is only a
worm!"

Job

26 Then Job replied:

2 "How you have helped the powerless!
How you have saved the arm that is
feeble!
3 What advice you have offered to one
without wisdom!
And what great insight you have
displayed!
4 Who has helped you utter these
words?
And whose spirit spoke from your
mouth?
5 "The dead are in deep anguish,
those beneath the waters and all
that live in them.
6 The realm of the dead is naked before
God;
Destruction[a] lies uncovered.
7 He spreads out the northern skies
over empty space;
he suspends the earth over
nothing.
8 He wraps up the waters in his
clouds,
yet the clouds do not burst under
their weight.
9 He covers the face of the full
moon,
spreading his clouds over it.
10 He marks out the horizon on the face
of the waters
for a boundary between light and
darkness.
11 The pillars of the heavens quake,
aghast at his rebuke.
12 By his power he churned up the sea;
by his wisdom he cut Rahab to
pieces.
13 By his breath the skies became
fair;
his hand pierced the gliding
serpent.
14 And these are but the outer fringe of
his works;
how faint the whisper we hear of
him!
Who then can understand the
thunder of his power?"

Job's Final Word to His Friends

27 And Job continued his discourse:

2 "As surely as God lives, who has
  denied me justice,
  the Almighty, who has made my life
  bitter,
3 as long as I have life within me,
  the breath of God in my nostrils,
4 my lips will not say anything wicked,
  and my tongue will not utter lies.
5 I will never admit you are in the
  right;
  till I die, I will not deny my integrity.
6 I will maintain my innocence and never
  let go of it;
  my conscience will not reproach me
  as long as I live.

7 "May my enemy be like the wicked,
  my adversary like the unjust!
8 For what hope have the godless when
  they are cut off,
  when God takes away their life?
9 Does God listen to their cry
  when distress comes upon them?
10 Will they find delight in the Almighty?
  Will they call on God at all times?

11 "I will teach you about the power of
  God;
  the ways of the Almighty I will not
  conceal.
12 You have all seen this yourselves.
  Why then this meaningless talk?

13 "Here is the fate God allots to the
  wicked,
  the heritage a ruthless man
  receives from the Almighty:
14 However many his children, their fate
  is the sword;
  his offspring will never have enough
  to eat.
15 The plague will bury those who survive
  him,
  and their widows will not weep for
  them.
16 Though he heaps up silver like dust
  and clothes like piles of clay,
17 what he lays up the righteous will
  wear,
  and the innocent will divide his
  silver.

18 The house he builds is like a moth's
  cocoon,
  like a hut made by a watchman.
19 He lies down wealthy, but will do so no
  more;
  when he opens his eyes, all is
  gone.
20 Terrors overtake him like a flood;
  a tempest snatches him away in the
  night.
21 The east wind carries him off, and he
  is gone;
  it sweeps him out of his place.
22 It hurls itself against him without
  mercy
  as he flees headlong from its
  power.
23 It claps its hands in derision
  and hisses him out of his
  place."

Interlude: Where Wisdom Is Found

28 There is a mine for silver
  and a place where gold is
  refined.
2 Iron is taken from the earth,
  and copper is smelted from ore.
3 Mortals put an end to the darkness;
  they search out the farthest
  recesses
  for ore in the blackest darkness.
4 Far from human dwellings they cut a
  shaft,
  in places untouched by human
  feet;
  far from other people they dangle
  and sway.
5 The earth, from which food comes,
  is transformed below as by fire;
6 lapis lazuli comes from its rocks,
  and its dust contains nuggets of
  gold.
7 No bird of prey knows that hidden
  path,
  no falcon's eye has seen it.
8 Proud beasts do not set foot on it,
  and no lion prowls there.
9 People assault the flinty rock with
  their hands
  and lay bare the roots of the
  mountains.
10 They tunnel through the rock;
  their eyes see all its treasures.

BREAK THROUGH!

Falcon
(JOB 28:7-8)
This is a bird of prey. It's like an eagle, but smaller.

---

¹¹ They search[a] the sources of the rivers
    and bring hidden things to light.

¹² But where can wisdom be found?
    Where does understanding dwell?
¹³ No mortal comprehends its worth;
    it cannot be found in the land of the
        living.
¹⁴ The deep says, "It is not in me";
    the sea says, "It is not with me."
¹⁵ It cannot be bought with the finest
        gold,
    nor can its price be weighed out in
        silver.
¹⁶ It cannot be bought with the gold of
        Ophir,
    with precious onyx or lapis lazuli.
¹⁷ Neither gold nor crystal can compare
        with it,
    nor can it be had for jewels of
        gold.
¹⁸ Coral and jasper are not worthy of
        mention;
    the price of wisdom is beyond
        rubies.
¹⁹ The topaz of Cush cannot compare
        with it;
    it cannot be bought with pure gold.

²⁰ Where then does wisdom come
        from?
    Where does understanding dwell?
²¹ It is hidden from the eyes of every
        living thing,
    concealed even from the birds in
        the sky.
²² Destruction[b] and Death say,
    "Only a rumor of it has reached our
        ears."
²³ God understands the way to it
    and he alone knows where it
        dwells,
²⁴ for he views the ends of the earth
    and sees everything under the
        heavens.
²⁵ When he established the force of the
        wind
    and measured out the waters,
²⁶ when he made a decree for the rain
    and a path for the thunderstorm,
²⁷ then he looked at wisdom and
        appraised it;
    he confirmed it and tested it.

---

[a] 11 Septuagint, Aquila and Vulgate; Hebrew *They dam up*
[b] 22 Hebrew *Abaddon*

BREAK THROUGH!

Coral, jasper and topaz
(JOB 28:18-19)
Coral is a kind of sea plant that's very expensive. Jasper and topaz are gemstones used for jewelry.

²⁸ And he said to the human race,
"The fear of the Lord—that is
wisdom,
and to shun evil is understanding."

Job's Final Defense

29 Job continued his discourse:

² "How I long for the months gone by,
for the days when God watched over
me,
³ when his lamp shone on my head
and by his light I walked through
darkness!
⁴ Oh, for the days when I was in my
prime,
when God's intimate friendship
blessed my house,
⁵ when the Almighty was still with me
and my children were around me,
⁶ when my path was drenched with
cream
and the rock poured out for me
streams of olive oil.

⁷ "When I went to the gate of the city
and took my seat in the public
square,
⁸ the young men saw me and stepped
aside
and the old men rose to their feet;
⁹ the chief men refrained from speaking
and covered their mouths with their
hands;
¹⁰ the voices of the nobles were hushed,
and their tongues stuck to the roof
of their mouths.
¹¹ Whoever heard me spoke well of me,
and those who saw me commended
me,
¹² because I rescued the poor who cried
for help,
and the fatherless who had none to
assist them.
¹³ The one who was dying blessed me;
I made the widow's heart sing.
¹⁴ I put on righteousness as my clothing;
justice was my robe and my
turban.
¹⁵ I was eyes to the blind
and feet to the lame.
¹⁶ I was a father to the needy;
I took up the case of the stranger.

¹⁷ I broke the fangs of the wicked
and snatched the victims from their
teeth.

¹⁸ "I thought, 'I will die in my own house,
my days as numerous as the grains
of sand.
¹⁹ My roots will reach to the water,
and the dew will lie all night on my
branches.
²⁰ My glory will not fade;
the bow will be ever new in my hand.'

²¹ "People listened to me expectantly,
waiting in silence for my counsel.
²² After I had spoken, they spoke no
more;
my words fell gently on their ears.
²³ They waited for me as for showers
and drank in my words as the spring
rain.
²⁴ When I smiled at them, they scarcely
believed it;
the light of my face was precious to
them.^a
²⁵ I chose the way for them and sat as
their chief;
I dwelt as a king among his troops;
I was like one who comforts
mourners.

30 "But now they mock me,
men younger than I,
whose fathers I would have disdained
to put with my sheep dogs.
² Of what use was the strength of their
hands to me,
since their vigor had gone from
them?
³ Haggard from want and hunger,
they roamed^b the parched land
in desolate wastelands at night.
⁴ In the brush they gathered salt herbs,
and their food^c was the root of the
broom bush.
⁵ They were banished from human
society,
shouted at as if they were thieves.
⁶ They were forced to live in the dry
stream beds,
among the rocks and in holes in the
ground.

---

^a 24 The meaning of the Hebrew for this clause is
uncertain.   ^b 3 Or *gnawed*   ^c 4 Or *fuel*

7 They brayed among the bushes
and huddled in the undergrowth.
8 A base and nameless brood,
they were driven out of the land.

9 "And now those young men mock me
in song;
I have become a byword among
them.
10 They detest me and keep their
distance;
they do not hesitate to spit in my
face.
11 Now that God has unstrung my bow
and afflicted me,
they throw off restraint in my
presence.
12 On my right the tribe*a* attacks;
they lay snares for my feet,
they build their siege ramps against
me.
13 They break up my road;
they succeed in destroying me.
'No one can help him,' they say.
14 They advance as through a gaping
breach;
amid the ruins they come rolling in.
15 Terrors overwhelm me;
my dignity is driven away as by the
wind,
my safety vanishes like a cloud.

16 "And now my life ebbs away;
days of suffering grip me.
17 Night pierces my bones;
my gnawing pains never rest.
18 In his great power God becomes like
clothing to me*b*;
he binds me like the neck of my
garment.
19 He throws me into the mud,
and I am reduced to dust and
ashes.

20 "I cry out to you, God, but you do not
answer;
I stand up, but you merely look at
me.
21 You turn on me ruthlessly;
with the might of your hand you
attack me.
22 You snatch me up and drive me before
the wind;
you toss me about in the storm.

23 I know you will bring me down to
death,
to the place appointed for all the
living.

24 "Surely no one lays a hand on a
broken man
when he cries for help in his
distress.
25 Have I not wept for those in trouble?
Has not my soul grieved for the
poor?
26 Yet when I hoped for good, evil came;
when I looked for light, then came
darkness.
27 The churning inside me never stops;
days of suffering confront me.
28 I go about blackened, but not by the
sun;
I stand up in the assembly and cry
for help.
29 I have become a brother of jackals,
a companion of owls.
30 My skin grows black and peels;
my body burns with fever.
31 My lyre is tuned to mourning,
and my pipe to the sound of
wailing.

31 "I made a covenant with my eyes
not to look lustfully at a young
woman.
2 For what is our lot from God above,
our heritage from the Almighty on
high?
3 Is it not ruin for the wicked,
disaster for those who do wrong?
4 Does he not see my ways
and count my every step?

5 "If I have walked with falsehood
or my foot has hurried after
deceit—
6 let God weigh me in honest scales
and he will know that I am
blameless—
7 if my steps have turned from the path,
if my heart has been led by my
eyes,
or if my hands have been defiled,
8 then may others eat what I have sown,
and may my crops be uprooted.

---

a 12 The meaning of the Hebrew for this word is uncertain.
b 18 Hebrew; Septuagint *power he grasps my clothing*

9 "If my heart has been enticed by a
woman,
or if I have lurked at my neighbor's
door,
10 then may my wife grind another man's
grain,
and may other men sleep with her.
11 For that would have been wicked,
a sin to be judged.
12 It is a fire that burns to Destruction[a];
it would have uprooted my harvest.

13 "If I have denied justice to any of my
servants,
whether male or female,
when they had a grievance against
me,
14 what will I do when God confronts me?
What will I answer when called to
account?
15 Did not he who made me in the womb
make them?
Did not the same one form us both
within our mothers?

16 "If I have denied the desires of the
poor
or let the eyes of the widow grow
weary,
17 if I have kept my bread to myself,
not sharing it with the fatherless—
18 but from my youth I reared them as a
father would,
and from my birth I guided the
widow—
19 if I have seen anyone perishing for
lack of clothing,
or the needy without garments,
20 and their hearts did not bless me
for warming them with the fleece
from my sheep,
21 if I have raised my hand against the
fatherless,
knowing that I had influence in
court,
22 then let my arm fall from the shoulder,
let it be broken off at the joint.
23 For I dreaded destruction from
God,
and for fear of his splendor I could
not do such things.

24 "If I have put my trust in gold
or said to pure gold, 'You are my
security,'

25 if I have rejoiced over my great
wealth,
the fortune my hands had gained,
26 if I have regarded the sun in its
radiance
or the moon moving in splendor,
27 so that my heart was secretly enticed
and my hand offered them a kiss of
homage,
28 then these also would be sins to be
judged,
for I would have been unfaithful to
God on high.

29 "If I have rejoiced at my enemy's
misfortune
or gloated over the trouble that
came to him—
30 I have not allowed my mouth to sin
by invoking a curse against their
life—
31 if those of my household have never
said,
'Who has not been filled with Job's
meat?'—
32 but no stranger had to spend the night
in the street,
for my door was always open to the
traveler—
33 if I have concealed my sin as people
do,[b]
by hiding my guilt in my heart
34 because I so feared the crowd
and so dreaded the contempt of the
clans
that I kept silent and would not go
outside—

35 ("Oh, that I had someone to hear me!
I sign now my defense—let the
Almighty answer me;
let my accuser put his indictment in
writing.
36 Surely I would wear it on my shoulder,
I would put it on like a crown.
37 I would give him an account of my
every step;
I would present it to him as to a
ruler.)—

38 "if my land cries out against me
and all its furrows are wet with
tears,

---

[a] 12 Hebrew *Abaddon*   [b] 33 Or *as Adam did*

39 if I have devoured its yield without
        payment
    or broken the spirit of its tenants,
40 then let briers come up instead of
        wheat
    and stinkweed instead of barley."

The words of Job are ended.

Elihu

32 So these three men stopped an-
        swering Job, because he was righ-
teous in his own eyes. ²But Elihu son of
Barakel the Buzite, of the family of Ram,
became very angry with Job for justifying
himself rather than God. ³He was also angry with the three friends, because they
had found no way to refute Job, and yet
had condemned him.ᵃ ⁴Now Elihu had
waited before speaking to Job because
they were older than he. ⁵But when he
saw that the three men had nothing more
to say, his anger was aroused.

⁶So Elihu son of Barakel the Buzite said:

"I am young in years,
    and you are old;
that is why I was fearful,
    not daring to tell you what I know.
⁷I thought, 'Age should speak;
    advanced years should teach
        wisdom.'
⁸But it is the spiritᵇ in a person,
    the breath of the Almighty, that
        gives them understanding.
⁹It is not only the oldᶜ who are wise,
    not only the aged who understand
        what is right.

¹⁰ "Therefore I say: Listen to me;
    I too will tell you what I know.
¹¹ I waited while you spoke,
    I listened to your reasoning;
while you were searching for words,
¹²   I gave you my full attention.
But not one of you has proved Job
        wrong;
    none of you has answered his
        arguments.
¹³ Do not say, 'We have found wisdom;
    let God, not a man, refute him.'
¹⁴ But Job has not marshaled his words
        against me,
    and I will not answer him with your
        arguments.

¹⁵ "They are dismayed and have no more
        to say;
    words have failed them.
¹⁶ Must I wait, now that they are
        silent,
    now that they stand there with no
        reply?
¹⁷ I too will have my say;
    I too will tell what I know.
¹⁸ For I am full of words,
    and the spirit within me compels
        me;
¹⁹ inside I am like bottled-up wine,
    like new wineskins ready to burst.

ᵃ 3 Masoretic Text; an ancient Hebrew scribal tradition *Job,
and so had condemned God*   ᵇ 8 Or *Spirit*; also in
verse 18   ᶜ 9 Or *many*; or *great*

THE WITNESSES

✓ **ELIHU** (JOB 32:2)
In this book, this person represents young
people, and he explains their ideas to the older
people. His name means "he's my God."

²⁰I must speak and find relief;
    I must open my lips and reply.
²¹I will show no partiality,
    nor will I flatter anyone;
²²for if I were skilled in flattery,
    my Maker would soon take me
    away.

33 "But now, Job, listen to my words;
    pay attention to everything I say.
²I am about to open my mouth;
    my words are on the tip of my
    tongue.
³My words come from an upright
    heart;
    my lips sincerely speak what I know.
⁴The Spirit of God has made me;
    the breath of the Almighty gives me
    life.
⁵Answer me then, if you can;
    stand up and argue your case
    before me.
⁶I am the same as you in God's
    sight;
    I too am a piece of clay.
⁷No fear of me should alarm you,
    nor should my hand be heavy on
    you.

⁸"But you have said in my hearing—
    I heard the very words—
⁹'I am pure, I have done no wrong;
    I am clean and free from sin.
¹⁰Yet God has found fault with me;
    he considers me his enemy.
¹¹He fastens my feet in shackles;
    he keeps close watch on all my
    paths.'

¹²"But I tell you, in this you are not
    right,
    for God is greater than any mortal.
¹³Why do you complain to him
    that he responds to no one's
    words[a]?
¹⁴For God does speak—now one way,
    now another—
    though no one perceives it.
¹⁵In a dream, in a vision of the night,
    when deep sleep falls on people
    as they slumber in their beds,
¹⁶he may speak in their ears
    and terrify them with warnings,
¹⁷to turn them from wrongdoing
    and keep them from pride,

¹⁸to preserve them from the pit,
    their lives from perishing by the
    sword.[b]

¹⁹"Or someone may be chastened on a
    bed of pain
    with constant distress in their
    bones,
²⁰so that their body finds food repulsive
    and their soul loathes the choicest
    meal.
²¹Their flesh wastes away to nothing,
    and their bones, once hidden, now
    stick out.
²²They draw near to the pit,
    and their life to the messengers of
    death.[c]
²³Yet if there is an angel at their side,
    a messenger, one out of a
    thousand,
    sent to tell them how to be upright,
²⁴and he is gracious to that person and
    says to God,
    'Spare them from going down to the
    pit;
    I have found a ransom for them—
²⁵let their flesh be renewed like a
    child's;
    let them be restored as in the days
    of their youth'—
²⁶then that person can pray to God and
    find favor with him,
    they will see God's face and shout
    for joy;
    he will restore them to full well-
    being.
²⁷And they will go to others and say,
    'I have sinned, I have perverted
    what is right,
    but I did not get what I deserved.
²⁸God has delivered me from going
    down to the pit,
    and I shall live to enjoy the light of
    life.'

²⁹"God does all these things to a
    person—
    twice, even three times—
³⁰to turn them back from the pit,
    that the light of life may shine on
    them.

---

[a] 13 Or *that he does not answer for any of his actions*
[b] 18 Or *from crossing the river*   [c] 22 Or *to the place of the dead*

BREAK THROUGH!

Can an angel ask God to help us?

(JOB 33:23-25)

We really don't know. Here, Elihu is just giving an example of what he thinks. The word *angel* means "messenger," and it refers to any person that God sent, not necessarily a spirit or an angel.

---

31 "Pay attention, Job, and listen
       to me;
    be silent, and I will speak.
32 If you have anything to say, answer
       me;
    speak up, for I want to vindicate
       you.
33 But if not, then listen to me;
    be silent, and I will teach you
       wisdom."

34 Then Elihu said:

2 "Hear my words, you wise men;
    listen to me, you men of learning.
3 For the ear tests words
    as the tongue tastes food.
4 Let us discern for ourselves what is
       right;
    let us learn together what is good.

5 "Job says, 'I am innocent,
    but God denies me justice.

6 Although I am right,
    I am considered a liar;
 although I am guiltless,
    his arrow inflicts an incurable
       wound.'
7 Is there anyone like Job,
    who drinks scorn like water?
8 He keeps company with evildoers;
    he associates with the wicked.
9 For he says, 'There is no profit
    in trying to please God.'

10 "So listen to me, you men of
       understanding.
    Far be it from God to do evil,
    from the Almighty to do wrong.
11 He repays everyone for what they have
       done;
    he brings on them what their
       conduct deserves.
12 It is unthinkable that God would do
       wrong,
    that the Almighty would pervert
       justice.
13 Who appointed him over the earth?
    Who put him in charge of the whole
       world?
14 If it were his intention
    and he withdrew his spirit[a] and
       breath,
15 all humanity would perish together
    and mankind would return to the
       dust.

16 "If you have understanding, hear
       this;
    listen to what I say.
17 Can someone who hates justice
       govern?
    Will you condemn the just and
       mighty One?
18 Is he not the One who says to kings,
    'You are worthless,'
    and to nobles, 'You are wicked,'
19 who shows no partiality to princes
    and does not favor the rich over the
       poor,
    for they are all the work of his
       hands?
20 They die in an instant, in the middle
       of the night;
    the people are shaken and they
       pass away;

---

a 14 Or *Spirit*

the mighty are removed without
human hand.

21 "His eyes are on the ways of mortals;
he sees their every step.
22 There is no deep shadow, no utter
darkness,
where evildoers can hide.
23 God has no need to examine people
further,
that they should come before him
for judgment.
24 Without inquiry he shatters the mighty
and sets up others in their place.
25 Because he takes note of their deeds,
he overthrows them in the night and
they are crushed.
26 He punishes them for their
wickedness
where everyone can see them,
27 because they turned from following
him
and had no regard for any of his
ways.
28 They caused the cry of the poor to
come before him,
so that he heard the cry of the
needy.
29 But if he remains silent, who can
condemn him?
If he hides his face, who can see
him?
Yet he is over individual and nation
alike,
30 to keep the godless from ruling,
from laying snares for the people.

31 "Suppose someone says to God,
'I am guilty but will offend no more.
32 Teach me what I cannot see;
if I have done wrong, I will not do so
again.'
33 Should God then reward you on your
terms,
when you refuse to repent?
You must decide, not I;
so tell me what you know.

34 "Men of understanding declare,
wise men who hear me say to me,
35 'Job speaks without knowledge;
his words lack insight.'
36 Oh, that Job might be tested to the
utmost
for answering like a wicked man!

37 To his sin he adds rebellion;
scornfully he claps his hands
among us
and multiplies his words against
God."

35

Then Elihu said:

2 "Do you think this is just?
You say, 'I am in the right,
not God.'
3 Yet you ask him, 'What profit
is it to me,[a]
and what do I gain by not sinning?'

4 "I would like to reply to you
and to your friends with you.
5 Look up at the heavens and see;
gaze at the clouds so high
above you.
6 If you sin, how does that affect him?
If your sins are many, what does
that do to him?
7 If you are righteous, what do
you give to him,
or what does he receive from
your hand?
8 Your wickedness only affects humans
like yourself,
and your righteousness only
other people.

9 "People cry out under a load of
oppression;
they plead for relief from the arm
of the powerful.
10 But no one says, 'Where is God my
Maker,
who gives songs in the night,
11 who teaches us more than he
teaches[b] the beasts of the
earth
and makes us wiser than[c] the birds
in the sky?'
12 He does not answer when people
cry out
because of the arrogance of
the wicked.
13 Indeed, God does not listen to their
empty plea;
the Almighty pays no attention
to it.

---

a 3 Or you   b 10,11 Or night, / 11who teaches us by
c 11 Or us wise by

¹⁴ How much less, then, will he listen
when you say that you do not
see him,
that your case is before him
and you must wait for him,
¹⁵ and further, that his anger never
punishes
and he does not take the least
notice of wickedness.ᵃ
¹⁶ So Job opens his mouth with
empty talk;
without knowledge he multiplies
words."

36 Elihu continued:

² "Bear with me a little longer and I will
show you
that there is more to be said in
God's behalf.
³ I get my knowledge from afar;
I will ascribe justice to my Maker.
⁴ Be assured that my words are not
false;
one who has perfect knowledge is
with you.

⁵ "God is mighty, but despises no one;
he is mighty, and firm in his purpose.
⁶ He does not keep the wicked alive
but gives the afflicted their rights.
⁷ He does not take his eyes off the
righteous;
he enthrones them with kings
and exalts them forever.
⁸ But if people are bound in chains,
held fast by cords of affliction,
⁹ he tells them what they have done—
that they have sinned arrogantly.
¹⁰ He makes them listen to correction
and commands them to repent of
their evil.
¹¹ If they obey and serve him,
they will spend the rest of their days
in prosperity
and their years in contentment.
¹² But if they do not listen,
they will perish by the swordᵇ
and die without knowledge.

¹³ "The godless in heart harbor
resentment;
even when he fetters them, they do
not cry for help.

¹⁴ They die in their youth,
among male prostitutes of the
shrines.
¹⁵ But those who suffer he delivers in
their suffering;
he speaks to them in their affliction.

¹⁶ "He is wooing you from the jaws of
distress
to a spacious place free from
restriction,
to the comfort of your table laden
with choice food.
¹⁷ But now you are laden with the
judgment due the wicked;
judgment and justice have taken
hold of you.
¹⁸ Be careful that no one entices you by
riches;
do not let a large bribe turn you
aside.

ᵃ 15 Symmachus, Theodotion and Vulgate; the meaning of
the Hebrew for this word is uncertain.   ᵇ 12 Or *will cross
the river*

BREAK THROUGH!

Does God use suffering
to make us understand?
Isn't there some better way?
(JOB 36:15)

That was Elihu's opinion. But, of course,
there are other ways God can use to make us
understand, and sometimes he uses them.

¹⁹ Would your wealth or even all your
   mighty efforts
   sustain you so you would not be in
   distress?
²⁰ Do not long for the night,
   to drag people away from their
   homes.ᵃ
²¹ Beware of turning to evil,
   which you seem to prefer to
   affliction.

²² "God is exalted in his power.
   Who is a teacher like him?
²³ Who has prescribed his ways for him,
   or said to him, 'You have
   done wrong'?
²⁴ Remember to extol his work,
   which people have praised in song.
²⁵ All humanity has seen it;
   mortals gaze on it from afar.
²⁶ How great is God—beyond our
   understanding!
   The number of his years is past
   finding out.

²⁷ "He draws up the drops of water,
   which distill as rain to the streamsᵇ;
²⁸ the clouds pour down their moisture
   and abundant showers fall
   on mankind.
²⁹ Who can understand how he spreads
   out the clouds,
   how he thunders from his pavilion?
³⁰ See how he scatters his lightning
   about him,
   bathing the depths of the sea.
³¹ This is the way he governsᶜ
   the nations
   and provides food in abundance.
³² He fills his hands with lightning
   and commands it to strike its mark.
³³ His thunder announces the
   coming storm;
   even the cattle make known
   its approach.ᵈ

37 "At this my heart pounds
   and leaps from its place.
² Listen! Listen to the roar of his voice,
   to the rumbling that comes from his
   mouth.
³ He unleashes his lightning beneath
   the whole heaven
   and sends it to the ends of
   the earth.

⁴ After that comes the sound of
   his roar;
   he thunders with his majestic voice.
   When his voice resounds,
   he holds nothing back.
⁵ God's voice thunders in marvelous
   ways;
   he does great things beyond our
   understanding.
⁶ He says to the snow, 'Fall on
   the earth,'
   and to the rain shower, 'Be a mighty
   downpour.'
⁷ So that everyone he has made may
   know his work,
   he stops all people from their labor.ᵉ
⁸ The animals take cover;
   they remain in their dens.
⁹ The tempest comes out from its
   chamber,
   the cold from the driving winds.
¹⁰ The breath of God produces ice,
   and the broad waters become
   frozen.
¹¹ He loads the clouds with moisture;
   he scatters his lightning through
   them.
¹² At his direction they swirl around
   over the face of the whole earth
   to do whatever he commands them.
¹³ He brings the clouds to punish people,
   or to water his earth and show
   his love.

¹⁴ "Listen to this, Job;
   stop and consider God's wonders.
¹⁵ Do you know how God controls
   the clouds
   and makes his lightning flash?
¹⁶ Do you know how the clouds hang
   poised,
   those wonders of him who has
   perfect knowledge?
¹⁷ You who swelter in your clothes
   when the land lies hushed under
   the south wind,
¹⁸ can you join him in spreading out
   the skies,
   hard as a mirror of cast bronze?

ᵃ 20 The meaning of the Hebrew for verses 18-20 is
uncertain.   ᵇ 27 Or distill from the mist as rain
ᶜ 31 Or nourishes   ᵈ 33 Or announces his coming — /
the One zealous against evil   ᵉ 7 Or work, / he fills all
people with fear by his power

¹⁹ "Tell us what we should say to him;
    we cannot draw up our case
        because of our darkness.
²⁰ Should he be told that I want to speak?
    Would anyone ask to be
        swallowed up?
²¹ Now no one can look at the sun,
    bright as it is in the skies
        after the wind has swept them
        clean.
²² Out of the north he comes in golden
        splendor;
    God comes in awesome majesty.
²³ The Almighty is beyond our reach and
        exalted in power;
    in his justice and great
        righteousness, he
        does not oppress.
²⁴ Therefore, people revere him,
    for does he not have regard for all
        the wise in heart?^a"

The LORD Speaks

38 Then the LORD spoke to Job out of
    the storm. He said:

² "Who is this that obscures my plans
    with words without knowledge?
³ Brace yourself like a man;
    I will question you,
        and you shall answer me.

⁴ "Where were you when I laid the
        earth's foundation?
    Tell me, if you understand.
⁵ Who marked off its dimensions?
    Surely you know!
    Who stretched a measuring line
        across it?
⁶ On what were its footings set,
    or who laid its cornerstone—
⁷ while the morning stars sang together
    and all the angels^b shouted for joy?

⁸ "Who shut up the sea behind doors
    when it burst forth from the womb,
⁹ when I made the clouds its garment
    and wrapped it in thick darkness,
¹⁰ when I fixed limits for it
    and set its doors and bars in place,
¹¹ when I said, 'This far you may come
        and no farther;
    here is where your proud
        waves halt'?

¹² "Have you ever given orders to
        the morning,
    or shown the dawn its place,
¹³ that it might take the earth by
        the edges
    and shake the wicked out of it?
¹⁴ The earth takes shape like clay
        under a seal;
    its features stand out like those
        of a garment.
¹⁵ The wicked are denied their light,
    and their upraised arm is broken.

¹⁶ "Have you journeyed to the springs
        of the sea
    or walked in the recesses of
        the deep?
¹⁷ Have the gates of death been
        shown to you?
    Have you seen the gates of the
        deepest darkness?
¹⁸ Have you comprehended the vast
        expanses of the earth?
    Tell me, if you know all this.

¹⁹ "What is the way to the abode
        of light?
    And where does darkness reside?
²⁰ Can you take them to their places?
    Do you know the paths to their
        dwellings?
²¹ Surely you know, for you were
        already born!
    You have lived so many years!

²² "Have you entered the storehouses
        of the snow
    or seen the storehouses of
        the hail,
²³ which I reserve for times of trouble,
    for days of war and battle?
²⁴ What is the way to the place where
        the lightning is dispersed,
    or the place where the east winds
        are scattered over the earth?
²⁵ Who cuts a channel for the torrents
        of rain,
    and a path for the thunderstorm,
²⁶ to water a land where no one lives,
    an uninhabited desert,
²⁷ to satisfy a desolate wasteland
    and make it sprout with grass?

---

^a 24 Or for he does not have regard for any who think they
are wise.   ^b 7 Hebrew the sons of God

28 Does the rain have a father?
Who fathers the drops of dew?
29 From whose womb comes the ice?
Who gives birth to the frost from
the heavens
30 when the waters become hard as
stone,
when the surface of the deep
is frozen?

31 "Can you bind the chains*a* of the
Pleiades?
Can you loosen Orion's belt?
32 Can you bring forth the constellations
in their seasons*b*
or lead out the Bear*c* with its cubs?
33 Do you know the laws of the heavens?
Can you set up God's*d* dominion
over the earth?

34 "Can you raise your voice to
the clouds
and cover yourself with a
flood of water?
35 Do you send the lightning bolts on
their way?
Do they report to you,
'Here we are'?
36 Who gives the ibis wisdom*e*
or gives the rooster
understanding?*f*
37 Who has the wisdom to count
the clouds?
Who can tip over the water jars of
the heavens
38 when the dust becomes hard
and the clods of earth stick
together?

39 "Do you hunt the prey for the lioness
and satisfy the hunger of the lions
40 when they crouch in their dens
or lie in wait in a thicket?
41 Who provides food for the raven
when its young cry out to God
and wander about for lack of food?

39 "Do you know when the mountain
goats give birth?
Do you watch when the doe
bears her fawn?
2 Do you count the months till
they bear?
Do you know the time they
give birth?

3 They crouch down and bring forth
their young;
their labor pains are ended.
4 Their young thrive and grow strong in
the wilds;
they leave and do not return.

5 "Who let the wild donkey go free?
Who untied its ropes?
6 I gave it the wasteland as its home,
the salt flats as its habitat.
7 It laughs at the commotion in
the town;
it does not hear a driver's shout.
8 It ranges the hills for its pasture
and searches for any green thing.

9 "Will the wild ox consent to
serve you?
Will it stay by your manger
at night?

---

a 31 Septuagint; Hebrew *beauty*   *b* 32 Or *the morning
star in its season*   *c* 32 Or *out Leo*   *d* 33 Or *their*
e 36 That is, wisdom about the flooding of the Nile
f 36 That is, understanding of when to crow; the meaning
of the Hebrew for this verse is uncertain.

BREAK THROUGH!

Driver
(JOB 39:7)

In the past, and still today in some countries,
they used donkeys, mules and horses to carry
heavy loads. The people who guided these
animals were the drivers who had to shout at
them to make them go faster.

¹⁰Can you hold it to the furrow with a
harness?
Will it till the valleys behind you?
¹¹Will you rely on it for its great
strength?
Will you leave your heavy work to it?
¹²Can you trust it to haul in your grain
and bring it to your threshing floor?

¹³"The wings of the ostrich flap joyfully,
though they cannot compare
with the wings and feathers of
the stork.
¹⁴She lays her eggs on the ground
and lets them warm in the sand,
¹⁵unmindful that a foot may crush them,
that some wild animal may
trample them.
¹⁶She treats her young harshly, as if
they were not hers;
she cares not that her labor
was in vain,
¹⁷for God did not endow her with
wisdom
or give her a share of good sense.
¹⁸Yet when she spreads her feathers
to run,
she laughs at horse and rider.

¹⁹"Do you give the horse its strength
or clothe its neck with a flowing
mane?
²⁰Do you make it leap like a locust,
striking terror with its proud
snorting?
²¹It paws fiercely, rejoicing in its
strength,
and charges into the fray.
²²It laughs at fear, afraid of nothing;
it does not shy away from the
sword.
²³The quiver rattles against its side,
along with the flashing spear
and lance.
²⁴In frenzied excitement it eats up the
ground;
it cannot stand still when the
trumpet sounds.
²⁵At the blast of the trumpet it
snorts, 'Aha!'
It catches the scent of battle
from afar,
the shout of commanders and
the battle cry.

²⁶"Does the hawk take flight by
your wisdom
and spread its wings toward
the south?
²⁷Does the eagle soar at your command
and build its nest on high?
²⁸It dwells on a cliff and stays
there at night;
a rocky crag is its stronghold.
²⁹From there it looks for food;
its eyes detect it from afar.
³⁰Its young ones feast on blood,
and where the slain are, there it is."

40 The LORD said to Job:

² "Will the one who contends with the
Almighty correct him?
Let him who accuses God
answer him!"

³Then Job answered the LORD:

⁴ "I am unworthy—how can I reply
to you?
I put my hand over my mouth.
⁵I spoke once, but I have no answer—
twice, but I will say no more."

⁶Then the LORD spoke to Job out of the
storm:

⁷ "Brace yourself like a man;
I will question you,
and you shall answer me.

⁸ "Would you discredit my justice?
Would you condemn me to justify
yourself?
⁹Do you have an arm like God's,
and can your voice thunder like his?
¹⁰Then adorn yourself with glory
and splendor,
and clothe yourself in honor
and majesty.
¹¹Unleash the fury of your wrath,
look at all who are proud and
bring them low,
¹²look at all who are proud and
humble them,
crush the wicked where they stand.
¹³Bury them all in the dust together;
shroud their faces in the grave.
¹⁴Then I myself will admit to you
that your own right hand
can save you.

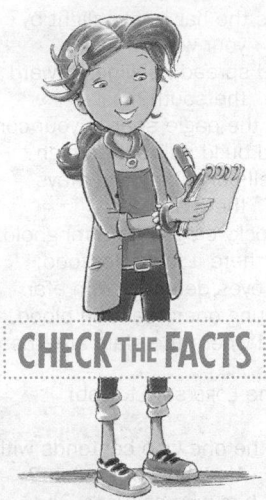

CHECK THE FACTS

**How did Job respond
to the Lord?**

A) Job began shouting at the Lord.

B) Job complained to his friends about
the Lord.

C) Job did not complain anymore, and put
his hand over his mouth.

CORRECT ANSWER: C

15 "Look at Behemoth,
    which I made along with you
    and which feeds on grass
        like an ox.
16 What strength it has in its loins,
    what power in the muscles of
        its belly!
17 Its tail sways like a cedar;
    the sinews of its thighs are
        close-knit.
18 Its bones are tubes of bronze,
    its limbs like rods of iron.
19 It ranks first among the works of God,
    yet its Maker can approach it with
        his sword.
20 The hills bring it their produce,
    and all the wild animals play
        nearby.
21 Under the lotus plants it lies,
    hidden among the reeds in
        the marsh.

22 The lotuses conceal it in their shadow;
    the poplars by the stream
        surround it.
23 A raging river does not alarm it;
    it is secure, though the Jordan
        should surge against its
        mouth.
24 Can anyone capture it by the eyes,
    or trap it and pierce its nose?

41 *a* "Can you pull in Leviathan with a
        fishhook
    or tie down its tongue with a rope?
2 Can you put a cord through its nose
    or pierce its jaw with a hook?
3 Will it keep begging you for mercy?
    Will it speak to you with gentle
        words?
4 Will it make an agreement with you
    for you to take it as your slave
        for life?

---

a In Hebrew texts 41:1-8 is numbered 40:25-32, and
41:9-34 is numbered 41:1-26.

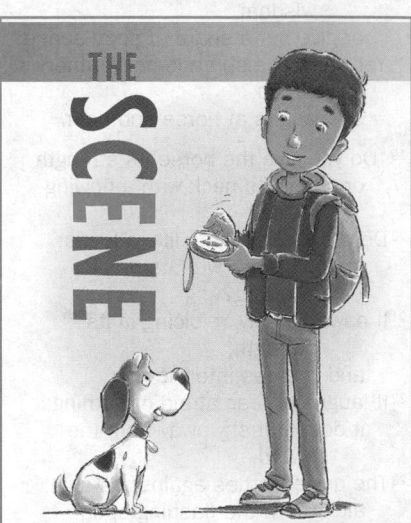

THE SCENE

JORDAN RIVER

(JOB 40:23)

The river that flows through
Palestine from north to south.
Its name means "rolling." It is
famous because Jesus was baptized
there.

⁵Can you make a pet of it like a bird
  or put it on a leash for the young
    women in your house?
⁶Will traders barter for it?
  Will they divide it up among the
    merchants?
⁷Can you fill its hide with harpoons
  or its head with fishing spears?
⁸If you lay a hand on it,
  you will remember the struggle and
    never do it again!
⁹Any hope of subduing it is false;
  the mere sight of it is overpowering.
¹⁰No one is fierce enough to rouse it.
  Who then is able to stand
    against me?
¹¹Who has a claim against me that
    I must pay?
  Everything under heaven
    belongs to me.

¹²"I will not fail to speak of Leviathan's
    limbs,
  its strength and its graceful form.
¹³Who can strip off its outer coat?
  Who can penetrate its double coat
    of armor*a*?
¹⁴Who dares open the doors of
    its mouth,
  ringed about with fearsome teeth?
¹⁵Its back has*b* rows of shields
  tightly sealed together;
¹⁶each is so close to the next
  that no air can pass between.
¹⁷They are joined fast to one another;
  they cling together and cannot
    be parted.
¹⁸Its snorting throws out flashes
    of light;
  its eyes are like the rays of dawn.
¹⁹Flames stream from its mouth;
  sparks of fire shoot out.
²⁰Smoke pours from its nostrils
  as from a boiling pot over
    burning reeds.
²¹Its breath sets coals ablaze,
  and flames dart from its mouth.
²²Strength resides in its neck;
  dismay goes before it.
²³The folds of its flesh are tightly joined;
  they are firm and immovable.
²⁴Its chest is hard as rock,
  hard as a lower millstone.

²⁵When it rises up, the mighty are
    terrified;
  they retreat before its thrashing.
²⁶The sword that reaches it has
    no effect,
  nor does the spear or the dart or
    the javelin.
²⁷Iron it treats like straw
  and bronze like rotten wood.
²⁸Arrows do not make it flee;
  slingstones are like chaff to it.
²⁹A club seems to it but a piece
    of straw;
  it laughs at the rattling of the
    lance.
³⁰Its undersides are jagged potsherds,
  leaving a trail in the mud like a
    threshing sledge.
³¹It makes the depths churn like a
    boiling caldron
  and stirs up the sea like a pot of
    ointment.
³²It leaves a glistening wake behind it;
  one would think the deep had
    white hair.
³³Nothing on earth is its equal—
  a creature without fear.
³⁴It looks down on all that are haughty;
  it is king over all that are proud."

Job

42

Then Job replied to the LORD:

²"I know that you can do all things;
  no purpose of yours can be
    thwarted.
³You asked, 'Who is this that obscures
    my plans without knowledge?'
  Surely I spoke of things I did not
    understand,
  things too wonderful for me
    to know.

⁴"You said, 'Listen now, and I
    will speak;
  I will question you,
    and you shall answer me.'
⁵My ears had heard of you
  but now my eyes have seen you.
⁶Therefore I despise myself
  and repent in dust and ashes."

---

a 13 Septuagint; Hebrew *double bridle*   *b* 15 Or *Its pride
is its*

Epilogue

⁷After the LORD had said these things to Job, he said to Eliphaz the Temanite, "I am angry with you and your two friends, because you have not spoken the truth about me, as my servant Job has. ⁸So now take seven bulls and seven rams and go to my servant Job and sacrifice a burnt offering for yourselves. My servant Job will pray for you, and I will accept his prayer and not deal with you according to your folly. You have not spoken the truth about me, as my servant Job has." ⁹So Eliphaz the Temanite, Bildad the Shuhite and Zophar the Naamathite did what the LORD told them; and the LORD accepted Job's prayer.

¹⁰After Job had prayed for his friends, the LORD restored his fortunes and gave him twice as much as he had before. ¹¹All his brothers and sisters and everyone who had known him before came and ate with him in his house. They comforted and consoled him over all the trouble the LORD had brought on him, and each one gave him a piece of silverᵃ and a gold ring.

¹²The LORD blessed the latter part of Job's life more than the former part. He had fourteen thousand sheep, six thousand camels, a thousand yoke of oxen and a thousand donkeys. ¹³And he also had seven sons and three daughters. ¹⁴The first daughter he named Jemimah, the second Keziah and the third Keren-Happuch. ¹⁵Nowhere in all the land were there found women as beautiful as Job's daughters, and their father granted them an inheritance along with their brothers.

¹⁶After this, Job lived a hundred and forty years; he saw his children and their children to the fourth generation. ¹⁷And so Job died, an old man and full of years.

ᵃ 11 Hebrew *him a kesitah*; a kesitah was a unit of money of unknown weight and value.

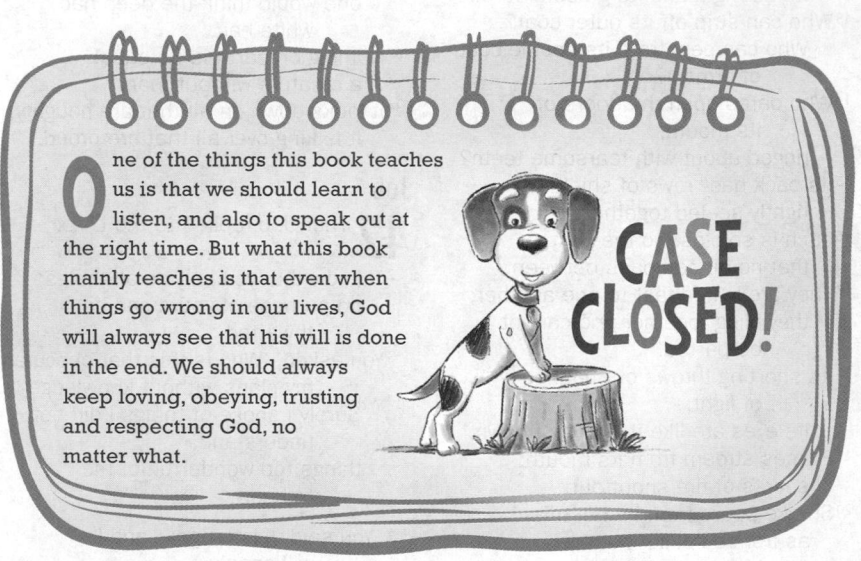

One of the things this book teaches us is that we should learn to listen, and also to speak out at the right time. But what this book mainly teaches is that even when things go wrong in our lives, God will always see that his will is done in the end. We should always keep loving, obeying, trusting and respecting God, no matter what.

CASE CLOSED!

PSALMS

THE EVIDENCE:

Psalms is a word that comes from the Greek and Latin languages and means "praise" or "song" with string instruments. So we could say that the book of Psalms is a song- or hymnbook. But there are also psalms that the people sang while they were on a pilgrimage (a kind of travel that many people do all together with a religious purpose) to Jerusalem. Throughout history, the psalms have really been sung more than they have been read.

WHO WROTE IT?

Isabella asked her dad if it's true that King David wrote them, because that's what we'd heard. And he told us that David did write many of them. But others were written by the sons of Korah and the sons of Asaph, and there is even a prayer of Moses.

HOW LONG AGO?

Not all of them were written during David's reign. The Psalms were collected over a period of time. Because a lot of them say "Psalm of David," the whole collection got to be known as Psalms of David.

WHAT'S IT ABOUT?

The Psalms are both songs and poems. Some are really joyful and others sound more like complaints. That's because different authors expressed different moods in their songs. Some writers were sad, some were persecuted, and others were sick, but they all asked for God's help. So a prayer can also be a song.

THE BEST PART

I like some Psalms more than others. But they all talk about the Word of God and his love and care for us. Perhaps Psalm 119 is the best, not just because it's the longest, but because the main idea is about the Word of God. This verse is very nice: "Your word is a lamp for my feet, a light on my path" (119:105).

BOOK I

Psalms 1 – 41

Psalm 1

¹ Blessed is the one
    who does not walk in step with the
        wicked
    or stand in the way that sinners
        take
    or sit in the company of mockers,
² but whose delight is in the law of the
        LORD,
    and who meditates on his law day
        and night.
³ That person is like a tree planted by
        streams of water,
    which yields its fruit in season
    and whose leaf does not wither—
        whatever they do prospers.

⁴ Not so the wicked!
    They are like chaff
        that the wind blows away.
⁵ Therefore the wicked will not stand in
        the judgment,
    nor sinners in the assembly of the
        righteous.

⁶ For the LORD watches over the way of
        the righteous,
    but the way of the wicked leads to
        destruction.

Psalm 2

¹ Why do the nations conspire[a]
    and the peoples plot in vain?
² The kings of the earth rise up
    and the rulers band together
    against the LORD and against his
        anointed, saying,
³ "Let us break their chains
    and throw off their shackles."

⁴ The One enthroned in heaven
        laughs;
    the Lord scoffs at them.
⁵ He rebukes them in his anger
    and terrifies them in his wrath,
        saying,
⁶ "I have installed my king
    on Zion, my holy mountain."

⁷ I will proclaim the LORD's decree:

He said to me, "You are my son;
    today I have become your father.
⁸ Ask me,
    and I will make the nations your
        inheritance,
    the ends of the earth your
        possession.
⁹ You will break them with a rod of iron[b];
    you will dash them to pieces like
        pottery."

¹⁰ Therefore, you kings, be wise;
    be warned, you rulers of the earth.
¹¹ Serve the LORD with fear
    and celebrate his rule with
        trembling.
¹² Kiss his son, or he will be angry
    and your way will lead to your
        destruction,
    for his wrath can flare up in a moment.
    Blessed are all who take refuge in
        him.

Psalm 3[c]

A psalm of David. When he fled
from his son Absalom.

¹ LORD, how many are my foes!
    How many rise up against me!
² Many are saying of me,
    "God will not deliver him."[d]

³ But you, LORD, are a shield around me,
    my glory, the One who lifts my head
        high.
⁴ I call out to the LORD,
    and he answers me from his holy
        mountain.

⁵ I lie down and sleep;
    I wake again, because the LORD
        sustains me.
⁶ I will not fear though tens of thousands
    assail me on every side.

⁷ Arise, LORD!
    Deliver me, my God!
    Strike all my enemies on the jaw;
    break the teeth of the wicked.

---

a 1 Hebrew; Septuagint *rage*   *b* 9 Or *will rule them with
an iron scepter* (see Septuagint and Syriac)   *c* In Hebrew
texts 3:1-8 is numbered 3:2-9.   *d* 2 The Hebrew has
Selah (a word of uncertain meaning) here and at the end of
verses 4 and 8.

THE
WITNESSES

✓ **DAVID** (PSALM 3)
He was an Israelite sheepherder who became the second king of Israel. He's accepted as the author of the psalms, although he really didn't compose all of them alone. His name means "beloved."

✓ **ABSALOM** (PSALM 3)
He was David's third son. His mother was Maakah. His name means "father of peace."

⁸ From the LORD comes deliverance.
　May your blessing be on your people.

Psalm 4[a]

For the director of music. With stringed
instruments. A psalm of David.

¹ Answer me when I call to you,
　my righteous God.
　Give me relief from my distress;
　　have mercy on me and hear my
　　prayer.

² How long will you people turn my glory
　into shame?
　How long will you love delusions
　　and seek false gods[b]?[c]
³ Know that the LORD has set apart his
　faithful servant for himself;
　the LORD hears when I call to him.

⁴ Tremble and[d] do not sin;
　when you are on your beds,
　search your hearts and be silent.
⁵ Offer the sacrifices of the righteous
　and trust in the LORD.

⁶ Many, LORD, are asking, "Who will bring
　us prosperity?"
　Let the light of your face shine on
　us.
⁷ Fill my heart with joy
　when their grain and new wine
　abound.

⁸ In peace I will lie down and sleep,
　for you alone, LORD,
　make me dwell in safety.

Psalm 5[e]

For the director of music. For pipes.
A psalm of David.

¹ Listen to my words, LORD,
　consider my lament.
² Hear my cry for help,
　my King and my God,
　for to you I pray.

³ In the morning, LORD, you hear my
　voice;
　in the morning I lay my requests
　before you
　and wait expectantly.
⁴ For you are not a God who is pleased
　with wickedness;
　with you, evil people are not
　welcome.
⁵ The arrogant cannot stand
　in your presence.
　You hate all who do wrong;
⁶ 　you destroy those who tell lies.
　The bloodthirsty and deceitful
　you, LORD, detest.

---

a In Hebrew texts 4:1-8 is numbered 4:2-9.　　b 2 Or seek
lies　　c 2 The Hebrew has Selah (a word of uncertain
meaning) here and at the end of verse 4.　　d 4 Or In your
anger (see Septuagint)　　e In Hebrew texts 5:1-12 is
numbered 5:2-13.

⁷ But I, by your great love,
  can come into your house;
  in reverence I bow down
  toward your holy temple.

⁸ Lead me, Lord, in your righteousness
  because of my enemies—
  make your way straight before me.
⁹ Not a word from their mouth can be
    trusted;
  their heart is filled with malice.
  Their throat is an open grave;
  with their tongues they tell lies.
¹⁰ Declare them guilty, O God!
  Let their intrigues be their downfall.
  Banish them for their many sins,
  for they have rebelled against you.
¹¹ But let all who take refuge in you be
    glad;
  let them ever sing for joy.
  Spread your protection over them,
  that those who love your name may
    rejoice in you.

¹² Surely, Lord, you bless the righteous;
  you surround them with your favor
  as with a shield.

Psalm 6 ᵃ

For the director of music. With stringed
instruments. According to *sheminith.* ᵇ
A psalm of David.

¹ Lord, do not rebuke me in your anger
  or discipline me in your wrath.
² Have mercy on me, Lord, for I am
    faint;
  heal me, Lord, for my bones are in
    agony.
³ My soul is in deep anguish.
  How long, Lord, how long?

⁴ Turn, Lord, and deliver me;
  save me because of your unfailing
    love.
⁵ Among the dead no one proclaims
    your name.
  Who praises you from the grave?

⁶ I am worn out from my groaning.

  All night long I flood my bed with
    weeping
  and drench my couch with tears.
⁷ My eyes grow weak with sorrow;
  they fail because of all my foes.

⁸ Away from me, all you who do evil,
  for the Lord has heard my weeping.
⁹ The Lord has heard my cry for
    mercy;
  the Lord accepts my prayer.
¹⁰ All my enemies will be overwhelmed
    with shame and anguish;
  they will turn back and suddenly be
    put to shame.

Psalm 7 ᶜ

A *shiggaion* ᵈ of David, which he sang to the
Lord concerning Cush, a Benjamite.

¹ Lord my God, I take refuge in you;
  save and deliver me from all who
    pursue me,
² or they will tear me apart like a lion
  and rip me to pieces with no one to
    rescue me.

³ Lord my God, if I have done this
  and there is guilt on my hands—
⁴ if I have repaid my ally with evil
  or without cause have robbed my
    foe—
⁵ then let my enemy pursue and
    overtake me;
  let him trample my life to the
    ground
  and make me sleep in the dust. ᵉ

⁶ Arise, Lord, in your anger;
  rise up against the rage of my
    enemies.
  Awake, my God; decree justice.
⁷ Let the assembled peoples gather
    around you,
  while you sit enthroned over them
    on high.
⁸   Let the Lord judge the peoples.
  Vindicate me, Lord, according to my
    righteousness,
  according to my integrity, O Most
    High.
⁹ Bring to an end the violence of the
    wicked
  and make the righteous secure—
  you, the righteous God
  who probes minds and hearts.

ᵃ In Hebrew texts 6:1-10 is numbered 6:2-11.   ᵇ Title:
Probably a musical term   ᶜ In Hebrew texts 7:1-17 is
numbered 7:2-18.   ᵈ Title: Probably a literary or musical
term   ᵉ 5 The Hebrew has *Selah* (a word of uncertain
meaning) here.

10 My shield[a] is God Most High,
　　who saves the upright in heart.
11 God is a righteous judge,
　　a God who displays his wrath every
　　　day.
12 If he does not relent,
　　he[b] will sharpen his sword;
　　he will bend and string his bow.
13 He has prepared his deadly weapons;
　　he makes ready his flaming arrows.

14 Whoever is pregnant with evil
　　conceives trouble and gives birth to
　　　disillusionment.
15 Whoever digs a hole and scoops it out
　　falls into the pit they have made.
16 The trouble they cause recoils on
　　　them;

THE
WITNESSES

✓ **CUSH** (PSALM 7)
The man Cush isn't mentioned anywhere else
in the Bible. He may have been trying to kill
David.

BREAK THROUGH!

Judging
(PSALM 7:8)
In the Psalms, sometimes God is seen like
a judge who can punish or forgive a guilty
person. In those cases, the decision of God is
called a "sentence."

their violence comes down on their
　　own heads.
17 I will give thanks to the LORD because
　　of his righteousness;
　　I will sing the praises of the name
　　of the LORD Most High.

Psalm 8[c]

For the director of music. According
to *gittith.*[d] A psalm of David.

1 LORD, our Lord,
　　how majestic is your name in all the
　　　earth!
　You have set your glory
　　in the heavens.
2 Through the praise of children and
　　　infants
　you have established a stronghold
　　against your enemies,
　　to silence the foe and the avenger.

---

[a] 10 Or *sovereign*　　[b] 12 Or *If anyone does not repent,* /
God　　[c] In Hebrew texts 8:1-9 is numbered 8:2-10.
[d] Title: Probably a musical term

BREAKTHROUGH!

Does God have a sword, a bow and weapons for killing?

(PSALM 7:12-13)

The poets used examples of things everybody was familiar with in order to talk about things they'd never seen. That's called "figurative language." Here, and in other Psalms too (for example, Psalm 17:13-14), God is talked about as a warrior and armed with a sword and a bow and arrows. That doesn't mean that God uses these weapons. It's just that the author of the Psalms uses this idea to explain God's power to us.

3 When I consider your heavens,
 the work of your fingers,
 the moon and the stars,
 which you have set in place,
4 what is mankind that you are mindful
 of them,
 human beings that you care for
 them?*a*

5 You have made them*b* a little lower
 than the angels*c*
 and crowned them*b* with glory and
 honor.
6 You made them rulers over the works
 of your hands;
 you put everything under their*d* feet:

7 all flocks and herds,
 and the animals of the wild,
8 the birds in the sky,
 and the fish in the sea,
 all that swim the paths of the seas.

9 LORD, our Lord,
 how majestic is your name in all the
 earth!

Psalm 9*e,f*

For the director of music. To the tune
of "The Death of the Son."
A psalm of David.

1 I will give thanks to you, LORD, with all
 my heart;
 I will tell of all your wonderful
 deeds.
2 I will be glad and rejoice in you;
 I will sing the praises of your name,
 O Most High.

3 My enemies turn back;
 they stumble and perish before you.
4 For you have upheld my right and my
 cause,
 sitting enthroned as the righteous
 judge.
5 You have rebuked the nations and
 destroyed the wicked;
 you have blotted out their name for
 ever and ever.
6 Endless ruin has overtaken my
 enemies,
 you have uprooted their cities;
 even the memory of them has
 perished.

7 The LORD reigns forever;
 he has established his throne for
 judgment.
8 He rules the world in righteousness
 and judges the peoples with
 equity.
9 The LORD is a refuge for the
 oppressed,
 a stronghold in times of trouble.

---

a 4 Or *what is a human being that you are mindful of him,* /
a son of man that you care for him?   *b* 5 Or *him*
c 5 Or *than God*   *d* 6 Or *made him ruler . . . ;* / *. . . his*
e Psalms 9 and 10 may originally have been a single
acrostic poem in which alternating lines began with the
successive letters of the Hebrew alphabet. In the
Septuagint they constitute one psalm.   *f* In Hebrew texts
9:1-20 is numbered 9:2-21.

¹⁰ Those who know your name trust in
you,
for you, LORD, have never forsaken
those who seek you.

¹¹ Sing the praises of the LORD,
enthroned in Zion;
proclaim among the nations what
he has done.

¹² For he who avenges blood remembers;
he does not ignore the cries of the
afflicted.

¹³ LORD, see how my enemies persecute
me!
Have mercy and lift me up from the
gates of death,

¹⁴ that I may declare your praises
in the gates of Daughter Zion,
and there rejoice in your salvation.

¹⁵ The nations have fallen into the pit
they have dug;
their feet are caught in the net they
have hidden.

¹⁶ The LORD is known by his acts of
justice;

BREAKTHROUGH!

Does God sit on a throne?

(PSALM 9:7)

Here, God is described as a king, so it says
he's ruling from on high, like sitting high up
on a throne.

the wicked are ensnared by the
work of their hands.^a

¹⁷ The wicked go down to the realm of
the dead,
all the nations that forget God.

¹⁸ But God will never forget the needy;
the hope of the afflicted will never
perish.

¹⁹ Arise, LORD, do not let mortals triumph;
let the nations be judged in your
presence.

²⁰ Strike them with terror, LORD;
let the nations know they are only
mortal.

Psalm 10^b

¹ Why, LORD, do you stand far off?
Why do you hide yourself in times of
trouble?

² In his arrogance the wicked man
hunts down the weak,
who are caught in the schemes he
devises.

³ He boasts about the cravings of his
heart;
he blesses the greedy and reviles
the LORD.

⁴ In his pride the wicked man does not
seek him;
in all his thoughts there is no room
for God.

⁵ His ways are always prosperous;
your laws are rejected by^c him;
he sneers at all his enemies.

⁶ He says to himself, "Nothing will ever
shake me."
He swears, "No one will ever do me
harm."

⁷ His mouth is full of lies and threats;
trouble and evil are under his
tongue.

⁸ He lies in wait near the villages;
from ambush he murders the
innocent.

---

^a 16 The Hebrew has *Higgaion* and *Selah* (words of
uncertain meaning) here; *Selah* occurs also at the end of
verse 20.   ^b Psalms 9 and 10 may originally have been
a single acrostic poem in which alternating lines began
with the successive letters of the Hebrew alphabet. In the
Septuagint they constitute one psalm.   ^c 5 See
Septuagint; Hebrew / *they are haughty, and your laws are
far from*

His eyes watch in secret for his
     victims;
9   like a lion in cover he lies in wait.
He lies in wait to catch the helpless;
     he catches the helpless and drags
     them off in his net.
10 His victims are crushed, they collapse;
     they fall under his strength.
11 He says to himself, "God will never
     notice;
     he covers his face and never sees."

12 Arise, LORD! Lift up your hand, O God.
     Do not forget the helpless.
13 Why does the wicked man revile
     God?
     Why does he say to himself,
     "He won't call me to account"?
14 But you, God, see the trouble of the
     afflicted;
     you consider their grief and take it
     in hand.
The victims commit themselves to
     you;
     you are the helper of the fatherless.
15 Break the arm of the wicked man;
     call the evildoer to account for his
     wickedness
     that would not otherwise be found
     out.

16 The LORD is King for ever and ever;
     the nations will perish from his
     land.
17 You, LORD, hear the desire of the
     afflicted;
     you encourage them, and you listen
     to their cry,
18 defending the fatherless and the
     oppressed,
     so that mere earthly mortals
     will never again strike terror.

Psalm 11

For the director of music. Of David.

1 In the LORD I take refuge.
     How then can you say to me:
     "Flee like a bird to your mountain.
2 For look, the wicked bend their bows;
     they set their arrows against the
     strings
to shoot from the shadows
     at the upright in heart.

3 When the foundations are being
     destroyed,
     what can the righteous do?"

4 The LORD is in his holy temple;
     the LORD is on his heavenly throne.
He observes everyone on earth;
     his eyes examine them.
5 The LORD examines the righteous,
     but the wicked, those who love
     violence,
     he hates with a passion.
6 On the wicked he will rain
     fiery coals and burning sulfur;
     a scorching wind will be their lot.

7 For the LORD is righteous,
     he loves justice;
     the upright will see his face.

Psalm 12 [a]

For the director of music. According
to *sheminith*. [b] A psalm of David.

1 Help, LORD, for no one is faithful
     anymore;
     those who are loyal have vanished
     from the human race.
2 Everyone lies to their neighbor;
     they flatter with their lips
     but harbor deception in their hearts.

3 May the LORD silence all flattering lips
     and every boastful tongue—
4 those who say,
     "By our tongues we will prevail;
     our own lips will defend us—who is
     lord over us?"

5 "Because the poor are plundered and
     the needy groan,
     I will now arise," says the LORD.
     "I will protect them from those who
     malign them."
6 And the words of the LORD are
     flawless,
     like silver purified in a crucible,
     like gold [c] refined seven times.

7 You, LORD, will keep the needy safe
     and will protect us forever from the
     wicked,

---

a In Hebrew texts 12:1-8 is numbered 12:2-9.   *b* Title:
Probably a musical term   *c* 6 Probable reading of the
original Hebrew text; Masoretic Text *earth*

8 who freely strut about
  when what is vile is honored by the
    human race.

Psalm 13 [a]

For the director of music.
A psalm of David.

1 How long, LORD? Will you forget me
    forever?
  How long will you hide your face
    from me?
2 How long must I wrestle with my
    thoughts
  and day after day have sorrow in my
    heart?
  How long will my enemy triumph
    over me?

3 Look on me and answer, LORD my God.
  Give light to my eyes, or I will sleep
    in death,
4 and my enemy will say, "I have
    overcome him,"
  and my foes will rejoice when I fall.

5 But I trust in your unfailing love;
  my heart rejoices in your salvation.
6 I will sing the LORD's praise,
  for he has been good to me.

Psalm 14

For the director of music. Of David.

1 The fool [b] says in his heart,
    "There is no God."
  They are corrupt, their deeds are
    vile;
  there is no one who does good.

2 The LORD looks down from heaven
    on all mankind
  to see if there are any who
    understand,
  any who seek God.
3 All have turned away, all have become
    corrupt;
  there is no one who does good,
    not even one.

4 Do all these evildoers know nothing?

  They devour my people as though
    eating bread;
  they never call on the LORD.

5 But there they are, overwhelmed with
    dread,
  for God is present in the company
    of the righteous.
6 You evildoers frustrate the plans of
    the poor,
  but the LORD is their refuge.

7 Oh, that salvation for Israel would
    come out of Zion!
  When the LORD restores his people,
  let Jacob rejoice and Israel be glad!

Psalm 15

A psalm of David.

1 LORD, who may dwell in your sacred
    tent?
  Who may live on your holy
    mountain?

2 The one whose walk is blameless,
    who does what is righteous,
    who speaks the truth from their
    heart;
3 whose tongue utters no slander,
    who does no wrong to a neighbor,
    and casts no slur on others;
4 who despises a vile person
    but honors those who fear the
    LORD;
  who keeps an oath even when it
    hurts,
    and does not change their mind;
5 who lends money to the poor without
    interest;
  who does not accept a bribe
    against the innocent.

  Whoever does these things
    will never be shaken.

Psalm 16

A *miktam* [c] of David.

1 Keep me safe, my God,
    for in you I take refuge.

2 I say to the LORD, "You are my Lord;
    apart from you I have no good
    thing."

---

a In Hebrew texts 13:1-6 is numbered 13:2-6.   *b* 1 The
Hebrew words rendered *fool* in Psalms denote one who is
morally deficient.   *c* Title: Probably a literary or musical
term

3 I say of the holy people who are in the
        land,
    "They are the noble ones in whom
        is all my delight."
4 Those who run after other gods will
        suffer more and more.
    I will not pour out libations of blood
        to such gods
    or take up their names on my lips.

5 Lord, you alone are my portion and my
        cup;
    you make my lot secure.
6 The boundary lines have fallen for me
        in pleasant places;
    surely I have a delightful
        inheritance.
7 I will praise the Lord, who counsels
        me;
    even at night my heart instructs me.
8 I keep my eyes always on the Lord.
    With him at my right hand, I will not
        be shaken.

9 Therefore my heart is glad and my
        tongue rejoices;
    my body also will rest secure,
10 because you will not abandon me to
        the realm of the dead,
    nor will you let your faithful a one
        see decay.
11 You make known to me the path of
        life;
    you will fill me with joy in your
        presence,
    with eternal pleasures at your right
        hand.

Psalm 17

A prayer of David.

1 Hear me, Lord, my plea is just;
    listen to my cry.
    Hear my prayer—
    it does not rise from deceitful lips.
2 Let my vindication come from you;
    may your eyes see what is right.

3 Though you probe my heart,
    though you examine me at night
        and test me,
    you will find that I have planned no
        evil;
    my mouth has not transgressed.

4 Though people tried to bribe me,
    I have kept myself from the ways of
        the violent
    through what your lips have
        commanded.
5 My steps have held to your paths;
    my feet have not stumbled.

6 I call on you, my God, for you will
        answer me;
    turn your ear to me and hear my
        prayer.
7 Show me the wonders of your great
        love,
    you who save by your right hand
    those who take refuge in you from
        their foes.
8 Keep me as the apple of your eye;
    hide me in the shadow of your
        wings
9 from the wicked who are out to
        destroy me,
    from my mortal enemies who
        surround me.

10 They close up their callous hearts,
    and their mouths speak with
        arrogance.
11 They have tracked me down, they now
        surround me,
    with eyes alert, to throw me to the
        ground.
12 They are like a lion hungry for prey,
    like a fierce lion crouching in cover.

13 Rise up, Lord, confront them, bring
        them down;
    with your sword rescue me from the
        wicked.
14 By your hand save me from such
        people, Lord,
    from those of this world whose
        reward is in this life.
    May what you have stored up for the
        wicked fill their bellies;
    may their children gorge themselves
        on it,
    and may there be leftovers for their
        little ones.

15 As for me, I will be vindicated and will
        see your face;
    when I awake, I will be satisfied with
        seeing your likeness.

_____
a 10 Or holy

Psalm 18 [a]

For the director of music. Of David the servant of the LORD. He sang to the LORD the words of this song when the LORD delivered him from the hand of all his enemies and from the hand of Saul. He said:

¹ I love you, LORD, my strength.

² The LORD is my rock, my fortress and
  my deliverer;
  my God is my rock, in whom I take
    refuge,
  my shield[b] and the horn[c] of my
    salvation, my stronghold.

³ I called to the LORD, who is worthy of
    praise,
  and I have been saved from my
    enemies.

⁴ The cords of death entangled me;
  the torrents of destruction
    overwhelmed me.

⁵ The cords of the grave coiled around
    me;
  the snares of death confronted me.

⁶ In my distress I called to the LORD;
  I cried to my God for help.
  From his temple he heard my
    voice;
  my cry came before him, into his
    ears.

⁷ The earth trembled and quaked,
  and the foundations of the
    mountains shook;
  they trembled because he was
    angry.

⁸ Smoke rose from his nostrils;
  consuming fire came from his
    mouth,
  burning coals blazed out of it.

⁹ He parted the heavens and came
    down;
  dark clouds were under his feet.

¹⁰ He mounted the cherubim and flew;
  he soared on the wings of the
    wind.

¹¹ He made darkness his covering, his
    canopy around him—
  the dark rain clouds of the sky.

¹² Out of the brightness of his presence
    clouds advanced,
  with hailstones and bolts of
    lightning.

¹³ The LORD thundered from heaven;
  the voice of the Most High
    resounded.[d]

¹⁴ He shot his arrows and scattered the
    enemy,
  with great bolts of lightning he
    routed them.

¹⁵ The valleys of the sea were exposed
  and the foundations of the earth
    laid bare
  at your rebuke, LORD,
  at the blast of breath from your
    nostrils.

¹⁶ He reached down from on high and
    took hold of me;
  he drew me out of deep waters.

¹⁷ He rescued me from my powerful
    enemy,
  from my foes, who were too strong
    for me.

¹⁸ They confronted me in the day of my
    disaster,
  but the LORD was my support.

¹⁹ He brought me out into a spacious
    place;
  he rescued me because he
    delighted in me.

²⁰ The LORD has dealt with me according
    to my righteousness;
  according to the cleanness of my
    hands he has rewarded me.

²¹ For I have kept the ways of the LORD;
  I am not guilty of turning from my
    God.

²² All his laws are before me;
  I have not turned away from his
    decrees.

²³ I have been blameless before him
  and have kept myself from sin.

²⁴ The LORD has rewarded me according
    to my righteousness,
  according to the cleanness of my
    hands in his sight.

²⁵ To the faithful you show yourself
    faithful,
  to the blameless you show yourself
    blameless,

---

[a] In Hebrew texts 18:1-50 is numbered 18:2-51.   [b] 2 Or
sovereign   [c] 2 Horn here symbolizes strength.
[d] 13 Some Hebrew manuscripts and Septuagint (see also
2 Samuel 22:14); most Hebrew manuscripts resounded, /
amid hailstones and bolts of lightning

26 to the pure you show yourself pure,
  but to the devious you show
  yourself shrewd.
27 You save the humble
  but bring low those whose eyes are
  haughty.
28 You, Lord, keep my lamp burning;
  my God turns my darkness into
  light.
29 With your help I can advance against a
  troop*a*;
  with my God I can scale a wall.

30 As for God, his way is perfect:
  The Lord's word is flawless;
  he shields all who take refuge in
  him.
31 For who is God besides the Lord?
  And who is the Rock except our
  God?
32 It is God who arms me with strength
  and keeps my way secure.
33 He makes my feet like the feet of a
  deer;
  he causes me to stand on the
  heights.
34 He trains my hands for battle;
  my arms can bend a bow of bronze.
35 You make your saving help my shield,
  and your right hand sustains me;
  your help has made me great.
36 You provide a broad path for my feet,
  so that my ankles do not give way.
37 I pursued my enemies and overtook
  them;
  I did not turn back till they were
  destroyed.
38 I crushed them so that they could not
  rise;
  they fell beneath my feet.
39 You armed me with strength for battle;
  you humbled my adversaries before
  me.
40 You made my enemies turn their
  backs in flight,
  and I destroyed my foes.
41 They cried for help, but there was no
  one to save them—
  to the Lord, but he did not answer.
42 I beat them as fine as windblown
  dust;
  I trampled them*b* like mud in the
  streets.

43 You have delivered me from the
  attacks of the people;
  you have made me the head of
  nations.
  People I did not know now serve me,
44   foreigners cower before me;
  as soon as they hear of me, they
  obey me.
45 They all lose heart;
  they come trembling from their
  strongholds.

46 The Lord lives! Praise be to my Rock!
  Exalted be God my Savior!
47 He is the God who avenges me,
  who subdues nations under me,
48   who saves me from my enemies.
  You exalted me above my foes;
  from a violent man you rescued me.
49 Therefore I will praise you, Lord,
  among the nations;
  I will sing the praises of your name.

50 He gives his king great victories;
  he shows unfailing love to his
  anointed,
  to David and to his descendants
  forever.

Psalm 19*c*

For the director of music.
A psalm of David.

1 The heavens declare the glory of God;
  the skies proclaim the work of his
  hands.
2 Day after day they pour forth speech;
  night after night they reveal
  knowledge.
3 They have no speech, they use no
  words;
  no sound is heard from them.
4 Yet their voice*d* goes out into all the
  earth,
  their words to the ends of the
  world.
  In the heavens God has pitched a tent
  for the sun.
5   It is like a bridegroom coming out of
  his chamber,

---

a 29 Or *can run through a barricade*   *b* 42 Many Hebrew
manuscripts, Septuagint, Syriac and Targum (see also
2 Samuel 22:43); Masoretic Text *I poured them out*   *c* In
Hebrew texts 19:1-14 is numbered 19:2-15.
d 4 Septuagint, Jerome and Syriac; Hebrew *measuring line*

like a champion rejoicing to run his
course.
⁶It rises at one end of the heavens
and makes its circuit to the other;
nothing is deprived of its warmth.

⁷The law of the Lᴏʀᴅ is perfect,
refreshing the soul.
The statutes of the Lᴏʀᴅ are
trustworthy,
making wise the simple.
⁸The precepts of the Lᴏʀᴅ are right,
giving joy to the heart.
The commands of the Lᴏʀᴅ are
radiant,
giving light to the eyes.
⁹The fear of the Lᴏʀᴅ is pure,
enduring forever.
The decrees of the Lᴏʀᴅ are firm,
and all of them are righteous.

¹⁰They are more precious than gold,
than much pure gold;
they are sweeter than honey,
than honey from the honeycomb.
¹¹By them your servant is warned;
in keeping them there is great
reward.
¹²But who can discern their own errors?
Forgive my hidden faults.
¹³Keep your servant also from willful
sins;
may they not rule over me.
Then I will be blameless,
innocent of great transgression.

¹⁴May these words of my mouth and
this meditation of my heart
be pleasing in your sight,
Lᴏʀᴅ, my Rock and my Redeemer.

Psalm 20ᵃ

For the director of music.
A psalm of David.

¹May the Lᴏʀᴅ answer you when you
are in distress;
may the name of the God of Jacob
protect you.
²May he send you help from the
sanctuary
and grant you support from Zion.
³May he remember all your sacrifices
and accept your burnt offerings.ᵇ

⁴May he give you the desire of your
heart
and make all your plans succeed.
⁵May we shout for joy over your
victory
and lift up our banners in the
name of our God.

May the Lᴏʀᴅ grant all your requests.

⁶Now this I know:
The Lᴏʀᴅ gives victory to his
anointed.
He answers him from his heavenly
sanctuary
with the victorious power of his right
hand.
⁷Some trust in chariots and some in
horses,
but we trust in the name of the Lᴏʀᴅ
our God.
⁸They are brought to their knees and
fall,
but we rise up and stand firm.
⁹Lᴏʀᴅ, give victory to the king!
Answer us when we call!

Psalm 21ᶜ

For the director of music.
A psalm of David.

¹The king rejoices in your strength,
Lᴏʀᴅ.
How great is his joy in the victories
you give!

²You have granted him his heart's
desire
and have not withheld the request
of his lips.ᵇ
³You came to greet him with rich
blessings
and placed a crown of pure gold on
his head.
⁴He asked you for life, and you gave it
to him—
length of days, for ever and ever.
⁵Through the victories you gave, his
glory is great;
you have bestowed on him splendor
and majesty.

ᵃ In Hebrew texts 20:1-9 is numbered 20:2-10.
ᵇ 3,2 The Hebrew has *Selah* (a word of uncertain meaning)
here. ᶜ In Hebrew texts 21:1-13 is numbered 21:2-14.

⁶Surely you have granted him unending
　　blessings
　　and made him glad with the joy of
　　　your presence.
⁷For the king trusts in the LORD;
　　through the unfailing love of the
　　　Most High
　　he will not be shaken.

⁸Your hand will lay hold on all your
　　enemies;
　　your right hand will seize your foes.
⁹When you appear for battle,
　　you will burn them up as in a
　　　blazing furnace.
The LORD will swallow them up in his
　　wrath,
　　and his fire will consume them.
¹⁰You will destroy their descendants
　　from the earth,
　　their posterity from mankind.
¹¹Though they plot evil against you
　　and devise wicked schemes, they
　　　cannot succeed.

BREAK THROUGH!

"You will burn them up as in a blazing furnace."

(PSALM 21:8-9)

When a person gets angry, it's said that his
anger is "red hot." Here, God is described as a
person, burning with anger and burning his
enemies up with fire.

¹²You will make them turn their backs
　　when you aim at them with drawn
　　　bow.
¹³Be exalted in your strength, LORD;
　　we will sing and praise your might.

Psalm 22ᵃ

For the director of music. To the tune
of "The Doe of the Morning."
A psalm of David.

¹My God, my God, why have you
　　forsaken me?
　Why are you so far from saving me,
　　so far from my cries of anguish?
²My God, I cry out by day, but you do
　　not answer,
　　by night, but I find no rest.ᵇ

³Yet you are enthroned as the Holy
　　One;
　　you are the one Israel praises.ᶜ
⁴In you our ancestors put their trust;
　　they trusted and you delivered
　　　them.
⁵To you they cried out and were saved;
　　in you they trusted and were not put
　　　to shame.

⁶But I am a worm and not a man,
　　scorned by everyone, despised by
　　　the people.
⁷All who see me mock me;
　　they hurl insults, shaking their
　　　heads.
⁸"He trusts in the LORD," they say,
　　"let the LORD rescue him.
　Let him deliver him,
　　since he delights in him."

⁹Yet you brought me out of the womb;
　　you made me trust in you, even at
　　　my mother's breast.
¹⁰From birth I was cast on you;
　　from my mother's womb you have
　　　been my God.

¹¹Do not be far from me,
　　for trouble is near
　　and there is no one to help.

¹²Many bulls surround me;
　　strong bulls of Bashan encircle me.

ᵃ In Hebrew texts 22:1-31 is numbered 22:2-32.　　ᵇ 2 Or
night, and am not silent　　ᶜ 3 Or Yet you are holy, /
enthroned on the praises of Israel

BREAK THROUGH!

Strong bulls of Bashan
(PSALM 22:12)
Bashan was a region of good pastureland, and the cows the people raised were famous for their strength.

13 Roaring lions that tear their prey
    open their mouths wide against me.
14 I am poured out like water,
    and all my bones are out of joint.
  My heart has turned to wax;
    it has melted within me.
15 My mouth[a] is dried up like a potsherd,
    and my tongue sticks to the roof of
      my mouth;
  you lay me in the dust of death.
16 Dogs surround me,
    a pack of villains encircles me;
  they pierce[b] my hands and my
      feet.
17 All my bones are on display;
    people stare and gloat over me.
18 They divide my clothes among them
    and cast lots for my garment.

19 But you, Lord, do not be far from me.
    You are my strength; come quickly
      to help me.
20 Deliver me from the sword,
    my precious life from the power of
      the dogs.

21 Rescue me from the mouth of the
      lions;
    save me from the horns of the wild
      oxen.

22 I will declare your name to my
      people;
    in the assembly I will praise
      you.
23 You who fear the Lord, praise him!
    All you descendants of Jacob,
      honor him!
  Revere him, all you descendants
    of Israel!
24 For he has not despised or scorned
    the suffering of the afflicted
      one;
  he has not hidden his face from
      him
  but has listened to his cry for
      help.
25 From you comes the theme of my
      praise in the great assembly;
    before those who fear you[c] I will
      fulfill my vows.
26 The poor will eat and be satisfied;
    those who seek the Lord will praise
      him—
  may your hearts live forever!
27 All the ends of the earth
    will remember and turn to the
      Lord,
  and all the families of the nations
    will bow down before him,
28 for dominion belongs to the Lord
    and he rules over the nations.

29 All the rich of the earth will feast and
      worship;
    all who go down to the dust will
      kneel before him—
  those who cannot keep themselves
    alive.
30 Posterity will serve him;
    future generations will be told about
      the Lord.
31 They will proclaim his righteousness,
    declaring to a people yet unborn:
  He has done it!

---

a 15 Probable reading of the original Hebrew text;
Masoretic Text *strength*   *b 16* Dead Sea Scrolls and
some manuscripts of the Masoretic Text, Septuagint and
Syriac; most manuscripts of the Masoretic Text *me, / like a
lion*   *c 25* Hebrew *him*

Psalm 23

A psalm of David.

1 The LORD is my shepherd, I lack
   nothing.
2   He makes me lie down in green
    pastures,
he leads me beside quiet waters,
3   he refreshes my soul.
He guides me along the right paths
   for his name's sake.
4 Even though I walk
   through the darkest valley,*a*
I will fear no evil,
   for you are with me;
your rod and your staff,
   they comfort me.

5 You prepare a table before me
   in the presence of my enemies.
You anoint my head with oil;
   my cup overflows.
6 Surely your goodness and love will
   follow me
   all the days of my life,
and I will dwell in the house of the
   LORD
   forever.

Psalm 24

Of David. A psalm.

1 The earth is the LORD's, and everything
   in it,
   the world, and all who live in it;
2 for he founded it on the seas
   and established it on the waters.

3 Who may ascend the mountain of the
   LORD?
   Who may stand in his holy place?
4 The one who has clean hands and a
   pure heart,
   who does not trust in an idol
   or swear by a false god.*b*

5 They will receive blessing from the
   LORD
   and vindication from God their
   Savior.
6 Such is the generation of those who
   seek him,
   who seek your face, God of
   Jacob.*c,d*

7 Lift up your heads, you gates;
   be lifted up, you ancient doors,
   that the King of glory may come in.
8 Who is this King of glory?
   The LORD strong and mighty,
   the LORD mighty in battle.
9 Lift up your heads, you gates;
   lift them up, you ancient doors,
   that the King of glory may come in.
10 Who is he, this King of glory?
   The LORD Almighty—
   he is the King of glory.

Psalm 25*e*

Of David.

1 In you, LORD my God,
   I put my trust.

2 I trust in you;
   do not let me be put to shame,
   nor let my enemies triumph
     over me.
3 No one who hopes in you
   will ever be put to shame,
but shame will come on those
   who are treacherous without
     cause.

4 Show me your ways, LORD,
   teach me your paths.
5 Guide me in your truth and teach me,
   for you are God my Savior,
   and my hope is in you all day long.
6 Remember, LORD, your great mercy and
   love,
   for they are from of old.
7 Do not remember the sins of my
   youth
   and my rebellious ways;
according to your love remember me,
   for you, LORD, are good.

8 Good and upright is the LORD;
   therefore he instructs sinners in his
     ways.
9 He guides the humble in what is
   right
   and teaches them his way.

---

a 4 Or *the valley of the shadow of death*   *b* 4 Or *swear falsely*   *c* 6 Two Hebrew manuscripts and Syriac (see also Septuagint); most Hebrew manuscripts *face, Jacob*   *d* 6 The Hebrew has *Selah* (a word of uncertain meaning) here and at the end of verse 10.   *e* This psalm is an acrostic poem, the verses of which begin with the successive letters of the Hebrew alphabet.

¹⁰ All the ways of the LORD are loving and
faithful
toward those who keep the
demands of his covenant.
¹¹ For the sake of your name, LORD,
forgive my iniquity, though it is great.

¹² Who, then, are those who fear the
LORD?
He will instruct them in the ways
they should choose.ᵃ
¹³ They will spend their days in
prosperity,
and their descendants will inherit
the land.
¹⁴ The LORD confides in those who fear
him;
he makes his covenant known to
them.
¹⁵ My eyes are ever on the LORD,
for only he will release my feet from
the snare.

¹⁶ Turn to me and be gracious to me,
for I am lonely and afflicted.
¹⁷ Relieve the troubles of my heart
and free me from my anguish.
¹⁸ Look on my affliction and my distress
and take away all my sins.
¹⁹ See how numerous are my enemies
and how fiercely they hate me!

²⁰ Guard my life and rescue me;
do not let me be put to shame,
for I take refuge in you.
²¹ May integrity and uprightness protect
me,
because my hope, LORD,ᵇ is in you.

²² Deliver Israel, O God,
from all their troubles!

Psalm 26

Of David.

¹ Vindicate me, LORD,
for I have led a blameless life;
I have trusted in the LORD
and have not faltered.
² Test me, LORD, and try me,
examine my heart and my mind;
³ for I have always been mindful of your
unfailing love
and have lived in reliance on your
faithfulness.

⁴ I do not sit with the deceitful,
nor do I associate with hypocrites.
⁵ I abhor the assembly of evildoers
and refuse to sit with the wicked.
⁶ I wash my hands in innocence,
and go about your altar, LORD,
⁷ proclaiming aloud your praise
and telling of all your wonderful
deeds.

⁸ LORD, I love the house where you live,
the place where your glory dwells.
⁹ Do not take away my soul along with
sinners,
my life with those who
are bloodthirsty,
¹⁰ in whose hands are wicked
schemes,
whose right hands are full of bribes.
¹¹ I lead a blameless life;
deliver me and be merciful to me.

¹² My feet stand on level ground;
in the great congregation I will
praise the LORD.

Psalm 27

Of David.

¹ The LORD is my light and my
salvation—
whom shall I fear?
The LORD is the stronghold of my life—
of whom shall I be afraid?

² When the wicked advance against me
to devourᶜ me,
it is my enemies and my foes
who will stumble and fall.
³ Though an army besiege me,
my heart will not fear;
though war break out against me,
even then I will be confident.

⁴ One thing I ask from the LORD,
this only do I seek:
that I may dwell in the house of the
LORD
all the days of my life,
to gaze on the beauty of the LORD
and to seek him in his temple.
⁵ For in the day of trouble
he will keep me safe in his dwelling;

ᵃ 12 Or *ways he chooses*   ᵇ 21 Septuagint; Hebrew
does not have LORD.   ᶜ 2 Or *slander*

he will hide me in the shelter of his
 sacred tent
 and set me high upon a rock.
⁶ Then my head will be exalted
 above the enemies who surround
 me;
 at his sacred tent I will sacrifice with
 shouts of joy;
 I will sing and make music to the
 LORD.

⁷ Hear my voice when I call, LORD;
 be merciful to me and answer me.
⁸ My heart says of you, "Seek his face!"
 Your face, LORD, I will seek.
⁹ Do not hide your face from me,
 do not turn your servant away in
 anger;
 you have been my helper.
 Do not reject me or forsake me,
 God my Savior.
¹⁰ Though my father and mother forsake
 me,
 the LORD will receive me.
¹¹ Teach me your way, LORD;
 lead me in a straight path
 because of my oppressors.
¹² Do not turn me over to the desire of
 my foes,
 for false witnesses rise up against
 me,
 spouting malicious accusations.

¹³ I remain confident of this:
 I will see the goodness of the LORD
 in the land of the living.
¹⁴ Wait for the LORD;
 be strong and take heart
 and wait for the LORD.

Psalm 28

Of David.

¹ To you, LORD, I call;
 you are my Rock,
 do not turn a deaf ear to me.
 For if you remain silent,
 I will be like those who go down to
 the pit.
² Hear my cry for mercy
 as I call to you for help,
 as I lift up my hands
 toward your Most Holy Place.

³ Do not drag me away with the wicked,
 with those who do evil,
 who speak cordially with their
 neighbors
 but harbor malice in their hearts.
⁴ Repay them for their deeds
 and for their evil work;
 repay them for what their hands have
 done
 and bring back on them what they
 deserve.
⁵ Because they have no regard for the
 deeds of the LORD
 and what his hands have done,
 he will tear them down
 and never build them up again.

⁶ Praise be to the LORD,
 for he has heard my cry for mercy.
⁷ The LORD is my strength and my
 shield;
 my heart trusts in him, and he
 helps me.
 My heart leaps for joy,
 and with my song I praise him.
⁸ The LORD is the strength of his
 people,
 a fortress of salvation for his
 anointed one.
⁹ Save your people and bless your
 inheritance;
 be their shepherd and carry them
 forever.

Psalm 29

A psalm of David.

¹ Ascribe to the LORD, you heavenly
 beings,
 ascribe to the LORD glory and
 strength.
² Ascribe to the LORD the glory due his
 name;
 worship the LORD in the splendor of
 his*ᵃ* holiness.

³ The voice of the LORD is over the
 waters;
 the God of glory thunders,
 the LORD thunders over the mighty
 waters.

ᵃ 2 Or LORD *with the splendor of*

4 The voice of the LORD is powerful;
  the voice of the LORD is majestic.
5 The voice of the LORD breaks the
        cedars;
  the LORD breaks in pieces the
        cedars of Lebanon.
6 He makes Lebanon leap like a calf,
  Sirion[a] like a young wild ox.
7 The voice of the LORD strikes
  with flashes of lightning.
8 The voice of the LORD shakes the
        desert;
  the LORD shakes the Desert of
        Kadesh.
9 The voice of the LORD twists the oaks[b]
  and strips the forests bare.
  And in his temple all cry, "Glory!"

10 The LORD sits enthroned over the
        flood;
  the LORD is enthroned as King
        forever.

THE SCENE

LEBANON

(PSALM 29:6)

Mount Lebanon is really a mountain range. It's famous for its many forests, with trees that are used to produce wood for building. Its name means "white," because its peaks are covered with snow year round.

11 The LORD gives strength to his
        people;
  the LORD blesses his people with
        peace.

Psalm 30[c]

A psalm. A song. For the dedication
of the temple.[d] Of David.

1 I will exalt you, LORD,
  for you lifted me out of the depths
  and did not let my enemies gloat
        over me.
2 LORD my God, I called to you for help,
  and you healed me.
3 You, LORD, brought me up from the
  realm of the dead;

THE SCENE

SIRION (ALSO CALLED HERMON)

(PSALM 29:6)

Mount Sirion is another mountain cluster. Together with Mount Lebanon, they form a big group of high mountains.

---

[a] 6 That is, Mount Hermon   [b] 9 Or LORD makes the
deer give birth   [c] In Hebrew texts 30:1-12 is numbered
30:2-13.   [d] Title: Or palace

you spared me from going down to
the pit.

4 Sing the praises of the LORD, you his
faithful people;
praise his holy name.
5 For his anger lasts only a moment,
but his favor lasts a lifetime;
weeping may stay for the night,
but rejoicing comes in the morning.

6 When I felt secure, I said,
"I will never be shaken."
7 LORD, when you favored me,
you made my royal mountain*a* stand
firm;
but when you hid your face,
I was dismayed.

8 To you, LORD, I called;
to the Lord I cried for mercy:
9 "What is gained if I am silenced,
if I go down to the pit?
Will the dust praise you?
Will it proclaim your faithfulness?
10 Hear, LORD, and be merciful to me;
LORD, be my help."

11 You turned my wailing into dancing;
you removed my sackcloth and
clothed me with joy,
12 that my heart may sing your praises
and not be silent.
LORD my God, I will praise you
forever.

Psalm 31 *b*

For the director of music. A psalm of David.

1 In you, LORD, I have taken refuge;
let me never be put to shame;
deliver me in your righteousness.
2 Turn your ear to me,
come quickly to my rescue;
be my rock of refuge,
a strong fortress to save me.
3 Since you are my rock and my
fortress,
for the sake of your name lead and
guide me.
4 Keep me free from the trap that is set
for me,
for you are my refuge.
5 Into your hands I commit my spirit;
deliver me, LORD, my faithful God.

6 I hate those who cling to worthless
idols;
as for me, I trust in the LORD.
7 I will be glad and rejoice in your love,
for you saw my affliction
and knew the anguish of my soul.
8 You have not given me into the hands
of the enemy
but have set my feet in a spacious
place.

9 Be merciful to me, LORD, for I am in
distress;
my eyes grow weak with sorrow,
my soul and body with grief.
10 My life is consumed by anguish
and my years by groaning;
my strength fails because of my
affliction,*c*
and my bones grow weak.
11 Because of all my enemies,
I am the utter contempt of my
neighbors
and an object of dread to my closest
friends—
those who see me on the street
flee from me.
12 I am forgotten as though I were
dead;
I have become like broken pottery.
13 For I hear many whispering,
"Terror on every side!"
They conspire against me
and plot to take my life.

14 But I trust in you, LORD;
I say, "You are my God."
15 My times are in your hands;
deliver me from the hands of my
enemies,
from those who pursue me.
16 Let your face shine on your servant;
save me in your unfailing love.
17 Let me not be put to shame, LORD,
for I have cried out to you;
but let the wicked be put to shame
and be silent in the realm of the
dead.
18 Let their lying lips be silenced,
for with pride and contempt
they speak arrogantly against the
righteous.

---

a 7 That is, Mount Zion   *b* In Hebrew texts 31:1-24 is
numbered 31:2-25.   *c* 10 Or *guilt*

19 How abundant are the good things
      that you have stored up for those
          who fear you,
  that you bestow in the sight of all,
      on those who take refuge in you.
20 In the shelter of your presence you
          hide them
      from all human intrigues;
  you keep them safe in your dwelling
      from accusing tongues.

21 Praise be to the LORD,
      for he showed me the wonders of
          his love
      when I was in a city under siege.
22 In my alarm I said,
      "I am cut off from your sight!"
  Yet you heard my cry for mercy
      when I called to you for help.

23 Love the LORD, all his faithful people!
      The LORD preserves those who are
          true to him,
      but the proud he pays back in full.
24 Be strong and take heart,
      all you who hope in the LORD.

Psalm 32

Of David. A *maskil*.[a]

1 Blessed is the one
      whose transgressions are forgiven,
      whose sins are covered.
2 Blessed is the one
      whose sin the LORD does not count
          against them
      and in whose spirit is no deceit.

3 When I kept silent,
      my bones wasted away
      through my groaning all day long.
4 For day and night
      your hand was heavy on me;
  my strength was sapped
      as in the heat of summer.[b]

5 Then I acknowledged my sin to you
      and did not cover up my iniquity.
  I said, "I will confess
      my transgressions to the LORD."
  And you forgave
      the guilt of my sin.

6 Therefore let all the faithful pray to you
      while you may be found;

surely the rising of the mighty waters
      will not reach them.
7 You are my hiding place;
      you will protect me from trouble
      and surround me with songs of
          deliverance.

8 I will instruct you and teach you in the
          way you should go;
      I will counsel you with my loving eye
          on you.
9 Do not be like the horse or the
          mule,
      which have no understanding
  but must be controlled by bit and
          bridle
      or they will not come to you.
10 Many are the woes of the wicked,
      but the LORD's unfailing love
      surrounds the one who trusts in
          him.

11 Rejoice in the LORD and be glad, you
          righteous;
      sing, all you who are upright in
          heart!

Psalm 33

1 Sing joyfully to the LORD, you righteous;
      it is fitting for the upright to praise
          him.
2 Praise the LORD with the harp;
      make music to him on the ten-
          stringed lyre.
3 Sing to him a new song;
      play skillfully, and shout for joy.

4 For the word of the LORD is right and
          true;
      he is faithful in all he does.
5 The LORD loves righteousness and
          justice;
      the earth is full of his unfailing love.

6 By the word of the LORD the heavens
          were made,
      their starry host by the breath of his
          mouth.
7 He gathers the waters of the sea into
          jars[c];
      he puts the deep into storehouses.

---

a Title: Probably a literary or musical term   *b* 4 The
Hebrew has *Selah* (a word of uncertain meaning) here and
at the end of verses 5 and 7.   *c* 7 Or *sea as into a heap*

⁸ Let all the earth fear the Lord;
　　let all the people of the world revere
　　　him.
⁹ For he spoke, and it came to be;
　　he commanded, and it stood firm.

¹⁰ The Lord foils the plans of the
　　　nations;
　　he thwarts the purposes of the
　　　peoples.
¹¹ But the plans of the Lord stand firm
　　　forever,
　　the purposes of his heart through
　　　all generations.

¹² Blessed is the nation whose God is
　　　the Lord,
　　the people he chose for his
　　　inheritance.
¹³ From heaven the Lord looks down
　　and sees all mankind;
¹⁴ from his dwelling place he watches
　　all who live on earth—
¹⁵ he who forms the hearts of all,
　　who considers everything they do.

¹⁶ No king is saved by the size of his
　　　army;

no warrior escapes by his great
　　strength.
¹⁷ A horse is a vain hope for deliverance;
　　despite all its great strength it
　　　cannot save.
¹⁸ But the eyes of the Lord are on those
　　who fear him,
　　on those whose hope is in his
　　　unfailing love,
¹⁹ to deliver them from death
　　and keep them alive in famine.

²⁰ We wait in hope for the Lord;
　　he is our help and our shield.
²¹ In him our hearts rejoice,
　　for we trust in his holy name.
²² May your unfailing love be with us,
　　　Lord,
　　even as we put our hope in you.

Psalm 34ᵃ,ᵇ

Of David. When he pretended to be insane
before Abimelek, who drove him away,
and he left.

¹ I will extol the Lord at all times;
　　his praise will always be on my
　　　lips.
² I will glory in the Lord;
　　let the afflicted hear and rejoice.
³ Glorify the Lord with me;
　　let us exalt his name together.

⁴ I sought the Lord, and he answered
　　　me;
　　he delivered me from all my fears.
⁵ Those who look to him are radiant;
　　their faces are never covered with
　　　shame.
⁶ This poor man called, and the Lord
　　　heard him;
　　he saved him out of all his troubles.
⁷ The angel of the Lord encamps
　　　around those who fear him,
　　and he delivers them.

⁸ Taste and see that the Lord is good;
　　blessed is the one who takes
　　　refuge in him.
⁹ Fear the Lord, you his holy people,
　　for those who fear him lack
　　　nothing.

BREAK THROUGH!

Reverence

(PSALM 33:8)

This is the same as showing respect, only for
God it's a bigger kind of respect. Of course,
God is the greatest!

ᵃ This psalm is an acrostic poem, the verses of which
begin with the successive letters of the Hebrew alphabet.
ᵇ In Hebrew texts 34:1-22 is numbered 34:2-23.

10 The lions may grow weak and hungry,
   but those who seek the Lord lack
      no good thing.
11 Come, my children, listen to me;
   I will teach you the fear of the Lord.
12 Whoever of you loves life
   and desires to see many good days,
13 keep your tongue from evil
   and your lips from telling lies.
14 Turn from evil and do good;
   seek peace and pursue it.

15 The eyes of the Lord are on the
     righteous,
   and his ears are attentive to their
     cry;
16 but the face of the Lord is against
     those who do evil,
   to blot out their name from the
     earth.

17 The righteous cry out, and the Lord
     hears them;
   he delivers them from all their
     troubles.
18 The Lord is close to the
     brokenhearted
   and saves those who are crushed in
     spirit.

19 The righteous person may have many
     troubles,
   but the Lord delivers him from them
     all;
20 he protects all his bones,
   not one of them will be broken.

21 Evil will slay the wicked;
   the foes of the righteous will be
     condemned.
22 The Lord will rescue his servants;
   no one who takes refuge in him will
     be condemned.

Psalm 35

Of David.

1 Contend, Lord, with those who
     contend with me;
   fight against those who fight
     against me.
2 Take up shield and armor;
   arise and come to my aid.
3 Brandish spear and javelin[a]
   against those who pursue me.

Say to me,
   "I am your salvation."

4 May those who seek my life
   be disgraced and put to shame;
   may those who plot my ruin
   be turned back in dismay.
5 May they be like chaff before the
     wind,
   with the angel of the Lord driving
     them away;
6 may their path be dark and slippery,
   with the angel of the Lord pursuing
     them.

7 Since they hid their net for me without
     cause
   and without cause dug a pit for me,
8 may ruin overtake them by surprise—
   may the net they hid entangle them,
   may they fall into the pit, to their
     ruin.
9 Then my soul will rejoice in the Lord
   and delight in his salvation.
10 My whole being will exclaim,
   "Who is like you, Lord?
   You rescue the poor from those too
     strong for them,
   the poor and needy from those who
     rob them."

11 Ruthless witnesses come forward;
   they question me on things I know
     nothing about.
12 They repay me evil for good
   and leave me like one bereaved.
13 Yet when they were ill, I put on
     sackcloth
   and humbled myself with fasting.
   When my prayers returned to me
     unanswered,
14   I went about mourning
   as though for my friend or brother.
   I bowed my head in grief
   as though weeping for my mother.
15 But when I stumbled, they gathered in
     glee;
   assailants gathered against me
     without my knowledge.
   They slandered me without ceasing.
16 Like the ungodly they maliciously
     mocked;[b]
   they gnashed their teeth at me.

---

[a] 3 Or *and block the way*   [b] 16 Septuagint; Hebrew may
mean *Like an ungodly circle of mockers,*

17 How long, Lord, will you look on?
　　Rescue me from their ravages,
　　my precious life from these lions.
18 I will give you thanks in the great
　　　assembly;
　　among the throngs I will praise you.
19 Do not let those gloat over me
　　who are my enemies without cause;
　　do not let those who hate me without
　　　reason
　　maliciously wink the eye.
20 They do not speak peaceably,
　　but devise false accusations
　　against those who live quietly in the
　　　land.
21 They sneer at me and say, "Aha! Aha!
　　With our own eyes we have seen it."

22 LORD, you have seen this; do not be
　　　silent.
　　Do not be far from me, Lord.
23 Awake, and rise to my defense!
　　Contend for me, my God and Lord.
24 Vindicate me in your righteousness,
　　LORD my God;
　　do not let them gloat over me.
25 Do not let them think, "Aha, just what
　　we wanted!"
　　or say, "We have swallowed him up."

26 May all who gloat over my distress
　　be put to shame and confusion;
　　may all who exalt themselves over me
　　be clothed with shame and
　　　disgrace.
27 May those who delight in my
　　　vindication
　　shout for joy and gladness;
　　may they always say, "The LORD be
　　　exalted,
　　who delights in the well-being of his
　　　servant."

28 My tongue will proclaim your
　　　righteousness,
　　your praises all day long.

Psalm 36[a]

For the director of music. Of David the
servant of the LORD.

1 I have a message from God in my heart
　concerning the sinfulness of the
　wicked:[b]

There is no fear of God
　before their eyes.

2 In their own eyes they flatter
　　themselves
　too much to detect or hate their sin.
3 The words of their mouths are wicked
　and deceitful;
　they fail to act wisely or do good.
4 Even on their beds they plot evil;
　they commit themselves to a sinful
　　course
　and do not reject what is wrong.

5 Your love, LORD, reaches to the
　　heavens,
　your faithfulness to the skies.
6 Your righteousness is like the highest
　　mountains,
　your justice like the great deep.
　You, LORD, preserve both people and
　　animals.
7 How priceless is your unfailing love,
　O God!
　People take refuge in the shadow of
　　your wings.
8 They feast on the abundance of your
　　house;
　you give them drink from your river
　　of delights.
9 For with you is the fountain of life;
　in your light we see light.

10 Continue your love to those who know
　　you,
　your righteousness to the upright in
　　heart.
11 May the foot of the proud not come
　　against me,
　nor the hand of the wicked drive me
　　away.
12 See how the evildoers lie fallen—
　thrown down, not able to rise!

Psalm 37[c]

Of David.

1 Do not fret because of those who are
　evil
　or be envious of those who do wrong;

---

[a] In Hebrew texts 36:1-12 is numbered 36:2-13.　　[b] 1 Or
A message from God: The transgression of the wicked /
resides in their hearts.　　[c] This psalm is an acrostic
poem, the stanzas of which begin with the successive
letters of the Hebrew alphabet.

2 for like the grass they will soon wither,
like green plants they will soon die
away.

3 Trust in the LORD and do good;
dwell in the land and enjoy safe
pasture.
4 Take delight in the LORD,
and he will give you the desires of
your heart.

5 Commit your way to the LORD;
trust in him and he will do this:
6 He will make your righteous reward
shine like the dawn,
your vindication like the noonday
sun.

7 Be still before the LORD
and wait patiently for him;
do not fret when people succeed in
their ways,
when they carry out their wicked
schemes.

8 Refrain from anger and turn from
wrath;
do not fret—it leads only to evil.
9 For those who are evil will be
destroyed,
but those who hope in the LORD will
inherit the land.

10 A little while, and the wicked will be no
more;
though you look for them, they will
not be found.
11 But the meek will inherit the land
and enjoy peace and prosperity.

12 The wicked plot against the righteous
and gnash their teeth at them;
13 but the Lord laughs at the wicked,
for he knows their day is coming.

14 The wicked draw the sword
and bend the bow
to bring down the poor and needy,
to slay those whose ways are
upright.
15 But their swords will pierce their own
hearts,
and their bows will be broken.

16 Better the little that the righteous
have
than the wealth of many wicked;

17 for the power of the wicked will be
broken,
but the LORD upholds the righteous.

18 The blameless spend their days under
the LORD's care,
and their inheritance will endure
forever.
19 In times of disaster they will not
wither;
in days of famine they will enjoy
plenty.

20 But the wicked will perish:
Though the LORD's enemies are like
the flowers of the field,
they will be consumed, they will go
up in smoke.

21 The wicked borrow and do not repay,
but the righteous give generously;
22 those the LORD blesses will inherit the
land,
but those he curses will be
destroyed.

23 The LORD makes firm the steps
of the one who delights in him;
24 though he may stumble, he will not
fall,
for the LORD upholds him with his
hand.

25 I was young and now I am old,
yet I have never seen the righteous
forsaken
or their children begging bread.
26 They are always generous and lend
freely;
their children will be a blessing.[a]

27 Turn from evil and do good;
then you will dwell in the land
forever.
28 For the LORD loves the just
and will not forsake his faithful ones.

Wrongdoers will be completely
destroyed[b];
the offspring of the wicked will
perish.
29 The righteous will inherit the land
and dwell in it forever.

---

*a 26 Or freely; / the names of their children will be used in
blessings (see Gen. 48:20); or freely; / others will see that
their children are blessed   b 28 See Septuagint; Hebrew
They will be protected forever*

30 The mouths of the righteous utter
wisdom,
and their tongues speak what is
just.
31 The law of their God is in their hearts;
their feet do not slip.
32 The wicked lie in wait for the
righteous,
intent on putting them to death;
33 but the Lord will not leave them in the
power of the wicked
or let them be condemned when
brought to trial.

34 Hope in the Lord
and keep his way.
He will exalt you to inherit the land;
when the wicked are destroyed, you
will see it.

35 I have seen a wicked and ruthless
man
flourishing like a luxuriant native
tree,
36 but he soon passed away and was no
more;
though I looked for him, he could
not be found.

37 Consider the blameless, observe the
upright;
a future awaits those who seek
peace.[a]
38 But all sinners will be destroyed;
there will be no future[b] for the
wicked.

39 The salvation of the righteous comes
from the Lord;
he is their stronghold in time of
trouble.
40 The Lord helps them and delivers
them;
he delivers them from the wicked
and saves them,
because they take refuge in him.

Psalm 38[c]

A psalm of David. A petition.

1 Lord, do not rebuke me in your anger
or discipline me in your wrath.
2 Your arrows have pierced me,
and your hand has come down
on me.

3 Because of your wrath there is no
health in my body;
there is no soundness in my bones
because of my sin.
4 My guilt has overwhelmed me
like a burden too heavy to bear.

5 My wounds fester and are loathsome
because of my sinful folly.
6 I am bowed down and brought very
low;
all day long I go about mourning.
7 My back is filled with searing pain;
there is no health in my body.
8 I am feeble and utterly crushed;
I groan in anguish of heart.

9 All my longings lie open before you,
Lord;
my sighing is not hidden from you.
10 My heart pounds, my strength
fails me;
even the light has gone from my
eyes.
11 My friends and companions avoid me
because of my wounds;
my neighbors stay far away.
12 Those who want to kill me set their
traps,
those who would harm me talk of
my ruin;
all day long they scheme and lie.

13 I am like the deaf, who cannot hear,
like the mute, who cannot speak;
14 I have become like one who does not
hear,
whose mouth can offer no reply.
15 Lord, I wait for you;
you will answer, Lord my God.
16 For I said, "Do not let them gloat
or exalt themselves over me when
my feet slip."

17 For I am about to fall,
and my pain is ever with me.
18 I confess my iniquity;
I am troubled by my sin.
19 Many have become my enemies
without cause[d];
those who hate me without reason
are numerous.

---

a 37 Or *upright;* / *those who seek peace will have posterity*
b 38 Or *posterity*   c In Hebrew texts 38:1-22 is
numbered 38:2-23.   d 19 One Dead Sea Scrolls
manuscript; Masoretic Text *my vigorous enemies*

20 Those who repay my good with
        evil
    lodge accusations against me,
    though I seek only to do what is
        good.
21 LORD, do not forsake me;
    do not be far from me, my God.
22 Come quickly to help me,
    my Lord and my Savior.

Psalm 39 [a]

For the director of music. For Jeduthun.
A psalm of David.

1 I said, "I will watch my ways
    and keep my tongue from sin;

THE
WITNESSES

✓ **JEDUTHUN** (PSALM 39; 77)
In King David's time, different groups of singers
were called by this name. It's used for the
director of a choir in the Psalms.

I will put a muzzle on my mouth
    while in the presence of the wicked."
2 So I remained utterly silent,
    not even saying anything good.
But my anguish increased;
3   my heart grew hot within me.
While I meditated, the fire burned;
    then I spoke with my tongue:

4 "Show me, LORD, my life's end
    and the number of my days;
    let me know how fleeting my life is.
5 You have made my days a mere
        handbreadth;
    the span of my years is as nothing
        before you.
Everyone is but a breath,
    even those who seem secure. [b]

6 "Surely everyone goes around like a
        mere phantom;
    in vain they rush about, heaping up
        wealth
    without knowing whose it will finally
        be.

7 "But now, Lord, what do I look for?
    My hope is in you.
8 Save me from all my transgressions;
    do not make me the scorn of fools.
9 I was silent; I would not open my
        mouth,
    for you are the one who has done
        this.
10 Remove your scourge from me;
    I am overcome by the blow of your
        hand.
11 When you rebuke and discipline
        anyone for their sin,
    you consume their wealth like a
        moth—
    surely everyone is but a breath.

12 "Hear my prayer, LORD,
    listen to my cry for help;
    do not be deaf to my weeping.
I dwell with you as a foreigner,
    a stranger, as all my ancestors
        were.
13 Look away from me, that I may enjoy
        life again
    before I depart and am no more."

---

a In Hebrew texts 39:1-13 is numbered 39:2-14.
b 5 The Hebrew has *Selah* (a word of uncertain meaning)
here and at the end of verse 11.

Psalm 40[a]

For the director of music. Of David.
A psalm.

[1] I waited patiently for the LORD;
　he turned to me and heard my cry.
[2] He lifted me out of the slimy pit,
　out of the mud and mire;
he set my feet on a rock
　and gave me a firm place to stand.
[3] He put a new song in my mouth,
　a hymn of praise to our God.
Many will see and fear the LORD
　and put their trust in him.

[4] Blessed is the one
　who trusts in the LORD,
who does not look to the proud,
　to those who turn aside to false
　　gods.[b]
[5] Many, LORD my God,
　are the wonders you have done,
　the things you planned for us.
None can compare with you;
　were I to speak and tell of your
　　deeds,
　they would be too many to declare.

[6] Sacrifice and offering you did not
　　desire—
　but my ears you have opened[c]—
　burnt offerings and sin offerings[d]
　　you did not require.
[7] Then I said, "Here I am, I have
　　come—
　it is written about me in the scroll.[e]
[8] I desire to do your will, my God;
　your law is within my heart."

[9] I proclaim your saving acts in the great
　　assembly;
　I do not seal my lips, LORD,
　as you know.
[10] I do not hide your righteousness in my
　　heart;
　I speak of your faithfulness and
　　your saving help.
I do not conceal your love and your
　　faithfulness
　from the great assembly.

[11] Do not withhold your mercy from me,
　LORD;
　may your love and faithfulness
　always protect me.

[12] For troubles without number surround
　　me;
　my sins have overtaken me, and I
　　cannot see.
They are more than the hairs of my
　　head,
　and my heart fails within me.
[13] Be pleased to save me, LORD;
　come quickly, LORD, to help me.

[14] May all who want to take my life
　be put to shame and confusion;
may all who desire my ruin
　be turned back in disgrace.
[15] May those who say to me, "Aha! Aha!"
　be appalled at their own shame.
[16] But may all who seek you
　rejoice and be glad in you;
may those who long for your saving
　　help always say,
　"The LORD is great!"

[17] But as for me, I am poor and
　　needy;
　may the Lord think of me.
You are my help and my deliverer;
　you are my God, do not delay.

Psalm 41[f]

For the director of music.
A psalm of David.

[1] Blessed are those who have regard for
　the weak;
　the LORD delivers them in times of
　　trouble.
[2] The LORD protects and preserves
　　them—
　they are counted among the
　　blessed in the land—
　he does not give them over to the
　　desire of their foes.
[3] The LORD sustains them on their
　　sickbed
　and restores them from their bed of
　　illness.

[4] I said, "Have mercy on me, LORD;
　heal me, for I have sinned against
　　you."

---

[a] In Hebrew texts 40:1-17 is numbered 40:2-18.　　[b] 4 Or
to lies　　[c] 6 Hebrew; some Septuagint manuscripts but a
body you have prepared for me　　[d] 6 Or purification
offerings　　[e] 7 Or come / with the scroll written for me
[f] In Hebrew texts 41:1-13 is numbered 41:2-14.

⁵My enemies say of me in malice,
  "When will he die and his name
    perish?"
⁶When one of them comes to see me,
  he speaks falsely, while his heart
    gathers slander;
  then he goes out and spreads it
    around.

⁷All my enemies whisper together
    against me;
  they imagine the worst for me,
    saying,
⁸"A vile disease has afflicted him;
  he will never get up from the place
    where he lies."
⁹Even my close friend,
  someone I trusted,
  one who shared my bread,
    has turned^a against me.

¹⁰But may you have mercy on me, Lord;
  raise me up, that I may repay
    them.
¹¹I know that you are pleased with me,
  for my enemy does not triumph
    over me.
¹²Because of my integrity you uphold me
  and set me in your presence
    forever.

¹³Praise be to the Lord, the God of Israel,
  from everlasting to everlasting.
    Amen and Amen.

BOOK II

Psalms 42–72

Psalm 42^b,c

For the director of music. A maskil^d
of the Sons of Korah.

¹As the deer pants for streams of water,
  so my soul pants for you, my God.
²My soul thirsts for God, for the living
    God.
  When can I go and meet with God?
³My tears have been my food
    day and night,
  while people say to me all day long,
    "Where is your God?"

⁴These things I remember
  as I pour out my soul:
  how I used to go to the house of God
  under the protection of the Mighty
    One^e
  with shouts of joy and praise
  among the festive throng.

⁵Why, my soul, are you downcast?
  Why so disturbed within me?
  Put your hope in God,
    for I will yet praise him,
    my Savior and my God.

---

^a 9 Hebrew has lifted up his heel   ^b In many Hebrew manuscripts Psalms 42 and 43 constitute one psalm.
^c In Hebrew texts 42:1-11 is numbered 42:2-12.   ^d Title: Probably a literary or musical term   ^e 4 See Septuagint and Syriac; the meaning of the Hebrew for this line is uncertain.

THE WITNESSES

✓ **KORAH** (**PSALM 42**)
A person whose descendants were a group of musicians, singers and authors of a number of Psalms.

⁶My soul is downcast within me;
    therefore I will remember you
from the land of the Jordan,
    the heights of Hermon—from
      Mount Mizar.
⁷Deep calls to deep
    in the roar of your waterfalls;
all your waves and breakers
    have swept over me.
    ⁸By day the LORD directs his
      love,
      at night his song is with
        me—
      a prayer to the God of my
        life.
⁹I say to God my Rock,
    "Why have you forgotten me?
Why must I go about mourning,
    oppressed by the enemy?"
¹⁰My bones suffer mortal agony
    as my foes taunt me,
saying to me all day long,
    "Where is your God?"

¹¹Why, my soul, are you downcast?
    Why so disturbed within me?
Put your hope in God,
    for I will yet praise him,
    my Savior and my God.

Psalm 43 [a]

¹Vindicate me, my God,
    and plead my cause
    against an unfaithful nation.
Rescue me from those who are
    deceitful and wicked.
²You are God my stronghold.
    Why have you rejected me?
Why must I go about mourning,
    oppressed by the enemy?
³Send me your light and your faithful
    care,
    let them lead me;
let them bring me to your holy
    mountain,
    to the place where you dwell.
⁴Then I will go to the altar of God,
    to God, my joy and my delight.
I will praise you with the lyre,
    O God, my God.

⁵Why, my soul, are you downcast?
    Why so disturbed within me?

Put your hope in God,
    for I will yet praise him,
    my Savior and my God.

Psalm 44 [b]

For the director of music. Of the Sons
of Korah. A *maskil*. [c]

¹We have heard it with our ears,
    O God;
our ancestors have told us
    what you did in their days,
    in days long ago.
²With your hand you drove out the
    nations
    and planted our ancestors;
you crushed the peoples
    and made our ancestors flourish.
³It was not by their sword that they won
    the land,
    nor did their arm bring them victory;
it was your right hand, your arm,
    and the light of your face, for you
      loved them.

⁴You are my King and my God,
    who decrees [d] victories for Jacob.
⁵Through you we push back our
    enemies;
    through your name we trample our
      foes.
⁶I put no trust in my bow,
    my sword does not bring me
      victory;
⁷but you give us victory over our
    enemies,
    you put our adversaries to shame.
⁸In God we make our boast all day
    long,
    and we will praise your name
      forever. [e]

⁹But now you have rejected and
    humbled us;
you no longer go out with our
    armies.
¹⁰You made us retreat before the enemy,
    and our adversaries have plundered
    us.

---

a In many Hebrew manuscripts Psalms 42 and 43
constitute one psalm.   *b* In Hebrew texts 44:1-26 is
numbered 44:2-27.   *c* Title: Probably a literary or
musical term   *d* 4 Septuagint, Aquila and Syriac; Hebrew
King, O God; / command   *e* 8 The Hebrew has *Selah*
(a word of uncertain meaning) here.

¹¹ You gave us up to be devoured like
sheep
and have scattered us among the
nations.
¹² You sold your people for a pittance,
gaining nothing from their sale.

¹³ You have made us a reproach to our
neighbors,
the scorn and derision of those
around us.
¹⁴ You have made us a byword among
the nations;
the peoples shake their heads
at us.
¹⁵ I live in disgrace all day long,
and my face is covered with shame
¹⁶ at the taunts of those who reproach
and revile me,
because of the enemy, who is bent
on revenge.

¹⁷ All this came upon us,
though we had not forgotten you;
we had not been false to your
covenant.
¹⁸ Our hearts had not turned back;
our feet had not strayed from your
path.
¹⁹ But you crushed us and made us a
haunt for jackals;
you covered us over with deep
darkness.

²⁰ If we had forgotten the name of our
God
or spread out our hands to a foreign
god,
²¹ would not God have discovered it,
since he knows the secrets of the
heart?
²² Yet for your sake we face death all day
long;
we are considered as sheep to be
slaughtered.

²³ Awake, Lord! Why do you sleep?
Rouse yourself! Do not reject us
forever.
²⁴ Why do you hide your face
and forget our misery and
oppression?

²⁵ We are brought down to the dust;
our bodies cling to the ground.

²⁶ Rise up and help us;
rescue us because of your unfailing
love.

Psalm 45ᵃ

For the director of music. To the tune of
"Lilies." Of the Sons of Korah. A *maskil*.ᵇ
A wedding song.

¹ My heart is stirred by a noble theme
as I recite my verses for the king;
my tongue is the pen of a skillful
writer.

² You are the most excellent of men
and your lips have been anointed
with grace,
since God has blessed you forever.

ᵃ In Hebrew texts 45:1-17 is numbered 45:2-18.
ᵇ Title: Probably a literary or musical term

Were these songs well known? Where were they sung?

(PSALM 45; 56; 58)

The psalms were sung, or almost chanted.
Some Psalms come with directions of how
to sing them and what musical instruments
were to be used. It seems that the tune of
"Lilies" as well as "A Dove on Distant Oaks"
were well-known melodies they used for
singing a number of Psalms.

³Gird your sword on your side, you
mighty one;
clothe yourself with splendor and
majesty.
⁴In your majesty ride forth victoriously
in the cause of truth, humility and
justice;
let your right hand achieve
awesome deeds.
⁵Let your sharp arrows pierce the
hearts of the king's enemies;
let the nations fall beneath your
feet.
⁶Your throne, O God,ᵃ will last for ever
and ever;
a scepter of justice will be the
scepter of your kingdom.
⁷You love righteousness and hate
wickedness;
therefore God, your God, has set
you above your companions
by anointing you with the oil of joy.
⁸All your robes are fragrant with myrrh
and aloes and cassia;
from palaces adorned with ivory
the music of the strings makes you
glad.
⁹Daughters of kings are among your
honored women;
at your right hand is the royal bride
in gold of Ophir.

¹⁰Listen, daughter, and pay careful
attention:
Forget your people and your father's
house.
¹¹Let the king be enthralled by your
beauty;
honor him, for he is your lord.
¹²The city of Tyre will come with a gift,ᵇ
people of wealth will seek your
favor.
¹³All glorious is the princess within her
chamber;
her gown is interwoven with gold.
¹⁴In embroidered garments she is led to
the king;
her virgin companions follow her—
those brought to be with her.
¹⁵Led in with joy and gladness,
they enter the palace of the king.

¹⁶Your sons will take the place of your
fathers;

THE SCENE

TYRE

(PSALM 45:12)

A Philistine city built on a rock
off the eastern coast of the
Mediterranean Sea. Its name
means precisely "rock." It was an
important military and money-making
port.

you will make them princes
throughout the land.
¹⁷I will perpetuate your memory through
all generations;
therefore the nations will praise you
for ever and ever.

Psalm 46ᶜ

For the director of music. Of the Sons
of Korah. According to *alamoth.*ᵈ A song.

¹God is our refuge and strength,
an ever-present help in trouble.
²Therefore we will not fear, though the
earth give way
and the mountains fall into the
heart of the sea,

ᵃ 6 Here the king is addressed as God's representative.
ᵇ 12 Or *A Tyrian robe is among the gifts*   ᶜ In Hebrew
texts 46:1-11 is numbered 46:2-12.   ᵈ Title: Probably a
musical term

3 though its waters roar and foam
and the mountains quake with their
surging.[a]

4 There is a river whose streams make
glad the city of God,
the holy place where the Most High
dwells.
5 God is within her, she will not fall;
God will help her at break of day.
6 Nations are in uproar, kingdoms fall;
he lifts his voice, the earth melts.

7 The Lord Almighty is with us;
the God of Jacob is our fortress.

8 Come and see what the Lord has
done,
the desolations he has brought on
the earth.
9 He makes wars cease
to the ends of the earth.
He breaks the bow and shatters the
spear;
he burns the shields[b] with fire.
10 He says, "Be still, and know that I am
God;
I will be exalted among the nations,
I will be exalted in the earth."

11 The Lord Almighty is with us;
the God of Jacob is our fortress.

Psalm 47[c]

For the director of music. Of the Sons
of Korah. A psalm.

1 Clap your hands, all you nations;
shout to God with cries of joy.

2 For the Lord Most High is awesome,
the great King over all the earth.
3 He subdued nations under us,
peoples under our feet.
4 He chose our inheritance for us,
the pride of Jacob, whom he loved.[d]

5 God has ascended amid shouts of
joy,
the Lord amid the sounding of
trumpets.
6 Sing praises to God, sing praises;
sing praises to our King, sing
praises.
7 For God is the King of all the earth;
sing to him a psalm of praise.

8 God reigns over the nations;
God is seated on his holy throne.
9 The nobles of the nations assemble
as the people of the God of
Abraham,
for the kings[e] of the earth belong to
God;
he is greatly exalted.

Psalm 48[f]

A song. A psalm of the Sons of Korah.

1 Great is the Lord, and most worthy of
praise,
in the city of our God, his holy
mountain.

2 Beautiful in its loftiness,
the joy of the whole earth,
like the heights of Zaphon[g] is Mount
Zion,
the city of the Great King.
3 God is in her citadels;
he has shown himself to be her
fortress.

4 When the kings joined forces,
when they advanced together,
5 they saw her and were astounded;
they fled in terror.
6 Trembling seized them there,
pain like that of a woman in
labor.
7 You destroyed them like ships of
Tarshish
shattered by an east wind.

8 As we have heard,
so we have seen
in the city of the Lord Almighty,
in the city of our God:
God makes her secure
forever.[d]

9 Within your temple, O God,
we meditate on your unfailing love.
10 Like your name, O God,
your praise reaches to the ends of
the earth;

---

[a] 3 The Hebrew has *Selah* (a word of uncertain meaning)
here and at the end of verses 7 and 11.   [b] 9 Or
chariots   [c] In Hebrew texts 47:1-9 is numbered 47:2-10.
[d] 4,8 The Hebrew has *Selah* (a word of uncertain meaning)
here.   [e] 9 Or *shields*   [f] In Hebrew texts 48:1-14 is
numbered 48:2-15.   [g] 2 *Zaphon* was the most sacred
mountain of the Canaanites.

your right hand is filled with
righteousness.
11 Mount Zion rejoices,
the villages of Judah are glad
because of your judgments.

12 Walk about Zion, go around her,
count her towers,
13 consider well her ramparts,
view her citadels,
that you may tell of them
to the next generation.

14 For this God is our God for ever and
ever;
he will be our guide even to the end.

Psalm 49[a]

For the director of music. Of the Sons
of Korah. A psalm.

1 Hear this, all you peoples;
listen, all who live in this world,
2 both low and high,
rich and poor alike:
3 My mouth will speak words of
wisdom;
the meditation of my heart will give
you understanding.
4 I will turn my ear to a proverb;
with the harp I will expound my
riddle:

5 Why should I fear when evil days
come,
when wicked deceivers surround
me—
6 those who trust in their wealth
and boast of their great riches?
7 No one can redeem the life of
another
or give to God a ransom for
them—
8 the ransom for a life is costly,
no payment is ever enough—
9 so that they should live on forever
and not see decay.
10 For all can see that the wise die,
that the foolish and the senseless
also perish,
leaving their wealth to others.
11 Their tombs will remain their houses[b]
forever,
their dwellings for endless
generations,

though they had[c] named lands after
themselves.

12 People, despite their wealth, do not
endure;
they are like the beasts that
perish.

13 This is the fate of those who trust in
themselves,
and of their followers, who approve
their sayings.[d]
14 They are like sheep and are destined
to die;
death will be their shepherd
(but the upright will prevail over
them in the morning).
Their forms will decay in the grave,
far from their princely mansions.
15 But God will redeem me from the
realm of the dead;
he will surely take me to himself.
16 Do not be overawed when others grow
rich,
when the splendor of their houses
increases;
17 for they will take nothing with them
when they die,
their splendor will not descend with
them.
18 Though while they live they count
themselves blessed—
and people praise you when you
prosper—
19 they will join those who have gone
before them,
who will never again see the light of
life.

20 People who have wealth but lack
understanding
are like the beasts that perish.

Psalm 50

A psalm of Asaph.

1 The Mighty One, God, the Lord,
speaks and summons the earth
from the rising of the sun to where
it sets.

---

[a] In Hebrew texts 49:1-20 is numbered 49:2-21.
[b] *11* Septuagint and Syriac; Hebrew *In their thoughts their
houses will remain*   [c] *11* Or *generations, / for they have*
[d] *13* The Hebrew has *Selah* (a word of uncertain meaning)
here and at the end of verse 15.

2 From Zion, perfect in beauty,
    God shines forth.
3 Our God comes
    and will not be silent;
  a fire devours before him,
    and around him a tempest
      rages.
4 He summons the heavens above,
    and the earth, that he may judge
      his people:
5 "Gather to me this consecrated
      people,
    who made a covenant with me by
      sacrifice."
6 And the heavens proclaim his
      righteousness,
    for he is a God of justice.[a,b]

7 "Listen, my people, and I will speak;
    I will testify against you, Israel:
    I am God, your God.
8 I bring no charges against you
      concerning your sacrifices
  or concerning your burnt offerings,
    which are ever before me.
9 I have no need of a bull from your
      stall
  or of goats from your pens,
10 for every animal of the forest is
      mine,
  and the cattle on a thousand hills.
11 I know every bird in the mountains,
    and the insects in the fields are
      mine.
12 If I were hungry I would not tell you,
    for the world is mine, and all that is
      in it.
13 Do I eat the flesh of bulls
  or drink the blood of goats?

14 "Sacrifice thank offerings to God,
    fulfill your vows to the Most High,
15 and call on me in the day of
      trouble;
    I will deliver you, and you will honor
      me."

16 But to the wicked person, God says:

"What right have you to recite my
      laws
  or take my covenant on your lips?
17 You hate my instruction
  and cast my words behind you.
18 When you see a thief, you join with
      him;
  you throw in your lot with adulterers.
19 You use your mouth for evil
  and harness your tongue to
      deceit.
20 You sit and testify against your
      brother
  and slander your own mother's
      son.
21 When you did these things and I kept
      silent,
    you thought I was exactly[c] like you.
But I now arraign you
    and set my accusations before you.

THE
WITNESSES

✓ **ASAPH** (PSALM 50; 74–83)
A person whose descendants were a group of
singers who also served as entrance guards
in the temple.

---

[a] 6 With a different word division of the Hebrew; Masoretic
Text *for God himself is judge*   [b] 6 The Hebrew has *Selah*
(a word of uncertain meaning) here.   [c] 21 Or *thought the
'I AM' was*

22 "Consider this, you who forget God,
  or I will tear you to pieces, with no
    one to rescue you:
23 Those who sacrifice thank offerings
    honor me,
  and to the blameless*a* I will show
    my salvation."

Psalm 51*b*

For the director of music. A psalm
of David. When the prophet Nathan
came to him after David had committed
adultery with Bathsheba.

1 Have mercy on me, O God,
    according to your unfailing love;
  according to your great compassion
    blot out my transgressions.
2 Wash away all my iniquity
    and cleanse me from my sin.

3 For I know my transgressions,
    and my sin is always before me.
4 Against you, you only, have I sinned
    and done what is evil in your sight;

BREAK THROUGH!

Adultery

(PSALM 51, INTRODUCTION)
The prophet Nathan scolded David because
he had slept with a married woman. That
means he had stolen another man's wife.
That's called *adultery*.

so you are right in your verdict
    and justified when you judge.
5 Surely I was sinful at birth,
    sinful from the time my mother
      conceived me.
6 Yet you desired faithfulness even
    in the womb;
  you taught me wisdom in that
    secret place.

7 Cleanse me with hyssop, and I will
    be clean;
  wash me, and I will be whiter than
    snow.
8 Let me hear joy and gladness;
  let the bones you have crushed
    rejoice.
9 Hide your face from my sins
    and blot out all my iniquity.

10 Create in me a pure heart,
      O God,
  and renew a steadfast spirit
    within me.
11 Do not cast me from your presence
    or take your Holy Spirit from me.
12 Restore to me the joy of your
      salvation
  and grant me a willing spirit, to
    sustain me.

13 Then I will teach transgressors your
      ways,
  so that sinners will turn back to
    you.
14 Deliver me from the guilt of
      bloodshed, O God,
  you who are God my Savior,
  and my tongue will sing of your
    righteousness.
15 Open my lips, Lord,
  and my mouth will declare your
    praise.
16 You do not delight in sacrifice, or I
      would bring it;
  you do not take pleasure in burnt
    offerings.
17 My sacrifice, O God, is*c* a broken
      spirit;
  a broken and contrite heart
    you, God, will not despise.

---

a 23 Probable reading of the original Hebrew text; the
meaning of the Masoretic Text for this phrase is uncertain.
b In Hebrew texts 51:1-19 is numbered 51:3-21.
c 17 Or *The sacrifices of God are*

THE WITNESSES

✓ **BATHSHEBA** (PSALM 51)
This name means "daughter of oath." She was David's wife and Solomon's mother. Before that, she was the wife of Uriah, a Hittite soldier who served King David.

✓ **NATHAN** (PSALM 51)
The Israelite prophet who scolded King David for taking his servant Uriah's wife.

✓ **DOEG** (PSALM 52)
King Saul's head sheepherder. He was also a spy. He betrayed David and killed the priests in the city of Nob.

✓ **AHIMELEK** (PSALM 52)
The priest who helped David when he was fleeing from King Saul. When Saul found out, he told Doeg to kill Ahimelek. His name means "my brother is king."

¹⁸ May it please you to prosper Zion,
   to build up the walls of Jerusalem.
¹⁹ Then you will delight in the sacrifices
      of the righteous,
   in burnt offerings offered whole;
   then bulls will be offered on your
      altar.

Psalm 52ᵃ

For the director of music. A *maskil*ᵇ
of David. When Doeg the Edomite
had gone to Saul and told him: "David has
gone to the house of Ahimelek."

¹ Why do you boast of evil, you mighty
      hero?
   Why do you boast all day long,
   you who are a disgrace in the eyes
      of God?
² You who practice deceit,
   your tongue plots destruction;
   it is like a sharpened razor.

³ You love evil rather than good,
   falsehood rather than speaking the
      truth.ᶜ
⁴ You love every harmful word,
   you deceitful tongue!

⁵ Surely God will bring you down to
      everlasting ruin:
   He will snatch you up and pluck
      you from your tent;
   he will uproot you from the land
      of the living.
⁶ The righteous will see and
      fear;
   they will laugh at you, saying,
⁷ "Here now is the man
   who did not make God his
      stronghold
   but trusted in his great wealth

ᵃ In Hebrew texts 52:1-9 is numbered 52:3-11.   ᵇ Title:
Probably a literary or musical term   ᶜ 3 The Hebrew has
Selah (a word of uncertain meaning) here and at the end of
verse 5.

and grew strong by destroying
others!"

8 But I am like an olive tree
flourishing in the house of
God;
I trust in God's unfailing love
for ever and ever.
9 For what you have done I will always
praise you
in the presence of your faithful
people.
And I will hope in your name,
for your name is good.

Psalm 53[a]

For the director of music. According
to *mahalath*.[b] A *maskil*[c] of David.

1 The fool says in his heart,
"There is no God."
They are corrupt, and their ways are
vile;
there is no one who does good.

2 God looks down from heaven
on all mankind
to see if there are any who
understand,
any who seek God.
3 Everyone has turned away, all have
become corrupt;
there is no one who does good,
not even one.

4 Do all these evildoers know
nothing?

They devour my people as though
eating bread;
they never call on God.
5 But there they are, overwhelmed with
dread,
where there was nothing to
dread.
God scattered the bones of those who
attacked you;
you put them to shame, for God
despised them.

6 Oh, that salvation for Israel would
come out of Zion!
When God restores his people,
let Jacob rejoice and Israel be
glad!

Psalm 54[d]

For the director of music. With stringed
instruments. A *maskil*[c] of David. When the
Ziphites had gone to Saul and said,
"Is not David hiding among us?"

1 Save me, O God, by your name;
vindicate me by your might.
2 Hear my prayer, O God;
listen to the words of my
mouth.

3 Arrogant foes are attacking me;
ruthless people are trying to kill
me—
people without regard for God.[e]

4 Surely God is my help;
the Lord is the one who sustains
me.

5 Let evil recoil on those who slander
me;
in your faithfulness destroy them.

6 I will sacrifice a freewill offering to
you;
I will praise your name, LORD, for it
is good.
7 You have delivered me from all my
troubles,
and my eyes have looked in triumph
on my foes.

Psalm 55[f]

For the director of music. With stringed
instruments. A *maskil*[c] of David.

1 Listen to my prayer, O God,
do not ignore my plea;
2   hear me and answer me.
My thoughts trouble me and I am
distraught
3   because of what my enemy is
saying,
because of the threats of the
wicked;
for they bring down suffering
on me
and assail me in their anger.

---

[a] In Hebrew texts 53:1-6 is numbered 53:2-7.   [b] Title:
Probably a musical term   [c] Title: Probably a literary or
musical term   [d] In Hebrew texts 54:1-7 is numbered
54:3-9.   [e] 3 The Hebrew has *Selah* (a word of uncertain
meaning) here.   [f] In Hebrew texts 55:1-23 is numbered
55:2-24.

⁴ My heart is in anguish within me;
   the terrors of death have fallen
     on me.
⁵ Fear and trembling have
     beset me;
   horror has overwhelmed me.
⁶ I said, "Oh, that I had the wings of a
     dove!
   I would fly away and be at rest.
⁷ I would flee far away
   and stay in the desert;ᵃ
⁸ I would hurry to my place of
     shelter,
   far from the tempest and storm."

⁹ Lord, confuse the wicked, confound
     their words,
   for I see violence and strife in the
     city.
¹⁰ Day and night they prowl about on its
     walls;
   malice and abuse are within it.
¹¹ Destructive forces are at work in the
     city;
   threats and lies never leave its
     streets.

¹² If an enemy were insulting me,
   I could endure it;
 if a foe were rising against me,
   I could hide.
¹³ But it is you, a man like myself,
   my companion, my close friend,
¹⁴ with whom I once enjoyed sweet
     fellowship
   at the house of God,
 as we walked about
   among the worshipers.

¹⁵ Let death take my enemies by
     surprise;
 let them go down alive to the realm
     of the dead,
 for evil finds lodging among
     them.

¹⁶ As for me, I call to God,
   and the LORD saves me.
¹⁷ Evening, morning and noon
   I cry out in distress,
   and he hears my voice.
¹⁸ He rescues me unharmed
   from the battle waged against me,
   even though many oppose me.

¹⁹ God, who is enthroned from of old,
   who does not change—
 he will hear them and humble them,
   because they have no fear of
     God.

²⁰ My companion attacks his
     friends;
   he violates his covenant.
²¹ His talk is smooth as butter,
   yet war is in his heart;
 his words are more soothing than
     oil,
   yet they are drawn swords.

²² Cast your cares on the LORD
   and he will sustain you;
 he will never let
   the righteous be shaken.
²³ But you, God, will bring down the
     wicked
 into the pit of decay;
 the bloodthirsty and deceitful
   will not live out half their
     days.

But as for me, I trust in you.

Psalm 56ᵇ

For the director of music. To the tune
of "A Dove on Distant Oaks." Of David.
A *miktam*.ᶜ When the Philistines
   had seized him in Gath.

¹ Be merciful to me, my God,
   for my enemies are in hot pursuit;
 all day long they press their
     attack.
² My adversaries pursue me all day
     long;
 in their pride many are attacking
     me.
³ When I am afraid, I put my trust in
     you.
⁴   In God, whose word I praise—
 in God I trust and am not afraid.
   What can mere mortals do
     to me?

⁵ All day long they twist my words;
   all their schemes are for my ruin.

ᵃ 7 The Hebrew has *Selah* (a word of uncertain meaning)
here and in the middle of verse 19.   ᵇ In Hebrew texts
56:1-13 is numbered 56:2-14.   ᶜ Title: Probably a
literary or musical term

⁶They conspire, they lurk,
   they watch my steps,
   hoping to take my life.
⁷Because of their wickedness do not*ᵃ*
   let them escape;
   in your anger, God, bring the nations
   down.

⁸Record my misery;
   list my tears on your scroll*ᵇ*—
   are they not in your record?
⁹Then my enemies will turn back
   when I call for help.
   By this I will know that God is for
   me.

¹⁰In God, whose word I praise,
   in the Lᴏʀᴅ, whose word I praise—
¹¹in God I trust and am not afraid.
   What can man do to me?

¹²I am under vows to you, my God;
   I will present my thank offerings to
   you.
¹³For you have delivered me from death
   and my feet from stumbling,
   that I may walk before God
   in the light of life.

Psalm 57*ᶜ*

For the director of music. To the tune
of "Do Not Destroy." Of David. A *miktam.ᵈ*
When he had fled from Saul into the cave.

¹Have mercy on me, my God, have
   mercy on me,
   for in you I take refuge.
I will take refuge in the shadow of your
   wings
   until the disaster has passed.

²I cry out to God Most High,
   to God, who vindicates me.
³He sends from heaven and saves me,
   rebuking those who hotly pursue
   me—*ᵉ*
God sends forth his love and his
   faithfulness.

⁴I am in the midst of lions;
   I am forced to dwell among
   ravenous beasts—
men whose teeth are spears and
   arrows,
   whose tongues are sharp swords.

⁵Be exalted, O God, above the
   heavens;
   let your glory be over all the earth.

⁶They spread a net for my feet—
   I was bowed down in distress.
They dug a pit in my path—
   but they have fallen into it
   themselves.

⁷My heart, O God, is steadfast,
   my heart is steadfast;
   I will sing and make music.
⁸Awake, my soul!
   Awake, harp and lyre!
   I will awaken the dawn.

⁹I will praise you, Lord, among the
   nations;
   I will sing of you among the
   peoples.
¹⁰For great is your love, reaching to the
   heavens;
   your faithfulness reaches to the
   skies.

¹¹Be exalted, O God, above the
   heavens;
   let your glory be over all the earth.

Psalm 58*ᶠ*

For the director of music. To the tune
of "Do Not Destroy." Of David. A *miktam.ᵈ*

¹Do you rulers indeed speak justly?
   Do you judge people with equity?
²No, in your heart you devise injustice,
   and your hands mete out violence
   on the earth.

³Even from birth the wicked go
   astray;
   from the womb they are wayward,
   spreading lies.
⁴Their venom is like the venom of a
   snake,
   like that of a cobra that has
   stopped its ears,
⁵that will not heed the tune of the
   charmer,

ᵃ 7 Probable reading of the original Hebrew text; Masoretic
Text does not have *do not*.   *ᵇ* 8 Or *misery; / put my tears
in your wineskin*   *ᶜ* In Hebrew texts 57:1-11 is numbered
57:2-12.   *ᵈ* Title: Probably a literary or musical term
ᵉ 3 The Hebrew has *Selah* (a word of uncertain meaning)
here and at the end of verse 6.   *ᶠ* In Hebrew texts
58:1-11 is numbered 58:2-12.

however skillful the enchanter
may be.
6 Break the teeth in their mouths,
O God;
Lord, tear out the fangs of those
lions!
7 Let them vanish like water that flows
away;
when they draw the bow, let their
arrows fall short.
8 May they be like a slug that melts
away as it moves along,
like a stillborn child that never sees
the sun.

9 Before your pots can feel the heat of
the thorns—
whether they be green or dry—the
wicked will be swept away.*a*
10 The righteous will be glad when they
are avenged,
when they dip their feet in the blood
of the wicked.
11 Then people will say,
"Surely the righteous still are
rewarded;
surely there is a God who judges
the earth."

Psalm 59*b*

For the director of music. To the tune
of "Do Not Destroy." Of David. A *miktam.c*
When Saul had sent men to watch
David's house in order to kill him.

1 Deliver me from my enemies,
O God;
be my fortress against those who
are attacking me.
2 Deliver me from evildoers
and save me from those who are
after my blood.

3 See how they lie in wait for me!
Fierce men conspire against me
for no offense or sin of mine,
Lord.
4 I have done no wrong, yet they are
ready to attack me.
Arise to help me; look on my
plight!
5 You, Lord God Almighty,
you who are the God of Israel,
rouse yourself to punish all the
nations;
show no mercy to wicked traitors.*d*
6 They return at evening,
snarling like dogs,
and prowl about the city.
7 See what they spew from their
mouths—
the words from their lips are sharp
as swords,
and they think, "Who can hear us?"
8 But you laugh at them, Lord;
you scoff at all those nations.

9 You are my strength, I watch for you;
you, God, are my fortress,
10 my God on whom I can rely.

God will go before me
and will let me gloat over those who
slander me.
11 But do not kill them, Lord our shield,*e*
or my people will forget.
In your might uproot them
and bring them down.
12 For the sins of their mouths,
for the words of their lips,
let them be caught in their pride.
For the curses and lies they utter,
13 consume them in your wrath,
consume them till they are no
more.
Then it will be known to the ends of
the earth
that God rules over Jacob.

14 They return at evening,
snarling like dogs,
and prowl about the city.
15 They wander about for food
and howl if not satisfied.
16 But I will sing of your strength,
in the morning I will sing of your
love;
for you are my fortress,
my refuge in times of trouble.

17 You are my strength, I sing praise to
you;
you, God, are my fortress,
my God on whom I can rely.

---

a 9 The meaning of the Hebrew for this verse is uncertain.
b In Hebrew texts 59:1-17 is numbered 59:2-18.
c Title: Probably a literary or musical term   *d* 5 The
Hebrew has *Selah* (a word of uncertain meaning) here and
at the end of verse 13.   *e* 11 Or *sovereign*

Psalm 60[a]

For the director of music. To the tune
of "The Lily of the Covenant." A *miktam*[b]
of David. For teaching. When he fought Aram
Naharaim[c] and Aram Zobah,[d] and when Joab
returned and struck down twelve thousand
Edomites in the Valley of Salt.

[1] You have rejected us, God, and burst
      upon us;
   you have been angry—now restore
      us!
[2] You have shaken the land and torn it
      open;
   mend its fractures, for it is
      quaking.
[3] You have shown your people
      desperate times;
   you have given us wine that makes
      us stagger.
[4] But for those who fear you, you have
      raised a banner
   to be unfurled against the bow.[e]

[5] Save us and help us with your right
      hand,

that those you love may be
      delivered.
[6] God has spoken from his
      sanctuary:
   "In triumph I will parcel out
      Shechem
   and measure off the Valley of
      Sukkoth.
[7] Gilead is mine, and Manasseh is
      mine;
   Ephraim is my helmet,
   Judah is my scepter.

---

[a] In Hebrew texts 60:1-12 is numbered 60:3-14.
[b] Title: Probably a literary or musical term   [c] Title: That
is, Arameans of Northwest Mesopotamia   [d] Title: That is,
Arameans of central Syria   [e] 4 The Hebrew has *Selah*
(a word of uncertain meaning) here.

BREAK THROUGH!

Edomites

(PSALM 60, INTRODUCTION)

The Edomites were a nation related to the
Israelites, because they were offspring of
Esau, Jacob's brother. Esau was also called
Edom.

THE WITNESSES

✓ JOAB (PSALM 60)

King David's nephew and commander of his
army. He was very faithful, although he later
helped Adonijah, David's son, who had rebelled.
Joab means "God is father."

8 Moab is my washbasin,
  on Edom I toss my sandal;
  over Philistia I shout in triumph."

9 Who will bring me to the fortified city?
  Who will lead me to Edom?
10 Is it not you, God, you who have now
    rejected us
  and no longer go out with our
    armies?
11 Give us aid against the enemy,
  for human help is worthless.
12 With God we will gain the victory,
  and he will trample down our
    enemies.

Psalm 61 [a]

For the director of music. With stringed
instruments. Of David.

1 Hear my cry, O God;
  listen to my prayer.

2 From the ends of the earth I call to
    you,
  I call as my heart grows faint;
  lead me to the rock that is higher
    than I.
3 For you have been my refuge,
  a strong tower against the foe.

4 I long to dwell in your tent forever
  and take refuge in the shelter of
    your wings. [b]
5 For you, God, have heard my vows;
  you have given me the heritage of
    those who fear your name.

6 Increase the days of the king's life,
  his years for many generations.
7 May he be enthroned in God's
    presence forever;
  appoint your love and faithfulness
    to protect him.

8 Then I will ever sing in praise of your
    name
  and fulfill my vows day after day.

Psalm 62 [c]

For the director of music. For Jeduthun.
A psalm of David.

1 Truly my soul finds rest in God;
  my salvation comes from him.

2 Truly he is my rock and my salvation;
  he is my fortress, I will never be
    shaken.

3 How long will you assault me?
  Would all of you throw me down—
  this leaning wall, this tottering
    fence?
4 Surely they intend to topple me
  from my lofty place;
  they take delight in lies.
  With their mouths they bless,
  but in their hearts they curse. [d]

5 Yes, my soul, find rest in God;
  my hope comes from him.
6 Truly he is my rock and my salvation;
  he is my fortress, I will not be
    shaken.
7 My salvation and my honor depend on
    God [e];
  he is my mighty rock, my refuge.
8 Trust in him at all times, you people;
  pour out your hearts to him,
  for God is our refuge.

9 Surely the lowborn are but a breath,
  the highborn are but a lie.
  If weighed on a balance, they are
    nothing;
  together they are only a breath.
10 Do not trust in extortion
  or put vain hope in stolen goods;
  though your riches increase,
  do not set your heart on them.

11 One thing God has spoken,
  two things I have heard:
  "Power belongs to you, God,
12   and with you, Lord, is unfailing love";
  and, "You reward everyone
  according to what they have done."

Psalm 63 [f]

A psalm of David. When he was
in the Desert of Judah.

1 You, God, are my God,
  earnestly I seek you;

---

[a] In Hebrew texts 61:1-8 is numbered 61:2-9.   [b] 4 The
Hebrew has *Selah* (a word of uncertain meaning) here.
[c] In Hebrew texts 62:1-12 is numbered 62:2-13.
[d] 4 The Hebrew has *Selah* (a word of uncertain meaning)
here and at the end of verse 8.   [e] 7 Or / *God Most High
is my salvation and my honor*   [f] In Hebrew texts 63:1-11
is numbered 63:2-12.

I thirst for you,
   my whole being longs for you,
in a dry and parched land
   where there is no water.

2 I have seen you in the sanctuary
   and beheld your power and your
     glory.
3 Because your love is better than life,
   my lips will glorify you.
4 I will praise you as long as I live,
   and in your name I will lift up my
     hands.
5 I will be fully satisfied as with the
     richest of foods;
   with singing lips my mouth will
     praise you.

6 On my bed I remember you;
   I think of you through the watches
     of the night.
7 Because you are my help,
   I sing in the shadow of your wings.
8 I cling to you;
   your right hand upholds me.

9 Those who want to kill me will be
     destroyed;
   they will go down to the depths of
     the earth.
10 They will be given over to the sword
   and become food for jackals.

11 But the king will rejoice in God;
   all who swear by God will glory in
     him,
   while the mouths of liars will be
     silenced.

Psalm 64 [a]

For the director of music. A psalm of David.

1 Hear me, my God, as I voice my
     complaint;
   protect my life from the threat of
     the enemy.
2 Hide me from the conspiracy of the
     wicked,
   from the plots of evildoers.
3 They sharpen their tongues like swords
   and aim cruel words like deadly
     arrows.
4 They shoot from ambush at the
     innocent;
   they shoot suddenly, without fear.

5 They encourage each other in evil
     plans,
   they talk about hiding their snares;
   they say, "Who will see it [b]?"
6 They plot injustice and say,
   "We have devised a perfect plan!"
   Surely the human mind and heart
     are cunning.

7 But God will shoot them with his
     arrows;
   they will suddenly be struck down.
8 He will turn their own tongues against
     them
   and bring them to ruin;
   all who see them will shake their
     heads in scorn.
9 All people will fear;
   they will proclaim the works of God
   and ponder what he has done.

10 The righteous will rejoice in the Lord
   and take refuge in him;
   all the upright in heart will glory in
     him!

Psalm 65 [c]

For the director of music.
A psalm of David. A song.

1 Praise awaits [d] you, our God, in Zion;
   to you our vows will be fulfilled.
2 You who answer prayer,
   to you all people will come.
3 When we were overwhelmed by sins,
   you forgave [e] our transgressions.
4 Blessed are those you choose
   and bring near to live in your
     courts!
We are filled with the good things of
     your house,
   of your holy temple.

5 You answer us with awesome and
     righteous deeds,
   God our Savior,
   the hope of all the ends of the earth
   and of the farthest seas,
6 who formed the mountains by your
     power,
   having armed yourself with strength,

---

a In Hebrew texts 64:1-10 is numbered 64:2-11.   b 5 Or
us   c In Hebrew texts 65:1-13 is numbered 65:2-14.
d 1 Or befits; the meaning of the Hebrew for this word is
uncertain.   e 3 Or made atonement for

⁷who stilled the roaring of the seas,
   the roaring of their waves,
   and the turmoil of the nations.
⁸The whole earth is filled with awe at
      your wonders;
   where morning dawns, where
      evening fades,
   you call forth songs of joy.

⁹You care for the land and water it;
   you enrich it abundantly.
The streams of God are filled with
      water
   to provide the people with grain,
   for so you have ordained it.ᵃ
¹⁰You drench its furrows and level its
      ridges;
   you soften it with showers and
      bless its crops.
¹¹You crown the year with your bounty,
   and your carts overflow with
      abundance.
¹²The grasslands of the wilderness
      overflow;
   the hills are clothed with gladness.
¹³The meadows are covered with flocks
   and the valleys are mantled with
      grain;
   they shout for joy and sing.

Psalm 66

For the director of music. A song. A psalm.

¹Shout for joy to God, all the earth!
²   Sing the glory of his name;
   make his praise glorious.
³Say to God, "How awesome are your
      deeds!
   So great is your power
   that your enemies cringe before
      you.
⁴All the earth bows down to you;
   they sing praise to you,
   they sing the praises of your
      name."ᵇ

⁵Come and see what God has done,
   his awesome deeds for mankind!
⁶He turned the sea into dry land,
   they passed through the waters on
      foot—
   come, let us rejoice in him.
⁷He rules forever by his power,
   his eyes watch the nations—

let not the rebellious rise up against
      him.
⁸Praise our God, all peoples,
   let the sound of his praise be
      heard;
⁹he has preserved our lives
   and kept our feet from slipping.
¹⁰For you, God, tested us;
   you refined us like silver.
¹¹You brought us into prison
   and laid burdens on our backs.
¹²You let people ride over our heads;
   we went through fire and water,
   but you brought us to a place of
      abundance.

¹³I will come to your temple with burnt
      offerings
   and fulfill my vows to you—
¹⁴vows my lips promised and my mouth
      spoke
   when I was in trouble.
¹⁵I will sacrifice fat animals to you
   and an offering of rams;
   I will offer bulls and goats.

¹⁶Come and hear, all you who fear God;
   let me tell you what he has done for
      me.
¹⁷I cried out to him with my mouth;
   his praise was on my tongue.
¹⁸If I had cherished sin in my heart,
   the Lord would not have listened;
¹⁹but God has surely listened
   and has heard my prayer.
²⁰Praise be to God,
   who has not rejected my prayer
   or withheld his love from me!

Psalm 67ᶜ

For the director of music. With stringed
instruments. A psalm. A song.

¹May God be gracious to us and
      bless us
   and make his face shine on us—ᵈ
²so that your ways may be known on
      earth,
   your salvation among all nations.

ᵃ 9 Or *for that is how you prepare the land*   ᵇ 4 The
Hebrew has *Selah* (a word of uncertain meaning) here and
at the end of verses 7 and 15.   ᶜ In Hebrew texts 67:1-7
is numbered 67:2-8.   ᵈ 1 The Hebrew has *Selah* (a word
of uncertain meaning) here and at the end of verse 4.

³ May the peoples praise you, God;
     may all the peoples praise you.
⁴ May the nations be glad and sing for
     joy,
     for you rule the peoples with equity
     and guide the nations of the earth.
⁵ May the peoples praise you, God;
     may all the peoples praise you.

⁶ The land yields its harvest;
     God, our God, blesses us.
⁷ May God bless us still,
     so that all the ends of the earth will
     fear him.

Psalm 68ᵃ

For the director of music. Of David.
A psalm. A song.

¹ May God arise, may his enemies be
     scattered;
     may his foes flee before him.
² May you blow them away like smoke—
     as wax melts before the fire,
     may the wicked perish before God.
³ But may the righteous be glad
     and rejoice before God;
     may they be happy and joyful.

⁴ Sing to God, sing in praise of his
     name,
     extol him who rides on the cloudsᵇ;
     rejoice before him—his name is
     the Lᴏʀᴅ.
⁵ A father to the fatherless, a defender
     of widows,
     is God in his holy dwelling.
⁶ God sets the lonely in families,ᶜ
     he leads out the prisoners with
     singing;
     but the rebellious live in a sun-
     scorched land.

⁷ When you, God, went out before your
     people,
     when you marched through the
     wilderness,ᵈ
⁸ the earth shook, the heavens poured
     down rain,
     before God, the One of Sinai,
     before God, the God of Israel.
⁹ You gave abundant showers, O God;
     you refreshed your weary
     inheritance.

¹⁰ Your people settled in it,
     and from your bounty, God, you
     provided for the poor.

¹¹ The Lord announces the word,
     and the women who proclaim it are
     a mighty throng:
¹² "Kings and armies flee in haste;
     the women at home divide the
     plunder.
¹³ Even while you sleep among the
     sheep pens,ᵉ
     the wings of my dove are sheathed
     with silver,
     its feathers with shining
     gold."
¹⁴ When the Almightyᶠ scattered the
     kings in the land,
     it was like snow fallen on Mount
     Zalmon.

ᵃ In Hebrew texts 68:1-35 is numbered 68:2-36.   ᵇ 4 Or *name, / prepare the way for him who rides through the deserts*   ᶜ 6 *Or the desolate in a homeland*   ᵈ 7 The Hebrew has *Selah* (a word of uncertain meaning) here and at the end of verses 19 and 32.   ᵉ 13 Or *the campfires; or the saddlebags*   ᶠ 14 Hebrew *Shaddai*

THE SCENE

MOUNT ZALMON

(PSALM 68:14)

A high mountain near the city of Sichem.

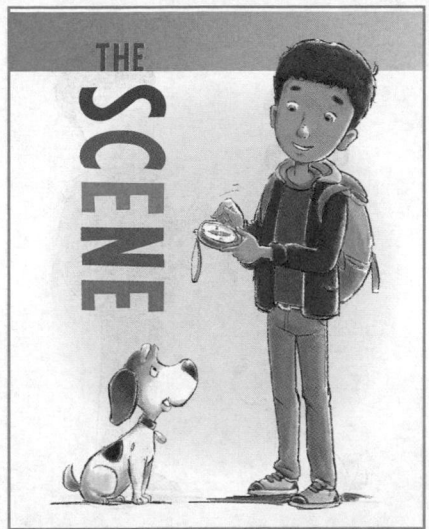

MOUNT BASHAN

(PSALM 68:15)

A range of high mountains that was a famous region because of the good cattle raised there.

15 Mount Bashan, majestic mountain,
   Mount Bashan, rugged mountain,
16 why gaze in envy, you rugged
         mountain,
   at the mountain where God chooses
         to reign,
   where the LORD himself will dwell
         forever?
17 The chariots of God are tens of
         thousands
   and thousands of thousands;
   the Lord has come from Sinai into
         his sanctuary.[a]
18 When you ascended on high,
   you took many captives;
   you received gifts from people,
   even from[b] the rebellious—
   that you,[c] LORD God, might dwell
         there.

19 Praise be to the Lord, to God our Savior,
   who daily bears our burdens.
20 Our God is a God who saves;
   from the Sovereign LORD comes
         escape from death.

21 Surely God will crush the heads of his
         enemies,
   the hairy crowns of those who go on
         in their sins.
22 The Lord says, "I will bring them from
         Bashan;
   I will bring them from the depths of
         the sea,
23 that your feet may wade in the blood
         of your foes,
   while the tongues of your dogs have
         their share."

24 Your procession, God, has come into
         view,

---

a 17 Probable reading of the original Hebrew text;
Masoretic Text *Lord is among them at Sinai in holiness*
b 18 Or *gifts for people, / even*   *c 18* Or *they*

"Surely God will crush the heads of his enemies ..."

(PSALM 68:21)

In the Old Testament and in this Psalm, there are expressions that are very harsh and violent (see Psalm 137:9). Bible experts say it has to do with the behaviors of people at that time, and that they exaggerated everything. It doesn't mean that God wanted to do that or that he likes to treat people that way. It was just the way those people expressed their anger.

the procession of my God and King
into the sanctuary.

25 In front are the singers, after them the
musicians;
with them are the young women
playing the timbrels.

26 Praise God in the great congregation;
praise the LORD in the assembly of
Israel.

27 There is the little tribe of Benjamin,
leading them,
there the great throng of Judah's
princes,
and there the princes of Zebulun
and of Naphtali.

28 Summon your power, God*a*;
show us your strength, our God, as
you have done before.

29 Because of your temple at Jerusalem
kings will bring you gifts.

30 Rebuke the beast among the
reeds,
the herd of bulls among the calves
of the nations.
Humbled, may the beast bring bars of
silver.
Scatter the nations who delight in
war.

31 Envoys will come from Egypt;
Cush*b* will submit herself to God.

32 Sing to God, you kingdoms of the
earth,
sing praise to the Lord,

33 to him who rides across the highest
heavens, the ancient heavens,
who thunders with mighty voice.

34 Proclaim the power of God,
whose majesty is over Israel,
whose power is in the heavens.

35 You, God, are awesome in your
sanctuary;
the God of Israel gives power and
strength to his people.

Praise be to God!

Psalm 69*c*

For the director of music. To the tune
of "Lilies." Of David.

1 Save me, O God,
for the waters have come up to my
neck.

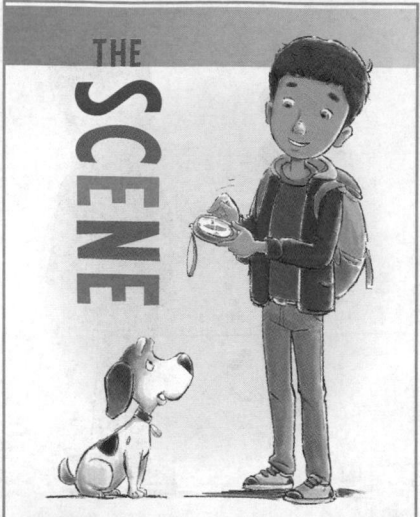

THE SCENE

CUSH

(PSALMS 68:31)

A lso called Ethiopia, it was a
country inhabited by warriors
in the region south of the Nile
River.

2 I sink in the miry depths,
where there is no foothold.
I have come into the deep waters;
the floods engulf me.

3 I am worn out calling for help;
my throat is parched.
My eyes fail,
looking for my God.

4 Those who hate me without reason
outnumber the hairs of my head;
many are my enemies without cause,
those who seek to destroy me.
I am forced to restore
what I did not steal.

5 You, God, know my folly;
my guilt is not hidden from you.

6 Lord, the LORD Almighty,
may those who hope in you
not be disgraced because of me;

---

a 28 Many Hebrew manuscripts, Septuagint and Syriac;
most Hebrew manuscripts *Your God has summoned power
for you*   *b* 31 That is, the upper Nile region   *c* In
Hebrew texts 69:1-36 is numbered 69:2-37.

God of Israel,
    may those who seek you
    not be put to shame because of me.
7 For I endure scorn for your sake,
    and shame covers my face.
8 I am a foreigner to my own family,
    a stranger to my own mother's
      children;
9 for zeal for your house consumes me,
    and the insults of those who insult
      you fall on me.
10 When I weep and fast,
    I must endure scorn;
11 when I put on sackcloth,
    people make sport of me.
12 Those who sit at the gate mock me,
    and I am the song of the drunkards.

13 But I pray to you, Lord,
    in the time of your favor;
in your great love, O God,
    answer me with your sure salvation.
14 Rescue me from the mire,
    do not let me sink;
deliver me from those who hate me,
    from the deep waters.
15 Do not let the floodwaters engulf me
    or the depths swallow me up
    or the pit close its mouth over me.

16 Answer me, Lord, out of the goodness
      of your love;
    in your great mercy turn to me.
17 Do not hide your face from your
      servant;
    answer me quickly, for I am in
      trouble.
18 Come near and rescue me;
    deliver me because of my foes.

19 You know how I am scorned, disgraced
      and shamed;
    all my enemies are before you.
20 Scorn has broken my heart
    and has left me helpless;
I looked for sympathy, but there was
      none,
    for comforters, but I found none.
21 They put gall in my food
    and gave me vinegar for my thirst.

22 May the table set before them
      become a snare;
    may it become retribution and[a] a
      trap.

23 May their eyes be darkened so they
      cannot see,
    and their backs be bent forever.
24 Pour out your wrath on them;
    let your fierce anger overtake them.
25 May their place be deserted;
    let there be no one to dwell in their
      tents.
26 For they persecute those you wound
    and talk about the pain of those you
      hurt.
27 Charge them with crime upon crime;
    do not let them share in your
      salvation.
28 May they be blotted out of the book of
      life
    and not be listed with the righteous.

29 But as for me, afflicted and in pain—
    may your salvation, God, protect me.

30 I will praise God's name in song
    and glorify him with thanksgiving.
31 This will please the Lord more than
      an ox,
    more than a bull with its horns and
      hooves.
32 The poor will see and be glad—
    you who seek God, may your hearts
      live!
33 The Lord hears the needy
    and does not despise his captive
      people.

34 Let heaven and earth praise him,
    the seas and all that move in them,
35 for God will save Zion
    and rebuild the cities of Judah.
Then people will settle there and
      possess it;
36   the children of his servants will
      inherit it,
    and those who love his name will
      dwell there.

Psalm 70[b]

For the director of music. Of David. A petition.

1 Hasten, O God, to save me;
    come quickly, Lord, to help me.

2 May those who want to take my life
    be put to shame and confusion;

---

a 22 Or *snare / and their fellowship become*   b In Hebrew
texts 70:1-5 is numbered 70:2-6.

may all who desire my ruin
  be turned back in disgrace.
3 May those who say to me, "Aha! Aha!"
  turn back because of their shame.
4 But may all who seek you
  rejoice and be glad in you;
may those who long for your saving
  help always say,
  "The Lord is great!"

5 But as for me, I am poor and needy;
  come quickly to me, O God.
You are my help and my deliverer;
  Lord, do not delay.

Psalm 71

1 In you, Lord, I have taken refuge;
  let me never be put to shame.
2 In your righteousness, rescue me and
  deliver me;
  turn your ear to me and save me.
3 Be my rock of refuge,
  to which I can always go;
give the command to save me,
  for you are my rock and my fortress.
4 Deliver me, my God, from the hand of
  the wicked,
  from the grasp of those who are evil
  and cruel.

5 For you have been my hope, Sovereign
  Lord,
  my confidence since my youth.
6 From birth I have relied on you;
  you brought me forth from my
  mother's womb.
  I will ever praise you.
7 I have become a sign to many;
  you are my strong refuge.
8 My mouth is filled with your praise,
  declaring your splendor all day
  long.

9 Do not cast me away when I am old;
  do not forsake me when my
  strength is gone.
10 For my enemies speak against me;
  those who wait to kill me conspire
  together.
11 They say, "God has forsaken him;
  pursue him and seize him,
  for no one will rescue him."
12 Do not be far from me, my God;
  come quickly, God, to help me.

13 May my accusers perish in shame;
  may those who want to harm me
  be covered with scorn and
  disgrace.

14 As for me, I will always have hope;
  I will praise you more and more.
15 My mouth will tell of your righteous
  deeds,
  of your saving acts all day long—
  though I know not how to relate
  them all.
16 I will come and proclaim your mighty
  acts, Sovereign Lord;
  I will proclaim your righteous deeds,
  yours alone.
17 Since my youth, God, you have taught
  me,
  and to this day I declare your
  marvelous deeds.
18 Even when I am old and gray,
  do not forsake me, my God,
till I declare your power to the next
  generation,
  your mighty acts to all who are to
  come.

19 Your righteousness, God, reaches to
  the heavens,
  you who have done great things.
  Who is like you, God?
20 Though you have made me see
  troubles,
  many and bitter,
  you will restore my life again;
from the depths of the earth
  you will again bring me up.
21 You will increase my honor
  and comfort me once more.

22 I will praise you with the harp
  for your faithfulness, my God;
I will sing praise to you with the
  lyre,
  Holy One of Israel.
23 My lips will shout for joy
  when I sing praise to you—
  I whom you have delivered.
24 My tongue will tell of your righteous
  acts
  all day long,
for those who wanted to harm me
  have been put to shame and
  confusion.

Psalm 72

Of Solomon.

¹ Endow the king with your justice,
O God,
the royal son with your
righteousness.
² May he judge your people in
righteousness,
your afflicted ones with justice.

³ May the mountains bring prosperity to
the people,
the hills the fruit of righteousness.
⁴ May he defend the afflicted among the
people
and save the children of the needy;
may he crush the oppressor.

⁵ May he endure[a] as long as the sun,
as long as the moon, through all
generations.
⁶ May he be like rain falling on a mown
field,
like showers watering the earth.
⁷ In his days may the righteous flourish
and prosperity abound till the moon
is no more.

⁸ May he rule from sea to sea
and from the River[b] to the ends of
the earth.
⁹ May the desert tribes bow before him
and his enemies lick the dust.
¹⁰ May the kings of Tarshish and of
distant shores
bring tribute to him.
May the kings of Sheba and Seba
present him gifts.
¹¹ May all kings bow down to him
and all nations serve him.

---

[a] 5 Septuagint; Hebrew *You will be feared*   [b] 8 That is,
the Euphrates

THE WITNESSES

✓ **SOLOMON** (PSALM 72)
Son of King David and Bathsheba. When David
died, Solomon became king of Israel.

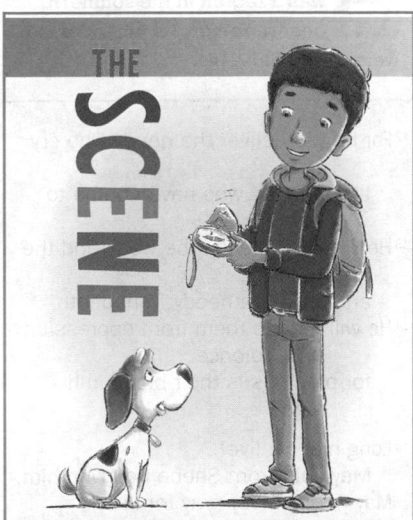

THE SCENE

TARSHISH

(PSALM 72:10)

A city on the western tip of the
Mediterranean Sea far from
the land of Israel.

SHEBA

(PSALM 72:10,15)

Home of the queen of Sheba. It was a region in the southern desert, Yemen. Its inhabitants were called Sabeans.

¹²For he will deliver the needy who cry
      out,
   the afflicted who have no one to
      help.
¹³He will take pity on the weak and the
      needy
   and save the needy from death.
¹⁴He will rescue them from oppression
      and violence,
   for precious is their blood in his
      sight.

¹⁵Long may he live!
   May gold from Sheba be given him.
May people ever pray for him
   and bless him all day long.
¹⁶May grain abound throughout the
      land;
   on the tops of the hills may it sway.
May the crops flourish like Lebanon
   and thrive^a like the grass of the
      field.
¹⁷May his name endure forever;
   may it continue as long as the sun.

Then all nations will be blessed
      through him,^b
   and they will call him blessed.

¹⁸Praise be to the LORD God, the God of
      Israel,
   who alone does marvelous
      deeds.
¹⁹Praise be to his glorious name
      forever;
   may the whole earth be filled with
      his glory.
         Amen and Amen.

²⁰This concludes the prayers of David
      son of Jesse.

---

^a 16 Probable reading of the original Hebrew text;
Masoretic Text *Lebanon, / from the city*   ^b 17 Or *will use
his name in blessings* (see Gen. 48:20)

THE
WITNESSES

✓ **JESSE (PSALM 72:20)**
King David's father.

BOOK III

Psalms 73 – 89

Psalm 73

A psalm of Asaph.

1 Surely God is good to Israel,
  to those who are pure in heart.

2 But as for me, my feet had almost
    slipped;
  I had nearly lost my foothold.
3 For I envied the arrogant
  when I saw the prosperity of the
    wicked.

4 They have no struggles;
  their bodies are healthy and
    strong.*a*
5 They are free from common human
    burdens;
  they are not plagued by human
    ills.
6 Therefore pride is their necklace;
  they clothe themselves with
    violence.
7 From their callous hearts comes
    iniquity*b*;
  their evil imaginations have no
    limits.
8 They scoff, and speak with malice;
  with arrogance they threaten
    oppression.
9 Their mouths lay claim to heaven,
  and their tongues take possession
    of the earth.
10 Therefore their people turn to them
  and drink up waters in abundance.*c*
11 They say, "How would God know?
  Does the Most High know
    anything?"

12 This is what the wicked are like—
  always free of care, they go on
    amassing wealth.

13 Surely in vain I have kept my heart
    pure
  and have washed my hands in
    innocence.
14 All day long I have been afflicted,
  and every morning brings new
    punishments.

15 If I had spoken out like that,
  I would have betrayed your children.
16 When I tried to understand all this,
  it troubled me deeply
17 till I entered the sanctuary of God;
  then I understood their final destiny.

18 Surely you place them on slippery
    ground;
  you cast them down to ruin.
19 How suddenly are they destroyed,
  completely swept away by terrors!
20 They are like a dream when one
    awakes;
  when you arise, Lord,
  you will despise them as fantasies.

21 When my heart was grieved
  and my spirit embittered,
22 I was senseless and ignorant;
  I was a brute beast before you.

23 Yet I am always with you;
  you hold me by my right hand.
24 You guide me with your counsel,
  and afterward you will take me into
    glory.
25 Whom have I in heaven but you?
  And earth has nothing I desire
    besides you.
26 My flesh and my heart may fail,
  but God is the strength of my heart
  and my portion forever.

27 Those who are far from you will perish;
  you destroy all who are unfaithful to
    you.
28 But as for me, it is good to be near
    God.
  I have made the Sovereign Lord my
    refuge;
  I will tell of all your deeds.

Psalm 74

A *maskil*[d] of Asaph.

1 O God, why have you rejected us
    forever?
  Why does your anger smolder against
    the sheep of your pasture?

---

a 4 With a different word division of the Hebrew; Masoretic
Text *struggles at their death; / their bodies are healthy*
b 7 Syriac (see also Septuagint); Hebrew *Their eyes bulge
with fat*   *c* 10 The meaning of the Hebrew for this
verse is uncertain.   *d* Title: Probably a literary or musical
term

2 Remember the nation you purchased
　　long ago,
　the people of your inheritance,
　　whom you redeemed—
　Mount Zion, where you dwelt.
3 Turn your steps toward these
　　everlasting ruins,
　all this destruction the enemy has
　　brought on the sanctuary.

4 Your foes roared in the place where
　　you met with us;
　they set up their standards as
　　signs.
5 They behaved like men wielding axes
　　to cut through a thicket of trees.
6 They smashed all the carved
　　paneling
　with their axes and hatchets.
7 They burned your sanctuary to the
　　ground;
　they defiled the dwelling place of
　　your Name.
8 They said in their hearts, "We will
　　crush them completely!"
　They burned every place where God
　　was worshiped in the land.

9 We are given no signs from God;
　no prophets are left,
　and none of us knows how long this
　　will be.
10 How long will the enemy mock you,
　　God?
　Will the foe revile your name
　　forever?
11 Why do you hold back your hand, your
　　right hand?
　Take it from the folds of your
　　garment and destroy them!

12 But God is my King from long ago;
　he brings salvation on the earth.

13 It was you who split open the sea by
　　your power;
　you broke the heads of the monster
　　in the waters.
14 It was you who crushed the heads of
　　Leviathan
　and gave it as food to the creatures
　　of the desert.
15 It was you who opened up springs and
　　streams;
　you dried up the ever-flowing rivers.

16 The day is yours, and yours also the
　　night;
　you established the sun and moon.
17 It was you who set all the boundaries
　　of the earth;
　you made both summer and winter.

18 Remember how the enemy has
　　mocked you, LORD,
　how foolish people have reviled your
　　name.
19 Do not hand over the life of your dove
　　to wild beasts;
　do not forget the lives of your
　　afflicted people forever.
20 Have regard for your covenant,
　because haunts of violence fill the
　　dark places of the land.
21 Do not let the oppressed retreat in
　　disgrace;
　may the poor and needy praise your
　　name.
22 Rise up, O God, and defend your
　　cause;
　remember how fools mock you all
　　day long.
23 Do not ignore the clamor of your
　　adversaries,
　the uproar of your enemies, which
　　rises continually.

Psalm 75 [a]

For the director of music. To the
tune of "Do Not Destroy."
A psalm of Asaph. A song.

1 We praise you, God,
　we praise you, for your Name is near;
　people tell of your wonderful deeds.

2 You say, "I choose the appointed time;
　it is I who judge with equity.
3 When the earth and all its people
　　quake,
　it is I who hold its pillars firm. [b]
4 To the arrogant I say, 'Boast no more,'
　and to the wicked, 'Do not lift up
　　your horns. [c]
5 Do not lift your horns against heaven;
　do not speak so defiantly.' "

---

[a] In Hebrew texts 75:1-10 is numbered 75:2-11.
[b] 3 The Hebrew has Selah (a word of uncertain meaning)
here.　[c] 4 Horns here symbolize strength; also in verses
5 and 10.

⁶No one from the east or the west
   or from the desert can exalt
      themselves.
⁷It is God who judges:
   He brings one down, he exalts
      another.
⁸In the hand of the Lᴏʀᴅ is a cup
   full of foaming wine mixed with
      spices;
   he pours it out, and all the wicked of
      the earth
   drink it down to its very dregs.

⁹As for me, I will declare this forever;
   I will sing praise to the God of
      Jacob,
¹⁰who says, "I will cut off the horns of
   all the wicked,
   but the horns of the righteous will
      be lifted up."

Psalm 76 *ᵃ*

For the director of music. With stringed
instruments. A psalm of Asaph. A song.

¹God is renowned in Judah;
   in Israel his name is great.
²His tent is in Salem,
   his dwelling place in Zion.
³There he broke the flashing arrows,
   the shields and the swords, the
      weapons of war.*ᵇ*
⁴You are radiant with light,
   more majestic than mountains rich
      with game.
⁵The valiant lie plundered,
   they sleep their last sleep;
   not one of the warriors
      can lift his hands.
⁶At your rebuke, God of Jacob,
   both horse and chariot lie still.

⁷It is you alone who are to be feared.
   Who can stand before you when you
      are angry?
⁸From heaven you pronounced
      judgment,
   and the land feared and was
      quiet—
⁹when you, God, rose up to judge,
   to save all the afflicted of the land.
¹⁰Surely your wrath against mankind
   brings you praise,

and the survivors of your wrath are
   restrained.*ᶜ*
¹¹Make vows to the Lᴏʀᴅ your God and
   fulfill them;
   let all the neighboring lands
   bring gifts to the One to be feared.
¹²He breaks the spirit of rulers;
   he is feared by the kings of the
      earth.

Psalm 77 *ᵈ*

For the director of music. For Jeduthun.
Of Asaph. A psalm.

¹I cried out to God for help;
   I cried out to God to hear me.
²When I was in distress, I sought the
      Lord;
   at night I stretched out untiring
      hands,
   and I would not be comforted.

³I remembered you, God, and I
      groaned;
   I meditated, and my spirit grew
      faint.*ᵉ*
⁴You kept my eyes from closing;
   I was too troubled to speak.
⁵I thought about the former days,
   the years of long ago;
⁶I remembered my songs in the night.
   My heart meditated and my spirit
      asked:

⁷"Will the Lord reject forever?
   Will he never show his favor again?
⁸Has his unfailing love vanished
      forever?
   Has his promise failed for all
      time?
⁹Has God forgotten to be merciful?
   Has he in anger withheld his
      compassion?"

¹⁰Then I thought, "To this I will appeal:
   the years when the Most High
      stretched out his right hand.

ᵃ In Hebrew texts 76:1-12 is numbered 76:2-13.
ᵇ 3 The Hebrew has *Selah* (a word of uncertain meaning)
here and at the end of verse 9.   *ᶜ 10* Or *Surely the*
wrath of mankind brings you praise, / and with the
remainder of wrath you arm yourself   *ᵈ* In Hebrew texts
77:1-20 is numbered 77:2-21.   *ᵉ 3* The Hebrew has
Selah (a word of uncertain meaning) here and at the end
of verses 9 and 15.

11 I will remember the deeds of the Lord;
    yes, I will remember your miracles
      of long ago.
12 I will consider all your works
    and meditate on all your mighty
      deeds."

13 Your ways, God, are holy.
    What god is as great as our God?
14 You are the God who performs
      miracles;
    you display your power among the
      peoples.
15 With your mighty arm you redeemed
      your people,
    the descendants of Jacob and
      Joseph.

16 The waters saw you, God,
    the waters saw you and writhed;
    the very depths were convulsed.
17 The clouds poured down water,
    the heavens resounded with
      thunder;
    your arrows flashed back and forth.
18 Your thunder was heard in the
      whirlwind,
    your lightning lit up the world;
    the earth trembled and quaked.
19 Your path led through the sea,
    your way through the mighty waters,
    though your footprints were not
      seen.

20 You led your people like a flock
    by the hand of Moses and Aaron.

Psalm 78

A *maskil*[a] of Asaph.

1 My people, hear my teaching;
    listen to the words of my mouth.
2 I will open my mouth with a parable;
    I will utter hidden things, things
      from of old—
3 things we have heard and known,
    things our ancestors have told us.
4 We will not hide them from their
      descendants;
    we will tell the next generation
    the praiseworthy deeds of the Lord,
    his power, and the wonders he has
      done.
5 He decreed statutes for Jacob
    and established the law in Israel,

which he commanded our ancestors
    to teach their children,
6 so the next generation would know
      them,
    even the children yet to be born,
    and they in turn would tell their
      children.
7 Then they would put their trust in
      God
    and would not forget his deeds
    but would keep his commands.
8 They would not be like their
      ancestors—
    a stubborn and rebellious
      generation,
    whose hearts were not loyal to God,
    whose spirits were not faithful to
      him.

9 The men of Ephraim, though armed
      with bows,
    turned back on the day of battle;
10 they did not keep God's covenant
    and refused to live by his law.
11 They forgot what he had done,
    the wonders he had shown them.
12 He did miracles in the sight of their
      ancestors
    in the land of Egypt, in the region of
      Zoan.
13 He divided the sea and led them
      through;
    he made the water stand up like a
      wall.
14 He guided them with the cloud by
      day
    and with light from the fire all
      night.
15 He split the rocks in the wilderness
    and gave them water as abundant
      as the seas;
16 he brought streams out of a rocky crag
    and made water flow down like
      rivers.

17 But they continued to sin against him,
    rebelling in the wilderness against
      the Most High.
18 They willfully put God to the test
    by demanding the food they craved.
19 They spoke against God;
    they said, "Can God really
      spread a table in the wilderness?

---

a Title: Probably a literary or musical term

20 True, he struck the rock,
and water gushed out,
streams flowed abundantly,
but can he also give us bread?
Can he supply meat for his
people?"
21 When the LORD heard them, he was
furious;
his fire broke out against Jacob,
and his wrath rose against
Israel,
22 for they did not believe in God
or trust in his deliverance.
23 Yet he gave a command to the skies
above
and opened the doors of the
heavens;
24 he rained down manna for the people
to eat,
he gave them the grain of heaven.
25 Human beings ate the bread of
angels;
he sent them all the food they could
eat.
26 He let loose the east wind from the
heavens
and by his power made the south
wind blow.
27 He rained meat down on them like
dust,
birds like sand on the seashore.
28 He made them come down inside their
camp,
all around their tents.
29 They ate till they were gorged—
he had given them what they
craved.
30 But before they turned from what they
craved,
even while the food was still in their
mouths,
31 God's anger rose against them;
he put to death the sturdiest among
them,
cutting down the young men of
Israel.

32 In spite of all this, they kept on
sinning;
in spite of his wonders, they did not
believe.
33 So he ended their days in futility
and their years in terror.

34 Whenever God slew them, they would
seek him;
they eagerly turned to him again.
35 They remembered that God was their
Rock,
that God Most High was their
Redeemer.
36 But then they would flatter him with
their mouths,
lying to him with their tongues;
37 their hearts were not loyal to him,
they were not faithful to his
covenant.
38 Yet he was merciful;
he forgave their iniquities
and did not destroy them.
Time after time he restrained his
anger
and did not stir up his full wrath.
39 He remembered that they were but
flesh,
a passing breeze that does not
return.

40 How often they rebelled against him in
the wilderness
and grieved him in the wasteland!
41 Again and again they put God to the
test;
they vexed the Holy One of Israel.
42 They did not remember his power—
the day he redeemed them from the
oppressor,
43 the day he displayed his signs in
Egypt,
his wonders in the region of Zoan.
44 He turned their river into blood;
they could not drink from their
streams.
45 He sent swarms of flies that devoured
them,
and frogs that devastated them.
46 He gave their crops to the
grasshopper,
their produce to the locust.
47 He destroyed their vines with hail
and their sycamore-figs with
sleet.
48 He gave over their cattle to the hail,
their livestock to bolts of
lightning.
49 He unleashed against them his hot
anger,

his wrath, indignation and
  hostility—
a band of destroying angels.
⁵⁰ He prepared a path for his anger;
  he did not spare them from death
  but gave them over to the plague.
⁵¹ He struck down all the firstborn of
  Egypt,
  the firstfruits of manhood in the
  tents of Ham.
⁵² But he brought his people out like a
  flock;
  he led them like sheep through the
  wilderness.
⁵³ He guided them safely, so they were
  unafraid;
  but the sea engulfed their enemies.
⁵⁴ And so he brought them to the border
  of his holy land,
  to the hill country his right hand had
  taken.
⁵⁵ He drove out nations before them
  and allotted their lands to them as
  an inheritance;
  he settled the tribes of Israel in
  their homes.

⁵⁶ But they put God to the test
  and rebelled against the Most High;
  they did not keep his statutes.
⁵⁷ Like their ancestors they were disloyal
  and faithless,
  as unreliable as a faulty bow.
⁵⁸ They angered him with their high
  places;
  they aroused his jealousy with their
  idols.
⁵⁹ When God heard them, he was
  furious;
  he rejected Israel completely.
⁶⁰ He abandoned the tabernacle of
  Shiloh,
  the tent he had set up among
  humans.
⁶¹ He sent the ark of his might into
  captivity,
  his splendor into the hands of the
  enemy.
⁶² He gave his people over to the sword;
  he was furious with his inheritance.
⁶³ Fire consumed their young men,
  and their young women had no
  wedding songs;

⁶⁴ their priests were put to the sword,
  and their widows could not weep.

⁶⁵ Then the Lord awoke as from sleep,
  as a warrior wakes from the stupor
  of wine.
⁶⁶ He beat back his enemies;
  he put them to everlasting shame.
⁶⁷ Then he rejected the tents of Joseph,
  he did not choose the tribe of
  Ephraim;
⁶⁸ but he chose the tribe of Judah,
  Mount Zion, which he loved.
⁶⁹ He built his sanctuary like the
  heights,
  like the earth that he established
  forever.
⁷⁰ He chose David his servant
  and took him from the sheep pens;
⁷¹ from tending the sheep he brought
  him
  to be the shepherd of his people
  Jacob,
  of Israel his inheritance.
⁷² And David shepherded them with
  integrity of heart;
  with skillful hands he led them.

Psalm 79

A psalm of Asaph.

¹ O God, the nations have invaded your
  inheritance;
  they have defiled your holy temple,
  they have reduced Jerusalem to
  rubble.
² They have left the dead bodies of your
  servants
  as food for the birds of the sky,
  the flesh of your own people for the
  animals of the wild.
³ They have poured out blood like water
  all around Jerusalem,
  and there is no one to bury the
  dead.
⁴ We are objects of contempt to our
  neighbors,
  of scorn and derision to those
  around us.

⁵ How long, Lᴏʀᴅ? Will you be angry
  forever?
  How long will your jealousy burn like
  fire?

6 Pour out your wrath on the nations
   that do not acknowledge you,
on the kingdoms
   that do not call on your name;
7 for they have devoured Jacob
   and devastated his homeland.

8 Do not hold against us the sins of
   past generations;
may your mercy come quickly to
   meet us,
for we are in desperate need.
9 Help us, God our Savior,
   for the glory of your name;
deliver us and forgive our sins
   for your name's sake.
10 Why should the nations say,
   "Where is their God?"

Before our eyes, make known among
   the nations
that you avenge the outpoured
   blood of your servants.
11 May the groans of the prisoners come
   before you;
with your strong arm preserve those
   condemned to die.
12 Pay back into the laps of our
   neighbors seven times
the contempt they have hurled at
   you, Lord.
13 Then we your people, the sheep of
   your pasture,
will praise you forever;
from generation to generation
   we will proclaim your praise.

Psalm 80 [a]

For the director of music. To the tune
of "The Lilies of the Covenant."
Of Asaph. A psalm.

1 Hear us, Shepherd of Israel,
   you who lead Joseph like a flock.
You who sit enthroned between the
   cherubim,
   shine forth 2 before Ephraim,
      Benjamin and Manasseh.
Awaken your might;
   come and save us.

3 Restore us, O God;
   make your face shine on us,
   that we may be saved.

4 How long, LORD God Almighty,
   will your anger smolder
   against the prayers of your people?
5 You have fed them with the bread of
   tears;
you have made them drink tears by
   the bowlful.
6 You have made us an object of
   derision [b] to our neighbors,
and our enemies mock us.

7 Restore us, God Almighty;
   make your face shine on us,
   that we may be saved.

8 You transplanted a vine from Egypt;
   you drove out the nations and
      planted it.
9 You cleared the ground for it,
   and it took root and filled the land.
10 The mountains were covered with its
   shade,
   the mighty cedars with its branches.

---

a In Hebrew texts 80:1-19 is numbered 80:2-20.
b 6 Probable reading of the original Hebrew text; Masoretic
Text *contention*

BREAKTHROUGH!

Does God get angry and punish?

(PSALM 80:4)

The Israelites thought of God as a father who corrects his children. That's why they thought that God also gets angry and punishes.

11 Its branches reached as far as the
Sea,[a]
     its shoots as far as the River.[b]

12 Why have you broken down its walls
     so that all who pass by pick its
     grapes?
13 Boars from the forest ravage it,
     and insects from the fields feed
     on it.
14 Return to us, God Almighty!
     Look down from heaven and see!
     Watch over this vine,
15   the root your right hand has
     planted,
     the son[c] you have raised up for
     yourself.

16 Your vine is cut down, it is burned with
     fire;
     at your rebuke your people perish.
17 Let your hand rest on the man at your
     right hand,
     the son of man you have raised up
     for yourself.
18 Then we will not turn away from you;
     revive us, and we will call on your
     name.

19 Restore us, Lord God Almighty;
     make your face shine on us,
     that we may be saved.

Psalm 81[d]

For the director of music. According
to gittith.[e] Of Asaph.

1 Sing for joy to God our strength;
     shout aloud to the God of Jacob!
2 Begin the music, strike the timbrel,
     play the melodious harp and lyre.

3 Sound the ram's horn at the New
     Moon,
     and when the moon is full, on the
     day of our festival;
4 this is a decree for Israel,
     an ordinance of the God of Jacob.
5 When God went out against Egypt,
     he established it as a statute for
     Joseph.

I heard an unknown voice say:

6 "I removed the burden from their
     shoulders;

BREAK THROUGH!

Timbrel and lyre
(PSALM 81:2)
The timbrel was a kind of tambourine. The
lyre was a musical instrument with strings. It
was kind of like a harp, but smaller.

     their hands were set free from the
     basket.
7 In your distress you called and I
     rescued you,
     I answered you out of a
     thundercloud;
     I tested you at the waters of
     Meribah.[f]
8 Hear me, my people, and I will warn
     you—
     if you would only listen to me,
     Israel!
9 You shall have no foreign god among
     you;
     you shall not worship any god other
     than me.
10 I am the Lord your God,
     who brought you up out of
     Egypt.
     Open wide your mouth and I will
     fill it.

---

[a] 11 Probably the Mediterranean   [b] 11 That is, the
Euphrates   [c] 15 Or branch   [d] In Hebrew texts 81:1-16
is numbered 81:2-17.   [e] Title: Probably a musical term
[f] 7 The Hebrew has Selah (a word of uncertain meaning)
here.

THE SCENE

WATERS OF MERIBAH

(PSALM 81:7)

When the Israelites left Egypt and crossed the Desert of Zin, they protested against God in the city of Kadesh. That's why Moses changed the name from Kadesh to Meribah, which means "quarrel."

11 "But my people would not listen
      to me;
   Israel would not submit to me.
12 So I gave them over to their stubborn
      hearts
   to follow their own devices.

13 "If my people would only listen to me,
   if Israel would only follow my ways,
14 how quickly I would subdue their
      enemies
   and turn my hand against their
      foes!
15 Those who hate the Lord would cringe
      before him,
   and their punishment would last
      forever.
16 But you would be fed with the finest
      of wheat;
   with honey from the rock I would
      satisfy you."

Psalm 82

A psalm of Asaph.

1 God presides in the great assembly;
   he renders judgment among the
      "gods":

2 "How long will you[a] defend the unjust
   and show partiality to the wicked?[b]
3 Defend the weak and the fatherless;
   uphold the cause of the poor and
      the oppressed.
4 Rescue the weak and the needy;
   deliver them from the hand of the
      wicked.

5 "The 'gods' know nothing, they
      understand nothing.
   They walk about in darkness;
   all the foundations of the earth are
      shaken.

6 "I said, 'You are "gods";
   you are all sons of the Most High.'

[a] 2 The Hebrew is plural.   [b] 2 The Hebrew has *Selah* (a word of uncertain meaning) here.

BREAKTHROUGH!

Are there other gods?

(PSALM 82:1; 138:1)

The Israelites saw that their neighbors worshiped other gods. They didn't turn their backs on them for that, but they did know that their God was really the true God.

⁷ But you will die like mere mortals;
  you will fall like every other ruler."

⁸ Rise up, O God, judge the earth,
  for all the nations are your
    inheritance.

Psalm 83*ᵃ*

A song. A psalm of Asaph.

¹ O God, do not remain silent;
  do not turn a deaf ear,
  do not stand aloof, O God.
² See how your enemies growl,
  how your foes rear their heads.
³ With cunning they conspire against
    your people;
  they plot against those you cherish.
⁴ "Come," they say, "let us destroy them
    as a nation,
  so that Israel's name is
    remembered no more."

⁵ With one mind they plot together;
  they form an alliance against you—
⁶ the tents of Edom and the
    Ishmaelites,
  of Moab and the Hagrites,
⁷ Byblos, Ammon and Amalek,
  Philistia, with the people of Tyre.
⁸ Even Assyria has joined them
  to reinforce Lot's descendants.*ᵇ*

⁹ Do to them as you did to Midian,
  as you did to Sisera and Jabin at
    the river Kishon,
¹⁰ who perished at Endor
  and became like dung on the
    ground.
¹¹ Make their nobles like Oreb and
    Zeeb,
  all their princes like Zebah and
    Zalmunna,
¹² who said, "Let us take possession
  of the pasturelands of God."

¹³ Make them like tumbleweed, my God,
  like chaff before the wind.
¹⁴ As fire consumes the forest
  or a flame sets the mountains
    ablaze,
¹⁵ so pursue them with your tempest
  and terrify them with your storm.
¹⁶ Cover their faces with shame, Lord,
  so that they will seek your name.

THE SCENE

MIDIAN

(PSALM 83:9)

The desert where Moses went when he fled from Egypt. It was inhabited by nomad tribes (people who move from one place to another) with whom the Israelites were at war.

¹⁷ May they ever be ashamed and
    dismayed;
  may they perish in disgrace.
¹⁸ Let them know that you, whose name
    is the Lord—
  that you alone are the Most High
    over all the earth.

Psalm 84*ᶜ*

For the director of music. According to *gittith.ᵈ*
  Of the Sons of Korah. A psalm.

¹ How lovely is your dwelling place,
  Lord Almighty!
² My soul yearns, even faints,
  for the courts of the Lord;
  my heart and my flesh cry out
    for the living God.

ᵃ In Hebrew texts 83:1-18 is numbered 83:2-19.
ᵇ 8 The Hebrew has *Selah* (a word of uncertain meaning)
here.   *ᶜ* In Hebrew texts 84:1-12 is numbered 84:2-13.
ᵈ Title: Probably a musical term

³Even the sparrow has found a home,
and the swallow a nest for herself,
where she may have her young—
a place near your altar,
LORD Almighty, my King and my God.
⁴Blessed are those who dwell in your
house;
they are ever praising you.ᵃ

⁵Blessed are those whose strength is
in you,
whose hearts are set on pilgrimage.
⁶As they pass through the Valley of
Baka,
they make it a place of springs;
the autumn rains also cover it with
pools.ᵇ
⁷They go from strength to strength,
till each appears before God in
Zion.

⁸Hear my prayer, LORD God Almighty;
listen to me, God of Jacob.
⁹Look on our shield,ᶜ O God;
look with favor on your anointed one.

¹⁰Better is one day in your courts
than a thousand elsewhere;
I would rather be a doorkeeper in the
house of my God
than dwell in the tents of the
wicked.
¹¹For the LORD God is a sun and shield;
the LORD bestows favor and honor;
no good thing does he withhold
from those whose walk is
blameless.

¹²LORD Almighty,
blessed is the one who trusts in you.

Psalm 85ᵈ

For the director of music. Of the Sons
of Korah. A psalm.

¹You, LORD, showed favor to your land;
you restored the fortunes of Jacob.
²You forgave the iniquity of your people
and covered all their sins.ᵉ
³You set aside all your wrath
and turned from your fierce anger.

⁴Restore us again, God our Savior,
and put away your displeasure
toward us.

⁵Will you be angry with us forever?
Will you prolong your anger through
all generations?
⁶Will you not revive us again,
that your people may rejoice in you?
⁷Show us your unfailing love, LORD,
and grant us your salvation.

⁸I will listen to what God the LORD says;
he promises peace to his people,
his faithful servants—
but let them not turn to folly.
⁹Surely his salvation is near those who
fear him,
that his glory may dwell in our land.

¹⁰Love and faithfulness meet together;
righteousness and peace kiss each
other.
¹¹Faithfulness springs forth from the
earth,
and righteousness looks down from
heaven.
¹²The LORD will indeed give what is
good,
and our land will yield its harvest.
¹³Righteousness goes before him
and prepares the way for his steps.

Psalm 86

A prayer of David.

¹Hear me, LORD, and answer me,
for I am poor and needy.
²Guard my life, for I am faithful to you;
save your servant who trusts in
you.
You are my God; ³have mercy on me,
Lord,
for I call to you all day long.
⁴Bring joy to your servant, Lord,
for I put my trust in you.

⁵You, Lord, are forgiving and good,
abounding in love to all who call to
you.
⁶Hear my prayer, LORD;
listen to my cry for mercy.
⁷When I am in distress, I call to you,
because you answer me.

ᵃ 4 The Hebrew has Selah (a word of uncertain meaning)
here and at the end of verse 8.   ᵇ 6 Or blessings
ᶜ 9 Or sovereign   ᵈ In Hebrew texts 85:1-13 is numbered
85:2-14.   ᵉ 2 The Hebrew has Selah (a word of
uncertain meaning) here.

⁸ Among the gods there is none like
    you, Lord;
  no deeds can compare with yours.
⁹ All the nations you have made
  will come and worship before you,
    Lord;
  they will bring glory to your name.
¹⁰ For you are great and do marvelous
    deeds;
  you alone are God.

¹¹ Teach me your way, LORD,
    that I may rely on your faithfulness;
  give me an undivided heart,
    that I may fear your name.
¹² I will praise you, Lord my God, with all
    my heart;
  I will glorify your name forever.
¹³ For great is your love toward me;
  you have delivered me from the
    depths,
    from the realm of the dead.

¹⁴ Arrogant foes are attacking me,
    O God;
  ruthless people are trying to kill
    me—
  they have no regard for you.
¹⁵ But you, Lord, are a compassionate
    and gracious God,
  slow to anger, abounding in love and
    faithfulness.
¹⁶ Turn to me and have mercy on me;
  show your strength in behalf of your
    servant;
  save me, because I serve you
    just as my mother did.
¹⁷ Give me a sign of your goodness,
    that my enemies may see it and be
    put to shame,
  for you, LORD, have helped me and
    comforted me.

Psalm 87

Of the Sons of Korah. A psalm. A song.

¹ He has founded his city on the holy
    mountain.
² The LORD loves the gates of Zion
  more than all the other dwellings of
    Jacob.

³ Glorious things are said of you,
  city of God:ᵃ

⁴ "I will record Rahabᵇ and Babylon
    among those who acknowledge
    me—
  Philistia too, and Tyre, along with
    Cushᶜ—
  and will say, 'This one was born in
    Zion.' "ᵈ
⁵ Indeed, of Zion it will be said,
  "This one and that one were born in
    her,
  and the Most High himself will
    establish her."
⁶ The LORD will write in the register of
    the peoples:
  "This one was born in Zion."

⁷ As they make music they will sing,
  "All my fountains are in you."

Psalm 88ᵉ

A song. A psalm of the Sons of Korah.
For the director of music. According
  to *mahalath leannoth.*ᶠ A *maskil*ᵍ
  of Heman the Ezrahite.

¹ LORD, you are the God who saves me;
  day and night I cry out to you.
² May my prayer come before you;
  turn your ear to my cry.

³ I am overwhelmed with troubles
  and my life draws near to death.
⁴ I am counted among those who go
    down to the pit;
  I am like one without strength.
⁵ I am set apart with the dead,
  like the slain who lie in the grave,
  whom you remember no more,
  who are cut off from your care.

⁶ You have put me in the lowest pit,
  in the darkest depths.
⁷ Your wrath lies heavily on me;
  you have overwhelmed me with all
    your waves.ʰ
⁸ You have taken from me my closest
    friends

ᵃ 3 The Hebrew has *Selah* (a word of uncertain meaning)
here and at the end of verse 6.   ᵇ 4 A poetic name for
Egypt   ᶜ 4 That is, the upper Nile region   ᵈ 4 Or "I will
record concerning those who acknowledge me: / 'This one
was born in Zion.' / Hear this, Rahab and Babylon, / and you
too, Philistia, Tyre and Cush."   ᵉ In Hebrew texts 88:1-18
is numbered 88:2-19.   ᶠ Title: Possibly a tune, "The
Suffering of Affliction"   ᵍ Title: Probably a literary or
musical term   ʰ 7 The Hebrew has *Selah* (a word of
uncertain meaning) here and at the end of verse 10.

and have made me repulsive to
them.
I am confined and cannot escape;
9 my eyes are dim with grief.

I call to you, LORD, every day;
I spread out my hands to you.
10 Do you show your wonders to the
dead?
Do their spirits rise up and praise
you?
11 Is your love declared in the grave,
your faithfulness in Destruction*a*?
12 Are your wonders known in the place
of darkness,
or your righteous deeds in the land
of oblivion?

13 But I cry to you for help, LORD;
in the morning my prayer comes
before you.
14 Why, LORD, do you reject me
and hide your face from me?

15 From my youth I have suffered and
been close to death;
I have borne your terrors and am
in despair.
16 Your wrath has swept over me;
your terrors have destroyed me.
17 All day long they surround me like a
flood;
they have completely engulfed me.
18 You have taken from me friend and
neighbor—
darkness is my closest friend.

Psalm 89*b*

A *maskil*c of Ethan the Ezrahite.

1 I will sing of the LORD's great love
forever;
with my mouth I will make your
faithfulness known
through all generations.
2 I will declare that your love stands
firm forever,
that you have established your
faithfulness in heaven itself.
3 You said, "I have made a covenant
with my chosen one,
I have sworn to David my
servant,

4 'I will establish your line forever
and make your throne firm through
all generations.' "d

5 The heavens praise your wonders,
LORD,
your faithfulness too, in the
assembly of the holy ones.
6 For who in the skies above can
compare with the LORD?
Who is like the LORD among the
heavenly beings?
7 In the council of the holy ones God is
greatly feared;
he is more awesome than all who
surround him.
8 Who is like you, LORD God Almighty?
You, LORD, are mighty, and your
faithfulness surrounds you.

9 You rule over the surging sea;
when its waves mount up, you still
them.
10 You crushed Rahab like one of the
slain;
with your strong arm you scattered
your enemies.
11 The heavens are yours, and yours also
the earth;
you founded the world and all that
is in it.
12 You created the north and the south;
Tabor and Hermon sing for joy at
your name.
13 Your arm is endowed with power;
your hand is strong, your right hand
exalted.

14 Righteousness and justice are the
foundation of your throne;
love and faithfulness go before you.
15 Blessed are those who have learned
to acclaim you,
who walk in the light of your
presence, LORD.
16 They rejoice in your name all day long;
they celebrate your righteousness.
17 For you are their glory and strength,
and by your favor you exalt our
horn.*e*

---

a 11 Hebrew *Abaddon*   *b* In Hebrew texts 89:1-52 is
numbered 89:2-53.   *c* Title: Probably a literary or
musical term   *d 4* The Hebrew has *Selah* (a word of
uncertain meaning) here and at the end of verses 37, 45
and 48.   *e 17* *Horn* here symbolizes strong one.

THE SCENE

TABOR

(PSALM 89:12)

A mountain in the center of a valley south of Jerusalem. Its name means "belly button." Now it's also called the Mount of Transfiguration.

¹⁸ Indeed, our shield^a belongs to the LORD,
   our king to the Holy One of Israel.

¹⁹ Once you spoke in a vision,
   to your faithful people you said:
"I have bestowed strength on a warrior;
   I have raised up a young man from among the people.
²⁰ I have found David my servant;
   with my sacred oil I have anointed him.
²¹ My hand will sustain him;
   surely my arm will strengthen him.
²² The enemy will not get the better of him;
   the wicked will not oppress him.
²³ I will crush his foes before him
   and strike down his adversaries.
²⁴ My faithful love will be with him,
   and through my name his horn^b will be exalted.

²⁵ I will set his hand over the sea,
   his right hand over the rivers.
²⁶ He will call out to me, 'You are my Father,
   my God, the Rock my Savior.'
²⁷ And I will appoint him to be my firstborn,
   the most exalted of the kings of the earth.
²⁸ I will maintain my love to him forever,
   and my covenant with him will never fail.
²⁹ I will establish his line forever,
   his throne as long as the heavens endure.

³⁰ "If his sons forsake my law
   and do not follow my statutes,
³¹ if they violate my decrees
   and fail to keep my commands,

---

^a 18 Or sovereign   ^b 24 Horn here symbolizes strength.

CHECK THE FACTS

Why is this book known as the Psalms of David?

A) Because many psalms have "A Psalm of David" as a title

B) Because David is the author of all the psalms

C) Because all the psalms talk about David

CORRECT ANSWER: A

32 I will punish their sin with the rod,
      their iniquity with flogging;
33 but I will not take my love from him,
      nor will I ever betray my
         faithfulness.
34 I will not violate my covenant
      or alter what my lips have
         uttered.
35 Once for all, I have sworn by my
         holiness—
      and I will not lie to David—
36 that his line will continue forever
      and his throne endure before me
         like the sun;
37 it will be established forever like the
         moon,
      the faithful witness in the sky."

38 But you have rejected, you have
         spurned,

BREAKTHROUGH!

Will the sun and moon disappear someday?
(PSALM 89:36–37)
Some versions of the Bible say "while the sun and moon exist." This version is very clear, and says "forever." It means that David's kingdom would last forever.

      you have been very angry with your
         anointed one.
39 You have renounced the covenant with
         your servant
      and have defiled his crown in the
         dust.
40 You have broken through all his walls
      and reduced his strongholds to
         ruins.
41 All who pass by have plundered him;
      he has become the scorn of his
         neighbors.
42 You have exalted the right hand of his
         foes;
      you have made all his enemies
         rejoice.
43 Indeed, you have turned back the
         edge of his sword
      and have not supported him in
         battle.
44 You have put an end to his splendor
      and cast his throne to the ground.
45 You have cut short the days of his
         youth;

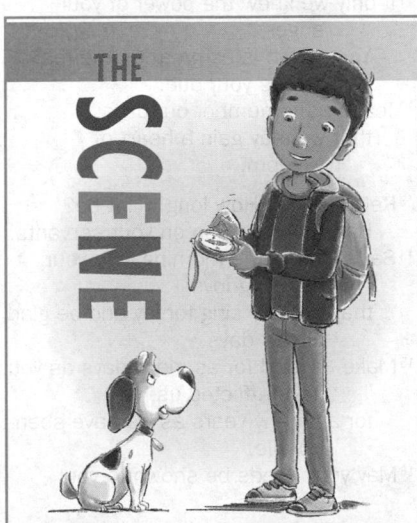

THE SCENE

OVER THE SEA ... OVER THE RIVERS

(PSALM 89:25)
This phrase describes how big the kingdom of David was. This was Mesopotamia, where the Assyrian empire was, and the Mediterranean Sea here was the money-making port.

you have covered him with a mantle
of shame.

⁴⁶ How long, Lᴏʀᴅ? Will you hide yourself
forever?
How long will your wrath burn like
fire?
⁴⁷ Remember how fleeting is my life.
For what futility you have created all
humanity!
⁴⁸ Who can live and not see death,
or who can escape the power of the
grave?
⁴⁹ Lord, where is your former great
love,
which in your faithfulness you swore
to David?
⁵⁰ Remember, Lord, how your servant
hasᵃ been mocked,
how I bear in my heart the taunts of
all the nations,
⁵¹ the taunts with which your enemies,
Lᴏʀᴅ, have mocked,
with which they have mocked every
step of your anointed one.

⁵² Praise be to the Lᴏʀᴅ forever!
Amen and Amen.

BOOK IV

Psalms 90 – 106

Psalm 90

A prayer of Moses the man of God.

¹ Lord, you have been our dwelling place
throughout all generations.
² Before the mountains were born
or you brought forth the whole
world,
from everlasting to everlasting you
are God.
³ You turn people back to dust,
saying, "Return to dust, you
mortals."
⁴ A thousand years in your sight
are like a day that has just gone by,
or like a watch in the night.
⁵ Yet you sweep people away in the
sleep of death—

they are like the new grass of the
morning:
⁶ In the morning it springs up new,
but by evening it is dry and
withered.

⁷ We are consumed by your anger
and terrified by your indignation.
⁸ You have set our iniquities before you,
our secret sins in the light of your
presence.
⁹ All our days pass away under your
wrath;
we finish our years with a moan.
¹⁰ Our days may come to seventy years,
or eighty, if our strength endures;
yet the best of them are but trouble
and sorrow,
for they quickly pass, and we fly
away.
¹¹ If only we knew the power of your
anger!
Your wrath is as great as the fear
that is your due.
¹² Teach us to number our days,
that we may gain a heart of
wisdom.

¹³ Relent, Lᴏʀᴅ! How long will it be?
Have compassion on your servants.
¹⁴ Satisfy us in the morning with your
unfailing love,
that we may sing for joy and be glad
all our days.
¹⁵ Make us glad for as many days as you
have afflicted us,
for as many years as we have seen
trouble.
¹⁶ May your deeds be shown to your
servants,
your splendor to their children.

¹⁷ May the favorᵇ of the Lord our God
rest on us;
establish the work of our hands for
us—
yes, establish the work of our
hands.

Psalm 91

¹ Whoever dwells in the shelter of the
Most High

ᵃ 50 Or *your servants have*   ᵇ 17 Or *beauty*

will rest in the shadow of the
Almighty.[a]
[2] I will say of the LORD, "He is my refuge
and my fortress,
my God, in whom I trust."

[3] Surely he will save you
from the fowler's snare
and from the deadly pestilence.
[4] He will cover you with his feathers,
and under his wings you will find
refuge;
his faithfulness will be your shield
and rampart.
[5] You will not fear the terror of night,
nor the arrow that flies by day,
[6] nor the pestilence that stalks in the
darkness,
nor the plague that destroys at
midday.
[7] A thousand may fall at your side,
ten thousand at your right hand,
but it will not come near you.
[8] You will only observe with your eyes
and see the punishment of the
wicked.

[9] If you say, "The LORD is my refuge,"
and you make the Most High your
dwelling,
[10] no harm will overtake you,
no disaster will come near your
tent.
[11] For he will command his angels
concerning you
to guard you in all your ways;
[12] they will lift you up in their hands,
so that you will not strike your foot
against a stone.
[13] You will tread on the lion and the
cobra;
you will trample the great lion and
the serpent.

[14] "Because he[b] loves me," says the
LORD, "I will rescue him;
I will protect him, for he
acknowledges my name.
[15] He will call on me, and I will answer
him;
I will be with him in trouble,
I will deliver him and honor him.
[16] With long life I will satisfy him
and show him my salvation."

Psalm 92[c]

A psalm. A song. For the Sabbath day.

[1] It is good to praise the LORD
and make music to your name,
O Most High,
[2] proclaiming your love in the morning
and your faithfulness at night,
[3] to the music of the ten-stringed
lyre
and the melody of the harp.

[4] For you make me glad by your deeds,
LORD;
I sing for joy at what your hands
have done.
[5] How great are your works, LORD,
how profound your thoughts!
[6] Senseless people do not know,
fools do not understand,
[7] that though the wicked spring up like
grass
and all evildoers flourish,
they will be destroyed forever.

[8] But you, LORD, are forever exalted.

[9] For surely your enemies, LORD,
surely your enemies will perish;
all evildoers will be scattered.
[10] You have exalted my horn[d] like that of
a wild ox;
fine oils have been poured
on me.
[11] My eyes have seen the defeat of my
adversaries;
my ears have heard the rout of my
wicked foes.

[12] The righteous will flourish like a palm
tree,
they will grow like a cedar of
Lebanon;
[13] planted in the house of the LORD,
they will flourish in the courts of our
God.
[14] They will still bear fruit in old age,
they will stay fresh and green,
[15] proclaiming, "The LORD is
upright;
he is my Rock, and there is no
wickedness in him."

---

[a] 1 Hebrew *Shaddai*   [b] 14 That is, probably the king
[c] In Hebrew texts 92:1-15 is numbered 92:2-16.
[d] 10 *Horn* here symbolizes strength.

Psalm 93

1 The LORD reigns, he is robed in
  majesty;
  the LORD is robed in majesty and
    armed with strength;
  indeed, the world is established,
    firm and secure.
2 Your throne was established long ago;
  you are from all eternity.

3 The seas have lifted up, LORD,
  the seas have lifted up their voice;
  the seas have lifted up their
    pounding waves.
4 Mightier than the thunder of the great
    waters,
  mightier than the breakers of the
    sea—
  the LORD on high is mighty.

5 Your statutes, LORD, stand firm;
  holiness adorns your house
    for endless days.

Psalm 94

1 The LORD is a God who avenges.
  O God who avenges, shine forth.
2 Rise up, Judge of the earth;
  pay back to the proud what they
    deserve.
3 How long, LORD, will the wicked,
  how long will the wicked be jubilant?

4 They pour out arrogant words;
  all the evildoers are full of
    boasting.
5 They crush your people, LORD;
  they oppress your inheritance.
6 They slay the widow and the
    foreigner;
  they murder the fatherless.
7 They say, "The LORD does not see;
  the God of Jacob takes no notice."

8 Take notice, you senseless ones
    among the people;
  you fools, when will you become
    wise?
9 Does he who fashioned the ear not
    hear?
  Does he who formed the eye not
    see?
10 Does he who disciplines nations not
    punish?

Does he who teaches mankind lack
    knowledge?
11 The LORD knows all human plans;
  he knows that they are futile.

12 Blessed is the one you discipline, LORD,
  the one you teach from your law;
13 you grant them relief from days of
    trouble,
  till a pit is dug for the wicked.
14 For the LORD will not reject his people;
  he will never forsake his
    inheritance.
15 Judgment will again be founded on
    righteousness,
  and all the upright in heart will
    follow it.

16 Who will rise up for me against the
    wicked?
  Who will take a stand for me
    against evildoers?
17 Unless the LORD had given me help,
  I would soon have dwelt in the
    silence of death.
18 When I said, "My foot is slipping,"
  your unfailing love, LORD, supported
    me.
19 When anxiety was great within me,
  your consolation brought me joy.

20 Can a corrupt throne be allied with
    you—
  a throne that brings on misery by its
    decrees?
21 The wicked band together against the
    righteous
  and condemn the innocent to
    death.
22 But the LORD has become my fortress,
  and my God the rock in whom I take
    refuge.
23 He will repay them for their sins
  and destroy them for their
    wickedness;
  the LORD our God will destroy them.

Psalm 95

1 Come, let us sing for joy to the LORD;
  let us shout aloud to the Rock of
    our salvation.
2 Let us come before him with
    thanksgiving
  and extol him with music and song.

³For the Lord is the great God,
the great King above all gods.
⁴In his hand are the depths of the
earth,
and the mountain peaks belong to
him.
⁵The sea is his, for he made it,
and his hands formed the dry
land.

⁶Come, let us bow down in worship,
let us kneel before the Lord our
Maker;
⁷for he is our God
and we are the people of his
pasture,
the flock under his care.

Today, if only you would hear his
voice,
⁸"Do not harden your hearts as you did
at Meribah,ᵃ
as you did that day at Massahᵇ in
the wilderness,

⁹where your ancestors tested me;
they tried me, though they had seen
what I did.
¹⁰For forty years I was angry with that
generation;
I said, 'They are a people whose
hearts go astray,
and they have not known my ways.'
¹¹So I declared on oath in my anger,
'They shall never enter my rest.'"

Psalm 96

¹Sing to the Lord a new song;
sing to the Lord, all the earth.
²Sing to the Lord, praise his name;
proclaim his salvation day after day.
³Declare his glory among the nations,
his marvelous deeds among all
peoples.

⁴For great is the Lord and most worthy
of praise;
he is to be feared above all gods.
⁵For all the gods of the nations are
idols,
but the Lord made the heavens.
⁶Splendor and majesty are before him;
strength and glory are in his
sanctuary.

⁷Ascribe to the Lord, all you families of
nations,
ascribe to the Lord glory and
strength.
⁸Ascribe to the Lord the glory due his
name;
bring an offering and come into his
courts.
⁹Worship the Lord in the splendor of
hisᶜ holiness;
tremble before him, all the earth.
¹⁰Say among the nations, "The Lord
reigns."
The world is firmly established, it
cannot be moved;
he will judge the peoples with
equity.
¹¹Let the heavens rejoice, let the earth
be glad;
let the sea resound, and all that is
in it.

THE SCENE

MASSAH

(PSALM 95:8)

A place in the Desert of Zin
where the Israelites rebelled
against Moses. Its name means
"to test."

ᵃ 8 *Meribah* means *quarreling*.   ᵇ 8 *Massah* means
testing.   ᶜ 9 Or Lord *with the splendor of*

¹²Let the fields be jubilant, and
    everything in them;
let all the trees of the forest sing
    for joy.
¹³Let all creation rejoice before the
    Lord, for he comes,
he comes to judge the earth.
He will judge the world in
    righteousness
and the peoples in his faithfulness.

Psalm 97

¹The Lord reigns, let the earth be
    glad;
let the distant shores rejoice.
²Clouds and thick darkness surround
    him;
righteousness and justice are the
    foundation of his throne.
³Fire goes before him
and consumes his foes on every
    side.
⁴His lightning lights up the world;
the earth sees and trembles.
⁵The mountains melt like wax before
    the Lord,
before the Lord of all the earth.
⁶The heavens proclaim his
    righteousness,
and all peoples see his glory.

⁷All who worship images are put to
    shame,
those who boast in idols—
worship him, all you gods!

⁸Zion hears and rejoices
and the villages of Judah are glad
because of your judgments, Lord.
⁹For you, Lord, are the Most High over
    all the earth;
you are exalted far above all gods.
¹⁰Let those who love the Lord hate
    evil,
for he guards the lives of his faithful
    ones
and delivers them from the hand of
    the wicked.
¹¹Light shines[a] on the righteous
and joy on the upright in heart.
¹²Rejoice in the Lord, you who are
    righteous,
and praise his holy name.

Psalm 98

A psalm.

¹Sing to the Lord a new song,
    for he has done marvelous things;
his right hand and his holy arm
    have worked salvation for him.
²The Lord has made his salvation known
    and revealed his righteousness to
     the nations.
³He has remembered his love
    and his faithfulness to Israel;
all the ends of the earth have seen
    the salvation of our God.

⁴Shout for joy to the Lord, all the earth,
    burst into jubilant song with music;
⁵make music to the Lord with the harp,
    with the harp and the sound of
     singing,
⁶with trumpets and the blast of the
    ram's horn—
shout for joy before the Lord, the
    King.

⁷Let the sea resound, and everything
    in it,
the world, and all who live in it.
⁸Let the rivers clap their hands,
    let the mountains sing together for
     joy;
⁹let them sing before the Lord,
    for he comes to judge the earth.
He will judge the world in
    righteousness
and the peoples with equity.

Psalm 99

¹The Lord reigns,
    let the nations tremble;
he sits enthroned between the
    cherubim,
    let the earth shake.
²Great is the Lord in Zion;
    he is exalted over all the nations.
³Let them praise your great and
    awesome name—
    he is holy.

⁴The King is mighty, he loves justice—
    you have established equity;

ᵃ 11 One Hebrew manuscript and ancient versions (see
also 112:4); most Hebrew manuscripts Light is sown

Cherubim
(PSALM 99:1)

In ancient Mesopotamia, the temples and palaces had images of lions with wings that protected the doors. The Israelites also had beings called cherubim that protected the ark of the covenant, the Garden of Eden, the king's palace and the temple. There were usually two cherubim.

in Jacob you have done
    what is just and right.
⁵ Exalt the LORD our God
    and worship at his footstool;
    he is holy.

⁶ Moses and Aaron were among his
    priests,
    Samuel was among those who
    called on his name;
they called on the LORD
    and he answered them.
⁷ He spoke to them from the pillar of
    cloud;
    they kept his statutes and the
    decrees he gave them.

⁸ LORD our God,
    you answered them;
you were to Israel a forgiving God,
    though you punished their
    misdeeds.ᵃ

⁹ Exalt the LORD our God
    and worship at his holy mountain,
    for the LORD our God is holy.

Psalm 100

A psalm. For giving grateful praise.

¹ Shout for joy to the LORD, all the earth.
²   Worship the LORD with gladness;
    come before him with joyful songs.
³ Know that the LORD is God.
    It is he who made us, and we are
    hisᵇ;
    we are his people, the sheep of his
    pasture.

⁴ Enter his gates with thanksgiving
    and his courts with praise;
    give thanks to him and praise his
    name.
⁵ For the LORD is good and his love
    endures forever;
    his faithfulness continues through
    all generations.

Psalm 101

Of David. A psalm.

¹ I will sing of your love and justice;
    to you, LORD, I will sing praise.
² I will be careful to lead a blameless
    life—
    when will you come to me?

I will conduct the affairs of my house
    with a blameless heart.
³ I will not look with approval
    on anything that is vile.

I hate what faithless people do;
    I will have no part in it.
⁴ The perverse of heart shall be far
    from me;
    I will have nothing to do with what is
    evil.

⁵ Whoever slanders their neighbor in
    secret,
    I will put to silence;
whoever has haughty eyes and a
    proud heart,
    I will not tolerate.

ᵃ 8 Or God, / an avenger of the wrongs done to them
ᵇ 3 Or and not we ourselves

⁶My eyes will be on the faithful in the
land,
that they may dwell with me;
the one whose walk is blameless
will minister to me.

⁷No one who practices deceit
will dwell in my house;
no one who speaks falsely
will stand in my presence.

⁸Every morning I will put to silence
all the wicked in the land;
I will cut off every evildoer
from the city of the LORD.

Psalm 102ᵃ

A prayer of an afflicted person who has
grown weak and pours out a lament
before the LORD.

¹Hear my prayer, LORD;
let my cry for help come to you.
²Do not hide your face from me
when I am in distress.
Turn your ear to me;
when I call, answer me quickly.

³For my days vanish like smoke;
my bones burn like glowing
embers.
⁴My heart is blighted and withered like
grass;
I forget to eat my food.
⁵In my distress I groan aloud
and am reduced to skin and bones.
⁶I am like a desert owl,
like an owl among the ruins.
⁷I lie awake; I have become
like a bird alone on a roof.
⁸All day long my enemies taunt me;
those who rail against me use my
name as a curse.
⁹For I eat ashes as my food
and mingle my drink with tears
¹⁰because of your great wrath,
for you have taken me up and
thrown me aside.
¹¹My days are like the evening
shadow;
I wither away like grass.

¹²But you, LORD, sit enthroned forever;
your renown endures through all
generations.

¹³You will arise and have compassion on
Zion,
for it is time to show favor to her;
the appointed time has come.
¹⁴For her stones are dear to your
servants;
her very dust moves them to pity.
¹⁵The nations will fear the name of the
LORD,
all the kings of the earth will revere
your glory.
¹⁶For the LORD will rebuild Zion
and appear in his glory.
¹⁷He will respond to the prayer of the
destitute;
he will not despise their plea.

¹⁸Let this be written for a future
generation,
that a people not yet created may
praise the LORD:
¹⁹"The LORD looked down from his
sanctuary on high,
from heaven he viewed the earth,
²⁰to hear the groans of the prisoners
and release those condemned to
death."
²¹So the name of the LORD will be
declared in Zion
and his praise in Jerusalem
²²when the peoples and the kingdoms
assemble to worship the LORD.

²³In the course of my lifeᵇ he broke my
strength;
he cut short my days.
²⁴So I said:
"Do not take me away, my God, in the
midst of my days;
your years go on through all
generations.
²⁵In the beginning you laid the
foundations of the earth,
and the heavens are the work of
your hands.
²⁶They will perish, but you remain;
they will all wear out like a
garment.
Like clothing you will change them
and they will be discarded.
²⁷But you remain the same,
and your years will never end.

ᵃ In Hebrew texts 102:1-28 is numbered 102:2-29.
ᵇ 23 Or *By his power*

²⁸The children of your servants will live
in your presence;
their descendants will be
established before you."

Psalm 103

Of David.

¹Praise the LORD, my soul;
all my inmost being, praise his holy
name.
²Praise the LORD, my soul,
and forget not all his benefits—
³who forgives all your sins
and heals all your diseases,
⁴who redeems your life from the pit
and crowns you with love and
compassion,
⁵who satisfies your desires with good
things
so that your youth is renewed like
the eagle's.

⁶The LORD works righteousness
and justice for all the oppressed.

⁷He made known his ways to Moses,
his deeds to the people of Israel:
⁸The LORD is compassionate and
gracious,
slow to anger, abounding in love.
⁹He will not always accuse,
nor will he harbor his anger forever;
¹⁰he does not treat us as our sins
deserve
or repay us according to our
iniquities.
¹¹For as high as the heavens are above
the earth,
so great is his love for those who
fear him;
¹²as far as the east is from the west,
so far has he removed our
transgressions from us.

¹³As a father has compassion on his
children,
so the LORD has compassion on
those who fear him;
¹⁴for he knows how we are formed,
he remembers that we are dust.
¹⁵The life of mortals is like grass,
they flourish like a flower of the
field;

¹⁶the wind blows over it and it is gone,
and its place remembers it no more.
¹⁷But from everlasting to everlasting
the LORD's love is with those who
fear him,
and his righteousness with their
children's children—
¹⁸with those who keep his covenant
and remember to obey his precepts.

¹⁹The LORD has established his throne in
heaven,
and his kingdom rules over all.

²⁰Praise the LORD, you his angels,
you mighty ones who do his bidding,
who obey his word.
²¹Praise the LORD, all his heavenly hosts,
you his servants who do his will.
²²Praise the LORD, all his works
everywhere in his dominion.

Praise the LORD, my soul.

Psalm 104

¹Praise the LORD, my soul.

LORD my God, you are very great;
you are clothed with splendor and
majesty.

²The LORD wraps himself in light as with
a garment;
he stretches out the heavens like a
tent
³   and lays the beams of his upper
chambers on their waters.
He makes the clouds his chariot
and rides on the wings of the wind.
⁴He makes winds his messengers,^a
flames of fire his servants.

⁵He set the earth on its foundations;
it can never be moved.
⁶You covered it with the watery depths
as with a garment;
the waters stood above the
mountains.
⁷But at your rebuke the waters fled,
at the sound of your thunder they
took to flight;
⁸they flowed over the mountains,
they went down into the valleys,
to the place you assigned for them.

---

^a 4 Or angels

9 You set a boundary they cannot cross;
  never again will they cover the
     earth.

10 He makes springs pour water into the
     ravines;
  it flows between the mountains.
11 They give water to all the beasts of
     the field;
  the wild donkeys quench their thirst.
12 The birds of the sky nest by the
     waters;
  they sing among the branches.
13 He waters the mountains from his
     upper chambers;
  the land is satisfied by the fruit of
     his work.
14 He makes grass grow for the cattle,
  and plants for people to cultivate—
  bringing forth food from the
     earth:
15 wine that gladdens human hearts,
  oil to make their faces shine,
  and bread that sustains their
     hearts.
16 The trees of the LORD are well
     watered,
  the cedars of Lebanon that he
     planted.
17 There the birds make their nests;
  the stork has its home in the
     junipers.
18 The high mountains belong to the wild
     goats;
  the crags are a refuge for the hyrax.
19 He made the moon to mark the
     seasons,
  and the sun knows when to go
     down.
20 You bring darkness, it becomes
     night,
  and all the beasts of the forest
     prowl.
21 The lions roar for their prey
  and seek their food from God.
22 The sun rises, and they steal away;
  they return and lie down in their
     dens.
23 Then people go out to their work,
  to their labor until evening.

24 How many are your works, LORD!
  In wisdom you made them all;
  the earth is full of your creatures.

25 There is the sea, vast and spacious,
  teeming with creatures beyond
     number—
  living things both large and small.
26 There the ships go to and fro,
  and Leviathan, which you formed to
     frolic there.

27 All creatures look to you
  to give them their food at the proper
     time.
28 When you give it to them,
  they gather it up;
  when you open your hand,
  they are satisfied with good things.
29 When you hide your face,
  they are terrified;
  when you take away their breath,
  they die and return to the dust.
30 When you send your Spirit,
  they are created,
  and you renew the face of the
     ground.

31 May the glory of the LORD endure
     forever;
  may the LORD rejoice in his works—
32 he who looks at the earth, and it
     trembles,
  who touches the mountains, and
     they smoke.

33 I will sing to the LORD all my life;
  I will sing praise to my God as long
     as I live.
34 May my meditation be pleasing to
     him,
  as I rejoice in the LORD.
35 But may sinners vanish from the
     earth
  and the wicked be no more.

  Praise the LORD, my soul.

  Praise the LORD.[a]

Psalm 105

1 Give praise to the LORD, proclaim his
     name;
  make known among the nations
     what he has done.
2 Sing to him, sing praise to him;
  tell of all his wonderful acts.

---

[a] 35 Hebrew *Hallelu Yah*; in the Septuagint this line stands
at the beginning of Psalm 105.

3 Glory in his holy name;
  let the hearts of those who seek
    the LORD rejoice.
4 Look to the LORD and his strength;
  seek his face always.

5 Remember the wonders he has done,
  his miracles, and the judgments he
    pronounced,
6 you his servants, the descendants of
    Abraham,
  his chosen ones, the children of
    Jacob.
7 He is the LORD our God;
  his judgments are in all the earth.

8 He remembers his covenant forever,
  the promise he made, for a
    thousand generations,
9 the covenant he made with Abraham,
  the oath he swore to Isaac.
10 He confirmed it to Jacob as a decree,
  to Israel as an everlasting covenant:
11 "To you I will give the land of Canaan
  as the portion you will inherit."

12 When they were but few in number,
  few indeed, and strangers in it,
13 they wandered from nation to nation,
  from one kingdom to another.
14 He allowed no one to oppress them;
  for their sake he rebuked kings:
15 "Do not touch my anointed ones;
  do my prophets no harm."

16 He called down famine on the land
  and destroyed all their supplies of
    food;
17 and he sent a man before them—
  Joseph, sold as a slave.
18 They bruised his feet with shackles,
  his neck was put in irons,
19 till what he foretold came to pass,
  till the word of the LORD proved him
    true.
20 The king sent and released him,
  the ruler of peoples set him free.
21 He made him master of his
    household,
  ruler over all he possessed,
22 to instruct his princes as he pleased
  and teach his elders wisdom.

23 Then Israel entered Egypt;
  Jacob resided as a foreigner in the
    land of Ham.

24 The LORD made his people very fruitful;
  he made them too numerous for
    their foes,
25 whose hearts he turned to hate his
    people,
  to conspire against his servants.
26 He sent Moses his servant,
  and Aaron, whom he had chosen.
27 They performed his signs among
    them,
  his wonders in the land of Ham.
28 He sent darkness and made the land
    dark—
  for had they not rebelled against his
    words?
29 He turned their waters into blood,
  causing their fish to die.
30 Their land teemed with frogs,
  which went up into the bedrooms of
    their rulers.
31 He spoke, and there came swarms of
    flies,
  and gnats throughout their country.
32 He turned their rain into hail,
  with lightning throughout their land;
33 he struck down their vines and fig
    trees
  and shattered the trees of their
    country.
34 He spoke, and the locusts came,
  grasshoppers without number;
35 they ate up every green thing in their
    land,
  ate up the produce of their soil.
36 Then he struck down all the firstborn
  in their land,
  the firstfruits of all their manhood.
37 He brought out Israel, laden with silver
    and gold,
  and from among their tribes no one
    faltered.
38 Egypt was glad when they left,
  because dread of Israel had fallen
    on them.

39 He spread out a cloud as a covering,
  and a fire to give light at night.
40 They asked, and he brought them
    quail;
  he fed them well with the bread of
    heaven.
41 He opened the rock, and water gushed
    out;
  it flowed like a river in the desert.

42 For he remembered his holy promise
given to his servant Abraham.
43 He brought out his people with
rejoicing,
his chosen ones with shouts of joy;
44 he gave them the lands of the nations,
and they fell heir to what others had
toiled for—
45 that they might keep his precepts
and observe his laws.

Praise the LORD.[a]

Psalm 106

1 Praise the LORD.[b]

Give thanks to the LORD, for he is
good;
his love endures forever.

2 Who can proclaim the mighty acts of
the LORD
or fully declare his praise?
3 Blessed are those who act justly,
who always do what is right.

4 Remember me, LORD, when you show
favor to your people,
come to my aid when you save
them,
5 that I may enjoy the prosperity of your
chosen ones,
that I may share in the joy of your
nation
and join your inheritance in giving
praise.

6 We have sinned, even as our
ancestors did;
we have done wrong and acted
wickedly.
7 When our ancestors were in Egypt,
they gave no thought to your
miracles;
they did not remember your many
kindnesses,
and they rebelled by the sea, the
Red Sea.[c]
8 Yet he saved them for his name's
sake,
to make his mighty power known.
9 He rebuked the Red Sea, and it
dried up;
he led them through the depths as
through a desert.

10 He saved them from the hand of the
foe;
from the hand of the enemy he
redeemed them.
11 The waters covered their adversaries;
not one of them survived.
12 Then they believed his promises
and sang his praise.

13 But they soon forgot what he had
done
and did not wait for his plan to
unfold.
14 In the desert they gave in to their
craving;
in the wilderness they put God to
the test.
15 So he gave them what they asked for,
but sent a wasting disease among
them.

16 In the camp they grew envious of
Moses
and of Aaron, who was consecrated
to the LORD.
17 The earth opened up and swallowed
Dathan;
it buried the company of Abiram.
18 Fire blazed among their followers;
a flame consumed the wicked.
19 At Horeb they made a calf
and worshiped an idol cast from
metal.
20 They exchanged their glorious God
for an image of a bull, which eats
grass.
21 They forgot the God who saved them,
who had done great things in Egypt,
22 miracles in the land of Ham
and awesome deeds by the Red
Sea.
23 So he said he would destroy them—
had not Moses, his chosen one,
stood in the breach before him
to keep his wrath from destroying
them.

24 Then they despised the pleasant
land;
they did not believe his promise.
25 They grumbled in their tents
and did not obey the LORD.

---

a 45 Hebrew Hallelu Yah   b 1 Hebrew Hallelu Yah; also
in verse 48   c 7 Or the Sea of Reeds; also in verses
9 and 22

26 So he swore to them with uplifted
hand
that he would make them fall in the
wilderness,
27 make their descendants fall among
the nations
and scatter them throughout the
lands.
28 They yoked themselves to the Baal of
Peor
and ate sacrifices offered to lifeless
gods;
29 they aroused the LORD's anger by their
wicked deeds,
and a plague broke out among
them.
30 But Phinehas stood up and
intervened,
and the plague was checked.
31 This was credited to him as
righteousness
for endless generations to come.
32 By the waters of Meribah they angered
the LORD,
and trouble came to Moses
because of them;
33 for they rebelled against the Spirit of
God,
and rash words came from Moses'
lips.*a*

34 They did not destroy the peoples
as the LORD had commanded them,
35 but they mingled with the nations
and adopted their customs.
36 They worshiped their idols,
which became a snare to them.
37 They sacrificed their sons
and their daughters to false gods.
38 They shed innocent blood,
the blood of their sons and
daughters,
whom they sacrificed to the idols of
Canaan,
and the land was desecrated by
their blood.
39 They defiled themselves by what they
did;
by their deeds they prostituted
themselves.
40 Therefore the LORD was angry with his
people
and abhorred his inheritance.

41 He gave them into the hands of the
nations,
and their foes ruled over them.
42 Their enemies oppressed them
and subjected them to their power.
43 Many times he delivered them,
but they were bent on rebellion
and they wasted away in their sin.
44 Yet he took note of their distress
when he heard their cry;
45 for their sake he remembered his
covenant
and out of his great love he
relented.
46 He caused all who held them captive
to show them mercy.

47 Save us, LORD our God,
and gather us from the nations,
that we may give thanks to your holy
name
and glory in your praise.

48 Praise be to the LORD, the God of
Israel,
from everlasting to everlasting.

Let all the people say, "Amen!"

Praise the LORD.

BOOK V

Psalms 107 – 150

Psalm 107

1 Give thanks to the LORD, for he is
good;
his love endures forever.

2 Let the redeemed of the LORD tell their
story—
those he redeemed from the hand
of the foe,
3 those he gathered from the lands,
from east and west, from north and
south.*b*

4 Some wandered in desert wastelands,
finding no way to a city where they
could settle.

---

a 33 Or *against his spirit, / and rash words came from his
lips*   *b* 3 Hebrew *north and the sea*

5 They were hungry and thirsty,
   and their lives ebbed away.
6 Then they cried out to the Lord in their
   trouble,
   and he delivered them from their
   distress.
7 He led them by a straight way
   to a city where they could settle.
8 Let them give thanks to the Lord for
   his unfailing love
   and his wonderful deeds for
   mankind,
9 for he satisfies the thirsty
   and fills the hungry with good
   things.

10 Some sat in darkness, in utter
   darkness,
   prisoners suffering in iron chains,
11 because they rebelled against God's
   commands
   and despised the plans of the Most
   High.
12 So he subjected them to bitter
   labor;
   they stumbled, and there was no
   one to help.
13 Then they cried to the Lord in their
   trouble,
   and he saved them from their
   distress.
14 He brought them out of darkness, the
   utter darkness,
   and broke away their chains.
15 Let them give thanks to the Lord for
   his unfailing love
   and his wonderful deeds for
   mankind,
16 for he breaks down gates of bronze
   and cuts through bars of iron.

17 Some became fools through their
   rebellious ways
   and suffered affliction because of
   their iniquities.
18 They loathed all food
   and drew near the gates of death.
19 Then they cried to the Lord in their
   trouble,
   and he saved them from their
   distress.
20 He sent out his word and healed
   them;
   he rescued them from the grave.

21 Let them give thanks to the Lord for
   his unfailing love
   and his wonderful deeds for
   mankind.
22 Let them sacrifice thank offerings
   and tell of his works with songs of
   joy.

23 Some went out on the sea in ships;
   they were merchants on the mighty
   waters.
24 They saw the works of the Lord,
   his wonderful deeds in the deep.
25 For he spoke and stirred up a
   tempest
   that lifted high the waves.
26 They mounted up to the heavens and
   went down to the depths;
   in their peril their courage melted
   away.
27 They reeled and staggered like
   drunkards;
   they were at their wits' end.
28 Then they cried out to the Lord in their
   trouble,
   and he brought them out of their
   distress.
29 He stilled the storm to a whisper;
   the waves of the sea[a] were hushed.
30 They were glad when it grew calm,
   and he guided them to their desired
   haven.
31 Let them give thanks to the Lord for
   his unfailing love
   and his wonderful deeds for
   mankind.
32 Let them exalt him in the assembly of
   the people
   and praise him in the council of the
   elders.

33 He turned rivers into a desert,
   flowing springs into thirsty ground,
34 and fruitful land into a salt waste,
   because of the wickedness of those
   who lived there.
35 He turned the desert into pools of
   water
   and the parched ground into flowing
   springs;
36 there he brought the hungry to live,
   and they founded a city where they
   could settle.

---

a 29 Dead Sea Scrolls; Masoretic Text / their waves

37 They sowed fields and planted
vineyards
that yielded a fruitful harvest;
38 he blessed them, and their numbers
greatly increased,
and he did not let their herds
diminish.

39 Then their numbers decreased, and
they were humbled
by oppression, calamity and sorrow;
40 he who pours contempt on nobles
made them wander in a trackless
waste.
41 But he lifted the needy out of their
affliction
and increased their families like
flocks.
42 The upright see and rejoice,
but all the wicked shut their
mouths.

43 Let the one who is wise heed these
things
and ponder the loving deeds of the
Lord.

Psalm 108 [a]

A song. A psalm of David.

1 My heart, O God, is steadfast;
I will sing and make music with all
my soul.
2 Awake, harp and lyre!
I will awaken the dawn.
3 I will praise you, Lord, among the
nations;
I will sing of you among the
peoples.
4 For great is your love, higher than the
heavens;
your faithfulness reaches to the
skies.
5 Be exalted, O God, above the
heavens;
let your glory be over all the earth.

6 Save us and help us with your right
hand,
that those you love may be
delivered.
7 God has spoken from his sanctuary:
"In triumph I will parcel out
Shechem

and measure off the Valley of
Sukkoth.
8 Gilead is mine, Manasseh is mine;
Ephraim is my helmet,
Judah is my scepter.
9 Moab is my washbasin,
on Edom I toss my sandal;
over Philistia I shout in triumph."

10 Who will bring me to the fortified city?
Who will lead me to Edom?
11 Is it not you, God, you who have
rejected us
and no longer go out with our
armies?
12 Give us aid against the enemy,
for human help is worthless.
13 With God we will gain the victory,
and he will trample down our
enemies.

Psalm 109

For the director of music.
Of David. A psalm.

1 My God, whom I praise,
do not remain silent,
2 for people who are wicked and
deceitful
have opened their mouths against
me;
they have spoken against me with
lying tongues.
3 With words of hatred they surround me;
they attack me without cause.
4 In return for my friendship they accuse
me,
but I am a man of prayer.
5 They repay me evil for good,
and hatred for my friendship.

6 Appoint someone evil to oppose my
enemy;
let an accuser stand at his right
hand.
7 When he is tried, let him be found
guilty,
and may his prayers condemn him.
8 May his days be few;
may another take his place of
leadership.
9 May his children be fatherless
and his wife a widow.

---

a In Hebrew texts 108:1-13 is numbered 108:2-14.

10 May his children be wandering
　　beggars;
　　may they be driven[a] from their
　　ruined homes.
11 May a creditor seize all he has;
　　may strangers plunder the fruits of
　　his labor.
12 May no one extend kindness to him
　　or take pity on his fatherless
　　children.
13 May his descendants be cut off,
　　their names blotted out from the
　　next generation.
14 May the iniquity of his fathers be
　　remembered before the Lord;
　　may the sin of his mother never be
　　blotted out.
15 May their sins always remain before
　　the Lord,
　　that he may blot out their name
　　from the earth.

16 For he never thought of doing a
　　kindness,
　　but hounded to death the poor
　　and the needy and the
　　brokenhearted.
17 He loved to pronounce a curse—
　　may it come back on him.
　　He found no pleasure in blessing—
　　may it be far from him.
18 He wore cursing as his garment;
　　it entered into his body like water,
　　into his bones like oil.
19 May it be like a cloak wrapped about
　　him,
　　like a belt tied forever around him.
20 May this be the Lord's payment to my
　　accusers,
　　to those who speak evil of me.

21 But you, Sovereign Lord,
　　help me for your name's sake;
　　out of the goodness of your love,
　　deliver me.
22 For I am poor and needy,
　　and my heart is wounded
　　within me.
23 I fade away like an evening shadow;
　　I am shaken off like a locust.
24 My knees give way from fasting;
　　my body is thin and gaunt.
25 I am an object of scorn to my
　　accusers;

when they see me, they shake their
　　heads.

26 Help me, Lord my God;
　　save me according to your unfailing
　　love.
27 Let them know that it is your hand,
　　that you, Lord, have done it.
28 While they curse, may you bless;
　　may those who attack me be put to
　　shame,
　　but may your servant rejoice.
29 May my accusers be clothed with
　　disgrace
　　and wrapped in shame as in a
　　cloak.

30 With my mouth I will greatly extol the
　　Lord;
　　in the great throng of worshipers I
　　will praise him.
31 For he stands at the right hand of the
　　needy,
　　to save their lives from those who
　　would condemn them.

Psalm 110

Of David. A psalm.

1 The Lord says to my lord:[b]

"Sit at my right hand
　　until I make your enemies
　　a footstool for your feet."

2 The Lord will extend your mighty
　　scepter from Zion, saying,
　　"Rule in the midst of your
　　enemies!"
3 Your troops will be willing
　　on your day of battle.
　　Arrayed in holy splendor,
　　your young men will come to you
　　like dew from the morning's womb.[c]

4 The Lord has sworn
　　and will not change his mind:
　　"You are a priest forever,
　　in the order of Melchizedek."

5 The Lord is at your right hand[d];
　　he will crush kings on the day of his
　　wrath.

---

[a] 10 Septuagint; Hebrew sought　　[b] 1 Or Lord　　[c] 3 The
meaning of the Hebrew for this sentence is uncertain.
[d] 5 Or My lord is at your right hand, Lord

6 He will judge the nations, heaping up
  the dead
and crushing the rulers of the whole
  earth.
7 He will drink from a brook along the
  way,[a]
and so he will lift his head high.

Psalm 111[b]

1 Praise the LORD.[c]

I will extol the LORD with all my
  heart
in the council of the upright and in
  the assembly.

2 Great are the works of the LORD;
  they are pondered by all who delight
  in them.
3 Glorious and majestic are his
  deeds,
  and his righteousness endures
  forever.
4 He has caused his wonders to be
  remembered;
  the LORD is gracious and
  compassionate.
5 He provides food for those who fear
  him;
  he remembers his covenant
  forever.
6 He has shown his people the power of
  his works,
  giving them the lands of other
  nations.
7 The works of his hands are faithful
  and just;
  all his precepts are trustworthy.
8 They are established for ever and
  ever,
  enacted in faithfulness and
  uprightness.
9 He provided redemption for his
  people;
  he ordained his covenant
  forever—
  holy and awesome is his name.
10 The fear of the LORD is the beginning
  of wisdom;
  all who follow his precepts have
  good understanding.
  To him belongs eternal praise.

Psalm 112[b]

1 Praise the LORD.[c]

Blessed are those who fear the
  LORD,
  who find great delight in his
  commands.

2 Their children will be mighty in the
  land;
  the generation of the upright will be
  blessed.
3 Wealth and riches are in their
  houses,
  and their righteousness endures
  forever.
4 Even in darkness light dawns for the
  upright,
  for those who are gracious and
  compassionate and
  righteous.
5 Good will come to those who are
  generous and lend freely,
  who conduct their affairs with
  justice.
6 Surely the righteous will never be
  shaken;
  they will be remembered
  forever.
7 They will have no fear of bad news;
  their hearts are steadfast, trusting
  in the LORD.
8 Their hearts are secure, they will have
  no fear;
  in the end they will look in triumph
  on their foes.
9 They have freely scattered their gifts
  to the poor,
  their righteousness endures
  forever;
  their horn[d] will be lifted high in
  honor.

10 The wicked will see and be
  vexed,
  they will gnash their teeth and
  waste away;
  the longings of the wicked will come
  to nothing.

---

[a] 7 The meaning of the Hebrew for this clause is
uncertain.   [b] This psalm is an acrostic poem, the lines
of which begin with the successive letters of the Hebrew
alphabet.   [c] 1 Hebrew *Hallelu Yah*   [d] 9 *Horn* here
symbolizes dignity.

Psalm 113

[1] Praise the LORD.[a]

Praise the LORD, you his servants;
    praise the name of the LORD.
[2] Let the name of the LORD be praised,
    both now and forevermore.
[3] From the rising of the sun to the place
      where it sets,
    the name of the LORD is to be
      praised.

[4] The LORD is exalted over all the nations,
    his glory above the heavens.
[5] Who is like the LORD our God,
    the One who sits enthroned on high,
[6] who stoops down to look
    on the heavens and the earth?

[7] He raises the poor from the dust
    and lifts the needy from the ash
      heap;
[8] he seats them with princes,
    with the princes of his people.
[9] He settles the childless woman in her
      home
    as a happy mother of children.

Praise the LORD.

Psalm 114

[1] When Israel came out of Egypt,
    Jacob from a people of foreign
      tongue,
[2] Judah became God's sanctuary,
    Israel his dominion.

[3] The sea looked and fled,
    the Jordan turned back;
[4] the mountains leaped like rams,
    the hills like lambs.

[5] Why was it, sea, that you fled?
    Why, Jordan, did you turn back?
[6] Why, mountains, did you leap like
      rams,
    you hills, like lambs?

[7] Tremble, earth, at the presence of the
      Lord,
    at the presence of the God of
      Jacob,
[8] who turned the rock into a pool,
    the hard rock into springs of water.

Psalm 115

[1] Not to us, LORD, not to us
    but to your name be the glory,
    because of your love and
      faithfulness.

[2] Why do the nations say,
    "Where is their God?"
[3] Our God is in heaven;
    he does whatever pleases him.
[4] But their idols are silver and gold,
    made by human hands.
[5] They have mouths, but cannot
      speak,
    eyes, but cannot see.
[6] They have ears, but cannot hear,
    noses, but cannot smell.
[7] They have hands, but cannot feel,
    feet, but cannot walk,
    nor can they utter a sound with their
      throats.
[8] Those who make them will be like
      them,
    and so will all who trust in them.

[9] All you Israelites, trust in the LORD—
    he is their help and shield.
[10] House of Aaron, trust in the LORD—
    he is their help and shield.
[11] You who fear him, trust in the LORD—
    he is their help and shield.

[12] The LORD remembers us and will
      bless us:
    He will bless his people Israel,
    he will bless the house of Aaron,
[13] he will bless those who fear the
      LORD—
    small and great alike.

[14] May the LORD cause you to flourish,
    both you and your children.
[15] May you be blessed by the LORD,
    the Maker of heaven and earth.

[16] The highest heavens belong to the
      LORD,
    but the earth he has given to
      mankind.
[17] It is not the dead who praise the
      LORD,
    those who go down to the place of
      silence;

---

[a] 1 Hebrew *Hallelu Yah*; also in verse 9

[18] it is we who extol the LORD,
  both now and forevermore.

Praise the LORD.[a]

Psalm 116

[1] I love the LORD, for he heard my voice;
  he heard my cry for mercy.
[2] Because he turned his ear to me,
  I will call on him as long as I live.

[3] The cords of death entangled me,
  the anguish of the grave came over
    me;
  I was overcome by distress and
    sorrow.
[4] Then I called on the name of the LORD:
  "LORD, save me!"

[5] The LORD is gracious and righteous;
  our God is full of compassion.
[6] The LORD protects the unwary;
  when I was brought low, he saved
    me.

[7] Return to your rest, my soul,
  for the LORD has been good to you.

[8] For you, LORD, have delivered me from
    death,
  my eyes from tears,
  my feet from stumbling,
[9] that I may walk before the LORD
  in the land of the living.

[10] I trusted in the LORD when I said,
  "I am greatly afflicted";
[11] in my alarm I said,
  "Everyone is a liar."

[12] What shall I return to the LORD
  for all his goodness to me?

[13] I will lift up the cup of salvation
  and call on the name of the LORD.
[14] I will fulfill my vows to the LORD
  in the presence of all his people.

[15] Precious in the sight of the LORD
  is the death of his faithful
    servants.
[16] Truly I am your servant, LORD;
  I serve you just as my mother did;
  you have freed me from my chains.

[17] I will sacrifice a thank offering to you
  and call on the name of the LORD.

[18] I will fulfill my vows to the LORD
  in the presence of all his people,
[19] in the courts of the house of the
    LORD—
  in your midst, Jerusalem.

Praise the LORD.[a]

Psalm 117

[1] Praise the LORD, all you nations;
  extol him, all you peoples.
[2] For great is his love toward us,
  and the faithfulness of the LORD
    endures forever.

Praise the LORD.[a]

Psalm 118

[1] Give thanks to the LORD, for he is
    good;
  his love endures forever.

[2] Let Israel say:
  "His love endures forever."
[3] Let the house of Aaron say:
  "His love endures forever."
[4] Let those who fear the LORD say:
  "His love endures forever."

[5] When hard pressed, I cried
    to the LORD;
  he brought me into a
    spacious place.
[6] The LORD is with me; I will not be
    afraid.
  What can mere mortals do to me?
[7] The LORD is with me; he is my
    helper.
  I look in triumph on my enemies.

[8] It is better to take refuge in the LORD
  than to trust in humans.
[9] It is better to take refuge in the LORD
  than to trust in princes.
[10] All the nations surrounded me,
  but in the name of the LORD I cut
    them down.
[11] They surrounded me on every side,
  but in the name of the LORD I cut
    them down.
[12] They swarmed around me like bees,
  but they were consumed as quickly
    as burning thorns;

---

[a] 18,19,2 Hebrew *Hallelu Yah*

in the name of the Lord I cut them
down.
¹³ I was pushed back and about to fall,
but the Lord helped me.
¹⁴ The Lord is my strength and my
defense[a];
he has become my salvation.

¹⁵ Shouts of joy and victory
resound in the tents of the
righteous:
"The Lord's right hand has done
mighty things!
¹⁶ The Lord's right hand is lifted high;
the Lord's right hand has done
mighty things!"
¹⁷ I will not die but live,
and will proclaim what the Lord has
done.
¹⁸ The Lord has chastened me severely,
but he has not given me over to
death.
¹⁹ Open for me the gates of the
righteous;
I will enter and give thanks to the
Lord.
²⁰ This is the gate of the Lord
through which the righteous may
enter.
²¹ I will give you thanks, for you
answered me;
you have become my salvation.

²² The stone the builders rejected
has become the cornerstone;
²³ the Lord has done this,
and it is marvelous in our eyes.
²⁴ The Lord has done it this very day;
let us rejoice today and be glad.

²⁵ Lord, save us!
Lord, grant us success!

²⁶ Blessed is he who comes in the name
of the Lord.
From the house of the Lord we
bless you.[b]
²⁷ The Lord is God,
and he has made his light shine on
us.
With boughs in hand, join in the festal
procession
up[c] to the horns of the altar.

²⁸ You are my God, and I will praise you;
you are my God, and I will exalt you.

²⁹ Give thanks to the Lord, for he is
good;
his love endures forever.

Psalm 119[d]

א Aleph

¹ Blessed are those whose ways are
blameless,
who walk according to the law of the
Lord.
² Blessed are those who keep his
statutes
and seek him with all their heart—
³ they do no wrong
but follow his ways.
⁴ You have laid down precepts
that are to be fully obeyed.
⁵ Oh, that my ways were steadfast
in obeying your decrees!
⁶ Then I would not be put to shame
when I consider all your commands.
⁷ I will praise you with an upright
heart
as I learn your righteous laws.
⁸ I will obey your decrees;
do not utterly forsake me.

ב Beth

⁹ How can a young person stay on the
path of purity?
By living according to your word.
¹⁰ I seek you with all my heart;
do not let me stray from your
commands.
¹¹ I have hidden your word in my heart
that I might not sin against you.
¹² Praise be to you, Lord;
teach me your decrees.
¹³ With my lips I recount
all the laws that come from your
mouth.
¹⁴ I rejoice in following your statutes
as one rejoices in great riches.
¹⁵ I meditate on your precepts
and consider your ways.
¹⁶ I delight in your decrees;
I will not neglect your word.

---

[a] 14 Or song   [b] 26 The Hebrew is plural.   [c] 27 Or
Bind the festal sacrifice with ropes / and take it   [d] This
psalm is an acrostic poem, the stanzas of which begin with
successive letters of the Hebrew alphabet; moreover, the
verses of each stanza begin with the same letter of the
Hebrew alphabet.

ג Gimel

¹⁷ Be good to your servant while I live,
     that I may obey your word.
¹⁸ Open my eyes that I may see
     wonderful things in your law.
¹⁹ I am a stranger on earth;
     do not hide your commands from me.
²⁰ My soul is consumed with longing
     for your laws at all times.
²¹ You rebuke the arrogant, who are
         accursed,
     those who stray from your
         commands.
²² Remove from me their scorn and
         contempt,
     for I keep your statutes.
²³ Though rulers sit together and
         slander me,
     your servant will meditate on your
         decrees.
²⁴ Your statutes are my delight;
     they are my counselors.

ד Daleth

²⁵ I am laid low in the dust;
     preserve my life according to your
         word.
²⁶ I gave an account of my ways and you
         answered me;
     teach me your decrees.
²⁷ Cause me to understand the way of
         your precepts,
     that I may meditate on your
         wonderful deeds.
²⁸ My soul is weary with sorrow;
     strengthen me according to your
         word.
²⁹ Keep me from deceitful ways;
     be gracious to me and teach me
         your law.
³⁰ I have chosen the way of faithfulness;
     I have set my heart on your laws.
³¹ I hold fast to your statutes, Lord;
     do not let me be put to shame.
³² I run in the path of your commands,
     for you have broadened my
         understanding.

ה He

³³ Teach me, Lord, the way of your
         decrees,
     that I may follow it to the end.^a

³⁴ Give me understanding, so that I may
         keep your law
     and obey it with all my heart.
³⁵ Direct me in the path of your
         commands,
     for there I find delight.
³⁶ Turn my heart toward your statutes
     and not toward selfish gain.
³⁷ Turn my eyes away from worthless
         things;
     preserve my life according to your
         word.^b
³⁸ Fulfill your promise to your servant,
     so that you may be feared.
³⁹ Take away the disgrace I dread,
     for your laws are good.
⁴⁰ How I long for your precepts!
     In your righteousness preserve my
         life.

ו Waw

⁴¹ May your unfailing love come to me,
         Lord,
     your salvation, according to your
         promise;
⁴² then I can answer anyone who
         taunts me,
     for I trust in your word.
⁴³ Never take your word of truth from my
         mouth,
     for I have put my hope in your laws.
⁴⁴ I will always obey your law,
     for ever and ever.
⁴⁵ I will walk about in freedom,
     for I have sought out your precepts.
⁴⁶ I will speak of your statutes before
         kings
     and will not be put to shame,
⁴⁷ for I delight in your commands
     because I love them.
⁴⁸ I reach out for your commands, which
         I love,
     that I may meditate on your
         decrees.

ז Zayin

⁴⁹ Remember your word to your servant,
     for you have given me hope.
⁵⁰ My comfort in my suffering is this:
     Your promise preserves my life.

---

^a 33 Or *follow it for its reward*   ^b 37 Two manuscripts
of the Masoretic Text and Dead Sea Scrolls; most
manuscripts of the Masoretic Text *life in your way*

51 The arrogant mock me unmercifully,
　　but I do not turn from your law.
52 I remember, LORD, your ancient laws,
　　and I find comfort in them.
53 Indignation grips me because of the
　　wicked,
　　who have forsaken your law.
54 Your decrees are the theme of my
　　song
　　wherever I lodge.
55 In the night, LORD, I remember your
　　name,
　　that I may keep your law.
56 This has been my practice:
　　I obey your precepts.

ח Heth

57 You are my portion, LORD;
　　I have promised to obey your
　　words.
58 I have sought your face with all my
　　heart;
　　be gracious to me according to your
　　promise.
59 I have considered my ways
　　and have turned my steps to your
　　statutes.
60 I will hasten and not delay
　　to obey your commands.
61 Though the wicked bind me with
　　ropes,
　　I will not forget your law.
62 At midnight I rise to give you thanks
　　for your righteous laws.
63 I am a friend to all who fear you,
　　to all who follow your precepts.
64 The earth is filled with your love,
　　LORD;
　　teach me your decrees.

ט Teth

65 Do good to your servant
　　according to your word, LORD.
66 Teach me knowledge and good
　　judgment,
　　for I trust your commands.
67 Before I was afflicted I went astray,
　　but now I obey your word.
68 You are good, and what you do is
　　good;
　　teach me your decrees.
69 Though the arrogant have smeared me
　　with lies,

　　I keep your precepts with all my
　　heart.
70 Their hearts are callous and unfeeling,
　　but I delight in your law.
71 It was good for me to be afflicted
　　so that I might learn your decrees.
72 The law from your mouth is more
　　precious to me
　　than thousands of pieces of silver
　　and gold.

י Yodh

73 Your hands made me and formed me;
　　give me understanding to learn your
　　commands.
74 May those who fear you rejoice when
　　they see me,
　　for I have put my hope in your word.
75 I know, LORD, that your laws are
　　righteous,
　　and that in faithfulness you have
　　afflicted me.
76 May your unfailing love be my comfort,
　　according to your promise to your
　　servant.
77 Let your compassion come to me that
　　I may live,
　　for your law is my delight.
78 May the arrogant be put to shame for
　　wronging me without cause;
　　but I will meditate on your precepts.
79 May those who fear you turn to me,
　　those who understand your
　　statutes.
80 May I wholeheartedly follow your
　　decrees,
　　that I may not be put to shame.

כ Kaph

81 My soul faints with longing for your
　　salvation,
　　but I have put my hope in your
　　word.
82 My eyes fail, looking for your promise;
　　I say, "When will you comfort me?"
83 Though I am like a wineskin in the
　　smoke,
　　I do not forget your decrees.
84 How long must your servant wait?
　　When will you punish my
　　persecutors?
85 The arrogant dig pits to trap me,
　　contrary to your law.

86 All your commands are trustworthy;
   help me, for I am being persecuted
   without cause.
87 They almost wiped me from the earth,
   but I have not forsaken your
   precepts.
88 In your unfailing love preserve my life,
   that I may obey the statutes of your
   mouth.

ל Lamedh

89 Your word, LORD, is eternal;
   it stands firm in the heavens.
90 Your faithfulness continues through all
   generations;
   you established the earth, and it
   endures.
91 Your laws endure to this day,
   for all things serve you.
92 If your law had not been my delight,
   I would have perished in my
   affliction.
93 I will never forget your precepts,
   for by them you have preserved my
   life.
94 Save me, for I am yours;
   I have sought out your precepts.
95 The wicked are waiting to destroy me,
   but I will ponder your statutes.
96 To all perfection I see a limit,
   but your commands are boundless.

מ Mem

97 Oh, how I love your law!
   I meditate on it all day long.
98 Your commands are always with me
   and make me wiser than my
   enemies.
99 I have more insight than all my
   teachers,
   for I meditate on your statutes.
100 I have more understanding than the
   elders,
   for I obey your precepts.
101 I have kept my feet from every evil
   path
   so that I might obey your word.
102 I have not departed from your laws,
   for you yourself have taught me.
103 How sweet are your words to my
   taste,
   sweeter than honey to my mouth!

104 I gain understanding from your
   precepts;
   therefore I hate every wrong path.

נ Nun

105 Your word is a lamp for my feet,
   a light on my path.
106 I have taken an oath and confirmed it,
   that I will follow your righteous
   laws.
107 I have suffered much;
   preserve my life, LORD, according to
   your word.
108 Accept, LORD, the willing praise of my
   mouth,
   and teach me your laws.
109 Though I constantly take my life in my
   hands,
   I will not forget your law.
110 The wicked have set a snare for me,
   but I have not strayed from your
   precepts.
111 Your statutes are my heritage
   forever;
   they are the joy of my heart.
112 My heart is set on keeping your
   decrees
   to the very end.[a]

ס Samekh

113 I hate double-minded people,
   but I love your law.
114 You are my refuge and my shield;
   I have put my hope in your word.
115 Away from me, you evildoers,
   that I may keep the commands of
   my God!
116 Sustain me, my God, according to your
   promise, and I will live;
   do not let my hopes be dashed.
117 Uphold me, and I will be delivered;
   I will always have regard for your
   decrees.
118 You reject all who stray from your
   decrees,
   for their delusions come to
   nothing.
119 All the wicked of the earth you discard
   like dross;
   therefore I love your statutes.
120 My flesh trembles in fear of you;
   I stand in awe of your laws.

---

[a] 112 Or decrees / for their enduring reward

ע Ayin

121I have done what is righteous and
   just;
   do not leave me to my oppressors.
122Ensure your servant's well-being;
   do not let the arrogant oppress me.
123My eyes fail, looking for your salvation,
   looking for your righteous promise.
124Deal with your servant according to
   your love
   and teach me your decrees.
125I am your servant; give me
   discernment
   that I may understand your
   statutes.
126It is time for you to act, LORD;
   your law is being broken.
127Because I love your commands
   more than gold, more than pure
   gold,
128and because I consider all your
   precepts right,
   I hate every wrong path.

פ Pe

129Your statutes are wonderful;
   therefore I obey them.
130The unfolding of your words gives
   light;
   it gives understanding to the
   simple.
131I open my mouth and pant,
   longing for your commands.
132Turn to me and have mercy on me,
   as you always do to those who love
   your name.
133Direct my footsteps according to your
   word;
   let no sin rule over me.
134Redeem me from human oppression,
   that I may obey your precepts.
135Make your face shine on your servant
   and teach me your decrees.
136Streams of tears flow from my eyes,
   for your law is not obeyed.

צ Tsadhe

137You are righteous, LORD,
   and your laws are right.
138The statutes you have laid down are
   righteous;
   they are fully trustworthy.

139My zeal wears me out,
   for my enemies ignore your words.
140Your promises have been thoroughly
   tested,
   and your servant loves them.
141Though I am lowly and despised,
   I do not forget your precepts.
142Your righteousness is everlasting
   and your law is true.
143Trouble and distress have come
   upon me,
   but your commands give me delight.
144Your statutes are always righteous;
   give me understanding that I may
   live.

ק Qoph

145I call with all my heart; answer me,
   LORD,
   and I will obey your decrees.
146I call out to you; save me
   and I will keep your statutes.
147I rise before dawn and cry for help;
   I have put my hope in your word.
148My eyes stay open through the
   watches of the night,
   that I may meditate on your
   promises.
149Hear my voice in accordance with your
   love;
   preserve my life, LORD, according to
   your laws.
150Those who devise wicked schemes
   are near,
   but they are far from your law.
151Yet you are near, LORD,
   and all your commands are true.
152Long ago I learned from your statutes
   that you established them to last
   forever.

ר Resh

153Look on my suffering and deliver me,
   for I have not forgotten your law.
154Defend my cause and redeem me;
   preserve my life according to your
   promise.
155Salvation is far from the wicked,
   for they do not seek out your
   decrees.
156Your compassion, LORD, is great;
   preserve my life according to your
   laws.

157Many are the foes who persecute me,
    but I have not turned from your
        statutes.
158I look on the faithless with loathing,
    for they do not obey your word.
159See how I love your precepts;
    preserve my life, LORD, in
        accordance with your love.
160All your words are true;
    all your righteous laws are
        eternal.

ש Sin and Shin

161Rulers persecute me without
        cause,
    but my heart trembles at your
        word.
162I rejoice in your promise
    like one who finds great spoil.
163I hate and detest falsehood
    but I love your law.
164Seven times a day I praise you
    for your righteous laws.
165Great peace have those who love your
        law,
    and nothing can make them
        stumble.
166I wait for your salvation, LORD,
    and I follow your commands.
167I obey your statutes,
    for I love them greatly.
168I obey your precepts and your
        statutes,
    for all my ways are known to you.

ת Taw

169May my cry come before you, LORD;
    give me understanding according to
        your word.
170May my supplication come before you;
    deliver me according to your
        promise.
171May my lips overflow with praise,
    for you teach me your decrees.
172May my tongue sing of your word,
    for all your commands are
        righteous.
173May your hand be ready to help me,
    for I have chosen your precepts.
174I long for your salvation, LORD,
    and your law gives me delight.
175Let me live that I may praise you,
    and may your laws sustain me.

176I have strayed like a lost sheep.
    Seek your servant,
    for I have not forgotten your
        commands.

Psalm 120

A song of ascents.

1I call on the LORD in my distress,
    and he answers me.
2Save me, LORD,
    from lying lips
    and from deceitful tongues.

3What will he do to you,
    and what more besides,
    you deceitful tongue?
4He will punish you with a warrior's
        sharp arrows,
    with burning coals of the broom
        bush.

5Woe to me that I dwell in Meshek,
    that I live among the tents of Kedar!
6Too long have I lived
    among those who hate peace.
7I am for peace;
    but when I speak, they are for war.

Psalm 121

A song of ascents.

1I lift up my eyes to the mountains—
    where does my help come from?
2My help comes from the LORD,
    the Maker of heaven and earth.

3He will not let your foot slip—
    he who watches over you will not
        slumber;
4indeed, he who watches over Israel
    will neither slumber nor sleep.

5The LORD watches over you—
    the LORD is your shade at your right
        hand;
6the sun will not harm you by day,
    nor the moon by night.

7The LORD will keep you from all
        harm—
    he will watch over your life;
8the LORD will watch over your coming
        and going
    both now and forevermore.

Psalm 122

A song of ascents. Of David.

1 I rejoiced with those who said to me,
   "Let us go to the house of the LORD."
2 Our feet are standing
   in your gates, Jerusalem.

3 Jerusalem is built like a city
   that is closely compacted together.
4 That is where the tribes go up—
   the tribes of the LORD—
   to praise the name of the LORD
   according to the statute given to
   Israel.
5 There stand the thrones for judgment,
   the thrones of the house of David.

6 Pray for the peace of Jerusalem:
   "May those who love you be secure.
7 May there be peace within your walls
   and security within your citadels."
8 For the sake of my family and friends,
   I will say, "Peace be within you."
9 For the sake of the house of the LORD
   our God,
   I will seek your prosperity.

Psalm 123

A song of ascents.

1 I lift up my eyes to you,
   to you who sit enthroned in heaven.
2 As the eyes of slaves look to the hand
   of their master,
   as the eyes of a female slave look
   to the hand of her mistress,
   so our eyes look to the LORD our God,
   till he shows us his mercy.

3 Have mercy on us, LORD, have mercy
   on us,
   for we have endured no end of
   contempt.
4 We have endured no end
   of ridicule from the arrogant,
   of contempt from the proud.

Psalm 124

A song of ascents. Of David.

1 If the LORD had not been on our
   side—
   let Israel say—
2 if the LORD had not been on our side
   when people attacked us,
3 they would have swallowed us alive
   when their anger flared against us;
4 the flood would have engulfed us,
   the torrent would have swept
   over us,
5 the raging waters
   would have swept us away.

6 Praise be to the LORD,
   who has not let us be torn by their
   teeth.
7 We have escaped like a bird
   from the fowler's snare;
   the snare has been broken,
   and we have escaped.
8 Our help is in the name of the LORD,
   the Maker of heaven and earth.

Psalm 125

A song of ascents.

1 Those who trust in the LORD are like
   Mount Zion,
   which cannot be shaken but
   endures forever.
2 As the mountains surround Jerusalem,
   so the LORD surrounds his people
   both now and forevermore.

3 The scepter of the wicked will not
   remain
   over the land allotted to the
   righteous,
   for then the righteous might use
   their hands to do evil.

4 LORD, do good to those who are good,
   to those who are upright in heart.
5 But those who turn to crooked ways
   the LORD will banish with the
   evildoers.

Peace be on Israel.

Psalm 126

A song of ascents.

1 When the LORD restored the fortunes
   of[a] Zion,
   we were like those who dreamed.[b]

---

a 1 Or LORD *brought back the captives to*   b 1 Or *those
restored to health*

2 Our mouths were filled with laughter,
   our tongues with songs of joy.
Then it was said among the nations,
   "The Lord has done great things for
      them."
3 The Lord has done great things
      for us,
   and we are filled with joy.

4 Restore our fortunes,*a* Lord,
   like streams in the Negev.
5 Those who sow with tears
   will reap with songs of joy.
6 Those who go out weeping,
   carrying seed to sow,
will return with songs of joy,
   carrying sheaves with them.

Psalm 127

A song of ascents. Of Solomon.

1 Unless the Lord builds the house,
   the builders labor in vain.
Unless the Lord watches over the city,
   the guards stand watch in vain.
2 In vain you rise early
   and stay up late,
toiling for food to eat—
   for he grants sleep to*b* those
      he loves.

3 Children are a heritage from the
      Lord,
   offspring a reward from him.
4 Like arrows in the hands of a warrior
   are children born in one's youth.
5 Blessed is the man
   whose quiver is full of them.
They will not be put to shame
   when they contend with their
      opponents in court.

Psalm 128

A song of ascents.

1 Blessed are all who fear the Lord,
   who walk in obedience to him.
2 You will eat the fruit of your labor;
   blessings and prosperity will be
      yours.
3 Your wife will be like a fruitful vine
   within your house;
your children will be like olive shoots
   around your table.

4 Yes, this will be the blessing
   for the man who fears the Lord.

5 May the Lord bless you from Zion;
   may you see the prosperity of
      Jerusalem
all the days of your life.
6 May you live to see your children's
      children—
   peace be on Israel.

Psalm 129

A song of ascents.

1 "They have greatly oppressed me from
      my youth,"
   let Israel say;
2 "they have greatly oppressed me from
      my youth,
   but they have not gained the victory
      over me.
3 Plowmen have plowed my back
   and made their furrows long.
4 But the Lord is righteous;
   he has cut me free from the cords
      of the wicked."

5 May all who hate Zion
   be turned back in shame.
6 May they be like grass on the roof,
   which withers before it can grow;
7 a reaper cannot fill his hands with it,
   nor one who gathers fill his arms.
8 May those who pass by not say to
      them,
   "The blessing of the Lord be on you;
   we bless you in the name of the
      Lord."

Psalm 130

A song of ascents.

1 Out of the depths I cry to you, Lord;
2   Lord, hear my voice.
Let your ears be attentive
   to my cry for mercy.

3 If you, Lord, kept a record of sins,
   Lord, who could stand?
4 But with you there is forgiveness,
   so that we can, with reverence,
      serve you.

---

a 4 Or *Bring back our captives*   *b* 2 Or *eat* — / *for while
they sleep he provides for*

⁵ I wait for the LORD, my whole being
 waits,
   and in his word I put my hope.
⁶ I wait for the Lord
   more than watchmen wait for the
    morning,
   more than watchmen wait for the
    morning.

⁷ Israel, put your hope in the LORD,
   for with the LORD is unfailing love
   and with him is full redemption.
⁸ He himself will redeem Israel
   from all their sins.

Psalm 131

A song of ascents. Of David.

¹ My heart is not proud, LORD,
   my eyes are not haughty;
 I do not concern myself with great
    matters
   or things too wonderful for me.
² But I have calmed and quieted
    myself,
   I am like a weaned child with its
    mother;
   like a weaned child I am content.

³ Israel, put your hope in the LORD
   both now and forevermore.

Psalm 132

A song of ascents.

¹ LORD, remember David
   and all his self-denial.

² He swore an oath to the LORD,
   he made a vow to the Mighty One of
    Jacob:
³ "I will not enter my house
   or go to my bed,
⁴ I will allow no sleep to my eyes
   or slumber to my eyelids,
⁵ till I find a place for the LORD,
   a dwelling for the Mighty One of
    Jacob."

⁶ We heard it in Ephrathah,
   we came upon it in the fields of
    Jaar:ᵃ
⁷ "Let us go to his dwelling place,
   let us worship at his footstool,
    saying,

THE SCENE

EPHRATHAH

(PSALM 132:6)

A city near Jerusalem. Its name
means "city of forests." The ark
of the covenant was there until
David took it to Jerusalem.

⁸ 'Arise, LORD, and come to your resting
    place,
   you and the ark of your might.
⁹ May your priests be clothed with your
    righteousness;
   may your faithful people sing for
    joy.' "

¹⁰ For the sake of your servant
    David,
   do not reject your anointed one.

¹¹ The LORD swore an oath to David,
   a sure oath he will not
    revoke:
 "One of your own descendants
   I will place on your throne.
¹² If your sons keep my covenant
   and the statutes I teach them,
 then their sons will sit
   on your throne for ever and ever."

ᵃ 6 Or *heard of it in Ephrathah, / we found it in the fields of
Jearim.* (See 1 Chron. 13:5,6) (And no quotation marks
around verses 7-9)

¹³ For the L<small>ORD</small> has chosen Zion,
  he has desired it for his dwelling,
    saying,
¹⁴ "This is my resting place for ever and
    ever;
  here I will sit enthroned, for I have
    desired it.
¹⁵ I will bless her with abundant
    provisions;
  her poor I will satisfy with food.
¹⁶ I will clothe her priests with
    salvation,
    and her faithful people will ever sing
      for joy.

¹⁷ "Here I will make a horn^a grow for
    David
  and set up a lamp for my anointed
    one.
¹⁸ I will clothe his enemies with shame,
  but his head will be adorned with a
    radiant crown."

Psalm 133

A song of ascents. Of David.

¹ How good and pleasant it is
  when God's people live together in
    unity!

² It is like precious oil poured on the
    head,
  running down on the beard,
  running down on Aaron's beard,
  down on the collar of his robe.
³ It is as if the dew of Hermon
  were falling on Mount Zion.
For there the L<small>ORD</small> bestows his
    blessing,
  even life forevermore.

Psalm 134

A song of ascents.

¹ Praise the L<small>ORD</small>, all you servants of
    the L<small>ORD</small>
  who minister by night in the house
    of the L<small>ORD</small>.
² Lift up your hands in the sanctuary
  and praise the L<small>ORD</small>.

³ May the L<small>ORD</small> bless you from Zion,
  he who is the Maker of heaven and
    earth.

Psalm 135

¹ Praise the L<small>ORD</small>.^b

Praise the name of the L<small>ORD</small>;
  praise him, you servants of the
    L<small>ORD</small>,
² you who minister in the house of the
    L<small>ORD</small>,
  in the courts of the house of our
    God.

³ Praise the L<small>ORD</small>, for the L<small>ORD</small> is good;
  sing praise to his name, for that is
    pleasant.
⁴ For the L<small>ORD</small> has chosen Jacob to be
    his own,
  Israel to be his treasured
    possession.

⁵ I know that the L<small>ORD</small> is great,
  that our Lord is greater than all
    gods.
⁶ The L<small>ORD</small> does whatever pleases him,
  in the heavens and on the earth,
  in the seas and all their depths.
⁷ He makes clouds rise from the ends
    of the earth;
  he sends lightning with the rain
  and brings out the wind from his
    storehouses.

⁸ He struck down the firstborn of
    Egypt,
  the firstborn of people and animals.
⁹ He sent his signs and wonders into
    your midst, Egypt,
  against Pharaoh and all his
    servants.
¹⁰ He struck down many nations
  and killed mighty kings—
¹¹ Sihon king of the Amorites,
  Og king of Bashan,
  and all the kings of Canaan—
¹² and he gave their land as an
    inheritance,
  an inheritance to his people Israel.

¹³ Your name, L<small>ORD</small>, endures forever,
  your renown, L<small>ORD</small>, through all
    generations.
¹⁴ For the L<small>ORD</small> will vindicate his people
  and have compassion on his
    servants.

---

^a 17 *Horn* here symbolizes strong one, that is, king.
^b 1 Hebrew *Hallelu Yah*; also in verses 3 and 21

¹⁵ The idols of the nations are silver and
   gold,
      made by human hands.
¹⁶ They have mouths, but cannot speak,
      eyes, but cannot see.
¹⁷ They have ears, but cannot hear,
      nor is there breath in their mouths.
¹⁸ Those who make them will be like
   them,
      and so will all who trust in them.

¹⁹ All you Israelites, praise the LORD;
      house of Aaron, praise the LORD;
²⁰ house of Levi, praise the LORD;
      you who fear him, praise the LORD.
²¹ Praise be to the LORD from Zion,
      to him who dwells in Jerusalem.

   Praise the LORD.

Psalm 136

¹ Give thanks to the LORD, for he is
   good.
      His love endures forever.
² Give thanks to the God of gods.
      His love endures forever.
³ Give thanks to the Lord of lords:
      His love endures forever.

⁴ to him who alone does great wonders,
      His love endures forever.
⁵ who by his understanding made the
   heavens,
      His love endures forever.
⁶ who spread out the earth upon the
   waters,
      His love endures forever.
⁷ who made the great lights—
      His love endures forever.
⁸ the sun to govern the day,
      His love endures forever.
⁹ the moon and stars to govern the
   night;
      His love endures forever.

¹⁰ to him who struck down the firstborn
   of Egypt
      His love endures forever.
¹¹ and brought Israel out from among
   them
      His love endures forever.
¹² with a mighty hand and outstretched
   arm;
      His love endures forever.

¹³ to him who divided the Red Seaᵃ
   asunder
      His love endures forever.
¹⁴ and brought Israel through the midst
   of it,
      His love endures forever.
¹⁵ but swept Pharaoh and his army into
   the Red Sea;
      His love endures forever.

¹⁶ to him who led his people through the
   wilderness;
      His love endures forever.

¹⁷ to him who struck down great kings,
      His love endures forever.
¹⁸ and killed mighty kings—
      His love endures forever.
¹⁹ Sihon king of the Amorites
      His love endures forever.

ᵃ *13* Or *the Sea of Reeds*; also in verse 15

BREAK THROUGH!

The God of gods

(PSALM 136:2)

This phrase is superlative. That means it's
like saying something is the most it can be.
It means that God is the best God, above all
other gods. There are other similar phrases
like "King of kings," "Lord of lords," and "Song
of songs." So that means the best king, the
most important Lord, the most beautiful
song. Do you catch on now?

²⁰ and Og king of Bashan—
  His love endures forever.
²¹ and gave their land as an inheritance,
  His love endures forever.
²² an inheritance to his servant Israel.
  His love endures forever.

²³ He remembered us in our low estate
  His love endures forever.
²⁴ and freed us from our enemies.
  His love endures forever.
²⁵ He gives food to every creature.
  His love endures forever.

²⁶ Give thanks to the God of heaven.
  His love endures forever.

Psalm 137

¹ By the rivers of Babylon we sat and
  wept
  when we remembered Zion.
² There on the poplars
  we hung our harps,
³ for there our captors asked us for
  songs,
  our tormentors demanded songs of
  joy;
  they said, "Sing us one of the songs
  of Zion!"

⁴ How can we sing the songs of the
  Lord
  while in a foreign land?
⁵ If I forget you, Jerusalem,
  may my right hand forget its skill.
⁶ May my tongue cling to the roof of my
  mouth
  if I do not remember you,
  if I do not consider Jerusalem
  my highest joy.

⁷ Remember, Lord, what the Edomites
  did
  on the day Jerusalem fell.
  "Tear it down," they cried,
  "tear it down to its foundations!"
⁸ Daughter Babylon, doomed to
  destruction,
  happy is the one who repays you
  according to what you have done
  to us.
⁹ Happy is the one who seizes your
  infants
  and dashes them against the rocks.

Psalm 138

Of David.

¹ I will praise you, Lord, with all my
  heart;
  before the "gods" I will sing your
  praise.
² I will bow down toward your holy
  temple
  and will praise your name
  for your unfailing love and your
  faithfulness,
  for you have so exalted your solemn
  decree
  that it surpasses your fame.
³ When I called, you answered me;
  you greatly emboldened me.

⁴ May all the kings of the earth praise
  you, Lord,
  when they hear what you have
  decreed.
⁵ May they sing of the ways of the Lord,
  for the glory of the Lord is great.

⁶ Though the Lord is exalted, he looks
  kindly on the lowly;
  though lofty, he sees them from
  afar.
⁷ Though I walk in the midst of trouble,
  you preserve my life.
  You stretch out your hand against the
  anger of my foes;
  with your right hand you save me.
⁸ The Lord will vindicate me;
  your love, Lord, endures forever—
  do not abandon the works of your
  hands.

Psalm 139

For the director of music. Of David. A psalm.

¹ You have searched me, Lord,
  and you know me.
² You know when I sit and when I rise;
  you perceive my thoughts from afar.
³ You discern my going out and my lying
  down;
  you are familiar with all my ways.
⁴ Before a word is on my tongue
  you, Lord, know it completely.
⁵ You hem me in behind and before,
  and you lay your hand upon me.

⁶ Such knowledge is too wonderful
   for me,
   too lofty for me to attain.

⁷ Where can I go from your Spirit?
   Where can I flee from your
      presence?
⁸ If I go up to the heavens, you are
      there;
   if I make my bed in the depths, you
      are there.
⁹ If I rise on the wings of the dawn,
   if I settle on the far side of the sea,
¹⁰ even there your hand will guide me,
   your right hand will hold me fast.
¹¹ If I say, "Surely the darkness will
      hide me
   and the light become night around
      me,"
¹² even the darkness will not be dark to
      you;
   the night will shine like the day,
   for darkness is as light to you.

¹³ For you created my inmost being;
   you knit me together in my mother's
      womb.
¹⁴ I praise you because I am fearfully
      and wonderfully made;
   your works are wonderful,
   I know that full well.
¹⁵ My frame was not hidden from you
   when I was made in the secret
      place,
   when I was woven together in the
      depths of the earth.
¹⁶ Your eyes saw my unformed body;
   all the days ordained for me were
      written in your book
   before one of them came to be.
¹⁷ How precious to me are your
      thoughts,ᵃ God!
   How vast is the sum of them!
¹⁸ Were I to count them,
   they would outnumber the grains of
      sand —
   when I awake, I am still with you.

¹⁹ If only you, God, would slay the
      wicked!
   Away from me, you who are
      bloodthirsty!
²⁰ They speak of you with evil intent;
   your adversaries misuse your name.

²¹ Do I not hate those who hate you,
      Lord,
   and abhor those who are in
      rebellion against you?
²² I have nothing but hatred for them;
   I count them my enemies.
²³ Search me, God, and know my heart;
   test me and know my anxious
      thoughts.
²⁴ See if there is any offensive way in me,
   and lead me in the way everlasting.

Psalm 140ᵇ

For the director of music. A psalm of David.

¹ Rescue me, Lord, from evildoers;
   protect me from the violent,
² who devise evil plans in their hearts
   and stir up war every day.
³ They make their tongues as sharp as
      a serpent's;
   the poison of vipers is on their
      lips.ᶜ

⁴ Keep me safe, Lord, from the hands
      of the wicked;
   protect me from the violent,
   who devise ways to trip my feet.
⁵ The arrogant have hidden a snare
      for me;
   they have spread out the cords of
      their net
   and have set traps for me along my
      path.

⁶ I say to the Lord, "You are my God."
   Hear, Lord, my cry for mercy.
⁷ Sovereign Lord, my strong deliverer,
   you shield my head in the day of
      battle.
⁸ Do not grant the wicked their desires,
      Lord;
   do not let their plans succeed.

⁹ Those who surround me proudly rear
      their heads;
   may the mischief of their lips engulf
      them.
¹⁰ May burning coals fall on them;
   may they be thrown into the fire,
   into miry pits, never to rise.

ᵃ 17 Or *How amazing are your thoughts concerning me*
ᵇ In Hebrew texts 140:1-13 is numbered 140:2-14.
ᶜ 3 The Hebrew has *Selah* (a word of uncertain meaning)
here and at the end of verses 5 and 8.

11 May slanderers not be established in
the land;
   may disaster hunt down the violent.
12 I know that the LORD secures justice
for the poor
   and upholds the cause of the
   needy.
13 Surely the righteous will praise your
name,
   and the upright will live in your
   presence.

Psalm 141

A psalm of David.

1 I call to you, LORD, come quickly to me;
   hear me when I call to you.
2 May my prayer be set before you like
incense;
   may the lifting up of my hands be
   like the evening sacrifice.

3 Set a guard over my mouth, LORD;
   keep watch over the door of my lips.
4 Do not let my heart be drawn to what
is evil
   so that I take part in wicked deeds
along with those who are evildoers;
   do not let me eat their delicacies.

5 Let a righteous man strike me—that
is a kindness;
   let him rebuke me—that is oil on
   my head.
My head will not refuse it,
   for my prayer will still be against the
   deeds of evildoers.

6 Their rulers will be thrown down from
the cliffs,
   and the wicked will learn that my
   words were well spoken.
7 They will say, "As one plows and
breaks up the earth,
   so our bones have been scattered
   at the mouth of the grave."

8 But my eyes are fixed on you,
Sovereign LORD;
   in you I take refuge—do not give
   me over to death.
9 Keep me safe from the traps set by
evildoers,
   from the snares they have laid for
   me.

10 Let the wicked fall into their own nets,
   while I pass by in safety.

Psalm 142 [a]

A maskil [b] of David. When he was
in the cave. A prayer.

1 I cry aloud to the LORD;
   I lift up my voice to the LORD for
   mercy.
2 I pour out before him my complaint;
   before him I tell my trouble.

3 When my spirit grows faint within me,
   it is you who watch over my way.
In the path where I walk
   people have hidden a snare for me.
4 Look and see, there is no one at my
right hand;
   no one is concerned for me.
I have no refuge;
   no one cares for my life.

5 I cry to you, LORD;
   I say, "You are my refuge,
   my portion in the land of the living."

6 Listen to my cry,
   for I am in desperate need;
rescue me from those who pursue me,
   for they are too strong for me.
7 Set me free from my prison,
   that I may praise your name.
Then the righteous will gather about
me
   because of your goodness to me.

Psalm 143

A psalm of David.

1 LORD, hear my prayer,
   listen to my cry for mercy;
in your faithfulness and righteousness
   come to my relief.
2 Do not bring your servant into
judgment,
   for no one living is righteous before
   you.
3 The enemy pursues me,
   he crushes me to the ground;
he makes me dwell in the darkness
   like those long dead.

---

[a] In Hebrew texts 142:1-7 is numbered 142:2-8.   [b] Title:
Probably a literary or musical term

4 So my spirit grows faint within me;
my heart within me is dismayed.
5 I remember the days of long ago;
I meditate on all your works
and consider what your hands have
done.
6 I spread out my hands to you;
I thirst for you like a parched land.[a]

7 Answer me quickly, LORD;
my spirit fails.
Do not hide your face from me
or I will be like those who go down
to the pit.
8 Let the morning bring me word of your
unfailing love,
for I have put my trust in you.
Show me the way I should go,
for to you I entrust my life.
9 Rescue me from my enemies, LORD,
for I hide myself in you.
10 Teach me to do your will,
for you are my God;
may your good Spirit
lead me on level ground.

11 For your name's sake, LORD, preserve
my life;
in your righteousness, bring me out
of trouble.
12 In your unfailing love, silence my
enemies;
destroy all my foes,
for I am your servant.

Psalm 144

Of David.

1 Praise be to the LORD my Rock,
who trains my hands for war,
my fingers for battle.
2 He is my loving God and my fortress,
my stronghold and my deliverer,
my shield, in whom I take refuge,
who subdues peoples[b] under me.

3 LORD, what are human beings that you
care for them,
mere mortals that you think of them?
4 They are like a breath;
their days are like a fleeting
shadow.

5 Part your heavens, LORD, and come
down;

touch the mountains, so that they
smoke.
6 Send forth lightning and scatter the
enemy;
shoot your arrows and rout them.
7 Reach down your hand from on high;
deliver me and rescue me
from the mighty waters,
from the hands of foreigners
8 whose mouths are full of lies,
whose right hands are deceitful.

9 I will sing a new song to you, my God;
on the ten-stringed lyre I will make
music to you,
10 to the One who gives victory
to kings,
who delivers his servant David.

From the deadly sword 11 deliver me;
rescue me from the hands of
foreigners
whose mouths are full of lies,
whose right hands are deceitful.

12 Then our sons in their youth
will be like well-nurtured plants,
and our daughters will be like pillars
carved to adorn a palace.
13 Our barns will be filled
with every kind of provision.
Our sheep will increase by thousands,
by tens of thousands in our fields;
14   our oxen will draw heavy loads.[c]
There will be no breaching of walls,
no going into captivity,
no cry of distress in our streets.
15 Blessed is the people of whom this is
true;
blessed is the people whose God is
the LORD.

Psalm 145[d]

A psalm of praise. Of David.

1 I will exalt you, my God the King;
I will praise your name for ever and
ever.

---

[a] 6 The Hebrew has *Selah* (a word of uncertain meaning)
here.   [b] 2 Many manuscripts of the Masoretic Text,
Dead Sea Scrolls, Aquila, Jerome and Syriac; most
manuscripts of the Masoretic Text *subdues my people*
[c] 14 Or *our chieftains will be firmly established*   [d] This
psalm is an acrostic poem, the verses of which (including
verse 13b) begin with the successive letters of the Hebrew
alphabet.

2 Every day I will praise you
　　and extol your name for ever
　　　and ever.

3 Great is the LORD and most worthy
　　of praise;
　　his greatness no one can fathom.
4 One generation commends your
　　works to another;
　　they tell of your mighty acts.
5 They speak of the glorious splendor
　　of your majesty—
　　and I will meditate on your
　　wonderful works.[a]
6 They tell of the power of your
　　awesome works—
　　and I will proclaim your great
　　deeds.
7 They celebrate your abundant
　　goodness
　　and joyfully sing of your
　　righteousness.

8 The LORD is gracious and
　　compassionate,
　　slow to anger and rich in love.

9 The LORD is good to all;
　　he has compassion on all he
　　has made.
10 All your works praise you, LORD;
　　your faithful people extol you.
11 They tell of the glory of your kingdom
　　and speak of your might,
12 so that all people may know of your
　　mighty acts
　　and the glorious splendor of your
　　kingdom.
13 Your kingdom is an everlasting
　　kingdom,
　　and your dominion endures through
　　all generations.

The LORD is trustworthy in all he
　　promises
　　and faithful in all he does.[b]
14 The LORD upholds all who fall
　　and lifts up all who are
　　bowed down.
15 The eyes of all look to you,
　　and you give them their food at the
　　proper time.
16 You open your hand
　　and satisfy the desires of every
　　living thing.

17 The LORD is righteous in all his ways
　　and faithful in all he does.
18 The LORD is near to all who call
　　on him,
　　to all who call on him in truth.
19 He fulfills the desires of those
　　who fear him;
　　he hears their cry and saves them.
20 The LORD watches over all who
　　love him,
　　but all the wicked he will destroy.

21 My mouth will speak in praise of
　　the LORD.
　　Let every creature praise his
　　holy name
　　for ever and ever.

Psalm 146

1 Praise the LORD.[c]

Praise the LORD, my soul.

2 I will praise the LORD all my life;
　　I will sing praise to my God as
　　long as I live.
3 Do not put your trust in princes,
　　in human beings, who
　　cannot save.
4 When their spirit departs, they return
　　to the ground;
　　on that very day their plans come
　　to nothing.
5 Blessed are those whose help is
　　the God of Jacob,
　　whose hope is in the
　　LORD their God.

6 He is the Maker of heaven and earth,
　　the sea, and everything in them—
　　he remains faithful forever.
7 He upholds the cause of the
　　oppressed
　　and gives food to the hungry.
　　The LORD sets prisoners free,
8 　the LORD gives sight to the blind,
　　the LORD lifts up those who are
　　bowed
　　down,
　　the LORD loves the righteous.

---

a 5 Dead Sea Scrolls and Syriac (see also Septuagint);
Masoretic Text *On the glorious splendor of your majesty /
and on your wonderful works I will meditate*　　*b* 13 One
manuscript of the Masoretic Text, Dead Sea Scrolls and
Syriac (see also Septuagint); most manuscripts of the
Masoretic Text do not have the last two lines of verse 13.
c 1 Hebrew *Hallelu Yah*; also in verse 10

9 The LORD watches over the foreigner
and sustains the fatherless and the
        widow,
but he frustrates the ways of
        the wicked.

10 The LORD reigns forever,
your God, O Zion, for all
        generations.

Praise the LORD.

Psalm 147

1 Praise the LORD.[a]

How good it is to sing praises to
        our God,
how pleasant and fitting to
        praise him!

2 The LORD builds up Jerusalem;
he gathers the exiles of Israel.
3 He heals the brokenhearted
and binds up their wounds.
4 He determines the number of
        the stars
and calls them each by name.
5 Great is our Lord and mighty
        in power;
his understanding has no limit.
6 The LORD sustains the humble
but casts the wicked to the
        ground.

7 Sing to the LORD with grateful
        praise;
make music to our God on the harp.

8 He covers the sky with clouds;
he supplies the earth with rain
and makes grass grow on the hills.
9 He provides food for the cattle
and for the young ravens when
        they call.

10 His pleasure is not in the strength
        of the horse,
nor his delight in the legs of
        the warrior;
11 the LORD delights in those who
        fear him,
who put their hope in his
        unfailing love.

12 Extol the LORD, Jerusalem;
praise your God, Zion.

13 He strengthens the bars of your gates
and blesses your people
        within you.
14 He grants peace to your borders
and satisfies you with the finest
        of wheat.

15 He sends his command to the earth;
his word runs swiftly.
16 He spreads the snow like wool
and scatters the frost like ashes.
17 He hurls down his hail like pebbles.
Who can withstand his icy blast?
18 He sends his word and melts them;
he stirs up his breezes, and the
        waters flow.

19 He has revealed his word to Jacob,
his laws and decrees to Israel.
20 He has done this for no
        other nation;
they do not know his laws.[b]

Praise the LORD.

Psalm 148

1 Praise the LORD.[c]

Praise the LORD from the heavens;
praise him in the heights above.
2 Praise him, all his angels;
praise him, all his heavenly hosts.
3 Praise him, sun and moon;
praise him, all you shining stars.
4 Praise him, you highest heavens
and you waters above the skies.

5 Let them praise the name of
        the LORD,
for at his command they were
        created,
6 and he established them for ever
        and ever—
he issued a decree that will never
        pass away.

7 Praise the LORD from the earth,
you great sea creatures and all
        ocean depths,
8 lightning and hail, snow and clouds,
stormy winds that do his
        bidding,

---

[a] 1 Hebrew *Hallelu Yah*; also in verse 20
[b] 20 Masoretic Text; Dead Sea Scrolls and Septuagint
nation; / he has not made his laws known to them
[c] 1 Hebrew *Hallelu Yah*; also in verse 14

⁹you mountains and all hills,
  fruit trees and all cedars,
¹⁰wild animals and all cattle,
  small creatures and flying
    birds,
¹¹kings of the earth and all nations,
  you princes and all rulers
    on earth,
¹²young men and women,
  old men and children.

¹³Let them praise the name of
    the LORD,
  for his name alone is exalted;
  his splendor is above the earth
    and the heavens.
¹⁴And he has raised up for his
    people a horn,ᵃ
  the praise of all his faithful
    servants,
  of Israel, the people close to
    his heart.

Praise the LORD.

Psalm 149

¹Praise the LORD.ᵇ

Sing to the LORD a new song,
  his praise in the assembly of his
    faithful people.

²Let Israel rejoice in their Maker;
  let the people of Zion be glad in
    their King.
³Let them praise his name with
    dancing
  and make music to him with
    timbrel and harp.
⁴For the LORD takes delight in his
    people;
  he crowns the humble with victory.
⁵Let his faithful people rejoice in
    this honor
  and sing for joy on their beds.

⁶May the praise of God be in their
    mouths
  and a double-edged sword in their
    hands,
⁷to inflict vengeance on the nations
  and punishment on the peoples,
⁸to bind their kings with fetters,
  their nobles with shackles
    of iron,
⁹to carry out the sentence written
    against them—
  this is the glory of all his faithful
    people.

Praise the LORD.

ᵃ 14 *Horn* here symbolizes strength.   ᵇ 1 Hebrew
Hallelu Yah; also in verse 9

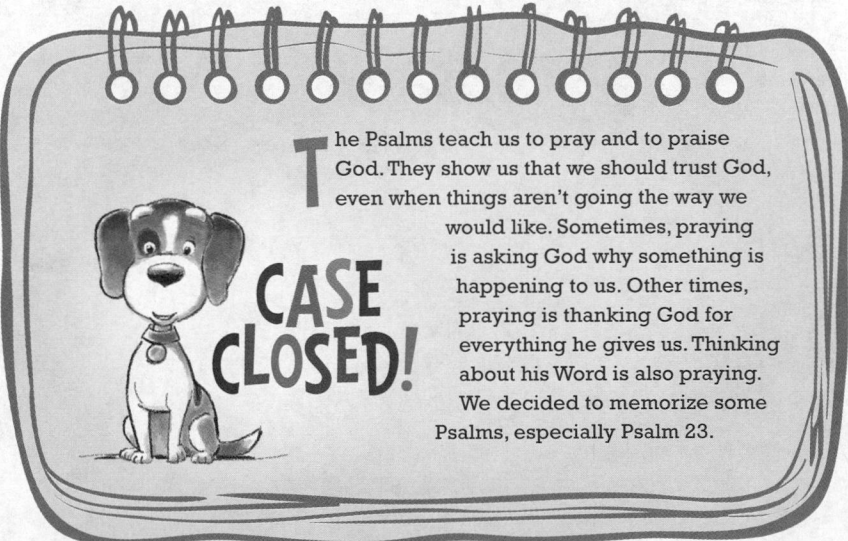

The Psalms teach us to pray and to praise
God. They show us that we should trust God,
even when things aren't going the way we
would like. Sometimes, praying
is asking God why something is
happening to us. Other times,
praying is thanking God for
everything he gives us. Thinking
about his Word is also praying.
We decided to memorize some
Psalms, especially Psalm 23.

CASE
CLOSED!

Psalm 150

[1] Praise the LORD.[a]

Praise God in his sanctuary;
 praise him in his mighty
  heavens.
[2] Praise him for his acts of power;
 praise him for his surpassing
  greatness.
[3] Praise him with the sounding of the
  trumpet,
 praise him with the harp and lyre,

[4] praise him with timbrel and
  dancing,
 praise him with the strings
  and pipe,
[5] praise him with the clash of cymbals,
 praise him with resounding
  cymbals.

[6] Let everything that has breath
  praise the LORD.

Praise the LORD.

---

[a] 1 Hebrew *Hallelu Yah*; also in verse 6

PROVERBS

THE EVIDENCE:

WHO WROTE IT?
In the very first words of this book, it says that it was written by Solomon, a very wise man who was king of Israel. So that's who wrote it. That said, Solomon wrote most of the book, but there are some Proverbs written by other wise men, like Agur and Lemuel (see Proverbs 30:1 and 31:1).

HOW LONG AGO?
King Solomon lived about 900 years before Christ. He was the one who started the writing of Proverbs, but the other collections were added many years later. That's why they say that Proverbs is the "wisdom of the centuries."

WHAT'S IT ABOUT?
Hmm, Proverbs ... What does *proverbs* mean? From what people who know a lot tell us, they are sayings or choruses that express facts and truths that everybody accepts. They're also statements that nobody can challenge. In other words, they're something like teachings. Some of the first words of this book say the purpose of these proverbs is "for giving [. . .] knowledge and discretion to the young."

THE BEST PART
All the proverbs teach something very valuable, but if we had to choose just one, we would choose this: "The fear of the LORD is the beginning of knowledge, but fools despise wisdom and instruction" (1:7).

Purpose and Theme

1 The proverbs of Solomon son of David,
king of Israel:

² for gaining wisdom and instruction;
  for understanding words of insight;
³ for receiving instruction in prudent
    behavior,
  doing what is right and just and fair;
⁴ for giving prudence to those who are
    simple,ᵃ

knowledge and discretion to the
    young—
⁵ let the wise listen and add to their
    learning,
  and let the discerning get guidance—
⁶ for understanding proverbs and
    parables,
  the sayings and riddles of the wise.ᵇ

ᵃ 4 The Hebrew word rendered *simple* in Proverbs denotes a person who is gullible, without moral direction and inclined to evil.   ᵇ 6 Or *understanding a proverb, namely, / a parable, / and the sayings of the wise, their riddles*

BREAK THROUGH!

What's the difference between knowledge and wisdom?

(PROVERBS 1 - 4)

Knowledge is about information. You know about things, or you might know people. Wisdom has to do with discerning or making a good decision. We often refer to people who are older as "wise," because they have a lot of life experience and can give good advice when it comes to making a hard decision.

⁷The fear of the LORD is the beginning of knowledge,
but fools*a* despise wisdom and instruction.

Prologue: Exhortations to Embrace Wisdom

Warning Against the Invitation of Sinful Men

⁸Listen, my son, to your father's instruction
and do not forsake your mother's teaching.
⁹They are a garland to grace your head
and a chain to adorn your neck.

¹⁰My son, if sinful men entice you,
do not give in to them.
¹¹If they say, "Come along with us;
let's lie in wait for innocent blood,
let's ambush some harmless soul;
¹²let's swallow them alive, like the grave,
and whole, like those who go down to the pit;
¹³we will get all sorts of valuable things
and fill our houses with plunder;
¹⁴cast lots with us;
we will all share the loot" —
¹⁵my son, do not go along with them,
do not set foot on their paths;
¹⁶for their feet rush into evil,
they are swift to shed blood.
¹⁷How useless to spread a net
where every bird can see it!
¹⁸These men lie in wait for their own blood;
they ambush only themselves!
¹⁹Such are the paths of all who go after ill-gotten gain;
it takes away the life of those who get it.

a 7 The Hebrew words rendered *fool* in Proverbs, and often elsewhere in the Old Testament, denote a person who is morally deficient.

BREAK THROUGH!

Proverbs

(PROVERBS 1:1)

The Proverbs are short lessons. Some people call them "wisdom in capsules."

Wisdom's Rebuke

20 Out in the open wisdom calls aloud,
  she raises her voice in the public
    square;
21 on top of the wall[a] she cries out,
  at the city gate she makes her
    speech:
22 "How long will you who are simple love
    your simple ways?
  How long will mockers delight in
    mockery
  and fools hate knowledge?
23 Repent at my rebuke!
  Then I will pour out my thoughts to
    you,
  I will make known to you my
    teachings.
24 But since you refuse to listen when I
    call
  and no one pays attention when I
    stretch out my hand,
25 since you disregard all my advice
  and do not accept my rebuke,
26 I in turn will laugh when disaster
    strikes you;

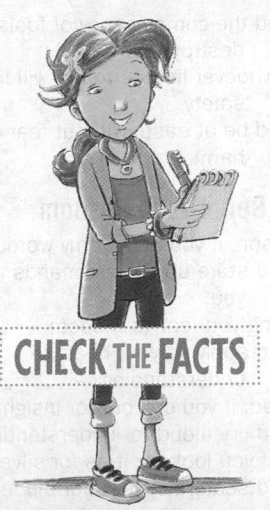

CHECK THE FACTS

What is a proverb?

A) A saying or a refrain

B) A lesson passed from parents to their children

C) A riddle

CORRECT ANSWER: A

BREAKTHROUGH!

Prudent behavior

(PROVERBS 1:2-4)

To be prudent is to make wise decisions. This means to have common sense and good judgment.

  I will mock when calamity overtakes
    you—
27 when calamity overtakes you like a
    storm,
  when disaster sweeps over you like
    a whirlwind,
  when distress and trouble
    overwhelm you.

28 "Then they will call to me but I will not
    answer;
  they will look for me but will not find
    me,
29 since they hated knowledge
  and did not choose to fear the LORD.
30 Since they would not accept my advice
  and spurned my rebuke,
31 they will eat the fruit of their ways
  and be filled with the fruit of their
    schemes.
32 For the waywardness of the simple will
    kill them,

---

a 21 Septuagint; Hebrew / at noisy street corners

and the complacency of fools will
destroy them;
33 but whoever listens to me will live in
safety
and be at ease, without fear of
harm."

Moral Benefits of Wisdom

2 My son, if you accept my words
and store up my commands within
you,
2 turning your ear to wisdom
and applying your heart to
understanding—
3 indeed, if you call out for insight
and cry aloud for understanding,
4 and if you look for it as for silver
and search for it as for hidden
treasure,
5 then you will understand the fear of
the LORD
and find the knowledge of God.
6 For the LORD gives wisdom;
from his mouth come knowledge
and understanding.
7 He holds success in store for the
upright,
he is a shield to those whose walk
is blameless,
8 for he guards the course of the just
and protects the way of his faithful
ones.

9 Then you will understand what is right
and just
and fair—every good path.
10 For wisdom will enter your heart,
and knowledge will be pleasant to
your soul.
11 Discretion will protect you,
and understanding will guard you.

12 Wisdom will save you from the ways of
wicked men,
from men whose words are
perverse,
13 who have left the straight paths
to walk in dark ways,
14 who delight in doing wrong
and rejoice in the perverseness of
evil,
15 whose paths are crooked
and who are devious in their
ways.

16 Wisdom will save you also from the
adulterous woman,
from the wayward woman with her
seductive words,
17 who has left the partner of her youth
and ignored the covenant she made
before God.ᵃ
18 Surely her house leads down to death
and her paths to the spirits of the
dead.
19 None who go to her return
or attain the paths of life.

20 Thus you will walk in the ways of the
good
and keep to the paths of the
righteous.
21 For the upright will live in the land,
and the blameless will remain in it;
22 but the wicked will be cut off from the
land,
and the unfaithful will be torn
from it.

Wisdom Bestows Well-Being

3 My son, do not forget my teaching,
but keep my commands in your
heart,
2 for they will prolong your life many
years
and bring you peace and
prosperity.

3 Let love and faithfulness never leave
you;
bind them around your neck,
write them on the tablet of your
heart.
4 Then you will win favor and a good
name
in the sight of God and man.

5 Trust in the LORD with all your heart
and lean not on your own
understanding;
6 in all your ways submit to him,
and he will make your paths
straight.ᵇ

7 Do not be wise in your own eyes;
fear the LORD and shun evil.
8 This will bring health to your body
and nourishment to your bones.

ᵃ 17 Or *covenant of her God*   ᵇ 6 Or *will direct your paths*

⁹Honor the LORD with your wealth,
  with the firstfruits of all your crops;
¹⁰then your barns will be filled to
    overflowing,
  and your vats will brim over with
    new wine.

¹¹My son, do not despise the LORD's
    discipline,
  and do not resent his rebuke,
¹²because the LORD disciplines those he
    loves,
  as a father the son he delights in.ᵃ

¹³Blessed are those who find wisdom,
  those who gain understanding,
¹⁴for she is more profitable than silver
  and yields better returns than gold.
¹⁵She is more precious than rubies;
  nothing you desire can compare
    with her.
¹⁶Long life is in her right hand;
  in her left hand are riches and
    honor.
¹⁷Her ways are pleasant ways,
  and all her paths are peace.
¹⁸She is a tree of life to those who take
    hold of her;
  those who hold her fast will be
    blessed.

¹⁹By wisdom the LORD laid the earth's
    foundations,
  by understanding he set the
    heavens in place;
²⁰by his knowledge the watery depths
    were divided,
  and the clouds let drop the dew.

²¹My son, do not let wisdom and
    understanding out of your
    sight,
  preserve sound judgment and
    discretion;
²²they will be life for you,
  an ornament to grace your neck.
²³Then you will go on your way in safety,
  and your foot will not stumble.
²⁴When you lie down, you will not be
    afraid;
  when you lie down, your sleep will
    be sweet.
²⁵Have no fear of sudden disaster
  or of the ruin that overtakes the
    wicked,

²⁶for the LORD will be at your side
  and will keep your foot from being
    snared.

²⁷Do not withhold good from those to
    whom it is due,
  when it is in your power to act.
²⁸Do not say to your neighbor,
  "Come back tomorrow and I'll give it
    to you"—
  when you already have it with you.
²⁹Do not plot harm against your
    neighbor,
  who lives trustfully near you.
³⁰Do not accuse anyone for no
    reason—
  when they have done you no harm.
³¹Do not envy the violent
  or choose any of their ways.

³²For the LORD detests the perverse
  but takes the upright into his
    confidence.
³³The LORD's curse is on the house of
    the wicked,
  but he blesses the home of the
    righteous.
³⁴He mocks proud mockers
  but shows favor to the humble and
    oppressed.
³⁵The wise inherit honor,
  but fools get only shame.

Get Wisdom at Any Cost

4 Listen, my sons, to a father's
    instruction;
  pay attention and gain
    understanding.
²I give you sound learning,
  so do not forsake my teaching.
³For I too was a son to my father,
  still tender, and cherished by my
    mother.
⁴Then he taught me, and he said to me,
  "Take hold of my words with all your
    heart;
  keep my commands, and you will
    live.
⁵Get wisdom, get understanding;
  do not forget my words or turn away
    from them.

ᵃ 12 Hebrew; Septuagint *loves, / and he chastens everyone
he accepts as his child*

6 Do not forsake wisdom, and she will
    protect you;
  love her, and she will watch over
    you.
7 The beginning of wisdom is this: Get*a*
    wisdom.
  Though it cost all you have,*b* get
    understanding.
8 Cherish her, and she will exalt you;
  embrace her, and she will honor
    you.
9 She will give you a garland to grace
    your head
  and present you with a glorious
    crown."

10 Listen, my son, accept what I say,
  and the years of your life will be
    many.
11 I instruct you in the way of wisdom
  and lead you along straight paths.
12 When you walk, your steps will not be
    hampered;
  when you run, you will not stumble.
13 Hold on to instruction, do not let it go;
  guard it well, for it is your life.
14 Do not set foot on the path of the
    wicked
  or walk in the way of evildoers.
15 Avoid it, do not travel on it;
  turn from it and go on your way.
16 For they cannot rest until they do evil;
  they are robbed of sleep till they
    make someone stumble.
17 They eat the bread of wickedness
  and drink the wine of violence.
18 The path of the righteous is like the
    morning sun,
  shining ever brighter till the full light
    of day.
19 But the way of the wicked is like deep
    darkness;
  they do not know what makes them
    stumble.

20 My son, pay attention to what I say;
  turn your ear to my words.
21 Do not let them out of your sight,
  keep them within your heart;
22 for they are life to those who find
    them
  and health to one's whole body.
23 Above all else, guard your heart,
  for everything you do flows from it.

24 Keep your mouth free of perversity;
  keep corrupt talk far from your lips.
25 Let your eyes look straight ahead;
  fix your gaze directly before you.
26 Give careful thought to the*c* paths for
    your feet
  and be steadfast in all your ways.
27 Do not turn to the right or the left;
  keep your foot from evil.

Warning Against Adultery

5 My son, pay attention to my wisdom,
  turn your ear to my words of insight,
2 that you may maintain discretion
  and your lips may preserve
    knowledge.
3 For the lips of the adulterous woman
    drip honey,
  and her speech is smoother than
    oil;
4 but in the end she is bitter as gall,
  sharp as a double-edged sword.
5 Her feet go down to death;
  her steps lead straight to the grave.
6 She gives no thought to the way of
    life;
  her paths wander aimlessly, but she
    does not know it.

7 Now then, my sons, listen to me;
  do not turn aside from what I say.
8 Keep to a path far from her,
  do not go near the door of her
    house,
9 lest you lose your honor to others
  and your dignity*d* to one who is
    cruel,
10 lest strangers feast on your wealth
  and your toil enrich the house of
    another.
11 At the end of your life you will groan,
  when your flesh and body are spent.
12 You will say, "How I hated discipline!
  How my heart spurned correction!
13 I would not obey my teachers
  or turn my ear to my instructors.
14 And I was soon in serious trouble
  in the assembly of God's people."

15 Drink water from your own cistern,
  running water from your own well.

---

a 7 Or *Wisdom is supreme; therefore get*   *b* 7 Or
wisdom. / Whatever else you get   *c* 26 Or *Make level*
d 9 Or *years*

Gall
(PROVERBS 5:4)
It's a very bitter material.

Warnings Against Folly

6 My son, if you have put up security
for your neighbor,
if you have shaken hands in pledge
for a stranger,
² you have been trapped by what you
said,
ensnared by the words of your
mouth.
³ So do this, my son, to free yourself,
since you have fallen into your
neighbor's hands:
Go—to the point of exhaustion—*ᵃ*
and give your neighbor no rest!
⁴ Allow no sleep to your eyes,
no slumber to your eyelids.
⁵ Free yourself, like a gazelle from the
hand of the hunter,
like a bird from the snare of the
fowler.

⁶ Go to the ant, you sluggard;
consider its ways and be wise!
⁷ It has no commander,
no overseer or ruler,
⁸ yet it stores its provisions in
summer
and gathers its food at harvest.

⁹ How long will you lie there, you
sluggard?
When will you get up from your
sleep?
¹⁰ A little sleep, a little slumber,
a little folding of the hands to
rest—
¹¹ and poverty will come on you like a
thief
and scarcity like an armed man.

¹² A troublemaker and a villain,
who goes about with a corrupt
mouth,
13　who winks maliciously with his eye,
signals with his feet
and motions with his fingers,
14　who plots evil with deceit in his
heart—
he always stirs up conflict.
¹⁵ Therefore disaster will overtake him in
an instant;
he will suddenly be destroyed—
without remedy.

ᵃ 3 Or Go and humble yourself,

¹⁶ Should your springs overflow in the
streets,
your streams of water in the public
squares?
¹⁷ Let them be yours alone,
never to be shared with
strangers.
¹⁸ May your fountain be blessed,
and may you rejoice in the wife of
your youth.
¹⁹ A loving doe, a graceful deer—
may her breasts satisfy you
always,
may you ever be intoxicated with her
love.
²⁰ Why, my son, be intoxicated with
another man's wife?
Why embrace the bosom of a
wayward woman?
²¹ For your ways are in full view of the
LORD,
and he examines all your paths.
²² The evil deeds of the wicked ensnare
them;
the cords of their sins hold them
fast.
²³ For lack of discipline they will die,
led astray by their own great folly.

16 There are six things the LORD hates,
  seven that are detestable to him:
17   haughty eyes,
  a lying tongue,
  hands that shed innocent blood,
18   a heart that devises wicked
    schemes,
  feet that are quick to rush into
    evil,
19   a false witness who pours out
    lies
  and a person who stirs up
    conflict in the community.

Warning Against Adultery

20 My son, keep your father's command
  and do not forsake your mother's
    teaching.
21 Bind them always on your heart;
  fasten them around your neck.
22 When you walk, they will guide you;
  when you sleep, they will watch over
    you;
  when you awake, they will speak to
    you.
23 For this command is a lamp,
  this teaching is a light,
  and correction and instruction
  are the way to life,
24 keeping you from your neighbor's wife,
  from the smooth talk of a wayward
    woman.

25 Do not lust in your heart after her
    beauty
  or let her captivate you with her
    eyes.
26 For a prostitute can be had for a loaf
    of bread,
  but another man's wife preys on
    your very life.
27 Can a man scoop fire into his lap
  without his clothes being burned?
28 Can a man walk on hot coals
  without his feet being scorched?
29 So is he who sleeps with another
    man's wife;
  no one who touches her will go
    unpunished.

30 People do not despise a thief if he
    steals
  to satisfy his hunger when he is
    starving.
31 Yet if he is caught, he must pay
    sevenfold,
  though it costs him all the wealth of
    his house.
32 But a man who commits adultery has
    no sense;
  whoever does so destroys himself.
33 Blows and disgrace are his lot,
  and his shame will never be wiped
    away.

34 For jealousy arouses a husband's fury,
  and he will show no mercy when he
    takes revenge.
35 He will not accept any compensation;
  he will refuse a bribe, however great
    it is.

Warning Against the Adulterous Woman

7 My son, keep my words
  and store up my commands within
    you.
2 Keep my commands and you will live;
  guard my teachings as the apple of
    your eye.
3 Bind them on your fingers;
  write them on the tablet of your
    heart.
4 Say to wisdom, "You are my sister,"
  and to insight, "You are my relative."
5 They will keep you from the adulterous
    woman,
  from the wayward woman with her
    seductive words.

6 At the window of my house
  I looked down through the lattice.
7 I saw among the simple,
  I noticed among the young men,
  a youth who had no sense.
8 He was going down the street near her
    corner,
  walking along in the direction of her
    house
9 at twilight, as the day was fading,
  as the dark of night set in.

10 Then out came a woman to meet
    him,
  dressed like a prostitute and with
    crafty intent.
11 (She is unruly and defiant,
  her feet never stay at home;

¹²now in the street, now in the squares,
at every corner she lurks.)
¹³She took hold of him and kissed him
and with a brazen face she said:

¹⁴"Today I fulfilled my vows,
and I have food from my fellowship
offering at home.
¹⁵So I came out to meet you;
I looked for you and have found you!
¹⁶I have covered my bed
with colored linens from Egypt.
¹⁷I have perfumed my bed
with myrrh, aloes and cinnamon.
¹⁸Come, let's drink deeply of love till
morning;
let's enjoy ourselves with love!
¹⁹My husband is not at home;
he has gone on a long journey.
²⁰He took his purse filled with money
and will not be home till full moon."

²¹With persuasive words she led him
astray;
she seduced him with her smooth
talk.
²²All at once he followed her
like an ox going to the slaughter,
like a deer*ᵃ* stepping into a noose*ᵇ*
²³   till an arrow pierces his liver,
like a bird darting into a snare,
little knowing it will cost him his life.

²⁴Now then, my sons, listen to me;
pay attention to what I say.
²⁵Do not let your heart turn to her ways
or stray into her paths.
²⁶Many are the victims she has brought
down;
her slain are a mighty throng.
²⁷Her house is a highway to the grave,
leading down to the chambers of
death.

Wisdom's Call

8 Does not wisdom call out?
Does not understanding raise her
voice?
²At the highest point along the way,
where the paths meet, she takes
her stand;
³beside the gate leading into the city,
at the entrance, she cries aloud:
⁴"To you, O people, I call out;
I raise my voice to all mankind.

⁵You who are simple, gain prudence;
you who are foolish, set your hearts
on it.*ᶜ*
⁶Listen, for I have trustworthy things to
say;
I open my lips to speak what is
right.
⁷My mouth speaks what is true,
for my lips detest wickedness.
⁸All the words of my mouth are just;
none of them is crooked or
perverse.
⁹To the discerning all of them are right;
they are upright to those who have
found knowledge.
¹⁰Choose my instruction instead of
silver,
knowledge rather than choice gold,
¹¹for wisdom is more precious than
rubies,
and nothing you desire can compare
with her.

¹²"I, wisdom, dwell together with
prudence;
I possess knowledge and
discretion.
¹³To fear the LORD is to hate evil;
I hate pride and arrogance,
evil behavior and perverse speech.
¹⁴Counsel and sound judgment are
mine;
I have insight, I have power.
¹⁵By me kings reign
and rulers issue decrees that are
just;
¹⁶by me princes govern,
and nobles—all who rule on earth.*ᵈ*
¹⁷I love those who love me,
and those who seek me find me.
¹⁸With me are riches and honor,
enduring wealth and prosperity.
¹⁹My fruit is better than fine gold;
what I yield surpasses choice silver.
²⁰I walk in the way of righteousness,
along the paths of justice,
²¹bestowing a rich inheritance on those
who love me
and making their treasuries full.

ᵃ 22 Syriac (see also Septuagint); Hebrew *fool*
ᵇ 22 The meaning of the Hebrew for this line is uncertain.
ᶜ 5 Septuagint; Hebrew *foolish, instruct your minds*
ᵈ 16 Some Hebrew manuscripts and Septuagint; other
Hebrew manuscripts *all righteous rulers*

22 "The LORD brought me forth as the
    first of his works,[a,b]
    before his deeds of old;
23 I was formed long ages ago,
    at the very beginning, when the
      world came to be.
24 When there were no watery depths, I
    was given birth,
    when there were no springs
      overflowing with water;
25 before the mountains were settled in
    place,
    before the hills, I was given birth,
26 before he made the world or its fields
    or any of the dust of the earth.
27 I was there when he set the heavens
    in place,
    when he marked out the horizon on
      the face of the deep,
28 when he established the clouds above
    and fixed securely the fountains of
      the deep,
29 when he gave the sea its boundary
    so the waters would not overstep
      his command,
    and when he marked out the
      foundations of the earth.
30   Then I was constantly[c] at his side.
    I was filled with delight day after day,
    rejoicing always in his presence,
31 rejoicing in his whole world
    and delighting in mankind.

32 "Now then, my children, listen to me;
    blessed are those who keep my
      ways.
33 Listen to my instruction and be wise;
    do not disregard it.
34 Blessed are those who listen to me,
    watching daily at my doors,
    waiting at my doorway.
35 For those who find me find life
    and receive favor from the LORD.
36 But those who fail to find me harm
    themselves;
    all who hate me love death."

Invitations of Wisdom and Folly

9 Wisdom has built her house;
    she has set up[d] its seven pillars.
2 She has prepared her meat and mixed
    her wine;
    she has also set her table.

3 She has sent out her servants, and
    she calls
    from the highest point of the city,
4   "Let all who are simple come to my
      house!"
    To those who have no sense she says,
5   "Come, eat my food
    and drink the wine I have mixed.
6 Leave your simple ways and you will
    live;
    walk in the way of insight."

7 Whoever corrects a mocker invites
    insults;
    whoever rebukes the wicked incurs
      abuse.
8 Do not rebuke mockers or they will
    hate you;
    rebuke the wise and they will love
      you.
9 Instruct the wise and they will be
    wiser still;
    teach the righteous and they will
      add to their learning.

10 The fear of the LORD is the beginning
    of wisdom,
    and knowledge of the Holy One is
      understanding.
11 For through wisdom[e] your days will be
    many,
    and years will be added to your life.
12 If you are wise, your wisdom will
    reward you;
    if you are a mocker, you alone will
      suffer.

13 Folly is an unruly woman;
    she is simple and knows nothing.
14 She sits at the door of her house,
    on a seat at the highest point of the
      city,
15 calling out to those who pass by,
    who go straight on their way,
16   "Let all who are simple come to my
      house!"
    To those who have no sense she
      says,
17   "Stolen water is sweet;
    food eaten in secret is delicious!"

---

[a] 22 Or *way*; or *dominion*   [b] 22 Or *The LORD possessed
me at the beginning of his work*; or *The LORD brought me
forth at the beginning of his work*   [c] 30 Or *was the
artisan*; or *was a little child*   [d] 1 Septuagint, Syriac and
Targum; Hebrew *has hewn out*   [e] 11 Septuagint, Syriac
and Targum; Hebrew *me*

¹⁸ But little do they know that the dead
are there,
that her guests are deep in the
realm of the dead.

Proverbs of Solomon

10 The proverbs of Solomon:

A wise son brings joy to his father,
but a foolish son brings grief to his
mother.

² Ill-gotten treasures have no lasting
value,
but righteousness delivers from
death.

³ The Lord does not let the righteous go
hungry,
but he thwarts the craving of the
wicked.

⁴ Lazy hands make for poverty,
but diligent hands bring wealth.

⁵ He who gathers crops in summer is a
prudent son,
but he who sleeps during harvest is
a disgraceful son.

⁶ Blessings crown the head of the
righteous,
but violence overwhelms the mouth
of the wicked.ᵃ

⁷ The name of the righteous is used in
blessings,ᵇ
but the name of the wicked will rot.

⁸ The wise in heart accept commands,
but a chattering fool comes to ruin.

⁹ Whoever walks in integrity walks
securely,
but whoever takes crooked paths
will be found out.

¹⁰ Whoever winks maliciously causes
grief,
and a chattering fool comes to ruin.

¹¹ The mouth of the righteous is a
fountain of life,
but the mouth of the wicked
conceals violence.

¹² Hatred stirs up conflict,
but love covers over all wrongs.

¹³ Wisdom is found on the lips of the
discerning,
but a rod is for the back of one who
has no sense.

¹⁴ The wise store up knowledge,
but the mouth of a fool invites ruin.

¹⁵ The wealth of the rich is their fortified
city,
but poverty is the ruin of the poor.

¹⁶ The wages of the righteous is life,
but the earnings of the wicked are
sin and death.

¹⁷ Whoever heeds discipline shows the
way to life,
but whoever ignores correction
leads others astray.

¹⁸ Whoever conceals hatred with lying
lips
and spreads slander is a fool.

¹⁹ Sin is not ended by multiplying words,
but the prudent hold their tongues.

²⁰ The tongue of the righteous is choice
silver,
but the heart of the wicked is of
little value.

²¹ The lips of the righteous nourish
many,
but fools die for lack of sense.

²² The blessing of the Lord brings
wealth,
without painful toil for it.

²³ A fool finds pleasure in wicked
schemes,
but a person of understanding
delights in wisdom.

²⁴ What the wicked dread will overtake
them;
what the righteous desire will be
granted.

²⁵ When the storm has swept by, the
wicked are gone,
but the righteous stand firm forever.

²⁶ As vinegar to the teeth and smoke to
the eyes,
so are sluggards to those who send
them.

ᵃ 6 Or *righteous, / but the mouth of the wicked conceals
violence*   ᵇ 7 See Gen. 48:20.

27 The fear of the Lord adds length to
   life,
     but the years of the wicked are cut
      short.

28 The prospect of the righteous is joy,
     but the hopes of the wicked come
      to nothing.

29 The way of the Lord is a refuge for the
     blameless,
     but it is the ruin of those who do
      evil.

30 The righteous will never be uprooted,
     but the wicked will not remain in the
      land.

31 From the mouth of the righteous
      comes the fruit of wisdom,
     but a perverse tongue will be
      silenced.

32 The lips of the righteous know what
      finds favor,
     but the mouth of the wicked only
      what is perverse.

11 The Lord detests dishonest
      scales,
     but accurate weights find favor
      with him.

2 When pride comes, then comes
      disgrace,
     but with humility comes wisdom.

3 The integrity of the upright guides
      them,
     but the unfaithful are destroyed by
      their duplicity.

4 Wealth is worthless in the day of
      wrath,
     but righteousness delivers from
      death.

5 The righteousness of the blameless
      makes their paths straight,
     but the wicked are brought down by
      their own wickedness.

6 The righteousness of the upright
      delivers them,
     but the unfaithful are trapped by evil
      desires.

7 Hopes placed in mortals die with
      them;

BREAK THROUGH!

Duplicity
(PROVERBS 11:3)
This is when a person lies or acts two different
ways to different people about the same
thing.

  all the promise of[a] their power
      comes to nothing.

8 The righteous person is rescued from
      trouble,
     and it falls on the wicked instead.

9 With their mouths the godless destroy
      their neighbors,
     but through knowledge the
      righteous escape.

10 When the righteous prosper, the city
      rejoices;
     when the wicked perish, there are
      shouts of joy.

11 Through the blessing of the upright a
      city is exalted,
     but by the mouth of the wicked it is
      destroyed.

12 Whoever derides their neighbor has no
      sense,
     but the one who has understanding
      holds their tongue.

---

a 7 Two Hebrew manuscripts; most Hebrew manuscripts,
Vulgate, Syriac and Targum *When the wicked die, their hope
perishes; / all they expected from*

¹³ A gossip betrays a confidence,
　　but a trustworthy person keeps a
　　secret.

¹⁴ For lack of guidance a nation falls,
　　but victory is won through many
　　advisers.

¹⁵ Whoever puts up security for a
　　stranger will surely suffer,
　　but whoever refuses to shake
　　hands in pledge is safe.

¹⁶ A kindhearted woman gains honor,
　　but ruthless men gain only
　　wealth.

¹⁷ Those who are kind benefit
　　themselves,
　　but the cruel bring ruin on
　　themselves.

¹⁸ A wicked person earns deceptive
　　wages,
　　but the one who sows
　　righteousness reaps a sure
　　reward.

¹⁹ Truly the righteous attain life,
　　but whoever pursues evil finds
　　death.

²⁰ The Lᴏʀᴅ detests those whose hearts
　　are perverse,
　　but he delights in those whose ways
　　are blameless.

²¹ Be sure of this: The wicked will not go
　　unpunished,
　　but those who are righteous will go
　　free.

²² Like a gold ring in a pig's snout
　　is a beautiful woman who shows no
　　discretion.

²³ The desire of the righteous ends only
　　in good,
　　but the hope of the wicked only in
　　wrath.

²⁴ One person gives freely, yet gains
　　even more;
　　another withholds unduly, but
　　comes to poverty.

²⁵ A generous person will prosper;
　　whoever refreshes others will be
　　refreshed.

²⁶ People curse the one who hoards
　　grain,
　　but they pray God's blessing on the
　　one who is willing to sell.

²⁷ Whoever seeks good finds favor,
　　but evil comes to one who searches
　　for it.

²⁸ Those who trust in their riches will fall,
　　but the righteous will thrive like a
　　green leaf.

²⁹ Whoever brings ruin on their family will
　　inherit only wind,
　　and the fool will be servant to the
　　wise.

³⁰ The fruit of the righteous is a tree of
　　life,
　　and the one who is wise saves lives.

³¹ If the righteous receive their due on
　　earth,
　　how much more the ungodly and
　　the sinner!

12 Whoever loves discipline loves
　　knowledge,
　　but whoever hates correction is
　　stupid.

BREAK THROUGH!

Day of wrath
(PROVERBS 11:4)
The time when God will judge everyone.

2 Good people obtain favor from the
   Lord,
  but he condemns those who devise
   wicked schemes.

3 No one can be established through
   wickedness,
  but the righteous cannot be
   uprooted.

4 A wife of noble character is her
   husband's crown,
  but a disgraceful wife is like decay
   in his bones.

5 The plans of the righteous are just,
  but the advice of the wicked is
   deceitful.

6 The words of the wicked lie in wait for
   blood,
  but the speech of the upright
   rescues them.

7 The wicked are overthrown and are no
   more,
  but the house of the righteous
   stands firm.

8 A person is praised according to their
   prudence,
  and one with a warped mind is
   despised.

9 Better to be a nobody and yet have a
   servant
  than pretend to be somebody and
   have no food.

10 The righteous care for the needs of
   their animals,
  but the kindest acts of the wicked
   are cruel.

11 Those who work their land will have
   abundant food,
  but those who chase fantasies have
   no sense.

12 The wicked desire the stronghold of
   evildoers,
  but the root of the righteous
   endures.

13 Evildoers are trapped by their sinful
   talk,
  and so the innocent escape
   trouble.

14 From the fruit of their lips people are
   filled with good things,
  and the work of their hands brings
   them reward.

15 The way of fools seems right to them,
  but the wise listen to advice.

16 Fools show their annoyance at once,
  but the prudent overlook an insult.

17 An honest witness tells the truth,
  but a false witness tells lies.

18 The words of the reckless pierce like
   swords,
  but the tongue of the wise brings
   healing.

19 Truthful lips endure forever,
  but a lying tongue lasts only a
   moment.

20 Deceit is in the hearts of those who
   plot evil,
  but those who promote peace have
   joy.

21 No harm overtakes the righteous,
  but the wicked have their fill of
   trouble.

22 The Lord detests lying lips,
  but he delights in people who are
   trustworthy.

23 The prudent keep their knowledge to
   themselves,
  but a fool's heart blurts out folly.

24 Diligent hands will rule,
  but laziness ends in forced labor.

25 Anxiety weighs down the heart,
  but a kind word cheers it up.

26 The righteous choose their friends
   carefully,
  but the way of the wicked leads
   them astray.

27 The lazy do not roast[a] any game,
  but the diligent feed on the riches
   of the hunt.

28 In the way of righteousness there is
   life;
  along that path is immortality.

---

a 27 The meaning of the Hebrew for this word is uncertain.

13 A wise son heeds his father's
instruction,
but a mocker does not respond to
rebukes.

2 From the fruit of their lips people enjoy
good things,
but the unfaithful have an appetite
for violence.

3 Those who guard their lips preserve
their lives,
but those who speak rashly will
come to ruin.

4 A sluggard's appetite is never filled,
but the desires of the diligent are
fully satisfied.

5 The righteous hate what is false,
but the wicked make themselves a
stench
and bring shame on themselves.

6 Righteousness guards the person of
integrity,
but wickedness overthrows the
sinner.

7 One person pretends to be rich, yet
has nothing;
another pretends to be poor, yet
has great wealth.

8 A person's riches may ransom their
life,
but the poor cannot respond to
threatening rebukes.

9 The light of the righteous shines
brightly,
but the lamp of the wicked is
snuffed out.

10 Where there is strife, there is pride,
but wisdom is found in those who
take advice.

11 Dishonest money dwindles away,
but whoever gathers money little by
little makes it grow.

12 Hope deferred makes the heart
sick,
but a longing fulfilled is a tree of
life.

13 Whoever scorns instruction will pay
for it,

but whoever respects a command is
rewarded.

14 The teaching of the wise is a fountain
of life,
turning a person from the snares of
death.

15 Good judgment wins favor,
but the way of the unfaithful leads
to their destruction.^a

16 All who are prudent act with^b
knowledge,
but fools expose their folly.

17 A wicked messenger falls into
trouble,
but a trustworthy envoy brings
healing.

18 Whoever disregards discipline comes
to poverty and shame,
but whoever heeds correction is
honored.

19 A longing fulfilled is sweet to the
soul,
but fools detest turning from evil.

20 Walk with the wise and become wise,
for a companion of fools suffers
harm.

21 Trouble pursues the sinner,
but the righteous are rewarded with
good things.

22 A good person leaves an inheritance
for their children's children,
but a sinner's wealth is stored up
for the righteous.

23 An unplowed field produces food for
the poor,
but injustice sweeps it away.

24 Whoever spares the rod hates their
children,
but the one who loves their children
is careful to discipline them.

25 The righteous eat to their hearts'
content,
but the stomach of the wicked goes
hungry.

---

^a 15 Septuagint and Syriac; the meaning of the Hebrew for
this phrase is uncertain.   ^b 16 Or *prudent protect*
themselves through

BREAKTHROUGH!

What does it mean when it says, "An unplowed field produces food for the poor"? Poor people don't always have fields, and they sometimes don't have food either.

(PROVERBS 13:23)

Keep on reading. Then the verse talks about injustice. Even an unplowed field can produce some food for the poor, however injustice can sweep even this small amount away.

14 The wise woman builds her house,
but with her own hands the foolish one tears hers down.

2 Whoever fears the LORD walks uprightly,
but those who despise him are devious in their ways.

3 A fool's mouth lashes out with pride,
but the lips of the wise protect them.

4 Where there are no oxen, the manger is empty,
but from the strength of an ox come abundant harvests.

5 An honest witness does not deceive,
but a false witness pours out lies.

6 The mocker seeks wisdom and finds none,
but knowledge comes easily to the discerning.

7 Stay away from a fool,
for you will not find knowledge on their lips.

8 The wisdom of the prudent is to give thought to their ways,
but the folly of fools is deception.

9 Fools mock at making amends for sin,
but goodwill is found among the upright.

10 Each heart knows its own bitterness,
and no one else can share its joy.

11 The house of the wicked will be destroyed,
but the tent of the upright will flourish.

12 There is a way that appears to be right,
but in the end it leads to death.

13 Even in laughter the heart may ache,
and rejoicing may end in grief.

14 The faithless will be fully repaid for their ways,
and the good rewarded for theirs.

15 The simple believe anything,
but the prudent give thought to their steps.

16 The wise fear the LORD and shun evil,
but a fool is hotheaded and yet feels secure.

17 A quick-tempered person does foolish things,
and the one who devises evil schemes is hated.

18 The simple inherit folly,
but the prudent are crowned with knowledge.

19 Evildoers will bow down in the presence of the good,
and the wicked at the gates of the righteous.

20 The poor are shunned even by their
    neighbors,
  but the rich have many friends.

21 It is a sin to despise one's neighbor,
  but blessed is the one who is kind
    to the needy.

22 Do not those who plot evil go astray?
  But those who plan what is good
    find[a] love and faithfulness.

23 All hard work brings a profit,
  but mere talk leads only to poverty.

24 The wealth of the wise is their crown,
  but the folly of fools yields folly.

25 A truthful witness saves lives,
  but a false witness is deceitful.

26 Whoever fears the LORD has a secure
    fortress,
  and for their children it will be a
    refuge.

27 The fear of the LORD is a fountain of
    life,
  turning a person from the snares of
    death.

28 A large population is a king's glory,
  but without subjects a prince is
    ruined.

29 Whoever is patient has great
    understanding,
  but one who is quick-tempered
    displays folly.

30 A heart at peace gives life to the body,
  but envy rots the bones.

31 Whoever oppresses the poor shows
    contempt for their Maker,
  but whoever is kind to the needy
    honors God.

32 When calamity comes, the wicked are
    brought down,
  but even in death the righteous
    seek refuge in God.

33 Wisdom reposes in the heart of the
    discerning
  and even among fools she lets
    herself be known.[b]

34 Righteousness exalts a nation,
  but sin condemns any people.

35 A king delights in a wise servant,
  but a shameful servant arouses his
    fury.

15 A gentle answer turns away wrath,
  but a harsh word stirs up anger.

2 The tongue of the wise adorns
    knowledge,
  but the mouth of the fool gushes
    folly.

3 The eyes of the LORD are everywhere,
  keeping watch on the wicked and
    the good.

4 The soothing tongue is a tree of life,
  but a perverse tongue crushes the
    spirit.

5 A fool spurns a parent's discipline,
  but whoever heeds correction
    shows prudence.

6 The house of the righteous contains
    great treasure,
  but the income of the wicked brings
    ruin.

7 The lips of the wise spread
    knowledge,
  but the hearts of fools are not
    upright.

8 The LORD detests the sacrifice of the
    wicked,
  but the prayer of the upright
    pleases him.

9 The LORD detests the way of the
    wicked,
  but he loves those who pursue
    righteousness.

10 Stern discipline awaits anyone who
    leaves the path;
  the one who hates correction will
    die.

11 Death and Destruction[c] lie open
    before the LORD—
  how much more do human
    hearts!

12 Mockers resent correction,
  so they avoid the wise.

---

a 22 Or *show*   *b 33* Hebrew; Septuagint and Syriac
discerning / but in the heart of fools she is not known
c 11 Hebrew *Abaddon*

¹³ A happy heart makes the face
   cheerful,
   but heartache crushes the spirit.

¹⁴ The discerning heart seeks
   knowledge,
   but the mouth of a fool feeds on
   folly.

¹⁵ All the days of the oppressed are
   wretched,
   but the cheerful heart has a
   continual feast.

¹⁶ Better a little with the fear of the LORD
   than great wealth with turmoil.

¹⁷ Better a small serving of vegetables
   with love
   than a fattened calf with hatred.

¹⁸ A hot-tempered person stirs up
   conflict,
   but the one who is patient calms a
   quarrel.

¹⁹ The way of the sluggard is blocked
   with thorns,
   but the path of the upright is a
   highway.

²⁰ A wise son brings joy to his father,
   but a foolish man despises his
   mother.

²¹ Folly brings joy to one who has no
   sense,
   but whoever has understanding
   keeps a straight course.

²² Plans fail for lack of counsel,
   but with many advisers they
   succeed.

²³ A person finds joy in giving an apt
   reply—
   and how good is a timely word!

²⁴ The path of life leads upward for the
   prudent
   to keep them from going down to
   the realm of the dead.

²⁵ The LORD tears down the house of the
   proud,
   but he sets the widow's boundary
   stones in place.

²⁶ The LORD detests the thoughts of the
   wicked,

but gracious words are pure in his
   sight.

²⁷ The greedy bring ruin to their
   households,
   but the one who hates bribes will
   live.

²⁸ The heart of the righteous weighs its
   answers,
   but the mouth of the wicked gushes
   evil.

²⁹ The LORD is far from the wicked,
   but he hears the prayer of the
   righteous.

³⁰ Light in a messenger's eyes brings joy
   to the heart,
   and good news gives health to the
   bones.

³¹ Whoever heeds life-giving correction
   will be at home among the wise.

³² Those who disregard discipline
   despise themselves,
   but the one who heeds correction
   gains understanding.

³³ Wisdom's instruction is to fear the
   LORD,
   and humility comes before honor.

16 To humans belong the plans of the
   heart,
   but from the LORD comes the proper
   answer of the tongue.

² All a person's ways seem pure to them,
   but motives are weighed by the
   LORD.

³ Commit to the LORD whatever you do,
   and he will establish your plans.

⁴ The LORD works out everything to its
   proper end—
   even the wicked for a day of
   disaster.

⁵ The LORD detests all the proud of
   heart.
   Be sure of this: They will not go
   unpunished.

⁶ Through love and faithfulness sin is
   atoned for;
   through the fear of the LORD evil is
   avoided.

7 When the LORD takes pleasure in
   anyone's way,
   he causes their enemies to make
   peace with them.

8 Better a little with righteousness
   than much gain with injustice.

9 In their hearts humans plan their
   course,
   but the LORD establishes their
   steps.

10 The lips of a king speak as an oracle,
   and his mouth does not betray
   justice.

11 Honest scales and balances belong to
   the LORD;
   all the weights in the bag are of his
   making.

12 Kings detest wrongdoing,
   for a throne is established through
   righteousness.

13 Kings take pleasure in honest lips;
   they value the one who speaks what
   is right.

14 A king's wrath is a messenger of
   death,
   but the wise will appease it.

15 When a king's face brightens, it
   means life;
   his favor is like a rain cloud in
   spring.

16 How much better to get wisdom than
   gold,
   to get insight rather than silver!

17 The highway of the upright avoids
   evil;
   those who guard their ways
   preserve their lives.

18 Pride goes before destruction,
   a haughty spirit before a fall.

19 Better to be lowly in spirit along with
   the oppressed
   than to share plunder with the
   proud.

20 Whoever gives heed to instruction
   prospers,[a]
   and blessed is the one who trusts
   in the LORD.

21 The wise in heart are called
   discerning,
   and gracious words promote
   instruction.[b]

22 Prudence is a fountain of life to the
   prudent,
   but folly brings punishment to fools.

23 The hearts of the wise make their
   mouths prudent,
   and their lips promote instruction.[c]

24 Gracious words are a honeycomb,
   sweet to the soul and healing to the
   bones.

25 There is a way that appears to be
   right,
   but in the end it leads to death.

26 The appetite of laborers works for
   them;
   their hunger drives them on.

27 A scoundrel plots evil,
   and on their lips it is like a
   scorching fire.

28 A perverse person stirs up conflict,
   and a gossip separates close
   friends.

29 A violent person entices their neighbor
   and leads them down a path that is
   not good.

30 Whoever winks with their eye is
   plotting perversity;
   whoever purses their lips is bent on
   evil.

31 Gray hair is a crown of splendor;
   it is attained in the way of
   righteousness.

32 Better a patient person than a warrior,
   one with self-control than one who
   takes a city.

33 The lot is cast into the lap,
   but its every decision is from the
   LORD.

17 Better a dry crust with peace and
     quiet
   than a house full of feasting, with
   strife.

---

a 20 Or *whoever speaks prudently finds what is good*
b 21 Or *words make a person persuasive*   c 23 Or
prudent / and make their lips persuasive

2 A prudent servant will rule over a
disgraceful son
and will share the inheritance as
one of the family.

3 The crucible for silver and the furnace
for gold,
but the Lord tests the heart.

4 A wicked person listens to deceitful
lips;
a liar pays attention to a destructive
tongue.

5 Whoever mocks the poor shows
contempt for their Maker;
whoever gloats over disaster will not
go unpunished.

6 Children's children are a crown to the
aged,
and parents are the pride of their
children.

7 Eloquent lips are unsuited to a
godless fool—
how much worse lying lips to a
ruler!

8 A bribe is seen as a charm by the one
who gives it;
they think success will come at
every turn.

9 Whoever would foster love covers over
an offense,
but whoever repeats the matter
separates close friends.

10 A rebuke impresses a discerning
person
more than a hundred lashes a fool.

11 Evildoers foster rebellion against
God;
the messenger of death will be sent
against them.

12 Better to meet a bear robbed of her
cubs
than a fool bent on folly.

13 Evil will never leave the house
of one who pays back evil for good.

14 Starting a quarrel is like breaching a
dam;
so drop the matter before a dispute
breaks out.

15 Acquitting the guilty and condemning
the innocent—
the Lord detests them both.

16 Why should fools have money in hand
to buy wisdom,
when they are not able to
understand it?

17 A friend loves at all times,
and a brother is born for a time of
adversity.

18 One who has no sense shakes hands
in pledge
and puts up security for a neighbor.

19 Whoever loves a quarrel loves sin;
whoever builds a high gate invites
destruction.

20 One whose heart is corrupt does not
prosper;
one whose tongue is perverse falls
into trouble.

21 To have a fool for a child brings grief;
there is no joy for the parent of a
godless fool.

22 A cheerful heart is good medicine,
but a crushed spirit dries up the
bones.

23 The wicked accept bribes in secret
to pervert the course of justice.

24 A discerning person keeps wisdom in
view,
but a fool's eyes wander to the ends
of the earth.

25 A foolish son brings grief to his
father
and bitterness to the mother who
bore him.

26 If imposing a fine on the innocent is
not good,
surely to flog honest officials is not
right.

27 The one who has knowledge uses
words with restraint,
and whoever has understanding is
even-tempered.

28 Even fools are thought wise if they
keep silent,

and discerning if they hold their tongues.

18 An unfriendly person pursues selfish ends
and against all sound judgment starts quarrels.

2 Fools find no pleasure in understanding
but delight in airing their own opinions.

3 When wickedness comes, so does contempt,
and with shame comes reproach.

4 The words of the mouth are deep waters,
but the fountain of wisdom is a rushing stream.

5 It is not good to be partial to the wicked
and so deprive the innocent of justice.

6 The lips of fools bring them strife,
and their mouths invite a beating.

7 The mouths of fools are their undoing,
and their lips are a snare to their very lives.

8 The words of a gossip are like choice morsels;
they go down to the inmost parts.

9 One who is slack in his work
is brother to one who destroys.

10 The name of the LORD is a fortified tower;
the righteous run to it and are safe.

11 The wealth of the rich is their fortified city;
they imagine it a wall too high to scale.

12 Before a downfall the heart is haughty,
but humility comes before honor.

13 To answer before listening—
that is folly and shame.

14 The human spirit can endure in sickness,
but a crushed spirit who can bear?

15 The heart of the discerning acquires knowledge,
for the ears of the wise seek it out.

16 A gift opens the way
and ushers the giver into the presence of the great.

17 In a lawsuit the first to speak seems right,
until someone comes forward and cross-examines.

18 Casting the lot settles disputes
and keeps strong opponents apart.

19 A brother wronged is more unyielding than a fortified city;
disputes are like the barred gates of a citadel.

20 From the fruit of their mouth a person's stomach is filled;
with the harvest of their lips they are satisfied.

21 The tongue has the power of life and death,
and those who love it will eat its fruit.

22 He who finds a wife finds what is good
and receives favor from the LORD.

23 The poor plead for mercy,
but the rich answer harshly.

24 One who has unreliable friends soon comes to ruin,
but there is a friend who sticks closer than a brother.

19 Better the poor whose walk is blameless
than a fool whose lips are perverse.

2 Desire without knowledge is not good—
how much more will hasty feet miss the way!

3 A person's own folly leads to their ruin,
yet their heart rages against the LORD.

4 Wealth attracts many friends,
but even the closest friend of the poor person deserts them.

⁵A false witness will not go
   unpunished,
and whoever pours out lies will not
   go free.

⁶Many curry favor with a ruler,
and everyone is the friend of one
   who gives gifts.

⁷The poor are shunned by all their
   relatives—
how much more do their friends
   avoid them!
Though the poor pursue them with
   pleading,
they are nowhere to be found.ᵃ

⁸The one who gets wisdom loves life;
the one who cherishes
   understanding will soon
   prosper.

⁹A false witness will not go
   unpunished,
and whoever pours out lies will
   perish.

¹⁰It is not fitting for a fool to live in
   luxury—
how much worse for a slave to rule
   over princes!

¹¹A person's wisdom yields patience;
it is to one's glory to overlook an
   offense.

¹²A king's rage is like the roar of a lion,
but his favor is like dew on the
   grass.

¹³A foolish child is a father's ruin,
and a quarrelsome wife is like
   the constant dripping of a leaky
   roof.

¹⁴Houses and wealth are inherited from
   parents,
but a prudent wife is from the Lord.

¹⁵Laziness brings on deep sleep,
and the shiftless go hungry.

¹⁶Whoever keeps commandments keeps
   their life,
but whoever shows contempt for
   their ways will die.

¹⁷Whoever is kind to the poor lends to
   the Lord,

and he will reward them for what
   they have done.

¹⁸Discipline your children, for in that
   there is hope;
do not be a willing party to their
   death.

¹⁹A hot-tempered person must pay the
   penalty;
rescue them, and you will have to
   do it again.

²⁰Listen to advice and accept discipline,
and at the end you will be counted
   among the wise.

²¹Many are the plans in a person's
   heart,
but it is the Lord's purpose that
   prevails.

²²What a person desires is unfailing
   loveᵇ;
better to be poor than a liar.

²³The fear of the Lord leads to life;
then one rests content, untouched
   by trouble.

²⁴A sluggard buries his hand in the
   dish;
he will not even bring it back to his
   mouth!

²⁵Flog a mocker, and the simple will
   learn prudence;
rebuke the discerning, and they will
   gain knowledge.

²⁶Whoever robs their father and drives
   out their mother
is a child who brings shame and
   disgrace.

²⁷Stop listening to instruction, my
   son,
and you will stray from the words of
   knowledge.

²⁸A corrupt witness mocks at justice,
and the mouth of the wicked gulps
   down evil.

²⁹Penalties are prepared for mockers,
and beatings for the backs of
   fools.

ᵃ 7 The meaning of the Hebrew for this sentence is
uncertain.   ᵇ 22 Or *Greed is a person's shame*

20 Wine is a mocker and beer a
brawler;
    whoever is led astray by them is not
wise.

2 A king's wrath strikes terror like the
roar of a lion;
    those who anger him forfeit their
lives.

3 It is to one's honor to avoid strife,
    but every fool is quick to quarrel.

4 Sluggards do not plow in season;
    so at harvest time they look but find
nothing.

5 The purposes of a person's heart are
deep waters,
    but one who has insight draws them
out.

6 Many claim to have unfailing love,
    but a faithful person who can find?

7 The righteous lead blameless lives;
    blessed are their children after
them.

8 When a king sits on his throne to
judge,
    he winnows out all evil with his
eyes.

9 Who can say, "I have kept my heart
pure;
    I am clean and without sin"?

10 Differing weights and differing
measures—
    the Lord detests them both.

11 Even small children are known by their
actions,
    so is their conduct really pure and
upright?

12 Ears that hear and eyes that see—
    the Lord has made them both.

13 Do not love sleep or you will grow
poor;
    stay awake and you will have food
to spare.

14 "It's no good, it's no good!" says the
buyer—
    then goes off and boasts about the
purchase.

15 Gold there is, and rubies in
abundance,
    but lips that speak knowledge are a
rare jewel.

16 Take the garment of one who puts up
security for a stranger;
    hold it in pledge if it is done for an
outsider.

17 Food gained by fraud tastes sweet,
    but one ends up with a mouth full of
gravel.

18 Plans are established by seeking
advice;
    so if you wage war, obtain guidance.

19 A gossip betrays a
confidence;
    so avoid anyone who
talks too much.

20 If someone curses their
father or mother,
    their lamp will be snuffed
out in pitch darkness.

21 An inheritance claimed too soon
    will not be blessed at the end.

22 Do not say, "I'll pay you back for this
wrong!"
    Wait for the Lord, and he will avenge
you.

23 The Lord detests differing weights,
    and dishonest scales do not please
him.

24 A person's steps are directed by the
Lord.
    How then can anyone understand
their own way?

25 It is a trap to dedicate something
rashly
    and only later to consider one's
vows.

26 A wise king winnows out the wicked;
    he drives the threshing wheel over
them.

27 The human spirit is[a] the lamp of the
Lord
    that sheds light on one's inmost
being.

---

[a] 27 Or *A person's words are*

28 Love and faithfulness keep a king
  safe;
  through love his throne is made
  secure.

29 The glory of young men is their
  strength,
  gray hair the splendor of the old.

30 Blows and wounds scrub away evil,
  and beatings purge the inmost
  being.

21 In the Lord's hand the king's heart
  is a stream of water
  that he channels toward all who
  please him.

2 A person may think their own ways are
  right,
  but the Lord weighs the heart.

3 To do what is right and just
  is more acceptable to the Lord than
  sacrifice.

4 Haughty eyes and a proud heart—
  the unplowed field of the wicked—
  produce sin.

5 The plans of the diligent lead to profit
  as surely as haste leads to poverty.

6 A fortune made by a lying tongue
  is a fleeting vapor and a deadly
  snare.[a]

7 The violence of the wicked will drag
  them away,
  for they refuse to do what is right.

8 The way of the guilty is devious,
  but the conduct of the innocent is
  upright.

9 Better to live on a corner of the roof
  than share a house with a
  quarrelsome wife.

10 The wicked crave evil;
  their neighbors get no mercy from
  them.

11 When a mocker is punished, the
  simple gain wisdom;
  by paying attention to the wise they
  get knowledge.

12 The Righteous One[b] takes note of the
  house of the wicked

and brings the wicked to ruin.

13 Whoever shuts their ears to the cry of
  the poor
  will also cry out and not be
  answered.

14 A gift given in secret soothes anger,
  and a bribe concealed in the cloak
  pacifies great wrath.

15 When justice is done, it brings joy to
  the righteous
  but terror to evildoers.

16 Whoever strays from the path of
  prudence
  comes to rest in the company of the
  dead.

17 Whoever loves pleasure will become
  poor;
  whoever loves wine and olive oil will
  never be rich.

18 The wicked become a ransom for the
  righteous,
  and the unfaithful for the upright.

19 Better to live in a desert
  than with a quarrelsome and
  nagging wife.

20 The wise store up choice food and
  olive oil,
  but fools gulp theirs down.

21 Whoever pursues righteousness and
  love
  finds life, prosperity[c] and honor.

22 One who is wise can go up against the
  city of the mighty
  and pull down the stronghold in
  which they trust.

23 Those who guard their mouths and
  their tongues
  keep themselves from calamity.

24 The proud and arrogant person—
  "Mocker" is his name—
  behaves with insolent fury.

25 The craving of a sluggard will be the
  death of him,
  because his hands refuse to work.

---

a 6 Some Hebrew manuscripts, Septuagint and Vulgate;
most Hebrew manuscripts vapor for those who seek death
b 12 Or The righteous person   c 21 Or righteousness

26 All day long he craves for more,
    but the righteous give without
      sparing.

27 The sacrifice of the wicked is
      detestable—
    how much more so when brought
      with evil intent!

28 A false witness will perish,
    but a careful listener will testify
      successfully.

29 The wicked put up a bold front,
    but the upright give thought to their
      ways.

30 There is no wisdom, no insight, no
      plan
    that can succeed against the Lord.

31 The horse is made ready for the day of
      battle,
    but victory rests with the Lord.

22 A good name is more desirable
      than great riches;
    to be esteemed is better than silver
      or gold.

2 Rich and poor have this in common:
    The Lord is the Maker of them all.

3 The prudent see danger and take
      refuge,
    but the simple keep going and pay
      the penalty.

4 Humility is the fear of the Lord;
    its wages are riches and honor and
      life.

5 In the paths of the wicked are snares
      and pitfalls,
    but those who would preserve their
      life stay far from them.

6 Start children off on the way they
      should go,
    and even when they are old they will
      not turn from it.

7 The rich rule over the poor,
    and the borrower is slave to the
      lender.

8 Whoever sows injustice reaps
      calamity,
    and the rod they wield in fury will be
      broken.

9 The generous will themselves be
      blessed,
    for they share their food with the
      poor.

10 Drive out the mocker, and out goes
      strife;
    quarrels and insults are ended.

11 One who loves a pure heart and who
      speaks with grace
    will have the king for a friend.

12 The eyes of the Lord keep watch over
      knowledge,
    but he frustrates the words of the
      unfaithful.

13 The sluggard says, "There's a lion
      outside!
    I'll be killed in the public square!"

14 The mouth of an adulterous woman is
      a deep pit;
    a man who is under the Lord's
      wrath falls into it.

15 Folly is bound up in the heart of a
      child,
    but the rod of discipline will drive it
      far away.

16 One who oppresses the poor to
      increase his wealth
    and one who gives gifts to the
      rich—both come to poverty.

Thirty Sayings of the Wise

Saying 1

17 Pay attention and turn your ear to the
      sayings of the wise;
    apply your heart to what I teach,

18 for it is pleasing when you keep them
      in your heart
    and have all of them ready on your
      lips.

19 So that your trust may be in the Lord,
    I teach you today, even you.

20 Have I not written thirty sayings for
      you,
    sayings of counsel and knowledge,

21 teaching you to be honest and to
      speak the truth,
    so that you bring back truthful
      reports
    to those you serve?

BREAK THROUGH!

Is it okay with God to hit children?

(PROVERBS 22:15; 29:15)

These proverbs recommend correcting stubborn or misbehaving children. Don't forget that everything was harder then than it is now. "The rod of discipline" here refers to the reality that children sometimes need to be disciplined so they avoid making bad mistakes. Discipline does not necessarily mean being hit. In fact, parents who hit their children might be abusing them rather than disciplining them. We all need to be corrected in a loving way. This passage reminds us of that.

Saying 2

22 Do not exploit the poor because they
          are poor
      and do not crush the needy in court,
23 for the LORD will take up their case
      and will exact life for life.

Saying 3

24 Do not make friends with a hot-
          tempered person,
      do not associate with one easily
          angered,
25 or you may learn their ways
      and get yourself ensnared.

Saying 4

26 Do not be one who shakes hands in
          pledge
      or puts up security for debts;
27 if you lack the means to pay,
      your very bed will be snatched from
          under you.

Saying 5

28 Do not move an ancient boundary
          stone
      set up by your ancestors.

BREAK THROUGH!

What does this advice mean: "Do not move an ancient boundary stone set up by your ancestors"? Is it bad to buy more land and want to get ahead?

(PROVERBS 22:28; 23:10)

This advice doesn't mean it's bad to buy more land or get ahead in life. It means it's bad to want more and more and never be satisfied. People often want more land, and don't respect the border they have with their neighbor. Increasing one's land by taking away land from another person is stealing. And that's injustice! The proverb is saying a person should be satisfied with the land he has received from his family.

Saying 6

²⁹ Do you see someone skilled in their
work?
They will serve before kings;
they will not serve before officials of
low rank.

Saying 7

23 When you sit to dine with a ruler,
note well what[a] is before you,
² and put a knife to your throat
if you are given to gluttony.
³ Do not crave his delicacies,
for that food is deceptive.

Saying 8

⁴ Do not wear yourself out to get
rich;
do not trust your own cleverness.
⁵ Cast but a glance at riches, and they
are gone,
for they will surely sprout wings
and fly off to the sky like an
eagle.

Saying 9

⁶ Do not eat the food of a begrudging
host,
do not crave his delicacies;
⁷ for he is the kind of person
who is always thinking about the
cost.[b]
"Eat and drink," he says to you,
but his heart is not with you.
⁸ You will vomit up the little you have
eaten
and will have wasted your
compliments.

Saying 10

⁹ Do not speak to fools,
for they will scorn your prudent
words.

Saying 11

¹⁰ Do not move an ancient boundary
stone
or encroach on the fields of the
fatherless,
¹¹ for their Defender is strong;
he will take up their case against
you.

Saying 12

¹² Apply your heart to instruction
and your ears to words of
knowledge.

Saying 13

¹³ Do not withhold discipline from a
child;
if you punish them with the rod,
they will not die.
¹⁴ Punish them with the rod
and save them from death.

Saying 14

¹⁵ My son, if your heart is wise,
then my heart will be glad indeed;
¹⁶ my inmost being will rejoice
when your lips speak what is right.

Saying 15

¹⁷ Do not let your heart envy sinners,
but always be zealous for the fear
of the LORD.
¹⁸ There is surely a future hope for you,
and your hope will not be cut off.

Saying 16

¹⁹ Listen, my son, and be wise,
and set your heart on the right
path:
²⁰ Do not join those who drink too much
wine
or gorge themselves on meat,
²¹ for drunkards and gluttons become
poor,
and drowsiness clothes them in
rags.

Saying 17

²² Listen to your father, who gave you
life,
and do not despise your mother
when she is old.
²³ Buy the truth and do not sell it—
wisdom, instruction and insight as
well.
²⁴ The father of a righteous child has
great joy;
a man who fathers a wise son
rejoices in him.

---

[a] 1 Or who   [b] 7 Or for as he thinks within himself, / so
he is; or for as he puts on a feast, / so he is

25 May your father and mother rejoice;
     may she who gave you birth be
     joyful!

Saying 18

26 My son, give me your heart
     and let your eyes delight in my
     ways,
27 for an adulterous woman is a deep pit,
     and a wayward wife is a narrow well.
28 Like a bandit she lies in wait
     and multiplies the unfaithful among
     men.

Saying 19

29 Who has woe? Who has sorrow?
     Who has strife? Who has
     complaints?
     Who has needless bruises? Who
     has bloodshot eyes?
30 Those who linger over wine,
     who go to sample bowls of mixed
     wine.
31 Do not gaze at wine when it is red,
     when it sparkles in the cup,
     when it goes down smoothly!
32 In the end it bites like a snake
     and poisons like a viper.
33 Your eyes will see strange sights,
     and your mind will imagine
     confusing things.
34 You will be like one sleeping on the
     high seas,
     lying on top of the rigging.
35 "They hit me," you will say, "but I'm
     not hurt!
     They beat me, but I don't feel it!
     When will I wake up
     so I can find another drink?"

Saying 20

24 Do not envy the wicked,
     do not desire their company;
2 for their hearts plot violence,
     and their lips talk about making
     trouble.

Saying 21

3 By wisdom a house is built,
     and through understanding it is
     established;
4 through knowledge its rooms are filled
     with rare and beautiful treasures.

Saying 22

5 The wise prevail through great power,
     and those who have knowledge
     muster their strength.
6 Surely you need guidance to wage
     war,
     and victory is won through many
     advisers.

Saying 23

7 Wisdom is too high for fools;
     in the assembly at the gate they
     must not open their mouths.

Saying 24

8 Whoever plots evil
     will be known as a schemer.
9 The schemes of folly are sin,
     and people detest a mocker.

Saying 25

10 If you falter in a time of trouble,
     how small is your strength!
11 Rescue those being led away to
     death;
     hold back those staggering toward
     slaughter.
12 If you say, "But we knew nothing about
     this,"
     does not he who weighs the heart
     perceive it?
     Does not he who guards your life
     know it?
     Will he not repay everyone
     according to what they have
     done?

Saying 26

13 Eat honey, my son, for it is good;
     honey from the comb is sweet to
     your taste.
14 Know also that wisdom is like honey
     for you:
     If you find it, there is a future hope
     for you,
     and your hope will not be cut off.

Saying 27

15 Do not lurk like a thief near the house
     of the righteous,
     do not plunder their dwelling place;
16 for though the righteous fall seven
     times, they rise again,

but the wicked stumble when
calamity strikes.

Saying 28

17 Do not gloat when your enemy falls;
when they stumble, do not let your
heart rejoice,
18 or the LORD will see and disapprove
and turn his wrath away from
them.

Saying 29

19 Do not fret because of evildoers
or be envious of the wicked,
20 for the evildoer has no future hope,
and the lamp of the wicked will be
snuffed out.

Saying 30

21 Fear the LORD and the king, my son,
and do not join with rebellious
officials,
22 for those two will send sudden
destruction on them,
and who knows what calamities
they can bring?

Further Sayings of the Wise

23 These also are sayings of the wise:

To show partiality in judging is not
good:
24 Whoever says to the guilty, "You are
innocent,"
will be cursed by peoples and
denounced by nations.
25 But it will go well with those who
convict the guilty,
and rich blessing will come on
them.

26 An honest answer
is like a kiss on the lips.

27 Put your outdoor work in order
and get your fields ready;
after that, build your house.

28 Do not testify against your neighbor
without cause—
would you use your lips to mislead?
29 Do not say, "I'll do to them as they
have done to me;
I'll pay them back for what they did."

30 I went past the field of a sluggard,
past the vineyard of someone who
has no sense;
31 thorns had come up everywhere,
the ground was covered with
weeds,
and the stone wall was in ruins.
32 I applied my heart to what I observed
and learned a lesson from what I
saw:
33 A little sleep, a little slumber,
a little folding of the hands to
rest—
34 and poverty will come on you like a
thief
and scarcity like an armed man.

More Proverbs of Solomon

25 These are more proverbs of Solomon, compiled by the men of Hezekiah king of Judah:

2 It is the glory of God to conceal a
matter;
to search out a matter is the glory
of kings.
3 As the heavens are high and the earth
is deep,
so the hearts of kings are
unsearchable.

4 Remove the dross from the silver,
and a silversmith can produce a
vessel;
5 remove wicked officials from the king's
presence,
and his throne will be established
through righteousness.

6 Do not exalt yourself in the king's
presence,
and do not claim a place among his
great men;
7 it is better for him to say to you,
"Come up here,"
than for him to humiliate you before
his nobles.

What you have seen with your eyes
8 do not bring[a] hastily to court,
for what will you do in the end
if your neighbor puts you to shame?

---

[a] *7,8 Or nobles / on whom you had set your eyes. /* [8]*Do
not go*

is a trustworthy messenger to the
one who sends him;
he refreshes the spirit of his
master.
14 Like clouds and wind without rain
is one who boasts of gifts never
given.
15 Through patience a ruler can be
persuaded,
and a gentle tongue can break a
bone.

a 11 Or possibly *apricots*

THE
WITNESSES

✓ **HEZEKIAH, KING OF JUDAH**
(PROVERBS 25:1)
This name means "the LORD is my strength."
Hezekiah ruled over Judah in the years 721 to
693 before Christ.

9 If you take your neighbor to court,
do not betray another's confidence,
10 or the one who hears it may shame
you
and the charge against you will
stand.
11 Like apples a of gold in settings of
silver
is a ruling rightly given.
12 Like an earring of gold or an ornament
of fine gold
is the rebuke of a wise judge to a
listening ear.
13 Like a snow-cooled drink at harvest
time

BREAKTHROUGH!

**What does this mean: "What
you have seen with your
eyes do not bring hastily to
court, for what will you do
in the end if your neighbor
puts you to shame?" What if
we see something that's not
right? Shouldn't we always
defend just causes?**

(PROVERBS 25:7‑8)
The proverb is recommending that we be
wise. It's good to defend just causes, but it's
also good to wait to be called as a witness. It
is one thing to be a witness. It's another thing
to be a gossip.

16 If you find honey, eat just enough—
     too much of it, and you will vomit.
17 Seldom set foot in your neighbor's
        house—
     too much of you, and they will hate
        you.
18 Like a club or a sword or a sharp
        arrow
     is one who gives false testimony
        against a neighbor.
19 Like a broken tooth or a lame foot
     is reliance on the unfaithful in a
        time of trouble.
20 Like one who takes away a garment
        on a cold day,
     or like vinegar poured on a wound,
     is one who sings songs to a heavy
        heart.
21 If your enemy is hungry, give him food
        to eat;
     if he is thirsty, give him water to
        drink.
22 In doing this, you will heap burning
        coals on his head,
     and the Lord will reward you.
23 Like a north wind that brings
        unexpected rain
     is a sly tongue—which provokes a
        horrified look.
24 Better to live on a corner of the roof
     than share a house with a
        quarrelsome wife.
25 Like cold water to a weary soul
     is good news from a distant land.
26 Like a muddied spring or a polluted
        well
     are the righteous who give way to
        the wicked.
27 It is not good to eat too much honey,
     nor is it honorable to search out
        matters that are too deep.
28 Like a city whose walls are broken
        through
     is a person who lacks self-control.

26 Like snow in summer or rain in
        harvest,
     honor is not fitting for a fool.
2 Like a fluttering sparrow or a darting
        swallow,

     an undeserved curse does not
        come to rest.
3 A whip for the horse, a bridle for the
        donkey,
     and a rod for the backs of fools!
4 Do not answer a fool according to his
        folly,
     or you yourself will be just like him.
5 Answer a fool according to his folly,
     or he will be wise in his own eyes.
6 Sending a message by the hands of a
        fool
     is like cutting off one's feet or
        drinking poison.
7 Like the useless legs of one who is
        lame
     is a proverb in the mouth of a fool.
8 Like tying a stone in a sling
     is the giving of honor to a fool.
9 Like a thornbush in a drunkard's
        hand
     is a proverb in the mouth of a fool.
10 Like an archer who wounds at
        random
     is one who hires a fool or any
        passer-by.
11 As a dog returns to its vomit,
     so fools repeat their folly.
12 Do you see a person wise in their own
        eyes?
     There is more hope for a fool than
        for them.
13 A sluggard says, "There's a lion in the
        road,
     a fierce lion roaming the streets!"
14 As a door turns on its hinges,
     so a sluggard turns on his bed.
15 A sluggard buries his hand in the dish;
     he is too lazy to bring it back to his
        mouth.
16 A sluggard is wiser in his own eyes
     than seven people who answer
        discreetly.
17 Like one who grabs a stray dog by the
        ears
     is someone who rushes into a
        quarrel not their own.
18 Like a maniac shooting
     flaming arrows of death
19 is one who deceives their neighbor
     and says, "I was only joking!"

20 Without wood a fire goes out;
    without a gossip a quarrel dies
        down.
21 As charcoal to embers and as wood to
        fire,
    so is a quarrelsome person for
        kindling strife.
22 The words of a gossip are like choice
        morsels;
    they go down to the inmost parts.

23 Like a coating of silver dross on
        earthenware
    are fervent[a] lips with an evil heart.
24 Enemies disguise themselves with
        their lips,
    but in their hearts they harbor
        deceit.
25 Though their speech is charming, do
        not believe them,
    for seven abominations fill their
        hearts.
26 Their malice may be concealed by
        deception,
    but their wickedness will be
        exposed in the assembly.
27 Whoever digs a pit will fall into it;
    if someone rolls a stone, it will roll
        back on them.
28 A lying tongue hates those it hurts,
    and a flattering mouth works ruin.

27 Do not boast about tomorrow,
    for you do not know what a day
        may bring.

2 Let someone else praise you, and not
        your own mouth;
    an outsider, and not your own lips.

3 Stone is heavy and sand a burden,
    but a fool's provocation is heavier
        than both.

4 Anger is cruel and fury overwhelming,
    but who can stand before jealousy?

5 Better is open rebuke
    than hidden love.

6 Wounds from a friend can be trusted,
    but an enemy multiplies kisses.

7 One who is full loathes honey from the
        comb,
    but to the hungry even what is bitter
        tastes sweet.

8 Like a bird that flees its nest
    is anyone who flees from home.

9 Perfume and incense bring joy to the
        heart,
    and the pleasantness of a friend
        springs from their heartfelt advice.

10 Do not forsake your friend or a friend
        of your family,
    and do not go to your relative's
        house when disaster strikes
        you—
    better a neighbor nearby than a
        relative far away.

11 Be wise, my son, and bring joy to my
        heart;
    then I can answer anyone who
        treats me with contempt.

12 The prudent see danger and take
        refuge,
    but the simple keep going and pay
        the penalty.

13 Take the garment of one who puts up
        security for a stranger;
    hold it in pledge if it is done for an
        outsider.

14 If anyone loudly blesses their neighbor
        early in the morning,
    it will be taken as a curse.

15 A quarrelsome wife is like the
        dripping
    of a leaky roof in a rainstorm;
16 restraining her is like restraining the
        wind
    or grasping oil with the hand.

17 As iron sharpens iron,
    so one person sharpens another.

18 The one who guards a fig tree will eat
        its fruit,
    and whoever protects their master
        will be honored.

19 As water reflects the face,
    so one's life reflects the heart.[b]

20 Death and Destruction[c] are never
        satisfied,
    and neither are human eyes.

---

[a] 23 Hebrew; Septuagint *smooth*   [b] 19 Or *so others
reflect your heart back to you*   [c] 20 Hebrew *Abaddon*

²¹ The crucible for silver and the furnace
for gold,
but people are tested by their
praise.
²² Though you grind a fool in a mortar,
grinding them like grain with a
pestle,
you will not remove their folly from
them.
²³ Be sure you know the condition of
your flocks,
give careful attention to your herds;
²⁴ for riches do not endure forever,
and a crown is not secure for all
generations.
²⁵ When the hay is removed and new
growth appears
and the grass from the hills is
gathered in,
²⁶ the lambs will provide you with
clothing,
and the goats with the price of a
field.
²⁷ You will have plenty of goats' milk to
feed your family
and to nourish your female
servants.

28 The wicked flee though no one
pursues,
but the righteous are as bold as a
lion.
² When a country is rebellious, it has
many rulers,
but a ruler with discernment and
knowledge maintains order.
³ A ruler*ᵃ* who oppresses the poor
is like a driving rain that leaves no
crops.
⁴ Those who forsake instruction praise
the wicked,
but those who heed it resist them.
⁵ Evildoers do not understand what is
right,
but those who seek the Lᴏʀᴅ
understand it fully.
⁶ Better the poor whose walk is
blameless
than the rich whose ways are
perverse.

⁷ A discerning son heeds instruction,
but a companion of gluttons
disgraces his father.
⁸ Whoever increases wealth by taking
interest or profit from the
poor
amasses it for another, who will be
kind to the poor.
⁹ If anyone turns a deaf ear to my
instruction,
even their prayers are detestable.
¹⁰ Whoever leads the upright along an
evil path
will fall into their own trap,
but the blameless will receive a
good inheritance.
¹¹ The rich are wise in their own eyes;
one who is poor and discerning
sees how deluded they are.
¹² When the righteous triumph, there is
great elation;
but when the wicked rise to power,
people go into hiding.
¹³ Whoever conceals their sins does not
prosper,
but the one who confesses and
renounces them finds mercy.
¹⁴ Blessed is the one who
always trembles
before God,
but whoever hardens their
heart falls into trouble.

¹⁵ Like a roaring lion or a charging bear
is a wicked ruler over a helpless
people.
¹⁶ A tyrannical ruler practices extortion,
but one who hates ill-gotten gain
will enjoy a long reign.
¹⁷ Anyone tormented by the guilt of
murder
will seek refuge in the grave;
let no one hold them back.
¹⁸ The one whose walk is blameless is
kept safe,
but the one whose ways are
perverse will fall into the pit.*ᵇ*

ᵃ 3 Or *A poor person*   *ᵇ 18* Syriac (see Septuagint);
Hebrew *into one*

19 Those who work their land will have
abundant food,
but those who chase fantasies will
have their fill of poverty.

20 A faithful person will be richly blessed,
but one eager to get rich will not go
unpunished.

21 To show partiality is not good—
yet a person will do wrong for a
piece of bread.

22 The stingy are eager to get rich
and are unaware that poverty awaits
them.

23 Whoever rebukes a person will in the
end gain favor
rather than one who has a flattering
tongue.

24 Whoever robs their father or mother
and says, "It's not wrong,"
is partner to one who destroys.

25 The greedy stir up conflict,
but those who trust in the Lord will
prosper.

26 Those who trust in themselves are
fools,
but those who walk in wisdom are
kept safe.

27 Those who give to the poor will lack
nothing,
but those who close their eyes to
them receive many curses.

28 When the wicked rise to power, people
go into hiding;
but when the wicked perish, the
righteous thrive.

29 Whoever remains stiff-necked after
many rebukes
will suddenly be destroyed—
without remedy.

2 When the righteous thrive, the people
rejoice;
when the wicked rule, the people
groan.

3 A man who loves wisdom brings joy to
his father,
but a companion of prostitutes
squanders his wealth.

4 By justice a king gives a country
stability,
but those who are greedy for[a]
bribes tear it down.

5 Those who flatter their neighbors
are spreading nets for their feet.

6 Evildoers are snared by their own sin,
but the righteous shout for joy and
are glad.

7 The righteous care about justice for
the poor,
but the wicked have no such
concern.

8 Mockers stir up a city,
but the wise turn away anger.

9 If a wise person goes to court with a
fool,
the fool rages and scoffs, and there
is no peace.

10 The bloodthirsty hate a person of
integrity
and seek to kill the upright.

11 Fools give full vent to their rage,
but the wise bring calm in the end.

12 If a ruler listens to lies,
all his officials become wicked.

13 The poor and the oppressor have this
in common:
The Lord gives sight to the eyes of
both.

14 If a king judges the poor with fairness,
his throne will be established
forever.

15 A rod and a reprimand impart wisdom,
but a child left undisciplined
disgraces its mother.

16 When the wicked thrive, so does
sin,
but the righteous will see their
downfall.

17 Discipline your children, and they will
give you peace;
they will bring you the delights you
desire.

18 Where there is no revelation, people
cast off restraint;

---

a 4 Or who give

but blessed is the one who heeds
    wisdom's instruction.
¹⁹ Servants cannot be corrected by mere
    words;
  though they understand, they will
    not respond.

²⁰ Do you see someone who speaks in
    haste?
  There is more hope for a fool than
    for them.

²¹ A servant pampered from youth
  will turn out to be insolent.

²² An angry person stirs up conflict,
  and a hot-tempered person commits
    many sins.

²³ Pride brings a person low,
  but the lowly in spirit gain honor.

²⁴ The accomplices of thieves are their
    own enemies;
  they are put under oath and dare
    not testify.

²⁵ Fear of man will prove to be a snare,
  but whoever trusts in the Lᴏʀᴅ is
    kept safe.

²⁶ Many seek an audience with a ruler,
  but it is from the Lᴏʀᴅ that one gets
    justice.

²⁷ The righteous detest the dishonest;
  the wicked detest the upright.

Sayings of Agur

30 The sayings of Agur son of Jakeh—
    an inspired utterance.

This man's utterance to Ithiel:

"I am weary, God,
  but I can prevail.ᵃ
² Surely I am only a brute, not a man;
  I do not have human understanding.
³ I have not learned wisdom,
  nor have I attained to the
    knowledge of the Holy One.
⁴ Who has gone up to heaven and come
    down?
  Whose hands have gathered up the
    wind?
  Who has wrapped up the waters in a
    cloak?

THE
WITNESSES

✓ **AGUR** (PROVERBS 30:1)
This man contributed a small group of proverbs
that appear in chapter 30. His name means
"hired worker."

Who has established all the ends of
    the earth?
What is his name, and what is the
    name of his son?
  Surely you know!

⁵ "Every word of God is flawless;
  he is a shield to those who take
    refuge in him.
⁶ Do not add to his words,
  or he will rebuke you and prove you
    a liar.

⁷ "Two things I ask of you, Lᴏʀᴅ;
  do not refuse me before I die:

ᵃ 1 With a different word division of the Hebrew; Masoretic
Text *utterance to Ithiel, / to Ithiel and Ukal:*

⁸Keep falsehood and lies far from me;
  give me neither poverty nor riches,
  but give me only my daily bread.
⁹Otherwise, I may have too much and
    disown you
  and say, 'Who is the Lᴏʀᴅ?'
Or I may become poor and steal,
  and so dishonor the name of my
    God.

¹⁰"Do not slander a servant to their
    master,
  or they will curse you, and you will
    pay for it.

¹¹"There are those who curse their
    fathers
  and do not bless their mothers;
¹²those who are pure in their own eyes
  and yet are not cleansed of their
    filth;
¹³those whose eyes are ever so
    haughty,
  whose glances are so disdainful;
¹⁴those whose teeth are swords
  and whose jaws are set with knives
to devour the poor from the earth
  and the needy from among
    mankind.

¹⁵"The leech has two daughters.
  'Give! Give!' they cry.

"There are three things that are never
    satisfied,
  four that never say, 'Enough!':
¹⁶the grave, the barren womb,
  land, which is never satisfied with
    water,
  and fire, which never says,
    'Enough!'

¹⁷"The eye that mocks a father,
  that scorns an aged mother,
will be pecked out by the ravens of the
    valley,
  will be eaten by the vultures.

¹⁸"There are three things that are too
    amazing for me,
  four that I do not understand:
¹⁹the way of an eagle in the sky,
  the way of a snake on a rock,
the way of a ship on the high seas,
  and the way of a man with a young
    woman.

²⁰"This is the way of an adulterous
    woman:
  She eats and wipes her mouth
  and says, 'I've done nothing wrong.'

²¹"Under three things the earth
    trembles,
  under four it cannot bear up:
²²a servant who becomes king,
  a godless fool who gets plenty to
    eat,
²³a contemptible woman who gets
    married,
  and a servant who displaces her
    mistress.

²⁴"Four things on earth are small,
  yet they are extremely wise:
²⁵Ants are creatures of little strength,
  yet they store up their food in the
    summer;
²⁶hyraxes are creatures of little power,
  yet they make their home in the
    crags;
²⁷locusts have no king,
  yet they advance together in ranks;

BREAK THROUGH!

Hyraxes
(PROVERBS 30:26)
Small animals sort of like rabbits 20–28
inches (50–70 cm) long. They live in the holes
they dig. They eat everything, but they're not
dangerous.

28 a lizard can be caught with the hand,
   yet it is found in kings' palaces.

29 "There are three things that are
      stately in their stride,
   four that move with stately bearing:
30 a lion, mighty among beasts,
   who retreats before nothing;
31 a strutting rooster, a he-goat,
   and a king secure against revolt.[a]

32 "If you play the fool and exalt yourself,
   or if you plan evil,
   clap your hand over your mouth!
33 For as churning cream produces
      butter,
   and as twisting the nose produces
      blood,
   so stirring up anger produces strife."

Sayings of King Lemuel

31 The sayings of King Lemuel—an in-
      spired utterance his mother taught
him.

2 Listen, my son! Listen, son of my
      womb!
   Listen, my son, the answer to my
      prayers!
3 Do not spend your strength[b] on
      women,
   your vigor on those who ruin kings.

4 It is not for kings, Lemuel—
   it is not for kings to drink wine,
   not for rulers to crave beer,
5 lest they drink and forget what has
      been decreed,
   and deprive all the oppressed of
      their rights.
6 Let beer be for those who are
      perishing,
   wine for those who are in anguish!
7 Let them drink and forget their
      poverty
   and remember their misery no
      more.

8 Speak up for those who cannot speak
      for themselves,
   for the rights of all who are destitute.
9 Speak up and judge fairly;
   defend the rights of the poor and
      needy.

Epilogue: The Wife of Noble Character

10 [c] A wife of noble character who can
      find?
   She is worth far more than rubies.
11 Her husband has full confidence in her
      and lacks nothing of value.
12 She brings him good, not harm,
      all the days of her life.
13 She selects wool and flax
      and works with eager hands.

---

[a] 31 The meaning of the Hebrew for this phrase is
uncertain.   [b] 3 Or wealth   [c] 10 Verses 10-31 are an
acrostic poem, the verses of which begin with the
successive letters of the Hebrew alphabet.

WITNESSES

✓ **KING LEMUEL** (PROVERBS 31)
The name of this king means "dedicated to
God." We don't know very much about him. It's
interesting that although he was a king, it was
his mother who taught him.

14 She is like the merchant ships,
　bringing her food from afar.
15 She gets up while it is still night;
　she provides food for her family
　and portions for her female
　　servants.
16 She considers a field and buys it;
　out of her earnings she plants a
　　vineyard.
17 She sets about her work vigorously;
　her arms are strong for her tasks.
18 She sees that her trading is profitable,
　and her lamp does not go out at
　　night.
19 In her hand she holds the distaff
　and grasps the spindle with her
　　fingers.
20 She opens her arms to the poor
　and extends her hands to the needy.
21 When it snows, she has no fear for
　　her household;
　for all of them are clothed in scarlet.
22 She makes coverings for her bed;
　she is clothed in fine linen and
　　purple.
23 Her husband is respected at the city
　　gate,
　where he takes his seat among the
　　elders of the land.

24 She makes linen garments and sells
　　them,
　and supplies the merchants with
　　sashes.
25 She is clothed with strength and
　　dignity;
　she can laugh at the days to
　　come.
26 She speaks with wisdom,
　and faithful instruction is on her
　　tongue.
27 She watches over the affairs of her
　　household
　and does not eat the bread of
　　idleness.
28 Her children arise and call her
　　blessed;
　her husband also, and he praises
　　her:
29 "Many women do noble things,
　but you surpass them all."
30 Charm is deceptive, and beauty is
　　fleeting;
　but a woman who fears the LORD is
　　to be praised.
31 Honor her for all that her hands have
　　done,
　and let her works bring her praise
　　at the city gate.

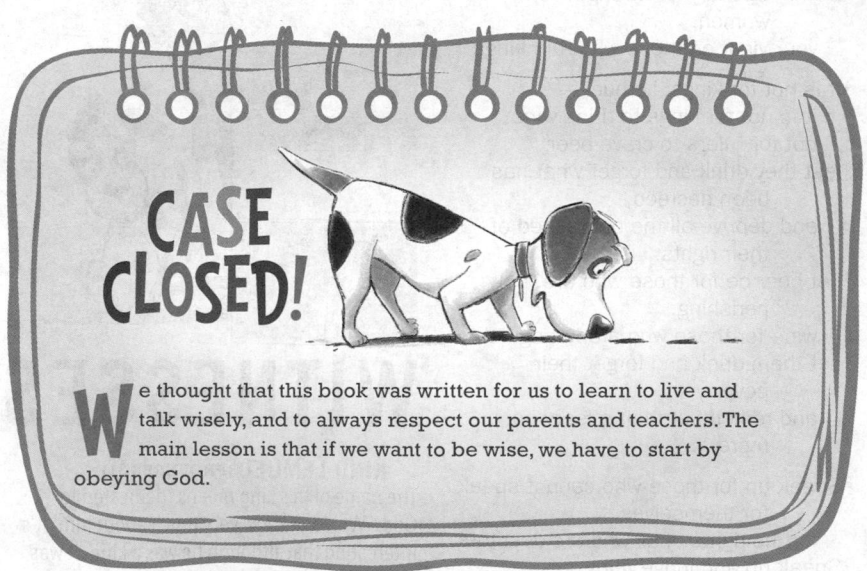

CASE CLOSED!

We thought that this book was written for us to learn to live and talk wisely, and to always respect our parents and teachers. The main lesson is that if we want to be wise, we have to start by obeying God.

ECCLESIASTES

THE EVIDENCE:

Now we're going to read a very interesting book—Ecclesiastes! And you're going to ask what's so interesting about it? Well, it's a book that has a lot to do with us.

WHO WROTE IT?

The author's name isn't in the book, but at the start it says "the words of the Teacher, son of David, king in Jerusalem." So it would seem that the author was King Solomon.

HOW LONG AGO?

If the author was King Solomon, then this book is almost 3,000 years old!

WHAT'S IT ABOUT?

The author complains about there being so much injustice in this life. He thinks it isn't fair that things go well for bad people and badly for good people. That's really unfair! We've always been taught that if we're good, good things will happen to us, and if we're bad, then bad things will happen. But in real life, that's not always true.

THE BEST PART

We think the best part is, well ... the whole book! Everything in this book is important, but the very most important lesson for us as kids is this: "Remember your Creator in the days of your youth ..." (12:1).

Everything Is Meaningless

1 The words of the Teacher,[a] son of David, king in Jerusalem:

2 "Meaningless! Meaningless!"
    says the Teacher.
  "Utterly meaningless!
    Everything is meaningless."

3 What do people gain from all their
      labors
    at which they toil under the sun?
4 Generations come and generations go,
    but the earth remains forever.
5 The sun rises and the sun sets,
    and hurries back to where it rises.
6 The wind blows to the south
      and turns to the north;
  round and round it goes,
      ever returning on its course.
7 All streams flow into the sea,
    yet the sea is never full.
  To the place the streams
      come from,
    there they return again.
8 All things are wearisome,
    more than one can say.
  The eye never has enough of
      seeing,
    nor the ear its fill of hearing.

---

[a] 1 Or the leader of the assembly; also in verses 2 and 12

⁹What has been will be again,
   what has been done will be done
      again;
   there is nothing new under the
      sun.
¹⁰Is there anything of which one can
      say,
   "Look! This is something new"?
   It was here already, long ago;
      it was here before our time.
¹¹No one remembers the former
      generations,
   and even those yet to come
   will not be remembered
      by those who follow them.

Wisdom Is Meaningless

¹²I, the Teacher, was king over Israel in Jerusalem. ¹³I applied my mind to study and to explore by wisdom all that is done under the heavens. What a heavy burden God has laid on mankind! ¹⁴I have seen all the things that are done under the sun; all of them are meaningless, a chasing after the wind.

Who is the Teacher?
(ECCLESIASTES 1:1-2)
The author doesn't give us his name on purpose. This word in Hebrew means "community of believers," and this writing is for the believers.

Doesn't anything make sense?
(ECCLESIASTES 1:1-2)
The author was writing in Hebrew. He refers to everything that happens in life when he says "utterly meaningless." He means that everything in life is kind of empty, and that's why it's "meaningless."

¹⁵What is crooked cannot be
      straightened;
   what is lacking cannot be counted.

¹⁶I said to myself, "Look, I have increased in wisdom more than anyone who has ruled over Jerusalem before me; I have experienced much of wisdom and knowledge." ¹⁷Then I applied myself to the understanding of wisdom, and also of madness and folly, but I learned that this, too, is a chasing after the wind.

¹⁸For with much wisdom comes much
      sorrow;
   the more knowledge, the more grief.

Pleasures Are Meaningless

2 I said to myself, "Come now, I will test you with pleasure to find out what is good." But that also proved to be meaningless. ²"Laughter," I said, "is madness. And what does pleasure accomplish?" ³I tried cheering myself with wine, and

BREAK THROUGH!

Why are things wearisome?

(ECCLESIASTES 1:8)

Because it's the same thing over and over, and nothing that happens is new. Everything repeats so much, it's boring.

embracing folly—my mind still guiding me with wisdom. I wanted to see what was good for people to do under the heavens during the few days of their lives. ⁴I undertook great projects: I built houses for myself and planted vineyards. ⁵I made gardens and parks and planted all kinds of fruit trees in them. ⁶I made reservoirs to water groves of flourishing trees. ⁷I bought male and female slaves and had other slaves who were born in my house. I also owned more herds and flocks than anyone in Jerusalem before me. ⁸I amassed silver and gold for myself, and the treasure of kings and provinces. I acquired male and female singers, and a harem*a* as well—the delights of a man's heart. ⁹I became greater by far than anyone in Jerusalem before me. In all this my wisdom stayed with me.

¹⁰I denied myself nothing my eyes
    desired;
    I refused my heart no pleasure.
My heart took delight in all my labor,
    and this was the reward for all my
    toil.

¹¹Yet when I surveyed all that my hands
    had done
and what I had toiled to achieve,
everything was meaningless, a
    chasing after the wind;
nothing was gained under the
    sun.

Wisdom and Folly Are Meaningless

¹²Then I turned my thoughts to consider
    wisdom,
and also madness and folly.
What more can the king's successor
    do
    than what has already been
    done?

---

a 8 The meaning of the Hebrew for this phrase is uncertain.

BREAK THROUGH!

The more knowledge, the more grief?

(ECCLESIASTES 1:18)

The author was a very wise person. He knew so much that he realized that knowing a lot involves a lot of responsibility. People who don't know much don't understand the problems there are in life, so they don't worry about them. But people who understand are concerned about their problems and the problems other people have. That can make them suffer a lot.

BREAK THROUGH!

Pleasures

(ECCLESIASTES 2:1)

Many people think that they should enjoy life. They spend a bunch of time eating a lot, drinking a lot, having fun, spending money, buying jewelry and houses and cars. The Teacher also tried that. Then he finally realized that's not what really gives us true "pleasure."

---

13 I saw that wisdom is better than
　　folly,
　　　just as light is better than
　　　　darkness.
14 The wise have eyes in their heads,
　　while the fool walks in the
　　　darkness;
　　but I came to realize
　　　that the same fate overtakes them
　　　　both.

15 Then I said to myself,

"The fate of the fool will overtake me
　　also.
　　What then do I gain by being wise?"
I said to myself,
　　"This too is meaningless."
16 For the wise, like the fool, will not be
　　long remembered;
　　the days have already come when
　　　both have been forgotten.
Like the fool, the wise too must die!

Toil Is Meaningless

17 So I hated life, because the work that is done under the sun was grievous to me. All of it is meaningless, a chasing after the wind. 18 I hated all the things I had toiled for under the sun, because I must leave them to the one who comes after me. 19 And who knows whether that person will be wise or foolish? Yet they will have control over all the fruit of my toil into which I have poured my effort and skill under the sun. This too is meaningless. 20 So my heart began to despair over all my toilsome labor under the sun. 21 For a person may labor with wisdom, knowledge and skill, and then they must leave all they own to another who has not toiled for it. This too is meaningless and a great misfortune. 22 What do people get for all the toil and anxious striving with which they labor under the sun? 23 All their days their work is grief and pain; even at night their minds do not rest. This too is meaningless.

24 A person can do nothing better than to eat and drink and find satisfaction in their own toil. This too, I see, is from the hand of God, 25 for without him, who can eat or find enjoyment? 26 To the person who pleases him, God gives wisdom, knowledge and happiness, but to the sinner he gives the task of gathering and storing up wealth to hand it over to the one who pleases God. This too is meaningless, a chasing after the wind.

A Time for Everything

3 There is a time for everything,
　　and a season for every activity
　　　under the heavens:

2 　　a time to be born and a time to die,
　　a time to plant and a time to uproot,
3 　　a time to kill and a time to heal,
　　a time to tear down and a time to
　　　build,
4 　　a time to weep and a time to laugh,
　　a time to mourn and a time to
　　　dance,
5 　　a time to scatter stones and a time
　　　to gather them,
　　a time to embrace and a time to
　　　refrain from embracing,

⁶ a time to search and a time to give
up,
a time to keep and a time to throw
away,
⁷ a time to tear and a time to mend,
a time to be silent and a time to
speak,
⁸ a time to love and a time to hate,
a time for war and a time for
peace.

⁹What do workers gain from their toil? ¹⁰I have seen the burden God has laid on the human race. ¹¹He has made everything beautiful in its time. He has also set eternity in the human heart; yet[a] no one can fathom what God has done from beginning to end. ¹²I know that there is nothing better for people than to be happy and to do good while they live. ¹³That each of them may eat and drink, and find satisfaction in all their toil—this is the gift of God. ¹⁴I know that everything God does will endure forever; nothing can be added to it and nothing taken from it. God does it so that people will fear him.

¹⁵Whatever is has already been,
and what will be has been before;
and God will call the past to
account.[b]

¹⁶And I saw something else under the sun:

In the place of judgment—wickedness
was there,
in the place of justice—wickedness
was there.

¹⁷I said to myself,

"God will bring into judgment
both the righteous and the wicked,
for there will be a time for every
activity,
a time to judge every deed."

¹⁸I also said to myself, "As for humans, God tests them so that they may see that they are like the animals. ¹⁹Surely the fate of human beings is like that of the animals; the same fate awaits them both: As one dies, so dies the other. All have the same breath[c]; humans have no advantage over animals. Everything is meaningless. ²⁰All go to the same place; all come from dust, and to dust all return. ²¹Who knows if the human spirit rises upward and if the spirit of the animal goes down into the earth?"

²²So I saw that there is nothing better for a person than to enjoy their work, because that is their lot. For who can bring them to see what will happen after them?

Oppression, Toil, Friendlessness

4 Again I looked and saw all the oppression that was taking place under the sun:

I saw the tears of the oppressed—
and they have no comforter;
power was on the side of their
oppressors—
and they have no comforter.
² And I declared that the dead,
who had already died,
are happier than the living,
who are still alive.
³ But better than both
is the one who has never been
born,
who has not seen the evil
that is done under the sun.

⁴And I saw that all toil and all achievement spring from one person's envy of another. This too is meaningless, a chasing after the wind.

⁵ Fools fold their hands
and ruin themselves.
⁶ Better one handful with tranquillity
than two handfuls with toil
and chasing after the wind.

⁷Again I saw something meaningless under the sun:

⁸ There was a man all alone;
he had neither son nor brother.
There was no end to his toil,
yet his eyes were not content with
his wealth.
"For whom am I toiling," he asked,
"and why am I depriving myself of
enjoyment?"
This too is meaningless—
a miserable business!

---

^a 11 Or also placed ignorance in the human heart, so that
^b 15 Or God calls back the past   ^c 19 Or spirit

⁹ Two are better than one,
    because they have a good return for
        their labor:
¹⁰ If either of them falls down,
    one can help the other up.
But pity anyone who falls
    and has no one to help them up.
¹¹ Also, if two lie down together, they will
        keep warm.
But how can one keep warm alone?
¹² Though one may be overpowered,
    two can defend themselves.
A cord of three strands is not quickly
    broken.

Advancement Is Meaningless

¹³ Better a poor but wise youth than an old but foolish king who no longer knows how to heed a warning. ¹⁴ The youth may have come from prison to the kingship, or he may have been born in poverty within his kingdom. ¹⁵ I saw that all who lived and walked under the sun followed the youth, the king's successor. ¹⁶ There was no end to all the people who were before them. But those who came later were not pleased with the successor. This too is meaningless, a chasing after the wind.

Fulfill Your Vow to God

5 ᵃ Guard your steps when you go to the house of God. Go near to listen rather than to offer the sacrifice of fools, who do not know that they do wrong.

² Do not be quick with your mouth,
    do not be hasty in your heart
    to utter anything before God.
God is in heaven
    and you are on earth,
    so let your words be few.
³ A dream comes when there are many
        cares,
    and many words mark the speech
        of a fool.

⁴ When you make a vow to God, do not delay to fulfill it. He has no pleasure in fools; fulfill your vow. ⁵ It is better not to make a vow than to make one and not fulfill it. ⁶ Do not let your mouth lead you into sin. And do not protest to the temple messenger, "My vow was a mistake." Why should God be angry at what you say and destroy the work of your hands? ⁷ Much dreaming and many words are meaningless. Therefore fear God.

Riches Are Meaningless

⁸ If you see the poor oppressed in a district, and justice and rights denied, do not be surprised at such things; for one official is eyed by a higher one, and over them both are others higher still. ⁹ The increase from the land is taken by all; the king himself profits from the fields.

¹⁰ Whoever loves money never has
        enough;
    whoever loves wealth is never
        satisfied with their income.
This too is meaningless.

¹¹ As goods increase,
    so do those who consume them.
And what benefit are they to the owners
    except to feast their eyes on them?

¹² The sleep of a laborer is sweet,
    whether they eat little or much,
but as for the rich, their abundance
    permits them no sleep.

¹³ I have seen a grievous evil under the sun:

wealth hoarded to the harm of its
        owners,
¹⁴   or wealth lost through some
        misfortune,
so that when they have children
    there is nothing left for them to
        inherit.
¹⁵ Everyone comes naked from their
        mother's womb,
    and as everyone comes, so they
        depart.
They take nothing from their toil
    that they can carry in their hands.

¹⁶ This too is a grievous evil:

As everyone comes, so they depart,
    and what do they gain,
    since they toil for the wind?
¹⁷ All their days they eat in darkness,
    with great frustration, affliction and
        anger.

ᵃ In Hebrew texts 5:1 is numbered 4:17, and 5:2-20 is numbered 5:1-19.

perity and does not receive proper burial, I say that a stillborn child is better off than he. ⁴It comes without meaning, it departs in darkness, and in darkness its name is shrouded. ⁵Though it never saw the sun or knew anything, it has more rest than does that man— ⁶even if he lives a thousand years twice over but fails to enjoy his prosperity. Do not all go to the same place?

⁷Everyone's toil is for their mouth,
　　yet their appetite is never
　　　satisfied.
⁸What advantage have the wise over
　　fools?
What do the poor gain
　　by knowing how to conduct
　　　themselves before others?
⁹Better what the eye sees
　　than the roving of the appetite.
This too is meaningless,
　　a chasing after the wind.

¹⁰Whatever exists has already been
　　named,
　　and what humanity is has been
　　　known;
no one can contend
　　with someone who is stronger.
¹¹The more the words,
　　the less the meaning,
　　and how does that profit anyone?

¹²For who knows what is good for a person in life, during the few and meaningless days they pass through like a shadow? Who can tell them what will happen under the sun after they are gone?

Wisdom

7 A good name is better than fine
　　perfume,
　　and the day of death better than the
　　　day of birth.
²It is better to go to a house of
　　mourning
　　than to go to a house of feasting,
for death is the destiny of everyone;
　　the living should take this to heart.
³Frustration is better than laughter,
　　because a sad face is good for the
　　　heart.
⁴The heart of the wise is in the house
　　of mourning,

Is it bad to save a lot of money?
(ECCLESIASTES 5:13)

Saving money to use it later when we might need it isn't bad. But many people save it just to say they have a lot of money. And the more money they have, the more money they want. That's what's bad.

¹⁸This is what I have observed to be good: that it is appropriate for a person to eat, to drink and to find satisfaction in their toilsome labor under the sun during the few days of life God has given them— for this is their lot. ¹⁹Moreover, when God gives someone wealth and possessions, and the ability to enjoy them, to accept their lot and be happy in their toil—this is a gift of God. ²⁰They seldom reflect on the days of their life, because God keeps them occupied with gladness of heart.

6 I have seen another evil under the sun, and it weighs heavily on mankind: ²God gives some people wealth, possessions and honor, so that they lack nothing their hearts desire, but God does not grant them the ability to enjoy them, and strangers enjoy them instead. This is meaningless, a grievous evil.

³A man may have a hundred children and live many years; yet no matter how long he lives, if he cannot enjoy his pros

BREAKTHROUGH!

Everything has a name?
(ECCLESIASTES 6:10)

Long ago, the Hebrews thought that people's names were the same as the people themselves. No one could be different from their name or act differently. For example, if your name was Isaac, which means "laughter," then you would always be smiling. If your name was Jacob, with means "tricky," then you would always be tricking other people. For the Hebrews, a person's name showed the personality of that person. A person's personality was a gift from God.

but the heart of fools is in the
house of pleasure.
5 It is better to heed the rebuke of a
wise person
than to listen to the song of
fools.
6 Like the crackling of thorns under
the pot,
so is the laughter of fools.
This too is meaningless.

7 Extortion turns a wise person into a
fool,
and a bribe corrupts the heart.

8 The end of a matter is better than its
beginning,
and patience is better than pride.

9 Do not be quickly provoked in your
spirit,
for anger resides in the lap of fools.

10 Do not say, "Why were the old days
better than these?"
For it is not wise to ask such
questions.

11 Wisdom, like an inheritance, is a good
thing
and benefits those who see the
sun.
12 Wisdom is a shelter
as money is a shelter,
but the advantage of knowledge is
this:
Wisdom preserves those who
have it.

13 Consider what God has done:

Who can straighten
what he has made crooked?
14 When times are good, be happy;
but when times are bad, consider
this:
God has made the one
as well as the other.
Therefore, no one can discover
anything about their future.

15 In this meaningless life of mine I have
seen both of these:

the righteous perishing in their
righteousness,
and the wicked living long in their
wickedness.
16 Do not be overrighteous,
neither be overwise—
why destroy yourself?
17 Do not be overwicked,
and do not be a fool—
why die before your time?
18 It is good to grasp the one
and not let go of the other.
Whoever fears God will avoid all
extremes.[a]

19 Wisdom makes one wise person more
powerful
than ten rulers in a city.

20 Indeed, there is no one on earth who
is righteous,

---

a 18 Or will follow them both

no one who does what is right and
never sins.
21 Do not pay attention to every word
people say,
or you may hear your servant
cursing you—
22 for you know in your heart
that many times you yourself have
cursed others.

23 All this I tested by wisdom and I said,
"I am determined to be wise"—
but this was beyond me.
24 Whatever exists is far off and most
profound—
who can discover it?
25 So I turned my mind to understand,
to investigate and to search out
wisdom and the scheme of
things
and to understand the stupidity of
wickedness
and the madness of folly.

26 I find more bitter than death
the woman who is a snare,
whose heart is a trap
and whose hands are chains.
The man who pleases God will escape
her,
but the sinner she will ensnare.

27 "Look," says the Teacher,[a] "this is
what I have discovered:

"Adding one thing to another to
discover the scheme of
things—
28   while I was still searching
but not finding—
I found one upright man among a
thousand,
but not one upright woman among
them all.
29 This only have I found:
God created mankind upright,
but they have gone in search of
many schemes."

8 Who is like the wise?
Who knows the explanation of
things?
A person's wisdom brightens their
face
and changes its hard appearance.

BREAKTHROUGH!

Why does it say, "I found ... not one upright woman"?
(ECCLESIASTES 7:28)
That's impossible—that's unfair! But the
Teacher can't help but think the way his
people think. In the Hebrew culture, women
were considered less than men. That's really
injustice! So, if the Teacher thought that
finding one good man in a thousand was
hard, then finding a good woman would have
been totally impossible!

Obey the King

2 Obey the king's command, I say, because you took an oath before God. 3 Do
not be in a hurry to leave the king's presence. Do not stand up for a bad cause,
for he will do whatever he pleases. 4 Since
a king's word is supreme, who can say to
him, "What are you doing?"

5 Whoever obeys his command will
come to no harm,
and the wise heart will know the
proper time and procedure.
6 For there is a proper time and
procedure for every matter,
though a person may be weighed
down by misery.

a 27 Or the leader of the assembly

⁷Since no one knows the future,
  who can tell someone else what is
    to come?
⁸As no one has power over the wind to
  contain it,
  so*ᵃ* no one has power over the time
    of their death.
As no one is discharged in time of war,
  so wickedness will not release
    those who practice it.

⁹All this I saw, as I applied my mind to everything done under the sun. There is a time when a man lords it over others to his own*ᵇ* hurt. ¹⁰Then too, I saw the wicked buried—those who used to come and go from the holy place and receive praise*ᶜ* in the city where they did this. This too is meaningless.

¹¹When the sentence for a crime is not quickly carried out, people's hearts are filled with schemes to do wrong. ¹²Although a wicked person who commits a hundred crimes may live a long time, I know that it will go better with those who fear God, who are reverent before him. ¹³Yet because the wicked do not fear God, it will not go well with them, and their days will not lengthen like a shadow.

¹⁴There is something else meaningless that occurs on earth: the righteous who get what the wicked deserve, and the wicked who get what the righteous deserve. This too, I say, is meaningless. ¹⁵So I commend the enjoyment of life, because there is nothing better for a person under the sun than to eat and drink and be glad. Then joy will accompany them in their toil all the days of the life God has given them under the sun.

¹⁶When I applied my mind to know wisdom and to observe the labor that is done on earth—people getting no sleep day or night— ¹⁷then I saw all that God has done. No one can comprehend what goes on under the sun. Despite all their efforts to search it out, no one can discover its meaning. Even if the wise claim they know, they cannot really comprehend it.

A Common Destiny for All

9 So I reflected on all this and concluded that the righteous and the wise and

what they do are in God's hands, but no one knows whether love or hate awaits them. ²All share a common destiny— the righteous and the wicked, the good and the bad,*ᵈ* the clean and the unclean, those who offer sacrifices and those who do not.

As it is with the good,
  so with the sinful;
as it is with those who take oaths,
  so with those who are afraid to take
    them.

³This is the evil in everything that happens under the sun: The same destiny overtakes all. The hearts of people, moreover, are full of evil and there is madness in their hearts while they live, and

---

ᵃ 8 Or *over the human spirit to retain it, / and so*   *ᵇ 9* Or *to their*   *ᶜ 10* Some Hebrew manuscripts and Septuagint (Aquila); most Hebrew manuscripts *and are forgotten* *ᵈ 2* Septuagint (Aquila), Vulgate and Syriac; Hebrew does not have *and the bad.*

BREAK THROUGH!

Why does it say that being good or bad makes no difference?

(ECCLESIASTES 9:2)

For the Teacher, life ends with death. So if good people die just like bad people, then the Teacher doesn't feel that good people have any advantage over bad people.

afterward they join the dead. ⁴Anyone who is among the living has hope^a—even a live dog is better off than a dead lion!

⁵For the living know that they will die,
   but the dead know nothing;
they have no further reward,
   and even their name is forgotten.
⁶Their love, their hate
   and their jealousy have long since
     vanished;
never again will they have a part
   in anything that happens under the
     sun.

⁷Go, eat your food with gladness, and drink your wine with a joyful heart, for God has already approved what you do. ⁸Always be clothed in white, and always anoint your head with oil. ⁹Enjoy life with your wife, whom you love, all the days of this meaningless life that God has given you under the sun—all your meaningless days. For this is your lot in life and in your toilsome labor under the sun. ¹⁰Whatever your hand finds to do, do it with all your might, for in the realm of the dead, where you are going, there is neither working nor planning nor knowledge nor wisdom.

¹¹I have seen something else under the sun:

The race is not to the swift
   or the battle to the strong,
nor does food come to the wise
   or wealth to the brilliant
   or favor to the learned;
but time and chance happen to them
   all.

¹²Moreover, no one knows when their hour will come:

As fish are caught in a cruel net,
   or birds are taken in a snare,
so people are trapped by evil times
   that fall unexpectedly upon them.

Wisdom Better Than Folly

¹³I also saw under the sun this example of wisdom that greatly impressed me: ¹⁴There was once a small city with only a few people in it. And a powerful king came against it, surrounded it and built huge siege works against it. ¹⁵Now there lived in that city a man poor but wise, and he saved the city by his wisdom. But nobody remembered that poor man. ¹⁶So I said, "Wisdom is better than strength." But the poor man's wisdom is despised, and his words are no longer heeded.

¹⁷The quiet words of the wise are more
   to be heeded
than the shouts of a ruler of fools.
¹⁸Wisdom is better than weapons of war,
   but one sinner destroys much good.

10 As dead flies give perfume a bad
   smell,
so a little folly outweighs wisdom
   and honor.
²The heart of the wise inclines to the
   right,
but the heart of the fool to the left.
³Even as fools walk along the road,
   they lack sense
and show everyone how stupid they
   are.
⁴If a ruler's anger rises against you,
   do not leave your post;
calmness can lay great offenses to
   rest.

⁵There is an evil I have seen under the
   sun,
   the sort of error that arises from a
     ruler:
⁶Fools are put in many high positions,
   while the rich occupy the low ones.
⁷I have seen slaves on horseback,
   while princes go on foot like slaves.

⁸Whoever digs a pit may fall into it;
   whoever breaks through a wall may
     be bitten by a snake.
⁹Whoever quarries stones may be
   injured by them;
whoever splits logs may be
   endangered by them.
¹⁰If the ax is dull
   and its edge unsharpened,
more strength is needed,
   but skill will bring success.

¹¹If a snake bites before it is charmed,
   the charmer receives no fee.

---

^a 4 Or What then is to be chosen? With all who live, there is hope

12 Words from the mouth of the wise are
gracious,
  but fools are consumed by their
own lips.
13 At the beginning their words are folly;
  at the end they are wicked
madness—
14   and fools multiply words.

No one knows what is coming—
  who can tell someone else what will
happen after them?

15 The toil of fools wearies them;
  they do not know the way to town.

16 Woe to the land whose king was a
servant[a]
  and whose princes feast in the
morning.
17 Blessed is the land whose king is of
noble birth
  and whose princes eat at a proper
time—
  for strength and not for
drunkenness.

18 Through laziness, the rafters sag;
  because of idle hands, the house
leaks.

19 A feast is made for laughter,
  wine makes life merry,
  and money is the answer for
everything.

20 Do not revile the king even in your
thoughts,
  or curse the rich in your bedroom,
because a bird in the sky may carry
your words,
  and a bird on the wing may report
what you say.

Invest in Many Ventures

11 Ship your grain across the sea;
  after many days you may receive a
return.
2 Invest in seven ventures, yes, in
eight;
  you do not know what disaster may
come upon the land.

3 If clouds are full of water,
  they pour rain on the earth.
Whether a tree falls to the south or to
the north,

in the place where it falls, there it
will lie.
4 Whoever watches the wind will not
plant;
  whoever looks at the clouds will not
reap.

5 As you do not know the path of the
wind,
  or how the body is formed[b] in a
mother's womb,
so you cannot understand the work of
God,
  the Maker of all things.

6 Sow your seed in the morning,
  and at evening let your hands not
be idle,
for you do not know which will
succeed,
  whether this or that,
  or whether both will do equally well.

Remember Your Creator While Young

7 Light is sweet,
  and it pleases the eyes to see the
sun.
8 However many years anyone may live,
  let them enjoy them all.
But let them remember the days of
darkness,
  for there will be many.
Everything to come is meaningless.

9 You who are young, be happy while
you are young,
  and let your heart give you joy in the
days of your youth.
Follow the ways of your heart
  and whatever your eyes see,
but know that for all these things
  God will bring you into judgment.
10 So then, banish anxiety from your
heart
  and cast off the troubles of your
body,
for youth and vigor are meaningless.

12 Remember your Creator
  in the days of your youth,
before the days of trouble come

---

[a] 16 Or *king is a child*   [b] 5 Or *know how life* (or *the spirit*)
/ *enters the body being formed*

BREAK THROUGH!

What are the days of trouble?

(ECCLESIASTES 12:1)

For the Teacher, the "days of trouble" are when you get old, because then you get weak. That's why he recommends that young people remember God when they're young and not just wait until they get old.

and the years approach when you
    will say,
"I find no pleasure in them"—
² before the sun and the light
    and the moon and the stars grow
        dark,
    and the clouds return after the
        rain;
³ when the keepers of the house
        tremble,
    and the strong men stoop,
when the grinders cease because they
        are few,
    and those looking through the
        windows grow dim;
⁴ when the doors to the street are
        closed
    and the sound of grinding fades;
when people rise up at the sound of
        birds,
    but all their songs grow faint;
⁵ when people are afraid of heights
    and of dangers in the streets;

when the almond tree blossoms
    and the grasshopper drags itself
        along
    and desire no longer is stirred.
Then people go to their eternal home
    and mourners go about the streets.

⁶ Remember him—before the silver
        cord is severed,
    and the golden bowl is broken;
before the pitcher is shattered at the
        spring,
    and the wheel broken at the well,
⁷ and the dust returns to the ground it
        came from,
    and the spirit returns to God who
        gave it.

⁸ "Meaningless! Meaningless!" says the
        Teacher.*a*
    "Everything is meaningless!"

---

a 8 Or *the leader of the assembly*; also in verses 9 and 10

CHECK THE FACTS

According to the Teacher, when should we remember our Creator?

A) When we're about to die

B) When we're young

C) When we're afraid

CORRECT ANSWER: B

Why is he so gloomy?

(ECCLESIASTES 12:8)

The Teacher is gloomy because he wanted to study everything to see if he could find something good. When he thought he hadn't found anything good, he was disappointed.

The Conclusion of the Matter

⁹Not only was the Teacher wise, but he also imparted knowledge to the people. He pondered and searched out and set in order many proverbs. ¹⁰The Teacher searched to find just the right words, and what he wrote was upright and true.

¹¹The words of the wise are like goads, their collected sayings like firmly embedded nails—given by one shepherd.ᵃ ¹²Be warned, my son, of anything in addition to them.

Of making many books there is no end, and much study wearies the body.

¹³ Now all has been heard;
    here is the conclusion of the
        matter:
Fear God and keep his
        commandments,
    for this is the duty of all mankind.
¹⁴ For God will bring every deed into
        judgment,
    including every hidden thing,
    whether it is good or evil.

ᵃ 11 Or *Shepherd*

Although the Teacher seems pessimistic, in the end he thinks that it's better to be wise and poor than to be rich and stupid. He misses his youth, but he's happy that he's lived to be old and wiser than other people. For the Teacher, being wise is very good, but being wise and young is even better. I think that's exactly what this lesson is about for us today.

SONG OF SONGS

THE EVIDENCE:

WHO WROTE IT?
Solomon. It starts by saying, "Solomon's Song of Songs" (1:1).

HOW LONG AGO?
Because of what the author says, we know it has been about 3,000 years since it was written.

WHAT'S IT ABOUT?
This poem is about the love of a young shepherd girl and a king. The lesson is that when there's love, the amount of money you have and color of your skin isn't important. The girl herself says that she's dark-skinned (1:5), but the idea is that the love of her life, the king, has light skin (5:10).

THE BEST PART
Isabella chose this part since Mateo wasn't very interested in this book. The whole poem is very beautiful, but if I have to choose, I'd say the part that says, "Love [...] burns like a blazing fire, like a mighty flame. Many waters cannot quench love; rivers cannot sweep it away" (8:6 – 7). How romantic!

---

1 Solomon's Song of Songs.

She[a]

2 Let him kiss me with the kisses of his
       mouth —
   for your love is more delightful than
       wine.
3 Pleasing is the fragrance of your
       perfumes;
   your name is like perfume poured
       out.
   No wonder the young women love
       you!
4 Take me away with you — let us
       hurry!
   Let the king bring me into his
       chambers.

Friends

   We rejoice and delight in you[b];
       we will praise your love more than
           wine.

She

   How right they are to adore you!

5 Dark am I, yet lovely,
       daughters of Jerusalem,
   dark like the tents of Kedar,
       like the tent curtains of
           Solomon.[c]

---

a The main male and female speakers (identified primarily on the basis of the gender of the relevant Hebrew forms) are indicated by the captions *He* and *She* respectively. The words of others are marked *Friends*. In some instances the divisions and their captions are debatable.   *b* 4 The Hebrew is masculine singular.   *c* 5 Or *Salma*

He

9 I liken you, my darling, to a mare
     among Pharaoh's chariot horses.
10 Your cheeks are beautiful with
     earrings,
     your neck with strings of jewels.
11 We will make you earrings of gold,
     studded with silver.

She

12 While the king was at his table,
     my perfume spread its fragrance.
13 My beloved is to me a sachet of myrrh
     resting between my breasts.
14 My beloved is to me a cluster of
     henna blossoms
     from the vineyards of En Gedi.

He

15 How beautiful you are, my darling!
     Oh, how beautiful!
     Your eyes are doves.

BREAK THROUGH!

What does "Song of Songs" mean exactly?

(SONG OF SONGS 1:1)

This is the way the Hebrew language uses the superlative — it's like exaggerating. They say "King of kings" to mean the king that is more king than others. Or "Lord of lords" means this Lord is more lord than other lords. So "Song of Songs" is the song that is the best song of all the other songs. It's the most beautiful.

6 Do not stare at me because I am dark,
     because I am darkened by the sun.
     My mother's sons were angry with me
     and made me take care of the
     vineyards;
     my own vineyard I had to neglect.
7 Tell me, you whom I love,
     where you graze your flock
     and where you rest your sheep at
     midday.
     Why should I be like a veiled woman
     beside the flocks of your friends?

Friends

8 If you do not know, most beautiful of
     women,
     follow the tracks of the sheep
     and graze your young goats
     by the tents of the shepherds.

BREAK THROUGH!

And other women love the girl's beloved?

(SONG OF SONGS 1:3)

Of course! Love is possible between different people. There's the love of engaged people. There's the love of married people. There's the love of brothers and sisters and friends. The girl knows that because her beloved is such a special person, everybody loves him.

THE
WITNESSES

✓ **SOLOMON** (SONG OF SONGS 1:1)
The name of David's son who became king of Israel. He is thought to be the author of Song of Songs.

She
16 How handsome you are, my beloved!
  Oh, how charming!
  And our bed is verdant.

He
17 The beams of our house are cedars;
  our rafters are firs.

She^a

2 I am a rose^b of Sharon,
  a lily of the valleys.

He
2 Like a lily among thorns
  is my darling among the young
    women.

She
3 Like an apple^c tree among the trees of
    the forest
  is my beloved among the young
    men.
 I delight to sit in his shade,
  and his fruit is sweet to my taste.
4 Let him lead me to the banquet
    hall,
  and let his banner over me be
    love.
5 Strengthen me with raisins,
  refresh me with apples,
  for I am faint with love.
6 His left arm is under my head,
  and his right arm embraces me.
7 Daughters of Jerusalem, I charge you
  by the gazelles and by the does of
    the field:
 Do not arouse or awaken love
  until it so desires.

---

^a Or He   ^b 1 Probably a member of the crocus family
^c 3 Or possibly *apricot*; here and elsewhere in Song of
Songs

THE
SCENE

JERUSALEM

(SONG OF SONGS 1:5)

Israel's most important city. It was the capital of the kingdom of Judah.

KEDAR

(SONG OF SONGS 1:5)

A nomad tribe (they moved from place to place frequently) in the Arabian Desert. Their camps could easily be distinguished in the desert because of the dark color of their tents.

EN GEDI

(SONG OF SONGS 1:14)

A spring in the Judean Desert near the Dead Sea. Since there was so much water there, there were many palm trees and grape vineyards. Did you know that it's still the same there nowadays?

⁸ Listen! My beloved!
  Look! Here he comes,
 leaping across the mountains,
  bounding over the hills.
⁹ My beloved is like a gazelle or a young
    stag.
  Look! There he stands behind our
    wall,
 gazing through the windows,
  peering through the lattice.
¹⁰ My beloved spoke and said
    to me,
  "Arise, my darling,
  my beautiful one, come with me.
¹¹ See! The winter is past;
  the rains are over and gone.
¹² Flowers appear on the earth;
  the season of singing has
    come,
 the cooing of doves
  is heard in our land.

¹³ The fig tree forms its early fruit;
  the blossoming vines spread their
    fragrance.
 Arise, come, my darling;
  my beautiful one, come
    with me."

He

¹⁴ My dove in the clefts of the
    rock,
  in the hiding places on the
    mountainside,
 show me your face,
  let me hear your voice;
 for your voice is sweet,
  and your face is lovely.
¹⁵ Catch for us the foxes,
  the little foxes
 that ruin the vineyards,
  our vineyards that are in
    bloom.

THE SCENE

SHARON

(SONG OF SONGS 2:1)

A very fertile valley between Mount Carmel and the Mediterranean coast. There was a lot of water there, so they could grow plants and have vineyards.

She

16 My beloved is mine and I am his;
  he browses among the lilies.
17 Until the day breaks
  and the shadows flee,
 turn, my beloved,
  and be like a gazelle
 or like a young stag
  on the rugged hills.[a]

3 All night long on my bed
  I looked for the one my heart
   loves;
  I looked for him but did not find
   him.
2 I will get up now and go about the
   city,
  through its streets and squares;
 I will search for the one my heart
   loves.
 So I looked for him but did not find
   him.

3 The watchmen found me
  as they made their rounds in the
   city.
 "Have you seen the one my heart
   loves?"
4 Scarcely had I passed them
  when I found the one my heart
   loves.
 I held him and would not let him go
  till I had brought him to my mother's
   house,
  to the room of the one who
   conceived me.
5 Daughters of Jerusalem, I charge
   you
  by the gazelles and by the does of
   the field:
 Do not arouse or awaken love
  until it so desires.

6 Who is this coming up from the
   wilderness
  like a column of smoke,
 perfumed with myrrh and incense
  made from all the spices of the
   merchant?
7 Look! It is Solomon's carriage,
  escorted by sixty warriors,
  the noblest of Israel,
8 all of them wearing the sword,
  all experienced in battle,
 each with his sword at his side,
  prepared for the terrors of the
   night.
9 King Solomon made for himself the
   carriage;
  he made it of wood from Lebanon.
10 Its posts he made of silver,
  its base of gold.
 Its seat was upholstered with
   purple,
  its interior inlaid with love.
 Daughters of Jerusalem, 11 come
   out,
  and look, you daughters of Zion.
 Look[b] on King Solomon wearing a
   crown,
  the crown with which his mother
   crowned him
 on the day of his wedding,
  the day his heart rejoiced.

---

[a] 17 Or the hills of Bether   [b] 10,11 Or interior lovingly
inlaid / by the daughters of Jerusalem. / 11 Come out, you
daughters of Zion, / and look

THE SCENE

LEBANON

(SONG OF SONGS 3:9)

The mountainous region near Syria that's very famous for its high mountains, large forests and snow.

He

4 How beautiful you are, my darling!
　　Oh, how beautiful!
　　Your eyes behind your veil are
　　　doves.
　Your hair is like a flock of goats
　　descending from the hills of Gilead.
² Your teeth are like a flock of sheep
　　just shorn,
　coming up from the washing.
　Each has its twin;
　　not one of them is alone.
³ Your lips are like a scarlet ribbon;
　your mouth is lovely.
　Your temples behind your veil
　　are like the halves of a
　　　pomegranate.
⁴ Your neck is like the tower of David,
　built with courses of stone[a];
　on it hang a thousand shields,
　　all of them shields of warriors.
⁵ Your breasts are like two fawns,
　like twin fawns of a gazelle

　that browse among the lilies.
⁶ Until the day breaks
　　and the shadows flee,
　I will go to the mountain of myrrh
　　and to the hill of incense.
⁷ You are altogether beautiful, my
　　darling;
　there is no flaw in you.

⁸ Come with me from Lebanon, my bride,
　come with me from Lebanon.
　Descend from the crest of Amana,
　　from the top of Senir, the summit of
　　　Hermon,
　from the lions' dens
　　and the mountain haunts of
　　　leopards.
⁹ You have stolen my heart, my sister,
　　my bride;
　you have stolen my heart

---

[a] 4 The meaning of the Hebrew for this phrase is uncertain.

THE SCENE

GILEAD

(SONG OF SONGS 4:1)

A mountainous region in northern Palestine. It's famous for its big forests and green pastureland that's ideal for raising cattle.

with every kind of incense tree,
    with myrrh and aloes
    and all the finest spices.
¹⁵ You areᵃ a garden fountain,
    a well of flowing water
    streaming down from Lebanon.

She

¹⁶ Awake, north wind,
    and come, south wind!
  Blow on my garden,
    that its fragrance may spread
      everywhere.
  Let my beloved come into his garden
    and taste its choice fruits.

He

5 I have come into my garden, my
    sister, my bride;
  I have gathered my myrrh with my
    spice.
  I have eaten my honeycomb and my
    honey;
  I have drunk my wine and my
    milk.

ᵃ 15 Or *I am* (spoken by *She*)

BREAKTHROUGH!

Tower of David

(SONG OF SONGS 4:4)

You know how people in love use pretty
words to talk about the person they love?
Here the man says "tower of David" to
describe the girl's long, thin neck.

with one glance of your eyes,
    with one jewel of your
      necklace.
¹⁰ How delightful is your love, my sister,
    my bride!
  How much more pleasing is your
    love than wine,
  and the fragrance of your perfume
    more than any spice!
¹¹ Your lips drop sweetness as the
    honeycomb, my bride;
  milk and honey are under your
    tongue.
  The fragrance of your garments
    is like the fragrance of Lebanon.
¹² You are a garden locked up, my sister,
    my bride;
  you are a spring enclosed, a sealed
    fountain.
¹³ Your plants are an orchard of
    pomegranates
    with choice fruits,
    with henna and nard,
¹⁴   nard and saffron,
    calamus and cinnamon,

BREAKTHROUGH!

Myrrh

(SONG OF SONGS 5:1)

A pleasant-smelling oil taken from thorny
trees in Arabia and the northern part of Africa.

Friends

Eat, friends, and drink;
  drink your fill of love.

She

² I slept but my heart was awake.
  Listen! My beloved is knocking:
"Open to me, my sister, my darling,
  my dove, my flawless one.
My head is drenched with dew,
  my hair with the dampness of the
      night."
³ I have taken off my robe—
  must I put it on again?
I have washed my feet—
  must I soil them again?
⁴ My beloved thrust his hand through
      the latch-opening;
  my heart began to pound for him.
⁵ I arose to open for my beloved,
  and my hands dripped with
      myrrh,
my fingers with flowing myrrh,
  on the handles of the bolt.

Topaz

(SONG OF SONGS 5:14)

Precious crystal stones used for jewelry. They are usually yellow and see-through.

⁶ I opened for my beloved,
  but my beloved had left; he was
      gone.
  My heart sank at his departure.ᵃ
I looked for him but did not find him.
  I called him but he did not answer.
⁷ The watchmen found me
  as they made their rounds in the
      city.
They beat me, they bruised me;
  they took away my cloak,
    those watchmen of the walls!
⁸ Daughters of Jerusalem, I charge
      you—
  if you find my beloved,
what will you tell him?
  Tell him I am faint with love.

Friends

⁹ How is your beloved better than
      others,
  most beautiful of women?
How is your beloved better than
      others,
  that you so charge us?

Bolt

(SONG OF SONGS 5:5)

A long time ago, they used iron bolts to lock the doors from inside. Sometimes it was also a heavy ring that hung on the door, and they used it to knock on the door.

ᵃ 6 Or *heart had gone out to him when he spoke*

Lapis lazuli
(SONG OF SONGS 5:14)
Precious crystal stones that are a bright blue,
and often have flecks that look like gold
inside them.

She
¹⁰ My beloved is radiant and ruddy,
        outstanding among ten thousand.
¹¹ His head is purest gold;
        his hair is wavy
        and black as a raven.
¹² His eyes are like doves
        by the water streams,
    washed in milk,
        mounted like jewels.
¹³ His cheeks are like beds of spice
        yielding perfume.
    His lips are like lilies
        dripping with myrrh.
¹⁴ His arms are rods of gold
        set with topaz.
    His body is like polished ivory
        decorated with lapis lazuli.
¹⁵ His legs are pillars of marble
        set on bases of pure gold.
    His appearance is like Lebanon,
        choice as its cedars.
¹⁶ His mouth is sweetness itself;
        he is altogether lovely.
    This is my beloved, this is my friend,
        daughters of Jerusalem.

Friends
6 Where has your beloved gone,
        most beautiful of women?
    Which way did your beloved turn,
        that we may look for him with you?

She
² My beloved has gone down to his
        garden,
        to the beds of spices,
    to browse in the gardens
        and to gather lilies.
³ I am my beloved's and my beloved is
        mine;
        he browses among the lilies.

He
⁴ You are as beautiful as Tirzah, my
        darling,
        as lovely as Jerusalem,
        as majestic as troops with banners.
⁵ Turn your eyes from me;
        they overwhelm me.
    Your hair is like a flock of goats
        descending from Gilead.
⁶ Your teeth are like a flock of sheep
        coming up from the washing.
    Each has its twin,
        not one of them is missing.
⁷ Your temples behind your veil
        are like the halves of a
        pomegranate.
⁸ Sixty queens there may be,
        and eighty concubines,
        and virgins beyond number;
⁹ but my dove, my perfect one, is
        unique,
        the only daughter of her
        mother,
        the favorite of the one who bore
        her.
    The young women saw her and called
        her blessed;
        the queens and concubines praised
        her.

Friends
¹⁰ Who is this that appears like the
        dawn,
        fair as the moon, bright as the sun,
        majestic as the stars in
        procession?

THE SCENE

TIRZAH

(SONG OF SONGS 6:4)

This place was very important, because several Israelite kings settled there. Jeroboam, Baasha, Zimri and Omri were just a few.

THE WITNESSES

✓ **SHULAMMITE** (SONG OF SONGS 6:13)
This is the name of the girl in this love poem. It means "woman from Shulem," but it's also a play on words based on the name of Solomon.

He

¹¹ I went down to the grove of nut trees
    to look at the new growth in the
        valley,
    to see if the vines had budded
        or the pomegranates were in
            bloom.
¹² Before I realized it,
    my desire set me among the royal
        chariots of my people.ᵃ

Friends

¹³ Come back, come back,
    O Shulammite;
    come back, come back, that we may
        gaze on you!

He

Why would you gaze on the Shulammite
    as on the dance of Mahanaim?ᵇ

7 ᶜ How beautiful your sandaled feet,
    O prince's daughter!

Your graceful legs are like jewels,
    the work of an artist's hands.
² Your navel is a rounded goblet
    that never lacks blended wine.
Your waist is a mound of wheat
    encircled by lilies.
³ Your breasts are like two fawns,
    like twin fawns of a gazelle.
⁴ Your neck is like an ivory tower.
Your eyes are the pools of Heshbon
    by the gate of Bath Rabbim.
Your nose is like the tower of
        Lebanon
    looking toward Damascus.

ᵃ 12 Or *among the chariots of Amminadab;* or *among the chariots of the people of the prince*   ᵇ 13 In Hebrew texts this verse (6:13) is numbered 7:1.   ᶜ In Hebrew texts 7:1-13 is numbered 7:2-14.

⁵Your head crowns you like Mount
Carmel.
Your hair is like royal tapestry;
the king is held captive by its
tresses.
⁶How beautiful you are and how
pleasing,
my love, with your delights!
⁷Your stature is like that of the
palm,
and your breasts like clusters of
fruit.
⁸I said, "I will climb the palm
tree;
I will take hold of its fruit."
May your breasts be like clusters of
grapes on the vine,
the fragrance of your breath like
apples,
⁹ and your mouth like the best
wine.

DAMASCUS

(SONG OF SONGS 7:4)

An ancient Armenian state in northern Palestine. Its capital city had the same name. Damascus was important, because it was on the road the caravans traveled between Assyria and Egypt.

HESHBON

(SONG OF SONGS 7:4)

The capital city of the Moabites, which was later given to the tribe of Gad. The two springs in this city were famous, so that's why the author compares them with the Shulammite's eyes.

She

May the wine go straight to my
beloved,
flowing gently over lips and
teeth.ᵃ
¹⁰I belong to my beloved,
and his desire is for me.
¹¹Come, my beloved, let us go to the
countryside,
let us spend the night in the
villages.ᵇ
¹²Let us go early to the vineyards
to see if the vines have
budded,
if their blossoms have opened,
and if the pomegranates are
in bloom—
there I will give you my love.

ᵃ 9 Septuagint, Aquila, Vulgate and Syriac; Hebrew *lips of sleepers*   ᵇ 11 Or *the henna bushes*

MOUNT CARMEL

(SONG OF SONGS 7:5)

A mountainous region several kilometers long between the Mediterranean Sea and the Valley of Jezreel that's famous for its large forests. The highest of all these mountains is also called by the same name, which means "God's vineyard."

13 The mandrakes send out their
        fragrance,
    and at our door is every delicacy,
both new and old,
    that I have stored up for you, my
        beloved.

8 If only you were to me like a
        brother,
    who was nursed at my mother's
        breasts!
Then, if I found you outside,
    I would kiss you,
    and no one would despise me.
2 I would lead you
    and bring you to my mother's
        house—
    she who has taught me.
I would give you spiced wine to
        drink,
    the nectar of my pomegranates.

3 His left arm is under my head
    and his right arm embraces me.
4 Daughters of Jerusalem, I charge
        you:
    Do not arouse or awaken love
    until it so desires.

Friends

5 Who is this coming up from the
        wilderness
    leaning on her beloved?

She

Under the apple tree I roused
        you;
    there your mother conceived
        you,
    there she who was in labor
        gave you birth.
6 Place me like a seal over your
        heart,
    like a seal on your arm;
for love is as strong as death,
    its jealousy[a] unyielding as the
        grave.
It burns like blazing fire,
    like a mighty flame.[b]
7 Many waters cannot quench love;
    rivers cannot sweep it away.
If one were to give
    all the wealth of one's house for
        love,
    it[c] would be utterly scorned.

Friends

8 We have a little sister,
    and her breasts are not yet
        grown.
What shall we do for our sister
    on the day she is spoken for?
9 If she is a wall,
    we will build towers of silver on
        her.
If she is a door,
    we will enclose her with panels of
        cedar.

She

10 I am a wall,
    and my breasts are like towers.

---

a 6 Or ardor   b 6 Or fire, / like the very flame of the LORD
c 7 Or he

Thus I have become in his eyes
   like one bringing contentment.
11 Solomon had a vineyard in Baal
      Hamon;
   he let out his vineyard to tenants.
   Each was to bring for its fruit
      a thousand shekels*a* of silver.
12 But my own vineyard is mine to
      give;
   the thousand shekels are for you,
      Solomon,
   and two hundred*b* are for those
      who tend its fruit.

He

13 You who dwell in the gardens
      with friends in attendance,
   let me hear your voice!

She

14 Come away, my beloved,
      and be like a gazelle
   or like a young stag
      on the spice-laden mountains.

---

a 11 That is, about 25 pounds or about 12 kilograms; also
in verse 12   *b* 12 That is, about 5 pounds or about
2.3 kilograms

This book teaches us a big lesson. The love between King Solomon and the Shulammite sheepherder girl shows us that when there's true love, differences aren't important—whether it's the color of someone's skin or if one is rich and the other is poor. Love is what's most important.

CASE CLOSED!

ISAIAH

THE EVIDENCE:

WHO WROTE IT?
By now, you're probably sure of one thing: this question about who wrote such an old book is always complicated! Experts who have spent time studying the book of Isaiah for years can't agree who wrote this. But, we'll tell you something: this book was probably written by the prophet Isaiah, who was the son of Amos. Some of Isaiah's followers may also have helped him write certain parts of the book.

HOW LONG AGO?
A very long time ago. Again, we have to say we can't be absolutely sure, but most of the book was probably written between 739 and 685 years before Christ. However, we have to say it again — we can't be sure. And besides, this book has probably been edited several times (meaning that it was written and then corrected several times).

WHAT'S IT ABOUT?
The book of Isaiah deals with several topics. There's a lot of concern with regard to the spiritual lives of the Israelites who were living in Judah. But Isaiah also sends warning messages to neighboring nations like Assyria, Egypt, Philistia, Moab, Babylonia and some others. God gives the Israelites a message of judgment as well as of hope.

THE BEST PART
The truth is that it's very hard to choose the best part of such a big book. There's one paragraph we like in chapter 61, verse 1. We think it's like the cherry on top of the icing on the cake!

> The Spirit of the Sovereign LORD is on me,
>   because the LORD has anointed me
>   to proclaim good news to the poor.
> He has sent me to bind up the
>   brokenhearted,
>   to proclaim freedom for the captives
>   and release from darkness for the
>   prisoners.

1 The vision concerning Judah and Jerusalem that Isaiah son of Amoz saw during the reigns of Uzziah, Jotham, Ahaz and Hezekiah, kings of Judah.

A Rebellious Nation

2 Hear me, you heavens! Listen, earth!
   For the Lord has spoken:
"I reared children and brought them up,
   but they have rebelled against me.
3 The ox knows its master,
   the donkey its owner's manger,
but Israel does not know,
   my people do not understand."

4 Woe to the sinful nation,
   a people whose guilt is great,
a brood of evildoers,
   children given to corruption!
They have forsaken the Lord;
   they have spurned the Holy One of Israel
   and turned their backs on him.

5 Why should you be beaten anymore?
   Why do you persist in rebellion?
Your whole head is injured,
   your whole heart afflicted.
6 From the sole of your foot to the top of your head
   there is no soundness—
only wounds and welts
   and open sores,
not cleansed or bandaged
   or soothed with olive oil.

7 Your country is desolate,
   your cities burned with fire;
your fields are being stripped by foreigners
   right before you,
   laid waste as when overthrown by strangers.

THE WITNESSES

✓ **ISAIAH** (ISAIAH 1:1)
This is the name of the prophet that God used to give a special message to the people of Israel. Isaiah's name means "the Lord is salvation."

✓ **UZZIAH** (ISAIAH 1:1)
He became the king of Judah when he was 16 years old.

✓ **JOTHAM** (ISAIAH 1:1)
He was Uzziah's son, and he also was king of Judah during a prosperous period.

✓ **AHAZ** (ISAIAH 1:1; 7:1)
He became king of Judah when he was 20 years old, and he ruled for 16 years.

✓ **HEZEKIAH** (ISAIAH 1:1)
Read about this king in 2 Kings 18 and Proverbs 25:1.

CHECK THE FACTS

Isaiah was a prophet of God, and he preached mostly in:

A) Judah

B) Babylon

C) Israel

CORRECT ANSWER: A

8 Daughter Zion is left
　like a shelter in a vineyard,
like a hut in a cucumber field,
　like a city under siege.
9 Unless the LORD Almighty
　had left us some survivors,
we would have become like
　　Sodom,
　we would have been like
　　Gomorrah.

10 Hear the word of the LORD,
　you rulers of Sodom;
listen to the instruction of our
　　God,
　you people of Gomorrah!
11 "The multitude of your sacrifices—
　what are they to me?" says the
　　LORD.
　"I have more than enough of burnt
　　offerings,
　　of rams and the fat of fattened
　　animals;

I have no pleasure
　in the blood of bulls and lambs and
　　goats.
12 When you come to appear before me,
　who has asked this of you,
　this trampling of my courts?
13 Stop bringing meaningless
　　offerings!
　Your incense is detestable
　　to me.
New Moons, Sabbaths and
　　convocations—
　I cannot bear your worthless
　　assemblies.
14 Your New Moon feasts and your
　　appointed festivals
　I hate with all my being.
They have become a burden to me;
　I am weary of bearing them.
15 When you spread out your hands in
　　prayer,
　I hide my eyes from you;
even when you offer many prayers,
　I am not listening.

Your hands are full of blood!

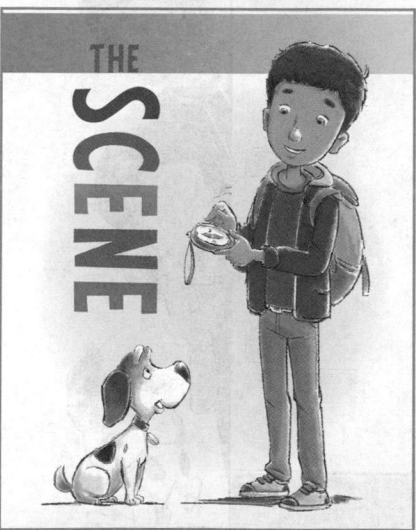

THE SCENE

SODOM AND GOMORRAH

(ISAIAH 1:9)

*Read what happened in
Genesis 19:1–29.*

BREAK THROUGH!

New Moons and Sabbaths
(ISAIAH 1:13-14)

The meaning of *Sabbath* is "to stop, to cease." It is when everybody had to rest. For Jews, it was on Saturday. The Israelites mixed worshiping God with worshiping other religions, and the prophet Isaiah says that's bad and doesn't serve any purpose.

¹⁶ Wash and make yourselves clean.
　　Take your evil deeds out of my sight;
　　stop doing wrong.
¹⁷ Learn to do right; seek justice.
　　Defend the oppressed.*ᵃ*
Take up the cause of the
　　fatherless;
　　plead the case of the widow.

¹⁸ "Come now, let us settle the
　　matter,"
　　says the LORD.
"Though your sins are like scarlet,
　　they shall be as white as snow;
though they are red as crimson,
　　they shall be like wool.
¹⁹ If you are willing and obedient,
　　you will eat the good things of
　　the land;
²⁰ but if you resist and rebel,
　　you will be devoured by the sword."
　　　　For the mouth of the LORD
　　　　　　has spoken.

²¹ See how the faithful city
　　has become a prostitute!
She once was full of justice;
　　righteousness used to dwell in
　　her—
　　but now murderers!
²² Your silver has become dross,
　　your choice wine is diluted with
　　water.
²³ Your rulers are rebels,
　　partners with thieves;
they all love bribes
　　and chase after gifts.
They do not defend the cause of the
　　fatherless;
　　the widow's case does not come
　　before them.

²⁴ Therefore the Lord, the LORD Almighty,
　　the Mighty One of Israel,
　　declares:
"Ah! I will vent my wrath on my
　　foes
　　and avenge myself on my enemies.
²⁵ I will turn my hand against you;*ᵇ*
　　I will thoroughly purge away your
　　dross
　　and remove all your impurities.
²⁶ I will restore your leaders as in days
　　of old,
　　your rulers as at the beginning.
Afterward you will be called
　　the City of Righteousness,
　　the Faithful City."

²⁷ Zion will be delivered with justice,
　　her penitent ones with
　　righteousness.
²⁸ But rebels and sinners will both be
　　broken,
　　and those who forsake the LORD will
　　perish.

²⁹ "You will be ashamed because of the
　　sacred oaks
　　in which you have delighted;
you will be disgraced because of the
　　gardens
　　that you have chosen.
³⁰ You will be like an oak with fading
　　leaves,
　　like a garden without water.

ᵃ 17 Or *justice. / Correct the oppressor*　　*ᵇ* 25 That is, against Jerusalem

³¹ The mighty man will become tinder
   and his work a spark;
both will burn together,
   with no one to quench the fire."

The Mountain of the Lord

2 This is what Isaiah son of Amoz saw
concerning Judah and Jerusalem:

² In the last days

the mountain of the Lord's temple will
   be established
as the highest of the mountains;
it will be exalted above the hills,
   and all nations will stream to it.

³ Many peoples will come and say,

"Come, let us go up to the mountain
   of the Lord,
to the temple of the God of
   Jacob.
He will teach us his ways,
   so that we may walk in his
   paths."
The law will go out from Zion,
   the word of the Lord from
   Jerusalem.
⁴ He will judge between the nations
   and will settle disputes for many
   peoples.
They will beat their swords into
   plowshares
   and their spears into pruning
   hooks.
Nation will not take up sword against
   nation,
   nor will they train for war anymore.

⁵ Come, descendants of Jacob,
   let us walk in the light of the Lord.

The Day of the Lord

⁶ You, Lord, have abandoned your
   people,
   the descendants of Jacob.
They are full of superstitions from the
   East;
   they practice divination like the
   Philistines
   and embrace pagan customs.
⁷ Their land is full of silver and gold;
   there is no end to their
   treasures.

Their land is full of horses;
   there is no end to their chariots.
⁸ Their land is full of idols;
   they bow down to the work of their
   hands,
   to what their fingers have made.
⁹ So people will be brought low
   and everyone humbled—
   do not forgive them.ᵃ

¹⁰ Go into the rocks, hide in the ground
   from the fearful presence of the
   Lord
   and the splendor of his majesty!
¹¹ The eyes of the arrogant will be
   humbled
   and human pride brought low;
the Lord alone will be exalted in that
   day.

¹² The Lord Almighty has a day in
   store
   for all the proud and lofty,

ᵃ 9 Or not raise them up

Will there be no wars?

(ISAIAH 2:4)

How wonderful it would be if there were no
more wars! But what the prophet is saying
is that this can happen only if everybody
obeys God and lets him give them what they
need.

BREAKTHROUGH!

Divination

(ISAIAH 2:6)

We have to be careful with this issue of divination and witchcraft! It is a practice that doesn't respect or take into account the true God. It's based on magic, on idols and on doing horrible things that God doesn't like.

for all that is exalted
(and they will be humbled),
13 for all the cedars of Lebanon, tall and
lofty,
and all the oaks of Bashan,
14 for all the towering mountains
and all the high hills,
15 for every lofty tower
and every fortified wall,
16 for every trading ship[a]
and every stately vessel.
17 The arrogance of man will be brought
low
and human pride humbled;
the LORD alone will be exalted in that
day,
18   and the idols will totally disappear.

19 People will flee to caves in the
rocks
and to holes in the ground
from the fearful presence of the LORD
and the splendor of his majesty,
when he rises to shake the earth.

20 In that day people will throw away
to the moles and bats
their idols of silver and idols of
gold,
which they made to worship.
21 They will flee to caverns in the
rocks
and to the overhanging crags
from the fearful presence of the
LORD
and the splendor of his majesty,
when he rises to shake the earth.

22 Stop trusting in mere humans,
who have but a breath in their
nostrils.
Why hold them in esteem?

Judgment on Jerusalem and Judah

3 See now, the Lord,
the LORD Almighty,
is about to take from Jerusalem and
Judah
both supply and support:
all supplies of food and all supplies
of water,
2   the hero and the warrior,
the judge and the prophet,
the diviner and the elder,
3 the captain of fifty and the man of
rank,
the counselor, skilled craftsman and
clever enchanter.

4 "I will make mere youths their
officials;
children will rule over
them."

5 People will oppress
each other—
man against man,
neighbor against
neighbor.
The young will rise up against the old,
the nobody against the honored.

6 A man will seize one of his brothers
in his father's house, and say,
"You have a cloak, you be our
leader;
take charge of this heap of ruins!"

---

a 16 Hebrew *every ship of Tarshish*

7 But in that day he will cry out,
    "I have no remedy.
  I have no food or clothing in my
      house;
    do not make me the leader of the
      people."

8 Jerusalem staggers,
    Judah is falling;
  their words and deeds are against the
      LORD,
    defying his glorious presence.
9 The look on their faces testifies
      against them;
    they parade their sin like Sodom;
      they do not hide it.
  Woe to them!
    They have brought disaster upon
      themselves.

10 Tell the righteous it will be well with
      them,
    for they will enjoy the fruit of their
      deeds.
11 Woe to the wicked!
    Disaster is upon them!
  They will be paid back
    for what their hands have done.

12 Youths oppress my people,
    women rule over them.
  My people, your guides lead you
      astray;
    they turn you from the path.

13 The LORD takes his place in court;
    he rises to judge the people.
14 The LORD enters into judgment
    against the elders and leaders of
      his people:
  "It is you who have ruined my
      vineyard;
    the plunder from the poor is in your
      houses.
15 What do you mean by crushing my
      people
  and grinding the faces of the poor?"
      declares the Lord,
      the LORD Almighty.

16 The LORD says,
    "The women of Zion are haughty,
  walking along with outstretched
      necks,
    flirting with their eyes,
  strutting along with swaying hips,
    with ornaments jingling on their
      ankles.
17 Therefore the Lord will bring sores
    on the heads of the women
      of Zion;
  the LORD will make their scalps
      bald."

18 In that day the Lord will snatch away
their finery: the bangles and headbands
and crescent necklaces, 19 the earrings
and bracelets and veils, 20 the headdress-
es and anklets and sashes, the perfume
bottles and charms, 21 the signet rings
and nose rings, 22 the fine robes and the
capes and cloaks, the purses 23 and mirrors, and the linen garments and tiaras
and shawls.

24 Instead of fragrance there will be a
      stench;
    instead of a sash, a rope;
  instead of well-dressed hair,
      baldness;
    instead of fine clothing, sackcloth;
    instead of beauty, branding.
25 Your men will fall by the sword,
    your warriors in battle.
26 The gates of Zion will lament and
      mourn;
    destitute, she will sit on the
      ground.

4 1 In that day seven women
    will take hold of one man
  and say, "We will eat our own food
    and provide our own clothes;
  only let us be called by your name.
    Take away our disgrace!"

The Branch of the LORD

2 In that day the Branch of the LORD will
be beautiful and glorious, and the fruit
of the land will be the pride and glory of
the survivors in Israel. 3 Those who are
left in Zion, who remain in Jerusalem,
will be called holy, all who are recorded
among the living in Jerusalem. 4 The Lord
will wash away the filth of the women
of Zion; he will cleanse the bloodstains
from Jerusalem by a spirit[a] of judgment
and a spirit[a] of fire. 5 Then the LORD will

---

a 4 Or the Spirit

create over all of Mount Zion and over those who assemble there a cloud of smoke by day and a glow of flaming fire by night; over everything the glory*a* will be a canopy. ⁶It will be a shelter and shade from the heat of the day, and a refuge and hiding place from the storm and rain.

The Song of the Vineyard

5 I will sing for the one I love
　　a song about his vineyard:
My loved one had a vineyard
　　on a fertile hillside.
²He dug it up and cleared it of stones
　　and planted it with the choicest
　　　vines.
He built a watchtower in it
　　and cut out a winepress as well.
Then he looked for a crop of good
　　　grapes,
　　but it yielded only bad fruit.

³ "Now you dwellers in Jerusalem and
　　　people of Judah,
　　judge between me and my
　　　vineyard.
⁴What more could have been done
　　　for my vineyard
　　than I have done for it?
When I looked for good grapes,
　　why did it yield only bad?
⁵Now I will tell you
　　what I am going to do to my
　　　vineyard:
I will take away its hedge,
　　and it will be destroyed;
I will break down its wall,
　　and it will be trampled.
⁶I will make it a wasteland,
　　neither pruned nor cultivated,
　　and briers and thorns will grow
　　　there.
I will command the clouds
　　not to rain on it."

⁷The vineyard of the Lord Almighty
　　is the nation of Israel,
and the people of Judah
　　are the vines he delighted in.
And he looked for justice, but saw
　　　bloodshed;
for righteousness, but heard cries
　　of distress.

Woes and Judgments

⁸Woe to you who add house to
　　house
　　and join field to field
till no space is left
　　and you live alone in the land.

⁹The Lord Almighty has declared in my hearing:

"Surely the great houses will become
　　desolate,
　　the fine mansions left without
　　　occupants.
¹⁰A ten-acre vineyard will produce only a
　　bath*b* of wine;
　　a homer*c* of seed will yield only an
　　　ephah*d* of grain."

---

a 5 Or *over all the glory there*　　*b* 10 That is, about 6 gallons or about 22 liters　　*c* 10 That is, probably about 360 pounds or about 160 kilograms　　*d* 10 That is, probably about 36 pounds or about 16 kilograms

Woes and judgments
(ISAIAH 5:8)

Have you noticed how sometimes our friends do crazy things? Well, sometimes big people start doing crazy things too, and that's not good. It's like they lose their heads and make many mistakes that, in the end, hurt them very much. That is what was happening to the Israelites.

¹¹ Woe to those who rise early in the
     morning
  to run after their drinks,
who stay up late at night
  till they are inflamed with wine.
¹² They have harps and lyres at their
     banquets,
  pipes and timbrels and wine,
but they have no regard for the deeds
     of the Lord,
  no respect for the work of his
     hands.
¹³ Therefore my people will go into exile
  for lack of understanding;
those of high rank will die of hunger
  and the common people will be
     parched with thirst.
¹⁴ Therefore Death expands its jaws,
  opening wide its mouth;
into it will descend their nobles and
     masses
  with all their brawlers and revelers.
¹⁵ So people will be brought low
  and everyone humbled,
  the eyes of the arrogant humbled.
¹⁶ But the Lord Almighty will be exalted
     by his justice,
  and the holy God will be proved holy
     by his righteous acts.
¹⁷ Then sheep will graze as in their own
     pasture;
  lambs will feed^a among the ruins of
     the rich.

¹⁸ Woe to those who draw sin along with
     cords of deceit,
  and wickedness as with cart ropes,
¹⁹ to those who say, "Let God hurry;
  let him hasten his work
  so we may see it.
The plan of the Holy One of Israel—
  let it approach, let it come into view,
  so we may know it."

²⁰ Woe to those who call evil good
     and good evil,
  who put darkness for light
     and light for darkness,
  who put bitter for sweet
     and sweet for bitter.

²¹ Woe to those who are wise in their
     own eyes
  and clever in their own sight.

²² Woe to those who are heroes at
     drinking wine
  and champions at mixing drinks,
²³ who acquit the guilty for a bribe,
  but deny justice to the innocent.
²⁴ Therefore, as tongues of fire lick up
     straw
  and as dry grass sinks down in the
     flames,
so their roots will decay
  and their flowers blow away like dust;
for they have rejected the law of the
     Lord Almighty
  and spurned the word of the Holy
     One of Israel.
²⁵ Therefore the Lord's anger burns
     against his people;
  his hand is raised and he strikes
     them down.
The mountains shake,
  and the dead bodies are like refuse
     in the streets.

Yet for all this, his anger is not turned
     away,
  his hand is still upraised.

²⁶ He lifts up a banner for the distant
     nations,
  he whistles for those at the ends of
     the earth.
Here they come,
  swiftly and speedily!
²⁷ Not one of them grows tired or
     stumbles,
  not one slumbers or sleeps;
not a belt is loosened at the waist,
  not a sandal strap is broken.
²⁸ Their arrows are sharp,
  all their bows are strung;
their horses' hooves seem like flint,
  their chariot wheels like a whirlwind.
²⁹ Their roar is like that of the lion,
  they roar like young lions;
they growl as they seize their prey
  and carry it off with no one to rescue.
³⁰ In that day they will roar over it
  like the roaring of the sea.
And if one looks at the land,
  there is only darkness and distress;
  even the sun will be darkened by
     clouds.

---

^a 17 Septuagint; Hebrew / strangers will eat

Isaiah's Commission

6 In the year that King Uzziah died, I saw the Lord, high and exalted, seated on a throne; and the train of his robe filled the temple. ²Above him were seraphim, each with six wings: With two wings they covered their faces, with two they covered their feet, and with two they were flying. ³And they were calling to one another:

> "Holy, holy, holy is the LORD
> > Almighty;
> > the whole earth is full of his
> > > glory."

⁴At the sound of their voices the doorposts and thresholds shook and the temple was filled with smoke.

⁵"Woe to me!" I cried. "I am ruined! For I am a man of unclean lips, and I live among a people of unclean lips, and my eyes have seen the King, the LORD Almighty."

Seraphim

(ISAIAH 6:2)

We really don't know much about what the seraphim are like. Obviously, they aren't human like us. They are beings that come from heaven, and they worship God. We should try to act like them in the way that they worship him.

Why did Isaiah think he was ruined?

(ISAIAH 6:5)

The situation was really scary. The temple was shaking, and it was full of smoke. Isaiah felt very small when faced with God's perfect holiness. Read the verse that comes just before this one.

⁶Then one of the seraphim flew to me with a live coal in his hand, which he had taken with tongs from the altar. ⁷With it he touched my mouth and said, "See, this has touched your lips; your guilt is taken away and your sin atoned for."

⁸Then I heard the voice of the Lord saying, "Whom shall I send? And who will go for us?"

And I said, "Here am I. Send me!"

⁹He said, "Go and tell this people:

> " 'Be ever hearing, but never
> > understanding;
> > be ever seeing, but never perceiving.'
¹⁰ Make the heart of this people
> > calloused;
> > make their ears dull
> > and close their eyes.ª

ª 9,10 Hebrew; Septuagint 'You will be ever hearing, but never understanding; / you will be ever seeing, but never perceiving.' / ¹⁰This people's heart has become calloused; / they hardly hear with their ears, / and they have closed their eyes

Otherwise they might see with their
     eyes,
   hear with their ears,
   understand with their hearts,
and turn and be healed."

[11]Then I said, "For how long, Lord?"
And he answered:

"Until the cities lie ruined
   and without inhabitant,
until the houses are left deserted
   and the fields ruined and ravaged,
[12]until the LORD has sent everyone far
     away
   and the land is utterly forsaken.
[13]And though a tenth remains in the
     land,
   it will again be laid waste.
But as the terebinth and oak
   leave stumps when they are cut
     down,
   so the holy seed will be the stump
     in the land."

The Sign of Immanuel

7 When Ahaz son of Jotham, the son of
Uzziah, was king of Judah, King Rezin
of Aram and Pekah son of Remaliah king
of Israel marched up to fight against Jerusalem, but they could not overpower it.
   [2]Now the house of David was told,
"Aram has allied itself with[a] Ephraim"; so
the hearts of Ahaz and his people were
shaken, as the trees of the forest are
shaken by the wind.
   [3]Then the LORD said to Isaiah, "Go out,
you and your son Shear-Jashub,[b] to meet
Ahaz at the end of the aqueduct of the
Upper Pool, on the road to the Launderer's Field. [4]Say to him, 'Be careful, keep
calm and don't be afraid. Do not lose
heart because of these two smoldering
stubs of firewood—because of the fierce
anger of Rezin and Aram and of the son
of Remaliah. [5]Aram, Ephraim and Remaliah's son have plotted your ruin, saying,
[6]"Let us invade Judah; let us tear it apart
and divide it among ourselves, and make
the son of Tabeel king over it." [7]Yet this is
what the Sovereign LORD says:

" 'It will not take place,
   it will not happen,

[8]for the head of Aram is Damascus,
   and the head of Damascus is only
     Rezin.
Within sixty-five years
   Ephraim will be too shattered to be
     a people.
[9]The head of Ephraim is Samaria,
   and the head of Samaria is only
     Remaliah's son.
If you do not stand firm in your faith,
   you will not stand at all.' "

[10]Again the LORD spoke to Ahaz, [11]"Ask
the LORD your God for a sign, whether
in the deepest depths or in the highest
heights."
   [12]But Ahaz said, "I will not ask; I will not
put the LORD to the test."

---

[a] 2 Or has set up camp in   *[b] 3 Shear-Jashub means a
remnant will return.*

THE SCENE

DAMASCUS

(ISAIAH 7:8)

This was a very important city.
In ancient times, it was also the
capital of the Aramean empire
(kingdom). Its location was very
important for all the business of the
ancient world. Today, it is the capital
of Syria.

THE SCENE

SAMARIA

(ISAIAH 7:9)

Read about this city in Jeremiah 23:13.

¹³Then Isaiah said, "Hear now, you house of David! Is it not enough to try the patience of humans? Will you try the patience of my God also? ¹⁴Therefore the Lord himself will give you*ᵃ* a sign: The virgin*ᵇ* will conceive and give birth to a son, and*ᶜ* will call him Immanuel.*ᵈ* ¹⁵He will be eating curds and honey when he knows enough to reject the wrong and choose the right, ¹⁶for before the boy knows enough to reject the wrong and choose the right, the land of the two kings you dread will be laid waste. ¹⁷The Lᴏʀᴅ will bring on you and on your people and on the house of your father a time unlike any since Ephraim broke away from Judah— he will bring the king of Assyria."

Assyria, the Lᴏʀᴅ's Instrument

¹⁸In that day the Lᴏʀᴅ will whistle for flies from the Nile delta in Egypt and for bees from the land of Assyria. ¹⁹They will all come and settle in the steep ravines and in the crevices in the rocks, on all the thornbushes and at all the water holes. ²⁰In that day the Lord will use a razor hired from beyond the Euphrates River—the king of Assyria—to shave your head and private parts, and to cut off your beard also. ²¹In that day, a person will keep alive a young cow and two goats. ²²And because of the abundance of the milk they give, there will be curds to eat. All who remain in the land will eat curds and honey. ²³In that day, in every place where there were a thousand vines worth a thousand silver shekels,*ᵉ* there will be only briers and thorns. ²⁴Hunters will go there with bow and arrow, for the land will be covered with briers and thorns. ²⁵As for all the hills once cultivated by the hoe, you will no longer go there for fear of the briers and thorns; they will become places where cattle are turned loose and where sheep run.

Isaiah and His Children as Signs

8 The Lᴏʀᴅ said to me, "Take a large scroll and write on it with an ordinary pen: Maher-Shalal-Hash-Baz."*ᶠ* ²So I called in Uriah the priest and Zechariah son of Jeberekiah as reliable witnesses for me. ³Then I made love to the prophetess, and she conceived and gave birth to a son. And the Lᴏʀᴅ said to me, "Name him Maher-Shalal-Hash-Baz. ⁴For before the boy knows how to say 'My father' or 'My mother,' the wealth of Damascus and the plunder of Samaria will be carried off by the king of Assyria."

⁵The Lᴏʀᴅ spoke to me again:

⁶"Because this people has rejected
    the gently flowing waters of Shiloah
and rejoices over Rezin
    and the son of Remaliah,
⁷therefore the Lord is about to bring
        against them
    the mighty floodwaters of the
        Euphrates—
    the king of Assyria with all his
        pomp.
It will overflow all its channels,
    run over all its banks

ᵃ 14 The Hebrew is plural.   *ᵇ 14 Or young woman*
ᶜ 14 Masoretic Text; Dead Sea Scrolls *son, and he* or
son, and they   ᵈ 14 Immanuel means *God with us.*
ᵉ 23 That is, about 25 pounds or about 12 kilograms
ᶠ 1 Maher-Shalal-Hash-Baz means *quick to the plunder, swift
to the spoil;* also in verse 3.

THE SCENE

SHILOAH

(ISAIAH 8:6)

Water for the city was stored here. The place was hidden from view so the enemies couldn't get to one of the Israelites' most important sources of water.

8 and sweep on into Judah, swirling
　　over it,
　　passing through it and reaching up
　　　　to the neck.
Its outspread wings will cover the
　　　　breadth of your land,
　　Immanuel[a]!"

9 Raise the war cry,[b] you nations, and
　　　　be shattered!
　　Listen, all you distant lands.
　　Prepare for battle, and be shattered!
　　Prepare for battle, and be
　　　　shattered!
10 Devise your strategy, but it will be
　　　　thwarted;
　　propose your plan, but it will not
　　　　stand,
　　for God is with us.[c]

11 This is what the LORD says to me with his strong hand upon me, warning me not to follow the way of this people:

12 "Do not call conspiracy
　　everything this people calls a
　　　　conspiracy;
　　do not fear what they fear,
　　and do not dread it.
13 The LORD Almighty is the one you are
　　　　to regard as holy,
　　he is the one you are to fear,
　　he is the one you are to dread.
14 He will be a holy place;
　　for both Israel and Judah he
　　　　will be
　　a stone that causes people to
　　　　stumble
　　and a rock that makes them fall.
　　And for the people of Jerusalem he
　　　　will be
　　a trap and a snare.
15 Many of them will stumble;
　　they will fall and be broken,
　　they will be snared and captured."

16 Bind up this testimony of warning
　　and seal up God's instruction
　　　　among my disciples.
17 I will wait for the LORD,
　　who is hiding his face from the
　　　　descendants of Jacob.
　　I will put my trust in him.

18 Here am I, and the children the LORD has given me. We are signs and symbols in Israel from the LORD Almighty, who dwells on Mount Zion.

The Darkness Turns to Light

19 When someone tells you to consult mediums and spiritists, who whisper and mutter, should not a people inquire of their God? Why consult the dead on behalf of the living? 20 Consult God's instruction and the testimony of warning. If anyone does not speak according to this word, they have no light of dawn. 21 Distressed and hungry, they will roam through the land; when they are famished, they will become enraged and, looking upward, will curse their king and their God. 22 Then they will look toward the earth and see only distress and darkness and fearful gloom, and they will be thrust into utter darkness.

---

[a] 8 Immanuel means God with us.　　[b] 9 Or Do your worst
[c] 10 Hebrew Immanuel

9 ^a Nevertheless, there will be no more gloom for those who were in distress. In the past he humbled the land of Zebulun and the land of Naphtali, but in the future he will honor Galilee of the nations, by the Way of the Sea, beyond the Jordan—

² The people walking in darkness
  have seen a great light;
on those living in the land of deep
    darkness
  a light has dawned.
³ You have enlarged the nation
  and increased their joy;
they rejoice before you
  as people rejoice at the harvest,
as warriors rejoice
  when dividing the plunder.
⁴ For as in the day of Midian's defeat,
  you have shattered
the yoke that burdens them,
  the bar across their shoulders,
  the rod of their oppressor.
⁵ Every warrior's boot used in battle
  and every garment rolled in blood
will be destined for burning,
  will be fuel for the fire.
⁶ For to us a child is born,
  to us a son is given,
  and the government will be on his
    shoulders.
And he will be called
  Wonderful Counselor, Mighty God,
  Everlasting Father, Prince of Peace.
⁷ Of the greatness of his government
    and peace
  there will be no end.
He will reign on David's throne
  and over his kingdom,
establishing and upholding it
  with justice and righteousness
  from that time on and forever.
The zeal of the LORD Almighty
  will accomplish this.

The LORD's Anger Against Israel

⁸ The Lord has sent a message against
    Jacob;
  it will fall on Israel.
⁹ All the people will know it—
  Ephraim and the inhabitants of
    Samaria—

who say with pride
  and arrogance of heart,
¹⁰ "The bricks have fallen down,
  but we will rebuild with dressed
    stone;
the fig trees have been felled,
  but we will replace them with
    cedars."
¹¹ But the LORD has strengthened Rezin's
    foes against them
  and has spurred their
    enemies on.
¹² Arameans from the east and
    Philistines from the west
  have devoured Israel with open
    mouth.

---

^a In Hebrew texts 9:1 is numbered 8:23, and 9:2-21 is numbered 9:1-20.

THE

WITNESSES

✓ **DAVID** (ISAIAH 9:7)
Remember who this king is by reading
1 Samuel 16:13.

BREAK THROUGH!

Fig trees and cedars

(ISAIAH 9:10)

These two kinds of trees grow in Israel and in countries north of Israel. The Israelites are thinking that if an enemy comes and cuts the fig trees in the northern part of Israel, they'll just plant cedar trees, because they're stronger and taller. However, the Israelites really couldn't do anything to protect themselves from an enemy like the strong Assyrians.

Yet for all this, his anger is not turned
    away,
    his hand is still upraised.

13 But the people have not returned to
    him who struck them,
    nor have they sought the Lord
      Almighty.
14 So the Lord will cut off from Israel
    both head and tail,
    both palm branch and reed in a
      single day;
15 the elders and dignitaries are the
    head,
    the prophets who teach lies are the
    tail.
16 Those who guide this people mislead
    them,
    and those who are guided are led
    astray.

17 Therefore the Lord will take no
    pleasure in the young men,
    nor will he pity the fatherless and
    widows,
    for everyone is ungodly and wicked,
    every mouth speaks folly.

Yet for all this, his anger is not turned
    away,
    his hand is still upraised.

18 Surely wickedness burns like a fire;
    it consumes briers and thorns,
    it sets the forest thickets ablaze,
    so that it rolls upward in a column
    of smoke.
19 By the wrath of the Lord Almighty
    the land will be scorched
    and the people will be fuel for the
    fire;
    they will not spare one another.
20 On the right they will devour,
    but still be hungry;
    on the left they will eat,
    but not be satisfied.
    Each will feed on the flesh of their
    own offspring[a]:
21   Manasseh will feed on Ephraim, and
    Ephraim on Manasseh;
    together they will turn against
    Judah.

Yet for all this, his anger is not turned
    away,
    his hand is still upraised.

10 Woe to those who make unjust
    laws,
    to those who issue oppressive
    decrees,
2 to deprive the poor of their rights
    and withhold justice from the
    oppressed of my people,
    making widows their prey
    and robbing the fatherless.
3 What will you do on the day of
    reckoning,
    when disaster comes from afar?
    To whom will you run for help?
    Where will you leave your riches?
4 Nothing will remain but to cringe
    among the captives
    or fall among the slain.

---

a 20 Or *arm*

Yet for all this, his anger is not turned
away,
his hand is still upraised.

God's Judgment on Assyria

⁵ "Woe to the Assyrian, the rod of my
anger,
in whose hand is the club of my
wrath!
⁶ I send him against a godless nation,
I dispatch him against a people who
anger me,
to seize loot and snatch plunder,
and to trample them down like mud
in the streets.
⁷ But this is not what he intends,
this is not what he has in mind;
his purpose is to destroy,
to put an end to many nations.
⁸ 'Are not my commanders all kings?'
he says.
⁹   'Has not Kalno fared like
Carchemish?
Is not Hamath like Arpad,
and Samaria like Damascus?
¹⁰ As my hand seized the kingdoms of
the idols,
kingdoms whose images excelled
those of Jerusalem and
Samaria—
¹¹ shall I not deal with Jerusalem and
her images
as I dealt with Samaria and her
idols?' "

¹²When the Lord has finished all his
work against Mount Zion and Jerusalem,
he will say, "I will punish the king of Assyria for the willful pride of his heart and the
haughty look in his eyes. ¹³For he says:

" 'By the strength of my hand I have
done this,
and by my wisdom, because I have
understanding.
I removed the boundaries of nations,
I plundered their treasures;
like a mighty one I subdued[a] their
kings.
¹⁴ As one reaches into a nest,
so my hand reached for the wealth
of the nations;
as people gather abandoned eggs,
so I gathered all the countries;

not one flapped a wing,
or opened its mouth to chirp.' "

¹⁵ Does the ax raise itself above the
person who swings it,
or the saw boast against the one
who uses it?
As if a rod were to wield the person
who lifts it up,
or a club brandish the one who is
not wood!
¹⁶ Therefore, the Lord, the Lᴏʀᴅ Almighty,
will send a wasting disease upon
his sturdy warriors;
under his pomp a fire will be kindled
like a blazing flame.
¹⁷ The Light of Israel will become a fire,
their Holy One a flame;
in a single day it will burn and
consume
his thorns and his briers.
¹⁸ The splendor of his forests and fertile
fields
it will completely destroy,
as when a sick person wastes away.
¹⁹ And the remaining trees of his forests
will be so few
that a child could write them down.

The Remnant of Israel

²⁰ In that day the remnant of Israel,
the survivors of Jacob,
will no longer rely on him
who struck them down
but will truly rely on the Lᴏʀᴅ,
the Holy One of Israel.
²¹ A remnant will return,[b] a remnant of
Jacob
will return to the Mighty God.
²² Though your people be like the sand
by the sea, Israel,
only a remnant will return.
Destruction has been decreed,
overwhelming and righteous.
²³ The Lord, the Lᴏʀᴅ Almighty, will carry
out
the destruction decreed upon the
whole land.

²⁴ Therefore this is what the Lord, the
Lᴏʀᴅ Almighty, says:

---

a 13 Or *treasures; / I subdued the mighty,*   *b 21* Hebrew
shear-jashub (see 7:3 and note); also in verse 22

"My people who live in Zion,
do not be afraid of the Assyrians,
who beat you with a rod
and lift up a club against you, as
Egypt did.
25 Very soon my anger against you will end
and my wrath will be directed to
their destruction."

26 The Lord Almighty will lash them with
a whip,
as when he struck down Midian at
the rock of Oreb;
and he will raise his staff over the
waters,
as he did in Egypt.
27 In that day their burden will be lifted
from your shoulders,
their yoke from your neck;
the yoke will be broken
because you have grown so fat.[a]

28 They enter Aiath;
they pass through Migron;
they store supplies at Mikmash.
29 They go over the pass, and say,
"We will camp overnight at Geba."
Ramah trembles;
Gibeah of Saul flees.
30 Cry out, Daughter Gallim!
Listen, Laishah!
Poor Anathoth!
31 Madmenah is in flight;
the people of Gebim take cover.
32 This day they will halt at Nob;
they will shake their fist
at the mount of Daughter Zion,
at the hill of Jerusalem.

33 See, the Lord, the Lord Almighty,
will lop off the boughs with great
power.
The lofty trees will be felled,
the tall ones will be brought low.
34 He will cut down the forest thickets
with an ax;
Lebanon will fall before the Mighty
One.

The Branch From Jesse

11 A shoot will come up from the
stump of Jesse;
from his roots a Branch will bear
fruit.

2 The Spirit of the Lord will rest on
him—
the Spirit of wisdom and of
understanding,
the Spirit of counsel and of might,
the Spirit of the knowledge and fear
of the Lord—
3 and he will delight in the fear of the
Lord.

He will not judge by what he sees with
his eyes,
or decide by what he hears with his
ears;
4 but with righteousness he will judge
the needy,
with justice he will give decisions
for the poor of the earth.
He will strike the earth with the rod of
his mouth;
with the breath of his lips he will
slay the wicked.
5 Righteousness will be his belt
and faithfulness the sash around
his waist.

6 The wolf will live with the lamb,
the leopard will lie down with the
goat,
the calf and the lion and the yearling[b]
together;
and a little child will lead them.
7 The cow will feed with the bear,
their young will lie down together,
and the lion will eat straw like
the ox.
8 The infant will play near the cobra's
den,
and the young child will put its hand
into the viper's nest.
9 They will neither harm nor destroy
on all my holy mountain,
for the earth will be filled with the
knowledge of the Lord
as the waters cover the sea.

10 In that day the Root of Jesse will
stand as a banner for the peoples; the
nations will rally to him, and his resting
place will be glorious. 11 In that day the
Lord will reach out his hand a second
time to reclaim the surviving remnant of

---

[a] 27 Hebrew; Septuagint *broken / from your shoulders*
[b] 6 Hebrew; Septuagint *lion will feed*

his people from Assyria, from Lower Egypt, from Upper Egypt, from Cush,[a] from Elam, from Babylonia,[b] from Hamath and from the islands of the Mediterranean.

12 He will raise a banner for the nations
  and gather the exiles of Israel;
  he will assemble the scattered people
    of Judah
  from the four quarters of the earth.
13 Ephraim's jealousy will vanish,
  and Judah's enemies[c] will be
    destroyed;
  Ephraim will not be jealous of Judah,
  nor Judah hostile toward Ephraim.
14 They will swoop down on the slopes of
    Philistia to the west;
  together they will plunder the
    people to the east.
  They will subdue Edom and Moab,
  and the Ammonites will be subject
    to them.
15 The LORD will dry up
  the gulf of the Egyptian sea;
  with a scorching wind he will sweep
    his hand

BREAK THROUGH!

Edom, Moab and the Ammonites
(ISAIAH 11:14)
You can read about them in
Jeremiah 9:25 – 26.

over the Euphrates River.
He will break it up into seven
  streams
  so that anyone can cross over in
    sandals.
16 There will be a highway for the
    remnant of his people
  that is left from Assyria,
  as there was for Israel
  when they came up from Egypt.

Songs of Praise

12 In that day you will say:

"I will praise you, LORD.
  Although you were angry with me,
your anger has turned away
  and you have comforted me.
2 Surely God is my salvation;
  I will trust and not be afraid.
The LORD, the LORD himself, is my
    strength and my defense[d];
  he has become my salvation."
3 With joy you will draw water
  from the wells of salvation.

4 In that day you will say:

"Give praise to the LORD, proclaim his
    name;
  make known among the nations
    what he has done,
  and proclaim that his name is
    exalted.
5 Sing to the LORD, for he has done
    glorious things;
  let this be known to all the world.
6 Shout aloud and sing for joy, people of
    Zion,
  for great is the Holy One of Israel
    among you."

A Prophecy Against Babylon

13 A prophecy against Babylon that Isaiah son of Amoz saw:

2 Raise a banner on a bare hilltop,
  shout to them;
beckon to them
  to enter the gates of the nobles.
3 I have commanded those I prepared
    for battle;

---

a 11 That is, the upper Nile region   b 11 Hebrew *Shinar*
c 13 Or *hostility*   d 2 Or *song*

I have summoned my warriors to
    carry out my wrath—
those who rejoice in my triumph.

⁴ Listen, a noise on the mountains,
    like that of a great multitude!
Listen, an uproar among the
    kingdoms,
    like nations massing together!
The Lord Almighty is mustering
    an army for war.
⁵ They come from faraway lands,
    from the ends of the heavens—
the Lord and the weapons of his
    wrath—
    to destroy the whole country.

⁶ Wail, for the day of the Lord is near;
    it will come like destruction from
    the Almighty.ᵃ
⁷ Because of this, all hands will go limp,
    every heart will melt with fear.
⁸ Terror will seize them,
    pain and anguish will grip them;
    they will writhe like a woman in
    labor.
They will look aghast at each other,
    their faces aflame.

⁹ See, the day of the Lord is coming
    —a cruel day, with wrath and fierce
    anger—
to make the land desolate
    and destroy the sinners within it.
¹⁰ The stars of heaven and their
    constellations
    will not show their light.
The rising sun will be darkened
    and the moon will not give its
    light.
¹¹ I will punish the world for its evil,
    the wicked for their sins.
I will put an end to the arrogance of
    the haughty
    and will humble the pride of the
    ruthless.
¹² I will make people scarcer than pure
    gold,
    more rare than the gold of Ophir.
¹³ Therefore I will make the heavens
    tremble;
    and the earth will shake from its
    place
at the wrath of the Lord Almighty,
    in the day of his burning anger.

BREAK THROUGH!

Will the sun and the moon stop shining someday?

(ISAIAH 13:10)

They're not really going to stop shining. Many people worship the sun, the moon and the stars as if they are gods. In this poem, the prophet is saying that someday people won't be worshiping the sun or the moon, but the true God instead.

¹⁴ Like a hunted gazelle,
    like sheep without a shepherd,
they will all return to their own people,
    they will flee to their native land.
¹⁵ Whoever is captured will be thrust
    through;
    all who are caught will fall by the
    sword.
¹⁶ Their infants will be dashed to pieces
    before their eyes;
    their houses will be looted and their
    wives violated.

¹⁷ See, I will stir up against them the
    Medes,
who do not care for silver
    and have no delight in gold.
¹⁸ Their bows will strike down the young
    men;
    they will have no mercy on infants,

ᵃ 6 Hebrew *Shaddai*

nor will they look with compassion
on children.
¹⁹ Babylon, the jewel of kingdoms,
the pride and glory of the
Babylonians,ᵃ
will be overthrown by God
like Sodom and Gomorrah.
²⁰ She will never be inhabited
or lived in through all generations;
there no nomads will pitch their tents,
there no shepherds will rest their
flocks.
²¹ But desert creatures will lie there,
jackals will fill her houses;
there the owls will dwell,
and there the wild goats will leap
about.
²² Hyenas will inhabit her strongholds,
jackals her luxurious palaces.
Her time is at hand,
and her days will not be prolonged.

14 The LORD will have compassion on
Jacob;
once again he will choose Israel
and will settle them in their own
land.
Foreigners will join them
and unite with the descendants of
Jacob.
² Nations will take them
and bring them to their own place.
And Israel will take possession of the
nations
and make them male and female
servants in the LORD's land.
They will make captives of their
captors
and rule over their oppressors.

³ On the day the LORD gives you relief
from your suffering and turmoil and from
the harsh labor forced on you, ⁴ you will
take up this taunt against the king of Babylon:

How the oppressor has come to an
end!
How his furyᵇ has ended!
⁵ The LORD has broken the rod of the
wicked,
the scepter of the rulers,
⁶ which in anger struck down peoples
with unceasing blows,

and in fury subdued nations
with relentless aggression.
⁷ All the lands are at rest and at peace;
they break into singing.
⁸ Even the junipers and the cedars of
Lebanon
gloat over you and say,
"Now that you have been laid low,
no one comes to cut us down."

⁹ The realm of the dead below is all
astir
to meet you at your coming;
it rouses the spirits of the departed to
greet you—
all those who were leaders in the
world;

ᵃ 19 Or *Chaldeans*   ᵇ 4 Dead Sea Scrolls, Septuagint
and Syriac; the meaning of the word in the Masoretic Text
is uncertain.

BREAK THROUGH!

Why will everybody be happy when Babylon is destroyed?

(ISAIAH 14:8)

Babylon was a powerful empire. It caused a
lot of damage and made people afraid. Many
people were made slaves, and families were
separated. Because of that, the poem says
that even the trees will be happy when this
enemy is conquered and is no longer a threat
to the rest of the world.

it makes them rise from their
thrones—
all those who were kings over the
nations.
¹⁰ They will all respond,
they will say to you,
"You also have become weak, as we
are;
you have become like us."
¹¹ All your pomp has been brought down
to the grave,
along with the noise of your harps;
maggots are spread out beneath you
and worms cover you.

¹² How you have fallen from heaven,
morning star, son of the dawn!
You have been cast down to the earth,
you who once laid low the nations!
¹³ You said in your heart,
"I will ascend to the heavens;
I will raise my throne
above the stars of God;
I will sit enthroned on the mount of
assembly,
on the utmost heights of Mount
Zaphon.ᵃ
¹⁴ I will ascend above the tops of the
clouds;
I will make myself like the Most
High."
¹⁵ But you are brought down to the realm
of the dead,
to the depths of the pit.

¹⁶ Those who see you stare at you,
they ponder your fate:
"Is this the man who shook the earth
and made kingdoms tremble,
¹⁷ the man who made the world a
wilderness,
who overthrew its cities
and would not let his captives go
home?"

¹⁸ All the kings of the nations lie in
state,
each in his own tomb.
¹⁹ But you are cast out of your tomb
like a rejected branch;
you are covered with the slain,
with those pierced by the sword,
those who descend to the stones of
the pit.
Like a corpse trampled underfoot,

²⁰ you will not join them in burial,
for you have destroyed your land
and killed your people.

Let the offspring of the wicked
never be mentioned again.
²¹ Prepare a place to slaughter his
children
for the sins of their ancestors;
they are not to rise to inherit the land
and cover the earth with their cities.

²² "I will rise up against them,"
declares the Lord Almighty.
"I will wipe out Babylon's name and
survivors,
her offspring and descendants,"
declares the Lord.
²³ "I will turn her into a place for owls
and into swampland;
I will sweep her with the broom of
destruction,"
declares the Lord Almighty.

²⁴ The Lord Almighty has sworn,

"Surely, as I have planned, so it will
be,
and as I have purposed, so it will
happen.
²⁵ I will crush the Assyrian in my land;
on my mountains I will trample him
down.
His yoke will be taken from my people,
and his burden removed from their
shoulders."

²⁶ This is the plan determined for the
whole world;
this is the hand stretched out over
all nations.
²⁷ For the Lord Almighty has purposed,
and who can thwart him?
His hand is stretched out, and who
can turn it back?

A Prophecy Against the Philistines

²⁸ This prophecy came in the year King
Ahaz died:

²⁹ Do not rejoice, all you Philistines,
that the rod that struck you is
broken;

ᵃ 13 Or of the north; Zaphon was the most sacred
mountain of the Canaanites.

from the root of that snake will spring
    up a viper,
    its fruit will be a darting, venomous
      serpent.
30 The poorest of the poor will find
    pasture,
    and the needy will lie down in
      safety.
But your root I will destroy by famine;
    it will slay your survivors.
31 Wail, you gate! Howl, you city!
    Melt away, all you Philistines!
A cloud of smoke comes from the
    north,
    and there is not a straggler in its
      ranks.
32 What answer shall be given
    to the envoys of that nation?
"The LORD has established Zion,
    and in her his afflicted people will
      find refuge."

A Prophecy Against Moab

15 A prophecy against Moab:

Ar in Moab is ruined,
    destroyed in a night!
Kir in Moab is ruined,
    destroyed in a night!
2 Dibon goes up to its temple,
    to its high places to weep;
    Moab wails over Nebo and Medeba.
Every head is shaved
    and every beard cut off.
3 In the streets they wear sackcloth;
    on the roofs and in the public
      squares
they all wail,
    prostrate with weeping.
4 Heshbon and Elealeh cry out,
    their voices are heard all the way to
      Jahaz.
Therefore the armed men of Moab cry
    out,
    and their hearts are faint.
5 My heart cries out over Moab;
    her fugitives flee as far as Zoar,
    as far as Eglath Shelishiyah.
They go up the hill to Luhith,
    weeping as they go;
on the road to Horonaim
    they lament their destruction.

6 The waters of Nimrim are dried up
    and the grass is withered;
the vegetation is gone
    and nothing green is left.
7 So the wealth they have acquired and
    stored up
they carry away over the Ravine of
    the Poplars.
8 Their outcry echoes along the border
    of Moab;
their wailing reaches as far as
    Eglaim,
their lamentation as far as Beer
    Elim.
9 The waters of Dimon*a* are full of blood,
    but I will bring still more upon
      Dimon*a* —
a lion upon the fugitives of Moab
    and upon those who remain in the
      land.

16 Send lambs as tribute
    to the ruler of the land,
from Sela, across the desert,
    to the mount of Daughter Zion.
2 Like fluttering birds
    pushed from the nest,
so are the women of Moab
    at the fords of the Arnon.

3 "Make up your mind," Moab says.
    "Render a decision.
Make your shadow like night —
    at high noon.
Hide the fugitives,
    do not betray the refugees.
4 Let the Moabite fugitives stay with
    you;
    be their shelter from the
      destroyer."

The oppressor will come to an end,
    and destruction will cease;
    the aggressor will vanish from the
      land.
5 In love a throne will be established;
    in faithfulness a man will sit
    on it —
one from the house*b* of David —
one who in judging seeks justice
    and speeds the cause of
      righteousness.

---

a 9 *Dimon*, a wordplay on *Dibon* (see verse 2), sounds like the Hebrew for *blood*.   *b* 5 Hebrew *tent*

THE SCENE

ARNON RIVER

(ISAIAH 16:2)

Again, you can see that water is something very important for the region the Israelites lived in. This river crossed through the country of Moab on the eastern side of Israel. For the Moabites, the water from this river was very valuable.

⁶We have heard of Moab's pride—
how great is her arrogance!—
of her conceit, her pride and her
insolence;
but her boasts are empty.
⁷Therefore the Moabites wail,
they wail together for Moab.
Lament and grieve
for the raisin cakes of Kir Hareseth.
⁸The fields of Heshbon wither,
the vines of Sibmah also.
The rulers of the nations
have trampled down the choicest
vines,
which once reached Jazer
and spread toward the desert.
Their shoots spread out
and went as far as the sea.*ᵃ*
⁹So I weep, as Jazer weeps,
for the vines of Sibmah.

Heshbon and Elealeh,
I drench you with tears!
The shouts of joy over your ripened
fruit
and over your harvests have been
stilled.
¹⁰Joy and gladness are taken away from
the orchards;
no one sings or shouts in the
vineyards;
no one treads out wine at the presses,
for I have put an end to the
shouting.
¹¹My heart laments for Moab like a
harp,
my inmost being for Kir Hareseth.
¹²When Moab appears at her high place,
she only wears herself out;
when she goes to her shrine to pray,
it is to no avail.

¹³This is the word the Lᴏʀᴅ has already spoken concerning Moab. ¹⁴But now the Lᴏʀᴅ says: "Within three years, as a servant bound by contract would count them, Moab's splendor and all her many people will be despised, and her survivors will be very few and feeble."

A Prophecy Against Damascus

17 A prophecy against Damascus:

"See, Damascus will no longer be a
city
but will become a heap of ruins.
²The cities of Aroer will be deserted
and left to flocks, which will lie
down,
with no one to make them afraid.
³The fortified city will disappear from
Ephraim,
and royal power from Damascus;
the remnant of Aram will be
like the glory of the Israelites,"
declares the Lᴏʀᴅ Almighty.

⁴"In that day the glory of Jacob will
fade;
the fat of his body will waste away.
⁵It will be as when reapers harvest the
standing grain,
gathering the grain in their arms—

ᵃ 8 Probably the Dead Sea

as when someone gleans heads of
grain
in the Valley of Rephaim.
⁶ Yet some gleanings will remain,
as when an olive tree is beaten,
leaving two or three olives on the
topmost branches,
four or five on the fruitful boughs,"
declares the LORD, the God
of Israel.
⁷ In that day people will look to their
Maker
and turn their eyes to the Holy One
of Israel.
⁸ They will not look to the altars,
the work of their hands,
and they will have no regard for the
Asherah poles*a*
and the incense altars their fingers
have made.

⁹ In that day their strong cities, which
they left because of the Israelites, will be
like places abandoned to thickets and undergrowth. And all will be desolation.

¹⁰ You have forgotten God your Savior;
you have not remembered the Rock,
your fortress.
Therefore, though you set out the
finest plants
and plant imported vines,
¹¹ though on the day you set them out,
you make them grow,
and on the morning when you plant
them, you bring them to bud,
yet the harvest will be as nothing
in the day of disease and incurable
pain.
¹² Woe to the many nations that rage—
they rage like the raging sea!
Woe to the peoples who roar—
they roar like the roaring of great
waters!
¹³ Although the peoples roar like the roar
of surging waters,
when he rebukes them they flee far
away,
driven before the wind like chaff on
the hills,
like tumbleweed before a gale.
¹⁴ In the evening, sudden terror!
Before the morning, they are gone!

This is the portion of those who
loot us,
the lot of those who plunder us.

A Prophecy Against Cush

18 Woe to the land of whirring wings*b*
along the rivers of Cush,*c*
² which sends envoys by sea
in papyrus boats over the water.

Go, swift messengers,
to a people tall and smooth-skinned,
to a people feared far and wide,
an aggressive nation of strange
speech,
whose land is divided by rivers.

³ All you people of the world,
you who live on the earth,
when a banner is raised on the
mountains,
you will see it,
and when a trumpet sounds,
you will hear it.
⁴ This is what the LORD says to me:
"I will remain quiet and will look on
from my dwelling place,
like shimmering heat in the
sunshine,
like a cloud of dew in the heat of
harvest."
⁵ For, before the harvest, when the
blossom is gone
and the flower becomes a ripening
grape,
he will cut off the shoots with pruning
knives,
and cut down and take away the
spreading branches.
⁶ They will all be left to the mountain
birds of prey
and to the wild animals;
the birds will feed on them all
summer,
the wild animals all winter.

⁷ At that time gifts will be brought to the
LORD Almighty

from a people tall and smooth-
skinned,
from a people feared far and wide,

---

a 8 That is, wooden symbols of the goddess Asherah
b 1 Or *of locusts*   *c* 1 That is, the upper Nile region

an aggressive nation of strange
speech,
whose land is divided by rivers —

the gifts will be brought to Mount Zion, the
place of the Name of the LORD Almighty.

A Prophecy Against Egypt

19 A prophecy against Egypt:

See, the LORD rides on a swift cloud
and is coming to Egypt.
The idols of Egypt tremble before him,
and the hearts of the Egyptians
melt with fear.

2 "I will stir up Egyptian against
Egyptian —
brother will fight against brother,
neighbor against neighbor,
city against city,
kingdom against kingdom.
3 The Egyptians will lose heart,
and I will bring their plans to
nothing;
they will consult the idols and the
spirits of the dead,
the mediums and the spiritists.
4 I will hand the Egyptians over
to the power of a cruel master,
and a fierce king will rule over them,"
declares the Lord, the LORD
Almighty.

5 The waters of the river will dry up,
and the riverbed will be parched and
dry.
6 The canals will stink;
the streams of Egypt will dwindle
and dry up.
The reeds and rushes will wither,
7 also the plants along the Nile,
at the mouth of the river.
Every sown field along the Nile
will become parched, will blow away
and be no more.
8 The fishermen will groan and lament,
all who cast hooks into the Nile;
those who throw nets on the water
will pine away.
9 Those who work with combed flax will
despair,
the weavers of fine linen will lose
hope.

10 The workers in cloth will be dejected,
and all the wage earners will be
sick at heart.
11 The officials of Zoan are nothing but
fools;
the wise counselors of Pharaoh give
senseless advice.
How can you say to Pharaoh,
"I am one of the wise men,
a disciple of the ancient kings"?
12 Where are your wise men now?
Let them show you and make known
what the LORD Almighty
has planned against Egypt.
13 The officials of Zoan have become
fools,
the leaders of Memphis are
deceived;
the cornerstones of her peoples
have led Egypt astray.
14 The LORD has poured into them
a spirit of dizziness;
they make Egypt stagger in all that
she does,
as a drunkard staggers around in
his vomit.
15 There is nothing Egypt can do —
head or tail, palm branch or reed.

16 In that day the Egyptians will become
weaklings. They will shudder with fear at
the uplifted hand that the LORD Almighty
raises against them. 17 And the land of Judah will bring terror to the Egyptians; everyone to whom Judah is mentioned will
be terrified, because of what the LORD Almighty is planning against them.
18 In that day five cities in Egypt will
speak the language of Canaan and swear
allegiance to the LORD Almighty. One of
them will be called the City of the Sun.*a*
19 In that day there will be an altar to the
LORD in the heart of Egypt, and a monument to the LORD at its border. 20 It will be
a sign and witness to the LORD Almighty
in the land of Egypt. When they cry out
to the LORD because of their oppressors,
he will send them a savior and defender,
and he will rescue them. 21 So the LORD will

---

a 18 Some manuscripts of the Masoretic Text, Dead Sea
Scrolls, Symmachus and Vulgate; most manuscripts of the
Masoretic Text *City of Destruction*

make himself known to the Egyptians, and in that day they will acknowledge the LORD. They will worship with sacrifices and grain offerings; they will make vows to the LORD and keep them. ²²The LORD will strike Egypt with a plague; he will strike them and heal them. They will turn to the LORD, and he will respond to their pleas and heal them. ²³In that day there will be a highway from Egypt to Assyria. The Assyrians will go to Egypt and the Egyptians to Assyria. The Egyptians and Assyrians will worship together. ²⁴In that day Israel will be the third, along with Egypt and Assyria, a blessing*a* on the earth. ²⁵The LORD Almighty will bless them, saying, "Blessed be Egypt my people, Assyria my handiwork, and Israel my inheritance."

A Prophecy Against Egypt and Cush

20 In the year that the supreme commander, sent by Sargon king of Assyria, came to Ashdod and attacked and captured it— ²at that time the LORD spoke through Isaiah son of Amoz. He said to him, "Take off the sackcloth from your body and the sandals from your feet." And he did so, going around stripped and barefoot. ³Then the LORD said, "Just as my servant Isaiah has gone stripped and barefoot for three years, as a sign and portent against Egypt and Cush,*b* ⁴so the king of Assyria will lead away stripped and barefoot the Egyptian captives and Cushite exiles, young and old, with buttocks bared—to Egypt's shame. ⁵Those who trusted in Cush and boasted in Egypt will be dismayed and put to shame. ⁶In that day the people who live on this coast will say, 'See what has happened to those we relied on, those we fled to for help and deliverance from the king of Assyria! How then can we escape?' "

A Prophecy Against Babylon

21 A prophecy against the Desert by the Sea:

Like whirlwinds sweeping through the
   southland,
an invader comes from the desert,
   from a land of terror.

²A dire vision has been shown to me:
   The traitor betrays, the looter takes
      loot.
Elam, attack! Media, lay siege!
   I will bring to an end all the groaning
      she caused.

³At this my body is racked with pain,
   pangs seize me, like those of a
      woman in labor;
I am staggered by what I hear,
   I am bewildered by what I see.
⁴My heart falters,
   fear makes me tremble;
the twilight I longed for
   has become a horror to me.

⁵They set the tables,
   they spread the rugs,
   they eat, they drink!
Get up, you officers,
   oil the shields!

---

a 24 Or *Assyria, whose names will be used in blessings* (see Gen. 48:20); or *Assyria, who will be seen by others as blessed*   *b 3* That is, the upper Nile region; also in verse 5

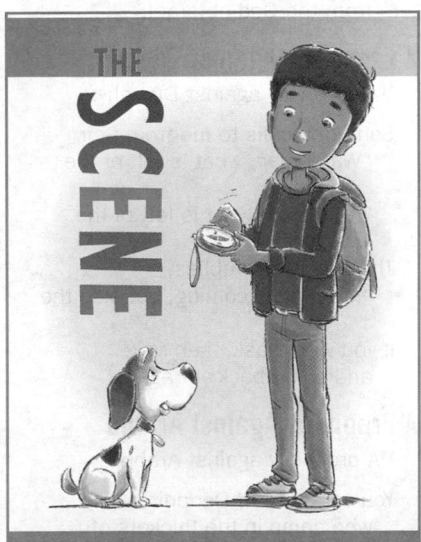

THE
SCENE

CUSH

(ISAIAH 20:3)

This country is in the northern part of Africa, very near Egypt.

⁶This is what the Lord says to me:

"Go, post a lookout
   and have him report what he sees.
⁷When he sees chariots
   with teams of horses,
riders on donkeys
   or riders on camels,
let him be alert,
   fully alert."

⁸And the lookout[a] shouted,

"Day after day, my lord, I stand on the
      watchtower;
   every night I stay at my post.
⁹Look, here comes a man in a chariot
   with a team of horses.
And he gives back the answer:
   'Babylon has fallen, has fallen!
All the images of its gods
   lie shattered on the ground!' "

¹⁰My people who are crushed on the
      threshing floor,
   I tell you what I have heard
from the LORD Almighty,
   from the God of Israel.

A Prophecy Against Edom

¹¹A prophecy against Dumah[b]:

Someone calls to me from Seir,
   "Watchman, what is left of the
      night?
   Watchman, what is left of the
      night?"
¹²The watchman replies,
   "Morning is coming, but also the
      night.
If you would ask, then ask;
   and come back yet again."

A Prophecy Against Arabia

¹³A prophecy against Arabia:

You caravans of Dedanites,
   who camp in the thickets of
      Arabia,
¹⁴   bring water for the thirsty;
you who live in Tema,
   bring food for the fugitives.
¹⁵They flee from the sword,
   from the drawn sword,
from the bent bow
   and from the heat of battle.

¹⁶This is what the Lord says to me:
"Within one year, as a servant bound by
contract would count it, all the splendor
of Kedar will come to an end. ¹⁷The survivors of the archers, the warriors of Kedar,
will be few." The LORD, the God of Israel,
has spoken.

A Prophecy About Jerusalem

22 A prophecy against the Valley of Vision:

What troubles you now,
   that you have all gone up on the
      roofs,
²you town so full of commotion,
   you city of tumult and revelry?
Your slain were not killed by the
      sword,
   nor did they die in battle.
³All your leaders have fled together;
   they have been captured without
      using the bow.
All you who were caught were taken
      prisoner together,
   having fled while the enemy was
      still far away.
⁴Therefore I said, "Turn away from me;
   let me weep bitterly.
Do not try to console me
   over the destruction of my people."

⁵The Lord, the LORD Almighty, has a
      day
   of tumult and trampling and terror
   in the Valley of Vision,
a day of battering down walls
   and of crying out to the mountains.
⁶Elam takes up the quiver,
   with her charioteers and horses;
Kir uncovers the shield.
⁷Your choicest valleys are full of
      chariots,
   and horsemen are posted at the
      city gates.

⁸The Lord stripped away the defenses
      of Judah,
   and you looked in that day
   to the weapons in the Palace of the
      Forest.

---

[a] 8 Dead Sea Scrolls and Syriac; Masoretic Text *A lion*
[b] 11 *Dumah*, a wordplay on *Edom*, means *silence* or
stillness.

BREAK THROUGH!

The Palace of the Forest

(ISAIAH 22:8)

Do you remember Solomon? He was the king who built the temple in Jerusalem. The Palace of the Forest was part of his palace that had decorative wood on the walls. Weapons and other very valuable things were stored in this section of the palace.

9 You saw that the walls of the City of David
   were broken through in many places;
you stored up water
   in the Lower Pool.
10 You counted the buildings in Jerusalem
   and tore down houses to strengthen the wall.
11 You built a reservoir between the two walls
   for the water of the Old Pool,
but you did not look to the One who made it,
   or have regard for the One who planned it long ago.

12 The Lord, the LORD Almighty,
   called you on that day
to weep and to wail,
   to tear out your hair and put on sackcloth.

13 But see, there is joy and revelry,
   slaughtering of cattle and killing of sheep,
   eating of meat and drinking of wine!
"Let us eat and drink," you say,
   "for tomorrow we die!"

14 The LORD Almighty has revealed this in my hearing: "Till your dying day this sin will not be atoned for," says the Lord, the LORD Almighty.

15 This is what the Lord, the LORD Almighty, says:

"Go, say to this steward,
   to Shebna the palace administrator:
16 What are you doing here and who gave you permission
   to cut out a grave for yourself here,

THE WITNESSES

✓ **SHEBNA** (ISAIAH 22:15)
He supervised everything in the king's house.

hewing your grave on the height
and chiseling your resting place in
the rock?

17 "Beware, the LORD is about to take
firm hold of you
and hurl you away, you mighty man.
18 He will roll you up tightly like a ball
and throw you into a large country.
There you will die
and there the chariots you were so
proud of
will become a disgrace to your
master's house.
19 I will depose you from your office,
and you will be ousted from your
position.

20 "In that day I will summon my servant, Eliakim son of Hilkiah. 21 I will clothe
him with your robe and fasten your sash
around him and hand your authority over
to him. He will be a father to those who
live in Jerusalem and to the people of Judah. 22 I will place on his shoulder the key
to the house of David; what he opens no
one can shut, and what he shuts no one
can open. 23 I will drive him like a peg into
a firm place; he will become a seat[a] of
honor for the house of his father. 24 All the
glory of his family will hang on him: its offspring and offshoots—all its lesser vessels, from the bowls to all the jars.

25 "In that day," declares the LORD Almighty, "the peg driven into the firm place
will give way; it will be sheared off and will
fall, and the load hanging on it will be cut
down." The LORD has spoken.

A Prophecy Against Tyre

23 A prophecy against Tyre:

Wail, you ships of Tarshish!
For Tyre is destroyed
and left without house or harbor.
From the land of Cyprus
word has come to them.

2 Be silent, you people of the island
and you merchants of Sidon,
whom the seafarers have
enriched.
3 On the great waters
came the grain of the Shihor;

THE SCENE

TYRE AND SIDON

(ISAIAH 23:1)

Read about them in Jeremiah 27:3.

the harvest of the Nile[b] was the
revenue of Tyre,
and she became the marketplace of
the nations.

4 Be ashamed, Sidon, and you fortress
of the sea,
for the sea has spoken:
"I have neither been in labor nor given
birth;
I have neither reared sons nor
brought up daughters."
5 When word comes to Egypt,
they will be in anguish at the report
from Tyre.

6 Cross over to Tarshish;
wail, you people of the island.
7 Is this your city of revelry,
the old, old city,
whose feet have taken her
to settle in far-off lands?
8 Who planned this against Tyre,
the bestower of crowns,

---

[a] 23 Or throne   [b] 2,3 Masoretic Text; Dead Sea Scrolls
Sidon, / who cross over the sea; / your envoys [3]are on the
great waters. / The grain of the Shihor, / the harvest of the
Nile,

THE SCENE

CYPRUS

(ISAIAH 23:1)

An island in the Mediterranean Sea. It's the third-largest island in the entire Mediterranean Sea.

whose merchants are princes,
    whose traders are renowned in the earth?
9 The LORD Almighty planned it,
    to bring down her pride in all her splendor
and to humble all who are renowned on the earth.
10 Till*a* your land as they do along the Nile,
Daughter Tarshish,
    for you no longer have a harbor.
11 The LORD has stretched out his hand over the sea
    and made its kingdoms tremble.
He has given an order concerning Phoenicia
    that her fortresses be destroyed.
12 He said, "No more of your reveling,
    Virgin Daughter Sidon, now crushed!

"Up, cross over to Cyprus;
    even there you will find no rest."

13 Look at the land of the Babylonians,*b*
    this people that is now of no account!
The Assyrians have made it
    a place for desert creatures;
they raised up their siege towers,
    they stripped its fortresses bare
    and turned it into a ruin.

14 Wail, you ships of Tarshish;
    your fortress is destroyed!

15 At that time Tyre will be forgotten for seventy years, the span of a king's life. But at the end of these seventy years, it will happen to Tyre as in the song of the prostitute:

16 "Take up a harp, walk through the city,
    you forgotten prostitute;
play the harp well, sing many a song,
    so that you will be remembered."

17 At the end of seventy years, the LORD will deal with Tyre. She will return to her lucrative prostitution and will ply her trade with all the kingdoms on the face of the earth. 18 Yet her profit and her earnings will be set apart for the LORD; they will not be stored up or hoarded. Her profits will go to those who live before the LORD, for abundant food and fine clothes.

The LORD's Devastation of the Earth

24 See, the LORD is going to lay waste
    the earth
    and devastate it;
he will ruin its face
    and scatter its inhabitants—
2 it will be the same
    for priest as for people,
    for the master as for his servant,
    for the mistress as for her servant,
    for seller as for buyer,
    for borrower as for lender,
    for debtor as for creditor.
3 The earth will be completely laid waste
    and totally plundered.
        The LORD has spoken this word.

4 The earth dries up and withers,
    the world languishes and withers,
    the heavens languish with the earth.

---

a 10 Dead Sea Scrolls and some Septuagint manuscripts; Masoretic Text *Go through*   *b* 13 Or *Chaldeans*

⁵ The earth is defiled by its people;
  they have disobeyed the laws,
  violated the statutes
  and broken the everlasting
    covenant.
⁶ Therefore a curse consumes the
    earth;
  its people must bear their guilt.
Therefore earth's inhabitants are
    burned up,
  and very few are left.
⁷ The new wine dries up and the vine
    withers;
  all the merrymakers groan.
⁸ The joyful timbrels are stilled,
  the noise of the revelers has
    stopped,
  the joyful harp is silent.
⁹ No longer do they drink wine with a
    song;
  the beer is bitter to its drinkers.
¹⁰ The ruined city lies desolate;
  the entrance to every house is
    barred.
¹¹ In the streets they cry out for wine;
  all joy turns to gloom,
  all joyful sounds are banished from
    the earth.
¹² The city is left in ruins,
  its gate is battered to pieces.
¹³ So will it be on the earth
  and among the nations,
as when an olive tree is beaten,
  or as when gleanings are left after
    the grape harvest.

¹⁴ They raise their voices, they shout for
    joy;
  from the west they acclaim the
    LORD's majesty.
¹⁵ Therefore in the east give glory to the
    LORD;
  exalt the name of the LORD, the God
    of Israel,
  in the islands of the sea.
¹⁶ From the ends of the earth we hear
    singing:
  "Glory to the Righteous One."

But I said, "I waste away, I waste away!
  Woe to me!
The treacherous betray!
  With treachery the treacherous
    betray!"

¹⁷ Terror and pit and snare await you,
  people of the earth.
¹⁸ Whoever flees at the sound of terror
  will fall into a pit;
whoever climbs out of the pit
  will be caught in a snare.
The floodgates of the heavens are
    opened,
  the foundations of the earth shake.
¹⁹ The earth is broken up,
  the earth is split asunder,
  the earth is violently shaken.
²⁰ The earth reels like a drunkard,
  it sways like a hut in the wind;
so heavy upon it is the guilt of its
    rebellion
  that it falls—never to rise again.

²¹ In that day the LORD will punish
  the powers in the heavens above
  and the kings on the earth below.
²² They will be herded together
  like prisoners bound in a dungeon;
they will be shut up in prison
  and be punished[a] after many days.
²³ The moon will be dismayed,
  the sun ashamed;
for the LORD Almighty will reign
  on Mount Zion and in Jerusalem,
  and before its elders—with great
    glory.

Praise to the LORD

25 LORD, you are my God;
  I will exalt you and praise your
    name,
for in perfect faithfulness
  you have done wonderful things,
  things planned long ago.
² You have made the city a heap of
    rubble,
  the fortified town a ruin,
the foreigners' stronghold a city no
    more;
  it will never be rebuilt.
³ Therefore strong peoples will honor you;
  cities of ruthless nations will revere
    you.
⁴ You have been a refuge for the poor,
  a refuge for the needy in their
    distress,

---

[a] 22 Or *released*

a shelter from the storm
and a shade from the heat.
For the breath of the ruthless
is like a storm driving against a
wall
5 and like the heat of the desert.
You silence the uproar of foreigners;
as heat is reduced by the shadow
of a cloud,
so the song of the ruthless is
stilled.

6 On this mountain the Lord Almighty
will prepare
a feast of rich food for all peoples,
a banquet of aged wine—
the best of meats and the finest of
wines.
7 On this mountain he will destroy
the shroud that enfolds all peoples,
the sheet that covers all nations;
8 he will swallow up death forever.
The Sovereign Lord will wipe away the
tears
from all faces;
he will remove his people's disgrace
from all the earth.
The Lord has spoken.

9 In that day they will say,

"Surely this is our God;
we trusted in him, and he saved us.
This is the Lord, we trusted in him;
let us rejoice and be glad in his
salvation."

10 The hand of the Lord will rest on this
mountain;
but Moab will be trampled in their
land
as straw is trampled down in the
manure.
11 They will stretch out their hands in it,
as swimmers stretch out their
hands to swim.
God will bring down their pride
despite the cleverness[a] of their
hands.
12 He will bring down your high fortified
walls
and lay them low;
he will bring them down to the
ground,
to the very dust.

A Song of Praise

26 In that day this song will be sung in
the land of Judah:

We have a strong city;
God makes salvation
its walls and ramparts.
2 Open the gates
that the righteous nation may
enter,
the nation that keeps faith.
3 You will keep in perfect peace
those whose minds are steadfast,
because they trust in you.
4 Trust in the Lord forever,
for the Lord, the Lord himself, is
the Rock eternal.
5 He humbles those who dwell on
high,
he lays the lofty city low;
he levels it to the ground
and casts it down to the dust.
6 Feet trample it down—
the feet of the oppressed,
the footsteps of the poor.

7 The path of the righteous is level;
you, the Upright One, make the
way of the righteous
smooth.
8 Yes, Lord, walking in the way of your
laws,[b]
we wait for you;
your name and renown
are the desire of our hearts.
9 My soul yearns for you in the night;
in the morning my spirit longs for
you.
When your judgments come upon the
earth,
the people of the world learn
righteousness.
10 But when grace is shown to the
wicked,
they do not learn righteousness;
even in a land of uprightness they go
on doing evil
and do not regard the majesty of
the Lord.
11 Lord, your hand is lifted high,
but they do not see it.

---

a 11 The meaning of the Hebrew for this word is uncertain.
b 8 Or judgments

Let them see your zeal for your people
    and be put to shame;
let the fire reserved for your
    enemies consume them.

12 LORD, you establish peace for us;
    all that we have accomplished you
    have done for us.
13 LORD our God, other lords besides you
    have ruled over us,
but your name alone do we honor.
14 They are now dead, they live no
    more;
    their spirits do not rise.
You punished them and brought them
    to ruin;
    you wiped out all memory of them.
15 You have enlarged the nation, LORD;
    you have enlarged the nation.
You have gained glory for yourself;
    you have extended all the borders
    of the land.

16 LORD, they came to you in their
    distress;
when you disciplined them,
    they could barely whisper a prayer.[a]
17 As a pregnant woman about to give
    birth
writhes and cries out in her pain,
    so were we in your presence, LORD.
18 We were with child, we writhed in
    labor,
    but we gave birth to wind.
We have not brought salvation to the
    earth,
    and the people of the world have
    not come to life.

19 But your dead will live, LORD;
    their bodies will rise—
let those who dwell in the dust
    wake up and shout for joy—
your dew is like the dew of the
    morning;
    the earth will give birth to her dead.

20 Go, my people, enter your rooms
    and shut the doors behind you;
hide yourselves for a little while
    until his wrath has passed by.
21 See, the LORD is coming out of his
    dwelling
    to punish the people of the earth
    for their sins.

The earth will disclose the blood shed
    on it;
    the earth will conceal its slain no
    longer.

Deliverance of Israel

27 In that day,

the LORD will punish with his sword—
    his fierce, great and powerful
    sword—
Leviathan the gliding serpent,
    Leviathan the coiling serpent;
he will slay the monster of the sea.

2 In that day—

"Sing about a fruitful vineyard:
3   I, the LORD, watch over it;
    I water it continually.
I guard it day and night
    so that no one may harm it.
4   I am not angry.
If only there were briers and thorns
    confronting me!
I would march against them in
    battle;
    I would set them all on fire.
5 Or else let them come to me for
    refuge;
    let them make peace with me,
    yes, let them make peace with me."

6 In days to come Jacob will take root,
    Israel will bud and blossom
    and fill all the world with fruit.

7 Has the LORD struck her
    as he struck down those who struck
    her?
Has she been killed
    as those were killed who killed
    her?
8 By warfare[b] and exile you contend with
    her—
    with his fierce blast he drives her
    out,
    as on a day the east wind blows.
9 By this, then, will Jacob's guilt be
    atoned for,
    and this will be the full fruit of the
    removal of his sin:

---

[a] 16 The meaning of the Hebrew for this clause is
uncertain.   [b] 8 See Septuagint; the meaning of the
Hebrew for this word is uncertain.

When he makes all the altar stones
  to be like limestone crushed to
  pieces,
no Asherah poles[a] or incense altars
  will be left standing.
10 The fortified city stands desolate,
  an abandoned settlement, forsaken
    like the wilderness;
there the calves graze,
  there they lie down;
  they strip its branches bare.
11 When its twigs are dry, they are broken
    off
  and women come and make fires
    with them.
For this is a people without
    understanding;
  so their Maker has no compassion
    on them,
  and their Creator shows them no
    favor.

12 In that day the LORD will thresh from
the flowing Euphrates to the Wadi of
Egypt, and you, Israel, will be gathered up
one by one. 13 And in that day a great trumpet will sound. Those who were perishing
in Assyria and those who were exiled in
Egypt will come and worship the LORD on
the holy mountain in Jerusalem.

Woe to the Leaders of Ephraim and Judah

28 Woe to that wreath, the pride of
    Ephraim's drunkards,
  to the fading flower, his glorious
    beauty,
set on the head of a fertile valley—
  to that city, the pride of those laid
    low by wine!
2 See, the Lord has one who is powerful
    and strong.
  Like a hailstorm and a destructive
    wind,
like a driving rain and a flooding
    downpour,
  he will throw it forcefully to the
    ground.
3 That wreath, the pride of Ephraim's
    drunkards,
  will be trampled underfoot.
4 That fading flower, his glorious beauty,
  set on the head of a fertile valley,

will be like figs ripe before harvest—
  as soon as people see them and
    take them in hand,
  they swallow them.

5 In that day the LORD Almighty
  will be a glorious crown,
a beautiful wreath
  for the remnant of his people.
6 He will be a spirit of justice
  to the one who sits in judgment,
a source of strength
  to those who turn back the battle at
    the gate.

7 And these also stagger from wine
  and reel from beer:
Priests and prophets stagger from
    beer
  and are befuddled with wine;
they reel from beer,
  they stagger when seeing visions,
  they stumble when rendering
    decisions.
8 All the tables are covered with vomit
  and there is not a spot without
    filth.

9 "Who is it he is trying to teach?
  To whom is he explaining his
    message?
To children weaned from their milk,
  to those just taken from the breast?
10 For it is:
  Do this, do that,
  a rule for this, a rule for that[b];
  a little here, a little there."

11 Very well then, with foreign lips and
    strange tongues
  God will speak to this people,
12 to whom he said,
  "This is the resting place, let the
    weary rest";
and, "This is the place of repose"—
  but they would not listen.
13 So then, the word of the LORD to them
    will become:
  Do this, do that,
  a rule for this, a rule for that;
  a little here, a little there—

---

[a] 9 That is, wooden symbols of the goddess Asherah
[b] 10 Hebrew / sav lasav sav lasav / kav lakav kav lakav
(probably meaningless sounds mimicking the prophet's
words); also in verse 13

so that as they go they will fall
    backward;
they will be injured and snared and
    captured.

14 Therefore hear the word of the Lord,
    you scoffers
who rule this people in Jerusalem.
15 You boast, "We have entered into a
    covenant with death,
with the realm of the dead we have
    made an agreement.
When an overwhelming scourge
    sweeps by,
it cannot touch us,
for we have made a lie our refuge
and falsehood[a] our hiding place."

16 So this is what the Sovereign Lord
says:

"See, I lay a stone in Zion, a tested
    stone,
a precious cornerstone for a sure
    foundation;
the one who relies on it
will never be stricken with panic.
17 I will make justice the measuring line
    and righteousness the plumb line;
hail will sweep away your refuge, the
    lie,
and water will overflow your hiding
    place.
18 Your covenant with death will be
    annulled;
your agreement with the realm of
    the dead will not stand.
When the overwhelming scourge
    sweeps by,
you will be beaten down by it.
19 As often as it comes it will carry you
    away;
morning after morning, by day and
    by night,
it will sweep through."

The understanding of this message
    will bring sheer terror.
20 The bed is too short to stretch out on,
the blanket too narrow to wrap
    around you.
21 The Lord will rise up as he did at
    Mount Perazim,
he will rouse himself as in the
    Valley of Gibeon—

to do his work, his strange work,
and perform his task, his alien
    task.
22 Now stop your mocking,
    or your chains will become heavier;
the Lord, the Lord Almighty, has
    told me
of the destruction decreed against
    the whole land.

23 Listen and hear my voice;
    pay attention and hear what I say.
24 When a farmer plows for planting,
    does he plow continually?
Does he keep on breaking up and
    working the soil?
25 When he has leveled the surface,
    does he not sow caraway and
    scatter cumin?
Does he not plant wheat in its place,[b]
    barley in its plot,[b]
    and spelt in its field?

---

[a] 15 Or false gods   [b] 25 The meaning of the Hebrew for
this word is uncertain.

MOUNT PERAZIM

(ISAIAH 28:21)

This is the mountain where
King David won his first battle
against the Philistines, who were
enemies of Israel.

THE SCENE

VALLEY OF GIBEON

(ISAIAH 28:21)

It was in this valley that Joshua won an important battle against some Canaanite kings.

26 His God instructs him
    and teaches him the right way.

27 Caraway is not threshed with a sledge,
    nor is the wheel of a cart rolled over
        cumin;
    caraway is beaten out with a rod,
    and cumin with a stick.
28 Grain must be ground to make bread;
    so one does not go on threshing it
        forever.
    The wheels of a threshing cart may be
        rolled over it,
    but one does not use horses to
        grind grain.
29 All this also comes from the LORD
        Almighty,
    whose plan is wonderful,
    whose wisdom is magnificent.

Woe to David's City

29 Woe to you, Ariel, Ariel,
    the city where David settled!
    Add year to year
        and let your cycle of festivals go on.

2 Yet I will besiege Ariel;
    she will mourn and lament,
    she will be to me like an altar
        hearth.[a]
3 I will encamp against you on all sides;
    I will encircle you with towers
    and set up my siege works against
        you.
4 Brought low, you will speak from the
        ground;
    your speech will mumble out of the
        dust.
Your voice will come ghostlike from
        the earth;
    out of the dust your speech will
        whisper.

5 But your many enemies will become
        like fine dust,
    the ruthless hordes like blown chaff.
Suddenly, in an instant,
6   the LORD Almighty will come
with thunder and earthquake and
        great noise,
    with windstorm and tempest and
        flames of a devouring fire.
7 Then the hordes of all the nations that
        fight against Ariel,
    that attack her and her fortress and
        besiege her,
will be as it is with a dream,
    with a vision in the night—
8 as when a hungry person dreams of
        eating,
    but awakens hungry still;
as when a thirsty person dreams of
        drinking,
    but awakens faint and thirsty still.
So will it be with the hordes of all the
        nations
    that fight against Mount Zion.

9 Be stunned and amazed,
    blind yourselves and be sightless;
be drunk, but not from wine,
    stagger, but not from beer.
10 The LORD has brought over you a deep
        sleep:
    He has sealed your eyes (the
        prophets);
    he has covered your heads (the
        seers).

_____
a 2 The Hebrew for altar hearth sounds like the Hebrew for Ariel.

¹¹For you this whole vision is nothing but words sealed in a scroll. And if you give the scroll to someone who can read, and say, "Read this, please," they will answer, "I can't; it is sealed." ¹²Or if you give the scroll to someone who cannot read, and say, "Read this, please," they will answer, "I don't know how to read."

¹³The Lord says:

"These people come near to me with
   their mouth
and honor me with their lips,
   but their hearts are far from me.
Their worship of me
   is based on merely human rules
   they have been taught.ᵃ
¹⁴Therefore once more I will astound
   these people
with wonder upon wonder;
   the wisdom of the wise will perish,
   the intelligence of the intelligent will
   vanish."
¹⁵Woe to those who go to great
   depths
to hide their plans from the LORD,
who do their work in darkness and
   think,
   "Who sees us? Who will know?"
¹⁶You turn things upside down,
   as if the potter were thought to be
   like the clay!
Shall what is formed say to the one
   who formed it,
   "You did not make me"?
Can the pot say to the potter,
   "You know nothing"?

¹⁷In a very short time, will not Lebanon
   be turned into a fertile field
   and the fertile field seem like a
   forest?
¹⁸In that day the deaf will hear the
   words of the scroll,
   and out of gloom and darkness
   the eyes of the blind will see.
¹⁹Once more the humble will rejoice in
   the LORD;
   the needy will rejoice in the Holy
   One of Israel.
²⁰The ruthless will vanish,
   the mockers will disappear,
   and all who have an eye for evil will
   be cut down—

²¹those who with a word make someone
   out to be guilty,
who ensnare the defender in court
   and with false testimony deprive the
   innocent of justice.

²²Therefore this is what the LORD, who redeemed Abraham, says to the descendants of Jacob:

"No longer will Jacob be ashamed;
   no longer will their faces grow
   pale.
²³When they see among them their
   children,
   the work of my hands,
they will keep my name holy;
   they will acknowledge the holiness
   of the Holy One of Jacob,
   and will stand in awe of the God of
   Israel.
²⁴Those who are wayward in spirit will
   gain understanding;
   those who complain will accept
   instruction."

Woe to the Obstinate Nation

30 "Woe to the obstinate children,"
   declares the LORD,
"to those who carry out plans that are
   not mine,
   forming an alliance, but not by my
   Spirit,
   heaping sin upon sin;
²who go down to Egypt
   without consulting me;
who look for help to Pharaoh's
   protection,
   to Egypt's shade for refuge.
³But Pharaoh's protection will be to
   your shame,
   Egypt's shade will bring you
   disgrace.
⁴Though they have officials in Zoan
   and their envoys have arrived in
   Hanes,
⁵everyone will be put to shame
   because of a people useless to
   them,
who bring neither help nor advantage,
   but only shame and disgrace."

ᵃ 13 Hebrew; Septuagint *They worship me in vain; / their
teachings are merely human rules*

⁶A prophecy concerning the animals of the Negev:

Through a land of hardship and
        distress,
    of lions and lionesses,
    of adders and darting snakes,
    the envoys carry their riches on
        donkeys' backs,
    their treasures on the humps of
        camels,
    to that unprofitable nation,
⁷   to Egypt, whose help is utterly
        useless.
    Therefore I call her
        Rahab the Do-Nothing.

⁸Go now, write it on a tablet for them,
    inscribe it on a scroll,
    that for the days to come
    it may be an everlasting witness.
⁹For these are rebellious people,
        deceitful children,
    children unwilling to listen to the
        LORD's instruction.
¹⁰They say to the seers,
        "See no more visions!"
    and to the prophets,
        "Give us no more visions of what is
            right!
    Tell us pleasant things,
        prophesy illusions.
¹¹Leave this way,
        get off this path,
    and stop confronting us
        with the Holy One of Israel!"

¹²Therefore this is what the Holy One
of Israel says:

"Because you have rejected this
        message,
    relied on oppression
    and depended on deceit,
¹³this sin will become for you
    like a high wall, cracked and
        bulging,
    that collapses suddenly, in an
        instant.
¹⁴It will break in pieces like pottery,
    shattered so mercilessly
    that among its pieces not a fragment
        will be found
    for taking coals from a hearth
    or scooping water out of a cistern."

¹⁵This is what the Sovereign LORD, the
Holy One of Israel, says:

"In repentance and rest is your
        salvation,
    in quietness and trust is your
        strength,
    but you would have none of it.
¹⁶You said, 'No, we will flee on horses.'
    Therefore you will flee!
    You said, 'We will ride off on swift
        horses.'
    Therefore your pursuers will be
        swift!
¹⁷A thousand will flee
    at the threat of one;
    at the threat of five
    you will all flee away,
    till you are left
    like a flagstaff on a mountaintop,
    like a banner on a hill."

¹⁸Yet the LORD longs to be gracious to
        you;
    therefore he will rise up to show you
        compassion.
    For the LORD is a God of justice.
    Blessed are all who wait for him!

¹⁹People of Zion, who live in Jerusalem, you will weep no more. How gracious he will be when you cry for help! As soon as he hears, he will answer you. ²⁰Although the Lord gives you the bread of adversity and the water of affliction, your teachers will be hidden no more; with your own eyes you will see them. ²¹Whether you turn to the right or to the left, your ears will hear a voice behind you, saying, "This is the way; walk in it." ²²Then you will desecrate your idols overlaid with silver and your images covered with gold; you will throw them away like a menstrual cloth and say to them, "Away with you!"

²³He will also send you rain for the seed you sow in the ground, and the food that comes from the land will be rich and plentiful. In that day your cattle will graze in broad meadows. ²⁴The oxen and donkeys that work the soil will eat fodder and mash, spread out with fork and shovel. ²⁵In the day of great slaughter, when the towers fall, streams of water will flow on

every high mountain and every lofty hill. ²⁶The moon will shine like the sun, and the sunlight will be seven times brighter, like the light of seven full days, when the LORD binds up the bruises of his people and heals the wounds he inflicted.

²⁷ See, the Name of the LORD comes
    from afar,
  with burning anger and dense
    clouds of smoke;
  his lips are full of wrath,
    and his tongue is a consuming fire.
²⁸ His breath is like a rushing torrent,
    rising up to the neck.
  He shakes the nations in the sieve of
    destruction;
  he places in the jaws of the
    peoples
    a bit that leads them astray.
²⁹ And you will sing
    as on the night you celebrate a holy
    festival;
  your hearts will rejoice
    as when people playing pipes go up
  to the mountain of the LORD,
    to the Rock of Israel.
³⁰ The LORD will cause people to hear his
    majestic voice
  and will make them see his arm
    coming down
  with raging anger and consuming fire,
    with cloudburst, thunderstorm and
    hail.
³¹ The voice of the LORD will shatter
    Assyria;
  with his rod he will strike them
    down.
³² Every stroke the LORD lays on them
    with his punishing club
  will be to the music of timbrels and
    harps,
    as he fights them in battle with the
    blows of his arm.
³³ Topheth has long been prepared;
    it has been made ready for the
    king.
  Its fire pit has been made deep and
    wide,
    with an abundance of fire and
    wood;
  the breath of the LORD,
    like a stream of burning sulfur,
    sets it ablaze.

Woe to Those Who Rely on Egypt

31 Woe to those who go down to
        Egypt for help,
  who rely on horses,
  who trust in the multitude of their
    chariots
  and in the great strength of their
    horsemen,
  but do not look to the Holy One of
    Israel,
    or seek help from the LORD.
² Yet he too is wise and can bring
    disaster;
  he does not take back his words.
  He will rise up against that wicked
    nation,
    against those who help evildoers.
³ But the Egyptians are mere mortals
    and not God;
  their horses are flesh and not spirit.
  When the LORD stretches out his hand,
    those who help will stumble,
    those who are helped will fall;
  all will perish together.

⁴ This is what the LORD says to me:

  "As a lion growls,
    a great lion over its prey—
  and though a whole band of shepherds
    is called together against it,
  it is not frightened by their shouts
    or disturbed by their clamor—
  so the LORD Almighty will come down
    to do battle on Mount Zion and on
    its heights.
⁵ Like birds hovering overhead,
    the LORD Almighty will shield
    Jerusalem;
  he will shield it and deliver it,
    he will 'pass over' it and will
    rescue it."

⁶Return, you Israelites, to the One you have so greatly revolted against. ⁷For in that day every one of you will reject the idols of silver and gold your sinful hands have made.

⁸ "Assyria will fall by no human sword;
    a sword, not of mortals, will devour
    them.
  They will flee before the sword
    and their young men will be put to
    forced labor.

⁹ Their stronghold will fall because of
     terror;
   at the sight of the battle standard
     their commanders will panic,"
declares the Lord,
   whose fire is in Zion,
   whose furnace is in Jerusalem.

The Kingdom of Righteousness

32 See, a king will reign in
     righteousness
   and rulers will rule with justice.
² Each one will be like a shelter from
     the wind
   and a refuge from the storm,
like streams of water in the desert
   and the shadow of a great rock in a
     thirsty land.

³ Then the eyes of those who see will
     no longer be closed,
   and the ears of those who hear will
     listen.
⁴ The fearful heart will know and
     understand,
   and the stammering tongue will be
     fluent and clear.
⁵ No longer will the fool be called noble
   nor the scoundrel be highly
     respected.
⁶ For fools speak folly,
   their hearts are bent on evil:
They practice ungodliness
   and spread error concerning the
     Lord;
the hungry they leave empty
   and from the thirsty they withhold
     water.
⁷ Scoundrels use wicked methods,
   they make up evil schemes
to destroy the poor with lies,
   even when the plea of the needy is
     just.
⁸ But the noble make noble plans,
   and by noble deeds they stand.

The Women of Jerusalem

⁹ You women who are so complacent,
   rise up and listen to me;
you daughters who feel secure,
   hear what I have to say!
¹⁰ In little more than a year
   you who feel secure will tremble;

   the grape harvest will fail,
   and the harvest of fruit will not come.
¹¹ Tremble, you complacent women;
   shudder, you daughters who feel
     secure!
Strip off your fine clothes
   and wrap yourselves in rags.
¹² Beat your breasts for the pleasant
     fields,
   for the fruitful vines
¹³ and for the land of my people,
   a land overgrown with thorns and
     briers—
yes, mourn for all houses of merriment
   and for this city of revelry.
¹⁴ The fortress will be abandoned,
   the noisy city deserted;
citadel and watchtower will become a
     wasteland forever,
   the delight of donkeys, a pasture for
     flocks,
¹⁵ till the Spirit is poured on us from on
     high,
   and the desert becomes a fertile
     field,
   and the fertile field seems like a
     forest.
¹⁶ The Lord's justice will dwell in the
     desert,
   his righteousness live in the fertile
     field.
¹⁷ The fruit of that righteousness will be
     peace;
   its effect will be quietness and
     confidence forever.
¹⁸ My people will live in peaceful dwelling
     places,
   in secure homes,
   in undisturbed places of rest.
¹⁹ Though hail flattens the forest
   and the city is leveled completely,
²⁰ how blessed you will be,
   sowing your seed by every stream,
   and letting your cattle and donkeys
     range free.

Distress and Help

33 Woe to you, destroyer,
   you who have not been destroyed!
Woe to you, betrayer,
   you who have not been betrayed!
When you stop destroying,
   you will be destroyed;

when you stop betraying,
   you will be betrayed.

[2] LORD, be gracious to us;
   we long for you.
Be our strength every morning,
   our salvation in time of distress.
[3] At the uproar of your army, the
      peoples flee;
   when you rise up, the nations
      scatter.
[4] Your plunder, O nations, is harvested
      as by young locusts;
   like a swarm of locusts people
      pounce on it.
[5] The LORD is exalted, for he dwells on
      high;
   he will fill Zion with his justice and
      righteousness.
[6] He will be the sure foundation for your
      times,
   a rich store of salvation and wisdom
      and knowledge;
   the fear of the LORD is the key to
      this treasure.[a]

[7] Look, their brave men cry aloud in the
      streets;
   the envoys of peace weep bitterly.
[8] The highways are deserted,
   no travelers are on the roads.
The treaty is broken,
   its witnesses[b] are despised,
   no one is respected.
[9] The land dries up and wastes away,
   Lebanon is ashamed and withers;
Sharon is like the Arabah,
   and Bashan and Carmel drop their
      leaves.

[10] "Now will I arise," says the LORD.
   "Now will I be exalted;
   now will I be lifted up.
[11] You conceive chaff,
   you give birth to straw;
   your breath is a fire that consumes
      you.
[12] The peoples will be burned to ashes;
   like cut thornbushes they will be set
      ablaze."

[13] You who are far away, hear what I have
      done;
   you who are near, acknowledge my
      power!

[14] The sinners in Zion are
      terrified;
   trembling grips the godless:
"Who of us can dwell with the
      consuming fire?
Who of us can dwell with everlasting
      burning?"
[15] Those who walk righteously
   and speak what is right,
who reject gain from extortion
   and keep their hands from
      accepting bribes,
who stop their ears against plots of
      murder
   and shut their eyes against
      contemplating evil—
[16] they are the ones who will dwell on
      the heights,
   whose refuge will be the mountain
      fortress.
Their bread will be supplied,
   and water will not fail them.

---

[a] 6 Or is a treasure from him   [b] 8 Dead Sea Scrolls;
Masoretic Text / the cities

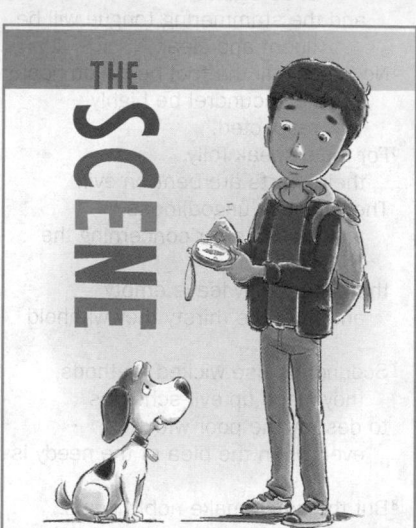

THE
SCENE

SHARON

(ISAIAH 33:9)

Sharon is a fertile valley on
the eastern coast of the
Mediterranean Sea.

MOUNT CARMEL

(ISAIAH 33:9)

The location of this mountain was important for the protection of Israel against its enemies.

17 Your eyes will see the king in his
    beauty
  and view a land that stretches afar.
18 In your thoughts you will ponder the
    former terror:
  "Where is that chief officer?
  Where is the one who took the
    revenue?
  Where is the officer in charge of the
    towers?"
19 You will see those arrogant people no
    more,
  people whose speech is obscure,
  whose language is strange and
    incomprehensible.

20 Look on Zion, the city of our festivals;
  your eyes will see Jerusalem,
  a peaceful abode, a tent that will
    not be moved;
  its stakes will never be pulled up,
  nor any of its ropes broken.
21 There the LORD will be our Mighty One.
  It will be like a place of broad rivers
    and streams.

  No galley with oars will ride them,
  no mighty ship will sail them.
22 For the LORD is our judge,
  the LORD is our lawgiver,
  the LORD is our king;
  it is he who will save us.

23 Your rigging hangs loose:
  The mast is not held secure,
  the sail is not spread.
  Then an abundance of spoils will be
    divided
  and even the lame will carry off
    plunder.
24 No one living in Zion will say, "I am
    ill";
  and the sins of those who dwell
    there will be forgiven.

Judgment Against the Nations

34 Come near, you nations, and listen;
  pay attention, you peoples!
  Let the earth hear, and all that is in it,
  the world, and all that comes out
    of it!
2 The LORD is angry with all nations;
  his wrath is on all their armies.
  He will totally destroy[a] them,
  he will give them over to slaughter.
3 Their slain will be thrown out,
  their dead bodies will stink;
  the mountains will be soaked with
    their blood.
4 All the stars in the sky will be
    dissolved
  and the heavens rolled up like a
    scroll;
  all the starry host will fall
  like withered leaves from the vine,
  like shriveled figs from the fig tree.

5 My sword has drunk its fill in the
    heavens;
  see, it descends in judgment on
    Edom,
  the people I have totally destroyed.
6 The sword of the LORD is bathed in
    blood,
  it is covered with fat—
  the blood of lambs and goats,
  fat from the kidneys of rams.

---

a 2 The Hebrew term refers to the irrevocable giving over of things or persons to the LORD, often by totally destroying them; also in verse 5.

For the L0RD has a sacrifice in Bozrah
and a great slaughter in the land of
Edom.
⁷ And the wild oxen will fall with them,
the bull calves and the great bulls.
Their land will be drenched with
blood,
and the dust will be soaked with fat.

⁸ For the L0RD has a day of vengeance,
a year of retribution, to uphold
Zion's cause.
⁹ Edom's streams will be turned into
pitch,
her dust into burning sulfur;
her land will become blazing pitch!
¹⁰ It will not be quenched night or day;
its smoke will rise forever.
From generation to generation it will
lie desolate;

no one will ever pass through it
again.
¹¹ The desert owlᵃ and screech owlᵃ will
possess it;
the great owlᵃ and the raven will
nest there.
God will stretch out over Edom
the measuring line of chaos
and the plumb line of desolation.
¹² Her nobles will have nothing there to
be called a kingdom,
all her princes will vanish away.
¹³ Thorns will overrun her citadels,
nettles and brambles her
strongholds.
She will become a haunt for jackals,
a home for owls.
¹⁴ Desert creatures will meet with hyenas,
and wild goats will bleat to each
other;
there the night creatures will also lie
down
and find for themselves places of
rest.
¹⁵ The owl will nest there and lay eggs,
she will hatch them, and care for
her young
under the shadow of her wings;
there also the falcons will gather,
each with its mate.

¹⁶ Look in the scroll of the L0RD and
read:

None of these will be missing,
not one will lack her mate.
For it is his mouth that has given the
order,
and his Spirit will gather them
together.
¹⁷ He allots their portions;
his hand distributes them by
measure.
They will possess it forever
and dwell there from generation to
generation.

Joy of the Redeemed

35 The desert and the parched land
will be glad;
the wilderness will rejoice and
blossom.

BREAK THROUGH!

Will God get even?

(ISAIAH 34:8)

We have to understand this correctly. If we
don't, we can do something wrong. First
of all, God's revenge is special. Not one of
us can get even in the same way. Secondly,
vengeance here means that God is going to
do what he promised. He is going to defend
weak, unprotected people, or people who
can't defend themselves. In other words, God
is correcting a bad situation.

ᵃ *11 The precise identification of these birds is uncertain.*

BREAKTHROUGH!

What is "the scroll of the Lord"?

(ISAIAH 34:15–16)

Well, the honest truth is that nobody really knows what the prophet was talking about when he said, "the scroll of the Lord." In the book of Psalms (56:8; 139:15–16), the poets say that God writes down everything we do in a book. It's a way to say that God knows everything.

Like the crocus, ²it will burst into bloom;
  it will rejoice greatly and shout for joy.
The glory of Lebanon will be given to it,
  the splendor of Carmel and Sharon;
they will see the glory of the Lord,
  the splendor of our God.
³Strengthen the feeble hands,
  steady the knees that give way;
⁴say to those with fearful hearts,
  "Be strong, do not fear;
your God will come,
  he will come with vengeance;
with divine retribution
  he will come to save you."

⁵Then will the eyes of the blind be opened

and the ears of the deaf unstopped.
⁶Then will the lame leap like a deer,
  and the mute tongue shout for joy.
Water will gush forth in the wilderness
  and streams in the desert.
⁷The burning sand will become a pool,
  the thirsty ground bubbling springs.
In the haunts where jackals once lay,
  grass and reeds and papyrus will grow.

⁸And a highway will be there;
  it will be called the Way of Holiness;
  it will be for those who walk on that Way.
The unclean will not journey on it;
  wicked fools will not go about on it.
⁹No lion will be there,
  nor any ravenous beast;
  they will not be found there.
But only the redeemed will walk there,
10 and those the Lord has rescued will return.
They will enter Zion with singing;
  everlasting joy will crown their heads.
Gladness and joy will overtake them,
  and sorrow and sighing will flee away.

Sennacherib Threatens Jerusalem

36 In the fourteenth year of King Hezekiah's reign, Sennacherib king of Assyria attacked all the fortified cities of Judah and captured them. ²Then the king of Assyria sent his field commander with a large army from Lachish to King Hezekiah at Jerusalem. When the commander stopped at the aqueduct of the Upper Pool, on the road to the Launderer's Field, ³Eliakim son of Hilkiah the palace administrator, Shebna the secretary, and Joah son of Asaph the recorder went out to him.

⁴The field commander said to them, "Tell Hezekiah:

" 'This is what the great king, the king of Assyria, says: On what are you basing this confidence of yours? ⁵You say you have counsel and might for war—but you speak only empty words. On whom are you depending, that you rebel against me? ⁶Look,

THE
WITNESSES

✓ **SENNACHERIB** (ISAIAH 36:1)
He was an Assyrian king who conquered several cities in the southern kingdom, called Judah. He wasn't able to conquer Jerusalem, which was the capital of Judah.

I know you are depending on Egypt, that splintered reed of a staff, which pierces the hand of anyone who leans on it! Such is Pharaoh king of Egypt to all who depend on him. ⁷But if you say to me, "We are depending on the LORD our God"—isn't he the one whose high places and altars Hezekiah removed, saying to Judah and Jerusalem, "You must worship before this altar"?

⁸"'Come now, make a bargain with my master, the king of Assyria: I will give you two thousand horses—if you can put riders on them! ⁹How then can you repulse one officer of the least of my master's officials, even though you are depending on Egypt for chariots and horsemen*a*? ¹⁰Furthermore, have I come to attack and destroy this land without the LORD? The LORD himself told me to march against this country and destroy it.' "

¹¹Then Eliakim, Shebna and Joah said to the field commander, "Please speak to your servants in Aramaic, since we understand it. Don't speak to us in Hebrew in the hearing of the people on the wall."

¹²But the commander replied, "Was it only to your master and you that my master sent me to say these things, and not to the people sitting on the wall—who, like you, will have to eat their own excrement and drink their own urine?"

¹³Then the commander stood and called out in Hebrew, "Hear the words of the great king, the king of Assyria! ¹⁴This is what the king says: Do not let Hezekiah deceive you. He cannot deliver you! ¹⁵Do not let Hezekiah persuade you to trust in the LORD when he says, 'The LORD will surely deliver us; this city will not be given into the hand of the king of Assyria.'

¹⁶"Do not listen to Hezekiah. This is what the king of Assyria says: Make peace with me and come out to me. Then each of you will eat fruit from your own vine and fig tree and drink water from your own cistern, ¹⁷until I come and take you to a land like your own—a land of grain and new wine, a land of bread and vineyards.

¹⁸"Do not let Hezekiah mislead you when he says, 'The LORD will deliver us.' Have the gods of any nations ever delivered their lands from the hand of the king of Assyria? ¹⁹Where are the gods of Hamath and Arpad? Where are the gods of Sepharvaim? Have they rescued Samaria from my hand? ²⁰Who of all the gods of these countries have been able to save their lands from me? How then can the LORD deliver Jerusalem from my hand?"

²¹But the people remained silent and said nothing in reply, because the king had commanded, "Do not answer him."

²²Then Eliakim son of Hilkiah the palace administrator, Shebna the secretary

---

a 9 Or *charioteers*

and Joah son of Asaph the recorder went to Hezekiah, with their clothes torn, and told him what the field commander had said.

Jerusalem's Deliverance Foretold

37 When King Hezekiah heard this, he tore his clothes and put on sackcloth and went into the temple of the Lord. ²He sent Eliakim the palace administrator, Shebna the secretary, and the leading priests, all wearing sackcloth, to the prophet Isaiah son of Amoz. ³They told him, "This is what Hezekiah says: This day is a day of distress and rebuke and disgrace, as when children come to the moment of birth and there is no strength to deliver them. ⁴It may be that the Lord your God will hear the words of the field commander, whom his master, the king of Assyria, has sent to ridicule the living God, and that he will rebuke him for the words the Lord your God has heard. Therefore pray for the remnant that still survives."

⁵When King Hezekiah's officials came to Isaiah, ⁶Isaiah said to them, "Tell your master, 'This is what the Lord says: Do not be afraid of what you have heard— those words with which the underlings of the king of Assyria have blasphemed me. ⁷Listen! When he hears a certain report, I will make him want to return to his own country, and there I will have him cut down with the sword.'"

⁸When the field commander heard that the king of Assyria had left Lachish, he withdrew and found the king fighting against Libnah.

⁹Now Sennacherib received a report that Tirhakah, the king of Cush,ᵃ was marching out to fight against him. When he heard it, he sent messengers to Hezekiah with this word: ¹⁰"Say to Hezekiah king of Judah: Do not let the god you depend on deceive you when he says, 'Jerusalem will not be given into the hands of the king of Assyria.' ¹¹Surely you have heard what the kings of Assyria have done to all the countries, destroying them completely. And will you be delivered? ¹²Did the gods of the nations that were destroyed by my predecessors deliver them—the gods of Gozan, Harran, Re-

zeph and the people of Eden who were in Tel Assar? ¹³Where is the king of Hamath or the king of Arpad? Where are the kings of Lair, Sepharvaim, Hena and Ivvah?"

Hezekiah's Prayer

¹⁴Hezekiah received the letter from the messengers and read it. Then he went up to the temple of the Lord and spread it out before the Lord. ¹⁵And Hezekiah prayed to the Lord: ¹⁶"Lord Almighty, the God of Israel, enthroned between the cherubim, you alone are God over all the kingdoms of the earth. You have made heaven and earth. ¹⁷Give ear, Lord, and hear; open your eyes, Lord, and see; listen to all the words Sennacherib has sent to ridicule the living God.

¹⁸"It is true, Lord, that the Assyrian kings have laid waste all these peoples and their lands. ¹⁹They have thrown their gods into the fire and destroyed them, for they were not gods but only wood and stone, fashioned by human hands. ²⁰Now, Lord our God, deliver us from his hand, so that all the kingdoms of the earth may know that you, Lord, are the only God.ᵇ"

Sennacherib's Fall

²¹Then Isaiah son of Amoz sent a message to Hezekiah: "This is what the Lord, the God of Israel, says: Because you have prayed to me concerning Sennacherib king of Assyria, ²²this is the word the Lord has spoken against him:

"Virgin Daughter Zion
  despises and mocks you.
Daughter Jerusalem
  tosses her head as you flee.
²³Who is it you have ridiculed and
    blasphemed?
Against whom have you raised your
    voice
and lifted your eyes in pride?
  Against the Holy One of Israel!
²⁴By your messengers
  you have ridiculed the Lord.
And you have said,
  'With my many chariots

ᵃ 9 That is, the upper Nile region   ᵇ 20 Dead Sea Scrolls (see also 2 Kings 19:19); Masoretic Text *you alone are the Lord*

I have ascended the heights of the
    mountains,
    the utmost heights of Lebanon.
I have cut down its tallest cedars,
    the choicest of its junipers.
I have reached its remotest heights,
    the finest of its forests.
²⁵ I have dug wells in foreign lands[a]
    and drunk the water there.
With the soles of my feet
    I have dried up all the streams of
    Egypt.'

²⁶ "Have you not heard?
    Long ago I ordained it.
In days of old I planned it;
    now I have brought it to pass,
that you have turned fortified cities
    into piles of stone.
²⁷ Their people, drained of power,
    are dismayed and put to shame.
They are like plants in the field,
    like tender green shoots,
like grass sprouting on the roof,
    scorched[b] before it grows up.

²⁸ "But I know where you are
    and when you come and go
    and how you rage against me.
²⁹ Because you rage against me
    and because your insolence has
    reached my ears,
I will put my hook in your nose
    and my bit in your mouth,
and I will make you return
    by the way you came.

³⁰ "This will be the sign for you, Hezekiah:

"This year you will eat what grows by
    itself,
    and the second year what springs
    from that.
But in the third year sow and reap,
    plant vineyards and eat their fruit.
³¹ Once more a remnant of the kingdom
    of Judah
    will take root below and bear fruit
    above.
³² For out of Jerusalem will come a
    remnant,
    and out of Mount Zion a band of
    survivors.
The zeal of the LORD Almighty
    will accomplish this.

³³ "Therefore this is what the LORD says
concerning the king of Assyria:

"He will not enter this city
    or shoot an arrow here.
He will not come before it with shield
    or build a siege ramp against it.
³⁴ By the way that he came he will
    return;
    he will not enter this city,"
                        declares the LORD.
³⁵ "I will defend this city and save it,
    for my sake and for the sake of
    David my servant!"

³⁶ Then the angel of the LORD went out
and put to death a hundred and eighty-five
thousand in the Assyrian camp. When the
people got up the next morning—there
were all the dead bodies! ³⁷ So Sennacherib king of Assyria broke camp and withdrew. He returned to Nineveh and stayed
there.

³⁸ One day, while he was worshiping in
the temple of his god Nisrok, his sons
Adrammelek and Sharezer killed him with
the sword, and they escaped to the land
of Ararat. And Esarhaddon his son succeeded him as king.

Hezekiah's Illness

38 In those days Hezekiah became ill
and was at the point of death. The
prophet Isaiah son of Amoz went to him
and said, "This is what the LORD says: Put
your house in order, because you are going to die; you will not recover."
²Hezekiah turned his face to the wall
and prayed to the LORD, ³ "Remember,
LORD, how I have walked before you faithfully and with wholehearted devotion and
have done what is good in your eyes." And
Hezekiah wept bitterly.

⁴ Then the word of the LORD came to Isaiah: ⁵ "Go and tell Hezekiah, 'This is what
the LORD, the God of your father David,
says: I have heard your prayer and seen
your tears; I will add fifteen years to your

ᵃ 25 Dead Sea Scrolls (see also 2 Kings 19:24);
Masoretic Text does not have *in foreign lands.*
ᵇ 27 Some manuscripts of the Masoretic Text, Dead Sea
Scrolls and some Septuagint manuscripts (see also
2 Kings 19:26); most manuscripts of the Masoretic Text
roof / and terraced fields

life. ⁶And I will deliver you and this city from the hand of the king of Assyria. I will defend this city.

⁷" 'This is the LORD's sign to you that the LORD will do what he has promised: ⁸I will make the shadow cast by the sun go back the ten steps it has gone down on the stairway of Ahaz.' " So the sunlight went back the ten steps it had gone down.

⁹A writing of Hezekiah king of Judah after his illness and recovery:

¹⁰I said, "In the prime of my life
    must I go through the gates of
        death
    and be robbed of the rest of my
        years?"

BREAK THROUGH!

What did Isaiah mean when he said, "I will make the shadow cast by the sun go back the ten steps it has gone down on the stairway of Ahaz"?

(ISAIAH 38:8)

Long ago, time was measured by the pyramid's shadow (all pyramids have a stairway). Isaiah was probably talking about that. What's important here is that this was the sign that God used to confirm that King Hezekiah was going to live 15 years longer.

¹¹I said, "I will not again see the LORD
        himself
    in the land of the living;
no longer will I look on my fellow man,
    or be with those who now dwell in
        this world.
¹²Like a shepherd's tent my house
    has been pulled down and taken
        from me.
Like a weaver I have rolled up my life,
    and he has cut me off from the loom;
    day and night you made an end
        of me.
¹³I waited patiently till dawn,
    but like a lion he broke all my
        bones;
    day and night you made an end
        of me.
¹⁴I cried like a swift or thrush,
    I moaned like a mourning dove.
My eyes grew weak as I looked to the
        heavens.
    I am being threatened; Lord, come
        to my aid!"

¹⁵But what can I say?
    He has spoken to me, and he
        himself has done this.
I will walk humbly all my years
    because of this anguish of my soul.
¹⁶Lord, by such things people live;
    and my spirit finds life in them too.
You restored me to health
    and let me live.
¹⁷Surely it was for my benefit
    that I suffered such anguish.
In your love you kept me
    from the pit of destruction;
you have put all my sins
    behind your back.
¹⁸For the grave cannot praise you,
    death cannot sing your praise;
those who go down to the pit
    cannot hope for your faithfulness.
¹⁹The living, the living—they praise you,
    as I am doing today;
parents tell their children
    about your faithfulness.

²⁰The LORD will save me,
    and we will sing with stringed
        instruments
all the days of our lives
    in the temple of the LORD.

²¹Isaiah had said, "Prepare a poultice of figs and apply it to the boil, and he will recover."

²²Hezekiah had asked, "What will be the sign that I will go up to the temple of the Lord?"

Envoys From Babylon

39 At that time Marduk-Baladan son of Baladan king of Babylon sent Hezekiah letters and a gift, because he had heard of his illness and recovery. ²Hezekiah received the envoys gladly and showed them what was in his storehouses—the silver, the gold, the spices, the fine olive oil—his entire armory and everything found among his treasures. There was nothing in his palace or in all his kingdom that Hezekiah did not show them.

³Then Isaiah the prophet went to King Hezekiah and asked, "What did those men say, and where did they come from?"

"From a distant land," Hezekiah replied. "They came to me from Babylon."

⁴The prophet asked, "What did they see in your palace?"

"They saw everything in my palace," Hezekiah said. "There is nothing among my treasures that I did not show them."

⁵Then Isaiah said to Hezekiah, "Hear the word of the Lord Almighty: ⁶The time will surely come when everything in your palace, and all that your predecessors have stored up until this day, will be carried off to Babylon. Nothing will be left, says the Lord. ⁷And some of your descendants, your own flesh and blood who will be born to you, will be taken away, and they will become eunuchs in the palace of the king of Babylon."

⁸"The word of the Lord you have spoken is good," Hezekiah replied. For he thought, "There will be peace and security in my lifetime."

Comfort for God's People

40 Comfort, comfort my people, says your God.
²Speak tenderly to Jerusalem,
 and proclaim to her
that her hard service has been
 completed,
 that her sin has been paid for,

that she has received from the Lord's
 hand
 double for all her sins.

³A voice of one calling:
 "In the wilderness prepare
 the way for the Lordᵃ;
 make straight in the desert
 a highway for our God.ᵇ
⁴Every valley shall be raised up,
 every mountain and hill made low;
the rough ground shall become level,
 the rugged places a plain.
⁵And the glory of the Lord will be
 revealed,
 and all people will see it together.
 For the mouth of the Lord
 has spoken."

⁶A voice says, "Cry out."
 And I said, "What shall I cry?"

"All people are like grass,
 and all their faithfulness is like the
 flowers of the field.
⁷The grass withers and the flowers
 fall,
 because the breath of the Lord
 blows on them.
 Surely the people are grass.
⁸The grass withers and the flowers
 fall,
 but the word of our God endures
 forever."

⁹You who bring good news to Zion,
 go up on a high mountain.
You who bring good news to
 Jerusalem,ᶜ
 lift up your voice with a shout,
lift it up, do not be afraid;
 say to the towns of Judah,
 "Here is your God!"
¹⁰See, the Sovereign Lord comes with
 power,
 and he rules with a mighty arm.
See, his reward is with him,
 and his recompense accompanies
 him.
¹¹He tends his flock like a shepherd:
 He gathers the lambs in his arms

ᵃ 3 Or A voice of one calling in the wilderness: / "Prepare the way for the Lord   ᵇ 3 Hebrew; Septuagint make straight the paths of our God   ᶜ 9 Or Zion, bringer of good news, / go up on a high mountain. / Jerusalem, bringer of good news

and carries them close to his
    heart;
he gently leads those that have
    young.

¹²Who has measured the waters in the
    hollow of his hand,
or with the breadth of his hand
    marked off the heavens?
Who has held the dust of the earth in
    a basket,
or weighed the mountains on the
    scales
and the hills in a balance?
¹³Who can fathom the Spirit[a] of the
    Lord,
or instruct the Lord as his
    counselor?
¹⁴Whom did the Lord consult to
    enlighten him,
and who taught him the right way?
Who was it that taught him knowledge,

BREAKTHROUGH!

Can God really measure the ocean in the hollow of his hand?

(ISAIAH 40:12)

We really don't know what God is like. This is
just a way of saying that God is all-powerful
and so great that the ocean isn't dangerous
for him.

or showed him the path of
    understanding?
¹⁵Surely the nations are like a drop in a
    bucket;
they are regarded as dust on the
    scales;
he weighs the islands as though
    they were fine dust.
¹⁶Lebanon is not sufficient for altar
    fires,
nor its animals enough for burnt
    offerings.
¹⁷Before him all the nations are as
    nothing;
they are regarded by him as
    worthless
and less than nothing.

¹⁸With whom, then, will you compare
    God?
To what image will you liken him?
¹⁹As for an idol, a metalworker
    casts it,
and a goldsmith overlays it with
    gold
and fashions silver chains for it.
²⁰A person too poor to present such an
    offering
selects wood that will not rot;
they look for a skilled worker
    to set up an idol that will not
    topple.

²¹Do you not know?
    Have you not heard?
Has it not been told you from the
    beginning?
Have you not understood since the
    earth was founded?
²²He sits enthroned above the circle of
    the earth,
and its people are like
    grasshoppers.
He stretches out the heavens like a
    canopy,
and spreads them out like a tent to
    live in.
²³He brings princes to naught
and reduces the rulers of this world
    to nothing.
²⁴No sooner are they planted,
    no sooner are they sown,

---

a 13 Or *mind*

no sooner do they take root in the
ground,
than he blows on them and they
wither,
and a whirlwind sweeps them away
like chaff.

25 "To whom will you compare me?
Or who is my equal?" says the Holy
One.
26 Lift up your eyes and look to the
heavens:
Who created all these?
He who brings out the starry host one
by one
and calls forth each of them by
name.
Because of his great power and
mighty strength,
not one of them is missing.

27 Why do you complain, Jacob?
Why do you say, Israel,
"My way is hidden from the LORD;
my cause is disregarded by my
God"?
28 Do you not know?
Have you not heard?
The LORD is the everlasting God,
the Creator of the ends of the
earth.
He will not grow tired or weary,
and his understanding no one can
fathom.
29 He gives strength to the weary
and increases the power of the
weak.
30 Even youths grow tired and weary,
and young men stumble and fall;
31 but those who hope in the LORD
will renew their strength.
They will soar on wings like
eagles;
they will run and not grow weary,
they will walk and not be faint.

The Helper of Israel

41 "Be silent before me, you
islands!
Let the nations renew their
strength!
Let them come forward and speak;
let us meet together at the place of
judgment.

THE
WITNESSES

✓ **"ONE FROM THE EAST"** (ISAIAH 41:2)
This person is Cyrus, king of Persia. You can read
about him in Ezra 1:1.

2 "Who has stirred up one from the
east,
calling him in righteousness to his
service[a]?
He hands nations over to him
and subdues kings before him.
He turns them to dust with his sword,
to windblown chaff with his bow.
3 He pursues them and moves on
unscathed,
by a path his feet have not traveled
before.
4 Who has done this and carried it
through,
calling forth the generations from
the beginning?

---

[a] 2 Or east, / whom victory meets at every step

I, the Lord—with the first of them
and with the last—I am he."

⁵ The islands have seen it and fear;
the ends of the earth tremble.
They approach and come forward;
⁶   they help each other
and say to their companions, "Be
strong!"
⁷ The metalworker encourages the
goldsmith,
and the one who smooths with the
hammer
spurs on the one who strikes the
anvil.
One says of the welding, "It is good."
The other nails down the idol so it
will not topple.

⁸ "But you, Israel, my servant,
Jacob, whom I have chosen,
you descendants of Abraham my
friend,
⁹ I took you from the ends of the earth,
from its farthest corners I called
you.
I said, 'You are my servant';
I have chosen you and have not
rejected you.
¹⁰ So do not fear, for I am with you;
do not be dismayed, for I am your
God.
I will strengthen you and help you;
I will uphold you with my righteous
right hand.

¹¹ "All who rage against you
will surely be ashamed and
disgraced;
those who oppose you
will be as nothing and perish.
¹² Though you search for your enemies,
you will not find them.
Those who wage war against you
will be as nothing at all.
¹³ For I am the Lord your God
who takes hold of your right hand
and says to you, Do not fear;
I will help you.
¹⁴ Do not be afraid, you worm Jacob,
little Israel, do not fear,
for I myself will help you," declares the
Lord,
your Redeemer, the Holy One of
Israel.

¹⁵ "See, I will make you into a threshing
sledge,
new and sharp, with many teeth.
You will thresh the mountains and
crush them,
and reduce the hills to chaff.
¹⁶ You will winnow them, the wind will
pick them up,
and a gale will blow them away.
But you will rejoice in the Lord
and glory in the Holy One of Israel.

¹⁷ "The poor and needy search for
water,
but there is none;
their tongues are parched with
thirst.
But I the Lord will answer them;
I, the God of Israel, will not forsake
them.
¹⁸ I will make rivers flow on barren
heights,
and springs within the valleys.
I will turn the desert into pools of
water,
and the parched ground into
springs.
¹⁹ I will put in the desert
the cedar and the acacia, the myrtle
and the olive.
I will set junipers in the wasteland,
the fir and the cypress together,
²⁰ so that people may see and know,
may consider and understand,
that the hand of the Lord has done
this,
that the Holy One of Israel has
created it.

²¹ "Present your case," says the Lord.
"Set forth your arguments," says
Jacob's King.
²² "Tell us, you idols,
what is going to happen.
Tell us what the former things were,
so that we may consider them
and know their final outcome.
Or declare to us the things to come,
²³   tell us what the future holds,
so we may know that you are
gods.
Do something, whether good or bad,
so that we will be dismayed and
filled with fear.

²⁴ But you are less than nothing
   and your works are utterly worthless;
   whoever chooses you is detestable.

²⁵ "I have stirred up one from the north,
      and he comes—
   one from the rising sun who calls
      on my name.
   He treads on rulers as if they were
      mortar,
      as if he were a potter treading the
         clay.
²⁶ Who told of this from the beginning,
      so we could know,
   or beforehand, so we could say, 'He
      was right'?
   No one told of this,
      no one foretold it,
      no one heard any words from you.
²⁷ I was the first to tell Zion, 'Look, here
      they are!'
   I gave to Jerusalem a messenger of
      good news.
²⁸ I look but there is no one—
   no one among the gods to give
      counsel,
   no one to give answer when I ask
      them.
²⁹ See, they are all false!
   Their deeds amount to nothing;
   their images are but wind and
      confusion.

The Servant of the LORD

42 "Here is my servant, whom I uphold,
      my chosen one in whom I delight;
   I will put my Spirit on him,
      and he will bring justice to the
         nations.
² He will not shout or cry out,
   or raise his voice in the streets.
³ A bruised reed he will not break,
   and a smoldering wick he will not
      snuff out.
   In faithfulness he will bring forth
      justice;
⁴   he will not falter or be discouraged
   till he establishes justice on earth.
      In his teaching the islands will put
         their hope."

⁵ This is what God the LORD says—
   the Creator of the heavens, who
      stretches them out,

who spreads out the earth with all
   that springs from it,
who gives breath to its people,
   and life to those who walk on it:
⁶ "I, the LORD, have called you in
      righteousness;
   I will take hold of your hand.
I will keep you and will make you
   to be a covenant for the people
   and a light for the Gentiles,
⁷ to open eyes that are blind,
   to free captives from prison
   and to release from the dungeon
      those who sit in darkness.

⁸ "I am the LORD; that is my name!
   I will not yield my glory to another
   or my praise to idols.
⁹ See, the former things have taken
      place,
   and new things I declare;
before they spring into being
   I announce them to you."

BREAK THROUGH!

Who is God's chosen one?

(ISAIAH 42:1)

As usual, many of these things are a mystery. Some people say that God's chosen one is Jesus. But since Jesus hadn't been born when this book was written, others think it might mean Isaiah himself. Others think that God's chosen one is the people of Israel.

Song of Praise to the LORD

¹⁰ Sing to the LORD a new song,
his praise from the ends of the
earth,
you who go down to the sea, and all
that is in it,
you islands, and all who live in
them.
¹¹ Let the wilderness and its towns raise
their voices;
let the settlements where Kedar
lives rejoice.
Let the people of Sela sing for joy;
let them shout from the
mountaintops.
¹² Let them give glory to the LORD
and proclaim his praise in the
islands.
¹³ The LORD will march out like a
champion,
like a warrior he will stir up his zeal;
with a shout he will raise the battle
cry
and will triumph over his enemies.

¹⁴ "For a long time I have kept silent,
I have been quiet and held myself
back.
But now, like a woman in childbirth,
I cry out, I gasp and pant.
¹⁵ I will lay waste the mountains and hills
and dry up all their vegetation;
I will turn rivers into islands
and dry up the pools.
¹⁶ I will lead the blind by ways they have
not known,
along unfamiliar paths I will guide
them;
I will turn the darkness into light
before them
and make the rough places smooth.
These are the things I will do;
I will not forsake them.
¹⁷ But those who trust in idols,
who say to images, 'You are our
gods,'
will be turned back in utter shame.

Israel Blind and Deaf

¹⁸ "Hear, you deaf;
look, you blind, and see!
¹⁹ Who is blind but my servant,
and deaf like the messenger I send?

Who is blind like the one in covenant
with me,
blind like the servant of the LORD?
²⁰ You have seen many things, but you
pay no attention;
your ears are open, but you do not
listen."
²¹ It pleased the LORD
for the sake of his righteousness
to make his law great and glorious.
²² But this is a people plundered and
looted,
all of them trapped in pits
or hidden away in prisons.
They have become plunder,
with no one to rescue them;
they have been made loot,
with no one to say, "Send them
back."

²³ Which of you will listen to this
or pay close attention in time to
come?
²⁴ Who handed Jacob over to become
loot,
and Israel to the plunderers?
Was it not the LORD,
against whom we have sinned?
For they would not follow his ways;
they did not obey his law.
²⁵ So he poured out on them his burning
anger,
the violence of war.
It enveloped them in flames, yet they
did not understand;
it consumed them, but they did not
take it to heart.

Israel's Only Savior

43 But now, this is what the LORD
says—
he who created you, Jacob,
he who formed you, Israel:
"Do not fear, for I have redeemed you;
I have summoned you by name; you
are mine.
² When you pass through the waters,
I will be with you;
and when you pass through the rivers,
they will not sweep over you.
When you walk through the fire,
you will not be burned;
the flames will not set you ablaze.

³For I am the LORD your God,
  the Holy One of Israel, your Savior;
I give Egypt for your ransom,
  Cushᵃ and Seba in your stead.
⁴Since you are precious and honored in
    my sight,
  and because I love you,
I will give people in exchange for you,
  nations in exchange for your life.
⁵Do not be afraid, for I am with you;
  I will bring your children from the
    east
and gather you from the west.
⁶I will say to the north, 'Give them up!'
  and to the south, 'Do not hold them
    back.'
Bring my sons from afar
  and my daughters from the ends of
    the earth—
⁷everyone who is called by my name,
  whom I created for my glory,
  whom I formed and made."

⁸Lead out those who have eyes but are
    blind,
  who have ears but are deaf.
⁹All the nations gather together
  and the peoples assemble.
Which of their gods foretold this
  and proclaimed to us the former
    things?
Let them bring in their witnesses to
    prove they were right,
  so that others may hear and say, "It
    is true."
¹⁰"You are my witnesses," declares the
    LORD,
  "and my servant whom I have
    chosen,
so that you may know and believe me
  and understand that I am he.
Before me no god was formed,
  nor will there be one after me.
¹¹I, even I, am the LORD,
  and apart from me there is no savior.
¹²I have revealed and saved and
    proclaimed—
  I, and not some foreign god among
    you.
You are my witnesses," declares the
    LORD, "that I am God.
¹³   Yes, and from ancient days I am he.
No one can deliver out of my hand.
  When I act, who can reverse it?"

God's Mercy and Israel's Unfaithfulness

¹⁴This is what the LORD says—
  your Redeemer, the Holy One of
    Israel:
"For your sake I will send to Babylon
  and bring down as fugitives all the
    Babylonians,ᵇ
  in the ships in which they took pride.
¹⁵I am the LORD, your Holy One,
  Israel's Creator, your King."

¹⁶This is what the LORD says—
  he who made a way through the sea,
  a path through the mighty waters,
¹⁷who drew out the chariots and horses,
  the army and reinforcements
    together,
and they lay there, never to rise again,
  extinguished, snuffed out like a
    wick:
¹⁸"Forget the former things;
  do not dwell on the past.
¹⁹See, I am doing a new thing!
  Now it springs up; do you not
    perceive it?
I am making a way in the wilderness
  and streams in the wasteland.
²⁰The wild animals honor me,
  the jackals and the owls,
because I provide water in the
    wilderness
  and streams in the wasteland,
to give drink to my people, my chosen,
²¹   the people I formed for myself
  that they may proclaim my praise.

²²"Yet you have not called on me, Jacob,
  you have not wearied yourselves
    forᶜ me, Israel.
²³You have not brought me sheep for
    burnt offerings,
  nor honored me with your sacrifices.
I have not burdened you with grain
    offerings
  nor wearied you with demands for
    incense.
²⁴You have not bought any fragrant
    calamus for me,
  or lavished on me the fat of your
    sacrifices.

ᵃ 3 That is, the upper Nile region   ᵇ 14 Or Chaldeans
ᶜ 22 Or Jacob; / surely you have grown weary of

But you have burdened me with your
　　sins
　　and wearied me with your offenses.
25 "I, even I, am he who blots out
　　your transgressions, for my own
　　　sake,
　　and remembers your sins no more.
26 Review the past for me,
　　let us argue the matter together;
　　state the case for your innocence.
27 Your first father sinned;
　　those I sent to teach you rebelled
　　　against me.
28 So I disgraced the dignitaries of your
　　　temple;
　　I consigned Jacob to destruction[a]
　　and Israel to scorn.

Israel the Chosen

44 "But now listen, Jacob, my servant,
　　Israel, whom I have chosen.
2 This is what the LORD says—
　　he who made you, who formed you
　　　in the womb,
　　and who will help you:
Do not be afraid, Jacob, my servant,
　　Jeshurun,[b] whom I have chosen.
3 For I will pour water on the thirsty
　　　land,
　　and streams on the dry ground;
I will pour out my Spirit on your
　　　offspring,
　　and my blessing on your
　　　descendants.
4 They will spring up like grass in a
　　　meadow,
　　like poplar trees by flowing streams.
5 Some will say, 'I belong to the LORD';
　　others will call themselves by the
　　　name of Jacob;
still others will write on their hand,
　　'The LORD's,'
　　and will take the name Israel.

The LORD, Not Idols

6 "This is what the LORD says—
　　Israel's King and Redeemer, the
　　　LORD Almighty:
I am the first and I am the last;
　　apart from me there is no God.
7 Who then is like me? Let him
　　proclaim it.

THE
WITNESSES

✓ **JACOB** (ISAIAH 44:5)
See who this is in Genesis 25:26.

Let him declare and lay out
　　before me
what has happened since I
　　established my ancient
　　people,
　　and what is yet to come—
　　yes, let them foretell what will
　　　come.
8 Do not tremble, do not be afraid.
　　Did I not proclaim this and foretell it
　　　long ago?
You are my witnesses. Is there any
　　God besides me?
　　No, there is no other Rock; I know
　　　not one."

---

a 28 The Hebrew term refers to the irrevocable giving over
of things or persons to the LORD, often by totally destroying
them.　　*b* 2 *Jeshurun* means *the upright one,* that is,
Israel.

9 All who make idols are nothing,
　and the things they treasure are
　　worthless.
Those who would speak up for them
　are blind;
they are ignorant, to their own
　shame.
10 Who shapes a god and casts an idol,
　which can profit nothing?
11 People who do that will be put to
　shame;
such craftsmen are only human
　beings.
Let them all come together and take
　their stand;
they will be brought down to terror
　and shame.

12 The blacksmith takes a tool
　and works with it in the coals;
he shapes an idol with hammers,
　he forges it with the might of his
　　arm.
He gets hungry and loses his
　strength;
he drinks no water and grows
　faint.
13 The carpenter measures with a line
　and makes an outline with a
　　marker;
he roughs it out with chisels
　and marks it with compasses.
He shapes it in human form,
　human form in all its glory,
　that it may dwell in a shrine.
14 He cut down cedars,
　or perhaps took a cypress or oak.
He let it grow among the trees of the
　forest,
or planted a pine, and the rain
　made it grow.
15 It is used as fuel for burning;
　some of it he takes and warms
　　himself,
he kindles a fire and bakes bread.
But he also fashions a god and
　worships it;
he makes an idol and bows down
　to it.
16 Half of the wood he burns in the fire;
　over it he prepares his meal,
　he roasts his meat and eats his fill.
He also warms himself and says,
　"Ah! I am warm; I see the fire."

17 From the rest he makes a god, his
　idol;
he bows down to it and worships.
He prays to it and says,
　"Save me! You are my god!"
18 They know nothing, they understand
　nothing;
their eyes are plastered over so
　they cannot see,
and their minds closed so they
　cannot understand.
19 No one stops to think,
　no one has the knowledge or
　understanding to say,
"Half of it I used for fuel;
　I even baked bread over its coals,
　I roasted meat and I ate.
Shall I make a detestable thing from
　what is left?
Shall I bow down to a block of
　wood?"
20 Such a person feeds on ashes; a
　deluded heart misleads him;
he cannot save himself, or say,
　"Is not this thing in my right hand a
　lie?"

21 "Remember these things, Jacob,
　for you, Israel, are my servant.
I have made you, you are my servant;
　Israel, I will not forget you.
22 I have swept away your offenses like a
　cloud,
　your sins like the morning mist.
Return to me,
　for I have redeemed you."

23 Sing for joy, you heavens, for the LORD
　has done this;
　shout aloud, you earth beneath.
Burst into song, you mountains,
　you forests and all your trees,
for the LORD has redeemed Jacob,
　he displays his glory in Israel.

Jerusalem to Be Inhabited

24 "This is what the LORD says—
　your Redeemer, who formed you in
　the womb:

I am the LORD,
　the Maker of all things,
who stretches out the heavens,
who spreads out the earth by
　myself,

25 who foils the signs of false prophets
and makes fools of diviners,
who overthrows the learning of the
wise
and turns it into nonsense,
26 who carries out the words of his
servants
and fulfills the predictions of his
messengers,

who says of Jerusalem, 'It shall be
inhabited,'
of the towns of Judah, 'They shall
be rebuilt,'
and of their ruins, 'I will restore
them,'
27 who says to the watery deep, 'Be dry,
and I will dry up your streams,'
28 who says of Cyrus, 'He is my shepherd
and will accomplish all that I
please;
he will say of Jerusalem, "Let it be
rebuilt,"
and of the temple, "Let its
foundations be laid." '

45 "This is what the LORD says to his
anointed,
to Cyrus, whose right hand I take
hold of
to subdue nations before him
and to strip kings of their armor,
to open doors before him
so that gates will not be shut:
2 I will go before you
and will level the mountains*a*;
I will break down gates of bronze
and cut through bars of iron.
3 I will give you hidden treasures,
riches stored in secret places,
so that you may know that I am the
LORD,
the God of Israel, who summons
you by name.
4 For the sake of Jacob my servant,
of Israel my chosen,
I summon you by name
and bestow on you a title of honor,
though you do not acknowledge me.
5 I am the LORD, and there is no other;
apart from me there is no God.
I will strengthen you,
though you have not acknowledged
me,

6 so that from the rising of the sun
to the place of its setting
people may know there is none
besides me.
I am the LORD, and there is no other.
7 I form the light and create darkness,
I bring prosperity and create
disaster;
I, the LORD, do all these things.

8 "You heavens above, rain down my
righteousness;
let the clouds shower it down.
Let the earth open wide,
let salvation spring up,
let righteousness flourish with it;
I, the LORD, have created it.

9 "Woe to those who quarrel with their
Maker,
those who are nothing but
potsherds
among the potsherds on the ground.

---

a 2 Dead Sea Scrolls and Septuagint; the meaning of the
word in the Masoretic Text is uncertain.

Does God cause disasters?

(ISAIAH 45:7)

God can cause disasters if he wants. But God
doesn't make all the disasters. In this verse,
the word *disaster* comes just before "I, the
LORD, do all these things." This shows that
God controls everything.

Does the clay say to the potter,
  'What are you making?'
Does your work say,
  'The potter has no hands'?
10 Woe to the one who says to a father,
  'What have you begotten?'
or to a mother,
  'What have you brought to birth?'

11 "This is what the LORD says—
  the Holy One of Israel, and its
    Maker:
Concerning things to come,
  do you question me about my
    children,
  or give me orders about the work of
    my hands?
12 It is I who made the earth
  and created mankind on it.
My own hands stretched out the
    heavens;
  I marshaled their starry hosts.
13 I will raise up Cyrus[a] in my
    righteousness:
  I will make all his ways straight.
He will rebuild my city
  and set my exiles free,
but not for a price or reward,
  says the LORD Almighty."

14 This is what the LORD says:

"The products of Egypt and the
    merchandise of Cush,[b]
  and those tall Sabeans—
they will come over to you
  and will be yours;
they will trudge behind you,
  coming over to you in chains.
They will bow down before you
  and plead with you, saying,
  'Surely God is with you, and there is
    no other;
  there is no other god.'"

15 Truly you are a God who has been
    hiding himself,
  the God and Savior of Israel.
16 All the makers of idols will be put to
    shame and disgraced;
  they will go off into disgrace
    together.
17 But Israel will be saved by the
    LORD
  with an everlasting salvation;

you will never be put to shame or
    disgraced,
  to ages everlasting.

18 For this is what the LORD says—
  he who created the heavens,
    he is God;
  he who fashioned and made the
    earth,
    he founded it;
  he did not create it to be empty,
    but formed it to be inhabited—
  he says:
  "I am the LORD,
    and there is no other.
19 I have not spoken in secret,
    from somewhere in a land of
      darkness;
  I have not said to Jacob's
    descendants,
    'Seek me in vain.'
  I, the LORD, speak the truth;
    I declare what is right.

20 "Gather together and come;
    assemble, you fugitives from the
      nations.
  Ignorant are those who carry about
    idols of wood,
  who pray to gods that cannot save.
21 Declare what is to be, present it—
    let them take counsel together.
  Who foretold this long ago,
    who declared it from the distant
      past?
  Was it not I, the LORD?
    And there is no God apart from me,
  a righteous God and a Savior;
    there is none but me.

22 "Turn to me and be saved,
    all you ends of the earth;
    for I am God, and there is no other.
23 By myself I have sworn,
    my mouth has uttered in all integrity
    a word that will not be revoked:
  Before me every knee will bow;
    by me every tongue will swear.
24 They will say of me, 'In the LORD alone
    are deliverance and strength.'"
  All who have raged against him
    will come to him and be put to
      shame.

---

a 13 Hebrew him   b 14 That is, the upper Nile region

25 But all the descendants of Israel
will find deliverance in the LORD
and will make their boast in him.

Gods of Babylon

46 Bel bows down, Nebo stoops low;
their idols are borne by beasts of
burden.[a]
The images that are carried about are
burdensome,
a burden for the weary.
2 They stoop and bow down together;
unable to rescue the burden,
they themselves go off into
captivity.

3 "Listen to me, you descendants of
Jacob,
all the remnant of the people of
Israel,
you whom I have upheld since your
birth,
and have carried since you were
born.
4 Even to your old age and gray hairs
I am he, I am he who will sustain
you.
I have made you and I will carry you;
I will sustain you and I will rescue
you.

5 "With whom will you compare me or
count me equal?
To whom will you liken me that we
may be compared?
6 Some pour out gold from their bags
and weigh out silver on the scales;
they hire a goldsmith to make it into a
god,
and they bow down and worship it.
7 They lift it to their shoulders and
carry it;
they set it up in its place, and there
it stands.
From that spot it cannot move.
Even though someone cries out to it,
it cannot answer;
it cannot save them from their
troubles.

8 "Remember this, keep it in mind,
take it to heart, you rebels.
9 Remember the former things, those of
long ago;

I am God, and there is no other;
I am God, and there is none
like me.
10 I make known the end from the
beginning,
from ancient times, what is still to
come.
I say, 'My purpose will stand,
and I will do all that I please.'
11 From the east I summon a bird of
prey;
from a far-off land, a man to fulfill
my purpose.
What I have said, that I will bring
about;
what I have planned, that I will do.
12 Listen to me, you stubborn-hearted,
you who are now far from my
righteousness.
13 I am bringing my righteousness near,
it is not far away;
and my salvation will not be
delayed.
I will grant salvation to Zion,
my splendor to Israel.

The Fall of Babylon

47 "Go down, sit in the dust,
Virgin Daughter Babylon;
sit on the ground without a throne,
queen city of the Babylonians.[b]
No more will you be called
tender or delicate.
2 Take millstones and grind flour;
take off your veil.
Lift up your skirts, bare your legs,
and wade through the streams.
3 Your nakedness will be exposed
and your shame uncovered.
I will take vengeance;
I will spare no one."

4 Our Redeemer—the LORD Almighty is
his name—
is the Holy One of Israel.

5 "Sit in silence, go into darkness,
queen city of the Babylonians;
no more will you be called
queen of kingdoms.
6 I was angry with my people
and desecrated my inheritance;

---

a 1 Or are but beasts and cattle   b 1 Or Chaldeans; also
in verse 5

I gave them into your hand,
   and you showed them no mercy.
Even on the aged
   you laid a very heavy yoke.
⁷ You said, 'I am forever—
   the eternal queen!'
But you did not consider these
      things
   or reflect on what might happen.

⁸ "Now then, listen, you lover of
      pleasure,
   lounging in your security
and saying to yourself,
   'I am, and there is none besides
      me.
I will never be a widow
   or suffer the loss of children.'
⁹ Both of these will overtake you
   in a moment, on a single day:
   loss of children and widowhood.

BREAK THROUGH!

Are spells bad?

(ISAIAH 47:9)

Do you like to watch a magic show? We do. It's
fun, and makes us curious. But here it's not
talking about tricks or optical illusions. It's
talking about witchcraft and real spells. These
things trap you and get you involved in the
dark things that God forbids. Then you can
end up trusting in magic instead of trusting
God, who created you and loves you.

They will come upon you in full
      measure,
   in spite of your many sorceries
   and all your potent spells.
¹⁰ You have trusted in your wickedness
   and have said, 'No one sees me.'
Your wisdom and knowledge mislead
      you
   when you say to yourself,
   'I am, and there is none besides
      me.'
¹¹ Disaster will come upon you,
   and you will not know how to
      conjure it away.
A calamity will fall upon you
   that you cannot ward off with a
      ransom;
a catastrophe you cannot foresee
   will suddenly come upon you.

¹² "Keep on, then, with your magic
      spells
   and with your many sorceries,
   which you have labored at since
      childhood.
Perhaps you will succeed,
   perhaps you will cause terror.
¹³ All the counsel you have received has
      only worn you out!
   Let your astrologers come
      forward,
those stargazers who make
      predictions month by month,
   let them save you from what is
      coming upon you.
¹⁴ Surely they are like stubble;
   the fire will burn them up.
They cannot even save themselves
   from the power of the flame.
These are not coals for warmth;
   this is not a fire to sit by.
¹⁵ That is all they are to you—
   these you have dealt with
   and labored with since childhood.
All of them go on in their error;
   there is not one that can save you.

Stubborn Israel

48 "Listen to this, you descendants
      of Jacob,
   you who are called by the name of
      Israel
   and come from the line of Judah,

you who take oaths in the name of the
LORD
and invoke the God of Israel—
but not in truth or righteousness—
2 you who call yourselves citizens of the
holy city
and claim to rely on the God of
Israel—
the LORD Almighty is his name:
3 I foretold the former things long ago,
my mouth announced them and I
made them known;
then suddenly I acted, and they
came to pass.
4 For I knew how stubborn you were;
your neck muscles were iron,
your forehead was bronze.
5 Therefore I told you these things long
ago;
before they happened I announced
them to you
so that you could not say,
'My images brought them about;
my wooden image and metal god
ordained them.'
6 You have heard these things; look at
them all.
Will you not admit them?

"From now on I will tell you of new
things,
of hidden things unknown to you.
7 They are created now, and not long
ago;
you have not heard of them before
today.
So you cannot say,
'Yes, I knew of them.'
8 You have neither heard nor
understood;
from of old your ears have not been
open.
Well do I know how treacherous you
are;
you were called a rebel from birth.
9 For my own name's sake I delay my
wrath;
for the sake of my praise I hold it
back from you,
so as not to destroy you completely.
10 See, I have refined you, though not as
silver;
I have tested you in the furnace of
affliction.

11 For my own sake, for my own sake,
I do this.
How can I let myself be defamed?
I will not yield my glory to another.

Israel Freed

12 "Listen to me, Jacob,
Israel, whom I have called:
I am he;
I am the first and I am the last.
13 My own hand laid the foundations of
the earth,
and my right hand spread out the
heavens;
when I summon them,
they all stand up together.

14 "Come together, all of you, and listen:
Which of the idols has foretold
these things?
The LORD's chosen ally
will carry out his purpose against
Babylon;
his arm will be against the
Babylonians.[a]
15 I, even I, have spoken;
yes, I have called him.
I will bring him,
and he will succeed in his mission.

16 "Come near me and listen to this:

"From the first announcement I have
not spoken in secret;
at the time it happens, I am there."

And now the Sovereign LORD has sent
me,
endowed with his Spirit.

17 This is what the LORD says—
your Redeemer, the Holy One of
Israel:
"I am the LORD your God,
who teaches you what is best for
you,
who directs you in the way you
should go.
18 If only you had paid attention to my
commands,
your peace would have been like a
river,
your well-being like the waves of the
sea.

---

a 14 Or Chaldeans; also in verse 20

19 Your descendants would have been
        like the sand,
    your children like its numberless
        grains;
    their name would never be blotted out
        nor destroyed from before me."

20 Leave Babylon,
        flee from the Babylonians!
    Announce this with shouts of joy
        and proclaim it.
    Send it out to the ends of the earth;
        say, "The LORD has redeemed his
        servant Jacob."
21 They did not thirst when he led them
        through the deserts;
    he made water flow for them from
        the rock;
    he split the rock
        and water gushed out.

22 "There is no peace," says the LORD,
        "for the wicked."

The Servant of the LORD

49 Listen to me, you islands;
        hear this, you distant nations:
    Before I was born the LORD
        called me;
    from my mother's womb he has
        spoken my name.
2 He made my mouth like a sharpened
        sword,
    in the shadow of his hand he hid
        me;
    he made me into a polished arrow
        and concealed me in his quiver.
3 He said to me, "You are my servant,
    Israel, in whom I will display my
        splendor."
4 But I said, "I have labored in vain;
    I have spent my strength for nothing
        at all.
    Yet what is due me is in the LORD's
        hand,
    and my reward is with my God."

5 And now the LORD says —
    he who formed me in the womb to
        be his servant
    to bring Jacob back to him
        and gather Israel to himself,
    for I am*a* honored in the eyes of the
        LORD

and my God has been my
        strength —
6 he says:
    "It is too small a thing for you to be
        my servant
    to restore the tribes of Jacob
        and bring back those of Israel I
        have kept.
    I will also make you a light for the
        Gentiles,
    that my salvation may reach to the
        ends of the earth."

7 This is what the LORD says —
    the Redeemer and Holy One of
        Israel —
    to him who was despised and
        abhorred by the nation,
    to the servant of rulers:
    "Kings will see you and stand up,
        princes will see and bow down,
    because of the LORD, who is faithful,
        the Holy One of Israel, who has
        chosen you."

Restoration of Israel

8 This is what the LORD says:

    "In the time of my favor I will answer
        you,
    and in the day of salvation I will
        help you;
    I will keep you and will make you
        to be a covenant for the people,
    to restore the land
        and to reassign its desolate
        inheritances,
9 to say to the captives, 'Come out,'
    and to those in darkness, 'Be free!'

    "They will feed beside the roads
        and find pasture on every barren
        hill.
10 They will neither hunger nor thirst,
    nor will the desert heat or the sun
        beat down on them.
    He who has compassion on them will
        guide them
    and lead them beside springs of
        water.
11 I will turn all my mountains into
        roads,
    and my highways will be raised up.

---

a 5 Or *him, / but Israel would not be gathered; / yet I will be*

¹²See, they will come from afar—
   some from the north, some from
      the west,
   some from the region of Aswan.ᵃ"

¹³Shout for joy, you heavens;
   rejoice, you earth;
   burst into song, you mountains!
For the LORD comforts his people
   and will have compassion on his
      afflicted ones.

¹⁴But Zion said, "The LORD has forsaken
      me,
   the Lord has forgotten me."

¹⁵"Can a mother forget the baby at her
      breast
   and have no compassion on the
      child she has borne?
Though she may forget,
   I will not forget you!
¹⁶See, I have engraved you on the palms
      of my hands;
   your walls are ever before me.
¹⁷Your children hasten back,
   and those who laid you waste
      depart from you.
¹⁸Lift up your eyes and look around;
   all your children gather and come to
      you.
As surely as I live," declares the
      LORD,
   "you will wear them all as
      ornaments;
   you will put them on, like a bride.

¹⁹"Though you were ruined and made
      desolate
   and your land laid waste,
now you will be too small for your
      people,
   and those who devoured you will be
      far away.
²⁰The children born during your
      bereavement
   will yet say in your hearing,
'This place is too small for us;
   give us more space to live in.'
²¹Then you will say in your heart,
   'Who bore me these?
I was bereaved and barren;
   I was exiled and rejected.
Who brought these up?

I was left all alone,
   but these—where have they come
      from?' "

²²This is what the Sovereign LORD says:

"See, I will beckon to the nations,
   I will lift up my banner to the
      peoples;
they will bring your sons in their arms
   and carry your daughters on their
      hips.
²³Kings will be your foster fathers,
   and their queens your nursing
      mothers.
They will bow down before you with
      their faces to the ground;
   they will lick the dust at your feet.
Then you will know that I am the LORD;
   those who hope in me will not be
      disappointed."

²⁴Can plunder be taken from warriors,
   or captives be rescued from the
      fierceᵇ?

²⁵But this is what the LORD says:

"Yes, captives will be taken from
      warriors,
   and plunder retrieved from the fierce;
I will contend with those who contend
      with you,
   and your children I will save.
²⁶I will make your oppressors eat their
      own flesh;
   they will be drunk on their own
      blood, as with wine.
Then all mankind will know
   that I, the LORD, am your Savior,
   your Redeemer, the Mighty One of
      Jacob."

Israel's Sin and the Servant's Obedience

50 This is what the LORD says:

"Where is your mother's certificate of
      divorce
   with which I sent her away?
Or to which of my creditors
   did I sell you?

ᵃ 12 Dead Sea Scrolls; Masoretic Text *Sinim*   ᵇ 24 Dead
Sea Scrolls, Vulgate and Syriac (see also Septuagint and
verse 25); Masoretic Text *righteous*

BREAKTHROUGH!

Why so much violence?

(ISAIAH 49:26)

Again, these words are symbols, and you mustn't read them exactly. In poetry, strong words are often used to give a strong message. Here, it's just saying that the people who were bad and conquered Israel will go through the same thing when God helps the people of Israel.

Because of your sins you were sold;
  because of your transgressions your
    mother was sent away.
2 When I came, why was there no one?
  When I called, why was there no
    one to answer?
Was my arm too short to deliver you?
  Do I lack the strength to rescue you?
By a mere rebuke I dry up the sea,
  I turn rivers into a desert;
their fish rot for lack of water
  and die of thirst.
3 I clothe the heavens with darkness
  and make sackcloth its covering."

4 The Sovereign LORD has given me a
    well-instructed tongue,
  to know the word that sustains the
    weary.
He wakens me morning by morning,
  wakens my ear to listen like one
    being instructed.

5 The Sovereign LORD has opened my
    ears;
  I have not been rebellious,
  I have not turned away.
6 I offered my back to those who beat
    me,
  my cheeks to those who pulled out
    my beard;
I did not hide my face
  from mocking and spitting.
7 Because the Sovereign LORD helps me,
  I will not be disgraced.
Therefore have I set my face like
    flint,
  and I know I will not be put to
    shame.
8 He who vindicates me is near.
  Who then will bring charges
    against me?
  Let us face each other!
Who is my accuser?
  Let him confront me!
9 It is the Sovereign LORD who
    helps me.
  Who will condemn me?
They will all wear out like a garment;
  the moths will eat them up.

10 Who among you fears the LORD
  and obeys the word of his
    servant?
Let the one who walks in the dark,
  who has no light,
trust in the name of the LORD
  and rely on their God.
11 But now, all you who light fires
  and provide yourselves with flaming
    torches,
go, walk in the light of your fires
  and of the torches you have set
    ablaze.
This is what you shall receive from my
    hand:
  You will lie down in torment.

Everlasting Salvation for Zion

51 "Listen to me, you who pursue
    righteousness
  and who seek the LORD:
Look to the rock from which you were
    cut
  and to the quarry from which you
    were hewn;

² look to Abraham, your father,
and to Sarah, who gave you birth.
When I called him he was only one
man,
and I blessed him and made him
many.
³ The Lᴏʀᴅ will surely comfort Zion
and will look with compassion on all
her ruins;
he will make her deserts like Eden,
her wastelands like the garden of
the Lᴏʀᴅ.
Joy and gladness will be found in her,
thanksgiving and the sound of
singing.

⁴ "Listen to me, my people;
hear me, my nation:
Instruction will go out from me;
my justice will become a light to the
nations.
⁵ My righteousness draws near speedily,
my salvation is on the way,
and my arm will bring justice to the
nations.
The islands will look to me
and wait in hope for my arm.
⁶ Lift up your eyes to the heavens,
look at the earth beneath;
the heavens will vanish like smoke,
the earth will wear out like a
garment
and its inhabitants die like flies.
But my salvation will last forever,
my righteousness will never fail.

⁷ "Hear me, you who know what is right,
you people who have taken my
instruction to heart:
Do not fear the reproach of mere
mortals
or be terrified by their insults.
⁸ For the moth will eat them up like a
garment;
the worm will devour them like wool.
But my righteousness will last forever,
my salvation through all
generations."

⁹ Awake, awake, arm of the Lᴏʀᴅ,
clothe yourself with strength!
Awake, as in days gone by,
as in generations of old.
Was it not you who cut Rahab to
pieces,

who pierced that monster through?
¹⁰ Was it not you who dried up the sea,
the waters of the great deep,
who made a road in the depths of the
sea
so that the redeemed might cross
over?
¹¹ Those the Lᴏʀᴅ has rescued will return.
They will enter Zion with singing;
everlasting joy will crown their
heads.
Gladness and joy will overtake them,
and sorrow and sighing will flee
away.

¹² "I, even I, am he who comforts you.
Who are you that you fear mere
mortals,
human beings who are but grass,
¹³ that you forget the Lᴏʀᴅ your Maker,
who stretches out the heavens
and who lays the foundations of the
earth,
that you live in constant terror every
day
because of the wrath of the
oppressor,
who is bent on destruction?
For where is the wrath of the
oppressor?
¹⁴   The cowering prisoners will soon be
set free;
they will not die in their dungeon,
nor will they lack bread.
¹⁵ For I am the Lᴏʀᴅ your God,
who stirs up the sea so that its
waves roar—
the Lᴏʀᴅ Almighty is his name.
¹⁶ I have put my words in your mouth
and covered you with the shadow of
my hand—
I who set the heavens in place,
who laid the foundations of the
earth,
and who say to Zion, 'You are my
people.' "

The Cup of the Lᴏʀᴅ's Wrath
¹⁷ Awake, awake!
Rise up, Jerusalem,
you who have drunk from the hand of
the Lᴏʀᴅ
the cup of his wrath,

you who have drained to its dregs
    the goblet that makes people
    stagger.
¹⁸ Among all the children she bore
    there was none to guide her;
among all the children she reared
    there was none to take her by the
    hand.
¹⁹ These double calamities have come
    upon you—
    who can comfort you?—
ruin and destruction, famine and
    sword—
    who can*a* console you?
²⁰ Your children have fainted;
    they lie at every street corner,
    like antelope caught in a net.
They are filled with the wrath of the
    LORD,
    with the rebuke of your God.
²¹ Therefore hear this, you afflicted one,
    made drunk, but not with wine.
²² This is what your Sovereign LORD says,
    your God, who defends his people:
"See, I have taken out of your hand
    the cup that made you stagger;
from that cup, the goblet of my wrath,
    you will never drink again.
²³ I will put it into the hands of your
    tormentors,
    who said to you,
    'Fall prostrate that we may walk on
    you.'
And you made your back like the
    ground,
    like a street to be walked on."

52 Awake, awake, Zion,
    clothe yourself with strength!
Put on your garments of splendor,
    Jerusalem, the holy city.
The uncircumcised and defiled
    will not enter you again.
² Shake off your dust;
    rise up, sit enthroned, Jerusalem.
Free yourself from the chains on your
    neck,
    Daughter Zion, now a captive.

³ For this is what the LORD says:

"You were sold for nothing,
    and without money you will be
    redeemed."

⁴ For this is what the Sovereign LORD
says:

"At first my people went down to Egypt
    to live;
    lately, Assyria has oppressed them.

⁵ "And now what do I have here?" declares the LORD.

"For my people have been taken away
    for nothing,
    and those who rule them mock,*b*"
                declares the LORD.
"And all day long
    my name is constantly blasphemed.
⁶ Therefore my people will know my
    name;
    therefore in that day they will know
    that it is I who foretold it.
    Yes, it is I."

⁷ How beautiful on the mountains
    are the feet of those who bring
    good news,
who proclaim peace,
    who bring good tidings,
    who proclaim salvation,
who say to Zion,
    "Your God reigns!"
⁸ Listen! Your watchmen lift up their
    voices;
    together they shout for joy.
When the LORD returns to Zion,
    they will see it with their own eyes.
⁹ Burst into songs of joy together,
    you ruins of Jerusalem,
for the LORD has comforted his
    people,
    he has redeemed Jerusalem.
¹⁰ The LORD will lay bare his holy arm
    in the sight of all the nations,
and all the ends of the earth will see
    the salvation of our God.

¹¹ Depart, depart, go out from there!
    Touch no unclean thing!
Come out from it and be pure,
    you who carry the articles of the
    LORD's house.
¹² But you will not leave in haste
    or go in flight;

---

a 19 Dead Sea Scrolls, Septuagint, Vulgate and Syriac;
Masoretic Text / how can I   *b* 5 Dead Sea Scrolls and
Vulgate; Masoretic Text wail

for the Lord will go before you,
   the God of Israel will be your rear
      guard.

The Suffering and Glory of the Servant

[13] See, my servant will act wisely[a];
   he will be raised and lifted up and
      highly exalted.
[14] Just as there were many who were
      appalled at him[b]—
   his appearance was so disfigured
      beyond that of any human
      being
   and his form marred beyond human
      likeness—
[15] so he will sprinkle many nations,[c]
   and kings will shut their mouths
      because of him.
For what they were not told, they will
   see,
   and what they have not heard, they
      will understand.

53 Who has believed our message
   and to whom has the arm of the
      Lord been revealed?
[2] He grew up before him like a tender
      shoot,
   and like a root out of dry ground.
He had no beauty or majesty to attract
   us to him,
   nothing in his appearance that we
      should desire him.
[3] He was despised and rejected by
      mankind,
   a man of suffering, and familiar with
      pain.
Like one from whom people hide their
   faces
   he was despised, and we held him
      in low esteem.

[4] Surely he took up our pain
   and bore our suffering,
yet we considered him punished by
   God,
   stricken by him, and afflicted.
[5] But he was pierced for our
      transgressions,
   he was crushed for our iniquities;
   the punishment that brought us peace
      was on him,
   and by his wounds we are healed.

[6] We all, like sheep, have gone astray,
   each of us has turned to our own
      way;
and the Lord has laid on him
   the iniquity of us all.

[7] He was oppressed and afflicted,
   yet he did not open his mouth;
he was led like a lamb to the
      slaughter,
   and as a sheep before its shearers
      is silent,
   so he did not open his mouth.
[8] By oppression[d] and judgment he was
      taken away.
   Yet who of his generation
      protested?
For he was cut off from the land of the
   living;
   for the transgression of my people
      he was punished.[e]
[9] He was assigned a grave with the
      wicked,
   and with the rich in his death,
though he had done no violence,
   nor was any deceit in his
      mouth.

[10] Yet it was the Lord's will to crush him
   and cause him to suffer,
   and though the Lord makes[f] his life
      an offering for sin,
he will see his offspring and prolong
   his days,
   and the will of the Lord will prosper
      in his hand.
[11] After he has suffered,
   he will see the light of life[g] and be
      satisfied[h];
by his knowledge[i] my righteous
      servant will justify many,
   and he will bear their iniquities.
[12] Therefore I will give him a portion
      among the great,[j]
   and he will divide the spoils with
      the strong,[k]

---

[a] 13 Or will prosper   [b] 14 Hebrew you   [c] 15 Or so will
many nations be amazed at him (see also Septuagint)
[d] 8 Or From arrest   [e] 8 Or generation considered / that
he was cut off from the land of the living, / that he was
punished for the transgression of my people?
[f] 10 Hebrew though you make   [g] 11 Dead Sea Scrolls
(see also Septuagint); Masoretic Text does not have the
light of life.   [h] 11 Or (with Masoretic Text) [11]He will see
the fruit of his suffering / and will be satisfied   [i] 11 Or by
knowledge of him   [j] 12 Or many   [k] 12 Or numerous

because he poured out his life unto
death,
and was numbered with the
transgressors.
For he bore the sin of many,
and made intercession for the
transgressors.

The Future Glory of Zion

54 "Sing, barren woman,
you who never bore a child;
burst into song, shout for joy,
you who were never in labor;
because more are the children of the
desolate woman
than of her who has a husband,"
says the Lord.
2 "Enlarge the place of your tent,
stretch your tent curtains wide,
do not hold back;
lengthen your cords,
strengthen your stakes.
3 For you will spread out to the right and
to the left;
your descendants will dispossess
nations
and settle in their desolate cities.

4 "Do not be afraid; you will not be put
to shame.
Do not fear disgrace; you will not be
humiliated.
You will forget the shame of your youth
and remember no more the
reproach of your widowhood.
5 For your Maker is your husband—
the Lord Almighty is his name—
the Holy One of Israel is your
Redeemer;
he is called the God of all the earth.
6 The Lord will call you back
as if you were a wife deserted and
distressed in spirit—
a wife who married young,
only to be rejected," says your God.
7 "For a brief moment I abandoned you,
but with deep compassion I will
bring you back.
8 In a surge of anger
I hid my face from you for a moment,
but with everlasting kindness
I will have compassion on you,"
says the Lord your Redeemer.

9 "To me this is like the days of Noah,
when I swore that the waters of
Noah would never again cover
the earth.
So now I have sworn not to be angry
with you,
never to rebuke you again.
10 Though the mountains be shaken
and the hills be removed,
yet my unfailing love for you will not be
shaken
nor my covenant of peace be
removed,"
says the Lord, who has compassion
on you.

11 "Afflicted city, lashed by storms and
not comforted,
I will rebuild you with stones of
turquoise,[a]
your foundations with lapis lazuli.
12 I will make your battlements of rubies,
your gates of sparkling jewels,
and all your walls of precious stones.
13 All your children will be taught by the
Lord,
and great will be their peace.
14 In righteousness you will be
established:
Tyranny will be far from you;
you will have nothing to fear.
Terror will be far removed;
it will not come near you.
15 If anyone does attack you, it will not
be my doing;
whoever attacks you will surrender
to you.

16 "See, it is I who created the blacksmith
who fans the coals into flame
and forges a weapon fit for its work.
And it is I who have created the
destroyer to wreak havoc;
17　no weapon forged against you will
prevail,
and you will refute every tongue that
accuses you.
This is the heritage of the servants of
the Lord,
and this is their vindication from
me,"
declares the Lord.

---

[a] 11 The meaning of the Hebrew for this word is uncertain.

Invitation to the Thirsty

55 "Come, all you who are thirsty,
come to the waters;
and you who have no money,
come, buy and eat!
Come, buy wine and milk
without money and without cost.
[2] Why spend money on what is not
bread,
and your labor on what does not
satisfy?
Listen, listen to me, and eat what is
good,
and you will delight in the richest of
fare.
[3] Give ear and come to me;
listen, that you may live.
I will make an everlasting covenant
with you,
my faithful love promised to David.
[4] See, I have made him a witness to the
peoples,
a ruler and commander of the
peoples.
[5] Surely you will summon nations you
know not,
and nations you do not know will
come running to you,
because of the Lord your God,
the Holy One of Israel,
for he has endowed you with
splendor."

[6] Seek the Lord while he may be
found;
call on him while he is near.
[7] Let the wicked forsake their ways
and the unrighteous their
thoughts.
Let them turn to the Lord, and he will
have mercy on them,
and to our God, for he will freely
pardon.
[8] "For my thoughts are not your
thoughts,
neither are your ways my ways,"
declares the Lord.
[9] "As the heavens are higher than the
earth,
so are my ways higher than your
ways
and my thoughts than your
thoughts.

[10] As the rain and the snow
come down from heaven,
and do not return to it
without watering the earth
and making it bud and flourish,
so that it yields seed for the sower
and bread for the eater,
[11] so is my word that goes out from my
mouth:
It will not return to me empty,
but will accomplish what I desire
and achieve the purpose for which I
sent it.
[12] You will go out in joy
and be led forth in peace;
the mountains and hills
will burst into song before you,
and all the trees of the field
will clap their hands.
[13] Instead of the thornbush will grow the
juniper,
and instead of briers the myrtle will
grow.
This will be for the Lord's renown,
for an everlasting sign,
that will endure forever."

Salvation for Others

56 This is what the Lord says:

"Maintain justice
and do what is right,
for my salvation is close at hand
and my righteousness will soon be
revealed.
[2] Blessed is the one who does this—
the person who holds it fast,
who keeps the Sabbath without
desecrating it,
and keeps their hands from doing
any evil."

[3] Let no foreigner who is bound to the
Lord say,
"The Lord will surely exclude me
from his people."
And let no eunuch complain,
"I am only a dry tree."

[4] For this is what the Lord says:

"To the eunuchs who keep my
Sabbaths,
who choose what pleases me
and hold fast to my covenant—

⁵to them I will give within my temple
and its walls
a memorial and a name
better than sons and daughters;
I will give them an everlasting name
that will endure forever.
⁶And foreigners who bind themselves
to the LORD
to minister to him,
to love the name of the LORD,
and to be his servants,
all who keep the Sabbath without
desecrating it
and who hold fast to my covenant—
⁷these I will bring to my holy mountain
and give them joy in my house of
prayer.
Their burnt offerings and sacrifices
will be accepted on my altar;
for my house will be called
a house of prayer for all nations."
⁸The Sovereign LORD declares—
he who gathers the exiles of Israel:
"I will gather still others to them
besides those already gathered."

God's Accusation Against the Wicked

⁹Come, all you beasts of the field,
come and devour, all you beasts of
the forest!
¹⁰Israel's watchmen are blind,
they all lack knowledge;
they are all mute dogs,
they cannot bark;
they lie around and dream,
they love to sleep.
¹¹They are dogs with mighty appetites;
they never have enough.
They are shepherds who lack
understanding;
they all turn to their own way,
they seek their own gain.
¹²"Come," each one cries, "let me get
wine!
Let us drink our fill of beer!
And tomorrow will be like today,
or even far better."

57 The righteous perish,
and no one takes it to heart;
the devout are taken away,
and no one understands

that the righteous are taken away
to be spared from evil.
²Those who walk uprightly
enter into peace;
they find rest as they lie in death.

³"But you—come here, you children of
a sorceress,
you offspring of adulterers and
prostitutes!
⁴Who are you mocking?
At whom do you sneer
and stick out your tongue?
Are you not a brood of rebels,
the offspring of liars?
⁵You burn with lust among the oaks
and under every spreading tree;
you sacrifice your children in the
ravines
and under the overhanging crags.
⁶The idols among the smooth stones of
the ravines are your portion;
indeed, they are your lot.
Yes, to them you have poured out
drink offerings
and offered grain offerings.
In view of all this, should I relent?
⁷You have made your bed on a high and
lofty hill;
there you went up to offer your
sacrifices.
⁸Behind your doors and your doorposts
you have put your pagan symbols.
Forsaking me, you uncovered your
bed,
you climbed into it and opened it
wide;
you made a pact with those whose
beds you love,
and you looked with lust on their
naked bodies.
⁹You went to Molek*ᵃ* with olive oil
and increased your perfumes.
You sent your ambassadors*ᵇ* far away;
you descended to the very realm of
the dead!
¹⁰You wearied yourself by such going
about,
but you would not say, 'It is
hopeless.'
You found renewal of your strength,
and so you did not faint.

ᵃ 9 Or *to the king*　　*ᵇ* 9 Or *idols*

BREAK THROUGH!

Sacrificing children
(ISAIAH 57:5)

Hey, you know what? This idea is very hard to understand. More than 2,000 years ago, some nations had some really strange beliefs. When they were going through tough times, they thought that if they killed a baby as an offering to the gods, their problem would be solved. This kind of sacrifice didn't happen very often, and it was when a situation was really, really terrible.

11 "Whom have you so dreaded and
          feared
      that you have not been true to me,
  and have neither remembered me
      nor taken this to heart?
  Is it not because I have long been
          silent
      that you do not fear me?
12 I will expose your righteousness and
          your works,
      and they will not benefit you.
13 When you cry out for help,
      let your collection of idols save
          you!
  The wind will carry all of them off,
      a mere breath will blow them
          away.
  But whoever takes refuge in me
      will inherit the land
      and possess my holy mountain."

Comfort for the Contrite
14 And it will be said:

  "Build up, build up, prepare the road!
      Remove the obstacles out of the
          way of my people."
15 For this is what the high and exalted
          One says—
      he who lives forever, whose name is
          holy:
  "I live in a high and holy place,
      but also with the one who is
          contrite and lowly in spirit,
  to revive the spirit of the lowly
      and to revive the heart of the
          contrite.
16 I will not accuse them forever,
      nor will I always be angry,
  for then they would faint away
          because of me—
      the very people I have created.
17 I was enraged by their sinful greed;
      I punished them, and hid my face
          in anger,
      yet they kept on in their willful
          ways.
18 I have seen their ways, but I will heal
          them;
      I will guide them and restore
          comfort to Israel's mourners,
19   creating praise on their lips.
  Peace, peace, to those far and near,"
      says the LORD. "And I will heal
          them."
20 But the wicked are like the tossing
          sea,
      which cannot rest,
      whose waves cast up mire and mud.
21 "There is no peace," says my God,
      "for the wicked."

True Fasting
58 "Shout it aloud, do not hold back.
      Raise your voice like a trumpet.
  Declare to my people their rebellion
      and to the descendants of Jacob
          their sins.
2 For day after day they seek me out;
      they seem eager to know my ways,
  as if they were a nation that does
          what is right
      and has not forsaken the
          commands of its God.

They ask me for just decisions
and seem eager for God to come
near them.
³ 'Why have we fasted,' they say,
'and you have not seen it?
Why have we humbled ourselves,
and you have not noticed?'

"Yet on the day of your fasting, you do
as you please
and exploit all your workers.
⁴ Your fasting ends in quarreling and
strife,
and in striking each other with
wicked fists.
You cannot fast as you do today
and expect your voice to be heard
on high.
⁵ Is this the kind of fast I have
chosen,
only a day for people to humble
themselves?
Is it only for bowing one's head like a
reed
and for lying in sackcloth and
ashes?
Is that what you call a fast,
a day acceptable to the Lord?

⁶ "Is not this the kind of fasting I have
chosen:
to loose the chains of injustice
and untie the cords of the yoke,
to set the oppressed free
and break every yoke?
⁷ Is it not to share your food with the
hungry
and to provide the poor wanderer
with shelter—
when you see the naked, to clothe
them,
and not to turn away from your own
flesh and blood?
⁸ Then your light will break forth like the
dawn,
and your healing will quickly appear;
then your righteousness*a* will go
before you,
and the glory of the Lord will be
your rear guard.
⁹ Then you will call, and the Lord will
answer;
you will cry for help, and he will say:
Here am I.

"If you do away with the yoke of
oppression,
with the pointing finger and
malicious talk,
¹⁰ and if you spend yourselves in behalf
of the hungry
and satisfy the needs of the
oppressed,
then your light will rise in the
darkness,
and your night will become like the
noonday.
¹¹ The Lord will guide you always;
he will satisfy your needs in a sun-
scorched land
and will strengthen your frame.
You will be like a well-watered garden,
like a spring whose waters never
fail.
¹² Your people will rebuild the ancient
ruins
and will raise up the age-old
foundations;
you will be called Repairer of Broken
Walls,
Restorer of Streets with Dwellings.

BREAKTHROUGH!

Fasting

(ISAIAH 58:3)

Read the reason for this in Esther 4:16 and
1 Samuel 7:6.

---

a 8 Or *your righteous One*

13 "If you keep your feet from breaking
the Sabbath
and from doing as you please on my
holy day,
if you call the Sabbath a delight
and the Lord's holy day
honorable,
and if you honor it by not going your
own way
and not doing as you please or
speaking idle words,
14 then you will find your joy in the
Lord,
and I will cause you to ride in
triumph on the heights of the
land
and to feast on the inheritance of
your father Jacob."
            For the mouth of the Lord
                      has spoken.

BREAK THROUGH!

The Sabbath, God's holy day
(ISAIAH 58:13)

Do you like to rest? We do, but sometimes we
prefer playing or doing something else. So
the Sabbath (Saturday for the Israelites, and
sometimes Saturday or Sunday for us) is a day
of the week when people should take time
out in order to rest and remember that God is
the Creator of everything. He should get our
special worship.

Sin, Confession and Redemption

59 Surely the arm of the Lord is not
too short to save,
nor his ear too dull to hear.
2 But your iniquities have separated
you from your God;
your sins have hidden his face from
you,
so that he will not hear.
3 For your hands are stained with blood,
your fingers with guilt.
Your lips have spoken falsely,
and your tongue mutters wicked
things.
4 No one calls for justice;
no one pleads a case with integrity.
They rely on empty arguments, they
utter lies;
they conceive trouble and give birth
to evil.
5 They hatch the eggs of vipers
and spin a spider's web.
Whoever eats their eggs will die,
and when one is broken, an adder
is hatched.
6 Their cobwebs are useless for
clothing;
they cannot cover themselves with
what they make.
Their deeds are evil deeds,
and acts of violence are in their
hands.
7 Their feet rush into sin;
they are swift to shed innocent
blood.
They pursue evil schemes;
acts of violence mark their ways.
8 The way of peace they do not know;
there is no justice in their paths.
They have turned them into crooked
roads;
no one who walks along them will
know peace.
9 So justice is far from us,
and righteousness does not
reach us.
We look for light, but all is darkness;
for brightness, but we walk in deep
shadows.
10 Like the blind we grope along the wall,
feeling our way like people without
eyes.

At midday we stumble as if it were
twilight;
among the strong, we are like the
dead.
11 We all growl like bears;
we moan mournfully like doves.
We look for justice, but find none;
for deliverance, but it is far away.

12 For our offenses are many in your
sight,
and our sins testify against us.
Our offenses are ever with us,
and we acknowledge our iniquities:
13 rebellion and treachery against the
LORD,
turning our backs on our God,
inciting revolt and oppression,
uttering lies our hearts have
conceived.
14 So justice is driven back,
and righteousness stands at a
distance;
truth has stumbled in the streets,
honesty cannot enter.
15 Truth is nowhere to be found,
and whoever shuns evil becomes a
prey.

The LORD looked and was displeased
that there was no justice.
16 He saw that there was no one,
he was appalled that there was no
one to intervene;
so his own arm achieved salvation for
him,
and his own righteousness
sustained him.
17 He put on righteousness as his
breastplate,
and the helmet of salvation on his
head;
he put on the garments of vengeance
and wrapped himself in zeal as in a
cloak.
18 According to what they have done,
so will he repay
wrath to his enemies
and retribution to his foes;
he will repay the islands their due.
19 From the west, people will fear the
name of the LORD,
and from the rising of the sun, they
will revere his glory.

For he will come like a pent-up flood
that the breath of the LORD drives
along.[a]
20 "The Redeemer will come to Zion,
to those in Jacob who repent of
their sins,"
declares the LORD.

21 "As for me, this is my covenant with
them," says the LORD. "My Spirit, who is
on you, will not depart from you, and my
words that I have put in your mouth will
always be on your lips, on the lips of your
children and on the lips of their descendants—from this time on and forever,"
says the LORD.

The Glory of Zion

60 "Arise, shine, for your light has
come,
and the glory of the LORD rises upon
you.
2 See, darkness covers the earth
and thick darkness is over the
peoples,
but the LORD rises upon you
and his glory appears over you.
3 Nations will come to your light,
and kings to the brightness of your
dawn.

4 "Lift up your eyes and look about
you:
All assemble and come to you;
your sons come from afar,
and your daughters are carried on
the hip.
5 Then you will look and be radiant,
your heart will throb and swell with
joy;
the wealth on the seas will be brought
to you,
to you the riches of the nations will
come.
6 Herds of camels will cover your land,
young camels of Midian and
Ephah.
And all from Sheba will come,
bearing gold and incense
and proclaiming the praise of the
LORD.

---

a 19 Or When enemies come in like a flood, / the Spirit of
the LORD will put them to flight

[7] All Kedar's flocks will be gathered to
you,
the rams of Nebaioth will serve you;
they will be accepted as offerings on
my altar,
and I will adorn my glorious temple.

[8] "Who are these that fly along like
clouds,
like doves to their nests?
[9] Surely the islands look to me;
in the lead are the ships of
Tarshish,[a]
bringing your children from afar,
with their silver and gold,
to the honor of the Lord your God,
the Holy One of Israel,
for he has endowed you with
splendor.

[10] "Foreigners will rebuild your walls,
and their kings will serve you.
Though in anger I struck you,
in favor I will show you compassion.
[11] Your gates will always stand open,
they will never be shut, day or night,
so that people may bring you the
wealth of the nations—
their kings led in triumphal
procession.
[12] For the nation or kingdom that will not
serve you will perish;
it will be utterly ruined.

[13] "The glory of Lebanon will come to
you,
the juniper, the fir and the cypress
together,
to adorn my sanctuary;
and I will glorify the place for my
feet.
[14] The children of your oppressors will
come bowing before you;
all who despise you will bow down
at your feet
and will call you the City of the Lord,
Zion of the Holy One of Israel.

[15] "Although you have been forsaken and
hated,
with no one traveling through,
I will make you the everlasting pride
and the joy of all generations.
[16] You will drink the milk of nations
and be nursed at royal breasts.

Then you will know that I, the Lord, am
your Savior,
your Redeemer, the Mighty One of
Jacob.
[17] Instead of bronze I will bring you gold,
and silver in place of iron.
Instead of wood I will bring you bronze,
and iron in place of stones.
I will make peace your governor
and well-being your ruler.
[18] No longer will violence be heard in
your land,
nor ruin or destruction within your
borders,
but you will call your walls Salvation
and your gates Praise.
[19] The sun will no more be your light by
day,
nor will the brightness of the moon
shine on you,
for the Lord will be your everlasting
light,
and your God will be your glory.
[20] Your sun will never set again,
and your moon will wane no more;
the Lord will be your everlasting light,
and your days of sorrow will end.
[21] Then all your people will be
righteous
and they will possess the land
forever.
They are the shoot I have planted,
the work of my hands,
for the display of my splendor.
[22] The least of you will become a
thousand,
the smallest a mighty nation.
I am the Lord;
in its time I will do this swiftly."

The Year of the Lord's Favor

61 The Spirit of the Sovereign Lord is
on me,
because the Lord has anointed me
to proclaim good news to the poor.
He has sent me to bind up the
brokenhearted,
to proclaim freedom for the
captives
and release from darkness for the
prisoners,[b]

---

[a] 9 Or the trading ships　　[b] 1 Hebrew; Septuagint the blind

² to proclaim the year of the Lord's favor
and the day of vengeance of our
God,
to comfort all who mourn,
³   and provide for those who grieve in
Zion—
to bestow on them a crown of beauty
instead of ashes,
the oil of joy
instead of mourning,
and a garment of praise
instead of a spirit of despair.
They will be called oaks of
righteousness,
a planting of the Lord
for the display of his splendor.

⁴ They will rebuild the ancient ruins
and restore the places long
devastated;
they will renew the ruined cities
that have been devastated for
generations.
⁵ Strangers will shepherd your flocks;
foreigners will work your fields and
vineyards.
⁶ And you will be called priests of the
Lord,
you will be named ministers of our
God.
You will feed on the wealth of
nations,
and in their riches you will boast.

⁷ Instead of your shame
you will receive a double portion,
and instead of disgrace
you will rejoice in your inheritance.
And so you will inherit a double
portion in your land,
and everlasting joy will be yours.

⁸ "For I, the Lord, love justice;
I hate robbery and wrongdoing.
In my faithfulness I will reward my
people
and make an everlasting covenant
with them.
⁹ Their descendants will be known
among the nations
and their offspring among the
peoples.
All who see them will acknowledge
that they are a people the Lord has
blessed."

¹⁰ I delight greatly in the Lord;
my soul rejoices in my God.
For he has clothed me with garments
of salvation
and arrayed me in a robe of his
righteousness,
as a bridegroom adorns his head like
a priest,
and as a bride adorns herself with
her jewels.
¹¹ For as the soil makes the sprout come
up
and a garden causes seeds to grow,
so the Sovereign Lord will make
righteousness
and praise spring up before all
nations.

Zion's New Name

62 For Zion's sake I will not keep
silent,
for Jerusalem's sake I will not
remain quiet,
till her vindication shines out like the
dawn,
her salvation like a blazing torch.
² The nations will see your vindication,
and all kings your glory;
you will be called by a new name
that the mouth of the Lord will
bestow.
³ You will be a crown of splendor in the
Lord's hand,
a royal diadem in the hand of your
God.
⁴ No longer will they call you Deserted,
or name your land Desolate.
But you will be called Hephzibah,ᵃ
and your land Beulahᵇ;
for the Lord will take delight in you,
and your land will be married.
⁵ As a young man marries a young
woman,
so will your Builder marry you;
as a bridegroom rejoices over his bride,
so will your God rejoice over you.
⁶ I have posted watchmen on your walls,
Jerusalem;
they will never be silent day or
night.

ᵃ 4 *Hephzibah* means *my delight is in her.*   ᵇ 4 *Beulah*
means *married.*

You who call on the LORD,
    give yourselves no rest,
[7] and give him no rest till he
        establishes Jerusalem
    and makes her the praise of the
        earth.

[8] The LORD has sworn by his right
        hand
    and by his mighty arm:
"Never again will I give your grain
        as food for your enemies,
    and never again will foreigners drink
        the new wine
    for which you have toiled;
[9] but those who harvest it will eat it
        and praise the LORD,
    and those who gather the grapes will
        drink it
    in the courts of my sanctuary."

[10] Pass through, pass through the
        gates!
    Prepare the way for the people.
    Build up, build up the highway!
    Remove the stones.
    Raise a banner for the nations.

[11] The LORD has made proclamation
        to the ends of the earth:
"Say to Daughter Zion,
    'See, your Savior comes!
    See, his reward is with him,
        and his recompense accompanies
            him.' "
[12] They will be called the Holy People,
        the Redeemed of the LORD;
    and you will be called Sought After,
        the City No Longer Deserted.

God's Day of Vengeance and Redemption

63 Who is this coming from Edom,
    from Bozrah, with his garments
        stained crimson?
Who is this, robed in splendor,
    striding forward in the greatness of
        his strength?

"It is I, proclaiming victory,
    mighty to save."

[2] Why are your garments red,
    like those of one treading the
        winepress?

[3] "I have trodden the winepress alone;
    from the nations no one was with
        me.
I trampled them in my anger
    and trod them down in my wrath;
their blood spattered my garments,
    and I stained all my clothing.
[4] It was for me the day of vengeance;
    the year for me to redeem had
        come.
[5] I looked, but there was no one to help,
    I was appalled that no one gave
        support;
so my own arm achieved salvation for
        me,
    and my own wrath sustained me.
[6] I trampled the nations in my anger;
    in my wrath I made them drunk
    and poured their blood on the
        ground."

Praise and Prayer

[7] I will tell of the kindnesses of the LORD,
    the deeds for which he is
        to be praised,
    according to all the LORD
        has done for us—
yes, the many good things
    he has done for Israel,
    according to his compassion and
        many kindnesses.
[8] He said, "Surely they are my people,
    children who will be true to me";
    and so he became their Savior.
[9] In all their distress he too was
        distressed,
    and the angel of his presence
        saved them.[a]
In his love and mercy he redeemed
        them;
    he lifted them up and carried them
        all the days of old.
[10] Yet they rebelled
    and grieved his Holy Spirit.
So he turned and became their enemy
    and he himself fought against them.

[11] Then his people recalled[b] the days of
        old,
    the days of Moses and his people—

---

[a] 9 Or Savior [9] in their distress. / It was no envoy or angel / but his own presence that saved them   [b] 11 Or But may he recall

where is he who brought them through
    the sea,
with the shepherd of his flock?
Where is he who set
    his Holy Spirit among them,
[12] who sent his glorious arm of power
    to be at Moses' right hand,
who divided the waters before them,
    to gain for himself everlasting
        renown,
[13] who led them through the depths?
Like a horse in open country,
    they did not stumble;
[14] like cattle that go down to the plain,
    they were given rest by the Spirit of
        the Lord.
This is how you guided your people
    to make for yourself a glorious
        name.

[15] Look down from heaven and see,
    from your lofty throne, holy and
        glorious.
Where are your zeal and your might?
    Your tenderness and compassion
    are withheld from us.
[16] But you are our Father,
    though Abraham does not
        know us
or Israel acknowledge us;
    you, Lord, are our Father,
    our Redeemer from of old is your
        name.
[17] Why, Lord, do you make us wander
    from your ways
and harden our hearts so we do not
    revere you?
Return for the sake of your servants,
    the tribes that are your inheritance.
[18] For a little while your people
        possessed your holy place,
    but now our enemies have trampled
        down your sanctuary.
[19] We are yours from of old;
    but you have not ruled over them,
    they have not been called[a] by your
        name.

64

[b] Oh, that you would rend the
    heavens and come down,
that the mountains would tremble
    before you!
[2] As when fire sets twigs ablaze
    and causes water to boil,

come down to make your name known
    to your enemies
and cause the nations to quake
    before you!
[3] For when you did awesome things that
    we did not expect,
    you came down, and the mountains
        trembled before you.
[4] Since ancient times no one has heard,
    no ear has perceived,
no eye has seen any God besides you,
    who acts on behalf of those who
        wait for him.
[5] You come to the help of those who
        gladly do right,
    who remember your ways.
But when we continued to sin against
        them,
    you were angry.
    How then can we be saved?
[6] All of us have become like one who is
        unclean,
    and all our righteous acts are like
        filthy rags;
we all shrivel up like a leaf,
    and like the wind our sins sweep us
        away.
[7] No one calls on your name
    or strives to lay hold of you;
for you have hidden your face from us
    and have given us over to[c] our sins.

[8] Yet you, Lord, are our Father.
    We are the clay, you are the potter;
    we are all the work of your hand.
[9] Do not be angry beyond measure,
        Lord;
    do not remember our sins forever.
Oh, look on us, we pray,
    for we are all your people.
[10] Your sacred cities have become a
        wasteland;
    even Zion is a wasteland, Jerusalem
        a desolation.
[11] Our holy and glorious temple, where
        our ancestors praised you,
    has been burned with fire,
    and all that we treasured lies in
        ruins.

---

[a] 19 Or We are like those you have never ruled, / like
those never called   [b] In Hebrew texts 64:1 is
numbered 63:19b, and 64:2-12 is numbered 64:1-11.
[c] 7 Septuagint, Syriac and Targum; Hebrew have made
us melt because of

¹²After all this, LORD, will you hold
  yourself back?
Will you keep silent and punish us
  beyond measure?

Judgment and Salvation

65 "I revealed myself to those who
  did not ask for me;
I was found by those who did not
  seek me.
To a nation that did not call on my
  name,
I said, 'Here am I, here am I.'
²All day long I have held out my hands
  to an obstinate people,
who walk in ways not good,
  pursuing their own imaginations—
³a people who continually provoke me
  to my very face,
offering sacrifices in gardens
  and burning incense on altars of
  brick;
⁴who sit among the graves
  and spend their nights keeping
  secret vigil;
who eat the flesh of pigs,
  and whose pots hold broth of
  impure meat;
⁵who say, 'Keep away; don't come near
  me,
for I am too sacred for you!'
Such people are smoke in my nostrils,
  a fire that keeps burning all day.

⁶"See, it stands written before me:
  I will not keep silent but will pay
  back in full;
I will pay it back into their laps—
⁷both your sins and the sins of your
  ancestors,"
  says the LORD.
"Because they burned sacrifices on
  the mountains
  and defied me on the hills,
I will measure into their laps
  the full payment for their former
  deeds."

⁸This is what the LORD says:

"As when juice is still found in a
  cluster of grapes
  and people say, 'Don't destroy it,
  there is still a blessing in it,'

so will I do in behalf of my servants;
  I will not destroy them all.
⁹I will bring forth descendants from
  Jacob,
  and from Judah those who will
  possess my mountains;
my chosen people will inherit them,
  and there will my servants live.
¹⁰Sharon will become a pasture for
  flocks,
  and the Valley of Achor a resting
  place for herds,
  for my people who seek me.

¹¹"But as for you who forsake the LORD
  and forget my holy mountain,
who spread a table for Fortune
  and fill bowls of mixed wine for
  Destiny,
¹²I will destine you for the sword,
  and all of you will fall in the
  slaughter;
for I called but you did not answer,
  I spoke but you did not listen.
You did evil in my sight
  and chose what displeases me."

¹³Therefore this is what the Sovereign
LORD says:

"My servants will eat,
  but you will go hungry;
my servants will drink,
  but you will go thirsty;
my servants will rejoice,
  but you will be put to shame.
¹⁴My servants will sing
  out of the joy of their hearts,
but you will cry out
  from anguish of heart
  and wail in brokenness of spirit.
¹⁵You will leave your name
  for my chosen ones to use in their
  curses;
the Sovereign LORD will put you to
  death,
  but to his servants he will give
  another name.
¹⁶Whoever invokes a blessing in the
  land
  will do so by the one true God;
whoever takes an oath in the land
  will swear by the one true God.
For the past troubles will be forgotten
  and hidden from my eyes.

New Heavens and a New Earth

17 "See, I will create
    new heavens and a new earth.
The former things will not be
    remembered,
    nor will they come to mind.
18 But be glad and rejoice forever
    in what I will create,
for I will create Jerusalem to be a
    delight
    and its people a joy.
19 I will rejoice over Jerusalem
    and take delight in my people;
the sound of weeping and of crying
    will be heard in it no more.

20 "Never again will there be in it
    an infant who lives but a few days,
    or an old man who does not live out
        his years;
the one who dies at a hundred
    will be thought a mere child;
the one who fails to reach[a] a hundred
    will be considered accursed.
21 They will build houses and dwell in
        them;
    they will plant vineyards and eat
        their fruit.
22 No longer will they build houses and
        others live in them,
    or plant and others eat.
For as the days of a tree,
    so will be the days of my people;
my chosen ones will long enjoy
    the work of their hands.
23 They will not labor in vain,
    nor will they bear children doomed
        to misfortune;
for they will be a people blessed by
    the LORD,
they and their descendants with
    them.
24 Before they call I will answer;
    while they are still speaking I will
        hear.
25 The wolf and the lamb will feed
        together,
    and the lion will eat straw like the
        ox,
    and dust will be the serpent's food.
They will neither harm nor destroy
    on all my holy mountain,"
                        says the LORD.

Judgment and Hope

66 This is what the LORD says:

"Heaven is my throne,
    and the earth is my footstool.
Where is the house you will build
    for me?
Where will my resting place be?
2 Has not my hand made all these
        things,
    and so they came into being?"
                        declares the LORD.

"These are the ones I look on with
        favor:
    those who are humble and contrite
        in spirit,
    and who tremble at my word.
3 But whoever sacrifices a bull
    is like one who kills a person,
and whoever offers a lamb
    is like one who breaks a dog's neck;
whoever makes a grain offering
    is like one who presents pig's
        blood,
and whoever burns memorial incense
    is like one who worships an idol.
They have chosen their own ways,
    and they delight in their
        abominations;
4 so I also will choose harsh treatment
    for them
    and will bring on them what they
        dread.
For when I called, no one answered,
    when I spoke, no one listened.
They did evil in my sight
    and chose what displeases me."

5 Hear the word of the LORD,
    you who tremble at his word:
"Your own people who hate you,
    and exclude you because of my
        name, have said,
'Let the LORD be glorified,
    that we may see your joy!'
    Yet they will be put to shame.
6 Hear that uproar from the city,
    hear that noise from the temple!
It is the sound of the LORD
    repaying his enemies all they
        deserve.

---

[a] 20 Or the sinner who reaches

⁷ "Before she goes into labor,
    she gives birth;
before the pains come upon her,
    she delivers a son.
⁸ Who has ever heard of such things?
    Who has ever seen things like this?
Can a country be born in a day
    or a nation be brought forth in a
        moment?
Yet no sooner is Zion in labor
    than she gives birth to her children.
⁹ Do I bring to the moment of birth
    and not give delivery?" says the
        Lord.
"Do I close up the womb
    when I bring to delivery?" says your
        God.
¹⁰ "Rejoice with Jerusalem and be glad
        for her,
    all you who love her;
rejoice greatly with her,
    all you who mourn over her.
¹¹ For you will nurse and be satisfied
    at her comforting breasts;
you will drink deeply

and delight in her overflowing
    abundance."

¹² For this is what the Lord says:

"I will extend peace to her like a river,
    and the wealth of nations like a
        flooding stream;
you will nurse and be carried on her
        arm
    and dandled on her knees.
¹³ As a mother comforts her child,
    so will I comfort you;
    and you will be comforted over
        Jerusalem."

¹⁴ When you see this, your heart will
        rejoice
    and you will flourish like grass;
the hand of the Lord will be made
        known to his servants,
    but his fury will be shown to his
        foes.
¹⁵ See, the Lord is coming with fire,
    and his chariots are like a
        whirlwind;

When we finished reading this very long and very difficult book, we realized that it's very clear that God judges. God doesn't accept injustice, and that's why he always sent his prophet to tell the people that they were doing bad things. But God is also love and wants to forgive his people. The only thing the people had to do was repent and be sorry, and look for him wholeheartedly. It's the same for us now. Let's always try to hear what God is saying to us through other people. Let's do what God wants, because God loves us very much. Everything he tells us is for our good.

CASE CLOSED!

he will bring down his anger with fury,
and his rebuke with flames of fire.
16 For with fire and with his sword
the LORD will execute judgment on
all people,
and many will be those slain by the
LORD.

17 "Those who consecrate and purify themselves to go into the gardens, following one who is among those who eat the flesh of pigs, rats and other unclean things—they will meet their end together with the one they follow," declares the LORD.

18 "And I, because of what they have planned and done, am about to come[a] and gather the people of all nations and languages, and they will come and see my glory.

19 "I will set a sign among them, and I will send some of those who survive to the nations—to Tarshish, to the Libyans[b] and Lydians (famous as archers), to Tubal and Greece, and to the distant islands that have not heard of my fame or seen my glory. They will proclaim my glory among the nations. 20 And they will bring all your people, from all the nations, to my holy mountain in Jerusalem as an offering to the LORD—on horses, in chariots and wagons, and on mules and camels," says the LORD. "They will bring them, as the Israelites bring their grain offerings, to the temple of the LORD in ceremonially clean vessels. 21 And I will select some of them also to be priests and Levites," says the LORD.

22 "As the new heavens and the new earth that I make will endure before me," declares the LORD, "so will your name and descendants endure. 23 From one New Moon to another and from one Sabbath to another, all mankind will come and bow down before me," says the LORD. 24 "And they will go out and look on the dead bodies of those who rebelled against me; the worms that eat them will not die, the fire that burns them will not be quenched, and they will be loathsome to all mankind."

---

[a] 18 The meaning of the Hebrew for this clause is uncertain.   [b] 19 Some Septuagint manuscripts *Put* (Libyans); Hebrew *Pul*

JEREMIAH

THE EVIDENCE:

WHO WROTE IT?

People who have studied the book of Jeremiah a lot think Jeremiah spoke the whole book to his secretary, Baruch, who wrote it down. At any rate, let's at least say that the person who thought about everything that's written in this book was Jeremiah. He was a very important prophet for the people of Israel. And being a prophet at that time was really hard and dangerous.

HOW LONG AGO?

Since this book was written many, many years ago, it's hard to know exactly when it was written. What we found out was that it was written around 600 years before Christ. That means it was created about 2,600 years ago.

WHAT'S IT ABOUT?

The book of Jeremiah deals with many subjects. It's a super complicated book, because Jeremiah liked poetry, stories, history and politics. He also always tried to write what God was telling him. But it seems to us that Jeremiah was one of those preachers who has a lot of passion. What he most wanted was for his people to be obedient to God. However, at that time, the people were very disobedient, and that made Jeremiah very sad.

THE BEST PART

You know what? As a prophet of God, Jeremiah said a lot of important things, but one of the things he said that we like best is in Jeremiah 33:3: "Call to me and I will answer you and tell you great and unsearchable things you do not know." God says this!

---

1 The words of Jeremiah son of Hilkiah, one of the priests at Anathoth in the territory of Benjamin. ²The word of the LORD came to him in the thirteenth year of the reign of Josiah son of Amon king of Judah, ³and through the reign of Jehoiakim son of Josiah king of Judah, down to the fifth month of the eleventh year of Zedekiah son of Josiah king of Judah, when the people of Jerusalem went into exile.

The Call of Jeremiah

⁴The word of the LORD came to me, saying,

⁵ "Before I formed you in the womb
   I knew*a* you,
   before you were born I set you apart;
   I appointed you as a prophet to the
      nations."

---

a 5 Or *chose*

THE
WITNESSES

✓ **JEREMIAH SON OF HILKIAH**
  (JEREMIAH 1:1)
Jeremiah was a prophet who announced
everything that God told him to say. His name
probably means "the LORD exalts," but we aren't
sure. His father was Hilkiah, who we know was
one of the priests who worked in the town of
Anathoth.

✓ **JOSIAH SON OF AMON (JEREMIAH 1:2)**
Josiah became king of Judah when he was
just a kid. Jeremiah was a prophet when Josiah
was king. Josiah was a very good king, but
he didn't live very long. The Egyptian pharaoh
(another word used to say *king*) Necho,
killed him in a battle when he was 39. The
people in Judah were very sad about that
because they loved Josiah very much. We
don't know for sure what his name means, but
it might be "to give."

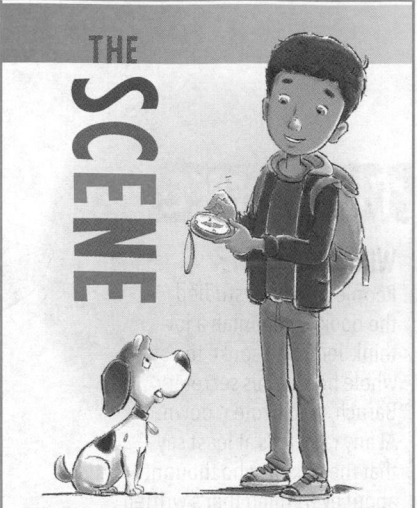

THE
SCENE

ANATHOTH

(JEREMIAH 1:1)

The town where Jeremiah was
born. This town doesn't exist
anymore, but it was probably
about 3 miles (5 km) northeast of
Jerusalem, the capital city. So it took
about an hour to walk from Anathoth
to Jerusalem. This fact is important,
because although Jeremiah wasn't
born in Jerusalem, he could see the
city from his town.

⁶"Alas, Sovereign LORD," I said, "I do not
know how to speak; I am too young."
⁷But the LORD said to me, "Do not say,
'I am too young.' You must go to everyone I send you to and say whatever I command you. ⁸Do not be afraid of them, for
I am with you and will rescue you," declares the LORD.
⁹Then the LORD reached out his hand
and touched my mouth and said to me, "I
have put my words in your mouth. ¹⁰See,
today I appoint you over nations and kingdoms to uproot and tear down, to destroy
and overthrow, to build and to plant."
¹¹The word of the LORD came to me:
"What do you see, Jeremiah?"

"I see the branch of an almond tree," I replied.

¹²The Lᴏʀᴅ said to me, "You have seen correctly, for I am watching*ᵃ* to see that my word is fulfilled."

¹³The word of the Lᴏʀᴅ came to me again: "What do you see?"

"I see a pot that is boiling," I answered. "It is tilting toward us from the north."

¹⁴The Lᴏʀᴅ said to me, "From the north disaster will be poured out on all who live in the land. ¹⁵I am about to summon all the peoples of the northern kingdoms," declares the Lᴏʀᴅ.

"Their kings will come and set up their
    thrones

in the entrance of the gates of
    Jerusalem;
they will come against all her
    surrounding walls
and against all the towns of
    Judah.
¹⁶I will pronounce my judgments on my
    people
because of their wickedness in
    forsaking me,
in burning incense to other gods
    and in worshiping what their hands
    have made.

¹⁷"Get yourself ready! Stand up and say to them whatever I command you. Do not be terrified by them, or I will terrify you before them. ¹⁸Today I have made you a fortified city, an iron pillar and a bronze wall to stand against the whole land—

ᵃ 12 The Hebrew for *watching* sounds like the Hebrew for *almond tree.*

JUDAH

(JEREMIAH 1:2–3)

Judah is the name the southern part of Israel got when the Israelites fought among themselves and divided the land into two parts. There were only two tribes in this region, but there were ten tribes in the north. The advantage that Judah had as a nation was that the capital city, Jerusalem, was in Judah.

BREAK THROUGH!

Exile

(JEREMIAH 1:3)

This word means "being forced to move." It is when a person is taken away and has to live in another country. In this book, it's talking about a time when the Babylonians (in modern-day Iraq) attacked Jerusalem. They destroyed it and took the Israelites to live in Babylon. Jeremiah lived there at that time.

CHECK THE FACTS

Who was Jeremiah?

A) A priest

B) A prophet

C) A sheepherder

CORRECT ANSWER: B

against the kings of Judah, its officials, its priests and the people of the land. ¹⁹They will fight against you but will not overcome you, for I am with you and will rescue you," declares the LORD.

Israel Forsakes God

2 The word of the LORD came to me: ²"Go and proclaim in the hearing of Jerusalem:

"This is what the LORD says:

" 'I remember the devotion of your
　　youth,
　how as a bride you loved me
and followed me through the
　　wilderness,
　through a land not sown.
³Israel was holy to the LORD,
　the firstfruits of his harvest;
all who devoured her were held
　　guilty,
　and disaster overtook them,' "
　　　　　　　declares the LORD.

⁴Hear the word of the LORD, you
　　descendants of Jacob,
　all you clans of Israel.

⁵This is what the LORD says:

"What fault did your ancestors find in
　　me,
　that they strayed so far from me?
They followed worthless idols
　and became worthless
　　themselves.
⁶They did not ask, 'Where is the LORD,
　who brought us up out of Egypt
and led us through the barren
　　wilderness,
　through a land of deserts and
　　ravines,
a land of drought and utter darkness,
　a land where no one travels and no
　　one lives?'

BREAKTHROUGH!

"Worshiping what their hands have made"

(JEREMIAH 1:16)

Jeremiah was talking about little statues. Many Israelites were worshiping these statues as if they were real gods. But they were totally wrong. Jeremiah tells the people very clearly that these statues were made by humans like you and me. They could never be gods.

⁷I brought you into a fertile land
  to eat its fruit and rich produce.
But you came and defiled my land
  and made my inheritance
    detestable.
⁸The priests did not ask,
  'Where is the LORD?'
Those who deal with the law did not
    know me;
  the leaders rebelled against me.
The prophets prophesied by
    Baal,
  following worthless idols.

⁹"Therefore I bring charges against you
    again,"
                    declares the LORD.
  "And I will bring charges against
    your children's children.
¹⁰Cross over to the coasts of Cyprus
    and look,
  send to Kedar[a] and observe closely;
  see if there has ever been anything
    like this:
¹¹Has a nation ever changed its gods?
  (Yet they are not gods at all.)
But my people have exchanged their
    glorious God
  for worthless idols.
¹²Be appalled at this, you heavens,
  and shudder with great horror,"
                    declares the LORD.
¹³"My people have committed two sins:
They have forsaken me,
  the spring of living water,
and have dug their own cisterns,
  broken cisterns that cannot hold
    water.
¹⁴Is Israel a servant, a slave by birth?
  Why then has he become plunder?
¹⁵Lions have roared;
  they have growled at him.
They have laid waste his land;
  his towns are burned and deserted.
¹⁶Also, the men of Memphis and
    Tahpanhes
  have cracked your skull.
¹⁷Have you not brought this on
    yourselves
  by forsaking the LORD your God
  when he led you in the way?
¹⁸Now why go to Egypt
  to drink water from the Nile[b]?

And why go to Assyria
  to drink water from the Euphrates?
¹⁹Your wickedness will punish you;
  your backsliding will rebuke you.
Consider then and realize
  how evil and bitter it is for you
when you forsake the LORD your
    God
  and have no awe of me,"
                    declares the Lord,
                    the LORD Almighty.

²⁰"Long ago you broke off your yoke
  and tore off your bonds;
  you said, 'I will not serve you!'

---

a 10 In the Syro-Arabian desert   *b* 18 Hebrew *Shihor*;
that is, a branch of the Nile

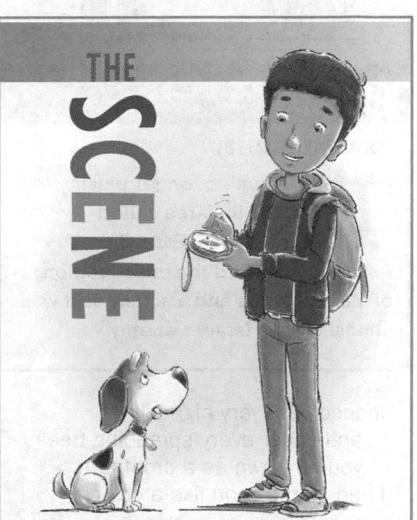

THE
SCENE

EGYPT

(JEREMIAH 2:18)

Egypt was and is a country in the northern part of the continent of Africa. So, it is southeast of the land of Israel. For many years, this nation was an enemy of the Israelites. This bad relationship between the Egyptians and the Israelites began more than 3,000 years ago, when the Egyptians kept the Israelites as slaves for 400 years.

THE SCENE

ASSYRIA

(JEREMIAH 2:18)

This nation no longer exists. It was in the area called Mesopotamia. For a time, Assyria controlled the entire region of Mesopotamia and also Israel. It was almost always Israel's enemy.

Indeed, on every high hill
and under every spreading tree
you lay down as a prostitute.
²¹ I had planted you like a choice
vine
of sound and reliable stock.
How then did you turn against me
into a corrupt, wild vine?
²² Although you wash yourself with
soap
and use an abundance of cleansing
powder,
the stain of your guilt is still before
me,"
declares the Sovereign LORD.
²³ "How can you say, 'I am not defiled;
I have not run after the Baals'?
See how you behaved in the valley;
consider what you have done.
You are a swift she-camel
running here and there,

²⁴ a wild donkey accustomed to the
desert,
sniffing the wind in her craving—
in her heat who can restrain
her?
Any males that pursue her need not
tire themselves;
at mating time they will find her.
²⁵ Do not run until your feet are bare
and your throat is dry.
But you said, 'It's no use!
I love foreign gods,
and I must go after them.'

²⁶ "As a thief is disgraced when he is
caught,
so the people of Israel are
disgraced—
they, their kings and their
officials,
their priests and their prophets.

BREAKTHROUGH!

The Baals

(JEREMIAH 2:23)

They were false gods. Sometimes, I think false gods are like pretend money—they're not worth anything. False gods are invented by people, and they don't have any strength or life or anything. They can't help you when you're sick or sad, because they really don't exist. They're just something people have invented.

27 They say to wood, 'You are my
        father,'
    and to stone, 'You gave me birth.'
  They have turned their backs to me
        and not their faces;
  yet when they are in trouble, they
        say,
    'Come and save us!'
28 Where then are the gods you made for
        yourselves?
    Let them come if they can save
        you
  when you are in trouble!
  For you, Judah, have as many gods
        as you have towns.

29 "Why do you bring charges against
        me?
    You have all rebelled against me,"
                declares the LORD.
30 "In vain I punished your people;
    they did not respond to correction.
  Your sword has devoured your
        prophets
    like a ravenous lion.

31 "You of this generation, consider the
  word of the LORD:

  "Have I been a desert to Israel
    or a land of great darkness?
  Why do my people say, 'We are free to
        roam;
    we will come to you no more'?
32 Does a young woman forget her
        jewelry,
    a bride her wedding ornaments?
  Yet my people have forgotten me,
    days without number.
33 How skilled you are at pursuing
        love!
    Even the worst of women can learn
        from your ways.
34 On your clothes is found
    the lifeblood of the innocent
        poor,
  though you did not catch them
        breaking in.
  Yet in spite of all this
35   you say, 'I am innocent;
        he is not angry with me.'
  But I will pass judgment on you
    because you say, 'I have not
        sinned.'

36 Why do you go about so much,
        changing your ways?
  You will be disappointed by
        Egypt
    as you were by Assyria.
37 You will also leave that place
    with your hands on your head,
  for the LORD has rejected those you
        trust;
    you will not be helped by
        them.

3 "If a man divorces his wife
    and she leaves him and marries
        another man,
  should he return to her again?
    Would not the land be completely
        defiled?

False gods and prostitution
(JEREMIAH 3)

Prostitution is when women sell themselves
to make money. They only value their lives
for the money they can make. The prophet
Jeremiah often compares the way the
Israelites were living to prostitution. Why?
Because the Israelites had forgotten the
true God, and they were worshiping other
gods that really weren't good for anything.
When the Israelites didn't love the God of life
anymore, they were acting like a person who
prostitutes.

But you have lived as a prostitute with
    many lovers—
would you now return to me?"
               declares the LORD.
2 "Look up to the barren heights and
    see.
Is there any place where you have
    not been ravished?
By the roadside you sat waiting for
    lovers,
    sat like a nomad in the desert.
You have defiled the land
    with your prostitution and
    wickedness.
3 Therefore the showers have been
    withheld,
    and no spring rains have fallen.
Yet you have the brazen look of a
    prostitute;
    you refuse to blush with shame.
4 Have you not just called to me:
    'My Father, my friend from my
    youth,
5 will you always be angry?
    Will your wrath continue forever?'
This is how you talk,
    but you do all the evil you can."

Unfaithful Israel

6 During the reign of King Josiah, the
LORD said to me, "Have you seen what
faithless Israel has done? She has gone
up on every high hill and under every
spreading tree and has committed adultery there. 7 I thought that after she had
done all this she would return to me but
she did not, and her unfaithful sister Judah saw it. 8 I gave faithless Israel her
certificate of divorce and sent her away
because of all her adulteries. Yet I saw
that her unfaithful sister Judah had no
fear; she also went out and committed
adultery. 9 Because Israel's immorality
mattered so little to her, she defiled the
land and committed adultery with stone
and wood. 10 In spite of all this, her unfaithful sister Judah did not return to me
with all her heart, but only in pretense,"
declares the LORD.

11 The LORD said to me, "Faithless Israel
is more righteous than unfaithful Judah.
12 Go, proclaim this message toward the
north:

" 'Return, faithless Israel,' declares
    the LORD,
'I will frown on you no longer,
for I am faithful,' declares the LORD,
    'I will not be angry forever.
13 Only acknowledge your guilt—
    you have rebelled against the LORD
    your God,
you have scattered your favors to
    foreign gods
under every spreading tree,
    and have not obeyed me,' "
               declares the LORD.

14 "Return, faithless people," declares
the LORD, "for I am your husband. I will
choose you—one from a town and two
from a clan—and bring you to Zion.
15 Then I will give you shepherds after my

THE SCENE

ZION

(JEREMIAH 3:14)

Zion is the city of Jerusalem we
know today. The old part still
exists, and people still live
there. It was the capital city of the
nation of Israel. It was founded by
David, the famous king, and it was
also God's chosen and preferred city
during the time of Jeremiah.

own heart, who will lead you with knowledge and understanding. ¹⁶In those days, when your numbers have increased greatly in the land," declares the Lᴏʀᴅ, "people will no longer say, 'The ark of the covenant of the Lᴏʀᴅ.' It will never enter their minds or be remembered; it will not be missed, nor will another one be made. ¹⁷At that time they will call Jerusalem The Throne of the Lᴏʀᴅ, and all nations will gather in Jerusalem to honor the name of the Lᴏʀᴅ. No longer will they follow the stubbornness of their evil hearts. ¹⁸In those days the people of Judah will join the people of Israel, and together they will come from a northern land to the land I gave your ancestors as an inheritance.

¹⁹"I myself said,

" 'How gladly would I treat you like my
      children
   and give you a pleasant land,
   the most beautiful inheritance of
      any nation.'
I thought you would call me
      'Father'
   and not turn away from following
      me.

Ark of the covenant
(JEREMIAH 3:16)
Read Numbers 10:33–36.

²⁰But like a woman unfaithful to her
      husband,
   so you, Israel, have been unfaithful
      to me,"
                  declares the Lᴏʀᴅ.

²¹A cry is heard on the barren heights,
   the weeping and pleading of the
      people of Israel,
because they have perverted their
      ways
   and have forgotten the Lᴏʀᴅ their
      God.

²²"Return, faithless people;
   I will cure you of backsliding."

"Yes, we will come to you,
   for you are the Lᴏʀᴅ our God.
²³Surely the idolatrous commotion on
      the hills
   and mountains is a deception;
surely in the Lᴏʀᴅ our God
   is the salvation of Israel.
²⁴From our youth shameful gods have
      consumed
   the fruits of our ancestors'
      labor—
their flocks and herds,
   their sons and daughters.
²⁵Let us lie down in our shame,
   and let our disgrace cover us.
We have sinned against the Lᴏʀᴅ our
      God,
   both we and our ancestors;
from our youth till this day
   we have not obeyed the Lᴏʀᴅ our
      God."

4 "If you, Israel, will return,
   then return to me,"
                  declares the Lᴏʀᴅ.
"If you put your detestable idols out of
      my sight
   and no longer go astray,
²and if in a truthful, just and righteous
      way
   you swear, 'As surely as the Lᴏʀᴅ
      lives,'
then the nations will invoke blessings
      by him
   and in him they will boast."

³This is what the Lᴏʀᴅ says to the people of Judah and to Jerusalem:

"Break up your unplowed ground
and do not sow among thorns.
4 Circumcise yourselves to the LORD,
circumcise your hearts,
you people of Judah and inhabitants
of Jerusalem,
or my wrath will flare up and burn like
fire
because of the evil you have
done—
burn with no one to quench it.

Disaster From the North

5 "Announce in Judah and proclaim in
Jerusalem and say:
'Sound the trumpet throughout the
land!'
Cry aloud and say:
'Gather together!
Let us flee to the fortified cities!'
6 Raise the signal to go to Zion!
Flee for safety without delay!
For I am bringing disaster from the
north,
even terrible destruction."

7 A lion has come out of his lair;
a destroyer of nations has set
out.
He has left his place
to lay waste your land.
Your towns will lie in ruins
without inhabitant.
8 So put on sackcloth,
lament and wail,
for the fierce anger of the LORD
has not turned away from us.

9 "In that day," declares the LORD,
"the king and the officials will lose
heart,
the priests will be horrified,
and the prophets will be appalled."

10 Then I said, "Alas, Sovereign LORD!
How completely you have deceived this
people and Jerusalem by saying, 'You will
have peace,' when the sword is at our
throats!"

11 At that time this people and Jerusalem will be told, "A scorching wind from
the barren heights in the desert blows
toward my people, but not to winnow
or cleanse; 12 a wind too strong for that

comes from me. Now I pronounce my
judgments against them."

13 Look! He advances like the clouds,
his chariots come like a
whirlwind,
his horses are swifter than eagles.
Woe to us! We are ruined!
14 Jerusalem, wash the evil from your
heart and be saved.
How long will you harbor wicked
thoughts?
15 A voice is announcing from Dan,
proclaiming disaster from the hills
of Ephraim.
16 "Tell this to the nations,
proclaim concerning Jerusalem:
'A besieging army is coming from a
distant land,
raising a war cry against the cities
of Judah.
17 They surround her like men guarding a
field,
because she has rebelled against
me,'"
declares the LORD.
18 "Your own conduct and actions
have brought this on you.
This is your punishment.
How bitter it is!
How it pierces to the heart!"

19 Oh, my anguish, my anguish!
I writhe in pain.
Oh, the agony of my heart!
My heart pounds within me,
I cannot keep silent.
For I have heard the sound of the
trumpet;
I have heard the battle cry.
20 Disaster follows disaster;
the whole land lies in ruins.
In an instant my tents are destroyed,
my shelter in a moment.
21 How long must I see the battle
standard
and hear the sound of the
trumpet?

22 "My people are fools;
they do not know me.
They are senseless children;
they have no understanding.
They are skilled in doing evil;
they know not how to do good."

THE SCENE

CITY OF DAN

(JEREMIAH 4:15)

Dan was a city at the northern border of the Israelite nation. It was near the source of the Jordan River. Although it doesn't exist now, archeological excavations show that it was important at Jeremiah's time, because it was from there that Israel could defend the nation against enemy attacks. The city is mentioned here because it was in a dangerous, emergency situation.

²³ I looked at the earth,
and it was formless and empty;
and at the heavens,
and their light was gone.
²⁴ I looked at the mountains,
and they were quaking;
all the hills were swaying.
²⁵ I looked, and there were no people;
every bird in the sky had flown
away.
²⁶ I looked, and the fruitful land was a
desert;
all its towns lay in ruins
before the LORD, before his fierce
anger.

²⁷ This is what the LORD says:

"The whole land will be ruined,
though I will not destroy it
completely.
²⁸ Therefore the earth will mourn
and the heavens above grow dark,
because I have spoken and will not
relent,
I have decided and will not turn
back."

²⁹ At the sound of horsemen and
archers
every town takes to flight.
Some go into the thickets;
some climb up among the rocks.
All the towns are deserted;
no one lives in them.

³⁰ What are you doing, you devastated
one?
Why dress yourself in scarlet
and put on jewels of gold?
Why highlight your eyes with
makeup?
You adorn yourself in vain.
Your lovers despise you;
they want to kill you.

³¹ I hear a cry as of a woman in labor,
a groan as of one bearing her first
child—
the cry of Daughter Zion gasping for
breath,
stretching out her hands and
saying,
"Alas! I am fainting;
my life is given over to murderers."

Not One Is Upright

5 "Go up and down the streets of
Jerusalem,
look around and consider,
search through her squares.
If you can find but one person
who deals honestly and seeks the
truth,
I will forgive this city.
² Although they say, 'As surely as the
LORD lives,'
still they are swearing falsely."

³ LORD, do not your eyes look for truth?
You struck them, but they felt no
pain;

you crushed them, but they refused
correction.
They made their faces harder than
stone
and refused to repent.
⁴I thought, "These are only the poor;
they are foolish,
for they do not know the way of the
LORD,
the requirements of their God.
⁵So I will go to the leaders
and speak to them;
surely they know the way of the LORD,
the requirements of their God."
But with one accord they too had
broken off the yoke
and torn off the bonds.
⁶Therefore a lion from the forest will
attack them,
a wolf from the desert will ravage
them,
a leopard will lie in wait near their
towns
to tear to pieces any who venture
out,
for their rebellion is great
and their backslidings many.

⁷"Why should I forgive you?
Your children have forsaken me
and sworn by gods that are not
gods.
I supplied all their needs,
yet they committed adultery
and thronged to the houses of
prostitutes.
⁸They are well-fed, lusty stallions,
each neighing for another man's
wife.
⁹Should I not punish them for this?"
declares the LORD.
"Should I not avenge myself
on such a nation as this?

¹⁰"Go through her vineyards and ravage
them,
but do not destroy them completely.
Strip off her branches,
for these people do not belong to
the LORD.
¹¹The people of Israel and the people of
Judah
have been utterly unfaithful to me,"
declares the LORD.

¹²They have lied about the LORD;
they said, "He will do nothing!
No harm will come to us;
we will never see sword or famine.
¹³The prophets are but wind
and the word is not in them;
so let what they say be done to
them."

¹⁴Therefore this is what the LORD God
Almighty says:

"Because the people have spoken
these words,
I will make my words in your mouth
a fire
and these people the wood it
consumes.
¹⁵People of Israel," declares the LORD,
"I am bringing a distant nation
against you—
an ancient and enduring nation,
a people whose language you do
not know,
whose speech you do not
understand.
¹⁶Their quivers are like an open
grave;
all of them are mighty warriors.
¹⁷They will devour your harvests and
food,
devour your sons and daughters;
they will devour your flocks and
herds,
devour your vines and fig trees.
With the sword they will destroy
the fortified cities in which you
trust.

¹⁸"Yet even in those days," declares the
LORD, "I will not destroy you completely.
¹⁹And when the people ask, 'Why has the
LORD our God done all this to us?' you will
tell them, 'As you have forsaken me and
served foreign gods in your own land, so
now you will serve foreigners in a land
not your own.'

²⁰"Announce this to the descendants of
Jacob
and proclaim it in Judah:
²¹Hear this, you foolish and senseless
people,
who have eyes but do not see,
who have ears but do not hear:

²² Should you not fear me?" declares the
       LORD.
    "Should you not tremble in my
       presence?
    I made the sand a boundary for the
       sea,
       an everlasting barrier it cannot
          cross.
    The waves may roll, but they cannot
       prevail;
       they may roar, but they cannot
          cross it.
²³ But these people have stubborn and
       rebellious hearts;
       they have turned aside and gone
          away.
²⁴ They do not say to themselves,
    'Let us fear the LORD our God,
    who gives autumn and spring rains in
       season,
       who assures us of the regular
          weeks of harvest.'
²⁵ Your wrongdoings have kept these
       away;
       your sins have deprived you of
          good.

²⁶ "Among my people are the wicked
       who lie in wait like men who snare
          birds
       and like those who set traps to
          catch people.
²⁷ Like cages full of birds,
       their houses are full of deceit;
    they have become rich and powerful
²⁸   and have grown fat and sleek.
    Their evil deeds have no limit;
       they do not seek justice.
    They do not promote the case of the
       fatherless;
       they do not defend the just cause of
          the poor.
²⁹ Should I not punish them for this?"
       declares the LORD.
    "Should I not avenge myself
       on such a nation as this?

³⁰ "A horrible and shocking thing
       has happened in the land:
³¹ The prophets prophesy lies,
       the priests rule by their own
          authority,
    and my people love it this way.
       But what will you do in the end?

Why does God call them foolish and senseless people?

(JEREMIAH 5:21)

God was trying to get the Israelites to listen
and obey him. So he called them foolish and
senseless to see if they'd pay attention. He
was trying to shake them up a bit. But it didn't
work, and the Israelites just didn't listen to
the true God.

Jerusalem Under Siege

6 "Flee for safety, people of Benjamin!
       Flee from Jerusalem!
    Sound the trumpet in Tekoa!
       Raise the signal over Beth Hakkerem!
    For disaster looms out of the north,
       even terrible destruction.
² I will destroy Daughter Zion,
       so beautiful and delicate.
³ Shepherds with their flocks will come
       against her;
       they will pitch their tents around
          her,
       each tending his own portion."

⁴ "Prepare for battle against her!
       Arise, let us attack at noon!
    But, alas, the daylight is fading,
       and the shadows of evening grow
          long.

⁵ So arise, let us attack at night
  and destroy her fortresses!"

⁶ This is what the Lᴏʀᴅ Almighty says:

"Cut down the trees
  and build siege ramps against
    Jerusalem.
This city must be punished;
  it is filled with oppression.
⁷ As a well pours out its water,
  so she pours out her wickedness.
Violence and destruction resound in
    her;
  her sickness and wounds are ever
    before me.
⁸ Take warning, Jerusalem,
  or I will turn away from you
and make your land desolate
  so no one can live in it."

⁹ This is what the Lᴏʀᴅ Almighty says:

"Let them glean the remnant of Israel
  as thoroughly as a vine;
pass your hand over the branches
    again,
  like one gathering grapes."

¹⁰ To whom can I speak and give warning?
  Who will listen to me?
Their ears are closed*a*
  so they cannot hear.
The word of the Lᴏʀᴅ is offensive to
    them;
  they find no pleasure in it.
¹¹ But I am full of the wrath of the Lᴏʀᴅ,
  and I cannot hold it in.

"Pour it out on the children in the
    street
  and on the young men gathered
    together;
both husband and wife will be caught
    in it,
  and the old, those weighed down
    with years.
¹² Their houses will be turned over to
    others,
  together with their fields and their
    wives,
when I stretch out my hand
  against those who live in the land,"
            declares the Lᴏʀᴅ.
¹³ "From the least to the greatest,
  all are greedy for gain;

prophets and priests alike,
  all practice deceit.
¹⁴ They dress the wound of my people
  as though it were not serious.
'Peace, peace,' they say,
  when there is no peace.
¹⁵ Are they ashamed of their detestable
    conduct?
  No, they have no shame at all;
  they do not even know how to
    blush.
So they will fall among the fallen;
  they will be brought down when
    I punish them,"
                says the Lᴏʀᴅ.

¹⁶ This is what the Lᴏʀᴅ says:

"Stand at the crossroads and look;
  ask for the ancient paths,
ask where the good way is, and walk
    in it,
  and you will find rest for your souls.
But you said, 'We will not walk in it.'
¹⁷ I appointed watchmen over you and
    said,
  'Listen to the sound of the
    trumpet!'
But you said, 'We will not listen.'
¹⁸ Therefore hear, you nations;
  you who are witnesses,
  observe what will happen to them.
¹⁹ Hear, you earth:
  I am bringing disaster on this
    people,
  the fruit of their schemes,
because they have not listened to my
    words
  and have rejected my law.
²⁰ What do I care about incense from
    Sheba
  or sweet calamus from a distant
    land?
Your burnt offerings are not
    acceptable;
  your sacrifices do not please me."

²¹ Therefore this is what the Lᴏʀᴅ says:

"I will put obstacles before this
    people.
  Parents and children alike will
    stumble over them;
  neighbors and friends will perish."

---

a 10 Hebrew *uncircumcised*

²²This is what the LORD says:

"Look, an army is coming
   from the land of the north;
a great nation is being stirred up
   from the ends of the earth.
²³They are armed with bow and spear;
   they are cruel and show no
      mercy.
They sound like the roaring sea
   as they ride on their horses;
they come like men in battle
      formation
   to attack you, Daughter Zion."

²⁴We have heard reports about them,
   and our hands hang limp.
Anguish has gripped us,
   pain like that of a woman in
      labor.

BREAK THROUGH!

Is it God who sends the disasters?

(JEREMIAH 6:19; 8:17; 9:9-11,15-16)

God is God. As the all-powerful God, he can send disasters if he wants to. But that doesn't mean God does that for fun. If God sends a disaster, it's because he wants to teach us something very important. God knew very well what was best for the Israelites. And he knows very well what's best for us today, although sometimes we don't understand.

THE SCENE

SHEBA

(JEREMIAH 6:20)

This kingdom was in the southwestern part of Arabia. It was a center of business where products were traded. In particular, incense and spices were sold there.

²⁵Do not go out to the fields
   or walk on the roads,
for the enemy has a sword,
   and there is terror on every side.
²⁶Put on sackcloth, my people,
   and roll in ashes;
mourn with bitter wailing
   as for an only son,
for suddenly the destroyer
   will come upon us.

²⁷"I have made you a tester of metals
   and my people the ore,
that you may observe
   and test their ways.
²⁸They are all hardened rebels,
   going about to slander.
They are bronze and iron;
   they all act corruptly.
²⁹The bellows blow fiercely
   to burn away the lead with fire,
but the refining goes on in vain;
   the wicked are not purged out.

30 They are called rejected silver,
　　because the LORD has rejected
　　　them."

False Religion Worthless

7 This is the word that came to Jeremiah from the LORD: 2 "Stand at the gate of the LORD's house and there proclaim this message:

" 'Hear the word of the LORD, all you people of Judah who come through these gates to worship the LORD. 3 This is what the LORD Almighty, the God of Israel, says: Reform your ways and your actions, and I will let you live in this place. 4 Do not trust in deceptive words and say, "This is the temple of the LORD, the temple of the LORD, the temple of the LORD!" 5 If you really change your ways and your actions and deal with each other justly, 6 if you do not oppress the foreigner, the fatherless or the widow and do not shed innocent blood in this place, and if you do not follow other gods to your own harm, 7 then I will let you live in this place, in the land I gave your ancestors for ever and ever. 8 But look, you are trusting in deceptive words that are worthless.

9 " 'Will you steal and murder, commit adultery and perjury,*a* burn incense to Baal and follow other gods you have not known, 10 and then come and stand before me in this house, which bears my Name, and say, "We are safe" — safe to do all these detestable things? 11 Has this house, which bears my Name, become a den of robbers to you? But I have been watching! declares the LORD.

12 " 'Go now to the place in Shiloh where I first made a dwelling for my Name, and see what I did to it because of the wickedness of my people Israel. 13 While you were doing all these things, declares the LORD, I spoke to you again and again, but you did not listen; I called you, but you did not answer. 14 Therefore, what I did to Shiloh I will now do to the house that bears my Name, the temple you trust in, the place I gave to you and your ancestors. 15 I will thrust you from my presence, just as I did all your fellow Israelites, the people of Ephraim.'

16 "So do not pray for this people nor offer any plea or petition for them; do not

THE
WITNESSES

✓ **BAAL** (JEREMIAH 7:9)

Let me remind you that this god wasn't real. Baal was a god the Canaanites invented. They lived where Israel is today. The Canaanites believed that Baal was the god of thunder and that he also helped them have children. The Israelites made lots of mistakes, and they worshiped this false god that didn't have the power to help them as the true God who created us does.

plead with me, for I will not listen to you. 17 Do you not see what they are doing in the towns of Judah and in the streets of Jerusalem? 18 The children gather wood, the fathers light the fire, and the women knead the dough and make cakes to offer to the Queen of Heaven. They pour out drink offerings to other gods to arouse my anger. 19 But am I the one they are provoking? declares the LORD. Are they not

---

a 9 Or *and swear by false gods*

rifices, 23but I gave them this command: Obey me, and I will be your God and you will be my people. Walk in obedience to all I command you, that it may go well with you. 24But they did not listen or pay attention; instead, they followed the stubborn inclinations of their evil hearts. They went backward and not forward. 25From the time your ancestors left Egypt until now, day after day, again and again I sent you my servants the prophets. 26But they did not listen to me or pay attention. They were stiff-necked and did more evil than their ancestors.'

27"When you tell them all this, they will not listen to you; when you call to them, they will not answer. 28Therefore say to them, 'This is the nation that has not obeyed the LORD its God or responded to correction. Truth has perished; it has vanished from their lips.

BREAK THROUGH!

Sanctuary of Shiloh
(JEREMIAH 7:14; 26:6)
The sanctuary of Shiloh was built about 400 years before Jeremiah's time. It was the place where the Israelites worshiped when they entered the land of Canaan after they were slaves in Egypt. The ark of the covenant and the Most Holy Place were kept in Shiloh. The Israelites started worshiping other gods there in Shiloh, so then that place was destroyed. Here, the prophet Jeremiah says that the same thing is going to happen to Jerusalem. God isn't tied down to just one place, and he won't allow his people to worship other gods.

rather harming themselves, to their own shame?

20" 'Therefore this is what the Sovereign LORD says: My anger and my wrath will be poured out on this place—on man and beast, on the trees of the field and on the crops of your land—and it will burn and not be quenched.

21" 'This is what the LORD Almighty, the God of Israel, says: Go ahead, add your burnt offerings to your other sacrifices and eat the meat yourselves! 22For when I brought your ancestors out of Egypt and spoke to them, I did not just give them commands about burnt offerings and sac-

BREAK THROUGH!

The Queen of Heaven
(JEREMIAH 7:18)
There's a lot of talk about who this Queen of Heaven is. It probably means the goddess Ishtar, which was worshiped in Babylonia and also in Assyria. Ishtar was the goddess of love and war for the Mesopotamian people. The problem for Jeremiah was that the Israelites were also worshiping Ishtar in addition to worshiping God.

29 " 'Cut off your hair and throw it away; take up a lament on the barren heights, for the Lord has rejected and abandoned this generation that is under his wrath.

The Valley of Slaughter

30 " 'The people of Judah have done evil in my eyes, declares the Lord. They have set up their detestable idols in the house that bears my Name and have defiled it. 31 They have built the high places of Topheth in the Valley of Ben Hinnom to burn their sons and daughters in the fire — something I did not command, nor did it enter my mind. 32 So beware, the days are coming, declares the Lord, when people will no longer call it Topheth or the Valley of Ben Hinnom, but the Valley of Slaughter, for they will bury the dead in Topheth until there is no more room. 33 Then the carcasses of this people will become food for the birds and the wild animals, and there will be no one to frighten them away. 34 I will bring an end to the sounds of joy and gladness and to the voices of bride and bridegroom in the towns of Judah and the streets of Jerusalem, for the land will become desolate.

8 " 'At that time, declares the Lord, the bones of the kings and officials of Judah, the bones of the priests and prophets, and the bones of the people of Jerusalem will be removed from their graves. 2 They will be exposed to the sun and the moon and all the stars of the heavens, which they have loved and served and which they have followed and consulted and worshiped. They will not be gathered up or buried, but will be like dung lying on the ground. 3 Wherever I banish them, all the survivors of this evil nation will prefer death to life, declares the Lord Almighty.'

Sin and Punishment

4 "Say to them, 'This is what the Lord says:

" 'When people fall down, do they not get up?
When someone turns away, do they not return?

BREAKTHROUGH!

Did they burn their children in the fire?

(JEREMIAH 7:31)

Don't get too scared, and let us explain. Although it does seem that some Israelites really did burn their children on an altar, this was not a common practice. We know it only happened in extreme situations. There are two things we can learn from this. First, God never told them to burn their children. Second, we can see what happens when the Israelites stop worshiping God and start worshiping other gods.

5 Why then have these people turned away?
Why does Jerusalem always turn away?
They cling to deceit;
they refuse to return.
6 I have listened attentively,
but they do not say what is right.
None of them repent of their wickedness,
saying, "What have I done?"
Each pursues their own course
like a horse charging into battle.
7 Even the stork in the sky
knows her appointed seasons,

and the dove, the swift and the
    thrush
        observe the time of their
            migration.
But my people do not know
    the requirements of the Lord.

8 " 'How can you say, "We are wise,
    for we have the law of the Lord,"
when actually the lying pen of the
        scribes
    has handled it falsely?
9 The wise will be put to shame;
    they will be dismayed and
        trapped.
Since they have rejected the word of
        the Lord,
    what kind of wisdom do they
        have?
10 Therefore I will give their wives to
        other men
    and their fields to new owners.
From the least to the greatest,
    all are greedy for gain;
prophets and priests alike,
    all practice deceit.
11 They dress the wound of my people
    as though it were not serious.

Swift
(JEREMIAH 8:7)
This is a long-winged bird, very similar to one
called a swallow.

Thrush
(JEREMIAH 8:7)
It's also a bird, a usually dull-colored
songbird. It can be found in many parts of
the world.

"Peace, peace," they say,
    when there is no peace.
12 Are they ashamed of their detestable
        conduct?
    No, they have no shame at all;
        they do not even know how to
            blush.
So they will fall among the fallen;
    they will be brought down when they
        are punished,
                    says the Lord.

13 " 'I will take away their harvest,
                    declares the Lord.
    There will be no grapes on the
        vine.
There will be no figs on the tree,
    and their leaves will wither.
What I have given them
    will be taken from them.ᵃ' "

14 Why are we sitting here?
    Gather together!
Let us flee to the fortified cities
    and perish there!

ᵃ 13 The meaning of the Hebrew for this sentence is
uncertain.

For the L<small>ORD</small> our God has doomed us
to perish
and given us poisoned water to
drink,
because we have sinned against
him.
¹⁵ We hoped for peace
but no good has come,
for a time of healing
but there is only terror.
¹⁶ The snorting of the enemy's horses
is heard from Dan;
at the neighing of their stallions
the whole land trembles.
They have come to devour
the land and everything in it,
the city and all who live there.

¹⁷ "See, I will send venomous snakes
among you,
vipers that cannot be charmed,
and they will bite you,"
declares the L<small>ORD</small>.

¹⁸ You who are my Comforter^a in sorrow,
my heart is faint within me.
¹⁹ Listen to the cry of my people
from a land far away:
"Is the L<small>ORD</small> not in Zion?
Is her King no longer there?"

"Why have they aroused my anger with
their images,
with their worthless foreign idols?"

²⁰ "The harvest is past,
the summer has ended,
and we are not saved."

²¹ Since my people are crushed, I am
crushed;
I mourn, and horror grips me.
²² Is there no balm in Gilead?
Is there no physician there?
Why then is there no healing
for the wound of my people?

9 ^b ¹ Oh, that my head were a spring of
water
and my eyes a fountain of tears!
I would weep day and night
for the slain of my people.
² Oh, that I had in the desert
a lodging place for travelers,
so that I might leave my people
and go away from them;

for they are all adulterers,
a crowd of unfaithful people.

³ "They make ready their tongue
like a bow, to shoot lies;
it is not by truth
that they triumph^c in the land.
They go from one sin to another;
they do not acknowledge me,"
declares the L<small>ORD</small>.
⁴ "Beware of your friends;
do not trust anyone in your clan.
For every one of them is a deceiver,^d
and every friend a slanderer.
⁵ Friend deceives friend,
and no one speaks the truth.
They have taught their tongues to
lie;
they weary themselves with
sinning.
⁶ You^e live in the midst of deception;
in their deceit they refuse to
acknowledge me,"
declares the L<small>ORD</small>.

⁷ Therefore this is what the L<small>ORD</small> Almighty says:

"See, I will refine and test them,
for what else can I do
because of the sin of my people?
⁸ Their tongue is a deadly arrow;
it speaks deceitfully.
With their mouths they all speak
cordially to their neighbors,
but in their hearts they set traps for
them.
⁹ Should I not punish them for this?"
declares the L<small>ORD</small>.
"Should I not avenge myself
on such a nation as this?"

¹⁰ I will weep and wail for the
mountains
and take up a lament concerning
the wilderness grasslands.
They are desolate and untraveled,
and the lowing of cattle is not
heard.
The birds have all fled
and the animals are gone.

---

^a 18 The meaning of the Hebrew for this word is uncertain.
^b In Hebrew texts 9:1 is numbered 8:23, and 9:2-26 is
numbered 9:1-25. ^c 3 Or lies; / they are not valiant for
truth ^d 4 Or a deceiving Jacob ^e 6 That is, Jeremiah
(the Hebrew is singular)

¹¹ "I will make Jerusalem a heap of
ruins,
a haunt of jackals;
and I will lay waste the towns of
Judah
so no one can live there."

¹²Who is wise enough to understand this? Who has been instructed by the LORD and can explain it? Why has the land been ruined and laid waste like a desert that no one can cross? ¹³The LORD said, "It is because they have forsaken my law, which I set before them; they have not obeyed me or followed my law. ¹⁴Instead, they have followed the stubbornness of their hearts; they have followed the Baals, as their ancestors taught them." ¹⁵Therefore this is what the LORD Almighty, the God of Israel, says: "See, I will make this people eat bitter food and drink poisoned water. ¹⁶I will scatter them among nations that neither they nor their ancestors have known, and I will pursue them with the sword until I have made an end of them."

¹⁷This is what the LORD Almighty says:

"Consider now! Call for the wailing
women to come;
send for the most skillful of
them.
¹⁸ Let them come quickly
and wail over us
till our eyes overflow with tears
and water streams from our
eyelids.
¹⁹ The sound of wailing is heard from
Zion:
'How ruined we are!
How great is our shame!
We must leave our land
because our houses are in ruins.' "

²⁰ Now, you women, hear the word of the
LORD;
open your ears to the words of his
mouth.
Teach your daughters how to wail;
teach one another a lament.
²¹ Death has climbed in through our
windows
and has entered our fortresses;

it has removed the children from the
streets
and the young men from the public
squares.

²²Say, "This is what the LORD declares:

" 'Dead bodies will lie
like dung on the open field,
like cut grain behind the reaper,
with no one to gather them.' "

²³This is what the LORD says:

"Let not the wise boast of their
wisdom
or the strong boast of their
strength
or the rich boast of their riches,
²⁴ but let the one who boasts boast
about this:
that they have the understanding to
know me,
that I am the LORD, who exercises
kindness,
justice and righteousness on
earth,
for in these I delight,"
declares the LORD.

²⁵ "The days are coming," declares the LORD, "when I will punish all who are circumcised only in the flesh— ²⁶Egypt, Judah, Edom, Ammon, Moab and all who live in the wilderness in distant places.^a For all these nations are really uncircumcised, and even the whole house of Israel is uncircumcised in heart."

God and Idols

10 Hear what the LORD says to you, people of Israel. ²This is what the LORD says:

"Do not learn the ways of the nations
or be terrified by signs in the
heavens,
though the nations are terrified by
them.
³ For the practices of the peoples are
worthless;
they cut a tree out of the forest,
and a craftsman shapes it with his
chisel.

---

^a 26 Or wilderness and who clip the hair by their foreheads

EDOM

(JEREMIAH 9:26)

Did you know that Edom means "red" or "reddish"? This country south of the Dead Sea got this name because the soil was reddish in color. Most of the time, Edom was an enemy of the Israelites. They wouldn't even let the Israelites pass through after they had been freed from slavery in Egypt and wanted to reach the promised land (Palestine).

⁴ They adorn it with silver and gold;
　　they fasten it with hammer and
　　　nails
　　so it will not totter.
⁵ Like a scarecrow in a cucumber field,
　　their idols cannot speak;
　they must be carried
　　because they cannot walk.
Do not fear them;
　　they can do no harm
　　nor can they do any good."

⁶ No one is like you, LORD;
　　you are great,
　　and your name is mighty in power.
⁷ Who should not fear you,
　　King of the nations?

This is your due.
Among all the wise leaders of the
　　nations
　and in all their kingdoms,
　　there is no one like you.

⁸ They are all senseless and foolish;
　　they are taught by worthless
　　　wooden idols.
⁹ Hammered silver is brought from
　　Tarshish
　and gold from Uphaz.
What the craftsman and goldsmith
　　have made
　is then dressed in blue and purple—
　　all made by skilled workers.
¹⁰ But the LORD is the true God;
　　he is the living God, the eternal
　　　King.
When he is angry, the earth trembles;
　　the nations cannot endure his
　　　wrath.

AMMON

(JEREMIAH 9:26)

Ammon was a country east of the Jordan River. It was located where Jordan is now. The inhabitants of Ammon usually joined other nations to fight against the Israelites.

11 "Tell them this: 'These gods, who did not make the heavens and the earth, will perish from the earth and from under the heavens.' "[a]

12 But God made the earth by his power;
he founded the world by his wisdom
and stretched out the heavens by his understanding.
13 When he thunders, the waters in the heavens roar;
he makes clouds rise from the ends of the earth.
He sends lightning with the rain
and brings out the wind from his storehouses.

14 Everyone is senseless and without knowledge;
every goldsmith is shamed by his idols.

The images he makes are a fraud;
they have no breath in them.
15 They are worthless, the objects of mockery;
when their judgment comes, they will perish.
16 He who is the Portion of Jacob is not like these,
for he is the Maker of all things,
including Israel, the people of his inheritance—
the LORD Almighty is his name.

Coming Destruction

17 Gather up your belongings to leave the land,
you who live under siege.
18 For this is what the LORD says:
"At this time I will hurl out
those who live in this land;
I will bring distress on them
so that they may be captured."

19 Woe to me because of my injury!
My wound is incurable!
Yet I said to myself,
"This is my sickness, and I must endure it."
20 My tent is destroyed;
all its ropes are snapped.
My children are gone from me and are no more;
no one is left now to pitch my tent
or to set up my shelter.
21 The shepherds are senseless
and do not inquire of the LORD;
so they do not prosper
and all their flock is scattered.
22 Listen! The report is coming—
a great commotion from the land of the north!
It will make the towns of Judah desolate,
a haunt of jackals.

Jeremiah's Prayer

23 LORD, I know that people's lives are not their own;
it is not for them to direct their steps.
24 Discipline me, LORD, but only in due measure—

THE SCENE

MOAB

(JEREMIAH 9:26)

This is another country that was east of the Jordan River. It was south of the country of Ammon, and they shared the border. The Moabites were enemies of the Israelites.

---

[a] 11 The text of this verse is in Aramaic.

not in your anger,
or you will reduce me to nothing.
²⁵Pour out your wrath on the nations
that do not acknowledge you,
on the peoples who do not call on
your name.
For they have devoured Jacob;
they have devoured him completely
and destroyed his homeland.

The Covenant Is Broken

11 This is the word that came to Jeremiah from the Lord: ²"Listen to the terms of this covenant and tell them to the people of Judah and to those who live in Jerusalem. ³Tell them that this is what the Lord, the God of Israel, says: 'Cursed is the one who does not obey the terms of this covenant— ⁴the terms I commanded your ancestors when I brought them out of Egypt, out of the iron-smelting furnace.' I said, 'Obey me and do everything I command you, and you will be my people, and I will be your God. ⁵Then I will fulfill the oath I swore to your ancestors, to give them a land flowing with milk and honey'—the land you possess today."

I answered, "Amen, Lord."

⁶The Lord said to me, "Proclaim all these words in the towns of Judah and in the streets of Jerusalem: 'Listen to the terms of this covenant and follow them. ⁷From the time I brought your ancestors up from Egypt until today, I warned them again and again, saying, "Obey me." ⁸But they did not listen or pay attention; instead, they followed the stubbornness of their evil hearts. So I brought on them all the curses of the covenant I had commanded them to follow but that they did not keep.' "

⁹Then the Lord said to me, "There is a conspiracy among the people of Judah and those who live in Jerusalem. ¹⁰They have returned to the sins of their ancestors, who refused to listen to my words. They have followed other gods to serve them. Both Israel and Judah have broken the covenant I made with their ancestors. ¹¹Therefore this is what the Lord says: 'I will bring on them a disaster they cannot escape. Although they cry out to me, I will not listen to them. ¹²The towns of Judah and the people of Jerusalem will go and

cry out to the gods to whom they burn incense, but they will not help them at all when disaster strikes. ¹³You, Judah, have as many gods as you have towns; and the altars you have set up to burn incense to that shameful god Baal are as many as the streets of Jerusalem.'

¹⁴"Do not pray for this people or offer any plea or petition for them, because I will not listen when they call to me in the time of their distress.

¹⁵"What is my beloved doing in my
temple
as she, with many others, works out
her evil schemes?
Can consecrated meat avert your
punishment?
When you engage in your wickedness,
then you rejoice.ᵃ"

¹⁶The Lord called you a thriving olive
tree
with fruit beautiful in form.
But with the roar of a mighty storm
he will set it on fire,
and its branches will be broken.

¹⁷The Lord Almighty, who planted you, has decreed disaster for you, because the people of both Israel and Judah have done evil and aroused my anger by burning incense to Baal.

Plot Against Jeremiah

¹⁸Because the Lord revealed their plot to me, I knew it, for at that time he showed me what they were doing. ¹⁹I had been like a gentle lamb led to the slaughter; I did not realize that they had plotted against me, saying,

"Let us destroy the tree and its fruit;
let us cut him off from the land of
the living,
that his name be remembered no
more."
²⁰But you, Lord Almighty, who judge
righteously
and test the heart and mind,
let me see your vengeance on them,
for to you I have committed my
cause.

ᵃ 15 Or *Could consecrated meat avert your punishment? /
Then you would rejoice*

²¹Therefore this is what the LORD says about the people of Anathoth who are threatening to kill you, saying, "Do not prophesy in the name of the LORD or you will die by our hands"— ²²therefore this is what the LORD Almighty says: "I will punish them. Their young men will die by the sword, their sons and daughters by famine. ²³Not even a remnant will be left to them, because I will bring disaster on the people of Anathoth in the year of their punishment."

Jeremiah's Complaint

12 You are always righteous, LORD,
    when I bring a case before you.
Yet I would speak with you about your
    justice:
    Why does the way of the wicked
      prosper?
    Why do all the faithless live at
      ease?
² You have planted them, and they have
    taken root;
    they grow and bear fruit.
You are always on their lips
    but far from their hearts.
³ Yet you know me, LORD;
    you see me and test my thoughts
      about you.
Drag them off like sheep to be
    butchered!
Set them apart for the day of
    slaughter!
⁴ How long will the land lie parched
    and the grass in every field be
      withered?
Because those who live in it are
    wicked,
    the animals and birds have
      perished.
Moreover, the people are saying,
    "He will not see what happens
      to us."

God's Answer

⁵ "If you have raced with men on foot
    and they have worn you out,
    how can you compete with
      horses?
If you stumble*ᵃ* in safe country,
    how will you manage in the thickets
      by*ᵇ* the Jordan?

⁶ Your relatives, members of your own
    family—
    even they have betrayed you;
    they have raised a loud cry against
      you.
Do not trust them,
    though they speak well of you.

⁷ "I will forsake my house,
    abandon my inheritance;
I will give the one I love
    into the hands of her enemies.
⁸ My inheritance has become
    to me
    like a lion in the forest.
She roars at me;
    therefore I hate her.
⁹ Has not my inheritance become to me
    like a speckled bird of prey
    that other birds of prey surround
      and attack?
Go and gather all the wild beasts;
    bring them to devour.
¹⁰ Many shepherds will ruin my vineyard
    and trample down my field;
    they will turn my pleasant field
      into a desolate wasteland.
¹¹ It will be made a wasteland,
    parched and desolate before me;
    the whole land will be laid waste
      because there is no one who cares.
¹² Over all the barren heights in the
    desert
    destroyers will swarm,
for the sword of the LORD will devour
    from one end of the land to the
      other;
    no one will be safe.
¹³ They will sow wheat but reap thorns;
    they will wear themselves out but
      gain nothing.
They will bear the shame of their
    harvest
    because of the LORD's fierce anger."

¹⁴This is what the LORD says: "As for all my wicked neighbors who seize the inheritance I gave my people Israel, I will uproot them from their lands and I will uproot the people of Judah from among them. ¹⁵But after I uproot them, I will again have compassion and will bring each of them back to their own inheritance and their own

---

ᵃ 5 Or *you feel secure only*   *ᵇ 5* Or *the flooding of* country. ¹⁶And if they learn well the ways of my people and swear by my name, saying, 'As surely as the LORD lives'—even as they once taught my people to swear by Baal—then they will be established among my people. ¹⁷But if any nation does not listen, I will completely uproot and destroy it," declares the LORD.

A Linen Belt

13 This is what the LORD said to me: "Go and buy a linen belt and put it around your waist, but do not let it touch water." ²So I bought a belt, as the LORD directed, and put it around my waist.

³Then the word of the LORD came to me a second time: ⁴"Take the belt you bought and are wearing around your waist, and go now to Perath*a* and hide it there in a crevice in the rocks." ⁵So I went and hid it at Perath, as the LORD told me.

⁶Many days later the LORD said to me, "Go now to Perath and get the belt I told you to hide there." ⁷So I went to Perath and dug up the belt and took it from the place where I had hidden it, but now it was ruined and completely useless.

⁸Then the word of the LORD came to me: ⁹"This is what the LORD says: 'In the same way I will ruin the pride of Judah and the great pride of Jerusalem. ¹⁰These wicked people, who refuse to listen to my words, who follow the stubbornness of their hearts and go after other gods to serve and worship them, will be like this belt—completely useless! ¹¹For as a belt is bound around the waist, so I bound all the people of Israel and all the people of Judah to me,' declares the LORD, 'to be my people for my renown and praise and honor. But they have not listened.'

Wineskins

¹²"Say to them: 'This is what the LORD, the God of Israel, says: Every wineskin should be filled with wine.' And if they say to you, 'Don't we know that every wineskin should be filled with wine?' ¹³then tell them, 'This is what the LORD says: I am going to fill with drunkenness all who live in this land, including the kings who sit on David's throne, the priests, the prophets and all those living in Jerusa-

BREAKTHROUGH!

Why did God have Jeremiah do such strange things?

(JEREMIAH 13:1-11; 25:15-38; 27:1-8)

It's really rather hard for us to understand these things. We wouldn't have wanted to be in Jeremiah's shoes. God's people, the Israelites, didn't want to listen to what God was saying. So God told Jeremiah to do some things that would get their attention.

lem. ¹⁴I will smash them one against the other, parents and children alike, declares the LORD. I will allow no pity or mercy or compassion to keep me from destroying them.'"

Threat of Captivity

¹⁵ Hear and pay attention,
     do not be arrogant,
     for the LORD has spoken.
¹⁶ Give glory to the LORD your God
     before he brings the darkness,
   before your feet stumble
     on the darkening hills.
   You hope for light,
     but he will turn it to utter darkness
     and change it to deep gloom.
¹⁷ If you do not listen,
     I will weep in secret
     because of your pride;

---

a 4 Or possibly *to the Euphrates*; similarly in verses 5-7

my eyes will weep bitterly,
   overflowing with tears,
   because the LORD's flock will be
      taken captive.

18 Say to the king and to the queen
      mother,
   "Come down from your thrones,
for your glorious crowns
   will fall from your heads."
19 The cities in the Negev will be shut up,
   and there will be no one to open
      them.
All Judah will be carried into exile,
   carried completely away.

20 Look up and see
   those who are coming from the
      north.
Where is the flock that was entrusted
      to you,
   the sheep of which you boasted?
21 What will you say when the LORD sets
      over you
   those you cultivated as your special
      allies?
Will not pain grip you
   like that of a woman in labor?
22 And if you ask yourself,
   "Why has this happened to me?" —
it is because of your many sins
   that your skirts have been torn off
   and your body mistreated.
23 Can an Ethiopian[a] change his skin
   or a leopard its spots?
Neither can you do good
   who are accustomed to doing evil.

24 "I will scatter you like chaff
   driven by the desert wind.
25 This is your lot,
   the portion I have decreed for
      you,"
                  declares the LORD,
"because you have forgotten me
   and trusted in false gods.
26 I will pull up your skirts over your face
   that your shame may be seen—
27 your adulteries and lustful neighings,
   your shameless prostitution!
I have seen your detestable acts
   on the hills and in the fields.
Woe to you, Jerusalem!
   How long will you be unclean?"

Drought, Famine, Sword

14 This is the word of the LORD that
   came to Jeremiah concerning the
drought:

2 "Judah mourns,
   her cities languish;
they wail for the land,
   and a cry goes up from Jerusalem.
3 The nobles send their servants for
      water;
   they go to the cisterns
   but find no water.
They return with their jars unfilled;
   dismayed and despairing,
   they cover their heads.
4 The ground is cracked
   because there is no rain in the land;
the farmers are dismayed
   and cover their heads.
5 Even the doe in the field
   deserts her newborn fawn
   because there is no grass.
6 Wild donkeys stand on the barren
      heights
   and pant like jackals;
their eyes fail
   for lack of food."

7 Although our sins testify against us,
   do something, LORD, for the sake of
      your name.
For we have often rebelled;
   we have sinned against you.
8 You who are the hope of Israel,
   its Savior in times of distress,
why are you like a stranger in the
      land,
   like a traveler who stays only a
      night?
9 Why are you like a man taken by
      surprise,
   like a warrior powerless to save?
You are among us, LORD,
   and we bear your name;
   do not forsake us!

10 This is what the LORD says about this
people:

"They greatly love to wander;
   they do not restrain their feet.

---

a 23 Hebrew *Cushite* (probably a person from the upper
Nile region)

So the LORD does not accept
them;
  he will now remember their
    wickedness
  and punish them for their sins."

¹¹Then the LORD said to me, "Do not pray for the well-being of this people. ¹²Although they fast, I will not listen to their cry; though they offer burnt offerings and grain offerings, I will not accept them. Instead, I will destroy them with the sword, famine and plague."

¹³But I said, "Alas, Sovereign LORD! The prophets keep telling them, 'You will not see the sword or suffer famine. Indeed, I will give you lasting peace in this place.' "

¹⁴Then the LORD said to me, "The prophets are prophesying lies in my name. I have not sent them or appointed them or spoken to them. They are prophesying to you false visions, divinations, idolatries[a] and the delusions of their own minds. ¹⁵Therefore this is what the LORD says about the prophets who are prophesying

BREAKTHROUGH!

Fasting
(JEREMIAH 14:12)
The problem here is that the people were fasting in order to try to control God. It's like they were trying to twist his arm. That's not the reason for fasting! Read more in Esther 4:16 and 1 Samuel 7:6.

in my name: I did not send them, yet they are saying, 'No sword or famine will touch this land.' Those same prophets will perish by sword and famine. ¹⁶And the people they are prophesying to will be thrown out into the streets of Jerusalem because of the famine and sword. There will be no one to bury them, their wives, their sons and their daughters. I will pour out on them the calamity they deserve.

¹⁷"Speak this word to them:

" 'Let my eyes overflow with tears
  night and day without ceasing;
for the Virgin Daughter, my people,
  has suffered a grievous wound,
  a crushing blow.
¹⁸If I go into the country,
  I see those slain by the sword;
if I go into the city,
  I see the ravages of famine.
Both prophet and priest
  have gone to a land they know
  not.' "

¹⁹Have you rejected Judah completely?
  Do you despise Zion?
Why have you afflicted us
  so that we cannot be healed?
We hoped for peace
  but no good has come,
for a time of healing
  but there is only terror.
²⁰We acknowledge our wickedness,
    LORD,
  and the guilt of our ancestors;
  we have indeed sinned against
    you.
²¹For the sake of your name do not
    despise us;
  do not dishonor your glorious
    throne.
Remember your covenant with us
  and do not break it.
²²Do any of the worthless idols of the
    nations bring rain?
  Do the skies themselves send down
    showers?
No, it is you, LORD our God.
  Therefore our hope is in you,
  for you are the one who does all
    this.

---

[a] 14 Or *visions, worthless divinations*

15 Then the Lord said to me: "Even if Moses and Samuel were to stand before me, my heart would not go out to this people. Send them away from my presence! Let them go! ²And if they ask you, 'Where shall we go?' tell them, 'This is what the Lord says:

     " 'Those destined for death, to death;
     those for the sword, to the sword;
     those for starvation, to starvation;
     those for captivity, to captivity.'

³"I will send four kinds of destroyers against them," declares the Lord, "the sword to kill and the dogs to drag away and the birds and the wild animals to devour and destroy. ⁴I will make them abhorrent to all the kingdoms of the earth because of what Manasseh son of Hezekiah king of Judah did in Jerusalem.

⁵"Who will have pity on you,
     Jerusalem?
     Who will mourn for you?
     Who will stop to ask how you are?
⁶You have rejected me," declares the
     Lord.
     "You keep on backsliding.
So I will reach out and destroy you;
     I am tired of holding back.
⁷I will winnow them with a winnowing
     fork
     at the city gates of the land.
I will bring bereavement and
     destruction on my people,
     for they have not changed their
     ways.
⁸I will make their widows more
     numerous
     than the sand of the sea.
At midday I will bring a destroyer
     against the mothers of their young
     men;
     suddenly I will bring down on them
     anguish and terror.
⁹The mother of seven will grow faint
     and breathe her last.
Her sun will set while it is still day;
     she will be disgraced and
     humiliated.
I will put the survivors to the sword
     before their enemies,"
                declares the Lord.

¹⁰Alas, my mother, that you gave me
     birth,
     a man with whom the whole land
     strives and contends!
I have neither lent nor borrowed,
     yet everyone curses me.

¹¹The Lord said,

"Surely I will deliver you for a good
     purpose;
     surely I will make your enemies
     plead with you
in times of disaster and times of
     distress.

¹²"Can a man break iron—
     iron from the north—or bronze?

¹³"Your wealth and your treasures
     I will give as plunder, without
     charge,
because of all your sins
     throughout your country.
¹⁴I will enslave you to your enemies
     in*a* a land you do not know,
for my anger will kindle a fire
     that will burn against you."

¹⁵Lord, you understand;
     remember me and care for me.
     Avenge me on my persecutors.
You are long-suffering—do not take
     me away;
     think of how I suffer reproach for
     your sake.
¹⁶When your words came, I ate them;
     they were my joy and my heart's
     delight,
for I bear your name,
     Lord God Almighty.
¹⁷I never sat in the company of
     revelers,
     never made merry with them;
I sat alone because your hand was
     on me
     and you had filled me with
     indignation.
¹⁸Why is my pain unending
     and my wound grievous and
     incurable?
You are to me like a deceptive brook,
     like a spring that fails.

---

a 14 Some Hebrew manuscripts, Septuagint and Syriac (see also 17:4); most Hebrew manuscripts *I will cause your enemies to bring you / into*

¹⁹Therefore this is what the Lord says:

"If you repent, I will restore you
   that you may serve me;
if you utter worthy, not worthless,
   words,
   you will be my spokesman.
Let this people turn to you,
   but you must not turn to them.
²⁰I will make you a wall to this people,
   a fortified wall of bronze;
they will fight against you
   but will not overcome you,
for I am with you
   to rescue and save you,"
                 declares the Lord.
²¹"I will save you from the hands of the
   wicked
   and deliver you from the grasp of
   the cruel."

Day of Disaster

16 Then the word of the Lord came to me: ²"You must not marry and have sons or daughters in this place." ³For this is what the Lord says about the sons and daughters born in this land and about the women who are their mothers and the men who are their fathers: ⁴"They will die of deadly diseases. They will not be mourned or buried but will be like dung lying on the ground. They will perish by sword and famine, and their dead bodies will become food for the birds and the wild animals."

⁵For this is what the Lord says: "Do not enter a house where there is a funeral meal; do not go to mourn or show sympathy, because I have withdrawn my blessing, my love and my pity from this people," declares the Lord. ⁶"Both high and low will die in this land. They will not be buried or mourned, and no one will cut themselves or shave their head for the dead. ⁷No one will offer food to comfort those who mourn for the dead — not even for a father or a mother — nor will anyone give them a drink to console them.

⁸"And do not enter a house where there is feasting and sit down to eat and drink. ⁹For this is what the Lord Almighty, the God of Israel, says: Before your eyes and in your days I will bring an end to the sounds of joy and gladness and to the voices of bride and bridegroom in this place.

¹⁰"When you tell these people all this and they ask you, 'Why has the Lord decreed such a great disaster against us? What wrong have we done? What sin have we committed against the Lord our God?' ¹¹then say to them, 'It is because your ancestors forsook me,' declares the Lord, 'and followed other gods and served and worshiped them. They forsook me and did not keep my law. ¹²But you have behaved more wickedly than your ancestors. See how all of you are following the stubbornness of your evil hearts instead of obeying me. ¹³So I will throw you out of this land into a land neither you nor your ancestors have known, and there you will serve other gods day and night, for I will show you no favor.'

¹⁴"However, the days are coming," declares the Lord, "when it will no longer be said, 'As surely as the Lord lives, who brought the Israelites up out of Egypt,' ¹⁵but it will be said, 'As surely as the Lord lives, who brought the Israelites up out of the land of the north and out of all the countries where he had banished them.' For I will restore them to the land I gave their ancestors.

¹⁶"But now I will send for many fishermen," declares the Lord, "and they will catch them. After that I will send for many hunters, and they will hunt them down on every mountain and hill and from the crevices of the rocks. ¹⁷My eyes are on all their ways; they are not hidden from me, nor is their sin concealed from my eyes. ¹⁸I will repay them double for their wickedness and their sin, because they have defiled my land with the lifeless forms of their vile images and have filled my inheritance with their detestable idols."

¹⁹Lord, my strength and my fortress,
   my refuge in time of distress,
to you the nations will come
   from the ends of the earth and say,
"Our ancestors possessed nothing
   but false gods,
   worthless idols that did them no
   good.

20 Do people make their own gods?
Yes, but they are not gods!"

21 "Therefore I will teach them—
this time I will teach them
my power and might.
Then they will know
that my name is the LORD.

17

"Judah's sin is engraved with an
iron tool,
inscribed with a flint point,
on the tablets of their hearts
and on the horns of their altars.
2 Even their children remember
their altars and Asherah poles[a]
beside the spreading trees
and on the high hills.
3 My mountain in the land
and your[b] wealth and all your
treasures
I will give away as plunder,
together with your high places,
because of sin throughout your
country.
4 Through your own fault you will lose
the inheritance I gave you.
I will enslave you to your enemies
in a land you do not know,
for you have kindled my anger,
and it will burn forever."

5 This is what the LORD says:

"Cursed is the one who trusts in man,
who draws strength from mere flesh
and whose heart turns away from
the LORD.
6 That person will be like a bush in the
wastelands;
they will not see prosperity when it
comes.
They will dwell in the parched places
of the desert,
in a salt land where no one lives.

7 "But blessed is the one who trusts in
the LORD,
whose confidence is in him.
8 They will be like a tree planted by the
water
that sends out its roots by the
stream.
It does not fear when heat comes;
its leaves are always green.

It has no worries in a year of
drought
and never fails to bear fruit."

9 The heart is deceitful above all things
and beyond cure.
Who can understand it?

10 "I the LORD search the heart
and examine the mind,
to reward each person according to
their conduct,
according to what their deeds
deserve."

11 Like a partridge that hatches eggs it
did not lay
are those who gain riches by unjust
means.
When their lives are half gone, their
riches will desert them,
and in the end they will prove to be
fools.

12 A glorious throne, exalted from the
beginning,
is the place of our sanctuary.
13 LORD, you are the hope of Israel;
all who forsake you will be put to
shame.
Those who turn away from you will be
written in the dust
because they have forsaken the
LORD,
the spring of living water.

14 Heal me, LORD, and I will be healed;
save me and I will be saved,
for you are the one I praise.
15 They keep saying to me,
"Where is the word of the LORD?
Let it now be fulfilled!"
16 I have not run away from being your
shepherd;
you know I have not desired the day
of despair.
What passes my lips is open before
you.
17 Do not be a terror to me;
you are my refuge in the day of
disaster.
18 Let my persecutors be put to shame,
but keep me from shame;

---

a 2 That is, wooden symbols of the goddess Asherah
b 2,3 Or hills / 3 and the mountains of the land. / Your

let them be terrified,
   but keep me from terror.
Bring on them the day of disaster;
   destroy them with double
      destruction.

Keeping the Sabbath Day Holy

¹⁹This is what the LORD said to me: "Go and stand at the Gate of the People,ᵃ through which the kings of Judah go in and out; stand also at all the other gates of Jerusalem. ²⁰Say to them, 'Hear the word of the LORD, you kings of Judah and all people of Judah and everyone living in Jerusalem who come through these gates. ²¹This is what the LORD says: Be careful not to carry a load on the Sabbath day or bring it through the gates of Jerusalem. ²²Do not bring a load out of your houses or do any work on the Sabbath, but keep the Sabbath day holy, as I commanded your ancestors. ²³Yet they did not listen or pay attention; they were stiff-necked and would not listen or respond to discipline. ²⁴But if you are careful to obey me, declares the LORD, and bring no load through the gates of this city on the Sabbath, but keep the Sabbath day holy by not doing any work on it, ²⁵then kings who sit on David's throne will come through the gates of this city with their officials. They and their officials will come riding in chariots and on horses, accompanied by the men of Judah and those living in Jerusalem, and this city will be inhabited forever. ²⁶People will come from the towns of Judah and the villages around Jerusalem, from the territory of Benjamin and the western foothills, from the hill country and the Negev, bringing burnt offerings and sacrifices, grain offerings and incense, and bringing thank offerings to the house of the LORD. ²⁷But if you do not obey me to keep the Sabbath day holy by not carrying any load as you come through the gates of Jerusalem on the Sabbath day, then I will kindle an unquenchable fire in the gates of Jerusalem that will consume her fortresses.' "

At the Potter's House

18 This is the word that came to Jeremiah from the LORD: ²"Go down to the potter's house, and there I will give you my message." ³So I went down to the potter's house, and I saw him working at the wheel. ⁴But the pot he was shaping from the clay was marred in his hands; so the potter formed it into another pot, shaping it as seemed best to him.

⁵Then the word of the LORD came to me. ⁶He said, "Can I not do with you, Israel, as this potter does?" declares the LORD. "Like clay in the hand of the potter, so are you in my hand, Israel. ⁷If at any time I announce that a nation or kingdom is to be uprooted, torn down and destroyed, ⁸and if that nation I warned repents of its evil, then I will relent and not inflict on it the disaster I had planned. ⁹And if at another time I announce that a nation or kingdom is to be built up and planted, ¹⁰and if it does evil in my sight and does not obey me, then I will reconsider the good I had intended to do for it.

¹¹"Now therefore say to the people of Judah and those living in Jerusalem, 'This is what the LORD says: Look! I am preparing a disaster for you and devising a plan against you. So turn from your evil ways, each one of you, and reform your ways and your actions.' ¹²But they will reply, 'It's no use. We will continue with our own plans; we will all follow the stubbornness of our evil hearts.' "

¹³Therefore this is what the LORD says:

"Inquire among the nations:
   Who has ever heard anything like
      this?
A most horrible thing has been done
   by Virgin Israel.
¹⁴Does the snow of Lebanon
   ever vanish from its rocky slopes?
Do its cool waters from distant
      sources
   ever stop flowing?ᵇ
¹⁵Yet my people have forgotten me;
   they burn incense to worthless
      idols,
which made them stumble in their
      ways,
   in the ancient paths.
They made them walk in byways,
   on roads not built up.

ᵃ 19 Or Army   ᵇ 14 The meaning of the Hebrew for this sentence is uncertain.

¹⁶Their land will be an object of horror
and of lasting scorn;
all who pass by will be appalled
and will shake their heads.
¹⁷Like a wind from the east,
I will scatter them before their
enemies;
I will show them my back and not my
face
in the day of their disaster."

¹⁸They said, "Come, let's make plans against Jeremiah; for the teaching of the law by the priest will not cease, nor will counsel from the wise, nor the word from the prophets. So come, let's attack him with our tongues and pay no attention to anything he says."

¹⁹Listen to me, Lord;
hear what my accusers are saying!
²⁰Should good be repaid with evil?
Yet they have dug a pit for me.
Remember that I stood before you
and spoke in their behalf
to turn your wrath away from them.
²¹So give their children over to famine;
hand them over to the power of the
sword.
Let their wives be made childless and
widows;
let their men be put to death,
their young men slain by the sword
in battle.
²²Let a cry be heard from their houses
when you suddenly bring invaders
against them,
for they have dug a pit to capture me
and have hidden snares for my feet.
²³But you, Lord, know
all their plots to kill me.
Do not forgive their crimes
or blot out their sins from your
sight.
Let them be overthrown before you;
deal with them in the time of your
anger.

19 This is what the Lord says: "Go and buy a clay jar from a potter. Take along some of the elders of the people and of the priests ²and go out to the Valley of Ben Hinnom, near the entrance of the Potsherd Gate. There proclaim the words

I tell you, ³and say, 'Hear the word of the Lord, you kings of Judah and people of Jerusalem. This is what the Lord Almighty, the God of Israel, says: Listen! I am going to bring a disaster on this place that will make the ears of everyone who hears of it tingle. ⁴For they have forsaken me and made this a place of foreign gods; they have burned incense in it to gods that neither they nor their ancestors nor the kings of Judah ever knew, and they have filled this place with the blood of the innocent. ⁵They have built the high places of Baal to burn their children in the fire as offerings to Baal — something I did not command or mention, nor did it enter my mind. ⁶So beware, the days are coming, declares the Lord, when people will no longer call this place Topheth or the Valley of Ben Hinnom, but the Valley of Slaughter.

⁷" 'In this place I will ruin^a the plans of Judah and Jerusalem. I will make them fall by the sword before their enemies, at the hands of those who want to kill them, and I will give their carcasses as food to the birds and the wild animals. ⁸I will devastate this city and make it an object of horror and scorn; all who pass by will be appalled and will scoff because of all its wounds. ⁹I will make them eat the flesh of their sons and daughters, and they will eat one another's flesh because their enemies will press the siege so hard against them to destroy them.'

¹⁰"Then break the jar while those who go with you are watching, ¹¹and say to them, 'This is what the Lord Almighty says: I will smash this nation and this city just as this potter's jar is smashed and cannot be repaired. They will bury the dead in Topheth until there is no more room. ¹²This is what I will do to this place and to those who live here, declares the Lord. I will make this city like Topheth. ¹³The houses in Jerusalem and those of the kings of Judah will be defiled like this place, Topheth — all the houses where they burned incense on the roofs to all

---

^a 7 The Hebrew for *ruin* sounds like the Hebrew for *jar* (see verses 1 and 10).

the starry hosts and poured out drink offerings to other gods.' "

¹⁴Jeremiah then returned from Topheth, where the LORD had sent him to prophesy, and stood in the court of the LORD's temple and said to all the people, ¹⁵"This is what the LORD Almighty, the God of Israel, says: 'Listen! I am going to bring on this city and all the villages around it every disaster I pronounced against them, because they were stiff-necked and would not listen to my words.' "

Jeremiah and Pashhur

20 When the priest Pashhur son of Immer, the official in charge of the temple of the LORD, heard Jeremiah prophesying these things, ²he had Jeremiah the prophet beaten and put in the stocks at the Upper Gate of Benjamin at the LORD's temple. ³The next day, when Pashhur released him from the stocks, Jeremiah said to him, "The LORD's name for you is not Pashhur, but Terror on Every Side. ⁴For this is what the LORD says: 'I will make you a terror to yourself and to all your friends; with your own eyes you will see them fall by the sword of their enemies. I will give all Judah into the hands of the king of Babylon, who will carry them away to Babylon or put them to the sword. ⁵I will deliver all the wealth of this city into the hands of their enemies—all its products, all its valuables and all the treasures of the kings of Judah. They will take it away as plunder and carry it off to Babylon. ⁶And you, Pashhur, and all who live in your house will go into exile to Babylon. There you will die and be buried, you and all your friends to whom you have prophesied lies.' "

Jeremiah's Complaint

⁷You deceived*ᵃ* me, LORD, and I was
      deceived*ᵃ*;
   you overpowered me and prevailed.
I am ridiculed all day long;
   everyone mocks me.
⁸Whenever I speak, I cry out
   proclaiming violence and
      destruction.
So the word of the LORD has brought
      me
   insult and reproach all day long.

⁹But if I say, "I will not mention his word
      or speak anymore in his name,"
his word is in my heart like a fire,
   a fire shut up in my bones.
I am weary of holding it in;
   indeed, I cannot.
¹⁰I hear many whispering,
   "Terror on every side!
   Denounce him! Let's denounce
      him!"
All my friends
   are waiting for me to slip, saying,
"Perhaps he will be deceived;
   then we will prevail over him
   and take our revenge on him."

¹¹But the LORD is with me like a mighty
      warrior;
   so my persecutors will stumble and
      not prevail.
They will fail and be thoroughly
      disgraced;
   their dishonor will never be
      forgotten.
¹²LORD Almighty, you who examine the
      righteous
   and probe the heart and mind,
let me see your vengeance on them,
   for to you I have committed my
      cause.

¹³Sing to the LORD!
   Give praise to the LORD!
He rescues the life of the needy
   from the hands of the wicked.

¹⁴Cursed be the day I was born!
   May the day my mother bore me not
      be blessed!
¹⁵Cursed be the man who brought my
      father the news,
   who made him very glad, saying,
   "A child is born to you—a son!"
¹⁶May that man be like the towns
   the LORD overthrew without pity.
May he hear wailing in the morning,
   a battle cry at noon.
¹⁷For he did not kill me in the womb,
   with my mother as my grave,
   her womb enlarged forever.
¹⁸Why did I ever come out of the womb
   to see trouble and sorrow
   and to end my days in shame?

ᵃ 7 Or persuaded

God Rejects Zedekiah's Request

21 The word came to Jeremiah from the LORD when King Zedekiah sent to him Pashhur son of Malkijah and the priest Zephaniah son of Maaseiah. They said: ² "Inquire now of the LORD for us because Nebuchadnezzar[a] king of Babylon is attacking us. Perhaps the LORD will perform wonders for us as in times past so that he will withdraw from us."

³ But Jeremiah answered them, "Tell Zedekiah, ⁴ 'This is what the LORD, the God of Israel, says: I am about to turn against you the weapons of war that are in your hands, which you are using to fight the king of Babylon and the Babylonians[b] who are outside the wall besieging you. And I will gather them inside this city. ⁵ I myself will fight against you with an outstretched hand and a mighty arm in furious anger and in great wrath. ⁶ I will strike down those who live in this city—both man and beast—and they will die of a terrible plague. ⁷ After that, declares the LORD, I will give Zedekiah king of Judah, his officials and the people in this city who survive the plague, sword and famine, into the hands of Nebuchadnezzar king of Babylon and to their enemies who want to kill them. He will put them to the sword; he will show them no mercy or pity or compassion.'

⁸ "Furthermore, tell the people, 'This is what the LORD says: See, I am setting before you the way of life and the way of death. ⁹ Whoever stays in this city will die by the sword, famine or plague. But whoever goes out and surrenders to the Babylonians who are besieging you will live; they will escape with their lives. ¹⁰ I have determined to do this city harm and not good, declares the LORD. It will be given into the hands of the king of Babylon, and he will destroy it with fire.'

¹¹ "Moreover, say to the royal house of Judah, 'Hear the word of the LORD. ¹² This is what the LORD says to you, house of David:

> " 'Administer justice every morning;
>   rescue from the hand of the
>   oppressor
>   the one who has been robbed,

or my wrath will break out and burn
      like fire
because of the evil you have done—
   burn with no one to quench it.
¹³ I am against you, Jerusalem,
   you who live above this valley
   on the rocky plateau, declares the
      LORD—

ᵃ 2 Hebrew *Nebuchadrezzar*, of which *Nebuchadnezzar* is a variant; here and often in Jeremiah and Ezekiel   ᵇ 4 Or *Chaldeans*; also in verse 9

THE
WITNESSES

✓ **NEBUCHADNEZZAR** (JEREMIAH 21:2)
We can tell you that Nebuchadnezzar was a very important king, and he had a lot of power. He was the king of Babylon 597 years before Christ, and he attacked and destroyed the city of Jerusalem and the temple. He also took many Israelites captive and made them slaves in Babylon. These Israelites suffered a lot, because they ended up living in a strange place and the Babylonians treated them badly.

you who say, "Who can come against
   us?
Who can enter our refuge?"
¹⁴I will punish you as your deeds
   deserve,
   declares the LORD.
I will kindle a fire in your forests
   that will consume everything around
   you.' "

Judgment Against Wicked Kings

22 This is what the LORD says: "Go
down to the palace of the king
of Judah and proclaim this message
there: ²'Hear the word of the LORD to
you, king of Judah, you who sit on David's throne — you, your officials and
your people who come through these
gates. ³This is what the LORD says: Do
what is just and right. Rescue from the
hand of the oppressor the one who has
been robbed. Do no wrong or violence to
the foreigner, the fatherless or the widow, and do not shed innocent blood in
this place. ⁴For if you are careful to carry
out these commands, then kings who sit
on David's throne will come through the
gates of this palace, riding in chariots
and on horses, accompanied by their officials and their people. ⁵But if you do
not obey these commands, declares the
LORD, I swear by myself that this palace
will become a ruin.' "

⁶For this is what the LORD says about
the palace of the king of Judah:

"Though you are like Gilead to me,
   like the summit of Lebanon,
I will surely make you like a
   wasteland,
   like towns not inhabited.
⁷I will send destroyers against you,
   each man with his weapons,
and they will cut up your fine cedar
   beams
   and throw them into the fire.

⁸"People from many nations will pass
by this city and will ask one another, 'Why
has the LORD done such a thing to this
great city?' ⁹And the answer will be: 'Because they have forsaken the covenant
of the LORD their God and have worshiped
and served other gods.' "

THE SCENE

GILEAD

(JEREMIAH 22:6)

This mountain still exists. It's
famous for its dense forests.

¹⁰Do not weep for the dead king or
   mourn his loss;
   rather, weep bitterly for him who is
     exiled,
because he will never return
   nor see his native land again.

¹¹For this is what the LORD says about
Shallum*a* son of Josiah, who succeeded
his father as king of Judah but has gone
from this place: "He will never return.
¹²He will die in the place where they have
led him captive; he will not see this land
again."

¹³"Woe to him who builds his palace by
   unrighteousness,
   his upper rooms by injustice,
making his own people work for
   nothing,
   not paying them for their labor.
¹⁴He says, 'I will build myself a great
   palace
   with spacious upper rooms.'

---

a 11 Also called *Jehoahaz*

So he makes large windows in it,
   panels it with cedar
   and decorates it in red.

15 "Does it make you a king
   to have more and more cedar?
Did not your father have food and
   drink?
He did what was right and just,
   so all went well with him.
16 He defended the cause of the poor
   and needy,
   and so all went well.
Is that not what it means to know me?"
   declares the LORD.
17 "But your eyes and your heart
   are set only on dishonest gain,
on shedding innocent blood
   and on oppression and extortion."

18 Therefore this is what the LORD says about Jehoiakim son of Josiah king of Judah:

"They will not mourn for him:
   'Alas, my brother! Alas, my sister!'
They will not mourn for him:
   'Alas, my master! Alas, his
     splendor!'
19 He will have the burial of a donkey—
   dragged away and thrown
   outside the gates of Jerusalem."

20 "Go up to Lebanon and cry out,
   let your voice be heard in Bashan,
cry out from Abarim,
   for all your allies are crushed.
21 I warned you when you felt secure,
   but you said, 'I will not listen!'
This has been your way from your
    youth;
   you have not obeyed me.
22 The wind will drive all your shepherds
    away,
   and your allies will go into exile.
Then you will be ashamed and
    disgraced
   because of all your wickedness.
23 You who live in 'Lebanon,ᵃ'
   who are nestled in cedar buildings,
how you will groan when pangs come
    upon you,
   pain like that of a woman in labor!

24 "As surely as I live," declares the LORD, "even if you, Jehoiachinᵇ son of Jehoiakim

king of Judah, were a signet ring on my right hand, I would still pull you off. 25 I will deliver you into the hands of those who want to kill you, those you fear—Nebuchadnezzar king of Babylon and the Babylonians.ᶜ 26 I will hurl you and the mother who gave you birth into another country, where neither of you was born, and there you both will die. 27 You will never come back to the land you long to return to."

28 Is this man Jehoiachin a despised,
   broken pot,
   an object no one wants?
Why will he and his children be hurled
    out,
   cast into a land they do not know?
29 O land, land, land,
   hear the word of the LORD!
30 This is what the LORD says:
"Record this man as if childless,
   a man who will not prosper in his
    lifetime,
for none of his offspring will prosper,
   none will sit on the throne of David
   or rule anymore in Judah."

The Righteous Branch

23 "Woe to the shepherds who are destroying and scattering the sheep of my pasture!" declares the LORD. 2 Therefore this is what the LORD, the God of Israel, says to the shepherds who tend my people: "Because you have scattered my flock and driven them away and have not bestowed care on them, I will bestow punishment on you for the evil you have done," declares the LORD. 3 "I myself will gather the remnant of my flock out of all the countries where I have driven them and will bring them back to their pasture, where they will be fruitful and increase in number. 4 I will place shepherds over them who will tend them, and they will no longer be afraid or terrified, nor will any be missing," declares the LORD.

5 "The days are coming," declares the
   LORD,
  "when I will raise up for Davidᵈ a
    righteous Branch,

ᵃ 23 That is, the palace in Jerusalem (see 1 Kings 7:2)
ᵇ 24 Hebrew *Koniah*, a variant of *Jehoiachin*; also in verse 28
ᶜ 25 Or *Chaldeans*   ᵈ 5 Or *up from David's line*

a King who will reign wisely
    and do what is just and right in the
    land.
⁶ In his days Judah will be saved
    and Israel will live in safety.
This is the name by which he will be
    called:
    The LORD Our Righteous Savior.

⁷ "So then, the days are coming," declares the LORD, "when people will no longer say, 'As surely as the LORD lives, who brought the Israelites up out of Egypt,' ⁸but they will say, 'As surely as the LORD lives, who brought the descendants of Israel up out of the land of the north and out of all the countries where he had banished them.' Then they will live in their own land."

Lying Prophets

⁹Concerning the prophets:

My heart is broken within me;
    all my bones tremble.
I am like a drunken man,
    like a strong man overcome by wine,
because of the LORD
    and his holy words.
¹⁰ The land is full of adulterers;
    because of the curseᵃ the land lies
        parched
    and the pastures in the wilderness
        are withered.
The prophets follow an evil course
    and use their power unjustly.

¹¹ "Both prophet and priest are godless;
    even in my temple I find their
        wickedness,"
                declares the LORD.
¹² "Therefore their path will become
        slippery;
    they will be banished to darkness
    and there they will fall.
I will bring disaster on them
    in the year they are punished,"
                declares the LORD.

¹³ "Among the prophets of Samaria
    I saw this repulsive thing:
They prophesied by Baal
    and led my people Israel astray.
¹⁴ And among the prophets of Jerusalem
    I have seen something horrible:
They commit adultery and live a lie.

They strengthen the hands of
    evildoers,
    so that not one of them turns from
        their wickedness.
They are all like Sodom to me;
    the people of Jerusalem are like
        Gomorrah."

¹⁵Therefore this is what the LORD Almighty says concerning the prophets:

"I will make them eat bitter
    food
    and drink poisoned water,
because from the prophets of
    Jerusalem
ungodliness has spread throughout
    the land."

ᵃ 10 Or *because of these things*

THE SCENE

SAMARIA

(JEREMIAH 23:13)

This city became the capital of Israel's northern kingdom. When the people of Israel divided, the ten northern tribes established their capital in Samaria. Samaria could be considered the city that competed with Jerusalem at that time.

¹⁶This is what the LORD Almighty says:

"Do not listen to what the prophets
   are prophesying to you;
   they fill you with false hopes.
They speak visions from their own
      minds,
   not from the mouth of the LORD.
¹⁷They keep saying to those who
      despise me,
   'The LORD says: You will have
      peace.'
And to all who follow the
      stubbornness of their hearts
   they say, 'No harm will come to you.'
¹⁸But which of them has stood in the
      council of the LORD
   to see or to hear his word?
   Who has listened and heard his
      word?
¹⁹See, the storm of the LORD
   will burst out in wrath,
a whirlwind swirling down
   on the heads of the wicked.
²⁰The anger of the LORD will not turn
      back
   until he fully accomplishes
      the purposes of his heart.
In days to come
   you will understand it clearly.
²¹I did not send these prophets,
   yet they have run with their
      message;
I did not speak to them,
   yet they have prophesied.
²²But if they had stood in my council,
   they would have proclaimed my
      words to my people
and would have turned them from
      their evil ways
   and from their evil deeds.

²³"Am I only a God nearby,"
                  declares the LORD,
"and not a God far away?
²⁴Who can hide in secret places
   so that I cannot see them?"
                  declares the LORD.
"Do not I fill heaven and earth?"
                  declares the LORD.

²⁵"I have heard what the prophets say
who prophesy lies in my name. They say,
'I had a dream! I had a dream!' ²⁶How
long will this continue in the hearts of
these lying prophets, who prophesy the
delusions of their own minds? ²⁷They
think the dreams they tell one another will
make my people forget my name, just as
their ancestors forgot my name through
Baal worship. ²⁸Let the prophet who has
a dream recount the dream, but let the
one who has my word speak it faithfully. For what has straw to do with grain?"
declares the LORD. ²⁹"Is not my word like
fire," declares the LORD, "and like a hammer that breaks a rock in pieces?

³⁰"Therefore," declares the LORD, "I
am against the prophets who steal from
one another words supposedly from me.
³¹Yes," declares the LORD, "I am against
the prophets who wag their own tongues
and yet declare, 'The LORD declares.' ³²Indeed, I am against those who prophesy
false dreams," declares the LORD. "They
tell them and lead my people astray with
their reckless lies, yet I did not send or
appoint them. They do not benefit these
people in the least," declares the LORD.

False Prophecy

³³"When these people, or a prophet
or a priest, ask you, 'What is the message from the LORD?' say to them, 'What
message? I will forsake you, declares the
LORD.' ³⁴If a prophet or a priest or anyone
else claims, 'This is a message from the
LORD,' I will punish them and their household. ³⁵This is what each of you keeps
saying to your friends and other Israelites: 'What is the LORD's answer?' or
'What has the LORD spoken?' ³⁶But you
must not mention 'a message from the
LORD' again, because each one's word becomes their own message. So you distort
the words of the living God, the LORD Almighty, our God. ³⁷This is what you keep
saying to a prophet: 'What is the LORD's
answer to you?' or 'What has the LORD
spoken?' ³⁸Although you claim, 'This is a
message from the LORD,' this is what the
LORD says: You used the words, 'This is
a message from the LORD,' even though
I told you that you must not claim, 'This
is a message from the LORD.' ³⁹Therefore,
I will surely forget you and cast you out
of my presence along with the city I gave
to you and your ancestors. ⁴⁰I will bring

on you everlasting disgrace—everlasting shame that will not be forgotten."

Two Baskets of Figs

24 After Jehoiachin[a] son of Jehoiakim king of Judah and the officials, the skilled workers and the artisans of Judah were carried into exile from Jerusalem to Babylon by Nebuchadnezzar king of Babylon, the LORD showed me two baskets of figs placed in front of the temple of the LORD. ²One basket had very good figs, like those that ripen early; the other basket had very bad figs, so bad they could not be eaten.

³Then the LORD asked me, "What do you see, Jeremiah?"

"Figs," I answered. "The good ones are very good, but the bad ones are so bad they cannot be eaten."

⁴Then the word of the LORD came to me: ⁵"This is what the LORD, the God of Israel, says: 'Like these good figs, I regard as good the exiles from Judah, whom I sent away from this place to the land of the Babylonians.[b] ⁶My eyes will watch over them for their good, and I will bring them back to this land. I will build them up and not tear them down; I will plant them and not uproot them. ⁷I will give them a heart to know me, that I am the LORD. They will be my people, and I will be their God, for they will return to me with all their heart.

⁸"'But like the bad figs, which are so bad they cannot be eaten,' says the LORD, 'so will I deal with Zedekiah king of Judah, his officials and the survivors from Jerusalem, whether they remain in this land or live in Egypt. ⁹I will make them abhorrent and an offense to all the kingdoms of the earth, a reproach and a byword, a curse[c] and an object of ridicule, wherever I banish them. ¹⁰I will send the sword, famine and plague against them until they are destroyed from the land I gave to them and their ancestors.'"

Seventy Years of Captivity

25 The word came to Jeremiah concerning all the people of Judah in the fourth year of Jehoiakim son of Josiah king of Judah, which was the first year of Nebuchadnezzar king of Babylon.

²So Jeremiah the prophet said to all the people of Judah and to all those living in Jerusalem: ³For twenty-three years—from the thirteenth year of Josiah son of Amon king of Judah until this very day—the word of the LORD has come to me and I have spoken to you again and again, but you have not listened.

⁴And though the LORD has sent all his servants the prophets to you again and again, you have not listened or paid any attention. ⁵They said, "Turn now, each of you, from your evil ways and your evil practices, and you can stay in the land the LORD gave to you and your ancestors for ever and ever. ⁶Do not follow other gods to serve and worship them; do not arouse my anger with what your hands have made. Then I will not harm you."

⁷"But you did not listen to me," declares the LORD, "and you have aroused my anger with what your hands have made, and you have brought harm to yourselves."

⁸Therefore the LORD Almighty says this: "Because you have not listened to my words, ⁹I will summon all the peoples of the north and my servant Nebuchadnezzar king of Babylon," declares the LORD, "and I will bring them against this land and its inhabitants and against all the surrounding nations. I will completely destroy[d] them and make them an object of horror and scorn, and an everlasting ruin. ¹⁰I will banish from them the sounds of joy and gladness, the voices of bride and bridegroom, the sound of millstones and the light of the lamp. ¹¹This whole country will become a desolate wasteland, and these nations will serve the king of Babylon seventy years.

¹²"But when the seventy years are fulfilled, I will punish the king of Babylon and his nation, the land of the Babylonians,[b] for their guilt," declares the LORD, "and will make it desolate forever. ¹³I will bring on that land all the things I have spoken against it, all that are written in this book

---

[a] 1 Hebrew *Jeconiah*, a variant of *Jehoiachin*   [b] 5,12 Or *Chaldeans*   [c] 9 That is, their names will be used in cursing (see 29:22); or, others will see that they are cursed.   [d] 9 The Hebrew term refers to the irrevocable giving over of things or persons to the LORD, often by totally destroying them.

and prophesied by Jeremiah against all the nations. [14]They themselves will be enslaved by many nations and great kings; I will repay them according to their deeds and the work of their hands."

The Cup of God's Wrath

[15]This is what the LORD, the God of Israel, said to me: "Take from my hand this cup filled with the wine of my wrath and make all the nations to whom I send you drink it. [16]When they drink it, they will stagger and go mad because of the sword I will send among them."

[17]So I took the cup from the LORD's hand and made all the nations to whom he sent me drink it: [18]Jerusalem and the towns of Judah, its kings and officials, to make them a ruin and an object of horror and scorn, a curse[a] — as they are today; [19]Pharaoh king of Egypt, his attendants, his officials and all his people, [20]and all the foreign people there; all the kings of Uz; all the kings of the Philistines (those of Ashkelon, Gaza, Ekron, and the people left at Ashdod); [21]Edom, Moab and Ammon; [22]all the kings of Tyre and Sidon; the kings of the coastlands across the sea; [23]Dedan, Tema, Buz and all who are in distant places[b]; [24]all the kings of Arabia and all the kings of the foreign people who live in the wilderness; [25]all the kings of Zimri, Elam and Media; [26]and all the kings of the north, near and far, one after the other — all the kingdoms on the face of the earth. And after all of them, the king of Sheshak[c] will drink it too.

[27]"Then tell them, 'This is what the LORD Almighty, the God of Israel, says: Drink, get drunk and vomit, and fall to rise no more because of the sword I will send among you.' [28]But if they refuse to take the cup from your hand and drink, tell them, 'This is what the LORD Almighty says: You must drink it! [29]See, I am beginning to bring disaster on the city that bears my Name, and will you indeed go unpunished? You will not go unpunished, for I am calling down a sword on all who live on the earth, declares the LORD Almighty.'

[30]"Now prophesy all these words against them and say to them:

" 'The LORD will roar from on high;
he will thunder from his holy
dwelling
and roar mightily against his
land.
He will shout like those who tread the
grapes,
shout against all who live on the
earth.
[31]The tumult will resound to the ends of
the earth,
for the LORD will bring charges
against the nations;
he will bring judgment on all
mankind
and put the wicked to the sword,' "
declares the LORD.

[32]This is what the LORD Almighty says:

"Look! Disaster is spreading
from nation to nation;
a mighty storm is rising
from the ends of the earth."

[33]At that time those slain by the LORD will be everywhere — from one end of the earth to the other. They will not be mourned or gathered up or buried, but will be like dung lying on the ground.

[34]Weep and wail, you shepherds;
roll in the dust, you leaders of the
flock.
For your time to be slaughtered has
come;
you will fall like the best of the
rams.[d]
[35]The shepherds will have nowhere to
flee,
the leaders of the flock no place to
escape.
[36]Hear the cry of the shepherds,
the wailing of the leaders of the
flock,
for the LORD is destroying their
pasture.
[37]The peaceful meadows will be laid
waste
because of the fierce anger of the
LORD.

---

a 18 That is, their names to be used in cursing (see 29:22); or, to be seen by others as cursed   *b 23* Or *who clip the hair by their foreheads*   *c 26 Sheshak* is a cryptogram for Babylon.   *d 34* Septuagint; Hebrew *fall and be shattered like fine pottery*

³⁸ Like a lion he will leave his lair,
   and their land will become
     desolate
because of the sword[a] of the
     oppressor
and because of the LORD's fierce
     anger.

Jeremiah Threatened With Death

26 Early in the reign of Jehoiakim son of Josiah king of Judah, this word came from the LORD: ² "This is what the LORD says: Stand in the courtyard of the LORD's house and speak to all the people of the towns of Judah who come to worship in the house of the LORD. Tell them everything I command you; do not omit a word. ³ Perhaps they will listen and each will turn from their evil ways. Then I will relent and not inflict on them the disaster I was planning because of the evil they have done. ⁴ Say to them, 'This is what the LORD says: If you do not listen to me and follow my law, which I have set before you, ⁵ and if you do not listen to the words of my servants the prophets, whom I have sent to you again and again (though you have not listened), ⁶ then I will make this house like Shiloh and this city a curse[b] among all the nations of the earth.' "

⁷ The priests, the prophets and all the people heard Jeremiah speak these words in the house of the LORD. ⁸ But as soon as Jeremiah finished telling all the people everything the LORD had commanded him to say, the priests, the prophets and all the people seized him and said, "You must die! ⁹ Why do you prophesy in the LORD's name that this house will be like Shiloh and this city will be desolate and deserted?" And all the people crowded around Jeremiah in the house of the LORD.

¹⁰ When the officials of Judah heard about these things, they went up from the royal palace to the house of the LORD and took their places at the entrance of the New Gate of the LORD's house. ¹¹ Then the priests and the prophets said to the officials and all the people, "This man should be sentenced to death because he has prophesied against this city. You have heard it with your own ears!"

¹² Then Jeremiah said to all the officials and all the people: "The LORD sent me to prophesy against this house and this city all the things you have heard. ¹³ Now reform your ways and your actions and obey the LORD your God. Then the LORD will relent and not bring the disaster he has pronounced against you. ¹⁴ As for me, I am in your hands; do with me whatever you think is good and right. ¹⁵ Be assured, however, that if you put me to death, you will bring the guilt of innocent blood on yourselves and on this city and on those who live in it, for in truth the LORD has sent me to you to speak all these words in your hearing."

¹⁶ Then the officials and all the people said to the priests and the prophets, "This man should not be sentenced to death! He has spoken to us in the name of the LORD our God."

¹⁷ Some of the elders of the land stepped forward and said to the entire assembly of people, ¹⁸ "Micah of Moresheth prophesied in the days of Hezekiah king of Judah. He told all the people of Judah, 'This is what the LORD Almighty says:

" 'Zion will be plowed like a field,
   Jerusalem will become a heap of
     rubble,
   the temple hill a mound overgrown
     with thickets.'[c]

¹⁹ "Did Hezekiah king of Judah or anyone else in Judah put him to death? Did not Hezekiah fear the LORD and seek his favor? And did not the LORD relent, so that he did not bring the disaster he pronounced against them? We are about to bring a terrible disaster on ourselves!"

²⁰ (Now Uriah son of Shemaiah from Kiriath Jearim was another man who prophesied in the name of the LORD; he prophesied the same things against this city and this land as Jeremiah did. ²¹ When King Jehoiakim and all his officers and officials heard his words, the king was determined to put him to death. But Uriah heard of it and fled in fear to Egypt. ²² King Jehoi-

---

a 38 Some Hebrew manuscripts and Septuagint (see also 46:16 and 50:16); most Hebrew manuscripts *anger*
b 6 That is, its name will be used in cursing (see 29:22); or, others will see that it is cursed.   *c 18* Micah 3:12

akim, however, sent Elnathan son of Akbor to Egypt, along with some other men. [23]They brought Uriah out of Egypt and took him to King Jehoiakim, who had him struck down with a sword and his body thrown into the burial place of the common people.)

[24]Furthermore, Ahikam son of Shaphan supported Jeremiah, and so he was not handed over to the people to be put to death.

Judah to Serve Nebuchadnezzar

27 Early in the reign of Zedekiah[a] son of Josiah king of Judah, this word came to Jeremiah from the LORD: [2]This is what the LORD said to me: "Make a yoke out of straps and crossbars and put it on your neck. [3]Then send word to the kings of Edom, Moab, Ammon, Tyre and Sidon through the envoys who have come to Jerusalem to Zedekiah king of Judah. [4]Give them a message for their masters and say, 'This is what the LORD Almighty, the God of Israel, says: "Tell this to your masters: [5]With my great power and outstretched arm I made the earth and its people and the animals that are on it, and I give it to anyone I please. [6]Now I will give all your countries into the hands of my servant Nebuchadnezzar king of Babylon; I will make even the wild animals subject to him. [7]All nations will serve him and his son and his grandson until the time for his land comes; then many nations and great kings will subjugate him.

[8]"'"If, however, any nation or kingdom will not serve Nebuchadnezzar king of Babylon or bow its neck under his yoke, I will punish that nation with the sword, famine and plague, declares the LORD, until I destroy it by his hand. [9]So do not listen to your prophets, your diviners, your interpreters of dreams, your mediums or your sorcerers who tell you, 'You will not serve the king of Babylon.' [10]They prophesy lies to you that will only serve to remove you far from your lands; I will banish you and you will perish. [11]But if any nation will bow its neck under the yoke of the king of Babylon and serve him, I will let that nation remain in its own land to till it and to live there, declares the LORD.'"'"

[12]I gave the same message to Zedekiah king of Judah. I said, "Bow your neck under the yoke of the king of Babylon;

---

[a] 1 A few Hebrew manuscripts and Syriac (see also 27:3,12 and 28:1); most Hebrew manuscripts *Jehoiakim* (Most Septuagint manuscripts do not have this verse.)

THE
WITNESSES

✓ MICAH OF MORESHETH
(JEREMIAH 26:18)
Check him out in Micah 1:1.

✓ HEZEKIAH (JEREMIAH 26:18)
Read about this king in 2 Kings 18.

✓ URIAH (JEREMIAH 26:20)
Uriah was a prophet who preached pretty much the same things as Jeremiah. These two prophets were very brave, because every time they preached against the governors, their lives were in danger. And you know what? Uriah got killed because he preached the word of God. They thought if they killed him, they could silence the word of God. How wrong they were!

serve him and his people, and you will live. ¹³Why will you and your people die by the sword, famine and plague with which the LORD has threatened any nation that will not serve the king of Babylon? ¹⁴Do not listen to the words of the prophets who say to you, 'You will not serve the king of Babylon,' for they are prophesying lies to you. ¹⁵'I have not sent them,' declares the LORD. 'They are prophesying lies in my name. Therefore, I will banish you and you will perish, both you and the prophets who prophesy to you.' "

¹⁶Then I said to the priests and all these people, "This is what the LORD says: Do not listen to the prophets who say, 'Very soon now the articles from the LORD's house will be brought back from Babylon.' They are prophesying lies to you. ¹⁷Do not listen to them. Serve the king of Babylon, and you will live. Why should this city become a ruin? ¹⁸If they are prophets and have the word of the LORD, let them plead with the LORD Almighty that the articles remaining in the house of the LORD and in the palace of the king of Judah and in Jerusalem not be taken to Babylon. ¹⁹For this is what the LORD Almighty says about the pillars, the bronze Sea, the movable stands and the other articles that are left in this city, ²⁰which Nebuchadnezzar king of Babylon did not take away when he carried Jehoiachin*ᵃ* son of Jehoiakim king of Judah into exile from Jerusalem to Babylon, along with all the nobles of Judah and Jerusalem— ²¹yes, this is what the LORD Almighty, the God of Israel, says about the things that are left in the house of the LORD and in the palace of the king of Judah and in Jerusalem: ²²'They will be taken to Babylon and there they will remain until the day I come for them,' declares the LORD. 'Then I will bring them back and restore them to this place.' "

The False Prophet Hananiah

28 In the fifth month of that same year, the fourth year, early in the reign of Zedekiah king of Judah, the prophet Hananiah son of Azzur, who was from Gibeon, said to me in the house of the LORD in the presence of the priests and all the people: ²"This is what the LORD Almighty, the God of Israel, says: 'I will break the yoke of the king of Babylon. ³Within two years I will bring back to this place all the articles of the LORD's house that Nebuchadnezzar king of Babylon removed from here and took to Babylon. ⁴I will also bring back to this place Jehoiachin*ᵃ* son of Jehoiakim king of Judah and all the other exiles from Judah who went to Babylon,' declares the LORD, 'for I will break the yoke of the king of Babylon.' "

⁵Then the prophet Jeremiah replied to the prophet Hananiah before the priests and all the people who were standing in

THE SCENE

TYRE AND SIDON

(JEREMIAH 27:3)

Tyre was a big city in the Phoenician empire. It was located on an island near the south of Lebanon, and it had two important ports where ships that sailed the Mediterranean Sea stopped to sell their goods. Sidon was another important city of the Phoenician empire. It was 22 miles (35 km) north of Tyre on the Mediterranean Sea coast, where Lebanon is today.

ᵃ 20,4 Hebrew Jeconiah, a variant of Jehoiachin

THE
WITNESSES

✓ **HANANIAH** (JEREMIAH 28:1)
Well, Hananiah was a big talker and a phony. So he was what's called a false prophet. Why? Because he preached lies. Hananiah said things that went against God's message. He also fought with Jeremiah, who really did preach what God wanted. Hananiah finally died because he was so against God.

the house of the LORD. ⁶He said, "Amen! May the LORD do so! May the LORD fulfill the words you have prophesied by bringing the articles of the LORD's house and all the exiles back to this place from Babylon. ⁷Nevertheless, listen to what I have to say in your hearing and in the hearing of all the people: ⁸From early times the prophets who preceded you and me have prophesied war, disaster and plague against many countries and great kingdoms. ⁹But the prophet who prophesies peace will be recognized as one truly sent

by the LORD only if his prediction comes true."

¹⁰Then the prophet Hananiah took the yoke off the neck of the prophet Jeremiah and broke it, ¹¹and he said before all the people, "This is what the LORD says: 'In the same way I will break the yoke of Nebuchadnezzar king of Babylon off the neck of all the nations within two years.' " At this, the prophet Jeremiah went on his way.

¹²After the prophet Hananiah had broken the yoke off the neck of the prophet Jeremiah, the word of the LORD came to Jeremiah: ¹³"Go and tell Hananiah, 'This is what the LORD says: You have broken a wooden yoke, but in its place you will get a yoke of iron. ¹⁴This is what the LORD Almighty, the God of Israel, says: I will put an iron yoke on the necks of all these nations to make them serve Nebuchadnezzar king of Babylon, and they will serve him. I will even give him control over the wild animals.' "

¹⁵Then the prophet Jeremiah said to Hananiah the prophet, "Listen, Hananiah! The LORD has not sent you, yet you have persuaded this nation to trust in lies. ¹⁶Therefore this is what the LORD says: 'I am about to remove you from the face of the earth. This very year you are going to die, because you have preached rebellion against the LORD.' "

¹⁷In the seventh month of that same year, Hananiah the prophet died.

A Letter to the Exiles

29 This is the text of the letter that the prophet Jeremiah sent from Jerusalem to the surviving elders among the exiles and to the priests, the prophets and all the other people Nebuchadnezzar had carried into exile from Jerusalem to Babylon. ²(This was after King Jehoiachin*ᵃ* and the queen mother, the court officials and the leaders of Judah and Jerusalem, the skilled workers and the artisans had gone into exile from Jerusalem.) ³He entrusted the letter to Elasah son of Shaphan and to Gemariah son of Hilkiah, whom Zedekiah king of Judah

---

ᵃ 2 Hebrew *Jeconiah,* a variant of *Jehoiachin*

sent to King Nebuchadnezzar in Babylon. It said:

⁴This is what the LORD Almighty, the God of Israel, says to all those I carried into exile from Jerusalem to Babylon: ⁵"Build houses and settle down; plant gardens and eat what they produce. ⁶Marry and have sons and daughters; find wives for your sons and give your daughters in marriage, so that they too may have sons and daughters. Increase in number there; do not decrease. ⁷Also, seek the peace and prosperity of the city to which I have carried you into exile. Pray to the LORD for it, because if it prospers, you too will prosper."

⁸Yes, this is what the LORD Almighty, the God of Israel, says: "Do not let the prophets and diviners among you deceive you. Do not listen to the dreams you encourage them to have.

BREAKTHROUGH!

Seventh month

(JEREMIAH 28:17)

By now, you know that the calendar of the Israelites wasn't the same as ours. Ours is based on the sun and theirs is based on the moon. The name of their seventh month was Ethanim. It was from the middle of September to the middle of October in our calendar.

⁹They are prophesying lies to you in my name. I have not sent them," declares the LORD.

¹⁰This is what the LORD says: "When seventy years are completed for Babylon, I will come to you and fulfill my good promise to bring you back to this place. ¹¹For I know the plans I have for you," declares the LORD, "plans to prosper you and not to harm you, plans to give you hope and a future. ¹²Then you will call on me and come and pray to me, and I will listen to you. ¹³You will seek me and find me when you seek me with all your heart. ¹⁴I will be found by you," declares the LORD, "and will bring you back from captivity.ᵃ I will gather you from all the nations and places where I have banished you," declares the LORD, "and will bring you back to the place from which I carried you into exile."

¹⁵You may say, "The LORD has raised up prophets for us in Babylon," ¹⁶but this is what the LORD says about the king who sits on David's throne and all the people who remain in this city, your fellow citizens who did not go with you into exile— ¹⁷yes, this is what the LORD Almighty says: "I will send the sword, famine and plague against them and I will make them like figs that are so bad they cannot be eaten. ¹⁸I will pursue them with the sword, famine and plague and will make them abhorrent to all the kingdoms of the earth, a curseᵇ and an object of horror, of scorn and reproach, among all the nations where I drive them. ¹⁹For they have not listened to my words," declares the LORD, "words that I sent to them again and again by my servants the prophets. And you exiles have not listened either," declares the LORD.

²⁰Therefore, hear the word of the LORD, all you exiles whom I have sent away from Jerusalem to Babylon. ²¹This is what the LORD Almighty, the

---

ᵃ 14 Or will restore your fortunes   ᵇ 18 That is, their names will be used in cursing (see verse 22); or, others will see that they are cursed.

God of Israel, says about Ahab son of Kolaiah and Zedekiah son of Maaseiah, who are prophesying lies to you in my name: "I will deliver them into the hands of Nebuchadnezzar king of Babylon, and he will put them to death before your very eyes. ²²Because of them, all the exiles from Judah who are in Babylon will use this curse: 'May the LORD treat you like Zedekiah and Ahab, whom the king of Babylon burned in the fire.' ²³For they have done outrageous things in Israel; they have committed adultery with their neighbors' wives, and in my name they have uttered lies—which I did not authorize. I know it and am a witness to it," declares the LORD.

Message to Shemaiah

²⁴Tell Shemaiah the Nehelamite, ²⁵"This is what the LORD Almighty, the God of Israel, says: You sent letters in your own name to all the people in Jerusalem, to the priest Zephaniah son of Maaseiah, and to all the other priests. You said to Zephaniah, ²⁶'The LORD has appointed you priest in place of Jehoiada to be in charge of the house of the LORD; you should put any maniac who acts like a prophet into the stocks and neck-irons. ²⁷So why have you not reprimanded Jeremiah from Anathoth, who poses as a prophet among you? ²⁸He has sent this message to us in Babylon: It will be a long time. Therefore build houses and settle down; plant gardens and eat what they produce.' "

²⁹Zephaniah the priest, however, read the letter to Jeremiah the prophet. ³⁰Then the word of the LORD came to Jeremiah: ³¹"Send this message to all the exiles: 'This is what the LORD says about Shemaiah the Nehelamite: Because Shemaiah has prophesied to you, even though I did not send him, and has persuaded you to trust in lies, ³²this is what the LORD says: I will surely punish Shemaiah the Nehelamite and his descendants. He will have no one left among this people, nor will he see the good things I will do for my people, declares the LORD, because he has preached rebellion against me.' "

Restoration of Israel

30 This is the word that came to Jeremiah from the LORD: ²"This is what the LORD, the God of Israel, says: 'Write in a book all the words I have spoken to you. ³The days are coming,' declares the LORD, 'when I will bring my people Israel and Judah back from captivity*a* and restore them to the land I gave their ancestors to possess,' says the LORD."

⁴These are the words the LORD spoke concerning Israel and Judah: ⁵"This is what the LORD says:

" 'Cries of fear are heard—
    terror, not peace.
⁶Ask and see:
    Can a man bear children?
Then why do I see every strong man
    with his hands on his stomach like
        a woman in labor,
    every face turned deathly pale?
⁷How awful that day will be!
    No other will be like it.
It will be a time of trouble for Jacob,
    but he will be saved out of it.

⁸ " 'In that day,' declares the LORD
        Almighty,
    'I will break the yoke off their
        necks
and will tear off their bonds;
    no longer will foreigners enslave
        them.
⁹Instead, they will serve the LORD their
        God
    and David their king,
    whom I will raise up for them.

¹⁰ " 'So do not be afraid, Jacob my
        servant;
    do not be dismayed, Israel,'
                declares the LORD.
    'I will surely save you out of a distant
        place,
    your descendants from the land of
        their exile.
Jacob will again have peace and
        security,
    and no one will make him afraid.
¹¹I am with you and will save you,'
    declares the LORD.

---

a 3 Or *will restore the fortunes of my people Israel and Judah*

'Though I completely destroy all the
nations
   among which I scatter you,
   I will not completely destroy you.
I will discipline you but only in due
   measure;
   I will not let you go entirely
      unpunished.'

¹² "This is what the LORD says:

" 'Your wound is incurable,
   your injury beyond healing.
¹³ There is no one to plead your cause,
   no remedy for your sore,
   no healing for you.
¹⁴ All your allies have forgotten you;
   they care nothing for you.
I have struck you as an enemy would
   and punished you as would the
      cruel,
because your guilt is so great
   and your sins so many.
¹⁵ Why do you cry out over your wound,
   your pain that has no cure?
Because of your great guilt and many
   sins
   I have done these things to you.

¹⁶ " 'But all who devour you will be
   devoured;
   all your enemies will go into exile.
Those who plunder you will be
   plundered;
   all who make spoil of you I will
      despoil.
¹⁷ But I will restore you to health
   and heal your wounds,'
                    declares the LORD,
'because you are called an outcast,
   Zion for whom no one cares.'

¹⁸ "This is what the LORD says:

" 'I will restore the fortunes of Jacob's
   tents
   and have compassion on his
      dwellings;
the city will be rebuilt on her ruins,
   and the palace will stand in its
      proper place.
¹⁹ From them will come songs of
   thanksgiving
   and the sound of rejoicing.
I will add to their numbers,
   and they will not be decreased;

I will bring them honor,
   and they will not be disdained.
²⁰ Their children will be as in days of
   old,
   and their community will be
      established before me;
   I will punish all who oppress them.
²¹ Their leader will be one of their own;
   their ruler will arise from among
      them.
I will bring him near and he will come
   close to me—
   for who is he who will devote
      himself
   to be close to me?'
                    declares the LORD.
²² " 'So you will be my people,
   and I will be your God.' "

²³ See, the storm of the LORD
   will burst out in wrath,
a driving wind swirling down
   on the heads of the wicked.
²⁴ The fierce anger of the LORD will not
   turn back
   until he fully accomplishes
   the purposes of his heart.
In days to come
   you will understand this.

31 "At that time," declares the LORD, "I
will be the God of all the families of
Israel, and they will be my people."

² This is what the LORD says:

"The people who survive the sword
   will find favor in the wilderness;
   I will come to give rest to Israel."

³ The LORD appeared to us in the past,[a]
saying:

"I have loved you with an everlasting
   love;
   I have drawn you with unfailing
      kindness.
⁴ I will build you up again,
   and you, Virgin Israel, will be
      rebuilt.
Again you will take up your timbrels
   and go out to dance with the
      joyful.
⁵ Again you will plant vineyards
   on the hills of Samaria;

---

a 3 Or LORD has appeared to us from afar

the farmers will plant them
and enjoy their fruit.
⁶ There will be a day when watchmen
cry out
on the hills of Ephraim,
'Come, let us go up to Zion,
to the LORD our God.' "

⁷ This is what the LORD says:

"Sing with joy for Jacob;
shout for the foremost of the
nations.
Make your praises heard, and say,
'LORD, save your people,
the remnant of Israel.'
⁸ See, I will bring them from the land of
the north
and gather them from the ends of
the earth.
Among them will be the blind and the
lame,
expectant mothers and women in
labor;
a great throng will return.
⁹ They will come with weeping;
they will pray as I bring them back.
I will lead them beside streams of
water
on a level path where they will not
stumble,
because I am Israel's father,
and Ephraim is my firstborn son.

¹⁰ "Hear the word of the LORD, you nations;
proclaim it in distant coastlands:
'He who scattered Israel will gather
them
and will watch over his flock like a
shepherd.'
¹¹ For the LORD will deliver Jacob
and redeem them from the hand of
those stronger than they.
¹² They will come and shout for joy on
the heights of Zion;
they will rejoice in the bounty of the
LORD—
the grain, the new wine and the olive
oil,
the young of the flocks and herds.
They will be like a well-watered garden,
and they will sorrow no more.
¹³ Then young women will dance and be
glad,
young men and old as well.

I will turn their mourning into
gladness;
I will give them comfort and joy
instead of sorrow.
¹⁴ I will satisfy the priests with
abundance,
and my people will be filled with my
bounty,"
declares the LORD.

¹⁵ This is what the LORD says:

"A voice is heard in Ramah,
mourning and great weeping,
Rachel weeping for her children
and refusing to be comforted,
because they are no more."

¹⁶ This is what the LORD says:

"Restrain your voice from weeping
and your eyes from tears,
for your work will be rewarded,"
declares the LORD.
"They will return from the land of
the enemy.
¹⁷ So there is hope for your
descendants,"
declares the LORD.
"Your children will return to their
own land.

¹⁸ "I have surely heard Ephraim's
moaning:
'You disciplined me like an unruly
calf,
and I have been disciplined.
Restore me, and I will return,
because you are the LORD my
God.
¹⁹ After I strayed,
I repented;
after I came to understand,
I beat my breast.
I was ashamed and humiliated
because I bore the disgrace of my
youth.'
²⁰ Is not Ephraim my dear son,
the child in whom I delight?
Though I often speak against him,
I still remember him.
Therefore my heart yearns for him;
I have great compassion for
him,"
declares the LORD.

²¹ "Set up road signs;
   put up guideposts.
Take note of the highway,
   the road that you take.
Return, Virgin Israel,
   return to your towns.
²² How long will you wander,
   unfaithful Daughter Israel?
The LORD will create a new thing on
      earth—
   the woman will return to*ᵃ* the man."

²³ This is what the LORD Almighty, the God of Israel, says: "When I bring them back from captivity,*ᵇ* the people in the land of Judah and in its towns will once again use these words: 'The LORD bless you, you prosperous city, you sacred mountain.' ²⁴ People will live together in Judah and all its towns—farmers and those who move about with their flocks. ²⁵ I will refresh the weary and satisfy the faint."

²⁶ At this I awoke and looked around. My sleep had been pleasant to me.

²⁷ "The days are coming," declares the LORD, "when I will plant the kingdoms of Israel and Judah with the offspring of people and of animals. ²⁸ Just as I watched over them to uproot and tear down, and to overthrow, destroy and bring disaster, so I will watch over them to build and to plant," declares the LORD. ²⁹ "In those days people will no longer say,

'The parents have eaten sour grapes,
   and the children's teeth are set
      on edge.'

³⁰ Instead, everyone will die for their own sin; whoever eats sour grapes—their own teeth will be set on edge.

³¹ "The days are coming," declares the
      LORD,
   "when I will make a new covenant
with the people of Israel
   and with the people of Judah.
³² It will not be like the covenant
   I made with their ancestors
when I took them by the hand
   to lead them out of Egypt,
because they broke my covenant,
   though I was a husband to*ᶜ* them,*ᵈ*"
      declares the LORD.

³³ "This is the covenant I will make with
      the people of Israel
   after that time," declares the
      LORD.
"I will put my law in their minds
   and write it on their hearts.
I will be their God,
   and they will be my people.
³⁴ No longer will they teach their
      neighbor,
   or say to one another, 'Know the
      LORD,'
because they will all know me,
   from the least of them to the
      greatest,"
            declares the LORD.
"For I will forgive their wickedness
   and will remember their sins no
      more."

³⁵ This is what the LORD says,

he who appoints the sun
   to shine by day,
who decrees the moon and stars
   to shine by night,
who stirs up the sea
   so that its waves roar—
   the LORD Almighty is his name:
³⁶ "Only if these decrees vanish from my
      sight,"
   declares the LORD,
"will Israel ever cease
   being a nation before me."

³⁷ This is what the LORD says:

"Only if the heavens above can be
      measured
   and the foundations of the earth
      below be searched out
will I reject all the descendants of
      Israel
   because of all they have done,"
            declares the LORD.

³⁸ "The days are coming," declares the LORD, "when this city will be rebuilt for me from the Tower of Hananel to the Corner Gate. ³⁹ The measuring line will stretch from there straight to the hill of Gareb and then turn to Goah. ⁴⁰ The whole valley where dead bodies and ashes are thrown,

---

ᵃ 22 Or *will protect*   *ᵇ 23* Or *I restore their fortunes*
ᶜ 32 Hebrew; Septuagint and Syriac */ and I turned away
from*   *ᵈ 32* Or *was their master*

and all the terraces out to the Kidron Valley on the east as far as the corner of the Horse Gate, will be holy to the LORD. The city will never again be uprooted or demolished."

Jeremiah Buys a Field

32 This is the word that came to Jeremiah from the LORD in the tenth year of Zedekiah king of Judah, which was the eighteenth year of Nebuchadnezzar. ²The army of the king of Babylon was then besieging Jerusalem, and Jeremiah the prophet was confined in the courtyard of the guard in the royal palace of Judah.

³Now Zedekiah king of Judah had imprisoned him there, saying, "Why do you prophesy as you do? You say, 'This is what the LORD says: I am about to give this city into the hands of the king of Babylon, and he will capture it. ⁴Zedekiah king of Judah will not escape the Babylonians*ᵃ* but will certainly be given into the hands of the king of Babylon, and will speak with him face to face and see him with his own eyes. ⁵He will take Zedekiah to Babylon, where he will remain until I deal with him, declares the LORD. If you fight against the Babylonians, you will not succeed.'"

⁶Jeremiah said, "The word of the LORD came to me: ⁷Hanamel son of Shallum your uncle is going to come to you and say, 'Buy my field at Anathoth, because as nearest relative it is your right and duty to buy it.'

⁸"Then, just as the LORD had said, my cousin Hanamel came to me in the courtyard of the guard and said, 'Buy my field at Anathoth in the territory of Benjamin. Since it is your right to redeem it and possess it, buy it for yourself.'

"I knew that this was the word of the LORD; ⁹so I bought the field at Anathoth from my cousin Hanamel and weighed out for him seventeen shekels*ᵇ* of silver. ¹⁰I signed and sealed the deed, had it witnessed, and weighed out the silver on the scales. ¹¹I took the deed of purchase— the sealed copy containing the terms and conditions, as well as the unsealed copy— ¹²and I gave this deed to Baruch son of Neriah, the son of Mahseiah, in the

THE
WITNESSES

✓ **BARUCH** (JEREMIAH 32:12; 36:4)
Do you have to take a lot of notes in school? Well, Baruch was kind of like Jeremiah's secretary, and he had to take notes. That meant that many times Jeremiah himself didn't write down what he said, he just told it to Baruch. Baruch wrote it on a leather scroll, which was what they used then instead of paper.

presence of my cousin Hanamel and of the witnesses who had signed the deed and of all the Jews sitting in the courtyard of the guard.

¹³"In their presence I gave Baruch these instructions: ¹⁴'This is what the LORD Almighty, the God of Israel, says: Take these documents, both the sealed and unsealed copies of the deed of purchase, and put them in a clay jar so they will last a long time. ¹⁵For this is what the

---

ᵃ 4 Or *Chaldeans*; also in verses 5, 24, 25, 28, 29 and 43
ᵇ 9 That is, about 7 ounces or about 200 grams

LORD Almighty, the God of Israel, says: Houses, fields and vineyards will again be bought in this land.'

¹⁶ "After I had given the deed of purchase to Baruch son of Neriah, I prayed to the LORD:

¹⁷ "Ah, Sovereign LORD, you have made the heavens and the earth by your great power and outstretched arm. Nothing is too hard for you. ¹⁸ You show love to thousands but bring the punishment for the parents' sins into the laps of their children after them. Great and mighty God, whose name is the LORD Almighty, ¹⁹ great are your purposes and mighty are your deeds. Your eyes are open to the ways of all mankind; you reward each person according to their conduct and as their deeds deserve. ²⁰ You performed signs and wonders in Egypt and have continued them to this day, in Israel and among all mankind, and have gained the renown that is still yours. ²¹ You brought your people Israel out of Egypt with signs and wonders, by a mighty hand and an outstretched arm and with great terror. ²² You gave them this land you had sworn to give their ancestors, a land flowing with milk and honey. ²³ They came in and took possession of it, but they did not obey you or follow your law; they did not do what you commanded them to do. So you brought all this disaster on them.

²⁴ "See how the siege ramps are built up to take the city. Because of the sword, famine and plague, the city will be given into the hands of the Babylonians who are attacking it. What you said has happened, as you now see. ²⁵ And though the city will be given into the hands of the Babylonians, you, Sovereign LORD, say to me, 'Buy the field with silver and have the transaction witnessed.' "

²⁶ Then the word of the LORD came to Jeremiah: ²⁷ "I am the LORD, the God of all mankind. Is anything too hard for me? ²⁸ Therefore this is what the LORD says: I am about to give this city into the hands of the Babylonians and to Nebuchadnezzar king of Babylon, who will capture it. ²⁹ The Babylonians who are attacking this city will come in and set it on fire; they will burn it down, along with the houses where the people aroused my anger by burning incense on the roofs to Baal and by pouring out drink offerings to other gods.

³⁰ "The people of Israel and Judah have done nothing but evil in my sight from their youth; indeed, the people of Israel have done nothing but arouse my anger with what their hands have made, declares the LORD. ³¹ From the day it was built until now, this city has so aroused my anger and wrath that I must remove it from my sight. ³² The people of Israel and Judah have provoked me by all the evil they have done — they, their kings and officials, their priests and prophets, the people of Judah and those living in Jerusalem. ³³ They turned their backs to me and not their faces; though I taught them again and again, they would not listen or respond to discipline. ³⁴ They set up their vile images in the house that bears my Name and defiled it. ³⁵ They built high places for Baal in the Valley of Ben Hinnom to sacrifice their sons and daughters to Molek, though I never commanded — nor did it enter my mind — that they should do such a detestable thing and so make Judah sin.

³⁶ "You are saying about this city, 'By the sword, famine and plague it will be given into the hands of the king of Babylon'; but this is what the LORD, the God of Israel, says: ³⁷ I will surely gather them from all the lands where I banish them in my furious anger and great wrath; I will bring them back to this place and let them live in safety. ³⁸ They will be my people, and I will be their God. ³⁹ I will give them singleness of heart and action, so that they will always fear me and that all will then go well for them and for their children after them. ⁴⁰ I will make an everlasting covenant with them: I will never stop doing good to them, and I will inspire them to fear me, so that they will never turn away from me. ⁴¹ I will rejoice in doing them good and will assuredly plant them in this land with all my heart and soul.

⁴²"This is what the LORD says: As I have brought all this great calamity on this people, so I will give them all the prosperity I have promised them. ⁴³Once more fields will be bought in this land of which you say, 'It is a desolate waste, without people or animals, for it has been given into the hands of the Babylonians.' ⁴⁴Fields will be bought for silver, and deeds will be signed, sealed and witnessed in the territory of Benjamin, in the villages around Jerusalem, in the towns of Judah and in the towns of the hill country, of the western foothills and of the Negev, because I will restore their fortunes,ᵃ declares the LORD."

Promise of Restoration

33 While Jeremiah was still confined in the courtyard of the guard, the word of the LORD came to him a second time: ²"This is what the LORD says, he who made the earth, the LORD who formed it and established it—the LORD is his name: ³'Call to me and I will answer you and tell you great and unsearchable things you do not know.' ⁴For this is what the LORD, the God of Israel, says about the houses in this city and the royal palaces of Judah that have been torn down to be used against the siege ramps and the sword ⁵in the fight with the Babyloniansᵇ: 'They will be filled with the dead bodies of the people I will slay in my anger and wrath. I will hide my face from this city because of all its wickedness.

⁶"'Nevertheless, I will bring health and healing to it; I will heal my people and will let them enjoy abundant peace and security. ⁷I will bring Judah and Israel back from captivityᶜ and will rebuild them as they were before. ⁸I will cleanse them from all the sin they have committed against me and will forgive all their sins of rebellion against me. ⁹Then this city will bring me renown, joy, praise and honor before all nations on earth that hear of all the good things I do for it; and they will be in awe and will tremble at the abundant prosperity and peace I provide for it.'

¹⁰"This is what the LORD says: 'You say about this place, "It is a desolate waste, without people or animals." Yet in the towns of Judah and the streets of Jerusalem that are deserted, inhabited by neither people nor animals, there will be heard once more ¹¹the sounds of joy and gladness, the voices of bride and bridegroom, and the voices of those who bring thank offerings to the house of the LORD, saying,

"Give thanks to the LORD Almighty,
　for the LORD is good;
　his love endures forever."

For I will restore the fortunes of the land as they were before,' says the LORD. ¹²"This is what the LORD Almighty says: 'In this place, desolate and without people or animals—in all its towns there will again be pastures for shepherds to rest their flocks. ¹³In the towns of the hill country, of the western foothills and of the Negev, in the territory of Benjamin, in the villages around Jerusalem and in the towns of Judah, flocks will again pass under the hand of the one who counts them,' says the LORD.

¹⁴"'The days are coming,' declares the LORD, 'when I will fulfill the good promise I made to the people of Israel and Judah.

¹⁵"'In those days and at that time
　I will make a righteous Branch
　　sprout from David's line;
　he will do what is just and right in
　　the land.
¹⁶In those days Judah will be saved
　and Jerusalem will live in safety.
This is the name by which itᵈ will be
　called:
　The LORD Our Righteous Savior.'

¹⁷For this is what the LORD says: 'David will never fail to have a man to sit on the throne of Israel, ¹⁸nor will the Levitical priests ever fail to have a man to stand before me continually to offer burnt offerings, to burn grain offerings and to present sacrifices.' "

¹⁹The word of the LORD came to Jeremiah: ²⁰"This is what the LORD says: 'If you can break my covenant with the day and my covenant with the night, so that day

---

ᵃ 44 Or will bring them back from captivity   ᵇ 5 Or Chaldeans   ᶜ 7 Or will restore the fortunes of Judah and Israel   ᵈ 16 Or he and night no longer come at their appointed time, [21]then my covenant with David my servant—and my covenant with the Levites who are priests ministering before me—can be broken and David will no longer have a descendant to reign on his throne. [22]I will make the descendants of David my servant and the Levites who minister before me as countless as the stars in the sky and as measureless as the sand on the seashore.'"

[23]The word of the LORD came to Jeremiah: [24]"Have you not noticed that these people are saying, 'The LORD has rejected the two kingdoms[a] he chose'? So they despise my people and no longer regard them as a nation. [25]This is what the LORD says: 'If I have not made my covenant with day and night and established the laws of heaven and earth, [26]then I will reject the descendants of Jacob and David my servant and will not choose one of his sons to rule over the descendants of Abraham, Isaac and Jacob. For I will restore their fortunes[b] and have compassion on them.'"

Warning to Zedekiah

34 While Nebuchadnezzar king of Babylon and all his army and all the kingdoms and peoples in the empire he ruled were fighting against Jerusalem and all its surrounding towns, this word came to Jeremiah from the LORD: [2]"This is what the LORD, the God of Israel, says: Go to Zedekiah king of Judah and tell him, 'This is what the LORD says: I am about to give this city into the hands of the king of Babylon, and he will burn it down. [3]You will not escape from his grasp but will surely be captured and given into his hands. You will see the king of Babylon with your own eyes, and he will speak with you face to face. And you will go to Babylon.

[4]"'Yet hear the LORD's promise to you, Zedekiah king of Judah. This is what the LORD says concerning you: You will not die by the sword; [5]you will die peacefully. As people made a funeral fire in honor of your predecessors, the kings who ruled before you, so they will make a fire in your honor and lament, "Alas, master!"

I myself make this promise, declares the LORD.'"

[6]Then Jeremiah the prophet told all this to Zedekiah king of Judah, in Jerusalem, [7]while the army of the king of Babylon was fighting against Jerusalem and the other cities of Judah that were still holding out—Lachish and Azekah. These were the only fortified cities left in Judah.

Freedom for Slaves

[8]The word came to Jeremiah from the LORD after King Zedekiah had made a covenant with all the people in Jerusalem to proclaim freedom for the slaves. [9]Everyone was to free their Hebrew slaves, both male and female; no one was to hold a fellow Hebrew in bondage. [10]So all the officials and people who entered into this covenant agreed that they would free their male and female slaves and no longer hold them in bondage. They agreed, and set them free. [11]But afterward they changed their minds and took back the slaves they had freed and enslaved them again.

[12]Then the word of the LORD came to Jeremiah: [13]"This is what the LORD, the God of Israel, says: I made a covenant with your ancestors when I brought them out of Egypt, out of the land of slavery. I said, [14]'Every seventh year each of you must free any fellow Hebrews who have sold themselves to you. After they have served you six years, you must let them go free.'[c] Your ancestors, however, did not listen to me or pay attention to me. [15]Recently you repented and did what is right in my sight: Each of you proclaimed freedom to your own people. You even made a covenant before me in the house that bears my Name. [16]But now you have turned around and profaned my name; each of you has taken back the male and female slaves you had set free to go where they wished. You have forced them to become your slaves again.

[17]"Therefore this is what the LORD says: You have not obeyed me; you have not proclaimed freedom to your own people.

---

[a] 24 Or families   [b] 26 Or will bring them back from captivity   [c] 14 Deut. 15:12

So I now proclaim 'freedom' for you, declares the LORD—'freedom' to fall by the sword, plague and famine. I will make you abhorrent to all the kingdoms of the earth. ¹⁸Those who have violated my covenant and have not fulfilled the terms of the covenant they made before me, I will treat like the calf they cut in two and then walked between its pieces. ¹⁹The leaders of Judah and Jerusalem, the court officials, the priests and all the people of the land who walked between the pieces of the calf, ²⁰I will deliver into the hands of their enemies who want to kill them. Their dead bodies will become food for the birds and the wild animals.

²¹"I will deliver Zedekiah king of Judah and his officials into the hands of their enemies who want to kill them, to the army of the king of Babylon, which has withdrawn from you. ²²I am going to give the order, declares the LORD, and I will bring them back to this city. They will fight against it, take it and burn it down. And I will lay waste the towns of Judah so no one can live there."

The Rekabites

35 This is the word that came to Jeremiah from the LORD during the reign of Jehoiakim son of Josiah king of Judah: ²"Go to the Rekabite family and invite them to come to one of the side rooms of the house of the LORD and give them wine to drink."

³So I went to get Jaazaniah son of Jeremiah, the son of Habazziniah, and his brothers and all his sons—the whole family of the Rekabites. ⁴I brought them into the house of the LORD, into the room of the sons of Hanan son of Igdaliah the man of God. It was next to the room of the officials, which was over that of Maaseiah son of Shallum the doorkeeper. ⁵Then I set bowls full of wine and some cups before the Rekabites and said to them, "Drink some wine."

⁶But they replied, "We do not drink wine, because our forefather Jehonadab*ᵃ* son of Rekab gave us this command: 'Neither you nor your descendants must ever drink wine. ⁷Also you must never build houses, sow seed or plant vine-

yards; you must never have any of these things, but must always live in tents. Then you will live a long time in the land where you are nomads.' ⁸We have obeyed everything our forefather Jehonadab son of Rekab commanded us. Neither we nor our wives nor our sons and daughters have ever drunk wine ⁹or built houses to live in or had vineyards, fields or crops. ¹⁰We have lived in tents and have fully obeyed everything our forefather Jehonadab commanded us. ¹¹But when Nebuchadnezzar king of Babylon invaded this land, we said, 'Come, we must go to Jerusalem to escape the Babylonian*ᵇ* and Aramean armies.' So we have remained in Jerusalem."

¹²Then the word of the LORD came to Jeremiah, saying: ¹³"This is what the LORD Almighty, the God of Israel, says: Go and tell the people of Judah and those living in Jerusalem, 'Will you not learn a lesson and obey my words?' declares the LORD. ¹⁴'Jehonadab son of Rekab ordered his descendants not to drink wine and this command has been kept. To this day they do not drink wine, because they obey their forefather's command. But I have spoken to you again and again, yet you have not obeyed me. ¹⁵Again and again I sent all my servants the prophets to you. They said, "Each of you must turn from your wicked ways and reform your actions; do not follow other gods to serve them. Then you will live in the land I have given to you and your ancestors." But you have not paid attention or listened to me. ¹⁶The descendants of Jehonadab son of Rekab have carried out the command their forefather gave them, but these people have not obeyed me.'

¹⁷"Therefore this is what the LORD God Almighty, the God of Israel, says: 'Listen! I am going to bring on Judah and on everyone living in Jerusalem every disaster I pronounced against them. I spoke to them, but they did not listen; I called to them, but they did not answer.'"

¹⁸Then Jeremiah said to the family of the Rekabites, "This is what the LORD

ᵃ 6 Hebrew *Jonadab*, a variant of *Jehonadab*; here and often in this chapter   *ᵇ 11* Or *Chaldean*

Almighty, the God of Israel, says: 'You have obeyed the command of your forefather Jehonadab and have followed all his instructions and have done everything he ordered.' ¹⁹Therefore this is what the LORD Almighty, the God of Israel, says: 'Jehonadab son of Rekab will never fail to have a descendant to serve me.' "

Jehoiakim Burns Jeremiah's Scroll

36 In the fourth year of Jehoiakim son of Josiah king of Judah, this word came to Jeremiah from the LORD: ²"Take a scroll and write on it all the words I have spoken to you concerning Israel, Judah and all the other nations from the time I began speaking to you in the reign of Josiah till now. ³Perhaps when the people of Judah hear about every disaster I plan to inflict on them, they will each turn from their wicked ways; then I will forgive their wickedness and their sin."

⁴So Jeremiah called Baruch son of Neriah, and while Jeremiah dictated all the words the LORD had spoken to him, Baruch wrote them on the scroll. ⁵Then Jeremiah told Baruch, "I am restricted; I am not allowed to go to the LORD's temple. ⁶So you go to the house of the LORD on a day of fasting and read to the people from the scroll the words of the LORD that you wrote as I dictated. Read them to all the people of Judah who come in from their towns. ⁷Perhaps they will bring their petition before the LORD and will each turn from their wicked ways, for the anger and wrath pronounced against this people by the LORD are great."

⁸Baruch son of Neriah did everything Jeremiah the prophet told him to do; at the LORD's temple he read the words of the LORD from the scroll. ⁹In the ninth month of the fifth year of Jehoiakim son of Josiah king of Judah, a time of fasting before the LORD was proclaimed for all the people in Jerusalem and those who had come from the towns of Judah. ¹⁰From the room of Gemariah son of Shaphan the secretary, which was in the upper courtyard at the entrance of the New Gate of the temple, Baruch read to all the people at the LORD's temple the words of Jeremiah from the scroll.

¹¹When Micaiah son of Gemariah, the son of Shaphan, heard all the words of the LORD from the scroll, ¹²he went down to the secretary's room in the royal palace, where all the officials were sitting: Elishama the secretary, Delaiah son of Shemaiah, Elnathan son of Akbor, Gemariah son of Shaphan, Zedekiah son of Hananiah, and all the other officials. ¹³After Micaiah told them everything he had heard Baruch read to the people from the scroll, ¹⁴all the officials sent Jehudi son of Nethaniah, the son of Shelemiah, the son of Cushi, to say to Baruch, "Bring the scroll from which you have read to the people and come." So Baruch son of Neriah went to them with the scroll in his hand. ¹⁵They said to him, "Sit down, please, and read it to us."

So Baruch read it to them. ¹⁶When they heard all these words, they looked at each other in fear and said to Baruch, "We must report all these words to the king." ¹⁷Then they asked Baruch, "Tell us, how did you come to write all this? Did Jeremiah dictate it?"

¹⁸"Yes," Baruch replied, "he dictated all these words to me, and I wrote them in ink on the scroll."

¹⁹Then the officials said to Baruch, "You and Jeremiah, go and hide. Don't let anyone know where you are."

²⁰After they put the scroll in the room of Elishama the secretary, they went to the king in the courtyard and reported everything to him. ²¹The king sent Jehudi to get the scroll, and Jehudi brought it from the room of Elishama the secretary and read it to the king and all the officials standing beside him. ²²It was the ninth month and the king was sitting in the winter apartment, with a fire burning in the firepot in front of him. ²³Whenever Jehudi had read three or four columns of the scroll, the king cut them off with a scribe's knife and threw them into the firepot, until the entire scroll was burned in the fire. ²⁴The king and all his attendants who heard all these words showed no fear, nor did they tear their clothes. ²⁵Even though Elnathan, Delaiah and Gemariah urged the king not to burn the scroll, he would not listen to them. ²⁶Instead, the king com-

manded Jerahmeel, a son of the king, Seraiah son of Azriel and Shelemiah son of Abdeel to arrest Baruch the scribe and Jeremiah the prophet. But the LORD had hidden them.

27After the king burned the scroll containing the words that Baruch had written at Jeremiah's dictation, the word of the LORD came to Jeremiah: 28"Take another scroll and write on it all the words that were on the first scroll, which Jehoiakim king of Judah burned up. 29Also tell Jehoiakim king of Judah, 'This is what the LORD says: You burned that scroll and said, "Why did you write on it that the king of Babylon would certainly come and destroy this land and wipe from it both man and beast?" 30Therefore this is what the LORD says about Jehoiakim king of Judah: He will have no one to sit on the throne of David; his body will be thrown out and exposed to the heat by day and the frost by night. 31I will punish him and his children and his attendants for their wickedness; I will bring

on them and those living in Jerusalem and the people of Judah every disaster I pronounced against them, because they have not listened.' "

32So Jeremiah took another scroll and gave it to the scribe Baruch son of Neriah, and as Jeremiah dictated, Baruch wrote on it all the words of the scroll that Jehoiakim king of Judah had burned in the fire. And many similar words were added to them.

Jeremiah in Prison

37 Zedekiah son of Josiah was made king of Judah by Nebuchadnezzar king of Babylon; he reigned in place of Jehoiachin*a* son of Jehoiakim. 2Neither he nor his attendants nor the people of the land paid any attention to the words the LORD had spoken through Jeremiah the prophet.

3King Zedekiah, however, sent Jehukal son of Shelemiah with the priest Zephaniah son of Maaseiah to Jeremiah the prophet with this message: "Please pray to the LORD our God for us."

4Now Jeremiah was free to come and go among the people, for he had not yet been put in prison. 5Pharaoh's army had marched out of Egypt, and when the Babylonians*b* who were besieging Jerusalem heard the report about them, they withdrew from Jerusalem.

6Then the word of the LORD came to Jeremiah the prophet: 7"This is what the LORD, the God of Israel, says: Tell the king of Judah, who sent you to inquire of me, 'Pharaoh's army, which has marched out to support you, will go back to its own land, to Egypt. 8Then the Babylonians will return and attack this city; they will capture it and burn it down.'

9"This is what the LORD says: Do not deceive yourselves, thinking, 'The Babylonians will surely leave us.' They will not! 10Even if you were to defeat the entire Babylonian*c* army that is attacking you and only wounded men were left in their tents, they would come out and burn this city down."

BREAK **THROUGH!**

Ninth month
(JEREMIAH 36:22)
The ninth month of the lunar calendar was called Kislev. That would be from the middle of November to the middle of December in our solar calendar.

---

a 1 Hebrew *Koniah*, a variant of *Jehoiachin*   *b* 5 Or *Chaldeans*; also in verses 8, 9, 13 and 14   *c* 10 Or *Chaldean*; also in verse 11

¹¹After the Babylonian army had withdrawn from Jerusalem because of Pharaoh's army, ¹²Jeremiah started to leave the city to go to the territory of Benjamin to get his share of the property among the people there. ¹³But when he reached the Benjamin Gate, the captain of the guard, whose name was Irijah son of Shelemiah, the son of Hananiah, arrested him and said, "You are deserting to the Babylonians!"

¹⁴"That's not true!" Jeremiah said. "I am not deserting to the Babylonians." But Irijah would not listen to him; instead, he arrested Jeremiah and brought him to the officials. ¹⁵They were angry with Jeremiah and had him beaten and imprisoned in the house of Jonathan the secretary, which they had made into a prison.

¹⁶Jeremiah was put into a vaulted cell in a dungeon, where he remained a long time. ¹⁷Then King Zedekiah sent for him and had him brought to the palace, where he asked him privately, "Is there any word from the LORD?"

"Yes," Jeremiah replied, "you will be delivered into the hands of the king of Babylon."

¹⁸Then Jeremiah said to King Zedekiah, "What crime have I committed against you or your attendants or this people, that you have put me in prison? ¹⁹Where are your prophets who prophesied to you, 'The king of Babylon will not attack you or this land'? ²⁰But now, my lord the king, please listen. Let me bring my petition before you: Do not send me back to the house of Jonathan the secretary, or I will die there."

²¹King Zedekiah then gave orders for Jeremiah to be placed in the courtyard of the guard and given a loaf of bread from the street of the bakers each day until all the bread in the city was gone. So Jeremiah remained in the courtyard of the guard.

Jeremiah Thrown Into a Cistern

38 Shephatiah son of Mattan, Gedaliah son of Pashhur, Jehukal*ᵃ* son of Shelemiah, and Pashhur son of Malkijah heard what Jeremiah was telling all the people when he said, ²"This is what the LORD says: 'Whoever stays in this city will die by the sword, famine or plague, but whoever goes over to the Babylonians*ᵇ* will live. They will escape with their lives; they will live.' ³And this is what the LORD says: 'This city will certainly be given into the hands of the army of the king of Babylon, who will capture it.' "

⁴Then the officials said to the king, "This man should be put to death. He is discouraging the soldiers who are left in this city, as well as all the people, by the things he is saying to them. This man is not seeking the good of these people but their ruin."

⁵"He is in your hands," King Zedekiah answered. "The king can do nothing to oppose you."

⁶So they took Jeremiah and put him into the cistern of Malkijah, the king's son, which was in the courtyard of the guard. They lowered Jeremiah by ropes into the cistern; it had no water in it, only mud, and Jeremiah sank down into the mud.

⁷But Ebed-Melek, a Cushite,*ᶜ* an official*ᵈ* in the royal palace, heard that they had put Jeremiah into the cistern. While the king was sitting in the Benjamin Gate, ⁸Ebed-Melek went out of the palace and said to him, ⁹"My lord the king, these men have acted wickedly in all they have done to Jeremiah the prophet. They have thrown him into a cistern, where he will starve to death when there is no longer any bread in the city."

¹⁰Then the king commanded Ebed-Melek the Cushite, "Take thirty men from here with you and lift Jeremiah the prophet out of the cistern before he dies."

¹¹So Ebed-Melek took the men with him and went to a room under the treasury in the palace. He took some old rags and worn-out clothes from there and let them down with ropes to Jeremiah in the cistern. ¹²Ebed-Melek the Cushite said to Jeremiah, "Put these old rags and worn-out clothes under your arms to pad the ropes." Jeremiah did so, ¹³and they pulled

---

ᵃ 1 Hebrew *Jukal,* a variant of *Jehukal*   *ᵇ 2* Or *Chaldeans;* also in verses 18, 19 and 23   *ᶜ 7* Probably from the upper Nile region   *ᵈ 7* Or *a eunuch* him up with the ropes and lifted him out of the cistern. And Jeremiah remained in the courtyard of the guard.

Zedekiah Questions Jeremiah Again

¹⁴Then King Zedekiah sent for Jeremiah the prophet and had him brought to the third entrance to the temple of the LORD. "I am going to ask you something," the king said to Jeremiah. "Do not hide anything from me."

¹⁵Jeremiah said to Zedekiah, "If I give you an answer, will you not kill me? Even if I did give you counsel, you would not listen to me."

¹⁶But King Zedekiah swore this oath secretly to Jeremiah: "As surely as the LORD lives, who has given us breath, I will neither kill you nor hand you over to those who want to kill you."

¹⁷Then Jeremiah said to Zedekiah, "This is what the LORD God Almighty, the God of Israel, says: 'If you surrender to the officers of the king of Babylon, your life will be spared and this city will not be burned down; you and your family will live. ¹⁸But if you will not surrender to the officers of the king of Babylon, this city will be given into the hands of the Babylonians and they will burn it down; you yourself will not escape from them.' "

¹⁹King Zedekiah said to Jeremiah, "I am afraid of the Jews who have gone over to the Babylonians, for the Babylonians may hand me over to them and they will mistreat me."

²⁰"They will not hand you over," Jeremiah replied. "Obey the LORD by doing what I tell you. Then it will go well with you, and your life will be spared. ²¹But if you refuse to surrender, this is what the LORD has revealed to me: ²²All the women left in the palace of the king of Judah will be brought out to the officials of the king of Babylon. Those women will say to you:

" 'They misled you and overcame
　　you—
　　those trusted friends of yours.
Your feet are sunk in the mud;
　　your friends have deserted
　　you.'

²³"All your wives and children will be brought out to the Babylonians. You yourself will not escape from their hands but will be captured by the king of Babylon; and this city willᵃ be burned down."

²⁴Then Zedekiah said to Jeremiah, "Do not let anyone know about this conversation, or you may die. ²⁵If the officials hear that I talked with you, and they come to you and say, 'Tell us what you said to the king and what the king said to you; do not hide it from us or we will kill you,' ²⁶then tell them, 'I was pleading with the king not to send me back to Jonathan's house to die there.' "

²⁷All the officials did come to Jeremiah and question him, and he told them everything the king had ordered him to say. So they said no more to him, for no one had heard his conversation with the king. ²⁸And Jeremiah remained in the courtyard of the guard until the day Jerusalem was captured.

The Fall of Jerusalem

This is how Jerusalem was taken:
39 ¹In the ninth year of Zedekiah king of Judah, in the tenth month, Nebuchadnezzar king of Babylon marched against Jerusalem with his whole army and laid siege to it. ²And on the ninth day of the fourth month of Zedekiah's eleventh year, the city wall was broken through. ³Then all the officials of the king of Babylon came and took seats in the Middle Gate: Nergal-Sharezer of Samgar, Nebo-Sarsekim a chief officer, Nergal-Sharezer a high official and all the other officials of the king of Babylon. ⁴When Zedekiah king of Judah and all the soldiers saw them, they fled; they left the city at night by way of the king's garden, through the gate between the two walls, and headed toward the Arabah.ᵇ

⁵But the Babylonianᶜ army pursued them and overtook Zedekiah in the plains of Jericho. They captured him and took him to Nebuchadnezzar king of Babylon at Riblah in the land of Hamath, where he pronounced sentence on him. ⁶There at Riblah the king of Babylon slaughtered

---

ᵃ 23 Or and you will cause this city to　ᵇ 4 Or the Jordan Valley　ᶜ 5 Or Chaldean the sons of Zedekiah before his eyes and also killed all the nobles of Judah. [7]Then he put out Zedekiah's eyes and bound him with bronze shackles to take him to Babylon.

[8]The Babylonians[a] set fire to the royal palace and the houses of the people and broke down the walls of Jerusalem. [9]Nebuzaradan commander of the imperial guard carried into exile to Babylon the people who remained in the city, along with those who had gone over to him, and the rest of the people. [10]But Nebuzaradan the commander of the guard left behind in the land of Judah some of the poor people, who owned nothing; and at that time he gave them vineyards and fields.

[11]Now Nebuchadnezzar king of Babylon had given these orders about Jeremiah through Nebuzaradan commander of the imperial guard: [12]"Take him and look after him; don't harm him but do for him whatever he asks." [13]So Nebuzaradan the commander of the guard, Nebushazban a chief officer, Nergal-Sharezer a high official and all the other officers of the king of Babylon [14]sent and had Jeremiah taken out of the courtyard of the guard. They turned him over to Gedaliah son of Ahikam, the son of Shaphan, to take him back to his home. So he remained among his own people.

[15]While Jeremiah had been confined in the courtyard of the guard, the word of the LORD came to him: [16]"Go and tell Ebed-Melek the Cushite, 'This is what the LORD Almighty, the God of Israel, says: I am about to fulfill my words against this city — words concerning disaster, not prosperity. At that time they will be fulfilled before your eyes. [17]But I will rescue you on that day, declares the LORD; you will not be given into the hands of those you fear. [18]I will save you; you will not fall by the sword but will escape with your life, because you trust in me, declares the LORD.'"

Jeremiah Freed

40 The word came to Jeremiah from the LORD after Nebuzaradan commander of the imperial guard had released him at Ramah. He had found Jeremiah bound in chains among all the captives from Jerusalem and Judah who were being carried into exile to Babylon. [2]When the commander of the guard found Jeremiah, he said to him, "The LORD your God decreed this disaster for this place. [3]And now the LORD has brought it about; he has done just as he said he would. All this happened because you people sinned against the LORD and did not obey him. [4]But today I am freeing you from the chains on your wrists. Come with me to Babylon, if you like, and I will look after you; but if you do not want to, then don't come. Look, the whole country lies before you; go wherever you please." [5]However, before Jeremiah turned to go,[b] Nebuzaradan added, "Go back to Gedaliah son of Ahikam, the son of Shaphan, whom the king of Babylon has appointed over the towns of Judah, and live with him among the people, or go anywhere else you please."

Then the commander gave him provisions and a present and let him go. [6]So Jeremiah went to Gedaliah son of Ahikam at Mizpah and stayed with him among the people who were left behind in the land.

Gedaliah Assassinated

[7]When all the army officers and their men who were still in the open country heard that the king of Babylon had appointed Gedaliah son of Ahikam as governor over the land and had put him in charge of the men, women and children who were the poorest in the land and who had not been carried into exile to Babylon, [8]they came to Gedaliah at Mizpah — Ishmael son of Nethaniah, Johanan and Jonathan the sons of Kareah, Seraiah son of Tanhumeth, the sons of Ephai the Netophathite, and Jaazaniah[c] the son of the Maakathite, and their men. [9]Gedaliah son of Ahikam, the son of Shaphan, took an oath to reassure them and their men. "Do not be afraid to serve the Babylonians,[d]" he said. "Settle down in the land and serve the king of Babylon, and it will go well with you. [10]I myself will stay at Mizpah to rep-

[a] 8 Or *Chaldeans*   [b] 5 Or *Jeremiah answered*
[c] 8 Hebrew *Jezaniah,* a variant of *Jaazaniah*   [d] 9 Or *Chaldeans;* also in verse 10

resent you before the Babylonians who come to us, but you are to harvest the wine, summer fruit and olive oil, and put them in your storage jars, and live in the towns you have taken over."

¹¹When all the Jews in Moab, Ammon, Edom and all the other countries heard that the king of Babylon had left a remnant in Judah and had appointed Gedaliah son of Ahikam, the son of Shaphan, as governor over them, ¹²they all came back to the land of Judah, to Gedaliah at Mizpah, from all the countries where they had been scattered. And they harvested an abundance of wine and summer fruit.

¹³Johanan son of Kareah and all the army officers still in the open country came to Gedaliah at Mizpah ¹⁴and said to him, "Don't you know that Baalis king of the Ammonites has sent Ishmael son of Nethaniah to take your life?" But Gedaliah son of Ahikam did not believe them.

¹⁵Then Johanan son of Kareah said privately to Gedaliah in Mizpah, "Let me go and kill Ishmael son of Nethaniah, and no one will know it. Why should he take your life and cause all the Jews who are gathered around you to be scattered and the remnant of Judah to perish?"

¹⁶But Gedaliah son of Ahikam said to Johanan son of Kareah, "Don't do such a thing! What you are saying about Ishmael is not true."

41 In the seventh month Ishmael son of Nethaniah, the son of Elishama, who was of royal blood and had been one of the king's officers, came with ten men to Gedaliah son of Ahikam at Mizpah. While they were eating together there, ²Ishmael son of Nethaniah and the ten men who were with him got up and struck down Gedaliah son of Ahikam, the son of Shaphan, with the sword, killing the one whom the king of Babylon had appointed as governor over the land. ³Ishmael also killed all the men of Judah who were with Gedaliah at Mizpah, as well as the Babylonianᵃ soldiers who were there.

⁴The day after Gedaliah's assassination, before anyone knew about it, ⁵eighty men who had shaved off their beards, torn their clothes and cut themselves came from Shechem, Shiloh and Samaria, bringing grain offerings and incense with them to the house of the LORD. ⁶Ishmael son of Nethaniah went out from Mizpah to meet them, weeping as he went. When he met them, he said, "Come to Gedaliah son of Ahikam." ⁷When they went into the city, Ishmael son of Nethaniah and the men who were with him slaughtered them and threw them into a cistern. ⁸But ten of them said to Ishmael, "Don't kill us! We have wheat and barley, olive oil and honey, hidden in a field." So he let them alone and did not kill them with the others. ⁹Now the cistern where he threw all the bodies of the men he had killed along with Gedaliah was the one King Asa had made as part of his defense against Baasha king of Israel. Ishmael son of Nethaniah filled it with the dead.

¹⁰Ishmael made captives of all the rest of the people who were in Mizpah—the king's daughters along with all the others who were left there, over whom

THE

SCENE

MIZPAH

(JEREMIAH 40:6)

Read more about Mizpah in Genesis 31:48–49.

ᵃ 3 Or *Chaldean*

Nebuzaradan commander of the imperial guard had appointed Gedaliah son of Ahikam. Ishmael son of Nethaniah took them captive and set out to cross over to the Ammonites.

[11] When Johanan son of Kareah and all the army officers who were with him heard about all the crimes Ishmael son of Nethaniah had committed, [12] they took all their men and went to fight Ishmael son of Nethaniah. They caught up with him near the great pool in Gibeon. [13] When all the people Ishmael had with him saw Johanan son of Kareah and the army officers who were with him, they were glad. [14] All the people Ishmael had taken captive at Mizpah turned and went over to Johanan son of Kareah. [15] But Ishmael son of Nethaniah and eight of his men escaped from Johanan and fled to the Ammonites.

Flight to Egypt

[16] Then Johanan son of Kareah and all the army officers who were with him led away all the people of Mizpah who had survived, whom Johanan had recovered from Ishmael son of Nethaniah after Ishmael had assassinated Gedaliah son of Ahikam—the soldiers, women, children and court officials he had recovered from Gibeon. [17] And they went on, stopping at Geruth Kimham near Bethlehem on their way to Egypt [18] to escape the Babylonians.[a] They were afraid of them because Ishmael son of Nethaniah had killed Gedaliah son of Ahikam, whom the king of Babylon had appointed as governor over the land.

42 Then all the army officers, including Johanan son of Kareah and Jezaniah[b] son of Hoshaiah, and all the people from the least to the greatest approached [2] Jeremiah the prophet and said to him, "Please hear our petition and pray to the LORD your God for this entire remnant. For as you now see, though we were once many, now only a few are left. [3] Pray that the LORD your God will tell us where we should go and what we should do."

[4] "I have heard you," replied Jeremiah the prophet. "I will certainly pray to the LORD your God as you have requested; I will tell you everything the LORD says and will keep nothing back from you."

[5] Then they said to Jeremiah, "May the LORD be a true and faithful witness against us if we do not act in accordance with everything the LORD your God sends you to tell us. [6] Whether it is favorable or unfavorable, we will obey the LORD our God, to whom we are sending you, so that it will go well with us, for we will obey the LORD our God."

[7] Ten days later the word of the LORD came to Jeremiah. [8] So he called together Johanan son of Kareah and all the army officers who were with him and all the people from the least to the greatest. [9] He said to them, "This is what the LORD, the God of Israel, to whom you sent me to present your petition, says: [10] 'If you stay in this land, I will build you up and not tear you down; I will plant you and not uproot you, for I have relented concerning the disaster I have inflicted on you. [11] Do not be afraid of the king of Babylon, whom you now fear. Do not be afraid of him, declares the LORD, for I am with you and will save you and deliver you from his hands. [12] I will show you compassion so that he will have compassion on you and restore you to your land.'

[13] "However, if you say, 'We will not stay in this land,' and so disobey the LORD your God, [14] and if you say, 'No, we will go and live in Egypt, where we will not see war or hear the trumpet or be hungry for bread,' [15] then hear the word of the LORD, you remnant of Judah. This is what the LORD Almighty, the God of Israel, says: 'If you are determined to go to Egypt and you do go to settle there, [16] then the sword you fear will overtake you there, and the famine you dread will follow you into Egypt, and there you will die. [17] Indeed, all who are determined to go to Egypt to settle there will die by the sword, famine and plague; not one of them will survive or escape the disaster I will bring on them.' [18] This is what the LORD Almighty, the God of Israel, says: 'As my anger and wrath have been poured out on those who lived in Jerusalem, so will my wrath be poured out on

---

[a] 18 Or *Chaldeans*   [b] 1 Hebrew; Septuagint (see also 43:2) *Azariah*

you when you go to Egypt. You will be a curse[a] and an object of horror, a curse[a] and an object of reproach; you will never see this place again.'

19 "Remnant of Judah, the Lord has told you, 'Do not go to Egypt.' Be sure of this: I warn you today 20 that you made a fatal mistake when you sent me to the Lord your God and said, 'Pray to the Lord our God for us; tell us everything he says and we will do it.' 21 I have told you today, but you still have not obeyed the Lord your God in all he sent me to tell you. 22 So now, be sure of this: You will die by the sword, famine and plague in the place where you want to go to settle.' "

43 When Jeremiah had finished telling the people all the words of the Lord their God—everything the Lord had sent him to tell them— 2 Azariah son of Hoshaiah and Johanan son of Kareah and all the arrogant men said to Jeremiah, "You are lying! The Lord our God has not sent you to say, 'You must not go to Egypt to settle there.' 3 But Baruch son of Neriah is inciting you against us to hand us over to the Babylonians,[b] so they may kill us or carry us into exile to Babylon."

4 So Johanan son of Kareah and all the army officers and all the people disobeyed the Lord's command to stay in the land of Judah. 5 Instead, Johanan son of Kareah and all the army officers led away all the remnant of Judah who had come back to live in the land of Judah from all the nations where they had been scattered. 6 They also led away all those whom Nebuzaradan commander of the imperial guard had left with Gedaliah son of Ahikam, the son of Shaphan—the men, the women, the children and the king's daughters. And they took Jeremiah the prophet and Baruch son of Neriah along with them. 7 So they entered Egypt in disobedience to the Lord and went as far as Tahpanhes.

8 In Tahpanhes the word of the Lord came to Jeremiah: 9 "While the Jews are watching, take some large stones with you and bury them in clay in the brick pavement at the entrance to Pharaoh's palace in Tahpanhes. 10 Then say to them, 'This is what the Lord Almighty, the God

of Israel, says: I will send for my servant Nebuchadnezzar king of Babylon, and I will set his throne over these stones I have buried here; he will spread his royal canopy above them. 11 He will come and attack Egypt, bringing death to those destined for death, captivity to those destined for captivity, and the sword to those destined for the sword. 12 He will set fire to the temples of the gods of Egypt; he will burn their temples and take their gods captive. As a shepherd picks his garment clean of lice, so he will pick Egypt clean and depart. 13 There in the temple of the sun[c] in Egypt he will demolish the sacred pillars and will burn down the temples of the gods of Egypt.' "

Disaster Because of Idolatry

44 This word came to Jeremiah concerning all the Jews living in Lower Egypt—in Migdol, Tahpanhes and Memphis—and in Upper Egypt: 2 "This is what the Lord Almighty, the God of Israel, says: You saw the great disaster I brought on Jerusalem and on all the towns of Judah. Today they lie deserted and in ruins 3 because of the evil they have done. They aroused my anger by burning incense to and worshiping other gods that neither they nor you nor your ancestors ever knew. 4 Again and again I sent my servants the prophets, who said, 'Do not do this detestable thing that I hate!' 5 But they did not listen or pay attention; they did not turn from their wickedness or stop burning incense to other gods. 6 Therefore, my fierce anger was poured out; it raged against the towns of Judah and the streets of Jerusalem and made them the desolate ruins they are today.

7 "Now this is what the Lord God Almighty, the God of Israel, says: Why bring such great disaster on yourselves by cutting off from Judah the men and women, the children and infants, and so leave yourselves without a remnant? 8 Why arouse my anger with what your hands have made, burning incense to other gods in Egypt, where you have come to live?

---

a 18 That is, your name will be used in cursing (see 29:22); or, others will see that you are cursed.　　*b 3* Or *Chaldeans*　　*c 13* Or *in Heliopolis*

You will destroy yourselves and make yourselves a curse[a] and an object of reproach among all the nations on earth. [9]Have you forgotten the wickedness committed by your ancestors and by the kings and queens of Judah and the wickedness committed by you and your wives in the land of Judah and the streets of Jerusalem? [10]To this day they have not humbled themselves or shown reverence, nor have they followed my law and the decrees I set before you and your ancestors.

[11]"Therefore this is what the LORD Almighty, the God of Israel, says: I am determined to bring disaster on you and to destroy all Judah. [12]I will take away the remnant of Judah who were determined to go to Egypt to settle there. They will all perish in Egypt; they will fall by the sword or die from famine. From the least to the greatest, they will die by sword or famine. They will become a curse and an object of horror, a curse and an object of reproach. [13]I will punish those who live in Egypt with the sword, famine and plague, as I punished Jerusalem. [14]None of the remnant of Judah who have gone to live in Egypt will escape or survive to return to the land of Judah, to which they long to return and live; none will return except a few fugitives."

[15]Then all the men who knew that their wives were burning incense to other gods, along with all the women who were present—a large assembly—and all the people living in Lower and Upper Egypt, said to Jeremiah, [16]"We will not listen to the message you have spoken to us in the name of the LORD! [17]We will certainly do everything we said we would: We will burn incense to the Queen of Heaven and will pour out drink offerings to her just as we and our ancestors, our kings and our officials did in the towns of Judah and in the streets of Jerusalem. At that time we had plenty of food and were well off and suffered no harm. [18]But ever since we stopped burning incense to the Queen of Heaven and pouring out drink offerings to her, we have had nothing and have been perishing by sword and famine."

[19]The women added, "When we burned incense to the Queen of Heaven and poured out drink offerings to her, did not our husbands know that we were making cakes impressed with her image and pouring out drink offerings to her?"

[20]Then Jeremiah said to all the people, both men and women, who were answering him, [21]"Did not the LORD remember and call to mind the incense burned in the towns of Judah and the streets of Jerusalem by you and your ancestors, your kings and your officials and the people of the land? [22]When the LORD could no longer endure your wicked actions and the detestable things you did, your land became a curse and a desolate waste without inhabitants, as it is today. [23]Because you have burned incense and have sinned against the LORD and have not obeyed him or followed his law or his decrees or his stipulations, this disaster has come upon you, as you now see."

[24]Then Jeremiah said to all the people, including the women, "Hear the word of the LORD, all you people of Judah in Egypt. [25]This is what the LORD Almighty, the God of Israel, says: You and your wives have done what you said you would do when you promised, 'We will certainly carry out the vows we made to burn incense and pour out drink offerings to the Queen of Heaven.'

"Go ahead then, do what you promised! Keep your vows! [26]But hear the word of the LORD, all you Jews living in Egypt: 'I swear by my great name,' says the LORD, 'that no one from Judah living anywhere in Egypt will ever again invoke my name or swear, "As surely as the Sovereign LORD lives." [27]For I am watching over them for harm, not for good; the Jews in Egypt will perish by sword and famine until they are all destroyed. [28]Those who escape the sword and return to the land of Judah from Egypt will be very few. Then the whole remnant of Judah who came to live in Egypt will know whose word will stand—mine or theirs.

[29]" 'This will be the sign to you that I will punish you in this place,' declares the LORD, 'so that you will know that my

---

[a] 8 That is, your name will be used in cursing (see 29:22); or, others will see that you are cursed; also in verse 12; similarly in verse 22.

threats of harm against you will surely stand.' ³⁰This is what the LORD says: 'I am going to deliver Pharaoh Hophra king of Egypt into the hands of his enemies who want to kill him, just as I gave Zedekiah king of Judah into the hands of Nebuchadnezzar king of Babylon, the enemy who wanted to kill him.' "

A Message to Baruch

45 When Baruch son of Neriah wrote on a scroll the words Jeremiah the prophet dictated in the fourth year of Jehoiakim son of Josiah king of Judah, Jeremiah said this to Baruch: ²"This is what the LORD, the God of Israel, says to you, Baruch: ³You said, 'Woe to me! The LORD has added sorrow to my pain; I am worn out with groaning and find no rest.' ⁴But the LORD has told me to say to you, 'This is what the LORD says: I will overthrow what I have built and uproot what I have planted, throughout the earth. ⁵Should you then seek great things for yourself? Do not seek them. For I will bring disaster on all people, declares the LORD, but wherever you go I will let you escape with your life.' "

A Message About Egypt

46 This is the word of the LORD that came to Jeremiah the prophet concerning the nations:

²Concerning Egypt:

This is the message against the army of Pharaoh Necho king of Egypt, which was defeated at Carchemish on the Euphrates River by Nebuchadnezzar king of Babylon in the fourth year of Jehoiakim son of Josiah king of Judah:

³ "Prepare your shields, both large and
        small,
    and march out for battle!
⁴ Harness the horses,
    mount the steeds!
Take your positions
    with helmets on!
Polish your spears,
    put on your armor!
⁵ What do I see?
    They are terrified,

they are retreating,
    their warriors are defeated.
They flee in haste
    without looking back,
    and there is terror on every
        side,"
                declares the LORD.
⁶ "The swift cannot flee
    nor the strong escape.
In the north by the River Euphrates
    they stumble and fall.

⁷ "Who is this that rises like the
        Nile,
    like rivers of surging waters?
⁸ Egypt rises like the Nile,
    like rivers of surging waters.
She says, 'I will rise and cover the
        earth;
    I will destroy cities and their
        people.'
⁹ Charge, you horses!
    Drive furiously, you charioteers!
March on, you warriors—men of
        Cush*ᵃ* and Put who carry
        shields,
    men of Lydia who draw the bow.
¹⁰ But that day belongs to the Lord, the
        LORD Almighty—
    a day of vengeance, for vengeance
        on his foes.
The sword will devour till it is
        satisfied,
    till it has quenched its thirst with
        blood.
For the Lord, the LORD Almighty, will
        offer sacrifice
    in the land of the north by the River
        Euphrates.

¹¹ "Go up to Gilead and get balm,
    Virgin Daughter Egypt.
But you try many medicines in vain;
    there is no healing for you.
¹² The nations will hear of your shame;
    your cries will fill the earth.
One warrior will stumble over another;
    both will fall down together."

¹³This is the message the LORD spoke to Jeremiah the prophet about the coming of Nebuchadnezzar king of Babylon to attack Egypt:

ᵃ 9 That is, the upper Nile region

¹⁴ "Announce this in Egypt, and proclaim
      it in Migdol;
  proclaim it also in Memphis and
      Tahpanhes:
  'Take your positions and get ready,
      for the sword devours those around
      you.'
¹⁵ Why will your warriors be laid low?
  They cannot stand, for the LORD will
      push them down.
¹⁶ They will stumble repeatedly;
      they will fall over each other.
  They will say, 'Get up, let us go back
      to our own people and our native
      lands,
      away from the sword of the
      oppressor.'
¹⁷ There they will exclaim,
  'Pharaoh king of Egypt is only a loud
      noise;
      he has missed his opportunity.'

¹⁸ "As surely as I live," declares the
      King,
  whose name is the LORD Almighty,
  "one will come who is like Tabor
      among the mountains,
      like Carmel by the sea.
¹⁹ Pack your belongings for exile,
      you who live in Egypt,
  for Memphis will be laid waste
      and lie in ruins without inhabitant.

²⁰ "Egypt is a beautiful heifer,
      but a gadfly is coming
      against her from the north.
²¹ The mercenaries in her ranks
      are like fattened calves.
  They too will turn and flee together,
      they will not stand their ground,
  for the day of disaster is coming upon
      them,
      the time for them to be punished.
²² Egypt will hiss like a fleeing serpent
      as the enemy advances in force;
  they will come against her with
      axes,
      like men who cut down trees.
²³ They will chop down her forest,"
                        declares the LORD,
  "dense though it be.
  They are more numerous than
      locusts,
      they cannot be counted.

²⁴ Daughter Egypt will be put to shame,
      given into the hands of the people
      of the north."

²⁵ The LORD Almighty, the God of Israel,
says: "I am about to bring punishment
on Amon god of Thebes, on Pharaoh, on
Egypt and her gods and her kings, and on
those who rely on Pharaoh. ²⁶ I will give
them into the hands of those who want
to kill them—Nebuchadnezzar king of
Babylon and his officers. Later, however,
Egypt will be inhabited as in times past,"
declares the LORD.

²⁷ "Do not be afraid, Jacob my
      servant;
  do not be dismayed, Israel.
  I will surely save you out of a distant
      place,
      your descendants from the land of
      their exile.
  Jacob will again have peace and
      security,
      and no one will make him afraid.
²⁸ Do not be afraid, Jacob my
      servant,
  for I am with you," declares the
      LORD.
  "Though I completely destroy all the
      nations
      among which I scatter you,
  I will not completely destroy
      you.
  I will discipline you but only in due
      measure;
  I will not let you go entirely
      unpunished."

A Message About the Philistines

47 This is the word of the LORD that
came to Jeremiah the prophet concerning the Philistines before Pharaoh attacked Gaza:

² This is what the LORD says:

  "See how the waters are rising in the
      north;
  they will become an overflowing
      torrent.
  They will overflow the land and
      everything in it,
      the towns and those who live in
      them.

The people will cry out;
   all who dwell in the land will wail
3 at the sound of the hooves of
      galloping steeds,
   at the noise of enemy chariots
      and the rumble of their
         wheels.
Parents will not turn to help their
      children;
   their hands will hang limp.
4 For the day has come
   to destroy all the Philistines
and to remove all survivors
   who could help Tyre and Sidon.
The LORD is about to destroy the
      Philistines,
   the remnant from the coasts of
      Caphtor.*a*
5 Gaza will shave her head in
      mourning;
   Ashkelon will be silenced.
You remnant on the plain,
   how long will you cut
      yourselves?

6 " 'Alas, sword of the LORD,
   how long till you rest?
Return to your sheath;
   cease and be still.'

Philistines
(JEREMIAH 47)
See who they were in Judges 14 – 15.

GAZA

(JEREMIAH 47:1)
Read what it says in Judges 1:18.

7 But how can it rest
   when the LORD has commanded it,
when he has ordered it
   to attack Ashkelon and the coast?"

A Message About Moab

48 Concerning Moab:

This is what the LORD Almighty, the God
of Israel, says:

"Woe to Nebo, for it will be ruined.
   Kiriathaim will be disgraced and
      captured;
   the stronghold*b* will be disgraced
      and shattered.
2 Moab will be praised no more;
   in Heshbon*c* people will plot her
      downfall:
   'Come, let us put an end to that
      nation.'
You, the people of Madmen,*d* will also
      be silenced;
   the sword will pursue you.

---

a 4 That is, Crete   *b 1* Or *captured; / Misgab*   *c 2* The
Hebrew for *Heshbon* sounds like the Hebrew for *plot*.
d 2 The name of the Moabite town *Madmen* sounds like
the Hebrew for *be silenced*.

BREAK THROUGH!

What did shaving their heads mean?

(JEREMIAH 47:5; 48:37)

Have you noticed that a lot of people shave their heads and go around looking bald now? Well, that's not what it's talking about. The reason they did that in Jeremiah's time was to show that they were suffering a lot because someone had died.

³ Cries of anguish arise from
        Horonaim,
    cries of great havoc and
        destruction.
⁴ Moab will be broken;
    her little ones will cry out.ᵃ
⁵ They go up the hill to Luhith,
    weeping bitterly as they go;
on the road down to Horonaim
    anguished cries over the
        destruction are heard.
⁶ Flee! Run for your lives;
    become like a bushᵇ in the desert.
⁷ Since you trust in your deeds and
        riches,
    you too will be taken captive,
and Chemosh will go into exile,
    together with his priests and
        officials.
⁸ The destroyer will come against every
        town,
    and not a town will escape.

The valley will be ruined
    and the plateau destroyed,
    because the Lᴏʀᴅ has spoken.
⁹ Put salt on Moab,
    for she will be laid wasteᶜ;
her towns will become desolate,
    with no one to live in them.

¹⁰ "A curse on anyone who is lax in doing
        the Lᴏʀᴅ's work!
    A curse on anyone who keeps their
        sword from bloodshed!

¹¹ "Moab has been at rest from youth,
    like wine left on its dregs,
not poured from one jar to
        another—
    she has not gone into exile.
So she tastes as she did,
    and her aroma is unchanged.
¹² But days are coming,"
    declares the Lᴏʀᴅ,
"when I will send men who pour from
        pitchers,
    and they will pour her out;
they will empty her pitchers
    and smash her jars.
¹³ Then Moab will be ashamed of
        Chemosh,
    as Israel was ashamed
    when they trusted in Bethel.

¹⁴ "How can you say, 'We are warriors,
    men valiant in battle'?
¹⁵ Moab will be destroyed and her towns
        invaded;
    her finest young men will go down
        in the slaughter,"
declares the King, whose name is
    the Lᴏʀᴅ Almighty.
¹⁶ "The fall of Moab is at hand;
    her calamity will come quickly.
¹⁷ Mourn for her, all who live around
        her,
    all who know her fame;
say, 'How broken is the mighty
        scepter,
    how broken the glorious staff!'

¹⁸ "Come down from your glory
    and sit on the parched ground,
    you inhabitants of Daughter
        Dibon,

ᵃ 4 Hebrew; Septuagint / *proclaim it to Zoar*   ᵇ 6 Or like
Aroer   ᶜ 9 Or *Give wings to Moab, / for she will fly away*

for the one who destroys Moab
    will come up against you
    and ruin your fortified cities.
¹⁹ Stand by the road and watch,
    you who live in Aroer.
Ask the man fleeing and the woman
        escaping,
    ask them, 'What has happened?'
²⁰ Moab is disgraced, for she is
        shattered.
    Wail and cry out!
    Announce by the Arnon
    that Moab is destroyed.
²¹ Judgment has come to the plateau—
    to Holon, Jahzah and Mephaath,
²² to Dibon, Nebo and Beth
        Diblathaim,
²³ to Kiriathaim, Beth Gamul and Beth
        Meon,
²⁴ to Kerioth and Bozrah—
    to all the towns of Moab, far and
        near.
²⁵ Moab's horn ᵃ is cut off;
    her arm is broken,"
                declares the LORD.

²⁶ "Make her drunk,
    for she has defied the LORD.
Let Moab wallow in her vomit;
    let her be an object of ridicule.
²⁷ Was not Israel the object of your
        ridicule?
Was she caught among thieves,
    that you shake your head in scorn
    whenever you speak of her?
²⁸ Abandon your towns and dwell among
        the rocks,
    you who live in Moab.
Be like a dove that makes its nest
    at the mouth of a cave.

²⁹ "We have heard of Moab's pride—
    how great is her arrogance!—
of her insolence, her pride, her
        conceit
    and the haughtiness of her heart.
³⁰ I know her insolence but it is futile,"
                declares the LORD,
    "and her boasts accomplish
        nothing.
³¹ Therefore I wail over Moab,
    for all Moab I cry out,
    I moan for the people of Kir
        Hareseth.

³² I weep for you, as Jazer weeps,
    you vines of Sibmah.
Your branches spread as far as the
        sea ᵇ;
    they reached as far as ᶜ Jazer.
The destroyer has fallen
    on your ripened fruit and grapes.
³³ Joy and gladness are gone
    from the orchards and fields of
        Moab.
I have stopped the flow of wine from
        the presses;
    no one treads them with shouts of
        joy.
Although there are shouts,
    they are not shouts of joy.

³⁴ "The sound of their cry rises
    from Heshbon to Elealeh and
        Jahaz,
from Zoar as far as Horonaim and
        Eglath Shelishiyah,
    for even the waters of Nimrim are
        dried up.
³⁵ In Moab I will put an end
    to those who make offerings on the
        high places
    and burn incense to their gods,"
                declares the LORD.
³⁶ "So my heart laments for Moab like
        the music of a pipe;
    it laments like a pipe for the people
        of Kir Hareseth.
The wealth they acquired is gone.
³⁷ Every head is shaved
    and every beard cut off;
every hand is slashed
    and every waist is covered with
        sackcloth.
³⁸ On all the roofs in Moab
    and in the public squares
there is nothing but mourning,
    for I have broken Moab
    like a jar that no one wants,"
                declares the LORD.
³⁹ "How shattered she is! How they wail!
    How Moab turns her back in shame!
Moab has become an object of
        ridicule,
    an object of horror to all those
        around her."

ᵃ 25 *Horn* here symbolizes strength.   ᵇ 32 Probably the
Dead Sea   ᶜ 32 Two Hebrew manuscripts and
Septuagint; most Hebrew manuscripts *as far as the Sea of*

⁴⁰This is what the LORD says:

"Look! An eagle is swooping down,
   spreading its wings over Moab.
⁴¹Kerioth^a will be captured
   and the strongholds taken.
In that day the hearts of Moab's
         warriors
   will be like the heart of a woman in
      labor.
⁴²Moab will be destroyed as a nation
   because she defied the LORD.
⁴³Terror and pit and snare await you,
   you people of Moab,"
                  declares the LORD.
⁴⁴"Whoever flees from the terror
   will fall into a pit,
whoever climbs out of the pit
   will be caught in a snare;
for I will bring on Moab
   the year of her punishment,"
                  declares the LORD.
⁴⁵"In the shadow of Heshbon
   the fugitives stand helpless,
for a fire has gone out from Heshbon,
   a blaze from the midst of Sihon;
it burns the foreheads of Moab,
   the skulls of the noisy boasters.
⁴⁶Woe to you, Moab!
   The people of Chemosh are
      destroyed;
your sons are taken into exile
   and your daughters into captivity.

⁴⁷"Yet I will restore the fortunes of Moab
   in days to come,"
                  declares the LORD.

Here ends the judgment on Moab.

A Message About Ammon

49 Concerning the Ammonites:

This is what the LORD says:

"Has Israel no sons?
   Has Israel no heir?
Why then has Molek^b taken
      possession of Gad?
   Why do his people live in its towns?
²But the days are coming,"
   declares the LORD,
"when I will sound the battle cry
   against Rabbah of the Ammonites;

it will become a mound of ruins,
   and its surrounding villages will be
      set on fire.
Then Israel will drive out
   those who drove her out,"
                  says the LORD.
³"Wail, Heshbon, for Ai is destroyed!
   Cry out, you inhabitants of Rabbah!
Put on sackcloth and mourn;
   rush here and there inside the
      walls,
for Molek will go into exile,
   together with his priests and
      officials.
⁴Why do you boast of your valleys,
   boast of your valleys so fruitful?
Unfaithful Daughter Ammon,
   you trust in your riches and say,
   'Who will attack me?'
⁵I will bring terror on you
   from all those around you,"
                  declares the Lord,
                  the LORD Almighty.
"Every one of you will be driven away,
   and no one will gather the fugitives.

⁶"Yet afterward, I will restore the
      fortunes of the Ammonites,"
                  declares the LORD.

A Message About Edom

⁷Concerning Edom:

This is what the LORD Almighty says:

"Is there no longer wisdom in Teman?
   Has counsel perished from the
      prudent?
   Has their wisdom decayed?
⁸Turn and flee, hide in deep caves,
   you who live in Dedan,
for I will bring disaster on Esau
   at the time when I punish him.
⁹If grape pickers came to you,
   would they not leave a few grapes?
If thieves came during the night,
   would they not steal only as much
      as they wanted?
¹⁰But I will strip Esau bare;
   I will uncover his hiding places,
      so that he cannot conceal himself.
His armed men are destroyed,
   also his allies and neighbors,

---

^a 41 Or The cities   ^b 1 Or their king; also in verse 3

so there is no one to say,
11 'Leave your fatherless children; I will
    keep them alive.
Your widows too can depend on
    me.' "

12 This is what the Lord says: "If those
who do not deserve to drink the cup must
drink it, why should you go unpunished?
You will not go unpunished, but must
drink it. 13 I swear by myself," declares
the Lord, "that Bozrah will become a ruin
and a curse,[a] an object of horror and reproach; and all its towns will be in ruins
forever."

14 I have heard a message from the
    Lord;
    an envoy was sent to the nations to
      say,
"Assemble yourselves to attack it!
    Rise up for battle!"

15 "Now I will make you small among the
    nations,
    despised by mankind.
16 The terror you inspire
    and the pride of your heart have
      deceived you,
you who live in the clefts of the rocks,
    who occupy the heights of the hill.
Though you build your nest as high as
      the eagle's,
    from there I will bring you down,"
                    declares the Lord.
17 "Edom will become an object of
    horror;
    all who pass by will be appalled and
      will scoff
    because of all its wounds.
18 As Sodom and Gomorrah were
    overthrown,
    along with their neighboring
      towns,"
                says the Lord,
"so no one will live there;
    no people will dwell in it.

19 "Like a lion coming up from Jordan's
    thickets
    to a rich pastureland,
I will chase Edom from its land in an
    instant.
Who is the chosen one I will appoint
    for this?

Who is like me and who can challenge
    me?
And what shepherd can stand
    against me?"

20 Therefore, hear what the Lord has
    planned against Edom,
what he has purposed against
    those who live in Teman:
The young of the flock will be dragged
    away;
    their pasture will be appalled at
      their fate.
21 At the sound of their fall the earth will
    tremble;
    their cry will resound to the Red
      Sea.[b]
22 Look! An eagle will soar and swoop
    down,
    spreading its wings over
      Bozrah.
In that day the hearts of Edom's
    warriors

THE SCENE

SODOM AND GOMORRAH

(JEREMIAH 49:18)

*Learn about these two cities in
Genesis 19:1–29.*

THE SCENE

DAMASCUS

(JEREMIAH 49:23)

*See what it says in Song of Songs 7:4;
Isaiah 7:8 and 17:1–3; and Amos 1:3.*

will be like the heart of a woman in labor.

A Message About Damascus

²³Concerning Damascus:

"Hamath and Arpad are dismayed,
    for they have heard bad news.
They are disheartened,
    troubled like[a] the restless sea.
²⁴Damascus has become feeble,
    she has turned to flee
    and panic has gripped her;
anguish and pain have seized her,
    pain like that of a woman in
        labor.
²⁵Why has the city of renown not been
        abandoned,
    the town in which I delight?
²⁶Surely, her young men will fall in the
        streets;
    all her soldiers will be silenced in
        that day,"
            declares the LORD Almighty.
²⁷"I will set fire to the walls of
        Damascus;

it will consume the fortresses of
    Ben-Hadad."

A Message About Kedar and Hazor

²⁸Concerning Kedar and the kingdoms
of Hazor, which Nebuchadnezzar king of
Babylon attacked:

This is what the LORD says:

"Arise, and attack Kedar
    and destroy the people of the East.
²⁹Their tents and their flocks will be
        taken;
    their shelters will be carried off
    with all their goods and camels.
People will shout to them,
    'Terror on every side!'
³⁰"Flee quickly away!
    Stay in deep caves, you who live in
        Hazor,"
            declares the LORD.
"Nebuchadnezzar king of Babylon has
        plotted against you;
    he has devised a plan against you.

³¹"Arise and attack a nation at ease,
    which lives in confidence,"
            declares the LORD,
"a nation that has neither gates nor
        bars;
    its people live far from danger.
³²Their camels will become plunder,
    and their large herds will be spoils
        of war.
I will scatter to the winds those who
    are in distant places[b]
and will bring disaster on them from
    every side,"
            declares the LORD.
³³"Hazor will become a haunt of jackals,
    a desolate place forever.
No one will live there;
    no people will dwell in it."

A Message About Elam

³⁴This is the word of the LORD that came
to Jeremiah the prophet concerning Elam,
early in the reign of Zedekiah king of Judah:

³⁵This is what the LORD Almighty says:

---

*a 23 Hebrew on or by   b 32 Or who clip the hair by their
foreheads*

"See, I will break the bow of Elam,
   the mainstay of their might.
³⁶ I will bring against Elam the four
     winds
   from the four quarters of heaven;
I will scatter them to the four
     winds,
   and there will not be a nation
   where Elam's exiles do not go.
³⁷ I will shatter Elam before their foes,
   before those who want to kill
     them;
I will bring disaster on them,
   even my fierce anger,"
               declares the Lord.
"I will pursue them with the sword
   until I have made an end of them.
³⁸ I will set my throne in Elam
   and destroy her king and officials,"
               declares the Lord.

³⁹ "Yet I will restore the fortunes of Elam
   in days to come,"
               declares the Lord.

A Message About Babylon

50 This is the word the Lord spoke through Jeremiah the prophet concerning Babylon and the land of the Babylonians^a:

² "Announce and proclaim among the
     nations,
   lift up a banner and proclaim it;
   keep nothing back, but say,
'Babylon will be captured;
   Bel will be put to shame,
   Marduk filled with terror.
Her images will be put to shame
   and her idols filled with terror.'
³ A nation from the north will attack her
   and lay waste her land.
No one will live in it;
   both people and animals will flee
     away.

⁴ "In those days, at that time,"
   declares the Lord,
"the people of Israel and the people
     of Judah together
will go in tears to seek the Lord
   their God.
⁵ They will ask the way to Zion
   and turn their faces toward it.

BREAKTHROUGH!

Who were Bel and Marduk?

(JEREMIAH 50:2; 51:44)

They were names of a god the Babylonians had invented. We told you these people lived in Mesopotamia, the land between two rivers. Marduk was the Babylonians' most important god. For a long time, he was considered the most powerful god. Sometimes they called him Bel, which means "Lord."

They will come and bind themselves to
   the Lord
   in an everlasting covenant
   that will not be forgotten.

⁶ "My people have been lost sheep;
   their shepherds have led them
     astray
   and caused them to roam on the
     mountains.
They wandered over mountain and hill
   and forgot their own resting place.
⁷ Whoever found them devoured
     them;
   their enemies said, 'We are not
     guilty,
for they sinned against the Lord, their
     verdant pasture,
   the Lord, the hope of their
     ancestors.'

^a 1 Or *Chaldeans*; also in verses 8, 25, 35 and 45

8 "Flee out of Babylon;
  leave the land of the Babylonians,
  and be like the goats that lead the
    flock.
9 For I will stir up and bring against
    Babylon
  an alliance of great nations from
    the land of the north.
They will take up their positions
    against her,
  and from the north she will be
    captured.
Their arrows will be like skilled
    warriors
  who do not return empty-handed.
10 So Babylonia*a* will be plundered;
  all who plunder her will have their
    fill,"
            declares the LORD.

11 "Because you rejoice and are glad,
  you who pillage my inheritance,
because you frolic like a heifer
    threshing grain
  and neigh like stallions,
12 your mother will be greatly ashamed;
  she who gave you birth will be
    disgraced.
She will be the least of the nations—
  a wilderness, a dry land, a desert.
13 Because of the LORD's anger she will
    not be inhabited
  but will be completely desolate.
All who pass Babylon will be appalled;
  they will scoff because of all her
    wounds.

14 "Take up your positions around
    Babylon,
  all you who draw the bow.
Shoot at her! Spare no arrows,
  for she has sinned against the
    LORD.
15 Shout against her on every side!
  She surrenders, her towers fall,
  her walls are torn down.
Since this is the vengeance of the
    LORD,
  take vengeance on her;
  do to her as she has done to
    others.
16 Cut off from Babylon the sower,
  and the reaper with his sickle at
    harvest.

Because of the sword of the
    oppressor
  let everyone return to their own
    people,
  let everyone flee to their own land.

17 "Israel is a scattered flock
  that lions have chased away.
The first to devour them
  was the king of Assyria;
the last to crush their bones
  was Nebuchadnezzar king of
    Babylon."

18 Therefore this is what the LORD Almighty, the God of Israel, says:

"I will punish the king of Babylon and
    his land
  as I punished the king of Assyria.
19 But I will bring Israel back to their own
    pasture,
  and they will graze on Carmel and
    Bashan;
their appetite will be satisfied
  on the hills of Ephraim and Gilead.
20 In those days, at that time,"
            declares the LORD,
"search will be made for Israel's
    guilt,
  but there will be none,
and for the sins of Judah,
  but none will be found,
  for I will forgive the remnant I spare.

21 "Attack the land of Merathaim
  and those who live in Pekod.
Pursue, kill and completely destroy*b*
    them,"
            declares the LORD.
"Do everything I have commanded
    you.
22 The noise of battle is in the land,
  the noise of great destruction!
23 How broken and shattered
  is the hammer of the whole
    earth!
How desolate is Babylon
  among the nations!
24 I set a trap for you, Babylon,
  and you were caught before you
    knew it;

---

a 10 Or *Chaldea*   *b 21* The Hebrew term refers to the
irrevocable giving over of things or persons to the LORD,
often by totally destroying them; also in verse 26.

you were found and captured
  because you opposed the LORD.
25 The LORD has opened his arsenal
  and brought out the weapons of his
    wrath,
  for the Sovereign LORD Almighty has
    work to do
  in the land of the Babylonians.
26 Come against her from afar.
  Break open her granaries;
  pile her up like heaps of grain.
  Completely destroy her
  and leave her no remnant.
27 Kill all her young bulls;
  let them go down to the slaughter!
  Woe to them! For their day has come,
  the time for them to be punished.
28 Listen to the fugitives and refugees
    from Babylon
  declaring in Zion
  how the LORD our God has taken
    vengeance,
  vengeance for his temple.

29 "Summon archers against Babylon,
  all those who draw the bow.
  Encamp all around her;
  let no one escape.
  Repay her for her deeds;
  do to her as she has done.
  For she has defied the LORD,
  the Holy One of Israel.
30 Therefore, her young men will fall in
    the streets;
  all her soldiers will be silenced in
    that day,"
                    declares the LORD.
31 "See, I am against you, you arrogant
    one,"
  declares the Lord, the LORD
    Almighty,
  "for your day has come,
  the time for you to be punished.
32 The arrogant one will stumble and
    fall
  and no one will help her up;
  I will kindle a fire in her towns
  that will consume all who are
    around her."

33 This is what the LORD Almighty says:

"The people of Israel are oppressed,
  and the people of Judah as well.

All their captors hold them fast,
  refusing to let them go.
34 Yet their Redeemer is strong;
  the LORD Almighty is his name.
  He will vigorously defend their cause
  so that he may bring rest to their
    land,
  but unrest to those who live in
    Babylon.

35 "A sword against the Babylonians!"
  declares the LORD—
  "against those who live in Babylon
  and against her officials and wise
    men!
36 A sword against her false prophets!
  They will become fools.
  A sword against her warriors!
  They will be filled with terror.
37 A sword against her horses and
    chariots
  and all the foreigners in her ranks!
  They will become weaklings.
  A sword against her treasures!
  They will be plundered.
38 A drought on[a] her waters!
  They will dry up.
  For it is a land of idols,
  idols that will go mad with terror.

39 "So desert creatures and hyenas will
    live there,
  and there the owl will dwell.
  It will never again be inhabited
  or lived in from generation to
    generation.
40 As I overthrew Sodom and Gomorrah
  along with their neighboring
    towns,"
                    declares the LORD,
  "so no one will live there;
  no people will dwell in it.

41 "Look! An army is coming from the
    north;
  a great nation and many kings
  are being stirred up from the ends
    of the earth.
42 They are armed with bows and
    spears;
  they are cruel and without mercy.
  They sound like the roaring sea
  as they ride on their horses;

---

a 38 Or A sword against

they come like men in battle
formation
to attack you, Daughter Babylon.
⁴³ The king of Babylon has heard reports
about them,
and his hands hang limp.
Anguish has gripped him,
pain like that of a woman in labor.
⁴⁴ Like a lion coming up from Jordan's
thickets
to a rich pastureland,
I will chase Babylon from its land in an
instant.
Who is the chosen one I will appoint
for this?
Who is like me and who can
challenge me?
And what shepherd can stand
against me?"

BREAK THROUGH!

King of Babylon

(JEREMIAH 50:43)

A long time ago, countries didn't have presidents like they do today. A president is usually a person the people elect to be political leader of their country. In Jeremiah's time, kings were the leaders of the nations, and they had all the power. They became king because their father had been the king, or because they won a battle against someone who also wanted to be king.

⁴⁵ Therefore, hear what the LORD has
planned against Babylon,
what he has purposed against the
land of the Babylonians:
The young of the flock will be dragged
away;
their pasture will be appalled at
their fate.
⁴⁶ At the sound of Babylon's capture the
earth will tremble;
its cry will resound among the
nations.

51 This is what the LORD says:

"See, I will stir up the spirit of a
destroyer
against Babylon and the people of
Leb Kamai.ᵃ
² I will send foreigners to Babylon
to winnow her and to devastate her
land;
they will oppose her on every side
in the day of her disaster.
³ Let not the archer string his bow,
nor let him put on his armor.
Do not spare her young men;
completely destroyᵇ her army.
⁴ They will fall down slain in Babylon,ᶜ
fatally wounded in her streets.
⁵ For Israel and Judah have not been
forsaken
by their God, the LORD Almighty,
though their landᵈ is full of guilt
before the Holy One of Israel.

⁶ "Flee from Babylon!
Run for your lives!
Do not be destroyed because of her
sins.
It is time for the LORD's vengeance;
he will repay her what she deserves.
⁷ Babylon was a gold cup in the LORD's
hand;
she made the whole earth drunk.
The nations drank her wine;
therefore they have now gone mad.
⁸ Babylon will suddenly fall and be
broken.
Wail over her!

ᵃ *1 Leb Kamai* is a cryptogram for Chaldea, that is, Babylonia.   ᵇ *3* The Hebrew term refers to the irrevocable giving over of things or persons to the LORD, often by totally destroying them.   ᶜ *4* Or *Chaldea*   ᵈ *5* Or *Almighty, / and the land of the Babylonians*

Get balm for her pain;
  perhaps she can be healed.
⁹ " 'We would have healed Babylon,
    but she cannot be healed;
  let us leave her and each go to our
    own land,
    for her judgment reaches to the
      skies,
    it rises as high as the heavens.'

¹⁰ " 'The LORD has vindicated us;
    come, let us tell in Zion
  what the LORD our God has done.'

¹¹ "Sharpen the arrows,
    take up the shields!
  The LORD has stirred up the kings of
    the Medes,
    because his purpose is to destroy
      Babylon.
  The LORD will take vengeance,
    vengeance for his temple.
¹² Lift up a banner against the walls of
    Babylon!
  Reinforce the guard,
  station the watchmen,
    prepare an ambush!

BREAK THROUGH!

Kings of the Medes
(JEREMIAH 51:11)
These kings ruled in the country of Media,
where the Medes lived. This country existed
many years ago, where Iran is today.

The LORD will carry out his purpose,
  his decree against the people of
    Babylon.
¹³ You who live by many waters
    and are rich in treasures,
  your end has come,
    the time for you to be destroyed.
¹⁴ The LORD Almighty has sworn by
      himself:
  I will surely fill you with troops, as
      with a swarm of locusts,
    and they will shout in triumph over
      you.

¹⁵ "He made the earth by his power;
    he founded the world by his wisdom
    and stretched out the heavens by
      his understanding.
¹⁶ When he thunders, the waters in the
      heavens roar;
    he makes clouds rise from the ends
      of the earth.
  He sends lightning with the rain
    and brings out the wind from his
      storehouses.

¹⁷ "Everyone is senseless and without
      knowledge;
    every goldsmith is shamed by his
      idols.
  The images he makes are a fraud;
    they have no breath in them.
¹⁸ They are worthless, the objects of
      mockery;
    when their judgment comes, they
      will perish.
¹⁹ He who is the Portion of Jacob is not
      like these,
    for he is the Maker of all things,
  including the people of his
      inheritance—
    the LORD Almighty is his name.

²⁰ "You are my war club,
    my weapon for battle—
  with you I shatter nations,
    with you I destroy kingdoms,
²¹ with you I shatter horse and rider,
    with you I shatter chariot and
      driver,
²² with you I shatter man and woman,
    with you I shatter old man and
      youth,
    with you I shatter young man and
      young woman,

²³ with you I shatter shepherd and
        flock,
    with you I shatter farmer and oxen,
    with you I shatter governors and
        officials.

²⁴ "Before your eyes I will repay Babylon
and all who live in Babylonia[a] for all the
wrong they have done in Zion," declares
the Lord.

²⁵ "I am against you, you destroying
        mountain,
    you who destroy the whole earth,"
                declares the Lord.
    "I will stretch out my hand against
        you,
    roll you off the cliffs,
    and make you a burned-out
        mountain.
²⁶ No rock will be taken from you for a
        cornerstone,
    nor any stone for a foundation,
    for you will be desolate forever,"
                declares the Lord.

²⁷ "Lift up a banner in the land!
    Blow the trumpet among the
        nations!
    Prepare the nations for battle against
        her;
    summon against her these
        kingdoms:
    Ararat, Minni and Ashkenaz.
    Appoint a commander against her;
    send up horses like a swarm of
        locusts.
²⁸ Prepare the nations for battle against
        her—
    the kings of the Medes,
    their governors and all their
        officials,
    and all the countries they rule.
²⁹ The land trembles and writhes,
    for the Lord's purposes against
        Babylon stand—
    to lay waste the land of Babylon
    so that no one will live there.
³⁰ Babylon's warriors have stopped
        fighting;
    they remain in their strongholds.
    Their strength is exhausted;
    they have become weaklings.
    Her dwellings are set on fire;
    the bars of her gates are broken.

³¹ One courier follows another
    and messenger follows
        messenger
    to announce to the king of
        Babylon
    that his entire city is captured,
³² the river crossings seized,
    the marshes set on fire,
    and the soldiers terrified."

³³ This is what the Lord Almighty, the
God of Israel, says:

    "Daughter Babylon is like a threshing
        floor
    at the time it is trampled;
    the time to harvest her will soon
        come."

³⁴ "Nebuchadnezzar king of Babylon has
        devoured us,
    he has thrown us into confusion,
    he has made us an empty jar.

---

a 24 Or *Chaldea*; also in verse 35

BREAK THROUGH!

Marshes
(JEREMIAH 51:32)

Did you know that it's a lot of fun to play in the
marshes? It's land where a lot of reeds grow.
It's easy to hide among the reeds, but they
also catch on fire really fast. That's why you
have to be careful if they're dry and it hasn't
rained for a long time.

Like a serpent he has swallowed us
    and filled his stomach with our
    delicacies,
    and then has spewed us out.
[35] May the violence done to our flesh[a] be
    on Babylon,"
    say the inhabitants of Zion.
"May our blood be on those who live
    in Babylonia,"
    says Jerusalem.

[36] Therefore this is what the LORD says:

"See, I will defend your cause
    and avenge you;
I will dry up her sea
    and make her springs dry.
[37] Babylon will be a heap of ruins,
    a haunt of jackals,
an object of horror and scorn,
    a place where no one lives.
[38] Her people all roar like young lions,
    they growl like lion cubs.
[39] But while they are aroused,
    I will set out a feast for them
    and make them drunk,
so that they shout with laughter—
    then sleep forever and not awake,"
                    declares the LORD.
[40] "I will bring them down
    like lambs to the slaughter,
    like rams and goats.

[41] "How Sheshak[b] will be captured,
    the boast of the whole earth
    seized!
How desolate Babylon will be
    among the nations!
[42] The sea will rise over Babylon;
    its roaring waves will cover her.
[43] Her towns will be desolate,
    a dry and desert land,
a land where no one lives,
    through which no one travels.
[44] I will punish Bel in Babylon
    and make him spew out what he
    has swallowed.
The nations will no longer stream to
    him.
And the wall of Babylon will fall.

[45] "Come out of her, my people!
    Run for your lives!
    Run from the fierce anger of the
    LORD.

[46] Do not lose heart or be afraid
    when rumors are heard in the land;
one rumor comes this year, another
    the next,
rumors of violence in the land
    and of ruler against ruler.
[47] For the time will surely come
    when I will punish the idols of
    Babylon;
her whole land will be disgraced
    and her slain will all lie fallen within
    her.
[48] Then heaven and earth and all that is
    in them
    will shout for joy over Babylon,
for out of the north
    destroyers will attack her,"
                    declares the LORD.

[49] "Babylon must fall because of Israel's
    slain,
    just as the slain in all the earth
    have fallen because of Babylon.
[50] You who have escaped the sword,
    leave and do not linger!
Remember the LORD in a distant land,
    and call to mind Jerusalem."

[51] "We are disgraced,
    for we have been insulted
    and shame covers our faces,
because foreigners have entered
    the holy places of the LORD's house."

[52] "But days are coming," declares the
    LORD,
    "when I will punish her idols,
and throughout her land
    the wounded will groan.
[53] Even if Babylon ascends to the
    heavens
    and fortifies her lofty stronghold,
    I will send destroyers against her,"
                    declares the LORD.

[54] "The sound of a cry comes from Babylon,
    the sound of great destruction
    from the land of the Babylonians.[c]
[55] The LORD will destroy Babylon;
    he will silence her noisy din.
Waves of enemies will rage like great
    waters;
    the roar of their voices will resound.

---

[a] 35 Or done to us and to our children   [b] 41 Sheshak is
a cryptogram for Babylon.   [c] 54 Or Chaldeans

⁵⁶A destroyer will come against Babylon;
   her warriors will be captured,
   and their bows will be broken.
For the Lᴏʀᴅ is a God of retribution;
   he will repay in full.
⁵⁷I will make her officials and wise men
      drunk,
   her governors, officers and warriors
      as well;
they will sleep forever and not awake,"
   declares the King, whose name is
      the Lᴏʀᴅ Almighty.

⁵⁸This is what the Lᴏʀᴅ Almighty says:

"Babylon's thick wall will be leveled
   and her high gates set on fire;
the peoples exhaust themselves for
      nothing,
   the nations' labor is only fuel for
      the flames."

⁵⁹This is the message Jeremiah the prophet gave to the staff officer Seraiah son of Neriah, the son of Mahseiah, when he went to Babylon with Zedekiah king of Judah in the fourth year of his reign. ⁶⁰Jeremiah had written on a scroll about all the disasters that would come upon Babylon—all that had been recorded concerning Babylon. ⁶¹He said to Seraiah, "When you get to Babylon, see that you read all these words aloud. ⁶²Then say, 'Lᴏʀᴅ, you have said you will destroy this place, so that neither people nor animals will live in it; it will be desolate forever.' ⁶³When you finish reading this scroll, tie a stone to it and throw it into the Euphrates. ⁶⁴Then say, 'So will Babylon sink to rise no more because of the disaster I will bring on her. And her people will fall.' "

The words of Jeremiah end here.

The Fall of Jerusalem

52 Zedekiah was twenty-one years old when he became king, and he reigned in Jerusalem eleven years. His mother's name was Hamutal daughter of Jeremiah; she was from Libnah. ²He did evil in the eyes of the Lᴏʀᴅ, just as Jehoiakim had done. ³It was because of the Lᴏʀᴅ's anger that all this happened to Jerusalem and Judah, and in the end he thrust them from his presence.

Now Zedekiah rebelled against the king of Babylon.

⁴So in the ninth year of Zedekiah's reign, on the tenth day of the tenth month, Nebuchadnezzar king of Babylon marched against Jerusalem with his whole army. They encamped outside the city and built siege works all around it. ⁵The city was kept under siege until the eleventh year of King Zedekiah.

⁶By the ninth day of the fourth month the famine in the city had become so severe that there was no food for the people to eat. ⁷Then the city wall was broken through, and the whole army fled. They left the city at night through the gate between the two walls near the king's garden, though the Babylonians[a] were surrounding the city. They fled toward the Arabah,[b] ⁸but the Babylonian[c] army pursued King Zedekiah and overtook him in the plains of Jericho. All his soldiers were separated from him and scattered, ⁹and he was captured.

---

[a] 7 Or Chaldeans; also in verse 17   [b] 7 Or the Jordan Valley   [c] 8 Or Chaldean; also in verse 14

Tenth month

(JEREMIAH 52:4)

The tenth month of the lunar calendar the Israelites used was called Tebet. It's from the middle of December to the middle of January in our calendar.

BREAKTHROUGH!

BREAK THROUGH!

Fourth month

(JEREMIAH 52:6)

It was called Tamuz in the Israelites' lunar calendar. It would be from mid-June to mid-July for us.

He was taken to the king of Babylon at Riblah in the land of Hamath, where he pronounced sentence on him. ¹⁰There at Riblah the king of Babylon killed the sons of Zedekiah before his eyes; he also killed all the officials of Judah. ¹¹Then he put out Zedekiah's eyes, bound him with bronze shackles and took him to Babylon, where he put him in prison till the day of his death.

¹²On the tenth day of the fifth month, in the nineteenth year of Nebuchadnezzar king of Babylon, Nebuzaradan commander of the imperial guard, who served the king of Babylon, came to Jerusalem. ¹³He set fire to the temple of the Lord, the royal palace and all the houses of Jerusalem. Every important building he burned down. ¹⁴The whole Babylonian army, under the commander of the imperial guard, broke down all the walls around Jerusalem. ¹⁵Nebuzaradan the commander of the guard carried into exile some of the poorest people and those who remained in the city, along with the rest of the craftsmen[a] and those who had deserted to the king of Babylon. ¹⁶But Nebuzaradan left

behind the rest of the poorest people of the land to work the vineyards and fields.

¹⁷The Babylonians broke up the bronze pillars, the movable stands and the bronze Sea that were at the temple of the Lord and they carried all the bronze to Babylon. ¹⁸They also took away the pots, shovels, wick trimmers, sprinkling bowls, dishes and all the bronze articles used in the temple service. ¹⁹The commander of the imperial guard took away the basins, censers, sprinkling bowls, pots, lampstands, dishes and bowls used for drink offerings—all that were made of pure gold or silver.

²⁰The bronze from the two pillars, the Sea and the twelve bronze bulls under it, and the movable stands, which King Solomon had made for the temple of the Lord, was more than could be weighed. ²¹Each pillar was eighteen cubits high and twelve cubits in circumference[b]; each was four fingers thick, and hollow. ²²The bronze capital on top of one pillar was

---

a 15 Or *the populace*   *b 21* That is, about 27 feet high and 18 feet in circumference or about 8.1 meters high and 5.4 meters in circumference

BREAK THROUGH!

Fifth month

(JEREMIAH 52:12)

It was called Ab in the Israelites' lunar calendar. It would be more or less from the middle of July to the middle of August for us.

five cubits*a* high and was decorated with a network and pomegranates of bronze all around. The other pillar, with its pomegranates, was similar. ²³There were ninety-six pomegranates on the sides; the total number of pomegranates above the surrounding network was a hundred.

²⁴The commander of the guard took as prisoners Seraiah the chief priest, Zephaniah the priest next in rank and the three doorkeepers. ²⁵Of those still in the city, he took the officer in charge of the fighting men, and seven royal advisers. He also took the secretary who was chief officer in charge of conscripting the people of the land, sixty of whom were found in the city. ²⁶Nebuzaradan the commander took them all and brought them to the king of Babylon at Riblah. ²⁷There at Riblah, in the land of Hamath, the king had them executed.

So Judah went into captivity, away from her land. ²⁸This is the number of the people Nebuchadnezzar carried into exile:

in the seventh year, 3,023 Jews;
²⁹ in Nebuchadnezzar's eighteenth year,
832 people from Jerusalem;
³⁰ in his twenty-third year,
745 Jews taken into exile by Nebuzaradan the commander of the imperial guard.
There were 4,600 people in all.

Jehoiachin Released

³¹In the thirty-seventh year of the exile of Jehoiachin king of Judah, in the year

a 22 That is, about 7 1/2 feet or about 2.3 meters

BREAKTHROUGH!

Twelfth month
(JEREMIAH 52:31)
This month was Adar in the lunar calendar. It's from the middle of February to the middle of March for us.

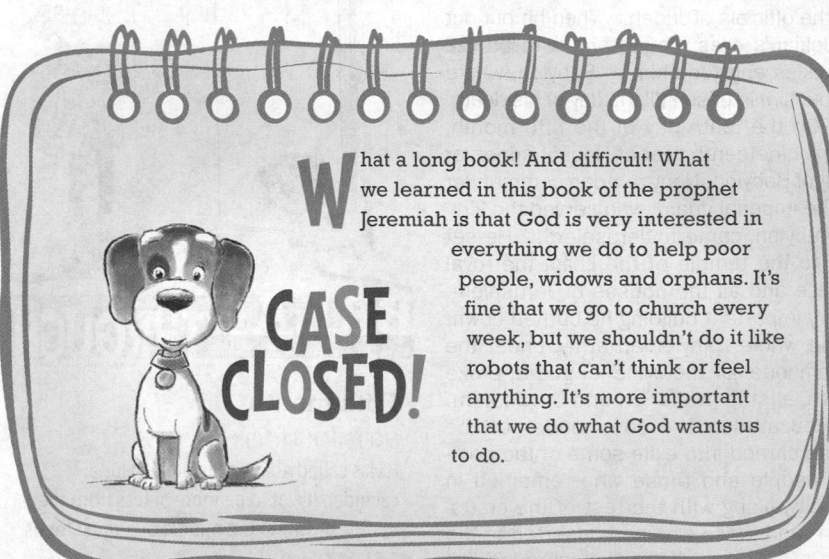

What a long book! And difficult! What we learned in this book of the prophet Jeremiah is that God is very interested in everything we do to help poor people, widows and orphans. It's fine that we go to church every week, but we shouldn't do it like robots that can't think or feel anything. It's more important that we do what God wants us to do.

CASE CLOSED!

Awel-Marduk became king of Babylon, on the twenty-fifth day of the twelfth month, he released Jehoiachin king of Judah and freed him from prison. [32]He spoke kindly to him and gave him a seat of honor higher than those of the other kings who were with him in Babylon. [33]So Jehoiachin put aside his prison clothes and for the rest of his life ate regularly at the king's table. [34]Day by day the king of Babylon gave Jehoiachin a regular allowance as long as he lived, till the day of his death.

LAMENTATIONS

THE EVIDENCE:

WHO WROTE IT?
Lamentations is a collection of the writings of several authors.

HOW LONG AGO?
It was probably written at the end of the 6th century (500s) before Christ.

WHAT'S IT ABOUT?
A lamentation is a sad song or poem. And that's what this book is. The city of Jerusalem had been attacked and destroyed by the Babylonian army. Then the Israelites had been captured and taken prisoner to Babylon. They spent about fifty years there, until King Cyrus of Persia let them go back to their own country. This book talks sadly about this terrible tragedy.

THE BEST PART
The whole book is pretty sad, so what we like best is where it says, "You came near when I called you, and you said, 'Do not fear'" (3:57).

1 ^a How deserted lies the city,
  once so full of people!
How like a widow is she,
  who once was great among the
    nations!
She who was queen among the
    provinces
  has now become a slave.

² Bitterly she weeps at night,
  tears are on her cheeks.
Among all her lovers
  there is no one to comfort her.
All her friends have betrayed her;
  they have become her enemies.

³ After affliction and harsh labor,
  Judah has gone into exile.
She dwells among the nations;
  she finds no resting place.
All who pursue her have overtaken her
  in the midst of her distress.

⁴ The roads to Zion mourn,
  for no one comes to her appointed
    festivals.
All her gateways are desolate,
  her priests groan,
her young women grieve,
  and she is in bitter anguish.

⁵ Her foes have become her
    masters;
  her enemies are at ease.
The Lord has brought her grief
  because of her many sins.
Her children have gone into exile,
  captive before the foe.

⁶ All the splendor has departed
  from Daughter Zion.
Her princes are like deer
  that find no pasture;

^a This chapter is an acrostic poem, the verses of which begin with the successive letters of the Hebrew alphabet.

in weakness they have fled
  before the pursuer.

⁷ In the days of her affliction and
      wandering
  Jerusalem remembers all the
      treasures
  that were hers in days of old.
  When her people fell into enemy
      hands,
  there was no one to help her.
  Her enemies looked at her
  and laughed at her destruction.

⁸ Jerusalem has sinned greatly
  and so has become unclean.
  All who honored her despise her,
    for they have all seen her naked;
  she herself groans
  and turns away.

⁹ Her filthiness clung to her skirts;
    she did not consider her future.
  Her fall was astounding;
    there was none to comfort her.
  "Look, Lᴏʀᴅ, on my affliction,
    for the enemy has triumphed."

THE SCENE

JERUSALEM

(LAMENTATIONS 1:7)

Remember that this city is explained in Nehemiah 2:12.

¹⁰ The enemy laid hands
    on all her treasures;
  she saw pagan nations
    enter her sanctuary—
  those you had forbidden
    to enter your assembly.

¹¹ All her people groan
    as they search for bread;
  they barter their treasures for food
    to keep themselves alive.
  "Look, Lᴏʀᴅ, and consider,
    for I am despised."

¹² "Is it nothing to you, all you who pass
      by?
  Look around and see.
  Is any suffering like my suffering
    that was inflicted on me,
  that the Lᴏʀᴅ brought on me
    in the day of his fierce anger?

¹³ "From on high he sent fire,
    sent it down into my bones.
  He spread a net for my feet
    and turned me back.
  He made me desolate,
    faint all the day long.

¹⁴ "My sins have been bound into a
      yokeᵃ;
    by his hands they were woven
      together.
  They have been hung on my neck,
    and the Lord has sapped my
      strength.
  He has given me into the hands
    of those I cannot withstand.

¹⁵ "The Lord has rejected
    all the warriors in my midst;
  he has summoned an army against me
    toᵇ crush my young men.
  In his winepress the Lord has
      trampled
    Virgin Daughter Judah.

¹⁶ "This is why I weep
    and my eyes overflow with tears.
  No one is near to comfort me,
    no one to restore my spirit.
  My children are destitute
    because the enemy has prevailed."

ᵃ *14* Most Hebrew manuscripts; many Hebrew manuscripts
and Septuagint *He kept watch over my sins*   ᵇ *15* Or *has
set a time for me / when he will*

17 Zion stretches out her hands,
      but there is no one to comfort her.
The LORD has decreed for Jacob
      that his neighbors become his foes;
Jerusalem has become
      an unclean thing among them.

18 "The LORD is righteous,
      yet I rebelled against his command.
Listen, all you peoples;
      look on my suffering.
My young men and young women
      have gone into exile.

19 "I called to my allies
      but they betrayed me.
My priests and my elders
      perished in the city
while they searched for food
      to keep themselves alive.

20 "See, LORD, how distressed I am!
      I am in torment within,
and in my heart I am disturbed,
      for I have been most rebellious.
Outside, the sword bereaves;
      inside, there is only death.

21 "People have heard my groaning,
      but there is no one to comfort me.
All my enemies have heard of my
            distress;
      they rejoice at what you have done.
May you bring the day you have
            announced
      so they may become like me.

22 "Let all their wickedness come before
            you;
      deal with them
as you have dealt with me
      because of all my sins.
My groans are many
      and my heart is faint."

2 *a* How the Lord has covered Daughter
            Zion
      with the cloud of his anger*b*!
He has hurled down the splendor of
            Israel
      from heaven to earth;
he has not remembered his footstool
      in the day of his anger.

2 Without pity the Lord has swallowed up
      all the dwellings of Jacob;

in his wrath he has torn down
      the strongholds of Daughter Judah.
He has brought her kingdom and its
            princes
      down to the ground in dishonor.

3 In fierce anger he has cut off
      every horn*c,d* of Israel.
He has withdrawn his right hand
      at the approach of the enemy.
He has burned in Jacob like a flaming
            fire
      that consumes everything around it.

4 Like an enemy he has strung his bow;
      his right hand is ready.
Like a foe he has slain
      all who were pleasing to the eye;
he has poured out his wrath like fire
      on the tent of Daughter Zion.

5 The Lord is like an enemy;
      he has swallowed up Israel.
He has swallowed up all her palaces
      and destroyed her strongholds.
He has multiplied mourning and
            lamentation
      for Daughter Judah.

6 He has laid waste his dwelling like a
            garden;
      he has destroyed his place of
            meeting.
The LORD has made Zion forget
      her appointed festivals and her
            Sabbaths;
in his fierce anger he has spurned
      both king and priest.

7 The Lord has rejected his altar
      and abandoned his sanctuary.
He has given the walls of her
            palaces
      into the hands of the enemy;
they have raised a shout in the house
            of the LORD
      as on the day of an appointed
            festival.

8 The LORD determined to tear down
      the wall around Daughter Zion.
He stretched out a measuring line

---

a This chapter is an acrostic poem, the verses of which
begin with the successive letters of the Hebrew alphabet.
b 1 Or *How the Lord in his anger / has treated Daughter
Zion with contempt*   *c* 3 Or *off / all the strength*; or *every
king*   *d* 3 *Horn* here symbolizes strength.

and did not withhold his hand from
  destroying.
He made ramparts and walls lament;
  together they wasted away.

⁹Her gates have sunk into the ground;
  their bars he has broken and
    destroyed.
Her king and her princes are exiled
  among the nations,
  the law is no more,
and her prophets no longer find
  visions from the Lᴏʀᴅ.

¹⁰The elders of Daughter Zion
  sit on the ground in silence;
they have sprinkled dust on their
    heads
  and put on sackcloth.
The young women of Jerusalem
  have bowed their heads to the
    ground.

¹¹My eyes fail from weeping,
  I am in torment within;
my heart is poured out on the ground
  because my people are destroyed,
because children and infants faint
  in the streets of the city.

¹²They say to their mothers,
  "Where is bread and wine?"
as they faint like the wounded
  in the streets of the city,
as their lives ebb away
  in their mothers' arms.

¹³What can I say for you?
  With what can I compare you,
  Daughter Jerusalem?
To what can I liken you,
  that I may comfort you,
  Virgin Daughter Zion?
Your wound is as deep as the sea.
  Who can heal you?

¹⁴The visions of your prophets
  were false and worthless;
they did not expose your sin
  to ward off your captivity.
The prophecies they gave you
  were false and misleading.

¹⁵All who pass your way
  clap their hands at you;
they scoff and shake their heads
  at Daughter Jerusalem:

"Is this the city that was called
  the perfection of beauty,
  the joy of the whole earth?"

¹⁶All your enemies open their mouths
  wide against you;
they scoff and gnash their teeth
  and say, "We have swallowed
    her up.
This is the day we have waited for;
  we have lived to see it."

¹⁷The Lᴏʀᴅ has done what he planned;
  he has fulfilled his word,
  which he decreed long ago.
He has overthrown you without pity,
  he has let the enemy gloat over you,
  he has exalted the horn[a] of your
    foes.

¹⁸The hearts of the people
  cry out to the Lord.
You walls of Daughter Zion,
  let your tears flow like a river
  day and night;
give yourself no relief,
  your eyes no rest.

¹⁹Arise, cry out in the night,
  as the watches of the night
    begin;
pour out your heart like water
  in the presence of the Lord.
Lift up your hands to him
  for the lives of your children,
who faint from hunger
  at every street corner.

²⁰"Look, Lᴏʀᴅ, and consider:
  Whom have you ever treated like
    this?
Should women eat their offspring,
  the children they have cared for?
Should priest and prophet be killed
  in the sanctuary of the Lord?

²¹"Young and old lie together
  in the dust of the streets;
my young men and young women
  have fallen by the sword.
You have slain them in the day of your
    anger;
  you have slaughtered them without
    pity.

---

a 17 Horn here symbolizes strength.

²² "As you summon to a feast day,
    so you summoned against me
        terrors on every side.
In the day of the Lᴏʀᴅ's anger
    no one escaped or survived;
those I cared for and reared
    my enemy has destroyed."

3 ᵃ I am the man who has seen
        affliction
    by the rod of the Lᴏʀᴅ's wrath.
² He has driven me away and made me
        walk
    in darkness rather than light;
³ indeed, he has turned his hand
        against me
    again and again, all day long.

⁴ He has made my skin and my flesh
        grow old
    and has broken my bones.
⁵ He has besieged me and surrounded
        me
    with bitterness and hardship.
⁶ He has made me dwell in darkness
    like those long dead.

⁷ He has walled me in so I cannot
        escape;
    he has weighed me down with
        chains.
⁸ Even when I call out or cry for help,
    he shuts out my prayer.
⁹ He has barred my way with blocks of
        stone;
    he has made my paths crooked.

¹⁰ Like a bear lying in wait,
    like a lion in hiding,
¹¹ he dragged me from the path and
        mangled me
    and left me without help.
¹² He drew his bow
    and made me the target for his
        arrows.

¹³ He pierced my heart
    with arrows from his quiver.
¹⁴ I became the laughingstock of all my
        people;
    they mock me in song all day long.
¹⁵ He has filled me with bitter herbs
    and given me gall to drink.

¹⁶ He has broken my teeth with gravel;
    he has trampled me in the dust.

¹⁷ I have been deprived of peace;
    I have forgotten what prosperity is.
¹⁸ So I say, "My splendor is gone
    and all that I had hoped from the
        Lᴏʀᴅ."

¹⁹ I remember my affliction and my
        wandering,
    the bitterness and the gall.
²⁰ I well remember them,
    and my soul is downcast within me.
²¹ Yet this I call to mind
    and therefore I have hope:

²² Because of the Lᴏʀᴅ's great love we
        are not consumed,
    for his compassions never fail.
²³ They are new every morning;
    great is your faithfulness.
²⁴ I say to myself, "The Lᴏʀᴅ is my
        portion;
    therefore I will wait for him."

²⁵ The Lᴏʀᴅ is good to those whose hope
        is in him,
    to the one who seeks him;
²⁶ it is good to wait quietly
    for the salvation of the Lᴏʀᴅ.
²⁷ It is good for a man to bear the yoke
    while he is young.

²⁸ Let him sit alone in silence,
    for the Lᴏʀᴅ has laid it on him.
²⁹ Let him bury his face in the dust—
    there may yet be hope.
³⁰ Let him offer his cheek to one who
        would strike him,
    and let him be filled with disgrace.

³¹ For no one is cast off
    by the Lord forever.
³² Though he brings grief, he will show
        compassion,
    so great is his unfailing love.
³³ For he does not willingly bring
        affliction
    or grief to anyone.

³⁴ To crush underfoot
    all prisoners in the land,
³⁵ to deny people their rights
    before the Most High,

ᵃ This chapter is an acrostic poem; the verses of each
stanza begin with the successive letters of the Hebrew
alphabet, and the verses within each stanza begin with the
same letter.

³⁶ to deprive them of justice —
would not the Lord see such
things?
³⁷ Who can speak and have it happen
if the Lord has not decreed it?
³⁸ Is it not from the mouth of the Most
High
that both calamities and good
things come?
³⁹ Why should the living complain
when punished for their sins?
⁴⁰ Let us examine our ways and test
them,
and let us return to the Lᴏʀᴅ.
⁴¹ Let us lift up our hearts and our
hands
to God in heaven, and say:
⁴² "We have sinned and rebelled
and you have not forgiven.

⁴³ "You have covered yourself with anger
and pursued us;
you have slain without pity.
⁴⁴ You have covered yourself with a
cloud
so that no prayer can get through.
⁴⁵ You have made us scum and refuse
among the nations.

⁴⁶ "All our enemies have opened their
mouths
wide against us.
⁴⁷ We have suffered terror and pitfalls,
ruin and destruction."
⁴⁸ Streams of tears flow from my eyes
because my people are destroyed.

⁴⁹ My eyes will flow unceasingly,
without relief,
⁵⁰ until the Lᴏʀᴅ looks down
from heaven and sees.
⁵¹ What I see brings grief to my soul
because of all the women of my
city.

⁵² Those who were my enemies without
cause
hunted me like a bird.
⁵³ They tried to end my life in a pit
and threw stones at me;
⁵⁴ the waters closed over my head,
and I thought I was about to perish.

⁵⁵ I called on your name, Lᴏʀᴅ,
from the depths of the pit.

⁵⁶ You heard my plea: "Do not close your
ears
to my cry for relief."
⁵⁷ You came near when I called you,
and you said, "Do not fear."

⁵⁸ You, Lord, took up my case;
you redeemed my life.
⁵⁹ Lᴏʀᴅ, you have seen the wrong done
to me.
Uphold my cause!
⁶⁰ You have seen the depth of their
vengeance,
all their plots against me.

⁶¹ Lᴏʀᴅ, you have heard their insults,
all their plots against me —
⁶² what my enemies whisper and mutter
against me all day long.
⁶³ Look at them! Sitting or standing,
they mock me in their songs.

⁶⁴ Pay them back what they deserve,
Lᴏʀᴅ,
for what their hands have done.
⁶⁵ Put a veil over their hearts,
and may your curse be on them!
⁶⁶ Pursue them in anger and destroy them
from under the heavens of the Lᴏʀᴅ.

4 ᵃ How the gold has lost its luster,
the fine gold become dull!
The sacred gems are scattered
at every street corner.

² How the precious children of Zion,
once worth their weight in gold,
are now considered as pots of clay,
the work of a potter's hands!

³ Even jackals offer their breasts
to nurse their young,
but my people have become heartless
like ostriches in the desert.

⁴ Because of thirst the infant's tongue
sticks to the roof of its mouth;
the children beg for bread,
but no one gives it to them.

⁵ Those who once ate delicacies
are destitute in the streets.
Those brought up in royal purple
now lie on ash heaps.

ᵃ This chapter is an acrostic poem, the verses of which
begin with the successive letters of the Hebrew alphabet.

⁶ The punishment of my people
  is greater than that of Sodom,
which was overthrown in a moment
  without a hand turned to help her.

⁷ Their princes were brighter than
    snow
  and whiter than milk,
their bodies more ruddy than rubies,
  their appearance like lapis lazuli.

⁸ But now they are blacker than soot;
  they are not recognized in the
    streets.
Their skin has shriveled on their
    bones;
  it has become as dry as a stick.

⁹ Those killed by the sword are better
    off
  than those who die of famine;
racked with hunger, they waste away
  for lack of food from the field.

¹⁰ With their own hands compassionate
    women
  have cooked their own children,
who became their food
  when my people were destroyed.

¹¹ The LORD has given full vent to his
    wrath;
  he has poured out his fierce anger.
He kindled a fire in Zion
  that consumed her foundations.

¹² The kings of the earth did not believe,
  nor did any of the peoples of the
    world,
that enemies and foes could enter
  the gates of Jerusalem.

¹³ But it happened because of the sins
    of her prophets
  and the iniquities of her priests,
who shed within her
  the blood of the righteous.

¹⁴ Now they grope through the streets
  as if they were blind.
They are so defiled with blood
  that no one dares to touch their
    garments.

¹⁵ "Go away! You are unclean!" people
    cry to them.
  "Away! Away! Don't touch us!"

When they flee and wander about,
  people among the nations say,
  "They can stay here no longer."

¹⁶ The LORD himself has scattered them;
  he no longer watches over them.
The priests are shown no honor,
  the elders no favor.

¹⁷ Moreover, our eyes failed,
  looking in vain for help;
from our towers we watched
  for a nation that could not
    save us.

¹⁸ People stalked us at every step,
  so we could not walk in our
    streets.
Our end was near, our days were
    numbered,
  for our end had come.

¹⁹ Our pursuers were swifter
  than eagles in the sky;
they chased us over the mountains
  and lay in wait for us in the desert.

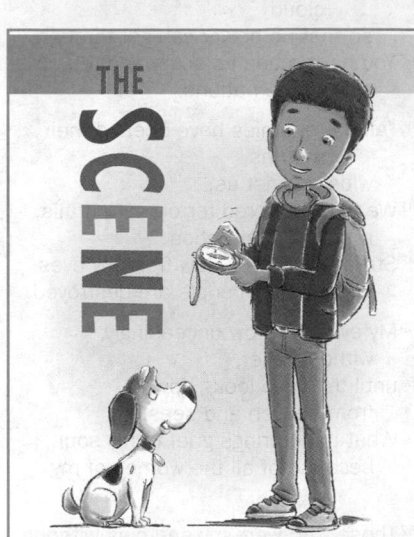

THE SCENE

DAUGHTER EDOM

(LAMENTATIONS 4:21)

This refers to the city of Edom.
Check this out in Jeremiah 9:26.

²⁰ The Lord's anointed, our very life breath,
 was caught in their traps.
We thought that under his shadow
 we would live among the nations.

²¹ Rejoice and be glad, Daughter Edom,
 you who live in the land of Uz.
But to you also the cup will be passed;
 you will be drunk and stripped naked.

²² Your punishment will end, Daughter Zion;
 he will not prolong your exile.
But he will punish your sin, Daughter Edom,
 and expose your wickedness.

5 Remember, Lord, what has happened to us;
 look, and see our disgrace.
² Our inheritance has been turned over to strangers,
 our homes to foreigners.

³ We have become fatherless,
 our mothers are widows.
⁴ We must buy the water we drink;
 our wood can be had only at a price.
⁵ Those who pursue us are at our heels;
 we are weary and find no rest.
⁶ We submitted to Egypt and Assyria
 to get enough bread.
⁷ Our ancestors sinned and are no more,
 and we bear their punishment.
⁸ Slaves rule over us,
 and there is no one to free us from their hands.
⁹ We get our bread at the risk of our lives
 because of the sword in the desert.
¹⁰ Our skin is hot as an oven,
 feverish from hunger.
¹¹ Women have been violated in Zion,
 and virgins in the towns of Judah.
¹² Princes have been hung up by their hands;
 elders are shown no respect.

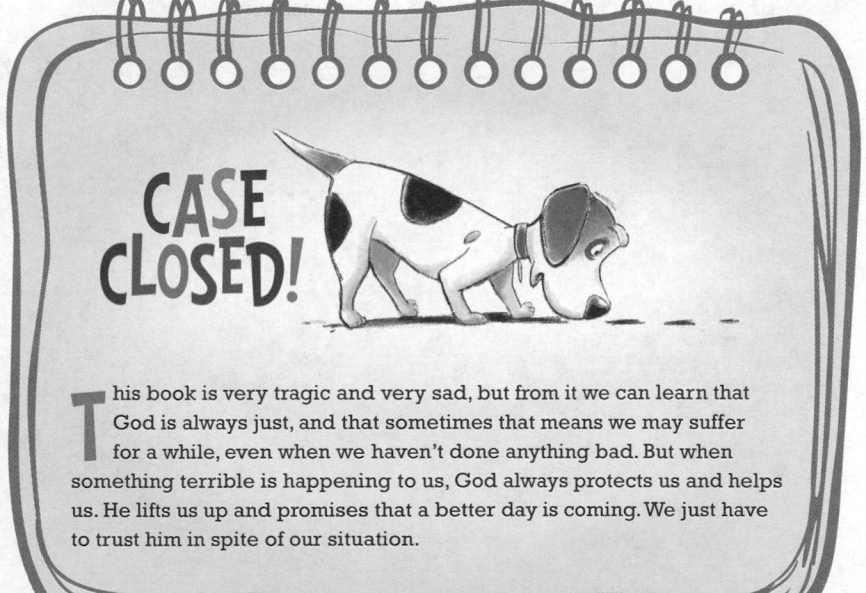

CASE CLOSED!

This book is very tragic and very sad, but from it we can learn that God is always just, and that sometimes that means we may suffer for a while, even when we haven't done anything bad. But when something terrible is happening to us, God always protects us and helps us. He lifts us up and promises that a better day is coming. We just have to trust him in spite of our situation.

CHECK THE FACTS

Who attacked and destroyed Jerusalem?

A) The French

B) The Babylonians

C) The Assyrians

CORRECT ANSWER: B

¹³ Young men toil at the millstones;
   boys stagger under loads of
      wood.
¹⁴ The elders are gone from the city
      gate;
   the young men have stopped their
      music.
¹⁵ Joy is gone from our hearts;
   our dancing has turned to
      mourning.
¹⁶ The crown has fallen from our head.
   Woe to us, for we have sinned!
¹⁷ Because of this our hearts are faint,
   because of these things our eyes
      grow dim
¹⁸ for Mount Zion, which lies desolate,
   with jackals prowling over it.

¹⁹ You, Lord, reign forever;
   your throne endures from
      generation to generation.
²⁰ Why do you always forget us?
   Why do you forsake us so long?
²¹ Restore us to yourself, Lord, that we
      may return;
   renew our days as of old
²² unless you have utterly rejected us
   and are angry with us beyond
      measure.

EZEKIEL

THE EVIDENCE:

This book is very important. When the people of Jerusalem thought everything was lost, Ezekiel showed up. He was a prophet who gave them a message of hope.

WHO WROTE IT?
Probably the prophet Ezekiel himself.

HOW LONG AGO?
About six centuries — or in other words, 600 years — before Jesus Christ was born.

WHAT'S IT ABOUT?
Ezekiel tells the people of Judah that they need to stop rebelling against God. He also says they can hope things are going to get better. The Babylonians had attacked the kingdom of Judah. They had destroyed the city of Jerusalem. They had taken almost all the people who were living in that kingdom and the king of Judah to Babylonia as prisoners. But that wasn't the end of Judah. While all this terrible tragedy was taking place, Ezekiel announced that the people of Judah, who seemed to be finished, would recover.

THE BEST PART
We thought it was exciting when Ezekiel had a vision and saw (obviously, it was a vision) a field full of dry bones that stood for the people of Judah. Then God gave him this message for the people: "Dry bones, hear the word of the LORD! This is what the Sovereign LORD says to these bones: I will make breath enter you, and you will come to life" (37:4–5).

Ezekiel's Inaugural Vision

1 In my thirtieth year, in the fourth month on the fifth day, while I was among the exiles by the Kebar River, the heavens were opened and I saw visions of God. 2 On the fifth of the month — it was the fifth year of the exile of King Jehoiachin — 3 the word of the LORD came to Ezekiel the priest, the son of Buzi, by the Kebar River in the land of the Babylonians.ᵃ There the hand of the LORD was on him.

4 I looked, and I saw a windstorm coming out of the north — an immense cloud with flashing lightning and surrounded by brilliant light. The center of the fire looked like glowing metal, 5 and in the fire was what looked like four living creatures. In appearance their form was human, 6 but each of them had four faces and four wings. 7 Their legs were straight; their feet were like those of a calf and

---

ᵃ 3 Or Chaldeans

BREAKTHROUGH!

Fourth month

(EZEKIEL 1:1)

It was called Tamuz in the Jewish lunar calendar. In our solar calendar, that is from the middle of June to the middle of July.

---

gleamed like burnished bronze. [8]Under their wings on their four sides they had human hands. All four of them had faces and wings, [9]and the wings of one touched the wings of another. Each one went straight ahead; they did not turn as they moved.

[10]Their faces looked like this: Each of the four had the face of a human being, and on the right side each had the face of a lion, and on the left the face of an ox; each also had the face of an eagle. [11]Such were their faces. They each had two wings spreading out upward, each wing touching that of the creature on either side; and each had two other wings covering its body. [12]Each one went straight ahead. Wherever the spirit would go, they would go, without turning as they went. [13]The appearance of the living creatures was like burning coals of fire or like torches. Fire moved back and forth among the creatures; it was bright, and lightning flashed out of it. [14]The creatures sped back and forth like flashes of lightning.

[15]As I looked at the living creatures, I saw a wheel on the ground beside each creature with its four faces. [16]This was the appearance and structure of the wheels: They sparkled like topaz, and all four looked alike. Each appeared to be made like a wheel intersecting a wheel. [17]As they moved, they would go in any one of the four directions the creatures faced; the wheels did not change direction as the creatures went. [18]Their rims were high and awesome, and all four rims were full of eyes all around.

[19]When the living creatures moved, the wheels beside them moved; and when the living creatures rose from the ground, the wheels also rose. [20]Wherever the spirit would go, they would go, and the wheels would rise along with them, because the spirit of the living creatures was in the wheels. [21]When the creatures moved, they also moved; when the creatures stood still, they also stood still; and when the creatures rose from the ground, the

THE SCENE

KEBAR RIVER

(EZEKIEL 1:1)

A river in Babylon. It's a branch of the Euphrates River.

wheels rose along with them, because the spirit of the living creatures was in the wheels.

²²Spread out above the heads of the living creatures was what looked something like a vault, sparkling like crystal, and awesome. ²³Under the vault their wings were stretched out one toward the other, and each had two wings covering its body. ²⁴When the creatures moved, I heard the

BREAK THROUGH!

Who were these four very strange creatures?

(EZEKIEL 1:5-24)

They are also known as cherubim. Images or statues of these cherubim were placed like guards at the doors of the ancient temples and palaces. In this book, they stand for God, who cannot be described with words.

THE
WITNESSES

✓ **EZEKIEL** (EZEKIEL 1:1-3)
He was a prophet. His name means "God gives me strength."

✓ **KING JEHOIACHIN** (EZEKIEL 1:1-3)
He was the second-to-last king of Judah. He ruled in Jerusalem for only three months. In the year 598 before Christ, he was taken prisoner to Babylon. In the year 561, he was set free by the Babylonian king Awel-Marduk, but then he didn't want to return to Jerusalem.

sound of their wings, like the roar of rushing waters, like the voice of the Almighty,ᵃ like the tumult of an army. When they stood still, they lowered their wings.

²⁵Then there came a voice from above the vault over their heads as they stood with lowered wings. ²⁶Above the vault over their heads was what looked like a throne of lapis lazuli, and high above on the throne was a figure like that of a man. ²⁷I saw that from what appeared to be his waist up he looked like glowing metal, as if full of fire, and that from there down he looked like fire; and brilliant light surrounded him. ²⁸Like the appearance of a rainbow in the clouds on a rainy day, so was the radiance around him.

This was the appearance of the likeness of the glory of the LORD. When I saw it, I fell facedown, and I heard the voice of one speaking.

ᵃ 24 Hebrew Shaddai

Ezekiel's Call to Be a Prophet

2 He said to me, "Son of man,[a] stand up on your feet and I will speak to you." ²As he spoke, the Spirit came into me and raised me to my feet, and I heard him speaking to me.

³He said: "Son of man, I am sending you to the Israelites, to a rebellious nation that has rebelled against me; they and their ancestors have been in revolt against me to this very day. ⁴The people to whom I am sending you are obstinate and stubborn. Say to them, 'This is what the Sovereign LORD says.' ⁵And whether they listen or fail to listen—for they are a rebellious people—they will know that a prophet has been among them. ⁶And you, son of man, do not be afraid of them or their words. Do not be afraid, though briers and thorns are all around you and you live among scorpions. Do not be afraid of what they say or be terrified by them, though they are a rebellious people. ⁷You must speak my words to them, whether they listen or fail to listen, for they are rebellious. ⁸But you, son of man, listen to what I say to you. Do not rebel like that rebellious people; open your mouth and eat what I give you."

⁹Then I looked, and I saw a hand stretched out to me. In it was a scroll, ¹⁰which he unrolled before me. On both sides of it were written words of lament and mourning and woe.

3 And he said to me, "Son of man, eat what is before you, eat this scroll; then go and speak to the people of Israel." ²So I opened my mouth, and he gave me the scroll to eat.

³Then he said to me, "Son of man, eat this scroll I am giving you and fill your stomach with it." So I ate it, and it tasted as sweet as honey in my mouth.

⁴He then said to me: "Son of man, go now to the people of Israel and speak my words to them. ⁵You are not being sent to a people of obscure speech and strange language, but to the people of Israel— ⁶not to many peoples of obscure speech and strange language, whose words you cannot understand. Surely if I had sent you to them, they would have listened to you. ⁷But the people of Israel are not willing to listen to you because they are not willing to listen to me, for all the Israelites are hardened and obstinate. ⁸But I will make you as unyielding and hardened as they are. ⁹I will make your forehead like the hardest stone, harder than flint. Do not be afraid of them or terrified by them, though they are a rebellious people."

¹⁰And he said to me, "Son of man, listen carefully and take to heart all the words I speak to you. ¹¹Go now to your people in exile and speak to them. Say to them, 'This is what the Sovereign LORD says,' whether they listen or fail to listen.

¹²Then the Spirit lifted me up, and I heard behind me a loud rumbling sound as the glory of the LORD rose from the place where it was standing.[b] ¹³It was

BREAKTHROUGH!

Son of man

(EZEKIEL 2:1)

This Hebrew expression is used a lot in this book when God talks to Ezekiel. It means that Ezekiel was a human being, fragile and mortal. God used him to carry out his plans and bring hope to the people of Judah.

---

a 1 The Hebrew phrase *ben adam* means *human being*. The phrase *son of man* is retained as a form of address here and throughout Ezekiel because of its possible association with "Son of Man" in the New Testament.
b 12 Probable reading of the original Hebrew text; Masoretic Text *sound*—may the glory of the LORD be praised from his place

the sound of the wings of the living creatures brushing against each other and the sound of the wheels beside them, a loud rumbling sound. ¹⁴The Spirit then lifted me up and took me away, and I went in bitterness and in the anger of my spirit, with the strong hand of the LORD on me. ¹⁵I came to the exiles who lived at Tel Aviv near the Kebar River. And there, where they were living, I sat among them for seven days—deeply distressed.

Ezekiel's Task as Watchman

¹⁶At the end of seven days the word of the LORD came to me: ¹⁷"Son of man, I have made you a watchman for the people of Israel; so hear the word I speak and give them warning from me. ¹⁸When I say to a wicked person, 'You will surely die,' and you do not warn them or speak out to dissuade them from their evil ways in order to save their life, that wicked person will die for*ᵃ* their sin, and I will hold you accountable for their blood. ¹⁹But if you do warn the wicked person and they do not turn from their wickedness or from their evil ways, they will die for their sin; but you will have saved yourself.

²⁰"Again, when a righteous person turns from their righteousness and does evil, and I put a stumbling block before them, they will die. Since you did not warn them, they will die for their sin. The righteous things that person did will not be remembered, and I will hold you accountable for their blood. ²¹But if you do warn the righteous person not to sin and they do not sin, they will surely live because they took warning, and you will have saved yourself."

²²The hand of the LORD was on me there, and he said to me, "Get up and go out to the plain, and there I will speak to you." ²³So I got up and went out to the plain. And the glory of the LORD was standing there, like the glory I had seen by the Kebar River, and I fell facedown. ²⁴Then the Spirit came into me and raised me to my feet. He spoke to me and said: "Go, shut yourself inside your house. ²⁵And you, son of man, they will tie with ropes; you will be bound so that you cannot go out among the people. ²⁶I

will make your tongue stick to the roof of your mouth so that you will be silent and unable to rebuke them, for they are a rebellious people. ²⁷But when I speak to you, I will open your mouth and you shall say to them, 'This is what the Sovereign LORD says.' Whoever will listen let them listen, and whoever will refuse let them refuse; for they are a rebellious people.

Siege of Jerusalem Symbolized

4 "Now, son of man, take a block of clay, put it in front of you and draw the city of Jerusalem on it. ²Then lay siege to it: Erect siege works against it, build a ramp up to it, set up camps against it and put battering rams around it. ³Then take an iron pan, place it as an iron wall between you and the city and turn your face toward it. It will be under siege, and you shall besiege it. This will be a sign to the people of Israel.

⁴"Then lie on your left side and put the sin of the people of Israel upon yourself.*ᵇ* You are to bear their sin for the number of days you lie on your side. ⁵I have assigned you the same number of days as the years of their sin. So for 390 days you will bear the sin of the people of Israel.

⁶"After you have finished this, lie down again, this time on your right side, and bear the sin of the people of Judah. I have assigned you 40 days, a day for each year. ⁷Turn your face toward the siege of Jerusalem and with bared arm prophesy against her. ⁸I will tie you up with ropes so that you cannot turn from one side to the other until you have finished the days of your siege.

⁹"Take wheat and barley, beans and lentils, millet and spelt; put them in a storage jar and use them to make bread for yourself. You are to eat it during the 390 days you lie on your side. ¹⁰Weigh out twenty shekels*ᶜ* of food to eat each day and eat it at set times. ¹¹Also measure out a sixth of a hin*ᵈ* of water and drink it at set times. ¹²Eat the food as you would a loaf of barley bread; bake it in the sight of the people, using human

---

ᵃ 18 Or *in; also in verses 19 and 20*   *ᵇ 4* Or *upon your side*   *ᶜ 10* That is, about 8 ounces or about 230 grams   *ᵈ 11* That is, about 2/3 quart or about 0.6 liter excrement for fuel." ¹³The Lᴏʀᴅ said, "In this way the people of Israel will eat defiled food among the nations where I will drive them."

¹⁴Then I said, "Not so, Sovereign Lᴏʀᴅ! I have never defiled myself. From my youth until now I have never eaten anything found dead or torn by wild animals. No impure meat has ever entered my mouth."

¹⁵"Very well," he said, "I will let you bake your bread over cow dung instead of human excrement."

¹⁶He then said to me: "Son of man, I am about to cut off the food supply in Jerusalem. The people will eat rationed food in anxiety and drink rationed water in despair, ¹⁷for food and water will be scarce. They will be appalled at the sight of each other and will waste away because of[a] their sin.

God's Razor of Judgment

5 "Now, son of man, take a sharp sword and use it as a barber's razor to shave your head and your beard. Then take a set of scales and divide up the hair. ²When the days of your siege come to an end, burn a third of the hair inside the city. Take a third and strike it with the sword all around the city. And scatter a third to the wind. For I will pursue them with drawn sword. ³But take a few hairs and tuck them away in the folds of your garment. ⁴Again, take a few of these and throw them into the fire and burn them up. A fire will spread from there to all Israel.

⁵"This is what the Sovereign Lᴏʀᴅ says: This is Jerusalem, which I have set in the center of the nations, with countries all around her. ⁶Yet in her wickedness she has rebelled against my laws and decrees more than the nations and countries around her. She has rejected my laws and has not followed my decrees.

⁷"Therefore this is what the Sovereign Lᴏʀᴅ says: You have been more unruly than the nations around you and have not followed my decrees or kept my laws. You have not even[b] conformed to the standards of the nations around you.

⁸"Therefore this is what the Sovereign Lᴏʀᴅ says: I myself am against you, Jerusalem, and I will inflict punishment on you in the sight of the nations. ⁹Because of all your detestable idols, I will do to you what I have never done before and will never do again. ¹⁰Therefore in your midst parents will eat their children, and children will eat their parents. I will inflict punishment on you and will scatter all your survivors to the winds. ¹¹Therefore as surely as I live, declares the Sovereign Lᴏʀᴅ, because you have defiled my sanctuary with all your vile images and detestable practices, I myself will shave you; I will not look on you with pity or spare you. ¹²A third of your people will die of the plague or perish by famine inside you; a third will fall by the sword outside your walls; and a third I will scatter to the winds and pursue with drawn sword.

¹³"Then my anger will cease and my wrath against them will subside, and I will be avenged. And when I have spent my wrath on them, they will know that I the Lᴏʀᴅ have spoken in my zeal.

¹⁴"I will make you a ruin and a reproach among the nations around you, in the sight of all who pass by. ¹⁵You will be a reproach and a taunt, a warning and an object of horror to the nations around you when I inflict punishment on you in anger and in wrath and with stinging rebuke. I the Lᴏʀᴅ have spoken. ¹⁶When I shoot at you with my deadly and destructive arrows of famine, I will shoot to destroy you. I will bring more and more famine upon you and cut off your supply of food. ¹⁷I will send famine and wild beasts against you, and they will leave you childless. Plague and bloodshed will sweep through you, and I will bring the sword against you. I the Lᴏʀᴅ have spoken."

Doom for the Mountains of Israel

6 The word of the Lᴏʀᴅ came to me: ²"Son of man, set your face against the mountains of Israel; prophesy against them ³and say: 'You mountains of Israel, hear the word of the Sovereign Lᴏʀᴅ. This is what the Sovereign Lᴏʀᴅ says to the mountains and hills, to

---

[a] 17 Or away in   [b] 7 Most Hebrew manuscripts; some Hebrew manuscripts and Syriac You have

the ravines and valleys: I am about to bring a sword against you, and I will destroy your high places. [4]Your altars will be demolished and your incense altars will be smashed; and I will slay your people in front of your idols. [5]I will lay the dead bodies of the Israelites in front of their idols, and I will scatter your bones around your altars. [6]Wherever you live, the towns will be laid waste and the high places demolished, so that your altars will be laid waste and devastated, your idols smashed and ruined, your incense altars broken down, and what you have made wiped out. [7]Your people will fall slain among you, and you will know that I am the LORD.

[8] " 'But I will spare some, for some of you will escape the sword when you are scattered among the lands and nations. [9]Then in the nations where they have been carried captive, those who escape will remember me — how I have been grieved by their adulterous hearts, which have turned away from me, and by their eyes, which have lusted after their idols. They will loathe themselves for the evil they have done and for all their detestable practices. [10]And they will know that I am the LORD; I did not threaten in vain to bring this calamity on them.

[11] " 'This is what the Sovereign LORD says: Strike your hands together and stamp your feet and cry out "Alas!" because of all the wicked and detestable practices of the people of Israel, for they will fall by the sword, famine and plague. [12]One who is far away will die of the plague, and one who is near will fall by the sword, and anyone who survives and is spared will die of famine. So will I pour out my wrath on them. [13]And they will know that I am the LORD, when their people lie slain among their idols around their altars, on every high hill and on all the mountaintops, under every spreading tree and every leafy oak — places where they offered fragrant incense to all their idols. [14]And I will stretch out my hand against them and make the land a desolate waste from the desert to Diblah[a] — wherever they live. Then they will know that I am the LORD.' "

The End Has Come

7 The word of the LORD came to me: [2]"Son of man, this is what the Sovereign LORD says to the land of Israel:

" 'The end! The end has come
    upon the four corners of the land!
[3]The end is now upon you,
    and I will unleash my anger against
        you.
I will judge you according to your
        conduct
    and repay you for all your detestable
        practices.
[4]I will not look on you with pity;
    I will not spare you.
I will surely repay you for your conduct
    and for the detestable practices
        among you.

" 'Then you will know that I am the LORD.'

[5]"This is what the Sovereign LORD says:

" 'Disaster! Unheard-of[b] disaster!
    See, it comes!
[6]The end has come!
    The end has come!
It has roused itself against you.
    See, it comes!
[7]Doom has come upon you,
    upon you who dwell in the land.
The time has come! The day is near!
    There is panic, not joy, on the
        mountains.
[8]I am about to pour out my wrath on
        you
    and spend my anger against you.
I will judge you according to your
        conduct
    and repay you for all your detestable
        practices.
[9]I will not look on you with pity;
    I will not spare you.
I will repay you for your conduct
    and for the detestable practices
        among you.

" 'Then you will know that it is I the LORD
    who strikes you.

[10] " 'See, the day!
    See, it comes!

---

[a] 14 Most Hebrew manuscripts; a few Hebrew manuscripts *Riblah*   [b] 5 Most Hebrew manuscripts; some Hebrew manuscripts and Syriac *Disaster after*

Doom has burst forth,
the rod has budded,
arrogance has blossomed!
[11] Violence has arisen,[a]
a rod to punish the wicked.
None of the people will be left,
none of that crowd—
none of their wealth,
nothing of value.
[12] The time has come!
The day has arrived!
Let not the buyer rejoice
nor the seller grieve,
for my wrath is on the whole crowd.
[13] The seller will not recover
the property that was sold—
as long as both buyer and seller
live.
For the vision concerning the whole
crowd
will not be reversed.
Because of their sins, not one of them
will preserve their life.

[14] " 'They have blown the trumpet,
they have made all things ready,
but no one will go into battle,
for my wrath is on the whole crowd.
[15] Outside is the sword;
inside are plague and famine.
Those in the country
will die by the sword;
those in the city
will be devoured by famine and
plague.
[16] The fugitives who escape
will flee to the mountains.
Like doves of the valleys,
they will all moan,
each for their own sins.
[17] Every hand will go limp;
every leg will be wet with urine.
[18] They will put on sackcloth
and be clothed with terror.
Every face will be covered with shame,
and every head will be shaved.

[19] " 'They will throw their silver into the
streets,
and their gold will be treated as a
thing unclean.
Their silver and gold
will not be able to deliver them
in the day of the Lord's wrath.

It will not satisfy their hunger
or fill their stomachs,
for it has caused them to stumble
into sin.
[20] They took pride in their beautiful jewelry
and used it to make their
detestable idols.
They made it into vile images;
therefore I will make it a thing
unclean for them.
[21] I will give their wealth as plunder to
foreigners
and as loot to the wicked of the
earth,
who will defile it.
[22] I will turn my face away from the
people,
and robbers will desecrate the
place I treasure.
They will enter it
and will defile it.

[23] " 'Prepare chains!
For the land is full of bloodshed,
and the city is full of violence.
[24] I will bring the most wicked of nations
to take possession of their houses.
I will put an end to the pride of the
mighty,
and their sanctuaries will be
desecrated.
[25] When terror comes,
they will seek peace in vain.
[26] Calamity upon calamity will come,
and rumor upon rumor.
They will go searching for a vision
from the prophet,
priestly instruction in the law will
cease,
the counsel of the elders will come
to an end.
[27] The king will mourn,
the prince will be clothed with
despair,
and the hands of the people of the
land will tremble.
I will deal with them according to their
conduct,
and by their own standards I will
judge them.

" 'Then they will know that I am the Lord.' "

---

[a] 11 Or *The violent one has become*

Idolatry in the Temple

8 In the sixth year, in the sixth month on the fifth day, while I was sitting in my house and the elders of Judah were sitting before me, the hand of the Sovereign LORD came on me there. ²I looked, and I saw a figure like that of a man.ᵃ From what appeared to be his waist down he was like fire, and from there up his appearance was as bright as glowing metal. ³He stretched out what looked like a hand and took me by the hair of my head. The Spirit lifted me up between earth and heaven and in visions of God he took me to Jerusalem, to the entrance of the north gate of the inner court, where the idol that provokes to jealousy stood. ⁴And there before me was the glory of the God of Israel, as in the vision I had seen in the plain.

⁵Then he said to me, "Son of man, look toward the north." So I looked, and in the entrance north of the gate of the altar I saw this idol of jealousy.

⁶And he said to me, "Son of man, do you see what they are doing—the utterly detestable things the Israelites are doing here, things that will drive me far from my sanctuary? But you will see things that are even more detestable."

⁷Then he brought me to the entrance to the court. I looked, and I saw a hole in the wall. ⁸He said to me, "Son of man, now dig into the wall." So I dug into the wall and saw a doorway there.

⁹And he said to me, "Go in and see the wicked and detestable things they are doing here." ¹⁰So I went in and looked, and I saw portrayed all over the walls all kinds of crawling things and unclean animals and all the idols of Israel. ¹¹In front of them stood seventy elders of Israel, and Jaazaniah son of Shaphan was standing among them. Each had a censer in his hand, and a fragrant cloud of incense was rising.

¹²He said to me, "Son of man, have you seen what the elders of Israel are doing in the darkness, each at the shrine of his own idol? They say, 'The LORD does not see us; the LORD has forsaken the land.' " ¹³Again, he said, "You will see them doing things that are even more detestable."

¹⁴Then he brought me to the entrance of the north gate of the house of the LORD, and I saw women sitting there, mourning the god Tammuz. ¹⁵He said to me, "Do you see this, son of man? You will see things that are even more detestable than this."

¹⁶He then brought me into the inner court of the house of the LORD, and there at the entrance to the temple, between the portico and the altar, were about twenty-five men. With their backs toward the temple of the LORD and their faces toward the east, they were bowing down to the sun in the east.

¹⁷He said to me, "Have you seen this, son of man? Is it a trivial matter for the people of Judah to do the detestable things they are doing here? Must they also fill the land with violence and continually arouse my anger? Look at them putting the branch to their nose! ¹⁸Therefore I will deal with them in anger; I will

BREAKTHROUGH!

Sixth month

(EZEKIEL 8:1)

This was Elul in the Jewish lunar calendar. In our solar calendar, that would be more or less from the middle of August to the middle of September.

ᵃ 2 Or *saw a fiery figure*

not look on them with pity or spare them. Although they shout in my ears, I will not listen to them."

Judgment on the Idolaters

9 Then I heard him call out in a loud voice, "Bring near those who are appointed to execute judgment on the city, each with a weapon in his hand." ²And I saw six men coming from the direction of the upper gate, which faces north, each with a deadly weapon in his hand. With them was a man clothed in linen who had a writing kit at his side. They came in and stood beside the bronze altar.

³Now the glory of the God of Israel went up from above the cherubim, where it had been, and moved to the threshold of the temple. Then the LORD called to the man clothed in linen who had the writing kit at his side ⁴and said to him, "Go throughout the city of Jerusalem and put a mark on the foreheads of those who grieve and lament over all the detestable things that are done in it."

⁵As I listened, he said to the others, "Follow him through the city and kill, without showing pity or compassion. ⁶Slaughter the old men, the young men and women, the mothers and children, but do not touch anyone who has the mark. Begin at my sanctuary." So they began with the old men who were in front of the temple.

⁷Then he said to them, "Defile the temple and fill the courts with the slain. Go!" So they went out and began killing throughout the city. ⁸While they were killing and I was left alone, I fell facedown, crying out, "Alas, Sovereign LORD! Are you going to destroy the entire remnant of Israel in this outpouring of your wrath on Jerusalem?"

⁹He answered me, "The sin of the people of Israel and Judah is exceedingly great; the land is full of bloodshed and the city is full of injustice. They say, 'The LORD has forsaken the land; the LORD does not see.' ¹⁰So I will not look on them with pity or spare them, but I will bring down on their own heads what they have done."

¹¹Then the man in linen with the writing kit at his side brought back word, saying, "I have done as you commanded."

God's Glory Departs From the Temple

10 I looked, and I saw the likeness of a throne of lapis lazuli above the vault that was over the heads of the cherubim. ²The LORD said to the man clothed in linen, "Go in among the wheels beneath the cherubim. Fill your hands with burning coals from among the cherubim and scatter them over the city." And as I watched, he went in.

³Now the cherubim were standing on the south side of the temple when the man went in, and a cloud filled the inner court. ⁴Then the glory of the LORD rose from above the cherubim and moved to the threshold of the temple. The cloud filled the temple, and the court was full of the radiance of the glory of the LORD. ⁵The sound of the wings of the cherubim could be heard as far away as the outer court, like the voice of God Almighty[a] when he speaks.

⁶When the LORD commanded the man in linen, "Take fire from among the wheels,

---

[a] 5 Hebrew *El-Shaddai*

BREAK THROUGH!

Lapis lazuli

(EZEKIEL 10:1)

A precious blue stone that is used for jewelry.

from among the cherubim," the man went in and stood beside a wheel. [7]Then one of the cherubim reached out his hand to the fire that was among them. He took up some of it and put it into the hands of the man in linen, who took it and went out. [8](Under the wings of the cherubim could be seen what looked like human hands.)

[9]I looked, and I saw beside the cherubim four wheels, one beside each of the cherubim; the wheels sparkled like topaz. [10]As for their appearance, the four of them looked alike; each was like a wheel intersecting a wheel. [11]As they moved, they would go in any one of the four directions the cherubim faced; the wheels did not turn about[a] as the cherubim went. The cherubim went in whatever direction the head faced, without turning as they went. [12]Their entire bodies, including their backs, their hands and their wings, were completely full of eyes, as were their four wheels. [13]I heard the wheels being called "the whirling wheels." [14]Each of the cherubim had four faces: One face was that of a cherub, the second the face of a human being, the third the face of a lion, and the fourth the face of an eagle.

[15]Then the cherubim rose upward. These were the living creatures I had seen by the Kebar River. [16]When the cherubim moved, the wheels beside them moved; and when the cherubim spread their wings to rise from the ground, the wheels did not leave their side. [17]When the cherubim stood still, they also stood still; and when the cherubim rose, they rose with them, because the spirit of the living creatures was in them.

[18]Then the glory of the LORD departed from over the threshold of the temple and stopped above the cherubim. [19]While I watched, the cherubim spread their wings and rose from the ground, and as they went, the wheels went with them. They stopped at the entrance of the east gate of the LORD's house, and the glory of the God of Israel was above them.

[20]These were the living creatures I had seen beneath the God of Israel by the Kebar River, and I realized that they were cherubim. [21]Each had four faces and four wings, and under their wings was what

looked like human hands. [22]Their faces had the same appearance as those I had seen by the Kebar River. Each one went straight ahead.

God's Sure Judgment on Jerusalem

11 Then the Spirit lifted me up and brought me to the gate of the house of the LORD that faces east. There at the entrance of the gate were twenty-five men, and I saw among them Jaazaniah son of Azzur and Pelatiah son of Benaiah, leaders of the people. [2]The LORD said to me, "Son of man, these are the men who are plotting evil and giving wicked advice in this city. [3]They say, 'Haven't our houses been recently rebuilt? This city is a pot, and we are the meat in it.' [4]Therefore prophesy against them; prophesy, son of man."

[5]Then the Spirit of the LORD came on me, and he told me to say: "This is what the LORD says: That is what you are saying, you leaders in Israel, but I know what is going through your mind. [6]You have killed many people in this city and filled its streets with the dead.

[7]"Therefore this is what the Sovereign LORD says: The bodies you have thrown there are the meat and this city is the pot, but I will drive you out of it. [8]You fear the sword, and the sword is what I will bring against you, declares the Sovereign LORD. [9]I will drive you out of the city and deliver you into the hands of foreigners and inflict punishment on you. [10]You will fall by the sword, and I will execute judgment on you at the borders of Israel. Then you will know that I am the LORD. [11]This city will not be a pot for you, nor will you be the meat in it; I will execute judgment on you at the borders of Israel. [12]And you will know that I am the LORD, for you have not followed my decrees or kept my laws but have conformed to the standards of the nations around you."

[13]Now as I was prophesying, Pelatiah son of Benaiah died. Then I fell facedown and cried out in a loud voice, "Alas, Sovereign LORD! Will you completely destroy the remnant of Israel?"

---

[a] 11 Or *aside*

The Promise of Israel's Return

¹⁴The word of the Lord came to me: ¹⁵"Son of man, the people of Jerusalem have said of your fellow exiles and all the other Israelites, 'They are far away from the Lord; this land was given to us as our possession.'

¹⁶"Therefore say: 'This is what the Sovereign Lord says: Although I sent them far away among the nations and scattered them among the countries, yet for a little while I have been a sanctuary for them in the countries where they have gone.'

¹⁷"Therefore say: 'This is what the Sovereign Lord says: I will gather you from the nations and bring you back from the countries where you have been scattered, and I will give you back the land of Israel again.'

¹⁸"They will return to it and remove all its vile images and detestable idols. ¹⁹I will give them an undivided heart and put a new spirit in them; I will remove from them their heart of stone and give them a heart of flesh. ²⁰Then they will follow my decrees and be careful to keep my laws. They will be my people, and I will be their God. ²¹But as for those whose hearts are devoted to their vile images and detestable idols, I will bring down on their own heads what they have done, declares the Sovereign Lord."

²²Then the cherubim, with the wheels beside them, spread their wings, and the glory of the God of Israel was above them. ²³The glory of the Lord went up from within the city and stopped above the mountain east of it. ²⁴The Spirit lifted me up and brought me to the exiles in Babylonia[a] in the vision given by the Spirit of God.

Then the vision I had seen went up from me, ²⁵and I told the exiles everything the Lord had shown me.

The Exile Symbolized

12 The word of the Lord came to me: ²"Son of man, you are living among a rebellious people. They have eyes to see but do not see and ears to hear but do not hear, for they are a rebellious people.

³"Therefore, son of man, pack your belongings for exile and in the daytime, as they watch, set out and go from where you are to another place. Perhaps they will understand, though they are a rebellious people. ⁴During the daytime, while they watch, bring out your belongings packed for exile. Then in the evening, while they are watching, go out like those who go into exile. ⁵While they watch, dig through the wall and take your belongings out through it. ⁶Put them on your shoulder as they are watching and carry them out at dusk. Cover your face so that you cannot see the land, for I have made you a sign to the Israelites."

⁷So I did as I was commanded. During the day I brought out my things packed for exile. Then in the evening I dug through the wall with my hands. I took my belongings out at dusk, carrying them on my shoulders while they watched.

⁸In the morning the word of the Lord came to me: ⁹"Son of man, did not the Israelites, that rebellious people, ask you, 'What are you doing?'

¹⁰"Say to them, 'This is what the Sovereign Lord says: This prophecy concerns the prince in Jerusalem and all the Israelites who are there.' ¹¹Say to them, 'I am a sign to you.'

"As I have done, so it will be done to them. They will go into exile as captives.

¹²"The prince among them will put his things on his shoulder at dusk and leave, and a hole will be dug in the wall for him to go through. He will cover his face so that he cannot see the land. ¹³I will spread my net for him, and he will be caught in my snare; I will bring him to Babylonia, the land of the Chaldeans, but he will not see it, and there he will die. ¹⁴I will scatter to the winds all those around him—his staff and all his troops—and I will pursue them with drawn sword.

¹⁵"They will know that I am the Lord, when I disperse them among the nations and scatter them through the countries. ¹⁶But I will spare a few of them from the sword, famine and plague, so that in the nations where they go they may acknowledge all their detestable practices. Then they will know that I am the Lord."

---

a 24 Or Chaldea

[17]The word of the Lord came to me: [18]"Son of man, tremble as you eat your food, and shudder in fear as you drink your water. [19]Say to the people of the land: 'This is what the Sovereign Lord says about those living in Jerusalem and in the land of Israel: They will eat their food in anxiety and drink their water in despair, for their land will be stripped of everything in it because of the violence of all who live there. [20]The inhabited towns will be laid waste and the land will be desolate. Then you will know that I am the Lord.'"

There Will Be No Delay

[21]The word of the Lord came to me: [22]"Son of man, what is this proverb you have in the land of Israel: 'The days go by and every vision comes to nothing'? [23]Say to them, 'This is what the Sovereign Lord says: I am going to put an end to this proverb, and they will no longer quote it in Israel.' Say to them, 'The days are near when every vision will be fulfilled. [24]For there will be no more false visions or flattering divinations among the people of Israel. [25]But I the Lord will speak what I will, and it shall be fulfilled without delay. For in your days, you rebellious people, I will fulfill whatever I say, declares the Sovereign Lord.'"

[26]The word of the Lord came to me: [27]"Son of man, the Israelites are saying, 'The vision he sees is for many years from now, and he prophesies about the distant future.'

[28]"Therefore say to them, 'This is what the Sovereign Lord says: None of my words will be delayed any longer; whatever I say will be fulfilled, declares the Sovereign Lord.'"

False Prophets Condemned

13 The word of the Lord came to me: [2]"Son of man, prophesy against the prophets of Israel who are now prophesying. Say to those who prophesy out of their own imagination: 'Hear the word of the Lord! [3]This is what the Sovereign Lord says: Woe to the foolish[a] prophets who follow their own spirit and have seen nothing! [4]Your prophets, Israel, are like jackals among ruins. [5]You have not gone up to the breaches in the wall to repair it for the people of Israel so that it will stand firm in the battle on the day of the Lord. [6]Their visions are false and their divinations a lie. Even though the Lord has not sent them, they say, "The Lord declares," and expect him to fulfill their words. [7]Have you not seen false visions and uttered lying divinations when you say, "The Lord declares," though I have not spoken?

[8]"'Therefore this is what the Sovereign Lord says: Because of your false words and lying visions, I am against you, declares the Sovereign Lord. [9]My hand will be against the prophets who see false visions and utter lying divinations. They will not belong to the council of my people or be listed in the records of Israel, nor will they enter the land of Israel. Then you will know that I am the Sovereign Lord.

[10]"'Because they lead my people astray, saying, "Peace," when there is no peace, and because, when a flimsy wall is built, they cover it with whitewash, [11]therefore tell those who cover it with whitewash that it is going to fall. Rain will come in torrents, and I will send hailstones hurtling down, and violent winds will burst forth. [12]When the wall collapses, will people not ask you, "Where is the whitewash you covered it with?"

[13]"'Therefore this is what the Sovereign Lord says: In my wrath I will unleash a violent wind, and in my anger hailstones and torrents of rain will fall with destructive fury. [14]I will tear down the wall you have covered with whitewash and will level it to the ground so that its foundation will be laid bare. When it[b] falls, you will be destroyed in it; and you will know that I am the Lord. [15]So I will pour out my wrath against the wall and against those who covered it with whitewash. I will say to you, "The wall is gone and so are those who whitewashed it, [16]those prophets of Israel who prophesied to Jerusalem and saw visions of peace for her when there was no peace, declares the Sovereign Lord."'

---

[a] 3 Or *wicked*   [b] 14 Or *the city*

17 "Now, son of man, set your face against the daughters of your people who prophesy out of their own imagination. Prophesy against them 18and say, 'This is what the Sovereign Lord says: Woe to the women who sew magic charms on all their wrists and make veils of various lengths for their heads in order to ensnare people. Will you ensnare the lives of my people but preserve your own? 19You have profaned me among my people for a few handfuls of barley and scraps of bread. By lying to my people, who listen to lies, you have killed those who should not have died and have spared those who should not live.

20 " 'Therefore this is what the Sovereign Lord says: I am against your magic charms with which you ensnare people like birds and I will tear them from your arms; I will set free the people that you ensnare like birds. 21I will tear off your veils and save my people from your hands, and they will no longer fall prey to your power. Then you will know that I am the Lord. 22Because you disheartened the righteous with your lies, when I had brought them no grief, and because you encouraged the wicked not to turn from their evil ways and so save their lives, 23therefore you will no longer see false visions or practice divination. I will save my people from your hands. And then you will know that I am the Lord.' "

Idolaters Condemned

14 Some of the elders of Israel came to me and sat down in front of me. 2Then the word of the Lord came to me: 3 "Son of man, these men have set up idols in their hearts and put wicked stumbling blocks before their faces. Should I let them inquire of me at all? 4Therefore speak to them and tell them, 'This is what the Sovereign Lord says: When any of the Israelites set up idols in their hearts and put a wicked stumbling block before their faces and then go to a prophet, I the Lord will answer them myself in keeping with their great idolatry. 5I will do this to recapture the hearts of the people of Israel, who have all deserted me for their idols.'

6 "Therefore say to the people of Israel, 'This is what the Sovereign Lord says: Repent! Turn from your idols and renounce all your detestable practices!

7 " 'When any of the Israelites or any foreigner residing in Israel separate themselves from me and set up idols in their hearts and put a wicked stumbling block before their faces and then go to a prophet to inquire of me, I the Lord will answer them myself. 8I will set my face against them and make them an example and a byword. I will remove them from my people. Then you will know that I am the Lord.

9 " 'And if the prophet is enticed to utter a prophecy, I the Lord have enticed that prophet, and I will stretch out my hand against him and destroy him from among my people Israel. 10They will bear their guilt—the prophet will be as guilty as the one who consults him. 11Then the people of Israel will no longer stray from me, nor will they defile themselves anymore with all their sins. They will be my people, and I will be their God, declares the Sovereign Lord.' "

Jerusalem's Judgment Inescapable

12The word of the Lord came to me: 13 "Son of man, if a country sins against me by being unfaithful and I stretch out my hand against it to cut off its food supply and send famine upon it and kill its people and their animals, 14even if these three men—Noah, Daniel[a] and Job—were in it, they could save only themselves by their righteousness, declares the Sovereign Lord.

15 "Or if I send wild beasts through that country and they leave it childless and it becomes desolate so that no one can pass through it because of the beasts, 16as surely as I live, declares the Sovereign Lord, even if these three men were in it, they could not save their own sons or daughters. They alone would be saved, but the land would be desolate.

17 "Or if I bring a sword against that country and say, 'Let the sword pass throughout the land,' and I kill its people and their animals, 18as surely as I live, de-

---

a 14 Or *Danel,* a man of renown in ancient literature; also in verse 20 clares the Sovereign LORD, even if these three men were in it, they could not save their own sons or daughters. They alone would be saved.

¹⁹"Or if I send a plague into that land and pour out my wrath on it through bloodshed, killing its people and their animals, ²⁰as surely as I live, declares the Sovereign LORD, even if Noah, Daniel and Job were in it, they could save neither son nor daughter. They would save only themselves by their righteousness.

²¹"For this is what the Sovereign LORD says: How much worse will it be when I send against Jerusalem my four dreadful judgments—sword and famine and wild beasts and plague—to kill its men and their animals! ²²Yet there will be some survivors—sons and daughters who will be brought out of it. They will come to you, and when you see their conduct and their actions, you will be consoled regarding the disaster I have brought on Jerusalem—every disaster I have brought on it. ²³You will be consoled when you see their conduct and their actions, for you will know that I have done nothing in it without cause, declares the Sovereign LORD."

Jerusalem as a Useless Vine

15 The word of the LORD came to me: ²"Son of man, how is the wood of a vine different from that of a branch from any of the trees in the forest? ³Is wood ever taken from it to make anything useful? Do they make pegs from it to hang things on? ⁴And after it is thrown on the fire as fuel and the fire burns both ends and chars the middle, is it then useful for anything? ⁵If it was not useful for anything when it was whole, how much less can it be made into something useful when the fire has burned it and it is charred?

⁶"Therefore this is what the Sovereign LORD says: As I have given the wood of the vine among the trees of the forest as fuel for the fire, so will I treat the people living in Jerusalem. ⁷I will set my face against them. Although they have come out of the fire, the fire will yet consume them. And when I set my face against them, you will know that I am the LORD. ⁸I will make the land desolate because

they have been unfaithful, declares the Sovereign LORD."

Jerusalem as an Adulterous Wife

16 The word of the LORD came to me: ²"Son of man, confront Jerusalem with her detestable practices ³and say, 'This is what the Sovereign LORD says to Jerusalem: Your ancestry and birth were in the land of the Canaanites; your father was an Amorite and your mother a Hittite. ⁴On the day you were born your cord was not cut, nor were you washed with water to make you clean, nor were you rubbed with salt or wrapped in cloths. ⁵No one looked on you with pity or had compassion enough to do any of these things for you. Rather, you were thrown out into the open field, for on the day you were born you were despised.

⁶"'Then I passed by and saw you kicking about in your blood, and as you lay there in your blood I said to you, "Live!"ᵃ ⁷I made you grow like a plant of the field. You grew and developed and entered puberty. Your breasts had formed and your hair had grown, yet you were stark naked.

⁸"'Later I passed by, and when I looked at you and saw that you were old enough for love, I spread the corner of my garment over you and covered your naked body. I gave you my solemn oath and entered into a covenant with you, declares the Sovereign LORD, and you became mine.

⁹"'I bathed you with water and washed the blood from you and put ointments on you. ¹⁰I clothed you with an embroidered dress and put sandals of fine leather on you. I dressed you in fine linen and covered you with costly garments. ¹¹I adorned you with jewelry: I put bracelets on your arms and a necklace around your neck, ¹²and I put a ring on your nose, earrings on your ears and a beautiful crown on your head. ¹³So you were adorned with gold and silver; your clothes were of fine linen and costly fabric and embroidered cloth. Your food was honey, olive oil and the finest flour. You became very beautiful

---

ᵃ 6 A few Hebrew manuscripts, Septuagint and Syriac; most Hebrew manuscripts repeat *and as you lay there in your blood I said to you, "Live!"*

and rose to be a queen. ¹⁴And your fame spread among the nations on account of your beauty, because the splendor I had given you made your beauty perfect, declares the Sovereign LORD.

¹⁵ " 'But you trusted in your beauty and used your fame to become a prostitute. You lavished your favors on anyone who passed by and your beauty became his. ¹⁶You took some of your garments to make gaudy high places, where you carried on your prostitution. You went to him, and he possessed your beauty.ᵃ ¹⁷You also took the fine jewelry I gave you, the jewelry made of my gold and silver, and you made for yourself male idols and engaged in prostitution with them. ¹⁸And you took your embroidered clothes to put on them, and you offered my oil and incense before them. ¹⁹Also the food I provided for you—the flour, olive oil and honey I gave you to eat—you offered as fragrant incense before them. That is what happened, declares the Sovereign LORD.

²⁰ " 'And you took your sons and daughters whom you bore to me and sacrificed them as food to the idols. Was your prostitution not enough? ²¹You slaughtered my children and sacrificed them to the idols. ²²In all your detestable practices and your prostitution you did not remember the days of your youth, when you were naked and bare, kicking about in your blood.

²³ " 'Woe! Woe to you, declares the Sovereign LORD. In addition to all your other wickedness, ²⁴you built a mound for yourself and made a lofty shrine in every public square. ²⁵At every street corner you built your lofty shrines and degraded your beauty, spreading your legs with increasing promiscuity to anyone who passed by. ²⁶You engaged in prostitution with the Egyptians, your neighbors with large genitals, and aroused my anger with your increasing promiscuity. ²⁷So I stretched out my hand against you and reduced your territory; I gave you over to the greed of your enemies, the daughters of the Philistines, who were shocked by your lewd conduct. ²⁸You engaged in prostitution with the Assyrians too, because you were insatiable; and even after that, you still

BREAKTHROUGH!

Assyrians
(EZEKIEL 16:28)
Warrior people from the region of Mesopotamia who were able to defeat other nations in that region, including the kingdom of Israel.

were not satisfied. ²⁹Then you increased your promiscuity to include Babylonia,ᵇ a land of merchants, but even with this you were not satisfied.

³⁰ " 'I am filled with fury against you,ᶜ declares the Sovereign LORD, when you do all these things, acting like a brazen prostitute! ³¹When you built your mounds at every street corner and made your lofty shrines in every public square, you were unlike a prostitute, because you scorned payment.

³² " 'You adulterous wife! You prefer strangers to your own husband! ³³All prostitutes receive gifts, but you give gifts to all your lovers, bribing them to come to you from everywhere for your illicit favors. ³⁴So in your prostitution you are the opposite of others; no one runs after you for your favors. You are the very opposite, for you give payment and none is given to you.

ᵃ 16 The meaning of the Hebrew for this sentence is uncertain.   ᵇ 29 Or *Chaldea*   ᶜ 30 Or *How feverish is your heart,*

³⁵" 'Therefore, you prostitute, hear the word of the LORD! ³⁶This is what the Sovereign LORD says: Because you poured out your lust and exposed your naked body in your promiscuity with your lovers, and because of all your detestable idols, and because you gave them your children's blood, ³⁷therefore I am going to gather all your lovers, with whom you found pleasure, those you loved as well as those you hated. I will gather them against you from all around and will strip you in front of them, and they will see you stark naked. ³⁸I will sentence you to the punishment of women who commit adultery and who shed blood; I will bring on you the blood vengeance of my wrath and jealous anger. ³⁹Then I will deliver you into the hands of your lovers, and they will tear down your mounds and destroy your lofty shrines. They will strip you of your clothes and take your fine jewelry and leave you stark naked. ⁴⁰They will bring a mob against you, who will stone you and hack you to pieces with their swords. ⁴¹They will burn down your houses and inflict punishment on you in the sight of many women. I will put a stop to your prostitution, and you will no longer pay your lovers. ⁴²Then my wrath against you will subside and my jealous anger will turn away from you; I will be calm and no longer angry.

⁴³" 'Because you did not remember the days of your youth but enraged me with all these things, I will surely bring down on your head what you have done, declares the Sovereign LORD. Did you not add lewdness to all your other detestable practices?

⁴⁴" 'Everyone who quotes proverbs will quote this proverb about you: "Like mother, like daughter." ⁴⁵You are a true daughter of your mother, who despised her husband and her children; and you are a true sister of your sisters, who despised their husbands and their children. Your mother was a Hittite and your father an Amorite. ⁴⁶Your older sister was Samaria, who lived to the north of you with her daughters; and your younger sister, who lived to the south of you with her daughters, was Sodom. ⁴⁷You not only followed their ways and copied their detestable practices, but in all your ways you soon became more depraved than they. ⁴⁸As surely as I live, declares the Sovereign LORD, your sister Sodom and her daughters never did what you and your daughters have done.

⁴⁹" 'Now this was the sin of your sister Sodom: She and her daughters were arrogant, overfed and unconcerned; they did not help the poor and needy. ⁵⁰They were haughty and did detestable things before me. Therefore I did away with them as you have seen. ⁵¹Samaria did not commit half the sins you did. You have done more detestable things than they, and have made your sisters seem righteous by all these things you have done. ⁵²Bear your disgrace, for you have furnished some justification for your sisters. Because your sins were more vile than theirs, they appear more righteous than you. So then, be ashamed and bear your disgrace, for you have made your sisters appear righteous.

⁵³" 'However, I will restore the fortunes of Sodom and her daughters and of

BREAK THROUGH!

Hittites
(EZEKIEL 16:45)

The Hittites were a small nation, but very powerful. They lived in what is now the western peninsula of Turkey. Since they were very good warriors, sometimes they served other countries and kingdoms.

Amorites
(EZEKIEL 16:45)
They were nomads (which means they moved around a lot) who lived in Canaan before the Israelites got there.

Samaria and her daughters, and your fortunes along with them, ⁵⁴so that you may bear your disgrace and be ashamed of all you have done in giving them comfort. ⁵⁵And your sisters, Sodom with her daughters and Samaria with her daughters, will return to what they were before; and you and your daughters will return to what you were before. ⁵⁶You would not even mention your sister Sodom in the day of your pride, ⁵⁷before your wickedness was uncovered. Even so, you are now scorned by the daughters of Edom*ᵃ* and all her neighbors and the daughters of the Philistines—all those around you who despise you. ⁵⁸You will bear the consequences of your lewdness and your detestable practices, declares the LORD.

⁵⁹" 'This is what the Sovereign LORD says: I will deal with you as you deserve, because you have despised my oath by breaking the covenant. ⁶⁰Yet I will remember the covenant I made with you in the days of your youth, and I will establish an everlasting covenant with you. ⁶¹Then you will remember your ways and be ashamed when you receive your sisters, both those who are older than you and those who are younger. I will give them to you as daughters, but not on the basis of my covenant with you. ⁶²So I will establish my covenant with you, and you will know that I am the LORD. ⁶³Then, when I make atonement for you for all you have done, you will remember and be ashamed and never again open your mouth because of your humiliation, declares the Sovereign LORD.' "

Two Eagles and a Vine

17 The word of the LORD came to me: ²"Son of man, set forth an allegory and tell it to the Israelites as a parable. ³Say to them, 'This is what the Sovereign LORD says: A great eagle with powerful wings, long feathers and full plumage of varied colors came to Lebanon. Taking hold of the top of a cedar, ⁴he broke off its topmost shoot and carried it away to a land of merchants, where he planted it in a city of traders.

⁵" 'He took one of the seedlings of the land and put it in fertile soil. He planted it like a willow by abundant water, ⁶and it sprouted and became a low, spreading vine. Its branches turned toward him, but its roots remained under it. So it became a vine and produced branches and put out leafy boughs.

⁷" 'But there was another great eagle with powerful wings and full plumage. The vine now sent out its roots toward him from the plot where it was planted and stretched out its branches to him for water. ⁸It had been planted in good soil by abundant water so that it would produce branches, bear fruit and become a splendid vine.'

⁹"Say to them, 'This is what the Sovereign LORD says: Will it thrive? Will it not be uprooted and stripped of its fruit so that it withers? All its new growth will wither. It will not take a strong arm or many people to pull it up by the roots. ¹⁰It has been planted, but will it thrive? Will it not wither completely when the east wind strikes it— wither away in the plot where it grew?' "

ᵃ 57 Many Hebrew manuscripts and Syriac; most Hebrew manuscripts, Septuagint and Vulgate *Aram*

¹¹Then the word of the LORD came to me: ¹²"Say to this rebellious people, 'Do you not know what these things mean?' Say to them: 'The king of Babylon went to Jerusalem and carried off her king and her nobles, bringing them back with him to Babylon. ¹³Then he took a member of the royal family and made a treaty with him, putting him under oath. He also carried away the leading men of the land, ¹⁴so that the kingdom would be brought low, unable to rise again, surviving only by keeping his treaty. ¹⁵But the king rebelled against him by sending his envoys to Egypt to get horses and a large army. Will he succeed? Will he who does such things escape? Will he break the treaty and yet escape?

¹⁶"'As surely as I live, declares the Sovereign LORD, he shall die in Babylon, in the land of the king who put him on the throne, whose oath he despised and whose treaty he broke. ¹⁷Pharaoh with his mighty army and great horde will be of no help to him in war, when ramps are built and siege works erected to destroy many lives. ¹⁸He despised the oath by breaking the covenant. Because he had given his hand in pledge and yet did all these things, he shall not escape.

¹⁹"'Therefore this is what the Sovereign LORD says: As surely as I live, I will repay him for despising my oath and breaking my covenant. ²⁰I will spread my net for him, and he will be caught in my snare. I will bring him to Babylon and execute judgment on him there because he was unfaithful to me. ²¹All his choice troops will fall by the sword, and the survivors will be scattered to the winds. Then you will know that I the LORD have spoken.

²²"'This is what the Sovereign LORD says: I myself will take a shoot from the very top of a cedar and plant it; I will break off a tender sprig from its topmost shoots and plant it on a high and lofty mountain. ²³On the mountain heights of Israel I will plant it; it will produce branches and bear fruit and become a splendid cedar. Birds of every kind will nest in it; they will find shelter in the shade of its branches. ²⁴All the trees of the forest will know that I the LORD bring down the tall tree and make the low tree grow tall. I dry up the green tree and make the dry tree flourish.

"'I the LORD have spoken, and I will do it.'"

The One Who Sins Will Die

18 The word of the LORD came to me: ²"What do you people mean by quoting this proverb about the land of Israel:

" 'The parents eat sour grapes,
    and the children's teeth are set on
        edge'?

³"As surely as I live, declares the Sovereign LORD, you will no longer quote this proverb in Israel. ⁴For everyone belongs to me, the parent as well as the child— both alike belong to me. The one who sins is the one who will die.

⁵"Suppose there is a righteous man
    who does what is just and right.
⁶He does not eat at the mountain
        shrines
    or look to the idols of Israel.
He does not defile his neighbor's wife
    or have sexual relations with a
        woman during her period.
⁷He does not oppress anyone,
    but returns what he took in pledge
        for a loan.
He does not commit robbery
    but gives his food to the hungry
    and provides clothing for the naked.
⁸He does not lend to them at interest
    or take a profit from them.
He withholds his hand from doing
        wrong
    and judges fairly between two
        parties.
⁹He follows my decrees
    and faithfully keeps my laws.
That man is righteous;
    he will surely live,
            declares the Sovereign LORD.

¹⁰"Suppose he has a violent son, who sheds blood or does any of these other things[a] ¹¹(though the father has done none of them):

"He eats at the mountain shrines.
He defiles his neighbor's wife.

---

a 10 Or things to a brother

¹²He oppresses the poor and needy.
He commits robbery.
He does not return what he took in
    pledge.
He looks to the idols.
He does detestable things.
¹³He lends at interest and takes a
    profit.

Will such a man live? He will not! Because he has done all these detestable things, he is to be put to death; his blood will be on his own head.

¹⁴"But suppose this son has a son who sees all the sins his father commits, and though he sees them, he does not do such things:

¹⁵"He does not eat at the mountain
    shrines
    or look to the idols of Israel.
He does not defile his neighbor's wife.
¹⁶He does not oppress anyone
    or require a pledge for a loan.
He does not commit robbery
    but gives his food to the hungry
    and provides clothing for the
    naked.
¹⁷He withholds his hand from
    mistreating the poor
    and takes no interest or profit from
    them.
He keeps my laws and follows my
    decrees.

He will not die for his father's sin; he will surely live. ¹⁸But his father will die for his own sin, because he practiced extortion, robbed his brother and did what was wrong among his people.

¹⁹"Yet you ask, 'Why does the son not share the guilt of his father?' Since the son has done what is just and right and has been careful to keep all my decrees, he will surely live. ²⁰The one who sins is the one who will die. The child will not share the guilt of the parent, nor will the parent share the guilt of the child. The righteousness of the righteous will be credited to them, and the wickedness of the wicked will be charged against them.

²¹"But if a wicked person turns away from all the sins they have committed and keeps all my decrees and does what is just and right, that person will surely live; they will not die. ²²None of the offenses they have committed will be remembered against them. Because of the righteous things they have done, they will live. ²³Do I take any pleasure in the death of the wicked? declares the Sovereign LORD. Rather, am I not pleased when they turn from their ways and live?

²⁴"But if a righteous person turns from their righteousness and commits sin and does the same detestable things the wicked person does, will they live? None of the righteous things that person has done will be remembered. Because of the unfaithfulness they are guilty of and because of the sins they have committed, they will die.

²⁵"Yet you say, 'The way of the Lord is not just.' Hear, you Israelites: Is my way unjust? Is it not your ways that are unjust? ²⁶If a righteous person turns from their righteousness and commits sin, they will die for it; because of the sin they have committed they will die. ²⁷But if a wicked person turns away from the wickedness they have committed and does what is just and right, they will save their life. ²⁸Because they consider all the offenses they have committed and turn away from them, that person will surely live; they will not die. ²⁹Yet the Israelites say, 'The way of the Lord is not just.' Are my ways unjust, people of Israel? Is it not your ways that are unjust?

³⁰"Therefore, you Israelites, I will judge each of you according to your own ways, declares the Sovereign LORD. Repent! Turn away from all your offenses; then sin will not be your downfall. ³¹Rid yourselves of all the offenses you have committed, and get a new heart and a new spirit. Why will you die, people of Israel? ³²For I take no pleasure in the death of anyone, declares the Sovereign LORD. Repent and live!

A Lament Over Israel's Princes

19 "Take up a lament concerning the princes of Israel ²and say:

" 'What a lioness was your mother
    among the lions!
She lay down among them
    and reared her cubs.

³ She brought up one of her cubs,
  and he became a strong lion.
He learned to tear the prey
  and he became a man-eater.
⁴ The nations heard about him,
  and he was trapped in their pit.
They led him with hooks
  to the land of Egypt.

⁵ " 'When she saw her hope unfulfilled,
  her expectation gone,
she took another of her cubs
  and made him a strong lion.
⁶ He prowled among the lions,
  for he was now a strong lion.
He learned to tear the prey
  and he became a man-eater.
⁷ He broke downᵃ their strongholds
  and devastated their towns.
The land and all who were in it
  were terrified by his roaring.
⁸ Then the nations came against him,
  those from regions round about.
They spread their net for him,
  and he was trapped in their pit.
⁹ With hooks they pulled him into a
      cage
  and brought him to the king of
      Babylon.
They put him in prison,
  so his roar was heard no longer
  on the mountains of Israel.

¹⁰ " 'Your mother was like a vine in your
      vineyardᵇ
  planted by the water;
it was fruitful and full of branches
  because of abundant water.
¹¹ Its branches were strong,
  fit for a ruler's scepter.
It towered high
  above the thick foliage,
conspicuous for its height
  and for its many branches.
¹² But it was uprooted in fury
  and thrown to the ground.
The east wind made it shrivel,
  it was stripped of its fruit;
its strong branches withered
  and fire consumed them.
¹³ Now it is planted in the desert,
  in a dry and thirsty land.
¹⁴ Fire spread from one of its mainᶜ
      branches

and consumed its fruit.
No strong branch is left on it
  fit for a ruler's scepter.'

"This is a lament and is to be used as a
lament."

Rebellious Israel Purged

20 In the seventh year, in the fifth
month on the tenth day, some of
the elders of Israel came to inquire of the
Lᴏʀᴅ, and they sat down in front of me.

² Then the word of the Lᴏʀᴅ came to me:
³ "Son of man, speak to the elders of Israel and say to them, 'This is what the
Sovereign Lᴏʀᴅ says: Have you come to
inquire of me? As surely as I live, I will not
let you inquire of me, declares the Sovereign Lᴏʀᴅ.'

⁴ "Will you judge them? Will you judge
them, son of man? Then confront them
with the detestable practices of their ancestors ⁵ and say to them: 'This is what

---

ᵃ 7 Targum (see Septuagint); Hebrew *He knew*
ᵇ 10 Two Hebrew manuscripts; most Hebrew manuscripts
your blood   ᶜ 14 Or *from under its*

Fifth month

(EZEKIEL 20:1)

In the Jewish lunar calendar, it was called Ab.
That would be from the middle of July to the
middle of August in our solar calendar.

the Sovereign LORD says: On the day I chose Israel, I swore with uplifted hand to the descendants of Jacob and revealed myself to them in Egypt. With uplifted hand I said to them, "I am the LORD your God." [6]On that day I swore to them that I would bring them out of Egypt into a land I had searched out for them, a land flowing with milk and honey, the most beautiful of all lands. [7]And I said to them, "Each of you, get rid of the vile images you have set your eyes on, and do not defile yourselves with the idols of Egypt. I am the LORD your God."

[8]" 'But they rebelled against me and would not listen to me; they did not get rid of the vile images they had set their eyes on, nor did they forsake the idols of Egypt. So I said I would pour out my wrath on them and spend my anger against them in Egypt. [9]But for the sake of my name, I brought them out of Egypt. I did it to keep my name from being profaned in the eyes of the nations among whom they lived and in whose sight I had revealed myself to the Israelites. [10]Therefore I led them out of Egypt and brought them into the wilderness. [11]I gave them my decrees and made known to them my laws, by which the person who obeys them will live. [12]Also I gave them my Sabbaths as a sign between us, so they would know that I the LORD made them holy.

[13]" 'Yet the people of Israel rebelled against me in the wilderness. They did not follow my decrees but rejected my laws—by which the person who obeys them will live—and they utterly desecrated my Sabbaths. So I said I would pour out my wrath on them and destroy them in the wilderness. [14]But for the sake of my name I did what would keep it from being profaned in the eyes of the nations in whose sight I had brought them out. [15]Also with uplifted hand I swore to them in the wilderness that I would not bring them into the land I had given them—a land flowing with milk and honey, the most beautiful of all lands— [16]because they rejected my laws and did not follow my decrees and desecrated my Sabbaths. For their hearts were devoted to their idols.

[17]Yet I looked on them with pity and did not destroy them or put an end to them in the wilderness. [18]I said to their children in the wilderness, "Do not follow the statutes of your parents or keep their laws or defile yourselves with their idols. [19]I am the LORD your God; follow my decrees and be careful to keep my laws. [20]Keep my Sabbaths holy, that they may be a sign between us. Then you will know that I am the LORD your God."

[21]" 'But the children rebelled against me: They did not follow my decrees, they were not careful to keep my laws, of which I said, "The person who obeys them will live by them," and they desecrated my Sabbaths. So I said I would pour out my wrath on them and spend my anger against them in the wilderness. [22]But I withheld my hand, and for the sake of my name I did what would keep it from being profaned in the eyes of the nations in whose sight I had brought them out. [23]Also with uplifted hand I swore to them in the wilderness that I would disperse them among the nations and scatter them through the countries, [24]because they had not obeyed my laws but had rejected my decrees and desecrated my Sabbaths, and their eyes lusted after their parents' idols. [25]So I gave them other statutes that were not good and laws through which they could not live; [26]I defiled them through their gifts—the sacrifice of every firstborn—that I might fill them with horror so they would know that I am the LORD.'

[27]"Therefore, son of man, speak to the people of Israel and say to them, 'This is what the Sovereign LORD says: In this also your ancestors blasphemed me by being unfaithful to me: [28]When I brought them into the land I had sworn to give them and they saw any high hill or any leafy tree, there they offered their sacrifices, made offerings that aroused my anger, presented their fragrant incense and poured out their drink offerings. [29]Then I said to them: What is this high place you go to?' " (It is called Bamah[a] to this day.)

---

[a] 29 *Bamah* means *high place*.

Rebellious Israel Renewed

[30] "Therefore say to the Israelites: 'This is what the Sovereign LORD says: Will you defile yourselves the way your ancestors did and lust after their vile images? [31]When you offer your gifts—the sacrifice of your children in the fire—you continue to defile yourselves with all your idols to this day. Am I to let you inquire of me, you Israelites? As surely as I live, declares the Sovereign LORD, I will not let you inquire of me.

[32] " 'You say, "We want to be like the nations, like the peoples of the world, who serve wood and stone." But what you have in mind will never happen. [33]As surely as I live, declares the Sovereign LORD, I will reign over you with a mighty hand and an outstretched arm and with outpoured wrath. [34]I will bring you from the nations and gather you from the countries where you have been scattered—with a mighty hand and an outstretched arm and with outpoured wrath. [35]I will bring you into the wilderness of the nations and there, face to face, I will execute judgment upon you. [36]As I judged your ancestors in the wilderness of the land of Egypt, so I will judge you, declares the Sovereign LORD. [37]I will take note of you as you pass under my rod, and I will bring you into the bond of the covenant. [38]I will purge you of those who revolt and rebel against me. Although I will bring them out of the land where they are living, yet they will not enter the land of Israel. Then you will know that I am the LORD.

[39] " 'As for you, people of Israel, this is what the Sovereign LORD says: Go and serve your idols, every one of you! But afterward you will surely listen to me and no longer profane my holy name with your gifts and idols. [40]For on my holy mountain, the high mountain of Israel, declares the Sovereign LORD, there in the land all the people of Israel will serve me, and there I will accept them. There I will require your offerings and your choice gifts,[a] along with all your holy sacrifices. [41]I will accept you as fragrant incense when I bring you out from the nations and gather you from the countries where you have been scat-

tered, and I will be proved holy through you in the sight of the nations. [42]Then you will know that I am the LORD, when I bring you into the land of Israel, the land I had sworn with uplifted hand to give to your ancestors. [43]There you will remember your conduct and all the actions by which you have defiled yourselves, and you will loathe yourselves for all the evil you have done. [44]You will know that I am the LORD, when I deal with you for my name's sake and not according to your evil ways and your corrupt practices, you people of Israel, declares the Sovereign LORD.' "

Prophecy Against the South

[45]The word of the LORD came to me: [46]"Son of man, set your face toward the south; preach against the south and prophesy against the forest of the southland. [47]Say to the southern forest: 'Hear the word of the LORD. This is what the Sovereign LORD says: I am about to set fire to you, and it will consume all your trees, both green and dry. The blazing flame will not be quenched, and every face from south to north will be scorched by it. [48]Everyone will see that I the LORD have kindled it; it will not be quenched.' "

[49]Then I said, "Sovereign LORD, they are saying of me, 'Isn't he just telling parables?' "[b]

Babylon as God's Sword of Judgment

21 [c] The word of the LORD came to me: [2]"Son of man, set your face against Jerusalem and preach against the sanctuary. Prophesy against the land of Israel [3]and say to her: 'This is what the LORD says: I am against you. I will draw my sword from its sheath and cut off from you both the righteous and the wicked. [4]Because I am going to cut off the righteous and the wicked, my sword will be unsheathed against everyone from south to north. [5]Then all people will know that I the LORD have drawn my sword from its sheath; it will not return again.'

---

[a] 40 Or *and the gifts of your firstfruits*   [b] 49 In Hebrew texts 20:45-49 is numbered 21:1-5.   [c] In Hebrew texts 21:1-32 is numbered 21:6-37.

⁶"Therefore groan, son of man! Groan before them with broken heart and bitter grief. ⁷And when they ask you, 'Why are you groaning?' you shall say, 'Because of the news that is coming. Every heart will melt with fear and every hand go limp; every spirit will become faint and every leg will be wet with urine.' It is coming! It will surely take place, declares the Sovereign LORD."

⁸The word of the LORD came to me: ⁹"Son of man, prophesy and say, 'This is what the Lord says:

" 'A sword, a sword,
   sharpened and polished—
¹⁰sharpened for the slaughter,
   polished to flash like lightning!

" 'Shall we rejoice in the scepter of my royal son? The sword despises every such stick.

¹¹ " 'The sword is appointed to be polished,
   to be grasped with the hand;
it is sharpened and polished,
   made ready for the hand of the slayer.
¹²Cry out and wail, son of man,
   for it is against my people;
it is against all the princes of Israel.
They are thrown to the sword
   along with my people.
Therefore beat your breast.

¹³ " 'Testing will surely come. And what if even the scepter, which the sword despises, does not continue? declares the Sovereign LORD.'

¹⁴ "So then, son of man, prophesy
   and strike your hands together.
Let the sword strike twice,
   even three times.
It is a sword for slaughter—
   a sword for great slaughter,
   closing in on them from every side.
¹⁵So that hearts may melt with fear
   and the fallen be many,
I have stationed the sword for slaughterᵃ
   at all their gates.
Look! It is forged to strike like lightning,
   it is grasped for slaughter.

¹⁶Slash to the right, you sword,
   then to the left,
   wherever your blade is turned.
¹⁷I too will strike my hands together,
   and my wrath will subside.
I the LORD have spoken."

¹⁸The word of the LORD came to me: ¹⁹"Son of man, mark out two roads for the sword of the king of Babylon to take, both starting from the same country. Make a signpost where the road branches off to the city. ²⁰Mark out one road for the sword to come against Rabbah of the Ammonites and another against Judah and fortified Jerusalem. ²¹For the king of Babylon will stop at the fork in the road, at the junction of the two roads, to seek an omen: He will cast lots with arrows, he will consult his idols, he will examine the liver. ²²Into his right hand will come the lot for Jerusalem, where he is to set up battering rams, to give the command to slaughter, to sound the battle cry, to set battering rams against the gates, to build a ramp and to erect siege works. ²³It will seem like a false omen to those who have sworn allegiance to him, but he will remind them of their guilt and take them captive.

²⁴"Therefore this is what the Sovereign LORD says: 'Because you people have brought to mind your guilt by your open rebellion, revealing your sins in all that you do—because you have done this, you will be taken captive.

²⁵ " 'You profane and wicked prince of Israel, whose day has come, whose time of punishment has reached its climax, ²⁶this is what the Sovereign LORD says: Take off the turban, remove the crown. It will not be as it was: The lowly will be exalted and the exalted will be brought low. ²⁷A ruin! A ruin! I will make it a ruin! The crown will not be restored until he to whom it rightfully belongs shall come; to him I will give it.'

²⁸"And you, son of man, prophesy and say, 'This is what the Sovereign LORD says about the Ammonites and their insults:

" 'A sword, a sword,
   drawn for the slaughter,

ᵃ 15 Septuagint; the meaning of the Hebrew for this word is uncertain.

polished to consume
and to flash like lightning!
²⁹ Despite false visions concerning you
and lying divinations about you,
it will be laid on the necks
of the wicked who are to be slain,
whose day has come,
whose time of punishment has
reached its climax.

³⁰ " 'Let the sword return to its sheath.
In the place where you were
created,
in the land of your ancestry,
I will judge you.
³¹ I will pour out my wrath on you
and breathe out my fiery anger
against you;
I will deliver you into the hands of
brutal men,
men skilled in destruction.
³² You will be fuel for the fire,
your blood will be shed in your land,
you will be remembered no more;
for I the LORD have spoken.' "

Judgment on Jerusalem's Sins

22 The word of the LORD came to me:

² "Son of man, will you judge her? Will you judge this city of bloodshed? Then confront her with all her detestable practices ³ and say: 'This is what the Sovereign LORD says: You city that brings on herself doom by shedding blood in her midst and defiles herself by making idols, ⁴ you have become guilty because of the blood you have shed and have become defiled by the idols you have made. You have brought your days to a close, and the end of your years has come. Therefore I will make you an object of scorn to the nations and a laughingstock to all the countries. ⁵ Those who are near and those who are far away will mock you, you infamous city, full of turmoil.

⁶ " 'See how each of the princes of Israel who are in you uses his power to shed blood. ⁷ In you they have treated father and mother with contempt; in you they have oppressed the foreigner and mistreated the fatherless and the widow. ⁸ You have despised my holy things

and desecrated my Sabbaths. ⁹ In you are slanderers who are bent on shedding blood; in you are those who eat at the mountain shrines and commit lewd acts. ¹⁰ In you are those who dishonor their father's bed; in you are those who violate women during their period, when they are ceremonially unclean. ¹¹ In you one man commits a detestable offense with his neighbor's wife, another shamefully defiles his daughter-in-law, and another violates his sister, his own father's daughter. ¹² In you are people who accept bribes to shed blood; you take interest and make a profit from the poor. You extort unjust gain from your neighbors. And you have forgotten me, declares the Sovereign LORD.

¹³ " 'I will surely strike my hands together at the unjust gain you have made and at the blood you have shed in your midst. ¹⁴ Will your courage endure or your hands be strong in the day I deal with you? I the LORD have spoken, and I will do it. ¹⁵ I will disperse you among the nations and scatter you through the countries; and I will put an end to your uncleanness. ¹⁶ When you have been defiled^a in the eyes of the nations, you will know that I am the LORD.' "

¹⁷ Then the word of the LORD came to me: ¹⁸ "Son of man, the people of Israel have become dross to me; all of them are the copper, tin, iron and lead left inside a furnace. They are but the dross of silver. ¹⁹ Therefore this is what the Sovereign LORD says: 'Because you have all become dross, I will gather you into Jerusalem. ²⁰ As silver, copper, iron, lead and tin are gathered into a furnace to be melted with a fiery blast, so will I gather you in my anger and my wrath and put you inside the city and melt you. ²¹ I will gather you and I will blow on you with my fiery wrath, and you will be melted inside her. ²² As silver is melted in a furnace, so you will be melted inside her, and you will know that I the LORD have poured out my wrath on you.' "

²³ Again the word of the LORD came to me: ²⁴ "Son of man, say to the land, 'You are a land that has not been cleansed or rained on in the day of wrath.' ²⁵ There is

^a 16 Or When I have allotted you your inheritance

a conspiracy of her princes^a within her like a roaring lion tearing its prey; they devour people, take treasures and precious things and make many widows within her. ²⁶Her priests do violence to my law and profane my holy things; they do not distinguish between the holy and the common; they teach that there is no difference between the unclean and the clean; and they shut their eyes to the keeping of my Sabbaths, so that I am profaned among them. ²⁷Her officials within her are like wolves tearing their prey; they shed blood and kill people to make unjust gain. ²⁸Her prophets whitewash these deeds for them by false visions and lying divinations. They say, 'This is what the Sovereign LORD says' — when the LORD has not spoken. ²⁹The people of the land practice extortion and commit robbery; they oppress the poor and needy and mistreat the foreigner, denying them justice.

³⁰"I looked for someone among them who would build up the wall and stand before me in the gap on behalf of the land so I would not have to destroy it, but I found no one. ³¹So I will pour out my wrath on them and consume them with my fiery anger, bringing down on their own heads all they have done, declares the Sovereign LORD."

Two Adulterous Sisters

23 The word of the LORD came to me: ²"Son of man, there were two women, daughters of the same mother. ³They became prostitutes in Egypt, engaging in prostitution from their youth. In that land their breasts were fondled and their virgin bosoms caressed. ⁴The older was named Oholah, and her sister was Oholibah. They were mine and gave birth to sons and daughters. Oholah is Samaria, and Oholibah is Jerusalem.

⁵"Oholah engaged in prostitution while she was still mine; and she lusted after her lovers, the Assyrians — warriors ⁶clothed in blue, governors and commanders, all of them handsome young men, and mounted horsemen. ⁷She gave herself as a prostitute to all the elite of the Assyrians and defiled herself with all the

idols of everyone she lusted after. ⁸She did not give up the prostitution she began in Egypt, when during her youth men slept with her, caressed her virgin bosom and poured out their lust on her.

⁹"Therefore I delivered her into the hands of her lovers, the Assyrians, for whom she lusted. ¹⁰They stripped her naked, took away her sons and daughters and killed her with the sword. She became

---

^a 25 Septuagint; Hebrew *prophets*

THE WITNESSES

✓ OHOLAH AND OHOLIBAH
(EZEKIEL 23:4)
Ezekiel uses these names to refer to Samaria and Jerusalem as if they were two rebellious sisters. *Oholah* means "her tent" and *Oholibah* may mean something like "my tent." In other words, the people of Samaria built their sanctuary just because they felt like it, but God himself built the sanctuary in Jerusalem.

a byword among women, and punishment was inflicted on her.

¹¹"Her sister Oholibah saw this, yet in her lust and prostitution she was more depraved than her sister. ¹²She too lusted after the Assyrians—governors and commanders, warriors in full dress, mounted horsemen, all handsome young men. ¹³I saw that she too defiled herself; both of them went the same way.

¹⁴"But she carried her prostitution still further. She saw men portrayed on a wall, figures of Chaldeans*ᵃ* portrayed in red, ¹⁵with belts around their waists and flowing turbans on their heads; all of them looked like Babylonian chariot officers, natives of Chaldea.*ᵇ* ¹⁶As soon as she saw them, she lusted after them and sent messengers to them in Chaldea. ¹⁷Then the Babylonians came to her, to the bed of love, and in their lust they defiled her. After she had been defiled by them, she turned away from them in disgust. ¹⁸When she carried on her prostitution openly and exposed her naked body, I turned away from her in disgust, just as I had turned away from her sister. ¹⁹Yet she became more and more promiscuous as she recalled the days of her youth, when she was a prostitute in Egypt. ²⁰There she lusted after her lovers, whose genitals were like those of donkeys and whose emission was like that of horses. ²¹So you longed for the lewdness of your youth, when in Egypt your bosom was caressed and your young breasts fondled.*ᶜ*

²²"Therefore, Oholibah, this is what the Sovereign Lᴏʀᴅ says: I will stir up your lovers against you, those you turned away from in disgust, and I will bring them against you from every side— ²³the Babylonians and all the Chaldeans, the men of Pekod and Shoa and Koa, and all the Assyrians with them, handsome young men, all of them governors and commanders, chariot officers and men of high rank, all mounted on horses. ²⁴They will come against you with weapons,*ᵈ* chariots and wagons and with a throng of people; they will take up positions against you on every side with large and small shields and with helmets. I will turn you over to them for punishment, and they will punish you according to their standards. ²⁵I will direct my jealous anger against you, and they will deal with you in fury. They will cut off your noses and your ears, and those of you who are left will fall by the sword. They will take away your sons and daughters, and those of you who are left will be consumed by fire. ²⁶They will also strip you of your clothes and take your fine jewelry. ²⁷So I will put a stop to the lewdness and prostitution you began in Egypt. You will not look on these things with longing or remember Egypt anymore.

²⁸"For this is what the Sovereign Lᴏʀᴅ says: I am about to deliver you into the hands of those you hate, to those you turned away from in disgust. ²⁹They will deal with you in hatred and take away everything you have worked for. They will leave you stark naked, and the shame of your prostitution will be exposed. Your lewdness and promiscuity ³⁰have brought this on you, because you lusted after the nations and defiled yourself with their idols. ³¹You have gone the way of your sister; so I will put her cup into your hand.

³²"This is what the Sovereign Lᴏʀᴅ says:

"You will drink your sister's cup,
    a cup large and deep;
it will bring scorn and derision,
    for it holds so much.
³³You will be filled with drunkenness
        and sorrow,
    the cup of ruin and desolation,
    the cup of your sister Samaria.
³⁴You will drink it and drain it dry
    and chew on its pieces—
    and you will tear your breasts.

I have spoken, declares the Sovereign Lᴏʀᴅ.

³⁵"Therefore this is what the Sovereign Lᴏʀᴅ says: Since you have forgotten me and turned your back on me, you must bear the consequences of your lewdness and prostitution."

ᵃ 14 Or *Babylonians*   *ᵇ 15* Or *Babylonia*; also in verse 16   *ᶜ 21* Syriac (see also verse 3); Hebrew *caressed because of your young breasts*   *ᵈ 24* The meaning of the Hebrew for this word is uncertain.

36 The LORD said to me: "Son of man, will you judge Oholah and Oholibah? Then confront them with their detestable practices, 37 for they have committed adultery and blood is on their hands. They committed adultery with their idols; they even sacrificed their children, whom they bore to me, as food for them. 38 They have also done this to me: At that same time they defiled my sanctuary and desecrated my Sabbaths. 39 On the very day they sacrificed their children to their idols, they entered my sanctuary and desecrated it. That is what they did in my house.

40 "They even sent messengers for men who came from far away, and when they arrived you bathed yourself for them, applied eye makeup and put on your jewelry. 41 You sat on an elegant couch, with a table spread before it on which you had placed the incense and olive oil that belonged to me.

42 "The noise of a carefree crowd was around her; drunkards were brought from the desert along with men from the rabble, and they put bracelets on the wrists of the woman and her sister and beautiful crowns on their heads. 43 Then I said about the one worn out by adultery, 'Now let them use her as a prostitute, for that is all she is.' 44 And they slept with her. As men sleep with a prostitute, so they slept with those lewd women, Oholah and Oholibah. 45 But righteous judges will sentence them to the punishment of women who commit adultery and shed blood, because they are adulterous and blood is on their hands.

46 "This is what the Sovereign LORD says: Bring a mob against them and give them over to terror and plunder. 47 The mob will stone them and cut them down with their swords; they will kill their sons and daughters and burn down their houses.

48 "So I will put an end to lewdness in the land, that all women may take warning and not imitate you. 49 You will suffer the penalty for your lewdness and bear the consequences of your sins of idolatry. Then you will know that I am the Sovereign LORD."

Jerusalem as a Cooking Pot

24 In the ninth year, in the tenth month on the tenth day, the word of the LORD came to me: 2 "Son of man, record this date, this very date, because the king of Babylon has laid siege to Jerusalem this very day. 3 Tell this rebellious people a parable and say to them: 'This is what the Sovereign LORD says:

" 'Put on the cooking pot; put it on
and pour water into it.
4 Put into it the pieces of meat,
all the choice pieces—the leg and
the shoulder.
Fill it with the best of these bones;
5 take the pick of the flock.
Pile wood beneath it for the bones;
bring it to a boil
and cook the bones in it.

6 " 'For this is what the Sovereign LORD says:

" 'Woe to the city of bloodshed,
to the pot now encrusted,
whose deposit will not go away!

BREAK THROUGH!

Tenth month
(EZEKIEL 24:1)
This month is called Tebeth in the Jewish lunar calendar. For us, that would be from the middle of December to the middle of January.

Take the meat out piece by piece
in whatever order it comes.

7 " 'For the blood she shed is in her
   midst:
   She poured it on the bare rock;
   she did not pour it on the ground,
   where the dust would cover it.
8 To stir up wrath and take revenge
   I put her blood on the bare rock,
   so that it would not be covered.

9 " 'Therefore this is what the Sovereign
Lord says:

" 'Woe to the city of bloodshed!
   I, too, will pile the wood high.
10 So heap on the wood
   and kindle the fire.
   Cook the meat well,
      mixing in the spices;
   and let the bones be charred.
11 Then set the empty pot on the coals
   till it becomes hot and its copper
      glows,
   so that its impurities may be melted
   and its deposit burned away.
12 It has frustrated all efforts;
   its heavy deposit has not been
      removed,
   not even by fire.

13 " 'Now your impurity is lewdness.
Because I tried to cleanse you but you
would not be cleansed from your impurity,
you will not be clean again until my wrath
against you has subsided.

14 " 'I the Lord have spoken. The time
has come for me to act. I will not hold
back; I will not have pity, nor will I relent.
You will be judged according to your conduct and your actions, declares the Sovereign Lord.' "

Ezekiel's Wife Dies

15 The word of the Lord came to me:
16 "Son of man, with one blow I am about
to take away from you the delight of your
eyes. Yet do not lament or weep or shed
any tears. 17 Groan quietly; do not mourn
for the dead. Keep your turban fastened
and your sandals on your feet; do not cover your mustache and beard or eat the
customary food of mourners."

18 So I spoke to the people in the morning, and in the evening my wife died. The
next morning I did as I had been commanded.

19 Then the people asked me, "Won't
you tell us what these things have to do
with us? Why are you acting like this?"

20 So I said to them, "The word of the
Lord came to me: 21 Say to the people of
Israel, 'This is what the Sovereign Lord
says: I am about to desecrate my sanctuary—the stronghold in which you take
pride, the delight of your eyes, the object
of your affection. The sons and daughters you left behind will fall by the sword.
22 And you will do as I have done. You will
not cover your mustache and beard or eat
the customary food of mourners. 23 You
will keep your turbans on your heads
and your sandals on your feet. You will
not mourn or weep but will waste away
because of[a] your sins and groan among
yourselves. 24 Ezekiel will be a sign to you;
you will do just as he has done. When
this happens, you will know that I am the
Sovereign Lord.'

25 "And you, son of man, on the day
I take away their stronghold, their joy
and glory, the delight of their eyes, their
heart's desire, and their sons and daughters as well— 26 on that day a fugitive will
come to tell you the news. 27 At that time
your mouth will be opened; you will speak
with him and will no longer be silent. So
you will be a sign to them, and they will
know that I am the Lord."

A Prophecy Against Ammon

25 The word of the Lord came to me:
2 "Son of man, set your face against
the Ammonites and prophesy against
them. 3 Say to them, 'Hear the word of the
Sovereign Lord. This is what the Sovereign Lord says: Because you said "Aha!"
over my sanctuary when it was desecrated and over the land of Israel when it was
laid waste and over the people of Judah
when they went into exile, 4 therefore I am
going to give you to the people of the East
as a possession. They will set up their
camps and pitch their tents among you;

---

a 23 Or away in

BREAK THROUGH!

Ammonites
(EZEKIEL 25:2)

These were neighbors of Israel. The Israelites didn't like them. This was because the Ammonites came from Ben-Ammi, who was the son Lot had with his younger daughter (Genesis 19:30–38).

they will eat your fruit and drink your milk. ⁵I will turn Rabbah into a pasture for camels and Ammon into a resting place for sheep. Then you will know that I am the LORD. ⁶For this is what the Sovereign LORD says: Because you have clapped your hands and stamped your feet, rejoicing with all the malice of your heart against the land of Israel, ⁷therefore I will stretch out my hand against you and give you as plunder to the nations. I will wipe you out from among the nations and exterminate you from the countries. I will destroy you, and you will know that I am the LORD.' "

A Prophecy Against Moab

⁸"This is what the Sovereign LORD says: 'Because Moab and Seir said, "Look, Judah has become like all the other nations," ⁹therefore I will expose the flank of Moab, beginning at its frontier towns— Beth Jeshimoth, Baal Meon and Kiriathaim—the glory of that land. ¹⁰I will give Moab along with the Ammonites to the

people of the East as a possession, so that the Ammonites will not be remembered among the nations; ¹¹and I will inflict punishment on Moab. Then they will know that I am the LORD.' "

A Prophecy Against Edom

¹²"This is what the Sovereign LORD says: 'Because Edom took revenge on Judah and became very guilty by doing so, ¹³therefore this is what the Sovereign LORD says: I will stretch out my hand against Edom and kill both man and beast. I will lay it waste, and from Teman to Dedan they will fall by the sword. ¹⁴I will take vengeance on Edom by the hand of my people Israel, and they will deal with Edom in accordance with my anger and my wrath; they will know my vengeance, declares the Sovereign LORD.' "

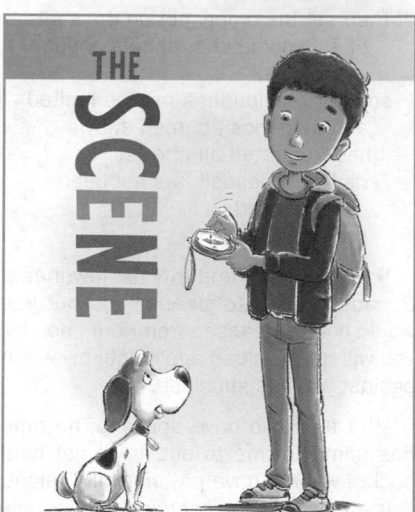

THE SCENE

MOAB
(EZEKIEL 25:8)

It's the name of a city formed by Moab, who was the son Lot had with his older daughter (Genesis 19:30–38). His descendants were neighbors of Israel. The Israelites didn't like them, because of their origins.

A Prophecy Against Philistia

15 "This is what the Sovereign Lord says: 'Because the Philistines acted in vengeance and took revenge with malice in their hearts, and with ancient hostility sought to destroy Judah, 16therefore this is what the Sovereign Lord says: I am about to stretch out my hand against the Philistines, and I will wipe out the Kerethites and destroy those remaining along the coast. 17I will carry out great vengeance on them and punish them in my wrath. Then they will know that I am the Lord, when I take vengeance on them.' "

A Prophecy Against Tyre

26 In the eleventh month of the twelfth*ª* year, on the first day of the month, the word of the Lord came to me: 2 "Son of man, because Tyre has said of Jerusalem, 'Aha! The gate to the nations is broken, and its doors have swung open

Eleventh month
(EZEKIEL 26:1)

This was called Shebat in the Jewish lunar calendar. That would be from the middle of January to the middle of February in our calendar.

to me; now that she lies in ruins I will prosper,' 3therefore this is what the Sovereign Lord says: I am against you, Tyre, and I will bring many nations against you, like the sea casting up its waves. 4They will destroy the walls of Tyre and pull down her towers; I will scrape away her rubble and make her a bare rock. 5Out in the sea she will become a place to spread fishnets, for I have spoken, declares the Sovereign Lord. She will become plunder for the nations, 6and her settlements on the mainland will be ravaged by the sword. Then they will know that I am the Lord.

7 "For this is what the Sovereign Lord says: From the north I am going to bring against Tyre Nebuchadnezzar*ᵇ* king of Babylon, king of kings, with horses and chariots, with horsemen and a great army. 8He will ravage your settlements on the

Philistines
(EZEKIEL 25:15)

A warrior people who lived on the eastern coast of the Mediterranean Sea. Their ships sailed out from there to carry on business with other countries. They did very good metal work. That always gave them the lead when they were fighting the Israelites.

ª 1 Probable reading of the original Hebrew text; Masoretic Text does not have month of the twelfth.   ᵇ 7 Hebrew Nebuchadrezzar, of which Nebuchadnezzar is a variant; here and often in Ezekiel and Jeremiah

THE SCENE

TYRE

(EZEKIEL 26:2)

A Philistine city built on a rock off the eastern coast of the Mediterranean Sea. Its name means "rock," and it was an important military and business port.

mainland with the sword; he will set up siege works against you, build a ramp up to your walls and raise his shields against you. ⁹He will direct the blows of his battering rams against your walls and demolish your towers with his weapons. ¹⁰His horses will be so many that they will cover you with dust. Your walls will tremble at the noise of the warhorses, wagons and chariots when he enters your gates as men enter a city whose walls have been broken through. ¹¹The hooves of his horses will trample all your streets; he will kill your people with the sword, and your strong pillars will fall to the ground. ¹²They will plunder your wealth and loot your merchandise; they will break down your walls and demolish your fine houses and throw your stones, timber and rubble into the sea. ¹³I will put an end to your noisy songs, and the music of your harps will be heard no more. ¹⁴I will make you a

bare rock, and you will become a place to spread fishnets. You will never be rebuilt, for I the LORD have spoken, declares the Sovereign LORD.

¹⁵"This is what the Sovereign LORD says to Tyre: Will not the coastlands tremble at the sound of your fall, when the wounded groan and the slaughter takes place in you? ¹⁶Then all the princes of the coast will step down from their thrones and lay aside their robes and take off their embroidered garments. Clothed with terror, they will sit on the ground, trembling every moment, appalled at you. ¹⁷Then they will take up a lament concerning you and say to you:

" 'How you are destroyed, city of renown,
    peopled by men of the sea!
You were a power on the seas,
    you and your citizens;
you put your terror
    on all who lived there.
¹⁸Now the coastlands tremble
    on the day of your fall;
the islands in the sea
    are terrified at your collapse.'

¹⁹"This is what the Sovereign LORD says: When I make you a desolate city, like cities no longer inhabited, and when I bring the ocean depths over you and its vast waters cover you, ²⁰then I will bring you down with those who go down to the pit, to the people of long ago. I will make you dwell in the earth below, as in ancient ruins, with those who go down to the pit, and you will not return or take your place[a] in the land of the living. ²¹I will bring you to a horrible end and you will be no more. You will be sought, but you will never again be found, declares the Sovereign LORD."

A Lament Over Tyre

27 The word of the LORD came to me: ²"Son of man, take up a lament concerning Tyre. ³Say to Tyre, situated at the gateway to the sea, merchant of peoples on many coasts, 'This is what the Sovereign LORD says:

---

a 20 Septuagint; Hebrew *return, and I will give glory*

" 'You say, Tyre,
"I am perfect in beauty."
⁴ Your domain was on the high seas;
    your builders brought your beauty to
        perfection.
⁵ They made all your timbers
    of juniper from Senirᵃ;
    they took a cedar from Lebanon
    to make a mast for you.
⁶ Of oaks from Bashan
    they made your oars;
    of cypress woodᵇ from the coasts of
        Cyprus
    they made your deck, adorned with
        ivory.
⁷ Fine embroidered linen from Egypt
    was your sail
    and served as your banner;
    your awnings were of blue and purple
    from the coasts of Elishah.
⁸ Men of Sidon and Arvad were your
        oarsmen;
    your skilled men, Tyre, were aboard
        as your sailors.
⁹ Veteran craftsmen of Byblos were on
        board
    as shipwrights to caulk your
        seams.
All the ships of the sea and their
        sailors
    came alongside to trade for your
        wares.

¹⁰ " 'Men of Persia, Lydia and Put
    served as soldiers in your army.
They hung their shields and helmets
        on your walls,
    bringing you splendor.
¹¹ Men of Arvad and Helek
    guarded your walls on every side;
    men of Gammad
    were in your towers.
They hung their shields around your
        walls;
    they brought your beauty to
        perfection.

¹² " 'Tarshish did business with you because of your great wealth of goods; they
exchanged silver, iron, tin and lead for
your merchandise.
¹³ " 'Greece, Tubal and Meshek did business with you; they traded human beings
and articles of bronze for your wares.

¹⁴ " 'Men of Beth Togarmah exchanged
chariot horses, cavalry horses and mules
for your merchandise.
¹⁵ " 'The men of Rhodesᶜ traded with
you, and many coastlands were your customers; they paid you with ivory tusks and
ebony.
¹⁶ " 'Aramᵈ did business with you because of your many products; they exchanged turquoise, purple fabric, embroidered work, fine linen, coral and rubies for
your merchandise.
¹⁷ " 'Judah and Israel traded with you;
they exchanged wheat from Minnith and
confections,ᵉ honey, olive oil and balm for
your wares.
¹⁸ " 'Damascus did business with you
because of your many products and great
wealth of goods. They offered wine from
Helbon, wool from Zahar ¹⁹ and casks of
wine from Izal in exchange for your wares:
wrought iron, cassia and calamus.
²⁰ " 'Dedan traded in saddle blankets
with you.
²¹ " 'Arabia and all the princes of Kedar
were your customers; they did business
with you in lambs, rams and goats.
²² " 'The merchants of Sheba and Raamah traded with you; for your merchandise they exchanged the finest of all
kinds of spices and precious stones, and
gold.
²³ " 'Harran, Kanneh and Eden and merchants of Sheba, Ashur and Kilmad traded with you. ²⁴ In your marketplace they
traded with you beautiful garments, blue
fabric, embroidered work and multicol-
ored rugs with cords twisted and tightly
knotted.

²⁵ " 'The ships of Tarshish serve
    as carriers for your wares.
You are filled with heavy cargo
    as you sail the sea.
²⁶ Your oarsmen take you
    out to the high seas.
But the east wind will break you to
        pieces
    far out at sea.

ᵃ 5 That is, Mount Hermon   ᵇ 6 Targum; the Masoretic
Text has a different division of the consonants.
ᶜ 15 Septuagint; Hebrew *Dedan*   ᵈ 16 Most Hebrew
manuscripts; some Hebrew manuscripts and Syriac *Edom*
ᵉ 17 The meaning of the Hebrew for this word is uncertain.

27 Your wealth, merchandise and wares,
   your mariners, sailors and
      shipwrights,
   your merchants and all your soldiers,
   and everyone else on board
   will sink into the heart of the sea
   on the day of your shipwreck.
28 The shorelands will quake
   when your sailors cry out.
29 All who handle the oars
   will abandon their ships;
   the mariners and all the sailors
   will stand on the shore.
30 They will raise their voice
   and cry bitterly over you;
   they will sprinkle dust on their heads
   and roll in ashes.
31 They will shave their heads because of
      you
   and will put on sackcloth.
   They will weep over you with anguish
      of soul
   and with bitter mourning.
32 As they wail and mourn over you,
   they will take up a lament
      concerning you:
   "Who was ever silenced like Tyre,
   surrounded by the sea?"
33 When your merchandise went out on
      the seas,
   you satisfied many nations;
   with your great wealth and your wares
   you enriched the kings of the earth.
34 Now you are shattered by the sea
   in the depths of the waters;
   your wares and all your company
   have gone down with you.
35 All who live in the coastlands
   are appalled at you;
   their kings shudder with horror
   and their faces are distorted with
      fear.
36 The merchants among the nations
      scoff at you;
   you have come to a horrible end
   and will be no more.' "

A Prophecy Against the King of Tyre

28 The word of the LORD came to me:
   2 "Son of man, say to the ruler of
Tyre, 'This is what the Sovereign LORD
says:

" 'In the pride of your heart
   you say, "I am a god;
I sit on the throne of a god
   in the heart of the seas."
But you are a mere mortal and not a
      god,
   though you think you are as wise as
      a god.
3 Are you wiser than Daniel[a]?
   Is no secret hidden from you?
4 By your wisdom and understanding
   you have gained wealth for yourself
and amassed gold and silver
   in your treasuries.
5 By your great skill in trading
   you have increased your wealth,
and because of your wealth
   your heart has grown proud.

6 " 'Therefore this is what the Sovereign
LORD says:

" 'Because you think you are wise,
   as wise as a god,
7 I am going to bring foreigners against
      you,
   the most ruthless of nations;
they will draw their swords against
      your beauty and wisdom
   and pierce your shining splendor.
8 They will bring you down to the pit,
   and you will die a violent death
   in the heart of the seas.
9 Will you then say, "I am a god,"
   in the presence of those who kill
      you?
You will be but a mortal, not a god,
   in the hands of those who slay you.
10 You will die the death of the
      uncircumcised
   at the hands of foreigners.

I have spoken, declares the Sovereign
LORD.' "

11 The word of the LORD came to me:
12 "Son of man, take up a lament concerning the king of Tyre and say to him: 'This
is what the Sovereign LORD says:

" 'You were the seal of perfection,
   full of wisdom and perfect in beauty.
13 You were in Eden,
   the garden of God;

---

[a] 3 Or *Danel*, a man of renown in ancient literature

every precious stone adorned you:
   carnelian, chrysolite and emerald,
   topaz, onyx and jasper,
   lapis lazuli, turquoise and beryl.[a]
Your settings and mountings[b] were
      made of gold;
   on the day you were created they
      were prepared.
[14] You were anointed as a guardian
      cherub,
   for so I ordained you.
You were on the holy mount of God;
   you walked among the fiery stones.
[15] You were blameless in your ways
   from the day you were created
   till wickedness was found in you.
[16] Through your widespread trade
   you were filled with violence,
   and you sinned.
So I drove you in disgrace from the
      mount of God,
   and I expelled you, guardian cherub,
   from among the fiery stones.
[17] Your heart became proud
   on account of your beauty,
and you corrupted your wisdom
   because of your splendor.
So I threw you to the earth;
   I made a spectacle of you before
      kings.
[18] By your many sins and dishonest trade
   you have desecrated your
      sanctuaries.
So I made a fire come out from you,
   and it consumed you,
and I reduced you to ashes on the
      ground
   in the sight of all who were
      watching.
[19] All the nations who knew you
   are appalled at you;
you have come to a horrible end
   and will be no more.' "

A Prophecy Against Sidon

[20] The word of the LORD came to me:
[21] "Son of man, set your face against Sidon; prophesy against her [22] and say:
'This is what the Sovereign LORD says:

   " 'I am against you, Sidon,
      and among you I will display my
         glory.

THE SCENE

SIDON

(EZEKIEL 28:21)

A Philistine city north of the city
of Tyre on the eastern coast
of the Mediterranean Sea. At
one time, it was more important and
stronger than the city of Tyre.

You will know that I am the LORD,
   when I inflict punishment on you
   and within you am proved to be
      holy.
[23] I will send a plague upon you
   and make blood flow in your
      streets.
The slain will fall within you,
   with the sword against you on every
      side.
Then you will know that I am the LORD.

[24] " 'No longer will the people of Israel
have malicious neighbors who are painful briers and sharp thorns. Then they will
know that I am the Sovereign LORD.

[25] " 'This is what the Sovereign LORD
says: When I gather the people of Israel
from the nations where they have been
scattered, I will be proved holy through

---

a 13 The precise identification of some of these precious
stones is uncertain.   *b* 13 The meaning of the Hebrew
for this phrase is uncertain.

them in the sight of the nations. Then they will live in their own land, which I gave to my servant Jacob. ²⁶They will live there in safety and will build houses and plant vineyards; they will live in safety when I inflict punishment on all their neighbors who maligned them. Then they will know that I am the LORD their God.' "

A Prophecy Against Egypt
Judgment on Pharaoh

29 In the tenth year, in the tenth month on the twelfth day, the word of the LORD came to me: ²"Son of man, set your face against Pharaoh king of Egypt and prophesy against him and against all Egypt. ³Speak to him and say: 'This is what the Sovereign LORD says:

" 'I am against you, Pharaoh king of
    Egypt,
you great monster lying among your
    streams.
You say, "The Nile belongs to me;
    I made it for myself."
⁴But I will put hooks in your jaws
    and make the fish of your streams
      stick to your scales.
I will pull you out from among your
    streams,
    with all the fish sticking to your
      scales.
⁵I will leave you in the desert,
    you and all the fish of your streams.
You will fall on the open field
    and not be gathered or picked up.
I will give you as food
    to the beasts of the earth and the
      birds of the sky.
⁶Then all who live in Egypt will know that I am the LORD.

" 'You have been a staff of reed for the people of Israel. ⁷When they grasped you with their hands, you splintered and you tore open their shoulders; when they leaned on you, you broke and their backs were wrenched.ᵃ

⁸" 'Therefore this is what the Sovereign LORD says: I will bring a sword against you and kill both man and beast. ⁹Egypt will become a desolate wasteland. Then they will know that I am the LORD.

" 'Because you said, "The Nile is mine; I made it," ¹⁰therefore I am against you and against your streams, and I will make the land of Egypt a ruin and a desolate waste from Migdol to Aswan, as far as the border of Cush.ᵇ ¹¹The foot of neither man nor beast will pass through it; no one will live there for forty years. ¹²I will make the land of Egypt desolate among devastated lands, and her cities will lie desolate forty years among ruined cities. And I will disperse the Egyptians among the nations and scatter them through the countries.

¹³" 'Yet this is what the Sovereign LORD says: At the end of forty years I will gather the Egyptians from the nations where they were scattered. ¹⁴I will bring them back from captivity and return them to Upper Egypt, the land of their ancestry. There they will be a lowly kingdom. ¹⁵It will be the lowliest of kingdoms and will never again exalt itself above the other nations. I will make it so weak that it will never again rule over the nations. ¹⁶Egypt will no longer be a source of confidence for the people of Israel but will be a reminder of their sin in turning to her for help. Then they will know that I am the Sovereign LORD.' "

Nebuchadnezzar's Reward

¹⁷In the twenty-seventh year, in the first month on the first day, the word of the LORD came to me: ¹⁸"Son of man, Nebuchadnezzar king of Babylon drove his army in a hard campaign against Tyre; every head was rubbed bare and every shoulder made raw. Yet he and his army got no reward from the campaign he led against Tyre. ¹⁹Therefore this is what the Sovereign LORD says: I am going to give Egypt to Nebuchadnezzar king of Babylon, and he will carry off its wealth. He will loot and plunder the land as pay for his army. ²⁰I have given him Egypt as a reward for his efforts because he and his army did it for me, declares the Sovereign LORD. ²¹"On that day I will make a hornᶜ grow for the Israelites, and I will open your mouth among them. Then they will know that I am the LORD."

ᵃ 7 Syriac (see also Septuagint and Vulgate); Hebrew *and you caused their backs to stand*   ᵇ 10 That is, the upper Nile region   ᶜ 21 *Horn* here symbolizes strength.

First month
(EZEKIEL 29:17)

This was Aviv in the Jewish lunar calendar. In our solar calendar, that is the time from the middle of March to the middle of April.

A Lament Over Egypt

30 The word of the Lord came to me: 2 "Son of man, prophesy and say: 'This is what the Sovereign Lord says:

" 'Wail and say,
"Alas for that day!"
3 For the day is near,
the day of the Lord is near—
a day of clouds,
a time of doom for the nations.
4 A sword will come against Egypt,
and anguish will come upon Cush.ᵃ
When the slain fall in Egypt,
her wealth will be carried away
and her foundations torn down.

5 Cush and Libya, Lydia and all Arabia, Kub and the people of the covenant land will fall by the sword along with Egypt.

6 " 'This is what the Lord says:

" 'The allies of Egypt will fall
and her proud strength will fail.
From Migdol to Aswan
they will fall by the sword within her,
declares the Sovereign Lord.

7 " 'They will be desolate
among desolate lands,
and their cities will lie
among ruined cities.
8 Then they will know that I am the Lord,
when I set fire to Egypt
and all her helpers are crushed.

9 " 'On that day messengers will go out from me in ships to frighten Cush out of her complacency. Anguish will take hold of them on the day of Egypt's doom, for it is sure to come.

10 " 'This is what the Sovereign Lord says:

" 'I will put an end to the hordes of Egypt
by the hand of Nebuchadnezzar king of Babylon.
11 He and his army—the most ruthless of nations—
will be brought in to destroy the land.
They will draw their swords against Egypt
and fill the land with the slain.
12 I will dry up the waters of the Nile
and sell the land to an evil nation;
by the hand of foreigners
I will lay waste the land and everything in it.

I the Lord have spoken.

13 " 'This is what the Sovereign Lord says:

" 'I will destroy the idols
and put an end to the images in Memphis.
No longer will there be a prince in Egypt,
and I will spread fear throughout the land.
14 I will lay waste Upper Egypt,
set fire to Zoan
and inflict punishment on Thebes.
15 I will pour out my wrath on Pelusium,
the stronghold of Egypt,
and wipe out the hordes of Thebes.
16 I will set fire to Egypt;
Pelusium will writhe in agony.

ᵃ 4 That is, the upper Nile region; also in verses 5 and 9

Thebes will be taken by storm;
    Memphis will be in constant
      distress.
¹⁷The young men of Heliopolis and
      Bubastis
    will fall by the sword,
    and the cities themselves will go
      into captivity.
¹⁸Dark will be the day at Tahpanhes
    when I break the yoke of Egypt;
    there her proud strength will come
      to an end.
She will be covered with clouds,
    and her villages will go into captivity.
¹⁹So I will inflict punishment on Egypt,
    and they will know that I am the
      Lord.' "

Pharaoh's Arms Are Broken

²⁰In the eleventh year, in the first month on the seventh day, the word of the Lord came to me: ²¹"Son of man, I have broken the arm of Pharaoh king of Egypt. It has not been bound up to be healed or put in a splint so that it may become strong enough to hold a sword. ²²Therefore this is what the Sovereign Lord says: I am against Pharaoh king of Egypt. I will break both his arms, the good arm as well as the broken one, and make the sword fall from his hand. ²³I will disperse the Egyptians among the nations and scatter them through the countries. ²⁴I will strengthen the arms of the king of Babylon and put my sword in his hand, but I will break the arms of Pharaoh, and he will groan before him like a mortally wounded man. ²⁵I will strengthen the arms of the king of Babylon, but the arms of Pharaoh will fall limp. Then they will know that I am the Lord, when I put my sword into the hand of the king of Babylon and he brandishes it against Egypt. ²⁶I will disperse the Egyptians among the nations and scatter them through the countries. Then they will know that I am the Lord."

Pharaoh as a Felled Cedar of Lebanon

31 In the eleventh year, in the third month on the first day, the word of the Lord came to me: ²"Son of man, say to Pharaoh king of Egypt and to his hordes:

BREAKTHROUGH!

Third month

(EZEKIEL 31:1)

The name in the Jewish lunar calendar is Sivan. In our solar calendar, that would be the period from the middle of May to the middle of June.

" 'Who can be compared with you in
      majesty?
³Consider Assyria, once a cedar in
      Lebanon,
    with beautiful branches
      overshadowing the forest;
it towered on high,
    its top above the thick foliage.
⁴The waters nourished it,
    deep springs made it grow
      tall;
their streams flowed
    all around its base
and sent their channels
    to all the trees of the field.
⁵So it towered higher
    than all the trees of the field;
its boughs increased
    and its branches grew long,
    spreading because of abundant
      waters.
⁶All the birds of the sky
    nested in its boughs,
all the animals of the wild
    gave birth under its branches;

all the great nations
   lived in its shade.
⁷It was majestic in beauty,
   with its spreading boughs,
for its roots went down
   to abundant waters.
⁸The cedars in the garden of God
   could not rival it,
nor could the junipers
   equal its boughs,
nor could the plane trees
   compare with its branches—
no tree in the garden of God
   could match its beauty.
⁹I made it beautiful
   with abundant branches,
the envy of all the trees of Eden
   in the garden of God.

¹⁰" 'Therefore this is what the Sovereign LORD says: Because the great cedar towered over the thick foliage, and because it was proud of its height, ¹¹I gave it into the hands of the ruler of the nations, for him to deal with according to its wickedness. I cast it aside, ¹²and the most ruthless of foreign nations cut it down and left it. Its boughs fell on the mountains and in all the valleys; its branches lay broken in all the ravines of the land. All the nations of the earth came out from under its shade and left it. ¹³All the birds settled on the fallen tree, and all the wild animals lived among its branches. ¹⁴Therefore no other trees by the waters are ever to tower proudly on high, lifting their tops above the thick foliage. No other trees so well-watered are ever to reach such a height; they are all destined for death, for the earth below, among mortals who go down to the realm of the dead.

¹⁵" 'This is what the Sovereign LORD says: On the day it was brought down to the realm of the dead I covered the deep springs with mourning for it; I held back its streams, and its abundant waters were restrained. Because of it I clothed Lebanon with gloom, and all the trees of the field withered away. ¹⁶I made the nations tremble at the sound of its fall when I brought it down to the realm of the dead to be with those who go down to the pit. Then all the trees of Eden, the choicest

and best of Lebanon, the well-watered trees, were consoled in the earth below. ¹⁷They too, like the great cedar, had gone down to the realm of the dead, to those killed by the sword, along with the armed men who lived in its shade among the nations.

¹⁸" 'Which of the trees of Eden can be compared with you in splendor and majesty? Yet you, too, will be brought down with the trees of Eden to the earth below; you will lie among the uncircumcised, with those killed by the sword.

" 'This is Pharaoh and all his hordes, declares the Sovereign LORD.' "

A Lament Over Pharaoh

32 In the twelfth year, in the twelfth month on the first day, the word of the LORD came to me: ²"Son of man, take up a lament concerning Pharaoh king of Egypt and say to him:

" 'You are like a lion among the
   nations;
you are like a monster in the seas
thrashing about in your streams,
   churning the water with your feet
   and muddying the streams.

³" 'This is what the Sovereign LORD says:

" 'With a great throng of
   people
I will cast my net over
   you,
and they will haul you
   up in my net.
⁴I will throw you on the land
   and hurl you on the open field.
I will let all the birds of the sky settle
   on you
and all the animals of the wild
   gorge themselves on you.
⁵I will spread your flesh on the
   mountains
and fill the valleys with your
   remains.
⁶I will drench the land with your flowing
   blood
all the way to the mountains,
   and the ravines will be filled with
   your flesh.

7 When I snuff you out, I will cover the
  heavens
  and darken their stars;
  I will cover the sun with a cloud,
  and the moon will not give its light.
8 All the shining lights in the heavens
  I will darken over you;
  I will bring darkness over your
  land,
      declares the Sovereign LORD.
9 I will trouble the hearts of many
  peoples
  when I bring about your destruction
  among the nations,
  among[a] lands you have not known.
10 I will cause many peoples to be
  appalled at you,
  and their kings will shudder with
  horror because of you
  when I brandish my sword before
  them.
On the day of your downfall
  each of them will tremble
  every moment for his life.

11 " 'For this is what the Sovereign LORD
says:

" 'The sword of the king of Babylon
  will come against you.
12 I will cause your hordes to fall
  by the swords of mighty men —
  the most ruthless of all nations.
They will shatter the pride of Egypt,
  and all her hordes will be
  overthrown.
13 I will destroy all her cattle
  from beside abundant waters
  no longer to be stirred by the foot of
  man
  or muddied by the hooves of cattle.
14 Then I will let her waters settle
  and make her streams flow like oil,
      declares the Sovereign LORD.
15 When I make Egypt desolate
  and strip the land of everything in it,
  when I strike down all who live there,
  then they will know that I am the
  LORD.'

16 "This is the lament they will chant
for her. The daughters of the nations will
chant it; for Egypt and all her hordes they
will chant it, declares the Sovereign LORD."

Egypt's Descent Into the Realm of the Dead

17 In the twelfth year, on the fifteenth
day of the month, the word of the LORD
came to me: 18 "Son of man, wail for the
hordes of Egypt and consign to the earth
below both her and the daughters of
mighty nations, along with those who go
down to the pit. 19 Say to them, 'Are you
more favored than others? Go down and
be laid among the uncircumcised.' 20 They
will fall among those killed by the sword.
The sword is drawn; let her be dragged
off with all her hordes. 21 From within the
realm of the dead the mighty leaders will
say of Egypt and her allies, 'They have
come down and they lie with the uncircumcised, with those killed by the sword.'

22 "Assyria is there with her whole army;
she is surrounded by the graves of all her
slain, all who have fallen by the sword.
23 Their graves are in the depths of the pit
and her army lies around her grave. All
who had spread terror in the land of the
living are slain, fallen by the sword.

24 "Elam is there, with all her hordes
around her grave. All of them are slain,
fallen by the sword. All who had spread
terror in the land of the living went down
uncircumcised to the earth below. They
bear their shame with those who go down
to the pit. 25 A bed is made for her among
the slain, with all her hordes around her
grave. All of them are uncircumcised,
killed by the sword. Because their terror
had spread in the land of the living, they
bear their shame with those who go down
to the pit; they are laid among the slain.

26 "Meshek and Tubal are there, with
all their hordes around their graves. All
of them are uncircumcised, killed by the
sword because they spread their terror in
the land of the living. 27 But they do not lie
with the fallen warriors of old,[b] who went
down to the realm of the dead with their
weapons of war — their swords placed under their heads and their shields[c] resting
on their bones — though these warriors
also had terrorized the land of the living.

---

[a] 9 Hebrew; Septuagint *bring you into captivity among the
nations, / to*   [b] 27 Septuagint; Hebrew *warriors who
were uncircumcised*   [c] 27 Probable reading of the
original Hebrew text; Masoretic Text *punishment*

28 "You too, Pharaoh, will be broken and will lie among the uncircumcised, with those killed by the sword.

29 "Edom is there, her kings and all her princes; despite their power, they are laid with those killed by the sword. They lie with the uncircumcised, with those who go down to the pit.

30 "All the princes of the north and all the Sidonians are there; they went down with the slain in disgrace despite the terror caused by their power. They lie uncircumcised with those killed by the sword and bear their shame with those who go down to the pit.

31 "Pharaoh—he and all his army—will see them and he will be consoled for all his hordes that were killed by the sword, declares the Sovereign Lord. 32 Although I had him spread terror in the land of the living, Pharaoh and all his hordes will be laid among the uncircumcised, with those killed by the sword, declares the Sovereign Lord."

Renewal of Ezekiel's Call as Watchman

33 The word of the Lord came to me: 2 "Son of man, speak to your people and say to them: 'When I bring the sword against a land, and the people of the land choose one of their men and make him their watchman, 3 and he sees the sword coming against the land and blows the trumpet to warn the people, 4 then if anyone hears the trumpet but does not heed the warning and the sword comes and takes their life, their blood will be on their own head. 5 Since they heard the sound of the trumpet but did not heed the warning, their blood will be on their own head. If they had heeded the warning, they would have saved themselves. 6 But if the watchman sees the sword coming and does not blow the trumpet to warn the people and the sword comes and takes someone's life, that person's life will be taken because of their sin, but I will hold the watchman accountable for their blood.'

7 "Son of man, I have made you a watchman for the people of Israel; so hear the word I speak and give them warning from

me. 8 When I say to the wicked, 'You wicked person, you will surely die,' and you do not speak out to dissuade them from their ways, that wicked person will die for[a] their sin, and I will hold you accountable for their blood. 9 But if you do warn the wicked person to turn from their ways and they do not do so, they will die for their sin, though you yourself will be saved.

10 "Son of man, say to the Israelites, 'This is what you are saying: "Our offenses and sins weigh us down, and we are wasting away because of[b] them. How then can we live?" ' 11 Say to them, 'As surely as I live, declares the Sovereign Lord, I take no pleasure in the death of the wicked, but rather that they turn from their ways and live. Turn! Turn from your evil ways! Why will you die, people of Israel?'

12 "Therefore, son of man, say to your people, 'If someone who is righteous disobeys, that person's former righteousness will count for nothing. And if someone who is wicked repents, that person's former wickedness will not bring condemnation. The righteous person who sins will not be allowed to live even though they were formerly righteous.' 13 If I tell a righteous person that they will surely live, but then they trust in their righteousness and do evil, none of the righteous things that person has done will be remembered; they will die for the evil they have done. 14 And if I say to a wicked person, 'You will surely die,' but they then turn away from their sin and do what is just and right— 15 if they give back what they took in pledge for a loan, return what they have stolen, follow the decrees that give life, and do no evil—that person will surely live; they will not die. 16 None of the sins that person has committed will be remembered against them. They have done what is just and right; they will surely live.

17 "Yet your people say, 'The way of the Lord is not just.' But it is their way that is not just. 18 If a righteous person turns from their righteousness and does evil, they will die for it. 19 And if a wicked person turns away from their wickedness and

---

a 8 Or in; also in verse 9   b 10 Or away in

does what is just and right, they will live by doing so. ²⁰Yet you Israelites say, 'The way of the Lord is not just.' But I will judge each of you according to your own ways."

Jerusalem's Fall Explained

²¹In the twelfth year of our exile, in the tenth month on the fifth day, a man who had escaped from Jerusalem came to me and said, "The city has fallen!" ²²Now the evening before the man arrived, the hand of the LORD was on me, and he opened my mouth before the man came to me in the morning. So my mouth was opened and I was no longer silent.

²³Then the word of the LORD came to me: ²⁴"Son of man, the people living in those ruins in the land of Israel are saying, 'Abraham was only one man, yet he possessed the land. But we are many; surely the land has been given to us as our possession.' ²⁵Therefore say to them, 'This is what the Sovereign LORD says: Since you eat meat with the blood still in it and look to your idols and shed blood, should you then possess the land? ²⁶You rely on your sword, you do detestable things, and each of you defiles his neighbor's wife. Should you then possess the land?'

²⁷"Say this to them: 'This is what the Sovereign LORD says: As surely as I live, those who are left in the ruins will fall by the sword, those out in the country I will give to the wild animals to be devoured, and those in strongholds and caves will die of a plague. ²⁸I will make the land a desolate waste, and her proud strength will come to an end, and the mountains of Israel will become desolate so that no one will cross them. ²⁹Then they will know that I am the LORD, when I have made the land a desolate waste because of all the detestable things they have done.'

³⁰"As for you, son of man, your people are talking together about you by the walls and at the doors of the houses, saying to each other, 'Come and hear the message that has come from the LORD.' ³¹My people come to you, as they usually do, and sit before you to hear your words, but they do not put them into practice. Their mouths speak of love, but their hearts are greedy for unjust gain. ³²Indeed, to them you are nothing more than one who sings love songs with a beautiful voice and plays an instrument well, for they hear your words but do not put them into practice.

³³"When all this comes true—and it surely will—then they will know that a prophet has been among them."

The LORD Will Be Israel's Shepherd

34 The word of the LORD came to me: ²"Son of man, prophesy against the shepherds of Israel; prophesy and say to them: 'This is what the Sovereign LORD says: Woe to you shepherds of Israel who only take care of yourselves! Should not shepherds take care of the flock? ³You eat the curds, clothe yourselves with the wool and slaughter the choice animals, but you do not take care of the flock. ⁴You have not strengthened the weak or healed the sick or bound up the injured. You have not brought back the strays or searched for the lost. You have ruled them harshly and brutally. ⁵So they were scattered because there was no shepherd, and when they were scattered they became food for all the wild animals. ⁶My sheep wandered over all the mountains and on every high hill. They were scattered over the whole earth, and no one searched or looked for them.

⁷" 'Therefore, you shepherds, hear the word of the LORD: ⁸As surely as I live, declares the Sovereign LORD, because my flock lacks a shepherd and so has been plundered and has become food for all the wild animals, and because my shepherds did not search for my flock but cared for themselves rather than for my flock, ⁹therefore, you shepherds, hear the word of the LORD: ¹⁰This is what the Sovereign LORD says: I am against the shepherds and will hold them accountable for my flock. I will remove them from tending the flock so that the shepherds can no longer feed themselves. I will rescue my flock from their mouths, and it will no longer be food for them.

¹¹" 'For this is what the Sovereign LORD says: I myself will search for my sheep and look after them. ¹²As a shepherd looks after his scattered flock when he is

with them, so will I look after my sheep. I will rescue them from all the places where they were scattered on a day of clouds and darkness. [13] I will bring them out from the nations and gather them from the countries, and I will bring them into their own land. I will pasture them on the mountains of Israel, in the ravines and in all the settlements in the land. [14] I will tend them in a good pasture, and the mountain heights of Israel will be their grazing land. There they will lie down in good grazing land, and there they will feed in a rich pasture on the mountains of Israel. [15] I myself will tend my sheep and have them lie down, declares the Sovereign Lord. [16] I will search for the lost and bring back the strays. I will bind up the injured and strengthen the weak, but the sleek and the strong I will destroy. I will shepherd the flock with justice.

[17] " 'As for you, my flock, this is what the Sovereign Lord says: I will judge between one sheep and another, and between rams and goats. [18] Is it not enough for you to feed on the good pasture? Must you also trample the rest of your pasture with your feet? Is it not enough for you to drink clear water? Must you also muddy the rest with your feet? [19] Must my flock feed on what you have trampled and drink what you have muddied with your feet?

[20] " 'Therefore this is what the Sovereign Lord says to them: See, I myself will judge between the fat sheep and the lean sheep. [21] Because you shove with flank and shoulder, butting all the weak sheep with your horns until you have driven them away, [22] I will save my flock, and they will no longer be plundered. I will judge between one sheep and another. [23] I will place over them one shepherd, my servant David, and he will tend them; he will tend them and be their shepherd. [24] I the Lord will be their God, and my servant David will be prince among them. I the Lord have spoken.

[25] " 'I will make a covenant of peace with them and rid the land of savage beasts so that they may live in the wilderness and sleep in the forests in safety. [26] I will make them and the places surrounding my hill a blessing.[a] I will send down showers in season; there will be showers of blessing. [27] The trees will yield their fruit and the ground will yield its crops; the people will be secure in their land. They will know that I am the Lord, when I break the bars of their yoke and rescue them from the hands of those who enslaved them. [28] They will no longer be plundered by the nations, nor will wild animals devour them. They will live in safety, and no one will make them afraid. [29] I will provide for them a land renowned for its crops, and they will no longer be victims of famine in the land or bear the scorn of the nations. [30] Then they will know that I, the Lord their God, am with them and that they, the Israelites, are my people, declares the Sovereign Lord. [31] You are my sheep, the sheep of my pasture, and I am your God, declares the Sovereign Lord.' "

A Prophecy Against Edom

35 The word of the Lord came to me: [2] "Son of man, set your face against Mount Seir; prophesy against it [3] and say: 'This is what the Sovereign Lord says: I am against you, Mount Seir, and I will stretch out my hand against you and make you a desolate waste. [4] I will turn your towns into ruins and you will be desolate. Then you will know that I am the Lord.

[5] " 'Because you harbored an ancient hostility and delivered the Israelites over to the sword at the time of their calamity, the time their punishment reached its climax, [6] therefore as surely as I live, declares the Sovereign Lord, I will give you over to bloodshed and it will pursue you. Since you did not hate bloodshed, bloodshed will pursue you. [7] I will make Mount Seir a desolate waste and cut off from it all who come and go. [8] I will fill your mountains with the slain; those killed by the sword will fall on your hills and in your valleys and in all your ravines. [9] I will make you desolate forever; your towns will not be inhabited. Then you will know that I am the Lord.

---

[a] 26 Or *I will cause them and the places surrounding my hill to be named in blessings* (see Gen. 48:20); or *I will cause them and the places surrounding my hill to be seen as blessed*

10 " 'Because you have said, "These two nations and countries will be ours and we will take possession of them," even though I the Lord was there, 11therefore as surely as I live, declares the Sovereign Lord, I will treat you in accordance with the anger and jealousy you showed in your hatred of them and I will make myself known among them when I judge you. 12Then you will know that I the Lord have heard all the contemptible things you have said against the mountains of Israel. You said, "They have been laid waste and have been given over to us to devour." 13You boasted against me and spoke against me without restraint, and I heard it. 14This is what the Sovereign Lord says: While the whole earth rejoices, I will make you desolate. 15Because you rejoiced when the inheritance of Israel became desolate, that is how I will treat you. You will be desolate, Mount Seir, you and all of Edom. Then they will know that I am the Lord.' "

Hope for the Mountains of Israel

36 "Son of man, prophesy to the mountains of Israel and say, 'Mountains of Israel, hear the word of the Lord. 2This is what the Sovereign Lord says: The enemy said of you, "Aha! The ancient heights have become our possession." ' 3Therefore prophesy and say, 'This is what the Sovereign Lord says: Because they ravaged and crushed you from every side so that you became the possession of the rest of the nations and the object of people's malicious talk and slander, 4therefore, mountains of Israel, hear the word of the Sovereign Lord: This is what the Sovereign Lord says to the mountains and hills, to the ravines and valleys, to the desolate ruins and the deserted towns that have been plundered and ridiculed by the rest of the nations around you— 5this is what the Sovereign Lord says: In my burning zeal I have spoken against the rest of the nations, and against all Edom, for with glee and with malice in their hearts they made my land their own possession so that they might plunder its pastureland.' 6Therefore prophesy concerning the land of Israel and say to the mountains and

hills, to the ravines and valleys: 'This is what the Sovereign Lord says: I speak in my jealous wrath because you have suffered the scorn of the nations. 7Therefore this is what the Sovereign Lord says: I swear with uplifted hand that the nations around you will also suffer scorn.

8 " 'But you, mountains of Israel, will produce branches and fruit for my people Israel, for they will soon come home. 9I am concerned for you and will look on you with favor; you will be plowed and sown, 10and I will cause many people to live on you—yes, all of Israel. The towns will be inhabited and the ruins rebuilt. 11I will increase the number of people and animals living on you, and they will be fruitful and become numerous. I will settle people on you as in the past and will make you prosper more than before. Then you will know that I am the Lord. 12I will cause people, my people Israel, to live on you. They will possess you, and you will be their inheritance; you will never again deprive them of their children.

13 " 'This is what the Sovereign Lord says: Because some say to you, "You devour people and deprive your nation of its children," 14therefore you will no longer devour people or make your nation childless, declares the Sovereign Lord. 15No longer will I make you hear the taunts of the nations, and no longer will you suffer the scorn of the peoples or cause your nation to fall, declares the Sovereign Lord.' "

Israel's Restoration Assured

16Again the word of the Lord came to me: 17"Son of man, when the people of Israel were living in their own land, they defiled it by their conduct and their actions. Their conduct was like a woman's monthly uncleanness in my sight. 18So I poured out my wrath on them because they had shed blood in the land and because they had defiled it with their idols. 19I dispersed them among the nations, and they were scattered through the countries; I judged them according to their conduct and their actions. 20And wherever they went among the nations they profaned my holy name, for it was said of them, 'These are the Lord's people, and yet they had to leave his land.' ²¹I had concern for my holy name, which the people of Israel profaned among the nations where they had gone.

²²"Therefore say to the Israelites, 'This is what the Sovereign LORD says: It is not for your sake, people of Israel, that I am going to do these things, but for the sake of my holy name, which you have profaned among the nations where you have gone. ²³I will show the holiness of my great name, which has been profaned among the nations, the name you have profaned among them. Then the nations will know that I am the LORD, declares the Sovereign LORD, when I am proved holy through you before their eyes.

²⁴" 'For I will take you out of the nations; I will gather you from all the countries and bring you back into your own land. ²⁵I will sprinkle clean water on you, and you will be clean; I will cleanse you from all your impurities and from all your idols. ²⁶I will give you a new heart and put a new spirit in you; I will remove from you your heart of stone and give you a heart of flesh. ²⁷And I will put my Spirit in you and move you to follow my decrees and be careful to keep my laws. ²⁸Then you will live in the land I gave your ancestors; you will be my people, and I will be your God. ²⁹I will save you from all your uncleanness. I will call for the grain and make it plentiful and will not bring famine upon you. ³⁰I will increase the fruit of the trees and the crops of the field, so that you will no longer suffer disgrace among the nations because of famine. ³¹Then you will remember your evil ways and wicked deeds, and you will loathe yourselves for your sins and detestable practices. ³²I want you to know that I am not doing this for your sake, declares the Sovereign LORD. Be ashamed and disgraced for your conduct, people of Israel!

³³" 'This is what the Sovereign LORD says: On the day I cleanse you from all your sins, I will resettle your towns, and the ruins will be rebuilt. ³⁴The desolate land will be cultivated instead of lying desolate in the sight of all who pass through it. ³⁵They will say, "This land that was laid waste has become like the garden of Eden; the cities that were lying in ruins,

desolate and destroyed, are now fortified and inhabited." ³⁶Then the nations around you that remain will know that I the LORD have rebuilt what was destroyed and have replanted what was desolate. I the LORD have spoken, and I will do it.'

³⁷"This is what the Sovereign LORD says: Once again I will yield to Israel's plea and do this for them: I will make their people as numerous as sheep, ³⁸as numerous as the flocks for offerings at Jerusalem during her appointed festivals. So will the ruined cities be filled with flocks of people. Then they will know that I am the LORD."

The Valley of Dry Bones

37 The hand of the LORD was on me, and he brought me out by the Spirit of the LORD and set me in the middle of a valley; it was full of bones. ²He led me back and forth among them, and I saw a great many bones on the floor of the valley, bones that were very dry. ³He asked me, "Son of man, can these bones live?"

I said, "Sovereign LORD, you alone know."

⁴Then he said to me, "Prophesy to these bones and say to them, 'Dry bones, hear the word of the LORD! ⁵This is what the Sovereign LORD says to these bones: I will make breath^a enter you, and you will come to life. ⁶I will attach tendons to you and make flesh come upon you and cover you with skin; I will put breath in you, and you will come to life. Then you will know that I am the LORD.' "

⁷So I prophesied as I was commanded. And as I was prophesying, there was a noise, a rattling sound, and the bones came together, bone to bone. ⁸I looked, and tendons and flesh appeared on them and skin covered them, but there was no breath in them.

⁹Then he said to me, "Prophesy to the breath; prophesy, son of man, and say to it, 'This is what the Sovereign LORD says: Come, breath, from the four winds and breathe into these slain, that they may live.' " ¹⁰So I prophesied as he commanded me, and breath entered them; they came to life and stood up on their feet— a vast army.

---

^a 5 The Hebrew for this word can also mean *wind* or *spirit* (see verses 6-14).

CHECK THE FACTS

What did the dry bones stand for in the vision God gave Ezekiel?

A) The Israelites

B) All the animals of the sacrifice

C) The priests

CORRECT ANSWER: A

[11]Then he said to me: "Son of man, these bones are the people of Israel. They say, 'Our bones are dried up and our hope is gone; we are cut off.' [12]Therefore prophesy and say to them: 'This is what the Sovereign LORD says: My people, I am going to open your graves and bring you up from them; I will bring you back to the land of Israel. [13]Then you, my people, will know that I am the LORD, when I open your graves and bring you up from them. [14]I will put my Spirit in you and you will live, and I will settle you in your own land. Then you will know that I the LORD have spoken, and I have done it, declares the LORD.' "

One Nation Under One King

[15]The word of the LORD came to me: [16]"Son of man, take a stick of wood and write on it, 'Belonging to Judah and the Israelites associated with him.' Then take another stick of wood, and write on it, 'Belonging to Joseph (that is, to Ephraim) and all the Israelites associated with him.' [17]Join them together into one stick so that they will become one in your hand.

[18]"When your people ask you, 'Won't you tell us what you mean by this?' [19]say to them, 'This is what the Sovereign LORD says: I am going to take the stick of Joseph—which is in Ephraim's hand—and of the Israelite tribes associated with him, and join it to Judah's stick. I will make them into a single stick of wood, and they will become one in my hand.' [20]Hold before their eyes the sticks you have written on [21]and say to them, 'This is what the Sovereign LORD says: I will take the Israelites out of the nations where they have gone. I will gather them from all around and bring them back into their own land. [22]I will make them one nation in the land, on the mountains of Israel. There will be one king over all of them and they will never again be two nations or be divided into two kingdoms. [23]They will no longer defile themselves with their idols and vile images or with any of their offenses, for I will save them from all their sinful backsliding,[a] and I will cleanse them. They will be my people, and I will be their God.

[24]" 'My servant David will be king over them, and they will all have one shepherd. They will follow my laws and be careful to keep my decrees. [25]They will live in the land I gave to my servant Jacob, the land where your ancestors lived. They and their children and their children's children will live there forever, and David my servant will be their prince forever. [26]I will make a covenant of peace with them; it will be an everlasting covenant. I will establish them and increase their numbers, and I will put my sanctuary among them forever. [27]My dwelling place will be with them; I will be their God, and they will be my people. [28]Then the nations will know that I the LORD make Israel holy, when my sanctuary is among them forever.' "

---

[a] 23 Many Hebrew manuscripts (see also Septuagint); most Hebrew manuscripts *all their dwelling places where they sinned*

The LORD's Great Victory Over the Nations

38 The word of the LORD came to me: 2 "Son of man, set your face against Gog, of the land of Magog, the chief prince of[a] Meshek and Tubal; prophesy against him 3 and say: 'This is what the Sovereign LORD says: I am against you, Gog, chief prince of[b] Meshek and Tubal. 4 I will turn you around, put hooks in your jaws and bring you out with your whole army—your horses, your horsemen fully armed, and a great horde with large and small shields, all of them brandishing their swords. 5 Persia, Cush[c] and Put will be with them, all with shields and helmets, 6 also Gomer with all its troops, and Beth Togarmah from the far north with all its troops—the many nations with you.

7 " 'Get ready; be prepared, you and all the hordes gathered about you, and take command of them. 8 After many days you will be called to arms. In future years you will invade a land that has recovered from war, whose people were gathered from many nations to the mountains of Israel, which had long been desolate. They had been brought out from the nations, and now all of them live in safety. 9 You and all your troops and the many nations with you will go up, advancing like a storm; you will be like a cloud covering the land.

10 " 'This is what the Sovereign LORD says: On that day thoughts will come into your mind and you will devise an evil scheme. 11 You will say, "I will invade a land of unwalled villages; I will attack a peaceful and unsuspecting people—all of them living without walls and without gates and bars. 12 I will plunder and loot and turn my hand against the resettled ruins and the people gathered from the nations, rich in livestock and goods, living at the center of the land.[d]" 13 Sheba and Dedan and the merchants of Tarshish and all her villages[e] will say to you, "Have you come to plunder? Have you gathered your hordes to loot, to carry off silver and gold, to take away livestock and goods and to seize much plunder?" '

14 "Therefore, son of man, prophesy and say to Gog: 'This is what the Sovereign LORD says: In that day, when my people Israel are living in safety, will you not take notice of it? 15 You will come from your place in the far north, you and many nations with you, all of them riding on horses, a great horde, a mighty army. 16 You will advance against my people Israel like a cloud that covers the land. In days to come, Gog, I will bring you against my land, so that the nations may know me when I am proved holy through you before their eyes.

17 " 'This is what the Sovereign LORD says: You are the one I spoke of in former days by my servants the prophets of Israel. At that time they prophesied for years that I would bring you against them. 18 This is what will happen in that day: When Gog attacks the land of Israel, my hot anger will be aroused, declares the Sovereign LORD. 19 In my zeal and fiery

THE SCENE

MAGOG

(EZEKIEL 38:2)

A nation in the Black Sea region. They were considered enemies of the people of God.

---

[a] 2 Or *the prince of Rosh,*   [b] 3 Or *Gog, prince of Rosh,*
[c] 5 That is, the upper Nile region   [d] 12 The Hebrew for this phrase means *the navel of the earth.*   [e] 13 Or *her strong lions*

wrath I declare that at that time there shall be a great earthquake in the land of Israel. ²⁰The fish in the sea, the birds in the sky, the beasts of the field, every creature that moves along the ground, and all the people on the face of the earth will tremble at my presence. The mountains will be overturned, the cliffs will crumble and every wall will fall to the ground. ²¹I will summon a sword against Gog on all my mountains, declares the Sovereign LORD. Every man's sword will be against his brother. ²²I will execute judgment on him with plague and bloodshed; I will pour down torrents of rain, hailstones and burning sulfur on him and on his troops and on the many nations with him. ²³And so I will show my greatness and my holiness, and I will make myself known in the sight of many nations. Then they will know that I am the LORD.'

39 "Son of man, prophesy against Gog and say: 'This is what the Sovereign LORD says: I am against you, Gog, chief prince of[a] Meshek and Tubal. ²I will turn you around and drag you along. I will bring you from the far north and send you against the mountains of Israel. ³Then I will strike your bow from your left hand and make your arrows drop from your right hand. ⁴On the mountains of Israel you will fall, you and all your troops and the nations with you. I will give you as food to all kinds of carrion birds and to the wild animals. ⁵You will fall in the open field, for I have spoken, declares the Sovereign LORD. ⁶I will send fire on Magog and on those who live in safety in the coastlands, and they will know that I am the LORD.

⁷" 'I will make known my holy name among my people Israel. I will no longer let my holy name be profaned, and the nations will know that I the LORD am the Holy One in Israel. ⁸It is coming! It will surely take place, declares the Sovereign LORD. This is the day I have spoken of.

⁹" 'Then those who live in the towns of Israel will go out and use the weapons for fuel and burn them up—the small and large shields, the bows and arrows, the war clubs and the spears. For seven years they will use them for fuel. ¹⁰They will not need to gather wood from the fields or cut it from the forests, because they will use the weapons for fuel. And they will plunder those who plundered them and loot those who looted them, declares the Sovereign LORD.

¹¹" 'On that day I will give Gog a burial place in Israel, in the valley of those who travel east of the Sea. It will block the way of travelers, because Gog and all his hordes will be buried there. So it will be called the Valley of Hamon Gog.[b]

¹²" 'For seven months the Israelites will be burying them in order to cleanse the land. ¹³All the people of the land will bury them, and the day I display my glory will be a memorable day for them, declares the Sovereign LORD. ¹⁴People will be continually employed in cleansing the land. They will spread out across the land and, along with others, they will bury any bodies that are lying on the ground.

" 'After the seven months they will carry out a more detailed search. ¹⁵As they go through the land, anyone who sees a human bone will leave a marker beside it until the gravediggers bury it in the Valley of Hamon Gog, ¹⁶near a town called Hamonah.[c] And so they will cleanse the land.'

¹⁷"Son of man, this is what the Sovereign LORD says: Call out to every kind of bird and all the wild animals: 'Assemble and come together from all around to the sacrifice I am preparing for you, the great sacrifice on the mountains of Israel. There you will eat flesh and drink blood. ¹⁸You will eat the flesh of mighty men and drink the blood of the princes of the earth as if they were rams and lambs, goats and bulls—all of them fattened animals from Bashan. ¹⁹At the sacrifice I am preparing for you, you will eat fat till you are glutted and drink blood till you are drunk. ²⁰At my table you will eat your fill of horses and riders, mighty men and soldiers of every kind,' declares the Sovereign LORD.

²¹"I will display my glory among the nations, and all the nations will see the punishment I inflict and the hand I lay on them. ²²From that day forward the people of Israel will know that I am the LORD their

---

a 1 Or Gog, prince of Rosh,　b 11 Hamon Gog means hordes of Gog.　c 16 Hamonah means horde.

God. ²³And the nations will know that the people of Israel went into exile for their sin, because they were unfaithful to me. So I hid my face from them and handed them over to their enemies, and they all fell by the sword. ²⁴I dealt with them according to their uncleanness and their offenses, and I hid my face from them.

²⁵ "Therefore this is what the Sovereign LORD says: I will now restore the fortunes of Jacob^a and will have compassion on all the people of Israel, and I will be zealous for my holy name. ²⁶They will forget their shame and all the unfaithfulness they showed toward me when they lived in safety in their land with no one to make them afraid. ²⁷When I have brought them back from the nations and have gathered them from the countries of their enemies, I will be proved holy through them in the sight of many nations. ²⁸Then they will know that I am the LORD their God, for though I sent them into exile among the nations, I will gather them to their own land, not leaving any behind. ²⁹I will no longer hide my face from them, for I will pour out my Spirit on the people of Israel, declares the Sovereign LORD."

The Temple Area Restored

40 In the twenty-fifth year of our exile, at the beginning of the year, on the tenth of the month, in the fourteenth year after the fall of the city—on that very day the hand of the LORD was on me and he took me there. ²In visions of God he took me to the land of Israel and set me on a very high mountain, on whose south side were some buildings that looked like a city. ³He took me there, and I saw a man whose appearance was like bronze; he was standing in the gateway with a linen cord and a measuring rod in his hand. ⁴The man said to me, "Son of man, look carefully and listen closely and pay attention to everything I am going to show you, for that is why you have been brought here. Tell the people of Israel everything you see."

The East Gate to the Outer Court

⁵I saw a wall completely surrounding the temple area. The length of the measuring rod in the man's hand was six long cubits,^b each of which was a cubit and a handbreadth. He measured the wall; it was one measuring rod thick and one rod high.

⁶Then he went to the east gate. He climbed its steps and measured the threshold of the gate; it was one rod deep. ⁷The alcoves for the guards were one rod long and one rod wide, and the projecting walls between the alcoves were five cubits^c thick. And the threshold of the gate next to the portico facing the temple was one rod deep.

⁸Then he measured the portico of the gateway; ⁹it^d was eight cubits^e deep and its jambs were two cubits^f thick. The portico of the gateway faced the temple.

¹⁰Inside the east gate were three alcoves on each side; the three had the same measurements, and the faces of the projecting walls on each side had the same measurements. ¹¹Then he measured the width of the entrance of the gateway; it was ten cubits and its length was thirteen cubits.^g ¹²In front of each alcove was a wall one cubit high, and the alcoves were six cubits square. ¹³Then he measured the gateway from the top of the rear wall of one alcove to the top of the opposite one; the distance was twenty-five cubits^h from one parapet opening to the opposite one. ¹⁴He measured along the faces of the projecting walls all around the inside of the gateway—sixty cubits.ⁱ The measurement was up to the portico^j facing the courtyard.^k ¹⁵The distance from the entrance of the gateway to the far end of its portico was fifty cubits.^l

^a 25 Or *now bring Jacob back from captivity*   ^b 5 That is, about 11 feet or about 3.2 meters; also in verse 12. The long cubit of about 21 inches or about 53 centimeters is the basic unit of measurement of length throughout chapters 40–48.   ^c 7 That is, about 8 3/4 feet or about 2.7 meters; also in verse 48   ^d 8,9 Many Hebrew manuscripts, Septuagint, Vulgate and Syriac; most Hebrew manuscripts *gateway facing the temple; it was one rod deep. 9Then he measured the portico of the gateway; it*   ^e 9 That is, about 14 feet or about 4.2 meters   ^f 9 That is, about 3 1/2 feet or about 1 meter   ^g 11 That is, about 18 feet wide and 23 feet long or about 5.3 meters wide and 6.9 meters long   ^h 13 That is, about 44 feet or about 13 meters; also in verses 21, 25, 29, 33 and 36   ⁱ 14 That is, about 105 feet or about 32 meters   ^j 14 Septuagint; Hebrew *projecting wall*   ^k 14 The meaning of the Hebrew for this verse is uncertain.   ^l 15 That is, about 88 feet or about 27 meters; also in verses 21, 25, 29, 33 and 36

16The alcoves and the projecting walls inside the gateway were surmounted by narrow parapet openings all around, as was the portico; the openings all around faced inward. The faces of the projecting walls were decorated with palm trees.

The Outer Court

17Then he brought me into the outer court. There I saw some rooms and a pavement that had been constructed all around the court; there were thirty rooms along the pavement. 18It abutted the sides of the gateways and was as wide as they were long; this was the lower pavement. 19Then he measured the distance from the inside of the lower gateway to the outside of the inner court; it was a hundred cubits*a* on the east side as well as on the north.

The North Gate

20Then he measured the length and width of the north gate, leading into the outer court. 21Its alcoves—three on each side—its projecting walls and its portico had the same measurements as those of the first gateway. It was fifty cubits long and twenty-five cubits wide. 22Its openings, its portico and its palm tree decorations had the same measurements as those of the gate facing east. Seven steps led up to it, with its portico opposite them. 23There was a gate to the inner court facing the north gate, just as there was on the east. He measured from one gate to the opposite one; it was a hundred cubits.

The South Gate

24Then he led me to the south side and I saw the south gate. He measured its jambs and its portico, and they had the same measurements as the others. 25The gateway and its portico had narrow openings all around, like the openings of the others. It was fifty cubits long and twenty-five cubits wide. 26Seven steps led up to it, with its portico opposite them; it had palm tree decorations on the faces of the projecting walls on each side. 27The inner court also had a gate facing south, and he measured from this gate to the outer gate on the south side; it was a hundred cubits.

The Gates to the Inner Court

28Then he brought me into the inner court through the south gate, and he measured the south gate; it had the same measurements as the others. 29Its alcoves, its projecting walls and its portico had the same measurements as the others. The gateway and its portico had openings all around. It was fifty cubits long and twenty-five cubits wide. 30(The porticoes of the gateways around the inner court were twenty-five cubits wide and five cubits deep.) 31Its portico faced the outer court; palm trees decorated its jambs, and eight steps led up to it.

32Then he brought me to the inner court on the east side, and he measured the gateway; it had the same measurements as the others. 33Its alcoves, its projecting walls and its portico had the same measurements as the others. The gateway and its portico had openings all around. It was fifty cubits long and twenty-five cubits wide. 34Its portico faced the outer court; palm trees decorated the jambs on either side, and eight steps led up to it.

35Then he brought me to the north gate and measured it. It had the same measurements as the others, 36as did its alcoves, its projecting walls and its portico, and it had openings all around. It was fifty cubits long and twenty-five cubits wide. 37Its portico*b* faced the outer court; palm trees decorated the jambs on either side, and eight steps led up to it.

The Rooms for Preparing Sacrifices

38A room with a doorway was by the portico in each of the inner gateways, where the burnt offerings were washed. 39In the portico of the gateway were two tables on each side, on which the burnt offerings, sin offerings*c* and guilt offerings were slaughtered. 40By the outside wall of the portico of the gateway, near the steps at the entrance of the north gateway were two tables, and on the other side of the steps were two tables. 41So there were four tables on one side of the gateway and four on the other—eight ta-

---

a 19 That is, about 175 feet or about 53 meters; also in verses 23, 27 and 47   *b 37* Septuagint (see also verses 31 and 34); Hebrew *jambs*   *c 39* Or *purification offerings* bles in all—on which the sacrifices were slaughtered. [42]There were also four tables of dressed stone for the burnt offerings, each a cubit and a half long, a cubit and a half wide and a cubit high.[a] On them were placed the utensils for slaughtering the burnt offerings and the other sacrifices. [43]And double-pronged hooks, each a handbreadth[b] long, were attached to the wall all around. The tables were for the flesh of the offerings.

The Rooms for the Priests

[44]Outside the inner gate, within the inner court, were two rooms, one[c] at the side of the north gate and facing south, and another at the side of the south[d] gate and facing north. [45]He said to me, "The room facing south is for the priests who guard the temple, [46]and the room facing north is for the priests who guard the altar. These are the sons of Zadok, who are the only Levites who may draw near to the LORD to minister before him."

[47]Then he measured the court: It was square—a hundred cubits long and a hundred cubits wide. And the altar was in front of the temple.

The New Temple

[48]He brought me to the portico of the temple and measured the jambs of the portico; they were five cubits wide on either side. The width of the entrance was fourteen cubits[e] and its projecting walls were[f] three cubits[g] wide on either side. [49]The portico was twenty cubits[h] wide, and twelve[i] cubits[j] from front to back. It was reached by a flight of stairs,[k] and there were pillars on each side of the jambs.

41 Then the man brought me to the main hall and measured the jambs; the width of the jambs was six cubits[l] on each side.[m] [2]The entrance was ten cubits[n] wide, and the projecting walls on each side of it were five cubits[o] wide. He also measured the main hall; it was forty cubits long and twenty cubits wide.[p]

[3]Then he went into the inner sanctuary and measured the jambs of the entrance; each was two cubits[q] wide. The entrance was six cubits wide, and the projecting walls on each side of it were

seven cubits[r] wide. [4]And he measured the length of the inner sanctuary; it was twenty cubits, and its width was twenty cubits across the end of the main hall. He said to me, "This is the Most Holy Place."

[5]Then he measured the wall of the temple; it was six cubits thick, and each side room around the temple was four cubits[s] wide. [6]The side rooms were on three levels, one above another, thirty on each level. There were ledges all around the wall of the temple to serve as supports for the side rooms, so that the supports were not inserted into the wall of the temple. [7]The side rooms all around the temple were wider at each successive level. The structure surrounding the temple was built in ascending stages, so that the rooms widened as one went upward. A stairway went up from the lowest floor to the top floor through the middle floor.

[8]I saw that the temple had a raised base all around it, forming the foundation of the side rooms. It was the length of the rod, six long cubits. [9]The outer wall of the side rooms was five cubits thick. The open area between the side rooms of the temple [10]and the priests' rooms was twenty cubits wide all around the temple. [11]There were entrances to the side rooms from the open area, one on the north and another on the south; and the base adjoining the open area was five cubits wide all around.

[a] 42 That is, about 2 2/3 feet long and wide and 21 inches high or about 80 centimeters long and wide and 53 centimeters high   [b] 43 That is, about 3 1/2 inches or about 9 centimeters   [c] 44 Septuagint; Hebrew *were rooms for singers, which were*   [d] 44 Septuagint; Hebrew *east*   [e] 48 That is, about 25 feet or about 7.4 meters   [f] 48 Septuagint; Hebrew *entrance was*   [g] 48 That is, about 5 1/4 feet or about 1.6 meters   [h] 49 That is, about 35 feet or about 11 meters   [i] 49 Septuagint; Hebrew *eleven*   [j] 49 That is, about 21 feet or about 6.4 meters   [k] 49 Hebrew; Septuagint *Ten steps led up to it*   [l] 1 That is, about 11 feet or about 3.2 meters; also in verses 3, 5 and 8   [m] 1 One Hebrew manuscript and Septuagint; most Hebrew manuscripts *side, the width of the tent*   [n] 2 That is, about 18 feet or about 5.3 meters   [o] 2 That is, about 8 3/4 feet or about 2.7 meters; also in verses 9, 11 and 12   [p] 2 That is, about 70 feet long and 35 feet wide or about 21 meters long and 11 meters wide   [q] 3 That is, about 3 1/2 feet or about 1.1 meters; also in verse 22   [r] 3 That is, about 12 feet or about 3.7 meters   [s] 5 That is, about 7 feet or about 2.1 meters

¹²The building facing the temple courtyard on the west side was seventy cubits*a* wide. The wall of the building was five cubits thick all around, and its length was ninety cubits.*b*

¹³Then he measured the temple; it was a hundred cubits*c* long, and the temple courtyard and the building with its walls were also a hundred cubits long. ¹⁴The width of the temple courtyard on the east, including the front of the temple, was a hundred cubits.

¹⁵Then he measured the length of the building facing the courtyard at the rear of the temple, including its galleries on each side; it was a hundred cubits.

The main hall, the inner sanctuary and the portico facing the court, ¹⁶as well as the thresholds and the narrow windows and galleries around the three of them—everything beyond and including the threshold was covered with wood. The floor, the wall up to the windows, and the windows were covered. ¹⁷In the space above the outside of the entrance to the inner sanctuary and on the walls at regular intervals all around the inner and outer sanctuary ¹⁸were carved cherubim and palm trees. Palm trees alternated with cherubim. Each cherub had two faces: ¹⁹the face of a human being toward the palm tree on one side and the face of a lion toward the palm tree on the other. They were carved all around the whole temple. ²⁰From the floor to the area above the entrance, cherubim and palm trees were carved on the wall of the main hall.

²¹The main hall had a rectangular doorframe, and the one at the front of the Most Holy Place was similar. ²²There was a wooden altar three cubits*d* high and two cubits square*e*; its corners, its base*f* and its sides were of wood. The man said to me, "This is the table that is before the LORD." ²³Both the main hall and the Most Holy Place had double doors. ²⁴Each door had two leaves—two hinged leaves for each door. ²⁵And on the doors of the main hall were carved cherubim and palm trees like those carved on the walls, and there was a wooden overhang on the front of the portico. ²⁶On the sidewalls of the portico were narrow windows with palm trees carved on each side. The side rooms of the temple also had overhangs.

The Rooms for the Priests

42 Then the man led me northward into the outer court and brought me to the rooms opposite the temple courtyard and opposite the outer wall on the north side. ²The building whose door faced north was a hundred cubits long and fifty cubits wide.*g* ³Both in the section twenty cubits*h* from the inner court and in the section opposite the pavement of the outer court, gallery faced gallery at the three levels. ⁴In front of the rooms was an inner passageway ten cubits wide and a hundred cubits*i* long.*j* Their doors were on the north. ⁵Now the upper rooms were narrower, for the galleries took more space from them than from the rooms on the lower and middle floors of the building. ⁶The rooms on the top floor had no pillars, as the courts had; so they were smaller in floor space than those on the lower and middle floors. ⁷There was an outer wall parallel to the rooms and the outer court; it extended in front of the rooms for fifty cubits. ⁸While the row of rooms on the side next to the outer court was fifty cubits long, the row on the side nearest the sanctuary was a hundred cubits long. ⁹The lower rooms had an entrance on the east side as one enters them from the outer court.

¹⁰On the south side*k* along the length of the wall of the outer court, adjoining the temple courtyard and opposite the outer wall, were rooms ¹¹with a passageway in front of them. These were like the rooms on the north; they had the same length and width, with similar exits and dimensions. Similar to the doorways on the north ¹²were the doorways of the rooms on the south. There was a doorway at the

---

a 12 That is, about 123 feet or about 37 meters   *b 12* That is, about 158 feet or about 48 meters   *c 13* That is, about 175 feet or about 53 meters; also in verses 14 and 15   *d 22* That is, about 5 1/4 feet or about 1.5 meters   *e 22* Septuagint; Hebrew *long*   *f 22* Septuagint; Hebrew *length*   *g 2* That is, about 175 feet long and 88 feet wide or about 53 meters long and 27 meters wide   *h 3* That is, about 35 feet or about 11 meters   *i 4* Septuagint and Syriac; Hebrew *and one cubit*   *j 4* That is, about 18 feet wide and 175 feet long or about 5.3 meters wide and 53 meters long   *k 10* Septuagint; Hebrew *Eastward* beginning of the passageway that was parallel to the corresponding wall extending eastward, by which one enters the rooms.

¹³Then he said to me, "The north and south rooms facing the temple courtyard are the priests' rooms, where the priests who approach the LORD will eat the most holy offerings. There they will put the most holy offerings—the grain offerings, the sin offerings[a] and the guilt offerings—for the place is holy. ¹⁴Once the priests enter the holy precincts, they are not to go into the outer court until they leave behind the garments in which they minister, for these are holy. They are to put on other clothes before they go near the places that are for the people."

¹⁵When he had finished measuring what was inside the temple area, he led me out by the east gate and measured the area all around: ¹⁶He measured the east side with the measuring rod; it was five hundred cubits.[b,c] ¹⁷He measured the north side; it was five hundred cubits[d] by the measuring rod. ¹⁸He measured the south side; it was five hundred cubits by the measuring rod. ¹⁹Then he turned to the west side and measured; it was five hundred cubits by the measuring rod. ²⁰So he measured the area on all four sides. It had a wall around it, five hundred cubits long and five hundred cubits wide, to separate the holy from the common.

God's Glory Returns to the Temple

43 Then the man brought me to the gate facing east, ²and I saw the glory of the God of Israel coming from the east. His voice was like the roar of rushing waters, and the land was radiant with his glory. ³The vision I saw was like the vision I had seen when he[e] came to destroy the city and like the visions I had seen by the Kebar River, and I fell facedown. ⁴The glory of the LORD entered the temple through the gate facing east. ⁵Then the Spirit lifted me up and brought me into the inner court, and the glory of the LORD filled the temple.

⁶While the man was standing beside me, I heard someone speaking to me from inside the temple. ⁷He said: "Son of man, this is the place of my throne and the place for the soles of my feet. This is where I will live among the Israelites forever. The people of Israel will never again defile my holy name—neither they nor their kings—by their prostitution and the funeral offerings[f] for their kings at their death.[g] ⁸When they placed their threshold next to my threshold and their doorposts beside my doorposts, with only a wall between me and them, they defiled my holy name by their detestable practices. So I destroyed them in my anger. ⁹Now let them put away from me their prostitution and the funeral offerings for their kings, and I will live among them forever.

¹⁰"Son of man, describe the temple to the people of Israel, that they may be ashamed of their sins. Let them consider its perfection, ¹¹and if they are ashamed of all they have done, make known to them the design of the temple—its arrangement, its exits and entrances—its whole design and all its regulations[h] and laws. Write these down before them so that they may be faithful to its design and follow all its regulations.

¹²"This is the law of the temple: All the surrounding area on top of the mountain will be most holy. Such is the law of the temple.

The Great Altar Restored

¹³"These are the measurements of the altar in long cubits,[i] that cubit being a cubit and a handbreadth: Its gutter is a cubit deep and a cubit wide, with a rim of one span[j] around the edge. And this is the height of the altar: ¹⁴From the gutter on the ground up to the lower ledge that goes around the altar it is two cubits high, and the ledge is a cubit wide.[k] From this lower

---

a 13 Or *purification offerings* *b* 16 See Septuagint of verse 17; Hebrew *rods*; also in verses 18 and 19. *c* 16 Five hundred cubits equal about 875 feet or about 265 meters; also in verses 17, 18 and 19. *d* 17 Septuagint; Hebrew *rods* *e* 3 Some Hebrew manuscripts and Vulgate; most Hebrew manuscripts *I* *f* 7 Or *the memorial monuments*; also in verse 9 *g* 7 Or *their high places* *h* 11 Some Hebrew manuscripts and Septuagint; most Hebrew manuscripts *regulations and its whole design* *i* 13 That is, about 21 inches or about 53 centimeters; also in verses 14 and 17. The long cubit is the basic unit for linear measurement throughout Ezekiel 40–48. *j* 13 That is, about 11 inches or about 27 centimeters *k* 14 That is, about 3 1/2 feet high and 1 3/4 feet wide or about 105 centimeters high and 53 centimeters wide ledge to the upper ledge that goes around the altar it is four cubits high, and that ledge is also a cubit wide.*a* 15Above that, the altar hearth is four cubits high, and four horns project upward from the hearth. 16The altar hearth is square, twelve cubits*b* long and twelve cubits wide. 17The upper ledge also is square, fourteen cubits*c* long and fourteen cubits wide. All around the altar is a gutter of one cubit with a rim of half a cubit.*d* The steps of the altar face east."

18Then he said to me, "Son of man, this is what the Sovereign Lord says: These will be the regulations for sacrificing burnt offerings and splashing blood against the altar when it is built: 19You are to give a young bull as a sin offering*e* to the Levitical priests of the family of Zadok, who come near to minister before me, declares the Sovereign Lord. 20You are to take some of its blood and put it on the four horns of the altar and on the four corners of the upper ledge and all around the rim, and so purify the altar and make atonement for it. 21You are to take the bull for the sin offering and burn it in the designated part of the temple area outside the sanctuary.

22"On the second day you are to offer a male goat without defect for a sin offering, and the altar is to be purified as it was purified with the bull. 23When you have finished purifying it, you are to offer a young bull and a ram from the flock, both without defect. 24You are to offer them before the Lord, and the priests are to sprinkle salt on them and sacrifice them as a burnt offering to the Lord.

25"For seven days you are to provide a male goat daily for a sin offering; you are also to provide a young bull and a ram from the flock, both without defect. 26For seven days they are to make atonement for the altar and cleanse it; thus they will dedicate it. 27At the end of these days, from the eighth day on, the priests are to present your burnt offerings and fellowship offerings on the altar. Then I will accept you, declares the Sovereign Lord."

The Priesthood Restored

44 Then the man brought me back to the outer gate of the sanctuary, the one facing east, and it was shut. 2The

Lord said to me, "This gate is to remain shut. It must not be opened; no one may enter through it. It is to remain shut because the Lord, the God of Israel, has entered through it. 3The prince himself is the only one who may sit inside the gateway to eat in the presence of the Lord. He is to enter by way of the portico of the gateway and go out the same way."

4Then the man brought me by way of the north gate to the front of the temple. I looked and saw the glory of the Lord filling the temple of the Lord, and I fell facedown.

5The Lord said to me, "Son of man, look carefully, listen closely and give attention to everything I tell you concerning all the regulations and instructions regarding the temple of the Lord. Give attention to the entrance to the temple and all the exits of the sanctuary. 6Say to rebellious Israel, 'This is what the Sovereign Lord says: Enough of your detestable practices, people of Israel! 7In addition to all your other detestable practices, you brought foreigners uncircumcised in heart and flesh into my sanctuary, desecrating my temple while you offered me food, fat and blood, and you broke my covenant. 8Instead of carrying out your duty in regard to my holy things, you put others in charge of my sanctuary. 9This is what the Sovereign Lord says: No foreigner uncircumcised in heart and flesh is to enter my sanctuary, not even the foreigners who live among the Israelites.

10"'The Levites who went far from me when Israel went astray and who wandered from me after their idols must bear the consequences of their sin. 11They may serve in my sanctuary, having charge of the gates of the temple and serving in it; they may slaughter the burnt offerings and sacrifices for the people and stand before the people and serve them. 12But because they served them in the presence of their idols and made the people of Israel fall into sin, therefore I have sworn

---

a 14 That is, about 7 feet high and 1 3/4 feet wide or about 2.1 meters high and 53 centimeters wide
b 16 That is, about 21 feet or about 6.4 meters
c 17 That is, about 25 feet or about 7.4 meters
d 17 That is, about 11 inches or about 27 centimeters
e 19 Or *purification offering*; also in verses 21, 22 and 25

with uplifted hand that they must bear the consequences of their sin, declares the Sovereign LORD. ¹³They are not to come near to serve me as priests or come near any of my holy things or my most holy offerings; they must bear the shame of their detestable practices. ¹⁴And I will appoint them to guard the temple for all the work that is to be done in it.

¹⁵ "'But the Levitical priests, who are descendants of Zadok and who guarded my sanctuary when the Israelites went astray from me, are to come near to minister before me; they are to stand before me to offer sacrifices of fat and blood, declares the Sovereign LORD. ¹⁶They alone are to enter my sanctuary; they alone are to come near my table to minister before me and serve me as guards.

¹⁷ "'When they enter the gates of the inner court, they are to wear linen clothes; they must not wear any woolen garment while ministering at the gates of the inner court or inside the temple. ¹⁸They are to wear linen turbans on their heads and linen undergarments around their waists. They must not wear anything that makes them perspire. ¹⁹When they go out into the outer court where the people are, they are to take off the clothes they have been ministering in and are to leave them in the sacred rooms, and put on other clothes, so that the people are not consecrated through contact with their garments.

²⁰ "'They must not shave their heads or let their hair grow long, but they are to keep the hair of their heads trimmed. ²¹No priest is to drink wine when he enters the inner court. ²²They must not marry widows or divorced women; they may marry only virgins of Israelite descent or widows of priests. ²³They are to teach my people the difference between the holy and the common and show them how to distinguish between the unclean and the clean.

²⁴ "'In any dispute, the priests are to serve as judges and decide it according to my ordinances. They are to keep my laws and my decrees for all my appointed festivals, and they are to keep my Sabbaths holy.

²⁵ "'A priest must not defile himself by going near a dead person; however, if the dead person was his father or mother, son or daughter, brother or unmarried sister, then he may defile himself. ²⁶After he is cleansed, he must wait seven days. ²⁷On the day he goes into the inner court of the sanctuary to minister in the sanctuary, he is to offer a sin offering[a] for himself, declares the Sovereign LORD.

²⁸ "'I am to be the only inheritance the priests have. You are to give them no possession in Israel; I will be their possession. ²⁹They will eat the grain offerings, the sin offerings and the guilt offerings; and everything in Israel devoted[b] to the LORD will belong to them. ³⁰The best of all the firstfruits and of all your special gifts will belong to the priests. You are to give them the first portion of your ground meal so that a blessing may rest on your household. ³¹The priests must not eat anything, whether bird or animal, found dead or torn by wild animals.

Israel Fully Restored

45 " 'When you allot the land as an inheritance, you are to present to the LORD a portion of the land as a sacred district, 25,000 cubits[c] long and 20,000[d] cubits[e] wide; the entire area will be holy. ²Of this, a section 500 cubits[f] square is to be for the sanctuary, with 50 cubits[g] around it for open land. ³In the sacred district, measure off a section 25,000 cubits long and 10,000 cubits[h] wide. In it will be the sanctuary, the Most Holy Place. ⁴It will be the sacred portion of the land for the priests, who minister in the sanctuary and who draw near to minister before the LORD. It will be a place for their houses as well as a holy place for the sanctuary. ⁵An area 25,000 cubits long and 10,000 cubits wide will belong to the Levites, who serve in the temple, as their possession for towns to live in.[i]

ᵃ 27 Or *purification offering*; also in verse 29   ᵇ 29 The Hebrew term refers to the irrevocable giving over of things or persons to the LORD.   ᶜ 1 That is, about 8 miles or about 13 kilometers; also in verses 3, 5 and 6
ᵈ 1 Septuagint (see also verses 3 and 5 and 48:9); Hebrew 10,000   ᵉ 1 That is, about 6 1/2 miles or about 11 kilometers   ᶠ 2 That is, about 875 feet or about 265 meters   ᵍ 2 That is, about 88 feet or about 27 meters   ʰ 3 That is, about 3 1/3 miles or about 5.3 kilometers; also in verse 5   ⁱ 5 Septuagint; Hebrew *temple; they will have as their possession 20 rooms*

6 " 'You are to give the city as its property an area 5,000 cubits*a* wide and 25,000 cubits long, adjoining the sacred portion; it will belong to all Israel.

7 " 'The prince will have the land bordering each side of the area formed by the sacred district and the property of the city. It will extend westward from the west side and eastward from the east side, running lengthwise from the western to the eastern border parallel to one of the tribal portions. 8This land will be his possession in Israel. And my princes will no longer oppress my people but will allow the people of Israel to possess the land according to their tribes.

9 " 'This is what the Sovereign Lord says: You have gone far enough, princes of Israel! Give up your violence and oppression and do what is just and right. Stop dispossessing my people, declares the Sovereign Lord. 10You are to use accurate scales, an accurate ephah*b* and an accurate bath.*c* 11The ephah and the bath are to be the same size, the bath containing a tenth of a homer and the ephah a tenth of a homer; the homer is to be the standard measure for both. 12The shekel*d* is to consist of twenty gerahs. Twenty shekels plus twenty-five shekels plus fifteen shekels equal one mina.*e*

13 " 'This is the special gift you are to offer: a sixth of an ephah*f* from each homer of wheat and a sixth of an ephah*g* from each homer of barley. 14The prescribed portion of olive oil, measured by the bath, is a tenth of a bath*h* from each cor (which consists of ten baths or one homer, for ten baths are equivalent to a homer). 15Also one sheep is to be taken from every flock of two hundred from the well-watered pastures of Israel. These will be used for the grain offerings, burnt offerings and fellowship offerings to make atonement for the people, declares the Sovereign Lord. 16All the people of the land will be required to give this special offering to the prince in Israel. 17It will be the duty of the prince to provide the burnt offerings, grain offerings and drink offerings at the festivals, the New Moons and the Sabbaths—at all the appointed festivals of Israel. He will provide the sin offerings,*i* grain offerings, burnt offerings and fellowship offerings to make atonement for the Israelites.

18 " 'This is what the Sovereign Lord says: In the first month on the first day you are to take a young bull without defect and purify the sanctuary. 19The priest is to take some of the blood of the sin offering and put it on the doorposts of the temple, on the four corners of the upper ledge of the altar and on the gateposts of the inner court. 20You are to do the same on the seventh day of the month for anyone who sins unintentionally or through ignorance; so you are to make atonement for the temple.

21 " 'In the first month on the fourteenth day you are to observe the Passover, a festival lasting seven days, during which you shall eat bread made without yeast. 22On that day the prince is to provide a bull as a sin offering for himself and for all the people of the land. 23Every day during the seven days of the festival he is to provide seven bulls and seven rams without defect as a burnt offering to the Lord, and a male goat for a sin offering. 24He is to provide as a grain offering an ephah for each bull and an ephah for each ram, along with a hin*j* of olive oil for each ephah.

25 " 'During the seven days of the festival, which begins in the seventh month on the fifteenth day, he is to make the same provision for sin offerings, burnt offerings, grain offerings and oil.

46 " 'This is what the Sovereign Lord says: The gate of the inner court facing east is to be shut on the six working days, but on the Sabbath day and on the day of the New Moon it is to be opened. 2The prince is to enter from the outside through the portico of the

---

a 6 That is, about 1 2/3 miles or about 2.7 kilometers
b 10 An ephah was a dry measure having the capacity of about 3/5 bushel or about 22 liters.   *c* 10 A bath was a liquid measure equaling about 6 gallons or about 22 liters.
d 12 A shekel weighed about 2/5 ounce or about 12 grams.   *e* 12 That is, 60 shekels; the common mina was 50 shekels. Sixty shekels were about 1 1/2 pounds or about 690 grams.   *f* 13 That is, probably about 6 pounds or about 2.7 kilograms   *g* 13 That is, probably about 5 pounds or about 2.3 kilograms   *h* 14 That is, about 2 1/2 quarts or about 2.2 liters   *i* 17 Or purification offerings; also in verses 19, 22, 23 and 25
j 24 That is, about 1 gallon or about 3.8 liters

BREAKTHROUGH!

Seventh month

(EZEKIEL 45:25)

This is called Ethanim in the Jewish lunar calendar. That's more or less from the middle of September to the middle of October.

gateway and stand by the gatepost. The priests are to sacrifice his burnt offering and his fellowship offerings. He is to bow down in worship at the threshold of the gateway and then go out, but the gate will not be shut until evening. ³On the Sabbaths and New Moons the people of the land are to worship in the presence of the LORD at the entrance of that gateway. ⁴The burnt offering the prince brings to the LORD on the Sabbath day is to be six male lambs and a ram, all without defect. ⁵The grain offering given with the ram is to be an ephah,ᵃ and the grain offering with the lambs is to be as much as he pleases, along with a hinᵇ of olive oil for each ephah. ⁶On the day of the New Moon he is to offer a young bull, six lambs and a ram, all without defect. ⁷He is to provide as a grain offering one ephah with the bull, one ephah with the ram, and with the lambs as much as he wants to give, along with a hin of oil for each ephah. ⁸When the prince enters, he is to go in through the portico of the gateway, and he is to come out the same way.

⁹ "'When the people of the land come before the LORD at the appointed festivals, whoever enters by the north gate to worship is to go out the south gate; and whoever enters by the south gate is to go out the north gate. No one is to return through the gate by which they entered, but each is to go out the opposite gate. ¹⁰The prince is to be among them, going in when they go in and going out when they go out. ¹¹At the feasts and the appointed festivals, the grain offering is to be an ephah with a bull, an ephah with a ram, and with the lambs as much as he pleases, along with a hin of oil for each ephah.

¹² "'When the prince provides a freewill offering to the LORD—whether a burnt offering or fellowship offerings—the gate facing east is to be opened for him. He shall offer his burnt offering or his fellowship offerings as he does on the Sabbath day. Then he shall go out, and after he has gone out, the gate will be shut.

¹³ "'Every day you are to provide a year-old lamb without defect for a burnt offering to the LORD; morning by morning you shall provide it. ¹⁴You are also to provide with it morning by morning a grain offering, consisting of a sixth of an ephahᶜ with a third of a hinᵈ of oil to moisten the flour. The presenting of this grain offering to the LORD is a lasting ordinance. ¹⁵So the lamb and the grain offering and the oil shall be provided morning by morning for a regular burnt offering.

¹⁶ "'This is what the Sovereign LORD says: If the prince makes a gift from his inheritance to one of his sons, it will also belong to his descendants; it is to be their property by inheritance. ¹⁷If, however, he makes a gift from his inheritance to one of his servants, the servant may keep it until the year of freedom; then it will revert to the prince. His inheritance belongs to his sons only; it is theirs. ¹⁸The prince must not take any of the inheritance of the people, driving them off their property.

ᵃ 5 That is, probably about 35 pounds or about 16 kilograms; also in verses 7 and 11   ᵇ 5 That is, about 1 gallon or about 3.8 liters; also in verses 7 and 11   ᶜ 14 That is, probably about 6 pounds or about 2.7 kilograms   ᵈ 14 That is, about 1 1/2 quarts or about 1.3 liters

He is to give his sons their inheritance out of his own property, so that not one of my people will be separated from their property.' "

[19] Then the man brought me through the entrance at the side of the gate to the sacred rooms facing north, which belonged to the priests, and showed me a place at the western end. [20] He said to me, "This is the place where the priests are to cook the guilt offering and the sin offering[a] and bake the grain offering, to avoid bringing them into the outer court and consecrating the people."

[21] He then brought me to the outer court and led me around to its four corners, and I saw in each corner another court. [22] In the four corners of the outer court were enclosed[b] courts, forty cubits long and thirty cubits wide;[c] each of the courts in the four corners was the same size. [23] Around the inside of each of the four courts was a ledge of stone, with places for fire built all around under the ledge. [24] He said to me, "These are the kitchens where those who minister at the temple are to cook the sacrifices of the people."

The River From the Temple

47 The man brought me back to the entrance to the temple, and I saw water coming out from under the threshold of the temple toward the east (for the temple faced east). The water was coming down from under the south side of the temple, south of the altar. [2] He then brought me out through the north gate and led me around the outside to the outer gate facing east, and the water was trickling from the south side.

[3] As the man went eastward with a measuring line in his hand, he measured off a thousand cubits[d] and then led me through water that was ankle-deep. [4] He measured off another thousand cubits and led me through water that was knee-deep. He measured off another thousand and led me through water that was up to the waist. [5] He measured off another thousand, but now it was a river that I could not cross, because the water had risen and was deep enough to swim in—a river

that no one could cross. [6] He asked me, "Son of man, do you see this?"

Then he led me back to the bank of the river. [7] When I arrived there, I saw a great number of trees on each side of the river. [8] He said to me, "This water flows toward the eastern region and goes down into the Arabah,[e] where it enters the Dead Sea. When it empties into the sea, the salty water there becomes fresh. [9] Swarms of living creatures will live wherever the river flows. There will be large numbers of fish, because this water flows there and makes the salt water fresh; so where the river flows everything will live. [10] Fishermen will stand along the shore; from En Gedi to En Eglaim there will be places for spreading nets. The fish will be of many kinds—like the fish of the Mediterranean Sea. [11] But the swamps and marshes will not become fresh; they will be left for salt. [12] Fruit trees of all kinds will grow on both banks of the river. Their leaves will not wither, nor will their fruit fail. Every month they will bear fruit, because the water from the sanctuary flows to them. Their fruit will serve for food and their leaves for healing."

The Boundaries of the Land

[13] This is what the Sovereign LORD says: "These are the boundaries of the land that you will divide among the twelve tribes of Israel as their inheritance, with two portions for Joseph. [14] You are to divide it equally among them. Because I swore with uplifted hand to give it to your ancestors, this land will become your inheritance.

[15] "This is to be the boundary of the land:

"On the north side it will run from the Mediterranean Sea by the Hethlon road past Lebo Hamath to Zedad, [16] Berothah[f] and Sibraim (which lies

---

[a] 20 Or *purification offering*   [b] 22 The meaning of the Hebrew for this word is uncertain.   [c] 22 That is, about 70 feet long and 53 feet wide or about 21 meters long and 16 meters wide   [d] 3 That is, about 1,700 feet or about 530 meters   [e] 8 Or *the Jordan Valley*   [f] 15,16 See Septuagint and 48:1; Hebrew *road to go into Zedad, 16Hamath, Berothah.*

on the border between Damascus and Hamath), as far as Hazer Hattikon, which is on the border of Hauran. ¹⁷The boundary will extend from the sea to Hazar Enan,ᵃ along the northern border of Damascus, with the border of Hamath to the north. This will be the northern boundary.

¹⁸ "On the east side the boundary will run between Hauran and Damascus, along the Jordan between Gilead and the land of Israel, to the Dead Sea and as far as Tamar.ᵇ This will be the eastern boundary.

¹⁹ "On the south side it will run from Tamar as far as the waters of Meribah Kadesh, then along the Wadi of Egypt to the Mediterranean Sea. This will be the southern boundary.

²⁰ "On the west side, the Mediterranean Sea will be the boundary to a point opposite Lebo Hamath. This will be the western boundary.

²¹ "You are to distribute this land among yourselves according to the tribes of Israel. ²²You are to allot it as an inheritance for yourselves and for the foreigners residing among you and who have children. You are to consider them as native-born Israelites; along with you they are to be allotted an inheritance among the tribes of Israel. ²³In whatever tribe a foreigner resides, there you are to give them their inheritance," declares the Sovereign Lᴏʀᴅ.

The Division of the Land

48 "These are the tribes, listed by name: At the northern frontier, Dan will have one portion; it will follow the Hethlon road to Lebo Hamath; Hazar Enan and the northern border of Damascus next to Hamath will be part of its border from the east side to the west side.

² "Asher will have one portion; it will border the territory of Dan from east to west.

³ "Naphtali will have one portion; it will border the territory of Asher from east to west.

⁴ "Manasseh will have one portion; it will border the territory of Naphtali from east to west.

⁵ "Ephraim will have one portion; it will

border the territory of Manasseh from east to west.

⁶ "Reuben will have one portion; it will border the territory of Ephraim from east to west.

⁷ "Judah will have one portion; it will border the territory of Reuben from east to west.

⁸ "Bordering the territory of Judah from east to west will be the portion you are to present as a special gift. It will be 25,000 cubitsᶜ wide, and its length from east to west will equal one of the tribal portions; the sanctuary will be in the center of it.

⁹ "The special portion you are to offer to the Lᴏʀᴅ will be 25,000 cubits long and 10,000 cubitsᵈ wide. ¹⁰This will be the sacred portion for the priests. It will be 25,000 cubits long on the north side, 10,000 cubits wide on the west side, 10,000 cubits wide on the east side and 25,000 cubits long on the south side. In the center of it will be the sanctuary of the Lᴏʀᴅ. ¹¹This will be for the consecrated priests, the Zadokites, who were faithful in serving me and did not go astray as the Levites did when the Israelites went astray. ¹²It will be a special gift to them from the sacred portion of the land, a most holy portion, bordering the territory of the Levites.

¹³ "Alongside the territory of the priests, the Levites will have an allotment 25,000 cubits long and 10,000 cubits wide. Its total length will be 25,000 cubits and its width 10,000 cubits. ¹⁴They must not sell or exchange any of it. This is the best of the land and must not pass into other hands, because it is holy to the Lᴏʀᴅ.

¹⁵ "The remaining area, 5,000 cubitsᵉ wide and 25,000 cubits long, will be for the common use of the city, for houses and for pastureland. The city will be in the center of it ¹⁶and will have these measurements: the north side 4,500 cubits,ᶠ the south side 4,500 cubits, the east side 4,500 cubits, and the west side 4,500 cubits. ¹⁷The pastureland for the city will

---

ᵃ 17 Hebrew *Enan*, a variant of *Enan*   ᵇ 18 See Syriac; Hebrew *Israel. You will measure to the Dead Sea.*
ᶜ 8 That is, about 8 miles or about 13 kilometers; also in verses 9, 10, 13, 15, 20 and 21   ᵈ 9 That is, about 3 1/3 miles or about 5.3 kilometers; also in verses 10, 13 and 18   ᵉ 15 That is, about 1 2/3 miles or about 2.7 kilometers   ᶠ 16 That is, about 1 1/2 miles or about 2.4 kilometers; also in verses 30, 32, 33 and 34

be 250 cubits[a] on the north, 250 cubits on the south, 250 cubits on the east, and 250 cubits on the west. [18]What remains of the area, bordering on the sacred portion and running the length of it, will be 10,000 cubits on the east side and 10,000 cubits on the west side. Its produce will supply food for the workers of the city. [19]The workers from the city who farm it will come from all the tribes of Israel. [20]The entire portion will be a square, 25,000 cubits on each side. As a special gift you will set aside the sacred portion, along with the property of the city.

[21]"What remains on both sides of the area formed by the sacred portion and the property of the city will belong to the prince. It will extend eastward from the 25,000 cubits of the sacred portion to the eastern border, and westward from the 25,000 cubits to the western border. Both these areas running the length of the tribal portions will belong to the prince, and the sacred portion with the temple sanctuary will be in the center of them. [22]So the property of the Levites and the property of the city will lie in the center of the area that belongs to the prince. The area belonging to the prince will lie between the border of Judah and the border of Benjamin.

[23]"As for the rest of the tribes: Benjamin will have one portion; it will extend from the east side to the west side.

[24]"Simeon will have one portion; it will border the territory of Benjamin from east to west.

[25]"Issachar will have one portion; it will border the territory of Simeon from east to west.

[26]"Zebulun will have one portion; it will border the territory of Issachar from east to west.

[27]"Gad will have one portion; it will border the territory of Zebulun from east to west.

[28]"The southern boundary of Gad will run south from Tamar to the waters of Meribah Kadesh, then along the Wadi of Egypt to the Mediterranean Sea.

[29]"This is the land you are to allot as an inheritance to the tribes of Israel, and these will be their portions," declares the Sovereign LORD.

The Gates of the New City

[30]"These will be the exits of the city: Beginning on the north side, which is 4,500 cubits long, [31]the gates of the city will be named after the tribes of Israel.

---

[a] 17 That is, about 440 feet or about 135 meters

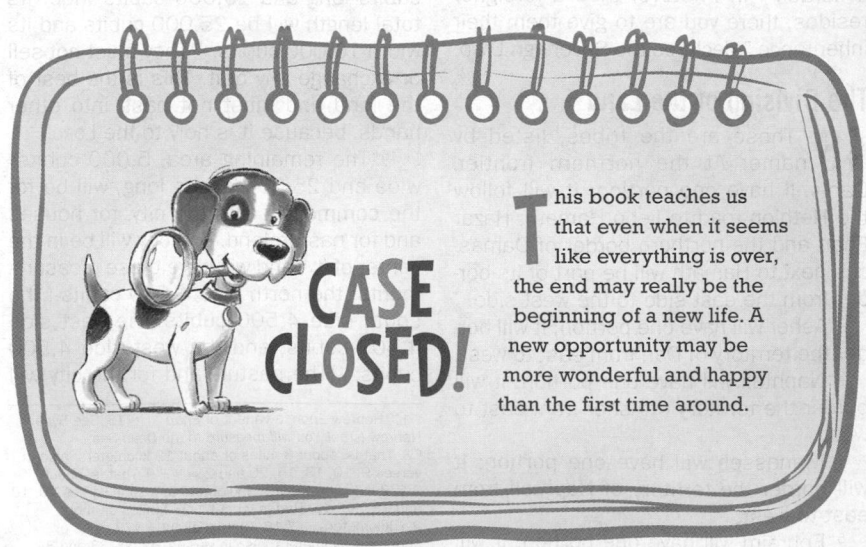

CASE CLOSED!

This book teaches us that even when it seems like everything is over, the end may really be the beginning of a new life. A new opportunity may be more wonderful and happy than the first time around.

The three gates on the north side will be the gate of Reuben, the gate of Judah and the gate of Levi.

32 "On the east side, which is 4,500 cubits long, will be three gates: the gate of Joseph, the gate of Benjamin and the gate of Dan.

33 "On the south side, which measures 4,500 cubits, will be three gates: the gate of Simeon, the gate of Issachar and the gate of Zebulun.

34 "On the west side, which is 4,500 cubits long, will be three gates: the gate of Gad, the gate of Asher and the gate of Naphtali.

35 "The distance all around will be 18,000 cubits.[a]

"And the name of the city from that time on will be:

THE LORD IS THERE."

---

[a] 35 That is, about 6 miles or about 9.5 kilometers

DANIEL

THE EVIDENCE:

WHO WROTE IT?
This book is the story of a boy named Daniel. He's the main character of the story. Since his name is the title of the book, it's believed that he's the author. However, it's also possible that somebody else wrote it and we don't know his name. That person may have called the book "Daniel" just because it was about Daniel!

HOW LONG AGO?
A long time ago, but Bible experts aren't totally sure when. Those who think Daniel wrote it say it was written while Daniel was a prisoner in Babylon. That was from the years 586 to 537 before Christ. Others think it was written later, maybe between 167 and 164 years before Christ.

WHAT'S IT ABOUT?
After he destroyed the city of Jerusalem, King Nebuchadnezzar took most of the people of Jerusalem to Babylon as prisoners. He took the "best" people — the smartest, those that had a job or those who were good for some kind of work. Daniel and three other boys were among this group — they were all really, really smart. This story shows that these kids were very obedient and faithful to God in spite of everything they had to go through.

THE BEST PART
The part where God saves Daniel from the lions is really good. Incredible! Some of the king's men accused Daniel unfairly, and Daniel was sentenced to die by being eaten by the lions. But God sent an angel to close the lions' mouths so they couldn't eat Daniel. When Daniel came out of the cave safe and sound, King Darius couldn't believe it! So then he understood that Daniel's God was the true God, and he said,

> "I issue a decree that in every part of my kingdom people must fear and reverence the God of Daniel.
>
> "For he is the living God
>   and he endures forever;
> his kingdom will not be destroyed,
>   his dominion will never end.
> He rescues and he saves;
>   he performs signs and wonders
>   in the heavens and on the earth.
> He has rescued Daniel
>   from the power of the lions" (6:26–27).

Daniel's Training in Babylon

1 In the third year of the reign of Jehoiakim king of Judah, Nebuchadnezzar king of Babylon came to Jerusalem and besieged it. ²And the Lord delivered Jehoiakim king of Judah into his hand, along with some of the articles from the temple of God. These he carried off to the temple of his god in Babylonia*a* and put in the treasure house of his god.

³Then the king ordered Ashpenaz, chief of his court officials, to bring into the king's service some of the Israelites from the royal family and the nobility — ⁴young men without any physical defect, handsome, showing aptitude for every kind of learning, well informed, quick to understand, and qualified to serve in the king's palace. He was to teach them the language and literature of the Babylonians.*b* ⁵The king assigned them a daily amount of food and wine from the king's table. They were to be trained for three years, and after that they were to enter the king's service.

⁶Among those who were chosen were some from Judah: Daniel, Hananiah, Mishael and Azariah. ⁷The chief official gave them new names: to Daniel, the name Belteshazzar; to Hananiah, Shadrach; to Mishael, Meshach; and to Azariah, Abednego.

⁸But Daniel resolved not to defile himself with the royal food and wine, and he asked the chief official for permission not to defile himself this way. ⁹Now God had caused the official to show favor and compassion to Daniel, ¹⁰but the official told Daniel, "I am afraid of my lord the king, who has assigned your*c* food and drink. Why should he see you looking worse than the other young men your age? The king would then have my head because of you."

¹¹Daniel then said to the guard whom the chief official had appointed over Daniel, Hananiah, Mishael and Azariah, ¹²"Please test your servants for ten days: Give us nothing but vegetables to eat and water to drink. ¹³Then compare our appearance with that of the young men who eat the royal food, and treat your ser-

vants in accordance with what you see." ¹⁴So he agreed to this and tested them for ten days.

---

a 2 Hebrew *Shinar*   *b 4* Or *Chaldeans*   *c 10* The Hebrew for *your* and *you* in this verse is plural.

THE

WITNESSES

✓ **NEBUCHADNEZZAR (DANIEL 1:1)**
Can you say this name right? You can read about him in Jeremiah 21:2.

✓ **KING JEHOIAKIM (DANIEL 1:1)**
Jehoiakim means "the Lord keeps me steady" and it's the name the Egyptian king Necho gave Eliakim, one of the last kings of Judah after Judah was conquered in the year 608 before Christ.

✓ **DANIEL, HANANIAH, MISHAEL AND AZARIAH (DANIEL 1:6)**
These are the Hebrew names of Daniel and his three friends. *Daniel* means "God is my judge." *Hananiah* means "the Lord is compassionate." *Mishael* means "Who is like God?" *Azariah* means "the Lord is my help."

¹⁵At the end of the ten days they looked healthier and better nourished than any of the young men who ate the royal food. ¹⁶So the guard took away their choice food and the wine they were to drink and gave them vegetables instead.

¹⁷To these four young men God gave knowledge and understanding of all kinds of literature and learning. And Daniel could understand visions and dreams of all kinds.

¹⁸At the end of the time set by the king to bring them into his service, the chief official presented them to Nebuchadnezzar. ¹⁹The king talked with them, and he found none equal to Daniel, Hananiah, Mishael and Azariah; so they entered the king's service. ²⁰In every matter of wisdom and understanding about which the king questioned them, he found them ten times better than all the magicians and enchanters in his whole kingdom.

²¹And Daniel remained there until the first year of King Cyrus.

Nebuchadnezzar's Dream

2 In the second year of his reign, Nebuchadnezzar had dreams; his mind was troubled and he could not sleep. ²So the king summoned the magicians, enchanters, sorcerers and astrologers[a] to tell him what he had dreamed. When they came in and stood before the king, ³he said to them, "I have had a dream that troubles me and I want to know what it means.[b]"

⁴Then the astrologers answered the king,[c] "May the king live forever! Tell your servants the dream, and we will interpret it."

⁵The king replied to the astrologers, "This is what I have firmly decided: If you do not tell me what my dream was and interpret it, I will have you cut into pieces and your houses turned into piles of rubble. ⁶But if you tell me the dream and explain it, you will receive from me gifts and rewards and great honor. So tell me the dream and interpret it for me."

⁷Once more they replied, "Let the king tell his servants the dream, and we will interpret it."

⁸Then the king answered, "I am certain that you are trying to gain time, because you realize that this is what I have firmly decided: ⁹If you do not tell me the dream, there is only one penalty for you. You have conspired to tell me misleading and wicked things, hoping the situation will change. So then, tell me the dream, and I will know that you can interpret it for me."

¹⁰The astrologers answered the king, "There is no one on earth who can do what the king asks! No king, however great and mighty, has ever asked such a thing of any magician or enchanter or astrologer. ¹¹What the king asks is too difficult. No one can reveal it to the king except the gods, and they do not live among humans."

THE WITNESSES

✓ **KING CYRUS** (DANIEL 1:21)
See Ezra 1:1.

---

a 2 Or Chaldeans; also in verses 4, 5 and 10   *b 3 Or was*   *c 4 At this point the Hebrew text has in Aramaic, indicating that the text from here through the end of chapter 7 is in Aramaic.*

Astrologers

(DANIEL 2:4)

These were men who studied the planets and stars and how they related to people. They were from a nation called Chaldea. This land was famous, because people there knew a lot about the stars, constellations and magic. At that time, saying "Chaldean" was like saying "wise." They spoke Aramaic because the Assyrians had ordered that language to be the official language in their kingdom. Aramaic was used for a long time after that, even until the time of Jesus.

¹²This made the king so angry and furious that he ordered the execution of all the wise men of Babylon. ¹³So the decree was issued to put the wise men to death, and men were sent to look for Daniel and his friends to put them to death.

¹⁴When Arioch, the commander of the king's guard, had gone out to put to death the wise men of Babylon, Daniel spoke to him with wisdom and tact. ¹⁵He asked the king's officer, "Why did the king issue such a harsh decree?" Arioch then explained the matter to Daniel. ¹⁶At this, Daniel went in to the king and asked for time, so that he might interpret the dream for him.

¹⁷Then Daniel returned to his house and explained the matter to his friends

Hananiah, Mishael and Azariah. ¹⁸He urged them to plead for mercy from the God of heaven concerning this mystery, so that he and his friends might not be executed with the rest of the wise men of Babylon. ¹⁹During the night the mystery was revealed to Daniel in a vision. Then Daniel praised the God of heaven ²⁰and said:

"Praise be to the name of God for
    ever and ever;
  wisdom and power are his.
²¹He changes times and seasons;
    he deposes kings and raises up
      others.
He gives wisdom to the wise
    and knowledge to the discerning.
²²He reveals deep and hidden things;
    he knows what lies in darkness,
    and light dwells with him.
²³I thank and praise you, God of my
    ancestors:
You have given me wisdom and
    power,
you have made known to me what we
    asked of you,
  you have made known to us the
    dream of the king."

Daniel Interprets the Dream

²⁴Then Daniel went to Arioch, whom the king had appointed to execute the wise men of Babylon, and said to him, "Do not execute the wise men of Babylon. Take me to the king, and I will interpret his dream for him."

²⁵Arioch took Daniel to the king at once and said, "I have found a man among the exiles from Judah who can tell the king what his dream means."

²⁶The king asked Daniel (also called Belteshazzar), "Are you able to tell me what I saw in my dream and interpret it?"

²⁷Daniel replied, "No wise man, enchanter, magician or diviner can explain to the king the mystery he has asked about, ²⁸but there is a God in heaven who reveals mysteries. He has shown King Nebuchadnezzar what will happen in days to come. Your dream and the visions that passed through your mind as you were lying in bed are these:

²⁹"As Your Majesty was lying there, your mind turned to things to come, and the revealer of mysteries showed you what is going to happen. ³⁰As for me, this mystery has been revealed to me, not because I have greater wisdom than anyone else alive, but so that Your Majesty may know the interpretation and that you may understand what went through your mind.

³¹"Your Majesty looked, and there before you stood a large statue—an enormous, dazzling statue, awesome in appearance. ³²The head of the statue was made of pure gold, its chest and arms of silver, its belly and thighs of bronze, ³³its legs of iron, its feet partly of iron and partly of baked clay. ³⁴While you were watching, a rock was cut out, but not by human hands. It struck the statue on its feet of iron and clay and smashed them. ³⁵Then the iron, the clay, the bronze, the silver and the gold were all broken to pieces and became like chaff on a threshing floor in the summer. The wind swept them away without leaving a trace. But the rock that struck the statue became a huge mountain and filled the whole earth.

³⁶"This was the dream, and now we will interpret it to the king. ³⁷Your Majesty, you are the king of kings. The God of heaven has given you dominion and power and might and glory; ³⁸in your hands he has placed all mankind and the beasts of the field and the birds in the sky. Wherever they live, he has made you ruler over them all. You are that head of gold.

³⁹"After you, another kingdom will arise, inferior to yours. Next, a third kingdom, one of bronze, will rule over the whole earth. ⁴⁰Finally, there will be a fourth kingdom, strong as iron—for iron breaks and smashes everything—and as iron breaks things to pieces, so it will crush and break all the others. ⁴¹Just as you saw that the feet and toes were partly of baked clay and partly of iron, so this will be a divided kingdom; yet it will have some of the strength of iron in it, even as you saw iron mixed with clay. ⁴²As the toes were partly iron and partly clay, so this kingdom will be partly strong and partly brittle. ⁴³And just as you saw the iron mixed with baked clay, so the people will be a mixture and will not remain united, any more than iron mixes with clay.

⁴⁴"In the time of those kings, the God of heaven will set up a kingdom that will never be destroyed, nor will it be left to another people. It will crush all those kingdoms and bring them to an end, but it will itself endure forever. ⁴⁵This is the meaning of the vision of the rock cut out of a mountain, but not by human hands—a rock that broke the iron, the bronze, the clay, the silver and the gold to pieces.

"The great God has shown the king what will take place in the future. The dream is true and its interpretation is trustworthy."

⁴⁶Then King Nebuchadnezzar fell prostrate before Daniel and paid him honor and ordered that an offering and incense be presented to him. ⁴⁷The king said to Daniel, "Surely your God is the God of gods and the Lord of kings and a revealer of mysteries, for you were able to reveal this mystery."

⁴⁸Then the king placed Daniel in a high position and lavished many gifts on him. He made him ruler over the entire province of Babylon and placed him in charge of all its wise men. ⁴⁹Moreover, at Daniel's request the king appointed Shadrach, Meshach and Abednego administrators over the province of Babylon, while Daniel himself remained at the royal court.

The Image of Gold and the Blazing Furnace

3 King Nebuchadnezzar made an image of gold, sixty cubits high and six cubits wide,ᵃ and set it up on the plain of Dura in the province of Babylon. ²He then summoned the satraps, prefects, governors, advisers, treasurers, judges, magistrates and all the other provincial officials to come to the dedication of the image he had set up. ³So the satraps, prefects, governors, advisers, treasurers, judges, magistrates and all the other provincial officials assembled for the dedication of the image that King Nebuchadnezzar had set up, and they stood before it.

ᵃ *1* That is, about 90 feet high and 9 feet wide or about 27 meters high and 2.7 meters wide

4Then the herald loudly proclaimed, "Nations and peoples of every language, this is what you are commanded to do: 5As soon as you hear the sound of the horn, flute, zither, lyre, harp, pipe and all kinds of music, you must fall down and worship the image of gold that King Nebuchadnezzar has set up. 6Whoever does not fall down and worship will immediately be thrown into a blazing furnace."

7Therefore, as soon as they heard the sound of the horn, flute, zither, lyre, harp and all kinds of music, all the nations and peoples of every language fell down and worshiped the image of gold that King Nebuchadnezzar had set up. 8At this time some astrologers[a] came forward and denounced the Jews. 9They said to King Nebuchadnezzar, "May the king live forever! 10Your Majesty has issued a decree that everyone who hears the sound of the horn, flute, zither, lyre, harp, pipe and all kinds of music must fall down and worship the image of gold, 11and that whoever does not fall down and worship will be thrown into a blazing furnace. 12But there are some Jews whom you have set over the affairs of the province of Babylon—Shadrach, Meshach and Abednego—who pay no attention to you, Your Majesty. They neither serve your gods nor worship the image of gold you have set up."

13Furious with rage, Nebuchadnezzar summoned Shadrach, Meshach and Abednego. So these men were brought before the king, 14and Nebuchadnezzar said to them, "Is it true, Shadrach, Meshach and Abednego, that you do not serve my gods or worship the image of gold I have set up? 15Now when you hear the sound of the horn, flute, zither, lyre, harp, pipe and all kinds of music, if you are ready to fall down and worship the image I made, very good. But if you do not worship it, you will be thrown immediately into a blazing furnace. Then what god will be able to rescue you from my hand?"

16Shadrach, Meshach and Abednego replied to him, "King Nebuchadnezzar, we do not need to defend ourselves before you in this matter. 17If we are thrown into the blazing furnace, the God we serve is able to deliver us from it, and he will deliver us[b] from Your Majesty's hand. 18But even if he does not, we want you to know, Your Majesty, that we will not serve your gods or worship the image of gold you have set up."

19Then Nebuchadnezzar was furious with Shadrach, Meshach and Abednego, and his attitude toward them changed. He ordered the furnace heated seven times hotter than usual 20and commanded some of the strongest soldiers in his army to tie up Shadrach, Meshach and Abednego and throw them into the blazing furnace. 21So these men, wearing their robes, trousers, turbans and other clothes, were bound and thrown into the blazing furnace. 22The king's command was so urgent and the furnace so hot that the flames of the fire killed the soldiers who took up Shadrach, Meshach and Abednego, 23and these three men, firmly tied, fell into the blazing furnace.

24Then King Nebuchadnezzar leaped to his feet in amazement and asked his advisers, "Weren't there three men that we tied up and threw into the fire?"

They replied, "Certainly, Your Majesty."

25He said, "Look! I see four men walking around in the fire, unbound and unharmed, and the fourth looks like a son of the gods."

26Nebuchadnezzar then approached the opening of the blazing furnace and shouted, "Shadrach, Meshach and Abednego, servants of the Most High God, come out! Come here!"

So Shadrach, Meshach and Abednego came out of the fire, 27and the satraps, prefects, governors and royal advisers crowded around them. They saw that the fire had not harmed their bodies, nor was a hair of their heads singed; their robes were not scorched, and there was no smell of fire on them.

28Then Nebuchadnezzar said, "Praise be to the God of Shadrach, Meshach and Abednego, who has sent his angel and rescued his servants! They trusted in him and defied the king's command and were

---

a 8 Or *Chaldeans*　　*b* 17 Or *If the God we serve is able to deliver us, then he will deliver us from the blazing furnace and* willing to give up their lives rather than serve or worship any god except their own God. ²⁹Therefore I decree that the people of any nation or language who say anything against the God of Shadrach, Meshach and Abednego be cut into pieces and their houses be turned into piles of rubble, for no other god can save in this way."

³⁰Then the king promoted Shadrach, Meshach and Abednego in the province of Babylon.

Nebuchadnezzar's Dream of a Tree

4 *ᵃ* King Nebuchadnezzar,

To the nations and peoples of every language, who live in all the earth:

May you prosper greatly!

²It is my pleasure to tell you about the miraculous signs and wonders that the Most High God has performed for me.

³How great are his signs,
   how mighty his wonders!
His kingdom is an eternal
   kingdom;
his dominion endures from
   generation to generation.

⁴I, Nebuchadnezzar, was at home in my palace, contented and prosperous. ⁵I had a dream that made me afraid. As I was lying in bed, the images and visions that passed through my mind terrified me. ⁶So I commanded that all the wise men of Babylon be brought before me to interpret the dream for me. ⁷When the magicians, enchanters, astrologers*ᵇ* and diviners came, I told them the dream, but they could not interpret it for me. ⁸Finally, Daniel came into my presence and I told him the dream. (He is called Belteshazzar, after the name of my god, and the spirit of the holy gods is in him.)

⁹I said, "Belteshazzar, chief of the magicians, I know that the spirit of the holy gods is in you, and no mystery is too difficult for you. Here is my dream; interpret it for me.

¹⁰These are the visions I saw while lying in bed: I looked, and there before me stood a tree in the middle of the land. Its height was enormous. ¹¹The tree grew large and strong and its top touched the sky; it was visible to the ends of the earth. ¹²Its leaves were beautiful, its fruit abundant, and on it was food for all. Under it the wild animals found shelter, and the birds lived in its branches; from it every creature was fed.

¹³"In the visions I saw while lying in bed, I looked, and there before me was a holy one, a messenger,*ᶜ* coming down from heaven. ¹⁴He called in a loud voice: 'Cut down the tree and trim off its branches; strip off its leaves and scatter its fruit. Let the animals flee from under it and the birds from its branches. ¹⁵But let the stump and its roots, bound with iron and bronze, remain in the ground, in the grass of the field.

" 'Let him be drenched with the dew of heaven, and let him live with the animals among the plants of the earth. ¹⁶Let his mind be changed from that of a man and let him be given the mind of an animal, till seven times*ᵈ* pass by for him.

¹⁷" 'The decision is announced by messengers, the holy ones declare the verdict, so that the living may know that the Most High is sovereign over all kingdoms on earth and gives them to anyone he wishes and sets over them the lowliest of people.'

¹⁸"This is the dream that I, King Nebuchadnezzar, had. Now, Belteshazzar, tell me what it means, for none of the wise men in my kingdom can interpret it for me. But you can, because the spirit of the holy gods is in you."

Daniel Interprets the Dream

¹⁹Then Daniel (also called Belteshazzar) was greatly perplexed for a

---

ᵃ In Aramaic texts 4:1-3 is numbered 3:31-33, and 4:4-37 is numbered 4:1-34.   *ᵇ* 7 Or *Chaldeans*   *ᶜ* 13 Or *watchman*; also in verses 17 and 23   *ᵈ* 16 Or *years*; also in verses 23, 25 and 32 time, and his thoughts terrified him. So the king said, "Belteshazzar, do not let the dream or its meaning alarm you."

Belteshazzar answered, "My lord, if only the dream applied to your enemies and its meaning to your adversaries! ²⁰The tree you saw, which grew large and strong, with its top touching the sky, visible to the whole earth, ²¹with beautiful leaves and abundant fruit, providing food for all, giving shelter to the wild animals, and having nesting places in its branches for the birds— ²²Your Majesty, you are that tree! You have become great and strong; your greatness has grown until it reaches the sky, and your dominion extends to distant parts of the earth.

²³"Your Majesty saw a holy one, a messenger, coming down from heaven and saying, 'Cut down the tree and destroy it, but leave the stump, bound with iron and bronze, in the grass of the field, while its roots remain in the ground. Let him be drenched with the dew of heaven; let him live with the wild animals, until seven times pass by for him.'

²⁴"This is the interpretation, Your Majesty, and this is the decree the Most High has issued against my lord the king: ²⁵You will be driven away from people and will live with the wild animals; you will eat grass like the ox and be drenched with the dew of heaven. Seven times will pass by for you until you acknowledge that the Most High is sovereign over all kingdoms on earth and gives them to anyone he wishes. ²⁶The command to leave the stump of the tree with its roots means that your kingdom will be restored to you when you acknowledge that Heaven rules. ²⁷Therefore, Your Majesty, be pleased to accept my advice: Renounce your sins by doing what is right, and your wickedness by being kind to the oppressed. It may be that then your prosperity will continue."

The Dream Is Fulfilled

²⁸All this happened to King Nebuchadnezzar. ²⁹Twelve months later, as the king was walking on the roof of the royal palace of Babylon, ³⁰he said, "Is not this the great Babylon I have built as the royal residence, by my mighty power and for the glory of my majesty?"

³¹Even as the words were on his lips, a voice came from heaven, "This is what is decreed for you, King Nebuchadnezzar: Your royal authority has been taken from you. ³²You will be driven away from people and will live with the wild animals; you will eat grass like the ox. Seven times will pass by for you until you acknowledge that the Most High is sovereign over all kingdoms on earth and gives them to anyone he wishes."

³³Immediately what had been said about Nebuchadnezzar was fulfilled. He was driven away from people and ate grass like the ox. His body was drenched with the dew of heaven until his hair grew like the feathers of an eagle and his nails like the claws of a bird.

³⁴At the end of that time, I, Nebuchadnezzar, raised my eyes toward heaven, and my sanity was restored. Then I praised the Most High; I honored and glorified him who lives forever.

His dominion is an eternal dominion;
    his kingdom endures from
        generation to generation.
³⁵All the peoples of the earth
    are regarded as nothing.
He does as he pleases
    with the powers of heaven
    and the peoples of the earth.
No one can hold back his hand
    or say to him: "What have you
        done?"

³⁶At the same time that my sanity was restored, my honor and splendor were returned to me for the glory of my kingdom. My advisers and nobles sought me out, and I was restored to

my throne and became even greater than before. [37]Now I, Nebuchadnezzar, praise and exalt and glorify the King of heaven, because everything he does is right and all his ways are just. And those who walk in pride he is able to humble.

The Writing on the Wall

5 King Belshazzar gave a great banquet for a thousand of his nobles and drank wine with them. [2]While Belshazzar was drinking his wine, he gave orders to bring in the gold and silver goblets that Nebuchadnezzar his father[a] had taken from the temple in Jerusalem, so that the king and his nobles, his wives and his concubines might drink from them. [3]So they brought in the gold goblets that had been taken from the temple of God in Jerusalem, and the king and his nobles, his wives and his concubines drank from them. [4]As they drank the wine, they praised the gods of gold and silver, of bronze, iron, wood and stone.

[5]Suddenly the fingers of a human hand appeared and wrote on the plaster of the wall, near the lampstand in the royal palace. The king watched the hand as it wrote. [6]His face turned pale and he was so frightened that his legs became weak and his knees were knocking.

[7]The king summoned the enchanters, astrologers[b] and diviners. Then he said to these wise men of Babylon, "Whoever reads this writing and tells me what it means will be clothed in purple and have a gold chain placed around his neck, and he will be made the third highest ruler in the kingdom."

[8]Then all the king's wise men came in, but they could not read the writing or tell the king what it meant. [9]So King Belshazzar became even more terrified and his face grew more pale. His nobles were baffled.

[10]The queen,[c] hearing the voices of the king and his nobles, came into the banquet hall. "May the king live forever!" she said. "Don't be alarmed! Don't look so pale! [11]There is a man in your kingdom who has the spirit of the holy gods in him. In the time of your father he was found to have insight and intelligence and wisdom like that of the gods. Your father, King Nebuchadnezzar, appointed him chief of the magicians, enchanters, astrologers and diviners. [12]He did this because Daniel, whom the king called Belteshazzar, was found to have a keen mind and knowledge and understanding, and also the ability to interpret dreams, explain riddles and solve difficult problems. Call for Daniel, and he will tell you what the writing means."

[13]So Daniel was brought before the king, and the king said to him, "Are you Daniel, one of the exiles my father the king brought from Judah? [14]I have heard that the spirit of the gods is in you and that you have insight, intelligence and outstanding wisdom. [15]The wise men and enchanters were brought before me to read this writing and tell me what it means, but they could not explain it. [16]Now I have heard that you are able to give interpretations and to solve difficult problems. If you can read this writing and tell me what it means, you will be clothed in purple and have a gold chain placed around your neck, and you will be made the third highest ruler in the kingdom."

[17]Then Daniel answered the king, "You may keep your gifts for yourself and give your rewards to someone else. Nevertheless, I will read the writing for the king and tell him what it means.

[18]"Your Majesty, the Most High God gave your father Nebuchadnezzar sovereignty and greatness and glory and splendor. [19]Because of the high position he gave him, all the nations and peoples of every language dreaded and feared him. Those the king wanted to put to death, he put to death; those he wanted to spare, he spared; those he wanted to promote, he promoted; and those he wanted to humble, he humbled. [20]But when his heart became arrogant and hardened with pride, he was deposed from his royal throne and stripped of his glory. [21]He was driven away from people and given the mind of an animal; he lived with the wild

---

[a] 2 Or *ancestor*; or *predecessor*; also in verses 11, 13 and 18   [b] 7 Or *Chaldeans*; also in verse 11   [c] 10 Or *queen mother*

donkeys and ate grass like the ox; and his body was drenched with the dew of heaven, until he acknowledged that the Most High God is sovereign over all kingdoms on earth and sets over them anyone he wishes.

22 "But you, Belshazzar, his son,[a] have not humbled yourself, though you knew all this. 23 Instead, you have set yourself up against the Lord of heaven. You had the goblets from his temple brought to you, and you and your nobles, your wives and your concubines drank wine from them. You praised the gods of silver and gold, of bronze, iron, wood and stone, which cannot see or hear or understand. But you did not honor the God who holds in his hand your life and all your ways. 24 Therefore he sent the hand that wrote the inscription.

25 "This is the inscription that was written:

      MENE, MENE, TEKEL, PARSIN

26 "Here is what these words mean:

    Mene[b]: God has numbered the days of your reign and brought it to an end.

27 *Tekel*[c]: You have been weighed on the scales and found wanting.

28 *Peres*[d]: Your kingdom is divided and given to the Medes and Persians."

29 Then at Belshazzar's command, Daniel was clothed in purple, a gold chain was placed around his neck, and he was proclaimed the third highest ruler in the kingdom.

30 That very night Belshazzar, king of the Babylonians,[e] was slain, 31 and Darius the Mede took over the kingdom, at the age of sixty-two.[f]

Daniel in the Den of Lions

6[g] It pleased Darius to appoint 120 satraps to rule throughout the kingdom, 2 with three administrators over them, one of whom was Daniel. The satraps were made accountable to them so that the king might not suffer loss. 3 Now Daniel so distinguished himself among the administrators and the satraps by his exceptional qualities that the king planned to set him over the whole kingdom. 4 At this, the administrators and the satraps tried

---

[a] 22 Or *descendant*; or *successor*   [b] 26 *Mene* can mean *numbered* or *mina* (a unit of money).   [c] 27 *Tekel* can mean *weighed* or *shekel*.   [d] 28 *Peres* (the singular of *Parsin*) can mean *divided* or *Persia* or *a half mina* or *a half shekel*.   [e] 30 Or *Chaldeans*   [f] 31 In Aramaic texts this verse (5:31) is numbered 6:1.   [g] In Aramaic texts 6:1-28 is numbered 6:2-29.

THE
WITNESSES

✓ **KING BELSHAZZAR** (DANIEL 5:1)
He was the son of Nabonidus, the last king of Babylonia. The book of Daniel calls him "king," but history tells us that he was just someone connected to the Babylonian kingdom but not the king. In the Acadian language, his name probably means "Bel (the god) protects the king."

✓ **DARIUS THE MEDE** (DANIEL 5:31)
He was king of Persia and successor of Cyrus and Cambyses. Darius let the Jews continue reconstructing the temple in Jerusalem.

to find grounds for charges against Daniel in his conduct of government affairs, but they were unable to do so. They could find no corruption in him, because he was trustworthy and neither corrupt nor negligent. ⁵Finally these men said, "We will never find any basis for charges against this man Daniel unless it has something to do with the law of his God."

⁶So these administrators and satraps went as a group to the king and said: "May King Darius live forever! ⁷The royal administrators, prefects, satraps, advisers and governors have all agreed that the king should issue an edict and enforce the decree that anyone who prays to any god or human being during the next thirty days, except to you, Your Majesty, shall be thrown into the lions' den. ⁸Now, Your Majesty, issue the decree and put it in writing so that it cannot be altered—in accordance with the law of the Medes and Persians, which cannot be repealed." ⁹So King Darius put the decree in writing.

BREAKTHROUGH!

The law of the Medes and Persians

(DANIEL 6:8)

We still use this phrase when we talk about something that can't be changed. It was a law that nobody — not even the king himself — could change for any reason.

¹⁰Now when Daniel learned that the decree had been published, he went home to his upstairs room where the windows opened toward Jerusalem. Three times a day he got down on his knees and prayed, giving thanks to his God, just as he had done before. ¹¹Then these men went as a group and found Daniel praying and asking God for help. ¹²So they went to the king and spoke to him about his royal decree: "Did you not publish a decree that during the next thirty days anyone who prays to any god or human being except to you, Your Majesty, would be thrown into the lions' den?"

The king answered, "The decree stands—in accordance with the law of the Medes and Persians, which cannot be repealed."

¹³Then they said to the king, "Daniel, who is one of the exiles from Judah, pays no attention to you, Your Majesty, or to the decree you put in writing. He still prays three times a day." ¹⁴When the king heard this, he was greatly distressed; he was determined to rescue Daniel and made every effort until sundown to save him.

¹⁵Then the men went as a group to King Darius and said to him, "Remember, Your Majesty, that according to the law of the Medes and Persians no decree or edict that the king issues can be changed."

¹⁶So the king gave the order, and they brought Daniel and threw him into the lions' den. The king said to Daniel, "May your God, whom you serve continually, rescue you!"

¹⁷A stone was brought and placed over the mouth of the den, and the king sealed it with his own signet ring and with the rings of his nobles, so that Daniel's situation might not be changed. ¹⁸Then the king returned to his palace and spent the night without eating and without any entertainment being brought to him. And he could not sleep.

¹⁹At the first light of dawn, the king got up and hurried to the lions' den. ²⁰When he came near the den, he called to Daniel in an anguished voice, "Daniel, servant of the living God, has your God, whom you serve continually, been able to rescue you from the lions?"

²¹Daniel answered, "May the king live forever! ²²My God sent his angel, and he shut the mouths of the lions. They have not hurt me, because I was found innocent in his sight. Nor have I ever done any wrong before you, Your Majesty."

²³The king was overjoyed and gave orders to lift Daniel out of the den. And when Daniel was lifted from the den, no wound was found on him, because he had trusted in his God.

²⁴At the king's command, the men who had falsely accused Daniel were brought in and thrown into the lions' den, along with their wives and children. And before they reached the floor of the den, the lions overpowered them and crushed all their bones.

²⁵Then King Darius wrote to all the nations and peoples of every language in all the earth:

"May you prosper greatly!

²⁶"I issue a decree that in every part of my kingdom people must fear and reverence the God of Daniel.

"For he is the living God
   and he endures forever;
his kingdom will not be destroyed,
   his dominion will never end.
²⁷He rescues and he saves;
   he performs signs and wonders
   in the heavens and on the earth.
He has rescued Daniel
   from the power of the lions."

²⁸So Daniel prospered during the reign of Darius and the reign of Cyrus[a] the Persian.

Daniel's Dream of Four Beasts

7 In the first year of Belshazzar king of Babylon, Daniel had a dream, and visions passed through his mind as he was lying in bed. He wrote down the substance of his dream.

²Daniel said: "In my vision at night I looked, and there before me were the four winds of heaven churning up the great sea. ³Four great beasts, each different from the others, came up out of the sea.

⁴"The first was like a lion, and it had the wings of an eagle. I watched until its wings were torn off and it was lifted from the ground so that it stood on two feet like a human being, and the mind of a human was given to it.

⁵"And there before me was a second beast, which looked like a bear. It was raised up on one of its sides, and it had three ribs in its mouth between its teeth. It was told, 'Get up and eat your fill of flesh!'

⁶"After that, I looked, and there before me was another beast, one that looked like a leopard. And on its back it had four wings like those of a bird. This beast had four heads, and it was given authority to rule.

⁷"After that, in my vision at night I looked, and there before me was a fourth beast—terrifying and frightening and very powerful. It had large iron teeth; it crushed and devoured its victims and trampled underfoot whatever was left. It was different from all the former beasts, and it had ten horns.

⁸"While I was thinking about the horns, there before me was another horn, a little one, which came up among them; and three of the first horns were uprooted before it. This horn had eyes like the eyes of a human being and a mouth that spoke boastfully.

⁹"As I looked,

"thrones were set in place,
   and the Ancient of Days took his
     seat.
His clothing was as white as snow;
   the hair of his head was white like
     wool.
His throne was flaming with fire,
   and its wheels were all ablaze.
¹⁰A river of fire was flowing,
   coming out from before him.
Thousands upon thousands attended
     him;
   ten thousand times ten thousand
     stood before him.
The court was seated,
   and the books were opened.

¹¹"Then I continued to watch because of the boastful words the horn was speaking.

ᵃ 28 Or *Darius, that is, the reign of Cyrus*

I kept looking until the beast was slain and its body destroyed and thrown into the blazing fire. 12(The other beasts had been stripped of their authority, but were allowed to live for a period of time.)

13"In my vision at night I looked, and there before me was one like a son of man,*a* coming with the clouds of heaven. He approached the Ancient of Days and was led into his presence. 14He was given authority, glory and sovereign power; all nations and peoples of every language worshiped him. His dominion is an everlasting dominion that will not pass away, and his kingdom is one that will never be destroyed.

The Interpretation of the Dream

15"I, Daniel, was troubled in spirit, and the visions that passed through my mind disturbed me. 16I approached one of those standing there and asked him the meaning of all this.

"So he told me and gave me the interpretation of these things: 17'The four great beasts are four kings that will rise from the earth. 18But the holy people of the Most High will receive the kingdom and will possess it forever—yes, for ever and ever.'

19"Then I wanted to know the meaning of the fourth beast, which was different from all the others and most terrifying, with its iron teeth and bronze claws—the beast that crushed and devoured its victims and trampled underfoot whatever was left. 20I also wanted to know about the ten horns on its head and about the other horn that came up, before which three of them fell—the horn that looked more imposing than the others and that had eyes and a mouth that spoke boastfully. 21As I watched, this horn was waging war against the holy people and defeating them, 22until the Ancient of Days came and pronounced judgment in favor of the holy people of the Most High, and the time came when they possessed the kingdom.

23"He gave me this explanation: 'The fourth beast is a fourth kingdom that will appear on earth. It will be different from all the other kingdoms and will devour the whole earth, trampling it down and crushing it. 24The ten horns are ten kings who will come from this kingdom. After them another king will arise, different from the earlier ones; he will subdue three kings. 25He will speak against the Most High and oppress his holy people and try to change the set times and the laws. The holy people will be delivered into his hands for a time, times and half a time.*b*

26"'But the court will sit, and his power will be taken away and completely destroyed forever. 27Then the sovereignty, power and greatness of all the kingdoms under heaven will be handed over to the holy people of the Most High. His kingdom will be an everlasting kingdom, and all rulers will worship and obey him.'

28"This is the end of the matter. I, Daniel, was deeply troubled by my thoughts, and my face turned pale, but I kept the matter to myself."

Daniel's Vision of a Ram and a Goat

8 In the third year of King Belshazzar's reign, I, Daniel, had a vision, after the one that had already appeared to me. 2In my vision I saw myself in the citadel of Susa in the province of Elam; in the vision I was beside the Ulai Canal. 3I looked up, and there before me was a ram with two horns, standing beside the canal, and the horns were long. One of the horns was longer than the other but grew up later. 4I watched the ram as it charged toward the west and the north and the south. No animal could stand against it, and none could rescue from its power. It did as it pleased and became great.

5As I was thinking about this, suddenly a goat with a prominent horn between its eyes came from the west, crossing the whole earth without touching the ground. 6It came toward the two-horned ram I had seen standing beside the canal and charged at it in great rage. 7I saw it attack the ram furiously, striking the ram

---

a 13 The Aramaic phrase *bar enash* means *human being.* The phrase *son of man* is retained here because of its use in the New Testament as a title of Jesus, probably based largely on this verse.   *b 25* Or *for a year, two years and half a year* and shattering its two horns. The ram was powerless to stand against it; the goat knocked it to the ground and trampled on it, and none could rescue the ram from its power. ⁸The goat became very great, but at the height of its power the large horn was broken off, and in its place four prominent horns grew up toward the four winds of heaven.

⁹Out of one of them came another horn, which started small but grew in power to the south and to the east and toward the Beautiful Land. ¹⁰It grew until it reached the host of the heavens, and it threw some of the starry host down to the earth and trampled on them. ¹¹It set itself up to be as great as the commander of the army of the Lᴏʀᴅ; it took away the daily sacrifice from the Lᴏʀᴅ, and his sanctuary was thrown down. ¹²Because of rebellion, the Lᴏʀᴅ's people*a* and the daily sacrifice were given over to it. It prospered in everything it did, and truth was thrown to the ground.

¹³Then I heard a holy one speaking, and another holy one said to him, "How long will it take for the vision to be fulfilled — the vision concerning the daily sacrifice, the rebellion that causes desolation, the surrender of the sanctuary and the trampling underfoot of the Lᴏʀᴅ's people?"

¹⁴He said to me, "It will take 2,300 evenings and mornings; then the sanctuary will be reconsecrated."

The Interpretation of the Vision

¹⁵While I, Daniel, was watching the vision and trying to understand it, there before me stood one who looked like a man. ¹⁶And I heard a man's voice from the Ulai calling, "Gabriel, tell this man the meaning of the vision."

¹⁷As he came near the place where I was standing, I was terrified and fell prostrate. "Son of man,"*b* he said to me, "understand that the vision concerns the time of the end."

¹⁸While he was speaking to me, I was in a deep sleep, with my face to the ground. Then he touched me and raised me to my feet.

¹⁹He said: "I am going to tell you what will happen later in the time of wrath,

THE
WITNESSES

✓ **GABRIEL** (DANIEL 8:16)
Gabriel is an angel or a messenger from God. His name means "God is a powerful warrior."

because the vision concerns the appointed time of the end.*c* ²⁰The two-horned ram that you saw represents the kings of Media and Persia. ²¹The shaggy goat is the king of Greece, and the large horn between its eyes is the first king. ²²The four horns that replaced the one that was broken off represent four kingdoms that will emerge from his nation but will not have the same power.

²³"In the latter part of their reign, when rebels have become completely wicked, a fierce-looking king, a master of intrigue, will arise. ²⁴He will become very strong,

---

a 12 Or *rebellion, the armies*   *b 17* The Hebrew phrase *ben adam* means *human being*. The phrase *son of man* is retained as a form of address here because of its possible association with "Son of Man" in the New Testament.
c 19 Or *because the end will be at the appointed time*

but not by his own power. He will cause astounding devastation and will succeed in whatever he does. He will destroy those who are mighty, the holy people. ²⁵He will cause deceit to prosper, and he will consider himself superior. When they feel secure, he will destroy many and take his stand against the Prince of princes. Yet he will be destroyed, but not by human power.

²⁶"The vision of the evenings and mornings that has been given you is true, but seal up the vision, for it concerns the distant future."

²⁷I, Daniel, was worn out. I lay exhausted for several days. Then I got up and went about the king's business. I was appalled by the vision; it was beyond understanding.

Daniel's Prayer

9 In the first year of Darius son of Xerxes ᵃ (a Mede by descent), who was made ruler over the Babylonian ᵇ kingdom— ²in the first year of his reign, I, Daniel, understood from the Scriptures, according to the word of the LORD given to Jeremiah the prophet, that the desolation of Jerusalem would last seventy years. ³So I turned to the Lord God and pleaded with him in prayer and petition, in fasting, and in sackcloth and ashes.

⁴I prayed to the LORD my God and confessed:

"Lord, the great and awesome God, who keeps his covenant of love with those who love him and keep his commandments, ⁵we have sinned and done wrong. We have been wicked and have rebelled; we have turned away from your commands and laws. ⁶We have not listened to your servants the prophets, who spoke in your name to our kings, our princes and our ancestors, and to all the people of the land.

⁷"Lord, you are righteous, but this day we are covered with shame—the people of Judah and the inhabitants of Jerusalem and all Israel, both near and far, in all the countries where you have scattered us because of our unfaithfulness to you. ⁸We and our kings, our princes and our ancestors are covered with shame, LORD, because we have sinned against you. ⁹The Lord our God is merciful and forgiving, even though we have rebelled against him; ¹⁰we have not obeyed the LORD our God or kept the laws he gave us through his servants the prophets. ¹¹All Israel has transgressed your law and turned away, refusing to obey you.

"Therefore the curses and sworn judgments written in the Law of Moses, the servant of God, have been poured out on us, because we have sinned against you. ¹²You have fulfilled the words spoken against us and against our rulers by bringing on us great disaster. Under the whole heaven nothing has ever been done like what has been done to Jerusalem. ¹³Just as it is written in the Law of Moses, all this disaster has come on us, yet we have not sought the favor of the LORD our God by turning from our sins and giving attention to your truth. ¹⁴The LORD did not hesitate to bring the disaster on us, for the LORD our God is righteous in everything he does; yet we have not obeyed him.

¹⁵"Now, Lord our God, who brought your people out of Egypt with a mighty hand and who made for yourself a name that endures to this day, we have sinned, we have done wrong. ¹⁶Lord, in keeping with all your righteous acts, turn away your anger and your wrath from Jerusalem, your city, your holy hill. Our sins and the iniquities of our ancestors have made Jerusalem and your people an object of scorn to all those around us.

¹⁷"Now, our God, hear the prayers and petitions of your servant. For your sake, Lord, look with favor on your desolate sanctuary. ¹⁸Give ear, our God, and hear; open your eyes and see the desolation of the city that bears your Name. We do not make

---

ᵃ 1 Hebrew Ahasuerus   ᵇ 1 Or Chaldean

requests of you because we are righteous, but because of your great mercy. ¹⁹Lord, listen! Lord, forgive! Lord, hear and act! For your sake, my God, do not delay, because your city and your people bear your Name."

The Seventy "Sevens"

²⁰While I was speaking and praying, confessing my sin and the sin of my people Israel and making my request to the LORD my God for his holy hill— ²¹while I was still in prayer, Gabriel, the man I had seen in the earlier vision, came to me in swift flight about the time of the evening sacrifice. ²²He instructed me and said to me, "Daniel, I have now come to give you insight and understanding. ²³As soon as you began to pray, a word went out, which I have come to tell you, for you are highly esteemed. Therefore, consider the word and understand the vision:

²⁴"Seventy 'sevens'ᵃ are decreed for your people and your holy city to finishᵇ transgression, to put an end to sin, to atone for wickedness, to bring in everlasting righteousness, to seal up vision and prophecy and to anoint the Most Holy Place.ᶜ

²⁵"Know and understand this: From the time the word goes out to restore and rebuild Jerusalem until the Anointed One,ᵈ the ruler, comes, there will be seven 'sevens,' and sixty-two 'sevens.' It will be rebuilt with streets and a trench, but in times of trouble. ²⁶After the sixty-two 'sevens,' the Anointed One will be put to death and will have nothing.ᵉ The people of the ruler who will come will destroy the city and the sanctuary. The end will come like a flood: War will continue until the end, and desolations have been decreed. ²⁷He will confirm a covenant with many for one 'seven.'ᶠ In the middle of the 'seven'ᶠ he will put an end to sacrifice and offering. And at the templeᵍ he will set up an abomination that causes desolation, until the end that is decreed is poured out on him.ʰ ⁱ

Daniel's Vision of a Man

10 In the third year of Cyrus king of Persia, a revelation was given to Daniel (who was called Belteshazzar). Its message was true and it concerned a great war.ʲ The understanding of the message came to him in a vision.

²At that time I, Daniel, mourned for three weeks. ³I ate no choice food; no meat or wine touched my lips; and I used no lotions at all until the three weeks were over.

⁴On the twenty-fourth day of the first month, as I was standing on the bank of the great river, the Tigris, ⁵I looked up and there before me was a man dressed in linen, with a belt of fine gold from Uphaz around his waist. ⁶His body was like topaz, his face like lightning, his eyes like flaming torches, his arms and legs like the gleam of burnished bronze, and his voice like the sound of a multitude.

⁷I, Daniel, was the only one who saw the vision; those who were with me did not see it, but such terror overwhelmed them that they fled and hid themselves. ⁸So I was left alone, gazing at this great vision; I had no strength left, my face turned deathly pale and I was helpless. ⁹Then I heard him speaking, and as I listened to him, I fell into a deep sleep, my face to the ground.

¹⁰A hand touched me and set me trembling on my hands and knees. ¹¹He said, "Daniel, you who are highly esteemed, consider carefully the words I am about to speak to you, and stand up, for I have now been sent to you." And when he said this to me, I stood up trembling.

¹²Then he continued, "Do not be afraid, Daniel. Since the first day that you set your mind to gain understanding and to humble yourself before your God, your words were heard, and I have come in response to them. ¹³But the prince of the Persian kingdom resisted me twenty-one days. Then Michael, one of the chief princes, came to help me, because I was detained there with the king of Persia. ¹⁴Now I have come to explain to you

---

ᵃ 24 Or 'weeks'; also in verses 25 and 26   ᵇ 24 Or restrain   ᶜ 24 Or the most holy One   ᵈ 25 Or an anointed one; also in verse 26   ᵉ 26 Or death and will have no one; or death, but not for himself   ᶠ 27 Or 'week'   ᵍ 27 Septuagint and Theodotion; Hebrew wing   ʰ 27 Or it   ⁱ 27 Or And one who causes desolation will come upon the wing of the abominable temple, until the end that is decreed is poured out on the desolated city   ʲ 1 Or true and burdensome what will happen to your people in the future, for the vision concerns a time yet to come."

¹⁵While he was saying this to me, I bowed with my face toward the ground and was speechless. ¹⁶Then one who looked like a man*a* touched my lips, and I opened my mouth and began to speak. I said to the one standing before me, "I am overcome with anguish because of the vision, my lord, and I feel very weak. ¹⁷How can I, your servant, talk with you, my lord? My strength is gone and I can hardly breathe."

¹⁸Again the one who looked like a man touched me and gave me strength. ¹⁹"Do not be afraid, you who are highly

BREAKTHROUGH!

Who are these princes?
(DANIEL 10:20-21)

Some translations of the Bible call them angels. They were like messengers. In ancient times, people thought that each country had its guardian angel or prince. It is possible that God sent angels or messengers to care for countries, but we don't know for sure.

THE
WITNESSES

✓ **MICHAEL** (DANIEL 10:13)
Michael is the angel or messenger of God who helped Daniel and who fought against the angel of Persia. His name means "Who is like God?"

esteemed," he said. "Peace! Be strong now; be strong."

When he spoke to me, I was strengthened and said, "Speak, my lord, since you have given me strength."

²⁰So he said, "Do you know why I have come to you? Soon I will return to fight against the prince of Persia, and when I go, the prince of Greece will come; ²¹but first I will tell you what is written in the Book of Truth. (No one supports me against them except Michael, your prince.

11 ¹And in the first year of Darius the Mede, I took my stand to support and protect him.)

The Kings of the South and the North

²"Now then, I tell you the truth: Three more kings will arise in Persia, and then

a 16 Most manuscripts of the Masoretic Text; one manuscript of the Masoretic Text, Dead Sea Scrolls and Septuagint *Then something that looked like a human hand* a fourth, who will be far richer than all the others. When he has gained power by his wealth, he will stir up everyone against the kingdom of Greece. ³Then a mighty king will arise, who will rule with great power and do as he pleases. ⁴After he has arisen, his empire will be broken up and parceled out toward the four winds of heaven. It will not go to his descendants, nor will it have the power he exercised, because his empire will be uprooted and given to others.

⁵"The king of the South will become strong, but one of his commanders will become even stronger than he and will rule his own kingdom with great power. ⁶After some years, they will become allies. The daughter of the king of the South will go to the king of the North to make an alliance, but she will not retain her power, and he and his power*ᵃ* will not last. In those days she will be betrayed, together with her royal escort and her father*ᵇ* and the one who supported her.

⁷"One from her family line will arise to take her place. He will attack the forces of the king of the North and enter his fortress; he will fight against them and be victorious. ⁸He will also seize their gods, their metal images and their valuable articles of silver and gold and carry them off to Egypt. For some years he will leave the king of the North alone. ⁹Then the king of the North will invade the realm of the king of the South but will retreat to his own country. ¹⁰His sons will prepare for war and assemble a great army, which will sweep on like an irresistible flood and carry the battle as far as his fortress.

¹¹"Then the king of the South will march out in a rage and fight against the king of the North, who will raise a large army, but it will be defeated. ¹²When the army is carried off, the king of the South will be filled with pride and will slaughter many thousands, yet he will not remain triumphant. ¹³For the king of the North will muster another army, larger than the first; and after several years, he will advance with a huge army fully equipped.

¹⁴"In those times many will rise against the king of the South. Those who are vi-olent among your own people will rebel in fulfillment of the vision, but without success. ¹⁵Then the king of the North will come and build up siege ramps and will capture a fortified city. The forces of the South will be powerless to resist; even their best troops will not have the strength to stand. ¹⁶The invader will do as he pleases; no one will be able to stand against him. He will establish himself in the Beautiful Land and will have the power to destroy it. ¹⁷He will determine to come with the might of his entire kingdom and will make an alliance with the king of the South. And he will give him a daughter in marriage in order to overthrow the kingdom, but his plans*ᶜ* will not succeed or help him. ¹⁸Then he will turn his attention to the coastlands and will take many of them, but a commander will put an end to his insolence and will turn his insolence back on him. ¹⁹After this, he will turn back toward the fortresses of his own country but will stumble and fall, to be seen no more.

²⁰"His successor will send out a tax collector to maintain the royal splendor. In a few years, however, he will be destroyed, yet not in anger or in battle.

²¹"He will be succeeded by a contemptible person who has not been given the honor of royalty. He will invade the kingdom when its people feel secure, and he will seize it through intrigue. ²²Then an overwhelming army will be swept away before him; both it and a prince of the covenant will be destroyed. ²³After coming to an agreement with him, he will act deceitfully, and with only a few people he will rise to power. ²⁴When the richest provinces feel secure, he will invade them and will achieve what neither his fathers nor his forefathers did. He will distribute plunder, loot and wealth among his followers. He will plot the overthrow of fortresses—but only for a time.

²⁵"With a large army he will stir up his strength and courage against the king of the South. The king of the South will wage war with a large and very powerful army,

---

ᵃ 6 Or *offspring*   *ᵇ* 6 Or *child* (see Vulgate and Syriac)
ᶜ 17 Or *but she*

but he will not be able to stand because of the plots devised against him. ²⁶Those who eat from the king's provisions will try to destroy him; his army will be swept away, and many will fall in battle. ²⁷The two kings, with their hearts bent on evil, will sit at the same table and lie to each other, but to no avail, because an end will still come at the appointed time. ²⁸The king of the North will return to his own country with great wealth, but his heart will be set against the holy covenant. He will take action against it and then return to his own country.

²⁹"At the appointed time he will invade the South again, but this time the outcome will be different from what it was before. ³⁰Ships of the western coastlands will oppose him, and he will lose heart. Then he will turn back and vent his fury against the holy covenant. He will return and show favor to those who forsake the holy covenant.

³¹"His armed forces will rise up to desecrate the temple fortress and will abolish the daily sacrifice. Then they will set up the abomination that causes desolation. ³²With flattery he will corrupt those who have violated the covenant, but the people who know their God will firmly resist him.

³³"Those who are wise will instruct many, though for a time they will fall by the sword or be burned or captured or plundered. ³⁴When they fall, they will receive a little help, and many who are not sincere will join them. ³⁵Some of the wise will stumble, so that they may be refined, purified and made spotless until the time of the end, for it will still come at the appointed time.

The King Who Exalts Himself

³⁶"The king will do as he pleases. He will exalt and magnify himself above every god and will say unheard-of things against the God of gods. He will be successful until the time of wrath is completed, for what has been determined must take place. ³⁷He will show no regard for the gods of his ancestors or for the one desired by women, nor will he regard any god, but will exalt himself above them all.

³⁸Instead of them, he will honor a god of fortresses; a god unknown to his ancestors he will honor with gold and silver, with precious stones and costly gifts. ³⁹He will attack the mightiest fortresses with the help of a foreign god and will greatly honor those who acknowledge him. He will make them rulers over many people and will distribute the land at a price.ᵃ

⁴⁰"At the time of the end the king of the South will engage him in battle, and the king of the North will storm out against him with chariots and cavalry and a great fleet of ships. He will invade many countries and sweep through them like a flood. ⁴¹He will also invade

---

ᵃ 39 Or *land for a reward*

the Beautiful Land. Many countries will fall, but Edom, Moab and the leaders of Ammon will be delivered from his hand. ⁴²He will extend his power over many countries; Egypt will not escape. ⁴³He will gain control of the treasures of gold and silver and all the riches of Egypt, with the Libyans and Cushites*ᵃ* in submission. ⁴⁴But reports from the east and the north will alarm him, and he will set out in a great rage to destroy and annihilate many. ⁴⁵He will pitch his royal tents between the seas at*ᵇ* the beautiful holy mountain. Yet he will come to his end, and no one will help him.

The End Times

12 "At that time Michael, the great prince who protects your people, will arise. There will be a time of distress such as has not happened from the beginning of nations until then. But at that time your people—everyone whose name is found written in the book—will be delivered. ²Multitudes who sleep in the dust of the earth will awake: some to everlasting life, others to shame and everlasting contempt. ³Those who are wise*ᶜ* will shine like the brightness of the heavens, and those who lead many to righteousness, like the stars for ever and ever. ⁴But

you, Daniel, roll up and seal the words of the scroll until the time of the end. Many will go here and there to increase knowledge."

⁵Then I, Daniel, looked, and there before me stood two others, one on this bank of the river and one on the opposite bank. ⁶One of them said to the man clothed in linen, who was above the waters of the river, "How long will it be before these astonishing things are fulfilled?"

⁷The man clothed in linen, who was above the waters of the river, lifted his right hand and his left hand toward heaven, and I heard him swear by him who lives forever, saying, "It will be for a time, times and half a time.*ᵈ* When the power of the holy people has been finally broken, all these things will be completed."

⁸I heard, but I did not understand. So I asked, "My lord, what will the outcome of all this be?"

⁹He replied, "Go your way, Daniel, because the words are rolled up and sealed until the time of the end. ¹⁰Many will be purified, made spotless and refined, but the wicked will continue to be wicked.

ᵃ 43 That is, people from the upper Nile region   *ᵇ 45* Or *the sea and*   *ᶜ 3* Or *who impart wisdom*   *ᵈ 7* Or *a year, two years and half a year*

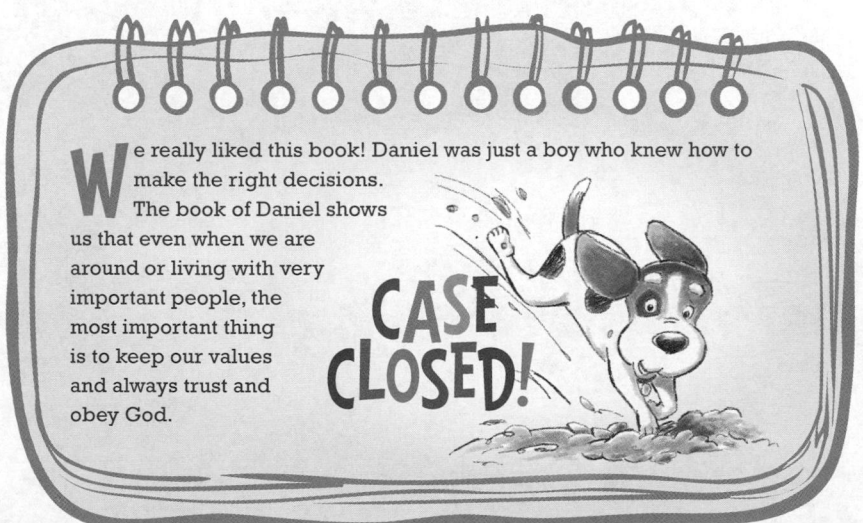

We really liked this book! Daniel was just a boy who knew how to make the right decisions. The book of Daniel shows us that even when we are around or living with very important people, the most important thing is to keep our values and always trust and obey God.

CASE CLOSED!

None of the wicked will understand, but those who are wise will understand.

[11] "From the time that the daily sacrifice is abolished and the abomination that causes desolation is set up, there will be 1,290 days. [12]Blessed is the one who waits for and reaches the end of the 1,335 days.

[13] "As for you, go your way till the end. You will rest, and then at the end of the days you will rise to receive your allotted inheritance."

HOSEA

THE EVIDENCE:

WHO WROTE IT?

We can't be sure about who wrote this book. Why? Well, because in the ancient world, they weren't very concerned about saying who had written a document or a book. But we think that although there isn't much information, this book was written by the prophet Hosea, because in the first part he appears as the main character.

HOW LONG AGO?

A really long time ago. We could say it was written about 2,700 years ago. This book of Hosea was written between the years 760 and 720 before Christ.

WHAT'S IT ABOUT?

We think (and many other people think) that this book is one of the most difficult to understand in the entire Bible. It's about the relationship God wants to have with his people Israel. In almost all of it, he talks to the northern kingdom — in other words, to the kingdom of Israel. But some of the messages are also for the southern kingdom, the kingdom of Judah. The main problem was that the Israelites were very disobedient toward God.

THE BEST PART

It's really very hard for us to choose just one verse. Hosea was a clever poet, and he has many clever sayings. So we'll share one that seems very, very important: "For I desire mercy, not sacrifice, and acknowledgment of God rather than burnt offerings" (6:6).

---

1 The word of the LORD that came to Hosea son of Beeri during the reigns of Uzziah, Jotham, Ahaz and Hezekiah, kings of Judah, and during the reign of Jeroboam son of Jehoash[a] king of Israel:

Hosea's Wife and Children

²When the LORD began to speak through Hosea, the LORD said to him, "Go, marry a promiscuous woman and have children with her, for like an adulterous wife this land is guilty of unfaithfulness to the LORD." ³So he married Gomer daughter of Diblaim, and she conceived and bore him a son.

⁴Then the LORD said to Hosea, "Call him Jezreel, because I will soon punish the house of Jehu for the massacre at Jezreel, and I will put an end to the kingdom of Israel. ⁵In that day I will break Israel's bow in the Valley of Jezreel."

⁶Gomer conceived again and gave birth to a daughter. Then the LORD said to Hosea, "Call her Lo-Ruhamah (which means

---

a 1 Hebrew *Joash*, a variant of *Jehoash*

Promiscuous woman

(HOSEA 1:2)

This is a woman who has many husbands and boyfriends without really loving any of them.

"not loved"), for I will no longer show love to Israel, that I should at all forgive them. ⁷Yet I will show love to Judah; and I will save them—not by bow, sword or battle, or by horses and horsemen, but I, the LORD their God, will save them."

⁸After she had weaned Lo-Ruhamah, Gomer had another son. ⁹Then the LORD said, "Call him Lo-Ammi (which means "not my people"), for you are not my people, and I am not your God.ᵃ

¹⁰"Yet the Israelites will be like the sand on the seashore, which cannot be measured or counted. In the place where it was said to them, 'You are not my people,' they will be called 'children of the living God.' ¹¹The people of Judah and the people of Israel will come together; they will appoint one leader and will come up out of the land, for great will be the day of Jezreel.ᵇ

2ᶜ "Say of your brothers, 'My people,' and of your sisters, 'My loved one.'

Israel Punished and Restored

² "Rebuke your mother, rebuke her,
    for she is not my wife,
    and I am not her husband.

Let her remove the adulterous look
    from her face
    and the unfaithfulness from
      between her breasts.
³Otherwise I will strip her naked
    and make her as bare as on the day
      she was born;
I will make her like a desert,
    turn her into a parched land,
    and slay her with thirst.
⁴I will not show my love to her
    children,
    because they are the children of
      adultery.

ᵃ 9 Or *your I* AM   ᵇ 11 In Hebrew texts 1:10,11 is numbered 2:1,2.   ᶜ In Hebrew texts 2:1-23 is numbered 2:3-25.

Why did God tell Hosea to go marry a promiscuous woman?

(HOSEA 1:2)

How strange! This is really a very interesting question. In order to understand this, first we have to understand that many times God acts like he is the husband of Israel. That's a way of saying that God loves Israel like a husband loves his wife. In this message, it's saying that Hosea is a husband like God is to Israel, and Israel is like a promiscuous woman or a prostitute.

THE
WITNESSES

✓ **HOSEA** (HOSEA 1:1)
This is the name of the prophet that God used to preach to the Israelites. His name may mean "the LORD has liberated."

✓ **JEROBOAM** (HOSEA 1:1)
He was the king who governed over the northern kingdom — the kingdom of Israel — during the years 783 to 743 before Christ. He ruled at the same time as King Uzziah in the southern kingdom. Jeroboam's name means "that the nation be great."

✓ **UZZIAH, JOTHAM, AHAZ AND HEZEKIAH** (HOSEA 1:1)
We talk about these kings in Isaiah 1:1 and 2 Kings 18.

✓ **GOMER** (HOSEA 1:3)
The name of the promiscuous woman. According to the story, Hosea had to marry her. This was a way of showing how much God loved his people even when they were unfaithful to him.

---

⁵ Their mother has been unfaithful
   and has conceived them in
      disgrace.
 She said, 'I will go after my lovers,
   who give me my food and my
      water,
   my wool and my linen, my olive oil
      and my drink.'
⁶ Therefore I will block her path with
      thornbushes;
   I will wall her in so that she cannot
      find her way.
⁷ She will chase after her lovers but not
      catch them;
   she will look for them but not find
      them.
 Then she will say,
   'I will go back to my husband as at
      first,
   for then I was better off than now.'
⁸ She has not acknowledged that I was
      the one
who gave her the grain, the new
      wine and oil,
who lavished on her the silver and
      gold —
   which they used for Baal.

⁹ "Therefore I will take away my grain
      when it ripens,
   and my new wine when it is ready.
 I will take back my wool and my linen,
   intended to cover her naked body.
¹⁰ So now I will expose her lewdness
   before the eyes of her lovers;
   no one will take her out of my
      hands.
¹¹ I will stop all her celebrations:
   her yearly festivals, her New Moons,
   her Sabbath days — all her
      appointed festivals.
¹² I will ruin her vines and her fig trees,
   which she said were her pay from
      her lovers;

THE SCENE

VALLEY OF JEZREEL

(HOSEA 1:4)

This is a very important valley in the northern part of Israel. The nation that controlled this valley had a big advantage over the other nations.

I will make them a thicket,
    and wild animals will devour them.
¹³ I will punish her for the days
    she burned incense to the Baals;
she decked herself with rings and
        jewelry,
    and went after her lovers,
    but me she forgot,"
                        declares the LORD.

¹⁴ "Therefore I am now going to allure
        her;
    I will lead her into the wilderness
    and speak tenderly to her.
¹⁵ There I will give her back her
        vineyards,
    and will make the Valley of Achor*a* a
        door of hope.
There she will respond*b* as in the days
        of her youth,
    as in the day she came up out of
        Egypt.

¹⁶ "In that day," declares the LORD,
    "you will call me 'my husband';
    you will no longer call me 'my
        master.*c*'
¹⁷ I will remove the names of the Baals
        from her lips;
    no longer will their names be
        invoked.
¹⁸ In that day I will make a covenant for
        them
    with the beasts of the field, the
        birds in the sky
    and the creatures that move along
        the ground.
Bow and sword and battle
    I will abolish from the land,
    so that all may lie down in
        safety.
¹⁹ I will betroth you to me forever;
    I will betroth you in*d* righteousness
        and justice,
    in*d* love and compassion.

---

a 15 *Achor* means *trouble.*   *b* 15 Or *sing*
c 16 Hebrew *baal*   *d* 19 Or *with*

BREAKTHROUGH!

What does this mean, that Israel has lovers?

(HOSEA 2:2-13)

It means that Israel isn't faithful to God and doesn't love him alone. The lovers are the idols or the false gods that Israel worships.

²⁰ I will betroth you in[a] faithfulness,
and you will acknowledge the LORD.

²¹ "In that day I will respond,"
declares the LORD—
"I will respond to the skies,
and they will respond to the earth;
²² and the earth will respond to the
grain,
the new wine and the olive oil,
and they will respond to Jezreel.[b]
²³ I will plant her for myself in the land;
I will show my love to the one I
called 'Not my loved one.'[c]
I will say to those called 'Not my
people,[d] 'You are my people';
and they will say, 'You are my God.' "

Hosea's Reconciliation With His Wife

3 The LORD said to me, "Go, show your
love to your wife again, though she is
loved by another man and is an adulteress. Love her as the LORD loves the Israelites, though they turn to other gods and
love the sacred raisin cakes."

² So I bought her for fifteen shekels[e] of
silver and about a homer and a lethek[f] of
barley. ³ Then I told her, "You are to live with
me many days; you must not be a prostitute or be intimate with any man, and I will
behave the same way toward you."

⁴ For the Israelites will live many days
without king or prince, without sacrifice or
sacred stones, without ephod or household gods. ⁵ Afterward the Israelites will
return and seek the LORD their God and
David their king. They will come trembling
to the LORD and to his blessings in the
last days.

The Charge Against Israel

4 Hear the word of the LORD, you
Israelites,
because the LORD has a charge to
bring
against you who live in the land:
"There is no faithfulness, no love,
no acknowledgment of God in the
land.
² There is only cursing,[g] lying and
murder,
stealing and adultery;

they break all bounds,
and bloodshed follows bloodshed.
³ Because of this the land dries up,
and all who live in it waste away;
the beasts of the field, the birds in the
sky
and the fish in the sea are swept
away.

⁴ "But let no one bring a charge,
let no one accuse another,
for your people are like those
who bring charges against a priest.
⁵ You stumble day and night,
and the prophets stumble with you.
So I will destroy your mother—
⁶ my people are destroyed from lack
of knowledge.

"Because you have rejected
knowledge,
I also reject you as my priests;
because you have ignored the law of
your God,
I also will ignore your children.
⁷ The more priests there were,
the more they sinned against me;
they exchanged their glorious God[h]
for something disgraceful.
⁸ They feed on the sins of my people
and relish their wickedness.
⁹ And it will be: Like people, like priests.
I will punish both of them for their
ways
and repay them for their deeds.

¹⁰ "They will eat but not have enough;
they will engage in prostitution but
not flourish,
because they have deserted the LORD
to give themselves ¹¹ to prostitution;
old wine and new wine
take away their understanding.
¹² My people consult a wooden idol,
and a diviner's rod speaks to them.
A spirit of prostitution leads them
astray;
they are unfaithful to their God.

---

[a] 20 Or *with*   [b] 22 *Jezreel* means *God plants.*
[c] 23 Hebrew *Lo-Ruhamah* (see 1:6)   [d] 23 Hebrew
Lo-Ammi (see 1:9)   [e] 2 That is, about 6 ounces or about
170 grams   [f] 2 A homer and a lethek possibly weighed
about 430 pounds or about 195 kilograms.   [g] 2 That is,
to pronounce a curse on   [h] 7 Syriac (see also an
ancient Hebrew scribal tradition); Masoretic Text *me; /
I will exchange their glory*

¹³They sacrifice on the mountaintops
  and burn offerings on the hills,
under oak, poplar and terebinth,
  where the shade is pleasant.
Therefore your daughters turn to
    prostitution
  and your daughters-in-law to
    adultery.

¹⁴"I will not punish your daughters
    when they turn to prostitution,
nor your daughters-in-law
    when they commit adultery,
because the men themselves consort
    with harlots
  and sacrifice with shrine
    prostitutes—
a people without understanding will
    come to ruin!

¹⁵"Though you, Israel, commit adultery,
  do not let Judah become guilty.

"Do not go to Gilgal;
  do not go up to Beth Aven.ᵃ

BREAK THROUGH!

Gilgal and Beth Aven
(HOSEA 4:15)
In the ancient world, idols or false gods were
associated with places. The Israelites would
go to Gilgal and Beth Aven (which meant
"house of evil") to worship the idols. They
were disobeying God.

And do not swear, 'As surely as the
    LORD lives!'
¹⁶The Israelites are stubborn,
  like a stubborn heifer.
How then can the LORD pasture them
  like lambs in a meadow?
¹⁷Ephraim is joined to idols;
  leave him alone!
¹⁸Even when their drinks are gone,
  they continue their prostitution;
  their rulers dearly love shameful
    ways.
¹⁹A whirlwind will sweep them away,
  and their sacrifices will bring them
    shame.

Judgment Against Israel

5 "Hear this, you priests!
  Pay attention, you Israelites!
Listen, royal house!
  This judgment is against you:
You have been a snare at Mizpah,
  a net spread out on Tabor.
²The rebels are knee-deep in
    slaughter.
  I will discipline all of them.
³I know all about Ephraim;
  Israel is not hidden from me.
Ephraim, you have now turned to
    prostitution;
  Israel is corrupt.

⁴"Their deeds do not permit them
  to return to their God.
A spirit of prostitution is in their
    heart;
  they do not acknowledge the LORD.
⁵Israel's arrogance testifies against
    them;
  the Israelites, even Ephraim,
    stumble in their sin;
  Judah also stumbles with them.
⁶When they go with their flocks and
    herds
  to seek the LORD,
they will not find him;
  he has withdrawn himself from
    them.
⁷They are unfaithful to the LORD;
  they give birth to illegitimate
    children.

ᵃ 15 *Beth Aven* means *house of wickedness* (a derogatory
name for Bethel, which means *house of God*).

When they celebrate their New Moon
        feasts,
    he will devour[a] their fields.

8 "Sound the trumpet in Gibeah,
    the horn in Ramah.
Raise the battle cry in Beth
        Aven[b];
    lead on, Benjamin.
9 Ephraim will be laid waste
        on the day of reckoning.
Among the tribes of Israel
    I proclaim what is certain.
10 Judah's leaders are like those
        who move boundary stones.
I will pour out my wrath on them
    like a flood of water.
11 Ephraim is oppressed,
    trampled in judgment,
    intent on pursuing idols.[c]
12 I am like a moth to Ephraim,
    like rot to the people of Judah.

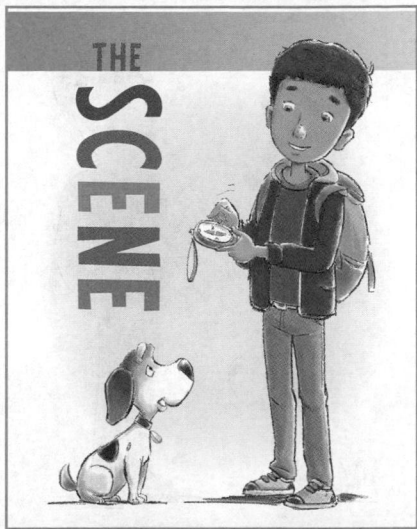

THE SCENE

RAMAH

(HOSEA 5:8)

This is one of the important cities
in the region of Benjamin. It
protected Jerusalem against
enemy nations.

BREAKTHROUGH!

Illegitimate children
(HOSEA 5:7)

This is something hard to express nowadays.
It refers to a son or daughter born of parents
who are not married to each other. Here,
the Lord is saying that Israel (the wife) is not
faithful to her husband (the Lord) and she
keeps on loving other "men," so her kids are
not legitimate.

13 "When Ephraim saw his sickness,
        and Judah his sores,
    then Ephraim turned to Assyria,
        and sent to the great king for
        help.
But he is not able to cure you,
    not able to heal your sores.
14 For I will be like a lion to Ephraim,
        like a great lion to Judah.
I will tear them to pieces and go
        away;
    I will carry them off, with no one to
        rescue them.
15 Then I will return to my lair
    until they have borne their
        guilt
    and seek my face—
in their misery
    they will earnestly seek me."

---

a 7 Or *Now their New Moon feasts / will devour them and*
b 8 *Beth Aven* means *house of wickedness* (a derogatory
name for Bethel, which means *house of God*).   c 11 The
meaning of the Hebrew for this word is uncertain.

THE SCENE

ASSYRIA

(HOSEA 5:13)

Read the explanation in Jeremiah 2:18.

Israel Unrepentant

6 "Come, let us return to the Lord.
He has torn us to pieces
but he will heal us;
he has injured us
but he will bind up our wounds.
2 After two days he will revive us;
on the third day he will restore us,
that we may live in his presence.
3 Let us acknowledge the Lord;
let us press on to acknowledge
him.
As surely as the sun rises,
he will appear;
he will come to us like the winter
rains,
like the spring rains that water the
earth."

4 "What can I do with you, Ephraim?
What can I do with you, Judah?
Your love is like the morning mist,
like the early dew that disappears.
5 Therefore I cut you in pieces with my
prophets,
I killed you with the words of my
mouth—

then my judgments go forth like the
sun.[a]
6 For I desire mercy, not sacrifice,
and acknowledgment of God rather
than burnt offerings.
7 As at Adam,[b] they have broken the
covenant;
they were unfaithful to me there.
8 Gilead is a city of evildoers,
stained with footprints of blood.
9 As marauders lie in ambush for a
victim,
so do bands of priests;
they murder on the road to
Shechem,
carrying out their wicked schemes.
10 I have seen a horrible thing in Israel:
There Ephraim is given to
prostitution,
Israel is defiled.

---

[a] 5 The meaning of the Hebrew for this line is uncertain.
[b] 7 Or *Like Adam*; or *Like human beings*

THE SCENE

GILEAD

(HOSEA 6:8)

Unfortunately, we can't be sure where this city was. What I can say is that it was a city where the people were pretty bad, and they were always rebelling against God.

11 "Also for you, Judah,
a harvest is appointed.

"Whenever I would restore the
fortunes of my people,
7 1 whenever I would heal Israel,
the sins of Ephraim are exposed
and the crimes of Samaria revealed.
They practice deceit,
thieves break into houses,
bandits rob in the streets;
2 but they do not realize
that I remember all their evil deeds.
Their sins engulf them;
they are always before me.

3 "They delight the king with their
wickedness,
the princes with their lies.
4 They are all adulterers,
burning like an oven
whose fire the baker need not stir
from the kneading of the dough till
it rises.
5 On the day of the festival of our king
the princes become inflamed with
wine,
and he joins hands with the
mockers.
6 Their hearts are like an oven;
they approach him with intrigue.
Their passion smolders all night;
in the morning it blazes like a
flaming fire.
7 All of them are hot as an oven;
they devour their rulers.
All their kings fall,
and none of them calls on me.

8 "Ephraim mixes with the nations;
Ephraim is a flat loaf not turned
over.
9 Foreigners sap his strength,
but he does not realize it.
His hair is sprinkled with gray,
but he does not notice.
10 Israel's arrogance testifies against
him,
but despite all this
he does not return to the LORD his God
or search for him.

11 "Ephraim is like a dove,
easily deceived and senseless—
now calling to Egypt,

now turning to Assyria.
12 When they go, I will throw my net over
them;
I will pull them down like the birds
in the sky.
When I hear them flocking together,
I will catch them.
13 Woe to them,
because they have strayed from
me!
Destruction to them,
because they have rebelled against
me!
I long to redeem them
but they speak about me falsely.
14 They do not cry out to me from their
hearts
but wail on their beds.
They slash themselves,[a] appealing to
their gods
for grain and new wine,
but they turn away from me.
15 I trained them and strengthened their
arms,
but they plot evil against me.
16 They do not turn to the Most High;
they are like a faulty bow.
Their leaders will fall by the sword
because of their insolent words.
For this they will be ridiculed
in the land of Egypt.

Israel to Reap the Whirlwind

8 "Put the trumpet to your lips!
An eagle is over the house of the
LORD
because the people have broken my
covenant
and rebelled against my law.
2 Israel cries out to me,
'Our God, we acknowledge you!'
3 But Israel has rejected what is good;
an enemy will pursue him.
4 They set up kings without my
consent;
they choose princes without my
approval.
With their silver and gold
they make idols for themselves
to their own destruction.

a 14 Some Hebrew manuscripts and Septuagint; most
Hebrew manuscripts *They gather together*

⁵ Samaria, throw out your calf-idol!
　My anger burns against them.
　How long will they be incapable of
　　purity?
⁶　They are from Israel!
　This calf—a metalworker has made it;
　　it is not God.
　It will be broken in pieces,
　　that calf of Samaria.

⁷ "They sow the wind
　and reap the whirlwind.
　The stalk has no head;
　　it will produce no flour.
　Were it to yield grain,
　　foreigners would swallow it up.
⁸ Israel is swallowed up;
　now she is among the nations
　like something no one wants.
⁹ For they have gone up to Assyria
　like a wild donkey wandering alone.
　Ephraim has sold herself to lovers.
¹⁰ Although they have sold themselves
　　among the nations,
　I will now gather them together.
　They will begin to waste away
　　under the oppression of the mighty
　　king.

BREAK THROUGH!

Calf-idol
(HOSEA 8:5-6)
The calf was an animal the Canaanites
worshiped because it stood for their god.

¹¹ "Though Ephraim built many altars for
　　sin offerings,
　these have become altars for
　　sinning.
¹² I wrote for them the many things of my
　　law,
　but they regarded them as
　　something foreign.
¹³ Though they offer sacrifices as gifts to
　　me,
　and though they eat the meat,
　　the LORD is not pleased with them.
　Now he will remember their
　　wickedness
　and punish their sins:
　They will return to Egypt.
¹⁴ Israel has forgotten their Maker
　and built palaces;
　Judah has fortified many towns.
　But I will send fire on their cities
　　that will consume their fortresses."

Punishment for Israel

9 Do not rejoice, Israel;
　　do not be jubilant like the other
　　nations.
　For you have been unfaithful to your
　　God;
　you love the wages of a prostitute
　　at every threshing floor.
² Threshing floors and winepresses will
　　not feed the people;
　the new wine will fail them.
³ They will not remain in the LORD's
　　land;
　Ephraim will return to Egypt
　and eat unclean food in Assyria.
⁴ They will not pour out wine offerings to
　　the LORD,
　nor will their sacrifices please him.
　Such sacrifices will be to them like the
　　bread of mourners;
　all who eat them will be unclean.
　This food will be for themselves;
　　it will not come into the temple of
　　the LORD.

⁵ What will you do on the day of your
　　appointed festivals,
　on the feast days of the LORD?
⁶ Even if they escape from destruction,
　Egypt will gather them,
　and Memphis will bury them.

Their treasures of silver will be taken
over by briers,
and thorns will overrun their tents.
⁷ The days of punishment are coming,
the days of reckoning are at hand.
Let Israel know this.
Because your sins are so many
and your hostility so great,
the prophet is considered a fool,
the inspired person a maniac.
⁸ The prophet, along with my God,
is the watchman over Ephraim,ᵃ
yet snares await him on all his paths,
and hostility in the house of his
God.
⁹ They have sunk deep into corruption,
as in the days of Gibeah.
God will remember their wickedness
and punish them for their sins.

¹⁰ "When I found Israel,
it was like finding grapes in the
desert;
when I saw your ancestors,
it was like seeing the early fruit on
the fig tree.
But when they came to Baal Peor,
they consecrated themselves to
that shameful idol
and became as vile as the thing
they loved.
¹¹ Ephraim's glory will fly away like a
bird—
no birth, no pregnancy, no
conception.
¹² Even if they rear children,
I will bereave them of every one.
Woe to them
when I turn away from them!
¹³ I have seen Ephraim, like Tyre,
planted in a pleasant place.
But Ephraim will bring out
their children to the slayer."

¹⁴ Give them, Lᴏʀᴅ—
what will you give them?
Give them wombs that miscarry
and breasts that are dry.
¹⁵ "Because of all their wickedness in
Gilgal,
I hated them there.
Because of their sinful deeds,
I will drive them out of my house.

I will no longer love them;
all their leaders are rebellious.
¹⁶ Ephraim is blighted,
their root is withered,
they yield no fruit.
Even if they bear children,
I will slay their cherished offspring."
¹⁷ My God will reject them
because they have not obeyed him;
they will be wanderers among the
nations.

10 Israel was a spreading vine;
he brought forth fruit for himself.
As his fruit increased,
he built more altars;
as his land prospered,
he adorned his sacred stones.
² Their heart is deceitful,
and now they must bear their guilt.
The Lᴏʀᴅ will demolish their altars
and destroy their sacred stones.

³ Then they will say, "We have no king
because we did not revere the
Lᴏʀᴅ.
But even if we had a king,
what could he do for us?"
⁴ They make many promises,
take false oaths
and make agreements;
therefore lawsuits spring up
like poisonous weeds in a plowed
field.
⁵ The people who live in Samaria fear
for the calf-idol of Beth Aven.ᵇ
Its people will mourn over it,
and so will its idolatrous priests,
those who had rejoiced over its
splendor,
because it is taken from them into
exile.
⁶ It will be carried to Assyria
as tribute for the great king.
Ephraim will be disgraced;
Israel will be ashamed of its foreign
alliances.
⁷ Samaria's king will be destroyed,
swept away like a twig on the
surface of the waters.

ᵃ 8 Or *The prophet is the watchman over Ephraim,* / *the
people of my God*   ᵇ 5 *Beth Aven* means *house of
wickedness* (a derogatory name for Bethel, which means
house of God).

⁸ The high places of wickedness[a] will be
destroyed—
it is the sin of Israel.
Thorns and thistles will grow up
and cover their altars.
Then they will say to the mountains,
"Cover us!"
and to the hills, "Fall on us!"
⁹ "Since the days of Gibeah, you have
sinned, Israel,
and there you have remained.[b]
Will not war again overtake
the evildoers in Gibeah?
¹⁰ When I please, I will punish them;
nations will be gathered against
them
to put them in bonds for their
double sin.
¹¹ Ephraim is a trained heifer
that loves to thresh;
so I will put a yoke
on her fair neck.
I will drive Ephraim,
Judah must plow,
and Jacob must break up the
ground.
¹² Sow righteousness for yourselves,
reap the fruit of unfailing love,
and break up your unplowed ground;
for it is time to seek the LORD,
until he comes
and showers his righteousness on
you.
¹³ But you have planted wickedness,
you have reaped evil,
you have eaten the fruit of
deception.
Because you have depended on your
own strength
and on your many warriors,
¹⁴ the roar of battle will rise against your
people,
so that all your fortresses will be
devastated—
as Shalman devastated Beth Arbel on
the day of battle,
when mothers were dashed to the
ground with their children.
¹⁵ So will it happen to you, Bethel,
because your wickedness is great.
When that day dawns,
the king of Israel will be completely
destroyed.

God's Love for Israel

11 "When Israel was a child, I loved
him,
and out of Egypt I called my son.
² But the more they were called,
the more they went away from me.[c]
They sacrificed to the Baals
and they burned incense to images.
³ It was I who taught Ephraim to walk,
taking them by the arms;
but they did not realize
it was I who healed them.
⁴ I led them with cords of human
kindness,
with ties of love.
To them I was like one who lifts
a little child to the cheek,
and I bent down to feed them.
⁵ "Will they not return to Egypt
and will not Assyria rule over them
because they refuse to repent?
⁶ A sword will flash in their cities;
it will devour their false prophets
and put an end to their plans.
⁷ My people are determined to turn from
me.
Even though they call me God Most
High,
I will by no means exalt them.
⁸ "How can I give you up, Ephraim?
How can I hand you over, Israel?
How can I treat you like Admah?
How can I make you like Zeboyim?
My heart is changed within me;
all my compassion is aroused.
⁹ I will not carry out my fierce anger,
nor will I devastate Ephraim
again.
For I am God, and not a man—
the Holy One among you.
I will not come against their cities.
¹⁰ They will follow the LORD;
he will roar like a lion.
When he roars,
his children will come trembling
from the west.
¹¹ They will come from Egypt,
trembling like sparrows,
from Assyria, fluttering like doves.

---

a 8 Hebrew *aven,* a reference to Beth Aven (a derogatory
name for Bethel); see verse 5.   *b 9* Or *there a stand was
taken*   *c 2* Septuagint; Hebrew *them*

I will settle them in their homes,"
declares the LORD.

Israel's Sin

¹²Ephraim has surrounded me with lies,
Israel with deceit.
And Judah is unruly against God,
even against the faithful Holy One.*ᵃ*

12 *ᵇ* ¹Ephraim feeds on the wind;
he pursues the east wind all day
and multiplies lies and violence.
He makes a treaty with Assyria
and sends olive oil to Egypt.
²The LORD has a charge to bring against
Judah;
he will punish Jacob*ᶜ* according to
his ways
and repay him according to his
deeds.
³In the womb he grasped his brother's
heel;
as a man he struggled with God.
⁴He struggled with the angel and
overcame him;
he wept and begged for his favor.
He found him at Bethel
and talked with him there—
⁵the LORD God Almighty,
the LORD is his name!
⁶But you must return to your God;
maintain love and justice,
and wait for your God always.

⁷The merchant uses dishonest
scales
and loves to defraud.
⁸Ephraim boasts,
"I am very rich; I have become
wealthy.
With all my wealth they will not find in
me
any iniquity or sin."

⁹"I have been the LORD your God
ever since you came out of Egypt;
I will make you live in tents again,
as in the days of your appointed
festivals.
¹⁰I spoke to the prophets,
gave them many visions
and told parables through them."

¹¹Is Gilead wicked?
Its people are worthless!

Do they sacrifice bulls in Gilgal?
Their altars will be like piles of
stones
on a plowed field.
¹²Jacob fled to the country of Aram*ᵈ*;
Israel served to get a wife,
and to pay for her he tended sheep.
¹³The LORD used a prophet to bring
Israel up from Egypt,
by a prophet he cared for him.
¹⁴But Ephraim has aroused his bitter
anger;
his Lord will leave on him the guilt
of his bloodshed
and will repay him for his contempt.

The LORD's Anger Against Israel

13 When Ephraim spoke, people
trembled;
he was exalted in Israel.
But he became guilty of Baal
worship and died.
²Now they sin more and more;
they make idols for themselves
from their silver,
cleverly fashioned images,
all of them the work of craftsmen.
It is said of these people,
"They offer human sacrifices!
They kiss*ᵉ* calf-idols!"
³Therefore they will be like the morning
mist,
like the early dew that disappears,
like chaff swirling from a threshing
floor,
like smoke escaping through a
window.

⁴"But I have been the LORD your God
ever since you came out of Egypt.
You shall acknowledge no God but me,
no Savior except me.
⁵I cared for you in the wilderness,
in the land of burning heat.
⁶When I fed them, they were satisfied;
when they were satisfied, they
became proud;
then they forgot me.

ᵃ 12 In Hebrew texts this verse (11:12) is numbered
12:1.   *ᵇ* In Hebrew texts 12:1-14 is numbered 12:2-15.
ᶜ 2 Jacob means *he grasps the heel,* a Hebrew idiom
for *he takes advantage of* or *he deceives.*   *ᵈ 12* That
is, Northwest Mesopotamia   *ᵉ 2* Or *"Men who
sacrifice / kiss*

⁷So I will be like a lion to them,
  like a leopard I will lurk by the path.
⁸Like a bear robbed of her cubs,
  I will attack them and rip them
    open;
like a lion I will devour them—
  a wild animal will tear them
    apart.

⁹"You are destroyed, Israel,
  because you are against me,
    against your helper.
¹⁰Where is your king, that he may save
    you?
  Where are your rulers in all your
    towns,
of whom you said,
  'Give me a king and princes'?
¹¹So in my anger I gave you a king,
  and in my wrath I took him away.
¹²The guilt of Ephraim is stored up,
  his sins are kept on record.
¹³Pains as of a woman in childbirth
    come to him,
  but he is a child without wisdom;
when the time arrives,
  he doesn't have the sense to come
    out of the womb.

¹⁴"I will deliver this people from the
    power of the grave;
  I will redeem them from death.
Where, O death, are your plagues?
  Where, O grave, is your destruction?

"I will have no compassion,
¹⁵ even though he thrives among his
    brothers.
An east wind from the LORD will
    come,
  blowing in from the desert;
his spring will fail
  and his well dry up.
His storehouse will be plundered
  of all its treasures.
¹⁶The people of Samaria must bear their
    guilt,
  because they have rebelled against
    their God.
They will fall by the sword;
  their little ones will be dashed to
    the ground,
  their pregnant women ripped
    open."ᵃ

BREAK THROUGH!

Why so much violence?

(HOSEA 13:16)

This isn't easy to understand. In the ancient world, when one nation beat another, the custom was to destroy everything and punish the nation with a lot of violence. Here, in Hosea, that image is used to explain how the Israelites were going to suffer at the hands of their enemies. All of this was because they weren't faithful to God.

Repentance to Bring Blessing

14 ᵇ Return, Israel, to the LORD your
      God.
    Your sins have been your downfall!
²Take words with you
    and return to the LORD.
  Say to him:
    "Forgive all our sins
  and receive us graciously,
    that we may offer the fruit of our
      lips.ᶜ
³Assyria cannot save us;
  we will not mount warhorses.
We will never again say 'Our gods'
  to what our own hands have made,
    for in you the fatherless find
      compassion."

ᵃ 16 In Hebrew texts this verse (13:16) is numbered 14:1.
ᵇ In Hebrew texts 14:1-9 is numbered 14:2-10.   ᶜ 2 Or
offer our lips as sacrifices of bulls

4 "I will heal their waywardness
  and love them freely,
    for my anger has turned away from them.
5 I will be like the dew to Israel;
  he will blossom like a lily.
Like a cedar of Lebanon
  he will send down his roots;
6   his young shoots will grow.
His splendor will be like an olive tree,
  his fragrance like a cedar of Lebanon.
7 People will dwell again in his shade;
  they will flourish like the grain,
they will blossom like the vine —
  Israel's fame will be like the wine of Lebanon.
8 Ephraim, what more have I[a] to do with idols?
  I will answer him and care for him.
I am like a flourishing juniper;
  your fruitfulness comes from me."

9 Who is wise? Let them realize these things.
  Who is discerning? Let them understand.
The ways of the LORD are right;
  the righteous walk in them,
  but the rebellious stumble in them.

a 8 Or Hebrew; Septuagint What more has Ephraim

This very complicated book teaches us something very important: God's love for us is gigantic. At the same time, God wants us to love him with all our life and with all our strength. God wants us to go to church and meet together to worship him, but not just out of habit. God cares much more about our loving him and showing it by the way we live.

CASE CLOSED!

JOEL

1 The word of the LORD that came to Joel son of Pethuel.

An Invasion of Locusts

² Hear this, you elders;
    listen, all who live in the land.
Has anything like this ever happened
        in your days
    or in the days of your ancestors?
³ Tell it to your children,
        and let your children tell it to their
            children,
        and their children to the next
            generation.
⁴ What the locust swarm has left
        the great locusts have eaten;
    what the great locusts have left
        the young locusts have
            eaten;
    what the young locusts have left
        other locusts[a] have eaten.

⁵ Wake up, you drunkards, and
        weep!
    Wail, all you drinkers of wine;
    wail because of the new wine,
        for it has been snatched from your
            lips.
⁶ A nation has invaded my land,
        a mighty army without number;
    it has the teeth of a lion,
        the fangs of a lioness.
⁷ It has laid waste my vines
        and ruined my fig trees.
    It has stripped off their bark
        and thrown it away,
        leaving their branches white.

---

[a] 4 The precise meaning of the four Hebrew words used here for locusts is uncertain.

the pomegranate, the palm and the
apple[a] tree—
all the trees of the field—are dried
up.
Surely the people's joy
is withered away.

A Call to Lamentation

13 Put on sackcloth, you priests, and
mourn;
wail, you who minister before the
altar.
Come, spend the night in sackcloth,
you who minister before my
God;

[a] 12 Or possibly apricot

BREAKTHROUGH!

Why is this book written like poetry?

(JOEL 1:1)

Poetry is often used to show deep feelings.
Sometimes romantic poetry talks about love
in a very special way. In Joel's case, the main
idea is very strong and is told much better in
a poem.

8 Mourn like a virgin in sackcloth
grieving for the betrothed of her
youth.
9 Grain offerings and drink offerings
are cut off from the house of the
Lord.
The priests are in mourning,
those who minister before the
Lord.
10 The fields are ruined,
the ground is dried up;
the grain is destroyed,
the new wine is dried up,
the olive oil fails.

11 Despair, you farmers,
wail, you vine growers;
grieve for the wheat and the
barley,
because the harvest of the field is
destroyed.
12 The vine is dried up
and the fig tree is withered;

THE WITNESSES

✓ JOEL (JOEL 1:1)

This name means "the Lord is God." He was a
prophet of God, the son of Pethuel, and he lived
in Jerusalem.

for the grain offerings and drink
      offerings
   are withheld from the house of your
      God.
¹⁴ Declare a holy fast;
   call a sacred assembly.
Summon the elders
   and all who live in the land
to the house of the LORD your God,
   and cry out to the LORD.

¹⁵ Alas for that day!
   For the day of the LORD is near;
   it will come like destruction from
      the Almighty.ᵃ

¹⁶ Has not the food been cut off
   before our very eyes—
joy and gladness
   from the house of our God?
¹⁷ The seeds are shriveled
   beneath the clods.ᵇ
The storehouses are in ruins,
   the granaries have been broken
      down,
   for the grain has dried up.
¹⁸ How the cattle moan!
   The herds mill about
because they have no pasture;
   even the flocks of sheep are
      suffering.

¹⁹ To you, LORD, I call,
   for fire has devoured the pastures
      in the wilderness
   and flames have burned up all the
      trees of the field.
²⁰ Even the wild animals pant for you;
   the streams of water have
      dried up
   and fire has devoured the pastures
      in the wilderness.

An Army of Locusts

2 Blow the trumpet in Zion;
   sound the alarm on my holy hill.

Let all who live in the land tremble,
   for the day of the LORD is coming.
It is close at hand—
²   a day of darkness and gloom,
      a day of clouds and blackness.
Like dawn spreading across the
      mountains
   a large and mighty army comes,

BREAK THROUGH!

Is the day of the LORD coming?

(JOEL 2:1)

In Joel's story, the day of the LORD is a day of judgment. The people aren't living by God's rules. In Joel's poem, we discover that God doesn't just judge, he forgives and is very kind.

such as never was in ancient times
   nor ever will be in ages to come.

³ Before them fire devours,
   behind them a flame blazes.
Before them the land is like the
      garden of Eden,
   behind them, a desert waste—
   nothing escapes them.
⁴ They have the appearance of horses;
   they gallop along like cavalry.
⁵ With a noise like that of chariots
   they leap over the mountaintops,
like a crackling fire consuming
      stubble,
   like a mighty army drawn up for
      battle.
⁶ At the sight of them, nations are in
      anguish;
   every face turns pale.

ᵃ 15 Hebrew *Shaddai*   ᵇ 17 The meaning of the Hebrew
for this word is uncertain.

BREAKTHROUGH!

An army of locusts?

(JOEL 2:1-11)

It's not that there's a real army of locusts. It's just a way to talk about the enemy army that's coming with all its strength to destroy.

⁷They charge like warriors;
    they scale walls like soldiers.
They all march in line,
    not swerving from their course.
⁸They do not jostle each other;
    each marches straight ahead.
They plunge through defenses
    without breaking ranks.
⁹They rush upon the city;
    they run along the wall.
They climb into the houses;
    like thieves they enter through the
        windows.

¹⁰Before them the earth shakes,
    the heavens tremble,
the sun and moon are darkened,
    and the stars no longer
        shine.
¹¹The Lᴏʀᴅ thunders
    at the head of his army;
his forces are beyond number,
    and mighty is the army that obeys
        his command.
The day of the Lᴏʀᴅ is great;
    it is dreadful.
Who can endure it?

Rend Your Heart

¹²"Even now," declares the Lᴏʀᴅ,
    "return to me with all your heart,
    with fasting and weeping and
        mourning."

¹³Rend your heart
    and not your garments.
Return to the Lᴏʀᴅ your God,
    for he is gracious and
        compassionate,
slow to anger and abounding in love,
    and he relents from sending
        calamity.
¹⁴Who knows? He may turn and relent
    and leave behind a blessing—
grain offerings and drink offerings
    for the Lᴏʀᴅ your God.

¹⁵Blow the trumpet in Zion,
    declare a holy fast,
    call a sacred assembly.
¹⁶Gather the people,
    consecrate the assembly;
bring together the elders,
    gather the children,
    those nursing at the breast.
Let the bridegroom leave his room
    and the bride her chamber.
¹⁷Let the priests, who minister before
        the Lᴏʀᴅ,
    weep between the portico and the
        altar.
Let them say, "Spare your people, Lᴏʀᴅ.
    Do not make your inheritance an
        object of scorn,
    a byword among the nations.
Why should they say among the
        peoples,
    'Where is their God?' "

The Lᴏʀᴅ's Answer

¹⁸Then the Lᴏʀᴅ was jealous for his land
    and took pity on his people.

¹⁹The Lᴏʀᴅ replied[a] to them:

"I am sending you grain, new wine and
        olive oil,
    enough to satisfy you fully;
never again will I make you
    an object of scorn to the nations.

---

[a] 18,19 Or *Lᴏʀᴅ will be jealous . . . / and take pity . . . /*
¹⁹*The Lᴏʀᴅ will reply*

²⁰ "I will drive the northern horde far
from you,
pushing it into a parched and
barren land;
its eastern ranks will drown in the
Dead Sea
and its western ranks in the
Mediterranean Sea.
And its stench will go up;
its smell will rise."

Surely he has done great things!
²¹ Do not be afraid, land of Judah;
be glad and rejoice.
Surely the LORD has done great things!
²² Do not be afraid, you wild animals,
for the pastures in the wilderness
are becoming green.
The trees are bearing their fruit;
the fig tree and the vine yield their
riches.
²³ Be glad, people of Zion,
rejoice in the LORD your God,
for he has given you the autumn rains
because he is faithful.
He sends you abundant showers,
both autumn and spring rains, as
before.
²⁴ The threshing floors will be filled with
grain;
the vats will overflow with new wine
and oil.

²⁵ "I will repay you for the years the
locusts have eaten—
the great locust and the young
locust,
the other locusts and the locust
swarm*—
my great army that I sent among you.
²⁶ You will have plenty to eat, until you
are full,
and you will praise the name of the
LORD your God,
who has worked wonders for you;
never again will my people be shamed.
²⁷ Then you will know that I am in Israel,
that I am the LORD your God,
and that there is no other;
never again will my people be shamed.

The Day of the LORD

²⁸ "And afterward,
I will pour out my Spirit on all people.

Your sons and daughters will
prophesy,
your old men will dream dreams,
your young men will see visions.
²⁹ Even on my servants, both men and
women,
I will pour out my Spirit in those
days.
³⁰ I will show wonders in the heavens
and on the earth,
blood and fire and billows of smoke.
³¹ The sun will be turned to darkness
and the moon to blood
before the coming of the great and
dreadful day of the LORD.

---

a 25 The precise meaning of the four Hebrew words used
here for locusts is uncertain.

BREAK THROUGH!

Will the sun really be turned to darkness and the moon to blood?

(JOEL 2:31)

Once again, it's the "figurative language"
used so much in poetry. Talking this way
usually makes more of an impact. It gets
a person's attention and causes very deep
feelings. The sun really won't stop shining
and the moon won't turn to blood. But for the
people who will be attacked, they'll feel like
that's happening because they won't be able
to save themselves.

³² And everyone who calls
   on the name of the L<small>ORD</small> will be
     saved;
for on Mount Zion and in Jerusalem
   there will be deliverance,
as the L<small>ORD</small> has said,
even among the survivors
   whom the L<small>ORD</small> calls.^a

The Nations Judged

3 ^b "In those days and at that time,
   when I restore the fortunes of
     Judah and Jerusalem,
² I will gather all nations
   and bring them down to the Valley
     of Jehoshaphat.^c
There I will put them on trial
   for what they did to my inheritance,
     my people Israel,
because they scattered my people
     among the nations
   and divided up my land.
³ They cast lots for my people
   and traded boys for prostitutes;
   they sold girls for wine to drink.

⁴ "Now what have you against me, Tyre and Sidon and all you regions of Philistia? Are you repaying me for something I have done? If you are paying me back, I will swiftly and speedily return on your own heads what you have done. ⁵ For you took my silver and my gold and carried off my finest treasures to your temples.^d ⁶ You sold the people of Judah and Jerusalem to the Greeks, that you might send them far from their homeland.

⁷ "See, I am going to rouse them out of the places to which you sold them, and I will return on your own heads what you have done. ⁸ I will sell your sons and daughters to the people of Judah, and they will sell them to the Sabeans, a nation far away." The L<small>ORD</small> has spoken.

⁹ Proclaim this among the nations:
   Prepare for war!
Rouse the warriors!
   Let all the fighting men draw near
     and attack.
¹⁰ Beat your plowshares into swords
   and your pruning hooks into spears.
Let the weakling say,
   "I am strong!"

THE SCENE

VALLEY OF JEHOSHAPHAT

(JOEL 3:2–3)

That phrase means "the valley where God judged," but there never was a valley with that name. God must have said it, because this valley was going to be the place where the nations would come to gather to be judged.

¹¹ Come quickly, all you nations from
     every side,
   and assemble there.

Bring down your warriors, L<small>ORD</small>!

¹² "Let the nations be roused;
   let them advance into the Valley of
     Jehoshaphat,
for there I will sit
   to judge all the nations on every side.
¹³ Swing the sickle,
   for the harvest is ripe.
Come, trample the grapes,
   for the winepress is full
   and the vats overflow—
so great is their wickedness!"

---

^a 32 In Hebrew texts 2:28-32 is numbered 3:1-5.
^b In Hebrew texts 3:1-21 is numbered 4:1-21.
^c 2 *Jehoshaphat* means *the L*<small>ORD</small> *judges*; also in verse 12.
^d 5 Or *palaces*

¹⁴ Multitudes, multitudes
    in the valley of decision!
  For the day of the LORD is near
    in the valley of decision.
¹⁵ The sun and moon will be darkened,
    and the stars no longer
        shine.
¹⁶ The LORD will roar from Zion
    and thunder from Jerusalem;
    the earth and the heavens will
        tremble.
  But the LORD will be a refuge for his
        people,
    a stronghold for the people of
        Israel.

Blessings for God's People

¹⁷ "Then you will know that I, the LORD
        your God,
    dwell in Zion, my holy hill.
  Jerusalem will be holy;
    never again will foreigners invade
        her.

¹⁸ "In that day the mountains will drip
        new wine,
    and the hills will flow with milk;
  all the ravines of Judah will run
    with water.

THE SCENE

VALLEY OF DECISION

(JOEL 3:14)

It's an imaginary valley to show that a quick decision has to be made because the enemy is going to invade.

This book is very important, because it teaches us two things about God that we need to know right now. First, God judges sin. God isn't unconcerned with the difference between right and wrong. No! God really notices what's wrong, and he punishes it. Second, Joel shows us that God is a God of concern and love. Therefore, he won't abandon his people (that's us!). If his people repent, then God will forgive them. That's good!

CASE CLOSED!

A fountain will flow out of the Lord's
    house
and will water the valley of acacias.[a]
19 But Egypt will be desolate,
    Edom a desert waste,
because of violence done to the
    people of Judah,
in whose land they shed innocent
    blood.

20 Judah will be inhabited forever
    and Jerusalem through all
    generations.
21 Shall I leave their innocent blood
    unavenged?
No, I will not."

The Lord dwells in Zion!

---

[a] 18 Or *Valley of Shittim*

AMOS

THE EVIDENCE:

WHO WROTE IT?
We're not real sure about this either, but it was probably written by Amos himself and some of his disciples.

HOW LONG AGO?
It seems that Amos was preaching between the years 767 and 753 before Christ, and the book was written sometime between the years 700 and 600 before Jesus.

WHAT'S IT ABOUT?
Amos accuses the leaders of the northern kingdom of being in favor of rich people and mistreating poor people. With all this going on, Amos also criticizes the worship of false gods and worshiping God in forbidden places. He also preaches the word of God to neighboring nations. He tells them that the true God is going to deal with them also.

THE BEST PART
The part we liked best is 5:24: "But let justice roll on like a river, righteousness like a never-failing stream!"

---

1 The words of Amos, one of the shepherds of Tekoa—the vision he saw concerning Israel two years before the earthquake, when Uzziah was king of Judah and Jeroboam son of Jehoash[a] was king of Israel.

² He said:

"The LORD roars from Zion
   and thunders from Jerusalem;
the pastures of the shepherds
      dry up,
   and the top of Carmel withers."

Judgment on Israel's Neighbors

³ This is what the LORD says:

"For three sins of Damascus,
   even for four, I will not relent.
Because she threshed Gilead
   with sledges having iron
      teeth,
⁴ I will send fire on the house of
      Hazael
   that will consume the fortresses of
      Ben-Hadad.
⁵ I will break down the gate of
      Damascus;
   I will destroy the king who is in[b] the
      Valley of Aven[c]
and the one who holds the scepter in
      Beth Eden.
   The people of Aram will go into exile
      to Kir,"
                              says the LORD.

---

*a 1 Hebrew Joash, a variant of Jehoash   b 5 Or the
inhabitants of   c 5 Aven means wickedness.*

THE
WITNESSES

✓ **AMOS** (AMOS 1:1)
This name means "he who is sustained by God."
He was a shepherd from the city of Tekoa, and
he spent time caring for sycamore-fig trees.
God called him to be a prophet in the northern
kingdom.

✓ **UZZIAH, KING OF JUDAH** (AMOS 1:1)
He was also called Azariah. He was king of Judah
between the years 783 and 742 before Christ.

✓ **JEROBOAM, SON OF JEHOASH
AND KING OF ISRAEL** (AMOS 1:1)
His name was Jeroboam II (the Second), and
while he ruled, Israel was prosperous and
enjoyed a lot of luxuries.

✓ **HAZAEL** (AMOS 1:4)
He was a powerful, evil king of Syria. He treated
the Israelites very badly and even wanted to
capture the city of Jerusalem. Amos uses him as
the symbol of a very bad person.

TEKOA
(AMOS 1:1)

It means "high place good for a
tent." It was the city where Amos
was born. It was in Judah, about
6 miles (10 km) south of Bethlehem
and 11 miles (18 km) from Jerusalem.

⁶This is what the LORD says:

"For three sins of Gaza,
    even for four, I will not relent.
Because she took captive whole
        communities
    and sold them to Edom,
⁷I will send fire on the walls of Gaza
    that will consume her fortresses.
⁸I will destroy the king[a] of Ashdod
    and the one who holds the scepter
        in Ashkelon.
I will turn my hand against Ekron,
    till the last of the Philistines are dead,"
        says the Sovereign LORD.

⁹This is what the LORD says:

"For three sins of Tyre,
    even for four, I will not relent.
Because she sold whole communities
        of captives to Edom,
    disregarding a treaty of brotherhood,

ᵃ 8 Or inhabitants

¹⁰I will send fire on the walls of
  Tyre
  that will consume her fortresses."

¹¹This is what the LORD says:

"For three sins of Edom,
  even for four, I will not relent.
Because he pursued his brother with
  a sword
  and slaughtered the women of the
  land,
because his anger raged continually
  and his fury flamed unchecked,
¹²I will send fire on Teman
  that will consume the fortresses
  of Bozrah."

¹³This is what the LORD says:

"For three sins of Ammon,
  even for four, I will not relent.

THE SCENE

DAMASCUS

(AMOS 1:3)

Did you know that this city is
thought to be the oldest city
in the world? It seems to have
existed many, many, many years ago,
and it was the capital of an important
city-state in Syria.

Because he ripped open the pregnant
  women of Gilead
  in order to extend his borders,
¹⁴I will set fire to the walls of Rabbah
  that will consume her fortresses
  amid war cries on the day of battle,
  amid violent winds on a stormy day.
¹⁵Her king[a] will go into exile,
  he and his officials together,"
  says the LORD.

2 This is what the LORD says:

"For three sins of Moab,
  even for four, I will not relent.
Because he burned to ashes
  the bones of Edom's king,
²I will send fire on Moab
  that will consume the fortresses of
  Kerioth.[b]
Moab will go down in great tumult
  amid war cries and the blast of the
  trumpet.
³I will destroy her ruler
  and kill all her officials with him,"
  says the LORD.

⁴This is what the LORD says:

"For three sins of Judah,
  even for four, I will not relent.
Because they have rejected the law of
  the LORD
  and have not kept his decrees,
because they have been led astray by
  false gods,[c]
  the gods[d] their ancestors followed,
⁵I will send fire on Judah
  that will consume the fortresses of
  Jerusalem."

Judgment on Israel

⁶This is what the LORD says:

"For three sins of Israel,
  even for four, I will not relent.
They sell the innocent for silver,
  and the needy for a pair of sandals.
⁷They trample on the heads of the poor
  as on the dust of the ground
  and deny justice to the oppressed.
Father and son use the same girl
  and so profane my holy name.

___

^a 15 Or / Molek   ^b 2 Or of her cities   ^c 4 Or by lies
^d 4 Or lies

8 They lie down beside every altar
  on garments taken in pledge.
In the house of their god
  they drink wine taken as fines.

9 "Yet I destroyed the Amorites before
    them,
  though they were tall as the cedars
    and strong as the oaks.
I destroyed their fruit above
  and their roots below.
10 I brought you up out of Egypt
  and led you forty years in the
    wilderness
  to give you the land of the
    Amorites.

11 "I also raised up prophets from among
    your children
  and Nazirites from among your
    youths.
Is this not true, people of Israel?"
                  declares the LORD.
12 "But you made the Nazirites drink
    wine
  and commanded the prophets not
    to prophesy.

13 "Now then, I will crush you
  as a cart crushes when loaded with
    grain.
14 The swift will not escape,
  the strong will not muster their
    strength,
  and the warrior will not save his life.
15 The archer will not stand his ground,
  the fleet-footed soldier will not get
    away,
  and the horseman will not save his
    life.
16 Even the bravest warriors
  will flee naked on that day,"
                  declares the LORD.

Witnesses Summoned Against Israel

3 Hear this word, people of Israel, the
  word the LORD has spoken against
you—against the whole family I brought
up out of Egypt:

2 "You only have I chosen
  of all the families of the earth;
therefore I will punish you
  for all your sins."

3 Do two walk together
  unless they have agreed to
    do so?
4 Does a lion roar in the thicket
  when it has no prey?
Does it growl in its den
  when it has caught nothing?
5 Does a bird swoop down to a trap on
    the ground
  when no bait is there?
Does a trap spring up from the
    ground
  if it has not caught anything?
6 When a trumpet sounds in a city,
  do not the people tremble?
When disaster comes to a city,
  has not the LORD caused it?

7 Surely the Sovereign LORD does
    nothing
  without revealing his plan
    to his servants the prophets.

BREAK THROUGH!

Is it God who makes bad things happen?

(AMOS 3:6)

This is a little complicated. When this verse talks about "disaster," it's talking about bad things for people. In real life, sometimes God does things that seem bad to us. For God, they're not bad, and he uses them to make people change for the better.

8 The lion has roared—
    who will not fear?
The Sovereign Lord has spoken—
    who can but prophesy?

9 Proclaim to the fortresses of
        Ashdod
    and to the fortresses of Egypt:
"Assemble yourselves on the
        mountains of Samaria;
    see the great unrest within her
    and the oppression among her
        people."

10 "They do not know how to do right,"
        declares the Lord,
    "who store up in their fortresses
    what they have plundered and
        looted."

11 Therefore this is what the Sovereign
Lord says:

"An enemy will overrun your land,
    pull down your strongholds
    and plunder your fortresses."

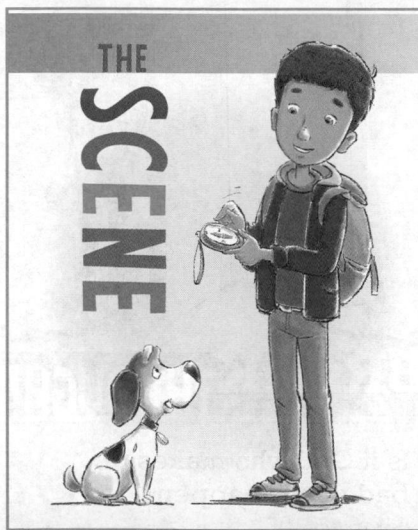

THE

SCENE

SAMARIA

(AMOS 3:9)

It was the capital of the northern
kingdom, and it was 42 miles
(67 km) north of Jerusalem.

12 This is what the Lord says:

"As a shepherd rescues from the
        lion's mouth
    only two leg bones or a piece of an
        ear,
so will the Israelites living in Samaria
        be rescued,
    with only the head of a bed
    and a piece of fabric*a* from a
        couch.*b*"

13 "Hear this and testify against the descendants of Jacob," declares the Lord,
the Lord God Almighty.

14 "On the day I punish Israel for her
        sins,
    I will destroy the altars of
        Bethel;
the horns of the altar will be cut
        off
    and fall to the ground.
15 I will tear down the winter house
        along with the summer house;
the houses adorned with ivory will be
        destroyed
    and the mansions will be
        demolished,"
                    declares the Lord.

Israel Has Not Returned to God

4 Hear this word, you cows of Bashan
        on Mount Samaria,
    you women who oppress the poor
        and crush the needy
    and say to your husbands, "Bring us
        some drinks!"
2 The Sovereign Lord has sworn by his
        holiness:
    "The time will surely come
when you will be taken away with
        hooks,
    the last of you with fishhooks.*c*
3 You will each go straight out
        through breaches in the wall,
    and you will be cast out toward
        Harmon,*d*"
                    declares the Lord.

a 12 The meaning of the Hebrew for this phrase is
uncertain.   *b 12* Or *Israelites be rescued, / those who sit
in Samaria / on the edge of their beds / and in Damascus
on their couches.*   *c 2* Or *away in baskets, / the last of
you in fish baskets*   *d 3* Masoretic Text; with a different
word division of the Hebrew (see Septuagint) *out, you
mountain of oppression*

⁴ "Go to Bethel and sin;
    go to Gilgal and sin yet more.
Bring your sacrifices every morning,
    your tithes every three years.ᵃ
⁵ Burn leavened bread as a thank
        offering
    and brag about your freewill
        offerings—
boast about them, you Israelites,
    for this is what you love to do,"
            declares the Sovereign Lord.
⁶ "I gave you empty stomachs in every
        city
    and lack of bread in every town,
    yet you have not returned to me,"
            declares the Lord.
⁷ "I also withheld rain from you
    when the harvest was still three
        months away.
I sent rain on one town,
    but withheld it from another.
One field had rain;
    another had none and dried up.
⁸ People staggered from town to town
        for water
    but did not get enough to drink,
    yet you have not returned to me,"
            declares the Lord.
⁹ "Many times I struck your gardens and
        vineyards,
    destroying them with blight and
        mildew.
Locusts devoured your fig and olive
        trees,
    yet you have not returned to me,"
            declares the Lord.
¹⁰ "I sent plagues among you
    as I did to Egypt.
I killed your young men with the sword,
    along with your captured horses.
I filled your nostrils with the stench of
        your camps,
    yet you have not returned to me,"
            declares the Lord.
¹¹ "I overthrew some of you
    as I overthrew Sodom and
        Gomorrah.
You were like a burning stick snatched
        from the fire,
    yet you have not returned to me,"
            declares the Lord.

¹² "Therefore this is what I will do to you,
        Israel,
    and because I will do this to you,
        Israel,
    prepare to meet your God."

¹³ He who forms the mountains,
    who creates the wind,
    and who reveals his thoughts to
        mankind,
who turns dawn to darkness,
    and treads on the heights of the
        earth—
    the Lord God Almighty is his name.

A Lament and Call to Repentance

5 Hear this word, Israel, this lament I
    take up concerning you:

² "Fallen is Virgin Israel,
    never to rise again,
deserted in her own land,
    with no one to lift her up."

³ This is what the Sovereign Lord says
to Israel:

"Your city that marches out a
        thousand strong
    will have only a hundred left;
your town that marches out a hundred
        strong
    will have only ten left."

⁴ This is what the Lord says to Israel:

"Seek me and live;
⁵   do not seek Bethel,
    do not go to Gilgal,
    do not journey to Beersheba.
For Gilgal will surely go into exile,
    and Bethel will be reduced to
        nothing."ᵇ
⁶ Seek the Lord and live,
    or he will sweep through the tribes
        of Joseph like a fire;
it will devour them,
    and Bethel will have no one to
        quench it.

⁷ There are those who turn justice into
        bitterness
    and cast righteousness to the
        ground.

ᵃ 4 Or days   ᵇ 5 Hebrew *aven*, a reference to Beth Aven
(a derogatory name for Bethel); see Hosea 4:15.

⁸ He who made the Pleiades and Orion,
　　who turns midnight into dawn
　　and darkens day into night,
　　who calls for the waters of the sea
　　and pours them out over the face of
　　　the land—
　　the Lᴏʀᴅ is his name.
⁹ With a blinding flash he destroys the
　　　stronghold
　　and brings the fortified city to ruin.

¹⁰ There are those who hate the one who
　　　upholds justice in court
　　and detest the one who tells the
　　　truth.
¹¹ You levy a straw tax on the poor
　　and impose a tax on their grain.
　　Therefore, though you have built stone
　　　mansions,
　　you will not live in them;
　　though you have planted lush
　　　vineyards,
　　you will not drink their wine.
¹² For I know how many are your
　　　offenses
　　and how great your sins.

There are those who oppress the
　　　innocent and take bribes
　　and deprive the poor of justice in
　　　the courts.
¹³ Therefore the prudent keep quiet in
　　　such times,
　　for the times are evil.

¹⁴ Seek good, not evil,
　　that you may live.
　　Then the Lᴏʀᴅ God Almighty will be
　　　with you,
　　just as you say he is.
¹⁵ Hate evil, love good;
　　maintain justice in the courts.
　　Perhaps the Lᴏʀᴅ God Almighty will
　　　have mercy
　　on the remnant of Joseph.

¹⁶ Therefore this is what the Lord, the
Lᴏʀᴅ God Almighty, says:

"There will be wailing in all the streets
　　and cries of anguish in every public
　　　square.
The farmers will be summoned to
　　　weep
　　and the mourners to wail.

¹⁷ There will be wailing in all the
　　　vineyards,
　　for I will pass through your
　　　midst,"
　　　　　　　　　　　　says the Lᴏʀᴅ.

The Day of the Lᴏʀᴅ

¹⁸ Woe to you who long
　　for the day of the Lᴏʀᴅ!
　　Why do you long for the day of the
　　　Lᴏʀᴅ?
　　That day will be darkness, not
　　　light.
¹⁹ It will be as though a man fled from a
　　　lion
　　only to meet a bear,
　　as though he entered his house
　　and rested his hand on the wall
　　only to have a snake bite him.
²⁰ Will not the day of the Lᴏʀᴅ be
　　　darkness, not light—
　　pitch-dark, without a ray of
　　　brightness?

²¹ "I hate, I despise your religious
　　　festivals;
　　your assemblies are a stench to
　　　me.
²² Even though you bring me burnt
　　　offerings and grain offerings,
　　I will not accept them.
　　Though you bring choice fellowship
　　　offerings,
　　I will have no regard for them.
²³ Away with the noise of your
　　　songs!
　　I will not listen to the music of your
　　　harps.
²⁴ But let justice roll on like a river,
　　righteousness like a never-failing
　　　stream!

²⁵ "Did you bring me sacrifices and
　　　offerings
　　forty years in the wilderness, people
　　　of Israel?
²⁶ You have lifted up the shrine of your
　　　king,
　　the pedestal of your idols,
　　the star of your god*ᵃ*—
　　which you made for yourselves.

---

*ᵃ 26 Or lifted up Sakkuth your king / and Kaiwan your idols,
/ your star-gods; Septuagint lifted up the shrine of Molek /
and the star of your god Rephan, / their idols*

BREAK THROUGH!

The star of your god

(AMOS 5:26)

Every group and every nation had its own gods. Of course, these gods were false. They didn't have anything to do with the true God. Here, it's talking about the gods they worshiped in Babylon and Assyria.

²⁷ Therefore I will send you into exile
       beyond Damascus,"
    says the LORD, whose name is God
       Almighty.

Woe to the Complacent

6 Woe to you who are complacent in
       Zion,
    and to you who feel secure on
       Mount Samaria,
    you notable men of the foremost
       nation,
    to whom the people of Israel
       come!
² Go to Kalneh and look at it;
    go from there to great Hamath,
    and then go down to Gath in
       Philistia.
    Are they better off than your two
       kingdoms?
    Is their land larger than yours?
³ You put off the day of disaster
    and bring near a reign of
       terror.

⁴ You lie on beds adorned with ivory
    and lounge on your couches.
 You dine on choice lambs
    and fattened calves.
⁵ You strum away on your harps like
       David
    and improvise on musical
       instruments.
⁶ You drink wine by the bowlful
    and use the finest lotions,
    but you do not grieve over the ruin
       of Joseph.
⁷ Therefore you will be among the first
       to go into exile;
    your feasting and lounging will
       end.

The Lord Abhors the Pride of Israel

⁸ The Sovereign LORD has sworn by himself—the LORD God Almighty declares:

    "I abhor the pride of Jacob
       and detest his fortresses;
    I will deliver up the city
       and everything in it."

⁹ If ten people are left in one house, they too will die. ¹⁰ And if the relative who comes to carry the bodies out of the house to burn them[a] asks anyone who might be hiding there, "Is anyone else with you?" and he says, "No," then he will go on to say, "Hush! We must not mention the name of the LORD."

¹¹ For the LORD has given the command,
    and he will smash the great house
       into pieces
    and the small house into bits.

¹² Do horses run on the rocky crags?
    Does one plow the sea[b] with oxen?
 But you have turned justice into
       poison
    and the fruit of righteousness into
       bitterness—
¹³ you who rejoice in the conquest of Lo
       Debar[c]
    and say, "Did we not take Karnaim[d]
       by our own strength?"

---

[a] 10 Or to make a funeral fire in honor of the dead
[b] 12 With a different word division of the Hebrew; Masoretic Text *plow there*   [c] 13 *Lo Debar* means *nothing*.   [d] 13 *Karnaim* means *horns*; *horn* here symbolizes strength.

14 For the Lord God Almighty
        declares,
"I will stir up a nation against you,
        Israel,
    that will oppress you all the way
        from Lebo Hamath to the valley of
        the Arabah."

Locusts, Fire and a Plumb Line

7 This is what the Sovereign Lord
   showed me: He was preparing swarms
of locusts after the king's share had been
harvested and just as the late crops were
coming up. ²When they had stripped the
land clean, I cried out, "Sovereign Lord,
forgive! How can Jacob survive? He is so
small!"

³So the Lord relented.

"This will not happen," the Lord said.

⁴This is what the Sovereign Lord
showed me: The Sovereign Lord was calling for judgment by fire; it dried up the
great deep and devoured the land. ⁵Then
I cried out, "Sovereign Lord, I beg you,
stop! How can Jacob survive? He is so
small!"

⁶So the Lord relented.

"This will not happen either," the Sovereign Lord said.

⁷This is what he showed me: The Lord
was standing by a wall that had been built
true to plumb,ᵃ with a plumb lineᵇ in his
hand. ⁸And the Lord asked me, "What do
you see, Amos?"

"A plumb line," I replied.

Then the Lord said, "Look, I am setting
a plumb line among my people Israel; I
will spare them no longer.

9 "The high places of Isaac will be
        destroyed
    and the sanctuaries of Israel will be
        ruined;
    with my sword I will rise against the
        house of Jeroboam."

Amos and Amaziah

¹⁰Then Amaziah the priest of Bethel
sent a message to Jeroboam king of Israel: "Amos is raising a conspiracy against
you in the very heart of Israel. The land
cannot bear all his words. ¹¹For this is
what Amos is saying:

" 'Jeroboam will die by the sword,
    and Israel will surely go into exile,
        away from their native land.' "

¹²Then Amaziah said to Amos, "Get out,
you seer! Go back to the land of Judah.
Earn your bread there and do your prophesying there. ¹³Don't prophesy anymore at
Bethel, because this is the king's sanctuary and the temple of the kingdom."

¹⁴Amos answered Amaziah, "I was neither a prophet nor the son of a prophet,
but I was a shepherd, and I also took care
of sycamore-fig trees. ¹⁵But the Lord took
me from tending the flock and said to me,
'Go, prophesy to my people Israel.' ¹⁶Now
then, hear the word of the Lord. You say,

" 'Do not prophesy against Israel,
    and stop preaching against the
        descendants of Isaac.'

¹⁷"Therefore this is what the Lord says:

" 'Your wife will become a prostitute in
        the city,
    and your sons and daughters will
        fall by the sword.
Your land will be measured and
        divided up,
    and you yourself will die in a paganᶜ
        country.
And Israel will surely go into exile,
    away from their native land.' "

A Basket of Ripe Fruit

8 This is what the Sovereign Lord
   showed me: a basket of ripe fruit.
²"What do you see, Amos?" he asked.

"A basket of ripe fruit," I answered.

Then the Lord said to me, "The time
is ripe for my people Israel; I will spare
them no longer.

³"In that day," declares the Sovereign
Lord, "the songs in the temple will turn
to wailing.ᵈ Many, many bodies—flung everywhere! Silence!"

4 Hear this, you who trample the
        needy
    and do away with the poor of the
        land,

ᵃ 7 The meaning of the Hebrew for this phrase is
uncertain.   ᵇ 7 The meaning of the Hebrew for this
phrase is uncertain; also in verse 8.   ᶜ 17 Hebrew an
unclean   ᵈ 3 Or "the temple singers will wail"

⁵saying,

"When will the New Moon be over
    that we may sell grain,
and the Sabbath be ended
    that we may market wheat?" —
skimping on the measure,
    boosting the price
    and cheating with dishonest
      scales,
⁶buying the poor with silver
    and the needy for a pair of
      sandals,
    selling even the sweepings with the
      wheat.

⁷The LORD has sworn by himself, the
Pride of Jacob: "I will never forget anything they have done.

⁸ "Will not the land tremble for this,
    and all who live in it mourn?
The whole land will rise like the Nile;
    it will be stirred up and then sink
    like the river of Egypt.

⁹ "In that day," declares the Sovereign
LORD,

"I will make the sun go down at noon
    and darken the earth in broad
      daylight.
¹⁰I will turn your religious festivals into
    mourning
    and all your singing into
      weeping.
I will make all of you wear sackcloth
    and shave your heads.
I will make that time like mourning for
    an only son
    and the end of it like a bitter
      day.

¹¹ "The days are coming," declares the
    Sovereign LORD,
    "when I will send a famine through
      the land—
not a famine of food or a thirst for
    water,
    but a famine of hearing the words
    of the LORD.
¹²People will stagger from sea to
    sea
    and wander from north to east,
searching for the word of the LORD,
    but they will not find it.

¹³ "In that day

"the lovely young women and strong
    young men
    will faint because of thirst.
¹⁴Those who swear by the sin of
    Samaria—
who say, 'As surely as your god
    lives, Dan,'
or, 'As surely as the godᵃ of
    Beersheba lives' —
they will fall, never to rise again."

Israel to Be Destroyed

9 I saw the Lord standing by the altar,
and he said:

"Strike the tops of the pillars
    so that the thresholds shake.
Bring them down on the heads of all
    the people;
    those who are left I will kill with the
      sword.
Not one will get away,
    none will escape.
² Though they dig down to the depths
    below,
    from there my hand will take
      them.
Though they climb up to the heavens
    above,
    from there I will bring them
      down.
³ Though they hide themselves on the
    top of Carmel,
    there I will hunt them down and
      seize them.
Though they hide from my eyes at the
    bottom of the sea,
    there I will command the serpent to
      bite them.
⁴ Though they are driven into exile by
    their enemies,
    there I will command the sword to
      slay them.

"I will keep my eye on them
    for harm and not for good."

⁵ The Lord, the LORD Almighty—
he touches the earth and it
    melts,
    and all who live in it mourn;

ᵃ 14 Hebrew *the way*

the whole land rises like the
    Nile,
  then sinks like the river of
    Egypt;
[6] he builds his lofty palace[a] in the
    heavens
  and sets its foundation[b] on the
    earth;
he calls for the waters of the sea
  and pours them out over the face
    of the land—
  the Lord is his name.

[7] "Are not you Israelites
  the same to me as the
    Cushites[c]?"
                 declares the Lord.
"Did I not bring Israel up from Egypt,
  the Philistines from Caphtor[d]
  and the Arameans from Kir?

BREAK THROUGH!

Did God free the Philistines and the Arameans too?

(AMOS 9:7)

This really means that Israel isn't the only nation under God's care. Many times, the Israelites thought they were better than anybody else. They thought that God was only for them. But that's not true. God is watching over all the other nations too. What a relief! If he didn't, then what would become of us because we're not Jewish?

[8] "Surely the eyes of the Sovereign
    Lord
  are on the sinful kingdom.
I will destroy it
  from the face of the earth.
Yet I will not totally destroy
  the descendants of Jacob,"
                declares the Lord.
[9] "For I will give the command,
  and I will shake the people of
    Israel
  among all the nations
as grain is shaken in a sieve,
  and not a pebble will reach the
    ground.
[10] All the sinners among my people
  will die by the sword,
all those who say,
  'Disaster will not overtake or
    meet us.'

Israel's Restoration

[11] "In that day

"I will restore David's fallen
    shelter—
  I will repair its broken walls
  and restore its ruins—
  and will rebuild it as it used
    to be,
[12] so that they may possess the remnant
    of Edom
  and all the nations that bear my
    name,[e]"
              declares the Lord,
              who will do these things.

[13] "The days are coming," declares the
Lord,

"when the reaper will be overtaken by
    the plowman
  and the planter by the one treading
    grapes.
New wine will drip from the
    mountains
  and flow from all the hills,
[14]   and I will bring my people Israel
    back from exile.[f]

---

[a] 6 The meaning of the Hebrew for this phrase is uncertain.   [b] 6 The meaning of the Hebrew for this word is uncertain.   [c] 7 That is, people from the upper Nile region   [d] 7 That is, Crete   [e] 12 Hebrew; Septuagint so that the remnant of people / and all the nations that bear my name may seek me   [f] 14 Or will restore the fortunes of my people Israel

"They will rebuild the ruined cities and
    live in them.
They will plant vineyards and drink
    their wine;
they will make gardens and eat their
    fruit.

15 I will plant Israel in their own
        land,
    never again to be uprooted
    from the land I have given them,"

                                        says the LORD your God.

What's most important about this book is that it teaches us how we
should act. It's not enough just to go to church, worship, pray and
read the Bible. That's all very good, but we also have to do things
that help to make things fair for people, and we need to treat foreigners,
poor people, widows and orphans right. In other words, God calls us to
care for people who are experiencing injustice. In that way, there will be
more justice in the world.

OBADIAH

THE EVIDENCE:

WHO WROTE IT?
Well, this time it's definite that nobody knows who wrote it!

HOW LONG AGO?
Obadiah was probably preaching in the year 586 before Christ, but the book was written a little later.

WHAT'S IT ABOUT?
This very short book talks about the destruction of the nation of Edom, the archenemy of Israel, and of all the other nations that made the Israelites suffer. But it also says that God would help his people.

THE BEST PART
We really like where it says, "But on Mount Zion will be deliverance; it will be holy, and Jacob will possess his inheritance" (v. 17).

Obadiah's Vision

¹The vision of Obadiah.

This is what the Sovereign LORD says about Edom—

We have heard a message from the
LORD:
An envoy was sent to the nations to
say,
"Rise, let us go against her for
battle"—

²"See, I will make you small among the
nations;
you will be utterly despised.
³The pride of your heart has deceived
you,
you who live in the clefts of the
rocks*a*
and make your home on the heights,
you who say to yourself,
'Who can bring me down to the
ground?'
⁴Though you soar like the eagle
and make your nest among the
stars,
from there I will bring you
down,"
declares the LORD.
⁵"If thieves came to you,
if robbers in the night—
oh, what a disaster awaits you!—
would they not steal only as much
as they wanted?
If grape pickers came to you,
would they not leave a few
grapes?
⁶But how Esau will be ransacked,
his hidden treasures pillaged!

---

a 3 Or of Sela

⁷All your allies will force you to the
  border;
  your friends will deceive and
    overpower you;
  those who eat your bread will set a
    trap for you,ᵃ
  but you will not detect it.

⁸"In that day," declares the LORD,
  "will I not destroy the wise men of
    Edom,
  those of understanding in the
    mountains of Esau?
⁹Your warriors, Teman, will be
    terrified,
  and everyone in Esau's mountains
    will be cut down in the slaughter.
¹⁰Because of the violence against your
    brother Jacob,
  you will be covered with shame;
  you will be destroyed forever.
¹¹On the day you stood aloof
  while strangers carried off his
    wealth
  and foreigners entered his gates
    and cast lots for Jerusalem,
  you were like one of them.
¹²You should not gloat over your
    brother
  in the day of his misfortune,
  nor rejoice over the people of Judah
  in the day of their destruction,
  nor boast so much
  in the day of their trouble.
¹³You should not march through the
    gates of my people
  in the day of their disaster,
  nor gloat over them in their
    calamity
  in the day of their disaster,
  nor seize their wealth
  in the day of their disaster.
¹⁴You should not wait at the
    crossroads
  to cut down their fugitives,
  nor hand over their survivors
  in the day of their trouble.

¹⁵"The day of the LORD is near
  for all nations.
  As you have done, it will be done to
    you;
  your deeds will return upon your
    own head.

THE
WITNESSES

✓ **OBADIAH** (OBADIAH v. 1)
This name means "servant of God." He was a man
who, with very few words, was able to preach a
very powerful message.

¹⁶Just as you drank on my holy hill,
  so all the nations will drink
    continually;
  they will drink and drink
  and be as if they had never been.
¹⁷But on Mount Zion will be
    deliverance;
  it will be holy,
  and Jacob will possess his
    inheritance.
¹⁸Jacob will be a fire
  and Joseph a flame;
  Esau will be stubble,
  and they will set him on fire and
    destroy him.

ᵃ 7 The meaning of the Hebrew for this clause is
uncertain.

THE SCENE

MOUNT ZION

(OBADIAH V. 17)

This refers to the city of Jerusalem.

There will be no survivors
from Esau."
The LORD has spoken.

19 People from the Negev will occupy
the mountains of Esau,
and people from the foothills will
possess
the land of the Philistines.
They will occupy the fields of Ephraim
and Samaria,
and Benjamin will possess
Gilead.
20 This company of Israelite exiles who
are in Canaan
will possess the land as far as
Zarephath;
the exiles from Jerusalem who are in
Sepharad
will possess the towns of the
Negev.
21 Deliverers will go up on*a* Mount
Zion
to govern the mountains of
Esau.
And the kingdom will be the
LORD's.

---

a 21 Or from

After reading this very short book carefully, we realized that its special message has to do with God's "sovereignty." What does "sovereignty" mean? It means that God is in control of everything, and that his power, his presence and his love are above everything. Nothing escapes God. That's great!

CASE CLOSED!

JONAH

THE EVIDENCE:

WHO WROTE IT?
We really don't know!

HOW LONG AGO?
It was probably written around the year 400 before Christ. That was a time when the Israelites hated the Assyrians because they had destroyed the Israelites' capital city, Samaria. At that time, the Assyrians had taken the Israelites as slaves to other countries.

WHAT'S IT ABOUT?
This is a nice book, because it shows that God cares about other nations too. God asks Jonah to take a message to the city of Nineveh so they will repent of their evil. But Jonah doesn't do as he's told. He tries to escape and get far away from God (as if that were possible!). After some really terrible things happen to him, Jonah decides to fulfill God's mission. The Ninevites apologize and God forgives them. But do you know what happened to Jonah then? He got angry with God!

THE BEST PART
We think this part is very powerful, when the king of Nineveh says, "Let everyone call urgently on God. Let them give up their evil ways and their violence. Who knows? God may yet relent and with compassion turn from his fierce anger so that we will not perish" (3:8-9).

Could it be that even when we mess up completely, we can change and start loving God?

Jonah Flees From the Lord

1 The word of the Lord came to Jonah son of Amittai: 2 "Go to the great city of Nineveh and preach against it, because its wickedness has come up before me."

3 But Jonah ran away from the Lord and headed for Tarshish. He went down to Joppa, where he found a ship bound for that port. After paying the fare, he went aboard and sailed for Tarshish to flee from the Lord.

4 Then the Lord sent a great wind on the sea, and such a violent storm arose that the ship threatened to break up. 5 All the sailors were afraid and each cried out to his own god. And they threw the cargo into the sea to lighten the ship.

But Jonah had gone below deck, where he lay down and fell into a deep sleep. 6 The captain went to him and said, "How can you sleep? Get up and call on your god! Maybe he will take notice of us so that we will not perish."

7 Then the sailors said to each other, "Come, let us cast lots to find out who is responsible for this calamity." They cast

sea," he replied, "and it will become calm. I know that it is my fault that this great storm has come upon you."

¹³Instead, the men did their best to row back to land. But they could not, for the sea grew even wilder than before. ¹⁴Then they cried out to the LORD, "Please, LORD, do not let us die for taking this man's life. Do not hold us accountable for killing an innocent man, for you, LORD, have done as you pleased." ¹⁵Then they took Jonah and threw him overboard, and the raging sea grew calm. ¹⁶At this the men greatly feared the LORD, and they offered a sacrifice to the LORD and made vows to him.

Jonah's Prayer

¹⁷Now the LORD provided a huge fish to swallow Jonah, and Jonah was in the belly of the fish three days and three nights.

THE WITNESSES

✓ **JONAH (JONAH 1:1)**
His name means "dove." He was from Judah, probably from Jerusalem.

lots and the lot fell on Jonah. ⁸So they asked him, "Tell us, who is responsible for making all this trouble for us? What kind of work do you do? Where do you come from? What is your country? From what people are you?"

⁹He answered, "I am a Hebrew and I worship the LORD, the God of heaven, who made the sea and the dry land."

¹⁰This terrified them and they asked, "What have you done?" (They knew he was running away from the LORD, because he had already told them so.)

¹¹The sea was getting rougher and rougher. So they asked him, "What should we do to you to make the sea calm down for us?"

¹²"Pick me up and throw me into the

THE SCENE

NINEVEH

(JONAH 1:2)

It was the capital of Assyria. The people there were very bad. The Assyrians were the people who had destroyed the northern kingdom and taken many Israelites as prisoners.

BREAKTHROUGH!

Why did Jonah run away from God? Why did he not do what God asked him to do?

(JONAH 1:3)

Being God's prophet isn't easy. The same thing happened to Moses, to Jeremiah and to others. Nobody really wanted to be a prophet, because it was risky. It also meant that he was going to suffer a lot.

THE SCENE

JOPPA

(JONAH 1:3)

It was the port on the Mediterranean Sea that was closest to Jerusalem.

2ᵃ ¹From inside the fish Jonah prayed to the Lᴏʀᴅ his God. ²He said:

"In my distress I called to the Lᴏʀᴅ,
    and he answered me.
From deep in the realm of the dead I
        called for help,
    and you listened to my cry.
³ You hurled me into the depths,
    into the very heart of the seas,
    and the currents swirled about me;
all your waves and breakers
    swept over me.
⁴ I said, 'I have been banished
    from your sight;
yet I will look again
    toward your holy temple.'
⁵ The engulfing waters threatened me,ᵇ
    the deep surrounded me;
    seaweed was wrapped around my
        head.

⁶ To the roots of the mountains I sank
        down;
    the earth beneath barred me in
        forever.
But you, Lᴏʀᴅ my God,
    brought my life up from the pit.

⁷ "When my life was ebbing away,
    I remembered you, Lᴏʀᴅ,
and my prayer rose to you,
    to your holy temple.

⁸ "Those who cling to worthless idols
    turn away from God's love for
        them.
⁹ But I, with shouts of grateful praise,
    will sacrifice to you.
What I have vowed I will make good.
    I will say, 'Salvation comes from the
        Lᴏʀᴅ.'"

¹⁰And the Lᴏʀᴅ commanded the fish, and it vomited Jonah onto dry land.

ᵃ In Hebrew texts 2:1 is numbered 1:17, and 2:1-10 is numbered 2:2-11.   ᵇ 5 Or *waters were at my throat*

Jonah Goes to Nineveh

3 Then the word of the LORD came to Jonah a second time: ²"Go to the great city of Nineveh and proclaim to it the message I give you."

³Jonah obeyed the word of the LORD and went to Nineveh. Now Nineveh was a very large city; it took three days to go through it. ⁴Jonah began by going a day's journey into the city, proclaiming, "Forty more days and Nineveh will be overthrown." ⁵The Ninevites believed God. A fast was proclaimed, and all of them, from the greatest to the least, put on sackcloth.

⁶When Jonah's warning reached the king of Nineveh, he rose from his throne, took off his royal robes, covered himself with sackcloth and sat down in the dust. ⁷This is the proclamation he issued in Nineveh:

"By the decree of the king and his nobles:

Do not let people or animals, herds or flocks, taste anything; do not let them eat or drink. ⁸But let people and animals be covered with sackcloth. Let everyone call urgently on God. Let them give up their evil ways and their violence. ⁹Who knows? God may yet relent and with compassion turn from his fierce anger so that we will not perish."

¹⁰When God saw what they did and how they turned from their evil ways, he relented and did not bring on them the destruction he had threatened.

Jonah's Anger at the LORD's Compassion

4 But to Jonah this seemed very wrong, and he became angry. ²He prayed to the LORD, "Isn't this what I said, LORD, when I was still at home? That is what I tried to forestall by fleeing to Tarshish. I knew that you are a gracious and compassionate God, slow to anger and abounding in love, a God who relents from sending calamity. ³Now, LORD, take away my life, for it is better for me to die than to live."

BREAKTHROUGH!

Sackcloth
(JONAH 3:5)
Clothes made from this material were worn to show sadness. It was so rough, it hurt the skin. It was also very ugly.

⁴But the LORD replied, "Is it right for you to be angry?"

⁵Jonah had gone out and sat down at a place east of the city. There he made himself a shelter, sat in its shade and waited to see what would happen to the city. ⁶Then the LORD God provided a leafy plant[a] and made it grow up over Jonah to give shade for his head to ease his discomfort, and Jonah was very happy about the plant. ⁷But at dawn the next day God provided a worm, which chewed the plant so that it withered. ⁸When the sun rose, God provided a scorching east wind, and the sun blazed on Jonah's head so that he grew faint. He wanted to die, and said, "It would be better for me to die than to live."

⁹But God said to Jonah, "Is it right for you to be angry about the plant?"

"It is," he said. "And I'm so angry I wish I were dead."

¹⁰But the LORD said, "You have been concerned about this plant, though

---

[a] 6 The precise identification of this plant is uncertain; also in verses 7, 9 and 10.

you did not tend it or make it grow. It sprang up overnight and died overnight. ¹¹And should I not have concern for the great city of Nineveh, in which there are more than a hundred and twenty thousand people who cannot tell their right hand from their left — and also many animals?"

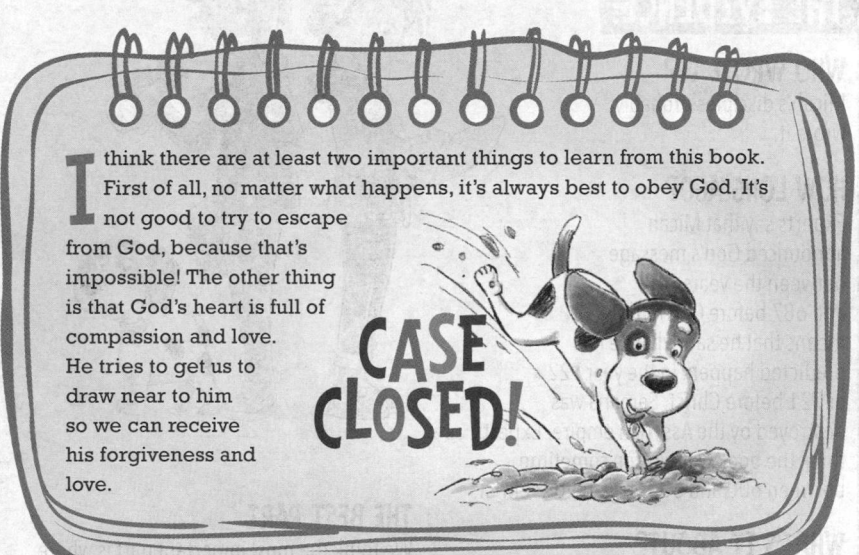

I think there are at least two important things to learn from this book. First of all, no matter what happens, it's always best to obey God. It's not good to try to escape from God, because that's impossible! The other thing is that God's heart is full of compassion and love. He tries to get us to draw near to him so we can receive his forgiveness and love.

CASE CLOSED!

MICAH

THE EVIDENCE:

WHO WROTE IT?
Micah's disciples probably wrote it.

HOW LONG AGO?
Experts say that Micah announced God's message between the years 742 and 687 before Christ. This means that he saw what he had predicted happen. In the year 722 or 721 before Christ, Samaria was destroyed by the Assyrian empire. Experts think the book was written sometime between 600 and 500 years before Christ.

WHAT'S IT ABOUT?
Micah tells the leaders of the people that they need to repent and change. This was because they were really powerful and were treating the poor people — and all the people, really — very badly. He also tells them that they should not worship other gods.

THE BEST PART
We think the most important part is where it says, "He has shown you, O mortal, what is good. And what does the LORD require of you? To act justly and to love mercy and to walk humbly with your God" (6:8).

---

1 The word of the LORD that came to Micah of Moresheth during the reigns of Jotham, Ahaz and Hezekiah, kings of Judah—the vision he saw concerning Samaria and Jerusalem.

² Hear, you peoples, all of you,
    listen, earth and all who live
        in it,
    that the Sovereign LORD may bear
        witness against you,
    the Lord from his holy temple.

Judgment Against Samaria and Jerusalem

³ Look! The LORD is coming from his
    dwelling place;

he comes down and treads on the
    heights of the earth.
⁴ The mountains melt beneath him
    and the valleys split apart,
like wax before the fire,
    like water rushing down a slope.
⁵ All this is because of Jacob's
        transgression,
    because of the sins of the people
        of Israel.
What is Jacob's transgression?
    Is it not Samaria?
What is Judah's high place?
    Is it not Jerusalem?

⁶ "Therefore I will make Samaria a heap
    of rubble,

I will howl like a jackal
  and moan like an owl.
⁹ For Samaria's plague is incurable;
  it has spread to Judah.
It has reached the very gate of my
    people,
  even to Jerusalem itself.
¹⁰ Tell it not in Gathᵃ;
  weep not at all.
In Beth Ophrahᵇ
  roll in the dust.
¹¹ Pass by naked and in shame,
  you who live in Shaphir.ᶜ
Those who live in Zaananᵈ
  will not come out.
Beth Ezel is in mourning;
  it no longer protects you.
¹² Those who live in Marothᵉ writhe in
    pain,
  waiting for relief,

ᵃ 10 *Gath* sounds like the Hebrew for *tell.*   ᵇ 10 *Beth
Ophrah* means *house of dust.*   ᶜ 11 *Shaphir* means
pleasant.   ᵈ 11 *Zaanan* sounds like the Hebrew for *come
out.*   ᵉ 12 *Maroth* sounds like the Hebrew for *bitter.*

THE
WITNESSES

✓ **MICAH** (MICAH 1:1)
We don't know how Micah received God's call.
Neither do we know what he did before he
started proclaiming God's message. We think
he was a man from the countryside, or maybe a
craftsman.

a place for planting vineyards.
I will pour her stones into the valley
  and lay bare her foundations.
⁷ All her idols will be broken to pieces;
  all her temple gifts will be burned
    with fire;
  I will destroy all her images.
Since she gathered her gifts from the
    wages of prostitutes,
  as the wages of prostitutes they will
    again be used."

Weeping and Mourning
⁸ Because of this I will weep and wail;
  I will go about barefoot and naked.

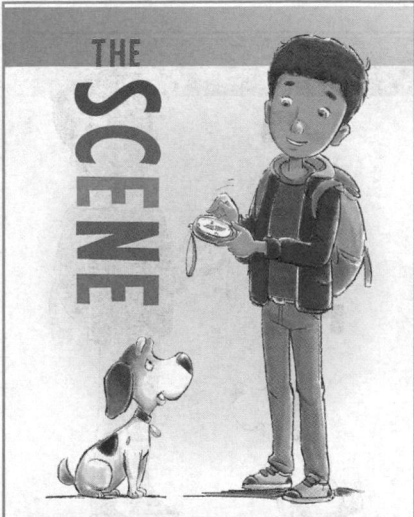

THE SCENE

MORESHETH

(MICAH 1:1)

This town was about 25 miles
(40 km) southwest of Jerusalem.
It was really called Moresheth-
Gath.

because disaster has come from the
　　LORD,
　　even to the gate of Jerusalem.
¹³ You who live in Lachish,
　　harness fast horses to the
　　　chariot.
You are where the sin of Daughter
　　Zion began,
　　for the transgressions of Israel were
　　　found in you.
¹⁴ Therefore you will give parting gifts
　　to Moresheth Gath.
The town of Akzib[a] will prove
　　deceptive
　　to the kings of Israel.
¹⁵ I will bring a conqueror against you
　　who live in Mareshah.[b]
The nobles of Israel
　　will flee to Adullam.
¹⁶ Shave your head in mourning
　　for the children in whom you
　　　delight;
make yourself as bald as the vulture,
　　for they will go from you into exile.

LACHISH

(MICAH 1:13)

A city with a fortress about 28 miles (45 km) southwest of Jerusalem.

Human Plans and God's Plans

2 Woe to those who plan iniquity,
　　to those who plot evil on their beds!
At morning's light they carry it out
　　because it is in their power to
　　　do it.
² They covet fields and seize them,
　　and houses, and take them.
They defraud people of their homes,
　　they rob them of their inheritance.

³ Therefore, the LORD says:

"I am planning disaster against this
　　people,
　　from which you cannot save
　　　yourselves.
You will no longer walk proudly,
　　for it will be a time of calamity.
⁴ In that day people will ridicule you;
　　they will taunt you with this
　　　mournful song:

GATH

(MICAH 1:10)

One of the five Philistine cities. The Philistines were enemies of Israel.

---

[a] 14 Akzib means deception.　[b] 15 Mareshah sounds like the Hebrew for conqueror.

'We are utterly ruined;
    my people's possession is divided
        up.
He takes it from me!
    He assigns our fields to traitors.' "

⁵ Therefore you will have no one in the
        assembly of the LORD
    to divide the land by lot.

False Prophets

⁶ "Do not prophesy," their prophets
        say.
    "Do not prophesy about these
        things;
    disgrace will not overtake us."
⁷ You descendants of Jacob, should it
        be said,
    "Does the LORD become*ᵃ* impatient?
    Does he do such things?"

"Do not my words do good
    to the one whose ways are upright?

BREAK THROUGH!

Why does he say they should shave their heads?

(MICAH 1:16)

It was to show that they were sad after someone died. Nowadays, many people in many countries wear black clothing to funerals or to show that someone they love has died.

⁸ Lately my people have risen up
    like an enemy.
You strip off the rich robe
    from those who pass by without a
        care,
    like men returning from battle.
⁹ You drive the women of my people
    from their pleasant homes.
You take away my blessing
    from their children forever.
¹⁰ Get up, go away!
    For this is not your resting place,
because it is defiled,
    it is ruined, beyond all remedy.
¹¹ If a liar and deceiver comes and says,
    'I will prophesy for you plenty of
        wine and beer,'
    that would be just the prophet for
        this people!

Deliverance Promised

¹² "I will surely gather all of you, Jacob;
    I will surely bring together the
        remnant of Israel.
I will bring them together like sheep in
        a pen,
    like a flock in its pasture;
    the place will throng with people.
¹³ The One who breaks open the way will
        go up before them;
    they will break through the gate and
        go out.
Their King will pass through before
        them,
    the LORD at their head."

Leaders and Prophets Rebuked

3 Then I said,

"Listen, you leaders of Jacob,
    you rulers of Israel.
Should you not embrace justice,
²   you who hate good and love evil;
who tear the skin from my people
    and the flesh from their bones;
³ who eat my people's flesh,
    strip off their skin
    and break their bones in pieces;
who chop them up like meat for the
        pan,
    like flesh for the pot?"

ᵃ 7 Or *Is the Spirit of the* LORD

⁴Then they will cry out to the Lord,
    but he will not answer them.
At that time he will hide his face from
    them
    because of the evil they have
      done.

⁵This is what the Lord says:

"As for the prophets
    who lead my people astray,
they proclaim 'peace'
    if they have something to eat,
but prepare to wage war against
    anyone
    who refuses to feed them.
⁶Therefore night will come over you,
    without visions,
    and darkness, without divination.
The sun will set for the prophets,
    and the day will go dark for
      them.
⁷The seers will be ashamed
    and the diviners disgraced.
They will all cover their faces
    because there is no answer from
      God."
⁸But as for me, I am filled with
    power,
    with the Spirit of the Lord,
    and with justice and might,
to declare to Jacob his transgression,
    to Israel his sin.

⁹Hear this, you leaders of Jacob,
    you rulers of Israel,
who despise justice
    and distort all that is right;
¹⁰who build Zion with bloodshed,
    and Jerusalem with wickedness.
¹¹Her leaders judge for a bribe,
    her priests teach for a price,
    and her prophets tell fortunes for
      money.
Yet they look for the Lord's support
    and say,
    "Is not the Lord among us?
    No disaster will come upon us."
¹²Therefore because of you,
    Zion will be plowed like a field,
Jerusalem will become a heap of
    rubble,
    the temple hill a mound overgrown
      with thickets.

The Mountain of the Lord

4 In the last days

the mountain of the Lord's temple will
    be established
    as the highest of the mountains;
it will be exalted above the hills,
    and peoples will stream to it.

²Many nations will come and say,

"Come, let us go up to the mountain
    of the Lord,
    to the temple of the God of Jacob.
He will teach us his ways,
    so that we may walk in his
      paths."
The law will go out from Zion,
    the word of the Lord from
      Jerusalem.
³He will judge between many peoples
    and will settle disputes for strong
      nations far and wide.
They will beat their swords into
    plowshares
    and their spears into pruning
      hooks.
Nation will not take up sword against
    nation,
    nor will they train for war anymore.
⁴Everyone will sit under their own
    vine
    and under their own fig tree,
and no one will make them afraid,
    for the Lord Almighty has
      spoken.
⁵All the nations may walk
    in the name of their gods,
but we will walk in the name of the
    Lord
    our God for ever and ever.

The Lord's Plan

⁶"In that day," declares the Lord,

"I will gather the lame;
    I will assemble the exiles
    and those I have brought to
      grief.
⁷I will make the lame my remnant,
    those driven away a strong nation.
The Lord will rule over them in Mount
    Zion
    from that day and forever.

8 As for you, watchtower of the flock,
  stronghold[a] of Daughter Zion,
the former dominion will be restored
    to you;
  kingship will come to Daughter
    Jerusalem."

9 Why do you now cry aloud—
  have you no king[b]?
Has your ruler[c] perished,
  that pain seizes you like that of a
    woman in labor?
10 Writhe in agony, Daughter Zion,
  like a woman in labor,
for now you must leave the city
  to camp in the open field.
You will go to Babylon;
  there you will be rescued.
There the LORD will redeem you
  out of the hand of your enemies.

11 But now many nations
  are gathered against you.
They say, "Let her be defiled,
  let our eyes gloat over Zion!"
12 But they do not know
  the thoughts of the LORD;
they do not understand his plan,
  that he has gathered them like
    sheaves to the threshing floor.
13 "Rise and thresh, Daughter Zion,
  for I will give you horns of iron;
I will give you hooves of bronze,
  and you will break to pieces many
    nations."
You will devote their ill-gotten gains to
    the LORD,
  their wealth to the Lord of all the
    earth.

A Promised Ruler From Bethlehem

5 [d] Marshal your troops now, city of
    troops,
  for a siege is laid against us.
They will strike Israel's ruler
  on the cheek with a rod.

2 "But you, Bethlehem Ephrathah,
  though you are small among the
    clans[e] of Judah,
out of you will come for me
  one who will be ruler over Israel,
whose origins are from of old,
  from ancient times."

3 Therefore Israel will be abandoned
  until the time when she who is in
    labor bears a son,
and the rest of his brothers return
  to join the Israelites.

4 He will stand and shepherd his flock
  in the strength of the LORD,
in the majesty of the name of the
    LORD his God.
And they will live securely, for then his
    greatness
  will reach to the ends of the earth.

5 And he will be our peace
  when the Assyrians invade our
    land
and march through our fortresses.
We will raise against them seven
    shepherds,
  even eight commanders,
6 who will rule[f] the land of Assyria with
    the sword,

---

[a] 8 Or hill   [b] 9 Or King   [c] 9 Or Ruler   [d] In Hebrew
texts 5:1 is numbered 4:14, and 5:2-15 is numbered
5:1-14.   [e] 2 Or rulers   [f] 6 Or crush

BREAK THROUGH!

Who was this important ruler who was going to be born?

(MICAH 5:2–6)

That ruler was Jesus! He was going to be born in Bethlehem, just like Micah says.

the land of Nimrod with drawn
    sword.ª
He will deliver us from the Assyrians
when they invade our land
and march across our borders.

⁷The remnant of Jacob will be
in the midst of many peoples
like dew from the LORD,
like showers on the grass,
which do not wait for anyone
or depend on man.
⁸The remnant of Jacob will be among
    the nations,
in the midst of many peoples,
like a lion among the beasts of the
    forest,
like a young lion among flocks of
    sheep,
which mauls and mangles as it goes,
and no one can rescue.
⁹Your hand will be lifted up in triumph
    over your enemies,
and all your foes will be destroyed.

¹⁰"In that day," declares the LORD,

"I will destroy your horses from among
    you
and demolish your chariots.
¹¹I will destroy the cities of your land
and tear down all your strongholds.
¹²I will destroy your witchcraft
and you will no longer cast spells.
¹³I will destroy your idols
and your sacred stones from among
    you;
you will no longer bow down
to the work of your hands.
¹⁴I will uproot from among you your
    Asherah polesᵇ
when I demolish your cities.
¹⁵I will take vengeance in anger and
    wrath
on the nations that have not obeyed
    me."

The LORD's Case Against Israel

6 Listen to what the LORD says:

"Stand up, plead my case before the
    mountains;
let the hills hear what you have to
    say.

²"Hear, you mountains, the LORD's
    accusation;
listen, you everlasting foundations
    of the earth.
For the LORD has a case against his
    people;
he is lodging a charge against
    Israel.

³"My people, what have I done to you?
How have I burdened you? Answer
    me.
⁴I brought you up out of Egypt
and redeemed you from the land of
    slavery.
I sent Moses to lead you,
also Aaron and Miriam.
⁵My people, remember
what Balak king of Moab plotted
and what Balaam son of Beor
    answered.
Remember your journey from Shittim
    to Gilgal,
that you may know the righteous
    acts of the LORD."

⁶With what shall I come before the
    LORD
and bow down before the exalted
    God?
Shall I come before him with burnt
    offerings,
with calves a year old?
⁷Will the LORD be pleased with
    thousands of rams,
with ten thousand rivers of olive
    oil?
Shall I offer my firstborn for my
    transgression,
the fruit of my body for the sin of my
    soul?
⁸He has shown you, O mortal, what is
    good.
And what does the LORD require of
    you?
To act justly and to love mercy
and to walk humblyᶜ with your God.

Israel's Guilt and Punishment

⁹Listen! The LORD is calling to the
    city—
and to fear your name is wisdom—

ª 6 Or *Nimrod in its gates*   ᵇ 14 That is, wooden
symbols of the goddess Asherah   ᶜ 8 Or *prudently*

BREAKTHROUGH!

What happened when they traveled from Shittim to Gilgal?

(MICAH 6:5)

Shittim was the last place Israel camped before going into the promised land. Gilgal was where they camped for the first time in their new land. God is reminding them that he was the one who helped them enter the promised land.

"Heed the rod and the One who
appointed it.*a*
¹⁰ Am I still to forget your ill-gotten
treasures, you wicked house,
and the short ephah,*b* which is
accursed?
¹¹ Shall I acquit someone with dishonest
scales,
with a bag of false weights?
¹² Your rich people are violent;
your inhabitants are liars
and their tongues speak deceitfully.
¹³ Therefore, I have begun to destroy
you,
to ruin*c* you because of your sins.
¹⁴ You will eat but not be satisfied;
your stomach will still be empty.*d*
You will store up but save nothing,
because what you save*e* I will give
to the sword.

¹⁵ You will plant but not harvest;
you will press olives but not use the
oil,
you will crush grapes but not drink
the wine.
¹⁶ You have observed the statutes of
Omri
and all the practices of Ahab's
house;
you have followed their traditions.
Therefore I will give you over to ruin
and your people to derision;
you will bear the scorn of the
nations.*f*"

Israel's Misery

7 What misery is mine!
I am like one who gathers summer
fruit
at the gleaning of the vineyard;
there is no cluster of grapes to
eat,
none of the early figs that I crave.
² The faithful have been swept from the
land;
not one upright person remains.
Everyone lies in wait to shed
blood;
they hunt each other with nets.
³ Both hands are skilled in doing evil;
the ruler demands gifts,
the judge accepts bribes,
the powerful dictate what they
desire—
they all conspire together.
⁴ The best of them is like a brier,
the most upright worse than a thorn
hedge.
The day God visits you has come,
the day your watchmen sound the
alarm.
Now is the time of your confusion.
⁵ Do not trust a neighbor;
put no confidence in a friend.
Even with the woman who lies in your
embrace
guard the words of your lips.

---

a 9 The meaning of the Hebrew for this line is uncertain.
b 10 An ephah was a dry measure.   *c 13* Or *Therefore, I
will make you ill and destroy you; / I will ruin*   *d 14* The
meaning of the Hebrew for this word is uncertain.
e 14 Or *You will press toward birth but not give birth, / and
what you bring to birth*   *f 16* Septuagint; Hebrew *scorn
due my people*

⁶For a son dishonors his father,
  a daughter rises up against her
    mother,
  a daughter-in-law against her mother-
    in-law—
  a man's enemies are the members
    of his own household.

⁷But as for me, I watch in hope for the
    LORD,
  I wait for God my Savior;
  my God will hear me.

Israel Will Rise

⁸Do not gloat over me, my enemy!
  Though I have fallen, I will rise.
  Though I sit in darkness,
    the LORD will be my light.
⁹Because I have sinned against
    him,
  I will bear the LORD's wrath,
  until he pleads my case
  and upholds my cause.
  He will bring me out into the light;
  I will see his righteousness.
¹⁰Then my enemy will see it
  and will be covered with
    shame,
  she who said to me,
  "Where is the LORD your God?"

My eyes will see her downfall;
  even now she will be trampled
    underfoot
  like mire in the streets.

¹¹The day for building your walls will
    come,
  the day for extending your
    boundaries.
¹²In that day people will come to you
  from Assyria and the cities of Egypt,
  even from Egypt to the Euphrates
  and from sea to sea
  and from mountain to mountain.
¹³The earth will become desolate
    because of its inhabitants,
  as the result of their deeds.

Prayer and Praise

¹⁴Shepherd your people with your staff,
  the flock of your inheritance,
  which lives by itself in a forest,
  in fertile pasturelands.ᵃ
  Let them feed in Bashan and Gilead
  as in days long ago.

¹⁵"As in the days when you came out of
    Egypt,
  I will show them my wonders."

ᵃ 14 Or *in the middle of Carmel*

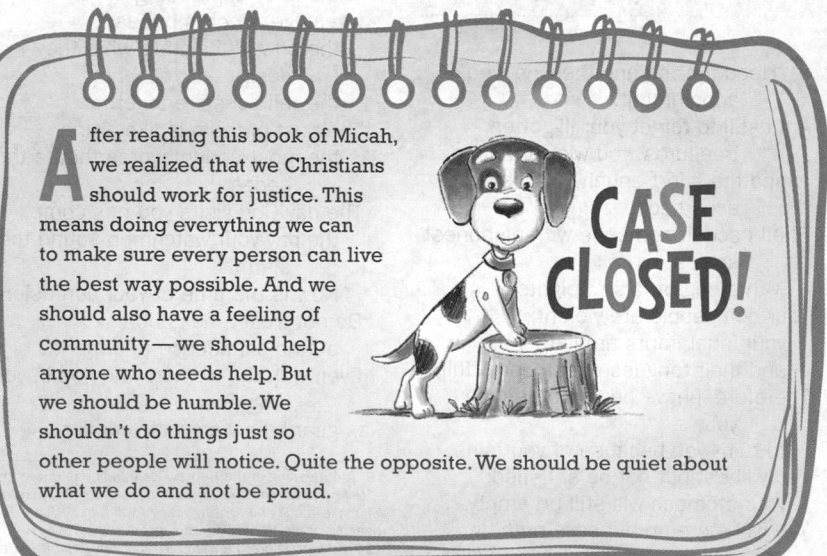

After reading this book of Micah, we realized that we Christians should work for justice. This means doing everything we can to make sure every person can live the best way possible. And we should also have a feeling of community—we should help anyone who needs help. But we should be humble. We shouldn't do things just so other people will notice. Quite the opposite. We should be quiet about what we do and not be proud.

CASE CLOSED!

¹⁶Nations will see and be
    ashamed,
  deprived of all their power.
  They will put their hands over their
    mouths
  and their ears will become
    deaf.
¹⁷They will lick dust like a snake,
  like creatures that crawl on the
    ground.
  They will come trembling out of their
    dens;
  they will turn in fear to the Lord our
    God
  and will be afraid of you.

¹⁸Who is a God like you,
  who pardons sin and forgives the
    transgression
  of the remnant of his inheritance?
  You do not stay angry forever
  but delight to show mercy.
¹⁹You will again have compassion on us;
  you will tread our sins underfoot
  and hurl all our iniquities into the
    depths of the sea.
²⁰You will be faithful to Jacob,
  and show love to Abraham,
  as you pledged on oath to our
    ancestors
  in days long ago.

NAHUM

THE EVIDENCE:

WHO WROTE IT?
We don't know who wrote this book.

HOW LONG AGO?
Nahum was probably preaching a short time before everything he's talking about happened. In other words, maybe in the years 650 to 620 before Jesus. The book was probably written a little later than that.

WHAT'S IT ABOUT?
The Assyrian empire was very powerful. They made a lot of people suffer. Nahum was really angry about how bad the Assyrians were. He preached against them, and he said that God would punish them because God is a just God who will not allow people to be so badly treated.

THE BEST PART
We thought that verse 15 of chapter 1 was very nice, because it says, "Look, there on the mountains, the feet of one who brings good news, who proclaims peace! Celebrate your festivals, Judah, and fulfill your vows. No more will the wicked invade you; they will be completely destroyed."

1 A prophecy concerning Nineveh. The book of the vision of Nahum the Elkoshite.

The Lord's Anger Against Nineveh

2 The Lord is a jealous and avenging God;
    the Lord takes vengeance and is filled with wrath.
The Lord takes vengeance on his foes
    and vents his wrath against his enemies.
3 The Lord is slow to anger but great in power;
    the Lord will not leave the guilty unpunished.

His way is in the whirlwind and the storm,
    and clouds are the dust of his feet.
4 He rebukes the sea and dries it up;
    he makes all the rivers run dry.
Bashan and Carmel wither
    and the blossoms of Lebanon fade.
5 The mountains quake before him
    and the hills melt away.
The earth trembles at his presence,
    the world and all who live in it.
6 Who can withstand his indignation?
    Who can endure his fierce anger?
His wrath is poured out like fire;
    the rocks are shattered before him.

BREAKTHROUGH!

Did everything Nahum predicted happen?
(NAHUM 1)

The city of Nineveh was finally destroyed, but it was a lot later. And the power of the Assyrians did come to an end.

---

⁷The LORD is good,
    a refuge in times of trouble.
He cares for those who trust in
    him,
⁸   but with an overwhelming flood
he will make an end of Nineveh;
    he will pursue his foes into the
        realm of darkness.

⁹Whatever they plot against the LORD
    he will bringᵃ to an end;
    trouble will not come a second
        time.
¹⁰They will be entangled among thorns
    and drunk from their wine;
    they will be consumed like dry
        stubble.ᵇ
¹¹From you, Nineveh, has one come
    forth
    who plots evil against the LORD
    and devises wicked plans.

¹²This is what the LORD says:

"Although they have allies and are
    numerous,

they will be destroyed and pass
    away.
Although I have afflicted you, Judah,
    I will afflict you no more.
¹³Now I will break their yoke from your
    neck
    and tear your shackles away."

¹⁴The LORD has given a command
        concerning you, Nineveh:
    "You will have no descendants to
        bear your name.
I will destroy the images and idols
    that are in the temple of your
        gods.

ᵃ 9 Or *What do you foes plot against the LORD? / He will bring it*   ᵇ 10 The meaning of the Hebrew for this verse is uncertain.

THE WITNESSES

✓ **NAHUM THE ELKOSHITE (NAHUM 1:1)**
Nahum may mean "comforted by God." Nahum was a great poet. We don't know much about where Elko was.

I will prepare your grave,
for you are vile."

15 Look, there on the mountains,
the feet of one who brings good
news,
who proclaims peace!
Celebrate your festivals, Judah,
and fulfill your vows.
No more will the wicked invade you;
they will be completely destroyed.*a*

Nineveh to Fall

2*b* An attacker advances against you,
   Nineveh.
Guard the fortress,
watch the road,
brace yourselves,
marshal all your strength!

2 The LORD will restore the splendor of
Jacob
like the splendor of Israel,
though destroyers have laid them
waste
and have ruined their vines.

3 The shields of the soldiers are red;
the warriors are clad in scarlet.
The metal on the chariots flashes
on the day they are made ready;
the spears of juniper are
brandished.*c*
4 The chariots storm through the
streets,
rushing back and forth through the
squares.
They look like flaming torches;
they dart about like lightning.

5 Nineveh summons her picked troops,
yet they stumble on their way.
They dash to the city wall;
the protective shield is put in
place.
6 The river gates are thrown open
and the palace collapses.
7 It is decreed*d* that Nineveh
be exiled and carried away.
Her female slaves moan like doves
and beat on their breasts.
8 Nineveh is like a pool
whose water is draining away.
"Stop! Stop!" they cry,
but no one turns back.

9 Plunder the silver!
Plunder the gold!
The supply is endless,
the wealth from all its treasures!
10 She is pillaged, plundered, stripped!
Hearts melt, knees give way,
bodies tremble, every face grows
pale.
11 Where now is the lions' den,
the place where they fed their
young,
where the lion and lioness went,
and the cubs, with nothing to fear?
12 The lion killed enough for his cubs
and strangled the prey for his
mate,
filling his lairs with the kill
and his dens with the prey.

13 "I am against you,"
declares the LORD Almighty.
"I will burn up your chariots in smoke,
and the sword will devour your
young lions.
I will leave you no prey on the
earth.
The voices of your messengers
will no longer be heard."

Woe to Nineveh

3 Woe to the city of blood,
   full of lies,
full of plunder,
never without victims!
2 The crack of whips,
the clatter of wheels,
galloping horses
and jolting chariots!
3 Charging cavalry,
flashing swords
and glittering spears!
Many casualties,
piles of dead,
bodies without number,
people stumbling over the
corpses —
4 all because of the wanton lust of a
prostitute,
alluring, the mistress of sorceries,

---

a 15 In Hebrew texts this verse (1:15) is numbered 2:1.
b In Hebrew texts 2:1-13 is numbered 2:2-14.
c 3 Hebrew; Septuagint and Syriac *ready; / the horsemen
rush to and fro.*   *d 7* The meaning of the Hebrew for this
word is uncertain.

who enslaved nations by her
  prostitution
and peoples by her witchcraft.

5 "I am against you," declares the LORD
  Almighty.
  "I will lift your skirts over your face.
I will show the nations your nakedness
  and the kingdoms your shame.
6 I will pelt you with filth,
  I will treat you with contempt
  and make you a spectacle.
7 All who see you will flee from you and
      say,
  'Nineveh is in ruins—who will
      mourn for her?'
  Where can I find anyone to comfort
      you?"

8 Are you better than Thebes,
  situated on the Nile,
  with water around her?
The river was her defense,
  the waters her wall.
9 Cush[a] and Egypt were her boundless
      strength;
  Put and Libya were among her allies.
10 Yet she was taken captive
  and went into exile.
Her infants were dashed to pieces
  at every street corner.
Lots were cast for her nobles,
  and all her great men were put in
      chains.

11 You too will become drunk;
  you will go into hiding
  and seek refuge from the enemy.

12 All your fortresses are like fig trees
  with their first ripe fruit;
when they are shaken,
  the figs fall into the mouth of the
      eater.
13 Look at your troops—
  they are all weaklings.
The gates of your land
  are wide open to your enemies;
  fire has consumed the bars of your
      gates.

14 Draw water for the siege,
  strengthen your defenses!
Work the clay,
  tread the mortar,
  repair the brickwork!

THE SCENE

THEBES

(NAHUM 3:8–10)

An ancient city in Egypt
416 miles (670 km) south of
Cairo.

15 There the fire will consume you;
  the sword will cut you down—
  they will devour you like a swarm of
      locusts.
Multiply like grasshoppers,
  multiply like locusts!
16 You have increased the number of
      your merchants
  till they are more numerous than
      the stars in the sky,
but like locusts they strip the land
  and then fly away.
17 Your guards are like locusts,
  your officials like swarms of locusts
  that settle in the walls on a cold
      day—
but when the sun appears they fly
      away,
  and no one knows where.

18 King of Assyria, your shepherds[b]
      slumber;
  your nobles lie down to rest.

---

[a] 9 That is, the upper Nile region   [b] 18 That is, rulers

Your people are scattered on the
mountains
with no one to gather them.
¹⁹ Nothing can heal you;
your wound is fatal.

All who hear the news about
you
clap their hands at your fall,
for who has not felt
your endless cruelty?

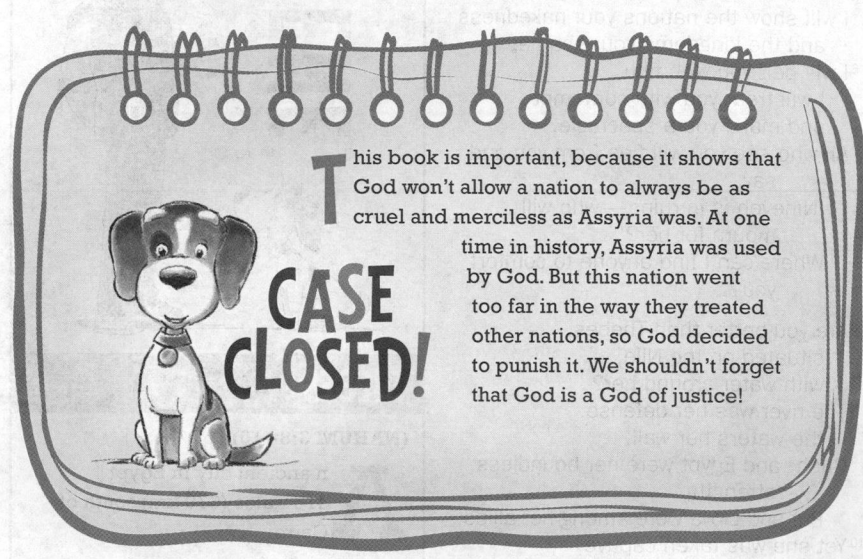

CASE CLOSED!

This book is important, because it shows that God won't allow a nation to always be as cruel and merciless as Assyria was. At one time in history, Assyria was used by God. But this nation went too far in the way they treated other nations, so God decided to punish it. We shouldn't forget that God is a God of justice!

HABAKKUK

THE EVIDENCE:

WHO WROTE IT?
This is another book where we don't know the author. Do you suppose it was Habakkuk himself?

HOW LONG AGO?
It was probably written at the end of the year 600 before Christ. According to the book, Habakkuk was preaching when the new Babylonian empire came into existence after the Assyrians were beaten. This big empire appeared in the year 626 or 625 before Christ. As a result, Habakkuk was preaching the word of God from 626 to 605 before Jesus.

WHAT'S IT ABOUT?
Habakkuk pleads with God to punish the evil of the people who live in Judah, because they don't respect God. God tells him that he's going to use the Babylonians to do that, but the Babylonians were even worse than the people in Judah! So God ends up punishing the Babylonians too!

THE BEST PART
We really liked this part: "The Sovereign LORD is my strength; he makes my feet like the feet of a deer, he enables me to tread on the heights" (3:19).

---

1 The prophecy that Habakkuk the prophet received.

Habakkuk's Complaint

2 How long, LORD, must I call for help,
   but you do not listen?
Or cry out to you, "Violence!"
   but you do not save?
3 Why do you make me look at injustice?
   Why do you tolerate wrongdoing?
Destruction and violence are before me;
   there is strife, and conflict abounds.
4 Therefore the law is paralyzed,
   and justice never prevails.
The wicked hem in the righteous,
   so that justice is perverted.

The LORD's Answer

5 "Look at the nations and watch—
   and be utterly amazed.
For I am going to do something in your days
   that you would not believe,
   even if you were told.
6 I am raising up the Babylonians,[a]
   that ruthless and impetuous people,
who sweep across the whole earth
   to seize dwellings not their own.

---

a 6 Or Chaldeans

THE
WITNESSES

✓ **HABAKKUK** (HABAKKUK 1:1)
This name comes from the Hebrew word that means "hug." We don't know very much about Habakkuk. He's called "prophet" in this book. He was probably a priest from the tribe of Levi.

⁷ They are a feared and dreaded
    people;
   they are a law to themselves
   and promote their own honor.
⁸ Their horses are swifter than leopards,
   fiercer than wolves at dusk.
   Their cavalry gallops headlong;
   their horsemen come from afar.
   They fly like an eagle swooping to
    devour;
⁹ they all come intent on violence.
   Their hordes*a* advance like a desert
    wind
   and gather prisoners like sand.
¹⁰ They mock kings
   and scoff at rulers.

They laugh at all fortified cities;
   by building earthen ramps they
    capture them.
¹¹ Then they sweep past like the wind
   and go on—
   guilty people, whose own strength is
    their god."

Habakkuk's Second Complaint

¹² Lord, are you not from everlasting?
   My God, my Holy One, you*b* will
    never die.
   You, Lord, have appointed them to
    execute judgment;
   you, my Rock, have ordained them
    to punish.
¹³ Your eyes are too pure to look on
    evil;
   you cannot tolerate wrongdoing.

---

a 9 The meaning of the Hebrew for this word is uncertain.
b 12 An ancient Hebrew scribal tradition; Masoretic Text we

BREAK THROUGH!

Why does he talk about God destroying and creating strife?

(HABAKKUK 1:3)
He was speaking the way people thought and spoke then. It isn't that God likes to kill and destroy. But that was the language the people understood, and the way they talked then.

Why then do you tolerate the
treacherous?
Why are you silent while the wicked
swallow up those more righteous
than themselves?
¹⁴You have made people like the fish in
the sea,
like the sea creatures that have no
ruler.
¹⁵The wicked foe pulls all of them up
with hooks,
he catches them in his net,
he gathers them up in his dragnet;
and so he rejoices and is glad.
¹⁶Therefore he sacrifices to his net
and burns incense to his
dragnet,
for by his net he lives in luxury
and enjoys the choicest food.
¹⁷Is he to keep on emptying his net,
destroying nations without mercy?

2 I will stand at my watch
and station myself on the ramparts;
I will look to see what he will say
to me,
and what answer I am to give to this
complaint.ᵃ

The Lᴏʀᴅ's Answer

²Then the Lᴏʀᴅ replied:

"Write down the revelation
and make it plain on tablets
so that a heraldᵇ may run with it.
³For the revelation awaits an appointed
time;
it speaks of the end
and will not prove false.
Though it linger, wait for it;
itᶜ will certainly come
and will not delay.

⁴"See, the enemy is puffed up;
his desires are not upright—
but the righteous person will live by
his faithfulnessᵈ—
⁵indeed, wine betrays him;
he is arrogant and never at rest.
Because he is as greedy as the
grave
and like death is never satisfied,
he gathers to himself all the nations
and takes captive all the peoples.

⁶"Will not all of them taunt him with ridicule and scorn, saying,

" 'Woe to him who piles up stolen
goods
and makes himself wealthy by
extortion!
How long must this go on?'
⁷Will not your creditors suddenly
arise?
Will they not wake up and make you
tremble?
Then you will become their prey.
⁸Because you have plundered many
nations,
the peoples who are left will plunder
you.
For you have shed human blood;
you have destroyed lands and cities
and everyone in them.

⁹"Woe to him who builds his house by
unjust gain,
setting his nest on high
to escape the clutches of ruin!
¹⁰You have plotted the ruin of many
peoples,
shaming your own house and
forfeiting your life.
¹¹The stones of the wall will cry out,
and the beams of the woodwork will
echo it.

¹²"Woe to him who builds a city with
bloodshed
and establishes a town by injustice!
¹³Has not the Lᴏʀᴅ Almighty determined
that the people's labor is only fuel
for the fire,
that the nations exhaust
themselves for nothing?
¹⁴For the earth will be filled with the
knowledge of the glory of the
Lᴏʀᴅ
as the waters cover the sea.

¹⁵"Woe to him who gives drink to his
neighbors,
pouring it from the wineskin till they
are drunk,
so that he can gaze on their naked
bodies!

ᵃ 1 Or and what to answer when I am rebuked   ᵇ 2 Or so
that whoever reads it   ᶜ 3 Or Though he linger, wait for
him; / he   ᵈ 4 Or faith

THE SCENE

REGION OF TEMAN

(HABAKKUK 3:3)

It was in Edom, but we don't know exactly where.

16 You will be filled with shame instead
   of glory.
   Now it is your turn! Drink and let
      your nakedness be exposed[a]!
   The cup from the LORD's right hand is
      coming around to you,
   and disgrace will cover your glory.
17 The violence you have done to
      Lebanon will overwhelm you,
   and your destruction of animals will
      terrify you.
   For you have shed human blood;
      you have destroyed lands and cities
      and everyone in them.

18 "Of what value is an idol carved by a
      craftsman?
   Or an image that teaches lies?
   For the one who makes it trusts in his
      own creation;
   he makes idols that cannot
      speak.
19 Woe to him who says to wood, 'Come
      to life!'
   Or to lifeless stone, 'Wake up!'

Can it give guidance?
   It is covered with gold and silver;
   there is no breath in it."

20 The LORD is in his holy temple;
   let all the earth be silent before
      him.

Habakkuk's Prayer

3 A prayer of Habakkuk the prophet. On
   shigionoth.[b]

2 LORD, I have heard of your fame;
   I stand in awe of your deeds, LORD.
   Repeat them in our day,
      in our time make them known;
   in wrath remember mercy.

3 God came from Teman,
   the Holy One from Mount Paran.[c]

---

a 16 Masoretic Text; Dead Sea Scrolls, Aquila, Vulgate and
Syriac (see also Septuagint) *and stagger*   *b 1* Probably
a literary or musical term   *c 3* The Hebrew has *Selah*
(a word of uncertain meaning) here and at the middle of
verse 9 and at the end of verse 13.

THE SCENE

MOUNT PARAN

(HABAKKUK 3:3)

A mountainous region north of Mount Sinai, where the Israelites camped when they were traveling to the promised land.

His glory covered the heavens
  and his praise filled the earth.
⁴His splendor was like the sunrise;
  rays flashed from his hand,
  where his power was hidden.
⁵Plague went before him;
  pestilence followed his steps.
⁶He stood, and shook the earth;
  he looked, and made the nations
    tremble.
The ancient mountains crumbled
  and the age-old hills collapsed—
  but he marches on forever.
⁷I saw the tents of Cushan in distress,
  the dwellings of Midian in
    anguish.

⁸Were you angry with the rivers, Lᴏʀᴅ?
  Was your wrath against the
    streams?
Did you rage against the sea
  when you rode your horses
  and your chariots to victory?
⁹You uncovered your bow,
  you called for many arrows.
You split the earth with rivers;
¹⁰ the mountains saw you and
    writhed.
Torrents of water swept by;
  the deep roared
  and lifted its waves on high.

¹¹Sun and moon stood still in the
    heavens
  at the glint of your flying arrows,
  at the lightning of your flashing
    spear.
¹²In wrath you strode through the earth
  and in anger you threshed the
    nations.
¹³You came out to deliver your people,
  to save your anointed one.
You crushed the leader of the land of
    wickedness,
  you stripped him from head to
    foot.
¹⁴With his own spear you pierced his
    head
  when his warriors stormed out to
    scatter us,
gloating as though about to devour
  the wretched who were in hiding.
¹⁵You trampled the sea with your
    horses,
  churning the great waters.

¹⁶I heard and my heart pounded,
  my lips quivered at the sound;
decay crept into my bones,
  and my legs trembled.
Yet I will wait patiently for the day of
    calamity
  to come on the nation invading us.

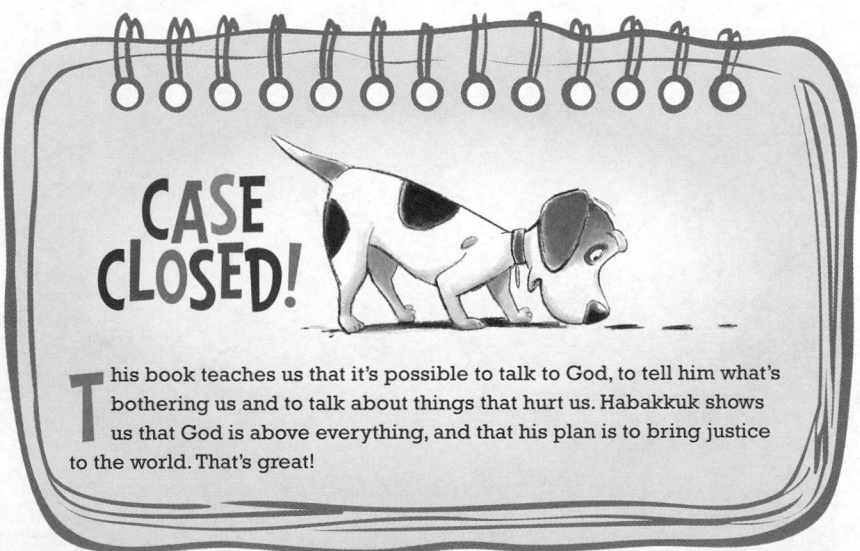

CASE CLOSED!

This book teaches us that it's possible to talk to God, to tell him what's bothering us and to talk about things that hurt us. Habakkuk shows us that God is above everything, and that his plan is to bring justice to the world. That's great!

¹⁷ Though the fig tree does not bud
    and there are no grapes on the vines,
  though the olive crop fails
    and the fields produce no food,
  though there are no sheep in the pen
    and no cattle in the stalls,
¹⁸ yet I will rejoice in the LORD,
    I will be joyful in God my Savior.

¹⁹ The Sovereign LORD is my strength;
    he makes my feet like the feet of a
    deer,
  he enables me to tread on the
    heights.

For the director of music. On my
  stringed instruments.

ZEPHANIAH

THE EVIDENCE:

WHO WROTE IT?
We don't know who wrote the book of Zephaniah.

HOW LONG AGO?
It was probably written at the end of the year 600 before Christ. By the time Zephaniah was preaching the word of God, the Assyrians had destroyed the northern kingdom and its capital city, Samaria. That's why he talks to the people in the southern kingdom (Judah).

WHAT'S IT ABOUT?
Zephaniah speaks for God, and he says punishment is coming for everybody. That punishment will come one day, and that will be the day God shows his anger. Only the people who look for God to protect them will escape God's day of punishment.

THE BEST PART
We think that the most important part of this book is in chapter 2, verse 3: "Seek the LORD, all you humble of the land, you who do what he commands. Seek righteousness, seek humility; perhaps you will be sheltered on the day of the LORD's anger."

---

1 The word of the LORD that came to Zephaniah son of Cushi, the son of Gedaliah, the son of Amariah, the son of Hezekiah, during the reign of Josiah son of Amon king of Judah:

Judgment on the Whole Earth in the Day of the LORD

² "I will sweep away everything
   from the face of the earth,"
                declares the LORD.
³ "I will sweep away both man and
      beast;
   I will sweep away the birds in the
      sky
   and the fish in the sea—
   and the idols that cause the wicked
      to stumble."[a]

"When I destroy all mankind
   on the face of the earth,"
                declares the LORD,
⁴ "I will stretch out my hand against
      Judah
   and against all who live in
      Jerusalem.
I will destroy every remnant of Baal
      worship in this place,
   the very names of the idolatrous
      priests—
⁵ those who bow down on the roofs
   to worship the starry host,
   those who bow down and swear by the
      LORD
   and who also swear by Molek,[b]

---

^a 3 The meaning of the Hebrew for this line is uncertain.
^b 5 Hebrew *Malkam*

The Lord has prepared a
    sacrifice;
  he has consecrated those he has
    invited.

⁸ "On the day of the Lord's sacrifice
  I will punish the officials
    and the king's sons
  and all those clad
    in foreign clothes.
⁹ On that day I will punish
  all who avoid stepping on the
    threshold,ᵃ
  who fill the temple of their gods
    with violence and deceit.

¹⁰ "On that day,"
    declares the Lord,
  "a cry will go up from the Fish
    Gate,
  wailing from the New Quarter,
    and a loud crash from the hills.
¹¹ Wail, you who live in the market
    districtᵇ;
  all your merchants will be wiped
    out,
  all who trade withᶜ silver will be
    destroyed.
¹² At that time I will search Jerusalem
    with lamps
  and punish those who are
    complacent,
  who are like wine left on its
    dregs,
  who think, 'The Lord will do nothing,
    either good or bad.'
¹³ Their wealth will be plundered,
    their houses demolished.
  Though they build houses,
    they will not live in them;
  though they plant vineyards,
    they will not drink the wine."

¹⁴ The great day of the Lord is near—
    near and coming quickly.
  The cry on the day of the Lord is
    bitter;
  the Mighty Warrior shouts his battle
    cry.
¹⁵ That day will be a day of wrath—
    a day of distress and anguish,
    a day of trouble and ruin,

THE
WITNESSES

✓ ZEPHANIAH (ZEPHANIAH 1:1)
This name means "God has hidden it." Maybe
it refers to God protecting him during the
reign of Manasseh, a very bad and violent
king. Zephaniah includes a list of his ancestors.
(We think he may have wanted to show that he
was related to the king's family.)

✓ JOSIAH SON OF AMON KING
OF JUDAH (ZEPHANIAH 1:1)
Josiah was the last good king of Judah. He
probably ruled between the years 640 and
609 before Christ.

⁶ those who turn back from following
    the Lord
  and neither seek the Lord nor
    inquire of him."

⁷ Be silent before the Sovereign
    Lord,
  for the day of the Lord is
    near.

ᵃ 9 See 1 Samuel 5:5.   ᵇ 11 Or the Mortar
ᶜ 11 Or in

Molek
(ZEPHANIAH 1:5)
Molek was a Canaanite god who was worshiped a lot in Ammon. He was a false god.

a day of darkness and gloom,
  a day of clouds and blackness—
¹⁶ a day of trumpet and battle
    cry
against the fortified cities
  and against the corner towers.

¹⁷ "I will bring such distress on all
    people
  that they will grope about like those
    who are blind,
because they have sinned against
    the LORD.
Their blood will be poured out like
    dust
  and their entrails like dung.
¹⁸ Neither their silver nor their
    gold
  will be able to save them
on the day of the LORD's
    wrath."

In the fire of his jealousy
  the whole earth will be
    consumed,
for he will make a sudden end
  of all who live on the earth.

Judah and Jerusalem Judged Along With the Nations
Judah Summoned to Repent
2 Gather together, gather yourselves
    together,
  you shameful nation,
² before the decree takes effect
  and that day passes like windblown
    chaff,
before the LORD's fierce anger
  comes upon you,
before the day of the LORD's wrath
  comes upon you.
³ Seek the LORD, all you humble of the
    land,
  you who do what he commands.
Seek righteousness, seek humility;
  perhaps you will be sheltered
  on the day of the LORD's anger.

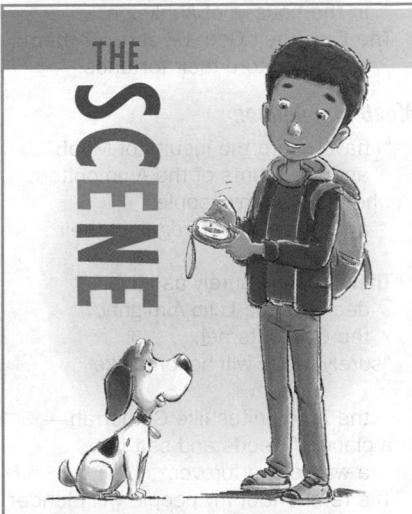

FISH GATE AND NEW QUARTER
(ZEPHANIAH 1:10–11)

Fish Gate was the name of one of the entrances into the city of Jerusalem. It got that name because there was a fish market there. We don't know much about the New Quarter.

Philistia

4 Gaza will be abandoned
and Ashkelon left in ruins.
At midday Ashdod will be emptied
and Ekron uprooted.
5 Woe to you who live by the sea,
you Kerethite people;
the word of the LORD is against you,
Canaan, land of the Philistines.
He says, "I will destroy you,
and none will be left."
6 The land by the sea will become
pastures
having wells for shepherds
and pens for flocks.
7 That land will belong
to the remnant of the people of
Judah;
there they will find pasture.
In the evening they will lie down
in the houses of Ashkelon.
The LORD their God will care for them;
he will restore their fortunes.[a]

Moab and Ammon

8 "I have heard the insults of Moab
and the taunts of the Ammonites,
who insulted my people
and made threats against their
land.
9 Therefore, as surely as I live,"
declares the LORD Almighty,
the God of Israel,
"surely Moab will become like
Sodom,
the Ammonites like Gomorrah—
a place of weeds and salt pits,
a wasteland forever.
The remnant of my people will plunder
them;
the survivors of my nation will
inherit their land."

10 This is what they will get in return for
their pride,
for insulting and mocking
the people of the LORD Almighty.
11 The LORD will be awesome to them
when he destroys all the gods of
the earth.
Distant nations will bow down to
him,
all of them in their own lands.

Cush

12 "You Cushites,[b] too,
will be slain by my sword."

Assyria

13 He will stretch out his hand against
the north
and destroy Assyria,
leaving Nineveh utterly desolate
and dry as the desert.
14 Flocks and herds will lie down there,
creatures of every kind.
The desert owl and the screech owl
will roost on her columns.
Their hooting will echo through the
windows,
rubble will fill the doorways,
the beams of cedar will be exposed.
15 This is the city of revelry
that lived in safety.
She said to herself,
"I am the one! And there is none
besides me."
What a ruin she has become,
a lair for wild beasts!
All who pass by her scoff
and shake their fists.

Jerusalem

3 Woe to the city of oppressors,
rebellious and defiled!
2 She obeys no one,
she accepts no correction.
She does not trust in the LORD,
she does not draw near to her God.
3 Her officials within her
are roaring lions;
her rulers are evening wolves,
who leave nothing for the morning.
4 Her prophets are unprincipled;
they are treacherous people.
Her priests profane the sanctuary
and do violence to the law.
5 The LORD within her is righteous;
he does no wrong.
Morning by morning he dispenses his
justice,
and every new day he does not fail,
yet the unrighteous know no
shame.

---

a 7 Or will bring back their captives   b 12 That is, people
from the upper Nile region

Jerusalem Remains Unrepentant

6 "I have destroyed nations;
   their strongholds are demolished.
I have left their streets deserted,
   with no one passing through.
Their cities are laid waste;
   they are deserted and empty.
7 Of Jerusalem I thought,
   'Surely you will fear me
   and accept correction!'
Then her place of refuge*a* would not
   be destroyed,
   nor all my punishments come upon*b*
   her.
But they were still eager
   to act corruptly in all they did.
8 Therefore wait for me,"
   declares the LORD,
   "for the day I will stand up to
   testify.*c*
I have decided to assemble the
   nations,
   to gather the kingdoms
and to pour out my wrath on them—
   all my fierce anger.
The whole world will be consumed
   by the fire of my jealous anger.

Restoration of Israel's Remnant

9 "Then I will purify the lips of the
   peoples,

that all of them may call on the
   name of the LORD
and serve him shoulder to shoulder.
10 From beyond the rivers of Cush*d*
   my worshipers, my scattered
   people,
   will bring me offerings.
11 On that day you, Jerusalem, will not be
   put to shame
   for all the wrongs you have done
   to me,
because I will remove from you
   your arrogant boasters.
Never again will you be haughty
   on my holy hill.
12 But I will leave within you
   the meek and humble.
The remnant of Israel
   will trust in the name of the LORD.
13 They will do no wrong;
   they will tell no lies.
A deceitful tongue
   will not be found in their mouths.
They will eat and lie down
   and no one will make them
   afraid."

14 Sing, Daughter Zion;
   shout aloud, Israel!

---

a 7 Or *her sanctuary*   *b* 7 Or *all those I appointed over*
c 8 Septuagint and Syriac; Hebrew *will rise up to plunder*
d 10 That is, the upper Nile region

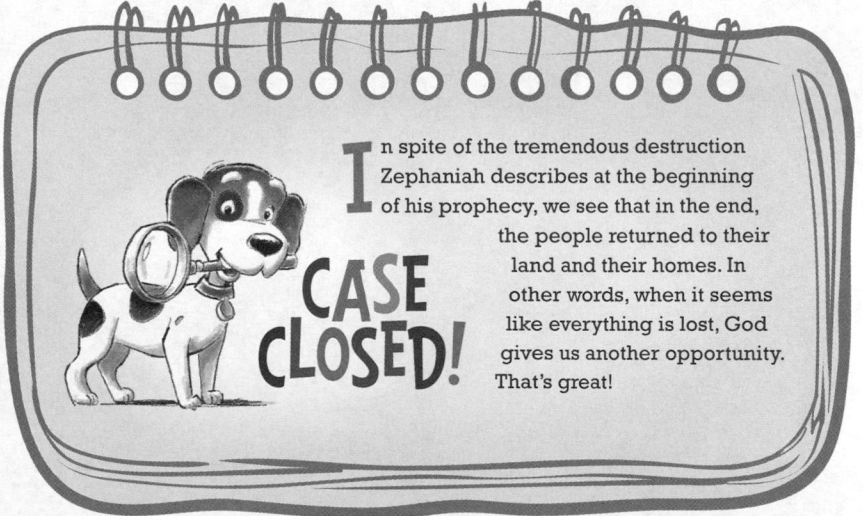

In spite of the tremendous destruction Zephaniah describes at the beginning of his prophecy, we see that in the end, the people returned to their land and their homes. In other words, when it seems like everything is lost, God gives us another opportunity. That's great!

CASE CLOSED!

Be glad and rejoice with all your
heart,
Daughter Jerusalem!
15 The Lord has taken away your
punishment,
he has turned back your enemy.
The Lord, the King of Israel, is with
you;
never again will you fear any
harm.
16 On that day
they will say to Jerusalem,
"Do not fear, Zion;
do not let your hands hang
limp.
17 The Lord your God is with you,
the Mighty Warrior who saves.
He will take great delight in you;
in his love he will no longer rebuke
you,
but will rejoice over you with
singing."

18 "I will remove from you
all who mourn over the loss of your
appointed festivals,
which is a burden and reproach for
you.
19 At that time I will deal
with all who oppressed you.
I will rescue the lame;
I will gather the exiles.
I will give them praise and honor
in every land where they have
suffered shame.
20 At that time I will gather you;
at that time I will bring you home.
I will give you honor and praise
among all the peoples of the
earth
when I restore your fortunes[a]
before your very eyes,"
says the Lord.

---

[a] 20 Or *I bring back your captives*

HAGGAI

THE EVIDENCE:

WHO WROTE IT?
We don't know.

HOW LONG AGO?
Haggai spoke God's message in the year 520 before Christ. It was probably written a little later, maybe at the end of the 6th century (500s) before Christ.

WHAT'S IT ABOUT?
Haggai stated the word of God in the city of Jerusalem. The people of God had returned from Babylon and they weren't slaves anymore. Now they needed to rebuild the temple of God, but they were more interested in rebuilding their own houses. Haggai scolds them, and he encourages them.

THE BEST PART
We love the part where God says, "This is what I covenanted with you when you came out of Egypt. And my Spirit remains among you. Do not fear" (2:5).

A Call to Build the House of the LORD

1 In the second year of King Darius, on the first day of the sixth month, the word of the LORD came through the prophet Haggai to Zerubbabel son of Shealtiel, governor of Judah, and to Joshua son of Jozadak,[a] the high priest:

² This is what the LORD Almighty says: "These people say, 'The time has not yet come to rebuild the LORD's house.' "

³ Then the word of the LORD came through the prophet Haggai: ⁴ "Is it a time for you yourselves to be living in your paneled houses, while this house remains a ruin?"

⁵ Now this is what the LORD Almighty says: "Give careful thought to your ways. ⁶ You have planted much, but harvested little. You eat, but never have enough. You drink, but never have your fill. You put on clothes, but are not warm. You earn wages, only to put them in a purse with holes in it."

⁷ This is what the LORD Almighty says: "Give careful thought to your ways. ⁸ Go up into the mountains and bring down timber and build my house, so that I may take pleasure in it and be honored," says the LORD. ⁹ "You expected much, but see, it turned out to be little. What you brought home, I blew away. Why?" declares the LORD Almighty. "Because of my house, which remains a ruin, while each of you is busy with your own house. ¹⁰ Therefore, because of you the heavens have withheld their dew and the earth its crops. ¹¹ I called for a drought on the fields and

---

a 1 Hebrew *Jehozadak*, a variant of *Jozadak*; also in verses 12 and 14

THE
WITNESSES

✓ **KING DARIUS** (HAGGAI 1:1)
Darius was the king of Persia. He was probably the king who put back into place King Cyrus' ruling that allowed the Israelite slaves in Babylon to go back to their land and homes and to be able to rebuild the temple.

✓ **HAGGAI** (HAGGAI 1:1)
He was a prophet of God. His name probably means that he was born on a Jewish holiday.

✓ **ZERUBBABEL SON OF SHEALTIEL** (HAGGAI 1:1)
His name means "seed of Babel." He was king of Judah. He paid attention to Haggai's message, and he worked hard at rebuilding God's temple.

✓ **JOSHUA SON OF JOZADAK** (HAGGAI 1:1)
He was the high priest of the people who returned from Babylon, where they were slaves.

the mountains, on the grain, the new wine, the olive oil and everything else the ground produces, on people and livestock, and on all the labor of your hands."

¹²Then Zerubbabel son of Shealtiel, Joshua son of Jozadak, the high priest, and the whole remnant of the people obeyed the voice of the Lᴏʀᴅ their God and the message of the prophet Haggai, because the Lᴏʀᴅ their God had sent him. And the people feared the Lᴏʀᴅ. ¹³Then Haggai, the Lᴏʀᴅ's messenger, gave this message of the Lᴏʀᴅ to the people: "I am with you," declares the Lᴏʀᴅ. ¹⁴So the Lᴏʀᴅ stirred up the spirit of Zerubbabel son of Shealtiel, governor of Judah, and the spirit of Joshua son of Jozadak, the high priest, and the spirit of the whole remnant of the people. They came and began to work on the house of the Lᴏʀᴅ Almighty, their God, ¹⁵on the twenty-fourth day of the sixth month.

The Promised Glory of the New House

In the second year of King Darius, **2** ¹on the twenty-first day of the seventh month, the word of the Lᴏʀᴅ came through the prophet Haggai: ²"Speak to Zerubbabel son of Shealtiel, governor of Judah, to Joshua son of Jozadak,ᵃ the high priest, and to the remnant of the people. Ask them, ³'Who of you is left who saw this house in its former glory? How does it look to you now? Does it not seem to you like nothing? ⁴But now be strong, Zerubbabel,' declares the Lᴏʀᴅ. 'Be strong, Joshua son of Jozadak, the high priest. Be strong, all you people of the land,' declares the Lᴏʀᴅ, 'and work. For I am with you,' declares the Lᴏʀᴅ Almighty. ⁵'This is what I covenanted with you when you came out of Egypt. And my Spirit remains among you. Do not fear.'

⁶"This is what the Lᴏʀᴅ Almighty says: 'In a little while I will once more shake the heavens and the earth, the sea and the dry land. ⁷I will shake all nations, and what is desired by all nations will come,

---

ᵃ 2 Hebrew *Jehozadak*, a variant of *Jozadak*; also in verse 4 mighty. ⁹'The glory of this present house will be greater than the glory of the former house,' says the LORD Almighty. 'And in this place I will grant peace,' declares the LORD Almighty."

Blessings for a Defiled People

¹⁰On the twenty-fourth day of the ninth month, in the second year of Darius, the word of the LORD came to the prophet Haggai: ¹¹"This is what the LORD Almighty says: 'Ask the priests what the law says: ¹²If someone carries consecrated meat in the fold of their garment, and that fold touches some bread or stew, some wine, olive oil or other food, does it become consecrated?' "

The priests answered, "No."

¹³Then Haggai said, "If a person defiled by contact with a dead body touches one of these things, does it become defiled?"

"Yes," the priests replied, "it becomes defiled."

¹⁴Then Haggai said, " 'So it is with this people and this nation in my sight,' declares the LORD. 'Whatever they do and whatever they offer there is defiled.

¹⁵" 'Now give careful thought to this from this day on*ᵃ*— consider how things

ᵃ 15 Or to the days past

BREAK THROUGH!

What "house in its former glory" are they talking about?

(HAGGAI 2:3)

The temple that Solomon had built when he was king of Israel.

and I will fill this house with glory,' says the LORD Almighty. ⁸'The silver is mine and the gold is mine,' declares the LORD Al-

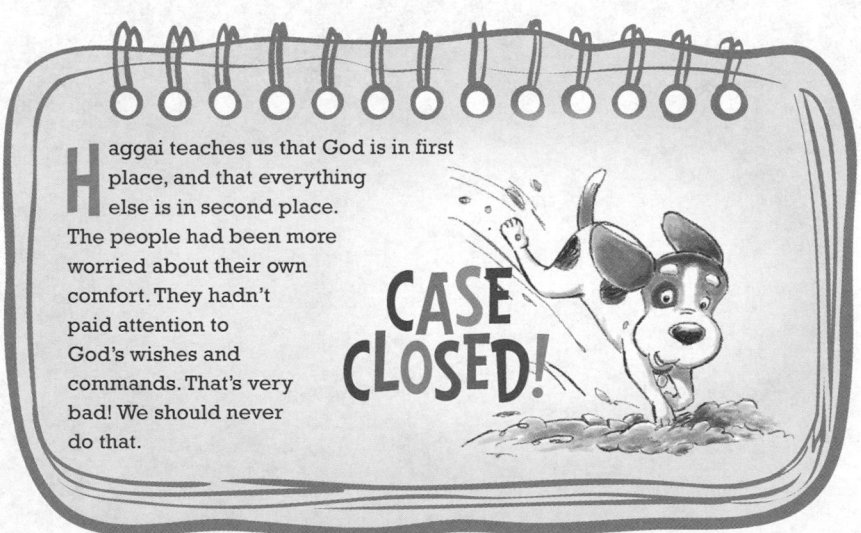

Haggai teaches us that God is in first place, and that everything else is in second place. The people had been more worried about their own comfort. They hadn't paid attention to God's wishes and commands. That's very bad! We should never do that.

CASE CLOSED!

were before one stone was laid on another in the LORD's temple. [16]When anyone came to a heap of twenty measures, there were only ten. When anyone went to a wine vat to draw fifty measures, there were only twenty. [17]I struck all the work of your hands with blight, mildew and hail, yet you did not return to me,' declares the LORD. [18]'From this day on, from this twenty-fourth day of the ninth month, give careful thought to the day when the foundation of the LORD's temple was laid. Give careful thought: [19]Is there yet any seed left in the barn? Until now, the vine and the fig tree, the pomegranate and the olive tree have not borne fruit.

" 'From this day on I will bless you.' "

Zerubbabel the LORD's Signet Ring

[20]The word of the LORD came to Haggai a second time on the twenty-fourth day of the month: [21]"Tell Zerubbabel governor of Judah that I am going to shake the heavens and the earth. [22]I will overturn royal thrones and shatter the power of the foreign kingdoms. I will overthrow chariots and their drivers; horses and their riders will fall, each by the sword of his brother.

[23]" 'On that day,' declares the LORD Almighty, 'I will take you, my servant Zerubbabel son of Shealtiel,' declares the LORD, 'and I will make you like my signet ring, for I have chosen you,' declares the LORD Almighty."

ZECHARIAH

THE EVIDENCE:

WHO WROTE IT?
It was probably written by Zechariah and some of his disciples.

HOW LONG AGO?
Zechariah says that God spoke to him during the second year of the reign of Darius the Persian. So that was during the year 520 before Christ. The part that Zechariah may have written was done in the 6th century (500s) before Christ and the rest was written by his disciples in the 2nd (100s) century before Christ.

WHAT'S IT ABOUT?
God sends visions to Zechariah. He tells him to warn the people and tell them to repent and obey him. If they did that, God would help so they could rebuild the temple and the city of Jerusalem as well.

THE BEST PART
We like 1:17, because there you can see how much God loved his city: "My towns will again overflow with prosperity, and the LORD will again comfort Zion and choose Jerusalem."

A Call to Return to the LORD

1 In the eighth month of the second year of Darius, the word of the LORD came to the prophet Zechariah son of Berekiah, the son of Iddo:

2 "The LORD was very angry with your ancestors. 3Therefore tell the people: This is what the LORD Almighty says: 'Return to me,' declares the LORD Almighty, 'and I will return to you,' says the LORD Almighty. 4Do not be like your ancestors, to whom the earlier prophets proclaimed: This is what the LORD Almighty says: 'Turn from your evil ways and your evil practices.' But they would not listen or pay attention to me, declares the LORD. 5Where are your ancestors now? And the prophets, do they live forever? 6But did not my words and my decrees, which I commanded my servants the prophets, overtake your ancestors?

"Then they repented and said, 'The LORD Almighty has done to us what our ways and practices deserve, just as he determined to do.' "

The Man Among the Myrtle Trees

7On the twenty-fourth day of the eleventh month, the month of Shebat, in the second year of Darius, the word of the LORD came to the prophet Zechariah son of Berekiah, the son of Iddo.

THE
WITNESSES

✓ **ZECHARIAH** (ZECHARIAH 1:1)
His name means "God has remembered." He was a prophet of God.

⁸During the night I had a vision, and there before me was a man mounted on a red horse. He was standing among the myrtle trees in a ravine. Behind him were red, brown and white horses.

⁹I asked, "What are these, my lord?"

The angel who was talking with me answered, "I will show you what they are."

¹⁰Then the man standing among the myrtle trees explained, "They are the ones the LORD has sent to go throughout the earth."

¹¹And they reported to the angel of the LORD who was standing among the myrtle trees, "We have gone throughout the earth and found the whole world at rest and in peace."

¹²Then the angel of the LORD said, "LORD Almighty, how long will you withhold mercy from Jerusalem and from the towns of Judah, which you have been angry with these seventy years?" ¹³So the LORD spoke kind and comforting words to the angel who talked with me.

¹⁴Then the angel who was speaking to me said, "Proclaim this word: This is what the LORD Almighty says: 'I am very jealous for Jerusalem and Zion, ¹⁵and I am very angry with the nations that feel secure. I was only a little angry, but they went too far with the punishment.'

¹⁶"Therefore this is what the LORD says: 'I will return to Jerusalem with mercy, and there my house will be rebuilt. And the measuring line will be stretched out over Jerusalem,' declares the LORD Almighty.

¹⁷"Proclaim further: This is what the LORD Almighty says: 'My towns will again overflow with prosperity, and the LORD will again comfort Zion and choose Jerusalem.' "

Four Horns and Four Craftsmen

¹⁸Then I looked up, and there before me were four horns. ¹⁹I asked the angel who was speaking to me, "What are these?"

He answered me, "These are the horns that scattered Judah, Israel and Jerusalem."

²⁰Then the LORD showed me four craftsmen. ²¹I asked, "What are these coming to do?"

He answered, "These are the horns that scattered Judah so that no one could raise their head, but the craftsmen have come to terrify them and throw down these horns of the nations who lifted up their horns against the land of Judah to scatter its people."ᵃ

A Man With a Measuring Line

2ᵇ Then I looked up, and there before me was a man with a measuring line in his hand. ²I asked, "Where are you going?"

He answered me, "To measure Jerusalem, to find out how wide and how long it is."

ᵃ 21 In Hebrew texts 1:18-21 is numbered 2:1-4.   ᵇ In Hebrew texts 2:1-13 is numbered 2:5-17.

³While the angel who was speaking to me was leaving, another angel came to meet him ⁴and said to him: "Run, tell that young man, 'Jerusalem will be a city without walls because of the great number of people and animals in it. ⁵And I myself will be a wall of fire around it,' declares the Lord, 'and I will be its glory within.'

⁶"Come! Come! Flee from the land of the north," declares the Lord, "for I have scattered you to the four winds of heaven," declares the Lord.

⁷"Come, Zion! Escape, you who live in Daughter Babylon!" ⁸For this is what the Lord Almighty says: "After the Glorious One has sent me against the nations that have plundered you—for whoever touches you touches the apple of his eye— ⁹I will surely raise my hand against them so that their slaves will plunder them.ᵃ Then you will know that the Lord Almighty has sent me.

¹⁰"Shout and be glad, Daughter Zion. For I am coming, and I will live among you," declares the Lord. ¹¹"Many nations will be joined with the Lord in that day and will become my people. I will live among you and you will know that the Lord Almighty has sent me to you. ¹²The Lord will inherit Judah as his portion in the holy land and will again choose Jerusalem. ¹³Be still before the Lord, all mankind, because he has roused himself from his holy dwelling."

Clean Garments for the High Priest

3 Then he showed me Joshua the high priest standing before the angel of the Lord, and Satanᵇ standing at his right side to accuse him. ²The Lord said to Satan, "The Lord rebuke you, Satan! The Lord, who has chosen Jerusalem, rebuke you! Is not this man a burning stick snatched from the fire?"

³Now Joshua was dressed in filthy clothes as he stood before the angel. ⁴The angel said to those who were standing before him, "Take off his filthy clothes."

Then he said to Joshua, "See, I have taken away your sin, and I will put fine garments on you."

BREAKTHROUGH!

Will other nations also be God's people?

(ZECHARIAH 2:11)

Yes, even if it's hard to believe. Other nations will also be God's people. God will live among people. In other words, people will worship and recognize God. In that way, God will be present among them.

⁵Then I said, "Put a clean turban on his head." So they put a clean turban on his head and clothed him, while the angel of the Lord stood by.

⁶The angel of the Lord gave this charge to Joshua: ⁷"This is what the Lord Almighty says: 'If you will walk in obedience to me and keep my requirements, then you will govern my house and have charge of my courts, and I will give you a place among these standing here.

⁸"'Listen, High Priest Joshua, you and your associates seated before you, who are men symbolic of things to come: I am going to bring my servant, the Branch. ⁹See, the stone I have set in front of Joshua! There are seven eyesᶜ on that one stone, and I will engrave an inscription on it,' says the Lord Almighty, 'and I will remove the sin of this land in a single day.

ᵃ 8,9 Or says after . . . eye: ⁹"I . . . plunder them."
ᵇ 1 Hebrew satan means adversary.   ᶜ 9 Or facets

BREAKTHROUGH!

Did God's angel forgive Joshua's sin?

(ZECHARIAH 3:4)

God forgave Joshua's sin. God's angel took the place of God at that moment. He spoke in the name of God.

10 " 'In that day each of you will invite your neighbor to sit under your vine and fig tree,' declares the LORD Almighty."

The Gold Lampstand and the Two Olive Trees

4 Then the angel who talked with me returned and woke me up, like someone awakened from sleep. 2 He asked me, "What do you see?"

I answered, "I see a solid gold lampstand with a bowl at the top and seven lamps on it, with seven channels to the lamps. 3 Also there are two olive trees by it, one on the right of the bowl and the other on its left."

4 I asked the angel who talked with me, "What are these, my lord?"

5 He answered, "Do you not know what these are?"

"No, my lord," I replied.

6 So he said to me, "This is the word of the LORD to Zerubbabel: 'Not by might nor by power, but by my Spirit,' says the LORD Almighty.

7 "What are you, mighty mountain? Before Zerubbabel you will become level ground. Then he will bring out the capstone to shouts of 'God bless it! God bless it!' "

8 Then the word of the LORD came to me: 9 "The hands of Zerubbabel have laid the foundation of this temple; his hands will also complete it. Then you will know that the LORD Almighty has sent me to you.

10 "Who dares despise the day of small things, since the seven eyes of the LORD that range throughout the earth will rejoice when they see the chosen capstone[a] in the hand of Zerubbabel?"

11 Then I asked the angel, "What are these two olive trees on the right and the left of the lampstand?"

12 Again I asked him, "What are these two olive branches beside the two gold pipes that pour out golden oil?"

13 He replied, "Do you not know what these are?"

"No, my lord," I said.

14 So he said, "These are the two who are anointed to[b] serve the Lord of all the earth."

The Flying Scroll

5 I looked again, and there before me was a flying scroll.

2 He asked me, "What do you see?"

I answered, "I see a flying scroll, twenty cubits long and ten cubits wide.[c]"

3 And he said to me, "This is the curse that is going out over the whole land; for according to what it says on one side, every thief will be banished, and according to what it says on the other, everyone who swears falsely will be banished. 4 The LORD Almighty declares, 'I will send it out, and it will enter the house of the thief and the house of anyone who swears falsely by my name. It will remain in that house and destroy it completely, both its timbers and its stones.' "

The Woman in a Basket

5 Then the angel who was speaking to me came forward and said to me, "Look up and see what is appearing."

---

a 10 Or *the plumb line*   *b 14* Or *two who bring oil and*
c 2 That is, about 30 feet long and 15 feet wide or about 9 meters long and 4.5 meters wide

⁶I asked, "What is it?" He replied, "It is a basket." And he added, "This is the iniquity*ᵃ* of the people throughout the land."

⁷Then the cover of lead was raised, and there in the basket sat a woman! ⁸He said, "This is wickedness," and he pushed her back into the basket and pushed its lead cover down on it.

⁹Then I looked up—and there before me were two women, with the wind in their wings! They had wings like those of a stork, and they lifted up the basket between heaven and earth.

¹⁰"Where are they taking the basket?" I asked the angel who was speaking to me.

¹¹He replied, "To the country of Babylonia*ᵇ* to build a house for it. When the house is ready, the basket will be set there in its place."

Four Chariots

6 I looked up again, and there before me were four chariots coming out from between two mountains—mountains of bronze. ²The first chariot had red horses, the second black, ³the third white, and the fourth dappled—all of them powerful. ⁴I asked the angel who was speaking to me, "What are these, my lord?"

⁵The angel answered me, "These are the four spirits*ᶜ* of heaven, going out from standing in the presence of the Lord of the whole world. ⁶The one with the black horses is going toward the north country, the one with the white horses toward the west,*ᵈ* and the one with the dappled horses toward the south."

⁷When the powerful horses went out, they were straining to go throughout the earth. And he said, "Go throughout the earth!" So they went throughout the earth.

⁸Then he called to me, "Look, those going toward the north country have given my Spirit*ᵉ* rest in the land of the north."

A Crown for Joshua

⁹The word of the Lord came to me: ¹⁰"Take silver and gold from the exiles Heldai, Tobijah and Jedaiah, who have arrived from Babylon. Go the same day to the house of Josiah son of Zephaniah. ¹¹Take the silver and gold and make a crown, and set it on the head of the high priest, Joshua son of Jozadak.*ᶠ* ¹²Tell him this is what the Lord Almighty says: 'Here is the man whose name is the Branch, and he will branch out from his place and build the temple of the Lord. ¹³It is he who will build the temple of the Lord, and he will be clothed with majesty and will sit and rule on his throne. And he*ᵍ* will be a priest on his throne. And there will be harmony between the two.' ¹⁴The crown will be given to Heldai,*ʰ* Tobijah, Jedaiah and Hen*ⁱ* son of Zephaniah as a memorial in the temple of the Lord. ¹⁵Those who are far away will come and help to build the temple of the Lord, and you will know that the Lord Almighty has sent me to you. This will happen if you diligently obey the Lord your God."

Justice and Mercy, Not Fasting

7 In the fourth year of King Darius, the word of the Lord came to Zechariah on the fourth day of the ninth month, the month of Kislev. ²The people of Bethel had sent Sharezer and Regem-Melek, together with their men, to entreat the Lord ³by asking the priests of the house of the Lord Almighty and the prophets, "Should I mourn and fast in the fifth month, as I have done for so many years?"

⁴Then the word of the Lord Almighty came to me: ⁵"Ask all the people of the land and the priests, 'When you fasted and mourned in the fifth and seventh months for the past seventy years, was it really for me that you fasted? ⁶And when you were eating and drinking, were you not just feasting for yourselves? ⁷Are these not the words the Lord proclaimed through the earlier prophets when Jerusalem and its surrounding towns were at rest and prosperous, and the Negev and the western foothills were settled?' "

⁸And the word of the Lord came again to Zechariah: ⁹"This is what the Lord Almighty said: 'Administer true justice;

ᵃ 6 Or appearance   ᵇ 11 Hebrew Shinar   ᶜ 5 Or winds   ᵈ 6 Or horses after them   ᵉ 8 Or spirit   ᶠ 11 Hebrew Jehozadak, a variant of Jozadak   ᵍ 13 Or there   ʰ 14 Syriac; Hebrew Helem   ⁱ 14 Or and the gracious one, the show mercy and compassion to one another. ¹⁰Do not oppress the widow or the fatherless, the foreigner or the poor. Do not plot evil against each other.'

¹¹"But they refused to pay attention; stubbornly they turned their backs and covered their ears. ¹²They made their hearts as hard as flint and would not listen to the law or to the words that the LORD Almighty had sent by his Spirit through the earlier prophets. So the LORD Almighty was very angry.

¹³" 'When I called, they did not listen; so when they called, I would not listen,' says the LORD Almighty. ¹⁴'I scattered them with a whirlwind among all the nations, where they were strangers. The land they left behind them was so desolate that no one traveled through it. This is how they made the pleasant land desolate.' "

The LORD Promises to Bless Jerusalem

8 The word of the LORD Almighty came to me. ²This is what the LORD Almighty says: "I am very jealous for Zion; I am burning with jealousy for her."

³This is what the LORD says: "I will return to Zion and dwell in Jerusalem. Then Jerusalem will be called the Faithful City, and the mountain of the LORD Almighty will be called the Holy Mountain."

⁴This is what the LORD Almighty says: "Once again men and women of ripe old age will sit in the streets of Jerusalem, each of them with cane in hand because of their age. ⁵The city streets will be filled with boys and girls playing there."

⁶This is what the LORD Almighty says: "It may seem marvelous to the remnant of this people at that time, but will it seem marvelous to me?" declares the LORD Almighty.

⁷This is what the LORD Almighty says: "I will save my people from the countries of the east and the west. ⁸I will bring them back to live in Jerusalem; they will be my people, and I will be faithful and righteous to them as their God."

⁹This is what the LORD Almighty says: "Now hear these words, 'Let your hands be strong so that the temple may be built.' This is also what the prophets said who were present when the foundation was laid for the house of the LORD Almighty. ¹⁰Before that time there were no wages for people or hire for animals. No one could go about their business safely because of their enemies, since I had turned everyone against their neighbor. ¹¹But now I will not deal with the remnant of this people as I did in the past," declares the LORD Almighty.

¹²"The seed will grow well, the vine will yield its fruit, the ground will produce its crops, and the heavens will drop their dew. I will give all these things as an inheritance to the remnant of this people. ¹³Just as you, Judah and Israel, have been a curse*ᵃ* among the nations, so I will save you, and you will be a blessing.*ᵇ* Do not be afraid, but let your hands be strong."

¹⁴This is what the LORD Almighty says: "Just as I had determined to bring disaster on you and showed no pity when your ancestors angered me," says the LORD Almighty, ¹⁵"so now I have determined to do good again to Jerusalem and Judah. Do not be afraid. ¹⁶These are the things you are to do: Speak the truth to each other, and render true and sound judgment in your courts; ¹⁷do not plot evil against each other, and do not love to swear falsely. I hate all this," declares the LORD.

¹⁸The word of the LORD Almighty came to me. ¹⁹This is what the LORD Almighty says: "The fasts of the fourth, fifth, seventh and tenth months will become joyful and glad occasions and happy festivals for Judah. Therefore love truth and peace."

²⁰This is what the LORD Almighty says: "Many peoples and the inhabitants of many cities will yet come, ²¹and the inhabitants of one city will go to another and say, 'Let us go at once to entreat the LORD and seek the LORD Almighty. I myself am going.' ²²And many peoples and powerful nations will come to Jerusalem to seek the LORD Almighty and to entreat him."

ᵃ 13 That is, your name has been used in cursing (see Jer. 29:22); or, you have been regarded as under a curse.
ᵇ 13 Or *and your name will be used in blessings* (see Gen. 48:20); or *and you will be seen as blessed*

²³This is what the LORD Almighty says: "In those days ten people from all languages and nations will take firm hold of one Jew by the hem of his robe and say, 'Let us go with you, because we have heard that God is with you.' "

Judgment on Israel's Enemies

9 A prophecy:

The word of the LORD is against the
land of Hadrak
and will come to rest on
Damascus—
for the eyes of all people and all the
tribes of Israel
are on the LORD—ᵃ
²and on Hamath too, which borders
on it,
and on Tyre and Sidon, though they
are very skillful.
³Tyre has built herself a stronghold;
she has heaped up silver like
dust,
and gold like the dirt of the
streets.
⁴But the Lord will take away her
possessions
and destroy her power on the sea,
and she will be consumed by fire.
⁵Ashkelon will see it and fear;
Gaza will writhe in agony,
and Ekron too, for her hope will
wither.
Gaza will lose her king
and Ashkelon will be deserted.
⁶A mongrel people will occupy
Ashdod,
and I will put an end to the pride of
the Philistines.
⁷I will take the blood from their mouths,
the forbidden food from between
their teeth.
Those who are left will belong to our
God
and become a clan in Judah,
and Ekron will be like the Jebusites.
⁸But I will encamp at my temple
to guard it against marauding
forces.
Never again will an oppressor overrun
my people,
for now I am keeping watch.

The Coming of Zion's King

⁹Rejoice greatly, Daughter Zion!
Shout, Daughter Jerusalem!
See, your king comes to you,
righteous and victorious,
lowly and riding on a donkey,
on a colt, the foal of a donkey.
¹⁰I will take away the chariots from
Ephraim
and the warhorses from Jerusalem,
and the battle bow will be broken.
He will proclaim peace to the nations.
His rule will extend from sea to sea
and from the Riverᵇ to the ends of
the earth.
¹¹As for you, because of the blood of my
covenant with you,
I will free your prisoners from the
waterless pit.
¹²Return to your fortress, you prisoners
of hope;
even now I announce that I will
restore twice as much to you.
¹³I will bend Judah as I bend my bow
and fill it with Ephraim.
I will rouse your sons, Zion,
against your sons, Greece,
and make you like a warrior's sword.

The LORD Will Appear

¹⁴Then the LORD will appear over them;
his arrow will flash like lightning.
The Sovereign LORD will sound the
trumpet;
he will march in the storms of the
south,
¹⁵   and the LORD Almighty will shield
them.
They will destroy
and overcome with slingstones.
They will drink and roar as with wine;
they will be full like a bowl
used for sprinklingᶜ the corners of
the altar.
¹⁶The LORD their God will save his
people on that day
as a shepherd saves his flock.
They will sparkle in his land
like jewels in a crown.

ᵃ 1 Or Damascus. / For the eye of the LORD is on all people, / as well as on the tribes of Israel,   ᵇ 10 That is, the Euphrates   ᶜ 15 Or bowl, / like

17 How attractive and beautiful they will
be!
Grain will make the young men
thrive,
and new wine the young women.

The Lord Will Care for Judah

10 Ask the Lord for rain in the
springtime;
it is the Lord who sends the
thunderstorms.
He gives showers of rain to all people,
and plants of the field to everyone.
2 The idols speak deceitfully,
diviners see visions that lie;
they tell dreams that are false,
they give comfort in vain.
Therefore the people wander like
sheep
oppressed for lack of a shepherd.

3 "My anger burns against the
shepherds,
and I will punish the leaders;
for the Lord Almighty will care
for his flock, the people of Judah,
and make them like a proud horse
in battle.
4 From Judah will come the cornerstone,
from him the tent peg,
from him the battle bow,
from him every ruler.
5 Together they*a* will be like warriors in
battle
trampling their enemy into the mud
of the streets.
They will fight because the Lord is
with them,
and they will put the enemy
horsemen to shame.

6 "I will strengthen Judah
and save the tribes of Joseph.
I will restore them
because I have compassion on
them.
They will be as though
I had not rejected them,
for I am the Lord their God
and I will answer them.
7 The Ephraimites will become like
warriors,
and their hearts will be glad as with
wine.

Their children will see it and be
joyful;
their hearts will rejoice in the Lord.
8 I will signal for them
and gather them in.
Surely I will redeem them;
they will be as numerous as
before.
9 Though I scatter them among the
peoples,
yet in distant lands they will
remember me.
They and their children will survive,
and they will return.
10 I will bring them back from Egypt
and gather them from Assyria.
I will bring them to Gilead and
Lebanon,
and there will not be room enough
for them.
11 They will pass through the sea of
trouble;
the surging sea will be subdued
and all the depths of the Nile will
dry up.
Assyria's pride will be brought down
and Egypt's scepter will pass
away.
12 I will strengthen them in the Lord
and in his name they will live
securely,"
declares the Lord.

11 Open your doors, Lebanon,
so that fire may devour your
cedars!
2 Wail, you juniper, for the cedar has
fallen;
the stately trees are ruined!
Wail, oaks of Bashan;
the dense forest has been cut
down!
3 Listen to the wail of the shepherds;
their rich pastures are destroyed!
Listen to the roar of the lions;
the lush thicket of the Jordan is
ruined!

Two Shepherds

4 This is what the Lord my God says:
"Shepherd the flock marked for slaughter. 5 Their buyers slaughter them and go

---

a 4,5 Or ruler, all of them together. / 5 They

unpunished. Those who sell them say, 'Praise the LORD, I am rich!' Their own shepherds do not spare them. ⁶For I will no longer have pity on the people of the land," declares the LORD. "I will give everyone into the hands of their neighbors and their king. They will devastate the land, and I will not rescue anyone from their hands."

⁷So I shepherded the flock marked for slaughter, particularly the oppressed of the flock. Then I took two staffs and called one Favor and the other Union, and I shepherded the flock. ⁸In one month I got rid of the three shepherds.

The flock detested me, and I grew weary of them ⁹and said, "I will not be your shepherd. Let the dying die, and the perishing perish. Let those who are left eat one another's flesh."

¹⁰Then I took my staff called Favor and broke it, revoking the covenant I had made with all the nations. ¹¹It was revoked on that day, and so the oppressed of the flock who were watching me knew it was the word of the LORD.

¹²I told them, "If you think it best, give me my pay; but if not, keep it." So they paid me thirty pieces of silver.

¹³And the LORD said to me, "Throw it to the potter"—the handsome price at which they valued me! So I took the thirty pieces of silver and threw them to the potter at the house of the LORD.

¹⁴Then I broke my second staff called Union, breaking the family bond between Judah and Israel.

¹⁵Then the LORD said to me, "Take again the equipment of a foolish shepherd. ¹⁶For I am going to raise up a shepherd over the land who will not care for the lost, or seek the young, or heal the injured, or feed the healthy, but will eat the meat of the choice sheep, tearing off their hooves.

¹⁷"Woe to the worthless shepherd,
   who deserts the flock!
May the sword strike his arm and his
   right eye!
May his arm be completely
   withered,
his right eye totally blinded!"

Jerusalem's Enemies to Be Destroyed

12 A prophecy: The word of the LORD concerning Israel.

The LORD, who stretches out the heavens, who lays the foundation of the earth, and who forms the human spirit within a person, declares: ²"I am going to make Jerusalem a cup that sends all the surrounding peoples reeling. Judah will be besieged as well as Jerusalem. ³On that day, when all the nations of the earth are gathered against her, I will make Jerusalem an immovable rock for all the nations. All who try to move it will injure themselves. ⁴On that day I will strike every horse with panic and its rider with madness," declares the LORD. "I will keep a watchful eye over Judah, but I will blind all the horses of the nations. ⁵Then the clans of Judah will say in their hearts, 'The people of Jerusalem are strong, because the LORD Almighty is their God.'

⁶"On that day I will make the clans of Judah like a firepot in a woodpile, like a flaming torch among sheaves. They will consume all the surrounding peoples right and left, but Jerusalem will remain intact in her place.

⁷"The LORD will save the dwellings of Judah first, so that the honor of the house of David and of Jerusalem's inhabitants may not be greater than that of Judah. ⁸On that day the LORD will shield those who live in Jerusalem, so that the feeblest among them will be like David, and the house of David will be like God, like the angel of the LORD going before them. ⁹On that day I will set out to destroy all the nations that attack Jerusalem.

Mourning for the One They Pierced

¹⁰"And I will pour out on the house of David and the inhabitants of Jerusalem a spirit[a] of grace and supplication. They will look on[b] me, the one they have pierced, and they will mourn for him as one mourns for an only child, and grieve bitterly for him as one grieves for a firstborn son. ¹¹On that day the weeping in

---

a 10 Or the Spirit   *b 10* Or to

Jerusalem will be as great as the weeping of Hadad Rimmon in the plain of Megiddo. ¹²The land will mourn, each clan by itself, with their wives by themselves: the clan of the house of David and their wives, the clan of the house of Nathan and their wives, ¹³the clan of the house of Levi and their wives, the clan of Shimei and their wives, ¹⁴and all the rest of the clans and their wives.

Cleansing From Sin

13 "On that day a fountain will be opened to the house of David and the inhabitants of Jerusalem, to cleanse them from sin and impurity.

²"On that day, I will banish the names of the idols from the land, and they will be remembered no more," declares the LORD Almighty. "I will remove both the prophets and the spirit of impurity from the land. ³And if anyone still prophesies, their father and mother, to whom they were born, will say to them, 'You must die, because you have told lies in the LORD's name.'

Hadad Rimmon

(ZECHARIAH 12:11)

He was the Phoenician god of plants. The plain of Megiddo is in the center of Israel, and it is very strategic. They performed rituals in the name of this god here in this flat land.

Then their own parents will stab the one who prophesies.

⁴"On that day every prophet will be ashamed of their prophetic vision. They will not put on a prophet's garment of hair in order to deceive. ⁵Each will say, 'I am not a prophet. I am a farmer; the land has been my livelihood since my youth.ᵃ' ⁶If someone asks, 'What are these wounds on your bodyᵇ?' they will answer, 'The wounds I was given at the house of my friends.'

The Shepherd Struck, the Sheep Scattered

⁷"Awake, sword, against my shepherd,
    against the man who is close to
        me!"
    declares the LORD Almighty.
"Strike the shepherd,
    and the sheep will be scattered,
    and I will turn my hand against the
        little ones.
⁸In the whole land," declares the
        LORD,
    "two-thirds will be struck down and
        perish;
    yet one-third will be left in it.
⁹This third I will put into the fire;
    I will refine them like silver
    and test them like gold.
They will call on my name
    and I will answer them;
I will say, 'They are my people,'
    and they will say, 'The LORD is our
        God.'"

The LORD Comes and Reigns

14 A day of the LORD is coming, Jerusalem, when your possessions will be plundered and divided up within your very walls.

²I will gather all the nations to Jerusalem to fight against it; the city will be captured, the houses ransacked, and the women raped. Half of the city will go into exile, but the rest of the people will not be taken from the city. ³Then the LORD will go out and fight against those nations, as he fights on a day of battle. ⁴On that

ᵃ 5 Or farmer; a man sold me in my youth   ᵇ 6 Or wounds between your hands

BREAKTHROUGH!

Will God himself fight against those nations?

(ZECHARIAH 14:3)

God usually uses another nation as his tool to fight against those nations.

day his feet will stand on the Mount of Olives, east of Jerusalem, and the Mount of Olives will be split in two from east to west, forming a great valley, with half of the mountain moving north and half moving south. ⁵You will flee by my mountain valley, for it will extend to Azel. You will flee as you fled from the earthquake*a* in the days of Uzziah king of Judah. Then the LORD my God will come, and all the holy ones with him.

⁶On that day there will be neither sunlight nor cold, frosty darkness. ⁷It will be a unique day—a day known only to the LORD—with no distinction between day and night. When evening comes, there will be light.

⁸On that day living water will flow out from Jerusalem, half of it east to the Dead Sea and half of it west to the Mediterranean Sea, in summer and in winter. ⁹The LORD will be king over the whole earth. On that day there will be one LORD, and his name the only name.

¹⁰The whole land, from Geba to Rimmon, south of Jerusalem, will become like the Arabah. But Jerusalem will be raised up high from the Benjamin Gate to the site of the First Gate, to the Corner Gate, and from the Tower of Hananel to the royal winepresses, and will remain in its place. ¹¹It will be inhabited; never again will it be destroyed. Jerusalem will be secure.

¹²This is the plague with which the LORD will strike all the nations that fought against Jerusalem: Their flesh will rot while they are still standing on their feet, their eyes will rot in their sockets, and their tongues will rot in their mouths. ¹³On that day people will be stricken by the LORD with great panic. They will seize each other by the hand and attack one another. ¹⁴Judah too will fight at Jerusalem. The wealth of all the surrounding nations will be collected—great quantities of gold

a 5 Or ⁵My mountain valley will be blocked and will extend to Azel. It will be blocked as it was blocked because of the earthquake

THE SCENE

MOUNT OF OLIVES

(ZECHARIAH 14:4)

This mountain is really covered with olive trees! It's 2.5 miles (4 km) long and rises above the eastern section of Jerusalem.

and silver and clothing. ¹⁵A similar plague will strike the horses and mules, the camels and donkeys, and all the animals in those camps.

¹⁶Then the survivors from all the nations that have attacked Jerusalem will go up year after year to worship the King, the LORD Almighty, and to celebrate the Festival of Tabernacles. ¹⁷If any of the peoples of the earth do not go up to Jerusalem to worship the King, the LORD Almighty, they will have no rain. ¹⁸If the Egyptian people do not go up and take part, they will have no rain. The LORD*ᵃ* will bring on them the plague he inflicts on the nations that do not go up to celebrate the Festival of Tabernacles. ¹⁹This will be the punishment of Egypt and the punishment of all the nations that do not go up to celebrate the Festival of Tabernacles.

²⁰On that day HOLY TO THE LORD will be inscribed on the bells of the horses, and the cooking pots in the LORD's house will be like the sacred bowls in front of the altar. ²¹Every pot in Jerusalem and Judah will be holy to the LORD Almighty, and all who come to sacrifice will take some of the pots and cook in them. And on that day there will no longer be a Canaaniteᵇ in the house of the LORD Almighty.

ᵃ 18 Or *part, then the* LORD   ᵇ 21 Or *merchant*

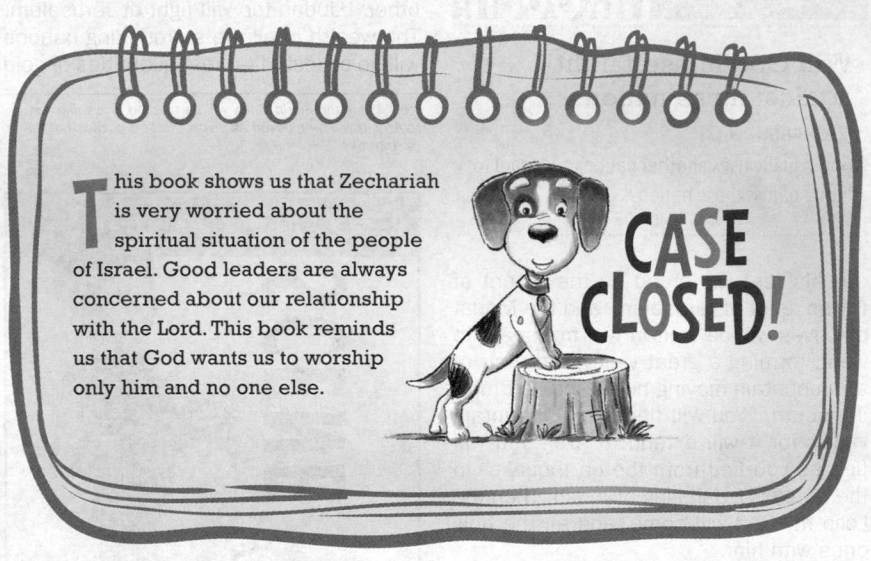

This book shows us that Zechariah is very worried about the spiritual situation of the people of Israel. Good leaders are always concerned about our relationship with the Lord. This book reminds us that God wants us to worship only him and no one else.

CASE CLOSED!

MALACHI

THE EVIDENCE:

WHO WROTE IT?
It seems that those who know lots of things about the Bible just don't know who wrote this book!

HOW LONG AGO?
This messenger of God lived at the same time as Nehemiah. It seems that he preached his message around the year 433 before Christ. The book was probably written between the years 520 and 450 before Jesus.

WHAT'S IT ABOUT?
The book begins by saying that God loves the Israelites. And then Malachi gives the priests a message, because they weren't doing their duty to teach God's law to the people. Malachi also scolds the people, because they were marrying people from other nations who didn't worship the true God.

THE BEST PART
I love it when God assures, "I the LORD do not change [...] Return to me, and I will return to you" (3:6–7).

---

1 A prophecy: The word of the LORD to Israel through Malachi.[a]

Israel Doubts God's Love

² "I have loved you," says the LORD.

"But you ask, 'How have you loved us?'

"Was not Esau Jacob's brother?" declares the LORD. "Yet I have loved Jacob, ³but Esau I have hated, and I have turned his hill country into a wasteland and left his inheritance to the desert jackals."

⁴Edom may say, "Though we have been crushed, we will rebuild the ruins."

But this is what the LORD Almighty says: "They may build, but I will demolish. They will be called the Wicked Land, a people always under the wrath of the LORD. ⁵You will see it with your own eyes and say, 'Great is the LORD—even beyond the borders of Israel!'

Breaking Covenant Through Blemished Sacrifices

⁶ "A son honors his father, and a slave his master. If I am a father, where is the honor due me? If I am a master, where is the respect due me?" says the LORD Almighty.

"It is you priests who show contempt for my name.

"But you ask, 'How have we shown contempt for your name?'

⁷ "By offering defiled food on my altar.

ᵃ 1 Malachi means my messenger.

hands. [11]My name will be great among the nations, from where the sun rises to where it sets. In every place incense and pure offerings will be brought to me, because my name will be great among the nations," says the LORD Almighty.

[12]"But you profane it by saying, 'The Lord's table is defiled,' and, 'Its food is contemptible.' [13]And you say, 'What a burden!' and you sniff at it contemptuously," says the LORD Almighty.

"When you bring injured, lame or diseased animals and offer them as sacrifices, should I accept them from your hands?" says the LORD. [14]"Cursed is the cheat who has an acceptable male in his flock and vows to give it, but then sacrifices a blemished animal to the Lord. For I am a great king," says the LORD Almighty, "and my name is to be feared among the nations.

Additional Warning to the Priests

2 "And now, you priests, this warning is for you. [2]If you do not listen, and if you do not resolve to honor my name," says the LORD Almighty, "I will send a curse on you, and I will curse your blessings. Yes, I have already cursed them, because you have not resolved to honor me.

[3]"Because of you I will rebuke your descendants[a]; I will smear on your faces the dung from your festival sacrifices, and you will be carried off with it. [4]And you will know that I have sent you this warning so that my covenant with Levi may continue," says the LORD Almighty. [5]"My covenant was with him, a covenant of life and peace, and I gave them to him; this called for reverence and he revered me and stood in awe of my name. [6]True instruction was in his mouth and nothing false was found on his lips. He walked with me in peace and uprightness, and turned many from sin.

[7]"For the lips of a priest ought to preserve knowledge, because he is the messenger of the LORD Almighty and people seek instruction from his mouth. [8]But you have turned from the way and

THE WITNESSES

✓ **MALACHI** (MALACHI 1:1)
The name means "my messenger."

"But you ask, 'How have we defiled you?'

"By saying that the LORD's table is contemptible. [8]When you offer blind animals for sacrifice, is that not wrong? When you sacrifice lame or diseased animals, is that not wrong? Try offering them to your governor! Would he be pleased with you? Would he accept you?" says the LORD Almighty.

[9]"Now plead with God to be gracious to us. With such offerings from your hands, will he accept you?" —says the LORD Almighty.

[10]"Oh, that one of you would shut the temple doors, so that you would not light useless fires on my altar! I am not pleased with you," says the LORD Almighty, "and I will accept no offering from your

---

[a] 3 Or will blight your grain

by your teaching have caused many to stumble; you have violated the covenant with Levi," says the LORD Almighty. ⁹"So I have caused you to be despised and humiliated before all the people, because you have not followed my ways but have shown partiality in matters of the law."

Breaking Covenant Through Divorce

¹⁰Do we not all have one Father[a]? Did not one God create us? Why do we profane the covenant of our ancestors by being unfaithful to one another? ¹¹Judah has been unfaithful. A detestable thing has been committed in Israel and in Jerusalem: Judah has desecrated the sanctuary the LORD loves by marrying women who worship a foreign god. ¹²As for the man who does this, whoever he may be, may the LORD remove him from the tents of Jacob[b] — even though he brings an offering to the LORD Almighty. ¹³Another thing you do: You flood the LORD's altar with tears. You weep and wail because he no longer looks with favor on your offerings or accepts them with pleasure from your hands. ¹⁴You ask, "Why?" It is because the LORD is the witness between you and the wife of your youth. You have been unfaithful to her, though she is your partner, the wife of your marriage covenant.

¹⁵Has not the one God made you? You belong to him in body and spirit. And what does the one God seek? Godly offspring.[c] So be on your guard, and do not be unfaithful to the wife of your youth.

¹⁶"The man who hates and divorces his wife," says the LORD, the God of Israel, "does violence to the one he should protect,"[d] says the LORD Almighty.

So be on your guard, and do not be unfaithful.

Breaking Covenant Through Injustice

¹⁷You have wearied the LORD with your words.

"How have we wearied him?" you ask.

By saying, "All who do evil are good in the eyes of the LORD, and he is pleased with them" or "Where is the God of justice?"

3 "I will send my messenger, who will prepare the way before me. Then suddenly the Lord you are seeking will come to his temple; the messenger of the covenant, whom you desire, will come," says the LORD Almighty.

²But who can endure the day of his coming? Who can stand when he appears? For he will be like a refiner's fire or a launderer's soap. ³He will sit as a refiner and purifier of silver; he will purify the Levites and refine them like gold and silver. Then the LORD will have men who will bring offerings in righteousness, ⁴and the offerings of Judah and Jerusalem will be acceptable to the LORD, as in days gone by, as in former years.

⁵"So I will come to put you on trial. I will be quick to testify against sorcerers,

Jackals
(MALACHI 1:3)
This is a medium-sized meat-eating animal that looks like a wolf. It's a scavenger. That means it eats rotten meat.

---

[a] 10 Or *father*   [b] 12 Or *12May the LORD remove from the tents of Jacob anyone who gives testimony in behalf of the man who does this*   [c] 15 The meaning of the Hebrew for the first part of this verse is uncertain.   [d] 16 Or *"I hate divorce," says the LORD, the God of Israel, "because the man who divorces his wife covers his garment with violence,"*

adulterers and perjurers, against those who defraud laborers of their wages, who oppress the widows and the fatherless, and deprive the foreigners among you of justice, but do not fear me," says the LORD Almighty.

Breaking Covenant by Withholding Tithes

⁶"I the LORD do not change. So you, the descendants of Jacob, are not destroyed. ⁷Ever since the time of your ancestors you have turned away from my decrees and have not kept them. Return to me, and I will return to you," says the LORD Almighty.

"But you ask, 'How are we to return?'

⁸"Will a mere mortal rob God? Yet you rob me.

"But you ask, 'How are we robbing you?'

"In tithes and offerings. ⁹You are under a curse—your whole nation—because you are robbing me. ¹⁰Bring the whole tithe into the storehouse, that there may be food in my house. Test me in this," says the LORD Almighty, "and see if I will not throw open the floodgates of heaven and pour out so much blessing that there will not be room enough to store it. ¹¹I will prevent pests from devouring your crops, and the vines in your fields will not drop their fruit before it is ripe," says the LORD Almighty. ¹²"Then all the nations will call you blessed, for yours will be a delightful land," says the LORD Almighty.

Israel Speaks Arrogantly Against God

¹³"You have spoken arrogantly against me," says the LORD.

"Yet you ask, 'What have we said against you?'

¹⁴"You have said, 'It is futile to serve God. What do we gain by carrying out his requirements and going about like mourners before the LORD Almighty? ¹⁵But now we call the arrogant blessed. Certainly evildoers prosper, and even when they put God to the test, they get away with it.'"

The Faithful Remnant

¹⁶Then those who feared the LORD talked with each other, and the LORD listened and heard. A scroll of remembrance was written in his presence concerning those who feared the LORD and honored his name.

¹⁷"On the day when I act," says the LORD Almighty, "they will be my treasured possession. I will spare them, just as a father has compassion and spares his son who serves him. ¹⁸And you will again see the distinction between the righteous and the wicked, between those who serve God and those who do not.

THE
WITNESSES

✓ **ELIJAH** (MALACHI 4:5)
He was the prophet of God who disappeared and went to heaven in a chariot of fire. The people of Israel were waiting for Elijah to come before the arrival of the Messiah, who God would send to save everyone. Now we know that is Jesus.

Judgment and Covenant Renewal

4 [a] "Surely the day is coming; it will burn like a furnace. All the arrogant and every evildoer will be stubble, and the day that is coming will set them on fire," says the LORD Almighty. "Not a root or a branch will be left to them. [2] But for you who revere my name, the sun of righteousness will rise with healing in its rays. And you will go out and frolic like well-fed calves. [3] Then you will trample on the wicked; they will be ashes under the soles of your feet on the day when I act," says the LORD Almighty.

[4] "Remember the law of my servant Moses, the decrees and laws I gave him at Horeb for all Israel.

[5] "See, I will send the prophet Elijah to you before that great and dreadful day of the LORD comes. [6] He will turn the hearts of the parents to their children, and the hearts of the children to their parents; or else I will come and strike the land with total destruction."

---

[a] In Hebrew texts 4:1-6 is numbered 3:19-24.

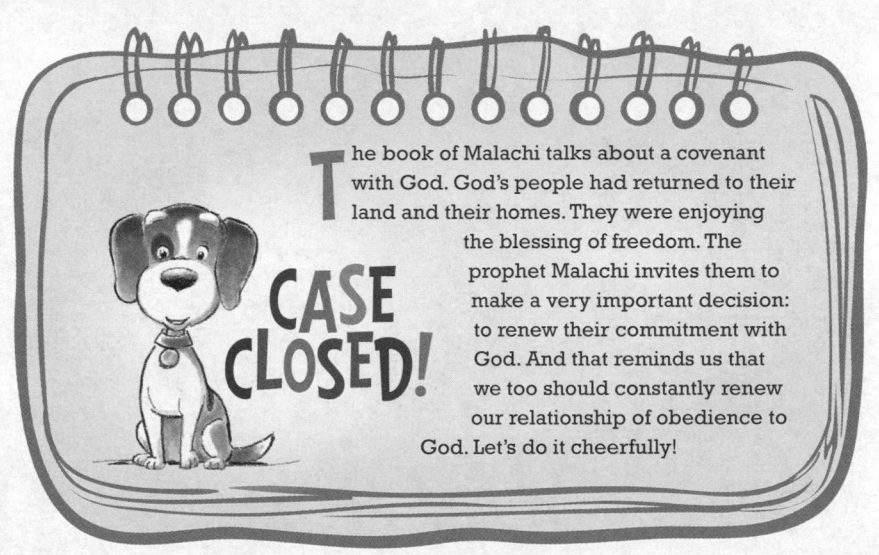

The book of Malachi talks about a covenant with God. God's people had returned to their land and their homes. They were enjoying the blessing of freedom. The prophet Malachi invites them to make a very important decision: to renew their commitment with God. And that reminds us that we too should constantly renew our relationship of obedience to God. Let's do it cheerfully!

CASE CLOSED!

NEW TESTAMENT

MATTHEW

THE EVIDENCE:

After Jesus went back to live with God in heaven, the people who had known him and had been living with him wanted to tell other people about all the wonderful things Jesus had taught them. That's why they wrote some books they called the Gospels, because that word means "good news." The good news of Jesus, the Son of God!

For example, this gospel that's called the "gospel of Matthew" tells the whole story of Jesus from the time he was a baby. It even tells who his grandparents were!

Matthew says that Jesus was a very important teacher, because he explained well what God wants us to know. That's why many people followed him. They would sit out on the grass to listen to what Jesus wanted to say to them.

WHO WROTE IT?

People who know a lot about the Bible aren't sure who wrote this gospel. Some think it was Matthew, the tax collector, but others think it was written by some of Matthew's friends, who learned everything Matthew had told them about Jesus.

HOW LONG AGO?

This book was written about 80 or 85 years after Christ (of course!). Jesus had already gone to heaven to be with God a long time before that, about 50 years or so. By that time, a lot of things had happened in Jerusalem. The Romans, who were governing at that time, had a powerful army, and they entered Jerusalem and destroyed everything. And they were so very, very bad that they stole all of God's things that were in the temple. Then they set fire to the temple and turned it to dust. The destruction of the temple was 70 years after Christ, so that means that it happened before this gospel was written.

WHAT'S IT ABOUT?

We thought that this book wants to tell us about all the things that Jesus taught. What's really most important is that the book says that Jesus is the Messiah. That means that God sent him so every person would be sorry for the bad things they do and they'd believe in God. That's what John the Baptist said!

THE BEST PART

The part in Matthew that we like best is called "the Beatitudes." It's really lovely! For example, we liked this part: "Blessed are the peacemakers, for they will be called children of God" (5:9).

The Genealogy of Jesus the Messiah

1 This is the genealogy[a] of Jesus the Messiah[b] the son of David, the son of Abraham:

2 Abraham was the father of Isaac,
Isaac the father of Jacob,
Jacob the father of Judah and his brothers,
3 Judah the father of Perez and Zerah, whose mother was Tamar,
Perez the father of Hezron,
Hezron the father of Ram,
4 Ram the father of Amminadab,
Amminadab the father of Nahshon,
Nahshon the father of Salmon,
5 Salmon the father of Boaz, whose mother was Rahab,
Boaz the father of Obed, whose mother was Ruth,
Obed the father of Jesse,
6 and Jesse the father of King David.

David was the father of Solomon, whose mother had been Uriah's wife,
7 Solomon the father of Rehoboam,
Rehoboam the father of Abijah,
Abijah the father of Asa,
8 Asa the father of Jehoshaphat,
Jehoshaphat the father of Jehoram,
Jehoram the father of Uzziah,
9 Uzziah the father of Jotham,
Jotham the father of Ahaz,
Ahaz the father of Hezekiah,
10 Hezekiah the father of Manasseh,
Manasseh the father of Amon,
Amon the father of Josiah,
11 and Josiah the father of Jeconiah[c] and his brothers at the time of the exile to Babylon.

12 After the exile to Babylon:
Jeconiah was the father of Shealtiel,
Shealtiel the father of Zerubbabel,
13 Zerubbabel the father of Abihud,
Abihud the father of Eliakim,
Eliakim the father of Azor,
14 Azor the father of Zadok,
Zadok the father of Akim,
Akim the father of Elihud,
15 Elihud the father of Eleazar,
Eleazar the father of Matthan,
Matthan the father of Jacob,
16 and Jacob the father of Joseph, the husband of Mary, and Mary was the mother of Jesus who is called the Messiah.

17 Thus there were fourteen generations in all from Abraham to David, fourteen from David to the exile to Babylon, and fourteen from the exile to the Messiah.

Joseph Accepts Jesus as His Son

18 This is how the birth of Jesus the Messiah came about[d]: His mother Mary

Genealogy
(MATTHEW 1:1)

This is a list of people who belong to the same family, starting with the oldest and going on down to the youngest. For example, I have my mother, she has her mother, who is my grandmother, and so on. And it means that when I have a son or a daughter, that child will be my descendant.

---

a 1 Or *is an account of the origin*   b 1 Or *Jesus Christ. Messiah* (Hebrew) and *Christ* (Greek) both mean *Anointed One*; also in verse 18.   c 11 That is, Jehoiachin; also in verse 12   d 18 Or *The origin of Jesus the Messiah was like this* was pledged to be married to Joseph, but before they came together, she was found to be pregnant through the Holy Spirit.

[19]Because Joseph her husband was faithful to the law, and yet[a] did not want to expose her to public disgrace, he had in mind to divorce her quietly.

[20]But after he had considered this, an angel of the Lord appeared to him in a dream and said, "Joseph son of David, do not be afraid to take Mary home as your wife, because what is conceived in her is from the Holy Spirit. [21]She will give birth to a son, and you are to give him the name Jesus,[b] because he will save his people from their sins."

[22]All this took place to fulfill what the Lord had said through the prophet: [23]"The virgin will conceive and give birth to a son,

---

[a] 19 Or *was a righteous man and*   [b] 21 *Jesus* is the Greek form of *Joshua,* which means *the Lord saves.*

THE
WITNESSES

✓ JESUS (MATTHEW 1:1)
The Son of God. But here, among the people, he was the son of Mary, and the adopted son of Joseph. His name means "God saves." What a lovely name!

✓ JOSEPH (MATTHEW 1:16)
He was Jesus' father. Well, he raised Jesus, because Jesus is the Son of God! Joseph was born in a village in Galilee called Nazareth and he was a craftsman. He probably was a carpenter who made things out of wood. But the nicest and most important thing the Bible says about Joseph is that he was good and obeyed God.

✓ MARY (MATTHEW 1:16)
She's Jesus' mother. She was born in Galilee, in a village called Nazareth.

BREAKTHROUGH!

Messiah
(MATTHEW 1:16)

That's an odd word! It's from another language, Hebrew. It appears a bunch of times in the Bible. It means "anointed" or "chosen," and that means that it's a person God has chosen to do something very, very special. For example, when God chose a king, they would say that king was "anointed." The most important messiah of all is Jesus, because he's more than a king — he's the Son of God! It says so in the Bible.

Generations

(MATTHEW 1:17)

Generations are groups of people more or less the same age. For example, my mom and dad belong to the same generation; my brother, my friends at school and my best friend in the neighborhood and I all belong to the same generation, but we don't belong to my parents' generation.

Angel

(MATTHEW 1:20)

How good to know that angels exist! Angels exist, but we don't often see them — like the wind! What's most important is that the angels always obey everything God tells them. The word *angel* means "messenger." Many times, angels come to deliver messages from God and help us make good decisions.

Sins

(MATTHEW 1:21)

These are things we do that don't please God. Or they're also things we don't do when God wants us to do them. For example, God wants us to be good friends. When we're not, that's a sin. Or, if I take something that belongs to a friend, that's stealing, and that's a sin.

and they will call him Immanuel"[a] (which means "God with us").

²⁴When Joseph woke up, he did what the angel of the Lord had commanded him and took Mary home as his wife. ²⁵But he did not consummate their marriage until she gave birth to a son. And he gave him the name Jesus.

The Magi Visit the Messiah

2 After Jesus was born in Bethlehem in Judea, during the time of King Herod, Magi[b] from the east came to Jerusalem ²and asked, "Where is the one who has been born king of the Jews? We saw his star when it rose and have come to worship him."

³When King Herod heard this he was disturbed, and all Jerusalem with him. ⁴When he had called together all the people's chief priests and teachers of the law, he asked them where the Messiah was to be born. ⁵"In Bethlehem in Judea," they replied, "for this is what the prophet has written:

⁶ " 'But you, Bethlehem, in the land of
        Judah,
    are by no means least among the
        rulers of Judah;

---

[a] 23 Isaiah 7:14   [b] 1 Traditionally *wise men*

for out of you will come a ruler
who will shepherd my people
Israel.'*ᵃ*"

⁷Then Herod called the Magi secretly and found out from them the exact time the star had appeared. ⁸He sent them to Bethlehem and said, "Go and search carefully for the child. As soon as you find him, report to me, so that I too may go and worship him."

⁹After they had heard the king, they went on their way, and the star they had seen when it rose went ahead of them until it stopped over the place where the child was. ¹⁰When they saw the star, they were overjoyed. ¹¹On coming to the house, they saw the child with his mother Mary, and they bowed down and worshiped him. Then they opened their

---

ᵃ 6 Micah 5:2,4

BREAKTHROUGH!

The virgin
(MATTHEW 1:23)
This is a person who is pure. Mary was probably about 14 or 15 years old when she was pregnant with Jesus.

Magi
(MATTHEW 2:1)
Now we call them "wise men." This is because they knew a whole lot about a certain topic. But long ago, they called the people who studied the stars and planets "Magi." They were astronomers; in other words, a person who studies the stars, the moon, the sun and the planets — everything out there in space. In Bible times, it was not easy to do this, because the telescope had not been invented yet. They simply watched the sky to see what happened. Nowadays, with a telescope, you can see a lot of stars and other things in the sky closer.

THE SCENE

BETHLEHEM

(MATTHEW 2:1)

This village is mentioned in the Bible and it's very important, because it is where Jesus was born. Bethlehem is a Hebrew name that means "house of bread." The western area of the land where Bethlehem is located is fertile and borders the Mediterranean Sea. The eastern area is dry and drops down to the Dead Sea. Bethlehem is 5.6 miles (9 km) south of Jerusalem, and now it belongs to a territory called the West Bank.

JUDEA

(MATTHEW 2:1)

It was part of the land God gave his people, the Jews. It's called Judea because it's inside the land that the tribe of Judah got. This mountainous region is south of Israel.

JERUSALEM

(MATTHEW 2:1)

In Jesus' time, Jerusalem was the capital of Judea. In other words, it was part of the land the tribe of Judah got. In Jesus' time, the Romans controlled the entire region.

Chief priests
(MATTHEW 2:4)
They were the people who were in charge of the other priests, and who made the most important decisions. They also were in charge of things in the temple, which is what we call church now.

Teachers of the law
(MATTHEW 2:4)
They were men who spent all their time studying the Bible. Well, not all of the Bible — just the part that's called the Old Testament, but they knew absolutely everything it said. Most importantly, they were the religious leaders who explained what the people should and shouldn't do.

treasures and presented him with gifts of gold, frankincense and myrrh. ¹²And having been warned in a dream not to go back to Herod, they returned to their country by another route.

The Escape to Egypt

¹³When they had gone, an angel of the Lord appeared to Joseph in a dream. "Get up," he said, "take the child and his mother and escape to Egypt. Stay there until I tell you, for Herod is going to search for the child to kill him."

¹⁴So he got up, took the child and his mother during the night and left for Egypt, ¹⁵where he stayed until the death of Herod. And so was fulfilled what the Lord had said through the prophet: "Out of Egypt I called my son."ᵃ

¹⁶When Herod realized that he had been outwitted by the Magi, he was fu-

ᵃ 15 Hosea 11:1

rious, and he gave orders to kill all the boys in Bethlehem and its vicinity who were two years old and under, in accordance with the time he had learned from the Magi. [17]Then what was said through the prophet Jeremiah was fulfilled:

[18] "A voice is heard in Ramah,
　　weeping and great mourning,
　Rachel weeping for her children
　　and refusing to be comforted,
　　because they are no more."[a]

The Return to Nazareth

[19]After Herod died, an angel of the Lord appeared in a dream to Joseph in Egypt [20]and said, "Get up, take the child and his mother and go to the land of Israel, for those who were trying to take the child's life are dead."

[21]So he got up, took the child and his mother and went to the land of Israel. [22]But when he heard that Archelaus was reigning in Judea in place of his father Herod, he was afraid to go there. Having been warned in a dream, he withdrew to the district of Galilee, [23]and he went and lived in a town called Nazareth. So was fulfilled what was said through the prophets, that he would be called a Nazarene.

John the Baptist Prepares the Way

3 In those days John the Baptist came, preaching in the wilderness of Judea

---

[a] 18 Jer. 31:15

THE
SCENE

EGYPT

(MATTHEW 2:13)

This country still exists. It's in Africa. It's one of the oldest countries in the world. Many, many years ago—about 1,300 years before Christ—the Jews were slaves in Egypt, but God freed them. He gave them a land of their own.

THE
WITNESSES

✓ **ARCHELAUS** **(MATTHEW 2:22)**
He was Herod the Great's son. When his father died, Archelaus became king of Samaria, Idumea and Judea.

THE SCENE

ISRAEL

(MATTHEW 2:20)

This is all the land God gave his people. Israel exists today, but it's smaller than it used to be.

GALILEE

(MATTHEW 2:22)

Galilee was an area west of the Jordan River, and the Sea of Galilee was in the northern part of Israel. It was the area the Jews lived in, where there weren't so many mountains. Over time, it was ruled by many different nations. For example, there were Assyrians, Babylonians, Persians and Greeks. In Jesus' time, it was the Romans.

²and saying, "Repent, for the kingdom of heaven has come near." ³This is he who was spoken of through the prophet Isaiah:

"A voice of one calling in the wilderness,
'Prepare the way for the Lord,
make straight paths for him.' "*a*

⁴John's clothes were made of camel's hair, and he had a leather belt around his waist. His food was locusts and wild honey. ⁵People went out to him from Jerusalem and all Judea and the whole region of the Jordan. ⁶Confessing their sins, they were baptized by him in the Jordan River.

⁷But when he saw many of the Pharisees and Sadducees coming to where he was baptizing, he said to them: "You brood of vipers! Who warned you to flee from the coming wrath? ⁸Produce fruit in keeping with repentance. ⁹And do not think you can say to yourselves, 'We have Abraham as our father.' I tell you that out

a 3 Isaiah 40:3

BREAKTHROUGH!

Baptize

(MATTHEW 3:6)

In the Bible, it says that we Christians have to be baptized so people will know that we believe in Jesus. In some churches, they do this the way it was in the Bible, so a person gets in the water and the pastor baptizes them. In other churches, the priest puts a little bit of water on the person's forehead. In some churches, people are baptized when they're babies. And in other churches, they wait until they're adults.

BREAKTHROUGH!

Pharisees
(MATTHEW 3:7)

They were a group of Jewish men who paid a lot of attention to doing everything like it said in the Bible, and they asked God to send the Messiah, who would be the man who would free them and get rid of the Romans who were ruling them. They would also go to the synagogues and teach what the Bible said so other people would obey. The problem was that they forgot what was most important, and they only taught the "external" things like rituals, customs and ceremonies. They were concerned with how the priest was doing his work in the temple and things like that. The name "Pharisee" meant "separate" or "pure."

The Baptism of Jesus

¹³Then Jesus came from Galilee to the Jordan to be baptized by John. ¹⁴But John tried to deter him, saying, "I need to be baptized by you, and do you come to me?"

¹⁵Jesus replied, "Let it be so now; it is proper for us to do this to fulfill all righteousness." Then John consented.

¹⁶As soon as Jesus was baptized, he went up out of the water. At that moment heaven was opened, and he saw the Spirit of God descending like a dove and

---

a 11 Or *in*

BREAKTHROUGH!

Sadducees
(MATTHEW 3:7)

These Jewish men were very good friends of the priests, because they were usually from the family of a priest named Zadok. They were the group that ruled mostly in Judea and in Jerusalem. They belonged to the class that had the most money and power in Jewish society. They read the Bible a lot, but they were mostly interested in the first five books, the ones called the Pentateuch. They weren't very interested in the spiritual or heavenly matters, just in what had to do with life on Earth. For example, they didn't believe in the resurrection of the dead.

---

of these stones God can raise up children for Abraham. ¹⁰The ax is already at the root of the trees, and every tree that does not produce good fruit will be cut down and thrown into the fire.

¹¹"I baptize you with*ᵃ* water for repentance. But after me comes one who is more powerful than I, whose sandals I am not worthy to carry. He will baptize you with*ᵃ* the Holy Spirit and fire. ¹²His winnowing fork is in his hand, and he will clear his threshing floor, gathering his wheat into the barn and burning up the chaff with unquenchable fire."

alighting on him. ¹⁷And a voice from heaven said, "This is my Son, whom I love; with him I am well pleased."

Jesus Is Tested in the Wilderness

4 Then Jesus was led by the Spirit into the wilderness to be tempted*ᵃ* by the devil. ²After fasting forty days and forty nights, he was hungry. ³The tempter came to him and said, "If you are the Son of God, tell these stones to become bread."

⁴Jesus answered, "It is written: 'Man shall not live on bread alone, but on every word that comes from the mouth of God.'*ᵇ*"

⁵Then the devil took him to the holy city and had him stand on the highest point of the temple. ⁶"If you are the Son of God," he said, "throw yourself down. For it is written:

" 'He will command his angels
      concerning you,
  and they will lift you up in their
      hands,
  so that you will not strike your foot
      against a stone.'*ᶜ*"

⁷Jesus answered him, "It is also written: 'Do not put the Lord your God to the test.'*ᵈ*"

⁸Again, the devil took him to a very high mountain and showed him all the kingdoms of the world and their splendor. ⁹"All this I will give you," he said, "if you will bow down and worship me."

¹⁰Jesus said to him, "Away from me, Satan! For it is written: 'Worship the Lord your God, and serve him only.'*ᵉ*"

¹¹Then the devil left him, and angels came and attended him.

Jesus Begins to Preach

¹²When Jesus heard that John had been put in prison, he withdrew to Galilee. ¹³Leaving Nazareth, he went and lived in Capernaum, which was by the lake in the area of Zebulun and Naphtali— ¹⁴to fulfill what was said through the prophet Isaiah:

¹⁵ "Land of Zebulun and land of
       Naphtali,
   the Way of the Sea, beyond the
       Jordan,
   Galilee of the Gentiles—

BREAK THROUGH!

Devil/Satan

(MATTHEW 4:1,10)

He's the worst. He's like an angel, but bad. He always does what God doesn't like, and he wants people to act like him too. What he likes best is stealing, killing and destroying.

¹⁶the people living in darkness
   have seen a great light;
 on those living in the land of the
     shadow of death
   a light has dawned."*ᶠ*

¹⁷From that time on Jesus began to preach, "Repent, for the kingdom of heaven has come near."

Jesus Calls His First Disciples

¹⁸As Jesus was walking beside the Sea of Galilee, he saw two brothers, Simon called Peter and his brother Andrew. They were casting a net into the lake, for they were fishermen. ¹⁹"Come, follow me," Jesus said, "and I will send you out to fish for people." ²⁰At once they left their nets and followed him.

²¹Going on from there, he saw two other brothers, James son of Zebedee and his brother John. They were in a boat with

---

ᵃ *1* The Greek for *tempted* can also mean *tested.*
ᵇ *4* Deut. 8:3   ᶜ *6* Psalm 91:11,12   ᵈ *7* Deut. 6:16
ᵉ *10* Deut. 6:13   ᶠ *16* Isaiah 9:1,2

their father Zebedee, preparing their nets. Jesus called them, ²²and immediately they left the boat and their father and followed him.

Jesus Heals the Sick

²³Jesus went throughout Galilee, teaching in their synagogues, proclaiming the good news of the kingdom, and healing every disease and sickness among the people. ²⁴News about him spread all over

THE SCENE

NAZARETH
(MATTHEW 4:13)

This is a very important city in Israel now, but in Jesus' time it was a little village in the region of Galilee. It was so small that the Bible mentions it only to say that Jesus lived there with his parents when he was young.

CAPERNAUM
(MATTHEW 4:13)

This was an important fishing village on the shores of the northwestern part of the Sea of Galilee. It was on a very important route that merchants used when they traveled from Egypt to Syria. In Jesus' time, there were barracks in Capernaum for Roman soldiers who were in charge of making all the people pay taxes.

THE WITNESSES

✓ **SIMON PETER** **(MATTHEW 4:18)**
Simon means "He (God) has heard," and Peter means "rock." He was a fisherman, just like his brother, Andrew, and his father's name was Jonah. Simon was a good friend of Jesus and followed him everywhere. Simon was the first person to realize that Jesus is the Son of God.

✓ **ANDREW** **(MATTHEW 4:18)**
Andrew was also one of Jesus' disciples, those twelve friends who went everywhere with him. But before that, he had learned a lot from John the Baptist. He was also Peter's brother, and they were both fishermen.

The good news
(MATTHEW 4:23)

There's a lot of good news in the Bible, but the best news is that Jesus was born and everything changed. That's because he's the Son of God, and he came to live like us in order to save us.

The kingdom
(MATTHEW 4:23)

Jesus talked a lot about the kingdom of God. The kingdom is wherever God rules. Sometimes we see the kingdom now, but we also hope that God's kingdom will come to places that still need to be saved.

The demon-possessed
(MATTHEW 4:24; 8:16)

Demons are like spirits, but we don't know for sure what they look like, because we can't see them. They always do what the devil tells them to do, and they don't do what God wants. That means they're bad. They also try to get other people to do bad things. That's why we shouldn't pay attention to them, and we should do just the opposite.

Syria, and people brought to him all who were ill with various diseases, those suffering severe pain, the demon-possessed, those having seizures, and the paralyzed; and he healed them. ²⁵Large crowds from Galilee, the Decapolis,ᵃ Jerusalem, Judea and the region across the Jordan followed him.

Introduction to the Sermon on the Mount

5 Now when Jesus saw the crowds, he went up on a mountainside and sat down. His disciples came to him, ²and he began to teach them.

The Beatitudes
He said:

³ "Blessed are the poor in spirit,
    for theirs is the kingdom of heaven.
⁴ Blessed are those who mourn,
    for they will be comforted.
⁵ Blessed are the meek,
    for they will inherit the earth.
⁶ Blessed are those who hunger and
        thirst for righteousness,
    for they will be filled.
⁷ Blessed are the merciful,
    for they will be shown mercy.
⁸ Blessed are the pure in heart,
    for they will see God.

ᵃ 25 That is, the Ten Cities

DECAPOLIS

(MATTHEW 4:25)

This is a Greek word that means "ten cities." It was a place east of the Sea of Galilee, where there really were ten cities that had been built in the same style as Greek cities.

9 Blessed are the peacemakers,
     for they will be called children of
        God.
10 Blessed are those who are persecuted
     because of righteousness,
     for theirs is the kingdom of heaven.

11 "Blessed are you when people insult you, persecute you and falsely say all kinds of evil against you because of me. 12 Rejoice and be glad, because great is your reward in heaven, for in the same way they persecuted the prophets who were before you.

Salt and Light

13 "You are the salt of the earth. But if the salt loses its saltiness, how can it be made salty again? It is no longer good for anything, except to be thrown out and trampled underfoot.

14 "You are the light of the world. A town built on a hill cannot be hidden. 15 Neither do people light a lamp and put it under a bowl. Instead they put it on its stand, and it gives light to everyone in the house. 16 In the same way, let your light shine before others, that they may see your good deeds and glorify your Father in heaven.

The Fulfillment of the Law

17 "Do not think that I have come to abolish the Law or the Prophets; I have not come to abolish them but to fulfill them. 18 For truly I tell you, until heaven and earth disappear, not the smallest letter, not the least stroke of a pen, will by any means disappear from the Law until everything is accomplished. 19 Therefore anyone who sets aside one of the least of these commands and teaches others accordingly will be called least in

BREAK THROUGH!

Disciples

(MATTHEW 5:1)

This is like saying "students." A long time ago, adults also had teachers who taught them important things about life. So a person who always followed a teacher was called a disciple. Jesus was a great teacher, and he had many students that he taught to live correctly.

the kingdom of heaven, but whoever practices and teaches these commands will be called great in the kingdom of heaven. [20]For I tell you that unless your righteousness surpasses that of the Pharisees and the teachers of the law, you will certainly not enter the kingdom of heaven.

Murder

[21]"You have heard that it was said to the people long ago, 'You shall not murder,[a] and anyone who murders will be subject to judgment.' [22]But I tell you that anyone who is angry with a brother or sister[b,c] will be subject to judgment. Again, anyone who says to a brother or sister, 'Raca,'[d] is answerable to the court. And anyone who says, 'You fool!' will be in danger of the fire of hell.

[23]"Therefore, if you are offering your gift at the altar and there remember that your brother or sister has something against you, [24]leave your gift there in front of the altar. First go and be reconciled to them; then come and offer your gift.

BREAKTHROUGH!

Hell
(MATTHEW 5:22)

Hell is being separated from God. Sometimes we choose this separation with our words or actions, but this is not what God wants for us. God is for us and wants to be with us.

[25]"Settle matters quickly with your adversary who is taking you to court. Do it while you are still together on the way, or your adversary may hand you over to the judge, and the judge may hand you over to the officer, and you may be thrown into prison. [26]Truly I tell you, you will not get out until you have paid the last penny.

Adultery

[27]"You have heard that it was said, 'You shall not commit adultery.'[e] [28]But I tell you that anyone who looks at a woman lustfully has already committed adultery with her in his heart. [29]If your right eye causes you to stumble, gouge it out and throw it away. It is better for you to lose one part of your body than for your whole body to be thrown into hell. [30]And if your right hand causes you to stumble, cut it off and throw it away. It is better for you to lose one part of your body than for your whole body to go into hell.

Divorce

[31]"It has been said, 'Anyone who divorces his wife must give her a certificate of divorce.'[f] [32]But I tell you that anyone who divorces his wife, except for sexual immorality, makes her the victim of adultery, and anyone who marries a divorced woman commits adultery.

Oaths

[33]"Again, you have heard that it was said to the people long ago, 'Do not break your oath, but fulfill to the Lord the vows you have made.' [34]But I tell you, do not swear an oath at all: either by heaven, for it is God's throne; [35]or by the earth, for it is his footstool; or by Jerusalem, for it is the city of the Great King. [36]And do not swear by your head, for you cannot make even one hair white or black. [37]All you need to say is simply 'Yes' or 'No'; anything beyond this comes from the evil one.[g]

[a] 21 Exodus 20:13   [b] 22 The Greek word for brother or sister (adelphos) refers here to a fellow disciple, whether man or woman; also in verse 23.   [c] 22 Some manuscripts brother or sister without cause   [d] 22 An Aramaic term of contempt   [e] 27 Exodus 20:14   [f] 31 Deut. 24:1   [g] 37 Or from evil

BREAKTHROUGH!

Certificate of divorce
(MATTHEW 5:31)

Divorce is when a man and woman who were married decide not to be married anymore. The certificate of divorce is a document that says that they're no longer husband and wife.

Eye for Eye

38 "You have heard that it was said, 'Eye for eye, and tooth for tooth.'ᵃ 39But I tell you, do not resist an evil person. If anyone slaps you on the right cheek, turn to them the other cheek also. 40And if anyone wants to sue you and take your shirt, hand over your coat as well. 41If anyone forces you to go one mile, go with them two miles. 42Give to the one who asks you, and do not turn away from the one who wants to borrow from you.

Love for Enemies

43 "You have heard that it was said, 'Love your neighborᵇ and hate your enemy.' 44But I tell you, love your enemies and pray for those who persecute you, 45that you may be children of your Father in heaven. He causes his sun to rise on the evil and the good, and sends rain on the righteous and the unrighteous. 46If you love those who love you, what re-

ward will you get? Are not even the tax collectors doing that? 47And if you greet only your own people, what are you doing more than others? Do not even pagans do that? 48Be perfect, therefore, as your heavenly Father is perfect.

Giving to the Needy

6 "Be careful not to practice your righteousness in front of others to be seen by them. If you do, you will have no reward from your Father in heaven.

2 "So when you give to the needy, do not announce it with trumpets, as the hypocrites do in the synagogues and on the streets, to be honored by others. Truly I tell you, they have received their reward in full. 3But when you give to the needy, do not let your left hand know what your right hand is doing, 4so that your giving may be in secret. Then your Father, who sees what is done in secret, will reward you.

_____
ᵃ 38 Exodus 21:24; Lev. 24:20; Deut. 19:21
ᵇ 43 Lev. 19:18

BREAKTHROUGH!

Adultery
(MATTHEW 5:32)

This is when a man or a woman is married, but then they fall in love with someone they're not married to.

¹²And forgive us our debts,
  as we also have forgiven our
    debtors.
¹³And lead us not into temptation,[a]
  but deliver us from the evil
    one.[b]'

¹⁴For if you forgive other people when they sin against you, your heavenly Father will also forgive you. ¹⁵But if you do not forgive others their sins, your Father will not forgive your sins.

Fasting

¹⁶"When you fast, do not look somber as the hypocrites do, for they disfigure their faces to show others they are fasting. Truly I tell you, they have received

[a] 13 The Greek for *temptation* can also mean *testing*.
[b] 13 Or *from evil*; some late manuscripts *one, / for yours is the kingdom and the power and the glory forever. Amen.*

BREAK THROUGH!

Hypocrites
(MATTHEW 6:2)

These are people who think one way but act differently. They appear to be something they're not. It's false and it's a lie. And it's a nasty attitude!

Prayer

⁵"And when you pray, do not be like the hypocrites, for they love to pray standing in the synagogues and on the street corners to be seen by others. Truly I tell you, they have received their reward in full. ⁶But when you pray, go into your room, close the door and pray to your Father, who is unseen. Then your Father, who sees what is done in secret, will reward you. ⁷And when you pray, do not keep on babbling like pagans, for they think they will be heard because of their many words. ⁸Do not be like them, for your Father knows what you need before you ask him.

⁹"This, then, is how you should pray:

" 'Our Father in heaven,
  hallowed be your name,
¹⁰your kingdom come,
  your will be done,
    on earth as it is in heaven.
¹¹Give us today our daily bread.

BREAK THROUGH!

Fasting
(MATTHEW 6:16)

It means not eating. But this not eating is not because you don't like the food. In the Bible, fasting means not eating in order to use a lot of strength to ask God for something we need. And simply not eating isn't enough. We also have to pray that God will hear us. In Bible times, people prayed and fasted quite often.

their reward in full. [17]But when you fast, put oil on your head and wash your face, [18]so that it will not be obvious to others that you are fasting, but only to your Father, who is unseen; and your Father, who sees what is done in secret, will reward you.

Treasures in Heaven

[19]"Do not store up for yourselves treasures on earth, where moths and vermin destroy, and where thieves break in and steal. [20]But store up for yourselves treasures in heaven, where moths and vermin do not destroy, and where thieves do not break in and steal. [21]For where your treasure is, there your heart will be also.

[22]"The eye is the lamp of the body. If your eyes are healthy,[a] your whole body will be full of light. [23]But if your eyes are unhealthy,[b] your whole body will be full of darkness. If then the light within you is darkness, how great is that darkness!

[24]"No one can serve two masters. Either you will hate the one and love the other, or you will be devoted to the one and despise the other. You cannot serve both God and money.

Do Not Worry

[25]"Therefore I tell you, do not worry about your life, what you will eat or drink; or about your body, what you will wear. Is not life more than food, and the body more than clothes? [26]Look at the birds of the air; they do not sow or reap or store away in barns, and yet your heavenly Father feeds them. Are you not much more valuable than they? [27]Can any one of you by worrying add a single hour to your life[c]?

[28]"And why do you worry about clothes? See how the flowers of the field grow. They do not labor or spin. [29]Yet I tell you that not even Solomon in all his splendor was dressed like one of these. [30]If that is how God clothes the grass of the field, which is here today and tomorrow is thrown into the fire, will he not much more clothe you—you of little

THE WITNESSES

✓ **SOLOMON** (MATTHEW 6:29)
He was one of King David's sons. Solomon was also king, but Solomon was best known for being considered the wisest and richest person living. He also built the temple in Jerusalem. Everything Solomon did is in the Bible in the book of 1 Kings.

faith? [31]So do not worry, saying, 'What shall we eat?' or 'What shall we drink?' or 'What shall we wear?' [32]For the pagans run after all these things, and your heavenly Father knows that you need them. [33]But seek first his kingdom and his righteousness, and all these things will be given to you as well. [34]Therefore do not worry about tomorrow, for tomorrow will worry about itself. Each day has enough trouble of its own.

---

[a] 22 The Greek for *healthy* here implies *generous*.
[b] 23 The Greek for *unhealthy* here implies *stingy*.
[c] 27 Or *single cubit to your height*

Judging Others

7 "Do not judge, or you too will be judged. ²For in the same way you judge others, you will be judged, and with the measure you use, it will be measured to you.

³"Why do you look at the speck of sawdust in your brother's eye and pay no attention to the plank in your own eye? ⁴How can you say to your brother, 'Let me take the speck out of your eye,' when all the time there is a plank in your own eye? ⁵You hypocrite, first take the plank out of your own eye, and then you will see clearly to remove the speck from your brother's eye.

⁶"Do not give dogs what is sacred; do not throw your pearls to pigs. If you do, they may trample them under their feet, and turn and tear you to pieces.

Ask, Seek, Knock

⁷"Ask and it will be given to you; seek and you will find; knock and the door will be opened to you. ⁸For everyone who asks receives; the one who seeks finds; and to the one who knocks, the door will be opened.

⁹"Which of you, if your son asks for bread, will give him a stone? ¹⁰Or if he asks for a fish, will give him a snake? ¹¹If you, then, though you are evil, know how to give good gifts to your children, how much more will your Father in heaven give good gifts to those who ask him! ¹²So in everything, do to others what you would have them do to you, for this sums up the Law and the Prophets.

The Narrow and Wide Gates

¹³"Enter through the narrow gate. For wide is the gate and broad is the road that leads to destruction, and many enter through it. ¹⁴But small is the gate and narrow the road that leads to life, and only a few find it.

True and False Prophets

¹⁵"Watch out for false prophets. They come to you in sheep's clothing, but inwardly they are ferocious wolves. ¹⁶By their fruit you will recognize them. Do people pick grapes from thornbushes, or figs from thistles? ¹⁷Likewise, every good tree bears good fruit, but a bad tree bears bad fruit. ¹⁸A good tree cannot bear bad fruit, and a bad tree cannot bear good fruit. ¹⁹Every tree that does not bear good fruit is cut down and thrown into the fire. ²⁰Thus, by their fruit you will recognize them.

True and False Disciples

²¹"Not everyone who says to me, 'Lord, Lord,' will enter the kingdom of heaven, but only the one who does the will of my Father who is in heaven. ²²Many will say to me on that day, 'Lord, Lord, did we not prophesy in your name and in your name drive out demons and in your name perform many miracles?' ²³Then I will tell them plainly, 'I never knew you. Away from me, you evildoers!'

BREAK THROUGH!

"The will of my Father"
(MATTHEW 7:21)

This will is what God wants us to do. "'Love the Lord your God with all your heart and with all your soul and with all your mind and with all your strength ... Love your neighbor as yourself.' There is no commandment greater than these." (Mark 12:30–31).

Miracle

(MATTHEW 7:22)

It's when God does something that really surprises us. This might be healing a sick person, or drying up a river so people can cross over without getting wet. They're things that people can't do — only God can do them, because he's super powerful! The Bible talks about a lot of miracles that God did.

The Wise and Foolish Builders

24"Therefore everyone who hears these words of mine and puts them into practice is like a wise man who built his house on the rock. 25The rain came down, the streams rose, and the winds blew and beat against that house; yet it did not fall, because it had its foundation on the rock. 26But everyone who hears these words of mine and does not put them into practice is like a foolish man who built his house on sand. 27The rain came down, the streams rose, and the winds blew and beat against that house, and it fell with a great crash."

28When Jesus had finished saying these things, the crowds were amazed at his teaching, 29because he taught as one who had authority, and not as their teachers of the law.

Jesus Heals a Man With Leprosy

8 When Jesus came down from the mountainside, large crowds followed him. 2A man with leprosy*a* came and knelt before him and said, "Lord, if you are willing, you can make me clean."

3Jesus reached out his hand and touched the man. "I am willing," he said. "Be clean!" Immediately he was cleansed of his leprosy. 4Then Jesus said to him, "See that you don't tell anyone. But go, show yourself to the priest and offer the gift Moses commanded, as a testimony to them."

The Faith of the Centurion

5When Jesus had entered Capernaum, a centurion came to him, asking for help.

a 2 The Greek word traditionally translated *leprosy* was used for various diseases affecting the skin.

Leprosy

(MATTHEW 8:2)

This is a disease that leaves pink-colored spots on the skin. Now it can be cured, but a very long time ago, it couldn't. It could spread to other people. That's why people were afraid to be near a person who had leprosy. These sick people had to live far away from the rest of the people.

⁶"Lord," he said, "my servant lies at home paralyzed, suffering terribly."

⁷Jesus said to him, "Shall I come and heal him?"

⁸The centurion replied, "Lord, I do not deserve to have you come under my roof. But just say the word, and my servant will be healed. ⁹For I myself am a man under authority, with soldiers under me. I tell this one, 'Go,' and he goes; and that one, 'Come,' and he comes. I say to my servant, 'Do this,' and he does it."

¹⁰When Jesus heard this, he was amazed and said to those following him, "Truly I tell you, I have not found anyone in Israel with such great faith. ¹¹I say to you that many will come from the east and the west, and will take their places at the feast with Abraham, Isaac and Jacob in the kingdom of heaven. ¹²But the subjects of the kingdom will be thrown outside, into the darkness, where there will be weeping and gnashing of teeth."

¹³Then Jesus said to the centurion, "Go! Let it be done just as you believed it would." And his servant was healed at that moment.

Jesus Heals Many

¹⁴When Jesus came into Peter's house, he saw Peter's mother-in-law lying in bed with a fever. ¹⁵He touched her hand and the fever left her, and she got up and began to wait on him.

¹⁶When evening came, many who were demon-possessed were brought to him, and he drove out the spirits with a word and healed all the sick. ¹⁷This was to fulfill what was spoken through the prophet Isaiah:

"He took up our infirmities
   and bore our diseases."ᵃ

The Cost of Following Jesus

¹⁸When Jesus saw the crowd around him, he gave orders to cross to the other side of the lake. ¹⁹Then a teacher of the law came to him and said, "Teacher, I will follow you wherever you go."

BREAKTHROUGH!

Son of Man

(MATTHEW 8:20; 9:6)

It's another way to talk about Jesus. When Jesus said he was the Son of Man, that meant he is God, but at the same time he was a person with a body like us.

²⁰Jesus replied, "Foxes have dens and birds have nests, but the Son of Man has no place to lay his head."

²¹Another disciple said to him, "Lord, first let me go and bury my father."

²²But Jesus told him, "Follow me, and let the dead bury their own dead."

Jesus Calms the Storm

²³Then he got into the boat and his disciples followed him. ²⁴Suddenly a furious storm came up on the lake, so that the waves swept over the boat. But Jesus was sleeping. ²⁵The disciples went and woke him, saying, "Lord, save us! We're going to drown!"

²⁶He replied, "You of little faith, why are you so afraid?" Then he got up and rebuked the winds and the waves, and it was completely calm.

²⁷The men were amazed and asked, "What kind of man is this? Even the winds and the waves obey him!"

ᵃ 17 Isaiah 53:4 (see Septuagint)

Jesus Restores Two Demon-Possessed Men

²⁸When he arrived at the other side in the region of the Gadarenes,^a two demon-possessed men coming from the tombs met him. They were so violent that no one could pass that way. ²⁹"What do you want with us, Son of God?" they shouted. "Have you come here to torture us before the appointed time?"

³⁰Some distance from them a large herd of pigs was feeding. ³¹The demons begged Jesus, "If you drive us out, send us into the herd of pigs."

³²He said to them, "Go!" So they came out and went into the pigs, and the whole herd rushed down the steep bank into the lake and died in the water. ³³Those tending the pigs ran off, went into the town and reported all this, including what had happened to the demon-possessed

THE SCENE

GADARENES

(MATTHEW 8:28)

This is one of the ten cities of Decapolis. It was located east of the Jordan River and south of the Sea of Galilee. Over time, it had several names, and now it's called Umm Qais and belongs to the country of Jordan.

men. ³⁴Then the whole town went out to meet Jesus. And when they saw him, they pleaded with him to leave their region.

Jesus Forgives and Heals a Paralyzed Man

9 Jesus stepped into a boat, crossed over and came to his own town. ²Some men brought to him a paralyzed man, lying on a mat. When Jesus saw their faith, he said to the man, "Take heart, son; your sins are forgiven."

³At this, some of the teachers of the law said to themselves, "This fellow is blaspheming!"

⁴Knowing their thoughts, Jesus said, "Why do you entertain evil thoughts in

BREAKTHROUGH!

"Let the dead bury their own dead."

(MATTHEW 8:22)

This is just a manner of speaking! It means that doing things for Jesus is what's most important. And it also means that for people who don't believe in God, it's like they're dead. They miss out on the nicest things in life!

---

^a 28 Some manuscripts *Gergesenes*; other manuscripts *Gerasenes*

your hearts? [5]Which is easier: to say, 'Your sins are forgiven,' or to say, 'Get up and walk'? [6]But I want you to know that the Son of Man has authority on earth to forgive sins." So he said to the paralyzed man, "Get up, take your mat and go home." [7]Then the man got up and went home. [8]When the crowd saw this, they were filled with awe; and they praised God, who had given such authority to man.

The Calling of Matthew

[9]As Jesus went on from there, he saw a man named Matthew sitting at the tax collector's booth. "Follow me," he told him, and Matthew got up and followed him.

[10]While Jesus was having dinner at Matthew's house, many tax collectors and sinners came and ate with him and his disciples. [11]When the Pharisees saw this, they asked his disciples, "Why does your teacher eat with tax collectors and sinners?"

[12]On hearing this, Jesus said, "It is not the healthy who need a doctor, but the sick. [13]But go and learn what this means: 'I desire mercy, not sacrifice.'[a] For I have not come to call the righteous, but sinners."

Jesus Questioned About Fasting

[14]Then John's disciples came and asked him, "How is it that we and the Pharisees fast often, but your disciples do not fast?"

[15]Jesus answered, "How can the guests of the bridegroom mourn while he is with them? The time will come when the bridegroom will be taken from them; then they will fast.

[16]"No one sews a patch of unshrunk cloth on an old garment, for the patch will pull away from the garment, making the tear worse. [17]Neither do people pour new wine into old wineskins. If they do, the skins will burst; the wine will run out and the wineskins will be ruined. No, they pour new wine into new wineskins, and both are preserved."

Jesus Raises a Dead Girl and Heals a Sick Woman

[18]While he was saying this, a synagogue leader came and knelt before him

THE
WITNESSES

✓ **MATTHEW** (MATTHEW 9:9)
He was one of Jesus' disciples, so he learned a lot from Jesus. The Bible says he worked as a tax collector. But he left that job because he decided to follow Jesus. *Matthew* means "gift of God."

and said, "My daughter has just died. But come and put your hand on her, and she will live." [19]Jesus got up and went with him, and so did his disciples.

[20]Just then a woman who had been subject to bleeding for twelve years came up behind him and touched the edge of his cloak. [21]She said to herself, "If I only touch his cloak, I will be healed."

[22]Jesus turned and saw her. "Take heart, daughter," he said, "your faith has healed you." And the woman was healed at that moment.

[a] 13 Hosea 6:6

BREAKTHROUGH!

Wineskins

(MATTHEW 9:17)

They didn't have glass or plastic bottles then, so they kept wine in leather bags.

²³When Jesus entered the synagogue leader's house and saw the noisy crowd and people playing pipes, ²⁴he said, "Go away. The girl is not dead but asleep." But they laughed at him. ²⁵After the crowd had been put outside, he went in and took the girl by the hand, and she got up. ²⁶News of this spread through all that region.

Jesus Heals the Blind and the Mute

²⁷As Jesus went on from there, two blind men followed him, calling out, "Have mercy on us, Son of David!"

²⁸When he had gone indoors, the blind men came to him, and he asked them, "Do you believe that I am able to do this?"

"Yes, Lord," they replied.

²⁹Then he touched their eyes and said, "According to your faith let it be done to you"; ³⁰and their sight was restored. Jesus warned them sternly, "See that no one knows about this." ³¹But they went out and spread the news about him all over that region.

³²While they were going out, a man who was demon-possessed and could not talk

was brought to Jesus. ³³And when the demon was driven out, the man who had been mute spoke. The crowd was amazed and said, "Nothing like this has ever been seen in Israel."

³⁴But the Pharisees said, "It is by the prince of demons that he drives out demons."

The Workers Are Few

³⁵Jesus went through all the towns and villages, teaching in their synagogues, proclaiming the good news of the kingdom and healing every disease and sickness. ³⁶When he saw the crowds, he had compassion on them, because they were harassed and helpless, like sheep without a shepherd. ³⁷Then he said to his disciples, "The harvest is plentiful but the workers are few. ³⁸Ask the Lord of the harvest, therefore, to send out workers into his harvest field."

CHECK THE FACTS

What was Jesus' disciple Matthew's job?

A) Carpenter

B) Fisherman

C) Tax collector

CORRECT ANSWER: C

THE
WITNESSES

✓ JAMES AND JOHN (MATTHEW 10:2)

These two guys were brothers, and their dad was Zebedee. They were both originally fishermen and they were always with Jesus, because they were his disciples. The names *James* and *Jacob* come from the same source, so sometimes people called James are also known as Jacob.

✓ PHILIP (MATTHEW 10:3)

He was one of Jesus' twelve friends who went around everywhere with him. Philip was born in a city called Bethsaida.

✓ BARTHOLOMEW (MATTHEW 10:3)

He was another friend and disciple of Jesus. It seems that he was also a good friend of Philip, because they were always together. *Bartholomew* means "son of Talmai."

✓ THOMAS (MATTHEW 10:3)

It seems that this disciple of Jesus had a twin brother, because *Thomas* means "twin." He was one of the twelve friends who went everywhere with Jesus.

✓ JAMES (MATTHEW 10:3)

This guy was another one of the twelve friends who followed Jesus everywhere. His father was Alphaeus, and his mother's name was Mary.

✓ THADDAEUS (MATTHEW 10:3)

What a nice name this disciple of Jesus had! It means "brave." He was also called Judas or Judas Thaddaeus.

✓ SIMON THE ZEALOT (MATTHEW 10:4)

He was another one of Jesus' twelve friends who always went along with him. His name was Simon, but they called him "the zealot" so as not to confuse him with the other Simon, who was Simon Peter. *Zealot* means "devoted to a cause."

Jesus Sends Out the Twelve

10 Jesus called his twelve disciples to him and gave them authority to drive out impure spirits and to heal every disease and sickness.

²These are the names of the twelve apostles: first, Simon (who is called Peter) and his brother Andrew; James son of Zebedee, and his brother John; ³Philip and Bartholomew; Thomas and Matthew the tax collector; James son of Alphaeus, and Thaddaeus; ⁴Simon the Zealot and Judas Iscariot, who betrayed him.

⁵These twelve Jesus sent out with the following instructions: "Do not go among the Gentiles or enter any town of the Samaritans. ⁶Go rather to the lost sheep of Israel. ⁷As you go, proclaim this message: 'The kingdom of heaven has come near.' ⁸Heal the sick, raise the dead, cleanse those who have leprosy,[a] drive out demons. Freely you have received; freely give.

⁹"Do not get any gold or silver or copper to take with you in your belts— ¹⁰no

---

[a] 8 The Greek word traditionally translated *leprosy* was used for various diseases affecting the skin.

TOWN OF THE SAMARITANS

(MATTHEW 10:5)

This was an ancient region on a hill east of the Jordan River, between Galilee and Judea. It was founded by King Omri, who is mentioned in the Old Testament. The Jews didn't like to pass through this area, because Jews and Samaritans were enemies.

bag for the journey or extra shirt or sandals or a staff, for the worker is worth his keep. ¹¹Whatever town or village you enter, search there for some worthy person and stay at their house until you leave. ¹²As you enter the home, give it your greeting. ¹³If the home is deserving, let your peace rest on it; if it is not, let your peace return to you. ¹⁴If anyone will not welcome you or listen to your words, leave that home or town and shake the dust off your feet. ¹⁵Truly I tell you, it will be more bearable for Sodom and Gomorrah on the day of judgment than for that town.

¹⁶"I am sending you out like sheep among wolves. Therefore be as shrewd as snakes and as innocent as doves. ¹⁷Be on your guard; you will be handed over to the local councils and be flogged in the synagogues. ¹⁸On my account you will be brought before governors and kings as witnesses to them and to the Gentiles. ¹⁹But when they arrest you, do not worry about what to say or how to say it. At that time you will be given what to say, ²⁰for it will not be you speaking, but the Spirit of your Father speaking through you.

²¹"Brother will betray brother to death, and a father his child; children will rebel against their parents and have them put to death. ²²You will be hated by everyone because of me, but the one who stands firm to the end will be saved. ²³When you are persecuted in one place, flee to another. Truly I tell you, you will not finish going through the towns of Israel before the Son of Man comes.

SODOM AND GOMORRAH

(MATTHEW 10:15)

These two cities existed many, many centuries ago. In Genesis, it says that the people who lived in those cities were so very, very bad that God destroyed them with fire. The only people who survived were Lot and his daughters.

24"The student is not above the teacher, nor a servant above his master. 25It is enough for students to be like their teachers, and servants like their masters. If the head of the house has been called Beelzebul, how much more the members of his household!

26"So do not be afraid of them, for there is nothing concealed that will not be disclosed, or hidden that will not be made known. 27What I tell you in the dark, speak in the daylight; what is whispered in your ear, proclaim from the roofs. 28Do not be afraid of those who kill the body but cannot kill the soul. Rather, be afraid of the One who can destroy both soul and body in hell. 29Are not two sparrows sold for a penny? Yet not one of them will fall to the ground outside your Father's care.*a* 30And even the very hairs of your head are all numbered. 31So don't be afraid; you are worth more than many sparrows.

32"Whoever acknowledges me before others, I will also acknowledge before my Father in heaven. 33But whoever disowns me before others, I will disown before my Father in heaven.

34"Do not suppose that I have come to bring peace to the earth. I did not come to bring peace, but a sword. 35For I have come to turn

" 'a man against his father,
    a daughter against her mother,
a daughter-in-law against her mother-in-law—
36   a man's enemies will be the
        members of his own
        household.'*b*

37"Anyone who loves their father or mother more than me is not worthy of me; anyone who loves their son or daughter more than me is not worthy of me. 38Whoever does not take up their cross and follow me is not worthy of me. 39Whoever finds their life will lose it, and whoever loses their life for my sake will find it.

40"Anyone who welcomes you welcomes me, and anyone who welcomes me welcomes the one who sent me. 41Whoever welcomes a prophet as a prophet will receive a prophet's reward, and whoever

THE
WITNESSES

✓ **ELIJAH** (MATTHEW 11:14)
This man lived a long, long time before Jesus. He was a prophet, so that means he talked to people about the message God had given him. There was a prophecy that said that Elijah would come to Earth before God's Day of Judgment (check it out in Malachi 4:5). The story of Elijah is in the Bible in the books called 1 and 2 Kings.

welcomes a righteous person as a righteous person will receive a righteous person's reward. 42And if anyone gives even a cup of cold water to one of these little ones who is my disciple, truly I tell you, that person will certainly not lose their reward."

Jesus and John the Baptist

11 After Jesus had finished instructing his twelve disciples, he went on from

---

a 29 Or *will;* or *knowledge*   *b* 36 Micah 7:6

there to teach and preach in the towns of Galilee.[a]

²When John, who was in prison, heard about the deeds of the Messiah, he sent his disciples ³to ask him, "Are you the one who is to come, or should we expect someone else?"

⁴Jesus replied, "Go back and report to John what you hear and see: ⁵The blind receive sight, the lame walk, those who have leprosy[b] are cleansed, the deaf hear, the dead are raised, and the good news is proclaimed to the poor. ⁶Blessed is anyone who does not stumble on account of me."

⁷As John's disciples were leaving, Jesus began to speak to the crowd about John: "What did you go out into the wilderness to see? A reed swayed by the wind? ⁸If not, what did you go out to see? A man dressed in fine clothes? No, those who wear fine clothes are in kings' palaces. ⁹Then what did you go out to see? A prophet? Yes, I tell you, and more than a prophet. ¹⁰This is the one about whom it is written:

" 'I will send my messenger ahead of
      you,
   who will prepare your way before
      you.'[c]

¹¹Truly I tell you, among those born of women there has not risen anyone greater than John the Baptist; yet whoever is least in the kingdom of heaven is greater than he. ¹²From the days of John the Baptist until now, the kingdom of heaven has been subjected to violence,[d] and violent people have been raiding it. ¹³For all the Prophets and the Law prophesied until John. ¹⁴And if you are willing to accept it, he is the Elijah who was to come. ¹⁵Whoever has ears, let them hear.

¹⁶"To what can I compare this generation? They are like children sitting in the marketplaces and calling out to others:

¹⁷" 'We played the pipe for you,
      and you did not dance;
   we sang a dirge,
      and you did not mourn.'

¹⁸For John came neither eating nor drinking, and they say, 'He has a demon.' ¹⁹The Son of Man came eating and drinking, and they say, 'Here is a glutton and a drunkard, a friend of tax collectors and sinners.' But wisdom is proved right by her deeds."

Woe on Unrepentant Towns

²⁰Then Jesus began to denounce the towns in which most of his miracles had been performed, because they did not repent. ²¹"Woe to you, Chorazin! Woe to you, Bethsaida! For if the miracles that were performed in you had been performed in Tyre and Sidon, they would have repented long ago in sackcloth and ashes. ²²But I tell you, it will be more bearable for Tyre and Sidon on the day of judgment than for you. ²³And you, Capernaum, will you be lifted to the heavens? No, you will go down to Hades.[e] For if the miracles that were performed in you had

---

[a] 1 Greek *in their towns*   [b] 5 The Greek word traditionally translated *leprosy* was used for various diseases affecting the skin.   [c] 10 Mal. 3:1
[d] 12 Or *been forcefully advancing*   [e] 23 That is, the realm of the dead

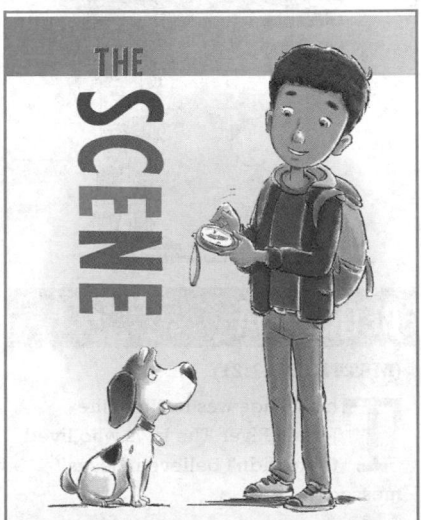

THE SCENE

CHORAZIN

(MATTHEW 11:21)

This was a village north of the Sea of Galilee. When Jesus preached in this village, the people didn't believe in him.

been performed in Sodom, it would have remained to this day. ²⁴But I tell you that it will be more bearable for Sodom on the day of judgment than for you."

The Father Revealed in the Son

²⁵At that time Jesus said, "I praise you, Father, Lord of heaven and earth, because you have hidden these things from the wise and learned, and revealed them to little children. ²⁶Yes, Father, for this is what you were pleased to do.

²⁷"All things have been committed to me by my Father. No one knows the Son

BETHSAIDA

(MATTHEW 11:21)

This village was north of the Jordan River. The Jews who lived there didn't believe in Jesus' message.

TYRE AND SIDON

(MATTHEW 11:21)

These two cities were very important a long time before Jesus was born. They were on the coast of the Mediterranean Sea.

except the Father, and no one knows the Father except the Son and those to whom the Son chooses to reveal him.

²⁸"Come to me, all you who are weary and burdened, and I will give you rest. ²⁹Take my yoke upon you and learn from me, for I am gentle and humble in heart, and you will find rest for your souls. ³⁰For my yoke is easy and my burden is light."

Jesus Is Lord of the Sabbath

12 At that time Jesus went through the grainfields on the Sabbath. His disciples were hungry and began to pick some heads of grain and eat them. ²When the Pharisees saw this, they said to him, "Look! Your disciples are doing what is unlawful on the Sabbath."

³He answered, "Haven't you read what David did when he and his companions were hungry? ⁴He entered the house of God, and he and his companions ate the consecrated bread—which was not lawful for them to do, but only for the priests. ⁵Or haven't you read in the Law that the priests on Sabbath duty in the temple desecrate the Sabbath and yet are innocent? ⁶I tell you that something greater than the temple is here. ⁷If you had known what these words mean, 'I desire mercy, not sacrifice,'ᵃ you would not have condemned the innocent. ⁸For the Son of Man is Lord of the Sabbath."

⁹Going on from that place, he went into their synagogue, ¹⁰and a man with a shriveled hand was there. Looking for a reason to bring charges against Jesus, they asked him, "Is it lawful to heal on the Sabbath?"

¹¹He said to them, "If any of you has a sheep and it falls into a pit on the Sabbath, will you not take hold of it and lift it out? ¹²How much more valuable is a person than a sheep! Therefore it is lawful to do good on the Sabbath."

¹³Then he said to the man, "Stretch out your hand." So he stretched it out and it was completely restored, just as sound as the other. ¹⁴But the Pharisees went out and plotted how they might kill Jesus.

ᵃ 7 Hosea 6:6

BREAKTHROUGH!

Sacrifice

(MATTHEW 12:7)

In the temple in Jerusalem, they sacrificed animals to ask for God's forgiveness or to give thanks for the nice things in their lives. That means that they would take little sheep or goats or bulls and kill them. Because Jesus died for us, we don't need to make sacrifices anymore.

God's Chosen Servant

¹⁵Aware of this, Jesus withdrew from that place. A large crowd followed him, and he healed all who were ill. ¹⁶He warned them not to tell others about him. ¹⁷This was to fulfill what was spoken through the prophet Isaiah:

¹⁸"Here is my servant whom I have chosen,
   the one I love, in whom I delight;
I will put my Spirit on him,
   and he will proclaim justice to the nations.
¹⁹He will not quarrel or cry out;
   no one will hear his voice in the streets.
²⁰A bruised reed he will not break,
   and a smoldering wick he will not snuff out,
till he has brought justice through to victory.

THE WITNESSES

✓ **BEELZEBUL** **(MATTHEW 12:24)**
This is the name of an ancient god, and it's also a name for the devil. The name means "Lord of the flies." How horrible!

21   In his name the nations will put
     their hope."^a

Jesus and Beelzebul

²²Then they brought him a demon-possessed man who was blind and mute, and Jesus healed him, so that he could both talk and see. ²³All the people were astonished and said, "Could this be the Son of David?"

²⁴But when the Pharisees heard this, they said, "It is only by Beelzebul, the prince of demons, that this fellow drives out demons."

²⁵Jesus knew their thoughts and said

^a 21 Isaiah 42:1-4

BREAK THROUGH!

Synagogue
(MATTHEW 12:9)

It was like a church. In Jesus' time, people met in the synagogues to pray or to read the Bible. Jesus went to the synagogue too.

to them, "Every kingdom divided against itself will be ruined, and every city or household divided against itself will not stand. ²⁶If Satan drives out Satan, he is divided against himself. How then can his kingdom stand? ²⁷And if I drive out demons by Beelzebul, by whom do your people drive them out? So then, they will be your judges. ²⁸But if it is by the Spirit of God that I drive out demons, then the kingdom of God has come upon you.

²⁹"Or again, how can anyone enter a strong man's house and carry off his possessions unless he first ties up the strong man? Then he can plunder his house.

³⁰"Whoever is not with me is against me, and whoever does not gather with me scatters. ³¹And so I tell you, every kind of sin and slander can be forgiven, but blasphemy against the Spirit will not be forgiven. ³²Anyone who speaks a word against the Son of Man will be forgiven, but anyone who speaks against the Holy Spirit will not be forgiven, either in this age or in the age to come.

³³"Make a tree good and its fruit will be good, or make a tree bad and its fruit will be bad, for a tree is recognized by its fruit. ³⁴You brood of vipers, how can you who are evil say anything good? For the mouth speaks what the heart is full of. ³⁵A good man brings good things out of the good stored up in him, and an evil man brings evil things out of the evil stored up in him. ³⁶But I tell you that everyone will have to give account on the day of judgment for every empty word they have spoken. ³⁷For by your words you will be acquitted, and by your words you will be condemned."

The Sign of Jonah

³⁸Then some of the Pharisees and teachers of the law said to him, "Teacher, we want to see a sign from you."

³⁹He answered, "A wicked and adulterous generation asks for a sign! But none will be given it except the sign of the prophet Jonah. ⁴⁰For as Jonah was three days and three nights in the belly of a huge fish, so the Son of Man will be three days and three nights in the heart of the earth. ⁴¹The men of Nineveh will stand up at the judgment with this generation and condemn it; for they repented at the preaching of Jonah, and now something greater than Jonah is here. ⁴²The Queen of the South will rise at the judgment with this generation and condemn it; for she came from the ends of the earth to listen to Solomon's wisdom, and now something greater than Solomon is here.

⁴³"When an impure spirit comes out of a person, it goes through arid places seeking rest and does not find it. ⁴⁴Then it says, 'I will return to the house I left.' When it arrives, it finds the house unoccupied, swept clean and put in order. ⁴⁵Then it goes and takes with it seven other spirits more wicked than itself, and they go in and live there. And the final condition of that person is worse than the first. That is how it will be with this wicked generation."

Jesus' Mother and Brothers

⁴⁶While Jesus was still talking to the crowd, his mother and brothers stood outside, wanting to speak to him. ⁴⁷Some-

one told him, "Your mother and brothers are standing outside, wanting to speak to you."

⁴⁸He replied to him, "Who is my mother, and who are my brothers?" ⁴⁹Pointing to his disciples, he said, "Here are my mother and my brothers. ⁵⁰For whoever does the will of my Father in heaven is my brother and sister and mother."

The Parable of the Sower

13 That same day Jesus went out of the house and sat by the lake. ²Such large crowds gathered around him that he got into a boat and sat in it, while all the people stood on the shore. ³Then he told them many things in parables, saying: "A farmer went out to sow his seed. ⁴As he was scattering the seed, some fell along the path, and the birds came and ate it up. ⁵Some fell on rocky places, where it did not have much soil. It sprang up quickly, because the soil was shallow. ⁶But when the sun came up, the plants were scorched, and they withered because they had no root. ⁷Other seed fell among thorns, which grew up and choked the plants. ⁸Still other seed fell on good soil, where it produced a crop—a hundred, sixty or thirty times what was sown. ⁹Whoever has ears, let them hear."

¹⁰The disciples came to him and asked, "Why do you speak to the people in parables?"

¹¹He replied, "Because the knowledge of the secrets of the kingdom of heaven has been given to you, but not to them. ¹²Whoever has will be given more, and they will have an abundance. Whoever does not have, even what they have will be taken from them. ¹³This is why I speak to them in parables:

"Though seeing, they do not see;
  though hearing, they do not hear or understand.

¹⁴In them is fulfilled the prophecy of Isaiah:

" 'You will be ever hearing but never understanding;
  you will be ever seeing but never perceiving.

¹⁵For this people's heart has become calloused;
  they hardly hear with their ears,
  and they have closed their eyes.
Otherwise they might see with their eyes,
  hear with their ears,
  understand with their hearts
and turn, and I would heal them.'ᵃ

¹⁶But blessed are your eyes because they see, and your ears because they hear. ¹⁷For truly I tell you, many prophets and righteous people longed to see what you

---

ᵃ *15* Isaiah 6:9,10 (see Septuagint)

BREAK THROUGH!

Sowing seed
(MATTHEW 13:3)

People used to eat a lot of wheat, because it's a very nutritious food. If they were going to plant it, they had to know if the weather was right. For planting, they used a rake or a shovel to leave the soil really, really soft. Then they'd bury each little seed about 2 inches (5 cm) deep in the ground. After that, they'd cover it with soil so the birds wouldn't eat it. Since it hardly ever rained in the country where Jesus was living, they had to water the plants by hand. If they didn't, nothing would grow.

BREAKTHROUGH!

Blessed

(MATTHEW 13:16)

This is like when we say nice things to someone. It's also when we say that God is good and wonderful. When we ask God to bless us, we're asking him to take care of us and protect us.

see but did not see it, and to hear what you hear but did not hear it.

¹⁸"Listen then to what the parable of the sower means: ¹⁹When anyone hears the message about the kingdom and does not understand it, the evil one comes and snatches away what was sown in their heart. This is the seed sown along the path. ²⁰The seed falling on rocky ground refers to someone who hears the word and at once receives it with joy. ²¹But since they have no root, they last only a short time. When trouble or persecution comes because of the word, they quickly fall away. ²²The seed falling among the thorns refers to someone who hears the word, but the worries of this life and the deceitfulness of wealth choke the word, making it unfruitful. ²³But the seed falling on good soil refers to someone who hears the word and understands it. This is the one who produces a crop, yielding a hundred, sixty or thirty times what was sown."

The Parable of the Weeds

²⁴Jesus told them another parable: "The kingdom of heaven is like a man who sowed good seed in his field. ²⁵But while everyone was sleeping, his enemy came and sowed weeds among the wheat, and went away. ²⁶When the wheat sprouted and formed heads, then the weeds also appeared.

²⁷"The owner's servants came to him and said, 'Sir, didn't you sow good seed in your field? Where then did the weeds come from?'

²⁸" 'An enemy did this,' he replied.

"The servants asked him, 'Do you want us to go and pull them up?'

²⁹" 'No,' he answered, 'because while you are pulling the weeds, you may uproot the wheat with them. ³⁰Let both grow together until the harvest. At that time I

BREAKTHROUGH!

Weed

(MATTHEW 13:25)

It's an undesirable or unwanted plant growing wild. Sometimes, it grows very tall. It's quite like the wheat, but you cannot eat it because it will make you sick with a stomachache. It is also bad for the crops, because it takes food or nourishment from them. And ... this is weird: nobody seeds the weed, it grows by itself!

will tell the harvesters: First collect the weeds and tie them in bundles to be burned; then gather the wheat and bring it into my barn.' "

The Parables of the Mustard Seed and the Yeast

31He told them another parable: "The kingdom of heaven is like a mustard seed, which a man took and planted in his field. 32Though it is the smallest of all seeds, yet when it grows, it is the largest of garden plants and becomes a tree, so that the birds come and perch in its branches."

33He told them still another parable: "The kingdom of heaven is like yeast that a woman took and mixed into about sixty pounds*a* of flour until it worked all through the dough."

34Jesus spoke all these things to the crowd in parables; he did not say anything to them without using a parable. 35So was fulfilled what was spoken through the prophet:

"I will open my mouth in parables,
    I will utter things hidden since the
    creation of the world."*b*

The Parable of the Weeds Explained

36Then he left the crowd and went into the house. His disciples came to him and said, "Explain to us the parable of the weeds in the field."

37He answered, "The one who sowed the good seed is the Son of Man. 38The field is the world, and the good seed stands for the people of the kingdom. The weeds are the people of the evil one, 39and the enemy who sows them is the devil. The harvest is the end of the age, and the harvesters are angels.

40"As the weeds are pulled up and burned in the fire, so it will be at the end of the age. 41The Son of Man will send out his angels, and they will weed out of his kingdom everything that causes sin and all who do evil. 42They will throw them into the blazing furnace, where there will be weeping and gnashing of teeth. 43Then the righteous will shine like the sun in the kingdom of their Father. Whoever has ears, let them hear.

The Parables of the Hidden Treasure and the Pearl

44"The kingdom of heaven is like treasure hidden in a field. When a man found it, he hid it again, and then in his joy went and sold all he had and bought that field.

45"Again, the kingdom of heaven is like a merchant looking for fine pearls. 46When he found one of great value, he went away and sold everything he had and bought it.

The Parable of the Net

47"Once again, the kingdom of heaven is like a net that was let down into the lake and caught all kinds of fish. 48When it was full, the fishermen pulled it up on the shore. Then they sat down and collected the good fish in baskets, but threw the bad away. 49This is how it will be at the end of the age. The angels will come and separate the wicked from the righteous 50and throw them into the blazing furnace, where there will be weeping and gnashing of teeth.

51"Have you understood all these things?" Jesus asked.

"Yes," they replied.

52He said to them, "Therefore every teacher of the law who has become a disciple in the kingdom of heaven is like the owner of a house who brings out of his storeroom new treasures as well as old."

A Prophet Without Honor

53When Jesus had finished these parables, he moved on from there. 54Coming to his hometown, he began teaching the people in their synagogue, and they were amazed. "Where did this man get this wisdom and these miraculous powers?" they asked. 55"Isn't this the carpenter's son? Isn't his mother's name Mary, and aren't his brothers James, Joseph, Simon and Judas? 56Aren't all his sisters with us? Where then did this man get all these things?" 57And they took offense at him.

---

a 33 Or about 27 kilograms   *b 35* Psalm 78:2

But Jesus said to them, "A prophet is not without honor except in his own town and in his own home."

58And he did not do many miracles there because of their lack of faith.

John the Baptist Beheaded

14 At that time Herod the tetrarch heard the reports about Jesus, 2and he said to his attendants, "This is John the Baptist; he has risen from the dead! That is why miraculous powers are at work in him."

3Now Herod had arrested John and bound him and put him in prison because of Herodias, his brother Philip's wife, 4for John had been saying to him: "It is not lawful for you to have her." 5Herod wanted to kill John, but he was afraid of the people, because they considered John a prophet.

6On Herod's birthday the daughter of Herodias danced for the guests and pleased Herod so much 7that he promised with an oath to give her whatever she asked. 8Prompted by her mother, she said, "Give me here on a platter the head of John the Baptist." 9The king was distressed, but because of his oaths and his dinner guests, he ordered that her request be granted 10and had John beheaded in the prison. 11His head was brought in on a platter and given to the girl, who carried it to her mother. 12John's disciples came and took his body and buried it. Then they went and told Jesus.

Jesus Feeds the Five Thousand

13When Jesus heard what had happened, he withdrew by boat privately to a solitary place. Hearing of this, the crowds followed him on foot from the towns. 14When Jesus landed and saw a large crowd, he had compassion on them and healed their sick.

15As evening approached, the disciples came to him and said, "This is a remote place, and it's already getting late. Send the crowds away, so they can go to the villages and buy themselves some food."

THE
WITNESSES

✓ **HEROD THE TETRARCH**
   (MATTHEW 14:1)

He was the son of a bad king who wanted to kill Jesus when he was a baby. Herod never became the king like his father, but he did rule in Galilee. And he was bad because he sent people to kill John the Baptist.

✓ **HERODIAS (MATTHEW 14:3–4)**
This woman was married to Herod the tetrarch. She was the one who gave Herod the idea of killing John the Baptist.

✓ **PHILIP (MATTHEW 14:3–4)**
This name means "lover of horses." He was another son of King Herod, the bad king who wanted to kill Jesus when he was a baby.

16Jesus replied, "They do not need to go away. You give them something to eat."

17"We have here only five loaves of bread and two fish," they answered.

¹⁸ "Bring them here to me," he said. ¹⁹And he directed the people to sit down on the grass. Taking the five loaves and the two fish and looking up to heaven, he gave thanks and broke the loaves. Then he gave them to the disciples, and the disciples gave them to the people. ²⁰They all ate and were satisfied, and the disciples picked up twelve basketfuls of broken pieces that were left over. ²¹The number of those who ate was about five thousand men, besides women and children.

Jesus Walks on the Water

²²Immediately Jesus made the disciples get into the boat and go on ahead of him to the other side, while he dismissed the crowd. ²³After he had dismissed them, he went up on a mountainside by himself to pray. Later that night, he was there alone, ²⁴and the boat was already a considerable distance from land, buffeted by the waves because the wind was against it.

²⁵Shortly before dawn Jesus went out to them, walking on the lake. ²⁶When the disciples saw him walking on the lake, they were terrified. "It's a ghost," they said, and cried out in fear.

²⁷But Jesus immediately said to them: "Take courage! It is I. Don't be afraid."

²⁸"Lord, if it's you," Peter replied, "tell me to come to you on the water."

²⁹"Come," he said.

Then Peter got down out of the boat, walked on the water and came toward Jesus. ³⁰But when he saw the wind, he was afraid and, beginning to sink, cried out, "Lord, save me!"

³¹Immediately Jesus reached out his hand and caught him. "You of little faith," he said, "why did you doubt?"

³²And when they climbed into the boat, the wind died down. ³³Then those who were in the boat worshiped him, saying, "Truly you are the Son of God."

³⁴When they had crossed over, they landed at Gennesaret. ³⁵And when the men of that place recognized Jesus, they sent word to all the surrounding country. People brought all their sick to him ³⁶and begged him to let the sick just touch the

THE SCENE

GENNESARET

(MATTHEW 14:34)

This village was northwest of the Sea of Galilee and south of Capernaum.

edge of his cloak, and all who touched it were healed.

That Which Defiles

15 Then some Pharisees and teachers of the law came to Jesus from Jerusalem and asked, ² "Why do your disciples break the tradition of the elders? They don't wash their hands before they eat!"

³Jesus replied, "And why do you break the command of God for the sake of your tradition? ⁴For God said, 'Honor your father and mother'ᵃ and 'Anyone who curses their father or mother is to be put to death.'ᵇ ⁵But you say that if anyone declares that what might have been used to help their father or mother is 'devoted to God,' ⁶they are not to 'honor their father or mother' with it. Thus you nullify the word of God for the sake of your tradition.

ᵃ 4 Exodus 20:12; Deut. 5:16   ᵇ 4 Exodus 21:17; Lev. 20:9

⁷You hypocrites! Isaiah was right when he prophesied about you:

⁸ " 'These people honor me with their lips,
  but their hearts are far from me.
⁹They worship me in vain;
  their teachings are merely human rules.'ᵃ"

¹⁰Jesus called the crowd to him and said, "Listen and understand. ¹¹What goes into someone's mouth does not defile them, but what comes out of their mouth, that is what defiles them."

¹²Then the disciples came to him and asked, "Do you know that the Pharisees were offended when they heard this?"

¹³He replied, "Every plant that my heavenly Father has not planted will be pulled up by the roots. ¹⁴Leave them; they are blind guides.ᵇ If the blind lead the blind, both will fall into a pit."

¹⁵Peter said, "Explain the parable to us."

¹⁶"Are you still so dull?" Jesus asked them. ¹⁷"Don't you see that whatever enters the mouth goes into the stomach and then out of the body? ¹⁸But the things that come out of a person's mouth come from the heart, and these defile them. ¹⁹For out of the heart come evil thoughts— murder, adultery, sexual immorality, theft, false testimony, slander. ²⁰These are what defile a person; but eating with unwashed hands does not defile them."

The Faith of a Canaanite Woman

²¹Leaving that place, Jesus withdrew to the region of Tyre and Sidon. ²²A Canaanite woman from that vicinity came to him, crying out, "Lord, Son of David, have mercy on me! My daughter is demon-possessed and suffering terribly."

²³Jesus did not answer a word. So his disciples came to him and urged him, "Send her away, for she keeps crying out after us."

²⁴He answered, "I was sent only to the lost sheep of Israel."

²⁵The woman came and knelt before him. "Lord, help me!" she said.

²⁶He replied, "It is not right to take the children's bread and toss it to the dogs."

²⁷"Yes it is, Lord," she said. "Even the dogs eat the crumbs that fall from their master's table."

²⁸Then Jesus said to her, "Woman, you have great faith! Your request is granted." And her daughter was healed at that moment.

Jesus Feeds the Four Thousand

²⁹Jesus left there and went along the Sea of Galilee. Then he went up on a mountainside and sat down. ³⁰Great crowds came to him, bringing the lame, the blind, the crippled, the mute and many others, and laid them at his feet; and he healed them. ³¹The people were amazed

---

ᵃ 9 Isaiah 29:13   ᵇ 14 Some manuscripts *blind guides of the blind*

BREAK THROUGH!

Canaanites

(MATTHEW 15:22)

These were people who lived in Canaan. It was a region between the Mediterranean Sea and the Jordan River. The encyclopedia says that the territory belongs to several different countries now. It's important to know that Jesus healed the daughter of a foreign woman, because that means that Jesus heals and protects anyone who believes in him, and it doesn't matter what country that person is from.

when they saw the mute speaking, the crippled made well, the lame walking and the blind seeing. And they praised the God of Israel.

³²Jesus called his disciples to him and said, "I have compassion for these people; they have already been with me three days and have nothing to eat. I do not want to send them away hungry, or they may collapse on the way."

³³His disciples answered, "Where could we get enough bread in this remote place to feed such a crowd?"

³⁴"How many loaves do you have?" Jesus asked.

"Seven," they replied, "and a few small fish."

³⁵He told the crowd to sit down on the ground. ³⁶Then he took the seven loaves and the fish, and when he had given thanks, he broke them and gave them to the disciples, and they in turn to the people. ³⁷They all ate and were satisfied. Afterward the disciples picked up seven basketfuls of broken pieces that were left over. ³⁸The number of those who ate was four thousand men, besides women and children. ³⁹After Jesus had sent the crowd away, he got into the boat and went to the vicinity of Magadan.

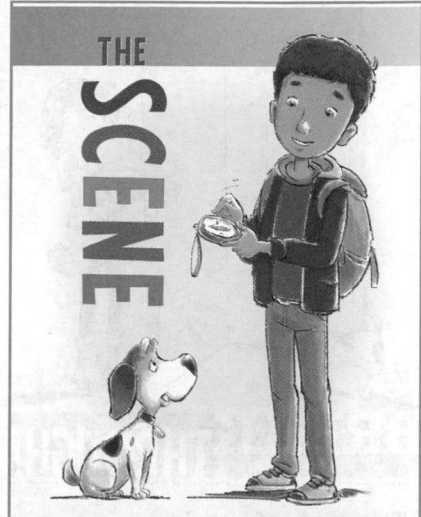

THE SCENE

MAGADAN

(MATTHEW 15:39)

Encyclopedias and atlases aren't able to explain where this village was. They think it might have been on the western coast of the Sea of Galilee.

The Demand for a Sign

16 The Pharisees and Sadducees came to Jesus and tested him by asking him to show them a sign from heaven.

²He replied, "When evening comes, you say, 'It will be fair weather, for the sky is red,' ³and in the morning, 'Today it will be stormy, for the sky is red and overcast.' You know how to interpret the appearance of the sky, but you cannot interpret the signs of the times.ª ⁴A wicked and adulterous generation looks for a sign, but none will be given it except the sign of Jonah." Jesus then left them and went away.

The Yeast of the Pharisees and Sadducees

⁵When they went across the lake, the disciples forgot to take bread. ⁶"Be careful," Jesus said to them. "Be on your guard against the yeast of the Pharisees and Sadducees."

⁷They discussed this among themselves and said, "It is because we didn't bring any bread."

⁸Aware of their discussion, Jesus asked, "You of little faith, why are you talking among yourselves about having no bread? ⁹Do you still not understand? Don't you remember the five loaves for the five thousand, and how many basketfuls you gathered? ¹⁰Or the seven loaves for the four thousand, and how many basketfuls you gathered? ¹¹How is it you don't understand that I was not talking to you about bread? But be on your guard against the yeast of the Pharisees and Sadducees." ¹²Then they understood that he was not telling them to guard against

---

ª 2,3 Some early manuscripts do not have *When evening comes . . . of the times.*

BREAKTHROUGH!

The sign of Jonah
(MATTHEW 16:4)

This story is in the Bible in the book called Jonah! God told Jonah to go to a city to talk about God and tell the people that they should ask forgiveness for their sins. But Jonah didn't want to go. He got on a boat and went in another direction. When the boat was out in the middle of the sea, there was a very bad storm. Then Jonah realized that God was angry because he had been disobedient. He told the sailors to toss him overboard so they would be saved. The sailors threw him into the sea, and a big fish swallowed him! But he didn't die, because the fish finally spit him out on the beach after three days. Jonah learned his lesson, and he never disobeyed God again. So the "sign" just means the story of Jonah.

the yeast used in bread, but against the teaching of the Pharisees and Sadducees.

Peter Declares That Jesus Is the Messiah

¹³When Jesus came to the region of Caesarea Philippi, he asked his disciples, "Who do people say the Son of Man is?" ¹⁴They replied, "Some say John the Baptist; others say Elijah; and still others, Jeremiah or one of the prophets."

¹⁵"But what about you?" he asked. "Who do you say I am?"

¹⁶Simon Peter answered, "You are the Messiah, the Son of the living God."

¹⁷Jesus replied, "Blessed are you, Simon son of Jonah, for this was not revealed to you by flesh and blood, but by my Father in heaven. ¹⁸And I tell you that you are Peter,ᵃ and on this rock I will build my church, and the gates of Hadesᵇ will not overcome it. ¹⁹I will give you the keys of the kingdom of heaven; whatever you

---

ᵃ 18 The Greek word for *Peter* means *rock.*   ᵇ 18 That is, the realm of the dead

THE SCENE

CAESAREA PHILIPPI

(MATTHEW 16:13)

This city is about 25 miles (40 km) north of the Sea of Galilee. It wasn't Jewish territory. The Greeks called this city *Paneas* in honor of the Greek god Pan. However, they later changed its name to honor the emperor, Caesar Augustus. In Caesarea Philippi, there was a natural spring of water, so that's why people went there to relax.

BREAK THROUGH!

Take up their cross

(MATTHEW 16:24)

It's just a manner of speaking! It means people stop doing what they want to do and start doing what God wants, even when they don't like it. It's like always obeying.

bind on earth will be[a] bound in heaven, and whatever you loose on earth will be[a] loosed in heaven." 20Then he ordered his disciples not to tell anyone that he was the Messiah.

Jesus Predicts His Death

21From that time on Jesus began to explain to his disciples that he must go to Jerusalem and suffer many things at the hands of the elders, the chief priests and the teachers of the law, and that he must be killed and on the third day be raised to life.

22Peter took him aside and began to rebuke him. "Never, Lord!" he said. "This shall never happen to you!"

23Jesus turned and said to Peter, "Get behind me, Satan! You are a stumbling block to me; you do not have in mind the concerns of God, but merely human concerns."

24Then Jesus said to his disciples, "Whoever wants to be my disciple must deny themselves and take up their cross and follow me. 25For whoever wants to save their life[b] will lose it, but whoever loses their life for me will find it. 26What good will it be for someone to gain the whole world, yet forfeit their soul? Or what can anyone give in exchange for their soul? 27For the Son of Man is going to come in his Father's glory with his angels, and then he will reward each person according to what they have done.

28"Truly I tell you, some who are standing here will not taste death before they see the Son of Man coming in his kingdom."

The Transfiguration

17 After six days Jesus took with him Peter, James and John the brother of James, and led them up a high mountain by themselves. 2There he was transfigured before them. His face shone like the sun, and his clothes became as white as the light. 3Just then there appeared before them Moses and Elijah, talking with Jesus.

4Peter said to Jesus, "Lord, it is good for us to be here. If you wish, I will put up three shelters—one for you, one for Moses and one for Elijah."

5While he was still speaking, a bright cloud covered them, and a voice from the cloud said, "This is my Son, whom I love; with him I am well pleased. Listen to him!"

6When the disciples heard this, they fell facedown to the ground, terrified. 7But Jesus came and touched them. "Get up," he said. "Don't be afraid." 8When they looked up, they saw no one except Jesus.

9As they were coming down the mountain, Jesus instructed them, "Don't tell anyone what you have seen, until the Son of Man has been raised from the dead."

10The disciples asked him, "Why then do the teachers of the law say that Elijah must come first?"

11Jesus replied, "To be sure, Elijah comes and will restore all things. 12But I tell you, Elijah has already come, and they

---

a 19 Or *will have been*   *b* 25 The Greek word means either *life* or *soul*; also in verse 26.

did not recognize him, but have done to him everything they wished. In the same way the Son of Man is going to suffer at their hands." ¹³Then the disciples understood that he was talking to them about John the Baptist.

Jesus Heals a Demon-Possessed Boy

¹⁴When they came to the crowd, a man approached Jesus and knelt before him. ¹⁵"Lord, have mercy on my son," he said. "He has seizures and is suffering greatly. He often falls into the fire or into the water. ¹⁶I brought him to your disciples, but they could not heal him."

¹⁷"You unbelieving and perverse generation," Jesus replied, "how long shall I stay with you? How long shall I put up with you? Bring the boy here to me." ¹⁸Jesus rebuked the demon, and it came out of the boy, and he was healed at that moment.

¹⁹Then the disciples came to Jesus in private and asked, "Why couldn't we drive it out?"

²⁰He replied, "Because you have so little faith. Truly I tell you, if you have faith as small as a mustard seed, you can say to this mountain, 'Move from here to there,' and it will move. Nothing will be impossible for you." [21]a

Jesus Predicts His Death a Second Time

²²When they came together in Galilee, he said to them, "The Son of Man is going to be delivered into the hands of men. ²³They will kill him, and on the third day he will be raised to life." And the disciples were filled with grief.

The Temple Tax

²⁴After Jesus and his disciples arrived in Capernaum, the collectors of the two-drachma temple tax came to Peter and asked, "Doesn't your teacher pay the temple tax?"

²⁵"Yes, he does," he replied.

When Peter came into the house, Jesus was the first to speak. "What do you think, Simon?" he asked. "From whom

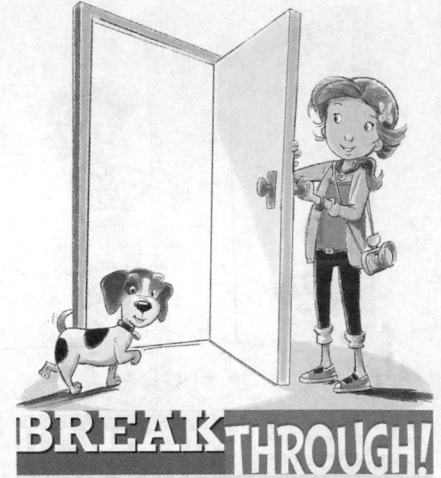

BREAKTHROUGH!

Temple tax

(MATTHEW 17:24)

In Jesus' time, people paid a tax, and the money was used in the temple to help the priest, because he had to do everything. He was in charge of the animal sacrifices. He didn't have time to be doing everything, so he needed help. In the Bible, the Old Testament says that the tax every person had to pay was the amount a working person would earn in two days.

do the kings of the earth collect duty and taxes—from their own children or from others?"

²⁶"From others," Peter answered.

"Then the children are exempt," Jesus said to him. ²⁷"But so that we may not cause offense, go to the lake and throw out your line. Take the first fish you catch; open its mouth and you will find a four-drachma coin. Take it and give it to them for my tax and yours."

The Greatest in the Kingdom of Heaven

18 At that time the disciples came to Jesus and asked, "Who, then, is the greatest in the kingdom of heaven?"

---

a 21 Some manuscripts include here words similar to Mark 9:29.

[2]He called a little child to him, and placed the child among them. [3]And he said: "Truly I tell you, unless you change and become like little children, you will never enter the kingdom of heaven. [4]Therefore, whoever takes the lowly position of this child is the greatest in the kingdom of heaven. [5]And whoever welcomes one such child in my name welcomes me.

Causing to Stumble

[6]"If anyone causes one of these little ones—those who believe in me—to stumble, it would be better for them to have a large millstone hung around their neck and to be drowned in the depths of the sea. [7]Woe to the world because of the things that cause people to stumble! Such things must come, but woe to the person through whom they come! [8]If your hand or your foot causes you to stumble, cut it off and throw it away. It is better for you to enter life maimed or crippled than to have two hands or two feet and be thrown into eternal fire. [9]And if your eye causes you to stumble, gouge it out and throw it away. It is better for you to enter life with one eye than to have two eyes and be thrown into the fire of hell.

The Parable of the Wandering Sheep

[10]"See that you do not despise one of these little ones. For I tell you that their angels in heaven always see the face of my Father in heaven. [11]a

[12]"What do you think? If a man owns a hundred sheep, and one of them wanders away, will he not leave the ninety-nine on the hills and go to look for the one that wandered off? [13]And if he finds it, truly I tell you, he is happier about that one sheep than about the ninety-nine that did not wander off. [14]In the same way your Father in heaven is not willing that any of these little ones should perish.

Dealing With Sin in the Church

[15]"If your brother or sister[b] sins,[c] go and point out their fault, just between the two of you. If they listen to you, you have won them over. [16]But if they will not listen, take one or two others along, so that 'every matter may be established by the testimony of two or three witnesses.'[d] [17]If they still refuse to listen, tell it to the church; and if they refuse to listen even to the church, treat them as you would a pagan or a tax collector.

[18]"Truly I tell you, whatever you bind on earth will be[e] bound in heaven, and whatever you loose on earth will be[e] loosed in heaven.

[19]"Again, truly I tell you that if two of you on earth agree about anything they ask for, it will be done for them by my Father in heaven. [20]For where two or three gather in my name, there am I with them."

BREAKTHROUGH!

"Cut it off and throw it away"

(MATTHEW 18:8)

How scary! We thought this was true, but it's really just a manner of speaking. We really don't have to cut off hands or take out eyes! It just means that we have to behave and not do bad things that God doesn't like.

---

a 11 Some manuscripts include here the words of Luke 19:10.   b 15 The Greek word for *brother or sister* (*adelphos*) refers here to a fellow disciple, whether man or woman; also in verses 21 and 35.   c 15 Some manuscripts *sins against you*   d 16 Deut. 19:15   e 18 Or *will have been*

The Parable of the Unmerciful Servant

²¹Then Peter came to Jesus and asked, "Lord, how many times shall I forgive my brother or sister who sins against me? Up to seven times?"

²²Jesus answered, "I tell you, not seven times, but seventy-seven times.ᵃ

²³"Therefore, the kingdom of heaven is like a king who wanted to settle accounts with his servants. ²⁴As he began the settlement, a man who owed him ten thousand bags of goldᵇ was brought to him. ²⁵Since he was not able to pay, the master ordered that he and his wife and his children and all that he had be sold to repay the debt.

²⁶"At this the servant fell on his knees before him. 'Be patient with me,' he

BREAKTHROUGH!

Sold to repay the debt

(MATTHEW 18:25)

In old times, some persons were slaves … How sad! They were people like us, but they couldn't do things they wanted to do or make their own decisions, because somebody had bought them as if they were a product! For example, if someone owed money to another person but couldn't pay, then he would become that person's slave. He had to do everything he was ordered to do.

begged, 'and I will pay back everything.' ²⁷The servant's master took pity on him, canceled the debt and let him go.

²⁸"But when that servant went out, he found one of his fellow servants who owed him a hundred silver coins.ᶜ He grabbed him and began to choke him. 'Pay back what you owe me!' he demanded.

²⁹"His fellow servant fell to his knees and begged him, 'Be patient with me, and I will pay it back.'

³⁰"But he refused. Instead, he went off and had the man thrown into prison until he could pay the debt. ³¹When the other servants saw what had happened, they were outraged and went and told their master everything that had happened.

³²"Then the master called the servant in. 'You wicked servant,' he said, 'I canceled all that debt of yours because you begged me to. ³³Shouldn't you have had mercy on your fellow servant just as I had on you?' ³⁴In anger his master handed him over to the jailers to be tortured, until he should pay back all he owed.

³⁵"This is how my heavenly Father will treat each of you unless you forgive your brother or sister from your heart."

Divorce

19 When Jesus had finished saying these things, he left Galilee and went into the region of Judea to the other side of the Jordan. ²Large crowds followed him, and he healed them there.

³Some Pharisees came to him to test him. They asked, "Is it lawful for a man to divorce his wife for any and every reason?"

⁴"Haven't you read," he replied, "that at the beginning the Creator 'made them male and female,'ᵈ ⁵and said, 'For this reason a man will leave his father and mother and be united to his wife, and the two will become one flesh'ᵉ? ⁶So they are no longer two, but one flesh. Therefore what God has joined together, let no one separate."

ᵃ 22 Or *seventy times seven*   ᵇ 24 Greek *ten thousand talents*; a talent was worth about 20 years of a day laborer's wages.   ᶜ 28 Greek *a hundred denarii*; a denarius was the usual daily wage of a day laborer (see 20:2).   ᵈ 4 Gen. 1:27   ᵉ 5 Gen. 2:24

⁷"Why then," they asked, "did Moses command that a man give his wife a certificate of divorce and send her away?"

⁸Jesus replied, "Moses permitted you to divorce your wives because your hearts were hard. But it was not this way from the beginning. ⁹I tell you that anyone who divorces his wife, except for sexual immorality, and marries another woman commits adultery."

¹⁰The disciples said to him, "If this is the situation between a husband and wife, it is better not to marry."

¹¹Jesus replied, "Not everyone can accept this word, but only those to whom it has been given. ¹²For there are eunuchs who were born that way, and there are eunuchs who have been made eunuchs by others—and there are those who choose to live like eunuchs for the sake of the kingdom of heaven. The one who can accept this should accept it."

The Little Children and Jesus

¹³Then people brought little children to Jesus for him to place his hands on them and pray for them. But the disciples rebuked them.

¹⁴Jesus said, "Let the little children come to me, and do not hinder them, for the kingdom of heaven belongs to such as these." ¹⁵When he had placed his hands on them, he went on from there.

The Rich and the Kingdom of God

¹⁶Just then a man came up to Jesus and asked, "Teacher, what good thing must I do to get eternal life?"

¹⁷"Why do you ask me about what is good?" Jesus replied. "There is only One who is good. If you want to enter life, keep the commandments."

¹⁸"Which ones?" he inquired.

Jesus replied, " 'You shall not murder, you shall not commit adultery, you shall not steal, you shall not give false testimony, ¹⁹honor your father and mother,'ᵃ and 'love your neighbor as yourself.'ᵇ"

²⁰"All these I have kept," the young man said. "What do I still lack?"

²¹Jesus answered, "If you want to be perfect, go, sell your possessions and give to the poor, and you will have treasure in heaven. Then come, follow me."

²²When the young man heard this, he went away sad, because he had great wealth.

²³Then Jesus said to his disciples, "Truly I tell you, it is hard for someone who is rich to enter the kingdom of heaven. ²⁴Again I tell you, it is easier for a camel to go through the eye of a needle than for someone who is rich to enter the kingdom of God."

²⁵When the disciples heard this, they were greatly astonished and asked, "Who then can be saved?"

²⁶Jesus looked at them and said, "With man this is impossible, but with God all things are possible."

²⁷Peter answered him, "We have left everything to follow you! What then will there be for us?"

²⁸Jesus said to them, "Truly I tell you, at the renewal of all things, when the Son of Man sits on his glorious throne, you who have followed me will also sit on twelve thrones, judging the twelve tribes of Israel. ²⁹And everyone who has left houses or brothers or sisters or father or mother or wifeᶜ or children or fields for my sake will receive a hundred times as much and will inherit eternal life. ³⁰But many who are first will be last, and many who are last will be first.

The Parable of the Workers in the Vineyard

20 "For the kingdom of heaven is like a landowner who went out early in the morning to hire workers for his vineyard. ²He agreed to pay them a denariusᵈ for the day and sent them into his vineyard.

³"About nine in the morning he went out and saw others standing in the marketplace doing nothing. ⁴He told them, 'You also go and work in my vineyard, and I will pay you whatever is right.' ⁵So they went.

"He went out again about noon and about three in the afternoon and did the

---

ᵃ 19 Exodus 20:12-16; Deut. 5:16-20   ᵇ 19 Lev. 19:18
ᶜ 29 Some manuscripts do not have or wife.
ᵈ 2 A denarius was the usual daily wage of a day laborer.

Throne

(MATTHEW 19:28)

This is the place where a king sits. It's a beautiful chair. Sometimes it's made of gold and is decorated with gemstones. It's usually placed up high—higher than the floor where people walk. Here it means that Jesus is King!

same thing. ⁶About five in the afternoon he went out and found still others standing around. He asked them, 'Why have you been standing here all day long doing nothing?'

⁷" 'Because no one has hired us,' they answered.

"He said to them, 'You also go and work in my vineyard.'

⁸"When evening came, the owner of the vineyard said to his foreman, 'Call the workers and pay them their wages, beginning with the last ones hired and going on to the first.'

⁹"The workers who were hired about five in the afternoon came and each received a denarius. ¹⁰So when those came who were hired first, they expected to receive more. But each one of them also received a denarius. ¹¹When they received it, they began to grumble against the landowner. ¹²'These who were hired last worked only one hour,' they said, 'and you have made us equal to us who have borne the burden of the work and the heat of the day.'

¹³"But he answered one of them, 'I am not being unfair to you, friend. Didn't you agree to work for a denarius? ¹⁴Take your pay and go. I want to give the one who was hired last the same as I gave you. ¹⁵Don't I have the right to do what I want with my own money? Or are you envious because I am generous?'

¹⁶"So the last will be first, and the first will be last."

Jesus Predicts His Death a Third Time

¹⁷Now Jesus was going up to Jerusalem. On the way, he took the Twelve aside and said to them, ¹⁸"We are going up to Jerusalem, and the Son of Man will be delivered over to the chief priests and the teachers of the law. They will condemn him to death ¹⁹and will hand him over to the Gentiles to be mocked and flogged and crucified. On the third day he will be raised to life!"

A Mother's Request

²⁰Then the mother of Zebedee's sons came to Jesus with her sons and, kneeling down, asked a favor of him.

²¹"What is it you want?" he asked.

She said, "Grant that one of these two sons of mine may sit at your right and the other at your left in your kingdom."

²²"You don't know what you are asking," Jesus said to them. "Can you drink the cup I am going to drink?"

"We can," they answered.

²³Jesus said to them, "You will indeed drink from my cup, but to sit at my right or left is not for me to grant. These places belong to those for whom they have been prepared by my Father."

²⁴When the ten heard about this, they were indignant with the two brothers. ²⁵Jesus called them together and said, "You know that the rulers of the Gentiles lord it over them, and their high officials exercise authority over them. ²⁶Not so with you. Instead, whoever wants to become great among you must be your servant, ²⁷and whoever wants to be first

must be your slave— ²⁸just as the Son of Man did not come to be served, but to serve, and to give his life as a ransom for many."

Two Blind Men Receive Sight

²⁹As Jesus and his disciples were leaving Jericho, a large crowd followed him. ³⁰Two blind men were sitting by the roadside, and when they heard that Jesus was going by, they shouted, "Lord, Son of David, have mercy on us!"

³¹The crowd rebuked them and told them to be quiet, but they shouted all the louder, "Lord, Son of David, have mercy on us!"

³²Jesus stopped and called them.

BREAK THROUGH!

Crucified

(MATTHEW 20:19)

A long, long time ago, the Romans killed criminals by hanging them on a cross. They would tie the criminal's hands and feet to some poles and let the person hang until he died. It was the worst way to die. They hung Jesus on a cross, and as if that wasn't bad enough, then they nailed him to the poles. That was because they wanted to show that they were treating him even worse than they would treat a thief. It was the way they treated murderers!

"What do you want me to do for you?" he asked.

³³"Lord," they answered, "we want our sight."

³⁴Jesus had compassion on them and touched their eyes. Immediately they received their sight and followed him.

Jesus Comes to Jerusalem as King

21 As they approached Jerusalem and came to Bethphage on the Mount of Olives, Jesus sent two disciples, ²saying to them, "Go to the village ahead of you, and at once you will find a donkey tied there, with her colt by her. Untie them and bring them to me. ³If anyone says anything to you, say that the Lord needs them, and he will send them right away."

⁴This took place to fulfill what was spoken through the prophet:

⁵ "Say to Daughter Zion,
  'See, your king comes to you,
    gentle and riding on a donkey,
      and on a colt, the foal of a donkey.' "ᵃ

⁶The disciples went and did as Jesus had instructed them. ⁷They brought the donkey and the colt and placed their cloaks on them for Jesus to sit on. ⁸A very large crowd spread their cloaks on the road, while others cut branches from the trees and spread them on the road. ⁹The crowds that went ahead of him and those that followed shouted,

  "Hosannaᵇ to the Son of David!"

  "Blessed is he who comes in the name of the Lord!"ᶜ

  "Hosannaᵇ in the highest heaven!"

¹⁰When Jesus entered Jerusalem, the whole city was stirred and asked, "Who is this?"

¹¹The crowds answered, "This is Jesus, the prophet from Nazareth in Galilee."

Jesus at the Temple

¹²Jesus entered the temple courts and drove out all who were buying and selling there. He overturned the tables of

---

ᵃ 5 Zech. 9:9   ᵇ 9 A Hebrew expression meaning "Save!" which became an exclamation of praise; also in verse 15   ᶜ 9 Psalm 118:25,26 the money changers and the benches of those selling doves. ¹³"It is written," he said to them, " 'My house will be called a house of prayer,'ᵃ but you are making it 'a den of robbers.'ᵇ"

¹⁴The blind and the lame came to him at the temple, and he healed them. ¹⁵But when the chief priests and the teachers of the law saw the wonderful things he did and the children shouting in the temple courts, "Hosanna to the Son of David," they were indignant.

¹⁶"Do you hear what these children are saying?" they asked him.

"Yes," replied Jesus, "have you never read,

" 'From the lips of children and infants
    you, Lord, have called forth your
        praise'ᶜ?"

¹⁷And he left them and went out of the city to Bethany, where he spent the night.

Jesus Curses a Fig Tree

¹⁸Early in the morning, as Jesus was on his way back to the city, he was hungry. ¹⁹Seeing a fig tree by the road, he went up to it but found nothing on it except leaves. Then he said to it, "May you never bear fruit again!" Immediately the tree withered.

²⁰When the disciples saw this, they were amazed. "How did the fig tree wither so quickly?" they asked.

²¹Jesus replied, "Truly I tell you, if you have faith and do not doubt, not only can you do what was done to the fig tree, but also you can say to this mountain, 'Go, throw yourself into the sea,' and it will be done. ²²If you believe, you will receive whatever you ask for in prayer."

The Authority of Jesus Questioned

²³Jesus entered the temple courts, and, while he was teaching, the chief priests and the elders of the people came to him. "By what authority are you doing these things?" they asked. "And who gave you this authority?"

²⁴Jesus replied, "I will also ask you one question. If you answer me, I will tell you by what authority I am doing these things. ²⁵John's baptism—where did it come from? Was it from heaven, or of human origin?"

They discussed it among themselves and said, "If we say, 'From heaven,' he will ask, 'Then why didn't you believe him?' ²⁶But if we say, 'Of human origin'—we are afraid of the people, for they all hold that John was a prophet."

²⁷So they answered Jesus, "We don't know."

Then he said, "Neither will I tell you by what authority I am doing these things.

The Parable of the Two Sons

²⁸"What do you think? There was a man who had two sons. He went to the first and said, 'Son, go and work today in the vineyard.'

²⁹" 'I will not,' he answered, but later he changed his mind and went.

³⁰"Then the father went to the other son and said the same thing. He answered, 'I will, sir,' but he did not go.

³¹"Which of the two did what his father wanted?"

"The first," they answered.

Jesus said to them, "Truly I tell you, the tax collectors and the prostitutes are entering the kingdom of God ahead of you. ³²For John came to you to show you the way of righteousness, and you did not believe him, but the tax collectors and the prostitutes did. And even after you saw this, you did not repent and believe him.

The Parable of the Tenants

³³"Listen to another parable: There was a landowner who planted a vineyard. He put a wall around it, dug a winepress in it and built a watchtower. Then he rented the vineyard to some farmers and moved to another place. ³⁴When the harvest time approached, he sent his servants to the tenants to collect his fruit.

³⁵"The tenants seized his servants; they beat one, killed another, and stoned a third. ³⁶Then he sent other servants

---

ᵃ *13* Isaiah 56:7   ᵇ *13* Jer. 7:11   ᶜ *16* Psalm 8:2
(see Septuagint)

to them, more than the first time, and the tenants treated them the same way. ³⁷Last of all, he sent his son to them. 'They will respect my son,' he said.

³⁸"But when the tenants saw the son, they said to each other, 'This is the heir. Come, let's kill him and take his inheritance.' ³⁹So they took him and threw him out of the vineyard and killed him.

⁴⁰"Therefore, when the owner of the vineyard comes, what will he do to those tenants?"

⁴¹"He will bring those wretches to a wretched end," they replied, "and he will rent the vineyard to other tenants, who will give him his share of the crop at harvest time."

⁴²Jesus said to them, "Have you never read in the Scriptures:

" 'The stone the builders rejected
   has become the cornerstone;
the Lord has done this,
   and it is marvelous in our eyes'[a]?

⁴³"Therefore I tell you that the kingdom of God will be taken away from you and given to a people who will produce its fruit. ⁴⁴Anyone who falls on this stone will be broken to pieces; anyone on whom it falls will be crushed."[b]

⁴⁵When the chief priests and the Pharisees heard Jesus' parables, they knew he was talking about them. ⁴⁶They looked for a way to arrest him, but they were afraid of the crowd because the people held that he was a prophet.

The Parable of the Wedding Banquet

22 Jesus spoke to them again in parables, saying: ²"The kingdom of heaven is like a king who prepared a wedding banquet for his son. ³He sent his servants to those who had been invited to the banquet to tell them to come, but they refused to come.

⁴"Then he sent some more servants and said, 'Tell those who have been invited that I have prepared my dinner: My oxen and fattened cattle have been butchered, and everything is ready. Come to the wedding banquet.'

⁵"But they paid no attention and went off—one to his field, another to his business. ⁶The rest seized his servants, mistreated them and killed them. ⁷The king was enraged. He sent his army and destroyed those murderers and burned their city.

⁸"Then he said to his servants, 'The wedding banquet is ready, but those I invited did not deserve to come. ⁹So go to the street corners and invite to the banquet anyone you find.' ¹⁰So the servants went out into the streets and gathered all the people they could find, the bad as well as the good, and the wedding hall was filled with guests.

¹¹"But when the king came in to see the guests, he noticed a man there who was not wearing wedding clothes. ¹²He asked, 'How did you get in here without wedding clothes, friend?' The man was speechless.

¹³"Then the king told the attendants, 'Tie him hand and foot, and throw him outside, into the darkness, where there will be weeping and gnashing of teeth.'

¹⁴"For many are invited, but few are chosen."

Paying the Imperial Tax to Caesar

¹⁵Then the Pharisees went out and laid plans to trap him in his words. ¹⁶They sent their disciples to him along with the Herodians. "Teacher," they said, "we know that you are a man of integrity and that you teach the way of God in accordance with the truth. You aren't swayed by others, because you pay no attention to who they are. ¹⁷Tell us then, what is your opinion? Is it right to pay the imperial tax[c] to Caesar or not?"

¹⁸But Jesus, knowing their evil intent, said, "You hypocrites, why are you trying to trap me? ¹⁹Show me the coin used for paying the tax." They brought him a denarius, ²⁰and he asked them, "Whose image is this? And whose inscription?"

²¹"Caesar's," they replied.

Then he said to them, "So give back

---

[a] 42 Psalm 118:22,23   [b] 44 Some manuscripts do not have verse 44.   [c] 17 A special tax levied on subject peoples, not on Roman citizens

to Caesar what is Caesar's, and to God what is God's."

²²When they heard this, they were amazed. So they left him and went away.

Marriage at the Resurrection

²³That same day the Sadducees, who say there is no resurrection, came to him with a question. ²⁴"Teacher," they said, "Moses told us that if a man dies without having children, his brother must marry the widow and raise up offspring for him. ²⁵Now there were seven brothers among

THE
WITNESSES

✓ **ABRAHAM, ISAAC AND JACOB**
  (MATTHEW 22:32)
These men were very important in the history of God's people. They were grandfather, father and son, and all of them obeyed God. Jacob had twelve sons and one daughter. You can read the story about these three men in the book of Genesis in the Bible.

us. The first one married and died, and since he had no children, he left his wife to his brother. ²⁶The same thing happened to the second and third brother, right on down to the seventh. ²⁷Finally, the woman died. ²⁸Now then, at the resurrection, whose wife will she be of the seven, since all of them were married to her?"

²⁹Jesus replied, "You are in error because you do not know the Scriptures or the power of God. ³⁰At the resurrection people will neither marry nor be given in marriage; they will be like the angels in heaven. ³¹But about the resurrection of the dead—have you not read what God said to you, ³²'I am the God of Abraham, the God of Isaac, and the God of Jacob'ᵃ? He is not the God of the dead but of the living."

³³When the crowds heard this, they were astonished at his teaching.

The Greatest Commandment

³⁴Hearing that Jesus had silenced the Sadducees, the Pharisees got together. ³⁵One of them, an expert in the law, tested him with this question: ³⁶"Teacher, which is the greatest commandment in the Law?"

³⁷Jesus replied: " 'Love the Lord your God with all your heart and with all your soul and with all your mind.'ᵇ ³⁸This is the first and greatest commandment. ³⁹And the second is like it: 'Love your neighbor as yourself.'ᶜ ⁴⁰All the Law and the Prophets hang on these two commandments."

Whose Son Is the Messiah?

⁴¹While the Pharisees were gathered together, Jesus asked them, ⁴²"What do you think about the Messiah? Whose son is he?"

"The son of David," they replied.

⁴³He said to them, "How is it then that David, speaking by the Spirit, calls him 'Lord'? For he says,

⁴⁴" 'The Lord said to my Lord:
    "Sit at my right hand
until I put your enemies
    under your feet." 'ᵈ

ᵃ 32 Exodus 3:6   ᵇ 37 Deut. 6:5   ᶜ 39 Lev. 19:18
ᵈ 44 Psalm 110:1

⁴⁵If then David calls him 'Lord,' how can he be his son?" ⁴⁶No one could say a word in reply, and from that day on no one dared to ask him any more questions.

A Warning Against Hypocrisy

23 Then Jesus said to the crowds and to his disciples: ²"The teachers of the law and the Pharisees sit in Moses' seat. ³So you must be careful to do everything they tell you. But do not do what they do, for they do not practice what they preach. ⁴They tie up heavy, cumbersome loads and put them on other people's shoulders, but they themselves are not willing to lift a finger to move them.

⁵"Everything they do is done for people to see: They make their phylacteries*ᵃ* wide and the tassels on their garments long; ⁶they love the place of honor at banquets and the most important seats in the synagogues; ⁷they love to be greeted with respect in the marketplaces and to be called 'Rabbi' by others.

⁸"But you are not to be called 'Rabbi,' for you have one Teacher, and you are all brothers. ⁹And do not call anyone on earth 'father,' for you have one Father, and he is in heaven. ¹⁰Nor are you to be called instructors, for you have one Instructor, the Messiah. ¹¹The greatest among you will be your servant. ¹²For those who exalt themselves will be humbled, and those who humble themselves will be exalted.

Seven Woes on the Teachers of the Law and the Pharisees

¹³"Woe to you, teachers of the law and Pharisees, you hypocrites! You shut the door of the kingdom of heaven in people's faces. You yourselves do not enter, nor will you let those enter who are trying to. [14]ᵇ

¹⁵"Woe to you, teachers of the law and Pharisees, you hypocrites! You travel over land and sea to win a single convert, and when you have succeeded, you make them twice as much a child of hell as you are.

¹⁶"Woe to you, blind guides! You say, 'If anyone swears by the temple, it means nothing; but anyone who swears by the gold of the temple is bound by that oath.'

¹⁷You blind fools! Which is greater: the gold, or the temple that makes the gold sacred? ¹⁸You also say, 'If anyone swears by the altar, it means nothing; but anyone who swears by the gift on the altar is bound by that oath.' ¹⁹You blind men! Which is greater: the gift, or the altar that makes the gift sacred? ²⁰Therefore, anyone who swears by the altar swears by it and by everything on it. ²¹And anyone who swears by the temple swears by it and by the one who dwells in it. ²²And anyone who swears by heaven swears by God's throne and by the one who sits on it.

²³"Woe to you, teachers of the law and Pharisees, you hypocrites! You give a tenth of your spices—mint, dill and cumin. But you have neglected the more important matters of the law—justice, mercy and faithfulness. You should have practiced the latter, without neglecting the former. ²⁴You blind guides! You strain out a gnat but swallow a camel.

²⁵"Woe to you, teachers of the law and Pharisees, you hypocrites! You clean the outside of the cup and dish, but inside they are full of greed and self-indulgence. ²⁶Blind Pharisee! First clean the inside of the cup and dish, and then the outside also will be clean.

²⁷"Woe to you, teachers of the law and Pharisees, you hypocrites! You are like whitewashed tombs, which look beautiful on the outside but on the inside are full of the bones of the dead and everything unclean. ²⁸In the same way, on the outside you appear to people as righteous but on the inside you are full of hypocrisy and wickedness.

²⁹"Woe to you, teachers of the law and Pharisees, you hypocrites! You build tombs for the prophets and decorate the graves of the righteous. ³⁰And you say, 'If we had lived in the days of our ancestors, we would not have taken part with them in shedding the blood of the prophets.' ³¹So you testify against yourselves that you are the descendants of those who murdered the prophets. ³²Go ahead, then, and complete what your ancestors started!

ᵃ 5 That is, boxes containing Scripture verses, worn on forehead and arm   *ᵇ 14* Some manuscripts include here words similar to Mark 12:40 and Luke 20:47.

33 "You snakes! You brood of vipers! How will you escape being condemned to hell? 34Therefore I am sending you prophets and sages and teachers. Some of them you will kill and crucify; others you will flog in your synagogues and pursue from town to town. 35And so upon you will come all the righteous blood that has been shed on earth, from the blood of righteous Abel to the blood of Zechariah son of Berekiah, whom you murdered between the temple and the altar. 36Truly I tell you, all this will come on this generation.

37 "Jerusalem, Jerusalem, you who kill the prophets and stone those sent to you, how often I have longed to gather your children together, as a hen gathers her chicks under her wings, and you were not willing. 38Look, your house is left to you desolate. 39For I tell you, you will not see me again until you say, 'Blessed is he who comes in the name of the Lord.'*a* "

The Destruction of the Temple and Signs of the End Times

24 Jesus left the temple and was walking away when his disciples came up to him to call his attention to its buildings. 2"Do you see all these things?" he asked. "Truly I tell you, not one stone here will be left on another; every one will be thrown down."

3As Jesus was sitting on the Mount of Olives, the disciples came to him privately. "Tell us," they said, "when will this happen, and what will be the sign of your coming and of the end of the age?"

4Jesus answered: "Watch out that no one deceives you. 5For many will come in my name, claiming, 'I am the Messiah,' and will deceive many. 6You will hear of wars and rumors of wars, but see to it that you are not alarmed. Such things must happen, but the end is still to come. 7Nation will rise against nation, and kingdom against kingdom. There will be famines and earthquakes in various places. 8All these are the beginning of birth pains.

9"Then you will be handed over to be persecuted and put to death, and you will be hated by all nations because of me.

10At that time many will turn away from the faith and will betray and hate each other, 11and many false prophets will appear and deceive many people. 12Because of the increase of wickedness, the love of most will grow cold, 13but the one who stands firm to the end will be saved. 14And this gospel of the kingdom will be preached in the whole world as a testimony to all nations, and then the end will come.

15"So when you see standing in the holy place 'the abomination that causes desolation,'*b* spoken of through the prophet Daniel—let the reader understand— 16then let those who are in Judea flee to the mountains. 17Let no one on the housetop go down to take anything out of the house. 18Let no one in the field go back to get their cloak. 19How dreadful it will be in those days for pregnant women and nursing mothers! 20Pray that your flight will not take place in winter or on the Sabbath. 21For then there will be great distress, unequaled from the beginning of the world until now—and never to be equaled again.

22"If those days had not been cut short, no one would survive, but for the sake of the elect those days will be shortened. 23At that time if anyone says to you, 'Look, here is the Messiah!' or, 'There he is!' do not believe it. 24For false messiahs and false prophets will appear and perform great signs and wonders to deceive, if possible, even the elect. 25See, I have told you ahead of time.

26"So if anyone tells you, 'There he is, out in the wilderness,' do not go out; or, 'Here he is, in the inner rooms,' do not believe it. 27For as lightning that comes from the east is visible even in the west, so will be the coming of the Son of Man. 28Wherever there is a carcass, there the vultures will gather.

29"Immediately after the distress of those days

" 'the sun will be darkened,
    and the moon will not give its light;
the stars will fall from the sky,
    and the heavenly bodies will be
       shaken.'*c*

---

a 39 Psalm 118:26   *b* 15 Daniel 9:27; 11:31; 12:11   *c* 29 Isaiah 13:10; 34:4

30 "Then will appear the sign of the Son of Man in heaven. And then all the peoples of the earth[a] will mourn when they see the Son of Man coming on the clouds of heaven, with power and great glory.[b] 31And he will send his angels with a loud trumpet call, and they will gather his elect from the four winds, from one end of the heavens to the other.

32 "Now learn this lesson from the fig tree: As soon as its twigs get tender and its leaves come out, you know that summer is near. 33Even so, when you see all these things, you know that it[c] is near, right at the door. 34Truly I tell you, this generation will certainly not pass away until all these things have happened. 35Heaven and earth will pass away, but my words will never pass away.

The Day and Hour Unknown

36 "But about that day or hour no one knows, not even the angels in heaven, nor the Son,[d] but only the Father. 37As it was in the days of Noah, so it will be at the coming of the Son of Man. 38For in the days before the flood, people were eating and drinking, marrying and giving in marriage, up to the day Noah entered the ark; 39and they knew nothing about what would happen until the flood came and took them all away. That is how it will be at the coming of the Son of Man. 40Two men will be in the field; one will be taken and the other left. 41Two women will be grinding with a hand mill; one will be taken and the other left.

42 "Therefore keep watch, because you do not know on what day your Lord will come. 43But understand this: If the owner of the house had known at what time of night the thief was coming, he would have kept watch and would not have let his house be broken into. 44So you also must be ready, because the Son of Man will come at an hour when you do not expect him.

45 "Who then is the faithful and wise servant, whom the master has put in charge of the servants in his household to give them their food at the proper time? 46It will be good for that servant whose master finds him doing so when he returns.

BREAKTHROUGH!

Possessions
(MATTHEW 24:47)

These are the valuable things that we have. For example, my possessions are my toys and my bracelets. An adult has things that are worth more—for example, houses, money and jewelry. The Bible says that there are people who are more worried about taking care of the things they have than taking care of their hearts and souls. That's not good!

47Truly I tell you, he will put him in charge of all his possessions. 48But suppose that servant is wicked and says to himself, 'My master is staying away a long time,' 49and he then begins to beat his fellow servants and to eat and drink with drunkards. 50The master of that servant will come on a day when he does not expect him and at an hour he is not aware of. 51He will cut him to pieces and assign him a place with the hypocrites, where there will be weeping and gnashing of teeth.

The Parable of the Ten Virgins

25 "At that time the kingdom of heaven will be like ten virgins who took their lamps and went out to meet the

---

a 30 Or *the tribes of the land*   *b 30* See Daniel 7:13-14.
c 33 Or *he*   *d 36* Some manuscripts do not have *nor the Son.*

BREAKTHROUGH!

Lamps
(MATTHEW 25:1)

Long ago, they couldn't just turn on a lamp and have a lightbulb light up like we do now. They had ceramic plates kind of like soup bowls, and those bowls had a lid that had a little hole for a string to be pulled through. They would put oil in the bowl, cover it and then burn the string, so that would give them light. They could carry these bowls around more or less like candles.

bridegroom. ²Five of them were foolish and five were wise. ³The foolish ones took their lamps but did not take any oil with them. ⁴The wise ones, however, took oil in jars along with their lamps. ⁵The bridegroom was a long time in coming, and they all became drowsy and fell asleep.

⁶"At midnight the cry rang out: 'Here's the bridegroom! Come out to meet him!'

⁷"Then all the virgins woke up and trimmed their lamps. ⁸The foolish ones said to the wise, 'Give us some of your oil; our lamps are going out.'

⁹"'No,' they replied, 'there may not be enough for both us and you. Instead, go to those who sell oil and buy some for yourselves.'

¹⁰"But while they were on their way to buy the oil, the bridegroom arrived. The

virgins who were ready went in with him to the wedding banquet. And the door was shut.

¹¹"Later the others also came. 'Lord, Lord,' they said, 'open the door for us!'

¹²"But he replied, 'Truly I tell you, I don't know you.'

¹³"Therefore keep watch, because you do not know the day or the hour.

The Parable of the Bags of Gold

¹⁴"Again, it will be like a man going on a journey, who called his servants and entrusted his wealth to them. ¹⁵To one he gave five bags of gold, to another two bags, and to another one bag,ᵃ each according to his ability. Then he went on his journey. ¹⁶The man who had received five bags of gold went at once and put his money to work and gained five bags more. ¹⁷So also, the one with two bags of gold gained two more. ¹⁸But the man who had received one bag went off, dug a hole in the ground and hid his master's money.

¹⁹"After a long time the master of those servants returned and settled accounts with them. ²⁰The man who had received five bags of gold brought the other five. 'Master,' he said, 'you entrusted me with five bags of gold. See, I have gained five more.'

²¹"His master replied, 'Well done, good and faithful servant! You have been faithful with a few things; I will put you in charge of many things. Come and share your master's happiness!'

²²"The man with two bags of gold also came. 'Master,' he said, 'you entrusted me with two bags of gold; see, I have gained two more.'

²³"His master replied, 'Well done, good and faithful servant! You have been faithful with a few things; I will put you in charge of many things. Come and share your master's happiness!'

²⁴"Then the man who had received one bag of gold came. 'Master,' he said, 'I knew that you are a hard man, harvesting where you have not sown and gathering where you have not scattered seed. ²⁵So

---

ᵃ 15 Greek *five talents . . . two talents . . . one talent*; also throughout this parable; a talent was worth about 20 years of a day laborer's wage.

I was afraid and went out and hid your gold in the ground. See, here is what belongs to you.'

26 "His master replied, 'You wicked, lazy servant! So you knew that I harvest where I have not sown and gather where I have not scattered seed? 27 Well then, you should have put my money on deposit with the bankers, so that when I returned I would have received it back with interest.

28 " 'So take the bag of gold from him and give it to the one who has ten bags. 29 For whoever has will be given more, and they will have an abundance. Whoever does not have, even what they have will be taken from them. 30 And throw that worthless servant outside, into the darkness, where there will be weeping and gnashing of teeth.'

The Sheep and the Goats

31 "When the Son of Man comes in his glory, and all the angels with him, he will sit on his glorious throne. 32 All the nations will be gathered before him, and he will separate the people one from another as a shepherd separates the sheep from the goats. 33 He will put the sheep on his right and the goats on his left.

34 "Then the King will say to those on his right, 'Come, you who are blessed by my Father; take your inheritance, the kingdom prepared for you since the creation of the world. 35 For I was hungry and you gave me something to eat, I was thirsty and you gave me something to drink, I was a stranger and you invited me in, 36 I needed clothes and you clothed me, I was sick and you looked after me, I was in prison and you came to visit me.'

37 "Then the righteous will answer him, 'Lord, when did we see you hungry and feed you, or thirsty and give you something to drink? 38 When did we see you a stranger and invite you in, or needing clothes and clothe you? 39 When did we see you sick or in prison and go to visit you?'

40 "The King will reply, 'Truly I tell you, whatever you did for one of the least of these brothers and sisters of mine, you did for me.'

41 "Then he will say to those on his left, 'Depart from me, you who are cursed, into the eternal fire prepared for the devil and his angels. 42 For I was hungry and you gave me nothing to eat, I was thirsty and you gave me nothing to drink, 43 I was a stranger and you did not invite me in, I needed clothes and you did not clothe me, I was sick and in prison and you did not look after me.'

44 "They also will answer, 'Lord, when did we see you hungry or thirsty or a stranger or needing clothes or sick or in prison, and did not help you?'

45 "He will reply, 'Truly I tell you, whatever you did not do for one of the least of these, you did not do for me.'

46 "Then they will go away to eternal punishment, but the righteous to eternal life."

The Plot Against Jesus

26 When Jesus had finished saying all these things, he said to his disciples, 2 "As you know, the Passover is two days away—and the Son of Man will be handed over to be crucified."

3 Then the chief priests and the elders of the people assembled in the palace of the high priest, whose name was Caiaphas, 4 and they schemed to arrest Jesus secretly and kill him. 5 "But not during the festival," they said, "or there may be a riot among the people."

Jesus Anointed at Bethany

6 While Jesus was in Bethany in the home of Simon the Leper, 7 a woman came to him with an alabaster jar of very expensive perfume, which she poured on his head as he was reclining at the table.

8 When the disciples saw this, they were indignant. "Why this waste?" they asked. 9 "This perfume could have been sold at a high price and the money given to the poor."

10 Aware of this, Jesus said to them, "Why are you bothering this woman? She has done a beautiful thing to me. 11 The poor you will always have with you,[a] but you will not always have me.

---

a 11 See Deut. 15:11.

¹²When she poured this perfume on my body, she did it to prepare me for burial. ¹³Truly I tell you, wherever this gospel is preached throughout the world, what she has done will also be told, in memory of her."

Judas Agrees to Betray Jesus

¹⁴Then one of the Twelve—the one called Judas Iscariot—went to the chief priests ¹⁵and asked, "What are you willing to give me if I deliver him over to you?" So they counted out for him thirty pieces of silver. ¹⁶From then on Judas watched for an opportunity to hand him over.

The Last Supper

¹⁷On the first day of the Festival of Unleavened Bread, the disciples came to Jesus and asked, "Where do you want us to make preparations for you to eat the Passover?"

¹⁸He replied, "Go into the city to a certain man and tell him, 'The Teacher says: My appointed time is near. I am going to celebrate the Passover with my disciples at your house.' " ¹⁹So the disciples did as Jesus had directed them and prepared the Passover.

²⁰When evening came, Jesus was reclining at the table with the Twelve. ²¹And while they were eating, he said, "Truly I tell you, one of you will betray me."

²²They were very sad and began to say to him one after the other, "Surely you don't mean me, Lord?"

²³Jesus replied, "The one who has dipped his hand into the bowl with me will betray me. ²⁴The Son of Man will go just as it is written about him. But woe to that man who betrays the Son of Man! It would be better for him if he had not been born."

²⁵Then Judas, the one who would betray him, said, "Surely you don't mean me, Rabbi?"

Jesus answered, "You have said so."

²⁶While they were eating, Jesus took bread, and when he had given thanks, he broke it and gave it to his disciples, saying, "Take and eat; this is my body."

²⁷Then he took a cup, and when he had given thanks, he gave it to them, saying, "Drink from it, all of you. ²⁸This is my blood of the[a] covenant, which is poured out for many for the forgiveness of sins. ²⁹I tell you, I will not drink from this fruit of the vine from now on until that day when I drink it new with you in my Father's kingdom."

³⁰When they had sung a hymn, they went out to the Mount of Olives.

Jesus Predicts Peter's Denial

³¹Then Jesus told them, "This very night you will all fall away on account of me, for it is written:

" 'I will strike the shepherd,
　　and the sheep of the flock will be
　　　　scattered.'[b]

³²But after I have risen, I will go ahead of you into Galilee."

BREAKTHROUGH!

Passover

(MATTHEW 26:2)

This is a very important Jewish celebration. It's to remember that a very, very long time ago, God brought the Jewish people out of a country called Egypt, where they had been slaves and had been treated very badly. God saw that and freed them. It's all told in a book of the Bible called Exodus. Jewish people still celebrate the Passover.

---

^a 28 Some manuscripts *the new*　　^b 31 Zech. 13:7

Zebedee along with him, and he began to be sorrowful and troubled. ³⁸Then he said to them, "My soul is overwhelmed with sorrow to the point of death. Stay here and keep watch with me."

³⁹Going a little farther, he fell with his face to the ground and prayed, "My Father, if it is possible, may this cup be taken from me. Yet not as I will, but as you will."

⁴⁰Then he returned to his disciples and found them sleeping. "Couldn't you men keep watch with me for one hour?" he asked Peter. ⁴¹"Watch and pray so that you will not fall into temptation. The spirit is willing, but the flesh is weak."

⁴²He went away a second time and prayed, "My Father, if it is not possible for this cup to be taken away unless I drink it, may your will be done."

THE
WITNESSES

✓ JUDAS ISCARIOT
(MATTHEW 10:4; 26:14)
This man was Jesus' friend. He was one of the group of twelve, but it seems that he didn't like Jesus so much, because in the end he delivered him to the enemy.

³³Peter replied, "Even if all fall away on account of you, I never will."

³⁴"Truly I tell you," Jesus answered, "this very night, before the rooster crows, you will disown me three times."

³⁵But Peter declared, "Even if I have to die with you, I will never disown you." And all the other disciples said the same.

Gethsemane

³⁶Then Jesus went with his disciples to a place called Gethsemane, and he said to them, "Sit here while I go over there and pray." ³⁷He took Peter and the two sons of

BREAK THROUGH!

"This is my body ... This is my blood"

(MATTHEW 26:26,28)
The Passover is that important time the Jews celebrate to remember that God took them out of Egypt. For that celebration, they used to sacrifice a little lamb to ask God to forgive their sins. Here, in this gospel, Jesus uses the bread and the wine to say that he is going to take the place of the little lamb so God will forgive all our sins forever.

⁴³When he came back, he again found them sleeping, because their eyes were heavy. ⁴⁴So he left them and went away once more and prayed the third time, saying the same thing.

⁴⁵Then he returned to the disciples and said to them, "Are you still sleeping and resting? Look, the hour has come, and the Son of Man is delivered into the hands of sinners. ⁴⁶Rise! Let us go! Here comes my betrayer!"

Jesus Arrested

⁴⁷While he was still speaking, Judas, one of the Twelve, arrived. With him was a large crowd armed with swords and clubs, sent from the chief priests and the elders of the people. ⁴⁸Now the betrayer had arranged a signal with them: "The one I kiss is the man; arrest him." ⁴⁹Going at once to Jesus, Judas said, "Greetings, Rabbi!" and kissed him.

⁵⁰Jesus replied, "Do what you came for, friend."*ᵃ*

Then the men stepped forward, seized Jesus and arrested him. ⁵¹With that, one of Jesus' companions reached for his sword, drew it out and struck the servant of the high priest, cutting off his ear.

⁵²"Put your sword back in its place," Jesus said to him, "for all who draw the sword will die by the sword. ⁵³Do you think I cannot call on my Father, and he will at once put at my disposal more than twelve legions of angels? ⁵⁴But how then would the Scriptures be fulfilled that say it must happen in this way?"

⁵⁵In that hour Jesus said to the crowd, "Am I leading a rebellion, that you have come out with swords and clubs to capture me? Every day I sat in the temple courts teaching, and you did not arrest me. ⁵⁶But this has all taken place that the writings of the prophets might be fulfilled." Then all the disciples deserted him and fled.

Jesus Before the Sanhedrin

⁵⁷Those who had arrested Jesus took him to Caiaphas the high priest, where the teachers of the law and the elders had assembled. ⁵⁸But Peter followed him

GETHSEMANE

(MATTHEW 26:36)

This is a garden. The name means "olive press." A press is a kind of metal container people fill with olives, and then they press down hard until oil comes out. Some people say they don't know where this place was, but other experts think it may have been east of Kidron Valley in an area near the Mount of Olives.

at a distance, right up to the courtyard of the high priest. He entered and sat down with the guards to see the outcome.

⁵⁹The chief priests and the whole Sanhedrin were looking for false evidence against Jesus so that they could put him to death. ⁶⁰But they did not find any, though many false witnesses came forward.

Finally two came forward ⁶¹and declared, "This fellow said, 'I am able to destroy the temple of God and rebuild it in three days.'"

⁶²Then the high priest stood up and said to Jesus, "Are you not going to answer? What is this testimony that these

---

ᵃ 50 Or "Why have you come, friend?"

men are bringing against you?" ⁶³But Jesus remained silent.

The high priest said to him, "I charge you under oath by the living God: Tell us if you are the Messiah, the Son of God."

⁶⁴"You have said so," Jesus replied. "But I say to all of you: From now on you will see the Son of Man sitting at the right hand of the Mighty One and coming on the clouds of heaven."ᵃ

⁶⁵Then the high priest tore his clothes and said, "He has spoken blasphemy! Why do we need any more witnesses? Look, now you have heard the blasphemy. ⁶⁶What do you think?"

"He is worthy of death," they answered.

⁶⁷Then they spit in his face and struck him with their fists. Others slapped him ⁶⁸and said, "Prophesy to us, Messiah. Who hit you?"

Peter Disowns Jesus

⁶⁹Now Peter was sitting out in the courtyard, and a servant girl came to him. "You also were with Jesus of Galilee," she said.

⁷⁰But he denied it before them all. "I don't know what you're talking about," he said.

⁷¹Then he went out to the gateway, where another servant girl saw him and said to the people there, "This fellow was with Jesus of Nazareth."

⁷²He denied it again, with an oath: "I don't know the man!"

⁷³After a little while, those standing there went up to Peter and said, "Surely you are one of them; your accent gives you away."

⁷⁴Then he began to call down curses, and he swore to them, "I don't know the man!"

Immediately a rooster crowed. ⁷⁵Then Peter remembered the word Jesus had spoken: "Before the rooster crows, you will disown me three times." And he went outside and wept bitterly.

Judas Hangs Himself

27 Early in the morning, all the chief priests and the elders of the people made their plans how to have Jesus executed. ²So they bound him, led him away and handed him over to Pilate the governor.

³When Judas, who had betrayed him, saw that Jesus was condemned, he was seized with remorse and returned the thirty pieces of silver to the chief priests and the elders. ⁴"I have sinned," he said, "for I have betrayed innocent blood."

ᵃ 64 See Psalm 110:1; Daniel 7:13.

THE WITNESSES

✓ **CAIAPHAS** (MATTHEW 26:57–58)
He was a temple priest and very important. When they took Jesus to the temple, Caiaphas was in charge there.

✓ **PILATE** (MATTHEW 27:2)
He was the Roman governor who was ruling in Judea. He was a good friend of Herod, so when he was visiting in Jerusalem, Herod let him stay in his house. Pilate didn't want to kill Jesus. He tried to avoid that, but he wasn't able to.

THE
WITNESSES

✓ **JEREMIAH** (**MATTHEW 27:9**)
This man was also a prophet. His father's name was Hilkiah. In the Bible, the book of Jeremiah talks about the messages God gave this man.

"What is that to us?" they replied. "That's your responsibility."

[5] So Judas threw the money into the temple and left. Then he went away and hanged himself.

[6] The chief priests picked up the coins and said, "It is against the law to put this into the treasury, since it is blood money." [7] So they decided to use the money to buy the potter's field as a burial place for foreigners. [8] That is why it has been called the Field of Blood to this day. [9] Then what was spoken by Jeremiah the prophet was fulfilled: "They took the thirty pieces of silver, the price set on him by the people of Israel, [10] and they used them to buy the potter's field, as the Lord commanded me."[a]

Jesus Before Pilate

[11] Meanwhile Jesus stood before the governor, and the governor asked him, "Are you the king of the Jews?"

"You have said so," Jesus replied.

[12] When he was accused by the chief priests and the elders, he gave no answer. [13] Then Pilate asked him, "Don't you hear the testimony they are bringing against you?" [14] But Jesus made no reply, not even to a single charge—to the great amazement of the governor.

[15] Now it was the governor's custom at the festival to release a prisoner chosen by the crowd. [16] At that time they had a well-known prisoner whose name was Jesus[b] Barabbas. [17] So when the crowd had gathered, Pilate asked them, "Which one do you want me to release to you: Jesus Barabbas, or Jesus who is called the Messiah?" [18] For he knew it was out of self-interest that they had handed Jesus over to him.

[19] While Pilate was sitting on the judge's seat, his wife sent him this message: "Don't have anything to do with that innocent man, for I have suffered a great deal today in a dream because of him."

[20] But the chief priests and the elders persuaded the crowd to ask for Barabbas and to have Jesus executed.

[21] "Which of the two do you want me to release to you?" asked the governor.

"Barabbas," they answered.

[22] "What shall I do, then, with Jesus who is called the Messiah?" Pilate asked.

They all answered, "Crucify him!"

[23] "Why? What crime has he committed?" asked Pilate.

But they shouted all the louder, "Crucify him!"

[24] When Pilate saw that he was getting nowhere, but that instead an uproar was starting, he took water and washed his hands in front of the crowd. "I am innocent of this man's blood," he said. "It is your responsibility!"

[25] All the people answered, "His blood is on us and on our children!"

[26] Then he released Barabbas to them.

---

[a] 10 See Zech. 11:12,13; Jer. 19:1-13; 32:6-9.
[b] 16 Many manuscripts do not have *Jesus*; also in verse 17.

But he had Jesus flogged, and handed him over to be crucified.

The Soldiers Mock Jesus

27Then the governor's soldiers took Jesus into the Praetorium and gathered the whole company of soldiers around him. 28They stripped him and put a scarlet robe on him, 29and then twisted together a crown of thorns and set it on his head. They put a staff in his right hand. Then they knelt in front of him and mocked him. "Hail, king of the Jews!" they said. 30They spit on him, and took the staff and struck him on the head again and again. 31After they had mocked him, they took off the robe and put his own clothes on him. Then they led him away to crucify him.

The Crucifixion of Jesus

32As they were going out, they met a man from Cyrene, named Simon, and they forced him to carry the cross. 33They came to a place called Golgotha (which means "the place of the skull"). 34There they offered Jesus wine to drink, mixed with gall; but after tasting it, he refused to drink it. 35When they had crucified him, they divided up his clothes by casting lots. 36And sitting down, they kept watch over him there. 37Above his head they placed the written charge against him: THIS IS JESUS, THE KING OF THE JEWS.

38Two rebels were crucified with him, one on his right and one on his left. 39Those who passed by hurled insults at him, shaking their heads 40and saying, "You who are going to destroy the temple and build it in three days, save yourself! Come down from the cross, if you are the Son of God!" 41In the same way the chief priests, the teachers of the law and the elders mocked him. 42"He saved others," they said, "but he can't save himself! He's the king of Israel! Let him come down now from the cross, and we will believe in him. 43He trusts in God. Let God rescue him now if he wants him, for he said, 'I am the Son of God.'" 44In the same way the rebels who were crucified with him also heaped insults on him.

The Death of Jesus

45From noon until three in the afternoon darkness came over all the land. 46About three in the afternoon Jesus cried out in a loud voice, *"Eli, Eli,ᵃ lema sabachthani?"* (which means "My God, my God, why have you forsaken me?").ᵇ

47When some of those standing there heard this, they said, "He's calling Elijah."

---

a 46 Some manuscripts *Eloi, Eloi*   *b 46* Psalm 22:1

CYRENE

(MATTHEW 27:32)

This Greek city was in northern Africa. It is now part of a country called Libya.

GOLGOTHA

(MATTHEW 27:33)

This was a hill outside the city of Jerusalem. The word *golgotha* means "place of the skull." Experts think that it got this name because it was near a big rock that looked like a skull. It was on this hill that the Romans crucified Jesus.

⁴⁸Immediately one of them ran and got a sponge. He filled it with wine vinegar, put it on a staff, and offered it to Jesus to drink. ⁴⁹The rest said, "Now leave him alone. Let's see if Elijah comes to save him."

⁵⁰And when Jesus had cried out again in a loud voice, he gave up his spirit.

⁵¹At that moment the curtain of the temple was torn in two from top to bottom. The earth shook, the rocks split ⁵²and the tombs broke open. The bodies of many holy people who had died were raised to life. ⁵³They came out of the tombs after Jesus' resurrection and*ᵃ* went into the holy city and appeared to many people.

⁵⁴When the centurion and those with him who were guarding Jesus saw the earthquake and all that had happened, they were terrified, and exclaimed, "Surely he was the Son of God!"

⁵⁵Many women were there, watching from a distance. They had followed Jesus from Galilee to care for his needs. ⁵⁶Among them were Mary Magdalene, Mary the mother of James and Joseph,*ᵇ* and the mother of Zebedee's sons.

ᵃ 53 Or *tombs, and after Jesus' resurrection they*
ᵇ 56 Greek *Joses*, a variant of *Joseph*

THE
WITNESSES

✓ MARY MAGDALENE (MATTHEW 27:56)
This woman learned everything Jesus taught, and she traveled with him everywhere, just like the disciples. *Magdalene* means "from the village of Migdal or Magdala."

✓ JOSEPH OF ARIMATHEA
(MATTHEW 27:57)
This man was very rich. When Jesus died, Joseph placed his body in a tomb that he had bought with silver. Joseph believed that Jesus was the Son of God. Arimathea was the village where he was living.

THE SCENE

ARIMATHEA

(MATTHEW 27:57)

This very small village in the mountainous region of Ephraim was about 20 miles (32 km) northwest of Jerusalem. It was also called Ramah.

The Burial of Jesus

⁵⁷As evening approached, there came a rich man from Arimathea, named Joseph, who had himself become a disciple of Jesus. ⁵⁸Going to Pilate, he asked for Jesus' body, and Pilate ordered that it be given to him. ⁵⁹Joseph took the body, wrapped it in a clean linen cloth, ⁶⁰and placed it in his own new tomb that he had cut out of the rock. He rolled a big stone in front of the entrance to the tomb and went away. ⁶¹Mary Magdalene and the other Mary were sitting there opposite the tomb.

The Guard at the Tomb

⁶²The next day, the one after Preparation Day, the chief priests and the Pharisees went to Pilate. ⁶³"Sir," they said, "we remember that while he was still alive that deceiver said, 'After three days I will rise again.' ⁶⁴So give the order for the tomb to be made secure until the third day. Otherwise, his disciples may come and steal the body and tell the people that he has been raised from the dead. This last deception will be worse than the first."

⁶⁵"Take a guard," Pilate answered. "Go, make the tomb as secure as you know how." ⁶⁶So they went and made the tomb secure by putting a seal on the stone and posting the guard.

Jesus Has Risen

28 After the Sabbath, at dawn on the first day of the week, Mary Magdalene and the other Mary went to look at the tomb.

²There was a violent earthquake, for an angel of the Lord came down from heaven and, going to the tomb, rolled back the stone and sat on it. ³His appearance was like lightning, and his clothes were white as snow. ⁴The guards were so afraid of him that they shook and became like dead men.

⁵The angel said to the women, "Do not be afraid, for I know that you are looking for Jesus, who was crucified. ⁶He is not here; he has risen, just as he said. Come and see the place where he lay. ⁷Then go quickly and tell his disciples: 'He has ris-

en from the dead and is going ahead of you into Galilee. There you will see him.' Now I have told you."

⁸So the women hurried away from the tomb, afraid yet filled with joy, and ran to tell his disciples. ⁹Suddenly Jesus met them. "Greetings," he said. They came to him, clasped his feet and worshiped him. ¹⁰Then Jesus said to them, "Do not be afraid. Go and tell my brothers to go to Galilee; there they will see me."

The Guards' Report

¹¹While the women were on their way, some of the guards went into the city and reported to the chief priests everything that had happened. ¹²When the chief priests had met with the elders and devised a plan, they gave the soldiers a large sum of money, ¹³telling them, "You are to say, 'His disciples came during the night and stole him away while we were

asleep.' [14]If this report gets to the governor, we will satisfy him and keep you out of trouble." [15]So the soldiers took the money and did as they were instructed. And this story has been widely circulated among the Jews to this very day.

The Great Commission

[16]Then the eleven disciples went to Galilee, to the mountain where Jesus had told them to go. [17]When they saw him, they worshiped him; but some doubted. [18]Then Jesus came to them and said, "All authority in heaven and on earth has been given to me. [19]Therefore go and make disciples of all nations, baptizing them in the name of the Father and of the Son and of the Holy Spirit, [20]and teaching them to obey everything I have commanded you. And surely I am with you always, to the very end of the age."

CASE CLOSED!

Mateo and I spent a lot of time thinking after we finished reading this book, and we decided that we liked a lot of it. We think the best part is at the end, when even after dying, Jesus is resurrected and shows us that there is life after death. And then he gave his friends an order. He said that then they had to tell everyone they knew about all the good things they had learned when they were with him. That's great!

MARK

THE EVIDENCE:

WHO WROTE IT?

Like the other authors of the Gospels, the person who wrote this book didn't sign it. So, we can't be sure who wrote it. But there was a man named Papias who wrote other things between the years 110 and 130 after Christ. He was the first person who thought that Mark wrote this book. Mark never knew Jesus personally. It seems he was just a kid when Jesus died, but it's thought that Peter, who definitely was with Jesus and was his friend and followed him everywhere, told Mark everything that had happened in Jesus' life. Then Mark wrote it all down.

Mark really had two names — he was called John Mark. We read that in another book of the New Testament, in Acts 12:12 and 25. John Mark was born in Jerusalem, and he was a friend of Paul and Barnabas, and for a time the three went around together talking to the people about Jesus.

HOW LONG AGO?

This is the shortest of the four Gospels. It has only 16 chapters, and it was the first gospel to be written. Some Bible experts think that Mark was in the city of Rome when he wrote this book about 65 years after Jesus was born.

WHAT'S IT ABOUT?

This book talks about Jesus and everything he did when he was here on Earth. (Well, not really everything, because he did a lot more, and they couldn't tell it all!) We liked reading it a lot, because Mark writes so clearly that we could understand everything. He talks about John the Baptist, who was a very brave man. And he tells how Jesus outsmarted the Pharisees when they tried to trick him. He was a genius!

THE BEST PART

Isabella thought the nicest part was near the end, when the women go to look for Jesus in the tomb and a man shows up and says, "He has risen! He is not here" (16:6).

The part Mateo liked best is in 10:14, where it says, "Let the little children come to me." That part is really nice because we're children, and that means that Jesus wants us to be at his side. That's great!

John the Baptist Prepares the Way

1 The beginning of the good news about Jesus the Messiah,[a] the Son of God,[b] [2]as it is written in Isaiah the prophet:

"I will send my messenger ahead of you,
who will prepare your way"[c]—
[3]"a voice of one calling in the wilderness,
'Prepare the way for the Lord,
make straight paths for him.'"[d]

[4]And so John the Baptist appeared in the wilderness, preaching a baptism of repentance for the forgiveness of sins. [5]The whole Judean countryside and all the people of Jerusalem went out to him. Confessing their sins, they were baptized by him in the Jordan River. [6]John wore clothing made of camel's hair, with a leather belt around his waist, and he ate locusts and wild honey. [7]And this was his message: "After me comes the one more powerful than I, the straps of

THE
WITNESSES

✓ **JOHN THE BAPTIST** (MARK 1:4)
The name *John* is from Hebrew and means "God was good." And I like that! He was a prophet who went from town to town preaching God's message and saying that Jesus was coming. He was Jesus' cousin.

BREAK THROUGH!

The Son of God / the Holy One of God
(MARK 1:1,24)
It's another way to talk about Jesus, because he's the true Son of God. It means that God chose him to be the true King of Israel.

whose sandals I am not worthy to stoop down and untie. [8]I baptize you with[e] water, but he will baptize you with[e] the Holy Spirit."

The Baptism and Testing of Jesus

[9]At that time Jesus came from Nazareth in Galilee and was baptized by John in the Jordan. [10]Just as Jesus was coming up out of the water, he saw heaven being torn open and the Spirit descending on

[a] 1 Or *Jesus Christ. Messiah* (Hebrew) and *Christ* (Greek) both mean *Anointed One.*   [b] 1 Some manuscripts do not have *the Son of God.*   [c] 2 Mal. 3:1   [d] 3 Isaiah 40:3   [e] 8 Or *in*

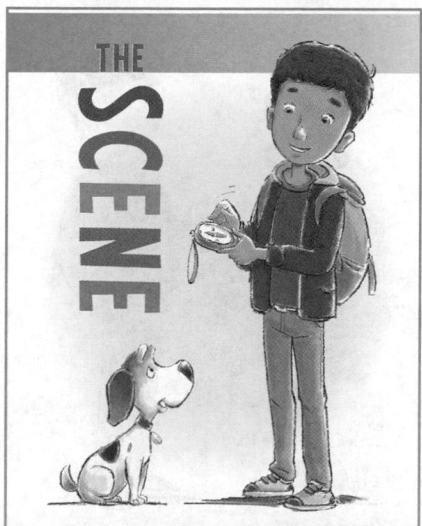

WILDERNESS

(MARK 1:4)

This is a region where plants and trees don't grow, because it hardly ever rains. It's hot during the day, and the nights can be very cold. In the region of Judea where John the Baptist lived, it was a desert. No one lived there, only some wild animals.

him like a dove. ¹¹And a voice came from heaven: "You are my Son, whom I love; with you I am well pleased."

¹²At once the Spirit sent him out into the wilderness, ¹³and he was in the wilderness forty days, being tempted*a* by Satan. He was with the wild animals, and angels attended him.

Jesus Announces the Good News

¹⁴After John was put in prison, Jesus went into Galilee, proclaiming the good news of God. ¹⁵"The time has come," he said. "The kingdom of God has come near. Repent and believe the good news!"

Jesus Calls His First Disciples

¹⁶As Jesus walked beside the Sea of Galilee, he saw Simon and his brother

Andrew casting a net into the lake, for they were fishermen. ¹⁷"Come, follow me," Jesus said, "and I will send you out to fish for people." ¹⁸At once they left their nets and followed him.

¹⁹When he had gone a little farther, he saw James son of Zebedee and his brother John in a boat, preparing their nets. ²⁰Without delay he called them, and they left their father Zebedee in the boat with the hired men and followed him.

Jesus Drives Out an Impure Spirit

²¹They went to Capernaum, and when the Sabbath came, Jesus went into the synagogue and began to teach. ²²The people were amazed at his teaching, because he taught them as one who had

---

a 13 The Greek for *tempted* can also mean *tested*.

JUDEAN COUNTRYSIDE

(MARK 1:5)

Read the explanation of Judea in Matthew 2:1.

JERUSALEM

(MARK 1:5)

Look this place up in Matthew 2:1.

Locusts and wild honey

(MARK 1:6)

A locust is a kind of grasshopper. In some places, they are also called crickets. John got his wild honey from the cracks of rocks. As he lived in the desert, he couldn't buy food at any shop, so he ate what he found. In the desert, there is almost no food at all.

The Spirit

(MARK 1:10)

It means the Holy Spirit, who also is God. But we can't see the Spirit. However, we can feel the Spirit. It's the Spirit of God who consoles us when we're sad, and it's the Spirit who gives us strength when we're tired.

JORDAN RIVER

(MARK 1:9)

This is the most important river in Palestine. It still exists and has the same name. It's super long! From beginning to end, it measures about 224 miles (360 km)! The river, which begins way up north, flows into the Sea of Galilee. That's where some of Jesus' friends would fish. From there, it continues on south and ends up in the Dead Sea. In the Bible, the Jordan River is very important, and it's there where Jesus was baptized.

authority, not as the teachers of the law. ²³ Just then a man in their synagogue who was possessed by an impure spirit cried out, ²⁴ "What do you want with us, Jesus of Nazareth? Have you come to destroy us? I know who you are—the Holy One of God!"

²⁵ "Be quiet!" said Jesus sternly. "Come out of him!" ²⁶ The impure spirit shook the man violently and came out of him with a shriek.

²⁷ The people were all so amazed that they asked each other, "What is this? A new teaching—and with authority! He even gives orders to impure spirits and they obey him." ²⁸ News about him spread quickly over the whole region of Galilee.

Jesus Heals Many

²⁹ As soon as they left the synagogue, they went with James and John to the home of Simon and Andrew. ³⁰ Simon's mother-in-law was in bed with a fever, and they immediately told Jesus about her. ³¹ So he went to her, took her hand and helped her up. The fever left her and she began to wait on them.

³²That evening after sunset the people brought to Jesus all the sick and demon-possessed. ³³The whole town gathered at the door, ³⁴and Jesus healed many who had various diseases. He also drove out many demons, but he would not let the demons speak because they knew who he was.

Jesus Prays in a Solitary Place

³⁵Very early in the morning, while it was still dark, Jesus got up, left the house and went off to a solitary place, where he prayed. ³⁶Simon and his companions went to look for him, ³⁷and when they found him, they exclaimed: "Everyone is looking for you!"

³⁸Jesus replied, "Let us go somewhere else—to the nearby villages—so I can preach there also. That is why I have come." ³⁹So he traveled throughout

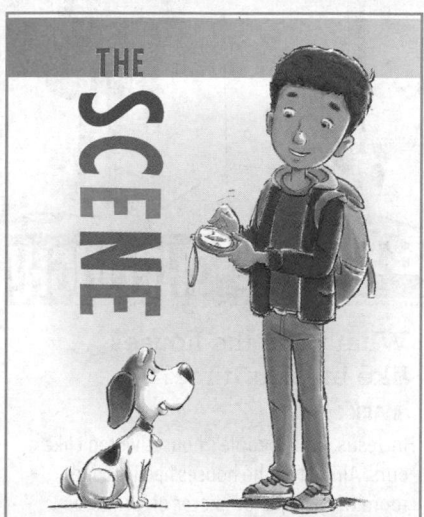

THE SCENE

SEA OF GALILEE

(MARK 1:16)

This is a big lake in the northern part of the Jordan Valley. The wind is often very strong over this lake, because it's surrounded by mountains. Sometimes it's also called the Lake of Gennesaret.

BREAKTHROUGH!

Sabbath

(MARK 1:21)

In the Bible, and for the Jews even today and for some Christians, Saturday is the day to rest and think only about God and study the Bible. God told the Jews to do this a very, very long time ago. It's also called the "day of rest."

Galilee, preaching in their synagogues and driving out demons.

Jesus Heals a Man With Leprosy

⁴⁰A man with leprosy[a] came to him and begged him on his knees, "If you are willing, you can make me clean."

⁴¹Jesus was indignant.[b] He reached out his hand and touched the man. "I am willing," he said. "Be clean!" ⁴²Immediately the leprosy left him and he was cleansed.

⁴³Jesus sent him away at once with a strong warning: ⁴⁴"See that you don't tell this to anyone. But go, show yourself to the priest and offer the sacrifices that Moses commanded for your cleansing, as a testimony to them." ⁴⁵Instead he went out and began to talk freely, spreading the news. As a result, Jesus could no longer enter a town openly but stayed outside in

---

[a] 40 The Greek word traditionally translated *leprosy* was used for various diseases affecting the skin.   [b] 41 Many manuscripts *Jesus was filled with compassion*

"Show yourself to the priest and offer the sacrifices ..."

(MARK 1:44)

In Bible times, the only person who could say a person had been cured of leprosy was the temple priest. This was very important, because if the priest didn't say he had been cured, this lonely person couldn't go back and live with his family.

lonely places. Yet the people still came to him from everywhere.

Jesus Forgives and Heals a Paralyzed Man

2 A few days later, when Jesus again entered Capernaum, the people heard that he had come home. ²They gathered in such large numbers that there was no room left, not even outside the door, and he preached the word to them. ³Some men came, bringing to him a paralyzed man, carried by four of them. ⁴Since they could not get him to Jesus because of the crowd, they made an opening in the roof above Jesus by digging through it and then lowered the mat the man was lying on. ⁵When Jesus saw their faith, he said to the paralyzed man, "Son, your sins are forgiven."

⁶Now some teachers of the law were sitting there, thinking to themselves, ⁷"Why does this fellow talk like that? He's blaspheming! Who can forgive sins but God alone?"

⁸Immediately Jesus knew in his spirit that this was what they were thinking in their hearts, and he said to them, "Why are you thinking these things? ⁹Which is easier: to say to this paralyzed man, 'Your sins are forgiven,' or to say, 'Get up, take your mat and walk'? ¹⁰But I want you to know that the Son of Man has authority on earth to forgive sins." So he said to the man, ¹¹"I tell you, get up, take your

What were the houses like in Jesus' time?

(MARK 2:1-12)

In Jesus' time, people's houses weren't like ours. Almost all the houses had just one room with only a few pieces of furniture. The walls were made of adobe (dry mud sometimes mixed with straw). Some houses had stone walls. The floors weren't made of wood, cement or tile — they were just really hard dirt, well crushed. The roofs were wood covered with dirt, so very often little plants would grow in the dirt and the people would have to pull those weeds out. All around the roof, there would be a railing to keep people from falling off.

mat and go home." ¹²He got up, took his mat and walked out in full view of them all. This amazed everyone and they praised God, saying, "We have never seen anything like this!"

Jesus Calls Levi and Eats With Sinners

¹³Once again Jesus went out beside the lake. A large crowd came to him, and he began to teach them. ¹⁴As he walked along, he saw Levi son of Alphaeus sitting at the tax collector's booth. "Follow me," Jesus told him, and Levi got up and followed him.

¹⁵While Jesus was having dinner at Levi's house, many tax collectors and sinners were eating with him and his disciples, for there were many who followed him. ¹⁶When the teachers of the law who were Pharisees saw him eating with the sinners and tax collectors, they asked his disciples: "Why does he eat with tax collectors and sinners?"

¹⁷On hearing this, Jesus said to them, "It is not the healthy who need a doctor, but the sick. I have not come to call the righteous, but sinners."

Jesus Questioned About Fasting

¹⁸Now John's disciples and the Pharisees were fasting. Some people came and asked Jesus, "How is it that John's disciples and the disciples of the Pharisees are fasting, but yours are not?"

¹⁹Jesus answered, "How can the guests of the bridegroom fast while he is with them? They cannot, so long as they have him with them. ²⁰But the time will come when the bridegroom will be taken from them, and on that day they will fast.

²¹"No one sews a patch of unshrunk cloth on an old garment. Otherwise, the

THE
WITNESSES

✓ **LEVI, SON OF ALPHAEUS** (MARK 2:14)
Matthew 9:9 calls this man Matthew. You can read who he was there.

BREAKTHROUGH!

Sinners
(MARK 2:17)
Everyone is sinful, because we are not perfect no matter how hard we try. But Jesus came for sinners. This is good news.

new piece will pull away from the old, making the tear worse. ²²And no one pours new wine into old wineskins. Otherwise, the wine will burst the skins, and both the wine and the wineskins will be ruined. No, they pour new wine into new wineskins."

Jesus Is Lord of the Sabbath

²³One Sabbath Jesus was going through the grainfields, and as his disciples walked along, they began to pick some heads of grain. ²⁴The Pharisees said to him, "Look, why are they doing what is unlawful on the Sabbath?"

²⁵He answered, "Have you never read what David did when he and his companions were hungry and in need? ²⁶In the days of Abiathar the high priest, he entered the house of God and ate the consecrated bread, which is lawful only for priests to eat. And he also gave some to his companions."

THE
WITNESSES

✓ **ABIATHAR** (MARK 2:26)
This man lived in the time of King David many years before Jesus. He was David's friend, and he gave David good advice. *Abiathar* means "father of abundance."

²⁷Then he said to them, "The Sabbath was made for man, not man for the Sabbath. ²⁸So the Son of Man is Lord even of the Sabbath."

Jesus Heals on the Sabbath

3 Another time Jesus went into the synagogue, and a man with a shriveled hand was there. ²Some of them were looking for a reason to accuse Jesus, so they watched him closely to see if he would heal him on the Sabbath. ³Jesus said to the man with the shriveled hand, "Stand up in front of everyone."

⁴Then Jesus asked them, "Which is lawful on the Sabbath: to do good or to

BREAKTHROUGH!

How was wine stored in Jesus' time?

(MARK 2:22)

In Jesus' time, people kept oil and wine in bottles made of clay. They also kept wine in bags made of leather, called wineskins. The people kept wine in these bags especially when they needed to travel.

BREAK THROUGH!

Shriveled hand

(MARK 3:1)

This means that the hand was rather dry and couldn't move, but Jesus healed it.

do evil, to save life or to kill?" But they remained silent.

⁵He looked around at them in anger and, deeply distressed at their stubborn hearts, said to the man, "Stretch out your hand." He stretched it out, and his hand was completely restored. ⁶Then the Pharisees went out and began to plot with the Herodians how they might kill Jesus.

Crowds Follow Jesus

⁷Jesus withdrew with his disciples to the lake, and a large crowd from Galilee followed. ⁸When they heard about all he was doing, many people came to him from Judea, Jerusalem, Idumea, and the regions across the Jordan and around Tyre and Sidon. ⁹Because of the crowd he told his disciples to have a small boat ready for him, to keep the people from crowding him. ¹⁰For he had healed many, so that those with diseases were pushing forward to touch him. ¹¹Whenever the impure spirits saw him, they fell down before him and cried out, "You are the Son of God." ¹²But he gave them strict orders not to tell others about him.

Jesus Appoints the Twelve

¹³Jesus went up on a mountainside and called to him those he wanted, and they came to him. ¹⁴He appointed twelve*ᵃ* that they might be with him and that he might send them out to preach ¹⁵and to have authority to drive out demons. ¹⁶These are the twelve he appointed: Simon (to whom he gave the name Peter), ¹⁷James son of Zebedee and his brother John (to them he gave the name Boanerges, which means "sons of thunder"), ¹⁸Andrew, Philip, Bartholomew, Matthew, Thomas, James son of Alphaeus, Thaddaeus, Simon the Zealot ¹⁹and Judas Iscariot, who betrayed him.

Jesus Accused by His Family and by Teachers of the Law

²⁰Then Jesus entered a house, and again a crowd gathered, so that he and

---

ᵃ 14 Some manuscripts *twelve — designating them apostles —*

BREAK THROUGH!

The Twelve

(MARK 3:13-19)

They were twelve friends of Jesus, who always went with him everywhere and learned everything that Jesus taught. When Jesus went to heaven, those twelve friends said that they were now in charge of teaching these same things to other people.

his disciples were not even able to eat. [21]When his family[a] heard about this, they went to take charge of him, for they said, "He is out of his mind."

[22]And the teachers of the law who came down from Jerusalem said, "He is possessed by Beelzebul! By the prince of demons he is driving out demons."

[23]So Jesus called them over to him and began to speak to them in parables: "How can Satan drive out Satan? [24]If a kingdom is divided against itself, that kingdom cannot stand. [25]If a house is divided against itself, that house cannot stand. [26]And if Satan opposes himself and is divided, he cannot stand; his end has come. [27]In fact, no one can enter a strong man's house without first tying him up. Then he can plunder the strong man's house. [28]Truly I tell you, people can be forgiven all their sins and every slander they utter, [29]but whoever blasphemes against the Holy Spirit will never be forgiven; they are guilty of an eternal sin."

[30]He said this because they were saying, "He has an impure spirit."

[31]Then Jesus' mother and brothers arrived. Standing outside, they sent someone in to call him. [32]A crowd was sitting around him, and they told him, "Your mother and brothers are outside looking for you."

[33]"Who are my mother and my brothers?" he asked.

[34]Then he looked at those seated in a circle around him and said, "Here are my mother and my brothers! [35]Whoever does God's will is my brother and sister and mother."

The Parable of the Sower

4 Again Jesus began to teach by the lake. The crowd that gathered around him was so large that he got into a boat and sat in it out on the lake, while all the people were along the shore at the water's edge. [2]He taught them many things by parables, and in his teaching said: [3]"Listen! A farmer went out to sow his seed. [4]As he was scattering the seed, some fell along the path, and the birds came and ate it up. [5]Some fell on rocky places, where it did not have much soil.

It sprang up quickly, because the soil was shallow. [6]But when the sun came up, the plants were scorched, and they withered because they had no root. [7]Other seed fell among thorns, which grew up and choked the plants, so that they did not bear grain. [8]Still other seed fell on good soil. It came up, grew and produced a crop, some multiplying thirty, some sixty, some a hundred times."

[9]Then Jesus said, "Whoever has ears to hear, let them hear."

[10]When he was alone, the Twelve and the others around him asked him about the parables. [11]He told them, "The secret of the kingdom of God has been given to you. But to those on the outside everything is said in parables [12]so that,

" 'they may be ever seeing but never
    perceiving,
and ever hearing but never
    understanding;
otherwise they might turn and be
    forgiven!'[b]"

[13]Then Jesus said to them, "Don't you understand this parable? How then will you understand any parable? [14]The farmer sows the word. [15]Some people are like seed along the path, where the word is sown. As soon as they hear it, Satan comes and takes away the word that was sown in them. [16]Others, like seed sown on rocky places, hear the word and at once receive it with joy. [17]But since they have no root, they last only a short time. When trouble or persecution comes because of the word, they quickly fall away. [18]Still others, like seed sown among thorns, hear the word; [19]but the worries of this life, the deceitfulness of wealth and the desires for other things come in and choke the word, making it unfruitful. [20]Others, like seed sown on good soil, hear the word, accept it, and produce a crop—some thirty, some sixty, some a hundred times what was sown."

A Lamp on a Stand

[21]He said to them, "Do you bring in a lamp to put it under a bowl or a bed? Instead, don't you put it on its stand? [22]For

---

[a] 21 Or his associates   [b] 12 Isaiah 6:9,10

whatever is hidden is meant to be disclosed, and whatever is concealed is meant to be brought out into the open. ²³If anyone has ears to hear, let them hear."

²⁴"Consider carefully what you hear," he continued. "With the measure you use, it will be measured to you—and even more. ²⁵Whoever has will be given more; whoever does not have, even what they have will be taken from them."

The Parable of the Growing Seed

²⁶He also said, "This is what the kingdom of God is like. A man scatters seed on the ground. ²⁷Night and day, whether he sleeps or gets up, the seed sprouts and grows, though he does not know how. ²⁸All by itself the soil produces grain—first the stalk, then the head, then the full kernel in the head. ²⁹As soon as the grain is ripe, he puts the sickle to it, because the harvest has come."

The Parable of the Mustard Seed

³⁰Again he said, "What shall we say the kingdom of God is like, or what parable shall we use to describe it? ³¹It is like a mustard seed, which is the smallest of all seeds on earth. ³²Yet when planted, it grows and becomes the largest of all garden plants, with such big branches that the birds can perch in its shade."

³³With many similar parables Jesus spoke the word to them, as much as they could understand. ³⁴He did not say anything to them without using a parable. But when he was alone with his own disciples, he explained everything.

Jesus Calms the Storm

³⁵That day when evening came, he said to his disciples, "Let us go over to the other side." ³⁶Leaving the crowd behind, they took him along, just as he was, in the boat. There were also other boats with him. ³⁷A furious squall came up, and the waves broke over the boat, so that it was nearly swamped. ³⁸Jesus was in the stern, sleeping on a cushion. The disciples woke him and said to him, "Teacher, don't you care if we drown?"

³⁹He got up, rebuked the wind and said to the waves, "Quiet! Be still!" Then the wind died down and it was completely calm.

⁴⁰He said to his disciples, "Why are you so afraid? Do you still have no faith?"

⁴¹They were terrified and asked each other, "Who is this? Even the wind and the waves obey him!"

Jesus Restores a Demon-Possessed Man

5 They went across the lake to the region of the Gerasenes.ᵃ ²When Jesus got out of the boat, a man with an impure spirit came from the tombs to meet him. ³This man lived in the tombs, and no one could bind him anymore, not even with a chain. ⁴For he had often been chained

---

ᵃ 1 Some manuscripts *Gadarenes*; other manuscripts *Gergesenes*

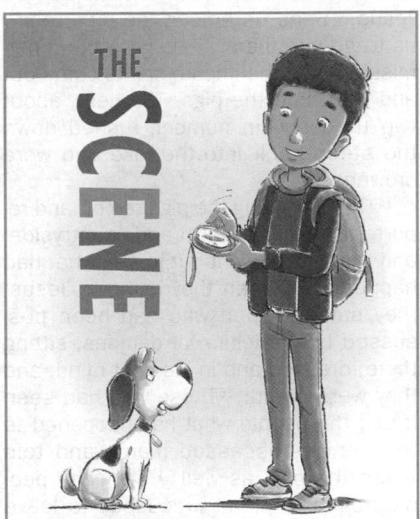

GERASENES

(MARK 5:1)

A city east of the Jordan River. Now it's called Jerash, and it's in the country of Jordan. There are still buildings there that date to Jesus' time.

hand and foot, but he tore the chains apart and broke the irons on his feet. No one was strong enough to subdue him. [5]Night and day among the tombs and in the hills he would cry out and cut himself with stones.

[6]When he saw Jesus from a distance, he ran and fell on his knees in front of him. [7]He shouted at the top of his voice, "What do you want with me, Jesus, Son of the Most High God? In God's name don't torture me!" [8]For Jesus had said to him, "Come out of this man, you impure spirit!"

[9]Then Jesus asked him, "What is your name?"

"My name is Legion," he replied, "for we are many." [10]And he begged Jesus again and again not to send them out of the area.

[11]A large herd of pigs was feeding on the nearby hillside. [12]The demons begged Jesus, "Send us among the pigs; allow us to go into them." [13]He gave them permission, and the impure spirits came out and went into the pigs. The herd, about two thousand in number, rushed down the steep bank into the lake and were drowned.

[14]Those tending the pigs ran off and reported this in the town and countryside, and the people went out to see what had happened. [15]When they came to Jesus, they saw the man who had been possessed by the legion of demons, sitting there, dressed and in his right mind; and they were afraid. [16]Those who had seen it told the people what had happened to the demon-possessed man—and told about the pigs as well. [17]Then the people began to plead with Jesus to leave their region.

[18]As Jesus was getting into the boat, the man who had been demon-possessed begged to go with him. [19]Jesus did not let him, but said, "Go home to your own people and tell them how much the Lord has done for you, and how he has had mercy on you." [20]So the man went away and began to tell in the Decapolis[a] how much Jesus had done for him. And all the people were amazed.

Jesus Raises a Dead Girl and Heals a Sick Woman

[21]When Jesus had again crossed over by boat to the other side of the lake, a large crowd gathered around him while he was by the lake. [22]Then one of the synagogue leaders, named Jairus, came, and when he saw Jesus, he fell at his feet. [23]He pleaded earnestly with him, "My little daughter is dying. Please come and put your hands on her so that she will be healed and live." [24]So Jesus went with him.

---

[a] 20 That is, the Ten Cities

THE
WITNESSES

✓ **JAIRUS** (MARK 5:22)
He was a Jew from the synagogue who believed in Jesus. His daughter was sick, and he asked Jesus to heal her. Jesus healed her because Jairus put his trust in him.

A large crowd followed and pressed around him. ²⁵And a woman was there who had been subject to bleeding for twelve years. ²⁶She had suffered a great deal under the care of many doctors and had spent all she had, yet instead of getting better she grew worse. ²⁷When she heard about Jesus, she came up behind him in the crowd and touched his cloak, ²⁸because she thought, "If I just touch his clothes, I will be healed." ²⁹Immediately her bleeding stopped and she felt in her body that she was freed from her suffering.

³⁰At once Jesus realized that power had gone out from him. He turned around in the crowd and asked, "Who touched my clothes?"

³¹"You see the people crowding against you," his disciples answered, "and yet you can ask, 'Who touched me?' "

³²But Jesus kept looking around to see who had done it. ³³Then the woman, knowing what had happened to her, came and fell at his feet and, trembling with fear, told him the whole truth. ³⁴He said to her, "Daughter, your faith has healed you. Go in peace and be freed from your suffering."

³⁵While Jesus was still speaking, some people came from the house of Jairus, the synagogue leader. "Your daughter is dead," they said. "Why bother the teacher anymore?"

³⁶Overhearing*ᵃ* what they said, Jesus told him, "Don't be afraid; just believe."

³⁷He did not let anyone follow him except Peter, James and John the brother of James. ³⁸When they came to the home of the synagogue leader, Jesus saw a commotion, with people crying and wailing loudly. ³⁹He went in and said to them, "Why all this commotion and wailing? The child is not dead but asleep." ⁴⁰But they laughed at him.

After he put them all out, he took the child's father and mother and the disciples who were with him, and went in where the child was. ⁴¹He took her by the hand and said to her, *"Talitha koum!"* (which means "Little girl, I say to you, get up!"). ⁴²Immediately the girl stood up and began to walk around (she was twelve years old). At this they were completely astonished. ⁴³He gave strict orders not to let anyone know about this, and told them to give her something to eat.

A Prophet Without Honor

6 Jesus left there and went to his hometown, accompanied by his disciples. ²When the Sabbath came, he began to teach in the synagogue, and many who heard him were amazed.

"Where did this man get these things?" they asked. "What's this wisdom that has been given him? What are these remarkable miracles he is performing? ³Isn't this the carpenter? Isn't this Mary's son and the brother of James, Joseph,ᵇ Judas and Simon? Aren't his sisters here with us?" And they took offense at him.

⁴Jesus said to them, "A prophet is not without honor except in his own

BREAKTHROUGH!

Did power come out of Jesus?

(MARK 5:30)

Yes, because Jesus is God and is all-powerful. Here, it means that Jesus realized that the woman was healed just by touching him and believing that he could heal her. God *is* all-powerful!

ᵃ 36 Or *Ignoring*   ᵇ 3 Greek *Joses*, a variant of *Joseph* dust off your feet as a testimony against them."

¹²They went out and preached that people should repent. ¹³They drove out many demons and anointed many sick people with oil and healed them.

John the Baptist Beheaded

¹⁴King Herod heard about this, for Jesus' name had become well known. Some were saying,ᵃ "John the Baptist has been raised from the dead, and that is why miraculous powers are at work in him."

ᵃ *14 Some early manuscripts He was saying*

BREAKTHROUGH!

The carpenter, Mary's son and the brother of James, Joseph, Judas and Simon

(MARK 6:3-4)

This is Jesus' family. He had sisters too, but their names are not in this list. The people around Jesus at that time couldn't believe that he could make such super powerful things happen, because they knew him and his family so well!

town, among his relatives and in his own home." ⁵He could not do any miracles there, except lay his hands on a few sick people and heal them. ⁶He was amazed at their lack of faith.

Jesus Sends Out the Twelve

Then Jesus went around teaching from village to village. ⁷Calling the Twelve to him, he began to send them out two by two and gave them authority over impure spirits.

⁸These were his instructions: "Take nothing for the journey except a staff— no bread, no bag, no money in your belts. ⁹Wear sandals but not an extra shirt. ¹⁰Whenever you enter a house, stay there until you leave that town. ¹¹And if any place will not welcome you or listen to you, leave that place and shake the

BREAKTHROUGH!

"Shake the dust off your feet"

(MARK 6:11)

This was a custom in the villages where Jesus lived. Since there weren't any hotels, if a traveler couldn't get back home because it was far away, he asked permission to stay in a house, and the owner almost always let him stay. But if the owners of the house were bad people and wouldn't let him stay, the traveler would take off his sandals and hit one against the other. Since they were full of dust from the road, the dust would fly off. This was a way of showing that the owners weren't polite and wouldn't help another person.

BREAKTHROUGH!

Oil

(MARK 6:13)

Long ago, people thought that oil could cure sickness, but it's really God who has the power to heal. People were healed because they had faith in God.

THE WITNESSES

[15]Others said, "He is Elijah."

And still others claimed, "He is a prophet, like one of the prophets of long ago."

[16]But when Herod heard this, he said, "John, whom I beheaded, has been raised from the dead!"

[17]For Herod himself had given orders to have John arrested, and he had him bound and put in prison. He did this because of Herodias, his brother Philip's wife, whom he had married. [18]For John had been saying to Herod, "It is not lawful for you to have your brother's wife." [19]So Herodias nursed a grudge against John and wanted to kill him. But she was not able to, [20]because Herod feared John and protected him, knowing him to be a righteous and holy man. When Herod heard John, he was greatly puzzled[a]; yet he liked to listen to him.

[21]Finally the opportune time came. On his birthday Herod gave a banquet for his high officials and military commanders and the leading men of Galilee. [22]When the daughter of[b] Herodias came in and

✓ KING HEROD (MARK 6:14)
Read the explanation in Matthew 14:1.

danced, she pleased Herod and his dinner guests.

The king said to the girl, "Ask me for anything you want, and I'll give it to you." [23]And he promised her with an oath, "Whatever you ask I will give you, up to half my kingdom."

[24]She went out and said to her mother, "What shall I ask for?"

"The head of John the Baptist," she answered.

[25]At once the girl hurried in to the king with the request: "I want you to give me right now the head of John the Baptist on a platter."

[26]The king was greatly distressed, but

---

[a] 20 Some early manuscripts *he did many things*
[b] 22 Some early manuscripts *When his daughter*

Prophets
(MARK 6:15)

In the Bible, prophets are people who hear a message that God gives them, and then they have to give this same message to other people or sometimes to an entire country.

Holy
(MARK 6:20)

It means that John the Baptist lived for God, because in the Bible, *holy* means set apart or separated for God.

because of his oaths and his dinner guests, he did not want to refuse her. [27]So he immediately sent an executioner with orders to bring John's head. The man went, beheaded John in the prison, [28]and brought back his head on a platter. He presented it to the girl, and she gave it to her mother. [29]On hearing of this, John's disciples came and took his body and laid it in a tomb.

Jesus Feeds the Five Thousand

[30]The apostles gathered around Jesus and reported to him all they had done and taught. [31]Then, because so many people were coming and going that they did not even have a chance to eat, he said to them, "Come with me by yourselves to a quiet place and get some rest."

[32]So they went away by themselves in a boat to a solitary place. [33]But many who saw them leaving recognized them and ran on foot from all the towns and got there ahead of them. [34]When Jesus landed and saw a large crowd, he had compassion on them, because they were like sheep without a shepherd. So he began teaching them many things.

[35]By this time it was late in the day, so his disciples came to him. "This is a remote place," they said, "and it's already very late. [36]Send the people away so that they can go to the surrounding countryside and villages and buy themselves something to eat."

[37]But he answered, "You give them something to eat."

They said to him, "That would take more than half a year's wages[a]! Are we to go and spend that much on bread and give it to them to eat?"

[38]"How many loaves do you have?" he asked. "Go and see."

When they found out, they said, "Five—and two fish."

[39]Then Jesus directed them to have all the people sit down in groups on the green grass. [40]So they sat down in groups of hundreds and fifties. [41]Taking the five loaves and the two fish and looking up to heaven, he gave thanks and broke the loaves. Then he gave them to his disciples to distribute to the people. He also divided the two fish among them all. [42]They all ate and were satisfied, [43]and the disciples picked up twelve basketfuls of broken pieces of bread and fish. [44]The number of the men who had eaten was five thousand.

Jesus Walks on the Water

[45]Immediately Jesus made his disciples get into the boat and go on ahead of him to Bethsaida, while he dismissed the crowd. [46]After leaving them, he went up on a mountainside to pray.

[47]Later that night, the boat was in the middle of the lake, and he was alone on

---

a 37 Greek *take two hundred denarii*

land. ⁴⁸He saw the disciples straining at the oars, because the wind was against them. Shortly before dawn he went out to them, walking on the lake. He was about to pass by them, ⁴⁹but when they saw him walking on the lake, they thought he was a ghost. They cried out, ⁵⁰because they all saw him and were terrified.

Immediately he spoke to them and said, "Take courage! It is I. Don't be afraid." ⁵¹Then he climbed into the boat with them, and the wind died down. They were completely amazed, ⁵²for they had not understood about the loaves; their hearts were hardened.

⁵³When they had crossed over, they landed at Gennesaret and anchored there. ⁵⁴As soon as they got out of the boat, people recognized Jesus. ⁵⁵They ran throughout that whole region and carried the sick on mats to wherever they heard he was. ⁵⁶And wherever he went—into villages, towns or countryside—they placed the sick in the marketplaces. They begged him to let them touch even the edge of his cloak, and all who touched it were healed.

BREAKTHROUGH!

"All who touched it were healed."

(MARK 6:56)

That's right, because they had faith in Jesus, and Jesus is God and is all-powerful.

That Which Defiles

7 The Pharisees and some of the teachers of the law who had come from Jerusalem gathered around Jesus ²and saw some of his disciples eating food with hands that were defiled, that is, unwashed. ³(The Pharisees and all the Jews do not eat unless they give their hands a ceremonial washing, holding to the tradition of the elders. ⁴When they come from the marketplace they do not eat unless they wash. And they observe many other traditions, such as the washing of cups, pitchers and kettles.ᵃ)

⁵So the Pharisees and teachers of the law asked Jesus, "Why don't your disciples live according to the tradition of the elders instead of eating their food with defiled hands?"

⁶He replied, "Isaiah was right when he prophesied about you hypocrites; as it is written:

" 'These people honor me with their lips,
    but their hearts are far from me.
⁷ They worship me in vain;
    their teachings are merely human rules.'ᵇ

⁸You have let go of the commands of God and are holding on to human traditions."

⁹And he continued, "You have a fine way of setting aside the commands of God in order to observeᶜ your own traditions! ¹⁰For Moses said, 'Honor your father and mother,'ᵈ and, 'Anyone who curses their father or mother is to be put to death.'ᵉ ¹¹But you say that if anyone declares that what might have been used to help their father or mother is Corban (that is, devoted to God)— ¹²then you no longer let them do anything for their father or mother. ¹³Thus you nullify the word of God by your tradition that you have handed down. And you do many things like that."

¹⁴Again Jesus called the crowd to him and said, "Listen to me, everyone, and understand this. ¹⁵Nothing outside a person

ᵃ 4 Some early manuscripts *pitchers, kettles and dining couches*   ᵇ 6,7 Isaiah 29:13   ᶜ 9 Some manuscripts *set up*   ᵈ 10 Exodus 20:12; Deut. 5:16   ᵉ 10 Exodus 21:17; Lev. 20:9

BREAK THROUGH!

"Anyone who curses his or her father or mother is to be put to death."
(MARK 7:10)

This law is in the Bible in the book of Leviticus. But for Jesus, that means that we have to be nice to our mom and dad and obey them. If we don't, that makes God sad, and we drift away from God.

can defile them by going into them. Rather, it is what comes out of a person that defiles them." [16]a

17After he had left the crowd and entered the house, his disciples asked him about this parable. 18"Are you so dull?" he asked. "Don't you see that nothing that enters a person from the outside can defile them? 19For it doesn't go into their heart but into their stomach, and then out of the body." (In saying this, Jesus declared all foods clean.)

20He went on: "What comes out of a person is what defiles them. 21For it is from within, out of a person's heart, that evil thoughts come — sexual immorality, theft, murder, 22adultery, greed, malice, deceit, lewdness, envy, slander, arrogance and folly. 23All these evils come from inside and defile a person."

Jesus Honors a Syrophoenician Woman's Faith

24Jesus left that place and went to the vicinity of Tyre.b He entered a house and did not want anyone to know it; yet he could not keep his presence secret. 25In fact, as soon as she heard about him, a woman whose little daughter was possessed by an impure spirit came and fell at his feet. 26The woman was a Greek, born in Syrian Phoenicia. She begged Jesus to drive the demon out of her daughter.

27"First let the children eat all they want," he told her, "for it is not right to take

a 16 Some manuscripts include here the words of 4:23.
b 24 Many early manuscripts Tyre and Sidon

THE SCENE

SYRIA

(MARK 7:26)

In Jesus' time, this was a huge territory that had been conquered by the Romans. As a result, it was a very important Roman province, and it grew to have a lot of inhabitants. If we look at a map of the world, we'll see that now that entire territory corresponds to parts of Syria, Libya, Israel and Turkey.

the children's bread and toss it to the dogs."

28 "Lord," she replied, "even the dogs under the table eat the children's crumbs."

29 Then he told her, "For such a reply, you may go; the demon has left your daughter."

30 She went home and found her child lying on the bed, and the demon gone.

Jesus Heals a Deaf and Mute Man

31 Then Jesus left the vicinity of Tyre and went through Sidon, down to the Sea of Galilee and into the region of the Decapolis.*a* 32 There some people brought to him a man who was deaf and could hardly talk, and they begged Jesus to place his hand on him.

33 After he took him aside, away from the crowd, Jesus put his fingers into the man's ears. Then he spit and touched the man's tongue. 34 He looked up to heaven and with a deep sigh said to him, *"Ephphatha!"* (which means "Be opened!"). 35 At this, the man's ears were opened, his tongue was loosened and he began to speak plainly.

36 Jesus commanded them not to tell anyone. But the more he did so, the more they kept talking about it. 37 People were overwhelmed with amazement. "He has done everything well," they said. "He even makes the deaf hear and the mute speak."

BREAKTHROUGH!

Why did Jesus command the people not to tell anyone?

(MARK 7:36)

Jesus didn't want people to talk about how he was healing sick people. He knew the priests would be jealous, and then they would try to send Jesus to jail. And Jesus didn't want people to follow him just because he was performing miracles. He wanted people to learn to live the way he was teaching them. But Jesus was still going to perform many more miracles anyway.

Jesus Feeds the Four Thousand

8 During those days another large crowd gathered. Since they had nothing to eat, Jesus called his disciples to him and said, 2 "I have compassion for these people; they have already been with me three days and have nothing to eat. 3 If I send them home hungry, they will collapse on the way, because some of them have come a long distance."

4 His disciples answered, "But where in this remote place can anyone get enough bread to feed them?"

5 "How many loaves do you have?" Jesus asked.

"Seven," they replied.

6 He told the crowd to sit down on the ground. When he had taken the seven loaves and given thanks, he broke them and gave them to his disciples to distribute to the people, and they did so. 7 They had a few small fish as well; he gave thanks for them also and told the disciples to distribute them. 8 The people ate and were satisfied. Afterward the disciples picked up seven basketfuls of broken pieces that were left over. 9 About four thousand were present. After he had sent them away, 10 he got into the boat with his disciples and went to the region of Dalmanutha.

11 The Pharisees came and began to question Jesus. To test him, they asked

---

a 31 That is, the Ten Cities

him for a sign from heaven. ¹²He sighed deeply and said, "Why does this generation ask for a sign? Truly I tell you, no sign will be given to it." ¹³Then he left them, got back into the boat and crossed to the other side.

The Yeast of the Pharisees and Herod

¹⁴The disciples had forgotten to bring bread, except for one loaf they had with them in the boat. ¹⁵"Be careful," Jesus warned them. "Watch out for the yeast of the Pharisees and that of Herod."

¹⁶They discussed this with one another and said, "It is because we have no bread."

¹⁷Aware of their discussion, Jesus asked them: "Why are you talking about having no bread? Do you still not see or understand? Are your hearts hardened? ¹⁸Do you have eyes but fail to see, and

BREAKTHROUGH!

The yeast of the Pharisees
(MARK 8:15)

This is just a way to explain something. Yeast is a dry powder, or sometimes a soft mass like butter that's mixed with flour to make the bread dough rise, or inflate. That's why Jesus says the Pharisees are like yeast. They were inflated and puffed up, because they thought they knew everything and were perfect.

ears but fail to hear? And don't you remember? ¹⁹When I broke the five loaves for the five thousand, how many basketfuls of pieces did you pick up?"

"Twelve," they replied.

²⁰"And when I broke the seven loaves for the four thousand, how many basketfuls of pieces did you pick up?"

They answered, "Seven."

²¹He said to them, "Do you still not understand?"

Jesus Heals a Blind Man at Bethsaida

²²They came to Bethsaida, and some people brought a blind man and begged Jesus to touch him. ²³He took the blind man by the hand and led him outside the village. When he had spit on the man's eyes and put his hands on him, Jesus asked, "Do you see anything?"

THE SCENE

DALMANUTHA
(MARK 8:10)

Nobody knows anything about this. They just say it was a city on the coast of the Sea of Galilee. Nothing more!

²⁴He looked up and said, "I see people; they look like trees walking around."

²⁵Once more Jesus put his hands on the man's eyes. Then his eyes were opened, his sight was restored, and he saw everything clearly. ²⁶Jesus sent him home, saying, "Don't even go into*ᵃ* the village."

Peter Declares That Jesus Is the Messiah

²⁷Jesus and his disciples went on to the villages around Caesarea Philippi. On the way he asked them, "Who do people say I am?"

²⁸They replied, "Some say John the Baptist; others say Elijah; and still others, one of the prophets."

²⁹"But what about you?" he asked. "Who do you say I am?"

Peter answered, "You are the Messiah."

³⁰Jesus warned them not to tell anyone about him.

Jesus Predicts His Death

³¹He then began to teach them that the Son of Man must suffer many things and be rejected by the elders, the chief priests and the teachers of the law, and that he must be killed and after three days rise again. ³²He spoke plainly about this, and Peter took him aside and began to rebuke him.

³³But when Jesus turned and looked at his disciples, he rebuked Peter. "Get behind me, Satan!" he said. "You do not have in mind the concerns of God, but merely human concerns."

The Way of the Cross

³⁴Then he called the crowd to him along with his disciples and said: "Whoever wants to be my disciple must deny themselves and take up their cross and follow me. ³⁵For whoever wants to save their life*ᵇ* will lose it, but whoever loses their life for me and for the gospel will save it. ³⁶What good is it for someone to gain the whole world, yet forfeit their soul? ³⁷Or what can anyone give in exchange for their soul? ³⁸If anyone

is ashamed of me and my words in this adulterous and sinful generation, the Son of Man will be ashamed of them when he comes in his Father's glory with the holy angels."

9 And he said to them, "Truly I tell you, some who are standing here will not taste death before they see that the kingdom of God has come with power."

The Transfiguration

²After six days Jesus took Peter, James and John with him and led them up a high mountain, where they were all alone. There he was transfigured before them. ³His clothes became dazzling white, whiter than anyone in the world could bleach them. ⁴And there appeared before them Elijah and Moses, who were talking with Jesus.

⁵Peter said to Jesus, "Rabbi, it is good for us to be here. Let us put up three shelters—one for you, one for Moses and one for Elijah." ⁶(He did not know what to say, they were so frightened.)

⁷Then a cloud appeared and covered them, and a voice came from the cloud: "This is my Son, whom I love. Listen to him!"

⁸Suddenly, when they looked around, they no longer saw anyone with them except Jesus.

⁹As they were coming down the mountain, Jesus gave them orders not to tell anyone what they had seen until the Son of Man had risen from the dead. ¹⁰They kept the matter to themselves, discussing what "rising from the dead" meant.

¹¹And they asked him, "Why do the teachers of the law say that Elijah must come first?"

¹²Jesus replied, "To be sure, Elijah does come first, and restores all things. Why then is it written that the Son of Man must suffer much and be rejected? ¹³But I tell you, Elijah has come, and they have done to him everything they wished, just as it is written about him."

ᵃ 26 Some manuscripts *go and tell anyone in*   *ᵇ 35* The Greek word means either *life* or *soul*; also in verses 36 and 37.

Jesus Heals a Boy Possessed by an Impure Spirit

14When they came to the other disciples, they saw a large crowd around them and the teachers of the law arguing with them. 15As soon as all the people saw Jesus, they were overwhelmed with wonder and ran to greet him.

16"What are you arguing with them about?" he asked.

17A man in the crowd answered, "Teacher, I brought you my son, who is possessed by a spirit that has robbed him of speech. 18Whenever it seizes him, it throws him to the ground. He foams at the mouth, gnashes his teeth and becomes rigid. I asked your disciples to drive out the spirit, but they could not."

19"You unbelieving generation," Jesus replied, "how long shall I stay with you? How long shall I put up with you? Bring the boy to me."

20So they brought him. When the spirit saw Jesus, it immediately threw the boy into a convulsion. He fell to the ground and rolled around, foaming at the mouth.

21Jesus asked the boy's father, "How long has he been like this?"

"From childhood," he answered. 22"It has often thrown him into fire or water to kill him. But if you can do anything, take pity on us and help us."

23"'If you can'?" said Jesus. "Everything is possible for one who believes."

24Immediately the boy's father exclaimed, "I do believe; help me overcome my unbelief!"

25When Jesus saw that a crowd was running to the scene, he rebuked the impure spirit. "You deaf and mute spirit," he said, "I command you, come out of him and never enter him again."

26The spirit shrieked, convulsed him violently and came out. The boy looked so much like a corpse that many said, "He's dead." 27But Jesus took him by the hand and lifted him to his feet, and he stood up.

28After Jesus had gone indoors, his disciples asked him privately, "Why couldn't we drive it out?"

29He replied, "This kind can come out only by prayer.[a]"

Jesus Predicts His Death a Second Time

30They left that place and passed through Galilee. Jesus did not want anyone to know where they were, 31because he was teaching his disciples. He said to them, "The Son of Man is going to be delivered into the hands of men. They will kill him, and after three days he will rise." 32But they did not understand what he meant and were afraid to ask him about it.

33They came to Capernaum. When he was in the house, he asked them, "What were you arguing about on the road?" 34But they kept quiet because on the way they had argued about who was the greatest.

35Sitting down, Jesus called the Twelve and said, "Anyone who wants to be first must be the very last, and the servant of all."

36He took a little child whom he placed among them. Taking the child in his arms, he said to them, 37"Whoever welcomes one of these little children in my name welcomes me; and whoever welcomes me does not welcome me but the one who sent me."

Whoever Is Not Against Us Is for Us

38"Teacher," said John, "we saw someone driving out demons in your name and we told him to stop, because he was not one of us."

39"Do not stop him," Jesus said. "For no one who does a miracle in my name can in the next moment say anything bad about me, 40for whoever is not against us is for us. 41Truly I tell you, anyone who gives you a cup of water in my name because you belong to the Messiah will certainly not lose their reward.

Causing to Stumble

42"If anyone causes one of these little

---

a 29 Some manuscripts prayer and fasting

ones—those who believe in me—to stumble, it would be better for them if a large millstone were hung around their neck and they were thrown into the sea. ⁴³If your hand causes you to stumble, cut it off. It is better for you to enter life maimed than with two hands to go into hell, where the fire never goes out. ⁽⁴⁴⁾ᵃ ⁴⁵And if your foot causes you to stumble, cut it off. It is better for you to enter life crippled than to have two feet and be thrown into hell. ⁽⁴⁶⁾ᵃ ⁴⁷And if your eye causes you to stumble, pluck it out. It is better for you to enter the kingdom of God with one eye than to have two eyes and be thrown into hell, ⁴⁸where

"'the worms that eat them do not die,
　and the fire is not quenched.'ᵇ

⁴⁹Everyone will be salted with fire.

⁵⁰"Salt is good, but if it loses its saltiness, how can you make it salty again? Have salt among yourselves, and be at peace with each other."

Divorce

10 Jesus then left that place and went into the region of Judea and across the Jordan. Again crowds of people came to him, and as was his custom, he taught them.

²Some Pharisees came and tested him by asking, "Is it lawful for a man to divorce his wife?"

³"What did Moses command you?" he replied.

⁴They said, "Moses permitted a man to write a certificate of divorce and send her away."

⁵"It was because your hearts were hard that Moses wrote you this law," Jesus replied. ⁶"But at the beginning of creation God 'made them male and female.'ᶜ ⁷'For this reason a man will leave his father and mother and be united to his wife,ᵈ ⁸and the two will become one flesh.'ᵉ So they are no longer two, but one flesh. ⁹Therefore what God has joined together, let no one separate."

ᵃ *44,46* Some manuscripts include here the words of verse 48.　ᵇ *48* Isaiah 66:24　ᶜ *6* Gen. 1:27　ᵈ *7* Some early manuscripts do not have *and be united to his wife.*　ᵉ *8* Gen. 2:24

Salted with fire
(MARK 9:49)
This expression is just figurative. Fire rids precious metals of any impurity and leaves them really, really clean. So this is like an example. It just means that God is going to make our hearts clean and pure.

Divorce
(MARK 10:2)
Read Matthew 5:31.

¹⁰When they were in the house again, the disciples asked Jesus about this. ¹¹He answered, "Anyone who divorces his wife and marries another woman commits adultery against her. ¹²And if she divorces her husband and marries another man, she commits adultery."

The Little Children and Jesus

¹³People were bringing little children to Jesus for him to place his hands on them, but the disciples rebuked them. ¹⁴When Jesus saw this, he was indignant. He said to them, "Let the little children come to me, and do not hinder them, for the kingdom of God belongs to such as these. ¹⁵Truly I tell you, anyone who will not receive the kingdom of God like a little child will never enter it." ¹⁶And he took the children in his arms, placed his hands on them and blessed them.

The Rich and the Kingdom of God

¹⁷As Jesus started on his way, a man ran up to him and fell on his knees before him. "Good teacher," he asked, "what must I do to inherit eternal life?"

¹⁸"Why do you call me good?" Jesus answered. "No one is good—except God alone. ¹⁹You know the commandments: 'You shall not murder, you shall not commit adultery, you shall not steal, you shall not give false testimony, you shall not defraud, honor your father and mother.'ᵃ"

²⁰"Teacher," he declared, "all these I have kept since I was a boy."

²¹Jesus looked at him and loved him. "One thing you lack," he said. "Go, sell everything you have and give to the poor, and you will have treasure in heaven. Then come, follow me."

²²At this the man's face fell. He went away sad, because he had great wealth.

²³Jesus looked around and said to his disciples, "How hard it is for the rich to enter the kingdom of God!"

²⁴The disciples were amazed at his words. But Jesus said again, "Children, how hard it isᵇ to enter the kingdom of God! ²⁵It is easier for a camel to go through the eye of a needle than for someone who is rich to enter the kingdom of God."

²⁶The disciples were even more amazed, and said to each other, "Who then can be saved?"

²⁷Jesus looked at them and said, "With man this is impossible, but not with God; all things are possible with God."

²⁸Then Peter spoke up, "We have left everything to follow you!"

²⁹"Truly I tell you," Jesus replied, "no one who has left home or brothers or sisters or mother or father or children or fields for me and the gospel ³⁰will fail to receive a hundred times as much in this present age: homes, brothers, sisters, mothers, children and fields—along with persecutions—and in the age to come eternal life. ³¹But many who are first will be last, and the last first."

Jesus Predicts His Death a Third Time

³²They were on their way up to Jerusalem, with Jesus leading the way, and the disciples were astonished, while those who followed were afraid. Again he took the Twelve aside and told them what was going to happen to him. ³³"We are going up to Jerusalem," he said, "and the Son of Man will be delivered over to the chief priests and the teachers of the law. They will condemn him to death and will hand him over to the Gentiles, ³⁴who will mock him and spit on him, flog him and kill him. Three days later he will rise."

The Request of James and John

³⁵Then James and John, the sons of Zebedee, came to him. "Teacher," they said, "we want you to do for us whatever we ask."

³⁶"What do you want me to do for you?" he asked.

³⁷They replied, "Let one of us sit at your right and the other at your left in your glory."

³⁸"You don't know what you are asking," Jesus said. "Can you drink the cup I drink or be baptized with the baptism I am baptized with?"

³⁹"We can," they answered.

ᵃ 19 Exodus 20:12-16; Deut. 5:16-20   ᵇ 24 Some manuscripts *is for those who trust in riches*

Jesus said to them, "You will drink the cup I drink and be baptized with the baptism I am baptized with, ⁴⁰but to sit at my right or left is not for me to grant. These places belong to those for whom they have been prepared."

⁴¹When the ten heard about this, they became indignant with James and John. ⁴²Jesus called them together and said, "You know that those who are regarded as rulers of the Gentiles lord it over them, and their high officials exercise authority over them. ⁴³Not so with you. Instead, whoever wants to become great among

THE
WITNESSES

✓ **BLIND BARTIMAEUS** (MARK 10:46–52)
Bartimaeus means "son of Timeaus." Because he was blind, he always sat in the same place. People would pass by and give him some coins because he couldn't work. But Jesus performed a miracle for Bartimaeus. Jesus healed Bartimaeus, and then he could see!

you must be your servant, ⁴⁴and whoever wants to be first must be slave of all. ⁴⁵For even the Son of Man did not come to be served, but to serve, and to give his life as a ransom for many."

Blind Bartimaeus Receives His Sight

⁴⁶Then they came to Jericho. As Jesus and his disciples, together with a large crowd, were leaving the city, a blind man, Bartimaeus (which means "son of Timaeus"), was sitting by the roadside begging. ⁴⁷When he heard that it was Jesus of Nazareth, he began to shout, "Jesus, Son of David, have mercy on me!"

⁴⁸Many rebuked him and told him to be quiet, but he shouted all the more, "Son of David, have mercy on me!"

⁴⁹Jesus stopped and said, "Call him."

So they called to the blind man, "Cheer up! On your feet! He's calling you." ⁵⁰Throwing his cloak aside, he jumped to his feet and came to Jesus.

⁵¹"What do you want me to do for you?" Jesus asked him.

The blind man said, "Rabbi, I want to see."

⁵²"Go," said Jesus, "your faith has healed you." Immediately he received his sight and followed Jesus along the road.

Jesus Comes to Jerusalem as King

11 As they approached Jerusalem and came to Bethphage and Bethany at the Mount of Olives, Jesus sent two of his disciples, ²saying to them, "Go to the village ahead of you, and just as you enter it, you will find a colt tied there, which no one has ever ridden. Untie it and bring it here. ³If anyone asks you, 'Why are you doing this?' say, 'The Lord needs it and will send it back here shortly.'"

⁴They went and found a colt outside in the street, tied at a doorway. As they untied it, ⁵some people standing there asked, "What are you doing, untying that colt?" ⁶They answered as Jesus had told them to, and the people let them go. ⁷When they brought the colt to Jesus and threw their cloaks over it, he sat on it. ⁸Many people spread their cloaks on the

CHECK THE FACTS

What was the name of the blind man that Jesus healed?

A) Bartimaeus

B) Bartholomew

C) Barnabas

CORRECT ANSWER: A

out if it had any fruit. When he reached it, he found nothing but leaves, because it was not the season for figs. ¹⁴Then he said to the tree, "May no one ever eat fruit from you again." And his disciples heard him say it.

¹⁵On reaching Jerusalem, Jesus entered the temple courts and began driving out those who were buying and selling there. He overturned the tables of the money changers and the benches of those selling doves, ¹⁶and would not allow anyone to carry merchandise through the temple courts. ¹⁷And as he taught them, he said, "Is it not written: 'My house will be called a house of prayer for all nations'ᶜ? But you have made it 'a den of robbers.'ᵈ"

ᵃ 9 A Hebrew expression meaning "Save!" which became an exclamation of praise; also in verse 10   ᵇ 9 Psalm 118:25,26   ᶜ 17 Isaiah 56:7   ᵈ 17 Jer. 7:11

road, while others spread branches they had cut in the fields. ⁹Those who went ahead and those who followed shouted,

"Hosanna!ᵃ"

"Blessed is he who comes in the name of the Lord!"ᵇ

¹⁰ "Blessed is the coming kingdom of our father David!"

"Hosanna in the highest heaven!"

¹¹Jesus entered Jerusalem and went into the temple courts. He looked around at everything, but since it was already late, he went out to Bethany with the Twelve.

Jesus Curses a Fig Tree and Clears the Temple Courts

¹²The next day as they were leaving Bethany, Jesus was hungry. ¹³Seeing in the distance a fig tree in leaf, he went to find

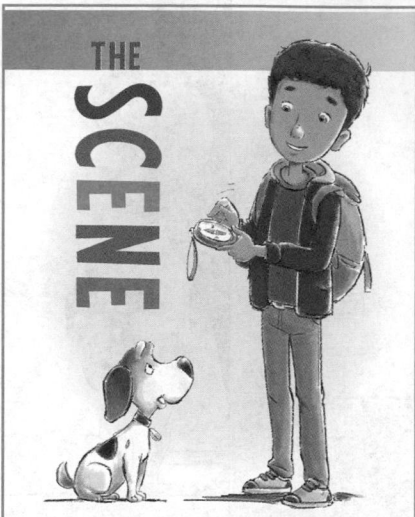

THE SCENE

MOUNT OF OLIVES

(MARK 11:1)

This is a hill in the Kidron Valley outside Jerusalem. It's an important place in the Bible. Jesus was praying there when soldiers arrived and arrested him. It's called "of olives" because there are olive trees all around.

BREAKTHROUGH!

Temple
(MARK 11:11)

According to the Bible, God had only one temple, and it was in Jerusalem. It was very, very beautiful. The walls were covered in gold, and people who were traveling into Jerusalem could see it shining from a distance. How pretty! Of course, the glory of God was there!

¹⁸The chief priests and the teachers of the law heard this and began looking for a way to kill him, for they feared him, because the whole crowd was amazed at his teaching.

¹⁹When evening came, Jesus and his disciples^a went out of the city.

²⁰In the morning, as they went along, they saw the fig tree withered from the roots. ²¹Peter remembered and said to Jesus, "Rabbi, look! The fig tree you cursed has withered!"

²²"Have faith in God," Jesus answered. ²³"Truly^b I tell you, if anyone says to this mountain, 'Go, throw yourself into the sea,' and does not doubt in their heart but believes that what they say will happen, it will be done for them. ²⁴Therefore I tell you, whatever you ask for in prayer, believe that you have received it, and it will be yours. ²⁵And when you stand praying, if you hold anything against anyone, forgive them, so that your Father in heaven may forgive you your sins." [26]^c

The Authority of Jesus Questioned

²⁷They arrived again in Jerusalem, and while Jesus was walking in the temple courts, the chief priests, the teachers of the law and the elders came to him. ²⁸"By what authority are you doing these things?" they asked. "And who gave you authority to do this?"

²⁹Jesus replied, "I will ask you one question. Answer me, and I will tell you by what authority I am doing these things. ³⁰John's baptism—was it from heaven, or of human origin? Tell me!"

³¹They discussed it among themselves and said, "If we say, 'From heaven,' he will ask, 'Then why didn't you believe him?' ³²But if we say, 'Of human origin' . . ." (They feared the people, for everyone held that John really was a prophet.)

³³So they answered Jesus, "We don't know."

Jesus said, "Neither will I tell you by what authority I am doing these things."

The Parable of the Tenants

12 Jesus then began to speak to them in parables: "A man planted a vineyard. He put a wall around it, dug a pit for the winepress and built a watchtower. Then he rented the vineyard to some farmers and moved to another place. ²At harvest time he sent a servant to the tenants to collect from them some of the fruit of the vineyard. ³But they seized him, beat him and sent him away empty-handed. ⁴Then he sent another servant to them; they struck this man on the head and treated him shamefully. ⁵He sent still another, and that one they killed. He sent many others; some of them they beat, others they killed.

⁶"He had one left to send, a son, whom he loved. He sent him last of all, saying, 'They will respect my son.'

⁷"But the tenants said to one another, 'This is the heir. Come, let's kill him, and

---

^a 19 Some early manuscripts *came, Jesus*
^b 22,23 Some early manuscripts *"If you have faith in God,"*
Jesus answered, ²³*"truly*   ^c 26 Some manuscripts include
here words similar to Matt. 6:15.

the inheritance will be ours.' ⁸So they took him and killed him, and threw him out of the vineyard.

⁹"What then will the owner of the vineyard do? He will come and kill those tenants and give the vineyard to others. ¹⁰Haven't you read this passage of Scripture:

" 'The stone the builders rejected
　has become the cornerstone;
¹¹the Lord has done this,
　and it is marvelous in our eyes'ᵃ?"

¹²Then the chief priests, the teachers of the law and the elders looked for a way to arrest him because they knew he had spoken the parable against them. But they were afraid of the crowd; so they left him and went away.

Paying the Imperial Tax to Caesar

¹³Later they sent some of the Pharisees and Herodians to Jesus to catch

THE WITNESSES

✓ CAESAR (MARK 12:14)
He was the emperor of Rome. He was more powerful than the governor, more powerful than the army general and more powerful than absolutely anybody else.

him in his words. ¹⁴They came to him and said, "Teacher, we know that you are a man of integrity. You aren't swayed by others, because you pay no attention to who they are; but you teach the way of God in accordance with the truth. Is it right to pay the imperial taxᵇ to Caesar or not? ¹⁵Should we pay or shouldn't we?"

But Jesus knew their hypocrisy. "Why are you trying to trap me?" he asked. "Bring me a denarius and let me look at it." ¹⁶They brought the coin, and he asked

BREAKTHROUGH!

Vineyard
(MARK 12:1)
This is a place where they grow a lot of grapes. There were vineyards all over Judea. The grape plant is called a vine. When there are many vines, that place is called a vineyard. They make wine from grapes.

ᵃ 11 Psalm 118:22,23　ᵇ 14 A special tax levied on subject peoples, not on Roman citizens them, "Whose image is this? And whose inscription?"

"Caesar's," they replied.

[17]Then Jesus said to them, "Give back to Caesar what is Caesar's and to God what is God's."

And they were amazed at him.

Marriage at the Resurrection

[18]Then the Sadducees, who say there is no resurrection, came to him with a question. [19]"Teacher," they said, "Moses wrote for us that if a man's brother dies and leaves a wife but no children, the man must marry the widow and raise up offspring for his brother. [20]Now there were seven brothers. The first one married and died without leaving any children. [21]The second one married the widow, but he also died, leaving no child. It was the same with the third. [22]In fact, none of the seven left any children. Last of all, the woman died too. [23]At the resurrection[a] whose wife will she be, since the seven were married to her?"

[24]Jesus replied, "Are you not in error because you do not know the Scriptures or the power of God? [25]When the dead rise, they will neither marry nor be given in marriage; they will be like the angels in heaven. [26]Now about the dead rising— have you not read in the Book of Moses, in the account of the burning bush, how God said to him, 'I am the God of Abraham, the God of Isaac, and the God of Jacob'[b]? [27]He is not the God of the dead, but of the living. You are badly mistaken!"

The Greatest Commandment

[28]One of the teachers of the law came and heard them debating. Noticing that Jesus had given them a good answer, he asked him, "Of all the commandments, which is the most important?"

[29]"The most important one," answered Jesus, "is this: 'Hear, O Israel: The Lord our God, the Lord is one.[c] [30]Love the Lord your God with all your heart and with all your soul and with all your mind and with all your strength.'[d] [31]The second is this: 'Love your neighbor as yourself.'[e] There is no commandment greater than these."

[32]"Well said, teacher," the man replied.

"You are right in saying that God is one and there is no other but him. [33]To love him with all your heart, with all your understanding and with all your strength, and to love your neighbor as yourself is more important than all burnt offerings and sacrifices."

[34]When Jesus saw that he had answered wisely, he said to him, "You are not far from the kingdom of God." And from then on no one dared ask him any more questions.

Whose Son Is the Messiah?

[35]While Jesus was teaching in the temple courts, he asked, "Why do the teachers of the law say that the Messiah is the son of David? [36]David himself, speaking by the Holy Spirit, declared:

" 'The Lord said to my Lord:
    "Sit at my right hand
until I put your enemies
    under your feet." '[f]

[37]David himself calls him 'Lord.' How then can he be his son?"

The large crowd listened to him with delight.

Warning Against the Teachers of the Law

[38]As he taught, Jesus said, "Watch out for the teachers of the law. They like to walk around in flowing robes and be greeted with respect in the marketplaces, [39]and have the most important seats in the synagogues and the places of honor at banquets. [40]They devour widows' houses and for a show make lengthy prayers. These men will be punished most severely."

The Widow's Offering

[41]Jesus sat down opposite the place where the offerings were put and watched the crowd putting their money into the temple treasury. Many rich people threw

---

a 23 Some manuscripts *resurrection, when people rise from the dead,*   *b 26* Exodus 3:6   *c 29* Or *The Lord our God is one Lord*   *d 30* Deut. 6:4,5   *e 31* Lev. 19:18   *f 36* Psalm 110:1

Jesus taught that the most important commandment is to love God. What is the second-most important commandment?

A) To love your mom and dad

B) To obey everything

C) To love our neighbor as much as we love ourselves

CORRECT ANSWER: C

in large amounts. ⁴²But a poor widow came and put in two very small copper coins, worth only a few cents.

⁴³Calling his disciples to him, Jesus said, "Truly I tell you, this poor widow has put more into the treasury than all the others. ⁴⁴They all gave out of their wealth; but she, out of her poverty, put in everything—all she had to live on."

The Destruction of the Temple and Signs of the End Times

13 As Jesus was leaving the temple, one of his disciples said to him, "Look, Teacher! What massive stones! What magnificent buildings!"

²"Do you see all these great build-

ings?" replied Jesus. "Not one stone here will be left on another; every one will be thrown down."

³As Jesus was sitting on the Mount of Olives opposite the temple, Peter, James, John and Andrew asked him privately, ⁴"Tell us, when will these things happen? And what will be the sign that they are all about to be fulfilled?"

⁵Jesus said to them: "Watch out that no one deceives you. ⁶Many will come in my name, claiming, 'I am he,' and will deceive many. ⁷When you hear of wars and rumors of wars, do not be alarmed. Such things must happen, but the end is still to come. ⁸Nation will rise against nation, and kingdom against kingdom. There will be earthquakes in various places, and famines. These are the beginning of birth pains.

⁹"You must be on your guard. You will be handed over to the local councils and flogged in the synagogues. On account of me you will stand before governors and kings as witnesses to them. ¹⁰And the gospel must first be preached to all nations. ¹¹Whenever you are arrested and brought to trial, do not worry beforehand about what to say. Just say whatever is given you at the time, for it is not you speaking, but the Holy Spirit.

¹²"Brother will betray brother to death, and a father his child. Children will rebel against their parents and have them put to death. ¹³Everyone will hate you because of me, but the one who stands firm to the end will be saved.

¹⁴"When you see 'the abomination that causes desolation'ᵃ standing where itᵇ does not belong—let the reader understand—then let those who are in Judea flee to the mountains. ¹⁵Let no one on the housetop go down or enter the house to take anything out. ¹⁶Let no one in the field go back to get their cloak. ¹⁷How dreadful it will be in those days for pregnant women and nursing mothers! ¹⁸Pray that this will not take place in winter, ¹⁹because those will be days of distress unequaled from the beginning, when God created the world, until now—and never to be equaled again.

ᵃ 14 Daniel 9:27; 11:31; 12:11   ᵇ 14 Or he

BREAKTHROUGH!

"The 'abomination that causes desolation' standing where it does not belong"

(MARK 13:14)

What Jesus was talking about has to do with something that's going to happen in the future. Jews weren't supposed to take just anything as an offering to God, only what God would accept. It's talking about something revolting here, because God won't accept it.

---

20 "If the Lord had not cut short those days, no one would survive. But for the sake of the elect, whom he has chosen, he has shortened them. 21 At that time if anyone says to you, 'Look, here is the Messiah!' or, 'Look, there he is!' do not believe it. 22 For false messiahs and false prophets will appear and perform signs and wonders to deceive, if possible, even the elect. 23 So be on your guard; I have told you everything ahead of time.

24 "But in those days, following that distress,

" 'the sun will be darkened,
    and the moon will not give its
      light;
25 the stars will fall from the sky,
    and the heavenly bodies will be
      shaken.'*a*

26 "At that time people will see the Son of Man coming in clouds with great power and glory. 27 And he will send his angels and gather his elect from the four winds, from the ends of the earth to the ends of the heavens.

28 "Now learn this lesson from the fig tree: As soon as its twigs get tender and its leaves come out, you know that summer is near. 29 Even so, when you see these things happening, you know that it*b* is near, right at the door. 30 Truly I tell you, this generation will certainly not pass away until all these things have happened. 31 Heaven and earth will pass away, but my words will never pass away.

The Day and Hour Unknown

32 "But about that day or hour no one knows, not even the angels in heaven, nor the Son, but only the Father. 33 Be on guard! Be alert*c*! You do not know when that time will come. 34 It's like a man going away: He leaves his house and puts his servants in charge, each with their assigned task, and tells the one at the door to keep watch.

35 "Therefore keep watch because you do not know when the owner of the house will come back—whether in the evening, or at midnight, or when the rooster crows, or at dawn. 36 If he comes suddenly, do not let him find you sleeping. 37 What I say to you, I say to everyone: 'Watch!' "

Jesus Anointed at Bethany

14 Now the Passover and the Festival of Unleavened Bread were only two days away, and the chief priests and the teachers of the law were scheming to arrest Jesus secretly and kill him. 2 "But not during the festival," they said, "or the people may riot."

3 While he was in Bethany, reclining at the table in the home of Simon the Leper, a woman came with an alabaster jar of very expensive perfume, made of pure nard. She broke the jar and poured the perfume on his head.

4 Some of those present were saying indignantly to one another, "Why this waste

---

a 25 Isaiah 13:10; 34:4   *b* 29 Or *he*   *c* 33 Some manuscripts *alert and pray* of perfume? ⁵It could have been sold for more than a year's wages*ª* and the money given to the poor." And they rebuked her harshly.

⁶"Leave her alone," said Jesus. "Why are you bothering her? She has done a beautiful thing to me. ⁷The poor you will always have with you,*ᵇ* and you can help them any time you want. But you will not always have me. ⁸She did what she could. She poured perfume on my body beforehand to prepare for my burial. ⁹Truly I tell you, wherever the gospel is preached throughout the world, what she has done will also be told, in memory of her."

¹⁰Then Judas Iscariot, one of the Twelve, went to the chief priests to betray Jesus to them. ¹¹They were delighted to hear this and promised to give him money. So he watched for an opportunity to hand him over.

BREAKTHROUGH!

Leper
(MARK 14:3)
Read the explanation for leprosy in Matthew 8.2.

Pouring perfume on a head
(MARK 14:3-9)
In Jesus' time, when a person died, they would place fragrant herbs and perfumes around the body before they wrapped it in a kind of sheet, like the Egyptian mummies! Then they would place the body in a tomb. This woman poured perfume on Jesus' head. But she didn't realize that she was more or less predicting that Jesus was going to die.

BREAKTHROUGH!

Festival of Unleavened Bread
(MARK 14:1)
This celebration was to remember that God brought the Jews out of Egypt, where they were slaves. The day that happened, they had to leave so fast they didn't have time to wait for the bread dough to rise. So they just baked it without yeast. The bread turned out flat, like a pancake or pita bread.

The Last Supper
¹²On the first day of the Festival of Unleavened Bread, when it was customary to sacrifice the Passover lamb, Jesus' disciples asked him, "Where do you want us to go and make preparations for you to eat the Passover?"

¹³So he sent two of his disciples, telling them, "Go into the city, and a man carrying a jar of water will meet you. Follow him. ¹⁴Say to the owner of the house he

---

ª 5 Greek *than three hundred denarii*   *ᵇ 7* See Deut. 15:11.

enters, 'The Teacher asks: Where is my guest room, where I may eat the Passover with my disciples?' ¹⁵He will show you a large room upstairs, furnished and ready. Make preparations for us there."

¹⁶The disciples left, went into the city and found things just as Jesus had told them. So they prepared the Passover.

¹⁷When evening came, Jesus arrived with the Twelve. ¹⁸While they were reclining at the table eating, he said, "Truly I tell you, one of you will betray me—one who is eating with me."

¹⁹They were saddened, and one by one they said to him, "Surely you don't mean me?"

²⁰"It is one of the Twelve," he replied, "one who dips bread into the bowl with me. ²¹The Son of Man will go just as it is written about him. But woe to that man who betrays the Son of Man! It would be better for him if he had not been born."

²²While they were eating, Jesus took bread, and when he had given thanks, he broke it and gave it to his disciples, saying, "Take it; this is my body."

²³Then he took a cup, and when he had given thanks, he gave it to them, and they all drank from it.

²⁴"This is my blood of the*a* covenant, which is poured out for many," he said to them. ²⁵"Truly I tell you, I will not drink again from the fruit of the vine until that day when I drink it new in the kingdom of God."

²⁶When they had sung a hymn, they went out to the Mount of Olives.

Jesus Predicts Peter's Denial

²⁷"You will all fall away," Jesus told them, "for it is written:

" 'I will strike the shepherd,
    and the sheep will be scattered.'*b*

²⁸But after I have risen, I will go ahead of you into Galilee."

²⁹Peter declared, "Even if all fall away, I will not."

³⁰"Truly I tell you," Jesus answered, "today—yes, tonight—before the rooster crows twice*c* you yourself will disown me three times."

³¹But Peter insisted emphatically, "Even

BREAK THROUGH!

Is bread the body and wine the blood of Jesus?

(MARK 14:22-25)

Read the explanation in Matthew 26:26,28.

if I have to die with you, I will never disown you." And all the others said the same.

Gethsemane

³²They went to a place called Gethsemane, and Jesus said to his disciples, "Sit here while I pray." ³³He took Peter, James and John along with him, and he began to be deeply distressed and troubled. ³⁴"My soul is overwhelmed with sorrow to the point of death," he said to them. "Stay here and keep watch."

³⁵Going a little farther, he fell to the ground and prayed that if possible the hour might pass from him. ³⁶"Abba,*d* Father," he said, "everything is possible for you. Take this cup from me. Yet not what I will, but what you will."

³⁷Then he returned to his disciples and found them sleeping. "Simon," he said to Peter, "are you asleep? Couldn't you keep watch for one hour? ³⁸Watch and pray so that you will not fall into temptation. The spirit is willing, but the flesh is weak."

---

a 24 Some manuscripts *the new*   *b 27* Zech. 13:7
c 30 Some early manuscripts do not have *twice.*
d 36 Aramaic for *father*

³⁹Once more he went away and prayed the same thing. ⁴⁰When he came back, he again found them sleeping, because their eyes were heavy. They did not know what to say to him.

⁴¹Returning the third time, he said to them, "Are you still sleeping and resting? Enough! The hour has come. Look, the Son of Man is delivered into the hands of sinners. ⁴²Rise! Let us go! Here comes my betrayer!"

Jesus Arrested

⁴³Just as he was speaking, Judas, one of the Twelve, appeared. With him was a crowd armed with swords and clubs, sent from the chief priests, the teachers of the law, and the elders.

⁴⁴Now the betrayer had arranged a signal with them: "The one I kiss is the man; arrest him and lead him away under guard." ⁴⁵Going at once to Jesus, Judas said, "Rabbi!" and kissed him. ⁴⁶The men seized Jesus and arrested him. ⁴⁷Then one of those standing near drew his sword and struck the servant of the high priest, cutting off his ear.

⁴⁸"Am I leading a rebellion," said Jesus, "that you have come out with swords and clubs to capture me? ⁴⁹Every day I was with you, teaching in the temple courts, and you did not arrest me. But the Scriptures must be fulfilled." ⁵⁰Then everyone deserted him and fled.

⁵¹A young man, wearing nothing but a linen garment, was following Jesus. When they seized him, ⁵²he fled naked, leaving his garment behind.

Jesus Before the Sanhedrin

⁵³They took Jesus to the high priest, and all the chief priests, the elders and the teachers of the law came together. ⁵⁴Peter followed him at a distance, right into the courtyard of the high priest. There he sat with the guards and warmed himself at the fire.

⁵⁵The chief priests and the whole Sanhedrin were looking for evidence against Jesus so that they could put him to death, but they did not find any. ⁵⁶Many testified

BREAK THROUGH!

Courtyard of the high priest
(MARK 14:54)
At that time, the high priest was a man named Caiaphas. He lived in a very nice place in Jerusalem, near the temple and the lovely palaces.

falsely against him, but their statements did not agree.

⁵⁷Then some stood up and gave this false testimony against him: ⁵⁸"We heard him say, 'I will destroy this temple made with human hands and in three days will build another, not made with hands.'" ⁵⁹Yet even then their testimony did not agree.

⁶⁰Then the high priest stood up before them and asked Jesus, "Are you not going to answer? What is this testimony that these men are bringing against you?" ⁶¹But Jesus remained silent and gave no answer.

Again the high priest asked him, "Are you the Messiah, the Son of the Blessed One?"

⁶²"I am," said Jesus. "And you will see the Son of Man sitting at the right hand of the Mighty One and coming on the clouds of heaven."

⁶³The high priest tore his clothes. "Why do we need any more witnesses?" he asked. ⁶⁴"You have heard the blasphemy. What do you think?"

They all condemned him as worthy of death. ⁶⁵Then some began to spit at him; they blindfolded him, struck him with their fists, and said, "Prophesy!" And the guards took him and beat him.

Peter Disowns Jesus

⁶⁶While Peter was below in the courtyard, one of the servant girls of the high priest came by. ⁶⁷When she saw Peter warming himself, she looked closely at him.

"You also were with that Nazarene, Jesus," she said.

⁶⁸But he denied it. "I don't know or understand what you're talking about," he said, and went out into the entryway.ᵃ

⁶⁹When the servant girl saw him there, she said again to those standing around, "This fellow is one of them." ⁷⁰Again he denied it.

After a little while, those standing near said to Peter, "Surely you are one of them, for you are a Galilean."

⁷¹He began to call down curses, and he swore to them, "I don't know this man you're talking about."

⁷²Immediately the rooster crowed the second time.ᵇ Then Peter remembered the word Jesus had spoken to him: "Before the rooster crows twiceᶜ you will disown me three times." And he broke down and wept.

Jesus Before Pilate

15 Very early in the morning, the chief priests, with the elders, the teachers of the law and the whole Sanhedrin, made their plans. So they bound Jesus, led him away and handed him over to Pilate.

²"Are you the king of the Jews?" asked Pilate.

"You have said so," Jesus replied.

³The chief priests accused him of many things. ⁴So again Pilate asked him, "Aren't you going to answer? See how many things they are accusing you of."

⁵But Jesus still made no reply, and Pilate was amazed.

⁶Now it was the custom at the festival to release a prisoner whom the people requested. ⁷A man called Barabbas was in prison with the insurrectionists who had committed murder in the uprising. ⁸The crowd came up and asked Pilate to do for them what he usually did.

⁹"Do you want me to release to you the king of the Jews?" asked Pilate, ¹⁰knowing it was out of self-interest that the chief priests had handed Jesus over to him. ¹¹But the chief priests stirred up the crowd to have Pilate release Barabbas instead.

¹²"What shall I do, then, with the one you call the king of the Jews?" Pilate asked them.

¹³"Crucify him!" they shouted.

¹⁴"Why? What crime has he committed?" asked Pilate.

But they shouted all the louder, "Crucify him!"

ᵃ 68 Some early manuscripts *entryway and the rooster crowed*   ᵇ 72 Some early manuscripts do not have *the second time.*   ᶜ 72 Some early manuscripts do not have *twice.*

BREAKTHROUGH!

"The king of the Jews"
(MARK 15:12)

The priests accused Jesus of wanting to be the king. That's why Pilate, who was Roman and was the ruling governor, asked them, "What shall I do, then, with the one you call the king of the Jews?" It was to mock and make fun of them. It made the priests angry.

¹⁵Wanting to satisfy the crowd, Pilate released Barabbas to them. He had Jesus flogged, and handed him over to be crucified.

The Soldiers Mock Jesus

¹⁶The soldiers led Jesus away into the palace (that is, the Praetorium) and called together the whole company of soldiers. ¹⁷They put a purple robe on him, then twisted together a crown of thorns and set it on him. ¹⁸And they began to call out to him, "Hail, king of the Jews!" ¹⁹Again and again they struck him on the head with a staff and spit on him. Falling on their knees, they paid homage to him. ²⁰And when they had mocked him, they took off the purple robe and put his own clothes on him. Then they led him out to crucify him.

The Crucifixion of Jesus

²¹A certain man from Cyrene, Simon, the father of Alexander and Rufus, was passing by on his way in from the country, and they forced him to carry the cross. ²²They brought Jesus to the place called Golgotha (which means "the place of the skull"). ²³Then they offered him wine mixed with myrrh, but he did not take it. ²⁴And they crucified him. Dividing up his clothes, they cast lots to see what each would get.

²⁵It was nine in the morning when they crucified him. ²⁶The written notice of the charge against him read: THE KING OF THE JEWS.

²⁷They crucified two rebels with him, one on his right and one on his left. [28]ᵃ ²⁹Those who passed by hurled insults at him, shaking their heads and saying, "So! You who are going to destroy the temple and build it in three days, ³⁰come down from the cross and save yourself!" ³¹In the same way the chief priests and the teachers of the law mocked him among themselves. "He saved others," they said, "but he can't save himself! ³²Let this Messiah, this king of Israel, come down now from the cross, that we may see and believe." Those crucified with him also heaped insults on him.

THE
WITNESSES

✓ **SIMON FROM CYRENE (MARK 15:21)**
This man had two sons, Alexander and Rufus. When Jesus was carrying his cross, Simon helped him carry it.

The Death of Jesus

³³At noon, darkness came over the whole land until three in the afternoon. ³⁴And at three in the afternoon Jesus cried out in a loud voice, *"Eloi, Eloi, lema sabachthani?"* (which means "My God, my God, why have you forsaken me?").ᵇ

³⁵When some of those standing near heard this, they said, "Listen, he's calling Elijah."

³⁶Someone ran, filled a sponge with wine vinegar, put it on a staff, and offered it to Jesus to drink. "Now leave him alone. Let's see if Elijah comes to take him down," he said.

ᵃ 28 Some manuscripts include here words similar to Luke 22:37.   ᵇ 34 Psalm 22:1

BREAK THROUGH!

Myrrh

(MARK 15:23)

This is an oil taken from a special tree, and it's like a lovely perfume. In order to get it, they have to cut the tree trunk a little bit and then wait until little yellow drops begin to seep out. That liquid is myrrh. In Jesus' time, they used it for many things, like perfume, toothpaste, and even to help with pain. The problem was that myrrh cost a lot of money.

[37] With a loud cry, Jesus breathed his last.

[38] The curtain of the temple was torn in two from top to bottom. [39] And when the centurion, who stood there in front of Jesus, saw how he died,[a] he said, "Surely this man was the Son of God!"

[40] Some women were watching from a distance. Among them were Mary Magdalene, Mary the mother of James the younger and of Joseph,[b] and Salome. [41] In Galilee these women had followed him and cared for his needs. Many other women who had come up with him to Jerusalem were also there.

The Burial of Jesus

[42] It was Preparation Day (that is, the day before the Sabbath). So as evening approached, [43] Joseph of Arimathea, a prominent member of the Council, who was himself waiting for the kingdom of God, went boldly to Pilate and asked for Jesus' body. [44] Pilate was surprised to hear that he was already dead. Summoning the centurion, he asked him if Jesus had already died. [45] When he learned from the centurion that it was so, he gave the body to Joseph. [46] So Joseph bought some linen cloth, took down the body, wrapped it in the linen, and placed it in a tomb cut out of rock. Then he rolled a stone against the entrance of the tomb. [47] Mary Magdalene and Mary the mother of Joseph saw where he was laid.

Jesus Has Risen

16 When the Sabbath was over, Mary Magdalene, Mary the mother of James, and Salome bought spices so that they might go to anoint Jesus' body. [2] Very early on the first day of the week,

---

[a] 39 Some manuscripts *saw that he died with such a cry*
[b] 40 Greek *Joses*, a variant of *Joseph*; also in verse 47

BREAK THROUGH!

Spices for anointing Jesus' body

(MARK 16:1)

When a person died in Palestine a long time ago, they would put perfume and a special oil on the body before wrapping it in white sheets. That was so the body would stay nice for longer.

just after sunrise, they were on their way to the tomb ³and they asked each other, "Who will roll the stone away from the entrance of the tomb?"

⁴But when they looked up, they saw that the stone, which was very large, had been rolled away. ⁵As they entered the tomb, they saw a young man dressed in a white robe sitting on the right side, and they were alarmed.

⁶"Don't be alarmed," he said. "You are looking for Jesus the Nazarene, who was crucified. He has risen! He is not here. See the place where they laid him. ⁷But go, tell his disciples and Peter, 'He is going ahead of you into Galilee. There you will see him, just as he told you.'"

⁸Trembling and bewildered, the women went out and fled from the tomb. They said nothing to anyone, because they were afraid.ᵃ

[The earliest manuscripts and some other ancient witnesses do not have verses 9–20.]

⁹When Jesus rose early on the first day of the week, he appeared first to Mary Magdalene, out of whom he had driven seven demons. ¹⁰She went and told those who had been with him and who were mourning and weeping. ¹¹When they heard that Jesus was alive and that she had seen him, they did not believe it.

¹²Afterward Jesus appeared in a different form to two of them while they were walking in the country. ¹³These returned and reported it to the rest; but they did not believe them either.

¹⁴Later Jesus appeared to the Eleven as they were eating; he rebuked them for their lack of faith and their stubborn refusal to believe those who had seen him after he had risen.

¹⁵He said to them, "Go into all the world and preach the gospel to all creation. ¹⁶Whoever believes and is baptized will be saved, but whoever does not believe will be condemned. ¹⁷And these signs will accompany those who believe: In my name they will drive out demons; they will speak in new tongues; ¹⁸they will pick up snakes with their hands; and when they drink deadly poison, it will not hurt them at all; they will place their hands on sick people, and they will get well."

¹⁹After the Lord Jesus had spoken to them, he was taken up into heaven and he sat at the right hand of God. ²⁰Then the disciples went out and preached everywhere, and the Lord worked with them and confirmed his word by the signs that accompanied it.

ᵃ 8 Some manuscripts have the following ending between verses 8 and 9, and one manuscript has it after verse 8 (omitting verses 9-20): *Then they quickly reported all these instructions to those around Peter. After this, Jesus himself also sent out through them from east to west the sacred and imperishable proclamation of eternal salvation. Amen.*

fter reading this book, Mateo and I decided that we have to learn from John the Baptist and Jesus. The Bible says they both were very obedient. Jesus teaches us that people and people's hearts are what's most important. That's why he wasn't bothered about what people might be saying, because he always did what God had told him to do. For example, he healed people on Saturday, although the Jews said that kind of work shouldn't be done on a Saturday.

CASE CLOSED!

LUKE

THE EVIDENCE:

WHO WROTE IT?

In the olden days many, many years ago, a lot of people who wrote books didn't put their names on them. That's why this book doesn't have the signature of its author either. However, many people who study the Bible say that the author of this gospel was Luke, and that he also wrote another book that's in the Bible. It's called Acts. Luke was from a city called Antioch in Syria, and he was a medical doctor. He didn't know Jesus personally, but people told him about Jesus, and that's how he could write everything he had heard from others who really had known Jesus.

HOW LONG AGO?

It's not easy to find out when Luke wrote this gospel. People who study the Bible think about a lot of details before they're ready to give a definite date for a book. Most of these people seem to think that Luke wrote his two books 80 to 85 years after Christ.

WHAT'S IT ABOUT?

Luke was a historian. We can see that because of the way he tells everything in order, starting at the beginning. He also spent time investigating. Everything he knew about Jesus was because he had asked a lot of questions to people who really did know him.

This gospel starts out just before Jesus' birth. We really like the part about the birth, because we can imagine what it was like in the manger, with all those animals there! The book also tells about when Mary and Joseph had to travel for the census, and when Jesus traveled from Galilee to Jerusalem.

THE BEST PART

For us, the nicest part was when we read the story of the loving father. Luke says this father loved his son so much that when the father saw him coming from far away, he ran so full of love to receive his son with hugs and kisses (15:20). It's really lovely to know that God loves us like that — the way that father loved his son!

Introduction

1 Many have undertaken to draw up an account of the things that have been fulfilled[a] among us, [2]just as they were handed down to us by those who from the first were eyewitnesses and servants of the word. [3]With this in mind, since I myself have carefully investigated everything from the beginning, I too decided to write an orderly account for you, most excellent Theophilus, [4]so that you may know the certainty of the things you have been taught.

The Birth of John the Baptist Foretold

[5]In the time of Herod king of Judea there was a priest named Zechariah, who belonged to the priestly division of Abijah; his wife Elizabeth was also a descendant of Aaron. [6]Both of them were righteous in the sight of God, observing all the Lord's commands and decrees blamelessly. [7]But they were childless because Elizabeth was not able to conceive, and they were both very old.

[8]Once when Zechariah's division was on duty and he was serving as priest before God, [9]he was chosen by lot, according to the custom of the priesthood, to go into the temple of the Lord and burn incense. [10]And when the time for the burning of incense came, all the assembled worshipers were praying outside.

[11]Then an angel of the Lord appeared to him, standing at the right side of the altar of incense. [12]When Zechariah saw him, he was startled and was gripped with fear. [13]But the angel said to him: "Do not be afraid, Zechariah; your prayer has been heard. Your wife Elizabeth will bear you a son, and you are to call him John. [14]He will be a joy and delight to you, and many will rejoice because of his birth, [15]for he will be great in the sight of the Lord. He is never to take wine or other fermented drink, and he will be filled with the Holy Spirit even before he is born. [16]He will bring back many of the people of Israel to the Lord their God. [17]And he will go on before the Lord, in the spirit and power of Elijah, to turn the hearts of the

BREAK THROUGH!

Burn incense

(LUKE 1:9)

Long ago, in the time of Jesus, they offered different things to God in the temple to show they were thankful and tell him how much they loved him. For example, they used incense that they could buy in little bars. When it burned, it smelled like a nice perfume. The idea was that God would smell it in heaven and know they were thanking him because he's good to people. In some churches today, Christians still use incense in some of their worship services.

parents to their children and the disobedient to the wisdom of the righteous—to make ready a people prepared for the Lord."

[18]Zechariah asked the angel, "How can I be sure of this? I am an old man and my wife is well along in years."

[19]The angel said to him, "I am Gabriel. I stand in the presence of God, and I have been sent to speak to you and to tell you this good news. [20]And now you will be silent and not able to speak until the day this happens, because you did not believe my words, which will come true at their appointed time."

---

[a] 1 Or been surely believed

THE WITNESSES

✓ **THEOPHILUS** (LUKE 1:3)
This name means "friend of God." What a lovely name! It seems he was a man who protected Luke, and that's why Luke calls him "most excellent."

✓ **ZECHARIAH** (LUKE 1:5)
This name means "the LORD remembers." Zechariah was a priest in the temple in Jerusalem. He was John the Baptist's father.

✓ **ELIZABETH** (LUKE 1:5)
She was the priest Zechariah's wife and John the Baptist's mother. She was also the cousin of Mary, the mother of Jesus. Her name means "my God is abundance."

✓ **ANGEL GABRIEL** (LUKE 1:11–20)
Angels are heavenly beings who follow God's orders and help him watch over us, although we can't see them. The angel Gabriel is an important angel. God sends him to Earth when he wants to transmit a special message. For example, the Bible says that God chose Gabriel to tell Mary that she was going to be Jesus' mother. The name Gabriel means "God is my strength."

21 Meanwhile, the people were waiting for Zechariah and wondering why he stayed so long in the temple. 22 When he came out, he could not speak to them. They realized he had seen a vision in the temple, for he kept making signs to them but remained unable to speak.

23 When his time of service was completed, he returned home. 24 After this his wife Elizabeth became pregnant and for five months remained in seclusion. 25 "The Lord has done this for me," she said. "In these days he has shown his favor and taken away my disgrace among the people."

The Birth of Jesus Foretold

26 In the sixth month of Elizabeth's pregnancy, God sent the angel Gabriel to Nazareth, a town in Galilee, 27 to a virgin pledged to be married to a man named Joseph, a descendant of David. The virgin's name was Mary. 28 The angel went to her and said, "Greetings, you who are highly favored! The Lord is with you."

29 Mary was greatly troubled at his words and wondered what kind of greeting this might be. 30 But the angel said to her, "Do not be afraid, Mary; you have found favor with God. 31 You will conceive and give birth to a son, and you are to call him Jesus. 32 He will be great and will be called the Son of the Most High. The Lord God will give him the throne of his father David, 33 and he will reign over Jacob's descendants forever; his kingdom will never end."

34 "How will this be," Mary asked the angel, "since I am a virgin?"

35 The angel answered, "The Holy Spirit will come on you, and the power of the Most High will overshadow you. So the holy one to be born will be called*a* the Son

a 35 Or So the child to be born will be called holy,

BREAKTHROUGH!

Pledged to be married
(LUKE 1:27)

In Bible times, when a boy or a girl were going to get married, their mom and dad chose their bride or groom. Then they had a party that made it official, and the boy promised to marry the girl. From that time on, they were officially engaged. After a year or so, everything was ready and they got married!

of God. 36Even Elizabeth your relative is going to have a child in her old age, and she who was said to be unable to conceive is in her sixth month. 37For no word from God will ever fail."

38"I am the Lord's servant," Mary answered. "May your word to me be fulfilled." Then the angel left her.

Mary Visits Elizabeth

39At that time Mary got ready and hurried to a town in the hill country of Judea, 40where she entered Zechariah's home and greeted Elizabeth. 41When Elizabeth heard Mary's greeting, the baby leaped in her womb, and Elizabeth was filled with the Holy Spirit. 42In a loud voice she exclaimed: "Blessed are you among women, and blessed is the child you will bear! 43But why am I so favored, that the mother of my Lord should come to me? 44As soon as the sound of your greeting reached my ears, the baby in my womb leaped for joy. 45Blessed is she who has believed that the Lord would fulfill his promises to her!"

Mary's Song

46And Mary said:

"My soul glorifies the Lord
47　and my spirit rejoices in God my
　　Savior,
48for he has been mindful
　　of the humble state of his servant.
From now on all generations will call
　　me blessed,
49　for the Mighty One has done great
　　things for me—
holy is his name.
50His mercy extends to those who fear
　　him,
　　from generation to generation.
51He has performed mighty deeds with
　　his arm;
　　he has scattered those who are
　　proud in their inmost thoughts.
52He has brought down rulers from their
　　thrones
　　but has lifted up the humble.
53He has filled the hungry with good
　　things
　　but has sent the rich away empty.
54He has helped his servant Israel,
　　remembering to be merciful
55to Abraham and his descendants
　　forever,
　　just as he promised our ancestors."

56Mary stayed with Elizabeth for about three months and then returned home.

The Birth of John the Baptist

57When it was time for Elizabeth to have her baby, she gave birth to a son. 58Her neighbors and relatives heard that the Lord had shown her great mercy, and they shared her joy.

59On the eighth day they came to circumcise the child, and they were going to name him after his father Zechariah, 60but his mother spoke up and said, "No! He is to be called John."

⁶¹They said to her, "There is no one among your relatives who has that name." ⁶²Then they made signs to his father, to find out what he would like to name the child. ⁶³He asked for a writing tablet, and to everyone's astonishment he wrote, "His name is John." ⁶⁴Immediately his mouth was opened and his tongue set free, and he began to speak, praising God. ⁶⁵All the neighbors were filled with awe, and throughout the hill country of Judea people were talking about all these things. ⁶⁶Everyone who heard this wondered about it, asking, "What then is this child going to be?" For the Lord's hand was with him.

Zechariah's Song

⁶⁷His father Zechariah was filled with the Holy Spirit and prophesied:

⁶⁸ "Praise be to the Lord, the God of Israel,
    because he has come to his people and redeemed them.
⁶⁹ He has raised up a horn*ᵃ* of salvation for us
    in the house of his servant David
⁷⁰ (as he said through his holy prophets of long ago),
⁷¹ salvation from our enemies
    and from the hand of all who hate us —
⁷² to show mercy to our ancestors
    and to remember his holy covenant,
⁷³   the oath he swore to our father Abraham:
⁷⁴ to rescue us from the hand of our enemies,
    and to enable us to serve him without fear
⁷⁵   in holiness and righteousness before him all our days.

⁷⁶ And you, my child, will be called a prophet of the Most High;
    for you will go on before the Lord to prepare the way for him,
⁷⁷ to give his people the knowledge of salvation
    through the forgiveness of their sins,

⁷⁸ because of the tender mercy of our God,
    by which the rising sun will come to us from heaven
⁷⁹ to shine on those living in darkness and in the shadow of death,
    to guide our feet into the path of peace."

⁸⁰And the child grew and became strong in spirit*ᵇ*; and he lived in the wilderness until he appeared publicly to Israel.

The Birth of Jesus

2 In those days Caesar Augustus issued a decree that a census should be taken of the entire Roman world. ²(This was the first census that took place while*ᶜ* Quirinius was governor of Syria.) ³And everyone went to their own town to register.

⁴So Joseph also went up from the town of Nazareth in Galilee to Judea, to Bethlehem the town of David, because he belonged to the house and line of David. ⁵He went there to register with Mary, who was pledged to be married to him and was expecting a child. ⁶While they were there, the time came for the baby to be born, ⁷and she gave birth to her firstborn, a son. She wrapped him in cloths and placed him in a manger, because there was no guest room available for them.

⁸And there were shepherds living out in the fields nearby, keeping watch over their flocks at night. ⁹An angel of the Lord appeared to them, and the glory of the Lord shone around them, and they were terrified. ¹⁰But the angel said to them, "Do not be afraid. I bring you good news that will cause great joy for all the people. ¹¹Today in the town of David a Savior has been born to you; he is the Messiah, the Lord. ¹²This will be a sign to you: You will find a baby wrapped in cloths and lying in a manger."

¹³Suddenly a great company of the heavenly host appeared with the angel, praising God and saying,

---

ᵃ 69 Horn here symbolizes a strong king.   *ᵇ 80* Or *in the Spirit*   *ᶜ 2* Or *This census took place before*

THE SCENE

THE ROMAN WORLD

(LUKE 2:1)

A very, very long time ago, Rome started out as just a little village. As time passed, it got bigger and bigger, until it was very large and strong and powerful. By Jesus' time, it had become the most powerful empire in the world. It ruled over almost all of Europe, part of Asia and part of Africa. So in Jesus' time, the Romans were ruling in Palestine.

14 "Glory to God in the highest heaven,
    and on earth peace to those on
        whom his favor rests."

¹⁵When the angels had left them and gone into heaven, the shepherds said to one another, "Let's go to Bethlehem and see this thing that has happened, which the Lord has told us about."

¹⁶So they hurried off and found Mary and Joseph, and the baby, who was lying in the manger. ¹⁷When they had seen him, they spread the word concerning what had been told them about this child, ¹⁸and all who heard it were amazed at what the shepherds said to them. ¹⁹But Mary treasured up all these things and pondered them in her heart. ²⁰The shepherds returned, glorifying and praising God for all the things they had heard and seen, which were just as they had been told.

²¹On the eighth day, when it was time to circumcise the child, he was named Jesus, the name the angel had given him before he was conceived.

Jesus Presented in the Temple

²²When the time came for the purification rites required by the Law of Moses,

BREAKTHROUGH!

Census

(LUKE 2:1)

In many countries the rulers wanted to know different things about the people who were living there. For example, they might want to know how many people were living in their territory. So a person who was working for the government would go from house to house and ask how many people were living in that house. They would ask who the father was, how old he was and how old his children were. This is still done in many countries, and it's called a "census." It serves several purposes. The rulers can find out how many people live in a city or a country, and how much money they are earning. They can also find out how many men are able to be soldiers if the country goes to war.

THE
WITNESSES

✓ CAESAR AUGUSTUS (LUKE 2:1)

This man was the emperor of Rome, so that means he was like a king who rules over an entire kingdom. The truth is his real name wasn't Augustus. His name was Gaius Julius Caesar Octavian Augustus. Wow! Now that's a name for you! "Augustus" was like a title, like saying "the Great," more or less. He was the emperor of Rome about 27 years before Jesus was born until 14 years after Christ. That means that Jesus was born when Caesar Augustus was the emperor.

✓ QUIRINIUS, GOVERNOR OF SYRIA (LUKE 2:2)

This man's full name was Publius Sulpicius Quirinius. Another good name! He was Roman and a friend of Emperor Tiberius. He was the governor of Syria in the year 6 before Christ. He ordered the census so they could count the number of people. He was very important because, besides being the governor of Syria, he also supervised the high priest of the temple.

Joseph and Mary took him to Jerusalem to present him to the Lord [23](as it is written in the Law of the Lord, "Every firstborn male is to be consecrated to the Lord"[a]), [24]and to offer a sacrifice in keeping with what is said in the Law of the Lord: "a pair of doves or two young pigeons."[b]

[25]Now there was a man in Jerusalem called Simeon, who was righteous and devout. He was waiting for the consolation of Israel, and the Holy Spirit was on him. [26]It had been revealed to him by the Holy Spirit that he would not die before he had seen the Lord's Messiah. [27]Moved by the Spirit, he went into the temple courts. When the parents brought in the child Jesus to do for him what the custom of the Law required, [28]Simeon took him in his arms and praised God, saying:

[29] "Sovereign Lord, as you have
        promised,
     you may now dismiss[c] your servant
        in peace.
[30] For my eyes have seen your salvation,
[31]   which you have prepared in the
        sight of all nations:
[32] a light for revelation to the Gentiles,
        and the glory of your people Israel."

[33]The child's father and mother marveled at what was said about him. [34]Then Simeon blessed them and said to Mary, his mother: "This child is destined to cause the falling and rising of many in Israel, and to be a sign that will be spoken against, [35]so that the thoughts of many hearts will be revealed. And a sword will pierce your own soul too."

---

[a] 23 Exodus 13:2,12   [b] 24 Lev. 12:8   [c] 29 Or
promised, / now dismiss

came strong; he was filled with wisdom, and the grace of God was on him.

The Boy Jesus at the Temple

⁴¹Every year Jesus' parents went to Jerusalem for the Festival of the Passover. ⁴²When he was twelve years old, they went up to the festival, according to the custom. ⁴³After the festival was over, while his parents were returning home, the boy Jesus stayed behind in Jerusalem, but they were unaware of it. ⁴⁴Thinking he was in their company, they traveled on for a day. Then they began looking for him among their relatives and friends. ⁴⁵When they did not find him, they went back to Jerusalem to look for him. ⁴⁶After three days they found him in the temple courts, sitting among the teachers, listening to them and asking them questions.

ᵃ 37 Or then had been a widow for eighty-four years.

BREAK THROUGH!

Firstborn
(LUKE 2:7)

Long ago, in Bible times, the first son who was born was very important. The whole family was very happy when a baby boy was born. This child was always treated in a special way. When the father died, this first son got twice as much inheritance as his younger brothers.

Manger
(LUKE 2:7)

It was like a wooden box where they put food, like straw, for the animals.

BREAK THROUGH!

The glory of the Lord
(LUKE 2:9)

It's a brilliant shining that comes from the presence of God. When God shows himself, it's called "theophany." Now that's a strange word! It means that God is present among the people. He appears in different forms, like a cloud, fire, or a very bright light, the way it happened here.

³⁶There was also a prophet, Anna, the daughter of Penuel, of the tribe of Asher. She was very old; she had lived with her husband seven years after her marriage, ³⁷and then was a widow until she was eighty-four.ᵃ She never left the temple but worshiped night and day, fasting and praying. ³⁸Coming up to them at that very moment, she gave thanks to God and spoke about the child to all who were looking forward to the redemption of Jerusalem.

³⁹When Joseph and Mary had done everything required by the Law of the Lord, they returned to Galilee to their own town of Nazareth. ⁴⁰And the child grew and be-

⁴⁷Everyone who heard him was amazed at his understanding and his answers. ⁴⁸When his parents saw him, they were astonished. His mother said to him, "Son, why have you treated us like this? Your father and I have been anxiously searching for you."

⁴⁹"Why were you searching for me?" he asked. "Didn't you know I had to be in my Father's house?"ᵃ ⁵⁰But they did not understand what he was saying to them.

⁵¹Then he went down to Nazareth with them and was obedient to them. But his

THE
WITNESSES

BREAK THROUGH!

"Circumcise the child"
(LUKE 2:21)

Circumcision is a Jewish custom, but it's also done in some other countries. When a baby boy is born, they cut off a little piece of skin that covers the end of the penis. This is a sign that the boy is Jewish. It's also a way to make sure that this part of the body is always clean.

Law of the Lord
(LUKE 2:23)

This would be the law that God gave Moses many years before Jesus was born. This law was really a bunch of rules to help the Jews live the way God likes people to live.

✓ **SIMEON** **(LUKE 2:25)**
This name is the same as Simon, and it means "God heard me."

✓ **ANNA** **(LUKE 2:36)**
This nice name means "grace."

mother treasured all these things in her heart. ⁵²And Jesus grew in wisdom and stature, and in favor with God and man.

John the Baptist Prepares the Way

3 In the fifteenth year of the reign of Tiberius Caesar—when Pontius Pilate was governor of Judea, Herod tetrarch of Galilee, his brother Philip tetrarch of Iturea and Traconitis, and Lysanias tetrarch of Abilene— ²during the high-priesthood of Annas and Caiaphas, the word of God came to John son of Zechariah in the wilderness. ³He went into all the country

---

ᵃ 49 Or be about my Father's business

THE SCENE

ISRAEL

(LUKE 2:34)

Israel is a country now, but in the Bible, Israel was originally the name of a man whose name had been Jacob. God changed his name and called him Israel. Later, Israel was the name of a kingdom they called the northern kingdom, and its capital was Samaria. Sometimes the word *Israel* is used to talk about the people who God loved very much, the "people of Israel."

around the Jordan, preaching a baptism of repentance for the forgiveness of sins. ⁴As it is written in the book of the words of Isaiah the prophet:

"A voice of one calling in the wilderness,
'Prepare the way for the Lord,
    make straight paths for him.
⁵Every valley shall be filled in,
    every mountain and hill made low.
The crooked roads shall become straight,
    the rough ways smooth.
⁶And all people will see God's salvation.' "ᵃ

⁷John said to the crowds coming out to be baptized by him, "You brood of vipers! Who warned you to flee from the coming wrath? ⁸Produce fruit in keeping with repentance. And do not begin to say to yourselves, 'We have Abraham as our father.' For I tell you that out of these stones God can raise up children for Abraham. ⁹The ax is already at the root of the trees, and every tree that does not produce good fruit will be cut down and thrown into the fire."

¹⁰"What should we do then?" the crowd asked.

¹¹John answered, "Anyone who has two shirts should share with the one who has none, and anyone who has food should do the same."

ᵃ 6 Isaiah 40:3-5

CHECK THE FACTS

Once when Jesus was 12 years old, he got separated from his mom and dad. Where did they find him, and what was he doing?

A) In the temple, talking to the teachers of the law

B) In the market, buying bread

C) In the village, playing with other children

CORRECT ANSWER: A

THE
WITNESSES

✓ TIBERIUS CAESAR (LUKE 3:1)
He was the emperor of Rome from the year 14 until the year 37 after Christ. His name was Tiberius Claudius Nero, but he was mostly called just Tiberius. Caesar Augustus adopted him as a son, so when Caesar Augustus died, Tiberius became the emperor.

✓ ANNAS (LUKE 3:2)
Now that's a nice name! It sounds like "Anna," and that name means "grace of God" or "God has had mercy." Annas was the high priest in the temple in Jerusalem.

✓ CAIAPHAS (LUKE 3:2)
His real name was Joseph, but they called him Caiaphas. Some say this means "the oppressor." Caiaphas married one of Annas' daughters. Caiaphas also was a high priest. It seems he didn't like Jesus, because he was one of the people who asked that Jesus be crucified.

¹²Even tax collectors came to be baptized. "Teacher," they asked, "what should we do?"

¹³"Don't collect any more than you are required to," he told them.

¹⁴Then some soldiers asked him, "And what should we do?"

He replied, "Don't extort money and don't accuse people falsely—be content with your pay."

¹⁵The people were waiting expectantly and were all wondering in their hearts if John might possibly be the Messiah. ¹⁶John answered them all, "I baptize you with^a water. But one who is more powerful than I will come, the straps of whose sandals I am not worthy to untie. He will baptize you with^a the Holy Spirit and fire. ¹⁷His winnowing fork is in his hand to clear his threshing floor and to gather the wheat into his barn, but he will burn up the chaff with unquenchable fire." ¹⁸And with many other words John exhorted the people and proclaimed the good news to them.

¹⁹But when John rebuked Herod the tetrarch because of his marriage to Herodias, his brother's wife, and all the other evil things he had done, ²⁰Herod added this to them all: He locked John up in prison.

The Baptism and Genealogy of Jesus

²¹When all the people were being baptized, Jesus was baptized too. And as he was praying, heaven was opened ²²and the Holy Spirit descended on him in bodily form like a dove. And a voice came from heaven: "You are my Son, whom I love; with you I am well pleased."

²³Now Jesus himself was about thirty years old when he began his ministry. He was the son, so it was thought, of Joseph,

the son of Heli, ²⁴the son of Matthat,
the son of Levi, the son of Melki,
the son of Jannai, the son of Joseph,
²⁵the son of Mattathias, the son of Amos,

---

a 16 Or in

BREAKTHROUGH!

"Gather the wheat into his barn, but he will burn up the chaff with unquenchable fire."

(LUKE 3:17)

It seems that Luke got this idea from the book of Isaiah. Truthfully, it's really hard to understand exactly what this means. Some people say that Luke was thinking about a place where they burned the city trash (a kind of dump or landfill). But other people think he wanted to talk about how forceful a big fire can be. For example, when dry branches catch fire, it's really hard to put the fire out. So it's like he's saying that bad people will burn up, but good people won't — to make it easier for people to understand.

the son of Nahum, the son of Esli,
the son of Naggai, ²⁶the son of Maath,
the son of Mattathias, the son of Semein,
the son of Josek, the son of Joda,
²⁷the son of Joanan, the son of Rhesa,
the son of Zerubbabel, the son of Shealtiel,
the son of Neri, ²⁸the son of Melki,
the son of Addi, the son of Cosam,
the son of Elmadam, the son of Er,

²⁹the son of Joshua, the son of Eliezer,
the son of Jorim, the son of Matthat,
the son of Levi, ³⁰the son of Simeon,
the son of Judah, the son of Joseph,
the son of Jonam, the son of Eliakim,
³¹the son of Melea, the son of Menna,
the son of Mattatha, the son of Nathan,
the son of David, ³²the son of Jesse,
the son of Obed, the son of Boaz,
the son of Salmon,ᵃ the son of Nahshon,
³³the son of Amminadab, the son of Ram,ᵇ
the son of Hezron, the son of Perez,
the son of Judah, ³⁴the son of Jacob,
the son of Isaac, the son of Abraham,
the son of Terah, the son of Nahor,
³⁵the son of Serug, the son of Reu,
the son of Peleg, the son of Eber,
the son of Shelah, ³⁶the son of Cainan,
the son of Arphaxad, the son of Shem,
the son of Noah, the son of Lamech,
³⁷the son of Methuselah, the son of Enoch,
the son of Jared, the son of Mahalalel,
the son of Kenan, ³⁸the son of Enosh,
the son of Seth, the son of Adam,
the son of God.

Jesus Is Tested in the Wilderness

4 Jesus, full of the Holy Spirit, left the Jordan and was led by the Spirit into the wilderness, ²where for forty days he was temptedᶜ by the devil. He ate nothing during those days, and at the end of them he was hungry.

³The devil said to him, "If you are the Son of God, tell this stone to become bread."

⁴Jesus answered, "It is written: 'Man shall not live on bread alone.'ᵈ"

⁵The devil led him up to a high place and showed him in an instant all the kingdoms of the world. ⁶And he said to him,

---

ᵃ 32 Some early manuscripts *Sala*   ᵇ 33 Some manuscripts *Amminadab, the son of Admin, the son of Arni*; other manuscripts vary widely.   ᶜ 2 The Greek for *tempted* can also mean *tested.*   ᵈ 4 Deut. 8:3

"I will give you all their authority and splendor; it has been given to me, and I can give it to anyone I want to. ⁷If you worship me, it will all be yours."

⁸Jesus answered, "It is written: 'Worship the Lord your God and serve him only.'ᵃ"

⁹The devil led him to Jerusalem and had him stand on the highest point of the temple. "If you are the Son of God," he said, "throw yourself down from here. ¹⁰For it is written:

" 'He will command his angels
    concerning you
    to guard you carefully;
¹¹they will lift you up in their hands,
    so that you will not strike your foot
    against a stone.'ᵇ"

¹²Jesus answered, "It is said: 'Do not put the Lord your God to the test.'ᶜ"

¹³When the devil had finished all this tempting, he left him until an opportune time.

Jesus Rejected at Nazareth

¹⁴Jesus returned to Galilee in the power of the Spirit, and news about him spread through the whole countryside. ¹⁵He was teaching in their synagogues, and everyone praised him.

¹⁶He went to Nazareth, where he had been brought up, and on the Sabbath day he went into the synagogue, as was his custom. He stood up to read, ¹⁷and the scroll of the prophet Isaiah was handed to him. Unrolling it, he found the place where it is written:

¹⁸ "The Spirit of the Lord is on me,
    because he has anointed me
    to proclaim good news to the
        poor.
He has sent me to proclaim freedom
        for the prisoners
    and recovery of sight for the blind,
    to set the oppressed free,
¹⁹   to proclaim the year of the Lord's
        favor."ᵈ

²⁰Then he rolled up the scroll, gave it back to the attendant and sat down. The eyes of everyone in the synagogue were fastened on him. ²¹He began by saying to them, "Today this scripture is fulfilled in your hearing."

²²All spoke well of him and were amazed at the gracious words that came from his lips. "Isn't this Joseph's son?" they asked.

²³Jesus said to them, "Surely you will quote this proverb to me: 'Physician, heal yourself!' And you will tell me, 'Do here in your hometown what we have heard that you did in Capernaum.' "

²⁴ "Truly I tell you," he continued, "no prophet is accepted in his hometown. ²⁵I assure you that there were many widows in Israel in Elijah's time, when the sky was shut for three and a half years and there was a severe famine throughout the land. ²⁶Yet Elijah was not sent to any of them, but to a widow in Zarephath in the region of Sidon. ²⁷And there were many in Israel with leprosyᵉ in the time of Elisha the prophet, yet not one of them was cleansed—only Naaman the Syrian."

²⁸All the people in the synagogue were furious when they heard this. ²⁹They got up, drove him out of the town, and took him to the brow of the hill on which the town was built, in order to throw him off the cliff. ³⁰But he walked right through the crowd and went on his way.

Jesus Drives Out an Impure Spirit

³¹Then he went down to Capernaum, a town in Galilee, and on the Sabbath he taught the people. ³²They were amazed at his teaching, because his words had authority.

³³In the synagogue there was a man possessed by a demon, an impure spirit. He cried out at the top of his voice, ³⁴ "Go away! What do you want with us, Jesus of Nazareth? Have you come to destroy us? I know who you are—the Holy One of God!"

³⁵ "Be quiet!" Jesus said sternly. "Come out of him!" Then the demon threw the man down before them all and came out without injuring him.

ᵃ 8 Deut. 6:13   ᵇ 11 Psalm 91:11,12
ᶜ 12 Deut. 6:16   ᵈ 19 Isaiah 61:1,2 (see Septuagint); Isaiah 58:6   ᵉ 27 The Greek word traditionally translated *leprosy* was used for various diseases affecting the skin.

[36]All the people were amazed and said to each other, "What words these are! With authority and power he gives orders to impure spirits and they come out!" [37]And the news about him spread throughout the surrounding area.

Jesus Heals Many

[38]Jesus left the synagogue and went to the home of Simon. Now Simon's mother-in-law was suffering from a high fever, and they asked Jesus to help her. [39]So he bent over her and rebuked the fever, and it left her. She got up at once and began to wait on them.

[40]At sunset, the people brought to Jesus all who had various kinds of sickness, and laying his hands on each one, he healed them. [41]Moreover, demons came out of many people, shouting, "You are the Son of God!" But he rebuked them and would not allow them to speak, because they knew he was the Messiah.

[42]At daybreak, Jesus went out to a solitary place. The people were looking for him and when they came to where he was, they tried to keep him from leaving them. [43]But he said, "I must proclaim the good news of the kingdom of God to the other towns also, because that is why I was sent." [44]And he kept on preaching in the synagogues of Judea.

Jesus Calls His First Disciples

5 One day as Jesus was standing by the Lake of Gennesaret,[a] the people were crowding around him and listening to the word of God. [2]He saw at the water's edge two boats, left there by the fishermen, who were washing their nets. [3]He got into one of the boats, the one belonging to Simon, and asked him to put out a little from shore. Then he sat down and taught the people from the boat.

[4]When he had finished speaking, he said to Simon, "Put out into deep water, and let down the nets for a catch."

[5]Simon answered, "Master, we've worked hard all night and haven't caught anything. But because you say so, I will let down the nets."

[6]When they had done so, they caught such a large number of fish that their nets began to break. [7]So they signaled their partners in the other boat to come and help them, and they came and filled both boats so full that they began to sink.

[8]When Simon Peter saw this, he fell at Jesus' knees and said, "Go away from me, Lord; I am a sinful man!" [9]For he and all his companions were astonished at the catch of fish they had taken, [10]and so were James and John, the sons of Zebedee, Simon's partners.

Then Jesus said to Simon, "Don't be afraid; from now on you will fish for people." [11]So they pulled their boats up on shore, left everything and followed him.

Jesus Heals a Man With Leprosy

[12]While Jesus was in one of the towns, a man came along who was covered with leprosy.[b] When he saw Jesus, he fell with his face to the ground and begged him, "Lord, if you are willing, you can make me clean."

[13]Jesus reached out his hand and touched the man. "I am willing," he said. "Be clean!" And immediately the leprosy left him.

[14]Then Jesus ordered him, "Don't tell anyone, but go, show yourself to the priest and offer the sacrifices that Moses commanded for your cleansing, as a testimony to them."

[15]Yet the news about him spread all the more, so that crowds of people came to hear him and to be healed of their sicknesses. [16]But Jesus often withdrew to lonely places and prayed.

Jesus Forgives and Heals a Paralyzed Man

[17]One day Jesus was teaching, and Pharisees and teachers of the law were sitting there. They had come from every village of Galilee and from Judea and Jerusalem. And the power of the Lord was with Jesus to heal the sick. [18]Some men came carrying a paralyzed man on a mat and tried to take him into the house to lay him before Jesus. [19]When they could not find a way to do this because of the

---

a 1 That is, the Sea of Galilee   *b 12* The Greek word traditionally translated *leprosy* was used for various diseases affecting the skin.

crowd, they went up on the roof and lowered him on his mat through the tiles into the middle of the crowd, right in front of Jesus.

²⁰When Jesus saw their faith, he said, "Friend, your sins are forgiven."

²¹The Pharisees and the teachers of the law began thinking to themselves, "Who is this fellow who speaks blasphemy? Who can forgive sins but God alone?"

²²Jesus knew what they were thinking and asked, "Why are you thinking these things in your hearts? ²³Which is easier: to say, 'Your sins are forgiven,' or to say, 'Get up and walk'? ²⁴But I want you to know that the Son of Man has authority on earth to forgive sins." So he said to the paralyzed man, "I tell you, get up, take your mat and go home." ²⁵Immediately he stood up in front of them, took what he had been lying on and went home praising God. ²⁶Everyone was amazed and gave praise to God. They were filled with awe and said, "We have seen remarkable things today."

Jesus Calls Levi and Eats With Sinners

²⁷After this, Jesus went out and saw a tax collector by the name of Levi sitting at his tax booth. "Follow me," Jesus said to him, ²⁸and Levi got up, left everything and followed him.

²⁹Then Levi held a great banquet for Jesus at his house, and a large crowd of tax collectors and others were eating with them. ³⁰But the Pharisees and the teachers of the law who belonged to their sect complained to his disciples, "Why do you eat and drink with tax collectors and sinners?"

³¹Jesus answered them, "It is not the healthy who need a doctor, but the sick. ³²I have not come to call the righteous, but sinners to repentance."

Jesus Questioned About Fasting

³³They said to him, "John's disciples often fast and pray, and so do the disciples of the Pharisees, but yours go on eating and drinking."

³⁴Jesus answered, "Can you make the friends of the bridegroom fast while he is with them? ³⁵But the time will come when the bridegroom will be taken from them; in those days they will fast."

³⁶He told them this parable: "No one tears a piece out of a new garment to patch an old one. Otherwise, they will have torn the new garment, and the patch from the new will not match the old. ³⁷And no one pours new wine into old wineskins. Otherwise, the new wine will burst the skins; the wine will run out and the wineskins will be ruined. ³⁸No, new wine must be poured into new wineskins. ³⁹And no one after drinking old wine wants the new, for they say, 'The old is better.' "

Jesus Is Lord of the Sabbath

6 One Sabbath Jesus was going through the grainfields, and his disciples began to pick some heads of grain, rub them in their hands and eat the kernels. ²Some of the Pharisees asked, "Why are you doing what is unlawful on the Sabbath?"

³Jesus answered them, "Have you never read what David did when he and his companions were hungry? ⁴He entered the house of God, and taking the consecrated bread, he ate what is lawful only for priests to eat. And he also gave some to his companions." ⁵Then Jesus said to them, "The Son of Man is Lord of the Sabbath."

⁶On another Sabbath he went into the synagogue and was teaching, and a man was there whose right hand was shriveled. ⁷The Pharisees and the teachers of the law were looking for a reason to accuse Jesus, so they watched him closely to see if he would heal on the Sabbath. ⁸But Jesus knew what they were thinking and said to the man with the shriveled hand, "Get up and stand in front of everyone." So he got up and stood there.

⁹Then Jesus said to them, "I ask you, which is lawful on the Sabbath: to do good or to do evil, to save life or to destroy it?"

¹⁰He looked around at them all, and then said to the man, "Stretch out your hand." He did so, and his hand was completely restored. ¹¹But the Pharisees and the teachers of the law were furious and

began to discuss with one another what they might do to Jesus.

The Twelve Apostles

¹²One of those days Jesus went out to a mountainside to pray, and spent the night praying to God. ¹³When morning came, he called his disciples to him and chose twelve of them, whom he also designated apostles: ¹⁴Simon (whom he named Peter), his brother Andrew, James, John, Philip, Bartholomew, ¹⁵Matthew, Thomas, James son of Alphaeus, Simon who was called the Zealot, ¹⁶Judas son of James, and Judas Iscariot, who became a traitor.

Blessings and Woes

¹⁷He went down with them and stood on a level place. A large crowd of his disciples was there and a great number of people from all over Judea, from Jerusalem, and from the coastal region around Tyre and Sidon, ¹⁸who had come to hear him and to be healed of their diseases. Those troubled by impure spirits were cured, ¹⁹and the people all tried to touch him, because power was coming from him and healing them all.

²⁰Looking at his disciples, he said:

"Blessed are you who are poor,
    for yours is the kingdom of God.
²¹Blessed are you who hunger now,
    for you will be satisfied.
Blessed are you who weep now,
    for you will laugh.
²²Blessed are you when people hate
        you,
    when they exclude you and insult
        you
    and reject your name as evil,
        because of the Son of Man.

²³"Rejoice in that day and leap for joy, because great is your reward in heaven. For that is how their ancestors treated the prophets.

²⁴"But woe to you who are rich,
    for you have already received your
        comfort.
²⁵Woe to you who are well fed now,
    for you will go hungry.

Woe to you who laugh now,
    for you will mourn and weep.
²⁶Woe to you when everyone speaks
        well of you,
    for that is how their ancestors
        treated the false prophets.

Love for Enemies

²⁷"But to you who are listening I say: Love your enemies, do good to those who hate you, ²⁸bless those who curse you, pray for those who mistreat you. ²⁹If someone slaps you on one cheek, turn to them the other also. If someone takes your coat, do not withhold your shirt from them. ³⁰Give to everyone who asks you, and if anyone takes what belongs to you, do not demand it back. ³¹Do to others as you would have them do to you.

³²"If you love those who love you,

BREAK THROUGH!

Zealot

(LUKE 6:15)

The Zealots belonged to a political party. They got that name because they had a lot of "zeal," a word that means enthusiasm. In other words, they were very patriotic. They defended everything the Jews had in Palestine, and they didn't want the Romans to rule their country.

what credit is that to you? Even sinners love those who love them. ³³And if you do good to those who are good to you, what credit is that to you? Even sinners do that. ³⁴And if you lend to those from whom you expect repayment, what credit is that to you? Even sinners lend to sinners, expecting to be repaid in full. ³⁵But love your enemies, do good to them, and lend to them without expecting to get anything back. Then your reward will be great, and you will be children of the Most High, because he is kind to the ungrateful and wicked. ³⁶Be merciful, just as your Father is merciful.

Judging Others

³⁷"Do not judge, and you will not be judged. Do not condemn, and you will not be condemned. Forgive, and you will be forgiven. ³⁸Give, and it will be given to you. A good measure, pressed down, shaken together and running over, will be poured into your lap. For with the measure you use, it will be measured to you."

³⁹He also told them this parable: "Can the blind lead the blind? Will they not both fall into a pit? ⁴⁰The student is not above the teacher, but everyone who is fully trained will be like their teacher.

⁴¹"Why do you look at the speck of sawdust in your brother's eye and pay no attention to the plank in your own eye? ⁴²How can you say to your brother, 'Brother, let me take the speck out of your eye,' when you yourself fail to see the plank in your own eye? You hypocrite, first take the plank out of your eye, and then you will see clearly to remove the speck from your brother's eye.

A Tree and Its Fruit

⁴³"No good tree bears bad fruit, nor does a bad tree bear good fruit. ⁴⁴Each tree is recognized by its own fruit. People do not pick figs from thornbushes, or grapes from briers. ⁴⁵A good man brings good things out of the good stored up in his heart, and an evil man brings evil things out of the evil stored up in his heart. For the mouth speaks what the heart is full of.

BREAKTHROUGH!

A plank in your eye?
(LUKE 6:41-42)

That was just a manner of speaking! It didn't mean that the person really had a big board or stick in his or her eye! It means that sometimes we criticize a person who does something wrong, but we don't realize that we're doing even worse things.

The Wise and Foolish Builders

⁴⁶"Why do you call me, 'Lord, Lord,' and do not do what I say? ⁴⁷As for everyone who comes to me and hears my words and puts them into practice, I will show you what they are like. ⁴⁸They are like a man building a house, who dug down deep and laid the foundation on rock. When a flood came, the torrent struck that house but could not shake it, because it was well built. ⁴⁹But the one who hears my words and does not put them into practice is like a man who built a house on the ground without a foundation. The moment the torrent struck that house, it collapsed and its destruction was complete."

The Faith of the Centurion

7 When Jesus had finished saying all this to the people who were listening, he entered Capernaum. ²There a centurion's servant, whom his master valued highly, was sick and about to die. ³The centurion heard of Jesus and sent some elders of the Jews to him, asking him to come and heal his servant. ⁴When they came to Jesus, they pleaded earnestly with him, "This man deserves to have you do this, ⁵because he loves our nation and has built our synagogue." ⁶So Jesus went with them.

He was not far from the house when the centurion sent friends to say to him: "Lord, don't trouble yourself, for I do not deserve to have you come under my roof. ⁷That is why I did not even consider myself worthy to come to you. But say the word, and my servant will be healed. ⁸For I myself am a man under authority, with soldiers under me. I tell this one, 'Go,' and he goes; and that one, 'Come,' and he comes. I say to my servant, 'Do this,' and he does it."

⁹When Jesus heard this, he was amazed at him, and turning to the crowd following him, he said, "I tell you, I have not found such great faith even in Israel." ¹⁰Then the men who had been sent returned to the house and found the servant well.

Jesus Raises a Widow's Son

¹¹Soon afterward, Jesus went to a town called Nain, and his disciples and a large crowd went along with him. ¹²As he approached the town gate, a dead person was being carried out—the only son of his mother, and she was a widow. And a large crowd from the town was with her. ¹³When the Lord saw her, his heart went out to her and he said, "Don't cry."

¹⁴Then he went up and touched the bier they were carrying him on, and the bearers stood still. He said, "Young man, I say to you, get up!" ¹⁵The dead man sat up and began to talk, and Jesus gave him back to his mother.

¹⁶They were all filled with awe and praised God. "A great prophet has appeared among us," they said. "God has come to help his people." ¹⁷This news about Jesus spread throughout Judea and the surrounding country.

THE SCENE

NAIN

(LUKE 7:11)

This city still exists, and its name now is Nein. It's in Galilee, very near Nazareth and Endor, about 25 miles (40 km) from Capernaum. Some ruins from the time of Jesus can be seen in Nein now.

Jesus and John the Baptist

¹⁸John's disciples told him about all these things. Calling two of them, ¹⁹he sent them to the Lord to ask, "Are you the one who is to come, or should we expect someone else?"

²⁰When the men came to Jesus, they said, "John the Baptist sent us to you to ask, 'Are you the one who is to come, or should we expect someone else?'"

²¹At that very time Jesus cured many who had diseases, sicknesses and evil spirits, and gave sight to many who were blind. ²²So he replied to the messengers, "Go back and report to John what you have seen and heard: The blind receive sight, the lame walk, those who have leprosy*a* are cleansed, the deaf hear, the dead are

---

a 22 The Greek word traditionally translated *leprosy* was used for various diseases affecting the skin.

raised, and the good news is proclaimed to the poor. ²³Blessed is anyone who does not stumble on account of me."

²⁴After John's messengers left, Jesus began to speak to the crowd about John: "What did you go out into the wilderness to see? A reed swayed by the wind? ²⁵If not, what did you go out to see? A man dressed in fine clothes? No, those who wear expensive clothes and indulge in luxury are in palaces. ²⁶But what did you go out to see? A prophet? Yes, I tell you, and more than a prophet. ²⁷This is the one about whom it is written:

> " 'I will send my messenger ahead of
> you,
> who will prepare your way before
> you.'ᵃ

²⁸I tell you, among those born of women there is no one greater than John; yet the one who is least in the kingdom of God is greater than he."

²⁹(All the people, even the tax collectors, when they heard Jesus' words, acknowledged that God's way was right, because they had been baptized by John. ³⁰But the Pharisees and the experts in the law rejected God's purpose for themselves, because they had not been baptized by John.)

³¹Jesus went on to say, "To what, then, can I compare the people of this generation? What are they like? ³²They are like children sitting in the marketplace and calling out to each other:

> " 'We played the pipe for you,
> and you did not dance;
> we sang a dirge,
> and you did not cry.'

³³For John the Baptist came neither eating bread nor drinking wine, and you say, 'He has a demon.' ³⁴The Son of Man came eating and drinking, and you say, 'Here is a glutton and a drunkard, a friend of tax collectors and sinners.' ³⁵But wisdom is proved right by all her children."

Jesus Anointed by a Sinful Woman

³⁶When one of the Pharisees invited Jesus to have dinner with him, he went to the Pharisee's house and reclined at the table. ³⁷A woman in that town who lived a sinful life learned that Jesus was eating at the Pharisee's house, so she came there with an alabaster jar of perfume. ³⁸As she stood behind him at his feet weeping, she began to wet his feet with her tears. Then she wiped them with her hair, kissed them and poured perfume on them.

³⁹When the Pharisee who had invited him saw this, he said to himself, "If this man were a prophet, he would know who is touching him and what kind of woman she is—that she is a sinner."

⁴⁰Jesus answered him, "Simon, I have something to tell you."

"Tell me, teacher," he said.

⁴¹"Two people owed money to a certain moneylender. One owed him five hundred denarii,ᵇ and the other fifty. ⁴²Neither of

---

ᵃ 27 Mal. 3:1   ᵇ 41 A denarius was the usual daily wage of a day laborer (see Matt. 20:2).

BREAK THROUGH!

What was money like in Jesus' time?

(LUKE 7:41)

At that time, there were many different kinds of coins, and each kind had a different value. Most coins had Latin writing and a picture of the emperor. The coin mentioned here in this text was called "denarii," and it was a silver coin. With 500 denarii, which is what this man owed, they could buy many things.

them had the money to pay him back, so he forgave the debts of both. Now which of them will love him more?"

⁴³Simon replied, "I suppose the one who had the bigger debt forgiven."

"You have judged correctly," Jesus said.

⁴⁴Then he turned toward the woman and said to Simon, "Do you see this woman? I came into your house. You did not give me any water for my feet, but she wet my feet with her tears and wiped them with her hair. ⁴⁵You did not give me a kiss, but this woman, from the time I entered, has not stopped kissing my feet. ⁴⁶You did not put oil on my head, but she has poured perfume on my feet. ⁴⁷Therefore, I tell you, her many sins have been forgiven—as her great love has shown. But whoever has been forgiven little loves little."

⁴⁸Then Jesus said to her, "Your sins are forgiven."

⁴⁹The other guests began to say among themselves, "Who is this who even forgives sins?"

⁵⁰Jesus said to the woman, "Your faith has saved you; go in peace."

The Parable of the Sower

8 After this, Jesus traveled about from one town and village to another, proclaiming the good news of the kingdom of God. The Twelve were with him, ²and also some women who had been cured of evil spirits and diseases: Mary (called Magdalene) from whom seven demons had come out; ³Joanna the wife of Chuza, the manager of Herod's household; Susanna; and many others. These women were helping to support them out of their own means.

⁴While a large crowd was gathering and people were coming to Jesus from town after town, he told this parable: ⁵"A farmer went out to sow his seed. As he was scattering the seed, some fell along the path; it was trampled on, and the birds ate it up. ⁶Some fell on rocky ground, and when it came up, the plants withered because they had no moisture. ⁷Other seed fell among thorns, which grew up with it and choked the plants. ⁸Still other seed fell on good soil. It came up and yielded

THE WITNESSES

✓ JOANNA (LUKE 8:3)
This name means "God has given his grace." Joanna was the wife of a man called Chuza, who was Herod's household manager. She believed in Jesus and went with Mary Magdalene when they put perfume on Jesus' body and to tell the disciples that Jesus had risen from the dead.

✓ SUSANNA (LUKE 8:3)
In Hebrew, this name means "lily." Susanna was a woman who accompanied Jesus, and she learned all the things that he taught.

a crop, a hundred times more than was sown."

When he said this, he called out, "Whoever has ears to hear, let them hear."

⁹His disciples asked him what this parable meant. ¹⁰He said, "The knowledge of the secrets of the kingdom of God has been given to you, but to others I speak in parables, so that,

" 'though seeing, they may not see;
though hearing, they may not
understand.'[a]

11 "This is the meaning of the parable: The seed is the word of God. 12 Those along the path are the ones who hear, and then the devil comes and takes away the word from their hearts, so that they may not believe and be saved. 13 Those on the rocky ground are the ones who receive the word with joy when they hear it, but they have no root. They believe for a while, but in the time of testing they fall away. 14 The seed that fell among thorns stands for those who hear, but as they go on their way they are choked by life's worries, riches and pleasures, and they do not mature. 15 But the seed on good soil stands for those with a noble and good heart, who hear the word, retain it, and by persevering produce a crop.

A Lamp on a Stand

16 "No one lights a lamp and hides it in a clay jar or puts it under a bed. Instead, they put it on a stand, so that those who come in can see the light. 17 For there is nothing hidden that will not be disclosed, and nothing concealed that will not be known or brought out into the open. 18 Therefore consider carefully how you listen. Whoever has will be given more; whoever does not have, even what they think they have will be taken from them."

Jesus' Mother and Brothers

19 Now Jesus' mother and brothers came to see him, but they were not able to get near him because of the crowd. 20 Someone told him, "Your mother and brothers are standing outside, wanting to see you."

21 He replied, "My mother and brothers are those who hear God's word and put it into practice."

Jesus Calms the Storm

22 One day Jesus said to his disciples, "Let us go over to the other side of the lake." So they got into a boat and set out. 23 As they sailed, he fell asleep. A squall came down on the lake, so that the boat

BREAKTHROUGH!

Who were Jesus' brothers?
(LUKE 8:19-21)
The Bible says that after Jesus was born, Mary and Joseph had other children. Jesus' brothers were named James, Joseph, Simon and Judas. We don't know the names of his sisters, but they're mentioned in other parts of the New Testament, like in Matthew 13:56 and Mark 6:3.

was being swamped, and they were in great danger.

24 The disciples went and woke him, saying, "Master, Master, we're going to drown!"

He got up and rebuked the wind and the raging waters; the storm subsided, and all was calm. 25 "Where is your faith?" he asked his disciples.

In fear and amazement they asked one another, "Who is this? He commands even the winds and the water, and they obey him."

Jesus Restores a Demon-Possessed Man

26 They sailed to the region of the Gerasenes,[b] which is across the lake from Galilee. 27 When Jesus stepped ashore,

---

[a] 10 Isaiah 6:9   [b] 26 Some manuscripts *Gadarenes*; other manuscripts *Gergesenes*; also in verse 37

he was met by a demon-possessed man from the town. For a long time this man had not worn clothes or lived in a house, but had lived in the tombs. ²⁸When he saw Jesus, he cried out and fell at his feet, shouting at the top of his voice, "What do you want with me, Jesus, Son of the Most High God? I beg you, don't torture me!" ²⁹For Jesus had commanded the impure spirit to come out of the man. Many times it had seized him, and though he was chained hand and foot and kept under guard, he had broken his chains and had been driven by the demon into solitary places.

³⁰Jesus asked him, "What is your name?"

"Legion," he replied, because many demons had gone into him. ³¹And they begged Jesus repeatedly not to order them to go into the Abyss.

³²A large herd of pigs was feeding there on the hillside. The demons begged Jesus to let them go into the pigs, and he gave them permission. ³³When the demons came out of the man, they went into the pigs, and the herd rushed down the steep bank into the lake and was drowned.

³⁴When those tending the pigs saw what had happened, they ran off and reported this in the town and countryside, ³⁵and the people went out to see what had happened. When they came to Jesus, they found the man from whom the demons had gone out, sitting at Jesus' feet, dressed and in his right mind; and they were afraid. ³⁶Those who had seen it told the people how the demon-possessed man had been cured. ³⁷Then all the people of the region of the Gerasenes asked Jesus to leave them, because they were overcome with fear. So he got into the boat and left.

³⁸The man from whom the demons had gone out begged to go with him, but Jesus sent him away, saying, ³⁹"Return home and tell how much God has done for you." So the man went away and told all over town how much Jesus had done for him.

Jesus Raises a Dead Girl and Heals a Sick Woman

⁴⁰Now when Jesus returned, a crowd welcomed him, for they were all expecting him. ⁴¹Then a man named Jairus, a synagogue leader, came and fell at Jesus' feet, pleading with him to come to his house ⁴²because his only daughter, a girl of about twelve, was dying.

As Jesus was on his way, the crowds almost crushed him. ⁴³And a woman was there who had been subject to bleeding for twelve years,ᵃ but no one could heal her. ⁴⁴She came up behind him and touched the edge of his cloak, and immediately her bleeding stopped.

⁴⁵"Who touched me?" Jesus asked.

When they all denied it, Peter said, "Master, the people are crowding and pressing against you."

⁴⁶But Jesus said, "Someone touched me; I know that power has gone out from me."

⁴⁷Then the woman, seeing that she could not go unnoticed, came trembling and fell at his feet. In the presence of all the people, she told why she had touched him and how she had been instantly healed. ⁴⁸Then he said to her, "Daughter, your faith has healed you. Go in peace."

⁴⁹While Jesus was still speaking, someone came from the house of Jairus, the synagogue leader. "Your daughter is dead," he said. "Don't bother the teacher anymore."

⁵⁰Hearing this, Jesus said to Jairus, "Don't be afraid; just believe, and she will be healed."

⁵¹When he arrived at the house of Jairus, he did not let anyone go in with him except Peter, John and James, and the child's father and mother. ⁵²Meanwhile, all the people were wailing and mourning for her. "Stop wailing," Jesus said. "She is not dead but asleep."

⁵³They laughed at him, knowing that she was dead. ⁵⁴But he took her by the hand and said, "My child, get up!" ⁵⁵Her spirit returned, and at once she stood up. Then Jesus told them to give her some-

---

ᵃ 43 Many manuscripts *years, and she had spent all she had on doctors* thing to eat. [56]Her parents were astonished, but he ordered them not to tell anyone what had happened.

Jesus Sends Out the Twelve

9 When Jesus had called the Twelve together, he gave them power and authority to drive out all demons and to cure diseases, [2]and he sent them out to proclaim the kingdom of God and to heal the sick. [3]He told them: "Take nothing for the journey—no staff, no bag, no bread, no money, no extra shirt. [4]Whatever house you enter, stay there until you leave that town. [5]If people do not welcome you, leave their town and shake the dust off your feet as a testimony against them." [6]So they set out and went from village to village, proclaiming the good news and healing people everywhere.

[7]Now Herod the tetrarch heard about all that was going on. And he was perplexed because some were saying that John had been raised from the dead, [8]others that Elijah had appeared, and still others that one of the prophets of long ago had come back to life. [9]But Herod said, "I beheaded John. Who, then, is this I hear such things about?" And he tried to see him.

Jesus Feeds the Five Thousand

[10]When the apostles returned, they reported to Jesus what they had done. Then he took them with him and they withdrew by themselves to a town called Bethsaida, [11]but the crowds learned about it and followed him. He welcomed them and spoke to them about the kingdom of God, and healed those who needed healing.

[12]Late in the afternoon the Twelve came to him and said, "Send the crowd away so they can go to the surrounding villages and countryside and find food and lodging, because we are in a remote place here."

[13]He replied, "You give them something to eat."

They answered, "We have only five loaves of bread and two fish—unless we go and buy food for all this crowd." [14](About five thousand men were there.)

But he said to his disciples, "Have them sit down in groups of about fifty each."

[15]The disciples did so, and everyone sat down. [16]Taking the five loaves and the two fish and looking up to heaven, he gave thanks and broke them. Then he gave them to the disciples to distribute to the people. [17]They all ate and were satisfied, and the disciples picked up twelve basketfuls of broken pieces that were left over.

Peter Declares That Jesus Is the Messiah

[18]Once when Jesus was praying in private and his disciples were with him, he asked them, "Who do the crowds say I am?"

[19]They replied, "Some say John the Baptist; others say Elijah; and still others, that one of the prophets of long ago has come back to life."

[20]"But what about you?" he asked. "Who do you say I am?"

Peter answered, "God's Messiah."

Jesus Predicts His Death

[21]Jesus strictly warned them not to tell this to anyone. [22]And he said, "The Son of Man must suffer many things and be rejected by the elders, the chief priests and the teachers of the law, and he must be killed and on the third day be raised to life."

[23]Then he said to them all: "Whoever wants to be my disciple must deny themselves and take up their cross daily and follow me. [24]For whoever wants to save their life will lose it, but whoever loses their life for me will save it. [25]What good is it for someone to gain the whole world, and yet lose or forfeit their very self? [26]Whoever is ashamed of me and my words, the Son of Man will be ashamed of them when he comes in his glory and in the glory of the Father and of the holy angels. [27]"Truly I tell you, some who are standing here will not taste death before they see the kingdom of God."

The Transfiguration

[28]About eight days after Jesus said this, he took Peter, John and James with him and went up onto a mountain to pray. [29]As he was praying, the appearance of

his face changed, and his clothes became as bright as a flash of lightning. ³⁰Two men, Moses and Elijah, appeared in glorious splendor, talking with Jesus. ³¹They spoke about his departure,ᵃ which he was about to bring to fulfillment at Jerusalem. ³²Peter and his companions were very sleepy, but when they became fully awake, they saw his glory and the two men standing with him. ³³As the men were leaving Jesus, Peter said to him, "Master, it is good for us to be here. Let us put up three shelters—one for you, one for Moses and one for Elijah." (He did not know what he was saying.)

³⁴While he was speaking, a cloud appeared and covered them, and they were afraid as they entered the cloud. ³⁵A voice came from the cloud, saying, "This is my Son, whom I have chosen; listen to him." ³⁶When the voice had spoken, they found that Jesus was alone. The disciples kept this to themselves and did not tell anyone at that time what they had seen.

Jesus Heals a Demon-Possessed Boy

³⁷The next day, when they came down from the mountain, a large crowd met him. ³⁸A man in the crowd called out, "Teacher, I beg you to look at my son, for he is my only child. ³⁹A spirit seizes him and he suddenly screams; it throws him into convulsions so that he foams at the mouth. It scarcely ever leaves him and is destroying him. ⁴⁰I begged your disciples to drive it out, but they could not."

⁴¹"You unbelieving and perverse generation," Jesus replied, "how long shall I stay with you and put up with you? Bring your son here."

⁴²Even while the boy was coming, the demon threw him to the ground in a convulsion. But Jesus rebuked the impure spirit, healed the boy and gave him back to his father. ⁴³And they were all amazed at the greatness of God.

Jesus Predicts His Death a Second Time

While everyone was marveling at all that Jesus did, he said to his disciples,

BREAKTHROUGH!

Shelters
(LUKE 9:33)

They were like huts made of branches and slim tree trunks. Sometimes they made them for a special celebration that was called the Feast of Booths, or the Festival of Tabernacles. This celebration was to remember that the Jews had lived in the desert for many years before they got to the land God had promised them.

⁴⁴"Listen carefully to what I am about to tell you: The Son of Man is going to be delivered into the hands of men." ⁴⁵But they did not understand what this meant. It was hidden from them, so that they did not grasp it, and they were afraid to ask him about it.

⁴⁶An argument started among the disciples as to which of them would be the greatest. ⁴⁷Jesus, knowing their thoughts, took a little child and had him stand beside him. ⁴⁸Then he said to them, "Whoever welcomes this little child in my name welcomes me; and whoever welcomes me welcomes the one who sent me. For it is the one who is least among you all who is the greatest."

⁴⁹"Master," said John, "we saw someone driving out demons in your name and

---

ᵃ 31 Greek exodos

we tried to stop him, because he is not one of us."

⁵⁰"Do not stop him," Jesus said, "for whoever is not against you is for you."

Samaritan Opposition

⁵¹As the time approached for him to be taken up to heaven, Jesus resolutely set out for Jerusalem. ⁵²And he sent messengers on ahead, who went into a Samaritan village to get things ready for him; ⁵³but the people there did not welcome him, because he was heading for Jerusalem. ⁵⁴When the disciples James and John saw this, they asked, "Lord, do you want us to call fire down from heaven to destroy them*ᵃ*?" ⁵⁵But Jesus turned and rebuked them. ⁵⁶Then he and his disciples went to another village.

The Cost of Following Jesus

⁵⁷As they were walking along the road, a man said to him, "I will follow you wherever you go."

⁵⁸Jesus replied, "Foxes have dens and birds have nests, but the Son of Man has no place to lay his head."

⁵⁹He said to another man, "Follow me."

But he replied, "Lord, first let me go and bury my father."

⁶⁰Jesus said to him, "Let the dead bury their own dead, but you go and proclaim the kingdom of God."

⁶¹Still another said, "I will follow you, Lord; but first let me go back and say goodbye to my family."

⁶²Jesus replied, "No one who puts a hand to the plow and looks back is fit for service in the kingdom of God."

Jesus Sends Out the Seventy-Two

10 After this the Lord appointed seventy-two*ᵇ* others and sent them two by two ahead of him to every town and place where he was about to go. ²He told them, "The harvest is plentiful, but the workers are few. Ask the Lord of the harvest, therefore, to send out workers into his harvest field. ³Go! I am sending you out like lambs among wolves. ⁴Do not take a purse or bag or sandals; and do not greet anyone on the road.

BREAKTHROUGH!

"Let the dead bury their own dead."

(LUKE 9:60)

This idea seems to have been difficult to understand, even for the people who study the Bible a lot, because they don't agree. Well, most of them think that "the dead" mentioned here means the people who don't obey God or believe in Jesus. Then "their own dead" means the people who have truly died. So then it would mean something like this: people who believe in Jesus have to tell the good news and do good things. The people who don't believe in Jesus can be in charge of doing all the other, everyday things.

⁵"When you enter a house, first say, 'Peace to this house.' ⁶If someone who promotes peace is there, your peace will rest on them; if not, it will return to you. ⁷Stay there, eating and drinking whatever they give you, for the worker deserves his wages. Do not move around from house to house.

⁸"When you enter a town and are welcomed, eat what is offered to you. ⁹Heal the sick who are there and tell them, 'The kingdom of God has come near to you.'

ᵃ 54 Some manuscripts *them, just as Elijah did*
ᵇ 1 Some manuscripts *seventy;* also in verse 17

¹⁰But when you enter a town and are not welcomed, go into its streets and say, ¹¹'Even the dust of your town we wipe from our feet as a warning to you. Yet be sure of this: The kingdom of God has come near.' ¹²I tell you, it will be more bearable on that day for Sodom than for that town.

¹³"Woe to you, Chorazin! Woe to you, Bethsaida! For if the miracles that were performed in you had been performed in Tyre and Sidon, they would have repented long ago, sitting in sackcloth and ashes. ¹⁴But it will be more bearable for Tyre and Sidon at the judgment than for you. ¹⁵And you, Capernaum, will you be lifted to the heavens? No, you will go down to Hades.ᵃ

¹⁶"Whoever listens to you listens to

BREAKTHROUGH!

The judgment
(LUKE 10:14)

The final judgment will be when Jesus comes to Earth a second time, but not as a baby. He will come in a glorious way as King of the World! That day, we will all become alive again, and God will ask us to explain everything. It'll be like a test of the things we did while we were alive. Jesus will look at the good things as well as the bad things to see if we acted out of love for other people or not.

me; whoever rejects you rejects me; but whoever rejects me rejects him who sent me."

¹⁷The seventy-two returned with joy and said, "Lord, even the demons submit to us in your name."

¹⁸He replied, "I saw Satan fall like lightning from heaven. ¹⁹I have given you authority to trample on snakes and scorpions and to overcome all the power of the enemy; nothing will harm you. ²⁰However, do not rejoice that the spirits submit to you, but rejoice that your names are written in heaven."

²¹At that time Jesus, full of joy through the Holy Spirit, said, "I praise you, Father, Lord of heaven and earth, because you have hidden these things from the wise and learned, and revealed them to little children. Yes, Father, for this is what you were pleased to do.

²²"All things have been committed to me by my Father. No one knows who the Son is except the Father, and no one knows who the Father is except the Son and those to whom the Son chooses to reveal him."

²³Then he turned to his disciples and said privately, "Blessed are the eyes that see what you see. ²⁴For I tell you that many prophets and kings wanted to see what you see but did not see it, and to hear what you hear but did not hear it."

The Parable of the Good Samaritan

²⁵On one occasion an expert in the law stood up to test Jesus. "Teacher," he asked, "what must I do to inherit eternal life?"

²⁶"What is written in the Law?" he replied. "How do you read it?"

²⁷He answered, " 'Love the Lord your God with all your heart and with all your soul and with all your strength and with all your mind'ᵇ; and, 'Love your neighbor as yourself.'ᶜ"

²⁸"You have answered correctly," Jesus replied. "Do this and you will live."

²⁹But he wanted to justify himself, so he asked Jesus, "And who is my neighbor?"

ᵃ 15 That is, the realm of the dead   ᵇ 27 Deut. 6:5
ᶜ 27 Lev. 19:18

³⁰In reply Jesus said: "A man was going down from Jerusalem to Jericho, when he was attacked by robbers. They stripped him of his clothes, beat him and went away, leaving him half dead. ³¹A priest happened to be going down the same road, and when he saw the man, he passed by on the other side. ³²So too, a Levite, when he came to the place and saw him, passed by on the other side. ³³But a Samaritan, as he traveled, came where the man was; and when he saw him, he took pity on him. ³⁴He went to him and bandaged his wounds, pouring on oil and wine. Then he put the man on his own donkey, brought him to an inn and took care of him. ³⁵The next day he took out two denarii*ᵃ* and gave them to the innkeeper. 'Look after him,' he said, 'and when I return, I will reimburse you for any extra expense you may have.'

³⁶"Which of these three do you think was a neighbor to the man who fell into the hands of robbers?"

³⁷The expert in the law replied, "The one who had mercy on him."

Jesus told him, "Go and do likewise."

At the Home of Martha and Mary

³⁸As Jesus and his disciples were on their way, he came to a village where a woman named Martha opened her home to him. ³⁹She had a sister called Mary, who sat at the Lord's feet listening to what he said. ⁴⁰But Martha was distracted by all the preparations that had to be made. She came to him and asked, "Lord, don't you care that my sister has left me to do the work by myself? Tell her to help me!"

⁴¹"Martha, Martha," the Lord answered, "you are worried and upset about many things, ⁴²but few things are needed—or indeed only one.*ᵇ* Mary has chosen what is better, and it will not be taken away from her."

Jesus' Teaching on Prayer

11 One day Jesus was praying in a certain place. When he finished, one of his disciples said to him, "Lord, teach us to pray, just as John taught his disciples."

BREAK THROUGH!

"...bandaged his wounds, pouring on oil and wine"
(LUKE 10:34)

In Bible times, wine and oil were used like medicine. They used wine to clean a wound so it wouldn't get infected. They used oil so the wound wouldn't hurt so much and the skin would get soft.

²He said to them, "When you pray, say:

" 'Father,*ᶜ*
hallowed be your name,
your kingdom come.*ᵈ*
³Give us each day our daily bread.
⁴Forgive us our sins,
     for we also forgive everyone who
          sins against us.*ᵉ*
And lead us not into temptation.*ᶠ* ' "

⁵Then Jesus said to them, "Suppose you have a friend, and you go to him at midnight and say, 'Friend, lend me three loaves of bread; ⁶a friend of mine on a journey has come to me, and I have no food to offer him.' ⁷And suppose the one inside answers, 'Don't bother me. The

ᵃ 35 A denarius was the usual daily wage of a day laborer (see Matt. 20:2).   *ᵇ 42* Some manuscripts *but only one thing is needed*   *ᶜ 2* Some manuscripts *Our Father in heaven*   *ᵈ 2* Some manuscripts *come. May your will be done on earth as it is in heaven.*   *ᵉ 4* Greek *everyone who is indebted to us*   *ᶠ 4* Some manuscripts *temptation, but deliver us from the evil one* door is already locked, and my children and I are in bed. I can't get up and give you anything.' ⁸I tell you, even though he will not get up and give you the bread because of friendship, yet because of your shameless audacity*a* he will surely get up and give you as much as you need.

⁹"So I say to you: Ask and it will be given to you; seek and you will find; knock and the door will be opened to you. ¹⁰For everyone who asks receives; the one who seeks finds; and to the one who knocks, the door will be opened.

¹¹"Which of you fathers, if your son asks for*b* a fish, will give him a snake instead? ¹²Or if he asks for an egg, will give him a scorpion? ¹³If you then, though you are evil, know how to give good gifts to your children, how much more will your Father in heaven give the Holy Spirit to those who ask him!"

Jesus and Beelzebul

¹⁴Jesus was driving out a demon that was mute. When the demon left, the man who had been mute spoke, and the crowd was amazed. ¹⁵But some of them said, "By Beelzebul, the prince of demons, he is driving out demons." ¹⁶Others tested him by asking for a sign from heaven.

¹⁷Jesus knew their thoughts and said to them: "Any kingdom divided against itself will be ruined, and a house divided against itself will fall. ¹⁸If Satan is divided against himself, how can his kingdom stand? I say this because you claim that I drive out demons by Beelzebul. ¹⁹Now if I drive out demons by Beelzebul, by whom do your followers drive them out? So then, they will be your judges. ²⁰But if I drive out demons by the finger of God, then the kingdom of God has come upon you.

²¹"When a strong man, fully armed, guards his own house, his possessions are safe. ²²But when someone stronger attacks and overpowers him, he takes away the armor in which the man trusted and divides up his plunder.

²³"Whoever is not with me is against me, and whoever does not gather with me scatters.

THE
WITNESSES

✓ **BEELZEBUL, THE PRINCE OF DEMONS** (LUKE 11:15)
This is a disgusting name! It means "Lord of the flies." This name comes from Baal, who was a god in the country called Canaan.

²⁴"When an impure spirit comes out of a person, it goes through arid places seeking rest and does not find it. Then it says, 'I will return to the house I left.' ²⁵When it arrives, it finds the house swept clean and put in order. ²⁶Then it goes and takes seven other spirits more wicked than itself, and they go in and live there. And the final condition of that person is worse than the first."

²⁷As Jesus was saying these things, a woman in the crowd called out, "Blessed is the mother who gave you birth and nursed you."

---

a 8 Or *yet to preserve his good name*   *b* 11 Some manuscripts *for bread, will give him a stone? Or if he asks for*

²⁸He replied, "Blessed rather are those who hear the word of God and obey it."

The Sign of Jonah

²⁹As the crowds increased, Jesus said, "This is a wicked generation. It asks for a sign, but none will be given it except the sign of Jonah. ³⁰For as Jonah was a sign to the Ninevites, so also will the Son of Man be to this generation. ³¹The Queen of the South will rise at the judgment with the people of this generation and condemn them, for she came from the ends of the earth to listen to Solomon's wisdom; and now something greater than Solomon is here. ³²The men of Nineveh will stand up at the judgment with this generation and condemn it, for they repented at the preaching of Jonah; and now something greater than Jonah is here.

The Lamp of the Body

³³"No one lights a lamp and puts it in a place where it will be hidden, or under a bowl. Instead they put it on its stand, so that those who come in may see the light. ³⁴Your eye is the lamp of your body. When your eyes are healthy,ᵃ your whole body also is full of light. But when they are unhealthy,ᵇ your body also is full of darkness. ³⁵See to it, then, that the light within you is not darkness. ³⁶Therefore, if your whole body is full of light, and no part of it dark, it will be just as full of light as when a lamp shines its light on you."

Woes on the Pharisees and the Experts in the Law

³⁷When Jesus had finished speaking, a Pharisee invited him to eat with him; so he went in and reclined at the table. ³⁸But the Pharisee was surprised when he noticed that Jesus did not first wash before the meal.

³⁹Then the Lord said to him, "Now then, you Pharisees clean the outside of the cup and dish, but inside you are full of greed and wickedness. ⁴⁰You foolish people! Did not the one who made the outside make the inside also? ⁴¹But now as for what is inside you—be generous to the poor, and everything will be clean for you.

⁴²"Woe to you Pharisees, because you give God a tenth of your mint, rue and all other kinds of garden herbs, but you neglect justice and the love of God. You should have practiced the latter without leaving the former undone.

⁴³"Woe to you Pharisees, because you love the most important seats in the synagogues and respectful greetings in the marketplaces.

⁴⁴"Woe to you, because you are like unmarked graves, which people walk over without knowing it."

⁴⁵One of the experts in the law answered him, "Teacher, when you say these things, you insult us also."

⁴⁶Jesus replied, "And you experts in the law, woe to you, because you load people down with burdens they can hardly carry, and you yourselves will not lift one finger to help them.

⁴⁷"Woe to you, because you build tombs for the prophets, and it was your ancestors who killed them. ⁴⁸So you testify that you approve of what your ancestors did; they killed the prophets, and you build their tombs. ⁴⁹Because of this, God in his wisdom said, 'I will send them prophets and apostles, some of whom they will kill and others they will persecute.' ⁵⁰Therefore this generation will be held responsible for the blood of all the prophets that has been shed since the beginning of the world, ⁵¹from the blood of Abel to the blood of Zechariah, who was killed between the altar and the sanctuary. Yes, I tell you, this generation will be held responsible for it all.

⁵²"Woe to you experts in the law, because you have taken away the key to knowledge. You yourselves have not entered, and you have hindered those who were entering."

⁵³When Jesus went outside, the Pharisees and the teachers of the law began to oppose him fiercely and to besiege him with questions, ⁵⁴waiting to catch him in something he might say.

ᵃ 34 The Greek for *healthy* here implies *generous*.
ᵇ 34 The Greek for *unhealthy* here implies *stingy*.

Warnings and Encouragements

12 Meanwhile, when a crowd of many thousands had gathered, so that they were trampling on one another, Jesus began to speak first to his disciples, saying: "Be*ᵃ* on your guard against the yeast of the Pharisees, which is hypocrisy. ²There is nothing concealed that will not be disclosed, or hidden that will not be made known. ³What you have said in the dark will be heard in the daylight, and what you have whispered in the ear in the inner rooms will be proclaimed from the roofs.

⁴"I tell you, my friends, do not be afraid of those who kill the body and after that can do no more. ⁵But I will show you whom you should fear: Fear him who, after your body has been killed, has authority to throw you into hell. Yes, I tell you, fear him. ⁶Are not five sparrows sold for two pennies? Yet not one of them is forgotten by God. ⁷Indeed, the very hairs of your head are all numbered. Don't be afraid; you are worth more than many sparrows.

⁸"I tell you, whoever publicly acknowledges me before others, the Son of Man will also acknowledge before the angels of God. ⁹But whoever disowns me before others will be disowned before the angels of God. ¹⁰And everyone who speaks a word against the Son of Man will be forgiven, but anyone who blasphemes against the Holy Spirit will not be forgiven.

¹¹"When you are brought before synagogues, rulers and authorities, do not worry about how you will defend yourselves or what you will say, ¹²for the Holy Spirit will teach you at that time what you should say."

The Parable of the Rich Fool

¹³Someone in the crowd said to him, "Teacher, tell my brother to divide the inheritance with me."

¹⁴Jesus replied, "Man, who appointed me a judge or an arbiter between you?" ¹⁵Then he said to them, "Watch out! Be on your guard against all kinds of greed; life does not consist in an abundance of possessions."

¹⁶And he told them this parable: "The ground of a certain rich man yielded an abundant harvest. ¹⁷He thought to himself, 'What shall I do? I have no place to store my crops.'

¹⁸"Then he said, 'This is what I'll do. I will tear down my barns and build bigger ones, and there I will store my surplus grain. ¹⁹And I'll say to myself, "You have plenty of grain laid up for many years. Take life easy; eat, drink and be merry."'

²⁰"But God said to him, 'You fool! This very night your life will be demanded from you. Then who will get what you have prepared for yourself?'

²¹"This is how it will be with whoever stores up things for themselves but is not rich toward God."

Do Not Worry

²²Then Jesus said to his disciples: "Therefore I tell you, do not worry about your life, what you will eat; or about your body, what you will wear. ²³For life is more than food, and the body more than clothes. ²⁴Consider the ravens: They do not sow or reap, they have no storeroom or barn; yet God feeds them. And how much more valuable you are than birds! ²⁵Who of you by worrying can add a single hour to your life*ᵇ*? ²⁶Since you cannot do this very little thing, why do you worry about the rest?

²⁷"Consider how the wild flowers grow. They do not labor or spin. Yet I tell you, not even Solomon in all his splendor was dressed like one of these. ²⁸If that is how God clothes the grass of the field, which is here today, and tomorrow is thrown into the fire, how much more will he clothe you—you of little faith! ²⁹And do not set your heart on what you will eat or drink; do not worry about it. ³⁰For the pagan world runs after all such things, and your Father knows that you need them. ³¹But seek his kingdom, and these things will be given to you as well.

³²"Do not be afraid, little flock, for your Father has been pleased to give you the kingdom. ³³Sell your possessions and give to the poor. Provide purses for your-

---

ᵃ 1 Or speak to his disciples, saying: "First of all, be
ᵇ 25 Or single cubit to your height

selves that will not wear out, a treasure in heaven that will never fail, where no thief comes near and no moth destroys. 34For where your treasure is, there your heart will be also.

Watchfulness

35"Be dressed ready for service and keep your lamps burning, 36like servants waiting for their master to return from a wedding banquet, so that when he comes and knocks they can immediately open the door for him. 37It will be good for those servants whose master finds them watching when he comes. Truly I tell you, he will dress himself to serve, will have them recline at the table and will come and wait on them. 38It will be good for those servants whose master finds them ready, even if he comes in the middle of the night or toward daybreak. 39But understand this: If the owner of the house had known at what hour the thief was coming, he would not have let his house be broken into. 40You also must be ready, because the Son of Man will come at an hour when you do not expect him."

41Peter asked, "Lord, are you telling this parable to us, or to everyone?"

42The Lord answered, "Who then is the faithful and wise manager, whom the master puts in charge of his servants to give them their food allowance at the proper time? 43It will be good for that servant whom the master finds doing so when he returns. 44Truly I tell you, he will put him in charge of all his possessions. 45But suppose the servant says to himself, 'My master is taking a long time in coming,' and he then begins to beat the other servants, both men and women, and to eat and drink and get drunk. 46The master of that servant will come on a day when he does not expect him and at an hour he is not aware of. He will cut him to pieces and assign him a place with the unbelievers.

47"The servant who knows the master's will and does not get ready or does not do what the master wants will be beaten with many blows. 48But the one who does not know and does things deserving pun-

ishment will be beaten with few blows. From everyone who has been given much, much will be demanded; and from the one who has been entrusted with much, much more will be asked.

Not Peace but Division

49"I have come to bring fire on the earth, and how I wish it were already kindled! 50But I have a baptism to undergo, and what constraint I am under until it is completed! 51Do you think I came to bring peace on earth? No, I tell you, but division. 52From now on there will be five in one family divided against each other, three against two and two against three. 53They will be divided, father against son and son against father, mother against daughter and daughter against mother, mother-in-law against daughter-in-law

"A treasure in heaven"
(LUKE 12:33)

Jesus tells his friends not to be worried about getting rich and richer, because God will take care of them and give them what they need. He also teaches them that the most important thing is to be good people, to believe in God and to behave. If our most important treasure is God's love, then in our hearts we'll always be thinking about him.

and daughter-in-law against mother-in-law."

Interpreting the Times

⁵⁴He said to the crowd: "When you see a cloud rising in the west, immediately you say, 'It's going to rain,' and it does. ⁵⁵And when the south wind blows, you say, 'It's going to be hot,' and it is. ⁵⁶Hypocrites! You know how to interpret the appearance of the earth and the sky. How is it that you don't know how to interpret this present time?

⁵⁷"Why don't you judge for yourselves what is right? ⁵⁸As you are going with your adversary to the magistrate, try hard to be reconciled on the way, or your adversary may drag you off to the judge, and the judge turn you over to the officer, and the officer throw you into prison. ⁵⁹I tell you, you will not get out until you have paid the last penny."

Repent or Perish

13 Now there were some present at that time who told Jesus about the Galileans whose blood Pilate had mixed with their sacrifices. ²Jesus answered, "Do you think that these Galileans were worse sinners than all the other Galileans because they suffered this way? ³I tell you, no! But unless you repent, you too will all perish. ⁴Or those eighteen who died when the tower in Siloam fell on them—do you think they were more guilty than all the others living in Jerusalem? ⁵I tell you, no! But unless you repent, you too will all perish."

⁶Then he told this parable: "A man had a fig tree growing in his vineyard, and he went to look for fruit on it but did not find any. ⁷So he said to the man who took care of the vineyard, 'For three years now I've been coming to look for fruit on this fig tree and haven't found any. Cut it down! Why should it use up the soil?'

⁸"'Sir,' the man replied, 'leave it alone for one more year, and I'll dig around it and fertilize it. ⁹If it bears fruit next year, fine! If not, then cut it down.'"

BREAKTHROUGH!

Sacrifices

(LUKE 13:1)

To sacrifice here means to kill, more or less. In Bible times, the Jews would go to the temple in Jerusalem, and they would take gifts for God. The gifts might be doves, a bull or a cow. The priest would sacrifice them. In other words, he would kill them. Those sacrifices were a way to ask for God's forgiveness or to give him thanks and worship him.

Jesus Heals a Crippled Woman on the Sabbath

¹⁰On a Sabbath Jesus was teaching in one of the synagogues, ¹¹and a woman was there who had been crippled by a spirit for eighteen years. She was bent over and could not straighten up at all. ¹²When Jesus saw her, he called her forward and said to her, "Woman, you are set free from your infirmity." ¹³Then he put his hands on her, and immediately she straightened up and praised God.

¹⁴Indignant because Jesus had healed on the Sabbath, the synagogue leader said to the people, "There are six days for work. So come and be healed on those days, not on the Sabbath."

¹⁵The Lord answered him, "You hypocrites! Doesn't each of you on the Sabbath untie your ox or donkey from the stall

and lead it out to give it water? ¹⁶Then should not this woman, a daughter of Abraham, whom Satan has kept bound for eighteen long years, be set free on the Sabbath day from what bound her?"

¹⁷When he said this, all his opponents were humiliated, but the people were delighted with all the wonderful things he was doing.

The Parables of the Mustard Seed and the Yeast

¹⁸Then Jesus asked, "What is the kingdom of God like? What shall I compare it to? ¹⁹It is like a mustard seed, which a man took and planted in his garden. It grew and became a tree, and the birds perched in its branches."

²⁰Again he asked, "What shall I compare the kingdom of God to? ²¹It is like yeast that a woman took and mixed into about sixty pounds*a* of flour until it worked all through the dough."

The Narrow Door

²²Then Jesus went through the towns and villages, teaching as he made his way to Jerusalem. ²³Someone asked him, "Lord, are only a few people going to be saved?"

He said to them, ²⁴"Make every effort to enter through the narrow door, because many, I tell you, will try to enter and will not be able to. ²⁵Once the owner of the house gets up and closes the door, you will stand outside knocking and pleading, 'Sir, open the door for us.'

"But he will answer, 'I don't know you or where you come from.'

²⁶"Then you will say, 'We ate and drank with you, and you taught in our streets.'

²⁷"But he will reply, 'I don't know you or where you come from. Away from me, all you evildoers!'

²⁸"There will be weeping there, and gnashing of teeth, when you see Abraham, Isaac and Jacob and all the prophets in the kingdom of God, but you yourselves thrown out. ²⁹People will come from east and west and north and south, and will take their places at the feast in the kingdom of God. ³⁰Indeed there are those who are last who will be first, and first who will be last."

Jesus' Sorrow for Jerusalem

³¹At that time some Pharisees came to Jesus and said to him, "Leave this place and go somewhere else. Herod wants to kill you."

³²He replied, "Go tell that fox, 'I will keep on driving out demons and healing people today and tomorrow, and on the third day I will reach my goal.' ³³In any case, I must press on today and tomorrow and the next day—for surely no prophet can die outside Jerusalem!

---

a 21 Or about 27 kilograms

SILOAM

(LUKE 13:4)

This word in Hebrew seems to mean "sent." In Bible times, there was a pool in Siloam. It was a big pond where the water gushed out of the ground. It was in Jerusalem, the area where the kings lived, and was called the "city of David." The tower Luke is talking about was near this pool, and one day it fell down and killed at least 18 people.

34 "Jerusalem, Jerusalem, you who kill the prophets and stone those sent to you, how often I have longed to gather your children together, as a hen gathers her chicks under her wings, and you were not willing. 35 Look, your house is left to you desolate. I tell you, you will not see me again until you say, 'Blessed is he who comes in the name of the Lord.'ᵃ"

Jesus at a Pharisee's House

14 One Sabbath, when Jesus went to eat in the house of a prominent Pharisee, he was being carefully watched. 2 There in front of him was a man suffering from abnormal swelling of his body. 3 Jesus asked the Pharisees and experts in the law, "Is it lawful to heal on the Sabbath or not?" 4 But they remained silent. So taking hold of the man, he healed him and sent him on his way.

5 Then he asked them, "If one of you has a childᵇ or an ox that falls into a well on the Sabbath day, will you not immediately pull it out?" 6 And they had nothing to say.

7 When he noticed how the guests picked the places of honor at the table, he told them this parable: 8 "When someone invites you to a wedding feast, do not take the place of honor, for a person more distinguished than you may have been invited. 9 If so, the host who invited both of you will come and say to you, 'Give this person your seat.' Then, humiliated, you will have to take the least important place. 10 But when you are invited, take the lowest place, so that when your host comes, he will say to you, 'Friend, move up to a better place.' Then you will be honored in the presence of all the other guests. 11 For all those who exalt themselves will be humbled, and those who humble themselves will be exalted."

12 Then Jesus said to his host, "When you give a luncheon or dinner, do not invite your friends, your brothers or sisters, your relatives, or your rich neighbors; if you do, they may invite you back and so you will be repaid. 13 But when you give a banquet, invite the poor, the crippled, the lame, the blind, 14 and you will be blessed. Although they cannot repay you, you will be repaid at the resurrection of the righteous."

The Parable of the Great Banquet

15 When one of those at the table with him heard this, he said to Jesus, "Blessed is the one who will eat at the feast in the kingdom of God."

16 Jesus replied: "A certain man was preparing a great banquet and invited many guests. 17 At the time of the banquet he sent his servant to tell those who had been invited, 'Come, for everything is now ready.'

18 "But they all alike began to make excuses. The first said, 'I have just bought a field, and I must go and see it. Please excuse me.'

19 "Another said, 'I have just bought five yoke of oxen, and I'm on my way to try them out. Please excuse me.'

20 "Still another said, 'I just got married, so I can't come.'

21 "The servant came back and reported this to his master. Then the owner of the house became angry and ordered his servant, 'Go out quickly into the streets and alleys of the town and bring in the poor, the crippled, the blind and the lame.'

22 " 'Sir,' the servant said, 'what you ordered has been done, but there is still room.'

23 "Then the master told his servant, 'Go out to the roads and country lanes and compel them to come in, so that my house will be full. 24 I tell you, not one of those who were invited will get a taste of my banquet.' "

The Cost of Being a Disciple

25 Large crowds were traveling with Jesus, and turning to them he said: 26 "If anyone comes to me and does not hate father and mother, wife and children, brothers and sisters — yes, even their own life — such a person cannot be my disciple. 27 And whoever does not carry their cross and follow me cannot be my disciple.

28 "Suppose one of you wants to build a tower. Won't you first sit down and esti-

---

ᵃ 35 Psalm 118:26   ᵇ 5 Some manuscripts donkey

mate the cost to see if you have enough money to complete it? ²⁹For if you lay the foundation and are not able to finish it, everyone who sees it will ridicule you, ³⁰saying, 'This person began to build and wasn't able to finish.'

³¹"Or suppose a king is about to go to war against another king. Won't he first sit down and consider whether he is able with ten thousand men to oppose the one coming against him with twenty thousand? ³²If he is not able, he will send a delegation while the other is still a long way off and will ask for terms of peace. ³³In the same way, those of you who do not give up everything you have cannot be my disciples.

³⁴"Salt is good, but if it loses its saltiness, how can it be made salty again? ³⁵It is fit neither for the soil nor for the manure pile; it is thrown out.

"Whoever has ears to hear, let them hear."

BREAK THROUGH!

Salt

(LUKE 14:34-35)

In Bible times, salt was used for many things, not just to flavor food. For example, salt was used to make food last longer. So here it means that Christians have to be like salt. They have to give the best "flavor" to life, and they should also help so people don't "spoil."

The Parable of the Lost Sheep

15 Now the tax collectors and sinners were all gathering around to hear Jesus. ²But the Pharisees and the teachers of the law muttered, "This man welcomes sinners and eats with them."

³Then Jesus told them this parable: ⁴"Suppose one of you has a hundred sheep and loses one of them. Doesn't he leave the ninety-nine in the open country and go after the lost sheep until he finds it? ⁵And when he finds it, he joyfully puts it on his shoulders ⁶and goes home. Then he calls his friends and neighbors together and says, 'Rejoice with me; I have found my lost sheep.' ⁷I tell you that in the same way there will be more rejoicing in heaven over one sinner who repents than over ninety-nine righteous persons who do not need to repent.

The Parable of the Lost Coin

⁸"Or suppose a woman has ten silver coins[a] and loses one. Doesn't she light a lamp, sweep the house and search carefully until she finds it? ⁹And when she finds it, she calls her friends and neighbors together and says, 'Rejoice with me; I have found my lost coin.' ¹⁰In the same way, I tell you, there is rejoicing in the presence of the angels of God over one sinner who repents."

The Parable of the Lost Son

¹¹Jesus continued: "There was a man who had two sons. ¹²The younger one said to his father, 'Father, give me my share of the estate.' So he divided his property between them.

¹³"Not long after that, the younger son got together all he had, set off for a distant country and there squandered his wealth in wild living. ¹⁴After he had spent everything, there was a severe famine in that whole country, and he began to be in need. ¹⁵So he went and hired himself out to a citizen of that country, who sent him to his fields to feed pigs. ¹⁶He longed

---

a 8 Greek *ten drachmas*, each worth about a day's wages

to fill his stomach with the pods that the pigs were eating, but no one gave him anything.

[17] "When he came to his senses, he said, 'How many of my father's hired servants have food to spare, and here I am starving to death! [18] I will set out and go back to my father and say to him: Father, I have sinned against heaven and against you. [19] I am no longer worthy to be called your son; make me like one of your hired servants.' [20] So he got up and went to his father.

"But while he was still a long way off, his father saw him and was filled with compassion for him; he ran to his son, threw his arms around him and kissed him.

[21] "The son said to him, 'Father, I have sinned against heaven and against you. I am no longer worthy to be called your son.'

[22] "But the father said to his servants, 'Quick! Bring the best robe and put it on him. Put a ring on his finger and sandals on his feet. [23] Bring the fattened calf and kill it. Let's have a feast and celebrate. [24] For this son of mine was dead and is alive again; he was lost and is found.' So they began to celebrate.

[25] "Meanwhile, the older son was in the field. When he came near the house, he heard music and dancing. [26] So he called one of the servants and asked him what was going on. [27] 'Your brother has come,' he replied, 'and your father has killed the fattened calf because he has him back safe and sound.'

[28] "The older brother became angry and refused to go in. So his father went out and pleaded with him. [29] But he answered his father, 'Look! All these years I've been slaving for you and never disobeyed your orders. Yet you never gave me even a young goat so I could celebrate with my friends. [30] But when this son of yours who has squandered your property with prostitutes comes home, you kill the fattened calf for him!'

[31] "'My son,' the father said, 'you are always with me, and everything I have is yours. [32] But we had to celebrate and be glad, because this brother of yours was dead and is alive again; he was lost and is found.'"

The Parable of the Shrewd Manager

16 Jesus told his disciples: "There was a rich man whose manager was accused of wasting his possessions. [2] So he called him in and asked him, 'What is this I hear about you? Give an account of your management, because you cannot be manager any longer.'

[3] "The manager said to himself, 'What shall I do now? My master is taking away my job. I'm not strong enough to dig, and I'm ashamed to beg— [4] I know what I'll do so that, when I lose my job here, people will welcome me into their houses.'

[5] "So he called in each one of his master's debtors. He asked the first, 'How much do you owe my master?'

[6] "'Nine hundred gallons[a] of olive oil,' he replied.

"The manager told him, 'Take your bill, sit down quickly, and make it four hundred and fifty.'

[7] "Then he asked the second, 'And how much do you owe?'

"'A thousand bushels[b] of wheat,' he replied.

"He told him, 'Take your bill and make it eight hundred.'

[8] "The master commended the dishonest manager because he had acted shrewdly. For the people of this world are more shrewd in dealing with their own kind than are the people of the light. [9] I tell you, use worldly wealth to gain friends for yourselves, so that when it is gone, you will be welcomed into eternal dwellings.

[10] "Whoever can be trusted with very little can also be trusted with much, and whoever is dishonest with very little will also be dishonest with much. [11] So if you have not been trustworthy in handling worldly wealth, who will trust you with true riches? [12] And if you have not been trustworthy with someone else's property, who will give you property of your own?

[13] "No one can serve two masters. Either you will hate the one and love the other, or you will be devoted to the one and despise the other. You cannot serve both God and money."

---

[a] 6 Or about 3,000 liters   [b] 7 Or about 30 tons

[14] The Pharisees, who loved money, heard all this and were sneering at Jesus. [15] He said to them, "You are the ones who justify yourselves in the eyes of others, but God knows your hearts. What people value highly is detestable in God's sight.

Additional Teachings

[16] "The Law and the Prophets were proclaimed until John. Since that time, the good news of the kingdom of God is being preached, and everyone is forcing their way into it. [17] It is easier for heaven and earth to disappear than for the least stroke of a pen to drop out of the Law.

[18] "Anyone who divorces his wife and marries another woman commits adultery, and the man who marries a divorced woman commits adultery.

The Rich Man and Lazarus

[19] "There was a rich man who was dressed in purple and fine linen and lived in luxury every day. [20] At his gate was laid a beggar named Lazarus, covered with sores [21] and longing to eat what fell from the rich man's table. Even the dogs came and licked his sores.

[22] "The time came when the beggar died and the angels carried him to Abraham's side. The rich man also died and was buried. [23] In Hades, where he was in torment, he looked up and saw Abraham far away, with Lazarus by his side. [24] So he called to him, 'Father Abraham, have pity on me and send Lazarus to dip the tip of his finger in water and cool my tongue, because I am in agony in this fire.'

[25] "But Abraham replied, 'Son, remember that in your lifetime you received your good things, while Lazarus received bad things, but now he is comforted here and you are in agony. [26] And besides all this, between us and you a great chasm has been set in place, so that those who want to go from here to you cannot, nor can anyone cross over from there to us.'

[27] "He answered, 'Then I beg you, father, send Lazarus to my family, [28] for I have five brothers. Let him warn them, so that they will not also come to this place of torment.'

[29] "Abraham replied, 'They have Moses and the Prophets; let them listen to them.'

[30] " 'No, father Abraham,' he said, 'but if someone from the dead goes to them, they will repent.'

[31] "He said to him, 'If they do not listen to Moses and the Prophets, they will not be convinced even if someone rises from the dead.' "

Sin, Faith, Duty

17 Jesus said to his disciples: "Things that cause people to stumble are bound to come, but woe to anyone through whom they come. [2] It would be better for them to be thrown into the sea with a millstone tied around their neck than to cause one of these little ones to stumble. [3] So watch yourselves.

"If your brother or sister[a] sins against you, rebuke them; and if they repent, forgive them. [4] Even if they sin against you seven times in a day and seven times come back to you saying 'I repent,' you must forgive them."

[5] The apostles said to the Lord, "Increase our faith!"

[6] He replied, "If you have faith as small as a mustard seed, you can say to this mulberry tree, 'Be uprooted and planted in the sea,' and it will obey you.

[7] "Suppose one of you has a servant plowing or looking after the sheep. Will he say to the servant when he comes in from the field, 'Come along now and sit down to eat'? [8] Won't he rather say, 'Prepare my supper, get yourself ready and wait on me while I eat and drink; after that you may eat and drink'? [9] Will he thank the servant because he did what he was told to do? [10] So you also, when you have done everything you were told to do, should say, 'We are unworthy servants; we have only done our duty.' "

Jesus Heals Ten Men With Leprosy

[11] Now on his way to Jerusalem, Jesus traveled along the border between Samaria and Galilee. [12] As he was going

---

[a] 3 The Greek word for *brother or sister* (*adelphos*) refers here to a fellow disciple, whether man or woman.

into a village, ten men who had leprosy[a] met him. They stood at a distance [13]and called out in a loud voice, "Jesus, Master, have pity on us!"

[14]When he saw them, he said, "Go, show yourselves to the priests." And as they went, they were cleansed.

[15]One of them, when he saw he was healed, came back, praising God in a loud voice. [16]He threw himself at Jesus' feet and thanked him—and he was a Samaritan.

[17]Jesus asked, "Were not all ten cleansed? Where are the other nine? [18]Has no one returned to give praise to God except this foreigner?" [19]Then he said to him, "Rise and go; your faith has made you well."

The Coming of the Kingdom of God

[20]Once, on being asked by the Pharisees when the kingdom of God would come, Jesus replied, "The coming of the kingdom of God is not something that can be observed, [21]nor will people say, 'Here it is,' or 'There it is,' because the kingdom of God is in your midst."[b]

[22]Then he said to his disciples, "The time is coming when you will long to see one of the days of the Son of Man, but you will not see it. [23]People will tell you, 'There he is!' or 'Here he is!' Do not go running off after them. [24]For the Son of Man in his day[c] will be like the lightning, which flashes and lights up the sky from one end to the other. [25]But first he must suffer many things and be rejected by this generation.

[26]"Just as it was in the days of Noah, so also will it be in the days of the Son of Man. [27]People were eating, drinking, marrying and being given in marriage up to the day Noah entered the ark. Then the flood came and destroyed them all.

[28]"It was the same in the days of Lot. People were eating and drinking, buying and selling, planting and building. [29]But the day Lot left Sodom, fire and sulfur rained down from heaven and destroyed them all.

[30]"It will be just like this on the day the Son of Man is revealed. [31]On that day no one who is on the housetop, with pos-

sessions inside, should go down to get them. Likewise, no one in the field should go back for anything. [32]Remember Lot's wife! [33]Whoever tries to keep their life will lose it, and whoever loses their life will preserve it. [34]I tell you, on that night two people will be in one bed; one will be taken and the other left. [35]Two women will be grinding grain together; one will be taken and the other left." [36][d]

[37]"Where, Lord?" they asked.

He replied, "Where there is a dead body, there the vultures will gather."

The Parable of the Persistent Widow

18 Then Jesus told his disciples a parable to show them that they should always pray and not give up. [2]He said: "In a certain town there was a judge who neither feared God nor cared what people thought. [3]And there was a widow in that town who kept coming to him with the plea, 'Grant me justice against my adversary.'

[4]"For some time he refused. But finally he said to himself, 'Even though I don't fear God or care what people think, [5]yet because this widow keeps bothering me, I will see that she gets justice, so that she won't eventually come and attack me!'"

[6]And the Lord said, "Listen to what the unjust judge says. [7]And will not God bring about justice for his chosen ones, who cry out to him day and night? Will he keep putting them off? [8]I tell you, he will see that they get justice, and quickly. However, when the Son of Man comes, will he find faith on the earth?"

The Parable of the Pharisee and the Tax Collector

[9]To some who were confident of their own righteousness and looked down on everyone else, Jesus told this parable: [10]"Two men went up to the temple to pray, one a Pharisee and the other a tax collec-

---

[a] 12 The Greek word traditionally translated *leprosy* was used for various diseases affecting the skin.   [b] 21 Or is *within you*   [c] 24 Some manuscripts do not have *in his day.*   [d] 36 Some manuscripts include here words similar to Matt. 24:40.

tor. [11]The Pharisee stood by himself and prayed: 'God, I thank you that I am not like other people—robbers, evildoers, adulterers—or even like this tax collector. [12]I fast twice a week and give a tenth of all I get.'

[13]"But the tax collector stood at a distance. He would not even look up to heaven, but beat his breast and said, 'God, have mercy on me, a sinner.'

[14]"I tell you that this man, rather than the other, went home justified before God. For all those who exalt themselves will be humbled, and those who humble themselves will be exalted."

The Little Children and Jesus

[15]People were also bringing babies to Jesus for him to place his hands on them. When the disciples saw this, they rebuked them. [16]But Jesus called the children to him and said, "Let the little children come to me, and do not hinder them, for the kingdom of God belongs to such as these. [17]Truly I tell you, anyone who will not receive the kingdom of God like a little child will never enter it."

The Rich and the Kingdom of God

[18]A certain ruler asked him, "Good teacher, what must I do to inherit eternal life?"

[19]"Why do you call me good?" Jesus answered. "No one is good—except God alone. [20]You know the commandments: 'You shall not commit adultery, you shall not murder, you shall not steal, you shall not give false testimony, honor your father and mother.'[a]"

[21]"All these I have kept since I was a boy," he said.

[22]When Jesus heard this, he said to him, "You still lack one thing. Sell everything you have and give to the poor, and you will have treasure in heaven. Then come, follow me."

[23]When he heard this, he became very sad, because he was very wealthy. [24]Jesus looked at him and said, "How hard it is for the rich to enter the kingdom of God! [25]Indeed, it is easier for a camel to go through the eye of a needle than for

someone who is rich to enter the kingdom of God."

[26]Those who heard this asked, "Who then can be saved?"

[27]Jesus replied, "What is impossible with man is possible with God."

[28]Peter said to him, "We have left all we had to follow you!"

[29]"Truly I tell you," Jesus said to them, "no one who has left home or wife or brothers or sisters or parents or children for the sake of the kingdom of God [30]will fail to receive many times as much in this age, and in the age to come eternal life."

Jesus Predicts His Death a Third Time

[31]Jesus took the Twelve aside and told them, "We are going up to Jerusalem, and everything that is written by the prophets about the Son of Man will be fulfilled. [32]He will be delivered over to the Gentiles. They will mock him, insult him and spit on him; [33]they will flog him and kill him. On the third day he will rise again."

[34]The disciples did not understand any of this. Its meaning was hidden from them, and they did not know what he was talking about.

A Blind Beggar Receives His Sight

[35]As Jesus approached Jericho, a blind man was sitting by the roadside begging. [36]When he heard the crowd going by, he asked what was happening. [37]They told him, "Jesus of Nazareth is passing by."

[38]He called out, "Jesus, Son of David, have mercy on me!"

[39]Those who led the way rebuked him and told him to be quiet, but he shouted all the more, "Son of David, have mercy on me!"

[40]Jesus stopped and ordered the man to be brought to him. When he came near, Jesus asked him, [41]"What do you want me to do for you?"

"Lord, I want to see," he replied.

---

[a] 20 Exodus 20:12-16; Deut. 5:16-20

[42]Jesus said to him, "Receive your sight; your faith has healed you." [43]Immediately he received his sight and followed Jesus, praising God. When all the people saw it, they also praised God.

Zacchaeus the Tax Collector

19 Jesus entered Jericho and was passing through. [2]A man was there by the name of Zacchaeus; he was a chief tax collector and was wealthy. [3]He wanted to see who Jesus was, but because he was short he could not see over the crowd. [4]So he ran ahead and climbed a sycamore-fig tree to see him, since Jesus was coming that way.

[5]When Jesus reached the spot, he looked up and said to him, "Zacchaeus, come down immediately. I must stay at your house today." [6]So he came down at once and welcomed him gladly.

[7]All the people saw this and began to mutter, "He has gone to be the guest of a sinner."

[8]But Zacchaeus stood up and said to the Lord, "Look, Lord! Here and now I give half of my possessions to the poor, and if I have cheated anybody out of anything, I will pay back four times the amount."

[9]Jesus said to him, "Today salvation has come to this house, because this man, too, is a son of Abraham. [10]For the Son of Man came to seek and to save the lost."

The Parable of the Ten Minas

[11]While they were listening to this, he went on to tell them a parable, because he was near Jerusalem and the people thought that the kingdom of God was going to appear at once. [12]He said: "A man of noble birth went to a distant country to have himself appointed king and then to return. [13]So he called ten of his servants and gave them ten minas.[a] 'Put this money to work,' he said, 'until I come back.'

[14]"But his subjects hated him and sent a delegation after him to say, 'We don't want this man to be our king.'

[15]"He was made king, however, and returned home. Then he sent for the servants to whom he had given the money, in order to find out what they had gained with it.

[16]"The first one came and said, 'Sir, your mina has earned ten more.'

[17]"'Well done, my good servant!' his master replied. 'Because you have been trustworthy in a very small matter, take charge of ten cities.'

[18]"The second came and said, 'Sir, your mina has earned five more.'

[19]"His master answered, 'You take charge of five cities.'

[20]"Then another servant came and said, 'Sir, here is your mina; I have kept it laid away in a piece of cloth. [21]I was afraid of you, because you are a hard man. You take out what you did not put in and reap what you did not sow.'

[22]"His master replied, 'I will judge you by your own words, you wicked servant! You knew, did you, that I am a hard man, taking out what I did not put in, and reaping what I did not sow? [23]Why then didn't you put my money on deposit, so that when I came back, I could have collected it with interest?'

[24]"Then he said to those standing by, 'Take his mina away from him and give it to the one who has ten minas.'

[25]"'Sir,' they said, 'he already has ten!'

[26]"He replied, 'I tell you that to everyone who has, more will be given, but as for the one who has nothing, even what they have will be taken away. [27]But those enemies of mine who did not want me to be king over them—bring them here and kill them in front of me.'"

Jesus Comes to Jerusalem as King

[28]After Jesus had said this, he went on ahead, going up to Jerusalem. [29]As he approached Bethphage and Bethany at the hill called the Mount of Olives, he sent two of his disciples, saying to them, [30]"Go to the village ahead of you, and as you enter it, you will find a colt tied there, which no one has ever ridden. Untie it and bring it here. [31]If anyone asks you, 'Why are you untying it?' say, 'The Lord needs it.'"

---

a 13 A mina was about three months' wages.

³²Those who were sent ahead went and found it just as he had told them. ³³As they were untying the colt, its owners asked them, "Why are you untying the colt?" ³⁴They replied, "The Lord needs it." ³⁵They brought it to Jesus, threw their cloaks on the colt and put Jesus on it. ³⁶As he went along, people spread their cloaks on the road.

³⁷When he came near the place where the road goes down the Mount of Olives, the whole crowd of disciples began joyfully to praise God in loud voices for all the miracles they had seen:

³⁸ "Blessed is the king who comes in the name of the Lord!"ᵃ

"Peace in heaven and glory in the highest!"

³⁹Some of the Pharisees in the crowd said to Jesus, "Teacher, rebuke your disciples!"

⁴⁰"I tell you," he replied, "if they keep quiet, the stones will cry out."

⁴¹As he approached Jerusalem and saw the city, he wept over it ⁴²and said, "If you, even you, had only known on this day what would bring you peace—but now it is hidden from your eyes. ⁴³The days will come upon you when your enemies will build an embankment against you and encircle you and hem you in on every side. ⁴⁴They will dash you to the ground, you and the children within your walls. They will not leave one stone on another, because you did not recognize the time of God's coming to you."

Jesus at the Temple

⁴⁵When Jesus entered the temple courts, he began to drive out those who were selling. ⁴⁶"It is written," he said to them, " 'My house will be a house of prayer'ᵇ; but you have made it 'a den of robbers.'ᶜ"

⁴⁷Every day he was teaching at the temple. But the chief priests, the teachers of the law and the leaders among the people were trying to kill him. ⁴⁸Yet they could not find any way to do it, because all the people hung on his words.

The Authority of Jesus Questioned

20 One day as Jesus was teaching the people in the temple courts and proclaiming the good news, the chief priests and the teachers of the law, together with the elders, came up to him. ²"Tell us by what authority you are doing these things," they said. "Who gave you this authority?"

³He replied, "I will also ask you a question. Tell me: ⁴John's baptism—was it from heaven, or of human origin?"

⁵They discussed it among themselves and said, "If we say, 'From heaven,' he will ask, 'Why didn't you believe him?' ⁶But if we say, 'Of human origin,' all the people will stone us, because they are persuaded that John was a prophet."

⁷So they answered, "We don't know where it was from."

⁸Jesus said, "Neither will I tell you by what authority I am doing these things."

The Parable of the Tenants

⁹He went on to tell the people this parable: "A man planted a vineyard, rented it to some farmers and went away for a long time. ¹⁰At harvest time he sent a servant to the tenants so they would give him some of the fruit of the vineyard. But the tenants beat him and sent him away empty-handed. ¹¹He sent another servant, but that one also they beat and treated shamefully and sent away empty-handed. ¹²He sent still a third, and they wounded him and threw him out.

¹³"Then the owner of the vineyard said, 'What shall I do? I will send my son, whom I love; perhaps they will respect him.'

¹⁴"But when the tenants saw him, they talked the matter over. 'This is the heir,' they said. 'Let's kill him, and the inheritance will be ours.' ¹⁵So they threw him out of the vineyard and killed him.

"What then will the owner of the vineyard do to them? ¹⁶He will come and kill those tenants and give the vineyard to others."

When the people heard this, they said, "God forbid!"

ᵃ 38 Psalm 118:26   ᵇ 46 Isaiah 56:7   ᶜ 46 Jer. 7:11

17 Jesus looked directly at them and asked, "Then what is the meaning of that which is written:

" 'The stone the builders rejected
   has become the cornerstone'[a]?

18 Everyone who falls on that stone will be broken to pieces; anyone on whom it falls will be crushed."

19 The teachers of the law and the chief priests looked for a way to arrest him immediately, because they knew he had spoken this parable against them. But they were afraid of the people.

Paying Taxes to Caesar

20 Keeping a close watch on him, they sent spies, who pretended to be sincere. They hoped to catch Jesus in something he said, so that they might hand him over to the power and authority of the governor. 21 So the spies questioned him: "Teacher, we know that you speak and teach what is right, and that you do not show partiality but teach the way of God in accordance with the truth. 22 Is it right for us to pay taxes to Caesar or not?"

23 He saw through their duplicity and said to them, 24 "Show me a denarius. Whose image and inscription are on it?"

"Caesar's," they replied.

25 He said to them, "Then give back to Caesar what is Caesar's, and to God what is God's."

26 They were unable to trap him in what he had said there in public. And astonished by his answer, they became silent.

The Resurrection and Marriage

27 Some of the Sadducees, who say there is no resurrection, came to Jesus with a question. 28 "Teacher," they said, "Moses wrote for us that if a man's brother dies and leaves a wife but no children, the man must marry the widow and raise up offspring for his brother. 29 Now there were seven brothers. The first one married a woman and died childless. 30 The second 31 and then the third married her, and in the same way the seven died, leaving no children. 32 Finally, the woman died too. 33 Now then, at the resurrection whose wife will she be, since the seven were married to her?"

34 Jesus replied, "The people of this age marry and are given in marriage. 35 But those who are considered worthy of taking part in the age to come and in the resurrection from the dead will neither marry nor be given in marriage, 36 and they can no longer die; for they are like the angels. They are God's children, since they are children of the resurrection. 37 But in the account of the burning bush, even Moses showed that the dead rise, for he calls the Lord 'the God of Abraham, and the God of Isaac, and the God of Jacob.'[b] 38 He is not the God of the dead, but of the living, for to him all are alive."

39 Some of the teachers of the law responded, "Well said, teacher!" 40 And no one dared to ask him any more questions.

Whose Son Is the Messiah?

41 Then Jesus said to them, "Why is it said that the Messiah is the son of David? 42 David himself declares in the Book of Psalms:

" 'The Lord said to my Lord:
   "Sit at my right hand
43 until I make your enemies
   a footstool for your feet." '[c]

44 David calls him 'Lord.' How then can he be his son?"

Warning Against the Teachers of the Law

45 While all the people were listening, Jesus said to his disciples, 46 "Beware of the teachers of the law. They like to walk around in flowing robes and love to be greeted with respect in the marketplaces and have the most important seats in the synagogues and the places of honor at banquets. 47 They devour widows' houses and for a show make lengthy prayers. These men will be punished most severely."

---

a 17 Psalm 118:22   *b* 37 Exodus 3:6
c 43 Psalm 110:1

The Widow's Offering

21 As Jesus looked up, he saw the rich putting their gifts into the temple treasury. ²He also saw a poor widow put in two very small copper coins. ³"Truly I tell you," he said, "this poor widow has put in more than all the others. ⁴All these people gave their gifts out of their wealth; but she out of her poverty put in all she had to live on."

The Destruction of the Temple and Signs of the End Times

⁵Some of his disciples were remarking about how the temple was adorned with beautiful stones and with gifts dedicated to God. But Jesus said, ⁶"As for what you see here, the time will come when not one stone will be left on another; every one of them will be thrown down."

⁷"Teacher," they asked, "when will these things happen? And what will be the sign that they are about to take place?"

⁸He replied: "Watch out that you are not deceived. For many will come in my name, claiming, 'I am he,' and, 'The time is near.' Do not follow them. ⁹When you hear of wars and uprisings, do not be frightened. These things must happen first, but the end will not come right away."

¹⁰Then he said to them: "Nation will rise against nation, and kingdom against kingdom. ¹¹There will be great earthquakes, famines and pestilences in various places, and fearful events and great signs from heaven.

¹²"But before all this, they will seize you and persecute you. They will hand you over to synagogues and put you in prison, and you will be brought before kings and governors, and all on account of my name. ¹³And so you will bear testimony to me. ¹⁴But make up your mind not to worry beforehand how you will defend yourselves. ¹⁵For I will give you words and wisdom that none of your adversaries will be able to resist or contradict. ¹⁶You will be betrayed even by parents, brothers and sisters, relatives and friends, and they will put some of you to death. ¹⁷Everyone will hate you because of me. ¹⁸But not a hair

of your head will perish. ¹⁹Stand firm, and you will win life.

²⁰"When you see Jerusalem being surrounded by armies, you will know that its desolation is near. ²¹Then let those who are in Judea flee to the mountains, let those in the city get out, and let those in the country not enter the city. ²²For this is the time of punishment in fulfillment of all that has been written. ²³How dreadful it will be in those days for pregnant women and nursing mothers! There will be great distress in the land and wrath against this people. ²⁴They will fall by the sword and will be taken as prisoners to all the nations. Jerusalem will be trampled on by the Gentiles until the times of the Gentiles are fulfilled.

²⁵"There will be signs in the sun, moon and stars. On the earth, nations will be in anguish and perplexity at the roaring and tossing of the sea. ²⁶People will faint from terror, apprehensive of what is coming on the world, for the heavenly bodies will be shaken. ²⁷At that time they will see the Son of Man coming in a cloud with power and great glory. ²⁸When these things begin to take place, stand up and lift up your heads, because your redemption is drawing near."

²⁹He told them this parable: "Look at the fig tree and all the trees. ³⁰When they sprout leaves, you can see for yourselves and know that summer is near. ³¹Even so, when you see these things happening, you know that the kingdom of God is near.

³²"Truly I tell you, this generation will certainly not pass away until all these things have happened. ³³Heaven and earth will pass away, but my words will never pass away.

³⁴"Be careful, or your hearts will be weighed down with carousing, drunkenness and the anxieties of life, and that day will close on you suddenly like a trap. ³⁵For it will come on all those who live on the face of the whole earth. ³⁶Be always on the watch, and pray that you may be able to escape all that is about to happen, and that you may be able to stand before the Son of Man."

³⁷Each day Jesus was teaching at the temple, and each evening he went out

BREAKTHROUGH!

The return of Jesus

(LUKE 21:25-28)

Many places in the Bible say that Jesus will return to Earth, not as a baby but as a powerful king. Jesus' power will be so powerful that even the sun, the moon and the stars will be aware of him. Luke also says that he will come from heaven in a cloud. He will come back to reward the people who believe in God and are good.

to spend the night on the hill called the Mount of Olives, 38and all the people came early in the morning to hear him at the temple.

Judas Agrees to Betray Jesus

22 Now the Festival of Unleavened Bread, called the Passover, was approaching, 2and the chief priests and the teachers of the law were looking for some way to get rid of Jesus, for they were afraid of the people. 3Then Satan entered Judas, called Iscariot, one of the Twelve. 4And Judas went to the chief priests and the officers of the temple guard and discussed with them how he might betray Jesus. 5They were delighted and agreed to give him money. 6He consented, and watched for an opportunity to hand Jesus over to them when no crowd was present.

The Last Supper

7Then came the day of Unleavened Bread on which the Passover lamb had to be sacrificed. 8Jesus sent Peter and John, saying, "Go and make preparations for us to eat the Passover."

9"Where do you want us to prepare for it?" they asked.

10He replied, "As you enter the city, a man carrying a jar of water will meet you. Follow him to the house that he enters, 11and say to the owner of the house, 'The Teacher asks: Where is the guest room, where I may eat the Passover with my disciples?' 12He will show you a large room upstairs, all furnished. Make preparations there."

13They left and found things just as Jesus had told them. So they prepared the Passover.

14When the hour came, Jesus and his apostles reclined at the table. 15And he said to them, "I have eagerly desired to eat this Passover with you before I suffer. 16For I tell you, I will not eat it again until it finds fulfillment in the kingdom of God."

17After taking the cup, he gave thanks and said, "Take this and divide it among you. 18For I tell you I will not drink again from the fruit of the vine until the kingdom of God comes."

19And he took bread, gave thanks and broke it, and gave it to them, saying, "This is my body given for you; do this in remembrance of me."

20In the same way, after the supper he took the cup, saying, "This cup is the new covenant in my blood, which is poured out for you.*a* 21But the hand of him who is going to betray me is with mine on the table. 22The Son of Man will go as it has been decreed. But woe to that man who betrays him!" 23They began to question among themselves which of them it might be who would do this.

24A dispute also arose among them as to which of them was considered to be greatest. 25Jesus said to them, "The kings of the Gentiles lord it over them; and those who exercise authority over

---

a 19,20 Some manuscripts do not have *given for you . . . poured out for you.*

them call themselves Benefactors. ²⁶But you are not to be like that. Instead, the greatest among you should be like the youngest, and the one who rules like the one who serves. ²⁷For who is greater, the one who is at the table or the one who serves? Is it not the one who is at the table? But I am among you as one who serves. ²⁸You are those who have stood by me in my trials. ²⁹And I confer on you a kingdom, just as my Father conferred one on me, ³⁰so that you may eat and drink at my table in my kingdom and sit on thrones, judging the twelve tribes of Israel.

³¹"Simon, Simon, Satan has asked to sift all of you as wheat. ³²But I have prayed for you, Simon, that your faith may not fail. And when you have turned back, strengthen your brothers."

³³But he replied, "Lord, I am ready to go with you to prison and to death."

³⁴Jesus answered, "I tell you, Peter, before the rooster crows today, you will deny three times that you know me."

³⁵Then Jesus asked them, "When I sent you without purse, bag or sandals, did you lack anything?"

"Nothing," they answered.

³⁶He said to them, "But now if you have a purse, take it, and also a bag; and if you don't have a sword, sell your cloak and buy one. ³⁷It is written: 'And he was numbered with the transgressors'ᵃ; and I tell you that this must be fulfilled in me. Yes, what is written about me is reaching its fulfillment."

³⁸The disciples said, "See, Lord, here are two swords."

"That's enough!" he replied.

Jesus Prays on the Mount of Olives

³⁹Jesus went out as usual to the Mount of Olives, and his disciples followed him. ⁴⁰On reaching the place, he said to them, "Pray that you will not fall into temptation." ⁴¹He withdrew about a stone's throw beyond them, knelt down and prayed, ⁴²"Father, if you are willing, take this cup from me; yet not my will, but yours be done." ⁴³An angel from heaven appeared to him and strengthened him. ⁴⁴And being in anguish, he prayed more earnestly, and

his sweat was like drops of blood falling to the ground.ᵇ

⁴⁵When he rose from prayer and went back to the disciples, he found them asleep, exhausted from sorrow. ⁴⁶"Why are you sleeping?" he asked them. "Get up and pray so that you will not fall into temptation."

Jesus Arrested

⁴⁷While he was still speaking a crowd came up, and the man who was called Judas, one of the Twelve, was leading them. He approached Jesus to kiss him, ⁴⁸but Jesus asked him, "Judas, are you betraying the Son of Man with a kiss?"

⁴⁹When Jesus' followers saw what was going to happen, they said, "Lord, should we strike with our swords?" ⁵⁰And one of them struck the servant of the high priest, cutting off his right ear.

⁵¹But Jesus answered, "No more of this!" And he touched the man's ear and healed him.

⁵²Then Jesus said to the chief priests, the officers of the temple guard, and the elders, who had come for him, "Am I leading a rebellion, that you have come with swords and clubs? ⁵³Every day I was with you in the temple courts, and you did not lay a hand on me. But this is your hour—when darkness reigns."

Peter Disowns Jesus

⁵⁴Then seizing him, they led him away and took him into the house of the high priest. Peter followed at a distance. ⁵⁵And when some there had kindled a fire in the middle of the courtyard and had sat down together, Peter sat down with them. ⁵⁶A servant girl saw him seated there in the firelight. She looked closely at him and said, "This man was with him."

⁵⁷But he denied it. "Woman, I don't know him," he said.

⁵⁸A little later someone else saw him and said, "You also are one of them."

"Man, I am not!" Peter replied.

⁵⁹About an hour later another asserted,

ᵃ 37 Isaiah 53:12   ᵇ 43,44 Many early manuscripts do not have verses 43 and 44.

"Certainly this fellow was with him, for he is a Galilean."

⁶⁰Peter replied, "Man, I don't know what you're talking about!" Just as he was speaking, the rooster crowed. ⁶¹The Lord turned and looked straight at Peter. Then Peter remembered the word the Lord had spoken to him: "Before the rooster crows today, you will disown me three times." ⁶²And he went outside and wept bitterly.

The Guards Mock Jesus

⁶³The men who were guarding Jesus began mocking and beating him. ⁶⁴They blindfolded him and demanded, "Prophesy! Who hit you?" ⁶⁵And they said many other insulting things to him.

Jesus Before Pilate and Herod

⁶⁶At daybreak the council of the elders of the people, both the chief priests and the teachers of the law, met together, and Jesus was led before them. ⁶⁷"If you are the Messiah," they said, "tell us."

Jesus answered, "If I tell you, you will not believe me, ⁶⁸and if I asked you, you would not answer. ⁶⁹But from now on, the Son of Man will be seated at the right hand of the mighty God."

⁷⁰They all asked, "Are you then the Son of God?"

He replied, "You say that I am."

⁷¹Then they said, "Why do we need any more testimony? We have heard it from his own lips."

23 Then the whole assembly rose and led him off to Pilate. ²And they began to accuse him, saying, "We have found this man subverting our nation. He opposes payment of taxes to Caesar and claims to be Messiah, a king."

³So Pilate asked Jesus, "Are you the king of the Jews?"

"You have said so," Jesus replied.

⁴Then Pilate announced to the chief priests and the crowd, "I find no basis for a charge against this man."

⁵But they insisted, "He stirs up the people all over Judea by his teaching. He started in Galilee and has come all the way here."

⁶On hearing this, Pilate asked if the man was a Galilean. ⁷When he learned that Jesus was under Herod's jurisdiction, he sent him to Herod, who was also in Jerusalem at that time.

⁸When Herod saw Jesus, he was greatly pleased, because for a long time he had been wanting to see him. From what he had heard about him, he hoped to see him perform a sign of some sort. ⁹He plied him with many questions, but Jesus gave him no answer. ¹⁰The chief priests and the teachers of the law were standing there, vehemently accusing him. ¹¹Then Herod and his soldiers ridiculed and mocked him. Dressing him in an elegant robe, they sent him back to Pilate. ¹²That day Herod and Pilate became friends — before this they had been enemies.

¹³Pilate called together the chief priests, the rulers and the people, ¹⁴and said to them, "You brought me this man as one who was inciting the people to rebellion. I have examined him in your presence and have found no basis for your charges against him. ¹⁵Neither has Herod, for he sent him back to us; as you can see, he has done nothing to deserve death. ¹⁶Therefore, I will punish him and then release him." [¹⁷]ᵃ

¹⁸But the whole crowd shouted, "Away with this man! Release Barabbas to us!" ¹⁹(Barabbas had been thrown into prison for an insurrection in the city, and for murder.)

²⁰Wanting to release Jesus, Pilate appealed to them again. ²¹But they kept shouting, "Crucify him! Crucify him!"

²²For the third time he spoke to them: "Why? What crime has this man committed? I have found in him no grounds for the death penalty. Therefore I will have him punished and then release him."

²³But with loud shouts they insistently demanded that he be crucified, and their shouts prevailed. ²⁴So Pilate decided to grant their demand. ²⁵He released the man who had been thrown into prison for insurrection and murder, the one they asked for, and surrendered Jesus to their will.

ᵃ 17 Some manuscripts include here words similar to Matt. 27:15 and Mark 15:6.

The Crucifixion of Jesus

²⁶As the soldiers led him away, they seized Simon from Cyrene, who was on his way in from the country, and put the cross on him and made him carry it behind Jesus. ²⁷A large number of people followed him, including women who mourned and wailed for him. ²⁸Jesus turned and said to them, "Daughters of Jerusalem, do not weep for me; weep for yourselves and for your children. ²⁹For the time will come when you will say, 'Blessed are the childless women, the wombs that never bore and the breasts that never nursed!' ³⁰Then

"'they will say to the mountains, "Fall on us!"
and to the hills, "Cover us!"'^a

³¹For if people do these things when the tree is green, what will happen when it is dry?"

³²Two other men, both criminals, were also led out with him to be executed. ³³When they came to the place called the Skull, they crucified him there, along with the criminals—one on his right, the other on his left. ³⁴Jesus said, "Father, forgive them, for they do not know what they are doing."^b And they divided up his clothes by casting lots.

³⁵The people stood watching, and the rulers even sneered at him. They said, "He saved others; let him save himself if he is God's Messiah, the Chosen One."

³⁶The soldiers also came up and mocked him. They offered him wine vinegar ³⁷and said, "If you are the king of the Jews, save yourself."

³⁸There was a written notice above him, which read: THIS IS THE KING OF THE JEWS.

³⁹One of the criminals who hung there hurled insults at him: "Aren't you the Messiah? Save yourself and us!"

⁴⁰But the other criminal rebuked him. "Don't you fear God," he said, "since you are under the same sentence? ⁴¹We are punished justly, for we are getting what our deeds deserve. But this man has done nothing wrong."

⁴²Then he said, "Jesus, remember me when you come into your kingdom.^c"

BREAKTHROUGH!

Why did they use a cross to kill Jesus?

(LUKE 23:33)

The cross was really just like a post or a big stake. It was a tall pole that had another pole crossing it at the top. It was used years ago to hang criminals. That was how the Romans killed people who had done bad things, like causing danger to the entire country or letting down the people in charge. It was a very painful way to kill, because the person was left hanging a long time, until, finally, he couldn't breathe anymore. They hung Jesus on a cross because they had accused him of saying that he was the King of the Jews. They thought he didn't respect the Roman emperor, who was ruler at that time, and that Jesus wanted to take his place.

⁴³Jesus answered him, "Truly I tell you, today you will be with me in paradise."

The Death of Jesus

⁴⁴It was now about noon, and darkness came over the whole land until three in the afternoon, ⁴⁵for the sun stopped shining. And the curtain of the temple was torn in two. ⁴⁶Jesus called out with a loud

^a 30 Hosea 10:8   ^b 34 Some early manuscripts do not have this sentence.   ^c 42 Some manuscripts *come with your kingly power*

THE SCENE

THE SKULL

(LUKE 23:33)

This is a mountain just outside Jerusalem. It probably got its name because its shape is rather like a skull. This is where Jesus was crucified, but the experts aren't really completely sure where this mountain is.

voice, "Father, into your hands I commit my spirit."[a] When he had said this, he breathed his last.

[47] The centurion, seeing what had happened, praised God and said, "Surely this was a righteous man." [48] When all the people who had gathered to witness this sight saw what took place, they beat their breasts and went away. [49] But all those who knew him, including the women who had followed him from Galilee, stood at a distance, watching these things.

The Burial of Jesus

[50] Now there was a man named Joseph, a member of the Council, a good and upright man, [51] who had not consented to their decision and action. He came from the Judean town of Arimathea, and he himself was waiting for the kingdom of God. [52] Going to Pilate, he asked for Jesus' body. [53] Then he took it down, wrapped it in linen cloth and placed it in a tomb cut in the rock, one in which no one had yet been laid. [54] It was Preparation Day, and the Sabbath was about to begin.

[55] The women who had come with Jesus from Galilee followed Joseph and saw the tomb and how his body was laid in it. [56] Then they went home and prepared spices and perfumes. But they rested on the Sabbath in obedience to the commandment.

Jesus Has Risen

24 On the first day of the week, very early in the morning, the women took the spices they had prepared and went to the tomb. [2] They found the stone rolled away from the tomb, [3] but when they entered, they did not find the body of the Lord Jesus. [4] While they were wondering about this, suddenly two men in clothes that gleamed like lightning stood beside them. [5] In their fright the women bowed down with their faces to the ground, but the men said to them, "Why do you look for the living among the dead? [6] He is not here; he has risen! Remember how he told you, while he was still with you in Galilee: [7] 'The Son of Man must be delivered over to the hands of sinners, be crucified and on the third day be raised again.' " [8] Then they remembered his words.

[9] When they came back from the tomb, they told all these things to the Eleven and to all the others. [10] It was Mary Magdalene, Joanna, Mary the mother of James, and the others with them who told this to the apostles. [11] But they did not believe the women, because their words seemed to them like nonsense. [12] Peter, however, got up and ran to the tomb. Bending over, he saw the strips of linen lying by themselves, and he went away, wondering to himself what had happened.

[a] 46 Psalm 31:5

On the Road to Emmaus

¹³Now that same day two of them were going to a village called Emmaus, about seven miles[a] from Jerusalem. ¹⁴They were talking with each other about everything that had happened. ¹⁵As they talked and discussed these things with each other, Jesus himself came up and walked along with them; ¹⁶but they were kept from recognizing him.

¹⁷He asked them, "What are you discussing together as you walk along?"

They stood still, their faces downcast. ¹⁸One of them, named Cleopas, asked him, "Are you the only one visiting Jerusalem who does not know the things that have happened there in these days?"

¹⁹"What things?" he asked.

"About Jesus of Nazareth," they replied. "He was a prophet, powerful in word and deed before God and all the people. ²⁰The chief priests and our rulers handed him over to be sentenced to death, and they crucified him; ²¹but we had hoped that he was the one who was going to redeem Israel. And what is more, it is the third day since all this took place. ²²In addition, some of our women amazed us. They went to the tomb early this morning ²³but didn't find his body. They came and told us that they had seen a vision of angels, who said he was alive. ²⁴Then some of our companions went to the tomb and found it just as the women had said, but they did not see Jesus."

²⁵He said to them, "How foolish you are, and how slow to believe all that the prophets have spoken! ²⁶Did not the Messiah have to suffer these things and then enter his glory?" ²⁷And beginning with Moses and all the Prophets, he explained to them what was said in all the Scriptures concerning himself.

²⁸As they approached the village to which they were going, Jesus continued on as if he were going farther. ²⁹But they urged him strongly, "Stay with us, for it is nearly evening; the day is almost over." So he went in to stay with them.

³⁰When he was at the table with them, he took bread, gave thanks, broke it and began to give it to them. ³¹Then their eyes were opened and they recognized him, and he disappeared from their sight. ³²They asked each other, "Were not our hearts burning within us while he talked with us on the road and opened the Scriptures to us?"

³³They got up and returned at once to Jerusalem. There they found the Eleven and those with them, assembled together ³⁴and saying, "It is true! The Lord has risen and has appeared to Simon." ³⁵Then the two told what had happened on the way, and how Jesus was recognized by them when he broke the bread.

ª 13 Or about 11 kilometers

BETHANY

(LUKE 24:50)

This was a village on the slopes of the Mount of Olives, near Jerusalem on the road to Jericho. Its name seems to mean "house of dates" or "poor person's house." Sometimes Jesus went to Bethany to visit his friends Lazarus, Martha and Mary. Now this village is called Al-Eizariya or al-Azariya, which means "the place of Lazarus."

Jesus Appears to the Disciples

[36]While they were still talking about this, Jesus himself stood among them and said to them, "Peace be with you."

[37]They were startled and frightened, thinking they saw a ghost. [38]He said to them, "Why are you troubled, and why do doubts rise in your minds? [39]Look at my hands and my feet. It is I myself! Touch me and see; a ghost does not have flesh and bones, as you see I have."

[40]When he had said this, he showed them his hands and feet. [41]And while they still did not believe it because of joy and amazement, he asked them, "Do you have anything here to eat?" [42]They gave him a piece of broiled fish, [43]and he took it and ate it in their presence.

[44]He said to them, "This is what I told you while I was still with you: Everything must be fulfilled that is written about me in the Law of Moses, the Prophets and the Psalms."

[45]Then he opened their minds so they could understand the Scriptures. [46]He told them, "This is what is written: The Messiah will suffer and rise from the dead on the third day, [47]and repentance for the forgiveness of sins will be preached in his name to all nations, beginning at Jerusalem. [48]You are witnesses of these things. [49]I am going to send you what my Father has promised; but stay in the city until you have been clothed with power from on high."

The Ascension of Jesus

[50]When he had led them out to the vicinity of Bethany, he lifted up his hands and blessed them. [51]While he was blessing them, he left them and was taken up into heaven. [52]Then they worshiped him and returned to Jerusalem with great joy. [53]And they stayed continually at the temple, praising God.

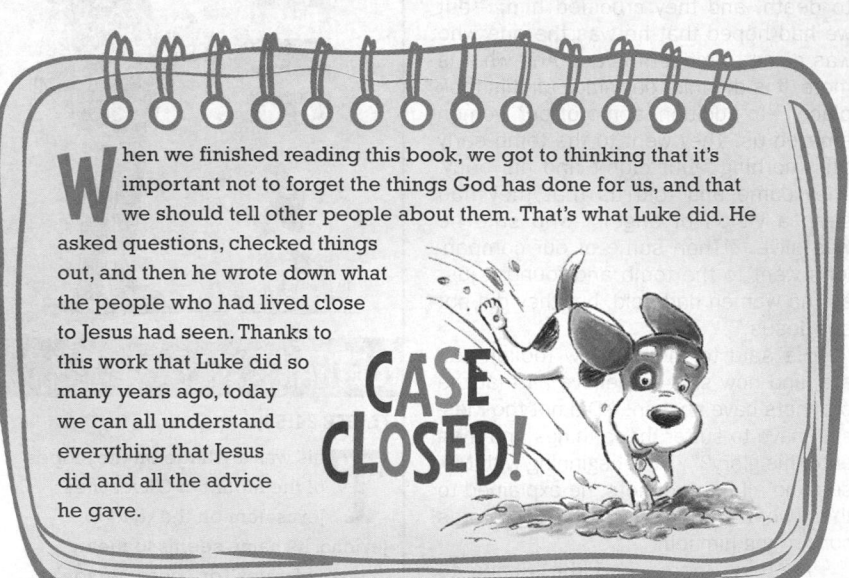

When we finished reading this book, we got to thinking that it's important not to forget the things God has done for us, and that we should tell other people about them. That's what Luke did. He asked questions, checked things out, and then he wrote down what the people who had lived close to Jesus had seen. Thanks to this work that Luke did so many years ago, today we can all understand everything that Jesus did and all the advice he gave.

CASE CLOSED!

JOHN

THE EVIDENCE:

WHO WROTE IT?
A long, long time ago, about two centuries after Christ, a man named Papias said that John wrote this book. John, the one Jesus loved very much. He learned everything Jesus taught and he followed him everywhere. He was even nearby when Jesus was crucified! John's father was Zebedee. Now, many Bible experts don't think that John wrote this book, so we aren't really sure about who wrote it. At any rate, it's been called "John" for many, many years.

HOW LONG AGO?
Everybody seems to agree about this. That's good! They say it was written at the end of the first century after Christ, between the years 90 and 100, when the emperor of Rome was a man called Domitian.

WHAT'S IT ABOUT?
The man who wrote this book says he wanted everybody to know that Jesus is the Son of God and that he is the Christ. That means that he is the person God had promised to send to save everyone. He also wanted everybody to know that Jesus is God. Jesus is a person who walked and ate and laughed and did everything just like us, except he never did anything bad.

THE BEST PART
We agree that what we like best is a promise Jesus made in John 14:3, when he said he was going to go to heaven to be with God, his Father. Jesus said, "I will come back and take you to be with me." We like that, because it means that Jesus is always thinking about each one of us. He's going to come to look for us so we'll not be separated anymore. That's wonderful!

The Word Became Flesh

1 In the beginning was the Word, and the Word was with God, and the Word was God. ²He was with God in the beginning. ³Through him all things were made; without him nothing was made that has been made. ⁴In him was life, and that life was the light of all mankind. ⁵The light shines in the darkness, and the darkness has not overcome[a] it.

⁶There was a man sent from God whose name was John. ⁷He came as a witness to testify concerning that light, so that through him all might believe. ⁸He himself was not the light; he came only as a witness to the light.

---

[a] 5 Or *understood*

about when I said, 'He who comes after me has surpassed me because he was before me.' ") ¹⁶Out of his fullness we have all received grace in place of grace already given. ¹⁷For the law was given through Moses; grace and truth came through Jesus Christ. ¹⁸No one has ever seen God, but the one and only Son, who is himself God and*a* is in closest relationship with the Father, has made him known.

---

a 18 Some manuscripts *but the only Son, who*

BREAKTHROUGH!

The Word

(JOHN 1:1)

Only John calls Jesus "Word." This means that Jesus is who was with God in the beginning when nothing else existed — only God existed. A very, very long time ago, God spoke to people through his Word. But here, John says that God was going to speak through a person. That means that the divine Word was going to become a man — and that was Jesus! So the gospel of John says that Jesus is God, and has existed forever.

⁹The true light that gives light to everyone was coming into the world. ¹⁰He was in the world, and though the world was made through him, the world did not recognize him. ¹¹He came to that which was his own, but his own did not receive him. ¹²Yet to all who did receive him, to those who believed in his name, he gave the right to become children of God— ¹³children born not of natural descent, nor of human decision or a husband's will, but born of God.

¹⁴The Word became flesh and made his dwelling among us. We have seen his glory, the glory of the one and only Son, who came from the Father, full of grace and truth.

¹⁵(John testified concerning him. He cried out, saying, "This is the one I spoke

THE WITNESSES

✓ JOHN (JOHN 1:6)

Here in this text, he's just called John, but in other books this same man is called John the Baptist. He was a prophet who went around the villages preaching God's message and announcing Jesus. In Hebrew, the name John means "God was good."

John the Baptist Denies Being the Messiah

¹⁹Now this was John's testimony when the Jewish leaders[a] in Jerusalem sent priests and Levites to ask him who he was. ²⁰He did not fail to confess, but confessed freely, "I am not the Messiah."

²¹They asked him, "Then who are you? Are you Elijah?"

He said, "I am not."

"Are you the Prophet?"

He answered, "No."

²²Finally they said, "Who are you? Give us an answer to take back to those who sent us. What do you say about yourself?"

²³John replied in the words of Isaiah the prophet, "I am the voice of one calling in the wilderness, 'Make straight the way for the Lord.'"[b]

²⁴Now the Pharisees who had been sent ²⁵questioned him, "Why then do you baptize if you are not the Messiah, nor Elijah, nor the Prophet?"

²⁶"I baptize with[c] water," John replied, "but among you stands one you do not know. ²⁷He is the one who comes after me, the straps of whose sandals I am not worthy to untie."

²⁸This all happened at Bethany on the other side of the Jordan, where John was baptizing.

John Testifies About Jesus

²⁹The next day John saw Jesus coming toward him and said, "Look, the Lamb of God, who takes away the sin of the world! ³⁰This is the one I meant when I said, 'A man who comes after me has surpassed me because he was before me.' ³¹I myself did not know him, but the reason I came baptizing with water was that he might be revealed to Israel."

³²Then John gave this testimony: "I saw the Spirit come down from heaven as a dove and remain on him. ³³And I myself did not know him, but the one who sent me to baptize with water told me, 'The man on whom you see the Spirit come down and remain is the one who will baptize with the Holy Spirit.' ³⁴I have seen and I testify that this is God's Chosen One."[d]

The Lamb of God

(JOHN 1:29)

This is another reference to Jesus. Some Bible experts think that this phrase relates Jesus with the little lamb that was offered as a sacrifice every day in the temple to ask forgiveness for sins.

John's Disciples Follow Jesus

³⁵The next day John was there again with two of his disciples. ³⁶When he saw Jesus passing by, he said, "Look, the Lamb of God!"

³⁷When the two disciples heard him say this, they followed Jesus. ³⁸Turning around, Jesus saw them following and asked, "What do you want?"

They said, "Rabbi" (which means "Teacher"), "where are you staying?"

³⁹"Come," he replied, "and you will see."

So they went and saw where he was staying, and they spent that day with him. It was about four in the afternoon.

⁴⁰Andrew, Simon Peter's brother, was one of the two who heard what John had

---

[a] *19* The Greek term traditionally translated *the Jews* (*hoi Ioudaioi*) refers here and elsewhere in John's Gospel to those Jewish leaders who opposed Jesus; also in 5:10, 15, 16; 7:1, 11, 13; 9:22; 18:14, 28, 36; 19:7, 12, 31, 38; 20:19.   [b] *23* Isaiah 40:3   [c] *26* Or *in*; also in verses 31 and 33 (twice)   [d] *34* See Isaiah 42:1; many manuscripts *is the Son of God*.

said and who had followed Jesus. 41The first thing Andrew did was to find his brother Simon and tell him, "We have found the Messiah" (that is, the Christ). 42And he brought him to Jesus.

Jesus looked at him and said, "You are Simon son of John. You will be called Cephas" (which, when translated, is Peter[a]).

Jesus Calls Philip and Nathanael

43The next day Jesus decided to leave for Galilee. Finding Philip, he said to him, "Follow me."

44Philip, like Andrew and Peter, was from the town of Bethsaida. 45Philip found Nathanael and told him, "We have found the one Moses wrote about in the Law, and about whom the prophets also wrote—Jesus of Nazareth, the son of Joseph."

46"Nazareth! Can anything good come from there?" Nathanael asked.

"Come and see," said Philip.

47When Jesus saw Nathanael approaching, he said of him, "Here truly is an Israelite in whom there is no deceit."

[a] 42 *Cephas* (Aramaic) and *Peter* (Greek) both mean *rock.*

THE WITNESSES

✓ CEPHAS (JOHN 1:42)
This is the same man who's called Peter in other places. Peter is a Greek name, and it means "rock." *Cephas* is a name in Aramaic that also means "rock." It's like the name *Mary* in English—in Spanish it's *Maria*, and in Hebrew it's *Miriam*. Three different names, but always the same person!

✓ JESUS OF NAZARETH (JOHN 1:45)
This is another way to refer to Jesus. At that time, the name Jesus was a pretty common name for Jewish boys. So to kind of distinguish one Jesus from another, they would say the name of the place where he was from. Since Jesus lived in Nazareth, they called him Jesus of Nazareth.

BREAKTHROUGH!

Why did they call him Rabbi?

(JOHN 1:38)

It's a Hebrew word that means "teacher." It's a title given to a person who had studied many years and was an expert. It was also used for a person who had disciples or followers.

BREAKTHROUGH!

The Christ

(JOHN 1:41)

The word *Christ* is Greek. In the Bible, this is the word used to mean the same as the Hebrew word *Messiah*. Christ, or Messiah, is the One God sent to save the world.

⁴⁸"How do you know me?" Nathanael asked.

Jesus answered, "I saw you while you were still under the fig tree before Philip called you."

⁴⁹Then Nathanael declared, "Rabbi, you are the Son of God; you are the king of Israel."

⁵⁰Jesus said, "You believe*ᵃ* because I told you I saw you under the fig tree. You will see greater things than that." ⁵¹He then added, "Very truly I tell you,*ᵇ* you*ᵇ* will see 'heaven open, and the angels of God ascending and descending on'*ᶜ* the Son of Man."

Jesus Changes Water Into Wine

2 On the third day a wedding took place at Cana in Galilee. Jesus' mother was there, ²and Jesus and his disciples had also been invited to the wedding. ³When the wine was gone, Jesus' mother said to him, "They have no more wine."

⁴"Woman,*ᵈ* why do you involve me?"

Jesus replied. "My hour has not yet come."

⁵His mother said to the servants, "Do whatever he tells you."

⁶Nearby stood six stone water jars, the kind used by the Jews for ceremonial washing, each holding from twenty to thirty gallons.*ᵉ*

ᵃ 50 Or *Do you believe . . . ?*   *ᵇ 51* The Greek is plural.
ᶜ 51 Gen. 28:12   *ᵈ 4* The Greek for *Woman* does not denote any disrespect.   *ᵉ 6* Or from about 75 to about 115 liters

THE SCENE

CANA

(JOHN 2:1)

This Hebrew word means "cane." There are two places in the Bible that have this name. In the New Testament, only John talks about Cana of Galilee. Now we can't be sure where this Cana is. Some people think it is the place now called Khirbet Qana, which is 7.5 miles (12 km) north of Nazareth. Other experts think that Cana of Galilee is what is now Kefr Kanna, 4.5 miles (7 km) northeast of Nazareth on the road that joins Tiberias with Capernaum. There are ruins from the time of Jesus in this place.

BREAKTHROUGH!

How did the Jews use these stone water jars for their ceremonies?

(JOHN 2:6)

In Bible times, wedding parties could last up to a whole week, and some of the guests would arrive before the others. The stone jars held water so the guests who came in off the street could wash their hands and arms, and other objects they brought along. These jars made of stone were usually used for wedding celebrations or cleansing rituals.

⁷Jesus said to the servants, "Fill the jars with water"; so they filled them to the brim.

⁸Then he told them, "Now draw some out and take it to the master of the banquet."

They did so, ⁹and the master of the banquet tasted the water that had been turned into wine. He did not realize where it had come from, though the servants who had drawn the water knew. Then he called the bridegroom aside ¹⁰and said, "Everyone brings out the choice wine first and then the cheaper wine after the guests have had too much to drink; but you have saved the best till now."

¹¹What Jesus did here in Cana of Galilee was the first of the signs through which he revealed his glory; and his disciples believed in him.

¹²After this he went down to Capernaum with his mother and brothers and his disciples. There they stayed for a few days.

Jesus Clears the Temple Courts

¹³When it was almost time for the Jewish Passover, Jesus went up to Jerusalem. ¹⁴In the temple courts he found people selling cattle, sheep and doves, and others sitting at tables exchanging money. ¹⁵So he made a whip out of cords, and drove all from the temple courts, both sheep and cattle; he scattered the coins of the money changers and overturned their tables. ¹⁶To those who sold doves he said, "Get these out of here! Stop turning my Father's house into a market!" ¹⁷His disciples remembered that it is written: "Zeal for your house will consume me."ᵃ

¹⁸The Jews then responded to him, "What sign can you show us to prove your authority to do all this?"

¹⁹Jesus answered them, "Destroy this temple, and I will raise it again in three days."

²⁰They replied, "It has taken forty-six years to build this temple, and you are going to raise it in three days?" ²¹But the temple he had spoken of was his body. ²²After he was raised from the dead, his disciples recalled what he had said. Then they believed the scripture and the words that Jesus had spoken.

²³Now while he was in Jerusalem at the Passover Festival, many people saw the signs he was performing and believed in his name.ᵇ ²⁴But Jesus would not entrust himself to them, for he knew all people. ²⁵He did not need any testimony about mankind, for he knew what was in each person.

Jesus Teaches Nicodemus

3 Now there was a Pharisee, a man named Nicodemus who was a member of the Jewish ruling council. ²He came to Jesus at night and said, "Rabbi, we know that you are a teacher who has come from

---

ᵃ 17 Psalm 69:9   ᵇ 23 Or *in him*

God. For no one could perform the signs you are doing if God were not with him."

³Jesus replied, "Very truly I tell you, no one can see the kingdom of God unless they are born again.ᵃ"

⁴"How can someone be born when they are old?" Nicodemus asked. "Surely they cannot enter a second time into their mother's womb to be born!"

⁵Jesus answered, "Very truly I tell you, no one can enter the kingdom of God unless they are born of water and the Spirit. ⁶Flesh gives birth to flesh, but the Spiritᵇ gives birth to spirit. ⁷You should not be surprised at my saying, 'Youᶜ must be born again.' ⁸The wind blows wherever it pleases. You hear its sound, but you cannot tell where it comes from or where it is going. So it is with everyone born of the Spirit."ᵈ

ᵃ 3 The Greek for *again* also means *from above*; also in verse 7.   ᵇ 6 Or *but spirit*   ᶜ 7 The Greek is plural.
ᵈ 8 The Greek for *Spirit* is the same as that for *wind*.

THE
WITNESSES

✓ NICODEMUS (JOHN 3:1)

This is a Greek name, and it means "conqueror of the people." He seems to have been a very important person in Israel. He was a teacher of the Law and he also belonged to a group of important people who made decisions about what was right and what was wrong in the Jewish religion. He went to visit Jesus in order to listen to his teachings. A few years later, when they were judging Jesus and were going to kill him, Nicodemus defended him, and then he provided some very expensive perfume to put on Jesus' body before he was placed in the tomb.

BREAK THROUGH!

Born of water and the Spirit
(JOHN 3:5)

Jesus taught Nicodemus what being born again means. For people who believe in God, it's like beginning life a new way by trusting in God and his power and doing what pleases God. That's why Jesus explains that it's necessary to be born of water. That means being baptized, since that's the way to show other people that the person being baptized is now living the kind of life that pleases God. Being born of the Spirit means that the person has changed in his or her heart. That's the most important kind of change.

⁹"How can this be?" Nicodemus asked.
¹⁰"You are Israel's teacher," said Jesus, "and do you not understand these things? ¹¹Very truly I tell you, we speak of what we know, and we testify to what we have seen, but still you people do not accept our testimony. ¹²I have spoken to you of earthly things and you do not believe; how then will you believe if I speak of heavenly things? ¹³No one has ever gone into heaven except the one who came from heaven—the Son of Man.ᵃ ¹⁴Just as Moses lifted up the snake in the wilderness, so the Son of Man must be lifted up,ᵇ ¹⁵that everyone who believes may have eternal life in him."ᶜ

¹⁶For God so loved the world that he gave his one and only Son, that whoever believes in him shall not perish but have eternal life. ¹⁷For God did not send his Son into the world to condemn the world, but to save the world through him. ¹⁸Whoever believes in him is not condemned, but whoever does not believe stands condemned already because they have not believed in the name of God's one and only Son. ¹⁹This is the verdict: Light has come into the world, but people loved darkness instead of light because their deeds were evil. ²⁰Everyone who does evil hates the light, and will not come into the light for fear that their deeds will be exposed. ²¹But whoever lives by the truth comes into the light, so that it may be seen plainly that what they have done has been done in the sight of God.

John Testifies Again About Jesus

²²After this, Jesus and his disciples went out into the Judean countryside, where he spent some time with them, and baptized. ²³Now John also was baptizing at Aenon near Salim, because there was plenty of water, and people were coming and being baptized. ²⁴(This was before John was put in prison.) ²⁵An argument developed between some of John's disciples and a certain Jew over the matter of ceremonial washing. ²⁶They came to John and said to him, "Rabbi, that man who was with you on the other side of the Jordan—the one you testified about—look, he is baptizing, and everyone is going to him."

BREAK THROUGH!

The snake

(JOHN 3:14)

The story of the snake is in the book called Numbers, and it's very interesting. When God's people were wandering around in the desert trying to get to the land God had promised them, they begin to complain and complain. Then God sent some poisonous snakes—the kind that kill you if they bite you. Soon, the people understood that they had sinned, and they asked God to forgive them. So God told Moses to make a snake out of bronze metal and put it up on a really high pole so everybody could see it. He said if a person that had been bitten by one of those poisonous snakes looked up and saw the bronze serpent, he or she would be cured. The story is in Numbers 21:4–9.

²⁷To this John replied, "A person can receive only what is given them from heaven. ²⁸You yourselves can testify that I said, 'I am not the Messiah but am sent ahead of him.' ²⁹The bride belongs to the bridegroom. The friend who attends the bridegroom waits and listens for him, and is full of joy when he hears the bride-

---

ᵃ 13 Some manuscripts *Man, who is in heaven*
ᵇ 14 The Greek for *lifted up* also means *exalted.*
ᶜ 15 Some interpreters end the quotation with verse 21.

groom's voice. That joy is mine, and it is now complete. [30]He must become greater; I must become less."[a]

[31]The one who comes from above is above all; the one who is from the earth belongs to the earth, and speaks as one from the earth. The one who comes from heaven is above all. [32]He testifies to what he has seen and heard, but no one accepts his testimony. [33]Whoever has accepted it has certified that God is truthful. [34]For the one whom God has sent speaks the words of God, for God[b] gives the Spirit without limit. [35]The Father loves the Son and has placed everything in his hands. [36]Whoever believes in the Son has eternal life, but whoever rejects the Son will not see life, for God's wrath remains on them.

Jesus Talks With a Samaritan Woman

4 Now Jesus learned that the Pharisees had heard that he was gaining and baptizing more disciples than John— [2]although in fact it was not Jesus who baptized, but his disciples. [3]So he left Judea and went back once more to Galilee.

[4]Now he had to go through Samaria. [5]So he came to a town in Samaria called Sychar, near the plot of ground Jacob had given to his son Joseph. [6]Jacob's well was there, and Jesus, tired as he was from the journey, sat down by the well. It was about noon.

[7]When a Samaritan woman came to draw water, Jesus said to her, "Will you give me a drink?" [8](His disciples had gone into the town to buy food.)

[9]The Samaritan woman said to him, "You are a Jew and I am a Samaritan woman. How can you ask me for a drink?" (For Jews do not associate with Samaritans.[c])

[10]Jesus answered her, "If you knew the gift of God and who it is that asks you for a drink, you would have asked him and he would have given you living water."

[11]"Sir," the woman said, "you have nothing to draw with and the well is deep. Where can you get this living water? [12]Are you greater than our father Jacob, who

BREAK THROUGH!

Eternal life
(JOHN 3:36)
This is the good news that Jesus brings to the people who believe in him. It has to do with the kind of life we live when we believe in Jesus. It doesn't mean that we won't die. It means that God has a better kind of life waiting for us after we die.

gave us the well and drank from it himself, as did also his sons and his livestock?"

[13]Jesus answered, "Everyone who drinks this water will be thirsty again, [14]but whoever drinks the water I give them will never thirst. Indeed, the water I give them will become in them a spring of water welling up to eternal life."

[15]The woman said to him, "Sir, give me this water so that I won't get thirsty and have to keep coming here to draw water."

[16]He told her, "Go, call your husband and come back."

[17]"I have no husband," she replied.

Jesus said to her, "You are right when you say you have no husband. [18]The fact is, you have had five husbands, and the man you now have is not your husband. What you have just said is quite true."

[a] 30 Some interpreters end the quotation with verse 36.
[b] 34 Greek he   [c] 9 Or do not use dishes Samaritans have used

BREAKTHROUGH!

Why didn't the Jews get along well with people from Samaria?

(JOHN 4:9)

A long time ago, the people who were living in Judea and in Samaria were enemies. It all started when they were returning from Babylon, where the Jews had been taken prisoners by force. One of the main reasons they couldn't get along was because the Samaritans built a temple to worship God on Mount Gerizim. The Judean people said that the only temple where God could be worshiped was in Jerusalem. Even though the Samaritan's temple didn't exist anymore, because it had been wrecked, the Samaritans and the Jews just kept on not liking each other. They didn't even talk to each other.

THE SCENE

WHAT WAS "THIS MOUNTAIN"?

(JOHN 4:20)

The woman is talking about Mount Gerizim, where the Samaritans built a temple to worship God. The problem was that the Jews at the time of Jesus said that the only temple where God could be worshiped was in Jerusalem. Mount Gerizim is one of the highest mountains in that region of Palestine. It's about a half a mile (880 meters) high.

---

19 "Sir," the woman said, "I can see that you are a prophet. 20 Our ancestors worshiped on this mountain, but you Jews claim that the place where we must worship is in Jerusalem."

21 "Woman," Jesus replied, "believe me, a time is coming when you will worship the Father neither on this mountain nor in Jerusalem. 22 You Samaritans worship what you do not know; we worship what we do know, for salvation is from the Jews. 23 Yet a time is coming and has now come when the true worshipers will worship the Father in the Spirit and in truth, for they are the kind of worshipers the Father seeks. 24 God is spirit, and his worshipers must worship in the Spirit and in truth."

25 The woman said, "I know that Messiah" (called Christ) "is coming. When he comes, he will explain everything to us."

26 Then Jesus declared, "I, the one speaking to you—I am he."

The Disciples Rejoin Jesus

27 Just then his disciples returned and were surprised to find him talking with a woman. But no one asked, "What do you want?" or "Why are you talking with her?"

28 Then, leaving her water jar, the woman went back to the town and said to the people, 29 "Come, see a man who told me everything I ever did. Could this be the Messiah?" 30 They came out of the town and made their way toward him.

31 Meanwhile his disciples urged him, "Rabbi, eat something."

32 But he said to them, "I have food to eat that you know nothing about."

33 Then his disciples said to each other, "Could someone have brought him food?"

34 "My food," said Jesus, "is to do the will of him who sent me and to finish his work. 35 Don't you have a saying, 'It's still four months until harvest'? I tell you, open your eyes and look at the fields! They are ripe for harvest. 36 Even now the one who reaps draws a wage and harvests a crop for eternal life, so that the sower and the reaper may be glad together. 37 Thus the saying 'One sows and another reaps' is true. 38 I sent you to reap what you have not worked for. Others have done the hard work, and you have reaped the benefits of their labor."

Many Samaritans Believe

39 Many of the Samaritans from that town believed in him because of the woman's testimony, "He told me everything I ever did." 40 So when the Samaritans came to him, they urged him to stay with them, and he stayed two days. 41 And because of his words many more became believers.

42 They said to the woman, "We no longer believe just because of what you said; now we have heard for ourselves, and we know that this man really is the Savior of the world."

Jesus Heals an Official's Son

43 After the two days he left for Galilee. 44 (Now Jesus himself had pointed out that a prophet has no honor in his own country.) 45 When he arrived in Galilee, the Galileans welcomed him. They had seen all that he had done in Jerusalem at the Passover Festival, for they also had been there.

46 Once more he visited Cana in Galilee, where he had turned the water into wine. And there was a certain royal official whose son lay sick at Capernaum. 47 When this man heard that Jesus had arrived in Galilee from Judea, he went to him and begged him to come and heal his son, who was close to death.

48 "Unless you people see signs and wonders," Jesus told him, "you will never believe."

49 The royal official said, "Sir, come down before my child dies."

50 "Go," Jesus replied, "your son will live."

The man took Jesus at his word and departed. 51 While he was still on the way, his servants met him with the news that his boy was living. 52 When he inquired as to the time when his son got better, they said to him, "Yesterday, at one in the afternoon, the fever left him."

53 Then the father realized that this was the exact time at which Jesus had said to him, "Your son will live." So he and his whole household believed.

54 This was the second sign Jesus performed after coming from Judea to Galilee.

The Healing at the Pool

5 Some time later, Jesus went up to Jerusalem for one of the Jewish festivals. 2 Now there is in Jerusalem near the Sheep Gate a pool, which in Aramaic is called Bethesda*a* and which is surrounded by five covered colonnades. 3 Here a great number of disabled people used to lie — the blind, the lame, the paralyzed. [4]*b* 5 One who was there had been an invalid for thirty-eight years. 6 When Jesus saw him lying there and learned that

---

a 2 Some manuscripts *Bethzatha*; other manuscripts *Bethsaida*   *b* 3,4 Some manuscripts include here, wholly or in part, *paralyzed — and they waited for the moving of the waters.* *4From time to time an angel of the Lord would come down and stir up the waters. The first one into the pool after each such disturbance would be cured of whatever disease they had.*

BREAKTHROUGH!

Sheep Gate

(JOHN 5:2)

Cities used to have thick walls that surrounded them. Those walls had gates that were opened during the day and closed at night so nobody could leave or enter the city after dark. The wall that went around Jerusalem had many gates. The one John is talking about was probably where they brought the animals in for the temple sacrifices.

he had been in this condition for a long time, he asked him, "Do you want to get well?"

7 "Sir," the invalid replied, "I have no one to help me into the pool when the water is stirred. While I am trying to get in, someone else goes down ahead of me."

8 Then Jesus said to him, "Get up! Pick up your mat and walk." 9 At once the man was cured; he picked up his mat and walked.

The day on which this took place was a Sabbath, 10 and so the Jewish leaders said to the man who had been healed, "It is the Sabbath; the law forbids you to carry your mat."

11 But he replied, "The man who made me well said to me, 'Pick up your mat and walk.' "

12 So they asked him, "Who is this fellow who told you to pick it up and walk?"

13 The man who was healed had no idea who it was, for Jesus had slipped away into the crowd that was there.

14 Later Jesus found him at the temple and said to him, "See, you are well again. Stop sinning or something worse may happen to you." 15 The man went away and told the Jewish leaders that it was Jesus who had made him well.

The Authority of the Son

16 So, because Jesus was doing these things on the Sabbath, the Jewish leaders began to persecute him. 17 In his defense Jesus said to them, "My Father is always at his work to this very day, and I too am working." 18 For this reason they tried all the more to kill him; not only was he breaking the Sabbath, but he was even calling God his own Father, making himself equal with God.

19 Jesus gave them this answer: "Very truly I tell you, the Son can do nothing by himself; he can do only what he sees his Father doing, because whatever the Father does the Son also does. 20 For the Father loves the Son and shows him all he does. Yes, and he will show him even greater works than these, so that you will be amazed. 21 For just as the Father raises the dead and gives them life, even so the Son gives life to whom he is pleased to give it. 22 Moreover, the Father judges no one, but has entrusted all judgment to the Son, 23 that all may honor the Son just as they honor the Father. Whoever does not honor the Son does not honor the Father, who sent him.

24 "Very truly I tell you, whoever hears my word and believes him who sent me has eternal life and will not be judged but has crossed over from death to life. 25 Very truly I tell you, a time is coming and has now come when the dead will hear the voice of the Son of God and those who hear will live. 26 For as the Father has life in himself, so he has granted the Son also to have life in himself. 27 And he has given him authority to judge because he is the Son of Man.

[28]"Do not be amazed at this, for a time is coming when all who are in their graves will hear his voice [29]and come out—those who have done what is good will rise to live, and those who have done what is evil will rise to be condemned. [30]By myself I can do nothing; I judge only as I hear, and my judgment is just, for I seek not to please myself but him who sent me.

Testimonies About Jesus

[31]"If I testify about myself, my testimony is not true. [32]There is another who testifies in my favor, and I know that his testimony about me is true.

[33]"You have sent to John and he has testified to the truth. [34]Not that I accept human testimony; but I mention it that you may be saved. [35]John was a lamp that burned and gave light, and you chose for a time to enjoy his light.

[36]"I have testimony weightier than that of John. For the works that the Father has given me to finish—the very works that I am doing—testify that the Father has sent me. [37]And the Father who sent me has himself testified concerning me. You have never heard his voice nor seen his form, [38]nor does his word dwell in you, for you do not believe the one he sent. [39]You study[a] the Scriptures diligently because you think that in them you have eternal life. These are the very Scriptures that testify about me, [40]yet you refuse to come to me to have life.

[41]"I do not accept glory from human beings, [42]but I know you. I know that you do not have the love of God in your hearts. [43]I have come in my Father's name, and you do not accept me; but if someone else comes in his own name, you will accept him. [44]How can you believe since you accept glory from one another but do not seek the glory that comes from the only God[b]?

[45]"But do not think I will accuse you before the Father. Your accuser is Moses, on whom your hopes are set. [46]If you believed Moses, you would believe me, for he wrote about me. [47]But since you do not believe what he wrote, how are you going to believe what I say?"

Jesus Feeds the Five Thousand

6 Some time after this, Jesus crossed to the far shore of the Sea of Galilee (that is, the Sea of Tiberias), [2]and a great crowd of people followed him because they saw the signs he had performed by healing the sick. [3]Then Jesus went up on a mountainside and sat down with his disciples. [4]The Jewish Passover Festival was near.

[5]When Jesus looked up and saw a great crowd coming toward him, he said to Philip, "Where shall we buy bread for these people to eat?" [6]He asked this only to test him, for he already had in mind what he was going to do.

[7]Philip answered him, "It would take more than half a year's wages[c] to buy enough bread for each one to have a bite!"

[8]Another of his disciples, Andrew, Simon Peter's brother, spoke up, [9]"Here is a boy with five small barley loaves and two small fish, but how far will they go among so many?"

[10]Jesus said, "Have the people sit down." There was plenty of grass in that place, and they sat down (about five thousand men were there). [11]Jesus then took the loaves, gave thanks, and distributed to those who were seated as much as they wanted. He did the same with the fish.

[12]When they had all had enough to eat, he said to his disciples, "Gather the pieces that are left over. Let nothing be wasted." [13]So they gathered them and filled twelve baskets with the pieces of the five barley loaves left over by those who had eaten.

[14]After the people saw the sign Jesus performed, they began to say, "Surely this is the Prophet who is to come into the world." [15]Jesus, knowing that they intended to come and make him king by force, withdrew again to a mountain by himself.

Jesus Walks on the Water

[16]When evening came, his disciples went down to the lake, [17]where they got

---

[a] 39 Or [39]Study   [b] 44 Some early manuscripts *the Only One*   [c] 7 Greek *take two hundred denarii*

BREAKTHROUGH!

Barley loaves

(JOHN 6:9)

Barley is a grain like wheat or corn. In Jesus' time, barley bread was the kind of bread poor people ate. It was cheaper than wheat bread. Barley was also used at that time as animal feed.

into a boat and set off across the lake for Capernaum. By now it was dark, and Jesus had not yet joined them. ¹⁸A strong wind was blowing and the waters grew rough. ¹⁹When they had rowed about three or four miles,ᵃ they saw Jesus approaching the boat, walking on the water; and they were frightened. ²⁰But he said to them, "It is I; don't be afraid." ²¹Then they were willing to take him into the boat, and immediately the boat reached the shore where they were heading.

²²The next day the crowd that had stayed on the opposite shore of the lake realized that only one boat had been there, and that Jesus had not entered it with his disciples, but that they had gone away alone. ²³Then some boats from Tiberias landed near the place where the people had eaten the bread after the Lord had given thanks. ²⁴Once the crowd realized that neither Jesus nor his disciples were there, they got into the boats and went to Capernaum in search of Jesus.

Jesus the Bread of Life

²⁵When they found him on the other side of the lake, they asked him, "Rabbi, when did you get here?"

²⁶Jesus answered, "Very truly I tell you, you are looking for me, not because you saw the signs I performed but because you ate the loaves and had your fill. ²⁷Do not work for food that spoils, but for food that endures to eternal life, which the Son of Man will give you. For on him God the Father has placed his seal of approval."

²⁸Then they asked him, "What must we do to do the works God requires?"

²⁹Jesus answered, "The work of God is this: to believe in the one he has sent."

³⁰So they asked him, "What sign then will you give that we may see it and believe you? What will you do? ³¹Our ancestors ate the manna in the wilderness; as it is written: 'He gave them bread from heaven to eat.'ᵇ"

³²Jesus said to them, "Very truly I tell you, it is not Moses who has given you the bread from heaven, but it is my Father who gives you the true bread from heaven. ³³For the bread of God is the bread that comes down from heaven and gives life to the world."

³⁴"Sir," they said, "always give us this bread."

³⁵Then Jesus declared, "I am the bread of life. Whoever comes to me will never go hungry, and whoever believes in me will never be thirsty. ³⁶But as I told you, you have seen me and still you do not believe. ³⁷All those the Father gives me will come to me, and whoever comes to me I will never drive away. ³⁸For I have come down from heaven not to do my will but to do the will of him who sent me. ³⁹And this is the will of him who sent me, that I shall lose none of all those he has given me, but raise them up at the last day. ⁴⁰For my Father's will is that everyone who looks to the Son and believes in him shall have eternal life, and I will raise them up at the last day."

⁴¹At this the Jews there began to grumble about him because he said, "I am the bread that came down from heaven."

ᵃ *19* Or about 5 or 6 kilometers   ᵇ *31* Exodus 16:4; Neh. 9:15; Psalm 78:24,25

⁴²They said, "Is this not Jesus, the son of Joseph, whose father and mother we know? How can he now say, 'I came down from heaven'?"

⁴³"Stop grumbling among yourselves," Jesus answered. ⁴⁴"No one can come to me unless the Father who sent me draws them, and I will raise them up at the last day. ⁴⁵It is written in the Prophets: 'They will all be taught by God.'ᵃ Everyone who has heard the Father and learned from him comes to me. ⁴⁶No one has seen the Father except the one who is from God; only he has seen the Father. ⁴⁷Very truly I tell you, the one who believes has eternal life. ⁴⁸I am the bread of life. ⁴⁹Your ancestors ate the manna in the wilderness, yet they died. ⁵⁰But here is the bread that comes down from heaven, which anyone may eat and not die. ⁵¹I am the living bread that came down from heaven. Whoever eats this bread will live forever. This bread is my flesh, which I will give for the life of the world."

⁵²Then the Jews began to argue sharply among themselves, "How can this man give us his flesh to eat?"

⁵³Jesus said to them, "Very truly I tell you, unless you eat the flesh of the Son of Man and drink his blood, you have no life in you. ⁵⁴Whoever eats my flesh and drinks my blood has eternal life, and I will raise them up at the last day. ⁵⁵For my flesh is real food and my blood is real drink. ⁵⁶Whoever eats my flesh and drinks my blood remains in me, and I in them. ⁵⁷Just as the living Father sent me and I live because of the Father, so the one who feeds on me will live because of me. ⁵⁸This is the bread that came down from heaven. Your ancestors ate manna and died, but whoever feeds on this bread will live forever." ⁵⁹He said this while teaching in the synagogue in Capernaum.

Many Disciples Desert Jesus

⁶⁰On hearing it, many of his disciples said, "This is a hard teaching. Who can accept it?"

⁶¹Aware that his disciples were grumbling about this, Jesus said to them, "Does this offend you? ⁶²Then what if you see the Son of Man ascend to where he was before! ⁶³The Spirit gives life; the flesh counts for nothing. The words I have spoken to you—they are full of the Spiritᵇ and life. ⁶⁴Yet there are some of you who do not believe." For Jesus had known from the beginning which of them did not believe and who would betray him. ⁶⁵He went on to say, "This is why I told you that no one can come to me unless the Father has enabled them."

⁶⁶From this time many of his disciples turned back and no longer followed him.

⁶⁷"You do not want to leave too, do you?" Jesus asked the Twelve.

⁶⁸Simon Peter answered him, "Lord, to whom shall we go? You have the words of eternal life. ⁶⁹We have come to believe and to know that you are the Holy One of God."

⁷⁰Then Jesus replied, "Have I not chosen you, the Twelve? Yet one of you is a devil!" ⁷¹(He meant Judas, the son of Simon Iscariot, who, though one of the Twelve, was later to betray him.)

Jesus Goes to the Festival of Tabernacles

7 After this, Jesus went around in Galilee. He did not wantᶜ to go about in Judea because the Jewish leaders there were looking for a way to kill him. ²But when the Jewish Festival of Tabernacles was near, ³Jesus' brothers said to him, "Leave Galilee and go to Judea, so that your disciples there may see the works you do. ⁴No one who wants to become a public figure acts in secret. Since you are doing these things, show yourself to the world." ⁵For even his own brothers did not believe in him.

⁶Therefore Jesus told them, "My time is not yet here; for you any time will do. ⁷The world cannot hate you, but it hates me because I testify that its works are evil. ⁸You go to the festival. I am notᵈ going up to this festival, because my time has not yet fully come." ⁹After he had said this, he stayed in Galilee.

ᵃ 45 Isaiah 54:13   ᵇ 63 Or are Spirit; or are spirit
ᶜ 1 Some manuscripts not have authority   ᵈ 8 Some manuscripts not yet

BREAKTHROUGH!

Festival of Tabernacles
(JOHN 7:2)

This festival was to remember when God brought the Israelite people out of Egypt. For a long time, they had to live in huts built with tree branches. It was the most spectacular of all their celebrations. Each family built a hut with branches all around Jerusalem, and they lived in it for about a week. During that time, the priest would also walk to Siloam every day, and the people would follow him. In this walk, the people would wave palm branches to the sound of a trumpet made of a ram's horn, which they called a shofar. They also sprinkled water on the temple altar, and they lit four golden candle holders in the part of the temple called the court of the women. These candle holders were so big, they lit up the entire city!

¹⁰However, after his brothers had left for the festival, he went also, not publicly, but in secret. ¹¹Now at the festival the Jewish leaders were watching for Jesus and asking, "Where is he?"

¹²Among the crowds there was widespread whispering about him. Some said, "He is a good man."

Others replied, "No, he deceives the people." ¹³But no one would say anything publicly about him for fear of the leaders.

Jesus Teaches at the Festival

¹⁴Not until halfway through the festival did Jesus go up to the temple courts and begin to teach. ¹⁵The Jews there were amazed and asked, "How did this man get such learning without having been taught?"

¹⁶Jesus answered, "My teaching is not my own. It comes from the one who sent me. ¹⁷Anyone who chooses to do the will of God will find out whether my teaching comes from God or whether I speak on my own. ¹⁸Whoever speaks on their own does so to gain personal glory, but he who seeks the glory of the one who sent him is a man of truth; there is nothing false about him. ¹⁹Has not Moses given you the law? Yet not one of you keeps the law. Why are you trying to kill me?"

²⁰"You are demon-possessed," the crowd answered. "Who is trying to kill you?"

²¹Jesus said to them, "I did one miracle, and you are all amazed. ²²Yet, because Moses gave you circumcision (though actually it did not come from Moses, but from the patriarchs), you circumcise a boy on the Sabbath. ²³Now if a boy can be circumcised on the Sabbath so that the law of Moses may not be broken, why are you angry with me for healing a man's whole body on the Sabbath? ²⁴Stop judging by mere appearances, but instead judge correctly."

Division Over Who Jesus Is

²⁵At that point some of the people of Jerusalem began to ask, "Isn't this the man they are trying to kill? ²⁶Here he is, speaking publicly, and they are not saying a word to him. Have the authorities really concluded that he is the Messiah? ²⁷But we know where this man is from; when the Messiah comes, no one will know where he is from."

²⁸Then Jesus, still teaching in the temple courts, cried out, "Yes, you know me, and you know where I am from. I am not here on my own authority, but he who sent me is true. You do not know him, ²⁹but I know him because I am from him and he sent me."

³⁰At this they tried to seize him, but

no one laid a hand on him, because his hour had not yet come. ³¹Still, many in the crowd believed in him. They said, "When the Messiah comes, will he perform more signs than this man?"

³²The Pharisees heard the crowd whispering such things about him. Then the chief priests and the Pharisees sent temple guards to arrest him.

³³Jesus said, "I am with you for only a short time, and then I am going to the one who sent me. ³⁴You will look for me, but you will not find me; and where I am, you cannot come."

³⁵The Jews said to one another, "Where does this man intend to go that we cannot find him? Will he go where our people live scattered among the Greeks, and teach the Greeks? ³⁶What did he mean when he said, 'You will look for me, but you will not find me,' and 'Where I am, you cannot come'?"

³⁷On the last and greatest day of the festival, Jesus stood and said in a loud voice, "Let anyone who is thirsty come to me and drink. ³⁸Whoever believes in me, as Scripture has said, rivers of living water will flow from within them."ᵃ ³⁹By this he meant the Spirit, whom those who believed in him were later to receive. Up to that time the Spirit had not been given, since Jesus had not yet been glorified.

⁴⁰On hearing his words, some of the people said, "Surely this man is the Prophet."

⁴¹Others said, "He is the Messiah."

Still others asked, "How can the Messiah come from Galilee? ⁴²Does not Scripture say that the Messiah will come from David's descendants and from Bethlehem, the town where David lived?" ⁴³Thus the people were divided because of Jesus. ⁴⁴Some wanted to seize him, but no one laid a hand on him.

Unbelief of the Jewish Leaders

⁴⁵Finally the temple guards went back to the chief priests and the Pharisees, who asked them, "Why didn't you bring him in?"

⁴⁶"No one ever spoke the way this man does," the guards replied.

⁴⁷"You mean he has deceived you also?" the Pharisees retorted. ⁴⁸"Have any of the rulers or of the Pharisees believed in him? ⁴⁹No! But this mob that knows nothing of the law — there is a curse on them."

⁵⁰Nicodemus, who had gone to Jesus earlier and who was one of their own number, asked, ⁵¹"Does our law condemn a man without first hearing him to find out what he has been doing?"

⁵²They replied, "Are you from Galilee, too? Look into it, and you will find that a prophet does not come out of Galilee."

[The earliest manuscripts and many other ancient witnesses do not have John 7:53 — 8:11. A few manuscripts include these verses, wholly or in part, after John 7:36, John 21:25, Luke 21:38 or Luke 24:53.]

8 ⁵³*Then they all went home,* ¹*but Jesus went to the Mount of Olives.*

²*At dawn he appeared again in the temple courts, where all the people gathered around him, and he sat down to teach them.* ³*The teachers of the law and the Pharisees brought in a woman caught in adultery. They made her stand before the group* ⁴*and said to Jesus, "Teacher, this woman was caught in the act of adultery.* ⁵*In the Law Moses commanded us to stone such women. Now what do you say?"* ⁶*They were using this question as a trap, in order to have a basis for accusing him.*

But Jesus bent down and started to write on the ground with his finger. ⁷*When they kept on questioning him, he straightened up and said to them, "Let any one of you who is without sin be the first to throw a stone at her."* ⁸*Again he stooped down and wrote on the ground.*

⁹*At this, those who heard began to go away one at a time, the older ones first, until only Jesus was left, with the woman still standing there.* ¹⁰*Jesus straightened up and asked her, "Woman, where are they? Has no one condemned you?"*

¹¹*"No one, sir," she said.*

"Then neither do I condemn you," Jesus declared. "Go now and leave your life of sin."

Dispute Over Jesus' Testimony

¹²When Jesus spoke again to the people, he said, "I am the light of the world.

ᵃ *37,38 Or me. And let anyone drink* ³⁸*who believes in me." As Scripture has said, "Out of him (or them) will flow rivers of living water."*

Whoever follows me will never walk in darkness, but will have the light of life."

¹³The Pharisees challenged him, "Here you are, appearing as your own witness; your testimony is not valid."

¹⁴Jesus answered, "Even if I testify on my own behalf, my testimony is valid, for I know where I came from and where I am going. But you have no idea where I come from or where I am going. ¹⁵You judge by human standards; I pass judgment on no one. ¹⁶But if I do judge, my decisions are true, because I am not alone. I stand with the Father, who sent me. ¹⁷In your own Law it is written that the testimony of two witnesses is true. ¹⁸I am one who testifies for myself; my other witness is the Father, who sent me."

¹⁹Then they asked him, "Where is your father?"

"You do not know me or my Father," Jesus replied. "If you knew me, you would know my Father also." ²⁰He spoke these words while teaching in the temple courts near the place where the offerings were put. Yet no one seized him, because his hour had not yet come.

Dispute Over Who Jesus Is

²¹Once more Jesus said to them, "I am going away, and you will look for me, and you will die in your sin. Where I go, you cannot come."

²²This made the Jews ask, "Will he kill himself? Is that why he says, 'Where I go, you cannot come'?"

²³But he continued, "You are from below; I am from above. You are of this world; I am not of this world. ²⁴I told you that you would die in your sins; if you do not believe that I am he, you will indeed die in your sins."

²⁵"Who are you?" they asked.

"Just what I have been telling you from the beginning," Jesus replied. ²⁶"I have much to say in judgment of you. But he who sent me is trustworthy, and what I have heard from him I tell the world."

²⁷They did not understand that he was telling them about his Father. ²⁸So Jesus said, "When you have lifted up*ᵃ* the Son of Man, then you will know that I am he and that I do nothing on my own but

speak just what the Father has taught me. ²⁹The one who sent me is with me; he has not left me alone, for I always do what pleases him." ³⁰Even as he spoke, many believed in him.

Dispute Over Whose Children Jesus' Opponents Are

³¹To the Jews who had believed him, Jesus said, "If you hold to my teaching, you are really my disciples. ³²Then you will know the truth, and the truth will set you free."

³³They answered him, "We are Abraham's descendants and have never been slaves of anyone. How can you say that we shall be set free?"

³⁴Jesus replied, "Very truly I tell you, everyone who sins is a slave to sin. ³⁵Now a slave has no permanent place in the family, but a son belongs to it forever. ³⁶So if the Son sets you free, you will be free indeed. ³⁷I know that you are Abraham's descendants. Yet you are looking for a way to kill me, because you have no room for my word. ³⁸I am telling you what I have seen in the Father's presence, and you are doing what you have heard from your father.*ᵇ*"

³⁹"Abraham is our father," they answered.

"If you were Abraham's children," said Jesus, "then you would*ᶜ* do what Abraham did. ⁴⁰As it is, you are looking for a way to kill me, a man who has told you the truth that I heard from God. Abraham did not do such things. ⁴¹You are doing the works of your own father."

"We are not illegitimate children," they protested. "The only Father we have is God himself."

⁴²Jesus said to them, "If God were your Father, you would love me, for I have come here from God. I have not come on my own; God sent me. ⁴³Why is my language not clear to you? Because you are unable to hear what I say. ⁴⁴You belong to your father, the devil, and you want to carry out your father's desires. He was a murderer

---

ᵃ 28 The Greek for *lifted up* also means *exalted.*
ᵇ 38 Or *presence. Therefore do what you have heard from the Father.*   *ᶜ 39* Some early manuscripts *"If you are Abraham's children," said Jesus, "then"*

from the beginning, not holding to the truth, for there is no truth in him. When he lies, he speaks his native language, for he is a liar and the father of lies. ⁴⁵Yet because I tell the truth, you do not believe me! ⁴⁶Can any of you prove me guilty of sin? If I am telling the truth, why don't you believe me? ⁴⁷Whoever belongs to God hears what God says. The reason you do not hear is that you do not belong to God."

Jesus' Claims About Himself

⁴⁸The Jews answered him, "Aren't we right in saying that you are a Samaritan and demon-possessed?"

⁴⁹"I am not possessed by a demon," said Jesus, "but I honor my Father and you dishonor me. ⁵⁰I am not seeking glory for myself; but there is one who seeks it, and he is the judge. ⁵¹Very truly I tell you, whoever obeys my word will never see death."

⁵²At this they exclaimed, "Now we know that you are demon-possessed! Abraham died and so did the prophets, yet you say that whoever obeys my word will never taste death. ⁵³Are you greater than our father Abraham? He died, and so did the prophets. Who do you think you are?"

⁵⁴Jesus replied, "If I glorify myself, my glory means nothing. My Father, whom you claim as your God, is the one who glorifies me. ⁵⁵Though you do not know him, I know him. If I said I did not, I would be a liar like you, but I do know him and obey his word. ⁵⁶Your father Abraham rejoiced at the thought of seeing my day; he saw it and was glad."

⁵⁷"You are not yet fifty years old," they said to him, "and you have seen Abraham!"

⁵⁸"Very truly I tell you," Jesus answered, "before Abraham was born, I am!" ⁵⁹At this, they picked up stones to stone him, but Jesus hid himself, slipping away from the temple grounds.

Jesus Heals a Man Born Blind

9 As he went along, he saw a man blind from birth. ²His disciples asked him, "Rabbi, who sinned, this man or his parents, that he was born blind?"

³"Neither this man nor his parents sinned," said Jesus, "but this happened so that the works of God might be displayed in him. ⁴As long as it is day, we must do the works of him who sent me. Night is coming, when no one can work. ⁵While I am in the world, I am the light of the world."

⁶After saying this, he spit on the ground, made some mud with the saliva, and put it on the man's eyes. ⁷"Go," he told him, "wash in the Pool of Siloam" (this word means "Sent"). So the man went and washed, and came home seeing.

⁸His neighbors and those who had formerly seen him begging asked, "Isn't this

POOL OF SILOAM

(JOHN 9:7)

This was a pool of natural water that came from a subterranean channel in the Gihon River, east of a hill called Ophel. The pool was inside the walls surrounding the city of Jerusalem, and it was about 22 yards (20 meters) long and 4 to 6 yards (4–5 meters) wide. The channel that carried the water from the hill to the pool was built by King Hezekiah many, many years before.

the same man who used to sit and beg?" ⁹Some claimed that he was.

Others said, "No, he only looks like him."

But he himself insisted, "I am the man."

¹⁰"How then were your eyes opened?" they asked.

¹¹He replied, "The man they call Jesus made some mud and put it on my eyes. He told me to go to Siloam and wash. So I went and washed, and then I could see." ¹²"Where is this man?" they asked him.

"I don't know," he said.

The Pharisees Investigate the Healing

¹³They brought to the Pharisees the man who had been blind. ¹⁴Now the day on which Jesus had made the mud and opened the man's eyes was a Sabbath. ¹⁵Therefore the Pharisees also asked him how he had received his sight. "He put mud on my eyes," the man replied, "and I washed, and now I see."

¹⁶Some of the Pharisees said, "This man is not from God, for he does not keep the Sabbath."

But others asked, "How can a sinner perform such signs?" So they were divided.

¹⁷Then they turned again to the blind man, "What have you to say about him? It was your eyes he opened."

The man replied, "He is a prophet."

¹⁸They still did not believe that he had been blind and had received his sight until they sent for the man's parents. ¹⁹"Is this your son?" they asked. "Is this the one you say was born blind? How is it that now he can see?"

²⁰"We know he is our son," the parents answered, "and we know he was born blind. ²¹But how he can see now, or who opened his eyes, we don't know. Ask him. He is of age; he will speak for himself." ²²His parents said this because they were afraid of the Jewish leaders, who already had decided that anyone who acknowledged that Jesus was the Messiah would be put out of the synagogue. ²³That was why his parents said, "He is of age; ask him."

²⁴A second time they summoned the man who had been blind. "Give glory to God by telling the truth," they said. "We know this man is a sinner."

²⁵He replied, "Whether he is a sinner or not, I don't know. One thing I do know. I was blind but now I see!"

²⁶Then they asked him, "What did he do to you? How did he open your eyes?"

²⁷He answered, "I have told you already and you did not listen. Why do you want to hear it again? Do you want to become his disciples too?"

²⁸Then they hurled insults at him and said, "You are this fellow's disciple! We are disciples of Moses! ²⁹We know that God spoke to Moses, but as for this fellow, we don't even know where he comes from."

³⁰The man answered, "Now that is remarkable! You don't know where he comes from, yet he opened my eyes. ³¹We know that God does not listen to sinners. He listens to the godly person who does his will. ³²Nobody has ever heard of opening the eyes of a man born blind. ³³If this man were not from God, he could do nothing."

³⁴To this they replied, "You were steeped in sin at birth; how dare you lecture us!" And they threw him out.

Spiritual Blindness

³⁵Jesus heard that they had thrown him out, and when he found him, he said, "Do you believe in the Son of Man?"

³⁶"Who is he, sir?" the man asked. "Tell me so that I may believe in him."

³⁷Jesus said, "You have now seen him; in fact, he is the one speaking with you."

³⁸Then the man said, "Lord, I believe," and he worshiped him.

³⁹Jesus said,ᵃ "For judgment I have come into this world, so that the blind will see and those who see will become blind."

⁴⁰Some Pharisees who were with him heard him say this and asked, "What? Are we blind too?"

⁴¹Jesus said, "If you were blind, you would not be guilty of sin; but now that you claim you can see, your guilt remains.

ᵃ 38,39 Some early manuscripts do not have *Then the man said . . . ³⁹Jesus said.*

BREAKTHROUGH!

Why did the Jews tell the blind man he was "steeped in sin at birth"?
(JOHN 9:34)
It was a way to insult the blind man Jesus had healed and say he didn't have any right to do what he had done. Back then, some people thought if a person was born with some disease or physical limitation, it was because the parents had sinned. Jesus taught that's not so.

The Good Shepherd and His Sheep

10 "Very truly I tell you Pharisees, anyone who does not enter the sheep pen by the gate, but climbs in by some other way, is a thief and a robber. ²The one who enters by the gate is the shepherd of the sheep. ³The gatekeeper opens the gate for him, and the sheep listen to his voice. He calls his own sheep by name and leads them out. ⁴When he has brought out all his own, he goes on ahead of them, and his sheep follow him because they know his voice. ⁵But they will never follow a stranger; in fact, they will run away from him because they do not recognize a stranger's voice." ⁶Jesus used this figure of speech, but the Pharisees did not understand what he was telling them.

⁷Therefore Jesus said again, "Very truly I tell you, I am the gate for the sheep. ⁸All who have come before me are thieves and robbers, but the sheep have not listened to them. ⁹I am the gate; whoever enters through me will be saved.ᵃ They will come in and go out, and find pasture. ¹⁰The thief comes only to steal and kill and destroy; I have come that they may have life, and have it to the full.

¹¹"I am the good shepherd. The good shepherd lays down his life for the sheep. ¹²The hired hand is not the shepherd and does not own the sheep. So when he sees the wolf coming, he abandons the sheep and runs away. Then the wolf attacks the flock and scatters it. ¹³The man

---

ᵃ 9 Or *kept safe*

BREAKTHROUGH!

The gate for the sheep
(JOHN 10:7)
When the author of this gospel wanted to talk about Jesus, many times he used examples of people, plants or everyday objects so the people could understand easily. Here, he uses the example of a gate. He means that a gate is made to walk through. So for people who believe in Jesus, it's like walking through a gate to enter a new life — eternal life — and receive forgiveness for sins.

runs away because he is a hired hand and cares nothing for the sheep.

¹⁴"I am the good shepherd; I know my sheep and my sheep know me— ¹⁵just as the Father knows me and I know the Father—and I lay down my life for the sheep. ¹⁶I have other sheep that are not of this sheep pen. I must bring them also. They too will listen to my voice, and there shall be one flock and one shepherd. ¹⁷The reason my Father loves me is that I lay down my life—only to take it up again. ¹⁸No one takes it from me, but I lay it down of my own accord. I have authority to lay it down and authority to take it up again. This command I received from my Father."

¹⁹The Jews who heard these words were again divided. ²⁰Many of them said, "He is demon-possessed and raving mad. Why listen to him?"

²¹But others said, "These are not the sayings of a man possessed by a demon. Can a demon open the eyes of the blind?"

Further Conflict Over Jesus' Claims

²²Then came the Festival of Dedication*a* at Jerusalem. It was winter, ²³and Jesus was in the temple courts walking in Solomon's Colonnade. ²⁴The Jews who were there gathered around him, saying, "How long will you keep us in suspense? If you are the Messiah, tell us plainly."

²⁵Jesus answered, "I did tell you, but you do not believe. The works I do in my Father's name testify about me, ²⁶but you do not believe because you are not my sheep. ²⁷My sheep listen to my voice; I know them, and they follow me. ²⁸I give them eternal life, and they shall never perish; no one will snatch them out of my hand. ²⁹My Father, who has given them to me, is greater than all*b*; no one can snatch them out of my Father's hand. ³⁰I and the Father are one."

³¹Again his Jewish opponents picked up stones to stone him, ³²but Jesus said to them, "I have shown you many good works from the Father. For which of these do you stone me?"

³³"We are not stoning you for any good

BREAKTHROUGH!

Solomon's Colonnade

(JOHN 10:23)

This was one of the gates in the wall around the temple in Jerusalem. This gate was on the east side. The sun rose from that side, and they were able to see the Kidron Valley. The columns that held up this big gate were built of very white stone. Each column was 11 yards (10 m) long and 3 yards (3 m) wide. It was the oldest gate of all the gates that didn't get destroyed when the newest temple was built. This was the place people preferred for their public meetings.

work," they replied, "but for blasphemy, because you, a mere man, claim to be God."

³⁴Jesus answered them, "Is it not written in your Law, 'I have said you are "gods"'*c*? ³⁵If he called them 'gods,' to whom the word of God came—and Scripture cannot be set aside— ³⁶what about the one whom the Father set apart as his very own and sent into the world? Why then do you accuse me of blasphemy because I said, 'I am God's Son'? ³⁷Do not believe me unless I do the works of my Father. ³⁸But if I do them, even though

---

a 22 That is, Hanukkah   *b 29* Many early manuscripts *What my Father has given me is greater than all*
c 34 Psalm 82:6

you do not believe me, believe the works, that you may know and understand that the Father is in me, and I in the Father." ³⁹Again they tried to seize him, but he escaped their grasp.

⁴⁰Then Jesus went back across the Jordan to the place where John had been baptizing in the early days. There he stayed, ⁴¹and many people came to him. They said, "Though John never performed a sign, all that John said about this man was true." ⁴²And in that place many believed in Jesus.

The Death of Lazarus

11 Now a man named Lazarus was sick. He was from Bethany, the village of Mary and her sister Martha. ²(This Mary, whose brother Lazarus now lay sick, was the same one who poured perfume on the Lord and wiped his feet with her hair.) ³So the sisters sent word to Jesus, "Lord, the one you love is sick."

⁴When he heard this, Jesus said, "This sickness will not end in death. No, it is for God's glory so that God's Son may be glorified through it." ⁵Now Jesus loved Martha and her sister and Lazarus. ⁶So when he heard that Lazarus was sick, he stayed where he was two more days, ⁷and then he said to his disciples, "Let us go back to Judea."

⁸"But Rabbi," they said, "a short while ago the Jews there tried to stone you, and yet you are going back?"

⁹Jesus answered, "Are there not twelve hours of daylight? Anyone who walks in the daytime will not stumble, for they see by this world's light. ¹⁰It is when a person walks at night that they stumble, for they have no light."

¹¹After he had said this, he went on to tell them, "Our friend Lazarus has fallen asleep; but I am going there to wake him up."

¹²His disciples replied, "Lord, if he sleeps, he will get better." ¹³Jesus had been speaking of his death, but his disciples thought he meant natural sleep.

¹⁴So then he told them plainly, "Lazarus is dead, ¹⁵and for your sake I am glad I was not there, so that you may believe. But let us go to him."

¹⁶Then Thomas (also known as Didymus[a]) said to the rest of the disciples, "Let us also go, that we may die with him."

Jesus Comforts the Sisters of Lazarus

¹⁷On his arrival, Jesus found that Lazarus had already been in the tomb for four days. ¹⁸Now Bethany was less than two miles[b] from Jerusalem, ¹⁹and many Jews had come to Martha and Mary to comfort them in the loss of their brother. ²⁰When Martha heard that Jesus was coming, she went out to meet him, but Mary stayed at home.

²¹"Lord," Martha said to Jesus, "if you had been here, my brother would not have died. ²²But I know that even now God will give you whatever you ask."

²³Jesus said to her, "Your brother will rise again."

²⁴Martha answered, "I know he will rise again in the resurrection at the last day."

²⁵Jesus said to her, "I am the resurrection and the life. The one who believes in me will live, even though they die; ²⁶and whoever lives by believing in me will never die. Do you believe this?"

²⁷"Yes, Lord," she replied, "I believe that you are the Messiah, the Son of God, who is to come into the world."

²⁸After she had said this, she went back and called her sister Mary aside. "The Teacher is here," she said, "and is asking for you." ²⁹When Mary heard this, she got up quickly and went to him. ³⁰Now Jesus had not yet entered the village, but was still at the place where Martha had met him. ³¹When the Jews who had been with Mary in the house, comforting her, noticed how quickly she got up and went out, they followed her, supposing she was going to the tomb to mourn there.

³²When Mary reached the place where Jesus was and saw him, she fell at his feet and said, "Lord, if you had been here, my brother would not have died."

³³When Jesus saw her weeping, and the Jews who had come along with her

---

a 16 Thomas (Aramaic) and Didymus (Greek) both mean twin.   *b 18* Or about 3 kilometers also weeping, he was deeply moved in spirit and troubled. ³⁴"Where have you laid him?" he asked.

"Come and see, Lord," they replied. ³⁵Jesus wept.

THE
WITNESSES

✓ **LAZARUS, MARY AND MARTHA**
(JOHN 11:1)
These sisters and their brother lived in a village called Bethany very near Jerusalem. All three were close friends of Jesus. One day, Lazarus got sick and died. Four days after they had placed his body in a tomb, Jesus arrived and brought him back to life. Lazarus was also called Eleazar, which means "God helped."

✓ **THOMAS, ALSO KNOWN AS DIDYMUS** (JOHN 11:16)
Didymus means "twin." He was one of Jesus' twelve closest friends that went everywhere with him and learned from him.

³⁶Then the Jews said, "See how he loved him!"

³⁷But some of them said, "Could not he who opened the eyes of the blind man have kept this man from dying?"

Jesus Raises Lazarus From the Dead

³⁸Jesus, once more deeply moved, came to the tomb. It was a cave with a stone laid across the entrance. ³⁹"Take away the stone," he said.

"But, Lord," said Martha, the sister of the dead man, "by this time there is a bad odor, for he has been there four days."

⁴⁰Then Jesus said, "Did I not tell you that if you believe, you will see the glory of God?"

⁴¹So they took away the stone. Then Jesus looked up and said, "Father, I thank you that you have heard me. ⁴²I knew that you always hear me, but I said this for the benefit of the people standing here, that they may believe that you sent me."

⁴³When he had said this, Jesus called in a loud voice, "Lazarus, come out!" ⁴⁴The dead man came out, his hands and feet wrapped with strips of linen, and a cloth around his face.

Jesus said to them, "Take off the grave clothes and let him go."

The Plot to Kill Jesus

⁴⁵Therefore many of the Jews who had come to visit Mary, and had seen what Jesus did, believed in him. ⁴⁶But some of them went to the Pharisees and told them what Jesus had done. ⁴⁷Then the chief priests and the Pharisees called a meeting of the Sanhedrin.

"What are we accomplishing?" they asked. "Here is this man performing many signs. ⁴⁸If we let him go on like this, everyone will believe in him, and then the Romans will come and take away both our temple and our nation."

⁴⁹Then one of them, named Caiaphas, who was high priest that year, spoke up, "You know nothing at all! ⁵⁰You do not realize that it is better for you that one man die for the people than that the whole nation perish."

⁵¹He did not say this on his own, but

Jesus was should report it so that they might arrest him.

Jesus Anointed at Bethany

12 Six days before the Passover, Jesus came to Bethany, where Lazarus lived, whom Jesus had raised from the dead. ²Here a dinner was given in Jesus' honor. Martha served, while Lazarus was among those reclining at the table with him. ³Then Mary took about a pint[a] of pure nard, an expensive perfume; she poured it on Jesus' feet and wiped his feet with her hair. And the house was filled with the fragrance of the perfume.

⁴But one of his disciples, Judas Iscariot, who was later to betray him, objected, ⁵"Why wasn't this perfume sold and the money given to the poor? It was worth a year's wages.[b] ⁶He did not say this because he cared about the poor but because he was a thief; as keeper of the money bag, he used to help himself to what was put into it.

⁷"Leave her alone," Jesus replied. "It was intended that she should save this perfume for the day of my burial. ⁸You will always have the poor among you,[c] but you will not always have me."

⁹Meanwhile a large crowd of Jews found out that Jesus was there and came, not only because of him but also to see Lazarus, whom he had raised from the dead. ¹⁰So the chief priests made plans to kill Lazarus as well, ¹¹for on account of him many of the Jews were going over to Jesus and believing in him.

Jesus Comes to Jerusalem as King

¹²The next day the great crowd that had come for the festival heard that Jesus was on his way to Jerusalem. ¹³They took palm branches and went out to meet him, shouting,

"Hosanna![d]"

"Blessed is he who comes in the name of the Lord!"[e]

"Blessed is the king of Israel!"

as high priest that year he prophesied that Jesus would die for the Jewish nation, ⁵²and not only for that nation but also for the scattered children of God, to bring them together and make them one. ⁵³So from that day on they plotted to take his life.

⁵⁴Therefore Jesus no longer moved about publicly among the people of Judea. Instead he withdrew to a region near the wilderness, to a village called Ephraim, where he stayed with his disciples.

⁵⁵When it was almost time for the Jewish Passover, many went up from the country to Jerusalem for their ceremonial cleansing before the Passover. ⁵⁶They kept looking for Jesus, and as they stood in the temple courts they asked one another, "What do you think? Isn't he coming to the festival at all?" ⁵⁷But the chief priests and the Pharisees had given orders that anyone who found out where

---

a 3 Or about 0.5 liter   *b 5* Greek *three hundred denarii*
c 8 See Deut. 15:11.   *d 13* A Hebrew expression
meaning "Save!" which became an exclamation of praise
e 13 Psalm 118:25,26

¹⁴Jesus found a young donkey and sat on it, as it is written:

¹⁵ "Do not be afraid, Daughter Zion;
　see, your king is coming,
　seated on a donkey's colt."ᵃ

¹⁶At first his disciples did not understand all this. Only after Jesus was glorified did they realize that these things had been written about him and that these things had been done to him. ¹⁷Now the crowd that was with him when he called Lazarus from the tomb and raised him from the dead continued to spread the word. ¹⁸Many people, because they had heard that he had performed this sign, went out to meet him. ¹⁹So the Pharisees said to one another, "See, this is getting us nowhere. Look how the whole world has gone after him!"

Jesus Predicts His Death

²⁰Now there were some Greeks among those who went up to worship at the festival. ²¹They came to Philip, who was from Bethsaida in Galilee, with a request. "Sir," they said, "we would like to see Jesus." ²²Philip went to tell Andrew; Andrew and Philip in turn told Jesus.

²³Jesus replied, "The hour has come for the Son of Man to be glorified. ²⁴Very truly I tell you, unless a kernel of wheat falls to the ground and dies, it remains only a single seed. But if it dies, it produces many seeds. ²⁵Anyone who loves their life will lose it, while anyone who hates their life in this world will keep it for eternal life. ²⁶Whoever serves me must follow me; and where I am, my servant also will be. My Father will honor the one who serves me. ²⁷"Now my soul is troubled, and what shall I say? 'Father, save me from this hour'? No, it was for this very reason I came to this hour. ²⁸Father, glorify your name!"

Then a voice came from heaven, "I have glorified it, and will glorify it again." ²⁹The crowd that was there and heard it said it had thundered; others said an angel had spoken to him.

³⁰Jesus said, "This voice was for your benefit, not mine. ³¹Now is the time for judgment on this world; now the prince of this world will be driven out. ³²And I, when I am lifted upᵇ from the earth, will draw all people to myself." ³³He said this to show the kind of death he was going to die.

³⁴The crowd spoke up, "We have heard from the Law that the Messiah will remain forever, so how can you say, 'The Son of Man must be lifted up'? Who is this 'Son of Man'?"

³⁵Then Jesus told them, "You are going to have the light just a little while longer. Walk while you have the light, before darkness overtakes you. Whoever walks in the dark does not know where they are going. ³⁶Believe in the light while you have the light, so that you may become children of light." When he had finished speaking, Jesus left and hid himself from them.

ᵃ 15 Zech. 9:9　　ᵇ 32 The Greek for *lifted up* also means *exalted.*

"The prince of this world"

(JOHN 12:31)

This is a way to talk about Satan. Many times, when John talks about the "world," he means the people who don't believe in Jesus. That's because for those people who don't believe in God, it's like they're managed by Satan. He tells them they have to do something bad, and the people believe him.

Belief and Unbelief Among the Jews

37 Even after Jesus had performed so many signs in their presence, they still would not believe in him. 38 This was to fulfill the word of Isaiah the prophet:

"Lord, who has believed our message
and to whom has the arm of the
Lord been revealed?" *a*

39 For this reason they could not believe, because, as Isaiah says elsewhere:

40 "He has blinded their eyes
and hardened their hearts,
so they can neither see with their
eyes,
nor understand with their hearts,
nor turn—and I would heal them." *b*

41 Isaiah said this because he saw Jesus' glory and spoke about him.

42 Yet at the same time many even among the leaders believed in him. But because of the Pharisees they would not openly acknowledge their faith for fear they would be put out of the synagogue; 43 for they loved human praise more than praise from God.

44 Then Jesus cried out, "Whoever believes in me does not believe in me only, but in the one who sent me. 45 The one who looks at me is seeing the one who sent me. 46 I have come into the world as a light, so that no one who believes in me should stay in darkness.

47 "If anyone hears my words but does not keep them, I do not judge that person. For I did not come to judge the world, but to save the world. 48 There is a judge for the one who rejects me and does not accept my words; the very words I have spoken will condemn them at the last day. 49 For I did not speak on my own, but the Father who sent me commanded me to say all that I have spoken. 50 I know that his command leads to eternal life. So whatever I say is just what the Father has told me to say."

Jesus Washes His Disciples' Feet

13 It was just before the Passover Festival. Jesus knew that the hour had come for him to leave this world and go to the Father. Having loved his own who were in the world, he loved them to the end.

2 The evening meal was in progress, and the devil had already prompted Judas, the son of Simon Iscariot, to betray Jesus. 3 Jesus knew that the Father had put all things under his power, and that he had come from God and was returning to God; 4 so he got up from the meal, took off his outer clothing, and wrapped a towel around his waist. 5 After that, he poured water into a basin and began to wash his disciples' feet, drying them with the towel that was wrapped around him.

6 He came to Simon Peter, who said to him, "Lord, are you going to wash my feet?"

7 Jesus replied, "You do not realize now what I am doing, but later you will understand."

8 "No," said Peter, "you shall never wash my feet."

Jesus answered, "Unless I wash you, you have no part with me."

9 "Then, Lord," Simon Peter replied, "not just my feet but my hands and my head as well!"

10 Jesus answered, "Those who have had a bath need only to wash their feet; their whole body is clean. And you are clean, though not every one of you." 11 For he knew who was going to betray him, and that was why he said not every one was clean.

12 When he had finished washing their feet, he put on his clothes and returned to his place. "Do you understand what I have done for you?" he asked them. 13 "You call me 'Teacher' and 'Lord,' and rightly so, for that is what I am. 14 Now that I, your Lord and Teacher, have washed your feet, you also should wash one another's feet. 15 I have set you an example that you should do as I have done for you. 16 Very truly I tell you, no servant is greater than his master, nor is a messenger greater than the one who sent him. 17 Now that you know these things, you will be blessed if you do them.

a 38 Isaiah 53:1   *b* 40 Isaiah 6:10

Jesus Predicts His Betrayal

¹⁸"I am not referring to all of you; I know those I have chosen. But this is to fulfill this passage of Scripture: 'He who shared my bread has turned*ᵃ* against me.'*ᵇ*

¹⁹"I am telling you now before it happens, so that when it does happen you will believe that I am who I am. ²⁰Very truly I tell you, whoever accepts anyone I send accepts me; and whoever accepts me accepts the one who sent me."

²¹After he had said this, Jesus was troubled in spirit and testified, "Very truly I tell you, one of you is going to betray me."

²²His disciples stared at one another, at a loss to know which of them he meant. ²³One of them, the disciple whom Jesus loved, was reclining next to him. ²⁴Simon Peter motioned to this disciple and said, "Ask him which one he means."

²⁵Leaning back against Jesus, he asked him, "Lord, who is it?"

BREAKTHROUGH!

"I am"

(JOHN 13:19)

In the Old Testament, God uses the phrase "I am" to speak to Moses. Later, Jesus used those same words to speak to the people and reveal that he is God. That's what John's gospel says.

²⁶Jesus answered, "It is the one to whom I will give this piece of bread when I have dipped it in the dish." Then, dipping the piece of bread, he gave it to Judas, the son of Simon Iscariot. ²⁷As soon as Judas took the bread, Satan entered into him.

So Jesus told him, "What you are about to do, do quickly." ²⁸But no one at the meal understood why Jesus said this to him. ²⁹Since Judas had charge of the money, some thought Jesus was telling him to buy what was needed for the festival, or to give something to the poor. ³⁰As soon as Judas had taken the bread, he went out. And it was night.

Jesus Predicts Peter's Denial

³¹When he was gone, Jesus said, "Now the Son of Man is glorified and God is glorified in him. ³²If God is glorified in him,*ᶜ* God will glorify the Son in himself, and will glorify him at once.

³³"My children, I will be with you only a little longer. You will look for me, and just as I told the Jews, so I tell you now: Where I am going, you cannot come.

³⁴"A new command I give you: Love one another. As I have loved you, so you must love one another. ³⁵By this everyone will know that you are my disciples, if you love one another."

³⁶Simon Peter asked him, "Lord, where are you going?"

Jesus replied, "Where I am going, you cannot follow now, but you will follow later."

³⁷Peter asked, "Lord, why can't I follow you now? I will lay down my life for you."

³⁸Then Jesus answered, "Will you really lay down your life for me? Very truly I tell you, before the rooster crows, you will disown me three times!

Jesus Comforts His Disciples

14 "Do not let your hearts be troubled. You believe in God*ᵈ*; believe also in me. ²My Father's house has many rooms; if that were not so, would I have told you that I am going there to prepare a place

---

ᵃ 18 Greek *has lifted up his heel*   *ᵇ* 18 Psalm 41:9
ᶜ 32 Many early manuscripts do not have *If God is glorified in him.*   *ᵈ* 1 Or *Believe in God*

for you? ³And if I go and prepare a place for you, I will come back and take you to be with me that you also may be where I am. ⁴You know the way to the place where I am going."

Jesus the Way to the Father

⁵Thomas said to him, "Lord, we don't know where you are going, so how can we know the way?"

⁶Jesus answered, "I am the way and the truth and the life. No one comes to the Father except through me. ⁷If you really know me, you will know*a* my Father as well. From now on, you do know him and have seen him."

⁸Philip said, "Lord, show us the Father and that will be enough for us."

⁹Jesus answered: "Don't you know me, Philip, even after I have been among you such a long time? Anyone who has seen me has seen the Father. How can you say, 'Show us the Father'? ¹⁰Don't you believe that I am in the Father, and that the Father is in me? The words I say to you I do not speak on my own authority. Rather, it is the Father, living in me, who is doing his work. ¹¹Believe me when I say that I am in the Father and the Father is in me; or at least believe on the evidence of the works themselves. ¹²Very truly I tell you, whoever believes in me will do the works I have been doing, and they will do even greater things than these, because I am going to the Father. ¹³And I will do whatever you ask in my name, so that the Father may be glorified in the Son. ¹⁴You may ask me for anything in my name, and I will do it.

Jesus Promises the Holy Spirit

¹⁵"If you love me, keep my commands. ¹⁶And I will ask the Father, and he will give you another advocate to help you and be with you forever— ¹⁷the Spirit of truth. The world cannot accept him, because it neither sees him nor knows him. But you know him, for he lives with you and will be*b* in you. ¹⁸I will not leave you as orphans; I will come to you. ¹⁹Before long, the world will not see me anymore, but you will see me. Because I live, you also will live. ²⁰On that day you will realize that

I am in my Father, and you are in me, and I am in you. ²¹Whoever has my commands and keeps them is the one who loves me. The one who loves me will be loved by my Father, and I too will love them and show myself to them."

²²Then Judas (not Judas Iscariot) said, "But, Lord, why do you intend to show yourself to us and not to the world?"

²³Jesus replied, "Anyone who loves me will obey my teaching. My Father will love them, and we will come to them and make

---

a 7 Some manuscripts *If you really knew me, you would know*   *b* 17 Some early manuscripts *and is*

THE
WITNESSES

✓ JUDAS, NOT JUDAS ISCARIOT
(JOHN 14:22)

Judas was a very common name in that time. This Judas was Jesus' friend. In another place in the Bible, he's called Thaddaeus. It seems he had a brother whose name was James. This Judas isn't the Judas who turned in Jesus.

our home with them. ²⁴Anyone who does not love me will not obey my teaching. These words you hear are not my own; they belong to the Father who sent me.

²⁵"All this I have spoken while still with you. ²⁶But the Advocate, the Holy Spirit, whom the Father will send in my name, will teach you all things and will remind you of everything I have said to you. ²⁷Peace I leave with you; my peace I give you. I do not give to you as the world gives. Do not let your hearts be troubled and do not be afraid.

²⁸"You heard me say, 'I am going away and I am coming back to you.' If you loved me, you would be glad that I am going to the Father, for the Father is greater than I. ²⁹I have told you now before it happens, so that when it does happen you will believe. ³⁰I will not say much more to you, for the prince of this world is coming. He has no hold over me, ³¹but he comes so that the world may learn that I love the Father and do exactly what my Father has commanded me.

"Come now; let us leave.

The Vine and the Branches

15 "I am the true vine, and my Father is the gardener. ²He cuts off every branch in me that bears no fruit, while every branch that does bear fruit he prunes[a] so that it will be even more fruitful. ³You are already clean because of the word I have spoken to you. ⁴Remain in me, as I also remain in you. No branch can bear fruit by itself; it must remain in the vine. Neither can you bear fruit unless you remain in me.

⁵"I am the vine; you are the branches. If you remain in me and I in you, you will bear much fruit; apart from me you can do nothing. ⁶If you do not remain in me, you are like a branch that is thrown away and withers; such branches are picked up, thrown into the fire and burned. ⁷If you remain in me and my words remain in you, ask whatever you wish, and it will be done for you. ⁸This is to my Father's glory, that you bear much fruit, showing yourselves to be my disciples.

⁹"As the Father has loved me, so have I loved you. Now remain in my love. ¹⁰If

you keep my commands, you will remain in my love, just as I have kept my Father's commands and remain in his love. ¹¹I have told you this so that my joy may be in you and that your joy may be complete. ¹²My command is this: Love each other as I have loved you. ¹³Greater love has no one than this: to lay down one's life for one's friends. ¹⁴You are my friends if you do what I command. ¹⁵I no longer call you servants, because a servant does not know his master's business. Instead, I have called you friends, for everything that I learned from my Father I have made known to you. ¹⁶You did not choose me, but I chose you and appointed you so that you might go and bear fruit—fruit that will last—and so that whatever you ask in my name the Father will give you. ¹⁷This is my command: Love each other.

The World Hates the Disciples

¹⁸"If the world hates you, keep in mind that it hated me first. ¹⁹If you belonged to the world, it would love you as its own. As it is, you do not belong to the world, but I have chosen you out of the world. That is why the world hates you. ²⁰Remember what I told you: 'A servant is not greater than his master.'[b] If they persecuted me, they will persecute you also. If they obeyed my teaching, they will obey yours also. ²¹They will treat you this way because of my name, for they do not know the one who sent me. ²²If I had not come and spoken to them, they would not be guilty of sin; but now they have no excuse for their sin. ²³Whoever hates me hates my Father as well. ²⁴If I had not done among them the works no one else did, they would not be guilty of sin. As it is, they have seen, and yet they have hated both me and my Father. ²⁵But this is to fulfill what is written in their Law: 'They hated me without reason.'[c]

The Work of the Holy Spirit

²⁶"When the Advocate comes, whom I will send to you from the Father—the Spirit of truth who goes out from the Father—

---

[a] 2 The Greek for *he prunes* also means *he cleans.*
[b] 20 John 13:16   [c] 25 Psalms 35:19; 69:4

he will testify about me. ²⁷And you also must testify, for you have been with me from the beginning.

16 "All this I have told you so that you will not fall away. ²They will put you out of the synagogue; in fact, the time is coming when anyone who kills you will think they are offering a service to God. ³They will do such things because they have not known the Father or me. ⁴I have told you this, so that when their time comes you will remember that I warned you about them. I did not tell you this from the beginning because I was with you, ⁵but now I am going to him who sent me. None of you asks me, 'Where are you going?' ⁶Rather, you are filled with grief because I have said these things. ⁷But very truly I tell you, it is for your good that I am going away. Unless I go away, the Advocate will not come to you; but if I go, I will send him to you. ⁸When he comes, he will prove the world to be in the wrong about sin and righteousness and judgment: ⁹about sin, because people do not believe in me; ¹⁰about righteousness, because I am going to the Father, where you can see me no longer; ¹¹and about judgment, because the prince of this world now stands condemned.

¹²"I have much more to say to you, more than you can now bear. ¹³But when he, the Spirit of truth, comes, he will guide you into all the truth. He will not speak on his own; he will speak only what he hears, and he will tell you what is yet to come. ¹⁴He will glorify me because it is from me that he will receive what he will make known to you. ¹⁵All that belongs to the Father is mine. That is why I said the Spirit will receive from me what he will make known to you."

The Disciples' Grief Will Turn to Joy

¹⁶Jesus went on to say, "In a little while you will see me no more, and then after a little while you will see me."

¹⁷At this, some of his disciples said to one another, "What does he mean by saying, 'In a little while you will see me no more, and then after a little while you will see me,' and 'Because I am going to the Father'?" ¹⁸They kept asking, "What does

he mean by 'a little while'? We don't understand what he is saying."

¹⁹Jesus saw that they wanted to ask him about this, so he said to them, "Are you asking one another what I meant when I said, 'In a little while you will see me no more, and then after a little while you will see me'? ²⁰Very truly I tell you, you will weep and mourn while the world rejoices. You will grieve, but your grief will turn to joy. ²¹A woman giving birth to a child has pain because her time has come; but when her baby is born she forgets the anguish because of her joy that a child is born into the world. ²²So with you: Now is your time of grief, but I will see you again and you will rejoice, and no one will take away your joy. ²³In that day you will no longer ask me anything. Very truly I tell you, my Father will give you whatever you ask in my name. ²⁴Until now you have not asked for anything in my name. Ask and you will receive, and your joy will be complete.

²⁵"Though I have been speaking figuratively, a time is coming when I will no longer use this kind of language but will tell you plainly about my Father. ²⁶In that day you will ask in my name. I am not saying that I will ask the Father on your behalf. ²⁷No, the Father himself loves you because you have loved me and have believed that I came from God. ²⁸I came from the Father and entered the world; now I am leaving the world and going back to the Father."

²⁹Then Jesus' disciples said, "Now you are speaking clearly and without figures of speech. ³⁰Now we can see that you know all things and that you do not even need to have anyone ask you questions. This makes us believe that you came from God."

³¹"Do you now believe?" Jesus replied. ³²"A time is coming and in fact has come when you will be scattered, each to your own home. You will leave me all alone. Yet I am not alone, for my Father is with me.

³³"I have told you these things, so that in me you may have peace. In this world you will have trouble. But take heart! I have overcome the world."

Jesus Prays to Be Glorified

17 After Jesus said this, he looked toward heaven and prayed:

"Father, the hour has come. Glorify your Son, that your Son may glorify you. [2]For you granted him authority over all people that he might give eternal life to all those you have given him. [3]Now this is eternal life: that they know you, the only true God, and Jesus Christ, whom you have sent. [4]I have brought you glory on earth by finishing the work you gave me to do. [5]And now, Father, glorify me in your presence with the glory I had with you before the world began.

Jesus Prays for His Disciples

[6]"I have revealed you[a] to those whom you gave me out of the world. They were yours; you gave them to me and they have obeyed your word. [7]Now they know that everything you have given me comes from you. [8]For I gave them the words you gave me and they accepted them. They knew with certainty that I came from you, and they believed that you sent me. [9]I pray for them. I am not praying for the world, but for those you have given me, for they are yours. [10]All I have is yours, and all you have is mine. And glory has come to me through them. [11]I will remain in the world no longer, but they are still in the world, and I am coming to you. Holy Father, protect them by the power of[b] your name, the name you gave me, so that they may be one as we are one. [12]While I was with them, I protected them and kept them safe by[c] that name you gave me. None has been lost except the one doomed to destruction so that Scripture would be fulfilled. [13]"I am coming to you now, but I say these things while I am still in the world, so that they may have the full measure of my joy within them. [14]I have given them your word and the world has hated them, for they are not of the world any more than I am of the world. [15]My prayer is not that you take them out of the world but that you protect them from the evil one. [16]They are not of the world, even as I am not of it. [17]Sanctify them by[d] the truth; your word is truth. [18]As you sent me into the world, I have sent them into the world. [19]For them I sanctify myself, that they too may be truly sanctified.

Jesus Prays for All Believers

[20]"My prayer is not for them alone. I pray also for those who will believe in me through their message, [21]that all of them may be one, Father, just as you are in me and I am in you. May they also be in us so that the world may believe that you have sent me. [22]I have given them the glory that you gave me, that they may be one as we are one— [23]I in them and you in me—so that they may be brought to complete unity. Then the world will know that you sent me and have loved them even as you have loved me.

[24]"Father, I want those you have given me to be with me where I am, and to see my glory, the glory you have given me because you loved me before the creation of the world. [25]"Righteous Father, though the world does not know you, I know you, and they know that you have sent me. [26]I have made you[a] known to them, and will continue to make you known in order that the love you have for me may be in them and that I myself may be in them."

Jesus Arrested

18 When he had finished praying, Jesus left with his disciples and crossed the Kidron Valley. On the other side there was a garden, and he and his disciples went into it.

[2]Now Judas, who betrayed him, knew the place, because Jesus had often met there with his disciples. [3]So Judas came to the garden, guiding a detachment of

---

[a] 6,26 Greek *your name*   [b] 11 Or *Father, keep them faithful to*   [c] 12 Or *kept them faithful to*   [d] 17 Or *them to live in accordance with*

THE SCENE

KIDRON VALLEY

(JOHN 18:1)

The Hebrew word *kidron* means "dark." It was a small orchard that was always dry, except during the heavy rains in the rainy season. It begins about 1 mile (2 km) north of Jerusalem and extends as far as the Dead Sea, passing by the city of David (Bethlehem), the temple and the Jerusalem of the kings.

soldiers and some officials from the chief priests and the Pharisees. They were carrying torches, lanterns and weapons.

⁴Jesus, knowing all that was going to happen to him, went out and asked them, "Who is it you want?"

⁵"Jesus of Nazareth," they replied.

"I am he," Jesus said. (And Judas the traitor was standing there with them.) ⁶When Jesus said, "I am he," they drew back and fell to the ground.

⁷Again he asked them, "Who is it you want?"

"Jesus of Nazareth," they said.

⁸Jesus answered, "I told you that I am he. If you are looking for me, then let these men go." ⁹This happened so that the words he had spoken would be ful-

filled: "I have not lost one of those you gave me."ᵃ

¹⁰Then Simon Peter, who had a sword, drew it and struck the high priest's servant, cutting off his right ear. (The servant's name was Malchus.)

¹¹Jesus commanded Peter, "Put your sword away! Shall I not drink the cup the Father has given me?"

¹²Then the detachment of soldiers with its commander and the Jewish officials arrested Jesus. They bound him ¹³and brought him first to Annas, who was the

ᵃ 9 John 6:39

THE WITNESSES

✓ MALCHUS (JOHN 18:10)

This man served Caiaphas, the priest. He went with a group of men to arrest Jesus. When Peter saw what he was going to do, Peter was angry and cut Malchus' ear off! But Jesus, who is always good, healed him.

father-in-law of Caiaphas, the high priest that year. ¹⁴Caiaphas was the one who had advised the Jewish leaders that it would be good if one man died for the people.

Peter's First Denial

¹⁵Simon Peter and another disciple were following Jesus. Because this disciple was known to the high priest, he went with Jesus into the high priest's courtyard, ¹⁶but Peter had to wait outside at the door. The other disciple, who was known to the high priest, came back, spoke to the servant girl on duty there and brought Peter in.

¹⁷"You aren't one of this man's disciples too, are you?" she asked Peter.

He replied, "I am not."

¹⁸It was cold, and the servants and officials stood around a fire they had made to keep warm. Peter also was standing with them, warming himself.

The High Priest Questions Jesus

¹⁹Meanwhile, the high priest questioned Jesus about his disciples and his teaching.

²⁰"I have spoken openly to the world," Jesus replied. "I always taught in synagogues or at the temple, where all the Jews come together. I said nothing in secret. ²¹Why question me? Ask those who heard me. Surely they know what I said."

²²When Jesus said this, one of the officials nearby slapped him in the face. "Is this the way you answer the high priest?" he demanded.

²³"If I said something wrong," Jesus replied, "testify as to what is wrong. But if I spoke the truth, why did you strike me?" ²⁴Then Annas sent him bound to Caiaphas the high priest.

Peter's Second and Third Denials

²⁵Meanwhile, Simon Peter was still standing there warming himself. So they asked him, "You aren't one of his disciples too, are you?"

He denied it, saying, "I am not."

²⁶One of the high priest's servants, a relative of the man whose ear Peter had cut off, challenged him, "Didn't I see you with him in the garden?" ²⁷Again Peter denied it, and at that moment a rooster began to crow.

Jesus Before Pilate

²⁸Then the Jewish leaders took Jesus from Caiaphas to the palace of the Roman governor. By now it was early morning, and to avoid ceremonial uncleanness they did not enter the palace, because they wanted to be able to eat the Passover. ²⁹So Pilate came out to them and asked, "What charges are you bringing against this man?"

³⁰"If he were not a criminal," they replied, "we would not have handed him over to you."

³¹Pilate said, "Take him yourselves and judge him by your own law."

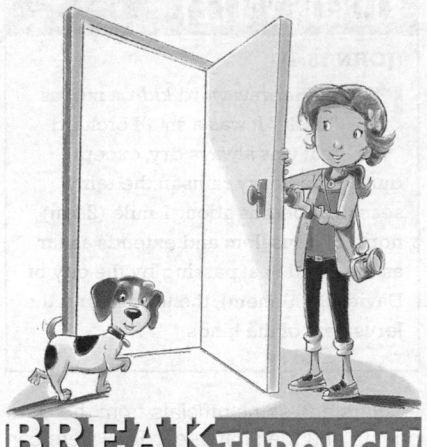

BREAKTHROUGH!

What was the detachment of soldiers?

(JOHN 18:12)

It was the agents of the Roman and Jewish rulers who arrested Jesus. The detachment probably consisted of 600 men, but sometimes there were fewer men in a detachment. There also was a temple guard (like police). Although the power was in Rome, the priests had their own police force in Palestine.

"But we have no right to execute any-one," they objected. ³²This took place to fulfill what Jesus had said about the kind of death he was going to die.

³³Pilate then went back inside the palace, summoned Jesus and asked him, "Are you the king of the Jews?"

³⁴"Is that your own idea," Jesus asked, "or did others talk to you about me?"

³⁵"Am I a Jew?" Pilate replied. "Your own people and chief priests handed you over to me. What is it you have done?"

³⁶Jesus said, "My kingdom is not of this world. If it were, my servants would fight to prevent my arrest by the Jewish leaders. But now my kingdom is from another place."

³⁷"You are a king, then!" said Pilate.

Jesus answered, "You say that I am a king. In fact, the reason I was born and came into the world is to testify to the truth. Everyone on the side of truth listens to me."

³⁸"What is truth?" retorted Pilate. With this he went out again to the Jews gathered there and said, "I find no basis for a charge against him. ³⁹But it is your custom for me to release to you one prisoner at the time of the Passover. Do you want me to release 'the king of the Jews'?"

⁴⁰They shouted back, "No, not him! Give us Barabbas!" Now Barabbas had taken part in an uprising.

Jesus Sentenced to Be Crucified

19 Then Pilate took Jesus and had him flogged. ²The soldiers twisted together a crown of thorns and put it on his head. They clothed him in a purple robe ³and went up to him again and again, saying, "Hail, king of the Jews!" And they slapped him in the face.

⁴Once more Pilate came out and said to the Jews gathered there, "Look, I am bringing him out to you to let you know that I find no basis for a charge against him." ⁵When Jesus came out wearing the crown of thorns and the purple robe, Pilate said to them, "Here is the man!"

⁶As soon as the chief priests and their officials saw him, they shouted, "Crucify! Crucify!"

But Pilate answered, "You take him and

BREAK THROUGH!

A purple robe

(JOHN 19:2)

In Jesus' time, dark red or purple clothes were very expensive, because it took a long time to dye fabric that color. As a result, only kings and very rich people could buy clothes that color. Here, they put a purple robe on Jesus just to make fun of him. Then, to make the joke complete, they put a crown made of thorns on his head instead of a gold crown like a real king would wear.

crucify him. As for me, I find no basis for a charge against him."

⁷The Jewish leaders insisted, "We have a law, and according to that law he must die, because he claimed to be the Son of God."

⁸When Pilate heard this, he was even more afraid, ⁹and he went back inside the palace. "Where do you come from?" he asked Jesus, but Jesus gave him no answer. ¹⁰"Do you refuse to speak to me?" Pilate said. "Don't you realize I have power either to free you or to crucify you?"

¹¹Jesus answered, "You would have no power over me if it were not given to you from above. Therefore the one who handed me over to you is guilty of a greater sin."

¹²From then on, Pilate tried to set Jesus free, but the Jewish leaders kept shouting, "If you let this man go, you are no

friend of Caesar. Anyone who claims to be a king opposes Caesar."

¹³When Pilate heard this, he brought Jesus out and sat down on the judge's seat at a place known as the Stone Pavement (which in Aramaic is Gabbatha). ¹⁴It was the day of Preparation of the Passover; it was about noon.

"Here is your king," Pilate said to the Jews.

¹⁵But they shouted, "Take him away! Take him away! Crucify him!"

"Shall I crucify your king?" Pilate asked.

"We have no king but Caesar," the chief priests answered.

¹⁶Finally Pilate handed him over to them to be crucified.

The Crucifixion of Jesus

So the soldiers took charge of Jesus. ¹⁷Carrying his own cross, he went out to the place of the Skull (which in Aramaic

BREAKTHROUGH!

The judge's seat

(JOHN 19:13)

This was really a chair that they called the "curule seat." The Roman rulers would sit on it during a legal trial. When the Jews saw that Pilate was sitting in the tribunal, they knew he was going to order a sentence (a punishment).

THE SCENE

GABBATHA

(JOHN 19:13)

This word in the Aramaic language means "high place." This is where Jesus was judged. People who study the Bible think it was a kind of room with a raised floor that was covered with something like cement or slabs, the way the Romans built floors. Some people think it was in a building called the Antonia Fortress, but others think it was the temple courtyard. What we know for sure is that Gabbatha was the place in Jerusalem where Pilate had his tribunal, and was where they took Jesus to judge him.

is called Golgotha). ¹⁸There they crucified him, and with him two others—one on each side and Jesus in the middle.

¹⁹Pilate had a notice prepared and fastened to the cross. It read: JESUS OF NAZARETH, THE KING OF THE JEWS. ²⁰Many of the Jews read this sign, for the place where Jesus was crucified was near the city, and the sign was written in Aramaic, Latin and Greek. ²¹The chief priests of the Jews protested to Pilate, "Do not write 'The King of

the Jews,' but that this man claimed to be king of the Jews."

²²Pilate answered, "What I have written, I have written."

²³When the soldiers crucified Jesus, they took his clothes, dividing them into four shares, one for each of them, with the undergarment remaining. This garment was seamless, woven in one piece from top to bottom.

²⁴"Let's not tear it," they said to one another. "Let's decide by lot who will get it."

This happened that the scripture might be fulfilled that said,

"They divided my clothes among them and cast lots for my garment."ᵃ

BREAKTHROUGH!

Why was the sign written in three languages?
(JOHN 19:20)

Pilate wanted everybody to know what Jesus had been accused of when he was judged. So he made sure everybody could read the sign they hung on the cross. That's why the sign was in three languages. Aramaic was the language of the people who were living there in Palestine. Latin was the official language that was spoken in Rome, and used in all the places that Rome had conquered. Greek was spoken by many people, especially if they were educated or were merchants.

So this is what the soldiers did.

²⁵Near the cross of Jesus stood his mother, his mother's sister, Mary the wife of Clopas, and Mary Magdalene. ²⁶When Jesus saw his mother there, and the disciple whom he loved standing nearby, he said to her, "Woman,ᵇ here is your son," ²⁷and to the disciple, "Here is your mother." From that time on, this disciple took her into his home.

The Death of Jesus

²⁸Later, knowing that everything had now been finished, and so that Scripture would be fulfilled, Jesus said, "I am thirsty." ²⁹A jar of wine vinegar was there, so they soaked a sponge in it, put the sponge on a stalk of the hyssop plant, and lifted it to Jesus' lips. ³⁰When he had received the drink, Jesus said, "It is finished." With that, he bowed his head and gave up his spirit.

³¹Now it was the day of Preparation, and the next day was to be a special Sabbath. Because the Jewish leaders did not want the bodies left on the crosses during the Sabbath, they asked Pilate to have the legs broken and the bodies taken down. ³²The soldiers therefore came and broke the legs of the first man who had been crucified with Jesus, and then those of the other. ³³But when they came to Jesus and found that he was already dead, they did not break his legs. ³⁴Instead, one of the soldiers pierced Jesus' side with a spear, bringing a sudden flow of blood and water. ³⁵The man who saw it has given testimony, and his testimony is true. He knows that he tells the truth, and he testifies so that you also may believe. ³⁶These things happened so that the scripture would be fulfilled: "Not one of his bones will be broken,"ᶜ ³⁷and, as another scripture says, "They will look on the one they have pierced."ᵈ

The Burial of Jesus

³⁸Later, Joseph of Arimathea asked Pilate for the body of Jesus. Now Joseph

---

ᵃ 24 Psalm 22:18   ᵇ 26 The Greek for *Woman* does not denote any disrespect.   ᶜ 36 Exodus 12:46; Num. 9:12; Psalm 34:20   ᵈ 37 Zech. 12:10

BREAKTHROUGH!

Why did they put wine vinegar on Jesus' lips?

(JOHN 19:29)

One of the terrible things a person being crucified suffers is thirst. Jesus was very thirsty while he was nailed on the cross. What the soldiers gave him probably wasn't pure vinegar, but rather vinegar mixed with water. They called it *posca*, and the soldiers drank it when they were thirsty.

was a disciple of Jesus, but secretly because he feared the Jewish leaders. With Pilate's permission, he came and took the body away. 39He was accompanied by Nicodemus, the man who earlier had visited Jesus at night. Nicodemus brought a mixture of myrrh and aloes, about seventy-five pounds.[a] 40Taking Jesus' body, the two of them wrapped it, with the spices, in strips of linen. This was in accordance with Jewish burial customs. 41At the place where Jesus was crucified, there was a garden, and in the garden a new tomb, in which no one had ever been laid. 42Because it was the Jewish day of Preparation and since the tomb was nearby, they laid Jesus there.

The Empty Tomb

20 Early on the first day of the week, while it was still dark, Mary Mag-

dalene went to the tomb and saw that the stone had been removed from the entrance. 2So she came running to Simon Peter and the other disciple, the one Jesus loved, and said, "They have taken the Lord out of the tomb, and we don't know where they have put him!"

3So Peter and the other disciple started for the tomb. 4Both were running, but the other disciple outran Peter and reached the tomb first. 5He bent over and looked in at the strips of linen lying there but did not go in. 6Then Simon Peter came along behind him and went straight into the tomb. He saw the strips of linen lying there, 7as well as the cloth that had been wrapped around Jesus' head. The cloth was still lying in its place, separate from the linen. 8Finally the other disciple, who had reached the tomb first, also went inside. He saw and believed. 9(They still did not understand from Scripture that Jesus had to rise from the dead.) 10Then the disciples went back to where they were staying.

Jesus Appears to Mary Magdalene

11Now Mary stood outside the tomb crying. As she wept, she bent over to look into the tomb 12and saw two angels in white, seated where Jesus' body had been, one at the head and the other at the foot.

13They asked her, "Woman, why are you crying?"

"They have taken my Lord away," she said, "and I don't know where they have put him." 14At this, she turned around and saw Jesus standing there, but she did not realize that it was Jesus.

15He asked her, "Woman, why are you crying? Who is it you are looking for?"

Thinking he was the gardener, she said, "Sir, if you have carried him away, tell me where you have put him, and I will get him."

16Jesus said to her, "Mary."

She turned toward him and cried out in Aramaic, "Rabboni!" (which means "Teacher").

17Jesus said, "Do not hold on to me, for I have not yet ascended to the Father. Go instead to my brothers and tell them,

<hr>

[a] 39 Or about 34 kilograms

'I am ascending to my Father and your Father, to my God and your God.' "

[18]Mary Magdalene went to the disciples with the news: "I have seen the Lord!" And she told them that he had said these things to her.

Jesus Appears to His Disciples

[19]On the evening of that first day of the week, when the disciples were together, with the doors locked for fear of the Jewish leaders, Jesus came and stood among them and said, "Peace be with you!" [20]After he said this, he showed them his hands and side. The disciples were overjoyed when they saw the Lord.

[21]Again Jesus said, "Peace be with you! As the Father has sent me, I am sending you." [22]And with that he breathed on them and said, "Receive the Holy Spirit. [23]If you forgive anyone's sins, their sins are forgiven; if you do not forgive them, they are not forgiven."

Jesus Appears to Thomas

[24]Now Thomas (also known as Didymus[a]), one of the Twelve, was not with the disciples when Jesus came. [25]So the other disciples told him, "We have seen the Lord!"

But he said to them, "Unless I see the nail marks in his hands and put my finger where the nails were, and put my hand into his side, I will not believe."

[26]A week later his disciples were in the house again, and Thomas was with them. Though the doors were locked, Jesus came and stood among them and said, "Peace be with you!" [27]Then he said to Thomas, "Put your finger here; see my hands. Reach out your hand and put it into my side. Stop doubting and believe."

[28]Thomas said to him, "My Lord and my God!"

[29]Then Jesus told him, "Because you have seen me, you have believed; blessed are those who have not seen and yet have believed."

The Purpose of John's Gospel

[30]Jesus performed many other signs in the presence of his disciples, which are not recorded in this book. [31]But these are written that you may believe[b] that Jesus is the Messiah, the Son of God, and that by believing you may have life in his name.

Jesus and the Miraculous Catch of Fish

21 Afterward Jesus appeared again to his disciples, by the Sea of Galilee.[c] It happened this way: [2]Simon Peter, Thomas (also known as Didymus[a]), Nathanael from Cana in Galilee, the sons of Zebedee, and two other disciples were together. [3]"I'm going out to fish," Simon Peter told them, and they said, "We'll go with you." So they went out and got into the boat, but that night they caught nothing.

[4]Early in the morning, Jesus stood on the shore, but the disciples did not realize that it was Jesus.

[5]He called out to them, "Friends, haven't you any fish?"

"No," they answered.

[6]He said, "Throw your net on the right side of the boat and you will find some." When they did, they were unable to haul the net in because of the large number of fish.

[7]Then the disciple whom Jesus loved said to Peter, "It is the Lord!" As soon as Simon Peter heard him say, "It is the Lord," he wrapped his outer garment around him (for he had taken it off) and jumped into the water. [8]The other disciples followed in the boat, towing the net full of fish, for they were not far from shore, about a hundred yards.[d] [9]When they landed, they saw a fire of burning coals there with fish on it, and some bread.

[10]Jesus said to them, "Bring some of the fish you have just caught." [11]So Simon Peter climbed back into the boat and dragged the net ashore. It was full of large fish, 153, but even with so many the net was not torn. [12]Jesus said to them, "Come and have breakfast." None of the disciples dared ask him, "Who are you?" They knew it was the Lord. [13]Jesus came, took the bread and

---

[a] 24,2 *Thomas* (Aramaic) and *Didymus* (Greek) both mean twin.   [b] 31 Or *may continue to believe*   [c] 1 Greek *Tiberias*   [d] 8 Or *about 90 meters*

gave it to them, and did the same with the fish. [14]This was now the third time Jesus appeared to his disciples after he was raised from the dead.

Jesus Reinstates Peter

[15]When they had finished eating, Jesus said to Simon Peter, "Simon son of John, do you love me more than these?"

"Yes, Lord," he said, "you know that I love you."

Jesus said, "Feed my lambs."

[16]Again Jesus said, "Simon son of John, do you love me?"

He answered, "Yes, Lord, you know that I love you."

Jesus said, "Take care of my sheep."

[17]The third time he said to him, "Simon son of John, do you love me?"

Peter was hurt because Jesus asked him the third time, "Do you love me?" He said, "Lord, you know all things; you know that I love you."

Jesus said, "Feed my sheep. [18]Very truly I tell you, when you were younger you dressed yourself and went where you wanted; but when you are old you will stretch out your hands, and someone else will dress you and lead you where you do not want to go." [19]Jesus said this to indicate the kind of death by which Peter would glorify God. Then he said to him, "Follow me!"

[20]Peter turned and saw that the disciple whom Jesus loved was following them. (This was the one who had leaned back against Jesus at the supper and had said, "Lord, who is going to betray you?") [21]When Peter saw him, he asked, "Lord, what about him?"

[22]Jesus answered, "If I want him to remain alive until I return, what is that to you? You must follow me." [23]Because of this, the rumor spread among the believers that this disciple would not die. But Jesus did not say that he would not die; he only said, "If I want him to remain alive until I return, what is that to you?"

[24]This is the disciple who testifies to these things and who wrote them down. We know that his testimony is true.

[25]Jesus did many other things as well. If every one of them were written down, I suppose that even the whole world would not have room for the books that would be written.

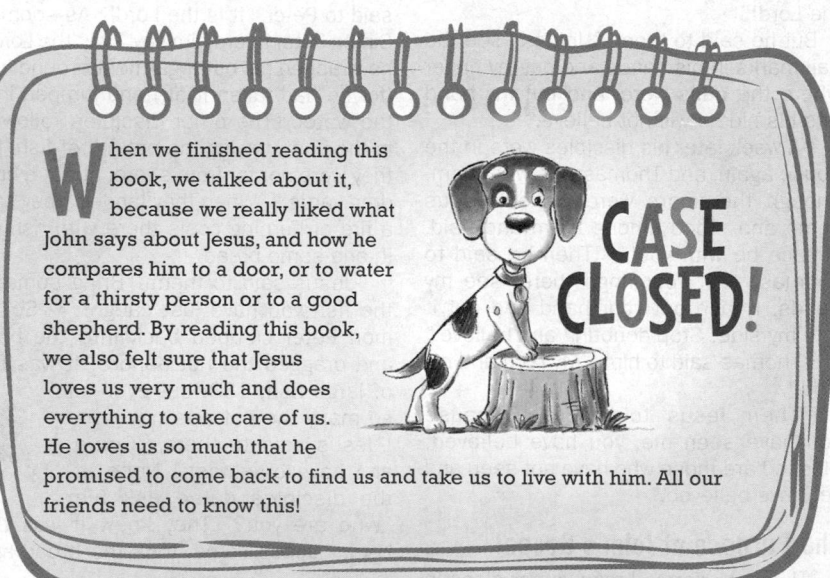

When we finished reading this book, we talked about it, because we really liked what John says about Jesus, and how he compares him to a door, or to water for a thirsty person or to a good shepherd. By reading this book, we also felt sure that Jesus loves us very much and does everything to take care of us. He loves us so much that he promised to come back to find us and take us to live with him. All our friends need to know this!

CASE CLOSED!

ACTS

THE EVIDENCE:

WHO WROTE IT?
Luke, the same man who wrote the gospel that has his name, wrote the book of Acts. It's almost like he wrote two volumes. Volume 1 would be the gospel of Luke and volume 2 would be Acts. He dedicated these two books to an important person called Theophilus.

HOW LONG AGO?
Luke was probably in Rome when he wrote Acts. He wrote it after the gospel of Luke. So it was probably about 85 years after Christ when he wrote it.

WHAT'S IT ABOUT?
This book isn't about Jesus' life like the Gospels are. It's about the lives of Jesus' friends and what happened after Jesus went to heaven to be with God. Some of these friends, like Peter, knew Jesus personally. But there were others, like Paul, who didn't know him. The book is very interesting, because those followers of Jesus went everywhere, telling people who Jesus is and how he changed their lives. The book tells about a lot of the things they did, but what's most important is that the Holy Spirit was always with them. They healed sick or afflicted people in the name of Jesus and they helped in the work of the churches.

THE BEST PART
We thought a lot before we decided what part we liked best. Finally, we agreed and we chose the story about when the Sanhedrin ordered Peter and John not to talk any more about Jesus, and they just answered very bravely, "We cannot help speaking about what we have seen and heard" (4:20).

Jesus Taken Up Into Heaven

1 In my former book, Theophilus, I wrote about all that Jesus began to do and to teach ²until the day he was taken up to heaven, after giving instructions through the Holy Spirit to the apostles he had chosen. ³After his suffering, he presented himself to them and gave many convincing proofs that he was alive. He appeared to them over a period of forty days and spoke about the kingdom of God. ⁴On one occasion, while he was eating with them, he gave them this command: "Do not leave Jerusalem, but wait for the gift my Father promised, which you have heard me speak about. ⁵For John baptized with^a water, but in a few days you will be baptized with^a the Holy Spirit."

⁶Then they gathered around him and

^a 5 Or in

THE
WITNESSES

✓ **THEOPHILUS** (ACTS 1:1)
Read the explanation in Luke 1:3.

✓ **JOHN** (ACTS 1:5)
Don't get confused. This is John the Baptist — it isn't the John who was Jesus' friend.

asked him, "Lord, are you at this time going to restore the kingdom to Israel?"

⁷He said to them: "It is not for you to know the times or dates the Father has set by his own authority. ⁸But you will receive power when the Holy Spirit comes on you; and you will be my witnesses in Jerusalem, and in all Judea and Samaria, and to the ends of the earth."

⁹After he said this, he was taken up before their very eyes, and a cloud hid him from their sight.

¹⁰They were looking intently up into the sky as he was going, when suddenly two men dressed in white stood beside

BREAKTHROUGH!

Baptized with the Holy Spirit
(ACTS 1:5)
This means that God himself fills us with his Spirit, which is he himself.

them. ¹¹"Men of Galilee," they said, "why do you stand here looking into the sky? This same Jesus, who has been taken from you into heaven, will come back in the same way you have seen him go into heaven."

Matthias Chosen to Replace Judas

¹²Then the apostles returned to Jerusalem from the hill called the Mount of Olives, a Sabbath day's walkᵃ from the city. ¹³When they arrived, they went upstairs to the room where they were staying. Those present were Peter, John, James and Andrew; Philip and Thomas, Bartholomew and Matthew; James son of Alphaeus and Simon the Zealot, and Judas son of James. ¹⁴They all joined together constantly in prayer, along with the women and Mary the mother of Jesus, and with his brothers.

¹⁵In those days Peter stood up among the believers (a group numbering about a hundred and twenty) ¹⁶and said, "Brothers

---

ᵃ 12 That is, about 5/8 mile or about 1 kilometer

and sisters,[a] the Scripture had to be fulfilled in which the Holy Spirit spoke long ago through David concerning Judas, who served as guide for those who arrested Jesus. [17]He was one of our number and shared in our ministry."

[18](With the payment he received for his wickedness, Judas bought a field; there he fell headlong, his body burst open and all his intestines spilled out. [19]Everyone in Jerusalem heard about this, so they called that field in their language Akeldama, that is, Field of Blood.)

[20]"For," said Peter, "it is written in the Book of Psalms:

" 'May his place be deserted;
    let there be no one to dwell in it,'[b]

and,

" 'May another take his place of
    leadership.'[c]

[21]Therefore it is necessary to choose one of the men who have been with us the whole time the Lord Jesus was living among us, [22]beginning from John's baptism to the time when Jesus was taken up from us. For one of these must become a witness with us of his resurrection."

[23]So they nominated two men: Joseph called Barsabbas (also known as Justus) and Matthias. [24]Then they prayed, "Lord, you know everyone's heart. Show us which of these two you have chosen [25]to take over this apostolic ministry, which Judas left to go where he belongs." [26]Then they cast lots, and the lot fell to Matthias; so he was added to the eleven apostles.

The Holy Spirit Comes at Pentecost

2 When the day of Pentecost came, they were all together in one place. [2]Suddenly a sound like the blowing of a violent wind came from heaven and filled the whole house where they were sitting. [3]They saw what seemed to be tongues of fire that separated and came to rest on each of them. [4]All of them were filled with the Holy Spirit and began to speak in other tongues[d] as the Spirit enabled them.

[5]Now there were staying in Jerusalem God-fearing Jews from every nation under heaven. [6]When they heard this sound, a

BREAK THROUGH!

Day of Pentecost
(ACTS 2:1)
God's people celebrated three very important feasts during the year. Pentecost was one of them. Pentecost comes from the Greek word for "fiftieth," and that was because this feast was 50 days after Passover. The celebration of Pentecost was just for one day. All the Israelite men had to go to Jerusalem to celebrate it in the temple. By the time the book of Acts was written, people from many parts of the world would arrive for this celebration too. At first, Pentecost was celebrated at the beginning of the harvest. Much later, it began to be related to the day God had given the Ten Commandments to Moses on Mount Sinai.

crowd came together in bewilderment, because each one heard their own language being spoken. [7]Utterly amazed, they asked: "Aren't all these who are speaking Galileans? [8]Then how is it that each of us hears them in our native language? [9]Parthians, Medes and Elamites; residents of Mesopotamia, Judea and Cappadocia, Pontus and Asia,[e] [10]Phrygia and

---

[a] 16 The Greek word for *brothers and sisters* (*adelphoi*) refers here to believers, both men and women, as part of God's family; also in 6:3; 11:29; 12:17; 16:40; 18:18, 27; 21:7, 17; 28:14, 15.   [b] 20 Psalm 69:25
[c] 20 Psalm 109:8   [d] 4 Or *languages*; also in verse 11
[e] 9 That is, the Roman province by that name

Pamphylia, Egypt and the parts of Libya near Cyrene; visitors from Rome ¹¹(both Jews and converts to Judaism); Cretans and Arabs—we hear them declaring the wonders of God in our own tongues!" ¹²Amazed and perplexed, they asked one another, "What does this mean?"

¹³Some, however, made fun of them and said, "They have had too much wine."

Peter Addresses the Crowd

¹⁴Then Peter stood up with the Eleven, raised his voice and addressed the crowd: "Fellow Jews and all of you who live in Jerusalem, let me explain this to

CHECK THE FACTS

What happened on the day of Pentecost while the disciples were praying together?

A) Jesus appeared risen from the dead.

B) The Holy Spirit came down upon them.

C) The Roman police came and took them to jail.

CORRECT ANSWER: B

BREAKTHROUGH!

Tongues of fire? What was that?

(ACTS 2:3)

Fire is a symbol of real cleanliness. Also, many times when God wanted to show that he was present in the midst of the people who obeyed and believed in him, he presented himself as fire or as wind. That's what happened when the Israelites were walking through the desert. At night, God went along with them as a column of fire so the people would know where they should walk. Jesus told his followers that they would be filled with the Holy Spirit, so that's shown here as "tongues of fire."

you; listen carefully to what I say. ¹⁵These people are not drunk, as you suppose. It's only nine in the morning! ¹⁶No, this is what was spoken by the prophet Joel:

¹⁷ " 'In the last days, God says,
  I will pour out my Spirit on all
    people.
  Your sons and daughters will
    prophesy,
  your young men will see visions,
  your old men will dream dreams.
¹⁸Even on my servants, both men and
    women,
  I will pour out my Spirit in those
    days,
  and they will prophesy.
¹⁹I will show wonders in the heavens
    above
  and signs on the earth below,
  blood and fire and billows of smoke.

BREAKTHROUGH!

Were they speaking in languages they didn't know?

(ACTS 2:7-12)

Yes. All of a sudden, and without ever having studied, Jesus' followers who were meeting there began to speak in other languages. The Holy Spirit (God) made them speak this way so all the people who had arrived in Jerusalem for the Feast of Pentecost would understand what they were saying when they were speaking about Jesus.

THE SCENE

PARTHIANS, MEDES, ELAMITES, ETC.

(ACTS 2:9-10)

People from cities and regions around the Mediterranean Sea and farther east. They all had their own languages and cultures.

---

20 The sun will be turned to darkness
and the moon to blood
before the coming of the great and
glorious day of the Lord.
21 And everyone who calls
on the name of the Lord will be
saved.'[a]

22 "Fellow Israelites, listen to this: Jesus of Nazareth was a man accredited by God to you by miracles, wonders and signs, which God did among you through him, as you yourselves know. 23 This man was handed over to you by God's deliberate plan and foreknowledge; and you, with the help of wicked men,[b] put him to death by nailing him to the cross. 24 But God raised him from the dead, freeing him from the agony of death, because it was impos-

sible for death to keep its hold on him. 25 David said about him:

" 'I saw the Lord always before me.
Because he is at my right hand,
I will not be shaken.
26 Therefore my heart is glad and my
tongue rejoices;
my body also will rest in hope,
27 because you will not abandon me to
the realm of the dead,
you will not let your holy one see
decay.
28 You have made known to me the
paths of life;
you will fill me with joy in your
presence.'[c]

29 "Fellow Israelites, I can tell you confidently that the patriarch David died and

---

[a] 21 Joel 2:28-32 [b] 23 Or of those not having the law
(that is, Gentiles) [c] 28 Psalm 16:8-11 (see Septuagint)

BREAK THROUGH!

If Peter had denied Jesus, then how is it that now he speaks so loudly about him, and to so many people?

(ACTS 2:14-40)

Well, Peter was afraid someone would hurt him before. But then the Holy Spirit, who is God, gave him the courage to speak about Jesus in front of so very many people. Then he didn't feel ashamed.

was buried, and his tomb is here to this day. ³⁰But he was a prophet and knew that God had promised him on oath that he would place one of his descendants on his throne. ³¹Seeing what was to come, he spoke of the resurrection of the Messiah, that he was not abandoned to the realm of the dead, nor did his body see decay. ³²God has raised this Jesus to life, and we are all witnesses of it. ³³Exalted to the right hand of God, he has received from the Father the promised Holy Spirit and has poured out what you now see and hear. ³⁴For David did not ascend to heaven, and yet he said,

" 'The Lord said to my Lord:
"Sit at my right hand
³⁵until I make your enemies
a footstool for your feet." 'ᵃ

³⁶"Therefore let all Israel be assured of this: God has made this Jesus, whom you crucified, both Lord and Messiah."

³⁷When the people heard this, they were cut to the heart and said to Peter and the other apostles, "Brothers, what shall we do?"

³⁸Peter replied, "Repent and be baptized, every one of you, in the name of Jesus Christ for the forgiveness of your sins. And you will receive the gift of the Holy Spirit. ³⁹The promise is for you and your children and for all who are far off— for all whom the Lord our God will call."

⁴⁰With many other words he warned them; and he pleaded with them, "Save yourselves from this corrupt generation." ⁴¹Those who accepted his message were baptized, and about three thousand were added to their number that day.

The Fellowship of the Believers

⁴²They devoted themselves to the apostles' teaching and to fellowship, to the breaking of bread and to prayer. ⁴³Everyone was filled with awe at the many wonders and signs performed by the apostles. ⁴⁴All the believers were together and had everything in common. ⁴⁵They sold property and possessions to give to anyone who had need. ⁴⁶Every day they continued to meet together in the temple courts. They broke bread in their homes and ate together with glad and sincere hearts, ⁴⁷praising God and enjoying the favor of all the people. And the Lord added to their number daily those who were being saved.

Peter Heals a Lame Beggar

3 One day Peter and John were going up to the temple at the time of prayer—at three in the afternoon. ²Now a man who was lame from birth was being carried to the temple gate called Beautiful, where he was put every day to beg from those going into the temple courts. ³When he saw Peter and John about to enter, he asked them for money. ⁴Peter looked straight at him, as did John. Then Peter said, "Look at us!" ⁵So the man

ᵃ 35 Psalm 110:1

Temple

(ACTS 3:2)

When the Bible talks about the temple, it's always referring to the temple that was in Jerusalem. Solomon built it, and it was very beautiful. But then it was destroyed and the people had to rebuild it. In Jesus' time, it was the second temple, which Herod had repaired and made very beautiful.

gave them his attention, expecting to get something from them.

⁶Then Peter said, "Silver or gold I do not have, but what I do have I give you. In the name of Jesus Christ of Nazareth, walk." ⁷Taking him by the right hand, he helped him up, and instantly the man's feet and ankles became strong. ⁸He jumped to his feet and began to walk. Then he went with them into the temple courts, walking and jumping, and praising God. ⁹When all the people saw him walking and praising God, ¹⁰they recognized him as the same man who used to sit begging at the temple gate called Beautiful, and they were filled with wonder and amazement at what had happened to him.

Peter Speaks to the Onlookers

¹¹While the man held on to Peter and John, all the people were astonished and came running to them in the place called Solomon's Colonnade. ¹²When Peter saw this, he said to them: "Fellow Israelites, why does this surprise you? Why do you stare at us as if by our own power or godliness we had made this man walk? ¹³The God of Abraham, Isaac and Jacob, the God of our fathers, has glorified his servant Jesus. You handed him over to be killed, and you disowned him before Pilate, though he had decided to let him go. ¹⁴You disowned the Holy and Righteous One and asked that a murderer be released to you. ¹⁵You killed the author of life, but God raised him from the dead. We are witnesses of this. ¹⁶By faith in the name of Jesus, this man whom you see and know was made strong. It is Jesus' name and the faith that comes through him that has completely healed him, as you can all see.

¹⁷"Now, fellow Israelites, I know that you acted in ignorance, as did your leaders. ¹⁸But this is how God fulfilled what he had foretold through all the prophets, saying that his Messiah would suffer. ¹⁹Repent, then, and turn to God, so that your sins may be wiped out, that times of refreshing may come from the Lord, ²⁰and that he may send the Messiah, who has been appointed for you—even Jesus. ²¹Heaven must receive him until the time comes for God to restore everything, as he promised long ago through his holy prophets. ²²For Moses said, 'The Lord your God will raise up for you a prophet like me from among your own people; you must listen to everything he tells you. ²³Anyone who does not listen to him will be completely cut off from their people.'[a]

²⁴"Indeed, beginning with Samuel, all the prophets who have spoken have foretold these days. ²⁵And you are heirs of the prophets and of the covenant God made with your fathers. He said to Abraham, 'Through your offspring all peoples on earth will be blessed.'[b] ²⁶When God raised up his servant, he sent him first to you to bless you by turning each of you from your wicked ways."

---

[a] 23 Deut. 18:15,18,19   [b] 25 Gen. 22:18; 26:4

Peter and John Before the Sanhedrin

4 The priests and the captain of the temple guard and the Sadducees came up to Peter and John while they were speaking to the people. ²They were greatly disturbed because the apostles were teaching the people, proclaiming in Jesus the resurrection of the dead. ³They seized Peter and John and, because it was evening, they put them in jail until the next day. ⁴But many who heard the message believed; so the number of men who believed grew to about five thousand.

⁵The next day the rulers, the elders and the teachers of the law met in Jerusalem. ⁶Annas the high priest was there, and so were Caiaphas, John, Alexander and others of the high priest's family. ⁷They had

Peter and John brought before them and began to question them: "By what power or what name did you do this?"

⁸Then Peter, filled with the Holy Spirit, said to them: "Rulers and elders of the people! ⁹If we are being called to account today for an act of kindness shown to a man who was lame and are being asked how he was healed, ¹⁰then know this, you and all the people of Israel: It is by the

THE WITNESSES

BREAKTHROUGH!

Sanhedrin

(ACTS 4:1 - 22)

This was a group of 71 Jewish men who were priests, teachers of the law and Pharisees. The most important person in this group was the high priest. The priests met in the temple to decide about things related to the temple, the synagogues, everyday life and things related to justice, like when someone had stolen something or killed someone. They also had a lot of policemen under their orders.

✓ **ANNAS THE HIGH PRIEST, CAIAPHAS, JOHN, ALEXANDER AND OTHERS OF THE HIGH PRIEST'S FAMILY** (ACTS 4:6)

Annas and Caiaphas were related, because Caiaphas was married to Annas' daughter. Annas was the high priest that year, but Caiaphas still had the title. The priests mentioned here are the ones who were on duty in the temple that day. We don't know anything about who John or Alexander were.

name of Jesus Christ of Nazareth, whom you crucified but whom God raised from the dead, that this man stands before you healed. ¹¹Jesus is

" 'the stone you builders rejected,
　　which has become the
　　　cornerstone.'ᵃ

¹²Salvation is found in no one else, for there is no other name under heaven given to mankind by which we must be saved."

¹³When they saw the courage of Peter and John and realized that they were unschooled, ordinary men, they were astonished and they took note that these men had been with Jesus. ¹⁴But since they could see the man who had been healed standing there with them, there was nothing they could say. ¹⁵So they ordered them to withdraw from the Sanhedrin and then conferred together. ¹⁶"What are we going to do with these men?" they asked. "Everyone living in Jerusalem knows they have performed a notable sign, and we cannot deny it. ¹⁷But to stop this thing from spreading any further among the people, we must warn them to speak no longer to anyone in this name."

¹⁸Then they called them in again and commanded them not to speak or teach at all in the name of Jesus. ¹⁹But Peter and John replied, "Which is right in God's eyes: to listen to you, or to him? You be the judges! ²⁰As for us, we cannot help speaking about what we have seen and heard."

²¹After further threats they let them go. They could not decide how to punish them, because all the people were praising God for what had happened. ²²For the man who was miraculously healed was over forty years old.

The Believers Pray

²³On their release, Peter and John went back to their own people and reported all that the chief priests and the elders had said to them. ²⁴When they heard this, they raised their voices together in prayer to God. "Sovereign Lord," they said, "you made the heavens and the earth and the sea, and everything in them. ²⁵You spoke

BREAKTHROUGH!

Does only Jesus have the power to save? What happens to people who follow the leaders of other religions?

(ACTS 4:12)

Yes, the Bible teaches us that the only one who can give us eternal life with God is Jesus. That's why he came to Earth. He died for us on the cross and then he lived again. Now he's in heaven, next to God the Father, and he's our Savior. The leaders of other religions were, or perhaps are, good people who have good intentions and good teachings, but they don't have the power to save.

by the Holy Spirit through the mouth of your servant, our father David:

" 'Why do the nations rage
　　and the peoples plot in vain?
²⁶The kings of the earth rise up
　　and the rulers band together
　against the Lord
　　and against his anointed one.'ᵇ'ᶜ

²⁷Indeed Herod and Pontius Pilate met together with the Gentiles and the people of Israel in this city to conspire against

---

ᵃ *11* Psalm 118:22   ᵇ *26* That is, Messiah or Christ
ᶜ *26* Psalm 2:1,2

your holy servant Jesus, whom you anointed. [28]They did what your power and will had decided beforehand should happen. [29]Now, Lord, consider their threats and enable your servants to speak your word with great boldness. [30]Stretch out your hand to heal and perform signs and wonders through the name of your holy servant Jesus."

[31]After they prayed, the place where they were meeting was shaken. And they were all filled with the Holy Spirit and spoke the word of God boldly.

The Believers Share Their Possessions

[32]All the believers were one in heart and mind. No one claimed that any of their possessions was their own, but they shared everything they had. [33]With great power the apostles continued to testify to the resurrection of the Lord Jesus. And God's grace was so powerfully at work in them all [34]that there were no needy persons among them. For from time to time those who owned land or houses sold them, brought the money from the sales [35]and put it at the apostles' feet, and it was distributed to anyone who had need.

[36]Joseph, a Levite from Cyprus, whom the apostles called Barnabas (which means "son of encouragement"), [37]sold a field he owned and brought the money and put it at the apostles' feet.

Ananias and Sapphira

5 Now a man named Ananias, together with his wife Sapphira, also sold a piece of property. [2]With his wife's full knowledge he kept back part of the money for himself, but brought the rest and put it at the apostles' feet.

[3]Then Peter said, "Ananias, how is it that Satan has so filled your heart that you have lied to the Holy Spirit and have kept for yourself some of the money you received for the land? [4]Didn't it belong to you before it was sold? And after it was sold, wasn't the money at your disposal? What made you think of doing such a thing? You have not lied just to human beings but to God."

THE WITNESSES

✓ ANANIAS AND SAPPHIRA
(ACTS 5:1–11)

Ananias is a Hebrew name that means "God has favored him." Sapphira is an Aramaic name that means "beautiful." What nice names for people who behaved so badly! Because this married couple that lived in Jerusalem lied, God was so angry with them that they fell down dead! So now we know—it's not good to lie. And worse if it's to God.

═══════════════════════════

[5]When Ananias heard this, he fell down and died. And great fear seized all who heard what had happened. [6]Then some young men came forward, wrapped up his body, and carried him out and buried him.

[7]About three hours later his wife came in, not knowing what had happened. [8]Peter asked her, "Tell me, is this the price you and Ananias got for the land?"

"Yes," she said, "that is the price."

⁹Peter said to her, "How could you conspire to test the Spirit of the Lord? Listen! The feet of the men who buried your husband are at the door, and they will carry you out also."

¹⁰At that moment she fell down at his feet and died. Then the young men came in and, finding her dead, carried her out and buried her beside her husband. ¹¹Great fear seized the whole church and all who heard about these events.

The Apostles Heal Many

¹²The apostles performed many signs and wonders among the people. And all the believers used to meet together in Solomon's Colonnade. ¹³No one else dared join them, even though they were highly regarded by the people. ¹⁴Nevertheless, more and more men and women believed in the Lord and were added to their number. ¹⁵As a result, people brought the sick into the streets and laid them on beds and mats so that at least Peter's shadow might fall on some of them as he passed by. ¹⁶Crowds gathered also from the towns around Jerusalem, bringing their sick and those tormented by impure spirits, and all of them were healed.

The Apostles Persecuted

¹⁷Then the high priest and all his associates, who were members of the party of the Sadducees, were filled with jealousy. ¹⁸They arrested the apostles and put them in the public jail. ¹⁹But during the night an angel of the Lord opened the doors of the jail and brought them out. ²⁰"Go, stand in the temple courts," he said, "and tell the people all about this new life."

²¹At daybreak they entered the temple courts, as they had been told, and began to teach the people.

When the high priest and his associates arrived, they called together the Sanhedrin—the full assembly of the elders of Israel—and sent to the jail for the apostles. ²²But on arriving at the jail, the officers did not find them there. So they went back and reported, ²³"We found

BREAKTHROUGH!

Why did they put the apostles in jail if they hadn't done anything bad?

(ACTS 5:18)

It was the priests who sent the apostles to jail, not the Roman police. It seems the priests were jealous because the apostles were healing the sick and many people were following them. Also, they didn't believe that Jesus was the Son of God. They thought that Jesus' followers would make problems, and then the Roman authorities would be angry with the Jews.

the jail securely locked, with the guards standing at the doors; but when we opened them, we found no one inside." ²⁴On hearing this report, the captain of the temple guard and the chief priests were at a loss, wondering what this might lead to.

²⁵Then someone came and said, "Look! The men you put in jail are standing in the temple courts teaching the people." ²⁶At that, the captain went with his officers and brought the apostles. They did not use force, because they feared that the people would stone them.

²⁷The apostles were brought in and made to appear before the Sanhedrin to be questioned by the high priest. ²⁸"We

gave you strict orders not to teach in this name," he said. "Yet you have filled Jerusalem with your teaching and are determined to make us guilty of this man's blood."

²⁹Peter and the other apostles replied: "We must obey God rather than human beings! ³⁰The God of our ancestors raised Jesus from the dead—whom you killed by hanging him on a cross. ³¹God exalted him to his own right hand as Prince and Savior that he might bring Israel to repentance and forgive their sins. ³²We are witnesses of these things, and so is the Holy Spirit, whom God has given to those who obey him."

³³When they heard this, they were furious and wanted to put them to death. ³⁴But a Pharisee named Gamaliel, a teacher of the law, who was honored by all the people, stood up in the Sanhedrin and ordered that the men be put outside for a little while. ³⁵Then he addressed the Sanhedrin: "Men of Israel, consider carefully what you intend to do to these men. ³⁶Some time ago Theudas appeared, claiming to be somebody, and about four hundred men rallied to him. He was killed, all his followers were dispersed, and it all came to nothing. ³⁷After him, Judas the Galilean appeared in the days of the census and led a band of people in revolt. He too was killed, and all his followers were scattered. ³⁸Therefore, in the present case I advise you: Leave these men alone! Let them go! For if their purpose or activity is of human origin, it will fail. ³⁹But if it is from God, you will not be able to stop these men; you will only find yourselves fighting against God."

⁴⁰His speech persuaded them. They called the apostles in and had them flogged. Then they ordered them not to speak in the name of Jesus, and let them go.

⁴¹The apostles left the Sanhedrin, rejoicing because they had been counted worthy of suffering disgrace for the Name. ⁴²Day after day, in the temple courts and from house to house, they never stopped teaching and proclaiming the good news that Jesus is the Messiah.

The Choosing of the Seven

6 In those days when the number of disciples was increasing, the Hellenistic Jews*ᵃ* among them complained against

ᵃ 1 That is, Jews who had adopted the Greek language and culture

THE
WITNESSES

✓ GAMALIEL (ACTS 5:34)
This Hebrew name means "God's reward." His father was Simon. Gamaliel was a famous Pharisee who knew a lot and taught the Bible. He was also a member of the Jewish Sanhedrin. He was a good person, and he saved the apostles from being condemned to death.

✓ STEPHEN (ACTS 6:5)
This name comes from the Greek word that means "crown." He was the first Christian who was killed because he believed in Jesus. That's why he's called the "first martyr." He was one of the people who worked a lot in the church in Jerusalem, and they chose him to help the apostles.

BREAKTHROUGH!

Hellenistic Jews? Hebraic Jews? What was the official language during Jesus' time?

(ACTS 6:1)

There were several different groups living in Palestine during Jesus' time. Each group spoke their own language. The "Hellenistic" group were the Jews who spoke Greek. The "Hebraic" group were the Jews who followed the traditions of their race and could speak and understand Hebrew, mostly when they read the Bible. Generally speaking, Jewish people spoke Aramaic. The authorities and Roman soldiers spoke Latin, because that was the official language of Rome. However, educated people knew a lot, so they often spoke Greek too.

the Hebraic Jews because their widows were being overlooked in the daily distribution of food. ²So the Twelve gathered all the disciples together and said, "It would not be right for us to neglect the ministry of the word of God in order to wait on tables. ³Brothers and sisters, choose seven men from among you who are known to be full of the Spirit and wisdom. We will turn this responsibility over to them ⁴and will give our attention to prayer and the ministry of the word."

⁵This proposal pleased the whole group. They chose Stephen, a man full of faith and of the Holy Spirit; also Philip, Procorus, Nicanor, Timon, Parmenas, and Nicolas from Antioch, a convert to Judaism. ⁶They presented these men to the apostles, who prayed and laid their hands on them.

⁷So the word of God spread. The number of disciples in Jerusalem increased rapidly, and a large number of priests became obedient to the faith.

Stephen Seized

⁸Now Stephen, a man full of God's grace and power, performed great wonders and signs among the people. ⁹Opposition arose, however, from members of the Synagogue of the Freedmen (as it was called) — Jews of Cyrene and Alexandria as well as the provinces of Cilicia and Asia — who began to argue with Stephen.

BREAKTHROUGH!

Synagogue of the Freedmen

(ACTS 6:9)

The synagogues were places where the Jews met to study the Bible and pray. There were synagogues in almost all the cities. The Synagogue of the Freedmen was a synagogue where Jews who had been slaves and then been freed went.

¹⁰But they could not stand up against the wisdom the Spirit gave him as he spoke.

¹¹Then they secretly persuaded some men to say, "We have heard Stephen speak blasphemous words against Moses and against God."

¹²So they stirred up the people and the elders and the teachers of the law. They seized Stephen and brought him before the Sanhedrin. ¹³They produced false witnesses, who testified, "This fellow never stops speaking against this holy place and against the law. ¹⁴For we have heard him say that this Jesus of Nazareth will destroy this place and change the customs Moses handed down to us."

¹⁵All who were sitting in the Sanhedrin looked intently at Stephen, and they saw that his face was like the face of an angel.

Stephen's Speech to the Sanhedrin

7 Then the high priest asked Stephen, "Are these charges true?"

²To this he replied: "Brothers and fathers, listen to me! The God of glory appeared to our father Abraham while he was still in Mesopotamia, before he lived in Harran. ³'Leave your country and your people,' God said, 'and go to the land I will show you.'ᵃ

⁴"So he left the land of the Chaldeans and settled in Harran. After the death of his father, God sent him to this land where you are now living. ⁵He gave him no inheritance here, not even enough ground to set his foot on. But God promised him that he and his descendants after him would possess the land, even though at that time Abraham had no child. ⁶God spoke to him in this way: 'For four hundred years your descendants will be strangers in a country not their own, and they will be enslaved and mistreated. ⁷But I will punish the nation they serve as slaves,' God said, 'and afterward they will come out of that country and worship me in this place.'ᵇ ⁸Then he gave Abraham the covenant of circumcision. And Abraham became the father of Isaac and circumcised him eight days after his birth. Later Isaac became the father of Jacob, and Jacob became the father of the twelve patriarchs.

⁹"Because the patriarchs were jealous of Joseph, they sold him as a slave into Egypt. But God was with him ¹⁰and rescued him from all his troubles. He gave Joseph wisdom and enabled him to gain the goodwill of Pharaoh king of Egypt. So Pharaoh made him ruler over Egypt and all his palace.

¹¹"Then a famine struck all Egypt and Canaan, bringing great suffering, and our ancestors could not find food. ¹²When Jacob heard that there was grain in Egypt, he sent our forefathers on their first visit. ¹³On their second visit, Joseph told his brothers who he was, and Pharaoh learned about Joseph's family. ¹⁴After this, Joseph sent for his father Jacob and his whole family, seventy-five in all. ¹⁵Then Jacob went down to Egypt, where he and our ancestors died. ¹⁶Their bodies were brought back to Shechem and placed in the tomb that Abraham had bought from the sons of Hamor at Shechem for a certain sum of money.

¹⁷"As the time drew near for God to fulfill his promise to Abraham, the number of our people in Egypt had greatly increased. ¹⁸Then 'a new king, to whom Joseph meant nothing, came to power in Egypt.'ᶜ ¹⁹He dealt treacherously with our people and oppressed our ancestors by forcing them to throw out their newborn babies so that they would die.

²⁰"At that time Moses was born, and he was no ordinary child.ᵈ For three months he was cared for by his family. ²¹When he was placed outside, Pharaoh's daughter took him and brought him up as her own son. ²²Moses was educated in all the wisdom of the Egyptians and was powerful in speech and action.

²³"When Moses was forty years old, he decided to visit his own people, the Israelites. ²⁴He saw one of them being mistreated by an Egyptian, so he went to his defense and avenged him by killing the Egyptian. ²⁵Moses thought that his own people would realize that God was using him to rescue them, but they did not. ²⁶The next day Moses came upon two Israelites who were fighting. He tried to recon-

---

ᵃ 3 Gen. 12:1   ᵇ 7 Gen. 15:13,14   ᶜ 18 Exodus 1:8
ᵈ 20 Or was fair in the sight of God

cile them by saying, 'Men, you are brothers; why do you want to hurt each other?'
²⁷"But the man who was mistreating the other pushed Moses aside and said, 'Who made you ruler and judge over us? ²⁸Are you thinking of killing me as you killed the Egyptian yesterday?'ᵃ ²⁹When Moses heard this, he fled to Midian, where he settled as a foreigner and had two sons.

³⁰"After forty years had passed, an angel appeared to Moses in the flames of a burning bush in the desert near Mount Sinai. ³¹When he saw this, he was amazed at the sight. As he went over to get a closer look, he heard the Lord say: ³²'I am the God of your fathers, the God of Abraham, Isaac and Jacob.'ᵇ Moses trembled with fear and did not dare to look.

³³"Then the Lord said to him, 'Take off your sandals, for the place where you are standing is holy ground. ³⁴I have indeed seen the oppression of my people in Egypt. I have heard their groaning and have come down to set them free. Now come, I will send you back to Egypt.'ᶜ

³⁵"This is the same Moses they had rejected with the words, 'Who made you ruler and judge?' He was sent to be their ruler and deliverer by God himself, through the angel who appeared to him in the bush. ³⁶He led them out of Egypt and performed wonders and signs in Egypt, at the Red Sea and for forty years in the wilderness.

³⁷"This is the Moses who told the Israelites, 'God will raise up for you a prophet like me from your own people.'ᵈ ³⁸He was in the assembly in the wilderness, with the angel who spoke to him on Mount Sinai, and with our ancestors; and he received living words to pass on to us.

³⁹"But our ancestors refused to obey him. Instead, they rejected him and in their hearts turned back to Egypt. ⁴⁰They told Aaron, 'Make us gods who will go before us. As for this fellow Moses who led us out of Egypt—we don't know what has happened to him!'ᵉ ⁴¹That was the time they made an idol in the form of a calf. They brought sacrifices to it and reveled in what their own hands had made. ⁴²But God turned away from them and gave them over to the worship of the sun, moon and stars. This agrees with what is written in the book of the prophets:

" 'Did you bring me sacrifices and
    offerings
forty years in the wilderness, people
    of Israel?
⁴³You have taken up the tabernacle of
    Molek
and the star of your god Rephan,
    the idols you made to worship.
Therefore I will send you into exile'ᶠ
    beyond Babylon.

⁴⁴"Our ancestors had the tabernacle of the covenant law with them in the wilderness. It had been made as God directed Moses, according to the pattern he had seen. ⁴⁵After receiving the tabernacle, our ancestors under Joshua brought it with them when they took the land from the nations God drove out before them. It remained in the land until the time of David, ⁴⁶who enjoyed God's favor and asked that he might provide a dwelling place for the God of Jacob.ᵍ ⁴⁷But it was Solomon who built a house for him.

⁴⁸"However, the Most High does not live in houses made by human hands. As the prophet says:

⁴⁹" 'Heaven is my throne,
    and the earth is my footstool.
What kind of house will you build for
    me?
                  says the Lord.
Or where will my resting place be?
⁵⁰Has not my hand made all these
    things?'ʰ

⁵¹"You stiff-necked people! Your hearts and ears are still uncircumcised. You are just like your ancestors: You always resist the Holy Spirit! ⁵²Was there ever a prophet your ancestors did not persecute? They even killed those who predicted the coming of the Righteous One. And now you have betrayed and murdered him— ⁵³you who have received the law that was given through angels but have not obeyed it."

ᵃ 28 Exodus 2:14   ᵇ 32 Exodus 3:6
ᶜ 34 Exodus 3:5,7,8,10   ᵈ 37 Deut. 18:15
ᵉ 40 Exodus 32:1   ᶠ 43 Amos 5:25-27 (see Septuagint)
ᵍ 46 Some early manuscripts *the house of Jacob*
ʰ 50 Isaiah 66:1,2

The Stoning of Stephen

⁵⁴When the members of the Sanhedrin heard this, they were furious and gnashed their teeth at him. ⁵⁵But Stephen, full of the Holy Spirit, looked up to heaven and saw the glory of God, and Jesus standing at the right hand of God. ⁵⁶"Look," he said, "I see heaven open and the Son of Man standing at the right hand of God."

⁵⁷At this they covered their ears and, yelling at the top of their voices, they all rushed at him, ⁵⁸dragged him out of the city and began to stone him. Meanwhile, the witnesses laid their coats at the feet of a young man named Saul.

BREAKTHROUGH!

Stoning

(ACTS 7:58)

Among the Jews, this was the way they punished people who had done something they considered very bad. For example, if a person worshiped an idol or stole something from the temple, they would kill them by stoning. They would take the person outside the city, and then a witness would throw a big stone against the person's chest to kill him or her. If the first stone didn't kill the person, other witnesses would throw more stones until the person died. That was the way they made sure that nobody would do something that was forbidden.

⁵⁹While they were stoning him, Stephen prayed, "Lord Jesus, receive my spirit." ⁶⁰Then he fell on his knees and cried out, "Lord, do not hold this sin against them." When he had said this, he fell asleep.

8 And Saul approved of their killing him.

The Church Persecuted and Scattered

On that day a great persecution broke out against the church in Jerusalem, and all except the apostles were scattered throughout Judea and Samaria. ²Godly men buried Stephen and mourned deeply for him. ³But Saul began to destroy the church. Going from house to house, he dragged off both men and women and put them in prison.

Philip in Samaria

⁴Those who had been scattered preached the word wherever they went. ⁵Philip went down to a city in Samaria and proclaimed the Messiah there. ⁶When the crowds heard Philip and saw the signs he performed, they all paid close attention to what he said. ⁷For with shrieks, impure spirits came out of many, and many who were paralyzed or lame were healed. ⁸So there was great joy in that city.

Simon the Sorcerer

⁹Now for some time a man named Simon had practiced sorcery in the city and amazed all the people of Samaria. He boasted that he was someone great, ¹⁰and all the people, both high and low, gave him their attention and exclaimed, "This man is rightly called the Great Power of God." ¹¹They followed him because he had amazed them for a long time with his sorcery. ¹²But when they believed Philip as he proclaimed the good news of the kingdom of God and the name of Jesus Christ, they were baptized, both men and women. ¹³Simon himself believed and was baptized. And he followed Philip everywhere, astonished by the great signs and miracles he saw.

¹⁴When the apostles in Jerusalem heard that Samaria had accepted the word of God, they sent Peter and John to

THE
WITNESSES

✓ SAUL/PAUL (ACTS 8:1–3)

This is the same person. It's just that Saul is Hebrew and Paul is Latin. The name means "small." Paul was born in Tarsus, a city in the Roman province of Cilicia. He was a Roman citizen, but he was Jewish and a Pharisee, so he had studied the Bible a lot. When he was young, he persecuted the Christians and got them put in jail. Then one day Jesus appeared to him, and he began to believe in Jesus.

Samaria. ¹⁵When they arrived, they prayed for the new believers there that they might receive the Holy Spirit, ¹⁶because the Holy Spirit had not yet come on any of them; they had simply been baptized in the name of the Lord Jesus. ¹⁷Then Peter and John placed their hands on them, and they received the Holy Spirit.

¹⁸When Simon saw that the Spirit was given at the laying on of the apostles' hands, he offered them money ¹⁹and said,

BREAKTHROUGH!

The church
(ACTS 8:3)

This word comes from the Greek word that means "to meet." In the Bible, the word *church* is used to talk about a group of Christians. But let me tell you something very interesting. In the Bible, *church* is never used to talk about a building where the believers met.

"Give me also this ability so that everyone on whom I lay my hands may receive the Holy Spirit."

²⁰Peter answered: "May your money perish with you, because you thought you could buy the gift of God with money! ²¹You have no part or share in this ministry, because your heart is not right before God. ²²Repent of this wickedness and pray to the Lord in the hope that he may forgive you for having such a thought in your heart. ²³For I see that you are full of bitterness and captive to sin."

²⁴Then Simon answered, "Pray to the Lord for me so that nothing you have said may happen to me."

²⁵After they had further proclaimed the word of the Lord and testified about Jesus, Peter and John returned to Jerusalem, preaching the gospel in many Samaritan villages.

Philip and the Ethiopian

26Now an angel of the Lord said to Philip, "Go south to the road—the desert road—that goes down from Jerusalem to Gaza." 27So he started out, and on his way he met an Ethiopian*a* eunuch, an important official in charge of all the treasury of the Kandake (which means "queen of the Ethiopians"). This man had gone to Jerusalem to worship, 28and on his way home was sitting in his chariot reading the Book of Isaiah the prophet. 29The Spirit told Philip, "Go to that chariot and stay near it."

30Then Philip ran up to the chariot and heard the man reading Isaiah the prophet. "Do you understand what you are reading?" Philip asked.

31"How can I," he said, "unless someone explains it to me?" So he invited Philip to come up and sit with him.

GAZA

(ACTS 8:26)

This Canaanite city was very, very old. It was on the commercial route between Egypt and Mesopotamia. It was destroyed and rebuilt several times. In the New Testament, it's mentioned only this once.

32This is the passage of Scripture the eunuch was reading:

"He was led like a sheep to the
    slaughter,
and as a lamb before its shearer is
    silent,
so he did not open his mouth.
33In his humiliation he was deprived of
    justice.
Who can speak of his descendants?
For his life was taken from the
    earth."*b*

34The eunuch asked Philip, "Tell me, please, who is the prophet talking about, himself or someone else?" 35Then Philip began with that very passage of Scripture and told him the good news about Jesus.

36As they traveled along the road, they came to some water and the eunuch said, "Look, here is water. What can stand in the way of my being baptized?" [37]*c* 38And he gave orders to stop the chariot. Then both Philip and the eunuch went down into the water and Philip baptized him. 39When they came up out of the water, the Spirit of the Lord suddenly took Philip away, and the eunuch did not see him again, but went on his way rejoicing. 40Philip, however, appeared at Azotus and traveled about, preaching the gospel in all the towns until he reached Caesarea.

Saul's Conversion

9 Meanwhile, Saul was still breathing out murderous threats against the Lord's disciples. He went to the high priest 2and asked him for letters to the synagogues in Damascus, so that if he found any there who belonged to the Way, whether men or women, he might take them as prisoners to Jerusalem. 3As he neared Damascus on his journey, suddenly a light from heaven flashed around him. 4He fell to the ground and heard a voice say to him, "Saul, Saul, why do you persecute me?"

5"Who are you, Lord?" Saul asked.

a 27 That is, from the southern Nile region
b 33 Isaiah 53:7,8 (see Septuagint)   *c* 37 Some manuscripts include here *Philip said, "If you believe with all your heart, you may." The eunuch answered, "I believe that Jesus Christ is the Son of God."*

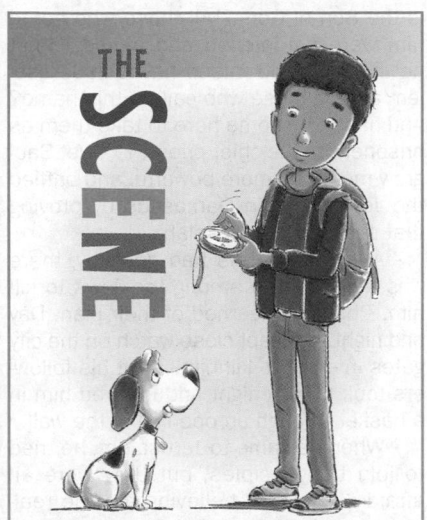

THE SCENE

DAMASCUS

(ACTS 9:1–2)

This was the capital of Syria. Since it was located at the crossroads of important roads, Damascus was always a busy city of business and culture. In Paul's time, Damascus was governed by the Romans.

"I am Jesus, whom you are persecuting," he replied. ⁶"Now get up and go into the city, and you will be told what you must do."

⁷The men traveling with Saul stood there speechless; they heard the sound but did not see anyone. ⁸Saul got up from the ground, but when he opened his eyes he could see nothing. So they led him by the hand into Damascus. ⁹For three days he was blind, and did not eat or drink anything.

¹⁰In Damascus there was a disciple named Ananias. The Lord called to him in a vision, "Ananias!"

"Yes, Lord," he answered.

¹¹The Lord told him, "Go to the house of Judas on Straight Street and ask for a man from Tarsus named Saul, for he is praying. ¹²In a vision he has seen a man named Ananias come and place his hands on him to restore his sight."

¹³"Lord," Ananias answered, "I have heard many reports about this man and all the harm he has done to your holy people in Jerusalem. ¹⁴And he has come here with authority from the chief priests to arrest all who call on your name."

¹⁵But the Lord said to Ananias, "Go! This man is my chosen instrument to proclaim my name to the Gentiles and their kings and to the people of Israel. ¹⁶I will show him how much he must suffer for my name."

¹⁷Then Ananias went to the house and

THE WITNESSES

✓ **ANANIAS** (ACTS 9:10)

He was a believer who lived in Damascus. One day, God gave him a vision, and he was told to help Paul. God used Ananias so Paul could get his eyesight back and receive the Holy Spirit and be baptized.

THE SCENE

TARSUS

(ACTS 9:11)

This was the biggest city in Cilicia in Asia Minor. It was in a fertile valley 10 miles (16 km) from the Mediterranean Sea. A Jewish colony settled there in the 4th century before Christ. In the 1st century, it became the capital of a province of the Roman empire. Some of the inhabitants of Tarsus (like Paul) were Roman citizens and had the same rights. The city belongs to Turkey now.

entered it. Placing his hands on Saul, he said, "Brother Saul, the Lord—Jesus, who appeared to you on the road as you were coming here—has sent me so that you may see again and be filled with the Holy Spirit." 18Immediately, something like scales fell from Saul's eyes, and he could see again. He got up and was baptized, 19and after taking some food, he regained his strength.

Saul in Damascus and Jerusalem

Saul spent several days with the disciples in Damascus. 20At once he began to preach in the synagogues that Jesus

is the Son of God. 21All those who heard him were astonished and asked, "Isn't he the man who raised havoc in Jerusalem among those who call on this name? And hasn't he come here to take them as prisoners to the chief priests?" 22Yet Saul grew more and more powerful and baffled the Jews living in Damascus by proving that Jesus is the Messiah.

23After many days had gone by, there was a conspiracy among the Jews to kill him, 24but Saul learned of their plan. Day and night they kept close watch on the city gates in order to kill him. 25But his followers took him by night and lowered him in a basket through an opening in the wall.

26When he came to Jerusalem, he tried to join the disciples, but they were all afraid of him, not believing that he really was a disciple. 27But Barnabas took him and brought him to the apostles. He told them how Saul on his journey had seen the Lord and that the Lord had spoken to him, and how in Damascus he had preached fearlessly in the name of Jesus. 28So Saul stayed with them and moved about freely in Jerusalem, speaking boldly in the name of the Lord. 29He talked and debated with the Hellenistic Jews,[a] but they tried to kill him. 30When the believers learned of this, they took him down to Caesarea and sent him off to Tarsus.

31Then the church throughout Judea, Galilee and Samaria enjoyed a time of peace and was strengthened. Living in the fear of the Lord and encouraged by the Holy Spirit, it increased in numbers.

Aeneas and Dorcas

32As Peter traveled about the country, he went to visit the Lord's people who lived in Lydda. 33There he found a man named Aeneas, who was paralyzed and had been bedridden for eight years. 34"Aeneas," Peter said to him, "Jesus Christ heals you. Get up and roll up your mat." Immediately Aeneas got up. 35All those who lived in Lydda and Sharon saw him and turned to the Lord.

36In Joppa there was a disciple named

---

a 29 That is, Jews who had adopted the Greek language and culture

Tabitha (in Greek her name is Dorcas); she was always doing good and helping the poor. ³⁷About that time she became sick and died, and her body was washed and placed in an upstairs room. ³⁸Lydda was near Joppa; so when the disciples heard that Peter was in Lydda, they sent two men to him and urged him, "Please come at once!"

³⁹Peter went with them, and when he arrived he was taken upstairs to the room. All the widows stood around him, crying and showing him the robes and other clothing that Dorcas had made while she was still with them.

BREAKTHROUGH!

What were the churches like at that time?

(ACTS 9:31)

At first, the people who believed in Jesus met in the synagogues, because they were Jews. Later, some Jews didn't want to meet with the Christians, so they wouldn't let them enter the synagogues. After that, Jesus' followers began to meet in the homes of different families, like that of Mary the mother of John Mark or Lydia's house. They would meet to pray, to read the Bible and study it, and to sing. A few years after the day of Pentecost, people started calling them "Christians," because they were following the teachings of Christ.

THE SCENE

JOPPA

(ACTS 9:36)

This ancient city had a wall all around it so enemies couldn't enter. It was 28 miles (45 km) south of Caesarea and 31 miles (50 km) northwest of Jerusalem. In Jesus' time, it was Jerusalem's main port. Now it's in Israel and its name is Jaffa.

⁴⁰Peter sent them all out of the room; then he got down on his knees and prayed. Turning toward the dead woman, he said, "Tabitha, get up." She opened her eyes, and seeing Peter she sat up. ⁴¹He took her by the hand and helped her to her feet. Then he called for the believers, especially the widows, and presented her to them alive. ⁴²This became known all over Joppa, and many people believed in the Lord. ⁴³Peter stayed in Joppa for some time with a tanner named Simon.

Cornelius Calls for Peter

10 At Caesarea there was a man named Cornelius, a centurion in what was known as the Italian Regiment. ²He and all his family were devout and men to Joppa to bring back a man named Simon who is called Peter. ⁶He is staying with Simon the tanner, whose house is by the sea."

⁷When the angel who spoke to him had gone, Cornelius called two of his servants and a devout soldier who was one of his attendants. ⁸He told them everything that had happened and sent them to Joppa.

Peter's Vision

⁹About noon the following day as they were on their journey and approaching the city, Peter went up on the roof to pray. ¹⁰He became hungry and wanted something to eat, and while the meal was being prepared, he fell into a trance. ¹¹He

THE

WITNESSES

✓ **CORNELIUS** (ACTS 10:1)
He was a captain of the Roman army and had 100 soldiers under his command. He lived in Caesarea. He was a good person and prayed to God every day. One afternoon, he had a vision, and God told him to look for Peter and ask him to explain what salvation through Jesus was about. After he listened to Peter, Cornelius believed in Jesus as his Savior. He received the Holy Spirit and was baptized.

God-fearing; he gave generously to those in need and prayed to God regularly. ³One day at about three in the afternoon he had a vision. He distinctly saw an angel of God, who came to him and said, "Cornelius!"

⁴Cornelius stared at him in fear. "What is it, Lord?" he asked.

The angel answered, "Your prayers and gifts to the poor have come up as a memorial offering before God. ⁵Now send

THE SCENE

CAESAREA

(ACTS 10:1)

This city was built by Herod the Great between the years 25 and 13 before Christ, and he gave it this name in honor of Caesar Augustus, the Roman emperor. It was on the Mediterranean Sea coast, 62 miles (100 km) from Jerusalem. Herod built an important seaport there. Caesarea belongs to Israel now.

saw heaven opened and something like a large sheet being let down to earth by its four corners. ¹²It contained all kinds of four-footed animals, as well as reptiles and birds. ¹³Then a voice told him, "Get up, Peter. Kill and eat."

¹⁴"Surely not, Lord!" Peter replied. "I have never eaten anything impure or unclean."

¹⁵The voice spoke to him a second time, "Do not call anything impure that God has made clean."

¹⁶This happened three times, and immediately the sheet was taken back to heaven.

¹⁷While Peter was wondering about the meaning of the vision, the men sent by Cornelius found out where Simon's house was and stopped at the gate. ¹⁸They called out, asking if Simon who was known as Peter was staying there.

¹⁹While Peter was still thinking about the vision, the Spirit said to him, "Simon, three*ᵃ* men are looking for you. ²⁰So get up and go downstairs. Do not hesitate to go with them, for I have sent them."

²¹Peter went down and said to the men, "I'm the one you're looking for. Why have you come?"

²²The men replied, "We have come from Cornelius the centurion. He is a righteous and God-fearing man, who is respected by all the Jewish people. A holy angel told him to ask you to come to his house so that he could hear what you have to say." ²³Then Peter invited the men into the house to be his guests.

Peter at Cornelius's House

The next day Peter started out with them, and some of the believers from Joppa went along. ²⁴The following day he arrived in Caesarea. Cornelius was expecting them and had called together his relatives and close friends. ²⁵As Peter entered the house, Cornelius met him and fell at his feet in reverence. ²⁶But Peter made him get up. "Stand up," he said, "I am only a man myself."

²⁷While talking with him, Peter went inside and found a large gathering of people. ²⁸He said to them: "You are well aware that it is against our law for a Jew

BREAKTHROUGH!

Why did the law say they couldn't eat certain animals?

(ACTS 10:14)

In a book called Leviticus, God gave the Israelite people some laws about what they could and couldn't eat. The animals they could eat were considered clean, and those they couldn't eat were considered not clean. Those unclean animals were rabbits, camels and pigs. A person who ate an animal that wasn't clean also became unclean. Later, Jesus told his disciples that what they ate wouldn't make them unclean, and that what really made a person unclean were bad thoughts.

to associate with or visit a Gentile. But God has shown me that I should not call anyone impure or unclean. ²⁹So when I was sent for, I came without raising any objection. May I ask why you sent for me?"

³⁰Cornelius answered: "Three days ago I was in my house praying at this hour, at three in the afternoon. Suddenly a man in shining clothes stood before me ³¹and said, 'Cornelius, God has heard your prayer and remembered your gifts to the poor. ³²Send to Joppa for Simon who is called Peter. He is a guest in the home of

---

ᵃ 19 One early manuscript *two*; other manuscripts do not have the number.

Simon the tanner, who lives by the sea.' ³³So I sent for you immediately, and it was good of you to come. Now we are all here in the presence of God to listen to everything the Lord has commanded you to tell us."

³⁴Then Peter began to speak: "I now realize how true it is that God does not show favoritism ³⁵but accepts from every nation the one who fears him and does what is right. ³⁶You know the message God sent to the people of Israel, announcing the good news of peace through Jesus Christ, who is Lord of all. ³⁷You know what has happened throughout the province of Judea, beginning in Galilee after the baptism that John preached— ³⁸how God anointed Jesus of Nazareth with the Holy Spirit and power, and how he went around doing good and healing all who were under the power of the devil, because God was with him.

³⁹"We are witnesses of everything he did in the country of the Jews and in Jerusalem. They killed him by hanging him on a cross, ⁴⁰but God raised him from the dead on the third day and caused him to be seen. ⁴¹He was not seen by all the people, but by witnesses whom God had already chosen—by us who ate and drank with him after he rose from the dead. ⁴²He commanded us to preach to the people and to testify that he is the one whom God appointed as judge of the living and the dead. ⁴³All the prophets testify about him that everyone who believes in him receives forgiveness of sins through his name."

⁴⁴While Peter was still speaking these words, the Holy Spirit came on all who heard the message. ⁴⁵The circumcised believers who had come with Peter were astonished that the gift of the Holy Spirit had been poured out even on Gentiles. ⁴⁶For they heard them speaking in tongues*ᵃ* and praising God.

Then Peter said, ⁴⁷"Surely no one can stand in the way of their being baptized with water. They have received the Holy Spirit just as we have." ⁴⁸So he ordered that they be baptized in the name of Jesus Christ. Then they asked Peter to stay with them for a few days.

Peter Explains His Actions

11 The apostles and the believers throughout Judea heard that the Gentiles also had received the word of God. ²So when Peter went up to Jerusalem, the circumcised believers criticized him ³and said, "You went into the house of uncircumcised men and ate with them."

⁴Starting from the beginning, Peter told them the whole story: ⁵"I was in the city of Joppa praying, and in a trance I saw a vision. I saw something like a large sheet being let down from heaven by its four corners, and it came down to where I was. ⁶I looked into it and saw four-footed animals of the earth, wild beasts, reptiles and birds. ⁷Then I heard a voice telling me, 'Get up, Peter. Kill and eat.'

⁸"I replied, 'Surely not, Lord! Nothing impure or unclean has ever entered my mouth.'

⁹"The voice spoke from heaven a second time, 'Do not call anything impure that God has made clean.' ¹⁰This happened three times, and then it was all pulled up to heaven again.

¹¹"Right then three men who had been sent to me from Caesarea stopped at the house where I was staying. ¹²The Spirit told me to have no hesitation about going with them. These six brothers also went with me, and we entered the man's house. ¹³He told us how he had seen an angel appear in his house and say, 'Send to Joppa for Simon who is called Peter. ¹⁴He will bring you a message through which you and all your household will be saved.'

¹⁵"As I began to speak, the Holy Spirit came on them as he had come on us at the beginning. ¹⁶Then I remembered what the Lord had said: 'John baptized with*ᵇ* water, but you will be baptized with*ᵇ* the Holy Spirit.' ¹⁷So if God gave them the same gift he gave us who believed in the Lord Jesus Christ, who was I to think that I could stand in God's way?"

¹⁸When they heard this, they had no further objections and praised God, saying, "So then, even to Gentiles God has granted repentance that leads to life."

ᵃ 46 Or other languages   ᵇ 16 Or in

THE
WITNESSES

✓ **CLAUDIUS** (ACTS 11:28)
Claudius was the fourth emperor of Rome. He ruled between the years 41 and 54 after Christ. In the year 49 after Christ, he made a law that said all the Jews had to leave Rome.

✓ **KING HEROD** (ACTS 12:1)
This was Herod Agrippa I (the First). He was a grandson of Herod the Great and the father of Herod Agrippa II (the Second). He was born about ten years before Christ. Herod Agrippa was a good friend of the Romans, and he won over the friendship of the Jews, especially that of the Pharisees. That's why he persecuted the Christians. Emperor Caligula declared him king of an area called Bataenea, and then Claudius, who was the emperor after Caligula, also made him king of Palestine, just as Herod Agrippa's grandfather had been.

The Church in Antioch

¹⁹Now those who had been scattered by the persecution that broke out when Stephen was killed traveled as far as Phoenicia, Cyprus and Antioch, spreading the word only among Jews. ²⁰Some of them, however, men from Cyprus and Cyrene, went to Antioch and began to speak to Greeks also, telling them the good news about the Lord Jesus. ²¹The Lord's hand was with them, and a great number of people believed and turned to the Lord.

²²News of this reached the church in Jerusalem, and they sent Barnabas to Antioch. ²³When he arrived and saw what the grace of God had done, he was glad and encouraged them all to remain true to the Lord with all their hearts. ²⁴He was a good man, full of the Holy Spirit and faith, and a great number of people were brought to the Lord.

²⁵Then Barnabas went to Tarsus to look for Saul, ²⁶and when he found him, he brought him to Antioch. So for a whole year Barnabas and Saul met with the church and taught great numbers of people. The disciples were called Christians first at Antioch.

²⁷During this time some prophets came down from Jerusalem to Antioch. ²⁸One of them, named Agabus, stood up and through the Spirit predicted that a severe famine would spread over the entire Roman world. (This happened during the reign of Claudius.) ²⁹The disciples, as each one was able, decided to provide help for the brothers and sisters living in Judea. ³⁰This they did, sending their gift to the elders by Barnabas and Saul.

Peter's Miraculous Escape From Prison

12 It was about this time that King Herod arrested some who belonged to the church, intending to persecute them. ²He had James, the brother of John, put to death with the sword. ³When he saw that this met with approval among the Jews, he proceeded to seize Peter also. This happened during the Festival of Unleavened Bread. ⁴After arresting him, he put him in prison, handing him over to be guarded by four squads of four soldiers each. Herod intended to bring him out for public trial after the Passover.

⁵So Peter was kept in prison, but the church was earnestly praying to God for him.

⁶The night before Herod was to bring him to trial, Peter was sleeping between two soldiers, bound with two chains, and

THE SCENE

CYPRUS AND ANTIOCH

(ACTS 11:19)

Cyprus is an island in the Mediterranean Sea, right between the Syrian and Sicilian coasts. In the year 58 before Christ, it became a Roman territory, but now it's a free country. In the Bible, there are two cities named Antioch. This one is called Antioch of Syria, and it's called that because in the year 65 before Christ, it became the capital of the province of Syria. Antioch was the third-most important city in Roman territory. That's where the first Christian church was formed by people who were not Jewish. It was in this city that Jesus' followers were first called "Christians."

BREAKTHROUGH!

Why did they send money to the elders in the church in Jerusalem?

(ACTS 11:30)

Around 40 to 50 years after Christ, there was a big famine (food shortage) in Palestine. That's why the Christians in Antioch gathered money and sent it to Jerusalem to help their Christian brothers and sisters who didn't have enough food to eat.

sentries stood guard at the entrance. ⁷Suddenly an angel of the Lord appeared and a light shone in the cell. He struck Peter on the side and woke him up. "Quick, get up!" he said, and the chains fell off Peter's wrists.

⁸Then the angel said to him, "Put on your clothes and sandals." And Peter did so. "Wrap your cloak around you and follow me," the angel told him. ⁹Peter followed him out of the prison, but he had no idea that what the angel was doing was really happening; he thought he was seeing a vision. ¹⁰They passed the first and second guards and came to the iron gate leading to the city. It opened for them by itself, and they went through it. When they had walked the length of one street, suddenly the angel left him.

¹¹Then Peter came to himself and said,

"Now I know without a doubt that the Lord has sent his angel and rescued me from Herod's clutches and from everything the Jewish people were hoping would happen."

¹²When this had dawned on him, he went to the house of Mary the mother of John, also called Mark, where many people had gathered and were praying. ¹³Peter knocked at the outer entrance, and a servant named Rhoda came to answer the door. ¹⁴When she recognized Peter's voice, she was so overjoyed she ran back without opening it and exclaimed, "Peter is at the door!"

¹⁵"You're out of your mind," they told her. When she kept insisting that it was so, they said, "It must be his angel."

¹⁶But Peter kept on knocking, and when they opened the door and saw him, they were astonished. ¹⁷Peter motioned with his hand for them to be quiet and described how the Lord had brought him out of prison. "Tell James and the other brothers and sisters about this," he said, and then he left for another place.

¹⁸In the morning, there was no small commotion among the soldiers as to what had become of Peter. ¹⁹After Herod had a thorough search made for him and did not find him, he cross-examined the guards and ordered that they be executed.

Herod's Death

Then Herod went from Judea to Caesarea and stayed there. ²⁰He had been quarreling with the people of Tyre and Sidon; they now joined together and sought an audience with him. After securing the support of Blastus, a trusted personal servant of the king, they asked for peace, because they depended on the king's country for their food supply.

²¹On the appointed day Herod, wearing his royal robes, sat on his throne and delivered a public address to the people. ²²They shouted, "This is the voice of a god, not of a man." ²³Immediately, because Herod did not give praise to God, an angel of the Lord struck him down, and he was eaten by worms and died.

²⁴But the word of God continued to spread and flourish.

THE
WITNESSES

✓ **RHODA** (ACTS 12:13)
In Greek, this name means "rose." She was a servant in the house of Mary, the mother of John Mark.

✓ **JOHN MARK** (ACTS 12:25)
He was Barnabas' cousin. His mother, Mary, opened her home in Jerusalem to receive the Christians so they could pray and talk about Jesus there. John Mark went with Barnabas and Paul on their first missionary journey to preach the good news that Jesus is the Savior. A very, very long time ago, it was decided that this Mark is the author of the gospel of Mark.

Barnabas and Saul Sent Off

²⁵When Barnabas and Saul had finished their mission, they returned from[a] Jerusalem, taking with them John, also

---

a 25 Some manuscripts to

13 called Mark. ¹Now in the church at Antioch there were prophets and teachers: Barnabas, Simeon called Niger, Lucius of Cyrene, Manaen (who had been brought up with Herod the tetrarch) and Saul. ²While they were worshiping the Lord and fasting, the Holy Spirit said, "Set apart for me Barnabas and Saul for the work to which I have called them." ³So after they had fasted and prayed, they placed their hands on them and sent them off.

On Cyprus

⁴The two of them, sent on their way by the Holy Spirit, went down to Seleucia and sailed from there to Cyprus. ⁵When they arrived at Salamis, they proclaimed the word of God in the Jewish synagogues. John was with them as their helper.

⁶They traveled through the whole island until they came to Paphos. There they met a Jewish sorcerer and false prophet named Bar-Jesus, ⁷who was an attendant of the proconsul, Sergius Paulus. The proconsul, an intelligent man, sent for Barnabas and Saul because he wanted to hear the word of God. ⁸But Elymas the sorcerer (for that is what his name means) opposed them and tried to turn the proconsul from the faith. ⁹Then Saul, who was also called Paul, filled with the Holy Spirit, looked straight at Elymas and said, ¹⁰"You are a child of the devil and an enemy of everything that is right! You are full of all kinds of deceit and trickery. Will you never stop perverting the right ways of the Lord? ¹¹Now the hand of the Lord is against you. You are going to be blind for a time, not even able to see the light of the sun."

Immediately mist and darkness came over him, and he groped about, seeking someone to lead him by the hand. ¹²When the proconsul saw what had happened, he believed, for he was amazed at the teaching about the Lord.

In Pisidian Antioch

¹³From Paphos, Paul and his companions sailed to Perga in Pamphylia, where John left them to return to Jerusalem. ¹⁴From Perga they went on to Pisidian Antioch. On the Sabbath they entered

THE SCENE

SALAMIS

(ACTS 13:5)

This city is on the west coast of the island of Cyprus. It became more important than Paphos, which was the capital of the island.

PAPHOS

(ACTS 13:6)

A seashore city. It was built by Augustus. It was the capital of the island of Cyprus, and the representative (proconsul) of the Roman empire lived there.

the synagogue and sat down. ¹⁵After the reading from the Law and the Prophets, the leaders of the synagogue sent word to them, saying, "Brothers, if you have a word of exhortation for the people, please speak."

¹⁶Standing up, Paul motioned with his hand and said: "Fellow Israelites and you Gentiles who worship God, listen to me! ¹⁷The God of the people of Israel chose our ancestors; he made the people prosper during their stay in Egypt; with mighty power he led them out of that country;

THE SCENE

PERGA

(ACTS 13:13)

This was the most important city in the region of Pamphylia in Asia Minor. It was the main center for worship of the goddess Artemis (called Diana by the Romans). Perga belongs to Turkey now.

¹⁸for about forty years he endured their conduct*a* in the wilderness; ¹⁹and he overthrew seven nations in Canaan, giving their land to his people as their inheritance. ²⁰All this took about 450 years.

"After this, God gave them judges until the time of Samuel the prophet. ²¹Then the people asked for a king, and he gave them Saul son of Kish, of the tribe of Benjamin, who ruled forty years. ²²After removing Saul, he made David their king. God testified concerning him: 'I have found David son of Jesse, a man after my own heart; he will do everything I want him to do.'

²³"From this man's descendants God has brought to Israel the Savior Jesus, as he promised. ²⁴Before the coming of Jesus, John preached repentance and baptism to all the people of Israel. ²⁵As John was completing his work, he said:

'Who do you suppose I am? I am not the one you are looking for. But there is one coming after me whose sandals I am not worthy to untie.'

²⁶"Fellow children of Abraham and you God-fearing Gentiles, it is to us that this message of salvation has been sent. ²⁷The people of Jerusalem and their rulers did not recognize Jesus, yet in condemning him they fulfilled the words of the prophets that are read every Sabbath. ²⁸Though they found no proper ground for a death sentence, they asked Pilate to have him executed. ²⁹When they had carried out all that was written about him, they took him down from the cross and laid him in a tomb. ³⁰But God raised him from the dead, ³¹and for many days he was seen by those who had traveled with him from Galilee to Jerusalem. They are now his witnesses to our people.

³²"We tell you the good news: What God promised our ancestors ³³he has fulfilled for us, their children, by raising up Jesus. As it is written in the second Psalm:

" 'You are my son;
    today I have become your father.'*b*

³⁴God raised him from the dead so that he will never be subject to decay. As God has said,

" 'I will give you the holy and sure
    blessings promised to David.'*c*

³⁵So it is also stated elsewhere:

" 'You will not let your holy one see
    decay.'*d*

³⁶"Now when David had served God's purpose in his own generation, he fell asleep; he was buried with his ancestors and his body decayed. ³⁷But the one whom God raised from the dead did not see decay.

³⁸"Therefore, my friends, I want you to know that through Jesus the forgiveness of sins is proclaimed to you. ³⁹Through him everyone who believes is set free from every sin, a justification you were not able to obtain under the law of Moses.

---

a 18 Some manuscripts *he cared for them*
b 33 Psalm 2:7   *c* 34 Isaiah 55:3   *d* 35 Psalm 16:10
(see Septuagint)

⁴⁰Take care that what the prophets have said does not happen to you:

⁴¹ " 'Look, you scoffers,
    wonder and perish,
  for I am going to do something in your
      days
    that you would never believe,
    even if someone told you.'ᵃ"

⁴²As Paul and Barnabas were leaving the synagogue, the people invited them to speak further about these things on the next Sabbath. ⁴³When the congregation was dismissed, many of the Jews and devout converts to Judaism followed Paul and Barnabas, who talked with them and urged them to continue in the grace of God.

⁴⁴On the next Sabbath almost the whole city gathered to hear the word of the Lord. ⁴⁵When the Jews saw the crowds, they were filled with jealousy. They began to contradict what Paul was saying and heaped abuse on him.

⁴⁶Then Paul and Barnabas answered them boldly: "We had to speak the word of God to you first. Since you reject it and do not consider yourselves worthy of eternal life, we now turn to the Gentiles. ⁴⁷For this is what the Lord has commanded us:

" 'I have made youᵇ a light for the
      Gentiles,
    that youᵇ may bring salvation to the
      ends of the earth.'ᶜ"

⁴⁸When the Gentiles heard this, they were glad and honored the word of the Lord; and all who were appointed for eternal life believed.

⁴⁹The word of the Lord spread through the whole region. ⁵⁰But the Jewish leaders incited the God-fearing women of high standing and the leading men of the city. They stirred up persecution against Paul and Barnabas, and expelled them from their region. ⁵¹So they shook the dust off their feet as a warning to them and went to Iconium. ⁵²And the disciples were filled with joy and with the Holy Spirit.

In Iconium

14 At Iconium Paul and Barnabas went as usual into the Jewish synagogue. There they spoke so effectively that a great number of Jews and Greeks believed. ²But the Jews who refused to believe stirred up the other Gentiles and poisoned their minds against the brothers. ³So Paul and Barnabas spent considerable time there, speaking boldly for the Lord, who confirmed the message of his grace by enabling them to perform signs and wonders. ⁴The people of the city were divided; some sided with the Jews, others with the apostles. ⁵There was a plot afoot among both Gentiles and Jews, together with their leaders, to mistreat them and stone them. ⁶But they found out about it and fled to the Lycaonian cities of Lystra and Derbe and to the surrounding country, ⁷where they continued to preach the gospel.

ᵃ 41 Hab. 1:5   ᵇ 47 The Greek is singular.
ᶜ 47 Isaiah 49:6

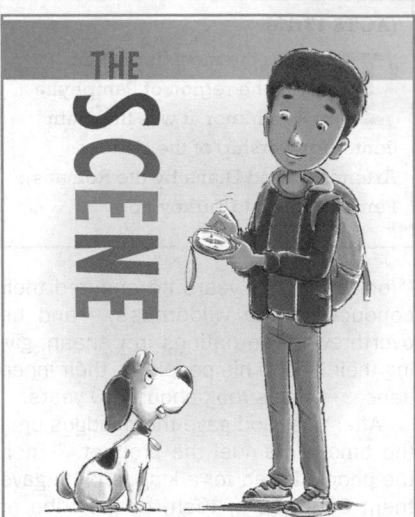

ICONIUM

(ACTS 14:1)

In the 1st century, this was one of the principal cities in the south of the Roman province of Galatia, 19 miles (30 km) from Lystra. It was on the main road between Ephesus and Tarsus. Now it belongs to Turkey.

In Lystra and Derbe

⁸In Lystra there sat a man who was lame. He had been that way from birth and had never walked. ⁹He listened to Paul as he was speaking. Paul looked directly at him, saw that he had faith to be healed ¹⁰and called out, "Stand up on your feet!" At that, the man jumped up and began to walk.

¹¹When the crowd saw what Paul had done, they shouted in the Lycaonian language, "The gods have come down to us in human form!" ¹²Barnabas they called Zeus, and Paul they called Hermes because he was the chief speaker. ¹³The priest of Zeus, whose temple was just outside the city, brought bulls and wreaths to the city gates because he and the crowd wanted to offer sacrifices to them.

¹⁴But when the apostles Barnabas and Paul heard of this, they tore their

THE SCENE

LYSTRA AND DERBE

(ACTS 14:6–7)

These two cities were in Lycaonia, in the Roman province of Galatia. The distance between Lystra and Derbe was about 56 miles (90 km). They belong to Turkey now.

THE WITNESSES

✓ **ZEUS AND HERMES** (ACTS 14:12)
Zeus was the most important Greek god. The Romans called him Jupiter. Hermes was the messenger of the gods, and the Romans called him Mercury.

clothes and rushed out into the crowd, shouting: ¹⁵"Friends, why are you doing this? We too are only human, like you. We are bringing you good news, telling you to turn from these worthless things to the living God, who made the heavens and the earth and the sea and everything in them. ¹⁶In the past, he let all nations go their own way. ¹⁷Yet he has not left himself without testimony: He has shown kindness by giving you rain from heaven and crops in their seasons; he provides you with plenty of food and fills your hearts with joy." ¹⁸Even with these words, they had difficulty keeping the crowd from sacrificing to them.

[19]Then some Jews came from Antioch and Iconium and won the crowd over. They stoned Paul and dragged him outside the city, thinking he was dead. [20]But after the disciples had gathered around him, he got up and went back into the city. The next day he and Barnabas left for Derbe.

The Return to Antioch in Syria

[21]They preached the gospel in that city and won a large number of disciples. Then they returned to Lystra, Iconium and Antioch, [22]strengthening the disciples and encouraging them to remain true to the faith. "We must go through many hardships to enter the kingdom of God," they said. [23]Paul and Barnabas appointed elders[a] for them in each church and, with prayer and fasting, committed them to the Lord, in whom they had put their trust. [24]After going through Pisidia, they came into Pamphylia, [25]and when they had preached the word in Perga, they went down to Attalia.

[26]From Attalia they sailed back to Antioch, where they had been committed to the grace of God for the work they had now completed. [27]On arriving there, they gathered the church together and reported all that God had done through them and how he had opened a door of faith to the Gentiles. [28]And they stayed there a long time with the disciples.

The Council at Jerusalem

15 Certain people came down from Judea to Antioch and were teaching the believers: "Unless you are circumcised, according to the custom taught by Moses, you cannot be saved." [2]This brought Paul and Barnabas into sharp dispute and debate with them. So Paul and Barnabas were appointed, along with some other believers, to go up to Jerusalem to see the apostles and elders about this question. [3]The church sent them on their way, and as they traveled through Phoenicia and Samaria, they told how the Gentiles had been converted. This news made all the believers very glad. [4]When they came to Jerusalem, they were welcomed by the church and the apostles and elders, to whom they reported everything God had done through them.

[5]Then some of the believers who belonged to the party of the Pharisees stood up and said, "The Gentiles must be circumcised and required to keep the law of Moses."

[6]The apostles and elders met to consider this question. [7]After much discussion, Peter got up and addressed them: "Brothers, you know that some time ago God made a choice among you that the Gentiles might hear from my lips the message of the gospel and believe. [8]God, who knows the heart, showed that he accepted them by giving the Holy Spirit to them, just as he did to us. [9]He did not discriminate between us and them, for he purified their hearts by faith. [10]Now then, why do you try to test God by putting on the necks of Gentiles a yoke that neither we nor our ancestors have been able to bear? [11]No! We believe it is through the grace of our Lord Jesus that we are saved, just as they are."

[12]The whole assembly became silent as they listened to Barnabas and Paul telling about the signs and wonders God had done among the Gentiles through them. [13]When they finished, James spoke up. "Brothers," he said, "listen to me. [14]Simon[b] has described to us how God first intervened to choose a people for his name from the Gentiles. [15]The words of the prophets are in agreement with this, as it is written:

[16] " 'After this I will return
    and rebuild David's fallen tent.
Its ruins I will rebuild,
    and I will restore it,
[17]that the rest of mankind may seek the Lord,
    even all the Gentiles who bear my name,
says the Lord, who does these things'[c]—
[18]   things known from long ago.[d]

---

[a] 23 Or *Barnabas ordained elders*; or *Barnabas had elders elected*   [b] 14 Greek *Simeon*, a variant of *Simon*; that is, Peter   [c] 17 Amos 9:11,12 (see Septuagint)   [d] 17,18 Some manuscripts *things'* — / [18]*the Lord's work is known to him from long ago*

THE
WITNESSES

✓ **JAMES** (ACTS 15:13)
The Bible says that Jesus had several brothers. One of them was James, who became the leader of the church in Jerusalem. He also is the author of the letter in the Bible that has his name.

---

19 "It is my judgment, therefore, that we should not make it difficult for the Gentiles who are turning to God. 20 Instead we should write to them, telling them to abstain from food polluted by idols, from sexual immorality, from the meat of strangled animals and from blood. 21 For the law of Moses has been preached in every city from the earliest times and is read in the synagogues on every Sabbath."

The Council's Letter to Gentile Believers

22 Then the apostles and elders, with the whole church, decided to choose some of their own men and send them to Antioch with Paul and Barnabas. They chose Judas (called Barsabbas) and Silas, men who were leaders among the believers. 23 With them they sent the following letter:

The apostles and elders, your brothers,

To the Gentile believers in Antioch, Syria and Cilicia:

Greetings.

24 We have heard that some went out from us without our authorization and disturbed you, troubling your minds by what they said. 25 So we all agreed to choose some men and send them to you with our dear friends Barnabas and Paul— 26 men who have risked their lives for the name of our Lord Jesus Christ. 27 Therefore we are sending Judas and Silas to confirm by word of mouth what we are writing. 28 It seemed good to the Holy Spirit and to us not to burden you with anything beyond the following requirements: 29 You are to abstain from food sacrificed to idols, from blood, from the meat of strangled animals and from sexual immorality. You will do well to avoid these things.

Farewell.

30 So the men were sent off and went down to Antioch, where they gathered the church together and delivered the letter. 31 The people read it and were glad for its encouraging message. 32 Judas and Silas, who themselves were prophets, said much to encourage and strengthen the believers. 33 After spending some time there, they were sent off by the believers with the blessing of peace to return to those who had sent them. [34]a 35 But Paul and Barnabas remained in Antioch, where they and many others taught and preached the word of the Lord.

---

a 34 Some manuscripts include here *But Silas decided to remain there.*

Disagreement Between Paul and Barnabas

36Some time later Paul said to Barnabas, "Let us go back and visit the believers in all the towns where we preached the word of the Lord and see how they are doing." 37Barnabas wanted to take John, also called Mark, with them, 38but Paul did not think it wise to take him, because he had deserted them in Pamphylia and had not continued with them in the work. 39They had such a sharp disagreement that they parted company. Barnabas took Mark and sailed for Cyprus, 40but Paul chose Silas and left, commended by the believers to the grace of the Lord. 41He went through Syria and Cilicia, strengthening the churches.

Timothy Joins Paul and Silas

16 Paul came to Derbe and then to Lystra, where a disciple named Timothy lived, whose mother was Jewish and a believer but whose father was a Greek. 2The believers at Lystra and Iconium spoke well of him. 3Paul wanted to take him along on the journey, so he circumcised him because of the Jews who lived in that area, for they all knew that his father was a Greek. 4As they traveled from town to town, they delivered the decisions reached by the apostles and elders in Jerusalem for the people to obey. 5So the churches were strengthened in the faith and grew daily in numbers.

Paul's Vision of the Man of Macedonia

6Paul and his companions traveled throughout the region of Phrygia and Galatia, having been kept by the Holy Spirit from preaching the word in the province of Asia. 7When they came to the border of Mysia, they tried to enter Bithynia, but the Spirit of Jesus would not allow them to. 8So they passed by Mysia and went down to Troas. 9During the night Paul had a vision of a man of Macedonia standing and begging him, "Come over to Macedonia and help us." 10After Paul had seen the vision, we got ready at once to leave for Macedonia, conclud-

THE SCENE

MACEDONIA

(ACTS 16:9)

The region of Macedonia in northern Greece became a Roman province in the year 148 before Christ. There were important cities there like Thessalonica, Berea and Philippi. Large cultural centers were established there.

ing that God had called us to preach the gospel to them.

Lydia's Conversion in Philippi

11From Troas we put out to sea and sailed straight for Samothrace, and the next day we went on to Neapolis. 12From there we traveled to Philippi, a Roman colony and the leading city of that district*a* of Macedonia. And we stayed there several days.

13On the Sabbath we went outside the city gate to the river, where we expected to find a place of prayer. We sat down and began to speak to the women who had gathered there. 14One of those

a 12 The text and meaning of the Greek for the leading city of that district are uncertain.

listening was a woman from the city of Thyatira named Lydia, a dealer in purple cloth. She was a worshiper of God. The Lord opened her heart to respond to Paul's message. ¹⁵When she and the members of her household were baptized, she invited us to her home. "If you consider me a believer in the Lord," she said, "come and stay at my house." And she persuaded us.

Paul and Silas in Prison

¹⁶Once when we were going to the place of prayer, we were met by a female slave who had a spirit by which she predicted the future. She earned a great deal of money for her owners by fortune-telling. ¹⁷She followed Paul and the rest of us, shouting, "These men are servants of the Most High God, who are telling you the way to be saved." ¹⁸She kept this up for many days. Finally Paul became so annoyed that he turned around and said to the spirit, "In the name of Jesus Christ I command you to come out of her!" At that moment the spirit left her.

¹⁹When her owners realized that their hope of making money was gone, they seized Paul and Silas and dragged them into the marketplace to face the authorities. ²⁰They brought them before the magistrates and said, "These men are Jews, and are throwing our city into an uproar ²¹by advocating customs unlawful for us Romans to accept or practice."

²²The crowd joined in the attack against Paul and Silas, and the magistrates ordered them to be stripped and beaten with rods. ²³After they had been severely flogged, they were thrown into prison, and the jailer was commanded to guard them carefully. ²⁴When he received these orders, he put them in the inner cell and fastened their feet in the stocks.

²⁵About midnight Paul and Silas were praying and singing hymns to God, and the other prisoners were listening to them. ²⁶Suddenly there was such a violent earthquake that the foundations of the prison were shaken. At once all the prison doors flew open, and everyone's chains came loose. ²⁷The jailer woke up, and when he saw the prison doors open,

he drew his sword and was about to kill himself because he thought the prisoners had escaped. ²⁸But Paul shouted, "Don't harm yourself! We are all here!"

²⁹The jailer called for lights, rushed in and fell trembling before Paul and Silas. ³⁰He then brought them out and asked, "Sirs, what must I do to be saved?"

³¹They replied, "Believe in the Lord Jesus, and you will be saved—you and your household." ³²Then they spoke the word of the Lord to him and to all the others in his house. ³³At that hour of the night the jailer took them and washed their wounds; then immediately he and all his household were baptized. ³⁴The jailer brought them into his house and set a meal before them; he was filled with joy because he had come to believe in God—he and his whole household.

³⁵When it was daylight, the magistrates sent their officers to the jailer with the order: "Release those men." ³⁶The jailer

BREAKTHROUGH!

Why did the jailer want to kill himself?

(ACTS 16:27)

Because he felt responsible for watching the prisoners, and he thought that Paul and Silas had escaped. He thought that when his bosses realized the two prisoners were gone, they would punish or kill him.

told Paul, "The magistrates have ordered that you and Silas be released. Now you can leave. Go in peace."

37 But Paul said to the officers: "They beat us publicly without a trial, even though we are Roman citizens, and threw us into prison. And now do they want to get rid of us quietly? No! Let them come themselves and escort us out."

38 The officers reported this to the magistrates, and when they heard that Paul and Silas were Roman citizens, they were alarmed. 39 They came to appease them and escorted them from the prison, requesting them to leave the city. 40 After Paul and Silas came out of the prison, they went to Lydia's house, where they met with the brothers and sisters and encouraged them. Then they left.

In Thessalonica

17 When Paul and his companions had passed through Amphipolis and Apollonia, they came to Thessalonica, where there was a Jewish synagogue. 2 As was

BREAKTHROUGH!

Being a Roman citizen
(ACTS 16:38; 22:25)

In New Testament times, being a Roman citizen had many benefits. There weren't many citizens in the entire Roman empire, but citizens were treated much better than other people. For example, a Roman citizen couldn't be arrested if there hadn't been a trial, and most definitely couldn't be beaten.

THE SCENE

THESSALONICA

(ACTS 17:1)

Read the explanation in 1 Thessalonians 2:1.

his custom, Paul went into the synagogue, and on three Sabbath days he reasoned with them from the Scriptures, 3 explaining and proving that the Messiah had to suffer and rise from the dead. "This Jesus I am proclaiming to you is the Messiah," he said. 4 Some of the Jews were persuaded and joined Paul and Silas, as did a large number of God-fearing Greeks and quite a few prominent women.

5 But other Jews were jealous; so they rounded up some bad characters from the marketplace, formed a mob and started ed a riot in the city. They rushed to Jason's house in search of Paul and Silas in order to bring them out to the crowd.[a] 6 But when they did not find them, they dragged Jason and some other believers before the city officials, shouting: "These men who have caused trouble all over the

---

[a] 5 Or *the assembly of the people*

world have now come here, ⁷and Jason has welcomed them into his house. They are all defying Caesar's decrees, saying that there is another king, one called Jesus." ⁸When they heard this, the crowd and the city officials were thrown into turmoil. ⁹Then they made Jason and the others post bond and let them go.

In Berea

¹⁰As soon as it was night, the believers sent Paul and Silas away to Berea.

On arriving there, they went to the Jewish synagogue. ¹¹Now the Berean Jews were of more noble character than those in Thessalonica, for they received the message with great eagerness and examined the Scriptures every day to see if what Paul said was true. ¹²As a result, many of them believed, as did also a number of prominent Greek women and many Greek men.

¹³But when the Jews in Thessalonica learned that Paul was preaching the word of God at Berea, some of them went there too, agitating the crowds and stirring them up. ¹⁴The believers immediately sent Paul to the coast, but Silas and Timothy stayed at Berea. ¹⁵Those who escorted Paul brought him to Athens and then left with instructions for Silas and Timothy to join him as soon as possible.

THE
WITNESSES

✓ **JASON** (ACTS 17:5)
He was a Jew who was born in Thessalonica. When Paul and Silas preached there, Jason became a Christian, and they stayed in his home. Later, when some Jews in the city created a scandal against Paul and his companion, they took Jason and some other Christians to the authorities, but they were all set free after they had posted bail.

BEREA

(ACTS 17:10)

I t was a big city with a lot of citizens in the province of Macedonia. There was an important Jewish community there. It was about 25 miles (40 km) from the Aegean Sea. Its name is Veria now.

In Athens

16While Paul was waiting for them in Athens, he was greatly distressed to see that the city was full of idols. 17So he reasoned in the synagogue with both Jews and God-fearing Greeks, as well as in the marketplace day by day with those who happened to be there. 18A group of Epicurean and Stoic philosophers began to debate with him. Some of them asked, "What is this babbler trying to say?" Others remarked, "He seems to be advocating foreign gods." They said this because Paul was preaching the good news about Jesus and the resurrection. 19Then they took him and brought him to a meeting of the Areopagus, where they said to him, "May we know what this new teaching is that you are presenting? 20You are bringing some strange ideas to our ears, and we would like to know what they mean." 21(All the Athenians and the foreigners who lived there spent their time doing nothing but talking about and listening to the latest ideas.)

22Paul then stood up in the meeting of the Areopagus and said: "People of Athens! I see that in every way you are very religious. 23For as I walked around and looked carefully at your objects of worship, I even found an altar with this inscription: TO AN UNKNOWN GOD. So you are ignorant of the very thing you worship—and this is what I am going to proclaim to you.

24"The God who made the world and everything in it is the Lord of heaven and earth and does not live in temples built by human hands. 25And he is not served by human hands, as if he needed anything. Rather, he himself gives everyone life and breath and everything else. 26From one man he made all the nations, that they should inhabit the whole earth; and he marked out their appointed times in history and the boundaries of their lands. 27God did this so that they would seek him and perhaps reach out for him and find him, though he is not far from any one of us. 28'For in him we live and move and have our being.'a As some of your own poets have said, 'We are his offspring.'b

THE SCENE

ATHENS

(ACTS 17:15)

It was the capital of the region of Attica, and now it's the capital of Greece. It was the most important cultural and religious center in the ancient world. There were statues and monuments all over the city, and many philosophers and wise men would go there. The Roman general Sulla captured Athens in the year 86 before Christ. Many ancient ruins can be seen there today.

29"Therefore since we are God's offspring, we should not think that the divine being is like gold or silver or stone—an image made by human design and skill. 30In the past God overlooked such ignorance, but now he commands all people everywhere to repent. 31For he has set a day when he will judge the world with justice by the man he has appointed. He has given proof of this to everyone by raising him from the dead."

32When they heard about the resurrection of the dead, some of them sneered,

---

a 28 From the Cretan philosopher Epimenides
b 28 From the Cilician Stoic philosopher Aratus

but others said, "We want to hear you again on this subject." ³³At that, Paul left the Council. ³⁴Some of the people became followers of Paul and believed. Among them was Dionysius, a member of the Areopagus, also a woman named Damaris, and a number of others.

In Corinth

18 After this, Paul left Athens and went to Corinth. ²There he met a Jew named Aquila, a native of Pontus, who had recently come from Italy with his wife Priscilla, because Claudius had ordered all Jews to leave Rome. Paul went to see them, ³and because he was a tentmaker as they were, he stayed and worked with them. ⁴Every Sabbath he reasoned in the synagogue, trying to persuade Jews and Greeks.

⁵When Silas and Timothy came from Macedonia, Paul devoted himself exclusively to preaching, testifying to the Jews that Jesus was the Messiah. ⁶But when they opposed Paul and became abusive, he shook out his clothes in protest and said to them, "Your blood be on your own heads! I am innocent of it. From now on I will go to the Gentiles."

⁷Then Paul left the synagogue and went next door to the house of Titius Justus, a worshiper of God. ⁸Crispus, the synagogue leader, and his entire household

THE
WITNESSES

✓ **AQUILA AND PRISCILLA** (ACTS 18:2)
They were a married couple. Priscilla comes from *prisca*, which means "antique," "previous" or "respectable." Aquila was born in Pontus in the northern part of Asia Minor. He was a tent maker. These two people helped Paul when he was preaching in Corinth and in Ephesus. Priscilla knew the Bible very well. It seems that Aquila and Priscilla had to flee from Rome when the Jews were persecuted by the emperor Claudius in the year 49 before Christ. It didn't take them long to become very important in the church in Corinth.

THE SCENE

CORINTH

(ACTS 18:1)

See the explanation in 1 Corinthians 1:2.

believed in the Lord; and many of the Corinthians who heard Paul believed and were baptized.

⁹One night the Lord spoke to Paul in a vision: "Do not be afraid; keep on speaking, do not be silent. ¹⁰For I am with you, and no one is going to attack and harm you, because I have many people in this city." ¹¹So Paul stayed in Corinth for a year and a half, teaching them the word of God.

¹²While Gallio was proconsul of Achaia, the Jews of Corinth made a united attack on Paul and brought him to the place of judgment. ¹³"This man," they charged, "is persuading the people to worship God in ways contrary to the law."

¹⁴Just as Paul was about to speak, Gallio said to them, "If you Jews were making a complaint about some misdemeanor or serious crime, it would be reasonable for me to listen to you. ¹⁵But since it involves questions about words and names and your own law—settle the matter yourselves. I will not be a judge of such things." ¹⁶So he drove them off. ¹⁷Then the crowd there turned on Sosthenes the synagogue leader and beat him in front of the proconsul; and Gallio showed no concern whatever.

Priscilla, Aquila and Apollos

¹⁸Paul stayed on in Corinth for some time. Then he left the brothers and sisters and sailed for Syria, accompanied by Priscilla and Aquila. Before he sailed, he had his hair cut off at Cenchreae because of a vow he had taken. ¹⁹They arrived at Ephesus, where Paul left Priscilla and Aquila. He himself went into the synagogue and reasoned with the Jews. ²⁰When they asked him to spend more time with them, he declined. ²¹But as he left, he promised, "I will come back if it is God's will." Then he set sail from Ephesus. ²²When he landed at Caesarea, he went up to Jerusalem and greeted the church and then went down to Antioch.

²³After spending some time in Antioch, Paul set out from there and traveled from place to place throughout the region of Galatia and Phrygia, strengthening all the disciples.

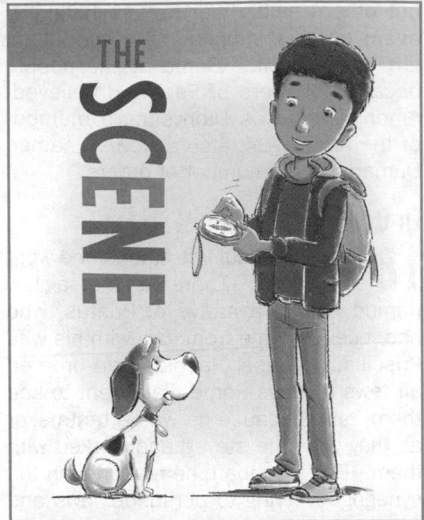

THE SCENE

EPHESUS

(ACTS 18:19)

Read the note at Ephesians 1:1.

²⁴Meanwhile a Jew named Apollos, a native of Alexandria, came to Ephesus. He was a learned man, with a thorough knowledge of the Scriptures. ²⁵He had been instructed in the way of the Lord, and he spoke with great fervor*a* and taught about Jesus accurately, though he knew only the baptism of John. ²⁶He began to speak boldly in the synagogue. When Priscilla and Aquila heard him, they invited him to their home and explained to him the way of God more adequately.

²⁷When Apollos wanted to go to Achaia, the brothers and sisters encouraged him and wrote to the disciples there to welcome him. When he arrived, he was a great help to those who by grace had believed. ²⁸For he vigorously refuted his Jewish opponents in public debate, proving from the Scriptures that Jesus was the Messiah.

Paul in Ephesus

19 While Apollos was at Corinth, Paul took the road through the interior

---

a 25 Or with fervor in the Spirit

and arrived at Ephesus. There he found some disciples [2]and asked them, "Did you receive the Holy Spirit when[a] you believed?"

They answered, "No, we have not even heard that there is a Holy Spirit."

[3]So Paul asked, "Then what baptism did you receive?"

"John's baptism," they replied.

[4]Paul said, "John's baptism was a baptism of repentance. He told the people to believe in the one coming after him, that is, in Jesus." [5]On hearing this, they were baptized in the name of the Lord Jesus. [6]When Paul placed his hands on them, the Holy Spirit came on them, and they spoke in tongues[b] and prophesied. [7]There were about twelve men in all.

THE SCENE

ACHAIA

(ACTS 18:27)

The Romans conquered Achaia and made it a province of the empire. Its territory extended from the south of Macedonia to Peloponnese, which is the most southern part of Greece. On the map, it looks like an open hand with its fingers stretching out into the sea. The capital of Achaia was Corinth.

[8]Paul entered the synagogue and spoke boldly there for three months, arguing persuasively about the kingdom of God. [9]But some of them became obstinate; they refused to believe and publicly maligned the Way. So Paul left them. He took the disciples with him and had discussions daily in the lecture hall of Tyrannus. [10]This went on for two years, so that all the Jews and Greeks who lived in the province of Asia heard the word of the Lord.

[11]God did extraordinary miracles through Paul, [12]so that even handkerchiefs and aprons that had touched him were taken to the sick, and their illnesses were cured and the evil spirits left them.

[13]Some Jews who went around driving out evil spirits tried to invoke the name of the Lord Jesus over those who were demon-possessed. They would say, "In the name of the Jesus whom Paul preaches, I command you to come out." [14]Seven sons of Sceva, a Jewish chief priest, were doing this. [15]One day the evil spirit answered them, "Jesus I know, and Paul I know about, but who are you?" [16]Then the man who had the evil spirit jumped on them and overpowered them all. He gave them such a beating that they ran out of the house naked and bleeding.

[17]When this became known to the Jews and Greeks living in Ephesus, they were all seized with fear, and the name of the Lord Jesus was held in high honor. [18]Many of those who believed now came and openly confessed what they had done. [19]A number who had practiced sorcery brought their scrolls together and burned them publicly. When they calculated the value of the scrolls, the total came to fifty thousand drachmas.[c] [20]In this way the word of the Lord spread widely and grew in power.

[21]After all this had happened, Paul decided[d] to go to Jerusalem, passing through Macedonia and Achaia. "After I have been there," he said, "I must visit Rome also." [22]He sent two of his helpers, Timothy and Erastus, to Macedonia, while he stayed in the province of Asia a little longer.

---

[a] 2 Or after   [b] 6 Or other languages   [c] 19 A drachma was a silver coin worth about a day's wages.   [d] 21 Or decided in the Spirit

The Riot in Ephesus

23About that time there arose a great disturbance about the Way. 24A silversmith named Demetrius, who made silver shrines of Artemis, brought in a lot of business for the craftsmen there. 25He called them together, along with the workers in related trades, and said: "You know, my friends, that we receive a good income from this business. 26And you see and hear how this fellow Paul has convinced and led astray large numbers of people here in Ephesus and in practically the whole province of Asia. He says that gods made by human hands are no gods at all. 27There is danger not only that our trade will lose its good name, but also that the temple of the great goddess Artemis will be discredited; and the goddess herself, who is worshiped throughout the province of Asia and the world, will be robbed of her divine majesty."

28When they heard this, they were furious and began shouting: "Great is Artemis of the Ephesians!" 29Soon the whole city was in an uproar. The people seized Gaius and Aristarchus, Paul's traveling companions from Macedonia, and all of them rushed into the theater together. 30Paul wanted to appear before the crowd, but the disciples would not let him. 31Even some of the officials of the province, friends of Paul, sent him a message begging him not to venture into the theater.

32The assembly was in confusion: Some were shouting one thing, some another. Most of the people did not even know why they were there. 33The Jews in the crowd pushed Alexander to the front, and they shouted instructions to him. He motioned for silence in order to make a defense before the people. 34But when they realized he was a Jew, they all shouted in unison for about two hours: "Great is Artemis of the Ephesians!"

35The city clerk quieted the crowd and said: "Fellow Ephesians, doesn't all the world know that the city of Ephesus is the guardian of the temple of the great Artemis and of her image, which fell from heaven? 36Therefore, since these facts are undeniable, you ought to calm down and not do anything rash. 37You have brought these men here, though they have neither robbed temples nor blasphemed our goddess. 38If, then, Demetrius and his fellow craftsmen have a grievance against anybody, the courts are open and there are proconsuls. They can press charges. 39If there is anything further you want to bring up, it must be settled in a legal assembly. 40As it is, we are in danger of being charged with rioting because of what happened today. In that case we would not be able to account for this commotion, since there is no reason for it." 41After he had said this, he dismissed the assembly.

Through Macedonia and Greece

20 When the uproar had ended, Paul sent for the disciples and, after encouraging them, said goodbye and set out for Macedonia. 2He traveled through that area, speaking many words of encouragement to the people, and finally arrived in Greece, 3where he stayed three months. Because some Jews had plotted against him just as he was about to sail for Syria, he decided to go back through Macedonia. 4He was accompanied by Sopater son of Pyrrhus from Berea, Aristarchus and Secundus from Thessalonica, Gaius from Derbe, Timothy also, and Tychicus and Trophimus from the province of Asia. 5These men went on ahead and waited for us at Troas. 6But we sailed from Philippi after the Festival of Unleavened Bread, and five days later joined the others at Troas, where we stayed seven days.

Eutychus Raised From the Dead at Troas

7On the first day of the week we came together to break bread. Paul spoke to the people and, because he intended to leave the next day, kept on talking until midnight. 8There were many lamps in the upstairs room where we were meeting. 9Seated in a window was a young man named Eutychus, who was sinking into a deep sleep as Paul talked on and on. When he was sound asleep, he fell to

GREECE

(ACTS 20:2)

This country is in eastern Europe. It's bordered by the Ionian Sea on the west, the Mediterranean Sea on the south and the Aegean Sea on the east. In New Testament times, Greece was part of the territory conquered by the Romans, but it had a much older and very important history. Greece was the birthplace of many philosophers, poets and politicians.

the ground from the third story and was picked up dead. ¹⁰Paul went down, threw himself on the young man and put his arms around him. "Don't be alarmed," he said. "He's alive!" ¹¹Then he went upstairs again and broke bread and ate. After talking until daylight, he left. ¹²The people took the young man home alive and were greatly comforted.

Paul's Farewell to the Ephesian Elders

¹³We went on ahead to the ship and sailed for Assos, where we were going to take Paul aboard. He had made this arrangement because he was going there

on foot. ¹⁴When he met us at Assos, we took him aboard and went on to Mitylene. ¹⁵The next day we set sail from there and arrived off Chios. The day after that we crossed over to Samos, and on the following day arrived at Miletus. ¹⁶Paul had decided to sail past Ephesus to avoid spending time in the province of Asia, for he was in a hurry to reach Jerusalem, if possible, by the day of Pentecost.

¹⁷From Miletus, Paul sent to Ephesus for the elders of the church. ¹⁸When they arrived, he said to them: "You know how I lived the whole time I was with you, from the first day I came into the province of Asia. ¹⁹I served the Lord with great humility and with tears and in the midst of severe testing by the plots of my Jewish opponents. ²⁰You know that I have not hesitated to preach anything that would be helpful to you but have taught you publicly and from house to house. ²¹I have declared to both Jews and Greeks that they must turn to God in repentance and have faith in our Lord Jesus.

²²"And now, compelled by the Spirit, I am going to Jerusalem, not knowing what will happen to me there. ²³I only know that in every city the Holy Spirit warns me that prison and hardships are facing me. ²⁴However, I consider my life worth nothing to me; my only aim is to finish the race and complete the task the Lord Jesus has given me—the task of testifying to the good news of God's grace.

²⁵"Now I know that none of you among whom I have gone about preaching the kingdom will ever see me again. ²⁶Therefore, I declare to you today that I am innocent of the blood of any of you. ²⁷For I have not hesitated to proclaim to you the whole will of God. ²⁸Keep watch over yourselves and all the flock of which the Holy Spirit has made you overseers. Be shepherds of the church of God,ᵃ which he bought with his own blood.ᵇ ²⁹I know that after I leave, savage wolves will come in among you and will not spare the flock. ³⁰Even from your own number men will arise and distort the truth in order to draw away disciples after them. ³¹So be on your

---

ᵃ 28 Many manuscripts *of the Lord*   ᵇ 28 Or *with the blood of his own Son.*

guard! Remember that for three years I never stopped warning each of you night and day with tears.

³²"Now I commit you to God and to the word of his grace, which can build you up and give you an inheritance among all those who are sanctified. ³³I have not coveted anyone's silver or gold or clothing. ³⁴You yourselves know that these hands of mine have supplied my own needs and the needs of my companions. ³⁵In everything I did, I showed you that by this kind of hard work we must help the weak, remembering the words the Lord Jesus himself said: 'It is more blessed to give than to receive.'"

³⁶When Paul had finished speaking, he knelt down with all of them and prayed. ³⁷They all wept as they embraced him and kissed him. ³⁸What grieved them most was his statement that they would never see his face again. Then they accompanied him to the ship.

On to Jerusalem

21 After we had torn ourselves away from them, we put out to sea and sailed straight to Kos. The next day we went to Rhodes and from there to Patara. ²We found a ship crossing over to Phoenicia, went on board and set sail. ³After sighting Cyprus and passing to the south of it, we sailed on to Syria. We landed at Tyre, where our ship was to unload its cargo. ⁴We sought out the disciples there and stayed with them seven days. Through the Spirit they urged Paul not to go on to Jerusalem. ⁵When it was time to leave, we left and continued on our way. All of them, including wives and children, accompanied us out of the city, and there on the beach we knelt to pray. ⁶After saying goodbye to each other, we went aboard the ship, and they returned home.

⁷We continued our voyage from Tyre and landed at Ptolemais, where we greeted the brothers and sisters and stayed with them for a day. ⁸Leaving the next day, we reached Caesarea and stayed at the house of Philip the evangelist, one of the Seven. ⁹He had four unmarried daughters who prophesied.

¹⁰After we had been there a number of days, a prophet named Agabus came down from Judea. ¹¹Coming over to us, he took Paul's belt, tied his own hands and feet with it and said, "The Holy Spirit says, 'In this way the Jewish leaders in Jerusalem will bind the owner of this belt and will hand him over to the Gentiles.'"

¹²When we heard this, we and the people there pleaded with Paul not to go up to Jerusalem. ¹³Then Paul answered, "Why are you weeping and breaking my heart? I am ready not only to be bound, but also to die in Jerusalem for the name of the Lord Jesus." ¹⁴When he would not be dissuaded, we gave up and said, "The Lord's will be done."

¹⁵After this, we started on our way up to Jerusalem. ¹⁶Some of the disciples from Caesarea accompanied us and brought us to the home of Mnason, where we were to stay. He was a man from Cyprus and one of the early disciples.

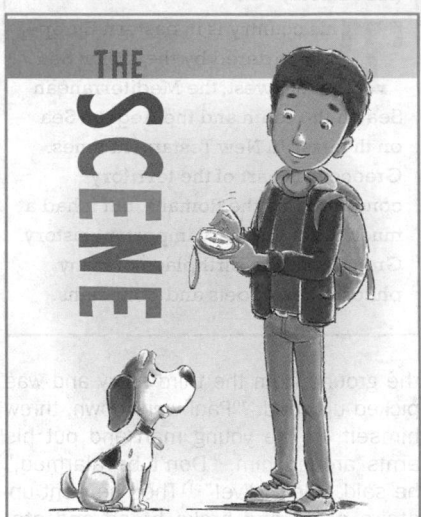

THE SCENE

TYRE

(ACTS 21:3)

This was an important Phoenician city. Over time, it was dominated by several empires. In the year 65 before Christ, it became part of the Roman territory.

Paul's Arrival at Jerusalem

¹⁷When we arrived at Jerusalem, the brothers and sisters received us warmly. ¹⁸The next day Paul and the rest of us went to see James, and all the elders were present. ¹⁹Paul greeted them and reported in detail what God had done among the Gentiles through his ministry.

²⁰When they heard this, they praised God. Then they said to Paul: "You see, brother, how many thousands of Jews have believed, and all of them are zealous for the law. ²¹They have been informed that you teach all the Jews who live among the Gentiles to turn away from Moses, telling them not to circumcise their children or live according to our customs. ²²What shall we do? They will certainly hear that you have come, ²³so do what we tell you. There are four men with us who have made a vow. ²⁴Take these men, join in their purification rites and pay their expenses, so that they can have their heads shaved. Then everyone will know there is no truth in these reports about you, but that you yourself are living in obedience to the law. ²⁵As for the Gentile believers, we have written to them our decision that they should abstain from food sacrificed to idols, from blood, from the meat of strangled animals and from sexual immorality."

²⁶The next day Paul took the men and purified himself along with them. Then he went to the temple to give notice of the date when the days of purification would end and the offering would be made for each of them.

Paul Arrested

²⁷When the seven days were nearly over, some Jews from the province of Asia saw Paul at the temple. They stirred up the whole crowd and seized him, ²⁸shouting, "Fellow Israelites, help us! This is the man who teaches everyone everywhere against our people and our law and this place. And besides, he has brought Greeks into the temple and defiled this holy place." ²⁹(They had previously seen Trophimus the Ephesian in the city with Paul and assumed that Paul had brought him into the temple.)

BREAK THROUGH!

Purification rites

(ACTS 21:24)

This was a ceremony ordered by the Law of Moses. The ceremony had several parts, which included washing the body a certain way and using certain oils. That ceremony was done to make a person clean or pure. For example, it was done when a person had come into contact with some object or person considered unclean or not pure. Every person who entered the temple had to be clean before entering.

³⁰The whole city was aroused, and the people came running from all directions. Seizing Paul, they dragged him from the temple, and immediately the gates were shut. ³¹While they were trying to kill him, news reached the commander of the Roman troops that the whole city of Jerusalem was in an uproar. ³²He at once took some officers and soldiers and ran down to the crowd. When the rioters saw the commander and his soldiers, they stopped beating Paul.

³³The commander came up and arrested him and ordered him to be bound with two chains. Then he asked who he was and what he had done. ³⁴Some in the crowd shouted one thing and some another, and since the commander could not get

at the truth because of the uproar, he ordered that Paul be taken into the barracks. [35]When Paul reached the steps, the violence of the mob was so great he had to be carried by the soldiers. [36]The crowd that followed kept shouting, "Get rid of him!"

Paul Speaks to the Crowd

[37]As the soldiers were about to take Paul into the barracks, he asked the commander, "May I say something to you?"

"Do you speak Greek?" he replied. [38]"Aren't you the Egyptian who started a revolt and led four thousand terrorists out into the wilderness some time ago?"

[39]Paul answered, "I am a Jew, from Tarsus in Cilicia, a citizen of no ordinary city. Please let me speak to the people."

[40]After receiving the commander's permission, Paul stood on the steps and motioned to the crowd. When they were all silent, he said to them in Aramaic[a]:

22 [1]"Brothers and fathers, listen now to my defense."

[2]When they heard him speak to them in Aramaic, they became very quiet.

Then Paul said: [3]"I am a Jew, born in Tarsus of Cilicia, but brought up in this city. I studied under Gamaliel and was thoroughly trained in the law of our ancestors. I was just as zealous for God as any of you are today. [4]I persecuted the followers of this Way to their death, arresting both men and women and throwing them into prison, [5]as the high priest and all the Council can themselves testify. I even obtained letters from them to their associates in Damascus, and went there to bring these people as prisoners to Jerusalem to be punished.

[6]"About noon as I came near Damascus, suddenly a bright light from heaven flashed around me. [7]I fell to the ground and heard a voice say to me, 'Saul! Saul! Why do you persecute me?'

[8]"'Who are you, Lord?' I asked.

"'I am Jesus of Nazareth, whom you are persecuting,' he replied. [9]My companions saw the light, but they did not understand the voice of him who was speaking to me.

[10]"'What shall I do, Lord?' I asked.

"'Get up,' the Lord said, 'and go into Damascus. There you will be told all that you have been assigned to do.' [11]My companions led me by the hand into Damascus, because the brilliance of the light had blinded me.

[12]"A man named Ananias came to see me. He was a devout observer of the law and highly respected by all the Jews living there. [13]He stood beside me and said, 'Brother Saul, receive your sight!' And at that very moment I was able to see him.

[14]"Then he said: 'The God of our ancestors has chosen you to know his will and to see the Righteous One and to hear words from his mouth. [15]You will be his witness to all people of what you have seen and heard. [16]And now what are you waiting for? Get up, be baptized and wash your sins away, calling on his name.'

[17]"When I returned to Jerusalem and was praying at the temple, I fell into a trance [18]and saw the Lord speaking to me. 'Quick!' he said. 'Leave Jerusalem immediately, because the people here will not accept your testimony about me.'

[19]"'Lord,' I replied, 'these people know that I went from one synagogue to another to imprison and beat those who believe in you. [20]And when the blood of your martyr[b] Stephen was shed, I stood there giving my approval and guarding the clothes of those who were killing him.'

[21]"Then the Lord said to me, 'Go; I will send you far away to the Gentiles.'"

Paul the Roman Citizen

[22]The crowd listened to Paul until he said this. Then they raised their voices and shouted, "Rid the earth of him! He's not fit to live!"

[23]As they were shouting and throwing off their cloaks and flinging dust into the air, [24]the commander ordered that Paul be taken into the barracks. He directed that he be flogged and interrogated in order to find out why the people were shouting at him like this. [25]As they stretched him out to flog him, Paul said to the centurion standing there, "Is it legal for you to flog a Roman citizen who hasn't even been found guilty?"

---

[a] 40 Or possibly *Hebrew*; also in 22:2   [b] 20 Or *witness*

THE
WITNESSES

✓ **HIGH PRIEST ANANIAS** (ACTS 23:2)
He was a priest between the years 47 and
58 after Christ. He was greedy and very proud,
and he accused Paul before Felix, the governor.
Later, in the year 66 after Christ, some Jews
accused Ananias of being a friend of the Romans,
and they killed him.

²⁶When the centurion heard this, he
went to the commander and reported it.
"What are you going to do?" he asked.
"This man is a Roman citizen."

²⁷The commander went to Paul and
asked, "Tell me, are you a Roman citizen?"

"Yes, I am," he answered.

²⁸Then the commander said, "I had to
pay a lot of money for my citizenship."

"But I was born a citizen," Paul replied.

²⁹Those who were about to interrogate
him withdrew immediately. The commander himself was alarmed when he realized

that he had put Paul, a Roman citizen, in
chains.

Paul Before the Sanhedrin

³⁰The commander wanted to find out
exactly why Paul was being accused by
the Jews. So the next day he released
him and ordered the chief priests and all
the members of the Sanhedrin to assemble. Then he brought Paul and had him
stand before them.

23 Paul looked straight at the Sanhedrin and said, "My brothers, I have
fulfilled my duty to God in all good conscience to this day." ²At this the high
priest Ananias ordered those standing
near Paul to strike him on the mouth.
³Then Paul said to him, "God will strike
you, you whitewashed wall! You sit there
to judge me according to the law, yet you
yourself violate the law by commanding
that I be struck!"

⁴Those who were standing near Paul
said, "How dare you insult God's high
priest!"

⁵Paul replied, "Brothers, I did not realize that he was the high priest; for it is
written: 'Do not speak evil about the ruler
of your people.'ᵃ"

⁶Then Paul, knowing that some of them
were Sadducees and the others Pharisees, called out in the Sanhedrin, "My
brothers, I am a Pharisee, descended
from Pharisees. I stand on trial because
of the hope of the resurrection of the
dead." ⁷When he said this, a dispute
broke out between the Pharisees and the
Sadducees, and the assembly was divided. ⁸(The Sadducees say that there is no
resurrection, and that there are neither
angels nor spirits, but the Pharisees believe all these things.)

⁹There was a great uproar, and some
of the teachers of the law who were Pharisees stood up and argued vigorously.
"We find nothing wrong with this man,"
they said. "What if a spirit or an angel has
spoken to him?" ¹⁰The dispute became
so violent that the commander was afraid
Paul would be torn to pieces by them. He
ordered the troops to go down and take

ᵃ 5 Exodus 22:28

him away from them by force and bring him into the barracks.

¹¹The following night the Lord stood near Paul and said, "Take courage! As you have testified about me in Jerusalem, so you must also testify in Rome."

The Plot to Kill Paul

¹²The next morning some Jews formed a conspiracy and bound themselves with an oath not to eat or drink until they had killed Paul. ¹³More than forty men were involved in this plot. ¹⁴They went to the chief priests and the elders and said, "We have taken a solemn oath not to eat anything until we have killed Paul. ¹⁵Now then, you and the Sanhedrin petition the commander to bring him before you on the pretext of wanting more accurate information about his case. We are ready to kill him before he gets here."

¹⁶But when the son of Paul's sister heard of this plot, he went into the barracks and told Paul.

¹⁷Then Paul called one of the centurions and said, "Take this young man to the commander; he has something to tell him." ¹⁸So he took him to the commander.

The centurion said, "Paul, the prisoner, sent for me and asked me to bring this young man to you because he has something to tell you."

¹⁹The commander took the young man by the hand, drew him aside and asked, "What is it you want to tell me?"

²⁰He said: "Some Jews have agreed to ask you to bring Paul before the Sanhedrin tomorrow on the pretext of wanting more accurate information about him. ²¹Don't give in to them, because more than forty of them are waiting in ambush for him. They have taken an oath not to eat or drink until they have killed him. They are ready now, waiting for your consent to their request."

²²The commander dismissed the young man with this warning: "Don't tell anyone that you have reported this to me."

Paul Transferred to Caesarea

²³Then he called two of his centurions and ordered them, "Get ready a detach-ment of two hundred soldiers, seventy horsemen and two hundred spearmen*ᵃ* to go to Caesarea at nine tonight. ²⁴Provide horses for Paul so that he may be taken safely to Governor Felix."

²⁵He wrote a letter as follows:

²⁶Claudius Lysias,

To His Excellency, Governor Felix:

Greetings.

²⁷This man was seized by the Jews and they were about to kill him, but I came with my troops and rescued him, for I had learned that he is a Roman citizen. ²⁸I wanted to know why they were accusing him, so I brought him to their Sanhedrin. ²⁹I found that the accusation had to do with questions about their law, but there was no charge against him that deserved death or imprisonment. ³⁰When I was informed of a plot to be carried out against the man, I sent him to you at once. I also ordered his accusers to present to you their case against him.

³¹So the soldiers, carrying out their orders, took Paul with them during the night and brought him as far as Antipatris. ³²The next day they let the cavalry go on with him, while they returned to the barracks. ³³When the cavalry arrived in Caesarea, they delivered the letter to the governor and handed Paul over to him. ³⁴The governor read the letter and asked what province he was from. Learning that he was from Cilicia, ³⁵he said, "I will hear your case when your accusers get here." Then he ordered that Paul be kept under guard in Herod's palace.

Paul's Trial Before Felix

24 Five days later the high priest Ananias went down to Caesarea with some of the elders and a lawyer named Tertullus, and they brought their charges against Paul before the governor. ²When Paul was called in, Tertullus presented his case before Felix: "We have enjoyed

---

ᵃ 23 The meaning of the Greek for this word is uncertain.

a long period of peace under you, and your foresight has brought about reforms in this nation. ³Everywhere and in every way, most excellent Felix, we acknowledge this with profound gratitude. ⁴But in order not to weary you further, I would request that you be kind enough to hear us briefly.

⁵"We have found this man to be a troublemaker, stirring up riots among the Jews all over the world. He is a ringleader of the Nazarene sect ⁶and even tried to

THE
WITNESSES

✓ **GOVERNOR FELIX** (ACTS 23:24)
Felix is a Latin name that means "happy." He was a freed man. That means he had been a slave in the emperor Claudius' house, but he had been freed. He was the governor of Palestine from the year 52 to the year 60 after Christ, and he was very authoritarian and cruel. During his government, the Jews began to really hate the Romans.

desecrate the temple; so we seized him. [7]ᵃ ⁸By examining him yourself you will be able to learn the truth about all these charges we are bringing against him."

⁹The other Jews joined in the accusation, asserting that these things were true.

¹⁰When the governor motioned for him to speak, Paul replied: "I know that for a number of years you have been a judge over this nation; so I gladly make my defense. ¹¹You can easily verify that no more than twelve days ago I went up to Jerusalem to worship. ¹²My accusers did not find me arguing with anyone at the temple, or stirring up a crowd in the synagogues or anywhere else in the city. ¹³And they cannot prove to you the charges they are now making against me. ¹⁴However, I admit that I worship the God of our ancestors as a follower of the Way, which they call a sect. I believe everything that is in accordance with the Law and that is written in the Prophets, ¹⁵and I have the same hope in God as these men themselves have, that there will be a resurrection of both the righteous and the wicked. ¹⁶So I strive always to keep my conscience clear before God and man.

¹⁷"After an absence of several years, I came to Jerusalem to bring my people gifts for the poor and to present offerings. ¹⁸I was ceremonially clean when they found me in the temple courts doing this. There was no crowd with me, nor was I involved in any disturbance. ¹⁹But there are some Jews from the province of Asia, who ought to be here before you and bring charges if they have anything against me. ²⁰Or these who are here should state what crime they found in me when I stood before the Sanhedrin— ²¹unless it was this one thing I shouted as I stood in their presence: 'It is concerning the resurrection of the dead that I am on trial before you today.'"

²²Then Felix, who was well acquainted with the Way, adjourned the proceedings. "When Lysias the commander comes,"

ᵃ 6-8 Some manuscripts include here *him, and we would have judged him in accordance with our law.* ⁷*But the commander Lysias came and took him from us with much violence,* ⁸*ordering his accusers to come before you.*

he said, "I will decide your case." ²³He ordered the centurion to keep Paul under guard but to give him some freedom and permit his friends to take care of his needs.

²⁴Several days later Felix came with his wife Drusilla, who was Jewish. He sent for Paul and listened to him as he spoke about faith in Christ Jesus. ²⁵As Paul talked about righteousness, self-control and the judgment to come, Felix was afraid and said, "That's enough for now! You may leave. When I find it convenient, I will send for you." ²⁶At the same time he was hoping that Paul would offer him a bribe, so he sent for him frequently and talked with him.

²⁷When two years had passed, Felix was succeeded by Porcius Festus, but because Felix wanted to grant a favor to the Jews, he left Paul in prison.

Paul's Trial Before Festus

25 Three days after arriving in the province, Festus went up from Caesarea to Jerusalem, ²where the chief priests and the Jewish leaders appeared before him and presented the charges against Paul. ³They requested Festus, as a favor to them, to have Paul transferred to Jerusalem, for they were preparing an ambush to kill him along the way. ⁴Festus answered, "Paul is being held at Caesarea, and I myself am going there soon. ⁵Let some of your leaders come with me, and if the man has done anything wrong, they can press charges against him there."

⁶After spending eight or ten days with them, Festus went down to Caesarea. The next day he convened the court and ordered that Paul be brought before him. ⁷When Paul came in, the Jews who had come down from Jerusalem stood around him. They brought many serious charges against him, but they could not prove them.

⁸Then Paul made his defense: "I have done nothing wrong against the Jewish law or against the temple or against Caesar."

⁹Festus, wishing to do the Jews a favor, said to Paul, "Are you willing to go up

THE
WITNESSES

✓ PORCIUS FESTUS (ACTS 24:27)
He was the governor of Palestine after Felix, around the year 60 after Christ. He wasn't governor long — only two years.

✓ KING AGRIPPA AND BERNICE (ACTS 25:13)
This is Herod Agrippa II (the Second). Bernice was his sister. They both lived and ruled in Chalcis. Before that, they were governors over a larger territory in the north part of Palestine. Bernice is a Greek name that means "who takes the victory." She was a very famous queen, and many historians have written about her.

to Jerusalem and stand trial before me there on these charges?"

¹⁰Paul answered: "I am now standing before Caesar's court, where I ought to be tried. I have not done any wrong to the Jews, as you yourself know very well. ¹¹If, however, I am guilty of doing anything

deserving death, I do not refuse to die. But if the charges brought against me by these Jews are not true, no one has the right to hand me over to them. I appeal to Caesar!"

¹²After Festus had conferred with his council, he declared: "You have appealed to Caesar. To Caesar you will go!"

Festus Consults King Agrippa

¹³A few days later King Agrippa and Bernice arrived at Caesarea to pay their respects to Festus. ¹⁴Since they were spending many days there, Festus discussed Paul's case with the king. He said: "There is a man here whom Felix left as a prisoner. ¹⁵When I went to Jerusalem, the chief priests and the elders of the Jews brought charges against him and asked that he be condemned.

¹⁶"I told them that it is not the Roman custom to hand over anyone before they have faced their accusers and have had an opportunity to defend themselves against the charges. ¹⁷When they came here with me, I did not delay the case, but convened the court the next day and ordered the man to be brought in. ¹⁸When his accusers got up to speak, they did not charge him with any of the crimes I had expected. ¹⁹Instead, they had some points of dispute with him about their own religion and about a dead man named Jesus who Paul claimed was alive. ²⁰I was at a loss how to investigate such matters; so I asked if he would be willing to go to Jerusalem and stand trial there on these charges. ²¹But when Paul made his appeal to be held over for the Emperor's decision, I ordered him held until I could send him to Caesar."

²²Then Agrippa said to Festus, "I would like to hear this man myself."

He replied, "Tomorrow you will hear him."

Paul Before Agrippa

²³The next day Agrippa and Bernice came with great pomp and entered the audience room with the high-ranking military officers and the prominent men of the city. At the command of Festus, Paul was brought in. ²⁴Festus said: "King Agrippa, and all who are present with us, you see this man! The whole Jewish community has petitioned me about him in Jerusalem and here in Caesarea, shouting that he ought not to live any longer. ²⁵I found he had done nothing deserving of death, but because he made his appeal to the Emperor I decided to send him to Rome. ²⁶But I have nothing definite to write to His Majesty about him. Therefore I have brought him before all of you, and especially before you, King Agrippa, so that as a result of this investigation I may have something to write. ²⁷For I think it is unreasonable to send a prisoner on to Rome without specifying the charges against him."

26 Then Agrippa said to Paul, "You have permission to speak for yourself."

So Paul motioned with his hand and began his defense: ²"King Agrippa, I consider myself fortunate to stand before you today as I make my defense against all the accusations of the Jews, ³and especially so because you are well acquainted with all the Jewish customs and controversies. Therefore, I beg you to listen to me patiently.

⁴"The Jewish people all know the way I have lived ever since I was a child, from the beginning of my life in my own country, and also in Jerusalem. ⁵They have known me for a long time and can testify, if they are willing, that I conformed to the strictest sect of our religion, living as a Pharisee. ⁶And now it is because of my hope in what God has promised our ancestors that I am on trial today. ⁷This is the promise our twelve tribes are hoping to see fulfilled as they earnestly serve God day and night. King Agrippa, it is because of this hope that these Jews are accusing me. ⁸Why should any of you consider it incredible that God raises the dead?

⁹"I too was convinced that I ought to do all that was possible to oppose the name of Jesus of Nazareth. ¹⁰And that is just what I did in Jerusalem. On the authority of the chief priests I put many of the Lord's people in prison, and when

they were put to death, I cast my vote against them. [11]Many a time I went from one synagogue to another to have them punished, and I tried to force them to blaspheme. I was so obsessed with persecuting them that I even hunted them down in foreign cities.

[12]"On one of these journeys I was going to Damascus with the authority and commission of the chief priests. [13]About noon, King Agrippa, as I was on the road, I saw a light from heaven, brighter than the sun, blazing around me and my companions. [14]We all fell to the ground, and I heard a voice saying to me in Aramaic,[a] 'Saul, Saul, why do you persecute me? It is hard for you to kick against the goads.'

[15]"Then I asked, 'Who are you, Lord?'

" 'I am Jesus, whom you are persecuting,' the Lord replied. [16]'Now get up and stand on your feet. I have appeared to you to appoint you as a servant and as a witness of what you have seen and will see of me. [17]I will rescue you from your own people and from the Gentiles. I am sending you to them [18]to open their eyes and turn them from darkness to light, and from the power of Satan to God, so that they may receive forgiveness of sins and a place among those who are sanctified by faith in me.'

[19]"So then, King Agrippa, I was not disobedient to the vision from heaven. [20]First to those in Damascus, then to those in Jerusalem and in all Judea, and then to the Gentiles, I preached that they should repent and turn to God and demonstrate their repentance by their deeds. [21]That is why some Jews seized me in the temple courts and tried to kill me. [22]But God has helped me to this very day; so I stand here and testify to small and great alike. I am saying nothing beyond what the prophets and Moses said would happen— [23]that the Messiah would suffer and, as the first to rise from the dead, would bring the message of light to his own people and to the Gentiles."

[24]At this point Festus interrupted Paul's defense. "You are out of your mind, Paul!" he shouted. "Your great learning is driving you insane."

[25]"I am not insane, most excellent Festus," Paul replied. "What I am saying is true and reasonable. [26]The king is familiar with these things, and I can speak freely to him. I am convinced that none of this has escaped his notice, because it was not done in a corner. [27]King Agrippa, do you believe the prophets? I know you do."

[28]Then Agrippa said to Paul, "Do you think that in such a short time you can persuade me to be a Christian?"

[29]Paul replied, "Short time or long—I pray to God that not only you but all who are listening to me today may become what I am, except for these chains."

[30]The king rose, and with him the governor and Bernice and those sitting with them. [31]After they left the room, they began saying to one another, "This man is not doing anything that deserves death or imprisonment."

[32]Agrippa said to Festus, "This man could have been set free if he had not appealed to Caesar."

Paul Sails for Rome

27 When it was decided that we would sail for Italy, Paul and some other prisoners were handed over to a centurion named Julius, who belonged to the Imperial Regiment. [2]We boarded a ship from Adramyttium about to sail for ports along the coast of the province of Asia, and we put out to sea. Aristarchus, a Macedonian from Thessalonica, was with us.

[3]The next day we landed at Sidon; and Julius, in kindness to Paul, allowed him to go to his friends so they might provide for his needs. [4]From there we put out to sea again and passed to the lee of Cyprus because the winds were against us. [5]When we had sailed across the open sea off the coast of Cilicia and Pamphylia, we landed at Myra in Lycia. [6]There the centurion found an Alexandrian ship sailing for Italy and put us on board. [7]We made slow headway for many days and had difficulty arriving off Cnidus. When the wind did not allow us to hold our course, we sailed to the lee of

---

[a] 14 Or *Hebrew*

THE SCENE

ITALY

(ACTS 27:1)

In New Testament times, when Paul was traveling around preaching about Jesus, Italy was more or less like it is now. Its capital was Rome, which was the political center of the monarchy, the republic and finally the Roman empire.

Crete, opposite Salmone. ⁸We moved along the coast with difficulty and came to a place called Fair Havens, near the town of Lasea.

⁹Much time had been lost, and sailing had already become dangerous because by now it was after the Day of Atonement.ᵃ So Paul warned them, ¹⁰"Men, I can see that our voyage is going to be disastrous and bring great loss to ship and cargo, and to our own lives also." ¹¹But the centurion, instead of listening to what Paul said, followed the advice of the pilot and of the owner of the ship. ¹²Since the harbor was unsuitable to winter in, the majority decided that we should sail on, hoping to reach Phoenix and winter there. This was a harbor in Crete, facing both southwest and northwest.

The Storm

¹³When a gentle south wind began to blow, they saw their opportunity; so they weighed anchor and sailed along the shore of Crete. ¹⁴Before very long, a wind of hurricane force, called the Northeaster, swept down from the island. ¹⁵The ship was caught by the storm and could not head into the wind; so we gave way to it and were driven along. ¹⁶As we passed to the lee of a small island called Cauda, we were hardly able to make the lifeboat secure, ¹⁷so the men hoisted it aboard. Then they passed ropes under the ship itself to hold it together. Because they were afraid they would run aground on the sandbars of Syrtis, they lowered the sea anchorᵇ and let the ship be driven along. ¹⁸We took such a violent battering from the storm that the next day they began to throw the cargo overboard. ¹⁹On the third day, they threw the ship's tackle overboard with their own hands. ²⁰When neither sun nor stars appeared for many days and the storm continued raging, we finally gave up all hope of being saved.

²¹After they had gone a long time without food, Paul stood up before them and said: "Men, you should have taken my advice not to sail from Crete; then you would have spared yourselves this damage and loss. ²²But now I urge you to keep up your courage, because not one of you will be lost; only the ship will be destroyed. ²³Last night an angel of the God to whom I belong and whom I serve stood beside me ²⁴and said, 'Do not be afraid, Paul. You must stand trial before Caesar; and God has graciously given you the lives of all who sail with you.' ²⁵So keep up your courage, men, for I have faith in God that it will happen just as he told me. ²⁶Nevertheless, we must run aground on some island."

The Shipwreck

²⁷On the fourteenth night we were still being driven across the Adriaticᶜ Sea,

---

ᵃ 9 That is, Yom Kippur   ᵇ 17 Or the sails
ᶜ 27 In ancient times the name referred to an area extending well south of Italy.

THE SCENE

ADRIATIC SEA

(ACTS 27:27)

This sea is east of Italy. In New Testament times, it also bordered the Ionian Sea (the southern part between Italy and Greece). It was very dangerous to navigate this sea in the months of November or March.

when about midnight the sailors sensed they were approaching land. ²⁸They took soundings and found that the water was a hundred and twenty feet*ᵃ* deep. A short time later they took soundings again and found it was ninety feet*ᵇ* deep. ²⁹Fearing that we would be dashed against the rocks, they dropped four anchors from the stern and prayed for daylight. ³⁰In an attempt to escape from the ship, the sailors let the lifeboat down into the sea, pretending they were going to lower some anchors from the bow. ³¹Then Paul said to the centurion and the soldiers, "Unless these men stay with the ship, you cannot be saved." ³²So the soldiers cut the ropes that held the lifeboat and let it drift away.

³³Just before dawn Paul urged them all to eat. "For the last fourteen days," he said, "you have been in constant suspense and have gone without food—you haven't eaten anything. ³⁴Now I urge you to take some food. You need it to survive. Not one of you will lose a single hair from his head." ³⁵After he said this, he took some bread and gave thanks to God in front of them all. Then he broke it and began to eat. ³⁶They were all encouraged and ate some food themselves. ³⁷Altogether there were 276 of us on board. ³⁸When they had eaten as much as they wanted, they lightened the ship by throwing the grain into the sea.

³⁹When daylight came, they did not recognize the land, but they saw a bay with a sandy beach, where they decided to run the ship aground if they could. ⁴⁰Cutting loose the anchors, they left them in the sea and at the same time untied the ropes that held the rudders. Then they hoisted the foresail to the wind and made for the beach. ⁴¹But the ship struck a sandbar and ran aground. The bow stuck fast and would not move, and the stern was broken to pieces by the pounding of the surf.

⁴²The soldiers planned to kill the prisoners to prevent any of them from swimming away and escaping. ⁴³But the centurion wanted to spare Paul's life and kept them from carrying out their plan. He ordered those who could swim to jump overboard first and get to land. ⁴⁴The rest were to get there on planks or on other pieces of the ship. In this way everyone reached land safely.

Paul Ashore on Malta

28 Once safely on shore, we found out that the island was called Malta. ²The islanders showed us unusual kindness. They built a fire and welcomed us all because it was raining and cold. ³Paul gathered a pile of brushwood and, as he put it on the fire, a viper, driven out by the heat, fastened itself on his hand. ⁴When the islanders saw the snake hanging from his hand, they said to each other, "This man must be a murderer; for though he escaped from the sea, the god-

---

ᵃ 28 Or about 37 meters   *ᵇ* 28 Or about 27 meters

dess Justice has not allowed him to live." ⁵But Paul shook the snake off into the fire and suffered no ill effects. ⁶The people expected him to swell up or suddenly fall dead; but after waiting a long time and seeing nothing unusual happen to him, they changed their minds and said he was a god.

⁷There was an estate nearby that belonged to Publius, the chief official of the island. He welcomed us to his home and showed us generous hospitality for three days. ⁸His father was sick in bed, suffering from fever and dysentery. Paul went in to see him and, after prayer, placed his hands on him and healed him. ⁹When this had happened, the rest of the sick on the island came and were cured. ¹⁰They honored us in many ways; and when we were ready to sail, they furnished us with the supplies we needed.

Paul's Arrival at Rome

¹¹After three months we put out to sea in a ship that had wintered in the island—it was an Alexandrian ship with the figurehead of the twin gods Castor and Pollux. ¹²We put in at Syracuse and stayed there three days. ¹³From there we set sail and arrived at Rhegium. The next day the south wind came up, and on the following day we reached Puteoli. ¹⁴There we found some brothers and sisters who invited us to spend a week with them. And so we came to Rome. ¹⁵The brothers and sisters there had heard that we were coming, and they traveled as far as the Forum of Appius and the Three Taverns to meet us. At the sight of these people Paul thanked God and was encouraged. ¹⁶When we got to Rome, Paul was allowed to live by himself, with a soldier to guard him.

Paul Preaches at Rome Under Guard

¹⁷Three days later he called together the local Jewish leaders. When they had assembled, Paul said to them: "My brothers, although I have done nothing against our people or against the customs of our ancestors, I was arrested in Jerusalem and handed over to the Romans. ¹⁸They examined me and wanted to release me, because I was not guilty of any crime deserving death. ¹⁹The Jews objected, so I was compelled to make an appeal to Caesar. I certainly did not intend to bring any charge against my own people. ²⁰For this reason I have asked to see you and talk with you. It is because of the hope of Israel that I am bound with this chain."

²¹They replied, "We have not received any letters from Judea concerning you, and none of our people who have come from there has reported or said anything bad about you. ²²But we want to hear what your views are, for we know that people everywhere are talking against this sect."

ISLAND OF MALTA

(ACTS 28:1)

This island is in the Mediterranean Sea, about 60 miles (96 km) south of Sicily. It was under Phoenician control for a long time, but in the year 218 before Christ, the Romans captured it and made it part of the Roman empire. Now it's free, and along with some other islands, it's part of the Republic of Malta.

23They arranged to meet Paul on a certain day, and came in even larger numbers to the place where he was staying. He witnessed to them from morning till evening, explaining about the kingdom of God, and from the Law of Moses and from the Prophets he tried to persuade them about Jesus. 24Some were convinced by what he said, but others would not believe. 25They disagreed among themselves and began to leave after Paul had made this final statement: "The Holy Spirit spoke the truth to your ancestors when he said through Isaiah the prophet:

26 " 'Go to this people and say,
    "You will be ever hearing but never
        understanding;

you will be ever seeing but never
    perceiving."
27 For this people's heart has become
    calloused;
    they hardly hear with their ears,
    and they have closed their eyes.
Otherwise they might see with their
        eyes,
    hear with their ears,
    understand with their hearts
and turn, and I would heal them.'a

28 "Therefore I want you to know that

---

a 27 Isaiah 6:9,10 (see Septuagint)

BREAKTHROUGH!

Gods Castor and Pollux
(ACTS 28:11)
Greek legends say that the twin brothers Castor and Pollux were sons of the god Zeus (the most powerful of all the gods) and a woman called Leda. They were born on a mountain in Sparta in the south of Greece. The sailors carrying Paul had carved images of Castor and Pollux on the bow, or front part, of their boats. They thought those false gods would protect them. Of course, we know that isn't true.

THE SCENE

ROME
(ACTS 28:14)
Rome is on the western coast of Italy, 10 miles (16 km) from the mouth of the Tiber River. At first, Rome was very small and poor, but the Romans made it larger as well as more beautiful and powerful. That's why it became a very, very important city, where the people who were governing the empire lived. Now you can see buildings in Rome that date back to that time, and they're still in good condition.

God's salvation has been sent to the Gentiles, and they will listen!" [29]a

30For two whole years Paul stayed there in his own rented house and welcomed all who came to see him. 31He proclaimed the kingdom of God and taught about the Lord Jesus Christ—with all boldness and without hindrance!

a 29 Some manuscripts include here *After he said this, the Jews left, arguing vigorously among themselves.*

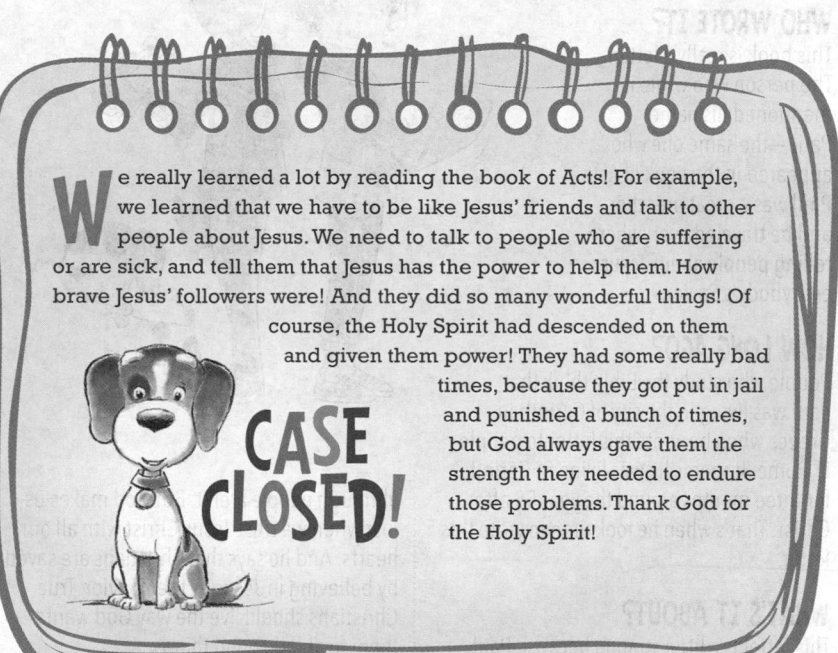

We really learned a lot by reading the book of Acts! For example, we learned that we have to be like Jesus' friends and talk to other people about Jesus. We need to talk to people who are suffering or are sick, and tell them that Jesus has the power to help them. How brave Jesus' followers were! And they did so many wonderful things! Of course, the Holy Spirit had descended on them and given them power! They had some really bad times, because they got put in jail and punished a bunch of times, but God always gave them the strength they needed to endure those problems. Thank God for the Holy Spirit!

CASE CLOSED!

ROMANS

THE EVIDENCE:

WHO WROTE IT?

This book is really a letter. The person who wrote it mentioned his name: Paul—the same one who appeared in the book of Acts. Paul was a great preacher, and he traveled everywhere, telling people about Jesus, everybody's Savior.

HOW LONG AGO?

People who study the Bible think that Paul was living in the city of Corinth in Greece when he wrote this letter to people in Rome. It seems he was living in Corinth for three months around the year 55 after Christ. That's when he took time to write this letter.

WHAT'S IT ABOUT?

This letter is a little strange because Paul writes to the Christians in the church in Rome, but he had never gone there before and he didn't really know what was happening there. In his letter, he says that the good news is that Jesus died and rose again and that he's the Savior of everyone, of the Jews and also of people who are not Jewish. He also says that God is just, although people aren't. But God makes us just when we trust Jesus Christ with all our hearts. And he says that Christians are saved by believing in Jesus as their Savior. True Christians should live the way God wants them to and do good things.

THE BEST PART

We agreed about this. The part we liked best is when Paul says, "For I am not ashamed of the gospel, because it is the power of God that brings salvation to everyone who believes" (1:16). Did you know that salvation is for everyone? How exciting!

---

1 Paul, a servant of Christ Jesus, called to be an apostle and set apart for the gospel of God— ²the gospel he promised beforehand through his prophets in the Holy Scriptures ³regarding his Son, who as to his earthly life*a* was a descendant of David, ⁴and who through the Spirit of holiness was appointed the Son of God in power*b* by his resurrection from the dead: Jesus Christ our Lord. ⁵Through him we received grace and apostleship to call all the Gentiles to the obedience that comes from*c* faith for his name's sake. ⁶And you also are among those Gentiles who are called to belong to Jesus Christ.

⁷To all in Rome who are loved by God and called to be his holy people:

---

a 3 Or *who according to the flesh*   *b 4* Or *was declared with power to be the Son of God*   *c 5* Or *that is* among you, just as I have had among the other Gentiles.

¹⁴I am obligated both to Greeks and non-Greeks, both to the wise and the foolish. ¹⁵That is why I am so eager to preach the gospel also to you who are in Rome.

¹⁶For I am not ashamed of the gospel, because it is the power of God that brings salvation to everyone who believes: first to the Jew, then to the Gentile. ¹⁷For in the gospel the righteousness of God is revealed—a righteousness that is by faith from first to last,ᵇ just as it is written: "The righteous will live by faith."ᶜ

ᵃ 13 The Greek word for *brothers and sisters* (*adelphoi*) refers here to believers, both men and women, as part of God's family; also in 7:1, 4; 8:12, 29; 10:1; 11:25; 12:1; 15:14, 30; 16:14, 17.   ᵇ 17 Or *is from faith to faith*
ᶜ 17 Hab. 2:4

Apostle
(ROMANS 1:1)

This is a word from the Greek language that means "a sent person." An apostle is like a disciple. Besides learning from a teacher, an apostle had to teach other people what the teacher had taught him.

Grace and peace to you from God our Father and from the Lord Jesus Christ.

Paul's Longing to Visit Rome

⁸First, I thank my God through Jesus Christ for all of you, because your faith is being reported all over the world. ⁹God, whom I serve in my spirit in preaching the gospel of his Son, is my witness how constantly I remember you ¹⁰in my prayers at all times; and I pray that now at last by God's will the way may be opened for me to come to you.

¹¹I long to see you so that I may impart to you some spiritual gift to make you strong— ¹²that is, that you and I may be mutually encouraged by each other's faith. ¹³I do not want you to be unaware, brothers and sisters,ᵃ that I planned many times to come to you (but have been prevented from doing so until now) in order that I might have a harvest

Were Roman people called to be "his holy people"?
(ROMANS 1:7)

Here, this doesn't mean that only the Romans are the people of God. Since the letter was for them, Paul wanted them to understand that God called them to be his children and fulfill his purposes. So "called" here means something like to be "appointed" or "designated" for some purpose or task.

God's Wrath Against Sinful Humanity

[18]The wrath of God is being revealed from heaven against all the godlessness and wickedness of people, who suppress the truth by their wickedness, [19]since what may be known about God is plain to them, because God has made it plain to them. [20]For since the creation of the world God's invisible qualities—his eternal power and divine nature—have been clearly seen, being understood from what has been made, so that people are without excuse.

[21]For although they knew God, they neither glorified him as God nor gave thanks to him, but their thinking became futile and their foolish hearts were darkened. [22]Although they claimed to be wise, they became fools [23]and exchanged the glory of the immortal God for images made to look like a mortal human being and birds and animals and reptiles.

[24]Therefore God gave them over in the sinful desires of their hearts to sexual

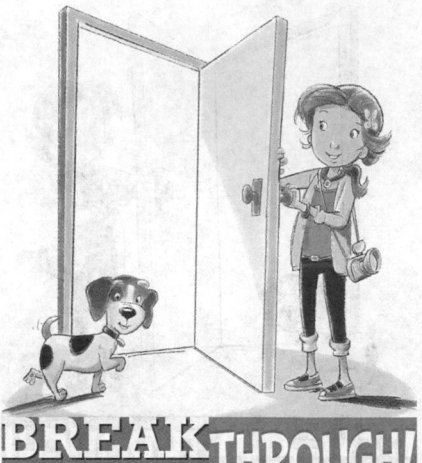

BREAK THROUGH!

Why does it always say "through Jesus Christ"?

(ROMANS 1:8)

Paul says this because Jesus is the Son of God and he rose from the dead in order to give us eternal life. Also, his name is powerful. Jesus had told his friends that it was in his name that they were going to do powerful things, like heal sick people and some other surprising things. Paul knew that, so he always says that's where the power comes from.

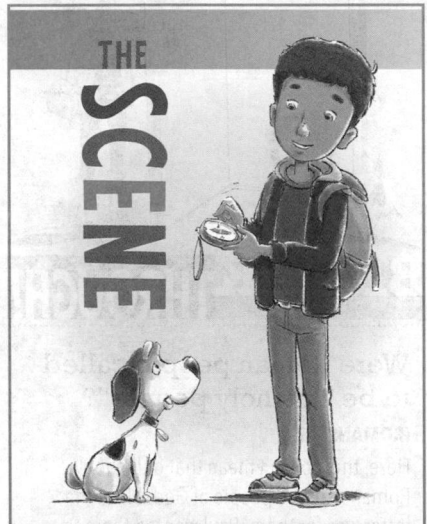

THE SCENE

ROME

(ROMANS 1:7)

Read what's written about this city in Acts 28:14.

impurity for the degrading of their bodies with one another. [25]They exchanged the truth about God for a lie, and worshiped and served created things rather than the Creator—who is forever praised. Amen.

[26]Because of this, God gave them over to shameful lusts. Even their women exchanged natural sexual relations for unnatural ones. [27]In the same way the men also abandoned natural relations with women and were inflamed with lust for one another. Men committed shameful acts with other men, and received in themselves the due penalty for their error.

[28]Furthermore, just as they did not think it worthwhile to retain the knowledge of God, so God gave them over to a depraved

BREAKTHROUGH!

Images

(ROMANS 1:23)

People from all over the world were living in Rome. They worshiped the gods of their own countries with images or idols. That's why Paul was scolding them. However, there are other ways to worship images, and it's always bad to do that. For example, anything that is more important to us than God can be like an image. There are people who are more worried about having more and more money, so then money becomes like an image or idol. Sometimes people spend so much time at the computer, they don't have time to go to church and pray. Then that becomes like an idol or image in our time.

mind, so that they do what ought not to be done. ²⁹They have become filled with every kind of wickedness, evil, greed and depravity. They are full of envy, murder, strife, deceit and malice. They are gossips, ³⁰slanderers, God-haters, insolent, arrogant and boastful; they invent ways of doing evil; they disobey their parents; ³¹they have no understanding, no fidelity, no love, no mercy. ³²Although they know God's righteous decree that those who do such things deserve death, they not only continue to do these very things but also approve of those who practice them.

God's Righteous Judgment

2 You, therefore, have no excuse, you who pass judgment on someone else, for at whatever point you judge another, you are condemning yourself, because you who pass judgment do the same things. ²Now we know that God's judgment against those who do such things is based on truth. ³So when you, a mere human being, pass judgment on them and yet do the same things, do you think you will escape God's judgment? ⁴Or do you show contempt for the riches of his kindness, forbearance and patience, not realizing that God's kindness is intended to lead you to repentance?

⁵But because of your stubbornness and your unrepentant heart, you are storing up wrath against yourself for the day of God's wrath, when his righteous judgment will be revealed. ⁶God "will repay each person according to what they have done."ᵃ ⁷To those who by persistence in doing good seek glory, honor and immortality, he will give eternal life. ⁸But for those who are self-seeking and who reject the truth and follow evil, there will be wrath and anger. ⁹There will be trouble and distress for every human being who does evil: first for the Jew, then for the Gentile; ¹⁰but glory, honor and peace for everyone who does good: first for the Jew, then for the Gentile. ¹¹For God does not show favoritism.

¹²All who sin apart from the law will also perish apart from the law, and all who sin under the law will be judged by the law. ¹³For it is not those who hear the law who are righteous in God's sight, but it is those who obey the law who will be declared righteous. ¹⁴(Indeed, when Gentiles, who do not have the law, do by nature things required by the law, they are a law for themselves, even though they do not have the law. ¹⁵They show that the requirements of the law are written on their hearts, their consciences also bearing witness, and their thoughts sometimes accusing them and at other times even defending them.) ¹⁶This will take place on the day when God judges people's

ᵃ 6 Psalm 62:12; Prov. 24:12

BREAKTHROUGH!

Who are the Jews?

(ROMANS 2-3)

Here it refers to common Jews. The Jews thought they were God's special people. They trusted the Law and thought they had to obey all the Laws of Moses and respect all the Jewish customs. They said that people who weren't Jewish and had become followers of Jesus also needed to accept their customs, even circumcision. Paul explains that Jesus did away with that law for all of us, and that we don't have to obey it anymore.

secrets through Jesus Christ, as my gospel declares.

The Jews and the Law

¹⁷Now you, if you call yourself a Jew; if you rely on the law and boast in God; ¹⁸if you know his will and approve of what is superior because you are instructed by the law; ¹⁹if you are convinced that you are a guide for the blind, a light for those who are in the dark, ²⁰an instructor of the foolish, a teacher of little children, because you have in the law the embodiment of knowledge and truth — ²¹you, then, who teach others, do you not teach yourself? You who preach against stealing, do you steal? ²²You who say that people should not commit adultery, do you

commit adultery? You who abhor idols, do you rob temples? ²³You who boast in the law, do you dishonor God by breaking the law? ²⁴As it is written: "God's name is blasphemed among the Gentiles because of you."ᵃ

²⁵Circumcision has value if you observe the law, but if you break the law, you have become as though you had not been circumcised. ²⁶So then, if those who are not circumcised keep the law's requirements, will they not be regarded as though they were circumcised? ²⁷The one who is not circumcised physically and yet obeys the law will condemn you who, even though you have theᵇ written code and circumcision, are a lawbreaker.

²⁸A person is not a Jew who is one only outwardly, nor is circumcision merely outward and physical. ²⁹No, a person is a Jew who is one inwardly; and circumcision is circumcision of the heart, by the Spirit, not by the written code. Such a person's praise is not from other people, but from God.

God's Faithfulness

3 What advantage, then, is there in being a Jew, or what value is there in circumcision? ²Much in every way! First of all, the Jews have been entrusted with the very words of God.

³What if some were unfaithful? Will their unfaithfulness nullify God's faithfulness? ⁴Not at all! Let God be true, and every human being a liar. As it is written:

"So that you may be proved right when you speak
and prevail when you judge."ᶜ

⁵But if our unrighteousness brings out God's righteousness more clearly, what shall we say? That God is unjust in bringing his wrath on us? (I am using a human argument.) ⁶Certainly not! If that were so, how could God judge the world? ⁷Someone might argue, "If my falsehood enhances God's truthfulness and so increases his glory, why am I still condemned as a sinner?" ⁸Why not say — as some slanderously claim that we say —

ᵃ 24 Isaiah 52:5 (see Septuagint); Ezek. 36:20,22
ᵇ 27 Or who, by means of a   ᶜ 4 Psalm 51:4

"Let us do evil that good may result"? Their condemnation is just!

No One Is Righteous

⁹What shall we conclude then? Do we have any advantage? Not at all! For we have already made the charge that Jews and Gentiles alike are all under the power of sin. ¹⁰As it is written:

> "There is no one righteous, not even one;
> ¹¹ there is no one who understands;
> there is no one who seeks God.
> ¹²All have turned away,
> they have together become worthless;
> there is no one who does good,
> not even one."ᵃ
> ¹³"Their throats are open graves;
> their tongues practice deceit."ᵇ
> "The poison of vipers is on their lips."ᶜ
> ¹⁴ "Their mouths are full of cursing and bitterness."ᵈ
> ¹⁵"Their feet are swift to shed blood;
> ¹⁶ ruin and misery mark their ways,
> ¹⁷and the way of peace they do not know."ᵉ
> ¹⁸ "There is no fear of God before their eyes."ᶠ

¹⁹Now we know that whatever the law says, it says to those who are under the law, so that every mouth may be silenced and the whole world held accountable to God. ²⁰Therefore no one will be declared righteous in God's sight by the works of the law; rather, through the law we become conscious of our sin.

Righteousness Through Faith

²¹But now apart from the law the righteousness of God has been made known, to which the Law and the Prophets testify. ²²This righteousness is given through faith inᵍ Jesus Christ to all who believe. There is no difference between Jew and Gentile, ²³for all have sinned and fall short of the glory of God, ²⁴and all are justified freely by his grace through the redemption that came by Christ Jesus. ²⁵God presented Christ as a sacrifice of atonement,ʰ through the shedding of his blood—to be received by faith. He did this to demonstrate his righteousness, because in his forbearance he had left the sins committed beforehand unpunished— ²⁶he did it to demonstrate his righteousness at the present time, so as to be just and the one who justifies those who have faith in Jesus.

²⁷Where, then, is boasting? It is excluded. Because of what law? The law that requires works? No, because of the law that requires faith. ²⁸For we maintain that a person is justified by faith apart from the works of the law. ²⁹Or is God the God of Jews only? Is he not the God of Gentiles too? Yes, of Gentiles too, ³⁰since there is only one God, who will justify the circumcised by faith and the uncircumcised through that same faith. ³¹Do we, then, nullify the law by this faith? Not at all! Rather, we uphold the law.

Abraham Justified by Faith

4 What then shall we say that Abraham, our forefather according to the flesh, discovered in this matter? ²If, in fact, Abraham was justified by works, he had something to boast about—but not before God. ³What does Scripture say? "Abraham believed God, and it was credited to him as righteousness."ⁱ

⁴Now to the one who works, wages are not credited as a gift but as an obligation. ⁵However, to the one who does not work but trusts God who justifies the ungodly, their faith is credited as righteousness. ⁶David says the same thing when he speaks of the blessedness of the one to whom God credits righteousness apart from works:

> ⁷"Blessed are those
> whose transgressions are forgiven,
> whose sins are covered.
> ⁸Blessed is the one
> whose sin the Lord will never count against them."ʲ

ᵃ 12 Psalms 14:1-3; 53:1-3; Eccles. 7:20
ᵇ 13 Psalm 5:9　ᶜ 13 Psalm 140:3
ᵈ 14 Psalm 10:7 (see Septuagint)
ᵉ 17 Isaiah 59:7,8　ᶠ 18 Psalm 36:1
ᵍ 22 Or through the faithfulness of　ʰ 25 The Greek for sacrifice of atonement refers to the atonement cover on the ark of the covenant (see Lev. 16:15,16).
ⁱ 3 Gen. 15:6; also in verse 22　ʲ 8 Psalm 32:1,2

⁹Is this blessedness only for the circumcised, or also for the uncircumcised? We have been saying that Abraham's faith was credited to him as righteousness. ¹⁰Under what circumstances was it credited? Was it after he was circumcised, or before? It was not after, but before! ¹¹And he received circumcision as a sign, a seal of the righteousness that he had by faith while he was still uncircumcised. So then, he is the father of all who believe but have not been circumcised, in order that righteousness might be credited to them. ¹²And he is then also the father of the circumcised who not only are circumcised but who also follow in the footsteps of the faith that our father Abraham had before he was circumcised.

¹³It was not through the law that Abraham and his offspring received the promise that he would be heir of the world, but through the righteousness that comes by faith. ¹⁴For if those who depend on the law are heirs, faith means nothing and the promise is worthless, ¹⁵because the law brings wrath. And where there is no law there is no transgression.

¹⁶Therefore, the promise comes by faith, so that it may be by grace and may be guaranteed to all Abraham's offspring—not only to those who are of the law but also to those who have the faith of Abraham. He is the father of us all. ¹⁷As it is written: "I have made you a father of many nations."ᵃ He is our father in the sight of God, in whom he believed—the God who gives life to the dead and calls into being things that were not.

¹⁸Against all hope, Abraham in hope believed and so became the father of many nations, just as it had been said to him, "So shall your offspring be."ᵇ ¹⁹Without weakening in his faith, he faced the fact that his body was as good as dead—since he was about a hundred years old—and that Sarah's womb was also dead. ²⁰Yet he did not waver through unbelief regarding the promise of God, but was strengthened in his faith and gave glory to God, ²¹being fully persuaded that God had power to do what he had promised. ²²This is why "it was credited to him as righteousness." ²³The words "it was

credited to him" were written not for him alone, ²⁴but also for us, to whom God will credit righteousness—for us who believe in him who raised Jesus our Lord from the dead. ²⁵He was delivered over to death for our sins and was raised to life for our justification.

Peace and Hope

5 Therefore, since we have been justified through faith, weᶜ have peace with God through our Lord Jesus Christ, ²through whom we have gained access by faith into this grace in which we now stand. And weᵈ boast in the hope of the glory of God. ³Not only so, but weᵈ also glory in our sufferings, because we know

---

ᵃ 17 Gen. 17:5   ᵇ 18 Gen. 15:5   ᶜ 1 Many manuscripts *let us*   ᵈ 2,3 Or *let us*

BREAKTHROUGH!

Are we happy because we're suffering? That doesn't make sense.

(ROMANS 5:3)

Paul is talking about suffering because a person is faithful to Jesus' teachings and obeys him. That's why we would be happy. Paul also says that it's God himself who gives us strength to continue loving him even when we are suffering. That's also why he has given us the Holy Spirit.

that suffering produces perseverance; [4]perseverance, character; and character, hope. [5]And hope does not put us to shame, because God's love has been poured out into our hearts through the Holy Spirit, who has been given to us.

[6]You see, at just the right time, when we were still powerless, Christ died for the ungodly. [7]Very rarely will anyone die for a righteous person, though for a good person someone might possibly dare to die. [8]But God demonstrates his own love for us in this: While we were still sinners, Christ died for us.

[9]Since we have now been justified by his blood, how much more shall we be saved from God's wrath through him! [10]For if, while we were God's enemies, we were reconciled to him through the death of his Son, how much more, having been reconciled, shall we be saved through his life! [11]Not only is this so, but we also boast in God through our Lord Jesus Christ, through whom we have now received reconciliation.

Death Through Adam, Life Through Christ

[12]Therefore, just as sin entered the world through one man, and death through sin, and in this way death came to all people, because all sinned—

[13]To be sure, sin was in the world before the law was given, but sin is not charged against anyone's account where there is no law. [14]Nevertheless, death reigned from the time of Adam to the time of Moses, even over those who did not sin by breaking a command, as did Adam, who is a pattern of the one to come.

[15]But the gift is not like the trespass. For if the many died by the trespass of the one man, how much more did God's grace and the gift that came by the grace of the one man, Jesus Christ, overflow to the many! [16]Nor can the gift of God be compared with the result of one man's sin: The judgment followed one sin and brought condemnation, but the gift followed many trespasses and brought justification. [17]For if, by the trespass of the one man, death reigned through that one

man, how much more will those who receive God's abundant provision of grace and of the gift of righteousness reign in life through the one man, Jesus Christ!

[18]Consequently, just as one trespass resulted in condemnation for all people, so also one righteous act resulted in justification and life for all people. [19]For just as through the disobedience of the one man the many were made sinners, so also through the obedience of the one man the many will be made righteous.

[20]The law was brought in so that the trespass might increase. But where sin increased, grace increased all the more, [21]so that, just as sin reigned in death, so also grace might reign through righteousness to bring eternal life through Jesus Christ our Lord.

Dead to Sin, Alive in Christ

6 What shall we say, then? Shall we go on sinning so that grace may increase? [2]By no means! We are those who have died to sin; how can we live in it any longer? [3]Or don't you know that all of us who were baptized into Christ Jesus were baptized into his death? [4]We were therefore buried with him through baptism into death in order that, just as Christ was raised from the dead through the glory of the Father, we too may live a new life.

[5]For if we have been united with him in a death like his, we will certainly also be united with him in a resurrection like his. [6]For we know that our old self was crucified with him so that the body ruled by sin might be done away with,[a] that we should no longer be slaves to sin— [7]because anyone who has died has been set free from sin.

[8]Now if we died with Christ, we believe that we will also live with him. [9]For we know that since Christ was raised from the dead, he cannot die again; death no longer has mastery over him. [10]The death he died, he died to sin once for all; but the life he lives, he lives to God.

[11]In the same way, count yourselves dead to sin but alive to God in Christ Jesus. [12]Therefore do not let sin reign in

---

[a] 6 Or be rendered powerless

your mortal body so that you obey its evil desires. ¹³Do not offer any part of yourself to sin as an instrument of wickedness, but rather offer yourselves to God as those who have been brought from death to life; and offer every part of yourself to him as an instrument of righteousness. ¹⁴For sin shall no longer be your master, because you are not under the law, but under grace.

Slaves to Righteousness

¹⁵What then? Shall we sin because we are not under the law but under grace? By no means! ¹⁶Don't you know that when you offer yourselves to someone as obedient slaves, you are slaves of the one you obey—whether you are slaves to sin, which leads to death, or to obedience, which leads to righteousness? ¹⁷But thanks be to God that, though you used to be slaves to sin, you have come to obey from your heart the pattern of teaching that has now claimed your allegiance. ¹⁸You have been set free from sin and have become slaves to righteousness.

¹⁹I am using an example from everyday life because of your human limitations. Just as you used to offer yourselves as slaves to impurity and to ever-increasing wickedness, so now offer yourselves as slaves to righteousness leading to holiness. ²⁰When you were slaves to sin, you were free from the control of righteousness. ²¹What benefit did you reap at that time from the things you are now ashamed of? Those things result in death! ²²But now that you have been set free from sin and have become slaves of God, the benefit you reap leads to holiness, and the result is eternal life. ²³For the wages of sin is death, but the gift of God is eternal life in*ᵃ* Christ Jesus our Lord.

Released From the Law, Bound to Christ

7 Do you not know, brothers and sisters—for I am speaking to those who know the law—that the law has authority over someone only as long as that person lives? ²For example, by law a married woman is bound to her husband as long as he is alive, but if her husband dies, she is released from the law that binds her to him. ³So then, if she has sexual relations with another man while her husband is still alive, she is called an adulteress. But if her husband dies, she is released from that law and is not an adulteress if she marries another man.

⁴So, my brothers and sisters, you also died to the law through the body of Christ, that you might belong to another, to him who was raised from the dead, in order that we might bear fruit for God. ⁵For when we were in the realm of the flesh,*ᵇ* the sinful passions aroused by the law were at work in us, so that we bore fruit for death. ⁶But now, by dying to what once bound us, we have been released from the law so that we serve in the new way of the Spirit, and not in the old way of the written code.

The Law and Sin

⁷What shall we say, then? Is the law sinful? Certainly not! Nevertheless, I would not have known what sin was had it not been for the law. For I would not have known what coveting really was if the law had not said, "You shall not covet."*ᶜ* ⁸But sin, seizing the opportunity afforded by the commandment, produced in me every kind of coveting. For apart from the law, sin was dead. ⁹Once I was alive apart from the law; but when the commandment came, sin sprang to life and I died. ¹⁰I found that the very commandment that was intended to bring life actually brought death. ¹¹For sin, seizing the opportunity afforded by the commandment, deceived me, and through the commandment put me to death. ¹²So then, the law is holy, and the commandment is holy, righteous and good.

¹³Did that which is good, then, become death to me? By no means! Nevertheless, in order that sin might be recognized as sin, it used what is good to bring about my death, so that through the commandment sin might become utterly sinful.

ᵃ 23 Or *through*   *ᵇ 5* In contexts like this, the Greek word for *flesh* (*sarx*) refers to the sinful state of human beings, often presented as a power in opposition to the Spirit.   *ᶜ 7* Exodus 20:17; Deut. 5:21

¹⁴We know that the law is spiritual; but I am unspiritual, sold as a slave to sin. ¹⁵I do not understand what I do. For what I want to do I do not do, but what I hate I do. ¹⁶And if I do what I do not want to do, I agree that the law is good. ¹⁷As it is, it is no longer I myself who do it, but it is sin living in me. ¹⁸For I know that good itself does not dwell in me, that is, in my sinful nature.ᵃ For I have the desire to do what is good, but I cannot carry it out. ¹⁹For I do not do the good I want to do, but the evil I do not want to do—this I keep on doing. ²⁰Now if I do what I do not want to do, it is no longer I who do it, but it is sin living in me that does it.

²¹So I find this law at work: Although I want to do good, evil is right there with me. ²²For in my inner being I delight in God's law; ²³but I see another law at work in me, waging war against the law of my mind and making me a prisoner of the law of sin at work within me. ²⁴What a wretched man I am! Who will rescue me from this body that is subject to death? ²⁵Thanks be to God, who delivers me through Jesus Christ our Lord!

So then, I myself in my mind am a slave to God's law, but in my sinful natureᵇ a slave to the law of sin.

Life Through the Spirit

8 Therefore, there is now no condemnation for those who are in Christ Jesus, ²because through Christ Jesus the law of the Spirit who gives life has set youᶜ free from the law of sin and death. ³For what the law was powerless to do because it was weakened by the flesh,ᵈ God did by sending his own Son in the likeness of sinful flesh to be a sin offering.ᵉ And so he condemned sin in the flesh, ⁴in order that the righteous requirement of the law might be fully met in us, who do not live according to the flesh but according to the Spirit.

⁵Those who live according to the flesh have their minds set on what the flesh desires; but those who live in accordance with the Spirit have their minds set on what the Spirit desires. ⁶The mind governed by the flesh is death, but the mind governed by the Spirit is life and peace. ⁷The mind governed by the flesh is hostile to God; it does not submit to God's law, nor can it do so. ⁸Those who are in the realm of the flesh cannot please God.

⁹You, however, are not in the realm of the flesh but are in the realm of the Spirit, if indeed the Spirit of God lives in you. And if anyone does not have the Spirit of Christ, they do not belong to Christ. ¹⁰But if Christ is in you, then even though your body is subject to death because of sin, the Spirit gives lifeᶠ because of righteousness. ¹¹And if the Spirit of him who raised Jesus from the dead is living in you, he who raised Christ from the dead will also give life to your mortal bodies because ofᵍ his Spirit who lives in you.

¹²Therefore, brothers and sisters, we have an obligation—but it is not to the flesh, to live according to it. ¹³For if you live according to the flesh, you will die; but if by the Spirit you put to death the misdeeds of the body, you will live.

¹⁴For those who are led by the Spirit of God are the children of God. ¹⁵The Spirit you received does not make you slaves, so that you live in fear again; rather, the Spirit you received brought about your adoption to sonship.ʰ And by him we cry, "Abba,ⁱ Father." ¹⁶The Spirit himself testifies with our spirit that we are God's children. ¹⁷Now if we are children, then we are heirs—heirs of God and co-heirs with Christ, if indeed we share in his sufferings in order that we may also share in his glory.

Present Suffering and Future Glory

¹⁸I consider that our present sufferings are not worth comparing with the glory that will be revealed in us. ¹⁹For the creation waits in eager expectation for the children of God to be revealed. ²⁰For the creation was subjected to frustration, not by its own choice, but by the

---

ᵃ 18 Or my flesh   ᵇ 25 Or in the flesh   ᶜ 2 The Greek is singular; some manuscripts me   ᵈ 3 In contexts like this, the Greek word for flesh (sarx) refers to the sinful state of human beings, often presented as a power in opposition to the Spirit; also in verses 4-13.   ᵉ 3 Or flesh, for sin   ᶠ 10 Or you, your body is dead because of sin, yet your spirit is alive   ᵍ 11 Some manuscripts bodies through   ʰ 15 The Greek word for adoption to sonship is a term referring to the full legal standing of an adopted male heir in Roman culture; also in verse 23.   ⁱ 15 Aramaic for father will of the one who subjected it, in hope [21]that[a] the creation itself will be liberated from its bondage to decay and brought into the freedom and glory of the children of God.

[22]We know that the whole creation has been groaning as in the pains of childbirth right up to the present time. [23]Not only so, but we ourselves, who have the firstfruits of the Spirit, groan inwardly as we wait eagerly for our adoption to sonship, the redemption of our bodies. [24]For in this hope we were saved. But hope that is seen is no hope at all. Who hopes for what they already have? [25]But if we hope for what we do not yet have, we wait for it patiently.

[26]In the same way, the Spirit helps us in our weakness. We do not know what we ought to pray for, but the Spirit himself intercedes for us through wordless groans. [27]And he who searches our hearts knows the mind of the Spirit, because the Spirit intercedes for God's people in accordance with the will of God.

[28]And we know that in all things God works for the good of those who love him, who[b] have been called according to his purpose. [29]For those God foreknew he also predestined to be conformed to the image of his Son, that he might be the firstborn among many brothers and sisters. [30]And those he predestined, he also called; those he called, he also justified; those he justified, he also glorified.

More Than Conquerors

[31]What, then, shall we say in response to these things? If God is for us, who can be against us? [32]He who did not spare his own Son, but gave him up for us all—how will he not also, along with him, graciously give us all things? [33]Who will bring any charge against those whom God has chosen? It is God who justifies. [34]Who then is the one who condemns? No one. Christ Jesus who died—more than that, who was raised to life—is at the right hand of God and is also interceding for us. [35]Who shall separate us from the love of Christ? Shall trouble or hardship or persecution or famine or nakedness or danger or sword? [36]As it is written:

"For your sake we face death all day long;
  we are considered as sheep to be slaughtered."[c]

[37]No, in all these things we are more than conquerors through him who loved us. [38]For I am convinced that neither death nor life, neither angels nor demons,[d] neither the present nor the future, nor any powers, [39]neither height nor depth, nor anything else in all creation, will be able to separate us from the love of God that is in Christ Jesus our Lord.

Paul's Anguish Over Israel

9 I speak the truth in Christ—I am not lying, my conscience confirms it through the Holy Spirit— [2]I have great sorrow and unceasing anguish in my heart. [3]For I could wish that I myself were cursed and cut off from Christ for the sake of my people, those of my own race, [4]the people of Israel. Theirs is the adoption to sonship; theirs the divine glory, the covenants, the receiving of the law, the temple worship and the promises. [5]Theirs are the patriarchs, and from them is traced the human ancestry of the Messiah, who is God over all, forever praised![e] Amen.

God's Sovereign Choice

[6]It is not as though God's word had failed. For not all who are descended from Israel are Israel. [7]Nor because they are his descendants are they all Abraham's children. On the contrary, "It is through Isaac that your offspring will be reckoned."[f] [8]In other words, it is not the children by physical descent who are God's children, but it is the children of the promise who are regarded as Abraham's offspring. [9]For this was how the promise was stated: "At the appointed time I will return, and Sarah will have a son."[g]

[10]Not only that, but Rebekah's children

---

[a] 20,21 Or subjected it in hope. [21]For   [b] 28 Or that all things work together for good to those who love God, who; or that in all things God works together with those who love him to bring about what is good—with those who
[c] 36 Psalm 44:22   [d] 38 Or nor heavenly rulers
[e] 5 Or Messiah, who is over all. God be forever praised! Or Messiah. God who is over all be forever praised!
[f] 7 Gen. 21:12   [g] 9 Gen. 18:10,14

THE
WITNESSES

✓ **ABRAHAM** (ROMANS 9:7)
Read about him in Genesis 11:26. He's called Abram there, because that was his name until God changed it.

were conceived at the same time by our father Isaac. ¹¹Yet, before the twins were born or had done anything good or bad—in order that God's purpose in election might stand: ¹²not by works but by him who calls—she was told, "The older will serve the younger."ᵃ ¹³Just as it is written: "Jacob I loved, but Esau I hated."ᵇ

¹⁴What then shall we say? Is God unjust? Not at all! ¹⁵For he says to Moses,

"I will have mercy on whom I have
        mercy,
    and I will have compassion on
        whom I have compassion."ᶜ

¹⁶It does not, therefore, depend on human desire or effort, but on God's mercy. ¹⁷For

Scripture says to Pharaoh: "I raised you up for this very purpose, that I might display my power in you and that my name might be proclaimed in all the earth."ᵈ ¹⁸Therefore God has mercy on whom he wants to have mercy, and he hardens whom he wants to harden.

¹⁹One of you will say to me: "Then why does God still blame us? For who is able to resist his will?" ²⁰But who are you, a human being, to talk back to God? "Shall what is formed say to the one who formed it, 'Why did you make me like this?' "ᵉ ²¹Does not the potter have the right to make out of the same lump of clay some pottery for special purposes and some for common use?

²²What if God, although choosing to show his wrath and make his power known, bore with great patience the objects of his wrath—prepared for destruction? ²³What if he did this to make the riches of his glory known to the objects of his mercy, whom he prepared in advance for glory— ²⁴even us, whom he also called, not only from the Jews but also from the Gentiles? ²⁵As he says in Hosea:

"I will call them 'my people' who are
        not my people;
    and I will call her 'my loved one'
        who is not my loved one,"ᶠ

²⁶and,

"In the very place where it was said to
        them,
    'You are not my people,'
    there they will be called 'children of
        the living God.' "ᵍ

²⁷Isaiah cries out concerning Israel:

"Though the number of the Israelites
        be like the sand by the sea,
    only the remnant will be saved.
²⁸For the Lord will carry out
    his sentence on earth with speed
        and finality."ʰ

²⁹It is just as Isaiah said previously:

ᵃ 12 Gen. 25:23   ᵇ 13 Mal. 1:2,3
ᶜ 15 Exodus 33:19   ᵈ 17 Exodus 9:16
ᵉ 20 Isaiah 29:16; 45:9   ᶠ 25 Hosea 2:23
ᵍ 26 Hosea 1:10   ʰ 28 Isaiah 10:22,23 (see Septuagint)

"Unless the Lord Almighty
   had left us descendants,
we would have become like Sodom,
   we would have been like
   Gomorrah."[a]

Israel's Unbelief

[30]What then shall we say? That the Gentiles, who did not pursue righteousness, have obtained it, a righteousness that is by faith; [31]but the people of Israel, who pursued the law as the way of righteousness, have not attained their goal. [32]Why not? Because they pursued it not by faith but as if it were by works. They stumbled over the stumbling stone. [33]As it is written:

"See, I lay in Zion a stone that causes
   people to stumble
and a rock that makes them fall,
and the one who believes in him will
   never be put to shame."[b]

10 Brothers and sisters, my heart's desire and prayer to God for the Israelites is that they may be saved. [2]For I can testify about them that they are zealous for God, but their zeal is not based on knowledge. [3]Since they did not know the righteousness of God and sought to establish their own, they did not submit to God's righteousness. [4]Christ is the culmination of the law so that there may be righteousness for everyone who believes.

[5]Moses writes this about the righteousness that is by the law: "The person who does these things will live by them."[c] [6]But the righteousness that is by faith says: "Do not say in your heart, 'Who will ascend into heaven?'"[d] (that is, to bring Christ down) [7]"or 'Who will descend into the deep?'"[e] (that is, to bring Christ up from the dead). [8]But what does it say? "The word is near you; it is in your mouth and in your heart,"[f] that is, the message concerning faith that we proclaim: [9]If you declare with your mouth, "Jesus is Lord," and believe in your heart that God raised him from the dead, you will be saved. [10]For it is with your heart that you believe and are justified, and it is with your mouth that you profess your faith and are saved.

[11]As Scripture says, "Anyone who believes in him will never be put to shame."[g] [12]For there is no difference between Jew and Gentile—the same Lord is Lord of all and richly blesses all who call on him, [13]for, "Everyone who calls on the name of the Lord will be saved."[h]

[14]How, then, can they call on the one they have not believed in? And how can they believe in the one of whom they have not heard? And how can they hear without someone preaching to them? [15]And how can anyone preach unless they are sent? As it is written: "How beautiful are the feet of those who bring good news!"[i]

[16]But not all the Israelites accepted the good news. For Isaiah says, "Lord, who has believed our message?"[j] [17]Consequently, faith comes from hearing the message, and the message is heard through the word about Christ. [18]But I ask: Did they not hear? Of course they did:

"Their voice has gone out into all the
   earth,
   their words to the ends of the
   world."[k]

[19]Again I ask: Did Israel not understand? First, Moses says,

"I will make you envious by those
   who are not a nation;
I will make you angry by a nation
   that has no understanding."[l]

[20]And Isaiah boldly says,

"I was found by those who did not
   seek me;
I revealed myself to those who did
   not ask for me."[m]

[21]But concerning Israel he says,

"All day long I have held out my
   hands
   to a disobedient and obstinate
   people."[n]

---

[a] 29 Isaiah 1:9   [b] 33 Isaiah 8:14; 28:16
[c] 5 Lev. 18:5   [d] 6 Deut. 30:12   [e] 7 Deut. 30:13
[f] 8 Deut. 30:14   [g] 11 Isaiah 28:16 (see Septuagint)
[h] 13 Joel 2:32   [i] 15 Isaiah 52:7   [j] 16 Isaiah 53:1
[k] 18 Psalm 19:4   [l] 19 Deut. 32:21
[m] 20 Isaiah 65:1   [n] 21 Isaiah 65:2

The Remnant of Israel

11 I ask then: Did God reject his people? By no means! I am an Israelite myself, a descendant of Abraham, from the tribe of Benjamin. [2]God did not reject his people, whom he foreknew. Don't you know what Scripture says in the passage about Elijah—how he appealed to God against Israel: [3]"Lord, they have killed your prophets and torn down your altars; I am the only one left, and they are trying to kill me"[a]? [4]And what was God's answer to him? "I have reserved for myself seven thousand who have not bowed the knee to Baal."[b] [5]So too, at the present time there is a remnant chosen by grace. [6]And if by grace, then it cannot be based on works; if it were, grace would no longer be grace.

[7]What then? What the people of Israel sought so earnestly they did not obtain. The elect among them did, but the others were hardened, [8]as it is written:

"God gave them a spirit of stupor,
      eyes that could not see
      and ears that could not hear,
to this very day."[c]

[9]And David says:

"May their table become a snare and
      a trap,
      a stumbling block and a retribution
      for them.
[10]May their eyes be darkened so they
      cannot see,
      and their backs be bent forever."[d]

Ingrafted Branches

[11]Again I ask: Did they stumble so as to fall beyond recovery? Not at all! Rather, because of their transgression, salvation has come to the Gentiles to make Israel envious. [12]But if their transgression means riches for the world, and their loss means riches for the Gentiles, how much greater riches will their full inclusion bring!

[13]I am talking to you Gentiles. Inasmuch as I am the apostle to the Gentiles, I take pride in my ministry [14]in the hope that I may somehow arouse my own people to envy and save some of them. [15]For if their rejection brought reconciliation to the world, what will their acceptance be but life from the dead? [16]If the part of the dough offered as firstfruits is holy, then the whole batch is holy; if the root is holy, so are the branches.

[17]If some of the branches have been broken off, and you, though a wild olive shoot, have been grafted in among the others and now share in the nourishing sap from the olive root, [18]do not consider yourself to be superior to those other branches. If you do, consider this: You do not support the root, but the root supports you. [19]You will say then, "Branches were broken off so that I could be grafted in." [20]Granted. But they were broken off because of unbelief, and you stand by faith. Do not be arrogant, but tremble. [21]For if God did not spare the natural branches, he will not spare you either.

[22]Consider therefore the kindness and sternness of God: sternness to those who fell, but kindness to you, provided that you continue in his kindness. Otherwise, you also will be cut off. [23]And if they do not persist in unbelief, they will be grafted in, for God is able to graft them in again. [24]After all, if you were cut out of an olive tree that is wild by nature, and contrary to nature were grafted into a cultivated olive tree, how much more readily will these, the natural branches, be grafted into their own olive tree!

All Israel Will Be Saved

[25]I do not want you to be ignorant of this mystery, brothers and sisters, so that you may not be conceited: Israel has experienced a hardening in part until the full number of the Gentiles has come in, [26]and in this way[e] all Israel will be saved. As it is written:

"The deliverer will come from Zion;
      he will turn godlessness away from
            Jacob.
[27]And this is[f] my covenant with them
      when I take away their sins."[g]

---

[a] 3 1 Kings 19:10,14   [b] 4 1 Kings 19:18
[c] 8 Deut. 29:4; Isaiah 29:10   [d] 10 Psalm 69:22,23
[e] 26 Or *and so*   [f] 27 Or *will be*   [g] 27 Isaiah 59:20,
21; 27:9 (see Septuagint); Jer. 31:33,34

28As far as the gospel is concerned, they are enemies for your sake; but as far as election is concerned, they are loved on account of the patriarchs, 29for God's gifts and his call are irrevocable. 30Just as you who were at one time disobedient to God have now received mercy as a result of their disobedience, 31so they too have now become disobedient in order that they too may now[a] receive mercy as a result of God's mercy to you. 32For God has bound everyone over to disobedience so that he may have mercy on them all.

Doxology

33Oh, the depth of the riches of the
    wisdom and[b] knowledge of God!
How unsearchable his judgments,
    and his paths beyond tracing out!
34"Who has known the mind of the Lord?
    Or who has been his counselor?"[c]
35"Who has ever given to God,
    that God should repay them?"[d]
36For from him and through him and for
    him are all things.
To him be the glory forever! Amen.

A Living Sacrifice

12 Therefore, I urge you, brothers and sisters, in view of God's mercy, to offer your bodies as a living sacrifice, holy and pleasing to God—this is your true and proper worship. 2Do not conform to the pattern of this world, but be transformed by the renewing of your mind. Then you will be able to test and approve what God's will is—his good, pleasing and perfect will.

Humble Service in the Body of Christ

3For by the grace given me I say to every one of you: Do not think of yourself more highly than you ought, but rather think of yourself with sober judgment, in accordance with the faith God has distributed to each of you. 4For just as each of us has one body with many members, and these members do not all have the same function, 5so in Christ we, though many, form one body, and each member belongs to all the others. 6We have different gifts,

according to the grace given to each of us. If your gift is prophesying, then prophesy in accordance with your[e] faith; 7if it is serving, then serve; if it is teaching, then teach; 8if it is to encourage, then give encouragement; if it is giving, then give generously; if it is to lead,[f] do it diligently; if it is to show mercy, do it cheerfully.

Love in Action

9Love must be sincere. Hate what is evil; cling to what is good. 10Be devoted to one another in love. Honor one another above yourselves. 11Never be lacking in zeal, but keep your spiritual fervor, serving the Lord. 12Be joyful in hope, patient in affliction, faithful in prayer. 13Share with the Lord's people who are in need. Practice hospitality.

14Bless those who persecute you; bless and do not curse. 15Rejoice with those who rejoice; mourn with those who mourn. 16Live in harmony with one another. Do not be proud, but be willing to associate with people of low position.[g] Do not be conceited.

17Do not repay anyone evil for evil. Be careful to do what is right in the eyes of everyone. 18If it is possible, as far as it depends on you, live at peace with everyone. 19Do not take revenge, my dear friends, but leave room for God's wrath, for it is written: "It is mine to avenge; I will repay,"[h] says the Lord. 20On the contrary:

"If your enemy is hungry, feed him;
    if he is thirsty, give him something
        to drink.
In doing this, you will heap burning
    coals on his head."[i]

21Do not be overcome by evil, but overcome evil with good.

Submission to Governing Authorities

13 Let everyone be subject to the governing authorities, for there is no authority except that which God has es-

---

[a] 31 Some manuscripts do not have *now*.   [b] 33 Or *riches and the wisdom and the*   [c] 34 Isaiah 40:13   [d] 35 Job 41:11   [e] 6 Or *the*   [f] 8 Or *to provide for others*   [g] 16 Or *willing to do menial work*   [h] 19 Deut. 32:35   [i] 20 Prov. 25:21,22

tablished. The authorities that exist have been established by God. [2]Consequently, whoever rebels against the authority is rebelling against what God has instituted, and those who do so will bring judgment on themselves. [3]For rulers hold no terror for those who do right, but for those who do wrong. Do you want to be free from fear of the one in authority? Then do what is right and you will be commended. [4]For the one in authority is God's servant for your good. But if you do wrong, be afraid, for rulers do not bear the sword for no reason. They are God's servants, agents of wrath to bring punishment on the wrongdoer. [5]Therefore, it is necessary to submit to the authorities, not only because of possible punishment but also as a matter of conscience.

[6]This is also why you pay taxes, for the authorities are God's servants, who give their full time to governing. [7]Give to everyone what you owe them: If you owe taxes, pay taxes; if revenue, then revenue; if respect, then respect; if honor, then honor.

Love Fulfills the Law

[8]Let no debt remain outstanding, except the continuing debt to love one another, for whoever loves others has fulfilled the law. [9]The commandments, "You shall not commit adultery," "You shall not murder," "You shall not steal," "You shall not covet,"[a] and whatever other command there may be, are summed up in this one command: "Love your neighbor as yourself."[b] [10]Love does no harm to a neighbor. Therefore love is the fulfillment of the law.

The Day Is Near

[11]And do this, understanding the present time: The hour has already come for you to wake up from your slumber, because our salvation is nearer now than when we first believed. [12]The night is nearly over; the day is almost here. So let us put aside the deeds of darkness and put on the armor of light. [13]Let us behave decently, as in the daytime, not in carousing and drunkenness, not in sexual immorality and debauchery, not in dissension and jealousy. [14]Rather, clothe your-

selves with the Lord Jesus Christ, and do not think about how to gratify the desires of the flesh.[c]

The Weak and the Strong

14 Accept the one whose faith is weak, without quarreling over disputable matters. [2]One person's faith allows them to eat anything, but another, whose faith is weak, eats only vegetables. [3]The one who eats everything must not treat with contempt the one who does not, and the one who does not eat everything must not judge the one who does, for God has accepted them. [4]Who are you to judge someone else's servant? To their own master, servants stand or fall. And they will stand, for the Lord is able to make them stand.

[5]One person considers one day more sacred than another; another considers every day alike. Each of them should be fully convinced in their own mind. [6]Whoever regards one day as special does so to the Lord. Whoever eats meat does so to the Lord, for they give thanks to God; and whoever abstains does so to the Lord and gives thanks to God. [7]For none of us lives for ourselves alone, and none of us dies for ourselves alone. [8]If we live, we live for the Lord; and if we die, we die for the Lord. So, whether we live or die, we belong to the Lord. [9]For this very reason, Christ died and returned to life so that he might be the Lord of both the dead and the living.

[10]You, then, why do you judge your brother or sister[d]? Or why do you treat them with contempt? For we will all stand before God's judgment seat. [11]It is written:

" 'As surely as I live,' says the Lord,
    'every knee will bow before me;
        every tongue will acknowledge
            God.' "[e]

---

[a] 9 Exodus 20:13-15,17; Deut. 5:17-19,21
[b] 9 Lev. 19:18   [c] 14 In contexts like this, the Greek word for *flesh* (*sarx*) refers to the sinful state of human beings, often presented as a power in opposition to the Spirit.   [d] 10 The Greek word for *brother or sister* (*adelphos*) refers here to a believer, whether man or woman, as part of God's family; also in verses 13, 15 and 21.   [e] 11 Isaiah 45:23

¹²So then, each of us will give an account of ourselves to God.

¹³Therefore let us stop passing judgment on one another. Instead, make up your mind not to put any stumbling block or obstacle in the way of a brother or sister. ¹⁴I am convinced, being fully persuaded in the Lord Jesus, that nothing is unclean in itself. But if anyone regards something as unclean, then for that person it is unclean. ¹⁵If your brother or sister is distressed because of what you eat, you are no longer acting in love. Do not by your eating destroy someone for whom Christ died. ¹⁶Therefore do not let what you know is good be spoken of as evil. ¹⁷For the kingdom of God is not a matter of eating and drinking, but of righteousness, peace and joy in the Holy Spirit, ¹⁸because anyone who serves Christ in this way is pleasing to God and receives human approval.

¹⁹Let us therefore make every effort to do what leads to peace and to mutual edification. ²⁰Do not destroy the work of God for the sake of food. All food is clean, but it is wrong for a person to eat anything that causes someone else to stumble. ²¹It is better not to eat meat or drink wine or to do anything else that will cause your brother or sister to fall.

²²So whatever you believe about these things keep between yourself and God. Blessed is the one who does not condemn himself by what he approves. ²³But whoever has doubts is condemned if they eat, because their eating is not from faith; and everything that does not come from faith is sin.ᵃ

15 We who are strong ought to bear with the failings of the weak and not to please ourselves. ²Each of us should please our neighbors for their good, to build them up. ³For even Christ did not please himself but, as it is written: "The insults of those who insult you have fallen on me."ᵇ ⁴For everything that was written in the past was written to teach us, so that through the endurance taught in the Scriptures and the encouragement they provide we might have hope.

⁵May the God who gives endurance and encouragement give you the same attitude of mind toward each other that Christ Jesus had, ⁶so that with one mind and one voice you may glorify the God and Father of our Lord Jesus Christ.

⁷Accept one another, then, just as Christ accepted you, in order to bring praise to God. ⁸For I tell you that Christ has become a servant of the Jewsᶜ on behalf of God's truth, so that the promises made to the patriarchs might be confirmed ⁹and, moreover, that the Gentiles might glorify God for his mercy. As it is written:

"Therefore I will praise you among the
    Gentiles;
I will sing the praises of your
    name."ᵈ

¹⁰Again, it says,

"Rejoice, you Gentiles, with his
    people."ᵉ

¹¹And again,

"Praise the Lord, all you
    Gentiles;
let all the peoples extol him."ᶠ

¹²And again, Isaiah says,

"The Root of Jesse will spring up,
    one who will arise to rule over the
        nations;
in him the Gentiles will hope."ᵍ

¹³May the God of hope fill you with all joy and peace as you trust in him, so that you may overflow with hope by the power of the Holy Spirit.

Paul the Minister to the Gentiles

¹⁴I myself am convinced, my brothers and sisters, that you yourselves are full of goodness, filled with knowledge and competent to instruct one another. ¹⁵Yet I have written you quite boldly on some points to remind you of them again, because of the grace God gave me ¹⁶to be a minister of Christ Jesus to the Gentiles. He gave me the priestly duty of proclaiming the gospel of God, so that

ᵃ 23 Some manuscripts place 16:25-27 here; others after 15:33.   ᵇ 3 Psalm 69:9   ᶜ 8 Greek *circumcision*   ᵈ 9 2 Samuel 22:50; Psalm 18:49   ᵉ 10 Deut. 32:43   ᶠ 11 Psalm 117:1   ᵍ 12 Isaiah 11:10 (see Septuagint) the Gentiles might become an offering acceptable to God, sanctified by the Holy Spirit.

¹⁷Therefore I glory in Christ Jesus in my service to God. ¹⁸I will not venture to speak of anything except what Christ has accomplished through me in leading the Gentiles to obey God by what I have said and done— ¹⁹by the power of signs and wonders, through the power of the Spirit of God. So from Jerusalem all the way around to Illyricum, I have fully proclaimed the gospel of Christ. ²⁰It has always been my ambition to preach the gospel where Christ was not known, so that I would not be building on someone else's foundation. ²¹Rather, as it is written:

> "Those who were not told about him
>   will see,
> and those who have not heard will
>   understand."ᵃ

²²This is why I have often been hindered from coming to you.

Paul's Plan to Visit Rome

²³But now that there is no more place for me to work in these regions, and since I have been longing for many years to visit you, ²⁴I plan to do so when I go to Spain. I hope to see you while passing through and to have you assist me on my journey there, after I have enjoyed your company for a while. ²⁵Now, however, I am on my way to Jerusalem in the service of the Lord's people there. ²⁶For Macedonia and Achaia were pleased to make a contribution for the poor among the Lord's people in Jerusalem. ²⁷They were pleased to do it, and indeed they owe it to them. For if the Gentiles have shared in the Jews' spiritual blessings, they owe it to the Jews to share with them their material blessings. ²⁸So after I have completed this task and have made sure that they have received this contribution, I will go to Spain and visit you on the way. ²⁹I know that when I come to you, I will come in the full measure of the blessing of Christ.

³⁰I urge you, brothers and sisters, by our Lord Jesus Christ and by the love of the Spirit, to join me in my struggle by praying to God for me. ³¹Pray that I may be kept safe from the unbelievers in Judea and that the contribution I take to Jerusalem may be favorably received by the Lord's people there, ³²so that I may come to you with joy, by God's will, and in your company be refreshed. ³³The God of peace be with you all. Amen.

Personal Greetings

16 I commend to you our sister Phoebe, a deaconᵇ,ᶜ of the church in Cenchreae. ²I ask you to receive her in the Lord in a way worthy of his people and to

ᵃ 21 Isaiah 52:15 (see Septuagint)   ᵇ 1 Or *servant*
ᶜ 1 The word *deacon* refers here to a Christian designated to serve with the overseers/elders of the church in a variety of ways; similarly in Phil. 1:1 and 1 Tim. 3:8,12.

THE SCENE

SPAIN

(ROMANS 15:24)

At that time, Spain wasn't a free country yet. It was a Roman province. In the year 19 after Christ, after some really long wars, it came under the power of Rome. At that time, Spain included the entire Iberian Peninsula, so it was the territory that is Spain and Portugal now.

THE
WITNESSES

Paul's letter to Rome. In Greek, Phoebe means "brilliant." How lovely!

✓ ANDRONICUS AND JUNIA
(ROMANS 16:7)

Andronicus was a Jew, but his name is Greek and it means "conqueror of men." Junia is the only woman in the entire New Testament that has the title of apostle. Andronicus and Junia were a married couple who became Christians before Paul did. They became missionaries, so they were traveling around telling people that Jesus is the Savior. Paul says they were his companions, and that all three were put in jail for talking about Jesus' love.

✓ RUFUS (ROMANS 16:13)

Some people think that this Rufus was the son of Simon from Cyrene mentioned in the gospel of Mark.

✓ TIMOTHY (ROMANS 16:21)

This name means "God fearing." He was a real help to Paul, because they made many missionary trips together. His mother was Jewish and she was a follower of Jesus, but his father wasn't Jewish. There are two letters in the New Testament named for Timothy.

✓ PHOEBE (ROMANS 16:1)

She was a leader in the church in Cenchreae. The word *deacon* in Greek refers to a person who is a leader in the church. We don't really know if she was married or if she had any children. Some experts think Phoebe was the person who took

✓ TERTIUS (ROMANS 16:22)

This name means "third." It was to this man that Paul dictated this letter for the people in Rome. Some people think Tertius was like Paul's secretary. Or maybe Paul couldn't see well and needed help to write his letters.

give her any help she may need from you, for she has been the benefactor of many people, including me.

³ Greet Priscilla*a* and Aquila, my co-workers in Christ Jesus. ⁴They risked their lives for me. Not only I but all the churches of the Gentiles are grateful to them.
⁵ Greet also the church that meets at their house.

Greet my dear friend Epenetus, who was the first convert to Christ in the province of Asia.
⁶ Greet Mary, who worked very hard for you.

⁷ Greet Andronicus and Junia, my fellow Jews who have been in prison with me. They are outstanding among*b* the apostles, and they were in Christ before I was.
⁸ Greet Ampliatus, my dear friend in the Lord.
⁹ Greet Urbanus, our co-worker in Christ, and my dear friend Stachys.
¹⁰ Greet Apelles, whose fidelity to Christ has stood the test.

Greet those who belong to the household of Aristobulus.

a 3 Greek Prisca, a variant of Priscilla   *b 7 Or are esteemed by*

THE SCENE

CENCHREAE

(ROMANS 16:1)

The city of Corinth had two nearby ports. One was on the Adriatic Sea and was called Lechaio, and the other was on the Aegean Sea and called Cenchreae, which was 5 miles (8 km) from Corinth, the capital.

¹¹ Greet Herodion, my fellow Jew.
Greet those in the household of Narcissus who are in the Lord.
¹² Greet Tryphena and Tryphosa, those women who work hard in the Lord.
Greet my dear friend Persis, another woman who has worked very hard in the Lord.
¹³ Greet Rufus, chosen in the Lord, and his mother, who has been a mother to me, too.
¹⁴ Greet Asyncritus, Phlegon, Hermes, Patrobas, Hermas and the other brothers and sisters with them.
¹⁵ Greet Philologus, Julia, Nereus and his sister, and Olympas and all the Lord's people who are with them.
¹⁶ Greet one another with a holy kiss.
All the churches of Christ send greetings.

¹⁷ I urge you, brothers and sisters, to watch out for those who cause divisions and put obstacles in your way that are contrary to the teaching you have learned. Keep away from them. ¹⁸ For such people are not serving our Lord Christ, but their own appetites. By smooth talk and flattery they deceive the minds of naive people. ¹⁹ Everyone has heard about your obedience, so I rejoice because of you; but I want you to be wise about what is good, and innocent about what is evil.

²⁰ The God of peace will soon crush Satan under your feet.

The grace of our Lord Jesus be with you.

²¹ Timothy, my co-worker, sends his greetings to you, as do Lucius, Jason and Sosipater, my fellow Jews.

²² I, Tertius, who wrote down this letter, greet you in the Lord.

²³ Gaius, whose hospitality I and the

CHECK THE FACTS

What was the name of Aquila's wife, the woman who preached, traveled and was even in prison with her husband and Paul?

A) Mary

B) Priscilla

C) Phoebe

CORRECT ANSWER: B

whole church here enjoy, sends you his greetings.

Erastus, who is the city's director of public works, and our brother Quartus send you their greetings. [24]a

25Now to him who is able to establish you in accordance with my gospel, the message I proclaim about Jesus Christ, in keeping with the revelation of the mystery hidden for long ages past, 26but now revealed and made known through the prophetic writings by the command of the eternal God, so that all the Gentiles might come to the obedience that comes from[b] faith— 27to the only wise God be glory forever through Jesus Christ! Amen.

---

[a] 24 Some manuscripts include here *May the grace of our Lord Jesus Christ be with all of you. Amen.*   [b] 26 Or that is

CASE CLOSED!

Paul left us thinking a lot about some very important things. First of all, that only Jesus saves people. It doesn't matter what country we're from or what race we belong to—Jesus can be our Savior. We also learned that we all sin, and that God looks on us with love because Jesus died on the cross and came alive again. God will accept us as his children if we believe in him. What good news!

1 CORINTHIANS

THE EVIDENCE:

WHO WROTE IT?
Paul, whose name was also Saul, wrote this letter. We know this because he says so at the very beginning of the letter.

HOW LONG AGO?
Paul wrote this letter while he was living in Ephesus between the years 54 and 57 after Christ. He says this himself in 16:8. He had already been in Corinth and he had met the Christians in the church in that city, because he was the first person who preached the love of Jesus to them.

WHAT'S IT ABOUT?
It seems there had been a lot of problems in the city of Corinth. The people there weren't acting in accordance with God. So Paul wrote to them and gave them some advice about how to live as Christians. He also scolded the people who weren't behaving right. It seems that the Christians in Corinth needed to think about some of the things they were doing in their worship services too. Paul also teaches them about the resurrection of the people who had died but had believed that Jesus Christ was their Savior.

THE BEST PART
We really like what Paul says in 2:9-10. This is really great, because God promises that we will see incredible things!

"What no eye has seen,
    what no ear has heard,
and what no human mind has conceived —
    the things God has prepared for those
        who love him —
these are the things God has revealed to
    us by his Spirit."

1 Paul, called to be an apostle of Christ Jesus by the will of God, and our brother Sosthenes,

² To the church of God in Corinth, to those sanctified in Christ Jesus and called to be his holy people, together with all those everywhere who call on the name of our Lord Jesus Christ—their Lord and ours:

³ Grace and peace to you from God our Father and the Lord Jesus Christ.

Thanksgiving

⁴ I always thank my God for you because of his grace given you in Christ Jesus. ⁵ For in him you have been enriched in every way—with all kinds of speech and with all knowledge— ⁶ God

THE SCENE

CORINTH

(1 CORINTHIANS 1:2)

Julius Caesar, the great Roman general, established a colony of military men there in the year 27 before Christ. At this time, it was the busy capital of the province of Achaia. Corinth was a very important city, because it was located on an isthmus—that's a narrow part of solid land. This isthmus joined the north and the south of Greece (the regions of Attica and Achaia). It separated the Aegean and Ionian Seas. During the time of the Roman empire, Corinth was a very important business center, because it joined Rome with the eastern part of the empire. The city had a bad name because there was a lot of corruption. Corinth belongs to Greece now.

thus confirming our testimony about Christ among you. ⁷Therefore you do not lack any spiritual gift as you eagerly wait for our Lord Jesus Christ to be revealed. ⁸He will also keep you firm to the end, so that you will be blameless on the day of our Lord Jesus Christ. ⁹God is faithful, who has called you into fellowship with his Son, Jesus Christ our Lord.

A Church Divided Over Leaders

¹⁰I appeal to you, brothers and sisters,ᵃ in the name of our Lord Jesus Christ, that all of you agree with one another in what you say and that there be no divisions among you, but that you be perfectly united in mind and thought. ¹¹My brothers and sisters, some from Chloe's household have informed me that there are quarrels among you. ¹²What I mean is this: One of you says, "I follow Paul"; another, "I follow Apollos"; another, "I follow Cephasᵇ"; still another, "I follow Christ."

¹³Is Christ divided? Was Paul crucified for you? Were you baptized in the name of Paul? ¹⁴I thank God that I did not baptize any of you except Crispus and Gaius, ¹⁵so no one can say that you were baptized in my name. ¹⁶(Yes, I also baptized the household of Stephanas; beyond that, I don't remember if I baptized anyone else.) ¹⁷For Christ did not send me to baptize, but to preach the gospel—not with wisdom and eloquence, lest the cross of Christ be emptied of its power.

Christ Crucified Is God's Power and Wisdom

¹⁸For the message of the cross is foolishness to those who are perishing, but to us who are being saved it is the power of God. ¹⁹For it is written:

"I will destroy the wisdom of the wise;
    the intelligence of the intelligent
    I will frustrate."ᶜ

²⁰Where is the wise person? Where is the teacher of the law? Where is the philosopher of this age? Has not God made foolish the wisdom of the world? ²¹For since in the wisdom of God the world through its wisdom did not know him, God was pleased through the foolishness of what was preached to save those who believe.

ᵃ 10 The Greek word for *brothers and sisters* (*adelphoi*) refers here to believers, both men and women, as part of God's family; also in verses 11 and 26; and in 2:1; 3:1; 4:6; 6:8; 7:24, 29; 10:1; 11:33; 12:1; 14:6, 20, 26, 39; 15:1, 6, 50, 58; 16:15, 20.   ᵇ 12 That is, Peter   ᶜ 19 Isaiah 29:14

THE
WITNESSES

✓ **SOSTHENES** (1 CORINTHIANS 1:1)
He was a Christian who was with Paul in
Ephesus. It's possible he's the same Sosthenes
who was the Jew in charge of the synagogue
in Corinth and was beaten by the Greeks there
when some Jews accused Paul before the
Roman tribunal.

✓ **CHLOE** (1 CORINTHIANS 1:11)
This Greek name means "green herb." It's
the name of a woman who was living in
Corinth.

✓ **APOLLOS** (1 CORINTHIANS 1:12)
He was a Jew from Alexandria, but he moved to
Ephesus. That's where he met Aquila, Priscilla
and Paul. Apollos was a great preacher who
could speak very well. He knew a lot about the
Bible, but he didn't know much about what
Jesus had taught. That's why Priscilla and
Aquila helped him understand those teachings
better.

²²Jews demand signs and Greeks look for
wisdom, ²³but we preach Christ crucified:
a stumbling block to Jews and foolishness
to Gentiles, ²⁴but to those whom God has
called, both Jews and Greeks, Christ the
power of God and the wisdom of God. ²⁵For
the foolishness of God is wiser than human wisdom, and the weakness of God is
stronger than human strength.

²⁶Brothers and sisters, think of what
you were when you were called. Not many
of you were wise by human standards; not
many were influential; not many were of
noble birth. ²⁷But God chose the foolish
things of the world to shame the wise;
God chose the weak things of the world
to shame the strong. ²⁸God chose the
lowly things of this world and the despised things—and the things that are
not—to nullify the things that are, ²⁹so
that no one may boast before him. ³⁰It
is because of him that you are in Christ
Jesus, who has become for us wisdom
from God—that is, our righteousness, holiness and redemption. ³¹Therefore, as it
is written: "Let the one who boasts boast
in the Lord."ᵃ

2 And so it was with me, brothers and
sisters. When I came to you, I did
not come with eloquence or human wisdom as I proclaimed to you the testimony about God.ᵇ ²For I resolved to know
nothing while I was with you except Jesus
Christ and him crucified. ³I came to you in
weakness with great fear and trembling.
⁴My message and my preaching were not
with wise and persuasive words, but with
a demonstration of the Spirit's power, ⁵so
that your faith might not rest on human
wisdom, but on God's power.

God's Wisdom Revealed
by the Spirit

⁶We do, however, speak a message of
wisdom among the mature, but not the
wisdom of this age or of the rulers of this
age, who are coming to nothing. ⁷No, we
declare God's wisdom, a mystery that has
been hidden and that God destined for
our glory before time began. ⁸None of the
rulers of this age understood it, for if they

ᵃ 31 Jer. 9:24   ᵇ 1 Some manuscripts *proclaimed to you
God's mystery*

had, they would not have crucified the Lord of glory. ⁹However, as it is written:

"What no eye has seen,
what no ear has heard,
and what no human mind has
    conceived"ᵃ—
the things God has prepared for
    those who love him—

¹⁰these are the things God has revealed to us by his Spirit.

The Spirit searches all things, even the deep things of God. ¹¹For who knows a person's thoughts except their own spirit within them? In the same way no one knows the thoughts of God except the Spirit of God. ¹²What we have received is not the spirit of the world, but the Spirit who is from God, so that we may understand what God has freely given us. ¹³This is what we speak, not in words taught us by human wisdom but in words taught by the Spirit, explaining spiritual realities with Spirit-taught words.ᵇ ¹⁴The person without the Spirit does not accept the things that come from the Spirit of God but considers them foolishness, and cannot understand them because they are discerned only through the Spirit. ¹⁵The person with the Spirit makes judgments about all things, but such a person is not subject to merely human judgments, ¹⁶for,

"Who has known the mind of the Lord
    so as to instruct him?"ᶜ

But we have the mind of Christ.

The Church and Its Leaders

3 Brothers and sisters, I could not address you as people who live by the Spirit but as people who are still worldly—mere infants in Christ. ²I gave you milk, not solid food, for you were not yet ready for it. Indeed, you are still not ready. ³You are still worldly. For since there is jealousy and quarreling among you, are you not worldly? Are you not acting like mere humans? ⁴For when one says, "I follow Paul," and another, "I follow Apollos," are you not mere human beings?

⁵What, after all, is Apollos? And what is Paul? Only servants, through whom you came to believe—as the Lord has as-

signed to each his task. ⁶I planted the seed, Apollos watered it, but God has been making it grow. ⁷So neither the one who plants nor the one who waters is anything, but only God, who makes things grow. ⁸The one who plants and the one who waters have one purpose, and they will each be rewarded according to their own labor. ⁹For we are co-workers in God's service; you are God's field, God's building.

¹⁰By the grace God has given me, I laid a foundation as a wise builder, and someone else is building on it. But each one should build with care. ¹¹For no one can lay any foundation other than the one already laid, which is Jesus Christ. ¹²If anyone builds on this foundation using gold, silver, costly stones, wood, hay or straw,

---

ᵃ 9 Isaiah 64:4   ᵇ 13 Or *Spirit, interpreting spiritual truths to those who are spiritual*   ᶜ 16 Isaiah 40:13

BREAKTHROUGH!

Who are the people that have the Spirit of God?

(1 CORINTHIANS 2:14-15)

They are the people who believe in Jesus as their Savior and are always ready to do what God likes. The Bible says that when we believe in Jesus and we're sorry for the bad things we've done, the Holy Spirit, who is God, comes to live in us.

BREAKTHROUGH!

Are we God's temple?

(1 CORINTHIANS 3:16)

It's just a manner of speaking! Of course, the Holy Spirit is in us. Since the Holy Spirit is God, then God lives in us. That's why our body is like a temple. We have to be very careful about what we do with our body and our heart.

13their work will be shown for what it is, because the Day will bring it to light. It will be revealed with fire, and the fire will test the quality of each person's work. 14If what has been built survives, the builder will receive a reward. 15If it is burned up, the builder will suffer loss but yet will be saved—even though only as one escaping through the flames.

16Don't you know that you yourselves are God's temple and that God's Spirit dwells in your midst? 17If anyone destroys God's temple, God will destroy that person; for God's temple is sacred, and you together are that temple.

18Do not deceive yourselves. If any of you think you are wise by the standards of this age, you should become "fools" so that you may become wise. 19For the wisdom of this world is foolishness in God's sight. As it is written: "He catches the wise in their craftiness"*a*; 20and again, "The Lord knows that the thoughts of

the wise are futile."*b* 21So then, no more boasting about human leaders! All things are yours, 22whether Paul or Apollos or Cephas*c* or the world or life or death or the present or the future—all are yours, 23and you are of Christ, and Christ is of God.

The Nature of True Apostleship

4 This, then, is how you ought to regard us: as servants of Christ and as those entrusted with the mysteries God has revealed. 2Now it is required that those who have been given a trust must prove faithful. 3I care very little if I am judged by you or by any human court; indeed, I do not even judge myself. 4My conscience is clear, but that does not make me innocent. It is the Lord who judges me. 5Therefore judge nothing before the appointed time; wait until the Lord comes. He will bring to light what is hidden in darkness and will expose the motives of the heart. At that time each will receive their praise from God.

6Now, brothers and sisters, I have applied these things to myself and Apollos for your benefit, so that you may learn from us the meaning of the saying, "Do not go beyond what is written." Then you will not be puffed up in being a follower of one of us over against the other. 7For who makes you different from anyone else? What do you have that you did not receive? And if you did receive it, why do you boast as though you did not?

8Already you have all you want! Already you have become rich! You have begun to reign—and that without us! How I wish that you really had begun to reign so that we also might reign with you! 9For it seems to me that God has put us apostles on display at the end of the procession, like those condemned to die in the arena. We have been made a spectacle to the whole universe, to angels as well as to human beings. 10We are fools for Christ, but you are so wise in Christ! We are weak, but you are strong! You are honored, we are dishonored! 11To this very hour we go hungry and thirsty, we are in rags, we are

a 19 Job 5:13   *b 20* Psalm 94:11   *c 22* That is, Peter brutally treated, we are homeless. ¹²We work hard with our own hands. When we are cursed, we bless; when we are persecuted, we endure it; ¹³when we are slandered, we answer kindly. We have become the scum of the earth, the garbage of the world—right up to this moment.

Paul's Appeal and Warning

¹⁴I am writing this not to shame you but to warn you as my dear children. ¹⁵Even if you had ten thousand guardians in Christ, you do not have many fathers, for in Christ Jesus I became your father through the gospel. ¹⁶Therefore I urge you to imitate me. ¹⁷For this reason I have sent to you Timothy, my son whom I love, who is faithful in the Lord. He will remind you of my way of life in Christ Jesus, which agrees with what I teach everywhere in every church.

¹⁸Some of you have become arrogant, as if I were not coming to you. ¹⁹But I will come to you very soon, if the Lord is willing, and then I will find out not only how these arrogant people are talking, but what power they have. ²⁰For the kingdom of God is not a matter of talk but of power. ²¹What do you prefer? Shall I come to you with a rod of discipline, or shall I come in love and with a gentle spirit?

Dealing With a Case of Incest

5 It is actually reported that there is sexual immorality among you, and of a kind that even pagans do not tolerate: A man is sleeping with his father's wife. ²And you are proud! Shouldn't you rather have gone into mourning and have put out of your fellowship the man who has been doing this? ³For my part, even though I am not physically present, I am with you in spirit. As one who is present with you in this way, I have already passed judgment in the name of our Lord Jesus on the one who has been doing this. ⁴So when you are assembled and I am with you in spirit, and the power of our Lord Jesus is present, ⁵hand this man over to Satan for the destruction of the flesh,ᵃ,ᵇ so that his spirit may be saved on the day of the Lord.

THE
WITNESSES

✓ **TIMOTHY** (1 CORINTHIANS 4:17; 16:10)
If you want to know who he was, then read the note near 1 Timothy 1:2.

⁶Your boasting is not good. Don't you know that a little yeast leavens the whole batch of dough? ⁷Get rid of the old yeast, so that you may be a new unleavened batch—as you really are. For Christ, our Passover lamb, has been sacrificed. ⁸Therefore let us keep the Festival, not with the old bread leavened with malice and wickedness, but with the unleavened bread of sincerity and truth.

⁹I wrote to you in my letter not to associate with sexually immoral people— ¹⁰not at all meaning the people of this world who are immoral, or the greedy and

---

ᵃ 5 In contexts like this, the Greek word for *flesh* (sarx) refers to the sinful state of human beings, often presented as a power in opposition to the Spirit.   ᵇ 5 Or *of his body* swindlers, or idolaters. In that case you would have to leave this world. [11]But now I am writing to you that you must not associate with anyone who claims to be a brother or sister[a] but is sexually immoral or greedy, an idolater or slanderer, a drunkard or swindler. Do not even eat with such people.

[12]What business is it of mine to judge those outside the church? Are you not to judge those inside? [13]God will judge those outside. "Expel the wicked person from among you."[b]

Lawsuits Among Believers

6 If any of you has a dispute with another, do you dare to take it before the ungodly for judgment instead of before the Lord's people? [2]Or do you not know that the Lord's people will judge the world? And if you are to judge the world, are you not competent to judge trivial cases? [3]Do you not know that we will judge angels? How much more the things of this life! [4]Therefore, if you have disputes about such matters, do you ask for a ruling from those whose way of life is scorned in the church? [5]I say this to shame you. Is it possible that there is nobody among you wise enough to judge a dispute between believers? [6]But instead, one brother takes another to court—and this in front of unbelievers!

[7]The very fact that you have lawsuits among you means you have been completely defeated already. Why not rather be wronged? Why not rather be cheated? [8]Instead, you yourselves cheat and do wrong, and you do this to your brothers and sisters. [9]Or do you not know that wrongdoers will not inherit the kingdom of God? Do not be deceived: Neither the sexually immoral nor idolaters nor adulterers nor men who have sex with men[c] [10]nor thieves nor the greedy nor drunkards nor slanderers nor swindlers will inherit the kingdom of God. [11]And that is what some of you were. But you were washed, you were sanctified, you were justified in the name of the Lord Jesus Christ and by the Spirit of our God.

Sexual Immorality

[12]"I have the right to do anything," you say—but not everything is beneficial. "I have the right to do anything"—but I will not be mastered by anything. [13]You say, "Food for the stomach and the stomach for food, and God will destroy them both." The body, however, is not meant for sexual immorality but for the Lord, and the Lord for the body. [14]By his power God raised the Lord from the dead, and he will raise us also. [15]Do you not know that your bodies are members of Christ himself? Shall I then take the members of Christ and unite them with a prostitute? Never! [16]Do you not know that he who unites himself with a prostitute is one with her in body? For it is said, "The two will become one flesh."[d] [17]But whoever is united with the Lord is one with him in spirit.[e]

[18]Flee from sexual immorality. All other sins a person commits are outside the body, but whoever sins sexually, sins against their own body. [19]Do you not know that your bodies are temples of the Holy Spirit, who is in you, whom you have received from God? You are not your own; [20]you were bought at a price. Therefore honor God with your bodies.

Concerning Married Life

7 Now for the matters you wrote about: "It is good for a man not to have sexual relations with a woman." [2]But since sexual immorality is occurring, each man should have sexual relations with his own wife, and each woman with her own husband. [3]The husband should fulfill his marital duty to his wife, and likewise the wife to her husband. [4]The wife does not have authority over her own body but yields it to her husband. In the same way, the husband does not have authority over his own body but yields it to his wife. [5]Do not deprive each other except perhaps by mutual consent and for a time, so that you may devote yourselves to prayer.

---

[a] 11 The Greek word for *brother or sister (adelphos)* refers here to a believer, whether man or woman, as part of God's family; also in 8:11, 13.   [b] 13 Deut. 13:5; 17:7; 19:19; 21:21; 22:21,24; 24:7   [c] 9 The words *men who have sex with men* translate two Greek words that refer to the passive and active participants in homosexual acts.   [d] 16 Gen. 2:24   [e] 17 Or *in the Spirit*

How can our bodies be members of Christ himself?

(1 CORINTHIANS 6:15)

Many times, we see that the Bible uses examples of things that are easy to understand in order to explain certain harder-to-understand things. This is one of those times. So our body has a head and it also has hands and feet. The head itself has ears and a mouth, but they all have to obey the head! So as Christians, we have one head, Jesus, and we obey him. But at the same time, we're all equally important. Each of us should serve the church with the skills and abilities we have so everybody can benefit. And everything we do should be by obeying the head — that's Jesus Christ.

Then come together again so that Satan will not tempt you because of your lack of self-control. ⁶I say this as a concession, not as a command. ⁷I wish that all of you were as I am. But each of you has your own gift from God; one has this gift, another has that.

⁸Now to the unmarried*ᵃ* and the widows I say: It is good for them to stay unmarried, as I do. ⁹But if they cannot control themselves, they should marry, for it is better to marry than to burn with passion.

¹⁰To the married I give this command (not I, but the Lord): A wife must not separate from her husband. ¹¹But if she does, she must remain unmarried or else be reconciled to her husband. And a husband must not divorce his wife.

¹²To the rest I say this (I, not the Lord): If any brother has a wife who is not a believer and she is willing to live with him, he must not divorce her. ¹³And if a woman has a husband who is not a believer and he is willing to live with her, she must not divorce him. ¹⁴For the unbelieving husband has been sanctified through his wife, and the unbelieving wife has been sanctified through her believing husband. Otherwise your children would be unclean, but as it is, they are holy.

¹⁵But if the unbeliever leaves, let it be so. The brother or the sister is not bound in such circumstances; God has called us to live in peace. ¹⁶How do you know, wife, whether you will save your husband? Or, how do you know, husband, whether you will save your wife?

Concerning Change of Status

¹⁷Nevertheless, each person should live as a believer in whatever situation the Lord has assigned to them, just as God has called them. This is the rule I lay down in all the churches. ¹⁸Was a man already circumcised when he was called? He should not become uncircumcised. Was a man uncircumcised when he was called? He should not be circumcised. ¹⁹Circumcision is nothing and uncircumcision is nothing. Keeping God's commands is what counts. ²⁰Each person should remain in the situation they were in when God called them.

²¹Were you a slave when you were called? Don't let it trouble you — although if you can gain your freedom, do so. ²²For the one who was a slave when called to faith in the Lord is the Lord's freed person; similarly, the one who was free when called is Christ's slave. ²³You were bought at a price; do not become slaves of human beings. ²⁴Brothers and sisters, each person, as responsible to God, should re-

ᵃ 8 Or widowers

main in the situation they were in when God called them.

Concerning the Unmarried

25Now about virgins: I have no command from the Lord, but I give a judgment as one who by the Lord's mercy is trustworthy. 26Because of the present crisis, I think that it is good for a man to remain as he is. 27Are you pledged to a woman? Do not seek to be released. Are you free from such a commitment? Do not look for a wife. 28But if you do marry, you have not sinned; and if a virgin marries, she has not sinned. But those who marry will face many troubles in this life, and I want to spare you this.

29What I mean, brothers and sisters, is that the time is short. From now on those who have wives should live as if they do not; 30those who mourn, as if they did not; those who are happy, as if they were not; those who buy something, as if it were not theirs to keep; 31those who use the things of the world, as if not engrossed in them. For this world in its present form is passing away.

32I would like you to be free from concern. An unmarried man is concerned about the Lord's affairs—how he can please the Lord. 33But a married man is concerned about the affairs of this world—how he can please his wife— 34and his interests are divided. An unmarried woman or virgin is concerned about the Lord's affairs: Her aim is to be devoted to the Lord in both body and spirit. But a married woman is concerned about the affairs of this world—how she can please her husband. 35I am saying this for your own good, not to restrict you, but that you may live in a right way in undivided devotion to the Lord.

36If anyone is worried that he might not be acting honorably toward the virgin he is engaged to, and if his passions are too strong*a* and he feels he ought to marry, he should do as he wants. He is not sinning. They should get married. 37But the man who has settled the matter in his own mind, who is under no compulsion but has control over his own will, and who has made up his mind not to marry the virgin—this man also does the right

BREAK THROUGH!

Does God like slavery?

(1 CORINTHIANS 7:21-22)

No! In Bible times, there were people who made other people be their slaves. That means they became the owners of those people—men, women and children who were forced to work. Many times the owners treated them badly, and the law did permit that. But Paul tells the people that if they were slaves but could get their freedom, then they should do that. Then he says that there's a different kind of freedom. That's the freedom a person has when he or she really believes in Jesus.

thing. 38So then, he who marries the virgin does right, but he who does not marry her does better.*b*

39A woman is bound to her husband as long as he lives. But if her husband dies, she is free to marry anyone she wishes, but he must belong to the Lord. 40In my judgment, she is happier if she stays as

a 36 Or if she is getting beyond the usual age for marriage
b 36-38 Or 36If anyone thinks he is not treating his daughter properly, and if she is getting along in years (or if her passions are too strong), and he feels she ought to marry, he should do as he wants. He is not sinning. He should let her get married. 37But the man who has settled the matter in his own mind, who is under no compulsion but has control over his own will, and who has made up his mind to keep the virgin unmarried—this man also does the right thing. 38So then, he who gives his virgin in marriage does right, but he who does not give her in marriage does better.

she is—and I think that I too have the Spirit of God.

Concerning Food Sacrificed to Idols

8 Now about food sacrificed to idols: We know that "We all possess knowledge." But knowledge puffs up while love builds up. [2]Those who think they know something do not yet know as they ought to know. [3]But whoever loves God is known by God.[a]

[4]So then, about eating food sacrificed to idols: We know that "An idol is nothing at all in the world" and that "There is no God but one." [5]For even if there are so-called gods, whether in heaven or on earth (as indeed there are many "gods" and many "lords"), [6]yet for us there is but one God, the Father, from whom all things came and for whom we live; and there is but one Lord, Jesus Christ, through whom all things came and through whom we live.

[7]But not everyone possesses this knowledge. Some people are still so accustomed to idols that when they eat sacrificial food they think of it as having been sacrificed to a god, and since their conscience is weak, it is defiled. [8]But food does not bring us near to God; we are no worse if we do not eat, and no better if we do.

[9]Be careful, however, that the exercise of your rights does not become a stumbling block to the weak. [10]For if someone with a weak conscience sees you, with all your knowledge, eating in an idol's temple, won't that person be emboldened to eat what is sacrificed to idols? [11]So this weak brother or sister, for whom Christ died, is destroyed by your knowledge. [12]When you sin against them in this way and wound their weak conscience, you sin against Christ. [13]Therefore, if what I eat causes my brother or sister to fall into sin, I will never eat meat again, so that I will not cause them to fall.

Paul's Rights as an Apostle

9 Am I not free? Am I not an apostle? Have I not seen Jesus our Lord? Are you not the result of my work in the Lord?

[2]Even though I may not be an apostle to others, surely I am to you! For you are the seal of my apostleship in the Lord.

[3]This is my defense to those who sit in judgment on me. [4]Don't we have the right to food and drink? [5]Don't we have the right to take a believing wife along with us, as do the other apostles and the Lord's brothers and Cephas[b]? [6]Or is it only I and Barnabas who lack the right to not work for a living?

[7]Who serves as a soldier at his own expense? Who plants a vineyard and does not eat its grapes? Who tends a flock and does not drink the milk? [8]Do I say this merely on human authority? Doesn't the Law say the same thing? [9]For it is written in the Law of Moses: "Do not muzzle an ox while it is treading out the grain."[c] Is it about oxen that God is concerned? [10]Surely he says this for us, doesn't he? Yes, this was written for us, because whoever plows and threshes should be able to do so in the hope of sharing in the harvest. [11]If we have sown spiritual seed among you, is it too much if we reap a material harvest from you? [12]If others have this right of support from you, shouldn't we have it all the more?

But we did not use this right. On the contrary, we put up with anything rather than hinder the gospel of Christ.

[13]Don't you know that those who serve in the temple get their food from the temple, and that those who serve at the altar share in what is offered on the altar? [14]In the same way, the Lord has commanded that those who preach the gospel should receive their living from the gospel.

[15]But I have not used any of these rights. And I am not writing this in the hope that you will do such things for me, for I would rather die than allow anyone to deprive me of this boast. [16]For when I preach the gospel, I cannot boast, since I am compelled to preach. Woe to me if I do not preach the gospel! [17]If I preach voluntarily, I have a reward; if not voluntarily, I am simply discharging the trust committed to me. [18]What then is my reward?

---

[a] 2,3 An early manuscript and another ancient witness think they have knowledge do not yet know as they ought to know. 3But whoever loves truly knows.   [b] 5 That is, Peter   [c] 9 Deut. 25:4

Just this: that in preaching the gospel I may offer it free of charge, and so not make full use of my rights as a preacher of the gospel.

Paul's Use of His Freedom

19Though I am free and belong to no one, I have made myself a slave to everyone, to win as many as possible. 20To the Jews I became like a Jew, to win the Jews. To those under the law I became like one under the law (though I myself am not under the law), so as to win those under the law. 21To those not having the law I became like one not having the law (though I am not free from God's law but am under Christ's law), so as to win those not having the law. 22To the weak I became weak, to win the weak. I have become all things to all people so that by all possible means I might save some. 23I do all this for the sake of the gospel, that I may share in its blessings.

The Need for Self-Discipline

24Do you not know that in a race all the runners run, but only one gets the prize? Run in such a way as to get the prize. 25Everyone who competes in the games goes into strict training. They do it to get a crown that will not last, but we do it to get a crown that will last forever. 26Therefore I do not run like someone running aimlessly; I do not fight like a boxer beating the air. 27No, I strike a blow to my body and make it my slave so that after I have preached to others, I myself will not be disqualified for the prize.

Warnings From Israel's History

10 For I do not want you to be ignorant of the fact, brothers and sisters, that our ancestors were all under the cloud and that they all passed through the sea. 2They were all baptized into Moses in the cloud and in the sea. 3They all ate the same spiritual food 4and drank the same spiritual drink; for they drank from the spiritual rock that accompanied them, and that rock was Christ. 5Nevertheless, God was not pleased with most of them; their bodies were scattered in the wilderness.

6Now these things occurred as examples to keep us from setting our hearts on evil things as they did. 7Do not be idolaters, as some of them were; as it is written: "The people sat down to eat and drink and got up to indulge in revelry."[a] 8We should not commit sexual immorality, as some of them did—and in one day twenty-three thousand of them died. 9We should not test Christ,[b] as some of them did—and were killed by snakes. 10And do not grumble, as some of them did—and were killed by the destroying angel.

11These things happened to them as examples and were written down as warnings for us, on whom the culmination of the ages has come. 12So, if you think you are standing firm, be careful that you don't fall! 13No temptation[c] has overtaken you except what is common to mankind. And God is faithful; he will not let you be tempted[c] beyond what you can bear. But when you are tempted,[c] he will also provide a way out so that you can endure it.

Idol Feasts and the Lord's Supper

14Therefore, my dear friends, flee from idolatry. 15I speak to sensible people; judge for yourselves what I say. 16Is not the cup of thanksgiving for which we give thanks a participation in the blood of Christ? And is not the bread that we break a participation in the body of Christ? 17Because there is one loaf, we, who are many, are one body, for we all share the one loaf.

18Consider the people of Israel: Do not those who eat the sacrifices participate in the altar? 19Do I mean then that food sacrificed to an idol is anything, or that an idol is anything? 20No, but the sacrifices of pagans are offered to demons, not to God, and I do not want you to be participants with demons. 21You cannot drink the cup of the Lord and the cup of demons too; you cannot have a part in both the Lord's table and the table of demons.

---

a 7 Exodus 32:6   *b* 9 Some manuscripts *test the Lord*
c 13 The Greek for *temptation* and *tempted* can also mean *testing* and *tested*.

²²Are we trying to arouse the Lord's jealousy? Are we stronger than he?

The Believer's Freedom

²³"I have the right to do anything," you say—but not everything is beneficial. "I have the right to do anything"—but not everything is constructive. ²⁴No one should seek their own good, but the good of others.

²⁵Eat anything sold in the meat market without raising questions of conscience, ²⁶for, "The earth is the Lord's, and everything in it."[a]

²⁷If an unbeliever invites you to a meal and you want to go, eat whatever is put before you without raising questions of conscience. ²⁸But if someone says to you, "This has been offered in sacrifice," then do not eat it, both for the sake of the one who told you and for the sake of conscience. ²⁹I am referring to the other person's conscience, not yours. For why is my freedom being judged by another's conscience? ³⁰If I take part in the meal with thankfulness, why am I denounced because of something I thank God for?

³¹So whether you eat or drink or whatever you do, do it all for the glory of God. ³²Do not cause anyone to stumble, whether Jews, Greeks or the church of God— ³³even as I try to please everyone in every way. For I am not seeking my own good but the good of many, so that they may be saved. ¹¹ ¹Follow my example, as I follow the example of Christ.

On Covering the Head in Worship

²I praise you for remembering me in everything and for holding to the traditions just as I passed them on to you. ³But I want you to realize that the head of every man is Christ, and the head of the woman is man,[b] and the head of Christ is God. ⁴Every man who prays or prophesies with his head covered dishonors his head. ⁵But every woman who prays or prophesies with her head uncovered dishonors her head—it is the same as having her head shaved. ⁶For if a woman does not cover her head, she might as well have her hair cut off; but if it is a disgrace for a

woman to have her hair cut off or her head shaved, then she should cover her head.

⁷A man ought not to cover his head,[c] since he is the image and glory of God; but woman is the glory of man. ⁸For man did not come from woman, but woman from man; ⁹neither was man created for woman, but woman for man. ¹⁰It is for this reason that a woman ought to have authority over her own[d] head, because of the angels. ¹¹Nevertheless, in the Lord woman is not independent of man, nor is man independent of woman. ¹²For as

---

[a] 26 Psalm 24:1   [b] 3 Or of the wife is her husband
[c] 4-7 Or ⁴Every man who prays or prophesies with long hair dishonors his head. ⁵But every woman who prays or prophesies with no covering of hair dishonors her head— she is just like one of the "shorn women." ⁶If a woman has no covering, let her be for now with short hair; but since it is a disgrace for a woman to have her hair shorn or shaved, she should grow it again. ⁷A man ought not to have long hair
[d] 10 Or have a sign of authority on her

BREAKTHROUGH!

What's all this about covering or uncovering one's head?

(1 CORINTHIANS 11:4–10)

It was a custom they had in the churches back then. Some people still do it. In Bible times, the Jews also covered their heads. But the Christians who weren't Jews weren't used to this custom, and some of them didn't want to do it.

woman came from man, so also man is born of woman. But everything comes from God. ¹³Judge for yourselves: Is it proper for a woman to pray to God with her head uncovered? ¹⁴Does not the very nature of things teach you that if a man has long hair, it is a disgrace to him, ¹⁵but that if a woman has long hair, it is her glory? For long hair is given to her as a covering. ¹⁶If anyone wants to be contentious about this, we have no other practice—nor do the churches of God.

Correcting an Abuse of the Lord's Supper

¹⁷In the following directives I have no praise for you, for your meetings do more harm than good. ¹⁸In the first place, I hear that when you come together as a church, there are divisions among you, and to some extent I believe it. ¹⁹No doubt there have to be differences among you to show which of you have God's approval. ²⁰So then, when you come together, it is not the Lord's Supper you eat, ²¹for when you are eating, some of you go ahead with your own private suppers. As a result, one person remains hungry and another gets drunk. ²²Don't you have homes to eat and drink in? Or do you despise the church of God by humiliating those who have nothing? What shall I say to you? Shall I praise you? Certainly not in this matter!

²³For I received from the Lord what I also passed on to you: The Lord Jesus, on the night he was betrayed, took bread, ²⁴and when he had given thanks, he broke it and said, "This is my body, which is for you; do this in remembrance of me." ²⁵In the same way, after supper he took the cup, saying, "This cup is the new covenant in my blood; do this, whenever you drink it, in remembrance of me." ²⁶For whenever you eat this bread and drink this cup, you proclaim the Lord's death until he comes.

²⁷So then, whoever eats the bread or drinks the cup of the Lord in an unworthy manner will be guilty of sinning against the body and blood of the Lord. ²⁸Everyone ought to examine themselves before they eat of the bread and drink from the

cup. ²⁹For those who eat and drink without discerning the body of Christ eat and drink judgment on themselves. ³⁰That is why many among you are weak and sick, and a number of you have fallen asleep. ³¹But if we were more discerning with regard to ourselves, we would not come under such judgment. ³²Nevertheless, when we are judged in this way by the Lord, we are being disciplined so that we will not be finally condemned with the world.

³³So then, my brothers and sisters, when you gather to eat, you should all eat together. ³⁴Anyone who is hungry should eat something at home, so that when you meet together it may not result in judgment.

And when I come I will give further directions.

Concerning Spiritual Gifts

12 Now about the gifts of the Spirit, brothers and sisters, I do not want you to be uninformed. ²You know that when you were pagans, somehow or other you were influenced and led astray to mute idols. ³Therefore I want you to know that no one who is speaking by the Spirit of God says, "Jesus be cursed," and no one can say, "Jesus is Lord," except by the Holy Spirit.

⁴There are different kinds of gifts, but the same Spirit distributes them. ⁵There are different kinds of service, but the same Lord. ⁶There are different kinds of working, but in all of them and in everyone it is the same God at work.

⁷Now to each one the manifestation of the Spirit is given for the common good. ⁸To one there is given through the Spirit a message of wisdom, to another a message of knowledge by means of the same Spirit, ⁹to another faith by the same Spirit, to another gifts of healing by that one Spirit, ¹⁰to another miraculous powers, to another prophecy, to another distinguishing between spirits, to another speaking in different kinds of tongues,ᵃ and to still another the interpretation of tongues.ᵃ ¹¹All these are the work of one and the same Spirit, and he distributes them to each one, just as he determines.

ᵃ *10* Or *languages; also in verse 28*

Unity and Diversity in the Body

¹²Just as a body, though one, has many parts, but all its many parts form one body, so it is with Christ. ¹³For we were all baptized by*ᵃ* one Spirit so as to form one body—whether Jews or Gentiles, slave or free—and we were all given the one Spirit to drink. ¹⁴Even so the body is not made up of one part but of many.

¹⁵Now if the foot should say, "Because I am not a hand, I do not belong to the body," it would not for that reason stop being part of the body. ¹⁶And if the ear should say, "Because I am not an eye, I do not belong to the body," it would not for that reason stop being part of the body. ¹⁷If the whole body were an eye, where would the sense of hearing be? If the whole body were an ear, where would the sense of smell be? ¹⁸But in fact God has placed the parts in the body, every one of them, just as he wanted them to be. ¹⁹If they were all one part, where would the body be? ²⁰As it is, there are many parts, but one body.

²¹The eye cannot say to the hand, "I don't need you!" And the head cannot say to the feet, "I don't need you!" ²²On the contrary, those parts of the body that seem to be weaker are indispensable, ²³and the parts that we think are less honorable we treat with special honor. And the parts that are unpresentable are treated with special modesty, ²⁴while our presentable parts need no special treatment. But God has put the body together, giving greater honor to the parts that lacked it, ²⁵so that there should be no division in the body, but that its parts should have equal concern for each other. ²⁶If one part suffers, every part suffers with it; if one part is honored, every part rejoices with it.

²⁷Now you are the body of Christ, and each one of you is a part of it. ²⁸And God has placed in the church first of all apostles, second prophets, third teachers, then miracles, then gifts of healing, of helping, of guidance, and of different kinds of tongues. ²⁹Are all apostles? Are all prophets? Are all teachers? Do all work miracles? ³⁰Do all have gifts of healing? Do all speak in tongues*ᵇ*? Do all interpret? ³¹Now eagerly desire the greater gifts.

BREAKTHROUGH!

What's the difference between an apostle, a prophet and a teacher?

(1 CORINTHIANS 12:28)

At first, the "apostles" were just Jesus' twelve friends who went everywhere with him. Later, they started saying that anybody who traveled from one place to another to talk about Jesus' love was an apostle. Prophets were people who got messages from God and passed them on to the church. And teachers were the people who taught the Bible.

Love Is Indispensable

And yet I will show you the most excellent way.

13 If I speak in the tongues*ᶜ* of men or of angels, but do not have love, I am only a resounding gong or a clanging cymbal. ²If I have the gift of prophecy and can fathom all mysteries and all knowledge, and if I have a faith that can move mountains, but do not have love, I am nothing. ³If I give all I possess to the poor and give over my body to hardship that I may boast,*ᵈ* but do not have love, I gain nothing.

⁴Love is patient, love is kind. It does not envy, it does not boast, it is not proud.

ᵃ 13 Or *with;* or *in*   *ᵇ 30* Or *other languages*   *ᶜ 1* Or *languages*   *ᵈ 3* Some manuscripts *body to the flames*

⁵It does not dishonor others, it is not self-seeking, it is not easily angered, it keeps no record of wrongs. ⁶Love does not delight in evil but rejoices with the truth. ⁷It always protects, always trusts, always hopes, always perseveres.

⁸Love never fails. But where there are prophecies, they will cease; where there are tongues, they will be stilled; where there is knowledge, it will pass away. ⁹For we know in part and we prophesy in part, ¹⁰but when completeness comes, what is in part disappears. ¹¹When I was a child, I talked like a child, I thought like a child, I reasoned like a child. When I became a man, I put the ways of childhood behind me. ¹²For now we see only a reflection as in a mirror; then we shall see face to face. Now I know in part; then I shall know fully, even as I am fully known.

¹³And now these three remain: faith, hope and love. But the greatest of these is love.

Intelligibility in Worship

14 Follow the way of love and eagerly desire gifts of the Spirit, especially prophecy. ²For anyone who speaks in a tongue*ᵃ* does not speak to people but to God. Indeed, no one understands them; they utter mysteries by the Spirit. ³But the one who prophesies speaks to people for their strengthening, encouraging and comfort. ⁴Anyone who speaks in a tongue edifies themselves, but the one who prophesies edifies the church. ⁵I would like every one of you to speak in tongues,*ᵇ* but I would rather have you prophesy. The one who prophesies is greater than the one who speaks in tongues,*ᵇ* unless someone interprets, so that the church may be edified.

⁶Now, brothers and sisters, if I come to you and speak in tongues, what good will I be to you, unless I bring you some revelation or knowledge or prophecy or word of instruction? ⁷Even in the case of lifeless things that make sounds, such as the pipe or harp, how will anyone know what tune is being played unless there is a distinction in the notes? ⁸Again, if the trumpet does not sound a clear call, who will get ready for battle? ⁹So it is with you. Unless you speak intelligible words with your tongue, how will anyone know what you are saying? You will just be speaking into the air. ¹⁰Undoubtedly there are all sorts of languages in the world, yet none of them is without meaning. ¹¹If then I do not grasp the meaning of what someone is saying, I am a foreigner to the speaker, and the speaker is a foreigner to me. ¹²So it is with you. Since you are eager for gifts of the Spirit, try to excel in those that build up the church.

¹³For this reason the one who speaks in a tongue should pray that they may interpret what they say. ¹⁴For if I pray in a tongue, my spirit prays, but my mind is

---

ᵃ 2 Or in another language; also in verses 4, 13, 14, 19, 26 and 27   ᵇ 5 Or in other languages; also in verses 6, 18, 22, 23 and 39

BREAKTHROUGH!

Speaking in a tongue
(1 CORINTHIANS 14:2-5)

The technical term is *glossolalia*. Now that's a strange word! It's like when the Holy Spirit made people start talking in other languages on the day of Pentecost. Here it's different, because it's talking about a language that only God can understand. It can also be that some other person in the church understands and then translates for the others.

unfruitful. ¹⁵So what shall I do? I will pray with my spirit, but I will also pray with my understanding; I will sing with my spirit, but I will also sing with my understanding. ¹⁶Otherwise when you are praising God in the Spirit, how can someone else, who is now put in the position of an inquirer,ᵃ say "Amen" to your thanksgiving, since they do not know what you are saying? ¹⁷You are giving thanks well enough, but no one else is edified.

¹⁸I thank God that I speak in tongues more than all of you. ¹⁹But in the church I would rather speak five intelligible words to instruct others than ten thousand words in a tongue.

²⁰Brothers and sisters, stop thinking like children. In regard to evil be infants, but in your thinking be adults. ²¹In the Law it is written:

"With other tongues
    and through the lips of foreigners

CHECK THE FACTS

**What's most important
for a Christian?**

A) To preach a lot

B) To never miss going to church

C) To love other people

CORRECT ANSWER: C

I will speak to this people,
    but even then they will not listen
        to me,
                    says the Lord."ᵇ

²²Tongues, then, are a sign, not for believers but for unbelievers; prophecy, however, is not for unbelievers but for believers. ²³So if the whole church comes together and everyone speaks in tongues, and inquirers or unbelievers come in, will they not say that you are out of your mind? ²⁴But if an unbeliever or an inquirer comes in while everyone is prophesying, they are convicted of sin and are brought under judgment by all, ²⁵as the secrets of their hearts are laid bare. So they will fall down and worship God, exclaiming, "God is really among you!"

Good Order in Worship

²⁶What then shall we say, brothers and sisters? When you come together, each of you has a hymn, or a word of instruction, a revelation, a tongue or an interpretation. Everything must be done so that the church may be built up. ²⁷If anyone speaks in a tongue, two—or at the most three—should speak, one at a time, and someone must interpret. ²⁸If there is no interpreter, the speaker should keep quiet in the church and speak to himself and to God.

²⁹Two or three prophets should speak, and the others should weigh carefully what is said. ³⁰And if a revelation comes to someone who is sitting down, the first speaker should stop. ³¹For you can all prophesy in turn so that everyone may be instructed and encouraged. ³²The spirits of prophets are subject to the control of prophets. ³³For God is not a God of disorder but of peace—as in all the congregations of the Lord's people.

³⁴Womenᶜ should remain silent in the churches. They are not allowed to speak, but must be in submission, as the law says. ³⁵If they want to inquire about something, they should ask their own husbands

---

ᵃ 16 The Greek word for *inquirer* is a technical term for someone not fully initiated into a religion; also in verses 23 and 24.   ᵇ 21 Isaiah 28:11,12   ᶜ 33,34 Or *peace. As in all the congregations of the Lord's people,* ³⁴*women* at home; for it is disgraceful for a woman to speak in the church.*a*

³⁶Or did the word of God originate with you? Or are you the only people it has reached? ³⁷If anyone thinks they are a prophet or otherwise gifted by the Spirit, let them acknowledge that what I am writing to you is the Lord's command. ³⁸But if anyone ignores this, they will themselves be ignored.*b*

³⁹Therefore, my brothers and sisters, be eager to prophesy, and do not forbid speaking in tongues. ⁴⁰But everything should be done in a fitting and orderly way.

The Resurrection of Christ

15 Now, brothers and sisters, I want to remind you of the gospel I preached to you, which you received and on which you have taken your stand. ²By this gospel you are saved, if you hold firmly to the word I preached to you. Otherwise, you have believed in vain.

³For what I received I passed on to you as of first importance*c*: that Christ died for our sins according to the Scriptures, ⁴that he was buried, that he was raised on the third day according to the Scriptures, ⁵and that he appeared to Cephas,*d* and then to the Twelve. ⁶After that, he appeared to more than five hundred of the brothers and sisters at the same time, most of whom are still living, though some have fallen asleep. ⁷Then he appeared to James, then to all the apostles, ⁸and last of all he appeared to me also, as to one abnormally born.

⁹For I am the least of the apostles and do not even deserve to be called an apostle, because I persecuted the church of God. ¹⁰But by the grace of God I am what I am, and his grace to me was not without effect. No, I worked harder than all of them—yet not I, but the grace of God that was with me. ¹¹Whether, then, it is I or they, this is what we preach, and this is what you believed.

The Resurrection of the Dead

¹²But if it is preached that Christ has been raised from the dead, how can some

BREAKTHROUGH!

Couldn't women speak in church?

(1 CORINTHIANS 14:34-35)

That's not fair! Why can't women speak in church? That can't be right! Well, we see that on the day of Pentecost, Peter was talking about a prophet in the Bible who said that God would make "men and women" talk for him. Also, Paul was Priscilla's and Junia's friend, and those two women knew a lot about the Bible and they preached. What Paul probably means is that women shouldn't be gossips and that they should listen to the teachings. Doesn't that make more sense? There were probably people in that church, many of them women, who talked too much and didn't pay attention to what was being taught!

of you say that there is no resurrection of the dead? ¹³If there is no resurrection of the dead, then not even Christ has been raised. ¹⁴And if Christ has not been raised, our preaching is useless and so is your faith. ¹⁵More than that, we are then found to be false witnesses about God, for we have testified about God that he raised Christ from the dead. But he did

---

a 34,35 In a few manuscripts these verses come after verse 40.   *b 38* Some manuscripts *But anyone who is ignorant of this will be ignorant*   *c 3* Or *you at the first*   *d 5* That is, Peter not raise him if in fact the dead are not raised. ¹⁶For if the dead are not raised, then Christ has not been raised either. ¹⁷And if Christ has not been raised, your faith is futile; you are still in your sins. ¹⁸Then those also who have fallen asleep in Christ are lost. ¹⁹If only for this life we have hope in Christ, we are of all people most to be pitied.

²⁰But Christ has indeed been raised from the dead, the firstfruits of those who have fallen asleep. ²¹For since death came through a man, the resurrection of the dead comes also through a man. ²²For as in Adam all die, so in Christ all will be made alive. ²³But each in turn: Christ, the firstfruits; then, when he comes, those who belong to him. ²⁴Then the end will come, when he hands over the kingdom to God the Father after he has destroyed all dominion, authority and power. ²⁵For he must reign until he has put all his enemies under his feet. ²⁶The last enemy to be destroyed is death. ²⁷For he "has put everything under his feet."ᵃ Now when it says that "everything" has been put under him, it is clear that this does not include God himself, who put everything under Christ. ²⁸When he has done this, then the Son himself will be made subject to him who put everything under him, so that God may be all in all.

²⁹Now if there is no resurrection, what will those do who are baptized for the dead? If the dead are not raised at all, why are people baptized for them? ³⁰And as for us, why do we endanger ourselves every hour? ³¹I face death every day — yes, just as surely as I boast about you in Christ Jesus our Lord. ³²If I fought wild beasts in Ephesus with no more than human hopes, what have I gained? If the dead are not raised,

"Let us eat and drink,
    for tomorrow we die."ᵇ

³³Do not be misled: "Bad company corrupts good character."ᶜ ³⁴Come back to your senses as you ought, and stop sinning; for there are some who are ignorant of God — I say this to your shame.

The Resurrection Body

³⁵But someone will ask, "How are the dead raised? With what kind of body will they come?" ³⁶How foolish! What you sow does not come to life unless it dies. ³⁷When you sow, you do not plant the body that will be, but just a seed, perhaps of wheat or of something else. ³⁸But God gives it a body as he has determined, and to each kind of seed he gives its own body. ³⁹Not all flesh is the same: People have one kind of flesh, animals have another, birds another and fish another. ⁴⁰There are also heavenly bodies and there are earthly bodies; but the splendor of the heavenly bodies is one kind, and the splendor of the earthly bodies is another. ⁴¹The sun has one kind of splendor, the moon another and the stars another; and star differs from star in splendor.

⁴²So will it be with the resurrection of the dead. The body that is sown is perishable, it is raised imperishable; ⁴³it is sown in dishonor, it is raised in glory; it is sown in weakness, it is raised in power; ⁴⁴it is sown a natural body, it is raised a spiritual body.

If there is a natural body, there is also a spiritual body. ⁴⁵So it is written: "The first man Adam became a living being"ᵈ; the last Adam, a life-giving spirit. ⁴⁶The spiritual did not come first, but the natural, and after that the spiritual. ⁴⁷The first man was of the dust of the earth; the second man is of heaven. ⁴⁸As was the earthly man, so are those who are of the earth; and as is the heavenly man, so also are those who are of heaven. ⁴⁹And just as we have borne the image of the earthly man, so shall weᵉ bear the image of the heavenly man.

⁵⁰I declare to you, brothers and sisters, that flesh and blood cannot inherit the kingdom of God, nor does the perishable inherit the imperishable. ⁵¹Listen, I tell you a mystery: We will not all sleep, but we will all be changed— ⁵²in a flash, in the twinkling of an eye, at the last trumpet. For the trumpet will sound, the dead will be raised

---

ᵃ 27 Psalm 8:6   ᵇ 32 Isaiah 22:13   ᶜ 33 From the Greek poet Menander   ᵈ 45 Gen. 2:7   ᵉ 49 Some early manuscripts so let us imperishable, and we will be changed. ⁵³For the perishable must clothe itself with the imperishable, and the mortal with immortality. ⁵⁴When the perishable has been clothed with the imperishable, and the mortal with immortality, then the saying that is written will come true: "Death has been swallowed up in victory."ᵃ

⁵⁵ "Where, O death, is your victory?
    Where, O death, is your sting?"ᵇ

⁵⁶The sting of death is sin, and the power of sin is the law. ⁵⁷But thanks be to God! He gives us the victory through our Lord Jesus Christ.

⁵⁸Therefore, my dear brothers and sisters, stand firm. Let nothing move you. Always give yourselves fully to the work of the Lord, because you know that your labor in the Lord is not in vain.

The Collection for the Lord's People

16 Now about the collection for the Lord's people: Do what I told the Galatian churches to do. ²On the first day of every week, each one of you should set aside a sum of money in keeping with your income, saving it up, so that when I come no collections will have to be made. ³Then, when I arrive, I will give letters of introduction to the men you approve and send them with your gift to Jerusalem. ⁴If it seems advisable for me to go also, they will accompany me.

Personal Requests

⁵After I go through Macedonia, I will come to you—for I will be going through Macedonia. ⁶Perhaps I will stay with you for a while, or even spend the winter, so that you can help me on my journey, wherever I go. ⁷For I do not want to see you now and make only a passing visit; I hope to spend some time with you, if the Lord permits. ⁸But I will stay on at Ephesus until Pentecost, ⁹because a great door for effective work has opened to me, and there are many who oppose me.

¹⁰When Timothy comes, see to it that he

ᵃ 54 Isaiah 25:8   ᵇ 55 Hosea 13:14

THE SCENE

MACEDONIA

(1 CORINTHIANS 16:5)

See Acts 16:9.

THE SCENE

EPHESUS

(1 CORINTHIANS 16:8)

Read about this city in Ephesians 1:1.

THE SCENE

ACHAIA

(1 CORINTHIANS 16:15)

Check out Acts 18:27 to learn more about it.

PROVINCE OF ASIA

(1 CORINTHIANS 16:19)

In New Testament times, it was a Roman province, and the person in charge there was called the "proconsul." The province was very large, and it was famous for being rich. It included all of the region west of Asia Minor along with Mysia, Lydda and many of the islands in the Aegean Sea. This province was one of the first to worship the emperor of Rome. When the Christians refused to worship him, they were persecuted and driven out. How wrong!

THE WITNESSES

✓ **STEPHANAS** **(1 CORINTHIANS 16:15)**
His name means "crowned" in Greek. He was an important person for the Christians in the church in Corinth. Paul baptized Stephanas.

---

¹²Now about our brother Apollos: I strongly urged him to go to you with the brothers. He was quite unwilling to go now, but he will go when he has the opportunity.

¹³Be on your guard; stand firm in the faith; be courageous; be strong. ¹⁴Do everything in love.

¹⁵You know that the household of Stephanas were the first converts in Achaia, and they have devoted themselves to the service of the Lord's people. I urge you, brothers and sisters, ¹⁶to submit to such people and to everyone who joins in the work and labors at it. ¹⁷I was glad when Stephanas, Fortunatus and Achaicus arrived, because they have

has nothing to fear while he is with you, for he is carrying on the work of the Lord, just as I am. ¹¹No one, then, should treat him with contempt. Send him on his way in peace so that he may return to me. I am expecting him along with the brothers.

supplied what was lacking from you. ¹⁸For they refreshed my spirit and yours also. Such men deserve recognition.

Final Greetings

¹⁹The churches in the province of Asia send you greetings. Aquila and Priscilla*ᵃ* greet you warmly in the Lord, and so does the church that meets at their house. ²⁰All the brothers and sisters here send you greetings. Greet one another with a holy kiss.

²¹I, Paul, write this greeting in my own hand.

²²If anyone does not love the Lord, let that person be cursed! Come, Lord*ᵇ*!

²³The grace of the Lord Jesus be with you.

²⁴My love to all of you in Christ Jesus. Amen.*ᶜ*

ᵃ 19 Greek *Prisca*, a variant of *Priscilla*　　*ᵇ 22* The Greek for *Come, Lord* reproduces an Aramaic expression (*Marana tha*) used by early Christians.　　*ᶜ 24* Some manuscripts do not have *Amen*.

CASE CLOSED!

In this letter, Paul teaches many things about how we should act as Christians. It's not just for the people of his time—it's for everybody, which means it's for us too. For example, we learned that God loves all of us equally. It doesn't matter if we're rich or poor, or if we're girls or boys. And we learned that Jesus rose from the dead and that we will too. We also learned to appreciate our pastors and our Bible teachers, because they explain the Bible and give us good advice, and they teach us about God.

2 CORINTHIANS

THE EVIDENCE:

WHO WROTE IT?
Paul wrote Romans and 1 Corinthians, and he wrote this letter too.

HOW LONG AGO?
People who know a lot about the Bible say that Paul wrote this letter shortly after he wrote 1 Corinthians. They think it was probably between 54 and 57 years after Christ. It was while he was in the region of Macedonia — perhaps he was in the city of Philippi.

WHAT'S IT ABOUT?
This is a very personal letter. Paul expresses all his love for the brethren in the church. However, he also defends himself from the attacks of other Christians in Corinth, who have made him very sad. In this letter, he talks about collecting money for the church in Jerusalem. He teaches the Corinthians to be generous with people who need help. The letter explains that some false teachers had inserted themselves in the church in Corinth. They were teaching things that went against what Paul had told them, so he sets them straight.

THE BEST PART
God "comforts us in all our troubles, so that we can comfort those in any trouble with the comfort we ourselves receive from God" (1:4). This verse is so very nice that we memorized it. It means that every time we have a problem, we should pray and ask for God to help us. Then we can help another person who is facing the same problem or something similar.

---

1 Paul, an apostle of Christ Jesus by the will of God, and Timothy our brother,

To the church of God in Corinth, together with all his holy people throughout Achaia:

²Grace and peace to you from God our Father and the Lord Jesus Christ.

Praise to the God of All Comfort

³Praise be to the God and Father of our Lord Jesus Christ, the Father of compassion and the God of all comfort, ⁴who comforts us in all our troubles, so that we can comfort those in any trouble with the comfort we ourselves receive from God. ⁵For just as we share abundantly in the sufferings of Christ, so also our comfort abounds through Christ. ⁶If we are distressed, it is for your comfort and salvation; if we are comforted, it is for your comfort, which produces in you patient

endurance of the same sufferings we suffer. ⁷And our hope for you is firm, because we know that just as you share in our sufferings, so also you share in our comfort.

⁸We do not want you to be uninformed, brothers and sisters,ᵃ about the troubles we experienced in the province of Asia. We were under great pressure, far beyond our ability to endure, so that we despaired of life itself. ⁹Indeed, we felt we had received the sentence of death. But this happened that we might not rely on ourselves but on God, who raises the dead. ¹⁰He has delivered us from such a deadly peril, and he will deliver us again. On him we have set our hope that he will continue to deliver us, ¹¹as you help us by your prayers. Then many will give thanks on our behalf for the gracious favor granted us in answer to the prayers of many.

Paul's Change of Plans

¹²Now this is our boast: Our conscience testifies that we have conducted ourselves in the world, and especially in our relations with you, with integrityᵇ and godly sincerity. We have done so, relying not on worldly wisdom but on God's grace. ¹³For we do not write you anything you cannot read or understand. And I hope that, ¹⁴as you have understood us in part, you will come to understand fully that you can boast of us just as we will boast of you in the day of the Lord Jesus.

¹⁵Because I was confident of this, I wanted to visit you first so that you might benefit twice. ¹⁶I wanted to visit you on my way to Macedonia and to come back to you from Macedonia, and then to have you send me on my way to Judea. ¹⁷Was I fickle when I intended to do this? Or do I make my plans in a worldly manner so that in the same breath I say both "Yes, yes" and "No, no"?

¹⁸But as surely as God is faithful, our message to you is not "Yes" and "No." ¹⁹For the Son of God, Jesus Christ, who was preached among you by us—by me and Silasᶜ and Timothy—was not "Yes" and "No," but in him it has always been "Yes." ²⁰For no matter how many promises God has made, they are "Yes" in Christ. And so through him the "Amen" is spoken

THE WITNESSES

✓ SILAS (2 CORINTHIANS 1:19)
He was also called Silvanus. He was a very important man and a prophet from the church in Jerusalem. He also accompanied Paul on his second trip when Paul went to preach about Jesus to the people in Syria, Asia Minor and Macedonia, where Silas stayed with Timothy. Later, he went around with Paul again. Silas was Jewish, and he was a Roman citizen.

✓ TIMOTHY (2 CORINTHIANS 1:19)
If you want to know who he was, check out 1 Timothy 1:2.

by us to the glory of God. ²¹Now it is God who makes both us and you stand firm in Christ. He anointed us, ²²set his seal of ownership on us, and put his Spirit in our

---

ᵃ 8 The Greek word for brothers and sisters (adelphoi) refers here to believers, both men and women, as part of God's family; also in 8:1; 13:11. ᵇ 12 Many manuscripts holiness ᶜ 19 Greek Silvanus, a variant of Silas

THE SCENE

JUDEA

(2 **CORINTHIANS** 1:16)

I n Old Testament times, Judea was more or less the region that belonged to Judah's sons, to his tribe. In Jesus' time, Judea was one of the main parts of Palestine, along with Samaria and Galilee. The area of Judea was pretty much mountainous, and the people raised sheep and goats. They also grew olives, figs and grapes.

hearts as a deposit, guaranteeing what is to come.

²³I call God as my witness—and I stake my life on it—that it was in order to spare you that I did not return to Corinth. ²⁴Not that we lord it over your faith, but we work with you for your joy, because it is by faith you stand firm. **2** ¹So I made up my mind that I would not make another painful visit to you. ²For if I grieve you, who is left to make me glad but you whom I have grieved? ³I wrote as I did, so that when I came I would not be distressed by those who should have made me rejoice. I had confidence in all of you, that you would all share my joy. ⁴For I wrote you out of great distress and anguish of heart and with many tears, not to grieve you but to let you know the depth of my love for you.

Forgiveness for the Offender

⁵If anyone has caused grief, he has not so much grieved me as he has grieved all of you to some extent—not to put it too severely. ⁶The punishment inflicted on him by the majority is sufficient. ⁷Now instead, you ought to forgive and comfort him, so that he will not be overwhelmed by excessive sorrow. ⁸I urge you, therefore, to reaffirm your love for him. ⁹Another reason I wrote you was to see if you would stand the test and be obedient in everything. ¹⁰Anyone you forgive, I also forgive. And what I have forgiven—if there was anything to forgive—I have forgiven in the sight of Christ for your sake, ¹¹in order that Satan might not outwit us. For we are not unaware of his schemes.

Ministers of the New Covenant

¹²Now when I went to Troas to preach the gospel of Christ and found that the Lord had opened a door for me, ¹³I still had no peace of mind, because I did not find my brother Titus there. So I said goodbye to them and went on to Macedonia.

¹⁴But thanks be to God, who always leads us as captives in Christ's triumphal procession and uses us to spread the aroma of the knowledge of him everywhere. ¹⁵For we are to God the pleasing aroma of Christ among those who are being saved and those who are perishing. ¹⁶To the one we are an aroma that brings death; to the other, an aroma that brings life. And who is equal to such a task? ¹⁷Unlike so many, we do not peddle the word of God for profit. On the contrary, in Christ we speak before God with sincerity, as those sent from God.

3 Are we beginning to commend ourselves again? Or do we need, like some people, letters of recommendation to you or from you? ²You yourselves are our letter, written on our hearts, known and read by everyone. ³You show that you are a letter from Christ, the result of our ministry, written not with ink but with the

Spirit of the living God, not on tablets of stone but on tablets of human hearts.

⁴Such confidence we have through Christ before God. ⁵Not that we are competent in ourselves to claim anything for ourselves, but our competence comes from God. ⁶He has made us competent as ministers of a new covenant—not of the letter but of the Spirit; for the letter kills, but the Spirit gives life.

The Greater Glory of the New Covenant

⁷Now if the ministry that brought death, which was engraved in letters on stone, came with glory, so that the Israelites could not look steadily at the face of

Why does Paul say that for people who don't believe we are "an aroma that brings death"?

(2 CORINTHIANS 2:16)

It's just a manner of speaking! He means that for people who believe in Jesus, it's like spraying a lovely perfume among the people who also believe. But for those who don't believe in Jesus, it's like they're smelling something bad when Christians are around. He accuses the people who smell death of choosing things that God doesn't like.

Not of the letter but of the Spirit

(2 CORINTHIANS 3:6)

Before Jesus' time, God had given the law so people would know what was right and what was wrong and what they had to do. But people were really breaking that law. The law wasn't bad, but it was just quite difficult to obey it. Then when Jesus came, he fulfilled all of that law. He always did what was pleasing to God, and he did it for us. Besides, he sent the Holy Spirit to help us obey and live in a way that is pleasing to God. So the "letter" means the "whole" law that was hard to live up to, and the "Spirit" is the new life Jesus gives.

Moses because of its glory, transitory though it was, ⁸will not the ministry of the Spirit be even more glorious? ⁹If the ministry that brought condemnation was glorious, how much more glorious is the ministry that brings righteousness! ¹⁰For what was glorious has no glory now in comparison with the surpassing glory. ¹¹And if what was transitory came with glory, how much greater is the glory of that which lasts!

¹²Therefore, since we have such a hope, we are very bold. ¹³We are not like Moses, who would put a veil over his face

to prevent the Israelites from seeing the end of what was passing away. ¹⁴But their minds were made dull, for to this day the same veil remains when the old covenant is read. It has not been removed, because only in Christ is it taken away. ¹⁵Even to this day when Moses is read, a veil covers their hearts. ¹⁶But whenever anyone turns to the Lord, the veil is taken away. ¹⁷Now the Lord is the Spirit, and where the Spirit of the Lord is, there is freedom. ¹⁸And we all, who with unveiled faces contemplate*ᵃ* the Lord's glory, are being transformed into his image with ever-increasing glory, which comes from the Lord, who is the Spirit.

Present Weakness and Resurrection Life

4 Therefore, since through God's mercy we have this ministry, we do not lose heart. ²Rather, we have renounced secret and shameful ways; we do not use deception, nor do we distort the word of God. On the contrary, by setting forth the truth plainly we commend ourselves to everyone's conscience in the sight of God. ³And even if our gospel is veiled, it is veiled to those who are perishing. ⁴The god of this age has blinded the minds of unbelievers, so that they cannot see the light of the gospel that displays the glory of Christ, who is the image of God. ⁵For what we preach is not ourselves, but Jesus Christ as Lord, and ourselves as your servants for Jesus' sake. ⁶For God, who said, "Let light shine out of darkness,"*ᵇ* made his light shine in our hearts to give us the light of the knowledge of God's glory displayed in the face of Christ.

⁷But we have this treasure in jars of clay to show that this all-surpassing power is from God and not from us. ⁸We are hard pressed on every side, but not crushed; perplexed, but not in despair; ⁹persecuted, but not abandoned; struck down, but not destroyed. ¹⁰We always carry around in our body the death of Jesus, so that the life of Jesus may also be revealed in our body. ¹¹For we who are alive are always being given over to death for Jesus' sake, so that his life may also be revealed

BREAKTHROUGH!

Why were they always in danger of dying for Jesus' sake?

(2 CORINTHIANS 4:11)

Many people were angry with the Christians who were talking about Jesus as Savior. They bullied them, and sometimes they put them in jail. But Paul and his friends obeyed God, and they all kept telling everyone about Jesus.

in our mortal body. ¹²So then, death is at work in us, but life is at work in you.

¹³It is written: "I believed; therefore I have spoken."*ᶜ* Since we have that same spirit of*ᵈ* faith, we also believe and therefore speak, ¹⁴because we know that the one who raised the Lord Jesus from the dead will also raise us with Jesus and present us with you to himself. ¹⁵All this is for your benefit, so that the grace that is reaching more and more people may cause thanksgiving to overflow to the glory of God.

¹⁶Therefore we do not lose heart. Though outwardly we are wasting away, yet inwardly we are being renewed day by day. ¹⁷For our light and momentary troubles are achieving for us an eternal glory

---

ᵃ 18 Or *reflect*   *ᵇ* 6 Gen. 1:3   *ᶜ* 13 Psalm 116:10
(see Septuagint)   *ᵈ* 13 Or *Spirit-given*

that far outweighs them all. [18]So we fix our eyes not on what is seen, but on what is unseen, since what is seen is temporary, but what is unseen is eternal.

Awaiting the New Body

5 For we know that if the earthly tent we live in is destroyed, we have a building from God, an eternal house in heaven, not built by human hands. [2]Meanwhile we groan, longing to be clothed instead with our heavenly dwelling, [3]because when we are clothed, we will not be found naked. [4]For while we are in this tent, we groan and are burdened, because we do not wish to be unclothed but to be clothed instead with our heavenly dwelling, so that what is mortal may be swallowed up by life. [5]Now the one who has fashioned us for this very purpose is God, who has given us the Spirit as a deposit, guaranteeing what is to come.

[6]Therefore we are always confident and know that as long as we are at home in the body we are away from the Lord. [7]For we live by faith, not by sight. [8]We are confident, I say, and would prefer to be away from the body and at home with the Lord. [9]So we make it our goal to please him, whether we are at home in the body or away from it. [10]For we must all appear before the judgment seat of Christ, so that each of us may receive what is due us for the things done while in the body, whether good or bad.

The Ministry of Reconciliation

[11]Since, then, we know what it is to fear the Lord, we try to persuade others. What we are is plain to God, and I hope it is also plain to your conscience. [12]We are not trying to commend ourselves to you again, but are giving you an opportunity to take pride in us, so that you can answer those who take pride in what is seen rather than in what is in the heart. [13]If we are "out of our mind," as some say, it is for God; if we are in our right mind, it is for you. [14]For Christ's love compels us, because we are convinced that one died for all, and therefore all died. [15]And he died for all, that those who live should

CHECK THE FACTS

According to this letter, what do we Christians live by?

A) We live by grace, not by works.

B) We live by faith, not by sight.

C) We live by the word of God.

CORRECT ANSWER: B

no longer live for themselves but for him who died for them and was raised again.

[16]So from now on we regard no one from a worldly point of view. Though we once regarded Christ in this way, we do so no longer. [17]Therefore, if anyone is in Christ, the new creation has come:[a] The old has gone, the new is here! [18]All this is from God, who reconciled us to himself through Christ and gave us the ministry of reconciliation: [19]that God was reconciling the world to himself in Christ, not counting people's sins against them. And he has committed to us the message of reconciliation. [20]We are therefore Christ's ambassadors, as though God were making his appeal through us. We implore you on Christ's behalf: Be reconciled to God. [21]God made him who had no sin to be sin[b] for us, so that in him we might become the righteousness of God.

---

[a] 17 Or *Christ, that person is a new creation.*   [b] 21 Or *be a sin offering*

6 As God's co-workers we urge you not to receive God's grace in vain. [2]For he says,

"In the time of my favor I heard you,
    and in the day of salvation I helped you."[a]

I tell you, now is the time of God's favor, now is the day of salvation.

Paul's Hardships

[3]We put no stumbling block in anyone's path, so that our ministry will not be discredited. [4]Rather, as servants of God we commend ourselves in every way: in great endurance; in troubles, hardships and distresses; [5]in beatings, imprisonments and riots; in hard work, sleepless nights and hunger; [6]in purity, understanding, patience and kindness; in the Holy Spirit and in sincere love; [7]in truthful speech and in the power of God; with weapons of righteousness in the right hand and in the left; [8]through glory and dishonor, bad report and good report; genuine, yet regarded as impostors; [9]known, yet regarded as unknown; dying, and yet we live on; beaten, and yet not killed; [10]sorrowful, yet always rejoicing; poor, yet making many rich; having nothing, and yet possessing everything.

[11]We have spoken freely to you, Corinthians, and opened wide our hearts to you. [12]We are not withholding our affection from you, but you are withholding yours from us. [13]As a fair exchange—I speak as to my children—open wide your hearts also.

Warning Against Idolatry

[14]Do not be yoked together with unbelievers. For what do righteousness and wickedness have in common? Or what fellowship can light have with darkness? [15]What harmony is there between Christ and Belial[b]? Or what does a believer have in common with an unbeliever? [16]What agreement is there between the temple of God and idols? For we are the temple of the living God. As God has said:

"I will live with them
    and walk among them,

and I will be their God,
    and they will be my people."[c]

[17]Therefore,

"Come out from them
    and be separate,
            says the Lord.
Touch no unclean thing,
    and I will receive you."[d]

[18]And,

"I will be a Father to you,
    and you will be my sons and daughters,
            says the Lord Almighty."[e]

7 Therefore, since we have these promises, dear friends, let us purify ourselves from everything that contaminates body and spirit, perfecting holiness out of reverence for God.

Paul's Joy Over the Church's Repentance

[2]Make room for us in your hearts. We have wronged no one, we have corrupted no one, we have exploited no one. [3]I do not say this to condemn you; I have said before that you have such a place in our hearts that we would live or die with you. [4]I have spoken to you with great frankness; I take great pride in you. I am greatly encouraged; in all our troubles my joy knows no bounds.

[5]For when we came into Macedonia, we had no rest, but we were harassed at every turn—conflicts on the outside, fears within. [6]But God, who comforts the downcast, comforted us by the coming of Titus, [7]and not only by his coming but also by the comfort you had given him. He told us about your longing for me, your deep sorrow, your ardent concern for me, so that my joy was greater than ever.

[8]Even if I caused you sorrow by my letter, I do not regret it. Though I did regret it—I see that my letter hurt you, but only for a little while— [9]yet now I am happy, not because you were made sorry, but because your sorrow led you to repentance.

---

[a] 2 Isaiah 49:8   [b] 15 Greek Beliar, a variant of Belial
[c] 16 Lev. 26:12; Jer. 32:38; Ezek. 37:27
[d] 17 Isaiah 52:11; Ezek. 20:34,41
[e] 18 2 Samuel 7:14; 7:8

THE
WITNESSES

✓ **TITUS** (2 CORINTHIANS 7:6)
Read about him in Titus 1:4.

For you became sorrowful as God intended and so were not harmed in any way by us. ¹⁰Godly sorrow brings repentance that leads to salvation and leaves no regret, but worldly sorrow brings death. ¹¹See what this godly sorrow has produced in you: what earnestness, what eagerness to clear yourselves, what indignation, what alarm, what longing, what concern, what readiness to see justice done. At every point you have proved yourselves to be innocent in this matter. ¹²So even though I wrote to you, it was neither on account of the one who did the wrong nor on account of the injured party, but rather that before God you could see for yourselves how devoted to us you are. ¹³By all this we are encouraged.

In addition to our own encouragement,

we were especially delighted to see how happy Titus was, because his spirit has been refreshed by all of you. ¹⁴I had boasted to him about you, and you have not embarrassed me. But just as everything we said to you was true, so our boasting about you to Titus has proved to be true as well. ¹⁵And his affection for you is all the greater when he remembers that you were all obedient, receiving him with fear and trembling. ¹⁶I am glad I can have complete confidence in you.

The Collection for the Lord's People

8 And now, brothers and sisters, we want you to know about the grace that God has given the Macedonian churches. ²In the midst of a very severe trial, their overflowing joy and their extreme poverty welled up in rich generosity. ³For I testify that they gave as much as they were able, and even beyond their ability. Entirely on their own, ⁴they urgently pleaded with us for the privilege of sharing in this service to the Lord's people. ⁵And they exceeded our expectations: They gave themselves first of all to the Lord, and then by the will of God also to us. ⁶So we urged Titus, just as he had earlier made a beginning, to bring also to completion this act of grace on your part. ⁷But since you excel in everything—in faith, in speech, in knowledge, in complete earnestness and in the love we have kindled in you[a]—see that you also excel in this grace of giving.

⁸I am not commanding you, but I want to test the sincerity of your love by comparing it with the earnestness of others. ⁹For you know the grace of our Lord Jesus Christ, that though he was rich, yet for your sake he became poor, so that you through his poverty might become rich.

¹⁰And here is my judgment about what is best for you in this matter. Last year you were the first not only to give but also to have the desire to do so. ¹¹Now finish the work, so that your eager willingness to do it may be matched by your completion of it, according to your means. ¹²For if the willingness is there, the gift is acceptable

---

a 7 Some manuscripts *and in your love for us*

BREAKTHROUGH!

Was Jesus rich?

(2 CORINTHIANS 8:9)

Of course, he was rich before he came to this world and was born as a baby! But when he came to Earth, he left everything he had before. He became poor and he lived among poor people. He did all that because he loved us, and so that we could become rich. But it wasn't to make us rich with money. It was to be rich in our hearts.

according to what one has, not according to what one does not have.

¹³Our desire is not that others might be relieved while you are hard pressed, but that there might be equality. ¹⁴At the present time your plenty will supply what they need, so that in turn their plenty will supply what you need. The goal is equality, ¹⁵as it is written: "The one who gathered much did not have too much, and the one who gathered little did not have too little."[a]

Titus Sent to Receive the Collection

¹⁶Thanks be to God, who put into the heart of Titus the same concern I have for you. ¹⁷For Titus not only welcomed our appeal, but he is coming to you with much enthusiasm and on his own initiative.

¹⁸And we are sending along with him the brother who is praised by all the churches for his service to the gospel. ¹⁹What is more, he was chosen by the churches to accompany us as we carry the offering, which we administer in order to honor the Lord himself and to show our eagerness to help. ²⁰We want to avoid any criticism of the way we administer this liberal gift. ²¹For we are taking pains to do what is right, not only in the eyes of the Lord but also in the eyes of man.

²²In addition, we are sending with them our brother who has often proved to us in many ways that he is zealous, and now even more so because of his great confidence in you. ²³As for Titus, he is my partner and co-worker among you; as for our brothers, they are representatives of the churches and an honor to Christ. ²⁴Therefore show these men the proof of your love and the reason for our pride in you, so that the churches can see it.

9 There is no need for me to write to you about this service to the Lord's people. ²For I know your eagerness to help, and I have been boasting about it to the Macedonians, telling them that since last year you in Achaia were ready to give; and your enthusiasm has stirred most of them to action. ³But I am sending the brothers in order that our boasting about you in this matter should not prove hollow, but that you may be ready, as I said you would be. ⁴For if any Macedonians come with me and find you unprepared, we—not to say anything about you—would be ashamed of having been so confident. ⁵So I thought it necessary to urge the brothers to visit you in advance and finish the arrangements for the generous gift you had promised. Then it will be ready as a generous gift, not as one grudgingly given.

Generosity Encouraged

⁶Remember this: Whoever sows sparingly will also reap sparingly, and whoever sows generously will also reap generously. ⁷Each of you should give what you have decided in your heart to give, not reluctantly or under compulsion, for God

---

a 15 Exodus 16:18

loves a cheerful giver. [8]And God is able to bless you abundantly, so that in all things at all times, having all that you need, you will abound in every good work. [9]As it is written:

"They have freely scattered their gifts
　to the poor;
their righteousness endures
　forever."[a]

[10]Now he who supplies seed to the sower and bread for food will also supply and increase your store of seed and will enlarge the harvest of your righteousness. [11]You will be enriched in every way so that you can be generous on every occasion, and through us your generosity will result in thanksgiving to God.

[12]This service that you perform is not only supplying the needs of the Lord's people but is also overflowing in many expressions of thanks to God. [13]Because of the service by which you have proved yourselves, others will praise God for the obedience that accompanies your confession of the gospel of Christ, and for your generosity in sharing with them and with everyone else. [14]And in their prayers for you their hearts will go out to you, because of the surpassing grace God has given you. [15]Thanks be to God for his indescribable gift!

Paul's Defense of His Ministry

10 By the humility and gentleness of Christ, I appeal to you—I, Paul, who am "timid" when face to face with you, but "bold" toward you when away! [2]I beg you that when I come I may not have to be as bold as I expect to be toward some people who think that we live by the standards of this world. [3]For though we live in the world, we do not wage war as the world does. [4]The weapons we fight with are not the weapons of the world. On the contrary, they have divine power to demolish strongholds. [5]We demolish arguments and every pretension that sets itself up against the knowledge of God, and we take captive every thought to make it obedient to Christ. [6]And we will be ready to punish every act of disobedience, once your obedience is complete.

[7]You are judging by appearances.[b] If anyone is confident that they belong to Christ, they should consider again that we belong to Christ just as much as they do. [8]So even if I boast somewhat freely about the authority the Lord gave us for building you up rather than tearing you down, I will not be ashamed of it. [9]I do not want to seem to be trying to frighten you with my letters. [10]For some say, "His letters are weighty and forceful, but in person he is unimpressive and his speaking amounts to nothing." [11]Such people should realize that what we are in our letters when we are absent, we will be in our actions when we are present.

[12]We do not dare to classify or compare ourselves with some who commend themselves. When they measure themselves by themselves and compare themselves with themselves, they are not wise. [13]We, however, will not boast beyond proper limits, but will confine our boasting to the sphere of service God himself has assigned to us, a sphere that also includes you. [14]We are not going too far in our boasting, as would be the case if we had not come to you, for we did get as far as you with the gospel of Christ. [15]Neither do we go beyond our limits by boasting of work done by others. Our hope is that, as your faith continues to grow, our sphere of activity among you will greatly expand, [16]so that we can preach the gospel in the regions beyond you. For we do not want to boast about work already done in someone else's territory. [17]But, "Let the one who boasts boast in the Lord."[c] [18]For it is not the one who commends himself who is approved, but the one whom the Lord commends.

Paul and the False Apostles

11 I hope you will put up with me in a little foolishness. Yes, please put up with me! [2]I am jealous for you with a godly jealousy. I promised you to one husband, to Christ, so that I might present you as a pure virgin to him. [3]But I am afraid that just as Eve was deceived by the serpent's cunning, your minds may

---

[a] 9 Psalm 112:9　　[b] 7 Or Look at the obvious facts
[c] 17 Jer. 9:24

somehow be led astray from your sincere and pure devotion to Christ. [4]For if someone comes to you and preaches a Jesus other than the Jesus we preached, or if you receive a different spirit from the Spirit you received, or a different gospel from the one you accepted, you put up with it easily enough.

[5]I do not think I am in the least inferior to those "super-apostles."[a] [6]I may indeed be untrained as a speaker, but I do have knowledge. We have made this perfectly clear to you in every way. [7]Was it a sin for me to lower myself in order to elevate you by preaching the gospel of God to you free of charge? [8]I robbed other churches by receiving support from them so as to serve you. [9]And when I was with you and needed something, I was not a burden to anyone, for the brothers who came from Macedonia supplied what I needed. I have kept myself from being a burden to you in any way, and will continue to do so. [10]As surely as the truth of Christ is in me, nobody in the regions of Achaia will stop this boasting of mine. [11]Why? Because I do not love you? God knows I do!

[12]And I will keep on doing what I am doing in order to cut the ground from under those who want an opportunity to be considered equal with us in the things they boast about. [13]For such people are false apostles, deceitful workers, masquerading as apostles of Christ. [14]And no wonder, for Satan himself masquerades as an angel of light. [15]It is not surprising, then, if his servants also masquerade as servants of righteousness. Their end will be what their actions deserve.

Paul Boasts About His Sufferings

[16]I repeat: Let no one take me for a fool. But if you do, then tolerate me just as you would a fool, so that I may do a little boasting. [17]In this self-confident boasting I am not talking as the Lord would, but as a fool. [18]Since many are boasting in the way the world does, I too will boast. [19]You gladly put up with fools since you are so wise! [20]In fact, you even put up with anyone who enslaves you or exploits you or takes advantage of you or puts

on airs or slaps you in the face. [21]To my shame I admit that we were too weak for that!

Whatever anyone else dares to boast about—I am speaking as a fool—I also dare to boast about. [22]Are they Hebrews? So am I. Are they Israelites? So am I. Are they Abraham's descendants? So am I. [23]Are they servants of Christ? (I am out of my mind to talk like this.) I am more. I have worked much harder, been in prison more frequently, been flogged more severely, and been exposed to death again and again. [24]Five times I received from the Jews the forty lashes minus one. [25]Three times I was beaten with rods, once I was pelted with stones, three times I was shipwrecked, I spent a night and a day in the open sea, [26]I have been constantly on the move. I have been in danger from rivers, in danger from bandits, in danger from my fellow Jews, in danger from Gentiles; in danger in the city, in danger in the country, in danger at sea; and in danger from false believers. [27]I have labored and toiled and have often gone without sleep; I have known hunger and thirst and have often gone without food; I have been cold and naked. [28]Besides everything else, I face daily the pressure of my concern for all the churches. [29]Who is weak, and I do not feel weak? Who is led into sin, and I do not inwardly burn?

[30]If I must boast, I will boast of the things that show my weakness. [31]The God and Father of the Lord Jesus, who is to be praised forever, knows that I am not lying. [32]In Damascus the governor under King Aretas had the city of the Damascenes guarded in order to arrest me. [33]But I was lowered in a basket from a window in the wall and slipped through his hands.

Paul's Vision and His Thorn

12 I must go on boasting. Although there is nothing to be gained, I will go on to visions and revelations from the Lord. [2]I know a man in Christ who fourteen years ago was caught up to the third heaven. Whether it was in the body or out of the body I do not know—God knows.

---

[a] 5 Or *to the most eminent apostles*

given a thorn in my flesh, a messenger of Satan, to torment me. [8]Three times I pleaded with the Lord to take it away from me. [9]But he said to me, "My grace is sufficient for you, for my power is made perfect in weakness." Therefore I will boast all the more gladly about my weaknesses, so that Christ's power may rest on me. [10]That is why, for Christ's sake, I delight in weaknesses, in insults, in hardships, in persecutions, in difficulties. For when I am weak, then I am strong.

Paul's Concern for the Corinthians

[11]I have made a fool of myself, but you drove me to it. I ought to have been commended by you, for I am not in the least inferior to the "super-apostles,"[a] even though I am nothing. [12]I persevered in demonstrating among you the marks of a true apostle, including signs, wonders and miracles. [13]How were you inferior to the other churches, except that I was

---

[a] 11 Or *the most eminent apostles*

THE
WITNESSES

✓ **KING ARETAS** (2 CORINTHIANS 11:32)
He was the king of a region called Nabataea, which would be more or less Arabia. In the year 106 after Christ, the emperor Trajan converted the Nabataean kingdom into the Roman province of Arabia.

BREAKTHROUGH!

Paradise

(2 CORINTHIANS 12:4)
This is the place where God lives, heaven. It's also where all of us who have believed in Jesus are going to live with him. We don't know where it is, but we're sure it exists!

[3]And I know that this man—whether in the body or apart from the body I do not know, but God knows— [4]was caught up to paradise and heard inexpressible things, things that no one is permitted to tell. [5]I will boast about a man like that, but I will not boast about myself, except about my weaknesses. [6]Even if I should choose to boast, I would not be a fool, because I would be speaking the truth. But I refrain, so no one will think more of me than is warranted by what I do or say, [7]or because of these surpassingly great revelations. Therefore, in order to keep me from becoming conceited, I was

never a burden to you? Forgive me this wrong!

¹⁴Now I am ready to visit you for the third time, and I will not be a burden to you, because what I want is not your possessions but you. After all, children should not have to save up for their parents, but parents for their children. ¹⁵So I will very gladly spend for you everything I have and expend myself as well. If I love you more, will you love me less? ¹⁶Be that as it may, I have not been a burden to you. Yet, crafty fellow that I am, I caught you by trickery! ¹⁷Did I exploit you through any of the men I sent to you? ¹⁸I urged Titus to go to you and I sent our brother with him. Titus did not exploit you, did he? Did we not walk in the same footsteps by the same Spirit?

¹⁹Have you been thinking all along that we have been defending ourselves to you? We have been speaking in the sight of God as those in Christ; and everything we do, dear friends, is for your strengthening. ²⁰For I am afraid that when I come I may not find you as I want you to be, and you may not find me as you want me to be. I fear that there may be discord, jealousy, fits of rage, selfish ambition, slander, gossip, arrogance and disorder. ²¹I am afraid that when I come again my God will humble me before you, and I will be grieved over many who have sinned earlier and have not repented of the impurity, sexual sin and debauchery in which they have indulged.

Final Warnings

13 This will be my third visit to you. "Every matter must be established by the testimony of two or three witnesses."ᵃ ²I already gave you a warning when I was with you the second time. I now repeat it while absent: On my return I will not spare those who sinned earlier or any of the others, ³since you are demanding proof that Christ is speaking through me. He is not weak in dealing with you, but is powerful among you. ⁴For to be sure, he was crucified in weakness, yet he lives by God's power. Likewise, we are weak in him, yet by God's power we will live with him in our dealing with you.

⁵Examine yourselves to see whether you are in the faith; test yourselves. Do you not realize that Christ Jesus is

---

ᵃ 1 Deut. 19:15

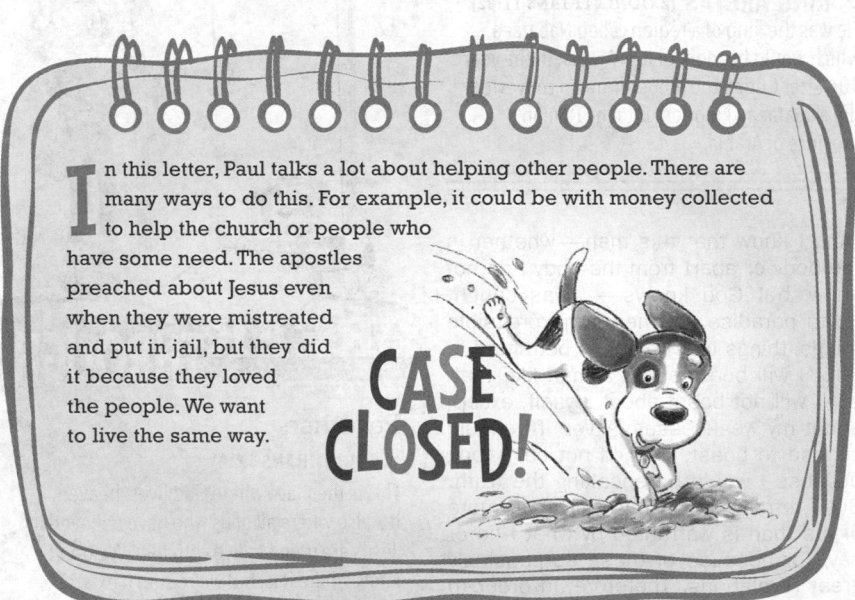

In this letter, Paul talks a lot about helping other people. There are many ways to do this. For example, it could be with money collected to help the church or people who have some need. The apostles preached about Jesus even when they were mistreated and put in jail, but they did it because they loved the people. We want to live the same way.

CASE CLOSED!

in you—unless, of course, you fail the test? ⁶And I trust that you will discover that we have not failed the test. ⁷Now we pray to God that you will not do anything wrong—not so that people will see that we have stood the test but so that you will do what is right even though we may seem to have failed. ⁸For we cannot do anything against the truth, but only for the truth. ⁹We are glad whenever we are weak but you are strong; and our prayer is that you may be fully restored. ¹⁰This is why I write these things when I am absent, that when I come I may not have to be harsh in my use of authority—the authority the

Lord gave me for building you up, not for tearing you down.

Final Greetings

¹¹Finally, brothers and sisters, rejoice! Strive for full restoration, encourage one another, be of one mind, live in peace. And the God of love and peace will be with you.

¹²Greet one another with a holy kiss. ¹³All God's people here send their greetings.

¹⁴May the grace of the Lord Jesus Christ, and the love of God, and the fellowship of the Holy Spirit be with you all.

GALATIANS

THE EVIDENCE:

WHO WROTE IT?
The apostle Paul wrote this letter too. The letter isn't addressed to just one church — it's for a group of churches in the region of Galatia (a region that belongs to Turkey now).

HOW LONG AGO?
Some experts think this letter was written around the year 54 after Christ. However, others think that maybe Paul wrote it a few years later, maybe in the year 56 after Christ. It's not certain where he was when he wrote it either. Some people think he was probably in Corinth, but others say maybe he was in Ephesus.

WHAT'S IT ABOUT?
Paul knew the members of those churches very well, because he had been in that region twice. He loved them very much, because the brethren in Galatia had been very nice to him. So, he was worried about them.

Paul wrote this letter to them because he had heard that some Jewish Christians were teaching the people to go back to their old ways of doing things. They were saying that the Old Testament ways were also for Christians who weren't Jews. As if Jesus hadn't saved everyone with his death and resurrection! How wrong! That wasn't good!

So Paul was upset with the people who were teaching these lies and with the people who wanted everybody to act like Jews. All the things they wanted the members of the churches to be doing was a real nuisance. Over and over, they were stuck with all those laws — and there were like millions of them!

That's why Paul tells them very clearly that salvation comes by trusting in Jesus.

THE BEST PART
"Because you are his sons, God sent the Spirit of his Son into our hearts, the Spirit who calls out, 'Abba, Father.' So you are no longer a slave, but God's child; and since you are his child, God has made you also an heir" (4:6 – 7).

We liked this verse, because it means that God loves us like a real dad. When we pray, we can call him Father and not be afraid to tell him everything.

1 Paul, an apostle—sent not from men nor by a man, but by Jesus Christ and God the Father, who raised him from the dead— ²and all the brothers and sisters[a] with me,

To the churches in Galatia:

³Grace and peace to you from God our Father and the Lord Jesus Christ, ⁴who gave himself for our sins to rescue us from the present evil age, according to the will of our God and Father, ⁵to whom be glory for ever and ever. Amen.

No Other Gospel

⁶I am astonished that you are so quickly deserting the one who called you to live in the grace of Christ and are turning to a different gospel— ⁷which is really no gospel at all. Evidently some people are throwing you into confusion and are trying to pervert the gospel of Christ. ⁸But even if we or an angel from heaven should preach a gospel other than the one we preached to you, let them be under God's curse! ⁹As we have already said, so now I say again: If anybody is preaching to you a gospel other than what you accepted, let them be under God's curse!

¹⁰Am I now trying to win the approval of

---

[a] 2 The Greek word for *brothers and sisters* (*adelphoi*) refers here to believers, both men and women, as part of God's family; also in verse 11; and in 3:15; 4:12, 28, 31; 5:11, 13; 6:1, 18.

BREAKTHROUGH!

Why did Jesus have to die so God would forgive our sins?

(GALATIANS 1:4)

Because we all do things that are bad, and we're disobedient. God had given the law so people would live like he wanted — knowing what was good and what was bad — but nobody could really live like the law said. That's why Jesus came, and he did it, all of it, for us. He could do exactly what God wanted and be obedient until the very end. He suffered the punishment we should have because of our naughtiness. He's like the lamb that the priests sacrificed in Old Testament times so God would forgive the sins of the people.

THE SCENE

GALATIA

(GALATIANS 1:2)

This is a region in Asia Minor, south of the central part of what is Turkey today. Paul had been there with Barnabas when they went to the cities of Iconium, Lystra and Derbe. This story is in Acts 14.

THE SCENE

ARABIA

(GALATIANS 1:17)

This is not the same territory we call Arabia now. In Paul's time, it was the region of the Nabataeans, which stretched to the southeast of Palestine and probably came close to Damascus.

THE SCENE

SYRIA

(GALATIANS 1:21)

The territory of Syria changed over the years, and there were different governors. In the year 64 before Christ, the Romans included it in their territory as a province. At that time, it extended from Egypt to the Taurus Mountains and from the Mediterranean Sea to the Euphrates River. Later on, it got smaller.

human beings, or of God? Or am I trying to please people? If I were still trying to please people, I would not be a servant of Christ.

Paul Called by God

¹¹I want you to know, brothers and sisters, that the gospel I preached is not of human origin. ¹²I did not receive it from any man, nor was I taught it; rather, I received it by revelation from Jesus Christ.

¹³For you have heard of my previous way of life in Judaism, how intensely I persecuted the church of God and tried to destroy it. ¹⁴I was advancing in Judaism beyond many of my own age among my people and was extremely zealous for the traditions of my fathers. ¹⁵But when God, who set me apart from my mother's womb and called me by his grace, was pleased ¹⁶to reveal his Son in me so that I

might preach him among the Gentiles, my immediate response was not to consult any human being. ¹⁷I did not go up to Jerusalem to see those who were apostles before I was, but I went into Arabia. Later I returned to Damascus.

¹⁸Then after three years, I went up to Jerusalem to get acquainted with Cephas[a] and stayed with him fifteen days. ¹⁹I saw none of the other apostles—only James, the Lord's brother. ²⁰I assure you before God that what I am writing you is no lie.

²¹Then I went to Syria and Cilicia. ²²I was personally unknown to the churches of Judea that are in Christ. ²³They only heard the report: "The man who formerly

---

a 18 That is, Peter

persecuted us is now preaching the faith he once tried to destroy." ²⁴And they praised God because of me.

Paul Accepted by the Apostles

2 Then after fourteen years, I went up again to Jerusalem, this time with Barnabas. I took Titus along also. ²I went in response to a revelation and, meeting privately with those esteemed as leaders, I presented to them the gospel that I preach among the Gentiles. I wanted to be sure I was not running and had not been running my race in vain. ³Yet not even Titus, who was with me, was compelled to be circumcised, even though he was a Greek. ⁴This matter arose because some false believers had infiltrated our ranks to spy on the freedom we have in Christ Jesus and to make us slaves. ⁵We did not give in to them for a moment, so that the truth of the gospel might be preserved for you.

THE SCENE

CILICIA

(GALATIANS 1:21)

This was a Roman province in the southeastern part of Asia Minor. Paul was born in its capital city, Tarsus.

BREAKTHROUGH!

Why so much mess with Jews and Gentiles?

(GALATIANS 2)

Because many Jews who had become Christians wanted everybody to continue the Jewish customs from before the time of Jesus. But then the question would be, why did Jesus die and sacrifice himself? In Jesus, we're forgiven when we repent because we haven't obeyed God. That's why if we go back to being controlled by the law, everything that Jesus did for us doesn't have any value. And that just can't be!

⁶As for those who were held in high esteem—whatever they were makes no difference to me; God does not show favoritism—they added nothing to my message. ⁷On the contrary, they recognized that I had been entrusted with the task of preaching the gospel to the uncircumcised,ᵃ just as Peter had been to the circumcised.ᵇ ⁸For God, who was at work in Peter as an apostle to the circumcised, was also at work in me as an apostle to the Gentiles. ⁹James, Cephasᶜ and John, those esteemed as pillars, gave me and Barnabas the right hand of fellowship when they recognized the grace given to

---

ᵃ 7 That is, Gentiles   ᵇ 7 That is, Jews; also in verses 8 and 9   ᶜ 9 That is, Peter; also in verses 11 and 14 me. They agreed that we should go to the Gentiles, and they to the circumcised. 10All they asked was that we should continue to remember the poor, the very thing I had been eager to do all along.

Paul Opposes Cephas

11When Cephas came to Antioch, I opposed him to his face, because he stood condemned. 12For before certain men came from James, he used to eat with the Gentiles. But when they arrived, he began to draw back and separate himself from the Gentiles because he was afraid of those who belonged to the circumci-

THE SCENE

ANTIOCH

(GALATIANS 2:11)

In ancient times, there were several cities that had this name. The one here was the capital of the Roman province of Syria. It was a very important business center, because it was located on the shores of the Orontes River. That made it easy for people to arrive from all directions to sell their products and buy other things. It was surrounded by mountains, and the weather was very nice.

sion group. 13The other Jews joined him in his hypocrisy, so that by their hypocrisy even Barnabas was led astray.

14When I saw that they were not acting in line with the truth of the gospel, I said to Cephas in front of them all, "You are a Jew, yet you live like a Gentile and not like a Jew. How is it, then, that you force Gentiles to follow Jewish customs?

15"We who are Jews by birth and not sinful Gentiles 16know that a person is not justified by the works of the law, but by faith in Jesus Christ. So we, too, have put our faith in Christ Jesus that we may be justified by faith in*a* Christ and not by the works of the law, because by the works of the law no one will be justified.

17"But if, in seeking to be justified in Christ, we Jews find ourselves also among the sinners, doesn't that mean that Christ promotes sin? Absolutely not! 18If I rebuild what I destroyed, then I really would be a lawbreaker.

19"For through the law I died to the law so that I might live for God. 20I have been crucified with Christ and I no longer live, but Christ lives in me. The life I now live in the body, I live by faith in the Son of God, who loved me and gave himself for me. 21I do not set aside the grace of God, for if righteousness could be gained through the law, Christ died for nothing!"*b*

Faith or Works of the Law

3 You foolish Galatians! Who has bewitched you? Before your very eyes Jesus Christ was clearly portrayed as crucified. 2I would like to learn just one thing from you: Did you receive the Spirit by the works of the law, or by believing what you heard? 3Are you so foolish? After beginning by means of the Spirit, are you now trying to finish by means of the flesh?*c* 4Have you experienced*d* so much in vain— if it really was in vain? 5So again I ask, does God give you his Spirit and work miracles among you by the works of the law, or by your believing what you heard? 6So

a 16 Or *but through the faithfulness of . . . justified on the basis of the faithfulness of*   *b* 21 Some interpreters end the quotation after verse 14.   *c* 3 In contexts like this, the Greek word for *flesh* (*sarx*) refers to the sinful state of human beings, often presented as a power in opposition to the Spirit.   *d* 4 Or *suffered*

CHECK THE FACTS

How is a person justified?

A) By loving their neighbors as themselves

B) By always giving their offerings and tithes to the church

C) By faith in Jesus Christ

CORRECT ANSWER: C

also Abraham "believed God, and it was credited to him as righteousness."[a]

[7]Understand, then, that those who have faith are children of Abraham. [8]Scripture foresaw that God would justify the Gentiles by faith, and announced the gospel in advance to Abraham: "All nations will be blessed through you."[b] [9]So those who rely on faith are blessed along with Abraham, the man of faith.

[10]For all who rely on the works of the law are under a curse, as it is written: "Cursed is everyone who does not continue to do everything written in the Book of the Law."[c] [11]Clearly no one who relies on the law is justified before God, because "the righteous will live by faith."[d] [12]The law is not based on faith; on the contrary, it says, "The person who does these things will live by them."[e] [13]Christ redeemed us from the curse of the law by becoming a curse for us, for it is written: "Cursed is everyone who is hung on a pole."[f] [14]He

redeemed us in order that the blessing given to Abraham might come to the Gentiles through Christ Jesus, so that by faith we might receive the promise of the Spirit.

The Law and the Promise

[15]Brothers and sisters, let me take an example from everyday life. Just as no one can set aside or add to a human covenant that has been duly established, so it is in this case. [16]The promises were spoken to Abraham and to his seed. Scripture does not say "and to seeds," meaning many people, but "and to your seed,"[g] meaning one person, who is Christ. [17]What I mean is this: The law, introduced 430 years later, does not set

[a] 6 Gen. 15:6   [b] 8 Gen. 12:3; 18:18; 22:18
[c] 10 Deut. 27:26   [d] 11 Hab. 2:4   [e] 12 Lev. 18:5
[f] 13 Deut. 21:23   [g] 16 Gen. 12:7; 13:15; 24:7

BREAK THROUGH!

What does Paul mean when he says, "I no longer live, but Christ lives in me"?

(GALATIANS 2:20)

It's just a manner of speaking, because Paul was definitely still alive. What he meant was that since he believes in Jesus, the most important thing for him is to do what pleases Jesus. It's like Paul doesn't live for himself anymore and that Jesus is living in Paul now.

aside the covenant previously established by God and thus do away with the promise. [18]For if the inheritance depends on the law, then it no longer depends on the promise; but God in his grace gave it to Abraham through a promise.

[19]Why, then, was the law given at all? It was added because of transgressions until the Seed to whom the promise referred had come. The law was given through angels and entrusted to a mediator. [20]A mediator, however, implies more than one party; but God is one.

[21]Is the law, therefore, opposed to the promises of God? Absolutely not! For if a law had been given that could impart life, then righteousness would certainly have come by the law. [22]But Scripture has locked up everything under the control of sin, so that what was promised, being given through faith in Jesus Christ, might be given to those who believe.

Children of God

[23]Before the coming of this faith,[a] we were held in custody under the law, locked up until the faith that was to come would be revealed. [24]So the law was our guardian until Christ came that we might be justified by faith. [25]Now that this faith has come, we are no longer under a guardian.

[26]So in Christ Jesus you are all children of God through faith, [27]for all of you who were baptized into Christ have clothed yourselves with Christ. [28]There is neither Jew nor Gentile, neither slave nor free, nor is there male and female, for you are all one in Christ Jesus. [29]If you belong to Christ, then you are Abraham's seed, and heirs according to the promise.

4 What I am saying is that as long as an heir is underage, he is no different from a slave, although he owns the whole estate. [2]The heir is subject to guardians and trustees until the time set by his father. [3]So also, when we were underage, we were in slavery under the elemental spiritual forces[b] of the world. [4]But when the set time had fully come, God sent his Son, born of a woman, born under the law, [5]to redeem those under the law, that we might receive adoption to sonship.[c] [6]Because you are his sons, God sent the

Spirit of his Son into our hearts, the Spirit who calls out, "Abba,[d] Father." [7]So you are no longer a slave, but God's child; and since you are his child, God has made you also an heir.

Paul's Concern for the Galatians

[8]Formerly, when you did not know God, you were slaves to those who by nature are not gods. [9]But now that you know God—or rather are known by God—how is it that you are turning back to those weak and miserable forces[e]? Do you wish to be enslaved by them all over again? [10]You are observing special days and months and seasons and years! [11]I fear for you, that somehow I have wasted my efforts on you.

[12]I plead with you, brothers and sisters, become like me, for I became like you. You did me no wrong. [13]As you know, it was because of an illness that I first preached the gospel to you, [14]and even though my illness was a trial to you, you did not treat me with contempt or scorn. Instead, you welcomed me as if I were an angel of God, as if I were Christ Jesus himself. [15]Where, then, is your blessing of me now? I can testify that, if you could have done so, you would have torn out your eyes and given them to me. [16]Have I now become your enemy by telling you the truth?

[17]Those people are zealous to win you over, but for no good. What they want is to alienate you from us, so that you may have zeal for them. [18]It is fine to be zealous, provided the purpose is good, and to be so always, not just when I am with you. [19]My dear children, for whom I am again in the pains of childbirth until Christ is formed in you, [20]how I wish I could be with you now and change my tone, because I am perplexed about you!

Hagar and Sarah

[21]Tell me, you who want to be under the law, are you not aware of what the law says? [22]For it is written that Abraham had two sons, one by the slave woman and the

---

[a] 22,23 Or through the faithfulness of Jesus . . . [23]Before faith came   [b] 3 Or under the basic principles   [c] 5 The Greek word for adoption to sonship is a legal term referring to the full legal standing of an adopted male heir in Roman culture.   [d] 6 Aramaic for Father   [e] 9 Or principles

other by the free woman. ²³His son by the slave woman was born according to the flesh, but his son by the free woman was born as the result of a divine promise. ²⁴These things are being taken figuratively: The women represent two covenants. One covenant is from Mount Sinai and bears children who are to be slaves: This is Hagar. ²⁵Now Hagar stands for Mount Sinai in Arabia and corresponds to the present city of Jerusalem, because she is in slavery with her children. ²⁶But the Jerusalem that is above is free, and she is our mother. ²⁷For it is written:

"Be glad, barren woman,
   you who never bore a child;
shout for joy and cry aloud,
   you who were never in labor;
because more are the children of the
     desolate woman
   than of her who has a husband."ᵃ

²⁸Now you, brothers and sisters, like Isaac, are children of promise. ²⁹At that time the son born according to the flesh persecuted the son born by the power of the Spirit. It is the same now. ³⁰But what does Scripture say? "Get rid of the slave woman and her son, for the slave woman's son will never share in the inheritance with the free woman's son."ᵇ ³¹Therefore, brothers and sisters, we are not children of the slave woman, but of the free woman.

Freedom in Christ

5 It is for freedom that Christ has set us free. Stand firm, then, and do not let yourselves be burdened again by a yoke of slavery.

²Mark my words! I, Paul, tell you that if you let yourselves be circumcised, Christ will be of no value to you at all. ³Again I declare to every man who lets himself be circumcised that he is obligated to obey the whole law. ⁴You who are trying to be justified by the law have been alienated from Christ; you have fallen away from grace. ⁵For through the Spirit we eagerly await by faith the righteousness for which we hope. ⁶For in Christ Jesus neither circumcision nor uncircumcision has any value. The only thing that counts is faith expressing itself through love.

⁷You were running a good race. Who cut in on you to keep you from obeying the truth? ⁸That kind of persuasion does not come from the one who calls you. ⁹"A little yeast works through the whole batch of dough." ¹⁰I am confident in the Lord that you will take no other view. The one who is throwing you into confusion, whoever that may be, will have to pay the penalty. ¹¹Brothers and sisters, if I am still preaching circumcision, why am I still being persecuted? In that case the offense of the cross has been abolished. ¹²As for those agitators, I wish they would go the whole way and emasculate themselves!

Life by the Spirit

¹³You, my brothers and sisters, were called to be free. But do not use your freedom to indulge the fleshᶜ; rather, serve one another humbly in love. ¹⁴For the entire law is fulfilled in keeping this one command: "Love your neighbor as yourself."ᵈ ¹⁵If you bite and devour each other, watch out or you will be destroyed by each other.

¹⁶So I say, walk by the Spirit, and you will not gratify the desires of the flesh. ¹⁷For the flesh desires what is contrary to the Spirit, and the Spirit what is contrary to the flesh. They are in conflict with each other, so that you are not to do whateverᵉ you want. ¹⁸But if you are led by the Spirit, you are not under the law.

¹⁹The acts of the flesh are obvious: sexual immorality, impurity and debauchery; ²⁰idolatry and witchcraft; hatred, discord, jealousy, fits of rage, selfish ambition, dissensions, factions ²¹and envy; drunkenness, orgies, and the like. I warn you, as I did before, that those who live like this will not inherit the kingdom of God.

²²But the fruit of the Spirit is love, joy, peace, forbearance, kindness, goodness, faithfulness, ²³gentleness and self-control. Against such things there is no law. ²⁴Those who belong to Christ

---

ᵃ 27 Isaiah 54:1   ᵇ 30 Gen. 21:10   ᶜ 13 In contexts like this, the Greek word for *flesh* (*sarx*) refers to the sinful state of human beings, often presented as a power in opposition to the Spirit; also in verses 16, 17, 19 and 24; and in 6:8.   ᵈ 14 Lev. 19:18   ᵉ 17 Or *you do not do what*

Jesus have crucified the flesh with its passions and desires. ²⁵Since we live by the Spirit, let us keep in step with the Spirit. ²⁶Let us not become conceited, provoking and envying each other.

Doing Good to All

6 Brothers and sisters, if someone is caught in a sin, you who live by the Spirit should restore that person gently. But watch yourselves, or you also may be tempted. ²Carry each other's burdens, and in this way you will fulfill the law of Christ. ³If anyone thinks they are something when they are not, they deceive themselves. ⁴Each one should test their own actions. Then they can take pride in themselves alone, without comparing themselves to someone else, ⁵for each one should carry their own load. ⁶Nevertheless, the one who receives instruction in the word should share all good things with their instructor.

⁷Do not be deceived: God cannot be mocked. A man reaps what he sows. ⁸Whoever sows to please their flesh, from the flesh will reap destruction; whoever sows to please the Spirit, from the Spirit will reap eternal life. ⁹Let us not become weary in doing good, for at the proper time we will reap a harvest if we do not give up. ¹⁰Therefore, as we have oppor-tunity, let us do good to all people, espe-cially to those who belong to the family of believers.

Not Circumcision but the New Creation

¹¹See what large letters I use as I write to you with my own hand!

¹²Those who want to impress people by means of the flesh are trying to compel you to be circumcised. The only reason they do this is to avoid being persecuted for the cross of Christ. ¹³Not even those who are circumcised keep the law, yet they want you to be circumcised that they may boast about your circumcision in the flesh. ¹⁴May I never boast except in the cross of our Lord Jesus Christ, through whichᵃ the world has been crucified to me, and I to the world. ¹⁵Neither circumci-sion nor uncircumcision means anything; what counts is the new creation. ¹⁶Peace and mercy to all who follow this rule—toᵇ the Israel of God.

¹⁷From now on, let no one cause me trouble, for I bear on my body the marks of Jesus.

¹⁸The grace of our Lord Jesus Christ be with your spirit, brothers and sisters. Amen.

ᵃ 14 Or whom   ᵇ 16 Or rule and to

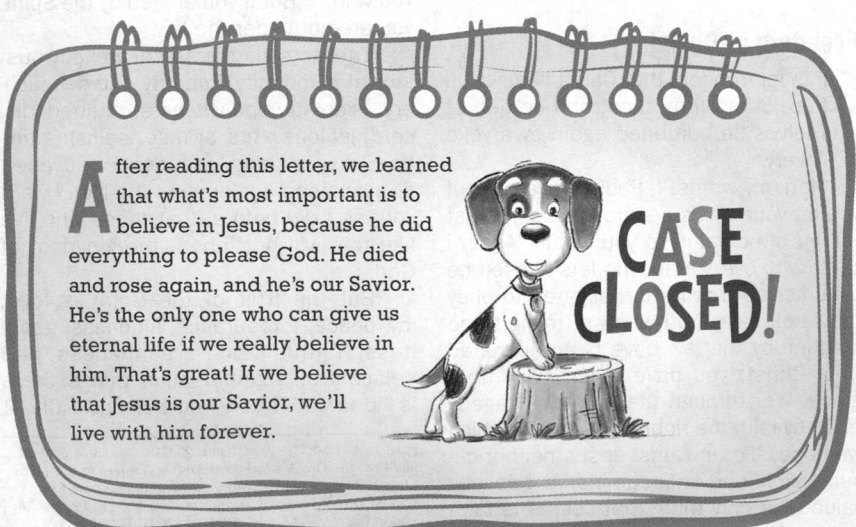

After reading this letter, we learned that what's most important is to believe in Jesus, because he did everything to please God. He died and rose again, and he's our Savior. He's the only one who can give us eternal life if we really believe in him. That's great! If we believe that Jesus is our Savior, we'll live with him forever.

CASE CLOSED!

EPHESIANS

THE EVIDENCE:

WHO WROTE IT?

We really can't know for sure who wrote this letter. Although the letter itself says that it was Paul, at that time it wasn't unusual for a follower to write about what his teacher thought and then use the name of the teacher as the author. However, many Bible experts say it really was Paul who wrote the letter. Since it's recognized as a letter from Paul, we'll call it that here.

HOW LONG AGO?

We don't know for sure when Paul wrote this letter. What is known is that he was in jail while he was writing. The problem is that Paul was in jail several times, so it's hard to know exactly which time this was. People who study the Bible think that Paul wrote this letter sometime between the years 55 and 64 after Christ.

WHAT'S IT ABOUT?

When we read this letter, we noticed that it deals with many things that have to do with the church. For example, God chose us to be like his adopted children. To God, we're all equally important, and it's not just the Jews who are special. It's also full of advice about how we should live as Christians and how we should behave with each other.

THE BEST PART

We really loved chapter 2, verses 4 – 5: "Because of his great love for us, God, who is rich in mercy, made us alive with Christ ..." How wonderful that God loves us so much!

---

1 Paul, an apostle of Christ Jesus by the will of God,

To God's holy people in Ephesus,*a* the faithful in Christ Jesus:

²Grace and peace to you from God our Father and the Lord Jesus Christ.

Praise for Spiritual Blessings in Christ

³Praise be to the God and Father of our Lord Jesus Christ, who has blessed us in the heavenly realms with every spiritual blessing in Christ. ⁴For he chose us in him before the creation of the world to be holy and blameless in his sight. In love ⁵he*b* predestined us for adoption to sonship*c* through Jesus Christ, in accordance with his pleasure and will— ⁶to the praise of his glorious grace, which he has freely given us in the One he loves. ⁷In him we have

a 1 Some early manuscripts do not have *in Ephesus.*
b 4,5 Or *sight in love.* ⁵*He*   *c 5* The Greek word for *adoption to sonship* is a legal term referring to the full legal standing of an adopted male heir in Roman culture.

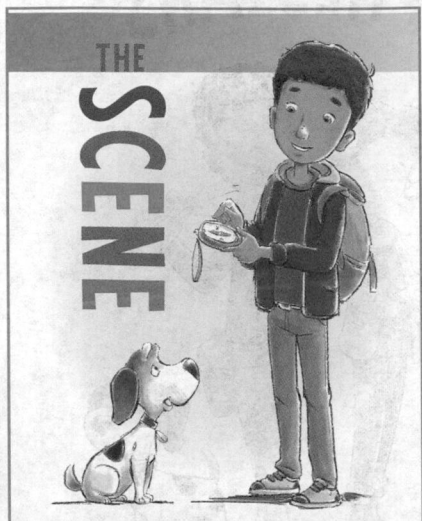

THE SCENE

EPHESUS

(EPHESIANS 1:1)

This city was the capital of the Roman province of Asia Minor (what is Turkey now). It was a very rich seaport where many ships arrived. It was also a very well-known city, and Paul started a church there. There was a very famous temple there dedicated to the goddess Artemis—also called Diana—and many people went to Ephesus to visit this temple. There were craftsmen who sold little statutes of that goddess. But Paul taught the people that those statues were just made of stone and they couldn't hear or see, because they weren't real gods.

redemption through his blood, the forgiveness of sins, in accordance with the riches of God's grace [8] that he lavished on us. With all wisdom and understanding, [9] he[a] made known to us the mystery of his will according to his good pleasure, which he purposed in Christ, [10] to be put into effect when the times reach their fulfillment— to bring unity to all things in heaven and on earth under Christ.

[11] In him we were also chosen,[b] having been predestined according to the plan of him who works out everything in conformity with the purpose of his will, [12] in order that we, who were the first to put our hope in Christ, might be for the praise of his glory. [13] And you also were included in Christ when you heard the message of truth, the gospel of your salvation. When you believed, you were marked in him with a seal, the promised Holy Spirit, [14] who is a deposit guaranteeing our inheritance until the redemption of those who are God's possession—to the praise of his glory.

Thanksgiving and Prayer

[15] For this reason, ever since I heard about your faith in the Lord Jesus and

---

a 8,9 Or us with all wisdom and understanding. 9And he
b 11 Or were made heirs

BREAKTHROUGH!

Why is Jesus called "Christ"?

(EPHESIANS 1:3)

The word *Christ* comes from Greek, and it's the translation of another Hebrew word that means "anointed" or "chosen." This refers to a person chosen by God for a very special mission. We call Jesus "Christ" because he was chosen by God for the super special mission of saving everyone.

may know the hope to which he has called you, the riches of his glorious inheritance in his holy people, ¹⁹and his incomparably great power for us who believe. That power is the same as the mighty strength ²⁰he exerted when he raised Christ from the dead and seated him at his right hand in the heavenly realms, ²¹far above all rule and authority, power and dominion, and every name that is invoked, not only in the present age but also in the one to come. ²²And God placed all things under his feet and appointed him to be head over everything for the church, ²³which is his body, the fullness of him who fills everything in every way.

---

a 17 Or *a spirit*

BREAKTHROUGH!

Redemption through his blood? Why did Jesus choose to save people by dying on the cross?

(EPHESIANS 1:7)

A very long time ago, God had sent the prophets to tell the people that they were doing bad things. If they would apologize and be sorry, then God would save them. But almost no one paid any attention to those messengers that God had sent. That's why Jesus needed to come. He is God made human in order to accept the punishment that all of us deserve. That's why he died on the cross. Now, since he has paid and received the punishment, we don't have to be punished. That's why we say that "Jesus saves us," because he took our place, and we don't have to do anything except trust in him and follow his rules. We know God loves us because he himself paid for us.

CHECK THE FACTS

When Paul prayed to God for the church in Ephesus, what did he ask for?

A) That they would be strong, so they could pray more

B) That God would give them the Spirit of wisdom and understanding, so that they may know him better

C) That God would make them rich, so they could give more offerings to the church

your love for all God's people, ¹⁶I have not stopped giving thanks for you, remembering you in my prayers. ¹⁷I keep asking that the God of our Lord Jesus Christ, the glorious Father, may give you the Spirit*a* of wisdom and revelation, so that you may know him better. ¹⁸I pray that the eyes of your heart may be enlightened in order that you

Made Alive in Christ

2 As for you, you were dead in your transgressions and sins, ²in which you used to live when you followed the ways of this world and of the ruler of the kingdom of the air, the spirit who is now at work in those who are disobedient. ³All of us also lived among them at one time, gratifying the cravings of our flesh*a* and following its desires and thoughts. Like the rest, we were by nature deserving of wrath. ⁴But because of his great love for us, God, who is rich in mercy, ⁵made us alive with Christ even when we were dead in transgressions—it is by grace you have been saved. ⁶And God raised us up with Christ and seated us with him in the heavenly realms in Christ Jesus, ⁷in order that in the coming ages he might show the incomparable riches of his grace, expressed in his kindness to us in Christ Jesus. ⁸For it is by grace you have been saved, through faith—and this is not from yourselves, it is the gift of God—⁹not by works, so that no one can boast. ¹⁰For we are God's handiwork, created in Christ Jesus to do good works, which God prepared in advance for us to do.

Jew and Gentile Reconciled Through Christ

¹¹Therefore, remember that formerly you who are Gentiles by birth and called "uncircumcised" by those who call themselves "the circumcision" (which is done in the body by human hands)—¹²remember that at that time you were separate from Christ, excluded from citizenship in Israel and foreigners to the covenants of the promise, without hope and without God in the world. ¹³But now in Christ Jesus you who once were far away have been brought near by the blood of Christ.

¹⁴For he himself is our peace, who has made the two groups one and has destroyed the barrier, the dividing wall of hostility, ¹⁵by setting aside in his flesh the law with its commands and regulations. His purpose was to create in himself one new humanity out of the two, thus making peace, ¹⁶and in one body to reconcile

BREAKTHROUGH!

If we are really, really good, can't we earn our salvation?

(EPHESIANS 2:8-9)

No, being good doesn't have anything to do with it. There isn't anybody, except Jesus, who has never done anything bad. The only one who can save us is Jesus—we cannot earn our own salvation. And we respond with thanks by doing good things and helping other people.

both of them to God through the cross, by which he put to death their hostility. ¹⁷He came and preached peace to you who were far away and peace to those who were near. ¹⁸For through him we both have access to the Father by one Spirit.

¹⁹Consequently, you are no longer foreigners and strangers, but fellow citizens with God's people and also members of his household, ²⁰built on the foundation of the apostles and prophets, with Christ Jesus himself as the chief cornerstone. ²¹In him the whole building is joined together and rises to become a holy temple in the Lord. ²²And in him you too are being built together to become a dwelling in which God lives by his Spirit.

a 3 In contexts like this, the Greek word for *flesh* (*sarx*) refers to the sinful state of human beings, often presented as a power in opposition to the Spirit.

God's Marvelous Plan for the Gentiles

3 For this reason I, Paul, the prisoner of Christ Jesus for the sake of you Gentiles—

2 Surely you have heard about the administration of God's grace that was given to me for you, 3 that is, the mystery made known to me by revelation, as I have already written briefly. 4 In reading this, then, you will be able to understand my insight into the mystery of Christ, 5 which was not made known to people in other generations as it has now been revealed by the Spirit to God's holy apostles and prophets. 6 This mystery is that through the gospel the Gentiles are heirs together with Israel, members together of one body, and sharers together in the promise in Christ Jesus.

7 I became a servant of this gospel by the gift of God's grace given me through the working of his power. 8 Although I am less than the least of all the Lord's people, this grace was given me: to preach to the Gentiles the boundless riches of Christ, 9 and to make plain to everyone the administration of this mystery, which for ages past was kept hidden in God, who created all things. 10 His intent was that now, through the church, the manifold wisdom of God should be made known to the rulers and authorities in the heavenly realms, 11 according to his eternal purpose that he accomplished in Christ Jesus our Lord. 12 In him and through faith in him we may approach God with freedom and confidence. 13 I ask you, therefore, not to be discouraged because of my sufferings for you, which are your glory.

A Prayer for the Ephesians

14 For this reason I kneel before the Father, 15 from whom every family[a] in heaven and on earth derives its name. 16 I pray that out of his glorious riches he may strengthen you with power through his Spirit in your inner being, 17 so that Christ may dwell in your hearts through faith. And I pray that you, being rooted and established in love, 18 may have power, together with all the Lord's holy people, to grasp how wide and long and high and deep is the love of Christ, 19 and to know this love that surpasses knowledge—that you may be filled to the measure of all the fullness of God.

20 Now to him who is able to do immeasurably more than all we ask or imagine, according to his power that is at work within us, 21 to him be glory in the church and in Christ Jesus throughout all generations, for ever and ever! Amen.

Unity and Maturity in the Body of Christ

4 As a prisoner for the Lord, then, I urge you to live a life worthy of the calling you have received. 2 Be completely humble and gentle; be patient, bearing with one another in love. 3 Make every effort to keep the unity of the Spirit through the bond of peace. 4 There is one body and one Spirit, just as you were called to one hope when you were called; 5 one Lord, one faith, one baptism; 6 one God and Father of all, who is over all and through all and in all.

7 But to each one of us grace has been given as Christ apportioned it. 8 This is why it[b] says:

"When he ascended on high,
    he took many captives
    and gave gifts to his people."[c]

9 (What does "he ascended" mean except that he also descended to the lower, earthly regions[d]? 10 He who descended is the very one who ascended higher than all the heavens, in order to fill the whole universe.) 11 So Christ himself gave the apostles, the prophets, the evangelists, the pastors and teachers, 12 to equip his people for works of service, so that the body of Christ may be built up 13 until we all reach unity in the faith and in the knowledge of the Son of God and become mature, attaining to the whole measure of the fullness of Christ.

14 Then we will no longer be infants, tossed back and forth by the waves, and

---

a 15 The Greek for *family* (*patria*) is derived from the Greek for *father* (*pater*).   b 8 Or *God*   c 8 Psalm 68:18
d 9 Or *the depths of the earth*

blown here and there by every wind of teaching and by the cunning and craftiness of people in their deceitful scheming. [15]Instead, speaking the truth in love, we will grow to become in every respect the mature body of him who is the head, that is, Christ. [16]From him the whole body, joined and held together by every supporting ligament, grows and builds itself up in love, as each part does its work.

Instructions for Christian Living

[17]So I tell you this, and insist on it in the Lord, that you must no longer live as the Gentiles do, in the futility of their thinking. [18]They are darkened in their understanding and separated from the life of God because of the ignorance that is in them due to the hardening of their hearts. [19]Having lost all sensitivity, they have given themselves over to sensuality so as to indulge in every kind of impurity, and they are full of greed.

[20]That, however, is not the way of life you learned [21]when you heard about Christ and were taught in him in accordance with the truth that is in Jesus. [22]You were taught, with regard to your former way of life, to put off your old self, which is being corrupted by its deceitful desires; [23]to be made new in the attitude of your minds; [24]and to put on the new self, created to be like God in true righteousness and holiness.

[25]Therefore each of you must put off falsehood and speak truthfully to your neighbor, for we are all members of one body. [26]"In your anger do not sin"[a]: Do not let the sun go down while you are still angry, [27]and do not give the devil a foothold. [28]Anyone who has been stealing must steal no longer, but must work, doing something useful with their own hands, that they may have something to share with those in need. [29]Do not let any unwholesome talk come out of your mouths, but only what is helpful for building others up according to their needs, that it may benefit those who listen. [30]And do not grieve the Holy Spirit of God, with whom you were sealed for the day of redemption. [31]Get rid of all bitterness, rage and anger, brawling and slander, along with every form of malice. [32]Be kind and compassionate to one another, forgiving each other, just as in Christ God forgave you. [1]Follow God's example, therefore, as dearly loved children [2]and walk in the way of love, just as Christ loved us and gave himself up for us as a fragrant offering and sacrifice to God.

[3]But among you there must not be even a hint of sexual immorality, or of any kind of impurity, or of greed, because these are improper for God's holy people. [4]Nor should there be obscenity, foolish talk or coarse joking, which are out of place, but rather thanksgiving. [5]For of this you can be sure: No immoral, impure or greedy person—such a person is an idolater—has any inheritance in the kingdom of Christ and of God.[b] [6]Let no one deceive you with empty words, for because of such things God's wrath comes on those who are disobedient. [7]Therefore do not be partners with them.

[8]For you were once darkness, but now you are light in the Lord. Live as children of light [9](for the fruit of the light consists in all goodness, righteousness and truth) [10]and find out what pleases the Lord. [11]Have nothing to do with the fruitless deeds of darkness, but rather expose them. [12]It is shameful even to mention what the disobedient do in secret. [13]But everything exposed by the light becomes visible—and everything that is illuminated becomes a light. [14]This is why it is said:

"Wake up, sleeper,
　rise from the dead,
　and Christ will shine on you."

[15]Be very careful, then, how you live—not as unwise but as wise, [16]making the most of every opportunity, because the days are evil. [17]Therefore do not be foolish, but understand what the Lord's will is. [18]Do not get drunk on wine, which leads to debauchery. Instead, be filled with the Spirit, [19]speaking to one another with psalms, hymns, and songs from the Spirit. Sing and make music from your heart to the Lord, [20]always giving thanks

---

[a] 26 Psalm 4:4 (see Septuagint)　　[b] 5 Or kingdom of the Messiah and God

to God the Father for everything, in the name of our Lord Jesus Christ.

Instructions for Christian Households

²¹Submit to one another out of reverence for Christ.

²²Wives, submit yourselves to your own husbands as you do to the Lord. ²³For the husband is the head of the wife as Christ is the head of the church, his body, of which he is the Savior. ²⁴Now as the church submits to Christ, so also wives should submit to their husbands in everything.

²⁵Husbands, love your wives, just as Christ loved the church and gave himself up for her ²⁶to make her holy, cleansing*a* her by the washing with water through the word, ²⁷and to present her to himself as a radiant church, without stain or wrinkle or any other blemish, but holy and blameless. ²⁸In this same way, husbands ought to love their wives as their own bodies.

_____

a 26 Or *having cleansed*

BREAKTHROUGH!

What does this mean, that wives have to submit to their husbands?

(EPHESIANS 5:22-33)

A long time ago, the law didn't give women any rights. But now we know that men and women are equal. Also, for Jesus, women are very important. He treated them just the same as men. It seems that in this church, they were having some problems with the attitude of some of the women. This letter is asking them to get things straight in the church. What Paul means is that there should be love and respect in families and everybody should be nice.

THE WITNESSES

✓ TYCHICUS (EPHESIANS 6:21–22)

This Greek name means "casual" or "unexpected." He was a Christian from Asia, and Paul's very good friend and helper. Some people think he was born in Ephesus. He was one of the people chosen by the churches to take an offering to the poor people in Jerusalem. He was in prison with Paul in Rome. He was also in charge of taking letters to the Ephesians and the Colossians.

He who loves his wife loves himself. ²⁹After all, no one ever hated their own body, but they feed and care for their body, just as Christ does the church— ³⁰for we are members of his body. ³¹"For this reason a man will leave his father and mother and be united to his wife, and the two will become one flesh."ᵃ ³²This is a profound mystery—but I am talking about Christ and the church. ³³However, each one of you also must love his wife as he loves himself, and the wife must respect her husband.

6 Children, obey your parents in the Lord, for this is right. ²"Honor your father and mother"—which is the first commandment with a promise— ³"so that it may go well with you and that you may enjoy long life on the earth."ᵇ

⁴Fathers,ᶜ do not exasperate your children; instead, bring them up in the training and instruction of the Lord.

⁵Slaves, obey your earthly masters with respect and fear, and with sincerity of heart, just as you would obey Christ. ⁶Obey them not only to win their favor when their eye is on you, but as slaves of Christ, doing the will of God from your heart. ⁷Serve wholeheartedly, as if you were serving the Lord, not people, ⁸because you know that the Lord will reward each one for whatever good they do, whether they are slave or free.

⁹And masters, treat your slaves in the same way. Do not threaten them, since you know that he who is both their Master and yours is in heaven, and there is no favoritism with him.

The Armor of God

¹⁰Finally, be strong in the Lord and in his mighty power. ¹¹Put on the full armor of God, so that you can take your stand against the devil's schemes. ¹²For our struggle is not against flesh and blood, but against the rulers, against the authorities, against the powers of this dark world and against the spiritual forces of evil in the heavenly realms. ¹³Therefore put on the full armor of God, so that when the day of evil comes, you may be able to stand your ground, and after you have done everything, to stand. ¹⁴Stand firm then, with the belt of truth buckled around your waist, with the breastplate of righteousness in place, ¹⁵and with your

---

ᵃ *31* Gen. 2:24   ᵇ *3* Deut. 5:16   ᶜ *4* Or *Parents*

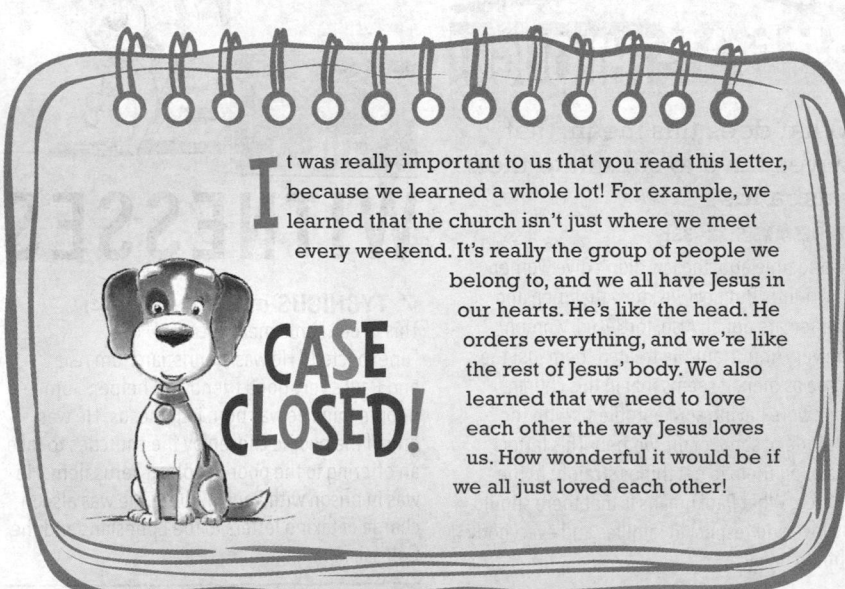

It was really important to us that you read this letter, because we learned a whole lot! For example, we learned that the church isn't just where we meet every weekend. It's really the group of people we belong to, and we all have Jesus in our hearts. He's like the head. He orders everything, and we're like the rest of Jesus' body. We also learned that we need to love each other the way Jesus loves us. How wonderful it would be if we all just loved each other!

CASE CLOSED!

feet fitted with the readiness that comes from the gospel of peace. [16]In addition to all this, take up the shield of faith, with which you can extinguish all the flaming arrows of the evil one. [17]Take the helmet of salvation and the sword of the Spirit, which is the word of God.

[18]And pray in the Spirit on all occasions with all kinds of prayers and requests. With this in mind, be alert and always keep on praying for all the Lord's people. [19]Pray also for me, that whenever I speak, words may be given me so that I will fearlessly make known the mystery of the gospel, [20]for which I am an ambassador in chains. Pray that I may declare it fearlessly, as I should.

Final Greetings

[21]Tychicus, the dear brother and faithful servant in the Lord, will tell you everything, so that you also may know how I am and what I am doing. [22]I am sending him to you for this very purpose, that you may know how we are, and that he may encourage you.

[23]Peace to the brothers and sisters,[a] and love with faith from God the Father and the Lord Jesus Christ. [24]Grace to all who love our Lord Jesus Christ with an undying love.[b]

---

[a] 23 The Greek word for *brothers and sisters* (*adelphoi*) refers here to believers, both men and women, as part of God's family.   [b] 24 Or *Grace and immortality to all who love our Lord Jesus Christ.*

PHILIPPIANS

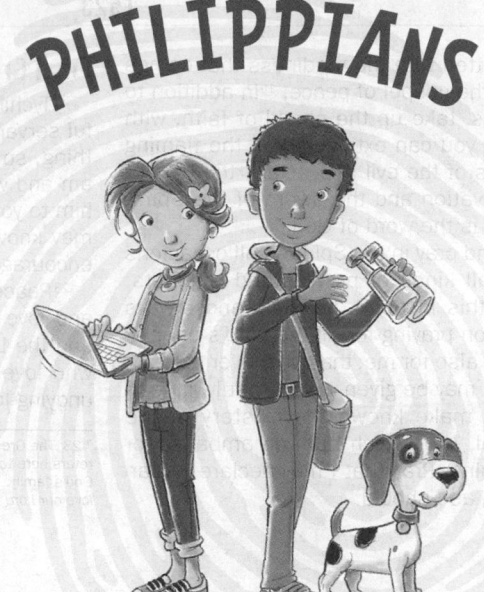

THE EVIDENCE:

WHO WROTE IT?
The letter starts out with Paul saying that he wrote it, and that Timothy was with him. Timothy was a very dear friend who was helping him preach about Jesus. Paul also says that he's in prison, but he doesn't say where (1:13–14).

HOW LONG AGO?
Since Paul was imprisoned several times (in Philippi, in Caesarea and in Rome), we don't really know which jail he was in when he wrote this letter. Some people think he was in Rome, but others say he was in Caesarea. If it was Rome, then it would have been between the years 60 and 62 after Christ. But if Paul wrote this letter from Caesarea, then it must have been between the years 56 and 59 after Christ.

WHAT'S IT ABOUT?
Paul established the church in Philippi on his second missionary journey. That's why he knew the Christians of that church so well. Paul loved them very much and he always prayed for them. In this letter, Paul thanks them for the help they sent to the prison, because that was a great help for him. They were good Christians, and Paul challenges them not to change. They should imitate Christ, who was faithful and obedient to God up until the end.

THE BEST PART
This letter is super nice, so it's hard to pick just one part. We like this good advice: "Do everything without grumbling or arguing, so that you may become blameless and pure, 'children of God without fault in a warped and crooked generation.' Then you will shine among them like stars in the sky …" (2:14–15).

---

1 Paul and Timothy, servants of Christ Jesus,

To all God's holy people in Christ Jesus at Philippi, together with the overseers and deacons[a]:

²Grace and peace to you from God our Father and the Lord Jesus Christ.

Thanksgiving and Prayer

³I thank my God every time I remember you. ⁴In all my prayers for all of you, I always pray with joy ⁵because of your partnership in the gospel from the first day until

[a] 1 The word deacons refers here to Christians designated to serve with the overseers/elders of the church in a variety of ways; similarly in Romans 16:1 and 1 Tim. 3:8,12.

now, ⁶being confident of this, that he who began a good work in you will carry it on to completion until the day of Christ Jesus.

⁷It is right for me to feel this way about all of you, since I have you in my heart and, whether I am in chains or defending and confirming the gospel, all of you share in God's grace with me. ⁸God can testify how I long for all of you with the affection of Christ Jesus.

⁹And this is my prayer: that your love may abound more and more in knowledge and depth of insight, ¹⁰so that you may be able to discern what is best and may be pure and blameless for the day of Christ, ¹¹filled with the fruit of righteousness that comes through Jesus Christ—to the glory and praise of God.

Paul's Chains Advance the Gospel

¹²Now I want you to know, brothers and sisters,ᵃ that what has happened to me

THE SCENE

PHILIPPI

(PHILIPPIANS 1:1)

It was an important city in the province of Macedonia. It was 7.5 miles (12 km) from the Aegean Sea coast. It was founded by Philip of Macedonia in the year 356 before Christ.

has actually served to advance the gospel. ¹³As a result, it has become clear throughout the whole palace guardᵇ and to everyone else that I am in chains for Christ. ¹⁴And because of my chains, most of the brothers and sisters have become confident in the Lord and dare all the more to proclaim the gospel without fear.

¹⁵It is true that some preach Christ out of envy and rivalry, but others out of goodwill. ¹⁶The latter do so out of love, knowing that I am put here for the defense of the gospel. ¹⁷The former preach Christ out of selfish ambition, not sincerely, supposing that they can stir up trouble for me while I am in chains. ¹⁸But what does it matter? The important thing is that in

BREAKTHROUGH!

Deacons

(PHILIPPIANS 1:1)

This word in Greek is used many times in the New Testament to talk about ministers in the church. They were people who shared the church work. For example, they helped with the Lord's Supper. They helped people who had problems.

ᵃ 12 The Greek word for *brothers and sisters* (*adelphoi*) refers here to believers, both men and women, as part of God's family; also in verse 14; and in 3:1, 13, 17; 4:1, 8, 21.   ᵇ 13 Or *whole palace*

Why didn't God set Paul free? Why didn't he do something if Paul hadn't done anything wrong?

(PHILIPPIANS 1:12-14)

Paul thought that prison was another place to preach the gospel. Since he was a good person and prayed, the jail keepers talked to each other about what a good prisoner he was. So he was a good example of how a Christian acts. Then there was another thing: after Paul was taken prisoner, other people felt encouraged to talk about Jesus and preach as well. Sometimes God allows us to go through hard situations, even when we haven't done anything bad. There's always something we or other people can learn from that situation.

Is suffering for Christ a good thing?

(PHILIPPIANS 1:29)

Yes. Paul thinks that being in jail because he preached the gospel is really a privilege. He doesn't mean that he's happy about this or that he wants to stay in jail. What Paul means is that he accepts what is happening to him because it's his way of giving his life to Jesus.

every way, whether from false motives or true, Christ is preached. And because of this I rejoice.

Yes, and I will continue to rejoice, ¹⁹for I know that through your prayers and God's provision of the Spirit of Jesus Christ what has happened to me will turn out for my deliverance.ᵃ ²⁰I eagerly expect and hope that I will in no way be ashamed, but will have sufficient courage so that now as always Christ will be exalted in my body, whether by life or by death. ²¹For to me, to live is Christ and to die is gain. ²²If I am to go on living in the body, this will mean fruitful labor for me. Yet what shall I choose? I do not know! ²³I am torn between the two: I desire to depart and be with Christ, which is better by far; ²⁴but it is more necessary for you that I remain in the body. ²⁵Convinced of this, I know that I will remain, and I will continue with all of you for your progress and joy in the faith, ²⁶so that through my being with you again your boasting in Christ Jesus will abound on account of me.

Life Worthy of the Gospel

²⁷Whatever happens, conduct yourselves in a manner worthy of the gospel

---

ᵃ *19* Or *vindication;* or *salvation*

of Christ. Then, whether I come and see you or only hear about you in my absence, I will know that you stand firm in the one Spirit,[a] striving together as one for the faith of the gospel [28]without being frightened in any way by those who oppose you. This is a sign to them that they will be destroyed, but that you will be saved—and that by God. [29]For it has been granted to you on behalf of Christ not only to believe in him, but also to suffer for him, [30]since you are going through the same struggle you saw I had, and now hear that I still have.

Imitating Christ's Humility

2 Therefore if you have any encouragement from being united with Christ, if any comfort from his love, if any common sharing in the Spirit, if any tenderness and compassion, [2]then make my joy complete by being like-minded, having the same love, being one in spirit and of one mind. [3]Do nothing out of selfish ambition or vain conceit. Rather, in humility value others above yourselves, [4]not looking to your own interests but each of you to the interests of the others.

[5]In your relationships with one another, have the same mindset as Christ Jesus:

[6]Who, being in very nature[b] God,
did not consider equality with God
something to be used to his
own advantage;
[7]rather, he made himself nothing
by taking the very nature[c] of a
servant,
being made in human likeness.
[8]And being found in appearance as a
man,
he humbled himself
by becoming obedient to death—
even death on a cross!
[9]Therefore God exalted him to the
highest place
and gave him the name that is
above every name,
[10]that at the name of Jesus every knee
should bow,
in heaven and on earth and under
the earth,
[11]and every tongue acknowledge that
Jesus Christ is Lord,
to the glory of God the Father.

Do Everything Without Grumbling

[12]Therefore, my dear friends, as you have always obeyed—not only in my presence, but now much more in my absence—continue to work out your salvation with fear and trembling, [13]for it is God who works in you to will and to act in order to fulfill his good purpose.

[14]Do everything without grumbling or arguing, [15]so that you may become blameless and pure, "children of God without fault in a warped and crooked generation."[d] Then you will shine among them like stars in the sky [16]as you hold firmly to the word of life. And then I will be able to boast on the day of Christ that I did not run or labor in vain. [17]But even if I am being poured out like a drink offering

CHECK THE FACTS

Who was the brother the Philippians sent to help Paul?

A) Timothy

B) Epaphroditus

C) Epaminondas

CORRECT ANSWER: B

---

[a] 27 Or *in one spirit*   [b] 6 Or *in the form of*   [c] 7 Or *the form*   [d] 15 Deut. 32:5

on the sacrifice and service coming from your faith, I am glad and rejoice with all of you. ¹⁸So you too should be glad and rejoice with me.

Timothy and Epaphroditus

¹⁹I hope in the Lord Jesus to send Timothy to you soon, that I also may be cheered when I receive news about you. ²⁰I have no one else like him, who will show genuine concern for your welfare. ²¹For everyone looks out for their own interests, not those of Jesus Christ. ²²But you know that Timothy has proved himself, because as a son with his father he has served with me in the work of the gospel. ²³I hope, therefore, to send him as soon as I see how things go with me. ²⁴And I am confident in the Lord that I myself will come soon.

²⁵But I think it is necessary to send back to you Epaphroditus, my brother, co-worker and fellow soldier, who is also your messenger, whom you sent to take care of my needs. ²⁶For he longs for all of you and is distressed because you heard he was ill. ²⁷Indeed he was ill, and almost died. But God had mercy on him, and not on him only but also on me, to spare me sorrow upon sorrow. ²⁸Therefore I am all the more eager to send him, so that when you see him again you may be glad and I may have less anxiety. ²⁹So then, welcome him in the Lord with great joy, and honor people like him, ³⁰because he almost died for the work of Christ. He risked his life to make up for the help you yourselves could not give me.

No Confidence in the Flesh

3 Further, my brothers and sisters, rejoice in the Lord! It is no trouble for me to write the same things to you again, and it is a safeguard for you. ²Watch out for those dogs, those evildoers, those mutilators of the flesh. ³For it is we who are the circumcision, we who serve God by his Spirit, who boast in Christ Jesus, and who put no confidence in the flesh— ⁴though I myself have reasons for such confidence.

If someone else thinks they have reasons to put confidence in the flesh, I have

more: ⁵circumcised on the eighth day, of the people of Israel, of the tribe of Benjamin, a Hebrew of Hebrews; in regard to the law, a Pharisee; ⁶as for zeal, persecuting the church; as for righteousness based on the law, faultless.

⁷But whatever were gains to me I now consider loss for the sake of Christ. ⁸What is more, I consider everything a loss because of the surpassing worth of knowing Christ Jesus my Lord, for whose sake I have lost all things. I consider them garbage, that I may gain Christ ⁹and be found in him, not having a righteousness of my own that comes from the law, but that which is through faith in[a] Christ—the righteousness that comes from God on the basis of faith. ¹⁰I want to know Christ—yes, to know the power of his resurrection and participation in his sufferings, becoming like him in his death, ¹¹and so, somehow, attaining to the resurrection from the dead.

---

[a] 9 Or *through the faithfulness of*

Being Hebrew

(PHILIPPIANS 3:5)

"Jewish" and "Hebrew" mean the same thing. The difference is that the Jews who were living outside their territory in another country were called "Hebrews." They spoke Aramaic and kept their Jewish customs.

THE
WITNESSES

✓ EPAPHRODITUS (PHILIPPIANS 2:25)

This Greek name means "handsome" or "charming." Epaphroditus was a Christian from the region of Macedonia. When Paul was in jail, the church in Philippi sent Epaphroditus to help Paul. While he was there with Paul, Epaphroditus got sick and had to stay longer than he had planned. Finally, he went back to Philippi with the letter that Paul wrote to the church there. Paul said that Epaphroditus was an excellent co-worker.

✓ EUODIA AND SYNTYCHE
(PHILIPPIANS 4:2)

What different names! *Syntyche* means "fortunate" and *Euodia* means "good road." These two women belonged to the church in Philippi. Paul liked them a lot, because they helped in the church and they had worked with him. However, it seems that they weren't getting along with each other, so Paul tells them they need to work things out.

---

¹²Not that I have already obtained all this, or have already arrived at my goal, but I press on to take hold of that for which Christ Jesus took hold of me. ¹³Brothers and sisters, I do not consider myself yet to have taken hold of it. But one thing I do: Forgetting what is behind and straining toward what is ahead, ¹⁴I press on toward the goal to win the prize for which God has called me heavenward in Christ Jesus.

Following Paul's Example

¹⁵All of us, then, who are mature should take such a view of things. And if on some point you think differently, that too God will make clear to you. ¹⁶Only let us live up to what we have already attained.

¹⁷Join together in following my example, brothers and sisters, and just as you have us as a model, keep your eyes on those who live as we do. ¹⁸For, as I have often told you before and now tell you again even with tears, many live as enemies of the cross of Christ. ¹⁹Their destiny is destruction, their god is their stomach, and their glory is in their shame. Their mind is set on earthly things. ²⁰But our citizenship is in heaven. And we eagerly await a Savior from there, the Lord Jesus Christ, ²¹who, by the power that enables him to bring everything under his control, will transform our lowly bodies so that they will be like his glorious body.

Closing Appeal for Steadfastness and Unity

4 Therefore, my brothers and sisters, you whom I love and long for, my joy and crown, stand firm in the Lord in this way, dear friends!

²I plead with Euodia and I plead with Syntyche to be of the same mind in the Lord. ³Yes, and I ask you, my true

companion, help these women since they have contended at my side in the cause of the gospel, along with Clement and the rest of my co-workers, whose names are in the book of life.

Final Exhortations

⁴Rejoice in the Lord always. I will say it again: Rejoice! ⁵Let your gentleness be evident to all. The Lord is near. ⁶Do not be anxious about anything, but in every situation, by prayer and petition, with thanksgiving, present your requests to God. ⁷And the peace of God, which transcends all understanding, will guard your hearts and your minds in Christ Jesus.

⁸Finally, brothers and sisters, whatever is true, whatever is noble, whatever is right, whatever is pure, whatever is lovely, whatever is admirable—if anything is excellent or praiseworthy—think about such things. ⁹Whatever you have learned or received or heard from me, or seen in me—put it into practice. And the God of peace will be with you.

Thanks for Their Gifts

¹⁰I rejoiced greatly in the Lord that at last you renewed your concern for me. Indeed, you were concerned, but you had no opportunity to show it. ¹¹I am not saying this because I am in need, for I have learned to be content whatever the circumstances. ¹²I know what it is to be in need, and I know what it is to have plenty. I have learned the secret of being content in any and every situation, whether well fed or hungry, whether living in plenty or in want. ¹³I can do all this through him who gives me strength.

¹⁴Yet it was good of you to share in my troubles. ¹⁵Moreover, as you Philippians know, in the early days of your acquaintance with the gospel, when I set out from Macedonia, not one church shared with me

CASE CLOSED!

Paul teaches us a whole lot of things in this letter. He says that being a Christian also means being a good person, helping others, loving everybody and not just the people in the church, preaching about Jesus and not fighting with anybody. We also need to accept the difficult situations that come our way because of believing in God. And we should always pray for each other. We need to learn that living for Jesus is like when an athlete is running a race. That means that we have to always do our best and keep our faith up in order to win the final race. Then God will give us the prize of belonging to him forever.

in the matter of giving and receiving, except you only; [16]for even when I was in Thessalonica, you sent me aid more than once when I was in need. [17]Not that I desire your gifts; what I desire is that more be credited to your account. [18]I have received full payment and have more than enough. I am amply supplied, now that I have received from Epaphroditus the gifts you sent. They are a fragrant offering, an acceptable sacrifice, pleasing to God. [19]And my God will meet all your needs according to the riches of his glory in Christ Jesus.

[20]To our God and Father be glory for ever and ever. Amen.

Final Greetings

[21]Greet all God's people in Christ Jesus. The brothers and sisters who are with me send greetings. [22]All God's people here send you greetings, especially those who belong to Caesar's household.

[23]The grace of the Lord Jesus Christ be with your spirit. Amen.[a]

---

[a] 23 Some manuscripts do not have *Amen*.

COLOSSIANS

WHO WROTE IT?

We don't know for sure who wrote this letter. The letter itself says it was Paul, and many Bible experts think that he is indeed the author. So we'll call him the author too. Together with Ephesians, Philippians and Philemon, Colossians make up a group of letters called "Letters from Prison," because Paul wrote all of them while he was in jail. We also know that Tychicus and Onesimus were sent to take the letter to the church in Colossae.

HOW LONG AGO?

Some Bible experts think that Paul wrote this letter from the jail in Rome between the years 61 and 63 after Christ. Others think that he was in Ephesus in the year 50 after Christ, and still others say that Paul was in Caesarea between the years 58 and 60 after Christ. However, the majority feels that he was in Rome when he wrote this letter.

WHAT'S IT ABOUT?

It's possible that Epaphras told Paul about the dangerous false teaching that was going on among the Colossians. It wasn't that there was fighting in the church. It was that they were confusing Christianity with other beliefs common at that time. They were beginning to believe that Christ wasn't the most important! They didn't want to forget Jesus Christ, they just wanted to add something extra to their worship. As if Jesus could be missing anything! So, this letter talks a lot about Christ.

THE BEST PART

We thought we should always remember this verse: "The Son is the image of the invisible God, the firstborn over all creation. For in him all things were created: things in heaven and on earth, visible and invisible" (1:15 – 16). Exactly!

---

1 Paul, an apostle of Christ Jesus by the will of God, and Timothy our brother,

² To God's holy people in Colossae, the faithful brothers and sisters *a* in Christ:

Grace and peace to you from God our Father. *b*

Thanksgiving and Prayer

³ We always thank God, the Father of our Lord Jesus Christ, when we pray for

a 2 The Greek word for *brothers and sisters (adelphoi)* refers here to believers, both men and women, as part of God's family; also in 4:15.   *b* 2 Some manuscripts *Father and the Lord Jesus Christ*

COLOSSAE

(COLOSSIANS 1:2)

This city was in the Lycus River Valley in the ancient province of Phrygia in Asia Minor. This land belongs to the country of Turkey now. Colossae was once a very important city. But when Paul wrote this letter, the city had gone downhill. There has been a really bad earthquake, and after that the city didn't recover very well. There was a pretty large Christian community in Colossae, and Philemon opened his home for worship services there. (Check out Philemon 1:2.)

you, 4because we have heard of your faith in Christ Jesus and of the love you have for all God's people— 5the faith and love that spring from the hope stored up for you in heaven and about which you have already heard in the true message of the gospel 6that has come to you. In the same way, the gospel is bearing fruit and growing throughout the whole world—just as it has been doing among you since the day you heard it and truly understood God's grace. 7You learned it

from Epaphras, our dear fellow servant,[a] who is a faithful minister of Christ on our[b] behalf, 8and who also told us of your love in the Spirit.

9For this reason, since the day we heard about you, we have not stopped praying for you. We continually ask God to fill you with the knowledge of his will through all the wisdom and understanding that the Spirit gives,[c] 10so that you may live a

---

[a] 7 Or slave　　[b] 7 Some manuscripts your　　[c] 9 Or all spiritual wisdom and understanding

THE
WITNESSES

✓ EPAPHRAS (COLOSSIANS 1:7)

This name is just short for Epaphroditus. It means "handsome" or "charming." But you shouldn't confuse it with another man in the Bible also called Epaphroditus. This man here was the pastor of the church in Colossae. He was a disciple of Paul and traveled with him as they preached. He was also in jail with Paul.

life worthy of the Lord and please him in every way: bearing fruit in every good work, growing in the knowledge of God, [11]being strengthened with all power according to his glorious might so that you may have great endurance and patience, [12]and giving joyful thanks to the Father, who has qualified you[a] to share in the inheritance of his holy people in the kingdom of light. [13]For he has rescued us from the dominion of darkness and brought us into the kingdom of the Son he loves, [14]in whom we have redemption, the forgiveness of sins.

The Supremacy of the Son of God

[15]The Son is the image of the invisible God, the firstborn over all creation. [16]For in him all things were created: things in heaven and on earth, visible and invisible, whether thrones or powers or rulers or authorities; all things have been created through him and for him. [17]He is before all things, and in him all things hold together. [18]And he is the head of the body, the church; he is the beginning and the firstborn from among the dead, so that in everything he might have the supremacy. [19]For God was pleased to have all his fullness dwell in him, [20]and through him to reconcile to himself all things, whether things on earth or things in heaven, by making peace through his blood, shed on the cross.

[21]Once you were alienated from God and were enemies in your minds because of[b] your evil behavior. [22]But now he has reconciled you by Christ's physical body through death to present you holy in his sight, without blemish and free from accusation— [23]if you continue in your faith, established and firm, and do not move from the hope held out in the gospel. This is the gospel that you heard and that has been proclaimed to every creature under heaven, and of which I, Paul, have become a servant.

Paul's Labor for the Church

[24]Now I rejoice in what I am suffering for you, and I fill up in my flesh what is still lacking in regard to Christ's afflictions, for the sake of his body, which is the church. [25]I have become its servant by the commission God gave me to present to you the word of God in its fullness— [26]the mystery that has been kept hidden for ages and generations, but is now disclosed to the Lord's people. [27]To them God has chosen to make known among the Gentiles the glorious riches of this mystery, which is Christ in you, the hope of glory.

[28]He is the one we proclaim, admonishing and teaching everyone with all wisdom, so that we may present everyone fully mature in Christ. [29]To this end I strenuously contend with all the energy Christ so powerfully works in me.

2 I want you to know how hard I am contending for you and for those at Laodicea, and for all who have not met me personally. [2]My goal is that they may be encouraged in heart and united in love, so that they may have the full riches of complete understanding, in order that they may know the mystery of God, namely, Christ, [3]in whom are hidden all the treasures of wisdom and knowledge. [4]I tell you this so that no one may deceive you by fine-sounding arguments. [5]For though I am absent from you in body, I am present with you in spirit and delight to see how disciplined you are and how firm your faith in Christ is.

Spiritual Fullness in Christ

[6]So then, just as you received Christ Jesus as Lord, continue to live your lives in him, [7]rooted and built up in him, strengthened in the faith as you were taught, and overflowing with thankfulness.

[8]See to it that no one takes you captive through hollow and deceptive philosophy, which depends on human tradition and the elemental spiritual forces[c] of this world rather than on Christ.

[9]For in Christ all the fullness of the Deity lives in bodily form, [10]and in Christ you have been brought to fullness. He is the head over every power and authority. [11]In him you were also circumcised

---

[a] 12 Some manuscripts *us*   [b] 21 Or *minds, as shown by*
[c] 8 Or *the basic principles; also in verse 20*

THE SCENE

LAODICEA

(COLOSSIANS 2:1)

This was an important city in the Roman province of Phrygia, in Asia Minor south of Colossae. It was famous for wool weavings and a medical center that specialized in treatments for eyesight problems. It was important because it was where two big highways met. It was called Laodicea in honor of Laodice, the wife of King Antioch II (the Second), who founded the city between the years 261 and 253 before Christ.

with a circumcision not performed by human hands. Your whole self ruled by the flesh[a] was put off when you were circumcised by[b] Christ, 12having been buried with him in baptism, in which you were also raised with him through your faith in the working of God, who raised him from the dead.

13When you were dead in your sins and in the uncircumcision of your flesh, God made you[c] alive with Christ. He forgave us all our sins, 14having canceled the charge of our legal indebtedness, which stood against us and condemned us; he has

taken it away, nailing it to the cross. 15And having disarmed the powers and authorities, he made a public spectacle of them, triumphing over them by the cross.[d]

Freedom From Human Rules

16Therefore do not let anyone judge you by what you eat or drink, or with regard to a religious festival, a New Moon celebration or a Sabbath day. 17These are a shadow of the things that were to come; the reality, however, is found in Christ. 18Do not let anyone who delights in false humility and the worship of angels disqualify you. Such a person also goes into great detail about what they have seen; they are puffed up with idle notions by their unspiritual mind. 19They have lost connection with the head, from whom the whole body, supported and held together by its ligaments and sinews, grows as God causes it to grow.

20Since you died with Christ to the elemental spiritual forces of this world, why, as though you still belonged to the world, do you submit to its rules: 21"Do not handle! Do not taste! Do not touch!"? 22These rules, which have to do with things that are all destined to perish with use, are based on merely human commands and teachings. 23Such regulations indeed have an appearance of wisdom, with their self-imposed worship, their false humility and their harsh treatment of the body, but they lack any value in restraining sensual indulgence.

Living as Those Made Alive in Christ

3 Since, then, you have been raised with Christ, set your hearts on things above, where Christ is, seated at the right hand of God. 2Set your minds on things above, not on earthly things. 3For you died, and your life is now hidden with Christ in God. 4When Christ, who is your[e] life, appears, then you also will appear with him in glory.

---

a 11 In contexts like this, the Greek word for *flesh* (*sarx*) refers to the sinful state of human beings, often presented as a power in opposition to the Spirit; also in verse 13.
b 11 Or *put off in the circumcision of*   *c* 13 Some manuscripts *us*   *d* 15 Or *them in him*   *e* 4 Some manuscripts *our*

Is Christ sitting at the right side of God, or is he everywhere?

(COLOSSIANS 3:1)

Since Christ is God, he is everywhere at the same time. As people, we can only be in one place at a time, because we have a body, but God is spirit. That's why he can do things that we humans can't. God is everywhere all the time. Paul also says in this letter that God lives in us, and that Christ is "at the right hand of God," which is a place of honor. A long time ago, kings and famous people always had important people sit on their right side.

⁵Put to death, therefore, whatever belongs to your earthly nature: sexual immorality, impurity, lust, evil desires and greed, which is idolatry. ⁶Because of these, the wrath of God is coming.ᵃ ⁷You used to walk in these ways, in the life you once lived. ⁸But now you must also rid yourselves of all such things as these: anger, rage, malice, slander, and filthy language from your lips. ⁹Do not lie to each other, since you have taken off your old self with its practices ¹⁰and have put on the new self, which is being renewed in knowledge in the image of its Creator. ¹¹Here there is no Gentile or Jew, circumcised or un-

circumcised, barbarian, Scythian, slave or free, but Christ is all, and is in all.

¹²Therefore, as God's chosen people, holy and dearly loved, clothe yourselves with compassion, kindness, humility, gentleness and patience. ¹³Bear with each other and forgive one another if any of you has a grievance against someone. Forgive as the Lord forgave you. ¹⁴And over all these virtues put on love, which binds them all together in perfect unity.

¹⁵Let the peace of Christ rule in your hearts, since as members of one body you were called to peace. And be thankful. ¹⁶Let the message of Christ dwell among you richly as you teach and admonish one another with all wisdom

---

ᵃ 6 Some early manuscripts *coming on those who are disobedient*

According to Paul's advice, how should we act toward our parents?

A) Obey them in everything

B) Obey them when we agree with what they want us to do

C) Do what we think best, because we need to live our own lives

CORRECT ANSWER: A

THE SCENE

HIERAPOLIS

(COLOSSIANS 4:13)

This name means "sacred city." It was a city in Phrygia in Asia Minor. Many tourists went there to bathe in the hot water springs that they considered good for their health. The city is in Turkey now.

through psalms, hymns, and songs from the Spirit, singing to God with gratitude in your hearts. ¹⁷And whatever you do, whether in word or deed, do it all in the name of the Lord Jesus, giving thanks to God the Father through him.

Instructions for Christian Households

¹⁸Wives, submit yourselves to your husbands, as is fitting in the Lord.

¹⁹Husbands, love your wives and do not be harsh with them.

²⁰Children, obey your parents in everything, for this pleases the Lord.

²¹Fathers,ᵃ do not embitter your children, or they will become discouraged.

²²Slaves, obey your earthly masters in everything; and do it, not only when their eye is on you and to curry their favor, but with sincerity of heart and reverence for the Lord. ²³Whatever you do, work at it with all your heart, as working for the Lord, not for human masters, ²⁴since you know that you will receive an inheritance from the Lord as a reward. It is the Lord Christ you are serving. ²⁵Anyone who does wrong will be repaid for their wrongs, and there is no favoritism.

ᵃ 21 Or *Parents*

CASE CLOSED!

After we finished reading this letter, we thought about everything we had learned. For example, we learned how to act at home, at church and with our friends. We also learned that we shouldn't let people trick us when they seem to know a lot about Jesus but don't teach what the Bible really says. We have to be very careful with them!

THE WITNESSES

✓ DEMAS (COLOSSIANS 4:14)
This is a Greek name that means "popular." Demas is short for Demetrius. He worked with Paul in Rome.

✓ ARCHIPPUS (COLOSSIANS 4:17)
Now that's an unusual name! It means "master of the horse" or "horse trainer." He was a kind of Bible teacher, and he taught the Christians in Colossae. He also preached the gospel with Paul.

4 Masters, provide your slaves with what is right and fair, because you know that you also have a Master in heaven.

Further Instructions

2Devote yourselves to prayer, being watchful and thankful. 3And pray for us, too, that God may open a door for our message, so that we may proclaim the mystery of Christ, for which I am in chains.

4Pray that I may proclaim it clearly, as I should. 5Be wise in the way you act toward outsiders; make the most of every opportunity. 6Let your conversation be always full of grace, seasoned with salt, so that you may know how to answer everyone.

Final Greetings

7Tychicus will tell you all the news about me. He is a dear brother, a faithful minister and fellow servant*a* in the Lord. 8I am sending him to you for the express purpose that you may know about our*b* circumstances and that he may encourage your hearts. 9He is coming with Onesimus, our faithful and dear brother, who is one of you. They will tell you everything that is happening here.

10My fellow prisoner Aristarchus sends you his greetings, as does Mark, the cousin of Barnabas. (You have received instructions about him; if he comes to you, welcome him.) 11Jesus, who is called Justus, also sends greetings. These are the only Jews*c* among my co-workers for the kingdom of God, and they have proved a comfort to me. 12Epaphras, who is one of you and a servant of Christ Jesus, sends greetings. He is always wrestling in prayer for you, that you may stand firm in all the will of God, mature and fully assured. 13I vouch for him that he is working hard for you and for those at Laodicea and Hierapolis. 14Our dear friend Luke, the doctor, and Demas send greetings. 15Give my greetings to the brothers and sisters at Laodicea, and to Nympha and the church in her house.

16After this letter has been read to you, see that it is also read in the church of the Laodiceans and that you in turn read the letter from Laodicea.

17Tell Archippus: "See to it that you complete the ministry you have received in the Lord."

18I, Paul, write this greeting in my own hand. Remember my chains. Grace be with you.

---

a 7 Or *slave*; also in verse 12   *b* 8 Some manuscripts *that he may know about your*   *c* 11 Greek *only ones of the circumcision group*

1 THESSALONIANS

THE EVIDENCE:

WHO WROTE IT?
Everybody agrees that Paul wrote this letter and that he was in Corinth when he wrote it. Timothy and Silas were with him. They were two Christians who worked very hard at preaching the gospel.

HOW LONG AGO?
All the people who study the Bible agree that this is the first letter Paul wrote. This is the oldest document in the New Testament. Almost everyone says that it was written around the year 51 after Christ.

WHAT'S IT ABOUT?
Paul had been in Thessalonica, but he had to leave the city because people began bullying the Jews. Paul was very worried about the Christians who were living there. That's why he sent Timothy to find out how they were. Timothy returned with good news. Paul was so happy that he wrote this letter so full of love and happiness. He was happy that the Thessalonians were continuing to live as faithful Christians in spite of the persecution.

Paul teaches several things in this letter. For example, he talks about what happens when people die and what will happen when Christ returns. The Thessalonians believed that Jesus was going to return very soon, so some of them had stopped working. But Paul tells them that nobody knows the day or the hour when Jesus will return. In the meantime, we need to preach the gospel, be obedient to God and keep on working in order to make a living and not have to ask other people to give us money.

THE BEST PART
The verse we liked best is very simple: "Rejoice always" (5:16). That's what God orders — that we be happy! That's great!

---

1 Paul, Silas[a] and Timothy,

To the church of the Thessalonians in God the Father and the Lord Jesus Christ:

Grace and peace to you.

Thanksgiving for the Thessalonians' Faith

[2]We always thank God for all of you and continually mention you in our prayers.

---

[a] 1 Greek *Silvanus*, a variant of *Silas*

³We remember before our God and Father your work produced by faith, your labor prompted by love, and your endurance inspired by hope in our Lord Jesus Christ.

⁴For we know, brothers and sisters[a] loved by God, that he has chosen you, ⁵because our gospel came to you not simply with words but also with power, with the Holy Spirit and deep conviction. You know how we lived among you for your sake. ⁶You became imitators of us and of the Lord, for you welcomed the message in the midst of severe suffering with the joy given by the Holy Spirit. ⁷And so you became a model to all the believers in Macedonia and Achaia. ⁸The Lord's message rang out from you not only in Macedonia and Achaia—your faith in God has become known everywhere. Therefore we do not need to say anything about it, ⁹for they themselves report what kind of reception you gave us. They tell how you turned to God from idols to serve the living and true God, ¹⁰and to wait for his Son from heaven, whom he raised from the dead—Jesus, who rescues us from the coming wrath.

Paul's Ministry in Thessalonica

2 You know, brothers and sisters, that our visit to you was not without results. ²We had previously suffered and been treated outrageously in Philippi, as you know, but with the help of our God we dared to tell you his gospel in the face of strong opposition. ³For the appeal we make does not spring from error or impure motives, nor are we trying to trick you. ⁴On the contrary, we speak as those approved by God to be entrusted with the gospel. We are not trying to please people but God, who tests our hearts. ⁵You know we never used flattery, nor did we put on a mask to cover up greed—God is our witness. ⁶We were not looking for praise from people, not from you or anyone else, even though as apostles of Christ we could have asserted our authority. ⁷Instead, we were like young children[b] among you.

Just as a nursing mother cares for her children, ⁸so we cared for you. Because

we loved you so much, we were delighted to share with you not only the gospel of God but our lives as well. ⁹Surely you remember, brothers and sisters, our toil and hardship; we worked night and day in order not to be a burden to anyone while we preached the gospel of God to you. ¹⁰You are witnesses, and so is God, of how holy, righteous and blameless we were among you who believed. ¹¹For you know that we dealt with each of you as a father deals with his own children, ¹²encouraging, comforting and urging you to live lives worthy of God, who calls you into his kingdom and glory.

¹³And we also thank God continually because, when you received the word of God, which you heard from us, you accepted it not as a human word, but as it actually is, the word of God, which is indeed at work in you who believe. ¹⁴For you, brothers and sisters, became imitators of God's churches in Judea, which are in Christ Jesus: You suffered from your own people the same things those churches suffered from the Jews ¹⁵who killed the Lord Jesus and the prophets and also drove us out. They displease God and are hostile to everyone ¹⁶in their effort to keep us from speaking to the Gentiles so that they may be saved. In this way they always heap up their sins to the limit. The wrath of God has come upon them at last.[c]

Paul's Longing to See the Thessalonians

¹⁷But, brothers and sisters, when we were orphaned by being separated from you for a short time (in person, not in thought), out of our intense longing we made every effort to see you. ¹⁸For we wanted to come to you—certainly I, Paul, did, again and again—but Satan blocked our way. ¹⁹For what is our hope, our joy, or the crown in which we will glory in the presence of our Lord Jesus when he comes? Is it not you? ²⁰Indeed, you are our glory and joy.

---

a 4 The Greek word for *brothers and sisters* (*adelphoi*) refers here to believers, both men and women, as part of God's family; also in 2:1, 9, 14, 17; 3:7; 4:1, 10, 13; 5:1, 4, 12, 14, 25, 27.   *b* 7 Some manuscripts *were gentle*   *c* 16 Or *them fully*

THE SCENE

THESSALONICA

(1 THESSALONIANS 2:1)

In New Testament times, this city was the capital of Macedonia's second district, on the coast of the Aegean Sea. The previous name of the city was Therma, because of the thermal springs where people liked to go for their health. Then it was called Thessalonica in honor of Thessalonike, the sister of Alexander the Great who was king of Macedonia. Now the city is called Saloniki. It was the first important city Paul visited on his second missionary trip. That was around the year 50 after Christ. Many Greeks, Romans and Jews were living in Thessalonica. In the year 42 after Christ, the Roman emperor ordered that the Thessalonians be considered free citizens. That was very important, because it gave them many rights. There were many businesses there, and a lot of goods from all over the Mediterranean region came through its port. The Jews had a synagogue there where they met to study the Old Testament and pray.

CHECK THE FACTS

What should we put on as a breastplate and a helmet?

A) Faith and love and the hope of salvation

B) Faith and good works and more knowledge

C) The Bible teachings Paul taught

CORRECT ANSWER: A

3 So when we could stand it no longer, we thought it best to be left by ourselves in Athens. ²We sent Timothy, who is our brother and co-worker in God's service in spreading the gospel of Christ, to strengthen and encourage you in your faith, ³so that no one would be unsettled by these trials. For you know quite well that we are destined for them. ⁴In fact, when we were with you, we kept telling you that we would be persecuted. And it turned out that way, as you well know. ⁵For this reason, when I could stand it no longer, I sent to find out about your faith. I was afraid that in some way the tempter had tempted you and that our labors might have been in vain.

Timothy's Encouraging Report

⁶But Timothy has just now come to us from you and has brought good news about your faith and love. He has told us that you always have pleasant memories

of us and that you long to see us, just as we also long to see you. [7]Therefore, brothers and sisters, in all our distress and persecution we were encouraged about you because of your faith. [8]For now we really live, since you are standing firm in the Lord. [9]How can we thank God enough for you in return for all the joy we have in the presence of our God because of you? [10]Night and day we pray most earnestly that we may see you again and supply what is lacking in your faith.

[11]Now may our God and Father himself and our Lord Jesus clear the way for us to come to you. [12]May the Lord make your love increase and overflow for each other and for everyone else, just as ours does for you. [13]May he strengthen your hearts so that you will be blameless and holy in the presence of our God and Father when our Lord Jesus comes with all his holy ones.

Living to Please God

4 As for other matters, brothers and sisters, we instructed you how to live in order to please God, as in fact you are living. Now we ask you and urge you in the Lord Jesus to do this more and more. [2]For you know what instructions we gave you by the authority of the Lord Jesus.

[3]It is God's will that you should be sanctified: that you should avoid sexual immorality; [4]that each of you should learn to control your own body[a] in a way that is holy and honorable, [5]not in passionate lust like the pagans, who do not know God; [6]and that in this matter no one should wrong or take advantage of a brother or sister.[b] The Lord will punish all those who commit such sins, as we told you and warned you before. [7]For God did not call us to be impure, but to live a holy life. [8]Therefore, anyone who rejects this instruction does not reject a human being but God, the very God who gives you his Holy Spirit.

[9]Now about your love for one another we do not need to write to you, for you yourselves have been taught by God to love each other. [10]And in fact, you do love all of God's family throughout Macedonia. Yet we urge you, brothers and sisters,

to do so more and more, [11]and to make it your ambition to lead a quiet life: You should mind your own business and work with your hands, just as we told you, [12]so that your daily life may win the respect of outsiders and so that you will not be dependent on anybody.

Believers Who Have Died

[13]Brothers and sisters, we do not want you to be uninformed about those who sleep in death, so that you do not grieve like the rest of mankind, who have no hope. [14]For we believe that Jesus died and rose again, and so we believe that God will bring with Jesus those who have

---

[a] 4 Or *learn to live with your own wife*; or *learn to acquire a wife*   [b] 6 The Greek word for *brother or sister* (*adelphos*) refers here to a believer, whether man or woman, as part of God's family.

Prophecies
(1 THESSALONIANS 5:20)
This is any prediction made by a prophet. Being able to prophesy is a gift that God gives some people so they can tell his message to a nation or to another person. Most of the time, the message is that the person or nation should ask forgiveness and go back to God. Sometimes, the message is for the future. For example, John the Baptist was a prophet of God.

fallen asleep in him. ¹⁵According to the Lord's word, we tell you that we who are still alive, who are left until the coming of the Lord, will certainly not precede those who have fallen asleep. ¹⁶For the Lord himself will come down from heaven, with a loud command, with the voice of the archangel and with the trumpet call of God, and the dead in Christ will rise first. ¹⁷After that, we who are still alive and are left will be caught up together with them in the clouds to meet the Lord in the air. And so we will be with the Lord forever. ¹⁸Therefore encourage one another with these words.

The Day of the Lord

5 Now, brothers and sisters, about times and dates we do not need to write to you, ²for you know very well that the day of the Lord will come like a thief in the night. ³While people are saying, "Peace and safety," destruction will come on them suddenly, as labor pains on a pregnant woman, and they will not escape.

⁴But you, brothers and sisters, are not in darkness so that this day should surprise you like a thief. ⁵You are all children of the light and children of the day. We do not belong to the night or to the darkness. ⁶So then, let us not be like others, who are asleep, but let us be awake and sober. ⁷For those who sleep, sleep at night, and those who get drunk, get drunk at night. ⁸But since we belong to the day, let us be sober, putting on faith and love as a breastplate, and the hope of salvation as a helmet. ⁹For God did not appoint us to suffer wrath but to receive salvation through our Lord Jesus Christ. ¹⁰He died for us so that, whether we are awake or asleep, we may live together with him. ¹¹Therefore encourage one another and build each other up, just as in fact you are doing.

Final Instructions

¹²Now we ask you, brothers and sisters, to acknowledge those who work hard among you, who care for you in the Lord and who admonish you. ¹³Hold them in the highest regard in love because of their work. Live in peace with each other. ¹⁴And

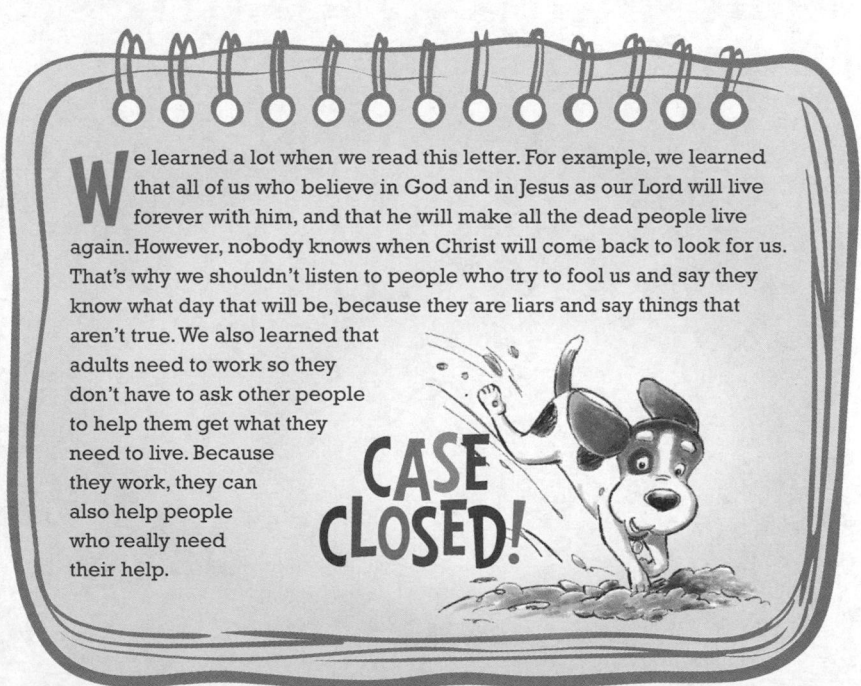

We learned a lot when we read this letter. For example, we learned that all of us who believe in God and in Jesus as our Lord will live forever with him, and that he will make all the dead people live again. However, nobody knows when Christ will come back to look for us. That's why we shouldn't listen to people who try to fool us and say they know what day that will be, because they are liars and say things that aren't true. We also learned that adults need to work so they don't have to ask other people to help them get what they need to live. Because they work, they can also help people who really need their help.

CASE CLOSED!

we urge you, brothers and sisters, warn those who are idle and disruptive, encourage the disheartened, help the weak, be patient with everyone. [15]Make sure that nobody pays back wrong for wrong, but always strive to do what is good for each other and for everyone else.

[16]Rejoice always, [17]pray continually, [18]give thanks in all circumstances; for this is God's will for you in Christ Jesus.

[19]Do not quench the Spirit. [20]Do not treat prophecies with contempt [21]but test them all; hold on to what is good, [22]reject every kind of evil.

[23]May God himself, the God of peace, sanctify you through and through. May your whole spirit, soul and body be kept blameless at the coming of our Lord Jesus Christ. [24]The one who calls you is faithful, and he will do it.

[25]Brothers and sisters, pray for us. [26]Greet all God's people with a holy kiss. [27]I charge you before the Lord to have this letter read to all the brothers and sisters. [28]The grace of our Lord Jesus Christ be with you.

BREAKTHROUGH!

A holy kiss

(1 THESSALONIANS 5:26)

This was a kiss on the cheek, like when we greet a family member or a friend. It was a very special way to greet people in those times.

2 THESSALONIANS

THE EVIDENCE:

WHO WROTE IT?
At the start of this letter, Paul says that he is the one writing. He also mentions that Timothy and Silas are helping him write it. However, there are Bible experts who think that maybe Paul really didn't write it. They think the writer was a person who admired Paul a lot and just used his name. Remember what we said in Ephesians about the writer of that letter? In the case of this letter, it says Paul was writing, so we're going to say he was the author.

HOW LONG AGO?
This letter was written a short time after the first letter to the Thessalonians. People who have studied these things think that if Paul wrote it, then it was written at the end of the year 51 after Christ or at the beginning of the year 52 after Christ.

WHAT'S IT ABOUT?
In this letter, Paul congratulates the Christians in Thessalonica because they were showing how much faith they had in spite of having to experience some very difficult times, like being bullied a lot. He also talks again about when Jesus would return. Paul says that nobody knows when that day will be. The people in Thessalonica thought that Jesus would come back to Earth any minute. Because they thought that way, many of them were leaving their jobs and weren't doing anything all day. That's not good! So Paul tells them not to be deceived and to go back to work. There will be signs that will announce Jesus' return, although nobody can know exactly when.

THE BEST PART
Isabella likes the part that says, "The Lord is faithful, and he will strengthen you and protect you from the evil one" (3:3). God always keeps his promises!

---

1 Paul, Silas[a] and Timothy,

To the church of the Thessalonians in God our Father and the Lord Jesus Christ:

[2] Grace and peace to you from God the Father and the Lord Jesus Christ.

Thanksgiving and Prayer

[3] We ought always to thank God for you, brothers and sisters,[b] and rightly so,

---

[a] 1 Greek Silvanus, a variant of Silas   [b] 3 The Greek word for brothers and sisters (adelphoi) refers here to believers, both men and women, as part of God's family; also in 2:1, 13, 15; 3:1, 6, 13.

because your faith is growing more and more, and the love all of you have for one another is increasing. ⁴Therefore, among God's churches we boast about your perseverance and faith in all the persecutions and trials you are enduring.

⁵All this is evidence that God's judgment is right, and as a result you will be counted worthy of the kingdom of God, for which you are suffering. ⁶God is just: He will pay back trouble to those who trouble you ⁷and give relief to you who are troubled, and to us as well. This will happen when the Lord Jesus is revealed from heaven in blazing fire with his powerful angels. ⁸He will punish those who do not know God and do not obey the gospel of our Lord Jesus. ⁹They will be punished with everlasting destruction and shut out from the presence of the Lord and from the glory of his might ¹⁰on the day he comes to be glorified in his holy people and to be marveled at among all those who have believed. This includes you, because you believed our testimony to you.

¹¹With this in mind, we constantly pray for you, that our God may make you worthy of his calling, and that by his power he may bring to fruition your every desire for goodness and your every deed prompted by faith. ¹²We pray this so that the name of our Lord Jesus may be glorified in you, and you in him, according to the grace of our God and the Lord Jesus Christ.ᵃ

The Man of Lawlessness

2 Concerning the coming of our Lord Jesus Christ and our being gathered to him, we ask you, brothers and sisters, ²not to become easily unsettled or alarmed by the teaching allegedly from us—whether by a prophecy or by word of mouth or by letter—asserting that the day of the Lord has already come. ³Don't let anyone deceive you in any way, for that day will not come until the rebellion occurs and the man of lawlessnessᵇ is revealed, the man doomed to destruction. ⁴He will oppose and will exalt himself over everything that is called God or is worshiped, so that he sets himself up in God's temple, proclaiming himself to be God.

BREAKTHROUGH!

Who is the "man of lawlessness"?

(2 THESSALONIANS 2:3)

There are two different opinions about this. Some experts think he is a person that is the enemy of Jesus and Christians. Other experts who study the Bible say it's not a person but rather a group, like a government, for example. It could be a group or even a spirit that makes many people go against Jesus. Everybody agrees that whatever it is, it's from the devil, who tries to trick Christians. But God will destroy this person or thing.

⁵Don't you remember that when I was with you I used to tell you these things? ⁶And now you know what is holding him back, so that he may be revealed at the proper time. ⁷For the secret power of lawlessness is already at work; but the one who now holds it back will continue to do so till he is taken out of the way. ⁸And then the lawless one will be revealed, whom the Lord Jesus will overthrow with the breath of his mouth and destroy by the splendor of his coming. ⁹The coming of the lawless one will be in accordance with how Satan works. He will use all

---

ᵃ 12 Or God and Lord, Jesus Christ   ᵇ 3 Some manuscripts sin

CHECK THE FACTS

What will happen to us when Jesus Christ comes?

A) We will be gathered to him.

B) We will be at home and see it all happen on TV.

C) We will go out and announce his return.

CORRECT ANSWER: A

sorts of displays of power through signs and wonders that serve the lie, [10]and all the ways that wickedness deceives those who are perishing. They perish because they refused to love the truth and so be saved. [11]For this reason God sends them a powerful delusion so that they will believe the lie [12]and so that all will be condemned who have not believed the truth but have delighted in wickedness.

Stand Firm

[13]But we ought always to thank God for you, brothers and sisters loved by the Lord, because God chose you as firstfruits[a] to be saved through the sanctifying work of the Spirit and through belief in the truth. [14]He called you to this through our gospel, that you might share in the glory of our Lord Jesus Christ.

[15]So then, brothers and sisters, stand firm and hold fast to the teachings[b] we passed on to you, whether by word of mouth or by letter.

[16]May our Lord Jesus Christ himself and God our Father, who loved us and by his grace gave us eternal encouragement and good hope, [17]encourage your hearts

---

[a] 13 Some manuscripts *because from the beginning God chose you*   [b] 15 Or *traditions*

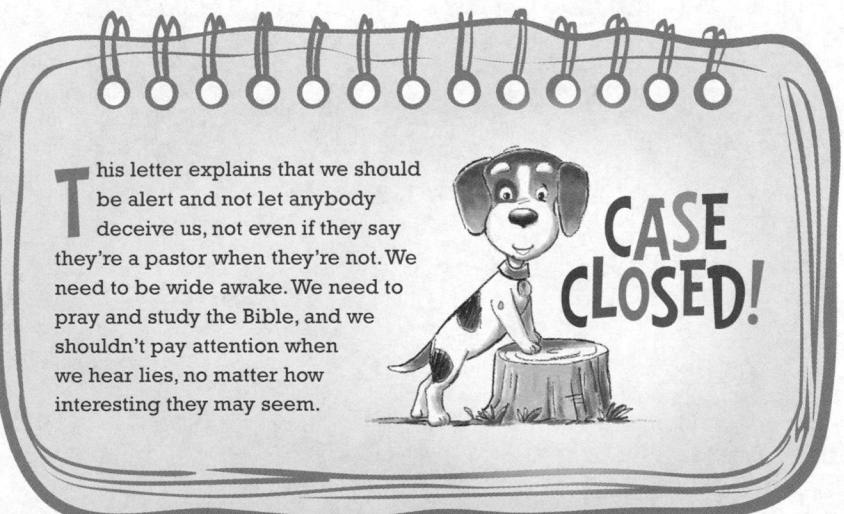

This letter explains that we should be alert and not let anybody deceive us, not even if they say they're a pastor when they're not. We need to be wide awake. We need to pray and study the Bible, and we shouldn't pay attention when we hear lies, no matter how interesting they may seem.

CASE CLOSED!

and strengthen you in every good deed and word.

Request for Prayer

3 As for other matters, brothers and sisters, pray for us that the message of the Lord may spread rapidly and be honored, just as it was with you. [2]And pray that we may be delivered from wicked and evil people, for not everyone has faith. [3]But the Lord is faithful, and he will strengthen you and protect you from the evil one. [4]We have confidence in the Lord that you are doing and will continue to do the things we command. [5]May the Lord direct your hearts into God's love and Christ's perseverance.

Warning Against Idleness

[6]In the name of the Lord Jesus Christ, we command you, brothers and sisters, to keep away from every believer who is idle and disruptive and does not live according to the teaching[a] you received from us. [7]For you yourselves know how you ought to follow our example. We were not idle when we were with you, [8]nor did we eat anyone's food without paying for it. On the contrary, we worked night and day, laboring and toiling so that we would not be a burden to any of you. [9]We did this, not because we do not have the right to such help, but in order to offer ourselves as a model for you to imitate. [10]For even when we were with you, we gave you this rule: "The one who is unwilling to work shall not eat."

[11]We hear that some among you are idle and disruptive. They are not busy; they are busybodies. [12]Such people we command and urge in the Lord Jesus Christ to settle down and earn the food they eat. [13]And as for you, brothers and sisters, never tire of doing what is good.

[14]Take special note of anyone who does not obey our instruction in this letter. Do not associate with them, in order that they may feel ashamed. [15]Yet do not regard them as an enemy, but warn them as you would a fellow believer.

Final Greetings

[16]Now may the Lord of peace himself give you peace at all times and in every way. The Lord be with all of you. [17]I, Paul, write this greeting in my own hand, which is the distinguishing mark in all my letters. This is how I write. [18]The grace of our Lord Jesus Christ be with you all.

---

a 6 Or *tradition*

1 TIMOTHY

1 Paul, an apostle of Christ Jesus by the command of God our Savior and of Christ Jesus our hope,

²To Timothy my true son in the faith:

Grace, mercy and peace from God the Father and Christ Jesus our Lord.

Timothy Charged to Oppose False Teachers

³As I urged you when I went into Macedonia, stay there in Ephesus so that you may command certain people not to teach false doctrines any longer ⁴or to devote themselves to myths and endless genealogies. Such things promote controversial speculations rather than advancing God's work—which is by faith. ⁵The goal of this command is love, which comes from a pure heart and a good conscience and a sincere faith. ⁶Some have departed from these and have turned to

Endless genealogies

(1 TIMOTHY 1:4)

The false teachers in Ephesus wanted the Christians to accept Jewish teachings and customs. But that wasn't right! If that was right, then what did Jesus die and rise from the dead for? Those lists of all those ancestors were a Jewish custom. The Jews kept a register of everybody, of every single ancestor — the grandfathers of the grandfathers and their grandfathers — to prove that they were true Jews. So that's why they thought they had more rights to land and to religious jobs. But that's just not so! Jesus saves us, and God accepts us all equally. It doesn't matter where we're from or who our parents are.

whatever else is contrary to the sound doctrine ¹¹that conforms to the gospel concerning the glory of the blessed God, which he entrusted to me.

The Lord's Grace to Paul

¹²I thank Christ Jesus our Lord, who has given me strength, that he considered me trustworthy, appointing me to his service. ¹³Even though I was once a blasphemer and a persecutor and a violent man, I was shown mercy because I acted in ignorance and unbelief. ¹⁴The grace of our Lord was poured out on me abundantly, along with the faith and love that are in Christ Jesus.

¹⁵Here is a trustworthy saying that deserves full acceptance: Christ Jesus came into the world to save sinners — of whom I am the worst. ¹⁶But for that very reason I was shown mercy so that in me, the worst of sinners, Christ Jesus might display his immense patience as an example for those who would believe in him and receive eternal life. ¹⁷Now to the King eternal, immortal, invisible, the only God, be honor and glory for ever and ever. Amen.

The Charge to Timothy Renewed

¹⁸Timothy, my son, I am giving you this command in keeping with the prophecies once made about you, so that by recalling them you may fight the battle well, ¹⁹holding on to faith and a good conscience, which some have rejected and so have suffered shipwreck with regard to the faith. ²⁰Among them are Hymenaeus and Alexander, whom I have handed over to Satan to be taught not to blaspheme.

Instructions on Worship

2 I urge, then, first of all, that petitions, prayers, intercession and thanksgiving be made for all people— ²for kings and all those in authority, that we may live peaceful and quiet lives in all godliness and holiness. ³This is good, and pleases God our Savior, ⁴who wants all people to be saved and to come to a knowledge of the truth. ⁵For there is one God and one mediator between God and mankind, the

meaningless talk. ⁷They want to be teachers of the law, but they do not know what they are talking about or what they so confidently affirm.

⁸We know that the law is good if one uses it properly. ⁹We also know that the law is made not for the righteous but for lawbreakers and rebels, the ungodly and sinful, the unholy and irreligious, for those who kill their fathers or mothers, for murderers, ¹⁰for the sexually immoral, for those practicing homosexuality, for slave traders and liars and perjurers—and for

THE
WITNESSES

✓ TIMOTHY (1 TIMOTHY 1:2)

He was born in Lystra. His mother was Eunice, and his grandmother was Lois. They taught him about God. Paul met him on his trip to Lystra, and after that, Timothy accompanied Paul when he traveled around preaching the gospel. Paul loved him like a son. Timothy was in charge of the church in Ephesus. There were problems there, so Paul tried to help him. Paul wrote two letters to Timothy to advise him on what to do as their pastor.

✓ HYMENAEUS AND ALEXANDER (1 TIMOTHY 1:20)

These are Greek names. The first one is quite rare. It was the name of a god of marriage celebrations. In this letter, it's the name of a man who was teaching lies against God and the faith in Jesus Christ. Alexander is also a Greek name, but it's more common. It means "defender of men." He was a false teacher too. It seems this is the same man mentioned in the second letter to Timothy in 4:14—a metalworker who did things to hurt Paul. They were such terrible liars and sinners that Paul expelled them from the church.

---

man Christ Jesus, ⁶who gave himself as a ransom for all people. This has now been witnessed to at the proper time. ⁷And for this purpose I was appointed a herald and an apostle—I am telling the truth, I am not lying—and a true and faithful teacher of the Gentiles.

⁸Therefore I want the men everywhere to pray, lifting up holy hands without anger or disputing. ⁹I also want the women to dress modestly, with decency and propriety, adorning themselves, not with elaborate hairstyles or gold or pearls or expensive clothes, ¹⁰but with good deeds, appropriate for women who profess to worship God.

¹¹A woman[a] should learn in quietness and full submission. ¹²I do not permit a woman to teach or to assume authority over a man;[b] she must be quiet. ¹³For Adam was formed first, then Eve. ¹⁴And Adam was not the one deceived; it was the woman who was deceived and became a sinner. ¹⁵But women[c] will be saved through childbearing—if they continue in faith, love and holiness with propriety.

Qualifications for Overseers and Deacons

3 Here is a trustworthy saying: Whoever aspires to be an overseer desires a noble task. ²Now the overseer is to be above reproach, faithful to his wife, temperate, self-controlled, respectable, hospitable, able to teach, ³not given to drunkenness, not violent but gentle, not quarrelsome, not a lover of money. ⁴He must manage his own family well and see that his children obey him, and he must do so in a manner worthy of full[d] respect.

---

a 11 Or *wife*; also in verse 12   *b* 12 Or *over her husband*
c 15 Greek *she*   *d* 4 Or *him with proper*

⁵(If anyone does not know how to manage his own family, how can he take care of God's church?) ⁶He must not be a recent convert, or he may become conceited and fall under the same judgment as the dev-

BREAKTHROUGH!

Weren't women allowed to teach in the churches?

(1 TIMOTHY 2:12)

This does seem unfair! Paul himself knew many women who were teaching in the churches and preaching about Jesus. Junia, Phoebe and Tabitha were women who did this, and there were others. Paul appreciated all of them and said they were good workers and were important for the churches. Some Bible experts think that this rule was just for the church in Ephesus, because the writer was afraid that the false teachers might be tricking the women. We have to remember that Timothy was in Ephesus, and the church there was having problems. Other experts think that women weren't allowed to teach men, because the writer was concerned about what people who weren't Christian might think about the church. That was because in the Greco-Roman community, only men could lead meetings. If they saw a woman doing this, they might think Christianity was a bad idea and reject it.

il. ⁷He must also have a good reputation with outsiders, so that he will not fall into disgrace and into the devil's trap.

⁸In the same way, deacons*a* are to be worthy of respect, sincere, not indulging in much wine, and not pursuing dishonest gain. ⁹They must keep hold of the deep truths of the faith with a clear conscience. ¹⁰They must first be tested; and then if there is nothing against them, let them serve as deacons.

¹¹In the same way, the women*b* are to be worthy of respect, not malicious talkers but temperate and trustworthy in everything.

¹²A deacon must be faithful to his wife and must manage his children and his household well. ¹³Those who have served well gain an excellent standing and great assurance in their faith in Christ Jesus.

Reasons for Paul's Instructions

¹⁴Although I hope to come to you soon, I am writing you these instructions so that, ¹⁵if I am delayed, you will know how people ought to conduct themselves in God's household, which is the church of the living God, the pillar and foundation of the truth. ¹⁶Beyond all question, the mystery from which true godliness springs is great:

He appeared in the flesh,
    was vindicated by the Spirit,*c*
was seen by angels,
    was preached among the nations,
was believed on in the world,
    was taken up in glory.

4 The Spirit clearly says that in later times some will abandon the faith and follow deceiving spirits and things taught by demons. ²Such teachings come through hypocritical liars, whose consciences have been seared as with a hot iron. ³They forbid people to marry and order them to abstain from certain foods, which God created to be received with thanksgiving by those who believe and who know the truth. ⁴For everything God

a 8 The word *deacons* refers here to Christians designated to serve with the overseers/elders of the church in a variety of ways; similarly in verse 12; and in Romans 16:1 and Phil. 1:1. *b* 11 Possibly deacons' wives or women who are deacons *c* 16 Or *vindicated in spirit* created is good, and nothing is to be rejected if it is received with thanksgiving, ⁵because it is consecrated by the word of God and prayer.

⁶If you point these things out to the brothers and sisters,ᵃ you will be a good minister of Christ Jesus, nourished on the truths of the faith and of the good teaching that you have followed. ⁷Have nothing to do with godless myths and old wives' tales; rather, train yourself to be godly. ⁸For physical training is of some value, but godliness has value for all things, holding promise for both the present life and the life to come. ⁹This is a trustworthy saying that deserves full acceptance. ¹⁰That is why we labor and strive, because we have put our hope in the living God, who is the Savior of all people, and especially of those who believe.

¹¹Command and teach these things. ¹²Don't let anyone look down on you because you are young, but set an example for the believers in speech, in conduct, in love, in faith and in purity. ¹³Until I come, devote yourself to the public reading of Scripture, to preaching and to teaching. ¹⁴Do not neglect your gift, which was given you through prophecy when the body of elders laid their hands on you.

¹⁵Be diligent in these matters; give yourself wholly to them, so that everyone may see your progress. ¹⁶Watch your life and doctrine closely. Persevere in them, because if you do, you will save both yourself and your hearers.

Widows, Elders and Slaves

5 Do not rebuke an older man harshly, but exhort him as if he were your father. Treat younger men as brothers, ²older women as mothers, and younger women as sisters, with absolute purity.

³Give proper recognition to those widows who are really in need. ⁴But if a widow has children or grandchildren, these should learn first of all to put their religion into practice by caring for their own family and so repaying their parents and grandparents, for this is pleasing to God. ⁵The widow who is really in need and left all alone puts her hope in God and continues night and day to pray and to ask God for help. ⁶But the widow who lives for pleasure is dead even while she lives. ⁷Give the people these instructions, so that no one may be open to blame. ⁸Anyone who does not provide for their relatives, and especially for their own household, has denied the faith and is worse than an unbeliever.

⁹No widow may be put on the list of widows unless she is over sixty, has been faithful to her husband, ¹⁰and is well known for her good deeds, such as bringing up children, showing hospitality, washing the feet of the Lord's people, helping those in trouble and devoting herself to all kinds of good deeds.

¹¹As for younger widows, do not put them on such a list. For when their sensual desires overcome their dedication

CHECK THE FACTS

What did Timothy need to train himself to be?

A) Godly

B) An athlete

C) Healthier

ᵃ 6 The Greek word for *brothers and sisters* (*adelphoi*) refers here to believers, both men and women, as part of God's family.

to Christ, they want to marry. [12]Thus they bring judgment on themselves, because they have broken their first pledge. [13]Besides, they get into the habit of being idle and going about from house to house. And not only do they become idlers, but also busybodies who talk nonsense, saying things they ought not to. [14]So I counsel younger widows to marry, to have children, to manage their homes and to give the enemy no opportunity for slander. [15]Some have in fact already turned away to follow Satan.

[16]If any woman who is a believer has widows in her care, she should continue to help them and not let the church be burdened with them, so that the church can help those widows who are really in need.

[17]The elders who direct the affairs of the church well are worthy of double honor, especially those whose work is preaching and teaching. [18]For Scripture says, "Do not muzzle an ox while it is treading out the grain,"[a] and "The worker deserves his wages."[b] [19]Do not entertain an accusation against an elder unless it is brought by two or three witnesses. [20]But those elders who are sinning you are to reprove before everyone, so that the others may take warning. [21]I charge you, in the sight of God and Christ Jesus and the elect angels, to keep these instructions without partiality, and to do nothing out of favoritism.

[22]Do not be hasty in the laying on of hands, and do not share in the sins of others. Keep yourself pure.

[23]Stop drinking only water, and use a little wine because of your stomach and your frequent illnesses.

[24]The sins of some are obvious, reaching the place of judgment ahead of them; the sins of others trail behind them. [25]In the same way, good deeds are obvious, and even those that are not obvious cannot remain hidden forever.

6 All who are under the yoke of slavery should consider their masters worthy of full respect, so that God's name and our teaching may not be slandered. [2]Those who have believing masters should not show them disrespect just be-cause they are fellow believers. Instead, they should serve them even better because their masters are dear to them as fellow believers and are devoted to the welfare[c] of their slaves.

False Teachers and the Love of Money

These are the things you are to teach and insist on. [3]If anyone teaches otherwise and does not agree to the sound instruction of our Lord Jesus Christ and to godly teaching, [4]they are conceited and understand nothing. They have an unhealthy interest in controversies and quarrels about words that result in envy, strife, malicious talk, evil suspicions [5]and constant friction between people of corrupt mind, who have been robbed of the truth and who think that godliness is a means to financial gain.

[6]But godliness with contentment is great gain. [7]For we brought nothing into the world, and we can take nothing out of it. [8]But if we have food and clothing, we will be content with that. [9]Those who want to get rich fall into temptation and a trap and into many foolish and harmful desires that plunge people into ruin and destruction. [10]For the love of money is a root of all kinds of evil. Some people, eager for money, have wandered from the faith and pierced themselves with many griefs.

Final Charge to Timothy

[11]But you, man of God, flee from all this, and pursue righteousness, godliness, faith, love, endurance and gentleness. [12]Fight the good fight of the faith. Take hold of the eternal life to which you were called when you made your good confession in the presence of many witnesses. [13]In the sight of God, who gives life to everything, and of Christ Jesus, who while testifying before Pontius Pilate made the good confession, I charge you [14]to keep this command without spot or blame until the appearing of our Lord Jesus Christ, [15]which God will bring about in his own

---

[a] 18 Deut. 25:4   [b] 18 Luke 10:7   [c] 2 Or and benefit from the service

time — God, the blessed and only Ruler, the King of kings and Lord of lords, [16]who alone is immortal and who lives in unapproachable light, whom no one has seen or can see. To him be honor and might forever. Amen.

[17]Command those who are rich in this present world not to be arrogant nor to put their hope in wealth, which is so uncertain, but to put their hope in God, who richly provides us with everything for our enjoyment. [18]Command them to do good, to be rich in good deeds, and to be generous and willing to share. [19]In this way they will lay up treasure for themselves as a firm foundation for the coming age, so that they may take hold of the life that is truly life.

[20]Timothy, guard what has been entrusted to your care. Turn away from godless chatter and the opposing ideas of what is falsely called knowledge, [21]which some have professed and in so doing have departed from the faith.

Grace be with you all.

This first letter to Timothy teaches us a lot about the history of the first Christian churches and the problems the first Christians had. We also learned how to recognize and deal with false teachers. This is very important, because there are still people today who try to teach lies in the churches and confuse people. That's why we need to really be careful and study the Bible a lot.

CASE CLOSED!

2 TIMOTHY

THE EVIDENCE:

WHO WROTE IT?
The situation is the same as for the first letter to Timothy: some experts think it was Paul and others say it wasn't. Because of what the text says, we say that it was Paul. This would be the last letter Paul wrote.

HOW LONG AGO?
Saying when this letter was written is a problem. Nobody really knows. The people who think that Paul is the author say it was written between the years 55 and 67 after Christ. The others who say he didn't write it think the letter was written much later, maybe around the year 100 after Christ.

WHAT'S IT ABOUT?
Paul was in jail in Rome when he wrote this letter. He was thinking that he was going to die soon. Consequently, he doesn't write to a church, as he usually did, but rather to one person. That was Timothy, the young man he loved as if he were his son. Timothy was in Ephesus. Paul talks about personal things, and he gives Timothy spiritual and pastoral advice. He tells him how to teach the Word of God correctly, to be careful not to be deceived by false teachers and to keep his faith in Jesus until the end. This letter is like the last words a father gives his son when he is trying to pass on his knowledge and wisdom.

THE BEST PART
We agreed about this. Here's our favorite part: "For the Spirit God gave us does not make us timid, but gives us power, love and self-discipline" (1:7).

---

1 Paul, an apostle of Christ Jesus by the will of God, in keeping with the promise of life that is in Christ Jesus,

² To Timothy, my dear son:

Grace, mercy and peace from God the Father and Christ Jesus our Lord.

Thanksgiving

³ I thank God, whom I serve, as my ancestors did, with a clear conscience, as night and day I constantly remember you in my prayers. ⁴ Recalling your tears, I long to see you, so that I may be filled with joy. ⁵ I am reminded of your sincere faith, which first lived in your grandmother Lois and in your mother Eunice and, I am persuaded, now lives in you also.

Appeal for Loyalty to Paul and the Gospel

⁶ For this reason I remind you to fan

into flame the gift of God, which is in you through the laying on of my hands. ⁷For the Spirit God gave us does not make us timid, but gives us power, love and self-discipline. ⁸So do not be ashamed of the testimony about our Lord or of me his prisoner. Rather, join with me in suffering for the gospel, by the power of God. ⁹He has saved us and called us to a holy life—not because of anything we have done but because of his own purpose and grace. This grace was given us in Christ Jesus before the beginning of time, ¹⁰but it has now been revealed through the appearing of our Savior, Christ Jesus, who has destroyed death and has brought life and immortality to light through the gospel. ¹¹And of this gospel I was appointed a herald and an apostle and a teacher. ¹²That is why I am suffering as I am. Yet this is no cause for shame, because I know whom I have believed, and am convinced that he is able to guard what I have entrusted to him until that day.

¹³What you heard from me, keep as the pattern of sound teaching, with faith and love in Christ Jesus. ¹⁴Guard the good deposit that was entrusted to you—guard it with the help of the Holy Spirit who lives in us.

Examples of Disloyalty and Loyalty

¹⁵You know that everyone in the province of Asia has deserted me, including Phygelus and Hermogenes. ¹⁶May the Lord show mercy to the household of Onesiphorus, because he often refreshed me and was not ashamed of my chains. ¹⁷On the contrary, when he was in Rome, he searched hard for me until he found me. ¹⁸May the Lord grant that he will find mercy from the Lord on that day! You know very well in how many ways he helped me in Ephesus.

The Appeal Renewed

2 You then, my son, be strong in the grace that is in Christ Jesus. ²And the things you have heard me say in the

THE
WITNESSES

✓ LOIS (2 TIMOTHY 1:5)
This is a Greek name, but we really don't know what it means. It might be a nickname for the Latin name Leticia, which means "happiness." She was Timothy's grandmother. She and Eunice were the first people who taught Timothy the Old Testament.

✓ EUNICE (2 TIMOTHY 1:5)
This name is Greek, and it means "good victory." Eunice was Timothy's mother. She was probably a Greek woman who decided to practice Judaism. She was living in Lystra and was married to a Greek man, but we don't know his name.

✓ ONESIPHORUS (2 TIMOTHY 1:16)
This Greek name means "beneficial" or "bringing advantage." He was a Christian who helped Paul in Ephesus. Later, he visited Paul in Rome when he was in jail. That's why Paul asks God to bless him.

presence of many witnesses entrust to reliable people who will also be qualified to teach others. ³Join with me in suffering, like a good soldier of Christ Jesus. ⁴No one serving as a soldier gets entangled in civilian affairs, but rather tries to please his commanding officer. ⁵Similarly, anyone who competes as an athlete does not receive the victor's crown except by competing according to the rules. ⁶The hardworking farmer should be the first to receive a share of the crops. ⁷Reflect on what I am saying, for the Lord will give you insight into all this.

⁸Remember Jesus Christ, raised from the dead, descended from David. This is my gospel, ⁹for which I am suffering even to the point of being chained like a criminal. But God's word is not chained. ¹⁰Therefore I endure everything for the sake of the elect, that they too may obtain the salvation that is in Christ Jesus, with eternal glory.

¹¹Here is a trustworthy saying:

If we died with him,
    we will also live with him;
¹²if we endure,
    we will also reign with him.
If we disown him,
    he will also disown us;
¹³if we are faithless,
    he remains faithful,
    for he cannot disown himself.

Dealing With False Teachers

¹⁴Keep reminding God's people of these things. Warn them before God against quarreling about words; it is of no value, and only ruins those who listen. ¹⁵Do your best to present yourself to God as one approved, a worker who does not need to be ashamed and who correctly handles the word of truth. ¹⁶Avoid godless chatter, because those who indulge in it will become more and more ungodly. ¹⁷Their teaching will spread like gangrene. Among them are Hymenaeus and Philetus, ¹⁸who have departed from the truth. They say that the resurrection has already taken place, and they destroy the faith of some. ¹⁹Nevertheless, God's solid foundation stands firm, sealed with this

BREAK THROUGH!

Parchments

(2 TIMOTHY 4:13)

In Bible times, the kind of paper we have now didn't exist. Also, only a few people knew how to write. The materials they needed for writing were very expensive. As a result, they only wrote things they considered really important. There were three different materials they used instead of paper. They would write words or short ideas on pieces of broken pottery, called *ostracon*. Another material was papyrus, which came from a cane-like plant that grew on the shores of the Nile River. This was used in Egypt. They would cut the stalks open and then stick them together to make a kind of sheet. The third material was parchment, which was the skin of an animal, maybe a sheep, a goat or a calf. They would pull the hair off the skin and put things on it to make the inside part very smooth so they could write on it. After they wrote on the parchment, they would roll it up, tie it and then store it. The good thing about parchment was that it could be made anywhere they had animals. Another good thing was that it is very, very tough. They could erase what they had written on it and then write on it again. When they did that, they called that parchment *palimpsest*. Now that's a word! Try to repeat it three times!

inscription: "The Lord knows those who are his," and, "Everyone who confesses the name of the Lord must turn away from wickedness."

20 In a large house there are articles not only of gold and silver, but also of wood and clay; some are for special purposes and some for common use. 21 Those who cleanse themselves from the latter will be instruments for special purposes, made holy, useful to the Master and prepared to do any good work.

22 Flee the evil desires of youth and pursue righteousness, faith, love and peace, along with those who call on the Lord out of a pure heart. 23 Don't have anything to do with foolish and stupid arguments, because you know they produce quarrels. 24 And the Lord's servant must not be quarrelsome but must be kind to everyone, able to teach, not resentful. 25 Opponents must be gently instructed, in the hope that God will grant them repentance leading them to a knowledge of the truth, 26 and that they will come to their senses and escape from the trap of the devil, who has taken them captive to do his will.

3 But mark this: There will be terrible times in the last days. 2 People will be lovers of themselves, lovers of money, boastful, proud, abusive, disobedient to their parents, ungrateful, unholy, 3 without love, unforgiving, slanderous, without self-control, brutal, not lovers of the good, 4 treacherous, rash, conceited, lovers of pleasure rather than lovers of God— 5 having a form of godliness but denying its power. Have nothing to do with such people.

6 They are the kind who worm their way into homes and gain control over gullible women, who are loaded down with sins and are swayed by all kinds of evil desires, 7 always learning but never able to come to a knowledge of the truth. 8 Just as Jannes and Jambres opposed Moses, so also these teachers oppose the truth. They are men of depraved minds, who, as far as the faith is concerned, are rejected. 9 But they will not get very far because, as in the case of those men, their folly will be clear to everyone.

A Final Charge to Timothy

10 You, however, know all about my teaching, my way of life, my purpose, faith, patience, love, endurance, 11 persecutions, sufferings—what kinds of things happened to me in Antioch, Iconium and Lystra, the persecutions I endured. Yet the Lord rescued me from all of them. 12 In fact, everyone who wants to live a godly life in Christ Jesus will be persecuted, 13 while evildoers and impostors will go from bad to worse, deceiving and being deceived. 14 But as for you, continue in what you have learned and have become convinced of, because you know those from whom you learned it, 15 and how from infancy you have known the Holy Scriptures, which are able to make you wise for salvation through faith in Christ Jesus. 16 All Scripture is God-breathed and is useful for teaching, rebuking, correcting and training in righteousness, 17 so that

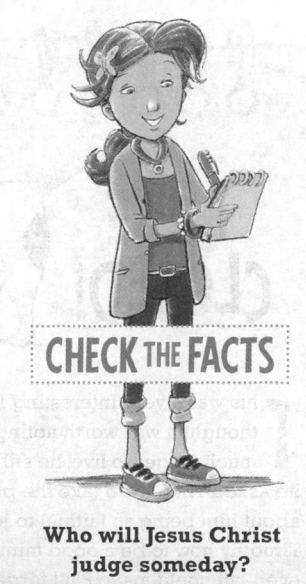

CHECK THE FACTS

Who will Jesus Christ judge someday?

A) Only bad people

B) The living and the dead

C) The Christians

CORRECT ANSWER: B

the servant of God[a] may be thoroughly equipped for every good work.

4 In the presence of God and of Christ Jesus, who will judge the living and the dead, and in view of his appearing and his kingdom, I give you this charge: ²Preach the word; be prepared in season and out of season; correct, rebuke and encourage—with great patience and careful instruction. ³For the time will come when people will not put up with sound doctrine. Instead, to suit their own desires, they will gather around them a great number of teachers to say what their itching ears want to hear. ⁴They will turn their ears away from the truth and turn aside to myths. ⁵But you, keep your head in all situations, endure hardship, do the work of an evangelist, discharge all the duties of your ministry.

⁶For I am already being poured out like a drink offering, and the time for my departure is near. ⁷I have fought the good fight, I have finished the race, I have kept the faith. ⁸Now there is in store for me the crown of righteousness, which the Lord, the righteous Judge, will award to me on that day—and not only to me, but also to all who have longed for his appearing.

Personal Remarks

⁹Do your best to come to me quickly, ¹⁰for Demas, because he loved this world, has deserted me and has gone to Thessalonica. Crescens has gone to Galatia, and Titus to Dalmatia. ¹¹Only Luke is with me. Get Mark and bring him with you, because he is helpful to me in my ministry. ¹²I sent Tychicus to Ephesus. ¹³When you come, bring the cloak that I left with Carpus at Troas, and my scrolls, especially the parchments.

---

[a] 17 Or that you, a man of God,

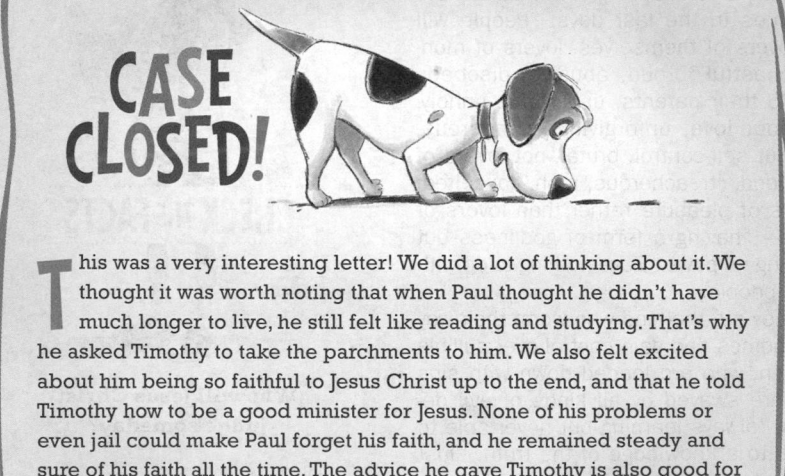

CASE CLOSED!

T his was a very interesting letter! We did a lot of thinking about it. We thought it was worth noting that when Paul thought he didn't have much longer to live, he still felt like reading and studying. That's why he asked Timothy to take the parchments to him. We also felt excited about him being so faithful to Jesus Christ up to the end, and that he told Timothy how to be a good minister for Jesus. None of his problems or even jail could make Paul forget his faith, and he remained steady and sure of his faith all the time. The advice he gave Timothy is also good for us now, because we should be careful about people who don't love God. We should also learn the Bible very well so false teachers can't fool us.

[14]Alexander the metalworker did me a great deal of harm. The Lord will repay him for what he has done. [15]You too should be on your guard against him, because he strongly opposed our message.

[16]At my first defense, no one came to my support, but everyone deserted me. May it not be held against them. [17]But the Lord stood at my side and gave me strength, so that through me the message might be fully proclaimed and all the Gentiles might hear it. And I was delivered from the lion's mouth. [18]The Lord will rescue me from every evil attack and will bring me safely to his heavenly kingdom. To him be glory for ever and ever. Amen.

Final Greetings

[19]Greet Priscilla[a] and Aquila and the household of Onesiphorus. [20]Erastus stayed in Corinth, and I left Trophimus sick in Miletus. [21]Do your best to get here before winter. Eubulus greets you, and so do Pudens, Linus, Claudia and all the brothers and sisters.[b]

[22]The Lord be with your spirit. Grace be with you all.

---

[a] 19 Greek *Prisca*, a variant of *Priscilla*   [b] 21 The Greek word for *brothers and sisters* (*adelphoi*) refers here to believers, both men and women, as part of God's family.

TITUS

THE EVIDENCE:

WHO WROTE IT?
This is just the same as for the letters to Timothy. Some experts say it was Paul, and others say it was another person, maybe one of his disciples whose name we don't know.

HOW LONG AGO?
Not much is known about when it was written. Some think it was around the year 65 after Christ, about the same time as the first letter to Timothy. What we can be sure about is that it was written before the second letter to Timothy, because it doesn't say that Paul was in jail in Rome.

WHAT'S IT ABOUT?
Titus was a man who began believing in Jesus when Paul talked to him about God's love. Then he became Paul's great helper as he preached the gospel, and he was put in charge of the church on the island of Crete. In this letter, Paul gives him pastoral advice so Titus will know how to choose helpers, how to be careful about false teachers and how good Christians should act.

THE BEST PART
We liked this verse in 2:11, because it's so very true: "The grace of God has appeared that offers salvation to all people." Yes, he definitely has shown us that! Jesus is the proof of how much God loves us.

---

1 Paul, a servant of God and an apostle of Jesus Christ to further the faith of God's elect and their knowledge of the truth that leads to godliness — ²in the hope of eternal life, which God, who does not lie, promised before the beginning of time, ³and which now at his appointed season he has brought to light through the preaching entrusted to me by the command of God our Savior,

⁴To Titus, my true son in our common faith:

Grace and peace from God the Father and Christ Jesus our Savior.

Appointing Elders Who Love What Is Good

⁵The reason I left you in Crete was that you might put in order what was left unfinished and appoint*a* elders in every town, as I directed you. ⁶An elder must be blameless, faithful to his wife, a man whose children believe*b* and are not open to the charge of being wild and disobedient. ⁷Since an overseer manages God's household, he must be blameless — not overbearing, not quick-tempered, not

---

a 5 Or ordain   *b* 6 Or children are trustworthy

given to drunkenness, not violent, not pursuing dishonest gain. [8]Rather, he must be hospitable, one who loves what is good, who is self-controlled, upright, holy and disciplined. [9]He must hold firmly to the trustworthy message as it has been taught, so that he can encourage others by sound doctrine and refute those who oppose it.

Rebuking Those Who Fail to Do Good

[10]For there are many rebellious people, full of meaningless talk and deception, especially those of the circumcision group. [11]They must be silenced, because

THE SCENE

CRETE

(TITUS 1:5)

Crete is a very large island in the Mediterranean Sea. It has extremely rocky soil. About 3,000 years before Christ, the Minoan civilization developed there. It was very important, and there are still many ruins of that civilization on the island to this day. In the year 140 before Christ, a very large Jewish colony settled there too.

THE WITNESSES

✓ TITUS (TITUS 1:4)

He was like a son to Paul, because he preached about Jesus. He was also Paul's good friend. Titus was Greek. Some think he was the brother of Luke, the person who wrote the gospel of Luke and the book of Acts, but we're not sure about that. Titus was the person who took Paul's second letter to the church in Corinth. Later, when Paul visited the island of Crete, he left Titus in charge of the church there.

they are disrupting whole households by teaching things they ought not to teach— and that for the sake of dishonest gain. [12]One of Crete's own prophets has said it: "Cretans are always liars, evil brutes, lazy gluttons."[a] [13]This saying is true. Therefore rebuke them sharply, so that they will be sound in the faith [14]and will pay no attention to Jewish myths or to the merely

[a] 12 From the Cretan philosopher Epimenides

human commands of those who reject the truth. ¹⁵To the pure, all things are pure, but to those who are corrupted and do not believe, nothing is pure. In fact, both their minds and consciences are corrupted. ¹⁶They claim to know God, but by their actions they deny him. They are detestable, disobedient and unfit for doing anything good.

Doing Good for the Sake of the Gospel

2 You, however, must teach what is appropriate to sound doctrine. ²Teach the older men to be temperate, worthy of respect, self-controlled, and sound in faith, in love and in endurance.

³Likewise, teach the older women to be reverent in the way they live, not to be slanderers or addicted to much wine, but to teach what is good. ⁴Then they can urge the younger women to love their hus-

NICOPOLIS

(TITUS 3:12)

In Greek, this word means "victorious city." Nicopolis was the capital of Epirus, in eastern Greece. Ruins of buildings from that time can still be seen there today.

CHECK THE FACTS

What church did Titus have to organize?

A) The church in Rome

B) The church in Crete

C) The church in Ephesus

bands and children, ⁵to be self-controlled and pure, to be busy at home, to be kind, and to be subject to their husbands, so that no one will malign the word of God.

⁶Similarly, encourage the young men to be self-controlled. ⁷In everything set them an example by doing what is good. In your teaching show integrity, seriousness ⁸and soundness of speech that cannot be condemned, so that those who oppose you may be ashamed because they have nothing bad to say about us.

⁹Teach slaves to be subject to their masters in everything, to try to please them, not to talk back to them, ¹⁰and not to steal from them, but to show that they can be fully trusted, so that in every way they will make the teaching about God our Savior attractive.

¹¹For the grace of God has appeared that offers salvation to all people. ¹²It teaches us to say "No" to ungodliness

and worldly passions, and to live self-controlled, upright and godly lives in this present age, [13]while we wait for the blessed hope—the appearing of the glory of our great God and Savior, Jesus Christ, [14]who gave himself for us to redeem us from all wickedness and to purify for himself a people that are his very own, eager to do what is good.

[15]These, then, are the things you should teach. Encourage and rebuke with all authority. Do not let anyone despise you.

Saved in Order to Do Good

3 Remind the people to be subject to rulers and authorities, to be obedient, to be ready to do whatever is good, [2]to slander no one, to be peaceable and considerate, and always to be gentle toward everyone.

[3]At one time we too were foolish, disobedient, deceived and enslaved by all kinds of passions and pleasures. We lived in malice and envy, being hated and hating one another. [4]But when the kindness and love of God our Savior appeared, [5]he saved us, not because of righteous things we had done, but because of his mercy. He saved us through the washing of rebirth and renewal by the Holy Spirit, [6]whom he poured out on us generously through Jesus Christ our Savior, [7]so that,

having been justified by his grace, we might become heirs having the hope of eternal life. [8]This is a trustworthy saying. And I want you to stress these things, so that those who have trusted in God may be careful to devote themselves to doing what is good. These things are excellent and profitable for everyone.

[9]But avoid foolish controversies and genealogies and arguments and quarrels about the law, because these are unprofitable and useless. [10]Warn a divisive person once, and then warn them a second time. After that, have nothing to do with them. [11]You may be sure that such people are warped and sinful; they are self-condemned.

Final Remarks

[12]As soon as I send Artemas or Tychicus to you, do your best to come to me at Nicopolis, because I have decided to winter there. [13]Do everything you can to help Zenas the lawyer and Apollos on their way and see that they have everything they need. [14]Our people must learn to devote themselves to doing what is good, in order to provide for urgent needs and not live unproductive lives.

[15]Everyone with me sends you greetings. Greet those who love us in the faith.

Grace be with you all.

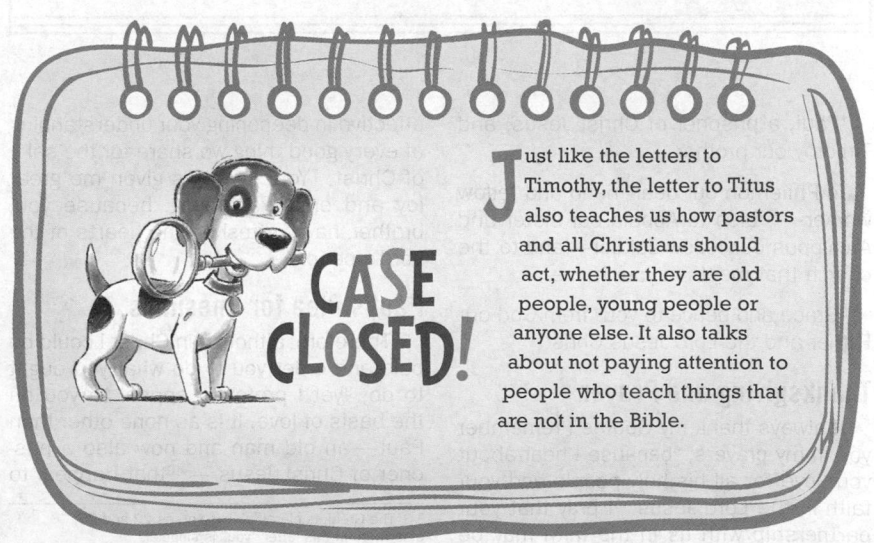

Just like the letters to Timothy, the letter to Titus also teaches us how pastors and all Christians should act, whether they are old people, young people or anyone else. It also talks about not paying attention to people who teach things that are not in the Bible.

CASE CLOSED!

PHILEMON

THE EVIDENCE:

WHO WROTE IT?
Paul wrote this letter. Nobody doubts that.

HOW LONG AGO?
Experts have several reasons for thinking that Paul wrote this letter about the same time he wrote the letter to the Colossians, which would be 50 to 63 years after Christ.

WHAT'S IT ABOUT?
This is a real letter, like the kind people used to write! Before telephones, the Internet and social networks existed, people wrote letters by hand and on paper. Here, Paul writes to Philemon about a personal matter. He talks about Philemon's slave named Onesimus. It just so happened that one day Onesimus escaped and went to Rome. Once in Rome, he met Paul. Since he was Philemon's slave, Onesimus must go back, because he could be punished if he didn't. So Paul wrote to Philemon to ask him to take Onesimus back with Christian love.

THE BEST PART
We liked this verse that's so full of love: "Grace and peace to you from God our Father and the Lord Jesus Christ" (1:3).

---

¹Paul, a prisoner of Christ Jesus, and Timothy our brother,

To Philemon our dear friend and fellow worker— ²also to Apphia our sister and Archippus our fellow soldier—and to the church that meets in your home:

³Grace and peace to you^a from God our Father and the Lord Jesus Christ.

Thanksgiving and Prayer

⁴I always thank my God as I remember you in my prayers, ⁵because I hear about your love for all his holy people and your faith in the Lord Jesus. ⁶I pray that your partnership with us in the faith may be effective in deepening your understanding of every good thing we share for the sake of Christ. ⁷Your love has given me great joy and encouragement, because you, brother, have refreshed the hearts of the Lord's people.

Paul's Plea for Onesimus

⁸Therefore, although in Christ I could be bold and order you to do what you ought to do, ⁹yet I prefer to appeal to you on the basis of love. It is as none other than Paul—an old man and now also a prisoner of Christ Jesus— ¹⁰that I appeal to

---

^a 3 The Greek is plural; also in verses 22 and 25; elsewhere in this letter "you" is singular.

you for my son Onesimus,[a] who became my son while I was in chains. [11]Formerly he was useless to you, but now he has become useful both to you and to me.

[12]I am sending him—who is my very heart—back to you. [13]I would have liked to keep him with me so that he could take your place in helping me while I am in chains for the gospel. [14]But I did not want to do anything without your consent, so that any favor you do would not seem forced but would be voluntary. [15]Perhaps the reason he was separated from you for a little while was that you might have him back forever— [16]no longer as a slave, but better than a slave, as a dear brother. He is very dear to me but even dearer to you, both as a fellow man and as a brother in the Lord.

[17]So if you consider me a partner, welcome him as you would welcome me. [18]If he has done you any wrong or owes you anything, charge it to me. [19]I, Paul, am writing this with my own hand. I will pay it back—not to mention that you owe me your very self. [20]I do wish, brother, that I may have some benefit from you in the Lord; refresh my heart in Christ. [21]Confident of your obedience, I write to you, knowing that you will do even more than I ask.

[22]And one thing more: Prepare a guest room for me, because I hope to be restored to you in answer to your prayers.

[23]Epaphras, my fellow prisoner in Christ Jesus, sends you greetings. [24]And so do Mark, Aristarchus, Demas and Luke, my fellow workers.

[25]The grace of the Lord Jesus Christ be with your spirit.

---

[a] 10 Onesimus means useful.

THE WITNESSES

✓ PHILEMON (PHILEMON 1:1)
This Greek name means "loving." We aren't sure if he was from Colossae or from Laodicea. He began to believe in Jesus Christ because Paul talked to him about Jesus. He held Christian meetings in his home, and he worked very hard for the church in his city.

✓ APPHIA AND ARCHIPPUS (PHILEMON 1:2)
About Apphia, we only know that she belonged to Philemon's house. Some experts think she was Philemon's wife. Archippus is a man's name. In Greek, it means "horse trainer." Some people think he was Philemon's son. The letter to the Colossians says he was a member of the churches of Colossae and Laodicea.

✓ ONESIMUS (PHILEMON 1:10)
He was Philemon's slave. His name means "useful." Onesimus had escaped and gone to Rome, where he met Paul and became a Christian. Paul sent him back to his owner with a letter so Philemon would receive him with love like a brother.

This letter teaches us about some of the customs in New Testament times, precisely about slavery. Paul didn't insist that Philemon free Onesimus, since the law prohibited that. If Paul had been openly against slavery, the Roman authorities would have considered Christianity a religion that went against society. However, Paul encouraged Philemon to love Onesimus like a brother in the faith, not like a slave. This is a clear demonstration that all of us who believe in Jesus are united by him, and it doesn't matter if we're rich or poor.

CASE CLOSED!

HEBREWS

THE EVIDENCE:

WHO WROTE IT?
Nobody knows who wrote Hebrews. A few people still think it was Paul, but now almost no one believes that. Over time, Bible experts have thought of different people in the Bible who could have been the author of Hebrews. For example, it could have been Luke, Barnabas, Apollos or Priscilla. The honest truth is that nobody really knows.

HOW LONG AGO?
This is another mystery! Since we don't know who wrote it, we can't know the date either. Because of a few things mentioned in the book, some experts say it had to have been written a little before the year 70 after Christ.

WHAT'S IT ABOUT?
This book is like a sermon we listen to in church, but then it ends just like the letters. Hebrews talks about several important things. It insists that we should be obedient to what God tells us. However, the most important topic is Jesus. The author knows the Old Testament very well, and in this sermon he says that Jesus is the great high priest. No other book in the New Testament says that!

THE BEST PART
We found a lot of nice verses in this book. We chose 13:6: "The Lord is my helper; I will not be afraid. What can mere mortals do to me?" I'm not afraid! God is with me!

God's Final Word: His Son

1 In the past God spoke to our ancestors through the prophets at many times and in various ways, ²but in these last days he has spoken to us by his Son, whom he appointed heir of all things, and through whom also he made the universe. ³The Son is the radiance of God's glory and the exact representation of his being, sustaining all things by his powerful word. After he had provided purification for sins, he sat down at the right hand of the Majesty in heaven. ⁴So he became as much superior to the angels as the name he has inherited is superior to theirs.

The Son Superior to Angels

⁵For to which of the angels did God ever say,

"You are my Son;
　　today I have become your Father"ᵃ?

ᵃ 5 Psalm 2:7

Or again,

"I will be his Father,
and he will be my Son"[a]?

6And again, when God brings his firstborn into the world, he says,

"Let all God's angels worship him."[b]

7In speaking of the angels he says,

"He makes his angels spirits,
and his servants flames of fire."[c]

8But about the Son he says,

"Your throne, O God, will last for ever
and ever;
a scepter of justice will be the
scepter of your kingdom.
9You have loved righteousness and
hated wickedness;
therefore God, your God, has set
you above your companions
by anointing you with the oil of joy."[d]

10He also says,

"In the beginning, Lord, you laid the
foundations of the earth,
and the heavens are the work of
your hands.
11They will perish, but you remain;
they will all wear out like a garment.
12You will roll them up like a robe;
like a garment they will be changed.
But you remain the same,
and your years will never end."[e]

13To which of the angels did God ever say,

"Sit at my right hand
until I make your enemies
a footstool for your feet"[f]?

14Are not all angels ministering spirits sent to serve those who will inherit salvation?

Warning to Pay Attention

2 We must pay the most careful attention, therefore, to what we have heard, so that we do not drift away. 2For since the message spoken through angels was binding, and every violation and disobedience received its just punishment, 3how shall we escape if we ignore so great a salvation? This salvation, which was first announced by the Lord, was confirmed to us by those who heard him. 4God also testified to it by signs, wonders and various miracles, and by gifts of the Holy Spirit distributed according to his will.

Jesus Made Fully Human

5It is not to angels that he has subjected the world to come, about which we are speaking. 6But there is a place where someone has testified:

"What is mankind that you are mindful
of them,
a son of man that you care for him?
7You made them a little[g] lower than the
angels;
you crowned them with glory and
honor
8   and put everything under their
feet."[h,i]

In putting everything under them,[j] God left nothing that is not subject to them.[j] Yet at present we do not see everything subject to them.[j] 9But we do see Jesus, who was made lower than the angels for a little while, now crowned with glory and honor because he suffered death, so that by the grace of God he might taste death for everyone.

10In bringing many sons and daughters to glory, it was fitting that God, for whom and through whom everything exists, should make the pioneer of their salvation perfect through what he suffered. 11Both the one who makes people holy and those who are made holy are of the same family. So Jesus is not ashamed to call them brothers and sisters.[k] 12He says,

"I will declare your name to my
brothers and sisters;
in the assembly I will sing your
praises."[l]

[a] 5 2 Samuel 7:14; 1 Chron. 17:13   [b] 6 Deut. 32:43
(see Dead Sea Scrolls and Septuagint)   [c] 7 Psalm 104:4
[d] 9 Psalm 45:6,7   [e] 12 Psalm 102:25-27
[f] 13 Psalm 110:1   [g] 7 Or them for a little while
[h] 6-8 Psalm 8:4-6   [i] 7,8 Or 7You made him a little lower
than the angels;/ you crowned him with glory and honor/
8and put everything under his feet."   [j] 8 Or him
[k] 11 The Greek word for brothers and sisters (adelphoi)
refers here to believers, both men and women, as part of
God's family; also in verse 12; and in 3:1, 12; 10:19;
13:22.   [l] 12 Psalm 22:22

¹³And again,

"I will put my trust in him."ᵃ

And again he says,

"Here am I, and the children God has
given me."ᵇ

¹⁴Since the children have flesh and
blood, he too shared in their humanity so
that by his death he might break the power of him who holds the power of death—
that is, the devil— ¹⁵and free those who
all their lives were held in slavery by their
fear of death. ¹⁶For surely it is not angels
he helps, but Abraham's descendants.
¹⁷For this reason he had to be made like
them,ᶜ fully human in every way, in order
that he might become a merciful and
faithful high priest in service to God, and
that he might make atonement for the
sins of the people. ¹⁸Because he himself
suffered when he was tempted, he is able
to help those who are being tempted.

Jesus Greater Than Moses

3 Therefore, holy brothers and sisters,
who share in the heavenly calling,
fix your thoughts on Jesus, whom we
acknowledge as our apostle and high
priest. ²He was faithful to the one who
appointed him, just as Moses was faithful in all God's house. ³Jesus has been
found worthy of greater honor than Moses, just as the builder of a house has
greater honor than the house itself. ⁴For
every house is built by someone, but God
is the builder of everything. ⁵"Moses was
faithful as a servant in all God's house,"ᵈ
bearing witness to what would be spoken
by God in the future. ⁶But Christ is faithful as the Son over God's house. And we
are his house, if indeed we hold firmly
to our confidence and the hope in which
we glory.

Warning Against Unbelief

⁷So, as the Holy Spirit says:

"Today, if you hear his voice,
⁸   do not harden your hearts
as you did in the rebellion,
during the time of testing in the
wilderness,

CHECK THE FACTS

**According to the author
of Hebrews, what should
we do if we hear the voice
of God today?**

A) Ask him to forgive our sins

B) Start praying right away

C) Do not harden our hearts

CORRECT ANSWER: C

⁹where your ancestors tested and
tried me,
though for forty years they saw what
I did.
¹⁰That is why I was angry with that
generation;
I said, 'Their hearts are always
going astray,
and they have not known my ways.'
¹¹So I declared on oath in my anger,
'They shall never enter my rest.' "ᵉ

¹²See to it, brothers and sisters, that
none of you has a sinful, unbelieving heart
that turns away from the living God. ¹³But
encourage one another daily, as long as it
is called "Today," so that none of you may
be hardened by sin's deceitfulness. ¹⁴We
have come to share in Christ, if indeed we

ᵃ 13 Isaiah 8:17   ᵇ 13 Isaiah 8:18   ᶜ 17 Or like his
brothers   ᵈ 5 Num. 12:7   ᵉ 11 Psalm 95:7-11

hold our original conviction firmly to the very end. [15]As has just been said:

"Today, if you hear his voice,
do not harden your hearts
as you did in the rebellion."[a]

[16]Who were they who heard and rebelled? Were they not all those Moses led out of Egypt? [17]And with whom was he angry for forty years? Was it not with those who sinned, whose bodies perished in the wilderness? [18]And to whom did God swear that they would never enter his rest if not to those who disobeyed? [19]So we see that they were not able to enter, because of their unbelief.

A Sabbath-Rest for the People of God

4 Therefore, since the promise of entering his rest still stands, let us be careful that none of you be found to have fallen short of it. [2]For we also have had the good news proclaimed to us, just as they did; but the message they heard was of no value to them, because they did not share the faith of those who obeyed.[b] [3]Now we who have believed enter that rest, just as God has said,

"So I declared on oath in my anger,
'They shall never enter my rest.' "[c]

And yet his works have been finished since the creation of the world. [4]For somewhere he has spoken about the seventh day in these words: "On the seventh day God rested from all his works."[d] [5]And again in the passage above he says, "They shall never enter my rest."

[6]Therefore since it still remains for some to enter that rest, and since those who formerly had the good news proclaimed to them did not go in because of their disobedience, [7]God again set a certain day, calling it "Today." This he did when a long time later he spoke through David, as in the passage already quoted:

"Today, if you hear his voice,
do not harden your hearts."[a]

[8]For if Joshua had given them rest, God would not have spoken later about another day. [9]There remains, then, a Sabbath-rest for the people of God; [10]for anyone who enters God's rest also rests from their works,[e] just as God did from his. [11]Let us, therefore, make every effort to enter that rest, so that no one will perish by following their example of disobedience.

[12]For the word of God is alive and active. Sharper than any double-edged sword, it penetrates even to dividing soul and spirit, joints and marrow; it judges the thoughts and attitudes of the heart. [13]Nothing in all creation is hidden from God's sight. Everything is uncovered and laid bare before the eyes of him to whom we must give account.

Jesus the Great High Priest

[14]Therefore, since we have a great high priest who has ascended into heaven,[f] Jesus the Son of God, let us hold firmly to the faith we profess. [15]For we do not have a high priest who is unable to empathize with our weaknesses, but we have one who has been tempted in every way, just as we are—yet he did not sin. [16]Let us then approach God's throne of grace with confidence, so that we may receive mercy and find grace to help us in our time of need.

5 Every high priest is selected from among the people and is appointed to represent the people in matters related to God, to offer gifts and sacrifices for sins. [2]He is able to deal gently with those who are ignorant and are going astray, since he himself is subject to weakness. [3]This is why he has to offer sacrifices for his own sins, as well as for the sins of the people. [4]And no one takes this honor on himself, but he receives it when called by God, just as Aaron was.

[5]In the same way, Christ did not take on himself the glory of becoming a high priest. But God said to him,

"You are my Son;
today I have become your Father."[g]

---

[a] 15,7 Psalm 95:7,8   [b] 2 Some manuscripts because those who heard did not combine it with faith
[c] 3 Psalm 95:11; also in verse 5   [d] 4 Gen. 2:2
[e] 10 Or labor   [f] 14 Greek has gone through the heavens
[g] 5 Psalm 2:7

Gifts and sacrifices

(HEBREWS 5:1)

In the old religion of the Israelite people, the priests had to present offerings and sacrifices (food and animals) on the altar of the temple in Jerusalem. This was so God would forgive the sins of all the people or the sins of just one person. However, those offerings and sacrifices were good for only a short time. They had to repeat them often. The author of Hebrews teaches us that when Jesus died on the cross, he offered himself as a sacrifice to God for our sins only once, and it lasts forever.

⁶And he says in another place,

"You are a priest forever,
in the order of Melchizedek." ᵃ

⁷During the days of Jesus' life on earth, he offered up prayers and petitions with fervent cries and tears to the one who could save him from death, and he was heard because of his reverent submission. ⁸Son though he was, he learned obedience from what he suffered ⁹and, once made perfect, he became the source of eternal salvation for all who obey him ¹⁰and was designated by God to be high priest in the order of Melchizedek.

Warning Against Falling Away

¹¹We have much to say about this, but it is hard to make it clear to you because you no longer try to understand. ¹²In fact, though by this time you ought to be teachers, you need someone to teach you the elementary truths of God's word all over again. You need milk, not solid food! ¹³Anyone who lives on milk, being still an infant, is not acquainted with the teaching about righteousness. ¹⁴But solid food is for the mature, who by constant use have trained themselves to distinguish good from evil.

6 Therefore let us move beyond the elementary teachings about Christ and be taken forward to maturity, not laying again the foundation of repentance from acts that lead to death,ᵇ and of faith in God, ²instruction about cleansing rites,ᶜ the laying on of hands, the resurrection of the dead, and eternal judgment. ³And God permitting, we will do so.

⁴It is impossible for those who have once been enlightened, who have tasted the heavenly gift, who have shared in the Holy Spirit, ⁵who have tasted the goodness of the word of God and the powers of the coming age ⁶and who have fallenᵈ away, to be brought back to repentance. To their loss they are crucifying the Son of God all over again and subjecting him to public disgrace. ⁷Land that drinks in the rain often falling on it and that produces a crop useful to those for whom it is farmed receives the blessing of God. ⁸But land that produces thorns and thistles is worthless and is in danger of being cursed. In the end it will be burned.

⁹Even though we speak like this, dear friends, we are convinced of better things in your case—the things that have to do with salvation. ¹⁰God is not unjust; he will not forget your work and the love you have shown him as you have helped his people and continue to help them. ¹¹We want each of you to show this same diligence to the very end, so that what you hope for may be fully realized. ¹²We do not want you to become lazy, but to

ᵃ 6 Psalm 110:4   ᵇ 1 Or from useless rituals   ᶜ 2 Or about baptisms   ᵈ 6 Or age, ⁶if they fall imitate those who through faith and patience inherit what has been promised.

The Certainty of God's Promise

¹³When God made his promise to Abraham, since there was no one greater for him to swear by, he swore by himself, ¹⁴saying, "I will surely bless you and give you many descendants."[a] ¹⁵And so after waiting patiently, Abraham received what was promised.

¹⁶People swear by someone greater than themselves, and the oath confirms what is said and puts an end to all argument. ¹⁷Because God wanted to make the unchanging nature of his purpose very clear to the heirs of what was promised, he confirmed it with an oath. ¹⁸God did this so that, by two unchangeable things in which it is impossible for God to lie, we who have fled to take hold of the hope set before us may be greatly encouraged. ¹⁹We have this hope as an anchor for the soul, firm and secure. It enters the inner sanctuary behind the curtain, ²⁰where our forerunner, Jesus, has entered on our behalf. He has become a high priest forever, in the order of Melchizedek.

Melchizedek the Priest

7 This Melchizedek was king of Salem and priest of God Most High. He met Abraham returning from the defeat of the kings and blessed him, ²and Abraham gave him a tenth of everything. First, the name Melchizedek means "king of righteousness"; then also, "king of Salem" means "king of peace." ³Without father or mother, without genealogy, without beginning of days or end of life, resembling the Son of God, he remains a priest forever.

⁴Just think how great he was: Even the patriarch Abraham gave him a tenth of the plunder! ⁵Now the law requires the descendants of Levi who become priests to collect a tenth from the people—that is, from their fellow Israelites—even though they also are descended from Abraham. ⁶This man, however, did not trace his descent from Levi, yet he collected a tenth from Abraham and blessed

THE
WITNESSES

✓ **ABRAHAM** (HEBREWS 6:13–15; 7:1–10; 11:8–19)

This name means "father of a multitude" in Hebrew. This man lived in Mesopotamia. God chose to make an agreement with him. As a result of this agreement (or covenant), we have all been blessed. How wonderful!

✓ **AARON** (HEBREWS 7:11)

He was Moses' brother. Together, they rescued the people of Israel from slavery and took them out of Egypt. Aaron was the first high priest in Israel. He was from the tribe of Levi.

him who had the promises. ⁷And without doubt the lesser is blessed by the greater. ⁸In the one case, the tenth is collected by people who die; but in the other case, by him who is declared to be living. ⁹One might even say that Levi, who collects the tenth, paid the tenth through Abraham,

[a] *14* Gen. 22:17

[10]because when Melchizedek met Abraham, Levi was still in the body of his ancestor.

Jesus Like Melchizedek

[11]If perfection could have been attained through the Levitical priesthood—and indeed the law given to the people established that priesthood—why was there still need for another priest to come, one in the order of Melchizedek, not in the order of Aaron? [12]For when the priesthood is changed, the law must be changed also. [13]He of whom these

BREAKTHROUGH!

Is Melchizedek still alive?

(HEBREWS 7:8)

That's a really odd name! It means "king of righteousness." The verse doesn't mean that he's still alive. It's just that the Bible never says when he died. Well, the fact is that the Bible really doesn't say very much about him at all. He just appeared and then suddenly disappeared! We only know that he was a priest and the king of Salem, a word that means "peace." We know that he met up with Abraham and blessed him, and that he received the tenth part of what Abraham had earned. You can read about that in Genesis 14:18–20.

things are said belonged to a different tribe, and no one from that tribe has ever served at the altar. [14]For it is clear that our Lord descended from Judah, and in regard to that tribe Moses said nothing about priests. [15]And what we have said is even more clear if another priest like Melchizedek appears, [16]one who has become a priest not on the basis of a regulation as to his ancestry but on the basis of the power of an indestructible life. [17]For it is declared:

> "You are a priest forever,
>   in the order of Melchizedek."[a]

[18]The former regulation is set aside because it was weak and useless [19](for the law made nothing perfect), and a better hope is introduced, by which we draw near to God.

[20]And it was not without an oath! Others became priests without any oath, [21]but he became a priest with an oath when God said to him:

> "The Lord has sworn
>   and will not change his mind:
>   'You are a priest forever.' "[a]

[22]Because of this oath, Jesus has become the guarantor of a better covenant.

[23]Now there have been many of those priests, since death prevented them from continuing in office; [24]but because Jesus lives forever, he has a permanent priesthood. [25]Therefore he is able to save completely[b] those who come to God through him, because he always lives to intercede for them.

[26]Such a high priest truly meets our need—one who is holy, blameless, pure, set apart from sinners, exalted above the heavens. [27]Unlike the other high priests, he does not need to offer sacrifices day after day, first for his own sins, and then for the sins of the people. He sacrificed for their sins once for all when he offered himself. [28]For the law appoints as high priests men in all their weakness; but the oath, which came after the law, appointed the Son, who has been made perfect forever.

---

[a] 17,21 Psalm 110:4   [b] 25 Or *forever*

The High Priest of a New Covenant

8 Now the main point of what we are saying is this: We do have such a high priest, who sat down at the right hand of the throne of the Majesty in heaven, ²and who serves in the sanctuary, the true tabernacle set up by the Lord, not by a mere human being.

³Every high priest is appointed to offer both gifts and sacrifices, and so it was necessary for this one also to have something to offer. ⁴If he were on earth, he would not be a priest, for there are already priests who offer the gifts prescribed by the law. ⁵They serve at a sanctuary that is a copy and shadow of what is in heaven. This is why Moses was warned when he was about to build the tabernacle: "See to it that you make everything according to the pattern shown you on the mountain."ᵃ ⁶But in fact the ministry Jesus has received is as superior to theirs as the covenant of which he is mediator is superior to the old one, since the new covenant is established on better promises.

⁷For if there had been nothing wrong with that first covenant, no place would have been sought for another. ⁸But God found fault with the people and saidᵇ:

"The days are coming, declares the Lord,
    when I will make a new covenant
with the people of Israel
    and with the people of Judah.
⁹It will not be like the covenant
    I made with their ancestors
when I took them by the hand
    to lead them out of Egypt,
because they did not remain faithful to
        my covenant,
    and I turned away from them,
                declares the Lord.
¹⁰This is the covenant I will establish
        with the people of Israel
    after that time, declares the Lord.
I will put my laws in their minds
    and write them on their hearts.
I will be their God,
    and they will be my people.
¹¹No longer will they teach their
            neighbor,
    or say to one another, 'Know the
            Lord,'
because they will all know me,
    from the least of them to the
            greatest.
¹²For I will forgive their wickedness
    and will remember their sins no
            more."ᶜ

¹³By calling this covenant "new," he has made the first one obsolete; and what is obsolete and outdated will soon disappear.

Worship in the Earthly Tabernacle

9 Now the first covenant had regulations for worship and also an earthly sanctuary. ²A tabernacle was set up. In its first room were the lampstand and the table

BREAKTHROUGH!

Sanctuary

(HEBREWS 8:2)

It was like a tent. It was a portable temple the Israelites used all the time they were traveling through the desert after they left Egypt up until Solomon built the temple building. This sanctuary could be taken down and set up again. They could carry it around from one place to another.

ᵃ 5 Exodus 25:40   ᵇ 8 Some manuscripts may be translated *fault and said to the people.*   ᶜ 12 Jer. 31:31-34 with its consecrated bread; this was called the Holy Place. ³Behind the second curtain was a room called the Most Holy Place, ⁴which had the golden altar of incense and the gold-covered ark of the covenant. This ark contained the gold jar of manna, Aaron's staff that had budded, and the stone tablets of the covenant. ⁵Above the ark were the cherubim of the Glory, overshadowing the atonement cover. But we cannot discuss these things in detail now.

⁶When everything had been arranged like this, the priests entered regularly into the outer room to carry on their ministry. ⁷But only the high priest entered the inner room, and that only once a year, and never without blood, which he offered for himself and for the sins the people had committed in ignorance. ⁸The Holy Spirit was showing by this that the way into the Most Holy Place had not yet been disclosed as long as the first tabernacle was still functioning. ⁹This is an illustration for the present time, indicating that the gifts and sacrifices being offered were not able to clear the conscience of the worshiper. ¹⁰They are only a matter of food and drink and various ceremonial washings — external regulations applying until the time of the new order.

The Blood of Christ

¹¹But when Christ came as high priest of the good things that are now already here,ᵃ he went through the greater and more perfect tabernacle that is not made with human hands, that is to say, is not a part of this creation. ¹²He did not enter by means of the blood of goats and calves; but he entered the Most Holy Place once for all by his own blood, thus obtainingᵇ eternal redemption. ¹³The blood of goats and bulls and the ashes of a heifer sprinkled on those who are ceremonially unclean sanctify them so that they are outwardly clean. ¹⁴How much more, then, will the blood of Christ, who through the eternal Spirit offered himself unblemished to God, cleanse our consciences from acts that lead to death,ᶜ so that we may serve the living God!

¹⁵For this reason Christ is the mediator of a new covenant, that those who are

BREAKTHROUGH!

Ceremonial washings
(HEBREWS 9:10)

The Jews performed many formal washings. They had to wash their hands and arms very well, and they also had to wash things they brought into their homes from outside. If those things weren't very clean, then they were considered dirty or impure, and they couldn't be used to worship God.

called may receive the promised eternal inheritance — now that he has died as a ransom to set them free from the sins committed under the first covenant.

¹⁶In the case of a will,ᵈ it is necessary to prove the death of the one who made it, ¹⁷because a will is in force only when somebody has died; it never takes effect while the one who made it is living. ¹⁸This is why even the first covenant was not put into effect without blood. ¹⁹When Moses had proclaimed every command of the law to all the people, he took the blood of calves, together with water, scarlet wool and branches of hyssop, and sprinkled the scroll and all the people. ²⁰He said, "This is the blood of the covenant, which God has commanded you to keep."ᵉ ²¹In

---

ᵃ 11 Some early manuscripts *are to come*   ᵇ 12 Or *blood, having obtained*   ᶜ 14 Or *from useless rituals*
ᵈ 16 Same Greek word as *covenant*; also in verse 17
ᵉ 20 Exodus 24:8

the same way, he sprinkled with the blood both the tabernacle and everything used in its ceremonies. 22In fact, the law requires that nearly everything be cleansed with blood, and without the shedding of blood there is no forgiveness.

23It was necessary, then, for the copies of the heavenly things to be purified with these sacrifices, but the heavenly things themselves with better sacrifices than these. 24For Christ did not enter a sanctuary made with human hands that was only a copy of the true one; he entered heaven itself, now to appear for us in God's presence. 25Nor did he enter heaven to offer himself again and again, the way the high priest enters the Most Holy Place every year with blood that is not his own. 26Otherwise Christ would have had to suffer many times since the creation of the world. But he has appeared once for all at the culmination of the ages to do away with sin by the sacrifice of himself. 27Just as people are destined to die once, and after that to face judgment, 28so Christ was sacrificed once to take away the sins of many; and he will appear a second time, not to bear sin, but to bring salvation to those who are waiting for him.

Christ's Sacrifice Once for All

10 The law is only a shadow of the good things that are coming—not the realities themselves. For this reason it can never, by the same sacrifices repeated endlessly year after year, make perfect those who draw near to worship. 2Otherwise, would they not have stopped being offered? For the worshipers would have been cleansed once for all, and would no longer have felt guilty for their sins. 3But those sacrifices are an annual reminder of sins. 4It is impossible for the blood of bulls and goats to take away sins.

5Therefore, when Christ came into the world, he said:

"Sacrifice and offering you did not
    desire,
    but a body you prepared for me;
6with burnt offerings and sin offerings
    you were not pleased.

7Then I said, 'Here I am—it is written
    about me in the scroll—
    I have come to do your will, my
    God.' "a

8First he said, "Sacrifices and offerings, burnt offerings and sin offerings you did not desire, nor were you pleased with them"—though they were offered in accordance with the law. 9Then he said, "Here I am, I have come to do your will." He sets aside the first to establish the second. 10And by that will, we have been made holy through the sacrifice of the body of Jesus Christ once for all.

11Day after day every priest stands and performs his religious duties; again and again he offers the same sacrifices, which can never take away sins. 12But when this priest had offered for all time one sacrifice for sins, he sat down at the right hand of God, 13and since that time he waits for his enemies to be made his footstool. 14For by one sacrifice he has made perfect forever those who are being made holy.

15The Holy Spirit also testifies to us about this. First he says:

16 "This is the covenant I will make with
    them
    after that time, says the Lord.
I will put my laws in their hearts,
    and I will write them on their
    minds."b

17Then he adds:

"Their sins and lawless acts
    I will remember no more."c

18And where these have been forgiven, sacrifice for sin is no longer necessary.

A Call to Persevere in Faith

19Therefore, brothers and sisters, since we have confidence to enter the Most Holy Place by the blood of Jesus, 20by a new and living way opened for us through the curtain, that is, his body, 21and since we have a great priest over the house of God, 22let us draw near to God with a sincere heart and with the full assurance that

---

a 7 Psalm 40:6-8 (see Septuagint)   b 16 Jer. 31:33
c 17 Jer. 31:34

faith brings, having our hearts sprinkled to cleanse us from a guilty conscience and having our bodies washed with pure water. ²³Let us hold unswervingly to the hope we profess, for he who promised is faithful. ²⁴And let us consider how we may spur one another on toward love and good deeds, ²⁵not giving up meeting together, as some are in the habit of doing, but encouraging one another—and all the more as you see the Day approaching.

²⁶If we deliberately keep on sinning after we have received the knowledge of the truth, no sacrifice for sins is left, ²⁷but only a fearful expectation of judgment and of raging fire that will consume the enemies of God. ²⁸Anyone who rejected the law of Moses died without mercy on the testimony of two or three witnesses. ²⁹How much more severely do you think someone deserves to be punished who has trampled the Son of God underfoot, who has treated as an unholy thing the blood of the covenant that sanctified them, and who has insulted the Spirit of grace? ³⁰For we know him who said, "It is mine to avenge; I will repay,"ᵃ and again, "The Lord will judge his people."ᵇ ³¹It is a dreadful thing to fall into the hands of the living God.

³²Remember those earlier days after you had received the light, when you endured in a great conflict full of suffering. ³³Sometimes you were publicly exposed to insult and persecution; at other times you stood side by side with those who were so treated. ³⁴You suffered along with those in prison and joyfully accepted the confiscation of your property, because you knew that you yourselves had better and lasting possessions. ³⁵So do not throw away your confidence; it will be richly rewarded.

³⁶You need to persevere so that when you have done the will of God, you will receive what he has promised. ³⁷For,

"In just a little while,
    he who is coming will come
    and will not delay."ᶜ

³⁸And,

"But my righteousᵈ one will live by
    faith.

And I take no pleasure
    in the one who shrinks back."ᵉ

³⁹But we do not belong to those who shrink back and are destroyed, but to those who have faith and are saved.

Faith in Action

11 Now faith is confidence in what we hope for and assurance about what we do not see. ²This is what the ancients were commended for.

³By faith we understand that the universe was formed at God's command, so that what is seen was not made out of what was visible.

⁴By faith Abel brought God a better offering than Cain did. By faith he was commended as righteous, when God spoke well of his offerings. And by faith Abel still speaks, even though he is dead. ⁵By faith Enoch was taken from this life, so that he did not experience death: "He could not be found, because God had taken him away."ᶠ For before he was taken, he was commended as one who pleased God. ⁶And without faith it is impossible to please God, because anyone who comes to him must believe that he exists and that he rewards those who earnestly seek him.

⁷By faith Noah, when warned about things not yet seen, in holy fear built an ark to save his family. By his faith he condemned the world and became heir of the righteousness that is in keeping with faith.

⁸By faith Abraham, when called to go to a place he would later receive as his inheritance, obeyed and went, even though he did not know where he was going. ⁹By faith he made his home in the promised land like a stranger in a foreign country; he lived in tents, as did Isaac and Jacob, who were heirs with him of the same promise. ¹⁰For he was looking forward to the city with foundations, whose architect and builder is God. ¹¹And by faith even Sarah, who was past childbearing age, was enabled to bear children because

---

ᵃ *30* Deut. 32:35   ᵇ *30* Deut. 32:36; Psalm 135:14
ᶜ *37* Isaiah 26:20; Hab. 2:3   ᵈ *38* Some early manuscripts *But the righteous*   ᵉ *38* Hab. 2:4 (see Septuagint)   ᶠ *5* Gen. 5:24

THE
WITNESSES

✓ ABEL AND CAIN (HEBREWS 11:4)

They were Adam and Eve's sons. One day, they presented their offerings to God. Cain was jealous of Abel, because God liked Abel's offering but he didn't like Cain's. Cain got very angry—so angry that he killed Abel. How terrible! That was the first murder in history.

she[a] considered him faithful who had made the promise. ¹²And so from this one man, and he as good as dead, came descendants as numerous as the stars in the sky and as countless as the sand on the seashore.

¹³All these people were still living by faith when they died. They did not receive the things promised; they only saw them and welcomed them from a distance, admitting that they were foreigners and strangers on earth. ¹⁴People who say such things show that they are looking for a country of their own. ¹⁵If they had been

thinking of the country they had left, they would have had opportunity to return. ¹⁶Instead, they were longing for a better country—a heavenly one. Therefore God is not ashamed to be called their God, for he has prepared a city for them.

¹⁷By faith Abraham, when God tested him, offered Isaac as a sacrifice. He who had embraced the promises was about to sacrifice his one and only son, ¹⁸even though God had said to him, "It is through Isaac that your offspring will be reckoned."[b] ¹⁹Abraham reasoned that God could even raise the dead, and so in a manner of speaking he did receive Isaac back from death.

²⁰By faith Isaac blessed Jacob and Esau in regard to their future.

²¹By faith Jacob, when he was dying, blessed each of Joseph's sons, and worshiped as he leaned on the top of his staff.

²²By faith Joseph, when his end was near, spoke about the exodus of the Israelites from Egypt and gave instructions concerning the burial of his bones.

²³By faith Moses' parents hid him for three months after he was born, because they saw he was no ordinary child, and they were not afraid of the king's edict.

²⁴By faith Moses, when he had grown up, refused to be known as the son of Pharaoh's daughter. ²⁵He chose to be mistreated along with the people of God rather than to enjoy the fleeting pleasures of sin. ²⁶He regarded disgrace for the sake of Christ as of greater value than the treasures of Egypt, because he was looking ahead to his reward. ²⁷By faith he left Egypt, not fearing the king's anger; he persevered because he saw him who is invisible. ²⁸By faith he kept the Passover and the application of blood, so that the destroyer of the firstborn would not touch the firstborn of Israel.

²⁹By faith the people passed through the Red Sea as on dry land; but when the Egyptians tried to do so, they were drowned.

³⁰By faith the walls of Jericho fell, after

---

a 11 Or *By faith Abraham, even though he was too old to have children—and Sarah herself was not able to conceive—was enabled to become a father because he* *b* 18 Gen. 21:12

the army had marched around them for seven days. [31]By faith the prostitute Rahab, because she welcomed the spies, was not killed with those who were disobedient.[a]

[32]And what more shall I say? I do not have time to tell about Gideon, Barak, Samson and Jephthah, about David and Samuel and the prophets, [33]who through faith conquered kingdoms, administered justice, and gained what was promised; who shut the mouths of lions, [34]quenched the fury of the flames, and escaped the edge of the sword; whose weakness was turned to strength; and who became powerful in battle and routed foreign armies. [35]Women received back their dead, raised to life again. There were others who were tortured, refusing to be released so that they might gain an even better resurrection. [36]Some faced jeers and flogging, and even chains and imprisonment. [37]They were put to death by stoning;[b] they were sawed in two; they were killed by the sword. They went about in sheepskins and goatskins, destitute, persecuted and mistreated— [38]the world was not worthy of them. They wandered in deserts and mountains, living in caves and in holes in the ground.

[39]These were all commended for their faith, yet none of them received what had been promised, [40]since God had planned something better for us so that only together with us would they be made perfect.

12 Therefore, since we are surrounded by such a great cloud of witnesses, let us throw off everything that hinders and the sin that so easily entangles. And let us run with perseverance the race marked out for us, [2]fixing our eyes on Jesus, the pioneer and perfecter of faith. For the joy set before him he endured the cross, scorning its shame, and sat down at the right hand of the throne of God. [3]Consider him who endured such opposition from sinners, so that you will not grow weary and lose heart.

God Disciplines His Children

[4]In your struggle against sin, you have not yet resisted to the point of shedding your blood. [5]And have you completely forgotten this word of encouragement that addresses you as a father addresses his son? It says,

"My son, do not make light of the
Lord's discipline,
and do not lose heart when he
rebukes you,
[6]because the Lord disciplines the one
he loves,
and he chastens everyone he
accepts as his son."[c]

[7]Endure hardship as discipline; God is treating you as his children. For what children are not disciplined by their father? [8]If you are not disciplined—and everyone undergoes discipline—then you are not legitimate, not true sons and daughters at all. [9]Moreover, we have all had human fathers who disciplined us and we respected them for it. How much more should we submit to the Father of spirits and live! [10]They disciplined us for a little while as they thought best; but God disciplines us for our good, in order that we may share in his holiness. [11]No discipline seems pleasant at the time, but painful. Later on, however, it produces a harvest of righteousness and peace for those who have been trained by it.

[12]Therefore, strengthen your feeble arms and weak knees. [13]"Make level paths for your feet,"[d] so that the lame may not be disabled, but rather healed.

Warning and Encouragement

[14]Make every effort to live in peace with everyone and to be holy; without holiness no one will see the Lord. [15]See to it that no one falls short of the grace of God and that no bitter root grows up to cause trouble and defile many. [16]See that no one is sexually immoral, or is godless like Esau, who for a single meal sold his inheritance rights as the oldest son. [17]Afterward, as you know, when he wanted to inherit this blessing, he was rejected. Even though he sought the blessing with tears, he could not change what he had done.

---

[a] 31 Or unbelieving   [b] 37 Some early manuscripts stoning; they were put to the test;   [c] 5,6 Prov. 3:11,12 (see Septuagint)   [d] 13 Prov. 4:26

The Mountain of Fear and the Mountain of Joy

¹⁸You have not come to a mountain that can be touched and that is burning with fire; to darkness, gloom and storm; ¹⁹to a trumpet blast or to such a voice speaking words that those who heard it begged that no further word be spoken to them, ²⁰because they could not bear what was commanded: "If even an animal touches the mountain, it must be stoned to death."ᵃ ²¹The sight was so terrifying that Moses said, "I am trembling with fear."ᵇ

²²But you have come to Mount Zion, to the city of the living God, the heavenly Jerusalem. You have come to thousands upon thousands of angels in joyful assembly, ²³to the church of the firstborn, whose names are written in heaven. You have come to God, the Judge of all, to the spirits of the righteous made perfect, ²⁴to Jesus the mediator of a new covenant, and to the sprinkled blood that speaks a better word than the blood of Abel.

²⁵See to it that you do not refuse him who speaks. If they did not escape when they refused him who warned them on earth, how much less will we, if we turn away from him who warns us from heaven? ²⁶At that time his voice shook the earth, but now he has promised, "Once more I will shake not only the earth but also the heavens."ᶜ ²⁷The words "once more" indicate the removing of what can be shaken—that is, created things—so that what cannot be shaken may remain.

²⁸Therefore, since we are receiving a kingdom that cannot be shaken, let us be thankful, and so worship God acceptably with reverence and awe, ²⁹for our "God is a consuming fire."ᵈ

Concluding Exhortations

13 Keep on loving one another as brothers and sisters. ²Do not forget to show hospitality to strangers, for by so doing some people have shown hospitality to angels without knowing it. ³Continue to remember those in prison as if you were together with them in prison, and those who are mistreated as if you yourselves were suffering.

⁴Marriage should be honored by all, and the marriage bed kept pure, for God will judge the adulterer and all the sexually immoral. ⁵Keep your lives free from the love of money and be content with what you have, because God has said,

"Never will I leave you;
    never will I forsake you."ᵉ

⁶So we say with confidence,

"The Lord is my helper; I will not
    be afraid.
What can mere mortals do
    to me?"ᶠ

ᵃ 20 Exodus 19:12,13   ᵇ 21 See Deut. 9:19.
ᶜ 26 Haggai 2:6   ᵈ 29 Deut. 4:24   ᵉ 5 Deut. 31:6
ᶠ 6 Psalm 118:6,7

What? Angels look like people?

(HEBREWS 13:2)

Well, it seems that sometimes they took on the form of people. But at the beginning of this same book, it says that angels are spirits (1:7). That means they are spiritual beings that don't have a body like ours. The word *angel* comes from Greek and means "messenger." They are beings created by God. This verse is saying that the people had received messengers but didn't know that God had sent them.

⁷Remember your leaders, who spoke the word of God to you. Consider the outcome of their way of life and imitate their faith. ⁸Jesus Christ is the same yesterday and today and forever.

⁹Do not be carried away by all kinds of strange teachings. It is good for our hearts to be strengthened by grace, not by eating ceremonial foods, which is of no benefit to those who do so. ¹⁰We have an altar from which those who minister at the tabernacle have no right to eat.

¹¹The high priest carries the blood of animals into the Most Holy Place as a sin offering, but the bodies are burned outside the camp. ¹²And so Jesus also suffered outside the city gate to make the people holy through his own blood. ¹³Let us, then, go to him outside the camp, bearing the disgrace he bore.

¹⁴For here we do not have an enduring city, but we are looking for the city that is to come.

¹⁵Through Jesus, therefore, let us continually offer to God a sacrifice of praise—the fruit of lips that openly profess his name. ¹⁶And do not forget to do good and to share with others, for with such sacrifices God is pleased.

¹⁷Have confidence in your leaders and submit to their authority, because they keep watch over you as those who must give an account. Do this so that their work will be a joy, not a burden, for that would be of no benefit to you.

¹⁸Pray for us. We are sure that we have a clear conscience and desire to live honorably in every way. ¹⁹I particularly urge you to pray so that I may be restored to you soon.

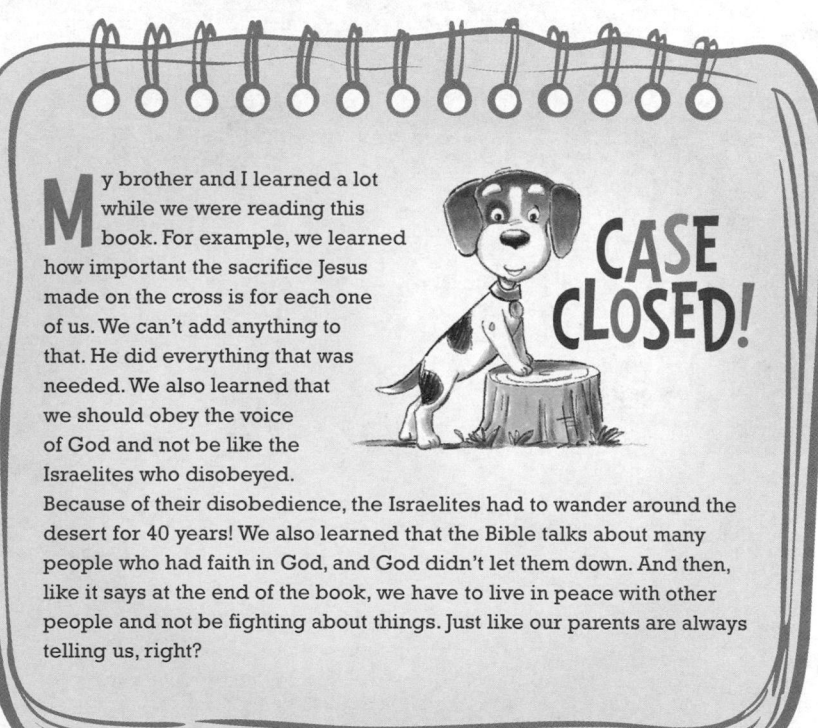

My brother and I learned a lot while we were reading this book. For example, we learned how important the sacrifice Jesus made on the cross is for each one of us. We can't add anything to that. He did everything that was needed. We also learned that we should obey the voice of God and not be like the Israelites who disobeyed. Because of their disobedience, the Israelites had to wander around the desert for 40 years! We also learned that the Bible talks about many people who had faith in God, and God didn't let them down. And then, like it says at the end of the book, we have to live in peace with other people and not be fighting about things. Just like our parents are always telling us, right?

Benediction and Final Greetings

20 Now may the God of peace, who through the blood of the eternal covenant brought back from the dead our Lord Jesus, that great Shepherd of the sheep, 21 equip you with everything good for doing his will, and may he work in us what is pleasing to him, through Jesus Christ, to whom be glory for ever and ever. Amen.

22 Brothers and sisters, I urge you to bear with my word of exhortation, for in fact I have written to you quite briefly. 23 I want you to know that our brother Timothy has been released. If he arrives soon, I will come with him to see you. 24 Greet all your leaders and all the Lord's people. Those from Italy send you their greetings.

25 Grace be with you all.

JAMES

THE EVIDENCE:

WHO WROTE IT?
This letter was probably written by James, Jesus' brother. Some people think that a disciple of James wrote it and used his teacher's name in order to teach what James thought. That way the letter would seem more official.

HOW LONG AGO?
If James, the brother of Jesus, really wrote this letter, then it was written between the years 57 and 66 after Christ. On the other hand, if one of his disciples wrote it, then it would have been later, probably between 70 and 100 years after Christ.

WHAT'S IT ABOUT?
The author of this letter writes "to the twelve tribes scattered among the nations" (1:1). He considers that the new people of Israel are the Christian church. He insists that a Christian shouldn't make differences between rich people and poor people, and they should obey the commandment to "love your neighbor as yourself" (2:8). He also says to be careful with one's tongue. We can cause a lot of problems when we gossip and hurt other people with what we say.

THE BEST PART
The part of this letter that we liked best is where it says, "Who is wise and understanding among you? Let them show it by their good life, by deeds done in the humility that comes from wisdom" (3:13). We know some people who think they know it all, but really they're just showing off. We should always be humble.

1 James, a servant of God and of the Lord Jesus Christ,

To the twelve tribes scattered among the nations:

Greetings.

Trials and Temptations

²Consider it pure joy, my brothers and sisters,ᵃ whenever you face trials of many kinds, ³because you know that the testing of your faith produces perseverance. ⁴Let perseverance finish its work so that you may be mature and complete, not lacking anything. ⁵If any of you lacks wisdom, you should ask God, who gives generously to all without finding fault, and it will be given to you. ⁶But when you ask, you

---

ᵃ 2 The Greek word for *brothers and sisters* (*adelphoi*) refers here to believers, both men and women, as part of God's family; also in verses 16 and 19; and in 2:1, 5, 14; 3:10, 12; 4:11; 5:7, 9, 10, 12, 19.

must believe and not doubt, because the one who doubts is like a wave of the sea, blown and tossed by the wind. [7]That person should not expect to receive anything from the Lord. [8]Such a person is double-minded and unstable in all they do.

[9]Believers in humble circumstances ought to take pride in their high position. [10]But the rich should take pride in their humiliation—since they will pass away like a wild flower. [11]For the sun rises with scorching heat and withers the plant; its blossom falls and its beauty is destroyed. In the same way, the rich will fade away even while they go about their business.

[12]Blessed is the one who perseveres under trial because, having stood the test, that person will receive the crown of life that the Lord has promised to those who love him.

[13]When tempted, no one should say, "God is tempting me." For God cannot be tempted by evil, nor does he tempt anyone; [14]but each person is tempted when they are dragged away by their own evil desire and enticed. [15]Then, after desire has conceived, it gives birth to sin; and sin, when it is full-grown, gives birth to death.

[16]Don't be deceived, my dear brothers and sisters. [17]Every good and perfect gift is from above, coming down from the Father of the heavenly lights, who does not change like shifting shadows. [18]He chose to give us birth through the word of truth, that we might be a kind of firstfruits of all he created.

Listening and Doing

[19]My dear brothers and sisters, take note of this: Everyone should be quick to listen, slow to speak and slow to become angry, [20]because human anger does not produce the righteousness that God desires. [21]Therefore, get rid of all moral filth and the evil that is so prevalent and humbly accept the word planted in you, which can save you.

[22]Do not merely listen to the word, and so deceive yourselves. Do what it says. [23]Anyone who listens to the word but does not do what it says is like someone who looks at his face in a mirror [24]and, after

THE
WITNESSES

✓ **JAMES** (JAMES 1:1)
This name comes from the Hebrew name Jacob. It got changed to James in English. The Bible says that Jesus had several brothers. One of them was James. He became a leader in the church in Jerusalem.

looking at himself, goes away and immediately forgets what he looks like. [25]But whoever looks intently into the perfect law that gives freedom, and continues in it—not forgetting what they have heard, but doing it—they will be blessed in what they do.

[26]Those who consider themselves religious and yet do not keep a tight rein on their tongues deceive themselves, and their religion is worthless. [27]Religion that God our Father accepts as pure and faultless is this: to look after orphans and widows in their distress and to keep oneself from being polluted by the world.

Favoritism Forbidden

2 My brothers and sisters, believers in our glorious Lord Jesus Christ must not show favoritism. ²Suppose a man comes into your meeting wearing a gold ring and fine clothes, and a poor man in filthy old clothes also comes in. ³If you show special attention to the man wearing fine clothes and say, "Here's a good seat for you," but say to the poor man, "You stand there" or "Sit on the floor by my feet," ⁴have you not discriminated among yourselves and become judges with evil thoughts?

⁵Listen, my dear brothers and sisters: Has not God chosen those who are poor in the eyes of the world to be rich in faith

BREAKTHROUGH!

Does God give eternal life to the person who endures under trial? I thought it was because we trust Jesus ...

(JAMES 1:12)

Well, eternal life comes by trusting in Jesus. Here, it means that if a person gets through a difficult situation, it's because he or she has trusted in Jesus. The reward is the crown of life, which is eternal life. That means that the person who really trusts Jesus is doing the right thing.

and to inherit the kingdom he promised those who love him? ⁶But you have dishonored the poor. Is it not the rich who are exploiting you? Are they not the ones who are dragging you into court? ⁷Are they not the ones who are blaspheming the noble name of him to whom you belong?

⁸If you really keep the royal law found in Scripture, "Love your neighbor as yourself," ᵃ you are doing right. ⁹But if you show favoritism, you sin and are convicted by the law as lawbreakers. ¹⁰For whoever keeps the whole law and yet stumbles at just one point is guilty of breaking all of it. ¹¹For he who said, "You shall not commit adultery," ᵇ also said, "You shall not murder." ᶜ If you do not commit adultery but do commit murder, you have become a lawbreaker.

¹²Speak and act as those who are going to be judged by the law that gives freedom, ¹³because judgment without mercy will be shown to anyone who has not been merciful. Mercy triumphs over judgment.

Faith and Deeds

¹⁴What good is it, my brothers and sisters, if someone claims to have faith but has no deeds? Can such faith save them? ¹⁵Suppose a brother or a sister is without clothes and daily food. ¹⁶If one of you says to them, "Go in peace; keep warm and well fed," but does nothing about their physical needs, what good is it? ¹⁷In the same way, faith by itself, if it is not accompanied by action, is dead.

¹⁸But someone will say, "You have faith; I have deeds."

Show me your faith without deeds, and I will show you my faith by my deeds. ¹⁹You believe that there is one God. Good! Even the demons believe that—and shudder.

²⁰You foolish person, do you want evidence that faith without deeds is useless ᵈ? ²¹Was not our father Abraham considered righteous for what he did when he offered his son Isaac on the altar? ²²You see that his faith and his actions were working together, and his faith was made

---

ᵃ 8 Lev. 19:18   ᵇ 11 Exodus 20:14; Deut. 5:18
ᶜ 11 Exodus 20:13; Deut. 5:17   ᵈ 20 Some early manuscripts *dead*

CHECK THE FACTS

How should we treat other people?

A) Rich people get everything first, because they can pay for the food poor people need.

B) We should treat all people the same.

C) Poor people are always the most important.

CORRECT ANSWER: B

complete by what he did. ²³And the scripture was fulfilled that says, "Abraham believed God, and it was credited to him as righteousness,"ᵃ and he was called God's friend. ²⁴You see that a person is considered righteous by what they do and not by faith alone.

²⁵In the same way, was not even Rahab the prostitute considered righteous for what she did when she gave lodging to the spies and sent them off in a different direction? ²⁶As the body without the spirit is dead, so faith without deeds is dead.

Taming the Tongue

3 Not many of you should become teachers, my fellow believers, because you know that we who teach will be judged more strictly. ²We all stumble in many ways. Anyone who is never at fault in what they say is perfect, able to keep their whole body in check.

³When we put bits into the mouths of horses to make them obey us, we can turn the whole animal. ⁴Or take ships as an example. Although they are so large and are driven by strong winds, they are steered by a very small rudder wherever the pilot wants to go. ⁵Likewise, the tongue is a small part of the body, but it makes great boasts. Consider what a great forest is set on fire by a small spark. ⁶The tongue also is a fire, a world of evil among the parts of the body. It corrupts the whole body, sets the whole course of one's life on fire, and is itself set on fire by hell.

⁷All kinds of animals, birds, reptiles and sea creatures are being tamed and have been tamed by mankind, ⁸but no human being can tame the tongue. It is a restless evil, full of deadly poison.

⁹With the tongue we praise our Lord and Father, and with it we curse human beings, who have been made in God's likeness. ¹⁰Out of the same mouth come praise and cursing. My brothers and sisters, this should not be. ¹¹Can both fresh water and salt water flow from the same spring? ¹²My brothers and sisters, can a fig tree bear olives, or a grapevine bear figs? Neither can a salt spring produce fresh water.

Two Kinds of Wisdom

¹³Who is wise and understanding among you? Let them show it by their good life, by deeds done in the humility that comes from wisdom. ¹⁴But if you harbor bitter envy and selfish ambition in your hearts, do not boast about it or deny the truth. ¹⁵Such "wisdom" does not come down from heaven but is earthly, unspiritual, demonic. ¹⁶For where you have envy and selfish ambition, there you find disorder and every evil practice.

¹⁷But the wisdom that comes from heaven is first of all pure; then peace-loving, considerate, submissive, full of mercy and good fruit, impartial and sincere.

ᵃ 23 Gen. 15:6

BREAK THROUGH!

Does wisdom in this world come from the devil?

(JAMES 3:15)

No, wisdom comes from God. We can study thousands of things, but in the end all that knowledge really comes from God. However, here it is talking about the wisdom of understanding things in life and knowing when we do right and when we do wrong. When what we know makes us think we're better than anyone else, then that feeling is what comes from the devil and not from God.

¹⁸Peacemakers who sow in peace reap a harvest of righteousness.

Submit Yourselves to God

4 What causes fights and quarrels among you? Don't they come from your desires that battle within you? ²You desire but do not have, so you kill. You covet but you cannot get what you want, so you quarrel and fight. You do not have because you do not ask God. ³When you ask, you do not receive, because you ask with wrong motives, that you may spend what you get on your pleasures.

⁴You adulterous people,ᵃ don't you know that friendship with the world means enmity against God? Therefore, anyone who chooses to be a friend of the world becomes an enemy of God. ⁵Or do you think Scripture says without reason that he jealously longs for the spirit he has caused to dwell in usᵇ? ⁶But he gives us more grace. That is why Scripture says:

"God opposes the proud
  but shows favor to the humble."ᶜ

⁷Submit yourselves, then, to God. Resist the devil, and he will flee from you. ⁸Come near to God and he will come near to you. Wash your hands, you sinners, and purify your hearts, you double-minded. ⁹Grieve, mourn and wail. Change your laughter to mourning and your joy to gloom. ¹⁰Humble yourselves before the Lord, and he will lift you up.

¹¹Brothers and sisters, do not slander one another. Anyone who speaks against a brother or sisterᵈ or judges them speaks against the law and judges it. When you judge the law, you are not keeping it, but sitting in judgment on it. ¹²There is only one Lawgiver and Judge, the one who is able to save and destroy. But you—who are you to judge your neighbor?

Boasting About Tomorrow

¹³Now listen, you who say, "Today or tomorrow we will go to this or that city, spend a year there, carry on business and make money." ¹⁴Why, you do not even know what will happen tomorrow. What is your life? You are a mist that appears for a little while and then vanishes. ¹⁵Instead, you ought to say, "If it is the Lord's will, we will live and do this or that." ¹⁶As it is, you boast in your arrogant schemes. All such boasting is evil. ¹⁷If anyone, then, knows the good they ought to do and doesn't do it, it is sin for them.

Warning to Rich Oppressors

5 Now listen, you rich people, weep and wail because of the misery that is coming on you. ²Your wealth has rotted, and moths have eaten your clothes. ³Your gold and silver are corroded. Their

---

ᵃ 4 An allusion to covenant unfaithfulness; see Hosea 3:1. ᵇ 5 Or that the spirit he caused to dwell in us envies intensely; or that the Spirit he caused to dwell in us longs jealously   ᶜ 6 Prov. 3:34   ᵈ 11 The Greek word for brother or sister (adelphos) refers here to a believer, whether man or woman, as part of God's family.

corrosion will testify against you and eat your flesh like fire. You have hoarded wealth in the last days. ⁴Look! The wages you failed to pay the workers who mowed your fields are crying out against you. The cries of the harvesters have reached the ears of the Lord Almighty. ⁵You have lived on earth in luxury and self-indulgence. You have fattened yourselves in the day of slaughter.ᵃ ⁶You have condemned and murdered the innocent one, who was not opposing you.

Patience in Suffering

⁷Be patient, then, brothers and sisters, until the Lord's coming. See how the farmer waits for the land to yield its valuable crop, patiently waiting for the autumn and spring rains. ⁸You too, be patient and stand firm, because the Lord's coming is near. ⁹Don't grumble against one another, brothers and sisters, or you will be judged. The Judge is standing at the door!

¹⁰Brothers and sisters, as an example of patience in the face of suffering, take the prophets who spoke in the name

ᵃ 5 Or *yourselves as in a day of feasting*

BREAKTHROUGH!

Anointing with oil
(JAMES 5:14)

In Bible times, they used oil like medicine. People would put some oil on the heads of sick people in order to cure them. Oil doesn't have the power to heal. God has that power, but they trusted God, and God healed them.

CASE CLOSED!

This letter teaches us that we should treat everyone the same way, and we shouldn't prefer rich people over poor people. That would really be bad! It also teaches us that we need to show our trust in God by doing good things. We shouldn't just say that we trust God. We need to act and do good things because we really believe in God.

of the Lord. [11]As you know, we count as blessed those who have persevered. You have heard of Job's perseverance and have seen what the Lord finally brought about. The Lord is full of compassion and mercy.

[12]Above all, my brothers and sisters, do not swear—not by heaven or by earth or by anything else. All you need to say is a simple "Yes" or "No." Otherwise you will be condemned.

The Prayer of Faith

[13]Is anyone among you in trouble? Let them pray. Is anyone happy? Let them sing songs of praise. [14]Is anyone among you sick? Let them call the elders of the church to pray over them and anoint them with oil in the name of the Lord. [15]And the prayer offered in faith will make the sick person well; the Lord will raise them up. If they have sinned, they will be forgiven. [16]Therefore confess your sins to each other and pray for each other so that you may be healed. The prayer of a righteous person is powerful and effective.

[17]Elijah was a human being, even as we are. He prayed earnestly that it would not rain, and it did not rain on the land for three and a half years. [18]Again he prayed, and the heavens gave rain, and the earth produced its crops.

[19]My brothers and sisters, if one of you should wander from the truth and someone should bring that person back, [20]remember this: Whoever turns a sinner from the error of their way will save them from death and cover over a multitude of sins.

1 PETER

THE EVIDENCE:

WHO WROTE IT?
It's possible that Peter wrote this letter while in Rome with the help of Silas, an old friend of the apostle Paul. This letter is written in very good Greek. Peter was just a fisherman in Galilee, so some experts think that Peter didn't write it. They think it is more probable that one of Peter's disciples wrote it. However, since the text says that Peter is the author, we'll let it go at that.

HOW LONG AGO?
If we accept Peter as the writer, then the date of the writing would be between 60 and 64 years after Christ. On the other hand, if one of his disciples wrote it, it could have been between 70 and 90 years after Christ.

WHAT'S IT ABOUT?
The first Christians were persecuted by the Roman authorities. That's why they got scattered all over the Roman empire. The apostle Peter writes this letter to those Christians. The whole letter is a series of recommendations about how to live the Christian life. Peter insists that they have to obey the emperor, the governors and all the authorities (2:13 – 14).

The Christians at that time believed that the end of the world was near (4:7). That's why Peter tells them to love each other and to receive other Christians in their homes and be ready to suffer for "being Christian."

THE BEST PART
There are several nice verses in this letter, but we chose 4:8, which says, "Above all, love each other deeply, because love covers over a multitude of sins." We agree. There's nothing to compare with love!

1 Peter, an apostle of Jesus Christ,

To God's elect, exiles scattered throughout the provinces of Pontus, Galatia, Cappadocia, Asia and Bithynia, ²who have been chosen according to the foreknowledge of God the Father, through the sanctifying work of the Spirit, to be obedient to Jesus Christ and sprinkled with his blood:

Grace and peace be yours in abundance.

Praise to God for a Living Hope
³Praise be to the God and Father of our Lord Jesus Christ! In his great mercy he has given us new birth into a living hope through the resurrection of Jesus Christ from the dead, ⁴and into an inheritance that can never perish, spoil or fade. This inheritance is kept in heaven for you, ⁵who through faith are shielded by God's power until the coming of the salvation that is ready to be revealed in the last time.

⁶In all this you greatly rejoice, though now for a little while you may have had to suffer grief in all kinds of trials. ⁷These have come so that the proven genuineness of your faith—of greater worth than gold, which perishes even though refined by fire—may result in praise, glory and honor when Jesus Christ is revealed. ⁸Though you have not seen him, you love him; and even though you do not see him now, you believe in him and are filled with an inexpressible and glorious joy, ⁹for you are receiving the end result of your faith, the salvation of your souls.

¹⁰Concerning this salvation, the prophets, who spoke of the grace that was to come to you, searched intently and with the greatest care, ¹¹trying to find out the time and circumstances to which the Spirit of Christ in them was pointing when he predicted the sufferings of the Messiah and the glories that would follow. ¹²It was revealed to them that they were not serving themselves but you, when they spoke of the things that have now been told you by those who have preached the gospel to you by the Holy Spirit sent from heaven. Even angels long to look into these things.

Be Holy

¹³Therefore, with minds that are alert and fully sober, set your hope on the grace to be brought to you when Jesus Christ is revealed at his coming. ¹⁴As obedient

THE WITNESSES

✓ PETER (1 PETER 1:1)
This name means "rock." Peter was one of Jesus' disciples. He was a fisherman, just like his brother, Andrew. Peter was a close friend of Jesus. He was the first person who was completely sure that Jesus was the Son of God.

BREAKTHROUGH!

Did God choose Christians to be his people?
(1 PETER 1:1-2)
God knows everything. If he didn't, then he wouldn't be God. He knew who was going to believe in him. So that's why the letter says that God decided to choose them according to his plan. He chose the people who believed. Does that make sense?

THE SCENE

PONTUS, GALATIA, CAPPADOCIA, ASIA AND BITHYNIA

(1 PETER 1:1)

These five Roman provinces were in the northern part of Asia Minor, where Turkey is now. It seems that the people who were living there had become Christians. Because of that, they had to flee from their countries. Peter thinks that Christians don't really belong to this world even if they're living in it. He says we belong to heaven, so that makes us something like "foreigners" in this world.

children, do not conform to the evil desires you had when you lived in ignorance. [15]But just as he who called you is holy, so be holy in all you do; [16]for it is written: "Be holy, because I am holy."[a]

[17]Since you call on a Father who judges each person's work impartially, live out your time as foreigners here in reverent fear. [18]For you know that it was not with perishable things such as silver or gold that you were redeemed from the empty way of life handed down to you from your ancestors, [19]but with the precious blood of Christ, a lamb without blemish or defect. [20]He was chosen before the creation of the world, but was revealed in these last times for your sake. [21]Through him you believe in God, who raised him from the dead and glorified him, and so your faith and hope are in God.

[22]Now that you have purified yourselves by obeying the truth so that you have sincere love for each other, love one another deeply, from the heart.[b] [23]For you have been born again, not of perishable seed, but of imperishable, through the living and enduring word of God. [24]For,

"All people are like grass,
   and all their glory is like the flowers
      of the field;
the grass withers and the flowers
      fall,
[25]   but the word of the Lord endures
      forever."[c]

And this is the word that was preached to you.

2 Therefore, rid yourselves of all malice and all deceit, hypocrisy, envy, and slander of every kind. [2]Like newborn babies, crave pure spiritual milk, so that by it you may grow up in your salvation, [3]now that you have tasted that the Lord is good.

The Living Stone and a Chosen People

[4]As you come to him, the living Stone—rejected by humans but chosen by God and precious to him— [5]you also, like living stones, are being built into a spiritual house[d] to be a holy priesthood, offering spiritual sacrifices acceptable to God through Jesus Christ. [6]For in Scripture it says:

"See, I lay a stone in Zion,
   a chosen and precious
      cornerstone,
and the one who trusts in him
   will never be put to shame."[e]

---

[a] 16 Lev. 11:44,45; 19:2   [b] 22 Some early manuscripts *from a pure heart*   [c] 25 Isaiah 40:6-8 (see Septuagint)   [d] 5 Or *into a temple of the Spirit*   [e] 6 Isaiah 28:16

[7]Now to you who believe, this stone is precious. But to those who do not believe,

"The stone the builders rejected
    has become the cornerstone,"[a]

[8]and,

"A stone that causes people to
    stumble
and a rock that makes them fall."[b]

They stumble because they disobey the message—which is also what they were destined for.

[9]But you are a chosen people, a royal priesthood, a holy nation, God's special possession, that you may declare the praises of him who called you out of darkness into his wonderful light. [10]Once you were not a people, but now you are the people of God; once you had not received mercy, but now you have received mercy.

Living Godly Lives in a Pagan Society

[11]Dear friends, I urge you, as foreigners and exiles, to abstain from sinful desires, which wage war against your soul. [12]Live such good lives among the pagans that, though they accuse you of doing wrong, they may see your good deeds and glorify God on the day he visits us.

[13]Submit yourselves for the Lord's sake to every human authority: whether to the emperor, as the supreme authority, [14]or to governors, who are sent by him to punish those who do wrong and to commend those who do right. [15]For it is God's will that by doing good you should silence the ignorant talk of foolish people. [16]Live as free people, but do not use your freedom as a cover-up for evil; live as God's slaves. [17]Show proper respect to everyone, love the family of believers, fear God, honor the emperor.

[18]Slaves, in reverent fear of God submit yourselves to your masters, not only to those who are good and considerate, but also to those who are harsh. [19]For it is commendable if someone bears up under the pain of unjust suffering because they are conscious of God. [20]But how is it to your credit if you receive a beating

BREAK THROUGH!

Should we always obey the people in charge, even when what they do is wrong?

(1 PETER 2:13-14)

Even when it seems that this isn't true, Peter says that God has given the people in charge their jobs, and that we should respect and obey them. However, when the laws that people have made force us to do something against God's laws, then we can disobey those laws while, at the same time, we continue to respect and pray for the people in charge.

for doing wrong and endure it? But if you suffer for doing good and you endure it, this is commendable before God. [21]To this you were called, because Christ suffered for you, leaving you an example, that you should follow in his steps.

[22]"He committed no sin,
    and no deceit was found in his
        mouth."[c]

[23]When they hurled their insults at him, he did not retaliate; when he suffered, he made no threats. Instead, he entrusted himself to him who judges justly. [24]"He

---

[a] 7 Psalm 118:22   [b] 8 Isaiah 8:14   [c] 22 Isaiah 53:9

himself bore our sins" in his body on the cross, so that we might die to sins and live for righteousness; "by his wounds you have been healed." [25]For "you were like sheep going astray,"[a] but now you have returned to the Shepherd and Overseer of your souls.

3 Wives, in the same way submit yourselves to your own husbands so that, if any of them do not believe the word, they may be won over without words by the behavior of their wives, [2]when they see the purity and reverence of your lives. [3]Your beauty should not come from outward adornment, such as elaborate hairstyles and the wearing of gold jewelry or fine clothes. [4]Rather, it should be that of your inner self, the unfading beauty of a gentle and quiet spirit, which is of great worth in God's sight. [5]For this is the way the holy women of the past who put their hope in God used to adorn themselves. They submitted themselves to their own husbands, [6]like Sarah, who obeyed Abraham and called him her lord. You are her daughters if you do what is right and do not give way to fear.

[7]Husbands, in the same way be considerate as you live with your wives, and treat them with respect as the weaker partner and as heirs with you of the gracious gift of life, so that nothing will hinder your prayers.

Suffering for Doing Good

[8]Finally, all of you, be like-minded, be sympathetic, love one another, be compassionate and humble. [9]Do not repay evil with evil or insult with insult. On the contrary, repay evil with blessing, because to this you were called so that you may inherit a blessing. [10]For,

"Whoever would love life
    and see good days
must keep their tongue from evil
    and their lips from deceitful speech.
[11]They must turn from evil and do good;
    they must seek peace and pursue it.
[12]For the eyes of the Lord are on the righteous
    and his ears are attentive to their prayer,

BREAKTHROUGH!

Should wives obey everything their husbands say?

(1 PETER 3:1)

We saw this in the letter to the Ephesians. It's just that the law didn't used to give women any rights. Now men and women are equal. In this letter, Peter is talking to the women who had husbands who didn't believe in Jesus. He tells them that they need to be a good example so their husbands will also begin to believe.

but the face of the Lord is against
    those who do evil."[b]

[13]Who is going to harm you if you are eager to do good? [14]But even if you should suffer for what is right, you are blessed. "Do not fear their threats[c]; do not be frightened."[d] [15]But in your hearts revere Christ as Lord. Always be prepared to give an answer to everyone who asks you to give the reason for the hope that you have. But do this with gentleness and respect, [16]keeping a clear conscience, so that those who speak maliciously against your good behavior in Christ may

---

[a] 24,25 Isaiah 53:4,5,6 (see Septuagint)
[b] 12 Psalm 34:12-16   [c] 14 Or fear what they fear
[d] 14 Isaiah 8:12

be ashamed of their slander. ¹⁷For it is better, if it is God's will, to suffer for doing good than for doing evil. ¹⁸For Christ also suffered once for sins, the righteous for the unrighteous, to bring you to God. He was put to death in the body but made alive in the Spirit. ¹⁹After being made alive,ᵃ he went and made proclamation to the imprisoned spirits — ²⁰to those who were disobedient long ago when God waited patiently in the days of Noah while the ark was being built. In it only a few people, eight in all, were saved through water, ²¹and this water symbolizes baptism that now saves you also — not the removal of dirt from the body but the pledge of a clear conscience toward God.ᵇ It saves you by the resurrection of Jesus Christ, ²²who has gone into heaven and is at God's right hand — with angels, authorities and powers in submission to him.

Living for God

4 Therefore, since Christ suffered in his body, arm yourselves also with the same attitude, because whoever suffers in the body is done with sin. ²As a result, they do not live the rest of their earthly lives for evil human desires, but rather for the will of God. ³For you have spent enough time in the past doing what pagans choose to do — living in debauchery, lust, drunkenness, orgies, carousing and detestable idolatry. ⁴They are surprised that you do not join them in their reckless, wild living, and they heap abuse on you. ⁵But they will have to give account to him who is ready to judge the living and the dead. ⁶For this is the reason the gospel was preached even to those who are now dead, so that they might be judged according to human standards in regard to the body, but live according to God in regard to the spirit.

⁷The end of all things is near. Therefore be alert and of sober mind so that you may pray. ⁸Above all, love each other deeply, because love covers over a multitude of sins. ⁹Offer hospitality to one another without grumbling. ¹⁰Each of you should use whatever gift you have received to serve others, as faithful stewards of God's grace in its various forms. ¹¹If anyone speaks, they should do so as one who speaks the very words of God. If anyone serves, they should do so with the strength God provides, so that in all things God may be praised through Jesus Christ. To him be the glory and the power for ever and ever. Amen.

Suffering for Being a Christian

¹²Dear friends, do not be surprised at the fiery ordeal that has come on you to test you, as though something strange were happening to you. ¹³But rejoice inasmuch as you participate in the sufferings of Christ, so that you may be overjoyed when his glory is revealed. ¹⁴If you are insulted because of the name of Christ, you are blessed, for the Spirit of glory and of God rests on you. ¹⁵If you suffer, it should

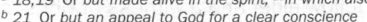

ᵃ 18,19 Or *but made alive in the spirit,* ¹⁹*in which also*
ᵇ 21 Or *but an appeal to God for a clear conscience*

What does it mean that "love covers over a multitude of sins"?

(1 PETER 4:8)

If we really love, then we won't be jealous or bitter. That's how love can "cover" sins. And since God is love, his love simply "covers" all our sins.

not be as a murderer or thief or any other kind of criminal, or even as a meddler. 16However, if you suffer as a Christian, do not be ashamed, but praise God that you bear that name. 17For it is time for judgment to begin with God's household; and if it begins with us, what will the outcome be for those who do not obey the gospel of God? 18And,

> "If it is hard for the righteous to be saved,
> what will become of the ungodly and the sinner?"*a*

19So then, those who suffer according to God's will should commit themselves to their faithful Creator and continue to do good.

To the Elders and the Flock

5 To the elders among you, I appeal as a fellow elder and a witness of Christ's sufferings who also will share in the glory to be revealed: 2Be shepherds of God's flock that is under your care, watching over them—not because you must, but because you are willing, as God wants you to be; not pursuing dishonest gain, but eager to serve; 3not lording it over those entrusted to you, but being examples to the flock. 4And when the Chief Shepherd appears, you will receive the crown of glory that will never fade away.

5In the same way, you who are younger, submit yourselves to your elders. All of you, clothe yourselves with humility toward one another, because,

> "God opposes the proud
> but shows favor to the humble."*b*

6Humble yourselves, therefore, under God's mighty hand, that he may lift you up in due time. 7Cast all your anxiety on him because he cares for you.

8Be alert and of sober mind. Your enemy the devil prowls around like a roaring lion looking for someone to devour. 9Resist him, standing firm in the faith, because you know that the family of believers throughout the world is undergoing the same kind of sufferings.

10And the God of all grace, who called

---

a 18 Prov. 11:31 (see Septuagint)   *b* 5 Prov. 3:34

Mateo and I read a lot of recommendations in this letter about how to live the Christian life. Even though the Christians at that time were being bullied by the Roman rulers, Peter tells them over and over that they should obey and respect those rulers. That couldn't have been easy. The most important thing was that Peter told them to love each other, to receive other Christians in their homes and to be happy even if they were suffering because they were Christians.

you to his eternal glory in Christ, after you have suffered a little while, will himself restore you and make you strong, firm and steadfast. [11]To him be the power for ever and ever. Amen.

Final Greetings

[12]With the help of Silas,[a] whom I regard as a faithful brother, I have written to you briefly, encouraging you and testifying that this is the true grace of God. Stand fast in it.

[13]She who is in Babylon, chosen together with you, sends you her greetings, and so does my son Mark. [14]Greet one another with a kiss of love.

Peace to all of you who are in Christ.

---

[a] 12 Greek Silvanus, a variant of Silas

2 PETER

THE EVIDENCE:

WHO WROTE IT?
This letter says it was written by Simon Peter. It's not addressed to any specific church, just to Christians in general. Most Bible experts think the author was really one of Peter's followers, who wrote in his name.

HOW LONG AGO?
The date of the writing is not known. It's possible that it was in the 2nd century (100s) after Christ.

WHAT'S IT ABOUT?
Everything the letter says deals with two main ideas: false teachings and Christ's return. In those days of the Roman empire, the Christians were persecuted, and there were also false teachers who confused the people with teachings that went against the true gospel. This letter says as well that Jesus would return soon, but it doesn't say when. His coming will be a surprise!

THE BEST PART
We think the nicest part is right at the end, where it says, "Grow in the grace and knowledge of our Lord and Savior Jesus Christ" (3:18). It's nice to know that with his love, we can become better people every day.

---

1 Simon Peter, a servant and apostle of Jesus Christ,

To those who through the righteousness of our God and Savior Jesus Christ have received a faith as precious as ours:

²Grace and peace be yours in abundance through the knowledge of God and of Jesus our Lord.

Confirming One's Calling and Election

³His divine power has given us everything we need for a godly life through our knowledge of him who called us by his own glory and goodness. ⁴Through these he has given us his very great and precious promises, so that through them you may participate in the divine nature, having escaped the corruption in the world caused by evil desires.

⁵For this very reason, make every effort to add to your faith goodness; and to goodness, knowledge; ⁶and to knowledge, self-control; and to self-control, perseverance; and to perseverance, godliness; ⁷and to godliness, mutual affection; and to mutual affection, love.

[8]For if you possess these qualities in increasing measure, they will keep you from being ineffective and unproductive in your knowledge of our Lord Jesus Christ. [9]But whoever does not have them is nearsighted and blind, forgetting that they have been cleansed from their past sins. [10]Therefore, my brothers and sisters,[a] make every effort to confirm your calling and election. For if you do these things, you will never stumble, [11]and you will receive a rich welcome into the eternal kingdom of our Lord and Savior Jesus Christ.

Prophecy of Scripture

[12]So I will always remind you of these things, even though you know them and are firmly established in the truth you now have. [13]I think it is right to refresh your memory as long as I live in the tent of this body, [14]because I know that I will soon put it aside, as our Lord Jesus Christ has made clear to me. [15]And I will make every effort to see that after my departure you will always be able to remember these things.

[16]For we did not follow cleverly devised stories when we told you about the coming of our Lord Jesus Christ in power, but we were eyewitnesses of his majesty. [17]He received honor and glory from God the Father when the voice came to him from the Majestic Glory, saying, "This is my Son, whom I love; with him I am well pleased."[b] [18]We ourselves heard this voice that came from heaven when we were with him on the sacred mountain.

[19]We also have the prophetic message as something completely reliable, and you will do well to pay attention to it, as to a light shining in a dark place, until the day dawns and the morning star rises in your hearts. [20]Above all, you must understand that no prophecy of Scripture came about by the prophet's own interpretation of things. [21]For prophecy never had its origin in the human will, but prophets, though human, spoke from God as they were carried along by the Holy Spirit.

False Teachers and Their Destruction

2 But there were also false prophets among the people, just as there will be false teachers among you. They will secretly introduce destructive heresies, even denying the sovereign Lord who bought them—bringing swift destruction on themselves. [2]Many will follow their depraved conduct and will bring the way of truth into disrepute. [3]In their greed these teachers will exploit you with fabricated stories. Their condemnation has long been hanging over them, and their destruction has not been sleeping.

[4]For if God did not spare angels when they sinned, but sent them to hell,[c] putting them in chains of darkness[d] to be held for judgment; [5]if he did not spare the ancient world when he brought the flood on its ungodly people, but protected Noah, a preacher of righteousness, and seven others; [6]if he condemned the cities of Sodom and Gomorrah by burning them to ashes, and made them an example of what is going to happen to the ungodly; [7]and if he rescued Lot, a righteous man, who was distressed by the depraved conduct of the lawless [8](for that righteous man, living among them day after day, was tormented in his righteous soul by the lawless deeds he saw and heard)— [9]if this is so, then the Lord knows how to rescue the godly from trials and to hold the unrighteous for punishment on the day of judgment. [10]This is especially true of those who follow the corrupt desire of the flesh[e] and despise authority.

Bold and arrogant, they are not afraid to heap abuse on celestial beings; [11]yet even angels, although they are stronger and more powerful, do not heap abuse on such beings when bringing judgment on them from[f] the Lord. [12]But these people blaspheme in matters they do not

BREAKTHROUGH!

Sacred mountain

(2 PETER 1:17-18)

This refers to the time when Jesus was "transfigured." That was when he showed all his glory and was shining like snow. Moses and Elijah also spoke with Jesus. Peter, James and John were with him at that moment, and they saw everything. It all happened on a mountain, but we don't know what mountain it was. (Read about this in Mark 9:2-9.)

understand. They are like unreasoning animals, creatures of instinct, born only to be caught and destroyed, and like animals they too will perish.

¹³They will be paid back with harm for the harm they have done. Their idea of pleasure is to carouse in broad daylight. They are blots and blemishes, reveling in their pleasures while they feast with you.ᵃ ¹⁴With eyes full of adultery, they never stop sinning; they seduce the unstable; they are experts in greed—an accursed brood! ¹⁵They have left the straight way and wandered off to follow the way of Balaam son of Bezer,ᵇ who loved the wages of wickedness. ¹⁶But he was rebuked for his wrongdoing by a donkey—an animal without speech—who spoke with a human voice and restrained the prophet's madness.

¹⁷These people are springs without water and mists driven by a storm. Blackest darkness is reserved for them. ¹⁸For they mouth empty, boastful words and, by appealing to the lustful desires of the flesh, they entice people who are just escaping from those who live in error. ¹⁹They promise them freedom, while they themselves are slaves of depravity—for "people are slaves to whatever has mastered them." ²⁰If they have escaped the corruption of the world by knowing our Lord and Savior Jesus Christ and are again entangled in it and are overcome, they are worse off at the end than they were at the beginning. ²¹It would have been better for them not to have known the way of righteousness, than to have known it and then to turn their backs on the sacred command that was passed on to them. ²²Of them the proverbs are true: "A dog returns to its vomit,"ᶜ and, "A sow that is washed returns to her wallowing in the mud."

The Day of the Lord

3 Dear friends, this is now my second letter to you. I have written both of them as reminders to stimulate you to wholesome thinking. ²I want you to recall the words spoken in the past by the holy prophets and the command given by our Lord and Savior through your apostles.

³Above all, you must understand that in the last days scoffers will come, scoffing and following their own evil desires. ⁴They will say, "Where is this 'coming' he promised? Ever since our ancestors died, everything goes on as it has since the beginning of creation." ⁵But they deliberately forget that long ago by God's word the heavens came into being and the earth was formed out of water and by water. ⁶By these waters also the world of that time was deluged and destroyed. ⁷By the same word the present heavens and earth are reserved for fire, being kept for the day of judgment and destruction of the ungodly.

⁸But do not forget this one thing, dear friends: With the Lord a day is like a thousand years, and a thousand years are like

---

ᵃ 13 Some manuscripts *in their love feasts*   ᵇ 15 Greek *Bosor*   ᶜ 22 Prov. 26:11

a day. ⁹The Lord is not slow in keeping his promise, as some understand slowness. Instead he is patient with you, not wanting anyone to perish, but everyone to come to repentance.

¹⁰But the day of the Lord will come like a thief. The heavens will disappear with a roar; the elements will be destroyed by fire, and the earth and everything done in it will be laid bare.ᵃ

¹¹Since everything will be destroyed in this way, what kind of people ought you to be? You ought to live holy and godly lives ¹²as you look forward to the day of God and speed its coming.ᵇ That day will bring about the destruction of the heavens by fire, and the elements will melt in the heat. ¹³But in keeping with his promise we are looking forward to a new heaven and a new earth, where righteousness dwells.

¹⁴So then, dear friends, since you are looking forward to this, make every effort to be found spotless, blameless and at peace with him. ¹⁵Bear in mind that our Lord's patience means salvation, just as our dear brother Paul also wrote you with the wisdom that God gave him. ¹⁶He writes the same way in all his letters, speaking in them of these matters. His letters contain some things that are hard to understand, which ignorant and unstable people distort, as they do the other Scriptures, to their own destruction.

¹⁷Therefore, dear friends, since you have been forewarned, be on your guard so that you may not be carried away by the error of the lawless and fall from your secure position. ¹⁸But grow in the grace and knowledge of our Lord and Savior Jesus Christ. To him be glory both now and forever! Amen.

ᵃ 10 Some manuscripts *be burned up*　ᵇ 12 Or *as you wait eagerly for the day of God to come*

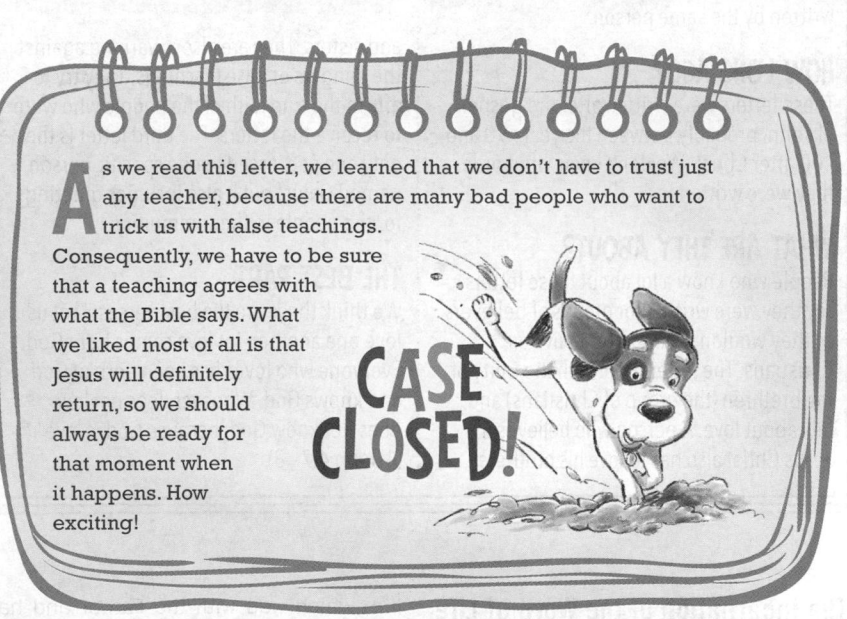

A s we read this letter, we learned that we don't have to trust just any teacher, because there are many bad people who want to trick us with false teachings. Consequently, we have to be sure that a teaching agrees with what the Bible says. What we liked most of all is that Jesus will definitely return, so we should always be ready for that moment when it happens. How exciting!

CASE CLOSED!

1 JOHN

INTRODUCTION FOR 1, 2 AND 3 JOHN

THE EVIDENCE:

WHO WROTE THEM?
The apostle John (Jesus' friend) probably wrote these letters, but it could have been someone who belonged to John's group. The writer calls himself "elder," which really means "leader" or "person in charge" (2 John 1:1). It is thought that the gospel of John and these three letters were all written by the same person.

HOW LONG AGO?
These letters were written after the gospel of John, probably between the years 90 and 100 after Christ. We don't know what order they were written in.

WHAT ARE THEY ABOUT?
People who know a lot about these letters say they were written for groups of believers so they wouldn't forget how to live as Christians. The letters deal with the unity of the brethren (the group of Christians) and talk about love. A person who believes in Jesus Christ also has to love his brothers and sisters. They are also a warning against the dangers of false teachings. They try to affirm the true faith of the people who were to receive the letters. The third letter is the only one addressed to one specific person, named Gaius, but it also includes greetings for the people in the community.

THE BEST PART
We think these are the best verses: "Let us love one another, for love comes from God. Everyone who loves has been born of God and knows God. Whoever does not love does not know God, because God is love" (1 John 4:7 – 8).

The Incarnation of the Word of Life

1 That which was from the beginning, which we have heard, which we have seen with our eyes, which we have looked at and our hands have touched—this we proclaim concerning the Word of life. ²The life appeared; we have seen it and testify to it, and we proclaim to you the eternal life, which was with the Father and has appeared to us. ³We proclaim to you what we have seen and heard, so that you also may have fellowship with us. And our fellowship is with the Father and with his Son, Jesus Christ. ⁴We write this to make our*a* joy complete.

---

a 4 Some manuscripts *your*

Light and Darkness, Sin and Forgiveness

⁵This is the message we have heard from him and declare to you: God is light; in him there is no darkness at all. ⁶If we claim to have fellowship with him and yet walk in the darkness, we lie and do not live out the truth. ⁷But if we walk in the light, as he is in the light, we have fellowship with one another, and the blood of Jesus, his Son, purifies us from all*ᵃ* sin.

⁸If we claim to be without sin, we deceive ourselves and the truth is not in us. ⁹If we confess our sins, he is faithful and just and will forgive us our sins and purify us from all unrighteousness. ¹⁰If we claim we have not sinned, we make him out to be a liar and his word is not in us.

2 My dear children, I write this to you so that you will not sin. But if anybody does sin, we have an advocate with the Father—Jesus Christ, the Righteous One. ²He is the atoning sacrifice for our sins, and not only for ours but also for the sins of the whole world.

Love and Hatred for Fellow Believers

³We know that we have come to know him if we keep his commands. ⁴Whoever says, "I know him," but does not do what he commands is a liar, and the truth is not in that person. ⁵But if anyone obeys his word, love for God*ᵇ* is truly made complete in them. This is how we know we are in him: ⁶Whoever claims to live in him must live as Jesus did.

⁷Dear friends, I am not writing you a new command but an old one, which you have had since the beginning. This old command is the message you have heard. ⁸Yet I am writing you a new command; its truth is seen in him and in you, because the darkness is passing and the true light is already shining.

⁹Anyone who claims to be in the light but hates a brother or sister*ᶜ* is still in the darkness. ¹⁰Anyone who loves their brother and sister*ᵈ* lives in the light, and there is nothing in them to make them stumble. ¹¹But anyone who hates a brother or sister is in the darkness and walks around

BREAK THROUGH!

The Word of life

(1 JOHN 1:1)

At the beginning of his gospel in the first chapter, John talked about the Word: "In the beginning was the Word, and the Word was with God, and the Word was God" (John 1:1). So we can say that the Word of life is Jesus, the Son of God who became a person.

in the darkness. They do not know where they are going, because the darkness has blinded them.

Reasons for Writing

¹²I am writing to you, dear children,
because your sins have been
forgiven on account of his
name.
¹³I am writing to you, fathers,
because you know him who is from
the beginning.
I am writing to you, young men,
because you have overcome the
evil one.

¹⁴I write to you, dear children,
because you know the Father.

ᵃ 7 Or *every   ᵇ 5* Or *word, God's love   ᶜ 9* The Greek word for *brother or sister* (*adelphos*) refers here to a believer, whether man or woman, as part of God's family; also in verse 11; and in 3:15, 17; 4:20; 5:16.   *ᵈ 10* The Greek word for *brother and sister* (*adelphos*) refers here to a believer, whether man or woman, as part of God's family; also in 3:10; 4:20, 21.

I write to you, fathers,
>because you know him who is from
>>the beginning.
>I write to you, young men,
>because you are strong,
>and the word of God lives in you,
>and you have overcome the evil one.

On Not Loving the World

¹⁵Do not love the world or anything in the world. If anyone loves the world, love for the Father*a* is not in them. ¹⁶For everything in the world—the lust of the flesh, the lust of the eyes, and the pride of life—comes not from the Father but from the world. ¹⁷The world and its desires pass away, but whoever does the will of God lives forever.

Warnings Against Denying the Son

¹⁸Dear children, this is the last hour; and as you have heard that the antichrist is coming, even now many antichrists have come. This is how we know it is the last hour. ¹⁹They went out from us, but they did not really belong to us. For if they had belonged to us, they would have remained with us; but their going showed that none of them belonged to us.

²⁰But you have an anointing from the Holy One, and all of you know the truth.*b* ²¹I do not write to you because you do not know the truth, but because you do know it and because no lie comes from the truth. ²²Who is the liar? It is whoever denies that Jesus is the Christ. Such a person is the antichrist—denying the Father and the Son. ²³No one who denies the Son has the Father; whoever acknowledges the Son has the Father also.

²⁴As for you, see that what you have heard from the beginning remains in you. If it does, you also will remain in the Son and in the Father. ²⁵And this is what he promised us—eternal life.

²⁶I am writing these things to you about those who are trying to lead you astray. ²⁷As for you, the anointing you received from him remains in you, and you do not need anyone to teach you. But as his anointing teaches you about all things and as that anointing is real, not

BREAK THROUGH!

Why does he say that we're living "the last hour"?

(1 JOHN 2:18)

Ever since Jesus rose from the dead and then said he would come back to Earth, we as Christians have been eagerly waiting for the Lord's return. Many people call this time between the resurrection and the second coming "the last days" or "the last hour." It means that with the second coming, it will be the end of the world as we know it. But we shouldn't be worried about this, because we know that we'll always be with God.

The antichrist

(1 JOHN 2:18)

This is someone who is against Christ. The writer sees the power of this enemy in the teachings of the false teachers and in the people who deny the true faith.

counterfeit—just as it has taught you, remain in him.

God's Children and Sin

²⁸And now, dear children, continue in him, so that when he appears we may be

---

a 15 Or *world, the Father's love*   *b* 20 Some manuscripts *and you know all things* confident and unashamed before him at his coming. [29]If you know that he is righteous, you know that everyone who does what is right has been born of him.

3 See what great love the Father has lavished on us, that we should be called children of God! And that is what we are! The reason the world does not know us is that it did not know him. [2]Dear friends, now we are children of God, and what we will be has not yet been made known. But we know that when Christ appears,[a] we shall be like him, for we shall see him as he is. [3]All who have this hope in him purify themselves, just as he is pure.

[4]Everyone who sins breaks the law; in fact, sin is lawlessness. [5]But you know that he appeared so that he might take away our sins. And in him is no sin. [6]No one who lives in him keeps on sinning. No one who continues to sin has either seen him or known him.

[7]Dear children, do not let anyone lead you astray. The one who does what is right is righteous, just as he is righteous. [8]The one who does what is sinful is of the devil, because the devil has been sinning from the beginning. The reason the Son of God appeared was to destroy the devil's work. [9]No one who is born of God will continue to sin, because God's seed remains in them; they cannot go on sinning, because they have been born of God. [10]This is how we know who the children of God are and who the children of the devil are: Anyone who does not do what is right is not God's child, nor is anyone who does not love their brother and sister.

More on Love and Hatred

[11]For this is the message you heard from the beginning: We should love one another. [12]Do not be like Cain, who belonged to the evil one and murdered his brother. And why did he murder him? Because his own actions were evil and his brother's were righteous. [13]Do not be surprised, my brothers and sisters,[b] if the world hates you. [14]We know that we have passed from death to life, because we love each other. Anyone who does not love remains in death. [15]Anyone who

hates a brother or sister is a murderer, and you know that no murderer has eternal life residing in him.

[16]This is how we know what love is: Jesus Christ laid down his life for us. And we ought to lay down our lives for our brothers and sisters. [17]If anyone has material possessions and sees a brother or sister in need but has no pity on them, how can the love of God be in that person? [18]Dear children, let us not love with words or speech but with actions and in truth.

[19]This is how we know that we belong to the truth and how we set our hearts at rest in his presence: [20]If our hearts condemn us, we know that God is greater than our hearts, and he knows everything. [21]Dear friends, if our hearts do not condemn us, we have confidence before God [22]and receive from him anything we ask, because we keep his commands and do what pleases him. [23]And this is his command: to believe in the name of his Son, Jesus Christ, and to love one another as he commanded us. [24]The one who keeps God's commands lives in him, and he in them. And this is how we know that he lives in us: We know it by the Spirit he gave us.

On Denying the Incarnation

4 Dear friends, do not believe every spirit, but test the spirits to see whether they are from God, because many false prophets have gone out into the world. [2]This is how you can recognize the Spirit of God: Every spirit that acknowledges that Jesus Christ has come in the flesh is from God, [3]but every spirit that does not acknowledge Jesus is not from God. This is the spirit of the antichrist, which you have heard is coming and even now is already in the world. [4]You, dear children, are from God and have overcome them, because the one who is in you is greater than the one who is in the world. [5]They are from the world and therefore speak from the viewpoint of the world, and the world listens to them.

---

[a] 2 Or *when it is made known*　　[b] 13 The Greek word for *brothers and sisters* (*adelphoi*) refers here to believers, both men and women, as part of God's family; also in verse 16.

⁶We are from God, and whoever knows God listens to us; but whoever is not from God does not listen to us. This is how we recognize the Spirit*ª* of truth and the spirit of falsehood.

God's Love and Ours

⁷Dear friends, let us love one another, for love comes from God. Everyone who loves has been born of God and knows God. ⁸Whoever does not love does not know God, because God is love. ⁹This is how God showed his love among us: He sent his one and only Son into the world that we might live through him. ¹⁰This is love: not that we loved God, but that he loved us and sent his Son as an atoning sacrifice for our sins. ¹¹Dear friends, since God so loved us, we also ought to love one another. ¹²No one has ever seen God; but if we love one another, God lives in us and his love is made complete in us. ¹³This is how we know that we live in him and he in us: He has given us of his Spirit. ¹⁴And we have seen and testify that the Father has sent his Son to be the Savior of the world. ¹⁵If anyone acknowledges that Jesus is the Son of God, God lives in them and they in God. ¹⁶And so we know and rely on the love God has for us.

God is love. Whoever lives in love lives in God, and God in them. ¹⁷This is how love is made complete among us so that we will have confidence on the day of judgment: In this world we are like Jesus. ¹⁸There is no fear in love. But perfect love drives out fear, because fear has to do with punishment. The one who fears is not made perfect in love.

¹⁹We love because he first loved us. ²⁰Whoever claims to love God yet hates a brother or sister is a liar. For whoever does not love their brother and sister, whom they have seen, cannot love God, whom they have not seen. ²¹And he has given us this command: Anyone who loves God must also love their brother and sister.

Faith in the Incarnate Son of God

5 Everyone who believes that Jesus is the Christ is born of God, and everyone who loves the father loves his child

BREAKTHROUGH!

Does it mean that a person who loves isn't afraid?

(1 JOHN 4:18)

Yes, that's right. People who love know that God loves them, because "he loved us first" (4:19). If we realize that God loves us, then we don't fear anything, because we are sure that God always takes care of us.

as well. ²This is how we know that we love the children of God: by loving God and carrying out his commands. ³In fact, this is love for God: to keep his commands. And his commands are not burdensome, ⁴for everyone born of God overcomes the world. This is the victory that has overcome the world, even our faith. ⁵Who is it that overcomes the world? Only the one who believes that Jesus is the Son of God.

⁶This is the one who came by water and blood—Jesus Christ. He did not come by water only, but by water and blood. And it is the Spirit who testifies, because the Spirit is the truth. ⁷For there are three that testify: ⁸the*ᵇ* Spirit, the water and the blood; and the three are in agreement.

ª 6 Or *spirit*   *ᵇ 7,8* Late manuscripts of the Vulgate *testify in heaven: the Father, the Word and the Holy Spirit, and these three are one.* ⁸*And there are three that testify on earth: the* (not found in any Greek manuscript before the fourteenth century)

⁹We accept human testimony, but God's testimony is greater because it is the testimony of God, which he has given about his Son. ¹⁰Whoever believes in the Son of God accepts this testimony. Whoever does not believe God has made him out to be a liar, because they have not believed the testimony God has given about his Son. ¹¹And this is the testimony: God has given us eternal life, and this life is in his Son. ¹²Whoever has the Son has life; whoever does not have the Son of God does not have life.

Concluding Affirmations

¹³I write these things to you who believe in the name of the Son of God so that you may know that you have eternal life. ¹⁴This is the confidence we have in approaching God: that if we ask anything according to his will, he hears us. ¹⁵And if we know that he hears us—whatever we ask—we know that we have what we asked of him.

¹⁶If you see any brother or sister commit a sin that does not lead to death, you should pray and God will give them life. I refer to those whose sin does not lead to death. There is a sin that leads to death. I am not saying that you should pray about that. ¹⁷All wrongdoing is sin, and there is sin that does not lead to death.

¹⁸We know that anyone born of God does not continue to sin; the One who was born of God keeps them safe, and the evil one cannot harm them. ¹⁹We know that we are children of God, and that the whole world is under the control of the evil one. ²⁰We know also that the Son of God has come and has given us

understanding, so that we may know him who is true. And we are in him who is true by being in his Son Jesus Christ. He is the true God and eternal life.

²¹Dear children, keep yourselves from idols.

BREAKTHROUGH!

What are the sins that lead to death?

(1 JOHN 5:16)

It's talking about the one sin that can't be forgiven. Jesus talked about this in Mark 3:28-29. This one sin is speaking badly against the Holy Spirit. It doesn't mean that God can't forgive a person who does this. What it means is that the person who talks against the Holy Spirit really doesn't want God's forgiveness.

2 JOHN

¹The elder,

To the lady chosen by God and to her children, whom I love in the truth— and not I only, but also all who know the truth— ²because of the truth, which lives in us and will be with us forever:

³Grace, mercy and peace from God the Father and from Jesus Christ, the Father's Son, will be with us in truth and love.

⁴It has given me great joy to find some of your children walking in the truth, just as the Father commanded us. ⁵And now, dear lady, I am not writing you a new command but one we have had from the beginning. I ask that we love one another. ⁶And this is love: that we walk in obedience to his commands. As you have heard from the beginning, his command is that you walk in love.

⁷I say this because many deceivers, who do not acknowledge Jesus Christ as coming in the flesh, have gone out into the world. Any such person is the deceiver and the antichrist. ⁸Watch out that you do not lose what we*a* have worked for, but that you may be rewarded fully. ⁹Anyone who runs ahead and does not continue in the teaching of Christ does not have God; whoever continues in the teaching has both the Father and the Son. ¹⁰If anyone comes to you and does not bring this teaching, do not take them into your house or welcome them. ¹¹Anyone who welcomes them shares in their wicked work.

¹²I have much to write to you, but I do not want to use paper and ink. Instead, I hope to visit you and talk with you face to face, so that our joy may be complete.

¹³The children of your sister, who is chosen by God, send their greetings.

---

a 8 Some manuscripts *you*

BREAKTHROUGH!

Is there a reward?

(2 JOHN 1:8)

The reward it's talking about here is also a gift. It is the gift that God gives us: eternal life.

Should we not welcome into our houses people who are not Christians?

(2 JOHN 1:10-11)

No, that's not what this is about. At the time this letter was written, greeting or welcoming a person into a home was a way of recognizing that a person was a believer and agreed with Christian teachings. That's not the way it is now. What it's saying here is that we can't accept the false teachings some people want us to believe.

3 JOHN

[1] The elder,

To my dear friend Gaius, whom I love in the truth.

[2] Dear friend, I pray that you may enjoy good health and that all may go well with you, even as your soul is getting along well. [3] It gave me great joy when some believers came and testified about your faithfulness to the truth, telling how you continue to walk in it. [4] I have no greater joy than to hear that my children are walking in the truth.

[5] Dear friend, you are faithful in what you are doing for the brothers and sisters,[a] even though they are strangers to you. [6] They have told the church about your love. Please send them on their way in a manner that honors God. [7] It was for the sake of the Name that they went out, receiving no help from the pagans. [8] We ought therefore to show hospitality to

---

[a] 5 The Greek word for *brothers and sisters* (*adelphoi*) refers here to believers, both men and women, as part of God's family.

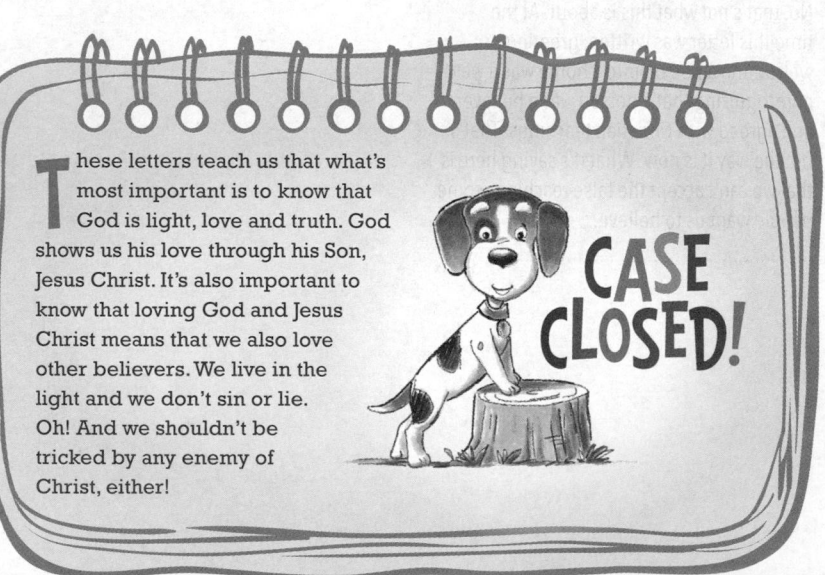

These letters teach us that what's most important is to know that God is light, love and truth. God shows us his love through his Son, Jesus Christ. It's also important to know that loving God and Jesus Christ means that we also love other believers. We live in the light and we don't sin or lie. Oh! And we shouldn't be tricked by any enemy of Christ, either!

CASE CLOSED!

such people so that we may work together for the truth.

⁹I wrote to the church, but Diotrephes, who loves to be first, will not welcome us. ¹⁰So when I come, I will call attention to what he is doing, spreading malicious nonsense about us. Not satisfied with that, he even refuses to welcome other believers. He also stops those who want to do so and puts them out of the church.

¹¹Dear friend, do not imitate what is evil but what is good. Anyone who does what is good is from God. Anyone who does what is evil has not seen God. ¹²Demetrius is well spoken of by everyone—and even by the truth itself. We also speak well of him, and you know that our testimony is true.

¹³I have much to write you, but I do not want to do so with pen and ink. ¹⁴I hope to see you soon, and we will talk face to face.

Peace to you. The friends here send their greetings. Greet the friends there by name.

THE
WITNESSES

✓ GAIUS (3 JOHN 1:1)
This is the person John is writing this third letter to. He probably was in charge of the Christian community the writer mentions, or he was an important person in that community.

✓ DIOTREPHES AND DEMETRIUS
(3 JOHN 1:9–12)
Diotrephes is another important person in that community, and both Gaius and John knew him. It seems that he was a rather difficult person, and that he liked "to be first" and was "spreading malicious nonsense" about John and his fellow workers. With regard to Demetrius, perhaps Gaius didn't know him. That's why the writer mentions that he is a good person.

JUDE

THE EVIDENCE:

WHO WROTE IT?
The writer says he is Jude, James' brother. That would make him Jesus' brother too. This Jude didn't believe in Jesus while Jesus was here on Earth.

HOW LONG AGO?
We don't know exactly when this letter was written. Some Bible experts say it was written between the years 70 and 81 after Christ. Others say it was between the years 95 and 105 after Christ.

WHAT'S IT ABOUT?
This is another letter that tries to make Christians aware of bad people who teach lies and go against the Bible. It insists that those false teachers will be destroyed, just like God did other times when people were very, very bad.

THE BEST PART
We really liked verse 24, which says, "To him who is able to keep you from stumbling ..." Thank you, Lord!

---

¹Jude, a servant of Jesus Christ and a brother of James,

To those who have been called, who are loved in God the Father and kept for[a] Jesus Christ:

²Mercy, peace and love be yours in abundance.

The Sin and Doom of Ungodly People

³Dear friends, although I was very eager to write to you about the salvation we share, I felt compelled to write and urge you to contend for the faith that was once for all entrusted to God's holy peo- ple. ⁴For certain individuals whose con- demnation was written about[b] long ago have secretly slipped in among you. They are ungodly people, who pervert the grace of our God into a license for immorality and deny Jesus Christ our only Sovereign and Lord.

⁵Though you already know all this, I want to remind you that the Lord[c] at one time delivered his people out of Egypt, but later destroyed those who did not believe. ⁶And the angels who did not keep their positions of authority but abandoned their proper dwelling—these he has kept in

---

ᵃ 1 Or by; or in for condemnation   ᵇ 4 Or individuals who were marked out   ᶜ 5 Some early manuscripts Jesus

THE
WITNESSES

✓ **JUDE** (JUDE 1:1)

It's thought that this Jude was Jesus' brother, and that he and Jesus also had another brother called James. At first, Jude and his other brothers didn't believe that Jesus was the Messiah, the one God had chosen to save us. But later, Jesus rose from the dead and appeared to James. That's probably when the brothers began to believe. The truth is that we really don't know, but we think it could have happened like that.

darkness, bound with everlasting chains for judgment on the great Day. ⁷In a similar way, Sodom and Gomorrah and the surrounding towns gave themselves up to sexual immorality and perversion. They serve as an example of those who suffer the punishment of eternal fire.

⁸In the very same way, on the strength of their dreams these ungodly people pollute their own bodies, reject authority and heap abuse on celestial beings. ⁹But even the archangel Michael, when he was disputing with the devil about the body of Moses, did not himself dare to condemn him for slander but said, "The Lord rebuke you!"ᵃ ¹⁰Yet these people slander whatever they do not understand, and the very things they do understand by instinct—as irrational animals do—will destroy them.

¹¹Woe to them! They have taken the way of Cain; they have rushed for profit into Balaam's error; they have been destroyed in Korah's rebellion.

¹²These people are blemishes at your love feasts, eating with you without the slightest qualm—shepherds who feed only themselves. They are clouds without rain, blown along by the wind; autumn trees, without fruit and uprooted—twice dead. ¹³They are wild waves of the sea, foaming up their shame; wandering stars, for whom blackest darkness has been reserved forever.

¹⁴Enoch, the seventh from Adam, prophesied about them: "See, the Lord is coming with thousands upon thousands of his holy ones ¹⁵to judge everyone, and to convict all of them of all the ungodly acts they have committed in their ungodliness, and of all the defiant words ungodly sinners have spoken against him."ᵇ ¹⁶These people are grumblers and faultfinders; they follow their own evil desires; they boast about themselves and flatter others for their own advantage.

A Call to Persevere

¹⁷But, dear friends, remember what the apostles of our Lord Jesus Christ foretold. ¹⁸They said to you, "In the last times there will be scoffers who will follow their own ungodly desires." ¹⁹These are the people who divide you, who follow mere natural instincts and do not have the Spirit.

²⁰But you, dear friends, by building yourselves up in your most holy faith and praying in the Holy Spirit, ²¹keep yourselves in God's love as you wait for the mercy of our Lord Jesus Christ to bring you to eternal life.

ᵃ 9 Jude is alluding to the Jewish *Testament of Moses* (approximately the first century A.D.).   ᵇ 14,15 From the Jewish *First Book of Enoch* (approximately the first century B.C.)

²²Be merciful to those who doubt; ²³save others by snatching them from the fire; to others show mercy, mixed with fear—hating even the clothing stained by corrupted flesh.ᵃ

Doxology

²⁴To him who is able to keep you from stumbling and to present you before his glorious presence without fault and with great joy— ²⁵to the only God our Savior be glory, majesty, power and authority, through Jesus Christ our Lord, before all ages, now and forevermore! Amen.

ᵃ 22,23 The Greek manuscripts of these verses vary at several points.

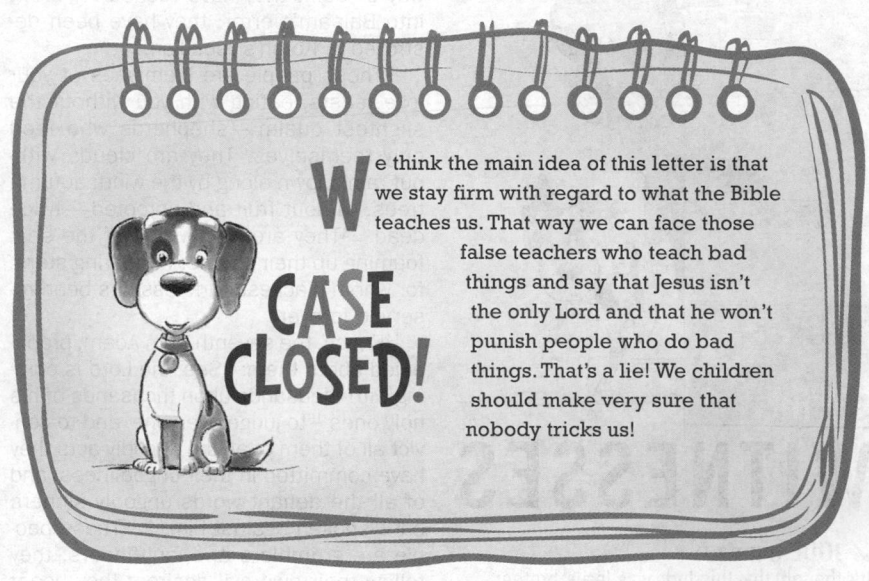

We think the main idea of this letter is that we stay firm with regard to what the Bible teaches us. That way we can face those false teachers who teach bad things and say that Jesus isn't the only Lord and that he won't punish people who do bad things. That's a lie! We children should make very sure that nobody tricks us!

CASE CLOSED!

REVELATION

WHO WROTE IT?
This book was written by a follower of Jesus whose name was John, the same name of the disciple of Jesus. Some people think he was the same person who wrote the gospel and the letters of John. Others think he was an important Christian leader in the 1st century after Christ and that he had the same name as that other John. At any rate, this John introduces himself simply as a servant.

HOW LONG AGO?
It was written at the end of the 1st century after Christ, which means about 60 or 70 years after Jesus was here on Earth.

WHAT'S IT ABOUT?
Many people are afraid of this book, but its main purpose is to encourage Christians who are having a hard time or having to face evil forces. The message is that Christ is coming soon and that God will conquer everything that's evil.

The author uses a lot of images to explain a very important idea. God has all the power, even when it seems like bad people are winning and Christians are being persecuted. In the end, God is always victorious even when we can't see it right away. People who are faithful to God will also be successful, and God will reward them with eternal life. In other words, we'll live with God forever. That's very good!

THE BEST PART
We agreed that the best part is 22:4, where it says, "They will see his face, and his name will be on their foreheads." How exciting! To see God face to face!

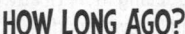

Prologue

1 The revelation from Jesus Christ, which God gave him to show his servants what must soon take place. He made it known by sending his angel to his servant John, ²who testifies to everything he saw—that is, the word of God and the testimony of Jesus Christ. ³Blessed is the one who reads aloud the words of this prophecy, and blessed are those who hear it and take to heart what is written in it, because the time is near.

Greetings and Doxology

⁴John,

To the seven churches in the province of Asia:

Grace and peace to you from him who is, and who was, and who is to come, and

THE
WITNESSES

✓ JOHN (REVELATION 1:1)

The name John means "grace of God." It's a way of saying that God gives his blessing and love. He gives us what we really don't deserve.

from the seven spirits[a] before his throne, [5]and from Jesus Christ, who is the faithful witness, the firstborn from the dead, and the ruler of the kings of the earth.

To him who loves us and has freed us from our sins by his blood, [6]and has made us to be a kingdom and priests to serve his God and Father—to him be glory and power for ever and ever! Amen.

[7] "Look, he is coming with the
　　clouds,"[b]
　and "every eye will see him,
　even those who pierced him";
　　and all peoples on earth "will
　　　mourn because of him."[c]
　　　　　So shall it be! Amen.

BREAK THROUGH!

What does *Revelation* mean?

(REVELATION 1:1)

The original Greek word means "take off the veil," which would be like seeing more clearly. It's like finding something that was hidden. In this case, God and Jesus make things clear to John.

[8] "I am the Alpha and the Omega," says the Lord God, "who is, and who was, and who is to come, the Almighty."

John's Vision of Christ

[9]I, John, your brother and companion in the suffering and kingdom and patient endurance that are ours in Jesus, was on the island of Patmos because of the word of God and the testimony of Jesus. [10]On the Lord's Day I was in the Spirit, and I heard behind me a loud voice like a trumpet, [11]which said: "Write on a scroll what you see and send it to the seven churches: to Ephesus, Smyrna, Pergamum, Thyatira, Sardis, Philadelphia and Laodicea."

[12]I turned around to see the voice that was speaking to me. And when I turned I saw seven golden lampstands, [13]and among the lampstands was someone like

---

[a] 4 That is, the sevenfold Spirit　　[b] 7 Daniel 7:13
[c] 7 Zech. 12:10

a son of man,ᵃ dressed in a robe reaching down to his feet and with a golden sash around his chest. ¹⁴The hair on his head was white like wool, as white as snow, and his eyes were like blazing fire. ¹⁵His feet were like bronze glowing in a furnace, and his voice was like the sound of rushing waters. ¹⁶In his right hand he held seven stars, and coming out of his mouth was a sharp, double-edged sword. His face was like the sun shining in all its brilliance.

¹⁷When I saw him, I fell at his feet as though dead. Then he placed his right hand on me and said: "Do not be afraid. I am the First and the Last. ¹⁸I am the Living One; I was dead, and now look, I am alive for ever and ever! And I hold the keys of death and Hades.

ᵃ *13* See Daniel 7:13.

ASIA

(REVELATION 1:4)

The Romans used to call the region that is Turkey now *Asia Minor.*

ISLAND OF PATMOS

(REVELATION 1:9)

This is a small, rocky island in the Aegean Sea, southwest of Ephesus in the south part of Turkey. The island is 7.5 miles (12 km) long and 4 miles (7 km) wide at one part. There are many volcanoes there, and the sea around it is very rough. The Romans would send prisoners there. They weren't really criminals. They were just people who had different opinions and were thought to be dangerous for the empire. This island belongs to Greece now.

BREAKTHROUGH!

Are there seven spirits in front of God's throne?

(REVELATION 1:4)

The number seven is very important for the writer of this book. This number shows something complete, finished, perfect, and it has to do with God. In Bible times, many people believed this about the number seven. So, saying that there are seven spirits means that the Spirit of God is complete and nothing is lacking. This is about the Spirit of God with all his power. It doesn't mean that God has a bunch of spirits and we can count them up to seven!

THE SCENE

EPHESUS

(REVELATION 1:11)

Read Ephesians 1:1.

SMYRNA

(REVELATION 1:11)

This was a city in the Roman province of Asia, on the coast of the Aegean Sea. Today, this is the western part of Turkey, and it's called Izmir. It's Turkey's second port. In ancient times, it was very famous for its beautiful buildings, and it even became a very powerful city in the Mediterranean Sea region.

[19] "Write, therefore, what you have seen, what is now and what will take place later. [20] The mystery of the seven stars that you saw in my right hand and of the seven golden lampstands is this: The seven stars are the angels[a] of the seven churches, and the seven lampstands are the seven churches.

To the Church in Ephesus

2 "To the angel[b] of the church in Ephesus write:

These are the words of him who holds the seven stars in his right hand and walks among the seven golden lampstands. [2] I know your deeds, your hard work and your perseverance. I know that you cannot tolerate wicked people, that you have tested those who claim to be apostles but are not, and have found them false. [3] You have persevered and have endured hardships for my name, and have not grown weary.

[4] Yet I hold this against you: You have forsaken the love you had at first. [5] Consider how far you have fallen! Repent and do the things you did at first. If you do not repent, I will come to you and remove your lampstand from its place. [6] But you have this in your favor: You hate the practices of the Nicolaitans, which I also hate.

[7] Whoever has ears, let them hear what the Spirit says to the churches. To the one who is victorious, I will give the right to eat from the tree of life, which is in the paradise of God.

To the Church in Smyrna

[8] "To the angel of the church in Smyrna write:

These are the words of him who is the First and the Last, who died and came to life again. [9] I know your afflictions and your poverty—yet you are rich! I know about the slander of those who say they are Jews and are not, but are a synagogue of Satan. [10] Do not be afraid of what you are about to suffer. I tell you, the devil will put some of you in prison to test you, and you will suffer persecution for ten days. Be faithful, even to the point of death, and I will give you life as your victor's crown.

[11] Whoever has ears, let them hear what the Spirit says to the churches. The one who is victorious will not be hurt at all by the second death.

---

[a] 20 Or *messengers*   [b] 1 Or *messenger*; also in verses 8, 12 and 18

To the Church in Pergamum

¹² "To the angel of the church in Pergamum write:

These are the words of him who has the sharp, double-edged sword. ¹³ I know where you live—where Satan has his throne. Yet you remain true to my name. You did not renounce your faith in me, not even in the days of Antipas, my faithful witness, who was put to death in your city—where Satan lives.

¹⁴ Nevertheless, I have a few things against you: There are some among you who hold to the teaching of Balaam, who taught Balak to entice the Israelites to sin so that they ate food sacrificed to idols and committed sexual immorality. ¹⁵ Likewise, you also have those who hold to the teaching of the Nicolaitans. ¹⁶ Repent therefore! Otherwise, I will soon come to you and will fight against them with the sword of my mouth.

¹⁷ Whoever has ears, let them hear what the Spirit says to the churches. To the one who is victorious, I will give some of the hidden manna. I will also give that person a white stone with a new name written on it, known only to the one who receives it.

To the Church in Thyatira

¹⁸ "To the angel of the church in Thyatira write:

These are the words of the Son of God, whose eyes are like blazing fire and whose feet are like burnished bronze. ¹⁹ I know your deeds, your love and faith, your service and perseverance, and that you are now doing more than you did at first.

²⁰ Nevertheless, I have this against you: You tolerate that woman Jezebel, who calls herself a prophet. By her teaching she misleads my servants into sexual immorality and the eating of food sacrificed to idols. ²¹ I have given her time to repent of her immorality, but she is unwilling. ²² So

THE WITNESSES

✓ **JEZEBEL (REVELATION 2:20)**
Her name means "Where is the prince?" She was a very bad queen. She was the daughter of Ethbaal, the king of the Sidonians who worshiped the god Baal. She married Ahab, who was the king of Israel. She persecuted the prophet Elijah for a long time and tried to kill him, because she didn't like that he was talking about God, and he had also told her that she was doing bad things.

I will cast her on a bed of suffering, and I will make those who commit adultery with her suffer intensely, unless they repent of her ways. ²³ I will strike her children dead. Then all the churches will know that I am he who searches hearts and minds, and I will repay each of you according to your deeds.

²⁴ Now I say to the rest of you in Thyatira, to you who do not hold to

BREAKTHROUGH!

Nicolaitans

(REVELATION 2:6)

Nobody seems to know exactly who they were. But it's clear that it was a group that was teaching incorrect things about faith in Christ and God. They had a way of thinking that made people want to stop following God. We don't know exactly what they thought or where they were meeting.

her teaching and have not learned Satan's so-called deep secrets, 'I will not impose any other burden on you, ²⁵except to hold on to what you have until I come.'

²⁶To the one who is victorious and does my will to the end, I will give authority over the nations— ²⁷that one 'will rule them with an iron scepter and will dash them to pieces like pottery'^a—just as I have received authority from my Father. ²⁸I will also give that one the morning star. ²⁹Whoever has ears, let them hear what the Spirit says to the churches.

To the Church in Sardis

3 "To the angel^b of the church in Sardis write:

^a 27 Psalm 2:9   ^b 1 Or messenger; also in verses 7 and 14

THE SCENE

PERGAMUM

(REVELATION 2:12)

This was a city in the Roman province of Asia, in the western part of what is Turkey today. Pergamum was very important for river trade in the large Caicus Valley, now called Bakir. The name Pergamum is related to the word for "parchment."

THYATIRA

(REVELATION 2:18)

Also a city in the Roman province of Asia, in the western part of what is Turkey today. It was very important in the highway system the Romans had built, because it was located between the cities of Pergamum and Laodicea. It was an important manufacturing center for wool products and fabric dying, as well as the production of ceramic objects.

These are the words of him who holds the seven spirits[a] of God and the seven stars. I know your deeds; you have a reputation of being alive, but you are dead. ²Wake up! Strengthen what remains and is about to die, for I have found your deeds unfinished in the sight of my God. ³Remember, therefore, what you have received and heard; hold it fast, and repent. But if you do not wake up, I will come like a thief, and you will not know at what time I will come to you.

⁴Yet you have a few people in Sardis who have not soiled their clothes. They will walk with me, dressed in white, for they are worthy. ⁵The one who is victorious will, like them, be dressed in white. I will never blot out the name of that person from the book of life, but will acknowledge that name before my Father and his angels. ⁶Whoever has ears, let them hear what the Spirit says to the churches.

To the Church in Philadelphia

⁷"To the angel of the church in Philadelphia write:

ᵃ *1* That is, the sevenfold Spirit

Hidden manna

(REVELATION 2:17)

This was the food that fell from the sky every day when the Hebrews were traveling to the promised land. God had told them that they had to keep some manna in a jar and place it in front of the ark of the covenant (Exodus 16:14–15,32–34; Hebrews 9:4). That was so God's people would never forget how God had taken care of them in the desert. The people believed that when the temple in Jerusalem was destroyed, Jeremiah hid that pot in a cave so it would still be there when the Messiah arrived. So the people were thinking that God would give them manna again in the future and it would appear in that hidden jar.

SARDIS

(REVELATION 3:1)

This was a city in the Roman province of Asia, in the western part of what is Turkey today. It was a very old city in the kingdom of Lydia. This kingdom existed before the arrival of the Greeks, who were later conquered by the Romans. Consequently, it wasn't founded by either Greeks or Romans.

These are the words of him who is holy and true, who holds the key of David. What he opens no one can shut, and what he shuts no one can open. [8]I know your deeds. See, I have placed before you an open door that no one can shut. I know that you have little strength, yet you have kept my word and have not denied my name. [9]I will make those who are of the synagogue of Satan, who claim to be Jews though they are not, but are liars—I will make them come and fall down at your feet and acknowledge that I have loved you. [10]Since you have kept my command to endure patiently, I will also keep you from the hour of trial that is going to come on the whole world to test the inhabitants of the earth.

[11]I am coming soon. Hold on to what you have, so that no one will take your crown. [12]The one who is victorious I will make a pillar in the temple of my God. Never again will they leave it. I will write on them the name of my God and the name of the city of my God, the new Jerusalem, which is coming down out of heaven from my God; and I will also write on them my new name. [13]Whoever has ears, let them hear what the Spirit says to the churches.

To the Church in Laodicea

[14]"To the angel of the church in Laodicea write:

These are the words of the Amen, the faithful and true witness, the ruler of God's creation. [15]I know your deeds, that you are neither cold nor hot. I wish you were either one or the other! [16]So, because you are lukewarm—neither hot nor cold—I am about to spit you out of my mouth. [17]You say, 'I am rich; I have acquired wealth and do not need a thing.' But you do not realize that you are wretched, pitiful, poor, blind and naked. [18]I counsel you to buy from me gold refined in the fire, so you can become rich; and white clothes to

PHILADELPHIA

(REVELATION 3:7)

This was a city in the Roman province of Asia, in the western part of what is Turkey today. It was founded by the king of the city of Pergamum. It was situated on a very fertile plain, so it became a rich region because of its agricultural production (crops). This city was famous for its many temples and the festivals of the different religions.

LAODICEA

(REVELATION 3:14)

Read Colossians 2:1.

wear, so you can cover your shameful nakedness; and salve to put on your eyes, so you can see.

[19]Those whom I love I rebuke and discipline. So be earnest and repent. [20]Here I am! I stand at the door and knock. If anyone hears my voice and opens the door, I will come in and eat with that person, and they with me. [21]To the one who is victorious, I

will give the right to sit with me on my throne, just as I was victorious and sat down with my Father on his throne. ²²Whoever has ears, let them hear what the Spirit says to the churches."

The Throne in Heaven

4 After this I looked, and there before me was a door standing open in heaven. And the voice I had first heard speaking to me like a trumpet said, "Come up here, and I will show you what must take place after this." ²At once I was in the Spirit, and there before me was a throne in heaven with someone sitting on it. ³And the one who sat there had the appearance of jasper and ruby. A rainbow that shone like an emerald encircled the throne. ⁴Surrounding the throne were twenty-four other thrones, and seated on them were twenty-four elders. They were dressed in white and had crowns of gold on their heads. ⁵From the throne came flashes of lightning, rumblings and peals of thunder. In front of the throne, seven lamps were blazing. These are the seven spirits[a] of God. ⁶Also in front of the throne there was what looked like a sea of glass, clear as crystal.

In the center, around the throne, were four living creatures, and they were covered with eyes, in front and in back. ⁷The first living creature was like a lion, the second was like an ox, the third had a face like a man, the fourth was like a flying eagle. ⁸Each of the four living creatures had six wings and was covered with eyes all around, even under its wings. Day and night they never stop saying:

> " 'Holy, holy, holy
> is the Lord God Almighty,'[b]
> who was, and is, and is to come."

⁹Whenever the living creatures give glory, honor and thanks to him who sits on the throne and who lives for ever and ever, ¹⁰the twenty-four elders fall down before him who sits on the throne and worship him who lives for ever and ever. They lay their crowns before the throne and say:

BREAK THROUGH!

Twenty-four elders

(REVELATION 4:4)

The Greek words of the Bible actually says *presbyters,* which means "old people." Those twenty-four old people that John saw in his vision probably stand for the people of God from the Old and New Testaments. In Old Testament times, the people of Israel were divided into twelve tribes. In New Testament times, Jesus chose twelve special men to belong to his group of friends. They were Jesus' twelve friends called the "apostles." So the number twenty-four could very well be the total of the twelve Old Testament leaders, plus Jesus' 12 friends. 12+12=24!

¹¹ "You are worthy, our Lord and God,
> to receive glory and honor and power,
> for you created all things,
> and by your will they were created
> and have their being."

The Scroll and the Lamb

5 Then I saw in the right hand of him who sat on the throne a scroll with writing on both sides and sealed with seven seals. ²And I saw a mighty angel proclaiming in a loud voice, "Who is

---

[a] 5 That is, the sevenfold Spirit   [b] 8 Isaiah 6:3

Four living creatures covered with eyes in front and in back

(REVELATION 4:6)

Nobody really knows what those four living creatures were. It is possible they were some kind of angels.

A scroll

(REVELATION 5:1)

A very, very long time ago, there were no books like the ones we have today, let alone an iPad! They used a kind of sheet made from animal skins or a plant called papyrus. Then they rolled those sheets up and called them *scrolls*. If what was written on a scroll was an important notice or a message for someone, they rolled it up and put a mark on it with wax and the seal of the person who was sending it. The person who wanted to read it had to break the seal in order to be able to read the "book." So that's why the book of Revelation talks about the seven seals that had to be broken!

worthy to break the seals and open the scroll?" ³But no one in heaven or on earth or under the earth could open the scroll or even look inside it. ⁴I wept and wept because no one was found who was worthy to open the scroll or look inside. ⁵Then one of the elders said to me, "Do not weep! See, the Lion of the tribe of Judah, the Root of David, has triumphed. He is able to open the scroll and its seven seals."

⁶Then I saw a Lamb, looking as if it had been slain, standing at the center of the throne, encircled by the four living creatures and the elders. The Lamb had seven horns and seven eyes, which are the seven spirits*a* of God sent out into all the earth. ⁷He went and took the scroll from the right hand of him who sat on the throne. ⁸And when he had taken it, the four living creatures and the twenty-four elders fell down before the Lamb. Each one had a harp and they were holding golden bowls full of incense, which are the prayers of God's people. ⁹And they sang a new song, saying:

> "You are worthy to take the scroll
>   and to open its seals,
> because you were slain,
>   and with your blood you purchased
>   for God
>   persons from every tribe and
>   language and people and
>   nation.

---

a 6 That is, the sevenfold Spirit

¹⁰ You have made them to be a kingdom
and priests to serve our God,
and they will reign*ᵃ* on the earth."

¹¹ Then I looked and heard the voice of many angels, numbering thousands upon thousands, and ten thousand times ten thousand. They encircled the throne and the living creatures and the elders. ¹² In a loud voice they were saying:

"Worthy is the Lamb, who was slain,
to receive power and wealth and
wisdom and strength
and honor and glory and praise!"

¹³ Then I heard every creature in heaven and on earth and under the earth and on the sea, and all that is in them, saying:

"To him who sits on the throne and to
the Lamb

be praise and honor and glory and
power,
for ever and ever!"

¹⁴ The four living creatures said, "Amen," and the elders fell down and worshiped.

The Seals

6 I watched as the Lamb opened the first of the seven seals. Then I heard

---

ᵃ 10 Some manuscripts *they reign*

Who is the Lamb?
(REVELATION 5:6)

In the Old Testament, God had told Moses that the Israelites had to kill a perfect lamb the night before they left Egypt. They had to rub the lamb's blood on the doors and windows to protect their children from the death angel who would pass through Egypt that night. In the New Testament, John the Baptist says that Jesus is the Lamb of God who comes to forgive the sins of the world (John 1:29). So in the same way each family sacrificed a lamb to free the people of Israel, Jesus sacrificed himself. That means that Jesus let himself be killed on the cross so we could be forgiven for sins. In the book of Revelation, John sees a lamb that stands for Jesus, and that reminds us that Jesus died on the cross.

Lion of the tribe of Judah
(REVELATION 5:5)

The "Lion of the tribe of Judah" and the "Root of David" are names for the Messiah, God's chosen One. David was the king of Israel who pleased God. Jesus came from the tribe of Judah just like David did. Jesus is the person who inherits everything that David meant to the people of Israel as their king and God's chosen person.

CHECK THE FACTS

Who is the Lamb who opens the scroll with the seven seals?

A) Jesus

B) Michael, the archangel

C) Rome

CORRECT ANSWER: A

one of the four living creatures say in a voice like thunder, "Come!" ²I looked, and there before me was a white horse! Its rider held a bow, and he was given a crown, and he rode out as a conqueror bent on conquest.

³When the Lamb opened the second seal, I heard the second living creature say, "Come!" ⁴Then another horse came out, a fiery red one. Its rider was given power to take peace from the earth and to make people kill each other. To him was given a large sword.

⁵When the Lamb opened the third seal, I heard the third living creature say, "Come!" I looked, and there before me was a black horse! Its rider was holding a pair of scales in his hand. ⁶Then I heard what sounded like a voice among the four living creatures, saying, "Two pounds[a] of wheat for a day's wages,[b] and six pounds[c] of barley for a day's wages,[b] and do not damage the oil and the wine!"

⁷When the Lamb opened the fourth seal, I heard the voice of the fourth living creature say, "Come!" ⁸I looked, and there before me was a pale horse! Its rider was named Death, and Hades was following close behind him. They were given power over a fourth of the earth to kill by sword, famine and plague, and by the wild beasts of the earth.

⁹When he opened the fifth seal, I saw under the altar the souls of those who had been slain because of the word of God and the testimony they had maintained. ¹⁰They called out in a loud voice, "How long, Sovereign Lord, holy and true, until you judge the inhabitants of the earth and avenge our blood?" ¹¹Then each of them was given a white robe, and they were told to wait a little longer, until the full number of their fellow servants, their brothers and sisters,[d] were killed just as they had been.

¹²I watched as he opened the sixth seal. There was a great earthquake. The sun turned black like sackcloth made of goat hair, the whole moon turned blood red, ¹³and the stars in the sky fell to earth, as figs drop from a fig tree when shaken by a strong wind. ¹⁴The heavens receded like a scroll being rolled up, and every mountain and island was removed from its place.

¹⁵Then the kings of the earth, the princes, the generals, the rich, the mighty, and everyone else, both slave and free, hid in caves and among the rocks of the mountains. ¹⁶They called to the mountains and the rocks, "Fall on us and hide us[e] from the face of him who sits on the throne and from the wrath of the Lamb! ¹⁷For the great day of their[f] wrath has come, and who can withstand it?"

144,000 Sealed

7 After this I saw four angels standing at the four corners of the earth, holding back the four winds of the earth to prevent any wind from blowing on the land or on the sea or on any tree. ²Then I saw another angel coming up from the east,

---

[a] 6 Or about 1 kilogram   [b] 6 Greek a *denarius*   [c] 6 Or about 3 kilograms   [d] 11 The Greek word for *brothers and sisters* (*adelphoi*) refers here to believers, both men and women, as part of God's family; also in 12:10; 19:10.   [e] 16 See Hosea 10:8.   [f] 17 Some manuscripts *his*

having the seal of the living God. He called out in a loud voice to the four angels who had been given power to harm the land and the sea: ³"Do not harm the land or the sea or the trees until we put a seal on the foreheads of the servants of our God." ⁴Then I heard the number of those who were sealed: 144,000 from all the tribes of Israel.

⁵From the tribe of Judah 12,000 were sealed,
from the tribe of Reuben 12,000,
from the tribe of Gad 12,000,
⁶from the tribe of Asher 12,000,
from the tribe of Naphtali 12,000,
from the tribe of Manasseh 12,000,
⁷from the tribe of Simeon 12,000,
from the tribe of Levi 12,000,
from the tribe of Issachar 12,000,
⁸from the tribe of Zebulun 12,000,
from the tribe of Joseph 12,000,
from the tribe of Benjamin 12,000.

The Great Multitude in White Robes

⁹After this I looked, and there before me was a great multitude that no one could count, from every nation, tribe, people and language, standing before the throne and before the Lamb. They were wearing white robes and were holding palm branches in their hands. ¹⁰And they cried out in a loud voice:

"Salvation belongs to our God,
who sits on the throne,
and to the Lamb."

¹¹All the angels were standing around the throne and around the elders and the four living creatures. They fell down on their faces before the throne and worshiped God, ¹²saying:

"Amen!
Praise and glory
and wisdom and thanks and honor
and power and strength
be to our God for ever and ever.
Amen!"

¹³Then one of the elders asked me, "These in white robes—who are they, and where did they come from?"

¹⁴I answered, "Sir, you know."

And he said, "These are they who have come out of the great tribulation; they have washed their robes and made them white in the blood of the Lamb. ¹⁵Therefore,

"they are before the throne of God
and serve him day and night in his
temple;
and he who sits on the throne
will shelter them with his presence.
¹⁶'Never again will they hunger;
never again will they thirst.
The sun will not beat down on them,'ᵃ
nor any scorching heat.
¹⁷For the Lamb at the center of the throne
will be their shepherd;
'he will lead them to springs of living
water.'ᵇ
'And God will wipe away every tear
from their eyes.'ᶜ"

The Seventh Seal and the Golden Censer

8 When he opened the seventh seal, there was silence in heaven for about half an hour.

²And I saw the seven angels who stand before God, and seven trumpets were given to them.

³Another angel, who had a golden censer, came and stood at the altar. He was given much incense to offer, with the prayers of all God's people, on the golden altar in front of the throne. ⁴The smoke of the incense, together with the prayers of God's people, went up before God from the angel's hand. ⁵Then the angel took the censer, filled it with fire from the altar, and hurled it on the earth; and there came peals of thunder, rumblings, flashes of lightning and an earthquake.

The Trumpets

⁶Then the seven angels who had the seven trumpets prepared to sound them.

⁷The first angel sounded his trumpet, and there came hail and fire mixed with blood, and it was hurled down on the earth. A third of the earth was burned up,

---

ᵃ 16 Isaiah 49:10   ᵇ 17 Isaiah 49:10
ᶜ 17 Isaiah 25:8

a third of the trees were burned up, and all the green grass was burned up.

⁸The second angel sounded his trumpet, and something like a huge mountain, all ablaze, was thrown into the sea. A third of the sea turned into blood, ⁹a third of the living creatures in the sea died, and a third of the ships were destroyed.

¹⁰The third angel sounded his trumpet, and a great star, blazing like a torch, fell from the sky on a third of the rivers and on the springs of water— ¹¹the name of the star is Wormwood.ᵃ A third of the waters turned bitter, and many people died from the waters that had become bitter.

¹²The fourth angel sounded his trumpet, and a third of the sun was struck, a third of the moon, and a third of the stars, so that a third of them turned dark. A third of the day was without light, and also a third of the night.

¹³As I watched, I heard an eagle that was flying in midair call out in a loud voice: "Woe! Woe! Woe to the inhabitants of the earth, because of the trumpet blasts about to be sounded by the other three angels!"

9 The fifth angel sounded his trumpet, and I saw a star that had fallen from the sky to the earth. The star was given the key to the shaft of the Abyss. ²When he opened the Abyss, smoke rose from it like the smoke from a gigantic furnace. The sun and sky were darkened by the smoke from the Abyss. ³And out of the smoke locusts came down on the earth and were given power like that of scorpions of the earth. ⁴They were told not to harm the grass of the earth or any plant or tree, but only those people who did not have the seal of God on their foreheads. ⁵They were not allowed to kill them but only to torture them for five months. And the agony they suffered was like that of the sting of a scorpion when it strikes. ⁶During those days people will seek death but will not find it; they will long to die, but death will elude them.

⁷The locusts looked like horses prepared for battle. On their heads they wore something like crowns of gold, and their faces resembled human faces. ⁸Their hair was like women's hair, and their teeth

BREAKTHROUGH!

Who were those strange locusts?

(REVELATION 9:3-11)

Nobody really knows. It's probably just a way of talking about bad spirits that bother human beings. The words talk about them like a combination of war horses, human beings and lions. That gives us the impression that it's a symbol. They stand for war and the evil that humans who are controlled by bad forces can cause on Earth. These humans will be destroyed by those locusts that have the Destroyer himself as their leader.

were like lions' teeth. ⁹They had breastplates like breastplates of iron, and the sound of their wings was like the thundering of many horses and chariots rushing into battle. ¹⁰They had tails with stingers, like scorpions, and in their tails they had power to torment people for five months. ¹¹They had as king over them the angel of the Abyss, whose name in Hebrew is Abaddon and in Greek is Apollyon (that is, Destroyer).

¹²The first woe is past; two other woes are yet to come.

¹³The sixth angel sounded his trumpet, and I heard a voice coming from the four

---

ᵃ 11 Wormwood is a bitter substance.

horns of the golden altar that is before God. [14]It said to the sixth angel who had the trumpet, "Release the four angels who are bound at the great river Euphrates." [15]And the four angels who had been kept ready for this very hour and day and month and year were released to kill a third of mankind. [16]The number of the mounted troops was twice ten thousand times ten thousand. I heard their number.

[17]The horses and riders I saw in my vision looked like this: Their breastplates were fiery red, dark blue, and yellow as sulfur. The heads of the horses resembled the heads of lions, and out of their mouths came fire, smoke and sulfur. [18]A third of mankind was killed by the three plagues of fire, smoke and sulfur that came out of their mouths. [19]The power of the horses was in their mouths and in their tails; for their tails were like snakes, having heads with which they inflict injury.

[20]The rest of mankind who were not killed by these plagues still did not repent of the work of their hands; they did not stop worshiping demons, and idols of gold, silver, bronze, stone and wood— idols that cannot see or hear or walk. [21]Nor did they repent of their murders, their magic arts, their sexual immorality or their thefts.

The Angel and the Little Scroll

10 Then I saw another mighty angel coming down from heaven. He was robed in a cloud, with a rainbow above his head; his face was like the sun, and his legs were like fiery pillars. [2]He was holding a little scroll, which lay open in his hand. He planted his right foot on the sea and his left foot on the land, [3]and he gave a loud shout like the roar of a lion. When he shouted, the voices of the seven thunders spoke. [4]And when the seven thunders spoke, I was about to write; but I heard a voice from heaven say, "Seal up what the seven thunders have said and do not write it down."

[5]Then the angel I had seen standing on the sea and on the land raised his right hand to heaven. [6]And he swore by him who lives for ever and ever, who created

the heavens and all that is in them, the earth and all that is in it, and the sea and all that is in it, and said, "There will be no more delay! [7]But in the days when the seventh angel is about to sound his trumpet, the mystery of God will be accomplished, just as he announced to his servants the prophets."

[8]Then the voice that I had heard from heaven spoke to me once more: "Go, take the scroll that lies open in the hand of the angel who is standing on the sea and on the land."

[9]So I went to the angel and asked him to give me the little scroll. He said to me, "Take it and eat it. It will turn your stomach sour, but 'in your mouth it will be as sweet as honey.'[a]" [10]I took the little scroll from the angel's hand and ate it. It tasted as sweet as honey in my mouth, but when I had eaten it, my stomach turned sour. [11]Then I was told, "You must prophesy again about many peoples, nations, languages and kings."

The Two Witnesses

11 I was given a reed like a measuring rod and was told, "Go and measure the temple of God and the altar, with its worshipers. [2]But exclude the outer court; do not measure it, because it has been given to the Gentiles. They will trample on the holy city for 42 months. [3]And I will appoint my two witnesses, and they will prophesy for 1,260 days, clothed in sackcloth." [4]They are "the two olive trees" and the two lampstands, and "they stand before the Lord of the earth."[b] [5]If anyone tries to harm them, fire comes from their mouths and devours their enemies. This is how anyone who wants to harm them must die. [6]They have power to shut up the heavens so that it will not rain during the time they are prophesying; and they have power to turn the waters into blood and to strike the earth with every kind of plague as often as they want.

[7]Now when they have finished their testimony, the beast that comes up from the Abyss will attack them, and overpower and kill them. [8]Their bodies will lie in

---

[a] 9 Ezek. 3:3   [b] 4 See Zech. 4:3,11,14.

the public square of the great city—which is figuratively called Sodom and Egypt—where also their Lord was crucified. [9]For three and a half days some from every people, tribe, language and nation will gaze on their bodies and refuse them burial. [10]The inhabitants of the earth will gloat over them and will celebrate by sending each other gifts, because these two prophets had tormented those who live on the earth.

[11]But after the three and a half days the breath[a] of life from God entered them, and they stood on their feet, and terror struck those who saw them. [12]Then they heard a loud voice from heaven saying to them, "Come up here." And they went up to heaven in a cloud, while their enemies looked on.

[13]At that very hour there was a severe earthquake and a tenth of the city collapsed. Seven thousand people were killed in the earthquake, and the survivors were terrified and gave glory to the God of heaven.

[14]The second woe has passed; the third woe is coming soon.

The Seventh Trumpet

[15]The seventh angel sounded his trumpet, and there were loud voices in heaven, which said:

"The kingdom of the world has become
    the kingdom of our Lord and of his
    Messiah,
and he will reign for ever and ever."

[16]And the twenty-four elders, who were seated on their thrones before God, fell on their faces and worshiped God, [17]saying:

"We give thanks to you, Lord God
    Almighty,
the One who is and who was,
because you have taken your great
    power
and have begun to reign.
[18]The nations were angry,
    and your wrath has come.
The time has come for judging the dead,
    and for rewarding your servants the
    prophets

and your people who revere your
    name,
    both great and small—
and for destroying those who destroy
    the earth."

[19]Then God's temple in heaven was opened, and within his temple was seen the ark of his covenant. And there came flashes of lightning, rumblings, peals of thunder, an earthquake and a severe hailstorm.

The Woman and the Dragon

12 A great sign appeared in heaven: a woman clothed with the sun, with the moon under her feet and a crown of twelve stars on her head. [2]She was pregnant and cried out in pain as she was about to give birth. [3]Then another sign appeared in heaven: an enormous red dragon with seven heads and ten horns and seven crowns on its heads. [4]Its tail swept a third of the stars out of the sky and flung them to the earth. The dragon stood in front of the woman who was about to give birth, so that it might devour her child the moment he was born. [5]She gave birth to a son, a male child, who "will rule all the nations with an iron scepter."[b] And her child was snatched up to God and to his throne. [6]The woman fled into the wilderness to a place prepared for her by God, where she might be taken care of for 1,260 days.

[7]Then war broke out in heaven. Michael and his angels fought against the dragon, and the dragon and his angels fought back. [8]But he was not strong enough, and they lost their place in heaven. [9]The great dragon was hurled down—that ancient serpent called the devil, or Satan, who leads the whole world astray. He was hurled to the earth, and his angels with him.

[10]Then I heard a loud voice in heaven say:

"Now have come the salvation and the
    power
    and the kingdom of our God,
    and the authority of his Messiah.

---

a 11 Or *Spirit* (see Ezek. 37:5,14)   *b* 5 Psalm 2:9

For the accuser of our brothers and
    sisters,
who accuses them before our God
    day and night,
has been hurled down.
¹¹They triumphed over him
    by the blood of the Lamb
    and by the word of their
        testimony;
they did not love their lives
    so much
    as to shrink from death.

BREAKTHROUGH!

A woman clothed with the sun

(REVELATION 12:1-18)

People who know a lot about symbols don't agree about what this woman stands for. Many think she's the people of Israel, because she's wearing a crown with twelve stars. Her son is the Messiah (12:5), and the rest of her offspring (12:17) are the followers of Christ. Then the twelve stars stand for the twelve tribes of Israel. But they could also stand for the twelve apostles. And if that's the case, then they could stand for the people of God, because the Messiah was to come from them. So the woman could be the church, which spreads the message of salvation through the people who believe in Christ.

¹²Therefore rejoice, you heavens
    and you who dwell in them!
But woe to the earth and the sea,
    because the devil has gone down to
        you!
He is filled with fury,
    because he knows that his time is
        short."

¹³When the dragon saw that he had been hurled to the earth, he pursued the woman who had given birth to the male child. ¹⁴The woman was given the two wings of a great eagle, so that she might fly to the place prepared for her in the wilderness, where she would be taken care of for a time, times and half a time, out of the serpent's reach. ¹⁵Then from his mouth the serpent spewed water like a river, to overtake the woman and sweep her away with the torrent. ¹⁶But the earth helped the woman by opening its mouth and swallowing the river that the dragon had spewed out of his mouth. ¹⁷Then the dragon was enraged at the woman and went off to wage war against the rest of her offspring—those who keep God's commands and hold fast their testimony about Jesus.

The Beast out of the Sea

13 The dragon[a] stood on the shore of the sea. And I saw a beast coming out of the sea. It had ten horns and seven heads, with ten crowns on its horns, and on each head a blasphemous name. ²The beast I saw resembled a leopard, but had feet like those of a bear and a mouth like that of a lion. The dragon gave the beast his power and his throne and great authority. ³One of the heads of the beast seemed to have had a fatal wound, but the fatal wound had been healed. The whole world was filled with wonder and followed the beast. ⁴People worshiped the dragon because he had given authority to the beast, and they also worshiped the beast and asked, "Who is like the beast? Who can wage war against it?"

⁵The beast was given a mouth to utter proud words and blasphemies and to

---

ª 1 Some manuscripts *And I*

exercise its authority for forty-two months. ⁶It opened its mouth to blaspheme God, and to slander his name and his dwelling place and those who live in heaven. ⁷It was given power to wage war against God's holy people and to conquer them. And it was given authority over every tribe, people, language and nation. ⁸All inhabitants of the earth will worship the beast—all whose names have not been written in the Lamb's book of life, the Lamb who was slain from the creation of the world.ᵃ

⁹Whoever has ears, let them hear.

¹⁰ "If anyone is to go into captivity,
      into captivity they will go.
   If anyone is to be killedᵇ with the
            sword,
      with the sword they will be killed."ᶜ

This calls for patient endurance and faithfulness on the part of God's people.

The Beast out of the Earth

¹¹Then I saw a second beast, coming out of the earth. It had two horns like a lamb, but it spoke like a dragon. ¹²It exercised all the authority of the first beast on its behalf, and made the earth and its inhabitants worship the first beast, whose fatal wound had been healed. ¹³And it performed great signs, even causing fire to come down from heaven to the earth in full view of the people. ¹⁴Because of the signs it was given power to perform on behalf of the first beast, it deceived the inhabitants of the earth. It ordered them to set up an image in honor of the beast who was wounded by the sword and yet lived. ¹⁵The second beast was given power to give breath to the image of the first beast, so that the image could speak and cause all who refused to worship the image to be killed. ¹⁶It also forced all people, great and small, rich and poor, free and slave, to receive a mark on their right hands or on their foreheads, ¹⁷so that they could not buy or sell unless they had the mark, which is the name of the beast or the number of its name.

¹⁸This calls for wisdom. Let the person who has insight calculate the number of the beast, for it is the number of a man.ᵈ That number is 666.

The Lamb and the 144,000

14 Then I looked, and there before me was the Lamb, standing on Mount Zion, and with him 144,000 who had his name and his Father's name written on their foreheads. ²And I heard a sound from heaven like the roar of rushing waters and like a loud peal of thunder. The sound I heard was like that of harpists playing their harps. ³And they sang a new song before the throne and before the four living creatures and the elders. No one could learn the song except the 144,000 who had been redeemed from the earth. ⁴These are those who did not

ᵃ 8 Or written from the creation of the world in the book of life belonging to the Lamb who was slain   ᵇ 10 Some manuscripts anyone kills   ᶜ 10 Jer. 15:2   ᵈ 18 Or is humanity's number

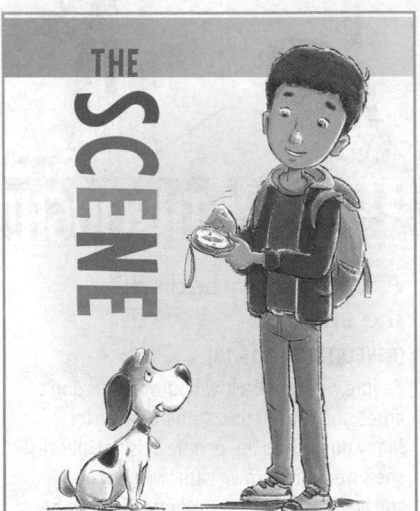

MOUNT ZION

(REVELATION 14:1)

Here, Mount Zion is a symbol of the heavenly Jerusalem. It is where the Messiah will appear at the end of time, when the believers will be reunited.

defile themselves with women, for they remained virgins. They follow the Lamb wherever he goes. They were purchased from among mankind and offered as first-fruits to God and the Lamb. [5]No lie was found in their mouths; they are blameless.

The Three Angels

[6]Then I saw another angel flying in mid-air, and he had the eternal gospel to proclaim to those who live on the earth—to every nation, tribe, language and people. [7]He said in a loud voice, "Fear God and give him glory, because the hour of his judgment has come. Worship him who made the heavens, the earth, the sea and the springs of water."

[8]A second angel followed and said, " 'Fallen! Fallen is Babylon the Great,'[a] which made all the nations drink the maddening wine of her adulteries."

[9]A third angel followed them and said in a loud voice: "If anyone worships the beast and its image and receives its mark on their forehead or on their hand, [10]they, too, will drink the wine of God's fury, which has been poured full strength into the cup of his wrath. They will be tormented with burning sulfur in the presence of the holy angels and of the Lamb. [11]And the smoke of their torment will rise for ever and ever. There will be no rest day or night for those who worship the beast and its image, or for anyone who receives the mark of its name." [12]This calls for patient endurance on the part of the people of God who keep his commands and remain faithful to Jesus.

[13]Then I heard a voice from heaven say, "Write this: Blessed are the dead who die in the Lord from now on."

"Yes," says the Spirit, "they will rest from their labor, for their deeds will follow them."

Harvesting the Earth and Trampling the Winepress

[14]I looked, and there before me was a white cloud, and seated on the cloud was one like a son of man[b] with a crown of gold on his head and a sharp sickle in his

Babylon the Great
(REVELATION 14:8)

Babylon was a very powerful country in Old Testament times. The Babylonians captured the southern part of Israel and took the Israelites as prisoners to Babylon. For the Jews, Babylon became the name of any power that was against the people of God. In the times of the book of Revelation, the Romans were in control of the region of the world where Israel is today. Therefore, it's not crazy to think that the author is referring to Rome as an evil city, because it was the center of the Roman empire. But he was talking in code so only the Christians would understand what he was talking about. Well, there are new "Babylons" in every age, and there are always new powers that go against God and his plan. However, we can always trust that God will help us.

hand. [15]Then another angel came out of the temple and called in a loud voice to him who was sitting on the cloud, "Take your sickle and reap, because the time to reap has come, for the harvest of the earth is ripe." [16]So he who was seated on the cloud swung his sickle over the earth, and the earth was harvested.

___

[a] 8 Isaiah 21:9   [b] 14 See Daniel 7:13.

[17]Another angel came out of the temple in heaven, and he too had a sharp sickle. [18]Still another angel, who had charge of the fire, came from the altar and called in a loud voice to him who had the sharp sickle, "Take your sharp sickle and gather the clusters of grapes from the earth's vine, because its grapes are ripe." [19]The angel swung his sickle on the earth, gathered its grapes and threw them into the great winepress of God's wrath. [20]They were trampled in the winepress outside the city, and blood flowed out of the press, rising as high as the horses' bridles for a distance of 1,600 stadia.[a]

Seven Angels With Seven Plagues

15 I saw in heaven another great and marvelous sign: seven angels with the seven last plagues—last, because with them God's wrath is completed. [2]And I saw what looked like a sea of glass glowing with fire and, standing beside the sea, those who had been victorious over the beast and its image and over the number of its name. They held harps given them by God [3]and sang the song of God's servant Moses and of the Lamb:

"Great and marvelous are your
        deeds,
    Lord God Almighty.
Just and true are your ways,
    King of the nations.[b]
[4]Who will not fear you, Lord,
    and bring glory to your name?
For you alone are holy.
All nations will come
    and worship before you,
for your righteous acts have been
        revealed."[c]

[5]After this I looked, and I saw in heaven the temple—that is, the tabernacle of the covenant law—and it was opened. [6]Out of the temple came the seven angels with the seven plagues. They were dressed in clean, shining linen and wore golden sashes around their chests. [7]Then one of the four living creatures gave to the seven angels seven golden bowls filled with the wrath of God, who lives for ever and ever. [8]And the temple was filled with smoke from the glory of God and from his power, and no one could enter the temple until the seven plagues of the seven angels were completed.

The Seven Bowls of God's Wrath

16 Then I heard a loud voice from the temple saying to the seven angels, "Go, pour out the seven bowls of God's wrath on the earth."

[2]The first angel went and poured out his bowl on the land, and ugly, festering sores broke out on the people who had the mark of the beast and worshiped its image.

[3]The second angel poured out his bowl on the sea, and it turned into blood like that of a dead person, and every living thing in the sea died.

[4]The third angel poured out his bowl on the rivers and springs of water, and they became blood. [5]Then I heard the angel in charge of the waters say:

"You are just in these judgments,
        O Holy One,
    you who are and who were;
[6]for they have shed the blood of your
        holy people and your prophets,
    and you have given them blood to
        drink as they deserve."

[7]And I heard the altar respond:

"Yes, Lord God Almighty,
    true and just are your judgments."

[8]The fourth angel poured out his bowl on the sun, and the sun was allowed to scorch people with fire. [9]They were seared by the intense heat and they cursed the name of God, who had control over these plagues, but they refused to repent and glorify him.

[10]The fifth angel poured out his bowl on the throne of the beast, and its kingdom was plunged into darkness. People gnawed their tongues in agony [11]and cursed the God of heaven because of their pains and their sores, but they refused to repent of what they had done.

---

[a] 20 That is, about 180 miles or about 300 kilometers   [b] 3 Some manuscripts ages   [c] 3,4 Phrases in this song are drawn from Psalm 111:2,3; Deut. 32:4; Jer. 10:7; Psalms 86:9; 98:2.

¹²The sixth angel poured out his bowl on the great river Euphrates, and its water was dried up to prepare the way for the kings from the East. ¹³Then I saw three impure spirits that looked like frogs; they came out of the mouth of the dragon, out of the mouth of the beast and out of the mouth of the false prophet. ¹⁴They are demonic spirits that perform signs, and they go out to the kings of the whole world, to gather them for the battle on the great day of God Almighty.

¹⁵"Look, I come like a thief! Blessed is the one who stays awake and remains clothed, so as not to go naked and be shamefully exposed."

¹⁶Then they gathered the kings together to the place that in Hebrew is called Armageddon.

¹⁷The seventh angel poured out his bowl into the air, and out of the temple came a loud voice from the throne, saying, "It is done!" ¹⁸Then there came flashes of lightning, rumblings, peals of thunder and a severe earthquake. No earthquake like it has ever occurred since mankind has been on earth, so tremendous was the quake. ¹⁹The great city split into three parts, and the cities of the nations collapsed. God remembered Babylon the Great and gave her the cup filled with the wine of the fury of his wrath. ²⁰Every island fled away and the mountains could not be found. ²¹From the sky huge hailstones, each weighing about a hundred pounds,ᵃ fell on people. And they cursed God on account of the plague of hail, because the plague was so terrible.

Babylon, the Prostitute on the Beast

17 One of the seven angels who had the seven bowls came and said to me, "Come, I will show you the punishment of the great prostitute, who sits by many waters. ²With her the kings of the earth committed adultery, and the inhabitants of the earth were intoxicated with the wine of her adulteries."

³Then the angel carried me away in the Spirit into a wilderness. There I saw

THE SCENE

ARMAGEDDON

(REVELATION 16:16)

This word means "Megiddo Mountain." Megiddo was a city where many Old Testament battles were fought. Consequently, it's not strange that in the book of Revelation we read that the final battle between good and evil will be precisely in that very famous place. Some people think it's just symbolic, meaning that it's a way of talking about the final battle between good and evil, when God will be the obvious winner. Others think it really means the territory of Megiddo, which is in the Carmel Mountain range, about 19 miles (30 km) southeast of the present port of Haifa in Jezreel Valley.

a woman sitting on a scarlet beast that was covered with blasphemous names and had seven heads and ten horns. ⁴The woman was dressed in purple and scarlet, and was glittering with gold, precious stones and pearls. She held a golden cup in her hand, filled with abominable things

---

ᵃ *21* Or about 45 kilograms

BREAKTHROUGH!

Who is the great prostitute who sits by many waters?

(REVELATION 17)

It's Rome, and this book calls it Babylon, but it's talking about the center of the Roman empire. God judges the powerful people who abuse those who are poor or weak. He did it with Babylon, like it says in Jeremiah 51:13. He would do it later with Rome, like it says in the book of Revelation. And yes, he will keep on doing this until the end of time.

and the filth of her adulteries. ⁵The name written on her forehead was a mystery:

BABYLON THE GREAT
THE MOTHER OF PROSTITUTES
AND OF THE ABOMINATIONS OF THE EARTH.

⁶I saw that the woman was drunk with the blood of God's holy people, the blood of those who bore testimony to Jesus.

When I saw her, I was greatly astonished. ⁷Then the angel said to me: "Why are you astonished? I will explain to you the mystery of the woman and of the beast she rides, which has the seven heads and ten horns. ⁸The beast, which you saw, once was, now is not, and yet will come up out of the Abyss and go to its destruction. The inhabitants of the earth whose names have not been writ-

ten in the book of life from the creation of the world will be astonished when they see the beast, because it once was, now is not, and yet will come.

⁹"This calls for a mind with wisdom. The seven heads are seven hills on which the woman sits. ¹⁰They are also seven kings. Five have fallen, one is, the other has not yet come; but when he does come, he must remain for only a little while. ¹¹The beast who once was, and now is not, is an eighth king. He belongs to the seven and is going to his destruction.

¹²"The ten horns you saw are ten kings who have not yet received a kingdom, but who for one hour will receive authority as kings along with the beast. ¹³They have one purpose and will give their power and authority to the beast. ¹⁴They will wage war against the Lamb, but the Lamb will triumph over them because he is Lord of lords and King of kings—and with him will be his called, chosen and faithful followers."

¹⁵Then the angel said to me, "The waters you saw, where the prostitute sits, are peoples, multitudes, nations and languages. ¹⁶The beast and the ten horns you saw will hate the prostitute. They will bring her to ruin and leave her naked; they will eat her flesh and burn her with fire. ¹⁷For God has put it into their hearts to accomplish his purpose by agreeing to hand over to the beast their royal authority, until God's words are fulfilled. ¹⁸The woman you saw is the great city that rules over the kings of the earth."

Lament Over Fallen Babylon

18 After this I saw another angel coming down from heaven. He had great authority, and the earth was illuminated by his splendor. ²With a mighty voice he shouted:

" 'Fallen! Fallen is Babylon the Great!'ᵃ
    She has become a dwelling for
        demons
and a haunt for every impure spirit,
    a haunt for every unclean bird,
    a haunt for every unclean and
        detestable animal.

ᵃ 2 Isaiah 21:9

³ For all the nations have drunk
the maddening wine of her
adulteries.
The kings of the earth committed
adultery with her,
and the merchants of the earth
grew rich from her excessive
luxuries."

Warning to Escape Babylon's Judgment

⁴ Then I heard another voice from heaven say:

" 'Come out of her, my people,'ᵃ
so that you will not share in her sins,
so that you will not receive any of
her plagues;
⁵ for her sins are piled up to heaven,
and God has remembered her
crimes.
⁶ Give back to her as she has given;
pay her back double for what she
has done.
Pour her a double portion from her
own cup.
⁷ Give her as much torment and grief
as the glory and luxury she gave
herself.
In her heart she boasts,
'I sit enthroned as queen.
I am not a widow;ᵇ
I will never mourn.'
⁸ Therefore in one day her plagues will
overtake her:
death, mourning and famine.
She will be consumed by fire,
for mighty is the Lord God who
judges her.

Threefold Woe Over Babylon's Fall

⁹ "When the kings of the earth who committed adultery with her and shared her luxury see the smoke of her burning, they will weep and mourn over her. ¹⁰ Terrified at her torment, they will stand far off and cry:

" 'Woe! Woe to you, great city,
you mighty city of Babylon!
In one hour your doom has come!'

¹¹ "The merchants of the earth will weep and mourn over her because no one buys their cargoes anymore— ¹²cargoes of gold, silver, precious stones and pearls; fine linen, purple, silk and scarlet cloth; every sort of citron wood, and articles of every kind made of ivory, costly wood, bronze, iron and marble; ¹³cargoes of cinnamon and spice, of incense, myrrh and frankincense, of wine and olive oil, of fine flour and wheat; cattle and sheep; horses and carriages; and human beings sold as slaves.

¹⁴ "They will say, 'The fruit you longed for is gone from you. All your luxury and splendor have vanished, never to be recovered.' ¹⁵The merchants who sold these things and gained their wealth from her will stand far off, terrified at her torment. They will weep and mourn ¹⁶and cry out:

" 'Woe! Woe to you, great city,
dressed in fine linen, purple and
scarlet,
and glittering with gold, precious
stones and pearls!
¹⁷ In one hour such great wealth has
been brought to ruin!'

"Every sea captain, and all who travel by ship, the sailors, and all who earn their living from the sea, will stand far off. ¹⁸When they see the smoke of her burning, they will exclaim, 'Was there ever a city like this great city?' ¹⁹They will throw dust on their heads, and with weeping and mourning cry out:

" 'Woe! Woe to you, great city,
where all who had ships on the sea
became rich through her wealth!
In one hour she has been brought to
ruin!'

²⁰ "Rejoice over her, you heavens!
Rejoice, you people of God!
Rejoice, apostles and prophets!
For God has judged her
with the judgment she imposed on
you."

The Finality of Babylon's Doom

²¹ Then a mighty angel picked up a boulder the size of a large millstone and threw it into the sea, and said:

ᵃ 4 Jer. 51:45   ᵇ 7 See Isaiah 47:7,8.

"With such violence
the great city of Babylon will be
thrown down,
never to be found again.
22 The music of harpists and musicians,
pipers and trumpeters,
will never be heard in you again.
No worker of any trade
will ever be found in you again.
The sound of a millstone
will never be heard in you again.
23 The light of a lamp
will never shine in you again.
The voice of bridegroom and bride
will never be heard in you again.
Your merchants were the world's
important people.
By your magic spell all the nations
were led astray.
24 In her was found the blood of
prophets and of God's holy
people,
of all who have been slaughtered
on the earth."

Threefold Hallelujah Over Babylon's Fall

19 After this I heard what sounded like
the roar of a great multitude in heav-
en shouting:

"Hallelujah!
Salvation and glory and power
belong to our God,
2   for true and just are his
judgments.
He has condemned the great
prostitute
who corrupted the earth by her
adulteries.
He has avenged on her the blood of
his servants."

3 And again they shouted:

"Hallelujah!
The smoke from her goes up for ever
and ever."

4 The twenty-four elders and the four
living creatures fell down and worshiped
God, who was seated on the throne. And
they cried:

"Amen, Hallelujah!"

5 Then a voice came from the throne,
saying:

"Praise our God,
all you his servants,
you who fear him,
both great and small!"

6 Then I heard what sounded like a great
multitude, like the roar of rushing waters
and like loud peals of thunder, shouting:

"Hallelujah!
For our Lord God Almighty reigns.
7 Let us rejoice and be glad
and give him glory!
For the wedding of the Lamb has come,
and his bride has made herself
ready.
8 Fine linen, bright and clean,
was given her to wear."
(Fine linen stands for the righteous acts
of God's holy people.)

9 Then the angel said to me, "Write this:
Blessed are those who are invited to the
wedding supper of the Lamb!" And he
added, "These are the true words of God."
10 At this I fell at his feet to worship him.
But he said to me, "Don't do that! I am
a fellow servant with you and with your
brothers and sisters who hold to the testimony of Jesus. Worship God! For it is the
Spirit of prophecy who bears testimony to
Jesus."

The Heavenly Warrior Defeats the Beast

11 I saw heaven standing open and there
before me was a white horse, whose rider is called Faithful and True. With justice
he judges and wages war. 12 His eyes are
like blazing fire, and on his head are many
crowns. He has a name written on him
that no one knows but he himself. 13 He is
dressed in a robe dipped in blood, and his
name is the Word of God. 14 The armies of
heaven were following him, riding on white
horses and dressed in fine linen, white
and clean. 15 Coming out of his mouth is
a sharp sword with which to strike down
the nations. "He will rule them with an
iron scepter."[a] He treads the winepress

---

a 15 Psalm 2:9

of the fury of the wrath of God Almighty. [16]On his robe and on his thigh he has this name written:

KING OF KINGS AND LORD OF LORDS.

[17]And I saw an angel standing in the sun, who cried in a loud voice to all the birds flying in midair, "Come, gather together for the great supper of God, [18]so that you may eat the flesh of kings, generals, and the mighty, of horses and their riders, and the flesh of all people, free and slave, great and small."

[19]Then I saw the beast and the kings of the earth and their armies gathered together to wage war against the rider on the horse and his army. [20]But the beast was captured, and with it the false prophet who had performed the signs on its behalf. With these signs he had deluded those who had received the mark of the beast and worshiped its image. The two of them were thrown alive into the fiery lake of burning sulfur. [21]The rest were killed with the sword coming out of the mouth of the rider on the horse, and all the birds gorged themselves on their flesh.

The Thousand Years

20 And I saw an angel coming down out of heaven, having the key to the Abyss and holding in his hand a great chain. [2]He seized the dragon, that ancient serpent, who is the devil, or Satan, and bound him for a thousand years. [3]He threw him into the Abyss, and locked and sealed it over him, to keep him from deceiving the nations anymore until the thousand years were ended. After that, he must be set free for a short time.

[4]I saw thrones on which were seated those who had been given authority to judge. And I saw the souls of those who had been beheaded because of their testimony about Jesus and because of the word of God. They[a] had not worshiped the beast or its image and had not received its mark on their foreheads or their hands. They came to life and reigned with Christ a thousand years. [5](The rest of the dead did not

come to life until the thousand years were ended.) This is the first resurrection. [6]Blessed and holy are those who share in the first resurrection. The second death has no power over them, but they will be priests of God and of Christ and will reign with him for a thousand years.

The Judgment of Satan

[7]When the thousand years are over, Satan will be released from his prison [8]and will go out to deceive the nations in the four corners of the earth—Gog and Magog—and to gather them for battle. In number they are like the sand on the seashore. [9]They marched across the breadth of the earth and surrounded the camp of God's people, the city he loves. But fire came down from heaven and devoured them. [10]And the devil, who deceived them, was thrown into the lake of burning sulfur, where the beast and the false prophet had been thrown. They will be tormented day and night for ever and ever.

The Judgment of the Dead

[11]Then I saw a great white throne and him who was seated on it. The earth and the heavens fled from his presence, and there was no place for them. [12]And I saw the dead, great and small, standing before the throne, and books were opened. Another book was opened, which is the book of life. The dead were judged according to what they had done as recorded in the books. [13]The sea gave up the dead that were in it, and death and Hades gave up the dead that were in them, and each person was judged according to what they had done. [14]Then death and Hades were thrown into the lake of fire. The lake of fire is the second death. [15]Anyone whose name was not found written in the book of life was thrown into the lake of fire.

A New Heaven and a New Earth

21 Then I saw "a new heaven and a new earth,"[b] for the first heaven

---

a 4 Or God; I also saw those who   *b 1 Isaiah 65:17*

and the first earth had passed away, and there was no longer any sea. ²I saw the Holy City, the new Jerusalem, coming down out of heaven from God, prepared as a bride beautifully dressed for her husband. ³And I heard a loud voice from the throne saying, "Look! God's dwelling place is now among the people, and he will dwell with them. They will be his people, and God himself will be with them and be their God. ⁴'He will wipe every tear from their eyes. There will be no more death'ᵃ or mourning or crying or pain, for the old order of things has passed away."

⁵He who was seated on the throne said, "I am making everything new!" Then he said, "Write this down, for these words are trustworthy and true."

⁶He said to me: "It is done. I am the Alpha and the Omega, the Beginning and the End. To the thirsty I will give water without cost from the spring of the water of life. ⁷Those who are victorious will inherit all this, and I will be their God and they will be my children. ⁸But the cowardly, the unbelieving, the vile, the murderers, the sexually immoral, those who practice magic arts, the idolaters and all liars— they will be consigned to the fiery lake of burning sulfur. This is the second death."

The New Jerusalem, the Bride of the Lamb

⁹One of the seven angels who had the seven bowls full of the seven last plagues came and said to me, "Come, I will show you the bride, the wife of the Lamb." ¹⁰And he carried me away in the Spirit to a mountain great and high, and showed me the Holy City, Jerusalem, coming down out of heaven from God. ¹¹It shone with the glory of God, and its brilliance was like that of a very precious jewel, like a jasper, clear as crystal. ¹²It had a great, high wall with twelve gates, and with twelve angels at the gates. On the gates were written the names of the twelve tribes of Israel. ¹³There were three gates on the east, three on the north, three on the south and three on the west. ¹⁴The wall of the city had twelve foundations, and on them were

the names of the twelve apostles of the Lamb.

¹⁵The angel who talked with me had a measuring rod of gold to measure the city, its gates and its walls. ¹⁶The city was laid out like a square, as long as it was wide. He measured the city with the rod and found it to be 12,000 stadiaᵇ in length, and as wide and high as it is long. ¹⁷The angel measured the wall using human measurement, and it was 144 cubitsᶜ thick.ᵈ ¹⁸The wall was made of jasper, and the city of pure gold, as pure as glass. ¹⁹The foundations of the city walls were decorated with every kind of precious stone. The first foundation was jasper, the second sapphire, the third agate, the fourth emerald, ²⁰the fifth onyx, the sixth ruby, the seventh chrysolite, the eighth beryl, the ninth topaz, the tenth turquoise, the eleventh jacinth, and the twelfth amethyst.ᵉ ²¹The twelve gates were twelve pearls, each gate made of a single pearl. The great street of the city was of gold, as pure as transparent glass.

²²I did not see a temple in the city, because the Lord God Almighty and the Lamb are its temple. ²³The city does not need the sun or the moon to shine on it, for the glory of God gives it light, and the Lamb is its lamp. ²⁴The nations will walk by its light, and the kings of the earth will bring their splendor into it. ²⁵On no day will its gates ever be shut, for there will be no night there. ²⁶The glory and honor of the nations will be brought into it. ²⁷Nothing impure will ever enter it, nor will anyone who does what is shameful or deceitful, but only those whose names are written in the Lamb's book of life.

Eden Restored

22 Then the angel showed me the river of the water of life, as clear as crystal, flowing from the throne of God and of the Lamb ²down the middle of the great street of the city. On each side of the river stood the tree of life, bearing twelve crops

---

ᵃ 4 Isaiah 25:8   ᵇ 16 That is, about 1,400 miles or about 2,200 kilometers   ᶜ 17 That is, about 200 feet or about 65 meters   ᵈ 17 Or high   ᵉ 20 The precise identification of some of these precious stones is uncertain.

of fruit, yielding its fruit every month. And the leaves of the tree are for the healing of the nations. ³No longer will there be any curse. The throne of God and of the Lamb will be in the city, and his servants will serve him. ⁴They will see his face, and his name will be on their foreheads. ⁵There will be no more night. They will not need the light of a lamp or the light of the sun, for the Lord God will give them light. And they will reign for ever and ever.

John and the Angel

⁶The angel said to me, "These words are trustworthy and true. The Lord, the God who inspires the prophets, sent his angel to show his servants the things that must soon take place."

⁷"Look, I am coming soon! Blessed is the one who keeps the words of the prophecy written in this scroll."

⁸I, John, am the one who heard and saw these things. And when I had heard and seen them, I fell down to worship at the feet of the angel who had been showing them to me. ⁹But he said to me, "Don't do that! I am a fellow servant with you and with your fellow prophets and with all who keep the words of this scroll. Worship God!"

¹⁰Then he told me, "Do not seal up the words of the prophecy of this scroll, because the time is near. ¹¹Let the one who does wrong continue to do wrong; let the vile person continue to be vile; let the one who does right continue to do right; and let the holy person continue to be holy."

Epilogue: Invitation and Warning

¹²"Look, I am coming soon! My reward is with me, and I will give to each person according to what they have done. ¹³I am

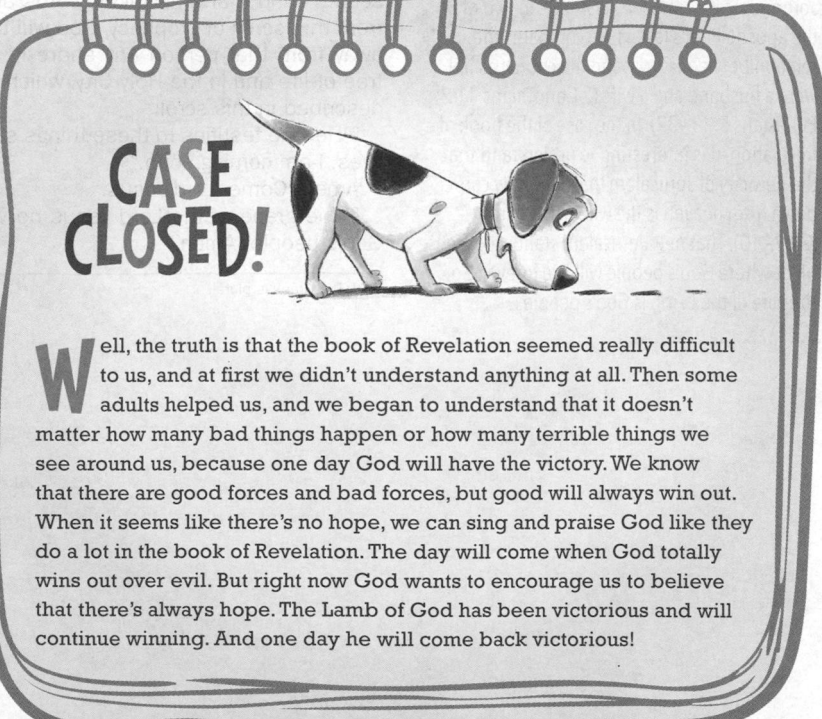

CASE CLOSED!

Well, the truth is that the book of Revelation seemed really difficult to us, and at first we didn't understand anything at all. Then some adults helped us, and we began to understand that it doesn't matter how many bad things happen or how many terrible things we see around us, because one day God will have the victory. We know that there are good forces and bad forces, but good will always win out. When it seems like there's no hope, we can sing and praise God like they do a lot in the book of Revelation. The day will come when God totally wins out over evil. But right now God wants to encourage us to believe that there's always hope. The Lamb of God has been victorious and will continue winning. And one day he will come back victorious!

The bride

(REVELATION 22:17)

Several books of prophets in the Old Testament talk about the nation of Israel as if it were the wife of God (Isaiah 54:5–6; 62:4–5; Jeremiah 2:2–3; Hosea 2:19–20). In two of the apostle Paul's letters, he compares the relation between Christ and the church as if it were a husband and a wife (2 Corinthians 11:2; Ephesians 5:23–32). In the case of the book of Revelation, it is interesting to understand that the new city of Jerusalem that John saw come down from heaven is the wife of the Lamb (21:9–10). That new Jerusalem stands for the place where God's people will live forever. So, the wife of the Lamb is God's people.

the Alpha and the Omega, the First and the Last, the Beginning and the End.

¹⁴"Blessed are those who wash their robes, that they may have the right to the tree of life and may go through the gates into the city. ¹⁵Outside are the dogs, those who practice magic arts, the sexually immoral, the murderers, the idolaters and everyone who loves and practices falsehood.

¹⁶"I, Jesus, have sent my angel to give you[a] this testimony for the churches. I am the Root and the Offspring of David, and the bright Morning Star."

¹⁷The Spirit and the bride say, "Come!" And let the one who hears say, "Come!" Let the one who is thirsty come; and let the one who wishes take the free gift of the water of life.

¹⁸I warn everyone who hears the words of the prophecy of this scroll: If anyone adds anything to them, God will add to that person the plagues described in this scroll. ¹⁹And if anyone takes words away from this scroll of prophecy, God will take away from that person any share in the tree of life and in the Holy City, which are described in this scroll.

²⁰He who testifies to these things says, "Yes, I am coming soon."

Amen. Come, Lord Jesus.

²¹The grace of the Lord Jesus be with God's people. Amen.

ᵃ 16 The Greek is plural.

TABLE OF WEIGHTS AND MEASURES

	Biblical Unit	Approximate American Equivalent	Approximate Metric Equivalent
WEIGHTS	talent (60 minas)	75 pounds	34 kilograms
	mina (50 shekels)	1 1/4 pounds	560 grams
	shekel (2 bekas)	2/5 ounce	11.5 grams
	pim (2/3 shekel)	1/4 ounce	7.8 grams
	beka (10 gerahs)	1/5 ounce	5.7 grams
	gerah	1/50 ounce	0.6 gram
	daric	1/3 ounce	8.4 grams
LENGTH	cubit	18 inches	45 centimeters
	span	9 inches	23 centimeters
	handbreadth	3 inches	7.5 centimeters
	stadion (pl. stadia)	600 feet	183 meters
CAPACITY			
Dry Measure	cor [homer] (10 ephahs)	6 bushels	220 liters
	lethek (5 ephahs)	3 bushels	110 liters
	ephah (10 omers)	3/5 bushel	22 liters
	seah (1/3 ephah)	7 quarts	7.5 liters
	omer (1/10 ephah)	2 quarts	2 liters
	cab (1/18 ephah)	1 quart	1 liter
Liquid Measure	bath (1 ephah)	6 gallons	22 liters
	hin (1/6 bath)	1 gallon	3.8 liters
	log (1/72 bath)	1/3 quart	0.3 liter

The figures of the table are calculated on the basis of a shekel equaling 11.5 grams, a cubit equaling 18 inches and an ephah equaling 22 liters. The quart referred to is either a dry quart (slightly larger than a liter) or a liquid quart (slightly smaller than a liter), whichever is applicable. The ton referred to in the footnotes is the American ton of 2,000 pounds. These weights are calculated relative to the particular commodity involved. Accordingly, the same measure of capacity in the text may be converted into different weights in the footnotes.

This table is based upon the best available information, but it is not intended to be mathematically precise; like the measurement equivalents in the footnotes, it merely gives approximate amounts and distances. Weights and measures differed somewhat at various times and places in the ancient world. There is uncertainty particularly about the ephah and the bath; further discoveries may shed more light on these units of capacity.

INDEX TO FEATURES

The Witnesses Feature

The Scene Feature

Check the Facts Feature

CONCORDANCE

The NIV Concordance, created by John R. Kohlenberger III, has been developed specifically for use with the New International Version (NIV). Like all concordances, it is a special index that contains an alphabetical listing of words used in the Bible text.

This concordance contains 2,474 word entries, with more than 10,000 Scripture references. Each word entry is followed by significant Scripture references in which that particular word is found, as well as by a brief excerpt from the surrounding context. In the context, the entry word is abbreviated by its first letter in bold print. Other forms of the entry word and related words indexed in this concordance are in parentheses.

This concordance also contains 155 biographical entries for significant people in the Bible. The descriptive phrases replace the brief context surrounding each occurrence of the name. In those instances where more than one Bible character has the same name, that name is placed under one block entry, and each person is given a number (1), (2), etc.

Two entries are marked with an asterisk (*). LORD* and LORD'S* list occurrences of the proper name of God, *Yahweh,* spelled "LORD" and "LORD's" in the NIV. These entries are distinguished from LORD and LORD'S, which list occurrences of the title "Lord" and "Lord's."

This concordance is a valuable tool for Bible study. While one of its key purposes is to help the reader find forgotten references to familiar verses, it can also be used to do word studies and to locate and trace biblical themes. Whenever you find a significant context, be sure to read at least the whole verse in the NIV to discover its fuller meaning in its larger context.

AARON
Priesthood of (Ex 28:1; Nu 17; Heb 5:1–4; 7), garments (Ex 28; 39), consecration (Ex 29), ordination (Lev 8).
Spokesman for Moses (Ex 4:14–16, 27–31; 7:1–2). Supported Moses' hands in battle (Ex 17:8–13). Built golden calf (Ex 32; Dt 9:20). Talked against Moses (Nu 12). Priesthood opposed (Nu 16); staff budded (Nu 17). Forbidden to enter land (Nu 20:1–12). Death (Nu 20:22–29; 33:38–39).

ABANDON
Dt	4: 31	he will not **a** or destroy you
1Ti	4: 1	in later times some will **a** the faith

ABBA
Ro	8: 15	And by him we cry, "**A**, Father."
Gal	4: 6	the Spirit who calls out, "**A**,

ABEL
Second son of Adam (Ge 4:2). Offered proper sacrifice (Ge 4:4; Heb 11:4). Murdered by Cain (Ge 4:8; Mt 23:35; Lk 11:51; 1Jn 3:12).

ABIGAIL
Wife of Nabal (1Sa 25:30); pled for his life with David (1Sa 25:14–35). Became David's wife (1Sa 25:36–42).

ABIJAH
Son of Rehoboam; king of Judah (1Ki 14:31—15:8; 2Ch 12:16—14:1).

ABILITY (ABLE)
Ezr	2: 69	According to their **a** they gave
2Co	1: 8	far beyond our **a** to endure,
	8: 3	were able, and even beyond their **a**.

ABIMELEK
1. King of Gerar who took Abraham's wife Sarah, believing her to be his sister (Ge 20). Later made a covenant with Abraham (Ge 21:22–33).

2. King of Gerar who took Isaac's wife Rebekah, believing her to be his sister (Ge 26:1–11). Later made a covenant with Isaac (Ge 26:12–31).

ABLE (ABILITY ENABLE ENABLED ENABLES)
Eze	7: 19	gold will not be **a** to deliver them
Da	3: 17	the God we serve is **a** to deliver us
Ro	8: 39	will be **a** to separate us
	14: 4	the Lord is **a** to make them stand.
	16: 25	to him who is **a** to establish you
2Co	9: 8	God is **a** to bless you abundantly,
Eph	3: 20	him who is **a** to do immeasurably
2Ti	1: 12	that he is **a** to guard what I have
	3: 15	which are **a** to make you wise
Heb	7: 25	he is **a** to save completely
Jude	: 24	To him who is **a** to keep you
Rev	5: 5	He is **a** to open the scroll and its

ABOLISH
Mt	5: 17	think that I have come to **a** the Law

ABOMINATION
Da	11: 31	set up the **a** that causes desolation.

ABOUND (ABOUNDING ABOUNDS)
2Co	9: 8	you will **a** in every good work.
Php	1: 9	your love may **a** more and more

ABOUNDING (ABOUND)
Ex	34: 6	to anger, **a** in love and faithfulness,
Ps	86: 5	**a** in love to all who call to you.

ABOUNDS (ABOUND)
2Co	1: 5	also our comfort **a** through Christ.

ABRAHAM
Covenant relation with the LORD (Ge 12:1–3; 13:14–17; 15; 17; 22:15–18; Ex 2:24; Ne 9:8; Ps 105; Mic 7:20; Lk 1:68–75; Ro 4; Heb 6:13–15).
Called from Ur, via Harran, to Canaan (Ge 12:1; Ac 7:2–4; Heb 11:8–10). Moved to Egypt, nearly lost Sarah to Pharoah (Ge 12:10–20). Divided the

land with Lot (Ge 13). Saved Lot from four kings (Ge 14;1–16), blessed by Melchizedek (Ge 14:17–20; Heb 7:1–20). Declared righteous by faith (Ge 15:6; Ro 4:3; Gal 3:6–9). Fathered Ishmael by Hagar (Ge 16). Name changed from Abram (Ge 17:5; Ne 9:7). Circumcised (Ge 17; Ro 4:9–12). Entertained three visitors (Ge 18); promised a son by Sarah (Ge 18:9–15; 17:16). Moved to Gerar; nearly lost Sarah to Abimelek (Ge 20). Fathered Isaac by Sarah (Ge 21:1–7; Ac 7:8; Heb 11:11–12); sent away Hagar and Ishmael (Ge 21:8–21; Gal 4:22–30). Tested by offering Isaac (Ge 22; Heb 11:17–19; Jas 2:21–24). Sarah died; bought field of Ephron for burial (Ge 23). Secured wife for Isaac (Ge 24). Death (Ge 25:7–11).

ABSALOM
Son of David by Maakah (2Sa 3:3; 1Ch 3:2). Killed Amnon for rape of his sister Tamar; banished by David (2Sa 13). Returned to Jerusalem; received by David (2Sa 14). Rebelled against David; seized kingdom (2Sa 15–17). Killed (2Sa 18).

ABSTAIN (ABSTAINS)
| 1Pe | 2: 11 | and exiles, to **a** from sinful desires, |

ABSTAINS (ABSTAIN)
| Ro | 14: 6 | and whoever **a** does so to the Lord |

ABUNDANCE (ABUNDANT)
| Lk | 12: 15 | not consist in an **a** of possessions." |
| Jude | : 2 | peace and love be yours in **a**. |

ABUNDANT (ABUNDANCE)
Dt	28: 11	will grant you **a** prosperity—
Ps	145: 7	They celebrate your **a** goodness
Pr	28: 19	work their land will have **a** food,
Ro	5: 17	who receive God's **a** provision

ABUSE
| 2Pe | 2: 11 | do not heap **a** on such beings |

ACCEPT (ACCEPTED ACCEPTS)
Ex	23: 8	"Do not **a** a bribe, for a bribe
Pr	10: 8	The wise in heart **a** commands,
	19: 20	Listen to advice and **a** discipline,
Ro	15: 7	**A** one another, then, just as Christ
Jas	1: 21	humbly **a** the word planted in you,

ACCEPTED (ACCEPT)
| Lk | 4: 24 | "no prophet is **a** in his hometown. |

ACCEPTS (ACCEPT)
| Ps | 6: 9 | the LORD **a** my prayer. |
| Jn | 13: 20 | whoever **a** anyone I send **a** me; |

ACCOMPANY
| Mk | 16: 17 | these signs will **a** those who believe: |

ACCOMPLISH
| Isa | 55: 11 | but will **a** what I desire and achieve |

ACCORD
| Nu | 24: 13 | not do anything of my own **a**, |
| Jn | 10: 18 | me, but I lay it down of my own **a**. |

ACCOUNT (ACCOUNTABLE)
Mt	12: 36	will have to give **a** on the day
Ro	14: 12	of us will give an **a** of ourselves
Heb	4: 13	of him to whom we must give **a**.

ACCOUNTABLE (ACCOUNT)
| Eze | 33: 6 | I will hold the watchman **a** for |
| Ro | 3: 19 | and the whole world held **a** to God. |

ACCUSATION (ACCUSE)
| 1Ti | 5: 19 | not entertain an **a** against an elder |

ACCUSE (ACCUSATION)
| Pr | 3: 30 | Do not **a** anyone for no reason— |
| Lk | 3: 14 | money and don't **a** people falsely— |

ACHAN
Sin at Jericho caused defeat at Ai; stoned (Jos 7; 22:20; 1Ch 2:7).

ACHE
| Pr | 14: 13 | Even in laughter the heart may **a**, |

ACKNOWLEDGE
Mt	10: 32	also **a** before my Father in heaven.
1Th	5: 12	**a** those who work hard among you,
Php	2: 11	every tongue **a** that Jesus Christ is
1Jn	4: 3	spirit that does not **a** Jesus is not

ACQUIT
| Ex | 23: 7 | to death, for I will not **a** the guilty. |

ACTION (ACTIONS ACTIVE ACTS)
| Jas | 2: 17 | if it is not accompanied by **a**, |

ACTIONS (ACTION)
| Gal | 6: 4 | Each one should test their own **a**. |
| Titus | 1: 16 | God, but by their **a** they deny him. |

ACTIVE (ACTION)
| Heb | 4: 12 | For the word of God is alive and **a**. |

ACTS (ACTION)
Ps	145: 12	people may know of your mighty **a**
	150: 2	Praise him for his **a** of power;
Isa	64: 6	all our righteous **a** are like filthy

ADAM
First man (Ge 1:26—2:25; Ro 5:14; 1Ti 2:13). Sin of (Ge 3; Hos 6:7; Ro 5:12–21). Children of (Ge 4:1—5:5). Death of (Ge 5:5; Ro 5:12–21; 1Co 15:22).

ADD
Dt	12: 32	do not **a** to it or take away from it.
Pr	30: 6	Do not **a** to his words, or he will
Lk	12: 25	by worrying can **a** a single hour
Rev	22: 18	them, God will **a** to that person

ADMIRABLE
| Php | 4: 8 | whatever is lovely, whatever is **a**— |

ADMONISH
| Col | 3: 16 | and **a** one another with all wisdom |

ADOPTION
| Ro | 8: 23 | wait eagerly for our **a** to sonship, |
| Eph | 1: 5 | he predestined us for **a** to sonship |

ADORE
| SS | 1: 4 | How right they are to **a** you! |

ADORNMENT (ADORNS)
| 1Pe | 3: 3 | should not come from outward **a**, |

ADORNS (ADORNMENT)
| Ps | 93: 5 | holiness **a** your house for endless |

ADULTERY
Ex	20: 14	"You shall not commit **a**.
Mt	5: 27	was said, 'You shall not commit **a**.'
	5: 28	lustfully has already committed **a**
	5: 32	a divorced woman commits **a**,
	15: 19	murder, **a**, sexual immorality, theft,

ADULTS
| 1Co | 14: 20 | but in your thinking be **a**. |

ADVANCED
| Job | 32: 7 | **a** years should teach wisdom.' |

ADVANTAGE
Ex	22: 22	"Do not take **a** of the widow
Dt	24: 14	Do not take **a** of a hired worker
1Th	4: 6	should wrong or take **a** of a brother

ADVERSITY
Pr	17: 17	a brother is born for a time of **a**.

ADVICE
1Ki	12: 8	Rehoboam rejected the **a** the elders
	12: 14	he followed the **a** of the young men
Pr	12: 5	but the **a** of the wicked is deceitful.
	12: 15	to them, but the wise listen to **a**.
	19: 20	Listen to **a** and accept discipline,
	20: 18	Plans are established by seeking **a**;

ADVOCATE
Jn	14: 16	he will give you another **a** to help
	14: 26	But the **A**, the Holy Spirit,
1Jn	2: 1	sin, we have an **a** with the Father—

AFFECTION
2Pe	1: 7	and to godliness, mutual **a**; and to mutual **a**, love.

AFFLICTION
Ro	12: 12	patient in **a**, faithful in prayer.

AFRAID (FEAR)
Ge	26: 24	Do not be **a**, for I am with you;
Ex	3: 6	because he was **a** to look at God.
Ps	27: 1	of my life—of whom shall I be **a**?
	56: 3	When I am **a**, I put my trust in
Pr	3: 24	you lie down, you will not be **a**;
Jer	1: 8	Do not be **a** of them, for I am
Mt	8: 26	of little faith, why are you so **a**?"
	10: 28	Do not be **a** of those who kill
	10: 31	So don't be **a**; you are worth more
Mk	5: 36	said, Jesus told him, "Don't be **a**;
Jn	14: 27	hearts be troubled and do not be **a**.
Heb	13: 6	Lord is my helper; I will not be **a**.

AGED
Job	12: 12	Is not wisdom found among the **a**?
Pr	17: 6	children are a crown to the **a**,

AGREE
Mt	18: 19	earth **a** about anything they ask for,
Ro	7: 16	want to do, I **a** that the law is good.

AHAB
Son of Omri; king of Israel (1Ki 16:28—22:40), husband of Jezebel (1Ki 16:31). Promoted Baal worship (1Ki 16:31–33); opposed by Elijah (1Ki 17:1; 18; 21), a prophet (1Ki 20:35–43), Micaiah (1Ki 22:1–28). Defeated Ben-Hadad (1Ki 20). Killed for failing to kill Ben-Hadad and for murder of Naboth (1Ki 20:35—21:40).

AHAZ
Son of Jotham; king of Judah, (2Ki 16; 2Ch 28; Isa 7).

AHAZIAH
1. Son of Ahab; king of Israel (1Ki 22:51–2Ki 1:18; 2Ch 20:35–37).
2. Son of Jehoram; king of Judah (2Ki 8:25–29; 9:14–29), also called Jehoahaz (2Ch 21:17—22:9; 25:23).

AIM
1Co	7: 34	Her **a** is to be devoted to the Lord

AIR
1Co	9: 26	not fight like a boxer beating the **a**.
Eph	2: 2	the ruler of the kingdom of the **a**,
1Th	4: 17	clouds to meet the Lord in the **a**.

ALABASTER
Mt	26: 7	him with an **a** jar of very expensive

ALERT
Jos	8: 4	far from it. All of you be on the **a**.
Mk	13: 33	Be **a**! You do not know
Eph	6: 18	be **a** and always keep on praying
1Pe	1: 13	with minds that are **a** and fully

ALIENATED
Gal	5: 4	the law have been **a** from Christ;

ALIVE (LIVE)
Ac	1: 3	convincing proofs that he was **a**.
Ro	6: 11	to sin but **a** to God in Christ Jesus.
1Co	15: 22	die, so in Christ all will be made **a**.
Heb	4: 12	the word of God is **a** and active.

ALMIGHTY (MIGHT)
Ge	17: 1	to him and said, "I am God **A**;
Job	11: 7	Can you probe the limits of the **A**?
	33: 4	the breath of the **A** gives me life.
Ps	91: 1	will rest in the shadow of the **A**.
Isa	6: 3	"Holy, holy, holy is the Lord **A**;

ALTAR
Ge	22: 9	Abraham built an **a** there
Ex	27: 1	"Build an **a** of acacia wood,
1Ki	18: 30	he repaired the **a** of the Lord,
2Ch	4: 1	a bronze **a** twenty cubits long,
	4: 19	the golden **a**; the tables

ALWAYS
Ps	16: 8	I keep my eyes **a** on the Lord.
	26: 3	for I have **a** been mindful of your
	51: 3	and my sin is **a** before me.
Mt	26: 11	The poor you will **a** have with you,
	28: 20	And surely I am with you **a**,
1Co	13: 7	It **a** protects, **a** trusts, **a** hopes,
Php	4: 4	Rejoice in the Lord **a**. I will say it
1Pe	3: 15	**A** be prepared to give an answer

AMAZIAH
Son of Joash; king of Judah (2Ki 14; 2Ch 25).

AMBASSADORS
2Co	5: 20	We are therefore Christ's **a**,

AMBITION
Ro	15: 20	It has always been my **a** to preach
1Th	4: 11	make it your **a** to lead a quiet life:

AMON
Son of Manasseh; king of Judah (2Ki 21:18–26; 1Ch 3:14; 2Ch 33:21–25).

ANANIAS
1. Husband of Sapphira; died for lying to God (Ac 5:1–11).
2. Disciple who baptized Saul (Ac 9:10–19).
3. High priest at Paul's arrest (Ac 22:30—24:1).

ANCESTORS
Heb	1: 1	spoke to our **a** through the prophets

ANCHOR
Heb	6: 19	We have this hope as an **a**

ANCIENT
Da	7: 9	and the **A** of Days took his seat.

ANDREW
Apostle; brother of Simon Peter (Mt 4:18; 10:2; Mk 1:16–18, 29; 3:18; 13:3; Lk 6:14; Jn 1:35–44; 6:8–9; 12:22; Ac 1:13).

ANGEL (ANGELS ARCHANGEL)
Ps	34: 7	The **a** of the Lord encamps

Ac 6: 15 his face was like the face of an **a**.
2Co 11: 14 Satan himself masquerades as an **a**
Gal 1: 8 or an **a** from heaven should preach

ANGELS (ANGEL)

Ps 8: 5 a little lower than the **a**
91: 11 command his **a** concerning you
Mt 18: 10 that their **a** in heaven always see
25: 41 fire prepared for the devil and his **a**.
Lk 20: 36 for they are like the **a**.
1Co 6: 3 you not know that we will judge **a**?
Heb 1: 4 the **a** as the name he has inherited
1: 14 Are not all **a** ministering spirits
2: 7 them a little lower than the **a**;
13: 2 hospitality to **a** without knowing it.
1Pe 1: 12 Even **a** long to look into these
2Pe 2: 4 if God did not spare **a** when they

ANGER (ANGERED ANGRY)

Ex 32: 10 that my **a** may burn against them
34: 6 slow to **a**, abounding in love
Dt 29: 28 In furious **a** and in great wrath
2Ki 22: 13 Great is the LORD's **a** that burns
Ps 30: 5 For his **a** lasts only a moment,
Pr 15: 1 wrath, but a harsh word stirs up **a**.

ANGERED (ANGER)

Pr 22: 24 do not associate with one easily **a**,
1Co 13: 5 it is not easily **a**, it keeps no record

ANGRY (ANGER)

Ps 2: 12 he will be **a** and your way will lead
Pr 29: 22 An **a** person stirs up conflict,
Jas 1: 19 to speak and slow to become **a**,

ANOINT

Ps 23: 5 You **a** my head with oil;
Jas 5: 14 **a** them with oil in the name

ANOTHER

1Pe 3: 8 love one **a**, be compassionate

ANT

Pr 6: 6 Go to the **a**, you sluggard;

ANTICHRIST

1Jn 2: 18 have heard that the **a** is coming,
2Jn : 7 person is the deceiver and the **a**.

ANTIOCH

Ac 11: 26 were called Christians first at **A**.

ANXIETY (ANXIOUS)

Pr 12: 25 **A** weighs down the heart,
1Pe 5: 7 Cast all your **a** on him because he

ANXIOUS (ANXIETY)

Php 4: 6 Do not be **a** about anything,

APOLLOS

Christian from Alexandria, learned in the Scriptures; instructed by Aquila and Priscilla (Ac 18:24–28). Ministered at Corinth (Ac 19:1; 1Co 1:12; 3; Titus 3:13).

APOSTLES

See also Andrew, Bartholomew, James, John, Judas, Matthew, Nathanael, Paul, Peter, Philip, Simon, Thaddaeus, Thomas.

Ac 1: 26 so he was added to the eleven **a**.
2: 43 and signs performed by the **a**.
1Co 12: 28 placed in the church first of all **a**,
15: 9 For I am the least of the **a** and do
2Co 11: 13 For such people are false **a**,
Eph 2: 20 built on the foundation of the **a**

APPEAR (APPEARANCE APPEARING)

Mk 13: 22 false prophets will **a** and perform
2Co 5: 10 we must all **a** before the judgment
Col 3: 4 you also will **a** with him in glory.
Heb 9: 24 now to **a** for us in God's presence.
9: 28 and he will **a** a second time,

APPEARANCE (APPEAR)

1Sa 16: 7 People look at the outward **a**,

APPEARING (APPEAR)

2Ti 4: 8 to all who have longed for his **a**.
Titus 2: 13 the **a** of the glory of our great God

APPLY

Pr 22: 17 **a** your heart to what I teach,
23: 12 **A** your heart to instruction and

APPROACH

Eph 3: 12 we may **a** God with freedom
Heb 4: 16 then **a** God's throne of grace

APPROVED

2Ti 2: 15 to present yourself to God as one **a**,

AQUILA

Husband of Priscilla; co-worker with Paul, instructor of Apollos (Ac 18; Ro 16:3; 1Co 16:19; 2Ti 4:19).

ARARAT

Ge 8: 4 to rest on the mountains of **A**.

ARCHANGEL (ANGEL)

1Th 4: 16 with the voice of the **a**
Jude : 9 But even the **a** Michael, when he

ARCHITECT

Heb 11: 10 whose **a** and builder is God.

ARGUING

Php 2: 14 everything without grumbling or **a**,

ARK

Ge 6: 14 So make yourself an **a** of cypress
Dt 10: 5 put the tablets in the **a** I had made,
2Ch 35: 3 "Put the sacred **a** in the temple
Heb 9: 4 This **a** contained the gold jar

ARM (ARMY)

Nu 11: 23 "Is the LORD's **a** too short?
1Pe 4: 1 **a** yourselves also with the same

ARMAGEDDON

Rev 16: 16 place that in Hebrew is called **A**.

ARMOR (ARMY)

1Ki 20: 11 his **a** should not boast like one who
Eph 6: 11 Put on the full **a** of God, so that
6: 13 Therefore put on the full **a** of God,

ARMS (ARMY)

Dt 33: 27 underneath are the everlasting **a**.
Ps 18: 32 It is God who **a** me with strength
Pr 31: 20 She opens her **a** to the poor
Isa 40: 11 He gathers the lambs in his **a**
Mk 10: 16 And he took the children in his **a**,

ARMY (ARM ARMOR ARMS)

Ps 33: 16 king is saved by the size of his **a**;
Rev 19: 19 the rider on the horse and his **a**.

AROMA

2Co 2: 15 the pleasing **a** of Christ among
2: 16 one we are an **a** that brings death;
2: 16 to the other, an **a** that brings life.

ARRAYED

Ps 110: 3 **A** in holy splendor, your young
Isa 61: 10 **a** me in a robe of his righteousness,

ARROGANT
Ro   11: 20   Do not be **a**, but tremble.

ARROWS
Eph   6: 16   can extinguish all the flaming **a**

ASA
King of Judah (1Ki 15:8–24; 1Ch 3:10; 2Ch 14–16).

ASCENDED
Eph   4:   8   "When he **a** on high, he took many

ASCRIBE
1Ch 16: 28   **A** to the LORD, all you families
        16: 28   **a** to the LORD glory and strength.
Job 36:   3   I will **a** justice to my Maker.
Ps   29:   2   **A** to the LORD the glory due his

ASHAMED (SHAME)
Lk   9: 26   Whoever is **a** of me and my words,
                   the Son of Man will be **a** of them
Ro   1: 16   For I am not **a** of the gospel,
2Ti   1:   8   So do not be **a** of the testimony
        2: 15   worker who does not need to be **a**

ASSIGNED
Mk   13: 34   each with their task, and tells
1Co   3:   5   as the Lord has **a** to each his task.
        7: 17   whatever situation the Lord has **a**

ASSOCIATE
Pr   22: 24   do not **a** with one easily angered,
Ro   12: 16   be willing to **a** with people of low
1Co   5: 11   you must not **a** with anyone who
2Th   3: 14   Do not **a** with them, in order

ASSURANCE
Heb 10: 22   and with the full **a** that faith brings,

ASTRAY
Pr   10: 17   ignores correction leads others **a**.
Isa 53:   6   have gone **a**, each of us has turned
Jer 50:   6   their shepherds have led them **a**
1Pe   2: 25   For "you were like sheep going **a**,"
1Jn   3:   7   do not let anyone lead you **a**.

ATHALIAH
Evil queen of Judah (2Ki 11; 2Ch 23).

ATHLETE
2Ti   2:   5   competes as an **a** does not receive

ATONEMENT
Ex   25: 17   "Make an **a** cover of pure gold—
        30: 10   Once a year Aaron shall make **a**
Lev 17: 11   blood that makes **a** for one's life.
        23: 27   this seventh month is the Day of **A**.
Nu   25: 13   God and made **a** for the Israelites."
Ro   3: 25   presented Christ as a sacrifice of **a**,
Heb   2: 17   that he might make **a** for the sins

ATTENTION
Pr   4:   1   pay **a** and gain understanding.
        5:   1   My son, pay **a** to my wisdom,
        22: 17   Pay **a** and turn your ear
Titus 1: 14   and will pay no **a** to Jewish myths

ATTITUDE (ATTITUDES)
Eph   4: 23   made new in the **a** of your minds;
1Pe   4:   1   yourselves also with the same **a**,

ATTITUDES (ATTITUDE)
Heb   4: 12   the thoughts and **a** of the heart.

ATTRACTIVE
Titus 2: 10   teaching about God our Savior **a**.

AUTHORITIES (AUTHORITY)
Ro   13:   5   it is necessary to submit to the **a**,
        13:   6   for the **a** are God's servants,
Titus 3:   1   to be subject to rulers and **a**,
1Pe   3: 22   **a** and powers in submission to him.

AUTHORITY (AUTHORITIES)
Mt   7: 29   he taught as one who had **a**,
        9:   6   the Son of Man has **a** on earth
        28: 18   "All **a** in heaven and on earth has
Ro   13:   1   for there is no **a** except
        13:   2   rebels against the **a** is rebelling
1Co 11: 10   ought to have **a** over her own head,
1Ti   2:   2   for kings and all those in **a**, that we
        2: 12   to teach or to assume **a** over a man;
Heb 13: 17   your leaders and submit to their **a**,

AVENGE (VENGEANCE)
Dt   32: 35   It is mine to **a**; I will repay.

AVOID
Pr   20:   3   It is to one's honor to **a** strife,
        20: 19   so **a** anyone who talks too much.
1Th   4:   3   you should **a** sexual immorality;
2Ti   2: 16   **A** godless chatter, because those
Titus 3:   9   But **a** foolish controversies

AWAKE
Ps   17: 15   when I **a**, I will be satisfied
1Th   5:   6   asleep, but let us be **a** and sober.

AWE (AWESOME)
Job 25:   2   "Dominion and **a** belong to God;
Ps 119:120   of you; I stand in **a** of your laws.
Isa 29: 23   will stand in **a** of the God of Israel.
Jer 33:   9   they will be in **a** and will tremble
Hab   3:   2   I stand in **a** of your deeds, LORD.
Mal   2:   5   me and stood in **a** of my name.
Mt   9:   8   saw this, they were filled with **a**;
Lk   7: 16   They were all filled with **a**
Ac   2: 43   Everyone was filled with **a**
Heb 12: 28   acceptably with reverence and **a**,

AWESOME (AWE)
Ge   28: 17   and said, "How **a** is this place!
Ex   15: 11   majestic in holiness, in glory,
Dt   7: 21   is among you, is a great and **a** God.
        10: 17   God, mighty and **a**, who shows no
        28: 58   revere this glorious and **a** name—
Jdg 13:   6   looked like an angel of God, very **a**.
Ne   1:   5   the great and **a** God, who keeps his
        9: 32   God, mighty and **a**, who keeps his
Job 10: 16   again display your **a** power against
        37: 22   God comes in **a** majesty.
Ps   45:   4   your right hand achieve **a** deeds.
        47:   2   For the LORD Most High is **a**,
        66:   5   has done, his **a** deeds for mankind!
        68: 35   You, God, are **a** in your sanctuary;
        89:   7   he is more **a** than all who surround
        99:   3   praise your great and **a** name—
        111:   9   holy and **a** is his name.
        145:   6   tell of the power of your **a** works—
Da   9:   4   the great and **a** God, who keeps his

BAAL
1Ki 18: 25   Elijah said to the prophets of **B**,

BAASHA
King of Israel (1Ki 15:16—16:7; 2Ch 16:1–6).

BABIES (BABY)
Lk   18: 15   bringing **b** to Jesus for him to place
1Pe   2:   2   Like newborn **b**, crave pure

BABY (BABIES)
Isa 49: 15   "Can a mother forget the **b** at her
Lk   1: 44   the **b** in my womb leaped for joy.

Lk   2: 12   You will find a **b** wrapped in cloths
Jn   16: 21   **b** is born she forgets the anguish

BABYLON
Ps 137:   1   By the rivers of **B** we sat and wept

BACKSLIDING
Jer   3: 22   I will cure you of **b**."
Eze 37: 23   save them from all their sinful **b**,

BAGS
Mt 25: 15   To one he gave five **b** of gold, to
               another two **b**, and to another one

BALAAM
Prophet who attempted to curse Israel (Nu 22–24;
Dt 23:4–5; 2Pe 2:15; Jude 11). Killed (Nu 31:8; Jos
13:22).

BALM
Jer   8: 22   Is there no **b** in Gilead? Is there no

BANISH
Jer 25: 10   will **b** from them the sounds of joy

BANQUET
SS   2:   4   Let him lead me to the **b** hall,
Lk   14: 13   But when you give a **b**,

BAPTIZE (BAPTIZED)
Mt   3: 11   "I **b** you with water for repentance.
      3: 11   He will **b** you with the Holy Spirit
Mk   1:   8   I **b** you with water, but he will **b**
1Co   1: 17   For Christ did not send me to **b**,

BAPTIZED (BAPTIZE)
Mt   3:   6   they were **b** by him in the Jordan.
Mk   1:   9   and was **b** by John in the Jordan.
     10: 38   be **b** with the baptism I am **b** with?"
     16: 16   believes and is **b** will be saved,
Jn   4:   2   in fact it was not Jesus who **b**,
Ac   1:   5   For John **b** with water, but in a few

BARABBAS
Mt 27: 17   release to you: Jesus **B**, or Jesus

BARBS
Nu 33: 55   remain will become **b** in your eyes

BARE
Heb   4: 13   and laid **b** before the eyes of him

BARNABAS
Disciple, originally Joseph (Ac 4:36), prophet (Ac
13:1), apostle (Ac 14:14). Brought Paul to apostles
(Ac 9:27), Antioch (Ac 11:22–29; Gal 2:1–13), on
the first missionary journey (Ac 13–14). Together at
Jerusalem Council, they separated over John Mark
(Ac 15). Later co-workers (1Co 9:6; Col 4:10).

BARTHOLOMEW
Apostle (Mt 10:3; Mk 3:18; Lk 6:14; Ac 1:13). Possibly also known as Nathanael (Jn 1:45–49; 21:2).

BATH
Jn 13: 10   who have had a **b** need only

BATHSHEBA
Wife of Uriah who committed adultery with and
became wife of David (2Sa 11), mother of Solomon
(2Sa 12:24; 1Ki 1–2; 1Ch 3:5).

BATTLE
2Ch 20: 15   For the **b** is not yours, but God's.
Ps   24:   8   mighty, the LORD mighty in **b**.
Ecc   9: 11   to the swift or the **b** to the strong,

BEAR (BEARING BIRTH BIRTHRIGHT BORE BORN
       FIRSTBORN NEWBORN)
Ge   4: 13   punishment is more than I can **b**.

Ps 38:   4   me like a burden too heavy to **b**.
Isa 53: 11   many, and he will **b** their iniquities.
Da   7:   5   beast, which looked like a **b**.
Mt   7: 18   A good tree cannot **b** bad fruit,
Jn 15:   2   branch that does **b** fruit he prunes
    15: 16   so that you might go and **b** fruit—
Ro 15:   1   We who are strong ought to **b**
1Co 10: 13   tempted beyond what you can **b**.
Col 3: 13   **B** with each other and forgive one

BEARING (BEAR)
Eph   4:   2   patient, **b** with one another in love.
Col   1: 10   **b** fruit in every good work,

BEAST
Rev 13: 18   calculate the number of the **b**, for it

BEAT (BEATING)
Isa   2:   4   They will **b** their swords
Joel 3: 10   **B** your plowshares into swords

BEATING (BEAT)
1Co   9: 26   I do not fight like a boxer **b** the air.
1Pe   2: 20   if you receive a **b** for doing wrong

BEAUTIFUL (BEAUTY)
Ge   6:   2   the daughters of humans were **b**,
     12: 11   "I know what a **b** woman you are.
     12: 14   saw that Sarai was a very **b** woman.
     24: 16   The woman was very **b**, a virgin;
     26:   7   of Rebekah, because she is **b**."
     29: 17   had a lovely figure and was **b**.
Pr   11: 22   snout is a **b** woman who shows no
Ecc   3: 11   He has made everything **b** in its
Isa   4:   2   the Branch of the LORD will be **b**
     52:   7   How **b** on the mountains are the
Eze 20:   6   and honey, the most **b** of all lands.
Zec   9: 17   How attractive and **b** they will be!
Mt 23: 27   which look **b** on the outside
     26: 10   She has done a **b** thing to me.
Ro 10: 15   "How **b** are the feet of those who

BEAUTY (BEAUTIFUL)
Ps 27:   4   to gaze on the **b** of the LORD
    45: 11   the king be enthralled by your **b**;
Pr 31: 30   is deceptive, and **b** is fleeting;
Isa 33: 17   Your eyes will see the king in his **b**
    53:   2   He had no **b** or majesty to attract
    61:   3   them a crown of **b** instead of ashes,
Eze 28: 12   full of wisdom and perfect in **b**.
1Pe 3:   4   unfading **b** of a gentle and quiet

BED
Heb 13:   4   and the marriage **b** kept pure,

BEELZEBUL
Lk 11: 15   said, "By **B**, the prince of demons,

BEER
Pr 20:   1   Wine is a mocker and **b** a brawler;

BEERSHEBA
Jdg 20:   1   all Israel from Dan to **B**

BEGINNING
Ge   1:   1   In the **b** God created the heavens
Ps 102: 25   In the **b** you laid the foundations
   111: 10   of the LORD is the **b** of wisdom;
Pr   1:   7   the LORD is the **b** of knowledge,
      4:   7   The **b** of wisdom is this:
Jn   1:   1   In the **b** was the Word,
1Jn   1:   1   That which was from the **b**,
Rev 21:   6   and the Omega, the **B** and the End.

BEHAVE (BEHAVIOR)
Ro 13: 13   us **b** decently, as in the daytime,

BEHAVIOR (BEHAVE)
Pr   1:   3   receiving instruction in prudent **b**,

BELIEVE (BELIEVED BELIEVER BELIEVERS
BELIEVES BELIEVING)

Pr	14:	15	The simple **b** anything,
Mt	18:	6	those who **b** in me—
	21:	22	If you **b**, you will receive whatever
Mk	1:	15	Repent and **b** the good news!"
	9:	24	the boy's father exclaimed, "I do **b**;
	16:	17	*accompany those who b:*
Lk	8:	50	just **b**, and she will be healed."
	24:	25	how slow to **b** all that the prophets
Jn	1:	7	so that through him all might **b**.
	3:	18	does not **b** stands condemned
	6:	29	to **b** in the one he has sent."
	10:	38	even though you do not **b** me,
	11:	27	"I **b** that you are the Messiah,
	14:	1	You **b** in God; **b** also in me.
	14:	11	**B** me when I say that I am
	16:	30	This makes us **b** that you came
	16:	31	"Do you now **b**?" Jesus replied.
	17:	21	the world may **b** that you have sent
	20:	27	into my side. Stop doubting and **b**."
	20:	31	may **b** that Jesus is the Messiah,
Ac	16:	31	They replied, "**B** in the Lord Jesus,
	24:	14	I **b** everything that is in accordance
Ro	3:	22	faith in Jesus Christ to all who **b**.
	4:	11	he is the father of all who **b**
	10:	9	**b** in your heart that God raised
	10:	14	how can they **b** in the one of whom
1Th	4:	14	For we **b** that Jesus died and rose
2Th	2:	11	delusion so that they will **b** the lie
1Ti	4:	10	and especially of those who **b**.
Titus	1:	6	a man whose children **b** and are
Heb	11:	6	comes to him must **b** that he exists
Jas	2:	19	You **b** that there is one God. Good!
			Even the demons **b** that—
1Jn	4:	1	Dear friends, do not **b** every spirit,

BELIEVED (BELIEVE)

Ge	15:	6	Abram **b** the Lord, and he
Jnh	3:	5	The Ninevites **b** God. A fast was
Jn	1:	12	to those who **b** in his name,
	2:	22	Then they **b** the scripture
	3:	18	already because they have not **b**
	20:	8	also went inside. He saw and **b**.
	20:	29	who have not seen and yet have **b**."
Ac	13:	48	were appointed for eternal life **b**.
Ro	4:	3	"Abraham **b** God, and it was
	10:	14	call on the one they have not **b** in?
1Co	15:	2	Otherwise, you have **b** in vain.
Gal	3:	6	So also Abraham "**b** God, and it
2Ti	1:	12	because I know whom I have **b**,
Jas	2:	23	that says, "Abraham **b** God, and it

BELIEVER (BELIEVE)

1Co	7:	12	brother has a wife who is not a **b**
2Co	6:	15	what does a **b** have in common

BELIEVERS (BELIEVE)

Ac	4:	32	All the **b** were one in heart
	5:	12	all the **b** used to meet together
1Co	6:	5	to judge a dispute between **b**?
1Ti	4:	12	set an example for the **b** in speech,
1Pe	2:	17	love the family of **b**, fear God,

BELIEVES (BELIEVE)

Mk	9:	23	is possible for one who **b**."
	11:	23	**b** that what they say will happen,
	16:	16	*Whoever b and is baptized*
Jn	3:	16	whoever **b** in him shall not perish
	3:	36	Whoever **b** in the Son has eternal
	5:	24	**b** him who sent me has eternal life
	6:	35	and whoever **b** in me will never be
	6:	40	and **b** in him shall have eternal life,
	6:	47	you, the one who **b** has eternal life.
	7:	38	Whoever **b** in me, as Scripture has
Ro	1:	16	salvation to everyone who **b**:

Ro	9:	33	the one who **b** in him will never be
	10:	4	righteousness for everyone who **b**.
1Jn	5:	1	Everyone who **b** that Jesus is
	5:	5	Only the one who **b** that Jesus is

BELIEVING (BELIEVE)

Jn	11:	26	whoever lives by **b** in me will never
	20:	31	by **b** you may have life in his name.

BELONG (BELONGS)

Dt	29:	29	The secret things **b** to the Lord
Job	25:	2	"Dominion and awe **b** to God;
Ps	47:	9	for the kings of the earth **b** to God;
	95:	4	and the mountain peaks **b** to him.
Jn	8:	44	You **b** to your father, the devil,
	15:	19	As it is, you do not **b** to the world,
Ro	1:	6	those Gentiles who are called to **b**
	7:	4	that you might **b** to another, to him
	14:	8	we live or die, we **b** to the Lord.
Gal	5:	24	Those who **b** to Christ Jesus have
1Th	5:	8	But since we **b** to the day, let us be

BELONGS (BELONG)

Job	41:	11	Everything under heaven **b** to me.
Ps	111:	10	To him **b** eternal praise.
Eze	18:	4	For everyone **b** to me, the parent as
Jn	8:	47	Whoever **b** to God hears what God
Ro	12:	5	each member **b** to all the others.

BELOVED (LOVE)

Dt	33:	12	"Let the **b** of the Lord rest
SS	2:	16	My **b** is mine and I am his;
	7:	10	I belong to my **b**, and his desire is

BELT

Isa	11:	5	Righteousness will be his **b**
Eph	6:	14	the **b** of truth buckled around your

BENEFICIAL (BENEFIT)

1Co	10:	23	but not everything is **b**.

BENEFIT (BENEFICIAL BENEFITS)

Ro	6:	22	the **b** you reap leads to holiness,
2Co	4:	15	All this is for your **b**,

BENEFITS (BENEFIT)

Ps	103:	2	my soul, and forget not all his **b**—
Jn	4:	38	and you have reaped the **b** of their

BENJAMIN

Twelfth son of Jacob by Rachel (Ge 35:16–24;
46:19–21; 1Ch 2:2). Jacob refused to send him to
Egypt, but relented (Ge 42–45).

BEREAN

Ac	17:	11	the **B** Jews were of more noble

BESTOWS

Ps	84:	11	the Lord **b** favor and honor;

BETHLEHEM

Mt	2:	1	After Jesus was born in **B** in Judea,

BETRAY

Pr	25:	9	do not **b** another's confidence,

BIND (BINDS)

Dt	6:	8	and **b** them on your foreheads.
Pr	6:	21	**B** them always on your heart;
Isa	61:	1	He has sent me to **b**
Mt	16:	19	whatever you **b** on earth will be

BINDS (BIND)

Ps	147:	3	and **b** up their wounds.
Isa	30:	26	when the Lord **b** up the bruises

BIRDS

Mt	8:	20	"Foxes have dens and **b** have nests,

BIRTH (BEAR)
Ps 58: 3 Even from **b** the wicked go astray;
Mt 1: 18 This is how the **b** of Jesus
1Pe 1: 3 great mercy he has given us new **b**

BIRTHRIGHT (BEAR)
Ge 25: 34 up and left. So Esau despised his **b**.

BLAMELESS
Ge 17: 1 walk before me faithfully and be **b**.
Job 1: 1 This man was **b** and upright;
Ps 84: 11 from those whose walk is **b**.
119: 1 are those whose ways are **b**,
Pr 19: 1 poor whose walk is **b** than a fool
1Co 1: 8 so that you will be **b** on the day
Eph 5: 27 any other blemish, but holy and **b**.
Php 2: 15 that you may become **b** and pure,
1Th 3: 13 your hearts so that you will be **b**
5: 23 body be kept **b** at the coming of
Titus 1: 6 An elder must be **b**, faithful to his
Heb 7: 26 one who is holy, **b**, pure, set apart
2Pe 3: 14 spotless, **b** and at peace with him.

BLASPHEMES
Mk 3: 29 whoever **b** against the Holy Spirit

BLEMISH
1Pe 1: 19 Christ, a lamb without **b** or defect.

BLESS (BLESSED BLESSING BLESSINGS)
Ge 12: 3 I will **b** those who **b** you,
Ro 12: 14 **B** those who persecute you;

BLESSED (BLESS)
Ge 1: 22 God **b** them and said, "Be fruitful
2: 3 Then God **b** the seventh day
22: 18 all nations on earth will be **b**,
Ps 1: 1 **B** is the one who does not walk
2: 12 **B** are all who take refuge in him.
33: 12 **B** is the nation whose God is
41: 1 **B** are those who have regard
84: 5 **B** are those whose strength is
106: 3 **B** are those who act justly,
112: 1 **B** are those who fear the LORD,
118: 26 **B** is he who comes in the name
Pr 29: 18 **b** is the one who heeds wisdom's
31: 28 Her children arise and call her **b**;
Mt 5: 3 "**B** are the poor in spirit, for theirs
5: 4 **B** are those who mourn, for they
5: 5 **B** are the meek, for they will
5: 6 **B** are those who hunger and thirst
5: 7 **B** are the merciful, for they will
5: 8 **B** are the pure in heart, for they
5: 9 **B** are the peacemakers, for they
5: 10 **B** are those who are persecuted
5: 11 "**B** are you when people insult you,
Lk 1: 48 on all generations will call me **b**,
Jn 12: 13 "**B** is he who comes in the name
Ac 20: 35 'It is more **b** to give than
Titus 2: 13 while we wait for the **b** hope—
Jas 1: 12 **B** is the one who perseveres
under
Rev 1: 3 **B** is the one who reads aloud
22: 14 "**B** are those who wash their
robes,

BLESSING (BLESS)
Eze 34: 26 there will be showers of **b**.

BLESSINGS (BLESS)
Pr 10: 6 **B** crown the head of the righteous,

BLIND
Mt 15: 14 If the **b** lead the **b**, both will fall
23: 16 "Woe to you, **b** guides! You say,
Jn 9: 25 I do know. I was **b** but now
I see!"

BLOOD
Ge 9: 6 "Whoever sheds human **b**, by
humans shall their **b** be shed;
Ex 12: 13 The **b** will be a sign for you
24: 8 "This is the **b** of the covenant
Lev 17: 11 For the life of a creature is in the **b**,
17: 11 it is the **b** that makes atonement
Ps 72: 14 for precious is their **b** in his sight.
Pr 6: 17 hands that shed innocent **b**,
Mt 26: 28 This is my **b** of the covenant,
Ro 3: 25 through the shedding of his **b**—
5: 9 have now been justified by his **b**,
1Co 11: 25 cup is the new covenant in my **b**;
Eph 1: 7 we have redemption through his **b**,
2: 13 brought near by the **b** of Christ.
Col 1: 20 by making peace through his **b**,
Heb 9: 12 once for all by his own **b**,
9: 22 everything be cleansed with **b**,
1Pe 1: 19 but with the precious **b** of Christ,
1Jn 1: 7 and the **b** of Jesus, his Son,
Rev 1: 5 has freed us from our sins by his **b**,
5: 9 with your **b** you purchased for God
7: 14 them white in the **b** of the Lamb.
12: 11 over him by the **b** of the Lamb

BLOT (BLOTS)
Ex 32: 32 **b** me out of the book you have
Ps 51: 1 to your great compassion **b** out my
Rev 3: 5 I will never **b** out the name

BLOTS (BLOT)
Isa 43: 25 "I, even I, am he who **b** out your

BLOWN
Eph 4: 14 and **b** here and there by every wind
Jas 1: 6 the sea, **b** and tossed by the wind.

BOAST
1Ki 20: 11 his armor should not **b** like one
Ps 44: 8 In God we make our **b** all day long,
Pr 27: 1 Do not **b** about tomorrow, for you
1Co 1: 31 "Let the one who boasts **b**
Gal 6: 14 May I never **b** except in the cross
Eph 2: 9 not by works, so that no one can **b**.

BOAZ
Wealthy Bethlehemite who showed favor to Ruth (Ru 2), married her (Ru 4). Ancestor of David (Ru 4:18–22; 1Ch 2:12–15), Jesus (Mt 1:5–16; Lk 3:23–32).

BODIES (BODY)
Ro 12: 1 to offer your **b** as a living sacrifice,
1Co 6: 15 not know that your **b** are members
6: 19 not know that your **b** are temples
Eph 5: 28 to love their wives as their own **b**.

BODY (BODIES)
Zec 13: 6 are these wounds on your **b**?'
Mt 10: 28 can destroy both soul and **b** in hell.
10: 28 be afraid of those who kill the **b**
26: 26 "Take and eat; this is my **b**."
Jn 13: 10 their whole **b** is clean.
1Co 11: 24 "This is my **b**, which is for you;
12: 12 Just as a **b**, though one, has many
Eph 5: 30 for we are members of his **b**.

BOLD (BOLDNESS)
Pr 21: 29 The wicked put up a **b** front,
28: 1 but the righteous are as **b** as
a lion.

BOLDNESS (BOLD)
Ac 4: 29 to speak your word with great **b**.

BONDAGE
Ezr 9: 9 God has not forsaken us in our **b**.

BOOK (BOOKS)
Jos	1:	8	Keep this **B** of the Law always
Ne	8:	8	They read from the **B** of the Law
Jn	20:	30	which are not recorded in this **b**.
Php	4:	3	whose names are in the **b** of life.
Rev	21:	27	are written in the Lamb's **b** of life.

BOOKS (BOOK)
Ecc	12:	12	Of making many **b** there is no end,

BORE (BEAR)
Isa	53:	4	up our pain and **b** our suffering,

BORN (BEAR)
Isa	9:	6	For to us a child is **b**, to us a son is
Jn	3:	7	my saying, 'You must be **b** again.'
1Pe	1:	23	For you have been **b** again,
1Jn	4:	7	Everyone who loves has been **b**
	5:	1	that Jesus is the Christ is **b** of God,

BORROWER
Pr	22:	7	and the **b** is slave to the lender.

BOUGHT
Ac	20:	28	which he **b** with his own blood.
1Co	6:	20	you were **b** at a price.
	7:	23	You were **b** at a price;
2Pe	2:	1	the sovereign Lord who **b** them—

BOUNDLESS
Eph	3:	8	the Gentiles the **b** riches of Christ,

BOW
Ps	95:	6	Come, let us **b** down in worship,
Isa	45:	23	Before me every knee will **b**;
Ro	14:	11	Lord, 'every knee will **b** before me;
Php	2:	10	name of Jesus every knee should **b**,

BRANCH (BRANCHES)
Isa	4:	2	that day the **B** of the Lᴏʀᴅ will be
Jer	33:	15	I will make a righteous **B** sprout

BRANCHES (BRANCH)
Jn	15:	5	"I am the vine; you are the **b**.

BRAVE
2Sa	2:	7	then, be strong and **b**, for Saul your

BREAD
Dt	8:	3	that man does not live on **b** alone
Pr	30:	8	riches, but give me only my daily **b**.
Isa	55:	2	spend money on what is not **b**,
Mt	4:	4	'Man shall not live on **b** alone,
	6:	11	Give us today our daily **b**.
Jn	6:	35	Jesus declared, "I am the **b** of life.
	21:	13	took the **b** and gave it to them,
1Co	11:	23	the night he was betrayed, took **b**,

BREAK (BREAKING BROKEN)
Nu	30:	2	he must not **b** his word but must
Jdg	2:	1	'I will never **b** my covenant
Ps	2:	9	You will **b** them with a rod of iron;
Isa	42:	3	A bruised reed he will not **b**,
Mt	12:	20	A bruised reed he will not **b**,

BREAKING (BREAK)
Jas	2:	10	just one point is guilty of **b** all of it.

BREASTPIECE (BREASTPLATE)
Ex	28:	15	"Fashion a **b** for making decisions

BREASTPLATE (BREASTPIECE)
Isa	59:	17	He put on righteousness as his **b**,
Eph	6:	14	the **b** of righteousness in place,
1Th	5:	8	putting on faith and love as a **b**,

BREATHED (GOD-BREATHED)
Ge	2:	7	**b** into his nostrils the breath of life,
Jn	20:	22	with that he **b** on them and said,

BRIBE
Ex	23:	8	"Do not accept a **b**, for a **b** blinds
Pr	6:	35	he will refuse a **b**, however great it

BRIDE
Rev	19:	7	and his **b** has made herself ready.

BRIGHTER (BRIGHTNESS)
Pr	4:	18	shining ever **b** till the full light

BRIGHTNESS (BRIGHTER)
2Sa	22:	13	Out of the **b** of his presence bolts
Da	12:	3	who are wise will shine like the **b**

BROAD
Mt	7:	13	gate and **b** is the road that leads

BROKEN (BREAK)
Ps	51:	17	My sacrifice, O God, is a **b** spirit;
Ecc	4:	12	of three strands is not quickly **b**.

BROKENHEARTED (HEART)
Ps	34:	18	The Lᴏʀᴅ is close to the **b**
	109:	16	the poor and the needy and the **b**.
	147:	3	He heals the **b** and binds up their
Isa	61:	1	He has sent me to bind up the **b**,

BROTHER (BROTHER'S BROTHERS)
Pr	17:	17	a **b** is born for a time of adversity.
	18:	24	a friend who sticks closer than a **b**.
Mt	18:	15	"If your **b** or sister sins,
Mk	3:	35	Whoever does God's will is my **b**
Lk	17:	3	"If your **b** or sister sins against you,
1Co	8:	13	if what I eat causes my **b** or sister
1Jn	2:	10	who loves their **b** and sister

BROTHER'S (BROTHER)
Ge	4:	9	"Am I my **b** keeper?"

BROTHERS (BROTHER)
Mt	25:	40	did for one of the least of these **b**
Mk	10:	29	"no one who has left home or **b**
Heb	13:	1	Keep on loving one another as **b**

BUILD (BUILDING BUILDS BUILT)
Mt	16:	18	on this rock I will **b** my church,
Ac	20:	32	which can **b** you up and give you
1Co	3:	10	But each one should **b** with care.
	14:	12	excel in those that **b** up the
			church.
1Th	5:	11	one another and **b** each other up,

BUILDING (BUILD)
1Co	3:	9	you are God's field, God's **b**.
2Co	5:	8	authority the Lord gave us for **b**
Eph	4:	29	only what is helpful for **b** others

BUILDS (BUILD)
Ps	127:	1	Unless the Lᴏʀᴅ **b** the house,
1Co	8:	1	puffs up while love **b** up.

BUILT (BUILD)
Mt	7:	24	is like a wise man who **b** his
			house
1Co	14:	26	so that the church may be **b** up.
Eph	2:	20	**b** on the foundation of the apostles
	4:	12	that the body of Christ may be **b**

BURDEN (BURDENED BURDENS)
Ps	38:	4	overwhelmed me like a **b** too heavy
Mt	11:	30	my yoke is easy and my **b** is light."

BURDENED (BURDEN)
Gal	5:	1	do not let yourselves be **b** again

BURDENS (BURDEN)
Ps	68:	19	our Savior, who daily bears our **b**.
Gal	6:	2	Carry each other's **b**, and in this

BURIED
Ro 6: 4 We were therefore **b** with him
1Co 15: 4 that he was **b**, that he was raised

BURNING
Lev 6: 9 the fire must be kept **b** on the altar.
Ro 12: 20 you will heap **b** coals on his head."

BUSINESS
Da 8: 27 got up and went about the king's **b**.
1Th 4: 11 You should mind your own **b**

BUSY
1Ki 20: 40 While your servant was **b** here
2Th 3: 11 are not **b**; they are busybodies.
Titus 2: 5 pure, to be **b** at home, to be kind,

CAESAR
Mt 22: 21 give back to **C** what is Caesar's,

CAIN
Firstborn of Adam (Ge 4:1), murdered brother Abel (Ge 4:1–16; 1Jn 3:12).

CALEB
Judahite who spied out Canaan (Nu 13:6); allowed to enter land because of faith (Nu 13:30—14:38; Dt 1:36). Possessed Hebron (Jos 14:6—15:19).

CALF
Ex 32: 4 into an idol cast in the shape of a **c**,
Lk 15: 23 Bring the fattened **c** and kill it.

CALL (CALLED CALLING CALLS)
Ps 145: 18 LORD is near to all who **c** on him,
Pr 31: 28 children arise and call her blessed;
Isa 5: 20 Woe to those who **c** evil good
55: 6 **c** on him while he is near.
65: 24 Before they **c** I will answer;
Jer 33: 3 '**C** to me and I will answer you
Mt 9: 13 I have not come to **c** the righteous,
Ro 10: 12 richly blesses all who **c** on him,
11: 29 gifts and his **c** are irrevocable.
1Th 4: 7 For God did not **c** us to be impure,

CALLED (CALL)
1Sa 3: 5 and said, "Here I am; you **c** me."
2Ch 7: 14 my people, who are **c** by my name,
Ps 34: 6 This poor man **c**, and the LORD
Mt 21: 13 " 'My house will be **c** a house
Ro 8: 30 And those he predestined, he also **c**; those he **c**, he also justified;
1Co 7: 15 God has **c** us to live in peace.
Gal 5: 13 and sisters, were **c** to be free.
1Pe 2: 9 the praises of him who **c** you

CALLING (CALL)
Jn 1: 23 voice of one **c** in the wilderness,
Ac 22: 16 your sins away, **c** on his name.'
Eph 4: 1 worthy of the **c** you have received.
2Pe 1: 10 every effort to confirm your **c**

CALLS (CALL)
Joel 2: 32 everyone who **c** on the name
Jn 10: 3 He **c** his own sheep by name
Ro 10: 13 "Everyone who **c** on the name

CALM
Pr 29: 11 but the wise bring **c** in the end.

CAMEL
Mt 19: 24 easier for a **c** to go through the eye
23: 24 strain out a gnat but swallow a **c**.

CANAAN
1Ch 16: 18 **C** as the portion you will inherit."

CANCELED
Col 2: 14 having **c** the charge of our legal

CAPITAL
Dt 21: 22 someone guilty of a **c** offense is put

CARE (CAREFUL CAREFULLY CARES CARING)
Ps 8: 4 human beings that you **c** for them?
Pr 29: 7 The righteous **c** about justice
Lk 10: 34 him to an inn and took **c** of him.
Jn 21: 16 Jesus said, "Take **c** of my sheep."
1Co 3: 10 But each one should build with **c**.
Eph 5: 29 but they feed and **c** for their body,
Heb 2: 6 a son of man that you **c** for him?
1Pe 5: 2 of God's flock that is under your **c**,

CAREFUL (CARE)
Ex 23: 13 "Be **c** to do everything I have said
Dt 6: 3 be **c** to obey so that it may go well
Jos 23: 6 be **c** to obey all that is written
23: 11 So be very **c** to love the LORD
Pr 13: 24 one who loves their children is **c**
Mt 6: 1 "Be **c** not to practice your
Ro 12: 17 Be **c** to do what is right in the eyes
1Co 8: 9 Be **c**, however, that the exercise of
Eph 5: 15 Be very **c**, then, how you live—

CAREFULLY (CARE)
Pr 12: 26 righteous choose their friends **c**,

CARES (CARE)
Ps 55: 22 Cast your **c** on the LORD and he
Na 1: 7 He **c** for those who trust in him,
1Th 2: 7 Just as a nursing mother **c** for her
1Pe 5: 7 on him because he **c** for you.

CARING (CARE)
1Ti 5: 4 practice by **c** for their own family

CARRIED (CARRY)
Ex 19: 4 and how I **c** you on eagles' wings
Heb 13: 9 Do not be **c** away by all kinds
2Pe 1: 21 God as they were **c** along

CARRIES (CARRY)
Dt 32: 11 to catch them and **c** them aloft.
Isa 40: 11 arms and **c** them close to his heart;

CARRY (CARRIED CARRIES)
Lk 14: 27 whoever does not **c** their cross
Gal 6: 2 **C** each other's burdens, and in this
6: 5 each one should **c** their own load.

CAST
Ps 22: 18 them and **c** lots for my garment.
55: 22 **C** your cares on the LORD and he
Jn 19: 24 them and **c** lots for my garment."
1Pe 5: 7 **C** all your anxiety on him because

CATTLE
Ps 50: 10 and the **c** on a thousand hills.

CAUGHT
1Th 4: 17 are left will be **c** up together

CAUSE (CAUSES)
Pr 24: 28 against your neighbor without **c**—
Ecc 8: 3 Do not stand up for a bad **c**, for he
Mt 18: 7 the things that **c** people to stumble!
Ro 14: 21 that will **c** your brother or sister
1Co 10: 32 Do not **c** anyone to stumble,

CAUSES (CAUSE)
Isa 8: 14 he will be a stone that **c** people
Mt 5: 6 "If anyone **c** one of these little

CEASE
Ps 46: 9 He makes wars **c** to the ends

CELEBRATE
Ps   2: 11   fear and **c** his rule with trembling.

CENSER
Lev 16: 12   is to take a **c** full of burning coals

CENTURION
Mt   8: 5   Capernaum, a **c** came to him,

CERTAINTY
Lk   1: 4   you may know the **c** of the things
Jn 17: 8   They knew with **c** that I came

CHAFF
Ps   1: 4   They are like **c** that the wind blows

CHAINED
2Ti   2: 9   But God's word is not **c**.

CHAMPION
Ps 19: 5   like a **c** rejoicing to run his course.

CHANGE (CHANGED)
1Sa 15: 29   does not lie or **c** his mind;
Ps 110: 4   has sworn and will not **c** his mind:
Jer   7: 5   If you really **c** your ways and your
Mal   3: 6   "I the Lᴏʀᴅ do not **c**. So you,
Mt 18: 3   unless you **c** and become like little
Heb   7: 21   has sworn and will not **c** his mind:
Jas   1: 17   lights, who does not **c** like shifting

CHANGED (CHANGE)
1Co 15: 51   not all sleep, but we will all be **c**—

CHARACTER
Ru   3: 11   that you are a woman of noble **c**.
Pr 31: 10   A wife of noble **c** who can find?
Ro   5: 4   perseverance, **c**; and **c**, hope.
1Co 15: 33   "Bad company corrupts good **c**."

CHARGE
Ro   8: 33   will bring any **c** against those
2Co 11: 7   the gospel of God to you free of **c**?
2Ti   4: 1   and his kingdom, I give you this **c**:

CHARIOTS
2Ki   6: 17   and **c** of fire all around Elisha.
Ps 20: 7   Some trust in **c** and some in horses

CHARM
Pr 31: 30   **C** is deceptive, and beauty is

CHASE
Pr 12: 11   who **c** fantasies have no sense.

CHATTER (CHATTERING)
1Ti   6: 20   Turn away from godless **c**
2Ti   2: 16   Avoid godless **c**, because those who

CHATTERING (CHATTER)
Pr 10: 8   but a **c** fool comes to ruin.
      10: 10   grief, and a **c** fool comes to ruin.

CHEAT (CHEATED)
Mal   1: 14   "Cursed is the **c** who has
1Co   6: 8   you yourselves **c** and do wrong,

CHEATED (CHEAT)
Lk 19: 8   if I have **c** anybody out of anything,
1Co   6: 7   Why not rather be **c**?

CHEEK
Mt   5: 39   turn to them the other **c** also.

CHEERFUL (CHEERS)
Pr 15: 13   A happy heart makes the face **c**,
      15: 15   the **c** heart has a continual feast.
      17: 22   A **c** heart is good medicine,
2Co   9: 7   for God loves a **c** giver.

CHEERS (CHEERFUL)
Pr 12: 25   the heart, but a kind word **c** it up.

CHILD (CHILDHOOD CHILDLESS CHILDREN)
Pr 22: 15   Folly is bound up in the heart of a **c**,
      23: 13   not withhold discipline from a **c**;
      29: 15   but a **c** left undisciplined disgraces
Isa   9: 6   For to us a **c** is born, to us a son is
      11: 6   and a little **c** will lead them.
      66: 13   As a mother comforts her **c**, so will
Mt 18: 2   He called a little **c** to him,
Lk   1: 42   and blessed is the **c** you will bear!
      1: 80   And the **c** grew and became strong
1Co 13: 11   When I was a **c**, I talked like a **c**,
1Jn   5: 1   loves the father loves his **c** as well.

CHILDHOOD (CHILD)
1Co 13: 11   I put the ways of **c** behind me.

CHILDLESS (CHILD)
Ps 113: 9   settles the **c** woman in her home

CHILDREN (CHILD)
Dt   4: 9   Teach them to your **c** and to their **c**
      11: 19   Teach them to your **c**,
Ps   8: 2   Through the praise of **c** and infants
Pr 13: 24   spares the rod hates their **c**,
      17: 6   parents are the pride of their **c**.
      20: 11   Even small **c** are known by their
      22: 6   Start **c** off on the way they should
      29: 17   Discipline your **c**, and they will
      31: 28   Her **c** arise and call her blessed;
Mt   7: 11   how to give good gifts to your **c**,
      11: 25   and revealed them to little **c**.
      18: 3   change and become like little **c**,
      19: 14   said, "Let the little **c** come to me,
      21: 16   " 'From the lips of **c** and infants
Mk   9: 37   these little **c** in my name welcomes
      10: 14   them, "Let the little **c** come to me,
      10: 16   And he took the **c** in his arms,
      13: 12   **C** will rebel against their parents
Lk 10: 21   and revealed them to little **c**.
      18: 16   said, "Let the little **c** come to me,
Jn 12: 36   so that you may become **c** of light."
Ro   8: 16   with our spirit that we are God's **c**.
2Co 12: 14   **c** should not have to save for
Eph   6: 1   **C**, obey your parents in the Lord,
      6: 4   Fathers, do not exasperate your **c**;
Col   3: 20   **C**, obey your parents in everything,
      3: 21   do not embitter your **c**, or they will
1Ti   3: 4   well and see that his **c** obey him,
      3: 12   and must manage his **c** and his
      5: 10   such as bringing up **c**,
Heb 12: 7   God is treating you as his **c**.
1Jn   3: 1   that we should be called **c** of God!

CHOOSE (CHOOSES CHOSE CHOSEN)
Dt 30: 19   Now **c** life, so that you and your
Jos 24: 15   **c** for yourselves this day whom you
Pr   8: 10   **c** my instruction instead of silver,
Jn 15: 16   You did not **c** me, but I chose you
Ac 15: 14   God first intervened to **c** a people

CHOOSES (CHOOSE)
Jn   7: 17   who **c** to do the will of God

CHOSE (CHOOSE)
Ge 13: 11   Lot **c** for himself the whole plain
Ps 33: 12   the people he **c** for his inheritance.
Jn 15: 16   but I **c** you and appointed you so
1Co   1: 27   But God **c** the foolish things
Eph   1: 4   For he **c** us in him before
2Th   2: 13   because God **c** you as firstfruits

CHOSEN (CHOOSE)
Isa 41: 8   whom I have **c**, you descendants
Mt 22: 14   many are invited, but few are **c**."

Lk	10: 42	Mary has **c** what is better, and it
	23: 35	if he is God's Messiah, the **C** One."
Jn	15: 19	but I have **c** you out of the world.
1Pe	1: 20	He was **c** before the creation
	2: 9	But you are a **c** people, a royal

CHRIST (CHRIST'S CHRISTIAN MESSIAH)

Jn	1: 41	found the Messiah" (that is, the **C**).
Ro	3: 22	faith in Jesus **C** to all who believe.
	5: 6	powerless, **C** died for the ungodly.
	5: 8	we were still sinners, **C** died for us.
	5: 17	life through the one man, Jesus **C**!
	6: 4	just as **C** was raised from the dead
	8: 1	for those who are in **C** Jesus,
	8: 9	does not have the Spirit of **C**, they do not belong to **C**.
	8: 35	separate us from the love of **C**?
	10: 4	**C** is the culmination of the law so
	14: 9	**C** died and returned to life so that
	15: 3	even **C** did not please himself but,
1Co	1: 23	but we preach **C** crucified:
	2: 2	while I was with you except Jesus **C**
	3: 11	one already laid, which is Jesus **C**.
	5: 7	For **C**, our Passover lamb, has been
	8: 6	Jesus **C**, through whom all things
	10: 4	them, and that rock was **C**.
	10: 9	We should not test **C**, as some
	11: 1	as I follow the example of **C**.
	11: 3	that the head of every man is **C**,
	11: 3	and the head of **C** is God.
	12: 27	Now you are the body of **C**,
	15: 3	that **C** died for our sins according
	15: 14	And if **C** has not been raised,
	15: 22	die, so in **C** all will be made alive.
	15: 57	victory through our Lord Jesus **C**.
2Co	3: 3	show that you are a letter from **C**,
	4: 5	but Jesus **C** as Lord, and ourselves
	5: 10	before the judgment seat of **C**,
	5: 17	if anyone is in **C**, the new creation
	11: 2	to **C**, so that I might present you as
Gal	2: 20	I have been crucified with **C**
	3: 13	**C** redeemed us from the curse
	6: 14	in the cross of our Lord Jesus **C**,
Eph	1: 3	and Father of our Lord Jesus **C**,
	3: 8	Gentiles the boundless riches of **C**,
	4: 13	whole measure of the fullness of **C**.
	5: 2	just as **C** loved us and gave himself
	5: 23	head of the wife as **C** is the head
	5: 25	just as **C** loved the church and gave
Php	1: 21	to live is **C** and to die is gain.
	1: 27	manner worthy of the gospel of **C**.
	4: 19	to the riches of his glory in **C** Jesus.
Col	1: 27	which is **C** in you, the hope
	1: 28	present everyone fully mature in **C**.
	2: 6	as you received **C** Jesus as Lord,
	2: 17	the reality, however, is found in **C**.
	3: 15	Let the peace of **C** rule in your
2Th	2: 1	the coming of our Lord Jesus **C**
1Ti	1: 15	**C** Jesus came into the world to save
	2: 5	and mankind, the man **C** Jesus,
2Ti	2: 3	like a good soldier of **C** Jesus.
	3: 15	salvation through faith in **C** Jesus.
Titus	2: 13	our great God and Savior, Jesus **C**,
Heb	3: 14	We have come to share in **C**,
	9: 14	will the blood of **C**, who through
	9: 15	For this reason **C** is the mediator
	9: 28	so **C** was sacrificed once to take
	10: 10	of the body of Jesus **C** once for all.
	13: 8	Jesus **C** is the same yesterday
1Pe	1: 19	but with the precious blood of **C**,
	2: 21	called, because **C** suffered for you,
	3: 18	For **C** also suffered once for sins,
	4: 14	insulted because of the name of **C**,
1Jn	2: 22	whoever denies that Jesus is the **C**.
	3: 16	Jesus **C** laid down his life for us.
	5: 1	who believes that Jesus is the **C**
Rev	20: 4	reigned with **C** a thousand years.

CHRISTIAN (CHRIST)

1Pe	4: 16	if you suffer as a **C**, do not be

CHRIST'S (CHRIST)

2Co	5: 14	For **C** love compels us, because we
	5: 20	We are therefore **C** ambassadors,
	12: 9	so that **C** power may rest on me.

CHURCH

Mt	16: 18	and on this rock I will build my **c**,
	18: 17	if they refuse to listen even to the **c**,
Ac	20: 28	Be shepherds of the **c** of God,
1Co	5: 12	mine to judge those outside the **c**?
	14: 4	one who prophesies edifies the **c**.
	14: 12	excel in those that build up the **c**.
	14: 26	done so that the **c** may be built up.
Eph	5: 23	wife as Christ is the head of the **c**,
Col	1: 24	the sake of his body, which is the **c**.

CIRCUMCISED

Ge	17: 10	Every male among you shall be **c**.
Gal	2: 8	in Peter as an apostle to the **c**,

CIRCUMSTANCES

Php	4: 11	to be content whatever the **c**.
1Th	5: 18	give thanks in all **c**; for this is God's

CITIZENS (CITIZENSHIP)

Eph	2: 19	but fellow **c** with God's people

CITIZENSHIP (CITIZENS)

Php	3: 20	But our **c** is in heaven.

CITY

Heb	13: 14	here we do not have an enduring **c**,

CIVILIAN

2Ti	2: 4	a soldier gets entangled in **c** affairs,

CLAIM (CLAIMS)

Pr	25: 6	do not **c** a place among his great
1Jn	1: 6	If we **c** to have fellowship with him
	1: 8	If we **c** to be without sin,
	1: 10	If we **c** we have not sinned,

CLAIMS (CLAIM)

Jas	2: 14	if someone **c** to have faith but has
1Jn	2: 6	Whoever **c** to live in him must live
	2: 9	Anyone who **c** to be in the light

CLAP

Ps	47: 1	**C** your hands, all you nations;
Isa	55: 12	trees of the field will **c** their hands.

CLAY

Isa	45: 9	Does the **c** say to the potter,
	64: 8	We are the **c**, you are the potter;
Jer	18: 6	"Like **c** in the hand of the potter,
La	4: 2	are now considered as pots of **c**,
Da	2: 33	of iron and partly of baked **c**.
Ro	9: 21	the same lump of **c** some pottery
2Co	4: 7	this treasure in jars of **c** to show
2Ti	2: 20	and silver, but also of wood and **c**;

CLEAN

Lev	16: 30	you will be **c** from all your sins.
Ps	24: 4	one who has **c** hands and a pure
Mt	12: 44	swept **c** and put in order.
	23: 25	You **c** the outside of the cup
Mk	7: 19	this, Jesus declared all foods **c**.)
Jn	13: 10	you are **c**, though not every one
	15: 3	You are already **c** because
Ac	10: 15	impure that God has made **c**."
Ro	14: 20	All food is **c**, but it is wrong

CLING

Ps	63: 8	I **c** to you; your right hand upholds
Ro	12: 9	Hate what is evil; **c** to what is good.

CLOAK
2Ki 4: 29 "Tuck your **c** into your belt,

CLOSE (CLOSER)
Ps 34: 18 The LORD is **c**
Isa 40: 11 and carries them **c** to his heart;
Jer 30: 21 near and he will come **c** to me—

CLOSER (CLOSE)
Ex 3: 5 "Do not come any **c**," God said.
Pr 18: 24 friend who sticks **c** than a brother.

CLOTHE (CLOTHED CLOTHES CLOTHING)
Ps 45: 3 **c** yourself with splendor
Isa 52: 1 Zion, **c** yourself with strength!
Ro 13: 14 **c** yourselves with the Lord Jesus
Col 3: 12 **c** yourselves with compassion,
1Pe 5: 5 **c** yourselves with humility toward

CLOTHED (CLOTHE)
Ps 30: 11 my sackcloth and **c** me with joy,
Pr 31: 25 She is **c** with strength and dignity;
Lk 24: 49 the city until you have been **c**

CLOTHES (CLOTHE)
Mt 6: 25 food, and the body more than **c**?
6: 28 "And why do you worry about **c**?
Jn 11: 44 "Take off the grave **c** and let him

CLOTHING (CLOTHE)
Dt 22: 5 nor a man wear women's **c**,
Mt 7: 15 They come to you in sheep's **c**,

CLOUD (CLOUDS)
Ex 13: 21 them in a pillar of **c** to guide them
Isa 19: 1 the LORD rides on a swift **c** and is
Lk 21: 27 of Man coming in a **c** with power
Heb 12: 1 by such a great **c** of witnesses,

CLOUDS (CLOUD)
Ps 104: 3 He makes the **c** his chariot and
Da 7: 13 man, coming with the **c** of heaven.
Mk 13: 26 Man coming in **c** with great power
1Th 4: 17 them in the **c** to meet the Lord

CO-HEIRS (INHERIT)
Ro 8: 17 heirs of God and **c** with Christ,

COALS
Pr 25: 22 will heap burning **c** on his head,
Ro 12: 20 this, you will heap burning **c** on his

COAT
Lk 6: 29 If someone takes your **c**, do not

COLD
Pr 25: 25 Like **c** water to a weary soul is
Mt 10: 42 anyone gives even a cup of **c** water
24: 12 the love of most will grow **c**,

COMFORT (COMFORTED COMFORTS)
Ps 23: 4 your rod and your staff, they **c** me.
119: 52 ancient laws, and I find **c** in them.
119: 76 May your unfailing love be my **c**,
Zec 1: 17 the LORD will again **c** Zion
1Co 14: 3 strengthening, encouraging and **c**.
2Co 1: 4 that we can **c** those in any trouble
2: 7 you ought to forgive and **c** him,

COMFORTED (COMFORT)
Mt 5: 4 who mourn, for they will be **c**.

COMFORTS (COMFORT)
Job 29: 25 I was like one who **c** mourners.
Isa 49: 13 For the LORD **c** his people
51: 12 "I, even I, am he who **c** you.
66: 13 As a mother **c** her child, so will I
2Co 1: 4 who **c** us in all our troubles,
7: 6 But God, who **c** the downcast,

COMMAND (COMMANDED COMMANDING COMMANDMENT COMMANDMENTS COMMANDS)
Ex 7: 2 You are to say everything I **c** you,
Nu 24: 13 to go beyond the **c** of the LORD—
Dt 4: 2 Do not add to what I **c** you and do
30: 16 For I **c** you today to love
32: 46 so that you may **c** your children
Ps 91: 11 he will **c** his angels concerning you
148: 5 for at his **c** they were created,
Pr 6: 23 For this **c** is a lamp, this teaching is
13: 13 whoever respects a **c** is rewarded.
Ecc 8: 2 Obey the king's **c**, I say,
Joel 2: 11 mighty is the army that obeys his **c**.
Jn 13: 34 "A new **c** I give you:
15: 12 My **c** is this: Love each other as I
1Co 14: 37 I am writing to you is the Lord's **c**.
Gal 5: 14 is fulfilled in keeping this one **c**:
1Ti 1: 5 The goal of this **c** is love,
Heb 11: 3 the universe was formed at God's **c**,
1Jn 3: 23 And this is his **c**: to believe
2Jn : 6 his **c** is that you walk in love.

COMMANDED (COMMAND)
Ps 33: 9 came to be; he **c**, and it stood firm.
Mt 28: 20 to obey everything I have **c** you.
1Co 9: 14 way, the Lord has **c** that those who
1Jn 3: 23 and to love one another as he **c** us.

COMMANDING (COMMAND)
2Ti 2: 4 rather tries to please his **c** officer.

COMMANDMENT (COMMAND)
Jos 22: 5 be very careful to keep the **c**
Mt 22: 38 This is the first and greatest **c**.
Ro 7: 12 and the **c** is holy,
Eph 6: 2 is the first **c** with a promise—

COMMANDMENTS (COMMAND)
Ex 20: 6 those who love me and keep my **c**.
34: 28 words of the covenant—the Ten **C**.
Dt 7: 9 those who love him and keep his **c**.
Ecc 12: 13 Fear God and keep his **c**, for this is
Da 9: 4 those who love him and keep his **c**,
Mt 22: 40 the Prophets hang on these two **c**."

COMMANDS (COMMAND)
Dt 11: 27 you obey the **c** of the LORD your
Ps 112: 1 who find great delight in his **c**.
119: 47 in your **c** because I love them.
119: 86 All your **c** are trustworthy;
119: 98 Your **c** are always with me
119:127 I love your **c** more than gold,
119:143 me, but your **c** give me delight.
119:172 word, for all your **c** are righteous.
Pr 3: 1 but keep my **c** in your heart,
10: 8 The wise in heart accept **c**,
Mt 5: 19 teaches these **c** will be called great
Jn 14: 15 "If you love me, keep my **c**.
14: 21 Whoever has my **c** and keeps them
Ac 17: 30 now he **c** all people everywhere
1Co 7: 19 Keeping God's **c** is what counts.
1Jn 5: 3 this is love for God: to keep his **c**. And his **c** are not burdensome,

COMMEND (COMMENDED COMMENDS)
Ecc 8: 15 So I **c** the enjoyment of life,
1Pe 2: 14 wrong and to **c** those who do right.

COMMENDED (COMMEND)
Ro 13: 3 do what is right and you will be **c**.
Heb 11: 39 These were all **c** for their faith,

COMMENDS (COMMEND)
2Co 10: 18 but the one whom the Lord **c**.

COMMIT (COMMITS COMMITTED)

Ex	20:	14	"You shall not **c** adultery.
Ps	37:	5	**C** your way to the LORD;
Mt	5:	27	was said, 'You shall not **c** adultery.'
Lk	23:	46	into your hands I **c** my spirit."
Ac	20:	32	"Now I **c** you to God
1Co	10:	8	We should not **c** sexual immorality,
1Pe	4:	19	to God's will should **c** themselves

COMMITS (COMMIT)

Pr	6:	32	a man who **c** adultery has no sense;
	29:	22	hot-tempered person **c** many sins.
Mt	19:	9	marries another woman **c** adultery."

COMMITTED (COMMIT)

Nu	5:	7	must confess the sin they have **c**.
1Ki	8:	61	may your hearts be fully **c**
2Ch	16:	9	those whose hearts are fully **c**
Mt	5:	28	lustfully has already **c** adultery
2Co	5:	19	And he has **c** to us the message
1Pe	2:	22	"He **c** no sin, and no deceit was

COMMON

Pr	22:	2	Rich and poor have this in **c**:
1Co	10:	13	has overtaken you except what is **c**
2Co	6:	14	and wickedness have in **c**?

COMPANION

Pr	13:	20	for a **c** of fools suffers harm.
	28:	7	a **c** of gluttons disgraces his father.
	29:	3	but a **c** of prostitutes squanders his

COMPANY

Pr	24:	1	the wicked, do not desire their **c**;
Jer	15:	17	I never sat in the **c** of revelers,
1Co	15:	33	"Bad **c** corrupts good character."

COMPARED (COMPARING)

Eze	31:	2	" 'Who can be **c** with you

COMPARING (COMPARED)

Ro	8:	18	present sufferings are not worth **c**
2Co	8:	8	of your love by **c** it
Gal	6:	4	without **c** themselves to someone

COMPASSION (COMPASSIONATE COMPASSIONS)

Ex	33:	19	I will have **c** on whom I will have **c**.
Ne	9:	19	your great **c** you did not abandon
	9:	28	in your **c** you delivered them time
Ps	51:	1	to your great **c** blot out my
	103:	4	pit and crowns you with love and **c**,
	103:	13	As a father has **c** on his children,
	145:	9	he has **c** on all he has made.
Isa	49:	13	will have **c** on his afflicted ones.
	49:	15	and have no **c** on the child she has
Hos	2:	19	and justice, in love and **c**.
	11:	8	all my **c** is aroused.
Jnh	3:	9	with **c** turn from his fierce anger so
Mt	9:	36	saw the crowds, he had **c** on them,
Mk	8:	2	"I have **c** for these people;
Ro	9:	15	I will have **c** on whom I have **c**."
Col	3:	12	clothe yourselves with **c**, kindness,
Jas	5:	11	The Lord is full of **c** and mercy.

COMPASSIONATE (COMPASSION)

Ne	9:	17	gracious and **c**, slow to anger
Ps	103:	8	The LORD is **c** and gracious,
	112:	4	for those who are gracious and **c**
Eph	4:	32	Be kind and **c** to one another,
1Pe	3:	8	love one another, be **c** and humble.

COMPASSIONS (COMPASSION)

La	3:	22	not consumed, for his **c** never fail.

COMPEL (COMPELLED COMPELS)

Lk	14:	23	lanes and **c** them to come in,

COMPELLED (COMPEL)

Ac	20:	22	"And now, **c** by the Spirit, I am
1Co	9:	16	boast, since I am **c** to preach.

COMPELS (COMPEL)

2Co	5:	14	For Christ's love **c** us, because we

COMPETENCE (COMPETENT)

2Co	3:	5	but our **c** comes from God.

COMPETENT (COMPETENCE)

Ro	15:	14	and **c** to instruct one another.
1Co	6:	2	are you not **c** to judge trivial cases?
2Co	3:	5	Not that we are **c** in ourselves
	3:	6	He has made us **c** as ministers

COMPETES

1Co	9:	25	Everyone who **c** in the games goes
2Ti	2:	5	anyone who **c** as an athlete does

COMPLACENT

Am	6:	1	Woe to you who are **c** in Zion,

COMPLETE

Jn	15:	11	in you and that your joy may be **c**.
	16:	24	will receive, and your joy will be **c**.
	17:	23	they may be brought to **c** unity.
Ac	20:	24	**c** the task the Lord Jesus has given
Php	2:	2	then make my joy **c** by being
Col	4:	17	it that you **c** the ministry you have
Jas	1:	4	so that you may be mature and **c**,
	2:	22	faith was made **c** by what he did.

CONCEAL (CONCEALED CONCEALS)

Ps	40:	10	I do not **c** your love and your
Pr	25:	2	It is the glory of God to **c** a matter;

CONCEALED (CONCEAL)

Jer	16:	17	me, nor is their sin **c** from my eyes.
Mt	10:	26	for there is nothing **c** that will not
Mk	4:	22	whatever is **c** is meant to be

CONCEALS (CONCEAL)

Pr	28:	13	Whoever **c** their sins does not

CONCEITED

Gal	5:	26	Let us not become **c**,
1Ti	6:	4	they are **c** and understand nothing.

CONCEIVE (CONCEIVED)

Isa	7:	14	The virgin will **c** and give birth
Mt	1:	23	"The virgin will **c** and give birth

CONCEIVED (CONCEIVE)

Mt	1:	20	because what is **c** in her is
1Co	2:	9	and what no human mind has **c**"—

CONCERN (CONCERNED)

Eze	36:	21	I had **c** for my holy name,
1Co	7:	32	I would like you to be free from **c**.
	12:	25	that its parts should have equal **c**
2Co	11:	28	of my **c** for all the churches.

CONCERNED (CONCERN)

Jnh	4:	10	"You have been **c** about this plant,
1Co	7:	32	An unmarried man is **c**

CONDEMN (CONDEMNATION CONDEMNED CONDEMNING CONDEMNS)

Job	40:	8	you **c** me to justify yourself?
Isa	50:	9	Who will **c** me? They will all wear
Lk	6:	37	Do not **c**, and you will not be
Jn	3:	17	Son into the world to **c** the world,
	12:	48	words I have spoken will **c** them
Ro	2:	27	yet obeys the law will **c** you who,
1Jn	3:	20	If our hearts **c** us, we know that

CONDEMNATION (CONDEMN)

Ro	5:	18	just as one trespass resulted in **c**
	8:	1	there is now no **c** for those who are
2Co	3:	9	that brought **c** was glorious,

CONDEMNED (CONDEMN)

Ps	34:	22	who takes refuge in him will be **c**.
Mt	12:	37	and by your words you will be **c**."
	23:	33	How will you escape being **c**
Jn	3:	18	Whoever believes in him is not **c**,
	16:	11	prince of this world now stands **c**.
Ro	14:	23	whoever has doubts is **c** if they eat,
1Co	11:	32	that we will not be finally **c**
Heb	11:	7	By his faith he **c** the world

CONDEMNING (CONDEMN)

Pr	17:	15	the guilty and **c** the innocent—
Ro	2:	1	you are **c** yourself, because you

CONDEMNS (CONDEMN)

Pr	14:	34	exalts a nation, but sin **c** any people
Ro	8:	34	Who then is the one who **c**?

CONDUCT

Pr	20:	11	is their **c** really pure and upright?
	21:	8	but the **c** of the innocent is upright.
Ecc	6:	8	how to **c** themselves before others?
Jer	4:	18	"Your own **c** and actions have
	17:	10	each person according to their **c**,
Eze	7:	3	I will judge you according to your **c**
1Ti	3:	15	how people ought to **c** themselves

CONFESS (CONFESSION)

Lev	16:	21	and **c** over it all the wickedness
	26:	40	if they will **c** their sins and the sins
Nu	5:	7	**c** the sin they have committed.
Ps	38:	18	I **c** my iniquity; I am troubled by
Jas	5:	16	Therefore **c** your sins to each other
1Jn	1:	9	If we **c** our sins, he is faithful

CONFESSION (CONFESS)

2Co	9:	13	accompanies your **c** of the gospel

CONFIDENCE

Ps	71:	5	LORD, my **c** since my youth.
Pr	11:	13	A gossip betrays a **c**,
	25:	9	to court, do not betray another's **c**,
	31:	11	Her husband has full **c** in her
Isa	32:	17	will be quietness and **c** forever.
Jer	17:	7	in the LORD, whose **c** is in him.
Php	3:	3	and who put no **c** in the flesh—
Heb	4:	16	God's throne of grace with **c**,
	10:	19	since we have **c** to enter the Most
	10:	35	So do not throw away your **c**;
	11:	1	Now faith is **c** in what we hope
	13:	17	Have **c** in your leaders and submit
1Jn	5:	14	This is the **c** we have

CONFIRM

2Pe	1:	10	make every effort to **c** your calling

CONFLICT

Pr	6:	14	his heart—he always stirs up **c**.
	6:	19	a person who stirs up **c**
	10:	12	Hatred stirs up **c**, but love covers
	15:	18	A hot-tempered person stirs up **c**,
	16:	28	A perverse person stirs up **c**,
	28:	25	The greedy stir up **c**,
	29:	22	An angry person stirs up **c**,

CONFORM (CONFORMED)

Ro	12:	2	not **c** to the pattern of this world,
1Pe	1:	14	do not **c** to the evil desires you had

CONFORMED (CONFORM)

Ro	8:	29	predestined to be **c** to the image

CONQUERORS

Ro	8:	37	are more than **c** through him who

CONSCIENCE (CONSCIENCES)

Ro	13:	5	but also as a matter of **c**.
1Co	8:	7	a god, and since their **c** is weak,
	8:	12	this way and wound their weak **c**,
	10:	25	without raising questions of **c**,
	10:	29	being judged by another's **c**?
Heb	10:	22	to cleanse us from a guilty **c**
1Pe	3:	16	keeping a clear **c**, so that those who

CONSCIENCES (CONSCIENCE)

Ro	2:	15	hearts, their **c** also bearing witness,
1Ti	4:	2	whose **c** have been seared as
Titus	1:	15	their minds and **c** are corrupted.
Heb	9:	14	cleanse our **c** from acts that lead

CONSCIOUS

Ro	3:	20	through the law we become **c** of
1Pe	2:	19	unjust suffering because they are **c**

CONSECRATE (CONSECRATED)

Ex	13:	2	"**C** to me every firstborn male.
Lev	20:	7	" '**C** yourselves and be holy,

CONSECRATED (CONSECRATE)

Ex	29:	43	and the place will be **c** by my glory.
1Ti	4:	5	because it is **c** by the word of God

CONSIDER (CONSIDERATE CONSIDERED CONSIDERS)

1Sa	12:	24	**c** what great things he has done
Job	37:	14	stop and **c** God's wonders.
Ps	8:	3	When I **c** your heavens, the work
	143:	5	and **c** what your hands have done.
Lk	12:	24	**C** the ravens: They do not sow
	12:	27	"**C** how the wild flowers grow.
Php	3:	8	I **c** everything a loss because
Heb	10:	24	And let us **c** how we may spur one
Jas	1:	2	**c** it pure joy, my brothers
	1:	26	Those who **c** themselves religious

CONSIDERATE (CONSIDER)

Titus	3:	2	to be peaceable and **c**, and always
Jas	3:	17	then peace-loving, **c**, submissive,
1Pe	2:	18	only to those who are good and **c**,
	3:	7	the same way be **c** as you live

CONSIDERED (CONSIDER)

Job	1:	8	"Have you **c** my servant Job?
	2:	3	"Have you **c** my servant Job?
Ps	44:	22	we are **c** as sheep to be slaughtered.
Isa	53:	4	yet we **c** him punished by God,
Ro	8:	36	all day long; we are **c** as sheep to be

CONSIDERS (CONSIDER)

Pr	31:	16	She **c** a field and buys it; out of her
Ro	14:	5	One person **c** one day more sacred

CONSIST

Lk	12:	15	life does not **c** in an abundance

CONSOLATION

Ps	94:	19	within me, your **c** brought me joy.

CONSTRUCTIVE

1Co	10:	23	but not everything is **c**.

CONSUME (CONSUMING)

Jn	2:	17	"Zeal for your house will **c** me."

CONSUMING (CONSUME)

Dt	4:	24	For the LORD your God is a **c** fire,
Heb	12:	29	for our "God is a **c** fire."

CONTAIN

1Ki	8:	27	the highest heaven, cannot **c** you.
2Pe	3:	16	His letters **c** some things that are

CONTAMINATES
2Co 7: 1 from everything that **c** body

CONTEMPLATE
2Co 3: 18 unveiled faces **c** the Lord's glory,

CONTEMPT
Pr 14: 31 oppresses the poor shows **c** for
17: 5 Whoever mocks the poor shows **c**
18: 3 so does **c**, and with shame comes
Da 12: 2 others to shame and everlasting **c**.
Ro 2: 4 do you show **c** for the riches of his
Gal 4: 14 did not treat me with **c** or scorn.
1Th 5: 20 Do not treat prophecies with **c**

CONTEND
Jude : 3 urge you to **c** for the faith that was

CONTENT (CONTENTMENT)
Pr 13: 25 The righteous eat to their hearts' **c**,
Php 4: 11 to be **c** whatever the circumstances.
4: 12 learned the secret of being **c** in any
1Ti 6: 8 clothing, we will be **c** with that.
Heb 13: 5 and be **c** with what you have,

CONTENTMENT (CONTENT)
1Ti 6: 6 But godliness with **c** is great gain.

CONTINUAL (CONTINUE)
Pr 15: 15 but the cheerful heart has a **c** feast.

CONTINUE (CONTINUAL)
Php 2: 12 **c** to work out your salvation
2Ti 3: 14 **c** in what you have learned and
1Jn 5: 18 born of God does not **c** to sin;
Rev 22: 11 let the one who does right **c** to do
22: 11 let the holy person **c** to be holy."

CONTRITE
Ps 51: 17 a broken and **c** heart you, God,
Isa 57: 15 and to revive the heart of the **c**.
66: 2 who are humble and **c** in spirit,

CONTROL (CONTROLLED SELF-CONTROL SELF-CONTROLLED)
1Co 7: 9 But if they cannot **c** themselves,
7: 37 but has **c** over his own will,
1Th 4: 4 should learn to **c** your own body

CONTROLLED (CONTROL)
Ps 32: 9 understanding but must be **c** by bit

CONTROVERSIES
Titus 3: 9 But avoid foolish **c** and genealogies

CONVERSATION
Col 4: 6 Let your **c** be always full of grace,

CONVERT
1Ti 3: 6 He must not be a recent **c**, or he

CONVICTION
Heb 3: 14 we hold our original **c** firmly

CONVINCED (CONVINCING)
Ro 8: 38 I am **c** that neither death nor life,
2Ti 1: 12 am **c** that he is able to guard what I
3: 14 have learned and have become **c** of,

CONVINCING (CONVINCED)
Ac 1: 3 and gave many **c** proofs that he was

CORNELIUS
Roman to whom Peter preached; first Gentile Christian (Ac 10).

CORNERSTONE (STONE)
Ps 118: 22 builders rejected has become the **c**;

Isa 28: 16 a precious **c** for a sure foundation;
Eph 2: 20 Christ Jesus himself as the chief **c**.
1Pe 2: 6 a chosen and precious **c**,
2: 7 rejected has become the **c**,"

CORRECT (CORRECTING CORRECTION CORRECTS)
2Ti 4: 2 **c**, rebuke and encourage—

CORRECTING (CORRECT)
2Ti 3: 16 **c** and training in righteousness,

CORRECTION (CORRECT)
Pr 10: 17 but whoever ignores **c** leads others
12: 1 but whoever hates **c** is stupid.
15: 5 whoever heeds **c** shows prudence.
15: 10 the one who hates **c** will die.

CORRECTS (CORRECT)
Job 5: 17 "Blessed is the one whom God **c**;
Pr 9: 7 Whoever **c** a mocker invites insults

CORRUPT (CORRUPTS)
Ge 6: 11 Now the earth was **c** in God's sight

CORRUPTS (CORRUPT)
Ecc 7: 7 into a fool, and a bribe **c** the heart.
1Co 15: 33 "Bad company **c** good character."
Jas 3: 6 It **c** the whole body, sets the whole

COST
Pr 4: 7 Though it **c** all you have,
Isa 55: 1 milk without money and without **c**.
Rev 21: 6 thirsty I will give water without **c**

COUNSEL (COUNSELOR)
1Ki 22: 5 "First seek the **c** of the Lord."
Pr 15: 22 Plans fail for lack of **c**,
Rev 3: 18 I **c** you to buy from me gold

COUNSELOR (COUNSEL)
Isa 9: 6 And he will be called Wonderful **C**,

COUNT (COUNTING COUNTS)
Ro 4: 8 Lord will never **c** against them."
6: 11 **c** yourselves dead to sin but alive

COUNTING (COUNT)
2Co 5: 19 not **c** people's sins against them.

COUNTRY
Jn 4: 44 prophet has no honor in his own **c**.

COUNTS (COUNT)
Jn 6: 63 the flesh **c** for nothing.
1Co 7: 19 God's commands is what **c**.
Gal 5: 6 **c** is faith expressing itself through

COURAGE (COURAGEOUS)
Ac 23: 11 stood near Paul and said, "Take **c**!

COURAGEOUS (COURAGE)
Dt 31: 6 Be strong and **c**. Do not be afraid
Jos 1: 6 Be strong and **c**, because you will
1Co 16: 13 firm in the faith; be **c**; be strong.

COURSE
Ps 19: 5 a champion rejoicing to run his **c**.
Pr 15: 21 understanding keeps a straight **c**.

COURTS
Ps 84: 10 your **c** than a thousand elsewhere;
100: 4 thanksgiving and his **c** with praise;

COVENANT (COVENANTS)
Ge 9: 9 "I now establish my **c** with you
Ex 19: 5 if you obey me fully and keep my **c**,
1Ch 16: 15 He remembers his **c** forever,
Job 31: 1 "I made a **c** with my eyes not

Jer 31: 31　I will make a new **c** with the people
1Co 11: 25　"This cup is the new **c** in my blood;
Gal 4: 24　One **c** is from Mount Sinai
Heb 9: 15　Christ is the mediator of a new **c**,

COVENANTS (COVENANT)

Ro 9: 4　the **c**, the receiving of the law,
Gal 4: 24　The women represent two **c**.

COVER (COVER-UP COVERED COVERS)

Ps 91: 4　He will **c** you with his feathers,
Jas 5: 20　and **c** over a multitude of sins.

COVERED (COVER)

Ps 32: 1　are forgiven, whose sins are **c**.
Isa 6: 2　With two wings they **c** their faces,
Ro 4: 7　are forgiven, whose sins are **c**.
1Co 11: 4　with his head **c** dishonors his head.

COVERS (COVER)

Pr 10: 12　conflict, but love **c** over all wrongs.
1Pe 4: 8　because love **c** over a multitude

COVER-UP (COVER)

1Pe 2: 16　do not use your freedom as a **c**

COVET

Ex 20: 17　"You shall not **c** your neighbor's
Ro 13: 9　"You shall not **c**," and whatever

COWARDLY

Rev 21: 8　But the **c**, the unbelieving, the vile,

CRAFTINESS (CRAFTY)

1Co 3: 19　"He catches the wise in their **c**";

CRAFTY (CRAFTINESS)

Ge 3: 1　the serpent was more **c** than any
2Co 12: 16　Yet, **c** fellow that I am, I caught you

CRAVE

Pr 23: 3　Do not **c** his delicacies, for that
1Pe 2: 2　babies, **c** pure spiritual milk,

CREATE (CREATED CREATION CREATOR)

Ps 51: 10　**C** in me a pure heart, O God,
Isa 45: 18　he did not **c** it to be empty,

CREATED (CREATE)

Ge 1: 1　In the beginning God **c** the
　　　　　heavens
　　1: 21　So God **c** the great creatures
　　1: 27　So God **c** mankind in his own
　　1: 27　male and female he **c** them.
Ps 148: 5　for at his command they were **c**,
Ro 1: 25　and served **c** things rather than
1Co 11: 9　neither was man **c** for woman,
Col 1: 16　For in him all things were **c**:
1Ti 4: 4　For everything God **c** is good,
Rev 10: 6　who **c** the heavens and all that is

CREATION (CREATE)

Mk 16: 15　*preach the gospel to all* **c**.
Jn 17: 24　because you loved me before the **c**
Ro 8: 19　For the **c** waits in eager expectation
　　8: 39　nor anything else in all **c**, will be
2Co 5: 17　is in Christ, the new **c** has come:
Col 1: 15　God, the firstborn over all **c**.
1Pe 1: 20　He was chosen before the **c**
Rev 13: 8　was slain from the **c** of the world.

CREATOR (CREATE)

Ge 14: 22　Most High, **C** of heaven and earth,
Isa 42: 5　Lord says—the **C** of the heavens,
Ro 1: 25　created things rather than the **C**—

CREATURE (CREATURES)

Lev 17: 11　For the life of a **c** is in the blood,

CREATURES (CREATURE)

Ge 6: 19　into the ark two of all living **c**,
Ps 104: 24　the earth is full of your **c**.

CREDIT (CREDITED)

Ro 4: 24　whom God will **c** righteousness—
1Pe 2: 20　it to your **c** if you receive a beating

CREDITED (CREDIT)

Ge 15: 6　and he **c** it to him as righteousness.
Ro 4: 5　their faith is **c** as righteousness.
Gal 3: 6　it was **c** to him as righteousness."
Jas 2: 23　it was **c** to him as righteousness,"

CRIED (CRY)

Ps 18: 6　I **c** to my God for help.

CRIMSON

Isa 1: 18　though they are red as **c**, they shall

CRIPPLED

Mk 9: 45　to enter life **c** than to have two feet

CRITICISM

2Co 8: 20　want to avoid any **c** of the way we

CROOKED

Pr 10: 9　whoever takes **c** paths will be
Php 2: 15　fault in a warped and **c** generation."

CROSS

Mt 10: 38　Whoever does not take up their **c**
Lk 9: 23　take up their **c** daily and follow me.
Ac 2: 23　to death by nailing him to the **c**.
1Co 1: 17　lest the **c** of Christ be emptied of
Gal 6: 14　in the **c** of our Lord Jesus Christ,
Php 2: 8　even death on a **c**!
Col 1: 20　through his blood, shed on the **c**.
　　2: 14　taken it away, nailing it to the **c**.
　　2: 15　triumphing over them by the **c**.
Heb 12: 2　joy set before him he endured the **c**,

CROWD

Ex 23: 2　pervert justice by siding with the **c**,

CROWN (CROWNED CROWNS)

Pr 4: 9　and present you with a glorious **c**."
　　10: 6　Blessings **c** the head
　　12: 4　noble character is her husband's **c**,
　　17: 6　Children's children are a **c**
Isa 61: 3　on them a **c** of beauty instead
Zec 9: 16　in his land like jewels in a **c**.
Mt 27: 29　then twisted together a **c** of thorns
1Co 9: 25　to get a **c** that will last forever.
2Ti 4: 8　store for me the **c** of righteousness,
Rev 2: 10　will give you life as your victor's **c**.

CROWNED (CROWN)

Ps 8: 5　the angels and **c** them with glory
Pr 14: 18　the prudent are **c** with knowledge.
Heb 2: 7　you **c** them with glory and honor

CROWNS (CROWN)

Rev 4: 10　They lay their **c** before the throne
　　19: 12　fire, and on his head are many **c**.

CRUCIFIED (CRUCIFY)

Mt 20: 19　to be mocked and flogged and **c**.
　　27: 38　Two rebels were **c** with him,
Lk 24: 7　be **c** and on the third day be raised
Jn 19: 18　they **c** him, and with him two
Ac 2: 36　Jesus, whom you **c**, both Lord
Ro 6: 6　that our old self was **c** with so
1Co 1: 23　but we preach Christ **c**:
　　2: 2　you except Jesus Christ and him **c**.
Gal 2: 20　I have been **c** with Christ and I no
　　5: 24　Christ Jesus have **c** the flesh with

CRUCIFY (CRUCIFIED CRUCIFYING)
Mt 27: 22 They all answered, "**C** him!"
27: 31 Then they led him away to **c** him.

CRUCIFYING (CRUCIFY)
Heb 6: 6 their loss they are **c** the Son of God

CRUSH (CRUSHED)
Ge 3: 15 he will **c** your head, and you will
Isa 53: 10 it was the LORD's will to **c** him
Ro 16: 20 peace will soon **c** Satan under your

CRUSHED (CRUSH)
Ps 34: 18 and saves those who are **c** in spirit.
Isa 53: 5 he was **c** for our iniquities;
2Co 4: 8 pressed on every side, but not **c**;

CRY (CRIED)
Ps 34: 15 and his ears are attentive to their **c**;
40: 1 he turned to me and heard my **c**.
130: 1 Out of the depths I **c** to you,

CULMINATION
Ro 10: 4 Christ is the **c** of the law so

CUP
Ps 23: 5 my head with oil; my **c** overflows.
Mt 10: 42 anyone gives even a **c** of cold water
23: 25 You clean the outside of the **c**
26: 39 may this **c** be taken from me.
1Co 11: 25 "This **c** is the new covenant in my

CURSE (CURSED)
Dt 11: 26 you today a blessing and a **c**—
21: 23 is hung on a pole is under God's **c**.
Lk 6: 28 bless those who **c** you,
Gal 1: 8 to you, let them be under God's **c**!
3: 13 redeemed us from the **c** of the law
by becoming a **c** for us,
Rev 22: 3 No longer will there be any **c**.

CURSED (CURSE)
Ge 3: 17 "**C** is the ground because of you;
Dt 27: 15 "**C** is anyone who makes an idol—
27: 16 "**C** is anyone who dishonors their
27: 17 "**C** is anyone who moves their
27: 18 "**C** is anyone who leads the blind
27: 19 "**C** is anyone who withholds justice
27: 20 "**C** is anyone who sleeps with his
27: 21 "**C** is anyone who has sexual
27: 22 "**C** is anyone who sleeps with his
27: 23 "**C** is anyone who sleeps with his
27: 24 "**C** is anyone who kills their
27: 25 "**C** is anyone who accepts a bribe
27: 26 "**C** is anyone who does not uphold
Ro 9: 3 I could wish that I myself were **c**
Gal 3: 10 "**C** is everyone who does not

CURTAIN
Ex 26: 33 Hang the **c** from the clasps
26: 33 The **c** will separate the Holy Place
Lk 23: 45 the **c** of the temple was torn in two.
Heb 10: 20 way opened for us through the **c**,

CYMBAL
1Co 13: 1 a resounding gong or a clanging **c**.

DANCE (DANCING)
Ecc 3: 4 a time to mourn and a time to **d**,
Mt 11: 17 the pipe for you, and you did not **d**;

DANCING (DANCE)
Ps 30: 11 You turned my wailing into **d**;
149: 3 Let them praise his name with **d**

DANGER
Pr 27: 12 The prudent see **d** and take refuge,
Ro 8: 35 or nakedness or **d** or sword?

DANIEL
Hebrew exile to Babylon, name changed to Belteshazzar (Da 1:6–7). Refused to eat unclean food (Da 1:8–21). Interpreted Nebuchadnezzar's dreams (Da 2; 4), writing on the wall (Da 5). Thrown into lions' den (Da 6). Visions of (Da 7–12).

DARK (DARKEST DARKNESS)
Ro 2: 19 a light for those who are in the **d**,
2Pe 1: 19 it, as to a light shining in a **d** place,

DARKEST (DARK)
Ps 23: 4 though I walk through the **d** valley,

DARKNESS (DARK)
Ge 1: 4 he separated the light from the **d**.
2Sa 22: 29 the LORD turns my **d** into light.
Job 34: 22 utter **d**, where evildoers can hide.
Jn 3: 19 but people loved **d** instead of light
2Co 6: 14 fellowship can light have with **d**?
Eph 5: 8 For you were once **d**, but now you
1Pe 2: 9 out of **d** into his wonderful light.
1Jn 1: 5 in him there is no **d** at all.
2: 9 a brother or sister is still in the **d**.

DAUGHTERS
Joel 2: 28 Your sons and **d** will prophesy,

DAVID
Son of Jesse (Ru 4:17–22; 1Ch 2:13–15), ancestor of Jesus (Mt 1:1–17; Lk 3:31).
Anointed king by Samuel (1Sa 16:1–13). Musician to Saul (1Sa 16:14–23; 18:10). Killed Goliath (1Sa 17). Relation with Jonathan (1Sa 18:1–4; 19–20; 23:16–18; 2Sa 1). Disfavor of Saul (1Sa 18:6—23:29). Spared Saul's life (1Sa 24; 26). Among Philistines (1Sa 21:10–14; 27–30). Lament for Saul and Jonathan (2Sa 1).
Anointed king of Judah (2Sa 2:1–11); of Israel (2Sa 5:1–4; 1Ch 11:1–3). Promised eternal dynasty (2Sa 7; 1Ch 17; Ps 132). Adultery with Bathsheba (2Sa 11–12). Absalom's revolt (2Sa 14–18). Last words (2Sa 23:1–7). Death (1Ki 2:10–12; 1Ch 29:28).

DAWN
Ps 37: 6 righteous reward shine like the **d**,

DAY (DAYS)
Ge 1: 5 God called the light "**d**,"
Ex 20: 8 "Remember the Sabbath **d**
Lev 23: 28 because it is the **D** of Atonement,
Nu 14: 14 them in a pillar of cloud by **d**
Jos 1: 8 meditate on it **d** and night,
Ps 84: 10 Better is one **d** in your courts than
96: 2 proclaim his salvation **d** after **d**.
118: 24 The LORD has done it this very **d**;
Pr 27: 1 do not know what a **d** may bring.
Joel 2: 31 great and dreadful **d** of the LORD.
Ob : 15 "The **d** of the LORD is near for all
Lk 11: 3 Give us each **d** our daily bread.
Ac 17: 11 examined the Scriptures every **d**
2Co 4: 16 we are being renewed **d** by **d**.
1Th 5: 2 the **d** of the Lord will come like
2Pe 3: 8 With the Lord a **d** is like a thousand

DAYS (DAY)
Dt 17: 19 he is to read it all the **d** of his life so
Ps 23: 6 love will follow me all the **d** of my
90: 10 Our **d** may come to seventy years,
Ecc 12: 1 Creator in the **d** of your youth,
Joel 2: 29 I will pour out my Spirit in those **d**.
Mic 4: 1 In the last **d** the mountain
Heb 1: 2 in these last **d** he has spoken to us
2Pe 3: 3 that in the last **d** scoffers will come,

DEACONS
1Ti 3: 8 way, **d** are to be worthy of respect,

DEAD (DIE)
Dt 18: 11 or spiritist or who consults the **d**.
Mt 28: 7 'He has risen from the **d** and is
Ro 6: 11 count yourselves **d** to sin but alive
Eph 2: 1 you were **d** in your transgressions
1Th 4: 16 and the **d** in Christ will rise first.
Jas 2: 17 is not accompanied by action, is **d**.
2: 26 so faith without deeds is **d**.

DEATH (DIE)
Nu 35: 16 the murderer is to be put to **d**.
Ps 116: 15 of the LORD is the **d** of his faithful
Pr 8: 36 all who hate me love **d**."
14: 12 right, but in the end it leads to **d**.
Ecc 7: 2 for **d** is the destiny of everyone;
Isa 25: 8 he will swallow up **d** forever.
53: 12 he poured out his life unto **d**,
Jn 5: 24 but has crossed over from **d** to life.
Ro 5: 12 **d** through sin, and in this way **d**
6: 23 For the wages of sin is **d**,
8: 13 Spirit you put to **d** the misdeeds
1Co 15: 21 For since **d** came through a man,
15: 31 I face **d** every day—yes, just as
15: 55 "Where, O **d**, is your victory?
1Pe 3: 18 He was put to **d** in the body
Rev 1: 18 I hold the keys of **d** and Hades.
20: 6 The second **d** has no power over
20: 14 The lake of fire is the second **d**.
21: 4 There will be no more **d**'

DEBAUCHERY
Ro 13: 13 not in sexual immorality and **d**,
Eph 5: 18 drunk on wine, which leads to **d**.

DEBORAH
Prophetess who led Israel to victory over Canaanites (Jdg 4–5).

DEBT (DEBTORS DEBTS)
Ro 13: 8 except the continuing **d** to love

DEBTORS (DEBT)
Mt 6: 12 as we also have forgiven our **d**.

DEBTS (DEBT)
Dt 15: 1 seven years you must cancel **d**.
Mt 6: 12 And forgive us our **d**, as we

DECAY
Ps 16: 10 will you let your faithful one see **d**.
Ac 2: 27 will not let your holy one see **d**.

DECEIT (DECEIVE)
Mk 7: 22 greed, malice, **d**, lewdness, envy,
1Pe 2: 1 yourselves of all malice and all **d**,
2: 22 and no **d** was found in his mouth."

DECEITFUL (DECEIVE)
Jer 17: 9 The heart is **d** above all things
2Co 11: 13 are false apostles, **d** workers,

DECEITFULNESS (DECEIVE)
Mk 4: 19 the **d** of wealth and the desires
Heb 3: 13 of you may be hardened by sin's **d**.

DECEIVE (DECEIT DECEITFUL DECEITFULNESS
DECEIVED DECEPTIVE)
Lev 19: 11 " 'Do not **d** one another.
Pr 14: 5 An honest witness does not **d**,
Mt 24: 5 am the Messiah,' and will **d** many.
Ro 16: 18 flattery they **d** the minds of naive
1Co 3: 18 Do not **d** yourselves. If any of you
Gal 6: 3 they are not, they **d** themselves.
Eph 5: 6 no one **d** you with empty words,
Jas 1: 22 to the word, and so **d** yourselves.
Jas 1: 26 rein on their tongues **d** themselves,
1Jn 1: 8 we **d** ourselves and the truth is not

DECEIVED (DECEIVE)
Ge 3: 13 said, "The serpent **d** me, and I ate."
Gal 6: 7 Do not be **d**: God cannot be
1Ti 2: 14 And Adam was not the one **d**; it was
the woman who was **d**
2Ti 3: 13 to worse, deceiving and being **d**.
Jas 1: 16 Don't be **d**, my dear brothers

DECENCY
1Ti 2: 9 modestly, with **d** and propriety,

DECEPTIVE (DECEIVE)
Pr 31: 30 Charm is **d**, and beauty is fleeting;
Col 2: 8 through hollow and **d** philosophy,

DECLARE (DECLARED DECLARING)
1Ch 16: 24 **D** his glory among the nations,
Ps 19: 1 The heavens **d** the glory of God;
96: 3 **D** his glory among the nations,
Isa 42: 9 taken place, and new things I **d**;
Ro 10: 9 If you **d** with your mouth, "Jesus is

DECLARED (DECLARE)
Mk 7: 19 saying this, Jesus **d** all foods clean.)
Ro 2: 13 the law who will be **d** righteous.
3: 20 no one will be **d** righteous

DECLARING (DECLARE)
Ps 71: 8 **d** your splendor all day long.
Ac 2: 11 hear them **d** the wonders of God

DECREED (DECREES)
La 3: 37 it happen if the Lord has not **d** it?
Lk 22: 22 Son of Man will go as it has been **d**.

DECREES (DECREED)
Lev 10: 11 Israelites all the **d** the LORD has
Ps 119:112 on keeping your **d** to the very end.

DEDICATE (DEDICATION)
Pr 20: 25 It is a trap to **d** something rashly

DEDICATION (DEDICATE)
1Ti 5: 11 sensual desires overcome their **d**

DEED (DEEDS)
Col 3: 17 whether in word or **d**, do it all

DEEDS (DEED)
1Sa 2: 3 knows, and by him **d** are weighed.
Ps 65: 5 us with awesome and righteous **d**,
66: 3 to God, "How awesome are your **d**!
78: 4 next generation the praiseworthy **d**
86: 10 you are great and do marvelous **d**;
92: 4 For you make me glad by your **d**,
111: 3 Glorious and majestic are his **d**,
Hab 3: 2 I stand in awe of your **d**, LORD.
Mt 5: 16 that they may see your good **d**
11: 19 wisdom is proved right by her **d**."
Ac 26: 20 their repentance by their **d**.
Jas 2: 14 claims to have faith but has no **d**?
2: 20 that faith without **d** is useless?
1Pe 2: 12 they may see your good **d**

DEEP (DEPTH)
1Co 2: 10 things, even the **d** things of God.
1Ti 3: 9 must keep hold of the **d** truths

DEER
Ps 42: 1 As the **d** pants for streams of water,

DEFEND (DEFENSE)
Ps 74: 22 Rise up, O God, and **d** your cause;
Pr 31: 9 **d** the rights of the poor and needy.
Jer 50: 34 He will vigorously **d** their cause so

DEFENSE (DEFEND)
Ps 35: 23 Awake, and rise to my **d**!
Php 1: 16 put here for the **d** of the gospel.

DEFERRED
Pr 13: 12 Hope **d** makes the heart sick,

DEFILE (DEFILED)
Da 1: 8 Daniel resolved not to **d** himself

DEFILED (DEFILE)
Isa 24: 5 The earth is **d** by its people;

DEFRAUD
Lev 19: 13 " 'Do not **d** or rob your neighbor.

DEITY
Col 2: 9 Christ all the fullness of the **D** lives

DELIGHT (DELIGHTS)
1Sa 15: 22 "Does the LORD **d** in burnt
Ps 1: 2 but whose **d** is in the law
16: 3 noble ones in whom is all my **d**."
35: 9 the LORD and **d** in his salvation.
37: 4 Take **d** in the LORD, and he will
43: 4 of God, to God, my joy and my **d**.
51: 16 You do not **d** in sacrifice,
119: 77 I may live, for your law is my **d**.
Isa 42: 1 my chosen one in whom I **d**;
55: 2 you will **d** in the richest of fare.
61: 10 I **d** greatly in the LORD;
Jer 9: 24 earth, for in these I **d**,"
15: 16 they were my joy and my heart's **d**,
Mic 7: 18 angry forever but **d** to show mercy.
Zep 3: 17 He will take great **d** in you;
Mt 12: 18 the one I love, in whom I **d**;
1Co 13: 6 Love does not **d** in evil but rejoices
2Co 12: 10 for Christ's sake, I **d** in weaknesses,

DELIGHTS (DELIGHT)
Ps 22: 8 deliver him, since he **d** in him."
35: 27 who **d** in the well-being of his
36: 8 them drink from your river of **d**.
Pr 3: 12 he loves, as a father the son
he **d** in.
12: 22 **d** in people who are trustworthy.
29: 17 will bring you the **d** you desire.

DELILAH
Woman who betrayed Samson (Jdg 16:4–22).

DELIVER (DELIVERANCE DELIVERED DELIVERER DELIVERS)
Ps 72: 12 he will **d** the needy who cry out,
79: 9 **d** us and forgive our sins for your
Da 3: 17 the God we serve is able to **d** us
Mt 6: 13 but **d** us from the evil one.'
2Co 1: 10 that he will continue to **d** us,

DELIVERANCE (DELIVER)
Ps 3: 8 From the LORD comes **d**.
32: 7 and surround me with songs of **d**.
33: 17 A horse is a vain hope for **d**;

DELIVERED (DELIVER)
Ps 34: 4 he **d** me from all my fears.
Ro 4: 25 He was **d** over to death for our sins

DELIVERER (DELIVER)
Ps 18: 2 is my rock, my fortress and my **d**;
40: 17 You are my help and my **d**;
140: 7 my strong **d**, you shield my head
144: 2 stronghold and my **d**, my shield,

DELIVERS (DELIVER)
Ps 34: 17 he **d** them from all their troubles.
34: 19 the LORD **d** him from them all;
37: 40 The LORD helps them and **d** them;

DEMANDED
Lk 12: 20 This very night your life will be **d**
12: 48 been given much, much will be **d**;

DEMONS
Mt 12: 27 And if I drive out **d** by Beelzebul,
Mk 5: 15 been possessed by the legion of **d**,
Ro 8: 38 life, neither angels nor **d**,
Jas 2: 19 Good! Even the **d** believe that—

DEMONSTRATE (DEMONSTRATES)
Ac 26: 20 **d** their repentance by their deeds.
Ro 3: 26 he did it to **d** his righteousness

DEMONSTRATES (DEMONSTRATE)
Ro 5: 8 God **d** his own love for us in this:

DEN
Da 6: 16 and threw him into the lions' **d**.
Mt 21: 13 but you are making it 'a **d**

DENARIUS
Mk 12: 15 "Bring me a **d** and let me look

DENIED (DENY)
1Ti 5: 8 has **d** the faith and is worse than

DENIES (DENY)
1Jn 2: 23 No one who **d** the Son has

DENY (DENIED DENIES DENYING)
Ex 23: 6 "Do not **d** justice to your poor
Job 27: 5 till I die, I will not **d** my integrity.
La 3: 35 **d** people their rights before the
Lk 9: 23 be my disciple must **d** themselves
Titus 1: 16 but by their actions they **d** him.

DENYING (DENY)
Eze 22: 29 the foreigner, **d** them justice.
2Ti 3: 5 a form of godliness but **d** its power.
2Pe 2: 1 even **d** the sovereign Lord who

DEPART (DEPARTED)
Ge 49: 10 The scepter will not **d** from Judah,
Job 1: 21 mother's womb, and naked I will **d**.
Mt 25: 41 to those on his left, 'D from me,
Php 1: 23 I desire to **d** and be with Christ,

DEPARTED (DEPART)
1Sa 4: 21 "The Glory has **d** from Israel"—
Ps 119:102 I have not **d** from your laws,

DEPOSIT
2Co 1: 22 put his Spirit in our hearts as a **d**,
5: 5 who has given us the Spirit as a **d**,
Eph 1: 14 who is a **d** guaranteeing our
2Ti 1: 14 Guard the good **d** that was entrusted

DEPRAVED (DEPRAVITY)
Ro 1: 28 God gave them over to a **d** mind,
2Pe 2: 7 was distressed by the **d** conduct

DEPRAVITY (DEPRAVED)
Ro 1: 29 of wickedness, evil, greed and **d**.

DEPRIVE
Dt 24: 17 Do not **d** the foreigner
Pr 18: 5 and so **d** the innocent of justice.
Isa 10: 2 to **d** the poor of their rights
29: 21 with false testimony **d** the innocent
1Co 7: 5 Do not **d** each other except

DEPTH (DEEP)
Ro 8: 39 neither height nor **d**, nor anything
11: 33 the **d** of the riches of the wisdom

DESERTED (DESERTS)
Mt 26: 56 all the disciples **d** him and fled.
2Ti 1: 15 in the province of Asia has **d** me,

DESERTING (DESERTS)
Gal 1: 6 you are so quickly **d** the one who

DESERTS (DESERTED DESERTING)
Zec 11: 17 shepherd, who **d** the flock!

DESERVE (DESERVES)
Ps 103: 10 he does not treat us as our sins **d**
Jer 21: 14 I will punish you as your deeds **d**,
Mt 22: 8 those I invited did not **d** to come.
Ro 1: 32 those who do such things **d** death,

DESERVES (DESERVE)
Lk 10: 7 for the worker **d** his wages.
1Ti 5: 18 and "The worker **d** his wages."

DESIRABLE (DESIRE)
Pr 22: 1 name is more **d** than great riches;

DESIRE (DESIRABLE DESIRES)
Ge 3: 16 Your **d** will be for your husband,
Dt 5: 21 You shall not set your **d** on your
Ps 40: 6 and offering you did not **d**—
40: 8 I **d** to do your will, my God;
73: 25 earth has nothing I **d** besides you.
Pr 3: 15 nothing you **d** can compare
10: 24 what the righteous **d** will be
11: 23 The **d** of the righteous ends only
19: 2 **D** without knowledge is not good
Isa 26: 8 and renown are the **d** of our hearts.
53: 2 appearance that we should **d** him.
55: 11 but will accomplish what I **d**
Hos 6: 6 For I **d** mercy, not sacrifice,
Mt 9: 13 'I **d** mercy, not sacrifice.'
Ro 7: 18 For I have the **d** to do what is good,
1Co 12: 31 Now eagerly **d** the greater gifts.
14: 1 and eagerly **d** gifts of the Spirit,
Php 1: 23 I **d** to depart and be with Christ,
Heb 13: 18 **d** to live honorably in every way.
Jas 1: 15 after **d** has conceived, it gives birth

DESIRES (DESIRE)
Ge 4: 7 it **d** to have you, but you must rule
1Ch 29: 18 keep these **d** and thoughts
Ps 34: 12 life and **d** to see many good days,
37: 4 will give you the **d** of your heart.
103: 5 who satisfies your **d** with good
145: 19 He fulfills the **d** of those who fear
Pr 11: 6 the unfaithful are trapped by evil **d**.
19: 22 What a person **d** is unfailing love;
Mk 4: 19 and the **d** for other things come
Ro 8: 5 minds set on what the Spirit **d**
13: 14 how to gratify the **d** of the flesh.
Gal 5: 16 and you will not gratify the **d**
5: 17 For the flesh **d** what is contrary
1Ti 3: 1 to be an overseer **d** a noble task.
6: 9 harmful **d** that plunge people
2Ti 2: 22 Flee the evil **d** of youth and pursue
Jas 1: 20 the righteousness that God **d**.
4: 1 from your **d** that battle within you?
1Pe 2: 11 to abstain from sinful **d**,
1Jn 2: 17 The world and its **d** pass away,

DESOLATE
Isa 54: 1 the children of the **d** woman than

DESPAIR
Isa 61: 3 of praise instead of a spirit of **d**.
2Co 4: 8 perplexed, but not in **d**;

DESPISE (DESPISED DESPISES)
Job 42: 6 Therefore I **d** myself and repent
Pr 1: 7 fools **d** wisdom and instruction.
3: 11 do not **d** the LORD's discipline,
14: 21 It is a sin to **d** one's neighbor,
15: 32 disregard discipline **d** themselves,
23: 22 do not **d** your mother when she is
Zec 4: 10 "Who dares **d** the day of small
Lk 16: 13 devoted to the one and **d** the other.
Titus 2: 15 Do not let anyone **d** you.

DESPISED (DESPISE)
Ge 25: 34 and left. So Esau **d** his birthright.
Isa 53: 3 He was **d** and rejected by mankind,
1Co 1: 28 of this world and the **d** things—

DESPISES (DESPISE)
Pr 15: 20 but a foolish man **d** his mother.

DESTINED (DESTINY)
Lk 2: 34 "This child is **d** to cause the falling

DESTINY (DESTINED PREDESTINED)
Ps 73: 17 then I understood their final **d**.
Ecc 7: 2 for death is the **d** of everyone;

DESTITUTE
Pr 31: 8 for the rights of all who are **d**.
Heb 11: 37 in sheepskins and goatskins, **d**,

DESTROY (DESTROYED DESTROYS DESTRUCTION)
Pr 1: 32 complacency of fools will **d** them;
11: 9 the godless **d** their neighbors,
Mt 10: 28 of the One who can **d** both soul

DESTROYED (DESTROY)
Job 19: 26 And after my skin has been **d**,
1Co 8: 11 is **d** by your knowledge.
15: 26 The last enemy to be **d** is death.
2Co 5: 1 if the earthly tent we live in is **d**,
Heb 10: 39 those who shrink back and are **d**,
2Pe 3: 10 the elements will be **d** by fire,

DESTROYS (DESTROY)
Pr 6: 32 whoever does so **d** himself.
18: 9 his work is brother to one who **d**.
28: 24 wrong," is partner to one who **d**.
Ecc 9: 18 but one sinner **d** much good.
1Co 3: 17 If anyone **d** God's temple, God will

DESTRUCTION (DESTROY)
Ps 1: 6 the way of the wicked leads to **d**.
Pr 16: 18 Pride goes before **d**, a haughty
Hos 13: 14 Where, O grave, is your **d**?
Mt 7: 13 broad is the road that leads to **d**,
Gal 6: 8 flesh, from the flesh will reap **d**;
2Th 1: 9 will be punished with everlasting **d**
1Ti 6: 9 that plunge people into ruin and **d**.
2Pe 2: 1 bringing swift **d** on themselves.
3: 16 other Scriptures, to their own **d**.

DETERMINED (DETERMINES)
Job 14: 5 A person's days are **d**;
Isa 14: 26 This is the plan **d** for the whole
Da 11: 36 what has been **d** must take place.

DETERMINES (DETERMINED)
Ps 147: 4 He **d** the number of the stars
1Co 12: 11 them to each one, just as he **d**.

DETESTABLE (DETESTS)
Pr 21: 27 The sacrifice of the wicked is **d**—
28: 9 even their prayers are **d**.
Isa 1: 13 Your incense is **d** to me.
Lk 16: 15 What people value highly is **d**
Titus 1: 16 They are **d**, disobedient and unfit

DETESTS (DETESTABLE)
Dt 22: 5 the LORD your God **d** anyone who
23: 18 the LORD your God **d** them both.
25: 16 the LORD your God **d** anyone who
Pr 11: 1 The LORD **d** dishonest scales,
12: 22 The LORD **d** lying lips, but he
15: 8 The LORD **d** the sacrifice
15: 9 The LORD **d** the way
15: 26 The LORD **d** the thoughts
16: 5 The LORD **d** all the proud

Pr 17: 15 the LORD **d** them both.
    20: 23 The LORD **d** differing weights,

DEVIL (DEVIL'S)
Mt 13: 39 the enemy who sows them is the **d**.
    25: 41 the eternal fire prepared for the **d**
Lk   4: 2 forty days he was tempted by the **d**.
     8: 12 then the **d** comes and takes away
Eph 4: 27 and do not give the **d** a foothold.
2Ti 2: 26 and escape from the trap of the **d**,
Jas 4: 7 Resist the **d**, and he will flee
1Pe 5: 8 Your enemy the **d** prowls around
1Jn 3: 8 who does what is sinful is of the **d**,
Rev 12: 9 that ancient serpent called the **d**,

DEVIL'S (DEVIL)
Eph 6: 11 your stand against the **d** schemes.
1Ti 3: 7 into disgrace and into the **d** trap.
1Jn 3: 8 was to destroy the **d** work.

DEVISED
2Pe 1: 16 we did not follow cleverly **d** stories

DEVOTE (DEVOTED DEVOTING DEVOTION DEVOUT)
Job 11: 13 "Yet if you **d** your heart to him
Jer 30: 21 who is he who will **d** himself to be
Col 4: 2 **D** yourselves to prayer,
1Ti 4: 13 **d** yourself to the public reading
Titus 3: 8 may be careful to **d** themselves

DEVOTED (DEVOTE)
Ezr 7: 10 For Ezra had **d** himself to the study
Ac   2: 42 They **d** themselves to the apostles'
Ro 12: 10 Be **d** to one another in love.
1Co 7: 34 Her aim is to be **d** to the Lord

DEVOTING (DEVOTE)
1Ti 5: 10 **d** herself to all kinds of good deeds.

DEVOTION (DEVOTE)
1Ch 28: 9 serve him with wholehearted **d**
1Co 7: 35 way in undivided **d** to the Lord.
2Co 11: 3 your sincere and pure **d** to Christ.

DEVOUR
2Sa 2: 26 to Joab, "Must the sword **d** forever?
Mk 12: 40 They **d** widows' houses
1Pe 5: 8 lion looking for someone to **d**.

DEVOUT (DEVOTE)
Lk   2: 25 Simeon, who was righteous and **d**.

DIE (DEAD DEATH DIED DIES)
Ge   2: 17 eat from it you will certainly **d**."
Ex 11: 5 Every firstborn son in Egypt will **d**,
Ru   1: 17 Where you **d** I will **d**, and there I
2Ki 14: 6 each will **d** for their own sin."
Pr   5: 23 For lack of discipline they will **d**,
    10: 21 many, but fools **d** for lack of sense.
    11: 7 placed in mortals **d** with them;
    15: 10 one who hates correction will **d**.
    23: 13 them with the rod, they will not **d**.
Ecc 3: 2 a time to be born and a time to **d**,
Isa 66: 24 the worms that eat them will
            not **d**,
Eze 3: 18 wicked person will **d** for their sin,
    18: 4 one who sins is the one who will **d**.
    33: 8 wicked person will **d** for their sin,
Mt 26: 52 all who draw the sword will **d**
Jn 11: 25 in me will live, even though they **d**;
    11: 26 by believing in me will never **d**.
Ro   5: 7 Very rarely will anyone **d**
    14: 8 and if we **d**, we **d** for the Lord.
1Co 15: 22 For as in Adam all **d**, so in Christ
Php 1: 21 to live is Christ and to **d** is gain.
Heb 9: 27 as people are destined to **d** once,
Rev 14: 13 Blessed are the dead who **d**

DIED (DIE)
Ro   5: 6 Christ **d** for the ungodly.
     6: 2 We are those who have **d** to sin;
     6: 8 Now if we **d** with Christ, we believe
    14: 15 someone for whom Christ **d**.
1Co 8: 11 for whom Christ **d**, is destroyed
    15: 3 that Christ **d** for our sins according
2Co 5: 14 one **d** for all, and therefore all **d**.
Col 3: 3 For you **d**, and your life is now
1Th 5: 10 He **d** for us so that, whether we are
2Ti 2: 11 If we **d** with him, we will also live
Heb 9: 15 that he has **d** as a ransom to set
Rev 2: 8 Last, who **d** and came to life again.

DIES (DIE)
Job 14: 14 If someone **d**, will they live again?
1Co 15: 36 does not come to life unless it **d**.

DIFFERENCE (DIFFERENT)
Ro 10: 12 For there is no **d** between Jew

DIFFERENT (DIFFERENCE)
1Co 12: 4 There are **d** kinds of gifts,
2Co 11: 4 or a **d** gospel from the one you

DIGNITY
Pr 31: 25 She is clothed with strength and **d**;

DIGS
Pr 26: 27 Whoever **d** a pit will fall into it;

DILIGENCE (DILIGENT)
Heb 6: 11 show this same **d** to the very end,

DILIGENT (DILIGENCE)
Pr 21: 5 The plans of the **d** lead to profit as
1Ti 4: 15 Be **d** in these matters;

DIRECT (DIRECTS)
Ps 119: 35 **D** me in the path of your
   119: 133 **D** my footsteps according to your
Jer 10: 23 it is not for them to **d** their steps.
2Th 3: 5 May the Lord **d** your hearts

DIRECTS (DIRECT)
Ps 42: 8 By day the LORD **d** his love,
Isa 48: 17 who **d** you in the way you should

DIRGE
Mt 11: 17 we sang a **d**, and you did not

DISAPPEAR
Mt   5: 18 until heaven and earth **d**,
Lk 16: 17 earth to **d** than for the least stroke

DISASTER
Ps 57: 1 your wings until the **d** has passed.
Pr   3: 25 Have no fear of sudden **d**
    17: 5 whoever gloats over **d** will not go
Isa 45: 7 I bring prosperity and create **d**;
Eze 7: 5 Unheard-of **d**! See, it comes!

DISCERN (DISCERNING)
Ps 19: 12 But who can **d** their own errors?
   139: 3 You **d** my going out and my lying
Php 1: 10 you may be able to **d** what is best

DISCERNING (DISCERN)
Pr 14: 6 knowledge comes easily to the **d**.
    15: 14 The **d** heart seeks knowledge,
    17: 10 A rebuke impresses a **d** person
    17: 24 A **d** person keeps wisdom in view,
    17: 28 and **d** if they hold their tongues.
    19: 25 rebuke the **d**, and they will gain
    28: 11 and **d** sees how deluded they are.

DISCIPLE (DISCIPLES)
Mt 10: 42 of these little ones who is my **d**,
Lk 14: 27 and follow me cannot be my **d**.

DISCIPLES (DISCIPLE)
Mt	28: 19	go and make **d** of all nations,
Jn	8: 31	my teaching, you are really my **d**.
	13: 35	will know that you are my **d**, if you
Ac	11: 26	The **d** were called Christians first

DISCIPLINE (DISCIPLINED DISCIPLINES)
Ps	38: 1	your anger or **d** me in your wrath.
	39: 11	rebuke and **d** anyone for their sin,
	94: 12	Blessed is the one you **d**, LORD,
Pr	3: 11	do not despise the LORD's **d**,
	5: 12	You will say, "How I hated **d**!
	5: 23	For lack of **d** they will die,
	10: 17	Whoever heeds **d** shows the way
	12: 1	Whoever loves **d** loves knowledge,
	13: 18	Whoever disregards **d** comes
	13: 24	their children is careful to **d** them.
	15: 5	A fool spurns a parent's **d**,
	15: 32	disregard **d** despise themselves,
	19: 18	**D** your children, for in that there is
	19: 20	Listen to advice and accept **d**,
	22: 15	the rod of **d** will drive it far away.
	23: 13	Do not withhold **d** from a child;
	29: 17	**D** your children, and they will give
Heb	12: 5	do not make light of the Lord's **d**,
	12: 7	Endure hardship as **d**;
	12: 11	No **d** seems pleasant at the time,
Rev	3: 19	Those whom I love I rebuke and **d**.

DISCIPLINED (DISCIPLINE)
Jer	31: 18	'You **d** me like an unruly calf,
1Co	11: 32	we are being **d** so that we will not
Col	2: 5	delight to see how **d** you are
Titus	1: 8	upright, holy and **d**.
Heb	12: 7	For what children are not **d** by

DISCIPLINES (DISCIPLINE)
Dt	8: 5	so the LORD your God **d** you.
Pr	3: 12	because the LORD **d** those he
Heb	12: 6	the Lord **d** the one he loves,
	12: 10	but God **d** us for our good,

DISCLOSED
Lk	8: 17	nothing hidden that will not be **d**,

DISCOURAGED
Jos	1: 9	do not be **d**, for the LORD your
	10: 25	"Do not be afraid; do not be **d**.
1Ch	28: 20	Do not be afraid or **d**,
Isa	42: 4	or be **d** till he establishes justice
Col	3: 21	children, or they will become **d**.

DISCREDITED
2Co	6: 3	so that our ministry will not be **d**.

DISCRETION
1Ch	22: 12	May the LORD give you **d**
Pr	1: 4	knowledge and **d** to the young—
	2: 11	**D** will protect you,
	5: 2	that you may maintain **d** and your
	8: 12	I possess knowledge and **d**.
	11: 22	beautiful woman who shows no **d**.

DISCRIMINATED
Jas	2: 4	have you not **d** among yourselves

DISFIGURED
Isa	52: 14	his appearance was so **d** beyond

DISGRACE (DISGRACEFUL DISGRACES)
Pr	11: 2	then comes **d**, but with humility
	19: 26	is a child who brings shame and **d**.
Ac	5: 41	worthy of suffering **d** for the Name.
Heb	13: 13	the camp, bearing the **d** he bore.

DISGRACEFUL (DISGRACE)
Pr	10: 5	sleeps during harvest is a **d** son.
	17: 2	servant will rule over a **d** son

DISGRACES (DISGRACE)
Pr	28: 7	companion of gluttons **d** his father.
	29: 15	left undisciplined **d** its mother.

DISGUISE
Pr	26: 24	Enemies **d** themselves with their

DISHONEST
Pr	11: 1	The LORD detests **d** scales,
	29: 27	The righteous detest the **d**;
Lk	16: 10	whoever is **d** with very little will
1Ti	3: 8	wine, and not pursuing **d** gain.

DISHONOR (DISHONORS)
Lev	18: 7	" 'Do not **d** your father by having
Pr	30: 9	and so **d** the name of my God.
1Co	13: 5	It does not **d** others, it is not
	15: 43	it is sown in **d**, it is raised in glory;

DISHONORS (DISHONOR)
Dt	27: 16	is anyone who **d** their father

DISMAYED
Isa	41: 10	do not be **d**, for I am your God.

DISOBEDIENCE (DISOBEY)
Ro	5: 19	as through the **d** of the one man
	11: 32	has bound everyone over to **d** so
Heb	2: 2	and **d** received its just punishment,
	4: 6	did not go in because of their **d**,
	4: 11	by following their example of **d**.

DISOBEDIENT (DISOBEY)
2Ti	3: 2	proud, abusive, **d** to their parents,
Titus	1: 6	to the charge of being wild and **d**.
	1: 16	**d** and unfit for doing anything

DISOBEY (DISOBEDIENCE DISOBEDIENT)
Dt	11: 28	the curse if you **d** the commands
2Ch	24: 20	'Why do you **d** the LORD's
Ro	1: 30	of doing evil; they **d** their parents;

DISORDER
1Co	14: 33	For God is not a God of **d**
2Co	12: 20	slander, gossip, arrogance and **d**.
Jas	3: 16	there you find **d** and every evil

DISOWN
Pr	30: 9	I may have too much and **d** you
Mt	10: 33	will **d** before my Father in heaven.
	26: 35	to die with you, I will never **d** you."
2Ti	2: 12	If we **d** him, he will also **d** us;

DISPLAY (DISPLAYS)
Eze	39: 21	"I will **d** my glory among
1Ti	1: 16	Christ Jesus might **d** his immense

DISPLAYS (DISPLAY)
Isa	44: 23	Jacob, he **d** his glory in Israel.

DISPUTE (DISPUTES)
Pr	17: 14	the matter before a **d** breaks out.
1Co	6: 1	If any of you has a **d** with another,

DISPUTES (DISPUTE)
Pr	18: 18	Casting the lot settles **d** and keeps

DISQUALIFIED
1Co	9: 27	I myself will not be **d** for the prize.

DISREGARD
Pr	15: 32	Those who **d** discipline despise

DISREPUTE
2Pe	2: 2	will bring the way of truth into **d**.

DISSENSION
Ro	13: 13	debauchery, not in **d** and jealousy.

DISTINGUISH
1Ki 3: 9   and to **d** between right and wrong.
Heb 5: 14   have trained themselves to **d** good

DISTORT
2Co 4: 2   nor do we **d** the word of God.
2Pe 3: 16   ignorant and unstable people **d**,

DISTRESS (DISTRESSED)
Ps 18: 6   In my **d** I called to the LORD;
Jnh 2: 2   "In my **d** I called to the LORD,
Jas 1: 27   and widows in their **d** and to keep

DISTRESSED (DISTRESS)
Ro 14: 15   sister is **d** because of what you eat,

DIVIDED (DIVISION)
Mt 12: 25   "Every kingdom **d** against itself
Lk 23: 34   **d** up his clothes by casting lots.
1Co 1: 13   Is Christ **d**? Was Paul crucified

DIVINATION
Lev 19: 26   " 'Do not practice **d** or seek

DIVINE
Ro 1: 20   his eternal power and **d** nature—
2Co 10: 4   they have **d** power to demolish
2Pe 1: 4   may participate in the **d** nature,

DIVISION (DIVIDED DIVISIONS DIVISIVE)
Lk 12: 51   peace on earth? No, I tell you, but **d**.
1Co 12: 25   there should be no **d** in the body,

DIVISIONS (DIVISION)
Ro 16: 17   to watch out for those who cause **d**
1Co 1: 10   and that there be no **d** among you,
     11: 18   as a church, there are **d** among you,

DIVISIVE (DIVISION)
Titus 3: 10   Warn a **d** person once,

DIVORCE (DIVORCES)
Mt 19: 3   for a man to **d** his wife for any
1Co 7: 11   a husband must not **d** his wife.

DIVORCES (DIVORCE)
Mal 2: 16   man who hates and **d** his wife,"

DOCTOR
Mt 9: 12   "It is not the healthy who need a **d**,

DOCTRINE
1Ti 4: 16   Watch your life and **d** closely.
Titus 2: 1   what is appropriate to sound **d**.

DOMINION
Ps 22: 28   for **d** belongs to the LORD and he

DOOR
Ps 141: 3   keep watch over the **d** of my lips.
Mt 6: 6   close the **d** and pray to your Father,
     7: 7   and the **d** will be opened to you.
Rev 3: 20   I stand at the **d** and knock.

DOORKEEPER
Ps 84: 10   I would rather be a **d** in the house

DOUBLE-EDGED
Heb 4: 12   Sharper than any **d** sword,
Rev 1: 16   of his mouth was a sharp, **d** sword.
     2: 12   of him who has the sharp, **d** sword.

DOUBLE-MINDED (MIND)
Ps 119:113   I hate **d** people, but I love your law.
Jas 1: 8   Such a person is **d** and unstable

DOUBT
Mt 14: 31   faith," he said, "why did you **d**?"
     21: 21   if you have faith and do not **d**,

Mk 11: 23   and does not **d** in their heart
Jas 1: 6   you must believe and not **d**,
Jude : 22   Be merciful to those who **d**;

DOWNCAST
Ps 42: 5   Why, my soul, are you **d**?
2Co 7: 6   who comforts the **d**, comforted us

DRAW (DRAWING DRAWS)
Mt 26: 52   "for all who **d** the sword will die
Jn 12: 32   earth, will **d** all people to myself."
Heb 10: 22   let us **d** near to God with a sincere

DRAWING (DRAW)
Lk 21: 28   your redemption is **d** near."

DRAWS (DRAW)
Jn 6: 44   the Father who sent me **d** them,

DREADFUL
Heb 10: 31   It is a **d** thing to fall into the hands

DRESS
1Ti 2: 9   want the women to **d** modestly,

DRINK (DRUNK DRUNKARDS DRUNKENNESS)
Pr 5: 15   **D** water from your own cistern,
Lk 12: 19   eat, **d** and be merry." '
Jn 7: 37   who is thirsty come to me and **d**.
1Co 12: 13   were all given the one Spirit to **d**.

DRIVES
1Jn 4: 18   But perfect love **d** out fear,

DROP
Pr 17: 14   so **d** the matter before a dispute
Isa 40: 15   Surely the nations are like a **d**

DRUNK (DRINK)
Eph 5: 18   Do not get **d** on wine, which leads

DRUNKARDS (DRINK)
Pr 23: 21   for **d** and gluttons become poor,
1Co 6: 10   the greedy nor **d** nor slanderers

DRUNKENNESS (DRINK)
Lk 21: 34   **d** and the anxieties of life,
Ro 13: 13   not in carousing and **d**,
Gal 5: 21   and envy; **d**, orgies, and the like.
1Pe 4: 3   living in debauchery, lust, **d**, orgies,

DRY
Isa 53: 2   and like a root out of **d** ground.
Eze 37: 4   bones and say to them, 'D bones,

DUST
Ge 2: 7   a man from the **d** of the ground
Ps 103: 14   he remembers that we are **d**.
Ecc 3: 20   come from **d**, and to **d** all return.

DUTY
Ecc 12: 13   for this is the **d** of all mankind.
Ac 23: 1   I have fulfilled my **d** to God in all
1Co 7: 3   husband should fulfill his marital **d**

DWELL (DWELLING DWELLS)
1Ki 8: 27   "But will God really **d** on earth?
Ps 23: 6   I will **d** in the house of the LORD
Isa 43: 18   do not **d** on the past.
Eph 3: 17   Christ may **d** in your hearts
Col 1: 19   to have all his fullness **d** in him,
     3: 16   of Christ **d** among you richly

DWELLING (DWELL)
Eph 2: 22   built together to become a **d**

DWELLS (DWELL)
1Co 3: 16   that God's Spirit **d** in your midst?

EAGER
Pr 31: 13   and flax and works with **e** hands.
1Pe 5: 2   dishonest gain, but **e** to serve;

EAGLE'S (EAGLES)
Ps 103: 5   your youth is renewed like the **e**.

EAGLES (EAGLE'S)
Isa 40: 31   They will soar on wings like **e**;

EAR (EARS)
1Co 2: 9   eye has seen, what no **e** has heard,
    12: 16   And if the **e** should say, "Because I

EARS (EAR)
Job 42: 5   My **e** had heard of you but now my
Ps 34: 15   and his **e** are attentive to their cry;
Pr 21: 13   Whoever shuts their **e** to the cry
2Ti 4: 3   to say what their itching **e** want

EARTH (EARTHLY)
Ge   1: 1   God created the heavens and the **e**.
Ps 24: 1   The **e** is the LORD's,
   108: 5   let your glory be over all the **e**.
Isa   6: 3   the whole **e** is full of his glory."
   51: 6   the **e** will wear out like a garment
   55: 9   the heavens are higher than the **e**,
   66: 1   throne, and the **e** is my footstool.
Jer 23: 24   "Do not I fill heaven and **e**?"
Hab 2: 20   let all the **e** be silent before him.
Mt   6: 10   will be done, on **e** as it is in heaven.
   16: 19   you bind on **e** will be bound
   24: 35   Heaven and **e** will pass away,
   28: 18   and on **e** has been given to me.
Lk   2: 14   on **e** peace to those on whom his
1Co 10: 26   for, "The **e** is the Lord's,
Php 2: 10   heaven and on **e** and under the **e**,
2Pe 3: 13   to a new heaven and a new **e**,

EARTHLY (EARTH)
Php 3: 19   Their mind is set on **e** things.
Col 3: 2   on things above, not on **e** things.

EAST
Ps 103: 12   as far as the **e** is from the west,

EASY
Mt 11: 30   For my yoke is **e** and my burden is

EAT (EATING)
Ge   2: 17   you must not **e** from the tree
Isa 55: 1   have no money, come, buy and **e**!
   65: 25   the lion will **e** straw like the ox,
Mt 26: 26   his disciples, saying, "Take and **e**;
Ro 14: 2   faith allows them to **e** anything,
1Co 8: 13   if what I **e** causes my brother
   10: 31   So whether you **e** or drink
2Th 3: 10   is unwilling to work shall not **e**."

EATING (EAT)
Ro 14: 17   kingdom of God is not a matter of **e**

EDICT
Heb 11: 23   they were not afraid of the king's **e**.

EDIFIES
1Co 14: 4   speaks in a tongue **e** themselves,

EFFECT
Isa 32: 17   its **e** will be quietness
Heb 9: 18   was not put into **e** without blood.

EFFORT
Lk 13: 24   "Make every **e** to enter through
Ro   9: 16   depend on human desire or **e**,
   14: 19   Let us therefore make every **e** to do
Eph 4: 3   Make every **e** to keep the unity
Heb 4: 11   make every **e** to enter that rest,
   12: 14   Make every **e** to live in peace

ELAH
Son of Baasha; king of Israel (1Ki 16:6–14).

ELDERLY (ELDERS)
Lev 19: 32   show respect for the **e** and revere

ELDERS (ELDERLY)
1Ti 5: 17   The **e** who direct the affairs

ELECTION
Ro   9: 11   God's purpose in **e** might stand:
2Pe 1: 10   to confirm your calling and **e**.

ELI
High priest in youth of Samuel (1Sa 1–4). Blessed Hannah (1Sa 1:12–18); raised Samuel (1Sa 2:11–26).

ELIJAH
Prophet; predicted famine in Israel (1Ki 17:1; Jas 5:17). Fed by ravens (1Ki 17:2–6). Raised Sidonian widow's son (1Ki 17:7–24). Defeated prophets of Baal at Carmel (1Ki 18:16–46). Ran from Jezebel (1Ki 19:1–9). Prophesied death of Azariah (2Ki 1). Succeeded by Elisha (1Ki 19:19–21; 2Ki 2:1–18). Taken to heaven in whirlwind (2Ki 2:11–12).

Return prophesied (Mal 4:5–6); equated with John the Baptist (Mt 17:9–13; Mk 9:9–13; Lk 1:17). Appeared with Moses in transfiguration of Jesus (Mt 17:1–8; Mk 9:1–8).

ELISHA
Prophet; successor of Elijah (1Ki 19:16–21); inherited his cloak (2Ki 2:1–18). Miracles of (2Ki 2–6).

ELIZABETH
Mother of John the Baptist, relative of Mary (Lk 1:5–58).

EMBITTER
Col 3: 21   Fathers, do not **e** your children,

EMPEROR
1Pe 2: 17   of believers, fear God, honor the **e**.

EMPTY
Mt 12: 36   for every **e** word they have spoken.
Eph 5: 6   no one deceive you with **e** words,
1Pe 1: 18   you were redeemed from the **e** way

ENABLE (ABLE)
Lk   1: 74   to **e** us to serve him without fear
Ac   4: 29   **e** your servants to speak your word

ENABLED (ABLE)
Lev 26: 13   **e** you to walk with heads held high.
Jn   6: 65   me unless the Father has **e** them."

ENABLES (ABLE)
Php 3: 21   by the power that **e** him to bring

ENCAMPS
Ps 34: 7   the LORD **e** around those who fear

ENCOURAGE (ENCOURAGEMENT ENCOURAGING)
Ps 10: 17   you **e** them, and you listen to their
Ac 15: 32   said much to **e** and strengthen
Ro 12: 8   if it is to **e**, then give
1Th 4: 18   Therefore **e** one another with these
2Ti 4: 2   correct, rebuke and **e**—
Titus 2: 6   Similarly, **e** the young men to be
Heb 3: 13   But **e** one another daily, as long as

ENCOURAGEMENT (ENCOURAGE)
Ac   4: 36   (which means "son of **e**"),

2Pe 1: 5   make every **e** to add to your faith
   3: 14   make every **e** to be found spotless,

Ro 15: 4 the **e** they provide we might have
   15: 5 **e** give you the same attitude of
Heb 12: 5 completely forgotten this word of **e**

ENCOURAGING (ENCOURAGE)
1Co 14: 3 their strengthening, **e** and comfort.
Heb 10: 25 habit of doing, but **e** one another—

END
Ps 119: 33 that I may follow it to the **e**.
Pr 14: 12 right, but in the **e** it leads to death.
   19: 20 the **e** you will be counted among
   23: 32 In the **e** it bites like a snake
Ecc 12: 12 making many books there is no **e**,
Mt 10: 22 stands firm to the **e** will be saved.
Lk 21: 9 but the **e** will not come right away."
1Co 15: 24 Then the **e** will come, when he

ENDURANCE (ENDURE)
Ro 15: 4 so that through the **e** taught
   15: 5 May the God who gives **e**
2Co 1: 6 you patient **e** of the same sufferings
Col 1: 11 might so that you may have great **e**
1Ti 6: 11 faith, love, **e** and gentleness.
Titus 2: 2 and sound in faith, in love and in **e**.

ENDURE (ENDURANCE ENDURES)
Ps 72: 17 May his name **e** forever;
Pr 12: 19 Truthful lips **e** forever, but a lying
   27: 24 for riches do not **e** forever,
Ecc 3: 14 everything God does will **e** forever;
Mal 3: 2 who can **e** the day of his coming?
2Ti 2: 12 if we **e**, we will also reign with him.
Heb 12: 7 **E** hardship as discipline;
Rev 3: 10 kept my command to **e** patiently,

ENDURES (ENDURE)
Ps 112: 9 poor, their righteousness **e** forever;
  136: 1 *His love **e** forever.*
Da 9: 15 yourself a name that **e** to this day,
1Pe 1: 25 but the word of the Lord **e** forever."

ENEMIES (ENEMY)
Ps 23: 5 before me in the presence of my **e**.
Mic 7: 6 a man's **e** are the members of his
Mt 5: 44 love your **e** and pray for those who
Lk 20: 43 until I make your **e** a footstool

ENEMY (ENEMIES ENMITY)
Pr 24: 17 Do not gloat when your **e** falls;
   25: 21 If your **e** is hungry, give him food
   27: 6 trusted, but an **e** multiplies kisses.
1Co 15: 26 The last **e** to be destroyed is death.
1Ti 5: 14 and to give the **e** no opportunity
Jas 4: 4 of the world becomes an **e** of God.

ENJOY (JOY)
Dt 6: 2 and so that you may **e** long life.
Eph 6: 3 and that you may **e** long life
Heb 11: 25 than to **e** the fleeting pleasures

ENJOYMENT (JOY)
Ecc 4: 8 why am I depriving myself of **e**?"
1Ti 6: 17 us with everything for our **e**.

ENLIGHTENED (LIGHT)
Eph 1: 18 eyes of your heart may be **e** in
Heb 6: 4 for those who have once been **e**,

ENMITY (ENEMY)
Ge 3: 15 I will put **e** between you

ENOCH
  Walked with God and taken by him (Ge 5:18–24; Heb 11:5). Prophet (Jude 14).

ENTANGLED (ENTANGLES)
2Ti 2: 4 soldier gets **e** in civilian affairs,
2Pe 2: 20 Jesus Christ and are again **e** in it

ENTANGLES (ENTANGLED)
Heb 12: 1 hinders and the sin that so easily **e**.

ENTER (ENTERED ENTERS)
Ps 100: 4 **E** his gates with thanksgiving
Mt 5: 20 will certainly not **e** the kingdom
   7: 13 "**E** through the narrow gate.
   18: 8 It is better for you to **e** life maimed
Mk 10: 15 like a little child will never **e** it."
   10: 23 the rich to **e** the kingdom of God!"

ENTERED (ENTER)
Ro 5: 12 just as sin **e** the world through one
Heb 9: 12 he **e** the Most Holy Place once

ENTERS (ENTER)
Mk 7: 18 that nothing that **e** a person
Jn 10: 2 The one who **e** by the gate is

ENTERTAIN
1Ti 5: 19 Do not **e** an accusation against

ENTHRALLED
Ps 45: 11 Let the king be **e** by your beauty;

ENTHRONED (THRONE)
1Sa 4: 4 who is **e** between the cherubim.
Ps 2: 4 The One **e** in heaven laughs;
  102: 12 But you, Lord, sit **e** forever;
Isa 40: 22 He sits **e** above the circle

ENTICE
Pr 1: 10 if sinful men **e** you, do not give
2Pe 2: 18 they **e** people who are just escaping

ENTIRE
Gal 5: 14 For the **e** law is fulfilled in keeping

ENTRUSTED (TRUST)
1Ti 6: 20 guard what has been **e** to your care.
2Ti 1: 12 to guard what I have **e** to him until
   1: 14 good deposit that was **e** to you—
Jude : 3 once for all **e** to God's holy people.

ENVY
Pr 3: 31 Do not **e** the violent or choose any
   14: 30 to the body, but **e** rots the bones.
1Co 13: 4 It does not **e**, it does not boast,

EPHRAIM
  1. Second son of Joseph (Ge 41:52; 46:20). Blessed as firstborn by Jacob (Ge 48).
  2. Synonymous with Northern Kingdom (Isa 7:17; Hos 5).

EQUAL
Isa 40: 25 Or who is my **e**?" says the Holy
Jn 5: 18 Father, making himself **e** with God.
1Co 12: 25 its parts should have **e** concern

EQUIP (EQUIPPED)
Eph 4: 12 to **e** his people for works of service,
Heb 13: 21 **e** you with everything good

EQUIPPED (EQUIP)
2Ti 3: 17 God may be thoroughly **e** for every

ERROR
Jas 5: 20 the **e** of their way will save them

ESAU
  Firstborn of Isaac, twin of Jacob (Ge 25:21–26). Also called Edom (Ge 25:30). Sold Jacob his birthright (Ge 25:29–34); lost blessing (Ge 27). Reconciled to Jacob (Gen 33).

ESCAPE (ESCAPING)
Ro 2: 3 think you will **e** God's judgment?
Heb 2: 3 how shall we **e** if we ignore so great

ESCAPING (ESCAPE)
1Co 3: 15 only as one **e** through the flames.

ESTABLISH (ESTABLISHED ESTABLISHES)
Ge   6: 18 But I will **e** my covenant with you,
1Ch 28: 7 I will **e** his kingdom forever if he is
Ro 10: 3 of God and sought to **e** their own,

ESTABLISHED (ESTABLISH)
Ps   8: 2 infants you have **e** a stronghold

ESTABLISHES (ESTABLISH)
Pr 16: 9 course, but the Lord **e** their steps.

ESTEEM (ESTEEMED)
Isa 53: 3 and we held him in low **e**.

ESTEEMED (ESTEEM)
Pr 22: 1 to be **e** is better than silver or gold.

ESTHER
Jewess who lived in Persia; cousin of Mordecai (Est 2:7). Chosen queen of Xerxes (Est 2:8–18). Foiled Haman's plan to exterminate the Jews (Est 3–4; 7–9).

ETERNAL (ETERNITY)
Ps 16: 11 with **e** pleasures at your right hand.
   111: 10 To him belongs **e** praise.
   119: 89 Your word, Lord, is **e**;
Isa 26: 4 the Lord himself, is the Rock **e**.
Mt 19: 16 good thing must I do to get **e** life?"
    25: 41 the **e** fire prepared for the devil
    25: 46 but the righteous to **e** life."
Jn   3: 15 who believes may have **e** life
     3: 16 him shall not perish but have **e** life.
     3: 36 believes in the Son has **e** life,
     4: 14 of water welling up to **e** life."
     5: 24 believes him who sent me has **e** life
     6: 47 the one who believes has **e** life.
     6: 68 You have the words of **e** life.
    10: 28 I give them **e** life, and they shall
    17: 3 Now this is **e** life: that they know
Ro   1: 20 his **e** power and divine nature—
     6: 23 of God is **e** life in Christ Jesus our
2Co 4: 17 for us an **e** glory that far outweighs
     4: 18 temporary, but what is unseen is **e**.
1Ti 1: 16 believe in him and receive **e** life.
     1: 17 Now to the King **e**, immortal,
Heb 9: 12 thus obtaining **e** redemption.
1Jn 5: 11 God has given us **e** life, and this life
     5: 13 you may know that you have **e** life.

ETERNITY (ETERNAL)
Ps 93: 2 you are from all **e**.
Ecc 3: 11 has also set **e** in the human heart;

ETHIOPIAN
Jer 13: 23 Can an **E** change his skin

EUNUCHS
Mt 19: 12 choose to live like **e** for the sake

EVANGELIST (EVANGELISTS)
2Ti 4: 5 do the work of an **e**, discharge all

EVANGELISTS (EVANGELIST)
Eph 4: 11 the **e**, the pastors and teachers,

EVE
2Co 11: 3 afraid that just as **E** was deceived
1Ti 2: 13 For Adam was formed first, then **E**.

EVEN-TEMPERED
Pr 17: 27 whoever has understanding is **e**.

EVER (EVERLASTING FOREVER)
Ex 15: 18 "The Lord reigns for **e** and **e**."
Dt   8: 19 you **e** forget the Lord your God

Ps   5: 11 you be glad; let them **e** sing for joy.
    10: 16 The Lord is King for **e** and **e**;
    25: 3 one who hopes in you will **e** be put
    45: 6 throne, O God, will last for **e** and **e**;
    52: 8 I trust in God's unfailing love for **e**
    89: 33 nor will I **e** betray my faithfulness.
   145: 1 I will praise your name for **e** and **e**.
Pr   4: 18 shining **e** brighter till the full light
     5: 19 may you **e** be intoxicated with her
Isa 66: 8 Who has **e** heard of such things?
Jer 31: 36 "will Israel **e** cease being a nation
Da   7: 18 possess it forever—yes, for **e** and **e**.'
    12: 3 like the stars for **e** and **e**.
Mk   4: 12 " 'they may be seeing but never
Jn   1: 18 No one has **e** seen God, but
Rev 1: 18 now look, I am alive for **e** and **e**!
    22: 5 And they will reign for **e** and **e**.

EVER-INCREASING (INCREASE)
Ro   6: 19 to impurity and to **e** wickedness,
2Co 3: 18 into his image with **e** glory,

EVERLASTING (EVER)
Dt 33: 27 and underneath are the **e** arms.
Ne   9: 5 your God, who is from **e** to **e**."
Ps 90: 2 world, from **e** to **e** you are God.
   139: 24 in me, and lead me in the way **e**.
Isa 9: 6 Mighty God, **E** Father,
    33: 14 of us can dwell with **e** burning?"
    35: 10 **e** joy will crown their heads.
    45: 17 by the Lord with an **e** salvation;
    54: 8 **e** kindness I will have compassion
    55: 3 I will make an **e** covenant with you,
    63: 12 them, to gain for himself **e** renown,
Jer 31: 3 "I have loved you with an **e** love;
Da   9: 24 to bring in **e** righteousness, to seal
    12: 2 some to **e** life, others to shame and **e** contempt.
2Th 1: 9 will be punished with **e** destruction
Jude : 6 bound with **e** chains for judgment

EVER-PRESENT
Ps 46: 1 and strength, an **e** help in trouble.

EVIDENCE (EVIDENT)
Jn 14: 11 on the **e** of the works themselves.

EVIDENT (EVIDENCE)
Php 4: 5 Let your gentleness be **e** to all.

EVIL (EVILDOER EVILDOERS)
Ge   2: 9 of the knowledge of good and **e**.
Job 1: 1 he feared God and shunned **e**.
     1: 8 a man who fears God and shuns **e**."
    34: 10 Far be it from God to do **e**,
Ps 23: 4 will fear no **e**, for you are with me;
    34: 14 Turn from **e** and do good;
    51: 4 and done what is **e** in your sight;
    97: 10 those who love the Lord hate **e**,
   101: 4 have nothing to do with what is **e**.
Pr   8: 13 To fear the Lord is to hate **e**;
    11: 27 **e** comes to one who searches for it.
Isa 5: 20 who call **e** good and good **e**,
    13: 11 I will punish the world for its **e**,
Hab 1: 13 Your eyes are too pure to look on **e**;
Mt   5: 45 He causes his sun to rise on the **e**
     6: 13 but deliver us from the **e** one.'
     7: 11 you are **e**, know how to give
    12: 35 an **e** man brings **e** things out of the **e**
Jn 17: 15 you protect them from the **e** one.
Ro   2: 9 for every human being who does **e**:
    12: 9 Hate what is **e**; cling to what is
    12: 17 Do not repay anyone **e** for **e**.
    16: 19 and innocent about what is **e**.
1Co 13: 6 Love does not delight in **e**
    14: 20 In regard to **e** be infants, but in

Eph	6:	16	all the flaming arrows of the **e** one.
1Th	5:	22	reject every kind of **e**.
1Ti	6:	10	of money is a root of all kinds of **e**.
2Ti	2:	22	Flee the **e** desires of youth
Jas	1:	13	For God cannot be tempted by **e**,
1Pe	2:	16	your freedom as a cover-up for **e**;
	3:	9	Do not repay **e** with **e** or insult
	3:	9	the contrary, repay **e** with blessing,

EVILDOER (EVIL)

Pr	24:	20	for the **e** has no future hope,

EVILDOERS (EVIL)

Pr	24:	19	Do not fret because of **e** or be

EXACT

Heb	1:	3	the **e** representation of his being,

EXALT (EXALTED EXALTS)

Ps	30:	1	I will **e** you, Lord, for you lifted
	34:	3	let us **e** his name together.
	118:	28	you are my God, and I will **e** you.
Isa	24:	15	**e** the name of the Lord, the God
Mt	23:	12	For those who **e** themselves will be

EXALTED (EXALT)

2Sa	22:	47	**E** be my God, the Rock, my Savior!
1Ch	29:	11	you are **e** as head over all.
Ne	9:	5	and may it be **e** above all blessing
Ps	21:	13	Be **e** in your strength, Lord;
	46:	10	I will be **e** among the nations,
	57:	5	Be **e**, O God, above the heavens;
	97:	9	you are **e** far above all gods.
	99:	2	he is **e** over all the nations.
	108:	5	Be **e**, O God, above the heavens;
	148:	13	the Lord, for his name alone is **e**;
Isa	6:	1	high and **e**, seated on a throne;
	12:	4	and proclaim that his name is **e**.
	33:	5	The Lord is **e**, for he dwells
Eze	21:	26	The lowly will be **e** and the **e** will
Mt	23:	12	who humble themselves will be **e**.
Php	1:	20	now as always Christ will be **e**
	2:	9	Therefore God **e** him to the highest

EXALTS (EXALT)

Ps	75:	7	He brings one down, he **e** another.
Pr	14:	34	Righteousness **e** a nation, but sin

EXAMINE (EXAMINED)

Ps	26:	2	try me, **e** my heart and my mind;
Jer	17:	10	search the heart and **e** the mind,
La	3:	40	Let us **e** our ways and test them,
1Co	11:	28	to **e** themselves before they eat
2Co	13:	5	**E** yourselves to see whether you

EXAMINED (EXAMINE)

Ac	17:	11	**e** the Scriptures every day to see

EXAMPLE (EXAMPLES)

Jn	13:	15	I have set you an **e** that you should
1Co	11:	1	Follow my **e**, as I follow the **e**
1Ti	4:	12	set an **e** for the believers in speech,
Titus	2:	7	everything set them an **e** by doing
1Pe	2:	21	leaving you an **e**, that you should

EXAMPLES (EXAMPLE)

1Co	10:	6	Now these things occurred as **e**
	10:	11	things happened to them as **e**
1Pe	5:	3	to you, but being **e** to the flock.

EXASPERATE

Eph	6:	4	Fathers, do not **e** your children;

EXCEL (EXCELLENT)

1Co	14:	12	try to **e** in those that build
2Co	8:	7	you also **e** in this grace of giving.

EXCELLENT (EXCEL)

1Co	12:	31	yet I will show you the most **e** way.
Php	4:	8	if anything is **e** or praiseworthy—
1Ti	3:	13	have served well gain an **e** standing
Titus	3:	8	These things are **e** and profitable

EXCHANGED

Ro	1:	23	**e** the glory of the immortal God
	1:	25	**e** the truth about God for a lie,

EXCUSE (EXCUSES)

Jn	15:	22	now they have no **e** for their sin.
Ro	1:	20	made, so that people are without **e**.

EXCUSES (EXCUSE)

Lk	14:	18	"But they all alike began to make **e**.

EXISTS

Heb	2:	10	and through whom everything **e**,
	11:	6	to him must believe that he **e**

EXPECT (EXPECTATION)

Mt	24:	44	at an hour when you do not **e** him.

EXPECTATION (EXPECT)

Ro	8:	19	waits in eager **e** for the children
Heb	10:	27	but only a fearful **e** of judgment

EXPEL

1Co	5:	13	"**E** the wicked person from among

EXPENSIVE

1Ti	2:	9	or gold or pearls or **e** clothes,

EXPLOIT

Pr	22:	22	Do not **e** the poor because they are
2Co	12:	17	I **e** you through any of the men

EXPOSE

1Co	4:	5	and will **e** the motives of the heart.
Eph	5:	11	of darkness, but rather **e** them.

EXTENDS

Pr	31:	20	poor and **e** her hands to the needy.
Lk	1:	50	His mercy **e** to those who fear him,

EXTINGUISHED

2Sa	21:	17	the lamp of Israel will not be **e**."

EXTOL

Job	36:	24	Remember to **e** his work,
Ps	34:	1	I will **e** the Lord at all times;
	68:	4	**e** him who rides on the clouds;
	95:	2	thanksgiving and **e** him with music
	109:	30	mouth I will greatly **e** the Lord;
	111:	1	I will **e** the Lord with all my
	115:	18	it is we who **e** the Lord,
	117:	1	**e** him, all you peoples.
	145:	2	and **e** your name for ever
	145:	10	your faithful people **e** you.
	147:	12	**E** the Lord, Jerusalem;

EXTORT

Lk	3:	14	"Don't **e** money and don't accuse

EYE (EYES)

Ex	21:	24	**e** for **e**, tooth for tooth,
Ps	94:	9	Does he who formed the **e** not see?
Mt	5:	29	If your right **e** causes you
	5:	38	have heard that it was said, '**E** for **e**,
	7:	3	speck of sawdust in your brother's **e**
1Co	2:	9	"What no **e** has seen, what no ear
Col	3:	22	not only when their **e** is on you
Rev	1:	7	and "every **e** will see him,

EYES (EYE)

Nu	33:	55	remain will become barbs in your **e**
Jos	23:	13	your backs and thorns in your **e**,

2Ch	16:	9	For the **e** of the Lord range
Job	31:	1	"I made a covenant with my **e** not
	36:	7	not take his **e** off the righteous;
Ps	119:	18	Open my **e** that I may see
	121:	1	I lift up my **e** to the mountains—
	141:	8	But my **e** are fixed on you,
Pr	3:	7	Do not be wise in your own **e**;
	4:	25	Let your **e** look straight ahead;
	15:	3	The **e** of the Lord are
Isa	6:	5	and my **e** have seen the King,
Hab	1:	13	Your **e** are too pure to look on
			evil;
Jn	4:	35	open your **e** and look at the fields!
2Co	4:	18	So we fix our **e** not on what is seen,
Heb	12:	2	fixing our **e** on Jesus, the pioneer
Jas	2:	5	who are poor in the **e** of the world
1Pe	3:	12	For the **e** of the Lord are
Rev	7:	17	away every tear from their **e**.' "
	21:	4	will wipe every tear from their **e**.

EZEKIEL
Priest called to be prophet to the exiles (Eze 1–3).

EZRA
Priest and teacher of the Law who led a return of exiles to Israel to reestablish temple and worship (Ezr 7–8). Corrected intermarriage of priests (Ezr 9–10). Read Law at celebration of Feast of Tabernacles (Neh 8).

FACE (FACES)
Ge	32:	30	"It is because I saw God **f** to **f**,
Ex	34:	29	that his **f** was radiant because he
Nu	6:	25	the Lord make his **f** shine on you
1Ch	16:	11	and his strength; seek his **f** always.
2Ch	7:	14	and seek my **f** and turn from their
Ps	4:	6	Let the light of your **f** shine on us.
	27:	8	My heart says of you, "Seek his **f**!"
	31:	16	Let your **f** shine on your servant;
	105:	4	and his strength; seek his **f** always.
	119:135		Make your **f** shine on your servant
Isa	50:	7	Therefore have I set my **f** like flint,
Mt	17:	2	His **f** shone like the sun, and his
1Co	13:	12	in a mirror; then we shall see **f** to **f**.
2Co	4:	6	glory displayed in the **f** of Christ.
1Pe	3:	12	the **f** of the Lord is against those
Rev	1:	16	His **f** was like the sun shining in all

FACES (FACE)
2Co	3:	18	unveiled **f** contemplate the Lord's

FACTIONS
Gal	5:	20	rage, selfish ambition, dissensions,

FADE
1Pe	5:	4	of glory that will never **f** away.

FAIL (FAILING FAILINGS FAILS)
1Ch	28:	20	He will not **f** you or forsake you
2Ch	34:	33	they did not **f** to follow the Lord,
Ps	89:	28	my covenant with him will never **f**.
Pr	15:	22	Plans **f** for lack of counsel,
Isa	51:	6	my righteousness will never **f**.
La	3:	22	for his compassions never **f**.
2Co	13:	5	unless, of course, you **f** the test?

FAILING (FAIL)
1Sa	12:	23	I should sin against the Lord by **f**

FAILINGS (FAIL)
Ro	15:	1	to bear with the **f** of the weak

FAILS (FAIL)
1Co	13:	8	Love never **f**. But where there are

FAINT
Isa	40:	31	weary, they will walk and not be **f**.

FAIR
Pr	1:	3	doing what is right and just and **f**;
Col	4:	1	your slaves with what is right and **f**,

FAITH (FAITHFUL FAITHFULLY FAITHFULNESS FAITHLESS)
2Ch	20:	20	Have **f** in the Lord your God
	20:	20	have **f** in his prophets
Mt	9:	29	"According to your **f** let it be done
	17:	20	if you have **f** as small as a mustard
	24:	10	many will turn away from the **f**
Mk	11:	22	"Have **f** in God," Jesus answered.
Lk	7:	9	I have not found such great **f** even
	12:	28	will he clothe you—you of little **f**!
	17:	5	said to the Lord, "Increase our **f**!"
	18:	8	comes, will he find **f** on the earth?"
Ac	14:	9	him, saw that he had **f** to be healed
	14:	27	how he had opened a door of **f**
Ro	1:	12	encouraged by each other's **f**.
	1:	17	"The righteous will live by **f**."
	1:	17	righteousness that is by **f** from first
	3:	22	righteousness is given through **f**
	3:	25	of his blood—to be received by **f**.
	4:	5	their **f** is credited as righteousness.
	5:	1	we have been justified through **f**,
	10:	17	**f** comes from hearing the message,
	14:	1	Accept the one whose **f** is weak,
	14:	23	that does not come from **f** is sin.
	16:	26	the obedience that comes from **f**—
1Co	13:	2	have a **f** that can move mountains,
	13:	13	three remain: **f**, hope and love.
	16:	13	stand firm in the **f**; be courageous;
2Co	5:	7	For we live by **f**, not by sight.
	13:	5	to see whether you are in the **f**;
Gal	2:	16	we may be justified by **f** in Christ
	2:	20	body, I live by **f** in the Son of God,
	3:	11	"the righteous will live by **f**."
	3:	24	that we might be justified by **f**.
Eph	2:	8	you have been saved, through **f**—
	4:	5	one Lord, one **f**, one baptism;
	6:	16	take up the shield of **f**,
Col	1:	23	if you continue in your **f**,
1Th	5:	8	be sober, putting on **f** and love as
1Ti	5:	8	if they continue in **f**,
	4:	1	later times some will abandon the **f**
	5:	8	has denied the **f** and is worse than
	6:	12	Fight the good fight of the **f**.
2Ti	3:	15	salvation through **f** in Christ Jesus.
	4:	7	finished the race, I have kept the **f**.
Phm	:	6	with us in the **f** may be effective
Heb	10:	38	my righteous one will live by **f**.
	11:	1	Now **f** is confidence in what we
	11:	3	By **f** we understand that the
	11:	5	By **f** Enoch was taken from this
	11:	6	without **f** it is impossible to please
	11:	7	By **f** Noah, when warned
	11:	7	By his **f** he condemned the world
	11:	8	By **f** Abraham, when called to go
	11:	8	By **f** Abraham, when God tested
	11:	20	By **f** Isaac blessed Jacob and Esau
	11:	21	By **f** Jacob, when he was dying,
	11:	22	By **f** Joseph, when his end was
	11:	24	By **f** Moses, when he had grown
	11:	31	By **f** the prostitute Rahab,
	12:	2	Jesus, the pioneer and perfecter of **f**.
Jas	2:	14	Can such **f** save them?
	2:	17	In the same way, **f** by itself, if it is
	2:	26	is dead, so **f** without deeds is dead.
2Pe	1:	5	effort to add to your **f** goodness;
1Jn	5:	4	overcome the world, even our **f**.
Jude	:	3	contend for the **f** that was once

FAITHFUL (FAITH)
Nu	12:	7	he is **f** in all my house.
Dt	7:	9	he is the **f** God, keeping his
	32:	4	A **f** God who does no wrong,

2Sa 22: 26   "To the **f** you show yourself **f**,
Ps 16: 10   will you let your **f** one see decay.
    25: 10   and **f** toward those who keep
    31: 23   Love the LORD, all his **f** people!
    33: 4   right and true; he is **f** in all he does.
    37: 28   just and will not forsake his **f** ones.
    97: 10   for he guards the lives of his **f** ones
  116: 15   is the death of his **f** servants.
  145: 13   all he promises and **f** in all he does.
  145: 17   in all his ways and **f** in all he does.
  146: 6   he remains **f** forever.
Pr 31: 26   and **f** instruction is on her tongue.
Mt 25: 21   'Well done, good and **f** servant!
    25: 21   You have been **f** with a few things;
Ro 12: 12   patient in affliction, **f** in prayer.
1Co 4: 2   been given a trust must prove **f**.
   10: 13   And God is **f**; he will not let you be
1Th 5: 24   The one who calls you is **f**, and he
1Ti 3: 2   to be above reproach, **f** to his wife,
2Ti 2: 13   he remains **f**, for he cannot disown
Heb 3: 6   Christ is **f** as the Son over God's
   10: 23   profess, for he who promised is **f**.
1Pe 4: 10   as **f** stewards of God's grace in its
    4: 19   themselves to their **f** Creator
1Jn 1: 9   he is **f** and just and will forgive us
Rev 1: 5   who is the **f** witness, the firstborn
    2: 10   Be **f**, even to the point of death,
   19: 11   whose rider is called **F** and True.

FAITHFULLY (FAITH)

Dt 11: 13   So if you **f** obey the commands
1Sa 12: 24   and serve him **f** with all your heart;
1Ki 2: 4   if they walk **f** before me with all

FAITHFULNESS (FAITH)

Ps 51: 6   you desired **f** even in the womb;
   57: 10   your **f** reaches to the skies.
   85: 10   Love and **f** meet together;
   86: 15   to anger, abounding in love and **f**.
   89: 1   make your **f** known through all
   89: 14   love and **f** go before you.
   91: 4   his **f** will be your shield
  117: 2   the **f** of the LORD endures forever.
  119: 75   and that in **f** you have afflicted me.
Pr   3: 3   Let love and **f** never leave you;
Isa 11: 5   and **f** the sash around his waist.
La   3: 23   new every morning; great is your **f**.
Hab 2: 4   righteous person will live by his **f**—
Ro   3: 3   their unfaithfulness nullify God's **f**?
Gal 5: 22   forbearance, kindness, goodness, **f**,

FAITHLESS (FAITH)

Ps 119:158   I look on the **f** with loathing,
Jer 3: 22   "Return, **f** people; I will cure you
2Ti 2: 13   if we are **f**, he remains faithful,

FALL (FALLEN FALLS)

Ps 37: 24   he will not **f**, for the LORD
   69: 9   of those who insult you **f** on me.
Pr 11: 28   who trust in their riches will **f**,
Lk 11: 17   a house divided against itself will **f**.
Jn 16: 1   you so that you will not **f** away.
Ro   3: 23   and **f** short of the glory of God,
   14: 4   own master, servants stand or **f**.

FALLEN (FALL)

2Sa 1: 19   How the mighty have **f**!
Isa 14: 12   How you have **f** from heaven,
1Co 15: 20   of those who have **f** asleep.
Gal 5: 4   you have **f** away from grace.
1Th 4: 15   precede those who have **f** asleep.
Heb 6: 6   and who have **f** away, to be brought

FALLS (FALL)

Pr 24: 17   Do not gloat when your enemy **f**;
Jn 12: 24   a kernel of wheat **f** to the ground

FALSE (FALSEHOOD FALSELY)

Ex 20: 16   shall not give **f** testimony against
   23: 1   "Do not spread **f** reports.
Pr 13: 5   The righteous hate what is **f**,
   19: 5   A **f** witness will not go unpunished,
Mt   7: 15   "Watch out for **f** prophets.
   19: 18   steal, you shall not give **f** testimony,
   24: 11   and many **f** prophets will appear
Php 1: 18   whether from **f** motives or true,
1Ti 1: 3   not to teach **f** doctrines any longer
2Pe 2: 1   there will be **f** teachers among you.

FALSEHOOD (FALSE)

Ps 119:163   and detest **f** but I love your law.
Pr 30: 8   Keep **f** and lies far from me;
Eph 4: 25   each of you must put off **f**

FALSELY (FALSE)

Lev 19: 12   " 'Do not swear **f** by my name
Lk   3: 14   money and don't accuse people **f**—
1Ti 6: 20   ideas of what is **f** called knowledge,

FALTER

Pr 24: 10   If you **f** in a time of trouble,
Isa 42: 4   he will not **f** or be discouraged till

FAMILIES (FAMILY)

Ps 68: 6   God sets the lonely in **f**, he leads

FAMILY (FAMILIES)

Pr 31: 15   she provides food for her **f**
Lk   9: 61   go back and say goodbye to my **f**."
   12: 52   in one **f** divided against each other,
1Ti 3: 4   He must manage his own **f** well
    3: 5   know how to manage his own **f**,
    5: 4   practice by caring for their own **f**

FAMINE

Ge 41: 30   seven years of **f** will follow them.
Am   8: 11   I will send a **f** through the land—
Ro   8: 35   or persecution or **f** or nakedness

FAN

2Ti 1: 6   this reason I remind you to **f**

FAST

Dt 13: 4   serve him and hold **f** to him.
Jos 22: 5   to hold **f** to him and to serve him
   23: 8   to hold **f** to the LORD your God,
Ps 119: 31   I hold **f** to your statutes, LORD;
  139: 10   me, your right hand will hold me **f**.
Mt   6: 16   "When you **f**, do not look somber
1Pe 5: 12   the true grace of God. Stand **f** in it.

FATHER (FATHER'S FATHERLESS FATHERS)

Ge   2: 24   That is why a man leaves his **f**
   17: 4   You will be the **f** of many nations.
Ex 20: 12   "Honor your **f** and your mother,
   21: 15   "Anyone who attacks their **f**
   21: 17   "Anyone who curses their **f**
Lev 18: 7   " 'Do not dishonor your **f**
   19: 3   must respect your mother and **f**,
Dt   5: 16   "Honor your **f** and your mother,
   21: 18   son who does not obey his **f**
Ps 27: 10   Though my **f** and mother forsake
   68: 5   A **f** to the fatherless, a defender
Pr 10: 1   A wise son brings joy to his **f**,
   23: 22   Listen to your **f**, who gave you life,
   23: 24   The **f** of a righteous child has great
   28: 7   of gluttons disgraces his **f**.
   29: 3   loves wisdom brings joy to his **f**,
Isa 9: 6   Everlasting **F**, Prince of Peace.
Mt   6: 9   " 'Our **F** in heaven, hallowed be
   10: 37   "Anyone who loves their **f**
   15: 4   said, 'Honor your **f** and mother'
   19: 5   this reason a man will leave his **f**

Lk 12: 53 f against son and son against f,
 23: 34 Jesus said, "F, forgive them,
Jn 6: 44 unless the F who sent me draws
 6: 46 from God; only he has seen the F.
 8: 44 You belong to your f, the devil,
 10: 30 I and the F are one."
 14: 6 comes to the F except through me.
 14: 9 who has seen me has seen the F.
Ro 4: 11 he is the f of all who believe
2Co 6: 18 And, "I will be a F to you, and you
Eph 6: 2 "Honor your f and mother"—
Heb 12: 7 are not disciplined by their f?

FATHER'S (FATHER)

Pr 13: 1 wise son heeds his f instruction,
 19: 13 A foolish child is a f ruin,
Lk 2: 49 know I had to be in my F house?"
Jn 2: 16 Stop turning my F house
 10: 29 can snatch them out of my F hand.
 14: 2 My F house has many rooms;

FATHERLESS (FATHER)

Dt 10: 18 He defends the cause of the f
 24: 17 the foreigner or the f of justice,
 24: 19 the foreigner, the f and the widow,
Ps 68: 5 A father to the f, a defender
Pr 23: 10 or encroach on the fields of the f,

FATHERS (FATHER)

Lk 11: 11 "Which of you f, if your son asks
Eph 6: 4 F, do not exasperate your children;
Col 3: 21 F, do not embitter your children,

FATHOM

Job 11: 7 "Can you f the mysteries of God?
Ps 145: 3 his greatness no one can f.
Ecc 3: 11 no one can f what God has done
Isa 40: 28 his understanding no one can f.
1Co 13: 2 of prophecy and can f all mysteries

FAULT (FAULTS)

Mt 18: 15 sins, go and point out their f,
Php 2: 15 of God without f in a warped
Jas 1: 5 generously to all without finding f,
Jude : 24 his glorious presence without f

FAULTFINDERS

Jude : 16 These people are grumblers and f;

FAULTS (FAULT)

Ps 19: 12 Forgive my hidden f.

FAVORITISM

Ex 23: 3 do not show f to a poor person
Lev 19: 15 to the poor or f to the great,
Ac 10: 34 true it is that God does not show f
Ro 2: 11 For God does not show f.
Gal 2: 6 God does not show f—
Eph 6: 9 heaven, and there is no f with him.
Col 3: 25 for their wrongs, and there is no f.
1Ti 5: 21 and to do nothing out of f.
Jas 2: 1 Lord Jesus Christ must not show f.
 2: 9 But if you show f, you sin and are

FEAR (AFRAID FEARS)

Dt 6: 13 F the LORD your God, serve him
 10: 12 you but to f the LORD your God,
 31: 12 learn to f the LORD your God
Ps 19: 9 The f of the LORD is pure,
 23: 4 the darkest valley, I will f no evil,
 27: 1 and my salvation—whom shall I f?
 91: 5 You will not f the terror of night,
 111: 10 The f of the LORD is
Pr 8: 13 To f the LORD is to hate evil;
 9: 10 The f of the LORD is
 10: 27 The f of the LORD adds length
 14: 27 The f of the LORD is a fountain

Pr 15: 33 instruction is to f the LORD,
 16: 6 through the f of the LORD evil is
 19: 23 The f of the LORD leads to life;
 29: 25 F of man will prove to be a snare,
Ecc 5: 7 Therefore f God.
Isa 11: 3 will delight in the f of the LORD.
 41: 10 So do not f, for I am with you;
Lk 12: 5 will show you whom you should f:
Php 2: 12 to work out your salvation with f
1Jn 4: 18 There is no f in love. But perfect love
     drives out f,

FEARS (FEAR)

Job 1: 8 a man who f God and shuns evil."
Ps 34: 4 he delivered me from all my f.
Pr 31: 30 a woman who f the LORD is to be
1Jn 4: 18 The one who f is not made perfect

FEED

Jn 21: 15 Jesus said, "F my lambs."
 21: 17 Jesus said, "F my sheep.
Ro 12: 20 "If your enemy is hungry, f him;
Jude : 12 shepherds who f only themselves.

FEET (FOOT)

Ps 8: 6 you put everything under their f:
 22: 16 they pierce my hands and my f.
 40: 2 he set my f on a rock and gave me
 110: 1 enemies a footstool for your f."
 119:105 Your word is a lamp to my f
Ro 10: 15 "How beautiful are the f of those
1Co 12: 21 And the head cannot say to the f,
 15: 25 has put all his enemies under his f.
Heb 12: 13 "Make level paths for your f,"

FELLOWSHIP

2Co 6: 14 f can light have with darkness?
 13: 14 the f of the Holy Spirit be with you
1Jn 1: 6 If we claim to have f with him
 1: 7 light, we have f with one another,

FEMALE

Ge 1: 27 male and f he created them.
Gal 3: 28 nor is there male and f, for you are

FERVOR

Ro 12: 11 but keep your spiritual f,

FIDELITY

Ro 1: 31 no understanding, no f, no love,

FIELD (FIELDS)

Mt 6: 28 See how the flowers of the f grow.
 13: 38 The f is the world, and the good
1Co 3: 9 you are God's f, God's building.

FIELDS (FIELD)

Lk 2: 8 shepherds living out in the f
Jn 4: 35 open your eyes and look at the f!

FIERY (FIRE)

1Pe 4: 12 do not be surprised at the f ordeal

FIG (FIGS)

Ge 3: 7 so they sewed f leaves together

FIGHT (FOUGHT)

Ex 14: 14 The LORD will f for you;
Dt 1: 30 is going before you, will f for you,
 3: 22 the LORD your God himself will f
Ne 4: 20 Our God will f for us!"
Ps 35: 1 f against those who f against me.
Jn 18: 36 my servants would f to prevent my
1Co 9: 26 I do not f like a boxer beating
2Co 10: 4 The weapons we f with are not
1Ti 1: 18 them you may f the battle well,
 6: 12 F the good f of the faith.
2Ti 4: 7 I have fought the good f, I have

FIGS (FIG)
Lk 6: 44 People do not pick **f**

FILL (FILLED FILLS FULL FULLNESS FULLY)
Ge 1: 28 **f** the earth and subdue it.
Ps 16: 11 you will **f** me with joy in your
81: 10 wide your mouth and I will **f** it.
Pr 28: 19 chase fantasies will have their **f**
Hag 2: 7 and I will **f** this house with glory,'
Jn 6: 26 you ate the loaves and had your **f**.
Ac 2: 28 you will **f** me with joy in your
Ro 15: 13 May the God of hope **f** you with all

FILLED (FILL)
Ps 72: 19 may the whole earth be **f** with his
119: 64 The earth is **f** with your love,
Isa 11: 9 for the earth will be **f**
Eze 43: 5 glory of the LORD **f** the temple.
Hab 2: 14 For the earth will be **f**
Lk 1: 15 he will be **f** with the Holy Spirit
1: 41 Elizabeth was **f** with the Holy Spirit.
Jn 12: 3 the house was **f** with the fragrance
Ac 2: 4 of them were **f** with the Holy Spirit
4: 8 Then Peter, **f** with the Holy Spirit,
9: 17 and be **f** with the Holy Spirit."
13: 9 called Paul, **f** with the Holy Spirit,
Eph 5: 18 Instead, be **f** with the Spirit,
Php 1: 11 **f** with the fruit of righteousness

FILLS (FILL)
Nu 14: 21 of the LORD **f** the whole earth,
Ps 107: 9 and **f** the hungry with good things.
Eph 1: 23 him who **f** everything in every way.

FILTHY
Isa 64: 6 all our righteous acts are like **f** rags;
Col 3: 8 and **f** language from your lips.

FIND (FINDS FOUND)
Nu 32: 23 be sure that your sin will **f** you out.
Dt 4: 29 you will **f** him if you seek him
1Sa 23: 16 and helped him **f** strength in God.
Ps 91: 4 under his wings you will **f** refuge;
112: 1 LORD, who **f** great delight in his
Pr 14: 22 those who plan what is good **f** love
31: 10 wife of noble character who can **f**?
Jer 6: 16 and you will **f** rest for your souls.
Mt 7: 7 seek and you will **f**;
11: 29 and you will **f** rest for your souls.
16: 25 loses their life for me will **f** it.
Lk 18: 8 will he **f** faith on the earth?"
Jn 10: 9 come in and go out, and **f** pasture.

FINDS (FIND)
Ps 62: 1 Truly my soul **f** rest in God;
119:162 promise like one who **f** great spoil.
Pr 18: 22 He who **f** a wife **f** what is good
Mt 7: 8 the one who seeks **f**; and to the one
10: 39 Whoever **f** their life will lose it,
Lk 12: 37 whose master **f** them watching
15: 4 go after the lost sheep until he **f** it?

FINISH (FINISHED)
Jn 4: 34 him who sent me and to **f** his work.
5: 36 that the Father has given me to **f**—
Ac 20: 24 my only aim is to **f** the race
2Co 8: 11 Now **f** the work, so that your eager
Gal 3: 3 are you now trying to **f** by means
Jas 1: 4 Let perseverance **f** its work so

FINISHED (FINISH)
Ge 2: 2 seventh day God had **f** the work he
Jn 19: 30 the drink, Jesus said, "It is **f**."
2Ti 4: 7 the good fight, I have **f** the race,

FIRE (FIERY)
Ex 13: 21 in a pillar of **f** to give them light,

Lev 6: 12 The **f** on the altar must be kept
Isa 30: 27 and his tongue is a consuming **f**.
Jer 23: 29 "Is not my word like **f**,"
Mt 3: 11 you with the Holy Spirit and **f**.
5: 22 will be in danger of the **f** of hell.
25: 41 the eternal **f** prepared for the devil
Mk 9: 43 hell, where the **f** never goes out.
Ac 2: 3 to be tongues of **f** that separated
1Co 3: 13 It will be revealed with **f**, and the **f**
Heb 12: 29 for our "God is a consuming **f**."
Jas 3: 5 what a great forest is set on **f**
2Pe 3: 10 the elements will be destroyed by **f**,
Jude : 23 by snatching them from the **f**;
Rev 20: 14 **f**. The lake of **f** is the second death.

FIRM
Ex 14: 13 Stand **f** and you will see
2Ch 20: 17 stand **f** and see the deliverance
Ps 33: 11 plans of the LORD stand **f** forever,
37: 23 The LORD makes **f** the steps
40: 2 and gave me a **f** place to stand.
89: 2 that your love stands **f** forever,
119: 89 it stands **f** in the heavens.
Zec 8: 23 nations will take **f** hold of one Jew
Mk 13: 13 the one who stands **f** to the end
1Co 16: 13 on your guard; stand **f** in the faith;
2Co 1: 24 because it is by faith you stand **f**.
Eph 6: 14 Stand **f** then, with the belt of truth
Col 4: 12 that you may stand **f** in all the will
2Th 2: 15 stand **f** and hold fast to the teachings
2Ti 2: 19 God's solid foundation stands **f**,
Heb 6: 19 anchor for the soul, **f** and secure.
1Pe 5: 9 Resist him, standing **f** in the faith,

FIRST
Isa 44: 6 I am the **f** and I am the last;
48: 12 I am the **f** and I am the last.
Mt 5: 24 **F** go and be reconciled to them;
6: 33 But seek **f** his kingdom and his
7: 5 **f** take the plank out of your own
20: 27 wants to be **f** must be your slave—
22: 38 This is the **f** and greatest
23: 26 **F** clean the inside of the cup
Mk 13: 10 the gospel must **f** be preached to all
Ac 11: 26 disciples were called Christians **f**
Ro 1: 16 **f** to the Jew, then to the Gentile.
1Co 12: 28 in the church **f** of all apostles,
2Co 8: 5 They gave themselves **f** of all
1Ti 2: 13 For Adam was formed **f**, then Eve.
Jas 3: 17 comes from heaven is **f** of all pure;
1Jn 4: 19 We love because he **f** loved us.
3Jn : 9 who loves to be **f**, will not welcome
Rev 1: 17 I am the **F** and the Last.
2: 4 have forsaken the love you had at **f**.

FIRSTBORN (BEAR)
Ex 11: 5 Every **f** son in Egypt will die,

FIRSTFRUITS
Ex 23: 19 "Bring the best of the **f** of your soil

FISH
Mk 1: 17 I will send you out to **f** for people."
Lk 5: 10 from now on you will **f** for people."

FITTING
Ps 33: 1 it is **f** for the upright to praise him.
147: 1 how pleasant and **f** to praise him!
Pr 19: 10 It is not **f** for a fool to live
26: 1 in harvest, honor is not **f** for a fool.
1Co 14: 40 everything should be done in a **f**
Col 3: 18 your husbands, as is **f** in the Lord.
Heb 2: 10 to glory, it was **f** that God,

FIX (FIXING)
Dt 11: 18 **F** these words of mine in your

Pr   4: 25   **f** your gaze directly before you.
2Co   4: 18   So we **f** our eyes not on what is
Heb   3:   1   calling, **f** your thoughts on Jesus,

FIXING (FIX)
Heb   12:   2   **f** our eyes on Jesus, the pioneer

FLAME (FLAMES FLAMING)
2Ti   1:   6   you to fan into **f** the gift of God,

FLAMES (FLAME)
1Co   3: 15   only as one escaping through the **f.**

FLAMING (FLAME)
Eph   6: 16   you can extinguish all the **f** arrows

FLASH
1Co   15: 52   in a **f**, in the twinkling of an eye,

FLATTER (FLATTERING FLATTERY)
Ps   12:   2   they **f** with their lips but harbor
Job   32: 21   no partiality, nor will I **f** anyone;
Jude   : 16   **f** others for their own advantage.

FLATTERING (FLATTER)
Ps   12:   3   May the LORD silence all **f** lips
Pr   26: 28   it hurts, and a **f** mouth works ruin.

FLATTERY (FLATTER)
Ro   16: 18   **f** they deceive the minds of naive
1Th   2:   5   You know we never used **f**, nor did

FLAWLESS
2Sa   22: 31   The LORD's word is **f**;
Job   11:   4   'My beliefs are **f** and I am pure
Ps   12:   6   And the words of the LORD are **f**,
      18: 30   The LORD's word is **f**;
Pr   30:   5   "Every word of God is **f**; he is
SS   5:   2   my darling, my dove, my **f** one.

FLEE
Ps   139:   7   Where can I **f** from your presence?
1Co   6: 18   **F** from sexual immorality.
      10: 14   my dear friends, **f** from idolatry.
1Ti   6: 11   man of God, **f** from all this,
2Ti   2: 22   **F** the evil desires of youth
Jas   4:   7   the devil, and he will **f** from you.

FLEETING
Ps   89: 47   Remember how **f** is my life.
Pr   31: 30   is deceptive, and beauty is **f**;

FLESH
Ge   2: 23   bone of my bones and **f** of my **f**;
       2: 24   to his wife, and they become one **f.**
Job   19: 26   yet in my **f** I will see God;
Eze   11: 19   of stone and give them a heart of **f.**
      36: 26   of stone and give you a heart of **f.**
Mt   26: 41   spirit is willing, but the **f** is weak."
Mk   10:   8   and the two will become one **f.**'
Jn   1: 14   The Word became **f** and made his
       6: 51   bread is my **f**, which I will give
Ro   8:   4   do not live according to the **f** but
       8:   8   realm of the **f** cannot please God.
1Co   6: 16   said, "The two will become one **f.**"
Gal   3:   3   trying to finish by means of the **f**?
       5: 19   The acts of the **f** are obvious:
       5: 24   crucified the **f** with its passions
Eph   5: 31   and the two will become one **f.**"
       6: 12   For our struggle is not against **f**

FLOCK (FLOCKS)
Isa   40: 11   He tends his **f** like a shepherd:
Eze   34:   2   not shepherds take care of the **f**?
Zec   11: 17   shepherd, who deserts the **f**!
Mt   26: 31   the sheep of the **f** will be scattered.'
Ac   20: 28   all the **f** of which the Holy Spirit
1Pe   5:   2   of God's **f** that is under your care,

FLOCKS (FLOCK)
Lk   2:   8   keeping watch over their **f** at night.

FLOG
Ac   22: 25   **f** a Roman citizen who hasn't even

FLOODGATES
Mal   3: 10   will not throw open the **f** of heaven

FLOURISHING
Ps   52:   8   am like an olive tree **f** in the house

FLOW (FLOWING)
Nu   13: 27   and it does **f** with milk and honey!
Jn   7: 38   of living water will **f** from within

FLOWERS
Isa   40:   7   The grass withers and the **f** fall,
Lk   12: 27   "Consider how the wild **f** grow.

FLOWING (FLOW)
Ex   3:   8   a land **f** with milk and honey—

FOLDING
Pr   6: 10   a little **f** of the hands to rest—

FOLLOW (FOLLOWS)
Ex   23:   2   "Do not **f** the crowd in doing
Lev   18:   4   laws and be careful to **f** my decrees.
Dt   5:   1   Learn them and be sure to **f** them.
Ps   23:   6   love will **f** me all the days of my
Mt   16: 24   and take up their cross and **f** me.
Jn   10:   4   his sheep **f** him because they know
1Co   14:   1   **F** the way of love and eagerly desire
Eph   5:   1   **F** God's example, therefore,
Rev   14:   4   They **f** the Lamb wherever he goes.

FOLLOWS (FOLLOW)
Jn   8: 12   Whoever **f** me will never walk

FOOD (FOODS)
Pr   20: 13   awake and you will have **f** to spare.
      22:   9   for they share their **f** with the poor.
      25: 21   enemy is hungry, give him **f** to eat;
      31: 15   she provides **f** for her family
Da   1:   8   to defile himself with the royal **f**
Jn   6: 27   Do not work for **f** that spoils, but for **f**
                 that endures to eternal life,
1Co   8:   8   **f** does not bring us near to God;
1Ti   6:   8   But if we have **f** and clothing,
Jas   2: 15   sister is without clothes and daily **f.**

FOODS (FOOD)
Mk   7: 19   this, Jesus declared all **f** clean.)

FOOL (FOOLISH FOOLISHNESS FOOLS)
Ps   14:   1   The **f** says in his heart, "There
Pr   15:   5   A **f** spurns a parent's discipline,
      26:   5   Answer a **f** according to his folly,
Mt   5: 22   And anyone who says, 'You **f**!'

FOOLISH (FOOL)
Pr   10:   1   a **f** son brings grief to his mother.
      17: 25   A **f** son brings grief to his father
Mt   7: 26   practice is like a **f** man who built
      25:   2   Five of them were **f** and five were
1Co   1: 27   God chose the **f** things of the world

FOOLISHNESS (FOOL)
1Co   1: 18   of the cross is **f** to those who are
       1: 25   the **f** of God is wiser than human
       2: 14   Spirit of God but considers them **f**,
       3: 19   of this world is **f** in God's sight.

FOOLS (FOOL)
Pr   14:   9   **F** mock at making amends for sin,
      17: 28   Even **f** are thought wise if they
      18:   2   **F** find no pleasure in understanding

Pr   28: 26   who trust in themselves are **f**,
1Co   4: 10   We are **f** for Christ, but you are so

FOOT (FEET FOOTHOLD)

Jos   1: 3   every place where you set your **f**,
Isa   1: 6   the sole of your **f** to the top of your
1Co 12: 15   Now if the **f** should say, "Because I

FOOTHOLD (FOOT)

Eph   4: 27   and do not give the devil a **f**.

FORBEARANCE

Ro   3: 25   his **f** he had left the sins committed
Gal   5: 22   love, joy, peace, **f**, kindness,

FORBID

1Co 14: 39   and do not **f** speaking in tongues.

FOREIGNER (FOREIGNERS)

Ex   22: 21   "Do not mistreat or oppress a **f**,

FOREIGNERS (FOREIGNER)

1Pe   2: 11   urge you, as **f** and exiles, to abstain

FOREKNEW (KNOW)

Ro   8: 29   those God **f** he also predestined
      11: 2   not reject his people, whom he **f**.

FOREVER (EVER)

1Ch 16: 15   He remembers his covenant **f**,
      16: 34   for he is good; his love endures **f**.
Ps   9: 7   The Lord reigns **f**;
      23: 6   dwell in the house of the Lord **f**.
      33: 11   plans of the Lord stand firm **f**,
      86: 12   I will glorify your name **f**.
      92: 8   But you, Lord, are **f** exalted.
     110: 4   "You are a priest **f**, in the order
     119:111   Your statutes are my heritage **f**;
Jn   6: 51   Whoever eats this bread will live **f**.
      14: 16   to help you and be with you **f**—
1Co   9: 25   do it to get a crown that will last **f**.
1Th   4: 17   And so we will be with the Lord **f**.
Heb 13: 8   the same yesterday and today
                and **f**.
1Pe   1: 25   the word of the Lord endures **f**."
1Jn   2: 17   does the will of God lives **f**.

FORFEIT

Lk   9: 25   and yet lose or **f** their very self?

FORGAVE (FORGIVE)

Ps   32: 5   And you **f** the guilt of my sin.
Lk   7: 42   him back, so he **f** the debts of both.
Eph   4: 32   other, just as in Christ God **f** you.
Col   2: 13   He **f** us all our sins,
      3: 13   Forgive as the Lord **f** you.

FORGET (FORGETS FORGETTING)

Dt   6: 12   that you do not **f** the Lord,
Ps 103: 2   my soul, and **f** not all his benefits—
     137: 5   If I **f** you, Jerusalem, may my right
Isa 49: 15   Though she may **f**, I will not **f** you!
Heb   6: 10   will not **f** your work and the love

FORGETS (FORGET)

Jn   16: 21   is born she **f** the anguish because
Jas   1: 24   immediately **f** what he looks like.

FORGETTING (FORGET)

Php   3: 13   **F** what is behind and straining

FORGIVE (FORGAVE FORGIVENESS FORGIVING)

2Ch   7: 14   and I will **f** their sin and will heal
Ps   19: 12   **F** my hidden faults.
Mt   6: 12   And **f** us our debts, as we also have
      6: 14   if you **f** other people when they sin
      18: 21   many times shall I **f** my brother
Mk   11: 25   anything against anyone, **f** them,

Lk   11: 4   **F** us our sins, for we also **f** everyone
      23: 34   "Father, **f** them, for they do not
Col   3: 13   **F** as the Lord forgave you.
1Jn   1: 9   and will **f** us our sins and purify

FORGIVENESS (FORGIVE)

Ps 130: 4   But with you there is **f**, so that we
Ac   10: 43   in him receives **f** of sins through
Eph   1: 7   through his blood, the **f** of sins,
Col   1: 14   we have redemption, the **f** of sins.
Heb   9: 22   the shedding of blood there is no **f**.

FORGIVING (FORGIVE)

Ne   9: 17   But you are a **f** God,
Eph   4: 32   to one another, **f** each other, just as

FORMED

Ge   2: 7   the Lord God **f** a man
Ps 103: 14   for he knows how we are **f**,
Isa 45: 18   be empty, but **f** it to be inhabited—
Ro   9: 20   what is **f** say to the one who **f** it,
1Ti   2: 13   For Adam was **f** first, then Eve.
Heb 11: 3   that the universe was **f** at God's

FORSAKE (FORSAKEN)

Jos   1: 5   I will never leave you nor **f** you.
      24: 16   us to **f** the Lord to serve other
2Ch 15: 2   you, but if you **f** him, he will **f** you.
Ps   27: 10   Though my father and mother **f** me,
Isa 55: 7   Let the wicked **f** their ways
Heb 13: 5   will I leave you; never will I **f** you."

FORSAKEN (FORSAKE)

Ezr   9: 9   God has not **f** us in our bondage.
Ps   22: 1   God, my God, why have you **f** me?
      37: 25   I have never seen the righteous **f**
Mt   27: 46   my God, why have you **f** me?").
Rev   2: 4   You have **f** the love you had at first.

FORTIFIED

Pr   18: 10   name of the Lord is a **f** tower;

FORTRESS

Ps   18: 2   is my rock, my **f** and my deliverer;
      71: 3   me, for you are my rock and my **f**.

FOUGHT (FIGHT)

2Ti   4: 7   I have **f** the good fight, I have

FOUND (FIND)

1Ch 28: 9   If you seek him, he will be **f** by you;
Isa 55: 6   Seek the Lord while he may be **f**;
Da   5: 27   on the scales and **f** wanting.
Lk   15: 6   I have **f** my lost sheep.'
      15: 9   I have **f** my lost coin.'
Ac   4: 12   Salvation is **f** in no one else,

FOUNDATION

Isa 28: 16   a precious cornerstone for a sure **f**;
1Co   3: 11   can lay any **f** other than the one
Eph   2: 20   built on the **f** of the apostles
2Ti   2: 19   God's solid **f** stands firm,

FOXES

Mt   8: 20   "**F** have dens and birds have nests,

FRANKINCENSE

Mt   2: 11   him with gifts of gold, **f** and myrrh.

FREE (FREED FREEDOM FREELY)

Ps 146: 7   The Lord sets prisoners **f**,
Jn   8: 32   truth, and the truth will set you **f**."
Ro   6: 18   You have been set **f** from sin
Gal   3: 28   neither slave nor **f**, nor is there
1Pe   2: 16   Live as **f** people, but do not use

FREED (FREE)

Rev   1: 5   has **f** us from our sins by his blood,

FREEDOM (FREE)
Ro	8: 21	brought into the **f** and glory
2Co	3: 17	the Spirit of the Lord is, there is **f**.
Gal	5: 13	But do not use your **f** to indulge
1Pe	2: 16	do not use your **f** as

FREELY (FREE)
Isa	55: 7	to our God, for he will **f** pardon.
Mt	10: 8	**F** you have received; **f** give.
Ro	3: 24	and all are justified **f** by his grace
Eph	1: 6	which he has **f** given us in the One

FRIEND (FRIENDS)
Ex	33: 11	face to face, as one speaks to a **f**.
Pr	17: 17	A **f** loves at all times, and a brother
	18: 24	there is a **f** who sticks closer than
	27: 6	Wounds from a **f** can be trusted,
	27: 10	Do not forsake your **f** or a **f** of your
Jas	4: 4	to be a **f** of the world becomes

FRIENDS (FRIEND)
Pr	16: 28	and a gossip separates close **f**.
	18: 24	who has unreliable **f** soon comes
Zec	13: 6	I was given at the house of my **f**.'
Jn	15: 13	to lay down one's life for one's **f**.

FRUIT (FRUITFUL)
Ps	1: 3	which yields its **f** in season
Pr	11: 30	The **f** of the righteous is a tree
Mt	7: 16	By their **f** you will recognize them.
Jn	15: 2	branch that does bear **f** he prunes
Gal	5: 22	But the **f** of the Spirit is love, joy,
Rev	22: 2	bearing twelve crops of **f**, yielding
		its **f** every month.

FRUITFUL (FRUIT)
Ge	1: 22	"Be **f** and increase in number
Ps	128: 3	wife will be like a **f** vine within
Jn	15: 2	so that it will be even more **f**.

FULFILL (FULFILLED FULFILLMENT)
Ps	116: 14	I will **f** my vows to the Lᴏʀᴅ
Mt	5: 17	to abolish them but to **f** them.
1Co	7: 3	The husband should **f** his marital

FULFILLED (FULFILL)
Pr	13: 19	A longing **f** is sweet to the soul,
Mk	14: 49	But the Scriptures must be **f**."
Ro	13: 8	whoever loves others has **f** the law.

FULFILLMENT (FULFILL)
Ro	13: 10	Therefore love is the **f** of the law.

FULL (FILL)
Ps	127: 5	Blessed is the man whose quiver is **f**
Pr	31: 11	Her husband has **f** confidence
		in her
Isa	6: 3	the whole earth is **f** of his glory."
Lk	6: 45	speaks what the heart is **f** of.
Jn	10: 10	may have life, and have it to the **f**.
Ac	6: 3	who are known to be **f** of the Spirit

FULLNESS (FILL)
Col	1: 19	to have all his **f** dwell in him,
	2: 9	in Christ all the **f** of the Deity lives

FULLY (FILL)
1Ki	8: 61	may your hearts be **f** committed
2Ch	16: 9	whose hearts are **f** committed
Ps	119: 4	precepts that are to be **f** obeyed.
	119:138	righteous; they are **f** trustworthy.
1Co	15: 58	Always give yourselves **f**

FUTURE
Ps	37: 37	a **f** awaits those who seek peace.
Pr	23: 18	There is surely a **f** hope for you,
Ro	8: 38	neither the present nor the **f**,

GABRIEL
Angel who interpreted Daniel's visions (Da 8:16–26; 9:20–27); announced births of John (Lk 1:11–20), Jesus (Lk 1:26–38).

GAIN (GAINED)
Ps	60: 12	With God we will **g** the victory,
Mk	8: 36	for someone to **g** the whole world,
1Co	13: 3	but do not have love, I **g** nothing.
Php	1: 21	me, to live is Christ and to die is **g**.
	3: 8	them garbage, that I may **g** Christ
1Ti	6: 6	with contentment is great **g**.
1Pe	5: 2	not pursuing dishonest **g**, but eager

GAINED (GAIN)
Ro	5: 2	through whom we have **g** access

GALILEE
Isa	9: 1	in the future he will honor **G**

GALL
Mt	27: 34	Jesus wine to drink, mixed with **g**;

GAP
Eze	22: 30	stand before me in the **g** on behalf

GARBAGE
Php	3: 8	I consider them **g**, that I may gain

GARDENER
Jn	15: 1	true vine, and my Father is the **g**.

GARMENT (GARMENTS)
Ps	102: 26	they will all wear out like a **g**.
Mt	9: 16	the patch will pull away from the **g**,
Jn	19: 23	This **g** was seamless, woven in one
	19: 24	them and cast lots for my **g**."

GARMENTS (GARMENT)
Ge	3: 21	The Lᴏʀᴅ God made **g** of skin
Isa	61: 10	For he has clothed me with **g**
	63: 1	with his **g** stained crimson?

GATE (GATES)
Mt	7: 13	"Enter through the narrow **g**.
Jn	10: 9	I am the **g**; whoever enters through

GATES (GATE)
Ps	100: 4	Enter his **g** with thanksgiving
Mt	16: 18	the **g** of Hades will not overcome

GATHER (GATHERS)
Zec	14: 2	I will **g** all the nations to Jerusalem
Mt	12: 30	and whoever does not **g** with me
	23: 37	longed to **g** your children together,

GATHERS (GATHER)
Isa	40: 11	He **g** the lambs in his arms
Mt	23: 37	as a hen **g** her chicks under her

GAVE (GIVE)
Ezr	2: 69	their ability they **g** to the treasury
Job	1: 21	The Lᴏʀᴅ **g** and the Lᴏʀᴅ has
Jn	3: 16	so loved the world that he **g** his
2Co	8: 5	They **g** themselves first of all
Gal	2: 20	loved me and **g** himself for me.
1Ti	2: 6	who **g** himself as a ransom for all

GAZE
Ps	27: 4	to **g** on the beauty of the Lᴏʀᴅ
Pr	4: 25	fix your **g** directly before you.

GENEALOGIES
1Ti	1: 4	themselves to myths and endless **g**.

GENERATIONS
Ps	22: 30	**g** will be told about the Lord.
	102: 12	renown endures through all **g**.

Ps 145: 13 dominion endures through all **g**.
Lk   1: 48 now on all **g** will call me blessed,
Eph 3: 5 other **g** as it has now been revealed

GENEROUS
Ps 112: 5 Good will come to those who are **g**
Pr 22: 9 The **g** will themselves be blessed,
2Co 9: 5 Then it will be ready as a **g** gift,
1Ti 6: 18 and to be **g** and willing to share.

GENTILE (GENTILES)
Ro   1: 16 first to the Jew, then to the **G**.
    10: 12 no difference between Jew and **G**—

GENTILES (GENTILE)
Isa 42: 6 for the people and a light for the **G**,
Ro   3: 9 **G** alike are all under the power
    11: 13 as I am the apostle to the **G**, I take
1Co 1: 23 block to Jews and foolishness to **G**,

GENTLE (GENTLENESS)
Pr 15: 1 A **g** answer turns away wrath,
Mt 11: 29 for I am **g** and humble in heart,
    21: 5 to you, **g** and riding on a donkey,
1Co 4: 21 I come in love and with a **g** spirit?
1Pe 3: 4 unfading beauty of a **g** and quiet

GENTLENESS (GENTLE)
2Co 10: 1 By the humility and **g** of Christ,
Gal 5: 23 **g** and self-control.
Php 4: 5 Let your **g** be evident to all.
Col 3: 12 kindness, humility, **g** and patience.
1Ti 6: 11 faith, love, endurance and **g**.
1Pe 3: 15 But do this with **g** and respect,

GETHSEMANE
Mt 26: 36 his disciples to a place called **G**,

GIDEON
Judge, also called Jerub-Baal; freed Israel from Midianites (Jdg 6–8; Heb 11:32). Given sign of fleece (Jdg 6:36–40).

GIFT (GIFTS)
Pr 21: 14 A **g** given in secret soothes anger,
Mt   5: 23 you are offering your **g** at the altar
Ac   2: 38 you will receive the **g** of the Holy
Ro   6: 23 the **g** of God is eternal life in Christ
1Co 7: 7 of you has your own **g** from God;
2Co 8: 12 the **g** is acceptable according
     9: 15 be to God for his indescribable **g**!
Eph 2: 8 yourselves, it is the **g** of God—
1Ti 4: 14 Do not neglect your **g**, which was
2Ti 1: 6 you to fan into flame the **g** of God,
Jas 1: 17 good and perfect **g** is from above,
1Pe 4: 10 should use whatever **g** you have

GIFTS (GIFT)
Ro 11: 29 for God's **g** and his call are
    12: 6 We have different **g**,
1Co 12: 4 There are different kinds of **g**,
    12: 31 Now eagerly desire the greater **g**.
    14: 1 and eagerly desire **g** of the Spirit,
    14: 12 Since you are eager for **g**

GILEAD
Jer 8: 22 Is there no balm in **G**? Is there no

GIVE (GAVE GIVEN GIVER GIVES GIVING)
Nu   6: 26 toward you and **g** you peace." '
1Sa 1: 11 forget your servant but **g** her a son,
     1: 11 I will **g** him to the LORD for all
2Ch 15: 7 be strong and do not **g** up, for your
Pr 21: 26 the righteous **g** without sparing.
    23: 26 **g** me your heart and let your eyes
    28: 27 Those who **g** to the poor will lack
    30: 8 but **g** me only my daily bread.

Eze 36: 26 I will **g** you a new heart and put
Mt   6: 11 **G** us today our daily bread.
    10: 8 Freely you have received; freely **g**.
    22: 21 them, "So **g** back to Caesar what is
Mk   8: 37 what can anyone **g** in exchange
Lk   6: 38 **G**, and it will be given to you.
    11: 13 Father in heaven **g** the Holy Spirit
Jn 10: 28 I **g** them eternal life, and they shall
    13: 34 "A new command I **g** you:
Ac 20: 35 'It is more blessed to **g** than
Ro 12: 8 encourage, then **g** encouragement;
    12: 8 if it is giving, then **g** generously;
    13: 7 **G** to everyone what you owe them:
    14: 12 then, each of us will **g** an account
2Co 9: 7 should **g** what you have decided
Rev 14: 7 voice, "Fear God and **g** him glory,

GIVEN (GIVE)
Nu   8: 16 Israelites who are to be **g** wholly
Ps 115: 16 but the earth he has **g** to mankind.
Isa 9: 6 a son is **g**, and the government
Mt   6: 33 all these things will be **g** to you as
     7: 7 "Ask and it will be **g** to you;
Lk 22: 19 saying, "This is my body **g** for you;
Jn   3: 27 can receive only what is **g** them
Ro   5: 5 Holy Spirit, who has been **g** to us.
1Co 4: 2 those who have been **g** a trust must
    12: 13 and we were all **g** the one Spirit
Eph 4: 7 of us grace has been **g** as Christ

GIVER (GIVE)
Pr 18: 16 ushers the **g** into the presence
2Co 9: 7 for God loves a cheerful **g**.

GIVES (GIVE)
Ps 119:130 unfolding of your words **g** light;
Pr 14: 30 A heart at peace **g** life to the body,
    15: 30 good news **g** health to the bones.
Isa 40: 29 He **g** strength to the weary
Mt 10: 42 anyone **g** even a cup of cold water
Jn   6: 63 The Spirit **g** life; the flesh counts
1Co 15: 57 He **g** us the victory through our
2Co 3: 6 the letter kills, but the Spirit **g** life.

GIVING (GIVE)
Ne   8: 8 **g** the meaning so that the people
Ps 19: 8 LORD are right, **g** joy to the heart.
Mt   6: 4 so that your **g** may be in secret.
2Co 8: 7 you also excel in this grace of **g**.

GLAD (GLADNESS)
Ps 31: 7 I will be **g** and rejoice in your love,
    46: 4 whose streams make **g** the city
    97: 1 LORD reigns, let the earth be **g**;
   118: 24 let us rejoice today and be **g**.
Zec 2: 10 "Shout and be **g**, Daughter Zion.
Mt   5: 12 Rejoice and be **g**, because great is

GLADNESS (GLAD)
Ps 45: 15 Led in with joy and **g**, they enter
    51: 8 Let me hear joy and **g**;
   100: 2 Worship the LORD with **g**;
Jer 31: 13 I will turn their mourning into **g**;

GLORIFIED (GLORY)
Jn 13: 31 "Now the Son of Man is **g** and God is **g** in him.
Ro   8: 30 those he justified, he also **g**.
2Th 1: 10 he comes to be **g** in his holy people

GLORIFY (GLORY)
Ps 34: 3 **G** the LORD with me; let us exalt
    86: 12 I will **g** your name forever.
Mt   5: 16 deeds and **g** your Father in heaven.
Jn 13: 32 God will **g** the Son in himself,
    17: 1 **G** your Son, that your Son may **g**

GLORIOUS (GLORY)

Ps	45:	13	All **g** is the princess within her
	111:	3	**G** and majestic are his deeds,
	145:	5	They speak of the **g** splendor
Isa	4:	2	the LORD will be beautiful and **g**,
	12:	5	LORD, for he has done **g** things;
	42:	21	to make his law great and **g**.
	63:	15	from your lofty throne, holy and **g**.
Mt	19:	28	Son of Man sits on his **g** throne,
Lk	9:	30	and Elijah, appeared in **g** splendor,
Ac	2:	20	of the great and **g** day of the Lord.
2Co	3:	8	of the Spirit be even more **g**?
Php	3:	21	so that they will be like his **g** body.
Jude	:	24	you before his **g** presence without

GLORY (GLORIFIED GLORIFY GLORIOUS)

Ex	15:	11	awesome in **g**, working wonders?
	33:	18	said, "Now show me your **g**."
1Sa	4:	21	"The **G** has departed from Israel"
1Ch	16:	24	Declare his **g** among the nations,
	16:	28	ascribe to the LORD **g**
	29:	11	power and the **g** and the majesty
Ps	8:	5	crowned them with **g** and honor.
	19:	1	The heavens declare the **g** of God;
	24:	7	that the King of **g** may come in.
	29:	1	beings, ascribe to the LORD **g**
	34:	2	I will **g** in the LORD;
	72:	19	the whole earth be filled with his **g**.
	96:	3	Declare his **g** among the nations,
Pr	19:	11	is to one's **g** to overlook an offense.
	25:	2	It is the **g** of God to conceal
	25:	2	a matter is the **g** of kings.
Isa	6:	3	the whole earth is full of his **g**."
	42:	8	I will not yield my **g** to another
	48:	11	I will not yield my **g** to another.
Eze	43:	2	and I saw the **g** of the God of Israel
Mt	24:	30	of heaven, with power and great **g**.
	25:	31	the Son of Man comes in his **g**,
Mk	8:	38	in his Father's **g** with the holy
	13:	26	in clouds with great power and **g**.
Lk	2:	9	and the **g** of the Lord shone around
	2:	14	"**G** to God in the highest heaven,
Jn	1:	14	have seen his **g**, the **g** of the one
	17:	5	your presence with the **g** I had
	17:	24	and to see my **g**, the **g** you have
Ac	7:	2	God of **g** appeared to our father
Ro	1:	23	exchanged the **g** of the immortal
	3:	23	and fall short of the **g** of God,
	8:	18	with the **g** that will be revealed
	9:	4	theirs the divine **g**, the covenants,
1Co	10:	31	you do, do it all for the **g** of God.
	11:	7	since he is the image and **g** of God;
	11:	7	but woman is the **g** of man.
	15:	43	sown in dishonor, it is raised in **g**;
2Co	3:	10	what was glorious has no **g** now
	3:	18	faces contemplate the Lord's **g**,
	4:	17	us an eternal **g** that far outweighs
Php	4:	19	the riches of his **g** in Christ Jesus.
Col	1:	27	is Christ in you, the hope of **g**.
	3:	4	you also will appear with him in **g**.
1Ti	3:	16	on in the world, was taken up in **g**.
Titus	2:	13	appearing of the **g** of our great God
Heb	1:	3	The Son is the radiance of God's **g**
	2:	7	crowned them with **g** and honor
1Pe	1:	24	all their **g** is like the flowers
Rev	4:	11	to receive **g** and honor and power,
	21:	23	for the **g** of God gives it light,

GLUTTONS

Titus	1:	12	always liars, evil brutes, lazy **g**."

GNASHING

Mt	8:	12	will be weeping and **g** of teeth."

GNAT

Mt	23:	24	You strain out a **g** but swallow

GOAL

2Co	5:	9	So we make it our **g** to please him,
Php	3:	14	on toward the **g** to win the prize

GOAT (GOATS SCAPEGOAT)

Isa	11:	6	leopard will lie down with the **g**,

GOATS (GOAT)

Nu	7:	17	five male **g** and five male lambs

GOD (GOD'S GODLINESS GODLY GODS)

Ge	1:	1	beginning **G** created the heavens
	1:	2	of **G** was hovering over the waters.
	1:	26	Then **G** said, "Let us make
	1:	27	So **G** created mankind in his own
	1:	31	**G** saw all that he had made, and it
	2:	3	Then **G** blessed the seventh day
	2:	22	the LORD **G** made a woman
	3:	21	The LORD **G** made garments
	3:	23	So the LORD **G** banished him
	5:	22	walked faithfully with **G** 300 years
	6:	2	sons of **G** saw that the daughters
	9:	16	everlasting covenant between **G**
	17:	1	to him and said, "I am **G** Almighty;
	21:	33	name of the LORD, the Eternal **G**.
	22:	8	"**G** himself will provide the lamb
	28:	12	the angels of **G** were ascending
	32:	28	because you have struggled with **G**
	32:	30	"It is because I saw **G** face to face,
	35:	10	**G** said to him, "Your name is
	41:	51	said, "It is because **G** has made me
	50:	20	me, but **G** intended it for good
Ex	2:	24	**G** heard their groaning and he
	3:	6	he said, "I am the **G** of your father,
	3:	6	because he was afraid to look at **G**.
	6:	7	know that I am the LORD your **G**,
	8:	10	is no one like the LORD our **G**.
	13:	18	So **G** led the people around
	15:	2	He is my **G**, and I will praise him,
	17:	9	with the staff of **G** in my hands."
	19:	3	Then Moses went up to **G**,
	20:	2	"I am the LORD your **G**,
	20:	5	the LORD your **G**, am a jealous **G**,
	20:	19	But do not have **G** speak to us
	22:	28	"Do not blaspheme **G** or curse
	31:	18	stone inscribed by the finger of **G**.
	34:	6	the compassionate and gracious **G**,
	34:	14	name is Jealous, is a jealous **G**.
Lev	18:	21	not profane the name of your **G**.
	19:	2	I, the LORD your **G**, am holy.
	26:	12	walk among you and be your **G**,
Nu	22:	38	I must speak only what **G** puts
	23:	19	**G** is not human, that he should lie,
Dt	1:	17	anyone, for judgment belongs to **G**.
	3:	22	the LORD your **G** himself will
	3:	24	For what **g** is there in heaven
	4:	24	**G** is a consuming fire, a jealous **G**.
	4:	31	the LORD your **G** is a merciful **G**;
	4:	39	day that the LORD is **G** in heaven
	5:	11	the name of the LORD your **G**,
	5:	14	is a sabbath to the LORD your **G**.
	5:	26	voice of the living **G** speaking
	6:	4	The LORD our **G**, the LORD is
	6:	5	Love the LORD your **G** with all
	6:	13	Fear the LORD your **G**, serve him
	6:	16	Do not put the LORD your **G**
	7:	9	is **G**; he is the faithful **G**,
	7:	12	the LORD your **G** will keep his
	7:	21	is a great and awesome **G**.
	8:	5	the LORD your **G** disciplines you.
	10:	12	what does the LORD your **G** ask you
			but to fear the LORD your **G**,
	10:	14	To the LORD your **G** belong
	10:	17	For the LORD your **G** is **G** of gods
	11:	13	to love the LORD your **G**
	13:	3	The LORD your **G** is testing you

Dt	13: 4	It is the LORD your **G** you must
	15: 6	the LORD your **G** will bless you
	19: 9	to love the LORD your **G**
	25: 16	the LORD your **G** detests anyone
	29: 29	things belong to the LORD our **G**,
	30: 2	return to the LORD your **G**
	30: 16	today to love the LORD your **G**,
	30: 20	you may love the LORD your **G**,
	31: 6	the LORD your **G** goes with you;
	32: 3	Oh, praise the greatness of our **G**!
	32: 4	A faithful **G** who does no wrong,
	33: 27	The eternal **G** is your refuge,
Jos	1: 9	the LORD your **G** will be with you
	14: 8	the LORD my **G** wholeheartedly.
	22: 5	to love the LORD your **G**, to walk
	22: 34	that the LORD is **G**.
	23: 11	careful to love the LORD your **G**.
	23: 14	the LORD your **G** gave you has
Jdg	16: 28	Please, **G**, strengthen me just once
Ru	1: 16	be my people and your **G** my **G**.
1Sa	2: 2	there is no Rock like our **G**.
	2: 3	for the LORD is a **G** who knows,
	2: 25	**G** may mediate for the offender;
	10: 26	men whose hearts **G** had touched.
	12: 12	the LORD your **G** was your king.
	17: 26	defy the armies of the living **G**?"
	17: 46	know that there is a **G** in Israel.
	30: 6	found strength in the LORD his **G**.
2Sa	14: 14	But that is not what **G** desires;
	22: 3	my **G** is my rock, in whom I take
	22: 31	"As for **G**, his way is perfect:
1Ki	4: 29	**G** gave Solomon wisdom and very
	8: 23	there is no **G** like you in heaven
	8: 27	"But will **G** really dwell on earth?
	8: 61	committed to the LORD our **G**,
	18: 21	If the LORD is **G**, follow him;
	18: 37	are **G**, and that you are turning
	20: 28	think the LORD is a **g** the hills
2Ki	19: 15	you alone are **G** over all
1Ch	16: 35	Cry out, "Save us, **G** our Savior;
	28: 2	for the footstool of our **G**, and I
	28: 9	acknowledge the **G** of your father,
	29: 10	LORD, the **G** of our father Israel,
	29: 17	my **G**, that you test the heart and
2Ch	2: 4	for the Name of the LORD my **G**
	5: 14	the LORD filled the temple of **G**.
	6: 18	will **G** really dwell on earth
	18: 13	can tell him only what my **G** says."
	20: 6	you not the **G** who is in heaven?
	25: 8	for **G** has the power to help
	30: 9	for the LORD your **G** is gracious
	33: 12	the favor of the LORD his **G**
Ezr	8: 22	"The gracious hand of our **G** is
	9: 6	my **G**, to lift up my face to you,
	9: 13	our **G**, you have punished us less
Ne	1: 5	the great and awesome **G**,
	8: 8	from the Book of the Law of **G**,
	9: 17	But you are a forgiving **G**,
	9: 32	"Now therefore, our **G**, the great **G**,
Job	1: 1	he feared **G** and shunned evil.
	2: 10	Shall we accept good from **G**,
	4: 17	mortal be more righteous than **G**?
	5: 17	is the one whom **G** corrects;
	11: 7	you fathom the mysteries of **G**?
	19: 26	yet in my flesh I will see **G**;
	22: 13	Yet you say, 'What does **G** know?
	25: 4	a mortal be righteous before **G**?
	33: 14	For **G** does speak—now one way,
	34: 12	unthinkable that **G** would do wrong,
	36: 26	How great is **G**—
	37: 22	**G** comes in awesome majesty.
Ps	18: 2	my **G** is my rock, in whom I take
	18: 28	my **G** turns my darkness into light.
	19: 1	The heavens declare the glory of **G**;
	22: 1	My **G**, my **G**, why have you
Ps	29: 3	the **G** of glory thunders, the LORD
	31: 14	I say, "You are my **G**."
	40: 3	mouth, a hymn of praise to our **G**.
	40: 8	I desire to do your will, my **G**;
	42: 2	My soul thirsts for **G**, for the living
	42: 2	When can I go and meet with **G**?
	42: 11	Put your hope in **G**, for I will yet
	45: 6	O **G**, will last for ever and ever;
	46: 1	**G** is our refuge and strength,
	46: 10	"Be still, and know that I am **G**;
	47: 7	For **G** is the King of all the earth;
	50: 3	Our **G** comes and will not be silent
	51: 1	O **G**, according to your unfailing
	51: 10	O **G**, and renew a steadfast spirit
	51: 17	sacrifice, O **G**, is a broken spirit;
	62: 7	and my honor depend on **G**;
	65: 5	and righteous deeds, **G** our Savior,
	66: 1	Shout for joy to **G**, all the earth!
	66: 16	Come and hear, all you who fear **G**;
	68: 6	**G** sets the lonely in families,
	71: 17	my youth, **G**, you have taught
	71: 19	Who is like you, **G**?
	71: 22	harp for your faithfulness, my **G**;
	73: 26	but **G** is the strength of my heart
	77: 13	What **g** is as great as our **G**?
	78: 19	They spoke against **G**;
	81: 1	Sing for joy to **G** our strength;
	84: 2	my flesh cry out for the living **G**.
	84: 10	the house of my **G** than dwell
	86: 12	you, Lord my **G**, with all my heart;
	89: 7	of the holy ones **G** is greatly feared;
	90: 2	to everlasting you are **G**.
	91: 2	fortress, my **G**, in whom I trust."
	95: 7	for he is our **G** and we are
	100: 3	Know that the LORD is **G**. It is he
	108: 1	My heart, O **G**, is steadfast;
	113: 5	Who is like the LORD our **G**,
	139: 23	Search me, **G**, and know my heart;
Pr	3: 4	a good name in the sight of **G**
	25: 2	It is the glory of **G** to conceal
	30: 5	"Every word of **G** is flawless;
Ecc	3: 11	can fathom what **G** has done
	11: 5	cannot understand the work of **G**,
	12: 13	of the matter: Fear **G** and keep his
Isa	9: 6	Mighty **G**, Everlasting Father,
	37: 16	you alone are **G** over all
	40: 3	in the desert a highway for our **G**.
	40: 8	the word of our **G** endures forever."
	40: 28	The LORD is the everlasting **G**,
	41: 10	not be dismayed, for I am your **G**.
	44: 6	apart from me there is no **G**.
	52: 7	who say to Zion, "Your **G** reigns!"
	55: 7	and to our **G**, for he will freely
	57: 21	says my **G**, "for the wicked."
	59: 2	have separated you from your **G**;
	61: 10	my soul rejoices in my **G**.
	62: 5	so will your **G** rejoice over you.
Jer	23: 23	"Am I only a **G** nearby,"
	31: 33	I will be their **G**, and they will be
	32: 27	the LORD, the **G** of all mankind.
Eze	28: 13	You were in Eden, the garden of **G**;
Da	3: 17	the **G** we serve is able to deliver us
	9: 4	the great and awesome **G**,
Hos	12: 6	But you must return to your **G**;
Joel	2: 13	Return to the LORD your **G**, for he
Am	4: 12	Israel, prepare to meet your **G**."
Mic	6: 8	and to walk humbly with your **G**.
Na	1: 2	is a jealous and avenging **G**;
Zec	14: 5	Then the LORD my **G** will come,
Mal	3: 8	"Will a mere mortal rob **G**?
Mt	1: 23	(which means "**G** with us").
	5: 8	pure in heart, for they will see **G**.
	6: 24	You cannot serve both **G**
	19: 6	Therefore what **G** has joined
	19: 26	but with **G** all things are possible."

Mt	22: 21	Caesar's, and to **G** what is God's."
	22: 37	" 'Love the Lord your **G** with all
	27: 46	(which means "My **G**, my **G**,
Mk	12: 29	The Lord our **G**, the Lord is one.
	16: 19	*at the right hand of* **G**.
Lk	1: 37	For no word from **G** will ever fail."
	1: 47	my spirit rejoices in **G** my Savior,
	10: 9	'The kingdom of **G** has come near
	10: 27	" 'Love the Lord your **G** with all
	18: 19	"No one is good—except **G** alone.
Jn	1: 1	and the Word was with **G**, and the Word was **G**.
	1: 18	No one has ever seen **G**, but
	1: 18	who is himself **G** and is in closest
	3: 16	For **G** so loved the world that he
	4: 24	**G** is spirit, and his worshipers must
	7: 17	to do the will of **G** will find
	14: 1	You believe in **G**;
	20: 28	said to him, "My Lord and my **G**!"
Ac	2: 24	But **G** raised him from the dead,
	5: 4	lied just to human beings but to **G**."
	5: 29	"We must obey **G** rather than
	7: 55	to heaven and saw the glory of **G**,
	17: 23	inscription: TO AN UNKNOWN **G**.
	20: 27	to you the whole will of **G**.
	20: 32	"Now I commit you to **G**
Ro	1: 17	righteousness of **G** is revealed—
	2: 11	For **G** does not show favoritism.
	3: 4	Let **G** be true, and every human
	3: 23	and fall short of the glory of **G**,
	4: 24	**G** will credit righteousness—
	5: 8	**G** demonstrates his own love for us
	6: 23	the gift of **G** is eternal life in Christ
	8: 28	in all things **G** works for the good
	11: 22	the kindness and sternness of **G**:
	14: 12	give an account of ourselves to **G**.
1Co	1: 20	not **G** made foolish the wisdom
	2: 9	the things **G** has prepared for those
	3: 6	it, but **G** has been making it grow.
	6: 20	Therefore honor **G** with your
	7: 24	they were in when **G** called them.
	8: 8	food does not bring us near to **G**;
	10: 13	**G** is faithful; he will not let you
	10: 31	you do, do it all for the glory of **G**.
	14: 33	For **G** is not a **G** of disorder
	15: 28	him, so that **G** may be all in all.
2Co	1: 9	not rely on ourselves but on **G**,
	2: 14	But thanks be to **G**, who always
	3: 5	our competence comes from **G**.
	4: 7	this all-surpassing power is from **G**
	5: 19	that **G** was reconciling the world
	5: 21	become the righteousness of **G**.
	6: 16	we are the temple of the living **G**.
	9: 7	for **G** loves a cheerful giver.
	9: 8	**G** is able to bless you abundantly,
Gal	2: 6	**G** does not show favoritism—
	6: 7	**G** cannot be mocked.
Eph	2: 10	**G** prepared in advance for us
	4: 6	one **G** and Father of all, who is
Php	2: 6	being in very nature **G**, did not consider equality with **G**
	4: 19	And my **G** will meet all your needs
1Th	2: 4	not trying to please people but **G**,
	4: 7	For **G** did not call us to be impure,
	4: 9	yourselves have been taught by **G**
	5: 9	For **G** did not appoint us to suffer
1Ti	2: 5	there is one **G** and one mediator
	4: 4	For everything **G** created is good,
	5: 4	for this is pleasing to **G**.
Titus	2: 13	of the glory of our great **G**
Heb	1: 1	the past **G** spoke to our ancestors
	4: 12	For the word of **G** is alive
	6: 10	**G** is not unjust; he will not forget
	10: 31	fall into the hands of the living **G**.
	11: 6	faith it is impossible to please **G**,

Heb	12: 10	but **G** disciplines us for our good,
	12: 29	for our "**G** is a consuming fire."
	13: 15	us continually offer to **G** a sacrifice
Jas	1: 13	For **G** cannot be tempted by evil,
	2: 19	You believe that there is one **G**.
	2: 23	"Abraham believed **G**, and it was
	4: 4	the world becomes an enemy of **G**.
	4: 8	Come near to **G** and he will come
1Pe	4: 11	who speaks the very words of **G**.
2Pe	1: 21	from **G** as they were carried along
1Jn	1: 5	him and declare to you: **G** is light;
	2: 5	love for **G** is truly made complete
	3: 20	that **G** is greater than our hearts,
	4: 7	another, for love comes from **G**.
	4: 7	has been born of **G** and knows **G**.
	4: 9	This is how **G** showed his love
	4: 11	Dear friends, since **G** so loved us,
	4: 12	No one has ever seen **G**; but if we
	4: 16	Whoever lives in love lives in **G**,
Rev	4: 8	holy is the Lord **G** Almighty,'
	7: 17	**G** will wipe away every tear
	19: 6	For our Lord **G** Almighty reigns.

GOD-BREATHED (BREATHED)

2Ti	3: 16	All Scripture is **G** and is useful

GODLINESS (GOD)

1Ti	2: 2	quiet lives in all **g** and holiness.
	4: 8	value, but **g** has value for all things,
	6: 6	**g** with contentment is great gain.
	6: 11	and pursue righteousness, **g**, faith,

GODLY (GOD)

2Co	7: 10	**G** sorrow brings repentance
	11: 2	jealous for you with a **g** jealousy.
2Ti	3: 12	live a **g** life in Christ Jesus will be
2Pe	3: 11	You ought to live holy and **g** lives

GOD'S (GOD)

2Ch	20: 15	For the battle is not yours, but **G**.
Job	37: 14	stop and consider **G** wonders.
Ps	52: 8	I trust in **G** unfailing love for ever
	69: 30	I will praise **G** name in song
Mk	3: 35	Whoever does **G** will is my brother
Jn	10: 36	because I said, 'I am **G** Son'?
Ro	2: 3	think you will escape **G** judgment?
	2: 4	that **G** kindness is intended
	3: 3	nullify **G** faithfulness?
	7: 22	my inner being I delight in **G** law;
	9: 16	desire or effort, but on **G** mercy.
	11: 29	for **G** gifts and his call are
	12: 2	test and approve what **G** will is—
	13: 6	for the authorities are **G** servants,
1Co	7: 19	Keeping **G** commands is what
2Co	6: 2	now is the time of **G** favor, now is
Eph	1: 7	with the riches of **G** grace
	5: 1	Follow **G** example, therefore,
1Th	4: 3	It is **G** will that you should be
	5: 18	for this is **G** will for you in Christ
1Ti	6: 1	so that **G** name and our teaching
2Ti	2: 19	**G** solid foundation stands firm,
Titus	1: 7	an overseer manages **G** household,
Heb	1: 3	The Son is the radiance of **G** glory
	9: 24	to appear for us in **G** presence,
	11: 3	was formed at **G** command,
1Pe	2: 15	For it is **G** will that by doing good
	3: 4	which is of great worth in **G** sight.

GODS (GOD)

Ex	20: 3	shall have no other **g** before me.
Ac	19: 26	by human hands are no **g** at all.

GOLD

Job	23: 10	tested me, I will come forth as **g**.
Ps	19: 10	precious than **g**, than much pure **g**;
	119:127	love your commands more than **g**,
Pr	22: 1	esteemed is better than silver or **g**.

GOLGOTHA

Jn 19: 17 (which in Aramaic is called **G**).

GOLIATH

Philistine giant killed by David (1Sa 17; 21:9).

GOOD

Ge	1: 4	God saw that the light was **g**,
	1: 31	he had made, and it was very **g**.
	2: 18	"It is not **g** for the man to be alone.
	50: 20	God intended it for **g**
Job	2: 10	Shall we accept **g** from God,
Ps	14: 1	there is no one who does **g**.
	34: 8	Taste and see that the LORD is **g**;
	37: 3	Trust in the LORD and do **g**;
	84: 11	no **g** thing does he withhold
	86: 5	are forgiving and **g**,
	103: 5	your desires with **g** things so
	119: 68	You are **g**, and what you do is **g**;
	133: 1	How **g** and pleasant it is
	147: 1	How **g** it is to sing praises to our
Pr	3: 4	and a **g** name in the sight of God
	11: 27	Whoever seeks **g** finds favor,
	13: 21	are rewarded with **g** things.
	17: 22	A cheerful heart is **g** medicine,
	18: 22	He who finds a wife finds what is **g**
	22: 1	A **g** name is more desirable than
	31: 12	She brings him **g**, not harm,
Isa	5: 20	Woe to those who call evil **g** and **g**
	52: 7	the feet of those who bring **g** news,
Jer	6: 16	ask where the **g** way is, and walk
Mic	6: 8	shown you, O mortal, what is **g**.
Mt	5: 45	sun to rise on the evil and the **g**,
	7: 17	Likewise, every **g** tree bears **g** fruit,
	12: 35	A **g** man brings **g** things out of the **g**
	19: 17	"There is only One who is **g**.
	25: 21	'Well done, **g** and faithful servant!
Mk	3: 4	to do **g** or to do evil, to save life
	8: 36	What **g** is it for someone to gain
Lk	6: 27	do **g** to those who hate you,
Jn	10: 11	"I am the **g** shepherd. The **g**
Ro	8: 28	for the **g** of those who love him,
	10: 15	feet of those who bring **g** news!"
	12: 9	Hate what is evil; cling to what is **g**.
1Co	10: 24	their own **g**, but the **g** of others.
	15: 33	company corrupts **g** character."
2Co	9: 8	you will abound in every **g** work.
Gal	6: 9	us not become weary in doing **g**,
	6: 10	let us do **g** to all people,
Eph	2: 10	in Christ Jesus to do **g** works,
Php	1: 6	he who began a **g** work in you will
1Th	5: 21	test them all; hold on to what is **g**,
2Th	3: 13	never tire of doing what is **g**.
1Ti	3: 7	have a **g** reputation with outsiders,
	4: 4	For everything God created is **g**,
	6: 12	Fight the **g** fight of the faith.
	6: 18	do **g**, to be rich in **g** deeds,
2Ti	3: 17	equipped for every **g** work.
	4: 7	I have fought the **g** fight, I have
Heb	12: 10	but God disciplines us for our **g**,
1Pe	2: 3	you have tasted that the Lord is **g**.
	2: 12	Live such **g** lives among the pagans

GOSPEL

Ro	1: 16	For I am not ashamed of the **g**,
	15: 16	duty of proclaiming the **g** of God,
1Co	1: 17	to baptize, but to preach the **g**—
	9: 16	Woe to me if I do not preach the **g**!
	15: 1	to remind you of the **g** I preached
Gal	1: 7	trying to pervert the **g** of Christ.
Php	1: 27	a manner worthy of the **g** of Christ.
	1: 27	as one for the faith of the **g**

GOSSIP

Pr	11: 13	A **g** betrays a confidence,
	16: 28	and a **g** separates close friends.

Pr	18: 8	of a **g** are like choice morsels;
	26: 20	without a **g** a quarrel dies down.
2Co	12: 20	slander, **g**, arrogance and disorder.

GOVERNED

Ro	8: 6	the mind **g** by the Spirit is life

GRACE (GRACIOUS)

Ps	45: 2	lips have been anointed with **g**,
Jn	1: 17	**g** and truth came through Jesus
Ac	20: 32	to God and to the word of his **g**,
Ro	3: 24	by his **g** through the redemption
	5: 15	that came by the **g** of the one man,
	5: 17	God's abundant provision of **g**
	5: 20	increased, **g** increased all the more,
	6: 14	are not under the law, but under **g**.
	11: 6	if it were, **g** would no longer be **g**.
2Co	6: 1	you not to receive God's **g** in vain.
	8: 9	you know the **g** of our Lord Jesus
	12: 9	to me, "My **g** is sufficient for you,
Gal	2: 21	I do not set aside the **g** of God,
	5: 4	you have fallen away from **g**.
Eph	1: 7	with the riches of God's **g**
	2: 5	it is by **g** you have been saved.
	2: 7	the incomparable riches of his **g**,
	2: 8	For it is by **g** you have been saved,
Php	1: 7	all of you share in God's **g** with me.
Col	4: 6	conversation be always full of **g**,
2Th	2: 16	**g** gave us eternal encouragement
2Ti	2: 1	be strong in the **g** that is in Christ
Titus	2: 11	For the **g** of God has appeared
	3: 7	having been justified by his **g**,
Heb	2: 9	the **g** of God he might taste death
	4: 16	approach God's throne of **g**
	4: 16	**g** to help us in our time of need.
Jas	4: 6	But he gives us more **g**. That is why
2Pe	3: 18	grow in the **g** and knowledge of

GRACIOUS (GRACE)

Nu	6: 25	face shine on you and be **g** to you;
Isa	30: 18	the LORD longs to be **g** to you;

GRAIN

Ecc	11: 1	Ship your **g** across the sea;
1Co	9: 9	an ox while it is treading out the **g**."

GRANTED

Php	1: 29	For it has been **g** to you on behalf

GRASS

Ps	103: 15	The life of mortals is like **g**,
1Pe	1: 24	the **g** withers and the flowers fall,

GRAVE (GRAVES)

Pr	7: 27	Her house is a highway to the **g**,
Hos	13: 14	Where, O **g**, is your destruction?

GRAVES (GRAVE)

Jn	5: 28	are in their **g** will hear his voice
Ro	3: 13	"Their throats are open **g**;

GREAT (GREATER GREATEST GREATNESS)

Ge	12: 2	"I will make you into a **g** nation,
Dt	10: 17	gods and Lord of lords, the **g** God,
2Sa	22: 36	your help has made me **g**.
Ps	19: 11	in keeping them there is **g** reward.
	89: 1	sing of the LORD's **g** love forever;
	103: 11	so **g** is his love for those who fear
	108: 4	For **g** is your love, higher than
	119:165	**G** peace have those who love your
	145: 3	**G** is the LORD and most worthy
Pr	23: 24	father of a righteous child has **g** joy
Isa	42: 21	his righteousness to make his law **g**
La	3: 23	**g** is your faithfulness.
Mk	10: 43	become **g** among you must be your
Lk	21: 27	in a cloud with power and **g** glory.
1Ti	6: 6	with contentment is **g** gain.

Titus 2: 13   appearing of the glory of our **g** God
Heb 2: 3   if we ignore so **g** a salvation?
1Jn 3: 1   See what **g** love the Father has

GREATER (GREAT)
Mk 12: 31   is no commandment **g** than these."
Jn 1: 50   You will see **g** things than that."
15: 13   **G** love has no one than this:
1Co 12: 31   Now eagerly desire the **g** gifts.
Heb 11: 26   as of **g** value than the treasures
1Jn 3: 20   that God is **g** than our hearts,
4: 4   is in you is **g** than the one who is

GREATEST (GREAT)
Mt 22: 38   is the first and **g** commandment.
Lk 9: 48   least among you all who is the **g**."
1Co 13: 13   But the **g** of these is love.

GREATNESS (GREAT)
Ps 145: 3   his **g** no one can fathom.
150: 2   praise him for his surpassing **g**.
Isa 9: 7   the **g** of his government and peace
63: 1   forward in the **g** of his strength?

GREED (GREEDY)
Lk 12: 15   guard against all kinds of **g**;
Ro 1: 29   wickedness, evil, **g** and depravity.
Eph 5: 3   or of **g**, because these are improper
Col 3: 5   desires and **g**, which is idolatry.
2Pe 2: 14   they are experts in **g**—

GREEDY (GREED)
Pr 15: 27   The **g** bring ruin to their
1Co 6: 10   thieves nor the **g** nor drunkards
Eph 5: 5   No immoral, impure or **g** person—

GREEN
Ps 23: 2   makes me lie down in **g** pastures,

GREW (GROW)
Lk 2: 52   And Jesus **g** in wisdom and stature,
Ac 16: 5   in the faith and **g** daily in numbers.

GRIEF (GRIEVE)
Ps 10: 14   you consider their **g** and take it
Pr 14: 13   ache, and rejoicing may end in **g**.
La 3: 32   Though he brings **g**, he will show
Jn 16: 20   grieve, but your **g** will turn to joy.
1Pe 1: 6   have had to suffer **g** in all kinds

GRIEVE (GRIEF)
Eph 4: 30   do not **g** the Holy Spirit of God,
1Th 4: 13   so that you do not **g** like the rest

GROUND
Ge 3: 17   it,' "Cursed is the **g** because of you;
Ex 3: 5   where you are standing is holy **g**."
Eph 6: 13   you may be able to stand your **g**,

GROW (GREW)
Pr 13: 11   money little by little makes it **g**.
1Co 3: 6   it, but God has been making it **g**.
2Pe 3: 18   But **g** in the grace and knowledge

GRUMBLE (GRUMBLING)
1Co 10: 10   do not **g**, as some of them did—
Jas 5: 9   Don't **g** against one another,

GRUMBLING (GRUMBLE)
Jn 6: 43   "Stop **g** among yourselves,"
1Pe 4: 9   hospitality to one another without **g**.

GUARANTEEING (GUARANTOR)
2Co 1: 22   as a deposit, **g** what is to come.
Eph 1: 14   is a deposit **g** our inheritance until

GUARANTOR (GUARANTEEING)
Heb 7: 22   Jesus has become the **g** of a better

GUARD (GUARDIAN, GUARDIAN-REDEEMER)
Ps 141: 3   Set a **g** over my mouth, LORD;
Pr 4: 23   Above all else, **g** your heart,
13: 3   Those who **g** their lips preserve
21: 23   Those who **g** their mouths and
Isa 52: 12   God of Israel will be your rear **g**.
Mk 13: 33   Be on **g**! Be alert! You do not know
1Co 16: 13   Be on your **g**; stand firm
Php 4: 7   will **g** your hearts and your minds
1Ti 6: 20   **g** what has been entrusted to your

GUARDIAN (GUARD)
Gal 3: 25   come, we are no longer under a **g**.

GUARDIAN-REDEEMER (GUARD)
Ru 3: 9   since you are a **g** of our family."

GUIDE
Ex 13: 21   of cloud to **g** them on their way
15: 13   In your strength you will **g** them
Ne 9: 19   cloud did not fail to **g** them on
Ps 25: 5   **G** me in your truth and teach me,
48: 14   he will be our **g** even to the end.
67: 4   and **g** the nations of the earth.
73: 24   You **g** me with your counsel,
139: 10   even there your hand will **g** me,
Pr 6: 22   When you walk, they will **g** you;
Isa 58: 11   The LORD will **g** you always;
Jn 16: 13   he will **g** you into all the truth.

GUILTY
Ex 34: 7   does not leave the **g** unpunished;
Jn 8: 46   Can any of you prove me **g** of sin?
Heb 10: 22   to cleanse us from a **g** conscience
Jas 2: 10   at just one point is **g** of breaking all

HADES
Mt 16: 18   the gates of **H** will not overcome it.
Lk 16: 23   In **H**, where he was in torment,

HAGAR
Servant of Sarah, wife of Abraham, mother of Ishmael (Ge 16:1–6; 25:12). Driven away by Sarah while pregnant (Ge 16:5–16); after birth of Isaac (Ge 21:9–21; Gal 4:21–31).

HAGGAI
Post-exilic prophet who encouraged rebuilding of the temple (Ezr 5:1; 6:14; Hag 1–2).

HAIR (HAIRS)
Lk 21: 18   not a **h** of your head will perish.
1Co 11: 6   for a woman to have her **h** cut off

HAIRS (HAIR)
Mt 10: 30   even the very **h** of your head are all

HALLELUJAH
Rev 19: 1,   multitude in heaven shouting: "**H**!

HALLOWED (HOLY)
Mt 6: 9   Father in heaven, **h** be your name,

HAND (HANDIWORK HANDS)
Ps 16: 8   With him at my right **h**, I will not
37: 24   the LORD upholds him with his **h**.
139: 10   even there your **h** will guide me,
Ecc 9: 10   Whatever your **h** finds to do, do it
Mt 6: 3   not let your left **h** know what your
right **h** is doing,
Jn 10: 28   one will snatch them out of my **h**.
1Co 12: 15   say, "Because I am not a **h**, I do not

HANDIWORK (HAND WORK)
Eph 2: 10   For we are God's **h**,

HANDS (HAND)
Ps 22: 16   they pierce my **h** and my feet.
24: 4   one who has clean **h** and a pure

Ps	31:	5	Into your **h** I commit my spirit;
	31:	15	My times are in your **h**;
Pr	10:	4	but diligent **h** bring wealth.
	31:	20	and extends her **h** to the needy.
Isa	55:	12	trees of the field will clap their **h**.
	65:	2	out my **h** to an obstinate people,
Lk	23:	46	into your **h** I commit my spirit."
1Th	4:	11	business and work with your **h**,
1Ti	2:	8	lifting up holy **h** without anger
	5:	22	not be hasty in the laying on of **h**,

HANNAH

Wife of Elkanah, mother of Samuel (1Sa 1). Prayer at dedication of Samuel (1Sa 2:1–10). Blessed (1Sa 2:18–21).

HAPPY

Ps	68:	3	may they be **h** and joyful.
Pr	15:	13	A **h** heart makes the face cheerful,
Ecc	3:	12	better for people than to be **h**
Jas	5:	13	Is anyone **h**? Let them sing songs

HARD (HARDEN HARDSHIP)

Ge	18:	14	Is anything too **h** for the LORD?
Ps	118:	5	When **h** pressed, I cried
Mt	19:	23	it is **h** for someone who is rich
1Co	4:	12	We work **h** with our own hands.
1Th	5:	12	those who work **h** among you,

HARDEN (HARD)

| Ro | 9: | 18 | he hardens whom he wants to **h**. |
| Heb | 3: | 8 | do not **h** your hearts as you did |

HARDHEARTED (HEART)

| Dt | 15: | 7 | do not be **h** or tightfisted toward |

HARDSHIP (HARD)

Ro	8:	35	Shall trouble or **h** or persecution
2Ti	4:	5	endure **h**, do the work
Heb	12:	7	Endure **h** as discipline;

HARM

Ps	121:	6	the sun will not **h** you by day,
Pr	3:	29	not plot **h** against your neighbor,
	31:	12	good, not **h**, all the days of her life.
Ro	13:	10	Love does no **h** to a neighbor.
1Jn	5:	18	and the evil one cannot **h** them.

HARMONY

| Ro | 12: | 16 | Live in **h** with one another. |
| 2Co | 6: | 15 | What **h** is there between Christ |

HARVEST

Mt	9:	37	"The **h** is plentiful but the workers
Jn	4:	35	at the fields! They are ripe for **h**.
Gal	6:	9	at the proper time we will reap a **h**
Heb	12:	11	it produces a **h** of righteousness

HASTE (HASTY)

| Pr | 21: | 5 | lead to profit as surely as **h** leads |
| | 29: | 20 | you see someone who speaks in **h**? |

HASTY (HASTE)

Pr	19:	2	how much more will **h** feet miss
Ecc	5:	2	do not be **h** in your heart to utter
1Ti	5:	22	Do not be **h** in the laying

HATE (HATED HATES HATRED)

Lev	19:	17	" 'Do not **h** a fellow Israelite
Ps	5:	5	You **h** all who do wrong;
	45:	7	righteousness and **h** wickedness;
	97:	10	those who love the LORD **h** evil,
	139:	21	Do I not **h** those who **h** you,
Pr	8:	13	To fear the LORD is to **h** evil; I **h**
Am	5:	15	**H** evil, love good;
Mt	5:	43	your neighbor and **h** your enemy.'
Lk	6:	27	do good to those who **h** you,
Ro	12:	9	**H** what is evil; cling to what is

HATED (HATE)

Mt	10:	22	be **h** by everyone because of me,
Ro	9:	13	"Jacob I loved, but Esau I **h**."
Eph	5:	29	all, no one ever **h** their own body,
Heb	1:	9	righteousness and **h** wickedness;

HATES (HATE)

Pr	6:	16	There are six things the LORD **h**,
	13:	24	spares the rod **h** their children,
Mal	2:	16	"The man who **h** and divorces his
Jn	3:	20	Everyone who does evil **h** the light,
1Jn	2:	9	to be in the light but **h** a brother

HATRED (HATE)

| Pr | 10: | 12 | **H** stirs up conflict, but love covers |

HAUGHTY

| Pr | 16: | 18 | destruction, a **h** spirit before a fall. |

HAY

| 1Co | 3: | 12 | costly stones, wood, **h** or straw, |

HEAD (HEADS HOTHEADED)

Ge	3:	15	he will crush your **h**, and you will
Ps	23:	5	You anoint my **h** with oil;
Pr	25:	22	will heap burning coals on his **h**,
Isa	59:	17	the helmet of salvation on his **h**;
Mt	8:	20	of Man has no place to lay his **h**."
Ro	12:	20	will heap burning coals on his **h**."
1Co	11:	3	the **h** of every man is Christ, and
			the **h** of the woman is man, and
			the **h** of Christ is God.
	12:	21	And the **h** cannot say to the feet,
Eph	5:	23	the husband is the **h** of the
			wife as Christ is the **h**
2Ti	4:	5	keep your **h** in all situations,
Rev	19:	12	fire, and on his **h** are many crowns.

HEADS (HEAD)

| Lev | 26: | 13 | you to walk with **h** held high. |
| Isa | 35: | 10 | everlasting joy will crown their **h**. |

HEAL (HEALED HEALING HEALS)

2Ch	7:	14	their sin and will **h** their land.
Ps	41:	4	**h** me, for I have sinned against
Mt	10:	8	**H** the sick, raise the dead,
Lk	4:	23	'Physician, **h** yourself!'
	5:	17	Lord was with Jesus to **h** the sick.

HEALED (HEAL)

Isa	53:	5	him, and by his wounds we are **h**.
Mt	9:	22	he said, "your faith has **h** you."
	14:	36	and all who touched it were **h**.
Ac	4:	10	that this man stands before you **h**.
	14:	9	saw that he had faith to be **h**
Jas	5:	16	each other so that you may be **h**.
1Pe	2:	24	"by his wounds you have been **h**."

HEALING (HEAL)

Eze	47:	12	for food and their leaves for **h**."
Mal	4:	2	righteousness will rise with **h** in its
1Co	12:	9	to another gifts of **h** by that one
	12:	30	Do all have gifts of **h**? Do all speak
Rev	22:	2	the tree are for the **h** of the
			nations.

HEALS (HEAL)

Ex	15:	26	for I am the LORD, who **h** you."
Ps	103:	3	your sins and **h** all your diseases,
	147:	3	He **h** the brokenhearted and binds

HEALTH (HEALTHY)

| Pr | 3: | 8 | This will bring **h** to your body |
| | 15: | 30 | good news gives **h** to the bones. |

HEALTHY (HEALTH)

| Mk | 2: | 17 | "It is not the **h** who need a doctor, |

HEAR (HEARD HEARING HEARS)

Dt	6:	4	**H**, O Israel: The Lᴏʀᴅ our God,
	31:	13	law, must **h** it and learn to fear
2Ch	7:	14	then I will **h** from heaven,
Ps	94:	9	he who fashioned the ear not **h**?
Isa	29:	18	day the deaf will **h** the words
	65:	24	they are still speaking I will **h**.
Mt	11:	15	Whoever has ears, let them **h**.
Jn	8:	47	The reason you do not **h** is that
2Ti	4:	3	what their itching ears want to **h**.

HEARD (HEAR)

Job	42:	5	My ears had **h** of you but now my
Isa	66:	8	Who has ever **h** of such things?
Mt	5:	21	"You have **h** that it was said
	5:	27	"You have **h** that it was said,
	5:	33	you have **h** that it was said
	5:	38	"You have **h** that it was said,
	5:	43	"You have **h** that it was said,
1Co	2:	9	what no ear has **h**, and what no
1Th	2:	13	which you **h** from us, you accepted
2Ti	1:	13	What you **h** from me, keep as
Jas	1:	25	not forgetting what they have **h**,

HEARING (HEAR)

Ro	10:	17	faith comes from **h** the message,

HEARS (HEAR)

Jn	5:	24	whoever **h** my word and believes
1Jn	5:	14	according to his will, he **h** us.
Rev	3:	20	If anyone **h** my voice and opens

HEART (BROKENHEARTED HARDHEARTED HEARTS WHOLEHEARTEDLY)

Ex	25:	2	everyone whose **h** prompts them
Lev	19:	17	not hate a fellow Israelite in your **h**.
Dt	4:	29	him if you seek him with all your **h**
	6:	5	Lᴏʀᴅ your God with all your **h**
	10:	12	Lᴏʀᴅ your God with all your **h**
	15:	10	and do so without a grudging **h**;
	30:	6	you may love him with all your **h**
	30:	10	Lᴏʀᴅ your God with all your **h**
Jos	22:	5	and to serve him with all your **h**
1Sa	13:	14	sought out a man after his own **h**
	16:	7	but the Lᴏʀᴅ looks at the **h**."
2Ki	23:	3	and decrees with all his **h** and
1Ch	28:	9	for the Lᴏʀᴅ searches every **h**
2Ch	7:	16	eyes and my **h** will always be there.
Job	22:	22	and lay up his words in your **h**.
	37:	1	"At this my **h** pounds and leaps
Ps	14:	1	says in his **h**, "There is no God."
	19:	14	this meditation of my **h** be pleasing
	37:	4	will give you the desires of your **h**.
	45:	1	My **h** is stirred by a noble theme as
	51:	10	Create in me a pure **h**, O God,
	51:	17	a broken and contrite **h** you, God,
	66:	18	If I had cherished sin in my **h**,
	86:	11	give me an undivided **h**, that I may
	119:	11	in my **h** that I might not sin against
	139:	23	Search me, God, and know my **h**;
Pr	3:	5	Trust in the Lᴏʀᴅ with all your **h**
	4:	21	sight, keep them within your **h**;
	4:	23	guard your **h**, for everything you
	7:	3	write them on the tablet of your **h**.
	13:	12	Hope deferred makes the **h** sick,
	14:	13	Even in laughter the **h** may ache,
	15:	30	eyes brings joy to the **h**, and good
	17:	22	A cheerful **h** is good medicine,
	24:	17	stumble, do not let your **h** rejoice,
	27:	19	the face, so one's life reflects the **h**.
Ecc	3:	11	also set eternity in the human **h**;
	8:	5	the wise **h** will know the proper
SS	4:	9	You have stolen my **h**, my sister,
Isa	40:	11	and carries them close to his **h**;
	57:	15	and to revive the **h** of the contrite.
Jer	17:	9	The **h** is deceitful above all things
	29:	13	when you seek me with all your **h**.

Eze	36:	26	I will give you a new **h** and put
Mt	5:	8	Blessed are the pure in **h**, for they
	6:	21	treasure is, there your **h** will be
	12:	34	mouth speaks what the **h** is full of.
	22:	37	the Lord your God with all your **h**
Lk	6:	45	mouth speaks what the **h** is full of.
Ro	2:	29	is circumcision of the **h**,
	10:	10	it is with your **h** that you believe
Eph	5:	19	music from your **h** to the Lord,
	6:	6	doing the will of God from your **h**.
Col	3:	23	you do, work at it with all your **h**,
1Pe	1:	22	one another deeply, from the **h**.

HEARTS (HEART)

Dt	11:	18	Fix these words of mine in your **h**
1Ki	8:	39	do, since you know their **h** (for you
	8:	61	may your **h** be fully committed
Ps	62:	8	pour out your **h** to him, for God is
Jer	31:	33	their minds and write it on their **h**.
Lk	16:	15	of others, but God knows your **h**.
	24:	32	"Were not our **h** burning within us
Jn	14:	1	"Do not let your **h** be troubled.
Ac	15:	9	for he purified their **h** by faith.
Ro	2:	15	of the law are written on their **h**,
1Co	14:	25	the secrets of their **h** are laid bare.
2Co	3:	2	written on our **h**, known and read
	3:	3	of stone but on tablets of human **h**.
	4:	6	shine in our **h** to give us the light
Eph	3:	17	may dwell in your **h** through faith.
Col	3:	1	Christ, set your **h** on things above,
Heb	3:	8	do not harden your **h** as you did
	10:	16	I will put my laws in their **h**, and I
1Jn	3:	20	that God is greater than our **h**,

HEAT

2Pe	3:	12	and the elements will melt in the **h**.

HEAVEN (HEAVENLY HEAVENS)

Ge	14:	19	Most High, Creator of **h** and earth.
1Ki	8:	27	even the highest **h**, cannot contain
2Ki	2:	1	take Elijah up to **h** in a whirlwind,
2Ch	7:	14	then I will hear from **h**, and I will
Isa	14:	12	How you have fallen from **h**,
	66:	1	"**H** is my throne, and the earth is
Da	7:	13	man, coming with the clouds of **h**.
Mt	6:	9	" 'Our Father in **h**, hallowed be
	6:	20	up for yourselves treasures in **h**,
	16:	19	you the keys of the kingdom of **h**,
	16:	19	bind on earth will be bound in **h**,
	19:	23	is rich to enter the kingdom of **h**.
	24:	35	**H** and earth will pass away, but my
	26:	64	and coming on the clouds of **h**."
	28:	18	"All authority in **h** and on earth has
Mk	16:	19	*was taken up into* **h**
Lk	15:	7	**h** over one sinner who repents
	18:	22	and you will have treasure in **h**.
Ro	10:	6	heart, 'Who will ascend into **h**?' "
2Co	5:	1	an eternal house in **h**, not built
	12:	2	ago was caught up to the third **h**.
Php	2:	10	in **h** and on earth and under
	3:	20	But our citizenship is in **h**.
1Th	1:	10	and to wait for his Son from **h**,
Heb	8:	5	a copy and shadow of what is in **h**.
	9:	24	he entered **h** itself, now to appear
2Pe	3:	13	we are looking forward to a new **h**
Rev	21:	1	I saw "a new **h** and a new earth,"

HEAVENLY (HEAVEN)

2Co	5:	2	clothed instead with our **h** dwelling,
Eph	1:	3	who has blessed us in the **h** realms
	1:	20	at his right hand in the **h** realms,
2Ti	4:	18	bring me safely to his **h** kingdom.
Heb	12:	22	of the living God, the **h** Jerusalem.

HEAVENS (HEAVEN)

Ge	1:	1	In the beginning God created the **h**
1Ki	8:	27	The **h**, even the highest heaven,

2Ch	2: 6	since the **h**, even the highest **h**,
Ps	8: 3	When I consider your **h**, the work
	19: 1	The **h** declare the glory of God;
	102: 25	the **h** are the work of your hands.
	108: 4	is your love, higher than the **h**;
	119: 89	it stands firm in the **h**.
	139: 8	If I go up to the **h**, you are there;
Isa	51: 6	the **h** will vanish like smoke,
	55: 9	"As the **h** are higher than the earth,
	65: 17	will create new **h** and a new earth.
Joel	2: 30	I will show wonders in the **h**
Eph	4: 10	ascended higher than all the **h**,
2Pe	3: 10	The **h** will disappear with a roar;

HEBREW
Ge	14: 13	and reported this to Abram the **H**.

HEEDS
Pr	13: 1	A wise son **h** his father's
	13: 18	whoever **h** correction is honored.
	15: 5	but whoever **h** correction shows
	15: 32	but the one who **h** correction gains

HEEL
Ge	3: 15	head, and you will strike his **h**."

HEIRS (INHERIT)
Ro	8: 17	**h** of God and co-heirs with Christ,
Gal	3: 29	and **h** according to the promise.
Eph	3: 6	gospel the Gentiles are **h** together
1Pe	3: 7	as **h** with you of the gracious gift

HELL
Mt	5: 22	will be in danger of the fire of **h**.
2Pe	2: 4	but sent them to **h**, putting them

HELMET
Isa	59: 17	and the **h** of salvation on his head;
Eph	6: 17	Take the **h** of salvation
1Th	5: 8	and the hope of salvation as a **h**.

HELP (HELPED HELPER HELPING HELPS)
2Sa	22: 36	You make your saving **h** my shield;
Ps	18: 6	I cried to my God for **h**.
	30: 2	called to you for **h**, and you healed
	46: 1	an ever-present **h** in trouble.
	70: 4	long for your saving **h** always say,
	79: 9	**H** us, God our Savior, for the glory
	121: 1	where does my **h** come from?
Isa	41: 10	I will strengthen you and **h** you;
Jnh	2: 2	the realm of the dead I called for **h**,
Mk	9: 24	**h** me overcome my unbelief!"
Ac	16: 9	over to Macedonia and **h** us."

HELPED (HELP)
1Sa	7: 12	"Thus far the Lord has **h** us."

HELPER (HELP)
Ge	2: 18	I will make a **h** suitable for him."
Ps	10: 14	you are the **h** of the fatherless.
Heb	13: 6	confidence, "The Lord is my **h**;

HELPING (HELP)
Ac	9: 36	always doing good and **h** the poor.
1Co	12: 28	gifts of healing, of **h**, of guidance,
1Ti	5: 10	**h** those in trouble and devoting

HELPS (HELP)
Ro	8: 26	the Spirit **h** us in our weakness.

HEN
Mt	23: 37	as a **h** gathers her chicks under her

HERITAGE (INHERIT)
Ps	127: 3	Children are a **h** from the Lord,

HEROD
1. King of Judea who tried to kill Jesus (Mt 2; Lk 1:5).

2. Son of 1. Tetrarch of Galilee who arrested and beheaded John the Baptist (Mt 14:1–12; Mk 6:14–29; Lk 3:1, 19–20; 9:7–9); tried Jesus (Lk 23:6–15).

3. Grandson of 1. King of Judea who killed James (Ac 12:2); arrested Peter (Ac 12:3–19). Death (Ac 12:19–23).

HERODIAS
Wife of Herod the Tetrarch who persuaded her daughter to ask for John the Baptist's head (Mt 14:1–12; Mk 6:14–29).

HEZEKIAH
King of Judah. Restored the temple and worship (2Ch 29–31). Sought the Lord for help against Assyria (2Ki 18–19; 2Ch 32:1–23; Isa 36–37). Illness healed (2Ki 20:1–11; 2Ch 32:24–26; Isa 38). Judged for showing Babylonians his treasures (2Ki 20:12–21; 2Ch 32:31; Isa 39).

HID (HIDE)
Ge	3: 8	they **h** from the Lord God among
Ex	2: 2	child, she **h** him for three months.
Jos	6: 17	because she **h** the spies we sent.
Heb	11: 23	faith Moses' parents **h** him for

HIDDEN (HIDE)
Ps	19: 12	Forgive my **h** faults.
	119: 11	I have **h** your word in my heart
Pr	2: 4	and search for it as for **h** treasure,
Isa	59: 2	your sins have **h** his face from you,
Mt	5: 14	A town built on a hill cannot be **h**.
	13: 44	heaven is like treasure **h** in a field.
Col	1: 26	that has been kept **h** for ages
	2: 3	in whom are **h** all the treasures
	3: 3	and your life is now **h** with Christ

HIDE (HID HIDDEN)
Ps	17: 8	**h** me in the shadow of your wings
	143: 9	Lord, for I **h** myself in you.

HIGH
Isa	57: 15	"I live in a **h** and holy place,

HILL (HILLS)
Mt	5: 14	town built on a **h** cannot be hidden.

HILLS (HILL)
Ps	50: 10	and the cattle on a thousand **h**.

HINDER (HINDERS)
1Sa	14: 6	Nothing can **h** the Lord
Mt	19: 14	do not **h** them, for the kingdom
1Co	9: 12	anything rather than **h** the gospel
1Pe	3: 7	so that nothing will **h** your prayers.

HINDERS (HINDER)
Heb	12: 1	let us throw off everything that **h**

HINT
Eph	5: 3	you there must not be even a **h**

HOLD
Ex	20: 7	Lord will not **h** anyone guiltless
Lev	19: 13	" 'Do not **h** back the wages
Jos	22: 5	to **h** fast to him and to serve him
Ps	73: 23	you **h** me by my right hand.
Pr	4: 4	"Take **h** of my words with all your
Isa	54: 2	tent curtains wide, do not **h** back;
Mk	11: 25	if you **h** anything against anyone,
Php	2: 16	as you **h** firmly to the word of life.
	3: 12	which Christ Jesus took **h** of me.
Col	1: 17	and in him all things **h** together.
1Th	5: 21	test them all; **h** on to what is good,
1Ti	6: 12	Take **h** of the eternal life
Heb	10: 23	Let us **h** unswervingly to the hope

HOLINESS (HOLY)

Ex	15:	11	majestic in **h**, awesome in glory,
Ps	29:	2	the LORD in the splendor of his **h**.
	96:	9	the LORD in the splendor of his **h**;
Ro	6:	19	to righteousness leading to **h**.
2Co	7:	1	perfecting **h** out of reverence
Eph	4:	24	God in true righteousness and **h**.
Heb	12:	10	in order that we may share in his **h**.
	12:	14	without **h** no one will see the Lord.

HOLY (HALLOWED HOLINESS)

Ex	19:	6	kingdom of priests and a **h** nation.'
	20:	8	the Sabbath day by keeping it **h**.
Lev	11:	44	and be **h**, because I am **h**.
	20:	7	yourselves and be **h**, because I am
	20:	26	You are to be **h** to me because I,
	21:	8	LORD am **h**—I who make you **h**.
	22:	32	Do not profane my **h** name,
Ps	24:	3	Who may stand in his **h** place?
	77:	13	Your ways, God, are **h**. What god is
	99:	3	great and awesome name—he is **h**.
	99:	5	worship at his footstool; he is **h**.
	99:	9	for the LORD our God is **h**.
	111:	9	**h** and awesome is his name.
Isa	5:	16	the **h** God will be proved **h** by his
	6:	3	"**H, h, h** is the LORD Almighty;
	40:	25	who is my equal?" says the **H** One.
	57:	15	who lives forever, whose name is **h**:
Eze	28:	25	I will be proved **h** through them
Da	9:	24	and to anoint the Most **H** Place.
Hab	2:	20	The LORD is in his **h** temple;
Ac	2:	27	will not let your **h** one see decay.
Ro	7:	12	the law is **h**, and the commandment is **h**,
	12:	1	sacrifice, **h** and pleasing to God—
2Th	1:	10	to be glorified in his **h** people
2Ti	1:	9	saved us and called us to a **h** life—
	3:	15	you have known the **H** Scriptures,
Titus	1:	8	upright, **h** and disciplined.
1Pe	1:	15	is **h**, so be **h** in all you do;
	1:	16	"Be **h**, because I am **h**."
	2:	9	a royal priesthood, a **h** nation,
2Pe	3:	11	You ought to live **h** and godly lives
Rev	4:	8	" '**H, h, h** is the Lord God

HOME (HOMES)

Dt	6:	7	Talk about them when you sit at **h**
Ps	84:	3	Even the sparrow has found a **h**,
Pr	3:	33	he blesses the **h** of the righteous.
Mk	10:	29	"no one who has left **h** or brothers
Jn	14:	23	and make our **h** with them.
Titus	2:	5	pure, to be busy at **h**, to be kind,

HOMES (HOME)

Ne	4:	14	daughters, your wives and your **h**."
1Ti	5:	14	to manage their **h** and to give

HOMOSEXUALITY

1Ti	1:	10	for those practicing **h**, for slave

HONEST

Lev	19:	36	**h** weights, an **h** ephah and an **h** hin.
Dt	25:	15	must have accurate and **h** weights
Job	31:	6	let God weigh me in **h** scales and
Pr	12:	17	An **h** witness tells the truth,

HONEY

Ex	3:	8	a land flowing with milk and **h**—
Ps	19:	10	they are sweeter than **h**, than **h**
	119:103		taste, sweeter than **h** to my mouth!

HONOR (HONORABLE HONORABLY HONORED HONORS)

Ex	20:	12	"**H** your father and your mother,
Nu	25:	13	he was zealous for the **h** of his God
Dt	5:	16	"**H** your father and your mother,

1Sa	2:	30	Those who **h** me I will **h**, but those
Ps	8:	5	crowned them with glory and **h**.
Pr	3:	9	**H** the LORD with your wealth,
	11:	16	A kindhearted woman gains **h**,
	15:	33	and humility comes before **h**.
	20:	3	It is to one's **h** to avoid strife,
	31:	31	**H** her for all that her hands have
Mt	15:	4	'**H** your father and mother'
Ro	12:	10	**H** one another above yourselves.
1Co	6:	20	Therefore **h** God with your bodies.
Eph	6:	2	"**H** your father and mother"—
1Ti	5:	17	church well are worthy of double **h**,
Heb	2:	7	crowned them with glory and **h**
Rev	4:	9	**h** and thanks to him who sits

HONORABLE (HONOR)

1Th	4:	4	body in a way that is holy and **h**,

HONORABLY (HONOR)

Heb	13:	18	and desire to live **h** in every way.

HONORED (HONOR)

Ps	12:	8	what is vile is **h** by the human race.
Pr	13:	18	but whoever heeds correction is **h**.
1Co	12:	26	if one part is **h**, every part rejoices
Heb	13:	4	Marriage should be **h** by all,

HONORS (HONOR)

Ps	15:	4	but **h** those who fear the LORD;
Pr	14:	31	is kind to the needy **h** God.
3Jn	:	6	their way in a manner that **h** God.

HOOKS

Isa	2:	4	and their spears into pruning **h**.
Joel	3:	10	and your pruning **h** into spears.

HOPE (HOPES)

Job	13:	15	he slay me, yet will I **h** in him;
Ps	42:	5	Put your **h** in God, for I will yet
	62:	5	rest in God; my **h** comes from him.
	119:	74	for I have put my **h** in your word.
	130:	7	Israel, put your **h** in the LORD,
	147:	11	put their **h** in his unfailing love.
Pr	13:	12	**H** deferred makes the heart sick,
Isa	40:	31	but those who **h** in the LORD will
Ro	5:	4	and character, **h**.
	8:	24	But **h** that is seen is no **h** at all.
	12:	12	Be joyful in **h**, patient in affliction,
	15:	4	they provide we might have **h**.
1Co	13:	13	three remain: faith, **h** and love.
	15:	19	for this life we have **h** in Christ,
Col	1:	27	is Christ in you, the **h** of glory.
1Th	5:	8	and the **h** of salvation as a helmet.
1Ti	6:	17	to put their **h** in God, who richly
Titus	2:	13	while we wait for the blessed **h**—
Heb	6:	19	We have this **h** as an anchor
	11:	1	faith is confidence in what we **h**
1Jn	3:	3	All who have this **h** in him purify

HOPES (HOPE)

1Co	13:	7	trusts, always **h**, always perseveres.

HORSE

Ps	147:	10	is not in the strength of the **h**,
Pr	26:	3	A whip for the **h**, a bridle
Zec	1:	8	me was a man mounted on a red **h**.
Rev	6:	2	and there before me was a white **h**!
	6:	4	Then another **h** came out, a fiery
	6:	5	and there before me was a black **h**!
	6:	8	and there before me was a pale **h**!
	19:	11	and there before me was a white **h**,

HOSANNA

Mt	21:	9	shouted, "**H** to the Son of David!"

HOSHEA

Last king of Israel (2Ki 15:30; 17:1–6).

HOSPITABLE (HOSPITALITY)
1Ti	3:	2	respectable, **h**, able to teach,
Titus	1:	8	he must be **h**, one who loves what

HOSPITALITY (HOSPITABLE)
Ro	12:	13	people who are in need. Practice **h**.
1Ti	5:	10	showing **h**, washing the feet
Heb	13:	2	shown **h** to angels without knowing
1Pe	4:	9	Offer **h** to one another without

HOSTILE
Ro	8:	7	governed by the flesh is **h** to God;

HOT
1Ti	4:	2	have been seared as with a **h** iron.
Rev	3:	15	that you are neither cold nor **h**.

HOT-TEMPERED
Pr	15:	18	A **h** person stirs up conflict,
	19:	19	A **h** person must pay the penalty;
	22:	24	not make friends with a **h** person,
	29:	22	and a **h** person commits many sins.

HOTHEADED (HEAD)
Pr	14:	16	but a fool is **h** and yet feels secure.

HOUR
Ecc	9:	12	one knows when their **h** will come:
Mt	6:	27	worrying add a single **h** to your life?
Lk	12:	40	an **h** when you do not expect him."
Jn	12:	23	"The **h** has come for the Son
	12:	27	this very reason I came to this **h**.

HOUSE (HOUSEHOLD HOUSEHOLDS STOREHOUSE)
Ex	20:	17	shall not covet your neighbor's **h**.
Ps	23:	6	in the **h** of the LORD forever.
	84:	10	in the **h** of my God than dwell
	122:	1	"Let us go to the **h** of the LORD."
	127:	1	Unless the LORD builds the **h**,
Pr	7:	27	Her **h** is a highway to the grave,
	21:	9	of the roof than share a **h**
Isa	56:	7	my **h** will be called a **h** of prayer
Zec	13:	6	I was given at the **h** of my friends.'
Mt	7:	24	is like a wise man who built his **h**
	12:	29	can anyone enter a strong man's **h**
	21:	13	"'My **h** will be called a **h**
Mk	3:	25	If a **h** is divided against itself, that **h**
Lk	11:	17	a **h** divided against itself will fall.
Jn	2:	16	Stop turning my Father's **h**
	12:	3	the **h** was filled with the fragrance
	14:	2	My Father's **h** has many rooms;
Heb	3:	3	of a **h** has greater honor than the **h**

HOUSEHOLD (HOUSE)
Jos	24:	15	But as for me and my **h**, we will
Mic	7:	6	are the members of his own **h**.
Mt	10:	36	will be the members of his own **h**.'
	12:	25	or **h** divided against itself will not
1Ti	3:	12	manage his children and his **h** well.
	3:	15	to conduct themselves in God's **h**,

HOUSEHOLDS (HOUSE)
Pr	15:	27	The greedy bring ruin to their **h**,

HUMAN (HUMANITY)
Ge	9:	6	"Whoever sheds **h** blood,
1Sa	15:	29	for he is not a **h** being, that he
Ac	5:	29	obey God rather than **h** beings!
2Pe	1:	21	never had its origin in the **h** will,

HUMANITY (HUMAN)
Heb	2:	14	he too shared in their **h** so

HUMBLE (HUMBLED HUMILIATE HUMILIATING HUMILITY)
2Ch	7:	14	will **h** themselves and pray and

Ps	25:	9	He guides the **h** in what is right
Pr	3:	34	favor to the **h** and oppressed.
Isa	66:	2	those who are **h** and contrite
Mt	11:	29	for I am gentle and **h** in heart,
Eph	4:	2	Be completely **h** and gentle;
Jas	4:	10	**H** yourselves before the Lord,
1Pe	5:	6	**H** yourselves, therefore,

HUMBLED (HUMBLE)
Mt	23:	12	who exalt themselves will be **h**,
Php	2:	8	he **h** himself by becoming obedient

HUMILIATE (HUMBLE)
Pr	25:	7	for him to **h** you before his nobles.

HUMILIATING (HUMBLE)
1Co	11:	22	God by **h** those who have nothing?

HUMILITY (HUMBLE)
Pr	11:	2	but with **h** comes wisdom.
	15:	33	LORD, and **h** comes before honor.
2Co	10:	1	the **h** and gentleness of Christ,
Php	2:	3	in **h** value others above yourselves,
1Pe	5:	5	with **h** toward one another,

HUNGRY
Ps	107:	9	and fills the **h** with good things.
	146:	7	oppressed and gives food to the **h**.
Pr	25:	21	If your enemy is **h**, give him food
Eze	18:	7	his food to the **h** and provides
Mt	25:	35	For I was **h** and you gave me
Lk	1:	53	has filled the **h** with good things
Jn	6:	35	comes to me will never go **h**,
Ro	12:	20	"If your enemy is **h**, feed him;

HURT (HURTS)
Ecc	8:	9	lords it over others to his own **h**.
Mk	16:	18	*it will not **h** them*
Rev	2:	11	one who is victorious will not be **h**

HURTS (HURT)
Ps	15:	4	who keeps an oath even when it **h**,
Pr	26:	28	A lying tongue hates those it **h**,

HUSBAND (HUSBAND'S HUSBANDS)
1Co	7:	3	The **h** should fulfill his marital
	7:	3	and likewise the wife to her **h**.
	7:	4	her own body but yields it to her **h**.
	7:	4	the **h** does not have authority over
	7:	10	wife must not separate from her **h**.
	7:	11	And a **h** must not divorce his wife.
	7:	13	And if a woman has a **h** who is not
	7:	39	But if her **h** dies, she is free
2Co	11:	2	I promised you to one **h**, to Christ,
Eph	5:	23	For the **h** is the head of the wife as
	5:	33	and the wife must respect her **h**.

HUSBAND'S (HUSBAND)
Pr	12:	4	of noble character is her **h** crown,

HUSBANDS (HUSBAND)
Eph	5:	22	yourselves to your own **h** as you do
	5:	25	**H**, love your wives, just as Christ
Titus	2:	4	the younger women to love their **h**
1Pe	3:	1	yourselves to your own **h** so that,
	3:	7	**H**, in the same way be considerate

HYMN
1Co	14:	26	each of you has a **h**, or a word

HYPOCRISY (HYPOCRITE HYPOCRITES)
Mt	23:	28	on the inside you are full of **h**
1Pe	2:	1	of all malice and all deceit, **h**, envy,

HYPOCRITE (HYPOCRISY)
Mt	7:	5	You **h**, first take the plank

HYPOCRITES (HYPOCRISY)
Ps   26:   4   deceitful, nor do I associate with **h.**
Mt   6:   5   do not be like the **h,** for they love

HYSSOP
Ps   51:   7   Cleanse me with **h,** and I will be

IDLE (IDLENESS)
1Th   5: 14   those who are **i** and disruptive,
2Th   3:   6   away from every believer who is **i**
1Ti   5: 13   they get into the habit of being **i**

IDLENESS (IDLE)
Pr   31: 27   and does not eat the bread of **i.**

IDOL (IDOLATRY IDOLS)
Isa 44: 17   From the rest he makes a god, his **i;**
1Co   8:   4   We know that "An **i** is nothing

IDOLATRY (IDOL)
Col   3:   5   evil desires and greed, which is **i.**

IDOLS (IDOL)
1Co   8:   1   Now about food sacrificed to **i:**

IGNORANT (IGNORE)
1Co 15: 34   there are some who are **i** of God—
Heb   5:   2   to deal gently with those who are **i**
1Pe   2: 15   good you should silence the **i** talk
2Pe   3: 16   **i** and unstable people distort,

IGNORE (IGNORANT IGNORES)
Dt   22:   1   not **i** it but be sure to take it back
Ps   9: 12   he does not **i** the cries
Heb   2:   3   escape if we **i** so great a salvation?

IGNORES (IGNORE)
Pr   10: 17   whoever **i** correction leads others

ILLUMINATED
Rev 18:   1   and the earth was **i** by his splendor.

IMAGE
Ge   1: 26   "Let us make mankind in our **i,**
      1: 27   God created mankind in his own **i,** in
               the **i** of God he created them;
Ro   8: 29   to be conformed to the **i** of his Son,
1Co 11:   7   since he is the **i** and glory of God;
2Co   3: 18   into his **i** with ever-increasing glory,
Col   1: 15   The Son is the **i** of the invisible
      3: 10   in knowledge in the **i** of its Creator.

IMAGINE
Eph   3: 20   more than all we ask or **i,**

IMITATE (IMITATORS)
1Co   4: 16   Therefore I urge you to **i** me.
Heb   6: 12   but to **i** those who through faith
     13:   7   of their way of life and **i** their faith.
3Jn   : 11   do not **i** what is evil but what is

IMITATORS (IMITATE)
1Th   1:   6   You became **i** of us and of the Lord,
      2: 14   became **i** of God's churches

IMMANUEL
Isa   7: 14   birth to a son, and will call him **I.**
Mt   1: 23   they will call him **I**" (which means

IMMORAL (IMMORALITY)
1Co   5:   9   to associate with sexually **i** people
      5: 10   the people of this world who are **i,**
      5: 11   or sister but is sexually **i** or greedy,
      6:   9   Neither the sexually **i** nor idolaters
Eph   5:   5   No **i,** impure or greedy person—
Heb 12: 16   See that no one is sexually **i,** or is
     13:   4   the adulterer and all the sexually **i.**
Rev 21:   8   the sexually **i,** those who practice
     22: 15   arts, the sexually **i,** the murderers,

IMMORALITY (IMMORAL)
Mt   5: 32   except for sexual **i,** makes her
     19:   9   except for sexual **i,** and marries
1Co   6: 13   is not meant for sexual **i**
      6: 18   Flee from sexual **i.** All other sins
     10:   8   We should not commit sexual **i,**
Gal   5: 19   sexual **i,** impurity and debauchery;
Eph   5:   3   must not be even a hint of sexual **i,**
1Th   4:   3   that you should avoid sexual **i;**
Jude   :   4   grace of our God into a license for **i**

IMMORTAL (IMMORTALITY)
Ro   1: 23   exchanged the glory of the **i** God
1Ti   1: 17   Now to the King eternal, **i,**
      6: 16   who alone is **i** and who lives

IMMORTALITY (IMMORTAL)
Ro   2:   7   and **i,** he will give eternal life.
1Co 15: 53   and the mortal with **i.**
2Ti   1: 10   and **i** to light through the gospel.

IMPERISHABLE
1Pe   1: 23   seed, but of **i,** through the living

IMPORTANCE (IMPORTANT)
1Co 15:   3   I passed on to you as of first **i:**

IMPORTANT (IMPORTANCE)
Mt   23: 23   have neglected the more **i** matters
Mk   12: 29   "The most **i** one," answered Jesus,
     12: 33   as yourself is more **i** than all burnt
Php   1: 18   The **i** thing is that in every way,

IMPOSSIBLE
Mt   17: 20   Nothing will be **i** for you."
Lk   18: 27   "What is **i** with man is possible
Heb   6: 18   in which it is **i** for God to lie,
     11:   6   without faith it is **i** to please God,

IMPROPER
Eph   5:   3   because these are **i** for God's holy

IMPURE (IMPURITY)
Ac   10: 15   "Do not call anything **i** that God
Eph   5:   5   No immoral, **i** or greedy person—
1Th   4:   7   For God did not call us to be **i,**
Rev 21: 27   Nothing **i** will ever enter it,

IMPURITY (IMPURE)
Ro   1: 24   hearts to sexual **i** for the degrading
Eph   5:   3   or of any kind of **i,** or of greed,

INCENSE
Ex   40:   5   Place the gold altar of **i** in front
Ps 141:   2   my prayer be set before you like **i;**

INCOME
Ecc   5: 10   is never satisfied with their **i.**
1Co 16:   2   of money in keeping with your **i,**

INCOMPARABLE
Eph   2:   7   ages he might show the **i** riches

INCREASE (EVER-INCREASING INCREASED
      INCREASING)
Ge   1: 22   "Be fruitful and **i** in number and
Ps   62: 10   though your riches **i,** do not set
Lk   17:   5   said to the Lord, "**I** our faith!"
1Th   3: 12   May the Lord make your love **i**

INCREASED (INCREASE)
Ac   6:   7   of disciples in Jerusalem **i** rapidly,
Ro   5: 20   where sin **i,** grace **i** all the more,

INCREASING (INCREASE)
Ac   6:   1   the number of disciples was **i,**
2Th   1:   3   all of you have for one another is **i.**
2Pe   1:   8   these qualities in **i** measure,

INDEPENDENT
1Co 11: 11   in the Lord woman is not **i** of man,
            nor is man **i** of woman.

INDESCRIBABLE
2Co 9: 15   Thanks be to God for his **i** gift!

INDISPENSABLE
1Co 12: 22   body that seem to be weaker are **i**,

INEFFECTIVE
2Pe 1: 8   they will keep you from being **i**

INEXPRESSIBLE
2Co 12: 4   up to paradise and heard **i** things,
1Pe 1: 8   are filled with an **i** and glorious joy,

INFANTS
Mt 21: 16   the lips of children and **i** you, Lord,
1Co 14: 20   In regard to evil be **i**, but in your

INHERIT (CO-HEIRS HEIRS HERITAGE INHERITANCE)
Ps 37: 11   the meek will **i** the land and enjoy
    37: 29   The righteous will **i** the land
Mt   5: 5   the meek, for they will **i** the earth.
Mk 10: 17   "what must I do to **i** eternal life?"
1Co 15: 50   cannot **i** the kingdom of God,

INHERITANCE (INHERIT)
Dt   4: 20   to be the people of his **i**, as you
Pr 13: 22   A good person leaves an **i** for their
Eph 1: 14   deposit guaranteeing our **i** until
     5: 5   has any **i** in the kingdom of Christ
Heb 9: 15   receive the promised eternal **i**—
1Pe 1: 4   This **i** is kept in heaven for you,

INIQUITIES (INIQUITY)
Ps 78: 38   he forgave their **i** and did not
   103: 10   or repay us according to our **i**.
Isa 59: 2   your **i** have separated you from
Mic 7: 19   hurl all our **i** into the depths

INIQUITY (INIQUITIES)
Ps 51: 2   Wash away all my **i** and cleanse me
Isa 53: 6   has laid on him the **i** of us all.

INJUSTICE
2Ch 19: 7   the LORD our God there is no **i**

INNOCENT
Pr 17: 26   a fine on the **i** is not good,
Mt 10: 16   shrewd as snakes and as **i** as doves.
    27: 4   said, "for I have betrayed **i** blood."
1Co 4: 4   clear, but that does not make me **i**.

INSCRIPTION
Mt 22: 20   image is this? And whose **i**?"

INSOLENT
Ro   1: 30   **i**, arrogant and boastful;

INSTITUTED
Ro 13: 2   is rebelling against what God has **i**,

INSTRUCT (INSTRUCTED INSTRUCTION)
Ps 32: 8   I will **i** you and teach you
Pr   9: 9   **i** the wise and they will be wiser
Ro 15: 14   and competent to **i** one another.

INSTRUCTED (INSTRUCT)
2Ti 2: 25   Opponents must be gently **i**,

INSTRUCTION (INSTRUCT)
Pr   1: 3   for receiving **i** in prudent behavior,
     1: 7   but fools despise wisdom and **i**.
     1: 8   your father's **i** and do not forsake
     4: 1   Listen, my sons, to a father's **i**;
     4: 13   Hold on to **i**, do not let it go;

Pr   6: 23   correction and **i** are the way to life,
     8: 10   Choose my **i** instead of silver,
     8: 33   Listen to my **i** and be wise;
    13: 1   A wise son heeds his father's **i**,
    13: 13   Whoever scorns **i** will pay for it,
    16: 20   Whoever gives heed to **i** prospers,
    16: 21   and gracious words promote **i**.
    23: 12   Apply your heart to **i** and your ears
    23: 23   wisdom, **i** and insight as well.
Isa 8: 20   Consult God's **i** and the testimony
1Co 14: 6   or prophecy or word of **i**?
    14: 26   hymn, or a word of **i**, a revelation,
Eph 6: 4   in the training and **i** of the Lord.
1Th 4: 8   who rejects this **i** does not reject
2Th 3: 14   anyone who does not obey our **i**
1Ti 6: 3   sound **i** of our Lord Jesus Christ
2Ti 4: 2   with great patience and careful **i**.

INSULT (INSULTS)
Pr 12: 16   but the prudent overlook an **i**.
Mt   5: 11   are you when people **i** you,
Lk   6: 22   when they exclude you and **i** you
1Pe 3: 9   not repay evil with evil or **i** with **i**.

INSULTS (INSULT)
Pr   9: 7   corrects a mocker invites **i**;

INTEGRITY
1Ki 9: 4   walk before me faithfully with **i**
Job 2: 3   And he still maintains his **i**,
    27: 5   till I die, I will not deny my **i**.
Pr 10: 9   Whoever walks in **i** walks securely,
    11: 3   The **i** of the upright guides them,
    29: 10   The bloodthirsty hate a person of **i**
Titus 2: 7   In your teaching show **i**,

INTELLIGENCE
Isa 29: 14   the **i** of the intelligent will vanish."
1Co 1: 19   the **i** of the intelligent I will

INTELLIGIBLE
1Co 14: 19   I would rather speak five **i** words

INTERCEDE (INTERCEDES INTERCESSION)
Heb 7: 25   him, because he always lives to **i**

INTERCEDES (INTERCEDE)
Ro   8: 26   the Spirit himself **i** for us through

INTERCESSION (INTERCEDE)
Isa 53: 12   and made **i** for the transgressors.
1Ti 2: 1   **i** and thanksgiving be made for all

INTEREST
Ne   5: 10   But let us stop charging **i**!

INTERESTS
1Co 7: 34   and his **i** are divided.
Php 2: 4   not looking to your own **i** but each of
             you to the **i** of the others.
     2: 21   everyone looks out for their own **i**,

INTERMARRY (MARRY)
Dt   7: 3   Do not **i** with them. Do not give

INVESTIGATED
Lk   1: 3   I myself have carefully **i** everything

INVISIBLE
Ro   1: 20   of the world God's **i** qualities—
Col 1: 15   The Son is the image of the **i** God,
1Ti 1: 17   eternal, immortal, **i**, the only God,

INVITE (INVITED INVITES)
Lk 14: 13   you give a banquet, **i** the poor,

INVITED (INVITE)
Mt 22: 14   "For many are **i**, but few are
    25: 35   I was a stranger and you **i** me in,

INVITES (INVITE)
1Co 10: 27 If an unbeliever **i** you to a meal

IRON
1Ti 4: 2 have been seared as with a hot **i**.
Rev 2: 27 'will rule them with an **i** scepter

IRREVOCABLE
Ro 11: 29 for God's gifts and his call are **i**.

ISAAC
Son of Abraham by Sarah (Ge 17:19; 21:1–7; 1Ch 1:28). Offered up by Abraham (Ge 22; Heb 11:17–19). Rebekah taken as wife (Ge 24). Fathered Esau and Jacob (Ge 25:19–26; 1Ch 1:34). Tricked into blessing Jacob (Ge 27). Father of Israel (Ex 3:6; Dt 29:13; Ro 9:10).

ISAIAH
Prophet to Judah (Isa 1:1). Called by the Lord (Isa 6).

ISHMAEL
Son of Abraham by Hagar (Ge 16; 1Ch 1:28). Blessed, but not son of covenant (Ge 17:18–21; Gal 4:21–31). Sent away by Sarah (Ge 21:8–21).

ISRAEL (ISRAELITES)
1. Name given to Jacob (see JACOB).
2. Corporate name of Jacob's descendants; often specifically Northern Kingdom.

Dt   6: 4 Hear, O **I**: The Lord our God,
1Sa 4: 21 "The Glory has departed from **I**"—
Isa 27: 6 **I** will bud and blossom and fill all
Jer 31: 10 'He who scattered **I** will gather
Eze 39: 23 that the people of **I** went into exile
Mk 12: 29 'Hear, O **I**: The Lord our God,
Lk 22: 30 judging the twelve tribes of **I**.
Ro   9: 6 all who are descended from **I** are **I**.
    11: 26 and in this way all **I** will be saved.
Eph 3: 6 Gentiles are heirs together with **I**,

ISRAELITES (ISRAEL)
Ex 14: 22 the **I** went through the sea on dry
    16: 35 The **I** ate manna forty years,
Hos 1: 10 "Yet the **I** will be like the sand
Ro   9: 27 number of the **I** be like the sand

ITCHING
2Ti 4: 3 say what their **i** ears want to hear.

JACOB
Second son of Isaac, twin of Esau (Ge 25:21–26; 1Ch 1:34). Bought Esau's birthright (Ge 25:29–34); tricked Isaac into blessing him (Ge 27:1–37). Abrahamic covenant perpetuated through (Ge 28:13–15; Mal 1:2). Vision at Bethel (Ge 28:10–22). Wives and children (Ge 29:1—30:24; 35:16–26; 1Ch 2–9). Wrestled with God; name changed to Israel (Ge 32:22–32). Sent sons to Egypt during famine (Ge 42–43). Settled in Egypt (Ge 46). Blessed Ephraim and Manasseh (Ge 48). Blessed sons (Ge 49:1–28; Heb 11:21). Death (Ge 49:29–33). Burial (Ge 50:1–14).

JAMES
1. Apostle; brother of John (Mt 4:21–22; 10:2; Mk 3:17; Lk 5:1–10). At transfiguration (Mt 17:1–13; Mk 9:1–13; Lk 9:28–36). Killed by Herod (Ac 12:2).
2. Apostle; son of Alphaeus (Mt 10:3; Mk 3:18; Lk 6:15).
3. Brother of Jesus (Mt 13:55; Mk 6:3; Lk 24:10; Gal 1:19) and Judas (Jude 1). With believers before Pentecost (Ac 1:13). Leader of church at Jerusalem (Ac 12:17; 15; 21:18; Gal 2:9, 12). Author of epistle (Jas 1:1).

JAPHETH
Son of Noah (Ge 5:32; 1Ch 1:4–5). Blessed (Ge 9:18–28).

JARS
2Co 4: 7 we have this treasure in **j** of clay

JEALOUS (JEALOUSY)
Ex 20: 5 am a **j** God, punishing the children
    34: 14 whose name is **J**, is a **j** God.
Dt   4: 24 God is a consuming fire, a **j** God.
Joel 2: 18 Then the Lord was **j** for his land
Zec 1: 14 I am very **j** for Jerusalem and Zion,
2Co 11: 2 am **j** for you with a godly jealousy.

JEALOUSY (JEALOUS)
1Co 3: 3 For since there is **j** and quarreling
2Co 11: 2 I am jealous for you with a godly **j**.
Gal 5: 20 hatred, discord, **j**, fits of rage,

JEHOAHAZ
1. Son of Jehu; king of Israel (2Ki 13:1–9).
2. Son of Josiah; king of Judah (2Ki 23:31–34; 2Ch 36:1–4).

JEHOASH
Son of Jehoahaz; king of Israel (2Ki 13–14; 2Ch 25).

JEHOIACHIN
Son of Jehoiakim; king of Judah exiled by Nebuchadnezzar (2Ki 24:8–17; 2Ch 36:8–10; Jer 22:24–30; 24:1). Raised from prisoner status (2Ki 25:27–30; Jer 52:31–34).

JEHOIAKIM
Son of Josiah; king of Judah (2Ki 23:34—24:6; 2Ch 36:4–8; Jer 22:18–23; 36).

JEHORAM
Son of Jehoshaphat; king of Judah (2Ki 8:16–24).

JEHOSHAPHAT
Son of Asa; king of Judah (1Ki 22:41–50; 2Ki 3; 2Ch 17–20).

JEHU
King of Israel (1Ki 19:16–19; 2Ki 9–10).

JEPHTHAH
Judge from Gilead who delivered Israel from Ammon (Jdg 10:6—12:7). Made rash vow concerning his daughter (Jdg 11:30–40).

JEREMIAH
Prophet to Judah (Jer 1:1–3). Called by the Lord (Jer 1). Put in stocks (Jer 20:1–3). Threatened for prophesying (Jer 11:18–23; 26). Opposed by Hananiah (Jer 28). Scroll burned (Jer 36). Imprisoned (Jer 37). Thrown into cistern (Jer 38). Forced to Egypt with those fleeing Babylonians (Jer 43).

JEROBOAM
1. Official of Solomon; rebelled to become first king of Israel (1Ki 11:26–40; 12:1–20; 2Ch 10). Idolatry (1Ki 12:25–33); judgment for (1Ki 13–14; 2Ch 13).
2. Son of Jehoash; king of Israel (1Ki 14:23–29).

JERUSALEM
2Ki 23: 27 and I will reject **J**, the city I chose,
2Ch 6: 6 now I have chosen **J** for my Name
Ne   2: 17 let us rebuild the wall of **J**,
Ps 122: 6 Pray for the peace of **J**:
   125: 2 As the mountains surround **J**,
   137: 5 If I forget you, **J**, may my right
Isa 40: 9 You who bring good news to **J**,
    65: 18 for I will create **J** to be a delight

Joel	3: 17	**J** will be holy; never again will
Zep	3: 16	On that day they will say to **J**,
Zec	2: 4	man, '**J** will be a city without walls
	8: 8	I will bring them back to live in **J**;
	14: 8	living water will flow out from **J**,
Mt	23: 37	"**J, J**, you who kill the prophets
Lk	13: 34	"**J, J**, you who kill the prophets
	21: 24	**J** will be trampled
Jn	4: 20	where we must worship is in **J**."
Ac	1: 8	and you will be my witnesses in **J**,
Gal	4: 25	to the present city of **J**,
Rev	21: 2	the new **J**, coming down

JESUS

LIFE: Genealogy (Mt 1:1–17; Lk 3:21–37). Birth announced (Mt 1:18–25; Lk 1:26–45). Birth (Mt 2:1–12; Lk 2:1–40). Escape to Egypt (Mt 2:13–23). As a boy in the temple (Lk 2:41–52). Baptism (Mt 3:13–17; Mk 1:9–11; Lk 3:21–22; Jn 1:32–34). Temptation (Mt 4:1–11; Mk 1:12–13; Lk 4:1–13). Ministry in Galilee (Mt 4:12—18:35; Mk 1:14—9:50; Lk 4:14—13:9; Jn 1:35—2:11; 4; 6), Transfiguration (Mt 17:1–8; Mk 9:2–8; Lk 9:28–36), on the way to Jerusalem (Mt 19–20; Mk 10; Lk 13:10—19:27), in Jerusalem (Mt 21–25; Mk 11–13; Lk 19:28—21:38; Jn 2:12—3:36; 5; 7–12). Last supper (Mt 26:17–35; Mk 14:12–31; Lk 22:1–38; Jn 13–17). Arrest and trial (Mt 26:36—27:31; Mk 14:43—15:20; Lk 22:39—23:25; Jn 18:1—19:16). Crucifixion (Mt 27:32–66; Mk 15:21–47; Lk 23:26–55; Jn 19:28–42). Resurrection and appearances (Mt 28; Mk 16; Lk 24; Jn 20–21; Ac 1:1–11; 7:56; 9:3–6; 1Co 15:1–8; Rev 1:1–20).

MIRACLES. Healings: official's son (Jn 4:43–54), demoniac in Capernaum (Mk 1:23–26; Lk 4:33–35), Peter's mother-in-law (Mt 8:14–17; Mk 1:29–31; Lk 4:38–39), leper (Mt 8:2–4; Mk 1:40–45; Lk 5:12–16), paralytic (Mt 9:1–8; Mk 2:1–12; Lk 5:17–26), cripple (Jn 5:1–9), shriveled hand (Mt 12:10–13; Mk 3:1–5; Lk 6:6–11), centurion's servant (Mt 8:5–13; Lk 7:1–10), widow's son raised (Lk 7:11–17), demoniac (Mt 12:22–23; Lk 11:14), Gadarene demoniacs (Mt 8:28–34; Mk 5:1–20; Lk 8:26–39), woman's bleeding and Jairus' daughter (Mt 9:18–26; Mk 5:21–43; Lk 8:40–56), blind man (Mt 9:27–31), mute man (Mt 9:32–33), Canaanite woman's daughter (Mt 15:21–28; Mk 7:24–30), deaf man (Mk 7:31–37), blind man (Mk 8:22–26), demoniac boy (Mt 17:14–18; Mk 9:14–29; Lk 9:37–43), ten lepers (Lk 17:11–19), man born blind (Jn 9:1–7), Lazarus raised (Jn 11), crippled woman (Lk 13:11–17), man with dropsy (Lk 14:1–6), two blind men (Mt 20:29–34; Mk 10:46–52; Lk 18:35–43), Malchus' ear (Lk 22:50–51). Other Miracles: water to wine (Jn 2:1–11), catch of fish (Lk 5:1–11), storm stilled (Mt 8:23–27; Mk 4:37–41; Lk 8:22–25), 5,000 fed (Mt 14:15–21; Mk 6:35–44; Lk 9:10–17; Jn 6:1–14), walking on water (Mt 14:25–33; Mk 6:48–52; Jn 6:15–21), 4,000 fed (Mt 15:32–39; Mk 8:1–9), money from fish (Mt 17:24–27), fig tree cursed (Mt 21:18–22; Mk 11:12–14), catch of fish (Jn 21:1–14).

MAJOR TEACHING: Sermon on the Mount (Mt 5–7; Lk 6:17–49), to Nicodemus (Jn 3), to Samaritan woman (Jn 4), Bread of Life (Jn 6:22–59), at Feast of Tabernacles (Jn 7–8), woes to Pharisees (Mt 23; Lk 11:37–54), Good Shepherd (Jn 10:1–18), Olivet Discourse (Mt 24–25; Mk 13; Lk 21:5–36), Upper Room Discourse (Jn 13–16).

PARABLES: Sower (Mt 13:3–23; Mk 4:3–25; Lk 8:5–18), seed's growth (Mk 4:26–29), wheat and weeds (Mt 13:24–30, 36–43), mustard seed (Mt 13:31–32; Mk 4:30–32), yeast (Mt 13:33; Lk 13:20–21), hidden treasure (Mt 13:44), valuable pearl (Mt 13:45–46), net (Mt 13:47–51), house owner (Mt 13:52), good Samaritan (Lk 10:25–37), unmerciful servant (Mt 18:15–35), lost sheep (Mt 18:10–14;

Lk 15:4–7), lost coin (Lk 15:8–10), prodigal son (Lk 15:11–32), dishonest manager (Lk 16:1–13), rich man and Lazarus (Lk 16:19–31), persistent widow (Lk 18:1–8), Pharisee and tax collector (Lk 18:9–14), payment of workers (Mt 20:1–16), tenants and the vineyard (Mt 21:28–46; Mk 12:1–12; Lk 20:9–19), wedding banquet (Mt 22:1–14), faithful servant (Mt 24:45–51), ten virgins (Mt 25:1–13), talents (Mt 25:1–30; Lk 19:12–27).

DISCIPLES see APOSTLES. Call of (Jn 1:35–51; Mt 4:18–22; 9:9; Mk 1:16–20; 2:13–14; Lk 5:1–11, 27–28). Named Apostles (Mk 3:13–19; Lk 6:12–16). Twelve sent out (Mt 10; Mk 6:7–11; Lk 9:1–5). Seventy sent out (Lk 10:1–24). Defection of (Jn 6:60–71; Mt 26:56; Mk 14:50–52). Final commission (Mt 28:16–20; Jn 21:15–23; Ac 1:3–8).

Ac	2: 32	God has raised this **J** to life, and we
	9: 5	Saul asked. "I am **J**, whom you are
	15: 11	of our Lord **J** that we are saved,
	16: 31	"Believe in the Lord **J**, and you will
Ro	3: 24	redemption that came by Christ **J**.
	5: 17	life through the one man, **J** Christ!
	8: 1	for those who are in Christ **J**,
1Co	2: 2	I was with you except **J** Christ
	8: 6	and there is but one Lord, **J** Christ,
	12: 3	and no one can say, "**J** is Lord,"
2Co	4: 5	but **J** Christ as Lord, and ourselves
Gal	2: 16	of the law, but by faith in **J** Christ.
	3: 28	for you are all one in Christ **J**.
	5: 6	in Christ **J** neither circumcision
Eph	2: 10	in Christ **J** to do good works,
	2: 20	with Christ **J** himself as the chief
Php	1: 6	until the day of Christ **J**.
	2: 5	have the same mindset as Christ **J**:
	2: 10	name of **J** every knee should bow,
Col	3: 17	do it all in the name of the Lord **J**,
2Th	2: 1	the coming of our Lord **J** Christ
1Ti	1: 15	**J** came into the world to save
2Ti	3: 12	life in Christ **J** will be persecuted,
Titus	2: 13	our great God and Savior, **J** Christ,
Heb	2: 9	But we do see **J**, who was made
	3: 1	fix your thoughts on **J**, whom we
	4: 14	into heaven, **J** the Son of God,
	7: 22	**J** has become the guarantor
	7: 24	but because **J** lives forever, he has
	12: 2	fixing our eyes on **J**, the pioneer
2Pe	1: 16	of our Lord **J** Christ in power,
1Jn	1: 7	and the blood of **J**, his Son,
	2: 1	**J** Christ, the Righteous One.
	2: 6	to live in him must live as **J** did.
	4: 15	acknowledges that **J** is the Son
Rev	22: 20	Amen. Come, Lord **J**.

JEW (JEWS JUDAISM)

Zec	8: 23	take firm hold of one **J** by the hem
Ro	1: 16	first to the **J**, then to the Gentile,
	10: 12	there is no difference between **J**
1Co	9: 20	To the Jews I became like a **J**,
Gal	3: 28	There is neither **J** nor Gentile,

JEWELRY (JEWELS)

1Pe	3: 3	wearing of gold **j** or fine clothes.

JEWELS (JEWELRY)

Isa	61: 10	as a bride adorns herself with her **j**.
Zec	9: 16	in his land like **j** in a crown.

JEWS (JEW)

Mt	2: 2	who has been born king of the **J**?
	27: 11	him, "Are you the king of the **J**?"
Jn	4: 22	know, for salvation is from the **J**.
Ro	3: 29	Or is God the God of **J** only?
1Co	1: 22	**J** demand signs and Greeks look
	9: 20	To the **J** I became like a Jew, to win
	12: 13	whether **J** or Gentiles,
Rev	3: 9	claim to be **J** though they are not,

JEZEBEL

Sidonian wife of Ahab (1Ki 16:31). Promoted Baal worship (1Ki 16:32–33). Killed prophets of the LORD (1Ki 18:4, 13). Opposed Elijah (1Ki 19:1–2). Had Naboth killed (1Ki 21). Death prophesied (1Ki 21:17–24). Killed by Jehu (2Ki 9:30–37).

JOASH

Son of Ahaziah; king of Judah. Sheltered from Athaliah by Jehoiada (2Ki 11; 2Ch 22:10—23:21). Repaired temple (2Ki 12; 2Ch 24).

JOB

Wealthy man from Uz; feared God (Job 1:1–5). Righteousness tested by disaster (Job 1:6–22), personal affliction (Job 2). Maintained innocence in debate with three friends (Job 3–31), Elihu (Job 32–37). Rebuked by the LORD (Job 38–41). Vindicated and restored to greater stature by the LORD (Job 42). Example of righteousness (Eze 14:14, 20).

JOHN

1. Son of Zechariah and Elizabeth (Lk 1). Called the Baptist (Mt 3:1–12; Mk 1:2–8). Witness to Jesus (Mt 3:11–12; Mk 1:7–8; Lk 3:15–18; Jn 1:6–35; 3:27–30; 5:33–36). Doubts about Jesus (Mt 11:2–6; Lk 7:18–23). Arrest (Mt 4:12; Mk 1:14). Execution (Mt 14:1–12; Mk 6:14–29; Lk 9:7–9). Ministry compared to Elijah (Mt 11:7–19; Mk 9:11–13; Lk 7:24–35).
2. Apostle; brother of James (Mt 4:21–22; 10:2; Mk 3:17; Lk 5:1–10). At transfiguration (Mt 17:1–13; Mk 9:1–13; Lk 9:28–36). Desire to be greatest (Mk 10:35–45). Leader of church at Jerusalem (Ac 4:1–3; Gal 2:9). Elder who wrote epistles (2Jn 1; 3Jn 1). Prophet who wrote Revelation (Rev 1:1; 22:8).
3. Cousin of Barnabas, co-worker with Paul, (Ac 12:12—13:13; 15:37), see MARK.

JOIN (JOINED)

Pr	23: 20	not **j** those who drink too much
	24: 21	do not **j** with rebellious officials,
Ro	15: 30	to **j** me in my struggle by praying
2Ti	1: 8	**j** with me in suffering
2Ti	2: 3	**J** with me in suffering, like a good

JOINED (JOIN)

Mt	19: 6	Therefore what God has **j** together,
Mk	10: 9	Therefore what God has **j** together,
Eph	2: 21	the whole building is **j** together
	4: 16	body, **j** and held together by every

JOINTS

| Heb | 4: 12 | soul and spirit, **j** and marrow; |

JOKING

| Eph | 5: 4 | foolish talk or coarse **j**, which are |

JONAH

Prophet in days of Jeroboam II (2Ki 14:25). Called to Nineveh; fled to Tarshish (Jnh 1:1–3). Cause of storm; thrown into sea (Jnh 1:4–16). Swallowed by fish (Jnh 1:17). Prayer (Jnh 2). Preached to Nineveh (Jnh 3). Attitude reproved by the LORD (Jnh 4). Sign of (Mt 12:39–41; Lk 11:29–32).

JONATHAN

Son of Saul (1Sa 13:16; 1Ch 8:33). Valiant warrior (1Sa 13–14). Relation to David (1Sa 18:1–4; 19–20; 23:16–18). Killed at Gilboa (1Sa 31). Mourned by David (2Sa 1).

JORAM

Son of Ahab; king of Israel (2Ki 3; 8–9; 2Ch 22).

JORDAN

Nu	34: 12	boundary will go down along the **J**
Jos	4: 22	'Israel crossed the **J** on dry ground.'
Mt	3: 6	baptized by him in the **J** River.

JOSEPH

1. Son of Jacob by Rachel (Ge 30:24; 1Ch 2:2). Favored by Jacob, hated by brothers (Ge 37:3–4). Dreams (Ge 37:5–11). Sold by brothers (Ge 37:12–36). Served Potiphar; imprisoned by false accusation (Ge 39). Interpreted dreams of Pharaoh's servants (Ge 40), of Pharaoh (Ge 41:4–40). Made great est in Egypt (Ge 41:41–57). Sold grain to brothers (Ge 42–45). Brought Jacob and sons to Egypt (Ge 46–47). Sons Ephraim and Manasseh blessed (Ge 48). Blessed (Ge 49:22–26; Dt 33:13–17). Death (Ge 50:22–26; Ex 13:19; Heb 11:22). 12,000 from (Rev 7:8).
2. Husband of Mary, mother of Jesus (Mt 1:16–24; 2:13–19; Lk 1:27; 2; Jn 1:45).
3. Disciple from Arimathea, who gave his tomb for Jesus' burial (Mt 27:57–61; Mk 15:43–47; Lk 23:50–53).
4. Original name of Barnabas (Ac 4:36).

JOSHUA

1. Son of Nun; name changed from Hoshea (Nu 13:8, 16; 1Ch 7:27). Fought Amalekites under Moses (Ex 17:9–14). Servant of Moses on Sinai (Ex 24:13; 32:17). Spied Canaan (Nu 13). With Caleb, allowed to enter land (Nu 14:6, 30). Succeeded Moses (Dt 1:38; 31:1–8; 34:9).

Charged Israel to conquer Canaan (Jos 1). Crossed Jordan (Jos 3–4). Circumcised sons of wilderness wanderings (Jos 5). Conquered Jericho (Jos 6), Ai (Jos 7–8), five kings at Gibeon (Jos 10:1–28), southern Canaan (Jos 10:29–43), northern Canaan (Jos 11–12). Defeated at Ai (Jos 7). Deceived by Gibeonites (Jos 9). Renewed covenant (Jos 8:30–35; 24:1–27). Divided land among tribes (Jos 13–22). Last words (Jos 23). Death (Jos 24:28–31).
2. High priest during rebuilding of temple (Hag 1–2; Zec 3:1–9; 6:11).

JOSIAH

Son of Amon; king of Judah (2Ki 22–23; 2Ch 34–35).

JOTHAM

Son of Azariah (Uzziah); king of Judah (2Ki 15:32–38; 2Ch 26:21—27:9).

JOY (ENJOY ENJOYMENT JOYFUL OVERJOYED REJOICE REJOICES REJOICING)

Dt	16: 15	hands, and your **j** will be complete.
1Ch	16: 27	and **j** are in his dwelling place.
Ne	8: 10	for the **j** of the LORD is your
Est	9: 22	their sorrow was turned into **j**
Job	38: 7	and all the angels shouted for **j**?
Ps	4: 7	Fill my heart with **j** when their
	21: 6	glad with the **j** of your presence.
	30: 11	sackcloth and clothed me with **j**,
	43: 4	God, to God, my **j** and my delight.
	51: 12	to me the **j** of your salvation
	66: 1	Shout for **j** to God, all the earth!
	96: 12	all the trees of the forest sing for **j**.
	107: 22	tell of his works with songs of **j**.
	119:111	forever; they are the **j** of my heart.
Pr	10: 1	A wise son brings **j** to his father,
	10: 28	The prospect of the righteous is **j**,
	12: 20	those who promote peace have **j**.
	15: 30	in a messenger's eyes brings **j**
Isa	35: 10	everlasting **j** will crown their heads
	51: 11	Gladness and **j** will overtake them,
	55: 12	You will go out in **j** and be led
Lk	1: 44	the baby in my womb leaped for **j**.
	2: 10	will cause great **j** for all the people.
Jn	15: 11	and that your **j** may be complete.
	16: 20	grieve, but your grief will turn to **j**.
2Co	8: 2	trial, their overflowing **j** and their
Php	2: 2	then make my **j** complete by being
	4: 1	love and long for, my **j** and crown,

1Th 2: 19 our **j**, or the crown in which we
Phm : 7 Your love has given me great **j**
Heb 12: 2 the **j** set before him he endured
Jas 1: 2 Consider it pure **j**, my brothers
1Pe 1: 8 an inexpressible and glorious **j**,
2Jn : 4 It has given me great **j** to find some
3Jn : 4 I have no greater **j** than to hear

JOYFUL (JOY)
Ps 100: 1 come before him with **j** songs.
Pr 23: 25 may she who gave you birth be **j**!
Hab 3: 18 I will be **j** in God my Savior.

JUDAH
1. Son of Jacob by Leah (Ge 29:35; 35:23; 1Ch 2:1). Tribe of blessed as ruling tribe (Ge 49:8–12; Dt 33:7).
2. Name used for people and land of Southern Kingdom.

Jer 13: 19 All **J** will be carried into exile,
Zec 10: 4 From **J** will come the cornerstone,
Heb 7: 14 that our Lord descended from **J**,

JUDAISM (JEW)
Gal 1: 13 of my previous way of life in **J**,

JUDAS
1. Apostle (Lk 6:16; Jn 14:22; Ac 1:13). Probably also called Thaddaeus (Mt 10:3; Mk 3:18).
2. Brother of James and Jesus (Mt 13:55; Mk 6:3), also called Jude (Jude 1).
3. Apostle, also called Iscariot, who betrayed Jesus (Mt 10:4; 26:14–56; Mk 3:19; 14:10–50; Lk 6:16; 22:3–53; Jn 6:71; 12:4; 13:2–30; 18:2–11). Suicide of (Mt 27:3–5; Ac 1:16–25).

JUDGE (JUDGED JUDGES JUDGING JUDGMENT)
Ge 18: 25 Will not the **J** of all the earth do
1Ch 16: 33 LORD, for he comes to **j** the earth.
Joel 3: 12 there I will sit to **j** all the nations
Mt 7: 1 "Do not **j**, or you too will be
Jn 7: 24 but instead **j** correctly."
12: 47 For I did not come to **j** the world,
Ac 17: 31 set a day when he will **j** the world
1Co 4: 3 indeed, I do not even **j** myself.
6: 2 the Lord's people will **j** the world?
2Ti 4: 1 who will **j** the living and the dead,
4: 8 the righteous **J**, will award to me
Jas 4: 12 who are you to **j** your neighbor?
Rev 20: 4 who had been given authority to **j**.

JUDGED (JUDGE)
Mt 7: 1 "Do not judge, or you too will be **j**.
Jn 5: 24 will not be **j** but has crossed over
Jas 3: 1 who teach will be **j** more strictly.
Rev 20: 12 The dead were **j** according to what

JUDGES (JUDGE)
Jdg 2: 16 Then the LORD raised up **j**,
Ps 9: 8 and **j** the peoples with equity.
58: 11 there is a God who **j** the earth."
Ro 2: 16 God people's secrets through Jesus
Heb 4: 12 it **j** the thoughts and attitudes
Rev 19: 11 With justice he **j** and wages war.

JUDGING (JUDGE)
Mt 19: 28 **j** the twelve tribes of Israel.
Jn 7: 24 Stop **j** by mere appearances,
2Co 10: 7 You are **j** by appearances.

JUDGMENT (JUDGE)
Dt 1: 17 of anyone, for **j** belongs to God.
Ps 1: 5 the wicked will not stand in the **j**,
119: 66 Teach me knowledge and good **j**,
Ecc 12: 14 God will bring every deed into **j**,
Isa 66: 16 his sword the LORD will execute **j**

Mt 5: 21 who murders will be subject to **j**.'
10: 15 Gomorrah on the day of **j** than
12: 36 the day of **j** for every empty word
Jn 5: 22 but has entrusted all **j** to the Son,
16: 8 about sin and righteousness and **j**:
Ro 14: 10 will all stand before God's **j** seat.
14: 13 Therefore let us stop passing **j**
1Co 11: 29 eat and drink **j** on themselves.
11: 31 we would not come under such **j**.
2Co 5: 10 we must all appear before the **j** seat
Heb 9: 27 to die once, and after that to face **j**,
10: 27 only a fearful expectation of **j**
1Pe 4: 17 For it is time for **j** to begin
Jude : 6 everlasting chains for **j** on the great

JUST (JUSTICE JUSTIFICATION JUSTIFIED JUSTIFY JUSTLY)
Dt 32: 4 are perfect, and all his ways are **j**.
Ps 37: 28 For the LORD loves the **j** and will
111: 7 of his hands are faithful and **j**;
Pr 1: 3 doing what is right and **j** and fair;
2: 8 for he guards the course of the **j**
Da 4: 37 does is right and all his ways are **j**.
Ro 3: 26 time, so as to be **j** and the one who
Heb 2: 2 received its **j** punishment,
1Jn 1: 9 he is faithful and **j** and will forgive
Rev 16: 7 true and **j** are your judgments."

JUSTICE (JUST)
Ex 23: 2 do not pervert **j** by siding
23: 6 "Do not deny **j** to your poor people
Job 37: 23 in his **j** and great righteousness,
Ps 9: 16 LORD is known by his acts of **j**;
11: 7 the LORD is righteous, he loves **j**;
45: 6 a scepter of **j** will be the scepter
101: 1 I will sing of your love and **j**;
Pr 21: 15 When **j** is done, it brings joy
29: 4 By **j** a king gives a country stability,
29: 26 is from the LORD that one gets **j**.
Isa 9: 7 and upholding it with **j**
28: 17 I will make **j** the measuring line
30: 18 For the LORD is a God of **j**.
42: 1 and he will bring **j** to the nations.
42: 4 be discouraged till he establishes **j**
56: 1 "Maintain **j** and do what is right,
61: 8 "For I, the LORD, love **j**;
Eze 34: 16 I will shepherd the flock with **j**.
Am 5: 15 maintain **j** in the courts.
5: 24 But let **j** roll on like a river,
Zec 7: 9 'Administer true **j**; show mercy
Lk 11: 42 you neglect **j** and the love of God.

JUSTIFICATION (JUST)
Ac 13: 39 sin, a **j** you were not able to obtain
Ro 4: 25 sins and was raised to life for our **j**.
5: 18 one righteous act resulted in **j**

JUSTIFIED (JUST)
Ro 3: 24 all are **j** freely by his grace through
3: 28 that a person is **j** by faith apart
5: 1 since we have been **j** through faith,
5: 9 Since we have now been **j** by his
8: 30 he called, he also **j**; those he **j**,
1Co 6: 11 you were **j** in the name of the Lord
Gal 2: 16 that a person is not **j** by the works
3: 11 relies on the law is **j** before God,
3: 24 came that we might be **j** by faith.

JUSTIFY (JUST)
Gal 3: 8 that God would **j** the Gentiles

JUSTLY (JUST)
Ps 106: 3 Blessed are those who act **j**,
Mic 6: 8 To act **j** and to love mercy

KEEP (KEEPER KEEPING KEEPS KEPT)
Ge 31: 49 "May the LORD **k** watch between

Ex	20:	6	love me and **k** my commandments.
Nu	6:	24	Lord bless you and **k** you;
Ps	18:	28	You, Lord, **k** my lamp burning;
	19:	13	**K** your servant also from willful
	121:	7	The Lord will **k** you from all
	141:	3	**k** watch over the door of my lips.
Pr	4:	24	**K** your mouth free of perversity;
	17:	28	are thought wise if they **k** silent,
Isa	26:	3	You will **k** in perfect peace those
Am	5:	13	Therefore the prudent **k** quiet
Mt	10:	10	staff, for the worker is worth his **k**.
Lk	12:	35	service and **k** your lamps burning,
Gal	5:	25	let us **k** in step with the Spirit.
Eph	4:	3	Make every effort to **k** the unity
1Ti	5:	22	the sins of others. **K** yourself pure.
2Ti	4:	5	you, **k** your head in all situations,
Heb	13:	5	**K** your lives free from the love
Jas	1:	26	and yet do not **k** a tight rein on
	2:	8	If you really **k** the royal law found
1Jn	5:	3	love for God: to **k** his commands.
Jude	:	24	To him who is able to **k** you

KEEPER (KEEP)

Ge	4:	9	"Am I my brother's **k**?"

KEEPING (KEEP)

Ex	20:	8	the Sabbath day by **k** it holy.
Ps	19:	11	in **k** them there is great reward.
Mt	3:	8	Produce fruit in **k** with repentance.
Lk	2:	8	**k** watch over their flocks at night.
1Co	7:	19	**K** God's commands is what counts.
2Pe	3:	9	Lord is not slow in **k** his promise,

KEEPS (KEEP)

1Co	13:	5	angered, it **k** no record of wrongs.
Jas	2:	10	For whoever **k** the whole law

KEPT (KEEP)

Ps	130:	3	Lord, **k** a record of sins, Lord,
2Ti	4:	7	finished the race, I have **k** the faith.
1Pe	1:	4	This inheritance is **k** in heaven

KEYS

Mt	16:	19	will give you the **k** of the kingdom

KILL (KILLS)

Mt	17:	23	will **k** him, and on the third day

KILLS (KILL)

Lev	24:	21	whoever **k** a human being is to be
2Co	3:	6	for the letter **k**, but the Spirit gives

KIND (KINDNESS KINDS)

Ge	1:	24	animals, each according to its **k**."
2Ch	10:	7	"If you will be **k** to these people
Pr	11:	17	Those who are **k** benefit themselves,
	12:	25	the heart, but a **k** word cheers it up.
	14:	21	blessed is the one who is **k**
	14:	31	whoever is **k** to the needy honors
	19:	17	Whoever is **k** to the poor lends
Da	4:	27	by being **k** to the oppressed.
Lk	6:	35	because he is **k** to the ungrateful
1Co	13:	4	Love is patient, love is **k**.
	15:	35	what **k** of body will they come?"
Eph	4:	32	Be **k** and compassionate to one
2Ti	2:	24	but must be **k** to everyone,
Titus	2:	5	to be **k**, and to be subject to their

KINDNESS (KIND)

Ac	14:	17	He has shown **k** by giving you rain
Ro	11:	22	but **k** to you, provided that you
			continue in his **k**.
Gal	5:	22	peace, forbearance, **k**, goodness,
Eph	2:	7	expressed in his **k** to us in Christ

KINDS (KIND)

1Co	12:	4	There are different **k** of gifts,
1Ti	6:	10	of money is a root of all **k** of evil.

KING (KINGDOM KINGS)

1. Kings of Judah and Israel: see Saul, David, Solomon.

2. Kings of Judah: see Rehoboam, Abijah, Asa, Jehoshaphat, Jehoram, Ahaziah, Athaliah (Queen), Joash, Amaziah, Uzziah, Jotham, Ahaz, Hezekiah, Manasseh, Amon, Josiah, Jehoahaz, Jehoiakim, Jehoiachin, Zedekiah.

3. Kings of Israel: see Jeroboam I, Nadab, Baasha, Elah, Zimri, Tibni, Omri, Ahab, Ahaziah, Joram, Jehu, Jehoahaz, Jehoash, Jeroboam II, Zechariah, Shallum, Menahem, Pekah, Pekahiah, Hoshea.

Jdg	17:	6	In those days Israel had no **k**;
1Sa	12:	12	'No, we want a **k** to rule over us'—
	12:	12	the Lord your God was your **k**.
Ps	24:	7	that the **K** of glory may come in.
Isa	32:	1	a **k** will reign in righteousness
Zec	9:	9	See, your **k** comes to you,
1Ti	6:	15	the **K** of kings and Lord of lords,
Rev	19:	16	thigh he has this name written: **K**

KINGDOM (KING)

Ex	19:	6	you will be for me a **k** of priests
1Ch	29:	11	Yours, Lord, is the **k**;
Ps	45:	6	justice will be the scepter of your **k**.
Da	4:	3	His **k** is an eternal **k**;
Mt	3:	2	for the **k** of heaven has come near."
	5:	3	spirit, for theirs is the **k** of heaven.
	6:	10	your **k** come, your will be done,
	6:	33	But seek first his **k** and his
	7:	21	Lord,' will enter the **k** of heaven,
	11:	11	the **k** of heaven is greater than he.
	13:	24	"The **k** of heaven is like a man who
	13:	31	"The **k** of heaven is like a mustard
	13:	33	"The **k** of heaven is like yeast
	13:	44	"The **k** of heaven is like treasure
	13:	45	the **k** of heaven is like a merchant
	13:	47	the **k** of heaven is like a net that
	16:	19	you the keys of the **k** of heaven;
	18:	23	the **k** of heaven is like a king who
	19:	24	who is rich to enter the **k** of God."
	24:	7	rise against nation, and **k** against **k**.
	24:	14	gospel of the **k** will be preached
	25:	34	the **k** prepared for you since
Mk	9:	47	you to enter the **k** of God with one
	10:	14	for the **k** of God belongs to such as
	10:	23	for the rich to enter the **k** of God!"
Lk	10:	9	'The **k** of God has come near
	12:	31	But seek his **k**, and these things
	17:	21	is,' because the **k** of God is in your
Jn	3:	5	one can enter the **k** of God unless
	18:	36	said, "My **k** is not of this world.
1Co	6:	9	wrongdoers will not inherit the **k**
	15:	24	when he hands over the **k** to God
Rev	1:	6	has made us to be a **k** and priests
	11:	15	"The **k** of the world has become

KINGS (KING)

Ps	2:	2	The **k** of the earth rise
	72:	11	May all **k** bow down to him and all
Da	7:	24	ten horns are ten **k** who will come
1Ti	2:	2	for **k** and all those in authority,
Rev	1:	5	and the ruler of the **k** of the earth.

KISS

Ps	2:	12	**K** his son, or he will be angry
Pr	24:	26	An honest answer is like a **k**
Lk	22:	48	the Son of Man with a **k**?"

KNEE (KNEES)

Isa	45:	23	Before me every **k** will bow;
Ro	14:	11	Lord, 'every **k** will bow before me;
Php	2:	10	name of Jesus every **k** should bow,

KNEES (KNEE)

Isa	35:	3	hands, steady the **k** that give way;
Heb	12:	12	your feeble arms and weak **k**.

KNEW (KNOW)

Job	23:	3	If only I **k** where to find him;
Jnh	4:	2	I **k** that you are a gracious
Mt	7:	23	tell them plainly, 'I never **k** you.

KNOCK

| Mt | 7: | 7 | **k** and the door will be opened |
| Rev | 3: | 20 | I stand at the door and **k**. |

KNOW (FOREKNEW KNEW KNOWING KNOWLEDGE KNOWN KNOWS)

Dt	18:	21	"How can we **k** when a message
Job	19:	25	I **k** that my redeemer lives,
	42:	3	things too wonderful for me to **k**.
Ps	46:	10	says, "Be still, and **k** that I am God;
	73:	11	Does the Most High **k** anything?"
	139:	1	LORD, and you **k** me.
	139:	23	Search me, God, and **k** my heart;
Pr	27:	1	you do not **k** what a day may bring.
Jer	24:	7	I will give them a heart to **k** me,
	31:	34	because they will all **k** me,
Mt	6:	3	let your left hand **k** what your right
	24:	42	because you do not **k** on what day
Lk	1:	4	so that you may **k** the certainty
Jn	3:	11	you, we speak of what we **k**, and we
	4:	22	worship what you do not **k**;
	9:	25	One thing I do **k**. I was blind
	10:	14	I **k** my sheep and my sheep **k** me—
	17:	3	that they **k** you, the only true God,
	21:	24	We **k** that his testimony is true.
Ac	1:	7	"It is not for you to **k** the times
Ro	6:	6	we **k** that our old self was crucified
	7:	18	I **k** that good itself does not dwell
	8:	28	we **k** that in all things God works
1Co	2:	2	I resolved to **k** nothing while I was
	6:	15	Do you not **k** that your bodies are
	6:	19	Do you not **k** that your bodies are
	8:	2	do not yet **k** as they ought to **k**.
	13:	12	Now I **k** in part; then I shall **k** fully,
	15:	58	because you **k** that your labor
Php	3:	10	I want to **k** Christ—yes, to **k**
2Ti	1:	12	because I **k** whom I have believed,
Jas	4:	14	do not even **k** what will happen
1Jn	2:	4	Whoever says, "I **k** him," but does
	3:	14	We **k** that we have passed
	3:	16	This is how we **k** what love is:
	5:	2	This is how we **k** that we love
	5:	13	may **k** that you have eternal life.

KNOWING (KNOW)

| Ge | 3: | 5 | will be like God, **k** good and evil." |
| Php | 3: | 8 | worth of **k** Christ Jesus my Lord, |

KNOWLEDGE (KNOW)

Ge	2:	9	the tree of the **k** of good and evil.
Job	42:	3	that obscures my plans without **k**?'
Ps	19:	2	night after night they reveal **k**.
	139:	6	Such **k** is too wonderful for me,
Pr	1:	7	of the LORD is the beginning of **k**,
	10:	14	The wise store up **k**, but the mouth
	12:	1	Whoever loves discipline loves **k**,
	13:	16	All who are prudent act with **k**,
	19:	2	Desire without **k** is not good—
Isa	11:	9	the **k** of the LORD as the waters
Hab	2:	14	will be filled with the **k** of the glory
Ro	11:	33	riches of the wisdom and **k** of God!
1Co	8:	1	But **k** puffs up while love builds up.
	8:	11	Christ died, is destroyed by your **k**.
	13:	2	can fathom all mysteries and all **k**,
2Co	2:	14	aroma of the **k** of him everywhere.
	4:	6	of the **k** of God's glory displayed
Eph	3:	19	know this love that surpasses **k**—
Col	2:	3	all the treasures of wisdom and **k**.
1Ti	6:	20	ideas of what is falsely called **k**,
2Pe	3:	18	grow in the grace and **k** of our Lord

KNOWN (KNOW)

Ps	16:	11	You make **k** to me the path of life;
	105:	1	make **k** among the nations what he
Isa	46:	10	I make **k** the end
Mt	10:	26	or hidden that will not be made **k**.
Ro	1:	19	since what may be **k** about God is
	11:	34	"Who has **k** the mind of the Lord?
	15:	20	the gospel where Christ was not **k**,
2Co	3:	2	our hearts, **k** and read by everyone.
2Pe	2:	21	than to have **k** it and then to turn

KNOWS (KNOW)

1Sa	2:	3	for the LORD is a God who **k**,
Job	23:	10	But he **k** the way that I take;
Ps	44:	21	since he **k** the secrets of the heart?
	94:	11	The LORD **k** all human plans; he **k**
Ecc	8:	7	Since no one **k** the future, who can
Mt	6:	8	your Father **k** what you need
	24:	36	about that day or hour no one **k**,
Ro	8:	27	searches our hearts **k** the mind
2Ti	2:	19	"The Lord **k** those who are his,"

LABAN

Brother of Rebekah (Ge 24:29–51), father of Rachel and Leah (Ge 29–31).

LABOR

Ex	20:	9	Six days you shall I and do all your
Isa	55:	2	your I on what does not satisfy?
Mt	6:	28	They do not I or spin.
1Co	3:	8	rewarded according to their own I.
	15:	58	know that your I in the Lord is not

LACK (LACKING LACKS)

| Pr | 15: | 22 | Plans fail for I of counsel, |
| Col | 2: | 23 | but they I any value in restraining |

LACKING (LACK)

| Ro | 12: | 11 | Never be I in zeal, but keep your |
| Jas | 1: | 4 | and complete, not I anything. |

LACKS (LACK)

| Jas | 1: | 5 | If any of you I wisdom, you should |

LAID (LAY)

Isa	53:	6	and the LORD has I on him
1Co	3:	11	other than the one already I,
1Jn	3:	16	Jesus Christ I down his life for us.

LAKE

| Rev | 19: | 20 | into the fiery I of burning sulfur. |
| | 20: | 14 | The I of fire is the second death. |

LAMB (LAMB'S LAMBS)

Ge	22:	8	"God himself will provide the I
Ex	12:	21	and slaughter the Passover I.
Isa	11:	6	The wolf will live with the I,
	53:	7	he was led like a I to the slaughter,
Jn	1:	29	"Look, the L of God, who takes
1Co	5:	7	our Passover I, has been sacrificed.
1Pe	1:	19	a I without blemish or defect.
Rev	5:	6	Then I saw a L, looking as if it had
	5:	12	"Worthy is the L, who was slain,
	14:	4	as firstfruits to God and the L.

LAMB'S (LAMB)

| Rev | 21: | 27 | names are written in the L book |

LAMBS (LAMB)

| Lk | 10: | 3 | you out like I among wolves. |
| Jn | 21: | 15 | Jesus said, "Feed my I." |

LAMENT

| 2Sa | 1: | 17 | took up this I concerning Saul |

LAMP (LAMPS)

| 2Sa | 22: | 29 | You, LORD, are my I; |

Ps 18: 28 You, Lᴏʀᴅ, keep my **l** burning;
    119:105 Your word is a **l** to my feet
Pr 31: 18 and her **l** does not go out at night.
Lk   8: 16 "No one lights a **l** and hides it
Rev 21: 23 gives it light, and the Lamb is its **l**.

LAMPS (LAMP)
Mt 25: 1 be like ten virgins who took their **l**
Lk 12: 35 service and keep your **l** burning,

LAND
Ge   1: 10 God called the dry ground "**l**,"
     1: 11 said, "Let the **l** produce vegetation:
    12: 7 your offspring I will give this **l**."
Ex   3: 8 a **l** flowing with milk and honey—
Nu 35: 33 Bloodshed pollutes the **l**,
Dt 34: 1 Lᴏʀᴅ showed him the whole **l**—
Jos 13: 2 "This is the **l** that remains:
    14: 4 Levites received no share of the **l**
2Ch 7: 14 their sin and will heal their **l**.
     7: 20 then I will uproot Israel from my **l**,
Eze 36: 24 bring you back into your own **l**.

LANGUAGE
Ge 11: 1 Now the whole world had one **l**
Jn   8: 44 speaks his native **l**, for he is a liar
Ac   2: 6 heard their own **l** being spoken.
Col 3: 8 slander, and filthy **l** from your lips.
Rev 5: 9 God persons from every tribe and **l**

LAST (LASTING LASTS LATTER)
2Sa 23: 1 These are the **l** words of David:
Isa 44: 6 I am the first and I am the **l**;
Mt 19: 30 But many who are first will be **l**,
Mk 10: 31 will be **l**, and the **l** first."
Jn 15: 16 fruit that will **l**—and so
Ro   1: 7 that is by faith from first to **l**,
2Ti 3: 1 will be terrible times in the **l** days.
2Pe 3: 3 in the **l** days scoffers will come,
Rev 1: 17 I am the First and the **L**.
    22: 13 the First and the **L**, the Beginning

LASTING (LAST)
Ex 12: 14 to the Lᴏʀᴅ—a **l** ordinance.
Lev 24: 8 of the Israelites, as a **l** covenant.
Nu 25: 13 have a covenant of a **l** priesthood,
Heb 10: 34 had better and **l** possessions.

LASTS (LAST)
Ps 30: 5 For his anger **l** only a moment,
2Co 3: 11 greater is the glory of that which **ll**!

LATTER (LAST)
Job 42: 12 The Lᴏʀᴅ blessed the **l** part

LAUGH (LAUGHS)
Ecc 3: 4 a time to weep and a time to **l**,

LAUGHS (LAUGH)
Ps   2: 4 The One enthroned in heaven **l**;
    37: 13 but the Lord **l** at the wicked, for he

LAVISHED
Eph 1: 8 that he **l** on us. With all wisdom
1Jn 3: 1 See what great love the Father has **l**

LAW (LAWS)
Dt 31: 11 you shall read this **l** before them
    31: 26 "Take this Book of the **L** and place
Jos 1: 8 Keep this Book of the **L** always
Ne   8: 8 from the Book of the **L** of God,
Ps   1: 2 delight is in the **l** of the Lᴏʀᴅ,
    19: 7 The **l** of the Lᴏʀᴅ is perfect,
    119: 18 may see wonderful things in your **l**.
    119: 72 The **l** from your mouth is more
    119: 97 Oh, how I love your **l**! I meditate
    119:165 peace have those who love your **l**,

Jer 31: 33 "I will put my **l** in their minds
Mt   5: 17 that I have come to abolish the **L**
     7: 12 you, for this sums up the **L**
    22: 40 All the **L** and the Prophets hang
Lk 16: 17 stroke of a pen to drop out of the **L**.
Jn   1: 17 For the **l** was given through Moses;
Ro   2: 12 All who sin apart from the **l** will
     2: 15 requirements of the **l** are written
     5: 13 account where there is no **l**.
     5: 20 The **l** was brought in so
     6: 14 because you are not under the **l**,
     7: 6 we have been released from the **l** so
     7: 12 So then, the **l** is holy,
     8: 3 For what the **l** was powerless to do
    10: 4 Christ is the culmination of the **l**
    13: 10 love is the fulfillment of the **l**.
Gal 3: 13 curse of the **l** by becoming a curse
     3: 24 So the **l** was our guardian until
     5: 3 he is obligated to obey the whole **l**.
     5: 4 by the **l** have been alienated
     5: 14 For the entire **l** is fulfilled
Heb 7: 19 (for the **l** made nothing perfect),
    10: 1 The **l** is only a shadow of the good
Jas 1: 25 the perfect **l** that gives freedom,
     2: 10 For whoever keeps the whole **l**

LAWLESSNESS
2Th 2: 3 occurs and the man of **l** is revealed,
     2: 7 the secret power of **l** is already
1Jn 3: 4 sins breaks the law; in fact, sin is **l**.

LAWS (LAW)
Lev 25: 18 and be careful to obey my **l**,
Ps 119: 30 I have set my heart on your **l**.
    119:120 fear of you; I stand in awe of your **l**.
Heb 8: 10 I will put my **l** in their minds
    10: 16 I will put my **l** in their hearts, and I

LAY (LAID LAYING)
Job 22: 22 and **l** up his words in your heart.
Isa 28: 16 "See, I **l** a stone in Zion, a tested
Mt   8: 20 of Man has no place to **l** his head."
Jn 10: 15 and I **l** down my life for the sheep.
    15: 13 to **l** down one's life for one's
1Co 3: 11 no one can **l** any foundation other
1Jn 3: 16 we ought to **l** down our lives for
Rev 4: 10 They **l** their crowns before

LAYING (LAY)
1Ti 5: 22 not be hasty in the **l** on of hands,
Heb 6: 1 not **l** again the foundation

LAZARUS
1. Poor man in Jesus' parable (Lk 16:19–31).
2. Brother of Mary and Martha whom Jesus raised from the dead (Jn 11:1—12:19).

LAZY
Pr 10: 4 **L** hands make for poverty,
Heb 6: 12 We do not want you to become **l**,

LEAD (LEADERS LEADS LED)
Ex 15: 13 love you will **l** the people you have
Ps 27: 11 **l** me in a straight path because
    61: 2 **l** me to the rock that is higher
                than I.
    139: 24 and **l** me in the way everlasting.
    143: 10 may your good Spirit **l** me on level
Ecc 5: 6 Do not let your mouth **l** you
Isa 11: 6 and a little child will **l** them.
Da 12: 3 those who **l** many to righteousness,
Mt   6: 13 And **l** us not into temptation,
1Jn 3: 7 do not let anyone **l** you astray.

LEADERS (LEAD)
Heb 13: 7 Remember your **l**, who spoke
    13: 17 Have confidence in your **l**

LEADS (LEAD)
Ps	23:	2	he I me beside quiet waters,
Pr	19:	23	The fear of the LORD I to life;
Isa	40:	11	he gently I those that have young.
Mt	7:	13	gate and broad is the road that I
Jn	10:	3	sheep by name and I them out.
Ro	14:	19	every effort to do what I to peace
2Co	2:	14	God, who always I us as captives

LEAH
Wife of Jacob (Ge 29:16–30); bore six sons and one daughter (Ge 29:31—30:21; 34:1; 35:23).

LEAN
Pr	3:	5	I not on your own understanding;

LEARN (LEARNED LEARNING)
Isa	1:	17	**L** to do right; seek justice.
Mt	11:	29	my yoke upon you and I from me,

LEARNED (LEARN)
Php	4:	11	I have I to be content whatever
2Ti	3:	14	know those from whom you I it,

LEARNING (LEARN)
Pr	1:	5	the wise listen and add to their I,
2Ti	3:	7	always I but never able to come

LED (LEAD)
Isa	53:	7	he was I like a lamb
Am	2:	10	I you forty years in the wilderness
Ro	8:	14	For those who are I by the Spirit

LEFT
Jos	1:	7	turn from it to the right or to the I,
Pr	4:	27	Do not turn to the right or the I;
Mt	6:	3	do not let your I hand know what
	25:	33	on his right and the goats on his I.

LEGION
Mk	5:	9	"My name is **L**," he replied,

LEND (LENDS)
Dt	15:	8	freely I them whatever they need.
Ps	37:	26	are always generous and I freely;
Lk	6:	34	Even sinners I to sinners,

LENDS (LEND)
Pr	19:	17	kind to the poor I to the LORD,

LENGTH (LONG)
Pr	10:	27	fear of the LORD adds I to life,

LEPROSY
2Ki	7:	3	Now there were four men with I

LETTER (LETTERS)
Mt	5:	18	not the smallest I, not the least
2Co	3:	2	You yourselves are our I,
	3:	6	not of the I but of the Spirit; for the I kills,
2Th	3:	14	not obey our instruction in this I.

LETTERS (LETTER)
2Co	3:	7	which was engraved in I on stone,
	10:	10	"His I are weighty and forceful,
2Pe	3:	16	He writes the same way in all his I,

LEVEL
Ps	143:	10	good Spirit lead me on I ground.
Isa	26:	7	The path of the righteous is I;
Heb	12:	13	"Make I paths for your feet,"

LEVI (LEVITES)
1. Son of Jacob by Leah (Ge 29:34; 46:11; 1Ch 2:1). Tribe of blessed (Ge 49:5–7; Dt 33:8–11), chosen as priests (Nu 3–4), numbered (Nu 3:39; 26:62), allotted cities, but not land (Nu 18; 35; Dt 10:9;

Jos 13:14; 21), land (Eze 48:8–22), 12,000 from (Rev 7:7).
2. See MATTHEW.

LEVITES (LEVI)
Nu	1:	53	The **L** are to be responsible
	8:	6	"Take the **L** from among all
	18:	21	"I give to the **L** all the tithes

LEWDNESS
Mk	7:	22	malice, deceit, I, envy, slander,

LIAR (LIE)
Pr	19:	22	better to be poor than a I.
Jn	8:	44	for he is a I and the father of lies.
Ro	3:	4	be true, and every human being a I.

LIBERATED
Ro	8:	21	the creation itself will be I from its

LIE (LIAR LIED LIES LYING)
Lev	19:	11	" 'Do not I. " 'Do not deceive
Nu	23:	19	that he should I, not a human
Dt	6:	7	when you I down and when you
Ps	23:	2	He makes me I down in green
Isa	11:	6	the leopard will I down
Eze	34:	14	There they will I down in good
Ro	1:	25	the truth about God for a I,
Col	3:	9	Do not I to each other, since you
Heb	6:	18	which it is impossible for God to I,

LIED (LIE)
Ac	5:	4	You have not I just to human

LIES (LIE)
Ps	34:	13	evil and your lips from telling I.
Jn	8:	44	for he is a liar and the father of I.

LIFE (LIVE)
Ge	2:	7	into his nostrils the breath of I,
	2:	9	of the garden were the tree of I
	9:	11	Never again will all I be destroyed
Ex	21:	23	injury, you are to take I for I,
Lev	17:	14	because the I of every creature is its
	24:	18	must make restitution—I for I.
Dt	30:	19	Now choose I, so that you and your
Ps	16:	11	make known to me the path of I;
	23:	6	will follow me all the days of my I,
	34:	12	Whoever of you loves I and desires
	39:	4	let me know how fleeting my I is.
	49:	7	one can redeem the I of another
	104:	33	I will sing to the LORD all my I;
Pr	6:	23	and instruction are the way to I,
	7:	23	little knowing it will cost him his I.
	8:	35	For those who find me find I
	11:	30	fruit of the righteous is a tree of I,
	21:	21	righteousness and love finds I,
Eze	37:	5	enter you, and you will come to I.
Da	12:	2	some to everlasting I,
Mt	6:	25	do not worry about your I,
	7:	14	and narrow the road that leads to I,
	10:	39	whoever loses their I for my sake
	16:	25	wants to save their I will lose it,
	20:	28	to give his I as a ransom for many."
Mk	10:	45	to give his I as a ransom for many."
Lk	12:	15	I does not consist in an abundance
	12:	22	do not worry about your I,
	14:	26	yes, even their own I—
Jn	1:	4	In him was I, and that I was the light
	3:	15	who believes may have eternal I
	3:	36	believes in the Son has eternal I,
	4:	14	of water welling up to eternal I."
	5:	24	has crossed over from death to I.
	6:	35	Jesus declared, "I am the bread of I.
	6:	47	the one who believes has eternal I.

Jn	6:	68	You have the words of eternal **l**.
	10:	10	I have come that they may have **l**,
	10:	15	and I lay down my **l** for the sheep.
	10:	28	I give them eternal **l**, and they shall
	11:	25	"I am the resurrection and the **l**.
	14:	6	am the way and the truth and the **l**.
	15:	13	lay down one's **l** for one's friends.
	20:	31	by believing you may have **l** in his
Ac	13:	48	appointed for eternal **l** believed.
Ro	4:	25	was raised to **l** for our justification.
	6:	13	have been brought from death to **l**;
	6:	23	God is eternal **l** in Christ Jesus our
	8:	38	convinced that neither death nor **l**,
1Co	15:	19	If only for this **l** we have hope
2Co	3:	6	the letter kills, but the Spirit gives **l**.
Gal	2:	20	The **l** I now live in the body, I live
Eph	4:	1	to live a **l** worthy of the calling you
Php	2:	16	as you hold firmly to the word of **l**.
Col	1:	10	you may live a **l** worthy of the Lord
1Th	4:	1	your daily **l** may win the respect
1Ti	4:	8	the present **l** and the **l** to come.
	4:	16	Watch your **l** and doctrine closely.
	6:	19	take hold of the **l** that is truly **l**.
2Ti	3:	12	live a godly **l** in Christ Jesus will be
Jas	1:	12	person will receive the crown of **l**
	3:	13	Let them show it by their good **l**,
1Pe	3:	10	"Whoever would love **l** and see
2Pe	1:	3	a godly **l** through our knowledge
1Jn	3:	14	we have passed from death to **l**,
	5:	11	God has given us eternal **l**, and this **l**
Rev	13:	8	written in the Lamb's book of **l**,
	20:	12	was opened, which is the book of **l**.
	21:	27	are written in the Lamb's book of **l**.
	22:	2	side of the river stood the tree of **l**,

LIFT (LIFTED LIFTING)

Ps	121:	1	I **l** up my eyes to the mountains—
	134:	2	**L** up your hands in the sanctuary
La	3:	41	Let us **l** up our hearts and our hands

LIFTED (LIFT)

Ps	40:	2	He **l** me out of the slimy pit,
Jn	3:	14	so the Son of Man must be **l** up,
	12:	32	I, when I am **l** up from the earth,

LIFTING (LIFT)

1Ti	2:	8	**l** up holy hands without anger

LIGHT (ENLIGHTENED)

Ge	1:	3	"Let there be **l**," and there was **l**.
2Sa	22:	29	Lord turns my darkness into **l**.
Job	38:	19	"What is the way to the abode of **l**?
Ps	4:	6	Let the **l** of your face shine on us.
	19:	8	are radiant, giving **l** to the eyes.
	27:	1	The Lord is my **l** and my
	56:	13	walk before God in the **l** of life.
	76:	4	You are radiant with **l**,
	104:	2	The Lord wraps himself in **l** as
	119:105		lamp to my feet and a **l** for my path.
	119:130		unfolding of your words gives **l**;
Isa	2:	5	let us walk in the **l** of the Lord.
	9:	2	in darkness have seen a great **l**;
	49:	6	also make you a **l** for the Gentiles,
Mt	4:	16	shadow of death a **l** has dawned."
	5:	16	way, let your **l** shine before others,
	11:	30	yoke is easy and my burden is **l**."
Jn	3:	19	**L** has come into the world,
	8:	12	he said, "I am the **l** of the world.
2Co	4:	6	made his **l** shine in our hearts
	6:	14	Or what fellowship can **l** have
	11:	14	masquerades as an angel of **l**.
1Ti	6:	16	and who lives in unapproachable **l**,
1Pe	2:	9	of darkness into his wonderful **l**.
1Jn	1:	5	God is **l**; in him there is no darkness
	1:	7	But if we walk in the **l**, as he is
Rev	21:	23	for the glory of God gives it **l**,

LIGHTNING

Da	10:	6	his face like **l**, his eyes like flaming
Mt	24:	27	For as **l** that comes from the east is
	28:	3	His appearance was like **l**, and his

LIKENESS

Ge	1:	26	in our **l**, so that they may rule over
Ps	17:	15	will be satisfied with seeing your **l**.
Isa	52:	14	his form marred beyond human **l**
Ro	8:	3	his own Son in the **l** of sinful flesh
Php	2:	7	a servant, being made in human **l**.
Jas	3:	9	who have been made in God's **l**.

LION

Isa	11:	7	and the **l** will eat straw like the ox.
1Pe	5:	8	around like a roaring **l** looking
Rev	5:	5	See, the **L** of the tribe of Judah,

LIPS

Ps	34:	1	his praise will always be on my **l**.
	119:171		May my **l** overflow with praise,
Pr	13:	3	who guard their **l** preserve their
	27:	2	an outsider, and not your own **l**.
Isa	6:	5	For I am a man of unclean **l**, and I
Mt	21:	16	read, " 'From the **l** of children
Col	3:	8	and filthy language from your **l**.

LISTEN (LISTENING)

Dt	30:	20	Lord your God, **l** to his voice,
Pr	1:	5	let the wise **l** and add to their
	12:	15	to them, but the wise **l** to advice.
Jn	10:	27	My sheep **l** to my voice;
Jas	1:	19	Everyone should be quick to **l**,
	1:	22	Do not merely **l** to the word,

LISTENING (LISTEN)

1Sa	3:	9	Lord, for your servant is **l**.' "
Pr	18:	13	To answer before **l**—that is folly

LIVE (ALIVE LIFE LIVES LIVING)

Ex	20:	12	that you may **l** long in the land
	33:	20	face, for no one may see me and **l**."
Dt	8:	3	that man does not **l** on bread alone
Job	14:	14	If someone dies, will they **l** again?
Ps	119:175		Let me **l** that I may praise you,
Isa	55:	3	come to me; listen, that you may **l**.
Eze	37:	3	"Son of man, can these bones **l**?"
Hab	2:	4	the righteous person will **l** by his
Mt	4:	4	'Man shall not **l** on bread alone,
Ac	17:	24	not **l** in temples built by human
	17:	28	'For in him we **l** and move and
Ro	1:	17	"The righteous will **l** by faith."
2Co	5:	7	For we **l** by faith, not by sight.
Gal	2:	20	The life I now **l** in the body,
	5:	25	Since we **l** by the Spirit, let us keep
Php	1:	21	me, to **l** is Christ and to die is gain.
1Th	5:	13	**L** in peace with each other.
2Ti	3:	12	who wants to **l** a godly life
Heb	12:	14	Make every effort to **l** in peace
1Pe	1:	17	**l** out your time as foreigners here

LIVES (LIVE)

Job	19:	25	I know that my redeemer **l**,
Pr	11:	30	and the one who is wise saves **l**.
Isa	57:	15	he who **l** forever, whose name is
Da	3:	28	to give up their **l** rather than serve
Jn	14:	17	he **l** with you and will be in you.
Gal	2:	20	I no longer live, but Christ **l** in me.
Heb	13:	5	Keep your **l** free from the love
2Pe	3:	11	You ought to live holy and godly **l**
1Jn	3:	16	to lay down our **l** for our brothers
	4:	16	Whoever **l** in love **l** in God,

LIVING (LIVE)

Ge	2:	7	life, and the man became a **l** being.
Jer	2:	13	the spring of **l** water, and have dug
Mt	22:	32	the God of the dead but of the **l**."

Jn	7: 38	said, rivers of **l** water will flow
Ro	12: 1	to offer your bodies as a **l** sacrifice,
Heb	10: 31	to fall into the hands of the **l** God.
Rev	1: 18	I am the **L** One; I was dead,

LOAD

Gal	6: 5	each one should carry their own **l**.

LOCUSTS

Mt	3: 4	His food was **l** and wild honey.

LOFTY

Ps	139: 6	for me, too **l** for me to attain.

LONELY

Ps	68: 6	God sets the **l** in families, he leads

LONG (LENGTH LONGED LONGING LONGS)

1Ki	18: 21	"How **l** will you waver between
Jn	9: 4	As **l** as it is day, we must do
Eph	3: 18	to grasp how wide and **l** and high
1Pe	1: 12	Even angels **l** to look into these

LONGED (LONG)

Mt	13: 17	righteous people **l** to see what you
	23: 37	how often I have **l** to gather your
2Ti	4: 8	to all who have **l** for his appearing.

LONGING (LONG)

Pr	13: 19	A **l** fulfilled is sweet to the soul,
2Co	5: 2	**l** to be clothed instead with our

LONGS (LONG)

Isa	30: 18	Yet the LORD **l** to be gracious

LOOK (LOOKING LOOKS)

Job	31: 1	my eyes not to **l** lustfully at a young
Ps	34: 5	Those who **l** to him are radiant;
Pr	4: 25	Let your eyes **l** straight ahead;
Isa	60: 5	Then you will **l** and be radiant,
Hab	1: 13	Your eyes are too pure to **l** on evil;
Zec	12: 10	They will **l** on me, the one they
Mk	13: 21	is the Messiah!' or, 'L, there he is!'
Lk	24: 39	**L** at my hands and my feet. It is I
Jn	1: 36	by, he said, "L, the Lamb of God!"
	4: 35	open your eyes and **l** at the fields!
	19: 37	"They will **l** on the one they have
Jas	1: 27	to **l** after orphans and widows
1Pe	1: 12	Even angels long to **l** into these

LOOKING (LOOK)

Rev	5: 6	a Lamb, **l** as if it had been slain,

LOOKS (LOOK)

1Sa	16: 7	but the LORD **l** at the heart."
Lk	9: 62	puts a hand to the plow and **l** back
Php	2: 21	everyone **l** out for their own interests,

LORD (LORD'S LORDING)

Ne	4: 14	Remember the **L**, who is great
Job	28: 28	human race, "The fear of the **L**—
Ps	54: 4	the **L** is the one who sustains me.
	62: 12	and with you, **L**, is unfailing love";
	86: 5	You, **L**, are forgiving and good,
	110: 1	The LORD says to my **l**:
	147: 5	Great is our **L** and mighty in power
Isa	6: 1	died, I saw the **L**, high and exalted,
Da	9: 4	"L, the great and awesome God,
Mt	3: 3	'Prepare the way for the **L**,
	4: 7	'Do not put the **L** your God
	7: 21	"Not everyone who says to me, 'L,
	22: 37	" 'Love the **L** your God with all
	22: 44	" 'The **L** said to my **L**: "Sit at my
Mk	12: 11	the **L** has done this, and it is
	12: 29	The **L** our God, the **L** is one.
Lk	2: 9	An angel of the **L** appeared to
	6: 46	"Why do you call me, 'L, L,'
	10: 27	" 'Love the **L** your God with all

Ac	2: 21	on the name of the **L** will be saved.'
	16: 31	"Believe in the **L** Jesus, and you
Ro	10: 9	"Jesus is **L**," and believe in your
	10: 13	the name of the **L** will be saved."
	12: 11	your spiritual fervor, serving the **L**.
	14: 8	we live or die, we belong to the **L**.
1Co	1: 31	the one who boasts boast in the **L**."
	3: 5	as the **L** has assigned to each his
	7: 34	to be devoted to the **L** in both body
	11: 23	The **L** Jesus, on the night he was
	12: 3	"Jesus is **L**," except by the Holy
	15: 57	victory through our **L** Jesus Christ.
	16: 22	let that person be cursed! Come, **L**!
2Co	3: 17	Now the **L** is the Spirit, and where
	8: 5	gave themselves first of all to the **L**,
	10: 17	the one who boasts boast in the **L**."
Gal	6: 14	in the cross of our **L** Jesus Christ,
Eph	4: 5	one **L**, one faith, one baptism;
	5: 10	and find out what pleases the **L**.
	5: 19	music from your heart to the **L**,
Php	2: 11	acknowledge that Jesus Christ is **L**,
	3: 1	and sisters, rejoice in the **L**!
	4: 4	Rejoice in the **L** always. I will say it
Col	2: 6	as you received Christ Jesus as **L**,
	3: 17	do it all in the name of the **L** Jesus,
	3: 23	working for the **L**, not for human
	4: 17	you have received in the **L**."
1Th	3: 12	May the **L** make your love increase
	5: 2	day of the **L** will come like a thief
	5: 23	at the coming of our **L** Jesus Christ.
2Th	2: 1	the coming of our **L** Jesus Christ
2Ti	2: 19	"The **L** knows those who are his,"
Heb	12: 14	holiness no one will see the **L**.
	13: 6	confidence, "The **L** is my helper;
Jas	4: 10	Humble yourselves before the **L**,
1Pe	1: 25	the word of the **L** endures forever."
	2: 3	you have tasted that the **L** is good.
	3: 15	in your hearts revere Christ as **L**.
2Pe	1: 16	the coming of our **L** Jesus Christ
	2: 1	sovereign **L** who bought them—
	3: 9	The **L** is not slow in keeping his
Jude	: 14	the **L** is coming with thousands
Rev	4: 8	holy is the **L** God Almighty,'
	4: 11	"You are worthy, our **L** and God,
	17: 14	triumph over them because he is **L**
	22: 20	Amen. Come, **L** Jesus.

LORD'S (LORD)

Ac	21: 14	up and said, "The **L** will be done."
1Co	10: 26	"The earth is the **L**, and everything
	11: 26	you proclaim the **L** death until he
2Co	3: 18	faces contemplate the **L** glory,
2Ti	2: 24	And the **L** servant must not be
Jas	4: 15	"If it is the **L** will, we will live

LORDING (LORD)

1Pe	5: 3	not **l** it over those entrusted to you,

LORD* (LORD'S*; this is the proper name of God, Yahweh, spelled "LORD" in the NIV)

Ge	2: 4	when the **L** God made the earth
	2: 7	the **L** God formed a man
	3: 21	The **L** God made garments of skin
	7: 16	Then the **L** shut him in.
	15: 6	Abram believed the **L**, and he
	18: 14	Is anything too hard for the **L**?
	31: 49	"May the **L** keep watch between
Ex	3: 2	There the angel of the **L** appeared
	9: 12	But the **L** hardened Pharaoh's heart
	14: 30	That day the **L** saved Israel
	20: 2	"I am the **L** your God, who
	33: 11	The **L** would speak to Moses face
	40: 34	glory of the **L** filled the tabernacle.
Lev	19: 2	'Be holy because I, the **L** your God,
Nu	8: 5	The **L** said to Moses:
	14: 21	glory of the **L** fills the whole earth,

Dt	2:	7	The **L** your God has blessed you
	5:	9	for I, the **L** your God, am a jealous
	6:	4	The **L** our God, the **L** is one.
	6:	5	Love the **L** your God with all your
	6:	16	Do not put the **L** your God
	10:	14	**L** your God belong the heavens,
	10:	17	For the **L** your God is God of gods
	11:	1	Love the **L** your God and keep his
	28:	1	If you fully obey the **L** your God
	30:	16	you today to love the **L** your God,
	30:	20	For the **L** is your life, and he will
	31:	6	for the **L** your God goes with you;
Jos	22:	5	to love the **L** your God, to walk
	24:	15	household, we will serve the **L**."
1Sa	1:	28	So now I give him to the **L**.
	2:	2	"There is no one holy like the **L**;
	7:	12	"Thus far the **L** has helped us."
	12:	22	his great name the **L** will not reject
	15:	22	as much as in obeying the **L**?
2Sa	22:	2	"The **L** is my rock, my fortress
1Ki	2:	3	and observe what the **L** your God
	8:	11	the glory of the **L** filled his temple.
	8:	61	fully committed to the **L** our God,
	18:	21	If the **L** is God, follow him;
2Ki	13:	23	But the **L** was gracious to them
1Ch	16:	8	Give praise to the **L**, proclaim his
	16:	23	Sing to the **L**, all the earth;
	28:	9	for the **L** searches every heart
	29:	11	Yours, **L**, is the kingdom;
2Ch	5:	14	the glory of the **L** filled the temple
	16:	9	the **L** range throughout the earth
	19:	6	for mere mortals but for the **L**,
	30:	9	for the **L** your God is gracious
Ne	1:	5	"**L**, the God of heaven, the great
Job	1:	21	The **L** gave and the **L** has taken
	38:	1	the **L** spoke to Job out of the storm.
	42:	9	did what the **L** told them;
Ps	1:	2	whose delight is in the law of the **L**,
	9:	9	The **L** is a refuge for the oppressed,
	12:	6	the words of the **L** are flawless,
	16:	8	I keep my eyes always on the **L**.
	19:	7	The law of the **L** is perfect,
	19:	14	heart be pleasing in your sight, **L**,
	23:	1	The **L** is my shepherd, I lack
	23:	6	dwell in the house of the **L** forever.
	27:	1	The **L** is the stronghold of my life
	27:	4	to gaze on the beauty of the **L**
	29:	1	ascribe to the **L** glory and strength.
	32:	2	one whose sin the **L** does not count
	33:	12	is the nation whose God is the **L**,
	33:	18	the eyes of the **L** are on those who
	34:	3	Glorify the **L** with me; let us exalt
	34:	7	of the **L** encamps around those
	34:	8	Taste and see that the **L** is good;
	34:	18	The **L** is close to the brokenhearted
	37:	4	Take delight in the **L**, and he will
	40:	1	I waited patiently for the **L**;
	47:	2	For the **L** Most High is awesome,
	48:	1	Great is the **L**, and most worthy
	55:	22	Cast your cares on the **L** and he
	75:	8	In the hand of the **L** is a cup full
	84:	11	For the **L** God is a sun and shield;
	86:	11	Teach me your way, **L**, that I may
	89:	5	heavens praise your wonders, **L**,
	95:	1	Come, let us sing for joy to the **L**;
	96:	1	Sing to the **L** a new song;
	98:	4	Shout for joy to the **L**, all the earth,
	100:	1	Shout for joy to the **L**, all the earth.
	103:	1	Praise the **L**, my soul; all my
	103:	8	The **L** is compassionate
	104:	1	Praise the **L**, my soul. **L** my God,
	107:	1	to the **L** for his unfailing love
	110:	1	The **L** says to my lord: "Sit at my
	113:	4	The **L** is exalted over all the nations
	115:	1	Not to us, **L**, not to us but to your
Ps	116:	15	the sight of the **L** is the death of his
	118:	1	Give thanks to the **L**, for he is good;
	118:	24	The **L** has done it this very day;
	121:	2	My help comes from the **L**,
	121:	5	The **L** watches over you—the **L** is
	125:	2	so the **L** surrounds his people both
	127:	1	Unless the **L** builds the house,
	127:	3	Children are a heritage from the **L**,
	130:	3	If you, **L**, kept a record of sins,
	135:	6	The **L** does whatever pleases him,
	136:	1	Give thanks to the **L**, for he is good.
	139:	1	You have searched me, **L**, and you
	144:	3	**L**, what are human beings that you
	145:	3	Great is the **L** and most worthy
	145:	18	The **L** is near to all who call on him,
Pr	1:	7	The fear of the **L** is the beginning
	3:	5	Trust in the **L** with all your heart
	3:	9	Honor the **L** with your wealth,
	3:	12	because the **L** disciplines those he
	3:	19	By wisdom the **L** laid the earth's
	5:	21	your ways are in full view of the **L**,
	6:	16	There are six things the **L** hates,
	10:	27	The fear of the **L** adds length to life,
	11:	1	The **L** detests dishonest scales,
	12:	22	The **L** detests lying lips, but he
	14:	26	Whoever fears the **L** has a secure
	15:	3	The eyes of the **L** are everywhere,
	16:	2	but motives are weighed by the **L**.
	16:	4	The **L** works out everything to its
	16:	9	but the **L** establishes their steps.
	16:	33	but its every decision is from the **L**.
	18:	10	name of the **L** is a fortified tower;
	18:	22	and receives favor from the **L**.
	19:	14	but a prudent wife is from the **L**,
	19:	17	is kind to the poor lends to the **L**,
	21:	3	acceptable to the **L** than sacrifice.
	21:	30	plan that can succeed against the **L**.
	21:	31	battle, but victory rests with the **L**.
	22:	2	The **L** is the Maker of them all.
	24:	18	or the **L** will see and disapprove
	31:	30	a woman who fears the **L** is to be
Isa	6:	3	holy, holy is the **L** Almighty;
	11:	2	The Spirit of the **L** will rest on him
	11:	9	of the **L** as the waters cover the sea.
	12:	2	The **L**, the **L** himself, is my strength
	24:	1	the **L** is going to lay waste the earth
	25:	8	The Sovereign **L** will wipe away
	29:	15	to hide their plans from the **L**,
	33:	6	the fear of the **L** is the key to this
	35:	10	those the **L** has rescued will return.
	40:	5	For the mouth of the **L** has spoken.
	40:	7	because the breath of the **L** blows
	40:	10	the Sovereign **L** comes with power,
	40:	28	The **L** is the everlasting God,
	40:	31	in the **L** will renew their strength.
	42:	8	"I am the **L**; that is my name!
	43:	11	I am the **L**, and apart from me
	44:	24	I am the **L**, the Maker of all things,
	45:	5	I am the **L**, and there is no other;
	45:	21	Was it not I, the **L**? And there is no
	51:	11	Those the **L** has rescued will return
	53:	6	the **L** has laid on him the iniquity
	53:	10	the will of the **L** will prosper in his
	55:	6	Seek the **L** while he may be found;
	58:	8	of the **L** will be your rear guard.
	58:	11	The **L** will guide you always;
	59:	1	the arm of the **L** is not too short
	61:	3	a planting of the **L** for the display
	61:	10	I delight greatly in the **L**;
Jer	1:	9	Then the **L** reached out his hand
	9:	24	in these I delight," declares the **L**.
	16:	19	**L**, my strength and my fortress,
	17:	7	is the one who trusts in the **L**,
La	3:	40	and let us return to the **L**.
Eze	1:	28	of the likeness of the glory of the **L**.

Hos	1: 7	but I, the **L** their God, will save
	3: 5	return and seek the **L** their God
	6: 1	"Come, let us return to the **L**.
Joel	2: 1	for the day of the **L** is coming.
	2: 11	The day of the **L** is great;
	3: 14	day of the **L** is near in the valley
Am	5: 18	you who long for the day of the **L**!
Jnh	1: 3	But Jonah ran away from the **L**
Mic	4: 2	the word of the **L** from Jerusalem.
	6: 8	what does the **L** require of you?
Na	1: 2	The **L** is a jealous and avenging
	1: 3	The **L** is slow to anger but great
Hab	2: 14	of the **L** as the waters cover the sea.
	2: 20	The **L** is in his holy temple;
Zep	3: 17	The **L** your God is with you,
Zec	1: 17	and the **L** will again comfort Zion
	9: 16	The **L** their God will save his people
	14: 5	Then the **L** my God will come,
	14: 9	On that day there will be one **L**,
Mal	4: 5	and dreadful day of the **L** comes.

LORD'S* (LORD*; this is the proper name of God, *Yahweh*, spelled "LORD's" in the NIV)

Ex	34: 34	he entered the **L** presence to speak
Nu	14: 41	you disobeying the **L** command?
Dt	6: 18	is right and good in the **L** sight,
	32: 9	For the **L** portion is his people,
Jos	21: 45	all the **L** good promises to Israel
Ps	24: 1	The earth is the **L**,
	32: 10	the **L** unfailing love surrounds
	89: 1	I will sing of the **L** great love
	103: 17	the **L** love is with those who fear
Pr	3: 11	do not despise the **L** discipline,
Isa	24: 14	west they acclaim the **L** majesty.
	62: 3	a crown of splendor in the **L** hand,
Jer	48: 10	who is lax in doing the **L** work!
La	3: 22	Because of the **L** great love we are
Mic	4: 1	the mountain of the **L** temple will

LOSE (LOSES LOSS LOST)

1Sa	17: 32	"Let no one **I** heart on account
Mt	10: 39	Whoever finds their life will **I** it,
Lk	9: 25	and yet **I** or forfeit their very self?
Jn	6: 39	that I shall **I** none of all those
Heb	12: 3	will not grow weary and **I** heart.
	12: 5	not **I** heart when he rebukes you,

LOSES (LOSE)

Mt	5: 13	But if the salt **I** its saltiness,
Lk	15: 4	a hundred sheep and **I** one of them.
	15: 8	has ten silver coins and **I** one.

LOSS (LOSE)

Ro	11: 12	their **I** means riches for the Gentiles,
1Co	3: 15	the builder will suffer **I** but yet will
Php	3: 8	I consider everything a **I** because

LOST (LOSE)

Ps	73: 2	I had nearly **I** my foothold.
Jer	50: 6	"My people have been **I** sheep;
Eze	34: 4	the strays or searched for the **I**.
	34: 16	I will search for the **I** and bring
Lk	15: 4	go after the **I** sheep until he finds
	15: 6	I have found my **I** sheep.'
	15: 9	I have found my **I** coin.'
	15: 24	he was **I** and is found.'
	19: 10	came to seek and to save the **I**."
Php	3: 8	for whose sake I have **I** all things.

LOT (LOTS)

Nephew of Abraham (Ge 11:27; 12:5). Chose to live in Sodom (Ge 13). Rescued from four kings (Ge 14). Rescued from Sodom (Ge 19:1–29; 2Pe 2:7). Fathered Moab and Ammon by his daughters (Ge 19:30–38).

Est	3: 7	the **I** was cast in the presence
	9: 24	the **I** for their ruin and destruction.

Pr	16: 33	The **I** is cast into the lap, but its
	18: 18	Casting the **I** settles disputes
Ecc	3: 22	their work, because that is their **I**.
Ac	1: 26	cast lots, and the **I** fell to Matthias;

LOTS (LOT)

Ps	22: 18	them and cast **I** for my garment.
Mt	27: 35	divided up his clothes by casting **I**.

LOVE (BELOVED LOVED LOVELY LOVER LOVERS LOVES LOVING)

Ge	22: 2	son, your only son, whom you **I**—
Ex	15: 13	In your unfailing **I** you will lead
	20: 6	showing **I** to a thousand generations
	34: 6	abounding in **I** and faithfulness,
Lev	19: 18	but **I** your neighbor as yourself.
	19: 34	**L** them as yourself, for you were
Nu	14: 18	abounding in **I** and forgiving sin
Dt	5: 10	showing **I** to a thousand generations
	6: 5	**L** the LORD your God with all
	7: 13	He will **I** you and bless you
	10: 12	to **I** him, to serve the LORD your
	11: 13	to **I** the LORD your God
	13: 6	or the wife you **I**, or your closest
	30: 6	you may **I** him with all your heart
Jos	22: 5	to **I** the LORD your God, to walk
1Ki	3: 3	Solomon showed his **I**
	8: 23	you who keep your covenant of **I**
2Ch	5: 13	his **I** endures forever."
Ne	1: 5	covenant of **I** with those who **I** him
Ps	18: 1	I **I** you, LORD, my strength.
	23: 6	I will follow me all the days of my
	25: 6	your great mercy and **I**, for they are
	31: 16	save me in your unfailing **I**.
	32: 10	LORD's unfailing **I** surrounds
	33: 5	the earth is full of his unfailing **I**.
	33: 18	whose hope is in his unfailing **I**,
	36: 5	Your **I**, LORD,
	36: 7	How priceless is your unfailing **I**,
	45: 7	You **I** righteousness and hate
	51: 1	God, according to your unfailing **I**;
	57: 10	For great is your **I**,
	63: 3	Because your **I** is better than life,
	66: 20	prayer or withheld his **I** from me!
	77: 8	his unfailing **I** vanished forever?
	85: 7	Show us your unfailing **I**, LORD,
	85: 10	**L** and faithfulness meet together;
	86: 13	For great is your **I** toward me;
	89: 1	sing of the LORD's great **I** forever;
	89: 33	but I will not take my **I** from him,
	92: 2	proclaiming your **I** in the morning
	94: 18	slipping," your unfailing **I**, LORD,
	100: 5	is good and his **I** endures forever;
	101: 1	I will sing of your **I** and justice;
	103: 4	crowns you with **I** and compassion,
	103: 8	slow to anger, abounding in **I**.
	103: 11	so great is his **I** for those who fear
	107: 8	to the LORD for his unfailing **I**
	108: 4	For great is your **I**, higher than
	116: 1	I **I** the LORD, for he heard my
	118: 1	he is good; his **I** endures forever.
	119: 47	your commands because I **I** them.
	119: 64	The earth is filled with your **I**,
	119: 76	May your unfailing **I** be my
	119: 97	Oh, how I **I** your law! I meditate
	119:119	dross; therefore I **I** your statutes.
	119:124	your servant according to your **I**
	119:132	do to those who **I** your name.
	119:159	See how I **I** your precepts;
	119:163	detest falsehood but I **I** your law.
	119:165	peace have those who **I** your law,
	122: 6	"May those who **I** you be secure.
	130: 7	for with the LORD is unfailing **I**
	136: 1	*His **I** endures forever.*
	143: 8	bring me word of your unfailing **I**,
	145: 8	slow to anger and rich in **I**.

Ps	145: 20	LORD watches over all who I him,
	147: 11	put their hope in his unfailing l.
Pr	3: 3	Let I and faithfulness never leave
	4: 6	I her, and she will watch over you.
	5: 19	you ever be intoxicated with her l.
	8: 17	I I those who I me, and those who
	9: 8	rebuke the wise and they will I you.
	10: 12	but I covers over all wrongs.
	14: 22	those who plan what is good find I
	15: 17	with I than a fattened calf
	17: 9	Whoever would foster I covers
	19: 22	a person desires is unfailing l;
	20: 6	Many claim to have unfailing l,
	20: 13	Do not I sleep or you will grow
	20: 28	L and faithfulness keep a king safe;
	21: 21	righteousness and I finds life,
	27: 5	is open rebuke than hidden l.
Ecc	9: 6	Their l, their hate and their
	9: 9	whom you l, all the days of this
SS	2: 4	and let his banner over me be l.
	8: 6	for I is as strong as death,
	8: 7	Many waters cannot quench l;
Isa	5: 1	sing for the one I I a song about his
	16: 5	In I a throne will be established;
	38: 17	In your I you kept me from the pit
	54: 10	yet my unfailing I for you will not
	55: 3	my faithful I promised to David.
	61: 8	"For I, the LORD, I justice;
	63: 9	In his I and mercy he redeemed
Jer	5: 31	and my people I it this way.
	31: 3	loved you with an everlasting l;
	32: 18	You show I to thousands but bring
	33: 11	his I endures forever."
La	3: 22	of the LORD's great I we are not
	3: 32	so great is his unfailing l.
Eze	33: 32	more than one who sings I songs
Da	9: 4	covenant of I with those who I him
Hos	2: 19	and justice, in I and compassion.
	3: 1	L her as the LORD loves
	11: 4	of human kindness, with ties of l.
	12: 6	maintain I and justice, and wait
Joel	2: 13	slow to anger and abounding in l,
Am	5: 15	Hate evil, I good; maintain justice
Mic	3: 2	you who hate good and I evil;
	6: 8	to I mercy and to walk humbly
Zep	3: 17	his I he will no longer rebuke you,
Zec	8: 19	Therefore I truth and peace."
Mt	3: 17	said, "This is my Son, whom I l;
	5: 44	I your enemies and pray for those
	6: 24	will hate the one and I the other,
	17: 5	said, "This is my Son, whom I l;
	19: 19	'I your neighbor as yourself.' "
	22: 37	" 'L the Lord your God with all
Lk	6: 32	"If you I those who I you,
	7: 42	which of them will I him more?"
	20: 13	I will send my son, whom I l;
Jn	13: 34	command I give you: L one another.
	13: 35	my disciples, if you I one another."
	14: 15	"If you I me, keep my commands.
	15: 13	Greater I has no one than this:
	15: 17	This is my command: L each other.
	21: 15	do you I me more than these?"
Ro	5: 5	because God's I has been poured
	5: 8	God demonstrates his own I for us
	8: 28	for the good of those who I him,
	8: 35	separate us from the I of Christ?
	8: 39	separate us from the I of God that
	12: 9	L must be sincere. Hate what is
	12: 10	Be devoted to one another in l.
	13: 8	continuing debt to I one another,
	13: 9	"L your neighbor as yourself."
	13: 10	Therefore I is the fulfillment
1Co	2: 9	prepared for those who I him—
	8: 1	puffs up while I builds up.
	13: 1	but do not have I, I am only
1Co	13: 2	but do not have I, I am nothing.
	13: 3	but do not have I, I gain nothing.
	13: 4	L is patient, I is kind. It does not
	13: 6	L does not delight in evil
	13: 8	L never fails. But where there are
	13: 13	these three remain: faith, hope and l.
		But the greatest of these is l.
	14: 1	Follow the way of I and eagerly
	16: 14	Do everything in l.
2Co	5: 14	For Christ's I compels us,
	8: 8	sincerity of your I by comparing it
	8: 24	show these men the proof of your I
Gal	5: 6	is faith expressing itself through l.
	5: 13	serve one another humbly in l.
	5: 22	But the fruit of the Spirit is l, joy,
Eph	1: 4	holy and blameless in his sight. In I
	2: 4	But because of his great I for us,
	3: 17	being rooted and established in l,
	3: 18	high and deep is the I of Christ,
	3: 19	and to know this I that surpasses
	4: 2	bearing with one another in l.
	4: 15	speaking the truth in l, we will
	5: 2	and walk in the way of l, just as
	5: 25	Husbands, I your wives, just as
	5: 28	to I their wives as their own bodies.
	5: 33	must I his wife as he loves himself,
Php	1: 9	that your I may abound more
	2: 2	having the same l, being one
Col	2: 5	I that spring from the hope stored
	2: 2	in heart and united in l,
	3: 14	And over all these virtues put on l,
	3: 19	I your wives and do not be harsh
1Th	1: 3	your labor prompted by l, and your
	4: 9	been taught by God to I each other.
	5: 8	on faith and I as a breastplate,
2Th	3: 5	Lord direct your hearts into God's I
1Ti	1: 5	The goal of this command is l,
	2: 15	faith, I and holiness with propriety.
	4: 12	conduct, in l, in faith and in purity.
	6: 10	For the I of money is a root of all
	6: 11	faith, l, endurance and gentleness.
2Ti	1: 7	us power, I and self-discipline.
	2: 22	faith, I and peace, along with those
	3: 10	faith, patience, l, endurance,
Titus	2: 4	women to I their husbands
Phm	: 9	to appeal to you on the basis of l.
Heb	6: 10	the I you have shown him as you
	10: 24	may spur one another on toward I
	13: 5	your lives free from the I of money
Jas	1: 12	has promised to those who I him.
	2: 5	he promised those who I him?
	2: 8	"L your neighbor as yourself,"
1Pe	1: 22	you have sincere I for each other,
	2: 17	everyone, the family of believers,
	3: 8	be sympathetic, I one another,
	3: 10	For, "Whoever would I life and see
	4: 8	Above all, I each other deeply,
	4: 8	because I covers over a multitude
	5: 14	Greet one another with a kiss of l.
2Pe	1: 7	and to mutual affection, l.
	1: 17	saying, "This is my Son, whom I I l;
1Jn	2: 5	I for God is truly made complete
	2: 15	Do not I the world or anything
	3: 1	See what great I the Father has
	3: 10	who does not I their brother
	3: 11	We should I one another.
	3: 14	to life, because I each other.
	3: 16	This is how we know what I is:
	3: 18	let us not I with words or speech
	3: 23	I one another as he commanded
	4: 7	one another, for I comes from God.
	4: 8	not know God, because God is l.
	4: 9	is how God showed his I among us:
	4: 10	This is l: not that we loved God,
	4: 11	us, we also ought to I one another.

1Jn	4:	12	but if we **l** one another, God lives
	4:	16	God is **l**. Whoever lives in **l** lives
	4:	17	This is how **l** is made complete
	4:	18	There is no fear in **l**. But perfect **l**
	4:	19	We **l** because he first loved us.
	4:	20	whoever does not **l** their brother
	4:	21	loves God must also **l** their brother
	5:	2	we know that we **l** the children
	5:	3	In fact, this is **l** for God: to keep his
2Jn	:	5	I ask that we **l** one another.
	:	6	his command is that you walk in **l**.
Jude	:	12	are blemishes at your **l** feasts,
	:	21	yourselves in God's **l** as you wait
Rev	2:	4	You have forsaken the **l** you had
	3:	19	Those whom **l l** I rebuke
	12:	11	they did not **l** their lives so much

LOVED (LOVE)

Ge	24:	67	she became his wife, and he **l** her;
	37:	3	Now Israel **l** Joseph more than any
Dt	7:	8	it was because the LORD **l** you
1Sa	1:	5	a double portion because he **l** her,
	20:	17	because he **l** him as he **l** himself.
Ps	44:	3	light of your face, for you **l** them.
Jer	2:	2	youth, how as a bride you **l** me
	31:	3	"I have **l** you with an everlasting
Hos	2:	23	to the one I called 'Not my **l** one.'
	3:	1	though she is **l** by another man
	9:	10	became as vile as the thing they **l**.
	11:	1	"When Israel was a child, **l l** him,
Mal	1:	2	"I have **l** you," says the LORD.
Mk	12:	6	one left to send, a son, whom he **l**.
Jn	3:	16	For God so **l** the world that he gave
	3:	19	people **l** darkness instead of light
	11:	5	Now Jesus **l** Martha and her sister
	12:	43	for they **l** human praise more than
	13:	1	in the world, he **l** them to the end.
	13:	23	the disciple whom Jesus **l**,
	13:	34	As I have **l** you, so you must love
	14:	21	The one who loves me will be **l**
	15:	9	"As the Father has **l** me, so have I **l**
	15:	12	Love each other as I have **l** you.
	19:	26	disciple whom he **l** standing
Ro	8:	37	conquerors through him who **l** us.
	9:	13	"Jacob **l** I, but Esau I hated."
	9:	25	'my **l** one' who is not my **l** one,"
	11:	28	they are **l** on account
Gal	2:	20	who **l** me and gave himself for me.
Eph	5:	2	just as Christ **l** us and gave himself
	5:	25	just as Christ **l** the church and gave
2Th	2:	16	who **l** us and by his grace gave us
2Ti	4:	10	for Demas, because he **l** this world,
Heb	1:	9	You have **l** righteousness and hated
1Jn	4:	10	not that we **l** God, but that he **l** us
	4:	11	since God so **l** us, we also ought
	4:	19	We love because he first **l** us.

LOVELY (LOVE)

Ps	84:	1	How **l** is your dwelling place,
SS	2:	14	voice is sweet, and your face is **l**.
	5:	16	sweetness itself; he is altogether **l**.
Php	4:	8	is pure, whatever is **l**, whatever is

LOVER (LOVE)

| 1Ti | 3: | 3 | not quarrelsome, not a **l** of money. |

LOVERS (LOVE)

2Ti	3:	2	People will be **l** of themselves,
	3:	3	brutal, not **l** of the good,
	3:	4	**l** of pleasure rather than **l** of God—

LOVES (LOVE)

| Ps | 11: | 7 | LORD is righteous, he **l** justice; |
| | 33: | 5 | The LORD **l** righteousness |

Ps	34:	12	Whoever of you **l** life and desires
	127:	2	for he grants sleep to those he **l**.
Pr	3:	12	the LORD disciplines those he **l**,
	12:	1	Whoever **l** discipline **l** knowledge,
	17:	17	A friend **l** at all times, and
	17:	19	Whoever **l** a quarrel **l** sin;
	22:	11	One who **l** a pure heart and who
Mt	10:	37	"Anyone who **l** their father
Lk	7:	47	has been forgiven little **l** little."
Jn	3:	35	The Father **l** the Son and has
	10:	17	The reason my Father **l** me is that I
	14:	21	The one who **l** me will be loved
	14:	23	"Anyone who **l** me will obey my
Ro	13:	8	for whoever **l** others has fulfilled
2Co	9:	7	for God **l** a cheerful giver.
Eph	5:	28	He who **l** his wife **l** himself.
	5:	33	must love his wife as he **l** himself,
Heb	12:	6	the Lord disciplines the one he **l**,
1Jn	4:	7	Everyone who **l** has been born
	5:	1	who **l** the father **l** his child
3Jn	:	9	but Diotrephes, who **l** to be first,
Rev	1:	5	To him who **l** us and has freed us

LOVING (LOVE)

Ps	25:	10	All the ways of the LORD are **l**
Heb	13:	1	Keep on **l** one another as brothers
1Jn	5:	2	by **l** God and carrying out his

LOWLY

Job	5:	11	The **l** he sets on high, and those
Pr	29:	23	low, but the **l** in spirit gain honor.
Isa	57:	15	to revive the spirit of the **l**
Eze	21:	26	The **l** will be exalted and
Mt	18:	4	whoever takes the **l** position
1Co	1:	28	God chose the **l** things of this

LUKE

Co-worker with Paul (Col 4:14; 2Ti 4:11; Phm 24).

LUKEWARM

| Rev | 3: | 16 | So, because you are **l**— |

LUST

Pr	6:	25	Do not **l** in your heart after her
Col	3:	5	impurity, **l**, evil desires and greed,
1Th	4:	5	not in passionate **l** like the pagans,
1Jn	2:	16	the **l** of the flesh, the **l** of the eyes,

LYING (LIE)

| Pr | 6: | 17 | haughty eyes, a **l** tongue, |
| | 26: | 28 | A **l** tongue hates those it hurts, |

MACEDONIA

| Ac | 16: | 9 | a vision of a man of **M** standing |

MADE (MAKE)

Ge	1:	16	God **m** two great lights—
	1:	25	God **m** the wild animals according
	2:	22	the LORD God **m** a woman
2Ki	19:	15	You have **m** heaven and earth.
Ps	95:	5	for he **m** it, and his hands formed
	100:	3	It is he who **m** us, and we are his;
	139:	14	I am fearfully and wonderfully **m**;
Ecc	3:	11	He has **m** everything beautiful in
Mk	2:	27	"The Sabbath was **m** for man,
Jn	1:	3	Through him all things were **m**;
Ac	17:	24	"The God who **m** the world
Heb	1:	2	whom also he **m** the universe.
Rev	14:	7	Worship him who **m** the heavens,

MAGI

| Mt | 2: | 1 | **M** from the east came to Jerusalem |

MAGOG

Eze	38:	2	of the land of **M**, the chief prince
	39:	6	I will send fire on **M** and on those
Rev	20:	8	Gog and **M**—and to gather them

MAIMED
Mt 18: 8   It is better for you to enter life **m**

MAJESTIC (MAJESTY)
Ex   15: 6   hand, Lord, was **m** in power.
     15: 11   **m** in holiness, awesome in glory,
Ps   8: 1   **m** is your name in all the earth!
     29: 4   the voice of the Lord is **m**.
    111: 3   Glorious and **m** are his deeds,
SS   6: 10   sun, **m** as the stars in procession?
2Pe   1: 17   came to him from the **M** Glory,

MAJESTY (MAJESTIC)
Ex   15: 7   your **m** you threw down those who
Dt   33: 26   and on the clouds in his **m**.
1Ch 16: 27   Splendor and **m** are before him;
Est   1: 4   the splendor and glory of his **m**.
Job 37: 22   God comes in awesome **m**.
     40: 10   clothe yourself in honor and **m**.
Ps   45: 4   In your **m** ride forth victoriously
     93: 1   Lord reigns, he is robed in **m**;
    145: 5   the glorious splendor of your **m**—
Isa 53: 2   beauty or **m** to attract us to him,
Eze 31: 2   can be compared with you in **m**?
2Pe   1: 16   but we were eyewitnesses of his **m**.
Jude : 25   only God our Savior be glory, **m**,

MAKE (MADE MAKER MAKES MAKING)
Ge   1: 26   "Let us **m** mankind in our image,
      2: 18   I will **m** a helper suitable for him."
     12: 2   "I will **m** you into a great nation,
Ex   22: 3   steals must certainly **m** restitution,
Nu   6: 25   the Lord **m** his face shine on you
Ps 108: 1   sing and **m** music with all my soul.
Isa 14: 14   I will **m** myself like the Most
     29: 16   formed it, "You did not **m** me"?
Jer 31: 31   "when I will **m** a new covenant
Mt   3: 3   Lord, **m** straight paths for him.' "
     28: 19   go and **m** disciples of all nations,
Lk   13: 24   "**M** every effort to enter through
Ro   14: 19   Let us therefore **m** every effort to
2Co   5: 9   So we **m** it our goal to please him,
Eph   4: 3   **M** every effort to keep the unity
Col   4: 5   **m** the most of every opportunity.
1Th   4: 11   **m** it your ambition to lead a quiet
Heb   4: 11   **m** every effort to enter that rest,
     12: 14   **M** every effort to live in peace
2Pe   1: 5   **m** every effort to add to your faith
      3: 14   **m** every effort to be found spotless,

MAKER (MAKE)
Job   4: 17   man be more pure than his **M**?
     36: 3   I will ascribe justice to my **M**.
Ps   95: 6   us kneel before the Lord our **M**;
Pr   22: 2   The Lord is the **M** of them all.
Isa 45: 9   to those who quarrel with their **M**,
     54: 5   For your **M** is your husband—
Jer 10: 16   these, for he is the **M** of all things,

MAKES (MAKE)
1Co   3: 7   but only God, who **m** things grow.

MAKING (MAKE)
Ps   19: 7   are trustworthy, **m** wise the simple.
Ecc 12: 12   Of **m** many books there is no end,
Jn   5: 18   Father, **m** himself equal with God.
Eph   5: 16   **m** the most of every opportunity,

MALE
Ge   1: 27   **m** and female he created them.
Gal   3: 28   nor free, nor is there **m** and female,

MALICE (MALICIOUS)
Ro   1: 29   envy, murder, strife, deceit and **m**.
Col   3: 8   anger, rage, **m**, slander, and filthy
1Pe   2: 1   rid yourselves of all **m** and all

MALICIOUS (MALICE)
1Ti   3: 11   not **m** talkers but temperate
      6: 4   envy, strife, **m** talk, evil suspicions

MAN (MANKIND MEN WOMAN WOMEN)
Ge   2: 7   the Lord God formed a **m**
      2: 18   not good for the **m** to be alone.
      2: 23   for she was taken out of **m**."
Dt   8: 3   **m** does not live on bread alone
1Sa 13: 14   sought out a **m** after his own heart
Ps 127: 5   Blessed is the **m** whose quiver is
Pr   30: 19   way of a **m** with a young woman.
Isa 53: 3   by mankind, a **m** of suffering,
Mt   19: 5   this reason a **m** will leave his father
Lk   4: 4   '**M** shall not live on bread alone.' "
Ro   5: 12   entered the world through one **m**,
1Co   7: 2   **m** should have sexual relations
     11: 3   that the head of every **m** is Christ,
     11: 3   and the head of the woman is **m**,
     13: 11   When I became a **m**, I put the ways
Php   2: 8   being found in appearance as a **m**,
1Ti   2: 5   and mankind, the **m** Christ Jesus,
      2: 12   or to assume authority over a **m**;

MANAGE
Jer 12: 5   how will you **m** in the thickets
1Ti   3: 4   He must **m** his own family well
      3: 12   to his wife and must **m** his children
      5: 14   to **m** their homes and to give

MANASSEH
   1. Firstborn of Joseph (Ge 41:51; 46:20). Blessed (Ge 48).
   2. Son of Hezekiah; king of Judah (2Ki 21:1–18; 2Ch 33:1–20).

MANGER
Lk   2: 12   in cloths and lying in a **m**."

MANKIND (MAN)
Ge   1: 26   "Let us make **m** in our image,

MANNA
Ex   16: 31   people of Israel called the bread **m**.
Dt   8: 16   He gave you **m** to eat
Jn   6: 49   Your ancestors ate the **m**
Rev   2: 17   I will give some of the hidden **m**.

MANNER
1Co 11: 27   in an unworthy **m** will be guilty
Php   1: 27   conduct yourselves in a **m** worthy

MARITAL (MARRY)
Ex   21: 10   of her food, clothing and **m** rights.
1Co   7: 3   husband should fulfill his **m** duty

MARK (MARKS)
   Cousin of Barnabas (Col 4:10; 2Ti 4:11; Phm 24; 1Pe 5:13), see JOHN.

Ge   4: 15   the Lord put a **m** on Cain so
Rev 13: 16   to receive a **m** on their right hands

MARKS (MARK)
Jn   20: 25   "Unless I see the nail **m** in his
Gal   6: 17   I bear on my body the **m** of Jesus.

MARRED
Isa 52: 14   and his form **m** beyond human

MARRIAGE (MARRY)
Mt   22: 30   neither marry nor be given in **m**;
     24: 38   marrying and giving in **m**,
Heb 13: 4   **M** should be honored by all,

MARRIED (MARRY)
Ro   7: 2   by law a **m** woman is bound to her
1Co   7: 33   But a **m** man is concerned
      7: 36   is not sinning. They should get **m**.

MARRIES (MARRY)
Mt 5: 32 anyone who **m** a divorced woman
19: 9 and **m** another woman commits
Lk 16: 18 the man who **m** a divorced woman

MARRY (INTERMARRY MARITAL MARRIAGE MARRIED MARRIES)
Mt 22: 30 people will neither **m** nor be given
1Co 7: 9 they should **m**, for it is better to **m**
1Ti 5: 14 So I counsel younger widows to **m**,

MARTHA
Sister of Mary and Lazarus (Lk 10:38–42; Jn 11; 12:2).

MARVELED
Lk 2: 33 mother **m** at what was said

MARY
1. Mother of Jesus (Mt 1:16–25; Lk 1:27–56; 2:1–40). With Jesus at temple (Lk 2:41–52), at the wedding in Cana (Jn 2:1–5), questioning his sanity (Mk 3:21), at the cross (Jn 19:25–27). Among disciples after Ascension (Ac 1:14).
2. Magdalene; former demoniac (Lk 8:2). Helped support Jesus' ministry (Lk 8:1–3). At the cross (Mt 27:56; Mk 15:40; Jn 19:25), burial (Mt 27:61; Mk 15:47). Saw angel after resurrection (Mt 28:1–10; Mk 16:1–9; Lk 24:1–12); also Jesus (Jn 20:1–18).
3. Sister of Martha and Lazarus (Jn 11). Washed Jesus' feet (Jn 12:1–8).

MASQUERADES
2Co 11: 14 for Satan himself **m** as an angel

MASTER (MASTERED MASTERS)
Mt 10: 24 teacher, nor a servant above his **m**.
24: 46 servant whose **m** finds him doing
25: 21 "His **m** replied, 'Well done,
Ro 6: 14 For sin shall no longer be your **m**,
14: 4 To their own **m**, servants stand
2Ti 2: 21 useful to the **M** and prepared to do

MASTERED (MASTER)
1Co 6: 12 but I will not be **m** by anything.
2Pe 2: 19 are slaves to whatever has **m** them."

MASTERS (MASTER)
Mt 6: 24 "No one can serve two **m**.
Eph 6: 5 obey your earthly **m** with respect
6: 9 **m**, treat your slaves in the same
Titus 2: 9 be subject to their **m** in everything,

MATTHEW
Apostle; former tax collector (Mt 9:9–13; 10:3; Mk 3:18; Lk 6:15; Ac 1:13). Also called Levi (Mk 2:14–17; Lk 5:27–32).

MATURE (MATURITY)
Eph 4: 13 of the Son of God and become **m**,
Php 3: 15 who are **m** should take such a view
Heb 5: 14 But solid food is for the **m**,
Jas 1: 4 its work so that you may be **m**

MATURITY (MATURE)
Heb 6: 1 Christ and be taken forward to **m**,

MEAL
1Co 10: 27 If an unbeliever invites you to a **m**
Heb 12: 16 single **m** sold his inheritance rights

MEANING
Ne 8: 8 and giving the **m** so that the people

MEANS
1Co 9: 22 by all possible **m** I might save some.

MEAT
Ro 14: 6 eats **m** does so to the Lord,
14: 21 It is better not to eat **m** or drink

MEDIATOR
1Ti 2: 5 one God and one **m** between God
Heb 8: 6 which he is **m** is superior to the old
9: 15 this reason Christ is the **m** of a new
12: 24 to Jesus the **m** of a new covenant,

MEDICINE
Pr 17: 22 A cheerful heart is good **m**,

MEDITATE (MEDITATES MEDITATION)
Jos 1: 8 **m** on it day and night, so that you
Ps 119: 15 I **m** on your precepts and consider
119: 78 but I will **m** on your precepts.
119: 97 I **m** on it all day long.
145: 5 I will **m** on your wonderful works.

MEDITATES (MEDITATE)
Ps 1: 2 who **m** on his law day and night.

MEDITATION (MEDITATE)
Ps 19: 14 this **m** of my heart be pleasing
104: 34 May my **m** be pleasing to him, as I

MEDIUM
Lev 20: 27 or woman who is a **m** or spiritist

MEEK
Ps 37: 11 But the **m** will inherit the land
Mt 5: 5 Blessed are the **m**, for they will

MEET (MEETING)
Ps 85: 10 Love and faithfulness **m** together;
Am 4: 12 Israel, prepare to **m** your God."
1Th 4: 17 the clouds to **m** the Lord in the air.

MEETING (MEET)
Heb 10: 25 not giving up **m** together, as some

MELCHIZEDEK
Ge 14: 18 **M** king of Salem brought out bread
Ps 110: 4 a priest forever, in the order of **M**."
Heb 7: 11 one in the order of **M**,

MELT
2Pe 3: 12 the elements will **m** in the heat.

MEMBERS
Mic 7: 6 a man's enemies are the **m** of his
Ro 12: 4 of us has one body with many **m**,
1Co 6: 15 your bodies are **m** of Christ
Eph 4: 25 for we are all **m** of one body.
Col 3: 15 since as **m** of one body you were

MEN (MAN)
Ro 1: 27 **M** committed shameful acts with other **m**,
1Ti 2: 8 Therefore I want the **m** everywhere

MENAHEM
King of Israel (2Ki 15:17–22).

MERCIFUL (MERCY)
Dt 4: 31 the LORD your God is a **m** God;
Ne 9: 31 for you are a gracious and **m** God.
Mt 5: 7 Blessed are the **m**, for they will be
Lk 6: 36 Be **m**, just as your Father is **m**.
Heb 2: 17 in order that he might become a **m**
Jude : 22 Be **m** to those who doubt;

MERCY (MERCIFUL)
Ex 33: 19 have **m** on whom I will have **m**,
Ps 25: 6 LORD, your great **m** and love,
Isa 63: 9 his love and **m** he redeemed them;
Hos 6: 6 For I desire **m**, not sacrifice,

Mic	6:	8	to love **m** and to walk humbly
Hab	3:	2	in wrath remember **m**.
Mt	12:	7	mean, 'I desire **m**, not sacrifice,'
	23:	23	justice, **m** and faithfulness.
Ro	9:	15	"I will have **m** on whom I have **m**,
Eph	2:	4	love for us, God, who is rich in **m**,
Jas	2:	13	**M** triumphs over judgment.
1Pe	1:	3	In his great **m** he has given us new

MESSAGE

Isa	53:	1	Who has believed our **m**
Jn	12:	38	who has believed our **m**
Ro	10:	17	faith comes from hearing the **m**,
1Co	1:	18	the **m** of the cross is foolishness
2Co	5:	19	to us the **m** of reconciliation.

MESSIAH (CHRIST MESSIAHS)

Mt	1:	16	of Jesus who is called the **M**.
	16:	16	"You are the **M**, the Son
	22:	42	"What do you think about the **M**?
Jn	1:	41	"We have found the **M**" (that is,
	4:	25	that **M**" (called Christ) "is coming.
	20:	31	may believe that Jesus is the **M**,
Ac	2:	36	you crucified, both Lord and **M**."
	5:	42	the good news that Jesus is the **M**.
	9:	22	by proving that Jesus is the **M**.
	17:	3	proving that the **M** had to suffer
	18:	28	the Scriptures that Jesus was the **M**.
	26:	23	that the **M** would suffer and,

MESSIAHS (MESSIAH)

Mt	24:	24	For false **m** and false prophets will

METHUSELAH

Ge	5:	27	**M** lived a total of 969 years,

MICHAEL

Archangel (Jude 9); warrior in angelic realm, protector of Israel (Da 10:13, 21; 12:1; Rev 12:7).

MIDWIVES

Ex	1:	17	The **m**, however, feared God

MIGHT (ALMIGHTY MIGHTY)

Jdg	16:	30	Then he pushed with all his **m**,
2Sa	6:	14	before the LORD with all his **m**,
Ps	21:	13	we will sing and praise your **m**.
Zec	4:	6	'Not by **m** nor by power, but by my
1Ti	6:	16	To him be honor and **m** forever.

MIGHTY (MIGHT)

Ex	6:	1	of my **m** hand he will let them go;
Dt	7:	8	he brought you out with a **m** hand
2Sa	1:	19	How the **m** have fallen!
	23:	8	the names of David's **m** warriors:
Ps	24:	8	and **m**, the LORD **m** in battle.
	50:	1	The **M** One, God, the LORD,
	89:	8	are **m**, and your faithfulness
	136:	12	a **m** hand and outstretched arm;
	147:	5	Great is our Lord and **m** in power;
Isa	9:	6	Wonderful Counselor, **M** God,
Zep	3:	17	you, the **M** Warrior who saves.
Eph	6:	10	in the Lord and in his **m** power.

MILE

Mt	5:	41	If anyone forces you to go one **m**,

MILK

Ex	3:	8	a land flowing with **m** and honey—
Isa	55:	1	buy wine and **m** without money
1Co	3:	2	I gave you **m**, not solid food,
Heb	5:	12	You need **m**, not solid food!
1Pe	2:	2	crave pure spiritual **m**, so that by it

MILLSTONE (STONE)

Lk	17:	2	with a **m** tied around their neck

MIND (DOUBLE-MINDED MINDFUL MINDS MINDSET)

1Sa	15:	29	does not lie or change his **m**;
1Ch	28:	9	devotion and with a willing **m**,
Ps	26:	2	me, examine my heart and my **m**;
Mt	22:	37	all your soul and with all your **m**.'
Ac	4:	32	believers were one in heart and **m**.
Ro	7:	25	then, I myself in my **m** am a slave
	8:	7	The **m** governed by the flesh is
	12:	2	by the renewing of your **m**.
1Co	2:	9	what no human **m** has conceived"
	14:	14	spirit prays, but my **m** is unfruitful.
2Co	13:	11	another, be of one **m**, live in peace.
Php	3:	19	Their **m** is set on earthly things.
1Th	4:	11	You should **m** your own business
Heb	7:	21	sworn and will not change his **m**:

MINDFUL (MIND)

Ps	8:	4	is mankind that you are **m** of them,
Lk	1:	48	he has been **m** of the humble state
Heb	2:	6	is mankind that you are **m** of them,

MINDS (MIND)

Ps	7:	9	the righteous God who probes **m**
Isa	26:	3	peace those whose **m** are steadfast,
Jer	31:	33	"I will put my law in their **m**
Eph	4:	23	new in the attitude of your **m**;
Col	3:	2	Set your **m** on things above,
Heb	8:	10	I will put my laws in their **m**
Rev	2:	23	he who searches hearts and **m**,

MINDSET (MIND)

Php	2:	5	have the same **m** as Christ Jesus:

MINISTERING (MINISTRY)

Heb	1:	14	Are not all angels **m** spirits sent

MINISTRY (MINISTERING)

Ac	6:	4	to prayer and the **m** of the word."
2Co	5:	18	gave us the **m** of reconciliation:
2Ti	4:	5	discharge all the duties of your **m**.

MIRACLES

1Ch	16:	12	done, his **m**, and the judgments he
Ps	77:	14	You are the God who performs **m**;
Mt	11:	20	most of his **m** had been performed,
	11:	21	the **m** that were performed in you
Mk	6:	2	What are these remarkable **m** he is
Ac	2:	22	accredited by God to you by **m**,
	19:	11	did extraordinary **m** through Paul,
1Co	12:	28	then **m**, then gifts of healing,
Heb	2:	4	wonders and various **m**, and by

MIRE

Ps	40:	2	slimy pit, out of the mud and **m**;
Isa	57:	20	whose waves cast up **m** and mud.

MIRIAM

Sister of Moses and Aaron (Nu 26:59). Led dancing at Red Sea (Ex 15:20–21). Struck with leprosy for criticizing Moses (Nu 12). Death (Nu 20:1).

MIRROR

Jas	1:	23	who looks at his face in a **m**

MISERY

Ex	3:	7	"I have indeed seen the **m** of my
Jdg	10:	16	he could bear Israel's **m** no longer.
Hos	5:	15	in their **m** they will earnestly seek
Ro	3:	16	ruin and **m** mark their ways,
Jas	5:	1	because of the **m** that is coming

MISLED

1Co	15:	33	Do not be **m**:

MISS

Pr	19:	2	more will hasty feet **m** the way!

MIST

| Hos | 6: | 4 | Your love is like the morning **m**, |
| Jas | 4: | 14 | You are a **m** that appears for a little |

MISUSE

Ex	20:	7	"You shall not **m** the name
Dt	5:	11	"You shall not **m** the name
Ps	139:	20	your adversaries **m** your name.

MOCK (MOCKED MOCKER MOCKERS MOCKING)

Ps	22:	7	All who see me **m** me;
Pr	14:	9	Fools **m** at making amends for sin,
Mk	10:	34	who will **m** him and spit on him,

MOCKED (MOCK)

Mt	27:	29	knelt in front of him and **m** him.
	27:	41	of the law and the elders **m** him.
Gal	6:	7	not be deceived: God cannot be **m**.

MOCKER (MOCK)

Pr	9:	7	corrects a **m** invites insults;
	9:	12	you are a **m**, you alone will suffer.
	20:	1	Wine is a **m** and beer a brawler;
	22:	10	Drive out the **m**, and out goes

MOCKERS (MOCK)

| Ps | 1: | 1 | take or sit in the company of **m**, |

MOCKING (MOCK)

| Isa | 50: | 6 | I did not hide my face from **m** |

MODEL

| 1Th | 1: | 7 | And so you became a **m** to all |
| 2Th | 3: | 9 | to offer ourselves as a **m** for you |

MOMENT

Job	20:	5	the joy of the godless lasts but a **m**.
Ps	30:	5	For his anger lasts only a **m**, but his
Isa	66:	8	a nation be brought forth in a **m**?
Gal	2:	5	We did not give in to them for a **m**,

MONEY

Ecc	5:	10	loves **m** never has enough;
Isa	55:	1	and you who have no **m**, come,
Mt	6:	24	You cannot serve both God and **m**.
Lk	9:	3	bag, no bread, no **m**, no extra shirt.
1Co	16:	2	you should set aside a sum of **m**
1Ti	3:	3	not quarrelsome, not a lover of **m**.
	6:	10	the love of **m** is a root of all kinds
2Ti	3:	2	themselves, lovers of **m**, boastful,
Heb	13:	5	your lives free from the love of **m**

MOON

Ps	121:	6	you by day, nor the **m** by night.
Joel	2:	31	the **m** to blood before the coming
1Co	15:	41	the **m** another and the stars

MORNING

Ge	1:	5	was evening, and there was **m**—
Dt	28:	67	In the **m** you will say, "If only it
Ps	5:	3	In the **m**, Lord, you hear my
2Pe	1:	19	and the **m** star rises in your hearts.
Rev	22:	16	of David, and the bright **M** Star."

MORTAL

| 1Co | 15: | 53 | and the **m** with immortality. |

MOSES

Levite; brother of Aaron (Ex 6:20; 1Ch 6:3). Put into basket into Nile; discovered and raised by Pharaoh's daughter (Ex 2:1–10). Fled to Midian after killing Egyptian (Ex 2:11–15). Married to Zipporah, fathered Gershom (Ex 2:16–22).

Called by the Lord to deliver Israel (Ex 3–4). Pharaoh's resistance (Ex 5). Ten plagues (Ex 7–11). Passover and Exodus (Ex 12–13). Led Israel through Red Sea (Ex 14). Song of deliverance (Ex 15:1–21).

Brought water from rock (Ex 17:1–7). Raised hands to defeat Amalekites (Ex 17:8–16). Delegated judges (Ex 18; Dt 1:9–18).

Received Law at Sinai (Ex 19–23; 25–31; Jn 1:17). Announced Law to Israel (Ex 19:7–8; 24; 35). Broke tablets because of golden calf (Ex 32; Dt 9). Saw glory of the Lord (Ex 33–34). Supervised building of tabernacle (Ex 36–40). Set apart Aaron and priests (Lev 8–9). Numbered tribes (Nu 1–4; 26). Opposed by Aaron and Miriam (Nu 12). Sent spies into Canaan (Nu 13). Announced forty years of wandering for failure to enter land (Nu 14). Opposed by Korah (Nu 16). Forbidden to enter land for striking rock (Nu 20:1–13; Dt 1:37). Lifted bronze snake for healing (Nu 21:4–9; Jn 3:14). Final address to Israel (Dt 1–33). Succeeded by Joshua (Nu 27:12–23; Dt 34). Death (Dt 34:5–12).

"Law of Moses" (1Ki 2:3; Ezr 3:2; Mk 12:26; Lk 24:44). "Book of Moses" (2Ch 25:12; Ne 13:1). "Song of Moses" (Ex 15:1–21; Rev 15:3). "Prayer of Moses" (Ps 90).

MOTHER (MOTHER'S)

Ge	2:	24	why a man leaves his father and **m**
	3:	20	because she would become the **m**
Ex	20:	12	"Honor your father and your **m**,
Lev	20:	9	they have cursed their father or **m**,
Dt	5:	16	"Honor your father and your **m**,
	21:	18	does not obey his father and **m**
	27:	16	who dishonors their father or **m**."
1Sa	2:	19	Each year his **m** made him a little
Ps	113:	9	her home as a happy **m** of children.
Pr	23:	25	May your father and **m** rejoice;
	29:	15	left undisciplined disgraces its **m**.
	31:	1	utterance his **m** taught him.
Isa	49:	15	"Can a **m** forget the baby at her
	66:	13	As a **m** comforts her child, so will I
Mt	10:	37	or **m** more than me is not worthy
	15:	4	said, 'Honor your father and **m**'
	19:	5	a man will leave his father and **m**
Mk	7:	10	'Honor your father and **m**,' and,
	10:	19	honor your father and **m**.'"
Jn	19:	27	to the disciple, "Here is your **m**."

MOTHER'S (MOTHER)

| Job | 1: | 21 | "Naked I came from my **m** womb, |
| Pr | 1: | 8 | do not forsake your **m** teaching. |

MOTHS

| Mt | 6: | 19 | where **m** and vermin destroy, |

MOTIVES

Pr	16:	2	but **m** are weighed by the Lord.
1Co	4:	5	and will expose the **m** of the heart.
Php	1:	18	way, whether from false **m** or true,
1Th	2:	3	not spring from error or impure **m**,
Jas	4:	3	because you ask with wrong **m**,

MOUNTAIN (MOUNTAINS)

| Mic | 4: | 2 | let us go up to the **m** of the Lord, |
| Mt | 17: | 20 | you can say to this **m**, |

MOUNTAINS (MOUNTAIN)

Isa	52:	7	beautiful on the **m** are the feet
	55:	12	the **m** and hills will burst into song
1Co	13:	2	if I have a faith that can move **m**,

MOURN (MOURNING)

Ecc	3:	4	a time to **m** and a time to dance,
Isa	61:	2	of our God, to comfort all who **m**,
Mt	5:	4	Blessed are those who **m**, for they
Ro	12:	15	**m** with those who **m**.

MOURNING (MOURN)

| Jer | 31: | 13 | I will turn their **m** into gladness; |
| Rev | 21: | 4 | There will be no more death' or **m** |

MOUTH

Ps	19:	14	May these words of my **m** and this
	40:	3	He put a new song in my **m**,
	119:103		taste, sweeter than honey to my **m**!
Pr	27:	2	praise you, and not your own **m**;
Isa	51:	16	I have put my words in your **m**
Mt	12:	34	the **m** speaks what the heart is full
	15:	11	but what comes out of their **m**,
Ro	10:	9	If you declare with your **m**,

MUD

Ps	40:	2	slimy pit, out of the **m** and mire;
Isa	57:	20	whose waves cast up mire and **m**.
2Pe	2:	22	returns to her wallowing in the **m**."

MULTITUDE (MULTITUDES)

Isa	31:	1	who trust in the **m** of their chariots
1Pe	4:	8	because love covers over a **m**
Rev	7:	9	there before me was a great **m**

MULTITUDES (MULTITUDE)

Joel	3:	14	**M, m** in the valley of decision!

MURDER (MURDERER MURDERERS)

Ex	20:	13	"You shall not **m**.
Mt	15:	19	**m**, adultery, sexual immorality,
Ro	13:	9	"You shall not **m**," "You shall not
Jas	2:	11	commit adultery but do commit **m**,

MURDERER (MURDER)

Nu	35:	16	a **m**; the **m** is to be put to death.
Jn	8:	44	He was a **m** from the beginning,
1Jn	3:	15	hates a brother or sister is a **m**,

MURDERERS (MURDER)

1Ti	1:	9	kill their fathers or mothers, for **m**,
Rev	21:	8	vile, the **m**, the sexually immoral,

MUSIC

Ps	27:	6	sing and make **m** to the LORD.
	95:	2	and extol him with **m** and song.
	98:	4	burst into jubilant song with **m**;
	108:	1	sing and make **m** with all my soul.
Eph	5:	19	make **m** from your heart to the Lord,

MUSTARD

Mt	13:	31	kingdom of heaven is like a **m** seed,
	17:	20	you have faith as small as a **m** seed,

MUZZLE

Dt	25:	4	Do not **m** an ox while it is treading
Ps	39:	1	I will put a **m** on my mouth while
1Co	9:	9	Do not **m** an ox while it is treading

MYRRH

Mt	2:	11	gifts of gold, frankincense and **m**.
Mk	15:	23	offered him wine mixed with **m**,

MYSTERY

Ro	16:	25	the revelation of the **m** hidden
1Co	15:	51	Listen, I tell you a **m**: We will not
Eph	5:	32	This is a profound **m**—but I am
Col	1:	26	the **m** that has been kept hidden
1Ti	3:	16	the **m** from which true godliness

MYTHS

1Ti	4:	7	Have nothing to do with godless **m**

NADAB

Son of Jeroboam I; king of Israel (1Ki 15:25–32).

NAIL (NAILING)

Jn	20:	25	"Unless I see the **n** marks in his

NAILING (NAIL)

Ac	2:	23	him to death by **n** him to the cross.
Col	2:	14	has taken it away, **n** it to the cross.

NAKED

Ge	2:	25	Adam and his wife were both **n**,
Job	1:	21	womb, and **n** I will depart.
Isa	58:	7	you see the **n**, to clothe them,
2Co	5:	3	are clothed, we will not be found **n**.

NAME

Ex	3:	15	"This is my **n** forever, the **n** you
	20:	7	"You shall not misuse the **n**
Dt	5:	11	"You shall not misuse the **n**
	28:	58	this glorious and awesome **n**—
1Ki	5:	5	will build the temple for my **N**.'
2Ch	7:	14	people, who are called by my **n**,
Ps	34:	3	let us exalt his **n** together.
	103:	1	my inmost being, praise his holy **n**.
	147:	4	the stars and calls them each by **n**.
Pr	22:	1	A good **n** is more desirable than
	30:	4	What is his **n**, and what is the **n**
Isa	40:	26	and calls forth each of them by **n**.
	57:	15	who lives forever, whose **n** is holy:
Jer	14:	7	LORD, for the sake of your **n**.
Da	12:	1	everyone whose **n** is found written
Joel	2:	32	the **n** of the LORD will be saved;
Zec	14:	9	one LORD, and his **n** the only **n**.
Mt	1:	21	you are to give him the **n** Jesus,
	6:	9	in heaven, hallowed be your **n**,
	18:	20	where two or three gather in my **n**,
Jn	10:	3	He calls his own sheep by **n**
	16:	24	not asked for anything in my **n**.
Ac	4:	12	is no other **n** under heaven given
Ro	10:	13	on the **n** of the Lord will be saved."
Php	2:	9	the **n** that is above every **n**,
Col	3:	17	do it all in the **n** of the Lord Jesus,
Heb	1:	4	the angels as the **n** he has inherited
Rev	20:	15	whose **n** was not found written

NAOMI

Mother-in-law of Ruth (Ru 1). Advised Ruth to seek marriage with Boaz (Ru 2–4).

NARROW

Mt	7:	13	"Enter through the **n** gate.

NATHANAEL

Apostle (Jn 1:45–49; 21:2). Probably also called Bartholomew (Mt 10:3).

NATION (NATIONS)

Ge	12:	2	"I will make you into a great **n**,
Ps	33:	12	Blessed is the **n** whose God is
Pr	14:	34	Righteousness exalts a **n**, but sin
Isa	65:	1	a **n** that did not call on my name,
1Pe	2:	9	a holy **n**, God's special possession,
Rev	7:	9	could count, from every **n**, tribe,

NATIONS (NATION)

Ge	17:	4	You will be the father of many **n**.
	18:	18	and all **n** on earth will be blessed
Ex	19:	5	of all **n** you will be my treasured
Ne	1:	8	I will scatter you among the **n**,
Ps	96:	3	Declare his glory among the **n**,
Isa	40:	15	Surely the **n** are like a drop
Eze	36:	23	has been profaned among the **n**,
Hag	2:	7	what is desired by all **n** will come,
Zec	8:	23	**n** will take firm hold of one Jew
	14:	2	I will gather all the **n** to Jerusalem
Mt	28:	19	go and make disciples of all **n**,
Rev	21:	24	The **n** will walk by its light,

NATURAL (NATURE)

1Co	15:	44	it is sown a **n** body, it is raised

NATURE (NATURAL)

Php	2:	6	Who, being in very **n** God, did not

NAZARENE

Mt	2:	23	that he would be called a **N**.

NAZIRITE
Jdg 13: 7 because the boy will be a **N** of God

NECESSARY
Ro 13: 5 it is **n** to submit to the authorities,

NEED (NEEDS NEEDY)
Mt 6: 8 knows what you **n** before you ask
Ro 12: 13 the Lord's people who are in **n**.
1Co 12: 21 say to the hand, "I don't **n** you!"
1Jn 3: 17 sister in **n** but has no pity on them,

NEEDLE
Mt 19: 24 to go through the eye of a **n** than

NEEDS (NEED)
Isa 58: 11 he will satisfy your **n**
Php 4: 19 God will meet all your **n** according

NEEDY (NEED)
Pr 14: 21 is the one who is kind to the **n**.
  14: 31 is kind to the **n** honors God.
  31: 20 and extends her hands to the **n**.
Mt 6: 2 "So when you give to the **n**, do not

NEGLECT (NEGLECTED)
Ne 10: 39 "We will not **n** the house of our
Ps 119: 16 I will not **n** your word.
Ac 6: 2 for us to **n** the ministry of the word
1Ti 4: 14 not **n** your gift, which was given

NEGLECTED (NEGLECT)
Mt 23: 23 But you have **n** the more important

NEHEMIAH
Cupbearer of Artaxerxes (Ne 2:1); governor of Israel (Ne 8:9). Returned to Jerusalem to rebuild walls (Ne 2–6). With Ezra, reestablished worship (Ne 8). Prayer confessing nation's sin (Ne 9). Dedicated wall (Ne 12).

NEIGHBOR (NEIGHBOR'S)
Ex 20: 16 give false testimony against your **n**.
Lev 19: 18 people, but love your **n** as yourself.
Pr 27: 10 better a **n** nearby than a relative far
Mt 19: 19 and 'love your **n** as yourself.'"
Lk 10: 29 asked Jesus, "And who is my **n**?"
Ro 13: 10 Love does no harm to a **n**.

NEIGHBOR'S (NEIGHBOR)
Ex 20: 17 "You shall not covet your **n** house.
Dt 5: 21 "You shall not covet your **n** wife.
  19: 14 not move your **n** boundary stone
Pr 25: 17 Seldom set foot in your **n** house—

NEW
Ps 40: 3 He put a **n** song in my mouth,
Ecc 1: 9 there is nothing **n** under the sun.
Isa 65: 17 I will create **n** heavens and a **n**
Jer 31: 31 I will make a **n** covenant
Eze 36: 26 I will give you a **n** heart and put a **n** spirit in you;
Mt 9: 17 they pour **n** wine into **n** wineskins,
Lk 22: 20 "This cup is the **n** covenant in my
2Co 5: 17 in Christ, the **n** creation has come:
Eph 4: 24 and to put on the **n** self,
2Pe 3: 13 to a **n** heaven and a **n** earth,
1Jn 2: 8 Yet I am writing you a **n** command;

NEWBORN (BEAR)
1Pe 2: 2 Like **n** babies, crave pure spiritual

NEWS
Isa 52: 7 the feet of those who bring good **n**,
Mk 1: 15 Repent and believe the good **n**!"
Lk 2: 10 I bring you good **n** that will cause
Ac 5: 42 proclaiming the good **n** that Jesus

Ac 17: 18 Paul was preaching the good **n**
Ro 10: 15 feet of those who bring good **n**!"

NICODEMUS
Pharisee who visited Jesus at night (Jn 3). Argued fair treatment of Jesus (Jn 7:50–52). With Joseph, prepared Jesus for burial (Jn 19:38–42).

NIGHT
Job 35: 10 Maker, who gives songs in the **n**,
Ps 1: 2 meditates on his law day and **n**.
  91: 5 You will not fear the terror of **n**,
Jn 3: 2 He came to Jesus at **n** and said,
1Th 5: 2 Lord will come like a thief in the **n**.
  5: 5 We do not belong to the **n**
Rev 21: 25 shut, for there will be no **n** there.

NOAH
Righteous man (Eze 14:14, 20) called to build ark (Ge 6–8; Heb 11:7; 1Pe 3:20; 2Pe 2:5). God's covenant with (Ge 9:1–17). Drunkenness of (Ge 9:18–23). Blessed sons, cursed Canaan (Ge 9:24–27).

NOBLE
Ru 3: 11 you are a woman of **n** character.
Ps 45: 1 by a **n** theme as I recite my verses
Pr 12: 4 **n** character is her husband's crown,
  31: 10 wife of **n** character who can find?
  31: 29 "Many women do **n** things, but
Isa 32: 8 But the **n** make **n** plans, and by **n**
Lk 8: 15 good soil stands for those with a **n**
Php 4: 8 whatever is **n**, whatever is right,

NOTHING
Ne 9: 21 they lacked **n**, their clothes did not
Jer 32: 17 **N** is too hard for you.
Jn 15: 5 apart from me you can do **n**.

NULLIFY
Ro 3: 31 we, then, **n** the law by this faith?

OATH
Dt 7: 8 and kept the **o** he swore to your

OBEDIENCE (OBEY)
2Ch 31: 21 of God's temple and in **o** to the law
Ro 1: 5 all the Gentiles to the **o** that comes
  6: 16 to death, or to **o**, which leads
2Jn : 6 that we walk in **o** to his commands.

OBEDIENT (OBEY)
Lk 2: 51 with them and was **o** to them.
Php 2: 8 himself by becoming **o** to death—
1Pe 1: 14 As **o** children, do not conform

OBEY (OBEDIENCE OBEDIENT OBEYED)
Ex 12: 24 "**O** these instructions as a lasting
Dt 6: 3 be careful to **o** so that it may go
  13: 4 Keep his commands and **o** him;
  21: 18 son who does not **o** his father
  30: 2 God and **o** him with all your heart
  32: 46 to **o** carefully all the words
1Sa 15: 22 To **o** is better than sacrifice,
Ps 119: 34 your law and **o** it with all my heart.
Mt 28: 20 to **o** everything I have commanded
Jn 14: 23 who loves me will **o** my teaching.
Ac 5: 29 must **o** God rather than human
Ro 6: 16 you are slaves of the one you **o**—
Gal 5: 3 he is obligated to **o** the whole law.
Eph 6: 1 **o** your parents in the Lord, for this
  6: 5 heart, just as you would **o** Christ.
Col 3: 20 **o** your parents in everything,
1Ti 3: 4 and see that his children **o** him,

OBEYED (OBEY)
Ps 119: 4 precepts that are to be fully **o**.
Jnh 3: 3 Jonah **o** the word of the LORD
Jn 17: 6 to me and they have **o** your word.

Heb 11:   8   as his inheritance, **o** and went,
1Pe 3:   6   who **o** Abraham and called him

OBLIGATED
Ro   1: 14   I am **o** both to Greeks
Gal 5:   3   that he is **o** to obey the whole law.

OBSCENITY
Eph 5:   4   Nor should there be **o**, foolish talk

OBSOLETE
Heb 8: 13   "new," he has made the first one **o**;

OBTAINED
Ro   9: 30   not pursue righteousness, have **o** it,
Php 3: 12   Not that I have already **o** all this,

OFFENSE (OFFENSIVE)
Pr 17:   9   would foster love covers over an **o**,
    19: 11   it is to one's glory to overlook an **o**.

OFFENSIVE (OFFENSE)
Ps 139: 24   See if there is any **o** way in me,

OFFER (OFFERED OFFERING OFFERINGS)
Ro 12:   1   **o** your bodies as a living sacrifice,
Heb 13: 15   let us continually **o** to God

OFFERED (OFFER)
Heb 7: 27   sins once for all when he **o** himself.

OFFERING (OFFER)
Ge 22:   8   provide the lamb for the burnt **o**,
Ps 40:   6   Sacrifice and **o** you did not desire
Isa 53: 10   the LORD makes his life an **o**
Mt   5: 23   if you are **o** your gift at the altar
Eph 5:   2   himself up for us as a fragrant **o**
Heb 10:   5   "Sacrifice and **o** you did not desire,

OFFERINGS (OFFER)
Mal 3:   8   we robbing you?' "In tithes and **o**.
Mk 12: 33   is more important than all burnt **o**

OFFICER
2Ti 2:   4   tries to please his commanding **o**.

OFFSPRING
Ge   3: 15   and between your **o** and hers;
    12:   7   "To your **o** I will give this land."

OIL
Ps 23:   5   You anoint my head with **o**;
Isa 61:   3   the **o** of joy instead of mourning,
Heb 1:   9   by anointing you with the **o** of joy."

OLIVE (OLIVES)
Zec 4:   3   Also there are two **o** trees by it,
Ro 11: 17   though a wild **o** shoot, have been
Rev 11:   4   They are "the two **o** trees"

OLIVES (OLIVE)
Jas 3: 12   can a fig tree bear **o**, or a grapevine

OMEGA
Rev 1:   8   "I am the Alpha and the **O**,"

OMRI
    King of Israel (1Ki 16:21–26).

OPINIONS
1Ki 18: 21   will you waver between two **o**?
Pr 18:   2   but delight in airing their own **o**.

OPPORTUNITY
Ro   7: 11   sin, seizing the **o** afforded
Gal 6: 10   as we have **o**, let us do good to all
Eph 5: 16   making the most of every **o**,
Col 4:   5   make the most of every **o**.
1Ti 5: 14   to give the enemy no **o** for slander.

OPPOSES
Jas 4:   6   "God **o** the proud but shows favor
1Pe 5:   5   "God **o** the proud but shows favor

OPPRESS (OPPRESSED)
Ex 22: 21   "Do not mistreat or **o** a foreigner,
Zec 7: 10   Do not **o** the widow

OPPRESSED (OPPRESS)
Ps   9:   9   The LORD is a refuge for the **o**,
Isa 53:   7   He was **o** and afflicted, yet he did
Zec 10:   2   the people wander like sheep **o**

ORDERLY
1Co 14: 40   be done in a fitting and **o** way.

ORGIES
Gal 5: 21   drunkenness, **o**, and the like.
1Pe 4:   3   lust, drunkenness, **o**,

ORIGIN
2Pe 1: 21   For prophecy never had its **o**

ORPHANS
Jn 14: 18   I will not leave you as **o**;
Jas 1: 27   to look after **o** and widows in their

OUTCOME
Heb 13:   7   Consider the **o** of their way of life
1Pe 4: 17   what will the **o** be for those who do

OUTSIDERS
Col 4:   5   wise in the way you act toward **o**;
1Th 4: 12   daily life may win the respect of **o**
1Ti 3:   7   also have a good reputation with **o**,

OUTSTANDING
SS   5: 10   and ruddy, **o** among ten thousand.
Ro 13:   8   Let no debt remain **o**,

OUTSTRETCHED
Ex   6:   6   I will redeem you with an **o** arm
Jer 27:   5   power and **o** arm I made the earth
Eze 20: 33   with a mighty hand and an **o** arm

OUTWEIGHS
2Co 4: 17   an eternal glory that far **o** them all.

OVERCOME (OVERCOMES)
Mt 16: 18   and the gates of Hades will not **o** it.
Mk   9: 24   help me **o** my unbelief!"
Jn 16: 33   But take heart! I have **o** the world."
Ro 12: 21   Do not be **o** by evil, but **o** evil
1Jn 5:   4   is the victory that has **o** the world,

OVERCOMES (OVERCOME)
1Jn 5:   4   everyone born of God **o** the world.
     5:   5   Who is it that **o** the world?

OVERFLOW (OVERFLOWS)
Ps 119:171   May my lips **o** with praise, for you
Ro 15: 13   so that you may **o** with hope
2Co 4: 15   may cause thanksgiving to **o**
1Th 3: 12   love increase and **o** for each other

OVERFLOWS (OVERFLOW)
Ps 23:   5   anoint my head with oil; my cup **o**.

OVERJOYED (JOY)
Da   6: 23   The king was **o** and gave orders
Mt   2: 10   they saw the star, they were **o**.
Jn 20: 20   disciples were **o** when they saw
Ac 12: 14   she was so **o** she ran back without
1Pe 4: 13   that you may be **o** when his glory

OVERSEER (OVERSEERS)
1Ti 3:   1   to be an **o** desires a noble task.
     3:   2   Now the **o** is to be above reproach,
Titus 1:   7   Since an **o** manages God's

OVERSEERS (OVERSEER)
Ac   20: 28   the Holy Spirit has made you **o**.
Php   1:   1   together with the **o** and deacons:

OVERWHELMED
Ps   38:   4   My guilt has **o** me like a burden
      65:   3   When we were **o** by sins,
Mt   26: 38   "My soul is **o** with sorrow
Mk   7: 37   People were **o** with amazement.

OWE
Ro   13:   7   Give to everyone what you **o** them:
Phm   : 19   that you **o** me your very self.

OX
Dt   25:   4   Do not muzzle an **o** while it is
Isa   11:   7   the lion will eat straw like the **o**.
1Co   9:   9   "Do not muzzle an **o** while it is

PAGANS
Mt   5: 47   Do not even **p** do that?
1Pe   2: 12   such good lives among the **p** that,

PAIN (PAINFUL PAINS)
Job 33: 19   on a bed of **p** with constant distress
Jn   16: 21   to a child has **p** because her time

PAINFUL (PAIN)
Ge   3: 17   through **p** toil you will eat food
Heb 12: 11   seems pleasant at the time, but **p**.

PAINS (PAIN)
Ge   3: 16   "I will make your **p** in childbearing

PALMS
Isa   49: 16   engraved you on the **p** of my hands

PANTS
Ps   42:   1   As the deer **p** for streams of water,
              so my soul **p** for you,

PARADISE
Lk   23: 43   today you will be with me in **p**."
2Co 12:   4   was caught up to **p** and heard
Rev   2:   7   tree of life, which is in the **p** of God.

PARALYZED
Mk   2:   3   bringing to him a **p** man,

PARDON (PARDONS)
Isa   55:   7   and to our God, for he will freely **p**.

PARDONS (PARDON)
Mic   7: 18   like you, who **p** sin and forgives

PARENT (PARENT'S PARENTS)
Pr   17: 21   is no joy for the **p** of a godless fool.

PARENT'S (PARENT)
     15:   5   A fool spurns a **p** discipline,

PARENTS (PARENT)
Ex   20:   5   for the sin of the **p** to the third
Pr   17:   6   **p** are the pride of their children.
Lk   18: 29   sisters or **p** or children for the sake
      21: 16   You will be betrayed even by **p**,
Ro   1: 30   of doing evil; they disobey their **p**;
2Co 12: 14   not have to save up for their **p**,
Eph   6:   1   Children, obey your **p** in the Lord,
Col   3: 20   obey your **p** in everything,
2Ti   3:   2   disobedient to their **p**, ungrateful,

PARTIALITY
Dt   10: 17   who shows no **p** and accepts no
2Ch 19:   7   our God there is no injustice or **p**
Lk   20: 21   that you do not show **p** but teach

PARTICIPATION
1Co 10: 16   bread that we break a **p** in the body

PASS
Ex   12: 13   I see the blood, I will **p** over you.
La   1: 12   nothing to you, all you who **p** by?
Lk   21: 33   but my words will never **p** away.
1Co 13:   8   there is knowledge, it will **p** away.

PASSION (PASSIONS)
1Co   7:   9   to marry than to burn with **p**.

PASSIONS (PASSION)
Gal   5: 24   have crucified the flesh with its **p**
Titus   2: 12   to ungodliness and worldly **p**,

PASSOVER
Ex   12: 11   Eat it in haste; it is the LORD's **P**.
Dt   16:   1   celebrate the **P** of the LORD your
1Co   5:   7   For Christ, our **P** lamb, has been

PAST
Isa   43: 18   do not dwell on the **p**.
Ro   15:   4   was written in the **p** was written
Heb   1:   1   the **p** God spoke to our ancestors

PASTORS
Eph   4: 11   the evangelists, the **p** and teachers,

PASTURE (PASTURES)
Ps   37:   3   dwell in the land and enjoy safe **p**.
     100:   3   are his people, the sheep of his **p**.
Jer 50:   7   their verdant **p**, the LORD,
Eze 34: 13   I will **p** them on the mountains
Jn   10:   9   come in and go out, and find **p**.

PASTURES (PASTURE)
Ps   23:   2   He makes me lie down in green **p**,

PATCH
Mt   9: 16   No one sews a **p** of unshrunk cloth

PATH (PATHS)
Ps   27: 11   me in a straight **p** because of my
     119:   9   person stay on the **p** of purity?
     119:105   to my feet and a light for my **p**.
Pr   15: 19   the **p** of the upright is a highway.
     15: 24   The **p** of life leads upward
Isa   26:   7   The **p** of the righteous is level;
Lk   1: 79   guide our feet into the **p** of peace."
2Co   6:   3   no stumbling block in anyone's **p**,

PATHS (PATH)
Ps   23:   3   He guides me along the right **p**
      25:   4   ways, LORD, teach me your **p**.
Pr   3:   6   and he will make your **p** straight.
Ro   11: 33   and his **p** beyond tracing out!
Heb 12: 13   "Make level **p** for your feet,"

PATIENCE (PATIENT)
Pr   19: 11   A person's wisdom yields **p**; it is
2Co   6:   6   understanding, **p** and kindness;
Col   1: 11   may have great endurance and **p**,
      3: 12   humility, gentleness and **p**.

PATIENT (PATIENCE PATIENTLY)
Pr   15: 18   the one who is **p** calms a quarrel.
Ro   12: 12   Be joyful in hope, **p** in affliction,
1Co 13:   4   Love is **p**, love is kind. It does not
Eph   4:   2   be **p**, bearing with one another
1Th   5: 14   help the weak, be **p** with everyone.

PATIENTLY (PATIENT)
Ps   40:   1   I waited **p** for the LORD;
Ro   8: 25   we do not yet have, we wait for it **p**.

PATTERN
Ro   5: 14   who is a **p** of the one to come.
     12:   2   not conform to the **p** of this world,
2Ti   1: 13   keep as the **p** of sound teaching,

PAUL

Also called Saul (Ac 13:9). Pharisee from Tarsus (Ac 9:11; Php 3:5). Apostle (Gal 1). At stoning of Stephen (Ac 8:1). Persecuted Church (Ac 9:1–2; Gal 1:13). Vision of Jesus on road to Damascus (Ac 9:4–9; 26:12–18). In Arabia (Gal 1:17). Preached in Damascus; escaped death through the wall in a basket (Ac 9:19–25). In Jerusalem; sent back to Tarsus (Ac 9:26–30).

Brought to Antioch by Barnabas (Ac 11:22–26). First missionary journey to Cyprus and Galatia (Ac 13–14). Stoned at Lystra (Ac 14:19–20). At Jerusalem council (Ac 15). Split with Barnabas over Mark (Ac 15:36–41).

Second missionary journey with Silas (Ac 16–20). Called to Macedonia (Ac 16:6–10). Freed from prison in Philippi (Ac 16:16–40). In Thessalonica (Ac 17:1–9). Speech in Athens (Ac 17:16–33). In Corinth (Ac 18). In Ephesus (Ac 19). Return to Jerusalem (Ac 20). Farewell to Ephesian elders (Ac 20:13–38). Arrival in Jerusalem (Ac 21:1–26). Arrested (Ac 21:27–36). Addressed crowds (Ac 22), Sanhedrin (Ac 23:1–11). Transferred to Caesarea (Ac 23:12–35). Trial before Felix (Ac 24), Festus (Ac 25:1–12). Before Agrippa (Ac 25:13—26:32). Voyage to Rome; shipwreck (Ac 27). Arrival in Rome (Ac 28).

PAY (REPAID REPAY)

Lev	26:	43	They will **p** for their sins because
Pr	22:	17	**P** attention and turn your ear
Mt	22:	17	Is it right to **p** the imperial tax
Ro	13:	6	This is also why you **p** taxes,
2Pe	1:	19	you will do well to **p** attention to it,

PEACE (PEACEMAKERS)

Nu	6:	26	toward you and give you **p**." '
Ps	34:	14	and do good; seek **p** and pursue it.
	85:	10	righteousness and **p** kiss each
	119:165		Great **p** have those who love your
	122:	6	Pray for the **p** of Jerusalem:
Pr	14:	30	A heart at **p** gives life to the body,
	17:	1	Better a dry crust with **p** and quiet
Isa	9:	6	Everlasting Father, Prince of **P**.
	26:	3	in perfect **p** those whose minds are
	48:	22	"There is no **p**," says the LORD,
Zec	9:	10	He will proclaim **p** to the nations.
Mt	10:	34	I did not come to bring **p**,
Lk	2:	14	and on earth **p** to those on whom
Jn	14:	27	**P** I leave with you; my **p** I give you.
	16:	33	so that in me you may have **p**.
Ro	5:	1	we have **p** with God through our
1Co	7:	15	God has called us to live in **p**.
	14:	33	is not a God of disorder but of **p**—
Gal	5:	22	Spirit is love, joy, **p**, forbearance,
Eph	2:	14	For he himself is our **p**, who has
Php	4:	7	the **p** of God, which transcends
Col	1:	20	by making **p** through his blood,
	3:	15	Let the **p** of Christ rule in your
1Th	5:	3	people are saying, "**P** and safety,"
2Th	3:	16	the Lord of **p** himself give you **p**
2Ti	2:	22	love and **p**, along with those who
1Pe	3:	11	they must seek **p** and pursue it.
Rev	6:	4	power to take **p** from the earth

PEACEMAKERS (PEACE)

Mt	5:	9	Blessed are the **p**, for they will be
Jas	3:	18	**P** who sow in peace reap a harvest

PEARL (PEARLS)

Rev	21:	21	each gate made of a single **p**.

PEARLS (PEARL)

Mt	7:	6	do not throw your **p** to pigs.
	13:	45	like a merchant looking for fine **p**.
1Ti	2:	9	or gold or **p** or expensive clothes,
Rev	21:	21	The twelve gates were twelve **p**,

PEKAH

King of Israel (2Ki 15:25–31; Isa 7:1).

PEKAHIAH

Son of Menahem; king of Israel (2Ki 15:22–26).

PEN

Mt	5:	18	not the least stroke of a **p**,

PENTECOST

Ac	2:	1	When the day of **P** came, they were

PEOPLE (PEOPLES)

Dt	32:	9	For the LORD's portion is his **p**,
Ru	1:	16	Your **p** will be my **p** and your God
2Ch	7:	14	if my **p**, who are called by my
Ps	133:	1	it is when God's **p** live together
Jer	24:	7	They will be my **p**, and I will be
Zec	2:	11	in that day and will become my **p**.
Mt	4:	19	I will send you out to fish for **p**."
Lk	2:	10	will cause great joy for all the **p**.
Jn	12:	32	earth, will draw all **p** to myself."
Ac	15:	14	to choose a **p** for his name
Ro	5:	12	and in this way death came to all **p**,
	8:	27	for God's **p** in accordance
1Co	9:	22	I have become all things to all **p** so
2Co	6:	16	their God, and they will be my **p**."
Eph	1:	18	glorious inheritance in his holy **p**,
	6:	18	keep on praying for all the Lord's **p**.
1Ti	2:	4	who wants all **p** to be saved
2Ti	2:	2	entrust to reliable **p** who will also
Titus	2:	14	himself a **p** that are his very own,
Heb	9:	27	Just as **p** are destined to die once,
1Pe	2:	9	But you are a chosen **p**, a royal
Rev	5:	8	which are the prayers of God's **p**.
	19:	8	the righteous acts of God's holy **p**.)
	21:	3	They will be his **p**, and God

PEOPLES (PEOPLE)

Da	7:	14	**p** of every language worshiped him
Mic	4:	1	the hills, and **p** will stream to it.

PERCEIVING

Isa	6:	9	be ever seeing, but never **p**.'

PERFECT (PERFECTER PERFECTION)

SS	6:	9	but my dove, my **p** one, is unique,
Isa	26:	3	in **p** peace those whose minds are
Mt	5:	48	Be **p**, therefore, as your heavenly Father is **p**.
Ro	12:	2	his good, pleasing and **p** will.
2Co	12:	9	my power is made **p** in weakness."
Col	3:	14	binds them all together in **p** unity.
Heb	9:	11	more **p** tabernacle that is not made
	10:	14	he has made **p** forever those who
Jas	1:	17	good and **p** gift is from above,
	1:	25	looks intently into the **p** law
	3:	2	never at fault in what they say is **p**,
1Jn	4:	18	But **p** love drives out fear,

PERFECTER (PERFECT)

Heb	12:	2	on Jesus, the pioneer and **p** of faith.

PERFECTION (PERFECT)

Ps	119:	96	To all **p** I see a limit, but your
Heb	7:	11	If **p** could have been attained

PERFORMS

Ps	77:	14	You are the God who **p** miracles;

PERISH (PERISHABLE)

Ps	102:	26	They will **p**, but you remain;
Lk	13:	3	you repent, you too will all **p**.
Jn	10:	28	eternal life, and they shall never **p**;
Col	2:	22	that are all destined to **p** with use,
Heb	1:	11	They will **p**, but you remain;
2Pe	3:	9	you, not wanting anyone to **p**,

PERISHABLE (PERISH)
1Co 15: 42   The body that is sown is **p**, it is

PERJURERS
1Ti 1: 10   for slave traders and liars and **p**—

PERMIT
1Ti 2: 12   I do not **p** a woman to teach

PERSECUTE (PERSECUTED PERSECUTION)
Mt   5: 11   **p** you and falsely say all kinds
Jn 15: 20   persecuted me, they will **p** you
Ac   9: 4   "Saul, Saul, why do you **p** me?"
Ro 12: 14   Bless those who **p** you; bless and

PERSECUTED (PERSECUTE)
1Co 4: 12   when we are **p**, we endure it;
2Ti 3: 12   godly life in Christ Jesus will be **p**,

PERSECUTION (PERSECUTE)
Ro   8: 35   trouble or hardship or **p** or famine

PERSEVERANCE (PERSEVERE)
Ro   5: 3   we know that suffering produces **p**;
     5: 4   **p**, character; and character, hope.
Heb 12: 1   let us run with **p** the race marked
Jas 1: 3   testing of your faith produces **p**.
2Pe 1: 6   and to self-control, **p**; and to **p**,

PERSEVERE (PERSEVERANCE PERSEVERED PERSEVERES)
1Ti 4: 16   **P** in them, because if you do,
Heb 10: 36   You need to **p** so that when you

PERSEVERED (PERSEVERE)
Heb 11: 27   he **p** because he saw him who is
Jas 5: 11   count as blessed those who have **p**.
Rev 2: 3   You have **p** and have endured

PERSEVERES (PERSEVERE)
1Co 13: 7   trusts, always hopes, always **p**.
Jas 1: 12   one who **p** under trial because,

PERSUADE
2Co 5: 11   to fear the Lord, we try to **p** others.

PERVERSION (PERVERT)
Lev 18: 23   sexual relations with it; that is a **p**.
Jude : 7   up to sexual immorality and **p**.

PERVERT (PERVERSION)
Gal 1: 7   are trying to **p** the gospel of Christ.

PESTILENCE
Ps 91: 6   the **p** that stalks in the darkness,

PETER
Apostle, brother of Andrew, also called Simon (Mt 10:2; Mk 3:16; Lk 6:14; Ac 1:13), and Cephas (Jn 1:42). Confession of Christ (Mt 16:13–20; Mk 8:27–30; Lk 9:18–27). At transfiguration (Mt 17:1–8; Mk 9:2–8; Lk 9:28–36; 2Pe 1:16–18). Caught fish with coin (Mt 17:24–27). Denial of Jesus predicted (Mt 26:31–35; Mk 14:27–31; Lk 22:31–34; Jn 13:31–38). Denied Jesus (Mt 26:69–75; Mk 14:66–72; Lk 22:54–62; Jn 18:15–27). Commissioned by Jesus to shepherd his flock (Jn 21:15–23).
Speech at Pentecost (Ac 2). Healed beggar (Ac 3:1–10). Speech at temple (Ac 3:11–26), before Sanhedrin (Ac 4:1–22). In Samaria (Ac 8:14–25). Sent by vision to Cornelius (Ac 10). Announced salvation of Gentiles in Jerusalem (Ac 11; 15). Freed from prison (Ac 12). Inconsistency at Antioch (Gal 2:11–21). At Jerusalem Council (Ac 15).

PHARISEES
Mt   5: 20   surpasses that of the **P**

PHILIP
1. Apostle (Mt 10:3; Mk 3:18; Lk 6:14; Jn 1:43–48; 14:8; Ac 1:13).
2. Deacon (Ac 6:1–7); evangelist in Samaria (Ac 8:4–25), to Ethiopian (Ac 8:26–40).

PHILOSOPHY
Col 2: 8   through hollow and deceptive **p**,

PHYLACTERIES
Mt 23: 5   They make their **p** wide

PHYSICAL
1Ti 4: 8   For **p** training is of some value,
Jas 2: 16   does nothing about their **p** needs,

PIECES
Ge 15: 17   and passed between the **p**.
Jer 34: 18   two and then walked between its **p**.

PIERCE (PIERCED)
Ps 22: 16   they **p** my hands and my feet.

PIERCED (PIERCE)
Isa 53: 5   he was **p** for our transgressions,
Zec 12: 10   the one they have **p**, and they will
Jn 19: 37   will look on the one they have **p**."

PIGS
Mt   7: 6   do not throw your pearls to **p**.

PILATE
Governor of Judea. Questioned Jesus (Mt 27:1–26; Mk 15:15; Lk 22:66—23:25; Jn 18:28—19:16); sent him to Herod (Lk 23:6–12); consented to his crucifixion when crowds chose Barabbas (Mt 27:15–26; Mk 15:6–15; Lk 23:13–25; Jn 19:1–10).

PILLAR
Ge 19: 26   back, and she became a **p** of salt.
Ex 13: 21   by night in a **p** of fire to give them
1Ti 3: 15   the **p** and foundation of the truth.

PIT
Ps 40: 2   He lifted me out of the slimy **p**,
    103: 4   who redeems your life from the **p**
Mt 15: 14   the blind, both will fall into a **p**."

PITIED
1Co 15: 19   we are of all people most to be **p**.

PLAGUE
2Ch 6: 28   famine or **p** comes to the land,

PLAIN
Ro   1: 19   God has made it **p** to them.

PLAN (PLANNED PLANS)
Pr 14: 22   those who **p** what is good find love
Eph 1: 11   to the **p** of him who works

PLANK
Mt   7: 3   attention to the **p** in your own eye?
Lk   6: 41   attention to the **p** in your own eye?

PLANNED (PLAN)
Ps 40: 5   have done, the things you **p** for us.
Isa 46: 11   what I have **p**, that I will do.
Heb 11: 40   since God had **p** something better

PLANS (PLAN)
Ps 20: 4   heart and make all your **p** succeed.
    33: 11   But the **p** of the LORD stand firm
Pr 20: 18   **P** are established by seeking advice;
Isa 32: 8   But the noble make noble **p**,

PLANTED (PLANTS)
Ps   1: 3   person is like a tree **p** by streams

Mt 15: 13 Father has not **p** will be pulled
1Co 3: 6 I **p** the seed, Apollos watered it,

PLANTS (PLANTED)

1Co 3: 7 neither the one who **p** nor the one
      9: 7 Who **p** a vineyard and does not eat

PLATTER

Mk 6: 25 head of John the Baptist on a **p**."

PLAYED

Lk 7: 32 " 'We **p** the pipe for you, and you
1Co 14: 7 what tune is being **p** unless there is

PLEADED

2Co 12: 8 Three times I **p** with the Lord

PLEASANT (PLEASE)

Ps 16: 6 lines have fallen for me in **p** places;
    133: 1 and **p** it is when God's people live
    147: 1 how **p** and fitting to praise him!
Heb 12: 11 No discipline seems **p** at the time,

PLEASE (PLEASANT PLEASED PLEASES PLEASING PLEASURE PLEASURES)

Pr 20: 23 and dishonest scales do not **p** him.
Jer 6: 20 your sacrifices do not **p** me."
Jn   5: 30 for I seek not to **p** myself but him
Ro   8: 8 realm of the flesh cannot **p** God.
    15: 2 Each of us should **p** our neighbors
1Co 7: 32 how he can **p** the Lord.
    10: 33 even as I try to **p** everyone in every
2Co 5: 9 So we make it our goal to **p** him,
Gal 1: 10 If I were still trying to **p** people,
1Th 4: 1 you how to live in order to **p** God,
2Ti 2: 4 tries to **p** his commanding officer.
Heb 11: 6 faith it is impossible to **p** God,

PLEASED (PLEASE)

Mt   3: 17 with him I am well **p**."
1Co 1: 21 God was **p** through the foolishness
Col 1: 19 God was **p** to have all his fullness
Heb 11: 5 commended as one who **p** God.
2Pe 1: 17 with him I am well **p**."

PLEASES (PLEASE)

Ps 135: 6 The Lord does whatever **p** him,
Pr 15: 8 the prayer of the upright **p** him.
Jn   3: 8 The wind blows wherever it **p**.
     8: 29 alone, for I always do what **p** him."
Col 3: 20 in everything, for this **p** the Lord.
1Ti 2: 3 is good, and **p** God our Savior,
1Jn 3: 22 his commands and do what **p** him.

PLEASING (PLEASE)

Ps 104: 34 May my meditation be **p** to him,
Ro 12: 1 living sacrifice, holy and **p** to God
Php 4: 18 an acceptable sacrifice, **p** to God.
Heb 13: 21 he work in us what is **p** to him,

PLEASURE (PLEASE)

Ps 147: 10 His **p** is not in the strength
Pr 21: 17 loves **p** will become poor;
Eze 18: 32 For I take no **p** in the death
Eph 1: 5 in accordance with his **p** and will—
     1: 9 of his will according to his good **p**,
2Ti 3: 4 lovers of **p** rather than lovers

PLEASURES (PLEASE)

Ps 16: 11 with eternal **p** at your right hand.
Heb 11: 25 than to enjoy the fleeting **p** of sin.
2Pe 2: 13 reveling in their **p** while they feast

PLENTIFUL

Mt   9: 37 "The harvest is **p** but the workers

PLOW (PLOWSHARES)

Lk   9: 62 "No one who puts a hand to the **p**

PLOWSHARES (PLOW)

Isa 2: 4 They will beat their swords into **p**
Joel 3: 10 Beat your **p** into swords and your

PLUNDER

Ex   3: 22 And so you will **p** the Egyptians."

POINT

Jas 2: 10 yet stumbles at just one **p** is guilty

POISON

Mk 16: 18 *and when they drink deadly p,*
Jas 3: 8 It is a restless evil, full of deadly **p**.

POLLUTE (POLLUTED)

Nu 35: 33 " 'Do not **p** the land where you
Jude : 8 these ungodly people **p** their own

POLLUTED (POLLUTE)

Ezr 9: 11 is a land **p** by the corruption
Pr 25: 26 a **p** well are the righteous who give
Ac 15: 20 to abstain from food **p** by idols,
Jas 1: 27 oneself from being **p** by the world.

PONDER

Ps 64: 9 of God and **p** what he has done.
    119: 95 me, but I will **p** your statutes.

POOR (POVERTY)

Dt 15: 4 need be no **p** people among you,
    15: 11 There will always be **p** people
Ps 34: 6 This **p** man called, and the Lord
    82: 3 uphold the cause of the **p**
    112: 9 freely scattered their gifts to the **p**,
Pr 13: 7 another pretends to be **p**, yet has
    14: 31 oppresses the **p** shows contempt
    19: 1 Better the **p** whose walk is
    19: 17 Whoever is kind to the **p** lends
    22: 2 Rich and **p** have this in common:
    22: 9 they share their food with the **p**.
    28: 6 Better the **p** whose walk is
    31: 20 She opens her arms to the **p**
Isa 61: 1 to proclaim good news to the **p**.
Mt   5: 3 "Blessed are the **p** in spirit,
    11: 5 good news is proclaimed to the **p**.
    19: 21 your possessions and give to the **p**,
    26: 11 The **p** you will always have
Mk 12: 42 a **p** widow came and put in two
Ac 10: 4 and gifts to the **p** have come up as
1Co 13: 3 If I give all I possess to the **p**
2Co 8: 9 yet for your sake he became **p**,
Jas 2: 2 and a **p** man in filthy old clothes

PORTION

Dt 32: 9 For the Lord's **p** is his people,
2Ki 2: 9 "Let me inherit a double **p** of your
La   3: 24 to myself, "The Lord is my **p**;

POSSESS (POSSESSING POSSESSION POSSESSIONS)

Nu 33: 53 for I have given you the land to **p**.

POSSESSING (POSSESS)

2Co 6: 10 nothing, and yet **p** everything.

POSSESSION (POSSESS)

Ge 15: 7 give you this land to take **p** of it."
Nu 13: 30 go up and take **p** of the land,
Eph 1: 14 of those who are God's **p**—

POSSESSIONS (POSSESS)

Lk 12: 15 not consist in an abundance of **p**."
2Co 12: 14 because what I want is not your **p**
1Jn 3: 17 If anyone has material **p** and sees

POSSIBLE

Mt 19: 26 but with God all things are **p**."

Mk   9: 23   "Everything is **p** for one who
      10: 27   all things are **p** with God."
Ro   12: 18   If it is **p**, as far as it depends on you
1Co   9: 22   by all **p** means I might save some.

POT (POTSHERDS POTTER POTTERY)
2Ki   4: 40   of God, there is death in the **p**!"
Jer 18: 4   the potter formed it into another **p**,

POTSHERDS (POT)
Isa 45: 9   but **p** among the **p** on the ground.

POTTER (POT)
Isa 29: 16   Can the pot say to the **p**,
      45: 9   Does the clay say to the **p**,
      64: 8   We are the clay, you are the **p**;
Jer 18: 6   do with you, Israel, as this **p** does?"
Ro   9: 21   Does not the **p** have the right

POTTERY (POT)
Ro   9: 21   of clay some **p** for special purposes

POUR (POURED)
Ps   62: 8   **p** out your hearts to him, for God
Joel 2: 28   I will **p** out my Spirit on all people.
Mal   3: 10   **p** out so much blessing that there
Ac   2: 17   I will **p** out my Spirit on all people.

POURED (POUR)
Ac   10: 45   the Holy Spirit had been **p** out
Ro   5: 5   because God's love has been **p**

POVERTY (POOR)
Pr   14: 23   but mere talk leads only to **p**.
      21: 5   profit as surely as haste leads to **p**.
      30: 8   give me neither **p** nor riches,
Mk   12: 44   she, out of her **p**, put in everything
2Co   8: 2   their extreme **p** welled up in rich
       8: 9   you through his **p** might become

POWER (POWERFUL POWERS)
1Ch 29: 11   greatness and the **p** and the glory
2Ch 32: 7   for there is a greater **p** with us than
Job 36: 22   "God is exalted in his **p**. Who is
Ps   63: 2   and beheld your **p** and your glory.
      68: 34   Proclaim the **p** of God,
     147: 5   Great is our Lord and mighty in **p**;
Pr   24: 5   The wise prevail through great **p**,
Isa 40: 10   Sovereign LORD comes with **p**,
Zec   4: 6   'Not by might nor by **p**, but by my
Mt   22: 29   the Scriptures or the **p** of God.
      24: 30   of heaven, with **p** and great glory.
Ac   1: 8   you will receive **p** when the Holy
       4: 33   With great **p** the apostles
      10: 38   with the Holy Spirit and **p**,
Ro   1: 16   because it is the **p** of God
1Co   1: 18   us who are being saved it is the **p**
      15: 56   is sin, and the **p** of sin is the law.
2Co 12: 9   so that Christ's **p** may rest on me.
Eph   1: 19   his incomparably great **p** for us
Php   3: 10   to know the **p** of his resurrection
Col   1: 11   strengthened with all **p** according
2Ti   1: 7   us timid, but gives us **p**,
Heb   7: 16   of the **p** of an indestructible life.
Rev   4: 11   to receive glory and honor and **p**,
      19: 1   glory and **p** belong to our God,
      20: 6   second death has no **p** over them,

POWERFUL (POWER)
Ps   29: 4   The voice of the LORD is **p**;
Lk   24: 19   in word and deed before God
2Th   1: 7   in blazing fire with his **p** angels.
Heb   1: 3   sustaining all things by his **p** word.
Jas   5: 16   prayer of a righteous person is **p**

POWERLESS
Ro   5: 6   when we were still **p**, Christ died
       8: 3   what the law was **p** to do because it

POWERS (POWER)
Ro   8: 38   present nor the future, nor any **p**,
1Co 12: 10   to another miraculous **p**,
Col   1: 16   whether thrones or **p** or rulers
       2: 15   And having disarmed the **p**

PRACTICE
Lev 19: 26   " 'Do not **p** divination or seek
Mt   23: 3   for they do not **p** what they preach.
Lk   8: 21   hear God's word and put it into **p**."
Ro   12: 13   who are in need. **P** hospitality.
1Ti   5: 4   put their religion into **p** by caring

PRAISE (PRAISED PRAISES PRAISING)
Ex   15: 2   and I will **p** him, my father's God,
Dt   32: 3   Oh, **p** the greatness of our God!
Ru   4: 14   "**P** be to the LORD, who this day
2Sa 22: 47   **P** be to my Rock!
1Ch 16: 25   the LORD and most worthy of **p**;
2Ch 20: 21   to **p** him for the splendor of his
Ps   8: 2   Through the **p** of children
      33: 1   it is fitting for the upright to **p** him.
      34: 1   his **p** will always be on my lips.
      40: 3   mouth, a hymn of **p** to our God.
      48: 1   and most worthy of **p**, in the city
      68: 19   **P** be to the Lord, to God our Savior,
      89: 5   The heavens **p** your wonders,
     100: 4   give thanks to him and **p** his name.
     105: 2   Sing to him, sing **p** to him;
     106: 1   **P** the LORD. Give thanks
     119:175   Let me live that I may **p** you,
     139: 14   I **p** you because I am fearfully
     145: 21   Let every creature **p** his holy name
     146: 1   **P** the LORD. **P** the LORD, my soul.
     150: 2   **p** him for his surpassing greatness.
     150: 6   Let everything that has breath **p** the
              LORD. **P** the LORD.
Pr   27: 2   Let someone else **p** you, and not
      27: 21   but people are tested by their **p**.
      31: 31   let her works bring her **p** at the city
Mt   21: 16   Lord, have called forth your **p**'?"
Jn   12: 43   they loved human **p** more than **p**
              from God.
Eph   1: 6   to the **p** of his glorious grace,
       1: 12   might be for the **p** of his glory.
       1: 14   to the **p** of his glory.
Heb 13: 15   offer to God a sacrifice of **p**—
Jas   5: 13   Let them sing songs of **p**.

PRAISED (PRAISE)
1Ch 29: 10   David **p** the LORD in the presence
Ne   8: 6   Ezra **p** the LORD, the great God;
Da   2: 19   Then Daniel **p** the God of heaven
Ro   9: 5   who is God over all, forever **p**!
1Pe   4: 11   God may be **p** through Jesus Christ

PRAISES (PRAISE)
2Sa 22: 50   I will sing the **p** of your name.
Ps   47: 6   Sing **p** to God, sing **p**; sing **p**
     147: 1   good it is to sing **p** to our God,
Pr   31: 28   her husband also, and he **p** her:

PRAISING (PRAISE)
Ac   10: 46   speaking in tongues and **p** God.
1Co 14: 16   when you are **p** God in the Spirit,

PRAY (PRAYED PRAYER PRAYERS PRAYING)
Dt   4: 7   our God is near us whenever we **p**
1Sa 12: 23   the LORD by failing to **p** for you.
2Ch   7: 14   will humble themselves and **p**
Job 42: 8   My servant Job will **p** for you,
Ps 122: 6   **P** for the peace of Jerusalem:
Mt   5: 44   and **p** for those who persecute you,
       6: 5   for they love to **p** standing
       6: 9   "This, then, is how you should **p**:
      26: 36   here while I go over there and **p**."

Lk	6: 28	you, **p** for those who mistreat you.
	18: 1	them that they should always **p**
	22: 40	them, "**P** that you will not fall
Ro	8: 26	not know what we ought to **p** for,
1Co	14: 13	in a tongue should **p** that they may
1Th	5: 17	**p** continually,
Jas	5: 13	Let them **p**. Is anyone happy?
	5: 16	**p** for each other so that you may be

PRAYED (PRAY)

1Sa	1: 27	I **p** for this child, and the LORD
Jnh	2: 1	From inside the fish Jonah **p**
Mk	14: 35	and **p** that if possible the hour

PRAYER (PRAY)

2Ch	30: 27	for their **p** reached heaven, his holy
Ezr	8: 23	about this, and he answered our **p**.
Ps	6: 9	the LORD accepts my **p**.
	86: 6	Hear my **p**, LORD; listen to my
Pr	15: 8	the **p** of the upright pleases him.
Isa	56: 7	house will be called a house of **p**
Mt	21: 13	house will be called a house of **p**,'
Mk	11: 24	whatever you ask for in **p**,
Jn	17: 15	My **p** is not that you take them
Ac	6: 4	will give our attention to **p**
Php	4: 6	every situation, by **p** and petition,
Jas	5: 15	the **p** offered in faith will make
1Pe	3: 12	and his ears are attentive to their **p**,

PRAYERS (PRAY)

1Ch	5: 20	He answered their **p**, because they
Mk	12: 40	and for a show make lengthy **p**.
1Pe	3: 7	so that nothing will hinder your **p**.
Rev	5: 8	which are the **p** of God's people.

PRAYING (PRAY)

Mk	11: 25	And when you stand **p**, if you hold
Jn	17: 9	I am not **p** for the world,
Ac	16: 25	Silas were **p** and singing hymns
Eph	6: 18	always keep on **p** for all the Lord's

PREACH (PREACHED PREACHING)

Mt	23: 3	they do not practice what they **p**.
Mk	16: 15	and **p** the gospel to all creation.
Ac	9: 20	At once he began to **p**
Ro	10: 15	how can anyone **p** unless they are
	15: 20	to **p** the gospel where Christ was
1Co	1: 17	to baptize, but to **p** the gospel—
	1: 23	but we **p** Christ crucified:
	9: 14	that those who **p** the gospel should
	9: 16	Woe to me if I do not **p** the gospel!
2Co	10: 16	so that we can **p** the gospel
Gal	1: 8	heaven should **p** a gospel other
2Ti	4: 2	**P** the word; be prepared in season

PREACHED (PREACH)

Mk	13: 10	the gospel must first be **p** to all
Ac	8: 4	who had been scattered **p** the word
1Co	9: 27	so that after I have **p** to others,
	15: 1	remind you of the gospel I **p** to you
2Co	11: 4	a Jesus other than the Jesus we **p**,
Gal	1: 8	a gospel other than the one we **p**
Php	1: 18	false motives or true, Christ is **p**.
1Ti	3: 16	angels, was **p** among the nations,

PREACHING (PREACH)

Ro	10: 14	can they hear without someone **p**
1Co	9: 18	in **p** the gospel I may offer it free
1Ti	4: 13	of Scripture, to **p** and to teaching.
	5: 17	especially those whose work is **p**

PRECEPTS

Ps	19: 8	The **p** of the LORD are right,
	111: 7	all his **p** are trustworthy.
	111: 10	all who follow his **p** have good
	119: 40	How I long for your **p**!

Ps	119: 69	I keep your **p** with all my heart.
	119:104	I gain understanding from your **p**;
	119:159	See how I love your **p**; preserve my

PRECIOUS

Ps	19: 10	They are more **p** than gold,
	116: 15	**P** in the sight of the LORD is
Pr	8: 11	for wisdom is more **p** than rubies,
Isa	28: 16	stone, a **p** cornerstone for a sure
1Pe	1: 19	but with the **p** blood of Christ,
	2: 6	a chosen and **p** cornerstone,
2Pe	1: 4	us his very great and **p** promises,

PREDESTINED (DESTINY)

Ro	8: 29	**p** to be conformed to the image
	8: 30	And those he **p**, he also called;
Eph	1: 5	he **p** us for adoption to sonship
	1: 11	been **p** according to the plan

PREDICTION

Jer	28: 9	LORD only if his **p** comes true."

PREPARE (PREPARED)

Ps	23: 5	You **p** a table before me
Am	4: 12	to you, Israel, **p** to meet your God."
Jn	14: 2	that I am going there to **p** a place

PREPARED (PREPARE)

Mt	25: 34	the kingdom **p** for you since
1Co	2: 9	the things God has **p** for those who
Eph	2: 10	which God **p** in advance for us
2Ti	4: 2	be **p** in season and out of season;
1Pe	3: 15	Always be **p** to give an answer

PRESENCE (PRESENT)

Ex	25: 30	Put the bread of the **P** on this table
Ezr	9: 15	not one of us can stand in your **p**."
Ps	31: 20	the shelter of your **p** you hide them
	89: 15	who walk in the light of your **p**,
	90: 8	secret sins in the light of your **p**.
	139: 7	Where can I flee from your **p**?
Jer	5: 22	"Should you not tremble in my **p**?
Heb	9: 24	now to appear for us in God's **p**.
Jude	: 24	before his glorious **p** without fault

PRESENT (PRESENCE)

2Co	11: 2	that I might **p** you as a pure virgin
Eph	5: 27	and to **p** her to himself as a radiant
2Ti	2: 15	Do your best to **p** yourself to God

PRESERVES

Ps	119: 50	Your promise **p** my life.

PRESS (PRESSED PRESSURE)

Php	3: 14	I **p** on toward the goal to win

PRESSED (PRESS)

Lk	6: 38	A good measure, **p** down,

PRESSURE (PRESS)

2Co	1: 8	We were under great **p**, far beyond
	11: 28	I face daily the **p** of my concern

PREVAILS

1Sa	2: 9	"It is not by strength that one **p**;

PRICE

Job	28: 18	the **p** of wisdom is beyond rubies.
1Co	6: 20	you were bought at a **p**.
	7: 23	You were bought at a **p**;

PRIDE (PROUD)

Pr	8: 13	I hate **p** and arrogance,
	16: 18	**P** goes before destruction,
Da	4: 37	those who walk in **p** he is able
Gal	6: 4	can take **p** in themselves alone,
Jas	1: 9	to take **p** in their high position.

PRIEST (PRIESTHOOD PRIESTS)
Heb 4: 14 a great high **p** who has ascended
 4: 15 do not have a high **p** who is unable
 7: 26 Such a high **p** truly meets our need
 8: 1 We do have such a high **p**, who sat

PRIESTHOOD (PRIEST)
Heb 7: 24 lives forever, he has a permanent **p**.
1Pe 2: 5 a spiritual house to be a holy **p**,
 2: 9 people, a royal **p**, a holy nation,

PRIESTS (PRIEST)
Ex 19: 6 you will be for me a kingdom of **p**
Rev 5: 10 a kingdom and **p** to serve our God,

PRINCE
Isa 9: 6 Everlasting Father, **P** of Peace.
Jn 12: 31 now the **p** of this world will be
Ac 5: 31 him to his own right hand as **P**

PRISON (PRISONER)
Isa 42: 7 blind, to free captives from **p**
Mt 25: 36 I was in **p** and you came to visit
Rev 20: 7 Satan will be released from his **p**

PRISONER (PRISON)
Ro 7: 23 making me a **p** of the law of sin
Eph 3: 1 the **p** of Christ Jesus for the sake

PRIVILEGE
2Co 8: 4 for the **p** of sharing in this service

PRIZE
1Co 9: 24 Run in such a way as to get the **p**.
Php 3: 14 on toward the goal to win the **p**

PROCLAIM (PROCLAIMED)
1Ch 16: 23 **p** his salvation day after day.
Ps 19: 1 the skies **p** the work of his hands.
 50: 6 the heavens **p** his righteousness,
 68: 34 **P** the power of God, whose majesty
 118: 17 will **p** what the LORD has done.
Zec 9: 10 He will **p** peace to the nations.
Ac 20: 27 I have not hesitated to **p** to you
Ro 10: 8 concerning faith that we **p**:
1Co 11: 26 cup, you **p** the Lord's death until

PROCLAIMED (PROCLAIM)
Ro 15: 19 I have fully **p** the gospel of Christ.
Col 1: 23 has been **p** to every creature under

PRODUCE (PRODUCES)
Mt 3: 8 **P** fruit in keeping with repentance.
 3: 10 does not **p** good fruit will be cut

PRODUCES (PRODUCE)
Pr 30: 33 so stirring up anger **p** strife."
Ro 5: 3 that suffering **p** perseverance;
Heb 12: 11 it **p** a harvest of righteousness

PROFANE
Lev 22: 32 Do not **p** my holy name, for I must

PROFESS
1Ti 2: 10 for women who **p** to worship God.
Heb 4: 14 let us hold firmly to the faith we **p**.
 10: 23 unswervingly to the hope we **p**,

PROMISE (PROMISED PROMISES)
1Ki 8: 20 LORD has kept the **p** he made:
Ac 2: 39 The **p** is for you and your children
Gal 3: 14 faith we might receive the **p**
1Ti 4: 8 holding **p** for both the present life
2Pe 3: 9 Lord is not slow in keeping his **p**,

PROMISED (PROMISE)
Ex 3: 17 I have **p** to bring you up out of
Dt 26: 18 his treasured possession as he **p**,

Ps 119: 57 I have **p** to obey your words.
Ro 4: 21 had power to do what he had **p**.
Heb 10: 23 we profess, for he who **p** is faithful.
2Pe 3: 4 say, "Where is this 'coming' he **p**?

PROMISES (PROMISE)
Jos 21: 45 of all the LORD's good **p** to Israel
Ro 9: 4 law, the temple worship and the **p**.
2Pe 1: 4 us his very great and precious **p**,

PROMPTED
1Th 1: 3 by faith, your labor **p** by love,
2Th 1: 11 and your every deed **p** by faith.

PROPHECIES (PROPHESY)
1Co 13: 8 But where there are **p**, they will
1Th 5: 20 Do not treat **p** with contempt

PROPHECY (PROPHESY)
1Co 14: 1 gifts of the Spirit, especially **p**.
2Pe 1: 20 that no **p** of Scripture came

PROPHESY (PROPHECIES PROPHECY PROPHESYING PROPHET PROPHETS)
Joel 2: 28 Your sons and daughters will **p**,
Mt 7: 22 did we not **p** in your name
1Co 14: 39 be eager to **p**, and do not forbid

PROPHESYING (PROPHESY)
Ro 12: 6 If your gift is **p**, then prophesy

PROPHET (PROPHESY)
Dt 18: 18 for them a **p** like you from among
Am 7: 14 neither a **p** nor the son of a **p**,
Mt 10: 41 Whoever welcomes a **p** as a **p** will
Lk 4: 24 "no **p** is accepted in his hometown.

PROPHETS (PROPHESY)
Ps 105: 15 do my **p** no harm."
Mt 5: 17 come to abolish the Law or the **P**;
 7: 12 for this sums up the Law and the **P**.
 24: 24 messiahs and false **p** will appear
Lk 24: 25 believe all that the **p** have spoken!
Ac 10: 43 All the **p** testify about him
1Co 12: 28 apostles, second **p**, third teachers,
 14: 32 The spirits of **p** are subject
Eph 2: 20 foundation of the apostles and **p**,
Heb 1: 1 ancestors through the **p** at many
1Pe 1: 10 the **p**, who spoke of the grace

PROSPER (PROSPERITY PROSPERS)
Pr 28: 25 who trust in the LORD will **p**.

PROSPERITY (PROSPER)
Ps 73: 3 when I saw the **p** of the wicked.

PROSPERS (PROSPER)
Ps 1: 3 whatever they do **p**.

PROSTITUTE (PROSTITUTES)
1Co 6: 15 of Christ and unite them with a **p**?

PROSTITUTES (PROSTITUTE)
Mt 21: 31 **p** are entering the kingdom of God
Lk 15: 30 your property with **p** comes home,

PROSTRATE
Dt 9: 18 again I fell **p** before the LORD

PROTECT (PROTECTS)
Ps 32: 7 you will **p** me from trouble
Pr 2: 11 Discretion will **p** you,
Jn 17: 11 **p** them by the power of your name,

PROTECTS (PROTECT)
1Co 13: 7 It always **p**, always trusts,

PROUD (PRIDE)
Pr 16: 5 The LORD detests all the **p**
Ro 12: 16 Do not be **p**, but be willing
1Co 13: 4 envy, it does not boast, it is not **p**.

PROVE
1Co 4: 2 been given a trust must **p** faithful.

PROVIDE (PROVIDED PROVIDES)
Ge 22: 8 "God himself will **p** the lamb
Isa 43: 20 because I **p** water in the wilderness
1Ti 5: 8 Anyone who does not **p** for their

PROVIDED (PROVIDE)
Jnh 1: 17 Now the LORD **p** a huge fish
     4: 6 the LORD God **p** a leafy plant
     4: 7 dawn the next day God **p** a worm,
     4: 8 rose, God **p** a scorching east wind,

PROVIDES (PROVIDE)
1Ti 6: 17 who richly **p** us with everything
1Pe 4: 11 do so with the strength God **p**,

PROVOKED
Ecc 7: 9 Do not be quickly **p** in your spirit,

PRUDENT
Pr 14: 15 the **p** give thought to their steps.
    19: 14 but a **p** wife is from the LORD.
Am   5: 13 Therefore the **p** keep quiet in such

PRUNING
Isa 2: 4 and their spears into **p** hooks.
Joel 3: 10 and your **p** hooks into spears.

PSALMS
Eph 5: 19 speaking to one another with **p**,
Col 3: 16 with all wisdom through **p**,

PUBLICLY
Ac 20: 20 have taught you **p** and from house

PUFFS
1Co 8: 1 knowledge **p** up while love builds

PUNISH (PUNISHED)
Ex 32: 34 to **p**, I will **p** them for their sin."
Pr 23: 13 if you **p** them with the rod,
Isa 13: 11 I will **p** the world for its evil,
1Pe 2: 14 by him to **p** those who do wrong

PUNISHED (PUNISH)
La   3: 39 should the living complain when **p**
2Th 1: 9 They will be **p** with everlasting
Heb 10: 29 to be **p** who has trampled the Son

PURE (PURIFIES PURIFY PURITY)
2Sa 22: 27 to the **p** you show yourself **p**,
Ps 24: 4 who has clean hands and a
               p heart,
    51: 10 Create in me a **p** heart, O God,
Pr 20: 9 can say, "I have kept my heart **p**;
Isa 52: 11 Come out from it and be **p**,
Hab 1: 13 Your eyes are too **p** to look on evil;
Mt   5: 8 Blessed are the **p** in heart, for they
2Co 11: 2 I might present you as a **p** virgin
Php 4: 8 whatever is **p**, whatever is lovely,
1Ti 5: 22 the sins of others. Keep yourself **p**.
Titus 1: 15 To the **p**, all things are **p**,
      2: 5 to be self-controlled and **p**, to be
Heb 13: 4 all, and the marriage bed kept **p**,
1Jn 3: 3 purify themselves, just as he is **p**.

PURGE
Pr 20: 30 and beatings **p** the inmost being.

PURIFIES (PURE)
1Jn 1: 7 of Jesus, his Son, **p** us from all sin.

PURIFY (PURE)
Titus 2: 14 to **p** for himself a people that are
1Jn 1: 9 and **p** us from all unrighteousness.
     3: 3 this hope in him **p** themselves,

PURITY (PURE)
Ps 119: 9 person stay on the path of **p**?
2Co 6: 6 in **p**, understanding,
1Ti 4: 12 conduct, in love, in faith and in **p**.

PURPOSE
Pr 19: 21 it is the LORD's **p** that prevails.
Isa 55: 11 achieve the **p** for which I sent it.
Ro   8: 28 been called according to his **p**.

PURSES
Lk 12: 33 Provide **p** for yourselves that will

PURSUE
Ps 34: 14 and do good; seek peace and **p** it.
2Ti 2: 22 of youth and **p** righteousness, faith,
1Pe 3: 11 they must seek peace and **p** it.

QUALITIES (QUALITY)
2Pe 1: 8 if you possess these **q** in increasing

QUALITY (QUALITIES)
1Co 3: 13 and the fire will test the **q** of each

QUARREL (QUARRELSOME)
Pr 15: 18 the one who is patient calms a **q**.
    17: 14 Starting a **q** is like breaching a dam
    17: 19 Whoever loves a **q** loves sin;

QUARRELSOME (QUARREL)
Pr 19: 13 **q** wife is like the constant dripping
1Ti 3: 3 gentle, not **q**, not a lover of money.
2Ti 2: 24 the Lord's servant must not be **q**

QUENCH
1Th 5: 19 Do not **q** the Spirit.

QUICK-TEMPERED
Titus 1: 7 not **q**, not given to drunkenness,

QUIET (QUIETNESS)
Ps 23: 2 he leads me beside **q** waters,
Lk 19: 40 "if they keep **q**, the stones will cry
1Ti 2: 2 peaceful and **q** lives in all godliness
1Pe 3: 4 beauty of a gentle and **q** spirit,

QUIETNESS (QUIET)
Isa 30: 15 in **q** and trust is your strength,
    32: 17 its effect will be **q** and confidence
1Ti 2: 11 woman should learn in **q** and full

QUIVER
Ps 127: 5 Blessed is the man whose **q** is full

RACE
Ecc 9: 11 The **r** is not to the swift or
1Co 9: 24 that in a **r** all the runners run,
2Ti 4: 7 I have finished the **r**, I have kept
Heb 12: 1 with perseverance the **r** marked

RACHEL
Daughter of Laban (Ge 29:16); wife of Jacob (Ge 29:28); bore two sons (Ge 30:22–24; 35:16–24; 46:19).

RADIANCE (RADIANT)
Heb 1: 3 The Son is the **r** of God's glory

RADIANT (RADIANCE)
Ex 34: 29 that his face was **r** because he had
Ps 34: 5 Those who look to him are **r**;
SS   5: 10 My beloved is **r** and ruddy,
Isa 60: 5 Then you will look and be **r**,
Eph 5: 27 her to himself as a **r** church,

RAIN (RAINBOW)
Mt   5: 45   and sends **r** on the righteous

RAINBOW (RAIN)
Ge   9: 13   I have set my **r** in the clouds, and it

RAISED (RISE)
Ro   4: 25   was **r** to life for our justification.
    10: 9   your heart that God **r** him
1Co 15: 4   he was **r** on the third day according

RAN (RUN)
Jnh   1: 3   But Jonah **r** away from the LORD

RANSOM
Mt 20: 28   to give his life as a **r** for many."
Heb 9: 15   he has died as a **r** to set them free

RAVENS
1Ki 17: 6   The **r** brought him bread and meat
Lk 12: 24   Consider the **r**: They do not sow

READ (READS)
Jos   8: 34   Joshua **r** all the words of the law—
Ne   8: 8   understood what was being **r**.
2Co 3: 2   hearts, known and **r** by everyone.

READS (READ)
Rev   1: 3   is the one who **r** aloud the words

REAL (REALITY)
Jn   6: 55   For my flesh is **r** food and my blood
             is **r** drink.

REALITY (REAL)
Col   2: 17   the **r**, however, is found in Christ.

REAP (REAPS)
Job   4: 8   evil and those who sow trouble **r** it.
2Co 9: 6   generously will also **r** generously.

REAPS (REAP)
Gal   6: 7   A man **r** what he sows.

REASON
1Pe   3: 15   asks you to give the **r** for the hope

REBEKAH
    Sister of Laban, secured as bride for Isaac (Ge 24). Mother of Esau and Jacob (Ge 25:19–26). Taken by Abimelek as sister of Isaac; returned (Ge 26:1–11). Encouraged Jacob to trick Isaac out of blessing (Ge 27:1–17).

REBEL
Mt 10: 21   children will **r** against their parents

REBUKE (REBUKING)
Pr   9: 8   **r** the wise and they will love you.
   27: 5   Better is open **r** than hidden love.
Lk 17: 3   or sister sins against you, **r** them;
2Ti 4: 2   correct, **r** and encourage—
Rev 3: 19   Those whom I love I **r**

REBUKING (REBUKE)
2Ti   3: 16   and is useful for teaching, **r**,

RECEIVE (RECEIVED RECEIVES)
Ac   1: 8   you will **r** power when the Holy
  20: 35   more blessed to give than to **r**.' "
2Co 6: 17   no unclean thing, and I will **r** you."
Rev 4: 11   to **r** glory and honor and power,

RECEIVED (RECEIVE)
Mt   6: 2   they have **r** their reward in full.
  10: 8   Freely you have **r**; freely give.
1Co 11: 23   For I **r** from the Lord what I
Col 2: 6   just as you **r** Christ Jesus as Lord,
1Pe 4: 10   should use whatever gift you have **r**

RECEIVES (RECEIVE)
Mt   7: 8   For everyone who asks **r**;
Ac 10: 43   who believes in him **r** forgiveness

RECKONING
Isa 10: 3   What will you do on the day of **r**,

RECOGNIZE (RECOGNIZED)
Mt   7: 16   By their fruit you will **r** them.

RECOGNIZED (RECOGNIZE)
Mt 12: 33   be bad, for a tree is **r** by its fruit.
Ro 7: 13   in order that sin might be **r** as sin,

RECOMPENSE
Isa 40: 10   him, and his **r** accompanies him.

RECONCILE (RECONCILED RECONCILIATION)
Eph   2: 16   and in one body to **r** both of them

RECONCILED (RECONCILE)
Mt   5: 24   First go and be **r** to them;
Ro 5: 10   were **r** to him through the death
2Co 5: 18   who **r** us to himself through Christ

RECONCILIATION (RECONCILE)
Ro   5: 11   whom we have now received **r**.
  11: 15   For if their rejection brought **r**
2Co 5: 18   and gave us the ministry of **r**:
  5: 19   committed to us the message of **r**.

RECORD
Ps 130: 3   you, LORD, kept a **r** of sins, Lord,

RED
Isa   1: 18   though they are **r** as crimson,

REDEEM (REDEEMED REDEEMER REDEMPTION)
2Sa   7: 23   out to **r** as a people for himself,
Ps 49: 7   No one can **r** the life of another
Gal 4: 5   to **r** those under the law, that we

REDEEMED (REDEEM)
Gal   3: 13   Christ **r** us from the curse of
           the law
1Pe 1: 18   you were **r** from the empty way

REDEEMER (REDEEM)
Job 19: 25   I know that my **r** lives,

REDEMPTION (REDEEM)
Ps 130: 7   love and with him is full **r**.
Lk 21: 28   because your **r** is drawing near."
Ro 8: 23   to sonship, the **r** of our bodies.
Eph 1: 7   we have **r** through his blood,
Col 1: 14   in whom we have **r**, the forgiveness
Heb 9: 12   blood, thus obtaining eternal **r**.

REFUGE
Nu 35: 11   some towns to be your cities of **r**,
Dt 33: 27   The eternal God is your **r**,
Ru 2: 12   wings you have come to take **r**."
Ps 46: 1   God is our **r** and strength,
  91: 2   "He is my **r** and my fortress,

REHOBOAM
    Son of Solomon (1Ki 11:43; 1Ch 3:10). Harsh treatment of subjects caused divided kingdom (1Ki 12:1–24; 14:21–31; 2Ch 10–12).

REIGN (REIGNS)
Ro   6: 12   not let sin **r** in your mortal body
1Co 15: 25   he must **r** until he has put all his
2Ti 2: 12   if we endure, we will also **r** with
Rev 20: 6   **r** with him for a thousand years.

REIGNS (REIGN)
Ex 15: 18   "The LORD **r** for ever and ever."

REJECTED (REJECTS)

Ps 118:	22	stone the builders r has become
Isa 53:	3	was despised and r by mankind,
1Ti 4:	4	nothing is to be r if it is received
1Pe 2:	4	r by humans but chosen by God
2:	7	stone the builders r has become

REJECTS (REJECTED)

Lk 10:	16	whoever r me r him who sent me."
Jn 3:	36	whoever r the Son will not see life,

REJOICE (JOY)

Ps 66:	6	come, let us r in him.
118:	24	let us r today and be glad.
Pr 5:	18	you r in the wife of your youth.
Lk 10:	20	but r that your names are written
15:	6	together and says, 'R with me;
Ro 12:	15	R with those who r;
Php 4:	4	R in the Lord always. I will say it again: R!

REJOICES (JOY)

Isa 61:	10	my soul r in my God.
Lk 1:	47	and my spirit r in God my Savior,
1Co 12:	26	is honored, every part r with it.
13:	6	delight in evil but r with the truth.

REJOICING (JOY)

Ps 30:	5	night, but r comes in the morning.
Lk 15:	7	the same way there will be more r
Ac 5:	41	r because they had been counted

RELIABLE

2Ti 2:	2	entrust to r people who will also be

RELIGION

1Ti 5:	4	of all to put their r into practice
Jas 1:	27	R that God our Father accepts as

REMAIN (REMAINS)

Nu 33:	55	you allow to r will become barbs
Jn 15:	7	If you r in me and my words r
Ro 13:	8	Let no debt r outstanding,
1Co 13:	13	And now these three r:

REMAINS (REMAIN)

Ps 146:	6	he r faithful forever.
2Ti 2:	13	if we are faithless, he r faithful,
Heb 7:	3	Son of God, he r a priest forever.

REMEMBER (REMEMBERS REMEMBRANCE)

Ex 20:	8	"R the Sabbath day by keeping it
1Ch 16:	12	R the wonders he has done,
Ecc 12:	1	R your Creator in the days of your
Jer 31:	34	and will r their sins no more."
Gal 2:	10	we should continue to r the poor,
Php 1:	3	I thank my God every time I r you.
Heb 8:	12	and will r their sins no more."

REMEMBERS (REMEMBER)

Ps 103:	14	are formed, he r that we are dust.
111:	5	he r his covenant forever.
Isa 43:	25	own sake, and r your sins no more.

REMEMBRANCE (REMEMBER)

1Co 11:	24	is for you; do this in r of me."

REMIND

Jn 14:	26	will r you of everything I have said

REMOVED

Ps 30:	11	you r my sackcloth and clothed me
103:	12	so far has he r our transgressions
Jn 20:	1	that the stone had been r

RENEW (RENEWED RENEWING)

Ps 51:	10	and r a steadfast spirit within me.
Isa 40:	31	in the LORD will r their strength.

RENEWED (RENEW)

Ps 103:	5	that your youth is r like the eagle's.
2Co 4:	16	yet inwardly we are being r day

RENEWING (RENEW)

Ro 12:	2	transformed by the r of your mind.

RENOUNCE (RENOUNCES)

Da 4:	27	R your sins by doing what is right,

RENOUNCES (RENOUNCE)

Pr 28:	13	confesses and r them finds mercy.

RENOWN

Isa 63:	12	to gain for himself everlasting r,
Jer 32:	20	have gained the r that is still yours.

REPAID (PAY)

Lk 14:	14	you will be r at the resurrection
Col 3:	25	Anyone who does wrong will be r

REPAY (PAY)

Dt 32:	35	It is mine to avenge; I will r.
Ru 2:	12	May the LORD r you for what you
Ro 12:	19	I will r," says the Lord.
1Pe 3:	9	the contrary, r evil with blessing,

REPENT (REPENTANCE REPENTS)

Job 42:	6	I despise myself and r in dust
Jer 15:	19	"If you r, I will restore you that you
Mt 4:	17	time on Jesus began to preach, "R,
Lk 13:	3	But unless you r, you too will all
17:	3	and if they r, forgive them.
Ac 2:	38	Peter replied, "R and be baptized,
17:	30	all people everywhere to r.

REPENTANCE (REPENT)

Lk 3:	8	Produce fruit in keeping with r.
5:	32	call the righteous, but sinners to r."
Ac 26:	20	demonstrate their r by their deeds.
2Co 7:	10	Godly sorrow brings r that leads

REPENTS (REPENT)

Lk 15:	10	of God over one sinner who r."

REPROACH

1Ti 3:	2	Now the overseer is to be above r,

REPUTATION

1Ti 3:	7	also have a good r with outsiders,

REQUESTS

Ps 20:	5	May the LORD grant all your r.
Php 4:	6	present your r to God.

REQUIRE

Mic 6:	8	what does the LORD r of you?

RESCUE (RESCUES)

Da 6:	20	been able to r you from the lions?"
2Pe 2:	9	the Lord knows how to r the godly

RESCUES (RESCUE)

1Th 1:	10	who r us from the coming wrath.

RESIST

Jas 4:	7	R the devil, and he will flee
1Pe 5:	9	R him, standing firm in the faith,

RESOLVED

Da 1:	8	Daniel r not to defile himself
1Co 2:	2	For I r to know nothing while I

RESPECT (RESPECTABLE)

Lev 19:	3	of you must r your mother
19:	32	show r for the elderly and revere
Mal 1:	6	a master, where is the r due me?"
1Th 4:	12	that your daily life may win the r

1Ti 3: 4 do so in a manner worthy of full **r**.
1Pe 2: 17 Show proper **r** to everyone,
     3: 7 them with **r** as the weaker partner

RESPECTABLE (RESPECT)
1Ti 3: 2 self-controlled, **r**, hospitable,

REST
Ex 31: 15 seventh day is a day of sabbath **r**,
Ps 91: 1 the Most High will **r** in the shadow
Jer 6: 16 and you will find **r** for your souls.
Mt 11: 28 burdened, and I will give you **r**.

RESTITUTION
Ex 22: 3 who steals must certainly make **r**,
Lev 6: 5 must make **r** in full, add a fifth

RESTORE
Ps 51: 12 **R** to me the joy of your salvation
Gal 6: 1 by the Spirit should **r** that person

RESURRECTION
Mt 22: 30 the **r** people will neither marry nor
Lk 14: 14 be repaid at the **r** of the righteous."
Jn 11: 25 said to her, "I am the **r** and the life.
Ro 1: 4 in power by his **r** from the dead:
1Co 15: 12 say that there is no **r** of the dead?
Php 3: 10 yes, to know the power of his **r**
Rev 20: 5 This is the first **r**.

RETRIBUTION
Jer 51: 56 For the LORD is a God of **r**;

RETURN
2Ch 30: 9 If you **r** to the LORD, then your
Ne 1: 9 but if you **r** to me and obey my
Isa 55: 11 It will not **r** to me empty, but will
Hos 6: 1 "Come, let us **r** to the LORD.
Joel 2: 12 "**r** to me with all your heart,

REVEALED (REVELATION)
Dt 29: 29 but the things **r** belong to us
Isa 40: 5 the glory of the LORD will be **r**,
Mt 11: 25 and **r** them to little children.
Ro 1: 17 the righteousness of God is **r**—
     8: 18 with the glory that will be **r** in us.

REVELATION (REVEALED)
Gal 1: 12 I received it by **r** from Jesus Christ.
Rev 1: 1 The **r** from Jesus Christ,

REVENGE (VENGEANCE)
Lev 19: 18 " 'Do not seek **r** or bear a grudge
Ro 12: 19 Do not take **r**, my dear friends,

REVERE (REVERENCE)
Ps 33: 8 all the people of the world **r** him.

REVERENCE (REVERE)
Lev 19: 30 and have **r** for my sanctuary.
Ps 5: 7 in **r** I bow down toward your holy
Col 3: 22 of heart and **r** for the Lord.
1Pe 3: 2 see the purity and **r** of your lives.

REVIVE
Ps 85: 6 Will you not **r** us again, that your
Isa 57: 15 to **r** the spirit of the lowly and to **r**

REWARD (REWARDED)
Ps 19: 11 in keeping them there is great **r**.
    127: 3 the LORD, offspring of a **r** from him.
Pr 19: 17 he will **r** them for what they have
    25: 22 head, and the LORD will **r** you.
Jer 17: 10 to **r** each person according to their
Mt 5: 12 because great is your **r** in heaven,
     6: 5 they have received their **r** in full.
    16: 27 he will **r** each person according
1Co 3: 14 the builder will receive a **r**.
Rev 22: 12 My **r** is with me, and I will give

REWARDED (REWARD)
Ru 2: 12 May you be richly **r** by the LORD,
Ps 18: 24 The LORD has **r** me according
Pr 14: 14 and the good **r** for theirs.
1Co 3: 8 and they will each be **r** according

RICH (RICHES)
Pr 23: 4 Do not wear yourself out to get **r**;
Jer 9: 23 or the **r** boast of their riches,
Mt 19: 23 for someone who is **r** to enter
2Co 6: 10 poor, yet making many **r**;
     8: 9 his poverty might become **r**.
1Ti 6: 17 Command those who are **r** in this

RICHES (RICH)
Ps 119: 14 statutes as one rejoices in great **r**.
Pr 30: 8 give me neither poverty nor **r**,
Isa 10: 3 Where will you leave your **r**?
Ro 9: 23 to make the **r** of his glory known
    11: 33 the depth of the **r** of the wisdom
Eph 2: 7 he might show the incomparable **r**
     3: 8 to the Gentiles the boundless **r**
Col 1: 27 among the Gentiles the glorious **r**

RID
Ge 21: 10 "Get **r** of that slave woman and her
1Co 5: 7 Get **r** of the old yeast, so that you
Gal 4: 30 "Get **r** of the slave woman and her

RIGHT (RIGHTS)
Ge 18: 25 not the Judge of all the earth do **r**?"
Ex 15: 26 God and do what is **r** in his eyes,
Dt 5: 32 do not turn aside to the **r**
Ps 6: 8 With him at my **r** hand, I will not
    19: 8 The precepts of the LORD are **r**,
    63: 8 your **r** hand upholds me.
    110: 1 "Sit at my **r** hand until I make your
Pr 4: 27 Do not turn to the **r** or the left;
    14: 12 There is a way that appears to be **r**,
Isa 1: 17 Learn to do **r**; seek justice.
Jer 23: 5 do what is just and **r** in the land.
Hos 14: 9 The ways of the LORD are **r**;
Mt 6: 3 know what your **r** hand is doing,
Jn 1: 12 he gave the **r** to become children
Ro 9: 21 Does not the potter have the **r**
    12: 17 careful to do what is **r** in the eyes
Eph 1: 20 and seated him at his **r** hand
Php 4: 8 whatever is **r**, whatever is pure,

RIGHTEOUS (RIGHTEOUSNESS)
Ps 34: 15 eyes of the LORD are on the **r**,
    37: 25 yet I have never seen the **r** forsaken
    119:137 You are **r**, LORD, and your laws
    143: 2 no one living is **r** before you.
Pr 3: 33 but he blesses the home of the **r**.
    11: 30 The fruit of the **r** is a tree of life,
    18: 10 the **r** run to it and are safe.
Isa 64: 6 all our **r** acts are like filthy rags;
Hab 2: 4 but the **r** person will live by his
Mt 5: 45 and sends rain on the **r**
     9: 13 For I have not come to call the **r**,
    13: 49 and separate the wicked from the **r**
    25: 46 but the **r** to eternal life."
Ro 1: 17 "The **r** will live by faith."
     3: 10 "There is no one **r**, not even one;
1Ti 1: 9 that the law is made not for the **r**
Jas 2: 24 is considered **r** by what they do
1Pe 3: 18 for sins, the **r** for the unrighteous,
1Jn 3: 7 is right is **r**, just as he is **r**.
Rev 19: 8 (Fine linen stands for the **r** acts

RIGHTEOUSNESS (RIGHTEOUS)
Ge 15: 6 and he credited it to him as **r**.
1Sa 26: 23 rewards everyone for their **r**
Ps 9: 8 He rules the world in **r** and judges
    45: 7 You love **r** and hate wickedness;

Ps 85: 10 **r** and peace kiss each other.
89: 14 **R** and justice are the foundation
111: 3 deeds, and his **r** endures forever.
Pr 14: 34 **R** exalts a nation, but sin
21: 21 Whoever pursues **r** and love finds
Isa 59: 17 He put on **r** as his breastplate,
Eze 18: 20 The **r** of the righteous will be
Da 9: 24 to bring in everlasting **r**, to seal
12: 3 and those who lead many to **r**,
Mal 4: 2 the sun of **r** will rise with healing
Mt 5: 6 those who hunger and thirst for **r**,
5: 20 you that unless your **r** surpasses
6: 1 practice your **r** in front of others
6: 33 seek first his kingdom and his **r**,
Ro 3: 25 He did this to demonstrate his **r**,
4: 3 and it was credited to him as **r**.”
4: 9 faith was credited to him as **r**.”
6: 13 to him as an instrument of **r**.
2Co 5: 21 we might become the **r** of God.
Gal 2: 21 **r** could be gained through the law,
3: 6 and it was credited to him as **r**.”
Eph 6: 14 with the breastplate of **r** in place,
Php 3: 9 not having a **r** of my own
2Ti 3: 16 correcting and training in **r**,
4: 8 is in store for me the crown of **r**,
Heb 11: 7 and became heir of the **r** that is
2Pe 2: 21 not to have known the way of **r**,

RIGHTS (RIGHT)
La 3: 35 deny people their **r** before the Most

RISE (RAISED)
Isa 26: 19 their bodies will **r**—let those who
Mt 27: 63 ‘After three days I will **r** again.’
Jn 5: 29 who have done what is good will **r**
1Th 4: 16 and the dead in Christ will **r** first.

ROAD
Mt 7: 13 gate and broad is the **r** that leads

ROBBERS
Jer 7: 11 Name, become a den of **r** to you?
Lk 19: 46 you have made it ‘a den of **r**.’ ”
Jn 10: 8 come before me are thieves and **r**,

ROCK
Ps 18: 2 The LORD is my **r**, my fortress
40: 2 he set my feet on a **r** and gave me
Mt 7: 24 man who built his house on the **r**.
16: 18 on this **r** I will build my church,
Ro 9: 33 and a **r** that makes them fall,
1Co 10: 4 them, and that **r** was Christ.

ROD
Ps 23: 4 your **r** and your staff, they comfort
Pr 13: 24 Whoever spares the **r** hates their
23: 13 if you punish them with the **r**,

ROOM (ROOMS)
Mt 6: 6 go into your **r**, close the door
Lk 2: 7 there was no guest **r** available
Jn 21: 25 the whole world would not have **r**

ROOMS (ROOM)
Jn 14: 2 My Father's house has many **r**;

ROOT
Isa 53: 2 and like a **r** out of dry ground.
1Ti 6: 10 the love of money is a **r** of all kinds

ROYAL
Jas 2: 8 If you really keep the **r** law found
1Pe 2: 9 are a chosen people, a **r** priesthood,

RUIN (RUINS)
Pr 18: 24 unreliable friends soon comes to **r**,
19: 3 person's own folly leads to their **r**,
1Ti 6: 9 desires that plunge people into **r**

RUINS (RUIN)
2Ti 2: 14 value, and only **r** those who listen.

RULE (RULER RULERS RULES)
1Sa 12: 12 ‘No, we want a king to **r** over us’—
Ps 119:133 to your word; let no sin **r** over me.
Zec 9: 10 His **r** will extend from sea to sea
Col 3: 15 peace of Christ **r** in your hearts,
Rev 2: 27 that one ‘will **r** them with an iron

RULER (RULE)
Eph 2: 2 of the **r** of the kingdom of the air,
1Ti 6: 15 the blessed and only **R**, the King

RULERS (RULE)
Ps 2: 2 and the **r** band together against
8: 6 You made them **r** over the works
Col 1: 16 or powers or **r** or authorities;

RULES (RULE)
Ps 103: 19 heaven, and his kingdom **r** over all.
Lk 22: 26 and the one who **r** like the one who
2Ti 2: 5 by competing according to the **r**.

RUMORS
Mt 24: 6 You will hear of wars and **r** of wars,

RUN (RAN)
Isa 40: 31 they will **r** and not grow weary,
1Co 9: 24 **R** in such a way as to get the prize.
Heb 12: 1 let us **r** with perseverance the race

RUTH
Moabitess; widow who went to Bethlehem with mother-in-law Naomi (Ru 1). Gleaned in field of Boaz; shown favor (Ru 2). Proposed marriage to Boaz (Ru 3). Married (Ru 4:1–12); bore Obed, ancestor of David (Ru 4:13–22), Jesus (Mt 1:5).

SABBATH
Ex 20: 8 “Remember the **S** day by keeping it
Dt 5: 12 “Observe the **S** day by keeping it
Col 2: 16 New Moon celebration or a **S** day.

SACKCLOTH
Mt 11: 21 would have repented long ago in **s**

SACRED
Mt 7: 6 “Do not give dogs what is **s**;
1Co 3: 17 for God's temple is **s**, and you

SACRIFICE (SACRIFICED)
Ge 22: 2 **S** him there as a burnt offering
Ex 12: 27 ‘It is the Passover **s** to the LORD,
1Sa 15: 22 To obey is better than **s**,
Ps 51: 17 My **s**, O God, is a broken spirit;
Hos 6: 6 not **s**, and acknowledgment of God
Mt 9: 13 ‘I desire mercy, not **s**.’
Ro 12: 1 to offer your bodies as a living **s**,
Heb 9: 26 away with sin by the **s** of himself.
13: 15 offer to God a **s** of praise—
1Jn 2: 2 He is the atoning **s** for our sins,

SACRIFICED (SACRIFICE)
1Co 5: 7 our Passover lamb, has been **s**.
8: 1 Now about food **s** to idols:
Heb 9: 28 so Christ was **s** once to take away

SADDUCEES
Mk 12: 18 Then the **S**, who say there is no

SAFE (SAVE)
Ps 37: 3 in the land and enjoy **s** pasture.
Pr 18: 10 the righteous run to it and are **s**.

SAFETY (SAVE)
Ps 4: 8 alone, LORD, make me dwell in **s**.
1Th 5: 3 “Peace and **s**,” destruction will

SAINTS See FAITHFUL, [GOD'S] PEOPLE

SAKE

Ps	44:	22	your **s** we face death all day long;
Php	3:	7	consider loss for the **s** of Christ.
Heb	11:	26	disgrace for the **s** of Christ as

SALT

| Ge | 19: | 26 | back, and she became a pillar of **s.** |
| Mt | 5: | 13 | "You are the **s** of the earth. |

SALVATION (SAVE)

Ex	15:	2	he has become my **s.**
1Ch	16:	23	proclaim his **s** day after day.
Ps	27:	1	The LORD is my light and my **s**—
	51:	12	Restore to me the joy of your **s**
	62:	2	Truly he is my rock and my **s**;
	85:	9	Surely his **s** is near those who fear
	96:	2	proclaim his **s** day after day.
Isa	25:	9	let us rejoice and be glad in his **s**."
	45:	17	the LORD with an everlasting **s**;
	51:	6	But my **s** will last forever,
	59:	17	and the helmet of **s** on his head;
	61:	10	has clothed me with garments of **s**
Jnh	2:	9	'**S** comes from the LORD.' "
Lk	2:	30	For my eyes have seen your **s**,
Jn	4:	22	we do know, for **s** is from the Jews.
Ac	4:	12	**S** is found in no one else, for there
	13:	47	that you may bring **s** to the ends
Ro	11:	11	**s** has come to the Gentiles to make
2Co	7:	10	brings repentance that leads to **s**
Eph	6:	17	Take the helmet of **s** and the sword
Php	2:	12	to work out your **s** with fear
1Th	5:	8	and the hope of **s** as a helmet.
2Ti	3:	15	make you wise for **s** through faith
Heb	2:	3	we escape if we ignore so great a **s**?
	6:	9	the things that have to do with **s.**
1Pe	1:	10	Concerning this **s**, the prophets,
	2:	2	by it you may grow up in your **s**,

SAMARITAN

| Lk | 10: | 33 | But a **S**, as he traveled, came where |

SAMSON

Danite judge. Birth promised (Jdg 13). Married to Philistine (Jdg 14). Vengeance on Philistines (Jdg 15). Betrayed by Delilah (Jdg 16:1–22). Death (Jdg 16:23–31). Feats of strength: killed lion (Jdg 14:6), 30 Philistines (Jdg 14:19), 1,000 Philistines with jawbone (Jdg 15:13–17), carried off gates of Gaza (Jdg 16:3), pushed down temple of Dagon (Jdg 16:25–30).

SAMUEL

Ephraimite judge and prophet (Heb 11:32). Birth prayed for (1Sa 1:10–18). Dedicated to temple by Hannah (1Sa 1:21–28). Raised by Eli (1Sa 2:11, 18–26). Called as prophet (1Sa 3). Led Israel to victory over Philistines (1Sa 7). Asked by Israel for a king (1Sa 8). Anointed Saul as king (1Sa 9–10). Farewell speech (1Sa 12). Rebuked Saul for sacrifice (1Sa 13). Announced rejection of Saul (1Sa 15). Anointed David as king (1Sa 16). Protected David from Saul (1Sa 19:18–24). Death (1Sa 25:1). Returned from dead to condemn Saul (1Sa 28).

SANCTIFIED (SANCTIFY)

Ac	20:	32	among all those who are **s.**
Ro	15:	16	to God, **s** by the Holy Spirit.
1Co	6:	11	you were **s**, you were justified
	7:	14	husband has been **s** through his
Heb	10:	29	blood of the covenant that **s** them,

SANCTIFY (SANCTIFIED SANCTIFYING)

| 1Th | 5: | 23 | peace, **s** you through and through. |

SANCTIFYING (SANCTIFY)

| 2Th | 2: | 13 | be saved through the **s** work |

SANCTUARY

| Ex | 25: | 8 | "Then have them make a **s** for me, |

SAND

| Ge | 22: | 17 | sky and as the **s** on the seashore. |
| Mt | 7: | 26 | man who built his house on **s.** |

SANDALS

| Ex | 3: | 5 | "Take off your **s**, for the place |
| Jos | 5: | 15 | "Take off your **s**, for the place |

SANG (SING)

| Job | 38: | 7 | while the morning stars **s** together |
| Rev | 5: | 9 | And they **s** a new song, saying: |

SARAH

Wife of Abraham, originally named Sarai; barren (Ge 11:29–31; 1Pe 3:6). Taken by Pharaoh as Abraham's sister; returned (Ge 12:10–20). Gave Hagar to Abraham; sent her away in pregnancy (Ge 16). Name changed; Isaac promised (Ge 17:15–21; 18:10–15; Heb 11:11). Taken by Abimelek as Abraham's sister; returned (Ge 20). Isaac born; Hagar and Ishmael sent away (Ge 21:1–21; Gal 4:21–31). Death (Ge 23).

SATAN

Job	1:	6	and **S** also came with them.
Zec	3:	2	to **S**, "The LORD rebuke you, **S**!
Mk	4:	15	**S** comes and takes away the word
2Co	11:	14	**S** himself masquerades as an angel
	12:	7	a messenger of **S**, to torment me.
Rev	12:	9	or **S**, who leads the whole world
	20:	2	**S**, and bound him for a thousand
	20:	7	**S** will be released from his prison

SATISFIED (SATISFY)

| Isa | 53: | 11 | he will see the light of life and be **s**; |

SATISFIES (SATISFY)

| Ps | 103: | 5 | **s** your desires with good things |

SATISFY (SATISFIED SATISFIES)

| Isa | 55: | 2 | and your labor on what does not **s**? |

SAUL

1. Benjamite; anointed by Samuel as first king of Israel (1Sa 9–10). Defeated Ammonites (1Sa 11). Rebuked for offering sacrifice (1Sa 13:1–15). Defeated Philistines (1Sa 14). Rejected as king for failing to annihilate Amalekites (1Sa 15). Soothed from evil spirit by David (1Sa 16:14–23). Sent David against Goliath (1Sa 17). Jealousy and attempted murder of David (1Sa 18:1–11). Gave David Michal as wife (1Sa 18:12–30). Second attempt to kill David (1Sa 19). Anger at Jonathan (1Sa 20:26–34). Pursued David: killed priests at Nob (1Sa 22), went to Keilah and Ziph (1Sa 23), life spared by David at En Gedi (1Sa 24) and in his tent (1Sa 26). Rebuked by Samuel's spirit for consulting witch at Endor (1Sa 28). Wounded by Philistines; took his own life (1Sa 31; 1Ch 10).
2. See PAUL

SAVE (SAFE SAFETY SALVATION SAVED SAVIOR)

Isa	63:	1	proclaiming victory, mighty to **s**."
Mt	1:	21	because he will **s** his people
	16:	25	wants to **s** their life will lose it,
Lk	19:	10	came to seek and to **s** the lost."
Jn	3:	17	but to **s** the world through him.
1Ti	1:	15	came into the world to **s** sinners—
Jas	5:	20	of their way will **s** them from death

SAVED (SAVE)

| Ps | 34: | 6 | he **s** him out of all his troubles. |
| Isa | 45: | 22 | "Turn to me and be **s**, all you ends |

Joel	2:	32	the name of the Lord will be **s**;
Mk	13:	13	stands firm to the end will be **s**.
	16:	16	*believes and is baptized will be* **s**,
Jn	10:	9	enters through me will be **s**.
Ac	4:	12	mankind by which we must be **s**."
	16:	30	"Sirs, what must I do to be **s**?"
Ro	9:	27	the sea, only the remnant will be **s**.
	10:	9	him from the dead, you will be **s**.
1Co	3:	15	will suffer loss but yet will be **s**—
	15:	2	By this gospel you are **s**, if you hold
Eph	2:	5	it is by grace you have been **s**.
	2:	8	For it is by grace you have been **s**,
1Ti	2:	4	who wants all people to be **s**

SAVIOR (SAVE)

Ps	89:	26	Father, my God, the Rock my **S**.'
Isa	43:	11	and apart from me there is no **s**.
Hos	13:	4	no God but me, no **S** except me.
Lk	1:	47	and my spirit rejoices in God my **S**,
	2:	11	town of David a **S** has been born
Jn	4:	42	that this man really is the **S**
Eph	5:	23	his body, of which he is the **S**.
1Ti	4:	10	God, who is the **S** of all people,
Titus	2:	10	about God our **S** attractive.
	2:	13	the glory of our great God and **S**,
	3:	4	and love of God our **S** appeared,
1Jn	4:	14	his Son to be the **S** of the world.
Jude	:	25	to the only God our **S** be glory,

SCALES

Lev	19:	36	Use honest **s** and honest weights,
Da	5:	27	You have been weighed on the **s**

SCAPEGOAT (GOAT)

Lev	16:	10	it into the wilderness as a **s**.

SCARLET

Isa	1:	18	"Though your sins are like **s**,

SCATTERED

Jer	31:	10	'He who **s** Israel will gather them
Ac	8:	4	who had been **s** preached the word

SCEPTER

Rev	19:	15	"He will rule them with an iron **s**."

SCHEMES

2Co	2:	11	For we are not unaware of his **s**.
Eph	6:	11	your stand against the devil's **s**.

SCOFFERS

2Pe	3:	3	that in the last days **s** will come,

SCORPION

Rev	9:	5	of the sting of a **s** when it strikes.

SCRIPTURE (SCRIPTURES)

Jn	10:	35	and **S** cannot be set aside—
1Ti	4:	13	yourself to the public reading of **S**,
2Ti	3:	16	All **S** is God-breathed and is useful
2Pe	1:	20	that no prophecy of **S** came

SCRIPTURES (SCRIPTURE)

Lk	24:	27	in all the **S** concerning himself.
Jn	5:	39	You study the **S** diligently because
Ac	17:	11	examined the **S** every day to see

SCROLL

Eze	3:	1	eat what is before you, eat this **s**;

SEA

Ex	14:	16	the Israelites can go through the **s**
Isa	57:	20	the wicked are like the tossing **s**,
Mic	7:	19	iniquities into the depths of the **s**.
Jas	1:	6	who doubts is like a wave of the **s**,
Rev	13:	1	I saw a beast coming out of the **s**.

SEAL (SEALS)

Jn	6:	27	God the Father has placed his **s**
2Co	1:	22	set his **s** of ownership on us,
Eph	1:	13	you were marked in him with a **s**,

SEALS (SEAL)

Rev	5:	2	"Who is worthy to break the **s**
	6:	1	opened the first of the seven **s**.

SEARCH (SEARCHED SEARCHES SEARCHING)

Ps	4:	4	beds, **s** your hearts and be silent.
	139:	23	**S** me, God, and know my heart;
Pr	2:	4	and **s** for it as for hidden treasure,
Jer	17:	10	"I the Lord **s** the heart
Eze	34:	16	I will **s** for the lost and bring back
Lk	15:	8	and **s** carefully until she finds it?

SEARCHED (SEARCH)

Ps	139:	1	You have **s** me, Lord, and you

SEARCHES (SEARCH)

Ro	8:	27	who **s** our hearts knows the mind
1Co	2:	10	The Spirit **s** all things, even the

SEARCHING (SEARCH)

Am	8:	12	east, **s** for the word of the Lord,

SEARED

1Ti	4:	2	whose consciences have been **s** as

SEASON

2Ti	4:	2	be prepared in **s** and out of **s**;

SEAT (SEATED SEATS)

Da	7:	9	and the Ancient of Days took his **s**.
2Co	5:	10	all appear before the judgment **s**

SEATED (SEAT)

Ps	47:	8	God is **s** on his holy throne.
Isa	6:	1	high and exalted, **s** on a throne;
Col	3:	1	Christ is, **s** at the right hand of God.

SEATS (SEAT)

Lk	11:	43	you love the most important **s**

SECRET (SECRETS)

Dt	29:	29	The **s** things belong to the Lord
Jdg	16:	6	"Tell me the **s** of your great
Ps	90:	8	you, our **s** sins in the light of your
Pr	11:	13	but a trustworthy person keeps a **s**.
Mt	6:	4	so that your giving may be in **s**.
2Co	4:	2	we have renounced **s** and shameful
Php	4:	12	have learned the **s** of being content

SECRETS (SECRET)

Ps	44:	21	since he knows the **s** of the heart?
1Co	14:	25	as the **s** of their hearts are laid bare.

SECURE (SECURITY)

Ps	112:	8	Their hearts are **s**, they will have
Heb	6:	19	an anchor for the soul, firm and **s**.

SECURITY (SECURE)

Job	31:	24	or said to pure gold, 'You are my **s**,'

SEED (SEEDS)

Lk	8:	11	The **s** is the word of God.
1Co	3:	6	I planted the **s**, Apollos watered it,
2Co	9:	10	he who supplies **s** to the sower
Gal	3:	29	you are Abraham's **s**, and heirs
1Pe	1:	23	again, not of perishable **s**,

SEEDS (SEED)

Jn	12:	24	But if it dies, it produces many **s**.
Gal	3:	16	Scripture does not say "and to **s**,"

SEEK (SEEKS SELF-SEEKING)

Dt	4:	29	you will find him if you **s** him
1Ch	28:	9	If you **s** him, he will be found

2Ch	7: 14	pray and **s** my face and turn
Ps	119: 10	I **s** you with all my heart; do not let
Isa	55: 6	**S** the LORD while he may be
	65: 1	found by those who did not **s** me.
Mt	6: 33	But **s** first his kingdom and his
Lk	19: 10	For the Son of Man came to **s**
Ro	10: 20	found by those who did not **s** me;
1Co	7: 27	Do not **s** to be released.

SEEKS (SEEK)

Jn 4: 23 the kind of worshipers the Father **s**.

SEER

1Sa 9: 9 of today used to be called a **s**.)

SELF-CONTROL (CONTROL)

1Co	7: 5	tempt you because of your lack of **s**.
Gal	5: 23	gentleness and **s**.
2Pe	1: 6	and to knowledge, **s**; and to **s**,

SELF-CONTROLLED (CONTROL)

1Ti	3: 2	his wife, temperate, **s**, respectable,
Titus	1: 8	what is good, who is **s**, upright,
	2: 2	worthy of respect, **s**, and sound
	2: 5	to be **s** and pure, to be busy
	2: 6	encourage the young men to be **s**.
	2: 12	to live **s**, upright and godly lives

SELF-INDULGENCE

Mt 23: 25 inside they are full of greed and **s**.

SELFISH

Ps	119: 36	statutes and not toward **s** gain.
Pr	18: 1	unfriendly person pursues **s** ends
Gal	5: 20	fits of rage, **s** ambition, dissensions,
Php	1: 17	preach Christ out of **s** ambition,
	2: 3	Do nothing out of **s** ambition
Jas	3: 14	envy and **s** ambition in your hearts,
	3: 16	you have envy and **s** ambition,

SELF-SEEKING (SEEK)

1Co 13: 5 it is not **s**, it is not easily angered,

SEND (SENDING SENT)

Isa	6: 8	And I said, "Here am I. **S** me!"
Mt	9: 38	to **s** out workers into his harvest
Jn	16: 7	but if I go, I will **s** him to you.

SENDING (SEND)

Jn 20: 21 the Father has sent me, I am
s you."

SENSES

Lk	15: 17	"When he came to his **s**, he said,
1Co	15: 34	Come back to your **s** as you ought,
2Ti	2: 26	that they will come to their **s**

SENSUAL

Col 2: 23 value in restraining **s** indulgence.

SENT (SEND)

Isa	55: 11	achieve the purpose for which I **s** it.
Mt	10: 40	me welcomes the one who **s** me.
Jn	4: 34	"is to do the will of him who **s** me
Ro	10: 15	anyone preach unless they are **s**?
1Jn	4: 10	**s** his Son as an atoning sacrifice

SEPARATE (SEPARATED SEPARATES)

Mt	19: 6	has joined together, let no one **s**."
Ro	8: 35	Who shall **s** us from the love
1Co	7: 10	A wife must not **s** from her
2Co	6: 17	"Come out from them and be **s**,

SEPARATED (SEPARATE)

Isa 59: 2 your iniquities have **s** you from

SEPARATES (SEPARATE)

Pr 16: 28 and a gossip **s** close friends.

SERPENT

Ge	3: 1	Now the **s** was more crafty than
Rev	12: 9	that ancient **s** called the devil,

SERVANT (SERVANTS)

1Sa	3: 10	"Speak, for your **s** is listening."
Mt	20: 26	great among you must be your **s**,
	25: 21	'Well done, good and faithful **s**!
Php	2: 7	by taking the very nature of a **s**,
2Ti	2: 24	And the Lord's **s** must not be

SERVANTS (SERVANT)

Lk	17: 10	do, should say, 'We are unworthy **s**;
Jn	15: 15	I no longer call you **s**,

SERVE (SERVICE SERVING)

Dt	10: 12	to **s** the LORD your God with all
Jos	22: 5	and to **s** him with all your heart
	24: 15	household, we will **s** the LORD."
Mt	4: 10	Lord your God, and **s** him only.' "
	6: 24	"No one can **s** two masters.
	6: 24	You cannot **s** both God and money.
	20: 28	but to **s**, and to give his life as
Eph	6: 7	**S** wholeheartedly, as if you were

SERVICE (SERVE)

1Co	12: 5	There are different kinds of **s**,
Eph	4: 12	to equip his people for works of **s**,

SERVING (SERVE)

Ro	12: 11	your spiritual fervor, **s** the Lord.
Eph	6: 7	as if you were **s** the Lord,
Col	3: 24	It is the Lord Christ you are **s**.
2Ti	2: 4	No one **s** as a soldier gets entangled

SEVEN (SEVENTH)

Ge	7: 2	Take with you **s** pairs of every kind
Jos	6: 4	march around the city **s** times,
1Ki	19: 18	Yet I reserve **s** thousand in Israel—
Pr	6: 16	hates, **s** that are detestable to him:
	24: 16	though the righteous fall **s** times,
Isa	4: 1	that day **s** women will take hold
Da	9: 25	comes, there will be **s** 'sevens,'
Mt	18: 21	sins against me? Up to **s** times?"
Lk	11: 26	takes **s** other spirits more wicked
Ro	11: 4	myself **s** thousand who have not
Rev	1: 4	To the **s** churches in the province
	1: 4	from the **s** spirits before his throne,
	6: 1	Lamb opened the first of the **s** seals.
	8: 2	I saw the **s** angels who stand before
	8: 2	and **s** trumpets were given to them.
	10: 4	And when the **s** thunders spoke,
	15: 7	to the **s** angels **s** golden bowls filled

SEVENTH (SEVEN)

Ge	2: 2	so on the **s** day he rested from all
Ex	23: 12	but on the **s** day do not work,

SEX (SEXUAL SEXUALLY)

1Co 6: 9 nor men who have **s** with men

SEXUAL (SEX)

Mt	5: 32	except for **s** immorality, makes her
	19: 9	except for **s** immorality,
1Co	6: 13	is not meant for **s** immorality
	6: 18	Flee from **s** immorality.
	7: 1	a man not to have **s** relations
	10: 8	should not commit **s** immorality,
Eph	5: 3	not be even a hint of **s** immorality,
1Th	4: 3	you should avoid **s** immorality;

SEXUALLY (SEX)

1Co	5: 9	associate with **s** immoral people—
	6: 18	but whoever sins **s**, sins against

SHADOW

Ps	36: 7	take refuge in the **s** of your wings.
Heb	10: 1	The law is only a **s** of the good

SHALLUM
King of Israel (2Ki 15:10–16).

SHAME (ASHAMED)
Ps	22:	5	they trusted and were not put to s.
	34:	5	faces are never covered with s.
Pr	13:	18	discipline comes to poverty and s,
Heb	12:	2	scorning its s, and sat down

SHARE (SHARED)
Ge	21:	10	that woman's son will never s
Lk	3:	11	who has two shirts should s
Gal	4:	30	the slave woman's son will never s
	6:	6	the word should s all good things
Eph	4:	28	they may have something to s
1Ti	6:	18	to be generous and willing to s.
Heb	12:	10	order that we may s in his holiness.
	13:	16	to do good and to s with others,

SHARED (SHARE)
Heb	2:	14	he too s in their humanity so

SHARON
SS	2:	1	I am a rose of S, a lily

SHARPER
Heb	4:	12	S than any double-edged sword,

SHED (SHEDDING)
Ge	9:	6	by humans shall their blood be s;
Col	1:	20	through his blood, s on the cross.

SHEDDING (SHED)
Heb	9:	22	without the s of blood there is no

SHEEP
Ps	100:	3	are his people, the s of his pasture.
	119:	176	I have strayed like a lost s.
Isa	53:	6	We all, like s, have gone astray,
Jer	50:	6	"My people have been lost s;
Eze	34:	11	I myself will search for my s
Mt	9:	36	helpless, like s without a shepherd.
Jn	10:	3	He calls his own s by name
	10:	15	and I lay down my life for the s.
	10:	27	My s listen to my voice;
	21:	17	Jesus said, "Feed my s.
1Pe	2:	25	For "you were like s going astray,"

SHELTER
Ps	61:	4	take refuge in the s of your wings.
	91:	1	in the s of the Most High will rest

SHEM
Son of Noah (Ge 5:32; 6:10). Blessed (Ge 9:26). Descendants (Ge 10:21–31; 11:10–32).

SHEPHERD (SHEPHERDS)
Ps	23:	1	The LORD is my s, I lack nothing.
Isa	40:	11	He tends his flock like a s;
Jer	31:	10	will watch over his flock like a s.'
Eze	34:	12	a s looks after his scattered flock
Zec	11:	17	"Woe to the worthless s,
Mt	9:	36	and helpless, like sheep without a s.
Jn	10:	11	"I am the good s. The good s lays
	10:	16	there shall be one flock and one s.
1Pe	5:	4	And when the Chief S appears,

SHEPHERDS (SHEPHERD)
Jer	23:	1	"Woe to the s who are destroying
Lk	2:	8	there were s living out in the fields
Ac	20:	28	Be s of the church of God,
1Pe	5:	2	Be s of God's flock that is under

SHIELD
Ps	28:	7	LORD is my strength and my s;
Eph	6:	16	take up the s of faith,

SHINE (SHONE)
Ps	4:	6	Let the light of your face s on us.
	80:	1	between the cherubim, s forth
Isa	60:	1	"Arise, s, for your light has come,
Da	12:	3	are wise will s like the brightness
Mt	5:	16	let your light s before others,
	13:	43	the righteous will s like the sun
2Co	4:	6	made his light s in our hearts
Eph	5:	14	the dead, and Christ will s on you."

SHIPWRECK (SHIPWRECKED)
1Ti	1:	19	so have suffered s with regard

SHIPWRECKED (SHIPWRECK)
2Co	11:	25	three times I was s, I spent a night

SHONE (SHINE)
Mt	17:	2	His face s like the sun, and his
Lk	2:	9	glory of the Lord s around them,
Rev	21:	11	It s with the glory of God, and its

SHORT
Isa	59:	1	of the LORD is not too s to save,
Ro	3:	23	and fall s of the glory of God,

SHOULDERS
Isa	9:	6	the government will be on his s.
Lk	15:	5	finds it, he joyfully puts it on his s

SHOWED
1Jn	4:	9	This is how God s his love among

SHREWD
Mt	10:	16	Therefore be as s as snakes and as

SHUN
Job	28:	28	and to s evil is understanding."
Pr	3:	7	fear the LORD and s evil.

SICK
Pr	13:	12	Hope deferred makes the heart s,
Mt	9:	12	who need a doctor, but the s.
	25:	36	I was s and you looked after me,
Jas	5:	14	Is anyone among you s?

SICKLE
Joel	3:	13	Swing the s, for the harvest is ripe.

SIDE
Ps	91:	7	A thousand may fall at your s,
	124:	1	the LORD had not been on our s—
2Ti	4:	17	Lord stood at my s and gave me

SIGHT
Ps	90:	4	years in your s are like a day
	116:	15	in the s of the LORD is the death
2Co	5:	7	For we live by faith, not by s.
1Pe	3:	4	which is of great worth in God's s.

SIGN (SIGNS)
Isa	7:	14	the Lord himself will give you a s:

SIGNS (SIGN)
Mt	24:	24	and perform great s and wonders
Mk	16:	17	these s will accompany those who
Jn	3:	2	could perform the s you are doing
	9:	16	can a sinner perform such s?"
	20:	30	Jesus performed many other s
1Co	1:	22	Jews demand s and Greeks look

SILENT
Pr	17:	28	are thought wise if they keep s,
Isa	53:	7	as a sheep before its shearers is s,
Hab	2:	20	let all the earth be s before him.
1Co	14:	34	Women should remain s

SILVER
Pr	25:	11	of s is a ruling rightly given.

Hag 2: 8 'The **s** is mine and the gold is
1Co 3: 12 on this foundation using gold, **s,**

SIMON
1. See PETER.
2. Apostle, called the Zealot (Mt 10:4; Mk 3:18; Lk 6:15; Ac 1:13).
3. Samaritan sorcerer (Ac 8:9–24).

SIN (SINFUL SINNED SINNER SINNERS SINNING SINS)
Nu   5: 7 and must confess the **s** they have
     32: 23 sure that your **s** will find you out.
Dt   24: 16 each will die for their own **s.**
1Ki   8: 46 there is no one who does not **s**—
2Ch   7: 14 I will forgive their **s** and will heal
Ps   4: 4 Tremble and do not **s**; when you
     32: 2 is the one whose **s** the LORD does
     32: 5 And you forgave the guilt of my **s.**
     51: 2 iniquity and cleanse me from my **s.**
     66: 18 If I had cherished **s** in my heart,
    119: 11 that I might not **s** against you.
    119:133 to your word; let no **s** rule over me.
Isa   6: 7 taken away and your **s** atoned for."
Mic   7: 18 you, who pardons **s** and forgives
Jn   1: 29 who takes away the **s** of the world!
      8: 34 everyone who sins is a slave to **s.**
Ro   5: 12 just as **s** entered the world through
      5: 20 But where **s** increased,
      6: 11 count yourselves dead to **s** but alive
      6: 23 For the wages of **s** is death,
     14: 23 that does not come from faith is **s.**
2Co   5: 21 God made him who had no **s** to be **s**
Gal   2: 17 if someone is caught in a **s,**
Heb   9: 26 to do away with **s** by the sacrifice
     11: 25 to enjoy the fleeting pleasures of **s.**
     12: 1 and the **s** that so easily entangles.
1Pe   2: 22 "He committed no **s,** and no deceit
1Jn   1: 8 If we claim to be without **s,**
      3: 4 in fact, **s** is lawlessness.
      3: 5 away our sins. And in him is no **s.**
      3: 9 is born of God will continue to **s,**
      5: 18 born of God does not continue to **s;**

SINCERE
Ro   12: 9 Love must be **s.** Hate what is evil;
Heb 10: 22 us draw near to God with a **s** heart

SINFUL (SIN)
Ps   51: 5 Surely I was **s** at birth,
Ro   7: 5 the **s** passions aroused by the law
1Pe   2: 11 to abstain from **s** desires,

SINFUL NATURE See FLESH

SING (SANG SINGING SONG SONGS)
Ps   30: 4 **S** the praises of the LORD, you his
     47: 6 **S** praises to God, **s** praises; **s**
              praises
     59: 16 in the morning I will **s** of your love
     89: 1 I will **s** of the LORD's great love
    101: 1 I will **s** of your love and justice;
Eph   5: 19 **S** and make music from your heart

SINGING (SING)
Ps   63: 5 **s** lips my mouth will praise you.
Ac   16: 25 were praying and **s** hymns to God,

SINNED (SIN)
2Sa 12: 13 "I have **s** against the LORD."
Job   1: 5 "Perhaps my children have **s**
Ps   51: 4 have I **s** and done what is evil
Da   9: 5 we have **s** and done wrong.
Mic   7: 9 Because I have **s** against him, I will
Lk   15: 18 I have **s** against heaven and against
Ro   3: 23 for all have **s** and fall short
1Jn   1: 10 If we claim we have not **s,** we make

SINNER (SIN)
Ecc   9: 18 war, but one **s** destroys much good.
Lk   15: 7 heaven over one **s** who repents
     18: 13 said, 'God, have mercy on me, a **s.'**
Jas   5: 20 Whoever turns a **s** from the error
1Pe   4: 18 become of the ungodly and the **s?"**

SINNERS (SIN)
Ps   1: 1 stand in the way that **s** take or sit
Pr   23: 17 Do not let your heart envy **s,**
Mt   9: 13 come to call the righteous, but **s."**
Ro   5: 8 While we were still **s,** Christ died
1Ti   1: 15 came into the world to save **s**—

SINNING (SIN)
Ex   20: 20 be with you to keep you from **s.**
1Co 15: 34 senses as you ought, and stop **s;**
Heb 10: 26 If we deliberately keep on **s** after
1Jn   3: 6 one who lives in him keeps on **s.**
      3: 9 they cannot go on **s,** because they

SINS (SIN)
Ezr   9: 6 because our **s** are higher than our
Ps   19: 13 your servant also from willful **s;**
     32: 1 are forgiven, whose **s** are covered.
    103: 3 who forgives all your **s** and heals
    130: 3 LORD, kept a record of **s,** Lord,
Pr   28: 13 Whoever conceals their **s** does not
Isa   1: 18 "Though your **s** are like scarlet,
     43: 25 and remembers your **s** no more.
     59: 2 your **s** have hidden his face
Eze 18: 4 The one who is the one who will
Mt   1: 21 will save his people from their **s."**
     18: 15 "If your brother or sister **s,**
Lk   11: 4 Forgive us our **s,** for we also forgive
              everyone who **s** against us.
     17: 3 your brother or sister **s** against you,
Ac   22: 16 be baptized and wash your **s** away,
1Co 15: 3 Christ died for our **s** according
Eph   2: 1 dead in your transgressions and **s,**
Col   2: 13 He forgave us all our **s,**
Heb   1: 3 he had provided purification for **s,**
      7: 27 He sacrificed for their **s** once for all
      8: 12 will remember their **s** no more."
     10: 12 for all time one sacrifice for **s,**
Jas   5: 16 Therefore confess your **s** to each
      5: 20 and cover over a multitude of **s.**
1Pe   2: 24 so that we might die to **s** and live
      3: 18 For Christ also suffered once for **s,**
1Jn   1: 9 If we confess our **s,** he is faithful
      1: 9 will forgive us our **s** and purify us
Rev   1: 5 freed us from our **s** by his blood,

SITS
Ps   99: 1 he **s** enthroned between
Isa 40: 22 He **s** enthroned above the circle
Mt   19: 28 Son of Man **s** on his glorious throne,
Rev   4: 9 thanks to him who **s** on the throne

SKIN
Job 19: 20 escaped only by the **s** of my teeth.
     19: 26 And after my **s** has been destroyed,
Jer 13: 23 Can an Ethiopian change his **s**

SLAIN (SLAY)
Rev   5: 12 who was **s,** to receive power

SLANDER (SLANDERED SLANDERERS)
Lev 19: 16 spreading **s** among your people.
1Ti   5: 14 the enemy no opportunity for **s.**
Titus 3: 2 to **s** no one, to be peaceable

SLANDERED (SLANDER)
1Co   4: 13 when we are **s,** we answer kindly.

SLANDERERS (SLANDER)
Ro   1: 30 **s,** God-haters, insolent,

1Co 6: 10 nor drunkards nor **s** nor swindlers
Titus 2: 3 not to be **s** or addicted to much

SLAUGHTER
Isa 53: 7 he was led like a lamb to the **s**,

SLAVE (SLAVERY SLAVES)
Ge 21: 10 "Get rid of that **s** woman and her
Mt 20: 27 wants to be first must be your **s**—
Jn   8: 34 everyone who sins is a **s** to sin.
1Co 12: 13 whether Jews or Gentiles, **s** or free
Gal 3: 28 Jew nor Gentile, neither **s** nor free,
     4: 30 the **s** woman's son will never share

SLAVERY (SLAVE)
Gal 4: 3 in **s** under the elemental spiritual

SLAVES (SLAVE)
Ro   6: 6 we should no longer be **s** to sin—
     6: 22 and have become **s** of God,
2Pe 2: 19 for "people are **s** to whatever has

SLAY (SLAIN)
Job 13: 15 Though he **s** me, yet will I hope

SLEEP (SLEEPING)
Ps 121: 4 Israel will neither slumber nor **s**.
1Co 15: 51 We will not all **s**, but we will all be

SLEEPING (SLEEP)
Mk 13: 36 do not let him find you **s**.

SLOW
Ex 34: 6 and gracious God, **s** to anger,
Jas 1: 19 **s** to speak and **s** to become angry,
2Pe 3: 9 The Lord is not **s** in keeping his

SLUGGARD (SLUGGARDS)
Pr   6: 6 Go to the ant, you **s**;

SLUGGARDS (SLUGGARD)
Pr 20: 4 **S** do not plow in season;

SLUMBER
Ps 121: 3 he who watches over you will not **s**;
Pr   6: 10 little **s**, a little folding of the hands
Ro 13: 11 for you to wake up from your **s**,

SNAKE (SNAKES)
Nu 21: 8 "Make a **s** and put it up on a pole;
Pr 23: 32 In the end it bites like a **s**
Jn   3: 14 lifted up the **s** in the wilderness,

SNAKES (SNAKE)
Mt 10: 16 Therefore be as shrewd as **s** and as
Mk 16: 18 *they will pick up* **s**

SNATCH (SNATCHING)
Jn 10: 28 no one will **s** them out of my hand.

SNATCHING (SNATCH)
Jude : 23 save others by **s** them from the fire;

SNOW
Ps 51: 7 me, and I will be whiter than **s**.

SOAR
Isa 40: 31 They will **s** on wings like eagles;

SODOM
Ge 19: 24 rained down burning sulfur on **S**
Ro   9: 29 we would have become like **S**,

SOIL
Ge   4: 2 kept flocks, and Cain worked the **s**.
Mt 13: 23 the seed falling on good **s** refers

SOLDIER
1Co 9: 7 Who serves as a **s** at his own
2Ti 2: 3 like a good **s** of Christ Jesus.

SOLE
Dt 28: 65 resting place for the **s** of your foot.
Isa 1: 6 From the **s** of your foot to the top

SOLID
2Ti 2: 19 God's **s** foundation stands firm,
Heb 5: 12 You need milk, not **s** food!

SOLOMON
   Son of David by Bathsheba; king of Judah (2Sa 12:24; 1Ch 3:5, 10). Appointed king by David (1Ki 1); adversaries Adonijah, Joab, Shimei killed by Benaiah (1Ki 2). Asked for wisdom (1Ki 3; 2Ch 1). Judged between two prostitutes (1Ki 3:16–28). Built temple (1Ki 5–7; 2Ch 2–5); prayer of dedication (1Ki 8; 2Ch 6). Visited by Queen of Sheba (1Ki 10; 2Ch 9). Wives turned his heart from God (1Ki 11:1–13). Jeroboam rebelled against (1Ki 11:26–40). Death (1Ki 11:41–43; 2Ch 9:29–31).
   Proverbs of (1Ki 4:32; Pr 1:1; 10:1; 25:1); psalms of (Ps 72; 127); song of (SS 1:1).

SON (SONS)
Ge 22: 2 said, "Take your **s**, your only **s**,
Ex 11: 5 Every firstborn **s** in Egypt will die,
Dt 21: 18 rebellious **s** who does not obey his
Ps   2: 7 He said to me, "You are my **s**;
     2: 12 Kiss his **s**, or he will be angry
Pr 10: 1 A wise **s** brings joy to his father,
Isa 7: 14 will conceive and give birth to a **s**,
Hos 11: 1 and out of Egypt I called my **s**.
Mt   2: 15 "Out of Egypt I called my **s**."
     3: 17 said, "This is my **S**, whom I love;
    11: 27 knows the **S** except the Father,
    11: 27 knows the Father except the **S**
    16: 16 Messiah, the **S** of the living God."
    17: 5 said, "This is my **S**, whom I love;
    20: 18 the **S** of Man will be delivered over
    24: 30 appear the sign of the **S** of Man
    24: 44 because the **S** of Man will come
    27: 54 "Surely he was the **S** of God!"
    28: 19 and of the **S** and of the Holy Spirit,
Mk 10: 45 even the **S** of Man did not come
    14: 62 you will see the **S** of Man sitting
Lk   9: 58 the **S** of Man has no place to lay his
    18: 8 when the **S** of Man comes, will he
    19: 10 For the **S** of Man came to seek
Jn   3: 14 so the **S** of Man must be lifted up,
     3: 16 that he gave his one and only **S**,
    17: 1 Glorify your **S**, that your **S** may
Ro   8: 29 conformed to the image of his **S**,
     8: 32 He who did not spare his own **S**,
1Co 15: 28 the **S** himself will be made subject
Gal 4: 30 for the slave woman's **s** will never
1Th 1: 10 and to wait for his **S** from heaven,
Heb 1: 2 days he has spoken to us by his **S**,
     10: 29 punished who has trampled the **S**
1Jn 1: 7 Jesus, his **S**, purifies us from all sin.
     4: 9 only **S** into the world that we might
     5: 5 believes that Jesus is the **S** of God.
     5: 11 eternal life, and this life is in his **S**.

SONG (SING)
Ps 40: 3 He put a new **s** in my mouth,
    96: 1 Sing to the LORD a new **s**;
   149: 1 Sing to the LORD a new **s**,
Isa 49: 13 burst into **s**, you mountains!
    55: 12 hills will burst into **s** before you,
Rev 5: 9 And they sang a new **s**, saying:
    15: 3 sang the **s** of God's servant Moses

SONGS (SING)
Job 35: 10 Maker, who gives **s** in the night,
Ps 100: 2 come before him with joyful **s**.
Eph 5: 19 hymns, and **s** from the Spirit.
Jas 5: 13 Let them sing **s** of praise.

SONS (SON)
Joel	2: 28	**s** and daughters will prophesy,
2Co	6: 18	you will be my **s** and daughters,

SORROW
Jer	31: 12	garden, and they will **s** no more.
Ro	9: 2	I have great **s** and unceasing
2Co	7: 10	Godly **s** brings repentance that

SOUL (SOULS)
Dt	6: 5	and with all your **s** and with all
	10: 12	all your heart and with all your **s**,
Jos	22: 5	all your heart and with all your **s**."
Ps	23: 3	he refreshes my **s**. He guides me
	42: 1	of water, so my **s** pants for you,
	42: 11	Why, my **s**, are you downcast?
	103: 1	Praise the Lᴏʀᴅ, my **s**;
Pr	13: 19	A longing fulfilled is sweet to the **s**,
Mt	10: 28	of the One who can destroy both **s**
	16: 26	the whole world, yet forfeit their **s**?
	22: 37	with all your **s** and with all your
Heb	4: 12	it penetrates even to dividing **s**

SOULS (SOUL)
Jer	6: 16	and you will find rest for your **s**.
Mt	11: 29	and you will find rest for your **s**.

SOUND
1Co	14: 8	the trumpet does not **s** a clear call,
	15: 52	the trumpet will **s**, the dead will
2Ti	4: 3	will not put up with **s** doctrine.

SOVEREIGN
Da	4: 25	Most High is **s** over all kingdoms

SOW (SOWS)
Job	4: 8	and those who **s** trouble reap it.
Mt	6: 26	they do not **s** or reap or store away
2Pe	2: 22	"A **s** that is washed returns to her

SOWS (SOW)
2Co	9: 6	and whoever **s** generously will

SPARE (SPARES)
Ro	8: 32	He who did not **s** his own Son,
	11: 21	God did not **s** the natural branches,

SPARES (SPARE)
Pr	13: 24	Whoever **s** the rod hates their

SPEARS
Isa	2: 4	and their **s** into pruning hooks.
Joel	3: 10	and your pruning hooks into **s**.
Mic	4: 3	and their **s** into pruning hooks.

SPECTACLE
1Co	4: 9	have been made a **s** to the whole
Col	2: 15	he made a public **s** of them,

SPIN
Mt	6: 28	They do not labor or **s**.

SPIRIT (SPIRITS SPIRITUAL)
Ge	1: 2	the **S** of God was hovering over
	6: 3	said, "My **S** will not contend
2Ki	2: 9	inherit a double portion of your **s**,"
Job	33: 4	The **S** of God has made me;
Ps	31: 5	Into your hands I commit my **s**;
	51: 10	and renew a steadfast **s** within me.
	51: 11	or take your Holy **S** from me.
	51: 17	My sacrifice, O God, is a broken **s**;
	139: 7	Where can I go from your **S**?
Isa	57: 15	to revive the **s** of the lowly
	63: 10	rebelled and grieved his Holy **S**.
Eze	11: 19	heart and put a new **s** in them;
	36: 26	a new heart and put a new **s** in you;
Joel	2: 28	I will pour out my **S** on all people.

Zec	4: 6	but by my **S**,' says the Lᴏʀᴅ
Mt	1: 18	to be pregnant through the Holy **S**.
	3: 11	He will baptize you with the Holy **S**
	3: 16	he saw the **S** of God descending
	4: 1	led by the **S** into the wilderness
	5: 3	"Blessed are the poor in **s**, for
	26: 41	The **s** is willing, but the flesh is
	28: 19	and of the Son and of the Holy **S**,
Lk	1: 80	child grew and became strong in **s**;
	11: 13	in heaven give the Holy **S** to those
Jn	4: 24	God is **s**, and his worshipers must
		worship in the **S**
	7: 39	that time the **S** had not been given,
	14: 26	the Holy **S**, whom the Father will
	16: 13	But when he, the **S** of truth, comes,
	20: 22	and said, "Receive the Holy **S**.
Ac	1: 5	will be baptized with the Holy **S**."
	2: 4	tongues as the **S** enabled them.
	2: 38	will receive the gift of the Holy **S**.
	6: 3	who are known to be full of the **S**
	19: 2	"Did you receive the Holy **S**
Ro	8: 9	if indeed the **S** of God lives in you.
	8: 26	the **S** helps us in our weakness.
1Co	2: 10	God has revealed to us by his **S**.
	2: 10	The **S** searches all things,
	2: 14	without the **S** does not accept
	3: 1	as people who live by the **S** but as
	6: 19	bodies are temples of the Holy **S**,
	12: 1	Now about the gifts of the **S**,
	12: 13	we were all baptized by one **S**
	12: 13	and we were all given the one **S**
	14: 1	and eagerly desire gifts of the **S**,
2Co	3: 6	the letter kills, but the **S** gives life.
	5: 5	who has given us the **S** as a deposit,
Gal	5: 16	say, walk by the **S**, and you will not
	5: 22	But the fruit of the **S** is love, joy,
	5: 25	Since we live by the **S**, let us keep
Gal	6: 1	who live by the **S** should restore
Eph	1: 13	with a seal, the promised Holy **S**,
	4: 30	do not grieve the Holy **S** of God,
	5: 18	Instead, be filled with the **S**,
	5: 19	hymns, and songs from the **S**.
	6: 17	of salvation and the sword of the **S**,
1Th	5: 19	Do not quench the **S**.
2Th	2: 13	the sanctifying work of the **S**
Heb	4: 12	even to dividing soul and **s**,
1Pe	3: 4	beauty of a gentle and quiet **s**,
2Pe	1: 21	were carried along by the Holy **S**.
1Jn	4: 1	do not believe every **s**, but test

SPIRITS (SPIRIT)
1Co	12: 10	another distinguishing between **s**,
	14: 32	The **s** of prophets are subject
1Jn	4: 1	but test the **s** to see whether they

SPIRITUAL (SPIRIT)
Ro	12: 11	but keep your **s** fervor,
1Co	2: 13	the Spirit, explaining **s** realities
	15: 44	a natural body, it is raised a **s** body.
Eph	1: 3	realms with every **s** blessing
	6: 12	against the **s** forces of evil
1Pe	2: 2	crave pure **s** milk, so that by it you
	2: 5	offering **s** sacrifices acceptable

SPLENDOR
1Ch	16: 29	the Lᴏʀᴅ in the **s** of his holiness.
	29: 11	glory and the majesty and the **s**,
Job	37: 22	of the north he comes in golden **s**;
Ps	29: 2	the Lᴏʀᴅ in the **s** of his holiness.
	45: 3	clothe yourself with **s** and majesty.
	96: 6	**S** and majesty are before him;
	96: 9	the Lᴏʀᴅ in the **s** of his holiness;
	104: 1	you are clothed with **s** and majesty.
	145: 5	of the glorious **s** of your majesty—
Isa	61: 3	the Lᴏʀᴅ for the display of his **s**.
	63: 1	robed in **s**, striding forward

Lk 9: 30 Elijah, appeared in glorious **s**,
2Th 2: 8 and destroy by the **s** of his coming.

SPOIL
Ps 119:162 promise like one who finds great **s**.

SPOTLESS
2Pe 3: 14 make every effort to be found **s**,

SPREAD (SPREADING)
Ac 12: 24 the word of God continued to **s**
19: 20 way the word of the Lord **s** widely

SPREADING (SPREAD)
1Th 3: 2 in God's service in **s** the gospel

SPRING
Jer 2: 13 forsaken me, the **s** of living water,
Jn 4: 14 in them a **s** of water welling
Jas 3: 12 can a salt **s** produce fresh water.

SPUR
Heb 10: 24 how we may **s** one another

SPURNS
Pr 15: 5 A fool **s** a parent's discipline,

STAFF
Ps 23: 4 your rod and your **s**, they comfort

STAKES
Isa 54: 2 your cords, strengthen your **s**.

STAND (STANDING STANDS)
Ex 14: 13 **S** firm and you will see
2Ch 20: 17 **s** firm and see the deliverance
Ps 1: 5 Therefore the wicked will not **s**
40: 2 rock and gave me a firm place to **s**.
119:120 fear of you; I **s** in awe of your laws.
Eze 22: 30 **s** before me in the gap on behalf
Zec 14: 4 day his feet will **s** on the Mount
Mt 12: 25 divided against itself will not **s**.
Ro 14: 10 we will all **s** before God's judgment
1Co 15: 58 dear brothers and sisters, **s** firm.
Eph 6: 14 **S** firm then, with the belt of truth
2Th 2: 15 firm and hold fast to the teachings
Jas 5: 8 be patient and **s** firm,
Rev 3: 20 I **s** at the door and knock.

STANDING (STAND)
Ex 3: 5 where you are **s** is holy ground."
Jos 5: 15 the place where you are **s** is holy."
1Pe 5: 9 Resist him, **s** firm in the faith,

STANDS (STAND)
Ps 89: 2 that your love **s** firm forever,
119: 89 it **s** firm in the heavens.
2Ti 2: 19 God's solid foundation **s** firm,

STAR (STARS)
Nu 24: 17 A **s** will come out of Jacob;
Rev 22: 16 David, and the bright Morning **S**."

STARS (STAR)
Da 12: 3 like the **s** for ever and ever.
Php 2: 15 you will shine among them like **s**

STEADFAST
Ps 51: 10 and renew a **s** spirit within me.
Isa 26: 3 peace those whose minds are **s**,
1Pe 5: 10 and make you strong, firm and **s**.

STEAL
Ex 20: 15 "You shall not **s**.
Mt 19: 18 you shall not **s**, you shall not give
Eph 4: 28 has been stealing must **s** no longer,

STEP (STEPS)
Gal 5: 25 let us keep in **s** with the Spirit.

STEPS (STEP)
Pr 16: 9 but the LORD establishes their **s**.
Jer 10: 23 it is not for them to direct their **s**.
1Pe 2: 21 that you should follow in his **s**.

STICKS
Pr 18: 24 there is a friend who **s** closer than

STIFF-NECKED
Ex 34: 9 Although this is a **s** people,

STILL
Ps 46: 10 "Be **s**, and know that I am God;
Zec 2: 13 Be **s** before the LORD,

STIRS
Pr 6: 19 a person who **s** up conflict
10: 12 Hatred **s** up conflict, but love
15: 1 wrath, but a harsh word **s** up anger.
29: 22 An angry person **s** up conflict,

STONE (CORNERSTONE MILLSTONE)
1Sa 17: 50 the Philistine with a sling and a **s**;
Isa 8: 14 and Judah he will be a **s** that causes
Eze 11: 19 remove from them their heart of **s**
Mk 16: 3 "Who will roll the **s** away
Lk 4: 3 God, tell this **s** to become bread."
Jn 8: 7 the first to throw a **s** at her."
2Co 3: 3 not on tablets of **s** but on tablets

STORE
Pr 10: 14 The wise **s** up knowledge,
Mt 6: 19 "Do not **s** up for yourselves

STOREHOUSE (HOUSE)
Mal 3: 10 Bring the whole tithe into the **s**,

STRAIGHT
Pr 3: 6 and he will make your paths **s**.
4: 25 Let your eyes look **s** ahead;
15: 21 understanding keeps a **s** course.
Jn 1: 23 'Make **s** the way for the Lord.' "

STRAIN
Mt 23: 24 You **s** out a gnat but swallow

STRANGER
Mt 25: 35 I was a **s** and you invited me in,
Jn 10: 5 But they will never follow a **s**;

STRAPS
Mk 1: 7 **s** of whose sandals I am not worthy

STREAMS
Ps 1: 3 person is like a tree planted by **s**
46: 4 a river whose **s** make glad the city
Ecc 1: 7 All **s** flow into the sea, yet the sea is

STRENGTH (STRONG)
Ex 15: 2 "The LORD is my **s** and my
Dt 6: 5 all your soul and with all your **s**.
2Sa 22: 33 It is God who arms me with **s**
Ne 8: 10 the joy of the LORD is your **s**."
Ps 28: 7 The LORD is my **s** and my shield;
46: 1 God is our refuge and **s**,
96: 7 ascribe to the LORD glory and **s**.
118: 14 The LORD is my **s** and my
147: 10 pleasure is not in the **s** of the horse,
Isa 40: 31 in the LORD will renew their **s**.
Mk 12: 30 all your mind and with all your **s**.'
1Co 1: 25 of God is stronger than human **s**.
Php 4: 13 this through him who gives me **s**.
1Pe 4: 11 do so with the **s** God provides,

STRENGTHEN (STRONG)
2Ch 16: 9 to **s** those whose hearts are fully
Ps 119: 28 **s** me according to your word.
Isa 35: 3 **S** the feeble hands, steady the
41: 10 I will **s** you and help you;

Eph	3:	16	of his glorious riches he may **s** you
2Th	2:	17	and **s** you in every good deed
Heb	12:	12	**s** your feeble arms and weak knees.

STRIFE

Pr	20:	3	It is to one's honor to avoid **s**,
	22:	10	out the mocker, and out goes **s**;

STRIKE

Ge	3:	15	your head, and you will **s** his heel."
Zec	13:	7	"**S** the shepherd, and the sheep will
Mt	26:	31	" 'I will **s** the shepherd,

STRONG (STRENGTH STRENGTHEN)

Dt	31:	6	Be **s** and courageous. Do not be
1Ki	2:	2	"So be **s**, act like a man,
Pr	31:	17	her arms are **s** for her tasks.
SS	8:	6	for love is as **s** as death, its jealousy
Lk	2:	40	And the child grew and became **s**;
Ro	15:	1	We who are **s** ought to bear
1Co	1:	27	things of the world to shame the **s**.
	16:	13	in the faith; be courageous; be **s**.
2Co	12:	10	For when I am weak, then I am **s**.
Eph	6:	10	be **s** in the Lord and in his mighty

STRUGGLE

Ro	15:	30	join me in my **s** by praying to God
Eph	6:	12	For our **s** is not against flesh
Heb	12:	4	In your **s** against sin, you have not

STUDY

Ezr	7:	10	Ezra had devoted himself to the **s**
Ecc	12:	12	end, and much **s** wearies the body.
Jn	5:	39	You **s** the Scriptures diligently

STUMBLE (STUMBLING)

Ps	37:	24	though he may **s**, he will not fall,
	119:	165	law, and nothing can make them **s**.
Isa	8:	14	be a stone that causes people to **s**
Jer	31:	9	a level path where they will not **s**,
Eze	7:	19	for it has caused them to **s** into sin.
1Co	10:	32	Do not cause anyone to **s**,
1Pe	2:	8	"A stone that causes people to **s**

STUMBLING (STUMBLE)

Ro	14:	13	your mind not to put any **s** block
1Co	8:	9	rights does not become a **s** block
2Co	6:	3	We put no **s** block in anyone's path,

SUBDUE

Ge	1:	28	fill the earth and **s** it.

SUBJECT (SUBJECTED)

1Co	14:	32	of prophets are **s** to the control
	15:	28	the Son himself will be made **s**
Titus	2:	5	and to be **s** to their husbands,
	2:	9	slaves to be **s** to their masters
	3:	1	Remind the people to be **s** to rulers

SUBJECTED (SUBJECT)

Ro	8:	20	the creation was **s** to frustration,

SUBMISSION (SUBMIT)

1Co	14:	34	but must be in **s**, as the law says.
1Ti	2:	11	learn in quietness and full **s**.

SUBMISSIVE (SUBMIT)

Jas	3:	17	considerate, **s**, full of mercy

SUBMIT (SUBMISSION SUBMISSIVE SUBMITS)

Ro	13:	5	necessary to **s** to the authorities,
1Co	16:	16	to **s** to such people and to everyone
Eph	5:	21	**S** to one another out of reverence
Col	3:	18	**s** yourselves to your husbands, as is
Heb	12:	9	How much more should we **s**
	13:	17	leaders and **s** to their authority,
Jas	4:	7	**S** yourselves, then, to God.
1Pe	2:	18	reverent fear of God **s** yourselves

SUBMITS (SUBMIT)

Eph	5:	24	Now as the church **s** to Christ,

SUCCESSFUL

Jos	1:	7	that you may be **s** wherever you go.
2Ki	18:	7	he was **s** in whatever he undertook.
2Ch	20:	20	in his prophets and you will be **s**."

SUFFER (SUFFERED SUFFERING SUFFERINGS SUFFERS)

Isa	53:	10	to crush him and cause him to **s**,
Mk	8:	31	Son of Man must **s** many things
Lk	24:	26	the Messiah have to **s** these things
	24:	46	The Messiah will **s** and rise
Php	1:	29	believe in him, but also to **s** for him,
1Pe	4:	16	if you **s** as a Christian, do not be

SUFFERED (SUFFER)

Heb	2:	9	and honor because he **s** death,
	2:	18	Because he himself **s** when he was
1Pe	2:	21	called, because Christ **s** for you,

SUFFERING (SUFFER)

Isa	53:	3	a man of **s**, and familiar with pain.
Ac	5:	41	been counted worthy of **s** disgrace
2Ti	1:	8	join with me in **s** for the gospel,

SUFFERINGS (SUFFER)

Ro	8:	17	if indeed we share in his **s** in order
	8:	18	that our present **s** are not worth
2Co	1:	5	share abundantly in the **s** of Christ,
Php	3:	10	and participation in his **s**,

SUFFERS (SUFFER)

Pr	13:	20	for a companion of fools **s** harm.
1Co	12:	26	If one part **s**, every part **s** with it;

SUFFICIENT

2Co	12:	9	said to me, "My grace is **s** for you,

SUITABLE

Ge	2:	18	I will make a helper **s** for him."

SUN

Ecc	1:	9	there is nothing new under the **s**.
Mal	4:	2	the **s** of righteousness will rise
Mt	5:	45	He causes his **s** to rise on the evil
	17:	2	His face shone like the **s**, and his
Rev	1:	16	His face was like the **s** shining in
	21:	23	The city does not need the **s**

SUPERIOR

Heb	1:	4	as the name he has inherited is **s**
	8:	6	he is mediator is **s** to the old one,

SUPREMACY

Col	1:	18	in everything he might have the **s**.

SURE

Nu	32:	23	you may be **s** that your sin will find
Dt	6:	17	Be **s** to keep the commands
	14:	22	Be **s** to set aside a tenth of all
Isa	28:	16	cornerstone for a **s** foundation;

SURPASS (SURPASSES SURPASSING)

Pr	31:	29	noble things, but you **s** them all."

SURPASSES (SURPASS)

Mt	5:	20	that unless your righteousness **s**
Eph	3:	19	to know this love that **s** knowledge

SURPASSING (SURPASS)

Ps	150:	2	praise him for his **s** greatness.
2Co	3:	10	in comparison with the **s** glory.
	9:	14	of the **s** grace God has given you.
Php	3:	8	a loss because of the **s** worth

SURROUNDED
Heb 12: 1 since we are **s** by such a great cloud

SUSPENDS
Job 26: 7 he **s** the earth over nothing.

SUSTAINING (SUSTAINS)
Heb 1: 3 **s** all things by his powerful word.

SUSTAINS (SUSTAINING)
Ps 18: 35 shield, and your right hand **s** me;
146: 9 the foreigner and **s** the fatherless
147: 6 The Lord **s** the humble but casts
Isa 50: 4 to know the word that **s** the weary.

SWALLOWED
1Co 15: 54 "Death has been **s** up in victory."
2Co 5: 4 so that what is mortal may be **s**

SWEAR
Mt 5: 34 I tell you, do not **s** an oath at all:

SWORD (SWORDS)
Ps 45: 3 Gird your **s** on your side,
Mt 10: 34 not come to bring peace, but a **s**.
26: 52 all who draw the **s** will die by the **s**.
Lk 2: 35 a **s** will pierce your own soul too."
Ro 13: 4 for rulers do not bear the **s** for no
Eph 6: 17 of salvation and the **s** of the Spirit,
Heb 4: 12 Sharper than any double-edged **s**,
Rev 1: 16 was a sharp, double-edged **s**.

SWORDS (SWORD)
Pr 12: 18 words of the reckless pierce like **s**,
Isa 2: 4 They will beat their **s**
Joel 3: 10 Beat your plowshares into **s**

SYMPATHETIC
1Pe 3: 8 be **s**, love one another,

SYNAGOGUE
Lk 4: 16 the Sabbath day he went into the **s**,
Ac 17: 2 Paul went into the **s**, and on three

TABERNACLE
Ex 40: 34 the glory of the Lord filled the **t**.

TABLE (TABLES)
Ps 23: 5 You prepare a **t** before me

TABLES (TABLE)
Ac 6: 2 word of God in order to wait on **t**.

TABLET (TABLETS)
Pr 3: 3 write them on the **t** of your heart.
7: 3 write them on the **t** of your heart.

TABLETS (TABLET)
Ex 31: 18 Sinai, he gave him the two **t**
Dt 10: 5 put the **t** in the ark I had made,
2Co 3: 3 not on **t** of stone but on **t** of human

TAKE (TAKEN TAKES TAKING TOOK)
Dt 12: 32 do not add to it or **t** away from it.
31: 26 "**T** this Book of the Law and place
Job 23: 10 But he knows the way that I **t**;
Ps 49: 17 for they will **t** nothing with them
51: 11 or **t** your Holy Spirit from me.
Mt 10: 38 Whoever does not **t** up their cross
11: 29 **T** my yoke upon you and learn
16: 24 deny themselves and **t** up their cross

TAKEN (TAKE)
Lev 6: 4 they have stolen or **t** by extortion,
Isa 6: 7 your guilt is **t** away and your sin
Mt 24: 40 one will be **t** and the other left.
Mk 16: 19 *them, he was **t** up into heaven*
1Ti 3: 16 on in the world, was **t** up in glory.

TAKES (TAKE)
1Ki 20: 11 not boast like one who **t** it off.' "
Jn 1: 29 who **t** away the sin of the world!
Rev 22: 19 if anyone **t** words away from this

TAKING (TAKE)
Php 2: 7 nothing by **t** the very nature

TALENT See BAGS

TAME
Jas 3: 8 no human being can **t** the tongue.

TASK
Mk 13: 34 each with their assigned **t**, and tells
Ac 20: 24 complete the **t** the Lord Jesus has
1Co 3: 5 the Lord has assigned to each his **t**.
2Co 2: 16 And who is equal to such a **t**?

TASTE (TASTED)
Ps 34: 8 **T** and see that the Lord is good;
Col 2: 21 Do not **t**! Do not touch!"?
Heb 2: 9 God he might **t** death for everyone.

TASTED (TASTE)
1Pe 2: 3 you have **t** that the Lord is good.

TAUGHT (TEACH)
Mt 7: 29 because he **t** as one who had
1Co 2: 13 but in words **t** by the Spirit,
Gal 1: 12 it from any man, nor was I **t** it;

TAX (TAXES)
Mt 22: 17 to pay the imperial **t** to Caesar

TAXES (TAX)
Ro 13: 7 you owe them: If you owe **t**, pay **t**;

TEACH (TAUGHT TEACHER TEACHERS TEACHES TEACHING)
Ex 33: 13 **t** me your ways so I may know you
Dt 4: 9 **T** them to your children and to
8: 3 to **t** you that man does not live
11: 19 **T** them to your children,
1Sa 12: 23 I will **t** you the way that is good
Ps 32: 8 **t** you in the way you should go;
51: 13 I will **t** transgressors your ways,
90: 12 **T** us to number our days, that we
143: 10 **T** me to do your will, for you are
Jer 31: 34 longer will they **t** their neighbor,
Lk 11: 1 "Lord, **t** us to pray, just as John
Jn 14: 26 will **t** you all things and will
1Ti 2: 12 I do not permit a woman to **t**
3: 2 respectable, hospitable, able to **t**,
Titus 2: 1 **t** what is appropriate to sound
Heb 8: 11 longer will they **t** their neighbor,
Jas 3: 1 that we who **t** will be judged more
1Jn 2: 27 you do not need anyone to **t** you.

TEACHER (TEACH)
Mt 10: 24 "The student is not above the **t**,
23: 8 for you have one **T**, and you are
Jn 13: 14 your Lord and **T**, have washed

TEACHERS (TEACH)
1Co 12: 28 prophets, third **t**, then miracles,
Eph 4: 11 the evangelists, the pastors and **t**,
Heb 5: 12 by this time you ought to be **t**,

TEACHES (TEACH)
1Ti 6: 3 If anyone **t** otherwise and does not

TEACHING (TEACH)
Pr 1: 8 and do not forsake your mother's **t**.
Mt 28: 20 **t** them to obey everything I have
Jn 7: 17 out whether my **t** comes from God
14: 23 who loves me will obey my **t**.
1Ti 4: 13 of Scripture, to preaching and to **t**.

2Ti 3: 16 is God-breathed and is useful for **t**,
Titus 2: 7 In your **t** show integrity,

TEAR (TEARS)
Rev 7: 17 God will wipe away every **t**

TEARS (TEAR)
Ps 126: 5 Those who sow with **t** will reap
Php 3: 18 and now tell you again even with **t**,

TEETH (TOOTH)
Mt 8: 12 will be weeping and gnashing of **t**."

TEMPERATE
1Ti 3: 2 reproach, faithful to his wife, **t**,
3: 11 not malicious talkers but **t**
Titus 2: 2 Teach the older men to be **t**,

TEMPEST
Ps 55: 8 shelter, far from the **t** and storm."

TEMPLE (TEMPLES)
1Ki 8: 27 How much less this **t** I have built!
Hab 2: 20 The LORD is in his holy **t**;
1Co 3: 16 that you yourselves are God's **t**
2Co 6: 16 For we are the **t** of the living God.

TEMPLES (TEMPLE)
Ac 17: 24 does not live in **t** built by human
1Co 6: 19 your bodies are **t** of the Holy Spirit,

TEMPT (TEMPTATION TEMPTED)
1Co 7: 5 Satan will not **t** you because of

TEMPTATION (TEMPT)
Mt 6: 13 lead us not into **t**, but deliver us
26: 41 pray so that you will not fall into **t**.
1Co 10: 13 No **t** has overtaken you except

TEMPTED (TEMPT)
Mt 4: 1 the wilderness to be **t** by the devil.
1Co 10: 13 not let you be **t** beyond what you
Heb 2: 18 he himself suffered when he was **t**,
2: 18 able to help those who are being **t**.
4: 15 but we have one who has been **t**
Jas 1: 13 For God cannot be **t** by evil,

TEN (TENTH TITHE TITHES)
Ex 34: 28 the **T** Commandments.
Ps 91: 7 side, **t** thousand at your right hand,
Mt 25: 28 give it to the one who has **t** bags.
Lk 15: 8 suppose a woman has **t** silver coins

TENTH (TEN)
Dt 14: 22 Be sure to set aside a **t** of all

TERRIBLE (TERROR)
2Ti 3: 1 There will be **t** times in the last

TERROR (TERRIBLE)
Ps 91: 5 You will not fear the **t** of night,
Lk 21: 26 People will faint from **t**,
Ro 13: 3 rulers hold no **t** for those who do

TEST (TESTED TESTS)
Dt 6: 16 your God to the **t** as you did
Ps 139: 23 **t** me and know my anxious
Ro 12: 2 you will be able to **t** and approve
1Co 3: 13 the fire will **t** the quality of each
1Jn 4: 1 **t** the spirits to see whether they are

TESTED (TEST)
Ge 22: 1 Some time later God **t** Abraham.
Job 23: 10 when he has **t** me, I will come forth
Pr 27: 21 but people are **t** by their praise.
1Ti 3: 10 They must first be **t**;

TESTIFY (TESTIMONY)
Jn 5: 39 These are the very Scriptures that **t**

TESTIMONY (TESTIFY)
Isa 8: 20 instruction and the **t** of warning.
Lk 18: 20 you shall not give false **t**,
2Ti 1: 8 be ashamed of the **t** about our Lord

TESTS (TEST)
Pr 17: 3 for gold, but the LORD **t** the heart.
1Th 2: 4 people but God, who **t** our hearts.

THADDAEUS
   Apostle (Mt 10:3; Mk 3:18); probably also known
as Judas son of James (Lk 6:16; Ac 1:13).

THANKFUL (THANKS)
Heb 12: 28 let us be **t**, and so worship God

THANKS (THANKFUL THANKSGIVING)
Ne 12: 31 assigned two large choirs to give **t**.
Ps 100: 4 give **t** to him and praise his name.
1Co 15: 57 But **t** be to God! He gives us
2Co 2: 14 But **t** be to God, who always leads
9: 15 **T** be to God for his indescribable
1Th 5: 18 give **t** in all circumstances;

THANKSGIVING (THANKS)
Ps 95: 2 Let us come before him with **t**
100: 4 Enter his gates with **t** and his
Php 4: 6 **t**, present your requests to God.
1Ti 4: 3 to be received with **t** by those who

THIEF (THIEVES)
1Th 5: 2 of the Lord will come like a **t**
Rev 16: 15 "Look, I come like a **t**!

THIEVES (THIEF)
1Co 6: 10 nor **t** nor the greedy nor drunkards

THINK (THOUGHT THOUGHTS)
Ro 12: 3 Do not **t** of yourself more highly
Php 4: 8 **t** about such things.

THIRST (THIRSTY)
Ps 69: 21 food and gave me vinegar for my **t**.
Mt 5: 6 hunger and **t** for righteousness,
Jn 4: 14 the water I give them will never **t**.

THIRSTY (THIRST)
Isa 55: 1 all you who are **t**,
Jn 7: 37 "Let anyone who is **t** come to me
Rev 22: 17 Let the one who is **t** come;

THOMAS
   Apostle (Mt 10:3; Mk 3:18; Lk 6:15; Jn 11:16;
14:5; 21:2; Ac 1:13). Doubted resurrection (Jn
20:24–28).

THORN (THORNS)
2Co 12: 7 I was given a **t** in my flesh,

THORNS (THORN)
Nu 33: 55 in your eyes and **t** in your sides.
Mt 27: 29 twisted together a crown of **t** and
Heb 6: 8 land that produces **t** and thistles is

THOUGHT (THINK)
Pr 14: 15 the prudent give **t** to their steps.
1Co 13: 11 I talked like a child, I **t** like a child,

THOUGHTS (THINK)
Ps 139: 23 test me and know my anxious **t**.
Isa 55: 8 "For my **t** are not your **t**, neither
Heb 4: 12 it judges the **t** and attitudes

THREE
Ecc 4: 12 of **t** strands is not quickly broken.
Mt 12: 40 the Son of Man will be **t** days and **t**
nights in the heart of the earth.
18: 20 where two or **t** gather in my name,
27: 63 said, 'After **t** days I will rise again.'

1Co 13: 13   And now these **t** remain:
    14: 27   or at the most **t**—should speak,
2Co 13: 1   testimony of two or **t** witnesses."

THRESHING

2Sa 24: 18   altar to the LORD on the **t** floor

THRONE (ENTHRONED)

2Sa 7: 16   your **t** will be established
Ps 45: 6   Your **t**, O God, will last for ever
    47: 8   God is seated on his holy **t**.
Isa 6: 1   high and exalted, seated on a **t**;
    66: 1   "Heaven is my **t**, and the earth is
Heb 4: 16   then approach God's **t** of grace
    12: 2   at the right hand of the **t** of God.
Rev 4: 10   They lay their crowns before the **t**
    20: 11   I saw a great white **t** and him who
    22: 3   The **t** of God and of the Lamb will

THROW

Jn 8: 7   the first to **t** a stone at her."
Heb 10: 35   So do not **t** away your confidence;
    12: 1   let us **t** off everything that hinders

THWART

Isa 14: 27   has purposed, and who can **t** him?

TIBNI

    King of Israel (1Ki 16:21–22).

TIME (TIMES)

Est 4: 14   royal position for such a **t** as this?"
Da 7: 25   be delivered into his hands for a **t**,
              times and half a **t**.
Hos 10: 12   for it is **t** to seek the LORD,
Ro 9: 9   "At the appointed **t** I will return,
Heb 9: 28   and he will appear a second **t**,
    10: 12   had offered for all **t** one sacrifice
1Pe 4: 17   For it is **t** for judgment to begin

TIMES (TIME)

Ps 9: 9   a stronghold in **t** of trouble.
    31: 15   My **t** are in your hands;
    62: 8   Trust in him at all **t**, you people;
Pr 17: 17   A friend loves at all **t**,
Am 5: 13   in such **t**, for the **t** are evil.
Mt 18: 21   sins against me? Up to seven **t**?"
Ac 1: 7   "It is not for you to know the **t**
Rev 12: 14   care of for a time, **t** and half a time,

TIMID

2Ti 1: 7   God gave us does not make us **t**,

TIMOTHY

    Believer from Lystra (Ac 16:1). Joined Paul on sec-
ond missionary journey (Ac 16–20). Sent to settle
problems at Corinth (1Co 4:17; 16:10). Led church
at Ephesus (1Ti 1:3). Co-writer with Paul (1Th 1:1;
2Th 1:1; Phm 1).

TIRE (TIRED)

2Th 3: 13   never **t** of doing what is good.

TIRED (TIRE)

Ex 17: 12   When Moses' hands grew **t**,
Isa 40: 28   He will not grow **t** or weary,

TITHE (TEN)

Lev 27: 30   " 'A **t** of everything
Dt 12: 17   your own towns the **t** of your grain
Mal 3: 10   Bring the whole **t**

TITHES (TEN)

Mal 3: 8   "In **t** and offerings.

TITUS

    Gentile co-worker of Paul (Gal 2:1–3; 2Ti 4:10);
sent to Corinth (2Co 2:13; 7–8; 12:18), Crete (Titus
1:4–5).

TODAY

Mt 6: 11   Give us **t** our daily bread.
Lk 23: 43   **t** you will be with me in paradise."
Heb 3: 13   as long as it is called "**T**,"
    13: 8   Christ is the same yesterday and **t**

TOIL

Ge 3: 17   through painful **t** you will eat food

TOLERATE

Hab 1: 13   then do you **t** the treacherous?
Rev 2: 2   that you cannot **t** wicked people,

TOMB

Mt 27: 65   make the **t** as secure as you know
Lk 24: 2   the stone rolled away from the **t**,

TOMORROW

Pr 27: 1   not boast about **t**, for you do not
Isa 22: 13   drink," you say, "for **t** we die!"
Mt 6: 34   do not worry about **t**, for **t**
Jas 4: 13   "Today or **t** we will go to this

TONGUE (TONGUES)

Ps 39: 1   my ways and keep my **t** from sin;
Pr 12: 18   but the **t** of the wise brings healing.
1Co 14: 2   who speaks in a **t** does not speak
    14: 4   speaks in a **t** edifies themselves,
    14: 13   one who speaks in a **t** should pray
    14: 19   than ten thousand words in a **t**.
Php 2: 11   and every **t** acknowledge that Jesus
Jas 3: 8   no human being can tame the **t**.

TONGUES (TONGUE)

Isa 28: 11   strange **t** God will speak to this
Mk 16: 17   they will speak in new **t**;
Ac 2: 4   other **t** as the Spirit enabled them.
    10: 46   For they heard them speaking in **t**
    19: 6   they spoke in **t** and prophesied.
1Co 12: 30   Do all speak in **t**? Do all interpret?
    14: 18   I speak in **t** more than all of you.
    14: 39   and do not forbid speaking in **t**.
Jas 1: 26   rein on their **t** deceive themselves,

TOOK (TAKE)

1Co 11: 23   the night he was betrayed, **t** bread,
Php 3: 12   which Christ Jesus **t** hold of me.

TOOTH (TEETH)

Ex 21: 24   eye for eye, **t** for **t**, hand for hand,
Mt 5: 38   was said, 'Eye for eye, and **t** for **t**.'

TORMENTED

Rev 20: 10   They will be **t** day and night

TORN

Gal 4: 15   you would have **t** out your eyes
Php 1: 23   I am **t** between the two: I desire

TOUCH (TOUCHED)

Ps 105: 15   "Do not **t** my anointed ones;
Lk 24: 39   **T** me and see; a ghost does not
2Co 6: 17   **T** no unclean thing, and I will
Col 2: 21   Do not taste! Do not **t**!"?

TOUCHED (TOUCH)

1Sa 10: 26   men whose hearts God had **t**.
Mt 14: 36   cloak, and all who **t** it were healed.

TOWER

Ge 11: 4   a **t** that reaches to the heavens,
Pr 18: 10   name of the LORD is a fortified **t**;

TOWN (TOWNS)

Mt 5: 14   **t** built on a hill cannot be hidden.

TOWNS (TOWN)

Nu 35: 2   to give the Levites **t** to live
    35: 15   These six **t** will be a place of refuge

TRACING
Ro 11: 33 and his paths beyond **t** out!

TRADITION
Mt 15: 6 word of God for the sake of your **t**.
Col 2: 8 which depends on human **t**

TRAINING
1Co 9: 25 in the games goes into strict **t**.
2Ti 3: 16 correcting and **t** in righteousness,

TRAMPLED
Lk 21: 24 Jerusalem will be **t**
Heb 10: 29 to be punished who has **t** the Son

TRANCE
Ac 10: 10 was being prepared, he fell into a **t**.

TRANSCENDS
Php 4: 7 God, which **t** all understanding,

TRANSFIGURED
Mt 17: 2 There he was **t** before them.

TRANSFORM (TRANSFORMED)
Php 3: 21 will **t** our lowly bodies so that they

TRANSFORMED (TRANSFORM)
Ro 12: 2 be **t** by the renewing of your mind.
2Co 3: 18 are being **t** into his image

TRANSGRESSION (TRANSGRESSIONS
    TRANSGRESSORS)
Isa 53: 8 **t** of my people he was punished.
Ro 4: 15 where there is no law there is no **t**.

TRANSGRESSIONS (TRANSGRESSION)
Ps 32: 1 is the one whose **t** are forgiven,
    51: 1 great compassion blot out my **t**.
    103: 12 so far has he removed our **t** from
Isa 53: 5 But he was pierced for our **t**,
Eph 2: 1 you were dead in your **t** and sins,

TRANSGRESSORS (TRANSGRESSION)
Ps 51: 13 Then I will teach **t** your ways,
Isa 53: 12 and was numbered with the **t**.
    53: 12 and made intercession for the **t**.

TREADING
Dt 25: 4 Do not muzzle an ox while it is **t**
1Co 9: 9 "Do not muzzle an ox while it is **t**

TREASURE (TREASURED TREASURES)
Isa 33: 6 of the LORD is the key to this **t**.
Mt 6: 21 where your **t** is, there your heart
2Co 4: 7 But we have this **t** in jars of clay

TREASURED (TREASURE)
Dt 7: 6 to be his people, his **t** possession.
Lk 2: 19 But Mary **t** up all these things

TREASURES (TREASURE)
Mt 6: 19 store up for yourselves **t** on earth,
Col 2: 3 in whom are hidden all the **t**
Heb 11: 26 of greater value than the **t** of Egypt,

TREAT
Lev 22: 2 sons to **t** with respect the sacred
1Ti 5: 1 **T** younger men as brothers,
1Pe 3: 7 **t** them with respect as the weaker

TREATY
Dt 7: 2 Make no **t** with them, and show

TREE
Ge 2: 9 of the garden were the **t** of life
    2: 9 and the **t** of the knowledge of good
Ps 1: 3 is like a **t** planted by streams

TREMBLE (TREMBLING)
Mt 3: 10 every **t** that does not produce good
    12: 33 for a **t** is recognized by its fruit.
Rev 22: 14 may have the right to the **t** of life

TREMBLE (TREMBLING)
1Ch 16: 30 **T** before him, all the earth!
Ps 114: 7 **T**, earth, at the presence of the Lord,

TREMBLING (TREMBLE)
Ps 2: 11 fear and celebrate his rule with **t**.
Php 2: 12 out your salvation with fear and **t**,

TRESPASS
Ro 5: 17 if, by the **t** of the one man,

TRIALS
1Th 3: 3 one would be unsettled by these **t**.
Jas 1: 2 whenever you face **t** of many kinds,
2Pe 2: 9 how to rescue the godly from **t**

TRIBES
Ge 49: 28 All these are the twelve **t** of Israel,
Mt 19: 28 judging the twelve **t** of Israel.

TRIBULATION
Rev 7: 14 who have come out of the great **t**;

TRIUMPHAL (TRIUMPHING)
Isa 60: 11 their kings led in **t** procession.
2Co 2: 14 as captives in Christ's **t** procession

TRIUMPHING (TRIUMPHAL)
Col 2: 15 of them, **t** over them by the cross.

TROUBLE (TROUBLED TROUBLES)
Job 14: 1 are of few days and full of **t**.
Ps 46: 1 strength, an ever-present help in **t**.
    107: 13 they cried to the LORD in their **t**,
Pr 24: 10 If you falter in a time of **t**,
Mt 6: 34 Each day has enough **t** of its own.
Jn 16: 33 In this world you will have **t**.
Ro 8: 35 Shall **t** or hardship or persecution

TROUBLED (TROUBLE)
Jn 14: 1 "Do not let your hearts be **t**.
    14: 27 Do not let your hearts be **t** and do

TROUBLES (TROUBLE)
1Co 7: 28 those who marry will face many **t**
2Co 1: 4 who comforts us in all our **t**,
    4: 17 momentary **t** are achieving for us

TRUE (TRUTH)
Dt 18: 22 does not take place or come **t**,
1Sa 9: 6 and everything he says comes **t**.
Ps 119:160 All your words are **t**; all your
Jn 17: 3 the only **t** God, and Jesus Christ,
Ro 3: 4 Let God be **t**, and every human
Php 4: 8 whatever is **t**, whatever is noble,
Rev 22: 6 These words are trustworthy and **t**.

TRUMPET
1Co 14: 8 if the **t** does not sound a clear call,
    15: 52 twinkling of an eye, at the last **t**.

TRUST (ENTRUSTED TRUSTED TRUSTWORTHY)
Ps 20: 7 we **t** in the name of the LORD our
    37: 3 **T** in the LORD and do good;
    56: 4 in God I **t** and am not afraid.
    119: 42 taunts me, for I **t** in your word.
Pr 3: 5 **T** in the LORD with all your heart
Isa 30: 15 in quietness and **t** is your strength,
1Co 4: 2 been given a **t** must prove faithful.

TRUSTED (TRUST)
Ps 26: 1 I have **t** in the LORD and have not
Isa 25: 9 we **t** in him, and he saved us.
Da 3: 28 They **t** in him and defied the king's
Lk 16: 10 "Whoever can be **t** with very little

TRUSTWORTHY (TRUST)

Ps 119:138 are righteous; they are fully **t**.
Pr 11: 13 but a **t** person keeps a secret.
Rev 22: 6 to me, "These words are **t** and true.

TRUTH (TRUE TRUTHFUL TRUTHS)

Isa 45: 19 I, the Lord, speak the **t**;
Zec 8: 16 Speak the **t** to each other,
Jn   4: 23 the Father in the Spirit and in **t**,
     8: 32 Then you will know the **t**, and the **t**
    14: 6 "I am the way and the **t** and the life.
    16: 13 he will guide you into all the **t**.
    18: 38 "What is **t**?" retorted Pilate.
Ro   1: 25 They exchanged the **t** about God
1Co 13: 6 in evil but rejoices with the **t**.
2Co 13: 8 against the **t**, but only for the **t**.
Eph 4: 15 Instead, speaking the **t** in love,
     6: 14 belt of **t** buckled around your waist,
2Th 2: 10 because they refused to love the **t**
1Ti 2: 4 to come to a knowledge of the **t**.
     3: 15 the pillar and foundation of the **t**.
2Ti 2: 15 correctly handles the word of **t**.
     3: 7 to come to a knowledge of the **t**.
Heb 10: 26 received the knowledge of the **t**,
1Pe 1: 22 by obeying the **t** so that you have
2Pe 2: 2 and will bring the way of **t**
1Jn 1: 6 we lie and do not live out the **t**.
     1: 8 ourselves and the **t** is not in us.

TRUTHFUL (TRUTH)

Jn   3: 33 it has certified that God is **t**.

TRUTHS (TRUTH)

1Ti 3: 9 keep hold of the deep **t** of the faith
Heb 5: 12 teach you the elementary **t** of God's

TRY (TRYING)

Ps 26: 2 and **t** me, examine my heart and
Isa 7: 13 Will you **t** the patience of my God
1Co 14: 12 **t** to excel in those that build
2Co 5: 11 the Lord, we **t** to persuade others.

TRYING (TRY)

2Co 5: 12 We are not **t** to commend ourselves
1Th 2: 4 We are not **t** to please people

TURN (TURNED TURNS)

Ex 32: 12 **T** from your fierce anger;
Dt   5: 32 do not **t** aside to the right
    28: 14 Do not **t** aside from any
Jos 1: 7 do not **t** from it to the right
2Ch 7: 14 face and **t** from their wicked ways,
    30: 9 He will not **t** his face from you
Ps 78: 6 they in **t** would tell their children.
Pr 22: 6 they are old they will not **t** from it.
Isa 29: 16 You **t** things upside down,
    30: 21 Whether you **t** to the right
    45: 22 "**T** to me and be saved, all you ends
    55: 7 Let them **t** to the Lord, and he
Eze 33: 11 they **t** from their ways and live.
Mal 4: 6 He will **t** the hearts of the parents
Mt   5: 39 to **t** to them the other cheek also.
    10: 35 to **t** " 'a man against his father,
Jn 12: 40 understand with their hearts, nor **t**
Ac   3: 19 and **t** to God, so that your sins may
    26: 18 and **t** them from darkness to light,
1Ti 6: 20 **T** away from godless chatter
1Pe 3: 11 must **t** from evil and do good;

TURNED (TURN)

Ps 30: 11 You **t** my wailing into dancing;
    40: 1 he **t** to me and heard my cry.
Isa 53: 6 each of us has **t** to our own way;
Hos 7: 8 Ephraim is a flat loaf not **t** over.
Joel 2: 31 The sun will be **t** to darkness
Ro   3: 12 All have **t** away, they have together

TURNS (TURN)

2Sa 22: 29 the Lord **t** my darkness
Pr 15: 1 A gentle answer **t** away wrath,
Isa 44: 25 of the wise and **t** it into nonsense,
Jas 5: 20 Whoever **t** a sinner from the error

TWELVE

Ge 49: 28 All these are the **t** tribes of Israel,
Mt 10: 1 Jesus called his **t** disciples to him

TWINKLING

1Co 15: 52 a flash, in the **t** of an eye, at the last

UNAPPROACHABLE

1Ti 6: 16 immortal and who lives in **u** light,

UNBELIEF (UNBELIEVER UNBELIEVERS UNBELIEVING)

Mk   9: 24 help me overcome my **u**!"
Ro 11: 20 they were broken off because of **u**,
Heb 3: 19 able to enter, because of their **u**.

UNBELIEVER (UNBELIEF)

1Co 7: 15 But if the **u** leaves, let it be so.
    10: 27 If an **u** invites you to a meal
    14: 24 if an **u** or an inquirer comes in
2Co 6: 15 have in common with an **u**?
1Ti 5: 8 the faith and is worse than an **u**.

UNBELIEVERS (UNBELIEF)

1Co 6: 6 and this in front of **u**!
2Co 6: 14 Do not be yoked together with **u**.

UNBELIEVING (UNBELIEF)

1Co 7: 14 the **u** husband has been sanctified
     7: 14 and the **u** wife has been sanctified
Rev 21: 8 But the cowardly, the **u**, the vile,

UNCERTAIN

1Ti 6: 17 which is so **u**, but to put their hope

UNCHANGEABLE

Heb 6: 18 that, by two **u** things in which it is

UNCIRCUMCISED

1Sa 17: 26 Who is this **u** Philistine that he
Col 3: 11 or Jew, circumcised or **u**,

UNCIRCUMCISION

1Co 7: 19 is nothing and **u** is nothing.
Gal 5: 6 neither circumcision nor **u** has any

UNCLEAN

Isa 6: 5 For I am a man of **u** lips, and I live
Ro 14: 14 Jesus, that nothing is **u** in itself.
2Co 6: 17 Touch no **u** thing, and I will

UNCONCERNED

Eze 16: 49 were arrogant, overfed and **u**;

UNCOVERED

Heb 4: 13 Everything is **u** and laid bare

UNDERSTAND (UNDERSTANDING UNDERSTANDS)

Job 42: 3 Surely I spoke of things I did not **u**,
Ps 73: 16 When I tried to **u** all this,
   119: 16 that I may **u** your statutes.
Lk 24: 45 so they could **u** the Scriptures.
Ac   8: 30 "Do you **u** what you are reading?"
Ro   7: 15 I do not **u** what I do. For what I
1Co 2: 14 and cannot **u** them because they
Eph 5: 17 but **u** what the Lord's will is,
2Pe 3: 16 some things that are hard to **u**,

UNDERSTANDING (UNDERSTAND)

Ps 119: 32 for you have broadened my **u**.
   119:104 I gain **u** from your precepts;
   147: 5 in power; his **u** has no limit.

Pr	3:	5	heart and lean not on your own **u**;
	4:	7	Though it cost all you have, get **u**.
	10:	23	a person of **u** delights in wisdom.
	11:	12	one who has **u** holds their tongue.
	15:	21	but whoever has **u** keeps a straight
	15:	32	one who heeds correction gains **u**.
Isa	40:	28	and his **u** no one can fathom.
Da	5:	12	a keen mind and knowledge and **u**,
Mk	4:	12	and ever hearing but never **u**;
	12:	33	with all your **u** and with all your
Php	4:	7	which transcends all **u**, will guard

UNDERSTANDS (UNDERSTAND)

| 1Ch | 28: | 9 | every heart and **u** every desire |

UNDIVIDED

1Ch	12:	33	to help David with **u** loyalty—
Ps	86:	11	give me an **u** heart, that I may fear
Eze	11:	19	I will give them an **u** heart and put
1Co	7:	35	in a right way in **u** devotion

UNDOING

| Pr | 18: | 7 | The mouths of fools are their **u**, |

UNDYING

| Eph | 6: | 24 | Lord Jesus Christ with an **u** love. |

UNFADING

| 1Pe | 3: | 4 | the **u** beauty of a gentle and quiet |

UNFAILING

Ps	33:	5	the earth is full of his **u** love.
	119:	76	May your **u** love be my comfort,
	143:	8	bring me word of your **u** love, for I
Pr	19:	22	What a person desires is **u** love;
La	3:	32	compassion, so great is his **u** love.

UNFAITHFUL

Lev	6:	2	is **u** to the Lord by deceiving
1Ch	10:	13	Saul died because he was **u**
Pr	3:	15	but the way of the **u** leads to their

UNFOLDING

| Ps | 119: | 130 | The **u** of your words gives light; |

UNGODLINESS

| Titus | 2: | 12 | It teaches us to say "No" to **u** |

UNITED (UNITY)

Ro	6:	5	For if we have been **u** with him
Php	2:	1	from being **u** with Christ, if any
Col	2:	2	encouraged in heart and **u** in love,

UNITY (UNITED)

Ps	133:	1	God's people live together in **u**!
Eph	4:	3	keep the **u** of the Spirit through
	4:	13	until we all reach **u** in the faith
Col	3:	14	them all together in perfect **u**.

UNIVERSE

| Heb | 1: | 2 | through whom also he made the **u**. |

UNKNOWN

| Ac | 17: | 23 | with this inscription: TO AN **U** GOD. |

UNLEAVENED

| Ex | 12: | 17 | "Celebrate the Festival of **U** Bread, |

UNPROFITABLE

| Titus | 3: | 9 | because these are **u** and useless. |

UNPUNISHED

| Ex | 34: | 7 | Yet he does not leave the guilty **u**; |
| Pr | 19: | 5 | A false witness will not go **u**, |

UNREPENTANT

| Ro | 2: | 5 | stubbornness and your **u** heart, |

UNRIGHTEOUS

Zep	3:	5	not fail, yet the **u** know no shame.
Mt	5:	45	rain on the righteous and the **u**.
1Pe	3:	18	the righteous for the **u**, to bring
2Pe	2:	9	to hold the **u** for punishment

UNSEARCHABLE

| Ro | 11: | 33 | How **u** his judgments, and his |

UNSEEN

| 2Co | 4: | 18 | temporary, but what is **u** is eternal. |

UNSTABLE

Jas	1:	8	double-minded and **u** in all they
2Pe	2:	14	they seduce the **u**; they are experts
	3:	16	ignorant and **u** people distort,

UNTHINKABLE

| Job | 34: | 12 | It is **u** that God would do wrong, |

UNVEILED

| 2Co | 3: | 18 | with **u** faces contemplate the Lord's |

UNWORTHY

| Job | 40: | 4 | "I am **u**—how can I reply to you? |
| Lk | 17: | 10 | do, should say, 'We are **u** servants; |

UPRIGHT

Job	1:	1	This man was blameless and **u**;
Pr	2:	7	He holds success in store for the **u**,
	15:	8	but the prayer of the **u** pleases him.
Titus	1:	8	who is self-controlled, **u**,
	2:	12	**u** and godly lives in this present

UPROOTED

| Jude | : | 12 | autumn trees, without fruit and **u** |

USEFUL

| 2Ti | 2: | 21 | **u** to the Master and prepared to do |
| | 3: | 16 | God-breathed and is **u** for teaching |

USELESS

| 1Co | 15: | 14 | our preaching is **u** and so is your |
| Jas | 2: | 20 | that faith without deeds is **u**? |

UZZIAH

Son of Amaziah; king of Judah also known as Azariah (2Ki 15:1–7; 1Ch 6:24; 2Ch 26).

VAIN

Ps	33:	17	A horse is a **v** hope for deliverance;
Isa	65:	23	They will not labor in **v**, nor will
1Co	15:	2	Otherwise, you have believed in **v**.
	15:	58	your labor in the Lord is not in **v**.
2Co	6:	1	you not to receive God's grace in **v**.

VALLEY

Ps	23:	4	I walk through the darkest **v**,
Isa	40:	4	Every **v** shall be raised up,
Joel	3:	14	Lord is near in the **v** of decision.

VALUABLE (VALUE)

| Lk | 12: | 24 | how much more **v** you are than |

VALUE (VALUABLE)

Mt	13:	46	When he found one of great **v**,
1Ti	4:	8	For physical training is of some **v**, but godliness has **v** for all things,
Heb	11:	26	as of greater **v** than the treasures

VEIL

| Ex | 34: | 33 | to them, he put a **v** over his face. |
| 2Co | 3: | 14 | to this day the same **v** remains |

VENGEANCE (AVENGE REVENGE)

| Isa | 34: | 8 | For the Lord has a day of **v**, |

VICTORIES (VICTORY)
Ps 18: 50   He gives his king great **v**;
    21: 1   great is his joy in the **v** you give!

VICTORIOUS (VICTORY)
Zec 9: 9   king comes to you, righteous
         and **v**,
Rev 2: 7   To the one who is **v**, I will give
    2: 11   The one who is **v** will not be hurt
    2: 17   To the one who is **v**, I will give
    2: 26   To the one who is **v** and does my
    3: 5   The one who is **v** will, like them,
    3: 12   The one who is **v** I will make
    3: 21   To the one who is **v**, I will give
   21: 7   Those who are **v** will inherit all

VICTORIOUSLY (VICTORY)
Ps 45: 4   In your majesty ride forth **v**

VICTORY (VICTORIES VICTORIOUS VICTORIOUSLY)
Ps 60: 12   With God we will gain the **v**,
1Co 15: 54   has been swallowed up in **v**."
   15: 57   He gives us the **v** through our
         Lord
1Jn 5: 4   This is the **v** that has overcome

VINDICATED
1Ti 3: 16   in the flesh, was **v** by the Spirit,

VINE
Jn 15: 1   "I am the true **v**, and my Father is

VINEGAR
Mk 15: 36   filled a sponge with wine **v**, put it

VIOLATION
Heb 2: 2   every **v** and disobedience received

VIOLENCE
Isa 60: 18   No longer will **v** be heard in your
Eze 45: 9   Give up your **v** and oppression

VIPERS
Ro 3: 13   "The poison of **v** is on their lips."

VIRGIN
Isa 7: 14   The **v** will conceive and give birth
Mt 1: 23   "The **v** will conceive and give birth
2Co 11: 2   I might present you as a pure **v**

VIRTUES
Col 3: 14   And over all these **v** put on love,

VISION
Ac 26: 19   disobedient to the **v** from heaven.

VOICE
Ps 95: 7   if only you would hear his **v**,
Isa 30: 21   your ears will hear a **v** behind you,
Jn 5: 28   are in their graves will hear his **v**
   10: 3   him, and the sheep listen to his **v**.
Heb 3: 7   "Today, if you hear his **v**,
Rev 3: 20   If anyone hears my **v** and opens

VOMIT
Pr 26: 11   As a dog returns to its **v**, so fools
2Pe 2: 22   "A dog returns to its **v**," and,

VOW
Nu 30: 2   a man makes a **v** to the Lord

WAGES
Lk 10: 7   you, for the worker deserves his **w**.
Ro 4: 4   **w** are not credited as a gift but as
    6: 23   the **w** of sin is death, but the gift

WAILING
Ps 30: 11   You turned my **w** into dancing;

WAIST
2Ki 1: 8   had a leather belt around his **w**."
Mt 3: 4   he had a leather belt around his **w**.

WAIT (WAITED WAITS)
Ps 27: 14   **W** for the Lord; be strong
  130: 5   I **w** for the Lord, my whole being
Isa 30: 18   Blessed are all who **w** for him!
Ac 1: 4   **w** for the gift my Father promised,
Ro 8: 23   groan inwardly as we **w** eagerly
1Th 1: 10   and to **w** for his Son from heaven,
Titus 2: 13   while we **w** for the blessed hope—

WAITED (WAIT)
Ps 40: 1   I **w** patiently for the Lord;

WAITS (WAIT)
Ro 8: 19   the creation **w** in eager expectation

WALK (WALKED)
Dt 11: 19   and when you **w** along the road,
Ps 1: 1   Blessed is the one who does not **w**
   23: 4   though I **w** through the darkest
   89: 15   **w** in the light of your presence,
Isa 2: 5   let us **w** in the light of the Lord.
   30: 21   saying, "This is the way; **w** in it."
   40: 31   weary, they will **w** and not be faint.
Jer 6: 16   and **w** in it, and you will find rest
Da 4: 37   those who **w** in pride he is able
Am 3: 3   Do two **w** together unless they
Mic 6: 8   and to **w** humbly with your God.
Mk 2: 9   say, 'Get up, take your mat and **w**'?
Jn 8: 12   Whoever follows me will never **w**
1Jn 1: 7   But if we **w** in the light, as he is
2Jn : 6   his command is that you **w** in love.

WALKED (WALK)
Ge 5: 24   Enoch **w** faithfully with God;
Jos 14: 9   which your feet have **w** will be
Mt 14: 29   **w** on the water and came toward

WALL
Jos 6: 20   gave a loud shout, the **w** collapsed;
Ne 2: 17   let us rebuild the **w** of Jerusalem,
Rev 21: 12   a great, high **w** with twelve gates,

WALLOWING
2Pe 2: 22   returns to her **w** in the mud."

WANT (WANTED WANTING WANTS)
1Sa 8: 19   they said. "We **w** a king over us.
Lk 19: 14   say, 'We don't **w** this man to be our
Ro 7: 15   For what I **w** to do I do not do,
Php 3: 10   I **w** to know Christ—yes, to know

WANTED (WANT)
1Co 12: 18   of them, just as he **w** them to be.

WANTING (WANT)
Da 5: 27   weighed on the scales and found **w**.
2Pe 3: 9   with you, not **w** anyone to perish,

WANTS (WANT)
Mt 20: 26   whoever **w** to become great among
Mk 8: 35   For whoever **w** to save their life
Ro 9: 18   on whom he **w** to have mercy,
    9: 18   he hardens whom he **w** to harden.
1Ti 2: 4   who **w** all people to be saved

WAR (WARS)
Isa 2: 4   nor will they train for **w** anymore.
Da 9: 26   **W** will continue until the end,
2Co 10: 3   we do not wage **w** as the world
Rev 19: 11   justice he judges and wages **w**.

WARN (WARNED WARNINGS)
Eze 3: 19   if you do **w** the wicked person
   33: 9   if you do **w** the wicked person

WARNED (WARN)
Ps 19: 11 By them your servant is **w**;

WARNINGS (WARN)
1Co 10: 11 and were written down as **w** for us,

WARS (WAR)
Ps 46: 9 He makes **w** cease to the ends
Mt 24: 6 will hear of **w** and rumors of **w**,

WASH (WASHED WASHING)
Ps 51: 7 **w** me, and I will be whiter than
Jn 13: 5 and began to **w** his disciples' feet,
Ac 22: 16 be baptized and **w** your sins away,
Rev 22: 14 are those who **w** their robes,

WASHED (WASH)
1Co 6: 11 But you were **w**, you were
Rev 7: 14 they have **w** their robes and made

WASHING (WASH)
Eph 5: 26 the **w** with water through the word,
Titus 3: 5 saved us through the **w** of rebirth

WATCH (WATCHES WATCHING WATCHMAN)
Ge 31: 49 the Lord keep **w** between you
Jer 31: 10 them and will **w** over his flock like
Mt 24: 42 "Therefore keep **w**, because you do
    26: 41 "**W** and pray so that you will not
Lk   2: 8 keeping **w** over their flocks at night
1Ti 4: 16 **W** your life and doctrine closely.

WATCHES (WATCH)
Ps   1: 6 For the Lord **w** over the way
   121: 3 he who **w** over you will not

WATCHING (WATCH)
Lk 12: 37 servants whose master finds them **w**

WATCHMAN (WATCH)
Eze 3: 17 I have made you a **w** for the people

WATER (WATERED WATERS)
Ps   1: 3 like a tree planted by streams of **w**,
    22: 14 I am poured out like **w**, and all my
Pr 25: 21 if he is thirsty, give him **w** to drink.
Isa 49: 10 and lead them beside springs of **w**.
Jer 2: 13 broken cisterns that cannot hold **w**.
Zec 14: 8 On that day living **w** will flow
Mk   9: 41 anyone who gives you a cup of **w**
Jn   4: 10 he would have given you living **w**."
     7: 38 rivers of living **w** will flow
Eph 5: 26 washing with **w** through the word,
1Pe 3: 21 this **w** symbolizes baptism that
Rev 21: 6 thirsty I will give **w** without cost

WATERED (WATER)
1Co 3: 6 I planted the seed, Apollos **w** it,

WATERS (WATER)
Ps 23: 2 he leads me beside quiet **w**,
Isa 58: 11 like a spring whose **w** never fail.
1Co 3: 7 nor the one who **w** is anything,

WAVE (WAVES)
Jas 1: 6 the one who doubts is like a **w**

WAVES (WAVE)
Isa 57: 20 whose **w** cast up mire and mud.
Mt   8: 27 the winds and the **w** obey him!"
Eph 4: 14 tossed back and forth by the **w**,

WAY (WAYS)
Dt   1: 33 to show you the **w** you should go.
2Sa 22: 31 "As for God, his **w** is perfect:
Job 23: 10 But he knows the **w** that I take;
Ps   1: 1 stand in the **w** that sinners take
    37: 5 Commit your **w** to the Lord;

Ps 139: 24 and lead me in the **w** everlasting.
Pr 14: 12 is a **w** that appears to be right,
    22: 6 off on the **w** they should go,
Isa 30: 21 behind you, saying, "This is the **w**;
    53: 6 of us has turned to our own **w**;
Mt   3: 3 'Prepare the **w** for the Lord,
Jn 14: 6 "I am the **w** and the truth
1Co 10: 13 provide a **w** out so that you can
    12: 31 I will show you the most excellent **w**.
Heb 4: 15 who has been tempted in every **w**,
     9: 8 the **w** into the Most Holy Place had
    10: 20 living **w** opened for us through

WAYS (WAY)
Ex 33: 13 teach me your **w** so I may know
Ps 25: 10 All the **w** of the Lord are loving
    51: 13 I will teach transgressors your **w**,
Pr   3: 6 in all your **w** submit to him, and he
    16: 17 who guard their **w** preserve their
Isa 55: 7 Let the wicked forsake their **w**
    55: 8 neither are your **w** my **w**,"
Jas 3: 2 We all stumble in many **w**."

WEAK (WEAKER WEAKNESS)
Mt 26: 41 spirit is willing, but the flesh is **w**."
Ro 14: 1 Accept the one whose faith is **w**,
1Co 1: 27 chose the **w** things of the world
     8: 9 a stumbling block to the **w**.
     9: 22 To the **w** I became **w**, to win the **w**.
2Co 12: 10 For when I am **w**, then I am strong.
Heb 12: 12 your feeble arms and **w** knees.

WEAKER (WEAK)
1Co 12: 22 seem to be **w** are indispensable,
1Pe 3: 7 them with respect as the **w** partner

WEAKNESS (WEAK)
Ro   8: 26 way, the Spirit helps us in our **w**.
1Co 1: 25 **w** of God is stronger than human
2Co 12: 9 my power is made perfect in **w**."
Heb 5: 2 since he himself is subject to **w**.

WEALTH
Pr   3: 9 Honor the Lord with your **w**,
Mk 10: 22 away sad, because he had great **w**.
Lk 15: 13 and there squandered his **w** in wild

WEAPONS
2Co 10: 4 The **w** we fight with are not the **w**

WEARIES (WEARY)
Ecc 12: 12 and much study **w** the body.

WEARY (WEARIES)
Isa 40: 31 they will run and not grow **w**,
Mt 11: 28 all you who are **w** and burdened,
Gal 6: 9 not become **w** in doing good,

WEDDING
Mt 22: 11 who was not wearing **w** clothes.
Rev 19: 7 For the **w** of the Lamb has come,

WEEP (WEEPING WEPT)
Ecc 3: 4 a time to **w** and a time to laugh,
Lk   6: 21 Blessed are you who **w** now, for

WEEPING (WEEP)
Ps 30: 5 **w** may stay for the night,
   126: 6 Those who go out **w**, carrying seed
Mt   8: 12 where there will be **w** and gnashing

WELCOMES
Mt 18: 5 **w** one such child in my name **w** me.
2Jn : 11 Anyone who **w** them shares in

WELL
Lk 17: 19 your faith has made you **w**."
Jas 5: 15 faith will make the sick person **w**;

WISE (WISDOM WISER)

1Ki	3:	12	I will give you a **w** and discerning
Job	5:	13	He catches the **w** in their craftiness,
Ps	19:	7	trustworthy, making **w** the simple.
Pr	3:	7	Do not be **w** in your own eyes;
	9:	8	rebuke the **w** and they will love
	10:	1	A **w** son brings joy to his father,
	11:	30	and the one who is **w** saves lives.
	13:	20	Walk with the **w** and become **w**,
	17:	28	Even fools are thought **w** if they
Da	12:	3	Those who are **w** will shine like
Mt	11:	25	hidden these things from the **w**
1Co	1:	27	things of the world to shame the **w**;
2Ti	3:	15	make you **w** for salvation through

WISER (WISE)

1Co	1:	25	of God is **w** than human wisdom,

WITHER (WITHERS)

Ps	1:	3	and whose leaf does not **w**—

WITHERS (WITHER)

Isa	40:	7	The grass **w** and the flowers fall,
1Pe	1:	24	the grass **w** and the flowers fall,

WITHHOLD

Ps	84:	11	no good thing does he **w** from
Pr	23:	13	Do not **w** discipline from a child;

WITNESS (WITNESSES)

Jn	1:	8	he came only as a **w** to the light.

WITNESSES (WITNESS)

Dt	19:	15	by the testimony of two or three **w**.
Ac	1:	8	and you will be my **w** in Jerusalem,

WIVES (WIFE)

Eph	5:	22	**W**, submit yourselves to your own
	5:	25	love your **w**, just as Christ loved
1Pe	3:	1	**W**, in the same way submit

WOE

Isa	6:	5	"**W** to me!" I cried. "I am ruined!

WOLF

Isa	65:	25	The **w** and the lamb will feed

WOMAN (MAN)

Ge	2:	22	the LORD God made a **w**
	3:	15	put enmity between you and the **w**,
Lev	20:	13	with a man as one does with a **w**,
Dt	22:	5	A **w** must not wear men's clothing,
Ru	3:	11	that you are a **w** of noble character.
Pr	31:	30	a **w** who fears the LORD is to be
Mt	5:	28	a **w** lustfully has already committed
Jn	8:	3	brought in a **w** caught
Ro	7:	2	by law a married **w** is bound to her
1Co	11:	3	and the head of the **w** is man,
	11:	13	Is it proper for a **w** to pray to God
1Ti	2:	11	A **w** should learn in quietness

WOMB

Job	1:	21	I came from my mother's **w**,
Jer	1:	5	I formed you in the **w** I knew you,
Lk	1:	44	the baby in my **w** leaped for joy.

WOMEN (MAN)

Lk	1:	42	"Blessed are you among **w**,
1Co	14:	34	**W** should remain silent
1Ti	2:	9	I also want the **w** to dress modestly,
Titus	2:	3	teach the older **w** to be reverent
1Pe	3:	5	the way the holy **w** of the past

WONDERFUL (WONDERS)

Job	42:	3	things too **w** for me to know.
Ps	119:	18	that I may see **w** things in your law.
	119:	27	I may meditate on your **w** deeds.

Ps	119:	129	statutes are **w**; therefore I obey
	139:	6	Such knowledge is too **w** for me,
Isa	9:	6	he will be called **W** Counselor,
1Pe	2:	9	out of darkness into his **w** light.

WONDERS (WONDERFUL)

Job	37:	14	stop and consider God's **w**.
Ps	17:	7	Show me the **w** of your great love,
	31:	21	for he showed me the **w** of his love
Joel	2:	30	I will show **w** in the heavens
Ac	2:	19	I will show **w** in the heavens

WOOD

Isa	44:	19	Shall I bow down to a block of **w**?"
1Co	3:	12	costly stones, **w**, hay or straw,

WORD (WORDS)

Dt	8:	3	but on every **w** that comes
2Sa	22:	31	The LORD's **w** is flawless;
Ps	119:	9	By living according to your **w**.
	119:	11	I have hidden your **w** in my heart
	119:	105	Your **w** is a lamp to my feet
Pr	12:	25	the heart, but a kind **w** cheers it up.
	30:	5	"Every **w** of God is flawless; he is
Isa	55:	11	so is my **w** that goes out from my
Jn	1:	1	In the beginning was the **W**, and the **W** was with God, and the **W** was God.
	1:	14	The **W** became flesh and made his
2Co	2:	17	we do not peddle the **w** of God
	4:	2	nor do we distort the **w** of God.
Eph	6:	17	of the Spirit, which is the **w** of God.
Php	2:	16	as you hold firmly to the **w** of life.
2Ti	2:	15	and who correctly handles the **w**
Heb	4:	12	the **w** of God is alive and active.
Jas	1:	22	Do not merely listen to the **w**,

WORDS (WORD)

Dt	11:	18	Fix these **w** of mine in your hearts
Ps	119:	103	How sweet are your **w** to my taste,
	119:	130	unfolding of your **w** gives light;
	119:	160	All your **w** are true; all your
Pr	30:	6	Do not add to his **w**, or he will
Jer	15:	16	When your **w** came, I ate them;
Mt	24:	35	but my **w** will never pass away.
Jn	6:	68	You have the **w** of eternal life.
	15:	7	in me and my **w** remain in you,
1Co	14:	19	rather speak five intelligible **w**
Rev	22:	19	if anyone takes **w** away from this

WORK (HANDIWORK WORKER WORKERS WORKING WORKS)

Ex	23:	12	but on the seventh day do not **w**,
Nu	8:	11	be ready to do the **w** of the LORD.
Dt	5:	14	On it you shall not do any **w**,
Jer	48:	10	who is lax in doing the LORD's **w**!
Jn	6:	27	Do not **w** for food that spoils,
	9:	4	is coming, when no one can **w**.
1Co	3:	13	test the quality of each person's **w**.
Php	1:	6	he who began a good **w** in you will
	2:	12	continue to **w** out your salvation
Col	3:	23	you do, **w** at it with all your heart,
1Th	5:	12	those who **w** hard among you,
2Th	3:	10	is unwilling to **w** shall not eat."
2Ti	3:	17	equipped for every good **w**
Heb	6:	10	he will not forget your **w**

WORKER (WORK)

Lk	10:	7	for the **w** deserves his wages.
1Ti	5:	18	and "The **w** deserves his wages."
2Ti	2:	15	a **w** who does not need to be

WORKERS (WORK)

Mt	9:	37	is plentiful but the **w** are few.
1Co	3:	9	For we are **c** in God's service;

WORKING (WORK)
Col   3: 23   all your heart, as **w** for the Lord,

WORKS (WORK)
Pr   31: 31   her **w** bring her praise at the city
Ro   8: 28   in all things God **w** for the good
Eph   2: 9   not by **w**, so that no one can boast.
      4: 12   to equip his people for **w** of service,

WORLD (WORLDLY)
Ps   50: 12   for the **w** is mine, and all that is
Isa 13: 11   I will punish the **w** for its evil,
Mt   5: 14   "You are the light of the **w**.
     16: 26   for someone to gain the whole **w**,
Mk   16: 15   "Go into all the **w** and preach
Jn   1: 29   who takes away the sin of the **w!**
      3: 16   God so loved the **w** that he gave his
      8: 12   he said, "I am the light of the **w**.
     15: 19   but I have chosen you out of the **w**.
              That is why the **w** hates you.
     16: 33   I have overcome the **w**."
     18: 36   said, "My kingdom is not of this **w**.
Ro   3: 19   and the whole **w** held accountable
1Co   3: 19   the wisdom of this **w** is foolishness
2Co   5: 19   that God was reconciling the **w**
     10: 3   For though we live in the **w**, we do
1Ti   6: 7   For we brought nothing into the **w**,
1Jn   2: 2   but also for the sins of the whole **w**.
      2: 15   not love the **w** or anything in the **w**.
Rev 13: 8   slain from the creation of the **w**.

WORLDLY (WORLD)
Titus 2: 12   to ungodliness and **w** passions,

WORMS
Mk   9: 48   where " 'the **w** that eat them do

WORRY (WORRYING)
Mt   6: 25   I tell you, do not **w** about your life,
     10: 19   do not **w** about what to say or how

WORRYING (WORRY)
Mt   6: 27   you by **w** add a single hour to your

WORSHIP
1Ch 16: 29   **W** the LORD in the splendor of his
Ps   95: 6   let us bow down in **w**, let us kneel
Mt   2: 2   it rose and have come to **w** him."
Jn   4: 24   his worshipers must **w** in the Spirit
Ro   12: 1   this is your true and proper **w**.

WORTH (WORTHY)
Job 28: 13   No mortal comprehends its **w;**
Pr   31: 10   She is **w** far more than rubies.
Mt   10: 31   you are **w** more than many
Ro   8: 18   sufferings are not **w** comparing
1Pe   1: 7   of greater **w** than gold,
      3: 4   which is of great **w** in God's sight.

WORTHLESS
Pr   11: 4   Wealth is **w** in the day of wrath,
Jas   1: 26   themselves, and their religion is **w**.

WORTHY (WORTH)
1Ch 16: 25   is the LORD and most **w** of praise;
Eph   4: 1   live a life **w** of the calling you have
Php   1: 27   in a manner **w** of the gospel
Rev   5: 2   "Who is **w** to break the seals

WOUNDS
Pr   27: 6   **W** from a friend can be trusted,
Isa 53: 5   and by his **w** we are healed.
Zec 13: 6   'What are these **w** on your body?'
1Pe   2: 24   "by his **w** you have been healed."

WRATH
2Ch 36: 16   at his prophets until the **w**

WORKING (continued)
Ps   2: 5   anger and terrifies them in his **w**,
     76: 10   Surely your **w** against mankind
Pr   15: 1   A gentle answer turns away **w**,
Jer 25: 15   cup filled with the wine of my **w**
Ro   1: 18   The **w** of God is being revealed
      5: 9   saved from God's **w** through him!
1Th   5: 9   God did not appoint us to suffer **w**
Rev   6: 16   and from the **w** of the Lamb!

WRESTLED
Ge   32: 24   a man **w** with him till daybreak.

WRITE (WRITING WRITTEN)
Dt   6: 9   **W** them on the doorframes of your
Pr   7: 3   **w** them on the tablet of your heart.
Heb   8: 10   minds and **w** them on their hearts.

WRITING (WRITE)
1Co 14: 37   what I am **w** to you is the Lord's

WRITTEN (WRITE)
Jos   1: 8   be careful to do everything **w** in it.
Da   12: 1   everyone whose name is found **w**
Lk   10: 20   that your names are **w** in heaven."
Jn   20: 31   these are **w** that you may believe
1Co   4: 6   "Do not go beyond what is **w**."
2Co   3: 3   **w** not with ink but with the Spirit
Heb 12: 23   whose names are **w** in heaven.

WRONG (WRONGDOING WRONGED WRONGS)
Ex   23: 2   not follow the crowd in doing **w**.
Nu   5: 7   restitution for the **w** they have
Job 34: 12   unthinkable that God would do **w**,
1Th   5: 15   that nobody pays back **w** for **w**,

WRONGDOING (WRONG)
Job   1: 22   not sin by charging God with **w**.

WRONGED (WRONG)
1Co   6: 7   Why not rather be **w**?

WRONGS (WRONG)
Pr   10: 12   conflict, but love covers over all **w**.
1Co 13: 5   angered, it keeps no record of **w**.

YEARS
Ps   90: 4   A thousand **y** in your sight are like
     90: 10   Our days may come to seventy **y**,
2Pe   3: 8   the Lord a day is like a thousand **y**,
Rev 20: 2   and bound him for a thousand **y**.

YESTERDAY
Heb 13: 8   Jesus Christ is the same **y** and today

YOKE (YOKED)
Mt   11: 29   Take my **y** upon you and learn

YOKED (YOKE)
2Co   6: 14   Do not be **y** together

YOUNG (YOUTH)
Ps 119: 9   can a **y** person stay on the path
1Ti   4: 12   down on you because you are **y**,

YOUTH (YOUNG)
Ps 103: 5   your **y** is renewed like the eagle's.
Ecc 12: 1   your Creator in the days of your **y**,
2Ti   2: 22   Flee the evil desires of **y** and

ZEAL
Jn   2: 17   **Z** for your house will consume me.
Ro   12: 11   Never be lacking in **z**, but keep

ZECHARIAH
1. Son of Jeroboam II; king of Israel (2Ki 15:8–12).
2. Post-exilic prophet who encouraged rebuilding of
temple (Ezr 5:1; 6:14; Zec 1:1).
3. Father of John the Baptist (Lk 1:13; 3:2).

ZEDEKIAH

Mattaniah, son of Josiah (1Ch 3:15), made king of Judah by Nebuchadnezzar (2Ki 24:17—25:7; 2Ch 36:10–14; Jer 37–39; 52:1–11).

ZERUBBABEL

Descendant of David (1Ch 3:19; Mt 1:3). Led return from exile (Ezr 2–3; Ne 7:7; Hag 1–2; Zec 4).

ZIMRI

King of Israel (1Ki 16:9–20).

ZION

Ps	137:	3	"Sing us one of the songs of **Z**!"
Jer	50:	5	They will ask the way to **Z** and
Ro	9:	33	I lay in **Z** a stone that causes people
	11:	26	"The deliverer will come from **Z**;

MAPS

WORLD OF THE PATRIARCHS

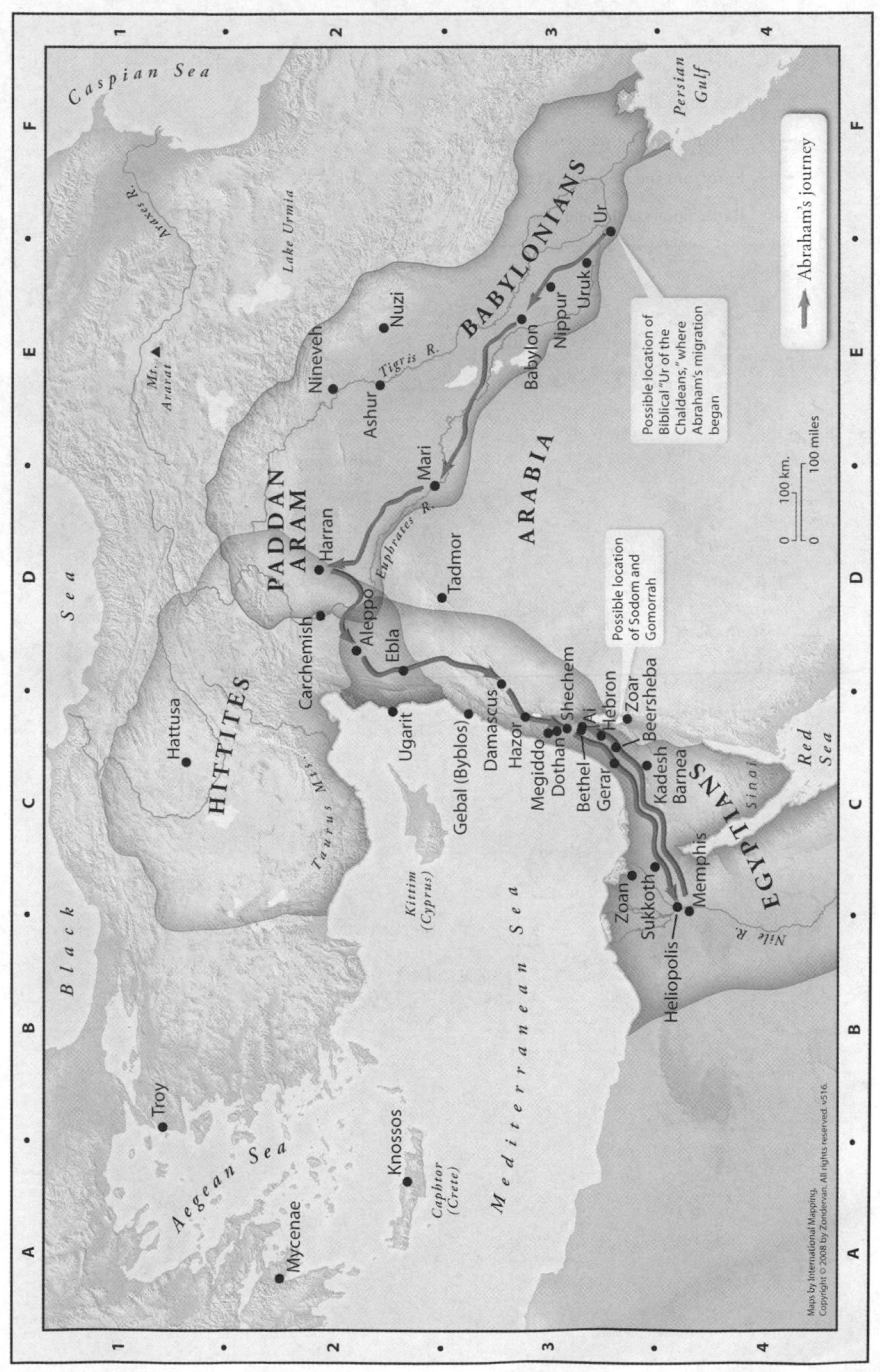

EXODUS AND CONQUEST OF CANAAN

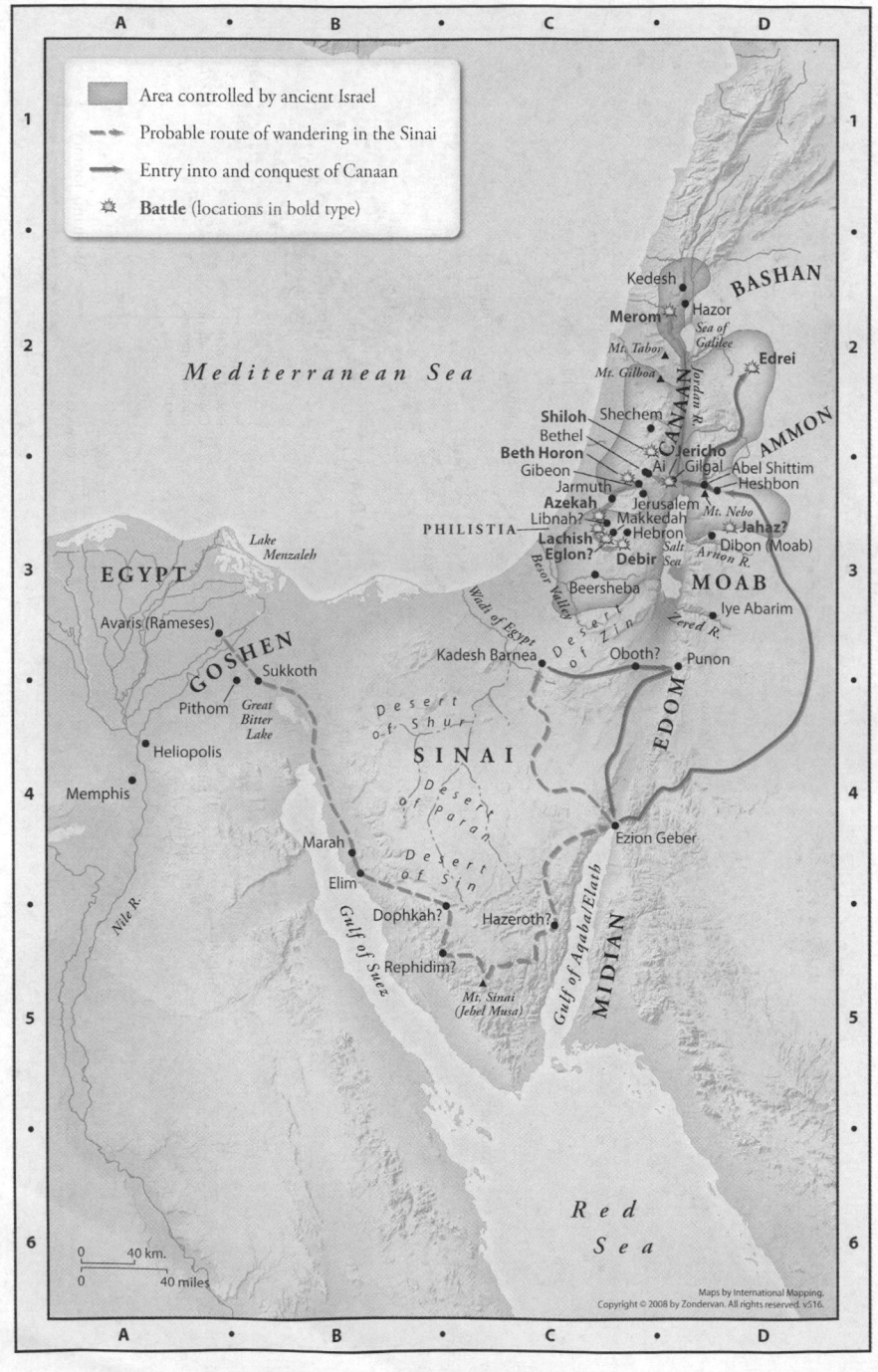

Legend:
- Area controlled by ancient Israel
- Probable route of wandering in the Sinai
- Entry into and conquest of Canaan
- ☼ **Battle** (locations in bold type)

Mediterranean Sea

BASHAN

Kedesh
Merom ☼   Hazor ☼
Sea of Galilee
Mt. Tabor ▲
Mt. Gilboa ▲   Edrei ☼

CANAAN

Shiloh   Shechem
Bethel
Beth Horon   ☼ Jericho
Gibeon   Ai   Gilgal   Abel Shittim
Jarmuth   Heshbon
Azekah   Jerusalem   Mt. Nebo
Libnah?   Makkedah   Jahaz? ☼
Lachish   Hebron   Dibon (Moab)
Eglon? ☼   Salt   Arnon R.
Debir   Sea
PHILISTIA
Beersheba   MOAB
Iye Abarim

AMMON

Jordan R.

EGYPT
Lake Menzaleh

Avaris (Rameses)
GOSHEN
Sukkoth
Pithom   Great Bitter Lake
Heliopolis

Memphis

Wadi of Egypt   Besor Valley   Desert of Zin
Kadesh Barnea   Oboth?   Punon
Desert of Shur
Desert of Paran
SINAI   EDOM
Desert of Sin
Marah
Elim   Ezion Geber
Dophkah?   Hazeroth?
Rephidim?   MIDIAN
Mt. Sinai (Jebel Musa)

Nile R.

Gulf of Suez
Gulf of Aqabat/Elath

Zered R.

Red Sea

0   40 km.
0   40 miles

LAND OF THE TWELVE TRIBES

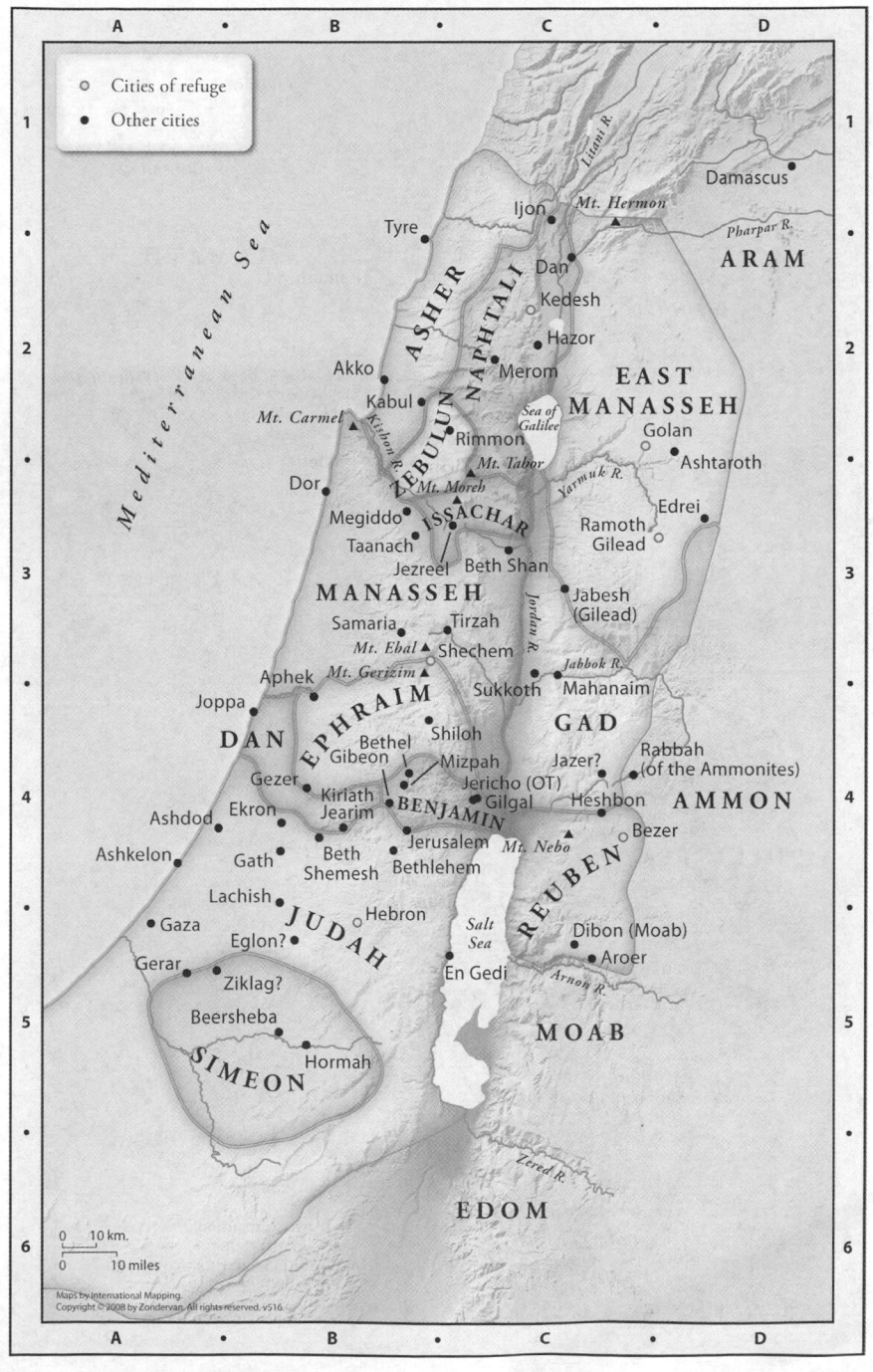

Cities of refuge

Other cities

Mediterranean Sea

Tyre

Ijon

Litani R.

Mt. Hermon

Damascus

ARAM

Pharpar R.

Dan

Kedesh

ASHER

NAPHTALI

Akko

Hazor

Kabul

Merom

Sea of Galilee

EAST MANASSEH

Mt. Carmel

Kishon R.

ZEBULUN

Rimmon

Golan

Ashtaroth

Dor

Mt. Tabor

Mt. Moreh

ISSACHAR

Yarmuk R.

Edrei

Megiddo

Taanach

Jezreel

Beth Shan

Ramoth Gilead

MANASSEH

Jordan R.

Jabesh (Gilead)

Samaria

Tirzah

Mt. Ebal

Shechem

Mt. Gerizim

Jabbok R.

Aphek

Sukkoth

Mahanaim

Joppa

EPHRAIM

DAN

Bethel

Shiloh

GAD

Gibeon

Mizpah

Jazer?

Rabbah (of the Ammonites)

Gezer

Jericho (OT)

Kirlath Jearim

BENJAMIN

Gilgal

Heshbon

AMMON

Ashdod

Ekron

Jerusalem

Mt. Nebo

Bezer

Ashkelon

Gath

Beth Shemesh

Bethlehem

REUBEN

Lachish

Hebron

Salt Sea

Dibon (Moab)

Gaza

Eglon?

JUDAH

Aroer

Gerar

Ziklag?

En Gedi

Arnon R.

Beersheba

MOAB

SIMEON

Hormah

Zered R.

EDOM

0   10 km.

0   10 miles

KINGDOM OF DAVID AND SOLOMON

Aleppo

Euphrates R.

Tiphsah

HAMATH

Orontes R.

Hamath

Kittim
(Cyprus)

Arvad

Qatna

Kedesh
(on the
Orontes)

Tadmor

Mediterranean Sea

Gebal
(Byblos)

Lebo Hamath

Berothah/Berothai

PHOENICIA

Litani R.

ARAM

Aramean
Desert

Sidon

Damascus

Tyre   Dan   Mt.
Hermon

Kedesh

Akko   Hazor

Sea of
Galilee

Ashtaroth

Megiddo   Mt.
Gilboa   Edrei

Taanach   Beth
Shan   Ramoth
Gilead

Shechem   Jordan R.

Joppa   Mahanaim

Rabbah (of the Ammonites)

PHILISTIA   Gezer   AMMON

Ashdod   Gibeah

Gath   Jerusalem   Medeba

Gaza   Hebron

Salt
Sea   Eastern Desert

Ziklag?   Beersheba   MOAB

EDOM

Kir
Hareseth

Tamar

Sinai

Wadi of Egypt

Kadesh Barnea

	Saul's kingdom
	David's expansion
	Additional territory controlled by Solomon

0   40 km.
0   40 miles

Ezion
Geber

Gulf of
Aqaba

JESUS' MINISTRY

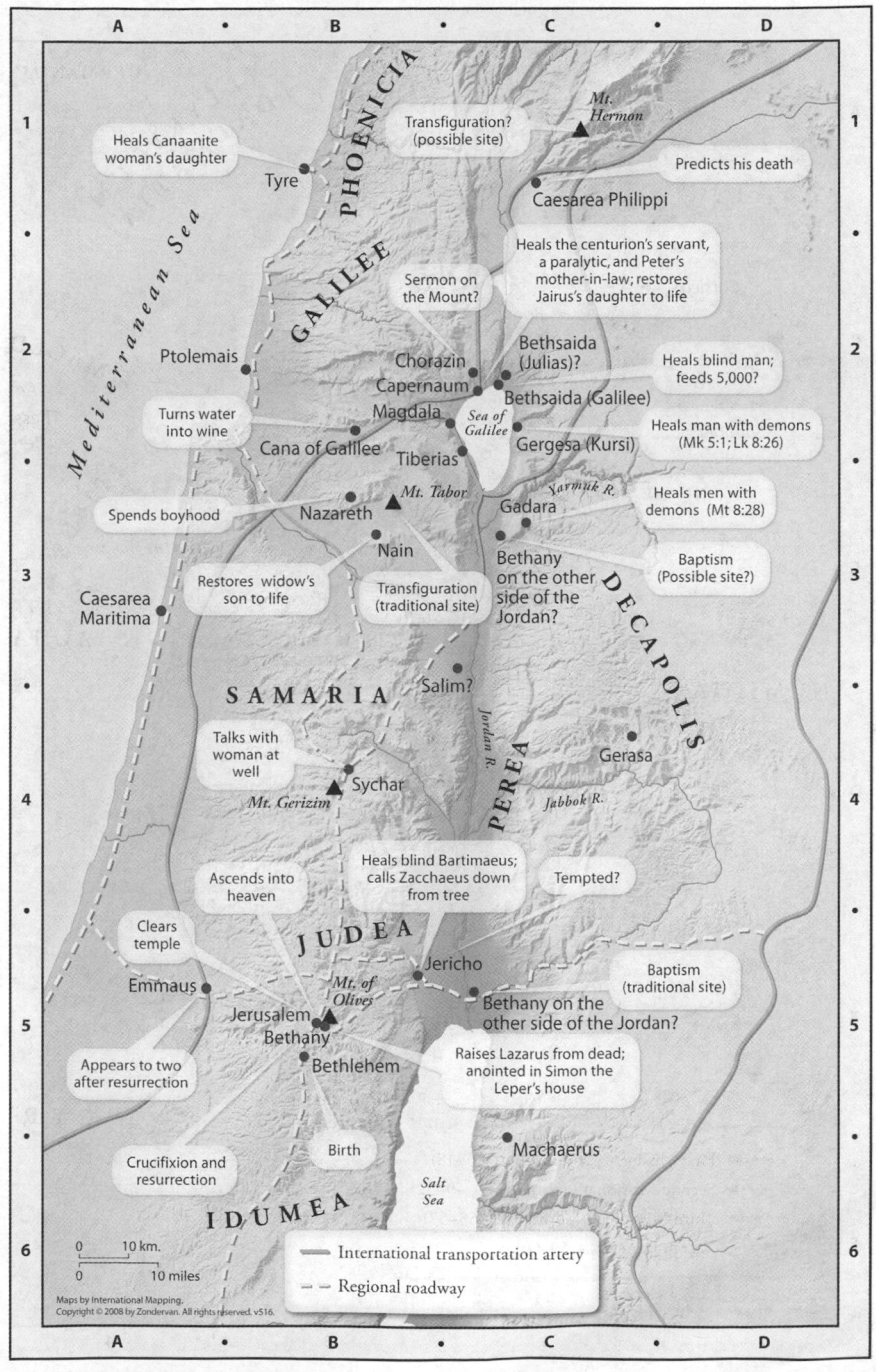

Heals Canaanite woman's daughter

Tyre

PHOENICIA

Mt. Hermon

Transfiguration? (possible site)

Predicts his death

Caesarea Philippi

GALILEE

Sermon on the Mount?

Heals the centurion's servant, a paralytic, and Peter's mother-in-law; restores Jairus's daughter to life

Mediterranean Sea

Ptolemais

Chorazin

Bethsaida (Julias)?

Heals blind man; feeds 5,000?

Capernaum

Turns water into wine

Magdala

Bethsaida (Galilee)

Cana of Galilee

Sea of Galilee

Gergesa (Kursi)

Heals man with demons (Mk 5:1; Lk 8:26)

Tiberias

Mt. Tabor

Yarmuk R.

Spends boyhood

Nazareth

Gadara

Heals men with demons (Mt 8:28)

Nain

Bethany on the other side of the Jordan?

Baptism (Possible site?)

DECAPOLIS

Restores widow's son to life

Transfiguration (traditional site)

Caesarea Maritima

SAMARIA

Salim?

Jordan R.

PEREA

Talks with woman at well

Sychar

Gerasa

Mt. Gerizim

Jabbok R.

Ascends into heaven

Heals blind Bartimaeus; calls Zacchaeus down from tree

Tempted?

Clears temple

JUDEA

Jericho

Baptism (traditional site)

Emmaus

Jerusalem

Mt. of Olives

Bethany on the other side of the Jordan?

Bethany

Appears to two after resurrection

Bethlehem

Raises Lazarus from dead; anointed in Simon the Leper's house

Crucifixion and resurrection

Birth

Machaerus

Salt Sea

IDUMEA

0   10 km.
0   10 miles

International transportation artery

Regional roadway

Maps by International Mapping.
Copyright © 2008 by Zondervan. All rights reserved. v516.

PAUL'S MISSIONARY JOURNEYS

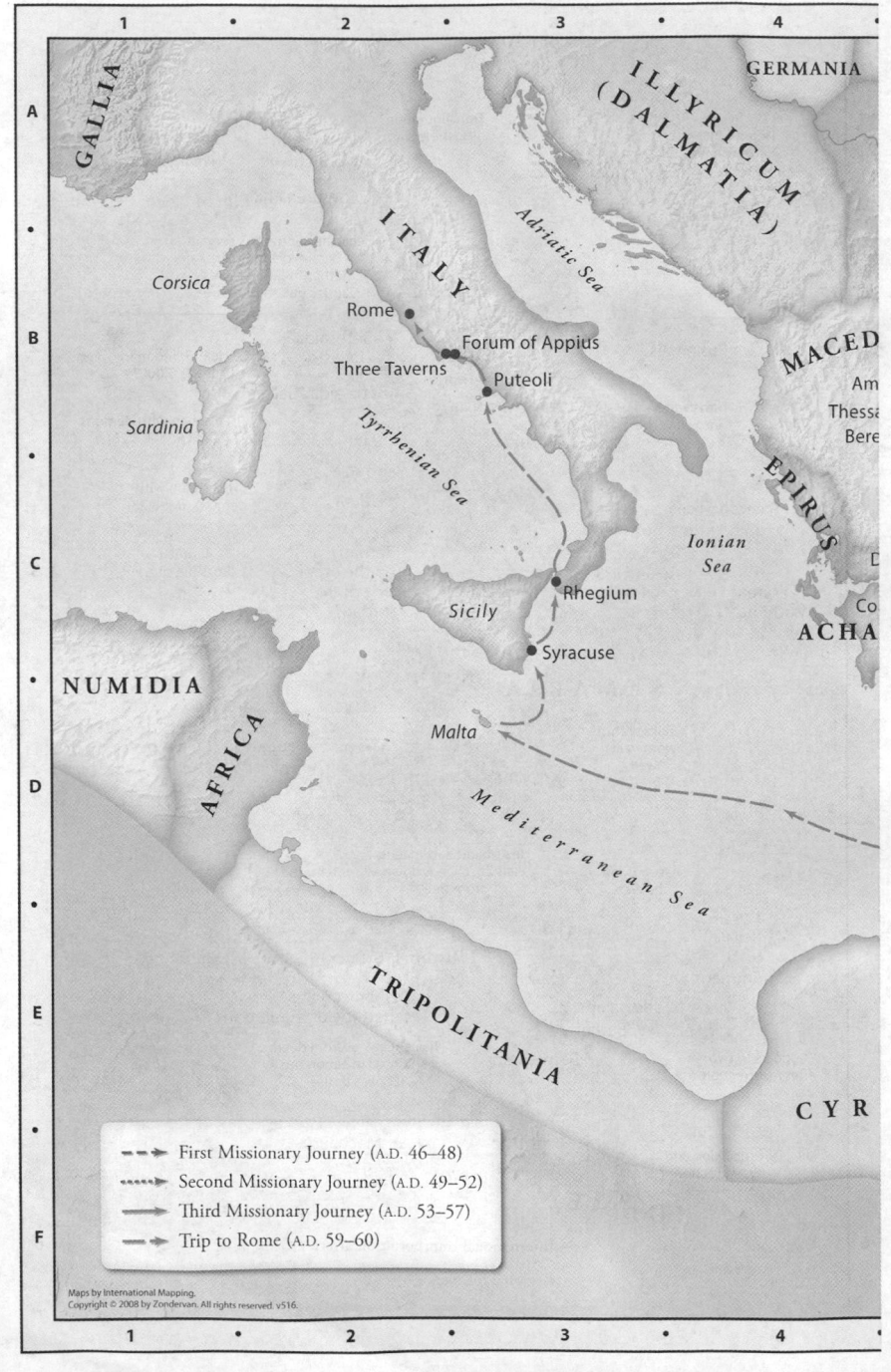

First Missionary Journey (A.D. 46–48)
Second Missionary Journey (A.D. 49–52)
Third Missionary Journey (A.D. 53–57)
Trip to Rome (A.D. 59–60)

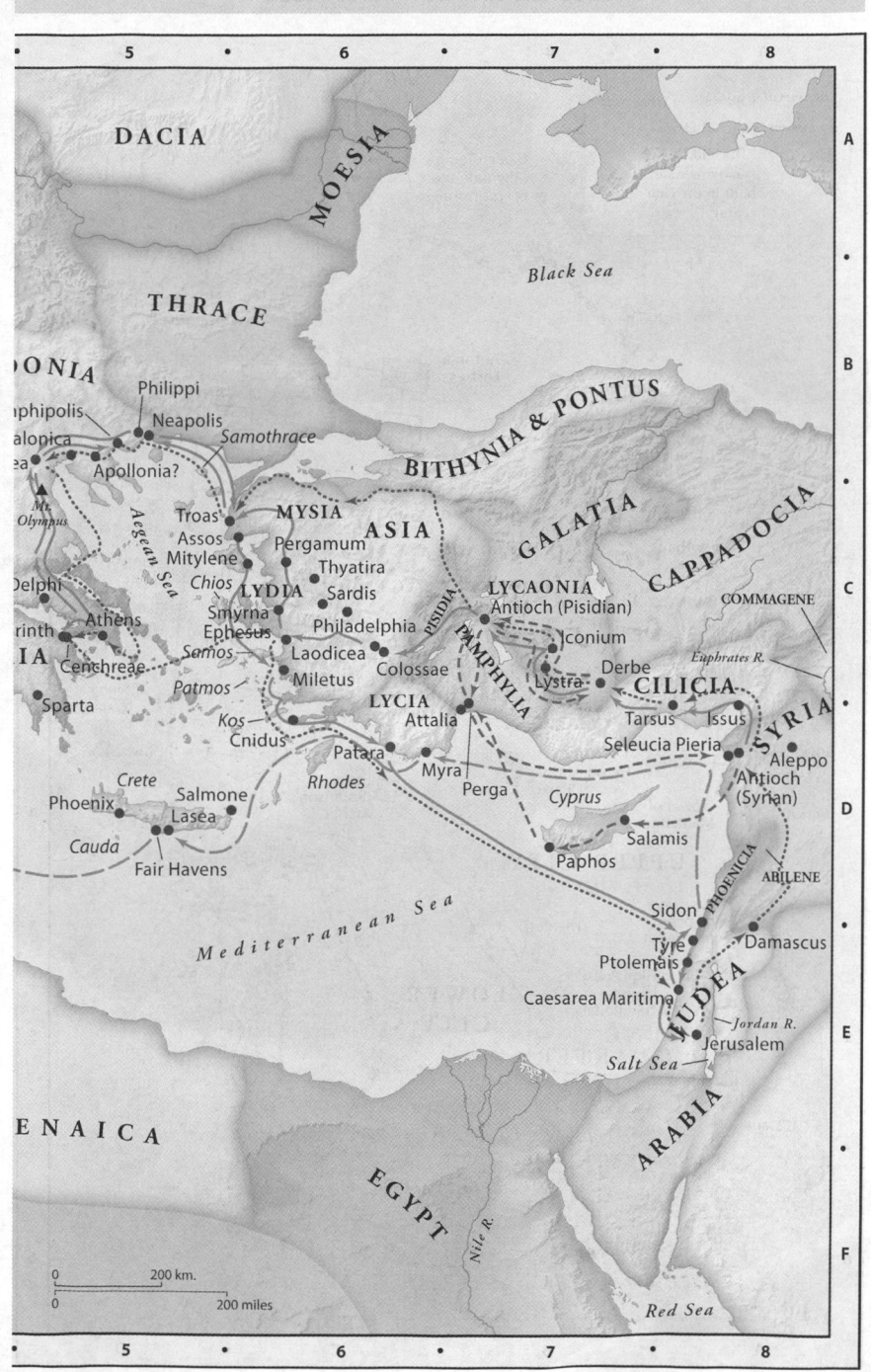

DACIA

MOESIA

THRACE

Black Sea

ONIA

Philippi

phipolis

Neapolis

alonica

Apollonia?

Samothrace

BITHYNIA & PONTUS

ea

Mt. Olympus

Troas

MYSIA

ASIA

GALATIA

CAPPADOCIA

Aegean Sea

Assos

Mitylene

Pergamum

Thyatira

Delphi

Chios

LYDIA

Sardis

LYCAONIA

COMMAGENE

rinth

Athens

Smyrna

Philadelphia

Antioch (Pisidian)

IA

Cenchreae

Ephesus

Laodicea

Iconium

Euphrates R.

Samos

Colossae

PAMPHYLIA

Derbe

CILICIA

Sparta

Patmos

Miletus

LYCIA

Lystra

SYRIA

Kos

Attalia

Tarsus

Issus

Cnidus

Patara

Perga

Seleucia Pieria

Aleppo

Crete

Salmone

Myra

Cyprus

Antioch (Syrian)

Phoenix

Lasea

Rhodes

ABILENE

Cauda

Fair Havens

Salamis

Paphos

Mediterranean Sea

Sidon

PHOENICIA

Damascus

Tyre

Ptolemais

Caesarea Maritima

JUDEA

Jordan R.

Jerusalem

ENAICA

Salt Sea

ARABIA

EGYPT

Nile R.

Red Sea

0   200 km.

0   200 miles

JERUSALEM IN THE TIME OF JESUS

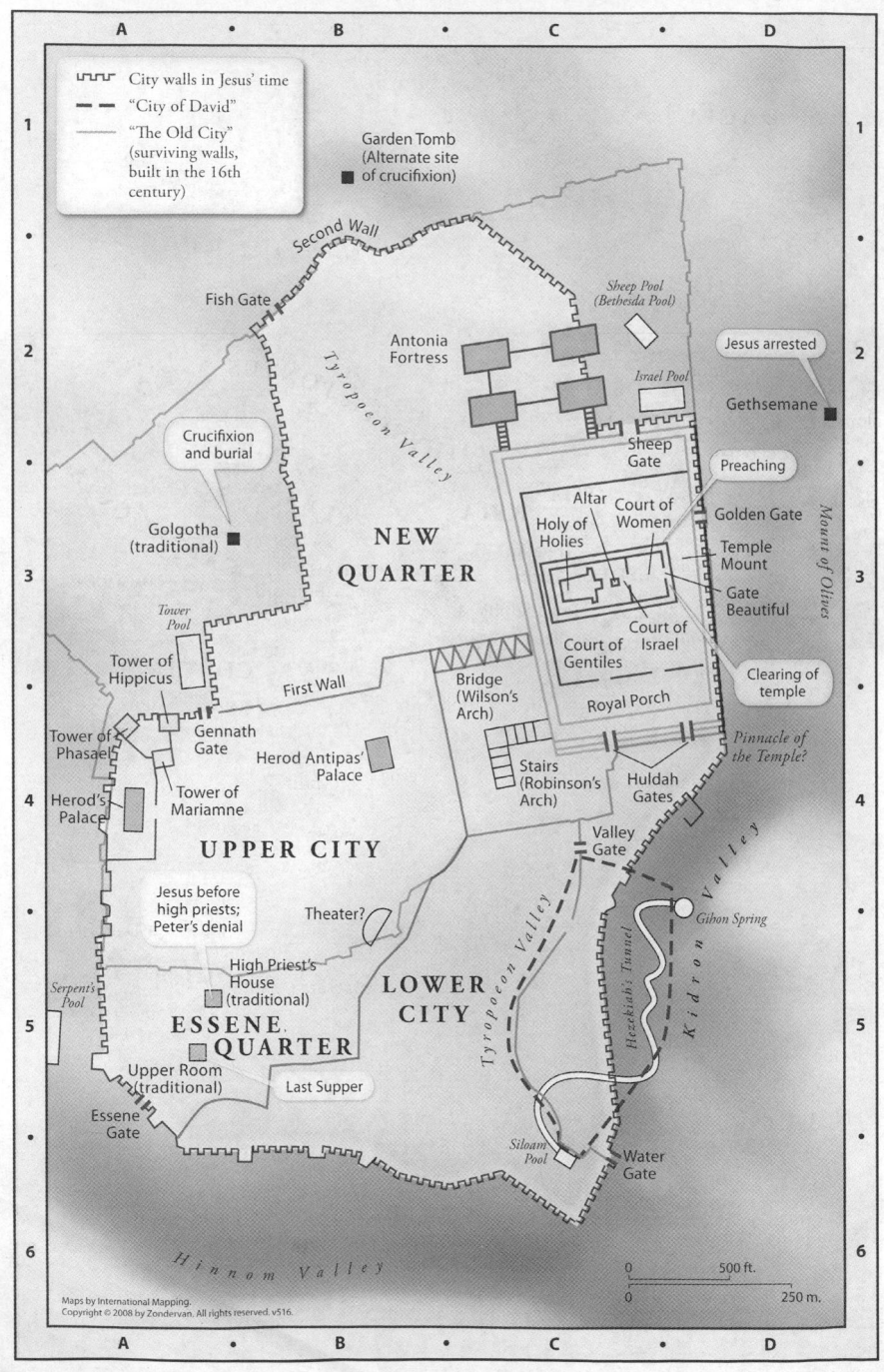

City walls in Jesus' time

"City of David"

"The Old City" (surviving walls, built in the 16th century)

Garden Tomb (Alternate site of crucifixion)

Second Wall

Fish Gate

Sheep Pool (Bethesda Pool)

Tyropoeon Valley

Antonia Fortress

Israel Pool

Jesus arrested

Gethsemane

Crucifixion and burial

Sheep Gate

Preaching

Golgotha (traditional)

NEW QUARTER

Altar

Court of Women

Holy of Holies

Golden Gate

Mount of Olives

Temple Mount

Tower Pool

Gate Beautiful

Tower of Hippicus

First Wall

Bridge (Wilson's Arch)

Court of Gentiles

Court of Israel

Clearing of temple

Royal Porch

Tower of Phasael

Gennath Gate

Herod Antipas' Palace

Stairs (Robinson's Arch)

Huldah Gates

Pinnacle of the Temple?

Herod's Palace

Tower of Mariamne

Valley Gate

UPPER CITY

Kidron Valley

Jesus before high priests; Peter's denial

Theater?

Gihon Spring

High Priest's House (traditional)

LOWER CITY

Serpent's Pool

Hezekiah's Tunnel

ESSENE QUARTER

Upper Room (traditional)

Last Supper

Tyropoeon Valley

Essene Gate

Siloam Pool

Water Gate

Hinnom Valley

0 — 500 ft.

0 — 250 m.

Maps by International Mapping.
Copyright © 2008 by Zondervan. All rights reserved. v516.